HANDBOOK OF LOGIC AND LANGUAGE

HANDBOOK OF LOGIC AND LANGUAGE

edited by

Johan van BENTHEM
University of Amsterdam & Stanford University
Alice ter MEULEN
Indiana University, Bloomington, Indiana

N·H

1997

ELSEVIER
AMSTERDAM · LAUSANNE · NEW YORK
OXFORD · SHANNON · TOKYO

1997

THE MIT PRESS
CAMBRIDGE, MASSACHUSETTS

ELSEVIER SCIENCE B.V.
Sara Burgerhartstraat 25
P.O. Box 211, 1000 AE Amsterdam, The Netherlands

Co-publishers for the United States and Canada:

The MIT Press
55 Hayward Street
Cambridge, MA 02142, U.S.A.

Library of Congress Cataloging-in-Publication Data

```
Handbook of logic and language / edited by Johan van Benthem, Alice
  ter Meulen.
      p.   cm.
    Includes bibliographical references and indexes.
    ISBN 0-444-81714-X (Elsevier). -- ISBN 0-262-22053-9 (MIT Press)
    1. Natural language processing (Computer science)  2. Logic,
  Symbolic and mathematical.  3. Semantics.  4. Linguistics.
  I. Benthem, J. F. A. K. van, 1949-   .  II. Meulen, Alice G. B. ter.
  QA76.9.N38H36  1996
  401'.5113--dc20                                            96-27559
                                                                  CIP
```

Elsevier Science B.V.
ISBN: 0-444-81714-X

The MIT Press
ISBN: 0-262-22053-9

This book is printed on acid-free paper.

Printed in The Netherlands

Preface

This Handbook documents the main currents in contemporary research at the interface of logic and natural language, including its broader ramifications in computer science, linguistic theory and cognitive science. The history of the combined study of "Logic and Language" goes back a long way, at least until the work of the scholastic philosophers in the Middle Ages. At the beginning of the twentieth century, the subject was revitalized through the pioneering efforts of Gottlob Frege, Bertrand Russell, and Polish philosophical logicians such as Kazimierz Ajdukiewicz. Around 1970, the landmark achievements of Richard Montague established a junction between state-of-the-art mathematical logic and generative linguistic theory, following Chomskyan standards of rigor. Over the subsequent decades, this enterprise of Montague Grammar has flourished, and diversified into a number of research programs with empirical and theoretical substance. Its current results are found in rapidly disseminated results concerning generalized quantifiers, categories and type theories, situations and partial logic, dynamic interpretation and inference, or feature structures and unification. Some of the material produced may be found in other handbooks on semantics or computer science. But most of it is scattered in research papers, preprints with only local accessibility, ftp-archives or limited editions of special-purpose collections. There is not even one main journal serving this emergent scientific community, even though "Linguistics and Philosophy", "The Journal of Philosophical Logic", "Natural Language Semantics" and "The Journal of Logic, Language and Information" collectively span a good deal of it. The current Handbook appears to be the first in putting the logic-language interface as such at center stage. We want to demonstrate both aspects of the interaction between logic and language, namely (1) how logical systems are designed and modified in response to linguistic needs, and (2) how mathematical theory arises in this process, and how it affects subsequent linguistic theory. This collection is not a textbook, however. The novice to the field should consult one of several available fine introductions with non-partisan coverage of basic assumptions, tools and results.

The primary purpose of this Handbook is to chart the scientific territory of this research community, serve as vademecum to its travelers and communicate its main results and achievements to its widening audience. Our choice of topics for the twenty chapters has been intended to demonstrate the strongest issues of 'ongoing concern', but also, to bring some new themes to the fore. The following working principles explain the principal architecture of this resulting volume.

Frameworks

"Logic and Language" used to be a loosely organized scholarly community, until a division into different schools became visible in the eighties, perhaps due to academic population growth or changing funding structures. These schools embodied certain valuable perspectives and methodologies, that we have chosen to represent here. There are the two classical paradigms of *Montague Grammar* and *Government Binding Theory*, which are still spawning modern manifestations to-day, such as 'dynamic' versions of the former, and 'minimalist' versions of the latter. Next, we have added two influential enterprises of the next generation in the 80s, viz. *Discourse Representation Theory* and *Categorial Grammar*. Finally, we have included two principal competitors, viz. *Game-Theoretical Semantics* and *Situation Theory*. Our sense is, however, that polemical scholarly divisions are on the wane. The six chapters in the Frameworks Part demonstrate broad approaches, rather than a scripture for narrow sects – and moreover, they interleave in various ways. It is our deep conviction that the logical study of natural language benefits from such methodological diversity, while keeping an open eye for universal topics of common concern. After all, even in the established sciences, the existence of different stances (say, 'discrete' or 'continuous', 'algebraic' or 'geometric') has long been a recognized as a beneficial aspect of our human repertoire of research strategies.

General topics

In this Part, we have collected some pervasive logical and mathematical themes across the study of linguistic phenomena. These have been chosen with various motivations in mind. First, the above frameworks use a number of different mathematical paradigms for their articulation. Montague Grammar and Categorial Grammar have been traditionally associated with the well-established fields of lambda calculus and *Type Theories*. On the other hand, Government Binding Theory as well as current 'unification grammars' tend toward some form of the newly emerging field of *Feature Logic*. Yet other mathematical paradigms are relevant, too. For example, game-theoretical semantics naturally involves mathematical game theory, and Situation Semantics has gone towards *Partial Logic*, often in combination with non-wellfounded set theories. These connections are not exclusive. For instance, the primordial formal question in linguistic semantics has been the quest for *Compositionality*, which is often pursued in a framework of universal algebra. Moreover, what is typical for mathematical approaches is the constant discovery of new connections. For instance, feature logics turn out to have many connections with the existing field of modal logic – and so do non-wellfounded set theories. (But even when existing mathematical paradigms are employed, the natural language connection may provide them with new twists.) A second source for logical theory has been the study of specific categories of linguistic expression. For instance, a recurrent topic is the structure of natural language quantification, which has inspired an independent theory of *Generalized Quantifiers*. Likewise, studies of anaphora and related phenomena (especially within discourse representation theory) have motivated a search for dynamic procedures for evaluating expressions, which finds its expression in the new topic of logical *Dynamics*. Thirdly, we have added some themes for other reasons. By and large, the logical emphasis in the study of natural language has been semantic. But the other main parts of logic, namely, proof theory and recursion theory, are becoming ever more relevant, too. The chapter on *Mathematical Linguistics and Proof Theory* demonstrates the first connection. It forms a natural pair with the Framework chapter on type-logical grammars, showing how significant proof-theoretic techniques can solve outstanding problems in mathematical linguistics, and how proof calculi and (algebraic) models are related at a meta-theoretic level after all. The chapter on *Formal Learning Theory* illustrates the second combinatorial connection, applying recursion-theoretic tools to important aspects of linguistic competence. Another common thread in much of this work are pervasive connections with the study of programming languages, data structures or knowledge representation in computer science. The chapter on *Nonmonotonicity in Linguistics* shows one striking instance where techniques and concerns from artificial intelligence are merging with those in "Logic and Language".

Descriptive themes

Finally, there is a group of chapters devoted to some major empirical phenomena in natural language that have inspired logical theory. The list is certainly not exhaustive from a linguistic (or even a more narrowly semantic) point of view, but we did try to cover most major areas in our chapters on *Quantifiers*, *Temporality*, *Plurals and Collectives*, and *Generics and Defaults*. To these, we added two chapters showing that the logical approach also extends to phenomena that are often considered part of pragmatics, such as *Presupposition* and *Questions*.

Evidently, other principles of division are possible for all this material. Therefore, an appended Glossary provides information about further ubiquitous notions in the field of "Logic and Language", that cut across chapters, such as 'anaphora', 'ambiguity' or 'inference'.

This is a rapidly developing field. In future editions, we may want to include new areas where logic and language meet, such as phonology, pragmatics and speech act theory, or discourse modeling. Also, the area of computational linguistics has been underrepresented (in part, to avoid overlap with other Handbooks) – so that we hardly deal with issues of efficiency or real-time performance for logical systems. Even so, no exclusions of principle underlie the present selection. For instance, even though our main emphasis here is semantic, we do include proof-theoretic and recursion-theoretic themes – and we even expect that proof-theoretic and indeed more general combinatorial concerns and results will grow in importance in the years to come.

Another development that we foresee is a confluence of concerns between this field and related areas within computer science and cognitive science. There are powerful analogies between studying, say, human conversation and information exchange between machines. Often, one common account of information structure may serve both descriptive and engineering needs. Various indications of this trend can already be observed in some of our chapters, witness the influence of dynamic programming paradigms, or the marriage between categorial analysis and type theories or linear logics prominent in program verification and synthesis. In the final analysis, this insight was already implicit in Montague's Thesis, when he stated that he saw no difference in principle between the study of formal and natural languages (and, we would add: programming languages).

This contact is also very much in evidence in the "European Summer Schools in Logic, Language and Information", which have served as a meeting place for the field for some eight years now. Their course curriculum brings together all the strands that we have touched upon: Logic, Language, Computation, Logic and Language, Logic and Computation, Language and Computation. We see this trend, not just as a technological fashion, but also as a welcome broadening of the scope and applicability of logico-linguistics – toward a general science of 'information systems' and cognitive processes. This field is so vast, that no methodological or ideological purity seems feasible or even desirable – and indeed, the recent literature shows ever changing constellations of syntax and semantics, model theory and proof theory. Finally, there is also a more descriptive perspective in this wider development. Both logical formalisms and computational ones are artifacts of human design. But logico-linguistic theories often deal with cognitive phenomena with independent empirical manifestations, which are also being studied by cognitive psychologists. We predict more intensive contacts here as well. For instance, the agenda of a semantic system might come to contain, not just the usual issues like correctness or completeness, but also the explanation of common mistakes, or other parts of human performance.

Our aim has been to demonstrate the interaction of logic and language, and the chapters of this Handbook should be assessed as the product of that contact: not exclusively on their linguistic or logical merit. Logico-linguistics is sui generis, even though we have emphasized its connections to its parent disciplines, as well as some broader interdisciplinary trends. Important contributions are not necessarily measured in terms of net weight in theorems, or baskets full of fresh empirical observations. They often consist in careful conceptual analysis, driven by empirical data, but using mathematical techniques to construct appropriate information models. Of course, contributions of this kind occasionally do affect the parent disciplines. Results obtained in generalized quantifier theory are currently interacting with more mathematical research, and the same can be observed or expected for other interfaces. (For instance, a case in point is that of temporal structure in natural languages, philosophy and computer science.) But the main point remains a certain 'feeling' and tolerance for different kinds of intellectual achievement. It is not at all easy to find the appropriate level of abstraction for logico-linguistic research. One is not after simplistic concrete notions like the ins and outs of 'grammatical wellformedness', but rather after deeper general mechanisms in cognition and information flow, such as 'collectivity', 'dependence' or 'polymorphism', and the cross-linguistic universals signaling their presence. It seems fair to say, though, that we do not yet have any good integrated architecture of this kind which would allow us to understand the structure and explain the efficiency (such as it is) of human cognitive processes.

Finally, let us formulate one more disclaimer. Aristotle once observed that it is the hallmark of an educated mind to give any subject of investigation no more formal structure than is germane to it. Many people have claimed that natural language is intrinsically unstable, and more 'artistic' then formal-mathematical in its character. From that viewpoint, logical analysis may not have enough of a foothold, and also, it may produce at best overly complex formalism. Evidently, the raison d'etre of the field represented here has a different presupposition. There is enough stable structure in natural language to support logical analysis and theory formation. This does not mean that every aspect of natural language is amenable to this style of analysis. It would be tedious to produce formal systems where a light essay would convey the main insights much more clearly. And indeed, the chapters in this Handbook show a great diversity of literary styles, reflecting the range of academic cultures meeting here. Incidentally, even the formal 'logical style' does not involve one uniform methodology. For instance, Montague advocated the complete formal specification of natural language fragments with fully determinate interpretations – which to some critics may seem like their terminal dissection and clinical death. But the methodology of the field has become much more diverse, as will be amply clear from the treatment of natural language structure and its uses in our various chapters. In this, it is quite similar to computer science, where the design of complete systems is just one way of approaching the study of computation. And with this much general philosophy, we invite the reader to take a look.

The diversity of perspectives that come together in this Handbook here will probably be reflected in that of its readership. Different digestive strategies may be advisable for linguists, logicians or computer scientists – and in any case, our chapters do not form a linear sequence. Some Framework chapters are good introductions to the kind of enterprise going on in this field, while those on Descriptive Topics present a lot of the typical data that must be accounted for. From a logician's viewpoint, there are yet other coherent subsets, including a type-theoretic track and a dynamic track. But it is by no means impractical to simply tackle the chapters in their own order, using the Glossary for occasional assistance.

Acknowledgement

For an enterprise of this scale to reach completion, a large number of colleagues have generously provided their assistance, ranging from an occasional bibliographic reference, via critical reading of early drafts or offering insightful advice on our coverage, to substantial contributions of material that went into chapter texts. Among these we would mention: *Greg Carlson, Gennaro Chierchia, the members of the FRACAS project, Josef von Genabit, Martin Kay, Monika Kiraly, Angelika Kratzer, Manfred Krifka, Sten Lindström, Godehard Link, Michael Morreau, Drew Moshier, Dick Oehrle, Barbara Partee, Jim Rogers, Krister Segerberg, Moshe Vardi, Frank Veltman.*

Various authors have profited importantly from comments and advice from their designated commentators, who are mentioned on the front leaf. We took this useful system from the various Handbooks produced by Dov Gabbay. Some commentators have become co-authors, witness several of our chapters. The Handbook and its editors have also been strengthened by early advice and support from *Stan Peters*. Despite this extensive support system, there have been set-backs. Planned chapters on "Unification Grammars", "Intensionality" and "Conditionals" had to be dropped at a late stage, for reasons entirely beyond the control of the editors. Some pointers to these areas have been moved into the Glossary. Finally, it is a pleasure to record a matter of intellectual credit. The idea for this Handbook was first conceived by *Arjen Sevenster* from Elsevier Science Publishers, who has been a pillar of support ever since. Elsevier has also provided funding for a successful start-up workshop on "Integrating Logic and Linguistics" (held at the University of Amsterdam, December 1992), as well as support for our editorial assistants *Martijn Spaan, Erik-Jan van der Linden*, and in the crucial final stages, especially the cool operator *Willem Groeneveld*, who also contributed the Glossary.

Johan van Benthem
Alice ter Meulen

Contents

List of Contributors

Nicholas Asher is Professor of Philosophy at the University of Texas at Austin. He has worked on various topics in the philosophy of language and formal semantics, including: propositional attitudes, Discourse Representation Theory, the paradox of the Liar, generics and nonmonotonic reasoning, discourse structure and dynamic semantics, temporal and pronominal anaphora, VP ellipsis, and lexical disambiguation.

Address: 316 Waggener Hall, The University of Texas, Austin, TX 78712, USA.
E-mail: nasher@bertie.la.utexas.edu

David Beaver is a Research Fellow at the Institute for Logic, Language and Computation at the University of Amsterdam. He studied Physics, Philosophy and Artificial Intelligence, and obtained a Ph.D. in Cognitive Science at the University of Edinburgh. His current research interests are spread across semantics, pragmatics, computational linguistics and logic.

Address: Institute for Logic, Language and Computation, Department of Philosophy, University of Amsterdam, Nieuwe Doelenstraat 15, 1012 CP Amsterdam, The Netherlands.
E-mail: dib@illc.uva.nl

Johan van Benthem is Professor of Logic at the University of Amsterdam (Department of Mathematics and Computer Science) as well as at Stanford University (Bonsall visiting chair, Department of Philosophy). His research interests include modal and dynamic logic, type-theoretic semantics, and proof-theoretic grammars.

Address: Department of Mathematics and Computer Science, University of Amsterdam, Plantage Muidergracht 24, 1018 TV Amsterdam, The Netherlands.
E-mail: johan@fwi.uva.nl, johan@csli.stanford.edu

Wojciech Buszkowski is Professor of Logic at the Adam Mickiewicz University. His research topics are mathematical logic, mathematical linguistics, categorial grammar, and the logical foundations of computer science.

Address: Faculty of Mathematics and Computer Science, Adam Mickiewicz University, Matejki 48/49, 60 769 Poznan, Poland.
E-mail: buszko@math.amu.edu.pl

Jan van Eijck is a Senior Researcher at CWI (Centre for Mathematics and Computer Science) in Amsterdam and professor of computational linguistics at OTS (Research Institute for Language and Speech) in Utrecht. His research concerns the logical aspects of computational linguistics.

Address: CWI, PO Box 94079, 1090 GB Amsterdam, The Netherlands.
E-mail: jve@cwi.nl
WWW: http://www.cwi.nl/~jve

Jens Erik Fenstad is Professor of Logic at the University of Oslo. His research concerns computability theory, non-standard analysis, and the semantics of natural language systems.

Address: Institute of Mathematics, University of Oslo, PO Box 1053, Blindern, 0316 Oslo, Norway.
E-mail: jfenstad@math.uio.no

Jeroen Groenendijk is Associate Professor of Logic and Linguistics, at the University of Amsterdam. His research interests concern the semantics and pragmatics of natural language, in particular questions, anaphora, coreference and modality, and dynamic semantics.

Address: Institute for Logic, Language and Computation, Department of Philosophy, University of Amsterdam, Nieuwe Doelenstraat 15, 1012 CP Amsterdam, The Netherlands.
E-mail: groenend@illc.uva.nl

Herman Hendriks is a Postdoctoral Fellow at the Research Institute for Language and Speech at Utrecht University. He wrote his dissertation on flexible type assignment and type-shifting operations in Montague Grammar and Categorial Grammer at Amsterdam University. His current research concerns (the linguistic realization of) information packaging, i.e. the pragmatic structuring of propositional content in function of the speaker's assumptions of the hearer's knowledge and attentional state.

Address: OTS, Utrecht University, Trans 10, 3512 JK Utrecht, The Netherlands.
E-mail: Herman.Hendriks@let.ruu.nl
WWW: http://wwwots.let.ruu.nl/cgi-bin/staff?hendriks

James Higginbotham is Professor of General Linguistics at the University of Oxford. He is the author of a number of articles on syntactic and semantic theory, and philosophy of language and mind. His current research is on semantics in generative grammar and the nature of conceptual and semantic competence.

Address: Centre for Linguistics and Philology, Walton Street, Oxford OX1 2HG, UK.
E-mail: higgy@ermine.ox.ac.uk

Jaako Hintikka is Professor of Philosophy at Boston University. His research concerns mathematical and philosophical logic, language theory, epistemology and philosophy of science, philosophy of mathematics, and history of philosophy.

Address: Boston University, Department of Philosophy, 745 Commonwealth Ave., Boston, MA 02215, USA.
E-mail: hintikka@acs.bu.edu

Theo M.V. Janssen is Assistant Professor of Computer Science at the University of Amsterdam. His research interests are on the borderline of natural language, logic, and computer science, in particular applications of universal algebra in natural language syntax and semantics. This involves foundational issues in Montague grammar and programming language semantics, and also machine translation, in particular the method of compositional translation.

Address: Department WINS, University of Amsterdam, Plantage Muidergracht 24, 1018 TV Amsterdam, The Netherlands.
E-mail: theo@fwi.uva.nl
WWW: http://turing.wins.uva.nl/~theo

Dick de Jongh is Associate Professor of Logic at the University of Amsterdam. His research has included intuitionistic logic, modal logic, and formalized arithmetic. Recent research involves the connection of the Osherson–Stob–Weinstein tradition of the study of identifiability of classes of r.e. languages with the Angluin tradition of the study of the identifiability of r.e. indexed classes of recursive languages and the characterization of such classes.

Address: Institute for Logic, Language and Computation, Plantage Muidergracht 24, 1024 TV Amsterdam, The Netherlands.
E-mail: dickdj@fwi.uva.nl

Hans Kamp is Professor of Logic and Philosophy of Language at University of Stuttgart. His research interests include: mathematical and philosophical logic; philosophy of language; logic and mind; semantics and pragmatics of natural language; computational linguistics and adjacent areas of computer science. Over the past 16 years he has devoted much time to the development of Discourse Representation Theory.

Address: Universität Stuttgart, Institut für Maschinelle Sprachverarbeitung, Azenbergstrasse 12, D-70174 Stuttgart, Germany.
E-mail: hans@ims.uni-stuttgart.de

Edward Keenan is Professor of Linguistics at the University of California at Los Angeles. He has worked mainly in syntactic typology and in formal semantics for natural language, which is his primary research interest. Here the emphasis in the last ten years has been on generalized quantifier theory, Boolean semantics, and recently also model theory.

Address: Department of Linguistics, University of California at Los Angeles, 405 Hilgard Avenue, Los Angeles, CA 90095-1543, USA.
E-mail: ekeenan@ucla.edu
WWW: http://www.humnet.ucla.edu./humnet/linguistics/people/keenan/keenan.tml

Jan Tore Lønning is Professor of Linguistics at the University of Oslo. He has mainly worked on the semantics and logic of noun phrases: plurals, mass terms and quantification. Currently, he is also interested in the relationship between formal semantics and computational linguistics.

Address: University of Oslo, Department of Linguistics, PO Box 1102, Blindern, 0317 Oslo, Norway.
E-mail: jtl@ilf.uio.no

Eric Martin is a researcher affiliated with the University Savoie. His research concerns theoretical frameworks for the problem of finding a set of rules to control a physical system by learning methods. This involves theoretical models of learning, scientific discovery, and inductive logic, and their links with belief revision theory.

Address: LAMII, Université de Savoie, 41, avenue de Savoie, B.P. 806, F 74 000 Annecy Cedex, France.
E-mail: martin@esia.univ-savoie.fr
WWW: ava.univ-savoie.fr

Alice ter Meulen is Professor of Philosophy and of Linguistics at Indiana University, Bloomington. Her research interest is in the interface of logic, language and metaphysics, and has been concerned with mass and amount terms in Montague grammar, and the semantics of tense and aspect in a dynamic system and its interaction with pronominal reference.

Address: Indiana University, Department of Philosophy, Sycamore Hall 026, Bloomington, IN 47405, USA.
E-mail: atm@phil.indiana.edu

Michael Moortgat is Professor of Computational Linguistics at Utrecht University. His research interests include categorial grammar, the logic of grammar architectures, and applications of proof theoretic techniques in natural language processing and understanding.

Address: Research Institute for Language and Speech (OTS), Trans 10, 3512 JK Utrecht, The Netherlands.
E-mail: michael.moortgat@let.ruu.nl

Larry Moss is Associate Professor of Mathematics at Indiana University. His research concerns several areas of applied logic close to computer science and linguistics, including the abstract theory of computation and abstract data type computability, the semantics of natural language, and frameworks for computational syntax based on relational grammar and on evolving algebras. Other work has been concerned with non-wellfounded sets, modal logic, and graph theory.

Address: Department of Mathematics, Indiana University, Bloomington, IN 47405, USA.
E-mail: lsm@cs.indiana.edu

Reinhard Muskens is Associate Professor of Logic at Tilburg University. His main interest is in the logic and semantics of natural language, including the foundations of Montague Grammar, Situation Semantics, and Discourse Representation Theory. He has made several proposals for unifying these three semantic frameworks. Currently he is also interested in underspecified representations for the meanings of natural language expressions.

Address: Department of Linguistics, Tilburg University, PO Box 90153, 5000 LE Tilburg, The Netherlands.
E-mail: r.a.muskens@kub.nl

Daniel Osherson is Director of the Laboratory of Cognitive Processes in Milan. His research is concerned with brain loci of rational thought, formal models of learning and scientific discovery, human judgment of uncertainty, and psychological structure of concepts.

Address: DIPSCO, Istituto San Raffaele, Via Olgettina 60, I-20132 Milano, Italy.
E-mail: osherson@ratio.hsr.it

Barbara H. Partee is Distinguished University Professor of Linguistics and Philosophy, University of Massachusetts at Amherst. The research interests of profesor Partee focus on semantics, including its foundations and its relation to syntax and to pragmatics, to logic and the philosophy of language, and to cognitive and representational theories of language. In recent years she has worked on type-shifting, on quantification, on topic-focus structure, on the formal structure of context-dependence, and on aspect and quantification in English and in the Slavic languages.

Address: Department of Linguistics, University of Massachusetts, Amherst, MA 01003-7130, USA.
E-mail: partee@cs.umass.edu
WWW: http://www-unix.oit.umass.edu/ osteele/lx/faculty/partee.html

Francis Jeffry Pelletier is Professor of Philosophy and Computer Science at the University of Alberta. His research includes formal semantics, philosophical logic, philosophy of language, computational linguistics, automated theorem proving, cognitive science, and artificial intelligence.

Address: Department of Philosophy, University of Alberta, Edmonton, Alta., Canada T6G 2E5.
E-mail: jeffp@cs.ualberta.ca
WWW: http://www.cs.ualberta.ca/˜jeffp

William C. Rounds is Professor of Computer Science at the University of Michigan. He is a theoretical computer scientist interested in logic and language. His research involves the use of sophisticated tools of theoretical computer science for making mathematical models of linguistic entities, ranging from grammars to semantics to complexity. Currently he is working on the subject of defaults in feature logic, using tools from domain theory.

Address: University of Michigan, 1101 Beal Avenue, Ann Arbor, MI 48109, USA.
E-mail: rounds@eecs.umich.edu
WWW: http://ai.eecs.umich.edu/people/rounds/index.html

Gabriel Sandu is Professor of Philosophy at the University of Helsinki. His main fields of interest are logical semantics for natural language, especially game-theoretical semantics, and the theory of generalized quantifiers. He is presently preparing a book on the partial interpretation of generalized quantifiers.

Address: Department of Philosophy, PO Box 24 (Unioninkatu 40) 00014 University of Helsinki, Finland.
E-mail: sandu@katk.helsinki.fi

Jerry Seligman is Associate Professor of Philosophy at the National Chung-Cheng University. His research is in the area of logic, language and information.

Address: Institute of Philosophy, National Chung-Cheng University, Min-Hsiung, Chia-Yi, Taiwan.
E-mail: jerry@phil.ccu.edu.tw
WWW: http://www.phil.indiana.edu/ jerry/home.html

Mark Steedman is Professor in the Department of Computer and Information Science at the University of Pennsylvania. His research interests cover issues in computational linguistics, artificial intelligence, computer science and cognitive science, including syntax and semantics of natural languages and programming languages, parsing and comprehension of natural language discourse by humans and by machine, natural language generation, and intonation in spoken discourse.

Address: University of Pennsylvania, Department of Computer and Information Science, Philadelphia, PA 19104, USA.
E-mail: steedman@cis.upenn.edu

Martin Stokhof is Associate Professor of Philosophy at the University of Amsterdam. His main areas of research include the semantics and pragmatics of natural language, in particular questions, anaphora, dynamic semantics; and philosophy of language, in particular the philosophy of Ludwig Wittgenstein.

Address: Institute for Logic, Language and Computation, Department of Philosophy, University of Amsterdam, Nieuwe Doelenstraat 15, 1012 CP Amsterdam, The Netherlands.
E-mail: stokhof@illc.uva.nl

Richmond H. Thomason is Professor of Linguistics, Intelligent Systems and Philosophy, at the University of Pittsburgh. He is a logician with long-term research interests in philosophical logic, philosophy of language, natural language semantics and pragmatics, knowledge representation, and computational linguistics. Recent and current research projects are: the theory of nonmonotonic inheritance networks; interactions between NL generation and interpretation; nonmonotonic reasoning in linguistic theory; formalizing semantic relations between words; action formalisms and reasoning about actions; qualitative decision theory.

Address: University of Pittsburgh, Pittsburgh, PA 15260, USA.
E-mail: thomason@isp.pitt.edu
WWW: http://www.pitt.edu/~thomason/thomason.html

Ray Turner is Professor of Computer Science at the University of Essex, UK. Research interests: Constructive Type Theories and Theories of Properties and their application to computation and semantics.

Address: Department of Computer Science, University of Essex, Essex, UK.
E-mail: turnr@essex.ac.uk

Albert Visser is Associate Professor of Philosophy at the University of Utrecht. His research focusses on three projects: a metamathematical investigation of dynamical systems like Dynamic Predicate Logic and Discourse Representation Theory; Intuitionistic Propositional Logic; the study of arithmetical interpretations of modal and intuitionistic propositional logic.

Address: Department of Philosophy, University of Utrecht, Heidelberglaan 8, 3584 CS Utrecht, The Netherlands.
E-mail: albert.visser@phil.ruu.nl
WWW:http://www.phil.ruu.nl/home/auto/albert.html

Scott Weinstein is Professor of Philosophy at the University of Pennsylvania. His research interests include computational learning theory, and applications of logic in computer science, especially descriptive complexity theory and finite model theory.

Address: Department of Philosophy, Suite 460, 3440 Market Street, University of Pennsylvania, Philadelphia, PA 19104-3325, USA.
E-mail: weinstein@cis.upenn.edu
WWW: http://www.cis.upenn.edu/~weinstein/home.html

Dag Westerståhl is Associate Professor of Philosophy at Stockholm University. His main area of research has been model theory and formal semantics for natural language, especially theory of generalized quantifiers. Recent work also concerns the issue of compositionality, and dynamic logic.

Address: Department of Philosophy, Stockholm University, 106 91 Stockholm, Sweden.
E-mail: dag.westerstahl@philosophy.su.se

Abbreviations of Journal Titles

ACM Comput. Surv.	ACM Computing Surveys
ACM SIGART Bull.	ACM SIGART Bulletin
Acta Philos. Fennica	Acta Philosophica Fennica
Amer. J. Math.	American Journal of Mathematics
Amer. Math. Monthly	American Mathematical Monthly
Amer. Philos. Q.	American Philosophical Quarterly
Ann. Math. Artif. Intell.	Annals of Mathematics and Artificial Intelligence
Ann. Math. Logic	Annals of Mathematical Logic
Ann. of Math.	Annals of Mathematics
Ann. Pure Appl. Logic	Annals of Pure and Applied Logic
Ann. Sci. École Norm. Sup.	Annales Scientifiques de l'École Normale Supérieure
Arch. Math. Logic	Archive for Mathematical Logic
Arch. Math. Logik Grundlagenforsch.	Archive für mathematische Logik und Grundlagenforschung
Artif. Intell.	Artificial Intelligence
Artif. Intell. Mag.	Artificial Intelligence Magazine
Australas. J. Philos.	Australasian Journal of Philosophy
Bull. Amer. Math. Soc.	Bulletin of the American Mathematical Society
Bull. IGPL	Bulletin of the Interest Group on Pure and Applied Logic
Bull. Polish Acad. Sci. Math.	Bulletin of the Polish Academy of Sciences. Mathematics
Bull. Res. Counc. Israel	Bulletin of the Research Council of Israel
Child Dev.	Child Development
Cogn. Psych.	Cognitive Psychology
Cogn. Science	Cognitive Science
Comm. ACM	Communications of the Association for Computing Machinery
Comput. Intell.	Computational Intelligence

Comput. Ling.	Computational Linguistics
Comput. Math. Appl.	Computational Mathematics and Applications
Duke Math. J.	Duke Mathematical Journal
Found. Lang.	Foundations of Language
Fund. Inform.	Fundamenta Informaticae
Fund. Math.	Fundamenta Mathematicae
History and Philos. of Logic	History and Philosophy of Logic
IEEE Trans. Inform. Theory	IEEE Transactions on Information Theory
Inform. and Comput.	Information and Computation
Inform. and Control	Information and Control
Inform. Process. Lett.	Information Processing Letters
Inform. Sci.	Information Sciences
Invent. Math.	Inventiones Mathematicae
Israel J. Math.	Israel Journal of Mathematics
J. Appl. Non-Classical Logics	Journal of Applied Non-Classical Logics
J. Artif. Intell. Math.	Journal of Artificial Intelligence and Mathematics
J. Assoc. Comput. Mach.	Journal of the Association for Computing Machinery
J. Automat. Reason.	Journal of Automated Reasoning
J. Child Lang.	Journal of Child Language
J. Comput. System Sci.	Journal of Computer and System Sciences
J. Ling.	Journal of Linguistics
J. Ling. Res.	Journal of Linguistic Research
J. Logic Comput.	Journal of Logic and Computation
J. Logic Programming	Journal of Logic Programming
J. Logic, Lang., Inform.	Journal of Logic, Language, and Information
J. Math. Psychol.	Journal of Mathematical Psychology
J. Math. Syst. Theory	Journal of the Mathematical Systems Theory
J. Philos.	The Journal of Philosophy
J. Philos. Logic	Journal of Philosophical Logic
J. Pragmatics	Journal of Pragmatics
J. Semantics	Journal of Semantics
J. Symb. Comput.	Journal of Symbolic Computation
J. Symb. Logic	Journal of Symbolic Logic
Ling. Anal.	Linguistic Analysis
Ling. and Philos.	Linguistics and Philosophy
Ling. Ber.	Linguistische Berichte
Ling. Inq.	Linguistic Inquiry

Ling. Rev.	Linguistic Review
Logic Comput.	Logic and Computation
Logique et Anal.	Logique et Analyse
Mach. Intell.	Machine Intelligence
Mach. Learning	Machine Learning
Mat. Sb.	Matematicheskii Sbornik
Math. Ann.	Mathematische Annalen
Math. Logic Q.	Mathematical Logic Quarterly
Math. Struct. Comput. Sci.	Mathematical Structures in Computer Science
Math. Z.	Mathematische Zeitschrift
Methodol. and Philos. Sci.	Methodology and Philosophy of Science
Monatsh. Math. Phys.	Monatshefte für Mathematik und Physik
Nat. Language and Ling. Theory	Natural Language and Linguistic Theory
Nat. Language Semantics	Natural Language Semantics
Notre Dame J. Formal Logic	Notre Dame Journal of Formal Logic
Papers Ling.	Papers in Linguistics
Perspect. Philos.	Perspectives in Philosophy
Philos. Phenomenolog. Res.	Philosophy and Phenomenological Research
Philos. Rev.	Philosophical Review
Philos. Sci.	Philosophy of Science
Philos. Stud.	Philosophical Studies
Proc. London Math. Soc.	Proceedings of the London Mathematical Society
Rev. Internat. Philos.	Revue Internationale de Philosophie
SIAM J. Computing	SIAM Journal of Computing
Stud. Lang.	Studies in Language
Stud. Logica	Studia Logica
Stud. Philos.	Studies in Philosophy
Theor. Ling.	Theoretical Linguistics
Theor. Comput. Sci.	Theoretical Computer Science
Trans. Amer. Math. Soc.	Transactions of the American Mathematical Society
Z. Math. Logik Grundlag. Math.	Zeitschrift für mathematische Logik und Grundlage der Mathematik
Z. Philos. Philosoph. Kritik	Zeitschrift für Philosophie und philosophishe Kritik

Part 1
Frameworks

Introduction

Perhaps, the need for a Part with this heading requires some explanation, as a great variety of 'frameworks' may look bewildering to readers from other disciplines. In the 70s, the interface between "Logic and Language" was a quiet scholarly field, with general issues on a common research agenda, such as intensionality, quantification or ambiguity. Logic played a general role as a model of elegance and clarity, with a pleasant interaction between philosophical logic and linguistic semantics. In the 80s, 'frameworks' started appearing trying to change and monopolize part of the research agenda, and authors felt the need to present their ideas more forcefully as 'theories' with appealing names, forming schools and proselytizing. Part of this may be symptomatic for a young emerging area trying to establish itself, a phenomenon well-documented in fields like linguistics and computer science. This trend toward separatism and rivaling research agendas, though it may have had positive effects in stimulating foundational discussions, has hampered communication, and generated much fortuitous competition. But by now, a more positive assessment of the current situation is certainly possible. Properly viewed, the frameworks in this Part represent compatible broad and exact strategies for dealing with the diversity of phenomena in natural language, mastery of which is an essential part of general education in the field. At least in this sense, they may be compared to competing 'schools' like logicism, intuitionism and formalism in the mathematical logic of the early 20th century, whose legacy is a range of widely applicable concerns, methods and results that are still highly relevant to-day.

Moreover, the presentation in this Part is 'open' in various ways. Authors have made their chapters non-ideological and non-polemical. We think that forging this peaceful co-existence is a valuable side-effect of this Handbook enterprise as such. Moreover, through these presentations, one can see many connections, collectively demonstrating the coherence of the field. Sometimes, even new results have been been found by authors searching for a broad presentation to outsiders, while new connections have become visible. We mention a number of these, in the form of clusters of techniques.

The first theme is that of logical *types*. Montague Grammar and Categorial Grammar have been explicitly type-based logical formalisms, which makes them part of the foundational tradition in mathematical logic since Russell and Ajdukiewicz. Types are also a lingua franca in large parts of computer science, which should facilitate interdisciplinary communication. But even newer frameworks may involve types in interesting ways. For instance, there are recent typed versions of DRT as well as dynamic semantics ('Dynamic Montague Grammar') which raise interesting new issues affecting type theory itself. Notably, from a dynamic point of view, the classical rule of alfa-conversion (which obliterates the identity of bound variables) must be rejected. Some of these themes are discussed in the chapter on Types in Part 2.

Another broad theme is that of feature structures and *unification*. Many grammatical and semantic frameworks use methods like this, deriving ultimately from Herbrand's work on reductions of logical validity, and the theorem-proving tradition since the 60s centered around Resolution. Stated polemically, unification is an alternative to function application as the main 'glue' for composing meanings. But many systems combine both (as happens in polymorphic type theories). In recent years, there has been a flourishing logical theory of unification over feature structures (cf. the relevant chapter in Part 2), which again enhances cohesion. For instance, feature models are a kind of information structures that are congenial to both Government Binding Theory and Categorial Grammar, and hence they reach out across quite different linguistic paradigms.

On the whole, we can see the role of technical foundational research in this area as a kind of 'federal agency', bringing up new cross-connections all the time. An interesting example are recent developments in *modal logic*. Feature-value structures are like Kripke models, and indeed many modal features are coming to light in the recent literature. Thus, we can also think of linguistic frameworks as defining classes of information structures (such as trees, graphs, ...). In standard logic, the issue is how to describe such classes, and at which level of expressive complexity. In particular, modal languages are small (usually decidable) fragments of the full first-order language over these models. Thus, we get a logical hierarchy for calibrating complexity of various linguistic theories: what is the minimal expressive power needed to describe their intended model classes? Such hierarchies may be compared with the usual more 'procedural' ones in terms of rewrite rules or various kinds of automata. Interestingly, similar topics are found in computer science. In particular, recent accounts of feature structures and their appropriate semantic equivalences show clear analogies with process equivalences in dynamic logic, and hence, again, we link up with a recent trend elsewhere in this Handbook.

We think of many of the themes identified in the above as interesting lines of research by themselves, which have by no means been explored to their full extent. In addition to the main business exposed in the separate chapters, it is a side-aim of this Handbook to suggest and further such connections between them.

Johan van Benthem
Alice ter Meulen

CHAPTER 1

Montague Grammar

Barbara H. Partee

University of Massachusetts, Department of Linguistics, Amherst, MA 01003, USA
E-mail: partee@coins.cs.umass.edu

with Herman L.W. Hendriks

Universiteit Utrecht, Research Institute for Language and Speech, Trans 10, 3512 JK Utrecht, The Netherlands
E-mail: herman.hendriks@let.ruu.nl

Commentator: T. Janssen

Contents

HANDBOOK OF LOGIC AND LANGUAGE
Edited by J. van Benthem and A. ter Meulen

1. Introduction

"Montague grammar" is a term that was first applied soon after the untimely death of Richard Montague (September 20, 1930 – March 7, 1971) to an approach to the syntax and semantics of natural languages based on Montague's last three papers (Montague, 1970b, 1970c, 1973). The term may be taken in a narrower or a broader sense, since continuing research has led to a variety of work that can be considered to involve either "developments of" or "departures from" Montague's original theory and practice. In its narrower sense, "Montague grammar", or "MG", means Montague's theory and those extensions and applications of it which remain consistent with most of the principles of that theory. But the boundaries are vague and if taken somewhat more broadly, as the present author (who I believe coined the term) is inclined to do, the term extends to a family of principles and practices which still constitute a large part of the common basis for the field of formal semantics.[1]

The term has never been restricted to Montague's work alone and it should not be, given that Montague was not single-handedly responsible for all of the ideas that were articulated in his papers; others such as David Lewis, Terry Parsons and Max Cresswell were contemporary contributors to more or less the same enterprise, as will be noted below. But Montague's work was particularly influential, in part because of the fact that the three papers just cited give a remarkably clear, concise, and complete statement of a powerful general theory, a good indication of a range of alternative more particular theories and formal tools and three different "fragments" of English that illustrate both the general theory and some of the choices that are available within it.

The plan of this article is to highlight the historical development of Montague grammar as both narrowly and broadly construed, with particular attention to the key ideas that led Montague's work to have such a great impact on subsequent developments. Section 2 outlines the historical context of Montague's work, describing earlier traditions in semantics in logic and philosophy that laid some of the foundations for Montague's work and the contrasting traditions in linguistics, against which Montague's work represented a fundamental and controversial change. Section 3 provides a selective overview of the basic principles and methodology of Montague grammar as laid out in "Universal Grammar" (Montague, 1970c) and some of the highlights of Montague's best-known and most influential paper, "The Proper Treatment of Quantification in Ordinary English" ("PTQ"; Montague, 1973), with brief remarks about Montague's two other fragments (Montague, 1970b, 1970c). In the final section of the paper we discuss the influence of Montague's work and Montague grammar on subsequent developments and theoretical innovations in linguistics and philosophy, illustrate the evolution from "Montague grammar" to a more heterogeneous but interrelated family of theoretical approaches by tracing progress in several key problem areas and venture an assessment of some of the main achievements and controversies that make up Montague's legacy.

[1] The term "formal semantics" has become the dominant name for the field, but is sometimes considered an unfortunate choice, insofar as the "formalist" tradition in logic and mathematics (associated with Hilbert) is a tradition that eschews model-theoretic semantics and pursues a purely syntactic and proof-theoretic approach. "Formal" semantics, like "formal" philosophy as Montague practiced it, is to be understood as contrasted with "informal". Other terms that are broadly applied to Montague grammar and its relatives are "model-theoretic semantics", "truth-conditional semantics", "logical semantics", "logical grammar".

2. Montague Grammar in historical context

It is important to look at the historical context in which Montague grammar developed, since the history of Montague grammar is also the history of the emergence of a new interdisciplinary field, formal semantics. One might reasonably speak of the Montagovian revolution in semantics as a landmark in the development of linguistics comparable to the Chomskyan revolution in generative grammar. The potential for fruitful interaction among linguists, philosophers and logicians had already existed for some time before Montague's work and some cross-fertilization had already taken place, but not until Montague made his foundational contributions was there a satisfactory systematic and comprehensive framework that could support the explosion of fruitful research on natural language semantics and the syntax-semantics interface that has occurred since the publication of his seminal papers.

2.1. Earlier traditions in semantics

Contemporary formal semantics has roots in several disciplines, most importantly logic, philosophy, and linguistics. The central figure in its recent history was Richard Montague, a logician and philosopher whose seminal works in this area date from the late 1960's and the beginning of the 1970's. But Montague's work did not occur in a vacuum, and the development of "Montague grammar" and of formal semantics more generally, has involved contributions from many sources before, during and after Montague's work, sometimes in separate historical strands and sometimes in the form of fruitful interdisciplinary collaboration among linguists, philosophers, logicians, and others, the fruits of which are evident in many of the other chapters in this Handbook.

At the time of Montague's work, semantics had been a lively and controversial field of research for centuries and radically different approaches to it could be found across various disciplines. One source of deep differences was (and still is) the selection of the object of study: there are at least as many different kinds of "central questions" as there are ways in which issues involving meaning may be relevant to a given discipline. Desiderata for a theory of meaning come out quite differently if one focuses on language and thought, or on language and communication, on language and truth, or on language "structure" per se. Here we will restrict our attention to the different traditions that fed into Montague grammar, principally logic, "formal philosophy", and generative grammar. The psychologism prevalent in much of linguistics and fundamental to the Chomskyan research program, contrasts with the anti-psychologism explicitly argued by Frege (1892) and prevalent in the traditions of philosophical logic and model theory from which Montague's work arose. This is bound to lead not only to differences in the nature of the questions being asked (although both are concerned with structure and the relation between form and meaning) but also to serious differences about the terms in which answers might be framed.

A more accidental but no less profound source of differences is the research methodology prevalent in the field within which one approaches questions of semantics. Thus Katz and J.A. Fodor (1963) in the early years of generative linguistics concentrated first on "semantic features", using methodology influenced by phonology to study questions of meaning and structure. Where the logician Quine would say: "Logic chases truth up the tree of grammar" (1970, p. 35), Katz and Fodor were equally seeking a compositional account of how the meanings of sentences were determined from the meanings of the smallest parts and the syntactic derivation of the whole from those parts, but they conceived of semantic projection rules chasing "features", not truth, up the tree of grammar, analyzing meanings as representable in terms of complexes of features rather than in terms of truth conditions. This was the practice David Lewis was deploring on the first page of his 1970 paper "General Semantics":

> But we can know the Markerese translation of an English sentence without knowing the first thing about the meaning of the English sentence: namely, the conditions under which it would be true. Semantics with no treatment of truth conditions is not semantics. Translation into Markerese is at best a substitute for real semantics, relying either on our tacit competence (at some future date) as speakers of Markerese or on our ability to do real semantics at least for the one language Markerese.

I believe linguists did presuppose tacit competence in Markerese and moreover took it to represent a hypothesis about a universal and innate representation, what Jerry (J.A.) Fodor later dubbed the Language of Thought (e.g., Fodor, 1975), and therefore not in need of further interpretation (see Jackendoff (1996) for a contemporary defense of a similar view). The problems that resulted and still result, however, from making up names for operators like "CAUSE" or features like "AGENT" without addressing the formidable problems of defining what they might mean, are evident whenever one looks at disputes that involve the "same" operators as conceived by different linguists or in the analysis of different languages or even different constructions in the same language.

To a philosopher like Vermazen (1967) or Lewis (1970), the language of "markerese" looked empty. To the generative linguist, the concern with truth seemed puzzling: the concern was with mental representation, because semantics was part of the language faculty, the explication of which was the linguist's central concern. The interpretation of (the innate) semantic primitives would be in terms of concepts and the study of details of such interpretation might relate to semantics in something like the way phonetics relates to phonology, involving an interface at which linguistic and non-linguistic (but still psychological) factors might intermingle. "Actual" truth was taken to be irrelevant to semantics and the richer conception behind the notion of truth *conditions* and entailment relations did not come to be widely appreciated within linguistics for some time. Linguists in the 1960's and early 1970's sought accounts of synonymy, antonymy, anomaly and ambiguity, structural notions that concerned such things as how many meanings a given sentence had and which meanings were shared by which sentences. These were kinds of questions which largely concerned sameness and difference of meaning and ways in which meanings are structured and therefore might be fruitfully addressed in terms of representations. Linguistic studies of lexical meaning were sometimes concerned with paraphrase and metonymy, but this did not generalize to any systematic attention to inference or entailment. The increasing influence of truth-conditional semantics on linguistics therefore led to a concomitant gradual shift in the nature of the questions linguists might ask about meanings and not only to a change in the arsenal of tools available for digging out answers.

The truth-conditional tradition in semantics has its source in the work of those logicians and philosophers of language who viewed semantics as the study of the relation between language on the one hand and whatever language is *about* on the other, some domain of interpretation which might be the real world or a part of it, or a hypothesized model of it, or some constructed model in the case of an artificial language. Such philosophers and logicians, at least since Frege, have tended strongly to view semantics non-psychologistically, making a distinction between language and our knowledge of it and generally taking such notions as reference, truth conditions and entailment relations as principal data a semantic description has to get right to reach even minimal standards of adequacy.

Before Montague, most logicians and most linguists (with important exceptions such as (Reichenbach, 1947)) had been agreed, for different reasons, that the apparatus developed by logicians for the syntax and semantics of formal languages was inapplicable to the analysis of natural languages. Logicians considered natural languages too unsystematic, too full of vagueness, ambiguity and irrelevant syntactic idiosyncracies to be amenable to formalization. Logicians also took to heart the warning of Tarski (1944) that natural languages contain their own truth predicate and his argument that such languages could not be consistently formalized.

Those linguists who took note of logicians' formalizations of the syntax and semantics of formal languages tended to reject the logicians' approach for either or both of two reasons: (i) because the formal languages invented and studied by the logicians appeared to be structurally so different from any natural language as to fall outside the bounds of the class of possible human languages and hence to be irrelevant to linguistics,[2] and (ii) because logicians generally eschewed the concern for psychological reality which is so important to most linguists; not only is this difference noticeable in what the notion of "possible language" means to a logician vs. a linguist, but it leads to opposite answers to the basic question of whether truth conditions and entailment relations are central to, or on the contrary irrelevant to, linguistics, given that speakers of a natural language do not always (in fact cannot always) have reliable intuitions about them.

2.2. Developments that made Montague grammar possible

2.2.1. The rise of model-theoretic semantics in philosophy and logic

Within philosophical logic, the foundational work of Frege, Carnap and Tarski led to a flowering in the middle third of this century of work on modal logic and on tense logic, on conditionals, on referential opacity, and on the analysis of other philosophically interesting natural language phenomena. The competition among different modal logics characterized by different axiom systems had led some philosophers like Quine to reject modal and intensional notions as incurably unclear; but the field was revolutionized when Kripke (1959), Kanger (1957a, 1957b), and Hintikka (1962) first provided a

[2] See the rebuff by Chomsky (1955) of the exhortation to collaboration made by Bar-Hillel (1954).

model-theoretic semantics for modal logic, a possible worlds semantics with differences in accessibility relations among worlds serving as the principal parameters distinguishing among different modal logics. Then necessity could be analyzed as truth in all accessible possible worlds and different sorts of accessibility relations (e.g., symmetrical or not, reflexive or not) could be plausibly correlated with different sorts of necessity (logical, deontic, epistemic, etc.), replacing arguments about which is "the right" modal logic with productive investigations of different modal logics and their applications. Carnap (1947) had earlier done something similar but not identical in analyzing (logically) necessary truth as truth in all models, but Kripke argued for the importance of distinguishing between possible models of a language (the basis for the semantical definition of entailment) and possible worlds (possible states of affairs, different ways things might be or might have been) as elements that should be included within a given model to be used in giving a model-theoretic semantics for modal notions.[3]

The distinction between models and worlds is an important one for the semantics of all intensional constructions, but one that is still not always clearly appreciated; see discussion in (Gamut, 1991, Volume II, Chapter 2). Part of the difficulty for students who come to semantics from linguistics rather than from logic is that logicians are accustomed to the freedom of designing formal languages with uninterpreted non-logical vocabulary; the stipulation of alternative models then provides alternative possible interpretations for a given language. Linguists, on the other hand, tend to presuppose that they are studying natural languages as independently existing empirical phenomena and the notion of alternative model-theoretic interpretations for one and the same language is therefore an unfamiliar and unnatural one. For that matter, the early philosophical literature did not always distinguish between Carnapian state descriptions as alternative interpretations for the non-logical vocabulary and as alternative ways the facts might have been. (The distinction between moments or intervals of time and models is intuitively much clearer and invites no such confusion, so it can be helpful to point out to students the analogy between the role of times as elements of models of tensed languages and the role of possible worlds as elements of models of modal languages, an analogy noted below as one of Montague's contributions to the field.)

The resulting extension of model-theoretic techniques into the realm of modal logic led to a great expansion of work in logic and the philosophy of language on quantified modal logic, tense logic, the logic of indexicals and demonstratives, studies of adjectives and adverbs, propositional attitude verbs, conditional sentences and intensionality more generally. With few exceptions, most of this work followed the earlier tradition of not formalizing the relation between the natural language constructions being studied and their logico-semantic analyses: the philosopher-analyst served as a bilingual speaker of both English and the formal language used for analysis; only the formal language would be provided with a model-theoretic semantics. Much insight into the semantic content of natural language expressions was achieved in these studies, but relatively little progress was made on systematically relating semantic content to syntactic structure. For those

[3] Quine was evidently not satisfied by these advances; Quine (1970) expresses as much aversion to intensions as Quine (1960) and Quine (1961), although possible-worlds semanticists generally considered it one of their major accomplishments to have satisfactorily answered the important concerns Quine had raised concerning quantifying into modal contexts.

natural language constructions where the semantically relevant syntactic structure was not perfectly straightforward (which were many), the strategy was "regimentation": the invention and analysis of formal languages which contained syntactically "transparent" analogs of the constructions of interest, languages which met the logician's criterion for being "logically perfect": unambiguous and describable with a unique semantic interpretation rule for each syntactic formation rule.

These developments went along with the rise of the tradition of "logical syntax", or "logical grammar" and the logicians' clean conception, going back to Peirce and Morris and Carnap, of the division of labor among syntax (well-formedness rules), semantics (compositional rules for specifying the truth-theoretic or model-theoretic interpretation of well-formed expressions) and pragmatics (rules or principles relating to the use of expressions in context). This tradition is nicely encapsulated in Donald Kalish's article "Semantics" in the *Encyclopedia of Philosophy* (1967). But although much work in that tradition is inspired by and concerned with issues in the semantics of ordinary language, relatively few attempts were made before Montague's work to apply the logicians' techniques directly and systematically to the grammatical analysis of natural language.

2.2.2. *The Chomskyan revolution*

In the meantime, the Chomskyan revolution in linguistics, commencing with the publication of Chomsky (1957) and in full swing by the mid-1960's, had led to what Bach (1989) has dubbed "Chomsky's Thesis", namely the thesis that English (and other natural languages) could be described on the syntactic level as a formal system. (Bach contrasts this with "Montague's Thesis", the thesis that English can be described as an *interpreted* formal system.) The previously prevalent view that natural languages were too unsystematic to be amenable to formal analysis came to be seen as a matter of not looking below the surface, not appreciating that the apparently bewildering complexity that meets the eye can be the result of the interaction of a complex but not unsystematic set of rules or principles.

Chomsky redefined the central task of linguistics as the explanation of the possibility of language acquisition by the child; as Davidson (1967) also emphasized, the fact that natural languages are infinite but learnable provides one of the most straightforward arguments for the thesis that they must be finitely characterizable. The form of that finite characterization, whether by something like a phrase structure or transformational grammar, a recursive definition, a set of simultaneously satisfied constraints, or something else and with exactly what aspects universal and what aspects subject to cross-linguistic variation, is the central subject matter of syntactic theory and subject to a great deal of ongoing debate and research.

The explosion of work in generative syntax starting in the late 1950's gradually gave rise to interest by linguists in issues of semantics, often driven by problems in syntax. A brief sketch of the situation in semantics within linguistics at the time that Montague's work began to be known to linguists is found in Section 2.4 below.

2.3. *Montague and the idea of "English as a Formal Language"*

Montague was himself an important contributor to the developments in philosophical logic, as well as to areas of mathematical logic such as axiomatic set theory and generalized recursion theory. Montague had been a student of Tarski's at UC Berkeley and as a faculty member at UCLA was a teacher and then a colleague of David Kaplan, co-authored a logic textbook with his colleague Donald Kalish and was an active part of a strong logic group spanning the departments of Philosophy and Mathematics.

Montague did not work single-handedly or in a vacuum: his students included Hans Kamp, Daniel Gallin, Nino Cocchiarella, Frank Vlach, Michael Bennett and Harry Deutsch; and his co-authors included Donald Kalish, Leon Henkin, Alfred Tarski, Robert Vaught, David Kaplan and Rolf Eberle. All of his papers on the development of pragmatics, intensional logic and his theory of grammar, however, are singly authored; but they include numerous acknowledgements to suggestions from others, especially Hans Kamp, David Kaplan, David Lewis and Dan Gallin; also Dana Scott, Rudolph Carnap, Alonzo Church, Yehoshua Bar-Hillel, Charles Chastain, Terence Parsons, the author and others.

Montague did important work on intensional logic, including the unification of tense logic and modal logic and more generally the unification of "formal pragmatics" with intensional logic (Montague, 1968, 1970a). This was accomplished in part by treating both worlds and times as components of "indices" and intensions as functions from indices (not just possible worlds) to extensions. He also generalized the intensional notions of property, proposition, individual concept, etc., into a fully typed intensional logic, extending the work of Carnap (1947), Church (1951) and Kaplan (1964), putting together the function-argument structure common to type theories since Russell with the treatment of intensions as functions to extensions.[4]

Although linguists have focused on Montague's last three papers and it is those that most directly set the framework for formal semantics, a considerable amount of Montague's earlier work was on areas of philosophical logic of direct relevance to issues in semantics and on the logico-philosophical analysis of various concepts that have traditionally been of concern in the philosophy of language: the logic of knowledge and belief, the interpretation of embedded **that**-clauses, syntactic vs. semantic analysis of modal operators, the analysis of events as properties of moments of time and the analysis of obligations and other "philosophical entities" discussed in (Montague, 1969).

It was reportedly[5] the experience of co-authoring Kalish and Montague (1964), a logic textbook, that gave Montague the idea that English should after all be amenable to the same kind of formal treatment as the formal languages of logic. Kalish and Montague took pains to give students explicit guidance in the process of translation from English to first-order logic: rather than the usual informal explanations and examples, they produced an algorithm for step-by-step conversion of sentences of (a subset of) English into formulas of first-order logic. Montague reportedly then reasoned that if translation from English into logic could be formalized, it must also be possible to formalize the

---

[4] The variant type system Ty2 of Gallin (1975) is a possibly more perspicuous version of Montague's typed intensional logic, especially with respect to explicitly showing the ubiquity of function-argument structure in the analysis of intensions. See Turner's "Type Theory" chapter in this Handbook for fuller discussion of type theories; particular issues will be mentioned at various points below.

[5] I recall learning this from one of Montague's UCLA colleagues or former students, but I no longer recall who: probably David Lewis or David Kaplan or Michael Bennett or Hans Kamp, but my misty memory makes a proper acknowledgement impossible.

syntax and semantics of English directly, without proceeding via an intermediate logical language. This led to the provocatively titled paper "English as a Formal Language" (EFL; Montague, 1970b), which contains the first statement of what Bach (1989) dubbed "Montague's Thesis", that English can be described as an interpreted formal system: EFL begins with the famous sentence "I reject the contention that an important theoretical difference exists between formal and natural languages" (Montague, 1974, p. 188). As noted by Bach, the term "theoretical" here must be understood from a logician's perspective and not from a linguist's. What Montague was denying was the logicians' and philosophers' common belief that natural languages were not directly amenable to formalization. What he was proposing, in this paper and even more systematically in (Montague, 1970c), was a framework for describing syntax and semantics and the relation between them that he considered compatible with existing practice for formal languages (in the tradition of "logical grammar" mentioned earlier) and an improvement on existing practice for the description of natural language.

Montague was aware of Chomsky's innovations in syntax but was puzzled and somewhat put off by the generative grammarians' practice of studying syntax without simultaneous attention to semantics. (See footnote 13 below for an excerpt from one of Montague's notorious footnotes offering his unsympathetic opinion of the Chomskyan enterprise.) While Montague's broad conception of "universal grammar" was closer to the notion of "logically possible grammar" than to the Chomskyan notion of universal grammar, which is tied to the aim of demarcating the humanly possible languages as a subset of the logically possible ones, linguists such as the present author argued that a linguistic conception of universal grammar could in principle be identified with a constrained subtheory of Montague's theory, the linguist's task being to identify further constraints on the syntactic and semantic rules and on the nature of the correspondence between them (Partee, 1976b, 1979a). Chomsky himself remained skeptical.[6] The central properties of Montague's framework are the subject of Section 3 and the impact of his work is discussed in Section 4.

2.4. *Semantics in linguistics before Montague and the introduction of Montague's work into linguistics*

Semantics in linguistics before the Chomskyan revolution, like semantics in parts of anthropology and psychology, was largely concerned with the decompositional analysis of lexical meaning. A central goal in such approaches to lexical semantics was and still is to identify semantic "distinctive features" or semantic "atoms" which combine to form lexical meanings, with heated but seemingly endless debates about whether total decomposability into such atoms is possible at all and about the universality or non-universality of the "semantic primitives" of natural languages. (A problem for such debates has been the difficulty of finding common starting points on which both sides

---

[6] There were no immediate reactions to Montague's work by Chomsky in print, but one can see a consistent line from Chomsky (1955) to the anti-compositionality arguments of Chomsky (1975); Chomsky may also have shared the general "East Coast" skepticism to possible-worlds semantics and intensional logic articulated by Quine and others.

might agree and the concomitant difficulty of identifying what kinds of empirical evidence could be brought to bear on the question.)

The increasingly dominant impact of syntax on the whole field soon led to focus on questions such as the relation between syntactic and semantic ambiguity, the issue of whether transformations preserve meaning and other such structural questions which can be explored relatively independently of the issue of "what meanings are"; semantic representations were often modeled on syntactic tree structures (sometimes influenced by the syntax of some logic) and in some theories were (and are) taken to be identical with some level of syntactic structures (e.g., the underlying structures of Generative Semantics or the level of Logical Form of GB syntax).

In the first years of generative grammar, as noted above, the key semantic properties of sentences were taken to be ambiguity, anomaly, and synonymy, analyzed in terms of how many readings a given sentence has and which sentences share which readings (Katz and J.A. Fodor, 1963; Chomsky, 1965).

The impact of philosophy and logic on semantics in linguistic work of the 1950's and 1960's was limited; many linguists knew some first-order logic, aspects of which began to be borrowed into linguists' "semantic representations" and there was gradually increasing awareness of the work of some philosophers of language.[7] While Chomsky alternated between general skepticism about the possibility of putting semantics on a rigorous footing and tentative endorsement of attempts by J.A. Fodor, Katz and Postal to map syntactic structures from one or more levels in some compositional way onto semantic representations, generative semanticists in the late 1960's and early 1970's in particular started giving serious attention to issues of "logical form" in relation to grammar and to propose ever more abstract underlying representations intended to serve simultaneously as unambiguous semantic representations and as input to the transformational mapping from meaning to surface form (see, for instance, Bach, 1968; Fillmore, 1968; Karttunen, 1969; Lakoff, 1968, 1971, 1972). But linguists' semantic representations were generally not suggested to be in need of further interpretation and truth conditions and entailment relations were never explicitly mentioned as an object of study in the indigenously linguistic traditions that existed before formal semantics came into linguistics in the 1970's.

By the late 1960's, linguists were intensely debating the question of what level or levels of syntactic representation should provide the input to semantic interpretation. The generative semanticists had rejected the idea that syntax should be studied independently of semantics and had moved almost to an opposite extreme which to some researchers appeared to give too little weight to syntactic evidence and too much weight to raw intuitions about underlying semantic structure, possibly influenced by the structure of first-order logic. Interpretive semantics, under the lead of Chomsky and Jackendoff, maintained the principle of the autonomy of syntax both in terms of grammatical description (syntax can be described without appeal to semantic notions) and in terms of

[7] See for instance the references to Lewis (1968) in (Lakoff, 1968), to Geach (1962) in (Karttunen, 1969), to Donnellan (1966) in (Partee, 1970a) and the evidence of awareness of logical and philosophical concerns in (Keenan, 1971a, 1971b; Karttunen, 1971; McCawley, 1971; Bach, 1968), and the volume (Davidson and Harman, 1972), in part a proceedings from one of the earliest linguistics and philosophy conferences (in 1969), one to which Montague was not invited.

argumentation (the choice among competing syntactic analyses can be made independently of evidence from semantics) and explored hypotheses about the syntactic input to semantics that ranged from surface structure only to multiple inputs from multiple syntactic levels.

Montague was doing his work on natural language at the height of the "linguistic wars" between generative and interpretive semantics (see J.D. Fodor, 1980; Newmeyer, 1980; Harris, 1993), though Montague and the semanticists in linguistics had no awareness of one another. (Montague was aware of Chomsky's work and respected its aim for rigor but was skeptical about the fruitfulness of studying syntax in isolation from semantics (see footnote 13 below).) As argued in (Partee, 1973b, 1975), one of the potential attractions of Montague's work for linguistics was that it offered an interestingly different view of the relation between syntax and semantics that might be able to accommodate the best aspects of both of the warring approaches. The PTQ instantiation of Montague's algebraic theory illustrates what Bach (1976) christened the "rule-by-rule" approach to the syntax-semantics correspondence: syntactic rules put expressions (or expressions-cum-structures, see Partee, 1975) together to form more complex expressions and corresponding semantic rules interpret the whole as a function of the interpretations of the corresponding parts. This is quite different from both generative and interpretive semantics, which were framed in terms of the prevailing conception of syntactic derivations from some kind of phrase-structure-generated underlying structures via transformations to surface structures, with the debate centered on which level(s) of syntactic representations provided the basis for semantic interpretation. The closest linguistic analog to Montague's rule-by-rule approach was in Katz and J.A. Fodor's (1963) proposal for compositional interpretation of Chomsky's T-markers (deep structure P-markers plus transformational history), but that approach was abandoned as too unrestrictive once Katz and Postal (1964) had introduced the hypothesis that transformations might be meaning-preserving, a hypothesis that in a sense defines generative semantics. Interpretive semantics did not go back to the derivational T-marker correspondence of early Katz and Fodor,[8] but rather focused on the level of surface structure and the question of what other levels of syntactic representation might have to feed into semantic interpretation (Jackendoff, 1972).

The earliest introduction of Montague's work to linguists came via Partee (1973a, 1973b, 1975) and Thomason (1974),[9] where it was argued that Montague's work might allow the syntactic structures generated to be relatively conservative ("syntactically motivated") and with relatively minimal departure from direct generation of surface structure, while offering a principled way to address the semantic concerns such as scope ambiguity that motivated some of the best work in generative semantics.

While "Montague grammar" was undoubtedly the principal vehicle by which the influence of model-theoretic semantics came into linguistics, there were other more or

[8] See Bach's (1976, 1979b) reexamination of generalized transformations in this context.

[9] The author sat in on some of Montague's seminars at UCLA along with David Lewis, who was very helpful in interpreting Montague to her, as was David Kaplan over the next several years. The 1970 two-part workshop at which Montague presented PTQ in September and Partee (1973a) was presented as commentary in December took place only months before Montague's untimely death. Partee and Thomason discussed potential linguistic applications of Montague grammar with each other and with other philosophers of language at an institute in philosophy of language and linguistics organized by Davidson and Harman at the University of California, Irvine in the summer of 1971.

less connected lines of similar research which contributed to the ensuing cooperative linguistics-philosophy enterprise. The work of David Lewis is important in this regard, both because Lewis, who knew the work of Chomsky and other linguists quite well, was an important influence on Montague's own work via conversations and his participation in Montague's seminars and because Lewis (1968, 1969, 1970) presented many of the same kinds of ideas in a form much more accessible to linguists. Cresswell (1973) was another related work, a book-length treatment of a similar semantic program, with a great deal of valuable discussion of both foundational issues and many specific grammatical constructions. Also Parsons (1972), Keenan (1971a, 1971b) and Thomason and Stalnaker (1973) were early and active contributors to linguistics-logic-philosophy exchanges. The 1973 conference at Cambridge University which led to the collection Keenan (ed.) (1975) was the first international meeting devoted to formal semantics and the 1977 conference at SUNY Albany which led to the collection Davis and Mithun (eds) (1979) was the first international formal semantics conference in the U.S. By the time of the latter conference, Montague grammar had become the dominant if not exclusive reference point for cooperative work by linguists, philosophers and logicians working on the formal semantics of natural language.

3. The theory and the substance

The paper of Montague's that had the most impact on linguists and on the subsequent development of formal semantics in general, was PTQ (Montague, 1973): 24 pages long, but densely packed. To many, "Montague Grammar" has probably meant what Montague did in the fragment in PTQ and the extensions of PTQ by subsequent linguists and philosophers with greater and lesser innovations, but it is the broader algebraic framework of "UG" ("Universal Grammar"; Montague, 1970c) that constitutes Montague's theory of grammar. We therefore begin this section with a discussion of the basic principles laid out in UG, concentrating on the implications of treating syntax and semantics as algebras and compositionality as the requirement of a homomorphism between them. In Section 3.2 we take up issues of model theory and the difference between direct model-theoretic interpretation and indirect interpretation via translation into an intermediate language such as the language of Montague's intensional logic (IL). Section 3.3 concerns issues of type theory, intensionality and choices of model structures. All of the issues discussed in these first three sections represent perspectives on semantics that were generally unknown to linguists (and even to many philosophers) before Montague's work but have become central to the foundations of contemporary formal semantics. In Section 3.4 we turn to the classic paper PTQ, focusing discussion on features of Montague's analysis that were particularly novel, either absolutely or for most working linguists, and which had a major impact on later work in the field. Finally, in Section 3.5, we include some brief notes on the fragments contained in Montague's two 1970 papers, EFL and UG, since a comparison of Montague's three fragments can be very helpful for distinguishing between general requirements of Montague's theoretical framework and particular choices made by Montague in PTQ and also because those often-neglected papers contain a number of ideas and analyses that are not duplicated in PTQ.

3.1. Universal Grammar: Syntax as algebra, semantics as algebra, compositionality as homomorphism

Montague's paper "Universal Grammar" (UG; Montague, 1970c) contains the most general statement of Montague's formal framework for the description of language.[10] The central idea is that anything that should count as a grammar should be able to be cast in the following form: the syntax is an algebra, the semantics is an algebra and there is a homomorphism mapping elements of the syntactic algebra onto elements of the semantic algebra.

The algebraic perspective is a generalization of the logician's approach to grammar in terms of recursive definitions. It is also a perspective which linguists should in principle find congenial, since it focuses on the structure of the syntax and of the semantics and of the relation between them, remaining quite neutral about the particulars of content, ontological commitment, epistemological grounding, etc. In principle it is a perspective that is entirely neutral with respect to whether grammars are in the head or are Platonic abstract entities, or other such foundational questions which may divide theorists who can nevertheless engage fruitfully in arguments about the syntax and semantics of various constructions.[11] The algebraic perspective therefore offers a good common ground, at least in principle, for logicians, linguists and philosophers of language and this aspect of Montague's contribution has indeed been valuable, even though relatively few researchers present analyses in explicitly algebraic form.

The syntactic algebra contains elements (expressions) and operations which apply to tuples of expressions to yield other expressions; the language, in the simplest case, is the set of all expressions which can be formed by starting from some basic expressions (the generators of the algebra) and applying operations in all possible ways; that is, it is the closure of the generator set under the operations of the algebra. The semantic algebra is similarly conceived. The homomorphism requirement is the compositionality requirement (more below); the fact that it is a homomorphism requirement and not an isomorphism requirement means that distinct syntactic expressions may have the same meaning, but each syntactic expression must have only one meaning. The requirement is thus that there be a many-one relationship between expressions and meanings and not a requirement of a one-one relationship, although the compositionality requirement has sometimes mistakenly been described this way (e.g., in Partee, 1973b). A brief pedagogical introduction to the algebraic formulation of the UG framework can be found in (Partee, Ter Meulen and Wall, 1990); more can be found in the three references cited in footnote 10.

[10] Three good references include Halvorsen and Ladusaw (1979), an early expository introduction for linguists; Link (1979), an introductory text in German which is particularly rich in showing how various familiar fragments would look when spelled out in the algebraic terms of UG; and Janssen (1986a, 1986b), in English, which includes a good discussion of exactly what the UG framework amounts to, what compositionality means in the theory of UG and what sorts of analyses the UG framework permits and excludes.

[11] When I once mentioned to Montague the linguist's preferred conception of universal grammar as the characterization of all and only possible human languages, his reaction was to express surprise that linguists should wish to disqualify themselves on principle from being the relevant scientists to call on if some extraterrestrial beings turn out to have some kind of language.

This very general definition leaves a great deal of freedom as to what sorts of things the elements and the operations of these algebras are. As for the syntactic algebra, in the case of a typical logical language the elements can be the well-formed expressions, but in the case of a natural language, ambiguity makes that impossible, since the homomorphism requirement means that each element of the syntactic algebra must be mapped onto a unique element of the semantic algebra[12] (the shorthand terminology for this is that the syntax must provide a "disambiguated language"). In the PTQ grammar for a fragment of English, the syntax is not explicitly presented as an algebra, but could be transformed into one; the elements of the syntactic algebra could not be the expressions, since many are ambiguous, but could be the analysis trees (Partee, 1973b). Montague allows for the grammar to include an "ambiguating relation" mapping elements of the syntactic algebra onto the actual ("surface") expressions of the language; as McCawley (1979) notes, if it were the case that a generative semantics deep structure were the right level to interpret compositionally, the entire transformational component mapping deep structures onto surface structures (plus a tree-wipeout rule to yield surface strings) could be the description of such an ambiguating relation.

The relation between a linguist's syntactic component and syntax as an algebra is not always easy to see and it can be non-trivial to determine whether and how a given syntax can be presented as an algebra, and more particularly, as an algebra homomorphic to a corresponding semantic algebra. The core issue is compositionality, since for Montague, the central function of syntax is not simply to generate the well-formed expressions of a language but to do so in such a way as to provide the necessary structural basis for their semantic interpretation.[13] Some kinds of non-transformational grammars such as Generalized Phrase Structure Grammar (Gazdar, Klein, Pullum and Sag, 1985), Head-Driven Phrase Structure Grammar (Pollard and Sag, 1987, 1994), and the various categorial grammar frameworks (see the chapter on Categorial Grammar in this Handbook) are among the clearest examples of "linguists' grammars" that are more or less consistent with the requirements of Montague's UG. A simple context-free grammar is the most

[12] Actually, there is a way of respecting the homomorphism requirement while working with semantically ambiguous expressions. It is standard in mathematics to turn a (one-many) relation into a function by making it a set-valued function. This method is employed, for instance, by Cooper (1975), who takes "sets of (standard) meanings" as the semantic objects, mapping each (possibly ambiguous) linguistic expression onto the semantic object which consists of all of its possible meanings; not all kinds of ambiguity are amenable in a natural way to this kind of treatment, but Cooper's device of "quantifier storage" for handling scope ambiguities for which there is no independent evidence of syntactic ambiguities is one of the serious options in this domain. The same general strategy for working directly with ambiguous expressions is employed by Hendriks (1988, 1993) to deal with the multiplicity of readings made available by type-lifting principles and in (Rosetta, 1994) to turn translations from English into Dutch and Spanish into functions. Thanks to Theo Janssen for pointing out to me the general principle behind all these cases.

[13] "It appears to me that the syntactical analyses of particular fragmentary languages that have been suggested by transformational grammarians, even if successful in correctly characterizing the declarative sentences of those languages, will prove to lack semantic relevance; and I fail to see any great interest in syntax except as a preliminary to semantics." (From the notorious footnote 2 of UG, p. 223 in (Montague, 1974).) Footnote 2, which goes on to criticize other aspects of "existing syntactical efforts by Chomsky and his associates", was not designed to endear Montague to generative linguists, although in the beginning of the paper he does present himself as agreeing more with Chomsky than with many philosophers about the goals of formal theories of syntax and semantics.

straightforward kind of grammar to convert to an equivalent algebra, since its surface phrase structure trees are isomorphic to its derivation trees.

The choice for the semantic elements is totally free, as long as they make up an algebra, i.e. as long as there is a well-defined set of elements and well-defined operations that have elements of the algebra as operands and values. The semantic elements, or "semantic values" as they are often called, could be taken to be the model-theoretic constructs of possible-worlds semantics as in Montague's fragments of English and most "classical" formal semantics, or the file change potentials of Heim (1982), or the game strategies of game-theoretical semantics, or the simple extensional domains of first-order logic, or hypothesized psychological concepts, or expressions in a "language of thought", or bundles of features, or anything else; what is constrained is not the "substance" of the semantics but some properties of its structure and of its relation to syntactic structure.

While there is no direct constraint on the kinds of things that make up the elements of a semantic algebra, there is nevertheless a further requirement that relates to truth conditions. An important guiding principle of the UG framework and at the heart of Montague's semantics, inherited from the traditions of logic and model theory and transmitted as one of the defining principles of formal semantics, is the principle that truth conditions and entailment relations are the basic semantic data, the phenomena that have to be accounted for to reach a minimal level of adequacy. Although UG gives a very unconstrained specification of the notion of a semantic algebra, under the heading "Theory of Meaning", it also provides, under the heading "Theory of Reference", a specification of the notion of a "Fregean interpretation"; a semantic algebra cannot form part of a Fregean interpretation unless it can be connected to an assignment of truth conditions in a specified way. An algebra whose elements were expressions in a "language of thought" would probably not directly be construable as properly semantic in that stronger sense and would probably fit better into the category of "intermediate language" in the sense of Section 3.2 below. The same is undoubtedly true *a fortiori* of a linguistic representational level such as the level of "LF" in a contemporary Chomskyan framework.

It is the homomorphism requirement, which is in effect the compositionality requirement, that provides one of the most important constraints on UG in Montague's sense and it is therefore appropriate that compositionality is frequently at the heart of controversies concerning formal semantics, including internal theoretical controversies concerning the appropriate formulation of the requirement and its implications for theories of formal semantics, external controversies concerning whether natural languages are best described or even reasonably described as compositional and "applications" controversies concerning whether a given analysis is or is not compositional (often a debate concerning whether a somewhat informally presented analysis could be given a compositional formulation).

The compositionality requirement, sometimes called Frege's principle (see Janssen, 1986a, for discussion) can be stated in plain language as follows:

> *The Principle of Compositionality*:
> The meaning of a complex expression is a function of the meanings of its parts and of the way they are syntactically combined.

Construed broadly and vaguely enough, the principle has sometimes seemed uncontroversial,[14] but Montague's precise version of it places strong constraints on admissible systems of syntax and semantics. As the wording given above suggests, the exact import of the compositionality principle depends on how one makes precise the notions of *meaning*, of *part* and of *syntactic combination*, as well as on the class of functions permitted to instantiate the "is a function of" requirement.

In the specification of formal languages, the compositionality principle is generally satisfied in the following way: the syntax is given by a recursive specification, starting with a stipulation of basic expressions of given categories and with recursive rules of the following sort:

> *Syntactic Rule n*:
> If α is a well-formed expression of category A and β is a well-formed expression of category B, then γ is a well-formed expression of category C, where $\gamma = F_i(\alpha, \beta)$.

In such a rule, F_i is a syntactic operation; it may be as simple as concatenation or, as far as the requirements of UG are concerned, arbitrarily complex and not even necessarily computable. It is the job of a linguistic theory of syntax to put further requirements on the nature of syntactic categories and syntactic operations.

The semantics is then given by a parallel recursive specification, including a stipulation of the semantic values for the basic expressions and for each syntactic rule n a single semantic rule of the following form:

> *Semantic Rule n*:
> If α is interpreted as α' and β is interpreted as β', then γ is interpreted as γ', where $\gamma' = G_k(\alpha', \beta')$.

In such a rule, G_k is a semantic operation; in typical examples it may be something like function-argument application, set intersection, or function composition, though that too is totally unconstrained by the theory of UG; it is up to a linguistic theory of semantics to specify the available semantic operations and any formal or substantive constraints on which semantic operations are used in the interpretation of which syntactic constructions.

This way of implementing the compositionality requirement in terms of corresponding recursive rule specifications of syntax and semantics has been dubbed by Bach (1976) the requirement of "rule-by-rule interpretation" and it is the form in which Montague grammars are most commonly instantiated.

When the systems of rules that make up the syntax and the semantics are recast as algebras, the requirement of rule-by-rule correspondence becomes the requirement of homomorphism. As the schematic illustration of the rule-by-rule correspondence requirement above illustrates, the homomorphism requirement applies at the level of rules, or

[14] But in fact even the most general form of the compositionality principle has been controversial; see discussion in Janssen's chapter on Compositionality.

derivation trees, not at the level of the particular syntactic or semantic operations employed in the rules. This is frequently a point of confusion for novices, understandably, since the *operations* of the syntactic algebra are the *rules* or *constructions* of the syntax and not what are normally referred to (including in the preceding paragraphs) as syntactic operations. But it is clear that while there may be a uniform compositional interpretation of the Subject-Predicate combining rule (that's a non-trivial challenge already!), there could not be not expected to be a uniform semantic interpretation of a syntactic operation such as concatenation, a syntactic operation which may be common to many rules. And of course it can make a big difference to the possibility of meeting the homomorphism requirement whether the elements of the syntactic algebra are taken to be strings, bracketed strings, labeled bracketed strings, or some other kind of abstract structures and what kinds of syntactic operations are allowed in the syntactic rules.

For a fuller discussion of the compositionality requirement, its various formulations, its place in various theories of formal syntax and semantics in addition to classical Montague grammar and discussion of its status as a methodological or an empirical principle, see the Compositionality chapter in this Handbook. With respect to the last point, most formal semanticists have come to agree with the claims of Gamut (1991) and Janssen (1986a) that the principle is so deeply constitutive of Montague grammar and most of its close relatives that it must be considered to be a methodological principle: there is no way to test it without testing an entire theory in which it is embedded. So the claim that natural languages have a compositional semantics amounts to a claim that natural languages can be fruitfully described with a theory that includes compositionality as one of its principles. (In this respect debates about compositionality are analogous to debates between transformational and non-transformational grammars, for instance; it is not that they can't be debated or that empirical evidence is not relevant, it is just that it is whole theories that must be evaluated.)

Some discussion of "external" controversies surrounding the Principle of Compositionality and initial skepticism among linguists, is found in Section 4.1. Some of the "internal" controversies will be touched on in various sections below in the context of discussions of specific constructions and of the development of various "post-Montague" theories.

Very few linguists and not very many philosophers or logicians have wrestled with the technically difficult presentation of Montague's theory as presented in "UG"; the author has made a few forays into the ring, but does not claim to have mastered it, relying for difficult points on the colleagues whose works are cited above.[15] Nevertheless, the basic ideas of the algebraic approach and the homomorphism requirement are not difficult to grasp and can be a very useful way to look at grammar. Partly similar approaches to looking at syntactic structure in terms of algebras, or derivational history, or analysis trees, or "constructions", can be found in the conception of T-markers noted in Section 2.4 above and at various points in the work of Zellig Harris, Hugh Matthews, Sebastian Shaumjan, Pavel Tichý and Prague school colleagues such as Pavel Materna and Petr Sgall and very clearly in the theory of Tree-Adjoining Grammars (TAGs) of Joshi and

[15] For that reason and also for the sake of brevity, the discussion of UG presented here is somewhat oversimplified. Issues left aside include the role of polynomials in stating the homomorphism requirement precisely, the distinctions among models, model structures and interpretations and of course all of the exact definitions.

his colleagues (Joshi, 1985; Joshi, Vijay-Shanker and Weir, 1991), where the difference between the derivation tree and the derived constituent structure tree is especially vivid. It is a conception that may be natural not only from a formal language point of view, but also from a typological perspective, since languages may often be fruitfully compared at the level of constructions, or rules in Montague's sense, in cases where the input and output categories for a family of counterpart constructions are the same and the semantic interpretation of these constructions in different languages is the same or similar, but the syntactic operations involved are different. For instance, "Yes-No questions" may be a common construction to find cross-linguistically but may be realized by the addition of a morpheme in one language, by reduplication of a specified part in another, by a rearrangement of word order in another, by application of a certain intonational contour in another, or by a composition of two or more such operations. Rosetta (1994), described briefly below in Section 3.4.7, discusses and demonstrates the fruitfulness of making explicit cross-linguistic correspondences at the level of derivation trees as part of a project of compositional translation.

3.2. Model theory; direct and indirect interpretation

"Universal Grammar" presents formal frameworks for both "direct" and "indirect" semantic interpretation, differing with respect to whether an "intermediate language" (such as the language of Montague's Intensional Logic) is employed or whether the language in question is given a direct model-theoretic interpretation. Relevant notions of compositionality are defined for each.

Direct interpretation is what was described in the preceding section, involving the homomorphic mapping of a syntactic algebra onto a semantic algebra. The semantic algebra in the normal case is a model-theoretic structure, containing domains with a typed structure. For each syntactic category, there must be a domain of possible interpretations for expressions of that category and the relation of syntactic categories to these semantic types must also be a homomorphism. For a simple formal language like the language of first-order logic, the semantic domains may consist just of a domain of entities, a domain of truth values and domains of sets of n-tuples of entities serving as the domains of possible interpretations of n-place predicates. In EFL, the only fragment in which Montague gave a direct model-theoretic interpretation of English, two basic semantic categories are used: a set of possible individuals as the domain of possible denotations of "name phrases", and a domain of sets of possible worlds, or propositions, as the domain for possible denotation of formulas; each of the other six semantic categories used for EFL is defined as the set of functions from an n-tuple (for a certain n) of particular semantic categories to a particular semantic category. (Examples of direct interpretation can also be found in the work of Cresswell, Von Stechow and Kratzer.)

Direct interpretation compositionally determines truth conditions for the expressions of the category "sentence" or "formula" and hence also determines entailment relations among the sentences or formulas of a given language. Indirect interpretation proceeds via translation into an intermediate language, as in Montague's grammars for fragments of English in UG and PTQ, where the intermediate language is a version of his Intensional Logic.

For "indirect" semantic interpretation, the notion of compositional translation is defined; as expected, this involves a requirement of homomorphism between two syntactic algebras, one for the source language and one for the target language, the intermediate language. The intermediate language must then be interpreted by means of a homomorphism from its own syntactic algebra to a semantic algebra in the earlier sense. Translation is iterable and any number of intermediate languages could be invoked, as long as the last in the chain is given a Fregean interpretation. (See the application of this idea in (Rosetta, 1994), where since the goal is actually translation from one natural language to another, the step of providing a Fregean interpretation is not included.)

When both the translation into an intermediate language and the semantic interpretation of that intermediate language are compositional, the intermediate language is in principle dispensable, since the composition of those two homomorphisms amounts to a direct compositional interpretation of the original language.

There may be various reasons for providing a semantics for a natural language via translation into an intermediate language. Montague viewed the use of an intermediate language as motivated by increased perspicuity in presentation and by the expectation (which has been amply realized in practice) that a sufficiently well-designed language such as his Intensional Logic with a known semantics could provide a convenient tool for giving the semantics of various fragments of various natural languages. Linguists with a Chomskyan background tend to be interested in the psychological reality of some level of "semantic representation" and hope to find evidence for or against the existence of some intermediate level and to discover its syntactic properties if it exists. Not surprisingly, direct empirical evidence for or against such levels is hard to find and the positing of an intermediate level is therefore another good candidate for a methodological principle rather than an empirical hypothesis. Linguists who work with a level of "LF" do not usually reach that level via a compositional translation from a disambiguated syntax, so the linguist's LF is not an intermediate language in the sense of UG.[16] Evidence for an intermediate language in the sense of UG would be particularly hard to find in any straightforward way, given that compositionality requirements force the intermediate language to be dispensable in principle.

3.3. Type theory and intensionality

Montague's general framework leaves wide latitude for choices at many points, including in particular many choices about the nature of the model structures which make up the semantic algebras. The choices involved in the semantic algebras are of two main sorts: structural and ontological. The structural choices involve the type theory and the choices of semantic operations; the ontological choices concern principally the nature of the

[16] Applications of formal semantics to theories including a Chomskyan level of LF usually take the language of LF as the language to be semantically interpreted; the LF language itself can be given a straightforward context-free grammar and can then be compositionally provided with a model-theoretic interpretation. Whether the rest of the syntax that pairs possible LFs with possible surface forms or phonological forms can be construed as a complex instantiation of Montague's "ambiguating relation" is an open question which to my knowledge is unexplored.

basic elements, such as a domain of entities or of possible entities, a domain of moments or intervals of time, a domain of truth values, a domain of possible worlds, etc.

Certain choices made by Montague have become conventionally associated with Montague grammar but are not essential to Montague's theory. The possible-worlds analysis of intensionality, for instance, while not essential to the algebraic conception of grammar presented in UG, was central to much of Montague's work, not only in his three "grammar" papers, and in practice is often regarded as if it were an inherent aspect of Montague grammar. Only in more recent times has there been a critical mass of researchers with enough background in both linguistics and model theory to begin to evaluate alternative choices in ways that are responsive to both linguistic and formal concerns.[17]

In this section we note some of the particular choices made by Montague in the realm of semantic structures that seem particularly interesting in hindsight, including the selection of model structures and their basic elements and issues of type theory, particularly Montague's use of functional types, which led to the heavy use of the lambda calculus in MG.

Montague did not present exactly the same type theory in all of his work, but the different systems are similar. What all type theories have in common is some selection of primitive types, some means for defining non-primitive types and a model-theoretic interpretation of the basic types and of the defined types.

Montague usually took as his primitive types the two types e and t, and his defined types always included some kinds of functional types and sometimes included a particular device for forming intensional types. The interpretation of the two basic types was different in different papers and even so did not exhaust the range of choices which could be made. Correspondence between Montague and Dana Scott[18] includes discussion of whether the domain corresponding to the type e should be a single world-independent domain of "possible individuals" (intuitively, the collection of all of the individuals that exist in any world), or whether there should be a domain of individuals assigned to each possible world; that issue was a matter of lively debate in the development of quantified modal logic (see Hughes and Cresswell, 1968; Chellas, 1980; and Gamut, 1991, Volume II, Chapter 3). Montague's eventual choice of working with a single domain of world-independent individuals seems to have been motivated in part by his desire to treat verbs such as **worship**, **remember** and **seek** as simple transitive verbs and names as rigid designators; he did not want to have to syntactically decompose sentences such as **Jones worships Zeus** or **Smith still remembers Einstein** with analyses involving embedded propositions with embedded modal operators and descriptions in place of the names.[19]

---

[17] In the early years of Montague grammar when linguists like the author were asked questions like "why do you used a typed rather than an untyped lambda calculus?", we did not have the training to answer and were completely dependent on choices made by our logician friends, who in turn were motivated by considerations that rested on a deep knowledge of logic but a shallow knowledge of linguistics. It is clearly important to localize at least some interdisciplinary competence inside single heads, as happens more frequently for these fields now.

[18] Part of Scott's side of that correspondence was presented in published form in (Scott, 1970); see also Hintikka (1970).

[19] But see Montague's footnote 8 in PTQ for a careful statement of division of labor between semantical analysis and philosophical argumentation: "If there are individuals that are only possible but not actual, A [i.e. the domain corresponding to the type e] is to contain them; but this is an issue on which it would be unethical for me as a logician (or linguist or grammarian or semanticist, for that matter) to take a stand".

But while most formal semanticists have followed Montague's practice of working with a single domain of world-independent individuals, the issues here remain difficult and complexly interwoven, including issues concerning existence and the interpretation of the existential operator, differences between verbs like **worship** and verbs like **seek** (Bennett, 1974), the semantics of proper names, the ontological status of "situations".[20]

The interpretation of the other basic type, t, is subject to well-known variation. In the systems of PTQ and UG, the associated domain is simply the two-element set consisting of the truth values 0 and 1; all intensional types are complex types of the form $\langle s, a\rangle$ for some type a. In the system of EFL, the universes of possible denotations corresponding to the two basic semantic categories are the set of possible individuals and the set of functions from possible worlds to truth values, or propositions. In the EFL system, as in Cresswell's lambda-categorial languages (Cresswell, 1973; and later works), the basic type t is interpreted as the type of propositions, which for Montague are again identified with functions from possible worlds to truth values.

It is frequently noted that the Boolean structure evident from the cross-categorial generality of **and**, **or** and **not** is good evidence that whatever the interpretation of type t is, it should form a Boolean structure and that, furthermore, the types of many other major syntactic categories should systematically reflect a similar Boolean structure (see Keenan and Faltz, 1985; Partee and Rooth, 1983). Both of Montague's choices, the set $\{0, 1\}$ and the set of functions from possible worlds to truth values, can be interpreted as Boolean algebras and the same holds for various other candidate interpretations for type t such as the set of sets of assignments (taking as the interpretation of a given formula the set of assignments that satisfy it). It is because of the need for Boolean structure that it is problematical to try to work with sets of truth values construed as real or rational numbers in the interval $[0, 1]$ (as has been proposed in some approaches to "fuzzy logic"), but there are other ways to structure analogs of "intermediate truth values" that do respect Boolean structure by working with "logical spaces" to which linear values can derivatively be assigned as measures (see Kamp and Partee, 1995).

For a natural language, the family of syntactic categories and corresponding semantic domains may be so rich that it is simplest to define an infinite system of domains recursively via a type theory and then only use the ones that are actually needed in a given fragment of grammar. In EFL, eight semantic domains were individually defined, although there was clearly a pattern evident, which was generalized in the systems of UG and PTQ. In UG and PTQ, Montague had two type-forming rules: a rule which would produce a functional type $\langle a, b\rangle$ from any two types a and b, with denotations as functions from type a to type b; and a rule which would produce an intensional type $\langle s, a\rangle$ from any type a, with denotations as functions from possible worlds (or more generally, indices, which might be worlds, times, world-time pairs, or other choices in a given interpretation) to denotations of type a. Both of these complex types are functional

[20] The widespread adoption of Montague's practice has not been the result of much explicit argument. Explicit argument on the side of adopting Lewis's counterpart theory and combining it with a theory of situations as parts of worlds can be found in (Kratzer, 1989) and the debates between Lewis (1973) and Kripke (1972), among others, concerning Lewis's counterpart theory with its world-bound individuals. There are also very interesting ontological issues that arise in applications of possible-worlds semantics in the field of poetics and the semantics of fictional language; see Parsons (1980), Pavel (1986).

types; the only difference is that the type s has no independent existence. Possible worlds are taken to be ingredients of model structures and tools for the definition of intensionality, but never themselves a domain of possible interpretations for any category of expressions.

An alternative closely related but interestingly different type structure is Gallin's Ty2: it differs from the type structure of Montague's intensional logic in taking e, t and s as basic types and having the formation of functional types $\langle a, b\rangle$ as the uniform means of forming complex types. A brief introduction into Ty2 can be found in (Gamut, 1991, Volume II, Chapter 5); the original reference is Gallin (1975). Ty2 is used in many of Groenendijk and Stokhof's papers and is discussed in (Janssen, 1986a). See also Zimmermann (1989) for an embedding of Ty2 into Montague's IL.

At the time of Montague's work, the use of type theory in the structuring of semantic domains was basically unknown in linguistics and not widespread within the philosophy of language, in part because of the dominance of first-order logic and modest extensions of it; a rich type theory is unnecessary if one is only working with a small number of types. Model theory and possible-worlds semantics were sometimes called "West Coast semantics", centered as they were in California institutions where Tarski and his students and colleagues (and Carnap in the later part of his career) were located, and that enterprise was looked upon with considerable skepticism by Quine and much of the "East Coast establishment". As a result of unfamiliarity with type theory, few early Montague grammarians were in a position to consider proposals for alternative type theories. Eventually variety in type theories became one of the dimensions in which theories might differ. Alternative modes of semantic combination such as function composition and corresponding enrichment of type structure, came to play a greater role as semanticists learned to appreciate the work that a powerful type theory could do; these developments will be touched on briefly in Section 4.4.

One important and lasting feature of Montague's type theory, one which has become so thoroughly absorbed into linguistics that its novelty in the early 1970's is easily forgotten, is the idea of seeing function-argument structure as the basic semantic glue by which meanings are combined. What did linguists think before that? In early work such as Katz and J.A. Fodor (1963) or Katz and Postal (1964) one sees attempts to represent meanings by means of bundles of features and meaning combination as the manipulations of such feature bundles; there were obvious problems with any semantic combinations that didn't amount to predicate-conjunction. Later logically-oriented linguists working on semantics invoked representations that looked more or less like first-order logic augmented by various "operators" (this was equally true for generative and interpretive semantics) and more generally the practice of linguists dealt in "semantic representations" without explicit attention to the interpretation of those representations. Therefore the issue of how semantic interpretations of parts are combined to make semantic interpretations of wholes did not really arise, since the semantic representations were not formally different in kind from syntactic representations.

The impact of seeing semantic interpretation as involving a great deal of function-argument structure (something also emphasized early by Lewis, Cresswell and Parsons and traceable to the work of Frege, Tarski and Carnap) was felt in linguistics most strongly in terms of its effect on the analysis of particular linguistic constructions, about which more will be said below. For example, the idea of an "intensional transitive verb" like Montague's treatment of **seek** had apparently not occurred to linguists or philosophers before: referential opacity was diagnosed as resulting from embedding under some sentential operator and to make the opacity of a verb like **seek** explicit required engaging in lexical decomposition (as suggested, for instance, in (Quine, 1960)) to make the opacity-producing operator overt (see Partee, 1974, for a discussion of the contrasting approaches). Similarly, linguists had never thought to analyze adjectives as functions applying to nouns. "Normal" adjectives were all assumed to originate as predicates and get to prenominal position via relative clause reduction (Bach (1968) went so far as to get nouns into their head positions via relative clause reduction as well, thereby providing a clausal structure that could contain temporal operators in order to account for temporal ambiguity in superficially tenseless expressions like **the president**) and linguists who noticed the non-predicate-like behavior of adjectives like **former** and **alleged** also noted the existence of cognate adverbs which were taken to be their sources through syntactically complex derivational relations (or equally complex derivations in an interpretivist treatment, where the "more logical" representation was derived, not underlying).

Function-argument structure and a rich type theory go naturally together in the treatment of natural language, given the fairly rich array of kinds of constituents that natural languages contain. Even if Chierchia (1984a) is correct in hypothesizing that the productive categories, those which have corresponding **wh**-words and/or pro-forms and are not limited to a small finite set of exemplars (criteria which may not always exactly agree, but a good start), are never higher than second-order in their types, that is still a much richer type structure than was found in classical predicate logic, which has so little diversity of types (sentence, entity and n-place first-order predicates) as to leave linguists who employed it unaware of types at all and to make it understandable why explicit semantics before Montague grammar seemed to require so much lexical decomposition. (See Dowty (1979) for illuminating discussion by a generative semanticist who became a leading Montague grammarian.)

3.4. The method of fragments

Each of Montague's three "grammar" papers contains a "fragment". The term was introduced in EFL, where it is used four times in the second paragraph, which begins (Montague, 1974, p. 188):

> In the present paper I shall accordingly present a precise treatment, culminating in a theory of truth, of a formal language that I believe may be reasonably regarded as a fragment of ordinary English.

The "method of fragments" was a feature of Montague's work which was novel to linguists and became quite influential methodologically as one of the hallmarks of Montague grammar; "fragment" has become almost a technical term of formal semantics. What is meant is simply writing a complete syntax and semantics for a specifiable subset ("fragment") of a language, rather than, say, writing rules for the syntax and semantics of relative clauses or some other construction of interest while making implicit assumptions about the grammar of the rest of the language. Linguists have traditionally given small (but interesting) fragments of analyses of various aspects of complete natural languages; Montague gave complete analyses of small (but interesting) fragments of natural languages.[21]

In this section we turn to the fragment of PTQ. Features of PTQ that will be discussed include the use of a version of categorial grammar in the syntax, the use of the lambda calculus, the interpretation of NPs as generalized quantifiers, the treatment of bound variable anaphora and scope phenomena and the role of analysis trees in capturing the relevant notion of "logical form". Discussion will be brief and will not recapitulate the content of PTQ; pedagogical introductions and fuller discussions are readily available elsewhere (e.g., Partee (1973b, 1975), Thomason (1974), Dowty, Wall and Peters (1981), Link (1979), Gamut (1991); see Zimmermann (1981) for an insightful review of three German Montague grammar textbooks including Link (1979)). The topics have been chosen for their importance to the subsequent development of the field of semantics and theories of the syntax-semantic interface. The discussion is partly from the perspective of the historical context in which PTQ made its first impact on linguistics. It is also partly retrospective, since it is impossible to discuss PTQ in the 1990's without thinking simultaneously about its impact on subsequent developments and about which of its features have had the most long-lasting significance.

3.4.1. Function-argument structure, category-type correspondences, modified categorial grammar and the lambda calculus

One of the noteworthy features of PTQ was the systematic correspondence between syntactic categories and semantic types. As in his other fragments, Montague used function-argument application as the most basic "semantic glue", employing it in the interpretation of virtually all basic grammatical relations (often composed with the operation of intensionalizing the argument). And as other philosophers and logicians such as Bar-Hillel, Curry, Lambek and David Lewis had realized, if there is to be a systematic correspondence between syntactic categories and semantic types and the non-basic semantic types are all constructed as functional types, then categorial grammar offers a good way to make the correspondence between syntax and semantics explicit in the very names of the syntactic categories. In PTQ it is not the case that all of the non-basic semantic types are functional types, because there are also the intensional types $\langle s, a\rangle$; but it is the case that all of the non-basic syntactic types are interpreted as functional types (see below), so a variant of the basic category-type correspondence of categorial grammar could be used in PTQ.

Strict classical categorial grammars use concatenation as the only syntactic operation and are equivalent to context-free grammars. Montague used the system of categories of categorial grammar and made a uniform category-type correspondence as in categorial

[21] There has not been much explicit discussion of pro's and con's of the method of fragments in theoretical linguistics and the methodological gap is in principle even wider now that some theories don't believe in rules at all. In practice the gap is not always unbridgeable, since, e.g., principles for interpreting LF tree structures can be comparable to descriptions of rules of a Montague grammar whose analysis trees those LFs resemble. To quote from Partee (1979a), "I would not recommend that one always work with the constraint of full explicitness. But I feel strongly that it is important to do so periodically, because otherwise it is extremely easy to think that you have a solution to a problem when in fact you don't".

grammar (with the addition of intensionalizing the type of the argument), but did not limit the syntactic operations to concatenation. If one works with a classical categorial grammar, the analysis tree which shows the rule-by-rule structure of a derivation is isomorphic to the surface syntactic structure of the generated expression; in PTQ, these structures are generally not isomorphic and it is the analysis tree which displays the semantically relevant syntactic structure.

An appreciation of the importance of function-argument structure, gained through experience with MG and related work, has helped linguists understand much more of the original motivation of categorial grammar, a formalism which had been dismissed by linguists as soon as it was proven to be equivalent in generative power to context-free phrase structure grammar. But since one of its central features is the way its category names encode an intimate correspondence between syntactic category and semantic type, categorial grammars are attractive from the point of view of compositionality. This had been pointed out by Lyons (1968) and Lewis (1970); Montague, as noted, used a modified categorial grammar for PTQ, and Cresswell (1973) used what he christened a lambda-categorial grammar. The problem of the (supposed) non-context-freeness of English and the context-freeness of standard categorial grammar was addressed in three different ways by those four authors. Lyons and Lewis added a (meaning-preserving) transformational component to a categorial base. Montague used categorial grammar nomenclature to establish the homomorphic category-type correspondence among generated expressions but allowed syntactic operations much more powerful than concatenation for putting expressions together (as with the Quantifying In rule and the relative clause rule mentioned in Section 3.4.1 below,[22] but the core "rules of functional application" did just use concatenation plus bits of morphology). Cresswell added free permutations to his categorial grammar, thereby generating a superset of English, with disclaimers about syntactic adequacy and suggestions about possible filters that might be added. (See also the chapter on Categorial Grammars in this Handbook.)

It was noted in Section 3.3 that the basic semantic types used in PTQ were e and t. The basic syntactic categories used in PTQ were also called e and t, with t the category of formulas (sentences) and e a "phantom" category that would have been the category of proper names and pronouns if all term phrases were not uniformly analyzed as generalized quantifiers (Section 3.4.2). The rest of the syntactic categories were all of the form A/B or A//B (an arbitrary distinction designed simply to distinguish syntactic categories that had the same semantic type), with corresponding semantic type $\langle\langle s, \tau(\mathrm{B})\rangle, \tau(\mathrm{A})\rangle$ (where τ is the type-assignment function): the type of functions from intensions of things of the type of Bs to things of the type of As.

Montague did not require every word and morpheme to be assigned to a syntactic category and semantic type. Words and morphemes could also be introduced as part of the effect of applying a syntactic rule, in which case they were not assigned any syntactic

[22] Janssen (1986a) shows that with the unrestricted power Montague allows for his syntactic rules, every recursively enumerable language can be generated and compositionally associated with any desired meaning assignment, i.e. that in the absence of any constraints on the power of syntactic rules, compositionality by itself does not formally limit the class of grammars in any serious way. See also Janssen's chapter "Compositionality" in this Handbook.

category, semantic type, or isolable meaning. Such expressions are called "syncategorematic"; relatively uncontroversial examples include the **to** of infinitives and the **that** of sentential complements. Montague treated most of the logical vocabulary of English syncategorematically, including not only the conjunctions **and** and **or**, but also the determiners **every**, **a/an** and **the**, each of which was introduced by a single syntactic rule which applied to a common noun phrase and yielded a term phrase. Subsequent work in Montague grammar quickly introduced the category of determiner phrases, replacing Montague's syncategorematic treatment of determiners with a categorematic one.

The PTQ type assignment was uniform, elegant and interestingly encoded the generalization that all function-argument-interpreted constructions included intensional examples, examples where the argument had to be interpreted as intensional (of which the **seek** case is an example for the verb-object construction; see Section 4.4.3 below for discussion of the "generalize to the worst case" strategy which dictated that the whole construction should therefore be treated as intensional). Nevertheless it became controversial whether the use Montague made of it for the treatment of nouns like **price** and **temperature** and intransitive verbs like **rise** and **change** was appropriate. Bennett (1974) therefore took as basic syntactic categories t, CN and IV, with the types $\langle e, t\rangle$ assigned to both of the latter;[23] for the remainder of the syntactic categories, Montague's categorial schema was used, resulting in types for the remaining categories that are identical to Montague's except that the "Bennett types" have simply e wherever Montague's original types have $\langle s, e\rangle$, the type of individual concepts. (See discussion in (Dowty, Wall and Peters, 1981) of the "temperature puzzle" and Montague's solution using individual concepts in PTQ. Dowty, Wall and Peters adopted the Bennett types, from which point they became widespread, but see Janssen (1984) for further discussion of the usefulness of individual concepts.)

A natural concomitant of the rich type structure of PTQ and the centrality of functional types in the PTQ analysis of English was the important use of the lambda calculus as a part of Montague's intensional logic, IL, the intermediate language used in the interpretation of PTQ. The lambda calculus gives one very good way to provide compositional names for functions and is therefore an important tool for making compositionality realizable. (If one uses direct rather than indirect interpretation, then where PTQ translates some grammatical construction as a lambda expression, direct interpretation will refer to "that function f such that ...", as one sees in the work of Cresswell and others, as well as in the fragment in EFL (Montague, 1970b).)

As illustrated in (Gallin, 1975), following Henkin (1963), it is possible to let abstraction, application and identity be the only primitive logical operators in a typed logic like Montague's IL and define both the propositional connectives and the existential and universal quantifiers in terms of these operators; it is not possible to take one of the quantifiers as primitive and define the lambda operators. So the lambda operators are more basic than the quantifiers, undoubtedly another reason for their importance in the development of Montague grammar and formal semantics more generally.

The lambda calculus embedded in the intensional logic used for PTQ is designed for unary functions only; the functional types in PTQ are all unary functions and the

[23] In PTQ these were categories $t//e$ and t/e, respectively, with type $\langle\langle s, e\rangle, t\rangle$.

analysis trees are all strictly binary branching (where branching at all). This is one of the choices in type structure that could have been different and it is a constraint that is not observed in all extensions of MG, although in subsequent years arguments in favor of binary branching structures have been made in a number of contexts.

The lambda vied with the unicorn as the "emblem" of Montague grammar, and both became famous among semanticists because of PTQ.[24] At the time of PTQ, the lambda calculus was virtually unknown among linguists and it is still not included in most introductory logic courses, although by now an elementary exposition of lambda abstraction and lambda conversion can be found in many introductions to semantics or to logic for linguists (see Partee, 1973b, 1975; Cresswell, 1973; Dowty, Wall and Peters, 1981; Gamut, 1991; Partee, Ter Meulen and Wall, 1990; Link, 1979; and other introductions to formal semantics).

It is of interest to recall briefly some of the principal uses for lambdas in PTQ which were excitingly innovative at the time; many of them have become more or less standard in the meantime or laid the groundwork for later analyses to be mentioned in later sections.

(i) *Conjunction*. Montague showed in PTQ how the lambda calculus could be used to specify meanings for constituent conjunction as in (1) and (2) below which met the principal desiderata of both the generative and the interpretive semanticists.

(1) **John and Bill love Mary.**

(2) **John walks and talks.**

The PTQ interpretation for the conjoined T phrase[25] in (1) is as in (3); the conjoined IVP in (2) is interpreted as in (4), where **John′** stands for the translation of **John**, etc.

(3) $\lambda P[\mathbf{John}'(P) \wedge \mathbf{Bill}'(P)]$.

(4) $\lambda x[\mathbf{walk}'(x) \wedge \mathbf{talk}'(x)]$.

As an interpretivist would wish, Montague's syntax generated the sentences directly in their surface form without a need for syntactic "conjunction reduction" from full conjoined sentences. As a generative semanticist would wish, Montague's semantic rules for constituent conjunction related the meanings clearly to the meanings of conjoined sentences. Empirically, Montague's proposal made, for the most part, correct predictions about the relative scopes of the connectives in conjoined constituents relative to one another and relative to quantifiers, negation and opacity-producing predicates that appeared in the sentence and did so more straightforwardly than any proposals then available in either generative or interpretive semantics, offering an elegant solution to the kinds of

[24] The unicorn is from Montague's example sentence **John seeks a unicorn**, used to illustrate his treatment of intensional transitive verbs; Bob Rodman chose the unicorn to illustrate the cover of the first collection of papers on Montague Grammar, Rodman (ed.) (1972) and Partee continued the tradition with the cover of Partee (ed.) (1976a).

[25] Actually, PTQ gave rules of disjunction with **or** for sentences, T phrases and IVPs, but rules of conjunction with **and** only for sentences and IVPs, in order to avoid having to introduce plurals.

problems debated in (Partee, 1970b) and (Lakoff, 1970), for example. PTQ did overgenerate in that there was no implementation of Ross's Coordinate Structure Constraint in the "Quantifying In rules"; see Rodman (1976) for an extension that implemented such a constraint uniformly for both **wh**-movement rules and for quantifying in.

The analysis of constituent conjunction in PTQ has been extended and generalized in various ways since PTQ and it has been noted that it is not always the only interpretation available (see Krifka (1990) for an analysis of "part-whole" based interpretations of **John and Mary**, **red and white**, **sing and dance**, etc.), but the basic analysis has proved very robust and has become standard. Later authors noted that the treatment of constituent conjunction in PTQ could be generalized into a schema and eventually argued for a cross-categorial treatment of **and** and **or** (and possibly **not**) that would make the explicit lambda formulas unnecessary; but the types needed in order to make a generalized cross-categorial **and** and **or** possible were not available directly in PTQ; cross-categorial **and** in PTQ terms would have to be an abbreviation for a recursively definable infinite family of meanings of an infinite family of types. (See von Stechow, 1974; Gazdar, 1980; Partee and Rooth, 1983; Keenan and Faltz, 1985.)

(ii) *Relative clauses.* As noted in (Partee, 1973a), the semantics of relative clauses, which is expressed by means of lambdas in PTQ, is not original with Montague; it can be found earlier in (Quine, 1960), where it is expressed in terms of simple set abstraction (equivalent to lambda abstraction when the "source" expression is of type t). The central idea is that relative clauses denote predicates formed from open sentences by abstracting on the relativized position. What was novel about the analysis at the time was not the use of lambdas *per se* but the insistence that restrictive relative clauses must be formed from open sentences and not from closed sentences. The Quine–Montague analysis, once it was acknowledged as the only way to interpret relative clauses compositionally, helped to bring about a shift in the way underlying structure was conceived and opened the way to the presence of variable-like elements in syntactic structures in many frameworks, whether expressed as the Montagovian **he**$_i$, by allowing variables like x_i in syntax, or with GB elements like traces, PRO and *pro*. Most of what had standardly been analyzed via some sort of deletion under identity in transformational grammar, including relative clause formation and "Equi-NP Deletion" in controlled infinitival constructions (with **force**, **persuade**, **promise**, etc.), was subsequently argued to semantically require that some relevant syntactic "part" of or input to the construction must be an "open" expression containing something interpreted as a free variable.

The Quine–Montague analysis of relative clauses has not been entirely uncontroversial, although its basic idea is now widely accepted. One ongoing issue has concerned the distinction between restrictive and non-restrictive relative clauses and how to analyze both kinds if the distinction between them is not always grammaticized (see Rodman, 1976; von Stechow, 1980) and whether restrictive relative clauses must be combined with CNPs or whether they can be combined with full T phrases (Bach and Cooper, 1978; von Stechow, 1980; Janssen, 1981).

(iii) *The interpretation of noun phrases as generalized quantifiers and the treatment of scope by "Quantifying In"*. The interpretation of NPs (Ts) as generalized quantifiers is the subject of Section 3.4.2 below and "Quantifying In" will be discussed along with the interpretation of bound variable anaphora in Section 3.4.3. In the present connection there are several relevant points to note about the importance of the lambdas in those analyses. In the first place, the NP interpretations are second order: sets of properties of individual concepts; the many puzzles resolved by that analysis provided the first really vivid evidence for linguists of the value of going beyond the more familiar territory of first-order logic. All NP interpretations begin with a lambda (although here too, since the "body" of the expression is of type t, that lambda is just a set abstractor). And in the compositional interpretation of NPs of any complexity, additional lambdas turn up repeatedly; they can be seen in PTQ in the rule that combines a relative clause with its head and in the conjoined and disjoined NPs discussed above; and lambdas that are not just set abstractors arise in the categorematic treatment of the three PTQ determiners (as in Dowty, Wall and Peters, 1981; Gamut, 1991) which Montague introduced syncategorematically.

Another important role for lambda abstraction in this area was its use in the interpretation of the Quantifying In rule. As with the relative clause rule, an important innovation (from a linguist's perspective) in Montague's Quantifying In rule was its crucial use of an open sentence as one constituent in a syntactic formation rule; the rule takes a term phrase and a sentence to make a sentence, but will apply vacuously unless the sentence contains a free variable (a **he**$_n$ in PTQ). The partial analysis tree in (5) illustrates the use of the rule.

(5) **John seeks a unicorn**, 10, 0
  / \
a unicorn, 2 **John seeks him**$_0$, 4

In the interpretation of the resulting sentence, in which the NP is substituted for the target free variable pronoun, the variable x_0 gets bound. By what? Not directly by the quantificational NP, as had been posited in the otherwise analogous proposals for "Quantifier Lowering" in generative semantics or in early versions of "Quantifier Raising" in later GB work by May and others; rather, by a lambda operator that is added as part of the interpretation of the rule. The NP **a unicorn** denotes a set of properties and must take a property expression as its argument. The semantic interpretation of Quantifying In involves the application of lambda abstraction to the open sentence (abstracting on the variable x_0) and applying an intension operator to that to form the property of being an x_0 such that John seeks x_0; the NP interpretation is then applied to that property, exactly as the interpretation of an NP subject is applied to the property which is the interpretation of the (intension of the) verb phrase.

3.4.2. NPs as generalized quantifiers

As noted in the previous section, a major legacy of PTQ has been the very important and influential analysis of noun phrases as denoting generalized quantifiers.[26] Part of the appeal of this analysis for linguists was that it allowed one to be explicit about the important semantic differences among NPs headed by different determiners, as in generative semantics treatments, while having a single semantic constituent corresponding to

[26] Although it was principally through PTQ that this analysis became influential in linguistics, this may be one of the ideas that Montague got from David Lewis, since it also appears in (Lewis, 1970), embedded in a theory which combined a categorial grammar phrase structure with a transformational component.

the syntactic NP constituent, unlike the distribution of pieces of NP-meanings all over the tree as required by the first-order-logic-like analyses linguists had been trying to work with (because linguists generally knew nothing about type theory, certainly nothing about generalized quantifiers). Dependence on first-order logic had made it impossible for linguists to imagine giving an explicit semantic interpretation for **the** or **a/an** or **every** or **no** that didn't require a great deal of structural decomposition into formulas with quantifiers and connectives, more or less the translations one finds in logic textbooks. The generative semanticists embraced such structures and made underlying structure look more like first-order logic, while the Chomskyites rejected such aspects of meaning as not belonging to any linguistic level and gave no explicit account of them at all. One can speculate that the rift might never have grown so large if linguists had known about generalized quantifiers earlier; the productive teamwork of Barwise and Cooper (1981) is a beautiful early example of how formal properties and linguistic constraints and explanations can be fruitfully explored in tandem with the combined insights and methdologies of model theory and linguistics, and generalized quantifiers have continued to be a fertile domain for further linguistically insightful work exploiting formal tools (see the chapter on Generalized Quantifiers by Keenan and Westerståhl in this Handbook).

A second important aspect of NP interpretation in PTQ is the handling of scope via differences in analysis trees. The treatment (and sometimes even the existence) of the scope ambiguity of (6) was a matter of considerable controversy in the interpretive/generative semantics debates. PTQ used a "Quantifying In" rule which resulted in a single syntactic tree structure for (6) but two different analysis trees,[27] an important illustration of the "rule-by-rule" approach.

(6) **A unicorn eats every fish.**

McCawley (1981) points out the similarity between Montague's Quantifying In rules and the generative semantics rule of Quantifier Lowering and there are indeed important similarities between what one might look at as a command relation in a Montagovian analysis tree and a command relation in a generative semantics underlying structure or a GB LF. The differences in conception are nevertheless interesting and important, with Montague's approach more like some structuralists' "item-and-process" (vs. "item-and-arrangement") grammars or like Zellig Harris's underappreciated algebraic work (e.g., Harris, 1968) which also treats structural similarity between languages in terms of derivational history rather than in terms of geometrical configurations at selected levels of representation. Montague's Quantifying In rule was in fact outside the bounds of what linguists would have called a single rule at the time, since it simultaneously substituted a full NP for one occurrence of a given variable/pronoun ($\mathbf{he}_i$) and pronouns of appropriate gender, case and number for all other occurrences of that same variable.

The proper treatment of scope ambiguity and the binding of pronouns is of course a continuing area of controversy with profound implications for the nature of the syntactic and semantic components of grammar and their interface and there is further discussion in Section 4 below.

[27] The generation of a syntactic tree structure assumes Partee's (1973b) amendment to the effect that the syntactic rules generate trees rather than strings. In fact, PTQ assigns not just two different analysis trees to (6) but infinitely many; see discussion in Section 3.4.5 below.

3.4.3. Bound variable anaphora

It is quite remarkable what a great role the analysis of anaphora and puzzles involving pronouns have played in arguments for choosing among theories of syntax and semantics over the last thirty-some years, before MG, in arguing for and against MG, post-MG and still now. Quantification and anaphora were very tightly connected in Montague grammar; that was not a consequence of Montague's general theory as spelled out in UG, but nevertheless closely associated with MG as a result of the legacy of PTQ.

In PTQ, the only pronouns explicitly treated were pronouns interpreted as bound variables; but every pronoun that might possibly be treated as a bound variable was so treated. One of the important insights that was gained from PTQ was that the possibility of interpreting a pronoun as a bound variable did not depend directly on the semantic properties of its antecedent NP, but rather on the construction by which it was introduced. With all NPs analyzed as generalized quantifiers, any NP could bind a bound-variable pronoun, including proper names or even other pronouns, since the binding is not actually by the NP itself, but by the lambda abstractor introduced in the Quantifying In rule, as noted in Section 3.4.1. This insight had a major impact on subsequent analyses of "strict-identity" and "sloppy-identity" puzzles in the interpretation of ellipsis in sentences like (7), discussed in Section 4.3 below.

(7) **Sam gave some fish to his dog and Sally did too.**

There are four rules in PTQ which effect the binding of pronouns: the three Quantifying In rules and the relative clause rule. In order for an NP to "bind" a pronoun, the NP has to be introduced via a Quantifying In rule, which as noted earlier introduces a lambda operator with scope over the expression being quantified into. And the relative clause rule also causes the relative pronoun and any further coindexed pronouns to be bound by a lambda operator.

The fact that PTQ treats only bound-variable uses of pronouns leads to a respect in which some "filtering" may be needed in the PTQ syntax. Subscripted pronouns $\mathbf{he}_i$, interpreted as free variables, are freely generated in NP positions; rules which have the semantic effect of binding them also have the syntactic effect of replacing them by non-subscripted pronouns of appropriate gender. Semantically this corresponds to Frege's insight that the recursive formation rules for generating closed quantified sentences need to work with open formulas as parts in order to support a compositional interpretation; the basic semantic valuation for formulas has to be truth relative to an assignment rather than truth simpliciter. But if the output of the grammar is to consist only of the closed sentences, then one must filter out of the final output any "sentences" that still contain free variables. The PTQ grammar does generate "sentences" that contain subscripted pronouns; semantically these are interpreted as open formulas rather than closed sentences. They may have different truth values relative to different assignments of variables, which is a useful property for their role as parts in the generation of other sentences, but it leads to an artificial treatment of assignment-independent truth, i.e. truth with respect to model, world and time, since in the system of PTQ, a formula is true with respect to a model, world and time if and only if it is true at that model, world and time with respect to *every* variable assignment. Thus a sentence containing a subscripted pronoun which happens to be true on some assignments and false on others is classified as false *simpliciter*, a counter-intuitive result. Montague said nothing explicit about these cases in PTQ; there have been two common proposals for how to view them. One possibility is simply to filter them out on the grounds that the subscripted pronouns are not really part of English but are just auxiliary expressions that are used in the derivation of real English expressions. The other possibility, and one which is explicitly worked out by Montague in UG, is to enrich the semantics into a formal pragmatic framework in which one treats subscripted pronouns that remain at the end of a derivation as demonstrative pronouns, letting "contexts of use" include assignments to variables. (In UG Montague had a slightly more intricate treatment of pronouns and their indices, treating the indices as basic entity-type expressions and introducing the pronouns syncategorematically, and using his "ambiguating relation" to delete "free" indices from the surface forms of the generated language.)

It was noted above that PTQ has three Quantifying In rules. These apply to quantification into sentences, IV-phrases (VPs) and CN-phrases. The idea that quantification could have scope other than sentence-size was also novel to linguists and is part of the package of ideas and techniques that opened up new debates about the division of labor between syntax and semantics and led over the course of a few years from the idea of constraining the role of transformations in a compositional theory to the possibility that a more adequate semantic component might make it possible to eliminate transformations altogether from the syntactic component. In an early and influential paper, Dowty (1978) showed that lexically governed transformations could be more appropriately replaced by lexical rules in a Montague grammar. Gazdar (1982) took the further step of arguing for the elimination of transformations altogether. Like cross-categorial conjunction and disjunction, cross-categorial Quantifying In rules helped to eliminate some of the earlier arguments for deriving infinitival complements from full sentences. Example (8) below, from Karttunen (1968), who attributes it to Baker (1966), presented one of the puzzles that Montague addressed in PTQ: how to account for the fact that there can be an anaphoric connection between **it** and **a fish** even when **a fish** is given a *de dicto* reading. Without a Quantifying In rule that can apply to the VP **catch him**$_0$ **and eat him**$_0$, one would either have to derive that VP from a full conjoined sentence (which would then also necessitate a conjunction-reduction transformation) or else quantify in at the top sentence level, deriving only a *de re* or "specific" reading.

(8) **John wants to catch a fish and eat it.**

The systematic similarity between quantification with sentence scope and quantification with VP scope is seen in the similarity of the translation rules and in the resulting patterns of logical entailment in those cases where there are relevant entailments. And as later noted in (Partee and Rooth, 1983), the three Quantifying In rules spelled out explicitly in PTQ can be seen as three instances of a recursively specificiable cross-categorial schema in which sentence-scope quantification may be taken as basic and the other rules are predictable from the semantic types of the categories being quantified into.[28]

[28] The reason for the presence of an explicit rule quantifying into CNs in PTQ is not clear; there would be a clearer need for such a rule in a fragment including expressions like **every search for a man with red hair** or **most pictures of two horses**, in which the head noun creates an opaque context for its complement much

Can all pronouns be treated as bound variables? That was a question which linguists were already debating at the time Montague was working (Karttunen, 1969; Partee, 1970a). But given the method of fragments, Montague did not have to address it in PTQ and he did not make any such claim. Among the problematic cases for a uniform treatment of pronouns as bound variables, some of which will be mentioned in Section 4.3 and later, are demonstrative and indexical uses of pronouns, "discourse" pronouns with explicit or implicit antecedents in other sentences, "donkey" pronouns and Karttunen's "paycheck" pronouns. An elegant treatment of demonstratives and indexicals was given in (Bennett, 1978); this work was not quickly integrated with work on pronouns as bound variables and fully unified approaches are only more recently being pursued. One important matter which Montague ignored in PTQ is the distinction between reflexive and non-reflexive pronouns; there is a footnote about that in EFL,[29] but in PTQ Montague simply used non-reflexive forms of pronouns in all cases, even where a reflexive form is obligatory.

A final note about the semantics of bound variable anaphora in PTQ. The interpretation of variables in PTQ is accomplished through the use of variable assignments g which are manipulated in basically the same way as in the classical model-theoretic semantics of quantification that goes back to Tarski. The variables that correspond to bound-variable pronouns are variables over a single world-independent and time-independent domain of individuals and the manipulation of the assignments g is completely insulated from the manipulation of world and time indices. The result is that in PTQ, pronouns are treated as "rigid" with respect to modal and temporal dimensions and so are the variables that correspond to positions that NPs are quantified into. This treatment represents a certain view about the semantics of quantified modal statements in ordinary English that has served well at least as a very good first approximation, but which may not adequately cover all pronoun occurrences. Janssen (1984) advocates the use of variables over individual concepts to account for cases where a bound pronoun has an index-dependent, non-rigid, interpretation, as in example (9) below. Other proposals have suggested treatments of some pronouns as disguised definite descriptions or as "Skolem functions", or as ranging over "guises".

(9) **This year the president is a Democrat, but next year he will be a Republican.**

The legacy of PTQ in its treatment of pronouns as bound variables bound by lambda operators introduced either in a Quantifying In rule or in the relative clause formation rule has been profound; even though other treatments of many pronouns have been and continue to be proposed, the PTQ treatment has the status of a kind of "standard", at least with respect to the semantics. Syntactically, the PTQ treatment is not completely

---

like an intensional transitive verb and for which one can distinguish three readings, in one of which the NP in the prepositional phrase has wider scope than the head noun but narrower scope than the top determiner. EFL included the expression **brother of** v_0 as a basic common noun phrase and the CN-quantification rule in PTQ may simply be a carry-over from EFL. Partee (1975) discusses some possible uses for the rule in PTQ in cases of an NP containing multiple relative clauses, citing an example from Joan Bresnan (p.c.): **Every girl who attended a women's college who made a large donation to it was included in the list.**

[29] See Bach and Partee (1980) for a treatment which builds on the idea in Montague's footnote 12 to EFL.

elegant and this is one domain in which the grammar does not generate surface structures directly. Some suggested alternatives will be discussed further below.

3.4.4. Scope and intensionality

Scope is not a notion that is explicitly defined in PTQ and I will not try to define it here; other than in the context of a specific formal language it seems not to be a perfectly simple or straightforward matter. Scope would be easier to define in IL than directly in the English fragment of PTQ and it may not even always make complete sense to try to define scope in a uniform way for natural language constructions if they are not all uniformly interpreted, e.g., as always involving function-argument application. The common sense notion that if A is in the scope of B, then the interpretation of A may depend on that of B but not vice versa, may be correct as far as it goes. But the same natural language construction may be subject to competing analyses of which part is the function and which the argument, as, e.g., in the case of the subject-predicate rule for which most analyses had traditionally treated the subject as an argument of the predicate but Montague treated the subject as the functor and the predicate as its argument, and therefore one cannot derive an unequivocal assignment of relative scopes to parts of an expression on the basis of such a notion in the absence of a specific formal analysis.

But as a fair approximation for PTQ one might venture the following. Given an analysis tree of an expression generated by PTQ, "higher in the tree" (assuming that trees are drawn with the root at the top) normally corresponds to "wider scope". Slightly more precisely, it probably makes sense to say that any expression interpreted as a function has scope over all parts of the expression interpreted as its argument. For the rules that involve the syncategorematic introduction of negation, auxiliary verbs expressing tense and aspect, **and** and **or** and the determiners **every**, **a/an**, and **the**, it is clearly in each case the syncategorematically introduced element that has scope over the other elements introduced in the same rule. This still does not cover every rule in PTQ; for instance, in the rule that combines a CNP with a relative clause, neither has scope over the other: the rule introduces a lambda abstractor which has scope over a conjunction which in turn has scope over both the CNP and the relative clause. And it also does not say anything directly about the sense in which the determiner in a subject NP has scope over the whole VP, since the determiner is the functor element in the NP interpretation and the VP is in turn the argument of the subject NP.

One of the consequences of the rich intensional type theory of Montague's IL and his exploitation of it in PTQ, is that matters of scope and scope ambiguities permeate the fragment. If one asks which are the scope-taking elements in PTQ, the answer is, "Almost all of them". Noun phrases, treated as generalized quantifiers, may take other expressions in their scope and may occur within the scope of other expressions. The usual sentential operators such as modals and tenses, negation and sentential adverbs like **necessarily** take scope in familiar ways even though some of them are introduced syncategorematically. But there are many other intensional constructions in which relative scope is also a significant phenomenon. Verbs like **believe** and **assert** take scope over their sentential complement; verbs like **try to** and **wish to** take scope over their infinitival complement; and intensional transitive verbs like **seek** and **conceive** take scope over their direct object. (In all of these cases, a given NP may "escape" out of the scope of a given scope-taking element if it is quantified in from a position "above" that element in the analysis tree, i.e. if it is introduced into the expression after the given scope-taking element has already been incorporated into the expression.) In fact, given Montague's uniform analysis, all transitive verbs take scope over their direct object; it only happens that in the case of the relation between an extensional transitive verb like **eat** and its object, the semantics of the verb (as constrained by a meaning postulate, see below) renders the issue of scope semantically inert. That is, whereas a sentence like (5) above, repeated below as (10), has different truth conditions depending on whether the NP object is generated *in situ* or quantified in, a sentence like (11) has the same truth conditions on either derivation.

(10) **John seeks a unicorn.**

(11) **John eats a fish.**

Other scope-taking elements in PTQ include the intransitive verbs **rise** and **change**, which Montague included in PTQ in order to treat the "temperature puzzle" illustrated by the invalid inference in (12) below,[30] whose invalidity needs to be explained.

(12) (a) **The temperature rises.**
(b) **The temperature is ninety.**
(c) **Therefore, ninety rises.** [INVALID]

But how can the intransitive verb be scope-taking if the generalized quantifier subject always has scope over the VP? This example illustrates the difficulty of talking unambiguously about the scopes of parts of natural language expressions. The generalized quantifier does indeed take scope over the intransitive verb, but its meaning is such that the verb takes scope over an individual concept expression that is "inside" the meaning of the generalized quantifier. The unreduced translation of (12c), $\mathbf{ninety}'(^\wedge\mathbf{rise}')$, is as in (12c′); but (12c′) is logically equivalent to the reduced translation (12c″).

(12) (c′) $[\lambda P[[^\vee P](^\wedge n)]](^\wedge\mathbf{rise}')$.
(c″) $\mathbf{rise}'(^\wedge n)$.

The scope-taking elements in PTQ include not only quantifiers, sentential (extended to be cross-categorial) operators of various sorts, and all the verbs, but also verb-phrase adverbs such as **voluntarily** and prepositions such as **about**. And in EFL Montague had also included prenominal adjectives like **alleged**, with scope over the CN phrase they combine with. (Scope arguments involving intensional adjectives like **alleged** and **former** were Montague's principal argument against the then-prevailing linguistic preference for deriving all prenominal adjectives from predicative ones, an early and strong instance of the use of the compositionality principle to choose between competing syntactic analyses.) In fact, given that in PTQ the sets of basic expressions of the two primitive categories

[30] Note that Montague treated simple present tense forms of verbs such as **rises** as having the kinds of meanings that often have to be conveyed in English with the use of a progressive form. This was a reasonable simplification, given that most Indo-European languages do use the simple present tense forms with such meaning.

e and t are empty, it follows that all of the basic lexical expressions of PTQ are of functional types and hence are the kinds of expressions that may in principle take scope over other expressions.

An *intensional* construction is one in which the determination of the extension of the whole depends not simply on the extensions of the parts but on the intension of at least one of the parts. Montague found instances of intensionality in virtually all of the basic grammatical relations of English and therefore constructed PTQ so that intensionality became the general case. For every syntactic category B/A or B//A, the corresponding semantic type $\tau(\mathrm{A}/\mathrm{B})$ or $\tau(\mathrm{A}//\mathrm{B})$ is not simply the type of functions from $\tau(\mathrm{A})$ to $\tau(\mathrm{B})$ but rather the type of functions from the intensional type $\langle s, \tau(\mathrm{A})\rangle$ to $\tau(\mathrm{B})$. Montague's use of his richly typed intensional logic contrasted sharply with more familiar analyses of intensionality which analyzed all intensional constructions as underlyingly sentential, involving some propositional operator or some predicate or relation that took a whole proposition as its argument. The arguments for such decompositional analyses, e.g., decomposing sentence (5), **John seeks a unicorn**, into something like "John endeavors that he find a unicorn" (Quine, 1960) had been largely semantic, often crucially resting on the assumption that intensionality must involve some sentence-scope operator or relation and many of those arguments dissolved once a richer semantics was available.

The treatment of **seeks** as a basic transitive verb (interpreted as applying to the intension of a generalized quantifier), for example, was a major innovation in Montague and sentence (5) became one of the most famous examples from PTQ, epitomizing the potential Montague offered for treating something very close to surface syntax as an optimal "logical form" and changing the methodology of semantics correspondingly. Instead of doing semantics by transforming natural language syntactic structures into structures dictated by some particular logical Procrustean bed, the task became one of identifying the right kind of logic and the right kind of semantic interpretations to be able to make sense of natural language syntax as it actually occurs. In this respect Montague grammar was in principle quite close in spirit to generative grammar; the syntax should be autonomously describable and the semantics should provide an interpretation of a given syntactic structure. The only respect in which the syntax is not autonomous in a Montague grammar, as noted earlier, is in respect of argumentation concerning the basis for choosing between alternative syntactic hypotheses, which in Montague grammar may include arguments from semantics and compositionality.

If Montague treated all basic grammatical relations as intensional in principle, how did he handle the extensional cases? By means of what have come to be called *meaning postulates* (after Carnap, 1952), restrictions on the interpretations of intensional logic which would be "reasonable candidates for interpretations of English" (Montague, 1974, p. 263). In choosing semantic types corresponding to syntactic categories, Montague followed the strategy of "generalizing to the worst case", with meaning postulates then guaranteeing that the "simpler" cases are indeed simpler. So, for example, the meaning postulate for the extensional transitive verbs **find**, **lose**, **eat**, **love**, **date** says that although their direct object is semantically an intension of a generalized quantifier and their subject an individual concept, they are in a well-defined sense equivalent to a relation between two entities. There are also meaning postulates guaranteeing the extensionality of the subject position of all PTQ verbs except **rise** and **change**, the extensionality of the preposition **in**, the rigidity of proper names, the constancy of the individual concepts in the extension of nouns other than **price** and **temperature**, and the truth-conditional equivalence of **seek** and **try to find**. Meaning postulates are in principle an important means for specifying linguistically significant aspects of the meanings of lexical items in a theory like Montague's in which lexical items are mostly treated as primitives rather than provided with explicit model-theoretic interpretations or "decomposed" into "semantic primitives". On the other hand, in the absence of a substantive theory constraining the class of possible meaning postulates, meaning postulates may sometimes be regarded as stipulating aspects of meanings of expressions without explaining them. For a linguist, meaning postulates might be thought of as supplying explicit model-theoretic content to "semantic features" which might be listed in lexical entries and it is an empirical question which semantic properties of a given lexical item should be so captured and included in the lexicon.

Montague unified tense logic and modal logic in a way which makes matters of scope with respect to intensionality very similar structurally to matters of quantifier scope. Tense and modal operators are interpreted as involving quantification over times and worlds and the "up" operator which yields an expression whose extension is the intension of the operand expression is semantically equivalent to a lambda abstractor over the world-time index. These structural parallels among intensional operators and quantification with NPs are somewhat more perspicuous in Gallin's Ty2 than in Montague's IL.

3.4.5. Disambiguated language. Analysis trees as logical form

In Section 3.1 above it was noted that Montague's general theory as spelled out in (Montague, 1970c) requires that the syntax provide a disambiguated language, since the homomorphism that maps the syntactic algebra onto the semantic algebra must be a (single-valued) function. It was noted there that this means that the elements of the syntactic algebra for PTQ cannot simply be the expressions generated by the given rules, since these are in many cases ambiguous. Nor can they be the constituent structures of the derived expressions (not explicitly given in PTQ, but they could and probably should be added; see Partee, 1973b), since an ambiguous sentence like (6), repeated here as (13), is not ambiguous with respect to its resulting constituent structure, a simplified representation of which is given in (14).

(13) **A unicorn eats every fish.**

(14)

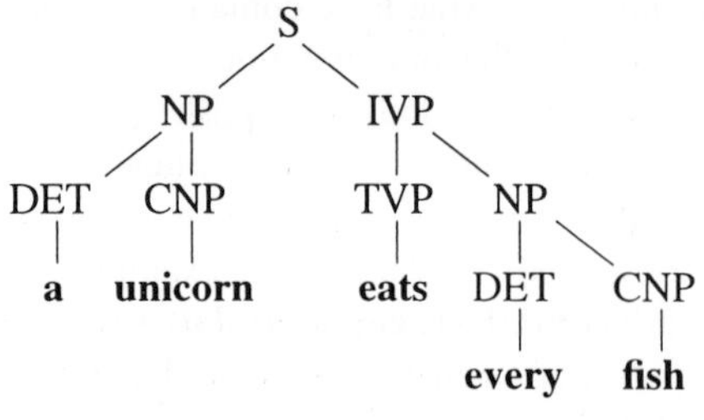

A novelty of PTQ with respect to most then-existing linguistic frameworks and a feature still not always fully understood, is that syntactic disambiguation is by means of a difference in the order of putting the parts together, a difference captured by "analysis trees" or "derivation trees". Two analysis trees for (13) are given below in (15).[31]

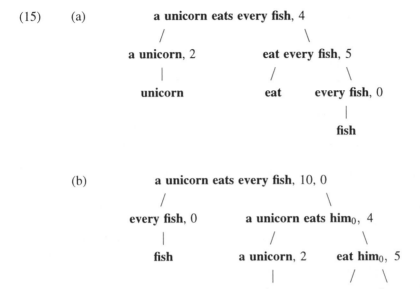

(15) (a)

a unicorn eats every fish, 4
/ \
a unicorn, 2 — **eat every fish**, 5
| — / \
unicorn — **eat** — **every fish**, 0
|
fish

(b)

a unicorn eats every fish, 10, 0
/ \
every fish, 0 — **a unicorn eats him**$_0$, 4
| — / \
fish — **a unicorn**, 2 — **eat him**$_0$, 5
| — / \
unicorn — **eat** — **he**$_0$

The analysis trees show the semantically relevant syntactic structure; the pairing of syntactic derivation rules with rules of translation into IL provides the basis for the homomorphic mapping from the PTQ syntax of English into (the polynomial closure of) the PTQ syntactic algebra for IL; and IL has its own pairing of syntactic and semantic rules leading to a homomorphic mapping onto the model-theoretic semantic algebra. The actual elements of the syntactic algebra for the English syntax of PTQ should therefore be taken to be the analysis trees. And each of the "syntactic rules" of PTQ provides an operation in the syntactic algebra, operating on one or two input analysis trees and yielding an analysis tree as result. (PTQ actually contains an infinite set of rules, finitely specified, since each of the three Quantifying In rules, as well as the relative clause rule, is actually a rule schema.)

The analysis trees are therefore the best candidates for a level of "logical form", if by "logical form" one means a structural representation of an expression from which its meaning is transparently derivable. While a translation of an expression into the logical

[31] There are actually infinitely many different analysis trees for (13), because of the free choice of variables in the positions to be quantified into and also because of the possibility of quantifying one variable in for another. But even if we regard analysis trees differing in only those ways as equivalent, there are still seven distinct equivalence classes of analysis trees for (13): Each NP can be generated *in situ* or quantified in; and the direct object NP can be quantified in with either S scope or VP scope. When both NPs are quantified in with S scope, they can be quantified in in either order. The reasonableness of such apparent overgeneration of syntactic analysis trees is discussed in various overview articles and textbooks, including Thomason (1974) and Dowty, Wall and Peters (1981, pp. 209–210). In the case of sentence (13), there are just two non-equivalent readings and I have selected the simplest analysis trees from among the several possible for each reading.

language IL might also be taken as a candidate for a "logical form" for the expression, there are two arguments against that choice: (i) given that the IL expression obtained directly by the translation rules is usually reducible to a sequence of progressively simpler logically equivalent expressions, differing significantly from one another in their form, a given expression on a given derivation would either have a multiplicity of logical forms, or some (non-obvious) means would have to be found to designate one of those many equivalent expressions as "the" logical form of the expression; and (ii) IL is a dispensable convenience ("probably more perspicuous", Montague, 1974, p. 256) with no serious theoretical status in PTQ; it is the analysis trees and the model-theoretic interpretations that are essential to the syntax and semantics respectively (see further discussion in (Gamut, 1991, Volume II, Section 6.5)).

The issue of "logical form" is related to the issue of ambiguity. How many ways ambiguous is sentence (13) in PTQ and how many distinct logical forms does it have? If one asks the ambiguity question about (13) in PTQ, the usual answer is "two", since all of the different possible syntactic derivations lead to one of two distinct truth conditions, i.e. one of two distinct model-theoretic objects. However, if one asks about logical forms, it seems that the only systematic answers are either "infinitely many" or "seven" (see footnote 31 above.) And on reflection, it would not be indefensible to say that sentence (13) is seven-ways structurally ambiguous in PTQ; it follows from the semantics of the particular lexical items chosen that those seven distinct structures collapse into two distinct truth conditions. Among sentences with the same structure, example (16) is truth-conditionally unambiguous, while example (17) has 3 truth-conditionally distinct readings.

(16) **John loves Mary.**

(17) **Every man seeks a unicorn.**

There is no sentence without further scope-bearing elements that has more than three truth-conditionally distinct readings. The distinction between VP-scope and S-scope for the direct object becomes crucial in the presence of additional VP-scope operators such as a VP-adverb or a verb taking an infinitival complement, as in example (8) in Section 3.4.3 and the distinction between *in situ* generation of the subject and quantifying it in becomes crucial only if either the object is quantified in or there is some additional S-scope element such as tense or negation in the sentence: an example such as **Every man will seek a unicorn**, with the addition of future tense, has seven non-equivalent readings. So one might want to argue that the sentences (13), (16) and (17) should have just three logical forms, which leads to a problem with taking the analysis trees as the level of logical form: which three and is there even any "formal" algorithm for determining how many logical forms a given expression has? However, all of the differences in the seven different derivation trees have semantic significance in other examples, as noted, so it seems reasonable to say that all of sentences (13), (16), (17) are seven ways structurally ambiguous in PTQ and all have seven logical forms.[32] The notion of structural ambiguity

[32] Tichý (1988) takes the fundamental semantic values of expressions to be not their intensions but "constructions" and a Tichý version of PTQ would accordingly treat all of these sentences as having seven distinct semantic interpretations, collapsing into a smaller number of readings only at the level of intensions. The same is presumably true for virtually any "structured meanings" approach and a similar idea can be traced back to Carnap's notion of "intensional isomorphism" (Carnap, 1947).

without truth-conditional difference is not without precedent; it applies to any simple sentence containing two universal or two existential quantifiers, where most analyses will necessarily provide a scope ambiguity which will happen to be semantically neutralized, as well as to the accidental neutralization of truth-conditional difference in sentence (18), an example in which we still strongly "feel" the ambiguity and have to "work" to compute the truth-conditional equivalence.[33]

(18) **They are visiting relatives.**

It should be noted, with respect to the questions raised about trying to pin down a notion of "logical form" that would have the properties that people seem to expect of it, that perhaps any lexical element whose interpretation is completely spelled out in the grammar, as that of **be** is in PTQ (see Section 3.4.6 below), should be considered a part of the logical form of any expression in which it occurs. Thus while two sentences that are alike except for a different choice of transitive verb, **eat** vs. **lose**, for instance, will be said to have the same logical form and only a lexical difference, it is not clear that the same would or should be said about two sentences differing with respect to **eat** vs. **be**. (But then it may have been a mistake to classify **be** as a transitive verb in the first place.) A similar issue arises with respect to the determiners, the adverb **necessarily**, etc. But we will not pursue the issue of logical form further here; our aim has been more to raise warning flags about the non-obviousness of the notion than to try to elucidate it and it is not a notion that Montague ever discussed explicitly, to the best of this author's knowledge.

3.4.6. Other choices made in design of PTQ

There are other specific choices made by Montague in constructing PTQ which deserve mention but do not fit under the general headings above. A few of them will be discussed briefly here.

As discussed by Thomason (1974), one important property of PTQ and of Montague's theory more generally is the separation of the lexicon from the grammar. While a linguistically more sophisticated treatment would have to pay more systematic attention to morphology, the central point is that whatever are taken to be the smallest semantically contentful units, whether words or morphemes, are treated as primitives with respect to the grammar. The only aspect of lexical meaning that is obligatorily included in giving a grammar in accordance with UG is that each basic expression must be assigned a specific semantic type; and the semantic types must in turn be homomorphically related to the syntactic categories: expressions assigned to the same syntactic category should be assigned the same semantic type. The meanings of some basic expressions may be further constrained by meaning postulates and for words or morphemes considered to have "logical" rather than "empirical" meanings, the meanings may be completely spelled out in the grammar, but in general lexical meanings are left unspecified. As Thomason puts it,

[33] I learned this example from Emmon Bach, who learned it from Janet (J.D.) Fodor; I don't know where it originated.

Montague considered the syntax, semantics and (formal) pragmatics of natural language to be branches of mathematics, but lexicography to be an empirical discipline.[34]

In the framework of Montague grammar, as in most frameworks, the line between lexicon and grammar may be debated. In PTQ, there are a fixed number of syntactic categories and the "lexicon" consists of the basic expressions of those categories. Elements which are not members of any category but are introduced syntactegorematically by the operation of some syntactic rule include the determiners **every**, **a**, **the**, the conjunctions **and**, **or**, the negative particle **not**, the auxiliary verbs **will**, **have**. While these elements are not themselves assigned meanings, the syntactic rules in which they occur are given semantic interpretations in which it is in fact quite clear what the semantic contributions of those elements is and in the textbook (Dowty, Wall and Peters, 1981) there are exercises which consist of giving alternative grammars in which such elements are treated either categorematically or syncategorematically. Of the mentioned elements, the determiners undoubtedly have the strongest claim to belonging to a syntactic category, since the class of determiner phrases may not be a closed class and it certainly contains non-basic elements such as **almost every**, **at most five**. Most formal semantic textbooks in fact follow Thomason (1976) and Dowty, Wall and Peters (1981) in recasting PTQ to include a category T/CN, i.e. DET.

One "logical" element which is treated categorematically in PTQ is **be**, which is analyzed as a transitive verb, but one whose semantics is completely spelled out. Montague gave a clever analysis of the semantics of **be**, given in two forms below as (19), which enabled him to give the correct semantics for both (20) and (21) without having to distinguish a "**be** of identity" from a "**be** of predication". The advantages and disadvantages of Montague's treatment of **be**, and a suggested alternative in which the meaning of English **be** is basically "Predicate!", as in (22), and Montague's (19) is reconstrued as a type-shifting operation that provides predicate meanings for full term phrases, are discussed in (Partee, 1987).

(19) (a) PTQ: $\mathbf{be}' = \lambda \mathbf{Q} \lambda x \big[[^\vee \mathbf{Q}](^\wedge \lambda y[^\vee x = ^\vee y])\big]$.

(b) Equivalently: $\mathbf{be}' = \lambda \mathbf{Q} \lambda x[^\wedge\{x\} \in ^\vee \mathbf{Q}]$.

(20) **Cicero is Tully.**

(21) **John is a man.**

(22) Alternative: $\mathbf{be}' = \lambda P \lambda x[[^\vee P](x)]$.

It is interesting to see what Montague did about one clear difference between English and the formal languages of logic. In any logic, the sentential operators like negation and the tense and modal operators are all recursive and there is no limit to the number of

[34] It is of course also an empirical matter to determine which particular syntax and semantic corresponds to the language of a particular speech community; this is discussed very clearly in (Lewis, 1969, 1975b). Montague, like others in the tradition of logic and model theory, saw the study of language and grammar as analogous to the study of geometry, separating the study of the platonic objects and their formal description from the study of the epistemological relation of humans to particular such abstract objects (including any questions of the "psychological reality" of any given formal description of the objects).

them that may be prefixed to a given sentence. In English, however, such elements are mainly limited to one per clause: this is certainly true of the tense-aspect-modal elements like **will**, **have** + − **en** and true (with certain caveats) of negation. In his earlier fragment in EFL, the trick Montague used for limiting negation to one occurrence per sentence was to "regiment" English into a form closer to a real historically earlier form, putting the **not** at the end of the sentence and limiting the rule to applying to sentences that do not already end with **not**. This was an expedient that made the fragment less like real English but allowed for a simple rule that had a sentence as its input and a sentence as its output, so that the corresponding semantic rule could just apply the usual logical negation operator to the corresponding proposition.

In PTQ, Montague chose a different solution for negation and his two auxiliary verbs. Instead of introducing them in "sentence-to-sentence" rules, he introduced them in a set of six rules all of which took as input a subject NP and a VP and gave as their outputs the six sentence forms "present affirmative", "present negative", "future affirmative", etc. Most linguists did not and do not regard this as an optimal solution to the problem of "sentence-scope operators" which do not apply recursively in natural languages; see Carlson (1983) for further discussion.

3.4.7. PTQ in retrospect

The discussion of PTQ above is already partly retrospective; in this short section we will focus more directly on two kinds of issues that are illuminated by the perspective of hindsight: (i) how some of the PTQ rules might be derivable from more general principles and how others might be modified, generalized, or questioned; and (ii) issues relating to Montague's type theory.

To a linguist, Montague's syntax in many points seemed somewhat primitive and highly unconstrained and stipulative. PTQ did however lead to the revival of categorial grammar that had been urged in the work of Lyons (1968) and Lewis (1970) and to an investigation of various versions of it and was also one important catalyst for the reintroduction of serious interest in "monostratal", or non-transformational, grammars, since it pointed the way to a conception of grammar in which more of the work of explaining relatedness between different expressions could be accomplished by the semantics.[35] And some other points of PTQ syntax were noted above to have had continuing influence: the idea that restrictive relative clauses should modify CNPs and not NPs, the idea that underlying structures should include "open" sentences containing (expressions to be interpreted as) free variables and most importantly the idea that it is the derivation tree, or analysis tree, that is the crucial semantically relevant syntactic structure rather than any level or levels of phrase structure.

One weakness of the PTQ syntax is that the grammar generates strings rather than bracketed strings or constituent structure trees and the syntactic operations are defined on strings. About the only place where this leads to an actual error in PTQ is in the interaction of subject-verb agreement with verb phrase conjunction rules, as noted in (Partee, 1973b). But most subsequent researchers have made the "friendly amendment"

[35] Gazdar (1982), who made one of the earliest of several kinds of proposals for a non-transformational phrase structure grammar in the 1970's and 1980's, used a semantics explicitly modeled on that of PTQ.

of having the rules generate bracketed strings or trees as a matter of course and Montague grammar is taught that way in (Dowty, Wall and Peters, 1981). (Gamut (1991) follows Montague in generating strings; the authors discuss the need for identifying the "main verb(s)" of a verb phrase in stating subject-verb agreement, but they do not define the notion "main verb" explicitly and it seems clear that doing so for a fragment that contains ambiguous strings like **try to walk and find a fish** will require either bracketing or reference to derivational history.)

More generally, linguists have from the start wanted to think about the syntactic rules of PTQ in terms of a theory of natural language syntax. As noted earlier, Montague put no constraints on the syntactic operations that could be used in a syntactic rule, not even a constraint of computability. A linguist wants a theory of syntax to specify the class of possible syntactic operations and to clarify what is universal and what is the minimum that must be stipulated in the grammar of a particular language. And many of Montague's syntactic rules combine syntactic concatenation with some morphological operations such as case-marking and agreement; some modularization of syntax proper and morphology is adopted in virtually all linguistically more sophisticated versions of Montague grammar. (But the notion of a "construction", which may involve function composition of several operations, may be a useful one, as noted above in Section 3.1.)

A linguist also wants a theory of syntax and semantics to specify whatever empirical generalizations there might be about the relation between the form of a given syntactic rule and the form of the corresponding semantic interpretation rule (see Partee 1976b, 1979a; Janssen, 1981; for some early suggestions in this direction). Thus, for example, it is probably no accident that PTQ's "Rules of Functional Application" cover virtually all of the basic grammatical relations instantiated in PTQ; one might hypothesize that the interpretation of all "X-bar" structures is by functional application: lexical heads applying to their subcategorized arguments, modifiers to their modifiees and specifiers to specifiees. Some directions in which linguistic theorizing has gone in this respect include the idea of "type-driven translation" (Klein and Sag, 1985) and the idea of "type shifting", discussed in Section 4.4.3 below, and the search for "natural functions" discussed in (Partee, 1987) as an alternative to Montague's strategy of always "generalizing to the worst case".

The rules in PTQ for conjunction and disjunction and the rules for quantifying in, are in retrospect just particular instances of cross-categorial schemas which call for "recursive types" and a recursive definition of both the syntactic and semantic rules; see Partee and Rooth (1983).

The rules for quantifying in and for the handling of pronominal anaphora are rules which work remarkably well as far as they go (although Montague made no attempt to capture "island constraints" or the distinction between reflexive and non-reflexive pronouns), but that is certainly one area in which there have been many other proposals before, simultaneously and since. Some discussion of alternatives is found in Sections 4.2 and 4.3.

Certain constructions which had been used in the transformational grammar literature to argue for the need for transformations and for their cyclic ordering were missing from the PTQ fragment and it was not obvious how to add them; in particular, there was no treatment of passive sentences, of existential **there** sentences, nor of "raising" constructions with **seem**, **appear**, etc., although examples of the latter were mentioned in

PTQ as a kind of sentence which could be accommodated directly in the UG fragment but would have to be treated "indirectly as paraphrases" (perhaps via transformations?) in PTQ. Explorations of extensions of PTQ to include such constructions included attempts to synthesize Montague grammar with transformational grammar (Partee, 1973b, 1975; Bennett, 1974; Bach, 1976, 1979b); further reflections on how best to constrain transformations to make them consistent with the requirements of compositionality led to proposals for eliminating them entirely, as discussed above in Section 3.4.3.

In contrast to approaches which have concentrated on minimizing or eliminating transformations, one noteworthy large-scale research effort, directed at the linguistic aspects of machine translation, has found that the factoring out of meaning-preserving transformations from the meaning-relevant construction rules of a grammar can be of great advantage in designing a compositional translation procedure. Rosetta (1994) describes the results of a seven-year project for translating among English, Dutch and Spanish; the system uses an interlingua which consists of semantic derivation trees and the grammars for the individual languages are of a form inspired by and very close to Montague grammar, with departures designed in part to capture linguistic generalizations within the individual languages and at the same time to make the transfer between languages as simple and systematic as possible. By separating the translation-relevant rules from the purely syntactic (and in general more language-specific) transformations, it proved feasible to make the grammars of the different languages isomorphic (in a precisely defined sense) with respect to the translation-relevant rules without having to complicate the grammars artificially. The translation-relevant rules in a number of cases introduce abstract elements which serve as triggers for transformations, a practice that recalls the work of Katz and Postal (1964), where the hypothesis that transformations should preserve meaning was first argued; the success of the Rosetta project suggests that that practice merits continued exploration in the context of Montague grammar (as was suggested by McCawley, 1979), as a competitor to the strategy of trying to generate and interpret surface structures as directly as possible.

In general, there has been much more lasting attachment to the principle of compositionality and to many aspects of Montague's semantics than to the manner in which Montague presented his syntax or to the particulars of his syntactic rules, although Montague's syntax was certainly of interest and has also influenced later developments in many ways.

3.5. The other two fragments: Brief notes

While a number of the ideas instantiated in PTQ, and particularly a great deal of the background of Montague's intensional logic IL, are developed in Montague's earlier papers (1959–1969), the two 1970 papers EFL and UG, corresponding to lectures and seminars given in 1966–1968 and 1969–1970 respectively, provide the most immediate background for PTQ, which was presented as a lecture in late 1970. EFL is particularly rich in discussion of particular grammatical constructions, sources and attributions for ideas about the handling of various phenomena, and informal descriptions of alternative ways things might be done or ways one might eliminate certain oversimplifications.

Both papers contain discussion that is relevant to a fuller understanding of some of the choices made in PTQ, discussion which is mostly not repeated in PTQ and it is therefore rewarding to read even just the prose parts of both papers.

EFL contains a fragment of English with a direct model-theoretic interpretation. In UG, in order to demonstrate the applicability of the general theory presented there (see Section 3.1 above) to both formal and natural languages, Montague presents the syntax and semantics of his intensional logic and the syntax and compositional translation into intensional logic of a fragment of English (plus meaning postulates cutting down the class of "logically possible models" for the fragment to a class of "strongly logically possible models"), thus illustrating the method of indirect interpretation also used in PTQ. In UG as in PTQ he emphasizes that the interpretation of English could have been done directly and that proceeding by way of translation into intensional logic is simply for the sake of greater perspicuity.

The fragments of EFL and UG contain many of the same parts of English that are treated in PTQ, with some differences of detail in the treatment in some points and with certain differences in the handling of the relation between extensions and intensions. EFL and UG both contain adjectives, absent from PTQ; they are less comprehensive than PTQ only in lacking infinitival complements, tenses other than the present and the nouns and verbs of the "temperature puzzle". EFL lacks intensional transitive verbs like **seeks** and non-intersective adjectives like **alleged**, **former**, but these are included in the UG fragment.

Besides using the method of direct interpretation, EFL also eliminates the distinction between extension and intension by treating sentences as denoting propositions and setting everything else up accordingly (verbs as denoting relations-in-intension, etc.). In UG, the distinction between sense and reference is reintroduced, as well as a further distinction between senses (functions from possible worlds or world-time pairs) and *meanings*, which serve as interpretations of expressions and are analyzed as functions from not only worlds or world-time pairs but also contexts of use (relevant for indexicals and other context-dependent expressions); Montague's meanings are thus similar in some respects to Kaplan's *characters* (Kaplan, 1979). For a discussion of the interdefinability of various ways of instantiating or eliminating the sense-reference distinction, see Lewis (1974). Montague intended for EFL to have a Part II which would include indexical expressions, among other extensions; that was never written, but many of Montague's ideas about the treatment of indexicals can be found in his papers on formal pragmatics and in UG, whose fragment includes "free variable pronouns" interpreted as demonstratives.

The treatment of anaphora, while semantically basically the same in EFL, UG and PTQ, is syntactically different in the three fragments; in all three, some kind of indexed variables are used in order to support a compositional interpretation, departing to this extent from the direct generation of surface expressions of English. In EFL, the category of "basic name phrases" contains both ordinary proper nouns of English and individual variables $v_0, \ldots, v_n, \ldots$, and the rules of quantification and relative clause formation replace occurrences of the relevant variables by anaphoric expressions of the form **that N**, where **N** is the head common noun of the quantified-in noun phrase and the head noun of the common noun phrase to which the relative clause is being attached, respectively. (Bound variable uses of the determiner **that** are in fact possible in English, although this analysis of Montague's has not been much followed up on.) Thus EFL contains derivations like those partially sketched in (23) and (24).

(23) **every tall man in Amsterdam loves a woman such that that woman loves that man**, 9

/ | \

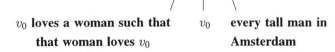

v_0 **loves a woman such that that woman loves** v_0 — v_0 — **every tall man in Amsterdam**

(24) **every man loves that man, 9**

/ | \

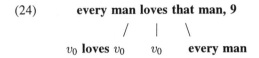

v_0 **loves** v_0 — v_0 — **every man**

As remarked earlier, Montague included a footnote in EFL about the fact that (24) would be more naturally expressed as "every man loves himself", with interesting ideas about how a reflexive rule might be formulated. But in fact in EFL there are no pronouns generated at all, either reflexive or plain; the "bound-variable" anaphoric expressions are all of the form **that N**.

In UG, the set of "basic individual expressions" no longer contains proper nouns, which are elevated to the status of "basic singular terms" and given intensional generalized quantifier interpretations as in PTQ, except for the addition of the intension operator and the omission of individual concepts. The set of basic individual expressions (which ends up being the set of all individual expressions; there are no non-basic ones) consists of the set of symbols v_{2n+1} for n a natural number. There is a syntactic rule that then says that if α is an individual expression, then **he** α is a term; compound expressions like **he** v_{2n+1} play the role in UG of subscripted pronouns like **he**$_n$ in PTQ, with the pronoun part serving as the locus of case marking and the variable part keeping the expressions disambiguated. The interpretation of that syntactic rule gives a term of the form **he** v_{2n+1} the intensional generalized quantifier meaning $^\wedge\lambda P[[^\vee P](v_{2n+1})]$, the intensional variant of the PTQ meaning of **he**$_n$ (modulo individual concepts). The variables stay in the expressions throughout a derivation, unlike the indices on the pronouns in PTQ and are eliminated at the very end as part of the operation of an "ambiguating" relation that also deletes certain parentheses that are introduced in the syntactic rules of UG.

The use of parentheses in UG is interesting; UG introduces certain marked parentheses in the course of the syntactic rules which serve the function served by introducing bracketing and defining the syntactic rules to operate on bracketed strings instead of strings. Montague in UG introduces such parentheses as parts of strings only where they are specifically needed and defines the rules on strings, referring to the parentheses where necessary. The definition of the main verb of a verb phrase is a recursive definition given as part of the grammar and involving such parenthesization and the agreement rules in UG correspondingly point the way to Montague's likely intended solution of the problem with the agreement rules of PTQ noted in Section 3.4.7.

It was noted earlier that lambda abstraction is a more basic variable-binding device than quantification. It is noteworthy in this respect that in UG, there is no quantifying in rule; the effects of PTQ's and EFL's quantifying in rules, including bound-variable anaphora and variations in quantifier scope, are all accomplished with the help of **such that** relative clauses and the "empty" noun **entity**. The proposition expressed by (25) in PTQ is expressed by (26) in UG ((26)a is generated and transformed by the ambiguating relation to (26)b) and corresponding to the ambiguous sentence (27) in PTQ are the two unambiguous sentences (28)a and (28)b in UG.[36] In UG the **such** (v_{2n+1}) **that** construction is analyzed as expressing predicate abstraction and the semantic interpretation associated with quantifying in in PTQ and EFL is more transparently expressed in UG by an English construction which, while stilted, is interestingly close in its surface syntax to the "logical form" displayed by the analysis trees of EFL or PTQ. The PTQ and EFL fragments, especially PTQ, associate what is basically the same semantic analysis with a more natural English syntax.

(25) **Every man loves a woman such that she loves him.**

(26) (a) **Every man is a(n) entity such v_1 that it v_1 loves a woman such v_3 that she v_3 loves it v_1.**

(b) **Every man is a(n) entity such that it loves a woman that she loves it.**

(27) **John seeks a unicorn.**

(28) (a) **John seeks a unicorn.**

(b) **A unicorn is a(n) entity such that John seeks it.**

The rule that forms **such that** relative clauses is the only variable binding rule in the grammar,[37] and it leaves the indexed pronoun expressions ungendered; it is the rule that combines those relative clauses with a common noun phrase that adjusts the gender of the relevant pronouns to correspond to the gender of the head noun of the common noun phrase. (And when that head noun is **entity**, the corresponding pronouns become **it**, which accounts for part of the stiltedness of (26).) Thomason (1976) made a related and even richer use of (sentential) "abstracts" in his early extension of Montague grammar.

One of the progressions that one sees in the three fragments is a drive toward finding general patterns in the syntactic and semantic rules and the relation between them. One instance of this is the gradual emptying out of the syntactic category of entity-expressions: in EFL that category included both proper names and variables; in UG, it still contained variables, but the proper names were put in the category of basic terms and the generated

[36] The example given in UG is **Jones seeks a horse such that it speaks**; unicorns make their first appearance in the examples of PTQ. But the lexicon of UG is open-ended, so the proper and common nouns of the explicit fragment of PTQ are also implicitly included in the fragment of UG.

[37] In EFL, Montague discusses the complications that would be involved in writing a rule for relative clauses headed simply by the complementizer **that**, with deletion of the appropriate variable inside the clause and pronominalization of subsequent ones; he notes some of the "island restrictions" that would have to be dealt with in such a rule and for that reason sticks to the syntactically simpler **such that** rule in all three fragments. See Rodman (1976) for the earliest Montague grammar of relative clauses with **that** and **which**.

"pronoun plus variable" complexes were also in the category of terms. In PTQ, there are no longer "variables" *per se* in the syntax, but indexed pronouns and these and the proper names are both in the category of basic terms. All terms and term phrases in PTQ belong to a single syntactic category and all are interpreted uniformly as generalized quantifiers. (The present move toward type multiplicity and type shifting may be seen in part as a way of reconciling the different motivations that may lie behind the different treatments in the three fragments, one being the wish to treat each kind of expression in the simplest way possible and another being the desire for uniformity of category-type correspondence without unnecessary multiplication of categories.)

Another interesting feature of the EFL and UG fragments is the treatment of adjectives. Montague followed ideas of Parsons and Kamp in interpreting adjectives as functions from properties to properties. In EFL he discussed the possibility of separating out subclasses of intersective and subsective adjectives but preferred for the sake of conceptual simplicity to keep a single class of adjectives. He did suggest the possibility of adding "postulates" to identify those subclasses, suggesting that a sentence might be called *analytic* with respect to a given analysis if it is a logical consequence of such postulates and noting that for some purposes we might be more concerned with analyticity than with logical truth. On the Parsons–Kamp–Montague treatment of adjectives, it is adnominal adjectives that are basic. In EFL, Montague also generated such adjectives in predicate position after **be** and there interpreted them as if they occurred in a full indefinite term phrase **an Adj entity**. (In UG, he omitted that additional rule; it was one of the few examples of the use of an interpretive analog of "abstract syntax" in Montague's work as opposed to a more direct interpretation of the actual surface forms.) In EFL, he remarked on the parallels between adjectival modification and adverbial modification; adverbial modification is included in both EFL and PTQ.

Some of the other interesting features of EFL and UG were noted in earlier sections: the "regimentation" of English negation in EFL (Section 3.4.6), the rich footnote concerning reflexive pronouns in the same paper (Section 3.4.3), the interpretation of "free variable pronouns" as demonstratives in UG (Section 3.4.3).

It was noted in Section 3.4.7 that work in the Montague tradition has been much more diverse in the degree to which it is influenced by Montague's syntax than in its continuity with Montague's semantics. Here we can add that the three fragments of EFL, UG and PTQ are themselves more diverse in their syntax than in their semantics. But all are compositional and the differences are interesting in illustrating some of the choices that may be made with respect to analyses of a given phenomenon within the overall theoretical framework of Montague's Universal Grammar.

4. The Montagovian revolution: Impact on linguistics and philosophy, further developments. Montague's legacy

In this section, we focus on a few selected topics to illustrate the impact Montague's work has had on linguistics and the philosophy of language and the progressive evolution of Montague grammar and formal semantics over the last 25 years, including a few of the main revisions that have largely supplanted aspects of Montague's theory. The topics that have been selected center around the domains of quantification, anaphora and type theory. The discussion is brief, with pointers to several other chapters in this Handbook which treat some of these topics in greater detail. As in the case of the Chomskyan revolution in syntax, the Montagovian revolution in semantics has had as its most lasting effect an exciting raising of expectations of what is possible, grounded on the foundations of a methodology, some powerful new tools and techniques, and some useful criteria for success. The richness of Montague's legacy can be seen not only in those specifics of Montague's theory or of specific aspects of his grammar fragments that have survived the test of time but also in the ease with which later researchers have been able to propose and debate alternative analyses and theoretical innovations within a common core of largely shared goals and standards for evaluating progress.

4.1. The Montagovian revolution. Initial impact

In the characterization of Bach (1989), the Chomskyan revolution had at its core the thesis that a natural language can be described as a formal system. Montague's revolutionary contribution was the thesis that a natural language can be described as an *interpreted* formal system, a thesis about which there had been skepticism from linguists and logicians alike (see Section 2.1) before Montague's demonstration of what could be accomplished with the skillful use of sophisticated tools.

The principal initial hurdles that had to be overcome in introducing Montague's ideas to the linguistics community were the historical skepticism just noted and the fact that on first exposure to Montague's work, many linguists were daunted by the heavy formalism and the high-powered typed intensional logic used by Montague; the reaction has been caricatured by the epithet "English as a Foreign Language"[38] applied to Montague's analysis of natural language. For some linguists, Montague grammar was simply somewhat unapproachable, since working with it required facility with logical tools that were previously unfamiliar. And among philosophers, there were many who followed Quine and Davidson in skepticism about possible-worlds semantics and about Montague's approach to intensionality. But among linguists and many philosophers of language, the central question was whether the theory's fruitfulness was worth the effort it took to learn it and for a critical mass of linguists and philosophers the answer was affirmative and within the decade of the 1970's Montague's semantics became a dominant (although by no means universally accepted) approach to semantics.

By the middle of the 1970's, Montague grammar and related work in formal semantics was flourishing as a cooperative linguistics-and-philosophy enterprise in parts of the U.S., the Netherlands, Germany, Scandinavia, and New Zealand. (By the late 1970's it was no longer possible to keep track.) The first published collection, Partee (ed.) (1976a), contained contributions by Lewis, Partee, Thomason, Bennett, Rodman, Delacruz, Dowty, Hamblin, Cresswell, Siegel and Cooper and Parsons; the first issue of *Linguistics and Philosophy* contained Karttunen (1977) as its first article; the biennial Amsterdam Colloquia, still a major forum for new results in formal semantics, started up in the mid-1970's

[38] The phrase was coined, I believe, by Emmon Bach, to use with students in sympathy with the formidable hurdle that the study of Montague grammar often seemed to present.

and opened its doors to scholars from outside Europe by the late 1970's. Other conferences and workshops on or including Montague grammar were held in various places in the U.S. and Europe from the mid-1970's onward.

Acceptance of Montague grammar was by no means universal, however; there was considerable skepticism among some linguists about compositionality and the applicability to natural language of truth-conditional model-theoretic tools (see Chomsky, 1975, for an important and influential example). And some philosophers have always considered Montague's intensional logic insufficiently intentional, given that all logically equivalent expressions are treated as semantically identical. Other linguists and philosophers had other reasons for pursuing different approaches, as always.

As time and theories have progressed, it is increasingly difficult to distinguish between theories that might be considered modified versions of Montague grammar, theories developed explicitly to provide alternatives to some aspect of Montague grammar and theories whose principal origins are different but which show the influence of some aspects of Montague grammar. The pedigrees are in any case not of substantive importance; the problem only arises when trying to decide what belongs in an article on "Montague grammar".

With respect to the dauntingness of Montague's formal tools, the main "antidote", besides good textbooks and added training in logic, has been the gradual progress in finding formal tools that are more and more closely adapted to the needs of natural language semantics, so that it is gradually less necessary to couch explanations of the semantics in terms of logics not well suited for that purpose. It will probably take more generations, however, before we have formal tools to work with which have both all of the advantages of explicitness and nice formal properties of logics like Montague's intensional logic and a very close and perspicuous relationship to the structures that are found in natural languages. And it will take even longer before any such formal tools gain the degree of familiarity and apparent "naturalness" now enjoyed by first-order logic.

4.2. Quantification

There are two convergent reasons for starting with a discussion of some of the salient points about analyses of quantificational phenomena since PTQ. One is that Montague, by his title, chose that as the most salient feature of the PTQ fragment; the other is that it has been an extremely fertile and richly cultivated area of semantic research in the last 25 years, involving productive interaction across the contributing disciplines. The discussion that follows will omit many specifics; see the chapter on Quantifiers in this Handbook by Keenan and Westerståhl, or a textbook such as Gamut (1991).

4.2.1. Generalized quantifiers

Montague's analysis of noun phrases as denoting generalized quantifiers was novel to linguists, but it was already a topic of research among logicians, who had long been aware that some kinds of quantificational expressions, like **most books**, are not first-order representable (see Barwise and Cooper, 1981) but can be satisfactorily analyzed as generalized quantifiers: the determiner **most** can be treated as a relation between two sets, or, equivalently, as a function mapping a set onto a set of sets. When the linguist Robin Cooper met the logician Jon Barwise at the University of Wisconsin in the late 1970's, a productive collaboration resulted which led to the now-classic paper Barwise and Cooper (1981). Another fruitful collaboration that began at about the same time was that between the linguist Ed Keenan and the logician Jonathan Stavi, leading to another highly influential paper, Keenan and Stavi (1986) (versions of which circulated several years earlier).

Barwise and Cooper started from Montague's analysis of NPs as generalized quantifiers, recast it in more directly model-theoretic terms and greatly expanded the range of determiners considered. One of their most important and influential contributions was the identification of a number of model-theoretic properties that could be used to classify determiners and NPs in ways that correlated interestingly with linguistic generalizations concerning the identified subclasses of determiners and NPs. Several of the particular properties that they isolated, including conservativity, monotonicity and the weak-strong distinction, continue to play a central role in the development of explanatory theories of the syntactic and semantic behavior of NPs and determiners. Even more important was the example they set of how one might search for linguistically significant model-theoretic properties of the interpretations of expressions, properties that might not have any direct representation in either "logical forms" or in "formal" properties of the expressions in some logic such as IL that might be used in an intermediate representation.

Barwise and Cooper suggested some properties that might be shared by all natural language determiners, though not by all logically possible meanings of the semantic type of determiners. The best-known of these is what is now called Conservativity, what Barwise and Cooper called the "lives-on" property. The statement that all natural language determiners live on their common noun set, or are conservative in their first argument, is formally captured by (29) and illustrated by the necessary truth of (30).

(29) A determiner meaning D lives on its first argument iff
for all sets A, B, it holds that $D(A)(B)$ iff $D(A)(A \cap B)$.

(30) **At most three horses are black if and only if**
at most three horses are horses that are black.

Barwise and Cooper also identified the properties "weak" and "strong" (see the Quantifier chapter) and showed their correlation with the classes of NPs subject to various "indefiniteness effects" and "definiteness effects", for some of which they were able to give a semantic account of the effects as well. Others since then have continued to explore alternative approaches to these and related properties and alternative analyses of the constructions in question, since this is an area where there are many significant linguistic phenomena to be explained and not all appear to be sensitive to exactly the same properties or to be analyzable by exactly the same means.

One interesting family of properties studied by Barwise and Cooper and further explored by subsequent scholars are the monotonicity properties, intimately related to the property of "downward-entailingness" identified by Ladusaw (1979) in what was probably the first clear example of a place where the model theory could do some explanatory work that could not be duplicated by logical forms or properties of logical formulas.

A function classified as downward-entailing by Ladusaw, given a suitable definition of a partial ordering "$\leqslant$" applicable to its domain and range, is a function f such that $f(y) \leqslant f(x)$ whenever $x \leqslant y$. Ladusaw showed that given the structure of the functional types of PTQ-like fragments, one can recursively define a partial order for most of the used types starting from the assumption that 0 (false) is less than 1 (true); the partial order's "$\leqslant$" corresponds to "$\subseteq$" on all the types whose domain are sets. And given those formal tools, Ladusaw was able to argue that the possibility of occurrence of negative polarity items like **any**, **ever**, **at all** is best explained in semantic terms: negative polarity items can occur within the arguments of downward- entailing (monotone decreasing) functions, an insight which had been suggested in earlier work of Gilles Fauconnier (1975a, 1975b); see the Quantifier chapter for further details.

Ladusaw's work was followed by a very interesting debate between Ladusaw and Linebarger, with Linebarger defending a syntactic account based on the triggering item being a C-commanding negative operator (Ladusaw, 1980, 1983; Linebarger, 1980, 1987). The debate illustrated the difficulty of settling arguments between a syntactic and a semantic account of a given phenomenon in any straightforwardly empirical way; it also illustrated both the advantages and the pitfalls of the method of fragments. Each account handled some of the same central cases adequately, each account had trouble with some kinds of "peripheral" cases, but the two accounts differed in other cases, handling different examples directly and requiring pragmatic augmentation for an account of some cases (different ones on the two approaches). But in any case, formal semanticists would agree that Ladusaw's work on polarity sensitivity as a semantic property was important and ground-breaking research which has served as a model for much that followed. Barwise and Cooper's investigation of monotonicity properties of determiners and NPs was a further development of the same sort.

Another major model-theoretic advance in the semantics of noun phrases and determiners came from the work of Godehard Link (1983), discussed in part in Lønning's chapter "Plurals and Collectivity" in this Handbook. Link proposed a treatment of the semantics of mass and plural nouns whose principal innovations rest on enriching the structure of the model by treating the domain of entities as a set endowed with a particular algebraic structure. In the model Link proposes, the domain of entities is not an unstructured set but contains subdomains which have the algebraic structure of semilattices. A distinction is made between *atomic* and *non-atomic* semilattices. Intuitively, atomic lattices have smallest discrete elements (their atoms), while non-atomic ones (really "not necessarily atomic") may not.

These atomic and non-atomic join semilattice structures, when used to provide structures for the domains of count and mass nouns respectively, give an excellent basis for showing both what properties mass and plural nouns share and how mass and count nouns differ, as well as for formally elucidating the parallelism between the mass/count distinction and the process/event distinction (Bach, 1986b). Some brief introductions to the main ideas can be found in (Bach, 1986b; Partee, 1992, 1993), and in Landman's contribution to Lappin (ed.) (1996); for more complete expositions, see Link (1983), Landman (1989a, 1989b, 1991).

A chief pay-off is that these lattice structures also make it possible to give a unified interpretation for those determiners (and other expressions) that are insensitive to atomicity, i.e. which can be used with what is intuitively a common interpretation for mass and count domains, such as **the**, **all**, **some** and **no**. **The**, for instance, can be elegantly and simply defined as a "supremum" operation that can be applied uniformly to atomic and non-atomic structures and to singular or plural entities within the atomic structures. "Count-only" determiners such as **three** and **every** have interpretations that inherently require an atomic semilattice structure.

Link's work, like that of Heim (discussed in the next subsection), adds support for the idea that the definite article is not primarily quantificational, contrary to Russell and contrary to Montague. Link's uniform analysis of **the** treats it as a supremum operator in the subsemilattice denoted by the common noun phrase it applies to; the semantic value of the result is an entity, not a generalized quantifier. Of course the resulting entity can always be "lifted" to the type of generalized quantifiers by the same means used for proper names and pronouns in PTQ, but the basic semantics of the definite determiner on Link's analysis is that it forms an individual-denoting expression rather than a quantifier phrase.

One of the most important features of this analysis is that the mass lattice structure emerges as unequivocally more general than the count noun structure, i.e. as the unmarked case. The domains of mass noun interpretations are simply join semilattices, unspecified as to atomicity. Atomic join semilattices are characterized as the same structures but with an added requirement, hence clearly a marked case. This means that languages without the mass/count distinction are describable as if all their nouns are *mass* nouns; we need not seek some alternative structure that is neutral between mass and count, since mass itself turns out to be the neutral case (see also Stein, 1981).

While some of these innovations naturally depart in various ways from Montague's work, they can all be seen as exploiting the possibility of finding model-theoretic bases for linguistic generalizations, removing some of the explanatory load from the syntactic component and showing that semantics is more than a matter of finding a symbolic "logical form". Link's work in particular shows the potential importance of uncovering further algebraic structure within the domains corresponding to simple types, an important step in the further integration of lexical semantic investigations into formal semantics, an enterprise which began with the work of Dowty (1979).

4.2.2. Kamp–Heim and non-uniform treatment of NPs

The work of Kamp and Heim beginning in the early 1980's was one of the major developments in the semantics of noun phrases, quantification and anaphora, and, more generally, influenced the shift from a "static" to a "dynamic" conception of meaning, discussed further in Sections 4.3 and 4.5 below. For substantive detail, see Heim (1982), Kamp (1981), Kamp and Reyle (1993) and the chapter on Discourse Representation Theory in this Handbook by Kamp and Van Eijck. Here we briefly underline some of the principal issues raised by their innovations in the context of Montague grammar, particularly their challenge to Montague's uniform interpretation of NPs as generalized quantifiers.

Kamp (1981) and Heim (1982) offered solutions to classic problems involving indefinite noun phrases and anaphora in multi-sentence discourses and in the famous "donkey-sentences" of Geach (1962) like (31) and (32).

(31) **Every farmer who owns a donkey beats it.**

(32) **If a farmer owns a donkey, he beats it.**

On their theories, indefinite (and in Heim's theory also definite) noun phrases are interpreted as variables (in the relevant argument position) plus open sentences, rather than as quantifier phrases. The puzzle about why an indefinite NP seems to be interpreted as existential in simple sentences but universal in the antecedents of conditionals stops being localized on the noun phrase itself; its apparently varying interpretations are explained in terms of the larger properties of the structures in which it occurs, which contribute explicit or implicit unselective binders that bind everything they find free within their scope.

Both Kamp and Heim make a major distinction between quantificational and non-quantificational NPs and the semantics they give to NPs varies with the internal structure of the NP. It is not straightforward to say what type is assigned to an indefinite NP on their approaches, given that the NP makes several separate contributions to the semantic interpretation of the larger expression in which it occurs. But in any case, the semantics of indefinites, definites, pronouns and names is on their analysis fundamentally different from the semantics of the "genuinely quantificational" NPs, represented in their original fragments by NPs headed by the determiner **every**.

A related innovation of Kamp's and Heim's work is their systematization of the similarities between adverbs of quantification and determiner quantifiers, starting from the classic paper Lewis (1975a) on adverbs of quantification as unselective binders. While not uncontroversial, their proposals opened up a rich line of research on quantificational structures of different kinds that has broadened into interesting typological research (see Section 4.6 below).

Both the diversification of NP semantics and the unification of some kinds of determiner quantification with adverbial quantification represented an important challenge to Montague's uniformity of assignment of semantic types to syntactic categories and in Kamp's presentation of DRT even an apparent challenge to compositionality. We return to these issues in Section 4.4.3 in our discussion of type flexibility. We will also briefly discuss the claim that Kamp's Discourse Representation Theory is insufficiently compositional, a concern which formed part of the motivation for the theory of "Dynamic Montague Grammar", developed by Groenendijk and Stokhof (1990, 1991) and extended by colleagues in Amsterdam and elsewhere (see especially the chapter on Dynamics in this Handbook).

4.2.3. Quantifier scope ambiguity

The analysis of quantifier scope ambiguity has been a perennial source of controversy. The heart of the problem is that in English and many other languages, sentences like (13), **A unicorn eats every fish**, which are ambiguous only with respect to quantifier scope, do not show any independent evidence of being syntactically ambiguous. The need to consider them syntactically ambiguous is purely a theoretical consequence of the acceptance of two assumptions: (i) the principle that semantic ambiguity must always be a result of lexical ambiguity or syntactic ambiguity (or both); and (ii) the assumption that quantifier scope ambiguity is an instance of semantic ambiguity that must be captured in a linguistic analysis.

Each of these principles is widely although not universally accepted. The principle stated in (i) is accepted by many theories and certainly must hold in any theory that accepts the principle of compositionality and therefore in most variants of Montague grammar. The assumption in (ii) contrasts with views which suggest that quantifier scope "ambiguity" is rather an instance of unspecificity, and that sentences with such "ambiguities" are to be given a single meaning which only in a given context of use may be further "specified"; but for theories which take truth conditions as an essential ingredient of linguistic meaning, it has proved very difficult to find an appropriate truth-conditional content which might be a plausible candidate for the "scope-neutral" content of such a sentence.

It therefore seems that any linguistic theory that includes a compositional truth-conditional semantics must analyze sentences like (13) as syntactically ambiguous. But there is tension from the fact that a sentence like (13) does not show any obvious signs of syntactic ambiguity, so a theoretical framework which wants to have an explanatorily as well as descriptively adequate syntax will prefer to regard (13) as syntactically unambiguous even at the cost of giving up or weakening compositionality. And even if one accepts the consequence that (13) must be syntactically ambiguous, there seems to be little syntactic evidence bearing on the question of what the nature of that ambiguity is, which is undoubtedly part of the reason why there have been and continue to be such a variety of proposals for dealing with them.

Some kinds of theories have proposed multiple levels of syntax, such that (13) has only a single syntactic structure on some levels (e.g., surface structure) and distinct structures on another, semantically relevant, level (e.g., "deep structure" on some theories, "logical form" on others). Thus May (1977, 1985) introduced Quantifier Raising, approximately the mirror image of the generative semantics rule of Quantifier Lowering, for deriving different logical forms from surface structures, but then made the startling proposal that (c-command at) the level of logical form does not in fact disambiguate quantifier scope.[39]

For Montague grammar, however, the principle of compositionality dictates that in all cases where a non-lexical ambiguity is found that cannot be traced to independently motivated differences of syntactic structure, there must nevertheless be two different syntactic derivations, two different routes of constructing one and the same expression (or surface syntactic structure, if one generates trees rather than strings). Montague, as described above, introduced Quantifying In rules for creating these derivational ambiguities. It was noted above that such Quantifying In rules, which simultaneously substitute a full NP and pronouns of appropriate case and gender for respective occurrences of a given syntactic variable $\mathbf{he}_n$, are in fact outside the bounds of what linguists would have called a single rule at the time. They are, moreover, the only rules in PTQ which give rise to syntactic derivations that do not respect the "intuitive" syntactic constituent structure and hence assign counterintuitive part/whole structures. The lack of "independent syntactic motivation" for Montague's Quantifying In rules has meant that even those linguists most sympathetic to many aspects of Montague's program have continued to

[39] Thereby abandoning the otherwise respected principle that the input to semantic interpretation must be a disambiguated syntax and that whatever "logical form" may mean, being truth-conditionally disambiguated is part of it. (See the discussion in (Chierchia, 1993).)

explore alternative treatments of quantifier scope ambiguities, starting from the earliest days of Montague grammar.

Cooper (1975, 1983) invented the alternative of "Cooper storage" as a means to avoid even a derivational ambiguity in a sentence such as (13), for which there is arguably no independent syntactic motivation for positing ambiguity. In the process of bottom-up compositional interpretation, whenever an NP is encountered, there is the option of either interpreting it *in situ* or of putting the NP meaning together with a chosen index into "storage" and putting the meaning of a correspondingly indexed pronoun into the interpretation in place of the given NP's meaning. The stored NP meaning is then "retrieved" into the sentence interpretation at any of the positions that correspond to possible scopes, i.e. any of the domains of Montague's Quantifying In rules; the stored index determines which variable is to be abstracted on in the accompanying lambda abstraction on the meaning with which the retrieved NP meaning is to be combined. (As noted in Section 3.1, this weakening of compositionality by permitting one syntactic structure to yield multiple meanings is only formal. The approach can be seen as compositional by taking the mapping from syntax to semantics to be a set-valued function.)

Scope ambiguity was the clearest phenomenon for which GPSG ("generalized phrase structure grammar"; see Gazdar, Klein, Pullum and Sag, 1985) had to choose between abandoning context-freeness or weakening compositionality; the latter option was chosen in quietly presupposing Cooper storage for quantifier scope. Cooper's mechanism of semantically storing quantifiers (and pronouns) avoids the "unintuitive" syntactic aspects of Montague's Quantifying-In, but accomplishes this at the expense of complicating the semantic component. Weighing the additional complexities of semantic interpretation against the simpler ambiguous syntax in his treatment of scope ambiguities, Cooper concludes: "What seems unappetizing about this system is not that we map into sets of meanings but that we have to map into sets of *sequences of sequences* of meanings" (Cooper, 1975, p. 160).

The "flexible Montague grammar" of Hendriks (1988, 1993) shares with Cooper's system the avoidance of a syntactic Quantifying In rule. It also represents quantifier (and coordination) scope ambiguities without syntactic repercussions such as "artificial" alternative ways of construction, but accounts for them by flexible type assignment, which affects the relationship between syntax and semantics: syntactic objects are associated with sets of systematically related interpretations of different types (see also Section 4.4.3 below). The flexible grammar can be shown to be fully compositional (i.e. in the single-valued sense), provided that its semantic "type-shifting" interpretation derivations are recast as unary syntactic/semantic rules. Since, moreover, all its syntactic operations respect the "intuitive" syntactic structure, so that constituent expressions are always real *parts*, the grammar also observes what Partee (1979b) called the "well-formedness constraint", i.e. the "most intuitive interpretation of the principle of compositionality, which says that the parts of a compound expression have to be *visible* parts of the compound expression" (Janssen, 1986a, pp. 65–66).

Other proposals for dealing with quantifier scope can be found in contemporary literature. Some scholars (see Szabolcsi (ed.) (forthcoming)) are putting more emphasis on the investigation of the semantics of individual determiners and noun phrases and the separate ingredients that go into the interpretation of quantificational expressions, such as distributivity and specificity or the lack of it. Some "classic" cases of scope ambiguity are being suggested not to involve scope ambiguity but other phenomena (see, e.g., Kratzer, 1995b) , and the study of the interaction of scope phenomena with topic-focus articulation and word-order phenomena in various languages is bringing new perspectives to bear on old problems.

Quantification and matters of scope have been and undoubtedly will continue to be an important arena for exploring consequences of rules and representations and the connections among them, as are the equally varied and controversial proposals concerning the syntax and semantics of pronouns and other "bindable" expressions.[40] These are areas in which the division of labor between syntax and semantics and even the question of whether that is a simple dichotomy, is particularly non-obvious.[41]

The integration of psycholinguistics and formal semantics requires some resolution of the problem of combinatorial explosion that comes with the disambiguation of such pervasive ambiguities as scope ambiguities; see Johnson-Laird (1983), J.D. Fodor (1982). It is hard to imagine all the ways in which recent linguistic history might be different if quantifier scope did not have to be worried about at all, but as long as systematic truth-conditional differences are regarded as semantic differences, quantifier scope possibilities must be accounted for.

4.3. Anaphora

Montague in PTQ treated only bound variable anaphora; in his earlier work developing pragmatics and intensional logic he treated indexical pronouns like **I** and demonstratives like **he**, **this**, **that**. At the time of Montague's work, linguists were already engaged in debates concerning how many and what kinds of uses of pronouns needed to be distinguished and to what extent these different uses could be unified or at least systematized. Karttunen (1969) considered the question of whether all non-demonstrative pronouns could be analyzed as bound variables and came up with some problematic examples that are still being debated, such as the "paycheck pronoun" **it** in (33).

(33) **The man who gave his paycheck to his wife was wiser than the man who gave it to his mistress.**

Partee (1970a) also explored the problem of trying to find a unified analysis of pronouns, with particular attention to cases that seem to require some kind of "pronoun

[40] Linguists not bound by a commitment to making truth conditions and entailment relations central to semantic adequacy criteria have the possibility of not representing scope as a linguistic ambiguity at all. This was a possibility sometimes entertained in Chomsky's earlier work, allowed for in current Prague school work such as Hajičová and Sgall (1987), explored in the context of parsing by Hindle and Rooth (1993) and in the context of Discourse Representation Theory by Reyle (1993); see also Poesio (1991, 1994).

[41] See, for instance, the "indexing mechanism" proposed by Williams (1988) as an alternative to Quantifier Raising and the similar indexing mechanism elaborated by Cooper and Parsons (1976); the status of an "indexed tree" with respect to syntax "or" semantics is not straightforward.

of laziness",[42] and to the problems raised by indefinite antecedents in particular. Other authors began to explore the possibility of pronouns sometimes being interpreted as "Skolem functions" with a hidden dependence on some non-overt variable as a possible solution to the paycheck pronouns and some other problematic cases.

As mentioned in Section 3.4.3 above, the insight that any NP, including a proper name, could be the antecedent of a bound-variable pronoun has had a major impact on subsequent discussions of the "strict"/"sloppy" identity puzzles in VP ellipsis in sentences like (7), repeated below.

(34) **Sam gave some fish to his dog and Sally did too.**

What had originally been seen as syntactic deletion of a VP under "sloppy" identity conditions (deleting **gave some fish to her dog** under "identity" with **gave some fish to his dog**) came to be seen instead as strict semantic identity of properties involving lambda binding of corresponding variables: $\lambda x[x$ **gave some fish to** x**'s dog**$]$. The difference between a proper name and a quantifier phrase like **every man** could then be argued to be that while both could be "antecedents" of bound variable pronouns (actually bound by a lambda operator), a proper name could also be "coreferential" with a non-bound-variable pronoun, while such coreference is not possible between a quantifier like **every man** and a singular pronoun like **he**.

The famous "donkey sentences" of Geach (1962), mentioned in Section 4.2.2 above and repeated below, were already beginning to receive some attention around the time of Montague's work, but it was not until after the importance of paying close attention to compositionality became more widely recognized by linguists that the real challenge of the donkey sentences was fully appreciated.

(35) **Every farmer who owns a donkey beats it.**

(36) **If a farmer owns a donkey, he beats it.**

The importance of donkey pronouns in the contemporary history of formal semantics could probably not have been predicted 25 years ago. The analysis of donkey-sentences and related problems remains at the time of writing this article a locus of intense unresolved arguments, arguments very important to competing views about issues of "logical form", compositionality, dynamics, the dispensability of intermediate levels of representation and other such key issues about the nature of semantics and its relation to syntax and to pragmatics.

In the following subsections, we mention briefly a small selection of the many issues and developments in the analysis of anaphora that have played an important role in the development of Montague grammar and "post-Montague grammar" over the last 25 years.

---

[42] The use of this term is not fully standardized; Partee (1970a) took the term from Geach (1962), but Geach (p.c.) took issue with Partee's usage of the term, arguing that in his original sense, there was never any shift of reference between the pronoun and its antecedent. Subsequent authors often use the term for any use of a pronoun which seems to be tantamount to a disguised definite description, which is closer to Partee's use than to the original Geach use.

4.3.1. Binding by lambda operators

One issue some of whose consequences were realized early although it has rarely had "center stage" in discussions of anaphora is the fact that on Montague's analysis in all three of his fragments of English, the binding of bound-variable pronouns is done not by the quantifier directly, but by the lambda operator that binds the "scope" expression that the quantifier applies to, as in the schematic translation (38) of (25), repeated here as (37), where not only the **she** in the relative clause but also the **him** whose antecedent is **every man** is bound by a lambda operator. It is true that after simplification steps, one may end up with a corresponding variable bound by a quantifier, as in (39), but (i) that is not true of the direct translation; and (ii) in a fragment with non-first-order generalized quantifiers like **most women**, there would not be any such reduction to a formula containing a first-order quantifier, so the variable corresponding to the pronoun would never be directly bound by a quantifier, but only by the lambda.

(37) **Every man loves a woman such that she loves him.**

(38) $\mathbf{every}'(^\wedge\mathbf{man}')\big(^\wedge\lambda x_1\big[\mathbf{love}'(^\wedge\mathbf{a}'(^\wedge\lambda x_3[\mathbf{woman}'(x_3)\wedge\mathbf{love}'_*(x_3,x_1)]))(x_1)\big]\big).$

(39) $\forall u\big[\mathbf{man}'_*(u)\to\exists v[\mathbf{woman}'_*(v)\wedge\mathbf{love}'_*(v,u)\wedge\mathbf{love}'_*(u,v)]\big].$

Recall the rather stilted structure (26)a, repeated here as (40), generated by the UG fragment before the disambiguating relation removes the variables.

(40) **Every man is a(n) entity such** v_1 **that it** v_1 **loves a woman such** v_3 **that she** v_3 **loves it** v_1**.**

The indirect relation between the actual binding of the pronoun and the assignment of a gender to the pronoun on the basis of the gender of its "antecedent" in the case of a Quantifying In rule and on the basis of the head noun of the relative clause containing the pronoun in the case of the relative clause rule creates both opportunities and problems.

One positive effect of lambda binding is that it allows us to see "sloppy identity", so called because of the apparently imperfect identity of **love her mother** and **love his mother** in the putative "VP-deletion" derivation of a sentence like (41), as strict semantic identity. There is no inherent gender in the property representable by the lambda expression in (42).

(41) **Mary loves her mother and John does too.**

(42) $\lambda x[\mathbf{love}(x, x\text{'s } \mathbf{mother})].$

The challenge is to figure out from this perspective what the right account of pronoun gender is, both in languages like English and in languages with "grammatical gender". See Dowty and Jacobson (1989) for relevant discussion. Montague's PTQ rules may seem clumsy and ad hoc with respect to the assignment of gender to pronouns, but they opened up new possibilities that linguists had not considered; the relationships among control, agreement and anaphora are currently under active exploration in many frameworks.

4.3.2. Evans and E-type pronouns

Montague in PTQ allowed quantification into coordinate structures with the possibility of an NP in one conjunct binding a pronoun in another conjunct, as in example (43), discussed earlier as (8), and as in example (44).

(43) **John wants to catch a fish and eat it.**

(44) **Mary catches a fish and John eats it.**

The semantic interpretation of (44) given by the Quantifying In rule is that there is at least one fish which Mary catches and John eats. Evans (1980) argued that this gives the wrong truth conditions for (44), that (44) implies that Mary caught just one fish (in the relevant context) and John ate the fish that Mary caught. Intuitions are even clearer with Evans's plural examples such as (45), which do clearly seem to imply that all of Jones's sheep were vaccinated, not just that there are some sheep owned by Jones that were vaccinated by Smith.

(45) **Jones owns some sheep and Smith vaccinated them.**

Evans therefore argued for an interpretation of the pronouns in these sentences that amounts to a definite description interpretation, the description to be systematically derived from the clause in which the antecedent occurs; (44) would then be interpreted in the same way as (46).

(46) **Mary catches a fish and John eats the fish that Mary catches.**

Evans called these pronouns "E-type" pronouns,[43] and versions of this kind of analysis continue to resurface as live candidates for some pronoun interpretations (see, e.g., Heim, 1990). The problem is always to figure out which pronouns can/must have such an analysis and how the appropriate interpretation, or possible interpretations, can be compositionally determined, or by what principles the right choice(s) might be narrowed down if the choice is grammatically non-deterministic.

4.3.3. Cooper pronouns

Cooper (1979) offered a theory of pronominal anaphora which was a Montague-grammar-oriented version of a theory combining Montague's treatment of bound variables with a generalization of theories like Evans's and other proposals for "pronouns as disguised definite descriptions", but which differed from most proposals of the latter type in relying on contextual/pragmatic rather than syntactic or explicit semantic principles for identifying the content of the "description"-type pronouns. Cooper's proposal was that a possible pronoun meaning was any meaning of the type of generalized quantifiers and of the form shown in the metalinguistic expression (47) below with the restriction that Π be a property-denoting expression containing only free variables and parentheses.

(47) $\lambda K \exists x \big[\forall y[[{}^{\vee}\Pi](y) \equiv y = x] \wedge K(x)\big].$

[43] It is not known, at least to this author and her colleagues, why he chose that term, but presumably not for "Evans".

Constraints on the possibilities on a given occasion of use of a given sentence are understood to be governed by the kinds of considerations that arise from the situation of speaker and hearer. We illustrate this idea briefly below.

Note first that Montague's pronoun meanings in PTQ are an instance of these Cooper pronouns. Their meanings are all of the form (48):

(48) $\lambda P[[{}^{\vee}P](x_i)]$.

(And if one follows the UG suggestion of allowing contexts of utterance to contain variable assignments, these same pronoun meanings can serve for bound-variable pronouns and pronouns whose referents are salient in the speech context.)

For a donkey pronoun or a paycheck pronoun, Cooper does not reconstruct pronoun meanings that are explicit descriptions like "the donkey he$_i$ owns" or "his$_i$ paycheck", but does provide pronoun meanings that are like those except for having free property or relation variables that are to be filled in contextually with salient properties and relations. A "paycheck pronoun" (see (33) above), for instance, is represented as in (49), where the relevant value of R would be "is the paycheck of" and the pronoun might be expected to be so understood if that relation were sufficiently salient to the hearer.

(49) $\lambda K \exists x \big[\forall y[[R(u)](y) \equiv y = x] \wedge K(x)\big]$.

The inclusion in the formula of u, a free variable that will be bound by the second occurrence of **the man**, is what lets this pronoun meaning be "functional", with its value dependent on the value of another bound variable in the sentence. Thus Cooper pronouns also subsume the idea of "Skolem-function pronouns".

Cooper pronouns offer a nice generalization of a number of proposals; but without more elaboration and auxiliary principles, the theory is too unrestrictive and allows too much. However, the continuing difficulty of devising an explicit theory which generates all and only the possible readings of pronouns leaves this approach an important live option.

4.3.4. Discourse referents and Kamp–Heim theories

As noted in Section 4.2.2, the interaction of indefinite noun phrases and anaphora raised the hardest puzzles about indefinites and some of the hardest puzzles about anaphora. The problem of donkey-sentences became particularly acute and well-defined in the context of PTQ, which did so many things nicely but did not offer a treatment of donkey-sentences and in the context of compositionality concerns more generally, which set high standards for the properties a genuine solution should have. (The best discussion of the problem and the inadequacy of previous approaches is found in the first chapter of Heim (1982).)

The other major puzzle, also well-described in (Heim, 1982), is the problem of "discourse anaphora", anaphora across sentences and the behavior of indefinite NPs in that phenomenon.

Kamp's and Heim's theories addressed both problems by offering a formalization of Karttunen's insight that indefinite NPs "introduce new discourse referents" in the process of interpreting a text and pronouns and definite NPs "refer to old discourse referents"; and that the "life span" of a discourse referent introduced by a given indefinite NP is determined by where in the structure the introducing NP occurs. The formalization of these insights required a shift from the usual "static" truth-conditional conception of meaning to a more dynamic conception.

Heim (1982) draws on the work of Stalnaker (1974, 1978), who characterized the function of assertion as the updating of the "common ground" of the participants in a conversation. Heim generalizes this conception and speaks of meaning as context-change potential; she shows how ordinary truth conditions can be defined in terms of context-change potential but not vice versa. Heim enriched the notion of common ground to include discourse referents as well as propositional information and Heim, Kamp and others since have enriched it further to serve as the locus of a variety of context-properties which show similarities in their formal behavior to the behavior of indefinites and anaphora.

Heim's and Kamp's theories are not formally identical and their worked-out fragments did not have exactly the same empirical coverage. Heim (1982) presented two alternative formalizations of her ideas, one, the Chapter II theory, with various kinds of explicit indexing carried out in the construction of "logical forms" and a rather standard semantic interpretation component applying to the output; the other, the Chapter III theory, involving a more basic semantic innovation, treating meaning as "context-change potential" and using the metaphor of "files", "file cards" and "file change" to describe the parts of the model structure and their formal manipulation in the process of interpretation. This second theory of Heim's often goes by the name of File Change Semantics. See Heim (1982), which by now is probably even more crucial as required reading for students of formal semantics than PTQ.

Kamp's theory, Discourse Representation Theory, described in the chapter of the same name in this Handbook, makes use of a novel "box language" (which can be converted to a linear representation if desired; see Zeevat, 1989; Chierchia, 1995) of Discourse Representations and Discourse Representation Structures; the semantics is presented in terms of recursive conditions of embeddability of such structures in a model. The details of the original presentation of Kamp's theory make it not obvious whether the theory is compositional; Zeevat (1989) explicitly provides a compositional version of the theory. Heim's theory is clearly compositional to begin with. The later versions of Kamp's work, including Kamp and Reyle (1993), again raise questions of compositionality which are not explicitly addressed. See the discussion and debate in (Groenendijk and Stokhof, 1991) and (Kamp, 1990).

4.3.5. Nominal and temporal anaphora

Another area that has been a rich one in the development of Montague grammar and formal semantics is the area of tense and aspect and temporal adverbials. This area, like many, is being almost entirely neglected in this article, but here we include a few words in connection with quantification and anaphora, partly in order to mention the impact Montague's contributions have had on more recent developments and partly because so much recent work has been concerned with the similarities and differences between entity-oriented language and event-oriented language, and this has been a major enrichment of the long history of work on anaphora and quantification.

The existence of parallels between expressions of quantification and anaphora in the noun phrase domain and in the temporal domain has long been recognized; entities, times and places and to some extent manners and degrees show similarities in having special **wh**-words, quantifier words like **everyone**, **everything**, **always**, **everywhere** and corresponding expressions with **some-**, **any-**, **no-**, deictic and demonstrative expressions, and anaphoric expressions. In pre-Montague days, linguists could only try to capture these similarities on some level of syntax or in first-order terms, invoking the existence of variables over times, places, degrees, etc. (see, e.g., Partee, 1973c).

Montague's unification of modal and tense logic and the indirect parallels between their quantificational interpretation in the model theory and their non-quantificational "operator" treatment in the object language, opened up a richer array of ways to see the similarities and differences between quantificational and anaphoric phenomena in the NP domain and partly similar phenomena in the domain of tense, aspect and temporal adverbials. The work of Dowty (1979, 1982), Bach (1980, 1981, 1986b), Hinrichs (1981, 1985, 1986), Krifka (1986, 1987), Partee (1984) and others built in increasingly rich ways on the model-theoretic perspective common to all of Montague grammar, on the integration of nominal and adverbial quantification offered by the Kamp–Heim perspective and on the richer algebraic structure imposed first on the domain of entities and then in a similar way on the domain of events on the basis of the work of Link (1983) as extended by Bach (1986b). The exploration of the similarities and differences between nominal and temporal quantification and nominal and temporal anaphora, and the mutual influences between aspectual properties of verb phrases and sentences (in a variety of languages) and quantificational properties of noun phrases, is a rich and growing area of research. See also the discussion in the chapter on Tense and Aspect in this Handbook.

4.3.6. Reflexives, 0-pronouns and ellipsis, control, traces

Most early work on anaphora in Montague grammar and much of the continuing work on anaphora in formal semantics more generally has focused on the properties of ordinary personal pronouns in English and related languages. There has, however, been increasing attention to questions concerning the variety of kinds of anaphoric elements that exist in English and in other languages and to the "anaphoric nature" of elements besides pronouns, elements ranging from "pro-forms" in other categories (**then**, **there**, **such**, **one**, etc.) to presuppositions, context-dependent words like **local**, **enemy** (Mitchell, 1986; Partee, 1989b) and focus-sensitive constructions (Rooth, 1992a; von Fintel, 1994).

Bach and Partee (1980) offered an account of the distribution of reflexive and non-reflexive pronouns in terms of a Montague Grammar making use of Cooper storage (Section 4.2.3) and following up on the idea of the importance of "co-arguments of the verb" discussed in Montague's footnote about reflexives in EFL; in their fragment, they built in a structural similarity between reflexivization and control phenomena, extending proposals that had been made by Bach (1979a). There is much current work and much current debate on the analysis of reflexive pronouns, both in formal semantics and in GB syntax and in approaches which blend the two; see, for instance, Reinhart and Reuland (1993).

Heim (1982) gave a unified account of the semantics of various elements that she included in the level of LF of GB theory, including ordinary pronouns, traces of NP movement and indices on NPs and on common nouns and relative pronouns.

With respect to the interpretation of ordinary pronouns, besides the continuing debates about the proper analysis of donkey pronouns and about the existence and nature of "functional" readings of some pronouns, both described above, there is also increasing attention to issues in the interpretation of plural pronouns, which raise a broader range of problems than singular pronouns because of the associated family of issues that arise in the interpretation of plural NPs more generally (see Kadmon, 1987, 1990; Kamp and Reyle, 1993; Landman, 1989a, 1989b; Schwarzschild, 1992; for a sample of relevant issues).

Other scholars have debated the semantic status of "zero pronouns" and "pro-drop" phenomena in various languages, tending toward the (still not completely clear) generalization that zero forms of pronouns are more likely to be obligatorily interpreted as bound variables than phonologically non-empty forms of pronouns. Debates concerning the semantics of various empty or abstract pronominal elements are intimately connected with debates concerning whether infinitival complements are to be analyzed as full sentences at some level of structure. Montague in PTQ showed that for many purposes a VP could simply be generated as a VP and Partee (1973b) showed how a "Derived Verb Phrase Rule" deriving a VP from an open sentence (with a free variable subject) could obviate the need for transformations like "Equi-NP Deletion"; subsequent work has gone back and forth with much debate on the question of whether some or all infinitival VPs still need to be analyzed as deriving from sentences on some level. See especially Chierchia (1984a, 1984b) for a defense of "VPs as VPs" and Chierchia and Jacobson (1986) for an argument that certain kinds of "Raising" constructions do have sentential sources for infinitival VPs.

The important domain of VP-anaphora (including so-called "VP-Deletion") interacts crucially with quantification and NP-anaphora and has also been the locus of much debate, particularly between approaches which analyze VP-deletion as involving identity of logical form and approaches which invoke identity of appropriate model-theoretic semantic objects. See, for a sample, Williams (1977), Sag (1976), Partee and Bach (1981), Rooth (1992b), Kratzer (1991).

Among approaches to VP-anaphora, the interesting new perspective of Dalrymple, Shieber and Pereira (1991) deserves mention: they propose to treat many kinds of anaphora as involving "solving for a missing variable". In particular, their approach is novel in providing for the ambiguity between strict- and sloppy-identity readings of (7), repeated here as (50), without requiring that the first clause, (51), be analyzed as itself ambiguous as between a bound-variable and a coreferential reading of the pronoun.

(50) **Sam gave some fish to his dog and Sally did too.**

(51) **Sam gave some fish to his dog.**

Whether the approach of Dalrymple, Shieber and Pereira can be expressed in a manner compatible with compositionality is an open question, but the proposal is attractive enough in many respects for its theoretical consequences to deserve serious attention.

4.3.7. Combinators and variable-free syntax

One novel development in the area of anaphora is the reinvigoration of the possibility that natural language pronouns might be analyzed in terms of "combinators" of combinatory logic in the context of an extended categorial grammar treatment of the syntax underlying a compositional semantics; see Szabolcsi (1987), Jacobson (1992, 1994, forthcoming), Dowty (1992). A "combinator" analysis of pronouns had been proposed in various forms at various times for reflexive pronouns, especially for languages in which reflexivization takes the form of a clitic on a verb rather than looking structurally like a normal NP: it is then natural to see the reflexive pronoun as a functor that applies to an n-place verb and identifies two of its arguments to yield an $(n - 1)$-place verb. Combinators were also heavily used in the unpublished but widely known semantics for a large fragment of English of Parsons (1972), but then were not reintroduced into formal semantics until the resurgence of categorial grammar in the 1980's (Bach, 1984; Zwarts, 1986; Oehrle, Bach and Wheeler (eds), 1988).

The recent work on pronouns as combinators raises the possibility of a "variable-free syntax" and the possibility of giving a compositional analysis of natural languages without requiring indices or variables as part of the natural language, hence the possibility of respecting what Partee (1979b) called the "well-formedness constraint" to a greater extent than previously imagined by most investigators. Advances in this direction are always welcome as support for the hypothesis that natural languages "wear their logical forms on their sleeve", i.e. that the actual syntactic structures of natural languages are well-designed vehicles for expressing their semantic content. (This hypothesis corresponds to a methodological principle: whenever the interpretation of a certain construction seems to require some transformation of the independently motivated syntactic structure into some differently structured "logical form", keep looking for different ways of assigning meanings to the parts or different semantic operations for putting meanings together in hopes of finding a way of interpreting the given syntactic structure more directly.)

4.4. Type theory, ontology, theoretical foundations

In this section we briefly review a few of the developments and controversial issues that have emerged in extensions of and reactions to Montague's work that bear on some of the more general features of Montague's framework. Many of these concern the choice of type theory and the generalizations concerning the type structure of natural languages. Some concern such foundational questions as the choice between set theory and some version of property theory at the very foundations of the formal system and the perennial issue of the epistemological relation of the language user to the language and to its grammar.

4.4.1. Basic ontology, basic types, philosophical underpinnings

It was noted above in Section 3.3 that various cross-categorial constructions seem to require that however one interprets the domain corresponding to the type of sentences, that domain should form a Boolean algebra (or some relevantly similar structure: perhaps lattices or semilattices would suffice; and it is also possible to work with a domain that is not itself a Boolean algebra but has a Boolean algebra lurking somewhere within it, e.g., a domain of functions whose range (codomain) is such an algebra). There are a variety of possible choices that can be and have been made for the model-theoretic domain corresponding to the basic type t in a Montague semantics. On the extensional side, the simplest choice is the two-element set of truth values; this is the domain corresponding to extensions of expressions of type t in PTQ. Another extensional choice is the set of sets of assignment functions: the extension of an expression of type t would then be the set of all assignments that satisfy it. (Such a choice relates to earlier work on the semantics of variables and variable-binding operators that interprets them in terms of cylindric algebras; see Janssen (1986a).) There also exist various proposals for countenancing domains of more than two "truth values", although there are disputes over whether those values should be called truth values; in any case, whether entertained in the context of considerations of presuppositionality or in the context of considerations of vagueness or "fuzziness", or in other contexts, it makes a big difference whether the domain in question is "Boolean-valued" or not; as long as it is, the extensions to cross-categorial versions of conjunction, quantification, etc. can be carried out straightforwardly by the kinds of pointwise lifting techniques described by Gazdar (1980), Partee and Rooth (1983), etc. and the arguments of Keenan and Faltz (1985) for seeing pervasive Boolean structure in natural language can be respected.[44]

It is equally common to take the extension of sentences to be an "intensional object" such as a proposition.[45] Montague in EFL, as noted earlier, took the extensions of sentences to be propositions, analyzed as functions from possible worlds to truth values and Cresswell did similarly in (Cresswell, 1973) (which also contains more explicit discussion of underlying ontological issues than is found in Montague's papers). It was also noted by Montague and others that one can generalize that notion and analyze propositions as functions from some richer "indices" that include not only possible worlds but times and perhaps other parameters of evaluation.

In early situation semantics as developed by Barwise and Perry, the basic semantic type of sentences was defined in terms of situations and/or "situation types". Barwise (1981) and Barwise and Perry (1983) argued that the use of possible worlds in traditional theories of meaning leads to a notion of intension that is too coarse-grained for adequately representing the meanings of sentences reporting propositional attitudes and neutral perceptions. For example, the sentences (52) and (53) are wrongly predicted to express the same proposition.

(52) **Mary sees John walk.**

(53) **Mary sees John walk and Bill talk or not talk.**

---

[44] For explicit arguments against the idea of letting "truth values" be elements of some linear scale such as real numbers in the interval [0, 1] as proposed in classic versions of fuzzy logic, see Kamp and Partee (1995).

[45] This is not a contradiction, although on some sloppy uses of the vocabulary of intensionality, including by the present author, it might seem to be. When we spoke above of verbs like **seek** taking intensions as arguments, that was an oversimplified way of speaking; the potential for confusion comes from the fact that in Montague's intensional logic, the extension of an expression of the form $^\wedge\alpha$ is the same as the intension of the expression α and it is common but sloppy practice to call $^\wedge\alpha$ itself (both the expression and its interpretation) "the intension of α". Speaking more accurately takes a lot more words and there is no standardized non-sloppy shorthand terminology. But it is reasonable to call the PTQ extension of expressions of type $\langle s, t\rangle$ "intensional objects" and to use that term for any model-theoretic object which consists of a function from possible worlds to something.

Accordingly, Barwise and Perry replace the concept of a possible world with that of a situation in their own theory of situation semantics. Barwise and Perry's challenge to possible world semantics is taken up by Muskens (1989), who shows that Montague grammar can be specified in terms of a relational formulation of the theory of types as given in (Orey, 1959) and that, moreover, this relational theory can serve as the basis of a partialization (i.e. technically, a four-valued generalization) which yields partially specified possible situations instead of completely defined possible worlds. The ensuing finer-grained notion of entailment can be put to use in an adequate account of the semantic phenomena brought up by Barwise and Perry.

The ontological status of Barwise and Perry's notion of situations and situation types became a matter of some controversy, especially with respect to those authors' avoidance of possible worlds or possible situations. Subsequent work by Kratzer and by some of her students has developed the possibility of letting situations, construed as parts of worlds, function both as individuals (analogous to events, playing a direct role in the interpretation of event nominals, for instance) and as "world-like" in that propositions are reinterpreted as sets of possible situations and expressions are evaluated at situations rather than at world-time pairs (see, e.g., Kratzer, 1989, 1995a; Berman, 1987; Portner, 1992; Zucchi, 1989). The rich research opened up by this development may shed light not only on the linguistic constructions under study but on properties of cognitive structurings of ontological domains which play a central role in human thought and language.

Attention to demonstratives, indexicals and other aspects of context has led researchers to at least two different strategies of enrichment of the type structure. One strategy, illustrated in (Lewis, 1970), is to enrich the "indices" to include not only possible worlds and times, but a speaker, a place of utterance and other contextual elements; Cresswell (1973) argues that there is no finite limit to the number of such elements that might be needed and so something like a single "context property" should be posited for that role. The other strategy, illustrated in (Kaplan, 1979) and developed as an extension of Montague grammar by Bennett (1978) (foreshadowed in Montague's UG and with similar proposals further developed in (Stalnaker, 1974, 1978)), is to distinguish "character" from "content", character capturing what different occurrences of a sentence like **I am here** share in common and "content" being the proposition (the intensional object) expressed by a given use of such a sentence in a given context. Characters are thus analyzed as functions from possible contexts of use to contents, which themselves are functions from indices of evaluation (e.g., world-time pairs) to truth values. See Lewis (1974) for further discussion of various permutations of such choices.

There are doubtless other choices possible for the basic semantic type of sentences; a rich variety of kinds of choices can be found in the literature on the formal semantics of programming languages, where special purposes may dictate specific sorts of semantic values and the commonalities of structural or algebraic properties across different choices become even more apparent. The type structure underlying various "dynamic" approaches is not reflected in the brief set of alternatives surveyed above, nor are the possibilities offered by replacing the background set theory by property theory (see Section 4.4.2 below).

Montague worked in a tradition in which linguistic objects were abstract objects and the basic conception was Platonistic, following Frege. As noted earlier, the question of "psychological reality" was not central in that tradition, particularly if formal languages and natural languages were being subsumed under a single larger category, as in Montague's work. The most explicit statement of the relation of a language to its users on such a conception is probably that found in the work of David Lewis (1969, 1975b), where a clear distinction is drawn between the investigation of a language as an abstract object and the investigation of the nature of the conventions of language users that form the basis for a claim that a particular language is the language of a given person or a given language community.

Nevertheless, it is of course to be expected that other researchers sympathetic to many of the goals and methods of Montague grammar or related work in formal semantics might prefer to investigate different kinds of foundations and that in some cases this might lead to differences in semantic analysis. One good example is the Data Semantics of Frank Veltman (Veltman, 1981, 1985a, 1985b) or its successor theory Update Semantics (Veltman, 1990), in which the epistemological relation of a speaker to her language and to her constantly changing "information state" is central. The change in philosophical underpinnings leads to changes in the semantics of modal verbs, of negation and of various other constructions. Ramifications for the interpretation of noun phrases as "partial objects" are explored in (Landman, 1986). The dynamic approach of Groenendijk and Stokhof (1990, 1991) draws together some of the motivations for Heim's and Kamp's "meanings as context-change potential" and Veltman's epistemological perspective.

Linguists in the generative grammar tradition following the seminal work of Chomsky (1957, 1965) generally share his concern with locating grammars in the heads of language users; some of the difficulties of combining such a view with a possible-worlds semantics like Montague's are explored in (Partee, 1979c, 1980, 1982), with some summary of the issues and of varieties of views about the nature of semantics in (Partee, 1989a). The viability of such an integration is challenged in (Schiffer, 1987), to which Partee (1988) is a disagreeing reply. See also Soames (1987). The nature of intensionality is a constant issue in such discussions.

4.4.2. Property theory vs. set theory as metalevel theoretical basis

Some philosophers still seriously defend the claim that intensions (truth conditions) adequately individuate propositions; most philosophers and linguists reject the idea that any two logically equivalent sentences express the same proposition, at least if propositions are to be, among other things, the objects of the propositional attitudes. Montague acknowledged the initially counterintuitive nature of that consequence of his treatment of belief as a relation between persons and propositions and the given analysis of propositions. In EFL he characterizes it as a conclusion he believes we should accept, pointing to discussion in (Montague, 1970a). Some of the most thoughtful defenses of a truth-conditional notion of proposition can be found in the work of Stalnaker (see Stalnaker, 1976, 1984).

One foundational development which could have a profound impact on this perennial problem and on the analysis of intensionality is the recent working out of several versions of *property theory* as candidate replacements for set theory in the foundations of formal semantics. The principal difference between all versions of set theory and all versions of property theory is the presence vs. absence of the axiom of extensionality. That axiom of set theory says that any two sets that contain exactly the same members are the same set. The absence of such an axiom in property theory allows distinct properties to apply to exactly the same individuals.

When set theory is given a foundational role in the reconstruction of mathematics and logic, as has been standard since the *Principia* (Russell and Whitehead, 1913), the axiom of extensionality has many repercussions. One result of extensionality is that when functions are reconstructed in set-theoretic terms, any two functions that have exactly the same set of input-output pairs (the same graph) are the same function. It may be argued that this is not a property of the working mathematician's notion of function; Moschovakis (1985) explores the possibility of a suitably intensional notion of function somewhere between the extensional standard notion and the very procedural notion of algorithm. In any case, with the standard extensional notion of function in the foundations that Montague (following common practice in logic and model theory) worked with, it followed that if propositions are analyzed as functions from possible worlds to truth values, then any two truth-conditionally equivalent propositions are analyzed as the same proposition.

But if one could replace set theory by a suitable property theory in the foundations (for various proposals, see Bealer, 1982; Cocchiarella, 1985; Jubien, 1985; Turner, 1987, 1989; Chierchia and Turner, 1988), then functions could be reconstructed as a species of relations-in-intension rather than as relations-in-extension, and propositions could be analyzed as functions from possible worlds to truth values without treating as identical all functions that happen to give the same values. That is, the analysis of propositions as functions from possible worlds (or possible situations) to truth values is not necessarily the culprit in giving us an insufficiently intensional notion of proposition; the fault may lie in the overly extensional notion of function we have been working with.

Other suggested solutions to the problem of an insufficient notion of intensionality have mostly involved trying to find ways to make meanings more "fine-grained", usually by adding some element of syntactic part-whole analysis to the truth-conditional content as standardly characterized. See the "constructions" of Tichý (1988), the "structured meanings" of David Lewis (1970) and the further development of the structured meanings approach of Cresswell and von Stechow (1982), von Stechow (1984), Cresswell (1985), among others. Other approaches treat propositional attitudes more like quotational contexts, sensitive to the linguistic form as well as the semantic content of their argument expressions. But the issues are large and have philosophical as well as semantic consequences and there is not space for a serious discussion of them here.

The possibility of a shift from set theory to property theory could have consequences for other parts of the semantics as well as for the basic analysis of intensionality. Chierchia (1982, 1985) and Chierchia and Turner (1988) explore the use of property theory in the analysis of nominalizations, exploiting the fact that properties may hold of themselves without the problem of paradox. There are a number of places where the imposition of a rigid type theory causes problems for the analysis of natural language, including the necessity to assign possibly infinitely many different types to a single expression like "has a property" (see Parsons, 1979).

4.4.3. Type shifting, coercion, flexibility

The type theory which Montague used in his intensional logic and indirectly or directly in the semantics of all three fragments was not an essential consequence of his general theory in Universal Grammar. Having some type theory is essential to that theory, but the range of kinds of type theories that are compatible with the principal constraints of Montague grammar has not been explored nearly as far as it could be. For that matter, the general theory permits having a trivial type theory with only one type.

Imposing a strong type theory on a semantics offers both advantages and disadvantages as a working methodology. Advantages include the explicitness of checking well-formedness of function-argument structure; without the discipline of type theory, it is easy to write down expressions that turn out to be difficult to interpret coherently. Type theory can also offer interesting perspectives on the correspondence between syntax and semantics, as witnessed in the renewal of active research in categorial grammar, a framework which takes type theory into its syntax even more systematically than Montague did in PTQ, where the syntactic categories are inspired by the work of Ajdukiewicz (1935), but the syntactic rules are much less constrained than in any systematic version of categorial grammar. Disadvantages come from the apparent great flexibility of natural language expressions to occur in a variety of types. More generally, it is not yet clear that natural languages really are as strongly typed as a strict type theory like Montague's would require. But as with other strong constraints of Montague's, trying to work within them is probably the best way to find out whether they are in the end reasonable or not.

Thus we saw above that in choosing semantic types corresponding to syntactic categories, Montague required that every category be associated with a single type, so that the interpretation of an expression of a category is always of the unique type assigned to that category. As a consequence, a strategy of "generalizing to the worst case" must be adopted: *all* expressions of a certain syntactic category have to be uniformly assigned an interpretation of the most complex type needed for *some* expression in that category and meaning postulates are necessary for guaranteeing that the "simpler" cases are indeed simpler. The latter means that this rigid category-type assignment entails a possible distortion of the semantics – a distortion which, as Bach (1980) argues, had not yet reached its full extent with PTQ. In itself, such a complication is not necessarily a defect, provided that it serves the empirical adequacy of the theory. But there is some evidence that Montague's strategy of generalizing to the worst case cannot be pursued successfully.

This has been claimed by, among others, Partee and Rooth (1983), whose starting point is a generalized, cross-categorial semantics for coordination by means of **and** and **or** (due to von Stechow, 1974; Gazdar, 1980; Keenan and Faltz, 1985), which is based on the set of "conjoinable types", i.e. the smallest set that contains the type of truth values as well as all types of functions from entities of some type to entities of a conjoinable type.[46] In consideration of the interpretation of sentences involving the coordination of extensional and intensional transitive and intransitive verbs, Partee and Rooth conclude that Montague's strategy should be given up. Instead, they enter each expression lexically in its minimal type and let type-shifting rules furnish a higher-type

[46] Note that the domain of the type of truth values constitutes a Boolean algebra. Hence all conjoinable types have domains that are Boolean algebras (cf. Keenan and Faltz, 1985).

homonym for lower-type expressions. In addition, a coercion principle ensures that all expressions are interpreted at the lowest type possible, invoking higher-type homonyms only when needed for type coherence: "try simplest types first". This is a reversal of Montague's strategy in the sense that the generalization is to the "best case" on the lexical level. Moreover, although there is still a "worst case" (most general case) in this set-up, one does not uniformly generalize to it, on account of the coercion principle.

The purpose of the coercion principle is the prevention of undesired readings, but, as Partee and Rooth note, it also precludes a use of type-shifting rules for the representation of ambiguities. They discuss an interesting example: the so-called *de dicto* wide scope-**or** reading of sentence (54), which is suggested by the continuation "...but I don't know which" and which is not accounted for in the PTQ fragment.[47]

(54) **The department is looking for a phonologist or a phonetician.**

Groenendijk and Stokhof (1984, 1989) argue that type-shifting rules are useful in the semantic description of various constructions involving interrogatives. They show that an extension of Partee and Rooth's rules to other categories allows for a representation of desired readings, and, furthermore, that certain intuitive entailments between (coordinated) interrogatives[48] can only be accounted for if it is assumed that a type-shifting rule admits of interpretations of interrogatives in higher types than their basic type. On the other hand, the basic type is needed as well, viz., for entailments between atomic interrogatives. Accordingly, Groenendijk and Stokhof liberalize interpretation of syntactic structures to a relation: coercion is replaced by the principle "anything goes that fits".

In order to be able to account for ambiguities by means of type-shifting rules, this principle of the survival of the fitting is also adopted in the fully explicit fragment of "flexible Montague grammar" of Hendriks (1988, 1993), where Montague's strategy of generalizing to the worst case fails, though for a different reason than in the grammar of Partee and Rooth. It fails, not because the worst case cannot always be generalized to, but simply because there *is* no such case. Expressions are assigned interpretation sets consisting of basic interpretations plus derived interpretations. Every lexical expression is assigned a "best case" basic interpretation of the minimal type available for that particular expression and generalized syntactic/semantic rules permit the compounding of all "mutually fitting" interpretations of constituent parts into basic translations of compound expressions. The derived interpretations are obtained by closing the set of basic interpretations under the generalized type-shifting rules of value raising, argument raising and argument lowering. The recursive nature of these rules precludes the existence of "worst case" interpretations. *De dicto* wide scope-**or** readings of increasingly complex sentences are adduced as evidence in defense of this feature. As noted, the type-shifting rules of Partee and Rooth (1983) can be used to represent some of these readings. In addition, the generalized rules are argued to yield a general account of natural language scope ambiguities that arise in the presence of quantifying and coordinating expressions:

[47] A sketch of an alternative treatment of wide scope-*or* along the lines of Kamp (1981) and Heim (1982, 1983) is given in (Rooth and Partee, 1982).

[48] Using a generalized notion of entailment according to which an interrogative A entails an interrogative B just in case every complete and true answer to A is a complete and true answer to B, so that a conjunction entails its conjuncts and a disjunction is entailed by its disjuncts.

the fragment represents coordination scope ambiguities beyond the reach of the original rules, and also the quantifier scope ambiguities and *de dicto/de re* ambiguities that gave rise to the rule of Quantifying In, as well as their mutual interactions.

Flexible type-assignment has been argued to lead to a more adequate division of labor between the syntactic and the semantic component, in that it eliminates the need for the arguably unintuitive syntactic and semantic devices of Quantifying In and Cooper storage for the representation of scope ambiguities. The representation of anaphoric pronouns, the second aspect of Quantifying In (and of Cooper storage), is also addressed by a flexible set-up: a flexible grammar which handles both anaphora and scope ambiguities is obtained by adding the generalized type-shifting mechanism to – a "best case" version of – the "dynamic Montague grammar" (DMG) of Groenendijk and Stokhof (1990). An interesting contribution in this respect is Dekker (1990, 1993). Focusing on the notion of negation in a dynamic Montague grammar, Dekker concludes that sentences should be assigned interpretations of a higher type than the type of sets of propositions, the type assigned to sentence interpretations in DMG. This claim is substantiated in the guise of a structural, conservative modification of DMG into the system DMG(2), where sentences are interpreted as generalized quantifiers over propositions. Dekker shows that the DMG(2)-style dynamic interpretations of expressions can actually be *obtained* in a systematic way from simple static interpretations, viz., by employing the generalized type-shifting system of flexible Montague grammar. The resulting flexible dynamic Montague grammar is shown to apply to an interesting range of examples that exhibit puzzling and complex anaphoric dependencies.

Partee (1987) employs type-shifting principles in an attempt to resolve the apparent conflict between Montague's uniform treatment of NPs as generalized quantifiers and approaches such as Kamp (1981) and Heim (1982, 1983), which distinguish among referring, predicative and quantificational NPs. In addition, it is shown that the availability of language-specific and universal type-shifting principles suggests a new perspective on the copula **be** and the determiners **a** and **the**, that may offer some help in explaining why certain semantic "functors" may be encoded either lexically or grammatically, or may not be explicitly marked at all in different natural languages. In this perspective, the meaning of English **be** is basically "Predicate!", as in (22) above, and Montague's meaning can be reconstructed as the result of subjecting this basic meaning to a type-shifting operation that provides predicate meanings for full term phrases. Type-shifting principles are also invoked cross-linguistically in the semantic theory of Bittner (1994). Some versions of categorial grammar make very heavy use of type-shifting operations in interesting explanations of subtle linguistic phenomena in terms of the possibilities allowed (see the chapter on Categorial Grammar in this Handbook).

Does formal semantics necessarily require attention to type theory? Not intrinsically, since one could have a trivial type theory with only one type. But most work so far has worked within some well-defined type theory and the results have been fruitful. It seems more likely that future work will see the enrichment of type theory and/or the addition of more attention to possibly cross-classifying sortal distinctions in addition to type distinctions, rather than the abandonment of type theory. See the chapters on Type Theory and on Categorial Grammar for more on these topics.

4.5. Context dependence and context change

As noted in Sections 4.2.2, 4.3.4 and 4.4.1 above, one of the major changes since Montague's work has been increased integration of context dependence and context-change potential into semantics. Montague helped to lay the foundations for these developments in his own work on formal pragmatics, which were further advanced by David Kaplan's seminal work on demonstratives, developed in a Montague grammar framework by Bennett (1978), and by Stalnaker's work on many issues at the borderline of semantics and pragmatics. The term "pragmatics" is becoming increasingly difficult to define as a consequence, since it had its origins as part of a partition of semiotics into syntax, semantics and pragmatics, and the line between the latter two is shifting in ways that make earlier definitions obsolete and new ones not yet stable. (So whatever is in the glossary of this Handbook should be taken with a grain of salt; that is probably true for all the theoretically interesting terms.)

From this perspective the Kamp–Heim theories brought with them important fundamental innovations, most centrally in the intimate integration of context dependence and context change in the recursive semantics of natural language. A related important innovation was Heim's successful formal integration of Stalnaker's (1978) context-change analysis of assertion with Karttunen's (1975) discourse-referent analysis of indefinite NPs.

Kamp's and Heim's work has led to a great deal of further research, applying it to other phenomena, extending and refining it in various directions and challenging it (see the DRT chapter). Heim herself has been one of the challengers, arguing for a revival of a modified version of Evans' (1980) "E-type pronouns" in (Heim, 1990), discussed further in Section 4.3 above. One line of research concerns the interaction of quantification and context-dependence, starting from the observation of Mitchell (1986) that open-class context-dependent predicates such as **local** and **enemy** behave like bound variables in that they can anchor not only to utterance contexts and constructed discourse contexts but also to "quantified contexts" as discussed in (Partee, 1989b).

There is still a need for a great deal more research on the linguistically significant structuring of various aspects of "context", and on the relationships among contexts of different sorts: the context of the speech act, narrative context in both fiction and ordinary dialogue and the very local context of a word within larger phrases. Here too there is a great deal of insightful work in other traditions that needs to be integrated with the approaches of formal semantics. What aspects of context should be reflected in the type structure of natural languages, if meanings are to be functions from contexts to contexts, is a major theoretical open issue, with ramifications for questions of "modularity" in the realm of semantics and pragmatics.

4.6. Typology and natural language metaphysics

Early work on Montague grammar focused largely on English. As with other kinds of linguistic research, attention to typologically diverse languages, now that it has gotten well underway, has been of great mutual benefit for the understanding of the semantics of those languages and for the development of semantic theory.

Montague himself speculated about the potential benefit for typological studies of a powerful formal semantic theory. Here is what he said on August 26, 1967:[49]

> Perhaps the most important applications of a formal treatment [of natural language along Montague's lines, that is – Th. E. Z.] will occur in the realm of prehistory. Indeed, certain pairs of natural languages, hitherto, on the basis of relatively superficial criteria, considered unrelated, appear now to exhibit identical idiosyncrasies in very basic formal features; it would be difficult to account for these similarities except on the hypothesis of a common origin or very early, as yet unsuspected, historical interaction.

But that speculation ("wild" speculation, some would undoubtedly say) was never followed up on, as far as we know.

More seriously: given that Montague grammar offers semantic tools that in many cases remove the need for "abstract syntax", it offers the potential for describing each language more "on its own terms" than theories that posit a more nearly universal level of semantic representation and a more indirect relation between syntactic structures and semantic representations, e.g., via a transformational mapping. It thus has become an interesting and important enterprise to figure out such things as the semantics of noun phrases in languages which lack articles; the semantics of tense and aspect in languages which mark more or fewer or very different distinctions from English; the difference, if any, between the semantics (and pragmatics) of focus in languages which mark focus principally by word order, languages which mark it by intonational prominence and languages which mark it with a specific syntactic position.

An early effort in this direction was the work of Stein (1981) on the semantics of Thai noun phrases. Thai is a classifier language that does not grammatically distinguish count/mass or singular/plural. Most of the earlier philosophical treatments of the semantics of mass nouns had presupposed that count nouns are more basic and better understood; this may have been yet another legacy of the virtually universal adoption of set theory (rather than some mereological system) as a metalanguage. It proved very difficult to construct on such a basis a semantics for Thai that faithfully reflected the lack of a count/mass distinction and made that seem "natural". Only after the introduction of Link's algebraic structuring of the entity domain (Link, 1983) did it become straightforward to view "mass" as the unmarked member of the mass/count opposition (see Section 4.2.1 above).

Such work falls in the realm of what Bach (1986a) called "natural language metaphysics", characterizing a linguistic concern which may or may not be distinct from metaphysics as a field of philosophy: that is a controversy among philosophers themselves (see Peregrin, 1995). Metaphysics is concerned with what there is and the structure of what there is; natural language metaphysics, Bach proposes, is concerned not with those questions in their pure form, but with the question of what metaphysical assumptions, if any, are presupposed by the semantics of natural languages (individually and universally). In the domain of time, one can ask whether a tense and aspect system requires any

[49] Thanks to Ede Zimmermann for this quotation from Staal (ed.) (1969).

assumptions about whether time is discrete or continuous, whether instants, intervals, or events are basic, whether the same "time line" must exist in every possible world, etc.

Link's work opened up interesting avenues of research in this area, suggesting the exploration of algebraically characterizable structures in various domains, structures that might differ from language to language. Bach (1986b) extended Link's algebra of mass and count domains to an algebra of processes and events and others have begun to explore how the relation between the semantics of noun phrases and the semantics of verb phrases and event expressions might be interestingly and differently connected in different languages (see Krifka, 1986, 1987; Filip, 1992, 1993).

Not surprisingly, since quantification has been the object of so much attention by formal semanticists, typological perspectives have become important in recent work. Bach, Kratzer and Partee (1989) hypothesized that adverbial quantification might be more widespread linguistically than the familiar noun phrase quantification of English described in PTQ; that hypothesis was confirmed first by Jelinek (1995), who showed that Straits Salish does not have noun phrases that are analyzed as generalized quantifiers. That and further typological issues are explored and richly illustrated in the collection (Bach, Jelinek, Kratzer and Partee, 1995).

Thematic roles and the structuring of lexical domains into semantic subclasses of various kinds is another area that is growing in importance and one where there is interesting potential for contact and mutual enrichment between formal semantics and other theories which have devoted much more attention to the structuring of lexical meanings (see Dowty, 1979; Chierchia, 1984a; Partee, 1995).

4.7. The naturalization of formal semantics and Montague's legacy

As formal semantics has come to be integrated more centrally into linguistic theory, especially in the United States, there has been a strong push to "naturalize" formal semantics (Partee, 1992). Whereas in the beginning, linguists were largely "consumers" of theories and formal tools developed by logicians and philosophers, now there is a much more symmetrical relationship, with linguists contributing actively to the specification of the properties an adequate theory of natural language semantics must have and to the development of such theories. These developments are beginning to have repercussions back into philosophy and logic and potentially on the design of artificial languages for computational purposes, as evidenced in diverse ways in the articles of this Handbook.

Within and around the field of formal semantics, there is currently a great deal of diversity, as the foregoing discussion and other articles in this Handbook make clear. At the same time, there is a sense of community among researchers working on formal semantics in different ways and from different disciplinary perspectives. Part of what makes discussion and debate possible and fruitful across considerable diversity is the existence of a common reference point, Montague Grammar, serving as a background and baseline for much of the work that has followed. No one of its properties is universally accepted by people who would be willing to identify themselves as doing formal semantics or model-theoretic semantics or "post-Montague" semantics, but there is a shared sense that Montague's work represented a fundamental advance, opening up new possibilities and setting new standards for the analysis of the semantics of natural languages, for linguistics as well as for philosophy. Montague's legacy endures in the continuing centrality of his theoretical contributions and the influence of his particular proposals about the semantics of natural language and probably even more strongly in harder-to-define ways that may be considered methodological, as reflected above in the discussion of compositionality, as well as in the mutual influences of linguists, philosophers and logicians on each other's thinking about semantics. While few would claim that the analysis of truth conditions (or context-change potential) exhausts the study of meaning, or that the tools of formal semantics can solve all of the linguistically interesting problems in semantics, the fruitfulness of research in Montague grammar and related theories has shown convincingly that this domain is a robust one and that the kind of approach which Montague illustrated so masterfully in his work has not come close to exhausting its potential usefulness for understanding natural language semantics and its relation to syntax.

Acknowledgements

There are several people whose help was crucial in the writing of this chapter, and to whom I am immensely grateful.

Theo Janssen was both an inspiration and a source of help of many kinds from the earliest conception of this project to its completion. Theo's own writings on Montague grammar, both technical and pedagogical, were among my principal starting points. And Theo, along with Alice ter Meulen, was persistent in encouraging me to keep trying to find time to write the chapter long after several initial deadlines had passed, encouragement that kept me from giving up on the project altogether. And when I was finally able to get down to the writing, in two major episodes separated by almost a year, Theo was always ready to provide helpful references, discuss questions, and read drafts and offer comments. Theo's very thoughtful and detailed comments on the penultimate draft were the principal basis for the final revisions. And not least, Theo's enthusiastic reaction to the first draft was one of the biggest emotional supports that kept me going through times when I feared I would never finish.

Emmon Bach read more successive drafts of this chapter than anyone else, and made many suggestions, from global organizational strategy to detailed comments on specific points, which led to a great many improvements and often helped me see the forest when I was in danger of being overwhelmed by the trees. I was fortunate to have the benefit of his excellent judgment about both the subject matter and how to write about it.

I also want to use this occasion to thank Herman Hendriks and comment on our non-standard semi-co-author status. It should be clear that I (BHP) am the principal author, responsible for choice and organization of content and for most of the writing; and wherever there is a detectable "authorial voice", it is mine. On the other hand, Herman's help was crucial and substantial. He did the writing of substantial parts of two subsections, 4.2.3. and 4.4.3; and he did a great deal of work, often at short notice and under great time pressure, with things that were crucial for pulling the chapter into final shape – not only did he catch and correct a number of potential errors in content and infelicities in expression, but he did all the work of putting the manuscript into LaTeX, including getting the formulas, the example numberings and the footnotes straight. He also did a very large amount of work on the bibliography, and provided other help at various times with reference searches, cross-references to other chapters, and proofreading. I suggested, and the editors of the volume agreed, that Herman deserved more than a mention in the acknowledgements, but that he was not a co-author in the standard sense. So we have appropriated the "with" that one sometimes finds, for instance, in a book written by a rock star "with" the help of a real writer. We don't pretend to be a rock star or a real writer respectively, but that "with" trick seems to fit here too.

Another crucial figure in the passage from possibility to actuality of this chapter was Alice ter Meulen. Alice was the one who really refused to give up on this chapter, and she has mastered the art of constructive nagging. She was always patient but persistent, ready with great positive feedback at any signs of life, and most importantly, constantly involved in the substance of the work. Alice and Johan van Benthem together did an excellent job of keeping authors informed about the potential relationships among the various chapters as the authors and commentators went through the many stages of planning and writing and commenting and revising. Alice was the shepherd for this chapter, and she made invaluable comments and suggestions at every stage from conception to final draft, and helped to coordinate communication with Herman and Theo as well. She is responsible for many improvements in the chapter as well as for making sure that we actually completed it.

All of the above helped to provide references when I needed help, which was often, since most of the writing was done while on sabbatical in northern British Columbia, away from any major research university or university library. For additional help in tracking down references, I am very grateful to Ede Zimmermann, Reinhard Muskens, Terry Parsons, and Nino Cocchiarella.

All of the many colleagues and students who were thanked in my earlier writings on Montague Grammar starting in the early 1970's should be thanked here too; they are too many to list, but they all helped to shape my understanding of Montague's work and of its potential usefulness for thinking about linguistic problems.

A few sections of this chapter overlap in content with some sections of the chapter "The development of formal semantics in linguistic theory", in Shalom Lappin (ed.), *The Handbook of Contemporary Semantic Theory*, Blackwell Handbooks in Linguistics Series, Blackwell, Oxford (1996), pp. 11–38.

Time to work was made available by a research leave from my department in the Fall of 1994 and a sabbatical leave from the University of Massachusetts in the Spring of 1995. For the most pleasant imaginable working environment as well as for his specific contributions to the chapter I am grateful to Emmon Bach, with thanks for inviting me to come with him to northern British Columbia, where the first substantial drafts were completed in the Fall 1994 semester, and the first near-complete draft was finished in the summer of 1995.

References

Ajdukiewicz, K. (1935), *Die syntaktische Konnexität*, Stud. Philos. **1**, 1–27. Translated as *Syntactic connexion*, Polish Logic, S. McCall, ed., (1967), Clarendon Press, Oxford, 207–231.

Bach, E. (1968), *Nouns and noun phrases*, Universals in Linguistic Theory, E. Bach and R.T. Harms, eds, Holt, Rinehart and Winston, New York, 91–124.

Bach, E. (1976), *An extension of classical transformational grammar*, Problems of Linguistic Metatheory, Proceedings of the 1976 Conference, Michigan State University.

Bach, E. (1979a), *Control in Montague grammar*, Ling. Inq. **10**, 515–531.

Bach, E. (1979b), *Montague grammar and classical transformational grammar*, S. Davis and M. Mithun, eds.

Bach, E. (1980), *Tenses and aspects as functions on verb-phrases*, Time, Tense and Quantifiers, C. Rohrer, ed., Max Niemeyer, Tübingen.

Bach, E. (1981), *On time, tense and aspect: An essay in English metaphysics*, Radical Pragmatics, P. Cole, ed., Academic Press, New York, 62–81.

Bach, E. (1984), *Some generalizations of categorial grammars*, Varieties of Formal Semantics, F. Landman and F. Veltman, eds, Foris, Dordrecht, 1–24.

Bach, E. (1986a), *Natural language metaphysics*, Logic, Methodology and Philosophy of Science VII, R.B. Marcus, G.J.W. Dorn and P. Weingartner, eds, North-Holland, Amsterdam, 573–595.

Bach, E. (1986b), *The algebra of events*, Ling. and Philos. **9**, 5–15.

Bach, E. (1989), *Informal Lectures on Formal Semantics*, State University of New York Press, Albany.

Bach, E. and Cooper, R. (1978), *The NP-S analysis of relative clauses and compositional semantics*, Ling. and Philos. **2**, 145–150.

Bach, E., Jelinek, E., Kratzer, A. and Partee, B.H. (eds) (1995), *Quantification in Natural Languages*, Kluwer, Dordrecht.

Bach, E., Kratzer, A. and Partee, B.H. (eds) (1989), *Papers in Quantification: Report to NSF*, Linguistics Department, University of Massachusetts, Amherst.

Bach, E. and Partee, B.H. (1980), *Anaphora and semantic structure*, Papers from the Parasession on Pronouns and Anaphora, J. Kreiman and A. Ojeda, eds, Chicago Linguistic Society, Chicago, 1–28.

Baker, C.L. (1966), *Definiteness and indefiniteness in English*, Unpublished Master's Thesis, University of Illinois.

Bar-Hillel, Y. (1954), *Logical syntax and semantics*, Language **30**, 230–237.

Barwise, J. (1981), *Scenes and other situations*, J. Philos. **78**, 369–397.

Barwise, J. and Cooper, R. (1981), *Generalized quantifiers and natural language*, Ling. and Philos. **4**, 159–219.

Barwise, J. and Perry, J. (1983), *Situations and Attitudes*, MIT Press, Cambridge, MA.

Bealer, G. (1982), *Quality and Concept*, Clarendon Press, Oxford.

Bennett, M. (1974), *Some extensions of a Montague fragment of English*, PhD Dissertation, University of California at Los Angeles, Indiana University Linguistics Club, Bloomington.

Bennett, M. (1976), *A variation and extension of a Montague fragment of English*, B. Partee, ed., 119–163.

Bennett, M. (1978), *Demonstratives and indexicals in Montague grammar*, Synthese **39**, 1–80.

Berman, S. (1987), *Situation-based semantics for adverbs of quantification*, University of Massachusetts Occasional Papers in Linguistics 1, University of Massachusetts, Umass Graduate Linguistics Students Association, Amherst, 45–68.

Bittner, M. (1994), *Cross-linguistic semantics*, Ling. and Philos. **17**, 53–108.

Carlson, G.N. (1983), *Marking constituents*, Linguistic Categories: Auxiliaries and Related Puzzles, vol. I: Categories, F. Heny and B. Richards, eds, Reidel, Dordrecht.

Carnap, R. (1947), *Meaning and Necessity. A Study in Semantics and Modal Logic*, Chicago Univ. Press, Chicago.

Carnap, R. (1952), *Meaning postulates*, Philos. Stud. **3**, 65–73.

Chellas, B. (1980), *Modal Logic: An Introduction*, Cambridge Univ. Press, Cambridge.

Chierchia, G. (1982), *Nominalization and Montague grammar*, Ling. and Philos. **5**, 303–354.

Chierchia, G. (1984a), *Topics in the syntax and semantics of infinitives and gerunds*, PhD Dissertation, University of Massachusetts, Amherst.

Chierchia, G. (1984b), *Anaphoric properties of infinitives and gerunds*, Proceedings of the West Coast Conference on Formal Linguistics vol. 3, M. Cobler, S. Mackaye and M. Wescoat, eds, Stanford Linguistics Association, Stanford University, 28–39.

Chierchia, G. (1985), *Formal semantics and the grammar of predication*, Ling. Inq. **16**, 417–443.

Chierchia, G. (1993), *Questions with quantifiers*, Nat. Language Semantics **1**, 181–234.

Chierchia, G. (1995), *Dynamics of Meaning. Anaphora, Presupposition and the Theory of Grammar*, Univ. of Chicago Press, Chicago and London.

Chierchia, G. and Jacobson, P. (1986), *Local and long distance control*, Papers from the Sixteenth Annual Meeting of the North Eastern Linguistic Society, S. Berman, J. Choe and J. McConough, eds, University of Massachusetts, Umass Graduate Linguistics Students Association, Amherst.

Chierchia, G. and Turner, R. (1988), *Semantics and property theory*, Ling. and Philos. **11**, 261–302.

Chomsky, N. (1955), *Logical syntax and semantics: Their linguistic relevance*, Language **31**, 36–45.

Chomsky, N. (1957), *Syntactic Structures*, Mouton, The Hague.

Chomsky, N. (1965), *Aspects of the Theory of Syntax*, MIT Press, Cambridge, MA.

Chomsky, N. (1975), *Questions of form and interpretation*, Ling. Anal. **1**, 75–109. Also: The Scope of American Linguistics, R. Austerlitz, ed., Peter de Ridder Press, Lisse, 159–196.

Church, A. (1951), *A formulation of the logic of sense and denotation*, Structure, Method and Meaning: Essays in Honor of H.M. Sheffer, P. Henle, H. Kallen and S. Langer, eds, New York.

Cocchiarella, N. (1985), *Frege's double correlation thesis and Quine's set-theories NF and ML*, J. Philos. Logic **14**, 1–39.

Cooper, R. (1975), *Montague's semantic theory and transformational syntax*, PhD Dissertation, University of Massachusetts, Umass Graduate Linguistics Students Association, Amherst.

Cooper, R. (1979), *The interpretation of pronouns*, Syntax and Semantics 10. Selections from the Third Groningen Round Table, F. Heny and H. Schnelle, eds, Academic Press, New York, 61–92.

Cooper, R. (1983), *Quantification and Syntactic Theory*, Reidel, Dordrecht.

Cooper, R. and Parsons, T. (1976), *Montague grammar, generative semantics and interpretive semantics*, B.H. Partee, ed., 311–362.

Cresswell, M.J. (1973), *Logics and Languages*, Methuen, London.

Cresswell, M.J. (1985), *Structured Meanings*, MIT Press, Cambridge, MA.

Cresswell, M.J. and von Stechow, A. (1982), *De re belief generalized*, Ling. and Philos. **5**, 503–535.

Dalrymple, M., Shieber, S.M. and Pereira, F.C.N. (1991), *Ellipsis and higher-order unification*, Ling. and Philos. **14**, 399–452.

Davidson, D. (1967), *The logical form of action sentences*, The Logic of Decision and Action, N. Rescher, ed., Univ. of Pittsburgh Press, Pittsburgh, 81–95.

Davidson, D. and Harman, G.F. (eds) (1972), *Semantics of Natural Language*, Reidel, Dordrecht.

Davis, S. and Mithun, M. (eds) (1979), *Linguistics, Philosophy and Montague Grammar*, Univ. of Texas Press, Austin.

Dekker, P. (1990), *The scope of negation in discourse. Towards a flexible dynamic Montague grammar*, Quantification and Anaphora I, J. Groenendijk, M. Stokhof and D. Beaver, eds, ESPRIT Basic Research Project 3175, Dynamic Interpretation of Natural Language, DYANA Deliverable R2.2A, 79–134.

Dekker, P. (1993), *Transsentential meditations. Ups and downs in dynamic semantics*, PhD Dissertation, ILLC Dissertation Series, University of Amsterdam.

Donnellan, K. (1966), *Reference and definite descriptions*, Philos. Rev. **75**, 281–304.

Dowty, D. (1978), *Governed transformations as lexical rules in a Montague grammar*, Ling. Inq. **9**, 393–426.

Dowty, D. (1979), *Word Meaning and Montague Grammar*, Reidel, Dordrecht.

Dowty, D. (1982), *Tenses, time adverbials and compositional semantic theory*, Ling. and Philos. **5**, 23–55.

Dowty, D. (1992), *Variable-free syntax, variable-binding syntax, the natural deduction Lambek calculus and the crossover constraint*, Proceedings of the 11th Meeting of the West Coast Conference on Formal Linguistics, CSLI Lecture Notes, Stanford.

Dowty, D. and Jacobson, P. (1989), *Agreement as a semantic phenomenon*, Proceedings of the Fifth Eastern States Conference on Linguistics, J. Powers and K. de Jong, eds, Ohio State University, Columbus.

Dowty, D., Wall, R. and Peters, S. (1981), *Introduction to Montague Semantics*, Reidel, Dordrecht.

Evans, G. (1980), *Pronouns*, Ling. Inq. **11**, 337–362.

Fauconnier, G. (1975a), *Pragmatic scales and logical structure*, Ling. Inq. **6**, 353–375.

Fauconnier, G. (1975b), *Polarity and the scale principle*, Papers from the Eleventh Meeting of the Chicago Linguistic Society, Chicago Linguistics Society, University of Chicago.

Filip, H. (1992), *Aspect and interpretation of nominal arguments*, Proceedings of the Twenty-Eighth Meeting of the Chicago Linguistic Society, C.P. Canakis, G.P. Chan and J.M. Denton, eds.

Filip, H. (1993), *Aspect, situation types and nominal reference*, Unpublished PhD Dissertation, University of California at Berkeley.

Fillmore, C. (1968), *The case for case*, Universals in Linguistic Theory, E. Bach and R. Harms, eds, Holt, Rinehart & Winston, New York, 1–88.

Fodor, J.A. (1975), *The Language of Thought*, Thomas Y. Crowell, New York.

Fodor, J.D. (1980), *Semantics: Theories of Meaning in Generative Grammar*, Harvard Univ. Press, Cambridge, MA.

Fodor, J.D. (1982), *The mental representation of quantifiers*, Processes, Beliefs and Questions, S. Peters and E. Saarinen, eds, Reidel, Dordrecht.

Frege, G. (1892), *Über Sinn und Bedeutung*, Z. Philos. Philosoph. Kritik **100**, 25–50. Translated as (1952), *On sense and reference*, Translations from the Philosophical Writings of Gottlob Frege, P.T. Geach and M. Black, eds, Blackwell, Oxford, 56–78.

Gallin, D. (1975), *Intensional and Higher-Order Modal Logic*, North-Holland, Amsterdam.

Gamut, L.T.F. (1991), *Logic, Language and Meaning*, vol. I: *Introduction to Logic*, vol. II: *Intensional Logic and Logical Grammar*, Univ. of Chicago Press, Chicago and London.

Gazdar, G. (1980), *A cross-categorial semantics for coordination*, Ling. and Philos. **3**, 407–410.

Gazdar, G. (1982), *Phrase structure grammar*, The Nature of Syntactic Representation, P. Jacobson and G. Pullum, eds, Reidel, Dordrecht, 131–186.

Gazdar, G., Klein, E., Pullum, G.K. and Sag, I.A. (1985), *Generalized Phrase Structure Grammar*, Basil Blackwell, Oxford; and Harvard Univ. Press, Cambridge, MA.

Geach, P.T. (1962), *Reference and Generality: An Examination of Some Medieval and Modern Theories*, Cornell Univ. Press, Ithaca.

Groenendijk, J. and Stokhof, M. (1984), *Studies on the semantics of questions and the pragmatics of answers*, PhD Dissertation, University of Amsterdam.

Groenendijk, J. and Stokhof, M. (1989), *Type-shifting rules and the semantics of interrogatives*, Properties, Types and Meaning, vol. II: Semantic Issues, G. Chierchia, B. Partee and R. Turner, eds, Kluwer, Dordrecht, 21–68.

Groenendijk, J. and Stokhof, M. (1990), *Dynamic Montague grammar*, Papers from the Second Symposium on Logic and Language, L. Kálmán and L. Pólos, eds, Akademiai Kiado, Budapest, 3–48.

Groenendijk, J. and Stokhof, M. (1991), *Dynamic predicate logic*, Ling. and Philos. **14**, 39–100.

Hajičová, E. and Sgall, P. (1987), *The ordering principle*, J. Pragmatics **11**, 435–454.

Halvorsen, P.-K. and Ladusaw, W.A. (1979), *Montague's "Universal Grammar". An introduction for the linguist*, Ling. and Philos. **3**, 185–223.

Harris, R.A. (1993), *The Linguistic Wars*, Oxford Univ. Press, New York and Oxford.

Harris, Z.S. (1968), *The Mathematics of Language*, Reidel, Dordrecht.

Heim, I. (1982), *The semantics of definite and indefinite noun phrases*, PhD Dissertation, University of Massachusetts, Umass Graduate Linguistics Students Association, Amherst.

Heim, I. (1983), *File change semantics and the familiarity theory of definiteness*, Meaning, Use and Interpretation of Language, R. Bäuerle, C. Schwarze and A. von Stechow, eds, Walter de Gruyter, Berlin, 164–189.

Heim, I. (1990), *E-type pronouns and donkey anaphora*, Ling. and Philos. **13**, 137–177.

Hendriks, H. (1988), *Type change in semantics: The scope of quantification and coordination*, Categories, Polymorphism and Unification, E. Klein and J. van Benthem, eds, Centre for Cognitive Science and Amsterdam: ITLI, University of Amsterdam, Edinburgh, 96–119.

Hendriks, H. (1993), *Studied flexibility. Categories and types in syntax and semantics*, PhD Dissertation, ILLC Dissertation Series, University of Amsterdam.

Henkin, L. (1963), *A theory of propositional types*, Fund. Math. **52**, 323–344.

Hindle, D. and Rooth, M. (1993), *Structural ambiguity and lexical relations*, Comput. Ling. **19**, 103–120.

Hinrichs, E. (1981), *Temporale Anaphora im Englischen*, Thesis, University of Tübingen.

Hinrichs, E. (1985), *A compositional semantics for aktionsarten and NP reference in English*, PhD Dissertation, Ohio State University.

Hinrichs, E. (1986), *Temporal anaphora in discourses of English*, Ling. and Philos. **9**, 63–82.

Hintikka, K.J.J. (1962), *Knowledge and Belief*, Cornell University Press, Ithaca.

Hintikka, K.J.J. (1970), *The semantics of modal notions*, Synthese **21**, 408–424. Reprinted: D. Davidson and G.F. Harman (eds) (1972); and (slightly revised) K.J.J. Hintikka (1975), *The Intentions of Intentionality and Other New Models for Modalities*, Reidel, Dordrecht.

Hughes, G. and Cresswell, M. (1968), *An Introduction to Modal Logic*, Methuen, London.

Jackendoff, R. (1972), *Semantic Interpretation in Generative Grammar*, MIT Press, Cambridge, MA.

Jackendoff, R. (1996), *Semantics and cognition*, S. Lappin, ed., 539–559.

Jacobson, P. (1992), *Bach–Peters sentences in a variable-free semantics*, Proceedings of the Eighth Amsterdam Colloquium, P. Dekker and M. Stokhof, eds, Institute for Logic, Language and Computation, University of Amsterdam, 283–302.

Jacobson, P. (1994), *i-within-i effects in a variable-free semantics and a categorial syntax*, Proceedings of the Ninth Amsterdam Colloquium, P. Dekker and M. Stokhof, eds, Institute for Logic, Language and Computation, University of Amsterdam, 349–368.

Jacobson, P. (forthcoming), *The locality of interpretation: The case of binding*, Proceedings of the Blaubeuren Symposium on Recent Developments in Natural Language Semantics, F. Hamm and A. von Stechow, eds, University of Tübingen, Tübingen.

Janssen, T.M.V. (1981), *Compositional semantics and relative clause formation in Montague grammar*, Formal Methods in the Study of Language, J. Groenendijk, T. Janssen and M. Stokhof, eds, Mathematisch Centrum, Amsterdam, 445–481.

Janssen, T.M.V. (1984), *Individual concepts are useful*, Varieties of Formal Semantics, F. Landman and F. Veltman, eds, Foris, Dordrecht, 171–192.

Janssen, T.M.V. (1986a), *Foundations and Applications of Montague Grammar*, part 1: *Foundations, Logic, Computer Science*, CWI Tracts no. 19, Centre for Mathematics and Computer Science, Amsterdam.

Janssen, T.M.V. (1986b), *Foundations and Applications of Montague Grammar*, part 2: *Applications to Natural Language*, CWI Tracts no. 28, Centre for Mathematics and Computer Science, Amsterdam.

Jelinek, E. (1995), *Quantification in straits salish*, Quantification in Natural Languages, E. Bach, E. Jelinek, A. Kratzer and B.H. Partee, eds, Kluwer, Dordrecht, 487–540.

Johnson-Laird, P.N. (1983), *Mental Models: Towards a Cognitive Science of Language, Inference and Consciousness*, Harvard Univ. Press, Cambridge, MA.

Joshi, A. (1985), *How much context-sensitivity is necessary for characterizing structural descriptions – tree adjoining grammars*, Natural Language Processing. Theoretical, Computational and Psychological Perspectives, D. Dowty, L. Karttunen and A. Zwicky, eds, Cambridge Univ. Press, Cambridge, MA.

Joshi, A., Vijay-Shanker, K. and Weir, D. (1991), *The convergence of mildly context-sensitive formalisms*, Processing of Linguistic Structure, P. Sells, S. Shieber, and T. Wasow, eds, MIT Press, Cambridge, MA. 31–81.

Jubien, M. (1985), *First-order property theory*, Manuscript, University of Massachusetts, Amherst.

Kadmon, N. (1987), *On unique and non-unique reference and asymmetric quantification*, PhD Dissertation, University of Massachusetts, Umass Graduate Linguistics Students Association, Amherst.

Kadmon, N. (1990), *Uniqueness*, Ling. and Philos. **13**, 273–324.

Kalish, D. (1967), *Semantics*, Encyclopedia of Philosophy, P. Edwards, ed., Macmillan, New York, 348–358.

Kalish, D. and Montague, R. (1964), *Logic: Techniques of Formal Reasoning*, Harcourt, Brace, Jovanovich, New York.

Kamp, H. (1981), *A theory of truth and semantic representation*, Formal Methods in the Study of Language: Proceedings of the Third Amsterdam Colloquium, J. Groenendijk, T. Janssen and M. Stokhof, eds, Mathematisch Centrum, Amsterdam. Reprinted: J. Groenendijk, T.M.V. Janssen and M. Stokhof (eds) (1984), *Truth, Interpretation and Information: Selected Papers from the Third Amsterdam Colloquium*, Foris, Dordrecht, 1–42.

Kamp, H. (1990), *Uniqueness presuppositions and plural anaphora in DTT and DRT*, Quantification and Anaphora I, J. Groenendijk, M. Stokhof and D. Beaver, eds, ESPRIT Basic Research Project 3175, Dynamic Interpretation of Natural Language, DYANA Deliverable R2.2A, 177–190.

Kamp, H. and Partee, B.H. (1995), *Property theory and compositionality*, Cognition **57**, 129–191.

Kamp, H. and Reyle, U. (1993), *From Discourse to Logic*, Kluwer, Dordrecht.

Kanger, S. (1957a), *The morning star paradox*, Theoria **23**, 1–11.

Kanger, S. (1957b), *A note on quantification and modalities*, Theoria **23**, 133–134.

Kaplan, D. (1964), *Foundations of intensional logic*, PhD Dissertation, University of California at Los Angeles.

Kaplan, D. (1979), *On the logic of demonstratives*, Contemporary Perspectives in the Philosophy of Language, P. French, Th. Uehling and H. Wettstein, eds, Univ. of Minnesota Press, Minneapolis.
Karttunen, L. (1968), *What do referential indices refer to?*, The Rand Corporation, Santa Monica, CA.
Karttunen, L. (1969), *Pronouns and variables*, Papers from the Fifth Regional Meeting of the Chicago Linguistic Society, R. Binnick et al., eds, University of Chicago Linguistics Department, 108–115.
Karttunen, L. (1971), *Implicative verbs*, Language **47**, 340–358.
Karttunen, L. (1975), *Discourse Referents*, Syntax and Semantics vol. 7, J. McCawley, ed., Academic Press, New York, 363–385.
Karttunen, L. (1977), *Syntax and semantics of questions*, Ling. and Philos. **1**, 3–44.
Katz, J.J. and Fodor, J.A. (1963), *The structure of a semantic theory*, Language **39**, 170–210.
Katz, J.J. and Postal, P.M. (1964), *An Integrated Theory of Linguistic Descriptions*, MIT Press, Cambridge, MA.
Keenan, E.L. (1971a), *Names, quantifiers and a solution to the sloppy identity problem*, Papers Ling. **4**.
Keenan, E.L. (1971b), *Quantifier structures in English*, Found. Lang. **7**, 225–284.
Keenan, E.L. (ed.) (1975), *Formal Semantics of Natural Language*, Cambridge Univ. Press, Cambridge, MA.
Keenan, E.L. and Faltz, L. (1985), *Boolean Semantics for Natural Language*, Reidel, Dordrecht.
Keenan, E.L. and Stavi, J. (1986), *A semantic characterization of natural language determiners*, Ling. and Philos. **9**, 253–326.
Klein, E. and Sag, I. (1985), *Type-driven translation*, Ling. and Philos. **8**, 163–201.
Kratzer, A. (1989), *An investigation of the lumps of thought*, Ling. and Philos. **12**, 607–653.
Kratzer, A. (1991), *The representation of focus*, Semantics: An International Handbook of Contemporary Research, A. von Stechow and D. Wunderlich, eds, Walter de Gruyter, Berlin, 825–834.
Kratzer, A. (1995a), *Stage-level and individual-level predicates*, The Generic Book, G.N. Carlson and F.J. Pelletier, eds, Univ. of Chicago Press, Chicago, 125–175.
Kratzer, A. (1995b), *Pseudoscope*, Manuscript, Amherst, MA.
Krifka, M. (1986), *Nominalreferenz und Zeitkonstitution. Zur Semantik von Massentermen, Pluraltermen und Aspektklassen*, PhD Dissertation, University of Munich. Published in 1989, Wilhelm Fink, Munich.
Krifka, M. (1987), *Nominal reference and temporal constitution: Towards a semantics of quantity*, Proceedings of the Sixth Amsterdam Colloquium, J. Groenendijk, M. Stokhof and F. Veltman, eds, 153–173.
Krifka, M. (1990), *Boolean and non-boolean And*, Papers from the Second Symposium on Logic and Language, L. Kálmán and L. Pólos, eds, Akademiai Kiado, Budapest.
Kripke, S. (1959), *A completeness theorem in modal logic*, J. Symb. Logic **24**, 1–14.
Kripke, S. (1972), *Naming and necessity*, D. Davidson and G.H. Harman, eds, 253–355, 763–769.
Ladusaw, G. (1979), *Polarity sensitivity as inherent scope relations*, PhD Dissertation, University of Texas at Austin, Indiana University Linguistics Club, Bloomington.
Ladusaw, G. (1980), *On the notion "affective" in the analysis of negative polarity items*, J. Ling. Res. **2**, 1–16.
Ladusaw, G. (1983), *Logical form and conditions on grammaticality*, Ling. and Philos. **6**, 373–392.
Lakoff, G. (1968), *Pronouns and reference. Parts I and II*, Indiana University Linguistics Club, Bloomington.
Lakoff, G. (1970), *Repartee*, Found. Lang. **6**, 389–422.
Lakoff, G. (1971), *On generative semantics*, Semantics. An Interdisciplinary Reader in Philosophy, Linguistics and Psychology, D. Steinberg and L. Jakobovits, eds, Cambridge Univ. Press, Cambridge, MA, 232–296.
Lakoff, G. (1972), *Linguistics and natural logic*, D. Davidson and G. Harman, eds, 545–665.
Landman, F. (1986), *Towards a theory of information: The status of partial objects in semantics*, PhD Dissertation, University of Amsterdam, Foris, Dordrecht.
Landman, F. (1989a), *Groups I*, Ling. and Philos. **12**, 559–605.
Landman, F. (1989b), *Groups II*, Ling. and Philos. **12**, 724–744.
Landman, F. (1991), *Structures for Semantics*, Kluwer, Dordrecht.
Landman, F. (1996), *Plurality*, S. Lappin, ed., 425–457.
Lappin, S. (ed.) (1996), *The Handbook of Contemporary Semantic Theory*, Blackwell, Dordrecht.
Lewis, D. (1968), *Counterpart theory and quantified modal logic*, J. Philos. **65**, 113–126.
Lewis, D. (1969), *Convention: A Philosophical Study*, Harvard Univ. Press, Cambridge, MA.
Lewis, D. (1970), *General semantics*, Synthese **22**, 18–67. Reprinted: D. Davidson and G. Harman (eds) (1972), 169–218.
Lewis, D. (1973), *Counterfactuals*, Basil Blackwell, Oxford.

Lewis, D. (1974), *Tensions*, Semantics and Philosophy, M. Munitz and P. Unger, eds, New York Univ. Press, New York.

Lewis, D. (1975a), *Adverbs of quantification*, Formal Semantics of Natural Language, E.L. Keenan, ed., Cambridge Univ. Press, Cambridge, MA.

Lewis, D. (1975b), *Languages and language*, Language, Mind and Knowledge, K. Gunderson, ed., Univ. of Minnesota Press, Minneapolis.

Linebarger, M. (1980), *The grammar of negative polarity*, PhD Dissertation, MIT, Cambridge, MA.

Linebarger, M. (1987), *Negative polarity and grammatical representation*, Ling. and Philos. **10**, 325–387.

Link, G. (1979), *Montague-Grammatik. Die logische Grundlagen*, Wilhelm Fink Verlag, Munich.

Link, G. (1983), *The logical analysis of plurals and mass terms: A lattice-theoretic approach*, Meaning, Use and Interpretation of Language, R. Bäuerle, C. Schwarze and A. von Stechow, eds, Walter de Gruyter, Berlin, 302–323.

Lyons, J. (1968), *Introduction to Theoretical Linguistics*, Cambridge Univ. Press, Cambridge, MA.

May, R. (1977), *The grammar of quantification*, PhD Dissertation, MIT, Cambridge, MA.

May, R. (1985), *Logical Form: Its Structure and Derivation*, MIT Press, Cambridge, MA.

McCawley, J.D. (1971), *Where do noun phrases come from?*, Semantics. An Interdisciplinary Reader in Philosophy, Linguistics and Psychology, D. Steinberg and L. Jakobovits, eds, Cambridge Univ. Press, Cambridge, MA, 217–231.

McCawley, J.D. (1979), *Helpful hints to the ordinary working Montague grammarian*, S. Davis and M. Mithun, eds, 103–125.

McCawley, J.D. (1981), *Everything that Linguists Have Always Wanted to Know About Logic But Were Ashamed to Ask*, Univ. of Chicago Press, Chicago.

Mitchell, J. (1986), *The formal semantics of point of view*, PhD Dissertation, University of Massachusetts, UMass Graduate Linguistics Students Association, Amherst.

Montague, R. (1968), *Pragmatics*, Contemporary Philosophy: A Survey, R. Klibansky, ed., La Nuova Italia Editrice, Florence, 102–122. Reprinted: Montague (1974), 95–118.

Montague, R. (1969), *On the nature of certain philosophical entities*, The Monist **53**, 159–194. Reprinted: Montague (1974), 148–187.

Montague, R. (1970a), *Pragmatics and intensional logic*, Synthese **22**, 68–94. Reprinted: Montague (1974), 119–147.

Montague, R. (1970b), *English as a formal language*, Linguaggi nella Società e nella Tecnica, B. Visentini et al., eds, Edizioni di Communità, Milan, 189–224. Reprinted: Montague (1974), 188–221.

Montague, R. (1970c), *Universal grammar*, Theoria **36**, 373–398. Reprinted: Montague (1974), 222–246.

Montague, R. (1973), *The proper treatment of quantification in ordinary English*, Approaches to Natural Language. Proceedings of the 1970 Stanford Workshop on Grammar and Semantics, K.J.J. Hintikka, J.M.E. Moravcsik and P. Suppes, eds, Reidel, Dordrecht, 221–242. Reprinted: Montague (1974), 247–270.

Montague, R. (1974), *Formal Philosophy: Selected Papers of Richard Montague, edited and with an introduction by Richmond Thomason*, Yale Univ. Press, New Haven, CT.

Moschovakis, Y. (1985), *Unpublished lecture notes*, CSLI-ASL Summer School on Logic, Language and Information, Stanford.

Muskens, R. (1989), *Meaning and partiality*, PhD Dissertation, University of Amsterdam.

Newmeyer, F.J. (1980), *Linguistic Theory in America*, Academic Press, New York.

Oehrle, R., Bach, E. and Wheeler, D. (eds) (1988), *Categorial Grammars and Natural Language Structures*, Reidel, Dordrecht.

Orey, S. (1959), *Model theory for the higher-order predicate calculus*, Trans. Amer. Math. Soc. **92**, 72–84.

Parsons, T. (1972), *An outline of a semantics for English*, Manuscript, Amherst, MA.

Parsons, T. (1979), *Type theory and ordinary language*, S. Davis and M. Mithun, eds.

Parsons, T. (1980), *Nonexistent Objects*, Yale Univ. Press, New Haven, CT.

Partee, B.H. (1970a), *Opacity, coreference and pronouns*, Synthese **21**, 359–385.

Partee, B.H. (1970b), *Negation, conjunction and quantifiers: Syntax vs. semantics*, Found. Lang. **6**, 153–165.

Partee, B.H. (1973a), *Comments on Montague's paper*, Approaches to Natural Language, K.J.J. Hintikka, J.M.E. Moravcsik and P. Suppes, eds, Reidel, Dordrecht, 243–258.

Partee, B.H. (1973b), *Some transformational extensions of Montague grammar*, J. Philos. Logic **2**, 509–534. Reprinted: B.H. Partee (ed.) (1976a), pp. 51–76.

Partee, B.H. (1973c), *Some structural analogies between tenses and pronouns in English*, J. Philos. **70**, 601–609.

Partee, B.H. (1974), *Opacity and scope*, Semantics and Philosophy, M. Munitz and P. Unger, eds, New York Univ. Press, New York.

Partee, B.H. (1975), *Montague grammar and transformational grammar*, Ling. Inq. **6**, 203–300.

Partee, B.H. (ed.) (1976a), *Montague Grammar*, Academic Press, New York.

Partee, B.H. (1976b), *Semantics and syntax: The search for constraints*, Georgetown University Roundtable on Languages and Linguistics, C. Rameh, ed., Georgetown University School of Languages and Linguistics, 99–110.

Partee, B.H. (1979a), *Constraining Montague grammar: A framework and a fragment*, S. Davis and M. Mithun, eds, 51–101.

Partee, B. (1979b), *Montague grammar and the well-formedness constraint*, Syntax and Semantics 10. Selections from the Third Groningen Round Table, F. Heny and H. Schnelle, eds, Academic Press, New York, 275–313.

Partee, B. (1979c), *Semantics – mathematics or psychology?*, Semantics from Different Points of View, R. Bäuerle, U. Egli and A. von Stechow, eds, Springer, Berlin, 1–14.

Partee, B. (1980), *Montague grammar, mental representation and reality*, Philosophy and Grammar, S. Ohman and S. Kanger, eds, Reidel, Dordrecht, 59–78. Reprinted: P. French et al. (eds) (1979), *Contemporary Perspectives in the Philosophy of Language*, Univ. of Minnesota Press, Minneapolis.

Partee, B. (1982), *Belief sentences and the limits of semantics*, Processes, Beliefs and Questions, S. Peters and E. Saarinen, eds, Reidel, Dordrecht, 87–106.

Partee, B. (1984), *Nominal and temporal anaphora*, Ling. and Philos. **7**, 243–286.

Partee, B. (1987), *Noun phrase interpretation and type-shifting principles*, Studies in Discourse Representation Theory and the Theory of Generalized Quantifiers, J. Groenendijk, D. de Jongh and M. Stokhof, eds, Foris, Dordrecht, 115–144.

Partee, B. (1988), *Semantic facts and psychological facts*, Mind & Language **3**, 43–52.

Partee, B. (1989a), *Possible worlds in model-theoretic semantics: A linguistic perspective*, Possible Worlds in Humanities, Arts and Sciences: Proceedings of Nobel Symposium 65, S. Allen, ed., Walter de Gruyter, Berlin and New York, 93–123.

Partee, B. (1989b), *Binding implicit variables in quantified contexts*, Papers from CLS 25, C. Wiltshire, B. Music and R. Graczyk, eds, Chicago Linguistic Society, Chicago, 342–365.

Partee, B. (1992), *Naturalizing formal semantics*, Proceedings of the XVth World Congress of Linguists: Texts of Plenary Sessions, Laval University, Quebec, 62–76.

Partee, B. (1993), *Semantic structures and semantic properties*, Knowledge and Language, vol. II: Lexical and Conceptual Structure, E. Reuland and W. Abraham, eds, Kluwer, Dordrecht, 7–29.

Partee, B. (1995), *Lexical semantics and compositionality*, Invitation to Cognitive Science, D. Osherson, ed. Second edition: L. Gleitman and M. Liberman (eds) (1995), *Part I: Language*, MIT Press, Cambridge, MA.

Partee, B. and Bach, E. (1981), *Quantification, pronouns and VP anaphora*, Formal Methods in the Study of Language: Proceedings of the Third Amsterdam Colloquium, J. Groenendijk, T. Janssen and M. Stokhof, eds, Mathematisch Centrum, Amsterdam. Reprinted: J. Groenendijk, T. Janssen and M. Stokhof (eds) (1984), *Truth, Information and Interpretation: Selected Papers from the Third Amsterdam Colloquium*, Foris, Dordrecht, 99–130.

Partee, B.H., Ter Meulen, A. and Wall, R.E. (1990), *Mathematical Methods in Linguistics*, Kluwer, Dordrecht.

Partee, B.H. and Rooth, M. (1983), *Generalized Conjunction and Type Ambiguity*, Meaning, Use and Interpretation of Language, R. Bäuerle, C. Schwarze and A. von Stechow, eds, Walter de Gruyter, Berlin, 361–383.

Pavel, T.G. (1986), *Fictional Worlds*, Harvard Univ. Press, Cambridge, MA.

Peregrin, J. (1995), *Doing Worlds and Words*, Kluwer, Dordrecht.

Poesio, M. (1991), *Relational semantics and scope ambiguity*, Situation Theory and Its Applications vol. 2, J. Barwise, J.M. Gawron, G. Plotkin and S. Tutiya, eds, CSLI, Stanford.

Poesio, M. (1994), *Discourse interpretation and the scope of operators*, PhD Dissertation, University of Rochester.

Pollard, C. and Sag, I.A. (1987), *Information-Based Syntax and Semantics*, vol. 1: *Fundamentals*, CSLI Lecture Notes, Stanford.

Pollard, C. and Sag, I.A. (1994), *Head-Driven Phrase Structure Grammar*, Center for the Study of Language and Information, Stanford; and Univ. of Chicago Press, Chicago and London.

Portner, P. (1992), *Situation theory and the semantics of propositional expressions*, PhD Dissertation, University of Massachusetts, Amherst.

Quine, W.V.O. (1960), *Word and Object*, MIT Press, Cambridge, MA.

Quine, W.V.O. (1961), *From a Logical Point of View*, MIT Press, Cambridge, MA.

Quine, W.V.O. (1970), *Philosophy of Logic*, Prentice-Hall, Englewood Cliffs, NJ.

Reichenbach, H. (1947), *Elements of Symbolic Logic*, Macmillan, New York.

Reinhart, T. and Reuland, E. (1993), *Reflexivity*, Ling. Inq. **24**, 657–720.

Reyle, U. (1993), *Dealing with Ambiguities by Underspecification: Construction, Representation and Deduction*, J. Semantics **10**, 123–179.

Rodman, R. (ed.) (1972), *Papers in Montague grammar*, Occasional Papers in Linguistics, Linguistics Department, UCLA, Los Angeles.

Rodman, R. (1976), *Scope phenomena, "movement transformations" and relative clauses*, B.H. Partee, ed., 165–176.

Rooth, M. (1992a), *A theory of focus interpretation*, Nat. Language Semantics **1**, 75–116.

Rooth, M. (1992b), *Ellipsis redundancy and reduction redundancy*, Manuscript, University of Stuttgart.

Rooth, M. and Partee, B. (1982), *Conjunction, type ambiguity and wide sope "or"*, Proceedings of the 1982 West Coast Conference on Formal Linguistics, D. Flickinger, M. Macken and N. Wiegand, eds, Stanford Linguistics Department, Stanford.

Rosetta, M.T. (1994), *Compositional Translation*, Kluwer, Dordrecht.

Russell, B. and Whitehead, A. (1913), *Principia Mathematica*, Cambridge Univ. Press, Cambridge, MA.

Sag, I.A. (1976), *Deletion and logical form*, PhD Dissertation, MIT, Cambridge, MA.

Schiffer, S. (1987), *Remnants of Meaning*, MIT Press, Cambridge, MA.

Schwarzschild, R. (1992), *Types of plural individuals*, Ling. and Philos. **15**, 641–675.

Scott, D. (1970), *Advice on modal logic*, Philosophical Problems in Logic, K. Lambert, ed., Dordrecht.

Soames, S. (1987), *Semantics and semantic competence*, Thought and Language: Second Arizona Colloquium in Cognitive Science, S. Schiffer and S. Steele, eds, Univ. of Arizona Press, Tucson.

Staal, J.F. (ed.) (1969), *Formal logic and natural languages: A symposium*, Found. Lang. **5**, 256–284.

Stalnaker, R. (1974), *Pragmatic presuppositions*, Semantics and Philosophy, M. Munitz and P. Unger, eds, New York Univ. Press, New York, 197–214.

Stalnaker, R. (1976), *Propositions*, Issues in the Philosophy of Language, A. Mackay and D. Merrill, eds, Yale Univ. Press, New Haven, CT, 79–91.

Stalnaker, R. (1978), *Assertion*, Syntax and Semantics, vol. 9: Pragmatics, P. Cole, ed., Academic Press, New York, 315–332.

Stalnaker, R. (1984), *Inquiry*, MIT Press, Cambridge, MA.

Stein, M. (1981), *Quantification in Thai*, PhD Dissertation, University of Massachusetts, Umass Graduate Linguistics Students Association, Amherst.

Szabolcsi, A. (1987), *Bound variables in syntax (are there any?)*, Proceedings of the Sixth Amsterdam Colloquium, J. Groenendijk, M. Stokhof and F. Veltman, eds, University of Amsterdam, 331–351.

Szabolcsi, A. (ed.) (forthcoming), *Ways of Scope Taking*, Kluwer, Dordrecht.

Tarski, A. (1944), *The semantic conception of truth and the foundations of semantics*, Philos. Phenomenolog. Res. **4**, 341–375.

Thomason, R. (1974), *Introduction*, in Montague, R. (1974), 1–69.

Thomason, R. (1976), *Some extensions of Montague grammar*, B.H. Partee, ed., 77–118.

Thomason, R. and Stalnaker, R. (1973), *A semantic theory of adverbs*, Ling. Inq. **4**, 195–220.

Tichý, P. (1988), *The Foundations of Frege's Logic*, Walter de Gruyter, Berlin.

Turner, R. (1987), *A theory of properties*, J. Symb. Logic **52**, 63–86.

Turner, R. (1989), *Two issues in the foundations of semantic theory*, Properties, Types and Meaning vol. 1, G. Chierchia, B. Partee and R. Turner, eds, Kluwer, Dordrecht.

Veltman, F. (1981), *Data semantics*, Formal Methods in the Study of Language: Proceedings of the Third Amsterdam Colloquium, J. Groenendijk, T. Janssen and M. Stokhof, eds, Mathematisch Centrum, Amsterdam. Reprinted: J. Groenendijk, T. Janssen and M. Stokhof (eds) (1984), *Truth, Information and Interpretation: Selected Papers from the Third Amsterdam Colloquium*, Foris, Dordrecht, 43–63.

Veltman, F. (1985a), *Logics for conditionals*, PhD Dissertation, University of Amsterdam.
Veltman, F. (1985b), *Data semantics and the pragmatics of indicative conditionals*, On Conditionals, E. Traugott et al., eds, Cambridge Univ. Press, Cambridge, MA.
Veltman, F. (1990), *Defaults in update semantics*, Conditionals, Defaults, and Belief Revision, H. Kamp, ed., DYANA Deliverable R2.5.A, Edinburgh. To appear in J. Philos. Logic.
Vermazen, B. (1967), *Review of J.J. Katz and P. Postal (1964), An Integrated Theory of Linguistic Descriptions and J.J. Katz (1966), The Philosophy of Language*, Synthese **17**, 350–365.
von Fintel, K. (1994), *Restrictions on quantifier domains*, PhD Dissertation, University of Massachusetts, Umass Graduate Linguistics Students Association, Amherst.
von Stechow, A. (1974), $\epsilon - \lambda$ *kontextfreie Sprachen: Ein Beitrag zu einer natürlichen formalen Semantik*, Ling. Ber. **34**, 1–34.
von Stechow, A. (1980), *Modification of noun phrases: A challenge for compositional semantics*, Theor. Ling. **7**, 57–110.
von Stechow, A. (1984), *Structured propositions and essential indexicals*, Varieties of Formal Semantics, F. Landman and F. Veltman, eds, Foris, Dordrecht, 385–403.
Williams, E. (1977), *Discourse and logical form*, Ling. Inq. **8**, 101–139.
Williams, E. (1988), *Is LF distinct from S-structure? A reply to May*, Ling. Inq. **19**, 135–146.
Zeevat, H. (1989), *A compositional approach to discourse representation theory*, Ling. and Philos. **12**, 95–131.
Zimmermann, T.E. (1981), *Einführungen in die Montague-Grammatik*, Ling. Ber. **75**, 26–40.
Zimmermann, T.E. (1989), *Intensional logic and two-sorted type theory*, J. Symb. Logic **54**, 65–77.
Zucchi, A. (1989), *The language of propositions and events: Issues in the syntax and semantics of nominalization*, PhD Dissertation, University of Massachusetts, Amherst.
Zwarts, F. (1986), *Categoriale grammatica en algebraïsche semantiek*, PhD Dissertation, Groningen University.

CHAPTER 2

Categorial Type Logics

Michael Moortgat

Research Institute for Language and Speech (OTS), Utrecht University, Trans 10, 3512 JK Utrecht, The Netherlands
E-mail: moortgat@let.ruu.nl

Commentator: G. Morrill

Contents

HANDBOOK OF LOGIC AND LANGUAGE
Edited by J. van Benthem and A. ter Meulen

Les quantités du langage et leurs rapports sont regulièrement exprimables dans leur nature fondamentale, par des formules mathématiques. ... L'expression simple [of linguistic concepts] *sera algébrique ou elle ne sera pas. ... On aboutit à des théorèmes qu'il faut démontrer.*

Ferdinand de Saussure[1]

This chapter describes the framework of categorial type logic, a grammar architecture that can be seen as the logical development of the categorial approach to natural language analysis initiated in the Thirties in the work of Ajdukiewicz (1935). The choice of grammatical number in the title stresses the pluralistic nature of the enterprise: this chapter systematically charts a *landscape* of systems of grammatical inference – the categorial counterpart of the Chomsky Hierarchy in the framework of phrase structure grammars.

The chapter has been written for two types of readers. For the reader with a background in *linguistics*, it tries to provide a useful compendium of the logical tools and results one needs to appreciate current categorial research. Such a compendium, we hope, will make the research literature more accessible. The reader with a *logic* background is justified in classifying the grammar formalism discussed here under the rubric Applied Logic. To measure progress in this field, then, one has to be in a position to evaluate the 'closeness of fit' between the formal systems proposed and the linguistic reality they intend to model. For the logical part of the audience, we try to provide enough linguistic background to make it possible to assess the motivation for categorial design choices.

In organizing the material one can opt for a 'historical' mode of development, or for a state-of-the-art presentation of the 'internal dynamics' of the field. Only the second approach adequately reveals the connections between linguistic composition and logical deduction. The major organizing principle for the chapter is the vocabulary of the 'logical constants' of grammatical reasoning, the type-forming operators. A brief preview is given below.

Multiplicative operators: $\Diamond$, $\Box^{\downarrow}$, $/$, $\bullet$, $\backslash$. The core part of the vocabulary. Unary and binary connectives dealing with grammatical composition in the form and meaning dimensions.

Boolean and/or additive operators: $\wedge$, $\vee$, $\sqcap$, $\sqcup$. Conjunctive/disjunctive type specifications, with set-theoretic or additive interpretation in the sense of Linear Logic.

Polymorphic types: first and second order quantification $\forall^1$, $\exists^1$, $\forall^2$, $\exists^2$. Dependent types and type schemata expressing generalizations across type assignments.

Given the space limitations of the handbook format, the information packaging of this chapter will be dense. Fortunately, we can refer the interested reader to a number of monographs that deal with logical and linguistic aspects of the type-logical approach in a more spacious manner. For the general logical background, *Language in Action* (Van Benthem, 1991, 1995) is essential reading. *Type Logical Grammar* (Morrill, 1994a) situates the type-logical approach within the framework of Montague's Universal Grammar

[1] N10 and N13a in R. Godel, *Les sources manuscrites du CLG de F. de Saussure*, Genève, 1957. Quoted without reference by Roman Jakobson in his introduction of Jakobson (1961).

and presents detailed linguistic analyses for a substantive fragment of syntactic and semantic phenomena in the grammar of English. *Type Logical Semantics* (Carpenter, 1996) offers a general introduction to natural language semantics studied from a type-logical perspective. Chapter 12 of this Handbook discusses categorial grammar logics from the perspective of mathematical linguistics and logical proof theory.

1. Introduction: Grammatical reasoning

The central objective of the type-logical approach is to develop a uniform *deductive* account of the composition of form and meaning in natural language: formal grammar is presented as a *logic* – a system for reasoning about structured linguistic resources. In the sections that follow, the model-theoretic and proof-theoretic aspects of this program will be executed in technical detail. First, we introduce the central concept of 'grammatical composition' in an informal way. It will be useful to distinguish two aspects of the composition relation: a fixed *logical* component, and a variable *structural* component. We discuss these in turn.

Grammatical composition: Logic. The categorial perspective on the form-meaning articulation in natural language is based on a distinction, which can be traced back to Frege, between 'complete' and 'incomplete' expressions. Such a distinction makes it possible to drastically simplify the traditional Aristotelian theory of categories (or types): one can reserve atomic category names for the complete expressions, and for the categorization of the incomplete expressions one inductively defines an infinite supply of category names out of the atomic types and a small number of type-forming connectives.

For the categorization of incomplete expressions, Ajdukiewicz in his seminal (Ajdukiewicz, 1935) used a fractional notation $\frac{A}{B}$, inspired by Husserl's Bedeutungskategorien and Russell's Theory of Types. The fractional notation immediately suggests the basic combination schema via an analogy with multiplication: $\frac{A}{B} \times B$ yields A. Bar-Hillel (see the papers in (Bar-Hillel, 1964)) refined the fractional categories by splitting up $\frac{A}{B}$ into a division from the left $B\backslash A$ and a division from the right A/B, in order to discriminate between incomplete expressions that will produce an expression of type A when composed with an arbitrary expression of type B to the left, and to the right, respectively. (The notation for directional fractions derives from Lambek (1958).)

It will be helpful for what follows to take a logical (rather than arithmetical) perspective on the category formulas, and read A/B, $B\backslash A$ as directionally-sensitive 'implications' – implications with respect to structural composition of linguistic material, rather than logical conjunction of propositions. Let us write $\Gamma \vdash A$ for the basic judgement of the grammar logic: the judgement that the structured configuration of linguistic expressions Γ can be categorized as a well-formed expression of type A. The inference pattern (1) tells us how to arrive at a grammaticality judgement for the composite structure Γ, Δ from judgements for the parts Γ and Δ – it tells us how we can *use* the implications $/$ and $\backslash$ in grammatical reasoning. Where the premises are immediate, the basic law of grammatical composition takes the form of a Modus Ponens inference: $A/B, B \vdash A$ and $B, B\backslash A \vdash A$.

(1)
$$\begin{array}{llll} \text{from } \Gamma \vdash A/B & \text{and} & \Delta \vdash B, & \text{infer } \Gamma, \Delta \vdash A, \\ \text{from } \Gamma \vdash B & \text{and} & \Delta \vdash B\backslash A, & \text{infer } \Gamma, \Delta \vdash A. \end{array}$$

In the example (2), one finds a little piece of grammatical reasoning leading from lexical categorizations to the conclusion that 'Kazimierz talks to the mathematician' is a well-formed sentence. In this example, sentences s, (proper) noun phrases np, common nouns n, and prepositional phrases pp are taken to be 'complete expressions', whereas the verb 'talk', the determiner 'the' and the preposition 'to' are categorized as incomplete with respect to these complete phrases. The sequence of Modus Ponens inference steps is displayed in Natural Deduction format in the style of Prawitz (1965), with labels [/E], [\E] for the 'elimination' of the implication connectives.

(2)
$$\dfrac{\dfrac{\text{Kazimierz}}{np} \quad \dfrac{\dfrac{\text{talks}}{((np\backslash s)/pp)} \quad \dfrac{\dfrac{\text{to}}{(pp/np)} \quad \dfrac{\dfrac{\text{the}}{(np/n)} \quad \dfrac{\text{mathematician}}{n}}{np}\,/E}{pp}\,/E}{(np\backslash s)}\,/E}{s}\,\backslash E$$

The inferences of (1) build more complex structural configurations out of their parts by using the grammatical implications. What about looking at grammatical structure from the opposite perspective? In other words: given information about the categorization of a composite structure, what conclusions could we draw about the categorization of its parts? Suppose we want to find out whether a structure Γ can be appropriately categorized as A/B. Given the interpretation we had in mind for the implication /, such a conclusion would be justified if we could show that Γ in construction with an arbitrary expression of type B can be categorized as an expression of type A. Similarly, from the grammaticality judgement that B in construction with Γ is of type A, we can conclude that Γ itself is of type $B\backslash A$. The inference patterns (3), introduced in (Lambek, 1958), tell us how to *prove* formulas A/B or $B\backslash A$, just as the (1) inferences told us how to *use* these implications.

(3)
$$\begin{array}{ll} \text{from } \Gamma, B \vdash A, & \text{infer } \Gamma \vdash A/B, \\ \text{from } B, \Gamma \vdash A, & \text{infer } \Gamma \vdash B\backslash A. \end{array}$$

In order to see where this type of 'deconstructive' reasoning comes into play, consider the relative clause example 'the mathematician whom Kazimierz talks to'. There is one new lexical item in this example: the relative pronoun *whom*. This item is categorized as incomplete: on the right, it wants to enter into composition with the relative clause body – an expression which we would like to assign to the category s/np.

(4)
$$\dfrac{\dfrac{\text{the}}{(np/n)} \quad \dfrac{\dfrac{\text{mathematician}}{n} \quad \dfrac{\dfrac{\text{whom}}{((n\backslash n)/(s/np))} \quad \dfrac{\dfrac{\dfrac{\text{Kazimierz}}{np} \quad \dfrac{\dfrac{\text{talks}}{((np\backslash s)/pp)} \quad \dfrac{\dfrac{\text{to}}{(pp/np)} \quad \overline{np}}{pp}\,/E}{(np\backslash s)}\,/E}{s}\,\backslash E}{(s/np)}\,/I}{(n\backslash n)}\,/E}{n}\,\backslash E}{np}\,/E$$

In order to show that 'Kazimierz talks to' is indeed of type s/np, we make a *hypothetical* assumption, and suppose we have an arbitrary np expression. With the aid of this hypothetical assumption, we derive s for 'Kazimierz talks to np', using the familiar Modus Ponens steps of inference. At the point where we have derived s, we withdraw the hypothetical np assumption, and conclude that 'Kazimierz talks to' can be categorized as s/np. This step is labeled [/I], for the 'introduction' of the implication connective, and the withdrawn assumption is marked by overlining.

The relation between the *wh* pronoun and the hypothetical np position which it preempts is often described metaphorically in terms of 'movement'. Notice that in our deductive setting we achieve the effects of 'movement' without adding anything to the theory of grammatical composition: there is no need for abstract syntactic place-holders (such as the 'empty' trace categories of Chomskyan syntax, or the $\mathbf{he}_i$ syntactic variables of Montague's PTQ), nor for extra combination schemata beyond Modus Ponens. The similarity between the Natural Deduction graphs and phrase structure trees, in other words, is misleading: what we have represented graphically are the steps in a deductive process – not to be confused with the construction of a syntactic tree.

In the above, we have talked about the *form* dimension of grammatical composition: about putting together linguistic resources into well-formed structural configurations. But a key point of the categorial approach is that one can simultaneously consider the types/categories, and hence grammatical composition, in the *meaning* dimension. From the semantic perspective, one fixes the kind of meaning objects one wants for the basic types that categorize complete expressions, and then interprets objects of types A/B, $B\backslash A$ as *functions* from B type objects to A type objects. Structural composition by means of Modus Ponens can then be naturally correlated with functional application, and Hypothetical Reasoning with functional abstraction in the semantic dimension. Composition of linguistic form and meaning composition thus become aspects of one and the same process of grammatical inference.

Grammatical composition: Structure. An aspect we have ignored so far in our discussion of the Modus Ponens and Hypothetical Reasoning inferences is the *management* of the linguistic resources – the manipulations we allow ourselves in using linguistic assumptions. Some aspects of resource management are explicitly encoded in the logical vocabulary – the distinction between the 'implications' / and \, for example, captures the fact that grammatical inference is sensitive to the linear order of the resources. But other equally important aspects of resource management have remained implicit. In the relative clause example, we inferred $\Gamma \vdash A/B$ from $\Gamma, B \vdash A$. In withdrawing the hypothetical B assumption, we did not take into account the *hierarchical embedding* of the B resource: we ignored its vertical nesting in the configuration of assumptions. Resource management, in other words, was implicitly taken to be *associative*: different hierarchical groupings over the same linear ordering of assumptions were considered as indistinguishable for the purposes of grammatical inference. On closer inspection, the implicit claim that restructuring of resources would not affect derivability (grammatical well-formedness) might be justified in some cases, whereas in other cases a more fine-grained notion of grammatical consequence might be appropriate. Similarly, the sensitivity to linear order, which restricts hypothetical reasoning to the withdrawal of a *peripheral* assumption, might be too strong in some cases. Compare (4) with the variant 'whom Kazimierz talked to yesterday', where one would like to withdraw a hypothetical np assumption from the non-peripheral position 'Kazimierz talked to np yesterday'. Switching to a commutative resource management regime would be too drastic – we would not be able anymore to deductively distinguish between the well-formed relative clause and its ill-formed permutations. In cases like this, one would like the grammar logic to provide facilities for *controlled modulation* of the management of linguistic resources, rather than to implement this in a global fashion as a hard-wired component of the type-forming connectives.

A brief history of types. The above discussion recapitulates the crucial phases in the historical development of the field. The Modus Ponens type of reasoning, with its functional application interpretation, provided the original motivation for the development of categorial grammar in (Ajdukiewicz, 1935). The insight that Modus Ponens and Hypothetical Reasoning are two inseparable aspects of the interpretation of the 'logical constants' /, \ is the key contribution of Lambek's work in the late Fifties. In the papers Lambek (1958, 1961) it is shown that attempts to generalize Modus Ponens in terms of extra rule schemata, such as Type Lifting or Functional Composition, are in fact weak approximations of Hypothetical Reasoning: viewing the type-forming operators as logical connectives, such schemata are reduced to *theorems*, given appropriate resource management choices. In retrospect, one can see that the core components of the type-logical architecture were worked out in 1958. But it took a quarter of a century before Lambek's work had a clear impact on the linguistic community. Contributions such as Lyons (1968), Lewis (1972), Geach (1972) are continuations of the rule-based Ajdukiewicz/Bar-Hillel tradition. Ironically, when linguists developed a renewed interest in categorial grammar in the early Eighties, they did not adopt Lambek's deductive view on grammatical composition, but fell back on an essentially rule-based approach. The framework of Combinatory Categorial Grammar (CCG, (Steedman, 1988)) epitomizes the rule-based generalized categorial architecture. In this framework, laws of type change and type combination are presented as theoretical primitives ('combinators') as a matter of methodological principle. For a good tutorial introduction to CCG, and a comparison with the deductive approach, we refer the reader to Steedman (1993).

The 1985 Tucson conference on Categorial Grammar brought together the adherents of the rule-based and the deductive traditions. In the proceedings of that conference, *Categorial Grammars and Natural Language Structures* (Oehrle, Bach and Wheeler, 1988) one finds a comprehensive picture of the varieties of categorial research in the Eighties.

Lambek originally presented his type logic as a calculus of *syntactic* types. Semantic interpretation of categorial deductions along the lines of the Curry–Howard correspondence was put on the categorial agenda in (Van Benthem, 1983). This contribution made it clear how the categorial type logics realize Montague's Universal Grammar program – in fact, how they improve on Montague's own execution of that program in offering an integrated account of the composition of linguistic meaning *and* form. Montague's adoption of a categorial syntax does not go far beyond notation: he was not interested in offering a principled theory of allowable 'syntactic operations' going with the category formalism.

The introduction of Linear Logic in (Girard, 1987) created a wave of research in the general landscape of 'substructural' logics: logics where structural rules of resource management are controlled rather than globally available. The importance of the distinction between the logical and the structural aspects of grammatical composition is a theme that directly derives from this research. The analysis of the linguistic ramifications of this distinction has guided the development of the present-day 'multimodal' type-logical architecture to be discussed in the pages that follow.

2. Linguistic inference: The Lambek systems

In the following sections we present the basic model-theory and proof-theory for the logical constants $/$, $\bullet$, $\backslash$, the so-called *multiplicative* connectives. On the model-theoretic level, we introduce abstract mathematical structures that capture the relevant aspects of grammatical composition. On the proof-theoretic level, we want to know how to perform valid inferences on the basis of the interpreted type language. We are not interested in syntax as the manipulation of meaningless symbols: we want the grammatical proof-theory to be sound and complete with respect to the abstract models of grammatical composition.

We proceed in two stages. In the present section, we develop a landscape of *simple* Lambek systems. Simple Lambek systems are obtained by taking the logic of residuation for a family of multiplicative connectives $/$, $\bullet$, $\backslash$, together with a package of structural postulates characterizing the resource management properties of the $\bullet$ connective. As resource management options, we consider Associativity and Commutativity. Different choices for these options yield the type logics known as **NL**, **L**, **NLP**, **LP**. Each of these systems has its virtues in linguistic analysis. But none of them in isolation provides a basis for a realistic theory of grammar. Mixed architectures, which overcome the limitations of the simple systems, are the subject of Section 4.

2.1. Modeling grammatical composition

Consider the language $\mathcal{F}$ of category formulae of a simple Lambek system. $\mathcal{F}$ is obtained by closing a set $\mathcal{A}$ of atomic formulae (or: basic types, prime formulae, e.g., $s, np, n, \ldots$) under binary connectives (or: type forming operators) $/$, $\bullet$, $\backslash$. We have already seen the connectives $/$, $\backslash$ at work in our informal introduction. The $\bullet$ connective will make it possible to explicitly refer to composed structures – in the introduction we informally used a comma for this purpose.

(5) $\mathcal{F} ::= \mathcal{A} \mid \mathcal{F}/\mathcal{F} \mid \mathcal{F} \bullet \mathcal{F} \mid \mathcal{F}\backslash\mathcal{F}.$

In this chapter we will explore a broad landscape of categorial type logics. On the semantic level, we are interested in a uniform model theory that naturally accommodates the subtle variations in categorial inference we want to study. A suitable level of abstraction can be obtained by viewing the categorial connectives as *modal* operators, and interpreting the type formulae in the powerset algebra of Kripke-style relational structures. The frame-based semantics for categorial logics is developed in (Došen, 1992), drawing on the literature on models for relevant logics, in particular Rontley and Meyer (1972). As will become clear later on, this type of semantics extends smoothly to the generalized and mixed architectures that form the core of this chapter. The 'modal' semantics also offers a suitable basis for comparison of the categorial systems with the feature-based grammar architectures studied in Chapter 8.

A modal frame, in general, is a set of 'worlds' W together with an $n+1$-ary 'accessibility relation' R for the n-ary modal operators. In the case of the binary categorial connectives, we interpret with respect to ternary relational structures and consider frames $\langle W, R^3 \rangle$. The domain W is to be thought of here as the set of *linguistic resources* (or: signs, form-meaning complexes of linguistic information). The ternary accessibility relation R models the core notion of grammatical composition. We obtain a model by adding a valuation v assigning subsets $v(p)$ of W to prime formulae p and satisfying the clauses of Definition 2.1 for compound formulae.

DEFINITION 2.1. Frame semantics: interpretation of compound formulae.

$$v(A \bullet B) = \{x \mid \exists y \exists z[Rxyz \ \&\ y \in v(A) \ \&\ z \in v(B)]\},$$
$$v(C/B) = \{y \mid \forall x \forall z[(Rxyz \ \&\ z \in v(B)) \Rightarrow x \in v(C)]\},$$
$$v(A\backslash C) = \{z \mid \forall x \forall y[(Rxyz \ \&\ y \in v(A)) \Rightarrow x \in v(C)]\}.$$

Notice that the categorial vocabulary is highly restricted in its expressivity. In contrast with standard Modal Logic, where the modal operators interact with the usual Boolean connectives, the formula language of the type logics we are considering here is *purely* modal. In Section 5.1 we will consider the addition of Boolean operations to the basic categorial language of (5).

We are interested in characterizing a relation of derivability between formulae such that $A \to B$ is provable iff $v(A) \subseteq v(B)$ for all valuations v over ternary frames. Consider the deductive system **NL**, given by the basic properties of the derivability relation REFL and TRANS, together with the so-called residuation laws RES establishing the relation between • and the two implications $/, \backslash$ with respect to derivability. Proposition 2.3 states the essential soundness and completeness result with respect to the frame semantics. (We write '$\mathcal{L} \vdash A \rightarrow B$' for '$A \rightarrow B$ is provable in logic $\mathcal{L}$'.)

DEFINITION 2.2. The pure logic of residuation **NL** (Lambek, 1961).

(REFL)	$A \rightarrow A$,
(TRANS)	if $A \rightarrow B$ and $B \rightarrow C$, then $A \rightarrow C$,
(RES)	$A \rightarrow C/B$ iff $A \bullet B \rightarrow C$ iff $B \rightarrow A\backslash C$.

PROPOSITION 2.3 (Došen, 1992). **NL** $\vdash A \rightarrow B$ *iff* $v(A) \subseteq v(B)$ *for every valuation* v *on every ternary frame.*

The proof of the $(\Rightarrow)$ soundness part is by induction on the length of the derivation of $A \rightarrow B$. For the $(\Leftarrow)$ completeness direction, one uses a simple *canonical* model, which effectively falsifies non-theorems. To show that the canonical model is adequate, one proves a Truth Lemma to the effect that, for any formula ϕ, $\mathcal{M}_K, A \models \phi$ iff **NL** $\vdash A \rightarrow \phi$. Due to the Truth Lemma we have that if **NL** $\nvdash A \rightarrow B$, then $A \in v_K(A)$ but $A \notin v_K(B)$, so $v_K(A) \nsubseteq v_K(B)$.

DEFINITION 2.4. Define the canonical model as $\mathcal{M}_K = \langle W_K, R^3_K, v_K \rangle$, where
(i) W_K is the set of formulae $\mathcal{F}$,
(ii) $R^3_K(A, B, C)$ iff **NL** $\vdash A \rightarrow B \bullet C$,
(iii) $A \in v_K(p)$ iff **NL** $\vdash A \rightarrow p$.

Structural postulates, constraints on frames. In Section 1, we gave a deconstruction of the notion of grammatical composition into a fixed 'logical' component and a variable 'structural' component. The pure logic of residuation **NL** captures the fixed logical component: the completeness result of Proposition 2.3 puts no interpretive constraints whatsoever on the grammatical composition relation. Let us turn now to the resource management component.

Starting from **NL** one can unfold a landscape of categorial type logics by gradually relaxing structure sensitivity in a number of linguistically relevant dimensions. Consider the dimensions of linear precedence (order sensitivity) and immediate dominance (constituent sensitivity). Adding structural postulates licensing associative or commutative resource management (or both) to the pure logic of residuation, one obtains the systems **L**, **NLP**, and **LP**. In order to maintain completeness in the presence of these structural postulates, one has to impose restrictions on the interpretation of the grammatical composition relation R^3. Below we give the postulates of Associativity and Commutativity with the corresponding frame constraints. The completeness result of Proposition 2.3 is then extended to the stronger logics by restricting the attention to the relevant classes of frames.

DEFINITION 2.5. Structural postulates and their frame conditions ($\forall x, y, z, u \in W$).

(ASS)	$(A \bullet B) \bullet C \leftrightarrow A \bullet (B \bullet C)$	$\exists t.Rtxy \;\&\; Rutz \Leftrightarrow \exists v.Rvyz \;\&\; Ruxv$,
(COMM)	$A \bullet B \rightarrow B \bullet A$	$Rxyz \Leftrightarrow Rxzy$.

PROPOSITION 2.6 (Došen, 1992). **L**, **NLP**, **LP** $\vdash A \to B$ *iff* $v(A) \subseteq v(B)$ *for every valuation* v *on every ternary frame satisfying* (ASS), (COMM), (ASS) + (COMM), *respectively.*

Correspondence theory. In the remainder of this chapter, we will consider more dimensions of linguistic structuring than those affected by the Associativity and Commutativity postulates. In (Kurtonina, 1995) it is shown that one can use the tools of modal Correspondence Theory (Van Benthem, 1984) to generalize the completeness results discussed above to these other dimensions. A useful class of structural postulates with pleasant completeness properties is characterized in Definition 2.7. The frame conditions for structural postulates of the required weak Sahlqvist form can be effectively computed using the Sahlqvist–Van Benthem algorithm as discussed in (Kurtonina, 1995).

DEFINITION 2.7. Weak Sahlqvist Axioms. A weak Sahlqvist axiom is an arrow of the form $\phi \to \psi$ where ϕ is a pure product formula, associated in any order, without repetition of proposition letters, and ψ is a pure product formula containing at least one $\bullet$, all of whose atoms occur in ϕ.

PROPOSITION 2.8. *Sahlqvist Completeness.* (Kurtonina, 1995). *If* P *is a weak Sahlqvist axiom, then* (i) $\mathbf{NL}+P$ *is frame complete for the first order frame condition corresponding to* P, *and* (ii) $\mathcal{L}+P$ *has a canonical model whenever* $\mathcal{L}$ *does.*

Specialized semantics. As remarked above, the choice for the modal frame semantics is motivated by the desire to have a *uniform* interpretation for the extended and mixed categorial architectures that form the core of this chapter. Grammatical composition is modeled in an abstract way, as a relation between grammatical processes. There is no trace, in this view, of what one could call 'syntactic representationalism'. As a matter of fact, the relational view on composition does not even require that for resources $y, z \in W$ there will always be a resource x such that $Rxyz$ (Existence), or if such an x exists, that it be unique (Uniqueness).

For many *individual* systems in the categorial hierarchy, completeness results have been obtained for more concrete models. The 'dynamic' interpretation of Lambek calculus interprets formulae with respect to *pairs* of points – transitions between information states. The $\bullet$ connective, in this setting, is seen as relational composition. In (Andréka and Mikulás, 1994), **L** is shown to be complete for this interpretation. In groupoid semantics, one considers structures $\langle W, \cdot \rangle$, which can be seen as specializations of the composition relation R^3: one now reads $Rxyz$ as $x = y \cdot z$, where '$\cdot$' is an arbitrary binary *operation*. Formulae are interpreted in the powerset algebra over these structures, with the simplified interpretation clauses of (6) for the connectives, because the properties of '$\cdot$' now guarantee Existence and Uniqueness.

$$
\begin{aligned}
& v(A \bullet B) = \{x \cdot y \mid x \in v(A) \ \& \ y \in v(B)\}, \\
(6) \qquad & v(C/B) = \{x \mid \forall y \in v(B) \ x \cdot y \in v(C)\}, \\
& v(A\backslash C) = \{y \mid \forall x \in v(A) \ x \cdot y \in v(C)\}.
\end{aligned}
$$

In the groupoid setting, options for resource management can be realized by attributing associativity and/or commutativity properties to the groupoid operation. Notice that the groupoid models are inappropriate if one wants to consider 'one-directional' structural postulates (e.g., one half of the Associativity postulate, $A\bullet(B\bullet C) \to (A\bullet B)\bullet C$, allowing restructuring of left-branching structures), unless one is willing to reintroduce abstractness in the form of a partial order on the resources W. See Došen (1992), Buszkowski (1986) and Chapter 12 for discussion.

Even more concrete are the *language models* or free semigroup semantics for **L**. In the language models, one takes W as V^+ (non-empty strings over the vocabulary) and $\cdot$ as string concatenation. This type of semantics turns out to be too specialized for our purposes: whereas Pentus (1994), with a quite intricate proof, has been able to establish completeness of **L** with respect to the free semigroup models, there is an *incompleteness* result for **NL** with respect to the corresponding free non-associative structures, viz. finite tree models. See Venema (1994b) for discussion.

General models versus specific grammars. In the discussion so far we have studied type-logical derivability in completely general terms, abstracting away from language-specific grammar specifications. Let us see then how we can relativize the general notions so as to take actual grammar specification into account. In accordance with the categorial tenet of *radical lexicalism*, we assume that the grammar for a language L is given by the conjunction of the general type logic $\mathcal{L}$ with a language-specific lexicon $\text{LEX}(L)$. The lexicon itself is characterized in terms of a type assignment function $f : V_L \mapsto \mathcal{P}(\mathcal{F})$, stipulating the primitive association of lexical resources V_L with their types. (We assume that for all lexical resources $x \in V_L$, the sets $f(x)$ are finite. In the so-called *rigid* categorial grammars, one further restricts the values of f to be *singletons*.)

For a general model $\mathcal{M} = \langle W, R^3, v\rangle$ to qualify as appropriate for a lexicon $\text{LEX}(L)$, we assume $V_L \subseteq W$, and we require the valuation v to be compatible with lexical type assignment, in the sense that, for all $x \in V_L$, $A \in f(x)$ implies $x \in v(A)$. Given this, we will say that the grammar assigns type B to a non-empty string of lexical resources $x_1 \cdots x_n \in V_L^+$, provided there are lexical type specifications $A_i \in f(x_i)$ such that we can deduce B from $\circ(A_1, \ldots, A_n)$ in the general type-logic $\mathcal{L}$. By $\circ(A_1, \ldots, A_n)$ we mean any of the possible products of the formulas $A_1, \ldots, A_n$, in that order.

Categorical combinators and CCG. To round off the discussion of the axiomatic presentation, we present the logics **NL, L, NLP, LP** with a proof term annotation, following Lambek (1988). The proof terms – categorical combinators – are motivated by Lambek's original category-theoretic interpretation of the type logics. The category-theoretic connection is not further explored here, but the combinator proof terms will be used in later sections as compact notation for complete deductions.

DEFINITION 2.9. Combinator proof terms (Lambek, 1988). Deductions of the form $f : A \to B$, where f is a process for deducing B from A.

$$1_A : A \to A \qquad \frac{f : A \to B \quad g : B \to C}{g \circ f : A \to C}$$

$$\frac{f : A \bullet B \to C}{\beta_{A,B,C}(f) : A \to C/B} \qquad \frac{f : A \bullet B \to C}{\gamma_{A,B,C}(f) : B \to A\backslash C}$$

$$\frac{g : A \to C/B}{\beta^{-1}_{A,B,C}(g) : A \bullet B \to C} \qquad \frac{g : B \to A\backslash C}{\gamma^{-1}_{A,B,C}(g) : A \bullet B \to C}$$

$$\alpha_{A,B,C} : A \bullet (B \bullet C) \leftrightarrow (A \bullet B) \bullet C : \alpha^{-1}_{A,B,C}$$

$$\pi_{A,B} : A \bullet B \to B \bullet A$$

EXAMPLE 2.10. Combinator proof terms for rightward functional application, and for leftward type lifting. (We omit the type subscripts where they are clear from context.) In the derivation of lifting, we write RA for $\beta^{-1}(1_{A/B})$.

$$\frac{1_{A/B} : A/B \to A/B}{\beta^{-1}(1_{A/B}) : A/B \bullet B \to A} \qquad \frac{\mathsf{RA} : A/B \bullet B \to A}{\gamma(\mathsf{RA}) : B \to (A/B)\backslash A}$$

This presentation makes obvious a variety of methods for creating fragments (subsystems) and extensions: restrict or extend the formula language; remove or add inference rules; remove or add structural postulates. The Ajdukiewicz/Bar-Hillel system (Ajdukiewicz, 1935; Bar-Hillel, 1964) appears in this guise as a subsystem lacking the hypothetical reasoning rules β and γ and the permutation rule π, but implicitly countenancing associativity. A more complex example is the rule-based approach of Combinatory Categorial Grammar (CCG, (Steedman, 1993)) where a finite collection of unary type transitions and binary type combinations (such as Lifting, Application) are postulated as *primitive* rule schemata. Within the CCG framework, Combinatory Logic (Curry and Feys, 1958) is put forward as the general theory for the class of grammatical operations natural languages draw upon. Combinatory Logic in itself, being equivalent with the full Lambda Calculus in its expressivity, is not very informative as to the fine-structure of grammatical inference. A decomposition of the CCG combinators in their logical and structural parts uncovers the hidden assumptions about grammatical resource management and makes it possible to situate the CCG systems within a more articulate landscape of grammatical inference. Comparing the CCG framework with the type-logical approach studied here, one should realize that CCG systems are, by necessity, only approximations of logics such as **L**, **LP**. These logics have been shown to be *not finitely axiomatizable* (see Zielonka, 1989; and Chapter 12), which means that no finite set of combinators in combination with Modus Ponens can equal their deductive strength.

2.2. *Gentzen calculus, cut elimination and decidability*

The axiomatic presentation is a proper vehicle for model-theoretic investigation of the logics we have considered: it closely follows the semantics, thus providing a suitable basis for 'easy' completeness results. But proof-theoretically the axiomatic presentation has a serious drawback: it does not offer an appropriate basis for proof search. The problematic rule of inference is TRANS, which is used to *compose* type transitions $A \to B$ and $B \to C$ into a transition $A \to C$. A type transition $A \to C$, in the presence of TRANS, could be effected with the aid of a formula B of which one finds no trace in the conclusion of the

TRANS inference. Since there is an infinity of candidate formulae B, exhaustive traversal of the search space for the auxiliary B formula in a TRANS inference is not an option.

For proof-theoretic investigation of the categorial type logics one introduces a Gentzen presentation which is shown to be equivalent to the axiomatic presentation. The main result for the Gentzen calculus (the *Hauptsatz* of Gentzen, 1934) then states that the counterpart of the TRANS rule, the Cut inference, can be eliminated from the logic without affecting the set of derivable theorems. An immediate corollary of this Cut Elimination Theorem is the *subformula property* which limits proof search to the subformulae of the theorem one wants to derive. In the absence of resource-affecting structural rules, decidability follows. The essential results for **L** have been established in (Lambek, 1958). They have been extended to the full landscape of type logics in (Kandulski, 1988; Došen, 1989).

In the axiomatic presentation, we considered derivability as a relation between formulae, i.e. we considered arrows $A \to B$ with $A, B \in \mathcal{F}$. In the Gentzen presentation, the derivability relation is stated to hold between a *term* $\mathcal{S}$ (the antecedent) and a type formula (the succedent). A Gentzen term is a structured configuration of formulae – a structured database, in the terminology of Gabbay (1994). The term language is defined inductively as $\mathcal{S} ::= \mathcal{F} \mid (\mathcal{S}, \mathcal{S})$. The binary structural connective $(\cdot, \cdot)$ in the term language tells you how structured databases Δ_1 and Δ_2 have been put together into a structured database (Δ_1, Δ_2). The structural connective mimics the logical connective $\bullet$ in the type language. A sequent is a pair (Γ, A) with $\Gamma \in \mathcal{S}$ and $A \in \mathcal{F}$, written as $\Gamma \Rightarrow A$.

To establish the equivalence between the two presentations, we define the formula translation Δ° of a structured database Δ: $(\Delta_1, \Delta_2)^\circ = \Delta_1^\circ \bullet \Delta_2^\circ$, and $A^\circ = A$, for $A \in \mathcal{F}$.

PROPOSITION 2.11 (Lambek, 1958). *For every arrow $f : A \to B$ there is a Gentzen proof of $A \Rightarrow B$, and for every proof of a sequent $\Gamma \Rightarrow B$ there is an arrow $f : \Gamma^\circ \to B$.*

DEFINITION 2.12. **NL**: Gentzen presentation. Sequents $\mathcal{S} \Rightarrow \mathcal{F}$ where $\mathcal{S} ::= \mathcal{F} \mid (\mathcal{S}, \mathcal{S})$. We write $\Gamma[\Delta]$ for a term Γ containing a distinguished occurrence of the subterm Δ. (The distinguished occurrences in premise and conclusion of an inference rule are supposed to occupy the same position within Γ.)

$$[\text{Ax}]\ \frac{}{A \Rightarrow A} \qquad \frac{\Delta \Rightarrow A \quad \Gamma[A] \Rightarrow C}{\Gamma[\Delta] \Rightarrow C}\ [\text{Cut}]$$

$$[/\text{R}]\ \frac{(\Gamma, B) \Rightarrow A}{\Gamma \Rightarrow A/B} \qquad \frac{\Delta \Rightarrow B \quad \Gamma[A] \Rightarrow C}{\Gamma[(A/B, \Delta)] \Rightarrow C}\ [/\text{L}]$$

$$[\backslash\text{R}]\ \frac{(B, \Gamma) \Rightarrow A}{\Gamma \Rightarrow B\backslash A} \qquad \frac{\Delta \Rightarrow B \quad \Gamma[A] \Rightarrow C}{\Gamma[(\Delta, B\backslash A)] \Rightarrow C}\ [\backslash\text{L}]$$

$$[\bullet\text{L}]\ \frac{\Gamma[(A, B)] \Rightarrow C}{\Gamma[A \bullet B] \Rightarrow C} \qquad \frac{\Gamma \Rightarrow A \quad \Delta \Rightarrow B}{(\Gamma, \Delta) \Rightarrow A \bullet B}\ [\bullet\text{R}]$$

As was the case for the axiomatic presentation of Definition 2.2, the Gentzen architecture of Definition 2.12 consists of three components: (i) [Ax] and [Cut] capture the basic properties of the derivability relation '$\Rightarrow$': reflexivity and contextualized transitivity for the Cut rule, (ii) each connective comes with two *logical rules*: a rule of use introducing the connective to the left of '$\Rightarrow$' and a rule of proof introducing it on the right of '$\Rightarrow$', finally (iii) there is a block of *structural rules*, empty in the case of **NL**, with different packages of structural rules resulting in systems with different resource management properties. (We should note here that sometimes the Cut rule is counted among the structural rules. We will reserve the term 'structural rule' for the Gentzen counterpart of the structural postulates governing the resource management properties of the composition operation.)

Structural rules. Structural postulates, in the axiomatic presentation, have been presented as transitions $A \to B$ where A and B are constructed out of formula variables $p_1, \ldots, p_n$ and the logical connective $\bullet$. For corresponding structure variables $\Delta_1, \ldots, \Delta_n$ and the structural connective $(\cdot, \cdot)$, define the structural equivalent $\sigma(A)$ of a formula A: $\sigma(p_i) = \Delta_i$, $\sigma(A \bullet B) = (\sigma(A), \sigma(B))$. The transformation of structural postulates into Gentzen rules allowing Cut Elimination is then straightforward: a postulate $A \to B$ translates as the Gentzen rule (7):

(7) $$\frac{\Gamma[\sigma(B)] \Rightarrow C}{\Gamma[\sigma(A)] \Rightarrow C}$$

To obtain the logics **L**, **NLP**, **LP** from **NL**, one thus adds the structural rules of Associativity and/or Permutation. Such additions result in less fine-grained notions of linguistic inference, where structural discrimination with respect to the dimensions of dominance and/or precedence is lost, as discussed above. (The double line in [A] stands for a two-way inference.)

(8) $$\frac{\Gamma[(\Delta_2, \Delta_1)] \Rightarrow A}{\Gamma[(\Delta_1, \Delta_2)] \Rightarrow A}\,[\mathrm{P}] \qquad \frac{\Gamma[((\Delta_1, \Delta_2), \Delta_3)] \Rightarrow A}{\Gamma[(\Delta_1, (\Delta_2, \Delta_3))] \Rightarrow A}\,[\mathrm{A}]$$

Sugaring. For the logics **L** and **LP** where $\bullet$ is associative, resp. associative and commutative, explicit application of the structural rules is generally compiled away by means of syntactic sugaring of the sequent language. Antecedent terms then take the form of sequences of formulae $A_1, \ldots, A_n$ where the comma is now of variable arity, rather than a binary connective. Reading these antecedents as sequences, one avoids explicit reference to the Associativity rule; reading them as multisets, one also makes Permutation implicit.

DEFINITION 2.13. Sugared Gentzen presentation: implicit structural rules. Sequents $\mathcal{S} \Rightarrow \mathcal{F}$ where $\mathcal{S} ::= \mathcal{F} \mid \mathcal{F}, \mathcal{S}$. **L**: implicit Associativity, interpreting $\mathcal{S}$ as a sequence.

LP: implicit Associativity + Permutation, interpreting $\mathcal{S}$ as a multiset. (The context variables Γ, Γ' can be empty.)

$$[\text{Ax}]\,\frac{}{A \Rightarrow A} \qquad \frac{\Delta \Rightarrow A \quad \Gamma, A, \Gamma' \Rightarrow C}{\Gamma, \Delta, \Gamma' \Rightarrow C}\,[\text{Cut}]$$

$$[/\text{R}]\,\frac{\Delta, B \Rightarrow A}{\Delta \Rightarrow A/B} \qquad \frac{\Delta \Rightarrow B \quad \Gamma, A, \Gamma' \Rightarrow C}{\Gamma, A/B, \Delta, \Gamma' \Rightarrow C}\,[/\text{L}]$$

$$[\backslash\text{R}]\,\frac{B, \Delta \Rightarrow A}{\Delta \Rightarrow B\backslash A} \qquad \frac{\Delta \Rightarrow B \quad \Gamma, A, \Gamma' \Rightarrow C}{\Gamma, \Delta, B\backslash A, \Gamma' \Rightarrow C}\,[\backslash\text{L}]$$

$$[\bullet\text{L}]\,\frac{\Gamma, A, B, \Gamma' \Rightarrow C}{\Gamma, A \bullet B, \Gamma' \Rightarrow C} \qquad \frac{\Delta \Rightarrow A \quad \Delta' \Rightarrow B}{\Delta, \Delta' \Rightarrow A \bullet B}\,[\bullet\text{R}]$$

Cut elimination and decidability. A categorial version of Gentzen's *Hauptsatz* is the core of Lambek (1958), who proves Cut Elimination for **L**, on the basis of the 'sugared' presentation introduced in Definition 2.13. In (Došen, 1989) the result is extended to the full landscape of categorial logics, using the structured term representation of antecedent databases, and explicit structural rules. It is important to carefully distinguish between an *admissible* rule of inference versus a *derived* one. We will see examples of derived rules of inference in Proposition 2.18: as the name indicates, one can deduce the derived inference rules using the basic logical rules for the connectives. The Cut rule cannot be so derived – it does not mention any logical connectives. But it is admissible in the sense that it does not increase the set of theorems that can already be derived without using Cut.

PROPOSITION 2.14. Cut Elimination (Lambek, 1958; Došen, 1989). *The Cut rule is admissible in* **NL**, **L**, **NLP**, **LP**: *every theorem has a cut-free proof.*

Below we present the general strategy for the cut elimination transformation, so that the reader can check how the various extensions of the type-logical vocabulary we will consider in the remainder of this chapter can be accommodated under the general cases of the elimination schema.

Cut elimination algorithm. The proof of the admissibility of the Cut rule is a constructive algorithm for a stepwise transformation of a derivation involving Cut inferences into a Cut-free derivation. Eliminability of the Cut rule is proved by induction on the complexity d of Cut inferences, measured in the number of connective occurrences. For the Cut rule of Definition 2.13, we have the following schema, with Cut complexity d defined as $d(\text{Cut}) = d(\Delta) + d(\Gamma) + d(\Gamma') + d(A) + d(B)$.

(9) $$\frac{\Delta \Rightarrow A \quad \Gamma, A, \Gamma' \Rightarrow B}{\Gamma, \Delta, \Gamma' \Rightarrow B}\ \text{Cut}$$

The targets for the elimination algorithm are instances of Cut which have themselves been derived without using the Cut rule. It is shown that in the derivation in question such a Cut inference can be replaced by one or two Cuts of lower degree. One repeats the process until all Cuts have been removed. The following main cases can be distinguished.

Case 1. The base case of the recursion: one of the Cut premises is an Axiom. In this case the other premise is identical to the conclusion, and the application of Cut can be pruned.

Case 2. Permutation conversions. In these cases, the active formula in the left or right premise of Cut is *not* the Cut formula. One shows that the logical rule introducing the main connective of the active formula and the Cut rule can be permuted, pushing the Cut inference upwards, with a decrease in degree because a connective is now introduced lower in the proof. (Explicit structural rules for the structured antecedent representation assimilate to this case: the Cut rule is permuted upwards over the structural rule.)

Case 3. Principal Cuts. The active formula in the left and right premise of Cut make up the Cut formula A. Here one reduces the degree by splitting the Cut formula up into its two immediate subformulae, and applying Cuts on these.

EXAMPLE 2.15. Case 2. The active formula in the left Cut premise is A'/A''. The Cut rule is moved upwards, permuting with the [/L] logical inference.

$$\dfrac{\dfrac{\Delta'' \Rightarrow A'' \quad \Delta, A', \Delta' \Rightarrow A}{\Delta, A'/A'', \Delta'', \Delta' \Rightarrow A}/L \quad \Gamma, A, \Gamma' \Rightarrow B}{\Gamma, \Delta, A'/A'', \Delta'', \Delta', \Gamma' \Rightarrow A}\text{Cut} \quad \leadsto$$

$$\dfrac{\Delta'' \Rightarrow A'' \quad \dfrac{\Delta, A', \Delta' \Rightarrow A \quad \Gamma, A, \Gamma' \Rightarrow B}{\Gamma, \Delta, A', \Delta', \Gamma' \Rightarrow B}\text{Cut}}{\Gamma, \Delta, A'/A'', \Delta'', \Delta', \Gamma' \Rightarrow B}/L$$

EXAMPLE 2.16. Case 3. Principal Cut on A'/A''. The Cut inference is replaced by two Cuts, on the subformulae A' and A''.

$$\dfrac{\dfrac{\Delta, A'' \Rightarrow A'}{\Delta \Rightarrow A'/A''}/R \quad \dfrac{\Delta' \Rightarrow A'' \quad \Gamma, A', \Gamma' \Rightarrow B}{\Gamma, A'/A'', \Delta', \Gamma' \Rightarrow B}/L}{\Gamma, \Delta, \Delta', \Gamma' \Rightarrow B}\text{Cut} \quad \leadsto$$

$$\dfrac{\Delta' \Rightarrow A'' \quad \dfrac{\Delta, A'' \Rightarrow A' \quad \Gamma, A', \Gamma' \Rightarrow B}{\Gamma, \Delta, A'', \Gamma' \Rightarrow B}\text{Cut}}{\Gamma, \Delta, \Delta', \Gamma' \Rightarrow B}\text{Cut}$$

Decidability, subformula property. In the case of **NL**, **L**, **NLP**, and **LP**, the Cut Elimination theorem immediately gives a decision procedure for theoremhood. One searches for a cut-free proof in a backward chaining manner, working from conclusion to premises. Every logical rule of inference removes a connective, breaking the selected active formula up into its immediate subformulae. The number of connectives of the goal sequent is finite. Exhaustive traversal of the finite cut-free search space will either produce a proof (a derivation tree the leaves of which are all instances of the Axiom schema), or it will fail to do so.

The important point about Cut Elimination and decidability is not so much to avoid the Cut rule altogether, but to restrict the attention to 'safe' cuts – instances of the Cut rule that do not affect the finiteness of the search space. The astute reader will have noticed that the left rules for the implications $A\backslash B$ (B/A) are in fact *compiled* Cut inferences on the basis of the subtypes A, B and Modus Ponens. These compiled Cuts are innocent: they preserve the complexity-decreasing property of the inference rules which guarantees decidability. The compilation of [\L] can be found below.

(10)
$$\dfrac{\dfrac{\Delta \Rightarrow B \qquad \dfrac{B \Rightarrow B \qquad A \Rightarrow A}{B, B\backslash A \Rightarrow A}/L}{\Delta, B\backslash A \Rightarrow A}[\mathrm{Cut}] \qquad \Gamma, A, \Gamma' \Rightarrow C}{\Gamma, \Delta, B\backslash A, \Gamma' \Rightarrow C}\mathrm{Cut} \quad \rightsquigarrow$$

$$\dfrac{\Delta \Rightarrow B \quad \Gamma, A, \Gamma' \Rightarrow C}{\Gamma, \Delta, B\backslash A, \Gamma' \Rightarrow C}\backslash L$$

Natural deduction. As a final item on the list of presentation formats for categorial derivations, Definition 2.17 gives the official definition of the Natural Deduction format used in Section 1. This style of presentation has Elimination rules and Introduction rules for the logical connectives: the Cut rule is not a part of the Natural Deduction format.

For the equivalence of the sequent and natural deduction styles the reader can turn to Girard, Taylor and Lafont (1989), where one finds explicit mappings relating the two presentations. The mapping from Gentzen proofs to natural deductions is *many-to-one* – there may be a number of Gentzen derivations for one and the same natural deduction. In this sense, natural deduction captures the 'essence' of a proof better than a Gentzen derivation, which allows irrelevant permutation alternatives in deriving a theorem. We will be in a better position to assess this spurious type of non-determinism of the sequent calculus after discussing the Curry–Howard interpretation of categorial deductions, which gives a precise answer to the question as to which derivations are 'essentially the same'. See Definition 3.5 and Section 7.1 for discussion.

DEFINITION 2.17 (*Natural deduction*). Sequent-style presentation. Notation: $\Gamma \vdash A$ for a deduction of the formula A from a configuration of undischarged assumptions Γ. Elimination/Introduction rules for **NL**. Structural rules as in (8).

$$A \vdash A$$

$$[/I]\frac{(\Gamma, B) \vdash A}{\Gamma \vdash A/B} \qquad \frac{\Gamma \vdash A/B \quad \Delta \vdash B}{(\Gamma, \Delta) \vdash A}[/E]$$

$$[\backslash I]\frac{(B, \Gamma) \vdash A}{\Gamma \vdash B\backslash A} \qquad \frac{\Gamma \vdash B \quad \Delta \vdash B\backslash A}{(\Gamma, \Delta) \vdash A}[\backslash E]$$

$$[\bullet I]\frac{\Gamma \vdash A \quad \Delta \vdash B}{(\Gamma, \Delta) \vdash A \bullet B} \qquad \frac{\Delta \vdash A \bullet B \quad \Gamma[(A, B)] \vdash C}{\Gamma[\Delta] \vdash C}[\bullet E]$$

2.3. *Discussion: Options for resource management*

In the previous sections, we have introduced the technical apparatus that is needed for a proper appreciation of the logics **NL**, **L**, **NLP**, **LP**. Let us turn now to the linguistic motivation for the different resource management regimes these logics represent. In order to compare the strengths and weaknesses of these individual systems, Proposition 2.18 gives a useful inventory of characteristic theorems and derived rules of inference for the logics in question. We leave their proof to the reader, who can test his or her understanding of the axiomatic and Gentzen presentations in deriving them.

PROPOSITION 2.18. *Characteristic theorems and derived inference rules for* **NL** (1–6); **L** (7–11), *plus* (1–6); **NLP** (12–14), *plus* (1–6); **LP** (15), *plus* (1–14).

1.	Application:	$A/B \bullet B \to A,\ B \bullet B\backslash A \to A$
2.	Co-application:	$A \to (A \bullet B)/B,\ A \to B\backslash(B \bullet A)$
3.	Monotonicity $\bullet$:	*if* $A \to B$ *and* $C \to D$, *then* $A \bullet C \to B \bullet D$
4.	Isotonicity $\cdot/C$, $C\backslash\cdot$:	*if* $A \to B$, *then* $A/C \to B/C$
		if $A \to B$, *then* $C\backslash A \to C\backslash B$
5.	Antitonicity $C/\cdot$, $\cdot\backslash C$:	*if* $A \to B$, *then* $C/B \to C/A$
		if $A \to B$, *then* $B\backslash C \to A\backslash C$
6.	Lifting:	$A \to B/(A\backslash B),\ A \to (B/A)\backslash B$
7.	Geach (main functor):	$A/B \to (A/C)/(B/C)$,
		$B\backslash A \to (C\backslash B)\backslash(C\backslash A)$
8.	Geach (secondary functor):	$B/C \to (A/B)\backslash(A/C)$,
		$C\backslash B \to (C\backslash A)/(B\backslash A)$
9.	Composition:	$A/B \bullet B/C \to A/C,\ C\backslash B \bullet B\backslash A \to C\backslash A$
10.	Restructuring:	$(A\backslash B)/C \leftrightarrow A\backslash(B/C)$
11.	(De)Currying:	$A/(B \bullet C) \leftrightarrow (A/C)/B$,
		$(A \bullet B)\backslash C \leftrightarrow B\backslash(A\backslash C)$
12.	Permutation:	*if* $A \to B\backslash C$ *then* $B \to A\backslash C$
13.	Exchange:	$A/B \leftrightarrow B\backslash A$
14.	Preposing/Postposing:	$A \to B/(B/A),\ A \to (A\backslash B)\backslash B$
15.	Mixed Composition:	$A/B \bullet C\backslash B \to C\backslash A,\ B/C \bullet B\backslash A \to A/C$

Items (1) to (6) are valid in the most discriminating logic **NL**. As shown in (Došen, 1989), the combination of (1)–(5) provides an alternative way of characterizing $(\bullet, /)$ and $(\bullet, \backslash)$ as residuated pairs, i.e. one can replace the RES inferences of Definition 2.2 by (1)–(5). The reader with a background in category theory recognizes the adjointness (1–2) and functoriality (3–5) laws. Lifting is the closest one can get to (2) in 'product-free' type languages, i.e. type languages where the role of the product operator (generally left implicit) is restricted to glue together purely implicational types on the left-hand side of the arrow. Items (7) to (11) mark the transition to **L**: their derivation involves the structural postulate of associativity for $\bullet$. Rule (12) is characteristic for systems with a commutative $\bullet$, **NLP** and **LP**. From (12) one immediately derives the collapse of the implications / and \, (13). As a result of this collapse, one gets variants of the earlier theorems obtained by substituting subtypes of the form A/B by $B\backslash A$ or vice versa. Examples are (14), an **NLP** variant of Lifting, or (15), an **LP** variant of Composition.

The pure logic of residuation. Let us look first at the most discriminating logic in the landscape, **NL**. In the absence of structural postulates for $\bullet$, grammatical inference is fully sensitive to both the horizontal and the vertical dimensions of linguistic structure: linear ordering and hierarchical grouping. As in classical Ajdukiewicz style categorial grammar, Application is the basic reduction law for this system. But the capacity for *hypothetical reasoning* already greatly increases the inferential strength of **NL** in comparison with the pure application fragment. The principles of Argument Lowering (e.g., $(s/(np\backslash s))\backslash s \to np\backslash s$) and Value Raising (e.g., $np/n \to (s/(np\backslash s))/n$), introduced as primitive postulates in (Partee and Rooth, 1983), turn out to be generally valid type change schemata, derivable from the combination of Lifting and the Isotonicity/Antitonicity laws for the implications. These type-changing laws play an important role in the semantic investigation of categorial type systems, as we will see in Section 3. On a more general level, it is pointed out in (Lambek, 1988) that Lifting is a closure operation, as it obeys the defining principles (11). (We write A^B for either $B/(A\backslash B)$ or $(B/A)\backslash B$.)

(11) $\quad A \to A^B, \qquad (A^B)^B \to A^B, \qquad \text{if } A \to C, \text{ then } A^B \to C^B.$

Associativity and flexible constituency. An essential limitation of the pure residuation logic is its rigid concept of constituency – a property which **NL** shares with conventional phrase structure grammars. The revival of interest in categorial grammar was inspired in the first place by a more flexible notion of constituent structure, depending on **L** theorems such as the Geach laws, Functional Composition, or its recursive generalization. These Geach and Composition principles are formulated as *implicational* laws, but with the interpretation of the type-logical connectives we have been assuming, the implicational laws and the product versions of the structural postulates are interderivable.

EXAMPLE 2.19. Deriving (one half of) Associativity from (one directional instantiation of) Geach. (We write **b** for the left-division variant of principle (7) in Proposition 2.18, and use X as an abbreviation for $A \bullet ((A\backslash(A \bullet B)) \bullet ((A \bullet B)\backslash((A \bullet B) \bullet C)))$.)

$$\dfrac{\dfrac{\mathbf{b} : A\backslash B \to (C\backslash A)\backslash(C\backslash B)}{\gamma^{-1}(\mathbf{b}) : C\backslash A \bullet A\backslash B \to C\backslash B}}{(\dagger)\ \gamma^{-1}(\gamma^{-1}(\mathbf{b})) : C \bullet (C\backslash A \bullet A\backslash B) \to B}$$

$$\dfrac{\dfrac{A \to A \quad \dfrac{(2) : B \to A\backslash(A \bullet B) \quad (2) : C \to (A \bullet B)\backslash((A \bullet B) \bullet C)}{(3) : B \bullet C \to (A\backslash(A \bullet B)) \bullet ((A \bullet B)\backslash((A \bullet B) \bullet C))}}{(3) : A \bullet (B \bullet C) \to X} \qquad (\dagger) : X \to (A \bullet B) \bullet C}{A \bullet (B \bullet C) \to (A \bullet B) \bullet C}$$

Associative resource management makes the grammar logic insensitive to hierarchical constituent structure: derivability of a sequent $\Gamma \Rightarrow A$ is preserved under arbitrary rebracketings of the antecedent assumptions Γ, a property which is referred to as the *structural completeness* of **L** (Buszkowski, 1988). The free availability of restructuring makes it possible to give alternative constituent analyses for expressions that would count as structurally unambiguous under rigid constituency assumptions, such as embodied by **NL**.

EXAMPLE 2.20. Restructuring: subject-(verb-object) versus (subject-verb)-object analysis. Derivation in CCG tree format, in terms of the combinators Lifting, Composition, and Application. One can see the CCG trees as concise representations of combinator proofs in the sense of Definition 2.9, given as compositions of 'primitive' CCG arrows.

$$\dfrac{\dfrac{\text{Mary}}{np} \quad \dfrac{\dfrac{\text{cooked}}{(np\backslash s)/np} \quad \dfrac{\text{the beans}}{np}}{np\backslash s}\,\mathbf{app}}{s}\,\mathbf{app} \qquad \dfrac{\dfrac{\dfrac{\dfrac{\text{Mary}}{np}}{s/(np\backslash s)}\,\mathbf{lift} \quad \dfrac{\text{cooked}}{(np\backslash s)/np}}{s/np}\,\mathbf{comp} \quad \dfrac{\text{the beans}}{np}}{s}\,\mathbf{app}$$

Coordination phenomena provide crucial motivation for associative resource management and the non-standard constituent analyses that come with it, cf. Steedman (1985), Dowty (1988), Zwarts (1986) for the original argumentation. On the assumption that coordination joins expressions of like category, theories of rigid constituency run into problems with cases of so-called non-constituent coordination, such as the Right Node Raising example below. With an associative theory of grammatical composition, non-constituent coordination can be reduced to standard coordination of phrases of like type. As will become clear in Section 3, the interpretation produced for the s/np instantiation of the coordination type is the appropriate one for a theory of generalized conjoinability such as Gazdar (1980), Keenan and Faltz (1985), Partee and Rooth (1983).

EXAMPLE 2.21. Conjunction of non-constituents. Natural Deduction format. See Section 5.2 for the type schema for 'and'.

$$\dfrac{\dfrac{\dfrac{\dfrac{\dfrac{\text{Kazimierz}}{np}\quad \dfrac{\dfrac{\text{loves}}{((np\backslash s)/np)}\quad \overline{np}}{(np\backslash s)}{\scriptstyle /E}}{s}{\scriptstyle \backslash E}}{(s/np)}{\scriptstyle /I} \qquad \dfrac{\dfrac{\dfrac{\text{and}}{\forall X.(X\backslash X)/X}}{(((s/np)\backslash(s/np))/(s/np))}{\scriptstyle \forall E} \quad \dfrac{\dfrac{\dfrac{\text{Ferdinand}}{np}\quad \dfrac{\dfrac{\text{hates}}{((np\backslash s)/np)}\quad \overline{np}}{(np\backslash s)}{\scriptstyle /E}}{s}{\scriptstyle \backslash E}}{(s/np)}{\scriptstyle /I}}{((s/np)\backslash(s/np))}{\scriptstyle /E}}{(s/np)}{\scriptstyle \backslash E} \qquad \dfrac{\text{Gottlob}}{np}}{s}{\scriptstyle /E}$$

Other types of argumentation for flexible constituency have been based on *processing* considerations (an associative regime can produce an *incremental* left-to-right analysis of a sentence, cf. Ades and Steedman (1982)), or *intonational structure* (distinct prosodic phrasing realizing alternative information packaging for the same truth conditional content, cf. Steedman (1991)).

Unfortunately, the strength of **L** is at the same time its weakness. Associative resource management *globally* destroys discrimination for constituency, not just where one would like to see a relaxation of structure sensitivity. Standard constituent analyses provide the proper basis for the characterization of domains of locality: in an associative setting, the constituent information is lost. As examples of the resulting overgeneration one can cite violations of the Coordinate Structure Constraint such as (12). The type assignment $(n\backslash n)/(s/np)$ to the relative pronoun requires 'Gottlob admired Kazimierz and Jim detested' to be of type s/np. With an instantiation $(s\backslash s)/s$ for the conjunction, and an associative regime of composition, there is nothing that can stop the derivation of (12), as pointed out in (Steedman, 1993), where this type of example is traced back to (Lambek, 1961).

(12) *(the mathematician) whom Gottlob admired Kazimierz and Jim detested

Discontinuous dependencies and restricted commutativity. The discussion above shows that **L** is too strong in that it fully ignores constituent information. But at the same time, the order sensitivity of this logic makes it too weak to handle discontinuous dependencies. A case in point are the crossed dependencies of the Dutch verb cluster. In the example below, the verb raising trigger 'wil' has to combine with the infinitival 'voeren' before the latter (a transitive verb) combines with its direct object.

EXAMPLE 2.22. Dutch verb clusters via Mixed Composition. (We write iv for infinitival verb phrases, vp for tensed ones.)

> (dat Marie) de nijlpaarden (np) wil (vp/iv) voeren ($np\backslash iv$),
> '(that Mary) the hippos wants feed' (= that M. wants to feed the hippos),
> $vp/iv, np\backslash iv \Rightarrow np\backslash vp$ (Mixed Composition),
> $A/B \to (C\backslash A)/(C\backslash B)$ (Mixed Geach, schematically).

In order to form the cluster 'wil voeren' in such a way that it 'inherits' the arguments of the embedded infinitive, composition laws (or their Geach generalizations) have been proposed (Steedman, 1984; Moortgat, 1988) that would combine functors with conflicting directionality requirements, so-called Mixed Composition. Clearly, with these laws, one goes beyond the inferential capacity of **L**. As the reader can check with the aid of Example 2.19, the product counterpart of the mixed Geach transition of Example 2.22 is $A \bullet (B \bullet C) \to B \bullet (A \bullet C)$, which together with Associativity introduces a contextualized form of Commutativity. The permutation side effects of Mixed Composition cause a damaging loss of control over the grammatical resources. Not surprisingly, then, the introduction of such combination schemata went hand in hand with the formulation of *extralogical* control principles. A more attractive alternative will be presented in Example 4.4.

Conclusion. Let us summarize this discussion. The individual simple Lambek systems each have their merits and their limitations when it comes to grammatical analysis. As a grammar writer, one would like to exploit the inferential capacities of a *combination* of different systems. Importing theorems from a system with more relaxed resource management into a logic with a higher degree of structural discrimination is not a viable strategy: it globally affects sensitivity for the relevant structural parameter of the more discriminating logic. In Section 4.1 we will develop a logical framework supporting a truly 'mixed' style of categorial inference. Structural collapse is avoided by moving to a multimodal architecture which is better adapted to deal with the fine-structure of grammatical composition. But first we discuss an aspect of grammatical inference which is of crucial importance for the categorial architecture but which has been ignored so far: the syntax-semantics interface.

3. The syntax-semantics interface: Proofs and readings

Categorial type logics offer a highly transparent view on the relation between form and meaning: semantic interpretation can be read off directly from the proof which establishes the well-formedness (derivability) of an expression. The principle of compositionality (see Chapters 1 and 7) is realized in a particularly stringent, purely deductive form, leaving no room for rule-to-rule stipulated meaning assignment.

In Section 1 we noticed that the categorial program ultimately has its ancestry in Russell's theory of types. In the original 'Polish' version of the program, categorial types were viewed simultaneously in the syntactic and in the semantic dimension. This unified perspective was lost in subsequent work: Lambek developed categorial calculi as theories of *syntactic* types, and Curry advocated the application of his *semantic* types of functionality in natural language analysis – a development which led up to Montague's use of type theory. The divergence can be traced back to Jakobson (1961), where Curry (1961) in fact criticizes Lambek (1961) for introducing the structural dimension of grammatical composition in his category concept. These divergent lines of research were brought together again in (Van Benthem, 1983), who established the connection between Lambek's categorial framework and the Curry–Howard 'formulas-as-types' program.

In the logical setting, the Curry–Howard program takes the form of an *isomorphism* between (Natural Deduction) proofs in the Positive Intuitionistic Propositional Logic and terms of the λ calculus. In the categorial application, one is interested in the Curry–Howard mapping as a *correspondence* rather than an isomorphism, in the sense that derivations for the various categorial logics are all associated with **LP** term recipes. The system **LP**, in this sense, plays the role of a general semantic composition language which abstracts away from syntactic fine-structure. As we have seen in Section 2, the form dimension of grammatical composition can be profitably studied in the context of the *frame semantics* for the type formulae: on that level, the structural postulates regulating sub-**LP** resource management naturally find their interpretation in terms of frame constraints.

The emphasis in this section is on the *limited semantic expressivity* of the categorial languages. With respect to the original intuitionistic terms, the **LP** fragment obeys linearity constraints reflecting the resource sensitivity of the categorial logic; moving on to more discriminating systems, the set of derivable readings further decreases. The price one pays for obtaining more fine-grained syntactic discrimination may be the loss of readings one would like to retain from a purely semantic point of view. This tension has played an important role in the development of the field. To regain lost readings one can enrich the logical vocabulary, and introduce more delicate type constructors compatible with both the structural and the semantic aspects of grammatical composition. And one can exploit the division of labor between *lexical* and *derivational* semantics. We discuss this theme in Section 3.2. In Section 3.1 we first introduce the necessary technical material, basing the exposition on Van Benthem (1991, 1995), Wansing (1992b), Hendriks (1993). Our treatment of term assignment focuses on the Gentzen presentation of the categorial calculi. For a parallel treatment in terms of Natural Deduction, the reader can turn to Chapter 12.

3.1. Term assignment for categorial deductions

We startour discussion of semantic term assignment with the system at the top of the categorial hierarchy – the system **LP**. Instead of sequents $A_1, \ldots, A_n \Rightarrow B$ we now consider annotated sequents $x_1 : A_1, \ldots, x_n : A_n \Rightarrow t : B$ where the type formulae are decorated with terms – distinct x_i for the assumptions and a term t constructed out of these x_i, in ways to be made precise below, for the goal. On the intuitive level, a derivation for an annotated sequent will represent the computation of a denotation recipe t of type B out of input parameters x_i of type A_i. Let us specify the syntax and semantics of the language of type formulae and term labels, and define the systematic association of the term labeling with the unfolding of a sequent derivation.

In the case of **LP**, we are considering a type language with formulae $\mathcal{F} ::= \mathcal{A} \mid \mathcal{F} \to \mathcal{F} \mid \mathcal{F} \circ \mathcal{F}$ (the two implications collapse in the presence of Permutation). The choice of primitive types $\mathcal{A}$ will depend on the application. A common choice would be e (the type of individual objects) and t (the type of truth values). In Section 3.2, we will encounter more elaborate inventories for the 'dynamic' approach to natural language semantics. For semantic interpretation of the type language, we consider frames $F = \{D_A\}_{A \in \mathcal{F}}$ based on some non-empty set E, the domain of discourse. Such frames consist of a family of semantic domains, one for each type $A \in \mathcal{F}$, such that

$$(13)\qquad \begin{array}{ll} D_{A \circ B} = D_A \times D_B & \text{(Cartesian product)},\\ D_{A \to B} = D_B^{D_A} & \text{(Function space)}. \end{array}$$

For the primitive types we can fix $D_e = E$ and $D_t = \{0, 1\}$ (the set of truth values).

We need a representation language to refer to the objects in our semantic structures. The language of the typed lambda calculus (with its familiar interpretation with respect to standard models) will serve this purpose.

DEFINITION 3.1. Syntax of typed lambda terms. Let $\mathcal{V}^A$ be the set of variables of type A. The set Λ of typed λ terms is $\{\mathcal{T}^A\}_{A \in \mathcal{F}}$, where for all $A, B \in \mathcal{F}$:

$$\begin{array}{l} \mathcal{T}^A ::= \mathcal{V}^A \mid \mathcal{T}^{B \to A}(\mathcal{T}^B) \mid (\mathcal{T}^{A \circ B})_0 \mid (\mathcal{T}^{B \circ A})_1,\\ \mathcal{T}^{A \to B} ::= \lambda \mathcal{V}^A \mathcal{T}^B, \qquad \mathcal{T}^{A \circ B} ::= \langle \mathcal{T}^A, \mathcal{T}^B \rangle. \end{array}$$

We now have all the ingredients for presenting term assignment to **LP** sequent proofs. We proceed in two stages: first we present the algorithm for decorating **LP** derivations with intuitionistic term labeling. For Intuitionistic Logic, there is a perfect correspondence between (Natural Deduction) proofs and Λ terms. But not every intuitionistic theorem is **LP** derivable. In the second stage, then, we identify a sublanguage $\Lambda(\mathbf{LP})$ of terms which effectively correspond to the resource-sensitive **LP** derivations.

DEFINITION 3.2. Term assignment for **LP**. Notation: x, y, z for variables, t, u, v for arbitrary terms; $u[t/x]$ for the substitution of term t for variable x in term u. In sequents $x_1 : A_1, \ldots, x_n : A_n \Rightarrow t : B$, the antecedent x_i are distinct. For the implication $\to$, the rule of use corresponds to functional application, the rule of proof to functional abstraction (λ binding). For $\circ$, the rule of proof corresponds to pairing, the rule of use to projection. The Cut rule corresponds to substitution.

$$\frac{}{x : A \Rightarrow x : A}\,(\mathrm{Ax}) \qquad \frac{\Gamma \Rightarrow t : A \quad x : A, \Delta \Rightarrow u : B}{\Gamma, \Delta \Rightarrow u[t/x] : B}\,(\mathrm{Cut})$$

$$\frac{\Gamma, x : A, y : B, \Delta \Rightarrow t : C}{\Gamma, y : B, x : A, \Delta \Rightarrow t : C}\,(\mathrm{P})$$

$$\frac{\Delta \Rightarrow t : A \quad \Gamma, x : B \Rightarrow u : C}{\Gamma, \Delta, y : A \to B \Rightarrow u[y(t)/x] : C}\,(\to L) \qquad \frac{\Gamma, x : A \Rightarrow t : B}{\Gamma \Rightarrow \lambda x.t : A \to B}\,(\to R)$$

$$\frac{\Gamma \Rightarrow t : A \quad \Delta \Rightarrow u : B}{\Gamma, \Delta \Rightarrow \langle t, u \rangle : A \circ B}\,(\circ R) \qquad \frac{\Gamma, x : A, y : B \Rightarrow t : C}{\Gamma, z : A \circ B \Rightarrow t[(z)_0/x, (z)_1/y] : C}\,(\circ L)$$

Unlike intuitionistic resource management, where the structural rules of Contraction and Weakening are freely available, the **LP** regime requires every resource in a proof to be used exactly once. For the implicational fragment, Proposition 3.4 indicates how the resource sensitivity of **LP** translates into the syntactic properties of its proof terms, as specified in Definition 3.3.[2]

DEFINITION 3.3. Let $\Lambda(\mathbf{LP})$ be the largest $\Gamma \subseteq \Lambda$ such that
(i) each subterm of $t \in \Gamma$ contains a free variable
(ii) no subterm of $t \in \Gamma$ contains more than one free occurrence of the same variable
(iii) each occurrence of the λ abstractor in $t \in \Gamma$ binds a variable within its scope

PROPOSITION 3.4 (Van Benthem, 1987; Buszkowski, 1987; Wansing, 1992b). *Correspondence between* **LP** *proofs and* $\Lambda(\mathbf{LP})$ *terms. Given an* **LP** *derivation of a sequent* $\sigma = A_1, \ldots, A_n \Rightarrow B$ *one can find a construction* $t^B \in \Lambda(\mathbf{LP})$ *of* σ*, and conversely (where a term* $t^B \in \Lambda(\mathbf{LP})$ *is called a construction of a sequent* $A_1, \ldots, A_n \Rightarrow B$ *iff* t *has exactly the free variable occurrences* $x_1^{A_1}, \ldots, x_n^{A_n}$*).*

Identifying proofs. So far we have been concerned with individual terms, not with relations of equivalence and reducibility between terms. Given the standard interpretation of the Λ term language, the Equations (E1) to (E4) of Definition 3.5 represent semantic equivalences of certain terms. Read from left (redex) to right (contractum), these equivalences can be seen as valid term reductions. From the Gentzen proof-theoretic perspective, it is natural to look for the operations on proofs that correspond to these term reductions.

DEFINITION 3.5. Term equations and their proof-theoretic reflexes (Lambek, 1993a; Wansing, 1992b). (E1) and (E3) correspond to β reduction, (E2) and (E4) to η reduction for function and product types, respectively.

(E1)	$(\lambda x^A.t^B)u = t[u/x]$	principal Cut on $A \to B$,
(E2)	$\lambda x^A.(tx)^B = t$	non-atomic axiom $A \to B$,
(E3)	$(\langle t^A, u^B\rangle)_0 = t \quad (\langle t, u\rangle)_1 = u$	principal Cut on $A \circ B$,
(E4)	$\langle (t^{A\circ B})_0, (t^{A\circ B})_1\rangle = t$	non-atomic axiom $A \circ B$.

The terms for cut-free proofs are in β-normal form: the principal Cut Elimination step replaces a redex by its contractum. Proofs restricted to atomic Axioms yield η-expanded terms. Such proofs can always be simplified by substituting complex Axioms for their unfoldings, yielding η-normal proof terms. The search space for Cut-free proofs is finite. Exhaustive Cut-free search produces the finite number of **LP** readings, thus providing a proof-theoretic perspective on the Finite Reading Property for **LP** established in (Van Benthem, 1983).

[2] For the product, one needs an auxiliary notion specifying what it means for the variables associated with the use of $\circ$ to be used 'exactly once', cf. Roorda (1991). In Linear Logic, alternative term assignment for the product is available in terms of a construct which directly captures the resource sensitivity of the proof regime: **let** s **be** $x \circ y$ **in** t. See Troelstra (1992).

EXAMPLE 3.6. Principal cut: β-conversion. Input:

$$\dfrac{\dfrac{\Gamma, x:B \Rightarrow t:A}{\Gamma \Rightarrow \lambda x.t:A/B}[R/] \quad \dfrac{\Delta' \Rightarrow u:B \quad \Delta, z:A, \Delta'' \Rightarrow v:C}{\Delta, y:A/B, \Delta', \Delta'' \Rightarrow v[y(u)/z]:C}[L/]}{\Delta, \Gamma, \Delta', \Delta'' \Rightarrow v[y(u)/z][\lambda x.t/y]:C}[Cut]$$

Output:

$$\dfrac{\dfrac{\Delta' \Rightarrow u:B \quad \Gamma, x:B \Rightarrow t:A}{\Gamma, \Delta' \Rightarrow t[u/x]:A}[Cut/] \quad \Delta, z:A, \Delta'' \Rightarrow v:C}{\Delta, \Gamma, \Delta', \Delta'' \Rightarrow v[t[u/x]/z]:C}[Cut]$$

EXAMPLE 3.7. Complex axioms: η-conversion.

$$\dfrac{\dfrac{x:B \Rightarrow x:B \quad y:A \Rightarrow y:A}{v:A/B, x:B \Rightarrow y[v(x)/y]:A}[L/]}{v:A/B \Rightarrow \lambda x.y[v(x)/y]:A/B}[R/] \quad \rightsquigarrow \quad \dfrac{}{v:A/B \Rightarrow v:A/B}[Ax]$$

Term assignment for syntactically more discriminating systems. In moving to the syntactically more discriminating inhabitants of the categorial landscape, we have two options for setting up the term assignment. The primary interest of the working linguist is not so much in the two-way correspondence between terms and proofs, but rather in the one-way computation of a meaning recipe as an automatic spin-off of proof search. From this perspective, one can be perfectly happy with **LP** term decoration also for the logics with a more developed structure-sensitivity. One relies here on a healthy division of labor between the syntactic and semantic dimensions of the linguistic resources. The role of the uniform Λ(**LP**) term labeling is to capture the composition of signs *qua* semantic objects. Linguistic composition in the form dimension is captured in the term structure over antecedent assumptions (or, alternatively, in terms of a *structural* term labeling discipline for type formulae as discussed in Definition 7.8). As the common denominator of the various calculi in the categorial hierarchy, **LP** can play the role of a general-purpose language of semantic composition. (In LFG, **LP** functions in a similar way as the semantic 'glue' language, cf. Lamping, Pereira and Saraswat (1995).)

In order to accommodate the dualism between syntactic and semantic types, we define a mapping $t:\mathcal{F} \mapsto \mathcal{F}'$ from syntactic to semantic types, which interprets complex types modulo directionality.

(14) $$t(A/B) = t(B\backslash A) = t(B) \to t(A), \qquad t(A \bullet B) = t(A) \circ t(B).$$

The primitive type inventory is a second source of divergence: categorizing signs in their syntactic and semantic dimensions may lead to different choices of atomic types. (For example, both common nouns (n) and verb phrases ($np\backslash s$) may be mapped to the semantic type $e \to t$ of properties.)

DEFINITION 3.8. Term assignment for 'sublinear' calculi **NL**, **L**, **NLP** using Λ(**LP**) as the language of semantic composition. Structural rules, if any, are neutral with respect to term assignment: they manipulate formulae with their associated term labels.

$$[\text{Ax}]\frac{}{x:A\Rightarrow x:A} \qquad \frac{\Delta\Rightarrow u:A \quad \Gamma[x:A]\Rightarrow t:C}{\Gamma[\Delta]\Rightarrow t[u/x]:C}[\text{Cut}]$$

$$[/\text{R}]\frac{(\Gamma,x:B)\Rightarrow t:A}{\Gamma\Rightarrow \lambda x.t:A/B} \qquad \frac{\Delta\Rightarrow t:B \quad \Gamma[x:A]\Rightarrow u:C}{\Gamma[(y:A/B,\Delta)]\Rightarrow u[y(t)/x]:C}[/\text{L}]$$

$$[\backslash\text{R}]\frac{(x:B,\Gamma)\Rightarrow t:A}{\Gamma\Rightarrow \lambda x.t:B\backslash A} \qquad \frac{\Delta\Rightarrow t:B \quad \Gamma[x:A]\Rightarrow u:C}{\Gamma[(\Delta,y:B\backslash A)]\Rightarrow u[y(t)/x]:C}[\backslash\text{L}]$$

$$[\bullet\text{L}]\frac{\Gamma[(x:A,y:B)]\Rightarrow t:C}{\Gamma[z:A\bullet B]\Rightarrow t[(z)_0/x,(z)_1/y]:C} \qquad \frac{\Gamma\Rightarrow t:A \quad \Delta\Rightarrow u:B}{(\Gamma,\Delta)\Rightarrow \langle t,u\rangle:A\bullet B}[\bullet\text{R}]$$

The alternative for the dualistic view is to equip the various inhabitants of the categorial landscape with more structured semantic term languages which directly reflect the syntactic resource management regime of the logics in question. In (Buszkowski, 1987; Wansing, 1992b; Hepple, 1994) one finds a term language which distinguishes left- and right oriented forms of abstraction λ^l, λ^r and application. These allow for a refinement of the term restrictions characterizing the $\Lambda(\mathbf{L})$ fragment and the two-way correspondence between term constructions and proofs: in the case of **L** the left (right) abstractors bind the leftmost (rightmost) free variable in their scope. In a similar vein, one could look for a structural characterization of the non-associativity of **NL**.

As long as the interpretation of the types is given in terms of function spaces and Cartesian products, the distinctions between left/right abstraction/application remain purely syntactic. For a more ambitious programme, see Abrusci (1996), who proposes a refinement of the notion 'meaning of proofs' in the context of a generalization of the coherence semantics for Linear Logic. One considers *bimodules* on coherent spaces and refines the class of linear functions into left-linear and right-linear functions. Interpreting A on the coherent space X and B on the coherent space Y, $D_{A\backslash B}$ (resp. $D_{B/A}$) is the coherent space of all the left-linear (resp. right-linear) functions from X to Y.

Natural deduction. For the display of sample derivations in the following section, we will continue to use the handy natural deduction format, which is presented below in its term-annotated form.

DEFINITION 3.9. Term assignment: (sequent-style) Natural Deduction. Notation: $\Gamma\vdash t:A$ for a deduction of the formula A decorated with term t from a structured configuration of undischarged term-decorated assumptions Γ.

$$x:A\vdash x:A$$

$$[/\text{I}]\frac{(\Gamma,x:B)\vdash t:A}{\Gamma\vdash \lambda x.t:A/B} \qquad \frac{\Gamma\vdash t:A/B \quad \Delta\vdash u:B}{(\Gamma,\Delta)\vdash t(u):A}[/\text{E}]$$

$$[\backslash I]\ \frac{(x:B,\Gamma)\vdash t:A}{\Gamma\vdash \lambda x.t:B\backslash A} \qquad \frac{\Gamma\vdash u:B \quad \Delta\vdash t:B\backslash A}{(\Gamma,\Delta)\vdash t(u):A}\ [\backslash E]$$

$$[\bullet I]\ \frac{\Gamma\vdash t:A \quad \Delta\vdash u:B}{(\Gamma,\Delta)\vdash \langle t,u\rangle:A\bullet B} \qquad \frac{\Delta\vdash u:A\bullet B \quad \Gamma[(x:A,y:B)]\vdash t:C}{\Gamma[\Delta]\vdash t[(u)_0/x,(u)_1/y]:C}\ [\bullet E]$$

3.2. Natural language interpretation: The deductive view

For an assessment of categorial type logics in the context of Montague's Universal Grammar program, it is instructive to compare the type-logical *deductive* view on the composition of linguistic meaning with the standard Montagovian *rule-to-rule* philosophy as discussed in Chapter 1. The rule-to-rule view on the syntax-semantics interface characterizes syntax in terms of a collection of syntactic rules (or rule schemata); for every syntactic rule, there is a corresponding semantic rule, specifying how the meaning of the whole is put together in terms of the meaning of the parts and the way they are put together. Apart from the homomorphism requirement for the syntactic and semantic algebras, compositionality, in its rule-to-rule implementation, does not impose any principled restrictions on exactly what operations in the semantic algebra one wants to line up with the syntactic algebra: the correlation between syntactic and semantic rules/operations can be entirely stipulative.

The type logical approach, as we have seen in Section 2 eliminates 'syntax' as a component of primitive rules. Instead of syntactic rules, one finds theorems – deductive consequences derived from the interpretation of the type-constructors. In the absence of syntactic rules, there can be no rule-to-rule stipulated assignment of meaning to derivations: rather, every theorem has to derive its meaning from its proof, again purely in terms of the semantic action of the type-constructors under the Curry–Howard correspondence.

EXAMPLE 3.10. Argument lowering (Partee and Rooth, 1983): the lexical type assignment for the verb 'needs', $(np\backslash s)/((s/np)\backslash s)$, can be lowered to $(np\backslash s)/np$. As discussed in Section 2, the principle is generally valid in the pure residuation logic **NL**.

$$\dfrac{\dfrac{\dfrac{\mathbf{needs}}{\text{needs}:(np\backslash s)/((s/np)\backslash s)} \quad \dfrac{\dfrac{\overline{x_1:s/np} \quad \overline{x_0:np}}{x_1(x_0):s}\ /E}{\lambda x_1.x_1(x_0):(s/np)\backslash s}\ \backslash I}{\text{needs}(\lambda x_1.x_1(x_0)):np\backslash s}\ /E}{\lambda x_0.\text{needs}(\lambda x_1.x_1(x_0)):(np\backslash s)/np}\ /I$$

Derivational ambiguity: Proofs and readings. The rule-to-rule implementation of compositionality requires there to be a unique meaning assignment for every syntactic rule. If one would like to associate different semantic effects with what looks like one and the same syntactic rule, one has to introduce diacritics in the syntax in order to keep the homomorphism requirement intact. In contrast, for the type-logical approach meaning resides in the *proof*, not in the type-change theorem that labels the conclusion of a proof. Different ways of proving one and the same goal sequent may, or may not, result in different readings.

EXAMPLE 3.11. As an example of derivational ambiguity, we consider the type-shifting principle known as Argument Raising (Partee and Rooth, 1983). The derivations below represent two semantically distinct **L** proofs of the theorem $(np\backslash s)/np \Rightarrow ((s/(np\backslash s))\backslash s)/((s/np)\backslash s)$, turning a simple first-order transitive verb into a third-order functor taking second-order generalized quantifier type arguments, encoding the subject wide scope reading (†) and object wide scope (‡) reading, respectively.

(†)

$$
\begin{prooftree}
\AxiomC{}
\UnaryInfC{$x_3 : s/(np\backslash s)$}
\AxiomC{}
\UnaryInfC{$x_0 : np$}
\AxiomC{$\mathbf{tv}$}
\UnaryInfC{$\mathbf{tv} : (np\backslash s)/np$}
\AxiomC{}
\UnaryInfC{$x_1 : np$}
\RightLabel{/E}
\BinaryInfC{$\mathbf{tv}(x_1) : np\backslash s$}
\RightLabel{$\backslash$E}
\BinaryInfC{$\mathbf{tv}(x_1)(x_0) : s$}
\RightLabel{/I}
\UnaryInfC{$\lambda x_1.\mathbf{tv}(x_1)(x_0) : s/np$}
\AxiomC{}
\UnaryInfC{$x_2 : (s/np)\backslash s$}
\RightLabel{$\backslash$E}
\BinaryInfC{$x_2(\lambda x_1.\mathbf{tv}(x_1)(x_0)) : s$}
\RightLabel{$\backslash$I}
\UnaryInfC{$\lambda x_0.x_2(\lambda x_1.\mathbf{tv}(x_1)(x_0)) : np\backslash s$}
\RightLabel{/E}
\BinaryInfC{$x_3(\lambda x_0.x_2(\lambda x_1.\mathbf{tv}(x_1)(x_0))) : s$}
\RightLabel{$\backslash$I}
\UnaryInfC{$\lambda x_3.x_3(\lambda x_0.x_2(\lambda x_1.\mathbf{tv}(x_1)(x_0))) : (s/(np\backslash s))\backslash s$}
\RightLabel{/I}
\UnaryInfC{$\lambda x_2 \lambda x_3.x_3(\lambda x_0.x_2(\lambda x_1.\mathbf{tv}(x_1)(x_0))) : ((s/(np\backslash s))\backslash s)/((s/np)\backslash s)$}
\end{prooftree}
$$

(‡)

$$
\begin{prooftree}
\AxiomC{}
\UnaryInfC{$x_2 : s/(np\backslash s)$}
\AxiomC{}
\UnaryInfC{$x_0 : np$}
\AxiomC{$\mathbf{tv}$}
\UnaryInfC{$\mathbf{tv} : (np\backslash s)/np$}
\AxiomC{}
\UnaryInfC{$x_1 : np$}
\RightLabel{/E}
\BinaryInfC{$\mathbf{tv}(x_1) : np\backslash s$}
\RightLabel{$\backslash$E}
\BinaryInfC{$\mathbf{tv}(x_1)(x_0) : s$}
\RightLabel{$\backslash$I}
\UnaryInfC{$\lambda x_0.\mathbf{tv}(x_1)(x_0) : np\backslash s$}
\RightLabel{/E}
\BinaryInfC{$x_2(\lambda x_0.\mathbf{tv}(x_1)(x_0)) : s$}
\RightLabel{/I}
\UnaryInfC{$\lambda x_1.x_2(\lambda x_0.\mathbf{tv}(x_1)(x_0)) : s/np$}
\AxiomC{}
\UnaryInfC{$x_3 : (s/np)\backslash s$}
\RightLabel{$\backslash$E}
\BinaryInfC{$x_3(\lambda x_1.x_2(\lambda x_0.\mathbf{tv}(x_1)(x_0))) : s$}
\RightLabel{$\backslash$I}
\UnaryInfC{$\lambda x_2.x_3(\lambda x_1.x_2(\lambda x_0.\mathbf{tv}(x_1)(x_0))) : (s/(np\backslash s))\backslash s$}
\RightLabel{/I}
\UnaryInfC{$\lambda x_3 \lambda x_2.x_3(\lambda x_1.x_2(\lambda x_0.\mathbf{tv}(x_1)(x_0))) : ((s/(np\backslash s))\backslash s)/((s/np)\backslash s)$}
\end{prooftree}
$$

Lexical versus derivational semantics. The derivational semantics of a sequent $\Gamma \Rightarrow t : A$ gives a meaning recipe t in terms of free variables x_i for the antecedent assumptions A_i in Γ, the 'parameters' of the recipe. In the actual computation of the meaning of a natural language expression, we substitute the *lexical* meanings of the words constituting the expression for these variables. For the logically more exciting part of the vocabulary, this will involve the substitution of a compound λ term representing the lexical meaning for a parameter in the proof term. The strict division of labor between the role assigned to derivational and lexical semantics realizes a fully modular implementation of compositionality, which has a number of pleasant consequences: on the level of individual lexical items, lexical semantics can overcome the expressive limitations of the resource-conscious derivational component; on a more global level, one can interface the neutral derivational semantics with one's favorite semantic theory via an appropriate category-to-type mapping and lexical meaning assignment. We illustrate these two aspects in turn.

Non-linear meaning recipes. We saw that the resource-sensitive **LP** terms have the property that every assumption is used exactly once: the lambda operator binds exactly one variable occurrence. Natural language semantics, in a variety of constructions, requires the identification of variables. Assigning multiple-bind terms to the relevant classes of lexical items one can realize variable-sharing while maintaining the resource-sensitivity of derivational semantics.

EXAMPLE 3.12. 'Everyone loves himself'. Proof term and substitution of lexical recipes. (Notice that reductions *after* lexical substitution can destructively affect the proof term, in the sense that the original proof term becomes irrecoverable after the 'lexical' β conversions.)

$$\text{himself}_{((np\backslash s)/np)\backslash(np\backslash s)} := \lambda x \lambda y.x(y)(y)$$
$$\text{everyone}_{s/(np\backslash s)} := \lambda x \forall y(\text{person}(y) \Rightarrow x(y)).$$

$$\dfrac{\dfrac{\textbf{everyone}}{\text{everyone} : s/(np\backslash s)} \quad \dfrac{\dfrac{\dfrac{}{x_0 : np} \quad \dfrac{\dfrac{\dfrac{\dfrac{\dfrac{}{x_1 : np} \quad \dfrac{\dfrac{\textbf{loves}}{\text{loves} : (np\backslash s)/np} \quad \dfrac{}{x_2 : np}}{\text{loves}(x_2) : np\backslash s}\,/E}{\text{loves}(x_2)(x_1) : s}\,\backslash E}{\lambda x_1.\text{loves}(x_2)(x_1) : np\backslash s}\,\backslash I}{\lambda x_2 \lambda x_1.\text{loves}(x_2)(x_1) : (np\backslash s)/np}\,/I \quad \dfrac{\textbf{himself}}{\text{himself} : ((np\backslash s)/np)\backslash(np\backslash s)}}{\text{himself}(\lambda x_2 \lambda x_1.\text{loves}(x_2)(x_1)) : np\backslash s}\,\backslash E}{\text{himself}(\lambda x_2 \lambda x_1.\text{loves}(x_2)(x_1))(x_0) : s}\,\backslash E}{\lambda x_0.\text{himself}(\lambda x_2 \lambda x_1.\text{loves}(x_2)(x_1))(x_0) : np\backslash s}\,\backslash I}{\text{everyone}(\lambda x_0.\text{himself}(\lambda x_2 \lambda x_1.\text{loves}(x_2)(x_1))(x_0)) : s}\,/E$$

$$\text{everyone}(\lambda x_0.\text{himself}(\lambda x_2 \lambda x_1.\text{loves}(x_2)(x_1))(x_0)) \rightarrow_\beta$$
$$\forall y.\text{person}(y) \Rightarrow \text{love}(y)(y).$$

Derivational semantics: Portability. The proof terms associated with categorial derivations relate structural composition in a systematic way to the composition of meaning. The derivational semantics is fully neutral with respect to the particular 'theory of natural language semantics' one wants to plug in: an attractive design property of the type-logical architecture when it comes to portability. An illustration can be found in (Muskens, 1994), who proposes a type-logical emulation of Discourse Representation Theory (cf. Chapter 3) driven by a categorial proof engine.

To obtain the combination, one starts from an appropriate primitive type inventory for dynamic semantics: e and t as before, plus s (program states) and d ('pigeon-holes' for discourse referents). The category-to-type map is set up in such a way that the syntactic categories get an interpretation in the appropriate semantic domains: $t(s) = t(txt) =$

$s \to s \to t$, $t(np) = d$, $t(n) = d \to (s \to (s \to t))$. Lexical recipes for a tiny corner of the DRT lexicon are given in (15).

$$(15)\quad \begin{array}{lll} \text{a}^n & (s/(np\backslash s))/n & \lambda P\lambda Q.[u_n \mid\ ]; P(u_n); Q(u_n) \\ \text{man, woman} & n & \lambda v.[\ \mid \text{MAN } v], \lambda v.[\ \mid \text{WOMAN } v] \\ \text{loves, hates} & (np\backslash s)/np & \lambda v\lambda w.[\ \mid v \text{ LOVES } w], \lambda v\lambda w.[\ \mid v \text{ HATES } w] \\ \text{he}^n, \text{she}^n & s/(np\backslash s) & \lambda P.P(u_n) \\ \text{him}^n, \text{her}^n & (s/np)\backslash s & \lambda P.P(u_n) \\ & s\backslash(txt/s), txt\backslash(txt/s) & \lambda p\lambda q.p;q \end{array}$$

The reader will be able to verify in Example 3.13 that the little discourse (a) is associated with proof term (b) which reduces to the discourse representation structure (c), using some notational sugaring, detailed below as far as relevant.

EXAMPLE 3.13. Type-driven composition of DRS's (Muskens, 1994). Notational abbreviations:

$$\phi\,;\psi = \lambda i\lambda j\exists k.\phi ik \wedge \psi ik \qquad \text{(dynamic discourse composition)},$$

$$[u_1 \cdots u_n \mid \gamma_1, \ldots, \gamma_n] = \lambda i\lambda j.i[u_1 \cdots u_n]j \wedge \gamma_1(j) \wedge \cdots \wedge \gamma_n(j)$$
$$\text{(box with conditions } \gamma_i\text{)},$$

$$[\vec{u} \mid \vec{\gamma}]; [\vec{u}' \mid \vec{\gamma}'] \rightsquigarrow [\vec{u}\,\vec{u}' \mid \vec{\gamma}\,\vec{\gamma}'] \quad \text{(merging boxes, provided the } \vec{u}' \text{ do not occur in any of the } \vec{\gamma}\text{)}.$$

(a) A^1man loves a^2 woman. She_2 hates him_1,
(b) $\cdot(\text{a}(\text{man})(\lambda x.\text{a}(\text{woman})(\lambda y.\text{loves}(y)(x))))(\text{she}(\lambda v.\text{him}(\lambda w.\text{hates}(w)(v))))$,
(c) $[u_1, u_2 \mid \text{MAN } u_1, \text{WOMAN } u_2, u_1 \text{ LOVES } u_2, u_2 \text{ HATES } u_1]$.

Discussion: Quantifier scope ambiguities
We close this section with a discussion of scope ambiguities involving generalized quantifier expressions: these phenomena nicely illustrate the tension between the composition of form and meaning, and the different strategies for resolving these tensions.

Consider generalized quantifier expressions like 'someone', 'everybody'. From the perspective of **LP**, we can study their semantic contribution via a standard Fregean type assignment $(e \to t) \to t$, with lexical recipes $\lambda x.\exists y[x(y)]$, $\lambda x.\forall y[x(y)]$. The **LP** notion of derivability, of course, is too crude to offer a unified deductive account of semantics in conjunction with syntax. Suppose we want to refine the **LP** type $(e \to t) \to t$ to take syntactic fine-structure into account. Within **L**, one can find two directional realizations compatible with the fact that generalized quantifiers occupy the positions of ordinary (proper noun) noun phrases: $s/(np\backslash s)$ and $(s/np)\backslash s$. But imposing order sensitivity in the type-assignment already causes the loss of scope readings one wants to preserve. Compare 'peripheral' versus 'medial' occurrences of generalized quantifiers. Given a 'direct object' assignment $(s/np)\backslash s$ to 'someone', both the (a) and (a′) readings are

L-derivable. Given a 'subject' assignment $s/(np\backslash s)$ the (b) reading is not derivable: in **L** one only derives the narrow scope reading (b′).

$$
(16) \quad
\begin{array}{ll}
\text{(a) Suzy thinks Mary loves someone} & \rightsquigarrow \text{someone}(\lambda x.\text{thinks}(\text{loves}(x)(\text{m}))(\text{s})), \\
\text{(a}') & \rightsquigarrow \text{thinks}(\text{someone}(\lambda x.\text{loves}(x)(\text{m})))(\text{s}), \\
\text{(b) Suzy thinks someone loves Mary} & \rightsquigarrow \text{someone}(\lambda x.\text{thinks}(\text{loves}(\text{m})(x))(\text{s})), \\
\text{(b}') & \rightsquigarrow \text{thinks}(\text{someone}(\lambda x.\text{loves}(\text{m})(x)))(\text{s}).
\end{array}
$$

The diagnosis of the problem is easy in the light of Section 2: the (b) reading would require the generalized quantifier expression to enter into structural composition with a *discontinuous* configuration of resources: such syntactic behaviour is beyond the expressivity of the **(N)L** connectives:

$$\boxed{\text{Suzy thinks}}\ \text{someone}\ \boxed{\text{loves Mary}}$$

We compare two strategies to resolve this problem: (i) in the *rule-based* approach, one postulates type-change axiom schemata to regain the lost readings, (ii) in the *deductive* approach, one enriches the vocabulary of connectives with logical constants such that these axiom schemata become derivable theorems. Flexible Montague Grammar (Hendriks, 1993), and the closely related polymorphic approach of Emms (1993b) (to be taken up in Section 5.2) are representatives of (i). The deductive alternative has been developed in (Moortgat, 1991; Morrill, 1995a; Carpenter 1996).

Flexible Montague grammar. Hendriks' proposal is formulated as a flexible version of Montague Grammar (FMG). For an assessment in the Montagovian context we refer to Chapter One. Our objective here is to give a type-logical reconstruction of the essential ideas. Syntactically, FMG is restricted to combine phrases by means of function application rule schemata. In order to accommodate quantificational scope ambiguities, the category-to-type mapping is relaxed to a relation rather than a function: a given syntactic type is associated with a set of semantic types. The semantic types are not unrelated: from a generator type an infinite number of semantic types (and the associated meaning recipes) are derived via the type-shifting rule schemata of Value Raising (VR), Argument Lowering (AL), and Argument Raising (AR).

Let us identify the pure application syntax of FMG as **NL**, and try to pinpoint exactly where the type-shifting schemata give a surplus inferential capacity. As we have seen in Section 2, Value Raising and Argument Lowering are universally valid already in the pure residuation logic **NL**: they reflect the monotonicity properties of the implicational type constructors. Argument Raising, as a semantic type-shifting rule, is schematically characterized in (17) (where $\vec{A} \to B$ abbreviates $A_1 \to \cdots \to A_n \to B$, and similarly for $\vec{x}$).

$$
(17) \quad
\begin{array}{ll}
\text{(AR)} & \vec{A} \to B \to \vec{C} \to D \Rightarrow \vec{A} \to ((B \to D) \to D) \to \vec{C} \to D \\
 & t \Rightarrow \lambda \vec{x}_{\vec{A}} \lambda w_{(B\to D)\to D} \lambda \vec{y}_{\vec{C}}.w(\lambda z_B.t(\vec{x})(z)(\vec{y})).
\end{array}
$$

Directional realizations of this schema are *not* generally valid. We saw two special cases in our Example 3.11: these happened to be derivable, in the associative setting of **L**, for generalized quantifiers occupying peripheral positions in their scopal domain. But what we would like to have in full generality is the possibility of having a generalized quantifier phrase at any np position, exerting its binding force at any s level of embedding.

As an illustration for the FMG type-shifting approach, take the sentence 'Kazimierz thinks someone left'. In (18) we list the necessary steps producing the wide scope reading for 'someone'. We give both the semantic shifts – abbreviating $A \to B$ as (AB) – and their directional counterpart. The (AR) transition for 'left', with the generalized quantifier variable x_2 in head position, is the critical one that cannot be obtained as a pure **NL** proof term. Combining the words (in their shifted types) by means of functional application produces the desired reading.

(18)

$$\begin{array}{ll}
\text{thinks } (np\backslash s)/s \Rightarrow (np\backslash s)/((s/s)\backslash s) & \text{left } np\backslash s \Rightarrow np\backslash((s/s)\backslash s) \\
(t(et)) \Rightarrow_{AR} ((tt)t)(et) & (et) \Rightarrow_{VR} (e((tt)t) \\
\text{thinks} \Rightarrow \lambda x_2 \lambda x_0 . x_2(\lambda x_1.\text{thinks}(x_1)(x_0)) & \text{left} \Rightarrow \lambda x_1 \lambda x_0 . x_0(\text{left}(x_1)) \quad (= \text{left}') \\
 & \\
 & np\backslash((s/s)\backslash s) \Rightarrow (s/(np\backslash s))\backslash((s/s)\backslash s) \\
 & (e((tt)t) \Rightarrow_{AR} ((et)t)((tt)t) \\
 & \text{left}' \Rightarrow \lambda x_2 \lambda x_0 . x_2(\lambda x_1 . x_0(\text{left}(x_1)))
\end{array}$$

A connective for binding. The deductive alternative is to investigate the theoretical space provided by the Lambek landscape in order to identify within this space a logical constant which renders the critical AR cases (the cases beyond the reach of **(N)L**) derivable.

DEFINITION 3.14. In situ binding $q(A, B, C)$ (Moortgat, 1991). Use of a formula $q(A, B, C)$ binds a variable x of type A, where the resource A is substituted for (takes the place of) $q(A, B, C)$ in the binding domain B. Using $q(A, B, C)$ turns the binding domain B into C. In the generalized quantifier case we have typing $q(np, s, s)$ where it happens that $B = C = s$. For the semantic term decoration of the rule of use $[qL]$, assume $t(q(A, B, C)) = (t(A) \to t(B)) \to t(C)$.

$$\frac{\Delta[x : A] \Rightarrow t : B \qquad \Gamma[y : C] \Rightarrow u : D}{\Gamma[\Delta[z : q(A, B, C)]] \Rightarrow u[z(\lambda x.t)/y] : D}\,(qL)$$

EXAMPLE 3.15. Direct cut-free proof search for 'Kazimierz thinks someone left', with wide scope 'someone'. (Compare: the FMG strategy of (18).)

$$\dfrac{\dfrac{\dfrac{np \Rightarrow np \quad s \Rightarrow s}{np, np\backslash s \Rightarrow s}(\backslash L) \quad \dfrac{np \Rightarrow np \quad s \Rightarrow s}{np, np\backslash s \Rightarrow s}(\backslash L)}{np, (np\backslash s)/s, \boxed{x : np}, np\backslash s \Rightarrow \boxed{u : s}}(/L) \qquad \boxed{y : s} \Rightarrow y : s}{np, (np\backslash s)/s, \boxed{\text{someone} : q(np, s, s)}, np\backslash s \Rightarrow \boxed{y[\text{someone}(\lambda x.u)/y] : s}}(qL)$$

$$u = \text{thinks}(\text{left}(x))(\text{k}), \quad y[\text{someone}(\lambda x.u)/y] = \text{someone}(\lambda x.\text{thinks}(\text{left}(x))(\text{k})).$$

Carpenter (1994, 1996) offers an in-depth discussion of the empirical range of the binding connective as compared with competing approaches to quantification, and an extension with a treatment of plurals. Notice finally the different 'heuristic' qualities of the connective-based and the rule-based type-shifting alternatives. The type-shifting approach is specifically designed to handle the semantics of quantificational phenomena and obtain minimal type assignment. The deductive approach introduces a *connective*, i.e. a fully general operation on types that cannot have a construction-specific limited range of application. Support for the generality of a connective for *in situ* binding can be found in the analyses of Pied-Piping (Morrill, 1995a), or *more* ... *than* comparative subdeletion (Hendriks, 1995).

We close this discussion with some open questions. With the $[qL]$ inference, we have given a rule of *use* – what about the rule of proof for the *in situ* binder? Also, the q connective was presented as a primitive connective, whereas the term assignment $z(\lambda x.t)$ shows the interaction of two implications – could we decompose the q connective into more elementary logical constants? In the context of the simple type logics we are discussing here, these questions must remain unanswered. In Section 4.1, multimodal type logics will be introduced which provide the tools to tackle these issues in a principled way.

4. Grammatical composition: Multimodal systems

In the present section we generalize the multiplicative vocabulary in a number of directions. The generalizations do not affect the overall model-theoretic or proof-theoretic properties of the categorial architecture in any essential sense. But they increase the linguistic sophistication in such a way that the limitations of the simple systems discussed in Section 2.3 are overcome.

In Section 4.1, simple type logics are put together into a mixed, *multimodal* system where distinct notions of grammatical composition coexist and communicate. The multimodal style of reasoning was developed in the work of Oehrle, Morrill, Hepple and the author, cf. Moortgat and Morrill (1991), Moortgat and Oehrle (1993, 1994), Hepple (1994). This development reintroduces in the type-logical discussion the theme of the 'multidimensionality' of grammatical composition that had been dealt with on a more philosophical level in earlier work such as Oehrle (1988), Bach (1984). Another antecedent is Dowty (1991), who distinguishes composition modes with different degrees of coherence.

In Section 4.2, the binary vocabulary is extended with a language of *unary* multiplicatives. The unary connectives play the role of *control* devices, with respect to both the static aspects of linguistic structure, and the dynamic aspects of putting this structure together. Unary operations entered the type-logical discussion in (Morrill, 1990a), who provides an analysis of semantic domains of intensionality in terms of a $\Box$ operator. The unary vocabulary soon found a variety of applications, including the syntactic domain modalities of Hepple (1990), the 'structural modalities' of Barry, Hepple, Leslie and Morrill (1991), and the 'bracket' operators of Morrill (1995a). Our treatment below systematizes and refines these earlier proposals.

As indicated in Section 1, the developments to be discussed here represent the categorial digestion of a number of themes in the field of Linear Logic and related substructural systems, and of Gabbay's general program for combining logics. The collection *Substructural Logics* (Došen and Schröder-Heister, 1993) and Gabbay (1994) offer useful background reading for these lines of research.

4.1. *Mixed inference: The modes of composition*

In Section 2 the type-forming connectives $/$, $\bullet$, $\backslash$ were interpreted in terms of a *single* notion of linguistic composition. In moving to a *multimodal* architecture the objective is to combine the virtues of the individual logics we have discussed so far, and to exploit new forms of grammatical inference arising from their communication. In merging different logics into a mixed system, we have to take care that their individual resource management properties are left intact. This can be done by relativizing linguistic composition to specific resource management *modes*. But also, we want the inferential capacity of the combined logic to be more than the sum of the parts. The extra expressivity comes from *interaction postulates* that hold when different modes are in construction with one another. The interaction postulates can apply in full generality, or can themselves be intrinsically controlled by exploiting mode distinctions, or by composition of modes.

On the syntactic level, the category formulae for the multimodal language are defined inductively on the basis of a set of category atoms $\mathcal{A}$ and a set of indices I. We refer to the $i \in I$ as *composition modes*, or modes for short.

(19) $$\mathcal{F} ::= \mathcal{A} \mid \mathcal{F}/_i\mathcal{F} \mid \mathcal{F} \bullet_i \mathcal{F} \mid \mathcal{F}\backslash_i\mathcal{F}.$$

The interpretation for the mixed language is a straightforward generalization of the semantics for the simple systems. Rather than interpret the multiplicatives in terms of *one* privileged notion of linguistic composition, we put together different forms of linguistic composition and interpret in multimodal frames $\langle W, \{R_i^3\}_{i\in I}\rangle$. The valuation v respects the structure of the complex formulae in the familiar way, interpreting each of the modes $i \in I$ in terms of its own composition relation R_i. The basic residuation laws (20) are *relativized* with respect to the composition modes.

DEFINITION 4.1. Interpretation in multimodal frames $\langle W, \{R_i^3\}_{i\in I}\rangle$.

$$v(A \bullet_i B) = \{x \mid \exists y \exists z[R_i xyz \ \&\ y \in v(A) \ \&\ z \in v(B)]\},$$
$$v(C/_i B) = \{y \mid \forall x \forall z[(R_i xyz \ \&\ z \in v(B)) \Rightarrow x \in v(C)]\},$$
$$v(A\backslash_i C) = \{z \mid \forall x \forall y[(R_i xyz \ \&\ y \in v(A)) \Rightarrow x \in v(C)]\},$$

(20) $$A \to C/_i B \quad \text{iff} \quad A \bullet_i B \to C \quad \text{iff} \quad B \to A\backslash_i C.$$

In sequent presentation, each residuated family of multiplicatives $\{/_i, \bullet_i, \backslash_i\}$ has a matching structural connective $(\cdot,\cdot)^i$. Logical rules insist that use and proof of connectives respect the resource management modes. The explicit construction of the antecedent database in terms of structural connectives derives directly from Belnap's (1982) work on Display Logic, where it serves the same purpose as it does here, viz. to combine logics with different resource management regimes. In (Kracht, 1993; Wansing, 1992a) one finds recent applications in the context of modal logic. More recently, the same idea has been introduced in Linear Logic in (Girard, 1993).

DEFINITION 4.2. Multimodal Gentzen calculus: logical rules. Structure terms $\mathcal{S} ::= \mathcal{F} \mid (\mathcal{S}, \mathcal{S})^i$.

$$[\mathrm{R}/_i]\ \frac{(\Gamma, B)^i \Rightarrow A}{\Gamma \Rightarrow A/_i B} \qquad \frac{\Gamma \Rightarrow B \quad \Delta[A] \Rightarrow C}{\Delta[(A/_i B, \Gamma)^i] \Rightarrow C}\ [\mathrm{L}/_i]$$

$$[\mathrm{R}\backslash_i]\ \frac{(B, \Gamma)^i \Rightarrow A}{\Gamma \Rightarrow B\backslash_i A} \qquad \frac{\Gamma \Rightarrow B \quad \Delta[A] \Rightarrow C}{\Delta[(\Gamma, B\backslash_i A)^i] \Rightarrow C}\ [\mathrm{L}\backslash_i]$$

$$[\mathrm{L}\bullet_i]\ \frac{\Gamma[(A, B)^i] \Rightarrow C}{\Gamma[A \bullet_i B] \Rightarrow C} \qquad \frac{\Gamma \Rightarrow A \quad \Delta \Rightarrow B}{(\Gamma, \Delta)^i \Rightarrow A \bullet_i B}\ [\mathrm{R}\bullet_i]$$

Notice that the mode specification can keep apart distinct forms of grammatical composition even if they have *the same* resource management properties. The dependency calculus of Moortgat and Morrill (1991) provides an example. By splitting up the product $\bullet$ in a left-headed $\bullet_l$ and a right-headed $\bullet_r$, these authors introduce a dimension of *dependency* structure next to the dimensions of precedence and dominance. The dependency products could both be non-associative operators; still, with the mode specification we would be able to distinguish left-headed structures from right-headed ones. Linguistic motivation for the dependency dimension can be found in (Barry, 1991; Barry and Pickering, 1990).

In addition to the residuation inferences (the fixed 'logical' component for all modes), we can now have mode-specific structural options. For a commutative mode c, for example, we would have the structural postulate (structural rule, in the Gentzen style) below, together with the matching frame constraint for the composition relation interpreting $\bullet_c$: $(\forall x, y, z \in W)\ R_c xyz \Rightarrow R_c xzy$. (Where there is an established notation, such as $\otimes$ in this case, we will often use the familiar symbol instead of the 'official' $\bullet_c$ notation.

(21) $$A \bullet_c B \leftrightarrow B \bullet_c A \qquad \frac{\Gamma[(\Delta_2, \Delta_1)^c] \Rightarrow A}{\Gamma[(\Delta_1, \Delta_2)^c] \Rightarrow A}\,[\mathrm{P}]$$

It is straightforward to extend the completeness results of Section 2 to the multimodal architecture, cf. Kurtonina (1995) for discussion. Semantic annotation of the multimodal derivations with λ term meaning recipes is implemented in exactly the same way as for the unimodal systems.

Multimodal communication. What we have done so far is simply put together the individual systems discussed before in isolation. This is enough to gain combined access to the inferential capacities of the component logics, and one avoids the unpleasant collapse into the least discriminating logic that results from putting together theorems from different simple logics without taking into account the mode distinctions, cf. our discussion in Section 2. But as things are, the borders between the constituting logics in our multimodal setting are still hermetically closed. Communication between composition relations R_i and R_j can be established in two ways.

Inclusion postulates. Postulates $A \bullet_i B \rightarrow A \bullet_j B$, with corresponding frame conditions $(\forall xyz \in W)\ R_i xyz \Rightarrow R_j xyz$, impose a 'specificity' order on composition modes $i,\ j$.

Interaction postulates. Postulates 'mixing' distinct modes i, j allow for the statement of distributivity principles regulating the communication between composition modes R_i, R_j. One obtains constrained multimodal forms of the resource management postulates of Section 2.

Inclusion principles. One can develop different perspectives on inclusion principles depending on the interpretation one has in mind for the ordering of the composition relations R_i, R_j involved. A natural candidate would be an ordering in terms of the information they provide about the structure of the linguistic resources. From this perspective, the non-commutative product $\bullet$ would count as more informative than the commutative product $\otimes$, since the former but not the latter is sensitive to the linear order of the resources. In terms of frame conditions, one imposes the constraint $R_\bullet xyz \Rightarrow R_\otimes xyz$, corresponding to the postulate $A \bullet B \rightarrow A \otimes B$. This perspective is taken in general terms in (Moortgat and Oehrle, 1993), where two products $\bullet_i$ and $\bullet_j$ are related by an inclusion principle $A \bullet_i B \rightarrow A \bullet_j B$ if the latter has greater freedom of resource management than the former. The opposite view is taken in (Hepple, 1995), where one finds a systematic reversal of the derivability arrows in the inclusion principles, e.g., $A \otimes B \rightarrow A \bullet B$. In (Kurtonina, 1995) it is shown that from the frame semantics point of view the two perspectives can be equally well accommodated: they reflect the choice for a 'conjunctive' versus 'disjunctive' reading of the commutative product.

Interaction principles. Among the multimodal interaction principles, we distinguish cases of weak and strong distributivity. The weak distributivity principles do not affect the multiplicity of the linguistic resources. They allow for the realization of mixed associativity or commutativity laws as the multimodal counterparts of the unimodal versions discussed above. Interaction principles of the strong distributivity type duplicate resources, thus giving access to mode-restricted forms of Contraction.

Weak distributivity. Consider first interaction of the weak distributivity type. Definition 4.3 states principles of *mixed* associativity and commutativity. Instead of the global associativity and commutativity options characterizing **L**, **NLP**, **LP**, these principles realize constrained forms of associativity/commutativity, restricted to the situation where modes i and j are in construction. (Symmetric duals can be added with the i mode distributing from the right, and one can split up the two-directional inferences in their one-directional components, if so required.)

DEFINITION 4.3. Mixed Associativity (MA), Mixed Commutativity (MP). Structural postulates, frame constraints, Gentzen rules.

$$\text{MP:} \quad A \bullet_i (B \bullet_j C) \leftrightarrow B \bullet_j (A \bullet_i C)$$
$$\exists t(R_i uxt \ \& \ R_j tyz) \Leftrightarrow \exists t'(R_j uyt' \ \& \ R_i t'xz)$$
$$\text{MA:} \quad A \bullet_i (B \bullet_j C) \leftrightarrow (A \bullet_i B) \bullet_j C$$
$$\exists t(R_i uxt \ \& \ R_j tyz) \Leftrightarrow \exists t'(R_j ut'z \ \& \ R_i t'xy)$$

$$\frac{\Gamma[(\Delta_2, (\Delta_1, \Delta_3)^i)^j] \Rightarrow A}{\Gamma[(\Delta_1, (\Delta_2, \Delta_3)^j)^i] \Rightarrow A}[\text{MP}] \qquad \frac{\Gamma[((\Delta_1, \Delta_2)^i, \Delta_3)^j] \Rightarrow A}{\Gamma[(\Delta_1, (\Delta_2, \Delta_3)^j)^i] \Rightarrow A}[\text{MA}]$$

For linguistic application of these general postulates, we turn to discontinuous dependencies. In the work of authors such as Bach (1984), Pollard (1984), Jacobson (1987), it has been argued that the discontinuous mode of combination ('wrapping') should be treated as a grammatical operation *sui generis*, rather than simulated in terms of the regular 'concatenation' mode. In the type-logical setting one can adopt this emancipated position with respect to wrapping operations, and formulate the logic of discontinuity in terms of multimodal interaction principles. Consider the Dutch Verb Raising construction. In Example 2.22 we saw that a *unimodal* 'Mixed Composition' law causes permutation disturbances in an otherwise order-sensitive grammar logic. With the aid of the MP/MA interaction principles, one obtains the multimodal version of Example 4.4.

EXAMPLE 4.4. Mixed Composition/Geach as a multimodal theorem (Moortgat and Oehrle, 1994). The MP interaction principle relates the head adjunction mode $\bullet_h$, which provides typing for the verb-raising triggers, and the dependency mode $\bullet_r$, which characterizes the head-final basic clausal structure of Dutch. (Compare $(vp/_h iv,\ np\backslash_r iv)^h \Rightarrow np\backslash_r vp$ with Example 2.22.)

$$\cfrac{\cfrac{\cfrac{\cfrac{\cfrac{C \Rightarrow C \quad B \Rightarrow B}{(C, C\backslash_r B)^r \Rightarrow B}\backslash_r L \quad A \Rightarrow A}{(A/_h B, (C, C\backslash_r B)^r)^h \Rightarrow A}/_h L}{(C, (A/_h B, C\backslash_r B)^h)^r \Rightarrow A}MP}{(A/_h B, C\backslash_r B)^h \Rightarrow C\backslash_r A}\backslash_r R}{A/_h B \Rightarrow (C\backslash_r A)/_h(C\backslash_r B)}/_h R$$

Notice that the order sensitivity of the individual modes $\bullet_r$ and $\bullet_h$ is respected: the valid forms of mixed composition form a subset of the composition laws derivable within unimodal **LP**. The principles of Directional Consistency and Directional Inheritance, introduced as theoretical primitives in the rule-based setting of CCG, can be seen here to follow automatically from the individual resource management properties of the modes involved and the distributivity principle governing their communication. Example 4.4 shows that it is *possible* to derive head adjunction. In order to *force* the formation of the verb cluster, the type language has to be further refined. See Moortgat and Oehrle (1994) for discussion, and Section 4.2 for the required logical vocabulary.

For a second illustration, we take up the discussion of *in situ* binding of Section 3. It is shown in (Morrill, 1994a) that the connective $q(A,B,C)$ can be *defined* in a multimodal system with three communicating modes: a (associative regime), n (non-associative regime), and w (wrapping). The crucial interaction principle is given in (22).

$$\text{(WN):}\quad (A \bullet_a B) \bullet_a C \leftrightarrow (A \bullet_n C) \bullet_w B$$

(22)

$$\frac{\Gamma[((\Delta_1, \Delta_3)^n, \Delta_2)^w] \Rightarrow A}{\Gamma[((\Delta_1, \Delta_2)^a, \Delta_3)^a] \Rightarrow A}\,[\text{WN}]$$

EXAMPLE 4.5. Multimodal deconstruction of $q(A,B,C)$ as $(B/_w A)\backslash_w C$. On the left the $[qL]$ rule of Definition 3.14. On the right the 'partial execution' compilation in terms of interaction principle (22).

$$\frac{\Delta[x:A] \Rightarrow t:B \qquad \Gamma[y:C] \Rightarrow u:D}{\Gamma[\Delta[z:q(A,B,C)]] \Rightarrow u[z(\lambda x.t)/y]:D}\,(qL)$$

$$\dfrac{\dfrac{\dfrac{\dfrac{(\Delta,(A,\Delta')^a)^a \Rightarrow B}{((\Delta,\Delta')^n, A)^w \Rightarrow B}\,WN}{(\Delta,\Delta')^n \Rightarrow B/_w A}\,/_w R \qquad \Gamma[C] \Rightarrow D}{\Gamma[((\Delta,\Delta')^n,(B/_w A)\backslash_w C)^w] \Rightarrow D}\,\backslash_w L}{\dfrac{\Gamma[((\Delta,(B/_w A)\backslash_w C)^a,\Delta')^a] \Rightarrow D}{\Gamma[((\Delta,q(A,B,C))^a,\Delta')^a] \Rightarrow D}\,(\text{def})}\,WN$$

The deconstruction of Example 4.5 partially answers the question raised in Section 3: for a default *associative* regime, it shows how one can define an *in situ* binding operator as $(s/_w np)\backslash_w s$. Associativity here is essential for obtaining access to arbitrary infixation points for the wrapping expression. A generalized multimodal wrapping operation, independent of associativity assumptions, is proposed in (Moortgat, 1996).

Interaction principles: Strong distributivity. As remarked above, the weak distributivity principles MP, MA keep us within the family of resource neutral logics: they do not affect the multiplicity of the resources in a configuration. Strong distributivity principles are not resource neutral: they duplicate resources. As an example, consider the interaction principle of Mixed Contraction in Definition 4.6, which strongly distributes mode j over mode i, thus copying a C datum. Rather than introducing global Contraction, this interaction principle allows for a constrained form of copying, restricted to the case where modes i and j are in construction.

DEFINITION 4.6. Restricted Contraction. Structural postulate, Gentzen rule, frame constraint.

$$\text{MC:} \quad (A \bullet_i B) \bullet_j C \to (A \bullet_j C) \bullet_i (B \bullet_j C)$$

$$\frac{\Gamma[((\Delta_1, \Delta_3)^j, (\Delta_2, \Delta_3)^j)^i] \Rightarrow A}{\Gamma[((\Delta_1, \Delta_2)^i, \Delta_3)^j] \Rightarrow A} MC$$

$$(R_i txy \ \&\ R_j utz) \Rightarrow \exists t' \exists t'' (R_j t'xz \ \&\ R_j t''yz \ \&\ R_i ut't'')$$

It has been argued that grammatical inference requires restricted access to Contraction for the analysis of the so-called parasitic gap constructions in (23) below. In this construction, one would like the abstractor associated with the *wh* element to bind multiple occurrences of the same variable, for the interpretation of the structural positions indicated by the underscores. Such multiple binding is beyond the scope of occurrence-sensitive logics we have considered so far. In the framework of CCG, parasitic gaps are handled by means of the combinator **S** which is introduced as a primitive for this purpose, cf. Szabolcsi (1987), Steedman (1987).

(23) **S**: $A/C, (A\backslash B)/C \Rightarrow B/C$

Which books did John (file _ without reading _)

In a multimodal framework, a mode-restricted form of the **S** combinator can be derived from the strong distributivity principle discussed above. In the Gentzen proof below, we give the relevant instance for the derivation of the example sentence (instantiate $A/_j C$ as $vp/_j np$ for *file*, and $(A\backslash_i B)/_j C$ as $(vp\backslash_i vp)/_j np$ for *without reading*). Mode j here would be the default mode by which the transitive verbs *file* and *read* consume their direct objects; the combination of the vp adjunct *without reading _* with the vp it modifies is given in terms of mode i, the 'parasitic' mode which licenses the secondary gap depending on the primary one, the argument of *file*.

EXAMPLE 4.7. Deriving the combinator **S** as a multimodal theorem.

$$\dfrac{\dfrac{\dfrac{\&c}{((A/_j C, C)^j, ((A\backslash_i B)/_j C, C)^j)^i \Rightarrow B}}{((A/_j C, (A\backslash_i B)/_j C)^i, C)^j \Rightarrow B} MC}{(A/_j C, (A\backslash_i B)/_j C)^i \Rightarrow B/_j C} /_j R$$

4.2. *Grammatical composition: Unary operations*

The language of binary multiplicative connectives is designed to talk about forms of linguistic composition where two resources are put together. It is not difficult to see how one could generalize the type language to n-ary multiplicatives, and interpret families of n-ary residuated connectives with respect to a composition relation of arity $n + 1$, in the setting of frame semantics. Writing $f_\bullet(A_1, \ldots, A_n)$ for an n-ary product and $f^i_\to(A_1, \ldots, A_n)$ for the i-th place residual, the basic residuation laws take the form shown in (24). For arities $2 \leqslant n$, an n-ary product connective would be interpreted with respect to a form of grammatical composition relating n 'component' resources to their 'fusion'. Such generalizations have been studied in a logical setting in (Dunn, 1993), and in the context of categorial grammar logics in (Buszkowski, 1984; Moortgat and Oehrle, 1993).

(24) $$f_\bullet(A_1, \ldots, A_n) \to B \text{ iff } A_i \to f^i_\to(A_1, \ldots, A_{i-1}, B, A_{i+1}, \ldots, A_n).$$

In this section we present the logic of *unary* residuated operations in the categorial type language. The need for unary complementation of the familiar binary vocabulary has long been felt: for arguments see Bach (1988), or Schmerling (1983), who relates the discussion to the 'item-and-arrangement' versus 'item-and-process' views on structuring linguistic resources. As remarked above, unary connectives were introduced in the type-logical discussion around 1990 in (Morrill, 1990a), and subsequent work of a number of Edinburgh researchers. A representative collection of papers can be found in (Barry and Morrill, 1990).

Our aim in this section is to systematize this area of research by developing a general framework that will naturally accommodate the various proposals for unary operators while at the same time providing more fine-grained notions of resource control. We extend the language of binary multiplicatives with a pair of unary residual operators $\Diamond$, $\Box^\downarrow$. Parallel to our treatment of the binary multiplicatives Section 2, we start from the most discriminating system, i.e. the pure logic of residuation for $\Diamond$, $\Box^\downarrow$. By gradually adding structural postulates, we obtain versions of these unary operators with a coarser resource management regime. We develop the model-theoretic and proof-theoretic technicalities in Section 4.2.1, drawing heavily on Moortgat (1995). In Section 4.2.2, we discuss the linguistic motivation for the various resource management options. Finally, in Section 4.2.3, we present a general theory of structural control in terms of embedding theorems connecting resource management regimes.

4.2.1. Unary connectives: logic and structure

Consider first the pure logic of residuation for a pair of unary type-forming operators $\Diamond$, $\Box^\downarrow$.

DEFINITION 4.8. Unary multiplicative connectives: the pure logic of residuation. Interpretation clauses. Residuation laws. Note that the interpretation of $\Diamond$ and $\Box^\downarrow$ 'moves' in opposite directions along the R^2 accessibility relation. (The downarrow on the universal operator is there to highlight this fact.)

$$v(\Diamond A) = \{x \mid \exists y(Rxy \wedge y \in v(A)\},$$
$$v(\Box^\downarrow A) = \{x \mid \forall y(Ryx \Rightarrow y \in v(A)\},$$

$$\Diamond A \to B \quad \text{iff} \quad A \to \Box^\downarrow B.$$

Completeness. The completeness result of Proposition 2.3 for the binary multiplicative language extends unproblematically to the language enriched with $\Diamond, \Box^{\downarrow}$. We interpret now with respect to mixed frames, where a binary and a ternary composition relation live together, and consider models $\mathcal{M} = \langle W, R^2, R^3, v\rangle$. In the formula-based canonical model construction of Definition 2.4, one defines $R^2(A, B)$ iff $\vdash A \to \Diamond B$. The Truth Lemma has to be checked for the new compound formulae $\Diamond A$, $\Box^{\downarrow}A$. The direction that requires a little thinking is dealt with below.

($\Diamond$) Assume $A \in v(\Diamond B)$. We have to show $\vdash A \to \Diamond B$. $A \in v(\Diamond B)$ implies $\exists A'$ such that R^2AA' and $A' \in v(B)$. By induction hypothesis, $\vdash A' \to B$. By Isotonicity for $\Diamond$ (cf. (26) below) this implies $\vdash \Diamond A' \to \Diamond B$. We have $\vdash A \to \Diamond A'$ by (Definition R^2) in the canonical frame. By Transitivity, $\vdash A \to \Diamond B$.

($\Box^{\downarrow}$) Assume $A \in v(\Box^{\downarrow}B)$. We have to show $\vdash A \to \Box^{\downarrow}B$. $A \in v(\Box^{\downarrow}B)$ implies that $\forall A'$ such that $R^2A'A$ we have $A' \in v(B)$. Let A' be $\Diamond A$. $R^2A'A$ holds in the canonical frame since $\vdash \Diamond A \to \Diamond A$. By induction hypothesis we have $\vdash A' \to B$, i.e. $\vdash \Diamond A \to B$. By Residuation this gives $\vdash A \to \Box^{\downarrow}B$.

Figure 1 may clarify the relation between the unary and the binary residuated pairs of connectives. Notice that if one were interpreting R^2 as temporal priority, $\Diamond$ and $\Box^{\downarrow}$ would be interpreted as past possibility and future necessity, respectively. But in the grammatical application, R^2 just like R^3 is to be interpreted in terms of structural composition. Where a ternary configuration $(xyz) \in R^3$ abstractly represents putting together the components y and z into a structured configuration x in the manner indicated by R^3, a binary configuration $(xy) \in R^2$ can be seen as the construction of the sign x out of a single structural component y in terms of the building instructions referred to by R^2. (An 'additive' alternative to the 'multiplicative' view on unary operators presented here, will be presented in Definition 5.6.)

In our discussion of the binary vocabulary in Section 2, we pointed out that one can characterize $/$, $\bullet$, $\backslash$ as a residuated family either in terms of the basic law RES of Definition 2.2, or in terms of the (Co-)Application and Monotonicity laws of Proposition 2.18. Similarly, for the unary connectives, we have the equivalent Lambek-style and Došen-style axiomatizations of Definition 4.9.

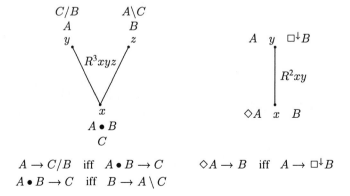

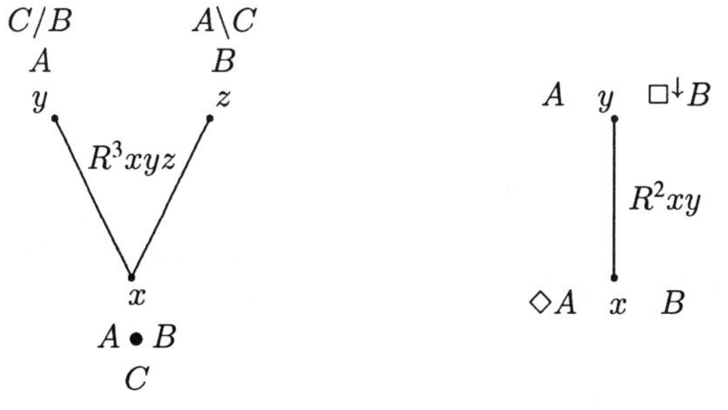

$A \to C/B$ iff $A \bullet B \to C$ $\qquad$ $\Diamond A \to B$ iff $A \to \Box^{\downarrow}B$

$A \bullet B \to C$ iff $B \to A \backslash C$

Fig. 1. Kripke graphs: binary and unary multiplicatives.

DEFINITION 4.9. Unary connectives: alternative combinator presentations. (†) Lambek-style in terms of Residuation. (‡) Došen-style in terms of the adjointness laws for the compositions $\Diamond\Box^{\downarrow}$, $\Box^{\downarrow}\Diamond$, and Isotonicity.

$$(\dagger)\quad \frac{f:\Diamond A\to B}{\mu(f):A\to\Box^{\downarrow}B}\qquad \frac{g:A\to\Box^{\downarrow}B}{\mu^{-1}(g):\Diamond A\to B}$$

$$(\ddagger)\quad \begin{array}{ll}\varepsilon_A: & \Diamond\Box^{\downarrow}A\to A\\ \eta_A: & A\to\Box^{\downarrow}\Diamond A\end{array}\qquad \frac{f:A\to B}{(f)^{\diamond}:\Diamond A\to\Diamond B}\qquad \frac{f:A\to B}{(f)^{\Box^{\downarrow}}:\Box^{\downarrow}A\to\Box^{\downarrow}B}$$

We take the Lambek-style presentation as our starting point here, and show for the extended system how from the residuation inferences μ,μ^{-1} we obtain the alternative axiomatization in terms of Isotonicity and the inequalities for the compositions $\Diamond\Box^{\downarrow}$ and $\Box^{\downarrow}\Diamond$ (Term decoration for the right column left to the reader).

$$(25)\qquad \frac{1_{\Box^{\downarrow}A}:\Box^{\downarrow}A\to\Box^{\downarrow}A}{\mu^{-1}(1_{\Box^{\downarrow}A}):\Diamond\Box^{\downarrow}A\to A}\qquad \frac{\Diamond A\to\Diamond A}{A\to\Box^{\downarrow}\Diamond A}$$

$$(26)\qquad \frac{\dfrac{f:A\to B\quad \dfrac{1_{\Diamond B}:\Diamond B\to\Diamond B}{\mu(1_{\Diamond B}):B\to\Box^{\downarrow}\Diamond B}}{\mu(1_{\Diamond B})\circ f:A\to\Box^{\downarrow}\Diamond B}}{\mu^{-1}(\mu(1_{\Diamond B})\circ f):\Diamond A\to\Diamond B}\qquad \frac{\dfrac{\dfrac{\Box^{\downarrow}A\to\Box^{\downarrow}A}{\Diamond\Box^{\downarrow}A\to A}\quad A\to B}{\Diamond\Box^{\downarrow}A\to B}}{\Box^{\downarrow}A\to\Box^{\downarrow}B}$$

Gentzen calculus. Following the agenda set out in Section 2 for the binary connectives, we introduce Gentzen sequent rules for the connectives $\Diamond$, $\Box^{\downarrow}$. Corresponding to the formula language $\mathcal{F}$ of (28) we have a language of Gentzen terms $\mathcal{S}$ for structured configurations of formulae. Gentzenization for the extended type language requires an n-ary structural operator for every family of n-ary logical operators: binary $(\cdot,\cdot)$ for the family $/$, $\bullet$, $\backslash$, and unary $(\cdot)^{\diamond}$ for the family $\Diamond$, $\Box^{\downarrow}$.

$$(27)\qquad \begin{array}{l}\mathcal{F}::=\mathcal{A}\mid\mathcal{F}/\mathcal{F}\mid\mathcal{F}\bullet\mathcal{F}\mid\mathcal{F}\backslash\mathcal{F}\mid\Diamond\mathcal{F}\mid\Box^{\downarrow}\mathcal{F},\\ \mathcal{S}::=\mathcal{F}\mid(\mathcal{S},\mathcal{S})\mid(\mathcal{S})^{\diamond}.\end{array}$$

DEFINITION 4.10. Unary connectives: Gentzen rules. Belnap-style antecedent punctuation, with *unary* structural connective $(\cdot)^{\diamond}$ matching the unary logical connective $\Diamond$.

$$\frac{\Gamma\Rightarrow A}{(\Gamma)^{\diamond}\Rightarrow\Diamond A}\,\Diamond R\qquad \frac{\Gamma[(A)^{\diamond}]\Rightarrow B}{\Gamma[\Diamond A]\Rightarrow B}\,\Diamond L$$

$$\frac{(\Gamma)^{\diamond}\Rightarrow A}{\Gamma\Rightarrow\Box^{\downarrow}A}\,\Box^{\downarrow}R\qquad \frac{\Gamma[A]\Rightarrow B}{\Gamma[(\Box^{\downarrow}A)^{\diamond}]\Rightarrow B}\,\Box^{\downarrow}L$$

As shown in (Moortgat, 1995), the Gentzen presentation is equivalent to the axiomatization of Definition 4.9, and it allows Cut Elimination with its pleasant corollaries: decidability and the subformula property.

Unary connectives: Structural postulates. Completeness for the pure logic of residuation for the unary family $\diamond, \Box^{\downarrow}$ does not depend on semantic restrictions on the R^2 composition relation. In addition to the fixed 'logical' part of the $\diamond$, $\Box^{\downarrow}$ connectives, we can consider various structural resource management options for the unary family $\diamond$, $\Box^{\downarrow}$ and its binary accessibility relation R^2, and for the mixed R^2, R^3 system.

The structural postulates in Definition 4.11 constrain R^2 to be transitive (4), or reflexive (T). Communication between R^2 and R^3 can be established via the 'percolation' principles $K(1,2)$. The strong distributivity postulate K distributes unary $\diamond$ over both components of a binary $\bullet$. The more constrained weak distributivity postulates $K1$, $K2$ make $\diamond$ select the left or right subtype of a product. The combination of the options $KT4$ gives an $S4$ modality with the logical rules of use and proof of the Linear Logic exponential '!'.

Observe that the postulates have the required Weak Sahlqvist form for the extended completeness result of Proposition 2.7. In (Moortgat, 1995), the Cut Elimination result for the pure residuation logic of Definition 4.10 is extended to cover the structural options of Definition 4.11. In a multimodal setting, one can further enhance the linguistic expressivity by combining different composition modes R^2_j for $\langle j \rangle, [j]^{\downarrow}$ in one logic. The multimodal generalization is completely standard.

DEFINITION 4.11. Unary connectives: resource management options. Structural postulates, frame constraints, Gentzen rules. (For $\Box^{\downarrow}$ duals of these postulates: replace $\diamond$ by $\Box^{\downarrow}$ and reverse the arrow.)

4:	$\diamond\diamond A \to \diamond A$	$(Rxy \;\&\; Ryz) \Rightarrow Rxz,$
T:	$A \to \diamond A$	$Rxx,$
$K1$:	$\diamond(A \bullet B) \to \diamond A \bullet B$	$(Rwx \;\&\; Rxyz) \Rightarrow \exists y'(Ry'y \;\&\; Rwy'z),$
$K2$:	$\diamond(A \bullet B) \to A \bullet \diamond B$	$(Rwx \;\&\; Rxyz) \Rightarrow \exists z'(Rz'z \;\&\; Rwyz'),$
K:	$\diamond(A \bullet B) \to \diamond A \bullet \diamond B$	$(Rwx \;\&\; Rxyz) \Rightarrow \exists y'\exists z'(Ry'y \;\&\; Rz'z \;\&\; Rwy'z').$

$$\frac{\Gamma[(\Delta)^{\diamond}] \Rightarrow A}{\Gamma[((\Delta)^{\diamond})^{\diamond}] \Rightarrow A}\,4 \qquad \frac{\Gamma[(\Delta)^{\diamond}] \Rightarrow A}{\Gamma[\Delta] \Rightarrow A}\,T$$

$$\frac{\Gamma[((\Delta_1)^{\diamond}, \Delta_2)] \Rightarrow A}{\Gamma[((\Delta_1, \Delta_2))^{\diamond}] \Rightarrow A}\,K1 \qquad \frac{\Gamma[((\Delta_1)^{\diamond}, (\Delta_2)^{\diamond})] \Rightarrow A}{\Gamma[((\Delta_1, \Delta_2))^{\diamond}] \Rightarrow A}\,K \qquad \frac{\Gamma[(\Delta_1, (\Delta_2)^{\diamond})] \Rightarrow A}{\Gamma[((\Delta_1, \Delta_2))^{\diamond}] \Rightarrow A}\,K2$$

S4: Compilation of structural rules. We saw in Definition 2.13 that in the presence of Associativity for $\bullet$, we have a sugared Gentzen presentation where the structural rule is compiled away, and the binary sequent punctuation $(\cdot, \cdot)$ omitted. Analogously, for $\Box^{\downarrow}$ with the combination $KT4$ (i.e. $S4$), we have a sugared version of the Gentzen rules, where the $KT4$ structural rules are compiled away, so that the unary $(\cdot)^{\diamond}$ punctuation can be omitted. In the sugared version, we recognize the rules of use and proof for the domain modalities of Morrill (1990a), Hepple (1990).

DEFINITION 4.12. Sugared presentation of $KT4$ modalities: compiling out the $(\cdot)^\diamond$ structural punctuation. We write $\Box^\downarrow\Gamma$, $(\Box^\downarrow)^\diamond\Gamma$, $(\Box^\downarrow\Box^\downarrow)^\diamond\Gamma$ for a term Γ of which the (pre)terminal subterms are all of the form $\Box^\downarrow A$, $(\Box^\downarrow A)^\diamond$, $(\Box^\downarrow\Box^\downarrow A)^\diamond$, respectively. The 4(Cut) step is a series of replacements (read bottom-up) of terminal $\Box^\downarrow A$ by $\Box^\downarrow\Box^\downarrow A$ via Cuts depending on 4.

$$\dfrac{\dfrac{\Gamma[A] \Rightarrow B}{\Gamma[(\Box^\downarrow A)^\diamond] \Rightarrow B}\ \Box^\downarrow L}{\Gamma[\Box^\downarrow A] \Rightarrow B}\ T \quad \rightsquigarrow \quad \dfrac{\Gamma[A] \Rightarrow B}{\Gamma[\Box^\downarrow A] \Rightarrow B}\ \Box^\downarrow L(S4)$$

$$\dfrac{\dfrac{\dfrac{\dfrac{\Box^\downarrow\Gamma \Rightarrow A}{(\Box^\downarrow\Box^\downarrow)^\diamond\Gamma \Rightarrow A}\ \Box^\downarrow L}{(\Box^\downarrow)^\diamond\Gamma \Rightarrow A}\ 4\,(\mathrm{Cut})}{(\Box^\downarrow\Gamma)^\diamond \Rightarrow A}\ K}{\Box^\downarrow\Gamma \Rightarrow \Box^\downarrow A}\ \Box^\downarrow R \quad \rightsquigarrow \quad \dfrac{\Box^\downarrow\Gamma \Rightarrow A}{\Box^\downarrow\Gamma \Rightarrow \Box^\downarrow A}\ \Box^\downarrow R(S4)$$

Situating unary operators. The above analysis of the unary vocabulary in its logical and structural components provides us with a tool to evaluate existing proposals for unary operators. In doing so, we follow the methodological 'minimality' principle adopted above in the discussion of the binary vocabulary, i.e. we try to pinpoint exactly which assumptions about the composition relation are necessary to achieve a certain grammatical effect.

At one end of the spectrum, the proposals that come closest to the pure logic of residuation for $\diamond, \Box^\downarrow$ are the 'bracket' operators of Morrill (1994a, 1995a). On the semantic level, the bracket operators are given an algebraic interpretation which, in the context of frame semantics, would amount to a functionality requirement for the accessibility relation R^2. The linguistic applications of the bracket operators as markers of locality domains can be recast straightforwardly in terms of the more discriminating pure residuation logic for $\diamond, \Box^\downarrow$ for which a sound and complete logic is available, imposing no functionality constraints on R^2.

At the other end of the spectrum, we find the domain modalities of Morrill (1990a), Hepple (1990), universal $\Box$ operators which assume the full set of postulates $KT4$, i.e. $S4$. Adding modally controlled structural rules, we obtain the structural modalities of Barry, Hepple, Leslie and Morrill (1991), Morrill (1994a). Like the exponentials of Linear Logic, the structural modalities license controlled access to resource management options that are not freely available. As we will see in Section 5, the $S4$ logical rules are *incomplete* with respect to the intended subalgebra semantics for these connectives. Again, we can scrutinize the $S4$ assumptions, and see whether a more delicate resource management regime can achieve the same effects.

In the framework presented here, where we consider a residuated *pair* of modalities $\diamond, \Box^\downarrow$ rather than a single modal operator $\Box$, we can *simulate* the T and 4 postulates proof-theoretically, without making Reflexivity or Transitivity assumptions about the R^2 composition relation. With the translation of Definition 4.13 the images of the T and 4 postulates for $\Box$ become valid type transitions in the pure residuation system for $\Diamond, \Box^{\downarrow}$, as the reader can check. For modally controlled structural rules, Definition 4.14 gives restricted versions of the global rules keyed to $\Diamond$ contexts; for communication between the unary and binary multiplicatives, one can rely on the K distributivity principles.

DEFINITION 4.13. Simulating T and 4 via compilation $(\Box A)^\sharp = \Diamond\Box^{\downarrow}(A)^\sharp$.

$$\begin{array}{llcl} T: & \Box A \to A & \rightsquigarrow & \Diamond\Box^{\downarrow}A \to A, \\ 4: & \Box A \to \Box\Box A & \rightsquigarrow & \Diamond\Box^{\downarrow}A \to \Diamond\Box^{\downarrow}\Diamond\Box^{\downarrow}A. \end{array}$$

DEFINITION 4.14. Modally restricted structural options: Commutativity ($P_\diamond$), Associativity ($A_\diamond$). Structural postulates, Gentzen rules. The side condition (†) requires one of the A_i (Δ_i) to be of the form $\Diamond A$ ($(\Delta)^\diamond$).

$$(P_\diamond): \Diamond A \bullet B \to B \bullet \Diamond A \qquad (A_\diamond): (A_1 \bullet A_2) \bullet A_3 \leftrightarrow A_1 \bullet (A_2 \bullet A_3)(\dagger)$$

$$\frac{\Gamma[((\Delta_2)^\diamond, \Delta_1)] \Rightarrow A}{\Gamma[(\Delta_1, (\Delta_2)^\diamond)] \Rightarrow A}(P_\diamond) \qquad (\dagger)\frac{\Gamma[((\Delta_1, \Delta_2), \Delta_3)] \Rightarrow A}{\Gamma[(\Delta_1, (\Delta_2, \Delta_3))] \Rightarrow A}(A_\diamond)$$

Term assignment: Unary connectives. To close this section, we present the term assignment for the unary connectives in an abstract format, with constructor/destructor operations in the term language matching rules of use and proof.

DEFINITION 4.15. Syntax of typed lambda terms: clauses for $\Diamond, \Box^{\downarrow}$. Destructors ${}^{\cup}\cdot$ and ${}^{\vee}\cdot$, corresponding to rules of use for $\Diamond$ and $\Box^{\downarrow}$. Constructors ${}^{\cap}\cdot$ and ${}^{\wedge}\cdot$, for rules of proof. Compare Definition 3.1 for the binary vocabulary.

$$\mathcal{T}^A ::= \cdots \mid {}^{\cup}(\mathcal{T}^{\Diamond A}) \mid {}^{\vee}(\mathcal{T}^{\Box^{\downarrow}A}),$$
$$\mathcal{T}^{\Diamond A} ::= {}^{\cap}(\mathcal{T}^A), \qquad \mathcal{T}^{\Box^{\downarrow}A} ::= {}^{\wedge}(\mathcal{T}^A).$$

DEFINITION 4.16. Term assignment. The $\Diamond, \Box^{\downarrow}$ cases.

$$\frac{\Gamma \Rightarrow t : A}{(\Gamma)^\diamond \Rightarrow {}^{\cap}t : \Diamond A}\Diamond R \qquad \frac{\Gamma[(y : A)^\diamond] \Rightarrow t : B}{\Gamma[x : \Diamond A] \Rightarrow t[{}^{\cup}x/y] : B}\Diamond L$$

$$\frac{(\Gamma)^\diamond \Rightarrow t : A}{\Gamma \Rightarrow {}^{\wedge}t : \Box^{\downarrow}A}\Box^{\downarrow}R \qquad \frac{\Gamma[y : A] \Rightarrow t : B}{\Gamma[(x : \Box^{\downarrow}A)^\diamond] \Rightarrow t[{}^{\vee}x/y] : B}\Box^{\downarrow}L$$

DEFINITION 4.17. Term equations and their Gentzen proof-theoretic reflexes. Compare the binary case in Definition 3.5.

$$^{\cup}(^{\cap}t) = t \;\rightsquigarrow\; \text{principal cut on } \Diamond A, \qquad ^{\vee}(^{\wedge}t) = t \;\rightsquigarrow\; \text{principal cut on } \Box^{\downarrow}A,$$
$$^{\cap}(^{\cup}t) = t \;\rightsquigarrow\; \text{non-atomic axiom } \Diamond A, \qquad ^{\wedge}(^{\vee}t) = t \;\rightsquigarrow\; \text{non-atomic axiom } \Box^{\downarrow}A.$$

Concrete realizations of the abstract term assignment schema will depend on the application. For an example, we refer to the type-logical implementation of Montague-style intensional semantics driven from an $S4$ universal modality in (Morrill, 1990a). Let us write the 'intensionality' type-forming operator as $\Box$. We interpret formulas $\Box A$ as functions from indices to the denotata of formulas A. Term assignment for the rules of use and proof for $\Box$ can then be given in terms of Montague's 'cup' and 'cap' operations, respectively. Cf. Chapter 1.

$$(28) \qquad \frac{\Box\Gamma \Rightarrow t : A}{\Box\Gamma \Rightarrow {}^{\wedge}t : \Box A}\,\Box R \qquad \frac{\Gamma, x : A, \Gamma' \Rightarrow t : B}{\Gamma, y : \Box A, \Gamma' \Rightarrow t[{}^{\vee}y/x] : B}\,\Box L$$

For another application, we refer to the work on information packaging in (Hendriks, 1994), where the term assignment for $\Diamond$ realizes the prosodic and pragmatic structuring of the text in terms of stress and given/new distinctions.

4.2.2. Applications: Imposing constraints, structural relaxation

One can develop two perspectives on controlling resource management, depending on the direction of communication. On the one hand, one would like to have control devices to license limited access to a more liberal resource management regime from within a system with a higher sense of structural discrimination. On the other hand, one would like to impose constraints on resource management in systems where such constraints are lacking by default.

Licensing structural relaxation. For the licensing type of communication, consider type assignment $r/(s/np)$ to relative pronouns like *that* in the sentences below.

(the book) that Kazimierz wrote,

(the book) that Kazimierz wrote yesterday,

$$(29) \qquad \begin{array}{rl} \mathbf{L} \vdash & r/(s/np), np, (np\backslash s)/np \Rightarrow r, \\ \mathbf{L} \nvdash & r/(s/np), np, (np\backslash s)/np, s\backslash s \Rightarrow r, \\ \mathbf{NL} \nvdash & (r/(s/np), (np, (np\backslash s)/np)) \Rightarrow r. \end{array}$$

Suppose first we are dealing with the associative regime of **L**. The first example is derivable, the second is not because the hypothetical np assumption in the subderivation 'Kazimierz wrote yesterday np' is not in the required position adjacent to the verb 'wrote'. We can refine the assignment to the relative pronoun to $r/(s/\Box_c np)$, where $\Box_c np$ is a noun phrase resource which has access to Permutation in virtue of its modal decoration. Similarly, if we change the default regime to **NL**, the first example already fails on the assignment $r/(s/np)$ with the indicated constituent bracketing: although the hypothetical np in the subcomputation '((Kazimierz wrote) np)' finds itself in the right position with respect to linear order requirements, it cannot satisfy the direct object role for 'wrote' being outside the clausal boundaries. A refined assignment $r/(s/\Box_a np)$ here could license the marked $\Box_a np$ a controlled access to the structural rule of Associativity which is absent in the **NL** default regime.

As remarked above, cases like these have been handled in terms of $S4$-style structural modalities in (Barry and Morrill, 1990; Morrill, 1994a). In (30), we illustrate the deconstruction of $\Box$ as $\Diamond\Box^{\downarrow}$ with the derivation of controlled rebracketing within **NL**.

(30)
$$\dfrac{\dfrac{\dfrac{\dfrac{\dfrac{\&c}{(np,(tv,np)) \Rightarrow s}}{(np,(tv,(\Box_a^{\downarrow} np)^{\diamond})) \Rightarrow s}\ \Box^{\downarrow}L}{((np,tv),(\Box_a^{\downarrow} np)^{\diamond}) \Rightarrow s}\ A_{\diamond}}{((np,tv),\Diamond_a \Box_a^{\downarrow} np) \Rightarrow s}\ \Diamond L}{(np,tv) \Rightarrow s/\Diamond_a \Box_a^{\downarrow} np}\ /R$$

Imposing structural constraints. For the other direction of communication, we return to the violations of the Coordinate Structure Constraint, discussed in Section 2 in connection with the overgeneration of **L**. Consider the relative clauses of Example 4.18. With the instantiation $X = s/np$ for the polymorphic conjunction particle, we can derive the (a) example. But, given Associativity and an instantiation $X = s$, nothing blocks the derivation of the ungrammatical (b) example.

EXAMPLE 4.18. Lexical projection of island constraints (Morrill, 1994a, 1995a).

(a) (the logician) whom Gottlob admired and Kazimierz detested,

$\mathbf{L} \vdash \quad r/(s/np), np, tv, (X\backslash X)/X, np, tv \Rightarrow r \quad (X = s/np),$

$\mathbf{L}\Diamond \vdash \quad r/(s/np), (np, tv, (X\backslash\Box^{\downarrow}X)/X, np, tv)^{\diamond} \Rightarrow r,$

(b) *(the logician) whom Gottlob admired Jim and Kazimierz detested,

$\mathbf{L} \vdash \quad r/(s/np), np, tv, np, (X\backslash X)/X, np, tv \Rightarrow r \quad (X = s),$

$\mathbf{L}\Diamond \nvdash \quad r/(s/np), (np, tv, np, (X\backslash\Box^{\downarrow}X)/X, np, tv)^{\diamond} \Rightarrow r.$

In (Morrill, 1994a, 1995a) it is shown that the coordinate structure domain can be lexically projected from a modal refinement of the assignment to 'and': $(X\backslash\Box^{\downarrow}X)/X$. (We recast the analysis in terms of the pure residuation logic for $\Diamond, \Box^{\downarrow}$.) The refined assignment allows the conjunction to combine with the left and right conjuncts in the associative mode. The resulting coordinate structure is of type $\Box^{\downarrow}X$. To eliminate the $\Box^{\downarrow}$ connective, we have to close off the coordinate structure with $\Diamond$ (or the corresponding structural operator $(\cdot)^{\diamond}$ in the Gentzen presentation) – recall the basic reduction $\Diamond\Box^{\downarrow}X \to X$. The Across-the-Board case of extraction (4.18a) works out fine, the island violation (4.18b) fails because the hypothetical gap np assumption finds itself outside the scope of the $(\cdot)^{\diamond}$ operator.

In (Versmissen, 1996), this use of modal decoration is generalized into a type-logical formulation of the theory of word-order domains of Reape (1989). The control operators $\Diamond, \Box^{\downarrow}$ provide a fully general vocabulary for projection and erasure of domains of locality, according to the following scheme distinguishing the antecedent (resource) versus succedent (goal) effects of $\Diamond, \Box^{\downarrow}$ decoration.

(31)

	RESOURCE	GOAL
$\Diamond$	domain-erasure	domain-projection
$\Box^{\downarrow}$	domain-projection	domain-erasure

Modalities as domains of locality. In (Morrill, 1990a), locality domains, in the sense of semantic intensionality, are characterized in terms of a uniform $S4$ $\Box$ decoration for the resources that make up a domain, cf. (28). Hepple (1990), dropping the semantic component of this proposal, uses the $\Box$ decoration to capture syntactic boundary effects. These applications are instructive because they crucially rely on the rule of *proof* for the $S4$ universal modality: as we have seen in Definition 4.12, this rule insists that all assumptions on which a $\Box A$ formula depends are themselves $\Box$ decorated.

Consider the constraint of clause-boundedness that governs the use of the English reflexive pronouns. In Example 3.12 we discussed an **L** type-assignment $((np\backslash s)/np)\backslash(np\backslash s)$ for 'himself' with meaning recipe $\lambda x\lambda y.x(y)(y)$. Within **L**, (a), (b) and (c) are all derivable: this system, because of the global availability of associativity, cannot discriminate between a lexical or complex clause-internal expression of type $((np\backslash s)/np)$ and a complex expression of that type which has been composed across clausal boundaries.

(32)
(a) David <u>admires</u> himself $\mathbf{L} \vdash \quad (np\backslash s)/np \Rightarrow (np\backslash s)/np,$
(b) David <u>cares for</u> himself $\mathbf{L} \vdash \quad (np\backslash s)/pp, pp/np \Rightarrow (np\backslash s)/np,$
(c) *David <u>thinks Emmy admires</u> himself $\mathbf{L} \vdash \quad (np\backslash s)/s, np, (np\backslash s)/np \Rightarrow (np\backslash s)/np.$

Within $\mathbf{L} + \Box$, appropriate modalization provides lexical control to make (a) and (b) derivable while ruling out (c). In moving from **L** to $\mathbf{L} + \Box$ lexical type assignments, one prefixes the original **L** lexical assignments with a $\Box$ operator, and further decorates with a $\Box$ every argument subtype that constitutes a locality domain. The effect of such modalization for the lexical resources of (32c) is shown in Example 4.19.

EXAMPLE 4.19. Blocking locality violations via $S4$ $\Box$ decoration (Morrill, 1990a, Hepple, 1990). The assignment to the verb 'think' marks its clausal complement as a locality domain. The derivation for the non-local reading (32c) fails, because the hypothetical direct object np assumption is not decorated with $\Box$, blocking application of the $[\Box R]$ inference, which requires all the antecedent assumptions on which it depends to be modally marked.

$$\dfrac{\dfrac{\dfrac{\dfrac{\dfrac{\dfrac{\dfrac{\text{FAIL}}{\Box np, \Box((np\backslash s)/np), np \Rightarrow \Box s} \quad \dfrac{\&c}{np, np\backslash s \Rightarrow s}}{np, (np\backslash s)/\Box s, \Box np, \Box((np\backslash s)/np), np \Rightarrow s}\,/L}{np, \Box((np\backslash s)/\Box s), \Box np, \Box((np\backslash s)/np), np \Rightarrow s}\,\Box L}{\Box((np\backslash s)/\Box s), \Box np, \Box((np\backslash s)/np) \Rightarrow (np\backslash s)/np}\,/R,\backslash R \quad \dfrac{\dfrac{\&c}{np, np\backslash s \Rightarrow s}}{\Box np, np\backslash s \Rightarrow s}\,\Box L}{\Box np, \Box((np\backslash s)/\Box s), \Box np, \Box((np\backslash s)/np), ((np \backslash s)/np) \backslash (np \backslash s) \Rightarrow s}\,\backslash L}{\Box np, \Box((np\backslash s)/\Box s), \Box np, \Box((np\backslash s)/np), \Box((np \backslash s)/np) \backslash (np \backslash s) \Rightarrow s}\,\Box L}{\Box np, \Box((np\backslash s)/\Box s), \Box np, \Box((np\backslash s)/np), \Box((np \backslash s)/np) \backslash (np \backslash s) \Rightarrow \Box s}\,\Box R$$

*David thinks Emmy loves himself.

A more elaborate account of syntactic island constraints is offered in (Hepple, 1990, 1992) in terms of a *polymodal* system with domain modalities $\{\Box_j\}_{j\in J}$. The domain modalities have an order defined on them, which allows for the characterization of syntactic boundaries of different strength. Island constraints are lexically controlled through the interplay of type-assignment to complement taking functors and 'extractable' elements. Take a relative pronoun with type $\Box((n\backslash n)/(s/\Box_i np))$ and a verb subcategorizing for a clausal complement, $\Box((np\backslash s)/\Box_j s)$. The relative pronoun will be extractable from the $\Box_j s$ embedded clause provided $\Box_i \preceq \Box_j$.

We have presented the analysis of locality domains in terms of the original $S4$ decoration of Hepple (1990). Decomposing the $S4$ account into its structural components, we see that the checking of uniform antecedent $\Box$ marking is taken care of by the K distributivity principle of Definition 4.11. In fact, with a slightly adapted modalization strategy which decorates the assignment to 'think' as $\Box^{\downarrow}(np\backslash s)/\Box^{\downarrow}s$, one can recast the above analysis in terms of K and the $\Diamond$, $\Box^{\downarrow}$ residuation logic, as the reader can check. The same combination of RES$\Diamond, \Box^{\downarrow} + K$ lies at the basis of an analysis of French clitic pronouns in (Kraak, 1995), and of the type-logical account of Linear Precedence constraints in (Versmissen, 1996).

4.2.3. Resource control: Faithful embeddings

In Section 4.2.2 we have presented analyses of a number of linguistic phenomena which rely on modally decorated type-assignments to obtain structural relaxation, or to impose structural constraints. These applications suggest a more fundamental logical question: Can one provide a *general* theory of resource control in terms of the unary vocabulary? The embedding theorems of Kurtonina and Moortgat (1995) answer this question in the affirmative: they show that the $\Diamond, \Box^{\downarrow}$ connectives provide a theory of systematic communication between the type logics of Figure 2. Below, we discuss the strategies for modal decoration realizing the embeddings, and reflect on general logical and linguistic aspects of this approach.

Figure 2 displays the resource logics one obtains in terms of the structural parameters of precedence (word-order), dominance (constituent structure) and dependency. The systems

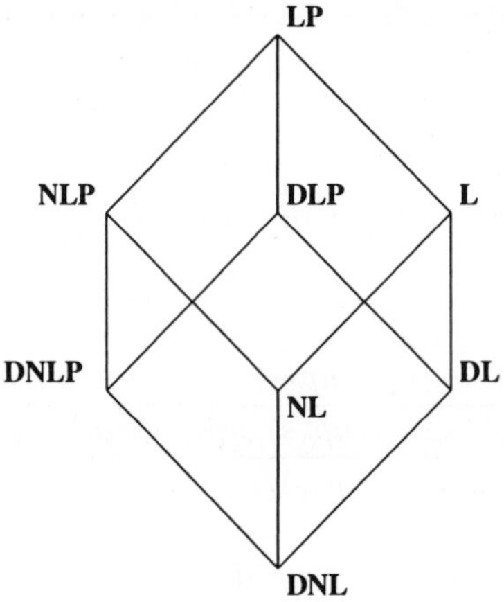

Fig. 2. Resource-sensitive logics: precedence, dominance, dependency.

occupying the upper plane of Figure 2 were the subject of Section 2. As we have seen in our discussion of Definition 4.2 each of these systems has a dependency variant, where the product is split up into a left-headed $\bullet_l$ and a right-headed $\bullet_r$ version.

Consider a pair of logics $\mathcal{L}_0, \mathcal{L}_1$ where $\mathcal{L}_0$ is a 'southern' neighbor of $\mathcal{L}_1$. Let us write $\mathcal{L}\diamond$ for the system $\mathcal{L}$ extended with the unary operators $\diamond, \Box^{\downarrow}$ with their minimal residuation logic. For the 12 edges of the cube of Figure 2, one can define *embedding translations* $(\cdot)^\flat : \mathcal{F}(\mathcal{L}_0) \mapsto \mathcal{F}(\mathcal{L}_1\diamond)$ which impose the structural discrimination of $\mathcal{L}_0$ in $\mathcal{L}_1$ with its more liberal resource management, and $(\cdot)^\sharp : \mathcal{F}(\mathcal{L}_1) \mapsto \mathcal{F}(\mathcal{L}_0\diamond)$ which license relaxation of structure sensitivity in $\mathcal{L}_0$ in such a way that one fully recovers the flexibility of the the coarser $\mathcal{L}_1$. The embedding translations decorate critical subformulae in the target logic with the operators $\diamond, \Box^{\downarrow}$. The translations are defined on the product $\bullet$ of the source logic: their action on the implicational formulas is fully determined by the residuation laws. For the $\cdot^\flat$ type of embedding, the modal decoration has the effect of blocking a structural rule that would be applicable otherwise. For the $\cdot^\sharp$ direction, the modal decoration gives access to a controlled version of a structural rule which is unavailable in its 'global' (non-decorated) version.

We illustrate the two-way structural control with the pair **NL** and **L**. Let us subscript the connectives in **NL** with 0 and those of **L** with 1. The embedding translations $\cdot^\flat$ and $\cdot^\sharp$ are given in Definition 4.20. For the two directions of communication, the same decoration schema can be used.

DEFINITION 4.20. Embedding translations $\cdot^\flat : \mathcal{F}(\mathbf{NL}) \mapsto \mathcal{F}(\mathbf{L}\diamond)$, and $\cdot^\sharp : \mathcal{F}(\mathbf{L}) \mapsto \mathcal{F}(\mathbf{NL}\diamond)$.

$$
\begin{aligned}
p^\flat &= p & p^\sharp &= p\\
(A \bullet_0 B)^\flat &= \diamond(A^\flat \bullet_1 B^\flat) & (A \bullet_1 B)^\sharp &= \diamond(A^\sharp \bullet_0 B^\sharp)\\
(A/_0 B)^\flat &= \Box^{\downarrow} A^\flat /_1 B^\flat & (A/_1 B)^\sharp &= \Box^{\downarrow} A^\sharp /_0 B^\sharp\\
(B\backslash_0 A)^\flat &= B^\flat \backslash_1 \Box^{\downarrow} A^\flat & (B\backslash_1 A)^\sharp &= B^\sharp \backslash_0 \Box^{\downarrow} A^\sharp
\end{aligned}
$$

The **L** system has an associative resource management which is insensitive to constituent bracketing. Extending **L** with the operators $\Diamond, \Box^{\downarrow}$ we can recover control over associativity in the sense of Proposition 4.21. A conjecture of embedding on the basis of $\cdot^{\flat}$ can be found in (Morrill, 1994b).

PROPOSITION 4.21. *Dominance structure: recovering control* (Kurtonina and Moortgat, 1995).

$$\mathbf{NL} \vdash A \to B \quad \textit{iff} \quad \mathbf{L}\Diamond \vdash A^{\flat} \to B^{\flat}.$$

Consider next the other direction of communication: suppose one wants to obtain the structural flexibility of **L** within the system **NL** with its rigid constituent sensitivity. This time, one achieves the desired embedding result by means of the embedding translation $\cdot^{\sharp}$ of Definition 4.20 together with a modally controlled version of the structural rule of Associativity, relativized to the critical $\Diamond$ decoration.

DEFINITION 4.22. Associativity. Global version (A) and its image under $(\cdot)^{\sharp}$, $(A_{\Diamond})$.

$$\begin{array}{ll} \mathcal{L}_1: & A \bullet_1 (B \bullet_1 C) \leftrightarrow (A \bullet_1 B) \bullet_1 C \quad (A) \\ \mathcal{L}_0: & \Diamond(A \bullet_0 \Diamond(B \bullet_0 C)) \leftrightarrow \Diamond(\Diamond(A \bullet_0 B) \bullet_0 C) \quad (A_{\Diamond}) \end{array}$$

PROPOSITION 4.23. *Dominance structure: licensing relaxation* (Kurtonina and Moortgat, 1995).

$$\mathbf{L} \vdash A \to B \quad \textit{iff} \quad \mathbf{NL}\Diamond + A_{\Diamond} \vdash A^{\sharp} \to B^{\sharp}.$$

The derivations of Example 4.24 illustrate the complementary strategies with the Geach rule, the characteristic theorem which differentiates **L** from **NL**. On the left, we try to derive the $\cdot^{\flat}$ translation of the Geach rule in $\mathbf{L}\Diamond$. The resource management regime is associative – still the derivation fails because of the structural $(\cdot)^{\Diamond}$ decoration which makes the C resource inaccessible for the functor $\Box^{\downarrow}B/_1C$. On the right one finds a successful derivation of the $\cdot^{\sharp}$ translation in $\mathbf{NL}\Diamond$. Although the resource management regime in this case does not allow free rebracketing, the $\Diamond$ decoration gives access to the modal version of the structural rule.

EXAMPLE 4.24. Imposing structural control versus relaxing structure sensitivity.

$$\dfrac{\dfrac{\dfrac{\dfrac{\dfrac{\text{FAIL}}{((((\Box^{\downarrow}A/_1B, \Box^{\downarrow}B/_1C)^1)^{\Diamond}, C)^1)^{\Diamond} \Rightarrow A}}{(((\Box^{\downarrow}A/_1B, \Box^{\downarrow}B/_1C)^1)^{\Diamond}, C)^1 \Rightarrow \Box^{\downarrow}A}\,\Box^{\downarrow}R}{((\Box^{\downarrow}A/_1B, \Box^{\downarrow}B/_1C)^1)^{\Diamond} \Rightarrow \Box^{\downarrow}A/_1C}\,/_1R}{(\Box^{\downarrow}A/_1B, \Box^{\downarrow}B/_1C)^1 \Rightarrow \Box^{\downarrow}(\Box^{\downarrow}A/_1C)}\,\Box^{\downarrow}R}{\Box^{\downarrow}A/_1B \Rightarrow \Box^{\downarrow}(\Box^{\downarrow}A/_1C)/_1(\Box^{\downarrow}B/_1C)}\,/_1R$$

$$\dfrac{\dfrac{\dfrac{\dfrac{\dfrac{\dfrac{\dfrac{C \Rightarrow C \quad \dfrac{B \Rightarrow B}{(\Box^{\downarrow}B)^{\Diamond} \Rightarrow B}\,\Box^{\downarrow}L}{((\Box^{\downarrow}B/_0C, C)^0)^{\Diamond} \Rightarrow B}\,/_0L \quad \dfrac{A \Rightarrow A}{(\Box^{\downarrow}A)^{\Diamond} \Rightarrow A}\,\Box^{\downarrow}L}{((\Box^{\downarrow}A/_0B, ((\Box^{\downarrow}B/_0C, C)^0)^{\Diamond})^0)^{\Diamond} \Rightarrow A}\,/_0L}{((((\Box^{\downarrow}A/_0B, \Box^{\downarrow}B/_0C)^0)^{\Diamond}, C)^0)^{\Diamond} \Rightarrow A}\,A_{\Diamond}}{(((\Box^{\downarrow}A/_0B, \Box^{\downarrow}B/_0C)^0)^{\Diamond}, C)^0 \Rightarrow \Box^{\downarrow}A}\,\Box^{\downarrow}R}{((\Box^{\downarrow}A/_0B, \Box^{\downarrow}B/_0C)^0)^{\Diamond} \Rightarrow \Box^{\downarrow}A/_0C}\,/_0R}{(\Box^{\downarrow}A/_0B, \Box^{\downarrow}B/_0C)^0 \Rightarrow \Box^{\downarrow}(\Box^{\downarrow}A/_0C)}\,\Box^{\downarrow}R}{\Box^{\downarrow}A/_0B \Rightarrow \Box^{\downarrow}(\Box^{\downarrow}A/_0C)/_0(\Box^{\downarrow}B/_0C)}\,/_0R$$

$$\mathbf{L}\Diamond \nvdash (A/_0B)^{\flat} \Rightarrow ((A/_0C)/_0(B/_0C))^{\flat}, \qquad \mathbf{NL}\Diamond + (A_{\Diamond}) \vdash (A/_1B)^{\sharp} \Rightarrow ((A/_1C)/_1(B/_1C))^{\sharp}.$$

Discussion. With respect to the theme of resource control it is instructive to contrast Linear Logic with the grammar logics discussed here. The theory of communication presented above uses the standard logical technique of embeddings. In Linear Logic, the unary 'exponentials' are designed to recover the expressivity of the structural rules of Contraction and Weakening in a controlled way. The modalities that achieve the desired embedding are governed by an $S4$-like regime. The 'sublinear' grammar logics exhibit a higher degree of structural organization. These more discriminating logics suggest more delicate instruments for obtaining structural control: as we have seen, the pure residuation logic for $\diamond, \Box^{\downarrow}$ does not depend on specific assumptions about the grammatical composition relation R^2, but it is expressive enough to obtain full control over grammatical resource management.[3] A second difference with the Linear Logic approach is the *bi-directionality* of the proposed communication: from the grammatical point of view, imposing structural constraints and licensing structural relaxation are equally significant forms of resource control.

On the level of actual grammar development, the embedding results provide a solution to the problem of 'mode proliferation' inherent in the multimodal approach of Section 4.1. The multimodal style of grammatical reasoning relies heavily on a (potentially unmanageable) inventory of primitive composition modes $\bullet_i$. The control operators $\diamond$, $\Box^{\downarrow}$ make it possible to reanalyse the various $\bullet_i$ as *defined* connectives, in terms of a familiar $\bullet$ and modal decoration. The dependency connectives $\bullet_l$, $\bullet_r$, for example, can be introduced as synthetic operators with definitions $(\diamond -) \bullet -$, and $- \bullet (\diamond -)$, respectively, with $\diamond$ marking the head component. This perspective suggests a global division of labor between 'syntax' and 'semantics', with **LP** playing the role of the default semantic composition language, and the pure residuation logic **NL** the default language of structural composition. The intermediate territory can be navigated by means of the modal control operators.

5. Reasoning about multiple type assignments

In the previous sections, we have discussed the multiplicative vocabulary, and its interpretation in terms of structural composition of grammatical resources. If we want to carry out the lexicalist program and account for the composition of form and meaning in purely deductive terms, it will often be necessary to associate grammatical resources with *multiple* types – types which are not related in terms of derivability. It is of vital importance, then, that the grammar logic also provides facilities for reasoning *about* such multiple type assignments. In the present section, we discuss two extensions of the type-logical vocabulary that serve this purpose. In Section 5.1, we introduce Boolean and additive type constructors for conjunctive/disjunctive types of reasoning. In Section 5.2, the type language is extended with first and second order quantifiers. These constructors express generalizations across types in terms of 'dependent' types and type schemata.

[3] It is interesting to note that for reasons different from ours, and for different types of models, a number of proposals in the field of Linear Logic have argued for a decomposition of the exponentials into more elementary operators (cf. Bucalo, 1994; Girard, 1995b).

5.1. Additive and Boolean operations

Let us extend the language of type formulae with logical constants $\sqcap, \sqcup$. A natural interpretation for formulas $A \sqcap B, A \sqcup B$ can be given in terms of the intersection and union of the interpretations of the subformulas A and B.

$$(33)\qquad \begin{aligned} v(A \sqcap B) &= \{x \mid x \in v(A) \wedge x \in v(B)\} = v(A) \cap v(B), \\ v(A \sqcup B) &= \{x \mid x \in v(A) \vee x \in v(B)\} = v(A) \cup v(B). \end{aligned}$$

In an axiomatic presentation of the type logic, one introduces appropriate axiom schemata and rules of inference for the new type constructors. It is shown in (Kurtonina, 1995) that with respect to the frame semantics for the multiplicatives, completeness is maintained when the $\sqcap, \sqcup$ connectives are added. Instead of the simple formula-based canonical model construction, the completeness proof now employs a hierarchy of filter constructions.

DEFINITION 5.1. Lattice operations. Axioms, rules of inference.

$$\pi^1_{A,B} : A \sqcap B \to A \qquad \pi^2_{A,B} : A \sqcap B \to B \qquad \frac{f : C \to A \quad g : C \to B}{\langle f, g\rangle : C \to A \sqcap B}$$

$$\kappa^1_{A,B} : A \to A \sqcup B \qquad \kappa^2_{A,B} : B \to A \sqcup B \qquad \frac{f : A \to C \quad g : B \to C}{[f, g] : A \sqcup B \to C}$$

As a first approximation of a Gentzen formulation, one could follow the usual route, replacing on the lefthand side of the derivability arrow formula variables by structure variables, and contextually embedding the π^i, $[f, g]$ schemata in such a way that the inference rules have the proper format for Cut Elimination. Cf. Došen (1989), Lambek (1993a). One obtains the sequent rules for the *additives* of Linear Logic.

DEFINITION 5.2. Gentzen rules: additives.

$$\frac{\Gamma[A] \Rightarrow C}{\Gamma[A \sqcap B] \Rightarrow C}\,\sqcap L \qquad \frac{\Gamma[B] \Rightarrow C}{\Gamma[A \sqcap B] \Rightarrow C}\,\sqcap L \qquad \frac{\Gamma \Rightarrow A \quad \Gamma \Rightarrow B}{\Gamma \Rightarrow A \sqcap B}\,\sqcap R$$

$$\frac{\Gamma \Rightarrow A}{\Gamma \Rightarrow A \sqcup B}\,\sqcup R \qquad \frac{\Gamma \Rightarrow B}{\Gamma \Rightarrow A \sqcup B}\,\sqcup R \qquad \frac{\Gamma[A] \Rightarrow C \quad \Gamma[B] \Rightarrow C}{\Gamma[A \sqcup B] \Rightarrow C}\,\sqcup L$$

The Curry–Howard interpretation for the extended vocabulary uses pairing and projection for term assignment to the $\sqcap$ connective,[4] and a disjoint sum and case construction

[4] Notice that the multiplicative product and additive $\sqcap$ are both interpreted in terms of pairing and projection. As pointed out in Section 3, categorial term assignment does not insist on an *isomorphism*, but on the weaker homomorphism requirement of the compositionality principle.

operation for the interpretation of $\sqcup$, cf. Troelstra (1992). (34) extends the syntax of lambda terms with clauses for the $\sqcup$ connective.

$$\text{(34)}\qquad \begin{aligned} &\mathcal{T}_A ::= \cdots \mid E^{\sqcup}_{\mathcal{V}_B,\mathcal{V}_C}(\mathcal{T}_{B\sqcup C}, \mathcal{T}_A, \mathcal{T}_A),\\ &\mathcal{T}_{A\sqcup B} ::= \kappa_1\mathcal{T}_A, \qquad \mathcal{T}_{B\sqcup A} ::= \kappa_2\mathcal{T}_A. \end{aligned}$$

The relevant term equations for disjoint sum and case construction are given below. In a term $E^{\sqcup}_{x,y}(s,t,u)$ the subscript on the constructor $E^{\sqcup}_{x,y}$ indicates that the variables x and y are bound in t and u, respectively.

$$\text{(35)}\qquad E^{\sqcup}_{x,y}(\kappa_1 s, t, u) = t[s/x], \qquad E^{\sqcup}_{x,y}(\kappa_2 s, t, u) = u[s/y].$$

DEFINITION 5.3. Term assignment for $\sqcup, \sqcap$ (Troelstra, 1992).

$$\frac{\Gamma \Rightarrow t : A}{\Gamma \Rightarrow \kappa_1 t : A \sqcup B}\ \sqcup R \qquad\qquad \frac{\Gamma \Rightarrow u : B}{\Gamma \Rightarrow \kappa_2 u : A \sqcup B}\ \sqcup R$$

$$\frac{\Gamma[x : A] \Rightarrow t : C \quad \Gamma[y : B] \Rightarrow u : C}{\Gamma[z : A \sqcup B] \Rightarrow \mathrm{E}^{\sqcup}_{x,y}(z, t, u) : C}\ \sqcup L$$

$$\frac{\Gamma[x : A] \Rightarrow t : C}{\Gamma[z : A \sqcap B] \Rightarrow t[(z)_0/x] : C}\ \sqcap L \qquad\qquad \frac{\Gamma[y : B] \Rightarrow t : C}{\Gamma[z : A \sqcap B] \Rightarrow t[(z)_1/y] : C}\ \sqcap L$$

$$\frac{\Gamma \Rightarrow t : A \quad \Gamma \Rightarrow u : B}{\Gamma \Rightarrow \langle t, u\rangle : A \sqcap B}\ \sqcap R$$

In (Morrill, 1994a), the interpretation for the additive connectives is further refined. The connectives are split up in a semantically *active* version $\sqcap, \sqcup$ with the above Curry–Howard interpretation, and a semantically *neutral* form $\sqcap', \sqcup'$ for the case where one and the same semantic recipe has two distinct syntactic type realizations. The range of application of the semantically neutral form $A \sqcap' B, A \sqcup' B$ is then naturally restricted to the case where $t(A) = t(B)$.

Lexical generalizations. Extension of the multiplicative vocabulary with the connectives $\sqcap, \sqcup$ provides type-logical facilities for expressing generalizations with respect to lexical type assignments – a categorial application of the lattice operations originally suggested in (Lambek, 1961). Such uses of the $\sqcap, \sqcup$ vocabulary have been explored for grammar development purposes in (Morrill, 1994a; Kanazawa, 1992; Hendriks, 1995), and in the context of a categorial learning theory in (Adriaans, 1992), where the meet and join connectives are used in formulating clustering operations of the learning algorithm.

On the most general level the conjunctive $\sqcap$ allows one to compress multiple assignment of types $A_1, \ldots, A_n$ to a vocabulary element into a single assignment of the form $A_1 \sqcap \cdots \sqcap A_n$. But in the case of assignments with shared structure, one can push the generalization further than the top-level conjunction. Given the theorems in (36), one can compress the left-hand side to the more economical right-hand side assignment.

(36)
$$(A/C) \sqcap (B/C) \leftrightarrow (A \sqcap B)/C,$$
$$(C/A) \sqcap (C/B) \leftrightarrow C/(A \sqcup B).$$

Notice that the generalization here is to be understood as economy of representation: the double arrow makes clear that on the denotational level, the redundant and the economical type formula are equivalent. Examples of this type of lexical generalization are easy to find. A preposition like *at* takes a noun phrase complement and functions in combination with it both as a nominal modifier (*the house at the corner*) and as a prepositional phrase complement (*laugh at Ferdinand*). The type $(pp \sqcap (n\backslash n))/np$ expresses this. A verb like *know* can be typed as $(np\backslash s)/(np \sqcup s)$: it takes either a sentential or a noun phrase complement to form a verb phrase (*know that he left* versus *know the answer*).

Coordination of unlike categories. The grammar logic can exploit the properties of the $\sqcap, \sqcup$ operations in combination with the built-in asymmetry of the derivability relation. Cases of coordination of 'unlike' categories illustrate this type of reasoning in terms of subsumption relations between types. For discussion, see Morrill (1990b, 1994a), Hendriks (1995), Bayer and Johnson (1995). Consider the following examples from Sag, Gazdar, Wasow and Weisler (1985). In (37a) we find coordination of an adjectival complement (*stupid*) with a noun phrase (*a liar*). The (37b) example shows that coordination of unlike categories does not come 'for free': the subcategorizational requirements of, in this case, the copula *be* license a form of coordination which, without this licensing factor, is ungrammatical.

(37)
(a) Pat is either stupid or a liar.
(b) *The longwinded and a bully man was my brother.

Suppose we assign *be* the type $(np\backslash s)/((n/n) \sqcup np)$. Now the coordination type schema $(X\backslash X)/X$ can be instantiated with $X = (n/n) \sqcup np$, and one can conjoin *stupid and a liar* as like categories. The lexical meaning recipe for the copula can be given in terms of a case construction keying the 'predicational' and the 'identificational' readings to the first and the second injections, respectively, as shown in (Morrill, 1994a). An attempt to derive the ungrammatical (37b) by means of a similar disjunctive instantiation of the coordination type schema leads to failure, as shown in (38). Given an instantiation $X = (n/n) \sqcup np$, one can conjoin *longwinded and a bully*, but the disjunctive type cannot be successfully used in the wider context of the noun phrase *the longwinded and a bully man*.

(38)
$$\frac{\dfrac{\text{OK}}{np/n, n/n, n \Rightarrow np} \qquad \dfrac{\text{FAIL}}{np/n, np, n \Rightarrow np}}{np/n, (n/n) \sqcup np, n \Rightarrow np} \sqcup L$$

Featural decomposition. Another suggested application of the Boolean type constructors relates to feature decomposition of categories, cf. Kanazawa (1992), Bayer and Johnson (1995). Suppose we want to distinguish plural and singular nominals. Introduction of new *atomic* types n_{sing} and n_{plur} misses the point that these types share the nominal information, while differing in their number properties. With the additive connectives, we could form the types $n \sqcap sing$ versus $n \sqcap plur$, where *sing* and *plur* now are taken to be 'feature' types. The determiner 'a', which requires a singular noun, can be typed $(np \sqcap sing)/(n \sqcap sing)$. The determiner 'the', which combines with either number, is typed simply as np/n.

The additive approach towards featural decomposition has a number of problematic aspects arising from the fact that 'syntactic' categories (like np) and featural information (like *sing*) are treated on a par. Because of the semantic associativity/commutativity of the additives, there is no guarantee that feature types will stay associated with the syntactic categories they are supposed to decorate. Consider an expression like 'her' which is both an accusative pronoun, say $np \sqcap acc \sqcap 3fem$, and a possessive pronoun, $(np/n) \sqcap 3fem$. Putting these two types together with '$\sqcap$', however, we cannot prevent the acc specification to reassociate with np/n. In the sections that follow, we will discuss some proposals that offer a more attractive perspective on the integration of feature information within the type-logical framework.

Recognizing capacity. The effects of additive enrichments of the type language on recognizing capacity have been studied by Kanazawa (1992), see Chapter 12 for discussion. Unconstrained addition of $\sqcap$ to **L** leads beyond context-free recognizing power. But one can constrain the interaction between the multiplicative and the additive vocabulary in such a way that the recognizing power is unaffected. One option is to impose a restriction on the distribution of the additive connectives in lexical assignments to the effect that only the rule of *use* for $\sqcap$ and the rule of *proof* for $\sqcup$ come into play (Kanazawa, 1992). A second option is to restrict the interaction between multiplicatives and additives to the level of atomic types, so that the $\sqcap, \sqcup$ operators never have scope over the multiplicatives (Dörre and Manandhar, 1995). For the grammar writer, such restrictions are not unreasonable.

Boolean resource management. As noted at the beginning of this section, the Gentzen rules of Definition 5.2 are only approximations of the Boolean intersection/union interpretation for $\sqcap, \sqcup$: the resource sensitive management of the Linear Logic database does not support full Boolean inference. For the distributivity law $A \sqcap (B \sqcup C) \leftrightarrow (A \sqcap B) \sqcup (A \sqcap C)$, the $\leftarrow$ direction is derivable, but the $\rightarrow$ direction is not, while it is valid for the intersection/union interpretation.

One can resolve this problem in two ways: one can keep the proof theory of Definition 5.2 as it is and refine the model theory, so that one indeed obtains completeness; or one can adjust the Gentzen proof rules, so that they are appropriate for the Boolean interpretation of $\sqcap, \sqcup$. For the first alternative, appropriate semantic structures are semilattice ordered groupoids (or 'resource algebras' cf. Došen (1989), Wansing (1992b)): structures $\langle W, \cdot, \cap, 1 \rangle$, where W is thought of as a set of information pieces, and where one has a notion of 'information growth' $x \leqslant y$, defined as $x = x \cap y$. The informational interpretation is quite natural, but it is not fully clear how one could reconcile this with our understanding of $\bullet$ as structural composition.

The second option is to maintain the Boolean interpretation, and make appropriate adjustments to the proof theory. Within the multimodal setting of Section 4.1, this option can be implemented without 'side-effects' on the interpretation of the multiplicative vocabulary, as has been shown in (Restall, 1994). One simply introduces a mode $(\cdot,\cdot)^2$ with Boolean resource management for the family of logical connectives $\sqcap, \sqcup$. The logical rules for $\sqcup$ can be taken over from Definition 5.2 and the logical rules for $\sqcap$ are replaced by the ones given in Definition 5.4. These rules are exactly the same as the multiplicative $\bullet$ rules except for the fact that they interpret $\sqcap$ in terms of the Boolean mode $(\cdot,\cdot)^2$. The connectives $\sqcap, \sqcup$ now derive their proper inferential capacities from the structural rule package that characterizes the $(\cdot,\cdot)^2$ mode. Apart from Associativity and Commutativity, this rule package contains mode-restricted Contraction and Weakening.

DEFINITION 5.4. Boolean resource management (Restall, 1994). Logical rules for $\sqcap$. Structural rules for the $(\cdot,\cdot)^2$ mode.

$$\frac{\Delta_1 \Rightarrow A \quad \Delta_2 \Rightarrow B}{(\Delta_1, \Delta_2)^2 \Rightarrow A \sqcap B}\ \sqcap R' \qquad \frac{\Gamma[(A,B)^2] \Rightarrow C}{\Gamma[A \sqcap B] \Rightarrow C}\ \sqcap L'$$

$$\frac{\Gamma[(\Delta,\Delta)^2] \Rightarrow A}{\Gamma[\Delta] \Rightarrow A}\ [\mathrm{C}] \qquad \frac{\Gamma[\Delta_1] \Rightarrow A}{\Gamma[(\Delta_1,\Delta_2)^2] \Rightarrow A}\ [\mathrm{W}]$$

$$\frac{\Gamma[(\Delta_2,\Delta_1)^2] \Rightarrow A}{\Gamma[(\Delta_1,\Delta_2)^2] \Rightarrow A}\ [\mathrm{P}] \qquad \frac{\Gamma[(\Delta_1,(\Delta_2,\Delta_3)^2)^2] \Rightarrow A}{\Gamma[((\Delta_1,\Delta_2)^2,\Delta_3)^2] \Rightarrow A}\ [\mathrm{A}]$$

We leave it as an exercise to show that the earlier $[\sqcap R]$ and $[\sqcap L]$ rules are derivable from $[\sqcap R']$ and $[\sqcap L']$, given the structural options of the $(\cdot,\cdot)^2$ mode. In is shown in (Restall, 1993) that the Cut rule is admissible in the multimodal system resulting from the combination of the above rules for $\sqcap, \sqcup$ with the standard Lambek-style multiplicatives, and that the system is decidable – the search space can be kept finite, in spite of the presence of the mode-restricted Contraction rule.

EXAMPLE 5.5. Deriving distributivity with Boolean resource management: the direction underivable under the additive regime.

$$\frac{\dfrac{\dfrac{\dfrac{A \Rightarrow A \quad B \Rightarrow B}{(A,B)^2 \Rightarrow A \sqcap B}\ \sqcap R'}{(A,B)^2 \Rightarrow (A \sqcap B) \sqcup (A \sqcap C)}\ \sqcup R \qquad \dfrac{\dfrac{A \Rightarrow A \quad C \Rightarrow C}{(A,C)^2 \Rightarrow A \sqcap C}\ \sqcap R'}{(A,C)^2 \Rightarrow (A \sqcap B) \sqcup (A \sqcap C)}\ \sqcup R}{(A,(B \sqcup C))^2 \Rightarrow (A \sqcap B) \sqcup (A \sqcap C)}\ \sqcup L}{A \sqcap (B \sqcup C) \Rightarrow (A \sqcap B) \sqcup (A \sqcap C)}\ \sqcap L'$$

Unary operators: Additive interpretation
In Section 4.2 we developed a *multiplicative* theory of the unary operators $\diamond$, $\Box^{\downarrow}$, presenting them as 'truncated' forms of $\bullet$ and a residual implication. In a language with $\sqcap$, one can develop an alternative *additive* account of the unary control operators. We present the proposals of Venema (1994a) for the introduction of a unary operator ∇, decomposable as $A \sqcap Q$, where Q is a type constant picking out a subset of the interpretation domain W – a subset of elements which count as 'special' in a sense indicated by the constant Q. The ∇ operator resolves model-theoretic problems for the 'subalgebra' interpretation of the categorial modalities, which we discuss below.

Modalities: Subalgebra interpretation. The frame semantics for $\diamond, \Box^{\downarrow}$ interprets the unary vocabulary in terms of a binary accessibility relation that models the relevant notion of multiplicative linguistic composition. The original Edinburgh interpretation for the $S4$-type $\Box$ operators discussed in Section 4.2 was presented in terms of groupoid, algebraic models for the multiplicative vocabulary. The semantics for the $\Box$ operator, attributed to Guy Barry in (Morrill, 1994a), is obtained by distinguishing within the default structural algebra $\langle W, \cdot \rangle$ a *subalgebra* $\langle W_{\Box}, \cdot \rangle$. The valuation is extended to $\Box$ formulae in the obvious way: $v(\Box A) = v(A) \cap W_{\Box}$. In the case of the *domain* modalities of Hepple (1990), the elements of $W_{\Box}$ do not have special resource management properties: one interprets $\Box A$ as the intersection of $v(A)$ with an arbitrary subalgebra. In the case of *structural* modalities for controlled resource management, the groupoid operation '$\cdot$' is governed by an appropriate set of structural equations explicitly restricted to elements of the subalgebra $W_{\Box}$. See Morrill (1994a) for discussion. For example, in the case of an operator $\Box_p$ for controlled permutation, the relevant equation would be: $\forall x \in W,\ \forall x' \in W_{\Box_p},\ x \cdot x' = x' \cdot x$.

Unfortunately, the $S4$ proof theory for $\Box$ is incomplete with respect to the intended subalgebra interpretation, for reasons discussed in (Vermissen, 1993). The origin of the problem is the condition on the rule of proof $[\Box R]$ which requires that *all* antecedent assumptions be modally decorated. For the subalgebra interpretation of the modalities, this condition is too strong: it rules out sequents that are generally valid. Compare the following sequents.

$$(39) \quad \begin{array}{lll} \text{(a)} & \mathbf{L}+\Box \vdash & \Box B/A, A \Rightarrow C/(A\backslash((\Box B/A)\backslash C)), \\ \text{(b)} & \mathbf{L}+\Box \nvdash & \Box B/A, A \Rightarrow \Box(C/(A\backslash((\Box B/A)\backslash C))). \end{array}$$

While (39a) is derivable, as the reader can check, (39b) is not, but it *is* generally valid. Pick arbitrary x, y with $x \in v(\Box B/A)$ and $y \in v(A)$. Derivability of (a) and soundness gives $(\dagger)$ $xy \in v(C/(A\backslash((\Box B/A)\backslash C)))$. But we know from the definition of v for the connective '/' that $(\ddagger)$ $xy \in v(\Box B) = v(B) \cap W_{\Box} \subseteq W_{\Box}$. The combination of $(\dagger, \ddagger)$ tells us that $xy \in v(C/(A\backslash((\Box B/A)\backslash C))) \cap W_{\Box}$. But by the definition of v for $\Box$ this means that $xy \in v(\Box(C/(A\backslash((\Box B/A)\backslash C))))$. It is clear why $[\Box R]$ causes the problem. If one could start the derivation of (39b) with $[\Box R]$, one obtains the derivable (39a) as the premise. But the condition on $[\Box R]$ prevents this: the A assumption is not modal.

Additive interpretation of the structural operators. The logic for the unary additive operator ∇ consists of three parts. First, there is the usual set of logical rules for use and proof of formulas ∇A. Secondly, the $[Q\circ]$ rule expresses the fact that the subset W_Q of the domain of interpretation is multiplicatively closed, i.e. that we deal with a subalgebra $\langle W_Q, \cdot \rangle$. (Notice that the rule $[Q\circ]$ is in fact a compiled Cut. But being a Cut on a constant, it does not threaten decidability.) Finally, there is a set of ∇-controlled structural rules. Controlled Permutation is given as an example.

DEFINITION 5.6. The additive structural operator ∇ (Venema, 1994a). Logical rules, structural rules ($i \in \{1,2\}$). The $[\nabla L i]$ and $[\nabla R]$ rules are derivable if one defines ∇A as $A \sqcap Q$.

$$[\nabla L1]\frac{\Gamma[A] \Rightarrow B}{\Gamma[\nabla A] \Rightarrow B} \qquad \frac{\Gamma[Q] \Rightarrow B}{\Gamma[\nabla A] \Rightarrow B}[\nabla L2] \qquad \frac{\Delta \Rightarrow A \quad \Delta \Rightarrow Q}{\Delta \Rightarrow \nabla A}[\nabla R]$$

$$\frac{\Delta_1 \Rightarrow Q \quad \Delta_2 \Rightarrow Q \quad \Gamma[Q] \Rightarrow A}{\Gamma[(\Delta_1, \Delta_2)] \Rightarrow A}[Q\circ] \qquad \frac{\Delta_i \Rightarrow Q \quad \Gamma[(\Delta_2, \Delta_1)] \Rightarrow A}{\Gamma[(\Delta_1, \Delta_2)] \Rightarrow A}[QP]$$

On the basis of the fixed core of logical rules $[\nabla L]$, $[\nabla R]$, one can design variants by modifying the other rules. The rule $[Q\circ]$ is appropriate in situations where putting together resources which are 'special' in the 'Q' sense produces a result which is also special. One can easily think of applications where putting together Q resources does not produce a new Q resource. (Using the Q constants for prosodic sorting, for example, the composition of two prosodic words might yield a phrase.) A second source of variation is the ∇ controlled structural rules. As presented above, the rules require *one* subterm of a structurally affected configuration to have the Q property – the subterm which then qualifies as the licensing factor for structural relaxation. Alternatively, one can formulate a version of the structural rules where relaxation requires *all* the immediate subterms of the target configuration to derive Q. See Versmissen (1996) for discussion.

Cut elimination, completeness, additive embeddings. Cut Elimination, and completeness of the ∇, Q extended language with respect to the subalgebra interpretation in semilattice ordered groupoids is proved in (Venema, 1994a). Venema also establishes general embedding results showing that the ∇ operator and the associated type constant Q allow one to fully recover the expressivity of a logic $\mathcal{L}$ with a more relaxed resource management regime from within a system $\mathcal{L}'$ with a more stringent form of structure sensitivity. The additive style of structural relaxation can be compared with the 'licensing' direction of the multiplicative embeddings discussed in Section 4.2. The existence of these alternative approaches suggests a more general question for future research: How does one draw the line between 'multiplicative' and 'additive' aspects of the grammatical composition relation?

5.2. Dependent types, type schemata

We move now to a first-order polymorphic type language where 'predicational' basic types take the place of propositional atoms, and to second-order polymorphic type schemata.

5.2.1. First-order polymorphism

The additive view on 'featurally' complex category formulas considers the basic types as unanalysed propositional atoms. But featural information can also be incorporated in the type system by moving from a propositional basis to a first-order predicational system. This view on categorial fine-structure is characteristic of the 'unification-based' versions of categorial grammar, which will be discussed more fully in Section 6, the section on hybrid architectures. In the type-logical setting proper, predicational types are discussed in (Morrill, 1994a). See also Carpenter (1992b), where the basic clausal structure of English is presented in terms of first-order basic type formulae.

Predicational basic types. Instead of the propositional basic types (such as np for noun phrases) we now take the atomic types to be predicates, and we introduce terms built up from feature constants and feature variables (and maybe feature function symbols) to fill the argument positions of the predicational types. For example: a noun phrase of feminine gender could be typed as $np(\mathit{fem})$; the type $np(3(\mathit{fem}))$ could serve for feminine noun phrases of the third person, etc. The Gentzen rules for dependent types are given in Definition 5.7. In symmetry with the treatment of $\sqcap, \sqcup$, Morrill (1994a) presents semantically inactive variants $\forall', \exists'$ in addition to the semantically active ones below.

DEFINITION 5.7. Dependent function types ($\forall$), dependent sum types ($\exists$) (Morrill, 1994a).

$$\frac{\Gamma[x\!:\!A[t/v]] \Rightarrow u\!:\!C}{\Gamma[y\!:\!\forall vA] \Rightarrow u[y(t)/x]\!:\!C}\ \forall L \qquad \frac{\Gamma \Rightarrow t\!:\!A}{\Gamma \Rightarrow \lambda v.t\!:\!\forall vA}\ \forall R \qquad (v \text{ not free in } \Gamma),$$

$$\frac{\Gamma \Rightarrow u\!:\!A[t/v]}{\Gamma \Rightarrow \langle t,u\rangle\!:\!\exists vA}\ \exists R \qquad \frac{\Gamma[x\!:\!A] \Rightarrow u\!:\!B}{\Gamma[z\!:\!\exists vA] \Rightarrow u[\pi_2 z/x]\!:\!B}\ \exists L \quad (v \text{ not free in } \Gamma,\ B).$$

Illustration: Unification/generalization through quantification. To express generalizations over feature information, we can now use the feature variables, and explicitly quantify over these. The definite determiner 'the', for example, could be typed as $\forall N.np(N)/n(N)$, where N is a variable over the number features. The proof rules for the universal quantifier then guarantee combination with singular as well as plural nominal arguments. In (Morrill, 1994a) it is shown how unification, underspecification and re-entrancy can be expressed type-logically through explicit universal quantification.

But the type-logical reanalysis is not just expressively equivalent to the conventional unification alternative. In the type-logical setting, the essential duality between universal and existential quantification suggests the possibility of assigning types with *existentially* bound feature variables. A problematic empirical area where existential binding seems to be required is the coordination of expressions with clashing feature specifications, e.g. 'boys and girls' where an $np(\mathit{masc})$ and an $np(\mathit{fem})$ have to be combined. Unification fails, but under the existential reading $\exists G.np(G)$ the conjuncts can be assigned a common type. What this example suggests is that explicit quantificational type assignments make it possible to trigger both unification and *generalization* as components of the process of linguistic composition.

5.2.2. *Second-order polymorphic systems*

In the *second order* polymorphic systems, the type language is extended with quantification over *type* variables. Definition 5.8 gives the sequent rules for **L2**, the second order polymorphic extension of **L**. For term assignment, one can draw on the constructs of the second order polymorphic λ calculus (Girard, Taylor and Lafont, 1989).

DEFINITION 5.8. Second order quantification in **L2** (Emms, 1993a). The side condition on $(\forall R)$ and $(\exists L)$ prohibits Y from being free in the conclusion, X in $QY.A$ (where Q is $\forall$ or $\exists$). Under these conditions $QX.A[X/Y]$ can count as an alphabetic variant of $QY.A$.

$$\frac{\Gamma, A[B/X], \Delta \Rightarrow C}{\Gamma, \forall X.A, \Delta \Rightarrow C}\ \forall L \qquad \frac{\Gamma \Rightarrow A}{\Gamma \Rightarrow \forall X.A[X/Y]}\ \forall R(\star)$$

$$\frac{\Gamma \Rightarrow A[B/X]}{\Gamma \Rightarrow \exists X.A}\ \exists R \qquad \frac{\Gamma, A, \Delta \Rightarrow C}{\Gamma, \exists X.A[X/Y], \Delta \Rightarrow B}\ \exists L(\star)$$

Chameleon words. Linguistic motivation for second order polymorphism comes from expressions with a chameleon-like behaviour. Coordinating particles *and, or* are cited by Lambek (1958) as prime examples. Resorting to multiple type assignment for the various manifestations of coordination would clearly miss a generalization. Rather, one would like to assign these particles a type schema $\forall X.(X\backslash X)/X$ generalizing over an infinite family of types. The type schema can then adapt to the context it finds itself in. Besides coordination particles, one can think here of negation $\forall X.X/X$, generalized quantifiers $\forall X.X/(np\backslash X)$, $\forall X.(X/np)\backslash X$, relative pronouns $\forall X.((n\backslash n)/(X\backslash s))/(X/np)$. Polymorphic accounts of these phenomena, and others, have been developed by Emms (1993b), in the context of **L2**. An illustration of the polymorphic account of relative clause formation is given in Example 5.9 (where r abbreviates $n\backslash n$). Notice that the reasoning about the type variables exploits the associativity of the underlying base logic: the relative clause body ('s missing an np') is broken in two pieces at the gap site – the part up to the gap is analyzed as X/np, the part after the gap site as $X\backslash s$.

EXAMPLE 5.9. Relativization with type assignment $\forall X.(r/(X\backslash s))/(X/np)$ for the relative pronoun (Emms, 1993a). Cf. '(the mathematician) whom Ferdinand considered intelligent'.[5]

$$\dfrac{\dfrac{\dfrac{\dfrac{\dfrac{\&c}{np, ((np\backslash s)/ap)/np, np, ap \Rightarrow s}}{np, ((np\backslash s)/ap)/np, np \Rightarrow s/ap}\ /R}{np, ((np\backslash s)/ap)/np \Rightarrow (s/ap)/np}\ /R \qquad \dfrac{\dfrac{\dfrac{\&c}{s/ap, ap \Rightarrow s}}{ap \Rightarrow (s/ap)\backslash s}\ \backslash R \quad r \Rightarrow r}{r/((s/ap)\backslash s), ap \Rightarrow r}\ /L}{(r/((s/ap)\backslash s))/((s/ap)/np), np, ((np\backslash s)/ap)/np, ap \Rightarrow r}\ /L}{\forall X.(r/(X\backslash s))/(X/np), np, ((np\backslash s)/ap)/np, ap \Rightarrow r}\ \forall L$$

[5] In order to cover cases of *peripheral* extraction with this relative pronoun type assignment, one has to lift the **L** prohibition of empty antecedents.

Derivational versus variable polymorphism. The way we have presented things above, the grammar writer will have recourse to polymorphic type assignment in cases where the built-in notion of type *derivability* of the system one is working with fails to capture a relevant generalization. There is a trade-off here between the degree of sophistication of the multiplicative vocabulary and the work-load one puts on polymorphic type schemata – between derivational and 'variable' polymorphism, to use the terminology of Van Benthem (1988a). Our discussion in the previous sections provides illustrations of the tension in question. In the case of coordination, deriving verb phrase $(np\backslash s)$ from sentential s coordination is beyond the reach of a Contraction-free grammar logic: generalized coordination then would qualify as genuinely polymorphic. But consider the case of generalized quantifier expressions. One can adopt a conservative attitude with respect to the multiplicative vocabulary and restrict this to the implicative operators of **L**. The inferential capacity of this system, as we have seen, is too limited to derive the appropriate range of scopal possibilities. In a polymorphic extension **L2** with double assignment $\forall X.X/(np\backslash X)$, $\forall X.(X/np)\backslash X$ to the generalized quantifiers one can overcome these limitations, as shown in (Emms, 1993b). Alternatively, one can move to a more articulate multiplicative language, and introduce a binding operator $q(A,B,C)$ (or the deconstruction of (22) in terms of wrapping). With this more refined vocabulary, the instantiations of the polymorphic type schemata for the generalized quantifier expressions are reduced to derivable type transitions.

The proper division of labor between multiplicative and polymorphic enhancements of the inferential capacity of the grammar logic cannot be decided *a priori* on grounds of semantic or structural expressivity. In fact, Definition 5.10 offers a systematic choice between the multiplicative and polymorphic strategies in terms of polymorphic *simulations* of multiplicative extensions of **L**. ($A \uparrow B$ and $A \downarrow B$ are the extraction and infixation connectives of Moortgat (1988), which, in the terminology of Section 4.2, can themselves be synthesized as $A/\Diamond\Box^{\downarrow}B$ and $\Diamond\Box^{\downarrow}(A/B)$, respectively, for a controlled Permutation $\Diamond$.)

DEFINITION 5.10. Polymorphic simulation of multiplicative extensions of **L** (Emms, 1994b).

$$
\begin{array}{lll}
p' = p & (A \uparrow B)' = \exists X.((X/B') \bullet (X\backslash A')) & \text{(extraction)},\\
(A/B)' = A'/B' & (A \downarrow B)' = \forall X.((X/A')/X\backslash B')) & \text{(infixation)},\\
(B\backslash A)' = B'\backslash A' & q(A,B,C)' = \forall X.(((X/A')\backslash C')/(X\backslash B')) & \text{('in situ' binding)}.
\end{array}
$$

Formal properties. General logical properties of **L2** have been studied in (Emms and Leiss, 1993; Emms, 1994c, 1995). On the model-theoretic level, Emms (1994c) investigates under what conditions one can obtain completeness results for **L2** with respect to the ternary relational models, and their specializations, residuated semigroups and free semigroups (string models). Proof-theoretically, Emms and Leiss (1993) show that the polymorphic system, both in its unrestricted form and with a restriction to outermost-only quantification, enjoys Cut Elimination. To establish the result for unrestricted second order quantifiers is more difficult, since the original Cut Elimination strategy with its induction on the complexity of the Cut formula cannot be used: the quantifier inferences may increase complexity. Still, the *resource sensitivity* of the categorial logic makes it possible to proceed by induction on the proof size.

In the case of the generalized Lambek calculi we have studied in Section 4.1, Cut Elimination went hand in hand with decidability. For **L2** this is not the case. Undecidability of **L2** has been established in (Emms, 1995) via a generalization of a recent result by Lincoln, Scedrov and Shankar (1995). These authors show that second order intuitionistic propositional logic ($LJ2$) – a system which is known to be undecidable – can be embedded into the multiplicative fragment of second order intuitionistic Linear Logic ($IMLL2$), i.e. **LP2**. The key idea of the embedding is to reintroduce the structural rules of Contraction and Weakening that differentiate between $LJ2$ and $IMLL2$ in the shape of second order $IMLL2$ *formulae* $\forall X.X \multimap (X \otimes X)$ and $\forall X.X \multimap I$. Emms extends this strategy to the structural rule that differentiates between $IMLL2$ and **L** – the rule of Permutation, which is reintroduced via the second order formula $\forall X \forall Y.((X \bullet Y)/X)/Y$.

The undecidability result suggests a general question in relation to the embeddings in Section 4.2.3: could one design a uniform embedding strategy based on second-order encoding of structural postulates such that the undecidability of $IMLL2$ would carry over to the polymorphic systems of the full sublinear landscape? The question remains open for the time being.

Parsing, recognizing capacity. The undecidability result for polymorphic **L** provides additional motivation for the search for restricted forms of categorial polymorphism with more pleasant computational properties. For a discussion of the options, see Barendregt (1992). Emms (1993a) has explored this issue in a discussion of parsing with **L2**. It turns out that for the actual linguistic uses of type schemata mentioned above, one can do with a very mild form of polymorphism where the universal quantifier is restricted to outermost position. Such a restricted version is closely related to the extension of Lambek Calculus with a Substitution Rule, discussed in (Van Benthem, 1988a), and used in (Moortgat, 1988) in a resolution-based treatment of generalized coordination. Emms (1993a) provides a terminating parsing algorithm for restricted **L2**. With respect to recognizing power, Emms (1994a) shows that extraction covering extensions of **L**, such as obtained via the $\uparrow$ operator of Definition 5.10 or its **L2** translation, have recognizing capacity beyond context-free.

6. Hybrid architectures

6.1. Combining type logic and feature logic

The additive type constructors and first or second order quantifiers of Section 5 offer a purely type-logical perspective on a number of issues that have played a central role in the development of unification formalisms. In this section, we consider the alternative approach of *hybrid* grammar architectures: frameworks based on an effective mixture of the categorial and unification formalisms. In the development of these hybrid frameworks, one can distinguish two phases.

'First generation' systems. Categorial Unification Grammar (CUG, (Uszkoreit, 1986; Bouma, 1988a)) and Unification Categorial Grammar (UCG, (Calder, Klein and Zeevat, 1988)). These systems were introduced a decade ago, during the initial wave of enthusiasm for unification-based grammar architectures. From a taxonomic perspective, CUG and UCG are unification grammars with a highly restricted categorial rule base (typically Functional Application, plus maybe some other rule schemata), and a categorially inspired make-up of the basic declarative unit, the 'sign'.

'Second generation' systems. A type-logical feature which the first generation systems lack is the ability for fully general hypothetical reasoning. Within the context of Gabbay's program for 'combining logics' (Gabbay, 1994), a number of proposals have recently been put forward for a genuine integration of type logic and feature logic. These second generation systems are designed so as to fully preserve the inferential capacities of the constituting logics. They offer a grammar logic with a categorial treatment of grammatical composition and its resource management, combined with a typed constraint-based account of internal categorial fine-structure. Exponents of this type of integration are Dörre and Manandhar (1995) and Dörre, Gabbay and König (1994).

First generation systems
The starting point for the CUG/UCG hybrids is an encoding of categorial type formulae in the attribute-value language of unification grammar. Such encodings can be implemented in a variety of ways. Ignoring matters of economy, one could use (following Bouma, 1988b) a feature CAT with atomic values for basic categories, or attribute-value specifications with attributes VAL (value), DIR (directionality), ARG (argument), in the case of compound (implicational) categories. In (40a) one finds the encoding of a transitive verb type $(np\backslash s)/np$, displayed as an attribute-value matrix. The category specification can be refined with phonological, semantic, or morphophonological information, by adding specifications for features PHON, SEM, AGR in addition to CAT, as in the (40b) specification for a third person singular noun phrase 'Ferdinand'.

$$(40)\quad \text{a.}\ \left[\text{CAT}: \begin{bmatrix} \text{VAL}: \left[\text{CAT}: \begin{bmatrix} \text{VAL}: [\text{CAT}: s] \\ \text{DIR}: \mathit{left} \\ \text{ARG}: [\text{CAT}: np] \end{bmatrix}\right] \\ \text{DIR}: \mathit{right} \\ \text{ARG}: [\text{CAT}: np] \end{bmatrix}\right] \qquad \text{b.}\ \begin{bmatrix} \text{CAT}: np \\ \text{PHON}: \text{'}\mathit{Ferdinand}\text{'} \\ \text{SEM}: f \\ \text{AGR}: \begin{bmatrix} \text{NUM}: \mathit{sing} \\ \text{PER}: 3 \end{bmatrix} \end{bmatrix}$$

Turning to the rule schemata of these systems, the basic law of categorial combination, Functional Application, is combined with the basic principle for fusing conglomerates of featural information: unification. In the Application reduction $A/B \bullet B' \to A'$, the types B, B', now considered as feature structures, are required to be unifiable rather than identical. Because there may be structure sharing between the A and B components of the functor A/B, the result of the combination A' may be affected by the unification of B and B' – a feature which is fully exploited to build up complex semantic or phonological representations via unification.

The unification-based extensions of categorial grammar, as appears from the above, rely on feature logic in two distinct areas: one concerns the internal informational make-up of signs, the other relates to their external combinatory potential. We discuss these two aspects in turn.

Categorial fine-structure and lexical organization. First and foremost, the language of feature logic can be used as a tool to obtain a decomposition of the crude 'atomic' category symbols of standard categorial grammar. Such decomposition allows for the expression of fine-grained distinctions in individual lexical entries, and of categorial generalizations relating classes of entries. We have seen that grammatical macro structure, in the categorial frameworks, is fully projected from the lexicon. With such a central role assigned to the lexicon, it is of crucial importance for realistic grammar development that the huge amounts of lexical information are *organized* in an efficient way. Within unification-based formalisms it has been customary to think of the lexicon as being structured using *templates* (or *macros*), cf. Shieber (1986). A template contains the information relevant for a class of lexical entries. Instead of fully specifying the information associated with a lexical entry, one assumes that the entry can 'inherit' from one or more templates (where inheritance amounts to (non-monotonic) unification). Thus, large amounts of information may be represented succinctly and a wide range of linguistic generalizations about the lexicon can be captured. Such aspects of lexical organization have been studied in depth in (Bouma, 1988a).

A second aspect of lexical organization concerns the *lexical rule* component. Lexical rules can capture relations between type assignments that are not covered by derivational laws. There is a question of balance here between the inferential capacity of the derivational system and the work load put on the lexical rule component. The inferential power of the derivational engine in the case of the unification-based categorial systems is limited, as we have seen. Consequently, lexical rules play an important role in these systems (as in HPSG, Pollard and Sag (1994)). In (Bouma and Van Noord, 1994), lexical polymorphism is implemented via recursive constraints. Techniques of delayed evaluation are employed to reason efficiently with such constraints. For a general assessment of the computational complexity of lexical rules in categorial or unification-based frameworks, the reader can turn to Carpenter (1991), who shows that the type of operations on subcategorization information actually used lead to Turing complexity. This makes the question of the division of labor between derivational polymorphism and lexical rules pregnant again, and shows the need for a restricted *theory* of lexical rules.

Unification-based grammatical composition. The combination of categorial reduction (Application) with unification makes it possible to rule out illformed expressions via unification clashes. A verb form like *runs*, for example, might be assigned a feature specification $\langle num\rangle \mathrm{sing} \wedge \langle person\rangle 3rd$ for its subject argument. Combination with the above entry for *Ferdinand* succeeds, but combination with a subject *they*, with specification $\langle num\rangle plur \wedge \langle person\rangle 3rd$ for its agreement features will fail because of the incompatibility of the constraints for the $\langle num\rangle$ attribute.

Although this picture of a unification-based refinement of categorial reduction works fine in the case of fully specified featural information, it runs into problems when *underspecification* comes into play. These problems have been highlighted in (Bayer and Johnson, 1995).

The feature structure encoding of categorial formulae, as given above, is not entirely faithful: it does not take into account the *polarity* of the subformulae. Categorial reasoning is sensitive to these polarity distinctions – the monotonicity inferences of Proposition 2.18 (3–5) license weakening of positive subformulae and strengthening of negative ones. Unification, being a symmetric operation, is ill-equipped to capture the polarity asymmetries that turn up in type-logical inference. The nature of the conflict can be illustrated with the case of conjunction of unlike categories, cf. (37). Consider the following (partial) lexical specifications (where COMPLEMENT stands for the path CAT | ARG | CAT in the transitive verb attribute-value matrix given above):

(41)
$$\textit{grew}: \left[\text{COMPLEMENT}: \begin{bmatrix}\text{NOUN}: + \\ \text{VERB}: +\end{bmatrix}\right] \quad \textit{became}: \left[\text{COMPLEMENT}: \left[\text{NOUN}: +\right]\right]$$
$$\textit{wealthy}: \begin{bmatrix}\text{VERB}: + \\ \text{NOUN}: +\end{bmatrix} \qquad \textit{a Republican}: \begin{bmatrix}\text{VERB}: - \\ \text{NOUN}: +\end{bmatrix}$$

Assume (with Sag, Gazdar, Wasow and Weisler, 1985; Shieber, 1992) an account of coordination where feature specification for the conjunction as a whole is the *generalization* of the specifications on the conjuncts, i.e. the most specific category which subsumes each conjunct. We can conjoin *wealthy and a Republican* in [NOUN: +], removing the conflicting constraint on the VERB attribute, and derive the well-formed *Kim became wealthy and a Republican*. But on the same account, *grew and remained* are conjoinable as [COMPLEMENT: [NOUN: +]], so that the ill-formed (42) cannot be blocked. Polymorphism here would demand a *conjunctive* effect in antecedents (ranges of lexical functors) but a *disjunctive* effect in succedents (domains of lexical functors). As we have seen in the discussion of (37), this can be achieved in the type-logical setting by having $\sqcap$ and $\sqcup$ (or explicit quantification $\forall$ and $\exists$) systematically alternating according to polarity of context.

(42) * Kim grew and remained wealthy and a republican

Second generation systems

The problems with the combination of unification and categorial derivability have led to the investigation of more delicate mixtures of type logic and feature logic. We briefly discuss the proposals of Dörre and Manandhar (1995) for 'layering' Lambek type logic over a base logic of feature formulas for the description of categorial fine-structure, and the 'fibered' combination of Dörre, Gabbay and König (1994) where feature formulas play the role of global constraints over type-logical derivations.

The layered architecture of Dörre and Manandhar (1995) realizes the interface between type logic and feature logic in terms of a *subtyping* discipline on the atomic types $\mathcal{A}$. In (Lambek, 1968), such an extension of the original calculus is shown to be decidable, cf. Buszkowski (1988) for discussion. The interpretation mapping respects the subtyping pre-order, i.e. $v(p) \subseteq v(q)$ whenever $p \preceq q$ for $p, q \in \mathcal{A}$. On the proof-theoretic level, one refines the Axiom schema to take into account the specificity ordering of the atomic types: $p \Rightarrow q$ holds, provided $p \preceq q$. The canonical model construction of Definition 2.4 readily accommodates the subtype ordering, and provides soundness/completeness for the $\preceq$ extensions of the various calculi in the categorial hierarchy.

From the type-logical perspective, the subtyping relation can be regarded as a 'black box'. One obtains the desired combination of type and feature logic by replacing the atomic formulae p, q of the Lambek component by feature-logic formulae ϕ, ψ, and interpreting the subtype ordering $\preceq$ as entailment checking $\phi \models \psi$. The design of the combination illustrates the philosophy of 'zooming-in, zooming-out' for mixed systems described in (Blackburn and De Rijke, 1994): as far as grammatical composition is concerned, Lambek type inference proceeds in the ordinary fashion until one reaches the atoms of the Lambek component. At that point, one 'zooms in' and switches to the feature logic which describes the internal fine-structure of these atoms. The interference of unification with categorial derivability is avoided: at the feature logical level, one performs *subsumption checking* rather than unification. In the Application case, a functor A/B can be freely applied to *subtypes* of B, not to supertypes.

Notice that the layered style of combination is modular in the sense that interaction between the type logic and feature logic components is restricted to the level of type-logical atoms. This has pleasant consequences for the formal power of the combination. It is shown in (Dörre and Manandhar, 1995) that the layered combination with **L** does not affect the context-free recognizing capacity, in contrast with the 'free' interleaving of multiplicatives and additives studied in (Kanazawa, 1992).

The pleasant modularity of the layered combination is at the same time its limitation: it does not provide the means of expressing featural structure-sharing (re-entrancy) between subtypes of a categorial formula. As we have seen, such re-entrancies are used for the unification-driven construction of semantic or phonological representations. In (Dörre, Gabbay and König, 1994), one finds a proposal for a complementary combination strategy which allows such structure sharing. In this 'fibered' architecture, one associates each atom of the categorial layer with a variable, and then imposes global feature constraints over these variables.

Background, further reading. Decidability aspects of the unification hybrids are discussed in (Van Benthem, 1991, 1995). The computational complexity of unification-based formalisms is studied in (Trautwein, 1995). Via simulations of CUG the NP-hard lower bound for that system is transferred to other formalisms in the unification-based family. The system LexGram (König, 1995) implements the hybridization strategies discussed above. Recent developments within $HPSG$ complement the categorially-inspired theory of subcategorization with simulations of principles such as Geach or Lifting, cf. the treatment of complement inheritance in (Hinrichs and Nakazawa, 1994), or the incorporation of adjuncts into SUBCAT of Miller (1992).

6.2. *Labeled Deductive Systems*

The program of Labeled Deductive Systems (Gabbay, 1994) provides a general framework for the design of hybrid logics, based on the technique of labeling. In labeled deduction, each occurrence of a formula is associated with a label yielding the pair $x : A$ with label x and formula A as the basic declarative unit. Correspondingly, consequence relations hold of structures of labeled formulas, so that in place of $A_1, \ldots, A_n \Rightarrow B$, we have $x_1 : A_1, \ldots, x_n : A_n \Rightarrow y : B$. And accordingly, rules of inference characterizing such consequence relations must specify how actions on formulas and actions on associated labels interact.

A familiar example of labeling is the Curry–Howard morphism, discussed in Section 3. Gabbay (1994) recognized the power and flexibility of the seemingly simple step of labeling and generalized its application across a diverse spectrum of logical problems. From this more abstract perspective, labels represent an extra 'informational resource' which is present in deduction and can play a variety of roles. One obtains a scala of labeling regimes depending on the degree of autonomy between the formula component and the label component of the basic declarative units. At the conservative end of the spectrum, the label simply keeps a passive record of inferential steps. Curry–Howard labeling is a case in point. In this simple situation, the labels provide no feedback to influence the deductive process. A more complex situation arises in cases in which the operations on labels are only partially defined: under these conditions, the labeling system acts as a *filter* on deduction, since an inference step requiring a label operation that cannot be carried out cannot go through. In more complex cases, there is a genuine two-way communication between labels and formulas. Initial investigations of such possibilities can be found in (Gabbay, 1994; Blackburn and De Rijke, 1994).

Within the categorial context, labeled deduction has appeared in a variety of different research directions. One focus of interest has been the use of labels to codify resource-management in different systems of proof, especially in adaptations of Girard's 'proof-nets' to various forms of categorial inference. We discuss this use in Section 7. Another focus of work on labeled deduction has been the investigation of how various logical systems are related to particular model structures. Already in 1986 (Buszkowski, 1986) employed λ-term labels in his study of completeness proofs for various members of the Lambek family of substructural logics. An LDS presentation of **NL** in (Venema, 1994b) forms the basis for completeness proofs for tree-based models. We have seen in Section 2 that the unlabeled system **NL** is incomplete for this type of semantics: labeling, in this case, makes an irreducible contribution to the deductive strength of the logic. In a similar vein, Kurtonina (1995) shows how the simple and multimodal Lambek systems of Sections 2 and 4.1 can be reconstructed in such a way that they share a common system of type-inference for formulas and distinct systems of resource-management involving only the associated labels, and provides completeness proofs for the appropriate ternary-relation frames. This direction of work illustrates a basic slogan of labeled deduction: 'bringing semantics into syntax'. The labels make it possible to discriminate among cases which the formula-language alone cannot tell apart.

The work just described reflects traditional logical questions of proof- and model-theory. But the study of labeled deduction for type-logical grammatical inference has intrinsic motivation as well: natural language (as stressed in (Oehrle, 1988)) is characteristically *multi-dimensional*, in a way that pairs phonological, syntactic, and interpretive information. Labeling can be used to explicitly manipulate these grammatical dimensions and their complex interactions. We mention some relevant studies. The system of 'Natural Logic' of Sanchez (1995) presents a combined calculus of categorial deduction and natural language inference: the inferential contribution of subexpressions is accounted for in terms of a labeling system decorating Lambek deductions with monotonicity markings. The work on ellipsis and cross-over phenomena of Gabbay and Kempson (1992) similarly exploits the structure of a labeled natural deduction system in order capture the context-dependency of natural language interpretation. This form of labeled deduction, and the systems proposed in (Oehrle, 1995) in studies of quantification and binding, essentially interleave phonological, syntactic, semantic and pragmatic information, and assign to the labels an active role in controlling and constraining the course of proof. Finally, the general framework of labeled deduction provides a unifying point of view in which to study different proposals concerning the multidimensional nature of linguistic structure, ranging from the sequential architecture of the Government & Binding school to the family of parallel architectures found in the 'sign'-based system of HPSG, the correspondences between f-structure, c-structure, and σ-structure of LFG, and various members of the family of Tree Adjoining Grammars. These systems can be simulated (at least partially) in the framework of labeled type-logical deduction, in a way that may reveal underlying points of similarity and sharpen understanding of points of essential difference. See Joshi and Kulick (1995) for an exploration of this perspective.

7. Categorial parsing as deduction

In this section we turn to the computational study of categorial type logics, and discuss some aspects of their algorithmic proof theory, under the slogan 'Parsing as Deduction' – a slogan which in the type-logical framework assumes a very literal interpretation. In Section 7.1 we return to a problem that was already signaled in Section 3: the many-to-one correspondence between Gentzen proofs and λ-term meaning recipes. We discuss the procedural control strategies that have been proposed to remove this source of 'spurious ambiguity' from Gentzen proof search. In Section 7.2, we present an attractive alternative for Gentzen proof search, inspired by what Girard (1995a) has called the Natural Deduction for resource logics – the 'proof nets' of Linear Logic. In the spirit of Section 6.2, we show how labeling can be used to implement an appropriate level of control over the linguistic resources.

7.1. Proof normalization in Gentzen calculus

From the literature on automated deduction, it is well known that Cut-free Gentzen proof search is still suboptimal from the efficiency perspective: there may be different (Cut-free!) derivations leading to one and the same proof term. Restricting ourselves to the implicational fragment, the spurious non-determinism in the search space has two causes (Wallen, 1990): (i) permutability of [L] and [R] inferences, and (ii) permutability of [L] inferences among themselves, i.e. non-determinism in the choice of the active formula in the antecedent. A so-called *goal-directed* (or: uniform) search regime performs the non-branching [R] inferences before the [L] inferences (re (i)), whereas *head-driven* search commits the choice of the antecedent active formula in terms of the goal formula (re (ii)). Such optimized search regimes have been proposed in the context of Linear Logic programming in (Hodas and Miller, 1994; Andreoli, 1992). In the categorial setting, goal-directed head-driven proof search for the implicational fragment **L** was introduced in (König, 1991) and worked out in (Hepple, 1990) who provided a proof of the safeness (no proof terms are lost) and non-redundancy (each proof term has a unique derivation) of the method. We present the search regime in the format of Hendriks (1993) with Curry–Howard semantic term labeling.

DEFINITION 7.1. Goal-directed head-driven search for product-free **L** (Hendriks, 1993).

$$[\mathrm{Ax}/\star\mathrm{L}]\frac{}{x:p^\star \Rightarrow x:p} \qquad \frac{\Gamma, u:B^\star, \Gamma' \Rightarrow t:p}{\Gamma, u:B, \Gamma' \Rightarrow t:p^\star}[\star\mathrm{R}]$$

$$[/\mathrm{R}]\frac{\Delta, x:B \Rightarrow t:A^\star}{\Delta \Rightarrow \lambda x.t:A/B^\star} \qquad \frac{\Delta \Rightarrow u:B^\star \quad \Gamma, x:A^\star, \Gamma' \Rightarrow t:C}{\Gamma, s:A/B^\star, \Delta, \Gamma' \Rightarrow t[su/x]:C}[/\mathrm{L}]$$

$$[\backslash\mathrm{R}]\frac{x:B, \Delta \Rightarrow t:A^\star}{\Delta \Rightarrow \lambda x.t:B\backslash A^\star} \qquad \frac{\Delta \Rightarrow u:B^\star \quad \Gamma, x:A^\star, \Gamma' \Rightarrow t:C}{\Gamma, \Delta, s:B\backslash A^\star, \Gamma' \Rightarrow t[su/x]:C}[\backslash\mathrm{L}]$$

The above **L*** calculus eliminates the spurious non-determinism of the original presentation **L** by annotating sequents with a procedural control operator '*'. Goal sequents $\Gamma \Rightarrow t:A$ in **L** are replaced by **L*** goal sequents $\Gamma \Rightarrow t:A^\star$. With respect to the first cause of spurious ambiguity (permutability of [L] and [R] inferences), the control part of the [R] inferences forces one to remove all connectives from the succedent until one reaches an atomic succedent. At that point, the '*' control is transmitted from succedent to antecedent: the [*R] selects an active antecedent formula the head of which ultimately, by force of the control version of the Axiom sequent [*L], will have to match the (now atomic) goal type. The [L] implication inferences initiate a '*' control derivation on the minor premise, and transmit the '*' active declaration from conclusion to major (right) premise. The effect of the flow of control information is to commit the search to the target type selected in the [*R] step. This removes the second source of spurious ambiguity: permutability of [L] inferences.

Proposition 7.2 sums up the situation with respect to proofs and readings in **L** and **L***. Syntactically, derivability in **L** and **L*** coincide. Semantically, the set of **L*** proof terms forms a subset of the **L** terms. But, modulo logical equivalence, no readings are lost in moving from **L** to **L***. Moreover, the **L*** system has the desired one-to-one correspondence between readings and proofs.

PROPOSITION 7.2. *Proofs and readings* (Hendriks, 1993).

1. $\mathbf{L}^\star \vdash \Gamma \Rightarrow A^\star$ *iff* $\mathbf{L} \vdash \Gamma \Rightarrow A$.
2. $\mathbf{L}^\star \vdash \Gamma \Rightarrow t:A^\star$ *implies* $\mathbf{L} \vdash \Gamma \Rightarrow t:A$.
3. $\mathbf{L} \vdash \Gamma \Rightarrow t:A$ *implies* $\exists t', t' = t$ *and* $\mathbf{L}^\star \vdash \Gamma \Rightarrow t':A^\star$.
4. *if* π_1 *is an* **L*** *proof of* $\Gamma \Rightarrow t:A$ *and* π_2 *is an* **L*** *proof of* $\Gamma \Rightarrow t':A$ *and* $t = t'$, *then* $\pi_1 = \pi_2$.

EXAMPLE 7.3. Without the constraint on uniform head-driven search, there are two **L** sequent derivations for the Composition law, depending on the choice of a/b or b/c as active antecedent type. They produce the same proof term. Of these two, only the first survives in the **L*** regime.

$$\dfrac{\dfrac{\dfrac{\dfrac{\dfrac{\dfrac{}{(c)^\star \Rightarrow c}\,\star L}{c \Rightarrow (c)^\star}\,\star R \quad \dfrac{}{(b)^\star \Rightarrow b}\,\star L}{(b/c)^\star, c \Rightarrow b}\,/L}{b/c, c \Rightarrow (b)^\star}\,\star R \quad \dfrac{}{(a)^\star \Rightarrow a}\,\star L}{\dfrac{\dfrac{(a/b)^\star, b/c, c \Rightarrow a}{a/b, b/c, c \Rightarrow (a)^\star}\,\star R}{a/b, b/c \Rightarrow (a/c)^\star}\,/R}\,/L
\qquad
\dfrac{\dfrac{\dfrac{}{(c)^\star \Rightarrow c}\,\star L}{c \Rightarrow (c)^\star}\,\star R \quad \dfrac{\text{FAIL}}{a/b, (b)^\star \Rightarrow a}}{\dfrac{\dfrac{a/b, (b/c)^\star, c \Rightarrow a}{a/b, b/c, c \Rightarrow (a)^\star}\,\star R}{a/b, b/c \Rightarrow (a/c)^\star}\,/R}\,/L$$

Uniform proof search: Modal control. The control operators $\Diamond, \Box^\downarrow$ make it possible to enforce the König–Hepple–Hendriks uniform head-driven search regime via a modal translation, as shown in (Moortgat, 1995). This illustrates a second type of control that can be logically implemented in terms of the unary vocabulary: a procedural/dynamic form of control rather than the structural/static control of Section 4.2.3. The $\Diamond$, $\Box^\downarrow$ annotation is a variation on the "lock-and-key" method of Lincoln, Scedrov and Shankar (1995): one forces a particular execution strategy for successful proof search by decorating formulae with the $\Box^\downarrow$ ('lock') and $\Diamond$ ('key') control operators. For the selection of the active formula, one uses the distributivity principles $K1, K2$, in combination with the base residuation logic for $\Diamond, \Box^\downarrow$. To establish the equivalence with **L*** search, one can use the sugared presentation of **L** where Associativity is compiled away so that *binary* punctuation $(\cdot\,,\cdot)$ can be omitted (but not the unary $(\cdot)^\diamond$!). This gives the following compiled format for $K1, K2$:

(43) $$\dfrac{\Gamma, (A)^\diamond, \Gamma' \Rightarrow B}{(\Gamma, A, \Gamma')^\diamond \Rightarrow B}\,[K'].$$

The mappings (44) $(\cdot)^1, (\cdot)^0 : \mathcal{F}(/,\backslash) \mapsto \mathcal{F}(/,\backslash,\Diamond,\Box^\downarrow)$, for antecedent and succedent formula occurrences, respectively, are defined as follows.

(44) $$\begin{array}{ll} (p)^1 = p & (p)^0 = \Box^\downarrow p \\ (A/B)^1 = (A)^1/(B)^0 & (A/B)^0 = (A)^0/\Box^\downarrow(B)^1 \\ (B\backslash A)^1 = (B)^0\backslash(A)^1 & (B\backslash A)^0 = \Box^\downarrow(B)^1\backslash(A)^0 \end{array}$$

We have the following proposition (Moortgat, 1995).

(45) $$\mathbf{L}^\star \vdash \Gamma \Rightarrow A^\star \quad \text{iff} \quad \mathbf{L}\Diamond\mathbf{K}' \vdash \Box^\downarrow(\Gamma)^1 \Rightarrow (A)^0.$$

EXAMPLE 7.4. Uniform head-driven search: modal control. We illustrate how a wrong identification of the antecedent head formula leads to failure. Below the modal translation of the crucial upper part of the failing **L*** derivation in Example 7.3.

$$\dfrac{\dfrac{\dfrac{\dfrac{\dfrac{\dfrac{\dfrac{\dfrac{c \Rightarrow c}{(c)^1 \Rightarrow c}\,(\cdot)^1}{(\Box^\downarrow(c)^1)^\diamond \Rightarrow c}\,\Box^\downarrow L}{\Box^\downarrow(c)^1 \Rightarrow \Box^\downarrow c}\,\Box^\downarrow R}{\Box^\downarrow(c)^1 \Rightarrow (c)^0}\,(\cdot)^0 \qquad \dfrac{\text{FAILS}}{\Box^\downarrow(a/b)^1, (b)^1 \Rightarrow a}\,\dagger}{\Box^\downarrow(a/b)^1, (b)^1/(c)^0, \Box^\downarrow(c)^1 \Rightarrow a}\,/L}{\Box^\downarrow(a/b)^1, (b/c)^1, \Box^\downarrow(c)^1 \Rightarrow a}\,(\cdot)^1}{\Box^\downarrow(a/b)^1, (\Box^\downarrow(b/c)^1)^\diamond, \Box^\downarrow(c)^1 \Rightarrow a}\,\Box^\downarrow L}{(\Box^\downarrow(a/b)^1, \Box^\downarrow(b/c)^1, \Box^\downarrow(c)^1)^\diamond \Rightarrow a}\,K'}{\Box^\downarrow(a/b)^1, \Box^\downarrow(b/c)^1, \Box^\downarrow(c)^1 \Rightarrow \Box^\downarrow a}\,\Box^\downarrow R$$

Consider first the interaction of [/R] rules and selection of the active antecedent type. Antecedent types all have $\Box^\downarrow$ as main connective. The $\Box^\downarrow$ acts as a *lock*: a $\Box^\downarrow A$ formula can only become active when it is *unlocked* by the key $\diamond$ (or $(\cdot)^\diamond$ in structural terms). The key becomes available only when the head of the goal formula is reached: through residuation, $[\Box^\downarrow R]$ transmits $\diamond$ to the antecedent, where it selects a formula via $[K']$. There is only *one* key $\diamond$ by residuation on the $\Box^\downarrow$ of the goal formula. As soon as it is used to unlock an antecedent formula, that formula has to remain active and connect to the Axiom sequent. In the derivation above, the key to unlock $\Box^\downarrow(a/b)^1$ has been spent on the wrong formula. As a result, the implication in $(a/b)^1$ cannot become active.

The normalization strategy for the implicational fragment can be extended to cover the $\bullet$ connective as well, as shown in Andreoli's 'focusing proofs' approach for **LP** (the multiplicative fragment of Linear Logic). But in the $\bullet$ case, a residue of 'spurious' non-determinism remains. Summarizing the above, we see that the Gentzen format has certain limitations as a vehicle for efficient categorial computation. To overcome these limitations, the above proposals *increase* the Gentzen bookkeeping by adding procedural control features. The alternative is to switch to a data structure for categorial derivations which effectively removes the sources of computational inefficiency. We turn to such an alternative below.

7.2. *Proof nets and labeled deduction*

In Sections 4.1 and 4.2 we have described the shift from the study of individual categorial systems to the mixed architecture of multimodal type logics. In this section, we consider the mixed architecture from a computational point of view. The central objective in this area is to develop a *general* algorithmic proof theory for the multimodal grammar logics. This is an active area of research (see a.o. Moortgat, 1992; Morrill, 1995c; Hepple, 1994; Oehrle, 1995) with an evolving methodology centering around the combination of the techniques of proof nets and labeled deduction, i.e. resolution theorem proving over labeled literals (rather than Gentzen style proof search over structured formula databases). Here are some desiderata that guide current work. In practice, one finds the expected tension between generality/expressivity and efficiency.

- soundness and completeness of the labeling regime w.r.t. the interpretation;
- expressivity: support for the full language $\Diamond$, $\Box^{\downarrow}$, $/$, $\bullet$, $\backslash$;
- modular treatment of 'logic' (residuation) and 'structure' (resource management);
- reversibility: neutrality w.r.t. parsing and generation;
- efficient compilation techniques.

In Linear Logic Girard (1987) has advocated 'proof nets' as the appropriate proof-theoretic framework for resource logics. The proof net approach has been studied in the context of categorial type logics in (Roorda, 1991). In this section, we first discuss semantic λ-term labeling for categorial proof nets. On the basis of the semantic labeling one can characterize the appropriate well-formedness conditions for proof nets and the correspondence between nets and **LP** sequent derivations. In order to capture the syntactic fine-structure of systems more discriminating than **LP**, and multimodal architectures with interacting unary and binary multiplicatives, we complement the semantic labeling with *structure* labeling. Both types of labeling 'bring semantics into the syntax', as the slogan has it: for the structure labeling, this is the semantics for the form dimension of the linguistic resources, as discussed in Section 2.

Semantic labeling. Building a proof net corresponding to a sequent $\Gamma \Rightarrow A$ is a three stage process. The first stage is deterministic and consists in unfolding the formula decomposition tree for the A_i antecedent terminal formulae and for the goal formula A. The unfolding keeps track of the antecedent/succedent occurrence of subformulae: we distinguish $(\cdot)^1$ (antecedent) from $(\cdot)^0$ (succedent) unfolding, corresponding to the sequent rules of use and proof for the connectives. We call the result of the unfolding a *proof frame*. The second stage, corresponding to the Axiom case in the Gentzen presentation, consists in linking the literals with opposite signature. We call an arbitrary linking connecting the leaves of the proof frame a *proof structure*. Not every proof structure corresponds to a sequent derivation. The final stage is to perform a wellformedness check on the proof structure graph in order to identify it as a *proof net*, i.e. a structure which effectively corresponds to a sequent derivation.

DEFINITION 7.5. Formula decomposition. Antecedent unfolding $(\cdot)^1$, succedent unfolding $(\cdot)^0$. $\exists$-type ($\Diamond$L, $\bullet$L, /R, \R) and $\forall$-type ($\Box^{\downarrow}$L, /L, \L, $\bullet$R) decomposition.

$$\frac{(A)^1 \quad (B)^0}{(A/B)^1}\,\forall \qquad \frac{(B)^1 \quad (A)^0}{(A/B)^0}\,\exists \qquad \frac{(B)^0 \quad (A)^1}{(B\backslash A)^1}\,\forall \qquad \frac{(A)^0 \quad (B)^1}{(B\backslash A)^0}\,\exists$$

$$\frac{(A)^1 \quad (B)^1}{(A\bullet B)^1}\,\exists \qquad \frac{(B)^0 \quad (A)^0}{(A\bullet B)^0}\,\forall$$

$$\frac{(A)^1}{(\Diamond A)^1}\,\exists \qquad \frac{(A)^0}{(\Diamond A)^0}\,\forall \qquad \frac{(A)^1}{(\Box^{\downarrow} A)^1}\,\forall \qquad \frac{(A)^0}{(\Box^{\downarrow} A)^0}\,\exists$$

For the checking of the well-formedness conditions, there are various alternatives, such as Girard's original 'long trip' condition, or the coloring algorithm of Roorda (1991). Here we develop a labeling approach, because it is naturally adaptable to the linguistic application of the type logics in parsing and generation. The purpose of the labeling regime in this case is to push all relevant information about the structure of the proof frame up to the atomic leaf literals, so that the wellformedness check can be formulated locally in terms of resolution on the axiom links.

DEFINITION 7.6. Labeled formula decomposition: semantic labeling. Positive (antecedent) unfolding $(\cdot)^1$, negative (succedent) unfolding $(\cdot)^0$. We use x, y, z (t, u, v) for object-level variables (terms), M, N for meta-level variables. Newly introduced object-level variables and metavariables in the rules below are chosen fresh.

$$\text{Axiom links} \quad \overline{t:(A)^1 \quad M:(A)^0} \qquad \overline{M:(A)^0 \quad t:(A)^1} \qquad \text{with } M := t$$

$$\frac{t(M):(A)^1 \quad M:(B)^0}{t:(A/B)^1} \qquad \frac{x:(B)^1 \quad N:(A)^0}{\lambda x.N:(A/B)^0}$$

$$\frac{M:(B)^0 \quad t(M):(A)^1}{t:(B\backslash A)^1} \qquad \frac{N:(A)^0 \quad x:(B)^1}{\lambda x.N:(B\backslash A)^0}$$

$$\frac{(t)_0:(A)^1 \quad (t)_1:(B)^1}{t:(A\bullet B)^1} \qquad \frac{N:(B)^0 \quad M:(A)^0}{\langle M,N\rangle:(A\bullet B)^0}$$

$$\frac{{}^{\cup}t:(A)^1}{t:(\Diamond A)^1} \qquad \frac{M:(A)^0}{{}^{\cap}M:(\Diamond A)^0} \qquad \frac{{}^{\vee}t:(A)^1}{t:(\Box^{\downarrow} A)^1} \qquad \frac{M:(A)^0}{{}^{\wedge}M:(\Box^{\downarrow} A)^0}$$

For the binary vocabulary, the wellformedness conditions of Definition 7.7 identify **LP** proof nets among the proof structures. Roorda also shows that one can narrow this class to the **L** proof nets by imposing an extra *planarity* constraint forbidding 'crossing' axiom linkings (interpreting the formula decomposition steps of Definition 7.6 in an order-sensitive way). Evaluating this proposal, Hendriks (1993) observes that don't care non-determinism is removed at the declarative level, *not* at the algorithmic/procedural level: the conditions act as filters, in the 'generate-and-test' sense, rejecting structures that have already been computed. In (Hendriks, 1993), the set of proof nets is defined in an alternative, purely inductive way, which does away with proof net conditions for rejecting structures that have already been computed.

DEFINITION 7.7. Proof net conditions (Roorda, 1991). Let t be the term assigned to the $(\cdot)^0$ goal formula.

(P1) there is precisely one terminal $(\cdot)^0$ formula,
(P2) all axiom substitutions can be performed,
(P3) if t contains a subterm $\lambda x.u$ then x occurs in u and x does not occur outside u,
(P4) every variable assigned to a terminal $(\cdot)^1$ formula occurs in t,
(P5) every subterm of t counts for one in t,
(P6) t has no closed subterms.

Structure labeling. The semantic labeling of Definition 7.6 checks for **LP** derivability, and relies on a geometric criterion (planarity) for the **L** refinement. It is not clear how the geometric approach would generalize to other systems in the categorial landscape, and to the multimodal systems. Below, we give a system of structure labeling, that functions with respect to the 'structural' interpretation of the type language. The labeling regime of Definition 7.8 is related to proposals in (Hepple, 1994; Morrill, 1995c; Oehrle, 1995), but makes adjustments for the full multimodal architecture.

DEFINITION 7.8. Structure labels: syntax. The labeling system uses atomic formula labels x and structure labels ${}^{\diamond}\sigma$, $(\sigma \circ \tau)$, for the $\forall$ formula decomposition nodes. For the $\exists$ nodes, we use *difference* structures: expressions that must be rewritten to structure/formula labels under the residuation reductions of Definition 7.9.

$$
\begin{array}{lllllll}
\sigma, \tau & \rightarrow & x & \text{(atoms)} & (\sigma \circ \tau) & \text{(constructor } \bullet\text{)}, \\
 & & {}^{\diamond}\sigma & \text{(constructor } \Diamond\text{)} & {}^{\triangleleft}(\sigma) & \text{(left-destructor } \bullet\text{)}, \\
 & & {}^{\sqcup}\sigma & \text{(destructor } \Diamond\text{)} & (\sigma)^{\triangleright} & \text{(right-destructor } \bullet\text{)}, \\
 & & {}^{\sqcap}\sigma & \text{(goal } \Box^{\downarrow}\text{)} & x \backslash \sigma & \text{(goal } \backslash\text{)}, \\
 & & & & \sigma / x & \text{(goal } /\text{)}.
\end{array}
$$

DEFINITION 7.9. Labeled formula decomposition and residuation term reductions (boxed). Positive (antecedent) unfolding $(\cdot)^1$, negative (succedent) unfolding $(\cdot)^0$. We use x, y, z (t, u, v) for object-level formula (structure) labels, Γ, Δ for meta-level structure label variables. Newly introduced formula labels and metavariables in the rules below are chosen fresh.

$$
\frac{(t \circ \Delta) : (A)^1 \quad \Delta : (B)^0}{t : (A/B)^1} \qquad \frac{x : (B)^1 \quad \Gamma : (A)^0}{\Gamma / x : (A/B)^0}
$$

$$
\boxed{(t \circ x)/x \succ t}
$$

$$
\frac{\Delta : (B)^0 \quad (\Delta \circ t) : (A)^1}{t : (B \backslash A)^1} \qquad \frac{\Gamma : (A)^0 \quad x : (B)^1}{x \backslash \Gamma : (B \backslash A)^0}
$$

$$
\boxed{x \backslash (x \circ t) \succ t}
$$

$$
\frac{{}^{\triangleleft}(t) : (A)^1 \quad (t)^{\triangleright} : (B)^1}{t : (A \bullet B)^1} \qquad \frac{\Delta : (B)^0 \quad \Gamma : (A)^0}{(\Gamma \circ \Delta) : (A \bullet B)^0}
$$

$$
\boxed{({}^{\triangleleft}(t) \circ (t)^{\triangleright}) \succ t}
$$

$$
\frac{{}^{\sqcup}t : (A)^1}{t : (\Diamond A)^1} \quad \frac{\Gamma : (A)^0}{{}^{\diamond}\Gamma : (\Diamond A)^0} \qquad \frac{{}^{\diamond}t : (A)^1}{t : (\Box^{\downarrow} A)^1} \quad \frac{\Gamma : (A)^0}{{}^{\sqcap}\Gamma : (\Box^{\downarrow} A)^0}
$$

$$
\boxed{{}^{\diamond\sqcup}t \succ t} \qquad \boxed{{}^{\sqcap\diamond}t \succ t}
$$

The basic residuation reductions in Definition 7.9 are dictated by the identities for complex formulae $\Diamond A$, $\Box^{\downarrow} A$, $A \bullet B$, A/B, $B \backslash A$. Structural postulates $A \to B$ translate to reductions $\sigma(B) \succ \sigma(A)$, where $\sigma(\cdot)$ is the structure label translation of a formula. The reduction for the distributivity postulate K is given as an illustration in (46). Notice that both residuation reductions and structural postulate reductions are asymmetric, capturing the asymmetry of the derivability relation.

$$(46) \qquad \Diamond(A \bullet B) \to \Diamond A \bullet \Diamond B \quad \overset{\sigma(\cdot)}{\rightsquigarrow} \quad ({}^{\diamond}t \circ {}^{\diamond}u) \succ {}^{\diamond}(t \circ u).$$

The parsing problem now assumes the following form. To determine whether a string $x_1, \ldots, x_n$ can be assigned the goal type B on the basis of a multiset of lexical assumptions $\Gamma = x_1 : A_1, \ldots, x_n : A_n$, one takes the formula decomposition of $(\Gamma)^1, (B)^0$, and resolves the literals $t : (p)^1$, $\Delta : (p)^0$, with matching $\Delta := t$ under the residuation and/or structural postulate rewritings. The string $x_1, \ldots, x_n$ has to be the yield of the structure label assigned to the goal type B.

EXAMPLE 7.10. Compare the unfoldings (†) for the theorem $A \to \Box^{\downarrow}\Diamond A$ and (‡) for the non-theorem $\Box^{\downarrow}\Diamond A \to A$. Matching $\underline{1}, \underline{2}$ gives the instantiation $\Delta := x$. For the goal type $(\Box^{\downarrow}\Diamond A)^0$ we get ${}^{\sqcap\diamond}\Delta = {}^{\sqcap\diamond}x \succ x$. In the case of (‡), matching $\underline{3}, \underline{4}$ yields $\Gamma := {}^{\sqcup\diamond}x$ which does not reduce to x.

$$(\dagger) \quad x : (A)^1 \ \underline{1} \quad \cfrac{\cfrac{\Delta : (A)^0 \ \underline{2}}{{}^{\diamond}\Delta : (\Diamond A)^0}}{{}^{\sqcap\diamond}\Delta : (\Box^{\downarrow}\Diamond A)^0} \qquad\qquad (\ddagger) \quad \cfrac{\cfrac{{}^{\sqcup\diamond}x : (A)^1 \ \underline{3}}{{}^{\diamond}x : (\Diamond A)^1}}{x : (\Box^{\downarrow}\Diamond A)^1} \quad \Gamma : (A)^0 \ \underline{4}$$

Efficient compilation techniques. The labeling regime of Definition 7.9 covers the multimodal architecture in a general fashion. In designing efficient compilation techniques one can exploit the properties of specific multimodal grammars. Such techniques have been developed in (Morrill, 1995b, 1995c) for the grammar fragment covered by Morrill (1994a) and some extensions. With a restriction on the use of the product connective, the compiler can translate lexical type assignments into a higher-order *clausal* fragment of linear logic. The clauses are processed by a linear-logical clausal engine and the normalized structure labels and semantic labels yielding the string are enumerated. The structural, sublinear properties, are represented by the term structure of the linear clauses. Satisfaction of constraints under associativity can be met not by enumerating and testing unifiers, but by propagating successive constraints through string position or difference list representations, as used in the compilation of context-free grammar. One thus obtains a linear logical programming paradigm for categorial grammar which is the counterpart of the logic programing paradigm for phrase structure grammar. But whereas the latter lacks resource-consciousness (in a derivation a rule may be used once, more than one, or not at all), sensitivity for the lexical resources processed is a built-in feature of the categorial paradigm.

8. Conclusions, directions for further research

If one compares the present state of the field with the situation as described seven years ago in the overview chapter of Moortgat (1988), one can qualify the changes as dramatic. On the level of 'empirical coverage', one has witnessed a strong increase in linguistic sophistication. On the level of 'logical foundations', Lambek's architecture for a grammar logic has been significantly generalized without sacrificing the attractive features of the original design. Below we summarize some key themes of the type-logical research that may facilitate comparison with related grammatical frameworks.

- Design of a specific *grammar logic*, i.e. a logic with a consequence relation attuned to the resource-sensitivity of grammatical inference – to be contrasted with 'general purpose' specification languages for grammar development, where such resource sensitivity has to be stipulated, e.g., the language of feature logic used in HPSG.
- A unified *deductive perspective* on the composition of form and meaning in natural language – to be contrasted with *rule-based* implementations of the compositionality principle.
- Radical lexicalism. Properties of the macro-grammatical organization are fully projected from lexical type declarations.
- Integration of the grammar logic in a wider landscape of reasoning systems, so that the transition between the formal systems characterizing 'knowledge of language' and the systems of inference underlying more general cognitive/reasoning capacities can be seen as gradual.

The change of emphasis from individual type logics to mixed architectures suggests new lines of research. The following themes, among others, would seem relevant for future exploration.

- Descriptive studies. Although, according to Carpenter (1996), the current descriptive coverage of type logical grammar rivals that of competing grammar formalisms, one can expect a wide range of further descriptive studies exploiting the expressivity of interactive modes of structural composition. Contrastive studies could deepen our understanding of the 'logical' perspective on parametric variation, characterized in terms of language specific structural rule packages.
- Formal learnability theory. From a cognitive point of view, the radical lexicalism of the type-logical approach makes the *acquisition problem* acute. This requires a theory explaining how multimodal type assignments (with their resource management properties) could be inferred from exposition to raw data. Learnability theory for the extended type logics can build on results that have been obtained for individual systems (e.g., Buszkowski and Penn, 1990; Kanazawa, 1992), but will have to remove the unrealistic input conditions for the learning algorithm assumed in these studies.
- Computational complexity. Even at the level of individual systems, our knowledge is partial, see Van Benthem (1991, 1995), Aarts (1994), Aarts and Trautwein (1995) for discussion and results. The context-free recognizing power result for **L** of Pentus (1993), for example, has not yielded a polynomial complexity result for this system. In the multimodal setting, one would like to have a systematic theory linking complexity to the algebraic properties of the characterizing rule packages.

- Connections between categorial type-logics and Linear Logic. In this chapter, we have presented an interpretation of the categorial formalism in terms of structural composition of grammatical resources. Recent studies of applications of Linear Logic in linguistic analysis suggest an interesting alternative interpretation in terms of temporal composition of grammatical processes. See Lecomte and Retoré (1995) for an illustration. An integration of these two complementary perspectives would offer a unified framework for the study of the static aspects of linguistic structure and the dynamics of natural language communication.

Acknowledgements

This chapter is based in part on work supported by the National Science Foundation under Grant No. SBR-9510706, and on research conducted in the context of the Esprit BRA project 6852 'Dynamic interpretation of natural language'. I thank the editors, Gosse Bouma and Martin Emms for comments on preliminary versions. The gestation period was somewhat longer than anticipated: it started with Moortgat and Oehrle (1993), and produced Moortgat (1995), Kurtonina and Moortgat (1995) as preparations for the final delivery. I am deeply indebted to Natasha Kurtonina, Dick Oehrle and Glyn Morrill: it was a pleasure to work together and exchange ideas with them over these years. The chapter has greatly benefited from their efforts. I also wish to thank Herman Hendriks for his meticulous comments which turned final drafts into prefinal ones. All remaining errors and imperfections are my own.

References

Aarts, E. (1994), *Proving theorems of the second order Lambek calculus in polynomial time*, Stud. Logica **53**, 373–387.

Aarts, E. and Trautwein, K. (1995), *Non-associative Lambek categorial grammar in polynomial time*, Math. Logic Q. **41**, 476–484.

Abrusci, M.V. (1996), *Semantics of proofs for noncommutative linear logic*, Preprint CILA, University of Bari.

Abrusci, M., Casadio, C. and Moortgat, M. (eds) (1994), *Linear logic and Lambek calculus*, Proceedings 1993 Rome Workshop. Esprit BRA 6852 Dyana-2 Occasional Publications, ILLC, Amsterdam.

Ades, A. and Steedman, K. (1982), *On the order of words*, Ling. and Philos. **4**, 517–558.

Adriaans, P. (1992), *Language learning from a categorial perspective*, PhD Dissertation, University of Amsterdam.

Ajdukiewicz, K. (1935), *Die syntaktische Konnexität*, Stud. Philos. **1**, 1–27. (English translation in Storrs McCall, ed., *Polish Logic*, 1920–1939. Oxford (1967), 207–231.)

Andréka, H. and Mikulás, S. (1994), *Lambek calculus and its relational semantics: Completeness and incompleteness*, J. Logic, Lang., Inform. **3**, 1–38.

Andreoli, J.-M. (1992), *Logic programming with focussing proofs in Linear Logic*, J. Logic Comput. **2**(3).

Bach, E. (1983a), *On the relationship between word-grammar and phrase-grammar*, Nat. Language and Ling. Theory **1**, 65–89.

Bach, E. (1983b), *Generalized categorial grammars and the English auxiliary*, Linguistic Categories. Auxiliaries and Related Puzzles vol. II, F. Heny and B. Richards, eds, Reidel, Dordrecht, 101–120.

Bach, E. (1984), *Some generalizations of categorial grammar*, Varieties of Formal Semantics, F. Landman and F. Veltman, eds, Foris, Dordrecht, 1–23.

Bach, E. (1988), *Categorial grammars as theories of language*, Categorial Grammars and Natural Language Structures, R.T. Oehrle, E. Bach and D. Wheeler, eds, Reidel, Dordrecht, 17–34.

Bar-Hillel, Y. (1964), *Language and Information*, Addison-Wesley, New York.

Barendregt, H. (1992), *λ-calculi with types*, Handbook of Logic in Computer Science vol. 2, S. Abramsky, D.M. Gabbay and T.E. Maibaum, eds, Oxford, 117–309.

Barry, G. (1991), *Derivation and structure in categorial grammar*, PhD Dissertation, Edinburgh.

Barry, G., Hepple, M., Leslie, N. and Morrill, G. (1991), *Proof figures and structural operators for categorial grammar*, Proceedings of the Fifth Conference of the European Chapter of the Association for Computational Linguistics, Berlin.

Barry, G. and Morrill, G. (eds) (1990), *Studies in categorial grammar*, Edinburgh Working Papers in Cognitive Science **5**, CCS, Edinburgh.

Barry, G. and Pickering, M. (1990), *Dependency and constituency in categorial grammar*, Studies in Categorial Grammar, G. Barry and G. Morrill, eds, CCS, Edinburgh, 23–45.

Bayer, S. and Johnson, M. (1995), *Features and agreement*, Proceedings ACL 1995, San Francisco, 70–76.

Belnap, N.D. (1982), *Display logic*, J. Philos. Logic **11**, 375–417.

Blackburn, P. and De Rijke, M. (1995), *Zooming-in, zooming-out*, Logic, Language, and Computation, J. Seligman and D. Westerståhl, eds, CSLI Lecture Notes, Chicago.

Bouma, G. (1988a), *Nonmonotonicity and categorial unification grammar*, PhD Dissertation, Groningen.

Bouma, G. (1988b), *Modifiers and specifiers in categorial unification grammar*, Linguistics **26**, 21–46.

Bouma, G. and Van Noord, G. (1994), *Constraint-based categorial grammar*, Proceedings ACL94.

Bucalo, A. (1994), *Modalities in Linear Logic weaker than the exponential "of course": Algebraic and relational semantics*, J. Logic, Lang., Inform. **3**, 211–232.

Buszkowski, W. (1984), *Fregean Grammar and residuated semigroups*, Frege Conference 1984, G. Wechsung, ed., Akademie-Verlag, Berlin.

Buszkowski, W. (1986), *Completeness results for Lambek syntactic calculus*, Z. Math. Logik Grundlag. Math. **32**, 13–28.

Buszkowski, W. (1987), *The logic of types*, Initiatives in Logic, J.T. Srzednicki, ed., Nijhoff, The Hague.

Buszkowski, W. (1988), *Generative power of categorial grammars*, Categorial Grammars and Natural Language Structures, R.T. Oehrle, E. Bach and D. Wheeler, eds, Reidel, Dordrecht, 69–94.

Buszkowski, W., Marciszewski, W. and Van Benthem, J. (eds) (1988), *Categorial Grammar*, Benjamin, Amsterdam.

Buszkowski, W. and Penn, G. (1990), *Categorial grammars determined from linguistic data by unification*, Stud. Logica **49**, 431–454.

Calder, J., Klein, E. and Zeevat, H. (1988), *Unification categorial grammar: A concise, extendable grammar for natural language processing*, Proceedings COLING 1988, Budapest, 83–86.

Carpenter, B. (1991), *The generative power of categorial grammars and head-driven phrase structure grammars with lexical rules*, Comput. Ling. **17**, 301–314.

Carpenter, B. (1992a), *Typed Feature Structures*, Cambridge.

Carpenter, B. (1992b), *Categorial grammars, lexical rules, and the English predicative*, Formal Grammar. Theory and Implementation, R. Levine, ed., Cambridge.

Carpenter, B. (1994), *Quantification and scoping: A deductive account*, Proceedings 13th West Coast Conference on Formal Linguistics, San Diego.

Carpenter, B. (1996), *Type-Logical Semantics*, MIT Press, Cambridge, MA.

Curry, H. (1961), *Some logical aspects of grammatical structure*, Structure of Language and Its Mathematical Aspects, R. Jakobson, ed., Providence, RI, 56–68.

Curry, H. and Feys, R. (1958), *Combinatory Logic*, vol. I, Amsterdam.

Dalrymple, M., Lamping, J., Pereira, F. and Saraswat, V. (1995), *Linear logic for meaning assembly*, Formal Grammar, G. Morrill and R.T. Oehrle (eds), Barcelona, 75–93.

Dörre, J., Gabbay, D. and König, E. (1994), *Fibered semantics for feature-based grammar logic*, Computational Aspects of Constraint-based Linguistic Description, J. Döre, ed., Esprit BRA Dyana-2 Deliverable R1.2.B. (To appear in J. Logic, Lang., Inform.)

Dörre, J. and Manandhar, S. (1995), *On constraint-based Lambek calculi*, Specifying Syntactic Structures, Blackburn and De Rijke, eds, CSLI Publications (to appear).

Došen, K. (1992), *A brief survey of frames for the Lambek calculus*, Z. Math. Logik Grundlag. Math. **38**, 179–187.

Došen, K. (1988, 1989), *Sequent systems and groupoid models*, Stud. Logica **47**, 353–385; **48**, 41–65.

Došen, K. and Schröder-Heister, P. (eds) (1993), *Substructural Logics*, Oxford.

Dowty, D. (1988), *Type-raising, functional composition, and non-constituent conjunction*, Categorial Grammars and Natural Language Structures, R.T. Oehrle, E. Bach and D. Wheeler, eds, Reidel, Dordrecht, 153–197.

Dowty, D. (1991), *Towards a minimalist theory of syntactic structure*, Discontinuous Constituency, W. Sijtsma and A. van Horck, eds, De Gruyter, Berlin (to appear).

Dunn, M. (1993), *Partial gaggles applied to logics with restricted structural rules*, Substructural Logics, K. Došen and P. Schröder-Heister, eds, Oxford, 63–108.

Emms, M. (1993a), *Parsing with polymorphism*, Proceedings of the Sixth Conference of the European ACL, Utrecht, 120–129.

Emms, M. (1993b), *Some applications of categorial polymorphism*, Polymorphic Treatments, M. Moortgat, ed., Esprit BRA 6852 Dyana-2 Deliverable R1.3.A, 1–52.

Emms, M. (1994a), *Extraction-covering extensions of the Lambek calculus are not CF*, Proceedings of the Ninth Amsterdam Colloquium, P. Dekker and M. Stokhof, eds, ILLC, Amsterdam, 269–286.

Emms, M. (1994b), *Movement in polymorphic and labelled calculi*, Linear Logic and Lambek Calculus, M. Abrusci, C. Casado and M. Moortgat, eds, ILLC, Amsterdam, 77–98.

Emms, M. (1994c), *Completeness results for polymorphic Lambek calculus*, Lambek Calculus, Multimodal and Polymorphic Extensions, M. Moortgat, ed., Esprit BRA 6852 Dyana-2 Deliverable R1.1.B, 73–100.

Emms, M. (1995), *An undecidability result for polymorphic Lambek calculus*, Logics of Structured Resources, M. Moortgat, ed., Esprit BRA 6852 Dyana-2 Deliverable R1.1.C, 59–77.

Emms, M. and Leiss, H. (1993), *The Cut-Elimination theorem for the second order Lambek calculus*, Categorial Parsing and Normalization, H. Leiss, ed., Esprit BRA 6852 Dyana-2 Deliverable R1.1.A, 77–100.

Gabbay, D. (1994), *LDS – Labeled Deductive Systems*, Report MPI-I-94-223, Max-Planck-Institut für Informatik, Saarbrücken. (To appear with Oxford Univ. Press.)

Gabbay, D. and Kempson, R. (1992), *Natural language content: A truth-theoretic perspective*, Proceedings Eighth Amsterdam Colloquium, P. Dekker and M. Stokhof, eds, ILLC, Amsterdam, 173–198.

Gazdar, G. (1980), *A cross-categorial semantics for coordination*, Linguist. and Philos. **3**, 407–410.

Geach, P. (1972), *A program for syntax*, Semantics of Natural Language, D. Davidson and G. Harman, eds, Reidel, Dordrecht, 483–497. Also in *Categorial Grammar*, W. Buszkowski, W. Marciszewski and J. van Benthem, eds, Amsterdam.

Gentzen, G. (1934), *Untersuchungen über das logische Schliessen*, Math. Z. **39**, 176–210; 405–431.

Girard, J.-Y. (1987), *Linear logic*, Theor. Comput. Sci. **50**, 1–102.

Girard, J.-Y. (1993), *On the unity of logic*, Ann. Pure Appl. Logic **59**, 201–217.

Girard, J.-Y. (1995a), *Geometry of interaction III: The general case*, Advances in Linear Logic, Girard, Lafont and Regnier, eds, Cambridge, 329–389.

Girard, J.-Y. (1995b), *Light linear logic*, Manuscript, LMD, Marseille.

Girard, J.-Y., Taylor, P. and Lafont, Y. (1989), *Proofs and Types*, Cambridge Tracts in Theoretical Computer Science vol. 7, Cambridge.

Hendriks, H. (1993), *Studied flexibility. Categories and types in syntax and semantics*, PhD Dissertation, ILLC, Amsterdam.

Hendriks, H. (1994), *Information packaging in a categorial perspective*, Integrating Information Structure into Constraint-Based and Categorial Approaches, E. Engdahl, ed., Esprit BRA 6852 Dyana-2 Deliverable R1.3.B, 89–116.

Hendriks, P. (1995), *Comparatives and categorial grammar*, PhD Dissertation, Groningen.

Hepple, M. (1990), *The grammar and processing of order and dependency*, PhD Dissertation, Edinburgh.

Hepple, M. (1992), *Command and domain constraints in a categorial theory of binding*, Proceedings Eighth Amsterdam Colloquium, 253–270.

Hepple, M. (1994), *Labelled deduction and discontinuous constituency*, Linear Logic and Lambek Calculus, M. Abrusci, C. Casadio and M. Moortgat, eds, ILLC, Amsterdam, 123–150.

Hepple, M. (1995), *Hybrid categorial logics*, Bull. IGPL (Special issue on Deduction and Language, R. Kempson, ed.) **3**(2,3), 343–355.

Hinrichs, E. and Nakazawa, T. (1994), *Linearizing AUXs in German verbal complexes*, German Grammar in HPSG, Nerbonne, Netter and Pollard, eds, CSLI Lecture Notes, Stanford, 11–38.

Hodas, J.S. and Miller, D. (1994), *Logic programming in a fragment of intuitionistic linear logic*, Inform. and Comput. **110**, 327–365.

Jacobson, P. (1987), *Phrase structure, grammatical relations, and discontinuous constituents*, Syntax and Semantics 20: Discontinuous Constituency, G.J. Huck and A.E. Ojeda, eds, Academic Press, New York, 27–69.

Jakobson, R. (ed.) (1961), *Structure of language and its mathematical aspects*, Proceedings of the Twelfth Symposium in Applied Mathematics, Providence, RI.

Joshi, A. and Kulick, S. (1995), *Partial proof trees as building blocks for a categorial grammar*, Formal Grammar, G. Morrill and R.T. Oehrle, eds, Barcelona, 138–149.

Kanazawa, M. (1992), *The Lambek calculus enriched with additional connectives*, J. Logic, Lang., Inform. **1**, 141–171.

Kanazawa, M. (1994), *Learnable classes of categorial grammars*, PhD Dissertation, Stanford.

Kandulski, W. (1988), *The non-associative Lambek calculus*, Categorical Grammar, W. Buszkowski, W. Marciszewski and J. van Benthem, eds, Amsterdam, 141–151.

Keenan, E.L. and Faltz, L. (1985), *Boolean Semantics for Natural Language*, Reidel, Dordrecht.

Kołowska-Gawiejnowics, M. (1995), *Powerset residuated algebras and generalized Lambek calculus*, Report 36/1995, Faculty of Mathematics and Computer Science, Adam Mickiewicz University, Poznán. (To appear in Math. Logic Q.)

König, E. (1991), *Parsing as natural deduction*, Proceedings of the 27th Annual Meeting of the ACL, Vancouver, 272–279.

König, E. (1995), *LexGram – a practical categorial grammar formalism*, Proceedings Computational Logic for Natural Language Processing, Edinburgh.

Kraak, E. (1995), *French object clitics: A multimodal analysis*, Formal Grammar, G. Morrill and R.T. Oehrle, eds, Barcelona, 166–180.

Kracht, M. (1993), *Power and weakness of the modal display calculus*, Manuscript, Freie Universität Berlin.

Kurtonina, N. (1995), *Frames and labels. A modal analysis of categorial inference*, PhD Dissertation, OTS Utrecht, ILLC Amsterdam.

Kurtonina, N. and Moortgat, M. (1995), *Structural control*, Logics of Structured Resources, M. Moortgat, ed., Esprit BRA 6852 Dyana-2 Deliverable R1.1.C. (To appear in P. Blackburn and M. de Rijke, eds, *Specifying Syntactic Structures*, CSLI Publications.)

Lambek, J. (1958), *The mathematics of sentence structure*, Amer. Math. Monthly **65**, 154–170.

Lambek, J. (1961), *On the calculus of syntactic types*, Structure of Language and Its Mathematical Aspects, R. Jakobson, ed., Providence, RI.

Lambek, J. (1968), *Deductive systems and categories, I*, J. Math. Syst. Theory **2**, 278–318.

Lambek, J. (1988), *Categorial and categorical grammar*, Categorial Grammars and Natural Language Structures, R.T. Oehrle, E. Bach and D. Wheeler, eds, Reidel, Dordrecht, 297–317.

Lambek, J. (1993a), *Logic without structural rules. (Another look at Cut Elimination)*, Substructural Logics, K. Došen and P. Schröder-Heister, eds, Oxford, 179–206.

Lambek, J. (1993b), *From categorial grammar to bilinear logic*, Substructural Logics, K. Došen and P. Schröder-Heister, eds, Oxford, 207–238.

Lecomte and Retoré (1995), *Pomset logic as an alternative categorial grammar*, Formal Grammar, G. Morrill and R.T. Oehrle, eds, Barcelona, 181–196.

Lewis, D. (1972), *General semantics*, Semantics of Natural Language, D. Davidson and G. Harman, eds, Reidel, Dordrecht, 169–218.

Lincoln, P., Scedrov, A. and Shankar, N. (1995), *Decision problems for second-order linear logic*, Proceedings of the Tenth Annual IEEE Symposium on Logic in Computer Science.

Lyons, J. (1968), *Theoretical Linguistics*, Cambridge.

Miller, Ph. (1992), *Clitics and Constituents in Phrase Structure Grammar*, Garland, New York.

Moortgat, M. (1988), *Categorial Investigations. Logical and Linguistic Aspects of the Lambek Calculus*, Foris, Dordrecht.

Moortgat, M. (1991), *Generalized quantification and discontinuous type constructors*. (To appear in W. Sijtsma and A. van Horck, eds, *Discontinuous Constituency*, De Gruyter, Berlin.)

Moortgat, M. (1992), *Labelled Deductive Systems for categorial theorem proving*, Proceedings Eighth Amsterdam Colloquium, ILLC, Amsterdam, 403–424.

Moortgat, M. (1995), *Multimodal linguistic inference*, Bull. IGPL (Special issue on Deduction and Language, R. Kempson, ed.) **3**(2,3), 371–401. (To appear in J. Logic, Lang., Inform.)

Moortgat, M. (1996), *In situ binding: A modal analysis*, Proceedings Tenth Amsterdam Colloquium, P. Dekker and M. Stokhof, eds, ILLC, Amsterdam, 539–549.

Moortgat, M. and Morrill, G. (1991), *Heads and phrases. Type calculus for dependency and constituent structure*, Manuscript, OTS Utrecht.

Moortgat, M. and Oehrle, R. (1993), *Logical parameters and linguistic variation. Lecture notes on categorial grammar*, Fifth European Summer School in Logic, Language and Information, Lisbon.

Moortgat, M. and Oehrle, R.T. (1994), *Adjacency, dependency and order*, Proceedings Ninth Amsterdam Colloquium, P. Dekker and M. Stokhof, eds, ILLC, Amsterdam, 447–466.

Morrill, G. (1990a), *Intensionality and Boundedness*, Ling. and Philos. **13**, 699–726.

Morrill, G. (1990b), *Grammar and logical types*, Proceedings of the Seventh Amsterdam Colloquium, M. Stokhof and L. Torenvliet, eds, ILLC, Amsterdam, 429–450.

Morrill, G. (1994a), *Type Logical Grammar. Categorial Logic of Signs*, Kluwer, Dordrecht.

Morrill, G. (1994b), *Structural facilitation and structural inhibition*, Linear Logic and Lambek Calculus, M. Abrusci, C. Casadio and M. Moortgat, eds, ILLC, Amsterdam, 183–210.

Morrill, G. (1995a), *Discontinuity in categorial grammar*, Ling. and Philos. **18**, 175–219.

Morrill, G. (1995b), *Higher-order linear logic programming of categorial deduction*, Proceedings of the European Chapter of the Association for Computational Linguistics, Dublin.

Morrill, G. (1995c), *Clausal proofs and discontinuity*, Bull. IGPL (Special issue on Deduction and Language, R. Kempson, ed.) **3**(2,3), 403–427.

Morrill, G. and Oehrle, R.T. (1995), *Formal grammar*, Proceedings of the Conference of the European Summer School in Logic, Language and Information, Barcelona.

Muskens, R. (1994), *Categorial grammar and discourse representation theory*, Proceedings COLING 94, Kyoto, 508–514.

Oehrle, R.T. (1988), *Multi-dimensional compositional functions as a basis for grammatical analysis*, Categorial Grammars and Natural Language Structures, R.T. Oehrle, E. Bach and D. Wheeler, eds, Reidel, Dordrecht, 349–389.

Oehrle, R.T. (1995), *Term-labeled categorial type systems*, Ling. and Philos. **17**, 633–678.

Oehrle, R.T., Bach, E. and Wheeler, D. (eds) (1988), *Categorial Grammars and Natural Language Structures*, Reidel, Dordrecht.

Partee, B. and Rooth, M. (1983), *Generalized conjunction and type ambiguity*, Meaning, Use, and Interpretation of Language, Bäuerle et al., eds, De Gruyter, Berlin, 361–383.

Pollard, C. (1984), *Head grammars, generalized phrase structure grammars, and natural language*, PhD Dissertation, Stanford.

Pollard, C. and Sag, I. (1994), *Head-Driven Phrase Structure Grammar*, Chicago.

Pentus, M. (1993), *Lambek grammars are context free*, Proceedings Eighth Annual IEEE Symposium on Logic in Computer Science, Montreal.

Pentus, M. (1994), *Language completeness of the Lambek calculus*, Proceedings Ninth Annual IEEE Symposium on Logic in Computer Science, Paris.

Prawitz, D. (1965), *Natural Deduction: A Proof-Theoretical Study*, Uppsala.

Reape, M. (1989), *A logical treatment of semi-free word order and bounded discontinuous constituency*, Proceedings of the Fourth Conference of the European Chapter of the Association for Computational Linguistics, Manchester, 103–115.

Restall, G. (1993), *Simplified semantics for relevant logics (and some of their rivals)*, J. Philos. Logic **22**, 279–303.

Restall, G. (1994), *A useful substructural logic*, Bull. IGPL **2**, 137–148.

Roorda, D. (1991), *Resource logics. Proof-theoretical investigations*, PhD Dissertation, Amsterdam.

Routley, R. and Meyer, R.K. (1972), *The semantics of entailment II*, J. Philos. Logic **1**, 53–73.

Sag, I., Gazdar, G., Wasow, Th. and Weisler, S. (1985), *Coordination and how to distinguish categories*, Nat. Language and Ling. Theory **3**, 117–171.

Sánchez Valencia, V. (1995), *Natural logic: Parsing driven inference*, To appear in Ling. Anal.

Shieber, S.M. (1986), *An Introduction to Unification-Based Approaches to Grammar*, CSLI Lecture Notes, Chicago.
Shieber, S.M. (1992), *Constraint-Based Grammar Formalisms. Parsing and Type Inference for Natural and Computer Languages*, MIT Press, Cambridge, MA.
Schmerling, S. (1983), *A new theory of English auxiliaries*, Linguistic Categories, Auxiliaries and Related Puzzles vol. II, F. Heny and B. Richards, eds, Reidel, Dordrecht, 1–53.
Steedman, M. (1984), *A categorial theory of intersecting dependencies in Dutch infinitival complements*, Proceedings of the International Conference on Complementation, De Geest and Putseys, eds, Foris, Dordrecht, 215–226.
Steedman, M. (1985), *Dependency and coordination in the grammar of Dutch and English*, Language **61**, 523–568.
Steedman, M. (1987), *Combinatory grammars and parasitic gaps*, Nat. Language and Ling. Theory **5**, 403–439.
Steedman, M. (1988), *Combinators and grammars*, Categorial Grammars and Natural Language Structures, R.T. Oehrle, E. Bach and D. Wheeler, eds, Reidel, Dordrecht, 417–442.
Steedman, M. (1991), *Structure and intonation*, Language **68**, 260–296.
Steedman, M. (1993), *Categorial grammar. Tutorial overview*, Lingua **90**, 221–258.
Steedman, M. (1994), *The grammar of intonation and focus*, Proceedings Ninth Amsterdam Colloquium, P. Dekker and M. Stokhof, eds, ILLC, Amsterdam, 17–33.
Szabolcsi, A. (1987), *On combinatory categorial grammar*, Proceedings of the Symposium on Logic and Language, Debrečen, Budapest, 151–162.
Trautwein, M. (1995), *Computational pitfalls in tractable grammar formalisms*, PhD Thesis, ILLC, Amsterdam.
Troelstra, A.S. (1992), *Lectures on Linear Logic*, CSLI Lecture Notes, Stanford.
Uszkoreit, H. (1986), *Categorial unification grammar*, Proceedings COLING 1986, Bonn, 187–194.
Van Benthem, J. (1983), *The semantics of variety in categorial grammar*, Report 83–29, Simon Fraser University, Burnaby (B.C.), Canada. (Revised version in W. Buszkowski, W. Marciszewski and J. van Benthem (eds) (1988), *Categorial Grammar*, Benjamin, Amsterdam.)
Van Benthem, J. (1984), *Correspondence theory*, Handbook of Philosophical Logic vol. II, D. Gabbay and F. Günthner, eds, Dordrecht, 167–247.
Van Benthem, J. (1987), *Categorial grammar and lambda calculus*, Mathematical Logic and Its Applications, D. Skordev, ed., Plenum, New York, 39–60.
Van Benthem, J. (1988a), *Categorial grammar meets unification*, Unification Formalisms: Syntax, Semantics and Implementation, J. Wedekind et al., eds.
Van Benthem, J. (1988b), *The Lambek calculus*, Categorial Grammars and Natural Language Structures, R.T. Oehrle, E. Bach and D. Wheeler, eds, Reidel, Dordrecht, 35–68.
Van Benthem, J. (1991, 1995), *Language in Action. Categories, Lambdas, and Dynamic Logic*, Studies in Logic, North-Holland, Amsterdam. (Student edition: (1995), MIT Press, Cambridge, MA.)
Venema, Y. (1994a), *Meeting strength in substructural logics*, Stud. Logica **53**, 3–32.
Venema, Y. (1994b), *Tree models and (labeled) categorial grammar*, Proceedings Ninth Amsterdam Colloquium, P. Dekker and M. Stokhof, eds, ILLC, Amsterdam, 703–722.
Versmissen, K. (1993), *Categorial grammar, modalities and algebraic semantics*, Proceedings EACL93, 377–383.
Versmissen, K. (1996), *Grammatical composition. Modes, models and modalities*, PhD Dissertation, OTS Utrecht.
Wallen, L.A. (1990), *Automated Deduction in Nonclassical Logics*, MIT Press, Cambridge, MA.
Wansing, H. (1992a), *Sequent calculi for normal modal propositional logics*, ILLC Report LP–92–12.
Wansing, H. (1992b), *Formulas-as-types for a hierarchy of sublogics of intuitionistic propositional logic*, Non-Classical Logics and Information Processing, D. Pearce and H. Wansing, eds, Springer Lecture Notes in AI 619, Berlin.
Wansing, H. (1992c), *The logic of information structures*, PhD Dissertation, Berlin.
Zielonka, W. (1989), *A simple and general method of solving the finite axiomatizability problems for Lambek's syntactic calculi*, Stud. Logica **48**, 35–39.
Zwarts, F. (1986), *Categoriale grammatica en algebraïsche semantiek*, PhD Dissertation, Groningen.

CHAPTER 3

Representing Discourse in Context*

Jan van Eijck

CWI, PO Box 94079, 1090 GB Amsterdam, The Netherlands
E-mail: jve@cwi.nl

Hans Kamp

Universität Stuttgart, Institut für Maschinelle Sprachverarbeitung, Azenbergstrasse 12, D-70174 Stuttgart, Germany
E-mail: hans@ims.uni-stuttgart.de

Commentator: Kees Vermeulen

Contents

*Financial support: LRE project FraCaS, NFI project NF 102/62-356.

HANDBOOK OF LOGIC AND LANGUAGE
Edited by J. van Benthem and A. ter Meulen

1. Introduction

The key idea behind the theory of the semantics of coherent multi-sentence discourse and text that is presented in this chapter – Discourse Representation Theory, or DRT for short – is that each new sentence S of a discourse is interpreted in the context provided by the sentences preceding it. The result of this interpretation is that the context is updated with the contribution made by S; often an important part of this process is that anaphoric elements of S are hooked up to elements that are present in the context. An implication of this conception of text interpretation is that one and the same structure serves simultaneously as content and as context – as content of the sentences that have been interpreted already and as context for the sentence that is to be interpreted next. This double duty imposes special constraints on logical form, which are absent when, as in most older conceptions of semantics and pragmatics, the contents and contexts are kept separate.

The initial problem that motivated the present theory is the interpretation of nominal and temporal anaphora in discourse. The key idea in the way of thinking about the semantics of discourse in context exemplified in (Heim, 1982) and (Kamp, 1981) is that each new sentence or phrase is interpreted as an addition to, or 'update' of, the context in which it is used and that this update often involves connections between elements from the sentence or phrase with elements from the context.

In the approach of Kamp (1981), which we will follow more closely here than the largely equivalent approach of Heim (1982), this idea is implemented in the form of interpretation rules – each associated with a particular lexical item or syntactic construction. When applied to a given sentence S, these rules identify the semantic contributions which S makes to the context C in which S is used and add these to C. In this way C is transformed into a new context, which carries the information contributed by S as well as the information that was part of the context already. The result can then serve as context for the interpretation of the sentence following S (in the given discourse or text), which leads to yet another context, and so on until the entire discourse or text has been interpreted.

An important aspect of this kind of updating of contexts is the introduction of elements – so-called reference markers or discourse referents – that can serve as antecedents to anaphoric expressions in subsequent discourse. These reference markers play a key part in the the context structures posited by DRT, the so-called Discourse Representation Structures or DRSs.

With its emphasis on representing and interpreting discourse in context, discourse representation theory has been instrumental in the emergence of a *dynamic perspective* on natural language semantics, where the center of the stage, occupied so long by the concept of truth with respect to appropriate models, has been replaced by context change conditions, with truth conditions defined in terms of those. Thus, under the influence of discourse representation theory, many traditional Montague grammarians have made the switch from static to dynamic semantics (see the Chapter on *Dynamics* in this Handbook). This shift has considerably enriched the enterprise of formal semantics, by bringing areas formerly belonging to informal pragmatics within its compass.

In the next section we will first look at some examples of DRSs and at the considerations which have led to their specific form. After that we will look more closely at the relationship between DRSs and the syntactic structure of sentences, discourses or texts from which they can be derived. This will lead us naturally to the much debated question whether the theory presented here is compositional. The compositionality issue will force us to look carefully at the operations by means of which DRSs can be put together from minimal building blocks. Next we will show, by developing a toy example, what a compositional discourse semantics for a fragment of natural language may look like. This is followed by sample treatments of quantification, tense and aspect. The chapter ends with some pointers to the literature on further extensions of the approach and to connections with related approaches.

2. The problem of anaphoric linking in context

The semantic relationship between personal pronouns and their antecedents was long perceived as being of two kinds: a pronoun either functions as an individual constant coreferential with its antecedent or it acts as a variable bound by its antecedent. However, in the examples (1)–(4) below, neither of these two possibilities seems to provide a correct account of how pronoun and antecedent are related.

(1) A man^1 entered. He_1 smiled.

(2) Every man who meets a nice woman^1 smiles at her_1.

(3) If a man^1 enters, he_1 smiles.

(4) Hob believes a witch^1 blighted his mare. Nob believes she_1 killed his sow.

In these examples we have used subscripts and superscripts to coindex anaphoric pronouns and their intended antecedents.

The first option – of pronoun and antecedent being coreferential – does not work for the simple reason that the antecedent does not refer (as there is no one particular thing that can be counted as the referent!); so a fortiori antecedent and pronoun cannot *co*refer (that is, refer to the same thing). The second option, the bound variable analysis, runs into problems because the pronoun seems to be outside the scope of its antecedent. For instance, in (1) the antecedent of the pronoun is an indefinite noun phrase occurring in the preceding sentence. In the approaches which see pronouns as either coreferring terms or bound variables, indefinite NPs are viewed as existential quantifiers whose scope does not extend beyond the sentence in which they occur. In such an approach there is no hope of the pronoun getting properly bound. Examples (2)–(4) present similar difficulties. Example (2) is arguably ambiguous in that *a nice woman* may be construed either as having wide or as having narrow scope with respect to *every man*. If *a nice woman* is construed as having narrow scope, i.e. as having its scope restricted to the relative clause, then the pronoun won't be bound; the phrase can bind the pronoun if it is given wide scope, as in that case its scope is the entire sentence, but this leads to an interpretation which, though perhaps marginally possible, is clearly not the preferred reading of (2). We find much the same problem with (3): in order that the indefinite *a man* bind the pronoun *he*, it must be construed as having scope over the conditional as a whole, and not just over the if-clause; but again, this yields a reading that is marginal at best, while the preferred reading is not available.

Sentences with the patterns of (2) and (3) have reached the modern semantic literature through Geach (1980), who traces them back to the Middle Ages and beyond. Geach's discussion revolves around examples with donkeys, so these sentences became known in the literature as *donkey sentences*. Also due to Geach are sentences like (4), which pose a binding problem across a sentential boundary, complicated by the fact that antecedent and anaphoric element occur in the scopes of different attitude predications, with distinct subjects.

Problems like the ones we encountered with (1)– (4) arise not just with pronouns. There are several other types of expressions with anaphoric uses that present essentially the same difficulties to the traditional ways of viewing the relationship between natural language and logic. First, there are other anaphoric noun phrases besides pronouns, viz. definite descriptions and demonstratives; and these also occur in the contexts where the problems we have just noted arise. Moreover, as was remarked already more than twenty years ago in (Partee, 1973), there are striking similarities in the behaviour of anaphoric pronouns and tenses, and it turns out that the interpretation of tense involves the same sort of anaphoric dependencies which (1)–(4) exhibit. More precisely, the past tense is often to be understood as referring to some particular time in the past (rather than meaning 'sometime in the past') and more often than not this particular time is to be recovered from the context in which the given past tense sentence is used.

(5) John entered the room. He switched on the light.

(6) Whenever John entered the room, he switched on the light.

In (5) the switching time is understood as temporally related to the time at which John entered the room (presumably the time of switching was directly after the time of entering) and a full interpretation of (5) needs to make this explicit. A quantificational sentence such as (6) suggests the same relationship between switching times and entering times; and insofar as the tense of the main clause is to be interpreted as anaphoric to that of the whenever-clause, this anaphoric connection raises the same questions as those of (2) and (3).

3. Basic ideas of discourse representation

The central concepts of DRT are best explained with reference to simple examples such as (1) in the previous section. The logical content of (1) appears to be that there was some man who entered and (then) smiled. That is, the content of (1) is what in standard predicate logic would be expressed by an existential quantification over material coming in part from the first and in another part from the second sentence of (1), roughly as in (7).

(7) $\exists x(\text{man}\ (x) \wedge \text{entered}\ (x) \wedge \text{smiled}\ (x)).$

As observed in the last section, according to DRT the interpretation of (1) results from a process in which an interpretation is obtained for the first sentence, which then serves as context for the interpretation of the second sentence. The interpretation of the second sentence transforms this context into a new context structure, the content of which is essentially that of (7).

The problem with (1) is that the first sentence has an existential interpretation and thus must in some way involve an existential quantifier, and that the contribution which the second sentence makes to the interpretation of (1) must be within the scope of that quantifier. Given the basic tenets of DRT, this means that (i) the first sentence of (1) must get assigned a representation, i.e. a DRS, K_1 which captures the existential interpretation of that sentence; and (ii) this DRS K_1 must be capable of acting as context for the interpretation of the second sentence in such a way that this second interpretation process transforms it into a DRS K_2 representing the truth conditions identified by (7). (i) entails that the reference marker introduced by the indefinite NP *a man* – let it be x – must get an existential interpretation within K_1; and (ii) entails that it is nevertheless available subsequently as antecedent for the pronoun *he*. Finally, after x has been so exploited in the interpretation of the second sentence, it must then receive once more an existential interpretation within the resulting DRS K_2.

Heim (1982) uses the metaphor of a filing cabinet for this process. The established representation structure K_1 is a set of file cards, and additions to the discourse effect a new structure K_2, which is the result of changing the file in the light of the new information. Here is how DRT deals with these desiderata. The DRS K_1 is as given in (8).

(8)

x
man x entered x

This can also be rendered in canonical set-theoretical notation, as in (9).

(9) $(\{\mathrm{x}\}, \{\mathrm{man\ x}, \mathrm{entered\ x}\})$.

Precisely how this DRS is derived from the syntactic structure of the first sentence of (1), and how DRS construction from sentences and texts works generally is discussed in Section 9. For now, suffice it to note that the reference marker x gets introduced when the NP *a man* is interpreted and that this interpretation also yields the two conditions *man(x)* and *entered(x)*, expressing that any admissible value a for x must be a man and that this man was one who entered.

A DRS like (8) can be viewed as a kind of 'model' of the situation which the represented discourse describes. The modeled situation contains at least one individual a, corresponding to the reference marker x, which satisfies the two conditions contained in (8), i.e. a is a man and a is someone who entered.

When a DRS is used as context in the interpretation of some sentence S, its reference markers may serve as antecedents for anaphoric NPs occurring in S. In the case of our example we have the following. (8), serving as context for the second sentence of (1), makes x available as antecedent for the pronoun *he*. That is, the interpretation of *he* links the reference marker it introduces, y say, to the marker x for the intended antecedent, something we express by means of the equational condition $y \doteq x$. In addition, the interpretation step yields, as in the case of the indefinite *a man*, a condition expressing the clausal predication which involves *he* as argument. Through the application of this principle (8) gets expanded to the DRS (10), which represents the content of all of (1).

(10)

x y
man x enter x $y \doteq x$ smiled y

DRS (10) models situations in which there is at least one individual that is a man, that entered and that smiled. It is easy to see that these are precisely the situations which satisfy the predicate formula (7). (This claim will be made formal by the model theory for DRSs, to be presented in Section 4.)

As illustrated by the above examples (8) and (10), a DRS generally consists of two parts, (i) a set of reference markers, the universe of the DRS, and (ii) a set of conditions, its condition set. There are some other general points which our example illustrates:

(i) The reference markers in the universe of a DRS all get an existential interpretation;

(ii) All reference markers in the universe of a context DRS are available as anaphoric antecedents to pronouns and other anaphoric expressions that are interpreted within this context;

(iii) The interpretation of a sentence S in the context provided by a DRS K results in a new DRS K', which captures not only the content represented by K but also the content of S, as interpreted with respect to K.

It should be clear that DRSs such as (8) and (10) can only represent information that has the logical form of an existentially quantified conjunction of atomic predications. But there is much information that is not of this form. This is so, in particular, for the information expressed by (3). So the DRS for (3) will have to make use of representational devices different from those that we have used up to this point.

The DRT conception of conditional information is this. The antecedent of a conditional describes a situation, and the conditional asserts that this situation must also satisfy the information specified in its consequent. When conditionals are seen from this perspective, it is not surprising that the interpretation of their consequents may use the interpretations of their antecedents as contexts much in the way the interpretation of a sentence S may build upon the interpretation assigned to the sentences preceding it in the discourse to which it belongs; for the consequent extends the situation description provided by the antecedent in essentially the same way in which S extends the situation described by its predecessors.

In the case of (3) this means that the DRS (8), which represents its antecedent (see the discussion of (1) above), can be exploited in the interpretation of the consequent, just as (8), as interpretation of the first sentence of (1), supported the interpretation of the second sentence of (1). To make this work out, we need a suitable representation for the consequent. This turns out to be (11).

(11)

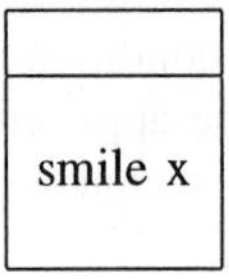

To obtain a representation of (3), (8) and (11) must be combined in a way which reveals the conditional connection between them. We represent this combination by a double arrow in between the two DRSs. The result $K \Rightarrow K'$, where K and K' are the two DRSs to be combined, is a DRS condition (a complex condition as opposed to the simple DRS conditions we have encountered so far). The DRS for a conditional sentence such as (3) will consist just of such a condition and nothing else.

Intuitively the meaning of a condition $K \Rightarrow K'$ is that a situation satisfying K also satisfies K'. This is indeed the semantics we adopt for such conditions (for details see Section 4). Applying this to the case of (3) we get the representation (12).

(12)

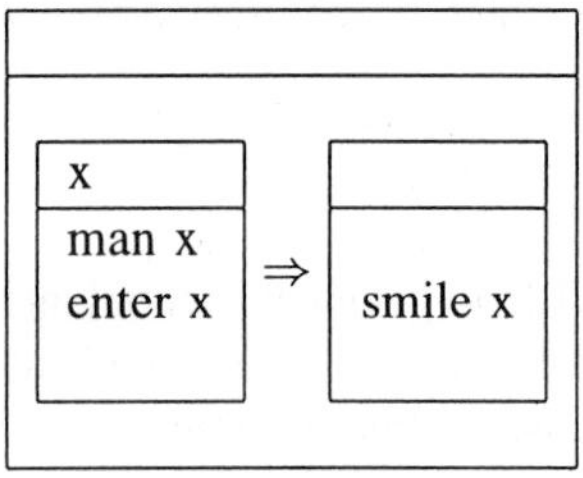

Conditions of the form $K \Rightarrow K'$ illustrate an important feature of DRT: The logical role played by a reference marker depends on the DRS-universe to which it belongs. Markers belonging to the universe of the main DRS get an existential interpretation – this is, we saw, a consequence of the principle that a DRS is true if it is possible to find individuals corresponding to the reference markers in the DRS universe which satisfy its conditions. This principle, however, applies only to the reference markers in the main DRS universe. The logic of reference markers in subordinate universes, such as for instance x in (12), is determined by the principles governing the complex DRS conditions to which they belong. Thus the semantics of conditions of the form $K \Rightarrow K'$ implies that for all individuals corresponding to reference markers in the universe of K which satisfy the conditions of K it is the case that K' is satisfiable as well. Thus the $\Rightarrow$-condition of (12) has the meaning that for every individual corresponding to the marker x – that is, for every man that enters – the right hand side DRS of (12) is satisfied, i.e. that individual smiles. Reference markers in the left hand side universe of an $\Rightarrow$- condition thus get a universal, not an existential interpretation.

It is worth noting explicitly the ingredients to this solution of the semantic dilemma posed by conditionals like (3). Crucial to the solution are:

(i) the combination of the principles of DRS construction, which assign to conditional sentences such as (3) representations such as (12), and

(ii) the semantics for $\Rightarrow$-conditions that has just been described.

Like any other DRS, (12) is a pair consisting of a set of reference markers and a set of conditions. But in (12) the first of these sets is empty. In particular, the reference marker x which does occur in (12) belongs not to the universe of the 'main' DRS of (12) but to that of a subordinate DRS, which itself is a constituent of some DRS condition occurring in (12). One important difference between reference markers in such subordinate positions and those belonging to the universe of the main DRS is that only the latter are accessible as antecedents for anaphoric pronouns in subsequent sentences. In general, in order that a reference marker can serve as antecedent to a subsequent pronoun, it must be accessible from the position that the pronoun occupies. Compare for instance the discourses (13) and (14).

(13) A man came in. He smiled. He was holding a flower in his right hand.

(14) If a man comes in, he smiles. ?He is holding a flower in his right hand.

While in (13) the second *he* is as unproblematic as the first *he*, in (14) the second *he* is hard or impossible to process. This difference is reflected by the fact that in the DRS for the first two sentences of (13) the reference marker for *a man* belongs to the universe of the main DRS and so is accessible to the pronoun of the last sentence, whereas in (14) this is not so.

The rules for processing sentences in the context of a representation structure impose formal constraints on availability of discourse referents for anaphoric linking. The set of available markers consists of the markers of the current structure, plus the markers of structures that can be reached from the current one by a series of steps in the directions *left*, (i.e. from the consequent of a pair $K \Rightarrow K'$ to the antecedent), and *up*, (i.e. from a structure to an encompassing structure).

For universally quantified sentences such as (2) DRT offers an analysis that closely resembles its treatment of conditionals. According to this analysis a universally quantifying NP imposes a conditional connection between its own descriptive content and the information expressed by the predication in which it participates as argument phrase; and this connection is interpreted in the same way as the $\Rightarrow$-conditions that the theory uses to represent conditional sentences. In particular, (2) gets an analysis in which any individual satisfying the descriptive content *man who meets a nice woman*, i.e. any individual corresponding to the reference marker x in the DRS (15), satisfies the DRS representing the main predication of (2). According to this way of looking at quantification, the descriptive content of the quantifying phrase can be taken as presupposed for purposes of interpreting the predication in which the phrase partakes, just as the antecedent of a conditional can be taken as given when interpreting its consequent. Thus, just as we saw for the consequent of the conditional (3), the construction of the DRS for the main predication of (2) may make use of information encoded in the 'descriptive content' DRS (15). The result is the DRS in (16).

(15)

x y
man x woman y nice y meet (x,y)

(16)

u
u $\doteq$ y smiles-at (x,u)

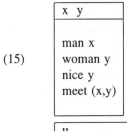

To get a representation of (2), DRSs (15) and (16) have to be combined into a single DRS condition. It is clear that $\Rightarrow$ has the desired effect. The result is (17).

(17)

x y		**u**
man x woman y nice y meet (x,y)	$\Rightarrow$	u $\doteq$ y smiles-at (x,u)

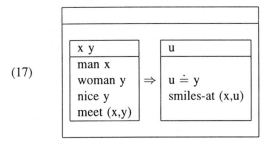

The constraints on marker accessibility are used to account for the awkwardness of anaphoric links as in (18).

(18) *If every man[1] meets a nice woman[2], he$_1$ smiles at her$_2$.

The difference between pronominal anaphora and the variable binding we find in classical logic is also nicely illustrated by anaphora involving the word *other*. Consider, e.g., (19).

(19) A man walked in. Another man followed him.

Here *another man* is anaphoric to *a man*, but the sense is that the two men should be different, not that they are the same. In other words, while any phrase of the form *another CN* must, just as an anaphorically used pronoun, find an antecedent in its context of interpretation, the semantic significance of the link is just the opposite here. The DRS for (19) is (20).

(20)

x y z
man x walk-in x y $\neq$ x man y z $\doteq$ x follow (y,z)

Note that the representation of *other*-anaphora always needs two reference markers, one introduced by the anaphoric NP itself and one for the antecedent; there is no question here of replacing the former marker by the latter (that is: eliminating the y at the top of (20) and the inequality $y \neq x$ and replacing the other occurrences of y by x), as that would force the two men to be the same, rather than different. In this regard *other*-anaphora differs from pronoun anaphora, for which the substitution treatment yields representations that are equivalent to the ones we have been constructing above.

One reason for preferring the treatment of pronoun anaphora we have adopted is that it brings out the similarity as well as the difference between pronouns and phrases with *other*: In both cases interpretation involves the choice of a suitable antecedent. But the 'links' between the chosen antecedent and the marker for the anaphoric NP are different in nature: they express equality in one case, inequality in the other.

We have said something about the interpretation of three kinds of NPs: indefinite descriptions, anaphoric pronouns and quantified NPs, and we have introduced *linking* as a central theme in DRT. More about quantification in Section 10. We will now briefly turn to definite descriptions. One of the most obvious facts about them, but a fact systematically ignored or played down in the classical theories of denoting phrases (Frege, 1892; Russell, 1905; Strawson, 1950), is that, like pronouns, definite descriptions often act as anaphoric expressions.

Indeed, there seems to be a kind of interchangeability in the use of pronouns and descriptions, with a description taking the place of a pronoun in positions where the latter would create an unwanted ambiguity; thus, in discourses like (21) the use of a definite description in the second sentence serves to disambiguate the intended anaphoric link.

(21) A man and a boy came in. The man/he(?) smiled.

Anaphoric definite descriptions are, like pronouns, linked to existing discourse referents, and thus, like pronouns, they impose certain conditions on the context in which they are used: the context must contain at least one discourse referent that can serve as an antecedent. In this sense both pronouns and anaphoric definite descriptions may be said to carry a certain presupposition: only when the context satisfies this presupposition is it possible to interpret the pronoun, or to interpret the description anaphorically. The descriptive content then serves as information to guide the anaphora resolution process. This will permit anaphora resolution in cases like (21).

Matters are not always this simple, however. Definite descriptions have uses that can hardly be described as anaphoric. For instance, in (22), the description *the street* is certainly not anaphoric in the strict sense of the word, for there is no antecedent part of the given discourse which has introduced an element that the description can be linked up with.

(22) A man was walking down the street. He was smiling.

It is argued in (Heim, 1982) that the use of a definite description is a means for the speaker to convey that he takes the referent of the description to be in some sense familiar. The hearer who is already acquainted with the street that is intended as the referent of *the street* by the speaker of (22) may be expected to interpret the description as referring to this street; in such cases speaker and hearer are said to *share a common ground* (see, e.g., Stalnaker, 1974) which includes the street in question, and it is this which enables the hearer to interpret the speaker's utterance as he meant it. Such common grounds can also be represented in the form of DRSs. Thus, the common ground just referred to will contain, at a minimum, a component of the form (23), where we assume that the marker u in (23) is *anchored* to a suitable object (the street that speaker and hearer have in mind).

(23)

u
street u

On the assumption of such a 'common ground DRS' (including a suitable anchor) it becomes possible to view the NP *the street* of (22) as anaphoric. Interpretation of (22) will then be relative to the context DRS (23) and the interpretation of its definite description will yield, by the same principle that governs the interpretation of *the man* in (21), a DRS like (24).

(24)

u x v y
street u
man x
$v \doteq u$
street v
was-walking-down (x,v)
$y \doteq x$
was-smiling y

This way of dealing with definite descriptions such as *the street* in (24) may seem to restore uniformity to the analysis of definites. An important difference between definite descriptions and pronouns remains, however. Definite descriptions can be linked much more easily than pronouns to objects that are implicit in the common ground, but have not been explicitly introduced by earlier parts of the same discourse.

To assimilate the use of definite descriptions as unique identifiers (the use that Frege and Russell focus on to the exclusion of all others) to the present anaphoric analysis one must allow for accommodation. When the context available to the hearer does not contain a representation of the referent of a definite description, he may accommodate this context so that it now does contain such a representation, and then proceed as if the representation had been there all along. However, under what conditions precisely accommodation is possible is still a largely unsolved problem.

Interesting cases where the anaphoric account and the unique identification account of definite description have to be combined are the so-called 'bridging descriptions', as in (25) and (26).

(25) (Yesterday) an M.P. was killed. The murderer got away.

(26) Usually when an M.P. is killed, the murderer gets away.

In (25) *the murderer* is naturally interpreted as referring to the murderer of the M.P. mentioned in the preceding sentence. In other words, the context provides a referent x, and the definite description is interpreted as *the unique individual who murdered x*. This account also works for (26), where x varies over murdered M.P.s, and the definite description ranges over the set of unique murderers for all those x.

We conclude with a brief remark on proper names. As has been emphasized in the philosophical literature (see in particular (Kripke, 1972)) a proper name has no descriptive content, or at any rate its descriptive content plays no essential part in the way it refers. One consequence of this is that a name cannot have more than one referential value (a point which should not be confused with the evident fact that many names – *Fred, Fido, John Smith, Fayetteville* – are many ways ambiguous). This means that a name cannot have the sort of anaphoric use which we found with *the murderer* in (25) and (26), and that the antecedent to which the reference marker for a name will have to be linked will always be a marker in the main universe of the context DRS. Logically speaking, therefore, a proper name will always have 'maximally wide scope'. One might think about this process in several ways. One might assume, as in the construction rule for proper names in (Kamp, 1981), that the processing of a proper name always leads to the introduction of a marker in the top DRS, even if the name gets processed in a subordinate DRS somewhere way down. Or one might assume an external element in the semantics of proper names, namely the presence of external anchors: reference markers that are already in place in the top box of a DRS. Any proper name, then, comes equipped with its fixed anaphoric index for linking the name to its anchor. This is the approach we will follow in Section 9.

4. Discourse representation structures

It is now time to turn to formal details. Let A be a set of constants, and U a set of reference markers or discourse referents (variables, in fact). We also assume that a set of predicate letters with their arities is given. In the following definition, c ranges over A, v over the set U, and P over the set of predicates.

DEFINITION 4.1 (*DRSs; preliminary definition*).

terms $t ::= v \mid c.$

conditions $C ::= \top \mid Pt_1 \cdots t_k \mid v \doteq t \mid v \neq t \mid \neg D.$

DRSs $D ::= (\{v_1, \ldots, v_n\}, \{C_1, \ldots, C_m\}).$

Note that this definition of the representation language is provisional; it will be modified in Section 6. We introduce the convention that $D_1 \Rightarrow D_2$ is shorthand for $\neg(\{v_1, \ldots, v_n\}, \{C_1, \ldots, C_m, \neg D_2\})$, where $D_1 = (\{v_1, \ldots, v_n\}, \{C_1, \ldots, C_m\})$.

As in the previous sections DRSs will sometimes be presented in the box notation:

$$\textbf{DRSs } D ::= \begin{array}{|c|}\hline v_1 \cdots v_n \\ \hline C_1 \\ \vdots \\ C_m \\ \hline \end{array}$$

The abbreviation $D_1 \Rightarrow D_2$ is rendered in box format by the agreement to write (27) as (28).

(27)

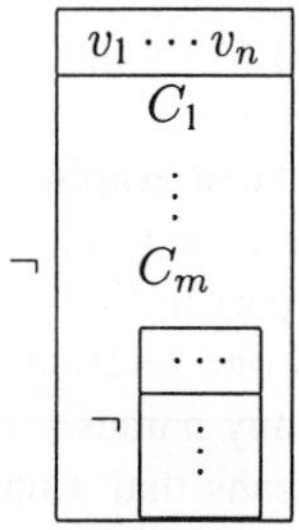

(28)

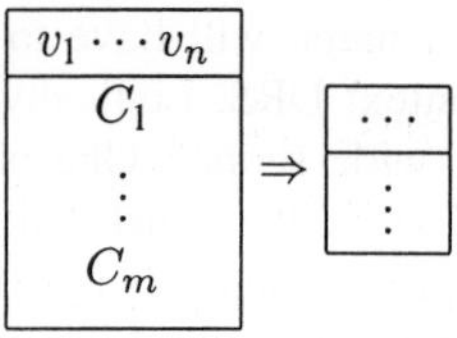

Conditions can be *atoms*, *links*, or *complex conditions*. Complex conditions are negations or implications. As the implications are abbreviations for special negations, we can assume that all complex conditions are negations.

An atom is the symbol $\top$ or a predicate name applied to a number of terms (constants or discourse referents), a link is an expression $v \doteq t$ or $v \neq t$, where v is a marker, and t is either a constant or a marker. The clause for complex conditions uses recursion: a complex condition is a condition of the form $\neg D$, where D is a discourse representation structure.

We will first give a static truth definition for discourse representation structures. Later on, when discussing the problem of compositionality for DRSs, we turn to a context change formulation of those same conditions. Call a first order model $\mathcal{M} = \langle M, I \rangle$ (we assume the domain M is non-empty) an *appropriate* model for DRS D if I maps the n-place predicate names in the atomic conditions of D to n-place relations on M, the individual constants occurring in the link conditions of D to members of M, and (here is the recursive part of the definition) $\mathcal{M}$ is also appropriate for the DRSs in the complex conditions of D.

Let $\mathcal{M} = \langle M, I \rangle$ be an appropriate model for DRS D. An assignment s for $\mathcal{M} = \langle M, I \rangle$ is a mapping of the set of reference markers U to elements of M. The term valuation determined by $\mathcal{M}$ and s is the function $V_{\mathcal{M},s}$ defined by $V_{\mathcal{M},s}(t) := I(t)$ if $t \in A$ and $V_{\mathcal{M},s}(t) := s(t)$ if $t \in U$. In the following definition we use $s[X]s'$ for: s' agrees with s except possibly on the values of the members of X.

DEFINITION 4.2 (*Assignments verifying a DRS*). An assignment s verifies $D = (\{v_1, \ldots, v_n\}, \{C_1, \ldots, C_m\})$ in $\mathcal{M}$ if there is an assignment s' with $s[\{v_1, \ldots, v_n\}]s'$ which satisfies every member of $\{C_1, \ldots, C_m\}$ in $\mathcal{M}$.

DEFINITION 4.3 (*Assignments satisfying a condition*).

(i) s always satisfies $\top$ in $\mathcal{M}$.

(ii) s satisfies $P(t_1, \ldots, t_n)$ in $\mathcal{M}$ iff $\langle V_{\mathcal{M},s}(t_1), \ldots, V_{\mathcal{M},s}(t_n)\rangle \in I(P)$.
(iii) s satisfies $v \doteq t$ in $\mathcal{M}$ iff $s(v) = V_{\mathcal{M},s}(t)$.
(iv) s satisfies $v \neq t$ in $\mathcal{M}$ iff $s(v) \neq V_{\mathcal{M},s}(t)$.
(v) s satisfies $\neg D$ in $\mathcal{M}$ iff s does not verify D in $\mathcal{M}$.

DEFINITION 4.4. Structure D is true in $\mathcal{M}$ if there is an assignment which verifies D in $\mathcal{M}$.

Note that it follows from Definition 4.4 that $(\{x\}, \{Pxy\})$ is true in $\mathcal{M}$ iff $(\{x, y\}, \{Pxy\})$ is true in $\mathcal{M}$. In other words: free variables are existentially quantified.

We leave it to the reader to check that the definition of verifying assignments yields the following requirement for conditions of the form $D_1 \Rightarrow D_2$:

- s satisfies $D_1 \Rightarrow D_2$ in $\mathcal{M}$, where $D_1 = (X, \{C_1, \ldots, C_k\})$, iff every assignment s' with $s[X]s'$ which satisfies $C_1, \ldots, C_k$ in $\mathcal{M}$ verifies D_2 in $\mathcal{M}$.

These definitions are easily modified to take anchors (partial assignments of values to fixed referents) into account. This is done by focusing on assignments extending a given anchor.

It is not difficult to see that the expressive power of basic DRT is the same as that of first order logic. In fact, there is an easy recipe for translating representation structures to formulae of predicate logic. Assuming that discourse referents can do duty as predicate logical variables, the atomic and link conditions of a representation structure are atomic formulae of predicate logic. The translation function $^\circ$ which maps representation structures to formulae of predicate logic is defined as follows:

DEFINITION 4.5 (*Translation from DRT to FOL*).

- For DRSs: if $D = (\{v_1, \ldots, v_n\}, \{C_1, \ldots, C_m\})$ then $D^\circ := \exists v_1 \cdots \exists v_n (C_1^\circ \wedge \cdots \wedge C_m^\circ)$.
- For atomic conditions (i.e. atoms or links): $C^\circ := C$.
- For negations: $(\neg D)^\circ := \neg D^\circ$.

It follows from this that the translation instruction for implications becomes (assume $D_1 = (\{v_1, \ldots, v_n\}, \{C_1, \ldots, C_m\})$)

- $(D_1 \Rightarrow D_2)^\circ := \forall v_1 \cdots \forall v_n ((C_1^\circ \wedge \cdots \wedge C_m^\circ) \to D_2^\circ)$.

The following is now easy to show:

PROPOSITION 4.6. *s verifies D in $\mathcal{M}$ iff $\mathcal{M}, s \models D^\circ$, where $\models$ is Tarski's definition of satisfaction for first order predicate logic.*

It is also not difficult to give a meaning preserving translation from first order predicate logic to basic DRT. In the following definition, $\phi^\bullet$ is the DRS corresponding to the predicate logical formula ϕ, and $\phi_1^\bullet$ and $\phi_2^\bullet$ are its first and second components.

DEFINITION 4.7 (*Translation from FOL to DRT*).

– For atomic formulas: $C^\bullet := (\emptyset, C)$.
– For conjunctions: $(\phi \wedge \psi)^\bullet := (\emptyset, \{\phi^\bullet, \psi^\bullet\})$.
– For negations: $(\neg\phi)^\bullet := (\emptyset, \neg\phi^\bullet)$.
– For quantifications: $(\exists v\phi)^\bullet := (\phi_1^\bullet \cup \{v\}, \phi_2^\bullet)$.

PROPOSITION 4.8. *$\mathcal{M}, s \models \phi$ iff s verifies $\phi^\bullet$ in $\mathcal{M}$, where $\models$ is Tarski's definition of satisfaction for first order predicate logic.*

The difference between first order logic and basic DRT has nothing to do with expressive power but resides entirely in the different way in which DRT handles context. The importance of this new perspective on context and context change is illustrated by the following examples with their DRS representations.

(29) Someone did not smile. He was angry.

(30) Not everyone smiled. *He was angry.

A suitable DRS representation (ignoring tense) for the first sentence of (29) is the following.

(31)
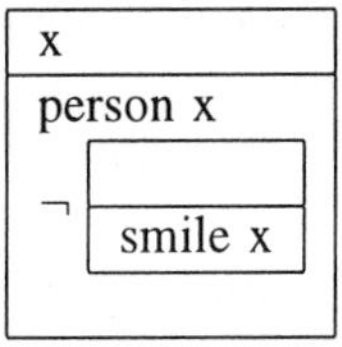

Here we see that the pronoun *he* in the next sentence of (29) can be resolved by linking it to the marker x occurring in the top box. The anaphoric possibilities of (30) are different, witness its DRS representation (32).

(32)
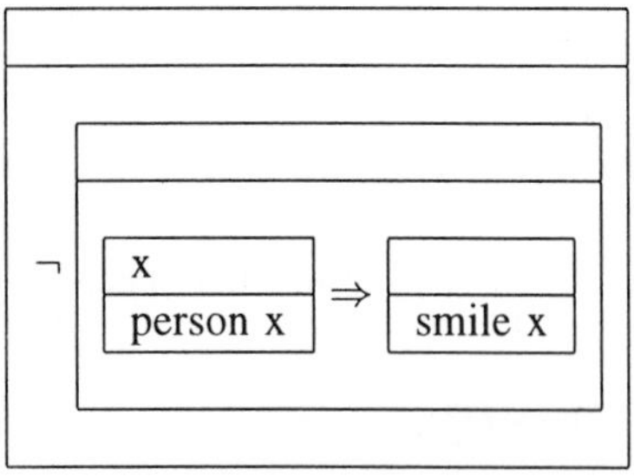

In this case there is no suitable marker available as an antecedent for *he* in the next sentence of (30).

What we see here is that DRSs with the same truth conditions, such as (31) and (32), may nevertheless be semantically different in an extended sense. The context change potentials of (31) and (32) are different, as the former creates a context for subsequent anaphoric links whereas the latter does not. This is as it should be, of course, as the pronoun in the second sentence of (29) can pick up the reference marker in the first sentence, but the pronoun in the second sentence of (30) cannot. The comparison of (31) and (32) illustrates that meaning in the narrow sense of truth conditions does not exhaust the concept of meaning for DRSs. The extended sense of meaning in which (31) and (32) are different can be informally phrased as follows: (31) creates a new context that can furnish an antecedent for a pronoun is subsequent discourse, (32) does not. This is because (31) *changes* the context, whereas (32) does not.

5. The static and dynamic meaning of representation structures

DRT has often been criticized for failing to be 'compositional'. It is important to see what this criticism could mean and to distinguish between two possible ways it could be taken. According to the first of these DRT fails to provide a direct compositional semantics for the natural language fragments to which it is applied. Given the form in which DRT was originally presented, this charge is justifiable, or at least it was so in the past. We will address it in Section 9. In its second interpretation the criticism pertains to the formalism of DRT itself. This objection is groundless. As Definitions 4.2 and 4.3 more or less directly imply, the formal language of Definition 4.1 is as compositional as standard predicate logic. We can make the point more explicit by rephrasing Definitions 4.2 and 4.3 as a definition of the semantic values $[\![\ ]\!]_{\mathcal{M}}$ that is assigned to each of the terms, conditions and DRSs of the DRT language by an appropriate model $\mathcal{M}$. As values for DRSs in $\mathcal{M}$ we use pairs $\langle X, F\rangle$ consisting of a finite set of reference markers $X \subseteq U$ and a set of functions $F \subseteq M^U$, and as meanings for conditions we use sets of assignments.

DEFINITION 5.1 (*Semantics of DRSs*).

$$[\![(\{v_1,\ldots,v_n\},\{C_1,\ldots,C_m\})]\!]_{\mathcal{M}} := (\{v_1,\ldots,v_n\},[\![C_1]\!]_{\mathcal{M}}\cap\cdots\cap[\![C_m]\!]_{\mathcal{M}}).$$

DEFINITION 5.2 (*Semantics of conditions*).

(i) $[\![P(t_1,\ldots,t_n)]\!]_{\mathcal{M}} := \{s \in M^U \mid \langle V_{\mathcal{M},s}(t_1),\ldots,V_{\mathcal{M},s}(t_n)\rangle \in I(P)\}$.

(ii) $[\![v \doteq t]\!]_{\mathcal{M}} := \{s \in M^U \mid s(v) = V_{\mathcal{M},s}(t)\}$.

(iii) $[\![v \neq t]\!]_{\mathcal{M}} := \{s \in M^U \mid s(v) \neq V_{\mathcal{M},s}(t)\}$.

(iv) $[\![\neg D]\!]_{\mathcal{M}} := \{s \in M^U \mid \text{ for no } s' \in M^U : s[X]s' \text{ and } s' \in F\}$,

where $(X, F) = [\![D]\!]_{\mathcal{M}}$.

To see the connection with the earlier definition of verification, 4.2, note that the following proposition holds:

PROPOSITION 5.3.

- *s verifies D in $\mathcal{M}$ iff $[\![D]\!]_{\mathcal{M}} = \langle X, F\rangle$ and there is an $s' \in M^U$ with $s[X]s'$ and $s' \in F$.*
- *D is true in $\mathcal{M}$ iff $[\![D]\!]_{\mathcal{M}} = \langle X, F\rangle$ and $F \neq \emptyset$.*

If one asks what are the DRS components of a DRS $(\{v_1,\ldots,v_n\},\{C_1,\ldots,C_m\})$, then the answer has to be: there aren't any. For those who do not like this answer, it turns out to be possible to view DRSs as built from atomic building blocks which are also DRSs. This was first pointed out by Zeevat(1989). The DRS language is now given in a slightly different way:

DEFINITION 5.4 (*Building DRSs from atomic DRSs*).

(i) If v is a reference marker, $(\{v\}, \emptyset)$ is a DRS.

(ii) If $(\emptyset, \{\top\})$ is a DRS.

(iii) If P is an n-ary predicate and $t_1, \ldots, t_n$ are terms, then $(\emptyset, \{P(t_1, \ldots, t_n)\})$ is a DRS.

(iv) If v is a reference marker and t is a term, then $(\emptyset, \{v \doteq t\})$ is a DRS.

(v) If v is a reference marker and t is a term, then $(\emptyset, \{v \neq t\})$ is a DRS.

(vi) If D is a DRS, then $(\emptyset, \neg D)$ is a DRS.

(vii) If $D = (X, C)$ and $D' = (X', C')$ are DRSs, then $(X \cup X', C \cup C')$ is a DRS.

(viii) Nothing else is a DRS.

It is clear that this defines the same DRS language. Let us use $-$ for the construction step that forms negated DRSs (that is, we use $-D$ for $(\emptyset, \neg D)$) and $\oplus$ for the operation of merging the universes and the constraint sets of two DRSs (that is, if $D = (X, C)$ and $D' = (X', C')$, then $D \oplus D' := (X \cup X', C \cup C')$).

Under this DRS definition, DRSs have become structurally ambiguous. DRS $(\{x\}, \{Px, Qx\})$, for example, has several possible construction histories:

- $(\{x\}, \emptyset) \oplus ((\emptyset, \{Px\}) \oplus (\emptyset, \{Qx\}))$,
- $(\{x\}, \emptyset) \oplus ((\emptyset, \{Qx\}) \oplus (\emptyset, \{Px\}))$,
- $((\{x\}, \emptyset) \oplus (\emptyset, \{Px\})) \oplus (\emptyset, \{Qx\})$,
- and so on.

The DRS semantics to be given next ensures that these structural ambiguities are harmless: the semantic operation corresponding to $\oplus$ is commutative and associative.

The following two semantic operations correspond to the syntactic operations $\oplus$, $-$ on DRSs (note that we overload the notation by calling the semantic operations by the same names as their syntactic counterparts):

$$\langle X, F\rangle \oplus \langle Y, G\rangle := \langle X \cup Y, F \cap G\rangle,$$
$$-\langle X, F\rangle := \langle \emptyset, \{g \in M^U \mid \neg\exists f \in F \text{ with } g[X]f\}\rangle.$$

The DRS semantics now looks like this:

DEFINITION 5.5.

(i) $[\![(\{v\}, \emptyset)]\!]_{\mathcal{M}} := (\{v\}, M^U)$.

(ii) $[\![(\emptyset, \{\top\})]\!]_{\mathcal{M}} := (\emptyset, M^U)$.

(iii) $[\![(\emptyset, \{Pt_1, \ldots, t_n\})]\!]_{\mathcal{M}} := (\emptyset, \{f \in M^U \mid \langle V_{\mathcal{M},f}(t_1), \ldots, V_{\mathcal{M},f}(t_n)\rangle \in I(P)\})$.

(iv) $[\![(\emptyset, \{v \doteq t\})]\!]_{\mathcal{M}} := (\emptyset, \{f \in M^U \mid f(v) = V_{\mathcal{M},f}(t)\})$.

(v) $[\![(\emptyset, \{v \neq t\})]\!]_{\mathcal{M}} := (\emptyset, \{f \in M^U \mid f(v) \neq V_{\mathcal{M},f}(t)\})$.

(vi) $[\![-D]\!]_{\mathcal{M}} := -[\![D]\!]_{\mathcal{M}}$.

(vii) $[\![D \oplus D']\!]_{\mathcal{M}} := [\![D]\!]_{\mathcal{M}} \oplus [\![D']\!]_{\mathcal{M}}$.

Clearly, this provides an elegant and compositional model- theoretic semantics for DRSs. Moreover, it is easily verified that Definition 5.5 is equivalent to Definitions 5.1 and 5.2

in the sense that if $[\![D]\!]_{\mathcal{M}} = \langle X, F \rangle$, then for any assignment s, $s \in F$ iff s verifies D in $\mathcal{M}$.

The semantics considered so far defines the *truth conditions* of DRSs. But as we noted at the end of Section 4, there is more to the meaning of a DRS than truth conditions alone. For DRSs which define the same truth conditions may still differ in their context change potentials.

To capture differences in context change potential, and not just in truth conditions, we need a different kind of semantics, which makes use of a more finely differentiated (and thus, necessarily, of a more complex) notion of semantic value. There are several ways in which this can be achieved. The one which we follow in the next definition defines the semantic value of a DRS as a relation between assignments – between *input assignments*, which verify the context to which the DRS is being evaluated, and *output assignments*, which reflect the way in which the DRS modifies this context. A semantics which characterizes the meaning of an expression in terms of its context change potential is nowadays usually referred to as *dynamic semantics*, while a semantics like that of the Definitions 4.2 and 4.3 or Definitions 5.1 and 5.2, whose central concern is with conditions of truth, is called *static*. The first explicit formulation of a dynamic semantics in this sense can be found in (Barwise, 1987). An elegant formulation is given in (Groenendijk and Stokhof, 1991).

Although they are quite different from a conceptual point of view, the dynamic and the static semantics for formalisms like those of DRT are nonetheless closely connected. Thus, if we denote the dynamic value of DRS D in model $\mathcal{M}$, – i.e. the relation between assignments of $\mathcal{M}$ which D determines – as ${}_s[\![D]\!]^{\mathcal{M}}_{s'}$, with s the input assignment and s' the output assignment, we have:

– If $D = (X, C)$ then: ${}_s[\![D]\!]^{\mathcal{M}}_{s'}$ iff $s[X]s'$ and s' verifies D in $\mathcal{M}$.

We can also characterize this relation directly, by a definition that is compositional in a similar spirit as Definition 5.5 in that it characterizes the dynamic value of a complex DRS in terms of the dynamic values of its constituents. It will be convenient to base this definition on a slightly different syntactic characterization of the DRS formalism than we have used hitherto, one in which the symmetric merge of Definition 5.5 is replaced by an asymmetric merge $\oslash$ defined as follows:

– If $D = (X, C)$ and $D' = (Y, C')$ then $D \oslash D' := (X, C \cup C')$ is a DRS.

It is clear that all DRSs can be built from atomic DRSs using $-$ and $\oslash$ (but note that $\oslash$ disregards the universe of its second argument).

The dynamic semantics is given as follows. We use ${}_s[\![D]\!]^{\mathcal{M}}_{s'}$ for s, s' is an input/output state pair for D in model $\mathcal{M}$, and $s[v]s'$ for: s and s' differ at most in the value for v.

DEFINITION 5.6.

(i) ${}_s[\![(\{v\}, \emptyset)]\!]^{\mathcal{M}}_{s'}$ iff $s[v]s'$.

(ii) ${}_s[\![(\emptyset, \{\top\})]\!]^{\mathcal{M}}_{s'}$ iff $s = s'$.

(iii) ${}_s[\![(\emptyset, \{Pt_1, \dots, t_n\})]\!]^{\mathcal{M}}_{s'}$ iff $s = s'$ and $\langle V_{\mathcal{M},s}(t_1), \dots, V_{\mathcal{M},s}(t_n)\rangle \in I(P)$.

(iv) ${}_s[\![(\emptyset, \{v \doteq t\})]\!]^{\mathcal{M}}_{s'}$ iff $s = s'$ and $s(v) = V_{\mathcal{M},s}(t)$.

(v) ${}_s[\![(\emptyset, \{v \neq t\})]\!]^{\mathcal{M}}_{s''}$ iff $s = s'$ and $s(v) \neq V_{\mathcal{M},s}(t)$.

(vi) ${}_s[\![-D]\!]^{\mathcal{M}}_{s'}$ iff $s = s'$ and for no s'' it is the case that ${}_s[\![D]\!]^{\mathcal{M}}_{s''}$.
(vii) ${}_s[\![D \oslash D']\!]^{\mathcal{M}}_{s'}$ iff ${}_s[\![D]\!]^{\mathcal{M}}_{s'}$ and ${}_{s'}[\![D']\!]^{\mathcal{M}}_{s'}$.

The static and the dynamic semantics of DRSs are equivalent, for we have the following proposition:

PROPOSITION 5.7. $[\![D]\!]_{\mathcal{M}} = \langle X, F\rangle$, $s[X]s'$, $s' \in F$ *iff* ${}_s[\![D]\!]^{\mathcal{M}}_{s'}$.

Still, the relation between static and dynamic semantics that we have given here leaves something to be desired. The composition operations for static semantics and dynamic semantics are different. The basic reason for this is that the dynamic semantics has a notion of sequentiality built in, a notion of processing in a given order. Therefore the commutative merge operation $\oplus$ does not quite fit the dynamic semantics: $\oplus$ is commutative, and sequential merging of DRSs intuitively is not. The operation $\oslash$ is not commutative, but it is unsatisfactory because it discards the dynamic effect of the second DRS (which is treated as if it had an empty universe).

To give a true account of the context change potential of DRSs one has to be able to answer the question how the context change potential of a DRS D_1 and that of a DRS D_2 which follows it determine the context change potential of their composition. This leads directly to the question how DRSs can be built from constituent DRSs by an operation of sequential merging.

6. Sequential composition of representation structures

Taking unions of universes and constraint sets is a natural commutative merge operation on DRSs, but it is not quite the operation on DRS meanings one would expect, given the dynamic perspective on DRS semantics. Intuitively, the process of gluing an existing DRS representing the previous discourse to a DRS representation for the next piece of natural language text is a process of sequential composition, a process which one would expect not to be commutative.

How should DRS meanings be composed sequentially? Before we address this question, it is convenient to switch to a slightly modified language for DRSs. It turns out that if one introduces a sequencing operator ; the distinction between DRSs and conditions can be dropped. This move yields the following language that we will call the language of proto-DRSs or pDRSs.

pDRSs $D ::= v \mid \top \mid Pt_1 \cdots t_n \mid v \doteq t \mid \neg D \mid (D_1; D_2)$.

In this language, a reference marker taken by itself is an atomic pDRS, and pDRSs are composed by means of ;. Thus, introductions of markers and conditions can be freely mixed. Although we drop the distinction between markers and conditions and that between conditions and pDRSs, a pDRS of the form v will still be called a marker, and one of the form $\top$, $Pt_1 \cdots t_n$, $v \doteq t$ or $\neg D$ a condition. Thus, a pDRS is a reference marker or an atomic condition or a negation or a ;-composition of pDRSs.

From now on, we will consider $v \not\doteq t$ as an abbreviation of $\neg v \doteq t$, and $D_1 \Rightarrow D_2$ as an abbreviation of $\neg(D_1; \neg D_2)$. It will turn out that the process of merging pDRSs with ';' is associative, so we will often drop parentheses where it does no harm, and write $D_1; D_2; D_3$ for both $((D_1; D_2); D_3)$ and $(D_1; (D_2; D_3))$.

It is possible to give a commutative semantics for pDRSs, by using the semantic operation $-$ to interpret $\neg$, and $\oplus$ to interpret ;.

DEFINITION 6.1 (*Commutative Semantics of pDRSs*).

(i) $[\![v]\!]_{\mathcal{M}} := \langle\{v\}, M^U\rangle$.

(ii) $[\![\top]\!]_{\mathcal{M}} := \langle\emptyset, M^U\rangle$.

(iii) $[\![Pt_1, \ldots, t_n]\!]_{\mathcal{M}} := \langle\emptyset, \{f \in M^U \mid \langle V_{\mathcal{M},f}(t_1), \ldots, V_{\mathcal{M},f}(t_n)\rangle \in I(P)\}\rangle$.

(iv) $[\![v \doteq t]\!]_{\mathcal{M}} := \langle\emptyset, \{f \in M^U \mid f(v) = V_{\mathcal{M},f}(t)\}\rangle$.

(v) $[\![\neg D]\!]_{\mathcal{M}} := -[\![D]\!]_{\mathcal{M}}$.

(vi) $[\![D; D']\!]_{\mathcal{M}} := [\![D]\!]_{\mathcal{M}} \oplus [\![D']\!]_{\mathcal{M}}$.

This interpretation of ; makes merging of pDRSs into a commutative operation. To see the effect of this, look for instance at examples (33) and (34).

(33) A man entered.

(34) A boy smiled.

How should pDRSs for these examples be merged? The commutative merge that we just defined gives the result (35).

(35)
$$\begin{array}{|l|}\hline \text{x} \\ \hline \text{man x} \\ \text{enter x} \\ \hline \end{array} \; ; \; \begin{array}{|l|}\hline \text{x} \\ \hline \text{boy x} \\ \text{smile x} \\ \hline \end{array} \; = \; \begin{array}{|l|}\hline \text{x} \\ \hline \text{man x} \\ \text{enter x} \\ \text{boy x} \\ \text{smile x} \\ \hline \end{array}$$

In the pDRT semantics the two discourse referents for *a man* and a *a boy* will be fused, for according to the operation $\oplus$ the fact that a marker is mentioned more than once is irrelevant. This shows that (35) cannot be the right translation of the sequential composition of (33) and (34).

A different approach to merging pDRSs is suggested by the fact that in a dynamic perspective merging in left to right order has a very natural relational meaning:

– ${}_s[\![D_1; D_2]\!]^{\mathcal{M}}_{s'}$ iff there is an assignment s'' with ${}_s[\![D_1]\!]^{\mathcal{M}}_{s''}$ and ${}_{s''}[\![D_2]\!]^{\mathcal{M}}_{s'}$.

This semantic clause complies with the intuition that the first pDRS is interpreted in an initial context s yielding a new context s'', and this new context serves as the initial context for the interpretation of the second pDRS.

Once we are here a natural way to extend the dynamic approach to the full language suggests itself, as was noted by Groenendijk and Stokhof (1991). Their observation is basically this. If we interpret the DRS conditions in terms of pairs of assignments, the dynamic semantic values of DRS conditions can be given in the same form as the dynamic values of DRSs.

At first sight, DRS conditions do not look like context changers. If (s, s') is a context pair for a condition, then always $s = s'$, representing the fact that the condition does not change anything. But who cares? If we allow degenerate context changers, we can drop the distinction between conditions and DRSs altogether. What is more, even the distinction between marker introductions and conditions is not essential, for the introduction of a marker u can also be interpreted in terms of context pairs, and the introduction of a list of markers can be obtained by merging the introductions of the components.

These considerations yield the following relational semantics for the pDRS format (this is in fact the semantic format of the dynamic version of first order predicate logic defined in (Groenendijk and Stokhof, 1991)):

DEFINITION 6.2 (*Relational Semantics of pDRSs*).
(i) ${}_s[\![v]\!]_{s'}^{\mathcal{M}}$ iff $s[v]s'$.
(ii) ${}_s[\![\top]\!]_{s'}^{\mathcal{M}}$ iff $s = s'$.
(iii) ${}_s[\![Pt_1, \ldots, t_n]\!]_{s'}^{\mathcal{M}}$ iff $s = s'$ and $\langle V_{\mathcal{M},s}(t_1), \ldots, V_{\mathcal{M},s}(t_n)\rangle \in I(P)$.
(iv) ${}_s[\![v \doteq t]\!]_{s'}^{\mathcal{M}}$ iff $s = s'$ and $s(v) = V_{\mathcal{M},s}(t)$.
(v) ${}_s[\![\neg D]\!]_{s'}^{\mathcal{M}}$ iff $s = s'$ and for no s'' it is the case that ${}_s[\![D]\!]_{s''}^{\mathcal{M}}$.
(vi) ${}_s[\![D; D']\!]_{s'}^{\mathcal{M}}$ iff there is an s'' with ${}_s[\![D]\!]_{s''}^{\mathcal{M}}$ and ${}_{s''}[\![D']\!]_{s'}^{\mathcal{M}}$.

Truth is defined in terms of this, as follows.

DEFINITION 6.3 (*Truth in relational semantics for pDRSs*). D is true in $\mathcal{M}$, given s, notation $\mathcal{M}, s \models D$, iff there is an s' with ${}_s[\![D]\!]_{s'}^{\mathcal{M}}$.

Note that the difference with the previous semantics (Definition 6.1) resides in the interpretation of ; and has nothing to do with with the static/dynamic opposition. To see that, observe that the relational semantics Definition 6.2 can also be given a static formulation. For that, the only change one has to make to Definition 6.1 is in the clause for $D_1; D_2$, by interpreting ; as the operation $\circ$ defined as follows:

$$\langle X, F\rangle \circ \langle X', F'\rangle := \langle X \cup X', \{f' \in F' \mid \exists f \in F \; f[X']f'\}\rangle.$$

Given this change to Definition 6.1, we have the following proposition:

PROPOSITION 6.4. *$\mathcal{M}, s \models D$ iff $[\![D]\!] = \langle X, F\rangle$ and $\exists f \in F$ with $s[X]f$.*

So we see that 6.2 can be given an equivalent static formulation. Conversely, it is not hard to give a relational clause for $\oplus$:

$$fR \oplus Sg \iff f[R^\bullet \cup S^\bullet]g \;\&\; g \in \text{rng}\,(R) \cap \text{rng}\,(S),$$

where $R^\bullet = \{v \in U \mid (f, g) \in R \;\&\; f(v) \neq g(v)\}$ (and similarly for $S^\bullet$).

According to the relational semantics of Definition 6.2, (36) and (37) have the same meanings.

(36) x; y; man x; woman y; love (x,y).

(37) x; man x; y; woman y; love (x,y).

This means that we can use the same box representation (38) for both:

(38)

x y
man x woman y love (x,y)

Unfortunately, other examples show that the box notation does not really fit the relational semantics for the pDRSs given in Definition 6.2. The use of collecting discourse referents in universes, as it is done in the box format, is that this allows one to see the anaphoric possibilities of a representation at a glance: the discourse referents in the top box are the markers available for subsequent anaphoric linking.

However, when the composition operation ; is interpreted as in Definition 6.2 (or, alternatively, as the operation $\circ$), the pDRS notation becomes capable of expressing distinctions that cannot be captured in the box notation we have been using. Note, for instance that the pDRSs in (39) and (40) are not equivalent with regard to the semantics of Definition 6.2, although they are equivalent with regard to that given by (the unmodified) Definitions 5.1 and 5.2.

(39) x; man x; dog y; y; woman y; love (x,y).

(40) x; y; man x; dog y; woman y; love (x,y).

To take this difference into account the box representation for (39) would have to be something like (41).

(41)

x	y
man x dog y	woman y love (x,y)

The vertical dividing line in (41) separates the occurrences of y that receive their interpretation from the previously given context from those that are linked to the new introduction.

Thus we see that the relational semantics for pDRSs provides a natural notion of sequential merging, which allows sharing of introduced markers between two DRSs. However, it distinguishes between different introductions of the same marker. This introduces a problem of *destructive assignment*: after a new introduction of a marker v that was already present, its previous value is lost. This feature of Definition 6.2 is the root cause of the mismatch between box representation and sequential presentation that we just noted. It is also the source of the non-equivalence of the commutative and the relational composition semantics for the pDRS format.

For a fruitful discussion of the problem of sequential merge, it is necessary to be clear about the nature of the different kinds of marker occurrences in a pDRS. In the following discussion we compare the role of reference markers with that of variables in classical logic and in programming languages. Classical logic has two kinds of variable occurrences: bound and free. In the dynamic logic that underlies DRT there are three kinds of variable or marker occurrences (see Visser, 1994b).

(i) marker occurrences that get their reference fixed by the larger context,
(ii) marker occurrences that get introduced in the current context,

(iii) markers occurrences that get introduced in a subordinate context.

We will call the first kind *fixed* marker occurrences, the second kind *introduced* marker occurrences, and the third kind *classically bound* marker occurrences. The first kind corresponds roughly to the free variable occurrences of classical logic, and the third kind to the bound variable occurrences of classical logic (hence the name). The second kind is altogether different: these are the markers that embody the context change potential of a given pDRS.

As the distinction between these three kinds of marker occurrences is given by 'dynamic' considerations, it is not surprising that there is a close connection with the various roles that variables can play in imperative programming. Here are the correspondences:

(i) Fixed markers correspond to variables in read memory.

(ii) Introduced markers correspond to variables in write memory.

(iii) Bound markers correspond to scratch memory (memory used for intermediate computations that are not part of the output of the program under consideration).

Due to the semantic motivation for this tripartite distinction, the formal definition will depend on the semantics for ; that we adopt. We will give the definition based on the relational semantics.

The set of discourse referents which have a fixed occurrence in a pDRS is given by a function $\mathit{fix} : \mathit{pDRSs} \to \mathcal{P}U$. The set of discourse referents which are introduced in a pDRS is given by a function $\mathit{intro} : \mathit{pDRSs} \to \mathcal{P}U$, and the set of discourse referents which have a classically bound occurrence in a pDRS is given by a function $\mathit{cbnd} : \mathit{pDRSs} \to \mathcal{P}U$. To define these functions, we first define a function *var* on the atomic conditions of a DRS.

$$\mathit{var}(Pt_1 \cdots t_n) := \{t_i \mid 1 \leqslant i \leqslant n,\ t_i \in U\},$$

$$\mathit{var}(v \doteq t) := \begin{cases} \{v, t\} & \text{if } t \in U, \\ \{v\} & \text{otherwise.} \end{cases}$$

DEFINITION 6.5 (*fix, intro, cbnd*).

– $\mathit{fix}(v) := \emptyset$, $\mathit{intro}(v) := \{v\}$, $\mathit{cbnd}(v) := \emptyset$.
– $\mathit{fix}(\top) := \emptyset$, $\mathit{intro}(\top) := \emptyset$, $\mathit{cbnd}(\top) := \emptyset$.
– $\mathit{fix}(Pt_1 \cdots t_n) := \mathit{var}(Pt_1 \cdots t_n)$, $\mathit{intro}(Pt_1 \cdots t_n) := \emptyset$, $\mathit{cbnd}(Pt_1 \cdots t_n) := \emptyset$.
– $\mathit{fix}(v \doteq t) := \mathit{var}(v \doteq t)$, $\mathit{intro}(v \doteq t) := \emptyset$, $\mathit{cbnd}(v \doteq t) := \emptyset$.
– $\mathit{fix}(\neg D) := \mathit{fix}(D)$, $\mathit{intro}(\neg D) := \emptyset$, $\mathit{cbnd}(\neg D) := \mathit{intro}(D) \cup \mathit{cbnd}(D)$.
– $\mathit{fix}(D_1; D_2) := \mathit{fix}(D_1) \cup (\mathit{fix}(D_2) - \mathit{intro}(D_1))$,
  $\mathit{intro}(D_1; D_2) := \mathit{intro}(D_1) \cup \mathit{intro}(D_2)$,
  $\mathit{cbnd}(D_1; D_2) := \mathit{cbnd}(D_1) \cup \mathit{cbnd}(D_2)$.

We will occasionally use $\mathit{activ}(D)$ for the set of markers $\mathit{fix}(D) \cup \mathit{intro}(D)$.

The set of conditions of a pDRS is given by the function $\mathit{cond} : \mathit{pDRSs} \to \mathcal{P}(\mathit{pDRSs})$, which collects the conditions of D together in a set:

DEFINITION 6.6 (*cond*).

(i) $\mathit{cond}(v) := \emptyset$.

(ii) $cond(\top) := \{\top\}$.
(iii) $cond(Pt_1 \cdots t_n) := \{Pt_1 \cdots t_n\}$.
(iv) $cond(v \doteq t) := \{v \doteq t\}$.
(v) $cond(\neg D) := \{\neg D\}$.
(vi) $cond(D_1; D_2) := cond(D_1) \cup cond(D_2)$.

Note that there are pDRSs D with $intro(D) \cap fix(D) \neq \emptyset$. An example is given in (42).

(42) $Px; x; Qx.$

Also, there are pDRSs D where a marker is introduced more than once. An example is given in (43).

(43) $x; Px; x; Qx.$

We will call a pDRS *proper* (or a DRS) if these situations do not occur. Thus, the set of DRSs is defined as follows:

DEFINITION 6.7 (*DRSs*).

- If v is a marker, then v is a DRS.
- $\top$ is a DRS.
- If $t_1, \ldots, t_n$ are terms and P is an n-place predicate letter, then $Pt_1 \cdots t_n$ is a DRS.
- If v is a marker and t is a term, then $v \doteq t$ is a DRS.
- If D is a DRS, then $\neg D$ is a DRS.
- If D_1, D_2 are DRSs, and $(fix(D_1) \cup intro(D_1)) \cap intro(D_2) = \emptyset$, then $D_1; D_2$ is a DRS.
- Nothing else is a DRS.

Note that examples (42) and (43) are not DRSs. Indeed, we have:

PROPOSITION 6.8. *For every DRS D*, $intro(D) \cap fix(D) = \emptyset$.

Proposition 6.8 entails that DRSs of the form $D; v$ are equivalent to $v; D$. This means that any DRS D can be written in box format (44) without change of meaning. Indeed, we can view the box format for DRSs as an abstract version of the underlying real syntax.

(44) 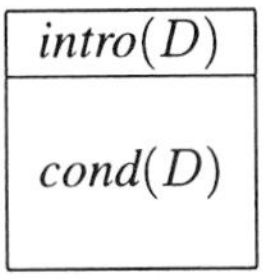

Note that if a DRS D has $intro(D) \neq \emptyset$ and $cond(D) \neq \emptyset$, then D must be of the form $D_1; D_2$, where $(fix(D_1) \cup intro(D_1)) \cap intro(D_2) = \emptyset$. We say that D is a simple merge of D_1 and D_2.

According to the DRS definition, DRSs are either of one of the forms in (45) or they are simple merges of two DRSs (but note that taking simple merges is a partial operation).

(45) 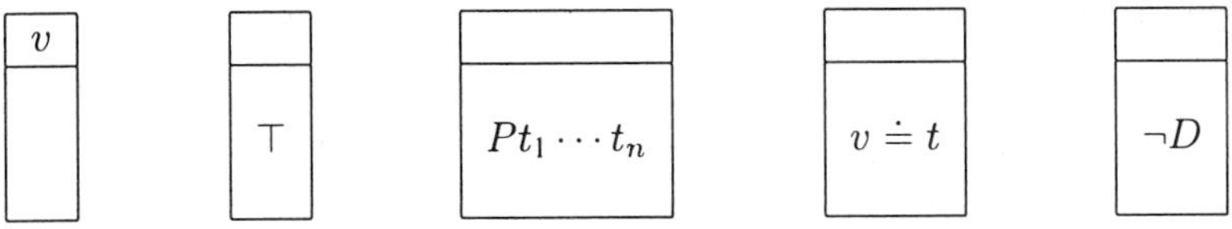

For DRSs, the truth conditions according to the commutative semantics coincide with those according to the relational semantics:

PROPOSITION 6.9. *For all models $\mathcal{M}$, all DRSs D:*

$$\text{if } [\![D]\!]_{\mathcal{M}} = \langle X, F\rangle \text{ then } {}_s[\![D]\!]^{\mathcal{M}}_{s'} \text{ iff } s[X]s' \text{ and } s' \in F.$$

7. Strategies for merging representation structures

To get a clear perspective on the problem of merging DRSs, note that the issue does not even occur in an approach where a natural language discourse is processed by means of a DRS construction algorithm that proceeds by 'deconstructing' natural language sentences in the context of a given DRS, as in (Kamp, 1981) or (Kamp and Reyle, 1993).

The problem emerges as soon as one modifies this architecture by switching to a set-up where representations for individual sentences are constructed first, and next these have to be merged in left to right order. Suppose we want to construct a DRS for the sequential composition of S_1 and S_2 on the basis of a DRS D_1 for S_1 and a DRS D_2 for S_2. Now it might happen that $D_1; D_2$ is not a DRS, because $(\mathit{fix}(D_1) \cup \mathit{intro}(D_1)) \cap \mathit{intro}(D_2) \neq \emptyset$. Our idea is to resolve this situation by applying a renaming strategy. In the example sentences given so far the problem has been avoided by a prudent choice of indices, but example (46) would pose such a conflict.

(46) A man[1] entered. A boy[1] smiled.

The initial representation for the sequential composition of D_1 and D_2 can be given by $D_1 \bullet D_2$. The problem of sequential merge now takes the form of finding strategies for reducing DRS-like expressions with occurrences of $\bullet$ to DRSs.

Before we list of a number of options for 'merge reduction', we define a class of reducible DRSs or RDRSs (assume D ranges over DRSs):

RDRSs $R ::= D \mid \neg R \mid (R_1 \bullet R_2)$.

Thus, RDRSs are compositions out of DRSs by means of $\neg$ and $\bullet$. It is useful to extend the definitions of *intro*, *fix* and *cbnd* to RDRSs:

DEFINITION 7.1 (*fix, intro, cbnd for RDRSs*).

– $\mathit{fix}(\neg R) := \mathit{fix}(R)$, $\mathit{intro}(\neg R) := \emptyset$, $\mathit{cbnd}(\neg R) := \mathit{intro}(R) \cup \mathit{cbnd}(R)$.
– $\mathit{fix}(R_1 \bullet R_2) := \mathit{fix}(R_1) \cup (\mathit{fix}(R_2) - \mathit{intro}(R_1))$,
$\mathit{intro}(R_1 \bullet R_2) := \mathit{intro}(R_1) \cup \mathit{intro}(R_2)$,
$\mathit{cbnd}(R_1 \bullet R_2) := \mathit{cbnd}(R_1) \cup \mathit{cbnd}(R_2)$.

We use $\bullet$ for sequential merge. The various options for how to merge DRSs all have a semantic and a syntactic side, for they must handle two questions:

(i) What is the semantics of $\bullet$?

(ii) How can RDRSs be reduced to DRSs?

In order to talk about these reductions in a sensible way, we must take negative context into account. Here is a definition of negative contexts (D ranges over DRSs, R over RDRSs).

Negative Contexts $N ::= \neg\Box \mid \neg N \mid (N; D) \mid (D; N) \mid (N \bullet R) \mid (R \bullet N)$.

Condition on $(N; D)$: $\mathit{activ}(N) \cap \mathit{intro}(D) = \emptyset$. Condition on $(D; N)$: $\mathit{activ}(D) \cap \mathit{intro}(N) = \emptyset$, where $\mathit{activ}(N)$ and $\mathit{intro}(N)$ are calculated on the basis of $\mathit{intro}(\Box) := \mathit{fix}(\Box) := \mathit{cbnd}(\Box) := \emptyset$.

What the definition says is that a negative context is an RDRS with one constituent RDRS immediately within the scope of a negation replaced by $\Box$. If N is a negative context, then $N[R]$ is the result of substituting RDRS R for $\Box$ in N. The definition of negative contexts allows us to single out an arbitrary negated sub-RDRS R of a given RDRS by writing that RDRS in the form $N[R]$.

Contexts $C ::= \Box \mid N$.

A context is either a $\Box$ or a negative context. If C is a context, then $C[R]$ is the result of substituting RDRS R for $\Box$ in N. Thus, if we want to say that a reduction rule applies to an RDRS R that may (but need not) occur immediately within the scope of a negation sign within a larger RDRS, we say that the rule applies to $C[R]$. If we specify a reduction rule

$$R \Longrightarrow R',$$

this is meant to be understood as licensing all reductions of the form:

$$C[R] \longrightarrow C[R'].$$

This format ensures that the rule can both apply at the top level and at a level bounded by a negation sign inside a larger RDRS.

We will now discuss several options for merge reduction: symmetric merge, prudent merge, destructive merge, deterministic merge with substitution, and indeterministic merge with substitution.

Symmetric merge. Interpret $\bullet$ as $\oplus$ and ; as $\circ$. The reduction rules that go with this are:

$$\begin{aligned}
(R \bullet v) &\Longrightarrow (v; R),\\
(R \bullet \top) &\Longrightarrow (R; \top),\\
(R \bullet Pt_1, \ldots, t_n) &\Longrightarrow (R; Pt_1, \ldots, t_n),\\
(R \bullet \neg R') &\Longrightarrow (R; \neg R'),\\
((R \bullet v) \bullet R') &\Longrightarrow ((v; R) \bullet R'),\\
((R \bullet \top) \bullet R') &\Longrightarrow ((R; \top) \bullet R'),
\end{aligned}$$

$$((R \bullet Pt_1, \dots, t_n) \bullet R') \Longrightarrow ((R; Pt_1, \dots, t_n) \bullet R'),$$
$$((R \bullet \neg R_1) \bullet R_2) \Longrightarrow ((R; \neg R') \bullet R_2),$$
$$(R \bullet (R_1; R_2)) \Longrightarrow ((R \bullet R_1) \bullet R_2),$$
$$(R \bullet (R_1 \bullet R_2)) \Longrightarrow ((R \bullet R_1) \bullet R_2).$$

Partial merge. Interpret $\bullet$ as a partial operation (see, e.g., Muskens, 1996) while retaining $\circ$ as the interpretation of ; (as we will do throughout the remainder of this section). To give the semantics, we have to take context into account. Assume that the semantics of a DRS D is given as a triple $\langle X, Y, F \rangle$, where $X = \mathit{fix}(D)$, $Y = \mathit{intro}(D)$ and F is a set of assignments, then the following partial operation gives the semantics of partial merge:

$$\langle X, Y, F \rangle \odot \langle X', Y', F' \rangle := \begin{cases} \langle X \cup X', Y \cup Y', F \cap F' \rangle \\ \quad \text{if } (X \cup Y) \cap Y' = \emptyset, \\ \uparrow \quad \text{otherwise.} \end{cases}$$

The reduction rules that go with this: same as above, except for the following change in the rules that handle marker introductions:

$$(R \bullet v) \Longrightarrow (R; v) \text{ if } v \notin \mathit{fix}(R) \cup \mathit{intro}(R),$$
$$(R \bullet v) \Longrightarrow \text{ERROR} \text{ if } v \in \mathit{fix}(R) \cup \mathit{intro}(R),$$
$$((R \bullet v) \bullet R') \Longrightarrow ((R; v) \bullet R') \text{ if } v \notin \mathit{fix}(R) \cup \mathit{intro}(R),$$
$$((R \bullet v) \bullet R') \Longrightarrow \text{ERROR} \text{ if } v \in \mathit{fix}(R) \cup \mathit{intro}(R).$$

Prudent merge. To give the semantics of prudent merging for $\bullet$ (see Visser, 1994b), one again has to take context fully into account.

$$\langle X, Y, F \rangle \odot \langle X', Y', F' \rangle := \langle X \cup (X' - Y), Y \cup (Y' - X), F \cap F' \rangle.$$

Reduction rules that go with this: same as above, except for the following change in the rules that handle marker introduction:

$$(R \bullet v) \Longrightarrow (R; v) \text{ if } v \notin \mathit{fix}(R) \cup \mathit{intro}(R),$$
$$(R \bullet v) \Longrightarrow R \text{ if } v \in \mathit{fix}(R) \cup \mathit{intro}(R),$$
$$((R \bullet v) \bullet R') \Longrightarrow (R; v) \bullet R') \text{ if } v \notin \mathit{fix}(R) \cup \mathit{intro}(R),$$
$$((R \bullet v) \bullet R') \Longrightarrow R \bullet R' \text{ if } v \in \mathit{fix}(R) \cup \mathit{intro}(R).$$

Destructive merge. Interpret $\bullet$ as $\circ$ (relational composition), and allow destructive assignment. The reduction rule that goes with this is very simple: replace all occurrences of $\bullet$ in one go by ;, and interpret ; as $\circ$. But of course, this reduction does not yield DRSs but only proto-DRSs.

For the next two perspectives on merging DRSs, we need to develop a bit of technique for handling substitution, or, more precisely, marker renamings.

DEFINITION 7.2. A marker renaming is a function $\theta : U \to U$, such that its domain $\text{Dom}(\theta) := \{v \in U \mid v \neq \theta(v)\}$ is finite. If θ is a renaming with $\text{Dom}(\theta) = \{v_1, \ldots, v_n\}$, then $\text{Rng}(\theta) := \{\theta(v_1), \ldots, \theta(v_n)\}$. A renaming θ avoids a set $X \subseteq U :\Leftrightarrow \text{Rng}(\theta) \cap X = \emptyset$. If θ is a renaming, then $\theta - v :=$ the renaming σ that is like θ but for the fact that $\sigma(v) = v$. If $X \subseteq U$ then $\theta X := \{\theta(x) \mid x \in X\}$. A marker renaming θ is injective on $X :\Leftrightarrow |X| = |\theta X|$.

We will refer to a renaming θ with domain $\{v_1, \ldots, v_n\}$ as $[\theta(v_1)/v_1, \ldots, \theta(v_n)/v_n]$. Thus, $[x/y]$ is the renaming θ with $\theta(u) = x$ if $u = y$ and $\theta(u) = u$ otherwise. This renaming is of course injective on $\{x\}$, but not on $\{x, y\}$. $[x/y, x/z]$ is a renaming which is not injective on $\{y, z\}$. $[x/y, x/z] - z = [x/y]$.

A renaming of a subset of *intro*(D) intuitively has as its semantic effect that the write memory of D gets shifted. Renaming in a dynamic system like DRT works quite differently from variable substitution in classical logic, because of the three kinds of marker occurrences that have to be taken into account: *fix*, *intro* and *cbnd*. In particular, a renaming of *intro*(D) has to satisfy the following requirements:

(i) it should be injective on *intro*(D),
(ii) it should avoid *fix*(D),
(iii) it should leave *cbnd*(D) untouched.

The first two of these requirements can be imposed globally. Requirement (iii) should be part of the definition of the effects of renamings on (R)DRSs: we will handle it by distinguishing between outer and inner renaming. For an outer renaming of RDRS R with θ we employ θR, for an inner renaming $\overline{\theta} R$. Inner renaming is renaming within a context where marker introductions act as classical binders, i.e. within the scope of an occurrence of $\neg$. For example, if $\theta = [v/x, w/y]$, then:

$$\theta(x; \neg(y; Rxy)) = v; \neg(y; Rvy).$$

A renaming θ induces functions from terms to terms as follows:

$$\theta(t) := \begin{cases} \theta(v) & \text{if } t = v \text{ with } v \in U, \\ t & \text{if } t \in C. \end{cases}$$

A renaming $\theta - v$ induces functions from terms to terms as follows:

$$\theta - v(t) := \begin{cases} \theta(w) & \text{if } t = w \neq v \text{ with } w \in U, \\ v & \text{if } t = v, \\ t & \text{if } t \in C. \end{cases}$$

The induced renaming functions from (R)DRSs to (R)DRSs are given by:

$$\begin{aligned}
\theta v &:= \theta(v),\\
\theta\top &:= \top,\\
\overline{\theta}\top &:= \top,\\
\theta(Pt_1\cdots t_n) &:= P\theta t_1\cdots\theta t_n,\\
\overline{\theta}(Pt_1\cdots t_n) &:= P\theta t_1\cdots\theta t_n,\\
\theta(v \doteq t) &:= \theta v \doteq \theta t,\\
\overline{\theta}(v \doteq t) &:= \theta v \doteq \theta t,\\
\theta(\neg R) &:= \neg\overline{\theta}R,\\
\overline{\theta}(\neg R) &:= \neg\overline{\theta}R,\\
\theta(v;R) &:= \theta v;\theta R,\\
\overline{\theta}(v;R) &:= v;\overline{\theta - v}R,\\
\theta(C;R) &:= \theta C;\theta R, \quad C\in\{Pt_1\cdots t_n, v\doteq t, \neg R'\},\\
\overline{\theta}(C;R) &:= \overline{\theta}C;\overline{\theta}R, \quad C\in\{Pt_1\cdots t_n, v\doteq t, \neg R'\},\\
\theta((R_1;R_2);R_3) &:= \theta(R_1;(R_2;R_3)),\\
\overline{\theta}((R_1;R_2);R_3) &:= \overline{\theta}(R_1;(R_2;R_3)),
\end{aligned}$$

plus rules for $\bullet$ exactly like those for ;.

For the semantics, let us again assume that a meaning for DRS D is a triple $\langle X, Y, F\rangle$, where $X = \mathit{fix}(D)$, $Y = \mathit{intro}(D)$, and F is the set of assignments satisfying $\mathit{cond}(D)$.

DEFINITION 7.3. θ is a proper renaming for DRS D :$\Leftrightarrow$

(i) $\mathrm{Dom}(\theta) \subseteq \mathit{intro}(D)$,

(ii) θ is injective on $\mathit{intro}(D)$,

(iii) $\mathrm{Rng}(\theta) \cap \mathit{fix}(D) = \emptyset$.

DEFINITION 7.4. If $F \subseteq M^U$, $\theta F := \{g \in M^U \mid g \circ \theta \in F\}$.

For example, if $F = \{f \in M^U \mid f(x) \in I(P)\}$, and $\theta = [y/x]$, then:

$$[y/x]F = \{g \in M^U \mid g \circ [y/x](x) \in I(P)\} = \{g \in M^U \mid g(y) \in I(P)\}.$$

PROPOSITION 7.5. *If θ is a proper renaming for D and $|D|^{\mathcal{M}} = \langle X, Y, F\rangle$ then $|\theta D|^{\mathcal{M}} = \langle X, \theta Y, \theta F\rangle$.*

The upshot if this proposition is that a proper renaming only changes the write memory of a DRS.

Deterministic merge with substitution. The sequence semantics for dynamic predicate logic defined in (Vermeulen, 1993) can be used as a semantics for a language of unreduced DRSs:

$$R ::= \text{PUSH } v \mid \top \mid Pt_1\cdots t_n \mid v \doteq t \mid \neg R \mid (R_1 \bullet R_2),$$

where v ranges over a set U of markers without indices. The meaning of a variable introduction v in sequence semantics is: push a new value for v on a stack of v values. Clearly, this prevents the destructive use of memory that we saw in connection with Definition 6.2. Suggestive notation for this: PUSH v.

We can reduce expressions of this language to a language of proper DRSs where the markers are taken from the set of indexed markers $U' := \{u_i \mid u \in U,\ i > 0\}$. The corresponding merge reduction rules for this use fully determined renamings, as follows.

First we do a global renaming, by replacing every occurrence of $v \in U$, except those immediately preceded by a PUSH, by $v_1 \in U'$. Next, assume that we are in a situation $D \bullet$ PUSH $v \bullet R$, where D is a DRS (no occurrences of PUSH in D, no occurrences of $\bullet$ in D). Then there are two cases to consider.

It may be that v_j does not occur in $\mathit{fix}(D) \cup \mathit{intro}(D)$, for any index j. In that case, rewrite as follows:

$$(D \bullet \text{PUSH } v) \bullet R \Longrightarrow (D; v_1); R.$$

It may also be that v_j does occur in $\mathit{fix}(D) \cup \mathit{intro}(D)$, for some index j. In that case, let i be $\sup(\{j \in I\!N \mid v_j \in \mathit{fix}(D) \cup \mathit{intro}(D)\})$, and rewrite as follows:

$$(D \bullet \text{PUSH } v) \bullet R \Longrightarrow (D; v_{i+1}); [v_{i+1}/v_i]R.$$

The idea behind these instructions is that if v_j does not occur in D, then v_1 can safely be introduced, and it will actively bind the occurrences of v_1 which occur in open position on the right. If v_j does occur in D, then the present push should affect the v-variables with the highest index in open position on the right. This is precisely what the renaming $[v_{i+1}/v_i]$ effects.

Indeterministic merge with substitution. Indeterministic merge does involve a family $\odot_\theta$ of merge operations, where θ is a renaming that is constrained by the two DRSs D_1 and D_2 to be merged, in the sense that θ is proper for D_2 and θ avoids the set $\mathit{intro}(D_1) \cup \mathit{fix}(D_1)$. If the interpretations of D_1 and D_2 are given by $\langle X_1, Y_1, F_1\rangle$ and $\langle X_2, Y_2, F_2\rangle$, respectively, then the interpretation of $D_1 \bullet_\theta D_2$ is given by:

$$\langle X_1 \cup X_2, Y_1 \cup \theta Y_2, F_1 \cap \theta F_2\rangle.$$

If θ is constrained in the way stated above this is a proper DRS denotation.

The rules for indeterministic merge reduction use renamings, as follows (we use $\mathit{activ}(R)$ for $\mathit{intro}(R) \cup \mathit{fix}(R)$):

$$(R \bullet v) \Longrightarrow \begin{cases} (R; v) & \text{if } v \notin \mathit{activ}(R), \\ (R; w) & \text{if } v \in \mathit{activ}(R), \\ & \quad w \notin \mathit{activ}(R), \end{cases}$$

$$(R \bullet \top) \Longrightarrow (R; \top),$$

$$(R \bullet Pt_1, \ldots, t_n) \Longrightarrow (R; Pt_1, \ldots, t_n),$$

$$(R \bullet \neg R') \Longrightarrow (R; \neg R'),$$

$$((R \bullet v) \bullet R') \Longrightarrow \begin{cases} ((R; v); R') & \text{if } v \notin \mathit{activ}(R), \\ ((R; w); [w/v]R' & \\ \quad \text{if } v \in \mathit{activ}(R),\ w \notin \mathit{activ}(R) \cup \mathit{activ}(R'), & \end{cases}$$

$$((R \bullet \top) \bullet R') \Longrightarrow ((R; \top) \bullet R'),$$

$$((R \bullet Pt_1, \ldots, t_n) \bullet R') \Longrightarrow ((R; Pt_1, \ldots, t_n) \bullet R'),$$

$$((R \bullet \neg R_1) \bullet R_2) \Longrightarrow ((R; \neg R_1) \bullet R_2),$$

$$(R \bullet (R_1; R_2)) \Longrightarrow ((R \bullet R_1) \bullet R_2),$$

$$(R \bullet (R_1 \bullet R_2)) \Longrightarrow ((R \bullet R_1) \bullet R_2).$$

Note that under the indeterministic merge regime, $\bullet$ does not get an independent semantics, so one cannot talk about 'the' meaning of $D \bullet D'$ anymore, only about its meaning modulo renaming of *intro*(D'). One can still prove that different reductions of R to normal form (i.e. to proper DRSs) are always write variants of one another, i.e. $R \twoheadrightarrow D$ and $R \twoheadrightarrow D'$ together entail that there is some proper renaming θ of D with $\theta D = D'$.

A set of RDRSs together with a set of merge reduction rules like the example sets given above is a so-called abstract reduction system (Klop, 1992), and the theory of abstract reduction systems can fruitfully be applied to their study. What all merge reduction rule sets above, with the exception of destructive merge, have in common is that they start out from reducible DRSs and produce proper DRSs as normal forms. They all take into account that the merge operation $\bullet$ should not destroy anaphoric links. Merge with substitution has as an additional feature that it preserves anaphoric sockets, and that is what we will use in the sequel. For practical reasons we opt for the indeterministic version, to avoid possible confusion due to the appearance of a new kind of indices (indicating stack depth).

The picture we end up with in indeterministic merge reduction is given in Figure 1. Each RDRS or DRS has a set of anaphoric plugs and a set of anaphoric sockets. The plugs anchor the representation structure to previous discourse or to contextually given antecedents. In both reduced and unreduced RDRSs, these plugs have fixed names, given by *fix*(R). The sockets are the anchoring ground for the next bit of discourse. In unreduced RDRSs, the sockets do not have fixed names yet, and they may not yet represent the

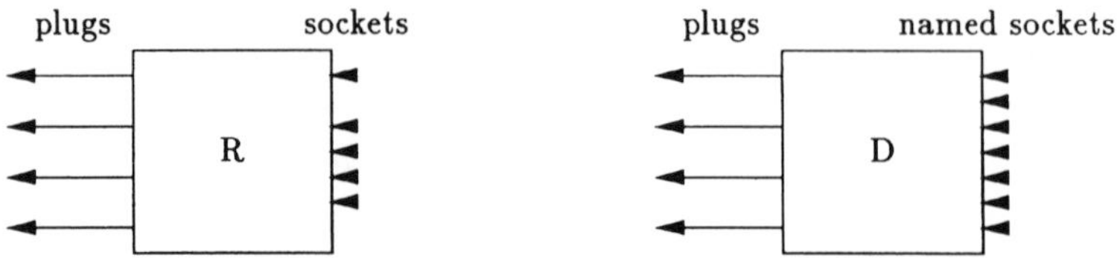

Fig. 1. Unreduced and reduced DRS, with plugs and sockets.

full set of anaphoric possibilities of the represented discourse. During the process of merge reduction, the internal wiring of the representation structure gets re-shuffled and some members of *intro*(R) may end up with a new name, to make room for extra sockets. If D is a fully reduced DRS, however, the sockets have fixed names, given by *intro*$(D) \cup$ *fix*(D), and this set of markers represents the full set of anaphoric possibilities for subsequent discourse.

Here is a concrete example of how disjoint merging according to the indeterministic merge regime works:

(47)

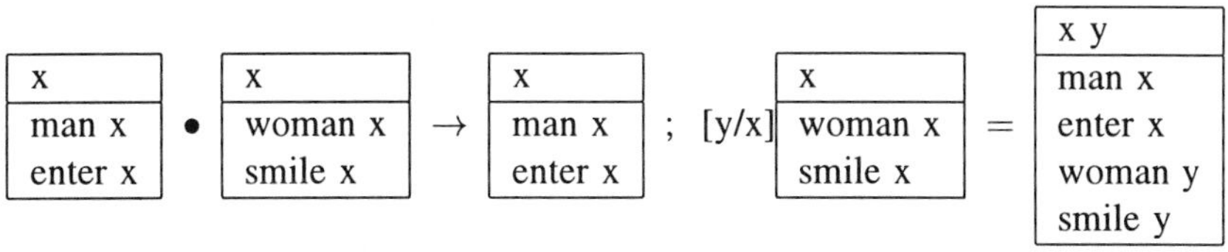

In DRT with indeterministic merge, introduced markers are always new, so no information is ever destroyed, and merging of representations preserves all anaphoric possibilities of the parts that are merged.

We now know what the basic building blocks of DRT are, namely structures as given in (45), and what is the glue that puts them together, namely the disjoint merge operation involving marker renaming. This concludes the discussion of compositionality for DRSs. Quite a few philosophical and technical questions concerning the natural notion of information ordering in DRT remain. See (Visser, 1994a) for illumination on these matters.

8. Disjoint merge and memory management

Reference markers are similar to variables, but differ from them in that they are not bound by logical operators in the usual sense. In fact, reference markers behave more like variables in programming languages than like variables in ordinary first order logic (Section 6 above).

Anaphoric links are created by linking new reference markers to available ones. How does one discard references? By de-allocating storage space on popping out of a 'subroutine'. The representation, in box format, for (3) is given in (48).

(48)

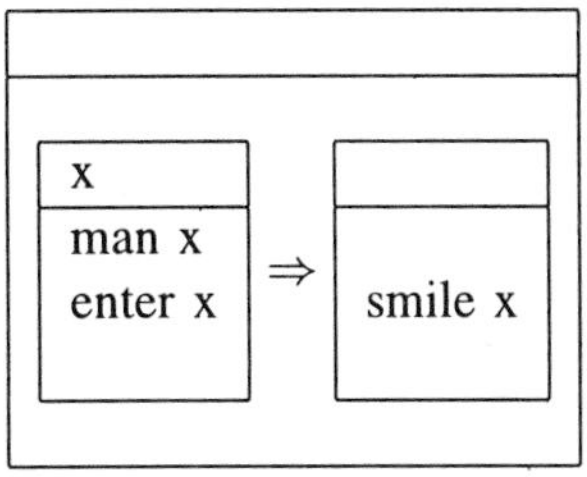

The semantic treatment of this uses a subroutine for checking if every way of making a reference to a man who enters (where the reference is established via marker x) makes the property given by the consequent of the clause succeed. Next the storage space for x

is de-allocated, which explains why an anaphoric link to *a man* in subsequent discourse is ruled out, or at least infelicitous (see example (49)).

(49) If a man[1] enters, he_1 smiles. *He_1 is happy.

Thus we see that anaphoric linking is not subsumed under variable binding, or at least not under variable binding perceived in a standard fashion, as in first order logic. The process is much more akin to variable binding in programming, where storage space is created and discarded dynamically, and where links to a variable remain possible until the space occupied by the variable gets de- allocated to be used for something else, so that further anaphoric links remain possible as long as the variable space for the antecedent remains accessible.

Reference markers, as we have seen, are allocated pieces of storage space for (representations of) things in the world. We can picture the building of a representation structure as an interactive process, where we give instructions to make memory reservations and to provide names for the allocated chunks of memory, as in (50).

(50) new(Var).

The system responds by allocating a chunk of memory of the correct size and by returning a name as value of *Var*, say $u385$, indicating that a piece of storage space is allocated and henceforth known under the name $u385$, where 385 presumably is the offset from the beginning of the piece of memory where the representation under construction is stored. Once storage space has been allocated to a discourse referent, it is useful to know the scope of the allocation. In DRT the scope of the introduction of a discourse referent is closed off by the closest $\neg$ operator (or the closest $\Rightarrow$ operator, in case $\Rightarrow$ is taken as a primitive) that has that introduction in its scope.

Of course, this interactive picture is an *inside* picture of what happens during the representation building process. We must also be able to look at the situation *from the outside*, and answer the question what happens if we assume that we have built and stored two representation structures D_1, D_2 in the memory of a computer, one after the other. Next, we want to store them in memory simultaneously, i.e. to merge them, where the merging has to preserve sequential order. This will in general involve changing the names of those variables declared in the second representation that would otherwise overwrite the area of memory already used by the first representation.

What if some very suspicious semanticist still has qualms about disjoint merge because of the indeterminism of the operation? We then would have to explain to him (or her) that the indeterminism is entirely natural, as it reflects the fact that the renaming operation is nothing but the familiar operation of copying variable values to a different (unused) part of memory before combining two memory states (Figure 2). Disjoint merge is indeterministic simply because any way of copying part of memory to a safe new location will do. This suggests that indeterminism is a strength rather than a weakness of the disjoint merge.

The story of a reasonable definition of merge is a story of memory management. Assuming we have an unlimited supply of memory available, we may picture the data part of memory where the active markers of representation structure D reside as an

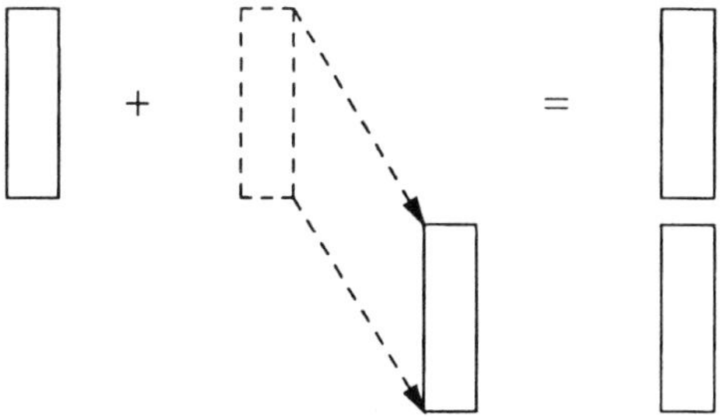

Fig. 2. Copying registers before merging memory states.

array $a[0], \ldots, a[i], \ldots$, where the $a[i]$ are the cells containing the referents (pointers to the individuals in the model under consideration). Where exactly in absolute memory representation structure D is stored is immaterial; we assume it is stored in relative memory, that is to say, at some unknown offset m from the start of the data part of memory. If the marker set *activ*(D) of structure D occupies k memory cells and is stored at offset m from the beginning of data memory, then the active markers of D range from $a[m]$ to $a[m+k]$.

As soon as we are willing to keep track of where in relative memory the result of merging representation structures D_1 and D_2 is going to reside, counting from the offset where D_1 is stored, a deterministic disjoint merge is readily available, in terms of a particular renaming θ determined by the memory locations. Now the story gets us down to the level of programming the bare silicon of the discourse representation machine, so to speak. Assuming the markers *activ*(D_1) of D_1 reside in memory at $u[0], \ldots, u[i]$ (where $u[0] = a[m]$, for some offset m), and the markers *activ*(D_2) of D_2 reside in some scratch part of memory $s[0], \ldots, s[j]$, then D_1 and D_2 can be merged after a renaming $\theta = [u[i+1]/s[0], \ldots, u[i+j+1]/s[j]]$, and *activ*$(D_1; \theta D_2)$ will reside in memory at $u[0], \ldots, u[i+j+1]$.

But once again, such a detailed description of the implementation of merge is really unnecessary. What we will need for the next section is the assumption that for all R_1, R_2, the merge $R_1 \bullet R_2$ is a well-defined (reducible) discourse representation structure, and that the result of merging R_1 and R_2 is independent of the choice of marker names, in the sense that the operation does not destroy anaphoric sockets due to variable name clashes. This is precisely what we have got in the definition of the merge operation provided by indeterministic merge.

What it all boils down to is this. Anaphoric links are essentially arrows pointing from anaphoric expressions to antecedents (Figure 3). Often these links can be represented by indices, as in (51).

(51) John^i hates a man^j who hates him$_i$ and another man$_j$ who does not.

The actual choice of the index numbers does not matter. What matters is the property of *having the same index*. In a slogan: anaphoric arrows are index pairs $({}^{i}\ {}_{i})$ *modulo renamings*. Of course, one might also assume that all indices have been picked appropriately

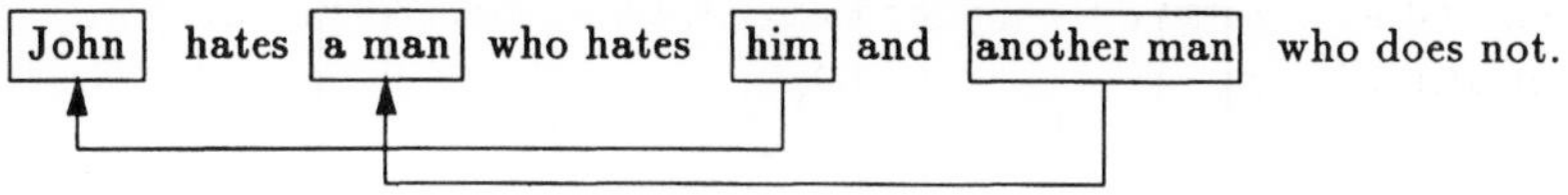

Fig. 3. Anaphoric links are arrows.

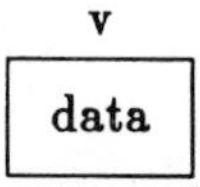

Fig. 4. Direct allocation of storage space to variable v.

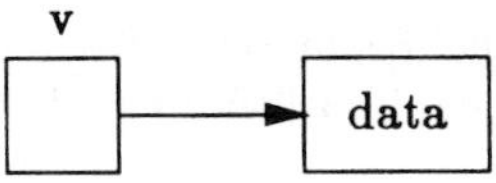

Fig. 5. Indirect allocation of storage space to variable v.

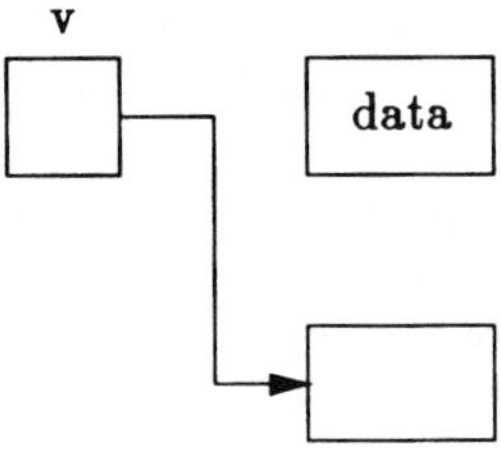

Fig. 6. Allocating new memory space to v without destroying old data.

from the start, but as a general strategy this would seem quite unrealistic; and in any case the point we want to make here is that that assumption is not necessary.

While we are at the topic of memory management, we might as well mention that there are at least two non-equivalent ways in which storage space for reference markers can get allocated. In the first variant, which we have assumed until now, on allocating memory and giving it a name v, v becomes the name of the piece of memory containing the data (Figure 4).

In the second variant, v refers to the data indirectly by pointing to a piece of storage space containing the data. This second variant allows much greater versatility in manipulating data structures. The name v might for instance be used to allocate and point to a new piece of memory, without destroying previous data (Figure 6). Indirect allocation ensures that old data are preserved in memory, although they may no longer be accessible under the old name (Figure 6). The development of a pointer semantics for DRT suggests the use of pointer stacks to keep track of referents that are contextually salient, allowing pointers to be set to nil to indicate that a referent has drifted out of focus, and so on.

For a detailed account of a pointer semantics for a variant of DRT we refer the reader to (Vermeulen, 1995).

9. Constructing DRSs for natural language fragments

As we have seen in Section 5, there is one sense in which the compositionality of DRT is unproblematic: the representation formalisms DRT proposes are as compositional as one could like. In fact, all semantic definitions we have considered in the last three sections, from Definition 5.1, onwards, have been essentially compositional: they either were, or else could readily be converted into, compositional definitions of the semantic values that expressions of these formalisms determine in a model. Moreover, in the last two sections we have looked at a number of merge operations for putting two DRSs together into a single one. These operations too, we found, can be given direct semantic interpretations which map the semantic values of the component DRSs into the semantic value of the compound.

But what about compositionality in the second sense? Does DRT provide a way of analyzing fragments of natural language which assigns these fragments a semantics that is compositional with respect to these fragments themselves, a semantics that is compositional with respect to a natural syntax for these fragments? The original formulation of DRT did not seem to provide such an analysis, and it was even suggested at the time that a compositional treatment of the natural language fragments then considered would be impossible. In the meantime we have, through the dynamic reformulation of DRT discussed in Sections 6, 7 and 8, come to see that such pessimism is not quite warranted: when applied judiciously, the traditional computational methods familiar from Montague Grammar can be made to work so that they assign sentences and texts from these fragments the same truth conditions as the original version of DRT. It suffices to define the building blocks of DRSs as suitably typed expressions of a typed language. In particular, each word of the natural language fragment in question can be assigned an expression of the typed language as its lexical entry, and these expressions can then be combined, by 'semantic' rules corresponding to syntactic composition rules, into representations of any given sentence or text of the fragment; by an entirely analogous process, one can compute the semantic value of the sentence or text directly from the semantic values of the (entries of) the words composing them.

Whether the compositional approach towards DRT, which operates under much stricter constraints than the original DRT approach (e.g., Kamp and Reyle, 1993), can handle all the purposes to which DRT has been put is a question to which there is at present no clear answer. We turn to this question briefly at the end of this section and again in Section 11.

A DRS construction algorithm for a given natural language fragment has to provide instructions for extending a given DRS with the information contained in a sentence from the fragment. This entails that the processing instructions for that sentence should take information from the previous representation into account. In practice, this is the list of available referents. Assuming that the representation of the previous discourse is in reduced form, we may take it that we have a list $u_1, \ldots, u_n$ available of reference

category	abbreviates
CN	S/E(*,*,*)
VP(*)	E(Nom,*,*)\S
NP(case,i,j)	S/(E(case,i,j)\S)
TV(tense)	VP(tense)/NP(Acc,*,*)
DET(i,j)	NP(*,i,j)/CN
AUX	VP(Tensed)/VP(Inf)
REL	(CN\CN)/VP(Tensed)

Fig. 7. Category abbreviations for a toy grammar.

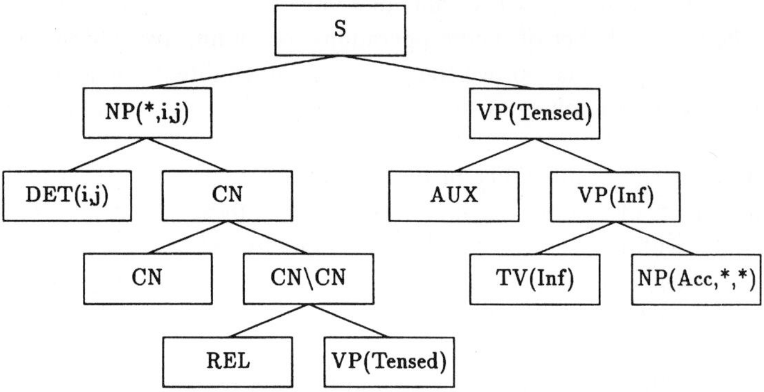

Fig. 8. Example of a possible sentence structure according to the toy grammar.

markers introduced by previous discourse. Pronouns may be resolved to any member of this list, and also to markers that get introduced by antecedents in the sentence under consideration.

The process of anaphoric resolution on the basis of available information from the representation of previous discourse poses a highly non-trivial challenge, and it is questionable if a real algorithm for this process is on the cards. The following problem is more manageable. Assuming that an anaphoric indexing for a sentence is given, and also that a decision has been made about the relative scopes of the operators (i.e. a *reading* of the sentence has been fixed by the sentence grammar), give an algorithm for updating an available representation structure with the information from that sentence. In fact, as we shall see, we get a lot of this for free because of the presence of the merge operation $\bullet$.

To illustrate the process of constructing DRSs for natural language fragments, we begin by defining a sentence grammar for a toy fragment. Basic categories are S (without features) for sentences, TXT (without features) for texts, and E (with features for case, antecedent index i, anaphoric index j), for markers for individual entities. We assume the category abbreviations given in Figure 7. Here the feature variable *tense* ranges over the values *Tensed* and *Inf*, the feature variable *case* ranges over the values *Nom* and *Acc*, and the index features range over the positive natural numbers. The example structure generated by this grammar given in Figure 8 illustrates how the grammar works.

expression	category	translates to	type
a^i	DET(i,*)	$\lambda P\lambda Q(u_i \bullet P(u_i) \bullet Q(u_i))$	((e,T),((e,T),T))
$every^i$	DET(i,*)	$\lambda P\lambda Q\neg((u_i \bullet P(u_i)) \bullet \neg Q(u_i))$	((e,T),((e,T),T))
no^i	DET(i,*)	$\lambda P\lambda Q\neg((u_i \bullet P(u_i)) \bullet Q(u_i))$	((e,T),((e,T),T))
$another^i_j$	DET(i,j)	$\lambda P\lambda Q(u_i; u_i \neq u_j \bullet P(u_i) \bullet Q(u_i))$	((e,T),((e,T),T))
the^i_j	DET(i,j)	$\lambda P\lambda Q(u_i; u_i \doteq u_j \bullet P(u_i) \bullet Q(u_i))$	((e,T),((e,T),T))
his^i_j	DET(i,j)	$\lambda P\lambda Q(u_i; poss\ (u_j, u_i) \bullet P(u_i) \bullet Q(u_i))$	((e,T),((e,T),T))
$Bill_i$	NP(*,*,i)	$\lambda P(u_i \doteq b \bullet P(u_i))$	((e,T),T)
who	REL	$\lambda P\lambda Q\lambda v(Q(v) \bullet P(v))$	((e,T),((e,T),(e,T)))
he_i	NP(nom,*,i)	$\lambda P(P(u_i))$	((e,T),T)
him_i	NP(acc,*,i)	$\lambda P(P(u_i))$	((e,T),T)
man	CN	$\lambda v(man\ (v))$	(e,T)
boy	CN	$\lambda v(boy\ (v))$	(e,T)
smiles	VP(Tensed)	$\lambda v(smile\ (v))$	(e,T)
smile	VP(Inf)	$\lambda v(smile\ (v))$	(e,T)
has	TV(Tensed)	$\lambda \mathcal{P}\lambda u(\mathcal{P}\lambda v(poss\ (u, v)))$	(((e,T),T),(e,T))
have	TV(Inf)	$\lambda \mathcal{P}\lambda u(\mathcal{P}\lambda v(poss\ (u, v)))$	(((e,T),T),(e,T))
hates	TV(Tensed)	$\lambda \mathcal{P}\lambda u(\mathcal{P}\lambda v(hate\ (u, v)))$	(((e,T),T),(e,T))
hate	TV(Inf)	$\lambda \mathcal{P}\lambda u(\mathcal{P}\lambda v(hate\ (u, v)))$	(((e,T),T),(e,T))
does not	AUX	$\lambda P\lambda v\neg P(v))$	((e,T),(e,T))
if	(S/S)/S	$\lambda p\lambda q(\neg(p \bullet \neg q))$	(T,(T,T))
.	S\(TXT/S)	$\lambda p\lambda q(p \bullet q)$	(T,(T,T))
.	TXT\(TXT/S)	$\lambda p\lambda q(p \bullet q)$	(T,(T,T))

Fig. 9. Lexical component of the toy fragment for English.

Further information about the categorial format with feature unification is provided in the Chapters on *Categorial Grammar* and on *Feature Structures* in this Handbook.

If we start out with basic types e for entities and T for state transitions (not truth values!), then the table given in Figure 9 defines the lexical component of a tiny fragment of English. Variables u, v range over type e, variables p, q over type T, variables P, Q over type (e, T), variables $\mathcal{P}$ over type $((e, T), T)$.

We distinguish between variables of the typed logic and reference markers (i.e. variables of the dynamic representation). Markers u_i are taken from a set U which we assume to be disjoint from the set V_e of variables of type e. Thus, from the perspective of the typed logic the reference markers behave like constants. A rather straightforward definition of the interpretation of a typed expression can now be given in terms of an interpretation function I, a (typed logic) variable assignment g, and a marker assignment f. This theme is played (sometimes with minor variations) in (Asher, 1993; Bos, Mastenbroek, McGlashan, Millies and Pinkal, 1994; Kuschert, 1995; and Muskens, 1996).

From the point of view of the dynamic logic reference markers are variables, to be sure, but, as we have seen, substitution for dynamic variables is handled quite differently from variable substitution in static logics. Another way of expressing the relation between typed variables and reference markers is by saying that β reduction (which affects typed variables) and merge reduction (which affects markers) are orthogonal: there is no interaction between the λ reduction rules and the $\bullet$ reduction rules.

The category table in the lexicon makes clear that example sentence (52) has the structure specified in Figure 8.

(52) The man who smiles does not hate Bill.

Some other sentences in the fragment are given in (53) and (54) (we use the particular nouns and verbs in the table as paradigms, of course).

(53) If a man hates Bill, he does not smile.

(54) If a bishop meets another bishop, he blesses him.

For convenience, we have assumed that the connective '.' serves as a discourse constructor. Example (55) gives a text which is in the fragment.

(55) The man who smiles does not hate Bill. He respects Bill.

Note that $\bullet$ is used for merging of structures in all those cases where renaming may still be necessary. The translations of *if* and *every* use $\neg(p \bullet \neg q)$ rather than $p \Rightarrow q$ to allow for the possibility of renaming during the merge of the components.

The composition of representation structures for these example sentences is a matter of routine. See Gamut (1991) for a didactic account of the general procedure, Asher (1993) and Muskens (1996) for applications in dynamic semantics, and Bouchez, Van Eijck and Istace (1993) for a description of an implementation of dynamic semantics using the technique.

As an example, let us go through the procedure of building a representation for (55). We assume the following indexing to indicate the intended anaphoric link.

(56) The [man who smiles]^1 does not hate Bill. He$_1$ respects Bill.

We also have to choose anaphoric indices for *the man who smiles* and *Bill*. Assume these to be 2 and 3, respectively. In the table we find translation $\lambda P \lambda Q \lambda v(Q(v) \bullet P(v))$ for *who*, while *smiles* translates as $\lambda v(\mathit{smile}\ (v))$. These combine by functional application, which gives (57) (after renaming of variables for perspicuity).

(57) $\lambda Q \lambda v(Q(v) \bullet \lambda w(\mathit{smile}\ (w))(v))$.

Expression (57) β reduces to (58).

(58) $\lambda Q \lambda v(Q(v) \bullet \mathit{smile}\ (v))$.

Combining (58) with the translation of *man*, we get (59).

(59) $\lambda v(\lambda w(\mathit{man}\ (w))(v) \bullet \mathit{smile}\ (v))$.

Expression (59) β reduces to (60).

(60) $\lambda v(\mathit{man}\ (v) \bullet \mathit{smile}\ (v))$.

Combining (60) with the translation of the_2^1 gives expression (61) as translation for the_2^1 *man who smiles*:

(61) $\lambda Q(u_1; u_1 \doteq u_2 \bullet \lambda w(\mathit{man}\ (w) \bullet \mathit{smile}\ (w))(u_1) \bullet Q(u_1))$.

Applying β reduction to expression (61) gives (62).

(62) $\lambda Q(u_1; u_1 \doteq u_2 \bullet \mathit{man}\ (u_1) \bullet \mathit{smile}\ (u_1) \bullet Q(u_1)).$

In a similar way, we get (63) for *does not hate* Bill^3_3.

(63) $\lambda u \neg (u_3 \doteq b \bullet \mathit{hate}\ (u, u_3)).$

Combining (62) and (63) gives the translation of the first sentence of (56):

(64) $(u_1; u_1 \doteq u_2 \bullet \mathit{man}\ (u_1) \bullet \mathit{smile}\ (u_1); \neg(u_3 \doteq b \bullet \mathit{hate}\ (u_1, u_3))).$

Merge reduction of (64) (with the identical renaming) gives:

(65) $(u_1; u_1 \doteq u_2; \mathit{man}\ (u_1); \mathit{smile}\ (u_1); \neg(u_3 \doteq b; \mathit{hate}\ (u_1, u_3))).$

In box format:

(66)
$$\begin{array}{|l|}\hline u_1 \\ \hline u_1 \doteq u_2 \\ \text{man } u_1 \\ \text{smile } u_1 \\ \neg \begin{array}{|l|}\hline \\ \hline u_3 \doteq b \\ \text{hate } (u_1, u_3) \\ \hline \end{array} \\ \\ \hline \end{array}$$

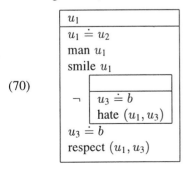

The translation of the second sentence of (56) is (67).

(67) $(u_3 \doteq b \bullet \mathit{respect}\ (u_1, u_3)).$

One merge reduction step, with identical renaming:

(68) $(u_3 \doteq b; \mathit{respect}\ (u_1, u_3)).$

The translation of discourse (56) is the result of applying the semantic operation for text composition (the semantics for '.' in the lexicon table) to (65) and (67), in that order:

(69) $\lambda p \lambda q(p \bullet q))(u_1; u_1 \doteq u_2; \mathit{man}\ (u_1); \mathit{smile}\ (u_1); \neg(u_3 \doteq b; \mathit{hate}\ (u_1, u_3)))$
$(u_3 \doteq b; \mathit{respect}\ (u_1, u_3)).$

Two β reductions and one further merge reduction with identical renaming gives the following result (in box format):

(70)
$$\begin{array}{|l|}\hline u_1 \\ \hline u_1 \doteq u_2 \\ \text{man } u_1 \\ \text{smile } u_1 \\ \neg \begin{array}{|l|}\hline \\ \hline u_3 \doteq b \\ \text{hate } (u_1, u_3) \\ \hline \end{array} \\ u_3 \doteq b \\ \text{respect } (u_1, u_3) \\ \hline \end{array}$$

The fact that no new discourse referent gets introduced for the proper name *Bill* is a reflection of our treatment of proper names. Here is the entry for proper names in the lexicon table again:

expression	category	translates to	type
Bill_i	NP(*,*,i)	$\lambda P(u_i \doteq b \bullet P(u_i))$	((e,T),T)

Here i is the index that links the constant b for the proper name to its external anchor. Anaphoric links involving proper names are insensitive to *where* the name gets introduced, for they are interpreted as links where the anaphor and the proper name are both anaphoric expressions with a common 'externally given' antecedent.

At this point a couple of remarks are in order about the rules of index assignment which are part of our present treatment. The first remark concerns the lower indices, which, we have been assuming, must be assigned not only to pronouns but in fact to definite noun phrases of any kind. The requirement that every definite NP must receive a lower index reflects the so-called *familiarity principle* (see Heim, 1982), according to which a definite NP is used felicitously only when the utterance context already contains a reference marker for its referent, which can then serve as 'anaphoric antecedent' for the NP. It is doubtful that the familiarity principle can be upheld in as rigid and comprehensive a form as this, in which it is taken to apply to every occurrence of every type of definite noun phrase. The definite description *the man who smiles* in (52) is a case in point. It would certainly be possible to use this phrase for picking out from a given crowd the unique person smiling, pretty much as many philosophers, from Frege and Russell onwards, have been claiming about definite descriptions. Such a use could easily occur in a context in which no reference marker for the smiling man had as yet been introduced. A treatment of definite descriptions which insists on the presence of antecedent reference markers for definites could still be saved by assuming that definite descriptions always come with a presupposition that the context contains such a reference marker, but that this presupposition can be easily accommodated when necessary. One may have one's doubts about the plausibility of this rescue strategy. But even if we go along with it, we will have to reformulate our semantics in such a way that it allows for such accommodations, and allows them to be made at those points where human interpreters would have to make them. In other words, the theory will have to be restated so that it can deal with aspects of presupposition. Unfortunately, this is a matter that we cannot go into for reasons of space. For the treatment of presupposition within DRT, see the bibliographical remarks in Section 13.

A similar remark is in order about the lower indices of proper names such as *John*. Does the use of a proper name presuppose that its referent is already represented in the given context? Perhaps, but if so, then 'context' needs to be construed in a quite liberal way. So, before such a treatment of proper names can be considered satisfactory, much more needs to be said about how the notion of context is to be construed – what kinds of information may contexts include, from what kinds of contexts can their information come, etc.

The second remark concerns the implicit assumption that the texts to which our theory is applied come fully equipped with all the necessary upper and lower indices and that

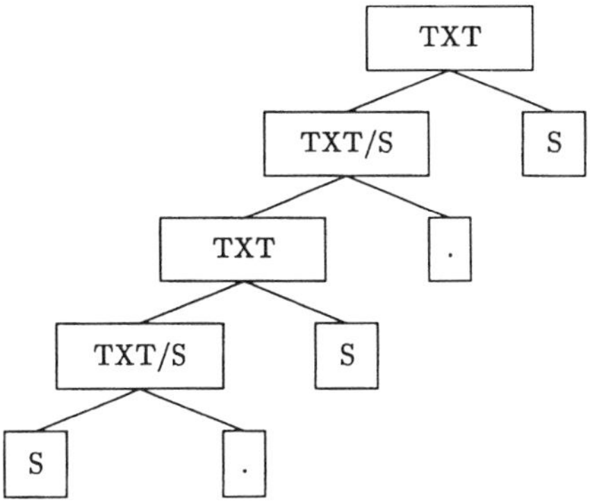

Fig. 10. The structure of a three sentence text in our grammar set-up.

all of these have been assigned in advance. One way in which this assumption gets us into difficulties shows up in the text (71), which has the structure indicated in Figure 10.

(71) A man^1 who mistrusted the assistant$^2_3$ walked in. He$_1$ asked for the manager$^2_4$. He$_2$ turned out to be on holiday.

As the text structure indicates, first representations are built for the first two sentences and these are merged together, and only then is a representation for the third sentence merged with the representation of the preceding discourse. Note that in this case the merge of the representations of the first and the second sentence would involve a renaming of the discourse referent for *the manager*, to avoid a clash with the marker for *the assistant* from the first sentence. This means that the anaphoric index 2 in the third sentence is not going to pick up a reference to *the manager* anymore, as was presumably intended.

The example points towards an aspect of DRT that deserves comment. DRT – this is as true of the form in which it was originally stated as it is of the dynamic formulation presented here – is not a theory of anaphora *resolution*: the theory itself tells us little about how to select the intended antecedent for a given anaphoric expression from among a number of possible candidates. The only substantive contribution which classical DRT makes to the problem of anaphora resolution consists in what it has to say about the 'accessibility' of reference markers that have been introduced in one part of a text to anaphoric expressions occurring elsewhere (see, e.g., Kamp and Reyle, 1993, Chapter 1.4); but this is only a small part of a comprehensive account of anaphora resolution capable of predicting the intended anaphoric connections in all cases in which these are evident to a human interpreter.

Arguably this is as it should be. It would be unreasonable to demand of a theory of *linguistic* semantics – and it is that which DRT originally aimed at – that it incorporate a detailed account of anaphora resolution, which would have to rely on a host of pragmatic principles as well as on an indefinite amount of world knowledge.

It seems *not* unreasonable, however, to demand of such a theory that it offer a suitable interface to other (pragmatic and/or extra-linguistic) components of a comprehensive theory of meaning which are designed to deal with anaphora resolution (see Sidner, 1979; Webber, 1979; Alshawi c.s., 1992, Chapter 10) and to allow these other components to come into action at those points when the information needed for anaphora resolution has become available and the resolution is necessary for interpretation to proceed. To insist that all upper and lower indexation take place in advance of interpretation would fly in the face of this demand. For as a rule it is only *through* and thus after interpretation of the earlier parts of a discourse that the correct links for subsequent anaphoric expressions can be established.

10. The proper treatment of quantification in DRT

As we have seen above, universal quantification can be treated in terms of $D \Rightarrow D'$, which can in turn be taken as an abbreviation of $\neg(D; \neg D')$. Look at the treatment of the quantifiers *every* and *no* in the fragment given above.

expression	category	translates to	type
every^i	DET(i,*)	$\lambda P \lambda Q \neg((u_i \bullet P(u_i)) \bullet \neg Q(u_i))$	((e,T),((e,T),T))
no^i	DET(i,*)	$\lambda P \lambda Q \neg((u_i \bullet P(u_i)) \bullet Q(u_i))$	((e,T),((e,T),T))

Working out an example like *Every man walks* on the basis of this gives the following representation (after merge reduction): $\neg(x; man\ x; \neg walk\ x)$. This is equivalent to: $(x; man\ x) \Rightarrow walk\ x$. In box notation:

(72)
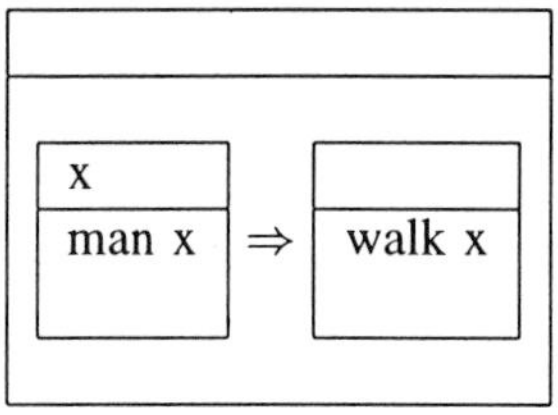

The treatment of *every* creates the impression that the quantificational force resides in the dynamic implication $\Rightarrow$. Note, by the way, that all occurrences of marker x in representation (72) are classically bound. The same holds for more complex examples like the representation for (73) in (74).

(73) Every man who meets a nice woman smiles at her.

(74)
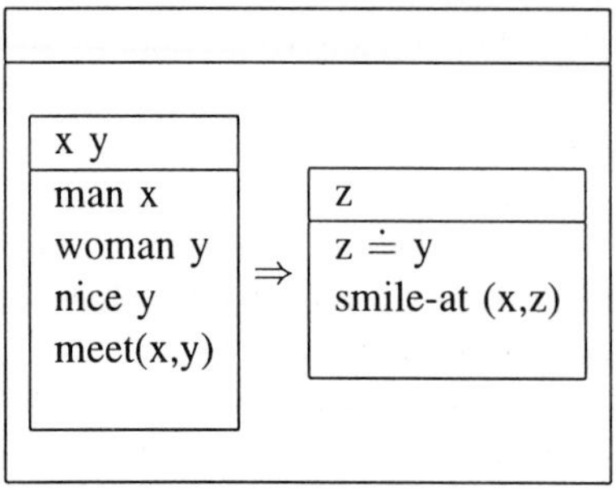

Now consider sentence (75).

(75) Most men who meet a nice woman smile at her.

This sentence is true if most individuals which satisfy the descriptive content of the subject NP also satisfy the VP, i.e. if most men who meet a nice woman have the property of smiling at her. Note that assessing the truth of (75) involves two classes of men, the class of men who meet a nice woman and the class of men who meet a nice woman and smile at her: the sentence is true, roughly, if the cardinality of the second class is more than half that of the first. Note that the truth conditions do not involve the comparison of two sets of pairs of individuals – they do not compare the set of pairs (a, b) such that a is a man, b a nice woman and a meets b with the set of pairs (a, b) such that a is a man, b a nice woman, a meets b and a smiles at b. One can see this by considering a situation in which one man meets lots of women and smiles at them all whereas the other men (say, there are 20 of them) meet very few women and never smile at any. With regard to such a situation intuition says that (75) is false, even though the pairs (a, b) such that a smiles at b may be a clear majority within the set of pairs (a, b) such that a is a man, b is a nice woman and a meets b.

Thus, while the treatment of universal quantification in (74) creates the impression that the quantificational force resides somehow in the dynamic implication $\Rightarrow$, we cannot hope that this can be extended to non-standard quantifiers by working out special variants of dynamic implication. For suppose that we represent (75) as (76).

(76)

x y   man x   woman y   nice y   meet(x,y) $\quad =_m\Rightarrow \quad$ z   z $\doteq$ y   smile-at (x,z)

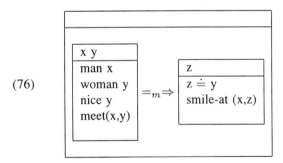

The semantics of $=_m\Rightarrow$ is given by:

– ${}_s[\![D_1 =_m\Rightarrow D_2]\!]^{\mathcal{M}}_{s'}$ iff $s = s'$ and for most assignments s_1 with ${}_s[\![D_1]\!]^{\mathcal{M}}_{s_1}$ there is an assignment s_2 with ${}_s[\![D_2]\!]^{\mathcal{M}}_{s_2}$.

Unfortunately, this analysis gives the wrong truth conditions. In the example case, it quantifies over man–woman pairs instead of individual men. This problem (called the *proportion problem* in the literature) suggests that generalized quantifiers be added explicitly to the representation language; see the Chapter on *Quantification* in this Handbook.

Assuming that what is true for *most* holds in essence also for *every*, the above considerations show that the roles which x and y play in (74) are not identical. The role played by x, the 'variable bound by the quantifier', is special in that it is x, and only x, which determines between which sets the generalized quantifier relation expressed by the determiner of the quantifying NP can be said to hold. A notation that singles out the variable of quantification achieves this. These considerations lead to the following Generalized Quantifier notation for (74) and (76).

(77)

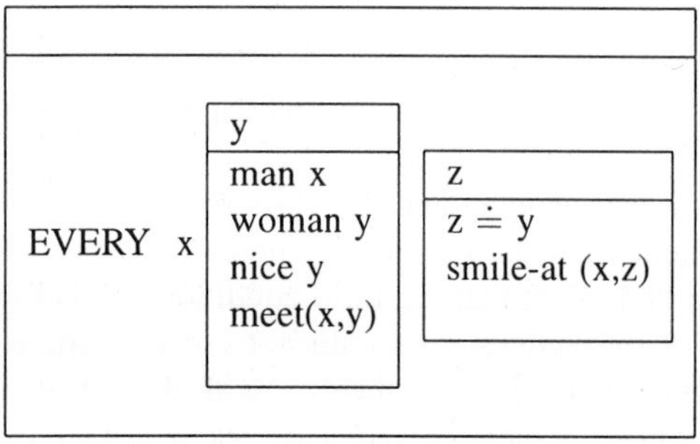

(78)

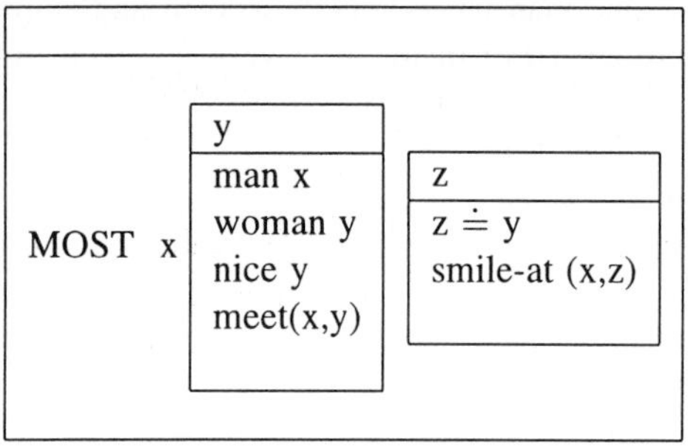

We can now revise the treatment of quantification in our fragment and extend the coverage to other non-standard quantifiers such as *most*, *at most half*, *at least seven*, as follows:

expression	category	translates to	type
every^i	DET(i,*)	$\lambda P \lambda Q(\mathit{EVERY}\ u_i(P(u_i), Q(u_i)))$	((e,T),((e,T),T))
no^i	DET(i,*)	$\lambda P \lambda Q(\mathit{NO}\ u_i(P(u_i), Q(u_i)))$	((e,T),((e,T),T))
most^i	DET(i,*)	$\lambda P \lambda Q(\mathit{MOST}\ u_i(P(u_i), Q(u_i)))$	((e,T),((e,T),T))
at least n^i	DET(i,*)	$\lambda P \lambda Q(\mathit{AT\ LEAST}\ n\ u_i(P(u_i), Q(u_i)))$	((e,T),((e,T),T))

The intended interpretation of this also takes care of the 'internal dynamics' of the quantification. We use $s[x]$ for an assignment which differs at most from s in the value assigned to x, and $\mathcal{M}, s \models D$ for truth in $\mathcal{M}$, given s.

(79) ${}_s[\![Qx(D_1, D_2)]\!]^{\mathcal{M}}_{s'}$ iff $s = s'$ and the set of assignments $s[x]$ for which $\mathcal{M}, s[x] \models D_1$ is Q-related to the set of assignments $s[x]$ for which $\mathcal{M}, s[x] \models D_1 \bullet D_2$.

Note the fact that the meaning of D_1 figures both in the definition of the restriction set R of the quantifier and in the definition of its body set B. The reason for this is that D_1 may introduce referents that have to be resolved in order to get at the meaning of the body set. In the example sentence we have to compare the set of men who meet a nice woman with the set of men who meet a nice woman at whom they smile. Saying that we want to compare the set of 'men who meet a nice woman' with that of 'men who smile at her' will not do, for the specification of the second set contains an unresolved pronominal reference.

It seems intuitively clear that the pronoun *her* is to be interpreted as anaphoric to the indefinite NP *a woman*. It is one of the central claims of DRT that this kind of anaphoric connection is possible because the material of the quantifying sentence that makes up the restrictor is also, implicitly, part of the quantifier's body. This principle also explains why natural language quantifiers are always *conservative*, i.e. express relations between sets with the property that for any sets A and B, A stands in the relation to B iff it stands in the relation to $A \cap B$. They satisfy this equation because a natural language quantification with restrictor condition P and body condition Q has a logical form to the effect that the quantifier relation holds between the extension of P and the extension of $P \wedge Q$. Conservativity is built directly into the logical form.

For the example sentence with *most*, (79) gives the following meaning: for most men who meet a nice woman it holds that they smile at at least one nice woman that they meet. This is called the *weak* reading of the dynamic generalized quantifier. Note that under the semantics given above, *EVERY* $x\ ((y; Rxy), Sxy)$ is not equivalent to $(x; y; Rxy) \Rightarrow Sxy$. In the first expression y has existential force, in the second, y has universal force. There is no perfect agreement among speakers whether (73) and (75) can be interpreted as having the weak reading. Some prefer the so-called *strong* reading:

(80) $_s[\![Qx(D_1, D_2)]\!]_{s'}^{\mathcal{M}}$ iff $s = s'$ and the set of assignments $s[x]$ for which $\mathcal{M}, s[x] \models D_1$ is Q-related to the set of assignments $s[x]$ for which $\mathcal{M}, s[x] \models \neg(D_1 \bullet \neg D_2)$.

Under this interpretation for the quantifiers,

$$\textit{EVERY}\,x\ ((y; Rxy), Sxy) \quad \text{and} \quad (x; y; Rxy) \Rightarrow Sxy$$

are equivalent.

In the definition of strong readings for the quantifiers, we again use the restriction set to resolve pronominal references in the specification of the body set, and again the conservativity property of the generalized quantifier denotation ensures that this does not change the truth conditions. In example case (78) the strong reading can be paraphrased as: for most men who meet a nice woman it holds that they smile at all the nice women that they meet. See the Chapter on *Quantification* in this Handbook for more information on how to choose between weak and strong readings of dynamic quantifiers.

11. Representing tense and aspect in texts

As was said in Section 2 above, discourse representation theory was motivated by a desire to give a systematic account of the interpretation of unbound nominal and temporal anaphora in context. In example (81), there is not only an intended anaphoric link between the indefinite subject of the first sentence and the pronominal subject of the second, but also between the tenses of the verbs in the two sentences.

(81) A man entered the White Hart. He smiled.

The events described in example (81) are naturally understood as sequential, with the event of entering preceding the event of smiling. Also, the past tense indicates that both events precede the time of speech. A plausible DRS representation for the example that makes this temporal anaphoric link explicit is given in (82).

(82)

$u_1\ u_2\ u_3\ e_1\ e_2$
man u_1
$u_2 \doteq WH$
enter (e_1, u_1, u_2)
$t(e_1) < n$
$u_3 \doteq u_1$
smile (e_2, u_3)
$t(e_1) < t(e_2)$
$t(e_2) < n$

In this representation we have given the verbs a Davidsonian event argument (Davidson, 1967), and we have assumed that $t(e)$ denotes the temporal interval during which the event e takes place. Also, we assume that n ('now') refers to an interval during which the text is uttered (the speech interval).

As the example representation indicates, we assume an ontology of events, with temporal intervals at which these take place. Furthermore, we assume that the set of temporal intervals is ordered by precedence $<$ and by temporal inclusion $\sqsubseteq$. We assume that $t_1 < t_2$ expresses that interval t_1 completely precedes t_2, i.e. the end of t_1 is before the beginning of t_2, while $t_1 \sqsubseteq t_2$ expresses that the beginning of t_2 is not later than the beginning of t_1 and the end of t_2 is not earlier than the end of t_1.

It is plausible to further assume that $<$ is irreflexive and transitive, while $\sqsubseteq$ is a partial order (reflexive and transitive). Also, the following are plausible interaction principles:

monotonicity $(x \sqsubseteq y \wedge y < z \wedge u \sqsubseteq z) \rightarrow x < u$.

convexity $(x \sqsubseteq u \wedge x < y \wedge y < z \wedge z \sqsubseteq u) \rightarrow y \sqsubseteq u$.

But we will not dwell on the underlying temporal ontology; for further information on the temporal logic of intervals we refer to the Chapter on *Temporality* of this Handbook and to (Van Benthem, 1982).

In (82) the smiling event e_2 is represented as following the entering event e_1. This is intuitively as it should be and has to do with the fact that in (81) the sentence reporting the smiling event comes after the one which reports the entering event. (Note that the interpretation given in (82) is not, or only barely, available when the sentences of (81) are reversed.) However, the order in which the sentences of a text appear is only one of several factors that determine the temporal relations between the events they mention. A second factor is aspect. For instance, when we replace the non-progressive *smiled* in (81) by the progressive *was smiling*, there is a strong tendency to understand the smiling as something that was going on *while* the man was entering the White Hart: the progressive of an activity verb like *smile* suggests, at least in narrative passages such as (81), simultaneity with the last mentioned event, rather than succession to it. Similarly, simultaneity rather than succession is suggested by a stative verb such as *like*. For instance in

(83) A man^1 entered the White Hart^2. He$_1$ smiled. He$_1$ liked the place$_2$.

The man's liking of the White Hart is not naturally interpreted as having been the case only *after his smiling*. Rather, it seems that the state of affairs of his liking the establishment obtained already as he was smiling, and possibly even before he came in. Thus, the representation of (83) should be as in (84):

(84)

$u_1\ u_2\ u_3\ u_4\ u_5\ e_1\ e_2\ e_3$	
man u_1	$u_2 \doteq WH$
enter (e_1, u_1, u_2)	$t(e_1) < n$
smile (e_2, u_3)	$u_3 \doteq u_1$
	$t(e_1) < t(e_2)$
	$t(e_2) < n$
	$u_4 \doteq u_1$
place (u_5)	$u_5 \doteq u_2$
like (e_3, u_4, u_5)	$t(e_2) \sqsubseteq t(e_3)$
	$t(e_3) < n$

When we consider the question whether one should assume that the man's liking the place in (83) anteceded his entering the White Hart, we perceive a further factor that is important for the interpretation of temporal relations. In order that a text is perceived as coherent, its successive sentences must be seen as standing in certain *rhetorical relations* to each other. (Halliday and Hasan, 1976; Mann and Thompson, 1987.) One such relation is *explanation*, a relation which holds between two neighboring sentences (or sometimes larger units, consisting of several sentences) when the later sentence or sentence group provides an explanation for what is claimed by the earlier sentence or group. Like many other rhetorical relations explanation carries certain implications for temporal order. For instance, when, say, two sentences S and S' are interpreted as standing in the explanation relation, with S' providing an explanation for what is said in S, the event or state described by S' cannot be later than that described in S. We see this when we look closely at (83): the man's liking the place can either be taken as an explanation of his smiling or as an explanation of why the man went to the White Hart in the first place. The first interpretation entails that his liking the place did not start after his smiling, but it leaves open whether he liked the place only upon entering it or already before. According to the second interpretation the man must have liked the place even before he went in.

We have dwelt on this dimension of the interpretation of the temporal relations in (83) to indicate how complicated the matter of interpreting temporal relations is and how much it depends on pragmatic factors such as discourse coherence and rhetorical relations. Just as with pronominal anaphora, linguistic form does in general no more than impose a frame of constraints within which the precise interpretation of temporal relations must be decided on other grounds.

For a presentation of the semantics of temporal reference within the very limited space available here this poses a dilemma. On the one hand, a presentation that does justice to what is now known about the interactions between the different factors mentioned above is out of the question. On the other, a general treatment of the purely grammatical constraints on temporal reference would, in view of its inevitable lack of specificity, be rather uninformative. We have therefore chosen to concentrate on a certain small subclass of texts, in which rhetorical relations are fully determined by linguistic form (by the order of the sentences in the text, by the tenses of the verbs and by their aspectual properties). (81) and (83) are both instances of this class.

The central idea behind the treatment we will present goes back to (Reichenbach, 1947). The interpretation of the tenses involves relating the event or state described to a *reference point*. For instance, for unembedded cases of the simple past tense, the reference point is provided by the context in which the given past tense sentence occurs. In texts of the kind to which our theory is intended to apply it is the immediately preceding sentence which supplies the reference point. How the reference point is used to temporally locate the event or state described by the sentence in question depends on whether the sentence has stative or non-stative aspect (or, what comes to the same in our terminology, whether what the sentence describes is a state or an event). For past tense sentences, the difference that aspect makes is illustrated by the distinct interpretations that are assigned to the second and the third sentence of (83) – the event described by the second sentence is interpreted as following the reference point by the preceding sentence, the state described by the third sentence as obtaining at the reference point provided by its predecessor. Moreover, an event sentence like the second sentence of (83) *resets* the reference point it inherits from the context to the event it itself introduces, whereas a stative sentence like the third one passes the reference point on to the next sentence unchanged. (To test this, see what happens when one adds a fourth sentence, stative or non-stative, on to (83).)

Besides playing a role in locating the described event or state in relation to the reference point, tense forms usually also have an 'absolute' semantic impact in that they relate the described state or event to the utterance time. For instance, unembedded occurrences of the past tense imply that the state or event lies before the utterance time and unembedded occurrences of the English present tense imply, with few exceptions, location at the utterance time.

For the limited domain to which our 'mini theory' is meant to apply, the use and modification of reference points can be elegantly handled along the lines proposed by Muskens (1995). As noted there, in a dynamic set-up it is natural to implement the reference interval as a register r to which a new value get assigned for a non-stative verb, while the value is unaffected for stative verbs. For instance, the lexical entry for *smiled* specifies that the interval of the smiling event is constrained to follow the current reference interval, that the reference interval is reset to the interval of the event, and that the event interval has to precede the interval of speech:

$$\lambda v(e; \mathit{smile}\ (e, v); r < t(e); r := t(e); r < n).$$

Here $r := t(e)$ is shorthand for $r; r \doteq t(e)$.

expression	category	translates to	type
does not	AUX	$\lambda P\lambda v\neg(P(v); r \sqsubseteq n)$	((e,T),(e,T))
did not	AUX	$\lambda P\lambda v\neg(P(v); r < n)$	((e,T),(e,T))
will	AUX	$\lambda P\lambda v(P(v); n < r)$	((e,T),(e,T))
will not	AUX	$\lambda P\lambda v\neg(P(v); n < r)$	((e,T),(e,T))
smiles	VP(Tensed)	$\lambda v(e; \mathit{smile}\ (e,v); r < t(e); r := t(e); r \sqsubseteq n)$	(e,T)
smiled	VP(Tensed)	$\lambda v(e; \mathit{smile}\ (e,v); r < t(e); r := t(e); r < n)$	(e,T)
smile	VP(Inf)	$\lambda v(e; \mathit{smile}\ (e,v); r < t(e); r := t(e))$	(e,T)
hates	TV(Tensed)	$\lambda\mathcal{P}\lambda u(\mathcal{P}\lambda v(e; \mathit{hate}\ (e,u,v); r \sqsubseteq t(e); r \sqsubseteq n))$	(((e,T),T),(e,T))
hated	TV(Tensed)	$\lambda\mathcal{P}\lambda u(\mathcal{P}\lambda v(e; \mathit{hate}\ (e,u,v); r \sqsubseteq t(e); r < n))$	(((e,T),T),(e,T))
hate	TV(Inf)	$\lambda\mathcal{P}\lambda u(\mathcal{P}\lambda v(e; \mathit{hate}\ (e,u,v); r \sqsubseteq t(e)))$	(((e,T),T),(e,T))
likes	TV(Tensed)	$\lambda\mathcal{P}\lambda u(\mathcal{P}\lambda v(e; \mathit{like}\ (e,u,v); r \sqsubseteq t(e); r \sqsubseteq n))$	(((e,T),T),(e,T))
liked	TV(Tensed)	$\lambda\mathcal{P}\lambda u(\mathcal{P}\lambda v(e; \mathit{like}\ (e,u,v); r \sqsubseteq t(e); r < n))$	(((e,T),T),(e,T))
like	TV(Inf)	$\lambda\mathcal{P}\lambda u(\mathcal{P}\lambda v(e; \mathit{like}\ (e,u,v); r \sqsubseteq t(e);))$	(((e,T),T),(e,T))

Fig. 11. Lexical entries for main and auxiliary verbs.

For verbs denoting stative events, the representation is the same, except for the fact that now the current reference interval has to be included in the event interval, and the reference interval is not reset. Here is a lexical entry for *liked*:

$$\lambda\mathcal{P}\lambda u(\mathcal{P}\lambda v(e; \mathit{like}\ (e,u,v); r \sqsubseteq t(e); r < n)).$$

Figure 11 gives a list of lexical entries for stative and non-stative main verbs and for temporal auxiliary verbs.

Note that in defining disjoint merge for fragments involving the markers r and n for the reference and the speech interval, we have to make sure that these never get renamed. For n, we get this for free, for an inspection of the lexical entries makes clear that n is a fixed marker of every DRS, as it never gets introduced. For r matters are different: $r := t(e)$ is shorthand for $r; r \doteq t(e)$, so r does get introduced. But we do not want $r := t(e_1); D_1 \bullet r := t(e_2); D_2$ to reduce to $r := t(e_1); D; r' := t(e_2); [r'/r]D_2$. To ensure that this does not happen, it is enough to exclude r from the set of reference markers; this guarantees that $r := t(e_1); D_1; r := t(e_2); D_2$ is a proper DRS if $D_1; D_2$ is one, because $r \notin \mathit{intro}(r := t(e_2); D_2)$.

Let us go through the procedure of building the representation for (83), assuming the antecedent and anaphoric indices to be as given in the example. The representation of *entered the White Hart* becomes (85).

(85) $$\lambda\mathcal{P}\lambda u(\mathcal{P}\lambda v(e; \mathit{enter}\ (e,u,v); r < t(e); r := t(e); r < n)) \\ (\lambda P(u_2 \doteq \mathit{WH} \bullet P(u_2))).$$

After β reduction:

(86) $$\lambda u(u_2 \doteq \mathit{WH} \bullet (e; \mathit{enter}\ (e,u,u_2); r < t(e); r := t(e); r < n)).$$

Combining with the translation of *a man* and reducing the result gives (87).

(87) $u_1 \bullet \mathit{man}\ u_1 \bullet (u_2 \doteq \mathit{WH} \bullet (e; \mathit{enter}\ (e, u_1, u_2); r < t(e); r := t(e); r < n)).$

Merge reduction with the identical renaming gives:

(88) $u_1; \mathit{man}\ u_1; u_2 \doteq \mathit{WH}; e; \mathit{enter}\ (e, u_1, u_2); r < t(e); r := t(e); r < n.$

Similarly, we get for *he smiled*, after β and merge reduction:

(89) $e; \mathit{smile}(e, u_1); r < t(e); r := t(e); r < n.$

The text consisting of the first two sentences gets the following translation after β reduction:

(90) $$u_1; \mathit{man}\ u_1; u_2 \doteq \mathit{WH}; e; \mathit{enter}\ (e, u_1, u_2); r < t(e); r := t(e); r < n \\ \bullet\ e; \mathit{smile}(e, u_1); r < t(e); r := t(e); r < n.$$

After merge reduction, this becomes:

(91) $$u_1; \mathit{man}\ u_1; u_2 \doteq \mathit{WH}; e; \mathit{enter}\ (e, u_1, u_2); r < t(e); r := t(e); r < n; \\ e_2; \mathit{smile}(e_2, u_1); r < t(e_2); r := t(e_2); r < n.$$

The translation of the third sentence from the discourse, after β and merge reduction:

(92) $u_3; u_3 \doteq u_2; \mathit{place}\ u_3; e; \mathit{like}(e, u_1, u_3); r \sqsubseteq t(e); r < n.$

The translation of the whole example, after β and merge reduction:

(93) $$u_1; \mathit{man}\ u_1; u_2 \doteq \mathit{WH}; e; \mathit{enter}\ (e, u_1, u_2); r < t(e); r := t(e); r < n; \\ e_2; \mathit{smile}(e_2, u_1); r < t(e_2); r := t(e_2); r < n; \\ u_3; u_3 \doteq u_2; \mathit{place}\ u_3; e_3; \mathit{like}(e_3, u_1, u_3); r \sqsubseteq t(e_3); r < n.$$

Evidently this treatment of temporal reference is to be seen as no more than a hint of the direction that a fully fledged account of tense and aspect for a language like English might take. One feature of our treatment that ought to be changed is the use of separate lexical entries for full forms of verbs, such as *smiled* and *smiles*. What one would like to have instead is specifications of the meaning and/or function of the different tenses, such that when these are applied to the entries for the infinitival forms of our mini-lexicon we get the entries of the corresponding full forms as results. For instance, one might consider assigning the Simple Past the following entry

expression	category	translates to	type
Simple Past	VP(Tensed)/VP(Perf)	$\lambda P \lambda v(P(v); r < n)$	((e,T),(e,T))

Indeed, applying this entry to the entries for *smile* and *like* produces the translations that our lexicon specifies for *smiled* and *liked*.

But here it behoves to repeat an earlier caveat. Tense forms do not always function in the same way. In particular, embedded occurrences of tenses often behave quite differently than when they occur in unembedded positions. (To cite just one example, involving the simple past, recall Baker's: "I thought you were going to say that you *had* only one trick to play." Here the past tense of *had* is compatible with the event in question being located in the future of the utterance time.) So, if we adopt the entry just proposed as entry for the 'Past Tense' in general, we will have to distinguish carefully between occurrences of the Past Tense in the semantic sense characterized by this entry on the one hand and, on the other hand, arbitrary occurrences of simple past tense morphology. But this is a distinction which requires a careful revision of the syntax-semantics interface used in our mini-fragment; and it is only one example among many which render such a revision necessary.

Another matter which seriously complicates the treatment of temporal reference is aspect. We already saw that the temporal relations between the states and events that are mentioned by sentences in a text depend in part on the aspectual properties of those sentences (i.e. in our terminology, on whether what they describe is a state or an event) and that the aspectual properties of those sentences depend in their turn on the aspectual properties of the verbs they contain. However, as noted explicitly first in (Verkuyl, 1972), the aspectual properties of a sentence depend not just on its verb but on several other factors as well. Prominent among those factors is the question whether the verb has been modified by some aspectual operator, such as the English perfect or progressive, or aspectual control verbs such as *begin*, *stop* or *go on*. It is natural to try and treat aspectual modifiers along the same lines as we have suggested for the tenses, viz by assigning them their own lexical entries, which then should combine systematically with the entry of any verb to which the operators can be applied (e.g. through functional application of the operator entry to the verb entry). But here we encounter a new difficulty, which is especially noticeable in relation to the progressive, and known in that context as the *imperfective paradox*. A simple-minded analysis of the progressive might treat it as transforming a given verb phrase VP into one which describes a process or state holding at precisely those times that fall within the duration of any state or event described by VP. With telic verbal predicates such as *cross the street*, however, this analysis breaks down, for a sentence involving the progressive of such a verb phrase can be true at times when an event described by the embedded VP did not actually happen. For instance, *The old lady was crossing the street* may be true with respect to times not included in the duration of any crossing-the-street event. For the lady may have changed her mind when she got halfway and turned around to the sidewalk from which she started, or she may have become a victim to the incalculable brutalities of motorized traffic.. Thus the semantic relation between progressives and their underlying VPs is in general an intensional rather than a purely extensional one, and a fully satisfactory analysis of this intensional relationship is still lacking.

Formulating an entry for the English perfect, which transforms a verb phrase VP into one which describes result states of events or states described by VP, may at first seem less problematic: the states described by the application of the perfect hold at precisely those times which follow a state or event of the type defined by the operand. But when one looks at the semantics of the perfect more closely, such simplicity proves illusory. It is part of the meanings of many perfects that the event of which the described state is understood to be the result did not just happen at some earlier time or other, but that it happened only recently, or that its influence is still tangible at the time of the result state; and these additional meaning components cannot be analyzed in purely extensional terms any more than the relationship between progressive and non-progressive uses of telic verb phrases.

For the perfect it is nevertheless possible to finesse the intensionality problem by assuming a relation $\rightsquigarrow$ between events and states which holds between e and e' when e' is the result state of e. We adopt the obvious assumption that $e \rightsquigarrow e'$ entails $t(e) < t(e')$. Using $\rightsquigarrow$, (94) might be represented as (95).

(94) Bill has smiled.

(95)
$$\begin{array}{|l|}\hline e_1\ e_2 \\ \hline u \doteq b \\ \text{smile}\ (e_1, u) \\ e_1 \rightsquigarrow e_2 \\ t(e_2) \sqsubseteq n \\ \hline \end{array}$$

This does not yet constrain the effect on the wider context. The effect is roughly this. First the current value of the reference interval is saved. Then r is reset to a value earlier than its old value. Next the verb is evaluated with respect to the shifted reference interval. Then the old value is restored, and finally the reference interval is located with respect to the speech interval (Muskens, 1995).

Using o as a store for the old value of r, we get the following DRS that also takes the external effects into account:

(96)
$$\begin{array}{|l|}\hline e_1\ e_2\ o \\ \hline u \doteq b \\ o \doteq r \\ \neg\neg \begin{array}{|l|}\hline \text{r} \\ \hline r < o \\ \text{smile}\ (e_1, u) \\ e_1 \rightsquigarrow e_2 \\ r < t(e_1) \\ \hline \end{array} \\ r := t(e_2) \\ r \sqsubseteq n \\ \hline \end{array}$$

For a compositional account, we have to assume that we can get access to the event parameter of a verb, so a typical entry for untensed verbs will now look like this:

expression	category	translates to	type
smile	VP(Inf)	$\lambda e \lambda v(\textit{smile}\ (e, v); r < t(e); r := t(e))$	(e,(e,T))

The entry of the perfective operator introduces two events: the verb phrase event and the consequent state (assume $\mathcal{R}$ ranges over type $(e, (e, T))$).

expression	category	translates to	type
PERF	VP(Perf)/ VP(Inf)	$\lambda \mathcal{R} \lambda v(e_1; e_2; o := r;$ $\neg\neg(r; r < o; \mathcal{R}(e_1)(v); e_1 \rightsquigarrow e_2);$ $r < t(e_2); r := t(e_2))$	((e,(e,T)), (e,T))

Temporal auxiliaries will now have the effect of putting further temporal constraints, as discussed above. For instance the present tense form *has* of the perfect auxiliary *have* could be given the following entry:

expression	category	translates to	type
has	VP(Tensed)/VP(Perf)	$\lambda P \lambda v(P(v); r \sqsubseteq n)$	((e,T),(e,T))

This section has presented a catalogue of problems rather than a list of fully satisfactory solutions. The emphasis on problems with the analysis of tense and aspect may have served to illustrate a dilemma that one faces in formal approaches to the semantics of natural language discourse such as DRT. The dilemma is this: the more closely one tries to stick to the ideal of strict compositionality when dealing with the manifold complexities of the syntax-semantics interface of natural languages, the trickier the analysis tends to become, especially if discourse effects are to be taken into account too.

There exists a good deal of work within DRT, current as well as past, which has been prepared to sacrifice certain aspects of this ideal in pursuit of a more flexible architecture that can be fitted more easily to the requirements that certain linguistic phenomena seem to impose. This does not mean that this work ignores the fundamental compositional imperative of explaining how grammars can be finitely encoded and languages can be used by beings whose knowledge of language takes this finitary form. In particular, a good part of the work within DRT on the problems of tense and aspect has opted for such a relaxation of strict compositionality. However, experience of the past ten years has shown that often, once the phenomena have been properly understood and have been given a systematic description using means that are not strictly compositional, it is then possible to also find a way of accounting for those phenomena that *is* strictly compositional, as well as attractive in other ways. Whether attractive strictly compositional solutions will become available in all cases is yet to be seen.

12. Extensions and variations

An important extension of the representation language concerns the singular/plural distinction. Singular and plural reference markers should be distinguished, and a constraint imposed that singular pronouns are linked to singular discourse referents, plural pronouns to plural reference markers. Accounting for plural anaphoric possibilities along these lines involves quite a lot of further work, however, as delicate issues concerning the formation of plurals by means of summation and abstraction, and the interpretation of dependent plurals have to be dealt with (Kamp and Reyle, 1993, Chapter 4).

Another fruitful application area for theories about the representation of discourse in context is the area of presupposition. Presuppositions can get cancelled or weakened by an evolving context; in other words, presupposition projection is a dynamic phenomenon. Approaches to presupposition in connection with discourse representation are of two kinds. The first kind exploits the representationalism inherent in the framework. See, e.g., (Van der Sandt, 1992), where the presupposition facts get accounted for in terms of manipulations of the representations. The second kind does not assume representationalism but exploits the dynamic aspect of the theory by providing a partial dynamic semantics fitting the presupposition facts. See, e.g., the account of the presuppositions of definite descriptions in (Van Eijck, 1993), which does not depend on properties of the representations, but only on the underlying 'error state' semantics. Further references in the Chapter on *Presupposition* in this Handbook.

A next extension concerns the representation of belief sentences. The Hob Nob sentence from Section 2 provides an example of a belief puzzle that seems amenable to solution within the present framework. A theory of representation of discourse in context holds a particular promise for the treatment of belief because the representation structures themselves could be viewed as a kind of mental representation language; thus a belief relation could typically be modeled as a relation between a subject and a representation structure (Asher, 1986).

The plausibility of using Discourse Representation Structures to model belief and other propositional attitudes is closely connected with the existence of cognitively plausible inference systems for DRSs. For work on proof theories for DRSs (see Sedogbo and Eytan, 1988; Saurer, 1993; Kamp and Reyle, 1991).

A different approach is reasoning about discourse structures with assertion logic and dynamic logic. Assume a language of quantified dynamic logic with discourse representation structures as program modalities $\langle \boldsymbol{D} \rangle$ and $[\boldsymbol{D}]$. Then $\langle \boldsymbol{D} \rangle \phi$ and $[\boldsymbol{D}]\phi$ get interpreted as follows:

- $\mathcal{M}, s \models \langle \boldsymbol{D} \rangle \phi$ iff there is an s' with ${}_s[\![D]\!]_{s'}^{\mathcal{M}}$ and $\mathcal{M}, s \models \phi$.
- $\mathcal{M}, s \models [\boldsymbol{D}]\phi$ iff for all s' with ${}_s[\![D]\!]_{s'}^{\mathcal{M}}$ it holds that $\mathcal{M}, s' \models \phi$.

An axiomatization of discourse representation theory along the same lines as the calculus for dynamic predicate logic (Groenendijk and Stokhof, 1991) given in (Van Eijck, 1994) is now readily available. Some example principles of this calculus are:

$$\langle \neg \boldsymbol{D} \rangle \phi \leftrightarrow ([\boldsymbol{D}]\bot \wedge \phi).$$

$$\langle \boldsymbol{D}_1 \Rightarrow \boldsymbol{D}_2 \rangle \phi \leftrightarrow ([\boldsymbol{D}_1]\langle \boldsymbol{D}_2 \rangle \top \wedge \phi).$$

$$\langle \boldsymbol{D}_1; \boldsymbol{D}_2 \rangle \phi \leftrightarrow \langle \boldsymbol{D}_1 \rangle \langle \boldsymbol{D}_2 \rangle \phi.$$

For marker introduction we have:

$$\langle \boldsymbol{u} \rangle \phi \leftrightarrow \exists u \phi,$$

or dually:

$$[\boldsymbol{u}]\phi \leftrightarrow \forall u \phi.$$

For atoms we have:

$$\langle \boldsymbol{P t}_1 \cdots \boldsymbol{t}_n \rangle \phi \leftrightarrow (P t_1 \cdots t_n \wedge \phi),$$

or dually:

$$[\boldsymbol{Pt_1 \cdots t_n}]\phi \leftrightarrow (Pt_1 \cdots t_n \rightarrow \phi).$$

The calculus nicely demonstrates the way in which discourse representation theory gives universal force to the markers introduced in the antecedent of an if–then clause.

(97) If a man greets a woman he smiles at her.

(98) $(x; Mx; y; Wy; Gxy) \Rightarrow Sxy.$

The truth conditions of (97), represented as (98), are given by the following calculation that uses the principles above.

$$\begin{aligned}
&\langle(\boldsymbol{x}; \boldsymbol{Mx}; \boldsymbol{y}; \boldsymbol{Wy}; \boldsymbol{Gxy}) \Rightarrow \boldsymbol{Sxy}\rangle\top\\
&\leftrightarrow [\boldsymbol{x}; \boldsymbol{Mx}; \boldsymbol{y}; \boldsymbol{Wy}; \boldsymbol{Gxy}]\langle\boldsymbol{Sxy}\rangle\top\\
&\leftrightarrow [\boldsymbol{x}][\boldsymbol{Mx}][\boldsymbol{y}][\boldsymbol{Wy}][\boldsymbol{Gxy}]\langle\boldsymbol{Sxy}\rangle\top\\
&\leftrightarrow \forall x([\boldsymbol{Mx}][\boldsymbol{y}][\boldsymbol{Wy}][\boldsymbol{Gxy}]\langle\boldsymbol{Sxy}\rangle\top)\\
&\leftrightarrow \cdots\\
&\leftrightarrow \forall x(Mx \rightarrow \forall y(Wy \rightarrow (Gxy \rightarrow Sxy))).
\end{aligned}$$

An important new direction is the theory of Underspecified Discourse Representation Structures which allows for representations that leave certain matters, such as scope relations between quantifiers and other operators, the distinction between distributive and collective readings of plural NPs, that between different readings of a given lexical item, etc. undecided. This work is of particular interest insofar as it has succeeded in developing proof theories that operate directly on the underspecified representations themselves (Reyle, 1993, 1995).

13. Further reading

Two key publications on discourse representation are Heim (1982) and Kamp (1981), which address themselves specifically to the problem of the interpretation of indefinite descriptions and their interaction with unbound and transsentential anaphora. Temporal anaphora, a kind of anaphora that is largely transsentential, is treated along the same lines in (Kamp and Rohrer, 1993). A systematic presentation of discourse representation theory including various later developments is given in (Kamp and Reyle, 1993). Asher (1993) extends DRT to a more comprehensive theory which among other things also takes discourse structure and rhetorical relations into account. The connections between the principles of DRT and those of generative syntax are explored in depth in (Chierchia, 1995). Questions of lexical semantics from a DR-theoretical perspective are explored in (Kamp and Rossdeutscher, 1994).

A precursor paper is Karttunen (1976). Examples of related approaches to semantics which have also advocated focusing on the discourse level are Seuren's discourse semantics (Seuren, 1986), Barwise's dynamic interpretation of anaphora (Barwise, 1987), and the game theoretical school of Hintikka c.s. (Hintikka and Kulas, 1985).

Further references on the connection with dynamic reasoning are given in the Chapter on *Dynamics* in this Handbook. Connections between discourse representation and type theory are sketched in (Ahn and Kolb, 1990). Connections between discourse representation and game theoretical semantics are given in (Van Benthem and Van Eijck, 1982).

References

Ahn, R. and Kolb, H.-P. (1990), *Discourse representation meets constructive mathematics*, Papers from the Second Symposium on Logic and Language, L. Kalman and L. Polos, eds, Akademiai Kiado, Budapest, 105–124.

Alshawi, H. (ed.) (1992), *The Core Language Engine*, MIT Press, Cambridge, MA, and London, England.

Asher, N. (1986), *Belief in discourse representation theory*, J. Philos. Logic **15**, 127–189.

Asher, N. (1993), *Reference to Abstract Objects in Discourse*, Kluwer, Dordrecht.

Barwise, J. (1987), *Noun phrases, generalized quantifiers and anaphora*, Generalized Quantifiers: Linguistic and Logical Approaches, P. Gärdenfors, ed., Reidel, Dordrecht, 1–30.

Blackburn, P., Gardent, C. and De Rijke, M. (1994), *Back and forth through time and events*, Proceedings 9th Amsterdam Colloquium, P. Dekker and M. Stokhof, eds, ILLC, Amsterdam, 161–174.

Bos, J., Mastenbroek, E., McGlashan, S., Millies, S. and Pinkal, M. (1994), *A compositional DRS-based formalism for NLP- applications*, Proceedings of the International Workshop on Computational Linguistics, University of Tilburg, 21–31.

Bouchez, O., Van Eijck, J. and Istace, O. (1993), *A strategy for dynamic interpretation: A fragment and an implementation*, Sixth Conference of the European Chapter of the Association for Computational Linguistics – Proceedings of the Conference, S. Krauwer, M. Moortgat and Louis des Tombe, eds, ACL, 61–70.

Chierchia, G. (1995), *The Dynamics of Meaning*, Univ. of Chicago Press, Chicago and London.

Davidson, D. (1967), *The logical form of action sentences*, The Logic of Decision and Action, N. Rescher, ed., The University Press, Pittsburgh, 81–95.

Frege, G. (1892), *Ueber Sinn und Bedeutung*, Translated as *On sense and reference* in Geach and Black (eds), *Translations from the Philosophical Writings of Gottlob Frege*, Blackwell, Oxford (1952).

Gamut, L.T.F. (1991), *Language, Logic and Meaning, Part* 2, Chicago Univ. Press, Chicago.

Geach, P.T. (1980), *Reference and Generality: An Examination of Some Medieval and Modern Theories*, Cornell Univ. Press, Ithaca, 1962 (Third rev. edition: 1980).

Groenendijk, J. and Stokhof, M. (1991), *Dynamic predicate logic*, Ling. and Philos. **14**, 39–100.

Halliday, M.A.K. and Hassan, R. (1976), *Cohesion in English*, Longman, London.

Heim, I. (1982), *The semantics of definite and indefinite noun phrases*, PhD Thesis, University of Massachusetts, Amherst.

Hintikka, J. and Kulas, J. (1985), *Anaphora and Definite Descriptions: Two Applications of Game-Theoretical Semantics*, Reidel, Dordrecht.

Kamp, H. (1981), *A theory of truth and semantic representation*, Formal Methods in the Study of Language, J. Groenendijk et al., eds, Mathematisch Centrum, Amsterdam.

Kamp, H. and Reyle, U. (1991), *A calculus for first order discourse representation structures*, Arbeitspapiere des Sonderforschungsbereichs 340, No. 16, IMS Stuttgart, Germany.

Kamp, H. and Reyle, U. (1993), *From Discourse to Logic*, Kluwer, Dordrecht.

Kamp, H. and Rohrer, C. (1993), *Tense in texts*, Meaning, Use and Interpretation of Language, Bäuerle, Schwarze, and von Stechow, eds, De Gruyter, Berlin, 250–269.

Kamp, H. and Rossdeutscher, A. (1994), *Remarks on lexical structure and DRS construction*, Theor. Ling. **20**(2/3).

Karttunen, L. (1976), *Discourse referents*, Syntax and Semantics vol. 7, J. McCawley, ed., Academic Press, New York, 363–385.

Klop, J.W. (1992), *Term rewriting systems*, Handbook of Logic in Computer Science, S. Abramski, D. Gabbay and T. Maibaum, eds, Oxford Univ. Press, Oxford, 1–116 .

Kripke, S.A. (1972), *Naming and Necessity, Semantics of Natural Language*, D. Davidson and G. Harman, eds, Reidel, Dordrecht, 253–355.

Kuschert, S. (1995), *Eine Erweiterung des λ-Kalküls um Diskursrepresentationsstrukturen*, Master's thesis, Universität des Saarlandes.

Mann, W. and Thompson, S. (1987), *Rhetorical structure theory: A theory of text organization*, ISI Reprint Series: ISI-RS-87-190.

Moens, M. and Steedman, M. (1988), *Temporal ontology and temporal reference*, Comput. Ling. **14**(2), 15–28.

Muskens, R. (1995), *Tense and the logic of change*, Lexical Knowledge in the Organisation of Language, U. Egli et al., eds, Benjamin, New York, 147–183.

Muskens, R. (1996), *Combining Montague semantics and discourse representation*, Ling. and Philos. **19**.

Partee, B. (1973), *Some structural analogies between tenses and pronouns in English*, J. Philos. **70**, 601–609.

Reichenbach, H. (1947), *Elements of Symbolic Logic*, Macmillan, London.

Reyle, U. (1993), *Dealing with ambiguities by underspecification: Construction, representation and deduction*, J. Semantics **10**, 123–179.

Reyle, U. (1995), *On reasoning with ambiguities*, Seventh Conference of the European Chapter of the Association for Computational Linguistics – Proceedings of the Conference, Dublin.

Russell, B. (1905), *On denoting*, Mind **14**, 479–493.

Saurer, W. (1993), *A natural deduction system of discourse representation theory*, J. Philos. Logic **22**(3), 249–302.

Sedogbo, C. and Eytan, M. (1988), *A tableau calculus for DRT*, Logique et Anal. **31**, 379–402.

Seuren, P. (1986), *Discourse Semantics*, Blackwell, Oxford.

Sidner, C.L. (1979), *Towards a computation theory of definite anaphora comprehension in English discourse*, PhD Thesis, MIT, Cambridge.

Smullyan, R. (1968), *First-Order Logic*, Springer, Berlin.

Stalnaker, R. (1974), *Pragmatic presuppositions*, Semantics and Philosophy, M.K. Munitz and P.K. Unger, eds, New York Univ. Press, New York, 197- -213.

Strawson, P.F. (1950), *On referring*, Mind **59**, 320–344.

Van Benthem, J. (1982), *The Logic of Time*, Reidel, Dordrecht.

Van Benthem, J. and Van Eijck, J. (1982), *The dynamics of interpretation*, J. Semantics **1**(1), 3–20.

Van der Sandt, R.A. (1992), *Presupposition projection as anaphora resolution*, J. Semantics **9**, 333–377. (Special Issue: Presupposition, Part 2.)

Van Eijck, J. (1993), *The dynamics of description*, J. Semantics **10**, 239–267.

Van Eijck, J. (1994), *Axiomatizing dynamic predicate logic with quantified dynamic logic*, Logic and Information Flow, J. van Eijck and A. Visser, eds, MIT Press, Cambridge, MA, 30–48.

Vendler, Z. (1967), *Linguistics and Philosophy*, Cornell Univ. Press, Ithaca, NY.

Verkuyl, H. (1972), *On the Compositional Nature of the Aspects*, Foundations of Language Supplementary Series vol. 15, Reidel, Dordrecht.

Vermeulen, C.F.M. (1993), *Sequence semantics for dynamic predicate logic*, J. Logic, Lang., Inform. **2**, 217–254.

Vermeulen, C.F.M. (1995), *Merging without mystery*, J. Philos. Logic **24**, 405–450.

Visser, A. (1994a), *Actions under presuppositions*, Logic and Information Flow, J. van Eijck and A. Visser, eds, MIT Press, Cambridge, MA, 196–233.

Visser, A. (1994b), *The Design of Dynamic Discourse Denotations*, Lecture Notes, Utrecht University, February, 1994.

Webber, B. (1979), *A Formal Approach to Discourse Anaphora*, Garland, New York.

Zeevat, H. (1989), *A compositional approach to discourse representation theory*, Ling. and Philos. **12**, 95–131.

CHAPTER 4

Situation Theory

Jerry Seligman

Institute of Philosophy, National Chung-Cheng University, Min-Hsiung, Chia-Yi, Taiwan
E-mail: jerry@phil.ccu.edu.tw

Lawrence S. Moss

Department of Mathematics, Indiana University, Bloomington, IN 47405, USA
E-mail: lsm@cs.indiana.edu

Contents

HANDBOOK OF LOGIC AND LANGUAGE
Edited by J. van Benthem and A. ter Meulen

1. Introduction

With the book *Situations and Attitudes*, Barwise and Perry (1983) initiated a program of research that has occupied a diverse group of researchers for many of the subsequent years. The original motivation was to provide a richer, more honest semantic theory of natural languages, one that called a spade a spade, a situation a situation, and (eventually) a proposition a proposition. The emphasis was on defending a naïve ontology containing all the entities to which linguistic expressions appear to refer.

A natural division of labor developed. Linguists were encouraged to provide semantic analyses that used whatever entities they needed, without worrying too much about the technical matter of how such entities should be modeled. Logicians were driven to investigate foundational questions about the emerging ontology, with the hope of providing a unified mathematical framework in which the linguists' work could be interpreted. The linguistic project became known as *Situation Semantics* and the logical project was called *Situation Theory*. Situation Theory was intended to stand to Situation Semantics as Type Theory stands to Montague Grammar.

This chapter is written as a self-contained introduction to the main themes and technical contributions of Situation Theory. We have not attempted to give a survey of Situation Semantics, although key references are included in the bibliography. This is a serious omission because many of the ideas in Situation Theory originated from linguistic considerations. One excuse is that neither of us is a linguist; a second is that the chapter is too long as it stands.

A more defensible excuse is that *Situations and Attitudes* was not only concerned with semantics. The program of research it initiated has spilled into many neighboring disciplines, such as philosophy, computer science, psychology, and even sociology. The influence of these other fields has been significant – so much so that it would be difficult to account for the purely linguistic factors.

In writing this chapter, we aimed both to present the existing literature on the subject and to provide a coherent statement of Situation Theory. Unfortunately, these goals conflict. The literature contains many technical contributions, some quite sophisticated; but they have not yet been put together. We judged that a mere survey of the existing results would be of limited interest, and decided to re-present the material in as coherent a way as possible.

In any foundational study one has to decide whether to build models or theories. The strategies are distinct if not divergent, and the ideal of a canonical theory is rarely achieved. Most of the research on Situation Theory has been directed towards constructing models. There are many models; they differ both on subject matter (which parts of the theory they model) and on substance (which axioms they satisfy), and no clear consensus has emerged. The work on developing a formal theory has been even less unified: approaches using classical logic, partial logic and even 'illative logic' have been tried. The subject matter of the theories and the models do not coincide completely, and when they do overlap there are many differences on matters of detail. In an effort to make this chapter compatible with all this, we have adopted a fairly abstract, loose approach. Axioms and models are discussed side by side.

In Section 2 we introduce the class of 'simple information structures'. Structures in this class are intended to provide a naïve model of the structure of information, as captured by the relational structures of first-order model theory. The class is axiomatized, and each of the axioms is discussed with a view to generalization. Many of the novelties of Situation Theory can be seen as generalizations of this sort.

Section 3 introduces techniques for constructing models of the generalizations considered in Section 2. All the techniques may be found in the literature but we have re-organized them into a framework called the Theory of Structural Relations. This is a new approach, with which those working on Situation Theory will be unfamiliar.

In Sections 2 and 3 the reader will not meet a single situation. Section 4 remedies the disappointment by introducing a host of ontological categories, including facts, restricted abstracts, situations, propositions, types, and constraints. The theory of structural relations is used throughout, but the focus in this section is on the motivation for diverging opinions in Situation Theory, critical evaluation, and pointers to open problems.

Finally, in Section 5 we give a brief guide to the literature on Situation Theory and related areas of research, followed by a selective bibliography.

2. The structure of information

Situation Theory has its fair share of neologisms, the most inspired of which is surely the term *infon*, coined by Keith Devlin. An infon is an item of information. The term is intended to be as neutral as possible about the form in which the information is represented. The common item of information separately conveyed by the statements made in the following little conversation is an example of an infon.

Raymond: (to Paul, displaying an omelette) I have cooked this for you.
Paul: (proudly, to Delia) Raymond cooked this omelette for me.
Delia: (to Albert) The chef cooked the omelette for Paul.

Of course, much more information can be gleaned about the situation from each of these statements, but that it is one in which the two people, Raymond and Paul, and an omelette stand in a certain relationship, that of Raymond having cooked the omelette for Paul, is information expressed by all three. The very same information may also be represented by other means, in a film, or a cartoon-strip, for example, or in the minds of Raymond, Paul, Delia and even Albert.[1]

The first goal of this chapter is to show how information of this simple form is modeled. To specify the structure of the infon in the example, we must say which individuals are involved and how they are related. We shall abbreviate 'Raymond' and 'Paul' to 'R' and 'P', and introduce the name 'O' to refer to the omelette. We use 'cooked' to name the relation that holds between a cook, a diner and a dish just in case the the cook has cooked the dish for the diner. Let I be information that R, P, and O stand in the relation cooked. The individuals R, P, and O are called *arguments* of the infon I, and the relation cooked, is called the *relation* of I.

[1] The reader may think to identify this item of information with the Russellian proposition expressed by 'R cooked O for P', with the understanding that 'R', 'O', and 'P' are proper names for Raymond, the omelette, and Paul, respectively. One branch of the theory follows this path (see Section 4) but the identification would be premature.

By specifying the relation and arguments of I we have done a lot toward characterizing everything of informational significance, but not quite all. Care must be taken to distinguish the information that Raymond cooked the omelette for Paul from the information that Paul cooked the omelette for Raymond. For this purpose, we require the concept of a *role*. In any infon involving the relation cooked there are three roles to be filled: that of the cook, the diner and the dish. In the present case, the cook is R, the diner is P, and the dish is O; if instead Paul cooked the omelette for Raymond, then the roles of cook and diner would be reversed. We say that an individual is an *argument* of an infon if it fills one of the infon's roles. The omelette O is an argument of the infon I by virtue of filling the dish role of I's relation cooked.

We have established that there are two basic ingredients determining the structure of I: that of cooked being the relation of I, and that of the three individuals R, P, and O filling the three roles of I, which we name cook, diner, and dish, respectively. We introduce the predicates 'Rel' and 'Arg' to denote these structural relations, writing 'Rel(cooked, I)' to mean that cooked is the relation of I, and 'Arg(O, dish, I)' to mean that O, the omelette, fills the dish role of our infon I.

More generally, we shall take simple infons like I to be 'structured' by the two relations, Rel and Arg. The first of these, Rel, determines the relation of the infon and the other, Arg, determines which arguments fill which roles. We define a 'simple infon' to be anything that has a relation or an argument. Similarly, a 'relation' is anything that is a relation of some infon, and a 'role' is anything that is filled by an argument in some infon. In other words,

σ is a *(simple) infon*	if $\exists r\ \mathsf{Rel}(r, \sigma)$ or $\exists a, i\ \mathsf{Arg}(a, i, \sigma)$,
r is a *relation*	if $\exists \sigma\ \mathsf{Rel}(r, \sigma)$, and
r is a *role*	if $\exists a, \sigma\ \mathsf{Arg}(a, i, \sigma)$.

These definitions form the basis of an abstract account of the structure of information that will be the focus of this section. The approach is 'abstract' because we consider any structure in which the predicates 'Rel' and 'Arg' are defined to be a candidate model for the theory of information, with the derived predicates 'relation', 'role' and 'infon' interpreted according to the above definitions. Our strategy is to isolate axioms describing those properties of infons that have been discussed in the literature on Situation Theory, generalizing from the properties of certain 'standard' models, to be introduced shortly.

First, a short digression.

2.1. Relational structures

It is a commonplace that in foundational theories one must be very careful to distinguish between meta-language and object-language. Situation Theory is no exception, and special difficulties arises with the word 'relation'. Before going further it will prove useful to make some preliminary definitions concerning relational structures. The following is slightly non-standard but enables us to avoid certain ambiguities with our use of 'relation' and similar words.

A (*relational*) *signature* is a function $\nu : S \to \mathbb{N}$ from a finite set S to the set $\mathbb{N}$ of positive integers. The elements of S are called *primitive relations* and the number $\nu(R)$ associated with a primitive relation R is a called its *arity*. A *relational structure* $\mathfrak{A}$ of signature ν consists of a class $|\mathfrak{A}|$, called the *universe* of $\mathfrak{A}$, and for each primitive relation R, a class $[\![R]\!]^{\mathfrak{A}}$ of finite sequences of elements of $|\mathfrak{A}|$, each of length $\nu(R)$, called the *extension* of R in $\mathfrak{A}$.[2] For example, we may model the situation of Raymond having cooked an omelette for Paul as a relational structure $\mathfrak{N}_1$ of signature $\nu : \{\mathsf{cooked}\} \to \mathbb{N}$ defined by $\nu(\mathsf{cooked}) = 3$, with universe $|\mathfrak{N}_1| = \{\mathsf{R}, \mathsf{P}, \mathsf{O}\}$ and $[\![\mathsf{cooked}]\!]^{\mathfrak{N}_1}$ containing, at least, the sequence ROP.

In discussing relational structures, we say that $\mathfrak{A}$ *is of type* $[A, R_1^{\nu_1}, \ldots, R_n^{\nu_n}]$ if $\mathfrak{A}$ has universe A and primitive relations $R_1, \ldots, R_n$, with arities $\nu_1, \ldots, \nu_n$ respectively. For example, $\mathfrak{N}_1$ is of type $[\{\mathsf{R}, \mathsf{P}, \mathsf{O}\}, \mathsf{cooked}^3]$. The notation is stretched to provide a way of saying that that one relational structure extends another. If $\mathfrak{A}$ is of type $[A, R_1^{\nu_1}, \ldots, R_n^{\nu_n}]$ and $n < m$ then we say that $\mathfrak{B}$ *is of type* $[\mathfrak{A}, R_{n+1}^{\nu_{n+1}}, \ldots, R_m^{\nu_m}]$ if it is of type $[A, R_1^{\nu_1}, \ldots, R_n^{\nu_n}, \ldots, R_m^{\nu_m}]$ and $[\![R_i]\!]^{\mathfrak{B}} = [\![R_i]\!]^{\mathfrak{A}}$ for $1 \leqslant i \leqslant n$.

We use the names of the primitive relations of a structure to form sentences about the structure as if they were predicates in a formal language. Given elements $a_1, \ldots, a_{\nu_i}$ of $|\mathfrak{A}|$, the sentence '$R_i(a_1, \ldots, a_{\nu_i})$' when used to describe the structure $\mathfrak{A}$, is true if and only if the finite sequence $a_1, \ldots, a_{\nu_i}$ lies in $[\![R_i]\!]^{\mathfrak{A}}$. For example, the sentence '$\mathsf{cooked}(\mathsf{R}, \mathsf{P}, \mathsf{O})$' provides yet another way of saying that Raymond cooked the omelette for Paul.

We also need to talk about specific elements of the universe of a relational structure. Given a set C, a relational structure *with constants* C is a relational structure $\mathfrak{A}$ together with an element $[\![c]\!]^{\mathfrak{A}}$ of $|\mathfrak{A}|$ for each $c \in C$.

Relational structures $\mathfrak{A}$ and $\mathfrak{B}$, both of signature $\nu : S \to \mathbb{N}$ and with constants C, are *isomorphic* if there is a bijective function $f : |\mathfrak{A}| \to |\mathfrak{B}|$ such that for each $R \in S$ and $a_1, \ldots, a_{\nu(R)} \in |\mathfrak{A}|$,

$$R(a_1, \ldots, a_{\nu(R)}) \text{ in } \mathfrak{A} \quad \text{iff} \quad R(f(a_1), \ldots, f(a_{\nu(R)})) \text{ in } \mathfrak{B}$$

and for each $c \in C$, $[\![c]\!]^{\mathfrak{B}} = f([\![c]\!]^{\mathfrak{A}})$.

2.2. *Simple information structures*

We are interested in relational structures in two quite different ways. First, we may use them to build models of a given situation. The structure $\mathfrak{N}_1$, defined in the previous section, models the situation discussed by Raymond and his friends in our initial example. It is the sort of model that underlies standard 'model-theoretic' semantics. In the manner of Tarski, we may provide a definition of truth in $\mathfrak{N}_1$ for a language having the predicate

[2] We allow relational structures whose universe is a proper class because models of Situation Theory are often very large. The exact meaning of the word 'set' will be discussed below, but for the moment the reader may assume that we are working with any theory of sets that accounts for their mundane properties, supports a distinction between 'set' and 'class', and allows collections of ordinary objects to be called 'sets'.

'cooked' and perhaps the names 'R', 'O', and 'P'. By virtue of this semantic function, structures like $\mathfrak{N}_1$ may also be thought to provide a model of the *information* conveyed in the conversation, but in this capacity they are rather limited. In constructing $\mathfrak{N}_1$ we are forced to determine the complete extension of cooked and so include more information than was conveyed. Consider the sequence ROR. If this lies in $[\![\mathsf{cooked}]\!]^{\mathfrak{N}_1}$ then the situation modeled is one in which Raymond also cooked the omelette for himself, and O is a two-person omelette. If, on the other hand, ROR is in not in $[\![\mathsf{cooked}]\!]^{\mathfrak{N}_1}$ then Paul has the feast to himself. The necessary overdetermination of information is one of the deficiencies that Situation Theory is intended to overcome.

The second, more important use of relational structures is as models of fragments of Situation Theory itself. Our strategy is to define successive classes of relational structures, that may be regarded as approximations to a suitable model for the theory as a whole. An example of the second use is given by our first substantial definition.

DEFINITION 2.1. A relational structure $\mathfrak{A}$ of type $[A, \mathsf{Rel}^2, \mathsf{Arg}^3]$ is a (*simple*) *information structure* if it satisfies the following conditions:

A1 *If* $\mathsf{Rel}(r, \sigma)$ *and* $\mathsf{Rel}(r', \sigma)$ *then* $r = r'$.
A2 *If* $\mathsf{Arg}(a, i, \sigma)$ *and* $\mathsf{Arg}(b, i, \sigma)$ *then* $a = b$.
A3 *No relation is a role.*
A4 *No role is an infon.*
A5 *No infon is a relation.*

Axioms A1 to A5 are not particularly stringent; they merely impose some discipline on the domain. Together, they say nothing more than that the relations, roles and infons form disjoint classes, and that infons may have at most one relation and at most one argument filling each role.

The previously mentioned ambiguity in the word 'relation' can be seen with the help of this definition.[3] Firstly, we use the word to talk about the relations of any relational structure. For example, the theoretical predicates 'Rel' and 'Arg' refer to the primitive *relations* of simple information structures. Relations of this kind will be dubbed '*external*'. Any other relation between elements of a relational structure whose extension is determined by our theoretical language is also called 'external'. Examples include relations defined from primitive relations, such as the property of being a simple infon.[4]

The second use of 'relation' is governed by the extension of Rel in a specific information structure. An element r of the universe of a simple information structure $\mathfrak{A}$ is an *internal* relation of $\mathfrak{A}$ if $\mathsf{Rel}(r, \sigma)$ for some infon σ. The ambiguity, once understood, should not cause the reader any difficulty. Where necessary the sense will be made clear using the adjectives 'internal' and 'external'.

Aside from illustrating ambiguities, simple information structures provide our first, crude approximation to the models of a fragment of Situation Theory. Their principal use

[3] Other words we use, such as 'role' and 'argument', have a similar ambiguity.

[4] Typically, an n-ary external relation is identified with its *graph*, the set, or class, of sequences $x_1, \ldots, x_n$ of objects that stand in the relation. We make no such assumption here. A meta-theory in which intensional distinctions are made between relations – as they are in our object-theory – is quite compatible with our approach.

is to show how the two ways in which we use relational structures are related. Suppose, for example, we use the structure $\mathfrak{N}_1$ to model the situation discussed by Raymond and his friends. There is a sense in which $\mathfrak{N}_1$ gives us all we need to know about the common informational content of the three culinary pronouncements. The relation of the infon, cooked, is included as a primitive relation of $\mathfrak{N}_1$; the three roles of this relation, cook, diner, and dish, are modeled by the first, second, and third positions in the sequences in the extension of cooked; and the arguments – Raymond, Paul and the omelette – are also directly included in the universe of $\mathfrak{N}_1$. The thought that we have thereby obtained a simple information structure is made more precise as follows.

CONSTRUCTION 2.1. Given a relational structure $\mathfrak{M}$ of type $[M, R_1^{\nu_1}, \ldots, R_n^{\nu_n}]$, possibly with constants, we construct an information structure $\mathrm{SInf}(\mathfrak{M})$. First, let

$$A_1 = \{1\} \times \{R_1, \ldots, R_n\},$$
$$A_2 = \{2\} \times \bigcup_{1 \leqslant i \leqslant n} \{1, \ldots, \nu_i\},$$
$$A_3 = \{\langle 3, R_i, \alpha\rangle \mid 1 \leqslant i \leqslant n \text{ and } \alpha\colon \{1, \ldots, \nu_i\} \to M\}.$$

The basic idea is to model simple infons as pairs of the form $\langle R_i, \alpha\rangle$ in which α is a function from $\{1, \ldots, \nu_i\}$ to the universe of $\mathfrak{M}$. But we must be careful to keep relations, roles and infons distinct, and so we also include a numerical prefix indicating the sort of object modeled: 1 for relations, 2 for roles, and 3 for simple infons. The information structure $\mathrm{SInf}^-(\mathfrak{M})$ has universe $M \cup A_1 \cup A_2 \cup A_3$ and the extensions of Rel and Arg given by

$$\begin{aligned} &\mathsf{Rel}(r, \sigma) && \text{iff} \quad \exists R, \alpha \text{ with } r = \langle 1, R\rangle \text{ and } \sigma = \langle 3, R, \alpha\rangle, \\ &\mathsf{Arg}(a, i, \sigma) && \text{iff} \quad \exists j, R, \alpha \text{ with } i = \langle 2, j\rangle,\ \sigma = \langle 3, R, \alpha\rangle, \text{and } \alpha(j) = a. \end{aligned}$$

The constants of $\mathrm{SInf}^-(\mathfrak{M})$ include all the constants of $\mathfrak{M}$. In addition, we take each primitive relation R of $\mathfrak{M}$ to be a constant denoting $\langle 1, R\rangle$. It is a simple matter to check that the resulting structure $\mathfrak{A}$ satisfies axioms A1 to A5.

A minor complication arises because of the need to ensure that isomorphic relational structures give rise to isomorphic information structures – we don't want accidental features of the representation to encode more information than there is in the original structure. We would get more if, for example, M happened to contain an element $m = \langle 1, R\rangle$ in which R is one of the primitive relations of $\mathfrak{M}$. In the structure $\mathrm{SInf}^-(\mathfrak{M})$, this pair would serve both as the object m of $\mathfrak{M}$ and as the internal relation denoted by the constant R.

We overcome this difficulty by first making a copy of $\mathfrak{M}$. Let $\mathfrak{M}_0$ be the isomorphic copy of $\mathfrak{M}$ in which each element m of M is replaced by the pair $\langle 0, m\rangle$, and let $\mathrm{SInf}(\mathfrak{M}) = \mathrm{SInf}^-(\mathfrak{M}_0)$. Unlike $\mathrm{SInf}^-(\mathfrak{M})$, the structure $\mathrm{SInf}(\mathfrak{M})$ keeps the old elements distinct from the newly constructed elements, and so our construction has the desired property of preserving isomorphism: if $\mathfrak{M}_1$ and $\mathfrak{M}_2$ are isomorphic, so are $\mathrm{SInf}(\mathfrak{M}_1)$ and $\mathrm{SInf}(\mathfrak{M}_2)$.[5]

For example, consider once again the model $\mathfrak{N}_1$. The information structure $\mathrm{SInf}(\mathfrak{N}_1)$ has individuals $\langle 0, \mathsf{R}\rangle$, $\langle 0, \mathsf{P}\rangle$, and $\langle 0, \mathsf{O}\rangle$, copied from $\mathfrak{N}_1$, a single relation $\langle 1, \mathsf{cooked}\rangle$, three roles $\langle 2, 1\rangle$, $\langle 2, 2\rangle$, and $\langle 2, 3\rangle$, and infons of the form $\langle 3, \langle \mathsf{cooked}, \alpha\rangle\rangle$, where α is a function from $\{1, 2, 3\}$ into $\{\langle 0, \mathsf{R}\rangle, \langle 0, \mathsf{P}\rangle, \langle 0, \mathsf{O}\rangle\}$. The structure also has a constant cooked that denotes the internal relation $\langle 1, \mathsf{cooked}\rangle$. The information that Raymond cooked the omelette O for Paul is modeled by the element $\langle 3, \langle \mathsf{cooked}, \alpha\rangle\rangle$ in which α is the function with domain $\{1, 2, 3\}$, and such that $\alpha(1) = \langle 0, \mathsf{R}\rangle$, $\alpha(2) = \langle 0, \mathsf{P}\rangle$, and $\alpha(3) = \langle 0, \mathsf{O}\rangle$.

Information structures constructed in this way serve as the starting point in our investigation into the structure of information. But we must proceed with care. Various aspects of the construction are artifacts of the set-theoretic tools used. For example, the choice of the numbers 0 to 3 as indicators of the sort of object modeled is quite arbitrary. In making theoretical claims about the properties of these structures we must consider only on the essential aspects of the construction. This is easily achieved by widening our focus to include all structures isomorphic to one obtained by Construction 2.1.

DEFINITION 2.2. A simple information structure is *standard* if it is isomorphic to $\mathrm{SInf}(\mathfrak{M})$ for some relational structure $\mathfrak{M}$.

In the remainder of Section 2 we shall study standard information structures in some detail. We shall see that some properties of the standard structures capture our basic intuitions about the structure of information, while others reflect only the limitations of the construction. By the end of the section we shall have a list of axioms characterizing the class of standard structures, and a number of alternative axioms designed to overcome their limitations.[6]

2.3. *Roles*

Suppose $\mathfrak{N}_2$ is a relational structure of type $[N_2, \mathsf{stir\text{-}fried}^2, \mathsf{braised}^2]$ and that R and P are elements of M. Let α_1 and α_2 be functions with domain $\{1, 2\}$ and such that $\alpha_1(1) = \mathsf{R}$ and $\alpha_2(1) = \mathsf{P}$. The information structure $\mathrm{SInf}(\mathfrak{N}_2)$ contains the simple infons $\sigma_1 = \langle 3, \mathsf{stir\text{-}fried}^2, \alpha_1\rangle$ and $\sigma_2 = \langle 3, \mathsf{braised}^2, \alpha_2\rangle$. Thus, in $\mathrm{SInf}(\mathfrak{N}_2)$, we have that

$$\mathsf{Arg}(\langle 0, \mathsf{R}\rangle, \langle 2, 1\rangle, \sigma_1) \quad \text{and} \quad \mathsf{Arg}(\langle 0, \mathsf{P}\rangle, \langle 2, 1\rangle, \sigma_2).$$

The elements $\langle 0, \mathsf{R}\rangle$ and $\langle 0, \mathsf{P}\rangle$ have the common property of filling the role $\langle 2, 1\rangle$. What, if anything, does this signify?

---

[5] The construction depends only on the type of the relational structure. If $\mathfrak{M}_1$ and $\mathfrak{M}_2$ are isomorphic relational structures of the same type then $\mathrm{SInf}(\mathfrak{M}_1) = \mathrm{SInf}(\mathfrak{M}_2)$.

[6] The axioms for standard information structures are labeled **A1**, **A2**, and so on. The alternatives to Axiom **A*n*** are labeled **A*n*.1**, **A*n*.2**, and so on. Some of the alternatives are weaker than the corresponding standard axioms, generalizing some aspect of standard structures. Others are stronger, asserting the existence of objects not present in standard structures.

In information structures obtained using Construction 2.1, roles are pairs of the form $\langle 2, n\rangle$, where n is a positive integer. These roles are simply indices recording the relative positions of arguments in the original relational structure, and it is difficult to see how the identity of roles – mere indices – in different infons can be given much import. Yet we must not be mislead by the peculiarities of the coding used in the construction. The statement that Raymond stir-fried the frogs' legs and Paul braised the monkfish implies that both Raymond and Paul are cooks; at least, it tells us that they played the role of cook in the situation described. Perhaps we can regard $\langle 2, 1\rangle$ as modeling this role in $\mathrm{SInf}(\mathfrak{M}_2)$.

Whatever the merits of this suggestion, the behaviour of roles in standard information structures is severely constrained. The roles of $\mathsf{stir\text{-}fried}$ and $\mathsf{braised}$ in $\mathfrak{M}_2$ are the same two, $\langle 2, 1\rangle$ and $\langle 2, 2\rangle$, not for culinary reasons but simply because both are binary relations and so we use the same numbers, 1 and 2, to index their arguments. This rather artificial limitation of standard structures is captured by the following rather artificial axiom.

A6 *If σ has a role that is not a role of τ, then every role of τ is a role of σ.*

In effect, Axiom A6 says that the sets of roles of infons are linearly ordered by inclusion. In moving away from standard structures, this axiom is sure to be dropped. Theoretical considerations concerning roles have been studied in connection with the linguistic concept of 'thematic role' by Engdahl (1990). Another restriction obeyed by standard structures is that

A7 *Each infon has only finitely many roles.*

Relations with infinite arities are conceivable, and perhaps of some theoretical use, but it is important to focus on those items of information that are finitely expressible. Indeed, it has been proposed (Devlin, 1991b) that the finiteness of infons is an essential characteristic. A much less reasonable restriction is that

A8 *There are only finitely many relations.*

This is satisfied by all standard information structures but it will be dropped when we generalize.

2.4. Identity

In all standard information structures, the following criterion of identity is satisfied.

A9 *Suppose σ and τ are infons and for all r, a, and i,*
1. $\mathsf{Rel}(r, \sigma)$ *iff* $\mathsf{Rel}(r, \tau)$, *and*
2. $\mathsf{Arg}(a, i, \sigma)$ *iff* $\mathsf{Arg}(a, i, \tau)$.

Then $\sigma = \tau$.

In many presentations of Situation Theory there is a further condition, relating to the 'polarity' of an infon. The infons expressed by 'Amelia is loquacious' and 'Amelia is not loquacious' are taken to be on an equal footing, instead of taking the negative form to be a constructed from the positive by an operation of negation, as is done in propositional logic. The infons have the same relation (being loquacious) and the same argument (Amelia) filling the same role. They are distinguished only by their *polarity*, which can be either *positive* or *negative*.

We can incorporate this proposal into the present account in various ways. For example, we could introduce a new unary relation, Pos, that holds of the positive infons only, and axioms to give the modified identity conditions and to ensure that for every positive infon there is a corresponding negative infon. For the moment, we shall keep our basic definitions uncluttered by matters of polarity; but we return to the topic when discussing complex infons in Section 3.6.

Considerations of polarity aside, Axiom A9 has found widespread support, partly because it allows the use of a convenient *functional notation*. For any finite infon σ there is a relation r and a finite sequence $\langle i_1, a_1\rangle, \ldots, \langle i_n, a_n\rangle$ of role-argument pairs, such that $\mathsf{Rel}(r, \sigma)$ and $\mathsf{Arg}(a_j, i_j, \sigma)$ for $1 \leqslant j \leqslant n$, and no other pair $\langle i, a\rangle$ is such that $\mathsf{Arg}(a, i, \sigma)$. Given Axiom A9, the identity of σ is completely determined by this information, and so we may write σ unambiguously as

$$\langle\!\langle r; i_1 : a_1, \ldots, i_n : a_n\rangle\!\rangle.$$

The set of role-argument pairs in a basic infon is called an *assignment*. Although confined by the linearity of text, the elements of the assignment are intended to be unordered, so that, for example, $\langle\!\langle r; i : a, j : b\rangle\!\rangle$ and $\langle\!\langle r; j : b, i : a\rangle\!\rangle$ denote the same infon – this follows from Axiom A9, of course.[7]

The functional notation and its variants are widely used. Indeed, it is tempting to base the subsequent development of Situation Theory on an infon-building *function* that maps each pair consisting of a relation r and an assignment $\langle\langle i_1, a_1\rangle, \ldots, \langle i_n, a_n\rangle\rangle$ to the infon $\langle\!\langle r; i_1 : a_1, \ldots, i_n : a_n\rangle\!\rangle$. A problem is that the infon-building function is partial. Even in standard information structures, not every relation-assignment pair determines an infon; an infon will result only if the length of assignment is the same as the arity of the relation.

Faced with partiality there are three natural responses. The first (Plotkin, 1990), is to have an infon-building function that is total but does not always deliver an infon. The advantage is an uncomplicated model; the disadvantage is the existence of many 'pseudo-objects' in the universe of the model that fail to model anything real. The second response (Plotkin, 1990; Barwise and Cooper, 1991) is to accept that the infon-building function is partial, and make do with a partial language (and logic) for describing situation-theoretic objects. The third response (Muskens, 1995; Cooper, 1991; and this chapter) is to base the theory on relations instead of functions. The advantage is that we retain the services of classical logic and our models remain uncomplicated. The disadvantage is that we must abandon the functional notation, at least for theoretical purposes.

In less formal discussions we shall still use terms of the form '$\langle\!\langle r; i : a, j : b\rangle\!\rangle$' with the presupposition that there is an infon to which the term refers. When the roles are clear from the context, or are numerical indices in the canonical order ($i = 1$, $j = 2$), we use the abbreviated form '$\langle\!\langle r; a, b\rangle\!\rangle$'.

---

[7] The use of angle brackets in the functional notation is suggestive of the set-theoretic model of infons used in Construction 2.1. It is important not to confuse the two.

The identity criteria discussed above are only intended to apply to infons of the simplest kind. Quite different criteria will be needed for complex infons, such as conjunctions and disjunctions. They will be discussed in Section 3.4.

2.5. *Arguments*

Standard information structures have the property that

A10 *No argument is an infon, relation or role.*

In other words, the information modeled is of a purely 'non-reflexive' kind: no information *about* infons, relations, or roles is included. This is a severe limitation that has motivated a number of important developments in Situation Theory.

A reason for rejecting Axiom A10 in favor of a more liberal framework is the need to express 'higher-order' information – information about infons. Ascriptions of propositional attitudes and conditionals are the obvious examples. For example, if σ is the information that Albert is replete, then the information that Delia knows that Albert is replete may be thought to involve some relation between Delia and σ. A first candidate for modeling this is an infon of the form $\langle\langle \mathsf{knows}; \mathsf{Delia}, \sigma\rangle\rangle$. Likewise, if τ is the information that Albert is snoring, then we might regard the conditional 'if Albert is snoring then he is replete' as expressing the information $\langle\langle \mathsf{if}; \sigma, \tau\rangle\rangle$.[8] We might also wish to model information about Situation Theory itself. For example, the information that r is the relation of σ may be modeled by an infon of the form $\langle\langle \mathsf{Rel}; r, \sigma\rangle\rangle$.

Recalling Construction 2.1, it is easy to see why Axiom A10 is satisfied. In $\mathrm{SInf}(\mathfrak{M})$ all arguments of infons are of the form $\langle 0, m\rangle$ but infons, relations and roles are of the form $\langle i, a\rangle$ for $i \neq 0$. As we have seen, these sortal restrictions are needed to ensure that the construction preserves isomorphism. They are enforced in the final move from $\mathrm{SInf}^-(\mathfrak{M})$ to $\mathrm{SInf}(\mathfrak{M})$ in which a copy is made of $|\mathfrak{M}|$. We can obtain models constraining higher-order infons by dropping this step. For example, suppose $\mathfrak{M}$ is of type $[M, R_1^1, R_2^2]$ and M happens to contain an element $\sigma = \langle 3, R_2, \alpha\rangle$, in which α is a function from $\{1, 2\}$ to M. Then σ is classified as an infon because of its set-theoretic form. But it is also an element of M and so may occur as a argument to another infon. If β is the function with domain $\{1\}$ and $\beta(1) = \sigma$ then $\tau = \langle 3, R_1, \beta\rangle$ is such a 'higher-order' infon. In the functional notation, $\tau = \langle\langle R_1; \sigma\rangle\rangle$. The nearest counterpart in $\mathrm{SInf}(\mathfrak{M})$ is $\langle\langle R_1; \langle 0, \sigma\rangle\rangle\rangle$, which is not the same thing at all.

The method may be made more systematic by iterating the construction of $\mathrm{SInf}^-(\mathfrak{M})$.

CONSTRUCTION 2.2. Given a relational structure $\mathfrak{M}$, we define an infinite sequence $\mathfrak{A}_0, \mathfrak{A}_1, \mathfrak{A}_2, \ldots$ of information structures as follows. Let $\mathfrak{A}_0$ be $\mathfrak{M}$, and for each integer n, let $\mathfrak{A}_{n+1}$ be $\mathrm{SInf}^-(\mathfrak{A}_n)$. Let $\mathfrak{A}$ be the 'iterated' structure defined by taking unions:

$$|\mathfrak{A}| = \bigcup_{n\in\mathbb{N}} |\mathfrak{A}_n|, \qquad [\![\mathsf{Rel}]\!]^{\mathfrak{A}} = \bigcup_{n\in\mathbb{N}} [\![\mathsf{Rel}]\!]^{\mathfrak{A}_n}, \qquad [\![\mathsf{Arg}]\!]^{\mathfrak{A}} = \bigcup_{n\in\mathbb{N}} [\![\mathsf{Arg}]\!]^{\mathfrak{A}_n}.$$

[8] Conditionals are reconsidered in Section 4.9.

It is simple to check that $\mathfrak{A}$ is an information structure, and that it is a fixed point: $\text{SInf}^-(\mathfrak{A}) = \mathfrak{A}$. Moreover, like Construction 2.1, this construction preserves isomorphism.

As intended, Axiom A10 fails in the iterated structures. In addition to the infons of $\text{SInf}(\mathfrak{M})$, the iterated structure contains infons of the forms $\langle\langle \mathsf{Rel}; r, \sigma\rangle\rangle$ and $\langle\langle \mathsf{Arg}; a, i, \sigma\rangle\rangle$. Other 'higher-order' infons can be incorporated by extending the definition of $\text{SInf}^-(\mathfrak{M})$ appropriately.[9]

2.6. *Circularity*

Despite escaping Axiom A10, the arguments of infons in iterated information structures are not entirely without restriction. The following axiom is satisfied by all iterated information structures, as well as by all standard ones.

A10.1 *There is no infinite sequence* $a_0, a_1, a_2, \ldots$ *such that, for each integer* n, a_{n+1} *is an argument of* a_n.

Axiom A10.1 is weaker than Axiom A10, which disallows even finite sequences of nested arguments, but it is strong enough to prohibit 'circular' information. For example, let σ be the information expressed by the following sentence: 'The information expressed by this sentence is expressible in English'. A simple-minded analysis of the structure of σ is that it has a relation expressible-in-English with a single role i, and is such that $\mathsf{Arg}(\sigma, i, \sigma)$. In other words, σ satisfies the equation

$$\sigma = \langle\langle \mathsf{expressible\text{-}in\text{-}English};\ \sigma\rangle\rangle,$$

and the infinite path $\sigma, \sigma, \sigma, \ldots$ is forbidden by Axiom A10.1. Infons with the self-referential properties that conflict with Axiom A10.1 have been called 'hyperinfons'. There are other examples.

Let τ be the information that the soufflé Paul cooked has failed to rise. If τ is common knowledge among Paul and Albert then they both know τ and each knows that the other knows τ. Moreover, each knows that the other knows that he knows τ – and so on, *ad infinitum*. Barwise (1987) notes that the shared information σ satisfies the following equation:

$$\sigma = \tau \wedge \langle\langle \mathsf{knows}, \mathsf{Albert}, \sigma\rangle\rangle \wedge \langle\langle \mathsf{knows}, \mathsf{Paul}, \sigma\rangle\rangle.$$

Next, suppose that being incorrect is a property of infons, and let 'incorrect' name this property. Any infon satisfying the equation

$$\sigma = \langle\langle \mathsf{incorrect};\ \sigma\rangle\rangle$$

[9] For example, in addition to A_1, A_2, and A_3, extend the universe to include

$$A_4 = \{\langle 4, \mathsf{knows}, \alpha\rangle \mid \alpha : \{1,2\} \to M \text{ and } \exists x, y\ \alpha(1) = \langle 0, x\rangle,\ \alpha(2) = \langle 3, y\rangle\} \text{ and}$$

$$A_5 = \{\langle 5, \mathsf{if}, \alpha\rangle \mid \alpha : \{1,2\} \to M \text{ and } \exists x, y\ \alpha(1) = \langle 3, x\rangle,\ \alpha(2) = \langle 3, y\rangle\}.$$

leads to some tricky problems for a theory of the relationship between information and truth (to be discussed in Section 4). One could claim that there are no such infons, but then it would be difficult to say what information is expressed by the statement that the information expressed by this statement is incorrect. Many similar puzzles are discussed in Barwise and Etchemendy (1987). Koons (1990, 1992) uses a similar approach to tackle doxastic puzzles involving self-reference.

The elucidation of the structure of hyperinfons and other 'circular phenomena' is one of Situation Theory's main achievements. It is also one of the main reasons for the present, relational approach. Although Axiom A10.1 is satisfied by all standard information structures, there are non-standard structures in which hyperinfons exist. This is easy to see: the structure $\mathfrak{A}_1$ with just three elements $\{a, r, i\}$ and with extensions $[\![\mathsf{Arg}]\!] = \{\langle a, i, a\rangle\}$ and $[\![\mathsf{Rel}]\!] = \{\langle r, a\rangle\}$ is a simple information structure in which the element a satisfies the equation $a = \langle\!\langle r; a\rangle\!\rangle$.

When Axiom A10.1 is dropped in order to model hyperinfons, Axiom A9 is no longer sufficient to determine identity. Consider the structure $\mathfrak{A}_2$ with universe $\{a, b, r, i\}$ and extensions $[\![\mathsf{Arg}]\!] = \{\langle a, i, a\rangle, \langle b, i, b\rangle\}$ and $[\![\mathsf{Rel}]\!] = \{\langle r, a\rangle, \langle r, b\rangle\}$. In this structure there are two infons, a and b, that satisfy the equation $\sigma = \langle\!\langle r; \sigma\rangle\!\rangle$. There is no difference in the structure of a and b, and yet they are distinct, despite the fact that Axiom A9 is satisfied. What went wrong?

The solution to this problem was a turning point in the development of Situation Theory. The crucial concept of 'bisimulation' first appeared in modal logic and in theoretical computer science, where it is used to define equivalence of processes. The latter lead directly to Aczel (1988), where it is used to formulate the Anti-Foundation Axiom (AFA), an alternative to the Axiom of Foundation in Set Theory. The resulting theory of sets offered a rich new class of structures with which to construct models of circular objects, such as hyperinfons. AFA is discussed further in Section 3.2.

Applied to simple information structures, 'bisimulation' is defined as follows.

DEFINITION 2.3. Given a simple information structure $\mathfrak{A}$, a binary relation R on A, is a *bisimulation* iff for all σ, τ in A, if $R(\sigma, \tau)$ then

1. if either σ or τ are not infons then $\sigma = \tau$,
2. if σ and τ are infons then they have the same relation and roles,
3. $\forall i, a, b$ if $\mathsf{Arg}(a, i, \sigma)$ and $\mathsf{Arg}(b, i, \tau)$ then $R(a, b)$, and
4. $R(\tau, \sigma)$.

For any elements a, b in A, we say that a is *bisimilar* to b iff there is a bisimulation R such that $R(a, b)$. It is easy to show that the relation of being bisimilar is itself a bisimulation, the largest bisimulation in $\mathfrak{A}$.

A more general definition of bisimulation is given in Section 3.1, but the one above will do for now. It allows use to state an improved principle of identity for infons:

A10.2 *If a is bisimilar to b then $a = b$.*

Returning to our example, we see that the structure $\mathfrak{A}_2$ fails to satisfy Axiom A10.2 because a and b are bisimilar but not identical. Axiom A10.2 is strictly stronger than Axiom A9, but equivalent to it when restricted to the class of structures satisfying Axiom A10.1, which includes the standard structures. At this stage it is important to realize that we have only shown the possibility of constructing models of some hyperinfons. The question of whether all 'circular phenomena' in Situation Theory can be modeled in this way is as yet undecided. A positive answer will be given in Section 3.2.

2.7. Appropriateness

Let's say that an object is *ordinary* if it is neither a role, nor an infon, nor a relation. In standard structures, for each relation r of arity n and each sequence $a_1, \dots, a_n$ of ordinary objects, the infon $\langle\!\langle r; 1 : a_1, \dots, n : a_n \rangle\!\rangle$ exists. We call this property of standard structures 'generality'. To state it precisely, we say that infons σ and τ each with role i are *i-variants* if for each role $j \neq i$ and each a, $\mathsf{Arg}(a, j, \sigma)$ iff $\mathsf{Arg}(a, j, \tau)$. With this terminology, the principle of generality, which is respected by all standard information structures, may be stated as follows.

A11 *For each infon σ with role i and each ordinary object a, there is an i-variant τ of σ such that* $\mathsf{Arg}(a, i, \tau)$.

There are reasons for thinking that Axiom A11 is both too weak and too strong. It is too weak because it says nothing about the appropriateness of arguments that are not ordinary. Removing the restriction to ordinary objects, we get the following:

A11.1 *For each infon σ with role i and each object a, there is an i-variant τ of σ such that* $\mathsf{Arg}(a, i, \tau)$.

Axiom A11.1 is not satisfied by standard information structures. The iterated structures of Construction 2.2 obey a version of the axiom restricted to infons with relation Rel or Arg.

Axioms A11 and A11.1 are both too strong because they do not permit sortal restrictions. For example, the information expressed by 'Albert tasted the *crème brûlée*' presupposes that Albert is an agent, perhaps even that he is subject of conscious experience. Good evidence for this is that 'Albert did not taste the *crème brûlée*' has the same presupposition; we would be surprised to the point of incomprehension if we were told later that Albert is a Moulinex food processor. An explanation for sortal presuppositions like these is that the argument roles of infons carry certain restrictions on what can fill them. The omelette O of our original example may be prevented from filling the role of cook played by Raymond by ensuring that there is no infon τ such that $\mathsf{Arg}(\mathsf{O}, \mathsf{cook}, \tau)$. Since there is an infon σ such that $\mathsf{Arg}(\mathsf{R}, \mathsf{cook}, \tau)$ and O is an ordinary object, this is inconsistent with Axiom A11.

We say that an object a is an *appropriate filler* of role i just in case there is an infon σ such that $\mathsf{Arg}(a, i, \sigma)$. To allow for role-linked sortal restrictions, we may modify Axiom A11 to get the principle of 'sortal generality':

A11.2 *For each infon σ with role i and each appropriate filler a of i, there is an i-variant τ of σ such that* $\mathsf{Arg}(a, i, \tau)$.

This is a great improvement. In effect, each role is associated with a class of appropriate fillers, and any argument may be replaced by any object in that set. In standard information structures, the class of appropriate fillers for each role is just the class of ordinary objects, but other structures may have different classes for different roles. The iterated structures of Construction 2.2 all satisfy Axiom A11.2. There are two classes of fillers: roles of the original structure may be filled by any ordinary object, and roles of infons whose relation is Arg of Rel may be filled by any object at all.

A theory of appropriateness, stating in general terms which arguments may fill which roles, has not yet been given. Axiom A11.2 is consistent with the way roles are usually thought to restrict their fillers, but there may be restrictions on the formation of infons that are not attributable to a single role. For example, a sketch of Paul and Raymond standing side-by-side conveys the information that Paul is standing next to Raymond; we can model this with an infon of the form $\langle\langle \mathsf{next\text{-}to}; \mathsf{P}, \mathsf{R}\rangle\rangle$. Arguably, the infon presupposes that there are *two* people rather than one. We could capture the presupposition by saying that the two roles of next-to place a joint restriction on their fillers, namely, that they cannot be filled by the same argument. This kind of restriction is not permitted by Axiom A11 or by Axiom A11.2.

2.8. *Partiality*

In standard information structures every infon has a relation and a set of roles determined by that relation. This is captured by the following two axioms.

A12 *For each infon σ there is a relation r such that* $\mathsf{Rel}(r, \sigma)$.
A13 *If* $\mathsf{Rel}(r, \sigma)$ *and* $\mathsf{Rel}(r, \tau)$ *and* $\mathsf{Arg}(a, i, \sigma)$ *then for some b,* $\mathsf{Arg}(b, i, \tau)$.

One reason for dropping these axioms is to allow infons to be *unsaturated*. For example, suppose you overhear someone saying 'Mary saw Elvis in Tokyo' but a distracting noise prevents you from hearing the word 'Elvis'. The information conveyed is unsaturated because the filler of one of the roles is missing. We may represent the unsaturated infon as $\langle\langle \mathsf{saw}; \mathsf{seer}: \mathsf{Mary}, \mathsf{location}: \mathsf{Tokyo}\rangle\rangle$, to be contrasted with the infon

$$\langle\langle \mathsf{saw}; \mathsf{seer}: \mathsf{Mary}, \mathsf{seen}: \mathsf{Elvis}, \mathsf{location}: \mathsf{Tokyo}\rangle\rangle,$$

which would have been conveyed had you heard the whole utterance. The coexistence of these infons is forbidden by Axiom A13. Another way in which an infon can be unsaturated is by lacking a relation – consider, for example, the information conveyed if the word 'saw' had been obscured. This possibility counts against Axiom A12.

In the absence of Axioms A12 and A13, it is useful to define an ordering of infons that captures the degree to which they are saturated.

DEFINITION 2.4. Infon σ is *part of* infon τ, written $\sigma \sqsubseteq \tau$, if
1. for all r, if $\mathsf{Rel}(r, \sigma)$ then $\mathsf{Rel}(r, \tau)$, and
2. for each role i and object a, if $\mathsf{Arg}(a, i, \sigma)$ then $\mathsf{Arg}(a, i, \tau)$.

An infon σ is *unsaturated* if there is another infon τ such that $\sigma \sqsubseteq \tau$. If there is no such infon, σ is *saturated*.

Despite the need for unsaturated infons, there is something to be said for the intuition that an infon *should* have a relation that determines its roles. We can recover the force of this idea by restricting Axioms A12 and A13 to apply only to saturated infons.

A13.1 *Every saturated infon has a relation.*

A13.2 *For saturated infons, σ and τ, having the same relation and for each object a and role i, if $\mathsf{Arg}(a, i, \sigma)$ then, for some b, $\mathsf{Arg}(b, i, \tau)$.*

Axioms A12 and A13 follow from A13.1 and A13.2 given the additional assumption that every infon is saturated. In this way, we see that the standard structures are a limiting special case.

The ordering $\sqsubseteq$ is clearly a pre-order of infons (reflexive and transitive). In information structures satisfying Axiom A9 it is a partial order (reflexive, transitive, and antisymmetric), and in standard structures it is trivial ($\sigma \sqsubseteq \tau$ iff $\sigma = \tau$) because every infon is saturated.

In non-standard information structures, we can ensure the existence of the greatest number of unsaturated infons with the following axiom:

A13.3 *For every set I of roles and every infon σ, there is an infon τ such that, for each role i and object a, $\mathsf{Arg}(a, i, \tau)$ iff $\mathsf{Arg}(a, i, \sigma)$ and $i \in I$.*

Axiom A13.3 entails that if $\langle\!\langle r; i : a, j : b \rangle\!\rangle$ exists then so do $\langle\!\langle r; i : a \rangle\!\rangle$, $\langle\!\langle r; j : b \rangle\!\rangle$ and even $\langle\!\langle r; \rangle\!\rangle$. In other words, it allows every infon to be broken up into smaller parts. The issue of whether and how the parts can be recombined is separate, and requires the following definition.

DEFINITION 2.5. Infons σ and τ are *compatible* if they have the same relation and for each role i and objects a and b, if $\mathsf{Arg}(a, i, \sigma)$ and $\mathsf{Arg}(b, i, \tau)$ then $a = b$. They are *unifiable* if they possess a least upper bound in the $\sqsubseteq$ ordering.[10]

For example, the information that Mary saw Elvis is compatible with the information that Elvis was seen in Tokyo. These two infons may be unified to produce the information that Mary saw Elvis in Tokyo.[11] This suggests the following unification axiom.

A13.4 *Every compatible pair of infons is unifiable.*

Questions concerning the order of infons become a lot more difficult to answer if the arguments of infons are also partial objects. This is unavoidable when we include 'higher-order' infons, as discussed in Section 2.5. There is a variety of ways of extending the order between infons by taking the order of arguments into account, but none of them is entirely satisfactory. Consider, for example, the idea that if $a \sqsubseteq a'$ then the infon $\langle\!\langle r; i : a, j : b \rangle\!\rangle$ is part of the infon $\langle\!\langle r; i : a', j : b \rangle\!\rangle$. This is initially plausible but has unattractive consequences when applied to higher-order infons, such as those of the conditional form $\langle\!\langle \mathsf{if}; \sigma, \tau \rangle\!\rangle$. If $\sigma \neq \sigma'$ then we would *not* wish to say that $\langle\!\langle \mathsf{if}; \sigma, \tau \rangle\!\rangle$ is part of $\langle\!\langle \mathsf{if}; \sigma', \tau \rangle\!\rangle$ even if $\sigma \sqsubseteq \sigma'$. Of course, one could take this as evidence against

[10] I.e. if $\exists x$ such that $\sigma \sqsubseteq x$, $\tau \sqsubseteq x$, and $\forall y$, if $\sigma \sqsubseteq y$ and $\tau \sqsubseteq y$, then $x \sqsubseteq y$.

[11] There is no requirement that the unification of two infons is 'entailed' by the infons being unified; just that the unification of the two infons is the least infon containing them.

modeling conditionals as infons of this form, instead of evidence against the proposed order-structure. As the issue is presently unressolved, we shall stick with the 'flat' order.

With discussions of unification, comparison with the literature on feature structures (cf. Chapter 8, this volume) is unavoidable. Indeed, it is easy to see how one can construct information structures using features structures to model the infons. Conversely, one can use information structures to model feature structures, by identifying features with roles and values with arguments. The order $\sqsubseteq$ defined for infons is relatively uninteresting when applied to feature structures, precisely because it does not take into account the order of arguments. Rounds (1991) discusses the relationship between the two subjects.

2.9. Representation theorems

In addition to the axioms discussed above, we need one more axiom to account for the behaviour of constants in standard information structures.

A14 *Every relation but no role and no infon is denoted by a constant.*

This axiom is entirely artificial, and of little consequence to the general theory.

THEOREM 2.1. *A simple information structure is standard if and only if it satisfies Axioms* A1 *to* A14.

PROOF. We have already seen that each of these axioms is satisfied by all standard information structures. For the converse, let $\mathfrak{A}$ be an information structure satisfying the axioms, with constants C. We shall construct a relational structure $\mathfrak{M}$ and an isomorphism $f: |\mathfrak{A}| \to |\,\mathrm{SInf}(\mathfrak{M})|$.

Let R be the class of relations in $\mathfrak{A}$, I the class of roles, Σ the class of infons, and M the class of ordinary objects. By Axioms A3 to A5, these four classes are pairwise disjoint and exhaust the universe of $\mathfrak{A}$.

The class R of relations is finite by Axiom A8. For each r in R, let

$$I_r = \{i \mid \exists a, \sigma\ \mathsf{Rel}(r, \sigma) \text{ and } \mathsf{Arg}(a, i, \sigma)\}.$$

We shall show that I_r is finite. For each infon σ of $\mathfrak{A}$, let $I_\sigma = \{i \mid \exists a\ \mathsf{Arg}(a, i, \sigma)\}$. By Axiom A13, for all infons σ and τ such that $\mathsf{Rel}(r, \sigma)$ and $\mathsf{Rel}(r, \tau)$, $I_\sigma = I_\tau$. Thus for each σ having relation r, $I_r = I_\sigma$. By Axiom A7, I_σ is finite for each infon σ, and so I_r is finite also.

Let $S \subseteq C$ be the class of those constants that denote relations in $\mathfrak{A}$. By Axiom A14, S is the same size as R. This enables us to define a relational signature ν with primitive relations S and such that for each R' in S, $\nu(R')$ is equal to the size of $I_{[\![R']\!]^{\mathfrak{A}}}$. Let $\mathfrak{M}$ be any relational structure with signature ν, universe M, and constants $C - S$, each with the same denotation it has in $\mathfrak{A}$; this is possible because these constants denote ordinary objects, by Axiom A14. We shall construct an isomorphism f from $\mathfrak{A}$ to $\mathrm{SInf}(\mathfrak{M})$.

First, we must enumerate the set I of roles of $\mathfrak{A}$. By Axioms A1 and A12, for each infon σ of $\mathfrak{A}$ there is a unique relation r_σ such that $\mathsf{Rel}(r_\sigma, \sigma)$. By the above, $I_\sigma = I_{r_\sigma}$. But there are only a finite number of relations (Axiom A8), and so there are only a finite number of sets of the form I_σ, even if the number of infons is infinite. Moreover, by Axiom A6, these sets are linearly ordered by inclusion. Consequently, there is an enumeration $r_1, \ldots, r_n$ of R such that $I_{r_k} \subseteq I_{r_{k+1}}$, for for $1 \leqslant k \leqslant n-1$. Now

$$I = I_{r_1} \cup \cdots \cup I_{r_n} = I_{r_1} \cup \cdots \cup (I_{r_{k+1}} - I_{r_k}) \cup \cdots \cup (I_{r_n} - I_{n-1})$$

and so we may enumerate I by enumerating each of the sets $(I_{r_{k+1}} - I_{r_k})$ in order, and without repetition. Let $i_1, \ldots, i_N$ be such an enumeration. It has the property that for $1 \leqslant k \leqslant n$, $I_{r_k} = \{i_1, \ldots, i_{\nu(r_k)}\}$.

Next, we must consider the arguments of infons. For each infon σ, we have seen that

$$I_\sigma = I_{r_\sigma} = \{i_1, \ldots, i_{\nu(r_\sigma)}\}$$

and by Axiom A2, for $1 \leqslant k \leqslant n$, there is a unique object a_k such that $\mathsf{Arg}(a_k, i_k, \sigma)$. By Axiom A10, a_k is ordinary and so is in M. Define the function $\alpha_\sigma : \{1, \ldots, \nu(r_\sigma)\} \to \{0\} \times M$ by $\alpha_\sigma(k) = \langle 0, a_k \rangle$.

Now we are ready to define the function f from $|\mathfrak{A}|$ to $|\operatorname{SInf}(\mathfrak{M})|$.

$$f(x) = \begin{cases} \langle 0, x \rangle & \text{if } x \text{ is in } M, \\ \langle 1, x \rangle & \text{if } x \text{ is in } R, \\ \langle 2, k \rangle & \text{if } x \text{ is in } I \text{ and } i_k = x, \\ \langle 3, \langle r_x, \alpha_x \rangle\rangle & \text{if } x \text{ is in } \Sigma. \end{cases}$$

This is a good definition, because every element of $|\mathfrak{A}|$ is in exactly one of the classes M, R, I or Σ, and for each x in I there is a unique k such that $i_k = x$. To show that f is one-one, suppose that $f(x) = f(y)$. We can show that $x = y$ by cases according to whether x and y are in M, R, I or Σ. The only non-trivial case is that in which x and y are infons. Then $f(x) = \langle 3, \langle r_x, \alpha_x \rangle\rangle$ and $f(y) = \langle 3, \langle r_y, \alpha_y \rangle\rangle$. Thus, $r_x = r_y$ and $\alpha_x = \alpha_y$, and so by Axiom A9, $x = y$, as required.

To show that f maps onto the universe of $\operatorname{SInf}(\mathfrak{M})$, consider any element $\langle j, x \rangle$ of that universe. We need to find a y such that $f(y) = \langle j, x \rangle$. The only non-trivial case is that in which $j = 3$. Then $x = \langle r, \alpha \rangle$ for some relation r and function $\alpha : \{1, \ldots, \nu(r)\} \to \{0\} \times M$. For $1 \leqslant k \leqslant \nu(r)$, let m_k be the element of M for which $\alpha(k) = \langle 0, m_k \rangle$. Now, r is a relation, so there is some infon σ of $\mathfrak{A}$ such that $\mathsf{Rel}(r, \sigma)$. The roles of σ are those in the set $I_\sigma = \{i_1, \ldots, i_{\nu(r)}\}$ and so, applying Axiom A11 repeatedly ($\nu(r)$ times), we obtain an infon σ' such that $\mathsf{Arg}(m_k, i_k, \sigma')$ for $1 \leqslant k \leqslant \nu(r)$. Spelling out the definition of $\alpha_{\sigma'}$ we see that this function is just α, so $\langle r_{\sigma'}, \alpha_{\sigma'} \rangle = \langle r, \alpha \rangle = x$, and so $f(\sigma') = \langle 3, \langle r_{\sigma'}, \alpha_{\sigma'} \rangle\rangle = \langle 3, x \rangle$, as required.

Finally, we must show that f preserves the structure of $\mathfrak{A}$. This follows from the following two chains of equivalences. Firstly for Rel:

$\mathsf{Rel}(f(r), f(\sigma))$ in $\operatorname{SInf}(\mathfrak{M})$ iff

$\mathsf{Rel}(\langle 1, r \rangle, \langle 3, \langle r_\sigma, \alpha_\sigma \rangle\rangle)$ in $\operatorname{SInf}(\mathfrak{M})$ iff

$r = r_\sigma$ iff

$\mathsf{Rel}(r, \sigma)$ in $\mathfrak{A}$.

And then for Arg:

$$\begin{aligned}&\mathsf{Arg}(f(m), f(i), f(\sigma)) \text{ in } \mathrm{SInf}(\mathfrak{M}) \text{ iff}\\&\mathsf{Arg}(\langle 0, m\rangle, \langle 2, k\rangle, \langle 3, \langle r_\sigma, \alpha_\sigma\rangle\rangle) \text{ in } \mathrm{SInf}(\mathfrak{M}) \text{ and } i_k = i \text{ iff}\\&\alpha_\sigma(k) = \langle 0, m\rangle \text{ and } i_k = i \text{ iff}\\&\mathsf{Arg}(m, i, \sigma) \text{ in } \mathfrak{A}.\end{aligned}$$

That f preserves the denotation of the constants in C follows from Axiom A14 and the definition of $\mathrm{SInf}(\mathfrak{M})$. □

So much for standard information structures. We have argued that these structures are too rigid to provide a comprehensive framework for modeling the structure of information, even information of the simple kind we have been considering. Nonetheless, several of the axioms of standard structures lead to attractive generalizations. Specifically, Axioms A10.2 and A11.2 provide a useful direction. Both will be explored in greater depth in the next section.

3. A theory of structural relations[12]

Information processed, inferred, conveyed, expressed, or otherwise represented need not be of the simple kind considered above; it may come in larger, more complex chunks.

Logical combinations present an obvious example: we need to account for conjunctions, disjunctions, and perhaps negations of infons. Yet even with the first item on the list there is a potential problem. The identity condition for well-founded simple infons was very clear: σ and τ are identical if and only if they have the same relation and the same arguments filling the same roles. It is much less clear what should be said about conjunctions. A strong condition, analogous to the one for basic infons, is that $\sigma_1 \wedge \tau_1$ is identical to $\sigma_2 \wedge \tau_2$ if and only if σ_1 is identical to σ_2 and τ_1 is identical to τ_2. The problem arises if we combine this condition with natural logically-motivated requirements on conjunction, such as commutativity, associativity and idempotence. For example, by idempotence, $\sigma \wedge \tau = (\sigma \wedge \tau) \wedge (\sigma \wedge \tau)$, and so, by the above condition, $\sigma = \sigma \wedge \tau = \tau$.

The heart of the problem is an inherent tension in the concept of information. On the one hand, information is *representation-independent*: the same information may be represented in many different ways. On the other hand, information is *fine-grained*: two pieces of information may be logically equivalent without being identical. Consequently, the identity conditions for information represented by complex signs must lie somewhere between those for the syntactic form of the sign and those for its semantic content. Striking the right balance is, in general, very difficult.

Another problem is that there has been little agreement as to which combinations of infons are needed. Finite conjunction and disjunction are commonly adopted; infinite

[12] In this section the theory of information structure introduced in Section 2 is developed in greater generality and depth. The reader impatient to find out about situations should jump ahead to Section 4.

conjunctions and disjunction, quantified infons (with variable binding), various negations and conditionals, have also been proposed. For applications in computer science other forms may be found useful. For example, it is not clear that the information stored as a list is simply a conjunction of the items of information stored in each cell, and even if it is some kind of conjunction, it is not clear that it is the same conjunction as expressed by an unordered set of the same items.

In view of the above, it would seem sensible to pursue a fairly open-minded policy about complex infons. The approach adopted here is intended to cover various proposals made in the literature, as well as offering a framework in which other approaches may be tried.

3.1. Extensional structures

Our idea is to generalize the notion of bisimulation to apply in a wider context. In the sequel, we will have (relational) structures of type

$$[A, S_1, \ldots, S_m; R_1, \ldots, R_n].$$

The relations in the first group, $S_1, \ldots, S_m$, are called *structural relations* because they capture the structure of elements of the domain. A structural relation S_i of arity $n+1$ is to be thought of as relating a list of n objects to a single structured object. If $S_i(x_1, \ldots, x_n, y)$ then y is a structured object with components $x_1, \ldots, x_n$, which may or may not be structured themselves.

More generally, we say that b is a *component* of a in $\mathfrak{A}$ if there is a structural relation S_i of arity $n+1$ and elements $x_1, \ldots, x_n$ of A such that $S_i(x_1, \ldots, x_n, a)$ and $x_j = b$ for some $1 \leqslant j \leqslant n$. For technical reasons, we require that the number of components of any object is not a proper class – that is to say, the class of all components of a given object can be placed in one-to-one correspondence with some set. An object a is an *atom* of $\mathfrak{A}$ if it has no components.

In an information structure, the only structured objects are the infons. Relations, roles and ordinary objects are all atomic, but infons have a component structure captured by the relations Rel and Arg. These are the structural relations of information structures. Information structures have no other primitive relations, but the defined relation $\sqsubseteq$ is an example of a non-structural relation – albeit one whose extension is determined by the structure of infons. The important distinction between Rel and Arg, on the one hand, and $\sqsubseteq$, on the other, is that the identity of infons is determined by the former by virtue of adherence to Axiom A10.2.

But now consider an arbitrary relational structure. What conditions must a relation satisfy to qualify as a structural relation? Our answer is based on the following definition.

DEFINITION 3.1. Given a relational structure $\mathfrak{A}$ of type $[A, S_1, \ldots, S_m; R_1, \ldots, R_n]$, a binary relation E on A is said to be a *bisimulation* on $\mathfrak{A}$ if for all $a, b \in A$, if $E(a, b)$ then the following three conditions hold:

1. if a is atomic then $a = b$,
2. for $1 \leqslant i \leqslant m$, if $\nu_i = k$ then, for all $y_1, \ldots, y_k$ such that $S_i(y_1, \ldots, y_k, a)$, there are $z_1, \ldots, z_k$ such that $S_i(z_1, \ldots, z_k, b)$ and $E(y_j, z_j)$ for $1 \leqslant j \leqslant k$, and
3. $E(b, a)$.

a is *bisimilar* to b in $\mathfrak{A}$ iff there is a bisimulation E of $\mathfrak{A}$ such that $E(a, b)$. The structure $\mathfrak{A}$ is *extensional* if it has no distinct bisimilar objects, i.e. if a is bisimilar to b in $\mathfrak{A}$ then $a = b$.

In an extensional structure, the non-atomic objects are individuated according to their structural properties alone. The extensionality condition is a form of Leibniz's Law: objects that are indistinguishable on the basis of their structural relationships are identical. The non-structural relations, $R_1, \ldots, R_n$, do not enter into the identity conditions of objects in the domain. They may be entirely determined by the structure of the objects they relate – $\sqsubseteq$ relation is an example of this – or they may capture genuinely non-structural properties.

Extensional structures will be used throughout the rest of this chapter to model a variety of situation-theoretic objects. Our strategy is to define different kinds of extensional structures to model different parts of the situation-theoretic universe, in a way that allows us to re-combine the parts easily.

DEFINITION 3.2. If $\mathfrak{A}$ is an extensional structure then, for each structural relation S of $\mathfrak{A}$, let S^* be the class of those objects a such that $S(\vec{x}, a)$ in $\mathfrak{A}$ for some sequence $\vec{x}$ (possibly empty) of elements of $|\mathfrak{A}|$. In other words, S^* is the projection of S along its last co-ordinate. We call these classes the *(structural) sorts* of $\mathfrak{A}$.

Every information structure satisfying Axiom A10.2 is an extensional structure with structural relations Rel and Arg. The standard structures and even the iterated structures are also well-founded, by Axiom A10.1. In a standard information structure $\mathsf{Rel}^* = \mathsf{Arg}^*$; and this is the class of infons, the only structured objects. In non-standard information structures, Rel^* and Arg^* may be slightly different if there are infons with a relation but no arguments or with arguments but no relation. In any case, the class of infons is $\mathsf{Rel}^* \cup \mathsf{Arg}^*$. The relations, roles and ordinary objects are all atoms.

Another, familiar example of an extensional structure is the structure $\mathfrak{V}$ of type $[V, \in^2;]$ where V is the class of all sets, and the extension of $\in$ is the binary relation of membership. The class $\in^*$ consists of all non-empty sets. Extensionality is assured by the set-theoretic axiom of the same name, together with the Axiom of Foundation or Anti-foundation, depending on whether V is assumed to satisfy the axioms of well-founded or anti-founded set theory.

DEFINITION 3.3. An extensional structure $\mathfrak{A}$ of of type $[A, \mathsf{Set}^1, \in^2;]$ is called a *set structure* if $\in^* \subseteq \mathsf{Set}^*$ and $\mathfrak{A}$ satisfies the axioms of ZFC^- with quantifiers restricted to Set^*.[13]

[13] ZFC^- is Zermelo–Frankel Set Theory with the Axiom of Choice, but without the Axiom of Foundation. See Section 3.2 for more details.

The ambiguity in our use of the word 'set' and the predicate '$\in$' is of the now familiar kind. Internal sets are those elements of the structure in Set*, which may or may not be (external) sets. But for any internal set a, we may define a corresponding external set $a^* = \{b \mid \in(b, a)\}$.

Our third example of an extensional structure presents functions as structured objects whose components are their arguments and values.

DEFINITION 3.4. An extensional structure $\mathfrak{A}$ of type $[A, \mathsf{App}^3, \mathsf{Fun}^1;]$ is a *function structure* if $\mathsf{App}^* \subseteq \mathsf{Fun}^*$ and, for all α, x, y and i in A, $\mathsf{App}(i, x, \alpha)$ iff $\mathsf{App}(i, y, \alpha)$, then $x = y$.

If $\alpha \in \mathsf{Fun}^*$ then α is an (internal) function of $\mathfrak{A}$. We associate it with an external function α^* whose domain consists of those elements i of A for which there is an x such that $\mathsf{App}(i, x, \alpha)$. For each such i, $\alpha^*(i)$ is the unique x such that $\mathsf{App}(i, x, \alpha)$.

The extensionality requirement on function structures means that different internal functions represent different external functions. For if $a^* = b^*$, then $I_A \cup \{\langle a, b\rangle, \langle b, a\rangle\}$ is a bisimulation relating a and b and so $a = b$. If the structure is *flat* (i.e. if no function is also an argument), then extensionality is equivalent to this condition; in other structures it is a stronger condition.

3.2. *Structural descriptions and anti-foundedness*

The extensionality condition ensures that our structures are not over-populated. In this section we guard against the danger of *under*-population, by showing how extensional structures can be populated to capacity.

Every object in an extensional structure can be identified by listing its structural relationships with other objects. Given an extensional structure $\mathfrak{A}$ and a 'parameter' x, which may be any object and not necessarily an element of $|\mathfrak{A}|$, a *unary structural description* T is a pair $\langle x, T_x\rangle$ consisting of a set T_x of tuples of the form $\langle S, b_1, \ldots, b_k\rangle$ where S is a structural relation of arity $k+1$ and each of $b_1, \ldots, b_k$ is either the parameter x or an object of $\mathfrak{A}$. For each a in $|\mathfrak{A}|$, we form the set $a.T$ of tuples of the form $\langle S, b_1[x/a], \ldots, b_k[x/a]\rangle$ for each $\langle S, b_1, \ldots, b_k\rangle$ in T_x, where $b_i[x/a] = a$ if $b_i = x$ and is b_i otherwise. The object a *satisfies* the description T if for all S and $b_1, \ldots, b_k$,

$$S(b_1, \ldots, b_k, a) \text{ in } \mathfrak{A} \quad \text{iff} \quad \langle S, b_1, \ldots, b_k\rangle \text{ is in } a.T.$$

For example, in a simple information structure $\mathfrak{A}$ the infon $\sigma = \langle\!\langle r; i : \sigma, j : a\rangle\!\rangle$ satisfies the description

$$T = \langle x, \{\langle \mathsf{Rel}, r\rangle, \langle \mathsf{Arg}, i, x\rangle, \langle \mathsf{Arg}, j, a\rangle\}\rangle$$

because

$$\sigma.T = \{\langle \mathsf{Rel}, r\rangle, \langle \mathsf{Arg}, i, \sigma\rangle, \langle \mathsf{Arg}, j, a\rangle\}$$

and $\mathsf{Rel}(r, \sigma)$, $\mathsf{Arg}(i, \sigma, \sigma)$, and $\mathsf{Arg}(j, a, \sigma)$ hold in $\mathfrak{A}$; and these are all the structural relationships in which σ participates.

Every object satisfies some description. An object a of $\mathfrak{A}$ satisfies the *canonical* description $\langle a, T_a \rangle$ where T_a is the set of tuples of the form $\langle S, b_1, \ldots, b_k \rangle$ such that $S(b_1, \ldots, b_k, a)$ in $\mathfrak{A}$.[14] By extensionality, no two objects satisfy the same canonical description, but in most cases there many more descriptions than there are objects described. The problem of under-population is that there may be too few objects to satisfy the descriptions used in Situation Theory. To solve it, the definition of 'structural description' must be extended to cover the polyadic case.

DEFINITION 3.5. Suppose $\mathfrak{A}$ is an extensional structure. A *structural description* T in $\mathfrak{A}$ is an indexed family $\{T_x\}_{x \in X}$ of sets T_x of tuples of the form $\langle S, b_1, \ldots, b_k \rangle$ such that S is a structural relation of $\mathfrak{A}$ of arity $k+1$ and $b_1, \ldots, b_k$ are elements of $|\mathfrak{A}| \cup X$. The elements of the index set X are called *parameters*. Given a mapping s from X to $|\mathfrak{A}|$ let $s.T$ be the family of sets $s.T_x$ of tuples of the form $\langle S, b_1[s], \ldots, b_k[s] \rangle$ for each $\langle S, b_1, \ldots, b_k \rangle$ in T_x where $b_i[s] = s(b_i)$ if b_i is in X and is b_i otherwise. The mapping s *satisfies* T if for each x in X, $s(x)$ satisfies the unary description $\langle s(x), s.T_x \rangle$.

To see how this definition works, consider its application to set structures. A set a satisfies the unary description T just in case

$$a.T = \{\langle \in, b \rangle \mid b \text{ in } a^*\} \cup \{\langle \mathsf{Set} \rangle\}.$$

Now, for each set U of tuples, let $U^* = \{b \mid \langle \in, b \rangle \text{ is in } U\}$. Then a satisfies T iff $a^* = (a.T)^*$. Likewise, if T is a polyadic structural description, then a mapping s satisfies T iff $s(x)^* = (s.T_x)^*$ for each parameter x of T. This relationship enables us to represent a structural description in a set structure as a system of simultaneous equations. For example, the system of equations shown on the left below corresponds to the structural description shown on the right.

$x = \{y, z\}$	$T_x = \{\langle \in, y \rangle, \langle \in, z \rangle, \langle \mathsf{Set} \rangle\}$,
$y = \emptyset$	$T_y = \{\langle \mathsf{Set} \rangle\}$,
$z = \{x, a\}$	$T_z = \{\langle \in, x \rangle, \langle \in, a \rangle, \langle \mathsf{Set} \rangle\}$.

A mapping s that satisfies the description on the right determines (and is determined by) a solution to the equations. It gives us sets $s(x)$, $s(y)$, and $s(z)$, such that $s(x) = \{s(y), s(z)\}$, $s(y) = \emptyset$ and $s(z) = \{s(x), a\}$.

Thus, in set structures the 'population density' is determined by the number of systems of equations that have solutions. Structural descriptions correspond to a wider range of systems of equations than one might expect. Consider $X = \{x, y\}$ and $e(x) = \{\langle x, y \rangle\}$, $e(y) = \{x, y, \emptyset\}$. This system is unlike the ones we've seen so far because $e(x)$ contains the *ordered pair* $\langle x, y \rangle$. In set theory, this pair is standardly taken to be $\{\{x\}, \{x, y\}\}$. To

[14] T_a cannot be a proper class because we have assumed that every object has only a set-sized class of components.

solve a system involving pairs, we must add more variables to X and more equations. Here we would take $X' = \{x, y, z_0, z_1, z_2\}$ and $e(x) = \{z_0\}$, $e(y) = \{x, y, \emptyset\}$, $e(z_0) = \{z_1, z_2\}$, $e(z_1) = \{x\}$, $e(z_2) = \{x, y\}$. A solution to the expanded system gives us a solution to the original system. This would be a map s defined on X with the property that $s(x) = \{\langle s(x), s(y)\rangle\}$ and $s(y) = \{s(x), s(y), \emptyset\}$. The usual models of Set Theory are rather sparse by this standard. The above system, for example, cannot be solved because any solution would conflict with the Foundation Axiom. If s is a solution, then there is an infinite descending sequence of elements: $s(x) \ni s(z) \ni \cdots \ni s(x) \ni s(z) \ni \cdots$.

Fortunately, Aczel (1988) showed that if the Foundation Axiom is dropped from Zermelo–Frankel Set Theory (ZFC), the resulting theory (ZFC$^-$) is consistent with the claim that *every* system of equations has a unique solution. That claim, called the Solution Lemma in Barwise and Etchemendy (1987), is equivalent to the Anti-Foundation Axiom (AFA) used by Aczel.[15] Aczel proposes ZFC$^-$ plus AFA as a new theory of sets, perhaps more suitable than ZFC when it comes to modeling the various circular phenomena encountered in applied logic.

Returning to the general case, we can formulate the two extremes of population density by generalizing Foundation and Anti-Foundation to apply to arbitrary extensional structures.

DEFINITION 3.6. An extensional structure $\mathfrak{A}$ is *well-founded* if there is no infinite sequence $a_1, a_2, \ldots$ of elements of A such that a_{n+1} is a component of a_n for each positive integer n. It is *anti-founded* if every structural description in $\mathfrak{A}$ is satisfied.

In particular, a set structure is well-founded if it satisfies the Foundation Axiom of ZFC and is anti-founded if it satisfies the Anti-Foundation Axiom. The well-founded extensional structures are those with the lowest population density: only those objects explicitly requested by other parts of the theory are required to be present. Anti-founded structures, by contrast, are full to the brim: any object you can describe is sure to be there. The next theorem shows that every extensional structure lies between these two such extremes.

THEOREM 3.1. *For every extensional structure $\mathfrak{A}$ there is a well-founded extensional structure $\mathfrak{A}_{\mathrm{wf}}$ and an anti-founded extensional structure $\mathfrak{A}_{\mathrm{af}}$ such that $\mathfrak{A}_{\mathrm{wf}}$ is isomorphically embedded in a $\mathfrak{A}$, and $\mathfrak{A}$ is isomorphically embedded $\mathfrak{A}_{\mathrm{af}}$.*

PROOF. The existence of a well-founded part of $\mathfrak{A}$ is easy to show. We can just restrict the structure to those objects that are not at the start of an infinitely descending chain of components, and check that the extensionality condition still holds. For the anti-founded extension of $\mathfrak{A}$, we shall assume that we are working in a universe of sets that satisfies ZFC$^-$+AFA, and that there is a proper class of ur-elements (non-sets) available.

---

[15] The Anti-Foundation Axiom is defined using 'decorations' of a pointed graph, rather than solutions of equations or the satisfiers of structural descriptions. Another approach is to look at the fixed points of monotone operators on an upper semi-lattice. We advise the interested reader to consult Aczel (1988) and Barwise and Moss (1996) for details. Aczel discusses the application of AFA to situation theory in Aczel (1996), and a more general framework for modeling structured objects is introduced in Aczel (1990). The approach taken here is also related to Fernando (1990).

With each structural relation S of $\mathfrak{A}$, we associate an ur-element z_s. We also associate an ur-element z_a with each atom of $\mathfrak{A}$. Let U be the collection of all these ur-elements. We assume that the association is one-to-one. For any set a, the 'support' of a is the set of objects b_0 for which there is a sequence $b_0 \in \cdots \in b_n$ with $b_n = a$. We assume that no ur-elements in U occur in the support of $|\mathfrak{A}|$.

From Aczel (1988) and Barwise and Moss (1996) we know that every system of equations in a model of ZFC$^-$+AFA has a unique solution.

DEFINITION 3.7. A *system of equations* is a function e whose domain is a set X of ur-elements with the property that for each x in X, $e(x)$ is a set (not an ur-element). A *solution* to e is a function s with domain X, such that for every x in X, $s(x) = \{a[s] \mid a \in e(x)\}$. The square-brackets operation is defined by: (i) $y[s] = s(y)$ for all y in X; (ii) $y[s] = y$ for all ur-elements y not in X; and (iii) $a[s] = \{b[s] \mid b \in a\}$ for sets b.[16]

Now, with each structural description T in $\mathfrak{A}$ with parameter set X_T, we associate the function e_T mapping each parameter x to the set

$$\{\langle z_s, b_1, \ldots, b_k\rangle \mid \langle S, b_1, \ldots, b_k\rangle \in T_x\}.$$

In other words, each structural relation S replaced by the corresponding z_s. As it stands, e_T is not a system of equations in the strict sense defined above because the elements of $e_T(x)$ are tuples of parameters and sets, rather than the parameters and sets themselves. Using the method illustrated earlier, e_T is easily converted into a system of equations e'_T with parameter set X'_T (containing X_T) such that a solution for e'_T is a solution for e_T and vice versa.

The system e'_T has a unique solution, s_T. Let

$$B = \{s_T(x) \mid T \text{ is a structural description in } \mathfrak{A} \text{ and } x \text{ is in } X'_T\}.$$

We'll soon see how to interpret the relations of $\mathfrak{A}$ on this set to get the desired structure $\mathfrak{A}_{\rm af}$, but first we need a subsidiary fact about structural descriptions.

Recall that each $a \in A$ satisfies a description T_a in one variable x. Let $i : A \to B$ be given by $i(a) = s_{T_a}(x)$ for a a non-atom of $\mathfrak{A}$, and $i(a) = z_a$ if a is an atom. Then is one-to-one: if $s_{T_a}(x) = s_{T_b}(x)$, then we could get a bisimulation relation on $\mathfrak{A}$ relating a and b. Since $\mathfrak{A}$ is extensional, we would have $a = b$. And if a is a non-atom, then $i(a)$ is a set, so it cannot equal $i(b) = z_b$ for b a non-atom

Now we can see how to make B into a structure $\mathfrak{A}_{\rm af}$ of the same type as $\mathfrak{A}$. Let S be a structural relation. We interpret it by

$$S(c_1, \ldots, c_n, c) \text{ in } \mathfrak{A}_{\rm af} \quad \text{iff} \quad \langle z_S, c_1, \ldots, c_n\rangle \in c.$$

The definition of the principal descriptions T_a implies that

$$S(b_1, \ldots, b_k, a) \text{ in } \mathfrak{A} \quad \text{iff} \quad S(i(b_1), \ldots, i(b_k), i(a)) \text{ in } \mathfrak{A}_{\rm af}.$$

[16] That $[s]$ is uniquely determined from s and these three conditions is also a consequence of AFA.

The non-structural relations extend to the image of $\mathfrak{A}$ via the isomorphism; we'll say that on tuples outside the image of i, each non-structural relation is false.

At this point we have $\mathfrak{A}_{\mathrm{af}}$. This structure is extensional by AFA. A bisimulation of structures relating c and c' would give us a bisimulation of *sets* doing the same thing. And according to AFA, bisimilar sets are equal.

Finally, we sketch a proof that $\mathfrak{A}_{\mathrm{af}}$ is anti-founded. Before we do this, we need to recall that for each $c \in B$ there is a structural description T_c over the original $\mathfrak{A}$ and a parameter x of T such that $s_T(x) = c$. Let T' be a structural description in $\mathfrak{A}_{\mathrm{af}}$. Now each T_y may contain elements $c \in |\mathfrak{A}_{\mathrm{af}}|$, so we replace each such c by a new ur-element (say z_c) and then adjoin all of the structural descriptions T_c to T. Of course, we must use new parameters to do this. In this way, T' is equivalent to a structural description in the original $\mathfrak{A}$. So by definition of $\mathfrak{A}_{\mathrm{af}}$, there is some $a \in |\mathfrak{A}_{\mathrm{af}}|$ instantiating T'. □

As a corollary, we apply this result to simple information structures. Suppose $\mathfrak{A}$ is a simple information structure with a set R of relations, a set I of roles, and a set O of ordinary objects. A structural description of an infon in $\mathfrak{A}$ with parameter set X is determined by a system of equations of the form $e(x) = \langle\langle r; i_1 : b_1, \ldots, i_n : b_n\rangle\rangle$ where $r \in R$, $i_j \in I$ and $b_i \in O \cup X$ for $1 \leqslant i \leqslant n$. Theorem 3.1 tells us that there is an anti-founded information structure $\mathfrak{A}_{\mathrm{af}}$ extending $\mathfrak{A}$. In this structure all structural descriptions are satisfied and so there are solutions to the equations. In particular, all the hyperinfons we care to define using relations R, roles I, and ordinary objects O can be found in this structure.

3.3. *Partiality and order*

We have seen how infons may be ordered according to their arguments and relations. In fact, the definition of $\sqsubseteq$ is quite general.

DEFINITION 3.8. Given an extensional structure $\mathfrak{A}$ of type

$$[A, S_1, \ldots, S_m; R_1, \ldots, R_n],$$

we define a relation $\sqsubseteq$ on the non-atomic elements of A as follows: $a \sqsubseteq b$ if for $1 \leqslant i \leqslant m$, and each sequence $\vec{x}$ of appropriate length, if $S_i(\vec{x}, a)$ then $S_i(\vec{x}, b)$.

For information structures, the definition of $\sqsubseteq$ agrees with our previous definition. For set structures, $a \sqsubseteq b$ iff $a^* \subseteq b^*$, and for function structures, it is the usual order on partial functions: $f \sqsubseteq g$ iff each i in the domain of f^* belongs to the domain of g^* and $f^*(i) = g^*(i)$. The relation $\sqsubseteq$ is a partial order on structured (non-atomic) objects.[17]

Other ordering of structured objects are possible and have been studied extensively. The most important of these is the 'hereditary' order, which takes into account the order of components. Roughly, an object a is a hereditary part of b if for every component a'

[17] It is clearly reflexive and transitive, and anti-symmetry follows from extensionality: if $a \sqsubseteq b$ and $b \sqsubseteq a$ then the union of $\{\langle a, b\rangle, \langle b, a\rangle\}$ and the identity relation is a bisimulation of $\mathfrak{A}$, and so $a = b$.

of a there is a component b' of b such that either $a' = b'$ or a' is a hereditary component of b'. Stated thus, the definition is circular. In some cases we can overcome the problem using an inductive layering of the domain. Say that an object is of order 0 if it is atomic, and of order $n+1$ if it has a component of order n but no components of order greater that n. This enables us to give a recursive definition of the hereditary order on objects of order n in terms of the hereditary order of objects of order less than n.

This strategy works for well-founded structures, in which every object has an order. But in structures with a 'circular' component relation there are objects that do not have an order. This is a common problem in the study of circular phenomena. The solution is as follows. First, we regard the 'definition' of the order as an operation on binary relations. Given one binary relation R, we let R^+ be defined by

> $R^+(a,b)$ if for every component a' of a there is a component b' of b such that either $a' = b'$ or $R(a', b')$.

Now, the operation taking R to R^+ is *monotone*: if $R \subseteq S$ then $R^+ \subseteq S^+$. A basic result of the theory of order is that every monotone operation has a *greatest fixed point*. In other words, there is an R such that $R^+ = R$ and for any S such that $S^+ = S$, $S \subseteq R$. This observation enables to define the hereditary order in the general case as follows.

DEFINITION 3.9. The *hereditary order*, $\sqsubseteq^h$, on an extensional structure $\mathfrak{A}$ of type $[A, S_1, \ldots, S_m; R_1, \ldots, R_n]$ is the largest binary relation between non-atomic objects of $\mathfrak{A}$ such that if $a \sqsubseteq^h b$ then for $1 \leqslant i \leqslant m$, if $S_i(x_1, \ldots, x_k, a)$ then there are $y_1, \ldots, y_k$ such that $S_i(y_1, \ldots, y_k, b)$ and $x_j \sqsubseteq^h y_j$ for each $1 \leqslant j \leqslant k$.

The hereditary order is a partial order on non-atomic objects for the same reason that $\sqsubseteq$ is. Other orders may be obtained by defining different monotone operations.

It is important to realize that both $\sqsubseteq$ and $\sqsubseteq^h$ are purely structural concepts. In the case of simple infons, if $\sigma \sqsubseteq \tau$ then it is possible to go further and interpret the order in terms of epistemological advantage: knowing σ is not as valuable as knowing τ. This interpretation is not available in the general case. For example, in Section 3.4 we show how to obtain a disjunction $\sigma_1 \vee \sigma_2$ whose components are σ_1 and σ_2, and is such that $\sigma_1 \vee \sigma_2 \sqsubseteq \sigma_1 \vee \sigma_2 \vee \sigma_3$. The question of how to relate the partiality of structure to logical operations is a difficult one; it is shared by those studying databases and feature logic (Rounds, 1991; and Chapter 8, this volume).

The discussion of unification in information structures may also be generalized, although no uniform definition of compatibility is available. Instead, we may introduce the following abstract version.

DEFINITION 3.10. An extensional structure $\mathfrak{A}$: $[A, S_1, \ldots, S_m; R_1, \ldots, R_n, C^2, P^2]$ is a *unification structure* with *order* P and *compatibility relation* C if

1. C is symmetric and reflexive on non-atoms,
2. P is a partial order of non-atoms, and
3. If $C(a, b)$ then a and b have a least upper bound in P.

For example, taking $C(\sigma, \tau)$ iff σ and τ are compatible simple infons, and $P(\sigma, \tau)$ iff $\sigma \sqsubseteq \tau$, we see that information structures obeying Axiom 13.4 are unification structures.

For set structures, take P to be $\sqsubseteq$ and C to be the universal relation on Set^*. Then the unification of any two sets is just their union. For function structures with P taken to be the $\sqsubseteq$ order, let $C(f, g)$ iff there is no i in the domains of both f^* and g^* and such that $f^*(i) \neq g^*(i)$. The hereditary orders may also be used to define unification structures with weaker, hereditary compatibility relations.

The converse of unification, imposed by Axiom 13.3 in the case of simple information structures, has no clear generalization to arbitrary extensional structures, but may be applied to function structures as follows. A function structure $\mathfrak{A}$ is *downwards-complete* if for each function f and each set I there is a function g such that for each i and a, $\mathsf{App}(i, a, g)$ iff $\mathsf{App}(i, a, f)$ and $i \in I$.

3.4. Complex infons

We have seen that infons, sets and functions may all be modeled using extensional structures. In each of these cases, the identity conditions are relatively straightforward. In this section we consider structured objects with more complicated identity conditions.

Suppose we wish to have a binary operation of conjunction with the following properties:

(commutativity) $\sigma \wedge \tau = \tau \wedge \sigma$,
(associativity) $\sigma \wedge (\tau_1 \wedge \tau_2) = (\sigma \wedge \tau_1) \wedge \tau_2)$, and
(idempotence) $\sigma \wedge \sigma = \sigma$.

Suppose that we already have a stock of infons Σ in some information structure $\mathfrak{A}$ from which to form conjunctions. Our task is to extend $\mathfrak{A}$ with new elements and relations designed to capture the structure of the conjunctions.

The solution is to define a new binary structural relation ConjunctOf that holds between conjuncts and their conjunction. Using this relation we can define the operation of conjunction: given infons σ and τ, the conjunction $\sigma \wedge \tau$ is the least x in the $\sqsubseteq$ order such that $\mathsf{ConjunctOf}(\sigma, x)$ and $\mathsf{ConjunctOf}(\tau, x)$.

In other words, $\sigma \wedge \tau$ is the structurally smallest conjunction containing σ and τ as conjuncts. Defined this way, conjunction is clearly commutative. Additional properties of $\wedge$ may be imposed by careful construction of ConjunctOf. By way of example, we show that it is possible to extend an information structure either with a conjunction that is associative and idempotent, or with one that has neither of these properties.

CONSTRUCTION 3.1. Let $\mathfrak{A}$ be an extensional structure with a class Σ of non-atomic objects, which we call 'infons'. We shall define an extensional structure $\mathfrak{B}$ extending $\mathfrak{A}$ with new elements and a new binary structural relation ConjunctOf such that the conjunction $\wedge$ defined, as above, on objects in Σ is both associative and idempotent. Let $B_0 = 0 \times (|\mathfrak{A}| - \Sigma)$, $B_1 = 1 \times \mathrm{pow}(\Sigma)$, and for each $a \in |\mathfrak{A}|$ let

$$a^* = \begin{cases} \langle 0, a \rangle & \text{if } a \notin \Sigma, \\ \langle 1, \{a\} \rangle & \text{if } a \in \Sigma. \end{cases}$$

Now let $\mathfrak{B}$ be the structure with universe $B_0 \cup B_1$, and with

$$R(a_1^*, \ldots, a_n^*) \text{ in } \mathfrak{B} \quad \text{iff} \quad R(a_1, \ldots, a_n) \text{ in } \mathfrak{A}$$

for each primitive relation R of $\mathfrak{A}$ and

$$\mathsf{ConjunctOf}(\langle 1, x\rangle, \langle 1, y\rangle) \quad \text{iff} \quad x \subseteq y.$$

The new relation ConjunctOf is treated as a structural relation of $\mathfrak{B}$ so we must check that $\mathfrak{B}$ is extensional.[18] The binary conjunction $\wedge$ is defined, as above, for all 'infons', which in this case refers to those objects in B_1. Now for any $x, y \subseteq \Sigma$, it is easily checked that $\langle 1, x\rangle \wedge \langle 1, y\rangle = \langle 1, x \cup y\rangle$. Thus conjunction is both idempotent and associative in $\mathfrak{B}$.

CONSTRUCTION 3.2. For the second construction, let $\mathfrak{A}$ and Σ be as before. Let $\Sigma_1 = \{1\} \times \mathrm{pow}(\{0\} \times \Sigma)$, $\Sigma_{(n+1)} = \Sigma_n \cup \{1\} \times \mathrm{pow}\, \Sigma_n$, and $\Sigma^* = \bigcup_{n=1}^{\omega} \Sigma_n$. Now let $\mathfrak{B}$ be the structure with universe $\Sigma^* \cup \{0\} \times |\mathfrak{A}|$, and with

$$R(\langle 0, a_1\rangle, \ldots, \langle 0, a_n\rangle) \text{ in } \mathfrak{B} \quad \text{iff} \quad R(a_1, \ldots, a_n), \text{ in } \mathfrak{A}$$

for each primitive relation R of $\mathfrak{A}$, and

$$\mathsf{ConjunctOf}(x, \langle 1, y\rangle) \quad \text{iff} \quad x \in y.$$

Again we must check that $\mathfrak{B}$ is extensional. The proof requires the notion of the 'rank' of an element of $|\mathfrak{B}|$. An element $b \in |\mathfrak{B}|$ is of rank 0 if $b = \langle 0, a\rangle$ for some $a \in |\mathfrak{A}|$ and is of rank $n > 0$ if $b \in \Sigma_n$ but $b \notin \Sigma_m$ for each $m < n$. We show that if a is bisimilar to b then $a = b$, by induction on the maximum of the ranks of a and b.[19] The 'infons' of $\mathfrak{B}$ are those objects of non-zero rank together with those objects of the form $\langle 0, x\rangle$ for

[18] If a is bisimilar to b then $a = \langle i, a_0\rangle$, $b = \langle j, b_0\rangle$ for some a_0 and b_0. First observe that $i = j$. For if $i \neq j$, say $i = 0$ and $j = 1$, then b_0 is a subset of Σ, and so $\mathsf{ConjunctOf}(\langle 1, \emptyset\rangle, b)$ whereas there is no x such that $\mathsf{ConjunctOf}(x, a)$, and this contradicts the assumption that a is bisimilar to b. In the case that $i = j = 0$, a_0 is bisimilar to b_0 in $\mathfrak{A}$, so $a_0 = b_0$ by the extensionality of $\mathfrak{A}$, and so $a = b$. And if $i = j = 1$ then for every $x \in a_0$, there is a $b_1 \subseteq b_0$ such that $\langle 1, \{x\}\rangle$ is bisimilar to $\langle 1, b_1\rangle$. Then for each $y \in b_1$, $\langle 1, \{y\}\rangle$ is bisimilar to $\langle 1, \{x\}\rangle$ – it cannot be bisimilar to $\langle 1, \emptyset\rangle$, the only other conjunct of $\langle 1, \{x\}\rangle$. But then either x and y are atoms of $\mathfrak{A}$, which is ruled out because $x, y \in \Sigma$, or x is bisimilar to y in $\mathfrak{A}$ and so $x = y$ by the extensionality of $\mathfrak{A}$. Thus $b_1 = \{x\}$ and so $a_0 \subseteq b_0$. By a symmetrical argument, it can be shown that $b_0 \subseteq a_0$, so $a_0 = b_0$ and so $a = b$.

[19] Suppose that a is bisimilar to b. There are three cases: (i) both x and y have rank 0; (ii) one of x or y has rank 0 and the other has rank greater than 0; and (iii) both x and y have ranks greater than 0. Case (i) is the base of the induction. In this case, $a = \langle 0, x\rangle$ and $b = \langle 0, y\rangle$ for some x and y, so x is bisimilar to y in $\mathfrak{A}$, so $x = y$ by the extensionality of $\mathfrak{A}$, and so $a = b$. Case (ii) is impossible. Suppose, for example, that $a = \langle 0, x\rangle$ and $b = \langle 1, y\rangle$. Then either y is empty, making b an atom of $\mathfrak{B}$ and so only bisimilar to itself, or y has an element y' and so $\mathsf{ConjunctOf}(y', b)$. There is no x' such that $\mathsf{ConjunctOf}(x', a)$, and so (ii) contradicts the assumption that a is bisimilar to b. Case (iii) is the inductive case. We may suppose that $a = \langle 1, x\rangle$ and $b = \langle 1, y\rangle$ for some x and y. Then for each $x' \in x$ there is a $y' \in y$ such that x' is bisimilar to y'. But the ranks of x' and y' are strictly less than those of x and y respectively, and so by the inductive hypothesis, $x' = y'$. Thus $x \subseteq y$, and by a similar argument $y \subseteq x$, so $x = y$, and so $a = b$.

which $x \in \Sigma$. It is easy to check that $a \wedge b = \langle 1, \{a, b\}\rangle$ and so conjunction is neither idempotent nor associative.

Both constructions give a commutative conjunction. In fact, commutativity follows from the definition of $\wedge$ from ConjunctOf. To get a non-commutative conjunction, we would need use different structural relations. For a non-associative, non-commutative conjunction we could use two binary structural relations, say, $\mathsf{ConjunctOf}_1$ and $\mathsf{ConjunctOf}_2$, with $\wedge$ defined such that $\mathsf{ConjunctOf}_1(\sigma, \sigma \wedge \tau)$ and $\mathsf{ConjunctOf}_2(\tau, \sigma \wedge \tau)$. For an associative, non-commutative conjunction, we could use a ternary structural relation $\mathsf{ConjunctOf}_*$, with integer roles, and $\wedge$ defined so that $\mathsf{ConjunctOf}_*(i, \sigma_i, (\sigma_1 \wedge \cdots \wedge \sigma_n))$.

The goal of defining a structural notion of conjunction is to capture those properties of conjunctive information that are immediately available to anyone receiving the information, without further reflection on the significance of the information itself. For this reason, conjunctive information represented in different forms may best be modeled by different conjunctions. For example, information about the relative heights of Indiana's Hoosiers may be conveyed in a list of sentences of the form 'x is taller than y', or by a team photograph. In the former case, the information conveyed may best be represented by a non-commutative, associative conjunction; in the latter case, a commutative, associative conjunction would be preferable.

Similar issues affect the choice of structural relations for modeling other complex infons such as disjunctions and conditionals. Negations may be modeled as complex infons, or as basic infons as indicated in Section 2.4. Constructions almost identical to Constructions 3.1 and 3.2 may be used for disjunctions. We simply re-name 'ConjunctOf' as 'DisjunctOf' and '$\wedge$' as '$\vee$' throughout. This further underlines the point that the issues are structural, not logical. Definitions of several kinds of structures having complex infons are given in Section 3.6, below.

The question of how to represent quantifiers is even more vexed (Robin Cooper, 1991; Richard Cooper, 1991). One approach is to use infinitary conjunctions and disjunctions. In Constructions 3.1 and 3.2 we may define an infinitary conjunction: given a set X of infons, the conjunction $\bigwedge X$ is the least x in the $\sqsubseteq$ order such that $\mathsf{ConjunctOf}(\sigma, x)$ for each $\sigma \in X$. This operation $\bigwedge$ has similar properties to the corresponding binary conjunction. In the structure defined in Construction 3.1 it is both associative an idempotent, but in that of Construction 3.2 it is neither.

Another approach is to model a quantified infon as a pair $\langle Q, \lambda x.\sigma\rangle$, in which Q is a quantifier and $\lambda x.\sigma$ is a 'infon-abstract'. We shall discuss abstracts in Section 3.7.

3.5. Substitution

In any extensional structure there is a well-defined operation of substitution. The following definition is influenced by the treatment of substitution in (Aczel, 1990) and (Aczel and Lunnon, 1991).

DEFINITION 3.11. Let $\mathfrak{A}$ be an extensional structure of type $[A, S_1, \ldots, S_m; R_1, \ldots, R_n]$. A function f is a *substitution* in $\mathfrak{A}$ if its arguments and values are all elements of A.

Given a substitution f, a binary relation E on A is an *f-simulation* if for all $a, b \in A$, if $E(a,b)$ then $b = f(a)$ if a is in the domain of f, and if a is not in the domain of f then

1. if a is atomic then $a = b$,
2. for $1 \leqslant i \leqslant m$, if S_i is of arity k then for all $x_1, \ldots, x_k$ such that $S_i(x_1, \ldots, x_k, a)$, there are $y_1, \ldots, y_k$ such that $S_i(y_1, \ldots, y_k, b)$, and $E(x_j, y_j)$ for $1 \leqslant j \leqslant k$, and
3. for $1 \leqslant i \leqslant m$, if S_i is of arity k then for all $y_1, \ldots, y_k$ such that $S_i(y_1, \ldots, y_k, b)$, there are $x_1, \ldots, x_k$ such that $S_i(x_1, \ldots, x_k, a)$, and $E(x_j, y_j)$ for $1 \leqslant j \leqslant k$.

b is *f-similar* to a in $\mathfrak{A}$ if there is an f-simulation E of $\mathfrak{A}$ such that $E(a,b)$. For a given f and a, there need not be an element of $\mathfrak{A}$ that is f-similar to a, but if there is one then there is only one, by the extensionality of $\mathfrak{A}$. We write $f.a$ for the unique element f-similar to a, should it exist. An extensional structure is a *substitution structure* if $f.a$ exists for every f and a.

For example, suppose that there are solutions to the equations

$$\begin{aligned}
v &= \langle\!\langle r; a, b\rangle\!\rangle,\\
w &= \langle\!\langle r; b, b\rangle\!\rangle,\\
x &= \langle\!\langle r; y, a\rangle\!\rangle,\\
y &= \langle\!\langle r; x, b\rangle\!\rangle,\\
z &= \langle\!\langle r; z, b\rangle\!\rangle,
\end{aligned}$$

in an extensional information structure $\mathfrak{A}$. Let $[a \mapsto b]$ be the function with domain $\{a\}$ such that $[a \mapsto b](a) = b$, and let E be the relation with graph

$$\{\langle v, w\rangle, \langle x, z\rangle, \langle y, z\rangle, \langle a, b\rangle\} \cup I_{\{b,r,z\}},$$

where $I_{\{b,r,z\}}$ is the identity relation on $\{b, r, z\}$. It is easy to check that E is an $[a \mapsto b]$-simulation on $\mathfrak{A}$, and so $[a \mapsto b].v = w$ and $[a \mapsto b].x = [a \mapsto b].y = z$.

Set structures are substitution structures, by the set-theoretic Axiom of Replacement, if they also satisfy either Foundation or Anti-Foundation. A simple information structure satisfying Axioms A7 (finite roles) and A10.2 (extensionality) is a substitution structure if and only if it satisfies the generality principle given in Axiom A11.1. The weaker principle of sortal generality, given by Axiom A11.2, is not sufficient. Nonetheless, all extensional structures are at least *partial* substitution structures and we can interpret the non-existence of $f.a$ as the inappropriateness of the substitution f for a.[20]

Next, we prove a result that shows us how to extend an arbitrary extensional structure to a substitution structure.

THEOREM 3.2. *Every anti-founded extensional structure is a substitution structure.*

[20] An interesting, weaker, substitutional property of extensional structures is as follows: if $f.a$ and $g.a$ both exist and f and g are compatible functions then $(f \sqcup g).a$ also exists. This is implied by sortal generality if the domains of f and g do not contain roles.

PROOF. Suppose that $\mathfrak{A}$ is an anti-founded extensional structure of type $[A, S_1, \ldots, S_m; R_1, \ldots, R_n]$ and that f is a substitution in $\mathfrak{A}$. Let X be the set $\{x_a : a \text{ a non-atom of } \mathfrak{A}\}$. We consider a structural description $T = \{T(x)\}_{x \in X}$, using x as the set of parameters.

For a non-atom a, $T(x_a)$ is obtained from the canonical description T_a. For each $\langle S, b_1, \ldots, b_k\rangle$ that holds in $\mathfrak{A}$, let $y_i = f(b_i)$ if b_i is in the domain of f and let $y_i = x_{b_i}$ if b_i is not in the domain of f. We put the corresponding tuple $\langle S, y_1, \ldots, y_k\rangle$ into $T(x_a)$. This defines the structural description T.

Since $\mathfrak{A}$ is anti-founded, let s satisfy T in $\mathfrak{A}$. For each $a \in \mathfrak{A}$, the construction has ensured that $s(x_a)$ is f-similar to a. This proves that $f.a$ exists. □

As an immediate corollary of Theorem 3.2 and Theorem 3.1, we see that every extensional may be extended to a substitution structure.

3.6. *Infon structures*

We are now in a position to improve our model of infons in a way that allows for the smooth incorporation of complex infons and a uniform treatment of abstraction (to be given in Section 3.7). An advantage of the models used in Section 2 – the 'simple information structures' – is their simplicity; they have only two structural relations. But there are disadvantages. First, the predicate 'infon', as applied to these structures, is defined in a way that presupposes that infons have a simple structure. This makes the move to structures containing complex infons a bit awkward. Second, the functions associating objects to roles in the infons of a simple information structure are not *internal* functions. This complicates the treatment of substitution and abstraction.

Now that we know how to represent the structure of functions using function structures, we can solve this problem. The basic idea is to represent the infon $\sigma = \langle\!\langle r; i : a, j : b, k : c\rangle\!\rangle$ as a pair consisting of the relation r and an internal function α with domain $\{i, j, k\}$ and such that $\alpha^*(i) = a$, $\alpha^*(j) = b$, and $\alpha^*(k) = c$. The function α is called the *assignment* of σ. We adapt the functional notation for use with assignments and write

$$\alpha = [i : a, j : b, k : c] \quad \text{and} \quad \sigma = \langle\!\langle r; \alpha\rangle\!\rangle.$$

The structure of infons can now be represented using three structural relations, Rel^2, Ass^2 and Inf^1, and one non-structural relation, Approp^1. $\mathsf{Inf}(\sigma)$ iff σ is an infon; $\mathsf{Rel}(r, \sigma)$ and $\mathsf{Ass}(\alpha, \sigma)$ iff $\sigma = \langle\!\langle r; \alpha\rangle\!\rangle$. An assignment $\alpha = [i : a, j : b, k : c]$ is represented as an internal function, so that $\mathsf{Fun}(\alpha)$ and $\mathsf{App}(i, a, \alpha)$, and α is appropriate iff $\mathsf{Approp}(\alpha)$.

DEFINITION 3.12. A function structure of type $[\mathfrak{A}, \mathsf{Ass}^2, \mathsf{Rel}^2, \mathsf{Inf}^1; \mathsf{Approp}^1]$ is an *infon structure* if it satisfies the following conditions:

1. (sorts) $\mathsf{Ass}^* \subseteq \mathsf{Inf}^*$, $\mathsf{Rel}^* \subseteq \mathsf{Inf}^*$, and $\mathsf{Fun}^* \cap \mathsf{Inf}^* = \emptyset$,
2. (basic infons) if $\mathsf{Rel}(r, \sigma)$ then $\exists\alpha\ \mathsf{Ass}(\alpha, \sigma)$,
3. (appropriateness) $\mathsf{Approp}(\alpha)$ iff $\exists\sigma\ \mathsf{Ass}(\alpha, \sigma)$, and
4. (substitution) if $\mathsf{Ass}(\alpha, \sigma)$ and if f is substitution such that $f.\alpha$ exists and $\mathsf{Approp}(f.\alpha)$, then $f.\sigma$ also exists.

An infon σ is *basic* if there is an α such that $\mathsf{Ass}(\alpha, \sigma)$. An infon structure is a *basic-infon structure* if every infon is basic. An object r is a *relation* if $\mathsf{Rel}(r, \sigma)$ for some σ; i is a *role* of σ if $\mathsf{App}(i, a, \alpha)$ and $\mathsf{Ass}(\alpha, \sigma)$ for some a; and an object is *ordinary* if it is neither an infon, a function, a role, nor a relation.

Clause 3 (appropriateness) links the appropriateness of an assignment to the existence of an infon with that assignment. If, for example, there is no infon in which a fills the role i then there is no α in Fun^* such that $\mathsf{Approp}(\alpha)$ and $\alpha^*(i) = a$. This is a generalization of the treatment of appropriateness in information structures. Clause 3.12 (substitution) ensures that the only issue governing substitution of infons is the appropriateness of the resulting assignment. This is an abstract form of the various principles of generality discussed in Section 2.7. To go further, we must look at the unification structure of appropriate assignments.

DEFINITION 3.13. A unification structure is an *infon unification structure* if it is an infon structure that satisfies the following conditions.

1. (Flatness) P is the 'flat' order: for every x and y, $P(x, y)$ iff $x \sqsubseteq y$.
2. (Function compatibility) If $\mathsf{Fun}(\alpha_1)$ and $\mathsf{Fun}(\alpha_2)$ then $C(\alpha_1, \alpha_2)$ iff the functions α_1^* and α_2^* agree, that is to say for every i, a and b, if $\mathsf{App}(i, a, \alpha_1)$ and $\mathsf{App}(i, b, \alpha_2)$ then $a = b$.
3. (Infon compatibility) If $\mathsf{Ass}(\alpha_1, \sigma_1)$, $\mathsf{Ass}(\alpha_2, \sigma_2)$, $\mathsf{Rel}(r_1, \sigma_1)$, and $\mathsf{Rel}(r_1, \sigma_1)$, then $C(\sigma_1, \sigma_2)$ iff $r_1 = r_2$ and $C(\alpha_1, \alpha_2)$.
4. (Unification of appropriate assignments) If $C(\alpha_1, \alpha_2)$, $\mathsf{Approp}(\alpha_1)$ and $\mathsf{Approp}(\alpha_2)$, then $\mathsf{Approp}(\alpha_1 \sqcup \alpha_2)$.

Infon unification structures give us our best theory of appropriateness. Clause 4 ensures that the appropriateness of assignments depends only on 'local' issues: if α_1 and α_2 are compatible appropriate assignments then so is $\alpha_1 \sqcup \alpha_2$; no additional grounds for inappropriateness can be introduced. Moreover, by clause 4 (substitution) of the definition of infon structures, substitutions that result in appropriate assignments may always be used to obtain new infons.

For example, given an infon $\sigma = \langle\langle r; \alpha \rangle\rangle$ and an assignment $\alpha = [i : a, j : b, k : c]$, let f be the function with domain $\{a, b\}$ such that $f(a) = x$ and $f(b) = y$, and let g be the function with domain $\{b, c\}$ such that $g(b) = y$ and $f(c) = z$. Suppose that $f.\alpha$ and $g.\alpha$ exist and are appropriate. Then $\mathsf{Approp}([i : x, j : y, k : c])$ and $\mathsf{Approp}([i : a, j : y, k : z])$, and so $[i : x, j : y, k : z]$ is an appropriate assignment (by unification of appropriate assignments) and the infon $f.\sigma = \langle\langle r; i : x, j : y, k : z \rangle\rangle$ exists (by substitution).

The implicit theory of appropriateness is still weaker than that given by the principle of sortal generality, according to which appropriateness is dependent only on restrictions applying to individual roles. Infon unification structures may restrict related roles, such as those discussed in the example of next-to at the send of Section 2.7. If next-to has roles nt_1 and nt_2, then we may deem assignments of the form $[\mathsf{nt}_1 : x, \mathsf{nt}_2 : x]$ inappropriate, without jeopardizing the unification principle. To obtain the principle of sortal generality we must insist that the structure is also downwards-complete and that appropriateness is inherited by parts: if $\mathsf{Approp}(\alpha_1)$ and $\alpha_2 \sqsubseteq \alpha_1$ then $\mathsf{Approp}(\alpha_2)$.

The second feature of infon structures not present in simple information structures, is the unary structural relation Inf. We say that σ is a *basic infon* if $\mathsf{Ass}(\alpha, \sigma)$ for some assignment α – by clause 2 of Definition 3.11 (basic infons) all infons having a relation are required to have an assignment, possibly the empty assignment [ ]. In simple information structures, by definition of the term 'infon', all infons are basic, but in infon structures we may have non-basic infons. Of course, by extensionality and clause 1 (sorts), if there are no more structural relations in $\mathfrak{A}$ then there is at most one non-basic infon. If there are more structural relations, such as $\mathsf{ConjunctOf}$, then we can add the axiom that $\mathsf{ConjunctOf}^* \subseteq \mathsf{Inf}^*$ without contradicting the axioms for infon structures.

This is a good example of how the 'holistic' nature of the extensionality property, which quantifies over *all* structural relations, allows a modular approach to the theory of structured objects. Another example is the treatment of polarity, discussed in Section 2.4. We need only add new structural relations to deal with polarity and the extensionality condition takes care of the rest.

DEFINITION 3.14. An infon structure of type $[\mathfrak{A}, \mathsf{Pos}^1, \mathsf{Neg}^1;]$ is *bi-polar* if it satisfies the following conditions:

1. σ is a basic infon iff either $\mathsf{Pos}(\sigma)$ or $\mathsf{Neg}(\sigma)$, and
2. if $\mathsf{Pos}(\sigma)$ then not $\mathsf{Neg}(\sigma)$.

Infons in Pos^* are *positive* and those in Neg^* are *negative*.[21]

Finite conjunctions and disjunctions are introduced effortlessly, as follows:

DEFINITION 3.15. An infon structure of type $[\mathfrak{A}, \mathsf{ConjunctOf}^2, \mathsf{DisjunctOf}^2;]$ is $\wedge\vee$*-closed* if it satisfies the following conditions:

1. $\mathsf{ConjunctOf}^* \subseteq \mathsf{Inf}^*$ and $\mathsf{DisjunctOf}^* \subseteq \mathsf{Inf}^*$,
2. if $\mathsf{Inf}(\sigma)$ and $\mathsf{Inf}(\tau)$ then there is a $\sqsubseteq$-minimal object $\sigma \wedge \tau$ such that $\mathsf{ConjunctOf}(\sigma, \sigma \wedge \tau)$ and $\mathsf{ConjunctOf}(\tau, \sigma \wedge \tau)$,
3. if $\mathsf{Inf}(\sigma)$ and $\mathsf{Inf}(\tau)$ then there is a $\sqsubseteq$-minimal object $\sigma \vee \tau$ such that $\mathsf{DisjunctOf}(\sigma, \sigma \vee \tau)$ and $\mathsf{DisjunctOf}(\tau, \sigma \vee \tau)$.

The principles of existence for infinite conjunctions and disjunctions are similar. We would like to say that for each set X of infons there is a conjunction $\bigwedge X$ and a disjunction $\bigvee X$ but this would be ambiguous. We must choose whether X is to be an internal or an external set. Here we follow the former, more cautious approach.

DEFINITION 3.16. An infon structure of type $[\mathfrak{A}, \mathsf{Set}^1, \in^2, \mathsf{ConjunctOf}^2, \mathsf{DisjunctOf}^2;]$ is $\bigwedge\bigvee$*-closed* if it is also a set structure, and

1. $\mathsf{ConjunctOf}^* \subseteq \mathsf{Inf}^*$ and $\mathsf{DisjunctOf}^* \subseteq \mathsf{Inf}^*$,
2. if $\mathsf{Set}(X)$ and $\mathsf{Inf}(\sigma)$ for each σ such that $\in(\sigma, X)$, then there is a $\sqsubseteq$-minimal object $\bigwedge X$ such that $\mathsf{ConjunctOf}(\sigma, \bigwedge X)$ for each σ such that $\in(\sigma, X)$, and

[21] For *bi-polar infon unification structures* we must modify clause 3 of the definition of infon unification structures to take polarity into account:

3′. If $\mathsf{Ass}(\alpha_1, \sigma_1)$, $\mathsf{Ass}(\alpha_2, \sigma_2)$, $\mathsf{Rel}(r_1, \sigma_1)$, and $\mathsf{Rel}(r_1, \sigma_1)$, then $C(\sigma_1, \sigma_2)$ iff $r_1 = r_2$, $C(\alpha_1, \alpha_2)$, and $\mathsf{Pos}(\sigma_1) \leftrightarrow \mathsf{Pos}(\sigma_2)$.

3. if $\mathsf{Set}(X)$ and $\mathsf{Inf}(\sigma)$ for each σ such that $\in(\sigma, X)$, then there is a $\sqsubseteq$-minimal object $\bigvee X$ such that $\mathsf{DisjunctOf}(\sigma, \bigvee X)$ for each σ such that $\in(\sigma, X)$.

Every $\bigwedge\bigvee$-closed infon structure is also $\wedge\vee$-closed because for infons σ and τ there is an internal set X with $X^* = \{\sigma, \tau\}$ and so $\sigma \wedge \tau = \bigwedge X$; and similarly for disjunction. The precise algebraic structure of $\bigwedge$ and $\bigvee$ is not determined by this definition; they may be associative and idempotent or not – see Section 3.4.

Negations may be modeled using a structural relation NegOf^2 with the following existence condition: if $\mathsf{Inf}(\sigma)$ then there is a unique object $\neg\sigma$ such that $\mathsf{NegOf}(\sigma, \neg\sigma)$. Another approach is to start with a bi-polar infon structure and treat NegOf^2 as a *non-structural* relation defined as follows:

DEFINITION 3.17. A bi-polar infon structure of type $[\mathfrak{A}; \mathsf{NegOf}]$ is a *de Morgan infon structure* if it is $\bigwedge\bigvee$-closed and satisfies the following conditions:
1. if $\mathsf{NegOf}(\sigma, \tau)$ then $\mathsf{Inf}(\sigma)$ and $\mathsf{Inf}(\tau)$,
2. if $\mathsf{NegOf}(\sigma, \tau)$ and $\mathsf{NegOf}(\sigma, \tau')$ then $\tau = \tau'$,
3. if $\mathsf{NegOf}(\sigma, \tau)$ then $\mathsf{NegOf}(\tau, \sigma)$,
4. if $\mathsf{Rel}(r, \sigma)$ and $\mathsf{Arg}(\alpha, \sigma)$ then there is an infon $\neg\sigma \neq \sigma$ such that $\mathsf{NegOf}(\sigma, \neg\sigma)$ $\mathsf{Rel}(r, \neg\sigma)$ and $\mathsf{Arg}(\alpha, \neg\sigma)$, and
5. if $\mathsf{Set}(X)$, $\mathsf{Set}(Y)$ and
   (a) for each $\sigma \in X^*$ there is a $\tau \in Y^*$ such that $\mathsf{NegOf}(\sigma, \tau)$,
   (b) for each $\tau \in Y^*$ there is a $\sigma \in X^*$ such that $\mathsf{NegOf}(\sigma, \tau)$,
then $\mathsf{NegOf}(\bigwedge X, \bigvee Y)$.[22]

A remaining question is how to distinguish between saturated and unsaturated infons in infon structures. In basic-infon structures, the answer is clear from the discussion in Section 2.8: saturated basic infons are those that are maximal in the $\sqsubseteq$-ordering. For complex infons, it is not so easy. In a $\wedge\vee$-closed infon structure, if σ and τ are distinct basic infon then $\sigma \sqsubseteq \sigma \wedge \tau$ and so σ is not maximal, no matter how many roles are filled. We decide the matter as follows.

DEFINITION 3.18. In an infon structure, an infon is *saturated* if it is the largest class $S \subseteq \mathsf{Inf}^*$ such that for each infon σ in S,
1. if σ is basic and $\sigma \sqsubseteq \tau$ then $\sigma = \tau$, and
2. if σ is non-basic then every infon component of σ is also in S.

By now, the reader will have an impression of some of the possibilities for modeling basic and complex infons using the theory of structural relations. Observers of the development of Situation Theory have been somewhat frustrated because of the lack of consensus on which structures – or even on which kinds of structures, obeying which axioms – are to be chosen for the theory (see Barwise, 1989a). We will see other reasons for diversity in Section 4, but the basic reason is clear from the above: logical and structural properties of infons are separate but interdependent, and striking the right balance is a difficult matter.

---

[22] No mention is made of polarities here, but from the definition of bi-polar infon structures we know that if σ is a basic infon then it is either positive or negative but not both, and from clause 4, $\sigma \neq \neg\sigma$; so if σ is positive then $\neg\sigma$ is negative, and vice versa.

3.7. Abstraction

Abstraction is a natural operation in semantics. By abstracting Paul from the information σ that Raymond cooked the omelette for Paul, we obtain the property of being someone for whom Raymond cooked the omelette. By abstracting both Paul and the omelette from σ, we obtain the relation that holds between x and y just in case Raymond cooked x for y. This relation and the previous property differ from the relations and properties we have considered so far in that they are not atomic. In this section we see how infon structures can be used to model these complex relations.[23]

There are two parts to abstraction over a structural object: the object after abstraction, which contains 'holes' where the abstracted object used to be, and something indicating where the holes are, so that subsequently they may be filled in. We call these the 'abstract' and the 'pointer', respectively.[24] The relationship between abstract and pointer may be captured by a binary structural relation Abs with $\mathsf{Abs}(a, x)$ meaning that x is a pointer to the abstract a.

DEFINITION 3.19. An *abstraction structure* is an extensional structure with structural relation Abs^2 such that if $\mathsf{Abs}(a, x)$ and $\mathsf{Abs}(a', x)$ then $a = a'$. The objects of sort Abs^* are called *pointers*. If $\mathsf{Abs}(a, x)$ then x is said to *point* to the *abstract* a.

The objects of interest in abstraction structures are the abstracts, but they do not form a structural sort; rather, it is the pointers that are structurally determined. The intention is that each pointer x of an abstract a is a hereditary component of a. We obtain the results of 'applying' an abstract a to some argument b by substituting b for a pointer x in a. To see how this achieves the desired effect we must consider how abstracts arise by abstraction from other objects in the domain.

Suppose, for example, that we want to abstract b from the infon $\sigma = \langle\!\langle r; i:b, j:c \rangle\!\rangle$. We would expect to obtain an abstract a with exactly one pointer x such that the result of substituting b for x in a is just σ. Furthermore, the result of substituting b' for x in a should be the infon $\langle\!\langle r; i:b', j:c \rangle\!\rangle$, if this infon exists. This is captured in the following definition.

DEFINITION 3.20. Suppose $\mathfrak{A}$ is an abstraction structure. Given elements a and b in $|\mathfrak{A}|$, an abstract $\lambda b.a$ is *the abstraction of* b *from* a if there is an x such that

1. $[b \mapsto x].a = \lambda b.a$,
2. $\mathsf{Abs}(\lambda b.a, x)$, and
3. the only sort of x is Abs^*.

The definite article is justified in the above definition because if $\mathsf{Abs}([b \mapsto x].a, x)$ and $\mathsf{Abs}([b \mapsto y].a, y)$ then, by extensionality, $x = y$. For example, if $\sigma = \langle\!\langle r; i:b, j:c \rangle\!\rangle$

[23] In Situation Theory, abstraction has been treated as a structural operation, and here we shall attempt to model it using structural relations. This goes against the dominant trend in semantics, which is to use functional types in a type theory described by means of the lambda-calculus (see Chapter 9, this volume). Interestingly, Lunnon (to appear), building on the work of Aczel and Lunnon, integrates these two approaches.

[24] Pointers are often called 'indeterminates' and 'parameters'; but that description of them is bad for the philosopher's digestion, and leaves a sour taste on the metaphysical palate.

and $\lambda b.\sigma$ exists, then there is an x such that $\mathsf{Abs}(\langle\!\langle r; i:x, j:c\rangle\!\rangle, x)$. But suppose there was a y such that $\mathsf{Abs}(\langle\!\langle r; i:y, j:c\rangle\!\rangle, y)$. Since Abs is the only structural relation determining x and y, they are obviously bisimilar and so equal. A similar argument shows that $\lambda b.\langle\!\langle r; i:b, j:c\rangle\!\rangle = \lambda b'.\langle\!\langle r; i:b', j:c\rangle\!\rangle$, assuming that b and b' are not hereditary components of r, i, j, or c. This is the expected principle of α-equivalence.

Notice also that under similar assumptions the order of abstraction is insignificant. If, for example, b and c are both atomic then $\lambda c.\lambda b.\langle\!\langle r; i:b, j:c\rangle\!\rangle = \lambda b.\lambda c.\langle\!\langle r; i:b, j:c\rangle\!\rangle$. In both cases, the abstract obtained has two pointers, pointing to the positions previously occupied by b and c respectively, but there nothing to distinguish the pointers apart from that, and so no trace of the order in which the abstraction was performed. This motivates a slightly more general notion of abstraction.

DEFINITION 3.21. Suppose $\mathfrak{A}$ is an abstraction structure. Given an element a of $|\mathfrak{A}|$ and a set B of elements of $|\mathfrak{A}|$, an abstract $\Lambda B.a$ is *the simultaneous abstraction of B from a* if there is an injective function $\pi : B \to |\mathfrak{A}|$ called the *pointer function* such that

1. $\pi.a = \Lambda B.a$,
2. $\mathsf{Abs}(\pi.a, \pi(b))$ for each $b \in B$, and
3. for each $b \in B$, the only sort of $\pi(b)$ is Abs^*.

Despite the previous observation about commuting lambdas, one should be careful to distinguish simultaneous abstraction from successive abstractions. When the elements of B are structurally dependent, the results obtained may differ (see Aczel and Lunnon, 1991); Ruhrberg, 1996). For example, if $\sigma = \langle\!\langle r; \tau_1, \tau_2\rangle\!\rangle$, $\tau_1 = \langle\!\langle s; \tau_2, a\rangle\!\rangle$, and $\tau_2 = \langle\!\langle s; \tau_1, b\rangle\!\rangle$ then

1. $\lambda\tau_1.\lambda\tau_2.\sigma = \langle\!\langle r; \langle\!\langle s; x, a\rangle\!\rangle, x\rangle\!\rangle$ with pointer x,
2. $\lambda\tau_2.\lambda\tau_1.\sigma = \langle\!\langle r; y, \langle\!\langle s; y, b\rangle\!\rangle\rangle\!\rangle$ with pointer y, and
3. $\Lambda\{\tau_1, \tau_2\}.\sigma = \langle\!\langle r; z_1, z_2\rangle\!\rangle$ with pointers z_1 and z_2.

Nonetheless, it is clear that simultaneous abstraction is a generalization of abstraction because $\lambda b.a = \Lambda\{b\}.a$.

We have already observed that abstraction obeys an identity principle analogous to α-equivalence in the λ-calculus, at least in special cases. To state the general result observe that if $\sigma = \langle\!\langle r; b, c\rangle\!\rangle$ and $\sigma' = \langle\!\langle r; b', c\rangle\!\rangle$ and b and b' are structurally independent then $[b \mapsto b'].\sigma = \sigma'$ and $[b' \mapsto b].\sigma' = \sigma$. These are the conditions needed to show that the two abstracts are bisimilar and so justify the claim that $\lambda b.\sigma = \lambda b'.\sigma'$. We state, without proof, the generalization of this result.

THEOREM 3.3 (α-identity). *If $\Lambda B.a$ and $\Lambda B'.a'$ exist in an abstraction structure and there is a one-to-one correspondence f between B and B' such that $f.a = a'$ and $f^{-1}.a' = a$ then $\Lambda B.a = \Lambda B'.a'$.*

We now show that extensional structures with abstraction really exist.

DEFINITION 3.22. An abstraction structure $\mathfrak{A}$ is a *Lambda structure* if for every element a of $|\mathfrak{A}|$ and a set B of elements of $|\mathfrak{A}|$, the simultaneous abstraction $\Lambda B.a$ exists.

THEOREM 3.4. *Every extensional structure can be extended to a Lambda structure.*

PROOF. Given an extensional structure $\mathfrak{A}$, extend it trivially to an abstraction structure by adding the structural relation Abs^2 with an empty extension. By Theorem 3.1 this can be extended to an anti-founded structure $\mathfrak{B}_0$. Throw away all pointers in this structure that point to more than one abstract to obtain an abstraction structure $\mathfrak{B}$. We show that $\mathfrak{B}$ contains a Lambda structure extending $\mathfrak{A}$. Suppose a is an element of $|\mathfrak{B}|$ and B is a set of elements of $|\mathfrak{B}|$. We exhibit a structural description whose satisfier gives the needed element $\lambda B.a$. For each $b \in B$, let $T_b = \{\langle \mathsf{Abs}, a\rangle\}$. Let H be the set of hereditary components of a that are not in B, and for each $c \in H$, let T_c be the canonical description of c in $\mathfrak{B}$. Now the structural description we want is $T = \{T_x\}_{x \in B \cup H}$. Since $\mathfrak{B}$ is contained in an anti-founded structure, there is a function s mapping into $\mathfrak{B}_0$ that satisfies T. But, clearly, the range of s does not contain any of the elements we threw away, so s maps into $\mathfrak{B}$. Thus for each b in B, $s(b)$ satisfies the description $s.T_b = \{\langle \mathsf{Abs}, s.a\rangle\}$ and so $\mathsf{Abs}(s.a, s(b))$. Moreover, $s(b)$ is only of sort Abs^*, and so $s.a$ is the required abstract $\Lambda B.a$. □

A short digression on the ontology of abstracts is in order. If σ is an infon with argument b then $\lambda b.\sigma$ is also of sort Inf^*. But, intuitively, it is a property not an infon. Moreover, it has a pointer as an argument, filling the role left by b, and so interfering with whatever implicit appropriateness conditions there may have been on this role. It is therefore useful to distinguish between genuine infons and these new entities, which we may call *infon abstracts*. Infon abstracts are just properties (or relations if they have more than one pointer) and so ontologically acceptable. That is not quite the end of the matter. Consider the infon $\tau = \langle\langle r, \sigma\rangle\rangle$ and the abstract $\lambda b.\tau$ with pointer x. The abstract $\lambda b.\tau$ is an infon abstract, not a genuine infon. But it has an argument $[b \mapsto x].\sigma$ that is also of sort Inf^* but neither an infon abstract nor, intuitively, a genuine infon. The only reasonable position to adopt is that $[b \mapsto x].\sigma$ is a *part* of an abstract. Fortunately, it is easily determined which abstract it is a part of, because the pointer x points to it. In this way, we may satisfy ourselves that no unexpected ontological categories have been created.[25]

3.8. *Application*

In the previous section we saw that an extensional structure may be extended with abstracts of the form $\Lambda B.a$, obtained by abstracting the elements of B from the object a. The purpose of these abstracts is to model generalizations across a class of structured objects. In particular, infon abstracts may be used to model properties and relations. To see how this works, we need an account of 'application'.

DEFINITION 3.23. Suppose $\mathfrak{A}$ is an abstraction structure. If a is an abstract then a function $f : X \to |\mathfrak{A}|$ is an (*external*) *assignment for* a if every x in X is a pointer of a. It is *appropriate for* a if $f.a$ exists. If f is appropriate for a then *the application of* a *to* f,

[25] The ontological status of 'parametric objects', which are closely related to our abstracts and their parts, is the subject of much debate. See, for example, Westerståhl (1990).

written $a^*(f)$, is $f.a$. In this way, every abstract a is associated with a (second-order) function a^* mapping appropriate assignments to elements of $|\mathfrak{A}|$.

THEOREM 3.5 (β-identity). *If $\Lambda B.a$ exists with pointer function π and f is an appropriate assignment for $\Lambda B.a$ then $(\Lambda B.a)^*(f) = f\pi.a$.*

PROOF. This follows directly from the definitions of simultaneous abstraction and application. □

How, then, should we incorporate complex properties and relations into infon structures? The key point is that the appropriateness conditions of infons having complex relations should be determined by those of basic infons.

DEFINITION 3.24. Let $\mathfrak{A}$ be an infon structure that is also an abstraction structure. $\mathfrak{A}$ has *coherent appropriateness conditions* if for each infon $\sigma = \langle\langle r; \alpha \rangle\rangle$ in $|\mathfrak{A}|$, if r is an infon abstract then α^* is an appropriate assignment for r. $\mathfrak{A}$ is *relation-closed* if for each infon σ and each set B of elements of $\mathfrak{A}$, the infon abstract $\Lambda B.\sigma$ exists and for each appropriate assignment f for $\Lambda B.\sigma$, there is an infon $\langle\langle \Lambda B.\sigma; \alpha \rangle\rangle$ with $\alpha^* = f$.

We state without proof the following result:

THEOREM 3.6. *Every infon structure is extendible to a relation-closed infon structure.*

By way of closing this section, we note that application has only been modeled in an 'external' way. We may ask what the properties of an 'internal' application operation should be. For more on this, see Aczel and Lunnon (1991), and Lunnon (to appear).

4. Truth and circumstance

Notoriously, the word 'information' is ambiguous. Traditionally, the possession of information that Smith is an anarchist like the knowledge of the same implies that Smith *is* an anarchist. With the advent of mechanisms for the gathering, storing and retrieval of large amounts of information, the word has taken on a more neutral meaning. According to more modern usage, to be adopted here, the information that Smith is an anarchist may be stored on a computer file in ASCII code, transmitted across the globe, converted to speech and heard over a loud speaker, without Smith's ever having had a subversive political thought in his life.

A problem with the modern usage is that a new word is required to separate genuine items of information, in the traditional, truth-implying sense, from mere infons. Provisionally, we will use the adjective 'factual' for this purpose. Thus, the infon $\langle\langle \mathsf{anarchist}; \mathsf{Smith} \rangle\rangle$ is *factual* just in case Smith is indeed an anarchist; otherwise it is non-factual, but information nonetheless.

The present use of the word 'factual' is provisional because the distinction on which it rests is an important contention in situation theory. No one would deny of the statement that Smith is an anarchist, that it is true if and only if Smith is an anarchist. It is less clear that this biconditional may be used to determine whether the corresponding infon is factual. To see the difficulty, let us suppose that Smith had a rebellious youth but has now settled down into conformist middle age. An utterance of 'Smith is an anarchist' during Smith's early period would have made a true statement, but an utterance of the same sentence today would not. On the assumption that both utterances express the infon ⟨⟨anarchist; Smith⟩⟩, we arrive at an impasse: which statement do we use to decide whether the infon is factual?

Of course, the problem can be resolved by denying the assumption that both utterances express the same information. We may say that the infons expressed by the two utterances are distinguished by a temporal role that is filled by the time of each utterance. Instead of one infon, we have two: ⟨⟨anarchist; subject: Smith, time: Friday 15th May, 1970⟩⟩ and ⟨⟨anarchist; subject: Smith, time: Monday 18th July, 1994⟩⟩.

The first infon is presumed to be factual, because of the truth of the statement made in 1970, and the second non-factual, because of the falsity of the statement made today. The ⟨⟨anarchist; Smith⟩⟩ is either excused from considerations of factuality because it is unsaturated, or supposed not to exist at all. We appropriate the terminology of Barwise and Etchemendy (1987) by calling this account *Russellian*.

A quite different solution is to take the truth or falsity of a statement to depend on more than just the information expressed. Following Austin (1961), two components of a statement are distinguished: the situation, event or state of affairs that the statement is about, and what is said about it. On this, the *Austinian* account, the difference between the two statements arises not because of a difference in the information they express, but because different situations are described: the utterance in 1970 correctly describes Smith's attitudes at that time, whereas today's utterance falsely describes his present state of bourgeois conformity.[26] The infon ⟨⟨anarchist; Smith⟩⟩ is factual if taken to be about Smith's beliefs and actions in 1970, but not if it is taken to be about his current views.

Proponents of both accounts agree that the common information expressed by the two utterances is neither factual nor straightforwardly non-factual. They differ on the reason for this failure. According to the Russellian, the infon ⟨⟨anarchist; Smith⟩⟩, if it exists at all, is merely the unsaturated common part of the distinct, saturated infons expressed by the two utterances. On the Austinian account, all claims to factuality if intelligible at all are relative to the situation the information is taken to be about. The infon ⟨⟨anarchist; Smith⟩⟩ is factual if it is taken to be information about the situation described by the first utterance, but not if it is taken to be about the situation described by the second.

On matters of detail, there is room for interplay between the two positions. For example, the Austinian may agree that the two statements express different information by virtue of the indexical nature of tense, but still maintain that the factual status of the information expressed is determined by the described situation. Moreover, the debate may be conducted in different areas. Instead of focusing on tense, the Austinian may claim an implicit relativity to a perspective from which the assessment of Smith's political views is to be made – it may be Smith's own, his fellow citizens', 'the authorities', or even that

[26] For Barwise and Etchemendy the terms 'Russellian' and 'Austinian' refer to different views about *propositions*, but the distinction is closely related to the present one. Propositions will be discussed in Section 4.8. Of course, neither Russell nor Austin were concerned with information *per se*, but basic infons play a very similar role in Situation Theory to the basic facts of Logical Atomism.

of the person making the statement. The Russellian account may respond by insisting either that the term 'anarchist' is ambiguous, or that the infon expressed has an extra role for the perspective from which the property of being an anarchist is judged.

In the next few sections we shall consider the Russellian account in more detail, before returning to the Austinian account in Section 4.5.

4.1. *Fact structures*

From a purely technical standpoint, the Russellian account is the more straightforward of the two. The information expressed by an unambiguous statement is modeled as a saturated infon, which may or may not be factual. If it is factual then the statement is true; if not, it is false. Those roles of the infon that are not filled by arguments given explicitly by linguistic features of a statement must be determined by other features of the context in which the statement is made. These additional roles are called 'hidden parameters'. For example, the temporal 'parameter' of the statement that Smith is an anarchist is filled by the time at which the statement is made. If there are further hidden parameters, such as the perspective from which this assessment is made, then the statement is either ambiguous or the additional role must be filled by some other aspect of the context.

This account can be modeled using a 'fact structures', defined as follows.

DEFINITION 4.1. An infon structure $\mathfrak{F}$ of type $[\mathfrak{A}; \mathsf{Fact}]$ is a *fact structure* if for each $\sigma \in A$, if $\mathsf{Fact}(\sigma)$ then σ is a saturated infon. An infon σ is a *fact* if $\mathsf{Fact}(\sigma)$. $\mathfrak{F}$ is *trivial* if every saturated infon is a fact.

Standard fact structure may be constructed from arbitrary relational structures in a straightforward manner. If $\mathfrak{M} = \langle M, R_1, \ldots, R_n \rangle$ is a relational structure and $\mathrm{SInf}(\mathfrak{M})$ is the information structure constructed from it using Construction 2.1, then let $F(\mathfrak{M})$ be the fact structure extending $\mathrm{SInf}(\mathfrak{M})$ with

$$\mathsf{Fact}(\langle 3, R_i, \alpha \rangle) \text{ iff } R_i(\alpha(1), \ldots, \alpha(\nu_i)) \text{ in } \mathfrak{M}_0$$

for each $i \leqslant n$ and each $\alpha : \{1, \ldots, \nu_i\} \to M$. Every infon in a standard structure is saturated, so there is nothing more to check. We call $F(\mathfrak{M})$ the *standard* fact structure generated by $\mathfrak{M}$.

The main problem for the Russellian is that there are many statements that would not usually be called ambiguous, but for which hidden parameters remain unfilled. These are statements that only express unsaturated information, even when all contextual factors are considered. They are more common that one might suspect. Suppose that in the course of telling the story of Smith's involvement in a riot, we say that he panicked and ran. Superficially, the content of the statement is the information that Smith panicked and ran, which might be modeled by the infon $\langle\!\langle \mathsf{panic}; \mathsf{Smith} \rangle\!\rangle \wedge \langle\!\langle \mathsf{run}; \mathsf{Smith} \rangle\!\rangle$.

This infon is unsaturated because panicking and running are events, and so occur at a particular time that has not yet been specified. Unlike in the previous example, the tense of the statement (simple past) is not sufficient to determine a saturated content. Unless there are aspects of the circumstances in which the statement is made that provide a way of saturating the infon, it is difficult to see how a truth-value is to be determined.

There are various ways in which the missing information may be provided. The date of Smith's alleged actions may be given explicitly at some earlier point in the narrative ("On the 15th May, 1970, Smith was involved in a riot...") or provided by some other means: the date of the riot may be common knowledge, or the narrator may have special access to the facts, perhaps by being witness to the original event.

The hunt for contextual factors that determine the content of statements is ultimately restricted by the lack of precision in ordinary language. A threat to the Russellian view is that suggestion that ordinary language is *indefinitely imprecise*: there are always ways of making a given statement more precise, with successive approximations to the 'missing' information, and no definite level of precision beyond which such improvements cannot be made.

For example, it there is no way of finding the exact date of the riot from the context – if for example, the context only specifies that it occurred in May, 1970 – then we would be forced to conclude that the statement is ambiguous. But even if the date is supplied by context, we may still be in trouble. Supposing the date to be determined to be 15 May, 1970, the content of the statement would be the infon

$$\langle\langle \mathsf{panic}; \mathsf{subject} : \mathsf{Smith}, \mathsf{date} : 5/15/70 \rangle\rangle \wedge \langle\langle \mathsf{run}; \mathsf{subject} : \mathsf{Smith}, \mathsf{date} : 5/15/70 \rangle\rangle.$$

Unfortunately, this infon is still unsaturated, as we can see by supposing that Smith was involved in two separate clashes with the police on the same day. On the first occasion, he bravely stood his ground; on the second he panicked and ran. The mere possibility of two clashes is sufficient to show that the infon is unsaturated and so the Russellian is left with ambiguity, even if there was only one clash.

In an effort to avoid the conclusion that there is widespread ambiguity in our use of ordinary language, we may search for more elaborate ways in which the context fills hidden parameters. If the exact time is not supplied in the linguistic context or by common knowledge, it may be determined by a causally related chain of events starting with Smith's actions in the riot.

The danger in this move is that information expressed by a statement may be unknown, even to the person who makes the statement. The narrator may well remember the day of the riot, and even whether it occurred in the morning or afternoon, but not the exact time. If this time is to be a component of the infon expressed by the statement then this is information that the narrator does not possess.

If, on the other hand, we are to resist the move to considering factors that go beyond the knowledge of the narrator, there are other problems. If we take the narrator's beliefs to determine the temporal parameter, then falsehoods are liable to appear in surprising places. Suppose, for example, that the narrator falsely believed the incident took place at around noon on the 15th May, 1970; in fact, it occurred at about 11 a.m. It is awkward to maintain that this false belief, which is otherwise irrelevant to the narrative, makes his statement that Smith panicked and ran false.

Finally, there is a problem in making the demand for ever-greater precision compatible with our somewhat roughshod ontology of events and processes. Although we think of the event of Smith panicking and running as having duration, it is not the sort of interval that can be measured in seconds.

We may hope that for each kind of description there is a fixed tolerance with which information about the values of hidden parameters must be specified. In this way, we could avoid the problems of requiring perfect precision. In many cases, the truth of a statement in which a time is not mentioned explicitly is fairly robust: small variations do not alter the truth-value. But there are circumstances in which small changes do matter – Smith's two clashes with the police may have happened within half-an-hour of each other – and so, the precision required for the saturation of a given piece of information is indefinite, depending on particular facts about the circumstances of the original event, and not just about the later circumstances in which the statement is made.

A way out of this web of difficulty is to embrace the conclusion that many, if not all, of the statements we make are ambiguous; or, better, to cut the link between lack of a truth-value and ambiguity. We may say that a statement is unambiguous if it expresses a determinate item of information, even if this information is unsaturated and the statement neither true nor false.

A quite different approach is to claim that an unsaturated infon is factual if there is some saturated fact of which it is a part. By quantifying over the possible ways of saturating the infon, we arrive at the rather charitable position that a statement is true just in case, in the circumstances, there is some way of construing it as expressing a saturated fact. This is reminiscent of Davidson's treatment (1967) of the same problem. There are two main difficulties with this solution. Firstly, an unrestricted quantification over possible arguments is clearly too generous. If in the course of discussing the riot in 1970 we state that Smith panicked and ran, then this statement cannot be made true by Smith's panicking and running last week. Thus, we must appeal to the context again, this time to provide suitable restrictions to the range of quantification. Secondly, the restrictions on quantifiers are often interdependent. For example, if in interpreting the text 'Smith panicked. He ran.' we may use of the quantificational strategy, then the restrictions on the possibly ways of saturating the two unsaturated infons $\langle\langle \mathsf{panic};\ \mathsf{Smith}\rangle\rangle$ and $\langle\langle \mathsf{run};\ \mathsf{Smith}\rangle\rangle$ must be related: if $\langle\langle \mathsf{panic};\ \mathsf{Smith},\ \mathsf{time}\colon t_1, \ldots\rangle\rangle$ and $\langle\langle \mathsf{run};\ \mathsf{Smith},\ \mathsf{time}\colon t_2, \ldots\rangle\rangle$ are among the permissible saturations then t_1 must be before t_2. Such technical obstacles are not insuperable (see Chapter 10, this volume) but introduce complications that we shall not go into here.[27]

4.2. *Logic in fact structures*

In Section 3.4 we showed how to model compound infons using the theory of structural relations. There we were concerned only with the structural properties of those objects; now we shall examine their logical properties. For example, any reasonable model of conjunctive facts should satisfy the condition that $\mathsf{Fact}(\sigma \wedge \tau)$ iff $\mathsf{Fact}(\sigma)$ and $\mathsf{Fact}(\tau)$. Certain special cases of this condition may be determined by structural properties of conjunction.

[27] The role of indexicals constituent of the content of statements is discussed in John Perry's seminal article Perry (1979), and something close to the Russellian approach is pursued by Perry and David Israel in a series of papers about information beginning with Israel and Perry (1990).

For example, in the infon structure of Construction 3.1 conjunction is idempotent, and so in any fact structure extending this, $\mathsf{Fact}(\sigma \wedge \sigma)$ iff $\mathsf{Fact}(\sigma)$. But structural properties alone will not usually suffice to determine every instance of the above condition, and so we shall need to impose additional axioms.

Typically, Situation Theory uses a de Morgan infon structure $\mathfrak{F}$ (from Section 3.6) that satisfies the following conditions:

1. $\mathsf{Fact}(\bigwedge \Sigma)$ iff $\mathsf{Fact}(\sigma)$ for each $\sigma \in \Sigma$, and
2. $\mathsf{Fact}(\bigvee \Sigma)$ iff $\mathsf{Fact}(\sigma)$ for some $\sigma \in \Sigma$.
3. $\mathsf{Fact}(\neg\sigma)$ iff $\mathsf{Inf}(\sigma)$ and not $\mathsf{Fact}(\sigma)$.

Let us say that a fact structure $\mathfrak{F}$ is *classical* if it does satisfy the above. The logical behaviour of abstract relations must also be considered. A fact structure that is also an abstraction structure should satisfy the

> *Principle of β-equivalence for Facts*: if $\langle\langle r, f\rangle\rangle$ is an infon whose relation r is an infon-abstract then $\mathsf{Fact}(\langle\langle r, f\rangle\rangle)$ iff $\mathsf{Fact}(r^*(f^*))$.

We could go on to define a host of different kinds of fact structures, catalogued by their logical properties. Such a list would be tediously long and necessarily incomplete, and so there is no merit in producing it here. In any case, we want to address not just the multitude of existing logics whose compounds have the familiar syntactic structure of (formal) sentences, but future logics that act on more intricate structures – circular structures, infinite structures, and anything else that can be modeled using the theory of structural relations. Our solution is to give a general method for imposing more or less arbitrary logical structure on fact structures.

Our work is based on the notion of a consequence relation, as it is studied in philosophical logic. For a survey of this large field, see Makinson (1994).

DEFINITION 4.2. A *consequence relation* $\vdash$ on a class C is a binary relation between subclasses of C such that $\Gamma \vdash \Delta$ iff $\Gamma' \vdash \Delta'$ for every partition $\langle \Gamma', \Delta' \rangle$ of C such that $\Gamma \subseteq \Gamma'$ and $\Delta \subseteq \Delta'$.[28] Given a fact structure $\mathfrak{F}$, a consequence relation $\vdash$ on the class of infons in $\mathfrak{F}$ is *sound* if whenever $\Gamma \vdash \Delta$ and every infon in Γ is a fact then some infon in Δ is a fact.

Consequence relations have the following familiar properties:

(identity) $\sigma \vdash \sigma$,

(weakening) if $\Gamma \vdash \Delta$ then $\Gamma', \Gamma \vdash \Delta, \Delta'$, and

(cut) if $\Gamma \vdash \Delta, \sigma$ and $\sigma, \Gamma \vdash \Delta$ then $\Gamma \vdash \Delta$.[29]

Moreover, if $\vdash$ is compact then these three conditions are jointly sufficient to ensure that $\vdash$ is a consequence relation (Barwise and Seligman, 1996).[30] Also note that a consequence relation is entirely determined by the class of partitions that lie in it. It is easy to see that a consequence relation is sound in a fact structure just in case the partition of Inf^* into facts and non-facts does not lie in the consequence relation.

[28] $\langle X, Y\rangle$ is a *partition* of C if $X \cup Y = C$ and $X \cap Y = \emptyset$.

[29] We use the usual abbreviations, e.g., Γ, σ stands for $\Gamma \cup \{\sigma\}$ when an argument of $\vdash$.

[30] $\vdash$ is *compact* if whenever $\Gamma \vdash \Delta$ there are finite sets $\Gamma_0 \subseteq \Gamma$ and $\Delta_0 \subseteq \Delta$ such that $\Gamma_0 \vdash \Delta_0$.

In any de Morgan infon structure $\mathfrak{F}$, if $\vdash$ is a sound consequence relation on Inf^* and $\mathfrak{F}$ is classical then $\vdash$ must satisfy the following conditions:

1. $\bigwedge\Sigma, \Gamma \vdash \Delta$ if $\Sigma, \Gamma \vdash \Delta$,
2. $\Gamma \vdash \Delta, \bigwedge\Sigma$ if $\Gamma \vdash \Delta, \sigma$ for each σ in Σ,
3. $\Gamma \vdash \Delta, \bigvee\Sigma$ if $\Gamma \vdash \Delta, \Sigma$,
4. $\bigvee\Sigma, \Gamma \vdash \Delta$ if $\sigma, \Gamma \vdash \Delta$ for each σ in Σ,
5. $\Gamma, \neg\sigma \vdash \Delta$ if $\Gamma \vdash \sigma, \Delta$,
6. $\Gamma \vdash \neg\sigma, \Delta$ if $\Gamma, \sigma \vdash \Delta$.

The conditions are analogues of the standard inference rules of the sequent calculus for (infinitary) classical propositional logic; let us say that $\vdash$ is *classical* if it satisfies all these conditions. Then it is easy to check that if $\mathfrak{F}$ is non-trivial and has a classical consequence relation then $\mathfrak{F}$ must be classical. These observations amount to the following characterization of de Morgan fact structures: a non-trivial de Morgan fact structure is classical iff it has a sound classical consequence relation.[31]

In this way, the logical properties of complex infons may be investigated by studying their consequence relations, without explicit reference to fact structures. A multitude of consequence relations have already been catalogued by logicians, and so we can import whichever logic we wish, defining the corresponding class of fact structures on which the consequence relation is sound.

4.3. Restriction

In Section 3.8 we saw that properties defined by means of abstraction inherit the appropriateness conditions of the infons over which they are defined. For example, the property $\lambda x.\langle\langle \mathsf{fed}; \mathsf{Martha}, x\rangle\rangle$ of being eaten by Martha is appropriate for just those objects a for which $\langle\langle \mathsf{fed}; \mathsf{Martha}, a\rangle\rangle$ is an infon.

For semantics, it has proved useful to introduce a more flexible notion of abstraction by which a much wider range of restrictions may be placed on appropriate assignments. On some semantic analyses, the information expressed by the sentence 'Martha fed him' is that the referent of 'him' has the property of being fed by Martha, modeled by the abstract $\lambda x.\langle\langle \mathsf{fed}; \mathsf{Martha}, x\rangle\rangle$. But the sentence also conveys the information that the person fed by Martha is male. One way of incorporating this information is to maintain that the abstract is restricted so that it may only be applied to males. In other words, we want a property p such that $\langle\langle p; a\rangle\rangle$ is

1. an infon iff a is male and $\langle\langle \mathsf{fed}; \mathsf{Martha}, a\rangle\rangle$ is an infon,
2. factual iff a is male and $\langle\langle \mathsf{fed}; \mathsf{Martha}, a\rangle\rangle$ is factual.

In some formulations, the restriction that a be male attaches to the abstracted variable (or 'parameter') x, and a theory of *restricted parameters* is developed (Gawron and Peters, 1990a; Fernando, 1990); in others, the situation-theoretic universe is extended to include *restricted objects* quite generally: such objects are identical to their unrestricted counterparts when the (often contingent) restricting condition is met, and are otherwise 'undefined' or of some other ontologically inferior status. Plotkin (1990) adapts Curry's

[31] Furthermore, there is a smallest classical consequence relation $\vdash_c$ on any de Morgan infon structure $\mathfrak{A}$, and so a non-trivial fact structure $\mathfrak{F}$ extending $\mathfrak{A}$ is classical iff $\vdash_c$ is sound on $\mathfrak{F}$.

'illative' approach to logic, treating restriction by means of a connective $\upharpoonright$ whose formation rules require that the restriction be met: if σ is an infon and τ is a fact then $\sigma \upharpoonright \tau$ is an infon; otherwise the expression '$\sigma \upharpoonright \tau$' is not even well-formed.

Barwise and Cooper (1993) introduce an elegant graphical notation for restrictions and abstracts called Extended Kamp Notation, in honor of Kamp's Discourse Representation Structures (see Chapter 3, this volume). They write situation theoretic objects as boxes. A box directly to the right of another box acts as a restriction, and a box directly above lists abstracted objects. For example, the restricted property p mentioned above would be written as

a	
$\langle\!\langle \mathsf{fed}; \mathsf{Martha}, a \rangle\!\rangle$	$\langle\!\langle \mathsf{male}; a \rangle\!\rangle$

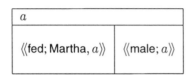

The approach adopted here is to extend the theory of abstraction and application developed in Sections 3.7 and 3.8.

DEFINITION 4.3. A fact structure $\mathfrak{F}$ has *restricted abstraction* if it is also an abstraction structure and has an additional structural relation Res^2, such that if $\mathsf{Res}(\sigma, a)$ then a is an abstract and for each assignment f for a, $f.\sigma$ is an infon. We say that a is a *restricted abstract* and that σ is a *restriction* of a. For each object a, set B of objects in $|\mathfrak{F}|$, and set Σ of infons in $|\mathfrak{F}|$, an object $\Lambda B[\Sigma].a$ is the *abstraction of B from a restricted by Σ* if there is a function $\pi : B \to |\mathfrak{A}|$ such that

1. $\mathsf{Abs}(\Lambda B[\Sigma].a, \pi(b))$ for each b in B,
2. for each b in B, $\pi(b)$ is only of sort Abs^*, and
3. $\Lambda B[\Sigma].a$ satisfies the description $\langle \Lambda B[\Sigma].a, T_{\pi.a} \cup \{\langle \mathsf{Res}, \pi.\sigma \rangle \mid \sigma \in \Sigma\}\rangle$.[32]

$\mathfrak{F}$ is a *restricted-Lambda structure* if $\Lambda B[\Sigma].a$ exists for each a, B, and Σ.

The above nails down the structure of restricted abstracts but we still need to say how they may be applied. For this the key definition is the following: an assignment f for a is *appropriate for a* if $f.a$ exists and $f.\sigma$ is a fact. As before, if f is appropriate for a then *the application of a to f*, written $a^*(f)$, is just $f.a$. $\mathfrak{F}$ has *coherent appropriateness conditions* if for each infon $\sigma = \langle\!\langle r; \alpha \rangle\!\rangle$, if r is a (restricted) infon abstract then α^* is an appropriate assignment for r. $\mathfrak{F}$ is *restricted-relation-closed* if for each infon σ, each set B of elements of $\mathfrak{A}$, and each set Σ of infons, the infon abstract $\Lambda B[\Sigma].\sigma$ exists and for each appropriate assignment f for $\Lambda B[\Sigma].\sigma$, there is an infon $\langle\!\langle \Lambda B[\Sigma].\sigma; \alpha \rangle\!\rangle$ for which $\alpha^* = f$.

Technically there are no difficulties here. Restricted Lambda structures and restricted-relation-closed structures may be constructed using methods similar to those used in Theorems 3.4 and 3.6.[33]

---

[32] This clause is slightly more complicated than the corresponding clause for unrestricted abstraction. It says that the restricted abstract $\Lambda B[\Sigma].a$ has the component structure of $\pi.a$, together with the additional structural relationships $\mathsf{Res}(\pi.\sigma, \Lambda B[\Sigma].a)$ for each σ in Σ.

[33] In the literature on Situation Theory, most authors have been concerned with objects restricted by true propositions rather than facts. We have explained the mechanism for the latter case only because we have yet to introduce propositions – see Section 4.8.

4.4. Internal definability

We have already seen how an internal function f represents an external function f^* in a function structure, and how in an abstraction structure an abstract a represents a second-order function a^* mapping assignments to objects of the domain. In fact structures, internal relations represent external relations. Suppose $\mathfrak{F}$ is a fact structure and R is an n-ary relation on $|\mathfrak{F}|$. The basic idea is that an internal relation r of $\mathfrak{F}$ represents R if for each $a_1, \ldots, a_n$ in $|\mathfrak{F}|$, there is a saturated infon $\langle\langle r; a_1, \ldots, a_n\rangle\rangle$ in $\mathfrak{F}$ and $R(a_1, \ldots, a_n)$ iff $\mathsf{Fact}(\langle\langle r; a_1, \ldots, a_n\rangle\rangle)$. There are, however, several complications. Firstly, our use of the functional notation for infons hides an assumed correlation between the roles of r and the integers $1, \ldots, n$; this must be made explicit. Secondly, the condition requires that the infon $\langle\langle r; a_1, \ldots, a_n\rangle\rangle$ exists for every sequence $a_1, \ldots, a_n$ of elements of $|\mathfrak{F}|$. This will rarely be satisfied because most internal relations have non-trivial appropriateness conditions – it fails even in standard fact structures because the relations of the underlying relational structure only take ordinary objects, not infons and roles, as appropriate arguments. The definition must be revised so that the domain of each relation is restricted in some way.

DEFINITION 4.4. Given a fact structure $\mathfrak{F}$, an n-ary external relation R on $|\mathfrak{F}|$ is *represented by* elements $r, i_1, \ldots, i_n$ of $|\mathfrak{F}|$ on the domain $A \subseteq |\mathfrak{F}|$ if for each (external) assignment f,

1. there is an infon $\langle\langle r; \alpha\rangle\rangle$ with $\alpha^* = f$ iff $f : \{i_1, \ldots, i_n\} \to A$, and
2. if $\mathsf{Inf}(\langle\langle r; \alpha\rangle\rangle)$ then $\mathsf{Fact}(\langle\langle r; f\rangle\rangle)$ iff $R(\alpha^*(i_1), \ldots, \alpha^*(i_n))$.

In standard fact structures, every relation r has a fixed finite arity, n say, and (by the generality principle) the infon $\langle\langle r; a_1, \ldots, a_n\rangle\rangle$ exists for each sequence $a_1, \ldots, a_n$ of ordinary objects. Thus every internal relation of a standard fact structure represents an external relation on the domain of ordinary objects.

In the non-standard fact structures, internal relations may fail to represent for a variety of reasons: they may have infinite or variable arity; they may generate unsaturated infons; or they may have sortal – or even more complex – appropriateness conditions. A simple generalization of the above definition handles the last of these cases.

DEFINITION 4.5. Given a fact structure $\mathfrak{F}$, an n-ary external relation R on $|\mathfrak{F}|$ is *represented by* elements $r, i_1, \ldots, i_n$ of $|\mathfrak{F}|$ *relative to* another n-ary relation D on $|\mathfrak{F}|$ if for each (external) assignment f,

1. there is an infon $\langle\langle r; \alpha\rangle\rangle$ with $\alpha^* = f$ iff f has domain $\{i_1, \ldots, i_n\}$ and $D(f(i_1), \ldots, f(i_n))$, and
2. if $\mathsf{Inf}(\langle\langle r; \alpha\rangle\rangle)$ then $\mathsf{Fact}(\langle\langle r; \alpha\rangle\rangle)$ iff $R(\alpha^*(i_1), \ldots, \alpha^*(i_n))$.

In effect r is taken to represent R only in the context of D; outside of D it does not matter which sequences are in R, and this is captured by making the corresponding assignments for r inappropriate. This gives three different ways of classifying a sequence $\vec{a}$: either $\vec{a}$ is in D and R, or $\vec{a}$ is in D but not in R, or $\vec{a}$ is not in D. Correspondingly, there are three ways of classifying an assignment α: either $\langle\langle r; \alpha\rangle\rangle$ is a fact, or $\langle\langle r; \alpha\rangle\rangle$ is not a fact, or there no infon of the form $\langle\langle r; \alpha\rangle\rangle$.

Another approach is to say that, in general, internal relations represent *partial* relations on $|\mathfrak{F}|$. A partial relation has an extension and an anti-extension that are disjoint but that need not exhaust the domain. Facts with relation r represent sequences lying in the extension of R, and infons that are not facts represent sequences lying in the anti-extension of R.

The issue of infinite and variable arities can be handled with similar generalizations of the meta-theoretic concept of 'relation'.[34] Whichever characterization of representation is adopted, it is natural to ask which external relations are represented in a given fact structure. For example, we may wonder if any of the structural relations Arg, Rel, Inf and Fact are represented.

Plotkin (1990) has various negative results. Suppose that Fact is represented by F in a Lambda structure with classical negation. Let p be the abstract $\lambda x.\neg\langle\langle \mathsf{F}; x\rangle\rangle$, which is sure to exist in such a structure. A simple argument shows that p cannot have a fixed point. Suppose that $\sigma = \neg\langle\langle \mathsf{F}; \sigma\rangle\rangle$. If σ is a fact then so is $\neg\langle\langle \mathsf{F}; \sigma\rangle\rangle$ and so $\langle\langle \mathsf{F}; \sigma\rangle\rangle$ is not a fact. This contradicts the assumption that F represents Fact and so σ must not be a fact. It follows that $\langle\langle \mathsf{F}; \sigma\rangle\rangle$ is not a fact and so that $\neg\langle\langle \mathsf{F}; \sigma\rangle\rangle$ is a fact. But $\sigma = \neg\langle\langle \mathsf{F}; \sigma\rangle\rangle$ and so we have shown that σ both is and is not a fact: a contradiction.

In the structures used by Plotkin, every abstract has a fixed point, and Fact cannot be represented unless at the expense of classical logic. Plotkin uses Frege structures (Aczel, 1980), which are constructed from models of the untyped λ-calculus in which fixed-point combinators such as Y exist. Similar problems arise in structures with internalized application, because they also contain fixed-point combinators. Even without such combinators fixed points will exist in any anti-founded fact structure. For example, the description $\langle x, \neg\langle\langle r; x\rangle\rangle\rangle$ is satisfied in any such structure, and this solution is a fixed point of p.

These considerations illustrate an important trade-off in the construction of models for Situation Theory. There are two ways in which we may measure the power of our structures as modeling tools. On the one hand, we may see which operations are possible, desiring closure under such operations as abstraction, infon-formation, and restricted abstraction. On the other hand, we may see which external entities are internalized, which functions and relations are represented, whether application can be internalized, and so on. We have seen in Section 3.2 that structures in which many descriptions are satisfied – in particular, anti-founded structures – are very useful for ensuring closure properties under structural operations. Unfortunately, the above results show that if too many descriptions are satisfied then some predicates may be not be representable. The goals of structural closure and internalization are in conflict. Where the boundary lies is still far from clear.

---

[34] In the most general case, an internal relation may be said to represent a partial predicate of indexed sets. First specify a class I of indices. Say that an *I-set* is an indexed set $\{x_j\}_{j\in J}$ for some $J \subseteq I$; equivalently, it is a function with domain J. Then say that r represents the partial predicate P of I-sets if there is a one-one function g from I to A such that the extension (anti-extension) of P consists of those I-sets $\{\alpha^*(g(j))\}_{j\in J}$ such that $\langle\langle r; \alpha\rangle\rangle$ is a fact (infon but not a fact) and $J = g^{-1}\operatorname{dom}\alpha^*$.

4.5. Situation structures

Sections 4.1 to 4.4 were primarily concerned with what we have called the Russellian approach to the relationship between information and truth. Now we turn to the alternative, Austinian approach.

Consider again the example of Smith's involvement in a riot. The straightforward analysis of the statement that Smith panicked and ran is that it expresses the information $\langle\langle \mathsf{panic}; \mathsf{Smith} \rangle\rangle \wedge \langle\langle \mathsf{run}; \mathsf{Smith} \rangle\rangle$. The puzzle is to identify the property of this infon that makes the statement true. To be a fact an infon must be saturated, but this infon is not. So, if the truth of the statement depends on its expressing a fact, the straightforward analysis cannot be correct. The Russellian solution is to claim that the statement, if it is unambiguous, expresses a saturated infon whose additional roles are filled by various contextually determined parameters. The task of identifying and cataloging the various contextual parameters is a matter for further semantic analysis.[35]

On the Austinian account, the gap between information and truth is attributed to the neglect of a fundamental component of descriptive statements: the described situation. The basic idea is that a statement using sentence S involves reference to a particular situation s, and that the truth-value of the statement depends on whether or not the S is a correct description of s. In our example, the described situation is a particular course of events twenty-six years ago in which Smith panicked and ran. The sentence 'Smith panicked and ran' is therefore a correct description of the described situation, and so the statement is true.

The same sentence may be used to describe other situations. For example, later in the narration we may be told of a second riot on the same day in which Smith participated but at which he stood his ground. This is obviously *not* correctly described by 'Smith panicked and ran', and so a statement using this sentence to describe the later situation would be false.

Another possibility is that the described situation is one that encompasses many different events, some correctly described and others not. In this case the statement may be genuinely ambiguous, or even unintelligible. Imagine an account of all the riotous events of 1970, including both the riot in which Smith panicked and the one in which he did not, and itemized by the people involved. If Smith's entry is the single sentence 'Smith panicked and ran', then it is difficult to assign any definite truth-value.

The different possibilities are accounted for by introducing a new predicate, 'supports', to refer to the relation holding between a situation and the information expressed by a true statement about it. In other words, a statement expressing the information σ made about a situation s is true if and only if s supports σ. The straightforward account of information is now sufficient. In our example, the statement that Smith panicked and ran expresses the information

$$\sigma = \langle\langle \mathsf{panic}; \mathsf{Smith} \rangle\rangle \wedge \langle\langle \mathsf{run}; \mathsf{Smith} \rangle\rangle$$

[35] An alternative is to explain semantic relationships directly in terms of information expressed rather than truth. This approach is summed up nicely by Barwise's slogan 'Information conditions not truth conditions' and has become a core idea in Dynamic Semantics (see Chapter 10, this volume).

and is true because the described situation – the course of events during the first riot – supports σ. A statement made about the second riot using the same sentence expresses the same information σ but is false because the situation to which it refers does not support σ.

The example shows why a simple distinction between fact and non-fact is not sufficient to accommodate the referential account. Two statements, one true and the other false, express the same information. Clearly no property of the information expressed will suffice to explain the difference in truth-value.

Criticism of the Austinian account has centered on two related problems. Firstly, it is difficult explain how reference to situations is achieved. Austin (1961) proposed that a statement is related to the situation it describes by 'demonstrative conventions', which he contrasted with the 'descriptive conventions' relating the statement to what it says about the situation – the information it expresses, in our terminology. In simple present tense statements about one's immediate surroundings, the relation may be akin to that relating demonstratives ('this', 'that', etc.) to their referents; but in general, the appeal to demonstration is clearly inadequate. The problem is especially acute if the described situation is temporally and spatially remote from the the person making the statement.

The determination of the reference of proper names is beset with similar difficulties, and so it is not surprising that solutions to the present problem parallel the familiar moves in the philosophy of language concerning singular reference. The intentions of the person making the statement may be involved; there may be some kind of causal relationship between the statement and described situation; and conventions within a linguistic community may be appealed to; but, in the end, no generally satisfactory account has been given, and this remains a serious lacuna of the theory. Special problems arise in the present case because the context of a statement has considerable importance in determining the situation to which it refers. A past tense sentence, such as the one we have been discussing, may well be referentially ambiguous when uttered out of context, attaining a definite reference only in the context of a discourse or narrative text (see Seligman and Ter Meulen, 1995).

The first problem is compounded by the second: that it is unclear to what a statement refers when reference is achieved. The word 'situation' is intended to be neutral between 'event' and 'state', so that it makes sense to speak both of the situation in Bosnia, meaning the war (an event or course of events), and the situation on Capitol Hill, meaning the state of deadlock over the budget. The theoretical uniformity of this terminology is bought at a price. Questions about the identity of situations appear much more pressing than the traditional (and equally baffling) metaphysical questions about the identity of material objects, persons and members of a host of other ontological categories.

A short, bold answer to the question of the identity of situations is that distinct situations support different infons. Contraposing we get the

> *Principle of Extensionality:* if for each infon σ, s supports σ iff s' supports σ, then $s = s'$.

If we accept this principle then we may think of situations, and model them, as structured objects whose structure is determined by the infons they support. This is the basis of a model of situations using the theory of structural relations. We introduce the structural relations Sit^1 of being a situation, and $\mathsf{HoldsIn}^2$, which holds between an infon and a situation just in case the situation supports the infon.

DEFINITION 4.6. An extensional structure $\mathfrak{S}$ of type $[\mathfrak{A}, \mathsf{HoldsIn}^2, \mathsf{Sit}^1;]$ is a *situation structure* if $\mathfrak{A}$ is an infon structure and the following conditions are satisfied:

1. if $\mathsf{HoldsIn}(\sigma, s)$ then $\mathsf{Inf}(\sigma)$ and $\mathsf{Sit}(s)$, and
2. if $\mathsf{Sit}(s)$ then s is an ordinary object of $\mathfrak{A}$.

The elements of Sit^* are called *situations*. We say that s *supports* σ, written $s \models \sigma$, if $\mathsf{HoldsIn}(\sigma, s)$. An *ordinary* object of $\mathfrak{S}$ is an ordinary object of $\mathfrak{A}$ that is not a situation.

The move from fact structures to situation structures is a generalization in two directions. First, the non-relational property of being factual is replaced by the relational property of holding in, or being supported by, a situation. Second, this property may be had by infons that are unsaturated. In other words, situations are *partial* in two respects: they need not support all of the facts, and the infons they do support may be only unsaturated parts of facts.

Any fact structure $\mathfrak{F}$ may be used to define a situation structure $\mathfrak{F}^{\#}$ by adding a new element s_Σ for each set Σ of facts, and defining: $\mathsf{HoldsIn}(\sigma, s_\Sigma)$ iff σ is in Σ. We say that a situation structure is *standard* if it is isomorphic to $\mathfrak{F}^{\#}$, for some standard fact structure $\mathfrak{F}$.

Standard situation structures depart from fact structures only in the first respect. Non-standard situation structures may be constructed by modeling situation using sets of infons taken from an infon structure with unsaturated infons. This is a very general method if we work with a theory of sets satisfying AFA, so that no problems are encountered with situations supporting infons about themselves. There are many examples, including Barwise (1987), Fernando (1990), Westerståhl (1990), Aczel (1990), Barwise and Cooper (1991). Here, as previously, we use the theory of structural relations to discuss these models at general level, without going in to the details of the constructions proposed in the literature.

4.6. *Parts of the world*

How smaller situations relate to larger situations is perhaps the most controversial issue in Situation Theory. To see why, consider the two riots, riot_1 and riot_2, in which Smith participated, and let riots be the larger situation that encompasses all of Smith's riotous activities that day. We have seen that the infon $\sigma = \langle\langle \mathsf{panic}; \mathsf{Smith} \rangle\rangle$ is supported by riot_1 but not by riot_2. Indeed, riot_2 supports the infon $\neg\sigma$. Clearly, the larger situation riots cannot support both σ and $\neg\sigma$, and so it does not support all of the infons supported by its parts.

If these intuitions are to be accepted, it follows that the part-whole relation between situations is not correctly modeled by the $\sqsubseteq$-order, obtained as an instance of the general theory of partiality in Section 3.3. According to this account, $s_1 \sqsubseteq s_2$ iff all infons holding in s_1 also hold in s_2. So, if $\mathsf{riot}_1 \sqsubseteq \mathsf{riots}$ and $\mathsf{riot}_2 \sqsubseteq \mathsf{riots}$ then riots would have to support the contradictory infons σ and $\neg\sigma$.

This difficulty may be resolved by supposing that riots supports the infons $\langle\langle \text{panic}; \text{Smith}, 10{:}15\text{am} \rangle\rangle$ and $\neg\langle\langle \text{panic}; \text{Smith}, 2{:}30\text{pm} \rangle\rangle$, which contain the infons σ and $\neg\sigma$ as parts. This suggests the following definition:

DEFINITION 4.7. s_1 is *a part of* s_2, written $s_1 \trianglelefteq s_2$, if for each infon σ, if $s_1 \models \sigma$ then there is an infon τ such that $s_2 \models \tau$ and $\sigma \sqsubseteq \tau$.

That $\text{riot}_1 \trianglelefteq \text{riots}$ and $\text{riot}_1 \trianglelefteq \text{riots}$ is consistent with the assumption that $\text{riot}_1 \models \sigma$ and $\text{riot}_1 \models \neg\sigma$, and so we see that riot_1 and riot_2 are compatible after all. Note that the $\trianglelefteq$-order satisfies the

Principle of Inclusion: if $s_1 \sqsubseteq s_2$ then $s_1 \trianglelefteq s_2$,

but not necessarily its converse, which is equivalent to the

Principle of Persistence: if $s_1 \trianglelefteq s_2$ and $s_1 \models \sigma$ then $s_2 \models \sigma$.

In every standard situation structure, Persistence is satisfied, making $\trianglelefteq$ equivalent to $\sqsubseteq$, but this is only because all infons are saturated in standard structures. If we consider situations modeled by sets of possibly unsaturated infons then Persistence may be violated, as it is in the above example. A consequence of Extensionality and Persistence is the

Principle of Anti-symmetry: if $s_1 \trianglelefteq s_2$ and $s_2 \trianglelefteq s_1$ then $s_1 = s_2$,

which makes $\trianglelefteq$ a partial order. This is a very desirable consequence because it ensures that the (partial) operation of joining two situations together is uniquely defined, as intuition demands it should be.

Anti-symmetry may be violated in non-standard situation structures that do not satisfy Persistence. For example, suppose that σ_1 is the information that Kara is eating and σ_2 is the information that Kara is eating that trout, so that $\sigma_1 \sqsubseteq \sigma_2$ but $\sigma_1 \neq \sigma_2$. If s_2 is the (necessarily unique) situation that supports only σ_2, and s_1 is the situation that supports only σ_1 and σ_2, then $s_1 \trianglelefteq s_2$ and $s_2 \trianglelefteq s_1$ but $s_1 \neq s_2$.

Even if one does not accept the Principle of Persistence, one might reject such counterexamples to Anti-symmetry as artificial. One way of ensuring that $\trianglelefteq$ is a partial order without a commitment to Persistence is to argue that all situations are *relatively saturated*: if s supports σ then there is no less saturated infon $\tau \sqsubseteq \sigma$ that is also supported by s, although such an infon may be supported by some other situation.

The discussion here must remain inconclusive. Definition 4.7 is by no means universally accepted as the correct definition of the part-whole relation between situations, and a number of theorists have either stuck with the $\sqsubseteq$-order or taken the part-whole relation to be a new primitive relation, not determined by the structural properties of situations, but perhaps constrained by one or more of the principles discussed above. In what follows we shall assume that $\trianglelefteq$ is used, but the questions we pose must be faced by all of the rival accounts.

Two situations are *compatible* if they have an upper bound in the $\trianglelefteq$-ordering. We shall consider several interpretations of compatibility below, but first some more definitions. We say that a situation s is *maximal* if for each situation s', if $s \trianglelefteq s'$ then $s = s'$. A set of situations may be *joined* if it has a least upper bound in the $\trianglelefteq$-ordering, called the *join* of S. The $\trianglelefteq$-ordering in a standard situation structure is relatively simple. Every standard situation structure satisfies the following conditions:

S1 any two situations are compatible,
S2 every set of pairwise-compatible situations may be joined, and so
S3 every set of situations may be joined.

In standard situation structures there is a simple relation between situations and facts: $\mathsf{Fact}(\sigma)$ iff $\exists s.s \models \sigma$. Moreover, if the class of facts is a set, there is a unique maximal situation w of which every other situation is a part and so $\mathsf{Fact}(\sigma)$ iff $w \models \sigma$. Non-standard situation structures are not so constrained, but to interpret them we must be able to make sense of incompatible situations. We shall consider two interpretations of compatibility that give rise to very different ways of understanding Situation Theory as a whole.

Compossibility interpretation. Maximal situations are completely saturated, in the sense that information about the filling of roles in infons is specified, and there is no compatible way of adding further infons. This suggests the interpretation of maximal situations as possible worlds. Under such an interpretation we would insist that

S4 every situation is part of some maximal situation.

Consequently, compatibility becomes compossibility: two situations are compossible iff they are part of the same possible world. Under this interpretation, one maximal situation w_a must be distinguished as the *actual world*, and the other incompatible maximal situations are ways the world might have been. There is a sharp metaphysical distinction between those situations that are part of w_a and those that are not: the former are *actual situations*; the latter are merely *possible situations*.

The compossibility interpretation allows one to introduce many of the tools of the theory of possible worlds.[36] For example, standard analyses of modality and conditionals may be given. Such analyses tend to run into difficulties because of the partiality of situations; we shall not go into the details here.

Relativist interpretation. Incompatible situations are regarded as embodiments of different perspectives on the same, actual world. For example, suppose we are facing each other across the dinner table, so that for you the salt is to the left of the pepper. The situation s_{you} concerning the arrangement of objects on the table from your perspective supports the infon $\langle\!\langle \mathsf{LeftOf}; \mathsf{salt}, \mathsf{pepper} \rangle\!\rangle$, whereas the situation s_{me} from my perspective supports $\langle\!\langle \mathsf{LeftOf}; \mathsf{pepper}, \mathsf{salt} \rangle\!\rangle$. On a relativist conception, these situations may be incompatible because they capture the structure of the world from essentially different

[36] Our construction of standard situation structures may be modified in a fairly obvious way to build standard 'modal' situation structures from first-order Kripke structures, by generating situations from sets of compossible facts.

perspectives. No one can see the objects on the table from a perspective from which the salt is to the left of the pepper and the pepper is to the left of the salt.

Whether or not the situations are incompatible depends on the substantial issue as to whether the relation expressed by the phrase 'to the left of' is a perspectival one or not; and, more generally, whether there are such things as perspectival facts. Without prejudging the outcome of metaphysical dispute on these matters, we can see that the present framework is able to make the pertinent distinctions.

For example, the perspectives on either side of the dinner table may be made compatible by appealing to a hidden parameter. If there are infons $\langle\langle \mathsf{LeftOf}; \mathsf{salt}, \mathsf{pepper}, \mathsf{me}\rangle\rangle$ and $\langle\langle \mathsf{LeftOf}; \mathsf{salt}, \mathsf{pepper}, \mathsf{you}\rangle\rangle$, in which a role for an egocentric frame of reference is filled by me and you respectively, then there could be a situation supporting both of these infons without conflict, and of which s_{you} and s_{me} would be parts. In this way, we can account for the fact that there are different perspectives in this example (s_{me} and s_{you} have no upper bound in the $\sqsubseteq$-ordering), while showing how the two perspectives can be reconciled using hidden parameters.[37]

4.7. Logic in situation structures

The use of consequence relations to capture logical structure (Section 4.2) may also be applied to situation structures. Given a consequence relation $\vdash$ on a class C, a class $X \subseteq C$ *respects* $\vdash$ if the partition $\langle X, C - X\rangle$ is not in $\vdash$. This is a slight generalization of soundness: if $\mathfrak{F}$ is a non-trivial fact structure then $\vdash$ is sound on $\mathfrak{F}$ iff Fact^* respects $\vdash$.

The way in which a logic with consequence relation is applied to a situation structure depends on selecting a class of infons to respect it. There are two obvious candidates: the infons supported by a single situation and the infons supported by some situation or other.

DEFINITION 4.8. Let $\mathfrak{S}$ be a situation structure and let $\vdash$ be a consequence relation on the class of infons of $\mathfrak{S}$. For each situation s, let F_s be the set of infons supported by s. The relation $\vdash$ is *locally sound* on $\mathfrak{S}$ if F_s respects $\vdash$, for each situation s. Let $\mathsf{F}_{\mathfrak{S}}$ be the class of infons supported by some situation in $\mathfrak{S}$. The relation $\vdash$ is *globally sound* on $\mathfrak{S}$ if $\mathsf{F}_{\mathfrak{S}}$ respects $\vdash$.

$\mathfrak{S}$ is *locally/globally classical* if there is a classical consequence relation that is locally/globally sound on $\mathfrak{S}$. From Section 4.2, we know that $\mathfrak{S}$ is locally classical if and only if it satisfies the following conditions:

1. $s \models \bigwedge \Sigma$ iff $s \models \sigma$ for each $\sigma \in \Sigma$,
2. $s \models \bigvee \Sigma$ iff $s \models \sigma$ for some $\sigma \in \Sigma$, and
3. $s \models \neg\sigma$ iff $s \not\models \sigma$.

For most applications these conditions are too strong. In particular, they imply that for each infon σ, every situation supports either σ or $\neg\sigma$, and this is quite contrary to the spirit of Situation Theory. Typically, the consequence relation chosen for local soundness

[37] For more discussion of perspectives, see Barwise (1989c) and Seligman (1990a, 1990b).

is that of a partial logic such as Kleene's strong three-valued logic. Another possibility, little studied in the literature but very appropriate to epistemological interpretations of Situation Theory (see Schultz, 1996), is that of taking a locally intuitionistic situation structure: structures for which the consequence relation for intuitionistic logic is locally sound. Both of these possibilities are consistent with the situation structure being globally classical.

There are many other ways of evaluating a consequence relation in a situation structure that are somewhere between the local and the global. For example, in order to make sense of classical reasoning on the compossibility interpretation, we may restrict the condition of local soundness to maximal situations. One could also involve the $\trianglelefteq$-order in a more direct way. For example, for each situation s, let E_s be the class of infons σ such that for each $s' \trianglerighteq s$ there is a $s'' \trianglerighteq s'$ such that $s'' \models \sigma$. A situation structure $\mathfrak{S}$ *eventually sound* if E_s respects $\vdash$, for each situation s in $\mathfrak{S}$. An attractive combination is for a situation structure to be both locally intuitionistic and eventually classical.

Space prohibits a more comprehensive treatment of logical matters, so we shall close this section by touching on a question that brings together logical and order-theoretic considerations: how many situations are there? Logical considerations tend to restrict the number of situations, eliminating arbitrary combinations of infons that do not respect the local consequence relation. Consideration of the $\trianglelefteq$-order has the opposite tendency: we are driven to claim the existence of the joins of existing situations or of parts that support some subset of the infons supported by an existing situation.

For example, if $\mathfrak{S}$ is a situation structure on which $\vdash$ is locally sound, then an example of a fairly generous existence principle compatible with logical considerations is the following: if Σ is a set of infons that respects $\vdash$ and there is a situation s such that for each σ in Σ there is a τ supported by s for which $\sigma \sqsubseteq \tau$, then there is a situation that supports all and only the infons in Σ. This principle can be used to establish the existence of joins of compatible situations. If s_1 and s_2 are compatible situations then there is a situation s of which both are parts. Let Σ be the smallest set of infons satisfying the conditions of the existence principle and such that for each infon τ supported by either s_1 or s_2 there is a infon σ in Σ such that $\tau \sqsubseteq \sigma$. Then the join of s_1 and s_2 is the situation supporting all and only the infons in Σ.

4.8. *Propositions*

On the Austinian account, the truth-value of a statement is determined by whether the described situation supports the information expressed. Truth is a property of statements but not of the information they express, which may be supported by some situations and not by others. To formulate a theory of truth it is therefore necessary to introduce a new kind of entity to which the property of being true may be predicated. Statements are the obvious choice, but statements have many contingent properties that are irrelevant to their truth value, including many of the details of their production, and – most seriously – the fact that they have to be made to exist. Statements not made do not exist and so cannot be true.

This problem is solved by introducing a new kind of abstract object: propositions. Despite its long philosophical pedigree, including an implied role as the object of propositional attitudes, the word 'proposition' is used in Situation Theory purely as a term denoting that by virtue of which a statement has the truth-value it does.

The proposition associated with a given statement is its *propositional content*. On the Russellian account, this is the infon expressed by the statement – fully saturated, possibly by hidden, contextual parameters – and so a *Russellian proposition* is just an infon. On the Austinian account, the truth of a statement is determined by the situation s it describes and the (possibly unsaturated) information σ it expresses. Its propositional content is the *Austinian proposition* $(s \vDash \sigma)$, an abstract entity that combines the two components in a structurally extensional manner: if $(s_1 \vDash \sigma_1) = (s_2 \vDash \sigma_2)$ then $s_1 = s_2$ and $\sigma_1 = \sigma_2$.

Truth is taken primarily to be a property of propositions: a statement is true if and only if its propositional content is true. Thus a Russellian proposition σ is true if and only if σ is a fact. The theory of Russellian propositions is therefore just the theory of facts, and so we shall consider them no further.

An Austinian proposition $(s \vDash \sigma)$ is true if and only if $s \vDash \sigma$. Austinian propositions were studied extensively by Barwise and Etchemendy (1987) and King (1994), and used to give an analysis of various semantic paradoxes. The Austinian proposition $(s \vDash \sigma)$ is usually modeled as the ordered pair $\langle s, \sigma \rangle$. It is easy to see how to characterize these models using structural relations, and so we shall skip over the details.

Austinian propositions are true or false absolutely but (Austinian) infons may only be evaluated relative to a situation. The contrast suggests an immediate generalization of Austinian propositions to include similarly 'absolute' propositions. For example, whether or not a given object σ is an infon is structurally determined and so does not depend on the situation in which the claim is evaluated. We introduce a new proposition $(\sigma : \mathsf{Inf})$ that is true if and only if $\mathsf{Inf}(\sigma)$. Although no typographical distinction is made, it is important to realize that the two occurrence of 'Inf' in the previous sentence are grammatically distinct. The latter refers to a structural (meta-theoretic) relation, whereas the former refers to a new abstract object: the *type* of infons.

Extending this idea to other structural relations, we write and $(\alpha : R)$ for the proposition that the objects in the sequence α stand in the structural relation R. The simple Austinian proposition $(s \vDash \sigma)$ is identified with the proposition $(s, \sigma : \mathsf{HoldsIn})$. This is modeled in a situation structure extended with structural relations Seq, Type, Prop, and a non-structural relation True, having the following interpretations:

$\mathsf{Seq}(\alpha, p)$	α is a sequence of objects in the basic proposition p,
$\mathsf{Type}(T, p)$	T is the type in the basic proposition p,
$\mathsf{Prop}(p)$	p is a proposition,
$\mathsf{True}(p)$	p is true.

The key to modeling propositions and types is to observe that the axioms governing the structure of propositions are exactly the same as those governing facts, with the following relabeling of primitive relations:

Seq	$\rightarrow$	Ass,
Type	$\rightarrow$	Rel,
Prop	$\rightarrow$	Inf,
True	$\rightarrow$	Fact.

With this in mind, we make the following definition.

DEFINITION 4.9. An extensional structure $\mathfrak{P}$ of type

$$[\mathfrak{A}, \mathsf{Seq}, \mathsf{Type}, \mathsf{Prop}; \mathsf{Approp}, \mathsf{True}]$$

is a *proposition structure* if the result of relabeling the primitive relations according to the above scheme is a fact structure in which each structural relation in $\mathfrak{A}$ is represented.

The requirement that each structural relation of $\mathfrak{A}$ is represented is exactly what is needed. For example, if $\mathfrak{A}$ is a situation structure then it will have a binary structural relation HoldsIn, and so there must be a type, also denoted by 'HoldsIn', roles $\mathsf{HoldsIn}_1$ and $\mathsf{HoldsIn}_2$, and for each situation s and infon σ, an appropriate assignment α such that $\mathsf{App}(\mathsf{HoldsIn}_1, \sigma, \alpha)$ and $\mathsf{App}(\mathsf{HoldsIn}_2, s, \alpha)$, and a proposition p such that $\mathsf{Seq}(\alpha, p)$ and $\mathsf{Type}(\mathsf{HoldsIn}, p)$, and $\mathsf{True}(p)$ iff $\mathsf{HoldsIn}(\sigma, s)$. This shows that $\mathfrak{P}$ contains all the Austinian propositions.

A proposition is *basic* if it has a type. Compound propositions, such as conjunctions, disjunctions and negations may be modeled in the same way as compound infons. In a Lambda structure there will also be *proposition-abstracts* of the form $\lambda x.p$ for each proposition p.[38] The structure is then *type-closed* if for each proposition-abstract T and appropriate assignment α, there is a proposition $(\alpha : T)$. Moreover, when these higher-order propositions exist, they should satisfy the

Principle of β-equivalence for Propositions: if $(\alpha : T)$ is a proposition whose type T is a proposition-abstract then $\mathsf{True}((\alpha : T))$ iff $\mathsf{True}(T^*(\alpha^*))$.

A common use of abstraction is the formation of 'situation types'. A *situation type* T is a type with a single argument role that forms a proposition when that argument role is assigned a situation. A situation s is *of type* T if $(s : T)$ is a true proposition.[39] In a Lambda proposition structure, we can form the situation type $\lambda x.(x \models \sigma)$ for any infon σ. β-equivalence for Propositions ensures that s is of type $\lambda x.(x \models \sigma)$ just in case $s \models \sigma$. A theoretical advantage of working with situation types and complex propositions is that it is possible to capture complex conditions on situations in a way that is independent of the structure of information. For example, suppose we are working with a model in which there is no conjunction of infons, and we need to internalize a condition of supporting both of the infons σ and τ. This can be done with the complex situation type $\lambda x.(x \models \sigma) \wedge (x \models \tau)$. A situation is of this type if and only if it supports both σ and τ.

Typically, situation theorists have proposed that the logic of propositions is classical.[40] This is compatible with any logic on infons, but a favorite combination is a classical proposition structure whose underlying situation structure locally respects a partial logic,

[38] The literature has a rich variety of notations for abstraction over propositions. In addition to the notations for abstraction mentioned earlier, '$[x|p]$' is quite common.

[39] We overload the notation for propositions by writing $(s : T)$ as an abbreviation for $([i \mapsto s] : T)$ where i is the unique role of T.

[40] In other words, the class of true propositions respects a classical consequence relation on the class of propositions.

such as Kleene's strong three-valued logic. To see that this is a coherent combination, note that the proposition $(s \models \sigma)$ is either true or not, and so in a classical proposition structure one of the propositions $(s \models \sigma)$ or $\neg(s \models \sigma)$ is true. If a situation s fails to support σ then $\neg(s \models \sigma)$ is true, but this does not imply that s supports $\neg\sigma$ unless the underlying situation structure is locally classical.

Another line of thought suggests that logical consequence is primarily a relation between propositions; they are the bearers of truth, after all. Some models of Situation Theory take infons to be basic infons only (possibly with complex relations) and model all logical combinations as yielding complex propositions. Whatever course is taken, the machinery of Section 3 can be adapted to provide the necessary structures and the approach to logic in fact structures (Section 4.2) can be applied to yield an appropriate definition of consequence.

The account of propositions summarized here suggests a two-storey residence for logical structure.

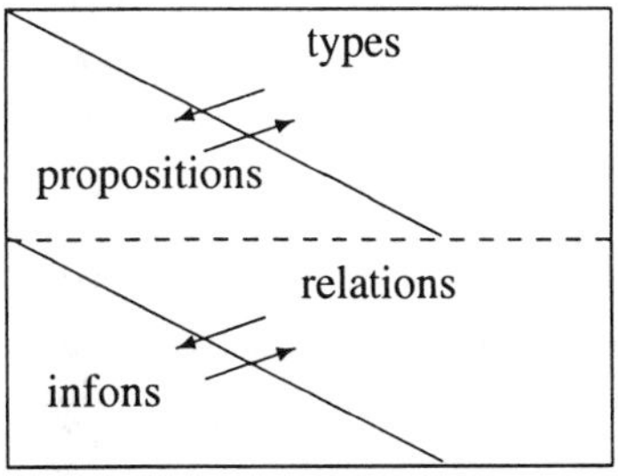

On the ground floor there are infons. Basic infons are made up of assignments and relations; compound infons are structured objects constructed from basic infons; and more complex relations are formed from infons by abstraction.

On the upper floor there are propositions. Basic propositions are made up of assignments and types; compound propositions are structured objects constructed from basic propositions; and more complex types are formed from propositions by abstraction.

The two floors may differ in matters of truth and factuality. Typically, the ground floor is *situated*. An infon needs a situation to determine if it is factual or not; likewise, the extension of a relation may vary from situation to situation. The upper floor is *absolute*, the lower *relative*. Propositions are either true or not, and types have a fixed extensions. The floors are linked by the relationship between a structural relation on the ground floor and the type that represents it on the upper floor.

Like all metaphors involving a duality, the two-storey picture raises a question of redundancy: can we make do with just one of the two, and if so which one? It should be clear that the notion of a proposition structure could serve as the basis for the whole theory. We could re-express the theory of infons and situations using types, with axioms involving constants referring to the internal representations of the structural relations Inf, Sit, and so on.

In the other direction we have an intriguing possibility. We have already observed that the same axioms govern infons and propositions, but so far we have regarded them as distinct kinds. The possibility of models in which the proposition $(\alpha : t)$ is *identical* to the infon $\langle\langle t, \alpha \rangle\rangle$ is open. In such a model, we would have to decide how the truth of propositions is related to their support by situations. Much would depend on whether we adopt a compossibility or a relativist interpretation of compatibility. On the relativist interpretation, there is no privileged perspective from which to judge the truth of perspective-independent truths, but we may require that they be recognized as true from all perspectives. This is in conflict with the partiality of situations, but the conflict can be overcome by resorting to the notion of eventual truth, introduced in Section 4.7, and claiming that a proposition is true if it is eventually supported by every situation.

On the compossibility interpretation, we could choose whether to interpret truth of a proposition as necessary truth – truth in all possible worlds – or as truth in the actual world. As we have seen, propositions are used to capture structural relationships, such as Inf and Rel, but also HoldsIn. If σ is an infon and r a relation, then surely they are necessarily so. It is less easy to evaluate the status of true Austinian propositions. On the one hand, they are true solely by virtue of structural relations holding between situations and the infons they support.[41] On the other hand, they are responsible for the truth of contingent statements, like 'Raymond cooked an omelette'. This points at another fundamental contention. Allegiance to the the Principle of Extensionality suggests that a situation's support of infons is essential: if s_1 supports σ and τ but no other infons, and s_2 supports only σ, then s_1 must support τ, for otherwise s_1 would be identical to s_2, by Extensionality.

This and many other important metaphysical issues raised by Situation Theory have yet to be debated seriously. In part this is because the development of technical tools has been slow. In a theory such as this, inconsistency lurks around every corner (as Plotkin (1990) has shown), and it is difficult to tell if a given list of axioms is consistent. For this reason, among others, research has focused on the construction of models.

Although many models of Situation Theory have been presented, it is in the nature of model-building that all decisions be made: the result is a concrete structure that represents the world in a particular way. Yet in Situation Theory, the decisions turn on significant philosophical issues that have yet to be considered in enough detail for us to be sure of the battle lines, let alone the outcome.

Those building models in this philosophical vacuum either have taken a particular line, contested by other proponents of Situation Theory, or have steered clear of the more contentious issues. Barwise's solution (1989a) was to give a list of 'branch points' at which critical decisions must be made. It is our hope that the model-construction tools are now sufficiently well understood to allow the looser, more abstract approach adopted in this chapter to be used to frame the important questions and sharpen the lines of future philosophical debate.

4.9. Constraints and the flow of information

Situations are user-friendly. Unlike worlds, situations may contain a limited amount of information, an amount that a person may acquire with limited resources. But information

[41] They are 'structurally determined' – see R.P. Cooper (1991).

is promiscuous. The limited information acquired in perception breeds in the fertile soil of a person's mind, and in the cognitive organization of any other well-adapted animal or machine. Information about one's immediate environment carries further information about the more remote and hidden parts of the world. The information that the sky is darkening may be acquired by visual perception, but the further information that a storm is coming, can not. The latter is not information about the immediate environment, and so not part of the information supported by that situation. We say that a situation s *carries* an infon σ, written $s \vDash \sigma$, if σ follows somehow from the information supported by s but is not necessarily supported by s; indeed, it may be information about a different situation altogether.

The responsibility for this 'flow of information' (Dretske, 1981) is placed on the existence of law-like relationships between situations called 'constraints'. Barwise and Perry (1983) placed considerable importance on the role of constraints. The appeal to constraints is central to the claim that Situation Theory is a viable foundation for semantics, significantly different from Montague's. It also lies behind the supposed affinity between Situation Theory and Gibsonian psychology and the approach to cognition urged by Barwise (1986) in his debate with Fodor (1985). More recently, constraints form an essential part of the theory of incremental information developed by Israel and Perry (1990, 1991). And, constraints are essential to applications of Situation Theory to semantics and AI, of the kind considered by Glasbey (1994, 1996) and Cavedon (1995, 1996).

Despite its importance, and considerable research effort, the theory of constraints has remained elusive. Recent developments (Seligman, 1991b; Barwise, 1991; Barwise and Seligman, 1994, 1996) suggest that a quite different outlook is required, one that has not yet been integrated with other parts of Situation Theory. For this reason, we content ourselves here with a exposition of some of the basic problem.

What are Constraints? Constraints have be categorized roughly as follows:

1. *Necessary Constraints*, including taxonomic relations between properties like 'moles are mammals', appropriateness conditions like 'sipping involves sipping something', incompatibility restrictions between properties like 'red things aren't green', or even between individuals like 'Kriesel is not Keisler', and mathematical constraints like '$5 + 7 = 12$';
2. *Conventional Constraints*, including linguistic rules, syntax and semantics, the rules of backgammon or the convention of driving on the right side on the road;
3. *Nomic Constraints*, including all laws of natures, both the commonplace – such as the law that unsupported coffee mugs fall to the floor, and that the radio works if you hit it – and the more esoteric laws about chemical valency or electromagnetism. Most notoriously, 'smoke means fire' expresses a nomic constraint.
4. *Meta-theoretic Constraints*, including all those laws that form a part of Situation Theory itself, such as the law that if $s \vDash \sigma$ then s is a situation and σ is an infon.

This list is haphazard, and there is little convergence on an answer to the question, 'What is a constraint?' Sentences, relations, rules, and laws are all given as examples. In semantics, constraints have been proposed as the referents of conditional and generic statements (see Barwise, 1985; Cavedon, 1995, 1996). The common thread is to be found in the epistemological role of constraints, and not their ontological status. A constraint is something that allows someone with information about one situation to gain information about a possibly different situation. It is because moles are mammals that a photograph of Ivor the mole carries the information that Ivor is warm-blooded, at least for anyone who knows than moles are warm-blooded. Likewise, it is the linguistic conventions of English-speaking sailors that ensure that the sentence 'Land ahoy!' carries the information that land has been sighted.

To model constraints we must decide where to put them in the universe of situation-theoretic entities. The simplest approach is to take constraints to be true propositions.[42] Many constraints concern the dependency between types of situations, and can be modeled by basic propositions of the form $(T_1, T_2 : \Rightarrow)$, abbreviated to $(T_1 \Rightarrow T_2)$, whose arguments T_1 and T_2 are situation types. If $(T_1 \Rightarrow T_2)$ is a constraint (true proposition) then we say that T_1 *involves* T_2. Such constraints constrain by satisfying the

Principle of Involvement: if s is a situation of type T_1 and T_1 involves T_2 then there is a compatible situation of type T_2.

Under the compossibility interpretation the reason for the restriction to compatible situations is clear: constraints only constrain situations in the same possible world. On the relativist interpretation, it ensures that constraints only apply within and not between irreconcilable perspectives. There may be constraints that relate different perspectives, but they are not of the simple form considered above.

The Principle of Involvement gives a necessary but not sufficient condition for the existence of a constraint. It is not for Situation Theory to decide what constraints there are in the world. Nonetheless, some sufficient conditions have been proposed, the foremost of which is the

Xerox Principle: if T_1 involves T_2 and T_2 involves T_3 then T_1 involves T_3.

The name is taken from Dretske's (1981) principle about information flow. According to Dretske, the transfer of information is an all-or-nothing affair with no degradation of quality, such as one would obtain from an ideal copying machine.[43] The link between constraints and information flow is given by the

Principle of Information Flow: s carries the information that σ if s is of some type T that involves $\lambda x.(x \models \sigma)$.

These two Principles account for the 'long range' of information flow: if s carries the information that σ and $\lambda x.(x \models \sigma)$ involves $\lambda x.(x \models \tau)$ then s carries the information that τ. For this reason, the information carried by a situation may far exceed the information it supports.[44]

---

[42] The choice is grammatically awkward because we talk of the *existence* of a constraint and not its *truth*. Other approaches include the following: constraints as facts; constraints as relations between situations, infons, or propositions; and constraints as sets of situations, worlds, infons or propositions. Some authors have used formal expressions purporting to refer to constraints without attempting to answer the ontological question.

[43] The Xerox Principle further constrains the distribution of information in the world: if s is of type T_1 then from the Principle of Involvement alone it follows that if T_1 involves T_2 and T_2 involves T_3 then there is a situation s' of type T_3, but not that s' is compatible with s – this requires the Xerox Principle.

[44] The information carried by a situation is supported by some situation, although possibly in a more saturated form: if $s \Vdash \sigma$ there there is a situation s' and an infon σ' such that $s \trianglelefteq s'$ and $\sigma \sqsubseteq \sigma'$ (by the Principles of Involvement and Information Flow).

Other constraints
Let us call the approach to information flow discussed above the *Theory of Involvement*. Before discussing the deficiencies of this theory, we shall consider briefly some other kinds of constraints considered in the literature.

Reflexive Constraints: The Principle of Involvement is too weak to capture the constraints governing the informational dependencies *within* a situation. If a constraint $(T_1 \Rightarrow T_2)$ is *reflexive* then every situation of type T_1 is also of type T_2. For example, the analytic constraint that if something is a square then it is a rectangle, may be considered to be reflexive. In that case, any situation supporting $\langle\langle \mathsf{square}; a\rangle\rangle$ also supports $\langle\langle \mathsf{rectangle}; a\rangle\rangle$. Reflexive constraints may also be used to internalize the logic of situations (Section 4.7). The local soundness of a consequence relation $\vdash$ can be captured with the condition that if $\Gamma \vdash \Delta$ then $(\wedge_\Gamma \Rightarrow \vee_\Delta)$ is a reflexive constraint, where $\wedge_\Gamma$ is the type of situations supporting every infon in Γ and $\vee_\Delta$ is the type of situations supporting at least one infon in Δ.

General Constraints: Let $\mathsf{kiss}(a, b)$ and $\mathsf{touch}(a, b)$ be the types of situation supporting the information that a kisses b and that a touches b, respectively. Then the constraint $(\mathsf{kiss}(a, b) \Rightarrow \mathsf{touch}(a, b))$ captures the dependency between a's kissing b and a's touching b, but not the general relationship between kissing and touching. An advantage of using propositions to model constraints is that the general constraint that kissing involves touching can be modeled as the complex proposition $\forall xy.(\mathsf{kiss}(x, y) \Rightarrow \mathsf{touch}(x, y))$. The logic of propositions together with the Principle of Involvement yield the desired relationship between kissing and touching.

Preclusion: Informational dependencies are not always positive. The information acquired in a given situation may rule out possibilities without indicating which of the remaining possibilities obtains. For example, the information that Helen's birthday is on a weekday precludes its being on a Saturday without determining the day of the week on which it falls. We may model a negative constraint as a proposition of the form $(T_1, T_2 : \perp)$, abbreviated to $(T_1 \perp T_2)$, and reported by saying that T_1 *precludes* T_2. The *Principle of Preclusion* is that if s is a situation of type T_1 and T_1 precludes T_2 then there is no compatible situation of type T_2.

The Problem of Specificity. The Theory of Involvement tells us that if a situation carries the information σ then there is a situation that supports σ, but it does not tell us which one.

On the Austinian approach to Situation Theory, the situation a statement is about is a very important factor in determining the truth of the statement. Comprehension may be severely restricted if one knows that a statement expresses the information σ without knowing which situation the statement is about. We have seen very different statement can be made using the sentence 'Smith panicked and ran', all of which express the same information. Likewise, knowing that a situation carries an infon σ may be of little significance unless one also knows which situation supports σ. On observing the darkening sky, we know more than that *some* situation is stormy; if we did not then this could not serve as a reason to take cover.

One approach to solving this problem is to model constraints as complex propositions. We can capture the dependency between a situation s_1 being of type T_1 and a situation s_2 being of type T_2 by means of a proposition of the form $(s_1 \models T_1) \rightarrow (s_2 \models T_2)$, in which '$\rightarrow$' is a binary propositional connective, modeled using structural relations in the obvious way. The Principle of Involvement is replaced by the principle that if $p_1 \rightarrow p_2$ and p_1 is true then so is p_2; and the new Principle of Information Flow states that a situation s carries the *proposition* p if there is type T such that $(s : T) \rightarrow p$. Call the result of these modifications the *Propositional Theory of Information Flow.*

The Propositional Theory over-compensates for the Theory of Involvement: it is *too* specific. One can understand a statement very well without knowing exactly which situation it is about, only that it lies within a certain range, or that it is the same situation that was described by an earlier statement. Likewise, the darkening sky does not indicate exactly which situation is stormy.

The middle ground has been explored by Seligman (1990a, 1991b), Barwise (1991), and Israel and Perry (1991). Each approach involves the addition of a parameter to capture the dependency between specific situations. Very roughly, we suppose that some situations are *connected,* while others are not. Then we modify the Principle of Involvement as follows: if a situation is of type T_1 and T_1 involves T_2 then there is a connected situation of type T_2. Clearly, which situations are 'connected' will vary greatly depending on the nature of the constraint. The connection between the observed situation in which the sky is darkening and the later, stormy situation is quite different from the connection between the statement that Smith panicked and the event of his panicking.

Another consideration that bears on this issue, and that the above accounts fail to address, is the limitations on a person's access to constraints. If every law-like regularity in the world is a constraint, then the world is a very constrained place, and just as 'connected'. Yet a person's information about the world at large is limited, not just by her observations but also by the constraints on which her knowledge is based. In determining the information carried by a situation some constraints must be excluded.

Barwise and Perry (1983) adopt the Gibsonian metaphor of *attunement* for this purpose. The ability of a person (animal or machine) to extract information from the environment is determined by the constraints to which that person is attuned. The mere existence of a constraint is not sufficient.

Conditional Constraints. The above discussion has proceeded on the assumption that constraints constrain without exception. This is a reasonable assumption for the necessary and meta-theoretic constraints of our original list, and perhaps for some of the nomic constraints concerned with fundamental laws of nature; but for the vast majority of constraints that underpin a person's beliefs and actions, the assumption is less secure. Smoke means fire only if there are no artificial smoke generators nearby; unsupported coffee mugs fall near the surface of the Earth but not in interstellar space; and an utterance of 'Land ahoy!' by a drunken sailor may not carry the information that land has been sighted.

Barwise and Perry (1983) introduced a separate category of constraint to account for information that flows only under special circumstances. A *conditional constraint* is a constraint that is only guaranteed to hold only when certain *background conditions* are met. For example, the background conditions of the constraint that smoke means fire must exclude those situations in which there are other sources of smoke nearby; those of the constraint that unsupported coffee mugs fall specify that the mug should be in the gravitational field of the Earth.

Continuing with the strategy of modeling constraints as true propositions, we take conditional constraints to be obtained from unconditional constraint by adding a *background situation type*. Conditional involvements are formed using a ternary type $\Rightarrow_c$ whose arguments are all situation types. The constraint $(T_1, T_2, B\colon \Rightarrow_c)$ is abbreviated to $(T_1 \Rightarrow T_2|B)$, and we say that *under conditions B, T_1 involves T_2*.[45] Such constraints conform to the

Principle of Conditional Involvement: if under conditions B, T_1 involves T_2, then for each situation s of type B, if s is of type T_1 then there is a compatible situation of type T_2.

For example, suppose that B is the type of situation in which smoke does indeed mean fire, and that smoky and firey are the types of smoky and firey situations, respectively. Then there is a conditional constraint of the form $(\mathsf{smoky} \Rightarrow \mathsf{firey}|B)$. By the Principle of Conditional Involvement, if s is a situation of type B and s is of type smoky then there is a situation s' of type firey and s' is compatible with s.

The Xerox Principle must also be modified for conditional constraints. The basic idea is that it should hold under fixed background conditions, but not when background conditions vary.

Conditional Xerox Principle: if $T_1 \Rightarrow T_2|B$ and $T_2 \Rightarrow T_3|B$ then $T_1 \Rightarrow T_3|B$.

This Principle was used by Barwise to explain the failure of inferences of the following form: from 'if φ then ψ' and 'if ψ then θ' infer 'if φ then θ'. The inference goes through only if the background conditions of the constraints denoted by each of the conditional statements are the same. Further connections between conditional logic and Situation Theory are discussed in Barwise (1985) and Cavedon (1995, 1996).

The Elusive Background Condition. The theory of conditional constraints faces a number of difficult problems. First, it is unclear how the background condition is specified. In psychological applications of constraints, the basic idea is that the background conditions of a constraints are those that hold in the 'environment' of the person (animal or machine) attuned to it, but that may fail to hold outside that environment. The background conditions are pre-conditions for the success of the organism's behaviour, and failure of a given response may therefore be attributed to the failure of the background conditions, rather than to a failure of attunement *per se*. Unfortunately, this idea has not been successfully incorporated into Situation Theory. In particular, the role of an 'environment' as the fixer of background conditions has proved very difficult to nail down.

In semantics, the determination of background conditions is just as mysterious. One idea is that they are fixed by the described situation, either as the 'environment' of that

---

[45] Conditional versions of reflexive constraints, general constraints and preclusions can be constructed similarly.

situation or as the situation itself.[46] But the relationship between a statement and the situation it describes (discussed in Section 4.5) is far from clear, and so no substantial progress is made.

A second problem is with the scope of background conditions. Consider the following example. A bathroom is wired so that a switch in the corridor outside may be used to control the light inside. If the switch is down then the light is on, and if the switch is up then light is off. These conditionals may be used by a person outside to know whether the light is on even when the door is closed. Let switch-down, switch-up, light-on, and light-off be the types of situations in which the switch and light are as indicated. The truth of the two conditional statements is attributed to the existence of constraints of the form (switch-down $\Rightarrow$ light-on $\mid B$) and (switch-up $\Rightarrow$ light-off $\mid B$), in which B is intended to capture the conditions under which the electrical circuit functions properly – no shorts, no loose wires, no blown fuses, etc.

Now suppose that Janet is outside the bathroom. The door is closed but she observes a situation s of type switch-down and infers that the light is on inside. Her conclusion that is warranted so long as s is of type B, even if Janet does not know that it is. It is difficult to see how the situation *outside* the bathroom can be of type B, a type that ensures the correct functioning of the wiring *inside*. A situation of type B must involve the whole system, within and without the bathroom walls, and perhaps incorporating components even further afield, such as the fuse box and the power supply. Such a situation may be comprehensive enough to ensure the success of Janet's inference, but it is not the situation she observes in the corridor outside the bathroom. Moreover, if the larger situation is large enough to guarantee that conditions are right, then it is difficult to see how it can fail to support the information that the light is on and the switch is down. In that case, even if Janet were able to observe it, and so obtain the information that the light is on, the conditional constraint would play no part in the process.

The problem of specificity, the need to consider connections between situations, the problems of identifying background conditions and determining their scope, and the need to incorporate a limitation on access suggest that there is a long way to go before Situation Theory is extended with a theory of constraints that satisfies the expectations raised by Barwise and Perry (1983).

Situation Theory, in its contemporary form, provides a rich, fine-grained ontology and the means of framing subtle questions about the the nature of truth and circumstance that could not otherwise be put. But it is a theory of stationary objects, of frozen structure, and has proved ill-suited for accounting for the flow of information. An alternative strategy is to aim for a theory of the flow of information that is not primarily concerned with its structure. In different ways, this strategy has been adopted in a number of contempory approaches, such as Dynamic Semantics (Chapter 10, this volume) and Channel Theory (Barwise and Seligman, 1994, 1996).

5. Guide to the literature

The bulk of research papers in Situation Theory and Situation Semantics are contained in the collections entitled *Situation Theory and its Applications*, Vols I to III, published

[46] Barwise (1989c) takes the background condition of a constraint to be a situation instead of a type of situation.

by CSLI. These contain selections of papers presented at a biannual conference. The name of the conference was changed in 1994 to 'Information-Theoretic Approaches to Logic, Language, and Computation'. We have listed in the references a number of papers from these volumes. For an introduction to Situation Semantics one could read Cooper (1991). Other source are the books Fenstad, Halvorsen, Langholm and Van Benthem (1987) and Gawron and Peters (1990a). The latter uses technically intricate concepts from Situation Theory, like restricted abstraction, to propose a theory of anaphora and quantification. In addition, Ter Meulen (1995) studies the representation of temporal information in a related framework, as does Seligman and Ter Meulen (1995). Conditionals are addressed in Barwise (1985) and Cavedon (1995, 1996).

Situation semantics has given rise to computational paradigms as well. For example, see Tin and Akman (1993) and Tin, Akman and Ersan (1995). The general theory has also lead to work in the social sciences; see Devlin and Rosenberg (1993) for the first paper in a series of explorations intended to give a foundation for ethnomethodology.

A good introduction to Situation Theory is Devlin (1991a) and the collection of papers by Barwise (1989b). Key philosophical works connected with Situation Theory are Barwise and Perry (1983), Barwise and Etchemendy (1987). Perhaps the closest in spirit to the approach taken here is that of Barwise and Etchemendy (1987); it was the first to consider circular structures and apply them in a diagnosis of the Liar Paradox. Barwise (1987) shows how to use circular structures to model common knowledge.

The seminal work on non-well-founded sets is Aczel (1988), supplemented more recently by Barwise and Moss (1996). The latter book has less of an emphasis on set theory, and covers many applications of bisimulations to logic and computer science. The role of bisimulation in modal logic is thoroughly explored in De Rijke (1995).

Recent work on anti-foundation has focused on sorted universes, abstraction and application. See, for example, Aczel and Lunnon (1991), Lunnon (to appear), and Aczel (1996). The guiding idea behind these developments is that one should be able to combine methods from set theory and the lambda calculus. The techniques developed by Aczel and Lunnon have been applied directly to Situation Theory by Barwise and Cooper (1991).

The concept of information employed in Situation Theory has developed from that used in Dretske (1981) and Barwise and Perry (1983). Israel and Perry (1990, 1991) have more to say on the subject. The importance of studying information *flow* has been voiced by many writers (see Chapter 10, this volume) and connections to relevant logic and the Lambek calculus have been brought out by Barwise (1993), Restall (1996) and Barwise, Gabbay and Hartonas (1994).

An recently culminating development is the theory of *channels* (Barwise and Seligman, 1996). The goal of this work is a framework for understanding how information flow results from law-like regularities in distributed systems. Key concerns are the modularity of information systems, the limitations imposed by an agent's perspective and the provision for an account of error. Early papers in this direction are Seligman (1990b) and Barwise (1991).

References

Aczel, P. (1980), *Frege structures and the notions of proposition, truth and set*, The Kleene Symposium, J. Baranse et al., eds, North-Holland, Amsterdam, 31–40.

Aczel, P. (1988), *Non-Well-Founded Sets*, CSLI Lecture Notes no. 14, CSLI Publications, Stanford.

Aczel, P. (1990), *Replacement systems and the axiomatization of situation theory*, See Cooper, Mukai and Perry (1990).

Aczel, P. (1996), *Generalized set theory*, See Seligman and Westerståhl (1996).

Aczel, P., Israel, D., Katagiri, Y. and Peters, S. (eds) (1993), *Situation Theory and Its Applications, III*, CSLI Lecture Notes no. 22, CSLI Publications, Stanford.

Aczel, P. and Lunnon, R. (1991), *Universes and parameters*, See Barwise, Gawron, Plotkin and Tutiya (1991).

Austin, J.L. (1961), *Truth*, Philosophical Papers, J.O. Urmson and G.J. Warnock, eds, Oxford Univ. Press, Oxford.

Barwise, J. (1981), *Scenes and other situations*, J. Philos. **78**, 369–397.

Barwise, J. (1985), *Conditionals and conditional information*, Technical report, CSLI. Reprinted in J. Barwise, 1989, 97–135.

Barwise, J. (1986), *Information and circumstance: A reply to Fodor*, Notre Dame J. Formal Logic **27**(3), 324–338.

Barwise, J. (1987), *Three views of common knowledge*, Theoretical Aspects of Reasoning about Knowledge, II, M. Vardi, ed., Morgan Kaufmann, Los Altos, CA. Reprinted with changes as *On the model theory of common knowledge*, J. Barwise (1989), 201–220.

Barwise, J. (1989a), *Notes on branch points in situation theory*, See Barwise (1989b), 255–276.

Barwise, J. (1989b), *The Situation in Logic*, CSLI Lecture Notes no. 17, CSLI Publications, Stanford, CA.

Barwise, J. (1989c), *Situations, facts, and true propositions*, See Barwise (1989b), 221–254.

Barwise, J. (1991), *Information links in domain theory*, Technical report, Indiana University Logic Group. Preprint #IULG-91-7.

Barwise, J. (1993), *Constraints, channels, and the flow of information*, See Aczel, Israel, Katagiri and Peters (1993), 3–27.

Barwise, J. and Cooper, R. (1991), *Simple situation theory and its graphical representation*, See Seligman (1991a). DYANA Deliverable R2.1.C.

Barwise, J. and Cooper, R. (1993), *Extended Kamp notation*, See Aczel, Israel, Katagiri and Peters (1993).

Barwise, J. and Etchemendy, J. (1987), *The Liar: An Essay on Truth and Circularity*, Oxford Univ. Press, New York.

Barwise, J. and Etchemendy, J. (1990), *Information, infons, and inference*, See Cooper, Mukai and Perry (1990), 33–78.

Barwise, J., Gabbay, D. and Hartonas, C. (1994), *On the logic of information flow*, Technical Report, Indiana University Logic Group.

Barwise, J., Gabbay, D. and Hartonas, C. (1996), *Information flow and the Lambek calculus*, See Seligman and Westerståhl (1996).

Barwise, J., Gawron, J.M., Plotkin, G. and Tutiya, S. (eds) (1991), *Situation Theory and Its Applications, II*, CSLI Lecture Notes no. 26, CSLI Publications, Stanford.

Barwise, J. and Moss, L.S. (1996), *Vicious Circles: On the Mathematics of Non-Wellfounded Phenomena*, CSLI Lecture Notes, CSLI Publications, Stanford.

Barwise, J. and Perry, J. (1983), *Situations and Attitudes*, MIT Press, Cambridge, MA.

Barwise, J. and Perry, J. (1985), *Shifting situations and shaken attitudes*, Ling. and Philos. **8**(1), 105–161.

Barwise, J. and Seligman, J. (1993), *Imperfect information flow*, Proceedings of the 8th Annual IEEE Symposium on Logic in Computer Science, M. Vardi, ed., IEEE Computer Society Press, Los Alamito, CA, 252–261.

Barwise, J. and Seligman, J. (1994), *The rights and wrongs of natural regularity*, Perspect. Philos. **8**, 331–364.

Barwise, J. and Seligman, J. (1996), *Information Flow: The Logic of Distributed Systems*, Tracts in Theoretical Computer Science, Cambridge Univ. Press, Cambridge.

Black, A.W. (1992), *A situation theoretic approach to computational semantics*, PhD Thesis, Department of Artificial Intelligence, University of Edinburgh.

Black, A.W. (1993), *An approach to computational situation semantics*, PhD Thesis, Department of Artificial Intelligence, University of Edinburgh, Edinburgh, UK.

Blackburn, P. and De Rijke, M. (1996), *Logical aspects of combined structures*, See Seligman and Westerståhl (1996).

Braisby, N. (1990), *Situation word meaning*, See Cooper, Mukai and Perry (1990), 315–341.

Braisby, N. and Cooper, R.P. (1996), *Naturalising constraints*, See Seligman and Westerståhl (1996).

Burke, T. (1990), *Dewey on defeasibility*, See Cooper, Mukai and Perry (1990), 233–268.

Cavedon, L. (1995), *A channel-theoretic approach to conditional reasoning*, PhD Thesis, Centre for Cognitive Science, University of Edinburgh.

Cavedon, L. (1996), *A channel-theoretic model for conditional logics*, See Seligman and Westerståhl (1996).

Cooper, R. (1986), *Tense and discourse location in situation semantics*, Ling. and Philos. **9**.

Cooper, R. (1991), *Three lectures on situation theoretic grammar*, Natural Language Processing: EAIA 90 Proceedings, M. Filgeiras, L. Damas, N. Moreira and A.P. Tomás, eds, Lecture Notes in Artif. Intell. vol. 476, Springer, New York, 101–140.

Cooper, R. (1992), *Situation theoretic discourse representation theory*, Manuscript, HCRC, Edinburgh.

Cooper, R. (1993), *Generalized quantifiers and resource situations*, See Aczel, Israel, Katagiri and Peters (1993), 191–211.

Cooper, R. (1996), *The attitudes in discourse representation theory and situation semantics*, See Seligman and Westerståhl (1996).

Cooper, R. and Ginzburg, J. (1996), *A compositional situation semantics for attitude reports*, See Seligman and Westerståhl (1996).

Cooper, R. and Kamp, H. (1991), *Negation in situation semantics and discourse representation theory*, See Barwise, Gawron, Plotkin and Tutiya (1991), 311–333.

Cooper, R., Mukai, K. and Perry, J. (eds) (1990), *Situation Theory and Its Applications, I*, CSLI Lecture Notes no. 22, CSLI Publications, Stanford.

Cooper, R.P. (1991), *Persistence and structural determination*, See Barwise, Gawron, Plotkin and Tutiya (1991), 295–309.

Davidson, D. (1967), *Truth and meaning*, Synthese **17**, 304–323.

De Rijke, M. (1995), *Modal model theory*, Technical Report No. CS-R9517, CWI, Amsterdam.

Devlin, K. (1990), *Infons and types in an information-based logic*, See Cooper, Mukai and Perry (1990), 79–95.

Devlin, K. (1991a), *Logic and Information*, Cambridge Univ. Press, Cambridge, UK.

Devlin, K. (1991b), *Situations as mathematical abstractions*, See Barwise, Gawron, Plotkin and Tutiya (1991), 25–39.

Devlin, K. and Rosenberg, D. (1993), *Situation theory and cooperative action*, See Aczel, Israel, Katagiri and Peters (1993), 213–267.

Dretske, F. (1981), *Knowledge and the Flow of Information*, MIT Press, Cambridge, MA.

Engdahl, E. (1990), *Argument roles and anaphora*, See Cooper, Mukai and Perry (1990), 379–393.

Fenstad, J.E., Halvorsen, P.-K., Langholm, T. and Van Benthem, J. (1987), *Situations, Language, and Logic*, Reidel, Dordrecht.

Fernando, T. (1990), *On the logic of situation theory*, See Cooper, Mukai and Perry (1990), 97–116.

Fernando, T. (1991), *Contributions to the foundations of situation theory*, PhD Thesis, Stanford University.

Fodor, J.D. (1985), *Situations and representation*, Ling. and Philos. **8**(1), 13–22.

Gawron, J.M. and Nerbonne, J. a. S.P. (1991), *The absorption principle and E-type anaphora*, See Barwise, Gawron, Plotkin and Tutiya (1991), 335–362.

Gawron, J.M. (1986), *Situations and prepositions*, Ling. and Philos. **9**, 327–382.

Gawron, J.M. and Peters, S. (1990a), *Anaphora and Quantification in Situation Semantics*, CSLI Lecture Notes no. 19, CSLI Publications, Stanford.

Gawron, J.M. and Peters, S. (1990b), *Some puzzles about pronouns*, See Cooper, Mukai and Perry (1990), 395–431.

Georgeff, M., Morley, D. and Rao, A. (1993), *Situation theory and its applications, III*, See Aczel, Israel, Katagiri and Peters (1993), 119–140.

Ginzburg, J. (1991), *Questions without answers, wh-phrases without scope: A semantics for direct wh-questions and their responses*, See Barwise, Gawron, Plotkin and Tutiya (1991), 363–404.

Glasbey, S. (1994), *Event structure in natural language discourse*, PhD Thesis, Centre for Cognitive Science, University of Edinburgh.

Glasbey, S. (1996), *Towards a channel-theoretic account of the progressive*, See Seligman and Westerståhl (1996).

Healey, P. and Vogel, C. (1993), *A situation theoretic model of dialogue*, Pragmatics in Dialogue Management, K. Jokinen, ed., Gothenburg Monographs in Linguistics.

Hintikka, J. (1983), *Situations, possible worlds, and attitudes*, Synthese **54**, 153–162.

Israel, D. and Perry, J. (1990), *What is information?*, Information, Language, and Cognition, P.P. Hanson, ed., The Univ. of British Columbia Press, Vancouver, Canada, 1–28.

Israel, D. and Perry, J. (1991), *Information and architecture*, See Barwise, Gawron, Plotkin and Tutiya (1991).

Katagiri, Y. (1991), *Perspectivity and the Japanese reflexive 'zibun'*, See Barwise, Gawron, Plotkin and Tutiya (1991), 425–447.

Katagiri, Y. (1996), *A distributed system model for actions of situated agents*, See Seligman and Westerståhl (1996).

King, P.J. (1994), *Reconciling Austinian and Russellian accounts of the Liar paradox*, J. Philos. Logic **23**, 451–494.

Koons, R. (1990), *Three indexical solutions to the Liar paradox*, See Cooper, Mukai and Perry (1990), 269–296.

Koons, R. (1992), *Paradoxes of Belief and Strategic Rationality*, Cambridge Univ. Press, Cambridge, UK.

Lewis, D.K. (1979), *Score keeping in a language game*, Semantics from Different Points of View, R. Bauerle, ed., Springer, New York, 172–187.

Lewis, D.K. (1983), *General semantics*, Philosophical Papers, vol. 1, Oxford Univ. Press, New York/Oxford, 233–249.

Lewis, M. (1991), *Visualization and situations*, See Barwise, Gawron, Plotkin and Tutiya (1991), 553–580.

Lunnon, R. (1991a), *Generalised universes*, PhD Thesis, Manchester University.

Lunnon, R. (1991b), *Many sorted universes, SRD's, and injective sums*, See Barwise, Gawron, Plotkin and Tutiya (1991), 51–79.

Lunnon, R. (to appear), *A theory of sets and functions*, J. Symb. Logic.

Makinson, D. (1994), *General non-monotonic logic*, Handbook of Logic in Artificial Intelligence and Logic Programming, vol. III, D. Gabbay, C. Hogger and J. Robinson, eds, Oxford Univ. Press, Oxford.

Mori, T. and Nakagawa, H. (1991), *A formalization of metaphor understanding in situation semantics*, See Barwise, Gawron, Plotkin and Tutiya (1991), 449–467.

Muskens, R. (1995), *Meaning and Partiality*, Studies in Logic, Language, and Information, CSLI Publications, Stanford.

Nakashima, H., Suzuki, H., Halvorsen, P.-K. and Peters, S. (1988), *Towards a computational interpretation of situation theory*, Proceedings of the International Conference on Fifth Generation Computer Systems, Institute for New Generation Computer Technology, Tokyo, Japan, 489–498.

Nakashima, H. and Tutiya, S. (1991), *Inferring in a situation about situations*, See Barwise, Gawron, Plotkin and Tutiya (1991), 215–227.

Perry, J. (1979), *The problem of the essential indexical*, Nous **13**, 3–21.

Perry, J. (1984), *Contradictory situations*, Varieties of Formal Semantics: Proceedings of the 4th Amsterdam Colloquium, F. Landman and F. Veltman, eds, Groningen–Amsterdam Series in Semantics, Foris, Dordrecht.

Perry, J. (1986), *From worlds to situations*, J. Philos. Logic **15**, 83–107.

Perry, J. (1993), *The Essential Indexical and Other Essays*, Oxford Univ. Press, New York.

Perry, J. and Macken, E. (1996), *Interfacing situations*, See Seligman and Westerståhl (1996).

Plotkin, G. (1990), *An illative theory of relations*, See Cooper, Mukai and Perry (1990), 133–146.

Poesio, M. (1991), *Relational semantics and scope ambiguity*, See Barwise, Gawron, Plotkin and Tutiya (1991), 469–497.

Poesio, M. (1993), *A situation-theoretic formalization of definite description interpretation in plan elaboration dialogues*, See Aczel, Israel, Katagiri and Peters (1993), 339–374.

Restall, G.A. (1996), *Information flow and relevant logics*, See Seligman and Westerståhl (1996).

Rounds, W.C. (1990), *The complexity of paradox*, See Cooper, Mukai and Perry (1990), 297–311.

Rounds, W.C. (1991), *Situation-theoretic aspects of databases*, See Barwise, Gawron, Plotkin and Tutiya (1991).

Rounds, W.C. and Zhang, G.-Q. (1996), *Attunement to constraints in non-monotonic reasoning*, See Seligman and Westerståhl (1996).

Ruhrberg, P. (1996), *A simultaneous abstraction calculus and theories of semantics*, See Seligman and Westerståhl (1996).

Schulz, S. (1996), *Minimal truth predicates and situation theory*, See Seligman and Westerståhl (1996).

Schütze, H. (1991), *The prosit language, version 0.4*, CSLI Memo, Center for the Study of Language and Information, Stanford University, Stanford, CA.

Seligman, J. (1990a), *Perspectives: A relativistic approach to the theory of information*, PhD Thesis, University of Edinburgh.

Seligman, J. (1990b), *Perspectives in situation theory*, See Cooper, Mukai and Perry (1990), 147–191.

Seligman, J. (ed.) (1991a), *Partial and Dynamic Semantics III*, Centre for Cognitive Science, University of Edinburgh. DYANA Deliverable R2.1.C.

Seligman, J. (1991b), *Physical situations and information flow*, See Barwise, Gawron, Plotkin and Tutiya (1991), 257–292.

Seligman, J. (1996), *The logic of correct description*, Advances in Modal Logic, M. de Rijke, ed., Kluwer, Dordrecht, 107–136.

Seligman, J. and Ter Meulen, A. (1995), *Dynamic aspect trees*, Applied Logic: How, What and Why, L. Pólos and M. Masuch, eds, Kluwer, Dordrecht.

Seligman, J. and Westerståhl, D. (eds) (1996), *Logic, Language and Computation*, CSLI Lecture Notes, CSLI Publications, Stanford.

Sem, H.F., Saebo, K.J., Verne, G.B. and Vestre, E.J. (1991), *Parameters: dependence and absorption*, See Barwise, Gawron, Plotkin and Tutiya (1991), 499–516.

Shin, S.-J. (1991), *A situation-theoretic account of valid reasoning with Venn diagrams*, See Barwise, Gawron, Plotkin and Tutiya (1991).

Stalnaker, R. (1986), *Possible worlds and situations*, J. Philos. Logic **15**, 109–123.

Suzuki, H. and Tutiya, S. (1991), *A strictly incremental approach to Japanese grammar*, See Barwise, Gawron, Plotkin and Tutiya (1991), 517–532.

Ter Meulen, A. (1995), *Representing Time in Natural Language. The Dynamic Interpretation of Tense and Aspect*, Bradford Books, MIT Press, Cambridge, MA.

Tin, E. and Akman, V. (1993), *BABY-SIT: A computational medium based on situations*, Proceedings of the 9th Amsterdam Colloquium, P. Dekker and M. Stokhof, eds, ILLC, Amsterdam.

Tin, E. and Akman, V. (1994a), *Computational situation theory*, ACM SIGART Bull. **5**(4), 4–17.

Tin, E. and Akman, V. (1994b), *Situated processing of pronominal anaphora*, Tagungsband KONVENS '94 Verarbeitung Natürlicher Sprache, H. Trost, ed., Vienna, Austria, Informatik Xpress, 369–378.

Tin, E. and Akman, V. (1996), *Information-oriented computation with BABY-SIT*, See Seligman and Westerståhl (1996).

Tin, E., Akman, V. and Ersan, M. (1995), *Towards situation-oriented programming languages*, ACM Sigplan Notices **30**(1), 27–36.

Tojo, S. and Wong, S. (1996), *A legal reasoning system based on situation theory*, See Seligman and Westerståhl (1996).

Vogel, C. (1992), *A situation theoretic model of inheritance reasoning*, Research Conference on Logic, Language, and Information: Toward an Integrated Theory of Linguistic Processing, European Science Foundation, December, 13–17.

Westerståhl, D. (1990), *Parametric types and propositions in first-order situation theory*, See Cooper, Mukai and Pery (1990).

Zadrozny, W. (1996), *From utterances to situations: Parsing with constructions in small domains*, See Seligman and Westerståhl (1996).

Zaefferer, D. (1991), *Probing the iroquoian perspective: Towards a situated inquiry of linguistic relativity*, See Barwise, Gawron, Plotkin and Tutiya (1991), 533–549.

Zalta, E. (1991), *A theory of situations*, See Barwise, Gawron, Plotkin and Tutiya (1991).

CHAPTER 5

GB Theory: An Introduction*

James Higginbotham

Centre for Linguistics and Philology, Walton Street, Oxford OX1 2HG, UK
E-mail: higgy@ermine.ox.ac.uk

Commentators: M. Kracht and E. Stabler

Contents

*This chapter would not have been possible without the assistance of my correspondents, Marcus Kracht and Edward Stabler, to whom I am much indebted both for comments and for advice on content. Errors remain my responsibility.

HANDBOOK OF LOGIC AND LANGUAGE
Edited by J. van Benthem and A. ter Meulen

"GB Theory" (or simply "GB"; we will use both terms) is the name commonly applied to the syntactic framework expounded in Chomsky (1981), with which is associated a looser set of considerations of a semantic nature. This framework represents a moment in the development of linguistic theory. At the same time, it continues several lines of thought that have been conspicuous in formal syntax since the inception of the subject in its modern form. Moreover, significant features of GB have been retained in subsequent work under the heading of "Minimalism" in the sense of Chomsky (1993, 1995); we consider this latter development briefly below.

This chapter is intended for persons with various backgrounds in linguistics (or even none at all) who are interested in becoming acquainted with the general features of the development and internal logic of GB and are ready to approach the subject from a somewhat abstract point of view. Hence we do not here assume prior acquaintance with GB theory, or for that matter with syntactic theory in general; but we do expound some of the concepts, and the axioms governing them, that would be wanted in a full exposition of the theory. Since the motivations both for general theoretical moves and for their specific modes of development can best be appreciated in the light of detailed arguments involving particular examples, we have chosen to concentrate on selected points rather than attempt an elementary survey. For this reason, many topics that would be discussed in any standard textbook (e.g., Freidin, 1992; Haegeman, 1994) are here omitted altogether. The points on which we concentrate have been chosen with an eye to the abstract properties of the theory, which have consequences for formalization and computational implementation. Reflection on examples, the stock in trade of professionals, is essential if a feeling for syntactic inquiry is to be imparted. We therefore encourage the reader to ponder the illustrations in what follows, testing them against his or her native language and judgments.

The extensive lore of GB contains relatively little in the nature of formalization. Although we do not attempt to fill the gap here, we have deemed it useful, especially in the context of this *Handbook*, to indicate some of the concepts and definitions that would form part of a formalization. The form chosen reflects to some degree the preferences of the present authors.[1]

Although the specific proposals characteristic of GB theory need not in themselves be seen as a part of psychological inquiry, the work of Chomsky, both early and late, has always been advanced as a fragment of a full theory of human linguistic knowledge, or *competence* in the sense of Chomsky (1965). Moreover, the theory of the competence of mature speakers of a language is itself to be part of a larger theory that addresses the question how that competence was acquired. Hence, among the criteria for the success of a full theory of syntax and interpretation is that of *learnability*: the theory must be such as to identify how a child can learn any language that it recognizes as a possible human language. The aim of describing competence, and the desideratum of learnability, often sit in the background of ongoing research, informing but not guiding: so it will be here.

Our discussion will follow a route that is both historical and analytical: historical in the sense that, beginning with the aspects of linguistic description first studied formally in the

[1] See note on the title page.

1950s (all of them characteristic of traditional grammatical studies, though informally and incompletely presented there), we proceed to the stage characteristic of GB, and thence to more recent work; analytical in the sense that the historical shifts are also points of progressive abstraction in the theory, advanced because of genuine problems of description or explanation within earlier stages.

1. Phrase structure

To bring out the fundamental and persistent themes that mark GB theory it is useful to begin farther back, with the explicit conception of sentence structure that is formulated in such works as Harris (1955) and Chomsky (1955).

The dawn of syntax is marked by the realization that the structure of sentences is *hierarchical*; that is, that behind the linear order of words and morphemes that is visible in natural languages there is another organization in terms of larger or smaller constituents nested one within another. Suppose that parts of speech have been distinguished as noun (N), verb (V), adjective (A), preposition (P), adverb (Adv), article (Art), and so forth. Then these elements may combine to make larger elements which themselves belong to linguistic categories. Common categorial membership is evidenced by *intersubstitutivity*, so that, for example, the expressions

London
the woman
the old man
the proud young child

may all be called nominal, since putting any one of them in a context like

_ is known to me

produces a grammatical sentence (and putting any one of them in a context like

That is known _ me

produces gibberish). In contemporary parlance such nominals are called noun phrases (NPs), on the grounds that the nominal words occurring in them are evidently what is responsible for their nominal behavior. The nominal word (for instance *child* in *the proud young child*) is said to be the *head* of the construction.

As the reader may verify at leisure, what has just been said of nouns and NPs applies equally to verbal elements. Thus

walked
is known to me
went slowly to London

are interchangeable in the context

John _

The heads are the verbs *walk, be*, and *go*, and the larger constituents are verb phrases (VPs). Prepositional phrases (PPs) are introduced similarly: they consist of a preposition followed by an NP, as in

with [the proud young child]

etc. Finally, adjective phrases (APs), although most of them consist of an adjective alone, or an adjective modified by an adverb, as in

tall
very tall

may include more material, as in comparatives

taller than John

There are also transitive adjectives, as in

proud of her sister

These admit adverbial modification, and the formation of comparatives, so that complex phrases like

very much prouder of her sister than of her brother

are also APs.

Diligent application of tests of substitutivity will produce compelling analyses of many complex sentences. Thus (1) may be broken down as consisting of the elements enumerated in (2):

(1) I went to London with the proud young child;

(2) The NP *I*;
the VP *went to London with the proud young child*;
the V *went* (which carries past tense);
the PP *to London*, consisting of the P *to* and the NP *London*;
the PP *with the proud young child*, consisting of the P *with* and the NP *the proud young child*, which consists in turn of the article *the* and the modified noun *proud young child*, which consists in turn of a sequence of adjectives followed by a head N.

The entire analysis may be displayed in the form of a labeled bracketing, as in (3), or in the form of a tree, as in (4), where S = *Sentence*:

(3) $[_S[_{NP}I][_{VP}[_V\text{went}][_{PP}[_P\text{to}][_{NP}\text{London}]]\ [_{PP}[_P\text{with}][_{NP}[_{\text{Article}}\text{the}][_N[_A\text{proud}]$
$[_A\text{young}]\ [_N\text{child}]]]]]]$

(4)

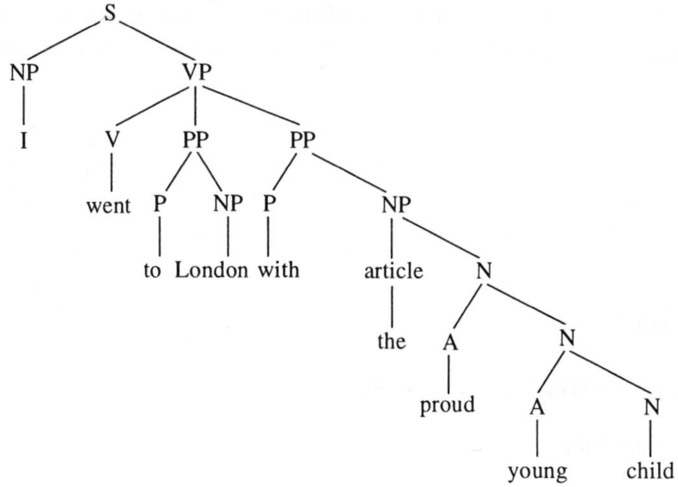

These analyses are said to give the *constituent structure* of a sentence, its representation at what Chomsky (1955) called the level of *phrase structure*. The object represented in (4) is a *phrase marker*; see further Section 5 below.

A crucial point in the development of theories of phrase structure is that phrases of a given kind can occur within others of the same kind; it is this recursive feature of language that enables sentences of arbitrary complexity to be constructed. The realization that phrase structure is recursive is very old. Thus Arnauld (1662) gives the examples (in Latin, but the point might as well have been made in English):

(5) $[_S$The divine law commands that $[_S$kings are to be honored]];

(6) $[_S[_{NP}$Men $[_S$who are pious]] are charitable];

remarking that in (5) the embedded element *kings are to be honored* is a sentence occurring within a sentence, and that in (6) the relative clause has all the structure of a sentence, except that the relative pronoun *who* has replaced the subject.

Supposing that the sentences of human languages all admit analyses in terms of phrase structure, how can the system that underlies a given language be made fully explicit? For English, we must take account of the following facts, among others:

(i) The combinations of categories that may make up a given, larger category are restricted in their nature. For instance, nouns combine with adjectives, as in *young child*, but not with adverbs, as we do not have

slowly child
child slowly

as Ns; articles combine with Ns but not with Vs as we have *the child* but not

I the walked

Following customary practice we annotate elements that do not belong to a given category with an asterisk *; omission of the asterisk indicates the judgment that at least appropriately selected elements can belong to the category. So in general we have, for English,

$*[_N\text{adverb } N]$
$[_N\text{adjective } N]$
$*[_V\text{article } V]$

and so forth.

(ii) Even when a certain combination of categories is permitted, the categories must be combined in certain orders. Since we do not have **tie white* as an English N, we must state that the tree has a linear orientation. In this respect we see at once that languages differ, since for instance in French we have

cravate blanche
*blanche cravate

The formalization that suggests itself for expressing categorial combinations consistently with both (i) and (ii) is that of the *inductive clause*, schematically as in (7):

(7) If X_1 is an A_1 and $\cdots$ and X_n is an A_n, then:
$X_1 \cdots X_n$ is a C

where the X_i are variables ranging over sequences of words, and $A_1, \ldots, A_n$ and C are categories. Such clauses enable us to say, for instance, that

If X is an A, and Y is an N, then XY is an N;
If X is an article and Y is an N, then XY is an NP;
If X is a V and Y and Z are PPs, then XYZ is a VP.

Besides inductive clauses we also require *basis clauses*, or assignments of primitive expressions to the categories to which they belong. The basis clauses underlying our examples could be simple lists, as in (8):

(8) *child* is an N
walk is a V

and so forth. The context-free grammars of Chapter XYZ of this *Handbook* are in effect inductive definitions of categorial membership, where basis and inductive clauses are expressed by rewriting rules. Thus the rule corresponding to (7) is (9):

(9) $C \to A_1 \cdots A_n.$

Below we express the rules in this format.

An important confirmation of the theory of phrase structure is that it yields an account of *structural ambiguity*, for instance as in (10):

(10) I bought a book to read.

The ambiguity in (10) is easy to spot: it can mean either that I bought a book with the intention of reading it, or that I bought a book that was suitable to be read. So the sequence *a book to read* is ambiguous. But no word in that sequence is ambiguous: such is the diagnostic for structural (rather than lexical) ambiguity. Structural ambiguities can normally be manipulated so that one or another interpretation stands out. Thus note that if we replace *a book* by a pronoun or title, we have only the first interpretation:

(11) I bought it/*War and Peace* to read.

Similarly, seeing that *a book* is the understood object of *read* in (10), we again have only this interpretation if we replace that object by a pronoun:

(12) I bought a book to read it.

Inversely, imagine *A* handing a book to *B* and saying:

(13) Here's a book to read.

A clearly must mean that the book is for reading, a meaning corresponding to the second interpretation of the sequence in (10). Finally, as would be expected, (14) is ungrammatical:

(14) *Here's a book to read it.

Especially with the contrasts in (11)–(14) in mind, the basis of the ambiguity of (10) is explained as follows. In the first interpretation, where it is said that I bought a book with the intention of reading it, we have a construction where the infinitive *to read* is separated from *a book*, and has only the function of indicating purpose. In the second interpretation the infinitive functions otherwise, as a relative clause modifying *a book*. In this case *a book to read* is an NP. But *it*, or *War and Peace* are, like proper names and pronouns generally, NPs that are not further modifiable; hence the following infinitive can only be a purpose clause, and (11) is unambiguous. Inversely, (13) presents no agent whose purpose can be to read the book; hence the infinitive is a modifier only, and the attempt to treat it as indicating purpose, as in (14), results in ungrammaticality. Combining the last two arguments, we deduce, correctly, that (15) is also ungrammatical:

(15) *Here's it to read.

2. Limitations of phrase-structure description

Chomsky (1955, 1957) contain a number of arguments pointing to the limitations of phrase structure description as conceived in the last section. In this section we consider three such arguments, representative but by no means exhaustive. On their basis Chomsky proposed a syntactic theory that is essentially *derivational*; that is, the phrase marker that underlies the heard string is the last member of a sequence of computations over phrase markers, each such computation being a *grammatical transformation*. We give the computations in question first in pre-GB and later in GB terms.

The arguments of this section leave open a number of questions about possible elaborations of phrase structure, and to that extent leave open the question whether there is a conception of phrase structure that can replace transformations, thus reverting again to a single level of syntactic description. The question of derivational versus non-derivational syntax will be taken up again in Section 7 below.

2.1. easy *and* eager

Against the background of the last section we may evaluate a classical discussion in Chomsky (1965), to the effect that phrase structure grammar will necessarily fail to contain certain information crucial to grammaticality, and will leave some general features of languages unaccounted for. The argument takes as its point of departure the pair of sentences (16)–(17):

(16) John is easy to please;

(17) John is eager to please.

At the level of phrase structure there is no apparent distinction between these sentences save for the choice of adjective. In each case the VP consists of a form of the verb *be*, inflected for present tense, followed by an A, followed by a so-called infinitival V *to please*, here dubbed INFV. The structure is (18):

(18) $[_S NP][_{VP} V\ A\ INFV]]$.

However, there is an obvious distinction between (16) and (17): in (16) the subject NP *John* is understood as the object of the V *please*, so that the sentence may be paraphrased as

It is easy for one to please John

but in (17) the subject NP is understood as the subject of *please*, so that the sentence may be paraphrased as

John is eager that he, John, should please (someone).

This distinction is correlated with several syntactic differences between the adjectives *easy* and *eager*:

(a) *easy*, but not *eager*, admits expletive (meaningless) subject *it*:

It is easy to please John (expletive *it*);
It is eager to please John (*it* must refer to something).

(b) *eager*, but not *easy*, admits the affix *-ness*, converting the A into an N, so that we have the possessive construction

John's eagerness to please.

However, we do not have

*John's easiness to please.

(c) *easy*, but not *eager*, admits infinitival subjects:

To please John is easy;
*To please John is eager.

It is a natural thought that these distinctions must be related to one another. For one thing, there are a number of As that belong to the *easy*-class, such as *tough*, *hard*, *difficult*, etc., and a number that belong to the *eager*-class, such as *anxious*, *ready*, *determined*, etc. For another, we should not expect that a person who grasps English has learned the facts (a)–(c) independently: the list is therefore unsatisfactory from the point of view of learnability. We are led, therefore, to consider the prospect of deriving all the distinctions from a common source. But no such source presents itself within phrase structure grammar.

In Chomsky (1965) the fundamental divergence between (16) and (17) was explained as follows (in simplified form). With each sentence is associated a *deep structure* and a *surface structure*. The surface structures of (16) and (17) are identical, except that (16) has the adjective *easy* where (17) has *eager*. At deep structure, however, (16) is represented as in (19):

(19) It $[_{VP}$is easy [one to please John]].

Two operations convert (19) into a surface structure (20):

(20) John $[_{VP}$is easy [to please]]

namely:
(i) *John* replaces the pleonastic subject *it*;
(ii) *One* becomes null.
The deep structure of (17) is (21):

(21) John $[_{VP}$is eager [John to please]]

with intransitive *please*, and this structure is converted to (22):

(22) John $[_{VP}$is eager [to please]]

by the single operation:
(iii) The second occurrence of *John* becomes null.
On this type of view, the distinction (or set of distinctions) between (16) and (17) is not revealed at the level of simple phrase structure description, but rather by deep structure representation, from which that description is derived.

The concept of a *derivational* syntax is thus intrinsic to the conception of grammar just sketched. As we will see below, the derivational histories of (16) and (17) according to GB are rather different.

2.2. *Long-distance dependencies*

A second type of example that argues for the necessity of departing from phrase structure grammar is that of *long-distance dependency*. To motivate examples of this type we first consider some simple dependencies between constituents.

(A) *Feature agreement*. In English, subject and verb agree visibly in number in the present tense; so we have *a man walks* (singular), but *men walk* (plural). Exceptionally, there is agreement in number between a V and post-verbal NP when the overt subject is existential *there*, as in (23):

(23) There is a man walking/There are men walking.

Agreement is obligatory: we do not have **There are a man walking*, or **There is men walking*. How can feature-agreement be expressed at the level of phrase structure? For the case of verbs and their subjects, we might try assuming complex categories, call them NP(sing) and NP(plural), V(sing) and V(plural) (though even here we are departing from the basic type of a phrase structure grammar, for which the categories do not have a compositional structure), and introduce in place of the simple rule

If X is an NP and Y is a VP, then XY is an S

the pair of rules

If X is an NP(sing) and Y is a VP(sing), then XY is an S;
If X is an NP(plural) and Y is a VP(plural), then XY is an S.

Since singular number is realized not on the VP but on the V this doubling-up must extend to the rules governing VP, of which one instance would be:

If X is a V(sing) and Y is an NP, then XY is a VP(sing).

Still more special rules would be needed for the case of number-agreement between V and the NP following V in the context of existential *there*. However these rules are specified, note that agreement is in a sense a *local* phenomenon. Local agreement is seen in (24), which shows the relevant parts of the phrase structure of the first sentence in (23):

(24)

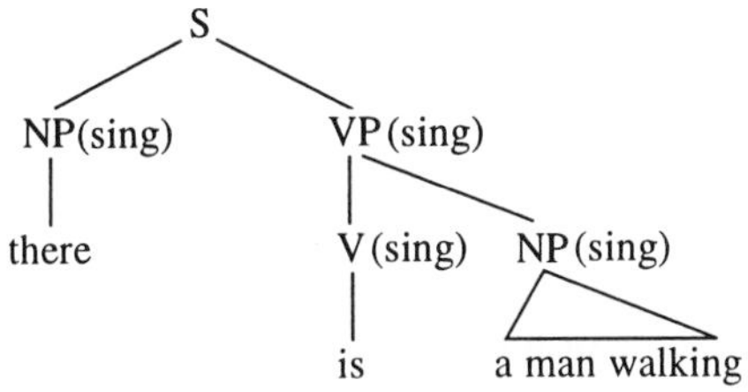

Now consider the examples (25)–(26):

(25) There seems to be *men/a man walking;

(26) There seem to be men/*a man walking.

These show agreement between the argument *men/a man* and the V *seems* of the main clause. But how are these elements able to communicate with one another? One explanation, practically dictated by the assumptions made above, has three parts, as follows:

(a) Expletive *there* shows number agreement with the post-verbal argument;

(b) (25) and (26) are derived by raising *there* from its initial position as the subject of *be* to the position of the subject of *seem* (where it receives nominative case from the tense on the main V);

(c) The raised element retains the features it had before movement, and they are checked against the features of *seem*.

Thus, starting from (27), we derive (28):

(27) seem(sing) [there(sing) [to be [a man](sing) in the garden]];

(28) [there(sing) seem(sing) [( ) to be [a man](sing) in the garden]];

with '()' marking the place from which the expletive subject moved. The long-distance agreement between the main V and the post-verbal NP of the embedded S is thus mediated by three more local relations, namely the two relations between *there* and the postverbal NP, and the fact that *there* "remembers" its features when it moves.

(B) *wh-movement.* Like many other, but by no means all, languages, English has a family of related words that serve to indicate positions of either modification or interrogation. These are referred to appropriately as *wh-expressions*, since a survey of examples shows that there is a significant part with that pronunciation. The examples include:

where, who, which, what, whether, why, ...

The contexts of interrogation are illustrated by (29), those of modification by (30):

(29) Where did Mary go?
Who solved the problem?
Which book did you give to John?

(30) [$_{NP}$the place [where Mary went]];
[$_{NP}$the person [who solved the problem]];
[$_{NP}$a book [which you gave to John]].

The operation that derives an element like

which you gave to John

is crudely describable as lifting a *wh*-expression from the position to which it is related (in this case the object position of *give*), and placing it at the front of the constituent that is to be an interrogative or a modifier: this is the operation of *wh-movement.* Phrase structure rules do not countenance operations of this sort.

A survey of examples of *wh*-movement in English quickly reveals that the crude description of *wh*-movement would allow the generation of many sentences that are in fact not possible. Thus, where the blank '___' indicates the position from which movement has occurred, we cannot have any of the examples in (31):

(31) (a) *Which book did the man who likes ___ talk to you?
(b) *What did you put the spoon or ___ on the plate?
(c) *How did Mary deny [$_S$you fixed the car ___].

(Note that the string *How did Mary deny you fixed the car* is grammatical with the interpretation, "How was Mary's denial made?" As the position of the blank within the sentential brackets indicates, however, the example is to be taken as, "By what means x did Mary deny that you fixed the car employing method x of car-fixing?" The question is then why the sentence *How did Mary deny you fixed the car?* fails to be structurally ambiguous.)

The conclusion to be drawn from these reflections is that, although it is easy to describe the basic operation of *wh*-movement, the conditions on well-formedness of its output are far from trivial. Especially since Ross (1967), inquiry has attempted to formulate the conditions under which the relation between *wh* and the position X of its origin is ill-formed. Any such condition is a *filter* Φ, ruling out certain otherwise possible structures, as in (32):

(32) $*[wh[...X...]]$ if Φ.

Local rules of agreement are likewise stateable as filters, ruling out, e.g., cases where a subject and its verb disagree in number (and, in some languages, in other features such as person and gender). Could phrase structure rules, of the simple kind that we have been considering, serve in principle to express some or all of the filters on *wh*-movement? In some cases they would. Suppose we allow the rules to "skip" an element that would otherwise be present, or to rewrite it as an "empty" element *e*. Then we might understand the first sentence in (29) (without the auxiliary) as generated in schematic form by

$$\mathrm{S}(wh) \rightarrow wh\mathrm{S}(e)$$
$$\mathrm{S}(e) \rightarrow \mathrm{NP\ VP}(e)$$
$$\mathrm{VP}(e) \rightarrow \mathrm{V}e$$

giving

$$[_{\mathrm{S}}(wh)\mathrm{where}\ [_{\mathrm{S}(e)}[_{\mathrm{NP}}\mathrm{Mary}]\ [_{\mathrm{VP}}[_{\mathrm{V}}\mathrm{go}]e]]]$$

where the information that the S contains a "gap" or unfilled position is passed down by features attaching to the grammatical categories. The rules introducing *e* would be restricted in their nature so that, for instance, it would not be possible to generate this element following the disjunction *or*, thus accounting for the ungrammaticality of (31b).[2] On the other hand, a survey of cases reveals that the information that must be drawn upon to decide whether an empty element in a position can or cannot be related to a given *wh*-expression is more extensive than any single, local condition will reveal. For instance, although (31c) is ungrammatical, (33), which differs only in choice of main V, is fully acceptable:

(33) How did Mary think [$_{\mathrm{S}}$you fixed the car ___].

[2] Proposals of this sort are (in their contemporary form at least) due to Gerald Gazdar; they still form a part of Head-Driven Phrase Structure Grammar (see Chapter YY). We do not consider any comparisons here. It should be noted, however, that developments of the alternative view involve composing categories, or combining them with features, and therefore constitutes a significant departure from simple phrase structure models. See further Section 7 below.

2.3. *Elements of a transformational grammar*

Examples such as the *easy-eager* distinction and long-distance dependencies such as *wh*-movement and remote number agreement are among those that motivated the conceptions of *grammatical transformation* that are to be found, in different forms, in the work of Harris and Chomsky in the 1950s. Summing up the lesson that they appear to teach, one conclusion is that a grammar consists at least of the following components:

(I) A system of constituent structure;

(II) Rules that allow elements to be moved from one position to another within such a structure;

(III) Filters (including rules of agreement) on constituent structures;

(IV) Principles regulating the types of rules under (II) and (III).

Let us compare the point that we have reached with the original starting point, the phrase structure grammar. Phrase structure grammars are very limited in their descriptive apparatus, and it is precisely this merit of theirs that allows decisive counterexamples either to their empirical adequacy or to their plausibility to be produced. A phrase structure grammar has a system as in (I) above, and it is not a radical departure to add agreement rules as in (III) so long as they are appropriately "local". However, once we allow elements to move within a phrase structure, and allow relations that are not local, the power of the descriptive apparatus is augmented enormously (indeed, it can be classically demonstrated that grammatical systems that merely have a system as in (I) and recursive relations (rules) as in II can generate any recursively enumerable language; see Peters and Ritchie (1971)). Again, whilst the evidence for phrase structure is quite overwhelming, it is a more complex theoretical question what rules there are as in (II) and (III), and still more what restrictions on them might be imposed as in (IV). For these reasons, no doubt among others, there is room for great diversity and development in grammatical theories that depart in any significant way from elementary phrase structure.

3. D-Structure and S-Structure

In this section we consider the synthesis represented in the exposition of GB in Chomsky (1981), *Lectures on Government and Binding*, hereafter the LGB theory, which provides a view of grammatical components answering to (I)–(IV) above.

3.1. *Heads, projections, and movement*

In the LGB theory, the fundamental system of constituent structure is provided by a system of lexical heads and admissible phrases of the same categories, their *projections*. In the case of nominals, for instance, it is supposed that the head N may be modified, perhaps more than once, producing a projection N′ (read "N-bar"). The projection is completed by an article (or a quantifier, such as *every*), so that one has NP = N″ with the structure

$$[_{N''}\text{Article } [_{N'}\text{modifier } [_{N}\text{head}]]].$$

The verbal projection is similar to the nominal, though here one must add that Vs are sorted according to the number and types of arguments that they take. The positions of arguments and modifiers are controlled by the relation of *government*, a traditional grammatical notion that may be given a precise interpretation in terms of the hierarchical structure of phrase markers. It will suffice for our purposes to note that Vs govern their complements (e.g., direct and indirect objects), but not their subjects, a point to which we shall return.

The system of projections of heads through modifiers and completion of phrases by articles or other expressions replaces the inductive clauses, or rewriting rules of earlier conceptions of phrase structure, in the sense that the rules are not arbitrary statements of the form

If X is a C_1 and Y is a C_2, then XY is a C

but instead assume the uniform shape

If X is a C_1^n and Y is of appropriate categorial type, then XY is a C_1^m

where $m = n$, or $m = n + 1$. The levels thus constructed are normally assumed to be only two beyond the lexical: thus $N^0 = N$ will be a nominal word, $N^1 = N'$ will be a modified N, and $N^2 = N''$ the final or *maximal* projection of the head N.

At the level where only the inductive principles are employed in building up phrase structures, the level of *D-Structure*, no syntactic movement has taken place. Thus in one of the examples under (29), repeated here as (34), we may propose a D-Structure as in (35):

(34) What did you give to John?

(35) [?[you [Tense [give what to John]]]];

where Tense in this case is realized as Past, and '?' is a feature in a higher position that indicates a question, and acts as an "attractant" for the *wh*-expression *what*. The derived structure shows the *wh*-expression *what* moving to the front, by hypothesis in fact to a designated position selected by '?', and Tense, which has likewise moved, supported by the "dummy V" *do*. The movement creating the derived structure leaves behind an element with no phonological content (though it may carry grammatical features) called the *trace* of the movement; moreover, the trace is related to the element whose trace it is by a relation on the derived structure. Indicating this relation by subscripting these items with the same index, the derived structure becomes (36):

(36) [What$_i$ [do + Tense$_j$ [you [t_j [give t_i [to John]]]]]].

The derived structure that is represented in the heard string of words and other morphemes is called *S-Structure*.[3] As can be seen even from our simple example, the linguistic level of S-Structure departs from traditional analysis in terms of phrase structure in a number of ways: S-Structure representations may contain phonologically empty elements; the

---

[3] This statement is not quite accurate, since there may be stylistic and other rules that rearrange elements prior to pronunciation. These cases, which are anyway marginal for the theory, will not be considered here.

constituents are not simply categories or morphemes but include sets of features; and, perhaps most significantly, there are systematic binary relations between constituents, and conditions governing their assignment.

In place of the single phrase markers of the simple phrase structure theory, sentences (and other categories) will now be associated with an ordered pair of phrase markers (Γ, Σ) where Γ is a D-Structure and Σ is an S-Structure representation, Σ being derived from Γ by a sequence of grammatical transformations (the principles under (II)), and with outputs subject to filters under (III).

3.2. Types of transformations

In the LGB theory the permissible types of syntactic movement are only two: *substitution*, which displaces an element to a designated position, and (left- or right-) *adjunction*, which inserts an element into a phrase marker above a designated position. Adjunction (here left-adjunction for illustrative purposes) of X to a position Y creates from

$$\ldots [_{\mathrm{Y}} \ldots \mathrm{X} \ldots$$

a phrase marker

$$\ldots [_{\mathrm{Y}} \mathrm{X}_i\ [_{\mathrm{Y}} \ldots t_i \ldots$$

The LGB theory thus places very strong constraints upon the rules as in (II) above, regulating syntactic movement. It places far weaker conditions on the filters under (III), a point to which we return in Section 6.2 below.

The reduction of transformation types in the manner suggested does away with most of the transformations of earlier periods of study. A classic example is the disappearance of the *passive transformation*, proposed in different forms by both Harris and Chomsky in early work, and relating active-passive pairs such as (37)–(38):[4]

(37) The boy broke the window;

(38) The window was broken by the boy.

Taking the structure of the active sentence

$$[_{\mathrm{S}}[_{\mathrm{NP}}\text{the boy}]\ [_{\mathrm{VP}}[_{\mathrm{V}}\text{broke}]\ [_{\mathrm{NP}}\text{the window}]]]$$

as given, the passive is derived (optionally), by (a) replacing the subject NP by the object, (b) postposing the subject, putting it as the object of the preposition *by*, and (c) introducing the copula bearing the tense of the active V (here, Past), and making the V a participle.

4 For Harris, transformations were relations between sentences; Chomsky's innovation was to think of them as relations between phrase markers used in the course of a derivation.

In LGB, the passive transformation cannot even be stated. The passive construction arises instead from an (obligatory) operation of substitution, putting the object of the participle into the empty subject position e of a structure

$$[_{S}e[_{VP}\text{be }[_{A'}\text{V} + en\text{ NP}]]]$$

with or without the added PP = *by* NP. Thus we derive, not (38), but (39), and also the form without expression of an agent, (40):

(39) The window was broken t by the boy;

(40) The window was broken t.

The passive construction is now seen as a special case of an operation moving an argument from one position to another, or *NP-movement* as it is called. Although we cannot go into the details here, we can point out that this operation will also be involved in the so-called "raising" constructions, as in (41), and the generalized movement constructions, which are like the passive except that the argument that moves is not an argument of the head whose subject it becomes, as in (42):

(41) John seems [t to be a nice fellow];

(42) Many people were believed [t to have voted for the proposal].

Notice that, although the passive morphology reflected in the change from *break* to *broken* forces movement of the argument *the window* to the subject position, it does not alter at all the grammatical relation between these items; we must, however, stipulate that the passive has the property that whatever could have appeared as the subject of the transitive form is optionally expressible as the object of the preposition *by*. This feature of the old passive transformation, expressed now as a reflex of a morphological change, survives in the new system.

3.3. Empty categories

The restrictions on transformations just outlined have gone together with a conception of syntactic movement, whether substitution or adjunction, as always leaving a trace t coindexed with the moved element, effectively marking the position from which movement took place. We shall survey some of the evidence for this point of view in Section 5.3 below. The introduction of unpronounced but syntactically present elements such as the trace invites further reflection on the system of constituent structure, item I in our enumeration of the components of a transformational grammar.

Supposing D-Structure to be prior to all movement, we have D-Structures paired with S-Structures as in (43)–(44), illustrating movement from a lower to a higher subject position, and also as in (45)–(46), illustrating movement of a *wh*-expression:

(43) e [was seen [the boy]];

(44) [the boy]$_i$ [was seen t_i];

(45) I know [? [you saw who]];

(46) I know [who$_i$ [you saw t_i]].

One and the same expression can undergo both types of movement: thus the D-Structure (47) will yield S-Structure (48):

(47) I know [? [you think [*e* was seen who]]];

(48) I know [who$_i$ [you think [t_i was seen t_i]]].

The theory thus allows sequences

$$\text{Moved Element} \ldots t_i^1 \ldots t_i^2 \ldots, \ldots t_i^n$$

where the position of the final trace t^n was occupied by the moved element at D-Structure, and is the position that determines the grammatical function of that element (object of *see* in our examples). But there are also cases where an overt element, occurring in one position, is clearly related to another position that is not occupied by any phonetically realized element, and where the grammatical function of the overt element must be located in both positions. Such cases include (49) and (50):

(49) Mary persuaded John [to go to college];

(50) Bill promised [to turn in the paper on time].

In traditional terms, the indirect object *John* in (49) is the understood subject of the infinitive *to go to college*; and the subject *Bill* of (50) is also the understood subject of *to turn in the paper on time*. Now, *promise* is evidently a two-place predicate, selecting a subject and an object; but then the subject *Bill* must have been present in the D-Structure of (50), and its S-Structure therefore does not involve movement (of this element). As for (49), we can verify that *persuade* is a three-place predicate: if we make the position of the clause indefinite, or existentially general, then we have sentences like (51):

(51) Mary persuaded John of something;

and expressions like (52) are nonsense, since the indirect object is missing:

(52) *Mary persuaded of something.

The position occupied by *John* in (49) was occupied by that expression even at D-Structure, so that we conclude in this case too that it has not undergone movement, and in particular has not moved from the subject position of the clause *to go to college*. But then, if every predicate must have its proper arguments present at D-Structure and at S-Structure, there must at D-Structure have been something that served as the subject of the infinitive, and continues at S-Structure to serve that function; at the same time, this element must be related to the overt element, for which it is understood. For (49)–(50), then, we have D- and S-Structures as in (53)–(54):

(53) Mary persuaded John$_i$ [e_i to go to college];

(54) John$_i$ promised [e_i to turn in the paper on time];

with e unpronounced, but syntactically present.[5]

We conclude that, alongside the trace t of movement, there must be another type of empty category. The type is dubbed PRO in the standard literature: it is distinguished from t in that it is related to another element not by movement but purely through coindexing. The distinction between trace and PRO is simply that whereas in relations

$$A_i \ldots t_i$$

the position of A is not selected by the predicate with which it occurs (but only the position of t is, so that A appeared there at D-Structure), in relations

$$A_i \ldots \mathrm{PRO}_i$$

both positions are selected, by their respective predicates. It follows that PRO and trace exclude each other: if one can occur in a given position, then the other cannot.[6]

The addition of PRO to the inventory of empty categories is a lexical extension of phrase structure: PRO is a word (although not pronounced). It is an argument, but in the cases we have discussed takes an antecedent, and is thus a kind of empty pronoun. Chomsky (1977) proposed that besides the empty argument PRO there was also an empty operator O, comparable to *wh*-expressions but like PRO unpronounced. Some evidence for O comes from comparative constructions in English, as in (55)–(56):

(55) Mary is taller than Susan is;

(56) Seals eat more fish than penguins do.

In these constructions the final predicate is reduced to null phonological shape; but the form of the auxiliary indicates that it is reduced from the predicate of the comparative, the adjective *tall* in the case of (55), or the VP *eat fish* in the case of (56). Chomsky (1977) suggests that the relation between the antecedent predicate and the deletion site is mediated by the empty operator O, which like *wh*-expressions has undergone movement, so that we have at S-Structure (57) and (58):

(57) Mary is taller than [O_i [Susan is t_i]];

(58) Seals eat more fish than [O_i [penguins do t_i]].

---

[5] The above deduction depends upon the assumption that understood elements are explicitly represented at each linguistic level; this is an informal version of the *projection principle* of Chomsky (1981).

[6] For suppose otherwise. Then we have S-Structures as in (i) and (ii):

(i) $[\ldots A_i \ldots P_1 \ldots t_i \ldots P_2 \ldots]$

(ii) $[\ldots A_i \ldots P_1 \ldots \mathrm{PRO}_i \ldots P_2 \ldots]$

(linear order irrelevant), where P_1 is the predicate hosting A_i and P_2 is the predicate hosting t_i or PRO_i. If (ii) is allowed, then A_i and PRO are independently selected by P_1 and P_2 respectively, or else selected in different positions of P_1 if $P_1 = P_2$. In either case the grammatical function of A_i in (i) is not exhausted by its role as a certain argument of P_2; so if (ii) is allowed then (i) is not.

Part of the evidence for this view comes from dialects of English where a *wh*-expression may actually appear in the position of *O*, as in (59)–(60):

(59) Mary is taller than what Susan is;

(60) Seals eat more fish than what penguins do.

Application of the theory extends far beyond these cases, and in particular to the case of *easy*-constructions, which we discuss immediately below. Assuming the account to this point, we have empty categories

t, PRO, *O*

each with its specific properties, as additions to the lexicon.

3.4. Analysis of easy *versus* eager

In light of our theoretical sketch, we return to the analysis of (16)–(17), repeated here:

(16) John is easy to please;
(17) John is eager to please;

the D-Structure of (16) will be as in (61):

(61) [John is [easy [PRO to please *O*]]];

with *O* an empty operator, and PRO an empty pronominal. The operator, like the *wh*-expression of a relative clause, moves to a position external to its clause, being interpreted through a relation with the subject *John*. We thus derive (62) at S-Structure:

(62) [John_i is [easy [O_i [PRO to please t_i]]]].

For (17), however, the D-Structure will be as in (63):

(63) [John is eager [PRO to please]];

with intransitive *please*. The subject PRO is obligatorily related to the matrix subject *John*, so that we have just (64):

(64) [John_i is eager [PRO_i to please]].

Turning now to the explanation of the grammatical divergences between the structures into which the roots *easy* and *eager* may respectively enter, we propose:

(a) *easy* is a one-place predicate, whose appearance with both a subject and an object in (16) is admitted only because the subject is related to the object position of the complement, as mediated by the empty operator. Hence *It is easy to please John* is grammatical, with the structure (65):

(65) [It is [easy [PRO to please John]]];

eager, however, is a two-place predicate, requiring both a subject and a complement, so that in (66) the word *it* will not be an expletive, and will in fact be related to PRO:

(66) [It$_i$ is [eager [PRO$_i$ to please John]]];

(b) The affix *-ness* when attached to an adjective does not disrupt the relation between the understood subject PRO and the subject of the underlying predicate, but in some way disrupts the communication between the operator *O* and the subject; thus we have *John's eagerness to please*, but not **John's easiness to please*. Compare also:

(67) the problem's hardness;

(68) *the problem's hardness to solve;

(c) Since *easy* is a one-place predicate, we can have *To please John is easy*, just as we have (65); but not **To please John is eager*, from which the subject has been omitted.

3.5. Long-distance dependencies in LGB

The representation of the long-distance dependency that consists in number agreement between a higher V and an NP related to an expletive *there* realized in the higher subject position, as in (25), repeated here, will now proceed as follows:

(25) There seems to be *men/a man walking.

First of all, there is no need to insert *there* at D-Structure, since its occurrence is predictable. We may have therefore the structure (69), with e an empty element in the subject positions of both higher and lower clauses:

(69) [*e* [seem [*e* to be [a man (sing)] in the garden]]].

Assume that there is number agreement between *a man* and the e of the lower clause.[7] That e then moves to the position of the higher *e*, carrying its singular number with it, and thus imposing agreement with the tensed main V *seem*. It also spells out in English as *there*. The long-distance dependency between singular *a man* and singular *seems* in (25) is therefore a product of three local processes: number agreement between *a man* and the *e* of the lower clause; movement, retaining the number feature; and number agreement between *seems* and the moved empty category.

The long-distance dependency exemplified by *wh*-movement is created by a movement transformation mapping D-Structure into S-Structure. Visibly, the movement is leftward. There are, however, considerations that suggest that we were right also to regard it as "upward", or to the higher position selected by '?' in (35), in a way to be characterized more fully below. Notice that the movement of embedded e in (69) is upward, the subject of a sentence being higher in the phrase structure than the subject of any sentence that it properly contains. Evidence that the leftward movement of *wh* shares this property is provided by the observation that *wh*-movement is suppletive with clause-introducing words of the type that Otto Jespersen called *complementizers*. English, for example, has relative clauses like (70) and (71), but never the likes of (72):

[7] The relation between these items is a special case of a *chain* in the sense of Chomsky (1981); for extensive discussion of chains of the expletive type, see particularly Safir (1985).

(70) the book (that) I read;

(71) the book which I read;

(72) *the book which that I read/the book that which I read.

The point continues to hold for embedded clauses. Thus we have embedded declaratives, as in (73) and embedded interrogatives as in (74), but their introducing words may not appear together, as in the ungrammatical (75):

(73) I know [that you read the book];

(74) I know [which book you read];

(75) *I know [that which book you read].

As shown especially in Bresnan (1972), these and similar facts follow at once if we but suppose that embedded clauses are introduced by the category C = complementizer, a designated position into which a *wh*-expression can move; and if we assume further that a *wh*-expression and an ordinary complementizer such as *that* cannot both occupy this position.[8]

The sense in which substitution and adjunction are always "upward" is explained more precisely in Section 5 below. In combination with the confinement of all syntactic movement to these two operations, the possibilities for syntactic movement are still further restricted.

4. Logical form

The notion of Logical Form (hereafter, LF), as proposed in Chomsky (1976) and subsequent work by him and many others, and incorporated as an intrinsic part of the LGB theory, is advanced with the thought that the levels of D-Structure and S-Structure may be insufficient for theoretical purposes. From a purely syntactic point of view there are two types of considerations that may support the thesis that a more abstract linguistic level, to which S-Structure representations constitute the input, is to be found in human language. First, there may be generalizations about given languages that are not stateable at the level of S-Structure, suggesting that a more abstract level of description is wanted. Second, the analysis of systematic similarities or differences among languages (or among dialects of given languages, or, still more finely, among styles of speech in particular speakers) may resist classification in terms of S-Structure distinctions. We give examples of both types.[9]

[8] In some languages, as in some dialects of Dutch, the latter condition does not always hold. If anything, however, this observation turns out to support Bresnan's analysis, since the differences between these dialects and other closely related ones is readily described, given that *wh*-movement (putting aside certain details) effectively a substitution or adjunction within a designated higher position.

[9] A guiding theme of research into LF is the thought that differences among languages that would mandate different semantic algorithms are wiped out at LF, so that there is effectively a unique interface between form and meaning; see Higginbotham (1985), among others. Here, however, we confine the discussion to considerations of a syntactic nature only. For an overview of proposals about LF, see especially Huang (1995).

4.1. Negative polarity

Considerable work has been devoted to the distribution in English and other languages of expressions that require to be hosted by negation or another appropriate "negative" element, the so-called *negative polarity items*. From English an example is afforded by the word *ever*, as it occurs in (76):

(76) Mary didn't ever go to France.

The meaning of *ever* is existential; that is, the interpretation of (76) is as in (77):[10]

(77) Not (for some past time τ) Mary goes to France at τ.

In (76), the existential is understood within the scope of negation, a necessary condition for the appearance of *ever* since scattered negations that do not take *ever* in their scope do not license it:

(78) *Mary ever didn't go to France.

Now, besides explicit negation, expressions with an appropriately "negative" meaning can host *ever*:

(79) I doubt/*believe that [Mary will ever go to France];

(80) Few people/*Many people thought that [Mary would ever go to France].

In these cases *ever* is interpreted within the scope of the negative element, *doubt* in the case of (79), *few people* in the case of (80). Now consider (81)–(82):

(81) Fathers of few children ever go to Euro-Disney;

(82) *Fathers with few children ever go to Euro-Disney;

(these are modeled after an original discussion due to Jackendoff (1972)). The negative *few children* in the subject NP of (81) is taken with scope over the whole sentence, but

---

[10] An alternative hypothesis, which would suffice for (76), is that *ever* represents a universal quantification taking wider scope than the negation. But this hypothesis is refuted by the consideration of contexts '. . . τ . . .' where the interpretation

(For all τ) Not . . . τ . . .

clearly fails to represent the meaning of the sentence

Not . . . ever . . .

For example, consider (i):

(i) Mary is not likely ever to go to France

Evidently, (i) does not have it that

(For all τ) Not (it is likely Mary goes to France at τ)

but rather that

Not (it is likely that (for some τ) Mary goes to France at τ)

In the text we cleave to simpler examples, for ease of exposition.

the same expression in (82) is interpreted within the NP; and the first but not the second can serve as host to the negative polarity item in the predicate.

The distinction between (81) and (82), and the condition on the distribution of the negative polarity item *ever*, is easily stated: this expression must occur within the scope of a negative element. But the condition is not represented at S-Structure, which does not relevantly distinguish the grammatical (81) from the ungrammatical (82). The hypothesis therefore suggests itself that (rather as *easy* and *eager* were distinguished at D-Structure and S-Structure, but not at the level of elementary phrase structure) there is a level of linguistic description at which scope is marked explicitly. This level will be distinct from S-Structure, in which such marking pays no role.[11]

4.2. Antecedent-contained deletion

A second notable example motivating LF is provided by the phenomenon of *antecedent-contained VP deletion*, exemplified by (83):

(83) John went everywhere that Bill did $\emptyset$.

The position marked by '$\emptyset$' is the site of ellipsis. Naturally, the sentence is understood as in (84):

(84) For every place x such that Bill went to x, John went to x.

But how is this interpretation arrived at? For cases like (85), we may suggest that the antecedent VP *went everywhere* is simply copied into the site marked by '$\emptyset$':

(85) John went everywhere, and then Bill did $\emptyset$.

But for (83) this cannot be: the ellipsis site is itself part of the VP that constitutes the antecedent. How, then, should the obvious principle governing VP-deletion, namely

Delete VP under conditions of identity with another VP

be stated in general? The evident solution, due in different forms to Sag (1976) and Williams (1977), and recently examined at length in Fiengo and May (1994), is to propose that the quantifier phrase *everywhere that Bill did* takes scope over the sentence, giving a structure we may represent as (86):

(86) [everywhere that Bill did $\emptyset$] [John went t];

with t the trace of abstract quantifier movement. At this point the antecedent of the ellipsis site is *went* t, which does not contain it. The resulting representation, (87), is easily understood as having the proper semantics as in (84):

[11] There are several ways of marking scope, which we do not distinguish here. It is sufficient for our purposes that there be syntactic phenomena that show the need to do so.

(87) [everywhere that Bill did go *t*] [John went *t*].

The crucial step in this derivation is the one that leads from the S-Structure representation of (83) to (86); the latter is not an S-Structure, but an element of LF. Thus the hypothesis that LF representations may be derived from S-Structure by such operations as indication of scope enables us to state quite generally the condition on well-formedness of sentences with negative polarity items, and the simple operation that restores ellipsis. At S-Structure no such simple statement is possible.[12]

We have considered two cases where generalizations about English, namely (i) that negative polarity items are licensed only within the scope of negative elements, and (ii) that VP-deletion is licensed under conditions of identity with another VP, are not stateable at S-Structure, but are stateable at a level LF, once scope has been explicitly assigned.

It was remarked above that although English showed *wh*-movement, many languages did not. In both Japanese and Chinese, for instance, the expressions whose meaning corresponds to that of English *wh*-expressions occur in all sentences in exactly the same positions where non-*wh*-expressions of the same types could go. For such languages, one might expect that the scopes of *wh*-expressions would be limited by sense only, and not also by formal grammar. However, studies of both (very different types of) languages have shown not only that there are formal limitations, but also that they differ among languages. Since these differences are evidently unpredictable from any simple properties of S-Structures, it is natural to take them as reflecting properties of LF.[13]

We thus arrive at the following picture: linguistic structures are generated initially from the lexicon, more inclusive structures being built up as they may be licensed by projection rules for modifiers and arguments. Movement (leaving trace), which is always to higher positions, is confined to substitution and adjunction. We have then partial responses to the requirements of a theory with components (I)–(III) enumerated above. After presenting a somewhat more formal treatment, we return to the question (IV), of limiting the scope of the principles involved.

5. Formal development and applications

In this section we develop some of the elements of a formal theory of phrase markers (with reference to S-Structure, although the theory could be applied to any of the levels discussed). Referring back to the examples given above, we see that a phrase marker has an hierarchical structure together with a linear ordering of elements, and that these elements carry grammatical information of various sorts. We develop these components in turn.

---

[12] Lasnik (1993) offers a different account of antecedent-contained deletion. Lappin (1995) surveys approaches to this and other cases of ellipsis, in some cases placing a heavy burden on semantic principles. All of these views, however, involve enrichment either of the syntax or of the (otherwise trivial) semantics for quantified sentences, and to that extent depart from the simplest assumptions.

[13] Seminal work in this area includes Huang (1982) on Chinese, Nishigauchi (1990) on Japanese, and Lasnik and Saito (1991) on the comparative syntax of (overt and abstract) *wh*-movement.

5.1. Trees, ordering, and labels

A *tree* is a partially ordered set $T = (X, \geqslant)$ such that, for each element x of X, $\{y\colon y \geqslant x\}$ is well-ordered by $\geqslant$ (in empirical linguistics one considers only finite trees, so that linear ordering is sufficient). The elements of T are the *points* or *nodes* of $(T, \geqslant)$. The relation $\geqslant$ is the relation of *domination*. The relation of *proper domination* is $>$, defined by

$$x > y \text{ iff } x \geqslant y \ \& \ x \neq y.$$

A *root* of a tree is a point x such that $x \geqslant y$ for every $y \in T$; since $\geqslant$ is a partial ordering, the root of a tree is unique if it exists. Linguistics generally considers only trees possessing roots, and we shall assume this restriction here. An *ordered* tree is a tree $(T, \geqslant)$ together with a linear ordering O_0 among the set of points that have no successors; i.e. points x such that $x \geqslant y$ implies $x = y$ (the *leaves*, to continue the arboreal terminology); this ordering is projected to the relation O defined by:

$$O(x, y) \text{ iff for every leaf } w \text{ such that } x \geqslant w \text{ and every leaf } u \text{ such that } y \geqslant u,\ O_0(w, u).$$

If T has the property that

$$x \ngeqslant y \ \& \ y \ngeqslant x \text{ implies } O(x, y) \vee O(y, x)$$

then T is *connected*, and the points of T are said to be *continuous*.[14]

The trees of linguistic theory are completed by the designation of their points as occupied by words or other expressions, including symbols for categories, drawn from the theoretical vocabulary. Formally, let Ω be a set of *labels*. A relation L contained in $X \times \Omega$ is a *labeling* of T. The labels represent predicates, true of the points that they occupy; the exact details will depend upon what conception of labels is in force.[15] Fully ticketed, then, a phrase marker is a structure

$$\mathbf{P} = (T, O, L)$$

[14] Trees with discontinuous points have been noted as a possibility for languages with relatively free word order, and for languages exhibiting basic orders that would disallow the types of constituency that are generally attested elsewhere. A canonical example of the latter type is Irish, whose basic order is Verb-Subject-Object. If Verb and Object form a constituent VP, however, the resulting tree must either be disconnected, or else the surface order must reflect an obligatory movement of one or more of S, V, and O. In fact there is evidence that the latter is the case (see for instance Speas (1992), which reviews work in this area): what is generated in phrase structure is in fact S-[V-O], and V subsequently moves to the left of S, giving rise to the observed ordering. For languages of the former type, with relatively free word order, similar "movement" solutions have been devised. On the other hand, it has been argued that there are exceptional constructions even in languages like English that do not in general permit discontinuous constituents: see McCawley (1982).

[15] The categorial labels, such as N, V, and their projections may be interpreted as predicates true of $x \in X$ meaning "x (or the subtree with root x) is a verb", or "...is a noun", and so forth. The labeling L is normally considered a function with respect to such labels; that is, at most one categorial label is available for a given point. This consideration in turn can be derived if one regards categories as sets of features (more primitive labels), assuming that feature sets may not conflict. However, there is nothing in principle that rules out non-functional labelings. Evidently, the choice of primitives, rather open at the present stage of inquiry, will be crucial for the abstract theory.

where T is a tree, O is the ordering projected from the initial ordering O_0 on the leaves of T, and L is the labeling relation.

Consider in the light of these definitions the example (4), reproduced here:

(4)

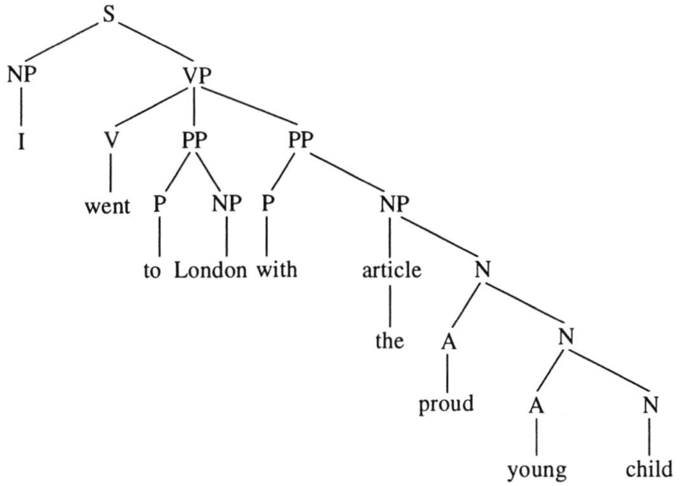

The ordering $\geqslant$ is displayed; the ordering O_0 is the order of the words as they would be spoken, and it is extended to an ordering that, e.g., puts the PP *to London* in the relation O to the N *proud young child.*

We have said that labels represent predicates of points, so that if the label P attaches to point x, then P is true of x. This understanding still leaves it open what to say if a point does not bear a certain label; here different conventions may be adopted. Questions arise also about *redundancy*; for linguistic principles may be such as to imply that a label P must attach to a point x. (4) already contains some possible examples. Thus the label VP attaching to the predecessor of V is predictable, since V are only heads, and never modifiers.

Besides the many details about the nature of labels that would have to be settled in a full formalization of elementary phrase structure with labeled trees, there arises the question whether, besides the one-place predicates that the labels signify, there are also two-place predicates, or linguistically significant binary relations between points in phrase structure. This question actually comes in two forms. First, there are relations definable in tree structures (definable, that is, in terms of $\geqslant$ and O and the resources of logic and set theory) and labels that may play a role; and second there may be specifically linguistic relations not so definable that should be posited to explain the phenomena of linguistic organization. We consider these in turn.

5.2. *Definable binary relations*

A central example of a definable binary relation is that of *c-command* (so named by Reinhart (1976), and superseding the closely related notion *in construction with*, due to Edward Klima). It is defined as follows:

> x c-commands y iff neither of x and y dominates the other, and the least point that properly dominates x and has more than one successor also dominates y.

This notion, call it CC, is (first-order) definable in terms of the primitive relation $\geqslant$. We define it in full by way of illustration. Put:

(i) y is a *successor* of $x =_{\mathrm{df}} x > y$ & $\neg(\mathbf{E}z)(x > z > y)$;
(ii) Px is a *branching point* $=_{\mathrm{df}}$ $(\mathbf{E}y)(\mathbf{E}z)(y \neq z$ & y and z are successors of $x)$.

Then:

(iii) $\mathrm{CC}(x, y) =_{\mathrm{df}} \neg(x \geqslant y)$ & $\neg(y \geqslant x)$
& $(\mathbf{A}w)$ (w is a branching point & $w > x \rightarrow w \geqslant z$).

Definability of linguistic relations of the sort discussed to this point (e.g., number- agreement) and below in this subsection is similarly straightforward.[16]

The c-command relation is exactly the conception of *scope* in standard formalized languages; thus a constituent x c-commands a constituent y if and only if y is within the scope of x. To see this point, notice that the common inductive definition governing quantifiers is:

If Φ is a formula and v is a variable, then

$$(\mathbf{E}v)\Phi$$

is a formula. This inductive clause corresponds to the licensing of a tree

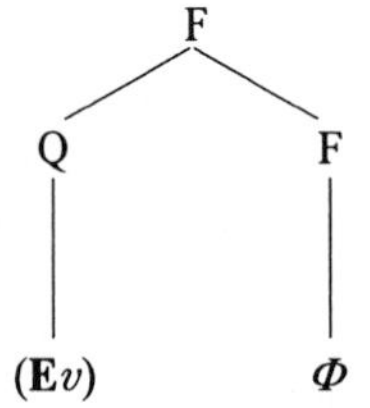

in which the quantifier label Q immediately dominating '$(\mathbf{E}v)$' c-commands Φ. The concept of scope has a semantic correlate, in that occurrences of a variable within the scope of a quantifier appearing with that variable are bound by the quantifier. A point of considerable interest is that c-command, or syntactic scope, has over a wide domain the semantic effects of scope in formalized languages. The discovery that a theory of binding can be constructed along these lines is one of the chief pillars of GB theory.

Various modifications of the fundamental c-command relation have been suggested for different purposes. One that we will employ below is that of *m-command*, defined by:

---

[16] The definition of c-command in terms of branching points is necessitated, on a classical conception, by the fact that an element can be simultaneously a lexical head X^0 and a maximal projection X'', so that structures $[_{X''}[_{X'}[_{X^0}]]]$ are possible. Where these elements are merged, and the lexical items occupying a point X^0 are part of its label, then every non-leaf is a branching point, and the extra information is not needed. Even so, some modified command relations will attend, given X and Y, to the least subtree dominating both.

> x m-commands y iff neither of x and y dominates the other, and every maximal projection that properly dominates x also dominates y.

The concepts of m-command and c-command are very close. If we assume that every non-lexical node branches; that every element other than the root is properly dominated by a maximal projection; and that maximal projections are of level no greater than 2, then m-command includes c-command, and only a little bit more. The case that we will employ in 7.2 below uses the fact that a head X^0 adjoined to a head Y^0 that c-commands it will m-command (though it will not c-command) its own trace, as in (88):

(88) $[_{Y''} \ldots [_{Y'} [^0_Y Y^0 + X^0] \ldots t_{X^0}]]]$.

Since Y is not a maximal projection, the least (and therefore every) maximal projection properly dominating X dominates t^0_X.

Aoun and Sportiche (1981) suggested that the relation of government could be defined as mutual m-command:

> x *governs* y iff x and y m-command each other.

On this definition, heads always govern their complements, but govern their subjects only if they are in the maximal projection, as shown in (89):

(89) $[_Z X [_{H'} H\ Y]]$.

Here H and Y are sisters, so that H governs Y necessarily; but H governs X if and only if H′ is not a maximal projection. Therefore, in the familiar

$$[_S NP [_{VP} V\ NP]]$$

where VP is maximal, V does not govern the subject NP.[17]

We said above that there were two allowable movement operations, substitution and adjunction. Suppose these operations must have the effect of putting the moved element into a position from which it c-commands the site from which it moved. Then, besides restricting allowable movements, we imply (a) that substitution of X for Y is possible only if Y c-commands X; and (b) that so far as the c-command requirement goes X may adjoin to a point Y if and only if Y dominates X. Point (a) is immediate. For (b), we observe that from a structure

$$\ldots [_Y \ldots X \ldots] \ldots$$

in which Y properly dominates X, adjunction of X to Y produces

$$\ldots [_Y X [_Y \ldots t_X \ldots]] \ldots$$

---

[17] For a systematization of various command relations see especially Barker and Pullum (1990), and further Kracht (1993).

so that X c-commands its trace; and that from a structure

$$\ldots [_Y \ldots] \ldots X \ldots$$

where Y does not dominate X, adjunction of X to Y produces

$$\ldots [_Y X [_Y \ldots]] \ldots t_X \ldots$$

where X c-commands only material within (the old) Y, hence not the trace t_X of X.

Consider in this light the operation of *wh*-movement discussed above. In ordinary English questions and in relative clauses the movement of some *wh* to the left periphery of the clause is obligatory: hence it is natural to regard it as a substitution operation. But then the restriction on movement imposed by the requirement that substitution be to a c-commanding position implies that the point of substitution c-commands the *wh*-expression, so that the input structure for the operation that produces the examples in (29) and (30) must be as in (90):

(90)

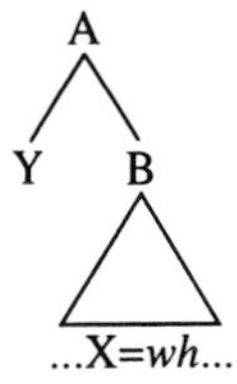

with X substituting in position Y. The point B will carry the label of a clause of some sort, and it may be taken as the complement of Y, acting as the head of the construction. If so, then A is Y′, and *wh*-movement carries an appropriate element into the position of a head, for reasons yet to be determined. The restrictions on movement imposed by c-command thus carry strong implications for input and derived structures under substitution, and the conclusion harmonizes with the idea that *wh*-movement is into the position of a complementizer, as suggested above, following Bresnan.

A similar point can be made about adjunction, at least if we assume that c-command in human languages is correlated with scope. Consider the ambiguous (91):

(91) John didn't go out because he (John) was sick.

The speaker of (91) may be affirming that John didn't go out, and stating that the reason for this was that he was sick; or may merely be denying that it was because he was sick that John went out. The ambiguity must be structural, and is determined by whether the subordinate clause *because he was sick* is outside the scope of negation, as in the first possibility, or within it, as in the second. The subordinate clause is a modifier in the broad sense; that is, the main clause *John didn't go out* is complete without it. Hence it is adjoined rather than a complement, and must in one interpretation not be c-commanded, and in the other be c-commanded, by the negation *not*. If the subordinate clause is proposed, then it may not be interpreted as within the scope of negation:

(92) Because he was sick, John didn't go out

an expected result, since the clause must now have adjoined to a position from which it c-commands the main clause, and the negation in particular. On the other hand, if we replace the subject in (91) by a *wh*-expression, we can see that the pronoun in the subordinate clause can be taken as bound to it, with either interpretation available:

(93) Who didn't go out because he was sick?

It follows that the *wh*-expression c-commands the pronoun *he*, and therefore that in the interpretation where *x*'s being sick is the reason for *x*'s not going out we shall have a structure as in (94):

(94)

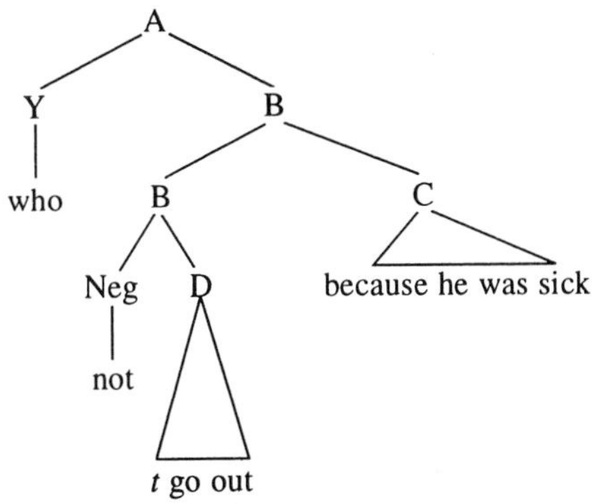

We have seen how the definable notion of c-command can be invoked as a general principle governing syntactic movement, thus partly responding to (IV) of the enumeration in Section 2 above. Our original description of the operation of *wh*-movement can now be refined as (95):

(95) Move a *wh*-expression into an appropriate complementizer.

However, we still do not have a sufficient restriction on *wh*-movement: recall that although all acceptable cases could be described in terms of movement to a left periphery (or now into the complementizer position, which in fact occurs there), not all cases of such movement were acceptable. To distinguish between the acceptable and unacceptable cases a number of conditions have been proposed, of which we outline the best known, based on Chomsky (1973), which itself endeavored to mold as far as possible into a single system the different constraints of Ross (1967).

Following a version of the original definition due to Chomsky (1973), say that a point x is *subjacent* to a point y in a phrase marker $\mathbf{P} = (T, O, L)$ if y c-commands x and the path consisting of the points in **P** lying between x and the least branching point dominating y contains at most one point bearing some label chosen from a set B of *barriers*.[18] Then given an interpretation of B, subjacency is definable in terms of domination. Suppose that

(96) If **P′** is immediately derived from **P** by moving a constituent X from a point x to a point y, then x is subjacent to y;

[18] The terminology here is anachronistic, but seems preferable to the older term *bounding nodes*. For a computational development of the theory of barriers in the contemporary sense, see Stabler (1992).

and furthermore that

(97) NP and S are barriers.

Then one immediately verifies that the examples in (29) and (30) satisfy (96)–(97), but those in (31) do not. For example, in the case of (31a), repeated here with traces and barriers shown as (98), the position of the trace *t* is not subjacent to the complementizer (in fact, three barriers intervene):

(98) [[Which book] [$_S$did [$_{NP}$the man who [$_S$$t'$ likes *t*]] talk to you]].

Now, it is possible to move *wh*-expressions over long distances, as in (99):

(99) [[Which book] [$_S$did John think [$_S$Mary said [$_S$I want [$_S$her to read *t*]]]]].

But in these cases it is supposed that the *wh*-expression moves step by step through the intervening complementizer positions, so that the structure is as in (100):

(100) [[Which book] [[$_S$did John think [*t*[$_S$Mary said [*t*[$_S$I want [*t*[$_S$her to read *t*]]]]]]]]];

and subjacency is preserved. No such movement is possible in (98), since (a) NP presumably lacks a complementizer position, and (b) the relative pronoun *who* fills the complementizer position in the relative clause. Similar reasoning serves to block (31b), repeated here with barriers shown:

(31) (b) *What [$_S$did you put [$_{NP}$the spoon or ___] on the plate].

The subjacency condition (96), then, is a prohibition against moving an element "too far" in a single step, where, crucially, "distance" is measured not in terms of the number of words (which may be arbitrarily long) but rather in terms of the number of phrasal points of specific types that are crossed. The ungrammaticality of (31c), repeated below, may then be owing to the fact that the *wh*-expression *how* cannot move through an intermediate position, the C of the complement to *deny*:

(31) (c) *How [$_S$did Mary deny [$_S$you fixed the car *t*]].

The subjacency condition is not sufficient to rule out all cases where movement is prohibited. In English in particular there is a particular case where even a "short" movement is prohibited, namely from the subject (but not the object) of a complement preceded by the complementizer *that*:

(101) Who do you think [that I saw *t*]?

(102) *Who do you think [that *t* saw me]?

If the complementizer is absent, then we have (103), which is fully grammatical:

(103) Who do you think [*t* saw me]?

The example (102) is the so-called "*that*-trace" effect, in the form in which it is seen in English; it is not a universal phenomenon, being absent for instance in Italian and many other languages. Although the diagnosis of the effect is still controversial, a descriptive point to which Chomsky (1981) called attention is that it may reflect the fact that subjects alone among the arguments of a V are not governed by V.

By the definition of government in terms of mutual m-command as given above, the V *see* governs the object in (101), but not the subject in (102). If traces are required to be governed, then (102) is ruled out; but so is (103), contrary to fact. However, recalling that *wh*-movement must proceed through the position C, what actually licenses *Who do you think saw me?* as a sentence is (104):

(104) Who [$_S$do you think [t[$_S t$ saw me]]]?

with an intermediate trace subjacent to *Who*, and incidentally a close relation between this trace and the trace of the subject. We might now suppose that the presence of the complementizer *that* disrupts this relation, producing ungrammaticality.[19]

5.3. *Introduced binary relations*

We have been examining the role of linguistic relations definable in terms of the given relations of domination and linear ordering, assuming some stock of labels (predicates) of points. Relations such as c-command (and other, closely related conceptions that have been prominent in the literature), subjacency, government and others are used to state conditions on well-formedness. Formally, these are either filters on single structures or conditions on the application of grammatical transformations. Traditional descriptive grammar contains many other examples of linguistic relations and conditions on well-formedness stateable in terms of such relations, and to the extent that these concepts and conditions are not superseded by the formalism of generative grammar we shall want to express them if possible within the apparatus given so far, and otherwise enrich the vocabulary of linguistic theory so as to accommodate them.

Consider in this regard the relation of subject to predicate. Chomsky (1965) argued that the notion

X is the subject of the sentence S

could be defined in terms of the properties of phrase markers, for instance by

X is the NP immediately dominated by S.

This definition is relative to a grammar *G*, but might hypothetically be extended to subjects cross-linguistically; and it can be extended to other categories than S by defining the subject of YP as the sister of the Y′ daughter of YP. The extension allows us to say,

[19] In LGB Chomsky suggested that the trace of *wh*-movement must be *properly governed*, where proper government amounted to (i) government by a lexical head (as in (101)), or (ii) *antecedent government* by a close element, as in (104). Especially in view of the cross-linguistic variability of the *that*-trace effect, modifications of this proposal have been suggested; again see Lasnik and Saito (1991) for a recent comparative analysis.

for instance, that in a nominalization such as (105) the phrase *the Romans* is the subject of NP:

(105) $[_{NP}$[the Romans'] $[_{N'}$destruction of Carthage]]

a result that accords with intuitive judgement, inasmuch as the semantic relation of the subject phrase to the N *destruction* is the same as that between subject and V in (106):

(106) The Romans destroyed Carthage.

The above definition of subject is too narrow to cover all cases, however. This point is most easily brought out by considering the converse relation of *predication*. A predicate may be predicated of a subject that is also the subject of another constituent, or indeed of one that is the object of a constituent. An example that admits both possibilities is (107):

(107) Mary left John [angry].

The predicate *angry* may be understood as predicated of the subject *Mary* or the object *John*: the choice is free. If we assume that the syntactic structure for (107) up to the relevant level of detail is just (108), then this fact is not represented:

(108) [Mary [left John angry]].

On the other hand, there are conditions that must be satisfied for a predicate to be predicated of a given constituent. Thus in (109) we cannot take *John* as subject of *angry*, although the meaning that would result from doing so, namely "Mary left John's mother when he, John, was angry", is perfectly in order:

(109) Mary left John's mother angry.

We cannot, therefore, simply omit to mention possibilities for predication in these cases.

Examples like (107) contain two predicates, namely *leave John*, unambiguously predicated of the subject *Mary*, and *angry*, which may be predicated either of the subject of the sentence or of its object. Following Rothstein (1983) we call the former the *primary* predicate, and the latter the *secondary* predicate of the construction. The subject of a primary predicate is determined by the phrase marker for the sentence in which it figures: it is the sister to the projection Y′ of the predicative head Y. But the subject of a secondary predicate is not so determined, though the candidate subjects are restricted in scope. In view of this indeterminacy Williams (1980) proposed that the relation of predication is in fact indicated in syntactic structures. This relation will not be definable, but a new primitive, subject to conditions stated in terms of the concepts already available. Examples like (109), where the subject of the secondary predicate *angry* can be the subject or object of the sentence, but not something contained within these, suggest that the c-command of predicate by subject is a necessary condition for predication. Since the subject of S and other categories c-commands the predicate, the condition is satisfied by all cases of primary predication, so that the original definition may stand for this case. But even if the range of permissible subjects for a secondary predicate is definable, secondary predication itself is not.

Besides predication, relations of co-interpretation, or *anaphora* in standard terminology, lead to an enrichment of the descriptive vocabulary for phrase markers. In general, an anaphoric relation is a relation between points in a tree that will be interpreted as expressing dependence of the interpretation of one element upon the interpretation of another. We have already seen such relations in our discussion of *easy* versus *eager*, where the subject of the complement of *eager*, and the object of the complement of *easy*, are understood as identical with the subject of the sentence. There are many similar examples. In these cases no ambiguity is possible; but with ordinary pronouns there are clear ambiguities, which there is to this point no way to represent.

Consider in this light the possible interpretations for (93), repeated here:

(93) Who didn't go out because he was sick?

In discussing this example above we were interested in the interpretation where the pronoun was taken as a variable bound to the *wh*-expression *who*. As we have already seen, the movement of the *wh*-expression in (93) is taken to leave a trace coindexed with the moved element. The coindexing represents an anaphoric relation, and it is natural to extend the relation to include optional relations such as that between the pronoun and the *wh*-expression. We would then derive the representation shown in (110), where both trace and pronoun are dependent upon the quasi-quantifier *who*:[20]

(110) [Who$_i$] [t_i didn't go out because he$_i$ was sick].

Anaphoric relations between pronouns and true quantifiers may be annotated in the same manner, as in (111):

(111) [Every boy]$_i$ loves his$_i$ mother.

In the context of this overview, the introduction of anaphoric relations should be seen as an essential enrichment of the theory of phrase markers, since these relations are not definable in terms of anything antecedently given. Supposing them introduced, the question arises what conditions if any there are on their structure, as determined by the linear or hierarchical properties of the trees in which they figure. Surveying the relations considered thus far, we see that coindexing has been licensed in the position occupied by X in trees such as (112):

(112)

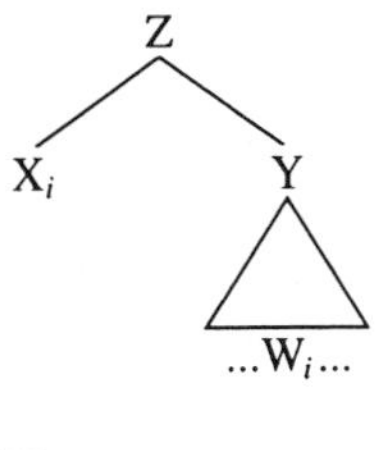

[20] The motivation given here for the explicit annotation of anaphoric relations actually reverses the historical order, inasmuch as coindexing was suggested as early as Chomsky (1965) (replacing earlier "pronominalization" theories of anaphora), antedating by some years the trace theory of movement rules.

Further inquiry reveals that we do not in general get coindexing licensed in arbitrary structures such as (113):

(113)

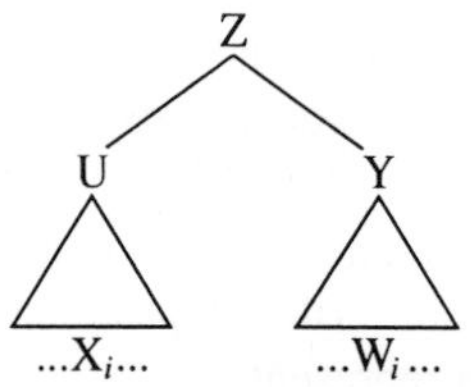

Moreover, it is a firm observation that subject pronominals may not be bound by the complements of their own predicates, or any arguments contained in those complements. Thus contrast (114) with (115):

(114) Who [t thinks [he is a nice fellow]];
(115) Who [does he think [t is a nice fellow]].

(114) can be interpreted as a general question, asking which persons x (in the relevant set) are of the opinion that x is a nice fellow. Not so (115), where the only interpretation is, for some indicated person α, the question which persons x are such that α is of the opinion that x is a nice fellow.

Suppose now that the relation of c-command governs coindexing, as suggested most prominently in Reinhart (1983). A signal feature of this concept is that it is completely indifferent to the linear order of expressions. Think of a linearly ordered tree as if it were a mobile, with elements free to spin, altering the order of constituents. A hierarchical structure such as (116) could then give rise to any of the orders in (117):

(116)

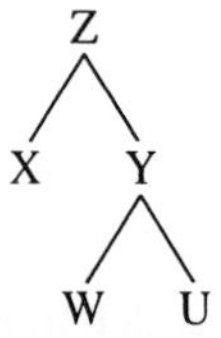

(117) XWU; XUW; WUX; UWX.

In (116), and likewise in all other linear arrangements, X c-commands U, but U does not c-command X.

Although linearity and c-command are fundamentally different notions, there is a specific case where they will coincide. Following standard terminology, say that a language is *right branching* if its system of phrasal projection, with hierarchical structure as in (116), always yields one of the orders XWU or XUW, and *left branching* if it yields WUX or UWX. It is easily seen that English (and for that matter most of the more familiar European languages) are right branching. In such languages, subjects precede objects (modulo stylistic or "scrambling" rules), and therefore a preceding argument will normally c-command a following one.

The c-command condition on coindexing, regulating anaphoric relations, led in the LGB theory to a systematic account of anaphora in English, the *binding theory* as it was called there. As originally presented, the theory divided expressions according to whether or not they had a *pronominal* character, and whether or not they were *anaphoric*. These terms overlap but do not coincide with the familiar notions of pronouns on the one hand, and elements that require antecedents on the other. Research since LGB has led to a number of modifications, both within English and cross-linguistically: we concentrate here on the abstract properties of the original theory, which it generally shares with its successors.

It is straightforward to confirm that in English the *reflexive* forms *herself, ourselves* etc. must (apart from a few isolated locutions, not considered here) have antecedents, and that their antecedents must not only c-command but also be sufficiently "close" to them; that ordinary pronominals *her, us* etc. may but need not have antecedents, and that these, if c-commanding, cannot be too "close" to them; and, finally, that elements such as names, definite descriptions, quantifiers and the like, dubbed *R-expressions* in LGB, cannot be related at all to elements that c-command them. Thus we have contrasts like those in (118), (119), and (120):

(118) (a) She saw herself in the mirror

(b) She saw her in the mirror (does not mean that she saw herself in the mirror)

(c) She saw Mary in the mirror (does not mean that Mary saw herself in the mirror)

(119) (a) *She wants them to visit herself

(b) She wants them to visit her (can mean that she is an x such that x wants them to visit x)

(c) She wants them to visit Mary (cannot mean that Mary is an x such that x wants them to visit x)

(120) (a) She wants herself to visit them

(b) She wants her to visit them (cannot mean that she is an x such that x wants x to visit them)

(c) She wants Mary to visit them (cannot mean that Mary is an x such that x wants x to visit them)

(118a) shows a reflexive with a close c-commanding antecedent, the subject *she*; in (118b), where the reflexive is replaced with an ordinary pronominal, the pronominal cannot have this antecedent; and where the object of *see* is occupied by an R-expression, *Mary*, the subject and object cannot be related (as indicated by the gloss). In (119a) there is a potential c-commanding antecedent for the reflexive, the subject *she*; but it is in some sense too far away; in (119b) an anaphoric relation between *her* and the subject is possible; but as (119c) shows the subject pronoun and an R-expression still cannot be related. Finally, (120a) shows that the antecedent of a reflexive need not (at least on the assumption that the complement of *wants* is the full infinitival clause *herself to visit them*) be an argument of the same predicate as the reflexive; (120b) that the complementarity between reflexives and pronominals holds also for this case; and (120c) that the embedded R-expression continues to resist any relation to the subject.

Say that X is *A(rgument)-bound* if it is c-commanded by and coindexed with an argument, and that it is *A(rgument)-free* otherwise, that an *anaphor* is an expression that is +anaphoric and −pronominal, a *pronominal* is −anaphoric and +pronominal, and an *R-expression* is −anaphoric and −pronominal. Then the general account of the distribution above is as in (A)–(C) below (simplified from Chomsky (1981)):

(A) An anaphor is locally A-bound;

(B) A pronominal is locally A-free;

(C) An R-expression is A-free.[21]

With these points to hand, we return to the examples (114)–(115), repeated here:

(114) Who [*t* thinks [he is a nice fellow]];

(115) Who [does he think [*t* is a nice fellow]].

It was remarked above that whereas (114) could be interpreted as a general question, with the pronoun *he* effectively functioning as a bound variable, (115) could not. For (114), we can recognize the trace *t* as the antecedent of the pronoun, just as the name *John* can serve as antecedent in (121):

(121) John_i thinks [he_i is a nice fellow].

For (115), we can take the step of assimilating the trace bound by an expression of generality (including ordinary quantifiers and *wh*) to R-expressions. That will imply that the representation (122), although perfectly meaningful (and in fact meaning the same thing as (114) with the pronoun and trace coindexed), is ungrammatical:

(122) Who_i [does he_i think [t_i is a nice fellow]].

In sum, the theory of anaphoric relations constitutes an intrinsic part of the theory of linguistic structures and their interpretations, one that interacts with but is not reducible to relations definable in terms of labels and configuration.

Resuming the question of the nature of phrase markers, we now recognize structures

$$\mathbf{P} = (T, O, L, R_1, \ldots, R_n)$$

where T, O, and L are as above, and the R_i are linguistic relations among the points of T, including at least the relation *predicate-of* and the relation *antecedent-of*, but perhaps involving others as well. Furthermore, we conceive the syntax of a human language to be derivational, mapping D-Structures into S-Structures via a restricted set of grammati-

[21] In LGB, locality was defined in terms of minimal categories dominating the pronoun or anaphor. In the rapid cross-linguistic development that followed, it was shown that if anaphoric forms were treated in this fashion, then languages diverged in various ways, notably in virtue of admitting in many cases "long-distance" anaphora, or reflexive forms that were not locally bound. These developments, however, have not disturbed the basic assumption that the acceptability of anaphora and antecedents for pronominal forms is in general configurationally determined.

cal transformations, and S-Structures into LF-representations by adjunction, determining relative scope.[22]

6. Beyond GB: Checking and copying

GB theory, with various modifications and emendations, retains several distinctive features, for each of which modifications have been suggested in recent work. In this section and the next we outline some of the points advanced in Chomsky (1993), which constitute important departures.

6.1. Morphosyntax and feature checking

In the above discussion we have considered as needed, and as customary in linguistic theory, both categorial labels and other features of points in phrase markers. It is possible to develop much of syntax as a theory of "communication" between such features, and we give a brief picture of the outline of such research.

The fundamental syntactic categories N, V, A, and P may be classified in terms of the features in the set $\{\pm N, \pm V\}$, with

$$N = \{+N, -V\}, \quad V = \{-N, +V\}, \quad A = \{+N, +V\},$$
$$\text{and} \quad P = \{-N, -V\}.$$

Besides these features, we have appealed to features for person, number, and gender. Nominative and other cases are features of heads, and nominative in particular is found in construction with tense. A label in the sense considered above may now be thought of as a set of features (in practice binary).

Particularly following the work of Baker (1988), Pollock (1989), and Chomsky (1986, 1993) we may regard tense or inflection INFL as itself a head, though one not occupied by a word but rather by an affix, and take it that subjects in ordinary tensed sentences

[22] Jaakko Hintikka especially has argued that classical conceptions of relative scope are inadequate to express all relative binding relations in natural language, and has proposed that branching or partially ordered quantifiers also be recognized. In the system of LF-representations, branching can be represented by allowing adjunction of two or more operators to the same position, as shown graphically in (i):

(i)
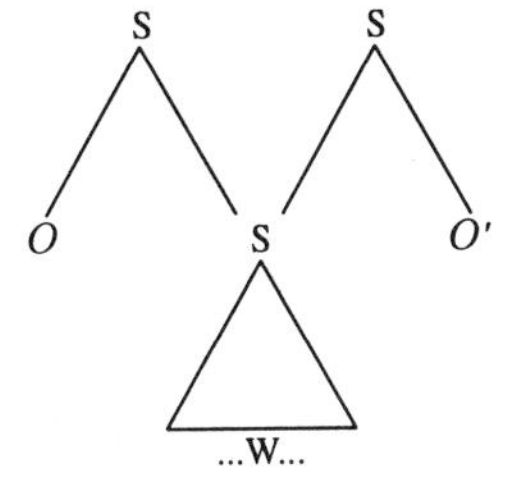

where the operators O and O' both c-command the lower S, but neither c-commands the other. If Hintikka's view is correct, then LF-representations would no longer consist exclusively of trees; but the departure from classical assumptions would be accommodated without great disruption to the system.

move to an external position so as to receive nominative case. Thus a sentence S may be regarded as a projection of INFL, so that we have the structure (123):

(123)

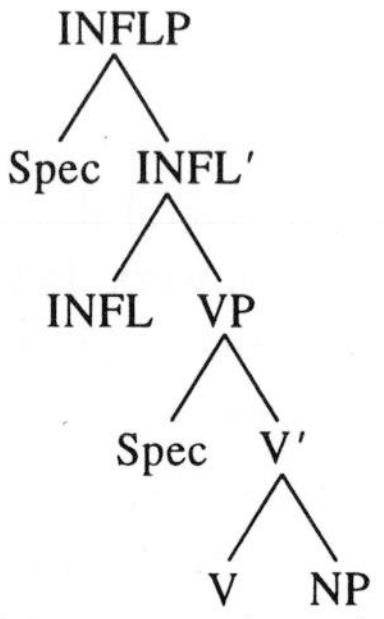

where the positions marked by 'Spec' ("specifier") are Spec(VP) = the underlying position of the subject, and Spec(IP), the position where nominative case is determined by agreement with INFL.

Contrast (123) with the LGB structure (124):

(124)

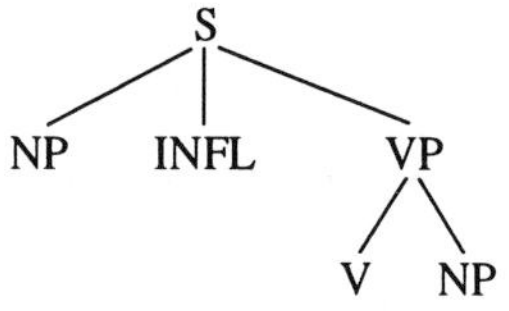

where in the simplest case INFL = Tense, as in examples given above. In both accounts the tense affix must meet up with its V somehow. But on (123) there is substantial syntactic movement even in the simplest sentences: the subject will move from Spec(VP) to Spec(INFLP), and V and INFL will combine as heads in some way to form a complex word (the present or past tense form attached to the verbal stem).

An important reason for proposing (124) as the structure for simple sentences, pointed out by Pollock (1989) following original research by Emonds (1978), is that the modes of combination of V and INFL seem to be different in different languages, with INFL "lowering" onto V in, e.g., English, and V "raising" to INFL in, e.g., French. The diagnostics for the difference include the placement of ordinary adverbs, which follow the inflected V in French, but precede it in English:

(125) (a) *John kisses often Mary;

(b) Jean embrasse souvent Marie;

(c) John often kisses Mary;

(d) *Jean souvent embrasse Marie;

(from Pollock (1989, p. 367)). Evidently, these data follow immediately if we suppose that adverbs are generated in the same positions in both languages, namely between INFL and V, but the combination V + INFL is realized by lowering INFL only in English. Pollock extends Emonds's proposal by "splitting" the inflectional head INFL into Agreement (AGR) and the Tense-bearing element I, with IP a complement of AGRP, and V in French moving through I (if it is present) to AGR, thus accounting for the fact that V-raising is required in French also for infinitives:

(126) parler à peine l'italien
to speak hardly Italian (= to hardly speak Italian).

Note that learnability considerations play a role here: the set of phrasal configurations is given once for all, and what must be learned is just the way that morphological complexes are formed.

Chomsky (1993) suggests that the principle requiring V-raising in French involves, not the movement of an uninflected V through I so as to receive inflection, but rather the movement of an inflected V (bearing Tense features) to I so as to "check" those features. All features must be checked eventually, at LF. Let a feature that requires such checking in the overt syntax be called *strong*, otherwise *weak*. The proposal then is that in both English and French the LF-representation for structures initially licensed by principles giving (123) is the same, with all V raising to I, but only in French is this movement carried out so as to be audible in the heard sentence.

We may pursue this theme more fully, but now in abstraction from actual lexical items. In English, as we saw in connection with examples like (25) and (26) above, there is "long-distance" agreement between V (but now as mediated through I)[23] and the "real" subject, even when the element occupying the surface subject position is expletive *there*. More fully, then, we might represent one of our examples above as (127):

(127) [There (α number) [$_{I}$(α number)[seems [t(α number)[to be
[[a man (α number)]walking]]];

where α = +plural or −plural. The requirement for feature sharing is simply that the value assigned to 'α number' be the same for all positions. But this requirement can be stated without mention of the specific items of vocabulary involved, so that the condition observed in (127) might ideally be expressed as (128):

(128) Spec(IP) agrees in number with its head.

Notice, however, that agreement with a head might in principle be realized without syntactic movement; i.e. without moving the entire bundle of features associated with a lexical item. Suppose, for instance, that we could detach the feature (α number) from the word *there*, and move it to Spec (IP). We would then obtain the ungrammatical (129):

(129) *Seems there to be a man walking.

That we cannot so detach features is an empirical fact, and it may be this fact, that feature bundles must move as wholes, that forces syntactic movement.

[23] Or, in fuller versions, through a special head for subject agreement; see Chomsky (1993). I pass over the extra complexity here, which would not affect the general point.

6.2. Movement and copying

Syntactic movement is a complex operation, which may in principle be broken down into several steps. In the theory with deep and surface structure, as in Chomsky (1965), it consisted of copying, followed by deletion of the copied element; on trace theory, the copied element is not deleted but replaced by a coindexed trace, syntactically visible although not itself pronounced. Yet another alternative is to retain in full the copied element, requiring only that in the two sites it occupies the pieces that are syntactically (and semantically) visible are complementary. A simple motivation for the latter view (originally pursued in a somewhat different manner in Wasow (1972)) has been suggested for the so-called problems of *reconstruction*, of which we give two canonical examples, both involving anaphora.

"Reconstruction" is a loose term, alluding to the variety of phenomena that seem to arise from the fact that a syntactic element that has undergone movement still behaves, as a whole or in part, as if it were still visible in the site from which it moved. Consider (130):

(130) Which picture of herself [did John think Mary liked *t*].

From clause (A) of the binding theory, the reflexive should not be acceptable, since its only admissible antecedent, the lower-clause subject *Mary*, does not c-command it following syntactic movement. However, the sentence is acceptable. The reflexive *herself* is in this respect behaving as though it had not moved from its underlying position, where the antecedent did indeed c-command it; it is, in other words, "reconstructed".

Barss (1986) formulated an account of such phenomena as the acceptable anaphora in (130). The account was in terms of complex conditions on S-Structure configurations, so-called "chain binding". One may suspect, however, that the complexity of these conditions is unilluminating, amounting to a way of somewhat artificially encoding the thought that it is "as if" the reflexive had not moved. Chomsky (1993) suggests that the "as if" formula be taken literally, in the sense that the output of movement is (131):

(131) Which picture of herself [did John think Mary liked [which picture of herself]].

We now consider two aspects of the structure: (i) its pronunciation, and (ii) its representation at LF.

(131) is pronounced such that the lower copy of the moved element is deleted. At LF, however, there are two options, one the structure (130), where the reflexive has no c-commanding potential antecedent, and the other (132), where it does:

(132) [Which] [did John think Mary liked [*t* picture of herself]].

The trace in (132) is the trace of the head *which* only; the remainder of the NP is in place. But now the reflexive is c-commanded by *Mary*, as desired.

Besides allowing otherwise impermissible cases of reflexive binding, the interpretation of reconstruction effects in terms of copying followed by selective deletion can capture some cases where anaphora are not possible. Recall that the condition that R-expressions be A-free was said to be responsible for the fact that the pronoun *he*, c-commanding the *wh*-trace t in (115), repeated here, could not be taken as bound to the *wh*-expression *who*:

(115) Who [does he think [t is a nice fellow]].

The condition is quite general, correctly disallowing anaphora in a number of cases. But compare (133) with (134), and these with (135) and (136), respectively:

(133) Which man [do you think [he likes t]];

(134) Which picture of which man [do you think [he likes t]];

(135) Which man [do you think [his mother likes]];

(136) Which picture of which man [do you think [his mother likes t]].

The third-person pronoun in (133) cannot be bound to *which man*, as expected. But the same is true in (134), where the pronoun c-commands, not the trace of *which man*, but rather the trace of the containing phrase *which picture of which man*; for that is the phrase that underwent syntactic movement. That it is c-command of the site of *wh*-movement by the pronoun that is playing a crucial role is seen by comparing these examples to (135)–(136), in each of which the relation of the pronoun to *which man*, although somewhat strained, is not out of the question.

Suppose now that the input structure for these binding-theoretic considerations is not the reduced structure (134), but rather the full "copied" structure (137):

(137) [Which picture of which man]$_i$ [do you think [he likes [which picture of which man]$_i$]].

In that case, the pronoun does c-command (one copy of) *which man*: and this, it may be proposed, is sufficient to block anaphora.[24]

It was suggested above that *wh*-expressions move in English, and comparable expressions in other languages, so as to realize agreement between the site of the complementizer and a feature of the clause it contains, call it +WH. But it is a striking fact that the movement of *wh*-expressions (understood now in a general sense, not confined to English) is in many languages optional, and in others impossible. Japanese is a case of the latter, where the expressions corresponding to English question words do not undergo *wh*-movement at all. It has been proposed that Japanese undergoes *wh*-movement at an abstract level, so that at LF the structures of, say, Japanese and English questions are effectively identical. But an alternative, first explored in Watanabe (1991), is that feature agreement comes about at LF without syntactic movement, either realized in the heard string, or abstract. At the abstract level a feature might as it were break apart from the bundle within which it occurs and attach itself to a higher position. So we might in principle have an abstract structure as in (138):

(138) [[+WH (α WH)] [. . . [α WH, β person, τ gender, . . .] . . .];

[24] This suggestion is different from the solution to (134) and like proposed in Chomsky (1993, pp. 48–49), and would require further elaboration of the structure of LF than can be provided here.

where the feature (α WH) is detached from its bundle and inserted for agreement in the complementizer position. The apparent difference between English and other languages showing *wh*-movement on the one hand and languages like Japanese on the other would now consist in the fact that in languages showing *wh*-movement the +WH feature hosts full syntactic items (it is a "strong" feature, like French INFL), whereas Japanese and other languages lacking *wh*-movement the feature cannot do this (it is a "weak" feature, like English INFL). Thus the theory of strong and weak features can be exploited for *wh*-movement as well as the V-to-I movement of the last subsection.

Pursuing other syntactic differences among languages along the lines just sketched for the comparative syntax of *wh*-movement, one might propose a syntactic theory consisting of the following components:

(I′) A universal system of features and their projection;

(II′) For a given language, a description of those that force syntactic movement for feature checking;

(III′) Rules governing the local conditions under which agreement takes place or features are checked;

(IV′) Principles that regulate the amount of variation that human languages may permit under (II′) and (III′).

Comparing this proposal with the research program sketched in (I)–(IV) of Section 2 above, we see important difference of detail, while the outline of requirements for obtaining an empirically adequate theory of given languages that is at the same time a theory of possible linguistic diversity remains the same. Ideally, the system of features will be small, and the conditions on feature checking reduced to highly local configurations, perhaps to be captured by a feature logic peculiar to the design of human language. Thus checking in local configurations would replace the open-ended set of filters of the LGB theory.

7. Minimalism and derivational and non-derivational syntax

In Section 2 above we presented some of the reasons for going beyond phrase structure description in an explicit syntax of English (similar arguments can be given for other languages). The type of phrase-structure descriptions considered, however, were themselves very restricted, and as we noted in passing it is possible to elaborate the level of phrase structure, thereby performing directly at least some of the work done by transformational rules.

Abstracting from the details of particular formulations, we may think of a grammar as having a *generative component*, consisting of the basis and inductive clauses that build phrase structure, and a *transformational component*, involving movement and deletion, of the types illustrated above. In the LGB theory the generative component consists exactly of the mechanisms yielding D-Structure configurations; the remainder of the grammar is derivational. The question arises, however, whether S-Structures might not be generated directly.

7.1. Generation of S-Structures

To appreciate the force of our question in the present context of inquiry, consider again the pair (16)–(17), reproduced here:

(16) John is easy to please;
(17) John is eager to please.

In Section 2 above we remarked that grammars of the type of Chomsky (1965) were intrinsically derivational, so that the distinction between (16) and (17) could not in those grammars be captured at a single, basic level of phrase structure. Now, the S-Structures of (16) and (17) in the LGB theory were (62) and (64) reproduced here:

(62) [John$_i$ is [easy [O_i [PRO to please t_i]]];
(64) [John$_i$ is [eager [PRO$_i$ to please]]].

These were derived from their respective D-Structures; but since they contain (through the traces, empty operators and coindexing shown) the information that is wanted to distinguish (16) from (17), they are not inadequate, as surface structures lacking these devices were, to express the distinction between the sentences.

Consider then the possibility of generating (62) and (63) by inductive clauses. Evidently, the relevant structures can be built up if the elements that combine are not merely categories but categories together with their labels; thus we might write for the complement of *easy*:

If C is a complementizer with the feature + operator, and
S (or IP) is a sentence, then C–S is a C′.

Especially if the outputs of the inductive clauses are subject to filters, there is no obvious bar to generating S-Structures directly in this way.

In GB, of course, there is no question of doing away with derivations altogether so long as the level LF is derived from S-Structure (and not identical to it); at the same time, syntacticians have in general been highly conservative about the admissibility of LF. Under Minimalism, as we saw above, a key feature of the use of LF is the capturing of reconstruction effects, a somewhat different territory from the scope-assignment algorithms that produced LF in the sense of Section 4 above; and it remains possible that these effects should be captured by conditions on the syntactic structures at a single linguistic level. For these reasons, the demonstration of the derivationality of syntax remains controversial.

Somewhat more abstractly, the derivationality of syntax involves above all the question of intermediate representations and principles that apply to them; that is, to representations that exist en route to the final configuration and are needed for the satisfaction of certain principles, but are destroyed in the final output. To give the reader a sample of the problems now under discussion, we consider in some detail one type of argument for intermediate representations under Minimalism, with reference to a typical example from German.

In German yes-no questions, the V, inflected for tense, comes in first position:

(139) Kennst du das Land?
Know you the land?
Do you know the land?

There is strong evidence that (139) and the like involve two steps of movement, one of the V to the position I of inflection, and the other of V + I to the complementizer position C. V, I, and C are the heads of their respective projections, and the operation is an instance of *head-to-head movement* in the sense of Baker (1988) and Travis (1984). The movement is a case of adjunction, of the moved head to the head at the landing site, so that we have, schematically:

(140) $[[_C X] \ldots [[_I Y] \ldots [_V Z]]]$;

and then, successively:

(141) $[[_C X] \ldots [[_I Y + Z] \ldots [_V t]]]$;

(142) $[[_C X [_I Y + Z]] \ldots [[_I t'] \ldots [_V t]]]$;

with t' the trace of Y + Z, and t the trace of Z.

What licenses the movement described? In earlier discussion we assumed that movement was licensed only by c-command, but it is evident that Z does not c-command its own trace, since it has adjoined to Y. But Y is a lexical head I^0, whose immediate predecessor is an I^1; therefore, I^0 is not maximal. It follows that Z m-commands its trace, and hence that if we weaken the c-command requirement to m-command, then the movement of Z adjoining to Y is licit; similarly for the movement of $[_I Y + Z]$ to X. Finally, in the ultimate structure (142), Z continues to m-command its trace, since the least maximal projection containing it lies outside the complementizer C.

Suppose now that in addition to observing m-command, head-to-head movement is required to obey a *shortest move* condition; i.e. each movement must be to the nearest c-commanding head, and none can be skipped.[25] The shortest move condition is satisfied in the operation that produces (141) from (140), and (142) from (141). If, however, the structure (142) were generated directly, without movement, it would be violated: for Z has "skipped over" the intermediate position I to move up to within C. Hence, on the assumptions stated, the grammar is derivational.

The above considerations were highly theory-internal, so that derivationality was a consequence of a number of theoretical propositions taken together. Alternatives that suggest themselves would include abstract conceptions of linking nodes one to another, perhaps in the manner of Head-Driven Phrase Structure Grammar (see Chapter XX of this *Handbook*).[26]

---

[25] This thesis is explored especially in Rizzi (1990).

[26] The linking established by the derivational theory of syntactic movement is more restricted than a theory of arbitrary links of features, however: as remarked in the last section, on a derivational theory whole bundles of features are constrained to move at once.

7.2. *Minimalist grammar: Induction over phrase markers*

Minimalism, or the Minimalist Program of Chomsky (1993) and (1995), incorporates the elements of feature-checking and the copy theory of movement described in Section 6, but remains a derivational grammar. Its specific linguistic features are described in Marantz (1995), and we concentrate here on the very general, formal description.

Recall that in a phrase structure grammar there were basis and inductive clauses where the former stipulated outright that certain items belonged to certain categories (e.g., *book* is a Noun), and the latter allowed the construction of constituents depending upon the categorial membership and linear order. Among the elaborations of this basic conception are (a) admitting other information than mere categorial membership into both basis and inductive clauses, and (b) allowing the formation of complex constituents only in certain linguistic environments, as in context-sensitive grammars. However, one may also suggest an inductive procedure where both basis and inductive clauses have for their arguments whole phrase markers rather than constituents and categories; these are *generalized transformations*, in the sense of Chomsky (1955, 1957). On this conception, an elementary structure, say $[_{V'}[_{V}\text{read}]\ [_{NP}\text{the book}]]$ will be built up by pairing the phrase markers

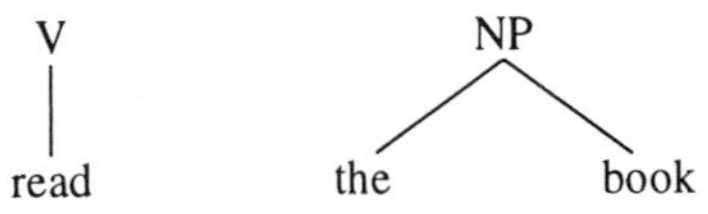

Similarly for more complex operations; see Chomsky (1995, Chapter 4) for considerable detail.

The inductive procedure ultimately yields an LF-representation for the structure computed. But D-Structure will now have disappeared, since the whole is not present until LF; and the unique significance of S-Structure disappears likewise, since the computation runs on unimpeded. Sentences and other linguistic objects are, however, pronounced: so at some point in the computation material is delivered to the articulatory system. Chomsky dubs this point *Spellout*. Spellout will continue to mark a transition in the computation (for instance, lexical material may be introduced at any point prior to Spellout, but at no point following); but there will be no special conditions attaching to representations there that are not derivable from the classification of features, attracting movement if they are strong, and repelling it if they are weak.

Is the resulting syntax derivational or not? There will be at least two levels of representation, but one can experiment with reductions even of these; and anyway there remains the question of intermediate representations, to which, for example, the argument from head-to-head movement of the last subsection applies, albeit highly theory-internally.

7.3. *Modes of formalization*

We conclude this chapter with a few remarks on the general project of formalizing GB or its descendants. The formalization of a linguistic theory requires an inventory of its primitives, among which we are given hierarchy, linear order, and labeling. Apart from the uncertainty about the inventory of possible labels, it was remarked in Section 3 above that phrase markers could, and arguably should, be enriched with binary relations not definable in terms of hierarchy, linear order, and labeling: these included at least the antecedent-anaphor relation, and the relation of predication. There are in fact a number of other anaphoric or quasi-anaphoric relations that have come to light in recent years, and it is unclear at this stage of theoretical development how far they may be assimilated and to what extent each is *sui generis*.[27] Setting this issue to one side, we may still ask what form a formalization should take.

The question of formalization is problematic in part because the domain of syntactic theory is itself less than clear. Some properties especially of coordinate structures and ellipsis may tap features of cognition that fall outside the central parts of grammatical competence. For example, it is no trivial problem to describe simple conjunction, *and*, for the natural hypothesis that only like elements may be conjoined, exemplified in (143)–(144), is conspicuously flouted in (145):

(143) I looked for [John and Mary];

(144) I sought my glasses [in and under] the bed;

(145) John is [honest and a good friend of mine].

The conjuncts in (145) are an adjective and an NP (a predicate nominative), respectively. Evidently, there is no way to assign a structure to the conjunction except by somehow conjoining unlike categories. But it is not evident that the relevant notion of a possible conjunction, in this case of predicates, is syntactic in the narrow sense.[28]

Wherever the line is drawn between grammatical and extra-grammatical processes, GB or Minimalist syntax may be formalized by a direct encoding of the derivational process; that is, by rendering all information and definitions in the first-order language of set theory, enriched with non-logical concepts. This course was pursued for a crucial part of GB in Stabler (1992) as part of the further project of providing a direct computational implementation of the theory, an important feature when one considers that syntactic theories are intricate and require long computations. Under such a formulation, however, the predictions of a theory can be accessed only by example and not globally, and theory comparison is correspondingly difficult. Furthermore, the quantificational complexity of any such formalization is formidable, and remains so even where quantification is bounded (consider, for example, spelling out the conditions on c-command and m-command as filters using the primitive notation). Among the logical approaches to more tractable formalization are Rogers (1994), who uses the monadic second-order

[27] There is at present no single presentation of these relations, which include, for example, association of words such as *only* with a focused constituent, as in (i):

(i) We only said that *John* was late

in the meaning, "John is the only person x such that we said x was late". See Rooth (1985) for an influential discussion.

[28] See especially Munn (1993) for a discussion of the issues within a GB framework. Processes of ellipsis and deletion, which we considered only in the special case of VP-deletion in English in Section 4 above, are in fact widespread and complex. See Fiengo and May (1995) and Lappin (1995) for recent discussion of some of the options.

logic of n-successor functions to formalize aspects of GB. In this system, however, the definable languages turn out to be context-free, and the phenomena that have been argued to take English or other natural languages outside the class of the context-free languages cannot be represented.[29] Kracht (1995) considers instead a dynamic modal logic over trees (phrase markers).

How much does computational tractability matter to a linguistic theory? Chomsky himself has generally been of the opinion has its importance has not been demonstrated; after all, the theory is a theory of linguistic knowledge, not of use, and the problems of linguistic description tend to remain where they were no matter what is said about decidability, or real-time computability in the limit. Indeed, Minimalism incorporates a notion of "economy of derivation", not considered here, that requires comparison of derivations as part of the determination of the grammatical status of linguistic expressions (including comparison with derivations that fail on other grounds: see Marantz (1995) for examples), and this notion adds a prima facie complexity to the computability problem. However, with a variety of avenues now being explored both in computational properties of grammars and empirically motivated theories of linguistic knowledge, we cannot with security predict where convergence may occur.

References

Aoun, J. and Sportiche, D. (1981), *On the formal theory of government*, Ling. Rev. **2**, 211–236.

Arnauld, A. (1662), *La Logique, ou L'Art de Penser*.

Baker, M. (1988), *Incorporation*, Univ. of Chicago Press, Chicago.

Barker, C. and Pullum, G. (1990), *A theory of command relations*, Ling. and Philos. **13**.

Barss, A. (1986), *Chains and anaphoric dependence: On reconstruction and its implications*, Unpublished doctoral dissertation, MIT, Cambridge, MA.

Bresnan, J. (1972), *Theory of complementation in English syntax*, Unpublished doctoral dissertation, MIT Press, Cambridge, MA.

Chomsky, N. (1955), *The Logical Structure of Linguistic Theory*, Mimeographed, Harvard University. Reprinted with additions: Plenum, New York, 1975.

Chomsky, N. (1957), *Syntactic Structures*, Mouton, The Hague.

Chomsky, N. (1965), *Aspects of the Theory of Syntax*, MIT Press, Cambridge, MA.

Chomsky, N. (1973), *Conditions on transformations*, A Festschrift for Morris Halle, S. Anderson and P. Kiparsky, eds, Reprinted: N. Chomsky, *Essays on Form and Interpretation*, North-Holland, Amsterdam, 25–59.

Chomsky, N. (1976), *Conditions on rules of grammar*, Ling. Anal. **2**, 4. Reprinted: N. Chomsky, *Essays on Form and Interpretation*, North-Holland, Amsterdam, 163–210.

Chomsky, N. (1977), *On WH-movement*, Formal Syntax, P. Culicover, T. Wasow and A. Akmajian, eds, Academic Press, New York, 71–132.

Chomsky, N. (1981), *Lectures on Government and Binding*, Foris, Dordrecht.

Chomsky, N. (1986), *Knowledge of Language*, Praeger, New York.

Chomsky, N. (1993), *A minimalist program for linguistic theory*, The View from Building 20: Essays in Linguistics in Honor of Sylvain Bromberger, K. Hale and S. Keyser, eds, MIT Press, Cambridge, MA, 1–52. Reprinted in Chomsky (1995).

Chomsky, N. (1995), *The Minimalist Program*, MIT Press, Cambridge, MA.

Emonds, J. (1978), *The verbal complex V'–V in French*, Ling. Inq. **9**, 151–175.

Fiengo, R. and May, R. (1994), *Indices and Identity*, MIT Press, Cambridge, MA.

[29] For a survey of such phenomena see Savitch, Bach, Marsh and Safran-Naveh (1987).

Fiengo, R. and May, R. (1995), *Anaphora and identity*, The Handbook of Contemporary Syntactic Theory, S. Lappin, ed., Basil Blackwell, Oxford, 117–144.

Freidin, R. (1992), *Foundations of Generative Syntax*, MIT Press, Cambridge, MA.

Haegeman, L. (1994), *Introduction to Government and Binding Theory*, 2nd edn, Basil Blackwell, Oxford.

Harris, Z. (1955), *Structural Linguistics*, Univ. of Chicago Press, Chicago.

Higginbotham, J. (1985), *On semantics*, Ling. Inq. **16**, 547–593.

Huang, C.-T. J. (1982), *Logical form in Chinese and the theory of grammar*, Unpublished doctoral dissertation, MIT, Cambridge, MA.

Huang, C.-T. J. (1995), *Logical form*, Government and Binding Theory and the Minimalist Program, G. Webelhuth, ed., Basil Blackwell, Oxford, 125–175.

Jackendoff, R. (1972), *Semantic Interpretation in Generative Grammar*, MIT Press, Cambridge, MA.

Kracht, M. (1993), *Mathematical aspects of command relations*, Proceedings of the EACL 1993, 240–249.

Kracht, M. (1995), *Is there a genuine modal perspective on feature structures?*, Ling. and Philos. **18**, 401–458.

Lappin, S. (1995), *The interpretation of ellipsis*, The Handbook of Contemporary Syntactic Theory, S. Lappin, ed., Basil Blackwell, Oxford, 145–176.

Lasnik, H. and Saito, M. (1991), *Move α*, MIT Press, Cambridge, MA.

Lasnik, H. (1993), *Lectures on minimalist syntax*, University of Connecticut Working Papers in Linguistics, University of Connecticut, Storrs, CT.

Marantz, A. (1995), *The minimalist program*, Government and Binding Theory and the Minimalist Program, G. Webelhuth, ed., Basil Blackwell, Oxford, 349–382.

McCawley, J. (1982), *Parentheticals and discontinuous constituent structure*, Ling. Inq. **13**, 91–106.

Munn, A. (1993), *Topics in the syntax and semantics of coordinate structures*, Unpublished doctoral dissertation, University of Maryland, College Park, MD.

Nishigauchi, T. (1990), *Quantification in the Theory of Grammar*, Kluwer, Dordrecht.

Peters, P.S. Jr. and Ritchie, R. (1971), *On restricting the base component of a transformational grammar*, Inform. and Control **18**, 483–501.

Pollock, J.-Y. (1989), *Verb movement, universal grammar, and the structure of IP*, Ling. Inq. **20**, 365–424.

Reinhart, T. (1976), *The syntactic domain of anaphora*, Unpublished doctoral dissertation, MIT, Cambridge, MA.

Reinhart, T. (1983), *Anaphora and Semantic Interpretation*, Croom Helm, London.

Rizzi, L. (1990), *Relativized Minimality*, MIT Press, Cambridge, MA.

Rogers, J. (1994), *Studies in the logic of trees, with applications to grammar formalisms*, Unpublished doctoral dissertation, University of Delaware.

Rooth, M. (1985), *Association with focus*, Unpublished doctoral dissertation, University of Massachusetts, Amherst.

Ross, J.R. (1967), *Constraints on variables in syntax*, Unpublished doctoral dissertation, MIT, Cambridge, MA.

Rothstein, S. (1983), *The syntactic forms of predication*, Unpublished doctoral dissertation, MIT, Cambridge, MA.

Safir, K. (1985), *Syntactic Chains*, Cambridge Univ. Press, Cambridge, MA.

Sag, I. (1976), *Deletion and logical form*, Unpublished doctoral dissertation, MIT, Cambridge, MA.

Savitch, W., Bach, E., Marsh, W. and Safran-Naveh, G. (eds) (1987), *The Formal Complexity of Natural Language*, Kluwer, Dordrecht.

Speas, M. (1992), *Phrase Structure in Natural Language*, Kluwer, Dordrecht.

Stabler, E. (1992), *The Logical Approach to Syntax*, MIT Press, Cambridge, MA.

Travis, L. (1984), *Parameters and effects of word order variation*, Unpublished doctoral dissertation, MIT, Cambridge, MA.

Wasow, T. (1972), *Anaphoric relations in English*, Unpublished doctoral dissertation, MIT, Cambridge, MA.

Watanabe, A. (1991), *S-Structure movement of Wh-in-situ*, MIT, Cambridge, MA, manuscript.

Williams, E. (1977), *Discourse and logical form*, Ling. Inq. **8**, 101–139.

Williams, E. (1980), *Predication*, Ling. Inq. **11**, 203–238.

CHAPTER 6

Game-Theoretical Semantics

Jaakko Hintikka

Boston University, Department of Philosophy, 745 Commonwealth Ave, Boston, MA 02215, USA
E-mail: hintikka@acs.bu.edu

Gabriel Sandu

University of Helsinki, Department of Philosophy, PO Box 24, 00014 Helsinki, Finland
E-mail: sandu@katk.helsinki.fi

Commentator: W. Hodges

Contents

HANDBOOK OF LOGIC AND LANGUAGE
Edited by J. van Benthem and A. ter Meulen

1. Formal languages

1.1. Background

The leading ideas of game-theoretical semantics (GTS) can be seen best from a special case. This special case is the semantics of quantifiers. In using quantifiers and in theorizing about them, it is hard not to use game-laden terms, especially if one thinks of seeking and finding as a game. In traditional informal mathematical jargon, quantifiers are routinely expressed by such phrases as "given any value of x, one can find a value of y such that". In several natural languages, existence is expressed by phrases translatable as "one can find".

As early as in C.S. Peirce, we find an explicit explanation of the meaning of quantifiers by reference to two-person games involving an interpreter and a respondent. (Cf. Hilpinen, 1982.) Later, mathematical logicians have spontaneously resorted to game-theoretical conceptualizations practically every time they have had to deal with a kind of logic where Tarski-type truth-definitions do not apply, including branching quantifier languages, game quantifier languages, and infinitely deep languages. (See Section 3, below.) Hence a game-theoretical treatment of quantification theory (first-order logic) is more of codification of natural and time-honored ways of thinking and speaking rather than a radical novelty.

Such a GTS for first-order languages can be implemented in a sample case as follows: We assume that we are given a first-order language L and a model M of L. M's being a model of L means that all the nonlogical constants of L are interpreted on M. This implies that any atomic sentence or identity involving the nonlogical vocabulary of L, plus names of the individuals in the domain $\mathrm{do}(M)$ of M, has a definite truth-value, true or false.

Consider now a sentence S of L. We define a certain two-persons semantical game $G(S; M)$ played with S on M. The players are called Myself (the initial verifier) and Nature (the initial falsifier). When the game starts, Myself has the role of verifier and Nature that of falsifier. At each stage of the game, intuitively speaking, the player who all that time is the verifier is trying to show that the sentence considered then is true and the falsifier is trying to show that it is false.

At each stage of a play of $G(S; M)$, the players are considering a sentence in an extension $L \cup \{c_a\colon a \in \mathrm{do}(M)\}$ of L, obtained by adding the new individual constants c_a as names of the individuals in the domain $\mathrm{do}(M)$ which do not have one. The game starts from S and is governed by the following rules:

(R. $\vee$) $G((S_1 \vee S_2); M)$ begins by the verifier's choice of $i = 1$ or $i = 2$. The game is continued as in $G(S_i; M)$.

(R. $\wedge$) $G((S_1 \wedge S_2); M)$ begins by the falsifier's choice of $i = 1$ or $i = 2$. The game is continued as in $G(S_i; M)$.

(R. $\exists$) $G((\exists x)S_0[x]; M)$ begins by the verifier's choice of an individual from $\mathrm{do}(M)$. Let its name be "c". The game is continued as in $G(S_0[c]; M)$.

(R. $\forall$) The rule for $G((\forall x)S_0[x]; M)$ is like (R. $\exists$), except that the falsifier makes the choice.

(R. $\neg$) $G(\neg S_0; M)$ is like $G(S_0; M)$, except that the roles of the two players are reversed.

(R. atom) If S is an atomic formula or an identity, the player who is then the verifier wins and that who is then the falsifier loses, if S is true in M. The player who is then the falsifier wins and that who is then the verifier loses if S is false in M.

Any play of a semantical game comes to an end after a finite number of moves, with one player winning and the other losing.

The distinctive feature of GTS is the definition of the central semantical notion of truth. The truth or falsity of S in M usually cannot be seen from any one play of $G(S; M)$. Rather, truth in M is defined by reference to what the initial verifier *can* do in $G(S; M)$. It refers to the strategies, in the sense of game theory, that Myself and Nature have available in $G(S; M)$. A strategy in this sense is a rule that tells a player what to do in every conceivable situation that might arise in a play of the given game. More exactly, a strategy for a player m (m is either Myself or Nature) in the game $G(S; M)$ is a set F_m of functions f_Q corresponding to different logical constants Q which can prompt a move by player m in $G(S; M)$. A winning strategy in a two-person zero-sum game is one which results in a win for that player no matter which strategy one's opponent uses.

The truth in M of a sentence S ($M \models_{\mathrm{GTS}} S^+$) can now be defined in a natural way:

DEFINITION 1.1. $M \models_{\mathrm{GTS}} S^+$ if and only if there exists a winning strategy for Myself in $G(S; M)$.

Falsity ($M \models_{GTS} S^-$) can be defined as the dual of truth:

DEFINITION 1.2. $M \models_{\mathrm{GTS}} S^-$ if and only if there exists a winning strategy for Nature in $G(S; M)$.

The following results are well known and will therefore be given here without proofs:

THEOREM 1.3 (Assuming the axiom of choice; (Hintikka, 1983; Hodges, 1989)). *For any first-order sentence S and model M, Tarski-type truth and GTS truth coincide, i.e.*

$$M \models_{\mathrm{Tarski}} S \quad \textit{if and only if} \quad M \models_{\mathrm{GTS}} S^+.$$

By quantifying explicitly over the functions in the set F_m we also obtain

THEOREM 1.4. *Every first-order sentence is equivalent with a second-order existential (i.e. Σ^1_1) sentence.*

The Σ^1_1 sentence $S^{(2)}$ equivalent with the given first-order one, say S, can be effectively formed as follows:

(i) Transform S to its negation normal form S_n.

(ii) For each variable x bound to an existential quantifier $(\exists x)$ in S_n, replace x by $f(y_1, y_2, \ldots)$, where f is a new function symbol (the Skolem function f connected with $(\exists x)$) and $(\forall y_1)$, $(\forall y_2), \ldots$ are all the universal quantifiers within the scope of which $(\exists x)$ occurs in S_n.

(iii) Each disjunction $(S_1 \vee S_2)$ is replaced by $(f(y_1, y_2, \ldots) = 0 \wedge S_1) \vee (f(y_1, y_2, \ldots) \neq 0 \wedge S_2)$, where f is a new function variable and $(\forall y_1), (\forall y_2), \ldots$ are all the universal quantifiers within the scope of which the disjunction occurs.

(iv) The function variables introduce in (ii)–(iii) are bound to sentence-initial existential quantifiers.

The equivalence of $S^{(2)}$ with S is a straightforward consequence of the axiom of choice.

We will extend the usual terminology somewhat and call all the functions introduced in (ii) and (iii) Skolem functions.

The argument selection for the different Skolem functions that occur in the Σ_1^1 translation of a given first-order sentence S shows graphically the different relations of dependence and independence between the corresponding quantifiers and connectives in S.

Later we will consider routinely first-order languages which also contain function symbols and which may contain an infinite number of nonlogical constants of different kinds. The treatment outlined in this section can be extended to them without any difficulties.

1.2. The strategic viewpoint

This treatment of first-order logic by means of game-theoretical concepts serves as a basis of extensions in several different directions. Some of these extensions are discussed in the next several sections. At the same time, the treatment of first-order logic can serve as an illustration of the rationale of GTS.

In most approaches to language and its logic in these days, language is considered as a rule-governed process. The explanatory arsenal of such an approach consists mainly of the move-by-move rules for certain processes, for instance for the generation of well-formed sentences or rules of semantical interpretation, for instance rules for a Tarski-type recursive determination of the truth-value of a given sentence.

In contrast, when language is considered in game-theoretical terms, it is viewed as a goal-directed process. This opens the door for conceptualizations and explanations which do not turn on step-by-step rules but rather on the strategies one can pursue throughout an entire process. (Indeed, the concept of strategy plays such a crucial role in game theory that it perhaps should be called strategy theory in the first place.) On the level of the explanation of actual linguistic phenomena, this facilitates a wealth of new avenues of conceptualization, explanation and understanding. For instance, instead of varying the move-by-move rules of our semantical games, we could vary the sets of strategies that are open to the two players. (Cf. Section 1.9 below.)

This reliance on strategies rather than move-by-move rules is in evidence in the game-theoretical definition of truth outlined above. Thus one way in which the game-theoretical approach can be developed is in the direction of new types of explanation. (Cf. Hintikka, 1991.)

1.3. The subgame interpretation and conditionals

An idea which goes back to Hintikka and Carlson (1979) is to divide certain semantical games into subgames, each played in its own right. This idea can be used on the sentence level, especially in the treatment of conditionals (see Section 2.6 below). It is also most useful in extending the concepts and results of GTS from the sentence level to discourse semantics, using the simple expedient of conceiving of discourse as a "supergame" consisting of subgames played with the successive sentences of the discourse. In either case, new conceptualizations are opened by the possibility of making different assumptions as to what information is transferred from an earlier subgame to a later one.

In this way, practically all the concepts and results concerning sentential anaphora that in the second part of this survey are registered on the sentential level are automatically extended to discourse anaphora without the need of any auxiliary assumptions.

Rules for formal conditionals will be discussed in Section 2.6 in connection with the corresponding rules for natural-language conditionals.

1.4. Extensions: Informational independence

There is an important feature of the usual first-order logic which usually passes unnoticed. It is an assumption concerning the kinds of dependence and independence between logical constants that is allowed in logic. It is built right into the usual logical notation. In that notation, each quantifier is associated with a segment of the formula as its scope. It is then required that these scopes are linearly ordered, that is, that the scopes of two different quantifiers must be either exclusive or else nested (i.e. the scope of one is included in the scope of the other).

On a closer look, alas, the requirement of (linear) ordering is seen to be unmotivated by any deeper theoretical reasons and hence dispensable. Every single explanation offered in introductory logic texts or anywhere else of the meaning of the notions of scope and quantifier is applicable irrespective of the restriction. The restriction, we are tempted to say, is simply an outright mistake on Frege's and Russell's part.

But what happens when this arbitrary stipulation is given up? Purely notationally, the use of parentheses as scope indicators becomes awkward, for it is not easy to perceive at once which parenthesis is to be paired with which, even if they are indexed. It is more convenient to introduce a special notation whose purpose is to exempt a quantifier (or other ingredient of a sentence) from the dependence of another one within whose scope it would otherwise be. For this purpose a slash notation will be used here. For instance, in the sentence

(4.1) $$(\forall x)(\forall z)(\exists y/\forall z)(\exists u/\forall x)R[x,z,y,u]$$

the idea is that the first existential quantifier depends on $(\forall x)$ but not on $(\forall z)$, while the second depends on $(\forall z)$ but not on $(\forall x)$.

An alternative notation would be to write the prefix of (4.1) in a *branching* form

(4.2) $$\begin{pmatrix} \forall x & \exists y \\ \forall z & \exists u \end{pmatrix} R[x,z,y,u]$$

which is taken to be equivalent with the second-order sentence

(4.3) $$(\exists f)(\exists g)(\forall x)(\forall z)R[x, z, f(x), g(z)].$$

The prefix of (4.2) is also known as a Henkin prefix (Henkin quantifier). It is well known that the logic with Henkin quantifiers is a non-axiomatizable, proper extension of first-order logic. If ordinary (contradictory) negation is used, this logic is also non-compact.

When the linear dependence of quantifiers on each other breaks down, then Tarskian truth definitions do not help us any longer. Consider for instance (4.1). A Tarskian truth definition does not work in this case, because it cannot avoid interpreting at least one of the existential quantifiers as semantically dependent upon both universal quantifiers. In contrast, a game-theoretical interpretation is readily available. We can simply associate with (4.1) a semantical game $G((4.1); M)$ which will consist of two moves by Nature prompted by the two universal quantifiers and two moves by Myself prompted by the two existential quantifiers. The idea that the existential quantifier $(\exists y)$ depends only on the universal quantifier $(\forall x)$ (and not on $(\forall z)$) and the quantifier $(\exists u)$ depends only on the universal quantifier $(\forall z)$ (and not on that $(\forall x)$) can be captured in GTS by requiring that the game in question is one of *imperfect information*. In this particular case, this means that Myself, at his first move, does not "know" Nature's second choice, and in his second move, Myself does not have access to Nature's first choice. We say in this case that the move prompted by $(\exists u)$ is *informationally independent* of the move prompted by $(\forall x)$, and similarly for $(\exists y)$ and $(\forall z)$. When game-theoretical semantics is used, our notions of informational dependence and independence thus become simply special cases of the namesake notions used in the mathematical theory of games.

The idea of informational independence can be extended to cover, not only quantifiers, but all the logical constants (and even the other ingredients of a sentence). The mild-looking extension of the usual first-order notation which is proposed here can be implemented by adding to the usual formation rules of first-order logic certain new ones, to be applied after the usual formation rules. The following are examples of such rules applied to formulas in negation normal form:

(a) If $(\exists x)$ occurs within the scope of the universal quantifiers $(\forall y_1), \ldots, (\forall y_k)$, among others, then it may be replaced by $(\exists x/\forall y_1, \ldots, \forall y_k)$.

(b) If $\vee$ occurs within the scope of the universal quantifiers $(\forall y_1), \ldots, (\forall y_k)$, among others, then it may be replaced by $(\vee/\forall y_1, \ldots, \forall y_k)$.

(c) If $(\forall x)$ occurs within the scope of the existential quantifiers $(\exists y_1), \ldots, (\exists y_k)$, among others, then it may be replaced by $(\forall x/\exists y_1, \ldots, \exists y_k)$.

(d) If $\wedge$ occurs within the scope of the universal quantifiers $(\exists y_1), \ldots, (\exists y_k)$, among others, then it may be replaced by $(\wedge/\exists y_1, \ldots, \exists y_k)$.

These two rules actually suffice for the simplest types of languages where informational independence is allowed. When needed, analogous rules can be formulated for other kinds of independence. Any number of applications of (a)–(d) may be made to a given first-order sentence and the slash notation may be extended to formulas which are not in negation normal form.

The game-theoretical interpretation we gave for the ordinary first-order languages can be extended to cover also the sentences of the new language. As a matter of fact, the game rules for the new language will be the same as the old ones. The only essential difference between the new and the old games is thus that the former are games of imperfect information.

The resulting logic will be called independence friendly (IF) first-order logic and the languages associated with it IF first-order languages. These languages were introduced in (Hintikka and Sandu, 1989). The IF first-order logic is a proper extension of first-order logic. This follows from the fact mentioned above that the Henkin quantifier is definable in this logic, i.e.

$$\text{(4.4)}\qquad \begin{pmatrix} \forall x & \exists y \\ \forall z & \exists u \end{pmatrix} R[x,z,y,u] \leftrightarrow (\forall x)(\forall z)(\exists y/\forall z)(\exists u/\forall x)R[x,z,y,u].$$

In fact the following holds:

THEOREM 4.1. *The IF first-order logic is a nonrecursively axiomatizable but compact extension of first-order logic.*

In order to prove Theorem 4.1 we note first that Theorem 1.4 extends to the IF first-order logic:

THEOREM 4.2 (Sandu, 1991; Hintikka, 1995). *Every IF first-order sentence is equivalent with a Σ^1_1 sentence.*

This Σ^1_1 sentence is formed in the same way as in ordinary first-order logic. (See Section 1.1 above.)

Enderton (1970) proved that every Σ^1_1 sentence is equivalent with a first-order sentence prefixed by a Henkin quantifier. Since the Henkin quantifier is definable in the IF logic, it follows that the converse of Theorem 4.2 holds too. The equivalence of IF first-order logic and Σ^1_1 logic has the consequence that the we get for the former all the metalogical properties of the latter: Compactness (i.e. Theorem 4.1), the Löwenheim–Skolem Property (cf. Ebbinghaus, Flum and Thomas, 1984, p. 195), and the following Separation Theorem:

THEOREM 4.3 (Analogue to Barwise, 1976). *Let K_1 and K_2 be two disjoint nonempty classes of structures definable by sentences of the IF first-order language. Then there is an elementary class K (definable by a single ordinary first-order formula) such that K contains K_1 and is disjoint from K_2.*

The IF languages have been introduced in (Hintikka and Sandu, 1989). They have somewhat longer ancestry, however. As we saw, IF first-order logic is closely related to the logic of partially ordered quantifiers. This study was begun by Henkin (1959), and among its milestones are the papers by Walkoe (1970), Enderton (1970), Krynicki and Lachlan (1979), Barwise (1979), Krynicki and Mostowski (1995). One novelty which is incorporated in the IF logic is that of partially ordered connectives. Such connectives are studied in (Sandu and Väänänen, 1992), and in (Hella and Sandu, 1995).

1.5. IF first-order logic and partiality

In the chapter on Partiality of this handbook, we saw what are the consequences of giving up the assumption of complete information with respect to a model. In that case, truth-value gaps arise already at the level of atomic sentences, and, through the inductive clauses, they are transmitted to the more complex sentence of the language in question.

In the case of IF first-order logic, the lack of complete information manifests itself at the level of the interpretation of the quantificational structure of a sentence. For this reason, truth-value gaps arise at a complex level of quantificational structure, i.e. a level involving at least two quantifiers. An illustrative example is the sentence $(\forall x)(\exists y/\forall x)\ [x = y]$ which fails to be true and fails to be false in any model which has at least two elements. (Cf. also our discussion in Section 1.8.) At the level of atomic sentences, IF first-order logic is classical.

In the chapter on Partiality it was shown that, if the models are partial, then the Boolean connectives in the underlying logic satisfy the Strong-Kleene valuation schema. In addition this logic is complete, compact and has the Interpolation Property. These properties follow automatically from the encoding of partial logic into classical logic.

We saw in the preceding section that all these results except completeness hold for the IF first-order logic, too. Next we will show that the Boolean connectives in IF first-order logic satisfy the Strong-Kleene valuation schema too. The proof of the next proposition is straightforward:

PROPOSITION 5.1. *Let S be an arbitrary IF first-order sentence. Then the following holds for any model M:*

(i) $M \vDash_{\mathrm{GTS}} (\neg S)^+$ *iff* $M \vDash_{\mathrm{GTS}} S^-$.
(ii) $M \vDash_{\mathrm{GTS}} (\neg S)^-$ *iff* $M \vDash_{\mathrm{GTS}} S^+$.
(iii) $M \vDash_{\mathrm{GTS}} (S \vee Q)^+$ *iff* $M \vDash_{\mathrm{GTS}} S^+$ *or* $M \vDash_{\mathrm{GTS}} Q^+$.
(iv) $M \vDash_{\mathrm{GTS}} (S \vee Q)^-$ *iff* $M \vDash_{\mathrm{GTS}} S^-$ *and* $M \vDash_{\mathrm{GTS}} Q^-$.
(v) $M \vDash_{\mathrm{GTS}} (S \wedge Q)^+$ *iff* $M \vDash_{\mathrm{GTS}} S^+$ *and* $M \vDash_{\mathrm{GTS}} Q^+$.
(vi) $M \vDash_{\mathrm{GTS}} (S \wedge Q)^-$ *iff* $M \vDash_{\mathrm{GTS}} S^-$ *or* $M \vDash_{\mathrm{GTS}} Q^-$.

Let us define $\|S\|^M$ (the truth-value of the L-sentence S in the model M) as

$$
\begin{array}{llllll}
\|S\|^M = 1, & \text{if} & M \vDash_{\mathrm{GTS}} S^+ & \text{(and not} & M \vDash_{\mathrm{GTS}} S^-). \\
\|S\|^M = 0, & \text{if} & M \vDash_{\mathrm{GTS}} S^- & \text{(and not} & M \vDash_{\mathrm{GTS}} S^+). \\
\|S\|^M = ?, & \text{if not} & M \vDash_{\mathrm{GTS}} S^+ & \text{and not} & M \vDash_{\mathrm{GTS}} S^-. \\
\|S\|^M = 10, & \text{if} & M \vDash_{\mathrm{GTS}} S^+ & \text{and} & M \vDash_{\mathrm{GTS}} S^-.
\end{array}
$$

($\|S\|^M = ?$ should be read as S is undefined in M, and $\|S\|^M = 10$ should be read as S is both true and false in M.)

It is straightforward to prove that for every IF first-order sentence S and model M, it cannot be the case that both $\|S\|^M = 1$ and $\|S\|^M = 0$. Thus the truth-value 10 does not actualize in IF first-order logic.

Using Proposition 5.1, it is straightforward to verify that the Boolean connectives satisfy the Strong-Kleene valuation schema.

1.6. IF first-order logic and the failure of compositionality

GTS is only one of the possible semantical (model-theoretical) treatments of first-order logic. In fact, it is not the most common one. The best known interpretation of ordinary first-order logic is given by Tarski-type truth-definitions. The essential difference between the two is that the latter is compositional while the former is not. However, Theorem 1.3 showed that they are equivalent (assuming the axiom of choice). This result does not extend to IF first-order logic, however. Let us be more specific about this question.

In its standard formulation, the principle of compositionality ("Frege's Principle") says that the meaning of a compound expression is a function of the meanings of its constituent parts and of the syntactic rules by which they are combined (cf. the chapter on compositionality in this handbook). What this comes down to in the case of Tarskian semantics is that the concepts of truth and satisfaction for a complex expression are defined recursively in terms of the truth and satisfaction of certain simpler expressions. This is also the basic reason why Tarski cannot define truth for first-order sentences directly, but has to draw in also the notion of satisfaction. For the relevant component expressions of a sentence (closed formula) are not always closed, but contain free variables. Since the concept of truth cannot be applied to open formulas, Tarski must resort to the concept of satisfaction.

But the principle of compositionality which is operative here presupposes a kind of semantical context-independence. If the meaning of a complex expression depends only on the meaning of its parts, it can never depend in its context on a still more comprehensive expression. Thus much of the actual force of the principle of compositionality lies in ruling out semantical context dependencies.

But the very idea of quantifier independence in IF logic violates the principle of compositionality. For the force of an independent quantifier (Q/Q_i) depends on another quantifier (Q_i) which occurs, not within the scope of the former, but outside its scope, in other words in the context of (Q/Q_i). This clearly violates compositionality, and it is the ultimate reason why Tarski-type truth-definitions do not work in an IF first-order logic (on the first-order level).

The impossibility of formulating Tarski-type truth-definitions for IF first-order languages may not be obvious. For instance why cannot we formulate a Tarski-type truth-condition for a sentence of the form

(6.1) $$(\forall x)(\exists y)(\forall z)(\exists w/\forall x)S[x, y, z, w]$$

by associating with its successive component formulas those classes of assignments which satisfy them in Tarski's sense? Let us try. Assuming that the satisfaction conditions for $S[x, y, z, w]$ have been determined, we must try to define the class of assignments which satisfy

(6.2) $$(\exists w/\forall x)S[x, y, z, w].$$

Here the independence of the choice of w from x can perhaps be taken into account. We can, for instance, not just say that an assignment g_0 satisfy (6.2) if and only if there is an evaluation g_1 which differs from g_0 only on w and which satisfies $S[x, y, z, w]$.

We can add that this different value of g_1 on w must be the same as soon as the values of y and z are the same. But this is not enough. We must also take into account possible dependencies of x, y, and z on each other. Neither kind of dependence or independence can be read off (6.2), not even the first kind, for we must consider choices of values of existentially quantified variables to be independent of each other.

In the chapter on compositionality of this handbook it is proved that any language that can be described by finite means can be described by a compositional grammar. This raises the question of what is a compositional semantics for the IF first-order languages described here.

A possible line of restoring compositionality for the IF first-order languages would be to take the whole prefix of quantifiers in, e.g., (6.1) as one full block, and introduce a generalized quantifier (called the Henkin quantifier), say $Hxyzw$, defined by

(6.3) $$HxyzwS[x,y,z,w] \Longleftrightarrow (\exists f)(\exists g)(\forall x)(\forall z)S[x,f(x),z,g(z)].$$

A similar move could be done for IF first-order sentences of the form

(6.4) $$(\forall x)(\exists y)(\forall z)(S_0(\vee/\forall x)S_1).$$

Here we could restore compositionality by introducing a generalized quantifier $Dxyz$ acting on two formulas defined by

(6.5) $$Dxyz(S_0, S_1) \Longleftrightarrow (\exists f)(\exists g)(\forall x)(\forall z)S_{g(z)}[x,f(x),z]$$

where g is a function from the domain to the set $\{0,1\}$. (Cf. the chapter on Generalized Quantifiers and Natural Language.)

The resulting semantics is, however, less natural than the game-theoretical semantics, since it introduces an analyzable notion as a primitive. In such a case, the definition of negation as role swapping loses its naturalness too.

The examples discussed here also clarify a point raised by Cresswell (1988). According to him, the advantages of GTS have the same source as those of Montague Grammar, viz. the use of higher-order entities. Even if this were correct, it would not be the whole story, since, as we saw, GTS is noncompositional while Montague Grammar relies essentially on compositionality.

Thus the study of IF first-order logic has a general methodological moral. It suggests that, even if there is always some way or another of restauring compositionality, there are cases in which the noncompositional semantics is more natural and finer grained than the compositional one. To the extent that we can argue that an IF logic is a better framework of semantical representation for natural languages than ordinary first-order logic, to the same extent the injunction against compositionality applies also to the semantical treatment of natural languages.

1.7. IF first-order logic and the failure of the substitutional account of quantification

In IF first-order logic, the substitutional interpretation of quantifiers does not work. According to this interpretation, an existentially quantified sentence

(7.1) $$(\exists x)S[x]$$

is true if and only if the substitution-instance $S[b]$ of its unquantified part $S[x]$ with respect to some individual constant b is true. The truth of universally quantified sentences is defined analogously. These definitions apply only to closed sentences. If $S[x]$ contains free individual variables other than x, $S[b]$ is open and hence cannot be either true or false. Hence the only way of basing one's conceptions of truth on the substitution idea is to use it to pare off one quantifier after another from outside in. But this procedure does not work in IF first-order languages. There we will eventually come to an expression of the form

$$(\exists x/\forall y)S[x] \tag{7.2}$$

where y does not occur in $S[x]$. Such an expression is not even a well-formed sentence of IF first-order language, and cannot be dealt with by the sole means of the substitution interpretation.

That this impossibility is not due to any notational peculiarity of IF logic is illustrated by the fact that the logical rule of inference known as existential instantiation fails in IF first-order logic. Or, rather, it does not do the whole job. The usual rule of universal instantiation entitles us to move from $(\exists x)S[x]$ to one of its substitution-instances $S[b]$ whenever b is a new individual constant. In IF logic, this can be strengthened to become a noncompositional rule that entitles us to move from a sentence (in negation normal form) of the form

$$S_0\big[(\exists x/\forall y_1, \forall y_2, \dots)S_1\big[x, y_1, y_2, \dots\big]\big] \tag{7.3}$$

to a sentence of the form

$$S_0\big[S_1\big[f(z_1, z_2, \dots), y_1, y_2, \dots\big]\big] \tag{7.4}$$

where f is a new function constant and $(\forall z_1), (\forall z_2), \dots$ are all the universal quantifiers other than $(\forall y_1), (\forall y_2), \dots$ within the scope of which

$$(\exists x/\forall y_1, \forall y_2, \dots)S_1\big[x, y_1, y_2, \dots\big] \tag{7.5}$$

occurs in (7.3) ($= S_0$). Moreover, this rule must not be applied after universal instantiation.

The need of such a contextual rule of existential instantiation illustrates the same failure of ordinary substitution to capture the force of informationally independent quantifiers as invalidated the substitutional interpretation of quantifiers and Tarski-type truth-definitions in IF first-order languages. In sum, the substitutional account of quantifiers does not work for IF first-order logic. This fact is of some interest, since it arises in a logic which is purely extensional and in which, according to Kripke, there should not be any difference between a substitutional and a referential account. For suppose that we restrict our models to those in which there is a name in the object language for each individual in the domain. In one trivial sense, in such languages "quantification into name position is also quantification over objects of the kind named", as Davis (1981, p. 143) puts it.

However, from the parallelism of names and individuals it simply does not follow that "there is indeed little difference between a substitutional quantifier and a referential [objectual] quantifier ranging over the set of denotata", as Kripke (1976, p. 351) claims, if this claim is extended to IF quantifiers. The hidden mistake here is that to think of quantifiers as merely "ranging over" a set of individuals. To do so is in effect to think that their semantics can be defined substitutionally. Hence Kripke's claim (1976, p. 383) that the real dispute is over the ranges of the variables of the object language is wrong. The real dispute is whether quantifiers should be interpreted as higher-order predicates or as codifying certain choice functions (Skolem functions).

1.8. The nature of negation

A pleasant feature of the GTS treatment of negation encoded in the rule (R. $\neg$) is its robustness. It allows us to make the same kind of distinction that was made in the chapter on Partiality between *non-true and false*. The former is the lack of a winning strategy for Myself, the latter is the existence of a winning strategy for Nature. Precisely, the same rule (R. $\neg$) can be used in ordinary first-order logic as well as in its IF variant.

Indeed, it is difficult to see how else negation could be treated game-theoretically. Furthermore, the way we defined truth and falsity preserves the usual symmetry between the two with respect to negation: S is true iff $\neg S$ is false; S is false iff $\neg S$ is true; S is undefined (neither true nor false) iff $\neg S$ is undefined.

All this is so natural that it might seem trivial. On closer inspection, however, certain striking consequences begin to come to light. One such striking consequence is the failure of the law of excluded middle.

Thus the IF negation $\neg$ is not contradictory negation, i.e. it does not always yield, when applied to an arbitrary IF first-order sentence S, the complement of the class of models in which S is true. What we have got in our logic is a much stronger negation than contradictory negation, i.e. a dual negation, as the next theorem shows.

DEFINITION 8.1. Let * be the following mapping which maps each IF first-order sentence S into its dual S^*:

$$S^* = \neg S,\ S \text{ atomic};$$
$$(\neg S)^* = S^*;$$
$$\big((\exists x/\forall y_1, \dots, \forall y_k)F\big)^* = \big(\forall x/\exists y_1, \dots, \exists y_k\big)F^*;$$
$$\big((\forall x/\exists y_1, \dots, \exists y_k)F\big)^* = \big(\exists x/\forall y_1, \dots, \forall y_k\big)F^*;$$
$$\big(F(\vee/\forall y_1, \dots, \forall y_k)G\big)^* = \big(F^*(\wedge/\exists y_1, \dots, \exists y_k)G^*\big);$$
$$\big(F(\wedge/\exists y_1, \dots, \exists y_k)G\big)^* = \big(F^*(\vee/\forall y_1, \dots, \forall y_k)G^*\big).$$

We call S^* the dual of S. The next theorem is proved by a straightforward induction on the length of S:

THEOREM 8.2. *For any* IF *first-order sentence S and model M:*

$$M \vDash_{\mathrm{GTS}} \neg S \quad \textit{iff} \quad M \vDash_{\mathrm{GTS}} S^*.$$

Weak (contradictory) negation $\neg_w$ can be introduced in our logic in a straightforward way. We first extend the IF first-order language to an extended IF first-order language ($\mathrm{IF}^{\mathrm{ext}}$ first-order language) which will contain the additional logical constant $\neg_w$. This is done by stipulating that for any arbitrary unextended IF first-order formula S, $\neg_w S$ is to be an $\mathrm{IF}^{\mathrm{ext}}$ formula. Thus weak negation can occur only sentence initially. Finally, we define:

DEFINITION 8.3. For any $\mathrm{IF}^{\mathrm{ext}}$ first-order sentence S and model M:
(i) $M \vDash_{\mathrm{GTS}} (\neg_w S)^+$ iff not $M \vDash_{\mathrm{GTS}} S^+$.
(ii) $M \vDash_{\mathrm{GTS}} (\neg_w S)^-$ iff not $M \vDash_{\mathrm{GTS}} S^-$.

Given Definitions 1.1 and 8.3, we get:

$$M \vDash_{\mathrm{GTS}} (\neg_w S)^+ \text{ iff Myself does not have a winning strategy in } G(S; M).$$

$$M \vDash_{\mathrm{GTS}} (\neg_w S)^- \text{ iff Nature does not have a winning strategy in } G(S; M).$$

The presence of weak negation in our logic has the consequence of introducing the truth-value 10 (both true and false) discussed in Section 1.5. The weak negation of sentences of the (restricted) IF first-order logic which are undefined turns out to be both true and false (denoted by 10). More generally, for every sentences S of the extended IF first-order sentence and model M, let

$$\begin{aligned} (8.1) \quad & \|S\|^M = 1, && \text{if} && M \vDash_{\mathrm{GTS}} S^+ && \text{and not} && M \vDash_{\mathrm{GTS}} S^-. \\ & \|S\|^M = 0, && \text{if} && M \vDash_{\mathrm{GTS}} S^- && \text{and not} && M \vDash_{\mathrm{GTS}} S^+. \\ & \|S\|^M = ?, && \text{if not} && M \vDash_{\mathrm{GTS}} S^+ && \text{and not} && M \vDash_{\mathrm{GTS}} S^-. \\ & \|S\|^M = 10, && \text{if} && M \vDash_{\mathrm{GTS}} S^+ && \text{and} && M \vDash_{\mathrm{GTS}} S^-. \end{aligned}$$

Then it can be checked that the weak negation has the following truth-table:

$$(8.2) \quad \|S\|^M = 1 \quad \text{iff} \quad \|\neg_w S\|^M = 0.$$

$$(8.3) \quad \|S\|^M = 0 \quad \text{iff} \quad \|\neg_w S\|^M = 1.$$

$$(8.4) \quad \|S\|^M = ? \quad \text{iff} \quad \|\neg_w S\|^M = 10.$$

$$(8.5) \quad \|S\|^M = 10 \quad \text{iff} \quad \|\neg_w S\|^M = ?.$$

Since an IF first-order sentence S is never true and false, it follows that $\|\neg_w S\|^M = ?$ is never the case.

Another consequence of the introduction of weak negation in our logic follows from the Separation Theorem:

THEOREM 8.4. *For any sentence S of an IF first-order language L, if $\neg_w S$ is representable in L (i.e. there is an L-sentence R such that S and R have the same models), then S is representable by an ordinary first-order sentence.*

What Theorem 8.4 shows is that the only sentences of an unextended IF first-order language to have their contradictory negations expressible in the same language are the usual first-order sentences (without slashes).

These observations put to a new light the behavior of negation in formal as well as natural languages. What one undoubtedly would like to express in one's favorite working language is the weak (contradictory) negation obeying the principle of excluded middle. But for such a negation we cannot give any reasonable semantical rules, let alone any proof rules. Basically the only thing you can say of this negation is Definition 8.1. Syntactically, weak negation can only occur sentence-initially. Game rules can only be formulated for the strong (dual) negation which does not obey the law of *tertium non datur*.

In natural languages negation normally expresses weak (contradictory) negation. However, its semantical behavior can only be understood by reference to another (strong or dual) negation which usually is not explicitly expressed in language. This explains why the rules for negation are as complex as they actually are in natural languages. It also helps to explain a number of regularities in languages like English. They are so to speak calculated to keep weak negation sentence initial, the reason being that it is interpretable only in such contexts.

In general, we can thus see that in sufficiently rich languages (natural or formal), there must be two different negations present. On the one hand, there must be the contradictory negation there, for it is presumably what we want to express by our negation. However, the contradictory negation cannot stand on its own feet. In order to be able to formulate rules for dealing with negation (semantical rules, deductive rules, game rules, or what not), we must also have the strong (dual) negation present, for satisfactory rules can be formulated only for it.

This general theoretical situation is reflected by specific regularities in natural languages. In Section 2.4 it will be seen that the interpretation of anaphoric pronouns relies conceptually on what happens in a play of the semantical game in question. But what has just been seen implies that sentences $\neg_w S$ with a contradictory negation $\neg_w$ are not interpreted through playing a semantical game. They say merely something about the game $G(S)$, viz. that the initial verifier does not have a winning strategy in $G(S)$. Thus we obtain the neat prediction that (contradictory) negation is a barrier to anaphora. This regularity has been noted before, and Heim (1982, pp. 114–117) has actually used its alleged inexplicability in GTS as a basis of criticizing the treatment of anaphora in GTS.

1.9. Constructivism and game strategies

We defined truth in GTS as the existence of a winning strategy for Myself and, as we saw, this strategy is codified by a set of functions. These functions can be assumed to be defined on the set of natural numbers but no other restriction has been put on them. However, it might seem that the class of such functions must be restricted, for it does not make sense to think of any actual player as following a nonconstructive (nonrecursive) strategy. How can I possibly follow in practice such a strategy when there is no effective way for me to find out in general what my next move will be? Hence the basic ideas of the entire game-theoretical approach apparently motivate an important change in the semantics of first-order languages (independence-friendly or not) and in their logic. The resulting semantics is just like the ordinary game-theoretical semantics, except that the strategies of Myself are restricted to recursive ones. This is a perfectly well-defined change. It leaves our notation completely unchanged (independently of whether the slash notation is present or not). It also leaves all the game rules for making moves in a semantical game untouched.

The change involved in the transition to the new version of GTS is motivated by the kind of argument that appeals to constructivists and according to them ought to appeal to everybody. For the basis of our argument was the requirement that the semantical games that are the foundations of our semantics and logic must be playable by actual human beings, at least in principle. The actual playability of our "language-games" is one of the most characteristic features of the thought of both Wittgenstein and Dummett.

The step from ordinary GTS to the constructivistic version makes a difference already in ordinary first-order logic. It is known that there are arithmetical sentences that are satisfiable in the domain of natural numbers but which do not have any recursive Skolem functions to satisfy them. This means that there are fewer arithmetical sentences true in the domain of natural numbers than before. On the other side, by a result of Vaught (1960), the set of first-order formulas valid in the class of countable models with constructive relations and operations is no longer effectively axiomatizable. There is thus an interesting interplay between the effectiveness of interpretation and the effectiveness of the resulting logic (cf. Van Benthem, 1988).

It is natural to define the falsity of a sentence in constructivistic GTS as the existence of a recursive winning strategy for Nature, i.e. a recursive strategy which wins against any strategy of the initial verifier. If so, there will be sentences of ordinary first-order logic which are neither true nor false in suitable models. Thus constructivists are not entirely wrong in focusing on the failure of *tertium non datur* as a possible symptom of a constructivist approach. However, as we saw, the law of excluded middle fails in perfectly classical nonconstructivist logic as soon as informational independence is allowed.

A definitive evaluation of the constructivistic version of GTS will not be attempted here.

1.10. Epistemic logic

One of the directions in which GTS can be extended is intensional logics. Here we will discuss the logic of knowledge as a representative special case.

The first step in the use of GTS in epistemic logic is an old hat. The basic new concept is *a knows that*, abbreviated by K_a. The appropriate model structure is a set of ordinary models (possible worlds), on which a three-place relation is defined. This relation associates with each world M_0 and each person b existing in M_0 a set of worlds, the epistemic b-alternatives to M_0. (The given model M_0 is assumed to be always among its own epistemic alternatives.) Such a structure of models might be called a *model structure*.

Then we can add the following clause to a usual Tarski-type truth-definition:

DEFINITION 10.1. Let Ω be a model structure and $M_0 \in \Omega$. Then $K_a S$ is true in M_0 if and only if for each epistemic a-alternative M_1 to M_0 in Ω, S is true in M_1.

This definition reflects the intuitive idea that to know something is to be able to restrict one's attention to a subset of all possibilities that *a priori* would have to be considered. From Definition 10.1 it is also seen that the epistemic operator K_a can be dealt with as a universal quantifier ranging over epistemic a-alternatives. This immediately shows a game-theoretical treatment can be extended to epistemic logic. At each stage of the game, the players now consider some one sentence in relation to some one "world" (model). The game rules are the same, *mutatis mutandis*, as in first-order languages, with a new one added:

(R. K) The game $G(K_a S; M_0)$ begins with the choice by the falsifier of an epistemic a-alternative M_1 to M_0. The game is then continued as in $G(S; M_1)$.

In order to analyze different kinds of knowledge statements, however, we need something more. *Knowing whether* S_1 or S_2 can be analyzed as

(10.1) $KS_1 \vee KS_2$

and a simple *knowing who* (or *knowing* + another *wh-word*) as

(10.2) $(\exists x) KS[x]$.

But no similar analysis works for constructions where the choice of the operator variable depends on the choice of a universal quantifier, as in

(10.3) It is known whom each person admires most.

It turns out that an adequate analysis of all the different knowledge statements requires the notion of informational independence. Thus the logical form of (10.3) is rather

(10.4) $K(\forall x)(\exists y/K)S[x, y]$.

By the same token (10.1) and (10.2) can be expressed as follows (respectively):

(10.5) $K(S_1(\vee/K)S_2)$,

(10.6) $K(\exists x/K)S[x]$.

The general form of a knowledge statement is

(10.7) KS

where S is a first-order statement (in negation normal form), except that a number of existential quantifiers $(\exists x)$ have been replaced by $(\exists x/K)$, and a number of disjunctions $(S_1 \vee S_2)$ by $(S_1(\vee/K)S_2)$.

Indeed, the logical counterpart of the question ingredient of an indirect question in natural language can be taken to be precisely $(\exists x/K)$ and $(\vee/K)$.

Such an analysis of different kinds of knowledge statements can be extended to an analysis of the main concepts relating to questions and answers.

(i) Any knowledge statement can serve as the *desideratum* of a direct question, i.e. as a description of the cognitive state the questioner wants to achieve by his or her question. Any number of the expressions $(\exists x/K)$ and $(\vee/K)$ can be questioned in asking the question. For instance, (10.4) is the desideratum of a question of the form

(10.8) Whom does each person admire most?

(ii) If the slash expression $/K$ is removed from the questioned ingredients, we obtain the *presupposition* of the question. For instance, the presuppositions of the questions whose desiderata are (10.4)–(10.6) are respectively

(10.9) $K(\forall x)(\exists y)S[x, y]$,

(10.10) $K(S_1 \vee S_2)$,

(10.11) $K(\exists x)S[x]$.

(iii) A *reply* to a question is like the desideratum, except that each variable x_i bound to a questioned ingredient like

(10.12) $(\exists x_i/K)$

is replaced by

(10.13) $f_i(y_1, y_2, \ldots, y_j)$

where each f_i is a function constant and $(\forall y_1), (\forall y_2), \ldots, (\forall y_j)$ are all the universal quantifiers in the scope of which (10.12) occurs in (10.7). Furthermore, each questioned disjunction

(10.14) $(S_1(\vee/K)S_2)$

is replaced by

(10.15) $(S_1 \wedge f_k(y_1, y_2, \ldots, y_j) = 0) \vee (S_2 \wedge f_k(y_1, y_2, \ldots, y_j) \neq 0)$

where f_k is a function constant and $(\forall y_1), (\forall y_2), \ldots, (\forall y_j)$ are all the universal quantifiers within the scope of which (10.14) occurs in (10.7).

(iv) The *conclusiveness conditions* of such a reply are the sentences

(10.16) $K(\forall y_1)(\forall y_2)\cdots(\forall y_j)(\exists x/K)(f_i(y_1, y_2, \ldots, y_j) = x)$,

(10.17) $K(\forall y_1)(\forall y_2)\cdots(\forall y_j)(\exists x/K)(f_k(y_1, y_2, \ldots, y_j) = x)$.

A reply plus the corresponding conclusiveness conditions logically imply the desideratum, which is not logically implied by the reply alone.

1.11. The definability of truth and its significance

It was shown by Tarski (1956) that, given certain assumptions, truth can be defined for a formal language only in a richer metalanguage. Tarski also argued that a complete and consistent notion of truth is impossible to apply to natural language (Tarski's "colloquial language").

Tarski's result and his pessimistic thesis are put to a new light by IF first-order logic. Given a sentence S of an IF first-order language, one can think of its second-order (Σ_1^1) translation as expressing its truth-condition. (Cf. Sections 1.1 and 1.4 above.) But the Σ_1^1 fragment of a second-order language can be translated back into the corresponding IF first-order language.

This observation can be converted into an actual truth-definition. First, we have to build up a modicum of arithmetic into an IF first-order language L in order to speak of the syntax of L in L itself. This can be done by means of the usual strategy of Gödel numbering. It is assumed here that this numbering is extended to the corresponding second-order language.

Then we can take a second-order predicate variable X and express the necessary and sufficient conditions for its being a truth-predicate, i.e. a predicate such that the sentence $X(n)$ is true if and only if the numeral n codifies the Gödel number of a true sentence of the language in question. This is a straightforward task for ordinary first-order language. All that needs to be done is to express the usual truth-conditions by means of the Gödel numbering, for instance that X applies to the Gödel number of a conjunction only if X applies to the Gödel number of both conjuncts, or that X applies to the Gödel number of an existentially quantified sentence $(\exists x)S[x]$ only if X applies to the Gödel number of at least one formula of the form $S[n]$, where n is a numeral.

The failure of compositionality in IF logic occasions a modification of this procedure. One can, for instance, do the following:

(i) Express the requirement that X applies to the Gödel number of a sentence S if and only if X applies to the Gödel number of the Skolem normal form of S.

(ii) Express the requirement that X applies to the Gödel number of a sentence in Skolem normal form

$$(\forall x_1)(\forall x_2)\cdots(\forall x_i)(\exists y_1/\forall x_{11},\forall x_{12},\ldots)(\exists y_2/\forall x_{21},\forall x_{22},\ldots)$$
$$\cdots(\exists y_j/\forall x_{j1},\forall x_{j2},\ldots)S[x_1,x_2,\ldots,x_i,y_1,y_2,\ldots,y_j]$$

(where each $\{x_{k1},x_{k2},\ldots\}\subseteq\{x_1,x_2,\ldots,x_i\}$) only if there are functions $f_1,f_2,\ldots,f_j$ such that X applies to the Gödel number of every sentence of the form $S[\mathbf{n}_1,\mathbf{n}_2,\ldots,$ $\mathbf{n}_i,\mathbf{m}_1,\mathbf{m}_2,\ldots,\mathbf{m}_j]$ where $\mathbf{n}_k$ is the numeral expressing the number n_k and $\mathbf{m}_l$ the numeral expressing the Gödel number of $f_l(n_{l_1},n_{l_2},\ldots)$.

It is not hard to prove that all these requirements are expressible by Σ_1^1-formulas. Let this conjunction be $Tr[X]$. Consider now the second-order formula

$$(\exists X)(Tr[X]\wedge X(y)).$$

It is obviously a perfectly good truth-predicate in the intended sense. It is equivalent to a Σ_1^1-sentence. Hence it has a translation to the corresponding IF first-order language. This translation is the desired truth predicate.

It is to be noticed that we do not claim that there exists an explicit definition of a truth predicate for IF first-order logic. The truth predicate just defined captures all and only true sentences. How it behaves with false and not true (not false) sentences is not being considered here.

No paradoxes arise because of the definability of truth for suitable IF first-order languages in these languages themselves. You can construct a Gödel type paradoxically looking sentence by the usual diagonal procedure and you will find that it is neither true nor false. And it was pointed out earlier without any fancy footwork that the law of excluded middle fails in IF first-order logic.

The possibility of defining a truth-predicate for IF languages in the language itself has striking suggestions for the general methodological situation in language theory.

(i) Since informational independence occurs in natural languages (cf. Section 2.3 below), there does not seem to be any good reasons to doubt the possibility of applying a consistent concept of truth to a natural language and even to discuss that concept in the natural language itself. There is hence no reason to exile the notion of truth from the semantical theory of natural languages.

(ii) All formal semantics and model theory has until now been under methodological suspicion. For what does it take to practice model theory, it may be asked. Two things are needed for the purpose in the case of any given language: (i) a set of models and (ii) a definition as to when a given sentence is true in a given model. The first requirement (i) need not detain us here. The second purpose (ii) has to be served by a suitable truth definition. But Tarski-type truth-definitions have to be formulated in a second-order language or else set-theoretically. In either case, the resulting theory of truth will be riddled by all the difficulties and uncertainties that are connected with the existence of sets and classes, complete with set-theoretical paradoxes, incompleteness of higher-order logics, difficulty of choosing between different set-theoretical assumptions, etc. Even though such problems do not affect actual linguistic theorizing, they cast a dark shadow on the entire enterprise of formal semantics methodologically and philosophically.

The possibility of self-applied truth-definitions on first-order level (viz. in IF first-order languages) removes most of these doubts. Whatever difficulties there may be about IF first-order languages, problems of set existence, set theoretical paradoxes or problems of infinity are not among them.

2. Natural languages

2.1. Game rules for quantifier phrases

In the tradition of generalized quantifiers started by Montague (cf. Thomason, 1974), a quantifier in English is taken to have the general structure:

(1.1) Quantifier = Determiner + Common Noun

where the category of determiners includes expressions such as *some, every, most*, etc. In what follows we will be even more liberal and take quantifier phrases to be expressions of the following forms: *some* X *who* Y, *an* X *who* Y, *every* X *who* Y, *any* X *who* Y, where X is a common noun and Y is a verb-phrase. Instead of *who* in the above phrase-forms, we could have any other wh-word.

When *who* does not occupy the subject position in *who* Y, this sentence can be thought of as having been derived from a string of the form

$$Y_1 - \text{someone} - Y_2$$

by wh-movement, resulting in $Y = \text{who} - Y_1 - \text{trace} - Y_2$.

Since there are no variables in natural languages, the procedure of substituting names of individuals for bound variables is not directly applicable in them. What we can do is to substitute proper names for such individuals for entire quantifier phrases. In addition, we stipulate that the individuals chosen in the course of a play of game $G(S; M)$ enter a certain *choice set* I_S. The choice set is not constant but changes when a play of the game progresses. The rationale of this is the presence of anaphoric expressions in natural language which forces us somehow to keep track of the individuals which might be potential "heads" for those anaphors.

As before, some basic vocabulary is assumed to be given and interpreted on a certain domain. The game rules for standard quantifiers will have then the following forms:

(R. some) If the game $G(S; M)$ has reached an expression of the form:

$$Z - \text{some } X \text{ who } Y - W$$

then the verifier may choose an individual from the appropriate domain, say b. The game is then continued as $G(Z - b - W,\ b \text{ is an } X \text{ and } b\ Y; M)$. The individual b is added to the choice set I_S.

When $Y = Y_1 - \text{trace} - Y_2$, the penultimate clause of the output sentence will be

$$Y_1 - b - Y_2.$$

(R. every) As in the corresponding case of (R. some), except that *every* replaces *some* in (*), that b is chosen by the falsifier, and that the game is continued with $G(Z - b - W, \text{ if } b \text{ is an } X \text{ and } b\ Y; M)$. The individual b is added to the choice set I_S.

(R. an) As in the corresponding case of (R. some), except that *an* replaces *some.*

(R. any) As in the corresponding case of (R. every), except that *any* replaces *every.*

In spite of their simplicity, these rules cover nontrivial cases. For instance, (R. any) incorporates the claim that *any* is univocal in English, always having basically the force of an universal quantifier. This is also the view of Quine (1960) and Lasnik (1975). In contrast, Davidson (1980) holds that *any* is invariably existential.

The rules for conjunction (R. and) and disjunction (R. or) are the analogues of the corresponding rules for formal languages. The rule for negation is defined in terms of role swapping, as in first-order logic:

(R. negation) If the game $G(S; M)$ has reached an expression $P^{(-)}$ which is the negation in English of P, then the players exchange roles, i.e. the verifier will become the falsifier and vice versa. The game goes on as $G(P; M)$.

Notice that the rule of negation is slightly different from its formal counterpart. It is intended to cover both internal, constituent negation (*do not, does not*, etc.) and external, sentential (*it is not true that, it is not the case that*, etc.). This rule presupposes a theory of negation in English, which is a project of not inconsiderable difficulty. However, for our purposes in this paper, the rule (R. negation) will do.

2.2. *The scope of scope*

If you examine the rules for quantifier expressions sketched above, you can see that they differ from the corresponding rules for formal languages in an interesting way. In formal languages, the first application of the rules for semantical games is always completely determined by the scopes of the different logical constants, e.g., quantifiers or connectives. These scopes are usually indicated by parentheses (brackets). The first rule application is always to the logical constant (or other logically active ingredient) with the widest scope. In contrast, different game rules (e.g., quantifier rules) can often be applied to one and the same natural-language sentence, and the same rule can often be applied to different ingredients of the same sentence. In the absence of scope-indicating parentheses, how is the order of different applications of rules determined in natural language?

It is easily seen that the job of parentheses is done by various *ordering principles* which govern the choice of the rule to be applied and the choice of its target. (Cf. Section 2.3 below.) They are a new element in the GTS for natural languages compared with formal languages. In a moment, their nature will be explained more fully.

Anticipating their formulation, an interesting fact about them can be noted. Some of them depend on the syntactical structure of the sentence in question. Others depend also on particular lexical items, e.g., on the choice between *any* and *every*. What they do not depend on is an assignment of a segment of the sentence or the discourse under scrutiny to each quantifier or connective as its "scope".

What this implies is that in formal languages the notion of scope does two things that do not always go together in natural languages. On the one hand, the so-called scopes indicate the relative priority of different logically active ingredients of a sentence. We might call this the *priority scope*. On the other hand, the scope of a quantifier is supposed to indicate the segment of a sentence (or discourse) where pronouns have that particular quantifier as its head or, as the saying goes, are bound to that particular quantifier. This might be called tentatively the *binding scope* of the quantifier.

There is no *a priori* reason (or *a posteriori* one, either) to claim that these two kinds of scope always go together in natural language, and some good reasons to claim that they do not go together in natural languages. Hence languages with the usual scope conventions cannot be expected to provide good models for natural language phenomena involving both senses of scope. This is one of the reasons why formal languages have been developed where the two scopes do not always coincide. (Cf. the chapter on Discourse Representation Theory and the chapter on Dynamics in this Handbook.)

Nor is this a mere theoretical possibility. It provides an instant analysis of the simplest puzzle examples called donkey sentences. They are exemplified by

(2.1) If Peter owns a donkey, he beats it.

The standard treatment of (2.1) makes it equivalent with

(2.2) $$(\forall x)\big((\text{Donkey}[x] \wedge \text{Own}\,[\text{Peter}, x]) \longrightarrow \text{Beat}\,[\text{Peter}, x]\big).$$

But by what rules do we get from (2.1) to (2.2)? Why does the prima facie existential quantifier *a* (as in *a donkey*) suddenly assume the force of a universal quantifier in (2.2)? (For such questions and related ones, see also the chapter on Discourse Representation Theory.)

The explanation is simpler if we deconstruct the notion of scope and distinguish the priority scope [ ] from the binding scope ( ). Then (2.1) will have the translation

(2.3) $$(\exists x)\big[(\text{Donkey}\,[x] \wedge \text{Own}\,[\text{Peter}, x]\big] \longrightarrow \text{Beat}\,[\text{Peter}, x]\big).$$

Since logical rules are governed by the priority scopes, (2.3) is equivalent with (2.2).

Another familiar example is:

(2.4) A man walks in the park. He whistles.

On the two-scopes analysis envisaged here this sentence will translate as:

(2.5) $$(\exists x)\big[(\text{Man}[x] \wedge \text{Walk}[x]\big] \wedge \text{Whistle}[x]\big).$$

In sum, the notion of scope, instead of being the simplest and unproblematic idea it is routinely taken to be, is in reality ambiguous. It must be handled with extreme caution when applied to natural language. A formal logic in which the two kinds of scope part company is Dynamic Predicate Logic. (See the chapter on Discourse Representation Theory and Dynamics.)

2.3. *Ordering principles*

In natural languages, the priority scope is handled by means of certain ordering principles which govern the order of application of the rules of semantical games to different expressions in language or in discourse.

In formal languages, the formula reached at a given stage of a game always determines what happens next. The order of application of the game rules is univocally determined by the syntactical structure of the sentence in question. Scope, in both of the two senses explained earlier is explicitly indicated. Actually, the only ordering principle which is needed and which has been applied tacitly over and over again in Section 1 is:

(O. LR) For any semantical game $G(S; M)$, the game rules are applied from left to right.

In contrast, in natural languages, the order of application of different rules has so far been left completely open. In such languages, the concept of scope does not even make sense. Instead of the notion of scope, we have to deal with the notion of rule ordering, which serves many of the same purposes that scope does in formal languages but which is essentially different from it. Some ordering principles are in fact fairly obvious and closely related to the phenomenon of governance studied intensively in linguistics.

There are two kinds of ordering principles in GTS, general principles and special ones. The general principles depend only on the syntactic structure of the sentence or sentences to whose ingredients a rule is to be applied. Special ordering principles depend also on the lexical items involved. The general principles are only two and extremely simple: (O. LR) mentioned above and (O. comm):

(O. comm) A game rule must not be applied to an ingredient of a lower clause if it can be applied to an ingredient of a higher one.

(A node N_1 is said to be in a higher clause than N_2 if the S-node immediately dominating N_1 also dominates N_2 but not vice versa.)

(Cf. Hintikka and Kulas, 1985.)

However, (O. LR) must be restricted so as to apply only to two ingredients of one and the same clause (i.e. ingredients governed by the same S-nodes). The general ordering principles are closely related to regularities known from the literature, such as the conditions on the possibility of anaphora.

The special ordering principles govern the relative ordering of two particular game rules. They overrule the general ordering principles. Here is one of them:

(O. any) (R. any) has priority over (R. negation), (R. or) and (R. conditional).

This principle assigns the right meaning to sentences like

(3.1) We haven't got any bananas.

Here, the normal order of application of the rules would be, by virtue of (O. LR): (R. not), (R. any). However, (O. LR) is overruled in this case by (O. any) and thus (R. any) will be applied first.

Related to ordering principles there is what has been called the Well-formedness Constraint (WFC):

WFC: The output sentence of the application of a game rule to a well formed input must be well-formed.

This constraint explains several phenomena. Among them is why certain readings of multiple questions are excluded in English. (See Hintikka, 1976). An example is the fact that, e.g., the reading of

(3.2) For whom did Mary buy what?

on which *what* governs *For whom*, is excluded (at least comparatively) in English.

Some ordering principles, e.g., (O. any) may be seen as directly derivable from WFC. A discussion of WFC and its consequences for GTS is contained in (Hand, 1987).

Finally, let us say something about quantifiers and informational independence in English. There are several different types of examples of informationally independent quantifiers in English. The following are instances of sentences involving irreducible informational independences (i.e. having no ordinary first-order equivalent):

(3.3) Everybody has a unique hobby.

(3.4) Some official of each company knows some aide of each senator.

(3.5) Some friend of each townsman and some neighbor of each villager envy each other.

Some of these types of examples have provoked lively discussion, especially sentences of the form (3.5). Stenius (1976) and Boolos (1984) claim that (3.5) has a first-order logical form. Hintikka (1974), Barwise (1978), and Carlson and Ter Meulen (1979) argue that (3.5) is essentially branching.

We think that, as soon as we understand the underlying mechanism of these sentences, we understand that some such sentences are less natural than others. Sentences of the form (3.4) have the logical form (using self-explanatory abbreviations)

(3.6) $$(\forall x)(\exists y)(\forall z)(\exists w/\forall x)\big((C[x] \wedge S[z]) \longrightarrow (O[y,x] \wedge A[w,z] \wedge C[y,w])\big)$$

which is equivalent with

(3.7) $$(\exists f)(\exists g)(\forall x)(\forall z)\big((C[x] \wedge S[z]) \longrightarrow (O[f(x),x] \wedge A[g(z),z] \wedge C[f(x),g(z)])\big).$$

They are more natural the easier it is to think of familiar functions that might serve as the truth-making values of f and g in (3.7).

2.4. *The treatment of pronouns in GTS*

Many linguists and logicians assimilate the typical *modus operandi* of anaphoric pronouns to that of the bound variables of quantification. For instance, Chomsky's LF is essentially a quantificational formula. (See the chapter on GB theory.) The motivation of such an approach springs from a general commitment to the principle of compositionality. For how else can an anaphoric pronoun be handled in a compositional semantics if not by construing it as a bound variable? Since GTS is a noncompositional semantics, we are not committed to such an approach. Instead, we shall construe them in a different way.

Very briefly, the basic idea of the theory of pronouns in GTS is that a pronoun is essentially like a hidden definite description, *he* like *the male, she* like *the female*, etc. Moreover, these definite descriptions can be treated like Russellian ones, with one major exception (and some minor ones). The major one is that quantifiers employed in Russellian analysis are taken to range over not the entire universe of discourse, or some context-independent part of it, but over the *choice set* I_S that we described in Section 2.1. As we said there, this set is not a constant but changes in the course of a play of a semantical game. The membership in I_S is determined by the course of a play of a semantical game $G(S;M)$ up to the time at which the pronoun in question is dealt with. As the first crude approximation, soon to be refined, it can be said that I_S consists of the individuals which the two players have picked out in the play of the game $G(S;M)$ before a rule is applied to the pronoun in question.

A sample game rule for pronouns might thus be somewhat like the following:

(R. he) When the game has reached a sentence of the form

$$X - \text{he} - Y,$$

the verifier may choose an individual, say b, from the choice set I_S, to be the value of the pronoun *he*, whereupon the falsifier chooses an individual d from I_S. The game is then continued with respect to

$$X - b - Y,\ b \text{ is a male, and if } d \text{ is a male then } d \text{ is the same as } b.$$

Similar rules can be formulated for the pronouns *she* and *it* as well as for pronouns in the object position, like *him, her*, etc.

For illustration, let us consider the following sentence:

(4.1) I met John and gave him a letter.

The choice set formed in the course of a semantical game played with (4.1) will contained all the individuals chosen by the two players. At the moment (R. him) is applied to *him*, an individual named by *John* has been already introduced in the choice set and is thus available to be picked by the the verifier as a value for *him.* The last clause of the game rule for pronouns ensures that this individual is the unique one satisfying (4.1).

This general idea leads to a number of insights, which at the same time show how it can (and must) be made more precise.

(i) This approach to pronouns is obviously quite intuitive. Why has it not been tried before? The reason why it cannot be formulated without the help of GTS is the dependence of the choice set I_S of the course taken by a play of the semantical game $G(S;M)$ and hence on this game. It does not depend only on the syntactical and on the semantical properties of the input sentence.

(ii) By the simple (and virtually inescapable) device of considering discourse as a succession of (sub)games, this theory is applicable also to discourse anaphora (cf. below). An additional pragmatic feature of the situation is then that speakers often tacitly drop individuals from I_S in the course of the discourse. In practice, the right value of a pronoun is therefore often the most conspicuous eligible individual rather than the unique eligible one.

(iii) The game rules for pronouns, like all other game rules, are subject to the ordering principles discussed earlier. These principles imply restrictions on the possible coreference between a pronoun P and a noun phrase NP occurring in the same sentence (or discourse). The value of NP can be also the value of P only if it is in I_S at the time a rule is applied to P. But that is possible only if a rule has been applied to NP earlier, i.e. only if the ordering principles allow a rule application to NP before a rule is applied to P.

For instance, the general ordering principle (O. comm) rules out applications to a lower clause if a rule application to a higher one is possible. This general principle, for which one can find a great deal of evidence independently of the treatment of pronouns, implies the familiar exclusion of coreference of a pronoun with a potential head located in a lower clause.

(iv) Besides individuals introduced into I_S by the players' moves, the choice set I_S may contain individuals introduced ostensively. This explains at once why anaphoric and deictic pronouns behave (by and large) in the same way semantically. Indeed, as separate rules are needed in GTS for deictic pronouns, merely a permission for the objects they refer to to enter the choice set I_S.

(v) Another dogma that is ready to be buried is that anaphora is essentially a matter of coreference. It is not. What is normally needed for an anaphoric pronoun P to be interpretable is the presence of a suitable individual b in I_S when a rule is applied to P. That individual b normally has been introduced as a value of some NP treated earlier. But a rule application to NP can introduce b even when b is not the reference of NP. A case in point is the following example:

(4.2) A couple were sitting on a bench. Suddenly he got up.

Here *A couple* is treated first. Whatever precisely the relevant rule is, an application introduces two individuals which on the most likely reading of the phrase are of different sexes. Hence by the time (R. he) is applied to *he*, there is in $I_{(4.2)}$ a unique male who therefore can serve as the (hopefully) winning value of *he*. Hence (4.2) is interpretable, and receives its normal sense in GTS. But of course, *he* is in no sense coreferential with *A couple*. In the sense illustrated by these observations, anaphora is a semantical phenomenon, not only a syntactical one.

(vi) It is not quite true that I_S consists only of individuals chosen earlier in the game. In the game rules which deals with successive subgames, it is often stipulated that a strategy function used by a player in an earlier subgame is available to the other player in a later subgame. Applied to a member of I_S, such functions yield further individuals as their values. All of them must be included in I_S. We can express this by saying that the "remembered" functions are included in I_S and that I_S must be closed with respect to functional applications. These locutions are made natural by the fact that a strategy function will sometimes reduce to a constant individual. For instance, consider the following simple variant of the so-called donkey sentences

(4.3) Peter owns *a donkey*. He beats *it*.

Here in the subgame with *Peter owns a donkey* the winning verifying strategy reduces to the choice of a donkey owned by Peter. This beast can serve as the value of *it* when (R. it) is applied to it in the second subgame.

Other cases, including more complex ones, will be treated in the next sections.

(vii) In natural languages, we encounter the distinction between normal and reflexive pronouns. This might seem a peculiarity of natural languages, without any deeper logical basis. In reality, the distinction is virtually predictable. In the logic of quantification, we have in principle a choice between two different readings of quantifiers. The difference is especially easy to explain in GTS. When a player chooses an individual to serve as a value of a variable of quantification, the question arises: Are the individuals chosen earlier still available later on for subsequent choices by one of the players? All the traditional treatments of quantification theory presuppose the affirmative answer. It is said to give rise to an inclusive interpretation of quantifiers. Yet the negative answer leads to a perfectly viable alternative to a logic of quantification for which rules are easily given. They can be said to codify an exclusive interpretation of quantifiers. The distinction is just like the contrast between draws from an urn with and without replacements in probability theory. An explicit logical treatment of the exclusive interpretation was first presented in (Hintikka, 1956).

Now in natural languages a version of the exclusive interpretation is usually assumed. This occasions in fact a correction to rules like (R. he). The choices by the two players in (R. he) must be restricted to a subset of the choice set I_S. This subset is obtained by omitting from I_S all individuals introduced by application of rules to expressions which were in the same clause as the he to which we are applying the rule (R. he).

But if so, we sometimes need a way of referring back to those excluded members of the choice set. That happens in natural language by means of reflexive pronouns. A rule for one of them, e.g., (R. himself) is just like the corresponding rule for the corresponding ordinary pronoun, (e.g., (R. he)), except that the players' choices are now restricted to those members of I_S which were excluded in the other one.

Thus the phenomenon of reflexive pronouns becomes understandable as a consequence of the general laws of the logical behavior of quantifiers. For instance, we can now put into a new theoretical perspective Chomsky's contrast between pronominals and anaphors. The GTS treatment also immediately yields verifiable predictions, for instance that reflexive pronouns cannot be deictic.

There are various kinds of evidence for the idea that anaphoric pronouns are interpreted by a game rule whose application depends on the earlier history of the game. An especially interesting item of evidence is the fact that ordinary contradictory negation is a barrier to anaphora. The explanation lies in the fact that a negated sentence $\neg_w S$ is not interpretable by reference to any semantical game which would facilitate the interpretation of an anaphoric pronoun occurring in S. It is interpreted only by reference to another game $G(S)$. But unless such a game is thought of as having been actually played, there is no play context available that would make possible an application of a rule like (R. he) or (R. she).

The theory of pronouns sketched above goes back to Hintikka and Kulas (1983, 1985).

2.5. *Comparisons with other approaches*

We will compare in this section the game-theoretical treatment of pronouns with that offered by other theories in this handbook. One such theory is Chomsky's Government and Binding theory (GB).

The GB theory divides pronouns into

(i) *Pure anaphors*, that is, reflexives (*himself, herself*, etc.) and reciprocals (*each other*);

(ii) *Pure pronominals*, that is, non-reflexive pronouns (*him, her*, etc.) (Chomsky, 1981.)

The behaviour of these pronouns is regulated by the following binding principles:

(A) An anaphor must be bound in its minimal governing category.

(B) Pronouns are generally free in precisely those contexts in which anaphors are bound. (Chomsky, 1986.)

For the notions of binding and government category, the reader is referred to the chapter on GB of the handbook.

Our first observation is that the binding principles (A) and (B) have a clear counterpart in GTS, viz. the following principles are direct consequences of the way the game rules (R. him) and (R. himself) have been formulated:

(A*) A reflexive must be coreferential with an NP occurring in the same clause.

(B*) The values of the pronouns *him* and *himself* occurring in the same place in otherwise similar sentences must come from mutually disjoint choice sets. (Hintikka and Kulas, 1985.)

The second observation is that, although the GB theory and GTS have some structural similarities as far as principles A and B are concerned, their explanatory mechanism is completely different. The binding principles refer to such notions as government category and context, while the corresponding principles in GTS refer to such notions as clause and choice set. These notions mean different things in the two theories. In the GB theory, they pertain to the initial syntactical structure of the sentence, while in GTS they are relative to the stage reached by the semantical game. From a GTS perspective, a GB theorist is trying to formulate all his or her rules by reference to the initial sentence of the entire semantical game in the course of which S makes its appearance. In contrast, a rule of GTS applies to the sentence which the players face at the time of the rule application. This makes a difference on more complex sentences where GTS and GB yield different predictions. (Cf. Hintikka and Sandu, 1991.)

Another major theory dealing with anaphora is the Discourse Representation Theory (DRT) of Kamp (1982) and its outgrowth, Dynamic Predicate Logic (DPL) developed by Groenendijk and Stokhof (1991).

The basic ideas of DRT are described in the chapter on Discourse Representation Theory. Essentially, the hearer of a sentence S possesses a sort of an algorithm with the help of which he processes S so as to determine the semantical information S conveys to him. This algorithm may be best introduced by an example. The sentence

(5.1) A farmer owns a donkey. He beats it

is processed in DRT in the following way: the two referring expressions of the first sentence of (5.1) are replaced by reference markers a and b; a is introduced for a *farmer*, and b for *a donkey*. Finally we write down explicitly the reference markers, the expressions for which we introduced them and the result of replacing every referring expression by its reference marker. We end up with the following discourse representation structure:

(5.2) $\big(a,\ b,\ \text{farmer}(a),\ \text{donkey}(b),\ \text{owns}(a,b)\big).$

The last three expressions are called conditions. We then go on and process the second sentence of (5.1). This means introducing new reference markers, one for *he*, say c, and another one for *it*, say, d. Since these pronouns are interpreted anaphorically, we also introduce the conditions $c = a$ and $d = b$. Thus we end up with the representation structure:

(5.3) $\big(a, b, c, d,\ \text{farmer}(a),\ \text{donkey}(b),\ \text{owns}(a,b),\ c = a,\ d = b,\ \text{beat}(c,d)\big).$

(5.1) is true just in case there are individuals a', b', c' and d' in the "real model" corresponding to the reference markers a, b, c, and d which satisfy the conditions of the representation structure (5.3).

The reader might have noticed that there are some important similarities between GTS and DRT, but also some important differences. For the sake of comparison, let us give a full description of the game G associated with (5.1).

The game G is divided into two subgames G_1 and G_2 associated with S_1 and S_2, that is, with the first and the second sentence of (5.1), respectively. G_1 starts with a choice of the verifier (Myself) of an individual who is given a name, say a and who is put into the choice set $I_{(5.1)}$. The game goes on with the sentence

(5.4) a is a farmer and a owns a donkey.

Next, in agreement with (R. and), the falsifier (Nature), chooses one of the conjuncts. If the conjunct so chosen is 'a is a farmer', G_1 stops here. If 'a is a farmer' is true in the model under consideration, then the verifier won this play of the game; otherwise the falsifier won. If the chosen conjunct is 'a owns a donkey', then the verifier (Myself) chooses an individual and gives it a name, say b. b is put into the choice set $I_{(5.1)}$, and the game goes on with

(5.5) a owns b and b is a donkey.

Finally, the falsifier (Nature) chooses a conjunct. In either case, the situation is analogous to the previous case. Only if Myself wins every possible play of the game, that is, only if all the atomic sentences 'a is a farmer', 'b is a donkey', and 'a owns b' are true in the model, Myself wins the whole game, and then the players move to play G_2. In that case Myself's winning strategy in G_1 enters the choice set $I_{(5.1)}$. Notice that this winning strategy amounts to the existence of two individuals a' and b' (which are the interpretations of a and b, respectively), which are already in $I_{(5.1)}$, and thus its structure remains unchanged.

In the subgame G_2 both the verifier (Myself) and the falsifier (Nature) chose individuals c and d, respectively, from $I_{(5.1)}$, and the game goes on with

(5.6) c beats it, and c is a male, and if d is a male then d is the same as c.

Now there are three possible plays of the game, depending on which of the three conjuncts Nature chooses. If the rightmost is chosen, then the game will go on with

(5.7) Either d is not a male or d is the same as c

which will prompt a move by Myself choosing one disjunct with which the game stops.

If the middle conjunct is chosen, the game stops. If the leftmost is chosen, the situation is similar to the case discussed above.

Notice that here too, in order for Myself to win the whole game, he will have to win all its possible plays. This would be possible only if Myself could find two individuals c and e from $I_{(5.1)}$ so that c is the same as a, e is the same as b and 'a beats e' is true.

We see that the way sentences are processed and reference markers are introduced in DRT is, somehow, similar to the choices made by the two players in GTS according to the game rules described at the beginning of this section. From the perspective of GTS, one can say that conceptualizations in DRT are formulated in terms of *one* player's (the text interpreter's) choices, while in GTS, having two players, one can bring more to the forefront the already existing resources of the well established mathematical and logical theory of games such as: the notions of winning strategy, information set, subgame, etc. An important consequence of this fact is the following.

The choice set I_S associated with a semantical game $G(S;M)$ collects all the "reference markers" introduced in the course of a play of G. However, in contradistinction to DRT, I_S collects more, i.e. it collects also verifying strategies. In other words, the information that is available in DRT from one sentence to the next one consists solely of individuals, while in GTS this information consists essentially of verifying strategies. This makes a difference in certain cases, as it will be seen below.

2.6. *Conditionals*

GTS facilitates several insights into the nature of conditionals. Formal and natural-language conditionals are naturally treated together. The treatment utilizes the subgame idea mentioned in the preceding section. Clearly, a conditional like

(6.1) If S_1, then S_2

asserts more than that either $\neg S_1$ (or perhaps $\neg_w S_1$) is true or S_2 is true. A conditional is supposed to provide a warrant for a passage from the truth of S_1 to the truth of S_2, that is, from a method of verifying S_1 to a method of verifying S_2. A way of implementing this idea is to introduce the following game rule for (1):

(R. cond) In $G_0 = G$ (If S_1 then $S_2; M$), the players first play $G(S_1; M)$ with their roles reversed. If Myself wins $G(S_1; M)$, she wins G_0. If Nature wins, the players move to play $G(S_2; M)$ (with their normal roles). In this subgame, Myself has access to Nature's strategy in $G(S_1; M)$. The player who wins $G(S_2; M)$ wins G_0.

The "access" mentioned here can be defined as membership of the strategy functions Nature used in $G(S_1; M)$ in the choice set of the whole game.

This rule implements the intuitions mentioned earlier in that according to it "the method of verifying S_2" (i.e. Myself's winning strategy in $G(S_2; M)$) depends on "the method of verifying S_1" (i.e. on Nature's strategy in $G(S_1; M)$ which led to a win in that game).

There are variants of this game rule depending on the information flow between $G(S_1; M)$ and $G(S_2; M)$. In the simple (R. cond), a player's access to the other player's strategy means of course that the first player's strategy is a function of the second one's strategy. This makes it possible to express formally different game rules for conditionals by using a device of Gödel and writing out the strategies used in a game with a sentence as if they were arguments of the sentence. If in this notation $F_0 = (\exists f)(\forall h)F[f, h]$ and $G_0 = (\exists g)(\forall i)G[g, i]$, then the rule (R. cond) can be expressed by saying that the interpretation of $(F_0 \rightarrow G_0)$ is

$$(\exists \gamma)(\exists h)(\forall f)(\forall i)(F[f, h] \longrightarrow G[\gamma(f), i]). \tag{6.2}$$

Other possible interpretations include the following

$$(\exists \eta)(\exists g)(\forall f)(\forall i)(F[f, \eta(i)] \longrightarrow G[g, i]), \tag{6.3}$$

$$(\exists \gamma)(\exists \eta)(\forall f)(\forall i)(F[f, \eta(i)] \longrightarrow G[\gamma(f), i]), \tag{6.4}$$

$$(\exists \gamma)(\exists \eta)(\forall f)(\forall i)(F[f, \eta(i, f)] \longrightarrow G[\gamma(f), i]). \tag{6.5}$$

We have formulated these rules for a formal language rather than a natural one but their applicability to the latter is obvious. However, in natural languages all these rules open up new possibilities of anaphoric coreference, and hence all of them make a difference. In formal languages, not all of the new rules result in an actually new interpretation. In formal languages, an additional element is the possibility of restricting the values of all higher-order quantifiers to recursive entities of the appropriate type. With this restriction, (6.5) becomes Gödel's interpretation of conditionals in his famous *Dialectica* paper.

Here we can indicate only some of the simplest facts about these different interpretations of conditionals. First, applied to natural-language conditionals, even the simplest interpretation provides, together with the usual rules for pronouns, an explanation of the so-called donkey sentences, e.g.,

(6.6) If Peter owns a donkey, he beats it.

(6.7) If you give each child a gift for Christmas, some child will open it today.

The treatment of (6.6) might run as follows:

The second subgame associated with *he beats* it is played only after Nature has verified the antecedent. Nature's winning strategy (if any) in the game with the antecedent of (6.6) reduces to two individuals, i.e. Peter and a donkey. This winning strategy is a verifying strategy and thus enters the choice set $I_{(6.6)}$ being available for the second subgame when the rules (R. he) and (R. it) are applied to the pronouns. The only possible values of the pronouns are the values of *Peter* and *a donkey* chosen by the initial falsifier in the first subgame. The whole sentence (6.6) will then say that any choices of the values of Peter and a donkey which verify the antecedent also verify the consequent. This is obviously the right meaning.

The second example is similar to (6.6), except that the "remembered" strategy function in the subgame associated with the consequent of (6.7) does not reduce to a single value. Here the choice set $I_{(6.7)}$ will contain (a) the verifying strategy function in the subgame associated with the antecedent of (6.7); (b) the value of *some child*; and (c) the individual resulting from the application of the function in (a) to the individual in (b) which will then serve as the truth-making value of *it*.

Second, the interpretation of natural-language conditionals varies between the truth-functional one and (6.2)–(6.5). It is affected by the left-to-right order of the antecedent and the conditional. Among other things, this explains the semantical difference between (6.6) and such examples as

(6.8) Peter will beat a donkey if he can find it.

Three, in formal languages, the new interpretations do not affect the coreference situation. Hence the interpretations (6.2)–(6.5) do not necessarily yield anything new. In some cases, only the additional requirement of recursivity makes a difference. However, (6.4) yields an irreducibly branching-quantifier sentence, and (6.5) together with the recursivity requirement yields Gödel's *Dialectica* interpretation of conditionals. Thus Gödel's ideas receive a natural (albeit minor) slot within the total structure of GTS.

2.7. Game rules for other expressions in English

A particularity of GTS is that almost every single lexical item occurring in a sentence S of English prompts a move in the semantical game $G(S; M)$. As an example of such rules we shall give the one dealing with prepositions. In addition to lexical items, also morphological constructions prompt moves in semantical games. Our sample rule will deal with possessives. However, before describing these rules, we shall treat briefly definite descriptions. A detailed exposition of the treatment of definite descriptions in GTS may be found in (Hintikka and Kulas, 1985).

The starting point of Hintikka–Kulas theory of descriptions is Russell's theory which, despite the criticisms it has encountered, remains still a natural starting point for any logics and semantics of definite descriptions. Roughly speaking, to say that "the F is G"

(where F and G are arbitrary predicate letters) is, according to Russell, to say three things

(7.1) There is at least one F,

(7.2) There is at most one F,

(7.3) Everything that is F is G.

The uses of definite descriptions Russell had primarily in mind are those occurring in context-independent sentences like

(7.4) The largest city in the world is Mexico City,

(7.5) The present president of France is F. Mitterand,

and not so much the anaphoric uses like

(7.6) If you are accosted by a stranger, don't talk to the man,

(7.7) A man was seen walking down the path, but soon the man turned back,

(7.8) If Bill owns a donkey, he beats the donkey.

In such cases, the use of the anaphoric *the*-phrase does not require uniqueness of reference in the sense of there existing only one individual of which the *the*-phrase is true. Instead, such a phrase is supposed to pick up some individual which has been introduced earlier in discourse. The similarity with anaphoric pronouns is obvious. In fact, the meanings of (7.6)–(7.8) remain unchanged if we replace the descriptions in them by the corresponding anaphoric pronouns. This fact by itself is enough to suggest what the game rule for anaphoric definite descriptions looks like: it will be almost identical with the rule (R. him) for pronouns we described in the previous section:

(R. the) When the game has reached a sentence of the form

$$X - \text{the } Y - W,$$

the verifier may choose an individual, say b, from the choice set I_S, to be the value of *the* Y, whereupon the falsifier chooses an individual d from I_S. The game is then continued with respect to

$$X - b - W,\ b \text{ is a } Y, \quad \text{and if } d \text{ is a } Y \text{ then } d \text{ is the same as } b.$$

That is, like anaphoric pronouns, anaphoric descriptions turn out to be quantifiers restricted to the choice set I_S formed in the course of the play of $G(S; M)$. And conversely, we see now validated the statement we made at the beginning of Section 2.4 to the effect that anaphoric pronouns turn out to be definite descriptions like the man or *the woman* restricted to the relevant choice set.

We have thus reached an unified treatment of both anaphoric pronouns and anaphorically used definite descriptions which puts into a new light anaphora in general. Expressions in English which apparently have nothing to do with each other turn out to have the same *modus operandi*. Recall, for instance, our discussion of anaphora in GB theory at the end of the previous section and the trichotomy of pronouns which is one of its by products: (i) deictic or referential pronouns, (ii) bound anaphors (that is, pronouns which are anaphoric on NP's and which are *c*-commanded by them), and (iii) unbound anaphors (pronouns which are anaphoric on NP's but which are not *c*-commanded by them) and which were assimilated by Neale to anaphoric definite descriptions. GTS shows that both (ii) and (iii) are Russellian definite descriptions in which the quantifiers are restricted to the relevant choice set (as it is at the time when a rule is applied to the pronoun.)

Studying the mechanism of coreference in GTS suggests the interesting prediction that almost any expression in English which prompts a choice of an individual from the domain of discourse might have an anaphoric interpretation, i.e. an interpretation in which the choice in question is restricted to the relevant choice set. Indeed, this prediction is confirmed: there are not only anaphoric pronouns and anaphorically used definite descriptions in English, but also anaphoric quantifiers:

(7.9) John bought *three donkeys. Two donkeys* died.

(7.10) Several *congressmen* arrived today. One was from France.

The quantifiers *two donkeys* and *one*, called choice set quantifiers, behave exactly like the other anaphoric expressions studied so far: their values are picked up from the choice set of the games associated with (7.9) and (7.10), respectively. In the case of, e.g., (7.9) this set will contain the verifying strategy from the first subgame, i.e. three individuals which are donkeys.

We can also sketch a lexical rule pertaining to prepositions and the morphological rule dealing with genitives:

(R. near) If the game has reached a sentence of the form

$$X - \text{near } Y - Z$$

the verifier may choose a location, say the one named b, and the game is continued with respect to

$$X - \text{prep} + b - Z \text{ and } b \text{ is near } Y.$$

We shall not try to specify here the choice of the preposition prep. In different examples, it can be *in*, *on*, *at*, etc.

The following can serve as an example:

(7.11) Near him, John sees a snake.

An application of (R. near) will take (7.11) to

(7.12) On the lawn, John sees a snake, and the lawn is near him.

(R. genitive) If the game has reached a sentence of the form

$$X - Y\text{'s } Z - W$$

then an individual is chosen by the verifier, say b and the game is continued with respect to

$$X - b - W \text{ and } b \text{ is an/the } Z \text{ of } Y.$$

2.8. Is *and Aristotelian categories*

The game rules for quantifier phrases in natural languages are worth a second and a third look. One thing that is revealed by such a re-examination are the much greater differences between the logic of natural language and the usual treatments of formal logic than many linguists seem to suspect.

For one thing, ever since Frege most linguists and logicians have believed that the English word *is* and its cognates are ambiguous between the *is* of identity, the *is* of predication, the *is* of existence, and the *is* of class-inclusion. That *is* has such different uses is unproblematic; the question is whether these differences have to be explained as being due to the ambiguity of a single word, rather than, e.g., a difference in context. It is of course true that the different uses of *is* have to be expressed differently in the usual first-order notation, the *is* of identity by =, the *is* of predication by filling the argument-place of a predicate letter by suitable singular terms, the *is* of existence by the existential quantifier, and the *is* of class-inclusion by a general implication of the form $(\forall x)(A[x] \to B[x])$. But the real question is how good the usual first-order logic is as a representation of natural language quantification.

In GTS, the Frege–Russell distinction becomes blurred and unnatural. Even more significantly, it is not needed in a game-theoretical approach. Examples can illustrate these facts. Consider, for instance, the sentence

(8.1) Jack is a boy who whistles.

Here *is* is usually taken to be the *is* of predication. Now an application of (R. an) takes (8.1) to a sentence of the form

(8.2) Jack is John Jr., John Jr. is a boy and John Jr. whistles.

Here the first *is* of (8.2) is the *alter ego* of the *is* in (8.1). But in (8.1) it is supposed to be an *is* of predication while in (8.2) it plays the role of an *is* of identity. Alternatively, one might view the *is* in (8.1) as an identity. But the closely related phrase *is a* in (8.2)

must be treated as expressing predication, on the pain of infinite regress. Thus the Frege–Russell distinction is shown to be virtually impossible to draw in GTS. This is of course not to say that a formal treatment of *is* as it is used in English is impossible, only that it must look quite different from traditional first-order logic.

Another difference between natural languages and formal first-order languages is that at best natural languages can be hoped to be many-sorted first-order languages. For instance, consider the game rule (R. some) above. Since the wh-word used there is *who*, the entity to be chosen as a value of a quantifier phrase must be a person. But if it had been *when*, the value would have been restricted to moments (or periods) of time; if *where*, to points (or regions of space, and so on). These alternative ranges of values of different quantifier phrases correspond to the different sorts of a many-sorted logic. They are thus indicated by the different question words (and some question phrases) in English.

But in some cases the entire wh-phrase may drop out. How can we then tell which sort the players have to make their choices from? Clearly the simple predicates that can occur in the place of the X in (R. some) must ultimately belong likewise to the corresponding classes. Hence we have at least a rough correspondence between four different distinctions:

(i) The largest classes that can be the value-ranges of a natural language quantifier phrases.

(ii) Different question words and question phrases in English.

(iii) Different classes of unanalyzable predicates.

(iv) Different means of *is* (occurring in the output of a quantifier rule application).

These correlated distinctions might repay a closer study. They are strongly reminiscent of Aristotelian categories. It is especially striking that Aristotle drew the distinction between the different categories in four different ways closely similar to (i)–(iv). For a further discussion of this matters, see Hintikka (1986b).

2.9. *Abstract vs. strategic meaning*

The game-theoretical truth-definition prompts at once a fundamental distinction which has so far not been exploited very much in the literature. The precise formulation of the truth-definition (cf. above Definition 1.1) has to be taken seriously. The truth of a given sentence S is defined as the existence of winning strategy for the initial verifier in the game $G(S; M)$. This does not imply that the verifier (or the falsifier) knows what such a winning strategy looks like. The definiens is a purely existential statement. Hence, according to strictly understood GTS, when somebody asserts an interpreted first-order statement, he or she merely asserts that there exists in mathematicians' Platonic realm of functions a set of functions codifying a strategy for the initial verifier in $G(S; M)$ such that it leads to a win for him (or her or it), no matter what strategy the initial falsifier opts for. The information so conveyed is called the abstract meaning of the sentence in question.

Yet in an act of asserting a sentence one often conveys to the hearer more than this abstract meaning. One conveys also some idea of what the winning strategy is supposed to be like. Such surplus meaning is called strategic meaning. It is not so much information about the world, as information about how a sentence can actually be verified.

These two kinds of meaning are both important in their basic nature. The best one can hope for of any formal semantics to accomplish directly is a contribution to the study of abstract meaning. That is also what our game-theoretical rules are calculated to do in the first place. It is possible, however, to put the apparatus of GTS to work for the purpose of elucidating strategic meaning. An example is in fact found in this article. In order to see it, consider what is meant from a game-theoretical viewpoint by saying that in the following sentence *her* "has its head" or "is coreferential with" *Mary* and that *him* is not coreferential with *Tom* but could be coreferential with *Dick*?

(9.1) Dick's friend Tom saw Mary and also saw a bench between her and him.

According to the analysis sketched above, the first statement means that the individual chosen by the verifier as the value of *her* when (R. she) is applied is *Mary*, i.e. the individual introduced into $I_{(9.1)}$ as a value of Mary. The second statement means that Tom is not chosen as the value of *him*, but that Dick might be. But speaking of "choosing" refers to some play of the game, connected with and starting with (9.1). Which play? And how do we know what choices the players will in fact make? Obviously what is meant is that the choices in question are a part of the verifier's winning strategy. She, he or it could have made other choices without violating any rules for making moves in a semantical game. But that could have led to a loss for the verifier.

What all this amounts to is that the theory of anaphoric cross-reference is a part of the study of strategic meaning not of abstract meaning. Yet it is seen from our examination of anaphoric pronouns that they can be analyzed and theorized about by means of the very same framework as was used to define abstract meaning.

This example shows that strategic meaning is not a merely pragmatic or psychological phenomenon that does not belong to the study of language, first impression notwithstanding.

Admittedly, other kinds of strategic meaning are more ephemeral, for instance, the circumlocutory use of quantifier expressions like *someone*, or *some people* to refer to someone present, e.g., in

(9.2) Some people have never learned how to behave in a civilized company.

2.10. De dicto *vs.* de re *distinction*

According to the GTS project, a game rule should be associated with each lexical item, not just with quantifiers, connectives and *knows that*. When this idea is applied successfully, the lexical item receives its semantics from the rule. What is more, its semantics becomes integrated into an overall theory, among other things, the new rule must obey the same general ordering principles as other rules because its specific ordering principles indirectly affect the meaning of other words and because these meaning-determining game rule automatically determine the rules for anaphora involving the expressions to be characterized. Likewise, the notion of information independence can in principle apply to any application of any rule for semantical games.

In fact, a game rule can be associated even with individual constant and predicate constants. Given an individuate constant b, the rule in question asks the verifier to assign a member of the domain of the relevant model to b as its value. Since it must be required that the individual chosen equals b, this rule – we shall call it (R. ind) – does not seem to matter for the interpretation of any sentence. In reality, the postulation of such a rule makes a great deal of sense. It must be subject to the same general ordering principles as other rules. These rules may in turn explain other phenomena, for instance, anaphora.

Examples are offered by pairs of sentences like

(10.1) John believes that he is clever.

(10.2) He believes that John is clever.

Because of (O. comm), in (10.1) *John* is treated before *he*. Hence *John* is a possible value of *he*, making coreference possible. In (10.2) *John* is in a lower clause, and hence cannot be available as a value of *he* in virtue of (O. comm).

Likewise, the notion of independence can apply to moves made in accordance with (R. ind). Consider, for the purpose of seeing what this may entail, the following formulas of epistemic logic:

(10.3) $K_a P(b)$

(10.4) $K_a P((b/K))$.

Here (10.3) says that a knows that (it is the case that) $P(b)$. But what does (10.4) say? In (10.4), the individual who is to serve as the value of b must be chosen independently of K_a, in other words, as being the same for all models compatible with what a knows. In still other words, a knows of the individual who is in fact b that that individual has the property P.

If you reflect on this distinction for a moment, you will see that is an instance of what is meant by the difference between the *de dicto* and *de re* readings of natural language sentences like

(10.5) Margaret knows that Lord Avon was indecisive.

Here what is meant may be that Margaret knows *de dicto* that the sentence

(10.6) Lord Avon was indecisive

is true, or that she knows of the gentleman who in fact was Lord Avon that he was indecisive, without knowing the noble title of the gentleman in question (perhaps she knows him only as Anthony Eden).

This explication of the famous distinction can be generalized to other cases. In spite of its simplicity, it has some remarkable consequences. For one thing, it shows that the *de dicto* vs. *de re* distinction is not unanalyzable, even if it is not signaled in English by any uniform syntactical device. As a consequence, the distinction does not involve any difference whatsoever between different kinds of knowledge. Both kinds of knowledge have precisely the same objects, in the sense that the same entities are involved in the models of either kind of knowledge statement. In general, the regularities governing the *de dicto* vs. *de re* distinction are consequences of the more general regularities governing informational independence.

The same distinction is found in other kinds of concepts, including functions and predicates. For instance, there is a difference between two readings of

(10.7) Tom knows that all Dick's friends are businessmen.

It can mean either that Tom knows the truth of the generalization

(10.8) $(\forall x)$ (x is a friend of Dick $\to x$ is a businessman)

or that Tom knows of each individual who happens to be (possibly unbeknowst to Tom) a friend of Dick that he is a businessman.

Likewise, our treatment of the *de dicto* vs. *de re* contrast applies *mutatis mutandis* to contexts other than the epistemic ones.

3. A survey of games in logic and in language theory

3.1. Games in logic

In order to put GTS into a perspective, and for the sake of the intrinsic interest of the subject, it is in order to survey the uses of game-theoretical ideas in logic and language-theory more generally.

In model theory, logicians have resorted to game-theoretical concepts whenever compositional truth-definitions elude them. This can happen in two different ways. Either there are actual semantical context-dependencies present, or else formulas need not be built recursively from atomic formulas, so that there are no starting points for inside-out truth-definitions.

The former predicament occurred for the first time when Henkin (1959) introduced branching quantifiers. Predictably, he characterized the truth of branching quantifier sentences by using game-theoretical concepts.

The latter predicament occurs in the study of infinitary languages. There the syntax of a formula need not be well-founded.

Needless to say, the natural truth-definitions for both kinds of languages are game-theoretical.

The motivation for using game-theoretical truth-definitions goes back to the work of Skolem (1920) who noticed that a sentence in prenex form, e.g., $\forall x \exists y \forall z \exists w S[x, y, z, w]$ is true in a model M if and only if there are (Skolem) functions f and g such that $\forall x \forall z S[x, f(x), z, g(x, z)]$ is true in M.

The connection between Skolem functions and games was made by Henkin (1959). He noticed that the truth of every sentence in prenex form in a model M can be characterized by a game of perfect information. The corresponding game is exactly like the semantical games of GTS. Henkin extended the game interpretation to sentences with quantifier-prefixes of countable length and noticed that the same could be done even for sentences $\cdots \exists y_3 \forall y_2 \exists y_1 \forall y_0 R[y_0, y_1, y_2, y_3, \ldots]$ in which the sequence of quantifiers in the prefix is not well-founded. The idea of extending the game interpretation to quantifier prefixes of arbitrary infinite length led to the study of game quantifiers. A survey of these quantifiers in the context of Abstract Model Theory is contained in (Kolaitis, 1985). (Cf. also Van Benthem, 1988; Hodges, forthcoming.)

In (Hintikka, 1974), the game interpretation of formulas was extended to formulas which are not prenex, that is, to the truth-functional connectives exactly as it is described in the first part of this article. As in the case of prenex formulas, the generalization of Hintikka's idea to the infinitary case led to the study of non-well-founded formulas which allow arbitrary alternating infinite sequences of quantifiers, conjunctions and disjunctions. They have been proposed for the first time in (Hintikka and Rantala, 1976) and thereafter studied by Joukko Väänänen and his associates, e.g., by Karttunen (1984), Hyttinen (1987) and Oikkonen (1988).

What is known as back-and-forth games were introduced by Ehrenfeucht (1961). The basic ideas of back-and-forth games nevertheless go back to Fraissé (1959) who did not used the game terminology. These games, usually denoted by $G(A, B)$, are used to compare two models M and N as to elementary equivalence. Here Nature tries to show that M and N are different (i.e. nonequivalent) and Myself tries to show that they are the same. Every move in the game consists of Nature choosing an element from one of the structures and Myself choosing an element from the other. Myself wins if, after a certain number of moves, the patterns of objects chosen in the two structures form an isomorphism. Natures wins if he can choose an element which Myself cannot match with the elements of the other structure. Elementary equivalence between the models is a necessary and sufficient condition for Myself winning the game $G(A, B)$ with countable moves. Hodges (forthcoming) contains a lively exposition of the ways in which these games can be generalized.

Another class of games used in logic deals with the construction of models. For instance, the Henkin-type construction of canonical models may be seen as a game of building models in which Nature formulates properties (via a language) to be realized or "enforced" in the model, and Myself adds witnessing constants, decompositions, etc. which makes the realization of the properties possible. (Cf. Van Benthem, 1988.)

Game-theoretical truth-definitions can also be used when the concept of model is extended in certain interesting ways. A case in point is the notion of urn model introduced by Rantala (1975). An urn model is like its namesake in probability theory: it can change between one's successive choices of elements from it. Those "choices" are of course but successive moves in a semantical game. Such urn models offers among other things a simple and natural way of reconciling a possible-worlds treatment of epistemic notions and the failure of "logical omniscience" (one does not know all the logical consequences of what one knows.) (See here Hintikka, 1975.)

One of the best known uses of game-theoretical ideas is in proof theory. The motivation for the game-theoretical interpretation came from the work of Hintikka (1955) and Beth (1955) on Gentzen-type proofs in first-order logic.

In the game-theoretical setting, we can think of the truth-tree method of a proof as a kind of game. A nice description of such games is contained in (Hodges, forthcoming).

In such a game, Myself wants to construct a model for a sentence S and Nature tries to show that there is no such model. For instance, if S is of the form $(R \wedge P)$, then

Nature challenges Myself to put both R and P on the table. If Myself cannot do this he loses the game. If S is $(R \vee P)$, then Nature challenges Myself to choose either one of the disjuncts and put it on the table. If S is $\exists x R(x)$, then Nature challenges Myself to find a name c and put $R(c)$ on the table. If Myself can comply with all of Nature's challenges, he wins the game. If a contradiction appears on the table, then Nature wins. These games are determinate. It is straightforward to show that Myself has a winning strategy in the game if and only if S has a model, and Nature has a winning strategy if and only if $\neg S$ has a proof. Actually a winning strategy for Nature turns out to be the same thing as a proof tableau for $\neg S$.

One of the interesting things about this game-theoretical setting in proof theory is that we can put all sorts of constraints on the moves of the players. For instance, we can require that the sentences challenged by Nature cannot be any longer used in the game, or that when challenging $(R \wedge P)$, Nature decides which one of R and P is put on the table. A suitable constraint on the moves of the players yields Lorenzen's dialogical logic.

Originally (cf. Lorenzen, 1961), Lorenzen offered an interpretation of the intuitionistic proof rules in first-order logic and in elementary arithmetic, including the uses of inductive definitions. His ideas were systematized and developed further by Lorenz (1961). The proof games they considered are identical with the ones illustrated above, except that they proceed through verbal "attacks" (*Angriffe*) and "defenses" (*Verteidigungen*).

Later, Lorenzen and Lorenz suggested another interpretation for closely related games (Lorenz, 1968; Lorenz and Lorenzen, 1978). These games were called material games in contradistinction to the earlier formal games, and they were supposed to serve as the semantical basis of the ordinary (interpreted, material) truth. The factual (nonlogical) element enters into these games through the assumptions that the truth-values of atomic sentences are fixed (and decidable).

Dialogue games inspired by Lorenzen's games and closely related to them have been constructed and studied by E.M. Barth and her associates; see, e.g., Krabbe (1982).

Lorenzen's games have also recently inspired Blass who presented a game semantics in the style of Lorenzen as an interpretation for Girard's linear logic. Essentially, a game interpretation assigns games to propositions, and operations on games to propositional connectives. The truth of a sentence in a game interpretation is defined as the existence of a winning strategy for the "defender" in the game assigned to it by the interpretation. Blass showed that under this interpretation, affine logic (i.e. linear logic plus the rule of weakening) is sound and complete (with certain restrictions). (Cf. Blass, 1992; Abramsky and Jagadeesan, 1992, for an improvement and refinement of Blass' results.)

Recently Aarne Ranta (1994) has sought to relate Martin-Löf's intuitionistic type theory to GTS. He tried to show that GTS can be understood constructively by interpreting games as propositions and winning strategies as proofs.

Occasionally, game-theoretical ideas have been used in the study of pragmatics, including conversational implicature. (See Parikh, 1992.)

3.2. *Games in philosophical language theory*

In philosophy, competitive question-answer games, modeled on the Socratic method of questioning, were cultivated in Plato's Academy. (Cf. Ryle, 1971; Hintikka, 1993a.) In the middle ages, a variety of question-answer disputation games, known as obligation games, was for a long time a central part of philosophical methodology. They are dealt with in detail in (Yrjönsuuri, 1994).

In our century, Wittgenstein's notion of language-game was the key concept in his later philosophy. The game idea was first introduced by him to illustrate the claim that language-world connections are mediated by certain human activities that are governed by rules just like games. Later, Wittgenstein came to assign to language-games a conceptual primacy over their rules. (See here Hintikka and Hintikka, 1986.)

More generally and much more loosely, analogy with games has been frequently employed by philosophers to illustrate the purely formal character of logical inference. In Wittgenstein, the emphasis is not on the formal character of game rules, but on the need for language users actually to do something.

Some philosophers have used game-theoretical concepts also in epistemology and spoken of of "games of exploring the world" (Ryle). One explicit form of such games are Hintikka's interrogative games, where the factual input into an inquirer's reasoning is conceptualized as nature's or some other "oracle's" answers to the inquirer's questions. (See Hintikka, 1988a.) These interrogative games are logically speaking closely related to Socratic games of questioning, with nature (or some other oracle) cast into the role of the inquirer's interlocutor. They can be used as a basis of a general logical theory of identification. (See Hintikka, 1991.)

3.3. *Differences between different games*

Some order can be created among this multitude by distinctions between different kinds of games. The following list of four kinds of games is not exhaustive:

(i) Games of verification and falsification.
(ii) Games of formal proof.
(iii) Games of inquiry.
(iv) Games of model construction.

Most of the applications of game-theoretical concepts mentioned above can easily find their niche in this classification.

The semantical games of GTS exemplify (i).

Many other games are simply special cases of semantical games, for instance Diophantine games and the games used in dealing with infinitary deep languages and with branching quantifiers. Diophantine games are especially interesting in a general theoretical perspective in that among them one soon runs into games in which there exists winning strategies for one of the players, but no recursive winning strategies. (Cf. Section 1.8, above, and (Matiyasevich, 1993, p. 183).)

Back-and-forth games are not literally special cases of semantical games. However, they are very closely related to semantical games played with the ingredients of distributive normal forms (Cf. Hintikka, 1953, 1994) called constituents. Then playing an Ehrenfeucht game $G_d(A, B)$ of length d on two models A and B is structurally related to playing a semantical game with a constituent of depth d. More generally, the entire back-and-forth technique can be considered as being tantamount to the technique of constituents and distributive normal forms.

The distinction between games of verification (i) and games of formal proof (ii) is important but is often overlooked. Yet the difference could not be more striking. Verification games serve to define truth; proof games aim at capturing all (and only) logical truths. Now truth and logical truth are categorially different. Truth presupposes a fixed interpretation and is relative to a single model. Logical truth means truth on any interpretation (in any model). Verification games are played among the objects one's language speaks of; proof games are played with pencil and paper (or on a computer).

The distinction between verification games and games of inquiry is even subtler. Games of inquiry model the ways in which sentences are actually found to be true, whereas semantical games are activities in terms of which the truth of sentences can be defined. In games of inquiry, there is an epistemic element present; such games are attempts to come to know a truth or an answer to some question. Games of inquiry have connections with learning theory (cf. Osherson's article in this volume.) They can serve to develop a general logical theory of identification. (Cf. Hintikka, 1991.) In contrast, in a semantical game, there may exist a winning strategy for the verifier without her knowing what it is or even knowing that such a strategy exists. In this sense our account of GTS differs significantly from Tennant's (1990) who speaks all the time about the players "possessing" strategies.

Games of model construction are becoming more and more important in logical theory. So far, they have not been related to language theory very closely.

Several other kinds of games used in model theory are either closely related to the semantical games of GTS or special cases of such games, for instance the Svenonius games defined in (Hodges, 1993, p. 112.)

All these types of games must be distinguished from still others:

(v) Disputation games.

(vi) Communication games.

Again there has been a great deal of confusion in the literature. Wittgenstein's language-games are sometimes taken to be games of communication whose "moves" are language acts, e.g., speech acts. This is a misinterpretation, as is shown in (Hintikka and Hintikka, 1986). Wittgenstein's first "calculi" were processes of verification and falsification, and even though the terms "language-game" came to cover a tremendous variety of different uses of language, the deep point in Wittgenstein is that even descriptive meaning is always mediated by those nonlinguistic activities he called "language-games".

3.4. Interrelations between different kinds of games

There is admittedly a fair amount of overlap between the different kinds of games (i)–(vi). For instance, dialogical games, including disputation games can involve question-answer sequences, which can likewise be used to model games of inquiry and even games of formal proof. It has been argued that the vagaries of medieval obligation-games reflect hesitation between the proof-interpretation and the inquiry-interpretation.

Likewise, and more obviously, the difficulty of understanding Lorenzen's games is due to the fact that they are tacitly supposed to do three different kinds of duty. His formal games are games of logical proof, but he claimed that the structurally similar material games can be used to define truth (material truth). In reality, Lorenzen's material games are not games of verification (i), but instead are very closely related to a special case of games of inquiry, viz. the case in which the only answers the inquirer has access to are atomic. It does not seem that one and the same kind of game can serve all these three purposes.

A link between (ii) and (iv) is established by the interpretation that was proposed by Hintikka (1955) and Beth (1955) on Gentzen-type proofs in first-order logic. Such proofs can be interpreted as frustrated attempts on the part of Myself to construct a countermodel (counter-example) to the sentence (or inference) to be proved. But then, recalling our discussion of proof games, if Myself cannot produce a model for $\neg S$, that is, if Myself does not have a winning strategy in the game $G(\neg S)$, then Nature has one, and this amounts, as we saw above to $\neg\neg S$ (S, in classical logic) having a proof.

Rules for such a procedure are naturally conditioned by the definitions of the truth and falsity, for the model is supposed to be one in which a certain sentence (or a set of sentences) is true. Hence, we have here also a link with games (i).

Another connection between different kinds of games is the close connection which exists between certain optimal strategies in games of deductive proof and optimal strategies in certain kinds of games of empirical inquiry (See Hintikka, 1989.)

The results of GTS help to clarify the roles of different kinds of games in language theory. They show that ordinary (descriptive) sentence meaning can be characterized in terms of semantical games (games of verification and falsification). However, different aspects of these games can all contribute to this meaning in different ways. For instance, while the difference between an universal quantifier and an existential quantifier is based on the game rule governing each of them separately, the difference between the English quantifier words *every* and *any* is based on the ordering principles that govern the priorities of their game rules in relation to other game rules. (Cf. Section 2.3 above.)

Normally, sentence meaning does not depend on games of inquiry. The only clear-cut exception that has come to light is the meaning of why-questions. (See here (Halonen and Hintikka, 1995).) Moreover, even though differences in the rules of formal proof may reflect differences between the different interpretations of a logical constant, there are no realistic examples where the interpretational difference can be characterized in any informative way by reference to the rules of formal proof.

3.5. What is essential about games?

In order to sort out the variety of uses of game concepts, it is also in order to ask what is essential about game-theoretical conceptualizations. What is essential is not the idea of competition, winning and losing. In the mathematical theory of games, one can study games of cooperation and not only competitive games, and there are "games against nature" where one of the players has a purely reactive role. What is essential is the notion of strategy. Game theory was born the moment John von Neumann (1929) formulated explicitly this notion. Hintikka (1990) has argued that the deeper significance of game-theoretical methods in language theory lies in the paradigm they represent. When they are used, language is considered a goal-directed rather than rule-governed activity.

Hintikka has also repeatedly emphasized the importance of strategic rules (or principles) as distinguished from definitory rules. The latter typically specify which particular moves are admissible. They specify the game tree (the extensive form of the game). In contrast, strategic rules deal with better and worse ways of playing the game (within the definitory rules). The truth-definition used in GTS is an example of a strategic conceptualization.

Thus the fact that Wittgensteinian language-games do not normally involve overt competition is thus no obstacle to treating them by game-theoretical means. The crucial question is, rather, what role is played by the notion of strategy in Wittgensteinian language-games. The conceptual priority which Wittgenstein assigned to entire language-games vis-à-vis their rules is in keeping with an emphasis on an essentially strategic viewpoint. Moreover, it is important to realize what kinds of games Wittgenstein had in mind. It turns out that during his formative period in 1929–1931, Wittgenstein was preoccupied with the activities ("games" or "calculi") of verification and falsification. In view of this fact, it is not unnatural to consider semantical games as a species of language-games in a Wittgensteinian sense.

How essential is the reliance on game-theoretical concepts in these various "games"? In many cases, as Hodges (forthcoming) points out, game-theoretical terminology is dispensable. One has to be careful here, however, for what is at issue is not mere terminology. It does not normally matter, for instance, whether we speak of Skolem functions, choice functions or functions codifying winning strategies in a semantical game, or whether we speak of back-and-forth games or of distributive normal forms. The interesting question is whether the structures that are characteristically game-theoretical are being utilized. Among them there is the notion of strategy and the notions depending on it.

A typical notion of that kind is the idea of determinacy. This notion is applicable to two-person zero-sum games. In such games, the question arises whether one or the other of the two players has a winning strategy in a given game. If and only if that is the case, the game is called determinate. It was seen in Section 1.8 above that the law of excluded middle is a determinacy assumption. From the set-theoretical assumption of determinacy (Fenstad, 1971) it is seen that determinacy assumptions can, in suitable circumstances, be very strong indeed.

When such typically game-theoretical ideas are used, the game-theoretical input can be taken to be essential.

Another kind of essential reliance on game-theoretical ideas is exemplified by the fact that GTS is independent of the assumption of compositionality, whereas several traditional methods, such as Tarski-type truth-definition, presuppose compositionality.

In the light of these remarks, it can be seen that the game element in games of formal proof is rather thin. At most, it amounts to an emphasis on the strategic aspects of logical proof. These strategic aspects are not very deeply connected with the question of whether a given formula is provable at all. For the very existence of a complete proof procedure means that it suffices to consider a single procedure in order to find a proof for a given sentence, if there exists one. In other words, we do not have to consider all the possible plays of a given game, as we have to do if the use of the concept of strategy is indispensable, as it is in the game-theoretical truth-definitions.

3.6. Games and nonclassical logic

These remarks can be illustrated by raising the question as to what the reasons are for opting for intuitionistic rules rather than classical ones. Some logicians, e.g., Lorenzen have claimed that the dialogical approach naturally leads to a nonclassical logic. This is dubious. The crucial restriction which leads to intuitionistic logic in Lorenzen's approach is that "attacks" and "defenses" of one of the players cannot be repeated arbitrarily, as they can be in the Lorenzenian version of classical logic (see Lorenz, 1961, Section 2.4). The motivation of that requirement is far from obvious, especially in the "material" games dealing with truth rather than provability.

By and large, nonclassical or nonclassical looking elements can enter into logical games in several different ways:

(i) When informational independence is allowed, the law of excluded middle fails.

It is important to see that this failure of the laws of classical logic has nothing to do with constructivistic or intuitionistic ideas. It cannot be captured by modifying classical proof procedures, for IF first-order logic is inevitably incomplete.

(ii) Constructivistic ideas are most naturally implemented by restricting the initial verifier's strategies in a semantical games to recursive ones. The resulting first-order logic is inevitably incomplete, however, and hence differs from Heyting's well-known axiomatization of intuitionistic first-order logic.

(iii) Games of inquiry involve an epistemic element. They are games of coming to know certain truths or of answering certain questions. If this epistemic element is not represented explicitly, the resulting rules will differ from classical ones, and at least in some cases agree with intuitionistic ones.

(iv) Nonclassical game rules can be given for propositional connectives, especially for conditional and negation. For negation, such rules were described in Section 1.8, and for the conditional in Section 2.6.

Sometimes game-theoretical concepts are used in a nontrivial way even when no overt game-terminology is employed. Thus Dana Scott (1993) has shown that Gödel's *Dialectica* interpretation (1958) of first-order logic and arithmetic can be given an elegant game-theoretical formulation. This way of looking at Gödel's interpretation has been examined further by Hintikka (1993b). Indeed, Gödel's interpretation turns out to exemplify several of the uses of game-theoretical concepts mentioned in this survey, including the constructivistic restriction of verificatory strategies to recursive ones and the nonstandard treatment of conditionals.

References

Abramsky, S. and Jagadeesan, R. (1992), *Games and full completeness for multiplicative linear logic*, Technical Report DoC 92/94, Imperial College of Science, Technology and Medicine, London.

Barwise, J. (1976), *Some applications of Henkin quantifiers*, Israel J. Math. **25**, 47–63.

Barwise, J. (1979), *On branching quantifiers in English*, J. Philos. Logic **8**, 47–80.

Beth, E.W. (1955), *Semantic entailment and formal derivability*, Mededelingen der Koninklijke Nederlandse Akademie van Wetenschappen, Afd. Letterkunde, n.s. **18**, 309–342.

Blass, A. (1992), *A game semantics for linear logic*, Ann. Pure Appl. Logic **56**, 183–220.

Boolos, G. (1984), *To be is to be the value of a variable (or to be the values of some variables)*, J. Philos. **10**, 430–449.

Carlson, L. and Ter Meulen, A. (1979), *Informational independence in intensional context*, Essays in Honor of Jaakko Hintikka on the Occasion of His Fiftieth Birthday on January 12, 1979, E. Saarinen, R. Hilpinen, I. Niiniluoto and M.B. Hintikka, eds, Reidel, Dordrecht, 61–74.

Chomsky, N. (1981), *Lectures on Government and Binding*, Foris, Dordrecht.

Chomsky, N. (1986), *Knowledge of Language*, Praeger, New York.

Conway, J.H. (1976), *On Numbers and Games*, Academic Press, London.

Cresswell, M.J. (1988), *Semantical Essays. Possible Worlds and Their Rivals*, Kluwer, Dordrecht.

Davidson, D. (1980), *Any as universal or existential?*, The Semantics of Determiners, J. van der Auwera, ed., Croon Helm, London.

Davis, M. (1981), *Meaning, Quantification, Necessity*, Routledge and Kegan Paul, London.

Ebbinghaus, H.D., Flum, J. and Thomas, W. (1984), *Mathematical Logic*, Springer, New York.

Ehrenfeucht, A. (1961), *An application of games to the completeness problem for formalized theories*, Fund. Math. **49**, 129–141.

Enderton, H.B. (1970), *Finite partially-ordered quantifiers*, Z. Math. Logik Grundlag. Math. **16**, 393–397.

Fenstad, J.E. (1971), *The axiom of determinateness*, Proceedings of the Second Scandinavian Logic Symposium, J.E. Fenstad, ed., North-Holland, Amsterdam, 41–62.

Fraissé, R. (1959), *Sur l'extension aux relations de quelques proprietés des ordres*, Ann. Sci. École Norm. Sup. **71**, 363–388.

Groenendijk, J. and Stokhof, M. (1991), *Dynamic predicate logic*, Ling. and Philos. **14**, 39–100.

Halonen, I. and Hintikka, J. (1955), *Semantics and pragmatics for why-questions*, J. Philos. **92**, 636–657.

Hand, M. *Vendlerian Quantification: A Unitary Semantics for Any*, Forthcoming.

Hand, M. (1987), *Semantical games, verification procedures, and wellformedness*, Philos. Stud. **51**, 271–284.

Heim, I.R. (1982), *The semantics of definite and indefinite noun phrases*, Dissertation at the University of Massachusetts.

Hella, L. and Sandu, G. (1995), *Partially ordered connectives and finite graphs*, Quantifiers, Generalizations, Extensions and Variants of Elementary Logic, M. Mostowski et al., eds, Kluwer, Dordrecht, 79–88.

Henkin, L. (1959), *Some remarks on infinitely long formulas*, Infinitistic Methods, Warsaw, 167–183.

Hilpinen, R. (1982), *On C.S. Peirce's theory of the proposition: Peirce as a precursor of game-theoretical semantics*, The Monist **62**, 182–189.

Hintikka, J. (1953), *Distributive normal forms in the calculus of predicates*, Acta Philos. Fennica **6**, Societas Philosophica Fennica, Helsinki.

Hintikka, J. (1955), *Form and content in quantification theory*, Two Papers on Symbolic Logic, Acta Philos. Fennica **8**, 7–55.

Hintikka, J. (1956), *Variables, identity and impredicative definitions*, J. Symb. Logic **21**, 225–245.

Hintikka, J. (1974), *Quantifiers vs. quantification theory*, Ling. Inq. **5**, 153–177.

Hintikka, J. (1975), *Impossible possible worlds vindicated*, J. Philos. Logic **4**, 475–484.

Hintikka, J. (1976), *The semantics of questions and the questions of semantics*, Acta Philos. Fennica **28**(4), Societas Philos. Fennica, Helsinki.

Hintikka, J. (1982), *Temporal discourse and semantical games*, Ling. and Philos. **5**, 3–22.

Hintikka, J. (1986a), *Is scope a viable concept in semantics?*, Proceedings of the Third Eastern State Conference in Semantics, ESCOL '86, F. Marshall et al., eds, The Ohio State University, Columbia, 259–270.

Hintikka, J. (1986b), *The varieties of being in Aristotle*, The Logic of Being, S. Knuuttila and J. Hintikka, eds, Reidel, Dordrecht, 81–114.

Hintikka, J. (1988a), *What is the logic of experimental inquiry?*, Synthese **74**, 173–190.

Hintikka, J. (1988b), *On the development of the model-theoretical tradition in logical theory*, Synthese **77**, 1–36.

Hintikka, J. (1989), *The role of logic in argumentation*, The Monist **72**(1), 3–24.

Hintikka, J. (1990), *Paradigms for language theory*, Language, Knowledge, and Intentionality: Perspectives on the Philosophy of Jaakko Hintikka, L. Haaparanta et. al., eds, Acta Philos. Fennica, **49**, Societas Philos. Fennica, Helsinki, 181–209.

Hintikka, J. (1991), *Towards a general theory of identification*, Definitions and Definability, J.H. Fetzer, D. Shatz and G.N. Schlesinger, eds, Kluwer, Dordrecht, 161–183.

Hintikka, J. (1991), *Defining truth, the whole truth and nothing but the truth*, Reports from the Department of Philosophy of the University of Helsinki, no. 2.

Hintikka, J. (1993a), *Gödel's functional interpretation in a wider perspective*, Kurt Gödel Society, Yearbook 1991, Vienna, 5–43.

Hintikka, J. (1993b), *Socratic questioning, logic and rhetoric*, Rev. Internat. Philos. **47**, 5–30.

Hintikka, J. (1994), *New foundations for mathematical theories*, Lecture Notes in Math. vol. 2.

Hintikka, J. (1995), *What is elementary logic? Independence-friendly logic as the true core area of logic*, Physics, Philosophy, and the Scientific Community, K. Gavroglu et al., eds, Kluwer, Dordrecht, 301–326.

Hintikka, J. and Carlson, L. (1979), *Conditionals, generic quantifiers, and other applications of subgames*, Meaning and Use, A. Margalit, ed., Reidel, Dordrecht, 57–92 (reprinted in Saarinen, 1979).

Hintikka, J. and Hintikka, M.B. (1986), *Investigating Wittgenstein*, Basil Blackwell, Oxford.

Hintikka, J. and Kulas, J. (1983), *The Game of Language*, Reidel, Dordrecht.

Hintikka, J. and Kulas, J. (1985), *Anaphora and Definite Descriptions*, Reidel, Dordrecht.

Hintikka, J. and Sandu, G. (1989), *Informational independence as a semantical phenomenon*, Logic, Methodology and Philosophy of Science VIII, J.E. Fenstad et al., eds, Elsevier, Amsterdam, 571–589.

Hintikka, J. and Sandu, G. (1991), *On the Methodology of Liguistics*, Basil Blackwell, Oxford.

Hodges, W. (1985), *Building Models by Games*, Cambridge Univ. Press, Cambridge, MA.

Hodges, W. (1993), *Model Theory*, Cambridge Univ. Press, Cambridge, MA.

Hodges, W. *Games in Model Theory*, Forthcoming.

Hodges, W. (1989), *Elementary predicate logic*, Handbook of Philosophical Logic I, D. Gabbay and F. Guenther, eds, Reidel, Dordrecht.

Hyttinen, T. (1987), *Games and infinitary languages*, Doctoral Dissertation, Annales Academiae Scientiarum Fennicae.

Jones, P.J. (1974), *Recursive undecidability – an exposition*, Amer. Math. Monthly **87**, 724–738.

Kamp, H. (1982), *A theory of truth and semantic representation*, Formal Methods in the Study of Language, J. Groenendijk et al., eds, Matematisch Centrum, Amsterdam, 277–322.

Karttunen, M. (1984), *Model theory for infinitary deep languages*, Ann. Acad. Sci. Fenn. ser. A I, Math. Dissertationes, 50.

Kolaitis, Ph.G. (1985), *Game quantification*, Model-Theoretical Logics, J. Barwise and S. Feferman, eds, Springer, New York, 365–421.

Krabbe, C.W.E. (1982), *Studies in dialogical logic*, Dissertation, University of Groningen.

Kripke, S. (1976), *Is there a problem about substitutional quantification?*, Truth and Meaning, G. Evans and J. McDowell, eds, Oxford Univ. Press, 325–419.

Krynicki, M. and Lachlan, A. (1979), *On the semantics of the Henkin quantifier*, J. Symb. Logic **44**, 184–200.

Krynicki, M. and Mostowski, M. (1995), *Henkin quantifiers*, Quantifiers: Logic, Models and Computation, vol. 1: Surveys, M. Krynicki, M. Mostowski and L. Szczerba, eds, Kluwer, Dordrecht, 193–262.

Kuhn, S.T. (1989), *Tense and time*, Handbook of Philosophical Logic IV, D. Gabbay and F. Guenther, eds, Reidel, Dordrecht, 552–573.

Lasnik, H. (1975), *On the semantics of negation*, Contemporary Research in Philosophical Logic and Linguistic Semantics, Hockney et. al., eds, Reidel, Dordrecht.

Lorenz, K. (1961), *Arithmetik und Logik als Spiele*, Dissertation, Kiel.

Lorenz, K. (1968), *Dialogspiele als semantische Grundlagen von Logikkalkülen*, Arch. Math. Logik und Grundlagenforschung **11**, 32–55, 73–100.

Lorenz, K. and Lorenzen, P. (1978), *Dialogische Logik*, Wissenschaftliche Buchgesellschaft, Darmstadt.

Lorenzen, P. (1960), *Logik und Agon*, Atti del XII Congresso Internationale di Filosofia vol. 4, Sansoni Editore, Firenze, 187–194.

Lorenzen, P. (1961), *Ein dialogisches Konstruktivitätskriterium*, Infinitistic Methods, Pergamon Press, Oxford, 193–200.

Makkai, M. (1977), *Admissible sets and infinitary logic*, Handbook of Mathematical Logic, J. Barwise, ed., North-Holland, Amsterdam, 233–282.

Matiyasevich, Y.M. (1993), *Hilbert's Tenth Problem*, MIT Press, Cambridge, MA.

May, R. (1985), *Logical Form, its Structure and Derivation*, MIT Press, Cambridge, MA.

Neale, S. (1990), *Descriptions*, MIT Press, Cambridge, MA.

Oikkonen, J. (1988), *How to obtain interpolation for* $L_{\kappa^+\kappa}$, Logic Colloquium '86, F. Drake and J. Thuss, eds, North-Holland, Amsterdam, 175–208.

Parikh, P. (1992), *A game-theoretic account of implicature*, Theoretical Aspects of Reasoning about Knowledge IV, Y. Moses, ed., Morgan Kaufmann, Los Altos, CA, 85–94.

Quine, W.V.O. (1960), *Word and Object*, MIT Press, Cambridge, MA.

Rabin, O.M. (1957), *Effective computability of winning strategies*, Contributions to the Theory of Games vol. III, A.W. Tucker and P. Wolf, eds, Ann. of Math. Stud. vol. 39, 147–157.

Ranta, A. (1994), *Type-Theoretical Grammar*, Oxford, Univ. Press.

Rantala, V. (1975), *Urn models*, J. Philos. Logic **4**, 455–474.

Reichenbach, H. (1947), *Elements of Symbolic Logic*, Macmillan, New York.

Reinhart, T. (1983), *Anaphora and Semantic Interpretation*, Croom Helm, London.

Ryle, G. (1971), *The Academy and dialectic*, Collected Papers vol. 1, Hutchinson, London, 89–115.

Saarinen, E. (ed.) (1979), *Game-Theoretical Semantics: Essays on Semantics by Hintikka, Carlson, Peacocke, Rantala, and Saarinen*, Reidel, Dordrecht.

Sandu, G. (1991), *Studies in game-theoretical logics and semantics*, Doctoral Dissertation, Department of Philosophy, University of Helsinki.

Sandu, G. (1993), *On the logic of informational independence and its applications*, J. Philos. Logic **22**, 29–60.

Sandu, G. and Väänänen, J. (1992), *Partially ordered connectives*, Z. Math. Logik Grundlag. Math. **38**, 361–372.

Scott, D. (1993), *A game-theoretical interpretation of logical formulae*, Kurt Gödel Society, Yearbook 1991, Vienna, 1993, 47–48. (Originally written in 1968.)

Sher, G. (1991), *The Bounds of Logic: A Generalized Viewpoint*, MIT Press, Cambridge, MA.

Skolem, T. (1920), *Logisch-kombinatorische Untersuchungen über die Erfüllbarkeit oder Beweisbarkeit mathematischer Sätze nebst einem Theoreme über dichte Mengen*, Videnskapsselskapets Skrifter, I. Matem.-naturv. Kl. I **4**, 1–36.

Stenius, E. (1976), *Comments on Jaakko Hintikka's paper "Quantification vs. Quantification Theory"*, Dialectica **30**, 67–88.

Thomason, R. (ed.) (1974), *Formal Philosophy: Selected Papers by Richard Montague*, Yale Univ. Press, New Haven, CT.

Tarski, A. (1956), *Logic, Semantics, and Metamathematics*, Clarendon Press, Oxford.

Tennant, N. (1990), *Natural Logic*, Edinburgh Univ. Press.

Tuuri, H. (1990), *Infinitary languages and Ehrenfeucht–Fraissé games*, Dissertation, University of Helsinki.

Van Benthem, J. (1988), *Games in logic*, Representation and Reasoning, J. Hoepelman, ed., Niemeyer Verlag, Tübingen, 3–15, 165–168.

Vaught, R.L. (1960), *Sentences true in all constructive models*, J. Symb. Logic **25**, 39–53.

von Neumann, J. (1929), *Zur Theorie der Gesellschaftsspiele*, Math. Ann. **100**, 295–320.

Walkoe, W. (1970), *Finite partially order quantification*, J. Symb. Logic **35**, 535–550.

Yrjönsuuri, M. (1994), *Obligationes: 14th Century Logic of Disputational Duties*, Societas Philos. Fennica, Acta Philos. Fennica **55**, Helsinki.

Part 2
General Topics

Introduction

This second Part deals with more specific issues than the first, though still with a general bent. The choice of topics in this Part reflects a logical frame of mind. That is, we have chosen broad issues that arise across linguistic applications. Nevertheless, our chapters do not just enumerate existing logical fields, such as modal logic or type theory: we have tried to arrange things around labels of greater relevance to natural language. Some of these have been around for many decades now, such as type structure or partiality – while others are quite new, such as feature logics or dynamics. What most of these chapters show is not just what standard logic has to offer, but also, how its agenda is affected by applications to, or rather, by shared concerns with linguistics.

Let us note a few striking general issues that arise. First, there are issues of *fine-structure*. The broad mathematical theory of the frameworks of Part 1 does not guide us to any special in-depth item in particular. But what has been typical for the "Logic and Language" interface since the eighties is an interest in the logico-linguistic fine-structure of categories of expression and communicative phenomena. This fine-structure has led to special-purpose theories of quantifiers, or temporality, or categorial combination. In particular, broad framework theories tend to work with overkill. They are powerful enough to perform every task, and hence they are informative about none. One virtue of logical formalisms is that they provide parameters for fine-structure, which may be tuned and varied. For instance, *how much* of a typed lambda calculus is needed to compose linguistic meanings? (Small 'linear' fragments turn out to do most of the job.) Or, how much expressive power of a first-order logic over trees is needed to describe grammatically relevant structures? (Small 'modal' fragments turn out to do most of the work at a context-free level.) Fine-structure, often coming in the form of natural *hierarchies* of expressive or computational power, has been a recurrent theme in the foundations of mathematics or computer science. It is equally significant here. For instance, natural logical levels defined by transitions from weaker to more powerful modalities throw an intriguing new light on the Chomsky Hierarchy, ascending from decidable to undecidable in related but interestingly different steps.

A counterpart to the first issue is that of linguistic *generality*. Contents of many chapters can be merged to address new concerns. For instance, with about every logical issue studied in isolation, there is an issue how it will function in the totality of natural language. Here is a paradigmatic case. Natural language quantifiers form just one category of expression (or perhaps, counting polyadics, a small family of these). One can give them a perspicuous semantics, and study their logical peculiarities. But this is not how we use quantifiers in successful ordinary communication. How do these properties *interact* with those of other expressions when all are put together to form meaningful assertions? This requires a type-theoretic stance, showing how quantifiers may be combined. But other paradigms could serve as well, such as the unification methods from logic programming that are employed in definite clause grammars.

Another virtue of formal analysis is that it brings out surprising analogies. One instance out of many is the following. Feature-value logics turn out to employ modal formalisms over trees or graphs. A grammar may be specified as a set of graphs, forming its potential analyses for linguistic expressions. (This view seems on the rise in linguistics generally: the information is not in the strings but in strings-plus-their-derivations.) But then, we are after 'strong recognizing capacity': and hence, the key issue is when we are to count two different graphs as representations of the same process. One answer coming up here, suggested partly by subsumption orders for unification, is that of various forms of 'bisimulation' respecting branching patterns on both sides. But then, the latter notion is precisely one of the central equivalences for dynamic processes found in the computational literature, and indeed, it also plays an important role in the logical dynamics underlying recent forms of dynamic semantics. Thus, at some conceptual level, are tree-based grammar formalisms and dynamic semantics developing the same idea about natural language from different perspectives? This illustrates the kind of question supervenient on our presentation, and it is also a crucial issue to be put on the agenda.

In practical settings, deeper connections between the various approaches in this Part may not be the first concern. As is well-known, the solution to large-scale engineering problems often involves workable *combination* of tools, rather than some grand unification of ideas. Such trends are visible in computational linguistics. Nevertheless, theoretical studies often provide ideas for harmless and useful combination. Indeed, there are several methodologies for this purpose. One of these is the method of *translation* into some next higher logical calculus. Originally inspired by translation methods from modal logic to classical first-order logic, these have now become a powerful general methodology combining, e.g., categorial grammar with discourse representation theory or dynamic semantics. Interestingly, translation methods have also become a major approach in the literature on theorem proving. But combination of logical systems as such is also becoming an active area of research, showing many analogies with the computational theory of abstract data types.

In all these topics, we have made passing reference to analogies with computer science. Indeed, it is hard to find a topic in "Logic and Language" which would not have some natural counterpart in the latter discipline. So far, we have mostly mentioned type theory, logic programming, and modal or dynamic logic – but it would be easy to continue this list ad libitum. Some further telling examples may be found in the chapters of this part. Feature-value logics turn out to be related to denotational semantics of programs, and in our third Part, we shall see analogies between the linguistic semantics of questions and the theory of queries to relational databases. To some extent, these are all semantic parallels. But also the core concern of computation itself may enter, witness our chapter on learning theory, which brings recursion theory to bear on the central phenomenon of language learning. To be sure, there are deep unresolved issues here, which mainly concern the earlier-mentioned programmatic analogy between natural languages and programming languages. Do natural language have genuine *recursion*, the central mechanism driving explicit computation? And if so, where? At a sentence level, or only at higher discourse levels? But semantics and algorithmics do not exhaust the computational interface. Another powerful influence is that emanating from Artificial Intelligence. We have even devoted a whole chapter to the penetration of non-monotonic logics from AI into linguistics. This illustrates both the utility of such non-standard tools in linguistic description, and a shared concern with various styles of reasoning, over and above classical logic.

Even as we close the books for this Handbook, new topics are emerging that might become nuclei for logical research. Some of these challenge the most basic conceptions of logical formalisms. An example is the current interest in *underspecification*. Linguistic expressions may be underspecified as to their syntax and semantics (e.g., the scopes of various operators may be underdetermined, and the same may hold for anaphoric connections). How can this be dealt with in a logical theory which does not reduce all this in computationally costly (and hence unrealistic) ways to sets of full alternatives in the old style?

Johan van Benthem
Alice ter Meulen

CHAPTER 7

Compositionality

Theo M.V. Janssen

Department of Computer Science, University of Amsterdam
Plantage Muidergracht 24, 1018 TV Amsterdam, The Netherlands
E-mail: theo@fwi.uva.nl

with an appendix by Barbara H. Partee

University of Massachusetts, Department of Linguistics, Amherst, MA 01003, USA
E-mail: partee@coins.cs.umass.edu

Commentators: T. Zimmermann and E. Goguen

Contents

HANDBOOK OF LOGIC AND LANGUAGE
Edited by J. van Benthem and A. ter Meulen

1. The principle of compositionality of meaning

1.1. The principle

The principle of compositionality reads, in its best known formulation:

> The meaning of a compound expression is a function of the meanings of its parts.

The principle of compositionality of meaning has immediate appeal, but at the same time it arouses many emotions. Does the principle hold for natural languages? This question cannot be answered directly, because the formulation of the principle is sufficiently vague, that anyone can put his own interpretation on the principle. One topic of investigation in this chapter is to provide a more precise interpretation of the principle, and developing a mathematical model for the principle. The second topic of investigation is to discuss challenges to the principle in the literature. It will be argued that the principle should not be considered an empirically verifiable restriction, but a methodological principle that describes how a system for syntax and semantics should be designed.

1.2. Occurrences of the principle

Compositionality of meaning is a standard principle in logic. It is hardly ever discussed there, and almost always adhered to. Propositional logic clearly satisfies the principle: the meaning of a formula is its truth value and the meaning of a compound formula is indeed a function of the truth values of its parts. The case of predicate logic will be discussed in more detail in Section 2.

The principle of compositionality is a well-known issue in philosophy of language, in particular it is the fundamental principle of Montague Grammar. The discussions in philosophy of language will be reviewed in several sections of this chapter. In linguistics the principle was put forward by Katz and Fodor (Katz, 1966, p. 152; Katz and Fodor, 1963, p. 503). They use it to design a finite system with infinite output: meanings for all sentences. There is also a psychological motivation in their argument, as, in their view, the principle can explain how a human being can understand sentences never heard before, an argument proposed by Frege much earlier (see Section 1.3); see also the discussion in Section 7.5.

The principle is also adhered to in computer science. Programming languages are not only used to instruct computers to perform certain tasks, but they are also used among scientists for the communication of algorithms. So they are languages with an (intended) meaning. To prove properties of programs, for example that the execution of the program terminates at some point, a formal semantics is required. A prominent school in this area, *Denotational Semantics*, follows the methods of logic, and espouses therefore compositionality as a fundamental principle, see Sections 4.2 and 10.1.

Another argument for working compositionally that is often put forward in computer science, is of a practical nature. A compositional approach enables the program designer to think of his system as a composite set of behaviors, which means that he can factorize his design problem into smaller problems which he can then handle one by one.

Above we have met occurrences of the principle of compositionality in rather different fields. They have a common characteristic. The problem to be dealt with is too difficult to tackle at once and in its entirety, therefore it is divided into parts and the solutions are combined. Thus compositionality forms a reformulation of old wisdom, attributed to Philippus of Macedonia: *divide et impera* (divide and conquer).

1.3. On the history of the principle

Many authors who mention compositionality call it *Frege's Principle*. Some assert that it originates with Frege (e.g., Dummett, 1973, p. 152), others inform their readers that it cannot be found in explicit form in his writings (Popper, 1976, p. 198). Below we will consider the situation in more detail.

In the introduction to *Grundlagen der Mathematik* (Frege, 1884, p. x), Frege presents a few principles he promises to follow, one being:

> One should ask for the meaning of a word only in the context of a sentence, and not in isolation.

Later this principle acquired the name of 'principle of contextuality'. Contextuality is repeated several times in his writings and ignoring this principle is, according to Frege, a source of many philosophical errors. The same opinion on these matters is held by Wittgenstein in his *Tractatus* (Wittgenstein, 1921).

Compositionality requires that words in isolation have a meaning and that from these meanings the meaning of a compound can be built. The formulation of contextuality given above disallows speaking about the meaning of words in isolation and is therefore incompatible with compositionality. This shows that Frege was (at the time he wrote these words) not an adherent of compositionality (for further arguments, see Janssen, 1986a). In (Dummett, 1973, pp. 192–193) it is tried to reconcile contextuality with compositionality.

In Frege's later writings one finds fragments that come close to what we call compositionality of meaning. The most convincing passage, from 'Compound thoughts' (Frege, 1923), is quoted here as it provides a clear illustration of Frege's attitude (in those days) with respect to compositionality. In the translation of Geach and Stoothoff:

> 'It is astonishing what language can do. With a few syllables it can express an incalculable number of thoughts, so that even a thought grasped by a terrestrial being for the very first time can be put into a form of words which will be understood by someone to whom the thought is entirely new. This would be impossible, were we not able to distinguish parts in the thoughts corresponding to the parts of a sentence, so that the structure of the sentence serves as the image of the structure of the thoughts.'

In this passage one could read the idea compositionality of meaning. Yet it is not the principle itself, as it is not presented as a principle but as an argument in a wider discussion. Furthermore, one notices that Frege does not require that the ultimate parts of the thought have an independently given meaning (which is an aspect of compositionality).

The conclusion is that Frege rejected the principle of compositionality in the period in which he wrote *Grundlagen der Mathematik*, but may have accepted the principle later on in his life. It seems that nowhere in his published works does he mention compositionality as a principle. It is, therefore, inaccurate to speak of 'Frege's principle'. Compositionality is not Frege's, but it it might be called 'Fregean' because it is in the spirit of his later writings.

2. Illustrations of compositionality

2.1. Introduction

In this section the principle of compositionality is illustrated with four examples, in later sections more complex examples will be considered. The examples are taken from natural language, programming language and logic. All cases concern a phenomenon that at a first sight might be considered as non-compositional. But it turns out that there is a perspective under which they are compositional.

2.2. Time dependence in natural language

The phrase *the queen of Holland* can be used to denote some person. Who this is depends on the time one is speaking about. Usually the linguistic context (tense, time adverbials) give sufficient information about whom is meant, as in (1) or (2):

(1) The Queen of Holland is married to Prince Claus.

(2) In 1910 the Queen of Holland was married to Prince Hendrik.

In (1) the present tense indicates that the present queen is meant: Queen Beatrix. In (2) Queen Wilhelmina is meant, because she was queen in the year mentioned.

These examples might suggest that the meaning of *the queen of Holland* varies with the time about which one is speaking. This is, however, not in accordance with compositionality, which requires that the phrase, when considered in isolation, has a meaning from which the meaning of (1) and (2) can be built. The solution that leads to a single meaning for the phrase is to incorporate the source of variation into the notion of meaning. Accordingly, the meaning of *the queen of Holland* is a function from moments of time to persons. For other expressions there may be other factors of influence (speaker, possible world, ...). Such factors are called *indices* and a function with indices as domain is called an *intension*. So compositionality leads us to consider intensions as meanings of natural language expressions. For a discussion, see Lewis (1970).

2.3. Identifiers in programming languages

Expressions like $x + 1$ are used in almost every programming language. The expression denotes a number; which number this is, depends on the contents of a certain cell in the memory of the computer. For instance, if the value 7 is stored for x in the memory, then $x + 1$ denotes the number 8. So one might say that the meaning of $x + 1$ varies, which is not in accordance with compositionality. As in the previous example, the source of variation can be incorporated in the notion of meaning, so that the meaning of an expression like $x + 1$ is a function from memory states of the computer to numbers. The same notion of meaning is given in the algebraic approach to semantics of programming languages, initiated by Goguen, Thatcher, Wagner and Wright (1977).

Interesting in the light of the present approach is a discussion in (Pratt, 1979). He distinguishes two notions of meaning: a static meaning (an expression gets a meaning once and for all) and a dynamic notion (the meaning of an expression varies). He argues that a static meaning has no practical purpose, because we frequently use expressions that are associated with different elements in the course of time. Therefore he developed a special language for the treatment of semantics of programming languages: dynamic logic. Compositionality requires that an expression has a meaning from which in all contexts the meaning of the compound can be built, hence a static notion of meaning. In this subsection we have seen that a dynamic aspect of meaning can be covered by a static logic by using a more abstract notion of meaning.

2.4. Tarski's interpretation of predicate logic

Compositionality requires that for each construction rule of predicate logic there is a semantic interpretation. It might not be obvious whether this is the case for predicate logic. Pratt (1979) even says that 'there is no function such that the meaning of $\forall x\phi$ can be specified with a constraint of the form $\mathcal{M}(\forall x\phi) = F(\mathcal{M}(\phi))$'. In a compositional approach such a meaning assignment $\mathcal{M}$ and an operator F on meanings has to be provided.

Let us consider Tarski's standard way of interpreting predicate logic in more detail. It roughly proceeds as follows. Let $\mathcal{A}$ be a model and g an $\mathcal{A}$-assignment. The interpretation in $\mathcal{A}$ of a formula ϕ with respect to g, denoted ϕ^g, is defined recursively. One of these clauses is:

$$[\phi \wedge \psi]^g \text{ is } \textit{true} \text{ iff } \phi^g \text{ is } \textit{true} \text{ and } \psi^g \text{ is } \textit{true}.$$

This suggests that the meaning of $\phi \wedge \psi$ is a truth value that is obtained from the truth values for ϕ and ψ. But another clause of the standard interpretation is not compatible with this idea:

$$[\exists x\phi]^g \text{ is } \textit{true} \text{ iff if there is a } g' \sim_x g \text{ such that } [\phi(x)]^{g'} \text{is } \textit{true}.$$

(Here $g' \sim_x g$ means that g' is the same assignment as g except for the possible difference that $g'(x) \neq g(x)$.) Since it obviously is not always possible to calculate the truth value of $\exists x\phi$ (for a given g) from the truth value of ϕ (for the same g), a compositional approach to predicate logic requires a more sophisticated notion of meaning.

Note that there is no single truth value which corresponds with $\phi(x)$. It depends on the interpretation of x, and in general on the interpretation of the free variables in ϕ, hence on g. In analogy with the previous example, we will incorporate the variable assignment into the notion of meaning. Then the meaning of a formula is a function from variable assignments to truth values, namely the function that yields true for an assignment in case the formula is true for that assignment. With this conception we can build the meaning of $\phi \wedge \psi$ from the meanings of ϕ and ψ: it is the function that yields true for an assignment if and only if both meanings of ϕ and ψ yield true for that assignment.

The situation becomes more transparent if we use an another perspective: the meaning of a formula is the set of assignments for which the formula is true. Let M denote the function that assigns meanings to formulas. Then we have: $\mathcal{M}(\phi \wedge \psi) = \phi \cap \psi$. For the other connectives there are related operations on sets. For existential quantification the operation is: $\mathcal{M}(\exists x\phi) = \{h \mid h \sim_x g \text{ and } g \in \mathcal{M}(\phi)\}$. Let C_x denote the semantic operation described at the right hand side of the $=$ sign, i.e. C_x is the operation 'extend the set of assignments with all x variants'. Thus the requirement of compositionality is satisfied: the syntactic operation of writing $\exists x$ in front of a formula has a semantic interpretation: apply C_x to the meaning of ϕ. This view on the meaning of predicate logic (sets of assignments) is explicit in some textbooks on logic (Monk, 1976, p. 196; Kreisel and Krivine, 1976, p. 17).

Note that same strategy can be followed for other logics. For instance, a compositional meaning assignment to propositional modal logic is obtained by defining the meaning of a proposition to be the set of possible worlds in which the proposition holds.

It is interesting to take another perspective on the conception of meaning besides as sets of variable assignments. An assignment can be seen as a infinite tuple of elements: the first element of the tuple being the value for the first variable, the second element for the second variable etc. So an assignment is a point in a infinite-dimensional space. If ϕ holds for a set of assignments, then the meaning of ϕ is a set of points in this space. The operator C_x applied to a point adds all points which differ from this point only in their x-coordinate. Geometrically speaking, a single point extends into an infinite line. When C_x is applied to a set consisting of a circle area, it is extended to a cylinder. Because of this effect, the operation C_x is called the xth cylindrification operation (see Figure 1).

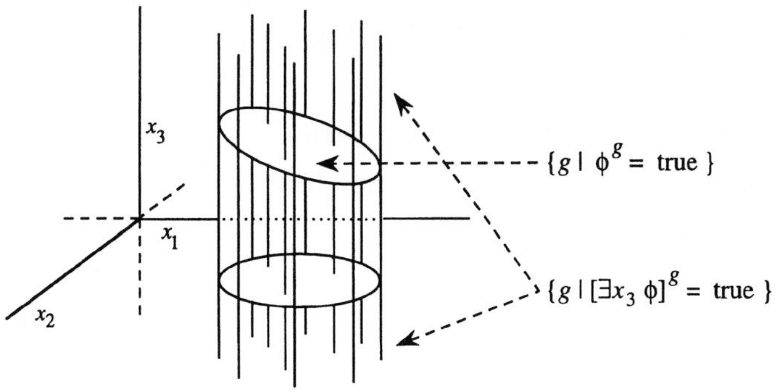

Fig. 1. The interpretation of $\exists x$ as a cylindrification operation.

The algebraic structure obtained for predicate logic with cylindrifications as operators, is called a cylindric algebra. The original motivation for studying cylindric algebras was a technical one: to make the powerful tools from algebra available for studying logic (Henkin, Monk and Tarski, 1971).

The discussion can be summarized as follows. The standard (Tarskian) interpretation of predicate logic is not a meaning assignment but a recursive, parameterized definition of truth for predicate logic. It can easily be turned into a compositional meaning assignment by incorporating the parameter (viz. the assignment to variables) into the concept of meaning. Then meaning becomes a function with assignments as domain.

2.5. *Situation semantics*

Situation Semantics (Barwise and Perry, 1983) presents an approach to meaning which differs from the traditional model-theoretic one. The basic new point is that a sentence conveys information (about the external world or about states of mind), formalized in their conception of meaning as a relation. The meaning of a declarative sentence is a relation between utterances of the sentence and the situation described by the utterance. More generally, the meaning of an expression is a relation between utterances and situations. The interpretation of an utterance at a specific occasion is the described situation.

To illustrate Situation Semantics, consider the following example (op. cit. p. 19):

(3) I am sitting.

The meaning of this sentence is a relation between utterance u and situation e which holds just in case there is a location l and an individual a such that a speaks at l, and in situation e this individual a is sitting at l. The parts of a sentence provide the following ingredients to build this meaning relation. The meaning of a referring noun phrase is a relation between an utterance and an individual; and the verb phrase is a relation between an utterance and a property. From the meanings of the subject and the verb phrase the meaning of the whole sentence is built in a systematic way. Thus, Situation Semantics satisfies the principle of compositionality of meaning.

This was a simple example because the domain of interpretation does not change. More challenging is sentence (4) with antecedent relations as indicated in (5) (Barwise and Perry, 1983, pp. 136–137):

(4) Joe admires Sarah and she admires him.

(5) Joe_1 admires Sarah_2 and she_2 admires him_1.

Sentence (4) has two parts (6) and (7):

(6) Joe admires Sarah.

(7) She admires him.

Sentence (7), when considered in isolation, has two free pronouns for which suitable connections must be found. This is not the case for the whole sentence (4); so (7) has another domain for the interpretation of pronouns than (4). For this reason, the statement made with (4) cannot be considered as just a conjunction of two independent statements: somehow the meaning of the first part has to influence the meaning of the second part.

The solution is based on the meaning of names. Initially (op. cit. p. 131), the meaning of a name β was defined as a relation that holds between an utterance u and an individual a_σ (in a discourse situation d) if and only if the speaker c of the utterance refers by β to that individual. For sentences like (4), the meaning of names is augmented to make them suitable antecedents for co-indexed pronouns (op. cit. p. 137), evoking a connection with the coindexed pronouns. In symbols:

$$d, c\big[[\beta_i]\big]a_\sigma, e \text{ iff } c(\beta_i) = a_\sigma,\ \ a_\sigma \text{ is named } \beta,$$
$$\text{and if } c(he_i) = b \text{ then } b = a_\sigma.$$

With this extension the meaning of a sentence of the form ϕ and ψ can be obtained from the meanings of ϕ and ψ in the following way:

$$d, c\big[[\phi \text{ and } \psi]\big]e \text{ iff there is an extension } c' \text{ of } c$$
$$\text{such that } d, c'\big[[\phi]\big]e \text{ and } d, c'\big[[\psi]\big]e.$$

Let us summarize the solution. The meaning of ϕ and ψ is a relation, and to find its value for the pair of coordinates d, c the value of the meanings of ϕ and ψ for these coordinates is not sufficient. Other coordinates c' have to be considered too, so the whole meaning relation has to be known. This illustrates that (op. cit. p. 32): 'a version of compositionality holds of meanings, but not of interpretations'. This is in analogy of the situation in Montague grammar, where there is compositionality of meaning, but not of extension.

This example illustrates that the relational approach to meaning is not an obstacle to compositional semantics. The problem was that the initial meaning of names was too poor to deal with coindexed pronouns, and the solution was to augment the concept of meaning. Again, the strategy was followed that if a given conception of meaning is not suitable for a compositional semantics, a richer conception of meaning is defined.

2.6. Conclusion

These examples illustrate that compositionality is not too narrow. Using a sufficiently abstract notion of meaning, it is flexible enough to cover many standard proposals in the field of semantics. The strategy was to incorporate a possible source of variation of meaning into a more abstract notion of meaning. In this way meanings not only capture the semantic intuitions, but do so in a compositional way. The classical advice of Lewis (1970, p. 5) is followed: 'In order to say what a meaning is, first ask what a meaning does, and then find something that does that'.

3. Towards formalization

3.1. Introduction

The principle of compositionality of meaning is not a formal statement. It contains several vague words which have to be made precise in order to give formal content to the principle. In this section the first steps in this direction are made, giving us ways to distinguish compositional and non-compositional proposals (in Section 4). In later sections (viz. 8, 9) mathematical formalizations are given, making it possible to prove certain consequences of the compositional approach.

Suppose that an expression E is constituted by the parts E_1 and E_2 (according to some syntactic rule). Then compositionality says that the meaning $M(E)$ of E can be found by finding the meanings $M(E_1)$ and $M(E_2)$ of respectively E_1 and E_2, and combining them (according to some semantic rule). Suppose moreover that E_1 is constituted by E_{1a} and E_{1b} (according to some syntactic rule, maybe another than the one used for E). Then the meaning $M(E_1)$ is in turn obtained from the meanings $M(E_{1a})$ and $M(E_{1b})$ (maybe according to another rule than the one combining $M(E_1)$ and $M(E_2)$). This situation is presented in Figure 2.

3.2. Assumptions

The interpretation in 3.1 is a rather straightforward explication of the principle, but there are several assumptions implicit in it. Most assumptions on compositionality are widely accepted, some will return in later sections. Notice that the assumptions give a gradually more abstract interpretation of the principle.

The assumptions are:

1. In a grammar the syntax and the semantics are distinguished components connected by the requirement of compositionality. This assumption excludes approaches, as in some variants of Transformational Grammar, with a series of intermediate levels between the syntax and the semantics.

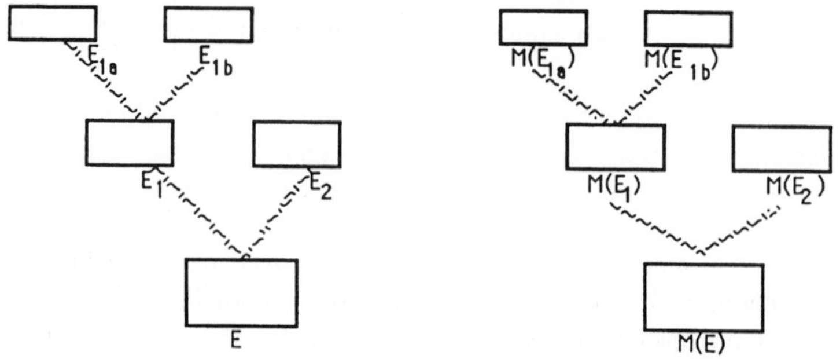

Fig. 2. Compositionality: the compositional formation of expression E from its parts and the compositional formation of the meaning of E from the meanings its parts.

2. It is assumed that the output of the syntax is the input for meaning assignment. This is for instance in contrast to the situation in Generative Semantics, where the syntactic form is projected from the meanings.
3. The rules specify how to combine the parts, i.e. they are instructions for combining expressions. So this gives a different perspective from the traditional view of a grammar as a rewriting system.
4. The grammar determines what the parts of an expression are. It depends on the rules whether *Mary does not cry* has two parts *Mary* and *does not cry*, or three *Mary, does not* and *cry*. This illustrates that **part** is a technical notion.
5. All expressions that arise as parts have meaning. This excludes systems in which only complete sentences can be assigned meaning (as in some variants of Transformational Grammar). Not only parts for which we have an intuitive meaning (as *loves* in *John loves Mary*), but also parts for which this is less intuitive (as *only* in *Only John loves Mary*). The choice what the meaning of a part is, might depend on what we consider a suitable ingredient for building the meaning of the whole expression.
6. The meaning of an expression is not only determined by the parts, but also by the rule which combines those parts. From the same collection of parts several sentences can be made with different meanings (e.g., *John loves Mary* vs. *Mary loves John*). Several authors make this explicit in their formulation of the principle, e.g., Partee, Ter Meulen and Wall (1990, p. 318):

   > The meaning of a compound expression is a function of the meanings of its parts and of the syntactic rule by which they are combined.

7. For each syntactic rule there is a semantic rule that describes its effect. In order to obtain this correspondence, the syntactic rules should be designed appropriately. For instance, semantic considerations may influence the design of syntactic rules. This correspondence leaves open the possibility that the semantic rule is a meaning-preserving rule (no change of meanings), or that different syntactic rules have the same meaning.
8. The meaning of an expression is determined by the way in which it is formed from its parts. The syntactic production process is, therefore, the only input to the process of determining its meaning. There is no other input, so no external factors can have an effect on the meaning of a sentence. If, for instance, discourse factors should contribute to meaning, the conception of meaning has to be enriched in order to capture this.
9. The production process is the input for the meaning assignment. Ambiguous expressions must have different derivations: i.e. a derivation with different rules, and/or with different basic expressions.

3.3. Options in syntax

In the above section it is not specified what the nature is of expressions and parts, i.e. what kind of objects are in the boxes in Figure 2. Such a decision has to be based upon linguistic insights. Below some important options are mentioned.

Concatenation of words
Close to the most naive conception of compositionality is that the boxes contain strings of words (the terminal boxes single words), and that the syntactic rules concatenate their contents. However, all important theories of natural language have a more sophisticated view. Classical Categorical Grammar and classical Generalized Phrase Structure grammar (GPSG) do not to use real words, but more abstract word-forms with features. In all these cases the structure from Figure 2 is isomorphic to the constituent structure of the involved expression.

Powerful operations on strings
In some theories the syntactic rules are more powerful than just concatenation. A small step is to allow a wrap-rule (a rule with two arguments, where the first argument is inserted in the second position of the second argument). In PTQ (Montague, 1973) the syntactic rules are very powerful, for instance there is a rule that substitutes a string for a pronoun (e.g., the wide scope reading of *Every man loves a woman* is obtained by substituting *a woman* for *him* in *every man loves him*). In these cases the grammar generates strings, and the derivation does not assign a constituent structure to them (since the parts are not constituent parts).

Operations on structures
Most theories concern structures. Tree Adjoining Grammar, for instance, assumes as its basic elements (small) trees, and two kinds of rules: adjunction and substitution. Another example are the M-grammars, introduced by Partee (1973), and used in the translation system (Rosetta, 1994). The boxes contain phrase-structure trees as in Transformational Grammar, and the rules are powerful operations on such trees. In this situation the tree that describes the derivation might differ considerably from the tree describing the structure of the string, as illustrated below.

Consider the following sentence:

(1) *John seeks a unicorn.*

There are semantic arguments for distinguishing two readings: the *de re* reading which implicates the existence of unicorns, and the *de dicto* reading which does not. But there are no syntactic arguments for distinguishing two different constituent structures. In an M-grammar this unique constituent structure can be derived in two ways, one for each meaning. In Figure 3 the derivation of the de re reading of (1) is given, using a tree-substitution rule.

3.4. Conclusion

Above it is argued that there are several options in syntax. In the previous section it has been shown that there are choices in defining what meanings are. The discussion whether natural language is compositional has to do with these options. If one has a definite opinion on what parts, meanings and rules should be like, then it may be doubted whether compositionality holds. But if one leaves one or more of these choices open, then the issue becomes: in which way can compositionality be obtained? These two positions will return in several discussions concerning the principle of compositionality.

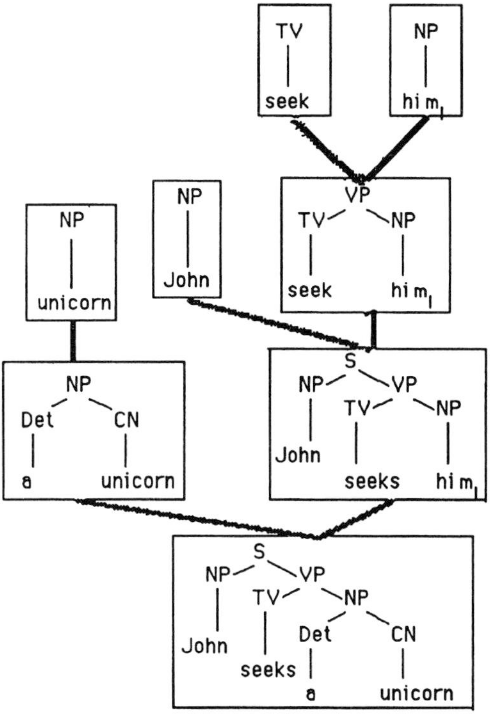

Fig. 3. The production of the *de dicto* reading of *John seeks a unicorn*. The resulting constituent structure is the same as the structure for the *de re* reading.

4. Examples of non-compositional semantics

4.1. Introduction

In this section examples of essentially non-compositional semantics are presented, where their non-compositional character is not caused by the nature of the phenomena, but by the fundamental aspects of the approach taken. It is not possible to turn these proposals into compositional ones without losing a fundamental aspect of the analysis. Thus the examples illustrate the demarcation line between compositional and non-compositional semantics. As in Section 2, the examples deal with several types of languages: programming languages, natural languages and logic.

4.2. Arrays in programming languages

In programming languages one finds expressions consisting of an array identifier with subscript, e.g., $a[7]$. Here a is an array identifier, it refers to a series of memory cells in the computer. Between the [-sign and] -sign the subscript is mentioned. That subscript tells which of the cells is to be considered, so the expression $a[7]$ refers to the contents of this cell (e.g., a number). The subscript can be a compound expression that denotes a number, e.g., $x + 1$, hence the syntax of this construction says that there are two parts: an array identifier, and an arithmetical expression.

In the semantics of programming languages one often interprets programs in an abstract computer with abstract memory cells. Then expressions like $a[7]$ and $a[x + 1]$ have as interpretation the value stored in such a memory cell (or alternatively a function to such a value). The array identifier itself cannot be given an interpretation, since in the abstract computer model there is nothing but cells and their contents, and a does not correspond to anyone of them. As a consequence every time the array identifier arises, it has to be accompanied by a subscript. This leads to complicated proof rules (e.g., in De Bakker, 1980).

This interpretation is not in accordance with compositionality, which requires that all parts have a meaning; in particular the array identifier should have a meaning. Although in the given computer model an appropriate meaning is not available, it is easy to define one: a function from numbers to cells. Changing the model in this way, allows a simpler reformulation of the proof rules, because array identifiers without subscripts can be used (see e.g., Janssen and Van Emde Boas, 1977).

4.3. Syntactic rules as conditions

In several theories syntactic rules are formulated as conditions, or they are accompanied by conditions. First we will consider a simple example. A context sensitive rule allows us to rewrite a symbol in a certain context. A context sensitive grammar is a grammar with such rules. An example is one with the rules $S \to AA$, $Ab \to bb$, $bA \to bb$. This grammar does not produce any strings, because after application of the first rule, no further rules are applicable. MacCawley (1986) proposed to consider context sensitive rules as 'node-admissability conditions'. These specify which configurations in trees are allowed. For instance, the last rule says that an b immediately dominated by an A is allowed, if there is an b immediately to the left of this b. With this interpretation, the tree in Figure 4 is allowed by the given grammar. So the string bb belongs to the language of the grammar, although it cannot be generated in the classical way. In this conception

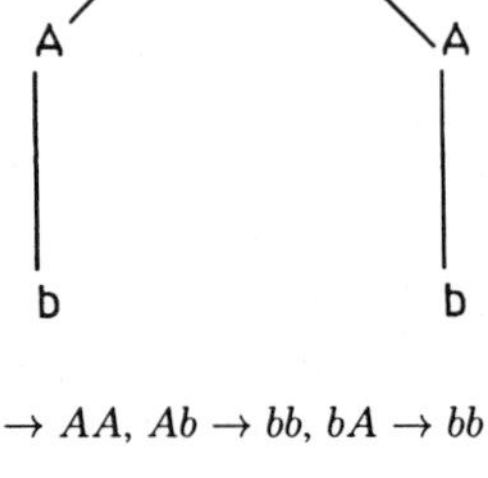

Fig. 4. The context sensitive rules $S \to AA$, $Ab \to bb$, $bA \to bb$ used as node admissibility conditions.

of grammar there are no rules, only conditions. Hence there is no syntactic algebra with operations, and an admissible structure has no derivation. Consequently, a compositional meaning assignment (in the sense of the principle) is not possible.

A similar situation arises in the variant of Transformational Grammar known as 'Principles and Parameters'. Conditions form also the central part of the theory, but formally the situation is slightly different. One single transformation, called *move* – α, can in principle move any constituent to any position controlled by various conditions on movement. So the interesting aspect of the theory does not lie in this transformation, but in the conditions. An algebraic formulation of this theory is possible, with one partial rule which takes one argument as input. Since this single rule has to account for all phenomena, there is no semantic counterpart for this rule. So 'Principles and Parameters' is a theory where compositionality of meaning is impossible.

In Generalized Phrase Structure Grammar (GPSG) syntactic rules are considered as expressing a tree admissibility condition, i.e. they say which trees are allowed given an ID-rule or an LP-rule. This form of admissibility conditions does not disturb compositionality: a rule can be considered as an abbreviation for a collection of rules, each generating one of the admissible structures, and all rules from the collection have the same semantic interpretation (the one associated with the original rule).

4.4. Discourse representation theory

Pronominal references in discourses may depend on previous sentences, as illustrated by the following two discourses which have identical second sentences.

(1) A man walks in the park. He whistles.

(2) Not all men do not walk in the park. He whistles.

In (1), the pronoun *he* in the second sentence is interpreted as anaphorically linked to the term *a man* in the first sentence. This is not possible in (2), where *he* has to refer to a third party. The meanings of discourses (1) and (2) are, therefore, different.

Since their second sentences are identical, their first sentence (3) and (4) must contain the source of the meaning difference.

(3) A man walks in the park.

(4) Not all men do not walk in the park.

However, (3) and (4) have identical truth-conditions, hence the discourses (1) and (2) seem to provide an argument against compositionality.

Discourse representation theory (henceforth 'DRT') is a theory about semantic representations of texts, especially concerning pronominal references in texts (Kamp, 1981; Kamp and Reyle, 1993). There are explicit rules how these representations are formed, and these rules follow the syntactic rules step by step. Parts of sentences provide building blocks for discourse representations. However, no semantic interpretation is provided for these parts of discourse representations. Furthermore, the instructions may require specific information concerning already built parts of representations, and may change them. So the representation plays an essential role in the system and cannot be eliminated. DRT is a system for compositionally constructing representations, but not for compositional semantics (then the representations should not be essential, see also the discussion in Section 5). This is intended: the name of the theory states explicitly that it is about representations, and claims psychological relevance of the representations. The solution DRT provides for the discourses we started with roughly is as follows. Different representations are assigned to (3) and (4), and the two negations in (4) cause a difference that triggers a difference in interpretation strategy, hence a difference in the pronominal reference.

However, a compositional treatment for this kind of discourse phenomena is quite feasible. In fact, the principle of compositionality itself points to a solution. Since (3) and (4) have identical truth-conditions, a richer notion of meaning is required if the principle of compositionality is to be saved for discourses. Truth-conditions of sentences (which involve possible worlds and assignments to free variables) are just one aspect of meaning. Another aspect is that the preceding discourse has a bearing on the interpretation of a sentence (and especially of the so called discourse pronouns). Moreover, the sentence itself extends this discourse and thus has a bearing on sentences that follow it. Hence a notion of meaning is required which takes the semantic contribution into account that a sentence makes to a discourse. Sentences (3) and (4) make different contributions to the meaning of the discourse, especially concerning the interpretation of later discourse pronouns. These ideas have led to Dynamic Predicate Logic (henceforth 'DPL'). It is a compositional theory that accounts not only for the phenomena that are treated in DRT, but for other phenomena as well, see Groenendijk and Stokhof (1991). Thus we see that the program to require compositionality has suggested a particular solution.

The difference in compositionality between DRT and DPL was initially a central point in the discussion, see Groenendijk and Stokhof (1991). Later developments made the difference less crucial, because several reformulation of DRT were given that adhered to compositionality. Examples are Zeevat (1989) and Muskens (1993), and the chapter in this Handbook on DRT. The concepts of meaning used in these proposals are illuminating. For instance, in Zeevat's proposal the meanings are pairs consisting of sets of assignments (as in predicate logic), and a set of variables (discourse markers). So syntactic symbols act as component in the semantics, which reflects the special role of representations in DRT.

4.5. Substitutional interpretation of quantifiers

For the interpretation of $\exists x\phi$ an alternative to the Tarskian interpretation has been proposed that is not compositional. It is called the *substitutional interpretation*, and says: $\exists x\phi(x)$ is true if and only if there is some substitution a for x such that $\phi(a)$ is true. Of course, the substitutional interpretation is only equivalent to the standard interpretation if there is a name for every element in the domain. The substitutional interpretation can be found in two rather divergent branches of logic: philosophical logic and in proof theory, both considered below.

In philosophical logic the substitutional interpretation is advocated by Marcus (1962) with an ontological motivation. Consider

(5) Pegasus is a winged horse.

Marcus argues that one might believe (5) without believing

(6) There exists at least one thing which is a winged horse.

At the same time she accepts that (5) entails (7):

(7) $\exists x$(x is a winged horse).

This view implies that the quantification in (7) cannot be considered quantification in the ontological sense. The substitutional interpretation of quantifiers allows us to accept (7) as a consequence of (5), without accepting (6) as a consequence.

The substitutional interpretation is discussed more formally by Kripke (1976). As a syntax for the logic he presents the traditional syntax: $\exists x\phi(x)$ is produced from $\phi(x)$ by placing the quantifier in front of it. According to that grammar $\phi(x)$ is a part of $\exists x\phi(x)$, and $\phi(a)$ is not a part of $\exists x\phi(x)$. Hence in this case the substitutional interpretation is not compositional: the meaning of $\exists x\phi(x)$ is not obtained from the meaning of its part $\phi(x)$.

In proof theory the substitutional interpretation is given by, e.g., Schütte (1977). According to his syntax $\forall x\phi(x)$ is formed from $\phi(a)$, where a is arbitrary. So the formula $\forall x\phi(x)$ is syntactically ambiguous: there are as many derivations as there are expressions of the form $\phi(a)$. It is in general not possible, given one such a, to find the interpretation of $\forall x\phi(x)$ from the interpretation of that $\phi(a)$, because $\forall x\phi(x)$ can be false, whereas $\phi(a)$ is true for some a's. Hence also in this case the substitutional interpretation does not satisfy the compositionality principle.

If one wishes to have the substitutional interpretation, and at the same time meet the principle of compositionality, then the syntax has to contain an infinitistic rule which says that all expressions of the form $\phi(a)$ are a part of $\forall x\phi(x)$. But such an infinitistic rule has not been proposed.

4.6. Conclusion

The examples illustrate that compositionality is a real restriction in the sense that there are theories that are essentially non-compositional. Moreover, it illustrates that compositionality is crucial in evaluating theories: not in the sense that it discriminates good from bad (such arguments are not given above, but will be given in later sections), but in the sense that it exhibits a special aspect of those theories. The fact that there was no compositional treatment of arrays exhibits that the semantic model used was ontologically sparse (or too poor, if you prefer). It exhibits that the substitutional interpretation of quantifiers avoids assignments to variables with the price of introducing an infinitistic aspect in the syntax. In DRT the rules refer in several ways to the particular form of the partial discourse representations that occur as their inputs. The compositional reformulations exhibit in which respect this is essential. This brings us to the following advice: if you encounter a new proposal, and wish to find the innovative or deviant aspect, then look for the point where it departs from compositionality.

5. Logic as auxiliary language

5.1. Introduction

The principle of compositionality of meaning expresses that meanings of parts are combined into the meaning of a compound expression. Since meanings are generally formalized as model-theoretic entities, such as truth values, sets of sets etc., functions have to be specified which operate on such meanings. An example of such an operation is (Montague, 1970a; Thomason, 1974, p. 194):

(1) G_3 is that function $f \in ((2^I)^{A \times A})^{A^\omega}$ such that, for all $x \in A^\omega$, all $u, t \in A$ and all $i \in I$: $f(x)(t, u)(i) = 1$ if and only if $t = u$.

Such descriptions are not easy to understand, nor convenient to work with. Therefore almost always a logical language is used to represent meanings and operations on meanings. The main exception is Montague (1970a). So in practice associating meanings with natural language amounts to translating sentences into logical formulas. The operation described above is represented in intensional logic with the formula $^\wedge\lambda t \lambda u[t = u]$. This is much easier to grasp than the formulation in (1). This example illustrates that such translations into logic are used for good reasons. In the present section the role of translations into a logical language is investigated.

5.2. Restriction on the use of logic

Working in accordance with compositionality of meaning puts a heavy restriction on the translations into logic, because the goal of the translations is to assign meanings. The logical representations are just a tool to reach this goal. The representations are not meanings themselves, and should not be confused with them. This means for instance, that two logically equivalent representations are equally good as representation of the associated meaning. A semantic theory cannot be based upon accidental properties of meaning representations, since it would then be a theory about representations, and not about the meanings themselves. Therefore the logical language should only be auxiliary tool and, in principle, be dispensable.

If one has a logic for representing meanings, this logic will probably not have all the operations on meanings one needs. For instance, logic usually has only one conjunction operator (between formulas of type t), whereas natural language requires several (not only between sentences, but also between verbs, nouns, etc.). So the logic has be extended with new operations. We will consider two methods.

A new semantic operation can be introduced by introducing a new basic operator symbol, together with a model theoretic interpretation for it. Such an interpretation can be given directly, speaking, e.g., about functions from functions to functions. Another method is to denote the intended interpretation with a logical expression. Then one should not forget that this expression stands for its interpretation, see the example below (in Section 5.3).

Another method is to describe the effects of the new operation using already available ones. An example we have met above (in Section 5.1) is $^\wedge\lambda t\lambda u[t = u]$. This is an example of the standard method (introduced by Montague, 1970b): using polynomials. Probably anyone has encountered polynomials in studying elementary mathematics; an example (with two variables) is $x_1^2 + x_1 + 3 \times x_2$. This polynomial defines a function on two arguments; the resulting value is obtained by substituting the arguments for the variables and evaluating the result. For the arguments 2 and 1 it yields $2^2 + 2 + 3 \times 1$, being 9. The method of polynomials can be used in logic as well. For instance, a polynomial over intensional logic with variables X_1 and X_2 is:

(2) $\lambda y[X_1(y) \wedge X_2(y)]$.

Note that y is not a variable in the sense of the polynomial. Polynomial (2) is an operation which takes two predicates as inputs and yields a predicate as result. It can be used to describe, for instance, the semantic effect of verb phrase conjunction. Usually Greek letters are used to indicate variables, in PTQ (Montague, 1973) one finds for the above polynomial:

(3) $\lambda y[\gamma'(y) \wedge \delta'(y)]$.

In Section 5.4 more examples of polynomials and non-polynomials will be given.

5.3. A new operator: *CAUSE*

Dowty (1976) presents a treatment of the semantics of factive constructions like *shake John awake*. For this purpose intensional logic is extended with an operator *CAUSE*. In order to define its interpretation the semantic apparatus is extended with a function that assigns to each well-formed formula ϕ and each possible world i a possible world $f(\phi, i)$. Intuitively speaking, $f(\phi, i)$ is the possible world that is most like i with the possible exception that ϕ is the case. Then the interpretation of *CAUSE* reads:

(4) If $\phi, \psi \in ME_t$ then $[\phi\, CAUSE\, \psi]^{\mathcal{A},i,j,g}$ is 1 if and only if $[\phi \wedge \psi]^{\mathcal{A},i,j,g}$ is 1 and $[\neg\phi]^{\mathcal{A},f(\neg\psi,i),j,g}$ is 1.

The first argument of f is a formula, and not the interpretation of this formula. Hence *CAUSE*, which is based upon this function, is an operator on formulas, and not on the meanings they represent. This suggests that the logic is not dispensable, that it is an essential stage and that the proposed solution is not compositional. This is shown as follows. Let f be such that $f(\neg[\phi \wedge \eta], i) \neq f(\neg[\eta \wedge \phi], i)$. Then it may be the case that $[(\phi \wedge \eta) CAUSE\, \psi]^{\mathcal{A},i,j,g}$ holds whereas this does not hold for $\eta \wedge \phi$. So the two equivalent formulas $\phi \wedge \eta$ and $\eta \wedge \phi$ cannot be substituted for each other without changing the resulting truth value; a consequence that was not intended. This illustrates that the introduction of a new operator in a way that violates compositionality bears the risk of being incorrect in the sense that the intended semantic operation is not defined.

The proposal can be corrected by defining f for the *meaning* of its first argument (i.e. its intension). Then the last clause of the definition becomes $[\neg\phi]^{\mathcal{A},k,j,g}$ is 1, where $k = f([^\wedge[\neg\eta \wedge \phi]]^{\mathcal{A},i,j,g}, i)$.

5.4. An operation on logic: Relative clause formation

The syntactic rule for restrictive relative clause formation in PTQ (Montague, 1973) roughly is as follows:

(5) $R_{3,n}$: If α is a CN and β a sentence, then α *such that* $\beta^\star$ is a CN, where $\beta^\star$ comes from β by replacing each occurrence of he_n by the appropriate pronoun.

The corresponding semantic rule reads (neglecting intensions and extensions):

(6) If α' is the translation of the common noun α, and β' of the sentence β, then the translation of the CN with relative clause is $\lambda x_n[\alpha'(x_n) \wedge \beta']$.

The rule above forms from *man* and *he*$_2$ *loves Mary* the common noun phrase *man such that he loves Mary*. Suppose that the meanings of these parts are represented by *man* and $love_*(x_2, j)$. Then the meaning of the common noun phrase is given correctly by $\lambda x_2[man(x_2) \wedge love_*(x_2, j)]$. However, the translation rule yields incorrect results in case the translation of the common noun contains the occurrence of a variable that becomes bound by the λ-operator introduced in the translation rule. In order to avoid this, the editor of the collection of Montague's work on philosophy of language, R.H. Thomason, gave in a footnote a correction (Thomason, 1974, p. 261):

(7) To avoid collision of variables, the translation must be $\lambda x_m[man(x_m) \wedge \psi)]$, where ψ is the result of replacing all occurrences of x_n in β' by occurrences of x_m, where m is the least even number such that x_m has no occurrences in either α' or β'.

This rule introduces an operation on expressions: the replacement of a variable by one with a special index. However, finding the least even index that is not yet used is an operation that essentially depends on the form of the formulas. This is illustrated by the two formulas $x_1 = x_1$ and $x_2 = x_2$, which are logically equivalent (they are tautologies), but have a different least index that is not yet used. So Thomason's reformulation is an operation on representations, and not on meanings.

Nevertheless, (7) is correct in the sense that it does correspond with an operation on meanings. The operation on meanings can be represented in a much simpler way, using a polynomial, viz.:

(8) $\lambda P[\lambda x_n[P(x_n) \wedge \beta']](\alpha')$.

This polynomial formulation avoids the binding of variables in α' by λx_n, so the complication of Montague's rule does not arise. Furthermore, it is much simpler than Thomason's correction of the rule.

5.5. Conclusion

These examples illustrate a method to find dangerous spots in a proposal: find the places where the translation into logic is not a polynomial. It is likely that compositionality is violated there. Either the proposal is incorrect in the sense that it makes unintended predictions, or it is correct, but can be improved (simplified) considerably by using a polynomial. The latter point, viz. that an operation on meanings can be expressed by means of a polynomial, (as illustrated in Section 5.3) can be given a mathematical basis (see Section 8). These applications of compositionality exhibit the benefits of compositionality as a heuristic method.

6. Counterexamples to compositionality

6.1. Introduction

In the present section we consider some examples from natural language that are used in the literature as arguments against compositionality. Several other examples could be given, see Partee (1984). The selection here suits to illustrate the methods available to obtain compositionality. The presentation of the examples follows closely the original argumentation; proposals for a compositional treatment are given afterwards. In the last section the methods to obtain compositional solutions are considered from a general perspective.

6.2. Counterexamples

6.2.1. Would

The need for the introduction of the *NOW*-operator was based upon the classical example (Kamp, 1971):

(1) A child was born that will become ruler of the world.

The following more complex variants are discussed by Saarinen (1979), who argues for other new tense operators.

(2) A child was born who would become ruler of the world.

(3) Joseph said that a child had been born who would become ruler of the world.

(4) Balthazar mentioned that Joseph said that a child was born who would become ruler of the world.

Sentence (2) is not ambiguous, the moment that the child becomes ruler of the world lies in the future of its birth. Sentence (3) is twofold ambiguous: the moment of becoming ruler can be in the future of the birth, but also in Joseph's future. And in (4) the child's becoming rules can even be in Balthazar's future. So the number of ambiguities increases with the length of the sentence. Therefore Hintikka (1983, pp. 276–279) presents (2)–(4) as arguments against compositionality.

6.2.2. Unless

Higginbotham (1986) presents arguments against compositionality; we discuss variants of his examples (from Pelletier, 1994a). In (5) and (6) *unless* has the meaning of a (non-exclusive) disjunction.

(5) John will eat steak unless he eats lobster.

(6) Every person will eat steak unless he eats lobster.

However, in (7) the situation is different.

(7) No person will eat steak unless he eats lobster.

This sentence is to be represented as

(8) [No: person] (x eat steak $\wedge \neg x$ eats lobster).

These examples show that the meaning of *unless* depends on the context of the sentence in which it occurs. Therefore compositionality does not hold.

6.2.3. Any

Hintikka (1983, pp. 266–267) presents several interesting sentences with *any* as challenges to compositionality. Consider

(9) Chris can win any match.

In this sentence it is expressed that for all matches it holds that Chris can win them, so *any* has the impact of a universal quantification. But in (10) it has the impact of an existential quantification.

(10) Jean doesn't believe that Chris can win any match.

Analogously for the pair (11) and (12), and for the pair (13) and (14):

(11) Anyone can beat Chris.

(12) I'd be greatly surprised if anyone can beat Chris.

(13) Chris will beat any opponent.

(14) Chris will not beat any opponent.

All these examples show that the meaning of the English determiner *any* depends on its environment.

The most exciting example is the one given below. As preparation, recall that Tarski required a theory of truth to result in T-schemes for all sentences:

(15) 'ϕ' is true if and only if ϕ is the case.

A classical example of this scheme is:

(16) *Snow is white* is true if and only if snow is white.

The next sentence is a counterexample against one half of the Tarskian T-scheme.

(17) *Anybody can become a millionaire* is true if anybody can become a millionaire.

This sentence happens to be false.

6.3. *Compositional solutions*

6.3.1. *Would*

A compositional analysis of (18) is indeed problematic if we assume that it has to be based on (19), because (18) is ambiguous and (19) is not.

(18) Joseph said that a child had been born who would become ruler of the world.

(19) A child was born who would become ruler of the world.

However, another approach is possible: there may be two derivations for (18). In the reading that 'becoming ruler' lies in the future of Joseph's saying it may have (20) as part.

(20) say that a child was born that will become ruler of the world.

The rule assigning past tense to the main clause should then deal with the 'sequence of tense' in the embedded clause, transforming *will* into *would.* The reading in which the time of becoming ruler lies in the future of the birth could then be obtained by building (18) from:

(21) say that a child was born who would become ruler of the world.

The strategy to obtain compositionality will now be clear: account for the ambiguities by using different derivations. In this way the parts of (18) are not necessarily identical to substrings of the sentences under consideration (the involved tenses may be different). Such an approach is followed for other scope phenomena with tenses in Janssen (1983).

6.3.2. *Unless*

Pelletier (1994a) discusses the arguments of Higginbotham (1986) concerning *unless*, and presents two proposals for a compositional solution.

The first solution is to consider the meaning of *unless* to be one out of a set of two meanings. If it is combined with a positive subject (as in *every person will eat steak unless he eats lobster*) then the meaning 'disjunction' is selected, and when combined with negative subject (as in *no person eats steak unless he eats lobster*) the other meaning is selected. For details of the solution, see Pelletier (1994a). So *unless* is considered as a single word, with a single meaning, offering a choice between two alternatives. In the same way as in Section 2 this can be defined by a function from contexts to values.

The second solution is to consider *unless* a homonym. So there are two words written as *unless*. The first one is $unless_{[-\text{neg}]}$, occurring only with subjects which bear (as is the case for *every person*) the syntactic feature [−neg], and having 'disjunction' as meaning. The second one is $unless_{[+\text{neg}]}$, which has the other meaning. Now *unless* is considered to be two words, each with its own meaning. The syntax determines which combinations are possible.

6.3.3. Any

Hintikka (1983, p. 280) is explicit about the fact that his arguments concerning the non-compositionality of *any*-sentences are based upon specific ideas about their syntactic structure. In particular it is assumed that (22) is a 'component part' of (23)

(22) Anyone can beat Chris.

(23) I'll be greatly surprised if anyone can beat Chris.

He claims that this analysis is in accordance with common sense, and in agreement with the best syntactic analysis. But, as he admits, other analyses cannot be excluded a priori; for instance that (24) is a component of (23).

(24) I'll be greatly surprised if – can beat Chris.

One might even be more radical in the syntax than Hintikka suggests, and introduce a rule that produces (23) from

(25) Someone can beat Chris.

Partee (1984) discusses the challenges of *any*. She shows that the situation is more complicated than suggested by the examples of Hintikka. Sentence (27) has two readings, only one of which can come from (26).

(26) Anyone can solve that problem.

(27) If anyone can solve that problem, I suppose John can.

Partee discusses the literature concerning the context-sensitivity of *any*, and concludes that here are strong arguments for two 'distinct' *any*'s: an *affective any* and a *free-choice any*.The two impose distinct (though overlapping) constraints on the contexts in which their semantic contributions 'make sense'. The constraints on affective *any* can be described in model-theoretic terms, whereas those of the free-choice *any* are less well understood. For references concerning this discussion see Partee (1984).

We conclude that the *any*-examples can be dealt with in a compositional way by distinguishing two *any*'s, with one or both readings eliminated when incompatible with the surrounding context.

6.4. General methods for compositionality

In this section we have encountered three methods to obtain compositionality:

1. New meanings.
   These are formed by the introduction of a new parameter, or alternatively, a function from such a parameter to old meanings. This was the first solution for *unless*.
2. New basic parts.
   Duplicate basic expressions, together with different meanings for the new expressions, or even new categories. This was the solution for *any*, and the second solution for *unless*.

3. New constructions.
   Use unorthodox parts, together with new syntactic rules forming those parts and rules operating on those parts. This approach may result in abstract parts, new categories, and new methods to form compound expressions. This was the solution for the *would* sentences.

For most of counterexamples several of these methods are in principle possible, and a choice must be motivated. That is not an easy task because the methods are not just technical tools to obtain compositionality: they raise fundamental questions concerning the syntax and semantics interface. If meanings include a new parameter, then meanings have this parameter in the entire grammar, and it must be decided what role the parameter plays. If new basic parts are introduced, then each part should have a meaning, and each part is available everywhere. If new constructions are introduced, they can be used everywhere. Other expressions may then be produced in new ways, and new ambiguities may arise. So adopting compositionality raises fundamental questions about what meanings are, what the basic building blocks are and what ways of construction are.

The real question is not whether a certain phenomenon can be analyzed compositionally, as enough methods are available, but what makes the overall theory (un)attractive or (un)acceptable. A case study which follows this line of argument is presented in Appendix B: a study by Partee concerning genitives.

7. Fundamental arguments against compositionality

7.1. Introduction

In the present section we discuss some arguments against compositionality which are not based upon the challenge of finding a compositional solution for certain phenomena, but arguments which concern issues of a more fundamental nature. The examples present the original arguments, immediately followed by discussion.

7.2. Ambiguity

Pelletier presents arguments against compositionality based upon its consequences for the analysis of ambiguities (Pelletier, 1993, 1994b). Some examples are:

(1) Every linguist knows two languages.

(2) John wondered when Alice said she would leave.

(3) The philosophers lifted the piano.

Sentence (1) is ambiguous regarding the total number of languages involved. In (2) the point is whether *when* asks for the time of departure, or the time of Alice's saying this, and in (3) the interpretation differs in whether they did it together or individually.

The above sentences contain no lexical ambiguity, and there are no syntactic arguments to assign them more than one constituent structure. Pelletier (1993) says: 'In order to maintain the Compositionality Principle, theorists have resorted to a number of devices which are all more or less unmotivated (except to maintain the Principle): Montagovian "quantifying-in" rules, "traces", "gaps", "Quantifier Raising", ... features, and many more'.

The issue raised by Pelletier with respect to (1) is a old one, and arises as well for the classical *de dicto – de re* ambiguity of:

(4) John seeks a unicorn.

Because the quantifying-in rules of Montague Grammar involve such a distortion from the surface form, various attempts have been made to avoid them. An influential proposal was to use Cooper storage (Cooper, 1983): the sentence is interpreted compositionally, but the *NP*s (*every linguist* and *two languages*) are exempted. Their interpretations are put in a storage, and can be retrieved out of storage at a suitable moment. The order in which they are retrieved reflects their relative scope. So Cooper storage introduces an interpretation procedure and an intermediate stage in the model. Perhaps it is a compositional process, but it is questionable whether it constitutes a compositional semantics, because of the essential role of the storage mechanism (see Chapter 1 of this Handbook for a discussion).

Other approaches try to eliminate the ambiguity. Linguists have argued that the scope order is the surface order. This is known as 'Jackendoff's principle' (Jackendoff, 1972). It has been said by semanticists that (1) has only one reading, viz. its weakest reading (*every* wide scope), and that the stronger reading is inferred, when additional information is available. Analogously for (4). These two approaches work well for simple sentences, but they are challenged by more complicated sentences in which the surface order is not a possible reading, or where the different scope readings are logically independent. The latest proposal for dealing with scope ambiguities is by means of 'lifting rules'. The meaning of a noun-phrase can, by means of rules, be 'lifted' to a more abstract level, and different levels yield different scope readings (Hendriks, 1993, Chapter 1).

No matter which approach is taken to quantifier scope, the situation remains the same with respect to other examples (as (2) and (3)). They are semantically ambiguous, even though there are no arguments for more than one syntactic structure.

The crucial assumption in Pelletier's arguments is that the derivation of a sentence describes its syntactic structure. But, as is explained in Section 3, this is not correct. The derivation tree specifies which rules are combined in what order and this derivation tree constitutes the input to the meaning assignment function. One should not call something 'syntactic structure' which is not intended as such and then refute it, because the notion so defined does not have the desired properties. The syntactic structure (constituent structure) is determined by the output of the syntactic rules. Different derivational processes may generate one and the same constituent structure, and in this way account for semantic ambiguities.

The distinction between derivation and resulting constituent structure is made in various grammatical theories. In Section 3 is illustrated how the quantifying-in rules in Montague grammar derive the *de re* version of (4) and how the rules produce a syntactic structure that differs formally from the derivation tree. In Tree Adjoining Grammars (TAG's) the different scope readings of (1) differ in the order in which the noun-phrases are substituted in the basic tree for *know*. In transformational grammar the two readings of (2) differ in their derivation: in the reading where *when* asks for the time of leaving, is formed from

(5) John wondered Alice said she would leave *when*.

Another classical example is:

(6) The shooting of the hunters was bloody.

For this sentence transformational grammar derives the two readings from two different sources: one in which *the hunters* is in subject position and one in which it is in object position.

7.3. Ontology

In (Hintikka, 1983, Chapter 10), an extended version of (Hintikka, 1981), the issue of compositionality is discussed. Besides counterexamples to compositionality (most have been considered in Section 6), he presents objections of a fundamental nature.

To illustrate Hintikka's arguments we consider an example involving branching quantifiers.

(7) Every villager has a friend and every townsman has a cousin who are members of the same party.

The meaning representation with branching quantifiers is:

(8)
$$\begin{matrix} \forall x \exists y \\ \\ \forall z \exists u \end{matrix} \Big\rangle M(x, y, z, u).$$

The representation indicates the dependency of the quantifiers: the choice of y depends only x, and of u only on z. Formula (8) is intended as an example from a formal language that does not adhere to compositionality. The information about the dependencies of the quantifiers would be lost in a first-order representation.

As Hintikka says, it is easy to provide a linear representation with compositional interpretation when Skolem functions are used:

(9) $\exists f \exists g \forall x \forall z M(x, f(x), z, g(z)).$

The connection with Hintikka's own (game-theoretical) treatment for (7) is that (9) can be interpreted as saying that Skolem functions exist which codify (partially) the winning strategy in the correlated game (op. cit. p. 281). See Chapter 6 of this Handbook, for more information on game theoretical semantics.

So compositionality can be maintained by replacing the first-order quantifiers by higher-order ones. About this, Hintikka (1983, p. 20) says 'It seems to me that this is the strategy employed by Montague Grammarians, who are in fact strongly committed to compositionality. However, the only way they can hope to abide by it is to make use of higher order conceptualizations. There is a price to be paid however. The higher order entities evoked in this "type theoretical ascent" are much less realistic philosophically and psycholinguistically than our original individuals. Hence the ascent is bound to detract from the psycholinguistic and methodological realism of one theory'. Furthermore (op. cit. p. 283): 'On a more technical level, the unnaturalness of this procedure is illustrated by the uncertainties that are attached to the interpretation of such higher order variables [...]'. Finally, (op. cit. 285): 'Moreover, the first order formulations have other advantages over higher order ones. In first-order languages we can achieve an axiomatization of logical truths and of valid inferences'.

Hintikka is completely right in his description of the attitudes of Montague Grammarians: they use higher-order objects without hesitation if this turns out to be useful. His objection against compositionality is in a nutshell objecting to the higher-order ontology required by compositionality.

Some comments here are in order (the first two originate from Groenendijk and Stokhof, pers. comm.).

1. If first-order analysis is so natural and psychologically realistic, it would be extremely interesting to have an explanation why it took more than two thousand years since Aristotle before the notion 'first order' was introduced by Frege. And it was presented in a notation that differs considerably from our current notation, as it was not linear.
2. It is difficult to see why the first-order notation matters. If there are ontological commitments, then the notions used in the interpretation of the logic, in the metatheory, are crucial, and not the notation itself. It is, for instance difficult to understand why a winning strategy for a game is more natural than a function from objects to objects (cf. Hintikka's comment on (9)).
3. If it is a point of axiomatizability, it would be interesting to have an axiomatization of game theoretical semantics. As concerns intensional logic, one might use generalized models; with respect to these models there is an axiomatization even for the case of higher-order logic (Gallin, 1975).

7.4. Synonymy

Pelletier discusses problems raised by the substitution of synonyms in belief-contexts (Pelletier, 1993, 1994b). Consider:

(10) Dentists usually need to hire an attorney.

(11) Tooth doctors commonly require the professional services of a lawyer.

Suppose that these two sentences are synonymous. If we assume that (12) and (13) are formed from respectively (10) and (11) by the same rules, then compositionality implies that (12) and (13) are synonymous.

(12) Kim believes that dentists usually need to hire an attorney.

(13) Kim believes that tooth doctors commonly require the professional services of a lawyer.

However, it easy to make up some story in which Kim believes the embedded sentence in (12), but not the one in (13). Pelletier formulates the following dilemma: either one has to state that (10) and (11) are not synonymous, and conclude that there are no synonymous sentences at all in natural language, or one has to give up compositionality.

Let us consider the situation in more detail. The standard model theoretic semantics says that the extension of *dentist* is a set of individuals; dependent on possible world and the time under consideration. So the meaning of *dentist* is a function from possible worlds and times. For most speakers the meaning of *tooth doctor* is the same function as for *dentist*. The source of the problem raised by Pelletier is that for Kim these meaning functions for *dentist* and *tooth doctor* might differ. This shows that the standard meaning notion is an abstraction that does not take into account that for someone the generally accepted synonymy might not hold. In order to account for this, the meaning function can be given the involved individual an additional argument. Then (10) and (11) are no longer synonymous, nor are (12) and (13). Thus there is no problem for compositionality: we have just found an additional factor.

Are we now claiming that, upon closer inspection, there are no synonymous sentences? The synonymy of belief-sentences is an old issue, and there is a lot of literature about it; for references see Partee (1982) and Salmon and Soames (1988). It seems that Mates (1950) already showed that almost any difference in the embedded clauses makes belief-sentences non-synonymous. But there are several cases of constructional (non-lexical) synonymy. Examples are (14) and (15), and (from Partee, 1982) sentences (16) and (17).

(14) Kim believes that John gives Mary a book.

(15) Kim believes that John gives a book to Mary.

(16) Mary believes that for John to leave now would be a mistake.

(17) Mary believes that it would be a mistake for John to leave now.

7.5. *Psychology*

An argument often put forward in defense of compositionality concerns its psychological motivation. The principle explains how a person can *understand* sentences he has never heard before (see also Sections 1.2 and 1.3). This psychological explanation is an important ingredient of the Gricean theory of meaning. However, this motivation for compositionality is rejected by Schiffer (1987). On the one hand he argues that compositionality is not needed in order to give an explanation for that power. On the other hand, he argues that such a compositional approach does not work. We will restrict our attention to this aspect of his book.

A compositional semantic analysis of

(18) Tanya believes that Gustav is a dog

assumes that belief is a relation between Tanya and some kind of proposition. There are several variants of the propositional theory of belief, some more representational, others more semantic. For all variants of these theories, Schiffer argues that they meet serious problems when they have to explain how Tanya might correctly come to the belief expressed in (18). As examples, we will consider two cases of semantic theories in which the proposition says that Gustav has the property of doghood (Schiffer, 1987, pp. 56–57). One approach is that doghood is defined by more or less observable properties. Then the problem arises that these properties are neither separately necessary, nor jointly sufficient, for being a dog. We might learn, for instance, that under illusive circumstances dogs do not have a doggy appearance. As Schiffer remarks, this theory was already demolished by Kripke (1972), and replaced by a theory which says that doghood means being an element of a natural kind. This kind most reasonably is the species 'Canis familiaris'. Membership of this kind is determined by some complex genetic property and it is not something we are directly acquainted with. Now suppose that we encounter a race of dogs we do not recognize as such, and decide that 'shmog' stands for any creature of the same biological species as those creatures. Then (18) can be true, while (19) is false because Tanya may fail to believe that shmogs are dogs.

(19) Tanya believes that Gustav is a shmog.

But in the explanation with natural kinds, the sentences have the same content.

Since none of the theories offer a plausible account of the role that *dog* plays in (18), there is no plausible account of the proposition that is supposed to be the content of Tanya's belief. Therefore there is nothing from which the meaning of (18) can be formed compositionally, so compositionality is not met.

Partee (1988) discusses Schiffer's arguments against compositionality, and I fully agree with her opinion that Schiffer does not make a sufficient distinction between semantic facts and psychological facts. There is a fundamental difference between semantic facts concerning belief contexts (as implication and synonymy), and questions that come closer to psychological processes (how can a person sincerely utter such a sentence). What Shiffer showed was that problems arise if one attempts to connect semantic theories with the relation between human beings and their language. Partee points out the analogy between these problems with belief and those with the semantics of proper names (how can one correctly use proper names without being acquainted with the referent). The latter is discussed and explained by Kripke (1972). Partee proposes to solve the problems of belief along the same lines. Her paper is followed by the reaction of Schiffer (Schiffer, 1988). However, he does not react to this suggestion, nor to the main point: that a semantic theory is to be distinguished from a psychological theory.

7.6. Flexibility

Partee argues that a finite complete compositional semantics that really deals with natural language is not possible (Partee, 1982, 1988). The reason is that compositional semantic theories are based upon certain simplifying assumptions concerning language, such as a closed language, closed world, a fixed set of semantic primitives and a fixed conceptual frame for the language users. The limitations of model theoretic semantics become clear when the relation is considered between the semantic theory and all the factors that play a role in the interpretation of natural language. The following cases can be distinguished.

1. For some parts of language the meaning can correctly be described as rigidly as just characterized. Examples are words like *and* and *rectangle*.
2. For other parts the semantics is jointly determined by the language users and the way the world is. The language users are only partially acquainted with the meanings. Examples are proper names and natural kinds.
3. There are parts of language where the speaker and hearer have to arrive at a mutually agreed interpretation. Examples are compounds like *boat train* and genitives like *John's team*, the resolution of demonstrative pronouns, and most lexical items.
4. For certain theory dependent terms, i.e. words like *socialism* or *semantics*, there is no expectation of the existence of a 'right' or 'best' interpretation. These terms constitute the main argument in (Partee, 1982).

Partee's position is the following. Compositional model-theoretic semantics is possible and important, but one should understand the limits of what it can do. In a system of compositional semantics the flexibility of language is abstracted away. Therefore it is too rigid to describe the real life process of communication, and limits the description of language users to creatures or machines whose minds are much more narrowly and rigidly circumscribed than those of human beings. This underscores the argument (mentioned above in the Section 7.5) that a theory of natural language semantics should be distinguished from a theory of natural language understanding.

The arguments of Partee describe limitations of the compositional possible world semantics. But most limitations are, in my opinion, just temporary, and not essential. There are several methods to deal compositionally with factors such as personal differences, linguistic context, situational context or vagueness. One may use additional parameters (as in Section 7.2 on ambiguity), context constants or variables (see Appendix B on genitives), the influence from discourse can be treated compositionally (see Section 4.4 on DRT), and vagueness by fuzzy logic. And if for some technical terms speaker and hearer have to come to agreement, and practically nothing can be said in general about their meaning, then we have not reached the limits of compositionality, but the limits of semantics (as is the title of Partee, 1982).

8. A mathematical model of compositionality

8.1. Introduction

In this section a mathematical model is developed that describes the essential aspects of compositional meaning assignment. The assumptions leading to this model have been discussed in Section 3. The model is closely related to the one presented in 'Universal Grammar' (Montague, 1970b). The mathematical tools used in this section are tools from *Universal Algebra*, a branch of mathematics that deals with general structures; a standard textbook is Graetzer (1979). For easy reference, the principle is repeated here:

> The meaning of a compound expression is a function of the meanings of its parts and of the syntactic rule by which they are combined.

8.2. *Algebra*

The first notion to be considered is *parts*. Since the information on how expressions are formed is given by the syntax of a language, the rules of the grammar determine what the parts of an expression are. The rules build new expressions from old expressions, so they are operators taking inputs and yielding an output. A syntax with this kind of rules is a specific example of what is called in mathematics an *algebra*. Informally stated, an algebra is a set with functions defined on that set. After the formal definitions some examples will be given.

DEFINITION 8.1. An *algebra* $\mathcal{A}$, consists of a set A called the *carrier* of the algebra, and a set F of functions defined on that set and yielding values in that set. So $\mathcal{A} = \langle A, F\rangle$. The elements of the carrier are called the *elements* of the algebra. Instead of the name function, often the name *operator* is used. If an operator is not defined on the whole carrier, it is called a *partial operator*. If $E = F(E_1, E_2, \ldots, E_n)$, then $E_1, E_2, \ldots$, and E_n are called *parts* of E. If an operator takes n arguments, it is called an *n-ary operator*.

The notion *set* is a very general notion, and so is the notion *algebra* which has a set as one of its basic ingredients. This abstractness makes algebras suitable models for compositionality, because it is abstracted from the particular grammatical theory. Three examples of a completely different nature will be considered.

1. The algebra $\langle \mathbf{N}, \{+, \times\}\rangle$ of natural numbers $\{1, 2, 3, \ldots\}$, with addition and multiplication as operators.
2. The set of trees (constituent structures) and the operation of making a new tree from two old ones by giving them a common root.
3. The carrier of the algebra consists of the words *boy, girl, apple, pear, likes, takes, the* and all possible strings that can be formed from them. There are two partial defined operations. R_{Def} forms from a common noun a noun-phrase by adding the article *the*. R_S forms a sentence from two noun-phrases and a verb. Examples of sentences are *The boy likes the apple* and *The pear takes the girl*.

In order to avoid the misconception that anything is an algebra, finally a *non*-example. Take the third algebra (finite strings of words with concatenation), and add an operator that counts the length of a string. This not an algebra any more, since the lengths (natural numbers) are not elements of the algebra.

8.3. *Generators*

Next we will define a subclass of the algebras, viz. the finitely generated algebras. To give an example, consider the subset $\{1\}$ in the algebra $\langle \mathbf{N}, \{+\}\rangle$ of natural numbers. By application of the operator $+$ to elements in this subset, that is by calculating $1 + 1$, one gets 2. Then 3 can be produced (by $2 + 1$, or $1 + 2$), and in this way the whole carrier can be obtained. Therefore the subset $\{1\}$ is called *a generating set* for this algebra. Since this algebra has a finite generating set, it is called a finitely generated algebra. If we have in the same algebra the subset $\{2\}$, then only the even numbers can be formed. Therefore the subset $\{2\}$ is *not* a generating subset of the algebra of natural numbers. On the other hand, the even numbers form an algebra, and $\{2\}$ is a generating set for that algebra. More generally, any subset is generating set for some algebra. This can be seen as follows. If one starts with some set, and adds all elements that can be produced from the given set and from already produced elements, then one gets a set that is closed under the given operators. Hence it is an algebra.

DEFINITION 8.2. Let $\mathcal{A} = \langle A, F\rangle$ be an algebra, and H be a subset of A. Then $\langle [H], F\rangle$ denotes the smallest algebra containing H, and is called the by H *generated algebra*. If $\langle [H], F\rangle = \langle A, F\rangle$, then H is called a generating set for $\mathcal{A}$. The elements of H are called *generators*. If H is finite, then $\mathcal{A}$ is called a *finitely generated* algebra.

The first example in Section 8.2 is a finitely generated algebra because

$$\langle \mathbf{N}, \{+, \times\}\rangle = \langle [\{1\}], \{+, \times\}\rangle.$$

The last example (with the set of strings over a lexicon) is finitely generated: the lexicon is the generating set. An algebra that is not finitely generated is $\langle \mathbf{N}, \{\times\}\rangle$, the natural numbers with multiplication (it is generated by the set of prime numbers).

A grammar that is suitable for a compositional meaning assignment has to be a generated algebra. Furthermore, some criterion is needed to select certain elements of the algebra as the generated language. For instance the expressions that are output of certain rules, or (if the grammar generates tree like structures) the elements with root labeled S.

DEFINITION 8.3. A compositional grammar is a pair $\langle \mathcal{A}, S\rangle$, where $\mathcal{A}$ is a generated algebra $\langle A, F\rangle$, and S a selection predicate that selects a subset of A, so $S(A) \subseteq A$.

8.4. *Terms*

In Section 3 it was argued that the *way of production* is crucial for the purpose of meaning assignment. Therefore it is useful to have a representation for such a production process or derivational history. In Section 3 we represented such a derivation by means of a tree. That is not the standard format. Let us first consider the linguistic example given in Section 8.2. By application of the operator R_{Def} to the noun *apple*, the noun phrase *the apple* is formed, and likewise *the boy* is formed by application of R_{Def} to *boy*. Next the operator R_S is applied to the just formed noun phrases and the verb *like*, yielding the sentence *the boy likes the apple*. This process is described by the following expression (sequence of symbols):

(1) $R_S\langle R_{\text{Def}}\langle boy\rangle, R_{\text{Def}}\langle apple\rangle, like\rangle.$

Such expressions are called *terms*. There is a simple relation of the terms to the elements in the original algebra. For instance, with the term $R_{\text{Def}}\langle apple\rangle$ corresponds an element which is found by evaluating the term (i.e. executing the operator on its arguments), viz. the string *the apple*. In principle, different terms may evaluate to the same element, and the evaluation of a term usually is very different from the term itself. Terms can be combined to form new terms: the term (1) above, is formed from the terms $R_{\text{Def}}\langle \textit{apple} \rangle$, $R_{\text{Def}}\langle \textit{boy} \rangle$ and *like*. Thus the terms over an algebra form an algebra themselves.

DEFINITION 8.4. Let $\mathcal{B} = \langle [B], F \rangle$ be an algebra. The set of *terms* over $\mathcal{B} = \langle [B], F \rangle$, denoted as $T_{B,F}$, is defined as follows:

1. For each element in B there is a new symbol $b \in T_{B,F}$.
2. For every operator in F there is a new symbol f. If f corresponds with a n-ary operator and $t_1, t_2, \ldots, t_n \in T_{B,F}$, then $f\langle t_1, t_2, \ldots, t_n \rangle \in T_{B,F}$.

The terms over $\mathcal{B} = \langle [B], F \rangle$ form an algebra with as operators combinations of terms according to the operators of $\mathcal{B}$. This algebra is called the *term algebra* over $\langle [B], F \rangle$. This term algebra is denoted $\mathcal{T}_{B,F}$, or shortly $\mathcal{T}_{\mathcal{B}}$.

In Section 3 it was argued that, according to the principle of compositionality of meaning, the derivation of an expression determines its meaning. Hence the meaning assignment is a function defined on the term algebra.

8.5. *Homomorphisms*

The principle of compositionality does not only tell us on which objects the meaning is defined (terms), but also in which way this has to be done. Suppose we have an expression obtained by application of operation f to arguments $a_1, \ldots, a_n$. Then its translation in algebra $\mathcal{B}$ should be obtained from the translations of its parts, hence by application of an operator g (corresponding with f) to the translations of $a_1, \ldots, a_n$. So, if we let Tr denote the translation function, we have

$$Tr\big(f\langle a_1, \ldots, a_n \rangle\big) = g\big(Tr(a_1), \ldots, Tr(a_n)\big).$$

Such a mapping is called a *homomorphism*. Intuitively speaking, a homomorphism h from an algebra $\mathcal{A}$ to algebra $\mathcal{B}$ is a mapping which respects the structure of $\mathcal{A}$ in the following way. If in $\mathcal{A}$ an element a is obtained by means of application of an operator f, then the image of a is obtained in $\mathcal{B}$ by application of an operator corresponding with f. The structural difference that may arise between $\mathcal{A}$ and $\mathcal{B}$ is that two distinct elements of $\mathcal{A}$ may be mapped to the same element of $\mathcal{B}$, and that two distinct operators of $\mathcal{A}$ may correspond with the same operator in $\mathcal{B}$.

DEFINITION 8.5. Let $\mathcal{A} = \langle A, F \rangle$ and $\mathcal{B} = \langle B, G \rangle$ be algebras. A mapping $h : \mathcal{A} \to \mathcal{B}$ is called a *homomorphism* if there is a mapping $h' : F \to G$ such that for all $f \in F$ and all $a_1, \ldots, a_n \in A$ holds $h(f(a_1, \ldots, a_n)) = h'(f)(h(a_1), \ldots, h(a_n))$.

Now that the notions 'terms' and 'homomorphisms' are introduced, all ingredients are present needed to formalize 'compositional meaning assignment'.

> A compositional meaning assignment for a language A in a model B is obtained by designing an algebra $\langle [G], F \rangle$ as syntax for A, an algebra $\langle [H], F \rangle$ for B, and by letting the meaning assignment be a homomorphism from the term algebra T_A to $\langle [H], G \rangle$.

8.6. *Polynomials*

Usually the meaning assignment is not directly given, but indirectly via a translation into a logical language. In Section 5 it is explained that the standard way to do this is by using polynomials. Here the algebraic background of this method will be investigated.

First the definition. A polynomial is term with variables, so

DEFINITION 8.6. Let $\mathcal{B} = \langle [B], F \rangle$ be an algebra. The set $Pol^n_{\langle [B],F \rangle}$ – *shortly* Pol^n – of *n-ary polynomial symbols*, or n-ary polynomials, over the algebra $\langle [B], F \rangle$ is defined as follows:

1. For every element in B there is a new symbol (a constant) $b \in Pol^n$.
2. For every i, with $1 \leqslant i \leqslant n$, there is a variable $x_i \in Pol^n$.
3. For every operator in F there is a new symbol. If f corresponds with a n-ary operator, and $p_1, p_2, \ldots, p_n \in Pol^n$ then also $f(p_1, p_2, \ldots, p_n) \in Pol^n$.

The set $Pol_{\langle [B],F \rangle}$ of *polynomial symbols* over algebra $\langle [B], F \rangle$ is defined as the union for all n of the n-ary polynomial symbols, shortly $Pol = \bigcup_n Pol^n$.

A polynomial symbol $p \in Pol^n$ defines an n-ary polynomial operator; its value for n given arguments is obtained by evaluating the term that is obtained by replacing x_1 by the first argument x_2 by the second, etc.

Given an algebra $\langle [B], F \rangle$ and a set P of polynomials over A, we obtain a new algebra $\langle [B], P \rangle$ by replacing the original set of operators by the polynomial operators. An algebra obtained in this way is a *polynomially derived algebra.*

If an operation is added to a given logic, it should be an operation on meanings. In other words, whatever the interpretation of the logic is, the new operator should have a unique semantic interpretation. This is expressed in the definition below, where h is a compositional meaning assignment to the original algebra, and h' describes the interpretation of new operators.

DEFINITION 8.7. Let $\langle [A], F \rangle$ be an algebra. A collection of operators G is called *safe* if for all algebras $\mathcal{B}$ and all surjective homomorphisms h from $\mathcal{A}$ onto $\mathcal{B}$ holds that there is a unique algebra $\mathcal{B}'$ such that the restriction h' of h to the elements of $\langle [A], G \rangle$ is a surjective homomorphism.

This definition is illustrated in Figure 5.

THEOREM 8.8 (Montague, 1970b). *Polynomial operators are safe.*

PROOF (*sketch*). Mimic the polynomial operators in the homomorphic image. □

There are of course other methods to define operations on logic, but safeness is then not guaranteed. Examples are

- Replaces all occurrences of x by y.
  There is no semantic interpretation for this operator because some of the new y's may become bound. So there is no algebra $\mathcal{B}'$ in the sense of the above theorem.

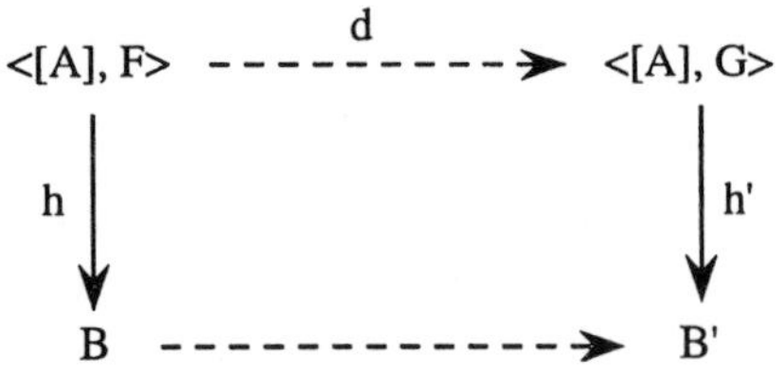

Fig. 5. G is safe if for all $\mathcal{B}$ there is a unique $\mathcal{B}'$ such that h', the restriction of h, is a surjective homomorphism.

- Replace all existential quantifiers by universal ones.
  For equivalent formulas (e.g., where one formula has $\forall$ and the other $\neg\exists\neg$) non-equivalent results are obtained.
- Recursion on the length of a formula.
  In the model for logic the notion length has no interpretation, hence the recursion is not well-founded in the model.

In Section 5 several examples were given which show that it is advisable to use only polynomial defined operators. This is not a restriction of the expressive power, as follows from the next theorem.

THEOREM 8.9. *Let $\langle A, F\rangle$ be an algebra with infinitely many generators, and G a collection of safe operators over $\langle A, F\rangle$. Then all elements of G are polynomially definable.*

PROOF. A proof for this theorem is given by Van Benthem (1979), and for many sorted algebras by F. Wiedijk in (Janssen, 1986a). □

Theorem 8.9 is important for applications since it justifies the restriction to polynomially defined operators. Suppose one introduces a new operator, then either it is safe, and polynomially definable, or it is not safe, and consequently should not be used. In applications the requirement of infinitely many generators is not a real restriction, since the logic usually has indexed variables $x_1, x_2, x_3, \ldots$. Furthermore it is claimed (Wiedijk pers. comm.) that the theorem holds for any algebra with at least two generators.

We may summarize the section by giving the formalization of the principle of compositionality of meaning.

> Let L be some language. A compositional meaning assignment to L is obtained as follows. We design for L a compositional grammar $\mathcal{A} = \langle\langle A_L, F_L\rangle, S_L\rangle$, and a compositional grammar $\mathcal{B} = \langle\langle B, G\rangle, S_B\rangle$ to represent the meanings, where B has a homomorphic interpretation in some model M. The meaning assignment for L is defined by a homomorphism on from T_A to an algebra that is polynomially derived from $\mathcal{B}$.

8.7. *Past and future of the model*

The algebraic framework presented here is almost the same as the one developed by Montague in Universal Grammar (Montague, 1970b). That article was written in a time that the mathematical theory of universal algebra was rather young (the first edition of the main textbook in the field (Graetzer, 1979) originates from 1968). The notions used in this section are the notions that are standard nowadays, and differ at some cases from the ones used by Montague. For instance, he uses a 'disambiguated language', where we use a 'term algebra', notions which, although closely related, differ not only by name. The algebraic model developed by Montague turned out to be the same as the model used in computer science in the approach to semantics called *initial algebra semantics* (Goguen, Thatcher and Wagner, 1978), as was noticed by Janssen and Van Emde Boas (1981).

Universal algebra became an important tool in computer science, and there the notions from universal algebra were refined further. Since concepts such as coercion, overloading, subtyping and modularization play a role not only in computer science, but also in natural language semantics, the model presented in this section can be refined further. For instance, in linguistic applications the involved algebra always is a many sorted algebra (Goguen, Thatcher, Wagner and Wright, 1977), and an order sorted algebra (Goguen and Diaconescu, 1994) seems a very appropriate concept to cover the linguistic concept of 'subcategorization'. Of course, the algebras have to be computable (see, e.g., Bergstra and Tucker, 1987). In Section 9.5 a restriction will be proposed that reduces the compositional grammars to parsible ones. Further, one might consider the consequences of partial rules. An overview of developments concerning universal algebra in computer science is given in (Wirsing, 1990). Montague's framework is redesigned using many sorted algebras in (Janssen, 1986a, 1986b); that framework is developed further for dealing with flexibility in (Hendriks, 1993).

9. The formal power of compositionality

9.1. Introduction

In the present section the power of the framework with respect to the generated language and the assigned meanings will be investigated. It will be shown that on the one hand compositionality is restrictive in the sense that, in some circumstances, a compositional analysis is impossible. On the other hand it will be shown that compositionality does not restrict the class of languages that can be analyzed, nor the meanings that can be assigned. Finally a restriction will be considered that guarantees recursiveness.

9.2. Not every grammar can be used

In the preceding sections examples are given which illustrate that not every grammar is suitable for a compositional meaning assignment. The example below gives a formal underpinning of this. A grammar for a language is given, together with the meanings for its expressions. It is proven that it is not possible to assign the given meanings in a compositional way to the given grammar.

EXAMPLE 9.1. The basic expressions are the digits: $\{0, 1, 2, 3, 4, 5, 6, 7, 8, 9\}$. There are two operations in the algebra. The first one makes from a digit a number name and is defined by $G_1(d) = d$. The second one makes from a digit and a number name a new number name by writing the digit in front of the number name: $G_2(d, n) = dn$. So $G_2(2, G_1(3)) = G_2(2, 3) = 23$, and $G_2(0, G_1(6)) = G_2(0, 6) = 06$. The meaning of an expression is the natural number it denotes, so 007 has the same meaning as 7. This meaning function is denoted by M.

FACT 9.2. *There is no function F such that $M(G_2(a, b)) = F(M(a), M(b))$.*

PROOF. Suppose that there was such an operation F. Since $M(7) = M(007)$, we would have

$$M(27) = M(G_2(2, 7)) = F(M(2), M(7)) = F(M(2), M(007))$$

$$= M(G_2(2, 007)) = M(2007).$$

This is a contradiction. Hence no such operation F can exist. □

This result is from (Janssen, 1986a); in (Zadrozny, 1994) a weaker result is proved, viz. that there does not exist a polynomial F with the required property.

A compositional treatment can be obtained by changing rule G_2. The digit should be written at the end of the already obtained number: $G_3(d, n) = nd$. Then there is a corresponding semantic operation F defined by $F(d, n) = 10 \times n + d$, for instance $M(07) = M(G_3(7, 0) = F(M(7), M(0)) = 10 \times M(0) + M(7)$. So a compositional assignment of the intended meaning is possible, but requires another syntax. This illustrates that compositionality becomes possible if semantic considerations influence the design of the syntactic rules.

9.3. *Power from syntax*

The next theme is the (generative) power of compositional grammars and of compositional meaning assignment. In this section we will consider the results of (Janssen, 1986a), and in the next section those of (Zadrozny, 1994).

In the theorem below it is proved that any recursively enumerable language can be generated by a compositional grammar. The recursively enumerable languages form the class of languages which can be generated by the most powerful kinds of grammars (unrestricted rewriting systems, transformational grammars, Turing machine languages etc.), or, more generally, by any kind of algorithm. Therefore, the theorem shows that if a language can be generated by any algorithm, it can be generated by a compositional grammar. The proof exploits the freedom of compositionality to choose some suitable grammar. The basic idea is that the rules of the grammar (operations of the algebra) can simulate a Turing Machine.

THEOREM 9.3. *Any recursively enumerable language can be generated by a compositional grammar.*

PROOF. In order to prove the theorem, we will simulate a nondeterministic Turing machine of the following type. The machine operates on a tape that has a beginning but no end, and it starts on an empty tape with its read/write head placed on the initial blank. The machine acts on the basis of its memory state and of the symbol read by the head. It may move right (R), left (L) or print a symbol, together with a change of memory state. Two examples of instructions are

I_1: $q_1 s q_2 R$(= if the Turing machine reads in state q_1 an s, then its state changes in q_2 and its head moves to the right).

I_2: $q_1 s q_2 t$(= if the Turing machine reads in state q_1 an s, then its state changes in q_2 and it writes an t).

The machine halts when no instruction is applicable. Then the string of symbols on the tape (neglecting the blanks) is the generated string. The set of all the strings the nondeterministic machine can generate, is the generated language.

A compositional grammar is of another nature than a Turing Machine. A grammar does not work with infinite tapes, and it has no memory. These features can be encoded by a finite string in the following way. In any stage of the calculations, the head of the Turing machine has passed only a finite number of positions on the tape. That finite string determines the whole tape, since the remainder is filled with blanks. The current memory state is inserted as an extra symbol in the string on a position to the left of the symbol that is currently scanned by the head. Such strings are elements of the algebra.

Each instruction of the Turing machine will be mimicked by an operation of the algebra. This will be shown below for the two examples mentioned before. Besides this, some additional operations are needed: operations that add additional blanks to the string if the head stands on the last symbol on the right and has to move to the right, and operations that remove at the end of the calculations the state symbol and the blanks from the string. These additional operations will not be described in further detail.

I_1: The corresponding operator F_1 is defined for strings of the form $w_1 q s w_2$ where w_1 and w_2 are arbitrary strings consisting of symbols from the alphabet and blanks. The effect of F_1 is defined by $F_1(w_1 q_1 s w_2) = w_1 s q_2 w_2$.

I_2: The corresponding operator F_2 is defined for strings of the form $F_2(w_1 q_1 s w_2) = w_1 q_2 t w_2$.

Since the algebra imitates the Turing machine, the generated language is the same. □

The above result can be extended to meanings. The theorem below says that any meaning can be assigned to any language in a compositional way.

THEOREM 9.4 (Any language, any meaning). *Let L be a recursively enumerable language, and $M : L \to D$ a computable function of the expressions of L into D. Then there are algebras for L and D with computable operations such that M is an homomorphism.*

PROOF. In the proof of Theorem 9.3 the existence is proven of an algebra $\mathcal{A}$ as syntax for the source language L. A variant $\mathcal{A}'$ of $\mathcal{A}$ is taken as grammar for L: the rules produce strings that end with a single #-sign, and an additional rule, say $R_{\#}$ removes that #. For the semantic algebra a copy of $\mathcal{A}'$ is taken, but instead of $R_{\#}$ there is a rule R_M that performs the meaning assignment M. Since M is computable, so is R_M. The syntactic rules of $\mathcal{A}'$ extended with $R_\#$ are in a one to one correspondence with the rules of $\mathcal{A}'$ extended with R_M. Hence the meaning assignment is an homomorphism. □

9.4. *Power from semantics*

Zadrozny proves that any semantics can be dealt with in a compositional way. He takes a version of compositionality that is most intuitive: in the syntax only concatenation of strings is used. On the other hand, he exploits the freedom to use unorthodox meanings. Let us quote his theorem (Zadrozny, 1994):

THEOREM 9.5. *Let M be an arbitrary set. Let A be an arbitrary alphabet. Let "$\cdot$" be a binary operation, and let S be the set closure of A under "$\cdot$". Let $m : S \to M$ be an arbitrary function. Then there is a set of functions M^* and a unique map $\mu : S \to M^*$ such that for all $s, t \in S$*

$$\mu(s.t) = \mu(s)(\mu(t)) \quad \textit{and} \quad \mu(s)(s) = m(s).$$

The first equality says that μ obeys compositionality, and the second equality says that from $\mu(s)$ the originally given meaning can be retrieved. The proof roughly proceeds as follows. The requirement of compositionality is formulated by an infinite set of equations concerning μ. Then a basic lemma from non-wellfounded set theory is evoked, the *solution lemma*. It guarantees that there is a unique solution for this set of equations – in non-wellfounded set theory. This non-wellfounded set theory is a recently developed model for set theory in which the axiom of foundation does not hold. Zadrozny claims that the result also holds if the involved functions are restricted to computable ones.

On the syntactic side this result is very attractive. It formalizes the intuitive version of compositionality: in the syntax there is concatenation of visible parts. However it remains to be investigated for which class of languages this result holds; with a partially defined computable concatenation operation, in any case, only recursive languages can be generated.

Zadrozny claims that the result also holds if the language is not specified by a (partial) concatenation operation, but by a Turing Machine. However, then the attractiveness of the result disappears (the intuitive form of compositionality), and the same result is obtained as described in the previous section (older and with standard mathematics).

On the semantic side some doubts can be raised. The given original meanings are encoded using non wellfounded sets. It is strange that synonymous sentences get different meanings. Furthermore it is unclear, given two meanings, how to define a useful entailment relation among them.

In spite of these critical comments, the result is a valuable contribution to the discussion of compositionality. It shows that if we restrict the syntax considerably, but are very liberal in the semantics, a lot more is possible than expected. In this way the result is complementary to the results in the previous section. Together the results of Janssen and Zadrozny illustrate that without constraints on syntax and semantics, there are no counterexamples to compositionality. This gives the pleasant feeling that a compositional treatment is somehow always possible.

It has been suggested that restrictions should be proposed because compositionality is now a vacuous principle. That is not the opinion of this author. The challenge of compositional semantics is not to prove the existence of such a semantics, but to obtain one. The formal results do no help in this respect because the proofs of the theorems assume that some meaning assigning function is already given, and then turn it into a compositional one. Compositionality is not vacuous, because we have no recipe to obtain a compositional meaning assignment, and because several proposals are ruled out by the principle. Restrictions should therefore have another motivation. The challenge of semantics is to design a function that assigns meanings, and the present paper argues that the best method is to do so in a compositional way. Compositionality is not an empirical principle, but a methodological one.

9.5. *Restriction to recursiveness*

In this section a restriction will be discussed that reduces the generative capacity of compositional grammar to recursive sets. The idea is to use rules that are reversible. If a rule is used to generate an expression, the reverse rule can be used to parse that expression. Let us consider an example.

Suppose that there is a rule specified by $R_1(\alpha, \beta, \gamma) = \alpha\ \beta s\ \gamma$. So:

$$R_1(\textit{every man, love, a woman}) = \textit{every man loves a woman}.$$

The idea is to introduce a rule R_1^{-1} such that

$$R_1^{-1}(\textit{every man loves a woman}) = \langle \textit{every man, love, a woman} \rangle.$$

In a next stage other reverse rules might investigate whether the first element of this tuple is a possible noun phrase, whether the second element is a transitive verb, and whether the third element is a noun phrase. A specification of R_1^{-1} might be: find a word ending on an s, consider the expression before the verb as the first element, the verb (without the s) as the second, and the expression after the verb as the third element. Using reverse rules, a parsing procedure can easily be designed.

The following complications may arise with R_1^{-1} or with another rule:

- **Ill-formed input**
  The input of the parsing process might be a string that is not a correct sentence, e.g., *John runs Mary*. Then the given specification of R_1^{-1} is applicable. It is not attractive to make the rule so restrictive that it cannot be applied to ill-formed sentences, because then rule R_1^{-1} would be as complicated as the whole grammar.
- **Applicable on several positions**
  An application of R_1^{-1} (with the given specification) to *The man who seeks Mary loves Suzy* can be applied both to *seeks*, and to *loves*. The information that *the man who* is not a noun-phrase can only be available when the rules for noun-phrase

formation are considered. As in the previous case, it is not attractive to make the formulation of R_1^{-1} that restrictive that is is only applicable to well-formed sentence.

- **Infinitely many sources**
A rule may remove information that is crucial for the reversion. Suppose that a rule deletes all words after the first word of the sentence. Then for a given output, there is an infinite collection of strings that has to be considered as possible inputs.

The above points illustrate that the reverse rule cannot be an inverse function in the mathematical sense. In order to account for the first two points, it is allowed that the reverse rule yields a set of expressions. In order to avoid the last point, it is required that it is a finite set.

Requiring that there is a reverse rule, is not sufficient to obtain a parsing algorithm. For instance, it may be the case the $y \in R_1^{-1}(y)$, and a loop arises. In order to avoid this, it is required that all the rules form expressions which are more complex (in some sense) than their inputs, and that the reverse rule yields expressions that are less complex than the input. Now there is a guarantee that the process of reversion terminates.

The above considerations lead to two restrictions on compositional grammars which together guarantee recursiveness of the generated language. The restrictions are a generalization of the ones in (Landsbergen, 1981), and provide the basis of the parsing algorithm of the machine translation system 'Rosetta' (see Rosetta, 1994) and of the parsing algorithm in (Janssen, 1989).

1. **Reversibility**
For each rule R there is a reverse rule R^{-1} such that
(a) For all y the set $R^{-1}(y)$ is finite.
(b) $y = R(x_1, x_2, \ldots, x_n)$ if and only if $\langle x_1, x_2, \ldots, x_n\rangle \in R^{-1}(y)$.
2. **Measure condition**
There is a computable function μ that assigns to an expression a natural number: its measure. Furthermore
(a) If $y = R(x_1, x_2, \ldots, x_n)$, then $\mu(y) > \max(\mu(x_1), \mu(x_2,), \ldots, \mu(x_n))$.
(b) If $\langle x_1, x_2, \ldots, x_n\rangle \in R^{-1}(y)$, then $\mu(y) > \max(\mu(x_1), \mu(x_2,), \ldots, \mu(x_n))$.

Assume a given grammar together with reverse rules and a computable measure condition. A parsing algorithm for M-grammars can be based upon the above two restrictions. Condition 1 makes it possible to find, given the output of a generative rule, potential inputs for the rule. Condition 2 guarantees termination of the recursive application of this search process. So the languages generated by grammars satisfying the requirements are decidable languages. Note that the grammar in the proof of Theorem 9.3 does not satisfy the requirements, since there is no sense in which the complexity increases, if the head moves to the right or the left.

10. Other applications of compositionality

10.1. Semantics of programming languages

In this section some issues that emerge in semantics of computer science are addressed because they are interesting as regards compositionality.

Environments
In most programming languages names (identifiers) have to be declared: their type has to be stated, in some cases they have to be initialized. Such names can only be used within a certain range: the scope of their declaration. Identifiers with a certain declaration can be hidden temporarily by a new declaration for the same identifier. So the meaning of an identifier depends on the context in which it arises.

Denotational Semantics (Stoy, 1977; De Bakker, 1980; Mosses, 1990, p. 586) follows the methods of logic, and has compositionality therefore as a fundamental principle. In this approach an abstraction is used by which a compositional meaning assignment becomes possible. The notion 'environment' encodes which declarations are valid on a certain moment, and the meaning of an identifier depends on (is a function of) the environment. So the same statement can get another effect, depending on the environment with respect to which it is evaluated. Thus they practiced a strategy discussed in Sections 2 and 7.

Jumps and continuations
Some programming languages have the instruction to jump to some other part of the program text. The effect of the jump instruction depends on what that other text means. Providing compositionally a meaning to the jumping instruction requires that it gets a meaning without having that other text of the program available. The solution provided in denotational semantics is to describe meanings with respect to possible 'continuations', i.e. with respect to all possible ways the computational process may continue.

Compositional proof systems
An important school is the Floyd–Hoare style of programming language semantics, which expresses meanings in terms of logical proofs (Floyd, 1976; Hoare, 1969). In doing so it makes use of another form of compositionality, viz. compositionality of proofs: proofs for subprograms can be combined into a proof for the whole program.

Parameter passing
There are several mechanisms for parameter passing; e.g., call by reference, call by value, and call by name. The last one is defined by means of syntactic substitution! In a compositional approach one would like to obtain the meaning of the entire construction by combining the meaning of the procedure name with the meaning of the parameter. Such a compositional analysis is given by Hung and Zucker (1991). They present a uniform semantic treatment for all those mechanisms.

Parallelism
In computer science the recent development of large networks of processors has focused attention on the behavior of such large systems with communicating processors. New theoretical concepts are needed as the size of the networks produces new problems and the individual processors can themselves become quite complex. In the theory of such systems, compositionality is an important factor: a proof concerning the behavior of the system as a whole should be a function of the proofs for the separate processors. Significant in this respect is the title of De Roever (1985): 'The quest for compositionality – A survey of proof systems for concurrency'.

10.2. Other translations

A we have seen in Section 5, a compositional meaning assignment is realized through compositional translation into logic. In other situations precisely the same happens – compositional translation – but the motivation is different. Below we consider translations between logics, between programming languages, and between natural languages.

Embedding logic

For many logical languages translations have been defined. The purpose is not to assign meanings, but to investigate the relation between the logics, for instance, their relative strength or their relative consistency. A famous example is Gödel's translation of intuitionistic logic into modal logic. It illustrates the method of using polynomially defined algebras.

In intuitionistic logic the connectives have a constructive interpretation. For instance $\phi \rightarrow \psi$ could be read as 'given a proof for ϕ, it can be transformed into a proof for ψ'. The disjunction $\phi \vee \psi$ is read as 'a proof for ϕ is available or a proof for ψ is available'. Since it may be the case that neither a proof for ϕ nor for $\neg\phi$ is available, it is explained why $\phi \vee \neg\phi$ is not a tautology in intuitionistic logic. These interpretations have a modal flavor, made explicit in the translation into modal logic.

Let us write *Tr* for the translation function. Then clauses of the translation are:

1. $Tr(p) = \Box p$, for p an atom.
2. $Tr(\phi \vee \psi) = Tr(\phi) \vee Tr(\psi)$.
3. $Tr(\phi \wedge \psi) = Tr(\phi) \wedge Tr(\psi)$.
4. $Tr(\phi \rightarrow \psi) = \Box[Tr(\phi) \rightarrow Tr(\psi)]$.

Thus one sees that the disjunction and conjunction operator in intuitionistic logic correspond to the same operator of modal logic, whereas the implication corresponds to a polynomially defined operator. Since $\neg\phi$ is an abbreviation for $\phi \rightarrow \bot$, the translation of $p \vee \neg p$ is $\Box p \vee \Box\neg\Box p$ (which is not a tautology in modal logic).

The above example illustrates that the Gödel translation is an example of the method of compositional translation. A large number of translations between logics is collected in (Epstein, 1990, Chapter 10: 'Translations between Logic', pp. 289–314). Almost all of them are compositional (there they are called 'grammatical translations'). The few that are not, are also in semantic respects deviant.

Compiler correctness

Compilation of a computer program can be viewed as a form of translation, viz. from a programming language to a more machine oriented language. The purpose is to instruct the machine how to execute the program. This translation has of course to respect the intended meaning of the programming language, an aim that is called 'compiler correctness'. It has been has been advocated that one can approach compiler correctness by using algebraic methods (Morris, 1973; Thatcher, Wagner and Wright, 1979), in other words, by working compositionally. Other arguments are given in (Rus, 1991).

Between natural languages
Translating from one natural language to another one is an action that should be meaning preserving. The machine translation project 'Rosetta' tries to reach this aim by following the principle of compositionality of translation. It reads (Rosetta, 1994, p. 17):

> Two expressions are each others translation if they are built up from parts which are each others translation, by means of rules with the same meaning.

11. Conclusion

The principle of compositionality of meaning really means something. It is a restriction that rules out several proposals in the literature, and is certainly not vacuous. On the other hand it was shown that there are several methods to obtain a compositional meaning assignment; so it is not an impossible task. For counterexamples to compositionality solutions were proposed, and fundamental arguments were answered.

This practical experience was supported by mathematical proofs that the sentences of any language can be assigned any meaning in a compositional way. However, the formal results do not make it any easier to obtain a compositional semantics, so these results form no reason for restrictions.

Compositionality is not a formal restriction on what can be achieved, but a methodology on how to proceed. The discussions in this chapter have pointed to several advantages of this methodology, in particular its heuristic value. It suggests solutions to semantic problems. It helps to find weak spots in non-compositional proposals; such proposals have a risk of being defective. Cases where an initially non-compositional proposal was turned into a compositional one, the analysis improved considerably.

Compositionality requires a decision on what in a given approach the basic semantic units are: if one has to build meanings from them, it has to be decided what these units are. Compositionality also requires a decision on what the basic units in syntax are, and how they are combined. If a proposal is not compositional, it is an indication that the fundamental question what the basic units are, is not answered satisfactorily. If such an answer is provided, the situation under discussion is better understood. So the main reason to follow this methodology, is that compositionality guides research in the right direction!

Acknowledgements

I am indebted to Yuri Engelhardt, Joseph Goguen, Willem Groeneveld, Herman Hendriks, Lex Hendriks, Barbara Partee, Jeff Pelletier, the participants of the 'handbook-workshop' and especially to Ede Zimmermann for their comments on the earlier versions of this chapter. I am very grateful to Barbara Partee for the permission to include her work on genitives as an appendix. Originally it was written as part of her paper on compositionality (Partee, 1984), but it was not included in the final version. It has, in mutual concert, slightly been edited and updated in order to fit in the present context. I thank Dag Westerståhl and Peter Pagin for their valuable help in obtaining an otherwise untraceable reference. For their stimulating guidance during the preparation of this chapter I thank the editors Johan van Benthem and Alice ter Meulen, who also turned my extraordinary English into intelligible prose.

Appendix A. Related principles

In this section we present shortly several principles which arise in discussions in the literature concerning compositionality. Some are variants of compositionality, others are alternatives, or are independent of compositionality.

Compositionality of meaning
The version one mostly finds in the literature is: *The meaning of a compound expression is built from the meanings of its parts.* A more precise version is (Partee, Ter Meulen and Wall, 1990, p. 318): *The meaning of a compound expression is a function of the meanings of its parts and of the syntactic rule by which they are combined.* This principle is main theme of this chapter.

Compositionality of translation
The translation of a compound expression is built from the translations of its parts. This principle was a guideline in the design of a variant of Eurotra (Arnold, Jaspaert, Johnson, Krauwer, Rosner, Des Tombes, Varile and Warwick, 1985; Arnold and Des Tombes, 1987). A symmetric and more precise version (see also Section 10.2) is given in (Rosetta, 1994, p. 17): *Two expressions are each other's translation if they are built up from parts which are each other's translation, by means of rules with the same meaning.* This principle is analogous to the compositionality principle.

Context independence thesis
The meaning of an expression should not depend on the context in which it occurs (Hintikka, 1983, p. 262). Closely related with the 'inside outside principle'. This thesis follows from the compositionality principle.

Contextuality principle
A word has a meaning only in the context of a sentence, not in separation (Frege, 1884, p. x). This principle seems to be the opposite of compositionality, see the discussion in Section 1.3.

Determinacy thesis
The meaning of E *must completely be determined by the meanings of the expressions* $E_1, E_2, \ldots, E_n$ *from which it constructed* (Hintikka, 1983, p. 264). This thesis follows from the compositionality principle.

Frege's principle
'Frege's Principle' is another name for the principle of compositionality. Whether the ascription to Frege is accurate, is discussed in Section 1.3.

Fully abstractness
A notion from computer science that is closely related to compositionality (Mosses, 1990, p. 586; Wirsing, 1990, p. 736). A meaning assignment is called 'fully abstract' in case *two expressions have the same meaning if and only if they are interchangeble in all contexts without changing the resulting meaning.*

Indifference principle
The semantic value of a constituent (phrase marker) does not depend upon what it is embedded in (Higginbotham, 1986). This is a consequence of compositionality.

Initial algebra semantics
In computer science a well known approach to semantics (Goguen, Thatcher, Wagner and Wright, 1977, 1978). It states that *the syntax is an initial algebra, the meanings form an algebra of the same type, and meaning assignment is a homomorphism.* Intuitively the notion 'initial' says that two elements in an algebra are different unless it is explicitly said that they are the same. A standard example of an initial algebra is a term algebra, hence compositionality of meaning is an example of initial algebra semantics.

Inside outside principle
The proper direction of a semantic analysis is from the inside out. (Hintikka, 1983, p. 262.) This principle follows from the compositionality principle.

Leibniz' principle
A well known principle concerning semantics of the philosopher Leibniz (Gerhardt, 1890, p. 228) *Eadem sunt, quorum substitui alteri, salva veritate.* (Those-the-same are, of-which is-substitutable for-the-other, with truth.)

The principle is understood as saying that two expressions refer to the same object if in all contexts they can be interchanged without changing the truth value. We may generalize it to all kinds of expressions, stating that two expressions have the same meaning if in all contexts the expressions can be interchanged without changing the truth value. This is the reverse of the consequences for meanings of the compositionality principle. Note that, according to our standards, this principle is sloppy formulated, because it confuses the things themselves, with the expressions to referring to them (see Church, 1956, p. 300; Quine, 1960, p. 116).

Rule to rule hypothesis
For each syntactic rule, which tells how a complex expression E is formed from simpler ones say $E_1, E_2, \ldots, E_n$, there is a corresponding semantic rule which tells how the meaning of E depends on the meanings of $E_1, E_2, \ldots, E_n$. The term 'rule to rule hypothesis' originates from (Bach, 1976), it is called **parallelism thesis** in (Hintikka, 1983). This hypothesis is the kernel of the compositionality principle.

Semantic groundedness
An alternative for compositionality proposed by Pelletier (1994b). It is, like compositionality, based on an inductively defined meaning assignment, The difference is that here

the induction does not follow the syntactic definition, but can be based on any other grounded ordering. An example is a definition of propositional logic in which the syntax forms the biimplication $\phi \leftrightarrow \psi$ from ϕ and ψ, but in which the meaning is defined by means of the two implications $\phi \rightarrow \psi$ and $\psi \rightarrow \phi$.

Surface compositionality
If expression E *is built from expressions* $E_1, E_1, \ldots, E_n$, *then these parts are actual parts of the resulting expression, they occur unchanged as subexpressions of* E. A further refinement of the principle and a grammar obeying the principle is given in (Hausser, 1984). It is called the **invariance thesis** by Hintikka (1983, p. 263). This is a very restricted version of the compositionality principle.

Appendix B. Genitives – A case study (by B. Partee)

B.1. Introduction

In this appendix we will consider a difficult case for compositionality: the variety of meanings of genitives. It will turn out that the problems can be solved compositionally by methods discussed before. The aim of this section is to illustrate that this is not the end of the story. Designing a compositional solution for a given phenomenon may implicate decisions that have consequences in other parts of the grammar, and these consequences have to be taken into account as well. It is possible that the new insights give an improvement of the grammar as a whole, but it may also be the case the system becomes unnecessarily complicated. If certain decisions can be given no other argumentation than to preserve compositionality, then we may have chosen the wrong solution, or we may be working with a too narrow conception of compositionality.

B.2. The problem

Here are some initial data:

(1) (a) John's team.
(b) A team of John's.
(c) That team is John's.

(2) (a) John's brother.
(b) A brother of John's.
(c) * That brother is John's.

(3) (a) John's favorite movie.
(b) A favorite movie of John's.
(c) * That favorite movie is John's.

Informally, we can give a unified description of the interpretation of the genitive phrase *John's* that applies to all these cases if we say that the genitive always expresses one argument of a relation (in intensional logic, something like $^{\vee}R(j)$). But the relation can come from any of the three sources:

1. The context. In (1), the most salient relevant relation might be "plays for", "owns", "has bet on", "writes about for the local newspaper", or any of an essentially open range of possibilities (henceforth the "free R" reading).
2. An inherently relational noun, like *brother* in (2).
3. A relational adjective, like *favorite* in (3).

I'll refer to the last two cases as the "inherent R" readings.

Compositionality asks for a uniform semantics of the genitive construction in syntax. Since not all examples contain a relational noun or adjective, the best hope for a unified analysis would clearly seem to be to try to assimilate all cases to the "free R case". This is in fact the strategy carried out by Hellan (1980). Simplifying his approach, we may say that he points out that an inherently relational noun can be presumed to make its associated relation salient in the context (while still being analyzed as a simple *CN* syntactically and a one-place predicate semantically).

Maybe this approach works for the given examples, but serious problems emerge if we consider the contrasts between *NP*-internal and predicative uses of genitives. In addition to the contrast among the (a) and (b) cases in (1)–(3) above, an interesting pattern of interpretations can be found in (Stockwell, Schachter and Partee, 1973). They give the following examples (the section on genitives was primarily done by Schachter and Frank Heny):

(4) (a) John's portrait. (*ambiguous*)
(b) (i) A portrait of John's. (*free R only*)
(ii) A portrait of John. (*inherent R only*)
(c) That portrait is John's. (*free R only*)

What emerges from these examples is that while predicative genitives (the (c) cases in (1)–(4)) are easily interpreted in terms of a free relation variable which can get its value from the context, they do not seem able to pick up a relation inherent within the subject-*NP* as a value for that variable. The postnominal genitive and non-genitive *of*-complements in (4b) seem to offer a minimal contrast which is neutralized in the prenominal genitive (4a), providing further evidence that the "free R" and the "inherent R" readings should be represented distinctly at some level within the grammar.

A caveat should be added concerning the predicative genitives. In some cases they appear to get an inherent relational reading, as in:

(5) I knew there were three grandmothers behind the curtain, but I didn't know one of them was mine.

We can understand *mine* in (5) as *my grandmother*; but I believe the complicating factor is a result of the phenomenon described in transformational terms as *one*(s) – deletion (Stockwell, Schachter and Partee, 1973). It seems that whenever a genuinely t/e-type genitive appears, it must be interpreted with a free R variable. In the present section the full-*NP* reading of bare genitives (of which (5) is an example) are omitted from further consideration.

B.3. A compositional analysis

Above we we have seen that the genitive construction seems to have two basic meanings. A strategy described in previous sections can be applied here: eliminating the ambiguity by introducing new parts. This is done by enriching the syntax to include a category *TCN* of "transitive common noun phrases", thus making the inherently relational nature overt in their syntactic category and semantic type. The basic idea is that there are two basic genitive constructions, a predicative one with a free R variable (context-dependent), and an adnominal one which applies to transitive common nouns and fills in an argument place, yielding an ordinary one-place *CN* as result. The predicative one also has a post-nominal counterpart, but of category *CN*/*CN*, and both have determiner counterparts of categories *NP*/*TCN* and *NP*/*CN* respectively.

Below a grammar for the genitive is presented; this grammar will be extended in the next section. Details of the analysis not immediately relevant to the genitive issue are not to be taken too seriously.

1. **Predicative genitives** (1c)–(4c)
   - Syntax: $[NP\text{'s}]_{t/e}$.
   - Semantics: $\lambda x[{}^{\vee}R_i(NP')(x)]$ or equivalently ${}^{\vee}R_i(NP')$.
   - Notes: The R_i in this interpretation is free; if context dependency should rather be treated by special constants, this would be one of those.

2. **Postnominal genitives** (1b)–(4b)

   (a) **Free R type**
   - Syntax: $[of\ NP\text{'s}]_{CN/CN}$.
   - Semantics: $\lambda P\lambda x[{}^{\vee}P(x) \wedge {}^{\vee}R_i(NP')(x)]$ or in the notation of Partee and Rooth (1983): $\lambda P[{}^{\vee}P \sqcap {}^{\vee}R_i(NP')]$.
   - Notes: This is exactly parallel to the conversion of t/e adjectives to *CN*/*CN* adjectives.

   (b) **Inherent R type**
   - Syntax: $[of\ NP\text{'s}]_{CN/TCN_{[+\text{gen}]}}$.
   - Semantics: $\lambda R\lambda x[{}^{\vee}R_i(NP')(x)]$.
   - Notes: The symbol $TCN_{[+\text{gen}]}$ is used to mark the subcategory of relational nouns which can take postnominal *of* + genitive (*brother*, *employee*, *enemy*, but not *portrait*, *description*, *height*); some relational nouns take *of* + accusative, some can take both. The data are messy; "heaviness" of the *NP* plays a role. Note that the agentive "by John" reading of (4b) counts as a free R reading; only the "of John" reading is blocked in (4b) and (4c).

3. **Prenominal genitives** (1a)–(4a)

   (a) **free R type**
   - Syntax: $[NP\text{'s}]_{NP/CN}$.

- Semantics: Tantamount roughly to the *the* + $[of\ NP\text{'s}]_{CN/CN}$, but see Notes below. Using Montague's treatment of *the*, this is:

$$\lambda Q \lambda P\big[NP'({}^\wedge\lambda z[\exists x[\forall y[[{}^\vee Q(y) \wedge {}^\vee R_i(y)(z)] \leftrightarrow y = x] \wedge {}^\vee P(x)]])\big].$$

- Notes: A quantifier in a prenominal genitive always has wide scope, while those in postnominal genitives seem to be ambiguous. The uniqueness condition this analysis imputes to *John's brother* is disputable, especially when the whole noun phrase occurs in predicate position.

(b) **Inherent R type**

- Syntax: $[NP\text{'s}]_{NP/TCN}$.
- Semantics: Similarly tantamount to the *the* + $[of\ NP\text{'s}]_{CN/TCN}$:

$$\lambda R \lambda P\big[NP'({}^\wedge\lambda z[\exists x[\forall y[{}^\vee R(z)(y) \leftrightarrow y = x] \wedge {}^\vee P(x)]])\big].$$

- Notes: The order of the arguments of R are reversed in the two determiners; this reflects the intuitive difference in natural paraphrases using, e.g., *owns* for the free R in *John's team* and *(is a) sister of* for *John's sister*. But this difference is not predicted or explained here, and to be fully consistent the arguments in the two other 'free R' genitives should be reversed as well.

B.4. Consequences for adjectives

In the previous section a compositional analysis is given for the genitive construction by distinguishing two types of common nouns. But having more types of common nouns, implicates more types of prenominal adjectives, viz. CN/CN, TCN/TCN and TCN/CN. We consider examples of adjectives of the new types.

1. TCN/CN: *favorite*$_1$, as in *John's favorite movie*.
   - Syntax: $[favorite]_{TCN/CN}$.
   - Semantics: Lexical; roughly

$$favorite'_1 = \lambda P[\lambda y[\lambda x[{}^\vee P(x)\ and\ y\ likes\ x\ best\ out\ of\ {}^\vee P]]].$$

2. TCN/TCN: *favorite*$_2$, as in *John's favorite brother*.
   - Syntax: $[favorite]_{TCN/TCN}$, probably derivable by lexical rule from *favorite*$_1$.
   - Semantics: lexical, but derivative; roughly

$$favorite'_2 = \lambda R[\lambda y[\lambda x[{}^\vee R(y)(x) \wedge favorite'_1({}^\wedge({}^\vee R(y)))(x)]]].$$

This analysis of inherently relational adjectives creates non-basic *TCN*'s which act just like basic *TCN*'s with respect to genitives. Once these categories are admitted, it appears that a number of traditionally CN/CN adjectives like *new* also fit here as well; we can distinguish four separate (but related) *new*'s as follows:

1. $[new_1]_{t/e}$ "hasn't existed long" (*a new movie*).

2. $[new_2]_{CN/CN}$ "hasn't been a *CN* long" (*a new movie star*).
3. $[new_3]_{TCN/TCN}$ "hasn't been a *TCN*-of long" (*my new friend*).
4. $[new_4]_{TCN/CN}$ "hasn't been in the (free) R_i-relation too long" (*John's new car is an old car*).

New$_4$ is definable in terms of *new*$_3$ and a free R as is shown in:

(6) $$new_4' = \lambda P[\lambda y[\lambda x[{}^\vee P(x) \wedge new_3' R(y)(x)]]].$$

Note the difference between $[favorite]_{TCN/CN}$ with an "inherent" R built into its meaning, and $[new]_{TCN/CN}$ which introduces a 'free R', which in turn acts as "inherent" for the genitive.

Thus the analysis of genitives has stimulated a more refined analysis of adjectives. The above treatment gives a reasonable account of the data: the distribution of 'inherent' and 'free' R readings is explained by treating the 'inherent R' genitive as something which must be in construction with a *TCN*, which can only happen within the *NP*, while the 'free R' genitive is basically a predicate. The fact that *TCN*'s can almost always be used as plain *CN*'s would be attributed to the existence of highly productive lexical rules which "detransitivize" *TCN*'s, interpreting the missing argument as existentially quantified or as an indexical or variable.

B.5. Doubts about the introduction of TCN's

Although the grammar from the previous two sections deals with the phenomena, and gives interesting insights, there can be serious reservations about introducing the category *TCN* into the syntax along with the associated distinctions in the categories of adjectives and determiners. The distinction between transitive and intransitive verbs has clear syntactic and morphological as well semantic motivation in many languages, while with nouns the motivation is almost entirely semantic. I believe that the analysis given above incorporates ingredients of a good explanation, but puts too much of it in the syntax.

Besides these general considerations, there are also phenomena which raise doubts. Consequences emerge when we consider what explanation to give of the semantics of *have* in sentences like (7)–(9).

(7) John has a car.

(8) John has a sister.

(9) John has three sisters and two brothers.

We could account for (7) and (8) by positing two *have*'s, one ordinary transitive verb (IV/*NP*) *have*$_1$ interpreted as a free variable R (with typical values such as 'own', but highly context dependent), plus a *have*$_2$ of category IV/*TCN* interpreted as in:

(10) $$have_2' = \lambda R \lambda x[\exists y R(x)(y)].$$

This requires us to treat *a sister* in (8) as not an *NP*, but a *TCN*, and similarly for even more complex indefinite noun phrases, as in (9). We could defend such a departure from apparent surface syntax, with arguments about the inadequacy of Montague's treatment of predicate nominals as ordinary *NP*'s and with appeals to the diversity and interrelatedness across languages of constructions expressing possession, existence, and location, justifying the singling out of *have* for special treatment along with *be*. But putting this in terms of categorial distinctions in the syntax would predict the impossibility of sentences like:

(11) John has piles of money and no living relatives.

(12) John has a tutor, a textbook, and a set of papers.

(13) John has a good job, a nice house, a beautiful wife, clever children, and plenty of money (and an ulcer).

Conjoinability is a very strong test of sameness of syntactic and semantic category, and in this case it supports the traditional assumption that these are all *NP*'s, and not a mixture of *NP*'s and *TCN*'s. This suggests that the interaction of the interpretation of *have* with relational nouns should not be dealt with by multiplying syntactic categories. And while the conjunction test does not give similarly clear evidence in the genitive construction, I expect that if we can find a way to treat the *have* data without *TCN*'s in the syntax, we will be able to extend it to a treatment of the genitives (probably still recognizing two genitives, but without invoking *TCN*'s to explain the difference).

B.6. Genitives and compositionality

There are several points at which the problems raised by the genitive construction relate to general issues concerning compositionality

1. If we were not committed to local and deterministic compositionality, we could extract a uniform core meaning that all the genitives described above share: [*NP*'s] means ${}^{\vee}R(NP')$. And we could, I think, describe general principles that dictate what more must be "filled in" for the postnominal and determiner uses, and whether the variable is to be left free or bound by a λR operator. This approach would couple a uniform interpretation of the genitive with a not totally implausible interpretation strategy that could be caricatured as "try to understand" (according to Bach a term originating from Philip Gouch). Arguments for such an interpretation strategy for semantically open-ended expressions are given in (Partee, 1988).
2. Montague's strategy for maintaining uniformity in the face of apparent diversity might be characterized as "generalize to the worst case". I don't think that will work for the analysis of the genitives, since trying to assimilate all genitives to the "free *R*" case gives the wrong result for the distribution of "inherent" readings. The only way I can see to give a *uniform* treatment of all genitives in English is to leave part of the meaning out of the grammar as sketched in paragraph 1) above. Perhaps a type-shifting along the lines of Partee (1987) could be explored.
3. If we do maintain the compositionality principle by building in the kind of multiple categorization described above, we simplify the process of determining semantic information from syntactic form, but complicate the task of parsing and ambiguity resolution, since we have simultaneously increased lexical and syntactic ambiguity.

4. The motivation for the introduction of *TCN*'s was a desire to make explicit the role of the implicit second argument of relational nouns in the interpretation of genitives. In quantificational genitives like *every woman's husband* and in similar cases with *have*, the implicit argument becomes a bound variable (for other examples of this phenomenon, see Section 4 in (Partee, 1984)). This seems to give an obstacle to a treatment which would absorb these implicit arguments into meanings of the predicates, namely the absence of any way to describe "variable binding" phenomena without an overt variable to bind. Since syntactic evidence goes rather strongly against introducing transitive common nouns, this adds to the motivation for seeking an alternative that would allow variable-like meanings as parts of predicate meanings, as argued in (Partee, 1989).
5. Although most of the above points suggest that the given treatment is not completely satisfactory, one aspect should be mentioned. For the compositional solution it is clear that it deals with the phenomena, how it would work out in a grammar, and how it would interact with other rules. For the suggested alternatives (interpretation strategy, partially unspecified meanings, new variable mechanisms) this is unclear.

References

Arnold, D. and Des Tombes, L. (1987), *Basic theory and methodology in EUROTRA*, Machine Translation. Theoretical and Methodological Issues, S. Nirenburg, ed., Cambridge Univ. Press, Cambridge, MA, 114–134.

Arnold, D.J., Jaspaert, L., Johnson, R.L., Krauwer, S., Rosner, M., Des Tombes, L., Varile, G.B. and Warwick, S. (1985), *A MU1 view of the CAT framework in EUROTRA*, Proceedings of the Conference on Theoretical and Methodological Issues in Machine Translation of Natural Languages, Colgate University, Hamilton, NY, 1–14.

Bach, E. (1976), *An extension of classical transformational grammar*, Problems in Linguistic Metatheory, Proceedings of the 1976 Conference, Michigan State University.

Barwise, J. and Perry, J. (1983), *Situations and Attitudes*, Bradford Books, Cambridge, MA.

Bergstra, J.A. and Tucker, J.V. (1987), *Algebraic specifications of computable and semicomputable data types*, Theor. Comput. Sci. **50**, 137–181.

Church, A. (1956), *Introduction to Mathematical Logic*, vol. 1, Princeton Univ. Press, Princeton, NJ.

Cooper, R. (1983), *Quantification and Syntactic Theory*, Synthese Language Library no. 21, Reidel, Dordrecht.

Davidson, D. and Harman, G. (eds) (1972), *Semantics of Natural Language*, Synthese Library no. 40, Reidel, Dordrecht.

De Bakker, J.W. (1980), *Mathematical Theory of Program Correctness*, Series in Computer Science, Prentice-Hall, London.

De Roever, W.P. (1985), *The quest for compositionality – a survey of proof systems for concurrency, part 1*, Proc. IFIP Working Group The role of abstract models in Computer Science, E.J. Neuhold, ed., North-Holland, Amsterdam.

Dowty, D.R. (1976), *Montague grammar and the lexical decomposition of causative verbs*, Montague Grammar, B. Partee, ed., Academic Press, New York, 201–245.

Dummett, M. (1973), *Frege. Philosophy of Language*, Duckworth, London.

Epstein, R.L. (1990), *The Semantic Foundation of Logic, Vol 1: Propositional Logic*, Nijhof International Philosophy Series no. 35, Nijhof, Dordrecht.

Floyd, R.W. (1976), *Assigning meanings to program*, Mathematical Aspects of Computer Science, J.T. Schwartz, ed., Proc. Symp. in Applied Mathematics no. 19, Amer. Math. Soc., Providence, RI, 19–32.

Frege, G. (1884), *Die Grundlagen der Arithmetik. Eine logisch-mathematische Untersuchung über den Begriff der Zahl*, W. Koebner, Breslau. Reprint published by: Georg Olms, Hildesheim, 1961.

Frege, G. (1923), *Logische Untersuchungen. Dritter Teil: Gedankenfüge*, Beiträge zur Philosophie des Deutschen Idealismus vol. III, 36–51. Reprinted: I. Angelelli (ed.) (1967), *Gottlob Frege. Kleine Schriften*, Georg Olms, Hildeheim, 378–394. Translated as *Compound thoughts, Logical Investigations*, Gottlob Frege, P.T. Geach and R.H. Stoothoff (transl.), Basil Blackwell, Oxford, 1977, pp. 55–78.

Gallin, D. (1975), *Intensional and Higher-Order Modal Logic*, Mathematics Studies no. 17, North-Holland, Amsterdam.

Gerhardt, C.I. (ed.) (1890), *Die philosphischen Schriften von Gottfried Wilhelm Leibniz*, vol. 7, Weidmannsche Buchhandlung, Berlin.

Goguen, J. and Diaconescu, R. (1994), *An Oxford survey of order sorted algebra*, Math. Struct. Comput. Sci. **4**, 363–392.

Goguen, J.A., Thatcher, J.W., Wagner, E.G. and Wright, J.B. (1977), *Initial algebra semantics and continuous algebras*, J. Assoc. Comput. Mach. **24**, 68–95.

Goguen, J.A., Thatcher, J.W. and Wagner, E.G. (1978), *An initial algebra approach to the specification, correctness and implementation of abstract data types*, Current Trends in Programming Methodology, R. Yeh, ed., Prentice-Hall, Englewood Cliffs, NJ, 80–149.

Graetzer, G. (1979), *Universal Algebra*, 2nd ed., Springer, New York. First edition published by Van Nostrand, Reinhold, Princeton, 1968.

Groenendijk, J. and Stokhof, M. (1991), *Dynamic predicate logic*, Ling. and Philos. **14**, 39–100.

Hausser, R.R. (1984), *Surface Compositional Grammar*, Studies in Theoretical Linguistics no. 4, Fink Verlag, München.

Hellan, L. (1980), *Toward an integrated theory of noun phrases*, Technical report, University of Trondheim.

Hendriks, H. (1993), *Studied flexibility. Categories and types in syntax and semantics*, PhD Thesis, ILLC dissertation Series 1993-5, University of Amsterdam.

Henkin, L., Monk, J.D. and Tarski, A. (1971), *Cylindric Algebras, Part I*, Studies in Logic and the Foundations of Mathematics no. 64, North-Holland, Amsterdam.

Higginbotham, J. (1986), *Linguistic theory and Davidson's program in semantics*, Truth and Interpretation. Perspectives on the Philosophy of Donald Davidson, E. le Pore, ed., Blackwell, Oxford, 29–48.

Hintikka, J. (1981), *Theories of truth and learnable languages*, Philosophy and Grammar: Papers on the Occasion of the Quincentennial of Uppsala University, S. Kanger and S. Ohman, eds, Reidel, Dordrecht, 37–57.

Hintikka, J. (1983), *The Game of Language. Studies in Game-Theoretical Semantics and Its Applications*, Synthese Language Library no. 22, Reidel, Dordrecht. In collaboration with J. Kulas.

Hoare, C.A.R. (1969), *An axiomatic base for computer programming*, Comm. ACM **12**, 576–580.

Hung, H.-K. and Zucker, J.I. (1991), *Semantics of pointers, referencing and dereferencing with intensional logic*, Proc. 6th Annual IEEE Symposium on Logic in Computer Science, IEEE Computer Society Press, Los Almolitos, CA, 127–136.

Jackendoff, R.S. (1972), *Semantic Interpretation in Generative Grammar*, MIT Press, Cambridge, MA.

Janssen, T.M.V. (1983), *Scope ambiguities of tense, aspect and negation*, Syntactic Categories: Auxiliaries and Related Puzzles, F. Heny and B. Richards, eds, Synthese Language Library no. 20, Reidel, Dordrecht, 55–99.

Janssen, T.M.V. (1986a), *Foundations and Applications of Montague Grammar, Part 1: Philosophy, Framework, Computer Science*, CWI Tracts no. 19, Centre for Mathematics and Computer Science, Amsterdam.

Janssen, T.M.V. (1986b), *Foundations and Applications of Montague Grammar, Part 2: Applications to Natural Language*, CWI Tracts no. 28, Centre for Mathematics and Computer Science, Amsterdam.

Janssen, T.M.V. (1989), *Towards a universal parsing algoritm for functional grammar*, Functional Grammar and the Computer, J.H. Conally and S.C. Dik, eds, Foris, Dordrecht, 65–75.

Janssen, T.M.V. and Van Emde Boas, P. (1977), *On the proper treatment of referencing, dereferencing and assignment*, Automata, Languages and Programming (Proc. 4th. Coll. Turku), A. Salomaa and M. Steinby, eds, Lecture Notes in Computer Science vol. 52, Springer, Berlin, 282–300.

Janssen, T.M.V. and Van Emde Boas, P. (1981), *Some remarks on compositional semantics*, Logic of Programs, D. Kozen, ed., Springer Lecture Notes in Computer Science vol. 131, Springer, Berlin, 137–149.

Kamp, H. (1971), *Formal properties of "now"*, Theoria **37**, 227–273.

Kamp, H. (1981), *A theory of truth and semantic representation*, A Theory of Truth and Semantic Representation, T.J. Groenendijk and M. Stokhof, eds, CWI, Amsterdam. Reprinted: J. Groenendijk, T. Janssen and M. Stokhof (eds) (1984), *Truth, Interpretation and Information*, Foris, Dordrecht.

Kamp, H. and Reyle, U. (1993), *From Discourse to Logic. Introduction to the Modeltheoretic Semantics of Natural Language*, Studies in Linguistics and Philosophy no. 42, Reidel, Dordrecht.

Katz, J.J. (1966), *The Philosophy of Language*, Harper & Row, London.

Katz, J.J. and Fodor, J.A. (1963), *The structure of a semantic theory*, Language **39**, 170–210.

Kreisel, G. and Krivine, J.L. (1976), *Elements of Mathematical Logic. Model Theory*, Studies in Logic and the Foundations of Mathematics no. 2, North-Holland, Amsterdam.

Kripke, S. (1972), *Naming and necessity*, Semantics of Natural Language, D. Davidson and G. Harman, eds, Reidel, Dordrecht, 253–355. Blackwell, 1980.

Kripke, S. (1976), *Is there a problem about substitutional quantification?*, Truth and Meaning. Essays in Semantics, G. Evans and J.H. McDowell, eds, Clarendon Press, Oxford, 325–419.

Landsbergen, J. (1981), *Adaption of Montague grammar to the requirements of parsing*, Formal Methods in the Study of Language. Proceedings of the Third Amsterdam Colloquium, J.A.G. Groenendijk, T.M.V. Janssen and M.B.J. Stokhof, eds, CWI Tracts, nos 135, 136, Centre for Mathematics and Computer Science, Amsterdam, 399–420.

Lewis, D. (1970), *General semantics*, Synthese **22**, 18–67. Reprinted: D. Davidson and G. Harman (eds) (1972), *Semantic of Naturale Language*, Reidel, Dordrecht, 169–248; and: B. Partee (ed.) (1976), *Montague Grammar*, Academic Press, New York, 1–50.

MacCawley, J.D. (1986), *Concerning the base component in a transformational grammar*, Found. Lang. **4**, 55–81.

Marcus, R.B. (1962), *Interpreting quantification*, Inquiry **5**, 252–259.

Mates, B. (1950), *Synonomy*, Meaning and Interpretation, Publications in Philosophy no. 25, Univ. of California, 201–226. Reprinted: L. Linsky (1952), *Semantics and the Philosophy of Language*, Univ. of Illinois Press, Urbana.

Monk, J.D. (1976), *Mathematical Logic*, Graduate Texts in Mathematics vol. 37, Springer, Berlin.

Montague, R. (1970a), *English as a formal language*, Linguaggi nella societa et nella technica, Visentini et al., eds, Edizioni di communita, Milan, 188–221. Reprinted: R.H. Thomason (1974), *Formal Philosophy. Selected Papers of Richard Montague*, Yale Univ. Press, New Haven, CT, 188–221.

Montague, R. (1970b), *Universal grammar*, Theoria **36**, 373–398. Reprinted: R.H. Thomason (1974), *Formal Philosophy. Selected Papers of Richard Montague*, Yale Univ. Press, New Haven, CT, 222–246.

Montague, R. (1973), *The proper treatment of quantification in ordinary English*, Approaches to Natural Language, Synthese Library 49, K.J.J. Hintikka, J.M.E. Moravcsik and P. Suppes, eds, Reidel, Dordrecht, 221–242. Reprinted: R.H. Thomason (1974), *Formal Philosophy. Selected Papers of Richard Montague*, Yale Univ. Press, New Haven, CT, 247–270.

Morris, F.L. (1973), *Advice on structuring compilers and proving them correct*, Proc. ACM, Symp. on Principles of Programming Languages, Boston, ACM, 144–152.

Mosses, P.D. (1990), *Denotational semantics*, Handbook of Theoretical Computer Science, vol. B, Formal Models and Semantics, J. van Leeuwen, ed., Elsevier, Amsterdam, 575–631.

Muskens, R. (1993), *A compositional discourse representation theory*, Proceedings 9th Amsterdam Colloquium. Part II, P. Dekker and M. Stokhof, eds, Institute for Language, Logic and Computation, University of Amsterdam, 467–486.

Partee, B. (1973), *Some transformational extensions of Montague grammar*, J. Philos. Logic **2**, 509–534. Reprinted: B. Partee (ed.) (1976), *Montague Grammar*, Academic Press, New York, 51–76.

Partee, B. (1982), *Believe-sentences and the limits of semantics*, Processes, Beliefs, and Questions, S. Peters and E. Saarinen, eds, Synthese Language Library, Reidel, Dordrecht, 87–106.

Partee, B. (1984), *Compositionality*, Varieties of Formal Semantics, F. Landman and F. Veltman, eds, GRASS no. 3, Foris, Dordrecht, 281–311.

Partee, B. (1987), *Noun phrase interpretation and type-shifting principles*, Studies in Discourse Representation Theory and the Theory of Generalized Quantifiers, J. Groenendijk, D. de Jongh and M. Stokhof, eds, GRASS no. 8, Foris, Dordrecht, 115–143.

Partee, B. (1988), *Semantic facts and psychological facts*, Mind and Language **3**, 43–52.

Partee, B. (1989), *Binding implicit variables in quantified contexts*, Papers from CLS 25, C. Wiltshire, B. Music, and R. Graczyk, eds, Chicago Linguistic Society, Chicago, 342–365.

Partee, B. and Rooth, M. (1983), *Generalized conjunction and type ambiguity*, Meaning, Use and Interpretation of Language, R. Bauerle, C. Schwartz, and A. von Stechow, eds, Walter de Gruyter, Berlin, 361–383.

Partee, B. (ed.) (1976), *Montague Grammar*, Academic Press, New York.
Partee, B., Ter Meulen, A. and Wall, R.E. (1990), *Mathematical Methods in Linguistics*, Studies in Linguistics and Philosophy no. 30, Kluwer, Dordrecht.
Pelletier, F.J. (1993), *Some issues involving internal and external semantics*, The Logical Foundations of Cognition, J. Macnamara and G. Reges, eds, Oxford Univ. Press, Oxford.
Pelletier, F.J. (1994a), *On an argument against semantic compositionality*, Logic, Methodology and Philosophy of Science, D. Westerståhl, ed., Kluwer, Dordrecht, 599–610.
Pelletier, F.J. (1994b), *The principle of semantic compositionality*, Topoi **13**, 11–24.
Popper, K. (1976), *Unended Quest. An Intellectual Autobiography*, Fontana.
Pratt, V.R. (1979), *Dynamic logic*, Foundations of Computer Science III, part 2, Languages, Logic, Semantics, De Bakker and Van Leeuwen, eds, CWI Tracts no. 100, Centre for Mathematics and Computer Science, Amsterdam, 53–82.
Quine, W.V.O. (1960), *Word and Object*, MIT Press, Cambridge, MA.
Rosetta, M.T. (1994), *Compositional Translation*, The Kluwer International Series in Engineering and Computer Science 230, Kluwer, Dordrecht.
Rus, T. (1991), *Algebraic construction of compilers*, Theor. Comput. Sci. 271–308.
Saarinen, E. (1979), *Backwards-looking operators in tense logic and in natural language*, Essays on Mathematical and Philosophical Logic. Proceedings of the 4th Scandinavian Logic Symposium, J. Hintikka, I. Niiniluotov and E. Saarinen, eds, Synthese Library no. 122, Kluwer, Dordrecht, 341–367.
Salmon, N. and Soames, S. (1988), *Propositions and Attitudes*, Oxford Readings in Philosophy, Oxford Univ. Press.
Schiffer, S. (1987), *Remnants of Meaning*, MIT Press, Cambridge, MA.
Schiffer, S. (1988), *Reply to comments*, Mind and Language **3**, 53–63.
Schütte, K. (1977), *Proof Theory*, Grundlehren der Mathematische Wissenschaften vol. 225, Springer, Berlin.
Stockwell, R., Schachter, P. and Partee, B.H. (1973), *The Major Syntactic Structures of English*, Holt, Rinehart, and Winston, New York.
Stoy, J.E. (1977), *Denotational Semantics: The Scott–Strachey Approach to Programming Language Theory*, MIT Press, Cambridge, MA.
Thatcher, J.W., Wagner, E.G. and Wright, J.B. (1979), *More on advice on structuring compilers and proving them correct*, Automata, languages and programming (Proc. 6th Coll. Graz), H.A. Maurer, ed., Lecture Notes in Computer Science vol. 71, Springer, Berlin.
Thomason, R.H. (1974), *Formal Philosophy. Selected Papers of Richard Montague*, Yale Univ. Press, New Haven, CT.
Van Benthem, J.F.A.K. (1979), *Universal algebra and model theory. Two excursions on the border*, Technical Report ZW-7908, Dept. of Mathematics, Groningen University.
Wirsing, M. (1990), *Algebraic specification*, Handbook of Theoretical Computer Science, vol. B, Formal Models and Semantics, J. van Leeuwen, ed., Elsevier, Amsterdam, 675–780.
Wittgenstein, L. (1921), *Tractatus logico-philosophicus. Logisch-philosophische Abhandlung*, Annalen der Naturphilosphie, Ostwald, ed., Reprint: (1959), Basil Blackwell, Oxford.
Zadrozny, W. (1994), *From compositional to systematic semantics*, Ling. and Philos. **17**, 329–342.
Zeevat, H. (1989), *A compositional approach to Kamp's DRT*, Ling. and Philos. **12**(1), 95–131.

CHAPTER 8

Feature Logics

William C. Rounds

Artificial Intelligence Laboratory, Department of Electrical Engineering and Computer Science, University of Michigan, Ann Arbor, MI 48109, USA
E-mail: rounds@eecs.umich.edu

Commentator: P. Blackburn

Contents

HANDBOOK OF LOGIC AND LANGUAGE
Edited by J. van Benthem and A. ter Meulen

1. Introduction

1.1. Overview

Feature logics form a class of specialized logics which have proven especially useful in classifying and constraining the linguistic objects known as feature structures. Linguistically, these structures have their origin in the work of the Prague school of linguistics, followed by the work of Chomsky and Halle in *The Sound Pattern of English* (Chomsky and Halle, 1957). Feature structures have been reinvented several times by computer scientists: in the theory of data structures, where they are known as record structures, in artificial intelligence, where they are known as frame or slot-value structures, in the theory of data bases, where they are called "complex objects", and in computational linguistics, where they arose as systems of "registers" in augmented transition networks for natural language parsing, and, quite incidentally, from logic-based approaches to parsing such as definite-clause grammars. Work on the subject has thus involved contributions from linguistics, logic, and computer science.

Before discussing the logic of feature structures, it would be well to understand feature structures themselves, as they are the linguistic objects being constrained by the logic. I will try to say very briefly what perspective is taken by various linguistic theories and computational frameworks on feature structures.

We will then embark on a survey of the various logical systems that have been proposed to constrain feature structures in the setting of grammar. Each logical system, like the linguistic theories, takes a slightly different view of its models. Partly the view is taken because of the particular linguistic theory into which a given logic is embedded, and partly the view is taken because of the model-theoretic and logical tools which can be used to understand the nature of feature structures and the expressive power of the descriptive formalism.

After that, I will discuss various properties of the logics and their models, including mathematical ways of modeling feature structures. An important point to remember is that there may well be no unique way to view the structures. Just as we can view a Boolean algebra as either an abstract algebra, a partially ordered set, or as a topological space, we can think about feature structures with respect to their algebraic properties, their order-theoretic properties, and their connections to set theory. Perhaps most importantly, there is also a dual view of feature logics as either logics or as type systems. It is the mark of a robust class of structures that there are several ways to see them mathematically. I hope also that the applications in linguistics and computer science will become clear as we proceed.

The chapter ends with a linguistic application, concerning the theory commonly known as relational grammar, and then a short discussion of possible future directions for the theory of feature systems and their logics.

1.2. Some background

One aim of feature logic is to make precise sense of notations like the one in Figure 1.

This notation, called a *feature matrix*, or *attribute-value matrix*, is common to a number of linguistic theories. It became well-known first in phonology, through the influential

$$\begin{bmatrix} \text{vp} & \\ \text{AGR} & \boxed{1}\begin{bmatrix}\text{NUM} & \text{sing}\\ \text{PERS} & \text{3rd}\end{bmatrix} \\ \text{SUBJ} & \boxed{1}\end{bmatrix}$$

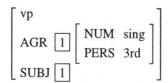

Fig. 1. A feature matrix.

work of Chomsky and Halle mentioned above. The descriptive notation continued in transformational theory (Chomsky, 1965), and became a *lingua franca* in the linguistic theories of Lexical-Functional Grammar (LFG) (Kaplan and Bresnan, 1982), Generalized Phrase-Structure Grammar (GPSG) (Gazdar, Klein, Pullum and Sag, 1985), and Head-driven Phrase-Structure Grammar (HPSG) (Pollard and Sag, 1987). The notation (and extensions thereof) is also the subject matter of the computational frameworks Functional Unification Grammar (FUG) (Kay, 1979) and PATR-II (Shieber, 1986), as well as mixed frameworks like Categorial Unification Grammar (see the Categorial Grammar chapter in this volume).

What use is made of these structures by each of these theories and frameworks? In LFG, the structures are called *f-structures*, and are viewed, along with trees, as linguistic descriptions. The role of a grammar is to constrain the descriptions; so they are thought of as model-theoretic objects which a grammar constrains by virtue of the conditions placed on functional roles (like SUBJECT). In GPSG, somewhat by contrast, the structures are regarded as giving an extended notion of linguistic category. So the above structure is a "more informative" kind of noun phrase. One aim of GPSG was to show that only a finite number of categories still suffice for natural language, so that in a weak sense, context-freeness of natural language still obtains. There was thus an effort made to limit the number of features (like SUBJECT) necessary for natural language description. On the way to this goal, though, GPSG introduced a logic for constraining the structures; one of the first explicit feature logics. (This was recognized as a true modal logic by Kracht (1989).) Finally, the theory of HPSG views feature structures as satisfiers of constraints as well. Here feature structures are used both for phrasal information and for other functional information. The kinds of feature structures vary: use is made of feature structures with set and sequence values embedded in them.

As for the computational frameworks, feature structures are used in Kay's FUG as representatives of linguistic *types*. We thus find the constraints of the grammar presented as type declarations, which means that disjunctive type restrictions are stated feature-theoretically. There is no separate use of a logic. We will see a formalization of this idea when we get to the order-theoretic aspects of the structures in Section 6. The other main computational framework, PATR-II, was instrumental in showing how *partial information* was encoded in feature structures, and how the *unification* of two structures encoded the sum of the information in both. It also emphasized the distinction between *extensional* versus *intensional* identity in the structures, by means of an explicit way to denote the sharing of structures. This kind of sharing is denoted in Figure 1 by the coreference markers like [1]. We should mention as well that the same ideas, though not the notation, appeared in the definite clause grammar (DCG) framework (Pereira and Warren, 1980). This system is rather obviously logic-based, as the control mechanism is a logic programming language.

There are feature constraints in other formalisms: for example, the current Chomskyan system of principles and parameters (the descendant of government-binding theory) (Haegeman, 1991), their role is somewhat limited. The general flavor of such systems is becoming increasingly like other constraint-based theories, though the details are quite different. In like manner, one uses feature constraints in the framework of tree adjoining grammars (Joshi and Schabes, 1992). Although the primary focus of TAG is tree-based, and purely generative, the addition of features makes the task of describing and generating actual language fragments much simpler (Vijay-Shanker, 1987).

Two other significant contributions to the theory of features must be mentioned. One important influence is Shieber's work on constraints in grammatical formalisms, started in his thesis (Shieber, 1989), and continued in his book (Shieber, 1992). Another is Mukai's work on the "Complex Indeterminate Language" CIL. (Mukai, 1990.) This latter was one of the pioneering computational efforts, and the theory is equally interesting. A theoretical summary can be found in (Mukai, 1991); this work is one of a few references I know of that mentions *coinductive* techniques for the semantics of Horn clause programs with feature constraints.

Finally, credit for the first complete integration of "feature logic" and linguistic theory may, I think, go to Johnson and Postal's *arc pair grammar* (Johnson and Postal, 1980). This is a fully formalized – in first-order logic – version of earlier work of Postal and Perlmutter on relational grammar. Arc pair grammar, in retrospect, was well ahead of its time. The ideas of DCG, for example, had not even been enunciated. GPSG, although under development, did not have a full logic to go with it. Furthermore, the idea of *constraints* or *principles* are very clear, and in some sense precede Chomsky's current theory. I will cover, as an application of feature logic, a current version of this theory due to Johnson and Moss (1993), called *stratified feature grammar.* To my mind this is the kind of synthesis of logic and linguistics that one hopes for when one proposes a theoretical framework like feature logic.

2. Formalizing feature systems

Our working hypothesis about objects like Figure 1 is that it is a readable notation for what computer scientists call a *data structure*. Such a data structure (here specialized to feature structures) earns an ontological equality with things like tree structures, which are well-understood linguistic objects. The kind of information contained in a feature structure is then information about the constituents of a typical utterance. Such information is constrained by the grammar of a language. So the grammar functions as a logical description language, and the feature structures associated with an utterance are limited by the "assertional constraints" of the grammar.

As with many data structures, including tree structures, however, one can give a mathematical specification in terms of abstract sets of objects. So, for example, tree structures can be defined as a certain kind of partially ordered set, perhaps with a labeling function to add information to the nodes, and so forth. The advantage of this is that we do not have to commit ourselves to a notation in advance, and we may find that there are many more useful examples than we had anticipated. We therefore begin with a noncommittal approach to feature structures, which first considers a type of algebraic structure, called a *feature system.* The class of feature structures themselves will be a subclass of this slightly more general class. It will eventually turn out that a feature structure can be considered as a feature system on its own, and also that the "set" of feature structures can be made into a feature system.

The general definition appears in (Blackburn and Spaan, 1993) and (Moshier, 1993). It unifies the definitions found in (Johnson, 1988) and (Smolka, 1992). We will later relate the definition to others found in the literature.

We begin with the notion of a signature:

DEFINITION 2.1. Let L be a set of **feature names**, and A be a set of **sort names**. We call the pair $\langle L, A \rangle$ a **feature signature**.

EXAMPLE 2.1. Referring to Figure 1, typical elements of L would be names like AGR or NUM. A typical sort name might be "vp".

DEFINITION 2.2 (*Feature system*). A feature system of signature $\langle L, A \rangle$ is a tuple

$$\mathcal{A} = \langle D, \{f_l\}_{l \in L}, \{D_a\}_{a \in A} \rangle,$$

where for each feature name l, f_l is a partial function on D, and for each sort name a, D_a is a subset of D.

The term *feature algebra* has been used to refer to similar systems by Smolka (1992). We do not use that term here, because technically, an algebra over some signature usually consists only of total operations on the carrier D. Because we have predicates D_a, our systems are somewhat more ontologically complex than algebras. Blackburn and Spaan call these structures either *attribute value structures* or *Kripke models*. (The last terminology reflects the fact that the structures are used to interpret the modal versions of feature logic.)

REMARK (*Notation*). We write function symbols for features on the right, so that $f(d)$ is written df. If f is defined at d, we write $df{\downarrow}$, and otherwise $df{\uparrow}$. We use p, q to denote strings of feature names, also known as *paths*, and if we write an equation $dp = eq$ it is intended that the appropriate composed function on the left side is defined; so is the composed function on the right, and the two values are equal. (This is not the standard convention for partial function equality, which regards the equation as true if both functions are undefined.)

EXAMPLE 2.2 (*Various feature systems*).

- The **Term system** $\mathbf{T}(\Sigma, X)$. Let Σ be a ranked alphabet of function symbols,[1] and X a countable set of variables or *parameters*. We make this set into a feature system of signature $\langle \mathbb{N}, \Sigma \rangle$, where $\mathbb{N}$ is the set of natural numbers. The elements of $\mathbf{T}(\Sigma, X)$ are first-order terms over Σ and X The features are the natural numbers $1, 2, \ldots$. The feature i gives us the ith argument term of a term, if it exists. For example, we have $(\sigma(x, \tau(a), b))2 = \tau(a)$, where σ has rank 3, and τ rank 1. For D_σ we take $\{\sigma(t_1, \ldots, t_n) \mid t_i \in \mathbf{T}(\Sigma, X)\}$. This example, due to Smolka (1992), arises from logic programming, where terms are used as information bearers. It also gives a model of tree structures *qua* feature system, as the correspondence between ordered, labeled trees and first-order terms is well-understood. Our next example is a variation on this theme.
- The **typed tree system** $\mathbf{T}(L, A)$. Consider L and A, the set of labels and types, as alphabets. Then the domain $D^{\mathbf{T}}$ of the tree system consists of all pairs (T, θ), where T is a nonempty, prefix-closed subset of of L^*, and θ is a partial function from T to A. If $(T, \theta) \in D^{\mathbf{T}}$, and $f \in L$, we define $Tf = \{p \mid fp \in T\}$, if this set is nonempty, and undefined otherwise. We also set $(\theta f)(p) = \theta(fp)$. In this system $D_a = \{T \mid \theta(\lambda) = a\}$ for $a \in A$, where λ is the null string.
- The **typed Nerode system** $\mathbf{N}(L, A)$. The domain D of this system consists of triples (T, N, θ), where T is as above, and N is a right-invariant equivalence relation on T respecting θ; that is, if p and q are strings in T, with $p\ N\ q$, and $pf \in T$ for a feature f, then (i) $qf \in T$ and $pf\ N\ qf$ (similarly if $qf \in T$); (ii) if $p\ N\ q$ and $\theta(p) = a$ then $\theta(q) = a$. We define $(T, N)f$ to be (Tf, Nf), where Tf and θf are as above, and Nf is given by $p\ (Nf)\ q$ if and only if $fp\ N\ fq$. We will use this system for representing abstract feature structures with structure-sharing.
- Consider a six-element domain consisting of Amy, Alice, Albert, and Anne, and the colors brown and red. Let $A = \{\text{TALL}, \text{HUNGRY}\}$. Take L to have one feature, HAIRCOLOR, with brown or red as a value. are atoms. The tall people are Amy and Albert. The hungry people are Anne, Albert, and Alice. Anne has brown hair, Amy and Albert have red hair, and Alice's hair color is not known. So, (*amy*) HAIRCOLOR = *red*, and so forth. This example is a more "real-life" one, which might arise in an AI situation.
- The **Feature Graph system F**. The elements of this system are pairs (G, n), where G is a finite directed graph, and n is a node of G. Nodes are taken from a fixed countable set; say the integers. Each arc is labeled with an element of L, and no two outgoing arcs are labeled with the same element of L. Nodes may optionally be labeled with elements of A. In this system, we interpret features f as follows: let $(G, n)f$ be the graph (G, nf), where nf is the unique node of G pointed to be the arc starting at n and labeled by f, if there is such an arc. We define, for $a \in A$, the set D_a to be the collection $\{(G, n) \mid \text{the label of } n \text{ is } a\}$.

We can think of attribute-value matrices as informal notations for feature graphs. Each submatrix of an AVM is in effect a node of the graph. Consider Figure 1. Coreference

[1] Rank is the same as arity.

markers like $\boxed{1}$ at the end of feature names like SUBJ indicate that the arc labeled SUBJ should point to the (unique) submatrix which is also tagged with that number, namely

$$\begin{bmatrix} \text{NUM} & \text{sing} \\ \text{PERS} & \text{3rd} \end{bmatrix}.$$

We continue with some useful concepts for the sequel.

DEFINITION 2.3. A *subsystem* of a feature system $\mathbf{A}$ consists of (i) a subset E of $D^{\mathbf{A}}$ such that if f is a feature, $d \in E$, and $df\downarrow$, then $df \in E$, and (ii) subsets E_a of D_a such that $E_a \subseteq E$. We also define the *principal subsystem* $P(d)$ generated by an element d of $D^{\mathbf{A}}$. The domain $E(d)$ of this subsystem is the set $\{d\pi \mid \pi \in L^* \wedge dp\downarrow\}$, and $E_a = D_a \cap E(d)$. A feature system is *point generated* or *principal* if $D = P(d_0)$ for some $d_0 \in D$. Another official name for such a system is *feature structure.*

We say that a feature system is finite if its domain is a finite set.

DEFINITION 2.4 (*Homomorphism*). A **homomorphism** between two feature systems $\mathcal{A}$ and $\mathcal{B}$ (of the same signature) is a total map γ between the two domains satisfying

(i) For any $d \in D^{\mathbf{A}}$ and $f \in L$, if $d\gamma\downarrow$ and $df^{\mathbf{A}}\downarrow$, then $df^{\mathbf{A}}\gamma = d\gamma f^{\mathbf{B}}$. (In particular, $d\gamma f^{\mathcal{B}}$ is defined.)

(ii) Whenever $d \in D_a^{\mathbf{A}}$, we have $d\gamma \in D_a^{\mathbf{B}}$.

DEFINITION 2.5. Let $\mathbf{A}$ be a feature system. The **subsumption preorder** $\sqsubseteq$ on $\mathbf{A}$ is defined as follows:

$$d \sqsubseteq e \iff \text{there is a homomorphism } \gamma : P(d) \to P(e), \text{ with } d\gamma = e.$$

We say that d *subsumes* e.

EXAMPLES.

- In the Term system, a term t subsumes a term u iff there is a substitution θ such that $t\theta = u$.
- In the (Amy, Alice, etc.) system above, Alice subsumes Anne, and no other relationships hold other than the identity; for example Anne does not subsume Alice because Anne's hair color is instantiated, whereas Alice's is not defined; Anne does not subsume Albert because Albert has red hair and Anne's is brown; and Anne does not subsume Amy because Amy is not hungry.

The intuitive idea behind the definition of subsumption is that of information content. If an element d subsumes an element e, then in some sense e bears at least as much information as d does.

3. Feature logics

We now introduce several logical languages which will be interpreted in variants of feature systems. All of these logics can be defined relative to the signature (L, A).

3.1. Kasper–Rounds logic

The language L(KR) was introduced in (Kasper and Rounds, 1986, 1990) to solve the problem of expressing disjunctive information in feature structures, while at the same time capturing the constraints implicit in Shieber's PATR-II (Shieber, 1986). The language L(KR) consists of *basic* and *compound* formulas. Assuming L and A as above, the basic formulas of L(KR) are as follows

- (Constants) a for each $a \in A$;
- (Truth) The special formula **true**;
- (Path equations) $p \doteq q$ for $p, q \in L^*$.

Then the compound formulas are given inductively. If φ and ψ are formulas, then so are

- $\varphi \wedge \psi$;
- $\varphi \vee \psi$;
- $l : \varphi$ for $l \in L$.

(In point of fact, Kasper and Rounds introduced, instead of path equations $p \doteq q$, finite sets E of paths as formulas, with the interpretation that all paths the set E were to be equal. We use the more readable notation here.)

A path equation models coreference constraints, as in PATR-II, and analogously in LFG. For example, we may have the PATR-II rule

$$\text{VP} \rightarrow \text{V NP}$$

with the constraint

$$\text{V agr} \doteq \text{NP agr.}$$

If we regard V, NP, and "agr" as feature names, then this equation says that the "V feature" of the VP shares agreement information with the "NP feature". Of course, in this case, the V and NP features refer to the actual constituents of the VP.

The semantics of Kasper–Rounds logic is straightforward given the concept of a feature system. Let **A** be such a feature system, fixed for the discussion. Let d range over elements in $D^{\mathbf{A}}$. Then we say

- $d \models a$ if $d \in D_a$;
- $d \models$ **true** always;
- $d \models p \doteq q$ if $dp = dq$;
- $d \models \varphi \wedge \psi$ if $d \models \varphi$ and $d \models \psi$;
- $d \models \varphi \vee \psi$ if $d \models \varphi$ or $d \models \psi$;
- $d \models l : \phi$ if $dl \models \varphi$ (implicitly dl is defined).

This definition is not quite the original semantics for the logic. There, the interpretation of a constant symbol a was required to be a set D_a consisting of just one element, and distinct constants received distinct interpretations. (Such a feature system is called a *feature algebra* in (Smolka, 1992; Dörre and Rounds, 1992).)

Kasper and Rounds provided a number of basic results about their logic, including an (almost) complete axiom system. We defer discussion of completeness results until later, and point out the connections between logical formulas and unification.

Consider the feature graph system **F**. An *isomorphism* of two graphs (G, n) and (H, m) is an ordinary graph isomorphism between the node sets of G and H, sending n to m. It is possible to show that the subsumption preorder on the feature graph algebra is a partial order, up to isomorphism. Further, if two graphs have an upper bound in this ordering, then they have a least such, up to isomorphism. This least upper bound (which can be calculated quite efficiently) is called the *unification* of the two graphs. (These results are due to Moshier (1988).)

Any formula in Kasper–Rounds logic has a finite number of subsumption-minimal satisfying feature graphs, again up to isomorphism. The basic fact about the logic is then that if (G, n) is a minimal satisfier of the formula φ, and (H, m) of ψ, then the unification of (G, m) and (H, n) is a minimal satisfier of the conjunction $\varphi \wedge \psi$. This fact makes it possible to compute the minimal satisfiers of the conjunction of two disjunctive formulas by pairwise unifying the minimal satisfiers of the two separate formulas, and thus leads to an elucidation of the "semantics of disjunctive feature structures" by regarding a disjunctive structure not as a semantic entity, but instead, a disjunctive formula – a description of a set of non-disjunctive structures.

Another distinguishing characteristic of Kasper–Rounds logic is *persistence*. Because the logic contains no negations, we have the fact that if an element d satisfies φ, and $d \sqsubseteq e$, then e satisfies φ too. Combined with the results in the previous paragraph, this means that the set of satisfiers of any Kasper–Rounds formula can be described as the upward closure, in the subsumption preorder, of the set of minimal satisfiers.

Finally, a remark on the connection of Kasper–Rounds to logics of programming is in order. Since feature graphs are essentially nothing more than the graphs of deterministic finite automata, it follows that Kasper–Rounds logic formulas describe possible transition systems of this type, albeit in a very limited way. The formulas of the form $l : \varphi$, in particular, describe the state of a system after an "action" l has been performed. So we can think of $l :$ as a kind of modal operator on formulas. This is the basic idea of dynamic logic (Pratt, 1976), where l in general could be a large program. The direct progenitor of Kasper–Rounds logic is, in fact, a modal logic due to Hennessy and Milner (1985), appropriate for describing nondeterministic transition systems.

3.2. Modal feature logics

Much has been made of the modal nature of Kasper–Rounds. Blackburn (1993), Blackburn and Spaan (1993), and Reape (1994) have investigated this direction extensively. In their formulation, the symbols a can be thought of as special propositional variables, perhaps rewritten as p_a. The modality $l : \varphi$ is written $\langle l \rangle \varphi$, and a negation operator $\neg\phi$ is included. The use of the $\langle\ \rangle$ notation is derived from the $\diamond$ or possibility modality in standard modal logic.

A feature system **A** can be rechristened a *Kripke model*, or *polyframe* in modal logic terminology. Now the elements $d \in D$ of the structure are thought of as possible worlds, and the interpretation of the arc labels l as unary partial functions give several accessibility relations between the worlds.

Blackburn (1993) shows how to treat path equations in the modal framework. He introduces *nominals*, an idea dating to Prior (1967). These are syntactic objects, written i, j, k (in effect constants in D) which are always interpreted as singleton subsets of D. So, instead of having path equations, one has instead basic formulas i, where i is a nominal. To get the effect of the equation $p \doteq q$, one writes instead $\langle p \rangle i \wedge \langle q \rangle i$, where i is a (fresh) nominal.

The distinction between the use of nominals and the use of path equations may not be obvious at first sight. However, notice that the formula $\langle p \rangle i \wedge \langle q \rangle i$ is not logically equivalent to the formula $\langle p \rangle j \wedge \langle q \rangle j$, where i and j are different nominals. This distinction shows up much more dramatically when the complexity issues for these logics are investigated. We will look at these problems below.

Blackburn and Spaan investigate various extensions of the basic modal formalism. The first of these is the *universal modality* $\Box$. Let φ be a formula of any of the types described so far. Then the semantics of $\Box\varphi$ is simply described as follows. Fix a Kripke model $\mathbf{A}$, and let $d \in D^{\mathbf{A}}$. Then

$$d \models \Box\varphi \iff (\forall e \in D)(e \models \varphi).$$

The universal modality finds application in GPSG: consider the *feature co-occurrence restriction*

$$[\text{VFORM}] \supset [-\text{N}, +\text{V}].$$

This says that any category classified as a verb form must have a positive "noun" and a negative "verb" quality. Phrased in modal feature logic, this would read

$$\Box(\text{vform: } \mathbf{true} \to \text{n: } + \wedge \text{ v: } -)$$

where VFORM, n, and v are attributes.

Another use of the modality would be to express the Head Feature Convention of GPSG and HPSG. This is a constraint which insists that the values of certain features occurring in constituents like verb phrases which are "headed" by verbs have the same values as features of the head as they do as features of the headed phrase. This would be expressed as a path equation in the scope of the universal modality.

Blackburn and Spaan cite the work of Evans (1988), where the $\Box$ modality is used in its dual form $\Diamond = \neg\Box\neg$ to express feature specification defaults. Specifically, the formula

$$(\Diamond\text{CASE: dat}) \to \text{CASE: dat}$$

is supposed to express that if it is consistent with known information that the case of a constituent is dative, then the case is dative. Unfortunately this use of the modality, when interpreted as the dual of the universal modality, does not express what is intended, as it says that if somewhere in a feature structure there is an occurrence of the CASE feature with a dative value, then there is an occurrence of the feature at the current level with the dative value. (Reparenthesizing the formula does not help, either, as the reader may check.) It seems that a more sophisticated approach to specifying defaults is necessary.

Gazdar, Pullum, Carpenter, Klein, Hukari and Levine (1988) also define a *master modality* $[*]\varphi$. The conditions for this are

$$d \models [*]\varphi \iff d \models \varphi \wedge dl \models [*]\varphi \text{ for all } l \in L \text{ such that } dl \text{ is defined.}$$

This definition is recursive, but plainly its force is the following, as pointed out by Blackburn and Spaan:

$$d \models \Box\varphi \quad \text{if } (\forall e \in P(d)(e \models \varphi)$$

where $P(d)$ is the set of all worlds reachable from d by any path (that is, the principal subsystem generated by d). This modality is very close to the universal modality in expressive power. The main interest is that it is defined recursively. This technique is of independent interest in feature logic, as we will see when we consider Moshier's fixed-point extensions. We should also mention that the master modality was studied in detail by Kracht (1989), and preceded the universal modality historically.

3.3. Heterogeneous modalities

We briefly look at the idea of *set-valued* feature systems. The basic idea in these systems is to notice that a set can be pictured graphically like a transition system. The elementhood relation is of course a binary relation on sets, so has a graph. Allowing this graph to have cycles leads to the idea of a non-well-founded set, and to the work of Aczel on the anti-foundation axiom (Aczel, 1988).

The simplest way to model feature structures with set values is to add a binary relation (representing set membership) to a feature system. If R is this binary relation, then by $d\,R\,e$ we mean that e is one of the members of d considered as a set. So an element of a feature system may have *attributes* (represented by feature arcs) as well as *members* (represented by R arcs). Obviously the relation R need not be functional, and obviously conditions on R will be required to make the extended graphs have set-like properties; in particular, to satisfy an extensionality property when sets can be non-well-founded.

Ignoring these difficulties for the moment, one way to give a modal feature logic encompassing set values is to add a new modality $\Box_s$ to our language. The semantics will be very simple:

$$d \models \Box_s\varphi \iff \text{for all } e \text{ with } dRe, e \models \varphi.$$

The logic obtained in this way is a combination of feature logic with the standard Kripke modal logic K, since there are no conditions on the relation R. Put another way, the following formulas are valid:

$$\Box_s\mathbf{true} \leftrightarrow \mathbf{true}$$

and

$$\Box_s(\varphi \wedge \psi) \leftrightarrow \Box_s\varphi \wedge \Box_s\psi.$$

This is observed by Moss (1991) in his paper on completeness theorems for feature logics. It is not the full story, however, since the relation R is not arbitrary, but has to satisfy extensionality conditions; more properly, to get a set theory out, one must axiomatize the relation between graphs and the sets they picture.

Some of the uses of set values arise when one is modeling linguistic objects containing a number of components, but in which the particular order or enumeration of the components is irrelevant. Consider, for example, of a list of NP conjuncts such as "apples and oranges". The situation in general is more complicated. Pollard and Moshier (1990) study the use of set values in HPSG. Consider the sentence "She likes him". This might be partially modeled by the following feature structure:

$$\begin{bmatrix} \text{CONTENT} & \begin{bmatrix} \text{EXPERIENCER } \boxed{1} \\ \text{THEME } \boxed{2} \end{bmatrix} \\ \text{CONTEXT} & .\{\boxed{1} \begin{bmatrix} \text{PERSON 3rd} \\ \text{NUMBER sing} \\ \text{GENDER fem} \end{bmatrix}, \boxed{2} \begin{bmatrix} \text{PERSON 3rd} \\ \text{NUMBER sing} \\ \text{GENDER masc} \end{bmatrix} .\} \end{bmatrix}$$

The value of the CONTEXT attribute is to be a set consisting of two parameters, each qualified to be of the appropriate person, number, and gender. These parameters are coreferential with the values of the EXPERIENCER and THEME attributes of the sentence.

Now we are faced with the problem of interpreting the "dotted brace" notation, and the notations within it. This is a problem independent of the logic used to describe such objects. The value of the CONTEXT attribute is a "set object", related by the relation R to the values of the EXPERIENCER and THEME attributes. For Pollard and Moshier, there cannot be more than two values in the set which is the value of the CONTEXT attribute. But, if this set value is merely a "partial set", one could hypothesize that potentially there could be more elements in the set. It all depends on the way one extends the idea of subsumption to set-valued attributes. We defer discussion until we have completed our survey of feature logics.

3.4. Reape's polyadic modal logic

We now come to a far-reaching generalization of feature logic. In fact, so much is contained in the generalization that the feature component of the logic is almost insignificant. This formalism is due to Reape (1994, especially Chapter 4).

Reape begins with the syntax of his logic, but it seems to be more perspicacious to start with the semantics. Assume that we are given a feature system $\mathbf{A}$. The set $D^{\mathbf{A}}$, in addition to being the domain of linguistic objects, may also possess additional mathematical structure. For example, D may be a Boolean algebra or a monoid. An example would be the case of set-valued feature structures, where we assume that the elements are sets (for the moment, let us say everything in D is a set). Then of course the set operations of union, intersection, and complement are available, as well as the membership relation.

Fix a feature signature as before, but augment the signature with function and relation symbols from some auxiliary set $\mathcal{R}$. So, in the set example, we use the signs for union, intersection, and complement, together with a function symbol $\{\cdot\}$ which takes an individual into the set consisting of that individual. Now the innovation in Reape's formalism is to regard these new symbols as modalities, just as features were regarded before. The feature matrix of Moshier and Pollard above, for example, can be thought of as a conjunctive formula read as follows:

$$\text{content: experiencer: } x \ \wedge \ \text{theme: } y \wedge \text{context: } \varphi$$

where φ is the formula

$$\{x \wedge \ \text{pers: } 3 \wedge \text{num: } \textit{sing} \wedge \text{gender: f}\} \\ \cup \{y \wedge \ \text{pers: } 3 \wedge \text{num: } \textit{sing} \wedge \text{gender: m}\}.$$

The difference between Reape's formalism and the structures of Moshier and Pollard then becomes one of the level at which one thinks of descriptions. For Moshier and Pollard, feature structures are semantic objects, to be further constrained by (an unspecified) logic. These semantic objects are themselves descriptive entities, furnishing partial information about an empirical domain. For Reape, the partiality enters at the level of syntax.

The full syntax of the Reape formalism is then as follows. Given a feature system $\mathbf{A}$ and auxiliary signature $\mathcal{R}$, we allow all the KR formulas, together with the rules that if $\varphi_1, \ldots, \varphi_n$ are formulas, then so are

$$r(\varphi_1, \ldots, \varphi_n),$$

for r an n-ary relation symbol, and

$$f(\varphi_1, \ldots, \varphi_n)$$

for f an auxiliary function symbol.

Turning to the formal semantics, the auxiliary functions are interpreted over $D^{\mathbf{A}}$ as usual: an n-ary function symbol is interpreted as an n-ary function on D. However, a relation symbol r is interpreted as an $(n+1)$-ary relation. The idea is that if $(d_1, \ldots, d_n, d)$ is in the interpretation of r, then the elements $d_1, \ldots, d_n$ stand in the relation r with respect to the current state d. An example will clarify this: instead of the union and set-former $\{\cdot\}$ of the above example, suppose instead we have the element-of relation $\textit{in}(x, z)$, indicating that x is a member of z. Then the above formula could be written

$$\text{content: experiencer: } x \wedge \ \text{theme: } y \ \wedge \ \text{context: } z \ \wedge \textit{in}(x, z) \wedge \textit{in}(y, z)$$

conjoined with the formula

$$x \wedge \text{pers: } 3 \wedge \text{ num: sing } \wedge \text{ sex: f} \wedge y \wedge \text{pers: } 3 \wedge \text{ num: sing } \wedge \text{ sex: m.}$$

(In fact, this new formula expresses something slightly different from the old one, in that it does not prevent the set z from having more members.)

Let the interpretation of r be $I(r)$ and of f be $I(f)$. As usual let $d \in d^{\mathbf{A}}$.

- $d \models f(\varphi_1, \ldots, \varphi_n)$ iff for some $d_1, \ldots, d_n \in D$, we have $I(f)(d_1, \ldots, d_n) = d$;
- $d \models r(\varphi_1, \ldots, \varphi_n)$ iff for some $d_1, \ldots, d_n \in D$, we have $I(r)(d_1, \ldots, d_n, d)$.

Notice the existential character of these polymodalities; also notice that if the formulas φ_i are nominals, then there will be a unique choice of the d_i in the above clauses. Finally, notice that if f is a unary function, then the interpretation of $f(\varphi)$ will not be the same as if f were considered a feature, and the formula were $f : \varphi$. In the first case, $d \models f(x)$ if for the element d_x interpreting the nominal x, we have $d = f(d_x)$. In the second case, $d \models f : x$ if $d_x = f(d)$. That is to say, the auxiliary function symbols are used as *constructors*, while the features are used as *selectors*.

Reape provides an axiom system and proof of completeness for his system, but does not investigate notions like subsumption. This seems to be because his semantic objects are total ones, not partial objects as in Kasper–Rounds and Moshier–Pollard. In fact, the view of feature structures as partial objects is not important for many of the modal logics extending Kasper–Rounds. What these logics bring is a wealth of techniques for understanding expressiveness, completeness, compactness, and complexity.

Bibliographic remarks on modal logics. Much more is known on polyadic modal logic in general. They have been extensively studied by Goldblatt (1989). Decidability results for KR logic, and indeed the logics in (Kracht, 1989) appear in much stronger form for *deterministic propositional dynamic logic* (Ben-Ari, Halpern and Pnueli, 1982).

3.5. Negation and implication

Now we consider adding connectives to Kasper–Rounds logic which (in the partial-description view) destroy persistence, at least if they are given a classical interpretation. Syntactically, we allow to form negations $\neg\varphi$ and $\varphi \to \psi$. The difficulty comes in giving the semantics.

One can, of course adopt the classical negation:

- $d \models \neg f$ iff not $d \models f$

with implication being defined as the standard material notion. This makes sense mathematically, especially if feature structures are regarded as total objects. However, consider what happens if feature structures are partial descriptions. Then if the feature l is not defined at a node d, it may be because we do not have the information at the present time that it is defined. Typically we get this behavior when we are parsing, and we do not know what the object of a verb might be, for example – even whether the verb will take an object. If we say $\neg$*person* : *third*, then according to the classical semantics, either the feature *person* is undefined at the current node, or it is defined, and the value is not "third". We really would rather have our specification mean this second possibility. As we have indicated, if features were always total functions, this is what we would get, but we do not wish features always to be total.

A simple way out of this difficulty was proposed by Dawar and Vijay-Shanker (1991). The basic idea is to adopt a strong Kleene three-valued semantics for feature logic. To express this concisely, we recall the truth tables for the Boolean connectives proposed by Kleene:

$\wedge$	**t**	**f**	**u**
t	**t**	**f**	**u**
f	**f**	**f**	**f**
u	**u**	**f**	**u**

$\vee$	**t**	**f**	**u**
t	**t**	**t**	**t**
f	**t**	**f**	**u**
u	**t**	**u**	**u**

p	$\neg p$
t	**f**
f	**t**
u	**u**

in which **u** stands for "undefined".

Let **A** be a feature system. If $d \in D^{\mathbf{A}}$, and φ is a feature logic formula with negation, we can define the *valuation* $[\![\varphi]\!](d)$ recursively on the structure of φ:

(i) $[\![\mathbf{true}]\!](d) = t$;

(ii) $[\![a]\!](d) = \begin{cases} t & \text{if } d \in D_a; \\ f & \text{otherwise.} \end{cases}$

(iii) $[\![p \doteq q]\!](d) = \begin{cases} t & \text{if } dp = dq; \\ f & \text{if } dp \text{ and } dq \text{ are both defined and unequal;} \\ u & \text{otherwise.} \end{cases}$

(iv) $[\![l : \varphi]\!](d) = \begin{cases} t & \text{if } [\![\varphi]\!](dl) = t; \\ f & \text{if } [\![\varphi]\!](dl) = f; \\ u & \text{otherwise.} \end{cases}$

(v) $[\![\varphi \wedge \psi]\!](d) = [\![\varphi]\!](d) \wedge [\![\psi]\!](d)$;

(vi) $[\![\varphi \vee \psi]\!](d) = [\![\varphi]\!](d) \vee [\![\psi]\!](d)$;

(vii) $[\![\neg\varphi]\!](d) = \neg[\![\varphi]\!](d)$,

where of course the functions $\wedge$, and so forth, on the right side are the Kleene three-valued functions.

One would like, with this definition, to recapture the persistence property of Kasper–Rounds logic augmented with negation. Stated again, if $[\![\varphi]\!](d) = t$, and $d \sqsubseteq e$, then $[\![\varphi]\!](e) = t$. Unfortunately this result does not quite go through, because of clause (iii) of the definition. To remedy this problem, Dawar and Vijay-Shanker replace the condition that *dp* and *dq* are both defined and unequal, by the condition that these elements are defined but not unifiable. Although this solves the problem, it requires that one literally interpret the logic in a feature system which supports unification, like the feature graph system or the Nerode system. The other problem with the three-valued interpretation above is that the formula $\neg l : \mathbf{true}$ is unsatisfiable, in fact logically equivalent to **false** =

$\neg$**true**. This means that if we define $\varphi \to \psi$ as the material conditional $\neg\varphi \vee \psi$ then we get intuitively incorrect behavior. For example, suppose we want to assert that if the feature l is defined at d, then the value of the *case* feature must be dative. One would naturally write

$$l : \mathbf{true} \to case : dat$$

but this formula is just equivalent to $case : dat$. Here the problem is that the material conditional is intuitively expressed, not with the strong Kleene negation, but with the weak version. A way out of the second difficulty is suggested by Dawar and Vijay-Shanker. In this approach, one looks not at the logic, but at the feature system definition itself. The idea is to specify in the semantics, the set of features which can *never* be defined at a node. If one does this, then the formula $\neg l :$ **true**, for example, could be satisfiable by a node where the feature l is prohibited.

This idea generalizes: the book by Carpenter (1992) shows how to assign types to nodes in such a way that the allowed features for a node are specified as part of the type. Typing also suggests a way out of the path equation persistence problem as well, and in fact Carpenter provides an elegant solution to the problem of negated path equations. We return to the logic of typed structures below.

3.6. *Intuitionistic logic*

The problem of saying that a feature can *never* become defined can, of course, be handled as a modal statement, and also by the idea implicit in intuitionistic logic that a negative statement is one that can be positively refuted. This chapter is not the place to review these well-known ideas, but this section is appropriate for mentioning the intuitionistic version of feature logic introduced by Moshier and Rounds (1987), in fact to recapture the persistence property of Kasper–Rounds while at the same time dealing with the problems mentioned in the section on three-valued systems.

The syntax of feature logic remains the same in this section; we have Kasper–Rounds augmented with negation and implication (and the formula **false**). However, we have a new kind of Kripke structure for interpreting formulae. We follow here the definition of Moss (1991), as it simplifies the notions in Moshier–Rounds considerably. In further point of fact, this presentation simplifies again Moss' definitions, while retaining the essential flavor.

The basic idea is to interpret formulae over a Kripke structure, where now in addition to the accessibilities provided by the features, we use the subsumption relation $\sqsubseteq$ as another accessibility notion. Moss does not work with the relation given above, but with a weaker notion: instead of using a homomorphism as a way to relate nodes d and e, he uses a more general relation. So let us say that a relation $\preceq$ on the nodes of a feature system $\mathbf{A}$ is an *approximation* if

$$d \preceq e \text{ and } dl \text{ is defined } \Rightarrow dl \preceq el$$

and

$$d \preceq e \text{ and } d \in D_a \Rightarrow e \in D_a.$$

To deal with preservation of path equalities, we also require

$$d \preceq e \text{ and } dp = dq \ \Rightarrow ep = eq.$$

By a Kripke structure we now mean a structure $(\mathbf{A}, \preceq)$ where $\mathbf{A}$ is a feature system and $\preceq$ is an approximation relation.

Instead of the satisfaction relation $\models$ used above, we now consider a forcing relation $\Vdash$ to interpret formulas. The clauses are as follows, where $\mathbf{A}$ is fixed and $d \in D^{\mathbf{A}}$:

- $d \Vdash a$ if $d \in D_a$;
- $d \Vdash$ **true** always;
- $d \Vdash$ **false** never;
- $d \Vdash p \doteq q$ if $dp = dq$;
- $d \Vdash \varphi \wedge \psi$ if $d \Vdash \varphi$ and $d \Vdash \psi$;
- $d \Vdash \varphi \vee \psi$ if $d \Vdash \varphi$ or $d \Vdash \psi$;
- $d \Vdash l : \phi$ if $dl \Vdash \varphi$ (implicitly dl is defined);
- $d \Vdash \varphi \to \psi$ if for all e such that $d \preceq e$, if $e \Vdash \varphi$, then $e \Vdash \psi$.

We do not need to include negation in this definition, since $\neg\varphi$ can be defined as $\varphi \to$ **false**.

Now notice that, as in the standard intuitionistic logics, that the law of the excluded middle may fail. Indeed, the formula l : **true** is not forced by a node with the feature l undefined, but neither is the formula $\neg(l$: **true**), as we may have another element e where the feature l is defined. But we now have persistence once again, and we do not have that l : **true** $\to$ *case* : *dat* is logically equivalent to *case* : *dat* (here, logical equivalence means forced equivalently over all Kripke structures).

Once again we defer the properties of such a system to a later section, and continue with our survey of feature logics.

3.7. *Fixed-point extensions*

We now come to another extension of Kasper–Rounds logic which arises from the desire to define formulas recursively. An example of this was the master modality of Gazdar, Pullum, Carpenter, Klein, Hukari and Levine (1988) which we saw in Section 3.2. This extension is due to Moshier (1988). If we use a strong logic of this form, then many of the ideas in Kay's *functional unification grammar* can be captured (for a preliminary attempt to do this, see Rounds and Manaster Ramer (1987)). The point is that a grammar can be viewed as a logic incorporating a natural recursion construct.

In the following, we will ignore some of the formula syntax introduced by Moshier. Instead we will concentrate on the recursive nature of the logic. We augment our syntax with a set of *variables* V. An interpretation $\mathbf{A}$ and an *environment* $\rho : V \to \mathrm{POW}(D^{\mathbf{A}})$

will be required to interpret formulas. The idea of an environment is first that variables intuitively represent "places" in a formula where other formulas can be substituted. Second, an environment will tell us, for one of these variables, what the set of satisfying nodes is for the formula that it stands for.

The syntax of Moshier's logic $\mathrm{L}(EKR1)$ is then the same as for Kasper–Rounds, with the addition of the following clauses:

- Every $v \in V$ is a formula;
- If $\varphi_1, \ldots, \varphi_n, \varphi$ are formulas, and $x_1, \ldots, x_n \in V$, then $[x_1 \leftarrow \varphi_1, \ldots, x_n \leftarrow \varphi_n]\varphi$ is a formula.

The idea of the recursion construct is that the formula φ will contain free occurrences of the x_i, and that successively repeating substitutions given in the bracketed part will lead to a kind of "infinitary" formula.

For example, consider the (as yet undefined) formula $\langle l^* \rangle a$, which, to be satisfied at a node, requires there to be some finite sequence of l's leading to a node satisfying a. This could be written as an infinitary formula

$$x = a \vee l : a \vee l : l : a \vee \cdots$$

Equivalently, it seemingly obeys the "equation"

$$x = a \vee l : x.$$

The intent of this is captured by the $\mathrm{L}(EKR1)$ formula

$$[x \leftarrow (a \vee l : x)]x$$

which could be thought of as a programming instruction to iteratively replace x by $a \vee l : x$. It turns out, however, that a more elegant semantics for the recursion operator can be given not by a notion of substitution, but by a compositional semantic definition making elementary use of fixed-point notions from recursion theory and computer science. This is in fact the way recursive constructs typically are defined in programming language semantics; the idea was pioneered in computer science by Scott (1982). The adaptation to feature logic follows work by Immerman (1982), Vardi (1982), and Blass and Gurevich (1987).

The semantics of $\mathrm{L}(EKR1)$ can be given by simple equations, but "unpacking" these equations leads to complexities, so we will be slow in our explanations. The basic idea is to define, for a formula φ and environment ρ, a subset $[\![\varphi]\!](\rho)$ of $D^{\mathbf{A}}$, where as usual $\mathbf{A}$ is a feature system. The set $[\![\varphi]\!](\rho)$ is the set of nodes which satisfy the formula φ, given that the set $\rho(x)$ is the set of nodes satisfying the "placeholder" formula x occurring free in φ. We therefore define (given a feature system $\mathbf{A}$) the *denotation* $[\![\varphi]\!]$ as a function from environments to subsets of $D^{\mathbf{A}}$, by induction on the structure of φ:

- $[\![a]\!](\rho) = D_a$;
- $[\![\mathbf{true}]\!](\rho) = D^{\mathbf{A}}$;
- $[\![p \doteq q]\!](\rho) = \{d \in D^{\mathbf{A}} \mid dp = dq\}$;

- $[\![x]\!](\rho) = \rho(x)$;
- $[\![l:\varphi]\!](\rho) = \{d \in D^{\mathbf{A}} \mid dl \in [\![\varphi]\!](\rho)\}$;
- $[\![\varphi \wedge \psi]\!](\rho) = [\![\varphi]\!](\rho) \cap [\![\psi]\!](\rho)$;
- $[\![\varphi \vee \psi]\!](\rho) = [\![\varphi]\!](\rho) \cup [\![\psi]\!](\rho)$;
- $[\![[x_1 \leftarrow \varphi_1, \ldots, x_n \leftarrow \varphi_n]\varphi]\!](\rho) = [\![\varphi]\!](\rho^*)$, where ρ^* is the *least fixed point* of a certain monotonic operator $T[x_1 \leftarrow \varphi_1, \ldots x_n \leftarrow \varphi_n; \rho]$ from environments to environments. The definition of T is

$$T[x_1 \leftarrow \varphi_1, \ldots, x_n \leftarrow \varphi_n; \rho](\tau)(x) = \begin{cases} [\![\varphi_1]\!](\tau)(x) & \text{if } x = x_1; \\ \vdots & \\ [\![\varphi_n]\!](\tau)(x) & \text{if } x = x_n; \\ \rho(x) & \text{otherwise.} \end{cases}$$

EXAMPLE 3.1. Consider the formula $\psi = [x_1 \leftarrow (a \vee l : x_1)]x_1$. We calculate the meaning $[\![\psi]\!]$ in the Feature Tree system (cf. Example 2.2). The formula is a fixpoint formula, satisfying the last clause of the inductive definition. So in this case, the definition of T reduces to:

$$T[x_1 \leftarrow (a \vee l : x_1); \rho](\tau)(x) = \begin{cases} [\![a \vee l : x_1]\!](\tau)(x) & \text{if } x = x_1; \\ \rho(x) & \text{otherwise.} \end{cases}$$

This in turn reduces to

$$T[x_1 \leftarrow (a \vee l : x_1); \rho](\tau)(x) = \begin{cases} \{a\} \cup \{t \mid t/l \in \tau(x)\} & \text{if } x = x_1; \\ \rho(x) & \text{otherwise.} \end{cases}$$

The least fixed point of this operator can be shown to be

$$\rho^*(x) = \begin{cases} \{a\} \cup \{t \mid (\exists n > 0)\,(t/(l^n) = a)\} & \text{if } x = x_1; \\ \rho(x) & \text{otherwise.} \end{cases}$$

The meaning of ψ is therefore

$$[\![x_1]\!](\rho^*) = \rho^*(x_1) = \{a\} \cup \{t \mid (\exists n > 0)\ \ (t/(l^n) = a)\}.$$

This is the set of all feature trees which are either the atom a or have a path of l's of some nonzero length leading to the leaf node labeled a, which accords exactly with the intuitive "infinitary" semantics proposed above.

What are these "least fixed points"? We still have to explain them, and demonstrate their existence. We will be using the classical theorem, variously attributed to Tarski, Knaster, and Kleene, that a monotonic operator F on a complete lattice $(R, \sqsubseteq)$ has a least fixed point: namely, an $x \in R$ such that $F(x) = x$ and for any other such y, we have $x \sqsubseteq y$. (To say that F is monotonic means that if $w \sqsubseteq z$ then $F(w) \sqsubseteq F(z)$.)

In our case, we take the lattice R to be the set of all environments ρ from the set of variables X to $\text{Pow}(D^{\mathbf{A}})$, and the ordering

$$\rho \sqsubseteq \tau \quad \text{iff} \quad \rho(x) \subseteq \tau(x) \text{ for all } x.$$

It remains to show that the operators T above are all actually monotonic. This is an easy consequence (in view of the definition of T) of the fact that the meaning $[\![\varphi]\!]$ is, for fixed φ, a monotonic function on environments. And the latter fact follows by induction on the structure of $\mathrm{L}(EKR1)$ formulas. Notice that here, by the way, is where the nonmonotonic operator of classical negation would invalidate the result.

The fixpoint existence theorem can be strengthened in special cases. If F is not only monotonic, but preserves all suprema of chains (i.e. is *continuous*) then there is a constructive way to calculate the least fixed point. Namely, the least fixed point x is given by

$$x = \bigvee_{i=1}^{\infty} F^n(\bot)$$

where $\bot$ is the least element of the lattice R, and F^n is the n-fold composition of F with itself. This formula was used to calculate ρ^* in the example above.

There are many properties of the $\mathrm{L}(EKR1)$ system. These include the usual logical properties, of which perhaps the most interesting is Moshier's result that $\mathrm{L}(EKR1)$ enjoys a finite model property. (Compare the analogous result, due to Fischer and Ladner (1979) for propositional dynamic logic (Pratt, 1976).) The result for $\mathrm{L}(EKR1)$ is possibly more complex, as more than just "regular" modalities can be introduced by fixpoint formulas.

Moshier applies his logic not only to the description of natural language syntax, but to computer language syntax as well. One example is the description of closed expressions of untyped lambda calculus. This formal language is not context-free, because of the problem of specifying variable binding. Its grammar, though, is naturally expressed in $\mathrm{L}(EKR1)$. Another example is the collection of all closed well-typable expressions of the untyped calculus. Here we must also ensure that occurrences of the same variable are all of the same type. However, not all programming languages are naturally specified in $\mathrm{L}(EKR1)$. The specification of polymorphic types, as in the programming language **ML**, seems to require an extension of $\mathrm{L}(EKR1)$ which allows the relation of subsumption to be a primitive relation of the language. These issues are beyond the scope of the chapter, but see Shieber (1992) for a discussion.

Recursion is also considered by Baader, Bürckert, Nebel, Nutt and Smolka (1991), and by Carpenter (1992). We turn now to a discussion of Carpenter's general treatment of feature logic.

3.8. The logic of typed feature structures

Carpenter's book *The Logic of Typed Feature Structures* (Carpenter, 1992, Chapter 6 ff.) involves making assumptions about feature structures themselves, as well as about their logic.

Carpenter is concerned with the use of feature structures in HPSG, and orients his discussion to the use HPSG will make of so-called *types*. According to the general theory, knowledge types of linguistic objects is what is shared by speakers of a language. So the problem of grammar is to specify the ways in which tokens of types may be produced and recognized.

To put type constraints on feature structures, Carpenter first assumes that there is a certain ordering relation prespecified on the sort set A. The reasons for this are partly computational and partly to accord with one of the usual notions in artificial intelligence: that of an *inheritance hierarchy*. This notion was spelled out in general for programming languages by Cardelli and Wegner (1985), where there are good reasons to associate types with each object. The first realization of typed feature structures themselves is probably due to Aït-Kaci (1984), in which the computational reasons for type checking via inheritance are made quite clear.

We already have a definition of feature structure as a principal or point-generated feature system. (Cf. Definition 2.3.) For the present, we only need to augment feature structures with a simple notion of type: when we say that a node d is of type a, where $a \in A$, then we mean that $d \in D_a$.

The technical condition placed on the type ordering $\sqsubseteq$ on A is that it be a *bounded complete partial order*, or *Scott domain*. For now we avoid certain complications by assuming that A is finite. The conditions then are that there be a least element $\bot$, which stands for the "most general" or "least informative" type, and that any two elements which have an upper bound in the ordering have a least or most general such. In this setting, the most general types appear at the bottom of the ordering, contrary to the usual practice in artificial intelligence. An example of such an ordering might place the type *sign* at the bottom, with *phrase* as a subtype being more specific, and thus "higher" in the ordering. The condition on upper bounds is made so that the result of unifying structures will be uniquely defined when it is possible to unify them.

The second kind of restriction placed on feature structures is called an *appropriateness condition*. For example, an attribute of *number* is not appropriate for the general type *sign*. But a feature which is appropriate for a type should be appropriate for any of its more specific subtypes. The idea of appropriateness is also a way of specifying negative information directly in feature structures. If a feature is not appropriate for a type, then it can never be defined at a node of a feature structure which has that type. Appropriateness is also a way of expressing at least some of the feature co-occurrence restrictions of GPSG.

Initially, adding the notion of appropriateness has little to do with feature logic itself. For example, Kasper–Rounds can be interpreted in the collection of typed feature structures. But it is clear that some of the validities of the logic will change. For instance, if a feature l is not appropriate for a type a then $a \wedge l : \mathbf{true}$ will be unsatisfiable.

Carpenter formalizes appropriateness restrictions as follows. Let $(A, \sqsubseteq)$ be the partially ordered set of sorts (primitive types.) An *appropriateness specification* is a partial function $Approp : L \times A \to A$ satisfying the following:

(i) For every feature $l \in L$, there is a most general type $Intro(l)$ such that $Approp(l, Intro(l))$ is defined;

(ii) If $Approp(l, a)$ is defined, and $a \sqsubseteq b$, then $Approp(l, b)$ is also defined and $Approp(l, a) \sqsubseteq Approp(l, b)$.

The intent of this definition is as follows. Think of the value of $Approp(l, a)$ as the most general type of value taken by feature f given that its argument is of type a. If the value is undefined, this means that the feature l is not appropriate for the type a. Then, condition (i) says that for each feature, there is a most general type for which it is appropriate. So if we know that a feature structure satisfies f : **true**, we can infer the most general type that can occur at the root of that structure. The second condition says that if a feature is appropriate for a type, then this is passed on to subtypes, and further, that the type of feature values for more specific kinds of inputs must be more specific than the general class of outputs. This is a standard requirement for most inheritance system specifications.

It should perhaps be pointed out that appropriateness specifications are analogous to the notion of *database schemata* in relational database theory. Such schemata determine the "shapes" of relations occurring in any databases using them. So for example, employees have certain attributes, such as *name, salary*, and so forth. The attribute *weight* would perhaps not be appropriate.

Appropriateness conditions are not the only place where types and typed feature structures can be useful, however. Carpenter has many other applications. We concentrate here on just one such: *recursive type constraint systems* (Carpenter, 1992, Chapter 15). These constraint systems form an interesting class of logical formulae which are connected on the one hand to $\mathrm{L}(EKR1)$ formulae, and on the other to the various kinds of master modalities. We begin with an example.

EXAMPLE 3.2. Suppose that *person* is a type, and consider the expression

$$person \Rightarrow adam \vee father : person.$$

Intuitively, this expresses a structured type, whose members are all those persons who have some chain of fathers leading back to Adam. In $\mathrm{L}(EKR1)$ this could be expressed by

$$[adam \vee father : x]x.$$

However, consider the closely related expression

$$person \Rightarrow employer : person.$$

We might wish the constraint to be satisfied by the cyclic feature structure consisting of one node of type *person*, with a single attribute *employer* pointing back to that same node.

But the corresponding $\mathrm{L}(EKR1)$ formula denotes the empty set of feature structures. And indeed, these cyclic structures are excluded from the set of structures satisfying the Biblical $EKR1$ formula above.

To allow such cyclic structures as solutions, Carpenter formalizes constraint systems as follows: Let $\mathrm{L}(KR)$ be the set of Kasper–Rounds formulae, and A be the set of sort symbols. A *constraint system* is then a mapping $C: A \to \mathrm{L}(KR)$. To deal with inheritance correctly, we then extend C as follows:

$$C^*(a) = \bigcap_{b \sqsubseteq a} C(b).$$

Now let $\mathbf{A}$ be a feature system, and $d \in D^{\mathbf{A}}$. Then d is said to be *resolved with respect to* C if for all $p \in l^*$ for which dp is defined, we have

$$dp \models C^*(a) \text{ for all } a \text{ such that } dp \in D_a.$$

This notion of "solution" is clearly related to the master modality described above in the section on modal logics. Suppose that we allow KR formulas of type $a \to \varphi$, where φ contained no implication signs, and $a \in A$. Then we could translate C into a conjunction of formulas

$$C^T = \bigwedge_{a \in A} (a \to \varphi_a).$$

We then apply the master modality:

$$[*]C^T.$$

The semantics of $a \to \varphi$ is straightforward: Given a feature system $\mathbf{A}$, and $d \in D^{\mathbf{A}}$, we say

$$d \models (a \Rightarrow \varphi) \iff d \notin D_a \text{ or } d \models \varphi.$$

If now $a \sqsubseteq b$ implies that $D_a \supseteq D_b$, then d is resolved with respect to C iff $d \models [*]C^T$.

3.9. *Attribute-value logics*

We next turn to a brand of feature logic much more closely related to standard first-order logic. This begins with Johnson's work on attribute-value logic, and is extended through the work of Smolka and others on "feature logic". Of course we have been treating "feature logic" all along, but in this section the term is reserved for the family of logics in the Johnson and Smolka tradition.

Johnson's work (1988) focuses on the concept of *attribute-value structures* as the semantic space over which logics are to be interpreted. The shape of these structures differs from feature systems, so let us give Johnson's own formulation:

DEFINITION 3.1. An **attribute-value** structure is a tuple $\langle F, C, \delta \rangle$, where F is a set (of attributes or features), C is a subset of F, and δ is a partial function from $F \times F$ into F. In addition $\delta(c, f)$ is required to be undefined whenever $c \in C$.

The idea is that $\delta(a, f)$ represents the value of attribute f on the element a. Notice here that F plays the role of L above, and C, the set of *constants*, are something like the set A above, where A can only label terminal nodes of a structure. A big difference in the formulation is that features can themselves be values of δ, a practice found in LFG, though not exemplified here.

Although δ can be a partial function, the view of AVS in Johnson is that of totally instantiated objects. Accordingly, the subsumption relation plays little role in his structures. Partiality is only used to rule out inappropriate features on certain objects (among those, no feature is defined on a constant). The interpretation of constants as constant types is also very restrictive: it is as if the sets D_c in feature systems were restricted to be singletons.

In Johnson's view, then, the usual attribute-value matrices are only a pictorial representation of attribute-value structures. Coindexed points in an AVM are a representation of actual path identity. We illustrate with an example. Consider the AVM

$$\begin{bmatrix} \text{SUBJ} & \boxed{1}\ [\text{PRED 'Tara'}] \\ \text{OBJ} & \boxed{2}\ [\text{PRED 'Louise'}] \\ \text{TENSE} & \text{PRES} \\ \text{PRED} & \text{'paint'} \\ \text{ACTOR}\ \boxed{1} & \\ \text{RECIPIENT}\ \boxed{2} & \end{bmatrix}$$

This is a pictorial representation of the following AVS:

- $F = \{a, b, c,$ paint, Tara, Louise, SUBJ, OBJ, PRED, TENSE, ACTOR, RECIPIENT, PRES$\}$;
- $C = \{$paint, Tara, Louise, PRES$\}$;
- $\delta(a,$ SUBJ$) = b$;
- $\delta(a,$ OBJ$) = c$;
- $\delta(a,$ TENSE$) =$ PRES;
- $\delta(a,$ PRED$) =$ paint;
- $\delta(a,$ ACTOR$) = b$;
- $\delta(a,$ RECIPIENT$) = c$;
- $\delta(b,$ PRED$) =$ Tara; $\delta(b,$ PRED$) =$ Louise.

Johnson introduces a formal language which will be interpreted using attribute-value structures. The interpretation shows how the language can be considered a "constraint language" for feature systems, and it reflects an orientation towards first-order models, in that it uses a classical treatment of negation.

Fix $\mathbf{C}$, a set of *constant symbols*, and $\mathbf{V}$, an (infinite) set of variables. Then the following grammar defines $\mathrm{L}(\mathbf{C}, \mathbf{V})$. It has two syntactic categories: terms and formulas.

- Variables and constant symbols are terms;
- If t_1 and t_2 are terms, then $t_1(t_2)$ is a term;
- If t_1 and t_2 are terms, then $t_1 \approx t_2$ is a formula;
- The special constants **true** and **false** are formulas;
- The formulas are recursively closed under the standard Boolean connectives.

The semantics of $\mathcal{L}$ is conditioned on having a way of interpreting constant symbols in an AVS (F, C, δ). This is an *injective* mapping

$$\xi : \mathbf{C} \to C.$$

The intent here is that distinct constants denote distinct constant elements of a structure, a typing notion common in LFG. Having said this, then the interpretation of terms and formulas is standard, modulo conventions on partiality. So, an interpretation is specified by giving ξ and an *environment* map $\rho : \mathbf{V} \to F$. We first define the denotation $[\![t]\!]$ of a term inductively.

- $[\![c]\!](\rho) = \xi(c)$ for constant symbol c;
- $[\![x]\!](\rho) = \rho(x)$ for variable $x \in V$;
- $[\![t_1(t_2)]\!] = \delta([\![t_1]\!], [\![t_2]\!])$, provided that the $[\![t_i]\!]$ are defined and that $\delta([\![t_1]\!], [\![t_2]\!])$ is also defined; otherwise this quantity is undefined.

This semantics, somewhat reminiscent of the λ-calculus, is occasioned by the fact that attributes can themselves be values. Most of the time, terms of a form such as $x(f)(g)(h)$ are considered, corresponding to applying the sequence of functions fgh to the variable quantity x. Then the semantics of the *satisfaction* relation is given, again relative to an interpretation $I = (\xi, \rho)$:

- $I \models$ **true** always and **false** never;
- $I \models t_1 = t_2$ if $[\![t_1]\!] = [\![t_2]\!]$ and both values are defined;
- The satisfaction of Boolean combinations, including negation, is classical.

From the second and third items, we get that for a constant c and variable x, that $I \models c(x) \neq c(x)$, a somewhat perplexing result, but one which represents the desire to restrict the equality relation to asserting "defined equality", and not to allow an "undefined element" $\perp$ as part of a model. This in turn reflects the desire to have linguistic objects (elements of a model) be *total descriptions*: the value of a feature should not be "undefined" if that feature is appropriate for a linguistic description. This requirement again has its source in LFG.

Johnson presents an axiomatic system for this logic, which he proves sound and complete in the usual sense of these terms. He also discusses the relationship of his logic to logics in the Kasper–Rounds style. In the course of this, he presents a translation of attribute-value logic to first-order logic of a restricted kind, and shows how techniques of first-order logic could be used to obtain results on compactness and complexity. Finally, he shows how to represent grammatical relations and constructions in the LFG style using his logic. This work thus represents a tying together of a full logical system with parts of a linguistic theory of syntax, one of the first such integrations, excepting perhaps the work of Montague (1974), and Johnson and Postal (1980).

3.10. Feature logics as constraint systems

The view of feature systems and feature logics as subsets of first-order logic is continued by Smolka (1992), and Nebel and Smolka (1989). Once again we explain the class of intended models, then move to the syntax.

Smolka considers the concept of *feature algebra*. This can be seen as a specialization of the concept of feature system that we have been considering. To give the precise definition: a feature algebra is a feature system $\mathbf{A}$ over L and A such that (i) D_a is a singleton for each $a \in A$; (ii) if $a \neq b$ then $D_a \neq D_b$; (iii) if $D_a = d$ then no feature is defined on d. Thus the elements of A denote primitive, unique atoms, and no feature can be defined on their interpretations.

Although a feature algebra can serve as a semantic model for a modal system, in the work of Smolka and Johnson it is considered more as a first-order structure. A feature is thought of as a relation which happens to be functional in nature. So, in the definition of Smolka's feature logic, the interpretation of negation is classical. Smolka also considers the addition of quantifiers.

The syntax of constraints requires again the introduction of variables in some set V. Recall also that p and q denote paths: strings of feature symbols. A feature constraint is then one of the following:

- $xp \doteq yq$ for variables x, y (path equation);
- $xp \doteq a$ for atom a (path equation and constant);
- $xp \uparrow$ (divergence);
- Boolean combinations of constraints;
- $\exists x\,(\varphi)$ where φ is a constraint.

By this time it is not necessary to spell out the semantics of such a system. It is done with respect to a feature algebra, using assignments from V to the elements of the carrier of the algebra. Quantification is expressed as usual in the standard Tarski semantics of first-order logic. Negation is treated classically.

The focus of Smolka's work is to give efficient algorithms for solving constraint systems, and not so much on the linguistic applications. He notes that it is possible to obtain a sound and complete axiom system for feature logic simply by regarding feature logic as a subsystem of first-order logic with equality, and by axiomatizing feature algebras as follows:

- For each set of distinct atoms $\{a, b\}$, add the constraint $\neg(a \doteq b)$.
- For each feature l, add the constraint

$$(xl \doteq y) \wedge (xl \doteq z) \rightarrow (y \doteq z).$$

– For each atom a and feature l add

$$\neg\exists x\,(al \doteq x).$$

A further section of Smolka's paper (Smolka, 1992) incorporates Kasper–Rounds formulae into constraints. Suppose one takes the basic Kasper–Rounds logic over the set A and the feature set L where now A may be interpreted as a general set of sorts, and for simplicity we do not allow negation or path equations. Then with respect to a feature system **A**, each KR formula denotes a subset of $D^{\mathbf{A}}$. So instead of thinking of a KR formula as a description of a linguistic object, we can think of it as defining an extended notion of type (i.e. an extension of the type system given by interpreting the sort symbols as subsets of D). Let S and T denote KR formulas (Smolka's word is *feature term*). Then we may add to our basic syntax of constraints the constraint $x : S$ where S is a feature term and x is a variable. Such a constraint will be satisfied in **A** by an assignment ρ to the variable x iff $\rho(x)$ is in the set $[\![S]\!]$, the set of elements "satisfying" the feature term S.

With sorts in place, Smolka considers the possibility of admitting recursive "definitions" of sorts; We compare his treatment with that of Carpenter, Moshier, and Gazdar et al. A *sort equation* is an expression

$$a \doteq S$$

where a is a primitive sort symbol, and S is a feature term. Of particular interest are *recursive* equations:

$$\mathit{person} \doteq \mathit{father} : \mathit{person}.$$

A sort equation may be considered as syntactic sugar for the constraint

$$\forall x\,(x : a \leftrightarrow x : S)$$

so that the notions of satisfiability and so forth carry over to constraint systems with sort equations. So, a recursive sort equation, like the one involving fatherhood above, may or not be satisfied in a particular feature system. In fact, the given sort equation is satisfied by any feature system interpreting *person* as the empty set, as well as by any system interpreting *person* as a one-element set $\{d\}$ with d's father being d himself. On the other hand (admitting negation for the moment) the sort equation

$$a \doteq \neg a$$

is not satisfiable.

Using the theory of definite relations, as given in (Höhfeld and Smolka, 1988), Smolka shows that any definite system of recursive sort equations will have a "least model". These notions need to be defined: "definite" refers to the feature term S on the right side of a sort equation. Each sort symbol in S must appear within the scope of an even number of negation signs. (We have ruled out negations for now, so that all of our feature terms are definite.) Then, the term "least model" refers to a partial ordering $\preceq$ on feature systems. We say $\mathbf{A} \preceq \mathbf{B}$ if A and B have the same domain D and the same interpretation of features, but that $D_a^{\mathbf{A}} \subseteq D_a^{\mathbf{B}}$ for every sort symbol a. As expected, the proof of the least-model theorem is an application of the same fixed point results as in Moshier's work. But Smolka's notion of sort equation allows cyclic solutions, whereas Moshier's notion rules them out by insisting on the least model as the meaning of the recursive definition of a predicate. These cyclic solutions are also allowed by Carpenter (who works in the algebra of feature structures) and by Gazdar.

We notice in passing that systems of sort definitions are crucial in the theory of *terminological logics* (Nebel and Smolka, 1989). Concept definitions (the Tbox component of KL-ONE-like knowledge representation systems (Brachman and Schmolze, 1985)) can be regarded as systems of sort equations. The idea of KR formulas as terms really occurred before the advent of KR formulae, in the work of Aït-Kaci (1984). Aït-Kaci's ψ-terms correspond to KR formulae without disjunction. In fact, the discovery of KR logic can be seen as an attempt to work out the properties of equations between Aït-Kaci's ε-terms, which are ψ-terms with the addition of disjunction. Both of the systems of Aït-Kaci were intended to model the type system in KL-ONE.

4. Logical properties: Soundness and completeness

The logics we have been discussing up to now, whether modal, intuitionistic, or first-order, all are subject to the usual logicians' questions about axiomatizability, soundness, completeness, and compactness. We will provide a representative sampling of results along this line, dividing between the three kinds of logical systems just mentioned. We will also present some work which unifies the various kinds of completeness results obtained for differing varieties of feature logics.

4.1. Axiomatizations for Kasper–Rounds-style logics

Kasper and Rounds presented an axiomatization of their original logic, which, we recall, involved acyclic feature structures with no sorts except for atoms at the leaf nodes of these structures, and did not involve negation. We are not going to give this axiomatization here in detail, but will present instead an axiomatic system given by Moss for KR logic augmented with negation. Moss' technique and axiom system are both much more elegant than the original formulation. The technique is an adaptation of the standard Henkin model-theoretic construction common in first-order logic. It is also very common in modal logic, where it usually is called a *canonical model* construction. The propositional nature of Kasper–Rounds makes the construction considerably simpler than in the full first-order case.

Before we begin, we should note that validity of a formula is not what is usually required in applications. Constraint-solving problems arise much more naturally in natural-language systems; such problems usually refer to satisfiability. However, one may wish to use an equational proof system, such as the one we are about to discuss, to replace a constraint formula by a logically equivalent one. It is handy to know when this is in general a correct step, especially in the initial design of constraints.

In the following, we make no assumptions about the nature of A; that is, D_a can be an arbitrary subset of $D^{\mathbf{A}}$ for an interpretation $\mathbf{A}$. So there will be no laws of the logic involving the sorts. We consider a Kasper–Rounds language with negation and path equations, and we seek a complete axiom system. It turns out that our axioms can be taken to be equational – that is, in the form of equivalences between Kasper–Rounds formulae. The following is Moss' axiom system. By $\varphi \supset \psi$ we mean the equation $\varphi \wedge \psi = \varphi$.

(i) The standard Boolean algebra equations;
(ii) $(l:\varphi) \wedge (l:\psi) = l:(\varphi \wedge \psi)$;
(iii) $l:\mathbf{true} = (l:\varphi) \vee (l:\neg\varphi)$;
(iv) $\mathbf{false} = l:\mathbf{false}$;
(v) $\mathbf{true} = (\lambda \doteq \lambda)$ (λ is the null string);
(vi) $(p \doteq q) \supset (q \doteq p)$;
(vii) $(p \doteq q) \wedge (q \doteq r) \supset (p \doteq r)$;
(viii) $(p \doteq q) \wedge (p:\varphi) \supset q:\varphi$;
(ix) $p:(q \doteq r) = (pq \doteq pr)$;
(x) $(p \doteq q) \wedge pr:\mathbf{true} \supset (pr \doteq qr)$;
(xi) $(p \doteq q) \supset p:\mathbf{true}$.

Here p, q are strings over L as usual.

The rules of proof for these axioms are the standard equational rules: the reflexive, symmetric, and transitive laws of $=$, together with the laws that make $=$ into a congruence relation. Our objective is now to show that every equation between KR formulae that is valid in all feature systems is provable in the above axiom system. (The converse, soundness, is straightforward by induction on equational proof length.)

Moss' core construction involves the ideas of *consistency* and *maximal consistency*. Say that a set S of KR formulae is *inconsistent* if there is a finite subset F of S such that the equation $\bigwedge F \supset \mathbf{false}$ is provable. Otherwise, say that S is *consistent*. Then S is *maximal consistent* if every proper superset of S is inconsistent. Finally, say that T is closed under deduction iff whenever $\varphi \in T$ and $\varphi = \psi$ is provable, then $\psi \in T$.

These definitions lead immediately to a completeness proof. The following is a combination of ideas from Moss' paper and from (Moshier, 1993).

Let T be a set of KR formulae. We construct a feature system $\mathcal{A}(T)$ based on T. The elements of $D^{\mathbf{A}(T)}$ will be equivalence classes in a certain subset P_T of L^*. We define

$$P_T = \{p \mid p:\mathbf{true} \in T\}.$$

Set $p \equiv_T q$ iff $(p \doteq q) \in T$. Then we have

LEMMA 4.1. *Suppose T is nonempty, consistent and closed under deduction. Then*
(i) *P_T is a nonempty, prefix-closed set of strings;*
(ii) *$\equiv_T$ is an equivalence relation on P_T;*
(iii) *If $p \equiv_T q$ and $pl \in P_T$ then $pl \equiv_T ql$;*

(iv) *If* $p \equiv_T q$ *and* $p{:}a \in T$ *then* $q{:}a \in T$.

The proof appeals mostly to the laws involving path equations. For example, $\varphi \supset \mathbf{t}$ is always provable, so **true** is in any nonempty closed T. So, to see that P_T is prefix-closed, suppose $(pr : \mathbf{true}) \in T$. Then $(pr \doteq pr) \in T$, so $p{:}(r \doteq r) \in T$. Since $(r \doteq r) \supset \mathbf{true}$ is provable, we have $p{:}\mathbf{true} \in T$. The other assertions follow similarly.

Now let T be nonempty, consistent, and closed. Define a feature system $\mathbf{A}(T)$ as follows: Take $D^{\mathbf{A}(T)}$ to be the collection of equivalence classes of P_T. If $[p]$ is such a class, let $[p]l$ be $[pl]$ if $pl \in P_T$, and otherwise undefined. Let $D_a = \{[p] \mid p{:}a \in T\}$. Then Lemma 4.1 above implies that $\mathbf{A}(T)$ is well-defined.

Our objective is now the following result. When we say $(\mathbf{A}, d) \models \varphi$ that we mean that the object d satisfies φ in the structure $\mathbf{A}$.

LEMMA 4.2 (Truth lemma). *Suppose φ is a KR formula. Then for any maximal consistent set T, we have $(\mathbf{A}(T), [\lambda]) \models \varphi$ if and only if $\varphi \in T$.*

The proof of this lemma is by induction on formulas φ. The base cases are direct from the definition of $\mathbf{A}(T)$, and the Boolean combinations follow from the Boolean laws. For the prefixing with labels case we need the next definitions and lemmas.

DEFINITION 4.3. Let T be a set of formulas, and $l \in L$. Define

$$l^{-1}(T) = \{\varphi \mid l{:}\varphi \in T\}.$$

Also, if $\mathbf{A}$ is a feature system, $d \in D^{\mathbf{A}}$, and $l \in L$, then $\mathbf{A}(d, l)$ is the principal subsystem $P(dl)$ of $\mathbf{A}$ generated by dl.

LEMMA 4.4. *If T is (maximal) consistent, and $l \in P_T$ then $l^{-1}(T)$ is also (maximal) consistent.*

For the proof, use the laws (2–4) involving prefixing.

LEMMA 4.5. *Let T be a closed theory, and $l \in P_T$. Then $\mathbf{A}(T)([\lambda], l)$ is isomorphic to $\mathbf{A}(l^{-1}(T))$.*

PROOF. Let $[p]$ be an equivalence class of $\mathbf{A}(l^{-1}(T))$. Let $h([p]) = [lp]_T$. It is easy to check that h is a well-defined bijection preserving structure. □

Now we can finish the proof of Lemma 4.2. We only check the case of $l : \phi$. We have

$$\begin{aligned}
(\mathbf{A}(T), [\lambda]_T) \models l{:}\varphi &\iff (\mathbf{A}(T), [l]) \models \varphi \\
&\iff (\mathbf{A}(T)([\lambda]_T, l), [\lambda]_T) \models \varphi \\
&\iff \mathbf{A}(l^{-1}(T), [\lambda]_{l^{-1}(T)}) \models \varphi \\
&\iff \varphi \in l^{-1}(T) \text{ (by induction)} \\
&\iff l{:}\varphi \in T.
\end{aligned}$$

The completeness of Moss' system now follows as a corollary of the truth lemma.

THEOREM 4.6. *Let S be a set of KR formulas. If for all $(\mathbf{A}, d)$ such that $d \models \sigma$ for all $\sigma \in S$, we have $(\mathbf{A}, d) \models \varphi$, then $S \vdash \varphi$.*

PROOF. Suppose not. Then $S \cup \{\neg\varphi\}$ is consistent. By Zorn's lemma, choose a maximal consistent T containing $S \cup \{\neg\varphi\}$. By the truth lemma, $(\mathbf{A}(T), [\lambda]) \models \sigma$ for all $\sigma \in S$, but $(\mathbf{A}(T), [\lambda])$ does not satisfy φ, in contradiction to the hypothesis of the theorem. □

4.2. *Axiomatizing intuitionistic feature logic*

Moss also uses similar model-theoretic apparatus to axiomatize his intuitionistic feature logic. Instead of presenting his axiom system, though, we move to a more general proof-theoretic setting, following the work of Moshier (1993). This involves the notion of a *sequent* and the notion of a Gentzen-style proof. (See (Takeuti, 1987) for a general introduction.)

The basic construct of a Gentzen-style proof system is the sequent. This we define to be a pair of finite sets of KR formulae (Γ, Δ), also written $\Gamma \vdash \Delta$. The intuitive meaning of such a sequent is that the conjunction of the formulas in Γ implies the disjunction of the formulas in Δ, in all feature systems. (We use sets instead of sequences of formulas to shorten assertions of commutativity and idempotence.) Then we have proof rules of the following forms.

– Unary schemata: of the form

$$\frac{\Gamma_0 \vdash \Delta_0}{\Gamma_1 \vdash \Delta_1}.$$

– Binary schemata: of the form

$$\frac{\Gamma_0 \vdash \Delta_0 \qquad \Gamma_1 \vdash \Delta_1}{\Gamma_2 \vdash \Delta_2}.$$

These are the general forms of any rule; a proof system will be a collection of such schemata together with a collection *Init* of initial sequents. A proof of a sequent $\Gamma \vdash \Delta$ will then be a finite tree whose root is labeled with $\Gamma \vdash \Delta$ and whose leaves are labeled with initial sequents. Typically the root of such a tree is at the bottom of the page.

Next we list rule schemata for the actual proof system F of feature logic. The first two are *structural schemata* which generally are included in any sequent-style proof system. Here LW and RW stand for the left and right *weakening* rules.

LW: $$\frac{\Gamma \vdash \Delta}{\Gamma, \varphi \vdash \Delta}$$ RW: $$\frac{\Gamma \vdash \Delta}{\Gamma \vdash \Delta, \varphi}$$

Cut: $$\frac{\Gamma \vdash \Delta, \varphi \qquad \varphi, \Gamma' \vdash \Delta'}{\Gamma, \Gamma' \vdash \Delta, \Delta'}$$

By Γ, ϕ we really mean $\Gamma \cup \{\phi\}$, and by Γ, γ' we mean $\Gamma \cup \Gamma'$. Also we omit braces around singleton sets. If we have blank space on the left or right of the sequent sign $\vdash$, then this means the empty set of formulae.

The second set of rules is for the propositional connectives. For intuitionistic calculus we include conjunction, disjunction, and implication.

- Conjunction:

Left: $\dfrac{\varphi, \Gamma \vdash \Delta}{\varphi \wedge \psi, \Gamma \vdash \Delta}$ $\quad$ $\dfrac{\psi, \Gamma \vdash \Delta}{\varphi \wedge \psi, \Gamma \vdash \Delta}$

and

Right: $\dfrac{\Gamma \vdash \Delta, \varphi \qquad \Gamma \vdash \Delta, \psi}{\Gamma \vdash \Delta, \varphi \wedge \psi}$

- Disjunction:

Right: $\dfrac{\Gamma \vdash \Delta, \varphi}{\Gamma \vdash \Delta, \varphi \vee \psi}$ $\quad$ $\dfrac{\Gamma \vdash \Delta, \psi}{\Gamma \vdash \Delta, \varphi \vee \psi}$

and

Left: $\dfrac{\Gamma, \varphi \vdash \Delta \qquad \Gamma, \psi \vdash \Delta}{\Gamma, \varphi \vee \psi \vdash \Delta}$

- Implication:

$$\frac{\varphi, \Gamma \vdash \psi}{\Gamma \vdash \varphi \supset \psi}$$

and

$$\frac{\Gamma \vdash \Delta, \varphi \qquad \psi, \Pi \vdash \Lambda}{\varphi \supset \psi, \Gamma, \Pi \vdash \Delta, \Lambda} .$$

We also include rules for dealing with the prefixing operation. If p is a path, then by $p : \Gamma$ we mean the set $\{p : \phi \mid \phi \in \Gamma\}$. Then the rule for prefixing reads

$$\frac{\Gamma \vdash \Delta}{p \doteq q, p : \Gamma \vdash q : \Delta} .$$

Besides the rules of inference for sequents, we have rules in *Init*. These include the *logical sequents* ($\vdash \mathbf{t}$), ($\mathbf{f} \vdash$), and ($\varphi \vdash \varphi$) for all atomic formulas φ. The also include the sequents particular to feature logic:

(i) $(\vdash \lambda \doteq \lambda)$, where λ is the null path;
(ii) $(p \doteq q,\ q \doteq r \vdash p \doteq r)$;
(iii) $(p \doteq q \vdash q \doteq p)$;
(iv) $(p : (q \doteq r) \vdash pq \doteq pr)$;
(v) $(pq \doteq pr \vdash p : (q \doteq r))$;
(vi) $(p \doteq q,\ pr : \mathbf{t} \vdash pr \doteq qr)$.

What do *soundness* and *completeness* mean in the setting of sequent calculi?

We need a notion of "valid sequent". If we were considering classical feature logic, then we could say that a sequent $\Gamma \vdash \Delta$ is valid if for all feature systems **A** (both finite and infinite) and $d \in D^{\mathbf{A}}$, we have that whenever $d \models \varphi$ for all $\varphi \in \Gamma$, then for some $\psi \in \Delta$, $d \models \psi$. Since we work intuitionistically, we use instead Moss' notion of forcing from Section 4.1.

Recall that a relation $\preceq$ on the nodes of a feature system **A** is an *approximation* if

$$d \preceq e \text{ and } dl \text{ is defined } \Rightarrow dl \preceq el$$

and

$$d \preceq e \text{ and } d \in D_a \Rightarrow e \in D_a.$$

To deal with preservation of path equalities, we also require

$$d \preceq e \text{ and } dp = dq \Rightarrow ep = eq.$$

A Kripke structure is a pair $(\mathbf{A}, \preceq)$ where **A** is a feature system and $\preceq$ is an approximation relation.

Instead of the satisfaction relation $\models$ used above, we consider a forcing relation $\Vdash$ to interpret formulas. The clauses are as follows, where $(\mathbf{A}, \preceq)$ is fixed and $d \in D^{\mathbf{A}}$:

- $d \Vdash a$ if $d \in D_a$;
- $d \Vdash$ **true** always;
- $d \Vdash$ **false** never;
- $d \Vdash p \doteq q$ if $dp = dq$;
- $d \Vdash \varphi \wedge \psi$ if $d \Vdash \varphi$ and $d \Vdash \psi$;
- $d \Vdash \varphi \vee \psi$ if $d \Vdash \varphi$ or $d \Vdash \psi$;
- $d \Vdash l : \phi$ if $dl \Vdash \varphi$ (implicitly dl is defined);
- $d \Vdash \varphi \to \psi$ if for all e such that $d \preceq e$, if $e \Vdash \varphi$, then $e \Vdash \psi$.

We can now define *validity* of a sequent: a sequent $\Gamma \vdash \Delta$ is valid if for all Kripke structures $(\mathbf{A}, \preceq)$ and $d \in D^{\mathbf{A}}$, we have that whenever $d \Vdash \varphi$ for all $\varphi \in \Gamma$, then for some $\psi \in \Delta$, $d \Vdash \psi$.

It is straightforward to show that the sequent proof system given above for feature systems is sound: Every provable sequent is valid. This follows by induction on the size of proof trees. The interesting question is the converse one. Moshier actually considers a strengthening of the converse. For this result, we need some preliminary notions.

The key to the result is the following definition.

DEFINITION 4.7 (*Saturation*). Let T be a set of intuitionistic KR formulas. We say that T is **saturated** if for any sequent $\Gamma \vdash \Delta$, such that $\Gamma \subseteq T$ and $\Gamma \vdash \Delta$ is provable, we have that $\Delta \cap T \neq \emptyset$.

The intuitive idea of this definition is that a saturated theory is rich enough to have witnesses for valid disjunctions: if a disjunctive formula is in a saturated closed theory, then one of the disjuncts is already in the theory. In fact, a *prime* theory in intuitionistic propositional calculus is a theory T such that whenever $(\varphi \vee \psi) \in T$, then one of φ or ψ must be in T (additionally T is closed under deduction and does not contain **false**). Notice also that in the classical setting, saturation corresponds to maximal consistency.

We need to relate saturated theories to models. In the setting of intuitionistic KR, we will take a model to be a tuple $((\mathbf{A}, \preceq), d)$, where $\mathbf{A}$ is a feature system, $\preceq$ is an approximation relation on $D^{\mathbf{A}}$, and $d \in D^{\mathbf{A}}$. Then we have the following results.

LEMMA 4.8 (Saturation lemma). *Suppose that (S, T) is a pair of sets of formulae, such that for every sequent $(\Gamma \vdash \Delta)$ with $\Gamma \subseteq S$ and $\Delta \subseteq T$, we have that $\Gamma \vdash \Delta$ is not provable. Then there is a saturated set $S' \supseteq S$ such that $S' \cap T = \emptyset$.*

We omit the proof. It involves some observations on provability using the cut rule, and an application of Zorn's lemma.

LEMMA 4.9 (Completeness criterion). *Suppose that for every saturated T there is a model $M = ((\mathbf{A}, \sqsubseteq), d)$ such that $T = \{\varphi \mid ((\mathbf{A}, \preceq), d) \models \varphi\}$. Then every valid sequent is provable.*

The lemma is immediate, because if there is a valid but unprovable $\Gamma \vdash \Delta$, we can apply the saturation lemma. We get a saturated T containing Γ and excluding Δ. By the hypothesis, there is an M such that $T = \{\varphi \mid M \models \varphi\}$. But such a model violates the validity of $\Gamma \vdash \Delta$.

LEMMA 4.10 (Truth lemma for Kripke structures). *There is a "universal" Kripke structure $(\mathbf{U}, \preceq)$ such that for each saturated T, there is a $d \in D^{\mathbf{U}}$ such that*

$$T = \{\varphi \mid ((\mathbf{U}, \preceq), d) \models \varphi\}.$$

We only sketch the proof of the lemma. We use the same equivalence relations $\equiv_T$ on strings as in the classical case. Then we can define a universal feature system $\mathbf{U}$ and approximation relation $\preceq$ as follows.

(i) $D^{\mathbf{U}}$ is the collection of pairs $(T, [p]_T)$, where T is a saturated theory and $[p]_T$ is an equivalence class of T;

(ii) $(T, [p]_T)l = [pl]_T$ provided $pl : \mathbf{true} \in T$;

(iii) $D_a = \{(T, [p]_T) \mid p : a \in T\}$;

(iv) $(T, [p]_T) \preceq (T', [p']_{T'})$ iff for some $u \in L^*$, $up' = p$ and $u^{-1}(T) \subseteq T'$, where as before

$$u^{-1}(T) = \{\varphi \mid u : \varphi \in T\}.$$

Then the basic claim is: for all formulas φ, all p and all saturated T,

$$((\mathbf{U}, \preceq), [p]_T) \models \varphi \iff p : \varphi \in T,$$

from which the lemma follows, taking $p = \lambda$. The claim is proved again by induction on φ. This time, instead of appealing to the equational proof system, we appeal to the sequent system; in particular *Init* and certain sequents easily provable from *Init*. The inductive cases follow from the proof rules for sequents involving the various connectives. Saturatedness is used to handle the case of implication. We give the proof for one direction of this case.

Suppose that $p:(\varphi \supset \psi)$ is not in T, where $p \in P_T$. Then every sequent $(\Gamma \vdash \Delta)$ such that $\Gamma \subseteq p^{-1}(T)$ and $\Delta = \{\psi\}$ is not provable, because $p:\mathbf{true}$ is in T. By the Saturation lemma, there is a saturated $T' \supseteq p^{-1}(T)$ so that $\varphi \in T'$ but $\psi \notin T'$. So $((\mathbf{U}, \preceq), (T, [p]_T)$ does not force $\varphi \supset \psi$.

REMARK. Moshier's techniques apply in a variety of other completeness proofs. He shows, for example, how to handle various assumptions about appropriateness conditions. He also deals with issues involving compactness and completeness, in a general setting for sequent proof systems which do not even involve feature logic. So I have included some of his work here, to point out a general logical technique which in the case of feature logic yields esthetically pleasing completeness results.

As a historical note, the axiomatization of Kasper and Rounds is an equational one, and in fact was the starting point for the discovery of feature logic in the first place. In work leading to the axiom system, the symbol $\wedge$ replaced the symbol $\oplus$, standing for "unification". That is, Kasper and Rounds were thinking of expressions involving disjunctive feature types, and simply wrote equations expressing desired validities between those expressions. The unification $\varphi \oplus \psi$ intuitively stood for the least type subsumed by both types φ and ψ. Only after these equations were written out did it become clear that they could be read as validities of feature logic, and that $\oplus$ was really $\wedge$.

4.3. *Axiomatizing other forms of feature logic*

After the excursion into sequent structures, we should also point out that standard methods of logic can be made to yield completeness results for feature logic. The idea is simply to choose a completeness technique from modal or first-order logic, and then to employ a translation method from feature logic into one of these systems, apply the completeness result, and infer a corresponding result for feature logic. Of course the term "feature logic" is ambiguous here, intentionally so. As an example, recall Smolka's constraint feature logic (Smolka, 1992).

A feature constraint is one of the following:

- $xp \doteq yq$ for variables x, y (path equation);
- $xp \doteq a$ for atom a (path equation and constant);
- $xp \uparrow$ (divergence);
- Boolean combinations of constraints;
- $\exists x\,(\varphi)$ where φ is a constraint.

The translation to first-order logic (with equality) is fairly simple. First axiomatize feature algebras as follows:

- For each set of distinct atoms $\{a, b\}$, add the constraint $\neg(a \doteq b)$.

- For each feature l, add the constraint

$$(xl \doteq y) \wedge (xl \doteq z) \to (y \doteq z).$$

- For each atom a and feature l add

$$\neg\exists x\,(al \doteq x).$$

Let F be the smallest set of constraints subject to these rules. Then the class of feature algebras, regarded as first-order structures, is exactly the class of structures satisfying every constraint of F.

We thus need to translate arbitrary feature constraints into formulas of first-order logic. Basic constraints (no connectives or quantifiers) are handled, for example, by replacing $xp \doteq yq$ by a conjunction of atomic constraints of the form $wl \doteq v$, where w and v (and so forth) are fresh variables, and then existentially quantifying over these new variables. So, for example, $xfg \doteq yh$ would transform into

$$(\exists uwv)\,(xf \doteq u \wedge ug \doteq v \wedge yh \doteq v).$$

Then each atomic constraint is a syntactic variant of the first-order formula $l(w, v)$ where l is a binary relation symbol. This relation is forced to be a partial function by the axiomatization F of feature algebras. Recall that atoms a are interpreted as singletons, so that they become constants in the translation to first-order logic. The translation of nonatomic constraints is then routine.

We get a sound and complete axiom system for constraints by choosing the axioms of F for nonlogical axioms, and adopting the usual first-order proof rules. The difficulty with this approach, of course, is that to work with arbitrary proof rules (such as generalization), proofs may need to go outside of the system of (translated) constraints. Thus such a deduction calculus need not be entirely self-contained. But it may be useful for deriving some of the other standard metamathematical properties of constraint theories such as compactness, decidability, or complexity.

Johnson's book (Johnson, 1988) uses similar techniques for his attribute-value system. We give an example of his techniques below, in the section on complexity issues. Johnson addresses the issues of *compactness* as well in his book. He shows from the translation into first-order logic that this attribute-value logic is compact (if every finite subset of a set of formulae is satisfiable, then so is the whole set). Compactness is a desirable property of a logic in that (informally) if a logic is not compact, then it does not admit of a finite axiom system; in general, infinitary proof rules tend to be required. Feature logics tend to be very "low-level" logics, so they do not often run into this problem. However, Moshier's recursive L($EKR1$) is not in fact compact.

Finally, we mention modal techniques. Reape's polyadic modal logic, for example, admits of complete axiomatizations relative to axiomatizing the arbitrary mathematical structures to which elements of a feature system belong. One thus gets a heterogeneous axiom system involving features and other classes of models (sets are just one example). As we have mentioned above, Kracht (1989) relates feature logics to other systems of modal logic, and adduces complete axiom systems as a result.

5. Complexity and decidability issues

The natural questions to answer here have to do with the satisfiability and validity problems for various feature logics. First let us ask where such questions might arise.

If one works in the constraint-based parsing mode, then one is led to ask whether or not a given string has a parse. This can be interpreted in several ways. The most obvious way to answer the question in many unification-based formalisms is to use the context-free base grammar to guide the search, in that a successful parse of a string will require the string to be the yield of some skeleton tree from the base grammar. Efficient methods, in particular chart-parsing methods, can be employed for this purpose. If the string has no underlying tree, then it has no parse. If it does have a tree, then one can (as in LFG) build a system of constraints among the feature paths. Here we find a special form of the satisfiability problem, for conjunctions of path equations in feature logic. These conjunctions can be solved efficiently by what is known as the unification algorithm, or in Smolka's terms, an incremental constraint-solving method. These algorithms are quite efficient, requiring linear time, or close-to-linear time for their implementation.

In practice, of course, life is not that simple. There are just too many possible parse trees which could potentially yield a given string. In general there could be infinitely many, because of productions of the form $A \to A$. Even if such productions are eliminated, we still face an exponentially difficult brute force elimination procedure. For this reason, chart parsing algorithms are typically interleaved with unification algorithms to reduce exponential search whenever possible. But at least, for reasonably well-designed grammars, there in principle is an algorithm for recognizing grammatical correctness.

There are, however, other sources of complexity – for example, when one has disjunctive feature information specified by the grammar; in particular, in the lexicon. (Think of multiple meanings for various words.) In this case, a natural constraint-solving method would try to extend unification to the case of disjunctive feature structures. It therefore becomes relevant to understand what the semantics of such structures is; and we have seen that disjunctive structures can be equivalently represented as disjunctive formulas. So, finding whether or not two disjunctive structures can be unified reduces to the question of satisfiability of two conjoined formulas, each containing disjunctions.

The complexity of this problem was determined by Kasper and Rounds. For KR formulas without negation, or even path equations, the satisfiability problem is *NP*-complete. This means that there is a nondeterministic algorithm that can guess a satisfying solution to a formula, in polynomial time in the size of the formula. But further, if there is a corresponding deterministic algorithm, then the complexity class P is equal to the class NP, a result widely conjectured to be untrue.

What about the validity problem for such a logic? With classical negation, the problem is easily seen to be "*co-NP*-complete". That is, validity is the complement of a problem in *NP*, and if the problem is actually polynomial, then the class P is equal to *co-NP*.

When we move to more complicated versions of feature logic, things get more interesting. Blackburn and Spaan (1993) have studied what happens when nominals are allowed, when one considers master modalities, and universal modalities. Since these modal logics admit classical negation, complexity results for validity are also not hard to derive.

One of Blackburn and Spaan's more surprising results is that the complexity of satisfiability for KR logic augmented with nominals and the universal modality is exponential-time complete, while the corresponding problem when we replace nominals by path equations is Π^0_1-complete; that is, co-semidecidable and Π^0_1-hard: every such problem reduces to this one.

The proof of the latter result is not too difficult. Blackburn and Spaan use a *tiling problem* (Harel, 1984) known to be hard for Π^0_1 (Robinson, 1971). Here I will prove undecidability of a slightly stronger result, using a technique of Smolka (1992). This involves the idea of *word problems for Thue systems.*

We need some preliminary definitions on such word problems. Given a finite alphabet L, consider the class Γ of semigroups finitely generated by L. An *equation* is a two-element set $\{p, q\}$, where p and q are nonempty strings over L. The *word problem* for semigroups is the following. Given a finite set $E = \{e_1, \ldots, e_n\}$ of equations, and a *test equation* $e = \{p, q\}$, is there a semigroup $S \in \Gamma$ satisfying all equations in E but not the test equation e? Analogously, the word problem for finite semigroups asks the same question when Γ is now the class of finite semigroups generated by L. Gurevich has shown that the word problem for finite semigroups is undecidable (Gurevich, 1966); this result holds with $|L| = 2$.

THEOREM 5.1. *Suppose* $|L| = 2$. *It is undecidable whether a formula* φ *in KR logic augmented by path equations and the universal modality is satisfiable in a finite feature system over* L.

PROOF. We reduce the word problem for finite semigroups to our desired one. Let $L = \{f, g\}$. Suppose given E and test equation $e = \{p, q\}$. Form the KR formula

$$\varphi_{E,e} = \Box\Big[f : \mathbf{true} \wedge g : \mathbf{true} \wedge \bigwedge_{\{p_i, q_i\} \in E} (p_i \doteq q_i)\Big] \wedge \neg(p \doteq q).$$

(Note that the scope of $\Box$ does not include the last subformula.) We claim that there is a finite feature system $\mathbf{A}$ and $d \in D^{\mathbf{A}}$ so that $d \models \varphi_{E,e}$ if and only if there is a finite semigroup S generated by L satisfying the equations in E but not the equation e.

To see one direction of the claim, let $\mathbf{A}$ and d be given satisfying $\varphi_{E,e}$. Then f and g, interpreted as functions on $P(d)$, are total. Since D is finite, the finite semigroup S generated by composing these functions (acting on $P(d)$) is a finite semigroup. By the universal modality, and by the third subformula of φ, the semigroup S satisfies the equations E. By the last subformula, S does not satisfy e.

Conversely, let S be a finite semigroup satisfying the condition. Adjoin an identity element λ to S if there is not one there already. Then S becomes a feature system under the feature definitions

$$sl = s * l,$$

where the $*$ on the right is multiplication in the semigroup. Choose the element $d \in S$ to be the identity element. Then trivially $d \models \varphi_{E,e}$. This proves the theorem. $\Box$

We remark that the use of negation in this result can be eliminated if we assume two disjoint sort symbols a and b, and replace the last subformula by $p:a \wedge q:b$. Of course a strictly positive formula, with no assumptions on sorts, can always be satisfied in a one-element system. Also, with negation, no sort symbols are necessary.

The above proof is an adaptation of one by Dörre and Rounds (1992), showing the unsolvability of *subsumption constraints*, a concept of Smolka which we will cover later in the section. The technique also leads to a proof, by further reductions, to a proof of the unsolvability of the *semi-unification* problem for *rational terms*. As such, this proof is an application of the theory of feature systems to a problem in computer science, arising from the need to perform type inference.

The original result of Blackburn and Spaan shows undecidability of the problem for finite or infinite feature systems, not just finite ones. Membership of that problem in Π_1^0 is shown by noting that the class of valid formulas can in fact be recursively enumerated. (An easy way to see this is to translate into first-order logic.) For just the case of finite structures, it is easy to see that the problem is in Σ_1^0, and it is not hard to check from Gurevich's result that the problem is complete for this class.

Now we turn to the case of nominals and the universal modality. Recall that nominals are special atomic sort symbols which can have only one node satisfying them. The force of the path equation $p \doteq q$ can be captured weakly by $p:i \wedge q:i$, where i is a fresh nominal. However, one would really like to say (and Smolka allows one to say) that $p \doteq q$ is expressed by $(\exists i)\,(p:i \wedge q:i)$. This is not allowed in $\mathrm{L}(KR)$ with nominals, and this is the source of the lessened difficulty of satisfiability, in the presence of the universal modality.

The proof that satisfiability of $\mathrm{L}(KR)$ with the universal modality and nominals is in exponential time is accomplished by a finite model argument: If a formula φ is satisfiable, then it is satisfiable in a model with at most c^n nodes, where $c > 1$ is a fixed constant, and n is the size of φ. This result follows from a filtration argument, which is fairly standard in modal logic. Given φ, one finds the set of all subformulas, and closes this under negation. Call this set $Cl(\varphi)$. Then if $\mathbf{A}$ is any structure and $d \in d^{\mathbf{A}}$ with $d \models \varphi$, we can construct an equivalence relation $\equiv_{\mathbf{A}}$ on$D$ by

$$d \equiv_{\mathbf{A}} e \iff (\forall \psi \in Cl\,(\varphi))(d \models \psi \iff e \models \psi).$$

The equivalence classes of this relation can then naturally be made into a structure satisfying φ, and there are at most exponentially many classes. It is only necessary to check that nominals denote singleton sets in the quotient structure.

The above argument only establishes a nondeterministic exponential time bound for satisfiability, as the decision procedure based on it requires guessing of the small model. The refinement of the argument to get a deterministic exponential procedure is more complex, and we omit the details here. Finally, the proof that the satisfiability problem is hard for exponential time requires an embedding of the corresponding problem for *propositional dynamic logic* (Fischer and Ladner, 1979). Details are again omitted.

The questions of satisfiability in a *finite* model for KR with path equations and the universal modality seems not to have been studied. Notice that the model constructed in the proof above is infinite. Below, though, I provide a short proof of undecidability in this case using a method of Smolka's. Let us then turn to some complexity results for the Smolka–Johnson class of attribute-value logics.

We recall Smolka's notion of *constraint*:

- $xp \doteq yq$ for variables x, y (path equation);
- $xp \doteq a$ for atom a (path equation and constant);
- $xp \uparrow$ (divergence);
- Boolean combinations of constraints;
- $\exists x\,(\varphi)$ where φ is a constraint.

From what we have seen on path equations and nominals, the following class of constraints is natural:

DEFINITION 5.2 (*Existential prenex constraints*). A constraint is in existential prenex form (EPF) if it is of the form

$$\exists x_1 \cdots \exists x_n\, \varphi,$$

where the constraint φ is quantifier-free.

Smolka gives a decision procedure, based on syntactic transformations, for checking satisfiability of EPF constraints. It relies on transforming the matrix of the constraint to disjunctive normal form, and in effect eliminating the initial existential quantifiers. Eventually, satisfiability reduces to considering *feature clauses* which are conjunctions of atomic constraints. Such a conjunction is said to have a solution if there is an assignment to its free variables (with respect to some feature system) making all of the conjuncts true. Existence of such a solution is shown to be decidable in at most quadratic time, again by a transformation method into what is called solved form.

Similar methods apply to *sorted* constraints, which, as we recall, allow constraints of the form $x : S$ where S is a feature term (Kasper–Rounds formula, Aït-Kaci ψ-term) over the sort alphabet A.

Smolka also provides an undecidability result for general feature logic, where universal quantification is allowed over variables involving path equations. This result is very much analogous to the undecidability result of Blackburn and Spaan for the universal modality. The technique was in fact shown in Theorem 5.1. This theme is continued in (Dörre and Rounds, 1992). There it is shown that systems of constraints including path constraints and *subsumption constraints*, of the form $xp \sqsubseteq yq$, where x and y are variables and p and q are paths, have an undecidable satisfiability problem (for the definition of $\sqsubseteq$, see Definition 2.4). A recent difficult positive decidability result on so-called *functional uncertainty constraints* has been shown by Backofen (1993). The form of such constraints is $x\alpha = y$, where α is a regular expression over the feature alphabet L. The interpretation in a feature system is that some path given by the expression leads from the element denoted by x to that denoted by y.

As a final excursion into complexity properties, we consider a method due to Johnson (1991a, 1991b). This relies on a "correspondence" theory between feature constraints and first order logic. The idea is to express natural feature constraints on first-order terms, but to rely on general decidability results for first order systems to derive them for feature constraint systems.

The observation in (Johnson, 1991b) is that feature constraints often translate into a special decidable subclass of first-order formulas: the *Schönfinkel–Bernays* class SB. A formula is in SB iff it is of the form

$$\exists x_1 \cdots x_m \forall y_1 \cdots y_n \varphi,$$

where φ contains no function symbols or quantifiers.

Following the methodology of his thesis and book, Johnson shows how to translate various assertions about features into the class SB. The first observation is that the functional nature of features can be captured by a formula of the class. In the following the three-place relation $arc(x, y, z)$ denotes a "feature arc" labeled by y connecting the nodes x and z. Then functionality is captured by the usual axiom

$$\forall x, a, y, z\, (arc(x, a, y) \wedge arc(x, a, z) \rightarrow y = z).$$

This is an SB formula.

Other constraints similarly can be translated. We content ourselves with examples.

(i) *Path equations.*

$$sem : swim \wedge \neg[agr : (num : sing \wedge person : 3)]$$

translates to

$$\begin{aligned} &arc(c, sem, swim) \wedge \exists v arc(c, agr, v) \\ &\qquad \wedge \neg[arc(v, num, sing) \wedge arc(v, person, 3)]. \end{aligned}$$

Perhaps the constant c should really be a free variable, but if the same "anonymous" constant is used to denote the "initial node" of a feature system, satisfiability of a conjunction of constraints in feature logics will reduce to satisfiability of a conjunction of SB formulae with no loss of expressive power.

(ii) *Extensionality*. This constraint says that no two distinct elements of the same sort have identical attribute values.

$$\begin{aligned} \forall x, y, u, v\ \ & A(x) \wedge arc(x, num, u) \wedge arc(x, person, v) \\ & \wedge A(y) \wedge arc(y, num, u) \wedge arc(y, person, v) \\ & \rightarrow x = y. \end{aligned}$$

(iii) *Definitions of predicates.* Suppose we have a formula which defines the predicate A:

$$\forall x\, (A(x) \leftrightarrow \Phi(x)),$$

where, say, Φ is a quantifier-free formula not involving A (the quantifier-free condition can be relaxed). As it stands, the definitional formula is not in SB. But if we are only concerned with satisfiability, then the formula may be replaced by the "one-sided" SB formula

$$\forall x\,(A(x) \to \Phi(x)).$$

It is then not hard to show that when the occurrences of A appear only positively inside another constraint Ψ, then the two-sided formula

$$\Psi(A) \wedge \forall x\,(A(x) \leftrightarrow \Phi(x))$$

is satisfiable if and only if the corresponding one-sided formula is. So, we still have a decision method for satisfiability in this case.

Johnson shows how to define certain formulae involving sets using the last item above. This entails the decidability of satisfiability for formulae involving such predicates, in the time necessary for the SB class. As to the complexity of deciding this problem, if the number of universal quantifiers is fixed, then the problem is *NP*-complete. The problem is in general complete for polynomial space if the number of such quantifiers is not fixed (Lewis, 1980). Johnson notes, however, that most of the linguistic uses require only fixed numbers of the quantifiers. This method thus does not lead to more complexity than in the original KR logic.

6. Order-theoretic aspects of feature structures

The unification method, alluded to in previous sections, is an efficient algorithm for constraint solving. Is there anything more to the method than this? Why is it that grammars with augmented with feature constraints are called "unification grammars"? We will look at ordering relations in feature systems to answer the question. In the process we will learn more about feature logics in the disguise of disjunctive type specifications. One of the principal tools we use is the theory of complete partially ordered sets, or *domain theory*. This theory is generally about constructive information-theoretic ordering relations. Only a few of the results are needed for our applications. On the other hand, feature systems provide a very nice illustration of some of the domain-theoretic constructions.

Historically, Pereira and Shieber (1984) were the first to suggest using domain theory to give a semantics of grammars. Their work preceded the introduction of feature logic, and appeared at about the same time as Aït-Kaci's work on what might be called feature types. Aït-Kaci uses domain-theoretic methods to construct disjunctive types (ε-terms) from conjunctive types (ψ-terms.) Pereira and Shieber suggest that types might be modeled by a so-called *powerdomain* construction.

Johnson (1988) also gives an interesting discussion on partiality issues for feature structures. His view, as we have mentioned, is that feature logic, without loss, can restrict itself to talking about total models. But the comparisons he makes between the two views are informative. In particular, partiality for Johnson, Smolka, and in fact the modal logicians resides in the logical theory, not in the models. Fenstad's chapter in this Handbook discusses the distinctions.

Carpenter's book on typed feature structures and their logic contains a detailed review of domain-theoretic ideas needed to understand these constructions. Here I will not be so thorough, but will use constructions as necessary to show how they arise in the task of modeling, say, disjunction. But we need to begin by examining how ordering is associated with the class of feature structures. For this, recall the definition of feature structure as a principal feature system as in Definition 2.3, and the definition of subsumption between two structures **A** and **B**, by means of a homomorphism of their domains (cf. Definition 2.4). In case **A** and **B** are feature structures, we require the mapping to preserve the generators.

EXAMPLE 6.1. Let $D^{\mathbf{A}} = \{d_0, d_1, d_2\}$, with $d_0 f = d_1$ and $d_0 g = d_2$. Let $D^{\mathbf{B}} = \{e_0, e_1\}$ with $e_0 f = e_0 g = e_1$. Then $\mathbf{A} \sqsubseteq \mathbf{B}$ via the map γ sending d_0 to e_0 and d_1 and d_2 to e_1.

It is easy to see that if there are two homomorphisms $\gamma : D^{\mathbf{A}} \to D^{\mathbf{B}}$ and $\gamma' : D^{\mathbf{B}} \to D^{\mathbf{A}}$, then these are mutual inverses, so that **A** and **B** are isomorphic. (The functional nature of the features makes this true.)

If $\mathbf{A} \sqsubseteq \mathbf{B}$, we regard **B** as *at least as informative* as **A**. In Example 6.1, the structure **B** is more informative, as it identifies two potentially different feature values. In this example, the structure **B** is *extensional*, as no two distinct elements have exactly the same features with the same values. This is not the case for **A**, as the elements d_0 and d_1 are distinct but indistinguishable. (We do not have space in the chapter to pursue the interesting topic of extensionality. Some discussion appears in (Carpenter, 1992, Chapter 8).)

The collection of isomorphism classes of feature structures is thus partially ordered by $\sqsubseteq$. In fact a better representation is available. Moshier, in his thesis (Moshier, 1988), shows that this collection is order-isomorphic to the partially ordered set of *abstract feature structures*. Such an abstract structure is a triple (P, N, V), where P is a nonempty, prefix-closed subset of L^*, N is a right-invariant equivalence relation[2] (a Nerode relation) on P, and V is a relation from P to A respecting the relation N; that is, if $p\ Va$ and $p\ N\ q$ then $q\ V\ a$.

Let $(\mathbf{N}, \sqsubseteq)$ be the poset of abstract feature structures, where $(P_1, N_1, V_1) \sqsubseteq (P_2, N_2, V_2)$ iff $P_1 \subseteq P_2$, $N_1 \subseteq N_2$, and $V_1 \subseteq V_2$ (this last as graphs of relations.) This poset is almost the same as the typed Nerode feature system in Example 2.2. It differs only in that V is relational, not functional.

Here, for example, is the representation of a concrete structure $(\mathbf{A}, d_0)$. We let

$$P = \{p \mid d_0 p{\downarrow}\}; \qquad N = \{(p, q) \mid d_0 p = d_0 q\};$$

and

$$V = \{(p, a) \mid d_0 p \in D_a\}.$$

[2] Recall from Section 2 that a relation N is right-invariant if whenever $d\ N\ e$ and $dl{\downarrow}$ then $el{\downarrow}$ and $dl\ N\ el$.

What kind of partially ordered set is the set of abstract feature structures? It turns out that (with proper assumptions on sorts, which we ignore for the moment) that **N** is a *Scott domain*. We review the necessary terminology.

DEFINITION 6.1 (*Domain-theoretic definitions*). A directed subset of a partial order $(U, \sqsubseteq)$ is a non-empty set $X \subseteq U$ such that for every $x, y \in X$, there is a $z \in X$ such that $x \sqsubseteq z$ and $y \sqsubseteq z$. A complete partial order (cpo) is a partial order which has a bottom element and least upper bounds of directed sets. A subset $X \subseteq U$ is bounded (or compatible, consistent) if it has an upper bound in U. An isolated (or compact, finite) element x of U is one such that whenever $x \sqsubseteq \bigsqcup X$ with X directed, we also have $x \sqsubseteq y$ for some $y \in X$. A cpo is algebraic if each element of which is the least upper bound of a set of isolated elements. A cpo is ω-algebraic if it is algebraic and the set of isolated elements is countable. A Scott domain is an ω-algebraic cpo in which every compatible subset has a least upper bound. Scott domains are somewhat more anonymously termed "bounded-complete partial orders" (BCPOs).

It is not too hard, using the set-theoretic definition of the partial order in **N**, to check that **N** in fact is a Scott domain, and that the finite feature structures are the compact elements. Notice that a finite feature structure is represented in **N** as a triple (P, N, V) where the equivalence relation N is of finite index.

Now it is possible to give an abstract characterization of *unification*. If x and y are elements of **N**, and $\{x, y\}$ is bounded above, then the least upper bound $x \sqcup y$ exists, and is called the *unification* of x and y. One can likewise form the least upper bound of any nonempty subset of **N** that is bounded above. Note also that the least upper bound of finite elements must be finite in any Scott domain; and one can find the *greatest lower bound* of an arbitrary nonempty subset. This latter is called the *generalization* of the subset.

Actually, the Scott domain determined by the class of all abstract feature structures, with no assumptions about the ordering of sorts, is uninteresting, because any two feature structures will be unifiable. In fact, the domain turns into a *complete lattice*, with the top element being the full tree on L, with all paths equivalent. So, we generally make sort assumptions, the most common of which is to assume a Scott ordering (also denoted by $\sqsubseteq$) on the sort symbols. We also typically limit the class of feature structures so that a given node is assigned a special type, which is thought of as the "most specific" type for that node. The following, for example, is Carpenter's definition of typed feature structure.

DEFINITION 6.2. A **typed** feature structure is a triple $(\mathbf{A}, d_0, \theta)$, where $(\mathbf{A}, d_0)$ is a feature structure, and $\theta : D^{\mathbf{A}} \to A$ is a total function. A node $d \in D_a$ if and only if $a \sqsubseteq \theta(d)$.

If **A** is a typed structure, then the sets D_a respect the ordering on sorts, but more general sorts denote bigger subsets: if $a \sqsubseteq b$, then $D_a \supseteq D_b$. (The reverse inclusion need not hold: Suppose archy is the only bug-author. He might be the only bug and the only author, but the type of authors need not subsume the type of bugs.)

For typed feature structures, a different definition of homomorphism is used: if $\gamma : D^{\mathbf{A}} \to D^{\mathbf{B}}$, then one requires $\theta(d) \sqsubseteq \theta(d\gamma)$. But this definition, in the case of typed structures, is really the same as the one we gave at the beginning of the section.

PROPOSITION 6.3. *For typed feature structures,*

$$\theta^{\mathbf{A}}(d) \sqsubseteq \theta^{\mathbf{B}}(d\gamma) \iff \{a \mid d \in D_a^{\mathbf{A}}\} \subseteq \{a \mid d\gamma \in D_a^{\mathbf{B}}\}.$$

PROOF. Assume the left side of the condition. Let a be such that $d \in D_a^{\mathbf{A}}$. Then $a \sqsubseteq \theta(d)$, so $a \sqsubseteq \theta(d\gamma)$. Therefore $d\gamma \in D_a^{\mathbf{B}}$. Conversely, let $a = \theta^{\mathbf{A}}(d)$. Then $a \in \{a \mid d \in D_a^{\mathbf{A}}\}$. So $a \in \{a \mid d\gamma \in D_a^{\mathbf{B}}\}$. This means $a \sqsubseteq \theta(d\gamma)$ as required. □

If we assume that all feature structures are typed, then we may equivalently represent the domain $\mathbf{N}$ of abstract feature structures over A and L as the set of all triples $f = (P, N, \theta)$ where P and N are as before, but now $\theta : P \to A$. The ordering relation $f_1 \sqsubseteq f_2$ still requires set containments for the P and N components but now requires $\theta_1(p) \sqsubseteq \theta_2(p)$ for all $p \in P_1$.

We assume for the rest of the section that feature structures are typed and that the underlying sort set A is a Scott domain. We can now tie feature logics to domain theory as follows. Consider Kasper–Rounds logic with path equations, but with only basic formulas and those involving prefixing, but not conjunction, negation, or disjunction. Call such formulas *extended basic*. For a feature structure $(\mathbf{A}, d_0)$, put

$$Th(\mathbf{A}) = \{\varphi \mid d_0 \models \varphi\},$$

where the φ are extended basic. It is straightforward to show the following:

THEOREM 6.4. $\mathbf{A} \sqsubseteq \mathbf{B}$ *if and only if* $Th(\mathbf{A}) \subseteq Th(\mathbf{B})$.

THEOREM 6.5. *Every satisfiable extended basic formula* φ *has a least satisfier* $\mathbf{A}_\varphi$ *in the subsumption order, up to isomorphism. In fact this satisfier is finite.*

We recall that KR logic without negation is *persistent*, so this last result tells us that an extended basic formula φ determines a *principal filter* in the poset $\mathbf{N}$. In fact it is a *compact filter*, being generated by a compact element.

When we allow conjunctions and disjunctions, we get the following result. It was originally shown by Kasper and Rounds, but only for the special kinds of structure they were considering.

THEOREM 6.6. *The collection of satisfiers of any KR formula without negation is a finite union of principal compact filters in the domain of feature structures.*

THEOREM 6.7. *Every compact element* $\mathbf{A}$ *in the domain of feature structures has a corresponding formula* $\varphi_{\mathbf{A}}$ *such that the principal filter generated by* $\mathbf{A}$ *is the filter of satisfiers of* $\varphi_{\mathbf{A}}$.

These results have the following significance: they show that negation-free KR logic, with no modalities other than prefixing, and with path equations, is in some sense the "natural" finite logic for the domain of feature structures. The reason is that every domain (in fact algebraic cpo) has a "natural" positive logic associated with it. This logic is given by the *Scott topology* of the domain.

DEFINITION 6.8. Let $(U, \sqsubseteq)$ be a cpo. A set $V \subseteq U$ is said to be **Scott open** if (i) U is upward-closed, and (ii) for any directed $D \subset U$, we have $\bigsqcup D \in U$ iff $U \cap D \neq \emptyset$.

(By "upward-closed", we mean that if $x \in U$ and $x \sqsubseteq y$, then $y \in U$.)

One checks readily that under this definition of "open", that the collection of open subsets of a cpo form a topological space. Such a space must contain $\emptyset$ and U, and be closed under finite intersections and arbitrary unions. Furthermore, we can regard open sets as being "properties" of domain elements. The definition says that if an element has a certain property, then we can discover that the property holds by testing a "sequence" of finite elements which "converges" to the given element. (In general, sequence really means directed set, and "converges to an element" means that the element is the least upper bound of the set.) After a finite time, we find that the element does indeed have the property. Such properties are sometimes called "affirmable" (Vickers, 1989).

It is straightforward to prove the following in any algebraic cpo U.

THEOREM 6.9 (Compactness in the Scott topology).

(i) *For each finite element $f \in U$, the principal compact filter $\uparrow f = \{u : f \sqsubseteq u\}$ is open.*

(ii) *Every open set V is the union of the principal compact filters generated by the compact elements of V.*

(iii) *Every compact open set X is a finite union of such compact principal filters.* (Compact here means the topological usage: every covering of X by open sets has a finite subcovering.)

We want to make a "logic" out of open sets in the domain **N**. To do this, we make the set **N** into a feature system. If $(P, N, \theta) \in \mathbf{N}$, and $l \in L$, then define $(P, N, V)l = (P/l, N/l\theta/l)$, where (i) $P/l = \{q \mid lq \in P\}$; (ii) $q\ N/l\ r$ iff $lq\ N\ lr$, and (iii) $\theta/l(q) = \theta(lq)$. For $a \in A$ we let $D_a = \{(P, N, \theta) \mid \theta(\lambda) \sqsubseteq a\}$. This in fact is the *Nerode system* in Example 3.2 of Section 3.

Now we can make a "logic" by using the following "syntax".

- **N** is a property;
- For $p, q \in L^*$, the set $\{f \in \mathbf{N} \mid fp = fq\}$ is a property;
- For $a \in A$, the set of feature structures $\{(P, N, \theta) \mid a \sqsubseteq \theta(\lambda)\}$ is a property;
- The empty set is a property;
- If $X \subseteq \mathbf{N}$ is a property and $l \in L$, then $\{f : fl \in X\}$ is a property;
- The union and intersection of two properties is a property.

"Satisfaction" in this "logic" is just membership: a feature structure $f \models X$ if and only if $f \in X$.

More properly, we define the class of properties to be the least class of subsets of **N** closed under the above operations. Then our results above tell us that the class of properties coincides with the sets definable as models of positive KR formulas, and further that these are exactly the compact open subsets of the domain of feature structures.

The Smyth powerdomain. We have not yet completed our promised task: to show how disjunctive types are modeled using domain-theoretic methods. Each finite feature structure (compact element) represents a conjunctive type. But we have not yet presented a domain construction such that an element of the domain represents a *disjunctive* type. One might think that the generalization of two feature structures represented the disjunction of their types, because the unification represents the conjunction. But this is easily seen to be incorrect, as generalization does not distribute over unification.

Fortunately we have done most of the work necessary to introduce disjunctive types, because we already have disjunction in our logic. The collection of all finite unions of compact principal filters is the set of compact elements of **N**. And each such finite union is really determined by a collection (antichain) of pairwise-incomparable compact elements; namely, the generators which do not subsume each other. So, we should take these collections as representatives of disjunctive types. Then the question becomes: how to order such antichains?

Remember that an antichain $\{f_1, \ldots, f_n\}$ represents the type of an object which is more specific than at least one of the f_i. We can thus increase the informativeness of the antichain by removing one or more of the elements, or by increasing the informativeness of one or more of the elements. So now if X and Y are compact antichains, we set $X \sqsubseteq_S Y$ (Smyth subsumption) iff for all $g \in Y$, there is some $f \in X$ with $g \sqsubseteq f$. It is easy to see that $\sqsubseteq_S$ is a partial order on antichains.

This construction actually does most of the work for us when we want to calculate with disjunctive types. It is possible to show (see, for example, Carpenter (1992, Chapter 12)) that the Smyth subsumption relation on compact antichains actually gives us a distributive lattice. So then, for example, to unify X and Y we form the set $\{x \sqcup y \mid x \in X;\ y \in y\}$ and remove non-minimal elements. The formula is expected given that the distributive law holds in the logic of the domain of feature structures. But in fact the construction is general.

As an aside, exactly these same methods were first used by Aït-Kaci (1984) to pass from conjunctive types to disjunctive ones. Aït-Kaci's syntax for conjunctive types is called the calculus of ψ-terms. In effect these are identifiable with, not so much conjunctive Kasper–Rounds formulae, but conjunctive Kasper–Rounds formulae without path equations and with nominals. So, for example, the type of people whose father is their employer is notated by Aït-Kaci as

$$\mathit{Person}(\mathit{father} \Rightarrow y; \mathit{employer} \Rightarrow y).$$

The translation of this should be clear; use *father* and *employer* as attributes, *Person* as a sort symbol, and y as a nominal. (These terms are very flexible. They form the basic data types in Aït-Kaci's logic programming language LIFE (Aït-Kaci and Podelski, 1990).) One can pass to disjunctive types (ε-terms) by introducing a connective for disjunctions and proceeding to give equational rules as suggested by the logic of feature structures.

In effect we have now constructed the set of compact elements of the Smyth powerdomain of the domain of feature structures. To generate the "complete" complete partial order "determined" by these compact elements, we use a domain-theoretic technique known as *ideal completion*. This is a general technique which always produces an algebraic cpo from a partially ordered set of elements, in such a way that all existing meets and joins are preserved. The details in general are as follows. Given a partially ordered set $(X, \preceq)$, we define an *ideal* of X to be a nonempty, directed, and downward-closed subset I of X. (The last condition just says that if $x \in X$ and $u \preceq x$ then $u \in X$.) Then the ideal completion of $(X, \preceq)$ is the collection of ideals of X, partially ordered by inclusion of sets.

We thus form the ideal completion of our set of compact Smyth elements, and arrive at the Smyth or *upper* powerdomain. It is possible to prove that if one starts with a Scott domain, then the Smyth powerdomain is again a Scott domain. And one can use other orderings on sets of domain elements to get new powerdomains. Two other very common constructions, for example, are the *Hoare* (lower) and the *Plotkin* (convex) powerdomains. See Gunter and Scott (1990) for a good survey; other references are Abramsky (1991), or Zhang (1991) for the details of passing to a logic from a domain.

At this point, we have digressed pretty much from linguistics. To return thereto, and to close out the subsection, we sketch the details of another powerdomain construction due to Pollard and Moshier (1990). It is one way in which *set values* might be handled order-theoretically.

Consider the following sentence.

He thinks he is smart.

The sentence has a *set* of referents, which might occur as the value of a CONTEXT feature. What should be the type for this set? The two occurrences could be coreferential or not. Otherwise, the two occurrences have identical features: third person masculine singular. Here is a feature structure proposed by Pollard and Moshier to account for the above sentence.

$$\begin{bmatrix} \text{CONTENT} & \begin{bmatrix} \text{EXPERIENCER}\ \boxed{1} \\ \text{THEME}\ \boxed{2} \end{bmatrix} \\ \\ \text{CONTEXT} & .\{\boxed{1}\begin{bmatrix} \text{PERSON} & \text{3rd} \\ \text{NUMBER} & \text{sing} \\ \text{GENDER} & \text{masc} \end{bmatrix}, \boxed{2}\begin{bmatrix} \text{PERSON} & \text{3rd} \\ \text{NUMBER} & \text{sing} \\ \text{GENDER} & \text{masc} \end{bmatrix}.\} \end{bmatrix}$$

The value of the CONTEXT attribute is to be a set consisting of two parameters, each qualified to be of the same type. These parameters are coreferential with the values of the EXPERIENCER and THEME attributes of the sentence. For sake of simplicity let us focus only on this "set node", ignoring coreferences within the structure:

$$.\{\begin{bmatrix} \text{PERSON} & \text{3rd} \\ \text{NUMBER} & \text{sing} \\ \text{GENDER} & \text{masc} \end{bmatrix}, \begin{bmatrix} \text{PERSON} & \text{3rd} \\ \text{NUMBER} & \text{sing} \\ \text{GENDER} & \text{masc} \end{bmatrix}.\}$$

We would like a "type" corresponding to this "set". Notice that since we have listed two identical feature structures in the "set", by the usual set theory extensionality laws, the set would only contain one element. So none of the usual powerdomain constructors will work, because the basis of compact generators is a set (antichain) of compact elements. Another problem is to make sure that no more than two individuals, but at least one individual, is represented.

Pollard and Moshier solve this problem by proposing a new powerdomain construction. One begins with the collection $K(U)$ of compact elements of the underlying domain $(U, \sqsubseteq)$ as before. However, for basis elements of the Pollard–Moshier powerdomain, one uses the collection of finite *multisets* X over K. (A finite multiset simply allows repetition of an element.) The relation $\sqsubseteq_{PM}$ is then the following: $X \sqsubseteq_{PM} Y$ iff there is an onto function $\mu : X \to Y$, such that

$$(\forall x \in X)\,(x \sqsubseteq \mu(x)).$$

This relation is reflexive and transitive, though not symmetric. But the ideal completion construction still works to give an algebraic cpo. In the example of the two pronoun occurrences, we see that the given multiset models those sets of individuals of the same type, consisting of either one or two members.

Our presentation of the Pollard–Moshier construction leaves out many other details of their set-valued feature structures. The point here is that not only does domain theory lead to new tools for understanding linguistic constructions, but also that linguistic examples suggest new definitions and results in the theory of domains.

7. An application

In this last technical section of the chapter we give an illustration of the use of feature logic: an application of the ideas to the topic of *multistratal grammar.* This subject emerged in the 1970's as *relational grammar*, principally through the work of Postal and Perlmutter (see, for example, Perlmutter, 1983; or Postal and Joseph, 1990, for representative work).

Multistratal grammar harks back to the early days of transformational theory. As we recall, the notion of a construction like "passive" in some intuitive sense identifies the surface subject *John* in the sentence *John was hit by Bill* with the "deep" or "initial" direct object. But whereas transformational theory represented this intuition by means of derivations, relational grammar took the position that a proper linguistic structure for a passive sentence would in fact record the information that the surface subject was once the direct object. The "stratal diagrams" of relational grammar are an attempt to do this, for example.

A consequence of this view of linguistic objects is that one can directly enunciate constructions like "passive" and "raising" as rules of grammar, in such a way that inspection of the structure guarantees that the rules have been satisfied. This is an idea which we see now in HPSG, but HPSG is *monostratal*, because there is no notion of an "earlier" stratum. Current versions of GB, by the same intuitive classification, could be said to be *bistratal* in that some constraints apply before the "move-α" transformation has taken place, and some after.

We will not dwell in this short exposition on the details of relational diagrams, or on the graphical versions formalized in *arc-pair grammar* (Johnson and Postal, 1980) or multigraph grammar (Postal, 1986). Instead we will illustrate a current version of the theory, due to Johnson and Moss (1993). *Stratified feature grammar* is a representation of multistratal grammar which integrates feature logic with the multistratal point of view. Feature logic is useful here because it allows for the natural expression of constructions working across strata, without having to adapt first-order logic for this purpose. It also shows how it might be possible to use some of the computational algorithms available in unification-based systems to actually parse in a multistratal style. And in fact, such a parser has been implemented (Johnson, Meyers and Moss, 1993).

What are the essential features of stratified feature grammars? There are two main innovations.

- To be able to capture the multistratal point of view, Johnson and Moss introduce structure on the label alphabet L. In typical linguistic analyses, labels stand for grammatical relations like "head", "comp", "patient", and the like. Call these feature names "R-signs" for the moment. Then, the labels on feature arcs in SFG are *sequences* of R-signs, standing for the role that a given constituent may have played at different strata. For example, $[2,1]$: **glass** tells us that the word "glass" is initially a direct object (2) and finally a subject (1). The label $[2,1]$ is not a path, but a single member of the label alphabet.
- Persistence in feature logics is in fact a persistent problem for linguistic analyses. A feature structure may, for example, satisfy $agr\!:\!per\!:\!3$, but if no restrictions are placed on the typing system, a feature structure with extra completely irrelevant arcs like $employer\!:\!IBM$ will also be allowed by the logic. But we certainly wish to rule out such irrelevant arcs. This is the reason that appropriateness conditions, for example, are introduced in Carpenter's typing system. Other systems place global conditions on models: typically that feature structures satisfying a formula be minimal in the subsumption ordering.
  In SFG, a new idea, called *justification*, is introduced to rule out, among other things, extraneous arcs. The difference between justification and a global minimality condition is that justification applies locally. In the example above, if $agr\!:\!per\!:\!3$ were a "rule", then it only would justify itself, or perhaps naturally co-occurring features, and not an irrelevant arc. So, the idea of justification is that each "local" piece of data occurring in a feature structure must be justified by some rule of the grammar, where "rule" is interpreted as a feature logic formula.

SFG independently adopts conventions that we have already seen in other systems of feature logic. Rules of the grammar are formulas of (stratified) feature logic, and a grammar is a conjunction of such rules. A stratified feature structure will satisfy a grammar only if at each node, all rules are satisfied. So, something like a universal modality is in effect, and rules typically have the form $a \to \psi$, where a is a fairly simple type, and ψ is a more complicated formula. Justification, in addition, requires the data at each node of a feature structure to be justified by some rule. (This is a very imprecise

$$\begin{bmatrix} [Cat] & \texttt{S} \\ [1] & \texttt{Joe} \\ [Head] & \texttt{breaks} \\ [2] & \texttt{the glass} \end{bmatrix}$$

Fig. 2. Joe breaks the glass.

rendering of the actual definition.) Word ordering is handled in SFG by *precedence constraints* on feature arcs. We will ignore word ordering in this overview.

Our presentation is by example, building on the illustrations of Johnson and Moss.

EXAMPLES.

- Consider the sentence *Joe breaks the glass*. This is diagrammed as a feature structure in Figure 2. We present an (oversimplified) SFG lexical rule, stated in logical format, which accounts for the sentence:

$$\texttt{breaks} \to [Head]^{-1} : \{[Cat] : \texttt{S} \wedge [1] : \mathbf{true} \wedge [2] : \mathbf{true}\}.$$

  This rule states that the head verb "breaks" occurs as the value of the attribute "Head" in a structure which also requires a subject [1] and a direct object [2]. It actually is a logic formula, but with a new "inverse label" modal connective. The semantics of such formulas is in general

$$d \models l^{-1} : \varphi \text{ iff there is a unique } e \in D \text{ such that } el = d \text{ and } e \models \varphi.$$

  We have other lexical entries for "glass" and "Joe". The entry for "Joe", for example, could be

$$\texttt{Joe} \to \mathbf{true}.$$

  This rule seems to be logically superfluous. However, it *justifies* the occurrence of "Joe" in Figure 2. And in a more detailed example, an entry would provide agreement and morphological information.
- Now we show how simple constructions combine with lexical rules. It also begins to explain the function of the stratified feature labels. Consider the "unaccusative" sentence *Glass breaks*. This is diagrammed in Figure 3. In this case, we need to recognize that "break" is a verb that may have no explicit agent. So an additional entry might be

$$\texttt{breaks} \to [Head]^{-1} : \{[Cat] : \texttt{S} \wedge \neg[1) : \mathit{true} \wedge [2) : \mathbf{true}\}.$$

  (The open and closed bracketing will be explained in a moment.)

$$\begin{bmatrix} [Cat] & S \\ [2,1] & \texttt{glass} \\ [Head] & \texttt{breaks} \end{bmatrix}$$

Fig. 3. Glass breaks.

$$\begin{bmatrix} [Cat] & \texttt{S} \\ [1] & \texttt{Joe} \\ [Head] & \texttt{gave} \\ [3,2] & \texttt{Mary} \\ [2,8] & \texttt{tea} \end{bmatrix}$$

Fig. 4. Joe gave Mary tea.

Next, there is a rule which embodies the unaccusative construction. This is a formula **Unacc**, defined to be

$$\neg[1): true \rightarrow \{(2): \mathbf{true} \rightarrow (2,1): \mathbf{true}\}.$$

This rule says that "if there is no initial subject, then assuming there is an initial object, that object can be "advanced" to be a subject at the next stratum. (In point of fact, these constructions are given by so-called "extension formulas", which have yet another semantics. But the formula above serves to show the idea.)
The feature structure in Figure 3 satisfies both these formulas. The reason it satisfies the lexical rule is that the label $[2)$ occurring in the lexical entry for "breaks" *extends to* the label $[2,1]$ occurring in the feature structure. Similarly $(2,1)$ in the unaccusative rule extends to $[2,1]$ in the feature structure. This explains the open and closed parentheses enclosing sequences of features; there is a natural partial ordering $\sqsubseteq$ (not, by the way, a Scott ordering) of the stratified label set L. For example $[2,1) \sqsubseteq [2,1,0)$ and $[2,1]$, but $[2,1]$ does not extend to anything but itself. The definition of satisfaction for such an ordered label set now reads

$$d \models l : \varphi \text{ iff for some unique } f \text{ with } l \sqsubseteq f,\ df \models \varphi.$$

It might be argued that the unaccusative rule is superfluous, since it is logically implied by the right side of the lexical rule. But the lexical rule does not *justify* the occurrence of $[2,1]$. It only justifies the occurrence of a $[2]$. The unaccusative rule does justify this occurrence.

– Here is another example showing the Dative construction. Consider the sentence *Joe gave Mary tea*. This appears in Figure 4. An entry for "gave" might be

$$\texttt{gave} \rightarrow [Head]^{-1} : \{[Cat] : \texttt{S} \wedge [1) : \mathbf{true} \wedge [2) : \mathbf{true} \wedge [3) : \mathbf{true}\}.$$

We also have a rule for Dative:

$$(3) : \mathbf{true} \wedge (2) : \mathbf{true} \mapsto (3,2) : \mathbf{true} \wedge (2,8) : \mathbf{true}.$$

This rule is an extension formula, and should not technically be read as an implication. The reasons are too detailed to cover here. The intent is certainly an implicational one: if there is an initial indirect object (3) and an initial direct object, then the indirect object gets "advanced" to a direct object, and the direct object becomes a "chômeur" (8).

– Constructions can interact. Consider a final example: *Mary was given tea by Joe*. This appears in Figure 5.
In this example nominals x, y are used to indicate sharing, though SFG uses path equations. The example shows a nontrivial clause structure (the value of [*Comp*]) and the interaction of Dative and Passive. I will not attempt to give all the rules involved in this structure. One other aspect of it needs to be pointed out: the occurrence of the "0" sign in the feature labels like $[1,8,0]$ and $[0, \mathit{Marked}]$. "0" is a special "null" relational sign. When it occurs at the end of a sequence, it means that the value of that attribute plays no role in the surface form of the sentence. Likewise, when 0 occurs at the beginning of a sequence, it means that the constituent plays no role in the "initial" or predicate-argument structure of the sentence.

The full notions of predicate-argument structure and surface-structure can also be illustrated by the last example. To get the predicate-argument structure for "Mary was

$$\begin{bmatrix} [\mathit{Cat}] & \mathtt{S} \\ [0,1] & (x)\ \mathtt{Mary} \\ [\mathit{Head}] & \mathtt{was} \\ [\mathit{Comp}] & \begin{bmatrix} [\mathit{Cat}] & \mathtt{VP} \\ [\mathit{Head}] & \mathtt{given} \\ [3,2,1,0] & (x) \\ [2,8] & \mathtt{tea} \\ [1,8,0] & (y) \\ [0,8] & \begin{bmatrix} [0,\mathit{Cat}] & \mathtt{PP} \\ [0,\mathit{Flag}] & \mathtt{by} \\ [0,\mathit{Marked}] & (y)\ \mathtt{Joe} \end{bmatrix} \end{bmatrix} \end{bmatrix}$$

Fig. 5. Mary was given tea by Joe.

given tea by Joe" we delete from the structure in Figure 5 all arcs beginning with a 0. In the remaining arcs, we remove every sign except the first. The result is the following.

$$\begin{bmatrix} [\mathit{Cat}] & \texttt{S} \\ [\mathit{Head}] & \texttt{was} \\ [\mathit{Comp}] & \begin{bmatrix} [\mathit{Cat}] & \texttt{VP} \\ [\mathit{Head}] & \texttt{given} \\ [3) & \texttt{Mary} \\ [2) & \texttt{tea} \\ [1) & \texttt{Joe} \end{bmatrix} \end{bmatrix}$$

Similarly, to get the surface structure, we remove all arcs ending in 0, and remove all signs in the remaining arcs except the last. We obtain

$$\begin{bmatrix} [\mathit{Cat}] & \texttt{S} \\ (1] & \texttt{Mary} \\ [\mathit{Head}] & \texttt{was} \\ [\mathit{Comp}] & \begin{bmatrix} [\mathit{Cat}] & \texttt{VP} \\ [\mathit{Head}] & \texttt{given} \\ (8] & \texttt{tea} \\ (8] & \begin{bmatrix} (\mathit{Cat}] & \texttt{PP} \\ (\mathit{Flag}] & \texttt{by} \\ (\mathit{Marked}] & \texttt{Joe} \end{bmatrix} \end{bmatrix} \end{bmatrix}$$

(Notice that there are two (8]'s in the complement, so this last structure is actually a set-valued structure.) From the surface structure, it is finally possible to get a terminal sentence. For this, the surface structure is required to be a tree. Ordering of the words is handled by the precedence relations, a part of SFG we do not cover here.

We also do not go into the full details of the SFG concept of *justification*. The data in a feature system justified by a formula of SFG logic can be given recursively simultaneously with the notion of satisfaction. Suffice it to say that this means that Boolean connectives now cannot be interdefined, even though the definition of satisfaction in SFG uses the classical interpretation of negation and implication. Intuitively speaking, justification introduces *nonmonotonicity* into feature logic. But a full explication of this has not, as far as I know, been undertaken.

To sum up: SFG extends ordinary feature logic by introducing stratified (in general partially ordered) labels, and by introducing some new connectives. It introduces non-persistence via the concept of justification. Rules are lexically based, and satisfaction is required to obey a "universal-modality" principle in that each node of a feature structure must satisfy all rules. In addition, each "core" node of a feature structure must be justified by some rule.

8. Conclusion and future work

I have attempted in the chapter to show how methods of logic, used initially to understand feature-theoretic representations in language, can lead to a development of the mathematics of those representations, and even further, to applications not only in linguistics, but to logic and computer science. In my view, there is still much work to be done both in applications and the theory itself.

Computer science applications that should be pursued more thoroughly, for example, include (i) the use of feature-theoretic ideas in the area of terminological logics for artificial intelligence, and (ii) applications to the design of data base systems and data base query languages. This last application has in a sense a long history, since record structures in the typical relational data bases are just flat feature structures. I will not attempt here to recount specific work on the subject. With regard to (i), we have already alluded to the work of Nebel and Smolka (1989). Work more in the spirit of domain theory, attempting to model subsumption in terminological systems, has been carried out by Dionne, Mays and Oles (1992).

Another extension of feature theory which is needed for linguistic applications is to give a treatment of *non-monotonic* phenomena. We have mentioned feature specification defaults in GPSG, for example. Johnson (1991b) shows how some of the non-monotonic phenomena in LFG can be modeled using first-order *circumscription* (McCarthy, 1987). Some results on unification of nonmonotonic structures can be found in Young (1992), which also refers to other work like that of Bouma (1992). Evans (1988) gives an extensive proposal for GPSG. A full treatment for feature logic has yet to appear, however. (The Handbook chapter by Thomason expands on these issues.)

A third objective for feature theory is to reconcile the distinction between the "total object" perspective of Smolka and Johnson, and the "partial object" view stemming from Kasper–Rounds, and earlier, from Pereira and Shieber. In fact, the theory to date raises more questions than it answers about the fundamental status of linguistic objects. If these objects can be partial, then what is their epistemological status?

Are they objectively existing entities? If so, then they should not have undefined appropriate attributes. If we allow such undefined attributes, then our objects may live in a kind of "third world" of descriptions, about which we speak with our grammars. Or, they may be regarded from a situation-theoretic perspective, which allows us the flexibility to look at worlds where not all issues are settled. These are quite general issues, as the chapter on partiality by Fenstad shows. The interesting point is that the issues are exemplified by such easily visualized objects as feature structures. So, we finally need to contrast feature *theory* with feature *logic*. As with ordinary mathematics, the subject matter is at least, if not more, interesting than the formal language we use to describe it.

References

Abramsky, A. (1991), *Domain theory in logical form*, Ann. Pure Appl. Logic **51**.

Aczel, P. (1988), *Non-Well-Founded Sets*, Center for Study of Language and Information Lecture Notes no. 14.

Aït-Kaci, H. (1984), *A lattice-theoretic approach to computation based on a calculus of partially ordered type structures*, PhD Thesis, University of Pennsylvania.

Aït-Kaci, H. and Podelski, A. (1990), *Is there a meaning to life?*, Proceedings of the International Conference on Logic Programming.

Baader, F., Bürckert, H.J., Nebel, B., Nutt, W. and Smolka, G. (1991), *On the expressivity of feature logics with negation, functional uncertainty, and sort equations*, Technical Report RR-91-01, DFKI.

Backofen, R. (1993), *On the decidability of functional uncertainty*, Proc. 31st Annual Meeting of the Association for Computational Linguistics, 201–208.

Ben-Ari, M., Halpern, J. and Pnueli, A. (1982), *Deterministic propositional dynamic logic: Finite models, complexity, and completeness*, J. Comput. System Sci. **25**, 402–417.

Blackburn, P. (1993), *Modal logic and attribute value structures*, Diamonds and Defaults, M. de Rijke, ed., Kluwer, Dordrecht.

Blackburn, P. and Spaan, E. (1993), *A modal perspective on the computational complexity of attribute value grammar*, J. Logic, Lang., Inform. **2**, 129–169.

Blass, A. and Gurevich, Y. (1987), *Existential fixed-point logic*, Computation Theory and Logic, E. Börger, ed., Lecture Notes 270, Springer, Berlin 20–36.

Bouma, G. (1992), *Feature structures and nonmonotonicity*, Comput. Ling. **18**, 183–203.

Brachman, R.J. and Schmolze, J. (1985), *An overview of the* KL-ONE *knowledge representation system*, Cogn. Science **9**(2), 171–216.

Cardelli, L. and Wegner, P. (1985), *On understanding types, data abstractions, and polymorphism*, ACM Comput. Surv. **17**(4), 471–522.

Carpenter, B. (1992), *The Logic of Typed Feature Structures*, Cambridge Univ. Press, Cambridge, MA.

Chomsky, N. (1965), *Aspects of the Theory of Syntax*, MIT Press, Cambridge, MA.

Chomsky, N. and Halle, M. (1957), *The Sound Pattern of English*, Harper and Row, New York.

Dawar, A. and Vijay-Shanker, K. (1991), *A three-valued interpretation of negation in feature structure descriptions*, Proceedings of 27th Annual meeting of the Association for Computational Linguistics.

Dionne, R., Mays, E. and Oles, F.J. (1992), *A non well founded approach to terminological cycles*, Proceedings of Tenth National Conference on Artificial Intelligence: AAAI 92, 761–766.

Dörre, J. and Rounds, W. (1992), *On subsumption and semiunification in feature algebras*, J. Symb. Comput. **13**, 441–461.

Evans, R. (1988), *Towards a formal specification for defaults in gpsg*, Categories, Polymorphism, and Unification, E. Klein and J. van Benthem, eds, Centre for Cognitive Science, Edinburgh.

Fischer, M.J. and Ladner, R.E. (1979), *Propositional dynamic logic of regular programs*, J. Comput. System Sci. **18**(2), 194–211.

Gazdar, G., Klein, E., Pullum, G. and Sag, I. (1985), *Generalized Phrase Structure Grammar*, Harvard Univ. Press.

Gazdar, G., Pullum, G., Carpenter, R., Klein, E., Hukari, T. and Levine, T. (1988), *Category structures*, Comput. Ling. **14**, 1–19.

Goldblatt, R.I. (1989), *Varieties of complex algebras*, Ann. Pure Appl. Logic **44**, 173–242.

Gunter, C.A. and Scott, D.S. (1990), *Semantic domains*, Handbook of Theoretical Computer Science, vol. B: Formal Models and Semantics, J. van Leeuwen, ed., Elsevier, Amsterdam, 633–674.

Gurevich, Y. (1966), *The word problem for certain classes of semigroups*, Algebra and Logic **5**, 25–35.

Haegeman, L. (1991), *Introduction to Government and Binding Theory*, Basil Blackwell, Oxford.

Harel, D. (1984), *Dynamic logic*, Handbook of Philosophical Logic vol. II, D. Gabbay and F. Guenthner, eds, Reidel, Dordrecht.

Hennessy, M. and Milner, R. (1985), *Algebraic laws for nondeterminism and concurrency*, J. Assoc. Comput. Mach. **32**(1), 137–161.

Höhfeld, M. and Smolka, G. (1988), *Definite relations over constraint languages*, Technical Report LILOG-REPORT 53, IBM Deutschland, Stuttgart.

Immerman, N. (1982), *Relational queries computable in polynomial time*, Proc. 14th ACM Symposium on the Theory of Computing, 147–152.

Johnson, D., Meyers, A. and Moss, L. (1993), *A unification-based parser for relational grammar*, Proc. 31st Annual Meeting of the Association for Computational Linguistics, 97–104.

Johnson, D. and Moss, L. (1993), *Some formal properties of stratified feature grammars*, Ann. Math. Artif. Intell. **8**.

Johnson, D.F. and Postal, P.M. (1980), *Arc Pair Grammar*, Princeton Univ. Press.

Johnson, M. (1988), *Attribute-Value Logic and the Theory of Grammar*, Center for Study of Language and Information.

Johnson, M. (1991a), *Features and formulae*, Comput. Ling. **17**, 131–152.

Johnson, M. (1991b), *Logic and feature structures*, Proceedings of IJCAI 91, 992–996.

Joshi, A.K. and Schabes, Y. (1992), *Tree adjoining grammars and lexicalized grammars*, Tree Automata and Languages, Elsevier, Amsterdam.

Kaplan, R. and Bresnan, J. (1982), *Lexical-functional grammar: A formal system for grammatical representations*, The Mental Representation of Grammatical Relations, J. Bresnan, ed., MIT Press, Cambridge, MA, 173–281.

Kasper, R. and Rounds, W. (1986), *A logical semantics for feature structures*, Proc. 24th Meeting of the Association for Computational Linguistics, 257–266.

Kasper, R. and Rounds, W. (1990), *The logic of unification in grammar*, Ling. and Philos. **13**, 33–58.

Kay, M. (1979), *Functional grammar*, Proceedings of the Fifth Annual Meeting of the Berkeley Linguist. Society, C. Chiarello, ed., 142–158.

Kracht, M. (1989), *On the logic of category definitions*, Comput. Ling. **15**, 111–113.

Lewis, H. (1980), *Complexity results for classes of quantificational formulae*, J. Comput. System Sci. **21**, 317–353.

McCarthy, J. (1987), *Circumscription – a form of non-monotonic reasoning*, Readings in Nonmonotonic Reasoning, M. Ginsberg, ed., Morgan Kauffman, 145–152.

Montague, R. (1974), *The proper treatment of quantification in ordinary English*, Formal Philosophy: Selected Writings of Richard Montague, R. Thomason, ed., Yale Univ. Press, 247–270.

Moshier, M.A. (1988), *Extensions to unification grammar for the description of programming languages*, PhD Thesis, University of Michigan.

Moshier, M.A. (1993), *Completeness theorems for logics of feature structures*, Ann. Math. Artif. Intell. **8**.

Moshier, M.A. and Rounds, W. (1987), *A logic for partially specified data structures*, Proceedings of 14th ACM Symposium on Principles of Programming Languages.

Moss, L. (1991), *Completeness theorems for logics of feature structures*, Proceedings of MSRI Workshop on Logic from Computer Science, Y. Moschovakis, ed., Springer, Berlin.

Mukai, K. (1990), *A system of logic programming for linguistic analysis*, Technical Report TR-540, ICOT, Tokyo.

Mukai, K. (1991), *Clp(afa): Coinductive semantics of horn clauses with compact constraints*, Situation Theory and its Applications, vol. 2, J. Gawron, G. Plotkin and S. Tutiya, eds, Center for Study of Language and Information, 179–214.

Nebel, B. and Smolka, G. (1989), *Representation and reasoning with attributive descriptions*, Sorts and Types in Artificial Intelligence, K.H. Bläsius, U. Hedstück and C.-R. Rollinger, eds, Lecture Notes in Artificial Intelligence 418, Springer, Berlin, 112–139.

Pereira, F. and Shieber, S. (1984), *The semantics of grammar formalisms seen as computer languages*, Proceedings of 10th International Conference on Computational Linguistics: COLING 84.

Pereira, F. and Warren, D.H.D. (1980), *Definite clause grammars for language analysis: A survey of the formalism and a comparison with augmented transition networks*, Artif. Intell. **13**, 231–278.

Perlmutter, D. (1983), *Studies in Relational Grammar I*, Chicago Univ. Press.

Pollard, C. and Moshier, M.A. (1990), *Unifying partial descriptions of sets*, Vancouver Studies in Cognitive Science: vol. I, P. Hansen, ed., Univ. British Columbia Press.

Pollard, C. and Sag, I. (1987), *Information-Based Syntax and Semantics: Volume I – Fundamentals*, CSLI Lecture Notes no. 13, Chicago Univ. Press.

Postal, P.M. (1986), *Studies of Passive Clauses*, State Univ. of New York Press.

Postal, P.M. and Joseph, B. (eds) (1990), *Studies in Relational Grammar III*, Chicago Univ. Press.

Pratt, V. (1976), *Semantical considerations on floyd-hoare logic*, Proceedings of the 17th IEEE Symposium on Foundations of Computer Science.

Prior, A. (1967), *Past, Present, and Future*, Oxford Univ. Press, Oxford.

Reape, M. (1994), *Introduction to Semantics of Unification-based Grammar Formalisms*, Kluwer, Dordrecht.

Robinson, R. (1971), *Undecidability and nonperiodicity for tilings of the plane*, Invent. Math. **12**, 177–209.

Rounds, W. and Manaster Ramer, R. (1987), *A logical version of functional grammar*, Proceedings of the 25th Annual Conference of the Association for Computational Linguistics.

Scott, D.S. (1982), *Domains for Denotational Semantics*, Lecture Notes in Comput. Sci. vol. 140.

Shieber, S. (1986), *The design of a computer language for linguistic information*, Proceedings of 12th COLING, 211–215.

Shieber, S. (1989), *Parsing and type inference for natural and computer languages*, PhD Thesis, Stanford University.

Shieber, S. (1992), *Constraint-Based Grammar Formalisms: Parsing and Type Inference for Natural and Computer Languages*, MIT Press, Cambridge, MA.

Smolka, G. (1992), *Feature constraint logics for unification grammars*, J. Logic Programming **12**, 51–87.

Takeuti, G. (1987), *Proof Theory*, North-Holland, Amsterdam.

Vardi, M. (1982), *The complexity of relational query languages*, Proceedings of the 14th ACM Symposium on the Theory of Computing, 137–146.

Vickers, S. (1989), *Topology via Logic*, Cambridge Univ. Press, Cambridge, MA.

Vijay-Shanker, K. (1987), *A study of tree-adjoining grammars*, PhD Thesis, University of Pennsylvania.

Young, M. (1992), *Non-monotonic sorts for feature structures*, Proceedings of Tenth National Conference on Artificial Intelligence: AAAI 92, 596–601.

Zhang, G.-Q. (1991), *Logic of Domains*, Birkhauser, Boston.

CHAPTER 9

Types

Raymond Turner

University of Essex, Department of Computer Science, Wivenhoe Park, Colchester, CO4 35Q, UK
E-mail: turnr@essex.ac.uk

Commentator: S. Feferman

Contents

HANDBOOK OF LOGIC AND LANGUAGE
Edited by J. van Benthem and A. ter Meulen

1. Categories, functions and types

Syntactic *categories* reflect distributional phenomena in natural language. *Types* are meant to play the role of their semantic counterparts. At least this is the traditional wisdom in that approach to semantic theory which has its historical roots in the philosophical logic of Frege and Russell. The objective of this paper is to study the various notions of *type* and *function* which are (or could be) employed in the semantic enterprise. In particular, we shall study various formulations of the typed lambda calculus and its logical extensions.

1.1. Functions and types in formal semantics

From Frege and Russell formal semantics inherited two crucial notions. Frege introduced the idea that certain natural language expressions (*predicative* expressions) should be semantically analyzed as mathematical functions. Of course, Frege's notion of function was the informal one of the contemporary mathematics of his time and the regimentation of that notion obtained by its formalization within axiomatic set-theory is of later origin. Nevertheless, it is this original conceptual insight which laid the groundwork for the development of a mathematical theory of natural language semantics.

The second important notion which underpins modern semantics is that of *type*. The original intention of Russell, in introducing both his *simple* and *ramified type* theories, concerned the paradoxes. His arguments for the necessity of some kind of typing regime were positive ones: he was not just concerned with blocking the paradoxes but with explaining the confusions in the conceptual systems that gave rise to them. His arguments concerned the illegitimacy of *impredicative* notions in mathematics and logic; his belief that a *type hierarchy* should be imposed upon any universe of discourse flows from these predicative strictures.

Semanticists, not primarily motivated by such philosophical scruples, nor with a burning concern with the paradoxes, have employed the notion of type as a form of mental hygiene; much like the role of dimensional analysis in elementary physics. Types are used as a semantic explanation for certain distributional phenomena in natural language. Roughly, the underlying syntactic structure is semantically explained in terms of the corresponding constraints imposed by the type structure.

1.2. Categories and types

The first systematic functional semantics for a reasonable fragment of English is due to Montague (1969, 1970). Within his system, expressions in the various natural language categories are semantically represented as objects of the corresponding type. For example, one possibility within the traditional Noun-phrase/Verb-phrase structure of sentences is to semantically unpack NP's as individuals and VP's as functions from individuals to propositions. The semantic value of the sentence (a *proposition*) is then computed via functional application. Alternatively, one might follow Montague's account and take the semantic type of NP's to be *high-order* functions whose domain is the set of functions

Table 1

Syntactic Category	Type
Sentences	Propositions
Common Nouns	Functions from individuals to propositions
Verb Phrases	Functions from individuals to propositions
Quantifier Phrases	Functions from, functions from individuals to propositions, to propositions

from individuals to propositions and whose range is the set of propositions. Application then operates in the opposite direction. This account has been taken to be necessary for a uniform treatment of NP's since under it both simple and complex NP's are assigned the same type. Whatever view is adopted the semantic correlate of complex category formation is functional application. As a consequence this correspondence rapidly generates functions of higher and higher type as Table 1 illustrates.

Modern formulations of categorial grammar are much more flexible than Montague's. We shall discuss the relationship between these grammars and the various formulations of type theory in the next section, although most of the emphasis of this paper will be on the type systems themselves. Categorial grammar has a chapter of its own.

1.3. The role of the typed lambda calculus

In Montague semantics, English sentences are directly interpreted as expressions of his *Intensional Logic*. This is a system of higher order modal logic whose underlying notion of function is supplied by the *typed lambda calculus*. In this paper we shall not be concerned with the modal notions embedded in his intensional logic but only with those aspects which pertain to the types and their calculi. Montague further supplied a set-theoretic interpretation of his intensional logic. While it is certainly the case that Montague saw this intermediate step via intensional logic as dispensable, since for him the primary semantic interpretation was to be a set-theoretic one, there are no compelling conceptual or formal reasons why this has to be so. All the lambda calculi we shall consider do admit of a set-theoretic interpretation but they can also be viewed as axiomatic theories of functions in there own right. This perspective will form one of the main thrust of the present paper and conforms to the original intuitions of Church in developing the lambda calculus.

> "Underlying the formal calculus we shall develop is the concept of a function, as it appears in various branches of mathematics, either under that name or under one of the synonymous names, "operation" or "transformation". Church (1941).[1]

2. The typed lambda calculus

This section is devoted to an exposition of the typed lambda Calculus. We shall consider three different versions of the typed lambda calculus which differ from each other according to the *rigidity* of the attachment between terms and types. In all three theories

[1] This quote refers to the *untyped* lambda calculus which we shall get to later.

the notion of type is the same: types are generated from a basic type (of *individuals*) by forming the type of *functions* from one type to a second. The language of type expressions thus takes the following form.

(i) I (type of individuals) is a type expression.

(ii) If T and S are type expressions then so is $T \Rightarrow S$ (the type of functions from T to S).

However, the way in which terms get assigned types in the three theories is different. In the first system the types are *hardwired* into the syntax of terms whereas the last two are less syntactically constrained in that the type information is not built into the syntax but supplied by *rules of type assignment.*

2.1. The Church calculus (CT)

Initially we study the original presentation of the typed lambda calculus due essentially to Church (1940). This corresponds to the form it takes within Montague's intensional logic.

2.1.1. The language of the Church system

In this formulation the syntax of terms is dictated by the types. There are variables (and optionally constants) for each type together with the operations of abstraction and application.

(i) Every variable, x^T, is a term of type T.

(ii) Every constant, c^T, is a term of type T.

(iii) If t is a term of type S then $\lambda x^T.t$ is a term of type $T \Rightarrow S$.

(iv) If t is a term of type T and s a term of type $T \Rightarrow S$ then st is a term of type S.

We shall write $s : E^T$ or s^T to indicate that s is a term of type T. We adopt the standard conventions regarding *free* and *bound* variables: in $\lambda x^T.t$, x is *bound* throughout the body t. The meta-expression $s[t/x]$ denotes the result of substituting t for each free occurrence of x in s with the proviso that no free variable of t becomes accidentally bound by the substitution. For more details of these syntactic conventions the reader should consult Hindley and Seldin (1986).

Under one interpretation of this calculus the lambda abstracts denote functions (in the set-theoretic sense) whose domains and ranges are dictated by their decorating types; the operation of application is then understood as functional application. We shall employ this informal set-theoretic interpretation in motivating the axioms of the theory; shortly, we shall provide a precise account of it.

2.1.2. Equality

The axioms and rules of the theory govern the basic assertion of equality: given $s : E^T$ and $t : E^T$,

$$s =_T t$$

asserts that s and t are equal objects of type T. We shall often drop the subscript on the equality symbol since it is a nuisance, and in any case is always recoverable from the terms themselves. The axioms and rules which govern this notion of equality are given as follows.

$$\lambda x^T.s = \lambda y^T.s[y/x] \quad y^T \text{ not free in } s \tag{α}$$

$$(\lambda x^T.t)s^T = t[s^T/x^T] \tag{β}$$

$$\frac{t =_{T\Rightarrow S} s \qquad u =_T \nu}{tu =_S s\nu} \tag{υ}$$

$$s = s \tag{ρ}$$

$$\frac{s = t}{t = s} \tag{σ}$$

$$\frac{s = t \qquad t = r}{s = r} \tag{τ}$$

We shall write $\vdash_{\mathbf{CT}} s =_T t$ if there is a derivation of $s =_T t$ from these axioms and rules.

There are further axioms which are suggested by the set-theoretic interpretation, namely the following axioms of *extensionality*.

$$\frac{t = s}{\lambda x^T.t = \lambda x^T.s} \tag{ξ}$$

$$\lambda x^T.tx^T = t \quad x^T \text{ not free in } t \tag{η}$$

$$\frac{t^{T\Rightarrow S}x^T = s^{T\Rightarrow S}x^T}{t^{T\Rightarrow S} = s^{T\Rightarrow S}} \tag{ext}$$

All the lambda calculi we shall consider are usually formulated with ξ (or its analogue) built in. This axiom is usually called a weak axiom of extensionality. The reason for this is best seen in its relationship to the strong axiom of extensionality, i.e. **ext**. The following is straightforward (see Barendregt, 1984).

PROPOSITION 2.1.2.1. $\mathbf{CT} + \eta + \xi$ *is equivalent to* $\mathbf{CT} + \mathbf{ext}$.

2.1.3. Set-theoretic models of the extensional theory

The set-theoretic interpretation is made precise in the following way. We first attach a set-theoretical meaning to the types by choosing some set D to stand proxy for the type of individuals; the function space types are then modeled by forming classical function spaces.

$$[\![I]\!] = D,$$
$$[\![T \Rightarrow S]\!] = [\![S]\!]^{[\![T]\!]} \quad \text{the class of functions from } [\![T]\!] \text{ to } [\![S]\!].$$

The terms are interpreted relative to an assignment function, g, which assigns a member of $[\![T]\!]$ to each variable of type T. The semantics of the pure term language then proceeds as follows.

$$[\![x^T]\!]_g = g(x^T),$$
$$[\![\lambda x^T.t^S]\!]_g = f \in [\![S]\!]^{[\![T]\!]} \quad \text{where for each } d \in [\![T]\!],\ f(d) = [\![t]\!]_{g(d/x^T)},$$
$$[\![t^{T \Rightarrow S} s^T]\!]_g = [\![t^{T \Rightarrow S}]\!]_g [\![s^T]\!]_g.$$

In the above, $g(d/x^T)$ is the same function as g except (perhaps) that x^T is assigned the value d. We shall say that $t =_T s$ is true in such a model if $[\![t]\!]_g = [\![s]\!]_g$, for all assignments g.

THEOREM 2.1.3.1. *If* $\vdash_{\mathrm{CT}+\eta+\xi} t =_T s$ *then* $t =_T s$ *is true in all set-theoretic models.*

PROOF. By induction on the derivations in Church system. All the cases are routine except the α and β-axioms. We illustrate with the latter. Observe that, $[\![(\lambda x^T.s)t^T]\!]_g = [\![s]\!]_{g([\![t]\!]g/x^T)}$ – by definition of $[\![\ ]\!]$. To complete the argument we require the following lemma. □

LEMMA 2.1.3.2. $[\![s]\!]_{g([\![t]\!]_g/x)} = [\![s[t/x]]\!]_g$.

PROOF. By induction on the terms. □

2.2. The loosely typed calculus (C)

Working with such a rigid syntax is often quite inconvenient. Indeed, we have already taken some liberties with the Church theory in that we have often not exhibited all the type information.The second theory can be seen as a further step in this direction. In this theory types get attached to terms in a less syntactic fashion via rules of type assignment.

2.2.1. The language of the theory

The terms are largely undecorated although we impose a minimal amount of type information. They take the following form.

(i) x a variable, is a term.
(ii) c a constant, is a term.
(iii) If t is a term, T a type expression and x a variable then $\lambda x \in T.t$ is a term.
(iv) If t and s are terms then so is st.

Notice that the type information is restricted to bound variables; free variables are untyped. As a consequence, $\lambda x \in T.xx$ and xx are syntactically well-formed, i.e. the theory admits terms which can be applied to themselves; however, it says nothing about them.

2.2.2. Type assignment

In the **CT** system there is only one basic judgement, namely, the equality of terms. In the **C** theory we require a further judgement of type membership which replaces the syntactic type impositions of **CT**. Indeed, we need to put this aspect of the theory in place before we can deal with equality. Type information is imposed via rules which facilitate the attachment of types to terms. The basic judgement of the system takes the form:

$$t \in T$$

i.e. the object t has type T. Moreover, such judgments are not made in isolation but take place relative to a *context* or basis B which consists of a set of statements of the form

$$\{x_1 \in T_1,\ x_2 \in T_2, \ldots,\ x_n \in T_n\}$$

– where no variable is assigned more than one type. Our type assignment system is then defined by the following axioms and rules. We shall often write $B, x \in T$ for the context $B \cup \{x \in T\}$.

$$B \vdash x \in T$$ **assump** whenever $x \in T$ is in B

$$\frac{B, x \in T \vdash t \in S}{B \vdash \lambda x \in T.t \in T \Rightarrow S}$$ **funi** function introduction rule

$$\frac{B \vdash t \in T \qquad B \vdash s \in T \Rightarrow S}{B \vdash st \in S}$$ **fune** function elimination rule

Not every term can be assigned a type. For example, $\lambda x \in T.xx$ is syntactically well-formed but cannot be assigned a type in any context. However, if a term can be assigned a type it is unique.

THEOREM 2.2.2.1. *If $B \vdash s \in S$ and $B \vdash s \in T$ then T and S are the same type expression.*

PROOF. By induction on the structure of s. The base case is clear. For application, suppose $B \vdash st \in T$ and $B \vdash st \in S$. This can only have arisen from derivations $B \vdash t \in U$ and $B \vdash s \in U \Rightarrow T$, on the one hand, and $B \vdash t \in V$ and $B \vdash s \in V \Rightarrow S$, on the other. By induction, $U = V$ and $V \Rightarrow S = U \Rightarrow T$. Hence $S = T$. For the case of abstraction, $B \vdash \lambda x \in T.t \in T \Rightarrow S$ can only have arisen by an application of the introduction rule from the premise $B, x \in T \vdash t \in S$. In which case, by induction, S must be unique. □

The system is *monomorphic*, i.e. every term can be assigned at most one type. This property is usually taken as the acid test of whether or not one has a genuine formulation of the typed lambda calculus. In the next system we consider, this property will fail. For more information on systems of type assignment see Barendregt (1991), Hindley (1969) and Hindley and Seldin (1986).

2.2.3. Equality

Type assignment is only part of the theory. By analogy with **CT**, we also require a notion of equality. Hence we introduce a second judgement which now interacts with the first. As with **CT**, the formula

$$t =_T s$$

asserts that t and s are equal objects of type T. However, in contrast to the **CT** theory, the judgement make sense for arbitrary terms; although it will only be true for terms which are provably of the same type. The axioms and rules for this notion parallel those of **CT** but now they require a context.

$$\frac{B, x \in T \vdash s \in S}{B \vdash \lambda x \in T.s =_{T \Rightarrow S} \lambda y \in T.s[y/x]} \quad y \text{ not free in } s \qquad (\alpha)$$

$$\frac{B, x \in R \vdash s \in T \qquad B \vdash t \in R}{B \vdash (\lambda x \in R.s)t =_T s[t/x]} \qquad (\beta)$$

$$\frac{B \vdash s \in T}{B \vdash s =_T s} \qquad (\rho)$$

$$\frac{B \vdash s =_T s'}{B \vdash s' =_T s} \qquad (\sigma)$$

$$\frac{B \vdash s =_T s' \qquad B \vdash s' =_T s''}{B \vdash s =_T s''} \qquad (\tau)$$

$$\frac{B \vdash s =_{T \Rightarrow R} s' \qquad B \vdash t =_T t'}{B \vdash st =_R s't'} \qquad (\upsilon)$$

We now have the complete system in place. We shall write $B \vdash_{\mathrm{C}} \theta$ (or just $B \vdash \theta$ if there is no danger of ambiguity) if θ (a conclusion of the form $t \in T$ or $t =_T s$) follows from the context B by the rules and axioms of type assignment and equality.

Our first result guarantees that two provably equal objects of type T are indeed objects of type T.

PROPOSITION 2.2.3.1. *If* $B \vdash s =_T t$ *then* $B \vdash s \in T$ *and* $B \vdash t \in T$.

PROOF. By induction on the derivations. By way of illustration, consider the β-rule. Given the premise, we can conclude that $B \vdash \lambda x \in R.s \in R \Rightarrow T$. It follows from the elimination rule that $(\lambda x \in R.s)t \in T$. For the other half, namely $s[t/x] \in T$, we require the following lemma. □

LEMMA 2.2.3.2. *If* $B, x \in T \vdash s \in S$ *and* $B \vdash t \in T$ *then* $B \vdash s[t/x] \in S$.

PROOF. By induction on s. If s is a variable the result is immediate. If it is an application it follows from the induction hypothesis and the definition of substitution. If it is an abstraction we employ induction, the definition of substitution and the introduction rule. □

We can add the extensionality axioms which, in the present context, take the following form. Since **ext** is equivalent to the other two, we just give them.

$$\frac{B, x \in T \vdash s =_R t}{B \vdash \lambda x \in T.s =_{T \Rightarrow R} \lambda x \in T.t} \qquad (\xi)$$

$$\frac{B \vdash t \in T \Rightarrow S}{B \vdash \lambda x \in T.tx =_{T \Rightarrow S} t} \quad x \text{ not free in } t \qquad (\eta)$$

Once again, when and if we use these we shall indicate the fact explicitly. We shall state the results with reference to the basic theory **C** but with the understanding that, unless we indicate to the contrary, they extend to the extensional theory.

2.2.4. Erasing and decorating

There is a systematic relationship between the two theories **CT** and **C** which concerns the *decorating* and *erasing* of type information. This is generated by two transformations: in the first we *erase* the types from the terms of the **CT** system and in the second we *decorate* the terms in the **C** system.

$$\text{erase}(x^T) \equiv x,$$
$$\text{erase}(ts) \equiv \text{erase}(t)\text{erase}(s),$$
$$\text{erase}(\lambda x^T.t) \equiv \lambda x \in T.\text{erase}(t).^2$$

LEMMA 2.2.4.1. $\text{erase}(t^S[s^T/x^T]) \equiv \text{erase}(t^S)[\text{erase}(s^T)/\text{erase}(x^T)]$.

PROOF. By induction on the typed terms: we employ only the definitions of erase and substitution. □

2 To avoid confusion, we shall often employ $\equiv$ for definitional equality.

For the reverse mapping we need to take the context into account: decorating is only well-formed on terms which are well-typed according to the typing rules. If $B \vdash r \in T$, we define decorate by recursion on the structure of r as follows.

$$\text{decorate}(B \vdash x \in T) \equiv x^T$$
$$\text{decorate}(B \vdash \lambda x \in T.t \in T \Rightarrow S) \equiv \lambda x^T.\text{decorate}(B, x \in T \vdash t \in S)$$
$$\text{decorate}(B \vdash st \in T) \equiv \text{decorate}(B \vdash s \in S \Rightarrow T)\text{decorate}(B \vdash t \in S)$$

where S is the unique type such that $B \vdash s \in S \Rightarrow T$ and $B \vdash t \in S$.

The last clause makes sense because of the monomorphic nature of type assignment. The following is also established by induction on the structure of terms; this time those of **C**.

LEMMA 2.2.4.2. *If* $B \vdash t[s/x] \in S$ *then*

$$\begin{aligned}&\text{decorate}(B \vdash t[s/x] \in S)\\ &\quad = \text{decorate}(B, x \in T \vdash t \in S)\left[\text{decorate}(B \vdash s \in T)/x^T\right].\end{aligned}$$

THEOREM 2.2.4.3.

(i) *For each* $t : E_T$, $B_t \vdash \text{erase}(t) \in T$ *where* $B_t = \{x \in T\colon x^T$ *is a free variable of* $t\}$. *Moreover, if* $\vdash_{\mathbf{CT}} s =_T t$ *then* $B_t \cup B_s \vdash_{\mathbf{C}} \text{erase}(t) =_T \text{erase}(s)$.

(ii) *If* $B \vdash_{\mathbf{C}} t \in T$ *then* $\text{decorate}(B \vdash t \in T) : E_T$. *Moreover, if* $B \vdash_{\mathbf{C}} t =_T s$ *then* $\vdash_{\mathbf{CT}} \text{decorate}(B \vdash t \in T) =_T \text{decorate}(B \vdash s \in T)$.

(iii) *If* $B \vdash_{\mathbf{C}} t \in T$ *then* $\text{erase}(\text{decorate}(B \vdash t \in T)) = t$. *Moreover, if* $t : E_T$ *then* $\text{decorate}(B_t \vdash \text{erase}(t) \in T) = t$.

PROOF.

(i) For the first part we employ induction on the terms of **CT**. We illustrate with abstraction. Suppose r is $\lambda x^T.s$ where $s : E_S$. By induction, $B_S \vdash \text{erase}(s) \in S$. Hence, $B_S - \{x \in T\} \vdash \lambda x \in T.\text{erase}(s) \in T \Rightarrow S$. For the second part we require the substitution Lemma 2.2.4.1.

(ii) By induction on the derivations in the **C** system. The first part is straightforward. For the second part we require the substitution Lemma 2.2.4.2.

(iii) Employ induction on the **CT** terms for the second part and induction on the **C** terms for the first.

□

Thus we have essentially the same theory under two different guises. However, the **C** formulation has the advantage of not demanding that every term be explicitly decorated with type information. It thus underwrites the practice of suppressing the type information. It also facilitates the exploration of the connections between the typed lambda calculus and categorial grammar; a topic we take up at the end of this section.

2.3. *The untyped lambda calculus*

In the final theory we remove all type information from the terms. Even the lambda abstracts are undecorated. As a result monomorphism will fail and we will not be able to decorate the terms in a unique way – no matter how much contextual information is given. This theory is usually called the Curry calculus (Curry, 1958, 1972). It is built upon the (*untyped*) lambda calculus **U** (Church, 1941). We shall devote this subsection to this. Our treatment will be brief since there are many excellent expositions available (e.g., Barendregt, 1984).

2.3.1. *Language*

Strictly speaking the *untyped lambda calculus* has no notion of type (except implicitly the type of everything). This is reflected in the fact that the basic judgement of equality is an absolute one which is made independently of any explicit notion of type and the terms are void of any type information.

(i) x, a variable, is a term.
(ii) c, a constant, is a term.
(iii) If t is a term and x a variable then $\lambda x.t$ is a term.
(iv) If t and s are terms then so is st.

The only difference between this syntax and that of the **C**-theory concerns the lambda abstracts but as we shall see it has some important implications.

2.3.2. *The formal system*

The formal system is constituted by the following axiom and rules of equality.

$$\lambda x.s = \lambda y.s[y/x] \quad y \text{ not free in } s \tag{α}$$

$$(\lambda x.s)t = s[t/x] \tag{β}$$

$$s = s \tag{ρ}$$

$$\frac{s = s'}{s' = s} \tag{σ}$$

$$\frac{s = s' \qquad s' = s''}{s = s''} \tag{τ}$$

$$\frac{s = s' \qquad t = t'}{st = s't'} \tag{υ}$$

We shall write $\vdash_{\mathbf{U}} t = s$ if $t = s$ follows from the rules and axioms of equality.[3]

[3] Approaches where equality is *partial* are also possible (see Feferman, 1975, 1979). Such approaches may prove attractive for dealing with partiality in natural language. For a version of type theory developed for semantic purposes see Muskens (1989). See also the discussion of Partiality (Fenstad) in this volume.

Strictly speaking, the untyped calculus usually has the ξ-rule built in and the η-axiom is optional. In the untyped calculus they take the following naked form.

$$\frac{s = t}{\lambda x.s = \lambda x.t} \qquad (\xi)$$

$$\lambda x.tx = t \quad x \text{ not free in } t \qquad (\eta)$$

The obvious formulation of **ext** is equivalent to $\xi + \eta$. Once again, if we employ any of the extensionality axioms, we shall explicitly say so.

2.3.3. The computational role of the untyped lambda calculus

Although we have approached the lambda calculi from the perspective of their role in natural language semantics any discussion of the lambda calculus would be incomplete without some mention of this computational aspect. We shall be brief and refer the reader to Barendregt (1984) for further details.

DEFINITION 2.3.3.1. We define three relations $\rightarrow_1$ (reduction in one step), $\twoheadrightarrow_\beta$ (reduction), $=_\beta$ (convertibility), by induction as follows

(i) (a) $(\lambda x.s)t \rightarrow_1 s[t/x]$
  (b) $t \rightarrow_1 s$ implies $rt \rightarrow_1 rs,\ tr \rightarrow_1 sr$ and $\lambda x.t \rightarrow_1 \lambda x.s$

(ii) (a) $t \twoheadrightarrow_\beta t$
  (b) $t \rightarrow_1 s$ implies $t \twoheadrightarrow_\beta s$
  (c) $t \twoheadrightarrow_\beta s$ and $s \twoheadrightarrow_\beta r$ implies $t \twoheadrightarrow_\beta r$

(iii) (a) $t \twoheadrightarrow_\beta s$ implies $t =_\beta s$
  (b) $t =_\beta s$ implies $s =_\beta t$
  (c) $t =_\beta s$ and $s =_\beta r$ implies $t =_\beta r$.

We can now link up the two notion of equivalence.

PROPOSITION 2.3.3.2. $\vdash_{\mathrm{U}+\xi}\ t = s$ *iff* $t =_\beta s$.

PROOF. From left to right is by induction on the derivations in $\mathbf{U} + \xi$. From right to left employ induction on the definition of $=_\beta$. □

DEFINITION 2.3.3.3. A *β-redex* is a term of the form $(\lambda x.s)t$. A term is in *β-normal form* if it does not have a β-redex as a subexpression. A term t has a *β-normal form* if $t =_\beta s$ for some term s in β-normal form.

The major theorem about reduction is the following. Elegant proofs of it and its corollaries can be found in (Barendregt, 1991).

THEOREM 2.3.3.4 (Church–Rosser). *If $s \twoheadrightarrow_\beta t$ and $s \twoheadrightarrow_\beta r$ then for some term k one has $t \twoheadrightarrow_\beta k$ and $r \twoheadrightarrow_\beta k$.*

COROLLARY 2.3.3.5. *If $s =_\beta t$ then there is a term r such that $s \twoheadrightarrow_\beta r$ and $t \twoheadrightarrow_\beta r$.*

COROLLARY 2.3.3.6. *If s has a β-normal form t then $s \twoheadrightarrow_\beta t$. Moreover every term has at most one β-normal form.*

One of the fundamental features of this calculus, which illustrates its essentially untyped nature and which is therefore not shared by its typed cousins, is the existence of a *fixpoint* operator. Consider the term

$$\mathbf{Y} = \lambda f.(\lambda x.f(xx))(\lambda x.f(xx)).$$

A little computation, using the rules and axioms, yields that, for any term t,

$$\vdash_{\mathrm{U}} \mathbf{Y}t = t(\mathbf{Y}t).$$

It is this feature which gives the calculus its computational power since it is the basis of the representation of the *general recursive* functions. It is also the feature which causes problems when one tries to base logic upon the untyped calculus; a topic we shall return to later.

2.3.4. *Models of the extensional calculus*

Models of the extensional theory are a little more difficult to come by. Indeed, there is a small academic industry involved in constructing and investigating models of the (extensional) untyped Lambda Calculus. The first two notions of model were discovered by Scott (1979), Plotkin (1980) and Scott (1981). We shall provide a brief introduction to these models but first we provide a general notion introduced by Meyer (1982).

DEFINITION 2.3.4.1. A *Functional model* is a structure of the form $\mathcal{D} = \langle D, [D \to D], f, h\rangle$ where D is a non-empty set, $[D \to D]$ is some class of functions from D to D and $f: D \to [D \to D]$, $h: [D \to D] \to D$ are functions such that for each $d \in D$, $h(f(d)) = d$.

The function f turns an arbitrary element of D into a function from D to D and the function h does the reverse. As a consequence each term of the calculus can be assigned an element of D as follows.

$$[\![x]\!]_g = g(x),$$
$$[\![\lambda x.t]\!]_g = h\big(\lambda d.[\![t]\!]_{g(d/x)}\big),$$
$$[\![ts]\!]_g = f([\![t]\!]_g)[\![s]\!]_g,$$

where g is an assignment of elements of D to variables.

THEOREM 2.3.4.2. *If $\vdash_{\mathrm{U}+\xi+\eta} t = s$ then, for each assignment g, $[\![t]\!]_g = [\![s]\!]_g$.*

PROOF. By induction on the derivations. The only non-trivial step involves the β-axiom and this requires the substitution result:

$$[\![t[s/x]]\!]_g = [\![t]\!]_{g([\![s]\!]_g/x)},$$

which is established by induction on the terms. □

This very general notion of model is not without its problems. Unless we insist that the functions

$$\lambda d.[\![t]\!]_{g(d/x)}$$

are in the class $[D \to D]$, the above interpretation is not well-defined. Mathematically, this is not a very attractive notion of model since the syntax of the theory is entering the definition of the model. Fortunately, there are models which satisfy this criterion and which are given in a syntax-independent way. We shall first deal with the so-called *Domain-Theoretic Models*. There are many variations on the notion of *domain*. A fairly minimal one is given as follows.

DEFINITION 2.3.4.3. A *Domain* is a partial-ordered set $\langle \mathcal{D}, \leqslant \rangle$ (with a least element $\perp$) which admits the least upper bounds of ω-sequences of the following form: $d_0 \leqslant d_1 \leqslant d_2 \leqslant d_3 \leqslant \cdots$. We shall write

$$\bigcup_{n \in \omega} d_n$$

for the least upper bound of such a sequence.

With this basic notion in place we construct a domain from the functions from one domain into a second. Such function spaces are restricted to monotone functions (i.e. $d \Rightarrow d' \to f(d) \subseteq' f(d')$) which are *continuous* in the sense that they preserve the least upper bounds of such ω-sequences, i.e.

$$f\Big(\bigcup_{n \in \omega} d_n\Big) = \bigcup_{n \in \omega}' f(d_n).$$

On this restricted class of functions $[D \to D']$ we impose an ordering.

$$f \leqslant g \quad \text{iff} \quad \forall d \in D.f(d) \leqslant' (f(d)),$$

which renders the function space a domain. Scott established the existence of a domain D such that D is continuously isomorphic to its own continuous function space. Moreover, all the functions $\lambda d.[\![t]\!]_{g(d/x)}$ are continuous. Hence, we have an example of a functional model which satisfies the closure conditions.

Our second example is the *Graph Model.* Let $\mathcal{P}(\omega)$ be the power set of the natural numbers partially ordered by inclusion. The construction of the model depends upon the fact that a continuous function on $\mathcal{P}(\omega)$ can be coded as a set. The underlying topology is determined by finite *information*: the sets

$$\mathcal{B}_E = \{B \in \mathcal{P}(\omega) \colon\ E \subseteq B\} \quad \text{where } E \text{ is finite}$$

form a basis for the topology. We next set up the following coding of ordered pairs and finite sets.

$$(n,m) = \tfrac{1}{2}(n+m)(n+m+1)+m,$$

$$e_n = \{k_0,\ldots,k_{m-1}\} \quad \text{where } k_0 < \cdots < k_{m-1} \text{ and } n = \sum_{i<m} 2^{k_i}.$$

A continuous function $f\colon \mathcal{P}(\omega) \to \mathcal{P}(\omega)$ is determined by its values on the finite sets. Hence, f can be coded as an element of $\mathcal{P}(\omega)$. This provides a continuous mapping

$$\mathit{graph}\colon [\mathcal{P}(\omega) \to \mathcal{P}(\omega)] \to \mathcal{P}(\omega) \text{ with an inverse}$$

$$\mathit{fun}\colon \mathcal{P}(\omega) \to [\mathcal{P}(\omega) \to \mathcal{P}(\omega)],$$

given as follows:

$$\mathit{graph}(f) = \{(n,m)\colon\ m \in f(e_n)\},$$

$$\mathit{fun}(u)x = \{m\colon\ \exists e_n \subseteq x.(n,m) \in u\}.$$

We thus have the required correspondence between the domain of the model and its continuous function space.

Both of these examples take place in a particular *Cartesian closed category* with *reflexive objects*. An general account of models in such categories can be found in (Barendregt, 1984).

2.4. *The Curry calculus (CU)*

Despite the fact that the untyped calculus has no built-in notion of type we can assign types to the terms in much the same way as with **CT**. The Curry calculus is obtained from the untyped calculus **U** by adding types and type assignment.

2.4.1. *Type assignment*

Indeed, the rules of type assignment are almost identical to those of the **C** system. The one difference concerns the introduction rule which now takes the following form.

$$\frac{B, x \in T \vdash t \in S}{B \vdash \lambda x.t \in T \Rightarrow S} \ \textbf{intro}.$$

However, as a consequence of this *small* modification, a term can now possess more than one type. For example, consider the following instance.

$$\frac{B, x \in T \vdash x \in T}{B \vdash \lambda x.x \in T \Rightarrow T}.$$

Thus, $\lambda x.x$ has all types of the form $T \Rightarrow T$. The theory is essentially *polymorphic*.[4]

We shall write $B \vdash_{\mathbf{CU}} t \in T$ (or just $B \vdash t \in T$) if $t \in T$ follows from the context B by the rules and axioms of type assignment.

We shall now examine the relationship between type assignment and reduction. In order to state the main theorem which connects type assignment and reduction we need the following notion.

DEFINITION 2.4.1.1. A term t is said to be *strongly normalizing* if all the reduction sequences starting with t terminate.

THEOREM 2.4.1.2.

(i) (Strong Normalization). *If $B \vdash t \in S$ then t is strongly normalizing*

(ii) (Subject Reduction). *If $B \vdash t \in S$ and $t \twoheadrightarrow_\beta s$ then $B \vdash s \in S$.*

The proof can be found in (Barendregt, 1991). The first part informs us a term which can be assigned a type must terminate – no matter how it is reduced. The subject reduction part ensures that type correctness of terms is preserved throughout their evaluation.

2.4.2. Models

We can easily extend the models of the untyped calculus to cater for type assignment. We illustrate with the general functional models. We interpret the types "internally", i.e. as subsets of the set D.

$$[\![I]\!] = D,$$
$$[\![T \Rightarrow S]\!] = \{d \in D\colon\ \forall e \in [\![T]\!].f(d)e \in [\![S]\!]\}.$$

An assignment function g is *consistent* with a context B if for each $x \in T$ which is a member of B, $g(x) \in [\![T]\!]$.

THEOREM 2.4.2.1 (Soundness). *For each term t, if $B \vdash t \in T$ and g is consistent with B, then*

$$[\![t]\!]_g \in [\![T]\!].$$

PROOF. By induction on the rules of type assignment. It is a simple matter to check that all the rules preserve soundness. □

An alternative view of types is supplied by the *quotient set semantics* (Scott, 1976; Hindley, 1983), in which the types are interpreted as partial equivalence relations.

[4] The term *polymorphism* in **CU** is being employed in a *schematic* sense. There is no explicit way of representing polymorphism as in *second-order lambda calculus* (e.g. Reynolds, 1974; Girard, 1972). See Section 5.3.1 for further discussion.

2.4.3. Erasing

We define the erasing mapping straight through from **CT** to **U**.

$$\text{erase}(x^T) \equiv x,$$
$$\text{erase}(ts) \equiv \text{erase}(t)\text{erase}(s),$$
$$\text{erase}(\lambda x^T.t) \equiv \lambda x.\text{erase}(t).$$

LEMMA 2.4.3.1. $\text{erase}(t^S[s^T/x^T]) \equiv \text{erase}(t^S)[\text{erase}(s^T)/x]$.

PROOF. By induction on the typed terms: we employ only the definitions of erase and substitution. □

Our first result establishes that the erasing transformation is *sound.*

THEOREM 2.4.3.2.
(i) *For each* $t : E_T$ *we have:* $B_t \vdash \text{erase}(t) \in T$.
(ii) *If* $\vdash_{\mathbf{CT}} s =_T t$ *then in* **U**, $\text{erase}(t) = \text{erase}(s)$.

PROOF. Part (i) is by induction on the **CT** terms. Part (ii) is by induction on the **CT** derivations. □

If we assume the extensionality axioms in the two theories the result remains intact. We also have a form of completeness for type assignment.

THEOREM 2.4.3.3. *If* $B \vdash t \in T$ *then there is a term* s^T *of* **CT** *such that* $\text{erase}(s^T) = t$.

PROOF. By induction on the Curry derivations. □

2.4.4. The rule of equality

Thus far the notions of *equality* and *type membership* are independent of each other; the axioms and rules of the two aspects of the theory have no overlap. In the **CT** system the judgement of equality can only be made with terms which are syntactically the same type. Moreover, the **C** system is monomorphic and, if two terms are equal with respect to a type, then they are members of that type. However, in the present theory the subject reduction theorem only applies to reduction not equality. Consequently, the principle that a type of a term should be preserved under equality has to be enforced.

$$\frac{s = t \qquad B \vdash s \in T}{B \vdash t \in T} \quad \mathbf{eq}$$

We shall write $B \vdash_{\mathbf{CU+eq}} t \in T$ if this follows from the axioms/rules of type assignment, equality and the **eq** rule. With this rule added we can formulate and prove a standard completeness result for the formal theory with respect to the above semantics (see Coppo, 1984). The soundness theorem for erasing is of course unaffected by the inclusion of **eq** but completeness for erasing fails. Indeed, **eq** has a non-effective nature which stems from the undecidability of the convertability relation. We can, however, postpone all applications of it to the final step in the deduction (see Barendregt, 1991).

THEOREM 2.4.4.1. *If there is a deduction of* $B \vdash_{\mathrm{CU}+\mathbf{eq}} t \in T$ *then there exists a term* s *such that* $t = s$ *and the sequent* $B \vdash_{\mathrm{CU}} s \in T$ *is derivable, i.e. without rule* **eq**.

This completes our rather brief exposition of the various forms of Lambda Calculi. Formal semantics has been based upon the first (**CT**). There is no reason why it could not be based on either of the other two. Indeed, the modern forms of *flexible* categorial grammar sit more naturally with these more liberated calculi.

2.5. *Categorial grammar and the typed lambda calculus*

Categorial grammar traditionally supplies the other half of the syntax/semantic pairing. In this section we introduce the basic ideas of categorial grammar. We shall only provide a brief introduction to this topic since it is covered at some length in Moortgat (this volume). Our main objective is to spell-out the relationships between the liberated typed lambda calculus and flexible categorial grammar.

2.5.1. *Basic categorial grammar*

The standard categorial grammars of Ajdukiewicz and Bar-Hillel are based on some fixed basic categories, which can be combined by a rule of functional application.

$$\frac{(a,b) \qquad a}{b}$$

For example, consider the complex expression "Every dog with a bone". Suppose that the lexical items are assigned the following categories

Every	(N,NP)	with	$(NP,(N,N))$	bone N
dog	N	a	(N,NP)	

Then the rule of functional application facilitates the following analysis of the complex expression.

$$\begin{array}{ccccc} \text{Every} & \text{dog} & \text{with} & \text{a} & \text{bone} \end{array}$$

$$\dfrac{(N,NP) \qquad \dfrac{N \qquad \dfrac{(NP,(N,N)) \qquad \dfrac{(N,NP) \qquad N}{NP}}{(N,N)}}{N}}{NP}$$

There are more sophisticated versions which contain directed versions of the rule of application but we shall not consider these here (see Moortgat (this volume)). Although

Table 2

Category	Type
Sentence	P
Proper name	I
Intransitive verb	$I \Rightarrow P$
Transitive verb	$I \Rightarrow (I \Rightarrow P)$
Complex noun phrase	$(I \Rightarrow P) \Rightarrow P$
Adverb	$(I \Rightarrow P) \Rightarrow (I \Rightarrow P)$
Preposition	$((I \Rightarrow P) \Rightarrow P) \Rightarrow (I \Rightarrow P) \Rightarrow (I \Rightarrow P)$
Nouns	$I \Rightarrow P$
Adjectives	$(I \Rightarrow P) \Rightarrow (I \Rightarrow P)$

categorial grammar is not committed to any particular correspondence between syntactic categories and semantic types the one given in Table 2 is the one that is most often encountered in the literature.

Notice that syntactic categories do not correspond one-one with semantic types. Indeed, this indicates a regularity of semantic behaviour between, for example, nouns and intransitive verbs in that they both semantically function as propositional functions.

2.5.2. *More flexible systems*

The main drawback with this simple picture concerns its rigidity. In the last twenty years versions of categorial grammar have been developed which enable a more flexible association between categories and types. New rules of combination have been added to the grammars which seem necessary to reflect the rich variety of combinations available in natural language syntax. These are essentially rules which force *type shifting*. Three of the most prominent are the following.

(i) *The Geach Rule* (Geach, 1972). Consider the following sentence. We employ basic categories i and p for proper names and sentences.

No man	loves	every woman
$((i,p),p)$	$(i,(i,p))$	$((i,p),p)$

As matters stand we cannot parse this sentence with the simple rule of categorial grammar since the categories do not match. One way forward is to add a rule which allows *categorial composition*.

$$\frac{(a,b) \qquad (b,c)}{(a,c)}.$$

(ii) *Montague Rule*. This is the well known strategy of Montague to upgrade simple proper names to noun phrases.

$$\frac{a}{((a,b),b)}.$$

So in particular, i is upgraded to $((i,p),p)$. Semantically, the type of a proper name is *type-shifted* to that of complex noun phrases.

(iii) *Argument Lowering* (Partee and Rooth, 1983). This has the general pattern

$$\frac{(((a,b),b),c)}{(a,c)}.$$

The standard example here is the lowering of complex intransitive verbs $(((i,p),p),p)$ to simple predicates (i,p). The general linguistic motivation for type-shifting seems overwhelming – see Montague Grammar (Partee [this volume]).

2.5.3. *Flexible grammars and the typed lambda calculus*

J. van Benthem (1991) offers a logical perspective on these flexible categorial grammars. He draws upon the analogy between derivations in the typed lambda calculus and derivations in categorial grammars. We can make the connection precise as follows. Let

$$a_1, \ldots, a_n \vdash a$$

be any derivable sequent (from the premises $a_1, \ldots, a_n$) in this enriched categorial grammar, i.e. with the basic rule of application together with the Geach, Montague and argument raising rules. We can interpret the categories as types in the obvious way – basic categories are assigned basic types and complex categories are interpreted as function spaces, i.e. (a,b) is interpreted as $A \Rightarrow B$.

THEOREM 2.5.3.1. *If* $a_1, \ldots, a_n \vdash a$ *then for some term* t, $[x_1 \in A_1, \ldots, x_n \in A_n] \vdash_{\mathbf{C}} t \in A$.

PROOF. By induction on the rules. The various cases are given as follows. For convenience, we employ a natural deduction style for type-assignment in **C**.

(i) Application

$$\frac{a \qquad (a,b)}{b} \qquad\qquad \frac{x \in A \qquad f \in A \Rightarrow B}{fx \in B}$$

(ii) Geach

$$\frac{(a,b) \qquad (b,c)}{(a,c)} \qquad\qquad \cfrac{f \in A \Rightarrow B \qquad \cfrac{g \in B \Rightarrow C \qquad \cfrac{[x \in A]}{}}{}}{}$$

$$\frac{f \in A \Rightarrow B \qquad g \in B \Rightarrow C \qquad [x \in A]}{\cfrac{fx \in B}{\cfrac{g(fx) \in C}{\lambda x \in A.g(fx) \in A \Rightarrow C}}}$$

(iii) Montague

$$\frac{a}{((a,b),b)} \qquad\qquad \cfrac{\cfrac{x \in A \qquad [f \in A \Rightarrow B]}{fx \in B}}{\lambda f \in A \Rightarrow B.fx \in (A \Rightarrow B) \Rightarrow B}$$

(iv) Argument Lowering

$$\frac{(((a,b),b),c)}{(a,c)} \qquad \cfrac{\cfrac{\cfrac{\cfrac{g \in ((A \Rightarrow B) \Rightarrow B) \Rightarrow C \qquad [f \in A \Rightarrow B] \qquad [x \in A]}{fx \in B}}{\lambda f \in A \Rightarrow B.fx \in (A \Rightarrow B) \Rightarrow B}}{g(\lambda f \in A \Rightarrow B.fx) \in C}}{\lambda x \in A.g(\lambda f \in A \Rightarrow B.fx) \in A \Rightarrow C}$$

□

Van Benthem (1991) suggests that this correspondence provides a way of proving an operational interpretation of these more flexible categorial grammars.

3. Higher-order logic

Our notion of type is far too impoverished to support any semantic application: the pure calculi do not have enough *logical* content. Indeed, in our discussion of the relationship between categorial grammars and type-systems we surreptitiously introduced the type P of propositions. In this section we put flesh on this introduction: we add a new basic type P (*propositions*) to stand proxy for the syntactic category of sentences. We shall explore all three approaches to the typed lambda calculus and extend them by the addition of this new type.This leads to the various formulations of higher order logic.

3.1. Church higher order logic

We begin with **CT**. This results in (standard) higher-order logic. This approach is the closest to that of Montague. It differs in that we take the type of *propositions* as primitive rather than unpacking it in terms of possible worlds.

3.1.1. The language of HOL

This is an extension of the language of **CT** obtained by adding a new basic type P of *propositions* together with logical connectives (implication and universal quantification). More precisely, the language of terms of **CT** is enriched as follows.

(ν) If ϕ and ψ are terms of type P and T is a type expression then $\phi \to \psi$ and $\forall x^T.\phi$ are terms of type P.

The other logical connectives are definable in the following way.

$$\phi \wedge \psi \equiv \forall z^P.(\phi \to (\psi \to z)) \to z,$$
$$\phi \vee \psi \equiv \forall z^P.((\phi \to z) \wedge (\psi \to z)) \to z,$$
$$\exists x^T.\phi \equiv \forall z^P.\forall y^T.(\phi[y/x] \to z) \to z,$$

$$\bot \equiv \forall z^P . z^P,$$

$$\sim\phi \equiv \phi \rightarrow \bot.$$

Indeed, the basic notions of typed equality and membership are also definable.

$$t =_T s \equiv \forall z^{T \Rightarrow P} . zt \rightarrow zs,$$

$$t \in T \equiv t =_T t.$$

There are formulations where the notion of equality is taken as primitive but the above better suits the development which follows. For more details of these other accounts see Andrews (1986).

3.1.2. Axioms and rules

The axioms/rules of the theory include the axioms and rules for equality α and β from the typed lambda calculus (**CT**) (the other axioms and rules, i.e. $\rho, \mu, \nu, \tau, \sigma$, are derivable from the definition of equality) together with the following rules of inference. A *context* B is now a finite set of wff.

$$\frac{B, \phi \vdash \psi}{B \vdash \phi \rightarrow \psi} \ (\rightarrow \mathbf{i}) \qquad \frac{B \vdash \phi \qquad B \vdash \phi \rightarrow \psi}{B \vdash \psi} \ (\rightarrow \mathbf{e})$$

$$\frac{B \vdash \phi[x^T]}{B \vdash \forall x^T . \phi} \ (\forall \mathbf{i}) \qquad \frac{B \vdash \forall x^T . \phi}{B \vdash \phi[t^T / x^T]} \ (\forall \mathbf{e})$$

We assume the normal side-conditions on the rules, i.e. in $(\forall \mathbf{i})$, x^T must not occur free in any assumption on which the premise depends. This already gets us an *intensional intuitionistic* system of higher-order logic (**IHOL**).

For the classical theory we add the following axiom.

LEM $\quad \forall u^P . u \vee \sim u.$

Finally, for the *extensional* version we add:

EXT (i) $\forall z^{T \Rightarrow S} . \forall y^{T \Rightarrow S} . (\forall x^T . zx =_S yx) \rightarrow z =_{T \Rightarrow S} y.$
(ii) $(\phi \leftrightarrow \psi) \rightarrow \phi =_P \psi.$

Notice that **EXT** yields the extensionality axioms of **CT**.

3.1.3. Models

At this point we ought to pause and ask for the intended interpretation of this theory. In the case of **CT**, under the set-theoretic interpretation, the non-primitive types were interpreted as function spaces. But how is the type of *propositions* to be interpreted? Within the formal semantic paradigm there are two common answers to this question: *truth-values* and sets of *possible worlds*. Both of these options face well-known difficulties. In Fregean terms the former fails to account for the distinction between the *sense* and the *reference* of a sentence. Frege took the *sense* of a sentence to be that aspect of its meaning which determined its truth-value (its *reference*). If *propositions* (*Fregean thoughts*) are taken as truth-values then there is no room for a difference between the *sense* of a sentence and its truth-value. Subsequently, we are unable to explain how two sentences with the same truth-value can express different *propositions*. This difficulty is somewhat circumvented within the Kripke–Hintikka–Montague tradition which takes *propositions* to be sets of *possible worlds*. This is a step forward in that for two sentences to express the same *proposition* they have to have the same truth-value in all possible worlds. However, it has been argued that this still does not leave enough room between *sense* and *reference*. This becomes critical when interpreting doxastic notions such as *belief* and *knowledge*. For example, under it all true assertions of mathematics denote the same proposition, hence believing one true proposition entails one believes them all. Neither space nor time permits a realistic discussion of these issues but for a strong defense of the possible world approach the reader should consult Stalnaker (1984). We shall remain neutral as to the nature of *propositions*: we shall not identify them with truth-values nor with sets of possible worlds – nor with any other more putatively primitive notion. However, the formal theory admits both the above interpretations. To see this we need to extend our classical set-theoretic models to this extended language. The notion of model for the **CT** has to be extended to include a basic set of *propositions*. In addition, we require operators which are the correlates of the logical constants. We provide a general notion which specializes to both the above examples but also admits of other more *fine-grained* interpretations.

DEFINITION 3.1.3.1. A *model* of **IHOL** is a structure

$$\mathcal{M} = \left\langle \mathbf{D}, \mathbf{P}, \mathbf{T}, ^{\rightarrow}, \prod\nolimits_T \right\rangle$$

where $\mathbf{D}, \mathbf{T}, \mathbf{P}$ are sets (with $\mathbf{T} \subseteq \mathbf{P}$, the *true* propositions), $^{\rightarrow}$ is a function from $\mathbf{P}$ to $\mathbf{P}^{\mathbf{P}}$ and, for each type symbol T, $\prod_T$ is a function from $\mathbf{P}^{[\![T]\!]}$ to $\mathbf{P}$. In addition, we have the following closure conditions on the set $\mathbf{T}$. In what follows we employ infix notation.

(i) If $d \in \mathbf{P}$ and $e \in \mathbf{P}$ then $d^{\rightarrow}e \in \mathbf{T}$ iff $d \in \mathbf{T}$ implies $e \in \mathbf{T}$

(ii) $d \in \mathbf{P}^{[\![T]\!]}$ then $\prod_T d \in \mathbf{T}$ iff for all $e \in [\![T]\!]$, $de \in \mathbf{T}$

The language is interpreted in such a model by extending the interpretation of **CT** as follows.

$$[\![\phi \rightarrow \psi]\!]_g^{\mathcal{M}} = [\![\phi]\!]_g^{\mathcal{M}\rightarrow} [\![\psi]\!]_g^{\mathcal{M}},$$

$$[\![\forall x^T.\phi]\!]_g^{\mathcal{M}} = \prod\nolimits_T \left(\lambda d \in [\![T]\!].[\![\phi]\!]_{g(d/x)}^{\mathcal{M}}\right).$$

In general, we shall say that ϕ is true in $\mathcal{M}$ if and only if $[\![\phi]\!]_g^{\mathcal{M}} \in \mathbf{T}$ for each assignment g.

THEOREM 3.1.3.2. **IHOL** *is sound in these models, i.e. if* $\vdash_{\mathbf{IHOL}} \phi$ *then* ϕ *is true in each such model.*

PROOF. We have only to check that the rules of inference preserve truth in the model. This is straightforward by induction on the proofs. □

If we wish to guarantee soundness for classical **HOL** we must first define $\neg$, a function from **P** to **P**, by

$$\neg p \equiv p \xrightarrow{} \Omega \quad \text{where } \Omega = \prod\nolimits_{\mathbf{P}} \lambda p \in \mathbf{P}.p,$$

and insist that, for $d \in \mathbf{P}$, $\neg d \in \mathbf{T}$ iff $d \notin \mathbf{T}$. There are two obvious examples of such models. Both satisfy the axioms of extensionality (**EXT**).

(i) *Standard models of HOL*

Here we take $\mathbf{P} = \{0, 1\}$ and $\mathbf{T} = \{1\}$. The operator $\xrightarrow{}$ is the classical truth function and $\prod_T d = 1$ iff for all $e \in [\![T]\!]$, $de = 1$.

(ii) *Possible worlds models of HOL*

Here we take $\mathbf{P} = \mathcal{P}(W)$, where W is some set (of *possible worlds*), and $\mathbf{T} = \{W\}$. The operator $\xrightarrow{}$ is the function which given two subsets of W (A and B, say), returns the set which is the union of $W - A$ and B. The function $\prod_T$, given a function f from $[\![T]\!]$ to $\mathcal{P}(W)$, returns W, if for all d in $[\![T]\!]$, $fd = W$, and the empty set otherwise. In this model we can add modal operators. For example, we can add $\Box$ with the interpretation that $\Box p = W$, if $p = W$, and the empty set of worlds otherwise. This yields **S5** modal logic. This is essentially the strategy adopted in Montague's intensional logic. We shall not pursue this further since we are primarily concerned with the notion of *type* not *modality*.

Our notion of model also admits of other interpretations where the notion of proposition is more *fine grained*. The *structured meanings* of Cresswell (1985) form one such example. Indeed, this more general notion of model forces no interpretation on the notion of proposition and is consistent with the view that they be taken as sui-generis. Such an approach is developed in (Thomason, 1980).

3.2. HOLC

We now develop the theory based upon the loosely typed lambda calculus. This will take us one step in the direction of *combinatory logic*.

3.2.1. Language

In the standard presentations of the first and higher-order predicate logic the language of wff is given via an explicit grammar. In contrast, within the **C** calculus the syntactic constraints are rather meagre and the rules of type assignment are employed to carve out the sensible objects. The same concept applies when we extend the **C** system of the typed lambda calculus by the addition of *propositions*. We shall use **HOL** as our guide in developing the theory in that we shall mirror (almost) the grammatically determined notion of *proposition* in **HOL** by rules of type assignment. To the language of **C** we add a new constant $\rightarrow$ (implication) and a family of constants Π_T (universal quantification). The other logical connectives and the standard representation of the quantifiers can be defined in a similar way to **HOL**. We again employ infix notation.

$$\forall x \in T.s \equiv \Pi_T(\lambda x \in T.s),$$

$$\wedge \equiv \lambda x \in P.\lambda y \in P.\forall z \in P.(x \rightarrow (y \rightarrow z)) \rightarrow z,$$

$$\vee \equiv \lambda x \in P.\lambda y \in P.\forall z \in P.(x \rightarrow z) \rightarrow ((y \rightarrow z) \rightarrow z),$$

$$\exists x \in T.s \equiv \forall z \in P.\forall y \in T.(s[y/x] \rightarrow z) \rightarrow z,$$

$$\bot \equiv \forall z \in P.z,$$

$$\sim \equiv \lambda x \in P.x \rightarrow \bot,$$

$$Q_T \equiv \lambda x \in T.\lambda y \in T.\forall z \in T \Rightarrow P.zx \rightarrow zy,$$

$$t \in T \equiv t =_T t,$$

where we write $Q_T\, ts$ as $t =_T s$. Judgements in the system are now made relative to a context $B = \{t_1, \ldots, t_n\}$ which is now a set of arbitrary terms. Since the assertion of membership is now itself a term, this generalizes the previous notion of context.

3.2.2. Axioms and rules

(*Intensional intuitionistic*) **HOLC** is defined by the following axioms and rules. The axioms/rules of the theory include the axioms and rules for equality α and β from **C** (the other axioms and rules, i.e. $\rho, \mu, \nu, \tau, \sigma$, are derivable from the definition of equality) and the rules **funi** and **fune** from **C**. Observe, that these are now to be understood with respect to the new notion of context. In addition, we have the following rules of inference.

$$\frac{B, s \vdash t \qquad B \vdash s \in P}{B \vdash s \rightarrow t} \ (\rightarrow \mathbf{i}) \qquad \frac{B, s \vdash t \in P \qquad B \vdash s \in P}{B \vdash (s \rightarrow t) \in P} \ (\rightarrow \mathbf{P})$$

$$\frac{B \vdash \forall x \in T.g \qquad B \vdash s \in T}{B \vdash g[s/x]} \ (\forall \mathbf{e}) \qquad \frac{B \vdash s \qquad B \vdash s \rightarrow t}{B \vdash t} \ (\rightarrow \mathbf{e})$$

$$\frac{B, x \in T \vdash t}{B \vdash \forall x \in T.t} \ (\forall \mathbf{i}) \qquad \frac{B, x \in T \vdash t \in P}{B \vdash \forall x \in T.t \in P} \ (\forall \mathbf{P})$$

$$\frac{B \vdash s}{B \vdash s \in P} \ (\mathbf{P})$$

We assume the normal side conditions on ($\forall$**i**) and ($\forall$**P**). Once again, this already gives us an intuitionistic theory. For (classical) **HOLC** we add the law of excluded middle as an axiom.

LEM $\quad \forall u \in P.u \vee \sim u.$

Finally, for an extensional theory, we add an axioms of extensionality for typed equality.

$$\textbf{EXT} \quad \text{(i)} \quad \forall z \in T \Rightarrow S.\forall y \in T \Rightarrow S.(\forall x \in T.zx =_S yx) \to z =_{T \Rightarrow S} y.$$

$$\text{(ii)} \quad \forall x \in P.\forall y \in P.(x \leftrightarrow y) \to x =_P y.$$

3.2.3. Erasing

We now explore the relationship between **HOL** and **HOLC** by extending the erasing transformation from the corresponding lambda calculi. This is achieved as follows:

$$\text{erase}(\forall x^T.\phi) \equiv \forall x \in T.\text{erase}(\phi),$$

$$\text{erase}(\phi \to \psi) \equiv \text{erase}(\phi) \to \text{erase}(\psi).$$

Our first result ensures that this mapping is *sound* in that typing and derivability in **HOL** are preserved by erasing. The second is its *completeness*. First we require the following.

LEMMA 3.2.3.1. $\text{erase}(t^S[s^T/x^T]) \equiv \text{erase}(t^S)[\text{erase}(s^T)/x]$.

PROOF. We extend the induction from the pure lambda calculus. □

THEOREM 3.2.3.2 (Soundness).

(i) *For each* t^T, $B_t \vdash_{\textbf{HOLC}} \text{erase}(t^T) \in T$ *where*

$$B_t = \{\text{erase}(x^T) \in T\text{: } x^T \textit{ is a free variable of } t\}.$$

(ii) *If* $\{\phi_1, \dots, \phi_n\} \vdash_{\textbf{HOL}} \phi$ *then* $\{\text{erase}(\phi_1), \dots, \text{erase}(\phi_n)\} \cup B_\phi \vdash_{\textbf{HOLC}} \text{erase}(\phi)$.

PROOF. (i) By induction on the terms of **HOL**. The only new cases to check are those for the logical connectives and these are entirely straightforward.

(ii) By induction on the derivations in **HOL**. We have only to check the rules for the logical connectives. These are routine but the universal elimination rule requires the substitution lemma. □

THEOREM 3.2.3.3 (Completeness). *Suppose* $B \vdash_{\textbf{HOLC}} t$, *where* $B = \{t_1, \dots, t_n\}$, *and there exists* $t_1^P, \dots, t_n^P$ *such that* $\text{erase}(t_i^P) \equiv t_i$, *for* $i = 1, \dots, n$. *Then there exists a term* t^P *such that* $\text{erase}(t^P) \equiv t$ *and* $\{t_1^P, \dots, t_n^P\} \vdash_{\textbf{HOL}} t^P$. *Furthermore, if* t *has the form* $s \in T$ *then there exists a term* s^T *such that* $\text{erase}(s^T) \equiv s$.

PROOF. By induction on the derivations in **HOLC**. We shall consider each of the axioms/rules in turn. We have only to check the new rules. For ($\to$ **i**), assume $B, t \vdash s$ and $B \vdash t \in P$. From the latter, by induction, there exists t^P such that $\text{erase}(t^P) \equiv t$. Hence, by induction, there exists a term s^P such that $\text{erase}(s^P) \equiv s$. Moreover, $\{t_1^P, \dots, t_n^P\}, t^P \vdash_{\textbf{HOL}} s^P$. Hence we have: $\{t_1^P, \dots, t_n^P\} \vdash_{\textbf{HOL}} t^P \to s^P$. Finally, observe that $\text{erase}(t^P \to s^P) \equiv t \to s$. For (**P**), assume that $B \vdash t$. By induction, there exists a term t^P such that $\text{erase}(t^P) \equiv t$. Since, $\text{erase}(t^P \in P) \equiv t \in P$ and, by definition, $\vdash_{\textbf{HOL}} t^P \in P$ we are done. For ($\to$ **e**), assume $B \vdash s$ and $B \vdash s \to t$. By induction and the assumption s, let erase$(s^P) \equiv s$ where $\{t_1^P, \ldots, t_n^P\} \vdash_{\mathbf{HOL}} s^P$. By induction and $B \vdash s \to t$, there exists some r^P such that erase$(r^P) \equiv s \to t \equiv$ erase$(s^P) \to t$. By definition of erase, r^P must have the form $s^P \to t^P$, where erase$(t^P) \equiv t$. By induction, we can conclude $\{t_1^P, \ldots, t_n^P\} \vdash_{\mathbf{HOL}} s^P \to t^P$. Consequently, $\{t_1^P, \ldots, t_n^P\} \vdash_{\mathbf{HOL}} t^P$. For ($\to$ **P**), assume that $B,\ t \vdash s \in P$ and $B \vdash t \in P$. By induction and the latter, there exists a term t^P such that erase$(t^P) \equiv t$. By $B, t \vdash s \in P$ and induction, there exists a term s^P such that erase$(s^P) \equiv s$ and $\{t_1^P, \ldots, t_n^P\} \vdash_{\mathbf{HOL}} (t^P \to s^P) \in P$. Finally, by definition, erase$((t^P \to s^P) \in P) \equiv (t \to s) \in P$. For ($\forall$**i**), assume $B, x \in T \vdash t$. Since we have erase$(x^T \in T) \equiv x \in T$, by induction, there exists a term t^P such that erase$(t^P) \equiv t$. Furthermore, $\{t_1^P, \ldots, t_n^P\} \vdash_{\mathbf{HOL}} t^P$. It follows in **HOL** that: $\{t_1^P, \ldots, t_n^P\} \vdash_{\mathbf{HOL}} \forall x^T.t^P$. Finally, observe that, by definition, erase$(\forall x^T.t^P) \equiv \forall x \in T.t$. For ($\forall$**P**), assume $B, x \in T \vdash t \in P$. Then, by induction, there exists a term t^P such that erase$(t^P) \equiv t$. By definition of membership in **HOL**: $\{t_1^P, \ldots, t_n^P\} \vdash_{\mathbf{HOL}} (\forall x^T.t^P) \in P$. Moreover, by definition, erase$(\forall x^T.t^P \in P) \equiv (\forall x \in T.t) \in P$. This leaves us to deal with ($\forall$**e**). Assume, $B \vdash \forall x \in T.g$ and $B \vdash s \in T$. By the first assumption and induction, there exists a term t^P such that erase$(t^P) \equiv \forall x \in T.g$ and $\{t_1^P, \ldots, t_n^P\} \vdash_{\mathbf{HOL}} t^P$. By the definition of erase, t^P must have the form $\forall x^T.\phi$ for some ϕ. Hence, g has the form erase(ϕ). By assumption, $s \in T$. By induction, there exists a term s^T such that erase$(s^T) \equiv s$. It follows that $\{t_1^P, \ldots, t_n^P\} \vdash_{\mathbf{HOL}} \phi[s^T/x^T]$. By the substitution lemma, erase$(\phi[s^T/x^T]) \equiv g[s/x]$. □

A consequence is the consistency of **HOLC**.

COROLLARY 3.2.3.4. **HOLC** *is consistent.*

PROOF. Absurdity in **HOLC** can only be (definitionally) the erased image of absurdity in **HOL**. Moreover, absurdity in **HOLC** is provably of type P. The result now follows from the completeness of erasing since, if absurdity is provable in **HOLC** it must be in **HOL**. □

3.3. Higher-order logic and the untyped calculus

Before we proceed with the Curry version we attempt to develop logic based upon the untyped calculus, i.e. with no notion of type. This will prove to be disastrous.

3.3.1. An untyped theory

Suppose we add one new logical constant $\to$ to the untyped calculus (**U**) together with its standard introduction and elimination rules.

$$\frac{s \vdash t}{s \to t} \qquad \frac{s \qquad s \to t}{t}$$

We also add the rule of equality.

$$\frac{t = s \qquad t}{s}\ \mathbf{eq}$$

3.3.2. The Curry paradox

Unfortunately, even this impoverished logical system is inconsistent. To see this fix a term t and let s be the term $\mathbf{Y}[\lambda x.x \to (x \to t)]$. Then consider the derivation

$t, t \to s \vdash s$	(i)	$\to$ elimination
$(t \to (t \to s)) \to (t \to s)$	(ii)	theorem
$s = s \to (s \to t)$	(iii)	properties of **Y**
$s = (s \to (s \to t)) \to (s \to t)$	(iv)	substitution from (iii)
$(s \to (s \to t)) \to (s \to t)$	(v)	from (ii)
$s \to (s \to t)$	(vi)	(iv) and rule **eq**
s	(vii)	(iii) and **eq**
$s \to t$	(viii)	(v), (vi) and (i)
t	(ix)	(vii), (i) and (viii)

Hence, this simple system is inconsistent: every term is derivable. We cannot add logical connectives to the untyped system and preserve consistency in this cavalier fashion.

3.4. The Curry theory

The moral of this is that not everything can function as a proposition and, in particular, be a bearer of truth. This has to be taken into account in developing the theory.

3.4.1. HOLCU

The theory is formulated in the untyped lambda calculus and includes the (non-redex) constants Π, P, I and $\to$.[5] The other logical connectives and quantifiers can be defined in a similar way to **HOL**. We again employ infix notation.

$$\forall x \in t.s \equiv \Pi t(\lambda x.s),$$
$$\wedge \equiv \lambda xy.\forall z \in P.(x \to (y \to z)) \to z,$$

[5] Implication is also definable but we shall not fuss over this. In any case one still has to postulate all the rules for implication except the elimination rule which is derivable.

$$\vee \equiv \lambda xy.\forall z \in P.(x \to z) \to ((y \to z) \to z),$$
$$\exists x \in t.s \equiv \forall z \in P.\forall y \in t.(s[y/x] \to z) \to z,$$
$$\bot \equiv \forall z \in P.z,$$
$$\sim \equiv \lambda x.x \to \bot.$$

Indeed in this theory the complex types themselves are definable. The types are formed from the basic types P and I by forming complex types via:

$$\Rightarrow \equiv \lambda xyz.\forall u \in x.y(zu).$$

We shall employ upper case T, S etc. for type terms. Consistent with the above quantifier notation, and to make the presentation a little more palatable, we shall often write $t \in T$ for Tt. Equality at each type is defined as:

$$Q_T \equiv \lambda xy.\forall z \in T \Rightarrow P.zx \to zy$$

which we shall write as infix $=_T$.

Intensional intuitionistic **HOLCU** is defined by the following axioms and rules. We assume the equality axioms and rules of the untyped lambda calculus (**U**)[6] together with the rules $\to$ **i**, $\to$ **e**, $\to$ **P**, $\forall$**i**, $\forall$**e**, $\forall$**P**, and **P**. Once again, this already gives us an intuitionistic theory. For (classical) **HOLCU** we add the law of excluded middle (**LEM**) as an axiom and for an extensional theory[7], we add the axioms of extensionality – both as in the theory **HOLC**.

3.4.2. *Erasing*

We extend the erasing transformation from the corresponding lambda calculi as follows.

$$\text{erase}(\forall x^T.\phi) \equiv \forall x \in T.\text{erase}(\phi),$$
$$\text{erase}(\phi \to \psi) \equiv \text{erase}(\phi) \to \text{erase}(\psi).$$

THEOREM 3.4.2.1 (Soundness).

If $\{t_1, \ldots, t_n\} \vdash_{\mathbf{HOL}} t$ *then* $\{\text{erase}(t_1), \ldots, \text{erase}(t_n)\} \cup B_t \vdash_{\mathbf{HOLCU}} \text{erase}(t)$.

PROOF. By induction on the derivations in **HOL**. □

We also have a completeness result which follows the same pattern as that for **HOLC**.

THEOREM 3.4.2.2 (Completeness). *Suppose* $B \vdash_{\mathbf{HOLCU}} t$, *where* $B = \{t_1, \ldots, t_n\}$, *and there exists* $t_1^P, \ldots, t_n^P$ *such that* $\text{erase}(t_i^P) \equiv t_i$, *for* $i = 1, \ldots, n$. *Then there exists a*

[6] Extensional versions (i.e. with respect to = in **U**) are also possible; we simply add the extensionality axioms ξ and η.

[7] *Extensional* with respect to the typed equality of the theory, i.e. not the underlying equality of the system **U**.

term t^P *such that* $\text{erase}(t^P) \equiv t$ *and* $\{t_1^P, \ldots, t_n^P\} \vdash_{\mathbf{HOL}} t^P$. *Furthermore, if* t *has the form* $s \in T$ *then there exists a term* s^T *such that* $\text{erase}(s^T) \equiv s$.

So this theory is consistent. However, as with the pure calculus, we have no link between what is provable via the rules of inference and the equality of **U**. To force this we require the following.

3.4.3. The **eq** *rule*

This now takes the following more general form.

$$\frac{B \vdash s = t \qquad B \vdash s}{B \vdash t} \quad (\mathbf{eq})$$

The addition of the rule yields one version of a *combinatory logic* (**HOPC**) due to Bunder (1983) – the version given in (Hindley and Seldin, 1986). As with the pure calculus completeness for erasing now fails. At present there is no strong consistency proof for the whole of **HOPC** (for some progress see Barendregt et al., forthcoming, JSL).

4. Universal types and nominalization

The theories of types of the previous section allow a degree of flexibility in assigning types to terms which goes beyond that of the simple Church formulations. However certain phenomena seem to require a more radical departure from the original formulations of type theory.

4.1. Nominalization

We first examine the process of nominalization in natural language. This is a fairly wide ranging topic so we shall concentrate on those aspects which seemingly cause trouble for the present theories.

4.1.1. Sentential complements and infinitives

Consider the following:

(1) John is strange.

(2) That John has arrived is strange.

On the standard analysis, predicative expressions such as *is strange* are assigned the type $I \Rightarrow P$ and proper names such as *John* are assigned the type I. The semantic analysis of (1) proceeds as normal but what are we to make of (2)? If the predicative expression *is strange* has type $I \Rightarrow P$ then *That John has arrived*, which is traditionally taken to be of type P, cannot be a legitimate argument.

Chierchia (1982) makes a similar point in the case of Infinitives, Gerunds, Bare-plurals and Mass terms. We shall only review the general form of his argument by reference to the former category. Consider the following sentences.

(3) To arrive late is strange.

(4) John is strange.

Since we have assigned the type $I \Rightarrow P$ to *is strange*, (4) is well-typed but (3) is problematic. There are at least two possible candidates for the semantic counterparts of infinitives. According to one analysis they represent propositions and according to the other propositional functions. However, Chierchia argues that the correct analysis is the latter. He does so on the basis of data of the following form:

(5)
Mary tries to read Principia
John tries whatever Mary tries

John tries to read Principia

The two proposals can be represented as follows:

$$(6)\qquad \frac{\mathrm{Try}(M, \lambda x.[RP(x)]) \qquad \forall x.\mathrm{Try}(M, x) \rightarrow \mathrm{Try}(J, x)}{\mathrm{Try}(J, \lambda x.[RP(x)])}$$

$$(7)\qquad \frac{\mathrm{Try}(M, RP(M)) \qquad \forall x.\mathrm{Try}(M, x) \rightarrow \mathrm{Try}(J, x)}{\mathrm{Try}(J, RP(J))}$$

Argument (6) is valid whereas (7) is not. From such data he argues that infinitives should be semantically analyzed as propositional functions but whichever analysis is adopted we have a problem.

There are two obvious remedies. One way out is duplicate all such predicates: in the case of sentential complements one could be semantically represented as a propositional function (i.e. of type $I \Rightarrow P$) and the other as a function from propositions to propositions (i.e. of type $P \Rightarrow P$). This, however, will result in a great deal of complexity since the duplication will have to be inherited by complex predicative expressions (e.g., those formed by VP-conjunction and disjunction). An alternative approach is the one which maintains the intuition that predicative expressions denote propositional functions but somehow allows them to take arguments of type other than I. In particular, any such analysis must facilitate their attachment to propositions and propositional functions themselves. It is our intention to explore such an approach. Theories which can handle this approach to these phenomena was the main motivation for the development of *theories of properties* (Turner, 1987; Chierchia and Turner, 1988). We shall not pursue these theories here but concentrate on those approaches which stem directly from the present theories of types. Before this we point out one other analogy between sentential complements and infinitives.

4.1.2. Intensionality

While it is commonly accepted that *that* generates intensional contexts it is not often observed that infinitive constructions do also. The inference (9) is intuitively invalid and the reason appears to be that extensional equivalence of the VP's is not sufficient to guarantee the validity of the inference.

$$(8) \qquad \begin{array}{l} \text{To run is fun} \\ \underline{\text{Everything dies iff it runs}} \\ \text{To die is fun} \end{array}$$

Hence, on this view infinitives and sentential complements seem to have a parallel behaviour: both can be seen to function as singular terms and both induce intensional contexts.

4.2. Universal types

We cannot formalize this analysis of nominalization and intensionality within the present theories of types. In the next two sections we present several theories in which these intuitions can be reflected. The first is essentially the theory of *Frege Structures.*

4.2.1. The theory F

The first theory we develop is a version of the Theory of *Frege Structures* (Aczel, 1980). The language of the theory is that of the untyped lambda calculus together with distinguished constants: $\wedge, \vee, \rightarrow, \forall, \exists, =, \Omega, P$. We define $\sim t$ as $t \rightarrow \Omega$. We shall also abbreviate $\forall\lambda x.t$ as $\forall x.t$ etc. The axioms and rules consist of those of **U** (extensionality is optional), the **eq** rule, plus the following rules.

$$\frac{B, s \vdash t \quad B \vdash Ps}{B \vdash s \rightarrow t}\ (\rightarrow \mathbf{i}) \qquad \frac{B, s \vdash Pt \quad B \vdash Ps}{B \vdash P(s \rightarrow t)}\ (\rightarrow \mathbf{P}) \qquad \frac{B \vdash s \quad B \vdash s \rightarrow t}{B \vdash t}\ (\rightarrow \mathbf{e})$$

$$\frac{B \vdash t \quad B \vdash s}{B \vdash s \wedge t}\ (\wedge \mathbf{i}) \qquad \frac{B \vdash Pt \quad B, t \vdash Ps}{B \vdash P(s \wedge t)}\ (\wedge \mathbf{P}) \qquad \frac{B \vdash t \wedge s}{B \vdash t}\ (\wedge \mathbf{e})$$

$$\frac{B \vdash t}{B \vdash s \vee t}\ (\vee \mathbf{i}) \qquad \frac{B \vdash Pt \quad B \vdash Ps}{B \vdash P(s \vee t)}\ (\vee \mathbf{P}) \qquad \frac{B \vdash s \vee t \quad B, s \vdash r \quad B, t \vdash r}{B \vdash r}\ (\vee \mathbf{e})$$

$$\frac{B \vdash t[x]}{B \vdash \exists x.t}\ (\exists \mathbf{i}) \qquad \frac{B \vdash \exists x, t \quad B, t[x] \vdash r}{B \vdash r}\ (\exists \mathbf{e}) \qquad \frac{B \vdash P(t[x])}{B \vdash P(\exists x.t)}\ (\exists \mathbf{P})$$

$$\frac{B \vdash \forall x.t}{B \vdash t[s/x]}\ (\forall \mathbf{e}) \qquad \frac{B \vdash t[x]}{B \vdash \forall x.t}\ (\forall \mathbf{i}) \qquad \frac{B \vdash P(t[x])}{B \vdash P(\forall x.t)}\ (\forall \mathbf{P})$$

$$\frac{B \vdash \Omega}{B \vdash t}\ (\Omega) \qquad \frac{B \vdash t}{B \vdash Pt}\ (\mathbf{P}) \qquad P(s = t)\ (= \mathbf{P})$$

Again we assume the normal side conditions on the rules: in $\exists$**e**, x is not free in t, r or any open assumption except the one shown: in $\exists$**P**, $\forall$**P** and $\forall$**i**, x not free in t or any open assumption. This provides an intuitionistic system. For the full classical theory (**F**) we add the rule of absurdity.

$$\frac{B \vdash Pt \qquad B, {\sim}t \vdash \Omega}{B \vdash t}$$

We shall write $B \vdash_{\mathbf{F}} t$ if t follows in **F** from the context B. We shall often write $t \in f$ for ft and abbreviate $\lambda x.t$ as $\{x : t\}$. With these conventions in place we can introduce bounded quantification as follows.

$$\forall x \in f.t \equiv \forall x.fx \to t, \qquad \exists x \in f.t \equiv \exists x.fx \wedge t.$$

4.2.2. Properties

Within this theory we can develop a theory of *properties* or *classes* where the notion of *property/class* is given as follows:

$$Pty(f) = \forall x.P(fx).$$

These properties are closed under a rather extensive class of operations. In particular, we have closure under *Cartesian products, disjoint unions, function spaces, intersections, unions, complements, dependent products/functions spaces* and *dependent sums.*

PROPOSITION 4.2.2.1. *If $Pty(f)$ and $Pty(g)$ then $Pty(f \otimes g)$, $Pty(f \oplus g)$, $Pty(f \Rightarrow g)$, $Pty(f \cap g)$, $Pty(f \cup g)$ and $Pty({\sim}f)$ where*

$$\begin{aligned}
&f \otimes g \equiv \{z\colon\ \exists x \in f.\exists y \in g.z = (x, y)\},\\
&f \oplus g \equiv \{z\colon\ \exists x \in f.(z = \mathbf{inl}\, x) \vee \exists x \in g.(z = \mathbf{inr}\, x)\},\\
&(f \Rightarrow g) \equiv \{z\colon\ \forall u \in f.zu \in g\},\\
&f \cap g \equiv \{y\colon\ fy \wedge gy\},\\
&f \cup g \equiv \{y\colon\ fy \vee gy\},\\
&{\sim}f \equiv \{y\colon\ {\sim}fy\},
\end{aligned}$$

where (x, y) and **inl** *and* **inr** *are any standard lambda calculus representations of pairing and injections.*

PROPOSITION 4.2.2.2. *Let $\Sigma fg = \{z\colon\ \exists x \in f.\exists y \in gx.z = (x, y)\}$ and $\Pi fg = \{z\colon \forall u \in f.zu \in gx\}$ then the following rules are derivable in* **F**

$$\frac{Pty(f) \qquad \forall x \in f.Pty(gx)}{Pty(\Pi fg)}, \qquad \frac{Pty(f) \qquad \forall x \in f.Pty(gx)}{Pty(\Sigma fg)}.$$

4.2.3. *Types*

The theory as presented above is in a sense *type-free*; there is no explicit notion of type. However, types can be defined within the theory. First observe that the type of individuals is definable.

$$I \equiv \{y\colon\ y = y\}.$$

By ($\mathbf{P} =$) this is a property. Moreover, this functions as a universal type. We also have P itself, built-in as a constant. Finally, we can form complex types via:

$$\Rightarrow \equiv \lambda xyz.\forall u.xu \to y(zu).$$

We shall employ upper case T, S etc. for types. It is easy to see that the introduction and elimination rules are derivable.

$$\frac{B, x \in T \vdash t \in S}{B \vdash \lambda x.t \in T \Rightarrow S}, \qquad \frac{B \vdash t \in T \qquad B \vdash s \in T \Rightarrow S}{B \vdash st \in S}.$$

As a consequence we can maintain the category type correspondence. For example, determiners have type $(I \Rightarrow P) \Rightarrow ((I \Rightarrow P) \Rightarrow P)$. In particular, **every** $= \lambda fg.\forall x \in f.x \in g$ and **some** $= \lambda fg.\exists x \in f.x \in g$, are provable of this type. However, the following rules are not derivable.

$$\frac{B, x \in T \vdash t \in P}{B \vdash (\forall x \in T.t) \in P}, \qquad \frac{B, x \in T \vdash t \in P}{B \vdash (\exists x \in T.t) \in P}.$$

Indeed, if they were then $r \equiv \lambda y.\exists x \in I \Rightarrow P.x \approx y \wedge {\sim}xy$ would be a property. Assume rr then for some $x \in I \Rightarrow P$ we have $x \approx r \wedge {\sim}xr$. Hence, ${\sim}rr$. Conversely, if ${\sim}rr$ then rr. Hence, if the theory is consistent, the above rules are not derivable. Hence, higher-order quantification is not *Internally Representable*: the theory is essentially first-order.

4.2.4. *Models*

The *type-free* nature of this theory may well dispose one to have doubts about its consistency. Fortunately models are relatively easy to come by. They are constructed via a simple inductive definition. We provide the bones of the idea. The present version is essentially that of Aczel (1980). Similar consistency proofs are due to Scott (1975) and Fitch (1963).

Let **D** be any model of the lambda calculus. Define

$$= \equiv \lambda x.y.\langle 0, x, y\rangle \qquad \forall \equiv \lambda x.\langle 6, x\rangle$$

$$P \equiv \lambda x.y.\langle 2, x, y\rangle \qquad \exists \equiv \lambda x.\langle 7, x\rangle$$

$$\vee \equiv \lambda x.y.\langle 3, x, y\rangle \qquad \Omega \equiv 8$$

$$\wedge \equiv \lambda x.y.\langle 4, x, y\rangle$$

$$\to \equiv \lambda x.y.\langle 5, x, y\rangle$$

where we assume some coding of tuples and the numerals in the lambda calculus – and hence in the model **D**. These objects possess an *independence property* in that we can never have for example, $\vee xy = \wedge xy$. Using these elements of the model we can now define two subsets **T** and **F** as the least fixed points of the following simultaneous inductive definition.

$$\frac{d \in D}{d = d \in \mathbf{T}} \qquad \frac{d \in D \quad e \in D \quad d \neq e}{d = e \in \mathbf{F}} \qquad \Omega \in \mathbf{F}$$

$$\frac{d \in \mathbf{T}}{Pd \in \mathbf{T}} \qquad \frac{d \in \mathbf{F}}{Pd \in \mathbf{T}}$$

$$\frac{d \in \mathbf{T}}{d \vee e \in \mathbf{T}} \quad \frac{e \in \mathbf{T}}{d \vee e \in \mathbf{T}} \qquad \frac{d \in \mathbf{F} \quad e \in \mathbf{F}}{d \vee e \in \mathbf{F}}$$

$$\frac{d \in \mathbf{T} \quad e \in \mathbf{T}}{d \wedge e \in \mathbf{T}} \qquad \frac{d \in \mathbf{F}}{d \wedge e \in \mathbf{F}} \quad \frac{e \in \mathbf{F}}{d \wedge e \in \mathbf{F}}$$

$$\frac{e \in \mathbf{T}}{d \to e \in \mathbf{T}} \quad \frac{d \in \mathbf{F}}{d \to e \in \mathbf{T}} \qquad \frac{d \in \mathbf{T} \quad e \in \mathbf{F}}{d \to e \in \mathbf{F}}$$

$$\frac{fe \in \mathbf{T},\ \text{for some } e \in D}{\exists f \in \mathbf{T}} \qquad \frac{fe \in \mathbf{F},\ \text{for all } e \in D}{\exists f \in \mathbf{F}}$$

$$\frac{fe \in \mathbf{T},\ \text{for all } e \in D}{\forall f \in \mathbf{T}} \qquad \frac{fe \in \mathbf{F},\ \text{for some } e \in D}{\forall f \in \mathbf{F}}$$

This is a monotone induction and so admits a least fixed point. It is easy to check that the least fixed point of this inductive definition is a model of the theory. Models of the form $\langle \mathbf{D}, \mathbf{T}, \mathbf{F} \rangle$ where $\mathbf{T}, \mathbf{F}$ satisfy the above definition are essentially Aczel's Frege Structures (Aczel, 1980). For further details about semantics in Frege structures the reader should consult (Kamareddine, 1992, 1993).

4.2.5. Is such a first-order theory enough?

One concern hinges on whether sentences such as:

Simon believes everything Mary does,

involve quantification over *propositions*. Implicitly, it clearly does. If we attempt to reflect this explicitly the appropriate formalization is:

$$\forall x \in P. \underset{m}{\text{Bel}}(x) \to \underset{s}{\text{Bel}}(x).$$

This cannot be proven to be a proposition in the present theory. This causes problems for nested belief contexts since, intuitively, in the following pair the embedded sentence is required to be a proposition.

John believes that Simon believes everything Mary does

$$\underset{j}{\text{Bel}}(\forall x \in P.\, \underset{m}{\text{Bel}}(x) \rightarrow \underset{s}{\text{Bel}}(x)).$$

The worry here seems to be that, in the present theory, we have no guarantee that what are truly believed are propositions. One way out is to impose some axiomatic constraints on the belief operator to the effect that $\text{Bel}(x) \rightarrow Px$ is taken as a axiom about belief. Alternatively, one might try to develop some aspects of higher-order quantification *internally* (see Kamareddine (1993) for such an approach).

4.3. Nominalized HOL (NHOL)

A rather different approach to the logic of nominalized predicates is that of (Cocchiarella, 1979). We first present his original second-order theory and then sketch how it can be extended to **HOL** itself.

4.3.1. Cocchiarella's logic of nominalized predicates

We shall adopt the following version of (classical) second-order logic (**SOL**). The language has individual variables (lower case x etc.) and n-place relation variables (upper case X^n $(n > 0)$). The wff are constructed as follows.

(i) $X^n(x_1, \ldots, x_n)$ is an atomic wff.

(ii) If ϕ and ψ are wff then so are $\sim\phi, \phi \wedge \psi, \forall x.\phi$ and $\forall X^n.\phi$.

The rules of the theory include those for negation, conjunction and universal quantification (both individual and relation) plus the following schemes of comprehension.

COMP For each wff ϕ and distinct variables $x_1, \ldots, x_n$
$$\exists Z^n.\forall x_1, \ldots, \forall x_n.Z(x_1, \ldots, x_n) \leftrightarrow \phi,$$
where Z is not free in ϕ.

Cocchiarella (1979) then allows relation variables to occupy individual positions in atomic wff. The theory T^* results from this addition to the language of **SOL** by extending all the axioms and rules of second-order logic to this new language (including the scheme of comprehension) and adding a basic ontological axiom which insists that every relation is indiscernible from an individual

ONT $\forall X^n.\exists x.x \cong X^n$,

where $\cong$ is indiscernability. **ONT** is actually equivalent to:

$$\forall x^I.\phi \rightarrow \forall x^T.\phi[x^T/x^I],$$

which is the form given by Cocchiarella. Given the desire to provide a logic of nominalized predicates this is a particularly natural theory. It does, however, have its oddities. Before we discuss them we briefly indicate how one can extend the treatment to the whole of **HOL**.

4.3.2. NHOL

In order to see how this might be possible we employ a more parsimonious version of **HOL**. This is essentially the version $\mathcal{F}^\omega$ given in (Andrews, 1986). We employ this version since it is much easier to grasp and investigate the inclusion of nominalized predicates. The language of types and terms is given as follows. We shall use lower case Greek letters for terms of type P.

(i) P is a type.
(ii) I is a type.
(iii) If $T_1, \ldots, T_n$ are types then $(T_1, \ldots, T_n)$ is a type $(n \geqslant 1)$.
(iv) A variable x^T is of type T.
(v) $x^{(T_1,\ldots,T_n)}(y^{T_1}, \ldots, y^{T_n})$ is of type P.
(vi) If ϕ and ψ are of type P then so are $\sim\phi$, $\phi \wedge \psi$ and $\forall x^T.\phi$.

Set-theoretically, $(T_1, \ldots, T_n)$ denotes the power set of the Cartesian product of $T_1, \ldots, T_n$. The rules of the theory include those for negation, conjunction and universal quantification as in (classical) **HOL** plus the following schemes of comprehension.

COMP (i) For each ϕ of type P with distinct variables $x^{T_1}, \ldots, x^{T_n}$
$$\exists z(T_1, \ldots, T_n).\forall x_1^{T_1} \ldots \forall x_n^{T_n}.z(x_1, \ldots, x_n) \leftrightarrow \phi,$$
where z is not free in ϕ.

(ii) $\exists z^P.z \leftrightarrow \phi$, where z is not free in ϕ.

For convenience, we shall continue to use **HOL** for this theory. The definitions of the other connectives and the relations of equality are as before. The extensional theory is obtained by adding the axioms of extensionality which now take the following form.

EXT (i) $\forall x_1^{T_1} \ldots \forall x_n^{T_n}.u^{(T_1,\ldots,T_n)}(x_1, \ldots, x_n) \leftrightarrow \nu^{(T_1,\ldots,T_n)}(x_1, \ldots, x_n) \to u =_{(T_1,\ldots,T_n)} \nu.$

(ii) $(\phi \leftrightarrow \psi) \to \phi =_P \psi.$

To this *version* of **HOL** we add nominalized predicates along the lines of Cocchiarella's second order theory. Clause (v) of the syntax is replaced by:

(v′) $x^{(T_1,\ldots,T_n)}(y^{S_1}, \ldots, y^{S_n})$ is of type P
where for $i = 1, \ldots, n$, if $T_i \neq I$ then $T_i = S_i$.

This allows nominalized items of all types to occur in individual position. All the rules/axioms remain as before but are extended to this new language. In addition we require the ontological axiom.

ONT $\forall x^T.\exists y^I.x =_I y.$

This completes the description of the intensional theory (**NHOL**). For the extensional version we add **EXT**.

This theory can be translated into **HOL**. The non-individual types and wff are translated as follows – the individual type evaporates under the translation. In what follows we assume that the variables are appropriately distinct in the concrete syntax. Notice that the translation only employs a fragment of **HOL** (i.e. that fragment known as *propositional higher-order logic*) where there is no individual quantification.

$$P^* = P$$

$$(T_1, \ldots, T_n)^* = (J_1^*, \ldots, J_m^*) \quad \text{if at least one of } T_i \neq I \text{ and where } J_1, \ldots, J_m \text{ are those elements of } \{T_1, \ldots, T_n\} \text{ not equal to } I$$

$$= P \quad \text{otherwise}$$

$$(x^{(T_1,\ldots,T_n)}(y^{S_1}, \ldots, y^{S_n}))^* = x^{(J_1^*,\ldots,J_m^*)}(y^{J_1^*}, \ldots, y^{J_m^*}) \quad \text{if at least one of } T_i \neq I$$

$$= x^P \quad \text{otherwise}$$

$$(\phi \wedge \psi)^* = \phi^* \wedge \psi^*$$

$$(\sim\phi)^* = \sim(\phi^*)$$

$$(\forall x^I.\phi)^* = \phi^*$$

$$(\forall x^T.\phi)^* = \forall x^{T^*}.\phi^* \quad \text{for } T \neq I$$

THEOREM 4.3.2.1. *If ϕ is provable in* (extensional) **NHOL** *then ϕ^* is provable in* (extensional) **HOL**.

PROOF. By induction on the proofs in **NHOL**. All the rules are routine to check. Consider the comprehension scheme: $\exists z^{(T_1,\ldots,T_n)}.\forall y^{T_1} \ldots \forall y^{T_n}.z(y^{T_1}, \ldots, y^{T_n}) \leftrightarrow \phi$. In the non-trivial case where at least one of $T_i \neq I$, this translates to: $\exists z^{(J_1^*,\ldots,J_m^*)}.\forall y^{J_1^*} \ldots \forall y^{J_m^*}.z(y^{J_1^*}, \ldots, y^{J_m^*}) \leftrightarrow \phi^*$, which is an instance of the scheme in **HPL**. Where all T_i are I it reduces to the second form of the scheme. **ONT** translates to an obvious logical truth. **EXT** translates to **EXT** in **HOL**. □

Despite its consistency this theory is not without its curiosities. In particular, given our observation about the intensional nature of nominalized items the following should hold.

$$\textbf{IT} \quad \forall x^T.\forall y^T.x =_I y \rightarrow x =_T y$$

Intuitively, if two items of type T are equal as individuals (i.e. *intensionally* the same) then they ought to equal as elements of type T. This is especially clear if the extensionality axioms are assumed. However, it is not derivable. Indeed its addition leads to inconsistency. Consider the following variation on the Russell property: $\phi[y^I] = \exists x^{(I)}.x =_I y \wedge \sim x(y)$. By comprehension, there exists $z^{(I)}$ such that $\forall y^I.z(y) \leftrightarrow \exists x^{(I)}.x =_I y \wedge \sim x(y)$. Assume $z(z)$. By **ONT**, $z(z) \leftrightarrow \exists x^{(I)}.x =_I z \wedge \sim x(z)$. By **IT**, $\exists x^{(I)}.x =_{(I)} z \wedge \sim x(z)$. Let $x^{(I)} =_{(I)} z \wedge \sim x(z)$. By comprehension, there exists $u^{((I))}$ such

$$u(y^{(I)}) \leftrightarrow (\forall w^I.y(w) \leftrightarrow x^{(I)}.(w)).$$

Since, $u(x^{(I)})$, we have $u(z)$. Hence, $\sim z(z)$. Conversely, if $\sim z(z)$ then clearly, $z(z)$. Hence, we cannot have **IT**. In particular, $x^{(T)} =_I y^{(T)}$ does not guarantee that $x^{(T)}$ and $y^{(T)}$ are extensionally equal.

4.3.3. A theory with equality

For a theory with such a notion of equality we must add it as a new primitive – just as in the case of first-order logic. To complete the picture we briefly illustrate how this might be achieved – for the second-order case. We add to the language of nominalized **SOL** a new atomic wff of equality

$$\xi = \xi'$$

where ξ, ξ' are variables of either kind (individual or relation). We assume the normal axioms for equality, i.e. reflexivity and replacement.

$$\textbf{ref} \quad \xi = \xi$$
$$\textbf{rep} \quad \xi = \xi' \to (\phi[\xi] \to \phi[\xi'])$$

All the proof rules of **SOL** are extended to this new language but the comprehension scheme is restricted to the wff of **SOL** itself (this is already enough for the application at hand). In addition, we assume the ontological axiom but now in the form with equality

$$\textbf{ONT} \quad \forall X^n.\exists x.x = X^n.$$

Models of this theory can be constructed along the lines given by Feferman for his theory of operations and classes $T_0 +$ *stratified* comprehension (Feferman, 1979). Alternatively the above theory can be easily translated into $T_0 +$ *stratified* comprehension. Beeson (1985) contains further information on Feferman's theories but restricts the theories to elementary or first-order comprehension.

5. Constructive type theories

Constructively, the meaning of a sentence is not given by spelling out its *truth conditions* but by indicating, for each sentence, what would count as a *witness* for its truth. Theories of meaning along these lines have been advocated and defended by Dummett (1975, 1976, 1991) and Sundholm (1986) – among others. In this chapter we shall develop type theories which are more in line with this approach to semantic theory.

5.1. Propositional theories

The idea behind all the theories we shall discuss is based on the so-called *Curry–Howard correspondence*. We first discuss the *correspondence* for propositional logic, beginning with implicational logic and its connection with the typed lambda calculus. We then examine its extension to deal with quantification – both first and higher-order.

5.1.1. Implicational logic and the typed lambda calculus
Implicational logic is determined by the following introduction and elimination rules.

$$\frac{B, \phi \vdash \psi}{B \vdash \phi \rightarrow \psi}, \qquad \frac{B \vdash \phi \rightarrow \psi \quad B \vdash \phi}{B \vdash \psi}.$$

The Curry–Howard correspondence between propositions and types is based upon the *constructive interpretation* of the connectives. In particular, the constructive interpretation of implication is given as follows.

(i) *t is witness for the truth of $\phi \rightarrow \psi$ iff t is an operation/function which given a witness for ϕ yields a witness for ψ.*

The second step is to set up the correspondence between *propositions* and the type of their witnessing data. For this we collect together the witnessing data for each proposition into a type. For implication, this takes the form of the *type* of functions from the type of witnesses for ϕ to the type of witnesses for ψ.

$$I[\phi \rightarrow \psi] \cong I[\phi] \Rightarrow I[\psi]$$

The correspondence between derivations in implicational logic and the typed lambda calculus (**C**) is then evident.

$$\frac{B^*, x \in I[\phi] \vdash t \in I[\psi]}{B^* \vdash \lambda x \in T.t \in I[\phi] \rightarrow I[\psi]}, \qquad \frac{B^* \vdash t \in I[\phi] \quad B^* \vdash s \in I[\phi] \Rightarrow I[\psi]}{B^* \vdash st \in I[\psi]}$$

where B^* contains the witnesses for the assumptions in B. Indeed, it is easy to see that this is a *sound* representation in the sense that if $B \vdash \phi$ then for some term t we have: $B^* \vdash_{\mathbf{C}} t \in I[\phi]$. This correspondence was also behind the scenes in our discussion of the relationship between categorial grammars and the typed calculus. Indeed, derivations in categorial grammar can be directly unpacked as derivations in implicational logic. Of course, for semantic purposes we require more than pure implicational logic.

5.1.2. Disjoint unions and Cartesian products
If we add disjunctions and conjunctions to our logical language we must match these with corresponding type constructors. To motivate these we first provide the informal constructive interpretation of these connectives.

(ii) t is a *witness for the truth of* $\phi \wedge \psi$ iff t is a pair (r, s) where r is a *witness* for ϕ and s is a witness for ψ.
(iii) t is a *witness for the truth of* $\phi \vee \psi$ iff either t is a left injection, **inl** r, where r is a *witness* for ϕ or t is a right injection, **inr** s, where s is a witness for ψ.

To extend the correspondence between propositions and types we need a parallel extension to the typed lambda calculus.We extend the type syntax of **C** as follows.

(iii) If T and S are type expressions then so is $T \otimes S$ (the *Cartesian product* of T and S).

(iv) If T and S are type expressions then so is $T \oplus S$ (the *disjoint union* of T and S).

We need also to add the *constructors* and *destructors* for these new types. The language of terms is enriched with *pairing, let-expressions, injections* and *case statements*.

(v) If t and s are terms then so is (t, s).
(vi) If t and s are terms and x and y variables then **let** (x, y) **be** t **in** s is a term.
(vii) If t is a term then so are **inl** t and **inr** t.
(viii) If t, s and r are terms and x and y variables then $\mathbf{case}_{xy}\, r$ **of** $[t, s]$ is a term.

The theory **C** is extended by providing introduction, elimination and equality rules for these types.

$$\frac{B \vdash t \in T}{B \vdash \mathbf{inl}_t \in T \oplus S} \qquad \frac{B \vdash t \in S}{B \vdash \mathbf{inr}\, t \in T \oplus S} \qquad \textbf{DUI}$$

$$\frac{B, x \in T \vdash t \in R \quad B, y \in S \vdash s \in R \quad B \vdash r \in T \oplus S}{B \vdash \mathbf{case}_{xy}\ r\ \mathbf{of}\ [t, s] \in R} \qquad \textbf{DUE}$$

$$\frac{B, x \in T \vdash t \in R \quad B, y \in S \vdash s \in R \quad B \vdash r \in T}{B \vdash \mathbf{case}_{xy}\ \mathbf{inl}\ r\ \mathbf{of}\ [t, s] =_R t[r/x]} \qquad \textbf{DUC1}$$

$$\frac{B, x \in T \vdash t \in R \quad B, y \in S \vdash s \in R \quad B \vdash r \in S}{B \vdash \mathbf{case}_{xy}\ \mathbf{inl}\ r\ \mathbf{of}\ [t, s] =_R s[r/x]} \qquad \textbf{DUC2}$$

$$\frac{B \vdash t \in T \quad B \vdash s \in S}{B \vdash (t, s) \in T \otimes S} \qquad \textbf{CPI}$$

$$\frac{B \vdash t \in T \otimes S \quad B, x \in T, y \in S \vdash s \in R}{B \vdash \mathbf{Let}\ (x, y)\ \mathbf{be}\ t\ \mathbf{in}\ s \in R} \qquad \textbf{CPE}$$

$$\frac{B \vdash (t, t') \in T \otimes S \quad B, x \in T, y \in S \vdash s \in R}{B \vdash \mathbf{Let}\ (x, y)\ \mathbf{be}\ (t, t')\ \mathbf{in}\ s =_R s[t/x, t'/y]} \qquad \textbf{CPC}$$

We also require a general rule of substitution[8] and general equality rules. In the rule of substitution, θ is a judgement of equality or membership.

$$\frac{B \vdash t =_T s \quad B \vdash \theta[t]}{B \vdash \theta[t]} \qquad \textbf{sub}$$

$$\frac{B \vdash t =_T t}{B \vdash t \in T} \qquad \frac{B \vdash t \in T}{B \vdash t =_T t} \qquad \textbf{ref}$$

$$\frac{B \vdash t =_T s}{B \vdash s =_T t}\ \textbf{sym} \qquad \frac{B \vdash t =_T s \quad B \vdash s =_T r}{B \vdash t =_T r}\ \textbf{trans}$$

[8] One also requires some general housekeeping rules such as a *cut* and *thinning* rules but we shall leave these to the readers imagination.

With this theory in place we can extend the *Curry–Howard* correspondence to the whole of the language of the propositional logic.

$$I[\phi \wedge \psi] \cong I[\phi] \otimes I[\psi].$$
$$I[\phi \vee \psi] \cong I[\phi] \oplus I[\psi].$$

If we add an *uninhabited* type to interpret absurdity we have an interpretation of the whole of the language of the propositional calculus where each wff is interpreted as a type – the type of *witnesses* for the proposition. Under this interpretation all the laws of intuitionistic logic are sound in the sense that if a formula is provable in intuitionistic logic then its witnessing type is inhabited, i.e. we can find a term which is in the type – and provable so within the extended type theory.

5.2. Dependent types

To achieve a similar correspondence for predicate logic we need to add types that stand proxy for the quantified wff and for atomic assertions. For simplicity we shall assume that the atomic assertions of the language are just equality assertions. Informally, the constructive interpretation of the equality assertions and the quantifiers is given as follows.

(iv) *t is witness for the truth of* $\forall x.\phi$ iff *t is a function which given d,* an element of the domain, yields a *witness for* $\phi[d]$.

(v) t is a *witness for the truth of* $\exists x.\phi$ iff t is a pair (d, s) where d is an element of the domain and s is a *witness* for $\phi[d]$.

(vi) t is *witness for the truth of* $s = t$ iff $s = t$.

Notice that atomic assertions are trivially witnessed or *realized.* To extend the correspondence for these types we must add new type constructors which collect together the witnessing information. Before this we need to say a little about the domains over which quantification is permitted.

> Wheresoever in logic the word *all* or every is used, this word, in order to make sense, tacitly involves the restriction: insofar as belonging to a mathematical structure which is supposed to be constructed beforehand. Brouwer (1975, p. 76).

According to "Brouwer's dictum" only bounded quantification is meaningful. One can only quantify over a domain which has already been constructed. If we follow this stricture then quantification (and presumably, equality) should be bounded. It is these two aspects – the Curry–Howard correspondence and the bounded nature of quantification – which lead to the following theory. The Theory (**M**) is based upon the theories of Martin-Löf (1975, 1979, 1982).[9] We shall not present the full details of his theories but merely sketch a theory which provides the flavor of his theories. We shall then indicate a possible empirical advantage of these theories.

---

[9] The major difference will be that the notion of type will be given as in the previous theories via an explicit syntax not by rules as in his theories. The contexts have also to allow for dependencies.

5.2.1. *The language of* **M**

We enrich the type theory of the previous section as follows.

(i) If T and S are type expressions then so are $T \oplus T$, $\Pi x \in T.S$ and $\Sigma x \in T.S$.
(ii) If T is a type and t and s are terms then $I[T, t, s]$ is a type.

The new types $I[T, t, t]$ are the *equality types* and $\Pi x \in T.S$ and $\Sigma x \in T.S$ the *dependent generalizations* of function spaces and Cartesian products, respectively. Apart from the terms of the previous theory we add a new term (**e**) for the equality types. Notice that via the equality types, type expressions can contain free variables – they have terms as components. Correspondingly, we write $T[s/x]$ for type substitution. In $\Pi x \in T.S$ and $\Sigma x \in T.S$ the variable x is bound. When T does not contain x free, we shall write $S \Rightarrow T$ (the *function space*) for $\Pi x \in S.T$ and $S \otimes T$ (the *Cartesian product*) for $\Sigma x \in S.T$. We have already seen such dependent types/properties in the last chapter.

5.2.2. *Rules*

The rules themselves are generalizations of the previous theory to allow for dependencies. We assume the general rules of equality and the rule of substitution, plus the following rules for the new type constructors.

$$\frac{B \vdash t =_T s}{B \vdash \mathbf{e} \in I(T, t, s)} \qquad \frac{B \vdash t \in I[T, s, t]}{B \vdash s =_T t} \qquad \frac{B \vdash t \in I[T, s, s']}{B \vdash t =_{I[T,s,s']} \mathbf{e}}$$

$$\frac{B \vdash t \in T}{B \vdash \mathbf{inl}\ t \in T \oplus S} \qquad \frac{B \vdash t \in S}{B \vdash \mathbf{inr}\ t \in T \oplus S}$$

$$\frac{B, x \in T \vdash t \in R[\mathbf{inl}\ x] \quad B, y \in S \vdash s \in R[\mathbf{inr}\ x] \quad B \vdash r \in T \oplus S}{B \vdash \mathbf{case}_{xy}\ r\ \mathbf{of}\ [t, s] \in R[r]}$$

$$\frac{B, x \in T \vdash t \in R[\mathbf{inl}\ x] \quad B, y \in S \vdash R[\mathbf{inr}\ x] \quad B \vdash r \in T}{B \vdash \mathbf{case}_{xy}\ \mathbf{inl}\ r\ \mathbf{of}\ [t, s] =_{R[\mathbf{inl}\ r]} t[r/x]}$$

$$\frac{B, x \in T \vdash t \in R[\mathbf{inl}\ x] \quad B, y \in S \vdash s \in R[\mathbf{inr}\ x] \quad B \vdash r \in S}{B \vdash \mathbf{case}_{xy}\ \mathbf{inr}\ r\ \mathbf{of}\ [t, s] =_{R[\mathbf{inr}\ r]} s[r/y]}$$

$$\frac{B, x \in S \vdash t \in T}{B \vdash \lambda x \in S.t \in \Pi x \in S.T} \qquad \frac{B \vdash s \in \Pi x \in S.T \quad B \vdash t \in S}{B \vdash st \in T[t]}$$

$$\frac{B, x \in S \vdash t \in T \quad B \vdash s \in S}{B \vdash (\lambda x \in S.t)s =_{T[s]} t[s/x]}$$

$$\frac{B \vdash t \in T \quad B \vdash s \in S[t/x]}{B \vdash (t, s) \in \Sigma x \in T.S}$$

$$\frac{B \vdash t \in \Sigma x \in T.S \quad B, x \in T, y \in S[x] \vdash s \in R[(x,y)]}{B \vdash \textbf{Let } (x,y) \textbf{ be } t \textbf{ in } s \in R[t]}$$

$$\frac{B \vdash (t,s) \in \Sigma x \in T.S \quad B, x \in T, y \in S[x] \vdash r \in R[(x,y)]}{B \vdash \textbf{Let } (x,y) \textbf{ be } (t,s) \textbf{ in } r =_{R[(t,s)]} r[t/x, s/y]}$$

This is a simplified version of Martin-Löf's theories. The crucial difference is that here the notion of type is given by an explicit syntax of type expressions. The above account is sufficient to illustrate the use of dependent types in semantics.

5.2.3. Application to semantics

Implicit in this theory is the identification of *propositions* and *types*. A proposition is taken to be true if one can construct an element of the proposition (as a type) via the rules of the theory. The identification has a surprising side effect. The richness of the type theory enables the expression of the logical form of certain sentences which seem impossible in the more traditional types theories. Consider the notorious *donkey sentence*.

Every man who owns a donkey beats it.

Ordinary predicate logic does not seem to provide an interpretation of this sentence. The best we can do is the following.

$$\forall x \in \text{Man}\,.(\exists y \in \text{Donkey}\,.(x,y) \in \text{Own}) \to (x, ?) \in \text{beat}\,.$$

Unfortunately, there is no way of filling the place marked with a ?; the variable y is not in scope. This has led to the development of Kamp's Discourse Representation theory (Kamp, this volume). However, in the present type theory we can employ the richness of the dependent types in conjunction with the identification of propositions and types to facilitate a representation:

$$\Pi z \in (\Sigma x \in \text{Man}\,.\Sigma y \in \text{Donkey}\,.\,\text{Own}(x,y)).\,\text{beat}(\mathbf{i}z, \mathbf{i}(\mathbf{r}z))$$

where we have used $T(x,y)$ as an abbreviation for the equality type $I[T,(x,y),(x,y)]$. Roughly, an object will be a member of this type if it is an operation which given an object which is a triple (the first member of which is a man, the second a donkey and the third which is a witness that the first owns the second), returns a witness that the first beats the second. This observation was made by Sundholm (1986). More systematic attempts at doing natural language semantics in constructive type theory can be found in (Ranta, 1991).

5.2.4. *An interpretation of* **M** *in* **F**

This theory can be interpreted in the theory **F**. Call the interpretation *. We inductively associate with each type T a property T^*. This is possible since the properties of **F** are closed under the type constructors of the present theory. The terms are mapped via * to their representation in the pure lambda calculus and equality is interpreted as follows.

$$(t =_T s)^* \equiv t^* = s^* \wedge t \in T^*.$$

It is then routine to check that all the rules are soundly interpreted in the theory **F**. In particular, the closure conditions for properties satisfy the closure conditions for types; indeed they satisfy the conditions of Martin-Löf's theory where the types themselves are given via proof rules. More details of this interpretation are given in (Smith, 1984).

Finally it is worth observing that the class of properties of theory **F** is closed under dependent properties; hence the representation of the donkey sentences is also possible in **F**.

5.3. *Second-order theories and beyond*

Can the Curry–Howard correspondence be extended to higher-order quantification? One might think that such impredicative systems are highly non-constructive so that even if this can be achieved it is philosophically irresponsible to do so. We shall not takes sides on this issue; our objective is merely to report on the type theories which can provide such an interpretation and indicate their semantic applications.

5.3.1. *Polymorphic lambda calculus*

We first examine a fragment of second-order logic and its constructive interpretation. The language of *minimal second-order logic* contains proposition variables and is closed under implication and universal quantification with respect to proposition variables. The logic contains the standard introduction and elimination rules for implication and (propositional) universal quantification. The type theory for this logic is the so-called *polymorphic lambda calculus*.

This can be motivated from a rather different perspective. We described the difference between the two theories **C** and **CU** by saying that the latter was implicitly *polymorphic* in that a term might be assigned more than one type. In the theory **C** we could recover the unique type of a term from the syntax. Moreover, in **CU** it is clear that the infinite number of types that a term might possess form a pattern. For example, $\lambda x.x$ has type $T \Rightarrow T$ for all type T. What we cannot do in **CU** is express this pattern.

In fact there are polymorphic extensions of all three theories but we illustrate with the theory **C**. This theory is due independently to Girard (1972) and Reynolds (1974). We enrich the language of types by introducing type variables X, Y, Z and increasing the stock of type expressions as follows.

(i) I (type of individuals) is a type expression.

(ii) If T and S are type expressions then so is $T \Rightarrow S$ (the type of functions from T to S).

(iii) If X is a type variable then X is a type expression.
(iv) If X is a type variable and T a type expression then $\Pi X.T$ is a type expression.

The language of terms is also an extension of that of **C**.

(i) x, a variable, is a term.
(ii) c, a constant, is a term.
(iii) If t is a term and x a variable and T a type then $\lambda x \in T.t$ is a term.
(iv) If t and s are terms then so is st.
(v) If t is a term and X a type variable then $\lambda X.t$ is a term.
(vi) If t is a term and T a type expression then $t.T$ is a term.

The rules of the theory **C** are enriched by the rules for polymorphic types.

$$\frac{B \vdash t \in T}{B \vdash \lambda X.t \in \Pi X.T}\ (\mathbf{PI}) \qquad \frac{B \vdash t \in \Pi X.T}{B \vdash t \cdot S \in T[S]}\ (\mathbf{PE})$$

$$\frac{B \vdash t \in T}{B \vdash (\lambda X.t) \cdot S =_{T[S/X]} t[S/X]}\ (\mathbf{PC})$$

Usually the Calculus is formulated as a type assignment system without the equality/conversion axiom.

The existence of polymorphism in natural language is not hard to illustrate. For example, the Boolean particles "not", "and" and "or" seem to be polymorphic. The type

$$\Pi X.(X \Rightarrow P) \Rightarrow (X \Rightarrow P)$$

seems to cover all cases for "not" (except sentential negation) but it also over-generates. However, even if we could make these instances work, they still do not support the full – impredicative theory: the polymorphism is *schematic* and there are no obvious examples of iterated applications of Π. Predicative theories seem to suffice (see Van Benthem, 1991, Chapter 13 for further discussion). However, the second-order calculus has found semantic application via the following extension.

5.3.2. The theory of constructions

The *Curry–Howard correspondence* extended to (intuitionistic) Higher-order (*propositional*) logic leads to the *theory of constructions* (Coquand, 1985, 1990). To complete the present picture we provide a brief sketch. Here we have two classes of types: those that provide the constructive analogues for the propositions of **HOL** and those which interpret the higher-order types of **HOL**. To provide a flavor of this theory we provide a syntax for the types and propositions as follows.

(i) If T and S are type expressions then so is $\Pi x \in T.S$.
(ii) If P is a proposition expression then P is a type expression.

(iii) If P is a proposition expressions and T is a type expression then $\Pi x \in T.P$ is a proposition expression.

Notice that this is a generalization of that which would arise naturally from **HOL** in that the types required to interpret the types of **HOL** would only require closure under function spaces, whereas we have closure under dependent function spaces. Observe also that implication is interpreted as the function space $P \Rightarrow Q$ which is a special case of $\Pi x \in P.Q$, where x is not free in Q. Given this syntax, and the familiarity with the systems so far constructed, the reader should be able to construct the rules of the theory. The rule for the dependent types parallel those for the theory **M** but of course the class of types is different. In particular, the polymorphism of the second-order calculus is given via the type $\Pi x \in P.T$. For an accessible exposition of the complete theory see Huet (1990). A good general and detailed introduction to higher-order type theories is (Barendregt, 1991).

As we said earlier, this theory has found some application in semantics: it has been employed to interpret Kamp's Discourse representation theory (Ahn, 1990). Whether the full power of this theory is necessary for this application remains to be seen. More details of this interpretation can be found in Kamp's paper (this volume).

6. Types in semantics, logic and computation

The majority of the type theories we have studied have been inspired by the foundations of computing science and mathematics. However, in our exposition we motivated matters from the perspective of natural language semantics. In this final section we draw some of the disparate strands together and briefly compare the role of types in these areas. This will set the scene for indicating more recent lines of research.

6.1. More flexible typing

Polymorphism comes in many flavors from *overloading* where the same symbol is employed with several different meanings, through to the *uniform polymorphism* of the second-order lambda calculus. Van Benthem (1991, Chapter 13) distinguishes between various forms of *polymorphism* (e.g., *variable, derivational, substitutional*) to cope with the variety of *type shifting* phenomena in natural language. All of these notions have their counterparts in computer science. In particular, the *substitutional* variety is essentially that of the programming languages ML and MIRANDA™. Hendriks (1993) develops a flexible Montague semantics in which each syntactic category is associated with a whole family of types: the families are inductively generated from some base types by closing under certain type constructors. Most of these forms of polymorphism can be represented in the second-order calculus. However, such representations are not *descriptively adequate* in the sense that the calculus goes way beyond the empirical data. This is true in both computer science and natural language. This leads to a further consideration which pertains to the design of a *sensible* theory of *polymorphic* typing.

6.2. Expressive power versus proof theoretic strength

The *expressive power* of a theory is often contrasted with its *proof-theoretic strength.* These dimensions of a theory are of central concern to mathematical foundations and, more recently, have become an issue in the foundations of computation (e.g., Feferman, 1990; Turner, 1996). In particular, Feferman demonstrates that one can design a theory (including a form of stratified polymorphism) which is expressive enough to capture computational practice but which has only the computational strength of primitive recursive arithmetic.[10] Thus far, these concerns have not been of major interest to semanticists. However, ever since the emergence of Montague semantics it has been clear that semantics does not require the full expressive power of higher-order intensional logic. More recently, Van Benthem (1991) has pointed out that one does not require the whole of the second order lambda calculus to capture the various forms of polymorphism implicit in natural language. Moreover, it is clear that one does not require the whole of the theory of constructions to capture discourse representation theory. A version of Martin-Löf's type theory with a universe would do; and this would be a theory proof-theoretically equivalent to first-order arithmetic.[11] More studies along these lines would be a welcome deterrent to the proliferation of ever stronger and, from the perspective of semantic and computational applications, hard to motivate systems. In both areas workers too often take the easy way out: expressive power is obtained by the brute force technique of increasing its proof-theoretic strength.

6.3. Unifying frameworks

The *Barendregt cube* (Barendregt, 1991) provides a framework in which many pure type systems can be accommodated. These include the simple type lambda calculus and progress through to the second-order calculus and eventually the theory of constructions. This has enabled a more systematic study of the various metamathematical properties of these systems. The cube also offers some further conceptual clarification of the theory of constructions itself. Recently, Borghuis (1994) has extended all these type systems to include modal operators and has introduced the *modal cube*. The motivation stems from the need for richer languages of knowledge representation which in particular allow for the representation of intensional notions. Kamareddine (1995) suggests a theory in which many of the current property theories (apparently) emerge as special cases.

6.4. Universal types

In natural language semantics the need for some form of universal type or property seems to arise in the semantics of nominalization. In computer science it emanates from the untyped lambda calculus. Moreover, many computational theories of types/classes, aimed at

[10] Practice would be even better served with systems the strength of polynomial arithmetic.

[11] Provided that induction is restricted to first-order types.

program development and analysis, admit a universal type (e.g., Feferman, 1990). However, this is largely for convenience and elegance in stating the theory. More explicitly, such theories are based upon a scheme of comprehension which admits a universal type as an instance. It is not clear that such types are useful or necessary in computational practice. Moreover, the usefulness of having logical theories like property theory as part of a computational logic is less than clear (see Kamareddine (1995) for an alternative view).

6.5. Dependent types

The term *Constructive Functional Programming* refers to the paradigm where the Curry–Howard correspondence between proofs and programs is employed to provide a foundation for the specification and development of provably correct programs. Dependent types have found application in unpacking the Curry–Howard correspondence. Thompson (1991) is a simple introduction to the use of Martin-Löf's type theory from the computational perspective. However, the role of these types in natural language semantics is quite different: they have been employed to model *discourse* phenomena. On the face of it, the constructive paradigm in semantics seems essential to this particular application. However, these types are available in certain property theories (e.g., Turner, 1987) and so, Sundholm's treatment of discourse, is also available here (see Fox, 1995).

6.6. Separation types

These types have been employed in the foundations of computation/constructive mathematics to *hide* information. Fox (1995) employs them in semantics to analyze discourse anaphora. Whether they can be employed to model underspecification e.g., underspecified discourse representations (Reyle, 1995) remains to be seen.

References

Aczel, P. (1980), *Frege structures and the notions of proposition, truth and set*, The Kleene Symposium, Baranse, Keister and Kunen, eds, North-Holland, Amsterdam, 31–40.

Ahn, R. and Kolb, H.P. (1990), *Discourse representation meets constructive mathematics*, Technical Report 16, ITK, Tilbury.

Andrews, P.B. (1986), *An Introduction to Mathematical Logic and Type Theory*, Academic Press, New York.

Barendregt, H. (1984), *The Lambda Calculus: Its Syntax and Semantics*, North-Holland Studies in Logic and the Foundations of Mathematics vol. 103.

Barendregt, H. (1991), *Lambda calculi with types*, Handbook of Logic in Computer Science, S. Abramsky, D.M. Gabbay and T.S.E. Maibaum, eds, Oxford Univ. Press, Oxford, 118–279.

Beeson, M. (1985), *Foundations of Constructive Mathematics*, Springer, Berlin.

Borghuis, T. (1994), *Coming to terms with modal logic*, PhD Thesis, University of Eindhoven.

Brouwer, L.E.J. (1975), *Collected Works*, vol. 1, A. Heyting, ed., North-Holland, Amsterdam.

Bunder, M.W.V. (1983), *Predicate calculus of arbitrarily high order*, Arch. Math. Logic **23**, 109–113.

Chierchia, G. (1982), *Nominalization and Montague grammar*, Ling. and Philos. **5**, 3.

Chierchia, G. and Turner, R. (1988), *Semantics and property theory*, Ling. and Philos. **11**, 261–302.

Church, A. (1940), *A formulation of the simple theory of types*, J. Symb. Logic **5**, 56–68.
Church, A. (1941), *The Calculi of Lambda Conversion*, Princeton Univ. Press.
Cocchiarella, N.B. (1979), *The theory of homogeneous simple types as a second order logic*, Notre Dame J. Formal Logic **20**, 505–524.
Coppo, M. (1984), *Completeness of type assignment in continuous lambda models*, Theor. Comput. Sci. **29**, 309–324.
Coquand, T. and Huet, G. (1985), *A theory of constructions*, Semantics of Data Types, Springer, Berlin.
Coquand, T. (1990), *Metamathematical investigations of the calculus of constructions*, Logic and Computer Science, P. Odifreddi, ed., Academic Press, New York.
Cresswell, M. (1985), *Structured Meanings*, MIT Press, Cambridge, MA.
Curry, H.B. and Feys, R. (1958), *Combinatory Logic*, North-Holland Studies in Logic vol. 1.
Curry, H.B., Hindley, R. and Seldin, J. (1972), *Combinatory Logic*, North-Holland Studies in Logic vol. 2.
Dummett, M. (1975), *What is a Theory of Meaning?: I*, Mind and Language, S. Guttenplan, ed., Oxford Univ. Press.
Dummett, M. (1976), *What is a Theory of Meaning?: II*, Truth and Meaning, E.G. Evans and J. McDowell, eds, Oxford Univ. Press.
Dummett, M. (1991), *The Logical Basis of Metaphysics*, Duckworth.
Feferman, S. (1975), *A language and axioms for explicit mathematics*, Algebra and Logic, Lecture Notes in Mathematics vol. 450, 87–139.
Feferman, S. (1979), *Constructive theories of functions and classes*, Logic Colloquium 78, North-Holland Studies in Logic and the Foundations of Mathematics, M. Boffa, D. Van-Dalen and K. McAloon, eds, 159–224.
Feferman, S. (1990), *Polymorphic typed Lambda Calculi in a type-free axiomatic framework*, Contemp. Math. vol. 106, 101–136.
Fitch, F.B. (1963), *The system CD of combinatory logic*, J. Symb. Logic **28**, 87–97.
Fox, C. (1995), *Representing discourse in property theory*, Internal report, University of Essex.
Geach, P. (1972), *A program for syntax*, Semantics of Natural Language, D. Davidson and G. Harman, eds, Reidel, Dordrecht, 483–497.
Girard, J.Y. (1972), *Interpretation fonctionnelle et elimination des coupures dans l'arithmetique d'ordre superieur*, These de doctorat d'etat, Universite Paris VII.
Hendriks, H. (1993), *Studied flexibility*, PhD Thesis, Department of Philosophy, University of Amsterdam. ILLC Dissertation Series 1993–5.
Hindley, J.R. (1969), *The principal type-scheme of an object in combinatory logics*, Trans. Amer. Math. Soc. **146**, 29–60.
Hindley, J.R. (1983), *The completeness theorem for typing lambda terms*, Theor. Comput. Sci. **22**, 1–17.
Hindley, J.R. and Seldin, J.P. (1986), *Introduction to Combinators and Lambda Calculus*, London Math. Soc. Students Texts vol. 1.
Huet, G. (1990), *A uniform approach to type theory*, Logical Foundations of Functional Programming, G. Huet, ed., Addison-Wesley, 337–399.
Kamareddine, F. (1992), *Set theory and nominalization, Part I*, J. Logic Comput. **2**(5).
Kamareddine, F. (1993), *Set theory and nominalization, Part II*, J. Logic Comput. **2**(6), 687–707.
Kamareddine, F. (1995), *Important issues in foundational formalism*, Bull. IGPL **3**(2.3), 291–319.
Martin-Löf, P. (1975), *An Intuitionistic Theory of Types: Predicative Part*, Logic Coll. 73, North-Holland, Amsterdam.
Martin-Löf, P. (1979), Preprint of (Martin-Löf, 1982), Report No. 11, University of Stockholm.
Martin-Löf, P. (1982), *Constructive mathematics and computer programming logic*, Methodol. and Philos. Sci. **6**, 153–179.
Meyer, A. (1982), *What is a model of the lambda calculus?*, Inform. and Control **52**, 87–122.
Montague, R. (1973), *The proper treatment of quantification in ordinary English*, Approaches to Natural Language, Hintikka et al., eds, Dordrecht.
Montague, R. (1970), *A Universal Grammar*, Theorem **36**, 373–390.
Muskens, R. (1989), *Meaning and partiality*, Dissertation, University of Amsterdam.
Partee, B.H. and Rooth, M. (1983), *Generalized conjunction and type ambiguity*, Meaning, Use and Interpretation of Language, R. Bauerle, C. Schwarz and A. von Stechow, eds, Walter de Gruyter, Berlin, 361–383.

Plotkin, G. (1972), *A set-theoretical definition of application*, Memo MIP-R-95, University of Edinburgh.

Ranta, A. (1991), *Intuitionistic categorial grammar*, Ling. and Philos. **14**, 203–239.

Reyle, U. (1995), *Underspecified discourse representation structures and their logic*, Bull. IGPL **3**(2.3), 473–489.

Reynolds, J.C. (1974), *Towards a theory of type structures*, Proc. Programming Symposium, Lecture Notes in Comput. Sci. vol. 19, Springer, Berlin.

Scott, D. (1973), *Models for various type-free calculi*, Logic, Methodology and Philosophy of Science IV, Seppos et al., eds, North-Holland Studies in Logic and Foundations of Mathematics, 157–187.

Scott, D.S. (1975), *Combinators and classes*, Lambda Calculus and Computer Science Theory, C. Bphm, ed., Lect. Notes in Comput. Sci. vol. 37, 1–26.

Scott, D.S. (1976), *Data types as lattices*, SIAM J. Computing **5**, 522–587.

Smith, J.M. (1984), *An interpretation of Martin-Löf's type theory in a type-free theory of propositions*, J. Symb. Logic **49**.

Stalnaker, R. (1984), *Inquiry*, MIT Press, Cambridge, MA.

Sundholm, G. (1986), *Proof theory and meaning*, Handbook of Philosophical Logic III, D. Gabbay and F. Guenthner, eds, Reidel, Dordrecht.

Thompson, S. (1991), *Type Theory and Functional Programming*, Addison-Wesley.

Turner, R. (1987), *A theory of properties*, J. Symb. Logic **52**, 445–472.

Turner, R. (1996), *Weak theories of operations and types*, J. Logic Comput. **6**(1), 5–31.

Thomason, R. (1980), *A model theory for the propositional attitudes*, Ling. and Philos. **4**, 47–70.

Van Benthem, J. (1991), *Language in Action*, North-Holland Studies in Logic.

CHAPTER 10

Dynamics

Reinhard Muskens

Department of Linguistics, Tilburg University, PO Box 90153, 5000 LE Tilburg, The Netherlands
E-mail: r.a.muskens@kub.nl

Johan van Benthem

University of Amsterdam, ILLC, Plantage Muidergracht 24, 1018 TV Amsterdam, The Netherlands
E-mail: johan@fwi.uva.nl, johan@csli.stonford.edu

Albert Visser

Department of Philosophy, Heidelberglaan 8, 3584 CS Utrecht, The Netherlands
E-mail: albert.visser@phil.ruu.nl

Commentator: D. McCarty

Contents

HANDBOOK OF LOGIC AND LANGUAGE
Edited by J. van Benthem and A. ter Meulen

0. Introduction

Intriguing parallels can be observed between the execution of computer programs and the interpretation of ordinary discourse. Various elements of discourse, such as assertions, suppositions and questions, may well be compared with statements or sequences of statements in an imperative program. Let us concentrate on assertions for the moment. Stalnaker (1979) sums up some of their more or less obvious characteristics in the following way.

> Let me begin with some truisms about assertions. First, assertions have content; an act of assertion is, among other things, the expression of a proposition – something that represents the world as being a certain way. Second, assertions are made in a context – a situation that includes a speaker with certain beliefs and intentions, and some people with their own beliefs and intentions to whom the assertion is addressed. Third, sometimes the content of the assertion is dependent on the context in which it is made, for example, on who is speaking or when the assertion takes place. Fourth, acts of assertion affect, and are intended to affect, the context, in particular the attitudes of the participants in the situation; how the assertion affects the context will depend on its content.

If we are prepared to think about assertions as if they were some special kind of programs, much of this behaviour falls into place. That assertions are made in a context may then be likened to the fact that execution of a program always starts in a given initial state; that the content of an assertion may depend on the context parallels the situation that the effect of a program will usually depend on this input state (for example, the effect of $x := y + 7$ will crucially depend on the value of y before execution); and that a program or part of a program will change and is intended to change the current program state is no less a truism as the contention that an act of assertion changes the context. After the change has taken place, the new state or the new context can serve as an input for the next part of the program or the next assertion.

The metaphor helps to explain some other features of discourse as well. For instance, it makes it easier to see why the meaning of a series of assertions is sensitive to order, why saying "John left. Mary started to cry." is different from saying "Mary started to cry. John left.". Clearly, the result of executing two programs will in general also depend on the order in which we run them. If we think about sequences of sentences as ordinary conjunctions on the other hand, this non-commutativity remains a puzzle. The picture also helps us see how it can be that some assertions are inappropriate in certain contexts, why we cannot say "Harry is guilty too" with a certain intonation just after it has been established that nobody else is guilty. This is like dividing by x just after x has been set to 0.

Discourse and programming then, seem to share some important structural properties, to the extent that one can serve as a useful metaphor for the other. We need not restrict application of the metaphor to that part of discourse that is expressed by overt linguistic means. Not only are assertions, suppositions and questions made in a context, other, non-verbal, contributions to conversation, such as gestures and gazes, are too. These non-verbal acts of communication likewise have a potential to change the current context state. A speaker may for instance introduce discourse referents into the conversation with the help of a gesture or a gaze, or may use such means (or more overt linguistic ones such as changes in tense and aspect or rise in pitch) to announce the introduction of a new 'discourse segment purpose' (Grosz and Sidner, 1986; Polanyi, 1985). Appropriateness conditions for gestures or gazes do not seem to differ in principle from those for linguistic acts: a case of pointing where there is nothing to be pointed at may be likened to saying "The king is bald" where there is no king, or the use of a variable that has not been declared.

But if even gestures and gazes share the structural properties that we have seen are common to computer programs and linguistic acts, then we may wonder whether the properties involved are not simply those that *all* actions (or at least all rule-based actions) have in common, and indeed we feel that this is the right level of abstraction to think about these matters. An action – whether it be a communicative act, the execution of an assignment statement, a move in chess, or simply the movement of an arm – is performed in a given situation, typically changes that situation, and is dependent upon that situation for the change that it brings about. The effect of castling is dependent on the previous configuration on the board and your friend's stepping forward may result in his stepping on your toe in some situations but not in others. The order in which we perform our actions will typically effect the result, as we are all aware, and in many situations an action may be inappropriate – you cannot move your rook if this exposes your king.

The similarity between linguistic acts and moves in a game was stressed by the philosopher Ludwig Wittgenstein (Wittgenstein, 1953), but the first paper with immediate relevance to theoretical linguistics that explicitly took such similarities as its point of departure was the influential Lewis (1979). In this article, which refers to Wittgenstein in its title, Lewis compares conversation with baseball and says that 'with any stage in a well-run conversation, there are many things analogous to the components of a baseball score'. The latter is defined as a septuple of numbers: the number of home team runs, the number of runs that the visiting team has, the half (1 or 2), and so on. And in a similar way Lewis lets conversational score consist of several components: a component that keeps track of the presuppositions at any moment of conversation, a component that ranks the objects in the domain of discourse according to salience, the point of reference, the possible worlds that are accessible at any given point, and many others. Just as the rules of baseball tell us how the actions of the players alter the baseball score, the rules of conversation specify the kinematics of context change. If you mention a particular cat during conversation, for example, the rules bring it about that that cat will become salient and that a subsequent use of the definite description "the cat" will most likely refer to it. And if you say "John went to Amsterdam", the point of reference will move to Amsterdam as well, so that if you continue by saying "Mary came the following day", it will be understood that Mary came to Amsterdam and not to any other place.

Clearly, Lewis' picture of a conversational scoreboard that gets updated through linguistic acts of the participants in a conversation has much in common with our previous computational picture. In fact, we can imagine the conversational scoreboard to be a list of variables that the agents may operate on by means of programs according to certain rules. But a caveat is in order, for although there are important structural similarities between games and programs on the one hand and discourse on the other, there are of course also many features that are particular to conversation and our metaphor is not intended to make us blind to these. An example is the phenomenon of *accommodation* that Lewis describes. If at some point during a conversation a contribution is made that, in order to be appropriate, requires some item of conversational score to have a certain value, that item will automatically assume that value. For instance, if you say "Harry is guilty too" in a situation where the presupposition component of conversational score does not entail that someone else is guilty (or that Harry has some salient property besides being guilty), that very presupposition will immediately come into existence. This accommodation does not seem to have a parallel in games or computing: trying to divide by x after this variable has been set to 0 will not reset x to another value and, to take an example used by Lewis, a batter's walking to first base after only three balls will not make it the case that there were four balls after all.

Such examples, however, need not change the basic picture. That conversation and other cognitive activities have many special properties besides the ones that they have in virtue of being examples of rule-governed activities in general need not surprise us. Accommodation can be thought of as such a special property and we may model it as one of the particular effects that the programs that model communicative acts have; one of the effects that they have in virtue of being a special kind of program rather than just any program. It is the logic of the general properties that we are after in this paper.

The paper is divided into two sections. In Section 1, without any attempt at giving a complete rubrication, we shall give an overview of some important dynamic theories in linguistics and artificial intelligence which have emerged in the last two decades and we shall see how these fit into the general perspective on communication sketched in this introduction. In Section 2 we shall offer some more general logical considerations on dynamic phenomena, discussing various ways to model their logic and discussing how the logic that emerges is related to its classical static predecessors.

1. Some specific dynamic systems

1.1. The kinematics of context change: Stalnaker, Karttunen, Heim and Veltman

Certain things can only be said if other things are taken for granted. For example, if you say (1a) you signal that you take the truth of (1b) for granted, and a similar relation obtains between (2a) and (2b) and between (3a) and (3b). The (b)-sentences are presuppositions of the (a)-sentences and in a situation where the falsity of any of the (b)-sentences is established, the corresponding (a)-sentence cannot be uttered felicitously (for an overview of theories of presupposition cf. Soames (1989), Beaver (1996), this Handbook).

(1a) The king of France likes bagels.
(1b) France has a king.
(2a) All of Jack's children are fools.
(2b) Jack has children.
(3a) John has stopped seeing your wife.
(3b) John was seeing your wife.

Stalnaker (1974) gives a rough definition of the notion of presupposition which runs as follows: *a speaker presupposes that P at a given moment in a conversation just in case he is disposed to act, in his linguistic behavior, as if he takes the truth of P for granted, and as if he assumes that his audience recognizes that he is doing so.* Note that this defines the notion of presupposition not only relative to a speaker and the assumptions that he makes regarding his audience, but also relative to a moment in conversation. This leaves open the possibility that the set of propositions that can be assumed to be taken for granted changes during discourse and indeed this is what normally happens. When you say: 'John was seeing your wife', you may from that moment on assume that your audience recognizes that you take it for granted that he did. Consequently, in order to be able to say (4) you need not assume in advance that your audience recognizes anything at all about your views on his wife's past fidelity; the necessary precondition for a felicitous uttering of the second conjunct will be in force from the moment on that the first conjunct has been uttered, regardless of the assumptions that were made beforehand.

(4) John was seeing your wife but he has stopped doing so.
(5) If France has a king, then the king of France likes bagels.
(6) Either Jack has no children or all of his children are fools.
(7) The king of France does not like bagels.

In (5) and in (6) something similar happens. If a speaker utters a conditional, his audience can be assumed to take the truth of the antecedent for granted during the evaluation of the consequent and hence a speaker need not presuppose that France has a king in order to utter (5) in a felicitous way. Similarly, when evaluating the second part of a disjunction, a hearer will conventionally take the falsity of the first part for granted and so (6) can be uttered by someone who does not presuppose that Jack has children. The presuppositions that a speaker must make in order to make a felicitous contribution to discourse with a negated sentence on the other hand do not seem to differ from those of the sentence itself and so (7) simply requires (1b) to be presupposed.

Such regularities suggest the possibility of calculating which presuppositions are in force at any given moment during the evaluation of a sentence and indeed rules for calculating these are given in (Karttunen, 1974). Let us call the set of sentences C that are being presupposed at the start of the evaluation of a given sentence S the *initial context* of S. Then we can assign local contexts $\mathrm{LC}(S')$ to all subclauses S' of S by letting $\mathrm{LC}(S) = C$ and, proceeding in a top-down fashion, by assigning local contexts to the proper subclauses of S with the help of the following rules.

(i) $\mathrm{LC}(\text{not}\, S) = C \Rightarrow \mathrm{LC}(S) = C$,
(ii) $\mathrm{LC}(\text{if } S \text{ then } S') = C \Rightarrow \mathrm{LC}(S) = C \;\&\; \mathrm{LC}(S') = C \cup \{S\}$,
(iii) $\mathrm{LC}(S \text{ and } S') = C \Rightarrow \mathrm{LC}(S) = C \;\&\; \mathrm{LC}(S') = C \cup \{S\}$,
(iv) $\mathrm{LC}(S \text{ or } S') = C \Rightarrow \mathrm{LC}(S) = C \;\&\; \mathrm{LC}(S') = C \cup \{\text{not } S\}$.

The local context of a clause consists of the presuppositions that are in force at the time the clause is uttered. The rules allow us to compute e.g. the local context of the first occurrence of S' in 'if (S and S') then (S'' or S')' as $C \cup \{S\}$, where C is the initial context, and the local context of the second occurrence of this sentence can be computed to be $C \cup \{S \text{ and } S',\ \text{not } S''\}$.

A speaker who presupposes an initial set of sentences C is now predicted to be able to utter a sentence S felicitously just in case the local context of each subclause of S entails all presuppositions that are triggered at the level of that subclause. If this is the case we say that C *admits* or *satisfies the presuppositions of* S. Since, e.g., C need not entail that Jack has children in order to admit (6) it is predicted that a speaker need not presuppose that he has in order to be able to make a suitable contribution to discourse with the help of this sentence.

Rules (i)–(iv) only allow us to compute the admittance conditions of sentences that are built from atomic clauses with the usual propositional connectives, but Karttunen also extends the theory to sentences constructed with complementizable verbs. The latter are divided into three: (a) verbs of saying such as *say, mention, warn, announce* and the like, which are called *plugs*; (b) verbs such as *believe, fear, think, doubt* and *want,* which are *filters*; and (c) verbs such as *know, regret, understand* and *force,* which are *holes.* Three extra rules are needed for assigning local contexts to the subclauses of sentences containing these constructions.

(v) $\mathrm{LC}(NP\ V_{\mathrm{plug}}S) = C \Rightarrow \mathrm{LC}(S) = \{\bot\}$,

(vi) $\mathrm{LC}(NP\ V_{\mathrm{filter}}S) = C \Rightarrow \mathrm{LC}(S) = \{S' \mid NP\ \textit{believes}\ S' \in C\}$,

(vii) $\mathrm{LC}(NP\ V_{\mathrm{hole}}S) = C \Rightarrow \mathrm{LC}(S) = C$.

For example, in (8) the local context for 'the king of France announced that John had stopped seeing his wife' is simply the initial context C, and so a speaker who is to utter (8) should presuppose that there is a king. But it need not be presupposed that John was seeing Bill's wife since the local context for the complement of *announce* is simply the falsum $\bot$, from which the required presupposition follows of course. With respect to (9) it is predicted that the initial context must entail that Sue believes there to be a king of France and that she believes that Jack has children for the utterance to be felicitous.

(8) Joe forced the king of France to announce that John had stopped seeing Bill's wife.

(9) Sue doubts that the king of France regrets that all of Jack's children are fools.

Karttunen's rules for the admittance conditions of a sentence are completely independent from the rules that determine its truth conditions (a feature of the theory criticized in (Gazdar, 1979)), but Heim (1983a) shows that there is an intimate connection. Many authors (e.g., Stalnaker, 1979) had already observed that a sequence of sentences $S_1, \ldots, S_n$ suggests a dynamic view of shrinking sets of possibilities $[S_1]$, $[S_1] \cap [S_2]$, $\ldots$, $[S_1] \cap \cdots \cap [S_n]$, where each $[S_i]$ denotes the possibilities that are compatible with sentence S_i. The idea is illustrated by the game of *Master Mind*, where some initial space of possibilities for a hidden sequence of colored pegs is reduced by successive answers to one's guesses, encodable in conjunctions of propositions like "either the green peg is in its correct position or the blue one is". Complete information corresponds to the case where just one possibility is left. Identifying the possibilities that are still open at any point with the local context C, we may let the *context change potential* $\|S\|$ of a sentence S be defined as the function that assigns $C \cap [S]$ to any C. Processing $S_1, \ldots, S_n$ will then reduce an initial context C to $\|S_1\| \circ \cdots \circ \|S_n\|(C)$, where $\circ$ denotes composition of functions.

This last set-up defines the context change potential of a sentence in terms of its truth conditions, but Heim takes the more radical approach of defining truth conditions in terms of context change potentials. The context change potential of a complex expression in her theory is a function of the context change potentials of its parts. In particular, she dynamicizes the interpretation of the propositional connectives by giving the following clauses for negation and implication.[1]

$$\|\text{not } S\|(C) = C - \|S\|(C),$$
$$\|\text{if } S \text{ then } S'\|(C) = C - (\|S\|(C) - \|S'\|(\|S\|(C)).$$

The functions $\|S\|$ considered here may be undefined on contexts C where the presuppositions of S fail to hold and it is to be understood that if an argument of a function is undefined, the value of that function also is. For example, $\|\text{if } S \text{ then } S'\|(C)$ is defined if and only if both $\|S\|(C)$ and $\|S'\|(\|S\|(C))$ are. This means that C acts as a local context of S, while $\|S\|(C)$ is the local context of S'. The local context for S in $\|\text{not } S\|(C)$ simply is C. Essentially then, Karttunen's local contexts for a sentence can be derived from the definition of its context change potential, but the definition also determines the sentence's truth conditions, as we may define S to be *true* in a point i iff $\|S\|(\{i\}) = \{i\}$ and *false* in i iff $\|S\|(\{i\}) = \emptyset$.[2] For sentences not containing any presupposition this is just the standard notion, but a sentence S may be neither true nor false in i if $\|S\|(\{i\})$ is undefined.

Heim's idea suggests adding a two-place presupposition connective / to the syntax of propositional logic, where φ/ψ is to mean that ψ holds but that φ is presupposed.[3] We shall interpret the resulting system dynamically, letting contexts be sets of ordinary valuations V, and defining context change potentials as follows.

(i) $\|p\|(C) = C \cap \{V \mid V(p) = 1\}$ if p is atomic,
(ii) $\|\neg\varphi\|(C) = C - \|\varphi\|(C)$,
(iii) $\|\varphi \wedge \psi\|(C) = \|\psi\|(\|\varphi\|(C))$,
(iv) $\|\varphi/\psi\|(C) = \|\psi\|(C)$ if $\|\varphi\|(C) = C$,
$= \text{undefined otherwise.}$

The demand that $\|\varphi\|(C) = C$ is a way to express admittance of φ by the context C (compare the notion of *acceptance* in (Veltman, 1991)). Again, it is to be understood that if an argument of a function is undefined, the value of that function also is. Implication and disjunction can be defined as usual, i.e. $\varphi \to \psi$ is to abbreviate $\neg(\varphi \wedge \neg\psi)$ and $\varphi \vee \psi$ is short for $\neg\varphi \to \psi$. The reader is invited to verify that the resulting logic gives us exactly the same admittance conditions as we had in (the propositional part of) Karttunen's theory. In particular, we may formalize sentences (4), (5) and (6) as $p \wedge (p/q)$, $p \to (p/q)$ and $\neg p \vee (p/q)$ respectively and see that these are admitted by any context.

---

[1] Heim writes $C + S$ where we prefer $\|S\|(C)$.

[2] Heim (1983a) and Heim (1982, p. 330) let a context (or a file) be true iff it is non-empty. A sentence S is then stipulated to be true with respect to a given C if $\|S\|(C)$ is true, and false with respect to C if C is true and $\|S\|(C)$ is false. The case where both C and $\|S\|(C)$ are false is not covered. Heim notices this and in (Heim, 1982) makes an effort to defend the definition. The present definition is more limited than Heim's original one, since it essentially instantiates C as $\{i\}$. But truth in i is always defined in our definition and the definition serves its purpose of showing that classical truth conditions can be derived from context change potentials.

[3] See Beaver (1992) for a unary presupposition connective ∂ which is interdefinable with /.

This then is a version of propositional logic which supports presuppositions and is truly dynamic, as its fundamental semantic notion is that of context change potential rather than truth. The reader be warned though that an alternative static definition gives exactly the same results. To see this, define the *positive extension* $[\varphi]^+$ and the *negative extension* $[\varphi]^-$ of each sentence φ as follows.

(i′) $[p]^+ = \{V \mid V(p) = 1\}$, $[p]^- = \{V \mid V(p) = 0\}$.

(ii′) $[\neg\varphi]^+ = [\varphi]^-$, $[\neg\varphi]^- = [\varphi]^+$.

(iii′) $[\varphi \wedge \psi]^+ = [\varphi]^+ \cap [\psi]^+$, $[\varphi \wedge \psi]^- = [\varphi]^- \cup ([\varphi]^+ \cap [\psi]^-)$.

(iv′) $[\varphi/\psi]^+ = [\varphi]^+ \cap [\psi]^+$, $[\varphi/\psi]^- = [\varphi]^+ \cap [\psi]^-$.

The connectives $\neg$ and $\wedge$ are essentially treated as in (Peters, 1975) here (see also Karttunen and Peters, 1979), while/is the so-called *transplication* of Blamey (1986). An induction on the complexity of φ will show for any C (a) that $\|\varphi\|(C)$ is defined iff $C \subseteq [\varphi]^+ \cup [\varphi]^-$ and (b) that $\|\varphi\|(C) = C \cap [\varphi]^+$ if $\|\varphi\|(C)$ is defined. This means that Heim's logic is not essentially dynamic after all, even if its dynamic formulation is certainly natural.

Essentially dynamic operators do exist, however. Let us call a total unary function F on some power set *continuous* if it commutes with arbitrary unions of its arguments, i.e. if for any indexed set $\{C_i \mid i \in I\}$ it holds that $\cup\{F(C_i) \mid i \in I\} = F(\cup\{C_i \mid i \in I\})$. Call F *introspective* if $F(C) \subseteq C$ for any C. Van Benthem (1986) shows that these two properties give a necessary and sufficient criterion for an operator to be static: F is continuous and introspective if and only if there is some P such that $F(C) = C \cap P$ for all C (see also Groenendijk, Stokhof and Veltman, 1996). This means that an essentially dynamic operator must either not be continuous or not be introspective. A key example of a non-continuous operator is Veltman's (1991) epistemic *might* in a theory called *Update Semantics*. A minimal version of Veltman's system can be obtained by taking propositional modal logic and interpreting it by adding the following clause to (i)–(iii) above.

$$\begin{aligned} \|\diamond\varphi\|(C) &= \emptyset \quad \text{if } \|\varphi\|(C) = \emptyset, \\ &\ C \quad \text{otherwise.} \end{aligned}$$

The operator helps explain the difference between the acceptability of discourses such as (10) and (11).

(10) Maybe it is raining. ... It is not raining.
(11) It is not raining. ... # Maybe it is raining.

A naive translation into modal logic would make this into the commutative pair $\diamond r \wedge \neg r$, $\neg r \wedge \diamond r$. But dynamically, there is a difference. In (10) the initial state can still be consistently updated with the information that it is raining. Only after the second sentence is processed this possibility is cut off. In (11), however, the information that it is not raining has been added at the start, after which the test for possibility of raining will fail. This modality is no longer a continuous function, and it does not reduce to classical propositions in an obvious way. Nevertheless, there are still strong connections with classical systems. Van Benthem (1988) provides a translation into monadic predicate logic computing the update transitions, and Van Eijck and De Vries (1995) improve this to a translation into the modal logic S5, where $\diamond$ behaves like a modality after all. This means that these systems are still highly decidable.

In addition to mere elimination of possibilities the update framework also supports other forms of movement through its phase space. A phrase like *unless* φ, for instance, may call for enlargement of the current state by reinstating those earlier situations where φ held. Other plausible revision operators which are not introspective in the sense given above are not hard to come by.

Clearly the picture of updating information that is sketched here, with contexts or information states being flatly equated with sets of valuations, gives an extremely simplified model of what goes on in actual natural language understanding and it is worthwhile to look for subtler definitions of the notion of information state and for operations on information states subtler than just taking away possibilities or adding them. Assertions, for example, may not only change our views as to which things are possible, they may also upgrade our preferences between possibilities, i.e. change our views as to which possibilities are more likely than others. The latter phenomenon may be represented in terms of preference relations between models, as it is currently done in Artificial Intelligence (Shoham, 1988) in a tradition that derives from Lewis's possible worlds semantics for conditional logic (cf. Lewis, 1973; Veltman, 1985). For instance, processing a conditional default rule *if A, then B* need not mean that any exceptions (i.e. A & *not* B worlds) are forcibly removed, but rather that the latter are downgraded in some sense. This idea has been proposed in (Spohn, 1988; Boutilier, 1993; Boutilier and Goldszmidt, 1993) – and most extensively, for natural language, in (Veltman, 1991). In the latter system, static operators may model adverbs like *presumably* or *normally*, whereas a default conditional leads to a change in expectation patterns. To simplify matters, in what follows, φ, ψ are classical formulas. States C now consist of a set of worlds plus a preference order $\leqslant$ over them, forming a so-called *expectation pattern*. Maximally preferred worlds in such patterns are called *normal*. Incoming propositions may either change the former 'factual' component, or the latter (or both). For instance, given C and φ we may define the upgrade C_φ as that expectation pattern which has the same factual component as C, but whose preference relation consists of $\leqslant$ with all pairs $\langle w, v\rangle$ taken out in which we have $v \models \varphi$ without $w \models \varphi$.

$$\begin{aligned}
\|\textit{normally } \varphi\|(C) &= C_\varphi \quad \text{if } \varphi \text{ is consistent with some normal world,} \\
& \emptyset \quad \text{otherwise.} \\
\|\textit{presumably } \varphi\|(C) &= C \quad \text{if } \varphi \text{ holds in all maximally preferred situations in } C, \\
& \emptyset \quad \text{otherwise.}
\end{aligned}$$

A much more complicated explication takes care of the binary operator *if* φ*, then* ψ. Cf. Veltman (1991) for details, basic theory and applications of the resulting system. In particular, this paper provides a systematic comparison of the predictions of this system against intuitions about natural default reasoning. A more abstract perspective on update semantics is provided in (Van Benthem, Van Eijck and Frolova, 1993), which also includes connections with dynamized versions of conditional logic.

1.2. Change of assignments: Heim, Kamp, Groenendijk and Stokhof

A person who is reading a text must keep track of the items that are being introduced, since these items may be referred to again at a later point. The first sentence of text (12), for example, requires its reader to set up *discourse referents* (the term and the idea are from (Karttunen, 1976)) for the indefinite noun phrases *a woman* and *a cat*. The anaphoric pronoun *it* in the second sentence can then be interpreted as picking up the discourse referent that was introduced for *a cat* and the pronoun *her* may pick up the referent for *a woman*. Thus, while you are reading, not only the set of sentences that you can be assumed to take for granted changes, but your set of discourse referents grows as well. This latter growth gives us another example of contextual change.

(12) A woman catches a cat. It scratches her.

There are many semantic theories that use this kind of change to explain the possibilities and impossibilities of anaphoric linking in natural language. Here we shall briefly discuss three important ones, *File Change Semantics* (FCS, Heim, 1982, 1983b), *Discourse Representation Theory* (DRT, Kamp, 1981; Kamp and Reyle, 1993; Van Eijck and Kamp, 1996; this Handbook), and *Dynamic Predicate Logic* (DPL, Groenendijk and Stokhof, 1991). The first two of these theories were formulated independently in the beginning of the eighties, address roughly the same questions and make roughly the same predictions (see also Seuren, 1975, 1985), the third was formulated at a later time and differs mainly from the first and second from a methodological point of view.

1.2.1. File change semantics

The basic metaphor underlying Heim's theory is a comparison between the reader of a text and a clerk who has to keep track of all that has been said by means of a file of cards. Each card in the file stands for a discourse referent and the information that is written on the cards tells us what we have learned about this discourse referent thus far. Reading text (12), for example, the clerk would first have to make a card for the indefinite noun phrase *a woman*.

x_1
x_1 is a woman

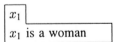

His next step would be to set up a card for *a cat*. His file now looks as follows.

x_1
x_1 is a woman

x_2
x_2 is a cat

The information that the woman catches the cat is now written upon both cards,

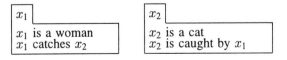

x_1
x_1 is a woman x_1 catches x_2

x_2
x_2 is a cat x_2 is caught by x_1

and finally the second sentence is interpreted. *It* is interpreted as x_2 and *her* is identified with x_1. This leads to the following file.

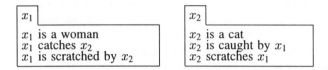

x_1
x_1 is a woman
x_1 catches x_2
x_1 is scratched by x_2

x_2
x_2 is a cat
x_2 is caught by x_1
x_2 scratches x_1

In this way our clerk proceeds, setting up a new card for each indefinite noun phrase that he encounters and identifying each definite noun phrase with a card that was already there. A file is said to be *true* if there is some way of assigning objects to the discourse referents occurring in it such that all the statements on the cards come out true, i.e. a file is true (in a given model) if there is some finite assignment satisfying all the open sentences in it, it is false if there is no such assignment. In fact, for the purposes at hand we can identify a file F with a pair $\langle Dom(F),\ Sat(F)\rangle$, where $Dom(F)$, the *domain* of F, is the set of all discourse referents (i.e. variables) occurring in F and $Sat(F)$, the *satisfaction set* of F, is the set of assignments with domain $Dom(F)$ which satisfy F. The meaning of a text is now identified with its *file change potential*, the way in which it alters the current file. Formally, it is a partial function from files to files.

Texts are connected to their file change potentials via a two-tier procedure in Heim's system. First, at the level of syntax, the text is associated with its so-called *logical form*. Logical forms are then interpreted compositionally by means of file change potentials. We shall look at each of these steps in a little detail.

The logical form of a sentence, which may be compared to the analysis tree that it gets in Montague Grammar, or to its logical form (LF) in contemporary generative grammar (cf. Higginbothan, this Handbook), is obtained from the syntactic structure of that sentence via three rules. The first, *NP Indexing*, assigns each NP a referential index. For ease of exposition we shall assume here that this index appears on the determiner of the noun phrase. If we apply NP Indexing to (14) (which for our purposes we may take to be the surface structure of (13)), for instance, (15) is a possible outcome. The second rule, *NP Prefixing*, adjoins every non-pronominal NP to S and leaves a coindexed empty NP behind. A possible result of this transformation when applied to (15) is (16), but another possibility (which will result in the wide scope reading for *a cat*) is (17). The last rule, *Quantifier Construal*, attaches each quantifier as a leftmost immediate constituent of S. Determiners such as *every, most* and *no* count as quantifiers in Heim's system, but the determiners *a* and *the* do not. The result of applying the transformation to (16) is (18) and applying it to (17) gives (19).

(13) Every woman catches a cat,

(14) $[_S[_{NP}\text{every woman}][_{VP}\text{catches}[_{NP}\text{a cat}]]]$,

(15) $[_S[_{NP}\text{every}_1\text{ woman}][_{VP}\text{catches}[_{NP}\text{a}_2\text{ cat}]]]$,

(16) $[_S[_{NP}\text{every}_1\text{ woman}][_S[_{NP}\text{a}_2\text{ cat}][_S e_1\text{ catches } e_2]]]$,

(17) $[_S[_{NP}\text{a}_2\text{ cat}][_S[_{NP}\text{every}_1\text{ woman}][_S e_1\text{ catches } e_2]]]$,

(18) $[_S\text{every}[_{NP}\text{–}_1\text{woman}][_S[_{NP}\text{a}_2\text{ cat}][_S e_1\text{ catches } e_2]]]$,

(19) $[_S[_{NP}a_2 \text{ cat}][_S\text{every}[_{NP-1}\text{woman}][_S e_1 \text{ catches } e_2]]]$.

The logical form of a text consisting of sentences $S_1, \ldots, S_n$ (in that order) will simply be $[_T\xi_1 \cdots \xi_n]$, where each of the ξ_i is the logical form of the corresponding S_i. For example, (20) will be the logical form of text (12).

(20) $[_T[_S[_{NP}a_1 \text{ woman}][_S[_{NP}a_2 \text{ cat}][_S e_1 \text{ catches } e_2]]][_S\text{it}_2 \text{ scratches her}_1]]$.

Logical forms such as (18), (19) and (20) can now be interpreted compositionally; each will be associated with a partial function from files to files. The smallest building blocks that the interpretation process will recognize are atoms such as $[_{NP}a_1 \text{ woman}]$, $[_{NP-1}\text{woman}]$, $[_S e_1 \text{ catches } e_2]$ and $[_S\text{it}_2 \text{ cratches her}_1]$, all of the form $[x_{i_1} R x_{i_2} \cdots x_{i_n}]$, with definite and indefinite determiners, pronouns, empty NP's and the trace – identified with variables x. We shall assume that indefinite determiners and the trace – carry a feature [−def] and that the other variables are [+def]. The following condition gives us the domain of the file change potential $\|[x_{i_1} R x_{i_2} \cdots x_{i_n}]\|$.

(i[a]) $\|[x_{i_1} R x_{i_2} \cdots x_{i_n}]\|(F)$ is defined iff for each x_{i_k} $(1 \leqslant k \leqslant n)$:
(Novelty) if x_{i_k} is [–def] then $x_{i_k} \notin \mathit{Dom}(F)$ and
(Familiarity) if x_{i_k} is [+def] then $x_{i_k} \in \mathit{Dom}(F)$.

This requirement, which Heim calls the *Novelty/Familiarity Condition*, corresponds to the file clerk's instruction to make a new card whenever he encounters an indefinite noun phrase but to update an old card whenever he encounters a definite NP.

In order to define what $\|[x_{i_1} R x_{i_2} \cdots x_{i_n}]\|(F)$ is in case the Novelty/Familiarity requirement is met, we suppose that a first-order model $M = \langle D, I\rangle$ that interprets the predicates of our language is given and stipulate the following.

(i[b]) If $\|[x_{i_1} R x_{i_2} \cdots x_{i_n}]\|(F)$ is defined then
$\mathit{Dom}(\|[x_{i_1} R x_{i_2} \cdots x_{i_n}]\|(F)) = \mathit{Dom}(F) \cup \{x_{i_1}, \ldots, x_{i_n}\}$
$\mathit{Sat}(\|[x_{i_1} R x_{i_2} \cdots x_{i_n}]\|(F)) = \{a \mid \mathit{dom}(a) = \mathit{Dom}(F) \cup \{x_{i_1}, \ldots, x_{i_n}\}$ &
$\exists b \subseteq a$: $b \in \mathit{Sat}(F)$ & $\langle a(x_{i_1}), \ldots, a(x_{i_n})\rangle \in I(R)\}$.

For example, if we apply $\|[_{NP}a_1 \text{ woman}]\|$ to the empty file $\langle\emptyset, \{\emptyset\}\rangle$, i.e. the file with empty domain and satisfaction set $\{\emptyset\}$, we obtain the file with domain $\{x_1\}$ and satisfaction set (21). If we apply $\|[_{NP}a_2 \text{ cat}]\|$ to the latter we get (22) as our new satisfaction set and $\{x_1, x_2\}$ as the new domain. Applying $\|[_S e_1 \text{ catches } e_2]\|$ to this file sets the satisfaction set to (23) and leaves the domain as it is. A last application of $\|[_S\text{it}_2 \text{ scratches her}_1]\|$ changes the satisfaction set to (24). Of course this set is non-empty if and only if (25) is true.

(21) $\{\{\langle x_1, d'\rangle\} \mid d' \in I(\text{woman})\}$,
(22) $\{\{\langle x_1, d'\rangle, \langle x_2, d''\rangle\} \mid d' \in I(\text{woman})\ \&\ d'' \in I(\text{cat})\}$,
(23) $\{\{\langle x_1, d'\rangle, \langle x_2, d''\rangle\} \mid d' \in I(\text{woman})\ \&\ d'' \in I(\text{cat})\ \&\ \langle d', d''\rangle \in I(\text{catches})\}$,
(24) $\{\{\langle x_1, d'\rangle, \langle x_2, d''\rangle\} \mid d' \in I(\text{woman})\ \&\ d'' \in I(\text{cat})\ \&\ \langle d', d''\rangle \in I(\text{catches})\ \&$
$\langle d'', d'\rangle \in I(\text{scratches})\}$,

(25) $\exists x_1 x_2(\text{woman } x_1 \wedge \text{cat } x_2 \wedge \text{catches } x_1 x_2 \wedge \text{scratches } x_2 x_1)$.

Thus by successively applying the atoms of (20) in a left-to-right fashion we have obtained its satisfaction set and thereby its truth conditions. Indeed, the general rule for obtaining the file change potential of two or more juxtaposed elements from the file change potentials of those elements is simply functional composition.

(ii) $\|[\xi_1 \cdots \xi_n]\|(F) = \|\xi_1\| \circ \cdots \circ \|\xi_n\|(F)$.

Note that the interpretation process of (20) would have broken down if $[_{\text{NP}}\text{a}_2 \text{ cat}]$ would have been replaced by $[_{\text{NP}}\text{a}_1 \text{ cat}]$ (a violation of the Novelty condition) or if, say, it_2 would have been replaced by it_6, which would violate Familiarity. Thus some ways to index NPs lead to uninterpretability.

With the help of rules (i) and (ii) we can only interpret purely existential texts; universals are treated somewhat differently. While an indefinite makes the domain of the current file grow, application of a universal sentence leaves it as it is. On the other hand, in general it will cause the satisfaction set to decrease. The following definition gives us the file change potential of a universal sentence.

(iii) $\mathit{Dom}(\|[\text{every } \xi\theta]\|(F)) = \mathit{Dom}(F)$,
$\mathit{Sat}(\|[\text{every } \xi\theta]\|(F)) = \{a \in \mathit{Sat}(F) \mid \forall b \supseteq a\colon\ b \in \mathit{Sat}(\|\xi\|(F)) \rightarrow$
$\exists c \supseteq b\colon\ c \in \mathit{Sat}(\|\xi\| \circ \|\theta\|(F))\}$.

Here it is understood that $\|[\text{every } \xi\theta]\|(F)$ is undefined iff $\|\xi\| \circ \|\theta\|(F)$ is. Applying this rule we can find truth conditions for logical forms (18) and (19): as the reader may verify, the value of $\|(18)\|$ applied to the empty file will have a non-empty satisfaction set if and only if (26) is true, and similarly $\mathit{Sat}(\|(19)\|(\langle\emptyset, \{\emptyset\}\rangle))$ will be non-empty iff (27) holds. A crucial difference between these two readings is their impact on the domain of any given file. While $\mathit{Dom}(\|(18)\|(F))$ will simply be $\mathit{Dom}(F)$ for any F, $\mathit{Dom}(\|(19)\|(F))$ will be $\mathit{Dom}(F) \cup \{x_2\}$, which makes it possible to pick up the discourse referent connected with *a cat* at a later stage in the conversation. And indeed (28) does not violate the Novelty/Familiarity constraint, provided that its first sentence is analyzed along the lines of (19), not along the lines of (18).

(26) $\forall x_1(\text{woman } x_1 \rightarrow \exists x_2(\text{cat } x_2 \wedge \text{catches } x_1 x_2))$.
(27) $\exists x_2(\text{cat } x_2 \wedge \forall x_1(\text{woman } x_1 \rightarrow \text{catches } x_1 x_2))$.
(28) Every_1 woman caught a_2 cat. The_2 cat scratched every_3 woman.

Thus rule (iii) predicts that a definite element can only be anaphorically related to an indefinite occurring within the scope of the quantifier *every* if the definite itself also occurs within that scope. If the first sentence of (28) is analyzed as (18), the universal quantifier blocks a coreferential interpretation of *a cat* and *the cat*, but in (29) we see that an anaphoric link between *a donkey* and *it* is possible since both elements are within the scope of *every* and, as the reader may verify, the file change potential of (30) is defined and leads to the truth conditions of (31).[4]

(29) Every farmer who owns a donkey beats it,

[4] Here $\|\text{who}\|$ may be interpreted as the identity function.

(30) $[_{S}\text{every}[_{NP}[_{NP-1}\text{ farmer}][_{S'}\text{who}[_{S}[_{NP}\text{a}_2\text{ donkey}][_{S}e_1\text{ owns }e_2]]]]\ [_{S}e_1\text{ beats it}_2]]$

(31) $\forall x_1 x_2((\text{farmer } x_1 \wedge \text{donkey } x_2 \wedge \text{owns } x_1 x_2) \rightarrow \text{beats } x_1 x_2)$.

(29) of course is one of Geach's famous "donkey" sentences and its treatment may serve to illustrate another important feature of Heim's system. Since rule (iii) involves a universal quantification over all extensions of the finite assignment a satisfying $\|\xi\|(F)$ and since indefinites in ξ will increase the domain of F, those indefinites will all be interpreted universally, not existentially. For a similar reason indefinites occurring in θ will get an existential interpretation. This explains the chameleontic behaviour of indefinites: if they are not within the scope of any operator they are interpreted existentially, within the "restrictor" ξ of a universal quantifier or the antecedent of an implication they behave universally, but occurring within the "nuclear scope" θ of a universal quantifier or within the consequent of an implication they are existentials again.

1.2.2. Discourse representation theory

The basic ideas of Heim's FCS and Kamp's Discourse Representation Theory (DRT) are very much the same. While in Heim's theory the reader or hearer of a text represents the information that he has obtained by means of a file, DRT lets him keep track of that information with the help of a *Discourse Representation Structure* (a *DRS* or *box* for short) and, just as a file is defined to be true iff some assignment satisfies all the open sentences in it, a box is also defined to be true iff it is satisfied by some assignment. Simple DRSs are much like files, be it that all information is written upon one card only. Thus the DRS corresponding to the first sentence of (12) is (32) and that corresponding to both sentences is (33). The variables written at the top of these boxes are called *discourse referents,* the open sentences underneath are called *conditions.*

(32)

$x_1 \quad x_2$
woman x_1 *cat* x_2 x_1 *catches* x_2

(33)

$x_1 \quad x_2$
woman x_1 *cat* x_2 x_1 *catches* x_2 x_2 *scratches* x_1

Boxes such as these are built from the discourses that they represent with the help of a *construction algorithm.* Box (32), for instance, can be obtained from the tree representing the surface structure of the first sentence in (12) by (a) putting this tree in an otherwise empty box and then (b) applying certain rules called *construction principles* until none of these principles is applicable any longer. Box (33) can then be obtained by extending (32) with a tree for the second sentence of the text and applying the construction principles again. A sentence can thus be interpreted as an instruction to update the current box, just as in FCS it can be interpreted as an instruction to change the current file.

Unlike Heim's files however, boxes can also directly represent universal information. (34), for instance, is a box that results from applying the construction algorithm to a tree for the surface structure of (13). It contains only one condition, an implication whose antecedent and consequent are themselves boxes, and it expresses that any way to satisfy the condition in the antecedent box can be extended to a way to satisfy the conditions in the consequent.

(34)
$$\boxed{\;\boxed{\begin{array}{c} x_1 \\ \\ \textit{woman } x_1 \end{array}} \Rightarrow \boxed{\begin{array}{c} x_2 \\ \\ \textit{cat } x_2 \\ x_1 \textit{ catches } x_2 \end{array}}\;}$$

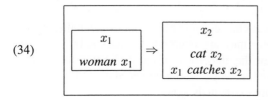

It would take us too far to spell out the construction principles that lead to boxes such as these in any detail here (see Kamp and Reyle (1993) for these), but it should be mentioned, firstly, that processing an indefinite noun phrase leads to the creation of a new discourse referent, and, secondly, that anaphoric pronouns must be linked to already existing discourse referents. However, not all existing discourse referents are *accessible* to a pronoun that is being processed at some level of embedding in the DRS. For example, no pronoun may be linked to a discourse referent that exists at some deeper level of embedding, a pronoun in the antecedent of an implication cannot be linked to a discourse referent in the consequent, and so on. With the help of such *accessibility conditions* DRT makes predictions about the possibilities and impossibilities of anaphoric linking that correspond to the predictions that are made by FCS by means of the Novelty/Familiarity condition.

While Discourse Representation Structures are being thought of as psychologically real, in the sense that a language user really creates representations analogous to them while interpreting a text, they also form the language of a logic that can be interpreted on first-order models in a more or less standard way. It is handy to linearize the syntax of this language. The following rules in Backus–Naur Form define the basic constructs, conditions (γ) and boxes (K), for the core part of DRT.

$$\gamma ::= Px \mid x_1 R x_2 \mid x_1 = x_2 \mid \neg K \mid K_1 \vee K_2 \mid K_1 \Rightarrow K_2,$$
$$K ::= [x_1 \cdots x_n \mid \gamma_1, \ldots, \gamma_m].$$

We can write (33) now more concisely as $[x_1 x_2 \mid \textit{woman } x_1,\ \textit{cat } x_2,\ x_1 \textit{ catches } x_2,\ x_2 \textit{ scratches } x_1]$ and (34) as $[\,\mid [x_1 \mid \textit{woman } x_1] \Rightarrow [x_2 \mid \textit{cat } x_2,\ x_1 \textit{ catches } x_2]]$. These, by the way, are examples of *closed* boxes, boxes containing no free discourse referents;[5] all boxes that result from the construction algorithm are closed.

The dynamic character of DRT does not only reside in the fact that the theory interprets sentences as instructions to change the current discourse representation, it also manifests itself in the formal evaluation of these discourse representations themselves.

[5] For the definition of a *free* discourse referent see Kamp and Reyle (1993).

For a discourse representation structure in its turn can very well be interpreted as an instruction to change the current context, contexts being formalized with the help of finite assignments here. Formally, we shall define the value $\|K\|^M$ of a box K on a first order model $M = \langle D, I\rangle$ (superscripts M will be suppressed) to be a binary relation between finite assignments, the idea being that if $\langle a, b\rangle \in \|K\|$, carrying out the instruction K with a as input may nondeterministically give us b as output.[6] The semantic value $\|\gamma\|$ of a condition γ will simply be a set of finite assignments for the given model. Clauses (i)–(iii) give a compositional definition of the intended meanings;[7] in the last clause we write $a[x_1 \cdots x_n]b$ for '$a \subseteq b$ and $dom(b) = dom(a) \cup \{x_1, \ldots, x_n\}$'.

(i) $\|Px\| = \{a \mid x \in dom(a)\ \&\ a(x) \in I(P)\}$,
$\|x_1 R x_2\| = \{a \mid x_1, x_2 \in dom(a)\ \&\ \langle a(x_1), a(x_2)\rangle \in I(R)\}$,
$\|x_1 = x_2\| = \{a \mid x_1, x_2 \in dom(a)\ \&\ a(x_1) = a(x_2)\}$.

(ii) $\|\neg K\| = \{a \mid \neg\exists b\ \langle a, b\rangle \in \|K\|\}$,
$\|K_1 \vee K_2\| = \{a \mid \exists b(\langle a, b\rangle \in \|K_1\| \vee \langle a, b\rangle \in \|K_2\|)\}$,
$\|K_1 \Rightarrow K_2\| = \{a \mid \forall b(\langle a, b\rangle \in \|K_1\| \rightarrow \exists c\ \langle b, c\rangle \in \|K_2\|)\}$.

(iii) $\|[x_1 \cdots x_n \mid \gamma_1, \ldots, \gamma_m]\| = \{\langle a, b\rangle \mid a[x_1 \cdots x_n]b\ \&\ b \in \|\gamma_1\| \cap \cdots \cap \|\gamma_m\|\}$.

A box K is defined to be *true in* a model M *under* an assignment a iff the domain of a consists of exactly those discourse referents that are free in K and there is an assignment b such that $\langle a, b\rangle \in \|K\|$. The reader may verify that the closed box (33) is true in any model iff (25) is, and that the truth conditions of (34) correspond to those of (26).

The semantic definition given here differs somewhat from the set-up in (Kamp and Reyle, 1993), but is in fact equivalent, as it is easy to show that a closed box is true in our set-up if and only if it is true in Kamp and Reyle's. A slightly different semantics for DRT is given in (Groenendijk and Stokhof, 1991). The Groenendijk and Stokhof semantics is obtained by letting a, b and c range over *total* assignments in the above definition and letting $a[x_1 \cdots x_n]b$ stand for '$a(y) = b(y)$ for all $y \notin \{x_1, \ldots, x_n\}$'. In later sections we will refer back to this definition as to the *total* semantics for DRT.

We have seen that DRT does not only predict certain possibilities of anaphoric linking, but, like Heim's FCS, also assigns truth conditions to the discourses that it considers. Both theories, moreover, to a certain extent fit within the framework of semantics that was laid out by Richard Montague in his 'Universal Grammar' (Montague, 1970). Both first replace the constructs of ordinary language by a 'disambiguated language', which is the language of logical forms in Heim's theory and the language of conditions and boxes in Kamp's case. The relation that connects ordinary language and unambiguous language (Montague's R) is given by a set of transformations in Heim's theory and a construction algorithm in Kamp's DRT. In both cases the 'disambiguated language' can be interpreted in a fully compositional way with the help of first-order models and assignments for these models.

---

[6] The first author to describe the dynamic potential of a discourse as a relation between finite variable assignments was Barwise in (Barwise, 1987), a paper which was presented at CSLI in the spring of 1984 and at the Lund meeting on generalized quantifiers in May 1985.

[7] The definition is formally equivalent to the one given in (Kamp and Reyle, 1993) but its form is inspired by the discussion in (Groenendijk and Stokhof, 1991). See especially Definition 26 of that paper.

1.2.3. Dynamic predicate logic

In an attempt to make the Kamp/Heim theory of discourse anaphora look even more like a conventional Montagovian theory, Jeroen Groenendijk and Martin Stokhof have published an alternative formulation called *Dynamic Predicate Logic* (DPL, Groenendijk and Stokhof, 1991), which offers a dynamic interpretation of the formulae of ordinary predicate logic and gives an interesting alternative to the Kamp/Heim approach.

The usual Tarski truth definition for predicate logic provides us with a three-place satisfaction relation $\models$ between models, formulae and assignments and we can identify the meaning of a formula in a model with the set of assignments that satisfy it in that model. But here too, the definition can be generalized so that the meaning of a formula is rendered as a binary relation between (total) assignments. The DPL definition runs as follows (we write $a[x]b$ for '$a(y) = b(y)$ for all $y \neq x$').

(i) $\|R(x_1, \ldots, x_n)\| = \{\langle a, a\rangle \mid \langle a(x_1), \ldots, a(x_n)\rangle \in I(R)\}$,
$\|x_1 = x_2\| = \{\langle a, a\rangle \mid a(x_1) = a(x_2)\}$.

(ii) $\|\neg\varphi\| = \{\langle a, a\rangle \mid \neg\exists b\ \langle a, b\rangle \in \|\varphi\|\}$,
$\|\varphi \vee \psi\| = \{\langle a, a\rangle \mid \exists b(\langle a, b\rangle \in \|\varphi\| \vee \langle a, b\rangle \in \|\psi\|)\}$,
$\|\varphi \to \psi\| = \{\langle a, a\rangle \mid \forall b(\langle a, b\rangle \in \|\varphi\| \to \exists c\ \langle b, c\rangle \in \|\psi\|)\}$,
$\|\varphi \wedge \psi\| = \{\langle a, c\rangle \mid \exists b(\langle a, b\rangle \in \|\varphi\|\ \&\ \langle b, c\rangle \in \|\psi\|)\}$.

(iii) $\|\exists x\varphi\| = \{\langle a, c\rangle \mid \exists b(a[x]b\ \&\ \langle b, c\rangle \in \|\varphi\|)\}$,
$\|\forall x\varphi\| = \{\langle a, a\rangle \mid \forall b(a[x]b \to \exists c\ \langle b, c\rangle \in \|\varphi\|)\}$.

A formula φ is defined to be *true under* an assignment a if $\langle a, b\rangle \in \|\varphi\|$ for some assignment b. Note that $\|\neg\varphi\|$ is given as the set of those $\langle a, a\rangle$ such that φ is not true under a, $\|\varphi \vee \psi\|$ as those $\langle a, a\rangle$ such that either φ or ψ is true under a. But the clause for implication is close to the corresponding DRT clause and conjunction is treated as relational composition. The value of $\exists x\varphi$ is in fact given as the relational composition of $\{\langle a, b\rangle \mid a[x]b\}$ (random assignment to x) and the value of φ; and $\forall x\varphi$ is treated as $\neg\exists x\neg\varphi$. Operators that have a semantics of the form $\{\langle a, a\rangle \mid \cdots\}$ are called *tests*.

By the associativity of relational composition we immediately see that $\exists x\varphi \wedge \psi$ is equivalent to $\exists x(\varphi \wedge \psi)$ in this set-up, *even if x is free in ψ*, and this enables Groenendijk and Stokhof to propose the following straightforward translation of text (12).

(35) $\exists x_1 x_2(\text{woman } x_1 \wedge \text{cat } x_2 \wedge \text{catches } x_1 x_2) \wedge \text{scratches } x_2 x_1$.

The first conjunct of this formula clearly corresponds to the first sentence of the text that is formalized, the second conjunct to the second sentence. But unlike in ordinary predicate logic, (35) is equivalent with (26), and since it is provable that truth conditions in DPL and ordinary logic correspond for closed sentences, the text gets the right truth conditions. In a similar way, since $\exists x\varphi \to \psi$ is equivalent with $\forall x(\varphi \to \psi)$, as the reader may verify, (29) can be rendered as (36), which is equivalent with (37) and hence with (31).

(36) $\forall x_1((\text{farmer } x_1 \wedge \exists x_2(\text{donkey } x_2 \wedge \text{owns } x_1 x_2)) \to \text{beats } x_1 x_2)$.

(37) $\forall x_1(\exists x_2(\text{farmer } x_1 \wedge \text{donkey } x_2 \wedge \text{owns } x_1 x_2) \to \text{beats } x_1 x_2)$.

Thus it is possible to give rather straightforward translations of texts into predicate logical formulae in DPL, while at the same time accounting for the possibility of anaphora between a pronoun and an indefinite in a preceding sentence, or between a pronoun in the consequence of an implication and an indefinite in the antecedent. Anaphoric linking is predicted to be impossible if any test intervenes. This conforms to the predictions that are made by Kamp and Heim's theories.

Extensions of DPL to dynamic theories of generalized quantifiers have been proposed in (Chierchia, 1988; Van Eijck and De Vries, 1992; Kanazawa, 1993b; Van der Does, 1992), and extensions to full type theories have been achieved in the Dynamic Montague Grammar of Groenendijk and Stokhof (1990), and the Compositional DRT of Muskens (1991, 1994, 1995a, 1995b) (see also Section 2.3.3). Extensions such as these raise the issue of systematic strategies of dynamization for existing systems of static semantics, which would somehow operate uniformly, while transforming the traditional semantic theory in systematic ways. For instance, in dynamic accounts of generalized quantifiers, a key role has been played by the fate of the Conservativity and Monotonicity principles that play such a prominent role in the standard theory (cf. Keenan and Westerståhl (1996), this Handbook).

Several variations have been investigated for the basic DPL framework. For instance, Van den Berg (1995) proposes a three-valued partial version, in which new operators appear (cf. also Beaver, 1992; Krahmer, 1995). This system allows for a distinction between 'false' transitions, such as staying in a state where an atomic test has failed, and merely 'inappropriate' ones, such as moving to a different state when testing. A more radical partialization, using analogies with partial functions in Recursion Theory, has been proposed in (Fernando, 1992). This will allow for a natural distinction between re-assignment to an old variable and pristine assignment to a new variable. Versions with still richer accounts of data structures, and thereby of the dynamic function of predicate-logical syntax, may be found in (Visser, 1994; Vermeulen, 1994).

1.2.4. Integrating dynamic predicate logic and update semantics

Natural language involves different dynamic mechanisms. For instance, DRT and DPL highlight changing anaphoric bindings, whereas Veltman's Update Semantics (US), described in Section 1.1 focuses on information flow and epistemic statements about its stages. Obviously, a combination of the two is desirable. There have been some technical obstacles to this endeavor, however, in that the two systems have different flavors of implementation. DPL involves an algebra of binary relations over assignments, and US rather a family of functions operating on sets of valuations. Various proposals have been made for a mathematical unification of the two, but the most sophisticated attempt is surely (Groenendijk, Stokhof and Veltman, 1996). The latter paper takes its empirical point of departure in the linguistic evidence which normally drives modal predicate logic. Here is a typical example. Consider the pair of sentences

(38) A man who might be wearing a blue sweater is walking in the park.
(39) A man is walking in the park. He might be wearing a blue sweater.

The relative clause in the first discourse expresses a property of the man introduced in the main clause: what we learn is that *he* might be wearing a blue sweater. But intuitively, Groenendijk, Stokhof and Veltman argue, this is not the function of the second sentence in the second discourse. The latter rather serves to express the possibility that some discourse individual introduced in the antecedent sentence might be wearing a blue sweater. A combined dynamic semantics will have to account for this. Since these two discourses are equivalent in standard DPL, some essential departure is needed from the latter system, in which antecedent existentials need no longer scope over free variables in succedents. The combined semantics is a more sophisticated follow-up to that of (Van Eijck and Cepparello, 1993), employing so-called 'referent systems' from (Vermeulen, 1994). In particular, the new information states consist of three components, namely: (1) an assignment of variables to 'pegs' (discourse individuals; as in (Landman, 1986)), (2) an assignment of pegs to individuals in some standard domain, (3) a set of possible worlds over that domain (encoding the current range of descriptive uncertainty). Updating will now combine several processes: such as elimination of possibilities and enrichment of assignments. One noticeable feature of this approach is its treatment of the existential quantifier. In DPL, $\exists x$ is essentially a single instruction for performing a random assignment. Thus, in the current setting, it would denote an enrichment for a given state so as to include every possible assignment of objects to (the peg associated with) the variable x. A compound formula $\exists x\varphi$ will then denote the composition of this move with the ordinary update for φ. But this account will yield unintuitive results on a modal statement like $\exists x \diamond Px$: the resulting state may still contain assignments to x denoting objects which cannot have the property P. Therefore, the new proposal is to make $\exists x\varphi$ a syncategorematic operation after all, whose update instruction is as follows: "Take the union of all actions $x := d\,; \varphi$ for all objects d in the domain". This will make an update for $\exists x \diamond Px$ end up with x assigned only to those objects which have P in some available possible world. In this richer setting, one can also review the vast semantic evidence surrounding the usual puzzles of modality and identity in the philosophical literature, and propose a dynamic cut on their solution. (Groenendijk, Stokhof and Veltman (1996) contains further innovations in its discussion of consistency and discourse coherence, which we must forego here.) Whatever technical theory exists for this paradigm is contained in this single reference (but cf. Cepparello, 1995).

1.3. Change of attentional state: Grosz and Sidner

Discourse Representation Theory models the way in which anaphoric elements can pick up accessible discourse referents, it tells us which referents are accessible at any given point of discourse, but it tells us little about the question which referent must be chosen if more than one of them is accessible. There are of course obvious linguistic clues that restrict the range of suitable antecedents for any given anaphoric element, such as the constraint that antecedent and anaphoric element must agree in gender and number, but it is also believed that the structure of discourse itself puts important further constraints on the use of referring expressions.

Thus theories of discourse structure, such as the ones discussed in (Polanyi, 1985; Scha and Polanyi, 1988; Grosz and Sidner, 1986), are a natural complement to the theories discussed in Section 1.2. Since these discourse theories are also good examples of dynamic modeling of natural language phenomena in linguistics, we shall have a closer look at one of them here. Of the theories mentioned, we shall choose Grosz and Sidner's, being the one that is most explicitly dynamic.

(a) E: First you have to remove the flywheel.
(b) A: How do I remove the flywheel?
(c) E: First, loosen the two allen head setscrews holding it to the shaft, then pull it off.
(d) A: OK.
(e) I can only find one screw. Where's the other one?
(f) E: On the hub of the flywheel.
(g) A: That's the one I found. Where's the other one?
(h) E: About ninety degrees around the hub from the first one.
(i) A: I don't understand. I can only find one. Oh wait, yes I think I was on the wrong wheel.
(j) E: Show me what you are doing.
(k) A: I was on the wrong wheel and I can find them both now.
DS2
(l) The tool I have is awkward. Is there another tool that I could use instead?
(m) E: Show me the tool you are using.
(n) A: OK.
(o) E: Are you sure you are using the right size key?
(p) A: I'll try some others.
(q) I found an angle I can get at it.
DS3
(r) The two screws are loose, but I'm having trouble getting the wheel off.
(s) E: Use the wheelpuller. Do you know how to use it?
(t) A: No.
(u) E: Do you know what it looks like?
(v) A: Yes.
(w) E: Show it to me please.
(x) A: OK.
(y) E: Good. Loosen the screw in the center and place the jaws around the hub of the wheel, then tighten the screw onto the center of the shaft. The wheel should slide off.
DS5 DS4 DS1

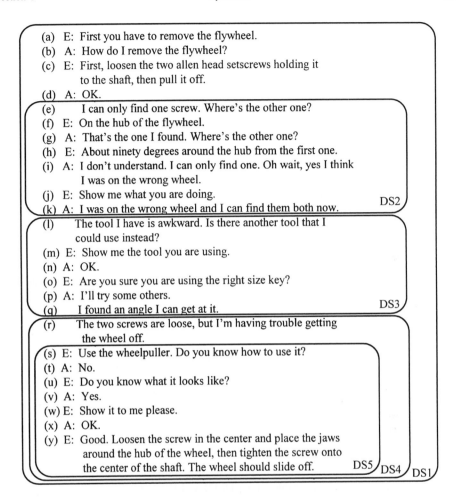

Fig. 1. A segment of a task oriented dialogue.

Grosz and Sidner distinguish three parts of discourse structure. The first of these, called *linguistic structure,* consists of a segmentation of any given discourse in various *discourse segments.* Experimental data suggest that a segmentation of this kind is present in discourses. Speakers, when asked to segment any given discourse, seem to do so more or less along the same lines. Moreover, the boundaries that are drawn between segments correspond to speech rate differences and differences in pause lengths when the text is read out aloud. There are also certain clue words that signal a discourse boundary. For example the expressions 'in the first place', 'in the second place' and 'anyway' are such clues. Changes in tense and aspect also indicate discourse boundaries.

In Figure 1 a segment of a dialogue between an expert (E) and an apprentice (A) is given and factored into further discourse segments. Each segment comes with a *discourse segment purpose* (DSP). The expert wants the apprentice to remove a flywheel and this,

DSP1:	E intends A to intend to remove the flywheel
DSP2:	A intends E to intend to tell him the location of the other setscrew
DSP3:	A intends E to intend to show him another tool
DSP4:	A intends E to intend to tell him how to get off the wheel
DSP5:	E intends A to know how to use the wheelpuller

Fig. 2. Discourse Segment Purposes connected to task oriented dialogue.

DSP1 dominates DSP2	DSP2 satisfaction-precedes DSP3
DSP1 dominates DSP3	DSP2 satisfaction-precedes DSP4
DSP1 dominates DSP4	DSP3 satisfaction-precedes DSP4
DSP4 dominates DSP5	

Fig. 3. Intentional structure for the task oriented dialogue.

or rather DSP1 in Figure 2, is the purpose of the discourse segment as a whole. The apprentice adopts the intention to remove the fly wheel, but in order to do this must perform certain subactions such as loosening screws and pulling off the wheel. In order to loosen the screws, he must first locate them, and, as it turns out that he can only find one, DSP2 is generated. This intention is connected to a discourse segment (DS2) that consists of utterances (e) to (k).

In the same manner two other discourse segment purposes that are connected to subtasks of the apprentice's task of removing the wheel come up, DSP3 and DSP4, and both intentions give rise to the creation of discourse segments (DS3 and DS4). The last, moreover, invokes DSP5 as a response from the expert, an intention related to DS5.

One discourse segment purpose may *dominate* another in the sense that satisfying the second segment's purpose provides part of the satisfaction of the first segment's purpose. For example, DSP4 in our example dominates DSP5. It may also occur that the satisfaction of one discourse segment purpose must precede another, it is then said to *satisfaction-precede* it. For example, since DSP2 and DSP3 both contribute to loosening the setscrews, DSP4 contributes to pulling off the wheel and, since world-knowledge tells us that the screws must be loosened before the wheel can be pulled off, it can be inferred that DSP2 and DSP3 satisfaction-precede DSP4. The relations of dominance and satisfaction-precedence constitute the second part of discourse structure which is identified by Grosz and Sidner, the *intentional state.* The intentional state connected with the discourse segment in Figure 1 consists of the seven statements given in Figure 3.

The third and last part of discourse structure, *attentional state,* is the part that is most truly dynamic. It consists of a stack of *focus spaces* containing the objects (discourse referents), properties, relations and discourse purposes that are salient at any given moment. Each focus space is connected to a discourse segment and contains its purpose. The closer a focus space is to the top of the stack, the more salient the objects in it are. Anaphoric expressions pick up the referent on the stack that is most salient, so if more than one focus space on the stack would contain, say, a pink elephant, then the definite description *the pink elephant* would refer to the elephant represented in the space that is nearer to the top of the stack.

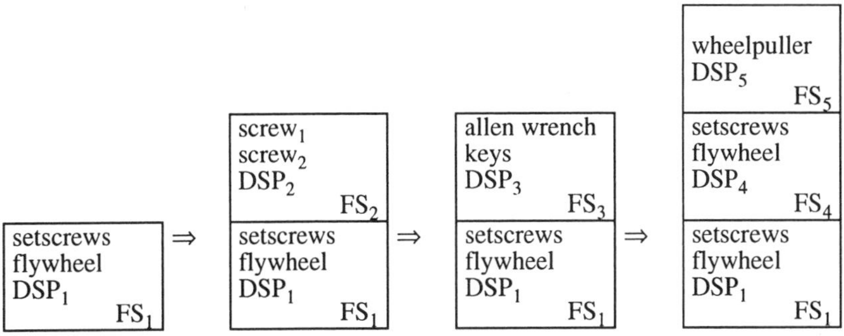

Fig. 4. Focus stack transitions leading up to utterance (y).

Change is brought about by pushing and popping the stack. Entering a discourse segment causes its focus space to be pushed onto the stack and leaving a segment causes its space to be popped. In Figure 4 a series of stacks leading up to the utterance in (y) is given. Note that the theory predicts that in DS5 no reference to the allen wrench is possible: its discourse referent was contained in FS3, which is popped from the stack at the time that DS5 is processed. Note also that the noun phrase *the screw in the center* refers to a screw on the wheelpuller, not to one of the two setscrews. Since the wheelpuller is in the focus space on top of the stack at the moment this noun phrase is uttered, its central screw is chosen as a referent instead of one of the setscrews that are in a lower focus space.

Two similarities strike us when we consider the Grosz and Sidner model of discourse. First there is a strong resemblance between the structure that the model assigns to ordinary discourse and the structure of programs in an imperative language such as PASCAL. The nested discourse segments of Figure 1 remind us of the nested loops and subloops that we find in a typical program. We can also compare the nested structure with the structure of procedures calling subroutines, which may in their turn also call subroutines etc. In this case the stack of focus spaces which constitutes attentional state finds its equivalent in the computer stack.

A second similarity that is to be noted is that between the structure of discourse and the structure of *proofs* in a natural deduction system. The discourse segments in figure 1 here compare to those fragments of a proof that start with the adoption of an assumption and end when that assumption is discharged. The *purpose* of such a segment may perhaps be compared with the conclusion it is intended to establish and there is a clear notion of *satisfaction-precedence* since one such segment may need the conclusion of another. That there is also a natural connection to the concept of a *stack* will be shown in the next section where we shall discuss the semantics of proofs.

1.4. Change of assumptions: Intuitionistic propositional logic in Zeinstra's style

Douglas Hofstadter, in his delightful (Hofstadter, 1980), gives an exposition of natural deduction systems using the idea of *fantasies*. Making an assumption is 'pushing into fantasy', discharging one is 'popping out of fantasy' in his terminology. Hofstadter's system has explicit push and pop operators, '[' and ']' respectively, and a simple derivation looks as follows.

[	push into fantasy,
p	assumption,
$\neg\neg p$	double negation rule,
]	pop out of fantasy.

The next step in this derivation would be an application of detachment (the 'fantasy rule' in Hofstadter's words) to obtain $p \to \neg\neg p$. It is usual of course to distinguish between the latter (object level) sentence and the (metalevel) derivation given above, which we shall write in linear form as $([p, \neg\neg p])$. For some purposes, however, one might want to have a system in which the distinction between metalevel entailment and object level implication is not made. Consider the following pair of texts.

(A) Suppose $x > 0$. Then $x + y > 0$.
(B) If $x > 0$, then $x + y > 0$.

The assertive production of (A) can be described as follows. First an assumption is introduced. Then a conclusion is drawn from it (possibly in combination with information derived from preceding text). Finally there is the hidden act of cancelling the assumption. The assertion of (B), on the other hand, on the classical account does not involve introducing, cancelling, etc. It is simply an utterance with assertive force of a sentence. What, then, are we to do with the strong intuition that (A) and (B) are 'assertively equivalent'?

The intuition that (A) and (B) should be treated on a par motivated (Zeinstra, 1990) to give a semantics for a simple propositional system which bases itself upon Hofstadter, has explicit push and pop operators, but retains the equivalence. The assertive utterance of a sentence is viewed – quite in the spirit of the more general dynamic program – as consisting of a sequence of all kinds of acts, and an utterance of *if* is taken as being just a variant of an utterance of *suppose*. Before we give an exposition of Zeinstra's logic, let us rehearse the Kripke semantics for the $\{\bot, \wedge, \to\}$ fragment of intuitionistic propositional logic (IPL$[\bot, \wedge, \to]$), as Zeinstra's system can be viewed as an extension of the latter. A *model* K for this logic is a triple $\langle W, \leqslant, V\rangle$ such that – in the present set-up – W, the set of worlds, contains the *absurd* world T; the relation $\leqslant$ is a reflexive and transitive ordering on W, such that $w \leqslant T$ for all $w \in W$; and V is a function sending propositional letters to subsets of W such that (a) $w \in V(p)$ implies $w' \in V(p)$ if $w \leqslant w'$ and (b) $T \in V(p)$ for each propositional letter p. The relation $w \models_K \varphi$ (φ is *true on* a model $K = \langle W, \leqslant, V\rangle$ *in* a world $w \in W$) is defined inductively as follows (we suppress subscripts K).

(i) $w \models p$ iff $w \in V(p)$, for propositional letters p,
(ii) $w \models \bot$ iff $w = T$,
(iii) $w \models \varphi \wedge \psi$ iff $w \models \varphi$ and $w \models \psi$,
(iv) $w \models \varphi \to \psi$ iff $\forall w' \geqslant w$: $w' \models \varphi \Rightarrow w' \models \psi$.

The language of Zeinstra's logic is given by the following Backus–Naur Form.

$$\varphi ::= p \mid \bot \mid \,]\, \mid \,[\, \mid (\varphi_1, \varphi_2) \mid \varphi_1 ; \varphi_2.$$

Here p stands for arbitrary propositional letters, $\bot$ is the falsum, $]$ and $[$ are the pop and push operators we have met before, (φ, ψ) is to be read as φ, *hence* ψ, and the semicolon is our sign for conjunction. We prefer the latter over the more conventional $\wedge$ since its semantics will be relational composition as in Groenendijk and Stokhof's system, not intersection or meet as in standard logic. We usually write $\varphi\psi$ for $\varphi ; \psi$. Since the negation $\neg\varphi$ of a formula φ can be considered to be an abbreviation of $([\varphi, \bot])$ the toy derivation in Hofstadter's system given above can now indeed be represented as $([p, \neg\neg p])$ or $([p, ([([p, \bot]), \bot])])$. The latter are examples of formulae in which the push and pop brackets are well-balanced, but in general no such condition need be imposed.

Kripke's semantics for IPL provides us with good candidates for the explication of Hofstadter's fantasies: fantasies are worlds. Since fantasies can be nested, we need stacks (sequences) of worlds for our semantics. For stacks $\sigma = \langle w_1, \ldots, w_n \rangle$ we demand that $w_i \leqslant w_{i+1}$, for all $i < n$, i.e. worlds that are higher in a stack, are also higher in the underlying model. We write $\mathrm{Last}(\langle w_1, \ldots, w_n \rangle)$ to refer to w_n and we write $\sigma \leqslant_1 \tau$ if $\sigma = \langle w_1, \ldots, w_n \rangle$ and $\tau = \langle w_1, \ldots, w_n, w \rangle$, i.e. if τ is a possible result of pushing the stack σ. The *meaning* $\|\varphi\|$ of a formula φ in Zeinstra's language is a binary relation between stacks of worlds in a Kripke model K, defined with the help of the following clauses.

(i) $\sigma\|p\|\tau$ iff $\sigma = \tau$ and $\mathrm{Last}(\sigma) \in V(p)$, for propositional p,
(ii) $\sigma\|\bot\|\tau$ iff $\sigma = \tau$ and $\mathrm{Last}(\sigma) = T$,
(iii) $\sigma\|\,[\,\|\tau$ iff $\sigma \leqslant_1 \tau$,
(iv) $\sigma\|\,]\,\|\tau$ iff $\tau \leqslant_1 \sigma$,
(v) $\sigma\|(\varphi, \psi)\|\tau$ iff $\exists\rho(\sigma\|\varphi\|\rho \;\&\; \rho\|\psi\|\tau)$ and $\forall\rho(\sigma\|\varphi\|\rho \Rightarrow \exists\nu\rho\|\psi\|\nu)$,
(vi) $\sigma\|\varphi;\psi\|\tau$ iff $\exists\rho(\sigma\|\varphi\|\rho \;\&\; \rho\|\psi\|\tau)$.

Truth is defined just as it was done in Discourse Representation Theory or in Dynamic Predicate Logic: in terms of the domain of the given relation. Formally, we write $K, \sigma \models \varphi$ if $\sigma\|\varphi\|\tau$ for some stack τ.

As an example of how this semantics works consider the formula $([p, q])$. We have:

$$\begin{aligned}
\sigma\|([p,q])\|\tau \quad &\text{iff} \quad \exists\rho(\sigma\|[p\|\rho \;\&\; \rho\|q]\|\tau) \text{ and } \forall\rho(\sigma\|[p\|\rho \Rightarrow \exists\nu\rho\|q]\|\nu),\\
&\text{iff} \quad \sigma = \tau \text{ and } \forall\rho(\sigma\|[p\|\rho \Rightarrow \exists\nu\rho\|q]\|\nu),\\
&\text{iff} \quad \sigma = \tau \text{ and } \forall\rho \geqslant_1 \sigma(\rho \models p \Rightarrow \rho \models q),\\
&\text{iff} \quad \sigma = \tau \text{ and } \forall w \geqslant \mathrm{Last}(\sigma)(w \models p \Rightarrow w \models q),\\
&\text{iff} \quad \sigma = \tau \text{ and } \mathrm{Last}(\sigma) \models p \rightarrow q.
\end{aligned}$$

The first equivalence is an instantiation of clause (v), the second follows since the required ρ in $\exists\rho(\sigma\|[p\|\rho \;\&\; \rho\|q]\|\tau)$ can simply be σ extended with T, and the last two equivalences are simple consequences of the definitions. It may amuse the reader to try her hand at $([p[q, r]s])$.

The equivalence given above shows a connection between the formula $([p, q])$ in Zeinstra's language and the implication $p \rightarrow q$ in IPL and indeed there is a more systematic connection between the two logics. Let $(\cdot)^\circ$ be the translation of IPL$[\bot, \wedge, \rightarrow]$ into Zeinstra's language such that $(p)^\circ = p$ for all propositional p, $(\bot)^\circ = \bot$, $(\varphi \wedge \psi)^\circ := \varphi^\circ; \psi^\circ$, and $(\varphi \rightarrow \psi)^\circ = ([\varphi^\circ, \psi^\circ])$. Then $K, \langle w \rangle \models \varphi^\circ$ iff $w \models_K \varphi$, for all formulae in IPL$[\bot, \wedge, \rightarrow]$, as the reader may care to verify. But a converse holds as well since Zeinstra has shown that for all formulae φ in her language such that the pop and push operators] and [are well-balanced in φ there is an IPL$[\bot, \wedge, \rightarrow]$ formula φ' such that $K, \langle w \rangle \models \varphi$ iff $w \models_K \varphi'$ for any K and w.

In essence then, the logic contains a fragment of well-balanced formulae which is equivalent to IPL$[\bot, \wedge, \rightarrow]$ and in which there is no longer a distinction between implication and entailment. But the logic is a true extension of that fragment, as it also gives a semantics for formulae that are not well-balanced. The latter correspond to almost arbitrary segments of proofs in which assumptions may be made without discharging them and where even pops may occur without the corresponding pushes.

1.5. Change of beliefs: Gärdenfors' theory of belief revision

Let us return to the Stalnaker–Karttunen theory of presuppositions temporarily and ask ourselves what will happen when a speaker utters a sentence A that carries a presupposition B which the hearer in fact does not take for granted. In many cases no problem will arise at all, because the very utterance of A will tell the hearer that B is presupposed by the speaker and the hearer may tacitly add B to his stock of beliefs or, in any case, he may pretend to do so. This process, which is called *accommodation* in (Lewis, 1979), allows a presupposition to spring into existence if it was not there when the sentence requiring it was uttered. But what if the required presupposition cannot be accommodated because it is not consistent with the hearer's existing set of beliefs? Karttunen (1973) remarks that this problem is reminiscent of a problem that arises in connection with conditionals. An influential theory about the evaluation of the latter, first proposed by Ramsey (1929), and later formalized in (Stalnaker, 1968) and (Lewis, 1973), wants you to hypothetically add the antecedent of a conditional to your stock of beliefs. If it turns out that the consequent of the conditional follows from this new set of beliefs, you may conclude that the conditional itself is true. Again the problem arises how consistency can be maintained. Disbelieving the antecedent of a counterfactual should not necessarily lead to acceptance of the counterfactual itself, simply because adding the antecedent to your stock of beliefs would lead to inconsistency. This means that some beliefs must be given up (hypothetically) before the (hypothetical) addition can take place. But not all ways to discard beliefs are equally rational; for instance, you do not want to end up with a proper subset of some set of beliefs that is consistent with the antecedent.

Of course the question how beliefs can be given up and how opinions can be revised rationally in the light of new evidence is a general one. The problem is central to an interesting research line that was initiated by Peter Gärdenfors and that is exemplified by papers such as (Makinson, 1985; Gärdenfors, 1988; Gärdenfors and Makinson, 1988; Rott, 1992). Suppose we have a set of beliefs K, which we may for present purposes take to be a deductively closed theory of predicate logic, and a new insight φ (a predicate logical sentence) and suppose we revise K in the light of φ, obtaining a new theory $K^*\varphi$.

What are the properties that $K^*\varphi$ should conform to? Gärdenfors gives eight postulates. Writing $K+\varphi$ for $\{\psi \mid K, \varphi \vdash \psi\}$ (the *expansion* of K by φ), he demands the following.

(*1) $K^*\varphi$ is deductively closed,
(*2) $\varphi \in K^*\varphi$,
(*3) $K^*\varphi \subseteq K + \varphi$,
(*4) If $K + \varphi$ is consistent then $K + \varphi \subseteq K^*\varphi$,
(*5) $K^*\varphi$ is consistent if $\{\varphi\}$ is consistent,
(*6) If φ is equivalent with ψ then $K^*\varphi = K^*\psi$,
(*7) $K^*\varphi \wedge \psi \subseteq (K^*\varphi) + \psi$,
(*8) If $(K^*\varphi) + \psi$ is consistent then $(K^*\varphi) + \psi \subseteq K^*\varphi \wedge \psi$.

We can think of the first of these postulates as being merely a matter of technical convenience: it allows us to formulate principles about $K^*\varphi$ instead of principles about its deductive closure. Postulates (*2)–(*6) seem reasonable in view of the intended meaning of $K^*\varphi$: (*2) states that after revising K in the light of φ we should come to believe φ, (*3) and (*4) that revising in the light of φ is just adding φ to one's set of beliefs, if this can be done consistently, (*5) is the requirement that consistency should be maintained if at all possible and (*6) demands that $K^*\varphi$ depends on the content rather than on the form of φ. Principles (*7) and (*8) are supplementary postulates about iterated revisions, the idea being that $K^*\varphi \wedge \psi$ ought to be the same as the expansion of $K^*\varphi$ by ψ, as long as ψ does not contradict the beliefs in $K^*\varphi$.

Gärdenfors also considers the process of giving up a belief, i.e. subtracting some belief φ from a set of beliefs K. The result $K \dot{-} \varphi$, the *contraction* of K with respect to φ, should conform to the following axioms.

($\dot{-}$1) $K \dot{-} \varphi$ is deductively closed,
($\dot{-}$2) $K \dot{-} \varphi \subseteq K$,
($\dot{-}$3) If $\varphi \notin K$ then $K \dot{-} \varphi = K$,
($\dot{-}$4) If $\varphi \in K \dot{-} \varphi$ then $\vdash \varphi$,
($\dot{-}$5) $K \subseteq (K \dot{-} \varphi) + \varphi$,
($\dot{-}$6) If φ is equivalent with ψ then $K \dot{-} \varphi = K \dot{-} \psi$,
($\dot{-}$7) $(K \dot{-} \varphi) \cap (K \dot{-} \psi) \subseteq K \dot{-} (\varphi \wedge \psi)$,
($\dot{-}$8) If $\varphi \notin K \dot{-} (\varphi \wedge \psi)$ then $K \dot{-} (\varphi \wedge \psi) \subseteq K \dot{-} \varphi$.

Again, motivations for the *basic* postulates ($\dot{-}$1)–($\dot{-}$6) follow readily from the intended meaning of $\dot{-}$. For a motivation of the (*supplementary*) postulates ($\dot{-}$7) and ($\dot{-}$8) see (Gärdenfors, 1988).

The operations $*$ and $\dot{-}$ are not unrelated, as revising in the light of φ can in fact be thought to consist of two operations, namely first contracting with respect to the negation of φ and then adding φ itself. Conversely, we may define the contraction with respect to φ as the set of those of our original beliefs that would still hold after a revision in the light of the negation of φ.

(Def L) $K^*\varphi := (K \dot{-} \neg\varphi) + \varphi$ (Levi Identity).
(Def H) $K \dot{-} \varphi := K \cap K^*\neg\varphi$ (Harper Identity).

Write L($\dot{-}$) for the revision function obtained from $\dot{-}$ by the Levi identity and H(*) for the contraction function obtained from * by the Harper identity. The following theorem (see Gärdenfors, 1988) connects revisions and contractions and states the duality of L and H.

THEOREM 1.1.
(i) *If* * *satisfies* (*1)–(*8) *then* H(*) *satisfies* ($\dot{-}$1)–($\dot{-}$8),
(ii) *If* $\dot{-}$ *satisfies* ($\dot{-}$1)–($\dot{-}$8) *then* L($\dot{-}$) *satisfies* (*1)–(*8),
(iii) *If* * *satisfies* (*1)–(*6) *then* L(H(*)) = *,
(iv) *If* $\dot{-}$ *satisfies* ($\dot{-}$1)–($\dot{-}$6) *then* H(L($\dot{-}$)) = $\dot{-}$.

In fact this theorem can be generalized to some degree since the number 8 can be replaced uniformly by 6 or 7 in each of the first two clauses. This is satisfactory as in both sets of postulates the first six seem to give some very general properties of the concept under investigation, while the last two more in particular pertain to conjunctions.

It is one thing to give a set of postulates for a concept and another to give structures which satisfy them. One need not go as far as Russell, who said that the method of postulation has 'the advantages of theft over honest toil' (the quote is from Makinson, 1985), to feel that an abstract set of postulates should be complemented with more explicit constructions if at all possible. But there are many ways to obtain constructs satisfying the Gärdenfors postulates and we shall consider three of them. The first construction – from Alchourrón, Gärdenfors and Makinson (1985) – takes $K \dot{-} \varphi$ to be the intersection of some maximal subsets of K that fail to imply φ. More precisely, let $K \bot \varphi$ (*K less φ*) be the set of all such maximal subsets, i.e. the set $\{X \subseteq K \mid X \nvdash \varphi \ \& \ \forall Y(X \subseteq Y \subseteq K \ \& \ Y \nvdash \varphi \Rightarrow X = Y)\}$, and let γ be a function such that $\gamma(K \bot \varphi) \neq \emptyset$, $\gamma(K \bot \varphi) \subseteq K \bot \varphi$ if $K \bot \varphi \neq \emptyset$ and $\gamma(K \bot \varphi) = \{K\}$ otherwise. Then the *partial meet contraction* $K \dot{-} \varphi$ can be defined as $\bigcap \gamma(K \bot \varphi)$. The following representation theorem holds.

THEOREM 1.2. *The operation of partial meet contraction satisfies* ($\dot{-}$1)–($\dot{-}$6). *Conversely, any operation that satisfies* ($\dot{-}$1)–($\dot{-}$6) *is itself a partial meet contraction operation.*

The theorem can be extended to a representation theorem for ($\dot{-}$1)–($\dot{-}$8) by placing extra conditions on γ. Of course, the Levi identity also allows us to obtain an operation of *partial meet revision* from the operation of partial meet contraction. This operation then satisfies (*1)–(*6), or (*1)–(*8) if extra conditions are added.

Another way to construct a contraction function makes use of the notion of *epistemic entrenchment*. Giving up some beliefs will have more drastic consequences as giving up others and consequently some beliefs have preferential status over others. Write $\varphi \leqslant \psi$ (*ψ is at least as epistemologically entrenched as φ*) if φ and ψ are both logical truths (and hence cannot be given up), or if φ is not believed at all, or if a need to give up one of φ or ψ will lead to discarding φ (or both). It seems reasonable to demand the following.

(EE1) If $\varphi \leqslant \psi$ and $\psi \leqslant \chi$, then $\varphi \leqslant \chi$,
(EE2) If $\varphi \vdash \psi$ then $\varphi \leqslant \psi$,

(EE3) $\varphi \leqslant \varphi \wedge \psi$ or $\psi \leqslant \varphi \wedge \psi$,
(EE4) If K is consistent then $\varphi \notin K$ iff $\varphi \leqslant \psi$ for all ψ,
(EE5) If $\varphi \leqslant \psi$ for all φ then $\vdash \psi$.

Transitivity of $\leqslant$ (EE1) must be required if $\leqslant$ is to be an ordering relation. If φ entails ψ, then ψ cannot be given up without giving up φ, whence (EE2). Since a choice between giving up φ or $\varphi \wedge \psi$ is in fact a choice between giving up φ or ψ, (EE3) in fact states that $\varphi \leqslant \psi$ or $\psi \leqslant \varphi$, a natural requirement. (EE4) identifies the sentences that are not believed with those that are least entrenched and the last requirement says that only logically valid sentences are maximal in $\leqslant$, i.e. that anything can be given up, logical truths excepted.

Given a contraction relation we can define a relation of epistemic entrenchment with the help of (C) below. Conversely, supposing that an entrenchment relation $\leqslant$ is given, then (E) defines a contraction relation in terms of it. ('$\varphi < \psi$' is defined as '$\varphi \leqslant \psi$ and not $\psi \leqslant \varphi$'.)

(C) $\varphi \leqslant \psi$ iff $\varphi \notin K \dot{-} (\varphi \wedge \psi)$ or $\vdash \varphi \wedge \psi$.
(E) $K \dot{-} \varphi = K \cap \{\psi \mid \varphi < \varphi \vee \psi\}$ if $\nvdash \varphi$,
$= K$ otherwise.

Write $\mathrm{C}(\leqslant)$ for the contraction function obtained from $\leqslant$ by (C) and $\mathrm{E}(\dot{-})$ for the relation of epistemic entrenchment obtained from $\dot{-}$ by def (E). The following representation theorem is proved in (Gärdenfors and Makinson, 1988).

THEOREM 1.3.
(i) *If* $\leqslant$ *satisfies* (EE1)–(EE5) *then* $\mathrm{C}(\leqslant)$ *satisfies* $(\dot{-}1)$–$(\dot{-}8)$.
(ii) *If* $\dot{-}$ *satisfies* $(\dot{-}1)$–$(\dot{-}8)$ *then* $\mathrm{E}(\dot{-})$ *satisfies* (EE1)–(EE5).
(iii) *If* $\leqslant$ *satisfies* (EE1)–(EE5) *then* $\mathrm{E}(\mathrm{C}(\leqslant)) = \leqslant$.
(iv) *If* $\dot{-}$ *satisfies* $(\dot{-}1)$–$(\dot{-}8)$ *then* $\mathrm{C}(\mathrm{E}(\dot{-})) = \dot{-}$.

A third way to construct operations satisfying the Gärdenfors postulates that we want to mention is the oldest of them all and in fact precedes the formulation of the postulates themselves. Gärdenfors (1988) notes that the *probability functions* that we find in the Bayesian tradition provide us with the necessary material to construct such operations. For example, the conditional probability functions axiomatized in (Popper, 1959) immediately give us revision functions satisfying $({*}1)$–$({*}8)$ above and again a representation theorem can be proved. For more details and a careful discussion see (Gärdenfors, 1988).

2. Logical observations

2.1. General dynamic logic

Dynamic semantics provides a fresh look at most aspects of logical theory. In this section we shall use the paradigm of Dynamic Logic (Pratt, 1976; Harel, 1984; Goldblatt, 1987; Harel and Kozen, 1994), broadly conceived, and twisted to suit our purposes wherever this is needed, for bringing out some of these. To appreciate what follows, there is a useful analogy with Generalized Quantifier Theory (cf. Keenan and Westerståhl, 1996; this Handbook): Dynamic Logic provides a broad logical space for dynamic operators and inference and this logical space may be contrasted fruitfully with the empirical space of what we find realized in natural language and human cognition. But the most fruitful analogy is the earlier one of the Introduction. Dynamic semantics has many counterparts in computer science, for obvious reasons. There are striking similarities between variable binding mechanisms in programming languages and what is currently being proposed for natural language. Similar observations may be made about Artificial Intelligence, witness the parallels in the study of default reasoning between Veltman (1991), Boutilier (1993), Boutilier and Goldszmidt (1993), and Van Benthem, Van Eijck and Frolova (1993). For our current purposes, we wish to emphasize the richer process theory available in the computational literature. We hope that, eventually, natural language semantics will come up with a similar refined view of its dynamic structures.

2.1.1. Dynamic logic

The expressions of Propositional Dynamic Logic (PDL) are divided in two categories: the category of *formulae*, which form the static part of the language, and the category of *programs,* the truly dynamic part. But formulae can be constructed from programs and vice versa, so that there is an active interplay between the two parts. The following Backus–Naur Form defines formulae (φ) and programs (π) from basic propositional letters (p) and atomic programs (α).

$$\varphi ::= p \mid \bot \mid \varphi_1 \rightarrow \varphi_2 \mid [\pi]\varphi,$$

$$\pi ::= \alpha \mid \varphi? \mid \pi_1 ; \pi_2 \mid \pi_1 \cup \pi_2 \mid \pi^*.$$

The intuitive meaning of $[\pi]\varphi$ is the statement that φ will be true after any successful execution of π. A *test* program $\varphi?$ tests whether φ is true, continues if it is, but fails if it is not. The *sequence* $\pi_1 ; \pi_2$ is an instruction to do π_1 and then π_2. The *choice* program $\pi_1 \cup \pi_2$ can be executed by either carrying out π_1 or by doing π_2 and the *iteration* π^* is an instruction to do π any number ($\geqslant 0$) of times.

The last two constructs introduce nondeterminism into the language. An execution of $p;p;q$ will count as an execution of $(p \cup q)^*$, but an execution of q alone, or of any finite sequence of p's and q's, will do as well. Programs are regular expressions and an execution of any sequence in the denotation of such an expression will count as an execution of the program itself.

The semantics of PDL is obtained by considering poly-modal Kripke models (also known as *labeled transition systems*) $\langle S, \{R_\alpha \mid \alpha \in \mathrm{AT}\}, V\rangle$, consisting of a set of abstract *program states* S, a set of binary relations R_α over S, indexed by the set of atomic programs AT, and a *valuation* function V which assigns a subset of S to each propositional letter in the language. In general, the meaning of a formula is identified with the set of all states where the formula is true, the meaning of a program with the set of pairs $\langle a, b\rangle$ such that the program, if started in state a, may end up in state b. Writing $R \circ R'$ for the relational composition of R and R' and $(R)^*$ for the reflexive transitive closure of R, we can define the meaning $\|\varphi\|^M$ of a formula φ and the meaning $\|\pi\|^M$ of a program π with respect to a given model $M = \langle S, \{R_\alpha \mid \alpha \in \mathrm{AT}\}, V\rangle$ as follows.

(i) $\|p\| = V(p)$,

(ii) $\|\bot\| = \emptyset$,
(iii) $\|\varphi_1 \to \varphi_2\| = (S - \|\varphi_1\|) \cup \|\varphi_2\|$,
(iv) $\|[\pi]\varphi\| = \{a \mid \forall b(\langle a, b\rangle \in \|\pi\| \to b \in \|\varphi\|)\}$,
(v) $\|\alpha\| = R_\alpha$,
(vi) $\|\varphi?\| = \{\langle a, a\rangle \mid a \in \|\varphi\|\}$,
(vii) $\|\pi_1;\pi_2\| = \|\pi_1\| \circ \|\pi_2\|$,
(viii) $\|\pi_1 \cup \pi_2\| = \|\pi_1\| \cup \|\pi_2\|$,
(ix) $\|\pi^*\| = (\|\pi\|)^*$.

We see that $[\pi]\varphi$ is in fact interpreted as a modal statement ('in all π-successors φ') with the modal accessibility relation given by the denotation of π and we may define a dual modality by letting $\langle\pi\rangle\varphi$ be an abbreviation of $\neg[\pi]\neg\varphi$. This new statement will then have the meaning that it is possible that φ will hold after execution of π. Abbreviations will also give us a host of constructs that are familiar from the usual imperative programming languages. For example, **while** φ **do** π **od** can be viewed as an abbreviation of $(\varphi?;\pi)^*;\neg\varphi?$; a little reflection will show that the latter has the intended input/output behaviour. Correctness statements (in Hoare's sense) about such programs can be formalized too; for example $\{\varphi\}\pi\{\psi\}$, the assertion that in any state where φ holds any successful execution of π will lead to a state where ψ holds, can be taken to be an abbreviation of $\varphi \to [\pi]\psi$.

A formula φ is said to be *universally valid* if $\|\varphi\| = S$ for each model $\langle S, \{R_\alpha \mid \alpha \in \mathrm{AT}\}, V\rangle$. Segerberg (1982) shows that this notion is axiomatizable by means of the following seven axiom schemes and two rules of inference.

(A1)	all instances of tautologies of the propositional calculus	
(A2)	$[\pi](\varphi \to \psi) \to ([\pi]\varphi \to [\pi]\psi)$	(Distribution)
(A3)	$[\varphi?]\psi \leftrightarrow (\varphi \to \psi)$	(Test axiom)
(A4)	$[\pi_1;\pi_2]\psi \leftrightarrow [\pi_1][\pi_2]\psi$	(Sequence axiom)
(A5)	$[\pi_1 \cup \pi_2]\psi \leftrightarrow ([\pi_1]\psi \wedge [\pi_2]\psi)$	(Choice axiom)
(A6)	$[\pi^*]\psi \leftrightarrow (\psi \wedge [\pi][\pi^*]\psi)$	(Iteration axiom)
(A7)	$(\varphi \wedge [\pi^*](\varphi \to [\pi]\varphi)) \to [\pi^*]\varphi$	(Induction axiom)
(MP)	from φ and $\varphi \to \psi$ to infer ψ	(Modus Ponens)
(N)	from φ to infer $[\pi]\varphi$	(Necessitation)

As a simple illustration we give a derivation of one of Hoare's rules of *Composition*, the rule that $\{\varphi\}\pi_1;\pi_2\{\chi\}$ can be inferred from $\{\varphi\}\pi_1\{\psi\}$ and $\{\psi\}\pi_2\{\chi\}$.

1. $\varphi \to [\pi_1]\psi$,
2. $\psi \to [\pi_2]\chi$,
3. $[\pi_1](\psi \to [\pi_2]\chi)$, necessitation, 2,
4. $[\pi_1]\psi \to [\pi_1][\pi_2]\chi$, distribution, 3,
5. $\varphi \to [\pi_1][\pi_2]\chi$, propositional logic, 1, 4,
6. $\varphi \to [\pi_1;\pi_2]\chi$, sequence axiom, 5.

We invite the reader to show that $\{\varphi\}$**while** ψ **do** π **od**$\{\varphi \wedge \neg\psi\}$ can be derived from $\{\varphi \wedge \psi\}\pi\{\varphi\}$.

The system of *Quantificational Dynamic Logic* (QDL) can be obtained from PDL by specifying the structure of atomic formulae and atomic programs. In particular, the atomic formulae of standard predicate logic will be atomic formulae of the new logic and *assignment statements* of the forms $x :=?$ (random assignment) and $x := t$ are its atomic programs. The following Backus–Naur Form gives a precise syntax.

$$\varphi ::= R(t_1, \ldots, t_n) \mid t_1 = t_2 \mid \bot \mid \varphi_1 \rightarrow \varphi_2 \mid [\pi]\varphi,$$
$$\pi ::= x := ? \mid x := t \mid \varphi? \mid \pi_1; \pi_2 \mid \pi_1 \cup \pi_2 \mid \pi^*.$$

The idea here is that $x := ?$ sets x to an arbitrary new value and that $x := t$ sets x to the current value of t. The semantics of this logic is given relative to ordinary first-order models $M = \langle D, I\rangle$ with the set of states S now being played by the set of all M-assignments, i.e. the set of all (total) functions from the variables in the language to D. Letting $\|t\|^a$ (the value of a term t under an assignment a) be defined as usual, we can define $\|\varphi\|^M$ and $\|\pi\|^M$ by taking the clauses for the PDL semantics given above, but replacing those for atomic formulae and programs by the following. (Here $a[x]b$ is to mean that $a(y) = b(y)$ if $x \neq y$.)

$$\|R(t_1, \ldots, t_n)\| = \{a \mid \langle \|t_1\|^a, \ldots, \|t_n\|^a\rangle \in I(R)\},$$
$$\|t_1 = t_2\| = \{a \mid \|t_1\|^a = \|t_2\|^a\},$$
$$\|x := ?\| = \{\langle a, b\rangle \mid a[x]b\},$$
$$\|x := t\| = \{\langle a, b\rangle \mid a[x]b \;\&\; b(x) = \|t\|^a\}.$$

We say that ψ *follows from* φ, $\varphi \models_{\mathrm{QDL}} \psi$, iff $\|\varphi\|^M \subseteq \|\psi\|^M$ for every model M. The logic thus obtained is a truly *quantificational* logic since $\forall x\varphi$ can taken to be an abbreviation of $[x := ?]\varphi$ and $\exists x\varphi$ of $\langle x := ?\rangle\varphi$. Note also that $[x := t]\varphi$ and $\langle x := t\rangle\varphi$ are both equivalent with the result of substitution of t for x in φ. However, the logic really extends first-order logic. Consider $[x := ?]\langle y := 0; (y := Sy)^*\rangle x = y$ in the language of Peano Arithmetic. Together with the usual first-order Peano axioms this sentence will characterize the natural numbers, a feat which first-order logic cannot perform.

The price that must be paid is non-axiomatizability of the system, of course. However, there is a simple proof system which is complete relative to structures containing a copy of the natural numbers (see Harel, 1984). Note that the iteration operator * is the sole culprit for non-axiomatizability: the Segerberg axioms (A3)–(A5) plus the equivalences between $[x :=?]\varphi$ and $\forall x\varphi$ and $[x := t]\varphi$ and $[t/x]\varphi$ provide an easy method to find a predicate logical equivalent for any formula $[\pi]\varphi$ not containing the star (see also the "weakest precondition" calculi in Section 2.3.4).

The interest of QDL for natural language semantics derives partly from the fact that the DRT and DPL systems that were considered in Section 1.2 can easily be shown to be fragments of the star free part of this logic. For example, we can translate DRT into QDL in the following way.

$$(\varphi)^\dagger = \varphi \quad \text{if } \varphi \text{ is atomic},$$
$$(\neg K)^\dagger = [K^\dagger]\bot,$$
$$(K_1 \vee K_2)^\dagger = \langle K_2^\dagger\rangle\top \vee \langle K_2^\dagger\rangle\top,$$

$$(K_1 \Rightarrow K_2)^\dagger = [K_1^\dagger]\langle K_2^\dagger\rangle\top,$$
$$([x_1,\dots,x_n \mid \varphi_1,\dots,\varphi_m])^\dagger = x_1 := ?\,;\dots;x_n := ?\,;\varphi_1^\dagger ?\,;\dots;\varphi_m^\dagger ?.$$

If we let DRT be interpreted by means of its total semantics (see Section 1.2.2), we have that $\|\delta\|^{\mathrm{DRT}} = \|\delta^\dagger\|^{\mathrm{QDL}}$ for any condition or DRS δ. If both DRT and QDL are provided with a semantics based on partial assignments an embedding is possible as well – see (Fernando, 1992). The reader will have no difficulty in defining a translation function from DPL to QDL either (see also Groenendijk and Stokhof, 1991).

2.1.2. Dynamization of classical systems

Systems of dynamic semantics may often be derived from static predecessors. For this purpose one has to identify parameters of change in classical systems, and then design dynamic logics exploiting these. For instance, consider Tarski's basic truth definition for a formula φ in a model $M = \langle D, I\rangle$ under some variable assignment a. Its atomic clause involves a static test whether some fact obtains. But intuitively, the clause for an existential quantifier $\exists x$ involves shifting an assignment value for x until some verifying object has been found. A system like DPL makes the latter process explicit, by assigning to each formula a binary relation consisting of those transitions between assignments which result in its successful verification. Entirely analogously, other components of the truth definition admit of such shifts too. For instance, shifting interpretation functions I are involved in questions (cf. Groenendijk and Stokhof, 1984) and ambiguity (Van Deemter, 1991), and shifting of individual domains D occurs with ranges for generalized quantifiers across sentences (Westerståhl, 1984).

In addition to these 'Tarskian Variations' for extensional logics (Van Benthem, 1991b), there are also 'Kripkean Variations' for intensional logics. Consider, e.g., the best-known classical information-oriented model structures, namely Kripke models for intuitionistic logic. Here, worlds stand for information states, ordered by a relation of growth $\subseteq$, which are traversed by a cognitive agent. Intuitively, intuitionistic formulas refer to transitions in this information pattern (cf. Troelstra and Van Dalen, 1988). For example, to see that $\neg\varphi$ holds, one has to inspect all possible extensions of the current state for absence of φ. Van Benthem (1991a) makes this dynamics into an explicit part of the logic, by creating a system of cognitive transitions, such as updates taking us to some minimal extension where a certain proposition has become true. While intuitionistic negation, which is expressible as $\lambda P\lambda x.\forall y(x \subseteq y \to \neg Py)$, takes us from sets of worlds to sets of worlds, Van Benthem is also interested in functions which take us from sets of worlds to binary relations between worlds, such as for example:

$\lambda P.\lambda xy.x \subseteq y \wedge Py$	(*loose updating*)
$\lambda P.\lambda xy.x \subseteq y \wedge Py \wedge \neg\exists z(x \subseteq z \subset y \wedge Pz)$	(*strict updating*)
$\lambda P.\lambda xy.y \subseteq x \wedge \neg Py$	(*loose downdating*)
$\lambda P.\lambda xy.y \subseteq x \wedge \neg Py \wedge \neg\exists z(y \subset z \subseteq x \wedge \neg Pz)$	(*strict downdating*)

Standard intuitionistic logic is a forward-looking system, but the full dynamic logic will include backward-looking downdates and revisions. The resulting Dynamic Modal Logic covers all cognitive tasks covered in the Gärdenfors theory of Section 1.5, and admits much more elaborate statements about them. The system has been studied extensively in (De Rijke, 1993), which has results on its expressive power and axiomatization and proves its undecidability. (Van Benthem (1993) presents a decidable reformulation.) Extensions of the formalism may be defined using operators from Temporal Logic. For instance, appropriate pre- and postconditions for strict updating and downdating will involve the well-known temporal operators *since* and *until*.

Other static systems which have been turned into dynamic ones include the theory of generalized quantifiers. There are many forms of change here: in bindings, ranges of quantification, drawing samples from domains, and model construction. (Cf. Van den Berg, 1995; Van Eijck and De Vries, 1992; Kanazawa, 1993b; Keenan and Westerståhl, 1996; Van Eijck and Kamp, 1996; Hintikka and Sandu, 1996.)

2.1.3. Dynamic constants as operators in relational algebra

Our general perspective employs the usual mathematical notion of a *state space* (i.e. poly-modal Kripke model) $\langle S, \{R_\alpha \mid \alpha \in \mathrm{AT}\}, V\rangle$. Over the atomic actions R_α, there is a procedural repertoire of operations creating compound actions. Examples of such procedural operations are sequential composition, choice, iteration as found in computer programs. Less standard examples include the DPL test negation:

$$\neg R = \{\langle x, x\rangle \mid \neg\exists y\langle x, y\rangle \in R\}$$

or the directed functions of categorial grammar (cf. Moortgat, 1996, this Handbook):

$$A\backslash B = \{\langle x, y\rangle \mid \forall z(\langle z, x\rangle \in A \to \langle z, y\rangle \in B)\},$$
$$B/A = \{\langle x, y\rangle \mid \forall z(\langle y, z\rangle \in A \to \langle x, z\rangle \in B)\}.$$

What we see here is a move from a standard Boolean Algebra of propositions to a Relational Algebra of procedures. The standard repertoire in relational algebras is:

Boolean operations: $-$ (complement) $\cap$ (intersection) $\cup$ (union)
Ordering operations: $\circ$ (composition) $^{\cup}$(converse)

with a distinguished diagonal Δ for the identity relation. These operations are definable in a standard predicate logic with variables over states:

$-R$	$\lambda xy.\neg Rxy,$
$R\cap S$	$\lambda xy.Rxy \wedge Sxy,$
$R\cup S$	$\lambda xy.Rxy \vee Sxy,$
$R\circ S$	$\lambda xy.\exists z(Rxz \wedge Szy),$
$R^{\cup}$	$\lambda xy.Ryx.$

This formalism can define many other procedural operators. In particular,

$$
\begin{array}{ll}
\neg R & \Delta \cap -(R \circ R^{\cup}), \\
A \backslash B & -(A^{\cup} \circ -B), \\
B/A & -(-B \circ A^{\cup}).
\end{array}
$$

The literature on Relational Algebra contains many relevant results concerning axiomatization of valid identities between such relational expressions, as well as expressive power of various choices of operators (see Németi, 1991). One natural measure of fine-structure here is the number of state variables needed in their definitions. This tells us the largest configuration of states involved in determining the action of the operator. The resulting Finite Variable Hierarchy of semantic complexity relates Relational Algebra with Modal Logic (cf. Andréka, Van Benthem and Németi, 1994). Its mathematical properties seem significant for dynamic logical operators in general: (1) the above vocabulary of Relational Algebra suffices for defining all relational operators with a 3-variable first-order definition (these include most common cases), (2) each n-variable level has a finite functionally complete set of operators, (3) there is no finite functionally complete set of algebraic operators for the whole hierarchy at once. The latter result shows how the logical space of dynamic propositional operators is much richer than that of classical Boolean Algebra.

2.1.4. Process equivalences and invariance

In order to understand a certain kind of process, one has to set up a criterion of identity among its different representations. One important notion to this effect is *bisimulation*, prominent in the computational literature, which tends to be richer in this respect than traditional logical semantics (cf. Milner, 1980; Hennessy and Milner, 1985). A bisimulation is a binary relation C between states in two 'labeled transition systems' (i.e. our dynamic transition models) $\langle S, \{R_\alpha \mid \alpha \in \mathrm{AT}\}, V\rangle$ and $\langle S', \{R'_\alpha \mid \alpha \in \mathrm{AT}\}, V'\rangle$ which connects only states with the same atomic valuation, and which satisfies the following back-and-forth clauses:

if xCx', $xR_\alpha y$, *then there exists some* y' *with* yCy', $x'R'_\alpha y'$,
if xCx', $x'R'_\alpha y'$, *then there exists some* y *with* yCy', $xR_\alpha y$.

This allows mutual tracing of the process in the two transition models, including its choice points. There are many other notions of process simulation: a coarser one is the 'trace equivalence' discussed in (Van Benthem and Bergstra, 1993), and a finer one is the'generated graph equivalence' discussed in the same paper.

There is a close connection between process equivalences and the design of a dynamic language. In particular, bisimulation is the key semantic invariance for a modal language describing labeled transition systems, which has the usual Boolean operators as well as indexed modalities $\langle a\rangle$ for each atomic action $a \in A$. Whenever C is a bisimulation between two models M, M' with sCs', we have

$$s \in \|\varphi\|^{M} \quad \textit{iff} \quad s' \in \|\varphi\|^{M'}, \quad \textit{for all modal formulas } \varphi.$$

This observation can be reversed:

> A first-order formula over labeled transition systems is invariant for bisimulation iff it is definable by means of a modal formula.

In propositional dynamic logic, this invariance persists for formulas, but there is also a new aspect. The above back-and-forth clauses in bisimulation are inherited by all program relations $\|\pi\|$, not just the atomic ones. More specifically, all regular program operations O are *safe for bisimulation*, in the sense that, whenever C is a bisimulation between two models with transition relations $R_1, \ldots, R_n$, it must also be a bisimulation for the transition relation $O(R_1, \ldots, R_n)$. This observation, too, can be reversed (Van Benthem, 1993):

> A first-order relational operation $O(R_1, \ldots, R_n)$ is safe for bisimulation iff it can be defined using atomic relations $R_\alpha xy$ and atomic tests $\alpha?$, using only the three relational operations of $\circ$ (composition), $\cup$ (union) and $\neg$ (DPL negation).

Thus, bisimulation seems very close to the mark for dynamic semantic operators with a modal flavor. Different outcomes will be obtained with coarser or finer notions of process equivalence. It would be of interest to see which level of invariance is plausible for the procedures involved in processing natural language.

2.1.5. Typology of dynamic procedures

Another source of more specific dynamic structure is the search for denotational constraints, suggested by semantic analysis of key linguistic items (cf. again the theory of generalized quantifiers). For instance, relational operators may obey various natural Boolean constraints (cf. Van Benthem, 1986; Keenan and Faltz, 1985), often of a computational character. One well-known example is *continuity* of an operator in one of its arguments:

$$O\Big(\ldots, \bigcup_{i \in I} R_i, \ldots\Big) = \bigcup_{i \in I} O(\ldots, R_i, \ldots).$$

Continuous operations compute their values locally, on single transitions (note that $R = \cup\{\{\langle x, y\rangle\} \mid Rxy\}$). Boolean intersection and union are continuous in both arguments, and so are relational composition and converse. A non-example is Boolean complement. This restriction has some bite. Van Benthem (1991a) proves that, for each fixed arity, there are only finitely many continuous permutation-invariant relational operators. (Belnap (1977) proposes a weaker notion of *Scott continuity* admitting more candidates.) Another source of constraints in dynamic semantics is the typology of cognitive actions themselves. For instance, updates are often taken to be idempotent: repeating them is unnecessary ($\forall xy(Rxy \to Ryy)$). Veltman (1991) wants them to be functions. Such basic choices will influence the choice of a procedural repertoire. For instance, if all admissible actions are to be idempotent, then composition is not a safe combination, while choice or iteration are. Likewise, special atomic repertoires may be of interest. For instance, the basic DPL actions R of propositional test and random assignment both satisfy the identity $R \circ R = R$, and both are symmetric relations. Other interesting denotational constraints of this kind occur in (Zeinstra, 1990) (cf. Section 1.4).

2.1.6. Styles of inference

We now turn from matters of dynamic vocabulary and expressive power to the issue of dynamic inference. The standard Tarskian explication of valid inference expresses transmission of truth: "in every situation where all premises are true, so is the conclusion". But what is the sense of this when propositions are procedures changing information states? There are plausible options here, and no single candidate has won universal favor so far. Here is a characteristic general feature. If premises and conclusions are instructions for achieving cognitive effects, then their presentation must be crucial, including sequential order, multiplicity of occurrences, and relevance of each move. This brings us into conflict with the basic structural rules of standard logic that allow us to disregard such aspects in classical reasoning (cf. Moortgat, 1996, this Handbook). Here are some dynamic styles of inference. The first employs fixed points for propositions (where their update procedure effects no state change) as approximations to classical truth, the second focuses on transitions to achieve an effect, and the third is a compromise between the two (Veltman, 1991; Van Benthem, 1991a).

test-test consequence

In all models, each state which is a fixed point for all premises is also a fixed point for the conclusion:

$$\varphi_1, \ldots, \varphi_n \models_{\text{test-test}} \psi \quad \text{iff} \quad \Delta \cap \|\varphi_1\|^M \cap \cdots \cap \|\varphi_n\|^M \subseteq \|\psi\|^M, \text{ for all models } M.$$

update-update consequence

in all models, each transition for the sequential composition of the premises is a transition for the conclusion:

$$\varphi_1, \ldots, \varphi_n \models_{\text{update-update}} \psi \quad \text{iff} \quad \|\varphi_1\|^M \circ \cdots \circ \|\varphi_n\|^M \subseteq \|\psi\|^M, \text{ for all models } M.$$

update-test consequence

in all models, each state reached after successful processing of the premises is a fixed point for the conclusion:

$$\varphi_1, \ldots, \varphi_n \models_{\text{update-test}} \psi \quad \text{iff} \quad \text{range}(\|\varphi_1\|^M \circ \cdots \circ \|\varphi_n\|^M) \subseteq \text{fix}(\|\psi\|^M), \text{ for all models } M.$$

Thus a variety of dynamic styles of inference emerges, reflecting different intuitions and possibly different applications. These show a certain coherence. For instance, Beaver (1992) analyzes presupposition as a test-update consequence stating that the premises can be processed only from states where the conclusion has a fixed point. Groenendijk and Stokhof (1991) require that the conclusion be processable after the premises have been processed successfully.

DPL consequence
in all models, in each state that is reached after successful processing of the premises, processing of the conclusion is possible:

$$\varphi_1, \ldots, \varphi_n \models_{\mathrm{DPL}} \psi \quad \text{iff} \quad \mathrm{range}(\|\varphi_1\|^M \circ \cdots \circ \|\varphi_n\|^M) \subseteq \mathrm{dom}(\|\psi\|^M), \text{ for all } M.$$

Here, the existential quantification for the conclusion takes care of free variables that are to be captured from the premises. (This "for all – there exists" format may also be observed with implications in DRT.) Van Eijck and de Vries (1995) require a converse, proposing that the domain of the composed premises be contained in the *domain* of the conclusion.

One way of defining a style of inference is through its general properties, expressed in structural rules. For instance, test-test consequence behaves like standard inference:

$$\varphi \Rightarrow \varphi, \qquad \textit{Reflexivity},$$

$$\frac{X \Rightarrow \varphi \quad Y, \varphi, Z \Rightarrow \psi}{Y, X, Z \Rightarrow \psi}, \qquad \textit{Cut Rule},$$

$$\frac{X, \varphi_1, \varphi_2, Y \Rightarrow \psi}{X, \varphi_2, \varphi_1, Y \Rightarrow \psi}, \qquad \textit{Permutation},$$

$$\frac{X, \varphi, Y, \varphi, Z \Rightarrow \psi}{X, \varphi, Y, Z \Rightarrow \psi}, \qquad \textit{Right Contraction},$$

$$\frac{X, \varphi, Y, \varphi, Z \Rightarrow \psi}{X, Y, \varphi, Z \Rightarrow \psi}, \qquad \textit{Left Contraction},$$

$$\frac{X, Y \Rightarrow \psi}{X, \varphi, Y \Rightarrow \psi}, \qquad \textit{Monotonicity}.$$

By contrast, update-update satisfies only Reflexivity and Cut. There are some exact representation results (Van Benthem, 1991a): (1) {*Monotonicity, Contraction, Reflexivity, Cut*} completely determine test-test consequence, (2) {*Reflexivity, Cut*} completely determine update-update inference. But this is not an all-or-nothing matter. Inferential styles may in fact modify standard structural rules, reflecting a more delicate handling of premises. Update-test consequence has none of the above structural properties, but it is completely characterized by

$$\frac{X \Rightarrow \psi}{\varphi, X \Rightarrow \psi}, \qquad \textit{Left Monotonicity},$$

$$\frac{X \Rightarrow \varphi \quad X, \varphi, Z \Rightarrow \psi}{X, Z \Rightarrow \psi}, \qquad \textit{Left Cut}.$$

The DPL style of inference is also non-classical, in that various structural rules from classical logic fail. For instance, it is

non-monotonic: $\exists x Ax \models_{\text{DPL}} Ax$, but not $\exists x Ax, \neg Ax \models_{\text{DPL}} Ax$,
non-contractive: $\exists x Ax, \neg Ax, \exists x Ax \models_{\text{DPL}} Ax$, but not $\exists x Ax, \neg Ax \models_{\text{DPL}} Ax$,
non-transitive: $\exists x Ax, \neg Ax \models_{\text{DPL}} \exists x Ax \models_{\text{DPL}} Ax$, but not $\exists x Ax, \neg Ax \models_{\text{DPL}} Ax$.

The only valid structural rule of inference is *Left Monotonicity*. It is not completely clear, however, that this is the last word. In practice, applications of DPL to natural language will use only very special 'decorations' of grammatical structures with individual variables. For instance, it seems reasonable to require that every quantifier have a unique bound variable associated with it. But then, the DPL *fragment* with this property may be shown to satisfy unrestricted monotonicity, allowing insertion of premises in arbitrary positions (Van Benthem, unpublished). Other well-behaved fragments may be relevant for natural language analysis, too.

Often, one inferential style can be simulated inside another, by adding suitable logical operators. Here is an illustration. Test-test consequence may be reduced to update-update consequence using a relational fixed point operator Φ sending relations R to their diagonal $\lambda xy.Rxy \wedge y = x$:

$$\varphi_1, \ldots, \varphi_n \models_{\text{test-test}} \psi \quad \text{iff} \quad \Phi(\varphi_1), \ldots, \Phi(\varphi_n) \models_{\text{update-update}} \Phi(\psi).$$

There is no similar faithful converse embedding. (This would imply Monotonicity for update-update consequence.) Another interplay between structural rules and logical constants arises as follows. Operators may license additional structural behaviour, not for all propositions, but for special kinds only (cf. Girard, 1987). For instance, in dynamic styles of inference, let O be some operator that is to admit of arbitrary monotonic insertion:

$$\frac{X, Y \Rightarrow \psi}{X, O(\varphi), Y \Rightarrow \psi}.$$

This can only be the case if $O(\varphi)$ is a test contained in the diagonal relation. It would be of interest to see how the linguistic formulation of actual arguments provides cues for adopting and switching between inferential styles.

Completeness theorems for dynamic styles of inference in various fragments of propositional dynamic logic may be found in (Kanazawa, 1993a; Blackburn and Venema, 1993). These results exemplify one direction of thinking in logic: from semantic notions of inference to their complete axiomatic description. Another line in the literature starts from given axiomatic properties of dynamic operators, and then determines corresponding complete semantics via representation theorems (cf. Alchourrón, Gärdenfors and Makinson (1985) and the ensuing tradition). Eventually, both logical treatments of dynamic inference may be too conservative. Perhaps, the very notion of formal proof needs re-thinking in a dynamic setting (a first attempt at defining 'proofs as texts' may be found in (Vermeulen, 1994)). Natural reasoning seems to involve the interplay of a greater variety of mechanisms at the same time (inferring, updating, querying, etcetera).

2.2. *Categories for dynamic semantics*

Dynamic logic is by no means the only mathematical paradigm for implementing the fundamental ideas of dynamic semantics. As a counterpoint to the preceding sections, we outline an alternative logical framework based on category theory, sometimes called the 'Utrecht approach'. Its basic tenet is this: the business of dynamic semantics is modeling interpretation processes. Thus, it is not sufficient to compositionally specify correct meanings: one should also specify these in a way that reflects temporal processes of interpretation. Category Theory provides the tools to do this.

Category theory is a branch of mathematics that is widely applied in both mathematics and computer science. (Some good textbooks are McLane, 1971; Manes and Arbib, 1975; Barr and Wells, 1989.) The uses of Category Theory in linguistics are less widespread, but multiplying. The reader is referred to (Reyes and Macnamara, 1994) for another application in linguistics.

2.2.1. *The program of monoidal updating*

The Utrecht approach develops radical versions of file-change semantics/DRT (see Visser and Vermeulen, 1995). Consider a simple sample sentence: *John cuts the bread with a sharp knife.* This will be analyzed as follows:

$$((subject\ John_j)\ cuts\ (object\ the_u\ bread)\ (with\ a_v\ sharp\ knife)).$$

Here, virtually all grammatical structure will be interpreted as semantic actions such as pushing a new file to a data stack or popping the last file from the stack. In an alternative notation:

> *push push subject* $John_j$ *pop cuts push object* the_u *bread pop push with* a_v *sharp knife pop pop.*

In other words, all grammatical structure gets a dynamic potential similar to the existential quantifier in DPL/DRT or to the dynamic *suppose* operator in Zeinstra's logic. As a consequence, the usual components of a sentence, such as (*object* the_u *bread*), are not necessarily the only possible inputs in a compositional interpretation. In fact, the meaning of any contiguous linguistic chunk of text can be specified. Thus, the source algebra of the interpretation is the language of arbitrary strings over an alphabet including such characters as *subject, with,* a_v, *pop*, whose basic operation is concatenation. This syntactic operation is matched at the semantic level with a dynamic operation, say *merge* or *composition*. This merge will be associative, thus reflecting the associativity of concatenation at the syntactic level. This has as a consequence, that the ambiguity of dividing up a sentence into chunks does not result in the assignment of different meanings. Components in the traditional sense, i.e. chunks with matching opening and closing brackets, correspond to *local files* that are introduced, used for some time and then discarded. (The words *subject, object,* and *with* contain machinery to arrange that the information of the discarded files is stored in the correct files associated with *cuts* at the sentence level.) So far, this semantics has been developed for narrative with existential quantifiers only. Even so, it exemplifies some broad programmatic features for a full-fledged dynamic semantics in the above sense.

In this approach, genuine grammaticality is decided at the semantic level, since the syntactic specification language does not have any interesting grammar at all. The fact that tasks that are traditionally assigned to grammar are now shifted to the semantic level, reflects a move that is typical in dynamic semantics: redivision of labor between syntax and semantics.

Since the semantic objects form a monoid (the basic operation is associative and there is a unit element), the semantics satisfies the *break-in principle*: any contiguous chunk of text can be assigned a meaning. As a result, one can process meanings *incrementally*. This seems a linguistically realistic, and hence desirable feature.

2.2.2. Meanings and contexts

Meanings in this approach are databases, just as in DRT. The main difference with ordinary DRT is that much more 'dynamic potential' is present in contexts. Contexts contain both global information connected to the anaphoric machinery ('variables') and local syntactic information (e.g., a file that stores local information about the subject of a sentence). Contexts regulate the way in which information is stored in case new information is added to a database.

Words like *with* and *object* stand for *argument places*. Their meanings are little machines that look for the place where information connected with the word (*with a knife*) is to be stored in the database that is being built. ("The knife is the *Instrument* of the cutting" – compare (Davidson, 1967; Parsons, 1990).) An anaphor like he_v links files introduced in the sentence (thematic roles such as *Agent* and *Instrument*) with files globally present in the discourse. In this way the chunk (*subj* he_v) ensures that the file locally known as the subject is connected to the file globally known as v. Thus, he_v gets the correct role in the semantics: it is a locus where local and global information are fused.

2.2.3. Diachronic information orderings as categories

Let us look at some chunks of our earlier example.

((*subject* $John_j$) *cuts* (*object*

and

the_u *bread*) (*with* a_v *sharp knife*)).

The meanings associated with these chunks are databases containing files/discourse objects. These databases have a layered structure that reflects some aspects of the local syntactic structure – e.g., the discourse objects are stored on the levels of a stack that represents part of the bracket structure. This structure on discourse objects occurs in the context part of the databases. Our problem now becomes *to describe what happens if two dynamic databases are 'clicked together'*. We do not only want to describe what the new object looks like, but also want to describe the *flow of files*: where do the files of the original databases re-occur in the new one? Apart from philosophical reasons to insist on describing the flow of files there is a pragmatic one: the description of the new meaning object and the verification that it has the desired properties quickly becomes too complicated if we do not have a principled way of describing the flow. This is where categories make their appearance: the flow of files is described by a *diachronic information ordering* and this ordering turns out to be a category.

One should distinguish (at least) two ways of ordering linguistic information. First, there is a *synchronic* ordering. For example, consider two slips of paper. One states *Jan is wearing something new*, the other *Jan is wearing a new hat*. Evidently, the first slip is less informative than the second. Whatever information state someone is in, being offered the second slip will make her at least as informed as being offered the first. So we compare the effects of pieces of information offered at the same time to the same person in different possible situations. The second ordering is the one we are after presently: the *diachronic* ordering, which looks at information as it occurs in time. Consider *Genever is a wonderful beverage. Not only the Dutch are fond of it*. The information content of these two statements forms an indissoluble whole, by virtue of their consecutive presentation. A mathematical analysis of the diachronic ordering $\leqslant$ leads to the core of the Utrecht approach. For a start, assume that $\leqslant$ is a pre-order, i.e. a transitive and reflexive binary relation. (There is no strong evidence for antisymmetry, and hence partial order.) But, there is further relevant dynamic structure. Consider this example:

(40) Genever is a wonderful beverage, I like it. Cognac is not too bad either. I like it too.

Here, the meaning of *I like it* is embedded in the meaning of the whole text twice. But not in the same way: the first *it* will be linked to *Genever*, the second one to *Cognac*. This suggests that the diachronic ordering should rather be a *labeled pre-ordering*, which adds information about the kind of embedding involved.

The preceding observation suggests a move to 'labeled transition systems' similar to those encountered in section Section 2.1 above. Such transition systems can be described in many ways. We describe them here as logical generalizations of partial pre-orders. We have structures $\langle O, L, R\rangle$, where O is a domain of *objects*, L a set of *labels*, and R a ternary relation between objects, labels and objects. A triple $\langle x, \lambda, y\rangle$ in R is called an *arrow*. We shall write $x \leqslant_\lambda y$ for: $\langle x, \lambda, y\rangle \in R$. Here are the analogues of the pre-order principles. Reflexivity says that everything can be embedded into itself *in a trivial way*. This requires a special label *id* such that, for every x, y in $O, x \leqslant_{\text{id}} y$ iff $x = y$. Next, transitivity says we can compose ways of embedding in suitable circumstances. Suppose we have $x \leqslant_\lambda y$ and $y \leqslant_\mu z$. Then $\lambda \circ \mu$ is defined and we have: $x \leqslant_{\lambda\circ\mu} z$. We demand that $id \circ \lambda = \lambda \circ id = \lambda$ and $\lambda \circ (\mu \circ \nu) = (\lambda \circ \mu) \circ \nu$. (Here an equation $\gamma = \delta$ states that γ is defined iff δ is, and that γ and δ are equal where defined.) Finally, for the sake of parsimony, we demand that every label is used at least once in some arrow. (There are obvious analogies here with Dynamic Logic and the Arrow Logic of Section 2.4.8.) Now, with the label *id* we can associate a function from objects to arrows. Moreover the partial operation $\circ$ on labels induces one on arrows. The resulting structure of objects and arrows is a *category* in the sense of Category Theory. (In fact our labeled pre-orderings have slightly more structure than a category.) Thus dynamic semantics can now avail itself of useful notions from an established mathematical discipline. (For instance, an arrow $x \leqslant_\lambda y$ is an *isomorphism* if there is an arrow $y \leqslant_\mu x$ such that $\lambda \circ \mu = \mu \circ \lambda = id$.)

The diachronic ordering may be viewed as a special kind of category, suitable for dynamic meanings. We already had a monoidal merge $\bullet$ on objects. We relax the notion of monoid by allowing that $(x \bullet y) \bullet z$ is not strictly identical to $x \bullet (y \bullet z)$, but that there is a standard isomorphism $\alpha(x, y, z)$ from $(x \bullet y) \bullet z$ to $x \bullet (y \bullet z)$. (This ensures category-theoretic *coherence*: see (McLane, 1971, pp. 161–176).) To make updating yield information growth along our ordering, we also assume standard embeddings of x and y into $x \bullet y$, say, via $\text{in}_1(x, y) : x \to x \bullet y$ and $\text{in}_2(x, y) : y \to x \bullet y$. For example, then, x may be embedded in $(x \bullet y) \bullet z$ as follows. First x is embedded in $x \bullet y$ by $\text{in}_1(x, y)$, and $(x \bullet y)$ in its turn is embedded in $(x \bullet y) \bullet z$ by $\text{in}_1(x \bullet y, z)$. Now $(x \bullet y) \bullet z$ is identified with $x \bullet (y \bullet z)$ by $\alpha(x, y, z)$. Alternatively, x is embedded in $x \bullet (y \bullet z)$ by $\text{in}_1(x, y \bullet z)$. Putting all this together, one obtains equalities like the following.

$$\begin{aligned}
&\text{in}_1(x, y) \circ \text{in}_1(x \bullet y, z) \circ \alpha(x, y, z) = \text{in}_1(x, y \bullet z).\\
&\text{in}_2(x, y) \circ \text{in}_1(x \bullet y, z) \circ \alpha(x, y, z) = \text{in}_1(y, z) \circ \text{in}_2(x, y \bullet z).\\
&\text{in}_2(x \bullet y, z) \circ \alpha(x, y, z) = \text{in}_2(y, z) \circ \text{in}_2(x, y \bullet z).
\end{aligned}$$

The resulting mathematical structures are called *m-categories*. m-categories are the natural medium for thinking about dynamic updating and dynamic contexts. Starting from simple m-categories that describe contexts and contents, we can now assemble meanings by the well-known categorical *Grothendieck construction* (see Barr and Wells, 1989; Visser and Vermeulen, 1995).

2.3. *Dynamics related to statics*

2.3.1. *Translations*

It is often useful to define functions from the expressions of one logic to those of another. If such a function preserves logical consequence it is called a *translation* and in the following section we shall define translations from PDL and QDL to classical logic. Our method will be to take the truth conditions of the source logics and transcribe them in the object language of the target logic. This is in fact an old procedure, as the so-called *standard translation* from modal logic into predicate logic may witness. To obtain this translation, associate a unary predicate symbol P with each propositional letter p of the modal language and let R be some binary relation symbol. Then define the translation ST, sending sentences from propositional modal logic to formulae of predicate logic having at most the fixed variable i free, as follows.

$$\begin{aligned}
\text{ST}(p) &= Pi,\\
\text{ST}(\bot) &= \bot,\\
\text{ST}(\varphi \to \psi) &= \text{ST}(\varphi) \to \text{ST}(\psi),\\
\text{ST}(\diamond\varphi) &= \exists j(Rij \wedge [j/i]\text{ST}(\varphi)).
\end{aligned}$$

Whether this function really preserves entailment depends on the modal system under investigation, of course. For the minimal modal logic K the translation will do as it stands, but for stronger logics we need to put additional constraints on the relation denoted by R. For many modal systems S a lemma of the following form will hold.

EMBEDDING LEMMA. $\varphi \models_S \psi$ *iff* $\mathrm{AX}, \mathrm{ST}(\varphi) \models \mathrm{ST}(\psi)$.

Here AX is some set of axioms putting extra requirements on R. For example, we can take AX to be the requirement that R be reflexive and transitive, while instantiating S as the system S4. In general, the correctness of a translation may require working with special classes of models.

There are various reasons why it is handy to have translations around whenever they are available. One reason is that it is often possible to derive information about the source logic of a translation from properties of the target logic that are already known. For example, the standard translation immediately tells us that the modal logics that can be treated in this way are recursively axiomatizable and will have the Löwenheim–Skolem property. Other translations often give us decidability of a system. Some information may not be obtainable in this easy way, of course. For example, although the above translation shows that there *are* recursive axiomatizations of the modal logics under consideration, it does not tell us what these axiomatizations look like. Moreover, some semantic characteristics of the original logic may be lost in translation. *Traduttore traditore,* not only in real life, but in logic as well.

Reasons for studying translation functions also include some of a more applied character. One is that a translation into classical logic will make it possible to use a general purpose classical theorem prover for the source logic. Another reason is that for applied purposes we often need to have many logics working in tandem. In linguistics, for example, we need logics that can deal with modalities, with temporal expressions, with verbs of perception, with propositional attitudes, with defaults, with dynamics, and with many other things. Trying to set up a logic that can simultaneously deal with all these things by adding up the characteristics of modal logic, temporal logic, default logic, dynamic logic, etc. will almost certainly result in disaster. Translating all these special logics into one common general purpose target logic may be a viable strategy, however.

2.3.2. *From dynamic logic to classical logic*

In this section we shall give translations of Dynamic Logic into classical logic. It will not be possible to let elementary predicate logic be our target language, because of the infinitary nature of the iteration operator. However, if we allow infinite disjunctions, and thus obtain the logic known as $L_{\omega_1\omega}$, translations are possible. The following function τ sends PDL constructs to classical formulae. The idea is that each PDL formula is translated as a formula which may have one variable i free and that a PDL program goes to a formula which may contain an additional free variable j. The variables i and j are fixed in advance, say as the first and second variables in some given ordering. Think of i as being the input state, of j as the output state. Each propositional letter p is associated with a unary predicate symbol P and each atomic program α with a binary relation symbol R_α. Let π^0 stand for $\top?$ (the **skip** command) and π^{n+1} for $\pi^n; \pi$.

$$\tau(p) = Pi,$$

$$\tau(\bot) = \bot,$$
$$\tau(\varphi \to \psi) = \tau(\varphi) \to \tau(\psi),$$
$$\tau([\pi]\varphi) = \forall k(\tau(\pi) \to [k/i]\tau(\varphi)), \text{ where } k \text{ is new},$$
$$\tau(\alpha) = R_\alpha ij,$$
$$\tau(\varphi?) = i = j \wedge \tau(\varphi),$$
$$\tau(\pi_1; \pi_2) = \exists k([k/j]\tau(\pi_1) \wedge [k/i]\tau(\pi_2)), \text{ where } k \text{ is new},$$
$$\tau(\pi_1 \cup \pi_2) = \tau(\pi_1) \vee \tau(\pi_2),$$
$$\tau(\pi^*) = \bigvee_n \tau(\pi^n).$$

This translation, which obviously follows the semantics for PDL given in Section 2.1.1 above, can be extended to a translation of QDL into $L_{\omega_1\omega}$ (cf. Harel, 1984). PDL may also be translated into second-order logic: with clauses as before, except that now

$$\tau(\pi^*) = \forall X\big((Xi \wedge \forall kh((Xk \wedge [k/i, h/j]\tau(\pi)) \to Xh) \to Xj\big),$$

where k and h are fresh variables and X varies over sets of states. The formula says that i and j are in the reflexive transitive closure of the denotation of π, which is true iff j is in all sets containing i which are closed under π successors.

We shall extend the last translation to a translation of QDL into three-sorted second order logic plus some axioms. There will be three types of objects: states, entities and registers. We use the following notation: u (with or without superscripts or subscripts) will be a constant that denotes a register; v will be a variable over registers; ρ will vary over terms of type register. The constant $\mathcal{V}$ will denote a two-place function from registers and states to entities; $\mathcal{V}(\rho, i)$ can be thought of as the value of register ρ in state i. We define $i[\rho_1 \cdots \rho_n]j$ to be short for $\forall v((\rho_1 \neq v \wedge \cdots \wedge \rho_n \neq v) \to \mathcal{V}(v, i) = \mathcal{V}(v, j))$ (i and j differ at most in $\rho_1, \ldots, \rho_n$). We require the following: for each state, each register and each entity, there must be a second state that is just like the first one, except that the given entity is a value of the given register. Moreover, we demand that different constants denote different registers.

AX1 $\forall i \forall v \forall x \exists j(i[v]j \wedge \mathcal{V}(v, j) = x)$,
AX2 $u \neq u'$ for each two syntactically different constants u and u'.

The translation is now obtained in the following way. We assume the set of QDL variables and the set of register constants to have a fixed ordering each. We let $\tau(x_n) = \mathcal{V}(u_n, i)$; $\tau(c) = c$, for each constant c and $\tau(f(t_1, \ldots, t_n)) = f(\tau(t_1), \ldots, \tau(t_n))$. Moreover, we let

$$\tau(R(t_1, \ldots, t_n)) = R(\tau(t_1), \ldots, \tau(t_n)),$$
$$\tau(t_1 = t_2) = \tau(t_1) = \tau(t_2),$$
$$\tau(x_n := ?) = i[u_n]j,$$
$$\tau(x_n := t) = i[u_n]j \wedge \mathcal{V}(u, j) = [j/i]\tau(t).$$

The remaining constructs of QDL are translated as before. It is not difficult to prove the following lemma.

EMBEDDING LEMMA. *Let $\models_2$ be the semantical consequence relation of three sorted second order logic, then*

$$\varphi \models_{\mathrm{QDL}} \psi \quad \textit{iff} \quad \mathrm{AX1}, \mathrm{AX2}, \tau(\varphi) \models_2 \tau(\psi).$$

Since we have already observed (in Section 2.1.1) that both DRT and DPL can be embedded in the star free part of QDL, this immediately gives us embeddings from DRT and DPL into (three-sorted) predicate logic; for each DRS K we have a predicate logical formula with at most the state variables i and j free which shows the same input/output behaviour as K. In the next section we shall see an application of this.

2.3.3. An application: Compositional DRT

Several researchers (e.g., Groenendijk and Stokhof, 1990; Asher, 1993; Bos, Mastenbroek, McGlashan, Millies and Pinkal, 1994) have stressed the desirability to combine the dynamic character of DRT and DPL with the possibility to interpret expressions compositionally as it is done in Montague Grammar (see also Van Eijck and Kamp, 1996, this Handbook). To this end one must have a logic that combines the constructs of DRT with lambda abstraction, but until recently no simple semantically interpreted system supporting full lambda conversion was forthcoming. Using the ideas from the previous section it is easy to define such a logic, however. We shall follow Muskens (1991, 1994, 1995a, 1995b) in giving an interpretation of DRT in the first-order part of classical type logic.

To get the required embedding, let $\mathcal{V}$ be a constant of type $\pi(se)$ (where π is the type of registers) and identify discourse referents with constants of type π. The original DRT constructs can now be obtained by means of the following abbreviations; conditions will be terms of type st DRSs terms of type $s(st)$.

Pu	*abbreviates*	$\lambda i.P(\mathcal{V}(u)(i))$,
$u_1 R u_2$	*abbreviates*	$\lambda i.R(\mathcal{V}(u_1)(i))(\mathcal{V}(u_2)(i))$,
u_1 **is** u_2	*abbreviates*	$\lambda i.(\mathcal{V}(u_1)(i)) = (\mathcal{V}(u_2)(i))$,
not K	*abbreviates*	$\lambda i \neg \exists j K(i)(j)$,
K_1 **or** K_2	*abbreviates*	$\lambda i \exists j (K_1(i)(j) \vee K_2(i)(j))$,
$K_1 \Rightarrow K_2$	*abbreviates*	$\lambda i \forall j (K_1(i)(j) \to \exists k K_2(j)(k))$,
$[u_1 \cdots u_n \mid \gamma_1, \ldots, \gamma_m]$	*abbreviates*	$\lambda i \lambda j.i[u_1, \ldots, u_n]j \wedge \gamma_1(j) \wedge \cdots \wedge \gamma_m(j)$,
$K_1; K_2$	*abbreviates*	$\lambda i \lambda j \exists k (K_1(i)(k) \wedge K_2(k)(j))$.

To allow for the possibility of compositional interpretation we have added the PDL sequencing operator (DPL conjunction) to the constructs under consideration. The following simple lemma is useful.

MERGING LEMMA. *If $u'_1, \ldots, u'_k$ do not occur in any of $\varphi_1, \ldots, \varphi_m$ then* $\models_{\mathrm{AX}} [u_1 \cdots u_n \mid \varphi_1, \ldots, \varphi_m]; [u'_1 \cdots u'_k \mid \gamma_1, \ldots, \gamma_r] = [u_1 \cdots u_n u'_1 \cdots u'_k \mid \varphi_1, \ldots, \varphi_m, \gamma_1, \ldots, \gamma_r]$.

We sketch the treatment of a small fragment of ordinary language in this system. It will be assumed that all determiners, proper names and anaphoric pronouns are indexed on the level of syntax. Here are translations for a limited set of basic expressions (variables P are of type $\pi(s(st))$, variables p and q of type $s(st)$ and variable Q is of type $(\pi(s(st)))(s(st)))$.

$\mathtt{a}^{\mathtt{n}}$	*translates as*	$\lambda P'\lambda P([u_n \mid\mid]\,;P'(u_n)\,;P(u_n))$,
$\mathtt{no}^{\mathtt{n}}$	*translates as*	$\lambda P'\lambda P[\mid \mathbf{not}([u_n \mid\mid]\,;P'(u_n)\,;P(u_n))]$,
$\mathtt{every}^{\mathtt{n}}$	*translates as*	$\lambda P'\lambda P[\mid ([u_n \mid\mid]\,;P'(u_n)) \Rightarrow P(u_n)]$,
$\mathtt{he}_{\mathtt{n}}$	*translates as*	$\lambda P(P(u_n))$,
`who`	*translates as*	$\lambda P'\lambda P\lambda v(P(v)\,;P'(v))$,
`man`	*translates as*	$\lambda v[\mid \mathit{man}\ v]$,
`woman`	*translates as*	$\lambda v[\mid \mathit{woman}\ v]$,
`stink`	*translates as*	$\lambda v[\mid \mathit{stinks}\ v]$,
`adore`	*translates as*	$\lambda Q\lambda v(Q(\lambda v'[\mid v\ \mathit{adores}\ v']))$,
`if`	*translates as*	$\lambda pq[\mid p \Rightarrow q]$.

Note that the translation of (say) $\mathtt{no}^3$ applied to the translation of `man` can be reduced to $\lambda P[\mid \mathbf{not}([u_3 \mid \mathit{man}\ u_3]\,;P(u_3))]$ with the help of lambda-conversion and the merging lemma. In a similar way the sentence $\mathtt{a}^1$ `man adores` $\mathtt{a}^2$ `woman` can be translated as suggested in the tree below.

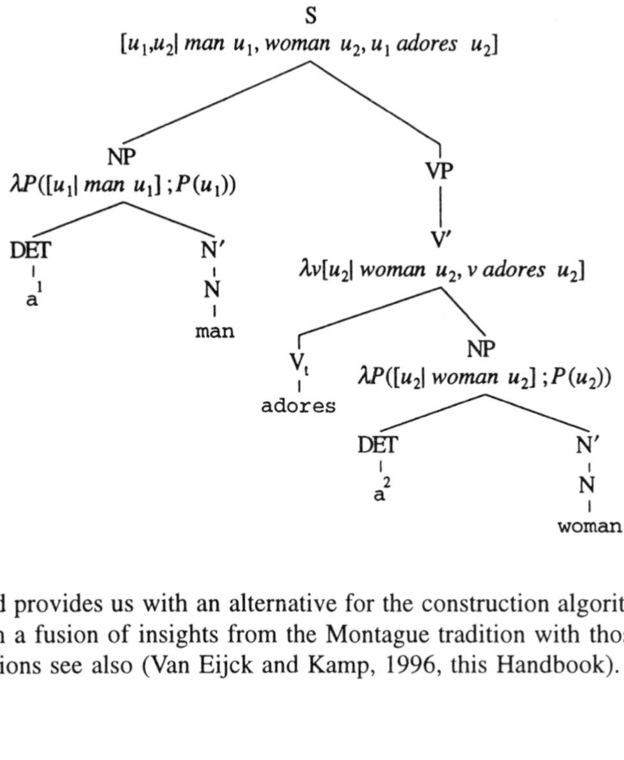

The method provides us with an alternative for the construction algorithm in standard DRT and with a fusion of insights from the Montague tradition with those of DRT. For more applications see also (Van Eijck and Kamp, 1996, this Handbook).

2.3.4. Two-level architecture and static tracing of dynamic procedures

The two-level approach of PDL suggests the following two-level architecture. Declarative propositions and dynamic procedures both have reasonable motivations. Presumably, actual inference is a mixture of more dynamic sequential short-term processes and more static long-term ones, not necessarily over the same representations. Thus, both systems must interact:

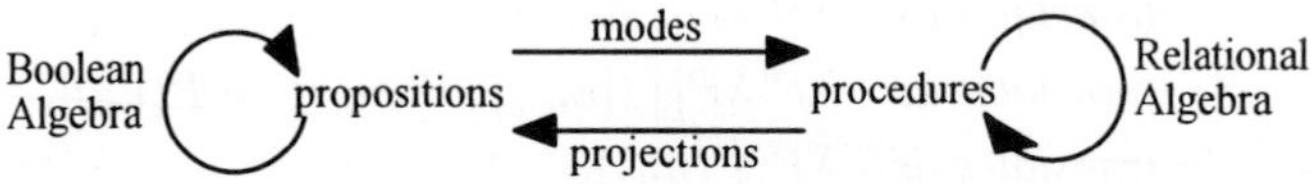

In such a picture, logical connections between the two levels become essential. There will be *modes* taking standard propositions to correlated procedures, such as 'updating' to make a proposition true, or 'testing' whether the proposition holds already. In the opposite direction, there are *projections* assigning to each procedure a standard proposition recording some essential feature of its action. Examples are the fixed point operator Φ giving the states where the procedure is already satisfied, or set-theoretic domain, giving the states where it can be performed at all. These new operators of 'logical management' may be analyzed technically much as those in Section 2.1, e.g., through type-theoretic analysis (cf. Turner, 1996, this Handbook). For instance, fixed-point is the only permutation-invariant projection that is a Boolean homomorphism (Van Benthem, 1991a). This style of analysis has been extended to eliminative update logic in (Van Benthem and Cepparello, 1994).

The above setting can also be analyzed using concepts from computer science. In particular, one can trace a dynamic process by means of propositions describing successive images of sets of states under its action. Define *strongest postconditions* and *weakest preconditions* as follows.

$$\mathrm{SP}(A,R) = R[A] \quad (= \{b \mid \exists a \in A\colon \langle a,b\rangle \in R\}),$$
$$\mathrm{WP}(R,A) = R^{-1}[A] \quad (= \{b \mid \exists a \in A\colon \langle b,a\rangle \in R\}).$$

The set $\mathrm{WP}(R,A)$ is also known as the *Peirce product* of R and A (cf. Brink, Britz and Schmidt, 1992). Note that $\|\langle\pi\rangle\varphi\| = \mathrm{WP}(\|\pi\|, \|\varphi\|)$. These notions may be used to render dynamic validity. For example, for update-update consequence, we have

$$\varphi_1, \ldots, \varphi_n \models_{\text{update-update}} \psi \quad \text{if and only if}$$
$$\mathrm{SP}(A, \|\varphi_1\| \circ \cdots \circ \|\varphi_n\|) \subseteq \mathrm{SP}(A, \|\psi\|) \quad \text{for arbitrary sets } A.$$

Moreover, there is an inductive calculus for computing weakest preconditions and strongest postconditions, with clauses such as:

$$\mathrm{SP}(A, R \circ S) = \mathrm{SP}(\mathrm{SP}(A,R), S),$$
$$\mathrm{WP}(R \circ S, A) = \mathrm{WP}(R, \mathrm{WP}(S,A)),$$

$$\begin{aligned}
\text{SP}(A, R \cup S) &= \text{SP}(A, R) \vee \text{SP}(A, S),\\
\text{WP}(R \cup S, A) &= \text{WP}(R, A) \vee \text{WP}(S, A),\\
\text{SP}(A, R^{\cup}) &= \text{WP}(R, A),\\
\text{WP}(R^{\cup}, A) &= \text{SP}(A, R).
\end{aligned}$$

As an application we give a weakest preconditions calculus which computes the truth conditions of any DRS or condition, given the total semantics for DRT discussed in Section 1.2.2. A simple induction will prove that $\text{TR}(\varphi)$ is a predicate logical formula which is true under the same assignments as the condition φ is and that $\text{WP}(K, \chi)$ is true under a iff there is some b such that $\langle a, b\rangle \in \|K\|$ and χ is true under b. In particular, $\text{WP}(K, \top)$ will give the truth conditions of K.

$$\begin{aligned}
&\text{TR}(\varphi) = \varphi \quad \text{if } \varphi \text{ is atomic},\\
&\text{TR}(\neg K) = \neg\text{WP}(K, \top),\\
&\text{TR}(K_1 \vee K_2) = \text{WP}(K_1, \top) \vee \text{WP}(K_2, \top),\\
&\text{TR}(K_1 \Rightarrow K_2) = \neg\text{WP}(K_1, \neg\text{WP}(K_2, \top)),\\
&\text{WP}([x_1, \ldots, x_n \mid \varphi_1, \ldots, \varphi_m], \chi) = \exists x_1 \cdots x_n(\text{TR}(\varphi_1) \wedge \cdots \wedge \text{TR}(\varphi_m) \wedge \chi).
\end{aligned}$$

A similar calculus can be given for DPL:

$$\begin{aligned}
&\text{WP}(\neg\varphi, \chi) = \neg\text{WP}(\varphi, \top) \wedge \chi,\\
&\text{WP}(\varphi \to \psi, \chi) = \neg\text{WP}(\varphi, \neg\text{WP}(\psi, \top)) \wedge \chi,\\
&\text{WP}(\varphi \wedge \psi, \chi) = \text{WP}(\varphi, \text{WP}(\psi, \chi)),\\
&\text{WP}(\exists x\varphi, \chi) = \exists x\text{WP}(\varphi, \chi), \text{ etc.}
\end{aligned}$$

And again $\text{WP}(\varphi, \top)$ gives φ's truth conditions. Van Eijck and De Vries (1992) extend a calculus such as this one with clauses for generalized quantifiers and a description operator (see also Van Eijck and De Vries, 1995; Van Eijck and Kamp, 1996, this Handbook, where the format of the Segerberg axioms of Section 2.1.1 is used).

2.4. *General perspectives*

In this final section, we summarize our main logical themes, and point out some further issues and lines of formal investigation in dynamic semantics.

2.4.1. *Models for dynamics*

Our main logical paradigm has been *Dynamic Logic*, broadly conceived (Harel, 1984), viewing procedures as sets of transitions over spaces of (information) states. Dynamic operators then resemble those found in the relation-algebraic literature. Alternative universal-algebraic approaches are *Process Algebra* (Baeten and Weyland, 1990) or *Arrow Logic* (Venema, 1994). More sensitive notions of computation might involve 'failure paths' (Segerberg, 1991) or 'trace models' (Vermeulen, 1994). These may suggest richer languages. With processes as sets of state transition sequences ('traces'), the proper formalism is a 'branching time logic' combining evaluation at states with that on traces ('epistemic histories'). But further mathematical paradigms were available. Gärdenfors' original theory of belief change (Section 1.5) uses *Category Theory*, with dynamic procedures as morphisms that can be combined via categorial limit constructions. Also, Arrow Logic has categorial models (Van Benthem, 1994). And we have seen some Utrecht-style examples of concrete category-theoretic analysis for anaphora. Clearly, this alternative route deserves exploration.

Dynamic semantic paradigms have proof-theoretic alternatives – with Curry–Howard–deBruyn isomorphisms assigning algorithmic procedures to derivations for assertions. (Cf. this Handbook, the chapters by Moortgat, Buszkowski, and Turner.) *Proof Theory* has been proposed as a general paradigm of linguistic meaning in (Kneale and Kneale, 1962; Dummett, 1976), as well as (Van Benthem, 1991a) (categorial logic and typed lambda calculus), (Ranta, 1991) (Martin-Löf style type theories), (Gabbay and Kempson, 1992) ('labeled deductive systems'). We also briefly considered *Game Theory* as yet another alternative (Hintikka and Sandu, 1996, this Handbook), which provides logical games for evaluating statements, comparing model structures, or carrying on debates, with suitably assigned roles for players and winning conventions (cf. the survey Van Benthem, 1988). Winning strategies in evaluation or debating games provide analyses for truth and consequence in the work of Lorenzen (1959), Hintikka (1973). For model-theoretic 'Ehrenfeucht Games', cf. (Doets, 1993).

The paradigms of programs, proofs and games are not mutually exclusive. All involve movement through a space of deductive stages, information states, or game configurations. This requires a repertoire of atomic moves over states, that can be combined into complex procedures through 'logical constructions'. Thus, proofs involve basic combinatorics for trees: 'combination', 'arguing by cases' and 'hypothesizing', creating a dynamic block structure. Programs involve the usual constructions for instructions or plans such as 'sequential composition', 'indeterministic choice' or 'iteration', possibly guided by 'control assertions'. Finally, game operations reflect roles of different players, such as conjunctions or disjunctions indicating their rights of choice and duties of response, as well as the notion of 'role change' (signaled by negation). Finally, all three paradigms involve an explicit interplay between actions changing states, and standard declarative statements about the states traversed by actions.

2.4.2. *Higher levels of aggregation*

Language use is guided by *global strategies*, such as 'preferring the more specific interpretation' (Kameyama (1992) has computational linguistic architectures reflecting this). Global strategies have been most prominent in the game-theoretical literature. As a result, one also needs *global structures*, viz. texts or theories, and the meta-rules that govern our activities at these higher levels. Early work on logical structure of scientific theories in the Philosophy of Science is suggestive here (cf. Suppe, 1977), as well as the analysis of global structures of definition, proof and refutation in (Lakatos, 1976), or recent computational work on structured data bases (cf. Ryan, 1992). But these have not yet been integrated with mainstream logic. Another global challenge is the fact that cognition is usually a social process with more than one participant. The role of *multiple agents* has been taken seriously in the game-theoretic approach, but hardly in the other two (but cf. Halpern and Moses, 1985). Many-person versions of dynamic theories are needed, replacing programs by protocols for a group of distributed agents, and proofs by more interactive formats of reasoning. (Jaspars (1994) is an exploration.)

2.4.3. Resources

Our 'dynamic turn' crucially involves cognitive *resources*. There are no unlimited supplies of information or 'deductive energy', and logical analysis should bring out which mechanisms are adopted, and which cost in resources is incurred. This requires management of *occurrences* of assertions or instructions in proofs, programs and games. Stating a formula twice in a proof means two calls to its evidence, repeating the same instruction in a program calls for two executions, and repeating it in the course of a game will signal a new obligation as to its defense or attack. (Unlimited energy or standing commitment must be encoded explicitly via a logical 'repetition operator': (Girard, 1987; Van Benthem, 1993).) Thus, many recent logics work with occurrences, at a finer level of detail than the usual classical or intuitionistic calculi. (Moortgat (1996) and Buszkowski (1996, this Handbook), provide detailed linguistic motivation for this shift in emphasis.) Another form of fine-structure is *dependence*. Standard logics assume that all individuals under discussion can be freely introduced into discourse. But in general, some objects may depend on others (cf. Fine, 1985; Meyer Viol, 1995; Hintikka and Sandu, 1996, this Handbook), either 'in nature' or procedurally, in the course of dynamic interpretation. This further degree of freedom has interesting consequences. For example, on the usual proof-theoretic account, non-standard generalized quantifiers like *most* or *many* are difficult to analyze (Sundholm, 1986). But Van Lambalgen (1991) gives a Gentzen calculus with 'dependence management' for variables in quantifier rules to provide complete logics for non-standard quantifiers, where the classical ones become the limiting case with 'unlimited access'. Alechina (1995) is a more systematic study of various current dependence semantics with a dynamic flavor.

2.4.4. States and atomic actions

In this chapter, we have tried to identify some general strands in a process theory for natural language, at a suitable level of abstraction. In particular, no single notion of cognitive state can serve all of natural language. For instance, the DRT/DPL treatment of anaphora uses (partial or total) Tarskian variable assignments. Dynamic accounts of learning or updating have used probability functions over propositions, sets of worlds, states in Kripke models, or data bases. More complex syntactic discourse states occur in the computational literature. Nevertheless, useful general distinctions have emerged, such as that between *constructive* and *eliminative* views of information processing (cf. Landman, 1986), where epistemic states become 'richer' under updating in the former case, but 'simpler', by dropping alternatives, in the latter. (The two viewpoints may be combined in a dynamic epistemic logic; cf. (Jaspars, 1994).) Another general feature is 'dynamization'. Many update calculi may be viewed as 'dynamizations' of ordinary modal logics (cf. Van Benthem, 1991a), and standard extensional or intensional semantics may dynamicized through their natural parameters of variation (Cepparello, 1995). A final interesting issue is *combination* of different notions of state, with the resulting marriage of the corresponding logics, as in the merges of DPL and Update Semantics mentioned in Section 1.2.4.

Atomic actions in linguistics include testing of propositions, as well as the updating, contracting and revision found in the computational literature. Other speech acts have only been touched upon, such as questions (cf. Groenendijk and Stokhof, 1984). There is little uniformity in basic actions for different notions of state (compare assignment change versus updating), unless we either (i) move to a higher level of abstraction, where pops or pushes are general computational moves (Visser, 1994), or (ii) analyze atomic actions into a combination of 'modes' plus resultative static propositions, such as *test*(φ), *achieve*(φ), *query*(φ), where modes may be uniform across many different situations (Van Benthem, 1991a).

2.4.5. Dynamic operators and invariance

Which dynamic operations construct complex programs, plans, actions? One can approach this question at the level of linguistic items (programs, scripts) or their denotations (executions). There is great diversity here, witness our earlier survey. The proper definition for various dynamic operators is still under debate, witness the extensive discussion of an appropriate dynamic negation for natural language in (Dekker, 1993). Moreover, different dynamic paradigms may cut the cake in different ways. For example negation is less at home in the proof-theoretic perspective, unless one treats refutation on a par with proof (cf. Wansing, 1992). Likewise, negation as complement of programs is a marginal operation ("avoidance") – but negation as role switching is a crucial element in games. Another difference occurs with quantifiers, which are no longer on a par with propositional connectives in some dynamic semantics. They rather signal atomic moves establishing some binding or drawing some object, plus (in some cases) some further assertion following these. Thus, the syntax of the usual formal languages may even be misleading, in that it does not allow us to regard, say, a prefix $\exists x$ as an independent instruction by itself (say, 'pick an object ($\exists$), and assign it a temporary name (x)'). A more sensitive account of quantificational activity, involving changing data structures and bindings, was found in Section 2.2.

What we have outlined in this chapter is a general framework for the whole logical space of possibilities. Dynamic logic is all about control operators that combine procedures. Much dynamic semantics investigates what standard logical constants mean when viewed as procedural combinators. But dynamics allows for finer distinctions than statics, so that there may not be any clear sense to this. Standard conjunction really collapses several notions: sequential composition, but also various forms of parallel composition. Likewise, standard negation may be either some test as in DPL, or merely an invitation to make any move refraining from some forbidden action ("you can do anything, but don't step on my blue suede shoes"). Some natural operators in dynamic logic even lack classical counterparts altogether, such as 'conversion' or 'iteration' of procedures. One general perspective of *semantic invariance* relates the static and dynamic notions (Sher, 1991; Van Benthem, 1989). Truly logical operators do not depend on specific individuals in their arguments. This is also true for procedural operators. What makes, say, a complement $-R$ a logical negation is that it works uniformly on all ordered pairs (or arrows) in R, unlike an adjective like "clever" which depends on the content of its relational arguments. The mathematical generalization is *invariance under permutations* π of the underlying universe of individuals (here, information states). Dynamic procedures denote binary relations between states, and hence procedural operators satisfy the commutation schema:

$$\pi[O(R, S, \ldots)] = O(\pi[R], \pi[S], \ldots).$$

For a general type-theoretic formulation of this notion, cf. (Van Benthem, 1991a).

Permutation invariance leaves infinitely many potential dynamic logical constants. There are several ways of tightening up. One insists on suitable forms of *linguistic definability*. For instance, many dynamic operators have first-order definitions with variables over states and binary relation letters for procedures. We shall encounter this view-point in the next section. Another strengthening increases the demands on invariance, by requiring commutation for much looser forms of process equivalence than isomorphism over the same base domain. A typical example was the 'safety for bisimulation' discussed earlier.

2.4.6. *Dynamic styles of inference*

We have identified several dynamic styles of inference. These may still vary according to one's dynamic paradigm. The proof-theoretic perspective justifies an inference by composing it as the result of a number of basic moves. For instance, the basic inference $A \vee B, \neg A/B$ is a combination of argument by cases and one basic negation step:

$$\frac{A \vee B \qquad \dfrac{A \quad \neg A}{B} \qquad B}{B}\;.$$

In the programming perspective, this same inference would rather be viewed as an procedural update instruction:

> Updating any information state by $A \vee B$ and then by $\neg A$ (given some suitable procedural meaning for these operations) leads to a new information state which may be tested to validate B.

In the context of games, the story is different again. For instance, the 'agonistic' Lorenzen style would express the relevant validity as follows:

> There exists a winning strategy for defending the claim B in a dialogue game against any opponent who has already granted the two concessions $A \vee B, \neg A$.

One locus of difference here lies in the *structural rules* governing inference. Important examples are the admissibility, without loss of previous conclusions, of shuffling premises by Permutation, or of adding new premises by Monotonicity (Section 2.1.6 provided detailed formulations). For instance, Permutation is reasonable on both proof-theoretic and game-theoretic views, whereas it seems unreasonable on the programming view, since the sequential order of instructions is usually crucial to their total intended effect. Likewise, Monotonicity is plausible in games (the more concessions from one's opponent the better), but less so on the other two accounts. Still, if premise ordering in a game encodes priority of commitments incurred, then Permutation loses its appeal in the latter model too.

But also, analyzing cognitive activity via different interacting mechanisms raises issues of *logical architecture*. What systematic methods are available for switching between components (proof-theoretic, algorithmic, game-theoretic – and within these, between different facilities), and how do we transport information from one to the other? In other words, what are natural constructions of heterogeneous logical calculi? Some relevant material on these issues exists in the logical literature (cf. Gabbay, 1996), but no general theory exists.

2.4.7. Connections with computer science

Process Algebra views the denotations of procedures, not as binary relations, but rather as labeled transition models themselves (identified modulo bisimulation, or some other appropriate semantic equivalence). Some key references in this extensive field are (Milner, 1980; Bergstra and Klop, 1984; Baeten and Weyland, 1990). The result is a family of equational calculi for operations on, rather than inside, labeled transition systems. These provide abstract algebraic axiomatizations for various program constructions, including a much richer repertoire than what has been considered in dynamic semantics. (Examples are various parallel merges, as well as operators for 'hiding' structure, or for performing recursion.) For connections between Process Algebra and Dynamic Logic, see (Hennessy and Milner, 1985; Van Benthem and Bergstra, 1993; Van Benthem, Van Eijck and Stebletsova, 1993; Van Benthem, 1994). An eventual process theory for natural language may well have to be of this level of semantic sophistication.

2.4.8. Lowering complexity: Arrow logic and modal state semantics

One immediate concern in dynamic semantics is computational complexity. Many systems in Section 1 are supposed to mirror mechanisms in human cognition, and presumably, these procedures are geared towards speed and efficiency. Nevertheless, little is known about the complexity of various procedural logics – and what little is known, often makes their behaviour more complex than that of standard static systems (cf. Harel, 1984). For example, static propositional logic is decidable, relational algebra is not. Some recent logical proposals exist for coming to terms with such apparent paradoxes. We mention two of these.

Relational Algebra is not the only candidate for analyzing dynamic procedures. Intuitively, the latter seem to consist of transitions or *arrows* as objects in their own right. This alternative view is brought out in Arrow Logic, a modal logic over *arrow frames* $\langle W, C, R, I\rangle$ with a set W of arrows, a ternary relation C of *composition*, a binary relation R of *reversal* and a set I of *identical* arrows. Formulas φ will describe sets of arrows $\|\varphi\|$, i.e. transition relations in the new sense. Some key clauses in the basic truth definition are as follows.

$$\|\varphi \cap \psi\| = \|\varphi\| \cap \|\psi\|,$$

$$\|\varphi \circ \psi\| = \{a \mid \exists bc(\langle a,b,c\rangle \in C \ \&\ b \in \|\varphi\| \ \&\ c \in \|\psi\|)\},$$
$$\|\varphi^{\cup}\| = \{a \mid \exists b(\langle a,b\rangle \in R \ \&\ b \in \|\varphi\|)\},$$
$$\|\Delta\| = I.$$

Arrow Logic is a minimal theory of composition of actions, which may be studied by well-known techniques from Modal Logic (cf. Van Benthem, 1991a; Venema, 1991, 1994). Standard principles of Relational Algebra then express constraints on arrow patterns, which can be determined via *frame correspondences* (Van Benthem, 1985; De Rijke, 1993). For instance, the algebraic law $(\varphi \cup \psi)^{\cup} = (\varphi^{\cup} \cup \psi^{\cup})$ is a universally valid principle of modal distribution on arrow frames, but $(\varphi \cap \psi)^{\cup} = (\varphi^{\cup} \cap \psi^{\cup})$ expresses the genuine constraint that the conversion relation be a partial function f, whose idempotence would be expressed by the modal axiom $\varphi^{\cup\cup} = \varphi$. As an illustration, basic categorial laws of natural language (cf. Moortgat, 1996, this Handbook) now acquire dynamic content.

$$A \bullet (A\backslash B) \Rightarrow B \quad \textit{expresses that } \forall abc(\langle a,b,c\rangle \in C \to \langle c, f(b), a\rangle \in C).$$
$$(B/A) \bullet A \Rightarrow B \quad \textit{expresses that } \forall abc(\langle a,b,c\rangle \in C \to \langle b, a, f(c)\rangle \in C).$$

In particular, one can now study dynamic counterparts of the Lambek Calculus (cf. Kurtonina (1995) for a full development).

More radically, one can take this same deconstructionist line with respect to first-order predicate logic, the lingua franca of modern semantics – which suffers from undecidability. What makes first-order predicate logic tick at an abstract computational level? As we saw, the basic Tarski truth definition makes choices that are inessential to a compositional semantics for first-order quantification. In particular, concrete assignments and the concrete relation $a[x]b$ between assignments are not needed to make the semantic recursion work. The abstract core pattern that is needed replaces assignments by abstract states and the relations $[x]$ by arbitrary binary relations R_x between states. Models will then be poly-modal Kripke models $\langle S, \{R_x\}_{x \in \mathrm{VAR}}, V\rangle$, where S is the set of states and the valuation function V assigns a subset of S to each atomic sentence $R(x_1, \ldots, x_n)$. The standard truth definition now generalizes to the following modal set-up.

(i′) $\|R(x_1, \ldots, x_n)\| = V(R(x_1, \ldots, x_n))$.

(ii′) $\|\neg\varphi\| = S - \|\varphi\|$,
$\|\varphi \vee \psi\| = \|\varphi\| \cup \|\psi\|$.

(iii′) $\|\exists x\varphi\| = \{a \in S \mid \exists b(aR_x b \ \&\ b \in \|\varphi\|)\}$.

This semantics treats existential quantifiers $\exists x$ as labeled modalities $\langle x\rangle$. Its universal validities constitute the well-known *minimal modal logic*, whose principles are (a) all classical propositional laws, (b) the axiom of Modal Distribution: $\exists x(\varphi \vee \psi) \leftrightarrow (\exists x\varphi \vee \exists x\psi)$, and (c) the rule of Modal Necessitation: *if* $\vdash \varphi$, *then* $\vdash \neg\exists x\neg\varphi$. A completeness theorem may be proved using the standard Henkin construction. This poly-modal logic can be analyzed in a standard fashion (Andréka, Van Benthem and Németi (1994) is a modern treatment), yielding the usual meta-properties such as the Craig Interpolation

Theorem, and the Łos–Tarski Preservation Theorem for submodels. In particular, the logic can be shown to be *decidable* via any of the usual modal techniques (such as filtration). This means that the particular set-theoretic implementation of the set S and the relations R_x that we find in the usual Tarski semantics can be diagnosed as the source of undecidability of elementary logic.

The modal perspective on classical logic uncovers a whole *fine-structure* of predicate-logical validity. The minimal predicate logic consists of those laws which are 'very much valid'. But we can analyze what other standard laws say too by the technique of modal *frame correspondence*. Here are some illustrations.

$(\varphi \wedge \exists x\varphi) \leftrightarrow \varphi$	*expresses that R_x is reflexive.*
$\exists x(\varphi \wedge \exists x\psi) \leftrightarrow (\exists x\varphi \wedge \exists x\psi)$	*expresses that R_x is transitive and euclidean,*
$\exists x\exists y\varphi \leftrightarrow \exists y\exists x\varphi$	*expresses that* $R_x \circ R_y = R_y \circ R_x$,
$\exists x\forall y\varphi \rightarrow \forall y\exists x\varphi$	*expresses that whenever aR_xbR_yc, there is a d such that aR_ydR_xc.*

The first two constraints make the R_x into equivalence relations, as with the modal logic S5. They do not impose existence of any particular states in frames. The third axiom, by contrast, is existential in nature; it says that sequences of state changes may be traversed in any order. Abstract state models need not have enough intermediate states to follow all alternative routes. The fourth example says that another well-known quantifier shift expresses a Church–Rosser property of computational processes. Thus, the valid laws of predicate logic turn have quite different dynamic content when analyzed in the light of this broader semantics.

We have found a minimal decidable system of predicate logic in addition to the standard undecidable one. Intermediate systems arise by varying requirements on states and updates R_x. Thus a whole landscape of intermediate predicate logics is opened up to us. Here, we seek expressive logics that share important properties with predicate logic (Interpolation, Effective Axiomatizability) and that even *improve* on this, preferably by being decidable. An attractive option, already known from Cylindric Algebra (cf. Henkin, Monk and Tarski, 1985; Németi, 1991) is CRS, the logic consisting of all predicate-logical validities in the state frames satisfying all *universal frame conditions* true in standard assignment models. These are the general logical properties of assignments that do not make existential demands on their supply. (The latter would be more 'mathematical' or 'set-theoretic'.) CRS is known to be decidable, though non-finitely axiomatizable. Moreover, its frame definition needs only universal *Horn* clauses, from which Craig Interpolation follows (Van Benthem, 1994). Another way of describing CRS has independent appeal. Consider state frames where S is a family of ordinary assignments (but not necessarily the full function space D^{VAR}), and the R_x are the standard relations $[x]$. Such frames admit 'assignment gaps', i.e. essentially they need not satisfy axiom AX1 of Section 2.3.2 above. This can be used to model dependencies between variables: changes in value for one variable x may induce, or be correlated with changes in value for another variable y (cf. our earlier discussion of resources). This phenomenon cannot be modeled in standard Tarskian semantics, the latter being a degenerate case where all interesting dependencies between variables have been suppressed. From CRS one can move upward in the hierarchy of logics by considering only families of assignments that satisfy natural closure conditions. Such further structure supports the introduction of further operators into the language (e.g., permutation or substitution operators). For the resulting logics, cf. (Marx, 1994; Mikulas, 1995).

2.4.9. Philosophical repercussions

We conclude with some sweeping thoughts. Dynamic paradigms suggest general cognitive claims. The programming model supports Church's Thesis which claims that any form of effective (cognitive) computation can be programmed on a Turing Machine, or some equivalent device from Recursion Theory. In its broader sense, the Turing Test is a well-known dramatized version. But similar claims can be made concerning proofs or games (in the setting of a suitably general Proof Theory or Game Theory), and that even in two ways. Church's Thesis may be interpreted as the *extensional* statement that the input-output behaviour of every effective function can be adequately programmed on some abstract machine. But it also has a stronger *intensional* version, stating that any algorithm can be reflected faithfully in some specific universal programming repertoire (cf. Moschovakis, 1991). This intensional question returns for proof-theoretic and game-theoretic approaches. What are their natural repertoires of logical constructions that should suffice for faithful modeling of any rational form of inference or cognitive play? (Compare the proof-theoretic functional completeness results in (Sundholm, 1986); or the hierarchies of programming operators in (Van Benthem, 1992).) There could also be 'Small Church Theses' at lower levels of computational complexity, closer to actual linguistic processing (cf. various equivalence results in (Kanovich, 1993)). Of course, one will have to analyze more carefully to which extent the computational metaphor is realistic for natural language (Fernando (1992) proposes recursion-theoretic models for this purpose). In this respect, another desideratum emerges. Our paradigms mostly provide *kinematics*: an extensional analysis of transitions made, whereas one eventually wants genuine *dynamics*: an account of the underlying processes, which explains observed transition behaviour. So far, much of logical semantics has had an extensional engineering flavor, following Lewis's (1972) dictum: *In order to say what a meaning* is, *we may first ask what a meaning* does, *and then find something that does that.*

References

Alchourrón, C., Gärdenfors, P. and Makinson, D. (1985), *On the logic of theory change: Partial meet functions for contraction and revision*, J. Symb. Logic **50**, 510–530.

Alechina, N. (1995), *Modal quantifiers*, Dissertation, Institute for Logic, Language and Computation, University of Amsterdam.

Andréka, H., Van Benthem, J. and Németi, I. (1994), *Back and forth between modal logic and classical logic*, Mathematical Institute, Hungarian Academy of Sciences, Budapest/Institute for Logic, Language and Computation, University of Amsterdam, Report ILLC-ML-95–04. (To appear in Bulletin of the Interest Group for Pure and Applied Logic, London and Saarbrücken, 1995.)

Asher, N. (1993), *Reference to Abstract Objects in Discourse*, Kluwer, Dordrecht.

Baeten, J. and Weyland, P. (1990), *Process Algebra*, Cambridge Univ. Press, Cambridge, MA.

Barr, M. and Wells, C. (1989), *Category Theory for Computing Science*, Prentice-Hall, New York.

Barwise, J. (1987), *Noun phrases, generalized quantifiers and anaphora*, Generalized Quantifiers. Logical and Linguistic Approaches, P. Gärdenfors, ed., Reidel, Dordrecht, 1–29.

Beaver, D. (1992), *The kinematics of presupposition*, Proceedings of the Eighth Amsterdam Colloquium, P. Dekker and M. Stokhof, eds, Institute for Logic, Language and Computation, University of Amsterdam, 17–36.

Beaver, D. (1996), *Presupposition*, This Handbook, Chapter 17.

Belnap, N. (1977), *A useful four-valued logic*, Modern Uses of Multiple-Valued Logics, J.M. Dunn and G. Epstein, eds, Reidel, Dordrecht, 8–37.

Bergstra, J. and Klop, J.-W. (1984), *Process algebra for synchronous communication*, Inform. and Control **60**, 109–137.

Blackburn, P. and Venema, Y. (1993), *Dynamic squares*, Logic Preprint 92, Department of Philosophy, University of Utrecht. (J. Philos. Logic, to appear.)

Blamey, S. (1986), *Partial logic*, Handbook of Philosophical Logic vol. III, D. Gabbay and F. Günthner, eds, 1–70.

Bos, J., Mastenbroek, E., McGlashan, S., Millies, S. and Pinkal, M. (1994), *A compositional DRS-based formalism for NLP applications*, Proceedings International Workshop on Computational Semantics, H. Bunt, R. Muskens and G. Rentier, eds, Institute for Language Technology and Artificial Intelligence, Tilburg, 21–31.

Boutilier, C. (1993), *Revision sequences and nested conditionals*, Proceedings of the 13th IJCAI, R. Bajcsy, ed., Morgan Kaufmann, Washington, DC, 519–525.

Boutilier, C. and Goldszmidt, M. (1993), *Revision by conditional beliefs*, Proceedings of the 11th National Conference on Artificial Intelligence (AAAI), Morgan Kaufmann, Washington, DC, 649–654.

Brink, C., Britz, K. and Schmidt, R. (1992), *Peirce algebras*, Report MPI-I-92-229, MPI, Saarbrücken.

Buszkowski, W. (1996), *Mathematical linguistics and proof theory*, This Handbook, Chapter 12.

Cepparello, G. (1995), *Dynamics: Logical design and philosophical repercussions*, Dissertation, Scuola Normale Superiore, Pisa.

Chierchia, G. (1988), *Dynamic Generalized Quantifiers and Donkey Anaphora*, Genericity in Natural Language, M. Krifka, ed., Tübingen, SNS, 53–84.

Davidson, D. (1967), *The Logical Form of Action Sentences*, Reprinted: D. Davidson, 1980, Essays on Actions and Events, Clarendon Press, Oxford.

Dekker, P. (1993), *Transsentential meditations*, ILLC Dissertation Series 1993-1, Institute for Logic, Language and Computation, University of Amsterdam.

Doets, K. (1993), *Model theory*, Lecture Notes for the Fifth European Summer School in Logic, Language and Information, University of Lisbon.

Dummett, M. (1976), *What is a theory of meaning?*, Truth and Meaning, G. Evans and J. McDowell, eds, Oxford Univ. Press, Oxford, 67–137.

Fernando, T. (1992), *Transition systems and dynamic semantics*, Logics in AI, LNCS 633, Springer, Berlin.

Fine, K. (1985), *Reasoning With Arbitrary Objects*, Blackwell, Oxford.

Gabbay, D. (1994), *Labeled Deductive Systems*, Oxford Univ. Press, Oxford. (To appear.)

Gabbay, D. and Kempson, R. (1992), *Natural language content: A proof-theoretic perspective*, Proceedings of the Eighth Amsterdam Colloquium, P. Dekker and M. Stokhof, eds, Institute for Logic, Language and Computation, University of Amsterdam, 173–195.

Gärdenfors, P. (1988), *Knowledge in Flux. Modelling the Dynamics of Epistemic States*, MIT Press, Cambridge, MA.

Gärdenfors, P. and Makinson, D. (1988), *Revisions of knowledge systems using epistemic entrenchment*, Theoretical Aspects of Reasoning about Knowledge, M. Vardi, ed., Morgan Kaufmann, Los Altos, CA, 83–95.

Gazdar, G. (1979), *Pragmatics*, Academic Press, New York.

Girard, J.-Y. (1987), *Linear logic*, Theor. Comput. Sci. **50**, 1–102.

Goldblatt, R. (1987), *Logics of Time and Computation*, CSLI Lecture Notes, Chicago Univ. Press, Chicago.

Groenendijk, J. and Stokhof, M. (1984), *Studies in the semantics of questions and the pragmatics of answers*, Doctoral Dissertation, University of Amsterdam.

Groenendijk, J. and Stokhof, M. (1990), *Dynamic Montague grammar*, Papers from the Second Symposium on Logic and Language, L. Kálmán and L. Pólos, eds, Akadémiai Kiadó, Budapest, 3–48.

Groenendijk, J. and Stokhof, M. (1991), *Dynamic predicate logic*, Ling. and Philos. **14**, 39–100.
Groenendijk, J., Stokhof, M. and Veltman, F. (1996), *Coreference and modality*, The Handbook of Contemporary Semantic Theory, S. Lappin, ed., Blackwell, Oxford, 179–214.
Grosz, B. and Sidner, C. (1986), *Attention, intention, and the structure of discourse*, Comput. Ling. **12**, 175–204.
Halpern, J. and Moses, Y. (1985), *Towards a theory of knowledge and ignorance*, Logics and Models of Concurrent Systems, K. Apt, ed., Springer, Berlin, 459–476.
Harel, D. (1984), *Dynamic logic*, Handbook of Philosophical Logic vol. II, D. Gabbay and F. Günthner, eds, Reidel, Dordrecht, 497–604.
Harel, D. and Kozen, D. (1994), *Dynamic logic*, Department of Computer Science, Technion, Haifa/Department of Computer Science, Cornell University.
Heim, I. (1982), *The semantics of definite and indefinite noun phrases*, Dissertation, Univ. of Massachusetts, Amherst, published in 1989 by Garland, New York.
Heim, I. (1983a), *On the projection problem for presuppositions*, Proceedings of the West Coast Conference on Formal Linguistics vol. II, Stanford Linguistic Association, Stanford, CA, 114–125, Reprinted in: S. Davies (ed.) (1991), *Pragmatics*, OUP, Oxford, 397–405.
Heim, I. (1983b), *File change semantics and the familiarity theory of definiteness*, Meaning, Use and Interpretation of Language, R. Bäuerle, C. Schwarze and von A. Stechow, eds, De Gruyter, Berlin.
Henkin, L., Monk, D. and Tarski, A. (1985), *Cylindric Algebra*, Part II, North-Holland, Amsterdam.
Hennessy, M. and Milner, R. (1985), *Algebraic laws for nondeterminism and concurrency*, J. Assoc. Comput. Mach. **32**, 137–161.
Hintikka, J. (1973), *Logic, Language Games and Information*, Clarendon Press, Oxford.
Hintikka, J. and Sandu, G. (1996), *Game-theoretical semantics*, This Handbook, Chapter 6.
Hofstadter, D. (1980), *Gödel, Escher, Bach: An Eternal Golden Braid*, Vintage Books, New York.
Jaspars, J. (1994), *Calculi for constructive communication*, ILLC Dissertation Series 1994-1, Institute for Logic, Language and Computation, University of Amsterdam/Institute for Language Technology and Artificial Intelligence, Tilburg University.
Kameyama, M. (1992), *The linguistic information in dynamic discourse*, Research Report CSLI-92-174, Center for the Study of Language and Information, Stanford University.
Kamp, H. (1981), *A theory of truth and semantic representation*, Truth, Interpretation and Information, J. Groenendijk et al., eds, Foris, Dordrecht, 1–41.
Kamp, H. and Reyle, U. (1993), *From Discourse to Logic*, Kluwer, Dordrecht.
Kanazawa, M. (1993a), *Completeness and decidability of the mixed style of inference with composition*, Proceedings of the Ninth Amsterdam Colloquium, P. Dekker and M. Stokhof, eds, Institute for Logic, Language and Computation, University of Amsterdam, 377–390.
Kanazawa, M. (1993b), *Dynamic generalized quantifiers and monotonicity*, Report LP-93-02, Institute for Logic, Language and Computation, University of Amsterdam.
Kanovich, M. (1993), *The expressive power of modalized purely implicational calculi*, Report CSLI-93-184, Center for the Study of Language and Information, Stanford University.
Karttunen, L. (1973), *Presuppositions of compound sentences*, Ling. Inq. **4**, 167–193.
Karttunen, L. (1974), *Presupposition and linguistic context*, Theor. Ling. **1**, 181–194.
Karttunen, L. (1976), *Discourse referents*, Syntax and Semantics 7: Notes from the Linguistic Underground, J. McCawley, ed., Academic Press, New York, 363–385.
Karttunen, L. and Peters, S. (1979), *Conventional implicature*, Syntax and Semantics 11: Presupposition, C.-K. Oh and D. Dinneen, eds, Academic Press, New York, 1–56.
Keenan, E. and Westerståhl, D. (1996), *Quantifiers*, This Handbook, Chapter 15.
Keenan, E. and Faltz, L. (1985), *Boolean Semantics for Natural Language*, Reidel, Dordrecht.
Kneale, W. and M. Kneale (1962), *The Development of Logic*, Clarendon Press, Oxford.
Krahmer, E. (1995), *Discourse and presupposition: From the man in the street to the king of France*, Doctoral Dissertation, Tilburg University.
Kurtonina, N. (1995), *Frames and labels. A logical investigation of categorial structure*, Dissertation, Onderzoeksinstituut voor Taal en Spraak, Universiteit Utrecht.
Lakatos, I. (1976), *Proofs and Refutations*, Cambridge Univ. Press, Cambridge.
Landman, F. (1986), *Towards a Theory of Information. The Status of Partial Objects in Semantics*, Foris, Dordrecht.

Lewis, D. (1972), *General semantics*, Semantics of Natural Language, D. Davidson and G. Harman, eds, Reidel, Dordrecht, 169–218.

Lewis, D. (1973), *Counterfactuals*, Blackwell, Oxford.

Lewis, D. (1979), *Score keeping in a language game*, J. Philos. Logic **8**, 339–359.

Lorenzen, P. (1959), *Ein dialogisches Konstruktivitätskriterium*, Lecture reprinted: Lorenzen, P. and Lorenz, K. (1978), *Dialogische Logik*, Wissenschaftliche Buchgesellschaft, Darmstadt.

Makinson, D. (1985), *How to give it up: A survey of some formal aspects of the logic of theory change*, Synthese **62**, 347–363.

Manes, E. and Arbib, M. (1975), *Arrows, Structures and Functors, the Categorical Imperative*, Academic Press, New York.

Marx, M. (1994), *Arrow logic and relativized algebras of relations*, Dissertation, CCSOM, Faculty of Social Sciences/Institute for Logic, Language and Computation, University of Amsterdam.

McLane, S. (1971), *Categories for the Working Mathematician*, Springer, Berlin.

Meyer Viol, W. (1995), *Instantial logic*, Dissertation, Onderzoeksinstituut voor Taal en Spraak, Universiteit Utrecht.

Milner, R. (1980), *A Calculus of Communicating Systems*, Springer, Berlin.

Montague, R. (1970), *Universal grammar*, Reprinted: Montague, R. (1974), *Formal Philosophy*, Yale Univ. Press, New Haven, CT, 222–246.

Moortgat, M. (1996), *Categorial grammar*, This Handbook, Chapter 2.

Moschovakis, Y. (1991), *Sense and reference as algorithm and value*, Department of Mathematics, University of California, Los Angeles.

Muskens, R. (1991), *Anaphora and the logic of change*, JELIA '90, European Workshop on Logics in AI, J. van Eijck, ed., Springer Lecture Notes, Springer, Berlin, 414–430.

Muskens, R. (1994), *Categorial grammar and discourse representation theory*, Proceedings of COLING 94, Kyoto, 508–514.

Muskens, R. (1995a), *Tense and the logic of change*, Lexical Knowledge in the Organization of Language, U. Egli, P.E. Pause, C. Schwarze, A. von Stechow and G. Wienold, eds, Benjamin, Amsterdam, 147–183.

Muskens, R. (1995b), *Combining Montague semantics and discourse representation*, Ling. and Philos. **19**, 143–186.

Németi, I. (1991), *Algebraizations of Quantifier Logics: An Introductory Overview*, Mathematical Institute, Hungarian Academy of Sciences, Budapest.

Parsons, T. (1990), *Events in the Semantics of English*, MIT Press, Cambridge, MA.

Peters, S. (1975), *A truth-conditional formulation of Karttunen's account of presuppositions*, Texas Linguistic Forum, University of Texas, Austin, TX, 137–149.

Polanyi, L. (1985), *A theory of discourse structure and discourse coherence*, Papers from the General Session of the Chicago Linguistic Society, CLS vol. 21, 306–322.

Popper, K. (1959), *The Logic of Scientific Discovery*, Hutchinson, London.

Pratt, V. (1976), *Semantical considerations on Floyd–Hoare logic*, Proc. 17th IEEE Symp. on Foundations of Computer Science, 109–121.

Ramsey, F.P. (1929), *General propositions and causality*, Reprinted: F.P. Ramsey, *Foundations: Essays in Philosophy, Logic, Mathematics and Economics*, Routledge and Kegan Paul, London, 1978.

Ranta, A. (1991), *Intuitionistic categorial grammar*, Ling. and Philos. **14**, 203–239.

Reyes, G.E. and Macnamara, J. (1994), *The Logical Foundations of Cognition*, Oxford Univ. Press, New York/Oxford.

De Rijke, M. (1993), *Extending modal logic*, Dissertation Series 1993–4, Institute for Logic, Language and Computation, University of Amsterdam.

Rott, H. (1992), *Preferential belief change using generalized epistemic entrenchment*, J. Logic, Lang., Inform. **1**, 45–78.

Ryan, M. (1992), *Ordered presentations of theories: Default reasoning and belief revision*, PhD Thesis, Department of Computing, Imperial College, University of London.

Scha, R. and Polanyi, L. (1988), *An augmented context free grammar for discourse*, Proceedings of the 12th International Conference on Computational Linguistics, Budapest.

Scott, D.S. (1982), *Domains for denotational semantics*, Proceedings 9th International Colloquium on Automata, Languages and Programming, M. Nelsen and E.T. Schmidt, eds, Lecture Notes Comput. Sci. vol. 140, Springer, Berlin, 577–613.

Segerberg, K. (1982), *A completeness theorem in the modal logic of programs*, Universal Algebra and Applications, T. Traczyk, ed., Banach Centre Publications 9, PWN – Polish Scientific, Warsaw, 31–46.
Segerberg, K. (1991), *Logics of action*, Abstracts 9th International Congress on Logic, Methodology and Philosophy of Science, Uppsala.
Seuren, P. (1975), *Tussen Taal en Denken*, Scheltema, Holkema en Vermeulen, Amsterdam.
Seuren, P. (1985), *Discourse Semantics*, Blackwell, Oxford.
Sher, G. (1991), *The Bounds of Logic. A Generalised Viewpoint*, Bradford Books/MIT Press, Cambridge, MA.
Shoham (1988), *Reasoning about Change. Time and causation from the standpoint of artificial intelligence*, Yale Univ. Press, New Haven, CT.
Soames, S. (1989), *Presupposition*, Handbook of Philosophical Logic vol. IV, D. Gabbay and F. Günthner, eds.
Spohn, W. (1988), *Ordinal conditional functions: A dynamic theory of epistemic states*, Causation in Decision, Belief Change and Statistics II, W.L. Harper et al., eds, Kluwer, Dordrecht, 105–134.
Stalnaker, R. (1968), *A theory of conditionals*, Studies in Logical Theory, N. Rescher, ed., Basil Blackwell, Oxford, 98–112.
Stalnaker, R. (1974), *Pragmatic presuppositions*, Semantics and Philosophy, M. Munitz and P. Unger, eds, New York Univ. Press, New York, 197–213.
Stalnaker, R. (1979), *Assertion*, Syntax and Semantics 9: Pragmatics, P. Cole, ed., Academic Press, New York, 315–332.
Sundholm, G. (1986), *Proof theory and meaning*, Handbook of Philosophical Logic vol. III, D. Gabbay and F. Guenthner, eds, Reidel, Dordrecht, 471–506.
Suppe, F. (1977), *The Structure of Scientific Theories*, Univ. of Illinois Press, Urbana, IL.
Troelstra, A. and Van Dalen, D. (1988), *Constructivism in Mathematics*, two volumes, North-Holland, Amsterdam.
Turner, R. (1996), *Types*, This Handbook, Chapter 9.
Van Benthem, J. (1986), *Essays in Logical Semantics*, Studies in Linguistics and Philosophy vol. 29, Reidel, Dordrecht.
Van Benthem, J. (1988), *Games in logic: A survey*, Representation and Reasoning, J. Hoepelman, ed., Niemeyer Verlag, Tübingen, 3–15.
Van Benthem, J. (1989), *Semantic parallels in natural language and computation*, Logic Colloquium. Granada 1987, H.-D. Ebbinghaus et al., eds, North-Holland, Amsterdam, 331–375.
Van Benthem, J. (1991), *Language in Action. Categories, Lambdas and Dynamic Logic*, North-Holland, Amsterdam.
Van Benthem, J. (1991a), *General dynamics*, Theor. Ling. **17**, 159–201.
Van Benthem, J. (1993), *Logic and the flow of information*, Proceedings 9th International Congress of Logic, Methodology and Philosophy of Science. Uppsala 1991, D. Prawitz, B. Skyrms and D. Westerståhl, eds, Elseviers, Amsterdam, 693–724.
Van Benthem, J. (1993a), *Modeling the kinematics of meaning*, Proceedings Aristotelean Society 1993, 105–122.
Van Benthem, J. (1993b), *Programming operations that are safe for bisimulation*, Report 93-179, Center for the Study of Language and Information, Stanford University. (To appear in *Logic Colloquium. Clermont-Ferrand 1994*, Elsevier, Amsterdam.)
Van Benthem, J. (1994a), *Dynamic Arrow logic*, Dynamic Logic and Information Flow, J. van Eijck and Visser, eds, MIT Press, Cambridge, MA.
Van Benthem, J. (1994b), *Modal foundations for predicate logic*, Research Report CSLI-94-191, Center for the Study of Language and Information, Stanford University.
Van Benthem, J. and Cepparello, G. (1994), *Tarskian variations. Dynamic parameters in classical semantics*, Technical Report CS-R9419, CWI, Amsterdam.
Van Benthem, J. and Bergstra, J. (1993), *Logic of transition systems*, Report CT-93–03, Institute for Logic, Language and Computation, University of Amsterdam. (To appear in J. Logic, Lang., Inform.)
Van Benthem, J., Van Eijck, J. and Frolova, A. (1993), *Changing preferences*, Technical Report CS-R9310, CWI, Amsterdam.
Van Benthem, J., Van Eijck, J. and Stebletsova, V. (1993), *Modal logic, transition systems and processes*, Logic Comput. **4**(5), 811–855.

Van den Berg, M. (1995), *Plural dynamic generalized quantifiers*, Dissertation, Institute for Logic, Language and Computation, University of Amsterdam.

Van Deemter, K. (1991), *On the composition of meaning*, Dissertation, Institute for Logic, Language and Information, University of Amsterdam.

Van der Does, J. (1992), *Applied quantifier logics*, Dissertation, Institute for Logic, Language and Computation, University of Amsterdam.

Van Eijck, J. and G. Cepparello (1994), *Dynamic modal predicate logic*, Dynamics, Polarity and Quantification, M. Kanazawa and C. Piñon, eds, CSLI, Stanford, 251–276.

Van Eijck, J. and Visser, A. (eds) (1994), *Dynamic Logic and Information Flow*, MIT Press, Cambridge, MA.

Van Eijck, J. and De Vries, F.-J. (1992), *Dynamic interpretation and Hoare deduction*, J. Logic, Lang., Inform. **1**, 1–44.

Van Eijck, J. and De Vries, F.-J. (1995), *Reasoning about update logic*, J. Philos. Logic **24**, 19–45.

Van Eijck, J. and Kamp, H. (1996), *Representing discourse in context*, This Handbook, Chapter 3.

Van Lambalgen, M. (1991), *Natural deduction for generalized quantifiers*, Generalized Quantifiers: Theory and Applications, J. van der Does and J. van Eijck, eds, Dutch PhD Network for Logic, Language and Information, Amsterdam, 143–154. (To appear with Cambridge Univ. Press.)

Veltman, F. (1985), *Logics for conditionals*, Dissertation, University of Amsterdam.

Veltman, F. (1991), *Defaults in update semantics*, Report LP-91-02, Institute for Logic, Language and Computation, University of Amsterdam. (To appear in the J. Philos. Logic.)

Venema, Y. (1991), *Many-dimensional modal logic*, Dissertation, Institute for Logic, Language and Computation, University of Amsterdam.

Venema, Y. (1994), *A crash course in Arrow logic*, Knowledge Representation and Reasoning under Uncertainty, Logic at Work, M. Masuch and L. Polos, eds, Lecture Notes in Artificial Intelligence vol. 808, Springer, Berlin.

Vermeulen, K. (1994), *Exploring the dynamic environment*, Dissertation, Onderzoeksinstituut voor Taal en Spraak, University of Utrecht.

Visser, A. (1994), *Actions under presuppositions*, Logic and Information Flow, J. van Eijck and A. Visser, eds, MIT Press, Cambridge, MA.

Visser, A. and Vermeulen, K. (1995), *Dynamic bracketing and discourse representation*, Logic Group Preprint Series 131, Department of Philosophy, University of Utrecht. (To appear in Notre Dame J. Formal Logic, special issue *Logical Aspects of Complex Structures*.)

Wansing, H. (1992), *The logic of information structures*, Dissertation, Department of Philosophy, Free University, Berlin.

Westerståhl, D. (1984), *Determiners and context sets*, Generalized Quantifiers in Natural Language, J. van Benthem and A. ter Meulen, eds, Foris, Dordrecht, 45–71.

Wittgenstein, L. (1953), *Philosophische Untersuchungen*, edited by G. Anscombe and R. Rhees with an English translation by G. Anscombe, Blackwell, Oxford.

Zeinstra, L. (1990), *Reasoning as discourse*, Master's Thesis, Department of Philosophy, University of Utrecht.

CHAPTER 11

Partiality

Jens Erik Fenstad

University of Oslo, Institute of Mathematics, PO Box 1053 Blindern, N-0316 Oslo, Norway
E-mail: jfenstad@math.uio.no

Commentator: L. Humberstone

Contents

HANDBOOK OF LOGIC AND LANGUAGE
Edited by J. van Benthem and A. ter Meulen

0. Introduction

Partiality is both complex and widespread. Aspects of it has been the object of intensive study in logic and mathematics. In this chapter our aim is to survey issues in partiality of possible relevance to theoretical and computational linguistics. Our exposition is aimed at an audience of linguists and, therefore, while technically sound, is not intended to be technically complete at every point.

The chapter is divided into three parts. In the first part we survey various *sources of partiality* arising from grammatical form, structure of knowledge, complexities of rule-following and the paradoxical properties of self-referential possibilities in natural languages.

In the second part we present in brief outline a *model for linguistic structure*. We do this, not in order to advocate the "correctness" of this particular model, but to use it as a vehicle to sort out some of the aspects of partiality identified in the first part.

In the final part we turn to *partiality and the structure of knowledge*. The focus of our discussion in this part will be the logic and model theory of partial structures, both propositional, first order and higher types. Although technical in form we shall not altogether lose sight of the connection to natural language modeling.

1. Sources of partiality

We start out with some observations on issues of partiality connected to *grammatical form*. We then turn to partiality and the *structure of knowledge*. This leads on to a discussion of some aspects of partiality related to *algorithms and rule-following*. We finish with a brief review of the complexities of *self-reference in natural language*.

1.1. Grammatical form

The Norwegian Prime Minister recently (i.e. early 1993) refused the publication of an interview with her. Not because anything incorrect was explicitly written or implied by the journalist, but because the journalist had been too correct, proposing to print exactly the "stream of utterances" of the prime minister during the interview. We sympathize with the prime minister, the partiality, even incoherence, of actual utterances rarely reproduce the meaning content of a communicative act.

The lesson to be learned is that the complexity of actual communication is too difficult for both the logician and the linguist; we shall, therefore, immediately abstract from reality and start from what is grammatically correct. But even in the domain of the grammatically correct there are issues of partiality.

1.1.1. Sortal incorrectness

One aspect of partiality is connected with *sortal incorrectness*. A favorite example of linguists is the following sentence:

Colorless green ideas sleep furiously.

This is taken as an example of a grammatically correct but meaningless sentence. The example is, perhaps, a bit too clever and confuses several issues. One is the predication of contradictory properties, such as colorless and green, to the same object. In most cases contradiction does not result in partiality, but in falsity, and this is of no further concern to us. We must, however, exercise some care; there are important examples, e.g., in connection with algorithms and rule-following, where contradiction is better resolved through partiality.

The oddness of the example (and in a sense the justification for the label of sortal incorrectness) lies in the combination of the noun phrase (NP) with the verb phrase (VP). An NP may play a large number of rôles, the VP may be more restrictive in calling for an actor for the rôle it describes. Thus there may even at the linguistic level be so-called selection rules, and violation of such rules may result in partiality, i.e. suspension in the assignment of truth-values, or of lack of meaning, rather than in claims of falsity.

1.1.2. Indexicals and definite descriptions

Another source of grammatical partiality is associated with the use of *indexicals*. Uttered among a crowd of mothers of school children,

she loves her children,

is underdetermined in the sense that *she* does not by itself pick out a unique referent. The same phenomenon may occur with *definite descriptions*, *the woman with the outrageous hat* is not a very appropriate mode of identification at Ascot. Definite descriptions may even fail to refer at all.

1.1.3. Presupposition

Sortal incorrectness and indexicals lead on to the broader topic of presuppositions which lives on the border line between grammatical form and semantical content where partiality or truth-value gaps may enter. An utterance of

Mary loves her children,

carries the presupposition that this particular Mary has children. So if our Mary has no children (born to her or legally adopted), we are at a loss of how to assign a truth value to what is expressed by the utterance. Note that a denial of the utterance is not necessarily a denial of the presuppositions of the utterance. We shall in later parts be dealing with issues concerning partiality of facts and partiality of information about facts. But the intricate interplay of presuppositions, assignment of truth-values and partiality, will be the topic of the chapter on *Presupposition.* The reader is also advised to consult the chapter on *Conditionals*.

Not every less-than-perfect feature of language should count as an example of partiality. There are a number of phenomena associated with, e.g., *quantifier scoping* and *ellipsis* which result in ambiguities and multiplicities of readings, but which we will not count as examples of partiality.

In Section 2 on models for linguistic structure we shall briefly return to some of the problems of this section and indicate how they can be accounted for. We now turn to some topics connected with knowledge and partiality.

1.2. The structure of knowledge

Even if its mechanisms are not well understood, we use language to express knowledge about the world. Thus there are cases where a sentence is *supported* by the world, i.e. there are facts in the world which show the correctness of the sentence. And there are cases where a sentence is *rejected* by the world, i.e. there are facts in the world which refute or contradict the sentence. Ordinarily, we strive for *coherence*, a sentence cannot at the same time and place be both supported and rejected by the facts of our world. We may wish for *completeness*, that a sentence is either supported or rejected by the facts, but this is not always to be obtained; we may be in a situation of "partial knowledge".

Note that this kind of partiality is different from those discussed in the previous section. No fact added to the world would resolve problems concerning sortal incorrectness, presuppositions and the use of indexicals.

1.2.1. Models

To make the above intuitive remarks more precise we shall follow a tradition from formal or mathematical logic. The development of a theory of semantics has a long history. One crucial step in this development was Tarski's work on *the notion of truth for formalized languages* in the early 1930's; see Tarski (1956). Truth, as conceived by Tarski, was a relation between a sentence of a language and the "world". To obtain technical results he replaced *language* by *formal* (first order or higher type) *language* and *world* by the set-theoretic notion of *model*.

A *model*, as understood by contemporary mathematical logic, is determined by a non-empty set, the *domain* of individuals/objects of the model, and a collection of *relations* and *functions*. An n-ary relation is at this level understood as a set of n-tuples from the domain, and functions are viewed as a special kind of relations. A model of a first order theory has a domain which is just a collection of individuals; higher-order theories require a type-theoretic structure on the domain. The relevance of this for linguistics will be the topic of later sections. Here we shall make some remarks on totality versus partiality in relation to model theory.

Models, including the "possible worlds" of intensional logic, have a certain *completeness property*, i.e. given any property (i.e. unary relation) P and individual a of the model, we have either the *positive fact* that a has the property P, or the *negative fact* that a does not have the property P. We have a partition of the domain into P's and non-P's. The model aims to capture all knowledge with respect to the relations and the individuals it contains.

This is a reasonable requirement if one starts, as did the pioneers of the development of formal logic in the first third of this century, with mathematical applications in mind, where the domain of a model might be the natural numbers or some other algebraic structure. This is not the only possibility, taking our clue from the history of logic and linguistics we could try to capture a different intuition. With respect to a language-user a "model" could try to capture his or her perspective in a particular utterance situation. In such a perspective a sentence uttered may or may not be supported or rejected by the facts available. This is an intuition which has always been present, but was neglected in the technical development of mathematical logic since "mathematical truths" do not seem to need a "speaker". We did, however, see various attempts in philosophical logic to add a dimension of *pragmatics* to the *syntax* and *semantics* of mathematical logicians; see the survey in Fenstad, Halvorsen, Langholm and Van Benthem (1987).

The use of small (e.g., finite) but standard (i.e. total) models is one way of capturing the partiality of one particular perspective on a "global" world. There are, however, more radical ways.

1.2.2. Situation theory

A more systematic attempt to capture the partiality of an utterance-situation within the semantics has recently been advocated by J. Barwise and J. Perry in their work on *Situation Theory*; see Barwise and Perry (1983), and Barwise (1989).

In their original set-up the starting point was a collection of facts. Facts are built out of *locations*, *relations* and *individuals*. *Locations* are taken as (connected) regions of space-time. *Relations* are understood as primitives or irreducibles, i.e. a relation is not given as a set of n-tuples of individuals. Relations may be used to classify individuals, but the "meaning" of the relation is not the resulting set theoretic construct. The notion of *individual* is quite liberal in order to account for the referential mechanisms of natural languages, e.g., facts can be arguments of relations inside other facts. Finally, facts come with a certain *polarity*, a fact is *positive* if it asserts of some individuals $a_1, \ldots, a_n$ that they stand in a relation r at some location l; it is *negative* if it asserts of some individuals $a_1, \ldots, a_n$ that they do not stand in the relation r at location l. Note that the denial of a positive fact is not the same as asserting the corresponding negative fact.

A *situation* is a collection of (located) facts with respects to some domain L of locations, R of relations and I of individuals. Thus a situation *supports* some facts (i.e. the positive facts in the situation) and *rejects* some facts (i.e. the negative facts in the situation). A situation may be *partial* in the sense that it need not contain either the positive or negative version of the facts possible with respect to the domains L, R and I.

Partial structures and their logic will be the topic of part three of this chapter. For the particular theory of *situation semantics* the reader is referred to the appropriate chapter of the Handbook. We shall, however, as part of our motivation for the use of partial structures, sketch an early analysis of the attitude verb "see" within situation semantics.

1.2.3. See

The relationship between logical entailment and sameness of meaning or synonomy in natural language is problematic. In standard logic we have the mutual entailment of

(i) *Mary walks.*

(ii) *Mary walks and Sue talks or does not talk.*

From this equivalence accepted principles of compositionality would give the further equivalence

(iii) *John sees Mary walk.*

(iv) *John sees Mary walk and Sue talk or not talk.*

This is odd, not only for the linguists but also for the logician. On the standard analysis (iv) would entail that John sees Sue. This is not entailed by (iii) since this sentence does not mention Sue. The situation can be saved in various ways. We can tamper with the notion of logical entailment, we can restrict the uses of compositionality, or we can let go the commitment to totality.

In the early framework of *Situation and Attitudes*, (Barwise and Perry, 1983), the problem was analyzed as follows. A situation s supports the sentence *John sees Mary walk* if there is some other situation s' such that s supports the fact that s' and John stand in the relation *see*, and s' support the fact that Mary walks. There may be no s' which in s stands in the relation *see* to John and which supports or reject the fact that Sue talks. Thus a situation s which supports (iii) need not support (iv). We are not forced on logical grounds alone to accept their equivalence.

The example shows that partiality has a role to play in the analysis of the relationship between language and the world. Not every fact, be it positive or negative, is present in every perspective on the world. Nevertheless, a particular perspective supports some and rejects other sentences. We conclude that partial models, whether they intend to model *the absence of facts* or *the lack of information about facts*, are useful constructs. With this disclaimer we shall abstain from further discussion if partiality is sometimes *natural*, i.e. a property of the world, or always *man-made*, i.e. a feature of our theories about the world.

1.2.4. Knowledge representation

An important trend in "applied logic" has been the use of model theory in the study of knowledge representation. In a certain sense, model theory *is* knowledge representation – the diagram of a (finite) model (i.e. the set of valid atomic or negated atomic statements) is a database representation; see, e.g., Gurevich (1987) and Makowsky (1984), for a sample of some recent results.

Partiality enters in a natural way from this perspective, partial databases are roughly the same as partial structures in our sense. For recent theory and applications see Minker (1988), and Doherty and Drainkov (forthcoming).

The study of partial structures and their associated logic will, as mentioned above, be the topic of Section 3 of this chapter. We conclude this section by some remarks on partiality *versus* issues of vagueness, fuzziness and probability.

Vagueness is an important source of indeterminateness in language use. It is, perhaps, mostly associated with the meaning of lexical items. Does or does not this entity fall under this concept, is or is not this colored patch green or blue? The polarities of situation theory (and of classical logic) are *sharp*. To the question "Does a have the property P?" the answer is *yes*, *no* or *neither*. The membership of a in P is never vague, fuzzy or probabilistic. The latter phenomena merit study, but they are not our concern in this chapter.

1.3. Rules

A system for natural language analysis must in some systematic way relate linguistic form and semantic content. If we want to be computational linguists, we must in addition insist that the relationship be algorithmic.

There are (at least) two sides to rule-following: *efficiency* and *limitations*. We shall not have much to add to the first topic. A great deal of effort has been spent within the computational linguistic community on the construction of efficient algorithms and on improving the performance of existing ones. This is still much of an art and therefore quite eclectic in methodology.

The situation changes when doubts arise about the existence of an algorithmic solution to a problem. The affirmative, i.e. the actual existence of an algorithm, is most convincingly proved through explicit construction, and there is no need to be too precise about the general notions. To prove non-existence is different. If you do not know what an algorithm is, how can you conclude that none exists; a general theory of algorithms is needed for this task.

In this section we shall make some brief remarks on the general notion of *algorithm*, connecting it to issues of *partiality* and *self-reference*. This will lead up to the discussion in the last section of this part on the paradoxial power of self-reference in natural languages.

1.3.1. Partial algorithms

We may "compute", i.e. perform effective operations, on objects of many kinds, such as syntactic structures and semantic representations, but familiar devices of coding always reduce such computations to computations with numbers. So let our computational domain be the natural numbers $0, 1, 2, \ldots$. Let us assume that our computations are performed by some "machine" M; we let $M(x_1, \ldots, x_n) \to y$ express the fact that the machine M when given the numbers $x_1, \ldots, x_n$ as *input* eventually produces the answer or *output* y. We use the arrow $\to$ instead of the equality symbol $=$ to emphasize that computations may fail, i.e. no output may be forthcoming. Most readers will be familiar with some concrete version of this notion, either through the theory of Turing Machines, general recursive functions, λ-definability, or one of the many other alternatives; a good survey is given in (Odifreddi, 1989).

A basic result of the theory is *the existence of a universal machine U* with the property that given any machine M there exists a number m such that $M(x) \simeq U(m, x)$ for all x. We use $\simeq$ to indicate that M and U are defined for exactly the same inputs x, and that they yield the same output whenever defined. We use $M(x){\downarrow}$ to express that the procedure M terminates for the input x, i.e. there exists a number y such that $M(x) \to y$.

One may conjecture that universal machines, encoding all possible forms of effective computations, must be monstrous creatures. We cannot resist including the following simple example of a universal machine (Fig. 1); see Aanderaa (1993).

But we warn the reader against using this machine for syntactic analysis.

The possibility of partiality was built into the definition of a computing device, and this for good reasons. We cannot impose totality. Suppose that we could, i.e. that we could replace $\to$ and $\simeq$ by $=$ and assume that any M is total. If there exists a total universal machine U, we can by diagonalization construct a new machine $U_1(x) = U(x, x)$; let $U_2(x) = U_1(x) + 1$ (i.e. U_2 is defined by feeding the output of U_1 into the successor function, which certainly is computable by some total machine S). By the universality of U we get a number m_0 such that $U_2(x) = U(m_0, x)$, for all x. Choose $x = m_0$ as input, then $U(m_0, m_0) = U_2(m_0) = U_1(m_0) + 1 = U(m_0, m_0) + 1$; a contradiction.

The only way out of this predicament is to deny the assumption of totality. To have an enumeration or universal function inside the class we need the extension from total to partial objects. But we have proved more. Given any specific version of the theory,

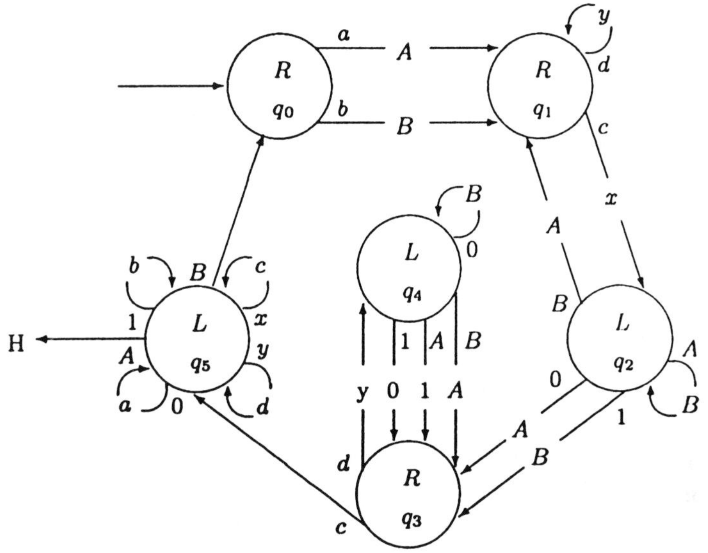

Fig. 1. Universal Turing machine: UTm.

a witness m_0 to partiality has been effectively found. Let us pursue this a bit further. A machine M is a description of an algorithm; the partiality of M means that there are inputs x such that $M(x)\downarrow$ is false. For the machine U_2 we can effectively compute an m_0 such that $U_2(m_0)$ is undefined. Can we more generally decide if algorithms converge? This is the famous Halting Problem.

1.3.2. The combinatorial core of undecidability

To answer this question we need one more notion. A set A of numbers is called *recursively enumerable* (r.e.) if it is the domain of some machine, i.e. $A = \{x \mid M(x)\downarrow\}$. A set is called *recursive* if and only if both it and its complement are r.e.

If a set A is recursive we can effectively decide for any x if $x \in A$ or $x \in \bar{A}$ ($\bar{A}$ being the complement of A in the domain of natural numbers): Since A is recursive there are machines M_1 and M_2 such that A is the domain of M_1 and $\bar{A}$ is the domain of M_2. For any number x we start the computations $M_1(x)$ and $M_2(x)$. Since x belongs to either A or $\bar{A}$, there is some y such that either $M_1(x) \to y$ or $M_2(x) \to y$. Since computations are finite, we will eventually know the answer.

Returning to the Halting Problem, let us take a closer look at the set $K = \{x \mid U(x,x)\downarrow\}$. We claim that K is not recursive. Suppose otherwise; then the complement $\overline{K}$ would be r.e., i.e. there is some number m_k such that $x \in \overline{K}$ if and only if $U(m_k, x)\downarrow$. This leads – once more – to a contradiction: $m_k \in \overline{K}$ iff $U(m_k, m_k)\downarrow$ iff $m_k \in K$. In this case $\overline{K}$ is really a Russellian paradoxical set since $\overline{K}$ is the set of all x such that x (as a code of a function) does not apply to itself (as an argument).

Simple as it is, the fact that K is r.e. but not recursive, is in a sense *the combinatorial core of undecidability results.* It basically asserts the undecidability of the Halting Problem. A number of algorithmic problems can be proved unsolvable by suitable reductions to this problem; for examples of relevance to linguistic theory, see Barton, Berwick and Ristad (1987).

Logicians and recursion theorists have learned to live with paradoxes and have occasionally been able to turn contradictions into technical tools. But, even if powerful and universal, computation theories are not all there is. In the next section we shall turn to self-reference in the broader context of natural languages and see how this is yet another source of partiality.

1.4. Self-reference

Human languages are in important respects *open systems*. There are, of course, rules of grammar and "correct usage", but language-in-use shows a remarkable creativity in circumventing such restrictions if that is necessary for enhancing its efficiency in human communication. Nevertheless, certain uses of language connected with fundamental properties of truth and reference seem to cross the boundary line of the paradoxical. If the "this" of "this is not true" refers to itself – and why should it not? – then this is not true if and only if it is true. Language in use is not free from contradictions, but when paradox emerges from "self-evident" properties of truth, reference and negation any linguist whose aim it is to explore the systematic connection between linguistic form and semantical content, must take notice.

1.4.1. The paradoxes

Logic has lived with paradox for a long time, the one just recalled, the *Liar Paradox*, has roots in antiquity. We must, with some regret, enter the story at the contemporary stage. Since Ramsey in 1925 it has been customary to make a distinction between *semantical paradoxes* dealing with notions such as truth, assertions and definitions and *mathematical or logical paradoxes*, dealing with membership, classes, functions – both types of paradoxes, however, involving notions of self-reference and negation.

We shall recall a few facts following an exposition of Feferman (1984).

To fix ideas assume that some logical formalism or language L is given with the usual apparatus of syntactic notions such as term, formula, sentence, free and bound variables etc. The presence of paradox depends upon what further assumptions we impose on the *language* L, the *logic* of L and the *basic principles* L admits concerning truth and set existence.

The Liar is the proto-type of a semantical paradox. In this case since we are discussing self-reference, we assume that the *language* of L has a naming mechanism, i.e. for every sentence A of L there is a closed term $\ulcorner A \urcorner$ which functions as the name of A in L. We also assume that L satisfies the basic property of self-reference, i.e. for every formula $B(x)$ there is a sentence A which is equivalent in L to $B(\ulcorner A \urcorner)$. The *logic* of L is assumed to be standard classical logic. Concerning *basic principles* we have the "truth"-principle which asserts that there is a truth predicate $Tr(x)$ in L such that for any sentence A of L, A is equivalent in L to $Tr(\ulcorner A \urcorner)$, i.e. we have a truth definition for L within L.

The construction of paradox is now straight forward. Take the formula $\neg Tr(x)$, by naming and self-reference there is a sentence A_0 in L equivalent to $\neg Tr(\ulcorner A_0 \urcorner)$ (i.e. the

Liar sentence). By the truth-principle A_0 is also equivalent to $Tr(\ulcorner A_0 \urcorner)$, i.e. A_0 is true if and only if it is not true. Since truth is a *complete* property, we have a paradox.

The Russell set, i.e. the set of all sets which are not element of themselves, is the proto-type of a mathematical paradox. In this case the basic relation of the *language* L is the membership relation $x \in y$ and the naming device allows for unrestricted set formation, i.e. for every formula $A(x)$ there is a set-term $\{x \mid A(x)\}$ with the intended meaning of naming the set of all x such that $A(x)$ is true in L. The *logic* of L is once more standard classical logic, and the *basic principle* is one which determines set membership: $a \in \{x \mid A(x)\}$ if and only if $A(a)$. The Russell set, $\{x \mid \neg(x \in x)\}$, immediately yields a contradiction, $a \in a$ if and only if $\neg(a \in a)$. Since the membership relation is *complete*, we have our paradox.

1.4.2. Paradoxes and partiality

In the previous section on algorithms and partiality we saw how the recursion theorist was able to find his way through the complexities of truth, self-reference and paradox. The Russell construction was used to prove the existence of a recursively enumerable but non-recursive set. The ability of the universal machine $U(m, x)$ to refer to itself did not lead to paradox, but to partiality.

The Gödel incompleteness theorem is another celebrated case where paradox has been put to constructive use. The witness to incompleteness of the provability predicate is a statement A which asserts its own unprovability. Here there is no paradox because of the difference between asserting the provability of $\neg A$ and the non-provability of A. This is a typical example of a *partial relation*. Let Pr be the set of all A provable in the system and $\overline{Pr}$ the set of all A such that $\neg A$ is provable in the system. The pair $\langle Pr, \overline{Pr} \rangle$ is a partial relation, in fact, the Gödel sentence A is neither in Pr nor in $\overline{Pr}$.

In a similar way, for the Liar Paradox, let Tr be the set of all A such that $Tr(\ulcorner A \urcorner)$ and $\overline{Tr}$ be the set of all A such that $Tr(\ulcorner \neg A \urcorner)$. Since the logic is classical the formula $A \vee \neg A$ is valid, hence by the basic truth-principle $\langle Tr, \overline{Tr} \rangle$ forms a complete pair, i.e. for any A, either $A \in Tr$ or $A \in \overline{Tr}$. In this case completeness enforces paradox.

The recursion theorist and the proof theorist have successfully met the challenge of the "paradoxes of self-application" and been able to turn contradiction into powerful techniques. For recursion theory this was evident already in Kleene's influential text-book from 1952. The step beyond Gödel took longer within the proof-theory community; for a recent survey of the history and of present applications, see Smorynski (1991). For us it remains to add some comments on responses and proposals in a wider context. First some remarks on the mathematical paradoxes.

1.4.3. Paradoxes and the foundation of mathematics

One observation on the Russell paradox is that it is made possible by the vagueness of the notion of set. Successful axiomatization is not a play with symbols and rules, but rests on sharp intuitions and a careful preformal analysis. This is indeed brought out by history. The axiomatization of set theory initiated by Zermelo, Fraenkel and Skolem and further developed by von Neumann and Bernays rests upon the intuition of sets being presented or constructed in stages. In the resulting "cumulative hierarchy" there will be no Russell set since every element of a set x must be "constructed" before x itself is secured. The condition $x \in x$ is contradictory and will give nothing but the empty set. A parallel analysis of functions and functional application including self-application has beyond recursion theory led to a rich theory of types and properties, both classical, constructive and partial.

This is the topic of the Chapter on *Type Structures*. Here we add a few words on a recent development which skirts close to the difficulties of the Russell paradox. In many branches of mathematics one would like to organize all structures of some given kind into a new mathematical structure with new operation and relations. These ideas was made precise in the early 1940 by Eilenberg and MacLane (for an introduction see MacLane, 1971), and the resulting theory, *category theory*, has proved to be a fruitful tool in many areas of mathematics. In the 1960 there was an interesting encounter of logic and category theory which has grown into a rich theory, see, e.g., Bell (1988).

But category theory rests on a different intuitive notion of set than the cumulative hierarchy of standard axiomatic set theory. The situation is complicated, but not untypical. Category theory is too useful to throw away, even if there could be paradoxes hiding behind "the category of all categories"; for a full discussion see MacLane and Moerdijk (1992).

1.4.4. Paradoxes and truth

It remains to conclude with some remarks on the Liar and related semantical paradoxes. As remarked the history of these paradoxes is old. With some justification we can date the modern development to Tarski's study on the concept of truth in formalized languages in the early 1930's; see Tarski (1956). The Liar paradox told us that truth of sentences in a formal language L is not definable in L. Tarski's response was to restrict the naming and self-referential strength of L. His proposal was to introduce an extension ML of L, ML being a "metalanguage" of L, which would allow for the naming of sentences of L, i.e. for each A of L there is a name (a closed term) $\lceil A \rceil$ of ML which serves as a name of A in ML. But there is in ML no general mechanism for introducing names for arbitrary formulas of ML. The basic truth-principle is retained by Tarski, i.e. for any sentence A of L, A is equivalent in ML to $Tr(\lceil A \rceil)$. By restricting the power of naming and self-reference there is no longer any paradox. But there is a price to pay, the truth predicate for ML is not definable in ML, but in a metalanguage of ML, i.e. in a meta-metalanguage of L. This leads to a hierarchy of languages of increasing strength.

From the point of view of mathematical logic there are no objections. The work of Tarski in the early 1930's lead in the late 1940's and early 1950's to a general development of model theory as a discipline at the interface of logic and mathematics; see Chang and Keisler (1977).

But neither for the philosopher of language nor the linguist is Tarski's analysis satisfactory. A major step forward was taken by Kripke (1957). There are two parts to his work, a critique in depth of the Tarskian approach and suggestions for a way out. As to the critique Kripke emphasized that the phenomenon of self-reference or circularity is so widespread in natural languages that no extension of the Tarskian trick of the language-metalanguage distinction would prove satisfactory. On the constructive side Kripke presented an analysis which allows for both self-reference and internal truth-definition. The price he paid was to turn the *total* truth predicate into a *partial* predicate

$\langle Tr, \overline{Tr} \rangle$, which would allow for truth-value gaps. In fact, the Liar sentence would belong to neither Tr nor $\overline{Tr}$ (under reasonable assumptions). The partial predicate $\langle Tr, \overline{Tr} \rangle$ was for the particular examples Kripke discussed, defined in stages $\langle Tr_\alpha, \overline{Tr}_\alpha \rangle$. Starting from a reasonable base pair $\langle Tr_0, \overline{Tr}_0 \rangle$, e.g., $\langle \emptyset, \emptyset \rangle$, one would pass from stage α to $\alpha + 1$ by stipulations such as putting $Tr(\ulcorner A \urcorner)$ into $Tr_{\alpha+1}$ and $\neg Tr(\ulcorner A \urcorner)$ into $\overline{Tr}_{\alpha+1}$ for any A true at stage α (i.e. $A \in Tr_\alpha$). Thus, in a sense, the Tarskian sequence of metalanguages, each extending its predecessor by adding the truth-definition, is internalized as a sequence of "approximations" to the full determination of truth and falsity for the language. Kripke shows for the examples that he considered, that there are fixed-points, i.e. pairs $\langle Tr_\gamma, \overline{Tr}_\gamma \rangle$ such that $Tr_\gamma = Tr_{\gamma+1}$ and $\overline{Tr}_\gamma = \overline{Tr}_{\gamma+1}$, and such that $Tr_\gamma \cap \overline{Tr}_\gamma = \emptyset$. A fixed-point provides a truth definition within the language and avoids the paradox of the Liar by the fact that the Liar sentence is neither in Tr_γ nor in $\overline{Tr}_\gamma$.

The pair $\langle Tr_\gamma, \overline{Tr}_\gamma \rangle$ is yet another example of a *partial predicate*. We shall not pursue the study of self-reference and paradoxes further in this chapter. An important post-Kripke paper is (Herzberger, 1982). There is a rich literature, some additional references are (Martin, 1981; Visser, 1989; Gupta and Belnap, 1993; Feferman, 1991). In Section 3 we shall return to a study of partial predicates, not in the context of paradoxes, but in connection with issues dealing with partiality of knowledge in the sense of Section 1.2.

1.4.5. Non-wellfounded structures

We conclude this section with a report on a different concept of set which has been used – among other things – to analyze the Liar Paradox. This is the concept of *non-well founded set*, i.e. a concept of set which admits sets A such that $A \in A$. This opens up for various direct ways of naming or coding with self-referential possibilities.

The notion of non-wellfounded set has an interesting history. A convenient contemporary starting point is the monograph by Aczel (1988), which also has some historical remarks. Aczel was motivated by the need for a mathematical analysis of (computational) *process which may apply to themselves*; such processes occurs naturally in parts of computer science. In graph theoretic terms these processes correspond to cyclic graphs (whereas the membership relation of a wellfounded set leads to an acyclic graph). Recasting the theory in terms of non-well founded sets opens up for an application of powerful set-theoretical techniques, in particular, fixed-point theorems.

This possibility was exploited by Barwise and Etchemendy (1987), in their analysis of the Liar Paradox. Lack of space prevents us from giving an account of their work. It is precisely a fixed-point construction which gives a Liar sentence with the right self-referential properties. On the surface there seems to be no need for coding and partiality. Coding is circumvented in the fixed-point construction because of non-wellfoundedness. However, partiality is implicitly present through the restricted power of the language to refer to the world. We must leave to the reader to decide if non-wellfoundedness adds more to the theory of cyclic graphs than set-theoretic techniques, i.e. if there is a "sharp" intuition of non-wellfounded membership.

This concludes our survey of sources of partiality. We next turn to a discussion of some issues of partiality in connection with linguistic form. This is a natural follow-up to the discussion in Section 1.1, but we shall also encounter some new aspects of partiality.

2. Partiality and models for linguistic structure

"... we have to make a distinction between a computational structure and a more or less independent conceptual structure ... The conceptual module includes what is often referred to as knowledge of the world, common sense and beyond. It also includes logical knowledge and knowledge of predicate-argument structure. The computational module concerns the constraints on our actual organization of discrete units, like morphemes and words, into phrases and constraints on relations between phrases" (Koster, 1989, p. 593). "If the two basic modules are autonomous and radically different in architecture and evolutionary origin, there must be ... an interface ... My hypothesis is that the interface we are looking for is the lexicon ..." (Koster, 1989, p. 598).

The point of view expressed by Koster is fairly conventional, there are two modules: *grammatical space* and *semantical space*. The link between the two could either be a logical formalism in the style of Montague or an attribute-value formalism in the style of Lexical-Functional Grammar. There are also intermediate forms such as the Discourse Representation Structures of Kamp; see Kamp (1981), Kamp and Reyle (1993) and the chapter on Discourse Representation Theory.

Not every approach adheres to the modular format. We specifically direct attention to the chapter on Game-Theoretical Semantics. A particular reason for doing so is the connection of this approach to the issue of partiality. The semantics is defined in terms of games and strategies. Games are not always determined, i.e. winning strategies may not always exist. This holds true for the games considered in the game-theoretical approach to natural language semantics. In particular, the law of excluded middle fails since there are easy and general examples when the associated game is not determined. We refer the reader to the game-theoretical chapter for a discussion of what this means for the notion of negation.

In this part we will choose an attribute-value formalism, but we will return to higher-order logic and partiality in Section 3. We emphasize, however, that the particular model chosen is just a vehicle used to sort out some of the aspects of partiality discussed in Section 1.

2.1. *Representional form*

Syntactic analysis aims to unravel the structure of a phrase. Part of this task consists in exhibiting the features and roles carried by or embedded into the phrase. Subparts of it may belong to different syntactic categories, they may function in a variety of roles such as subject, object, etc., and they may be marked for various types of agreement features. Such information can be conveniently represented in an *attribute-value format*.

Feature-value systems and their logic is the topic of other chapters of the Handbook, *Unification Grammars* by Martin Kay and *Feature Logics* by W.C. Rounds. Let us here remark that this format of analysis was pioneered within computational linguistics by Martin Kay. It was also the format chosen by Kaplan and Bresnan (1982), in their theory of *Lexical-Functional Grammar*, with an emphasis on grammatical attributes such as SUBJ, OBJ, TENSE, PRED, etc. In our theory of *Situation Schemata* we shifted from a focusing on grammatical roles to an emphasis of semantical roles such as REL, ARG, LOC; see Fenstad, Halvorsen, Langholm and Van Benthem (1987).

2.1.1. *A theory of signs*

From our point of view we can also view the class of Head-Driven Phrase Structure Grammars (HPSG) as attribute-value theories; see the basic text by Pollard and Sag (1987). HPSG is a *theory of signs*, where the basic format is

$$\begin{bmatrix} \text{PHON} & \cdots \\ \text{SYN} & \begin{bmatrix} \text{LOC} & \begin{bmatrix} \text{HEAD} & \cdots \\ \text{SUBCAT} & \cdots \\ \text{LEX} & \cdots \end{bmatrix} \\ \text{BIND} & \cdots \end{bmatrix} \\ \text{SEM} & \cdots \end{bmatrix}.$$

A sign can be phrasal or lexical, according to whether the LEX feature is unmarked or marked. Within this framework Pollard and Sag developed a rich theory of grammatical structure. We shall only comment on one aspect of relevance to partiality. The information carried by sign is possibly partial. A noun – or rather its sign – is not in itself complete or *saturated*, but calls for a determiner to form a full sign, an NP. In the same way a VP subcategorizes for an NP to form a full sign, in this case a sign of category S. In HPSG this process is governed by the *subcategorization principle*. In this way the theory is able to deal with partiality phenomena classified as sortal incorrectness; see Section 1.1.1.

We have dwelt upon this issue at some length in order to highlight the phenomenon of partiality associated with grammatical signs. In order to carry "meaning" (as in the case of a sign of category S) or "reference" (as in the case of a sign of category NP) the sign must be *saturated*.

2.1.2. *The algebra of signs*

This partiality is also reflected in the *algebraic theory of signs*. This theory can be cast in several different forms. In one version we look upon an attribute-value matrix as a *finite* or *partial function*, where complex matrices correspond to iterated functions. An approach along these lines has been developed by Johnson (1988); for a brief exposition see the chapter on *Feature Logics*. Alternatively, we can look upon attribute-value matrices as a *collection of paths*; see the pioneering work of Rounds and Kaspar (1986). In the following example

$$\begin{bmatrix} \text{SUBJ} & [\text{PRED} \quad \text{MARY}] \\ \text{OBJ} & [\text{PRED} \quad \text{JOHN}] \\ \text{PRED} & \text{KISS} \end{bmatrix}$$

we have a set $A = \{\text{MARY}, \text{JOHN}, \text{KISS}, \ldots\}$ of *atomic values* and a set $L = \{\text{SUBJ}, \text{OBJ}, \text{PRED}, \ldots\}$ of *labels*. The matrix can be redrawn as a graph

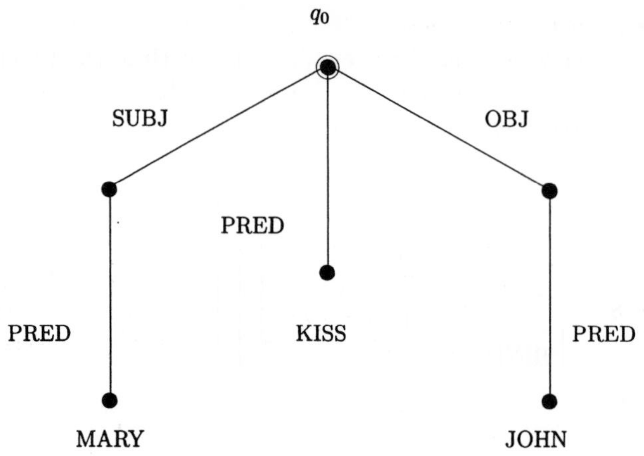

where we have six *nodes*, including an *initial node*; labels are attached to the arcs between nodes, and atomic values are assigned to some nodes. Formally a *complex feature structure* is defined as

$$M = \langle Q, q_0, \delta, \alpha \rangle,$$

where Q is the set of *nodes*; q_0 is the *initial node*; δ is a *transition function*, i.e. a *partial* function $\delta : Q \times L \to Q$; and α is an *assignment function*, i.e. a *partial* (and injective) function $\alpha : Q \to A$.

How the theory proceeds from this basis can be seen from chapter on *Feature Logics* of the Handbook; see also the expositions in Carpenter (1992) and Keller (1993). We have included this brief hint to highlight how partiality is present at a rather fundamental structural level in the theory of grammatical form. Signs need not be saturated but may only encode partial information. The transition and assignment functions of a complex feature-valued structure are *partial predicates* in the sense of Section 1. Lack of subsumption and failure of unification can be used to block the occurrence of sortal incorrectness.

We are still at the level of grammatical form; our next task is to discuss how to cope with problems of partiality associated with reference and indexicality. But the reader should bear in mind that this structure partiality has not called for a parallel partiality in the logic; for further discussion see Section 3.2.6.

2.2. *A relational theory of meaning*

The sentences of mathematics do not need a speaker. And since mathematical praxis had a decisive influence on the development of logic, we may well ask how appropriate the deductive chains and proof figures of formal logic are for "seeing" the validity of arguments in natural language contexts. We shall not discuss the adequacy of proof theory as a paradigm for natural language reasoning; see Barwise and Etchemendy (1991), for recent work see Allwein and Barwise (1993). Our problem is to account for the "I" and "you" of natural language use; i.e. how to include the speaker and hearer as part of the communicative act. To fix ideas we shall follow the approach of Fenstad, Halvorsen, Langholm, and Van Benthem (1987).

2.2.1. Situation schemata

A *situation schema* is an attribute-value matrix where the features have been chosen to reflect the primitives of situation theory; see Section 1.2.2. Thus we have a feature label REL corresponding to the set R of relations; we have feature labels IND corresponding to individuals in I or elements of L; labels LOC corresponding to the set of locations L; and a label POL to indicate the polarities of basic facts. The situation schema corresponding the sentence $A =$ *John is running* is

$$\text{SIT.A} = \begin{bmatrix} \text{REL} & \textit{run} \\ \text{ARG.1} & \textit{John} \\ \text{LOC} & \begin{bmatrix} \text{IND} & \text{IND.1} \\ \text{COND} & \begin{bmatrix} \text{REL} & o \\ \text{ARG.1} & \text{IND.1} \\ \text{ARG.2} & \text{IND.0} \end{bmatrix} \end{bmatrix} \\ \text{POL} & 1 \end{bmatrix}$$

The set L of locations consists of regions of space-time. L can be given a rich geometric structure, we always assume that we have the relations *precede* and *overlap* with respect to the time dimension.

2.2.2. A relational theory of meaning

The interpretation of a situation schema in a situation structure is always relative to an *utterance situation* u and a *described situation* s. Thus *meaning is relational* and we use the notation:

$$u[|\text{SIT.A}|]s$$

to express this fact. We shall use our simple example to illustrate the meaning relation; for details of the full theory see Fenstad, Halvorsen, Langholm and Van Benthem (1987).

The utterance situation is decomposed into two parts: the *discourse situation* d and the *speaker's connection* c. The former tells us who the speaker is, who the addressee is, the sentence uttered, and the discourse location in space and time. The latter determines the speaker's meaning of lexical items.

We return to SIT.A and to the explanation of its "meaning". The atomic values IND.0 and IND.1 in SIT.A are called *indeterminates*. A map g defined on the set of indeterminates of SIT.A.LOC (i.e. on the embedded attribute-value matrix which is the value of the feature LOC in SIT.A) is called an *anchor* on SIT.A.LOC relative to the utterance situation d, c if

$$g(\text{IND.0}) = l_d$$

and

$$g(\text{IND.1})\ \mathit{overlap}\ l_d,$$

where l_d is the discourse location determined by d, and where the "value" o in SIT.A (which is computed from the tense marker of the given sentence) is interpreted as the *overlap*-relation of L. Then

$$d, c[|\text{SIT.A}|]s$$

if and only if there exists an anchor g on SIT.A.LOC relative to d such that

$$\text{in } s : \text{at } g(\text{IND.1}) : c(\mathit{run}), c(\mathit{John}); 1,$$

i.e. "c(*John*) stands in the relation c(*run*) at the location g(IND.1)" is a positive fact in s. Observe the speaker's connection c is a map defined on parts of the expression A and with values in the appropriate domains, i.e. $c(\mathit{run})$ is in R and $c(\mathit{John})$ is in I.

Our example is simple, but the reader will appreciate how the mechanisms introduced above can be used to analyze *indexicals* and *definite descriptions*; see Barwise and Perry (1983). We should note that the partiality of situations is not an issue at this point. Situations could be complete; for a further discussion on the relationship of the present theory to other approaches the reader is referred to Sem (1988). Whether the same mechanisms are useful in the analysis of *conditionals* and *presuppositions* is more uncertain; the reader is referred to the appropriate chapters of the Handbook.

2.2.3. The geometry of models

Situation theory locates the basic entities of the meaning analysis in *the world*, i.e. situations, locations, relations and individuals are part of the actual world. In recent cognitive science there have been much written about "mental models" and how the basic constructs are cognitive structures in *the mind*. This is a topic beyond our brief in this chapter; for a few references see Johnson-Laird (1983) and Gärdenfors (forthcoming). However, much of the mathematics will remain the same whether the structures are in the world or in the mind. And on both approaches there is a need to supplement the standard model theory with a richer geometric structure on the semantical space. To put it in slogan form: The geometry of meaning is not a homomorphic image of the algebra of syntax; for an elaborations of this point of view, see Fenstad (forthcoming).

Let us briefly summarize the discussion so far. We have surveyed several sources of partiality of importance to theoretical and computational linguistics. We made a distinction between two modules in linguistic analysis, grammatical form and semantical content. Partiality enters at a *structural level* in both components, complex feature-value structures in connection with representational form and "situations" or partial models in connection with the theory of meaning. Many phenomena of partiality in linguistics can be "explained" in terms of this structural partiality. In addition we surveyed various issues of partiality in connection with computations and self-reference. From this the importance of the notion of *partial predicates* emerged. This will be a focus of attention in the last part of this chapter.

3. Partiality and the structure of knowledge

One lesson drawn from the introductory discussion in Section 1.2 was that *partial models*, whether they are intended to model *the absence of facts* or *the lack of information about facts*, are useful constructs. With respect to models of this class we have certain *positive facts*, i.e. facts *supported* by the model, and certain *negative facts*, i.e. *rejected* by the model. Since the model is partial there may be facts that are neither supported nor rejected. The logic of partial structures thus recognizes three possibilities, *true*, *false*, *neither*.

One domain of application where this is of particular importance, is the theory of partial recursive functions; see Section 1.3. Let us restrict attention to functions taking values 0 or 1. Any such function f defines a number-theoretic predicate P_f consisting of all $n \in \mathbf{N}$ such that $f(n) = 1$. If f is total, the complement of P_f in $\mathbf{N}$ is the set of all $n \in \mathbf{N}$ such that $f(n) = 0$. Conversely, any total predicate $P \subseteq \mathbf{N}$ determines a function f_P, defined by the requirements that $f_P(n) = 1$, if $n \in P$; and $f_P(n) = 0$, if $n \notin P$. f_P is called *the characteristic function* of P.

What happens when our characteristic functions are partial recursive functions? Any such function is given by a machine M; see Section 1.3. In this case the domain of definition of M, i.e. the set of all $n \in \mathbf{N}$ such that $M(n)\downarrow$, need not be all of $\mathbf{N}$. This leads to an associated partial predicate $\langle P_M, \overline{P}_M\rangle$, where $P_M \cup \overline{P}_M$ is the domain of definition of M; $n \in P_M$, if $M(n) \simeq 1$; and $n \in \overline{P}_M$, if $M(n) \simeq 0$. From this perspective the third possibility *neither* is different from the proper truth-values; it represents a "truth-value gap", in this case represented by the co-domain $\mathbf{N} - (P_M \cup \overline{P}_M)$, i.e. the set where M is not defined. We use the word *gap* to indicate the possibility of completion, e.g., if the domain of M is recursive, we can extend M to a total recursive function M' simply by setting

$$M'(n) = 1 \quad \text{for all } n \in \mathbf{N} - (P_M \cup \overline{P}_M).$$

This is justified by the simple fact that the complement of a recursive set is recursive.

Many-valued logic is a separate topic; for an introduction see Urquhart (1986). However, drawing the exact dividing line between partial logic and many-valued logic is not an easy task. The mathematics tends to be the same, it is the interpretation (truth-value gap versus a third truth value) and the questions asked which reflect a difference in perspective.

The remainder of this part will be somewhat technical. We first study *propositional connectives*, their semantics and axiomatization. Next we discuss *partial predicates*, both in the frame-work of first order theories and in higher types. The final topic concerns *reductions*. We have argued for the necessity of partial structures. But do partial structures need a special kind of partial logic?

3.1. Partiality and propositional logic

The classical truth functions are given by the tables:

$\neg Q$

Q	t	f
	f	t

$Q \vee R$

	R	t	f
Q	t	t	t
	f	t	f

$Q \wedge R$

	R	t	f
Q	t	t	f
	f	f	f

$Q \to R$

	R	t	f
Q	t	t	f
	f	t	t

In extending from total to partial predicates we have to account for the third possibility, *neither*. We shall use the case of partial recursive functions as our guiding example. We do this with some justification, since the extension that we are going to propose, was introduced by Kleene (1952) to handle exactly this case. There is also an added "moral lesson". Formal analysis is not an arbitrary play with symbols, but needs to be grounded in experience, insight and precise preformal analysis.

3.1.1. Partial connectives

Following Kleene, let us concentrate on the case of disjunction, $Q \vee R$. In this case, let Q be the proposition that $M_1(x) \simeq 1$, i.e. Q is the positive part of the partial predicate $\langle Q, \overline{Q}\rangle$ determined by the algorithm M_1; similarly, let R be the proposition that $M_2(x) \simeq 1$. We want $Q \vee R$ to be represented by an algorithm M; the problem is to decide how the behavior of M shall be determined by the behavior of M_1 and M_2. The already filled in parts of the truth table presents no problems: If for a given value of x, $M_1(x) \simeq 0$ and $M_2(x) \simeq 0$, then the predicates Q and R have the value f for this x. In this case we want $M(x) \simeq 0$, i.e. $Q \vee R$ to have the value f.

Suppose the algorithm for $Q \vee R$ is defined, say $M(x) \simeq 1$, giving the value t to $Q \vee R$, in a case where $M_1(x)$ is undefined. This means that M gives an answer without using any information about Q, but depends only on the information that $M_2(x) \simeq 1$. In this particular case, changing the Q-predicate to one giving the value t or f, would not change the computation of M as long as the value of R is kept fixed.

Carrying through this kind of analysis for all cases, we see that in order for the propositional connectives to reflect the behavior of partial recursive operation, they must be regular (in the following sense of Kleene, 1952): A given column (row) contains t in the u (undefined) row (column), only if the column (row) consists entirely of t's; similarly for f. The Kleene truth tables are the strongest possible regular extension of the total tables, i.e. they have a t or an f whenever it is compatible with being a regular extension. The reader may verify that this leads to the tables:

$\neg Q$

Q	t	f
	f	t
	u	u

$Q \vee R$

	R	t	f	u
Q	t	t	t	t
	f	t	f	u
	u	t	u	u

$Q \wedge R$

	R	t	f	u
Q	t	t	f	u
	f	f	f	f
	u	u	f	u

$Q \to R$

	R	t	f	u
Q	t	t	f	u
	f	t	t	t
	u	t	u	u

There are other connectives of interest in the study of partial logic. In addition to the *strong* (Kleene) *negation*, $\neg Q$, we can introduce a *"weak" negation*, $\sim Q$, given by the table

$\sim Q$

Q	t	f
	f	t
	u	t

which corresponds to a kind of denial, since to deny a positive fact is either to assert that the situation is not defined or, if defined, that the corresponding negative fact obtains. In terms of partial predicates $\langle P, \overline{P} \rangle$, *strong negation* interchanges P and $\overline{P}$, *weak negation* correspond to set-theoretic complement. There is also an alternative to the implication $Q \to R$, viz. $Q \supset R$ defined as $\sim Q \vee R$. Both $\sim$ and $\supset$ are *non-persistent*, i.e. adding new facts may change truth-values. We shall return to the topic of persistence in connection with the discussion of partial predicates.

The fact that we have written down truth-tables in the "values" t, f and u does not mean that we have changed from partiality to *many-valued logic*. If "values" were part of our calculus, we would have to show some care; there are, e.g., differences between partial functions $f : \mathbf{N} \to \{0, 1\}$ and total functions $f : \mathbf{N} \to \{0, 1, u\}$. This is well known to every recursion theorist; in our context we can refer to the system of Johnson (1988) mentioned in Section 2.1.5. We also need the perspective of partiality in the discussion of *persistence*, see Section 3.2.2.

There is a large body of results on connectives and definability in partial propositional logic. Particularity noteworthy are various results on functional completeness of sets of connectives. This is of great importance for the systematic study of partial logic, but may be of more marginal interest for the linguist. The reader is referred to the technical literature; some key references are Blamey (1986), Langholm (1988), Thijsse (1992) and Jaspars (1994).

3.1.2. Partiality and the consequence relation

Let us be a bit more precise about the technical machinery of propositional logic. *Formulas* ϕ, ψ are built from a finite set $P_1, \ldots, P_n$ of propositional variables using the connectives $\wedge, \vee, \neg, \to$. Occasionally we consider a larger set of connectives, e.g., the "weak" connectives $\sim$, $\supset$; this will always be explicitly mentioned. *Models* are valuations, i.e. maps from the set of propositional variables to the set of "truth"-values t, f and u, extended to the class of all formulas by the use of (Kleene's) truth-tables.

In the partial case we see that there is a difference between *non-true* and *false*, and between *non-false* and *true*. For let V be a valuation in which not $V(\phi) = t$, for some ϕ. This means that $V(\phi) = f$ or $V(\phi) = u$; thus non-truth of ϕ with respect to the model V does not imply the falsity of ϕ with respect to V (i.e. $V(\phi) = f$).

This distinction means that the notion of consequence splits into two versions when we pass from classical to partial logic. Let Γ and Δ be finite sets or sequences of formulas. (If we were to enter into the finer details of proof theory, we would have to be more careful about the nature of Γ and Δ, whether they be sets, sequences, multi-sets etc.; see Langholm (1989).) Let $\Gamma = \{\phi_1, \ldots, \phi_n\}$ and $\Delta = \{\psi\}$. The classical consequence relation $\Gamma \models \Delta$ is intended to express that the truth of ψ follows from the validity of all of $\phi_1, \ldots, \phi_n$, i.e. from the truth of the conjunction $\phi_1 \wedge \cdots \wedge \phi_n$. In the general case where $\Delta = \{\psi_1, \ldots, \psi_m\}$ the single formula ψ is replaced by the disjunction $\psi_1 \vee \cdots \vee \psi_m$. From the classical truth tables we conclude that $\Gamma \models \Delta$, if there is no valuation V such that $V(\phi_i) = t$, for all $i = 1, \ldots, n$ and $V(\psi_j) = f$, for all $j = 1, \ldots, m$. Since non-true is different from false in partial logic, the classical consequence relation splits into two parts:

$\Gamma \models_S \Delta$ *if and only if* there is no partial model (valuation) in which all formulas of Γ are true and all formulas of Δ are non-true.

$\Gamma \models_W \Delta$ *if and only if* there is no partial model (valuation) in which all formulas of Γ are true and all formulas of Δ are false.

The distinction between the two is easily seen, since we always have $\models_W \phi, \neg\phi$, but not always $\models_S \phi, \neg\phi$ – take a case where $V(\phi) = V(\neg\phi) = u$.

3.1.3. Validity

Langholm (1989) suggested how to combine the two versions into a single "figure" or consequence relation:

$$\begin{array}{c||c} \Gamma & \Delta \\ \hline \Pi & \Sigma \end{array} \qquad (*)$$

which is *valid*, if and only if there exists no model in which

all formulas of Γ are true;
all formulas of Δ are non-true;
all formulas of Π are false;
all formulas of Σ are non-false.

Thus $\models_S$ corresponds to

$$\begin{array}{c||c} \Gamma & \Delta \\ \hline & \end{array}$$

and $\models_W$ corresponds to

$$\begin{array}{c||c} \Gamma & \\ \hline \Delta & \end{array}$$

What we in fact have done is to replace the set of "truth"-values t, f and u (undefined) with the set t, f, nt and nf, where nt stands for non-true and nf for non-false. We see that old values correspond to pairs of new values, thus u corresponds to nt and nf; t corresponds to t and nf (but since t is stronger or more informative than nf, we shall omit the latter); and f corresponds to f and nt (where we for the same reason omit the nt-part of the pair).

3.1.4. Derivability

Corresponding to the validity relation we introduce the proof relation:

$$\begin{array}{c|c} \Gamma & \Delta \\ \hline \Pi & \Sigma \end{array} \tag{$**$}$$

We shall indicate in a few cases how to give axioms and rules for this proof relation. Of the six possible pairs of truth values three are allowed

$$t, nf \qquad f, nt \qquad nt, nf$$

and three are impossible

$$t, nt \qquad f, nf \qquad t, f.$$

The latter pairs translate into the following three axioms:

$$\begin{array}{c|c} \Gamma, \phi & \Delta, \phi \\ \hline \Pi & \Sigma \end{array} \qquad \begin{array}{c|c} \Gamma & \Delta \\ \hline \Pi, \phi & \Sigma, \phi \end{array} \qquad \begin{array}{c|c} \Gamma, \phi & \Delta \\ \hline \Pi, \phi & \Sigma \end{array}$$

which are all seen to be valid by the definition of $(*)$. The truth table for strong negation can be replaced by the following truth table

ϕ	$\neg\phi$
t	f
f	t
nt	nf
nf	nt

We see how the two tables correspond, t which is the same as the pair t and nf, is changed by $\neg$ to the pair f and nt. Likewise nt and nf is changed by $\neg$ to nf and nt, which corresponds to u being transformed to u by $\neg$.

The table translates into the following *rules*:

$$\begin{array}{c|c} \Gamma, \phi & \Delta \\ \hline \Pi & \Sigma \end{array} \qquad \begin{array}{c|c} \Gamma & \Delta \\ \hline \Pi, \phi & \Sigma \end{array} \qquad \begin{array}{c|c} \Gamma & \Delta, \phi \\ \hline \Pi & \Sigma \end{array} \qquad \begin{array}{c|c} \Gamma & \Delta \\ \hline \Pi & \Sigma, \phi \end{array}$$

$$\Downarrow \qquad\qquad \Downarrow \qquad\qquad \Downarrow \qquad\qquad \Downarrow$$

$$\begin{array}{c|c} \Gamma & \Delta \\ \hline \Pi, \neg\phi & \Sigma \end{array} \qquad \begin{array}{c|c} \Gamma, \neg\phi & \Delta \\ \hline \Pi & \Sigma \end{array} \qquad \begin{array}{c|c} \Gamma & \Delta \\ \hline \Pi & \Sigma, \neg\phi \end{array} \qquad \begin{array}{c|c} \Gamma & \Delta, \neg\phi \\ \hline \Pi & \Sigma \end{array}$$

We see how these rules preserve validity, e.g., in the first case, if there is no model in which ϕ is t, then there is no model in which $\neg\phi$ is f.

Let us have a brief look at conjunction. In this case the truth-table in t, f and u translates to the following table:

ϕ	ψ	$\phi \wedge \psi$
t	t	t
nt	$-$	nt
$-$	nt	nt
f	$-$	f
$-$	f	f
nf	nf	nf

(where a line – indicates that any of the values t, f, nt and nf can be inserted). We leave it to the reader to argue in detail how this table correspond to the table for conjunction in Section 3.1.1. Rules can now be extracted from the table; we indicate a few cases:

$$\begin{array}{c|c} \Gamma, \phi, \psi & \Delta \\ \hline \Pi & \Sigma \end{array}$$

$$\Downarrow$$

$$\begin{array}{c|c} \Gamma, (\phi \wedge \psi) & \Delta \\ \hline \Pi & \Sigma \end{array}$$

This is the rule corresponding to line one of the table. Matching lines two and three we get the rule:

$$\begin{array}{c|c} \Gamma & \Delta, \phi \\ \hline \Pi & \Sigma \end{array} \qquad \begin{array}{c|c} \Gamma & \Delta, \psi \\ \hline \Pi & \Sigma \end{array}$$

$$\Downarrow$$

$$\begin{array}{c|c} \Gamma & \Delta, (\phi \wedge \psi) \\ \hline \Pi & \Sigma \end{array}$$

Likewise lines four and five and line six allow us to introduce conjunction in the last two quadrants in complete symmetry to the two cases exhibited above.

3.1.5. Completeness

We shall not pursue the proof theory to any extent in this chapter; however, one remark on completeness. In $(*)$ and $(**)$ we have discussed certain *sequents* of formulas $\langle \Gamma, \Delta, \Pi, \Sigma \rangle$. In $(*)$ we introduced the notion of *validity* of a sequent. The axioms and rules developed in connection with $(**)$ leads to a notion of *derivability*. The way in which we have introduced axioms and rules leads almost directly to the following completeness result:

A sequent is derivable if and only if it is valid.

The format of analysis which we have used, was introduced by Langholm (1989); see also Langholm (forthcoming), where he presents a general scheme for the introductions of axioms and rules (of which we have given only some specific examples), and where he proves some general definability and completeness theorems.

The sequent formalism and the axioms and rules arising from it is particularity suitable for an *algorithmic analysis* of the derivability relation. If partial logic is to play any role in computational linguistics it must be as part of an *inference mechanism* for some natural-language system. We shall return to this point later.

3.1.6. Supervaluations and implicit truth

Before turning to partial predicates in first and higher-order logic there are a few remarks to be added. We have focused on the consequence relation associated with the strong Kleene truth tables and the corresponding proof theory. But this is not the only possible consequence relation in partial logic. Adding some weak connections such as $\sim$ and $\supset$ do not change the format of the analysis. There are, however, other more radical departures which we briefly touch.

If partiality is seen as lack of knowledge, we could suspend judgement and define truth in terms of all possible ways of completing our knowledge. To be a bit more precise, a valuation V can be seen as a partial map from propositional variables to the truth-values t and f. This means that the "value" u is now really taken as undefined. A partial V can be extended to a complete, i.e. totally defined, $\widehat{V}$ in many ways. This gives rise to a notion of *implicit truth*; we say that ϕ is *implicitly true* in a model V if $\widehat{V}(\phi) = t$ for all completions $\widehat{V}$ of V; ϕ is called *implicitly false* if $\widehat{V}(\phi) = f$ for all completions $\widehat{V}$ of V.

Implicit truth is not the same as true with respect to the model, e.g., $(\phi \wedge \psi) \vee (\phi \wedge \neg\psi)$ is *implicitly true* in any model V where ϕ is true and ψ is undefined, but it is *not true* in V. The notion of implicit truth (i.e. truth in every completion or *supervaluation*) was introduced by Van Fraassen (1986), with applications to free logic and to the analysis of the Liar Paradox. There is a rich theory concerning implicit truth and other truth definitions, the reader will find an introduction and technical discussions in the papers referred to in Section 3.1.1.

We must also mention another omission of this chapter. Partiality has been extended to modal notions. In addition to the intrinsic study of *partiality in modal logic*, his theory has been used to obtain many interesting results on definability and interpretability both in classical and partial logic; see Van Benthem (1985), Jaspars and Thijsse (forthcoming), Thijsse (1992), and Jaspars (1994).

Let us, however, add one remark concerning partiality, small models and modality. It would not be unreasonable to expect that with partiality one would in general have much smaller (minimal) models for a set of consistent sentences since there is no need to represent the undefined part by sets of total alternatives. Perhaps surprisingly, in partial model logic this need not be so. In worst cases minimal partial model structures may have to be larger than in the corresponding total semantics; see Thijsse (1992).

3.2. *Partial predicates*

Partiality can be introduced into first-order logic in a number of ways. We have repeatedly argued for the usefulness of *partial predicates* and shall in this section restrict partiality to precisely this point.

3.2.1. *Partiality and first order logic*

To keep technicalities to a minimum we assume that our *language* has variables, constants, relation symbols, some propositional connectives and the universal and existential quantifiers. *Formulas* are defined as usual. A *model* M is determined by a non-empty domain $D = D_M$ of individuals. M assigns to each constant c of the language an element $[|c|]_M \in D$. So far nothing is changed.

Relation symbols, however, will be interpreted as *partial relations*. Let R be an n-ary relation symbol of the language. M assigns to R a pair $\langle [|R|]_M^+, [|R|]_M^- \rangle$, where both the "positive part" $[|R|]_M^+$ and the "negative part" $[|R|]_M^-$ are subsets of the set D^n, the set of all n-tuples over D.

A formula ϕ of the language has a truth value t, f or u with respect to a model M and a variable assignment (which is a map from variables of the language to the domain D of M). The truth-definition is exactly as in the classical case, using the partial tables for propositional connections where the classical definition uses the two-valued ones. The only change comes with relation symbols. Let R be an n-ary relation symbol and $c_1, \ldots, c_n$ constants. The value of $R(c_1, \ldots, c_n)$ in the model M is

$$[|R(c_1, \ldots, c_n)|]_M = \begin{cases} t, & \text{if } \langle [|c_1|], \ldots, [|c_n|] \rangle \in [|R|]^+ \\ f, & \text{if } \langle [|c_1|], \ldots, [|c_n|] \rangle \in [|R|]^- \end{cases}$$

If $\langle [|c_1|], \ldots, [|c_n|] \rangle \in D^n - ([|R|]^+ \cup [|R|]^-)$, which well may happen, the value is u or undefined. (When the particular model M is clear from the context, we drop the subscript M on $[|\ |]_M$.) The analysis of the derivability notion, see $(**)$ of Section 3.1, easily extends to the first order case, and one has the "correct" completeness results. We shall not pursue the proof theory here, but touch a topic of relevance to the "growth of information" issue.

On the present perspective partiality is restricted to relation symbols only. This means that an assertion can change value from *undefined* to *true* or *false* only by adding new elements to either the positive or negative part of a partial relation. To illustrate let us assume that our languages for the remainder of this discussion contains the "weak" connectives $\sim\phi$, $\phi \supset \psi$ (defined as $\sim\phi \vee \psi$), and $\phi \equiv \psi$ (defined as $(\phi \supset \psi) \wedge (\psi \supset \phi)$) in addition to the strong connectives $\wedge, \vee, \neg$. Let $R(c_1, \ldots, c_n)$ be an atomic formula and M a model such that $[|R(c_1, \ldots, c_n)|]_M$ is undefined. It is then possible to extend M to models N_1 and N_2, where N_1 comes from M by adding $\langle [|c_1|]_M, \ldots, [|c_n|]_M \rangle$ to $[|R|]_M^+$, and N_2 comes from M by adding $\langle [|c_1|]_M, \ldots, [|c_n|]_M \rangle$ to $[|R|]_M^-$. Thus we have in N_1 the added information that $[|R(c_1, \ldots, c_n)|]_{N_1} = t$ and in N_2 that $[|R(c_1, \ldots, c_n)|]_{N_2} = f$.

The situation is more complicated when we look at the formula $\sim R(c_1, \ldots, c_n)$. In this case $[|\sim R(c_1, \ldots, c_n)|]_M = t$ (weak negation), but $[|\sim R(c_1, \ldots, c_n)|]_{N_1} = f$ for the extended model N_1. In this case we have a *revision* rather than an *extension* of information. Let us discuss the situation in some more details.

3.2.2. Persistence

Let M and N be two models for the language, we say that N *extends* M, in symbols,

$$M \sqsubseteq N,$$

if and only if:

(i) $D_M = D_N$;

(ii) $[|c|]_M = [|c|]_N$, for all constants c; and

(iii) $[|R|]^+_M \subseteq [|R|]^+_N$ and $[|R|]^-_M \subseteq [|R|]^-_N$, for all relation symbols R.

A sentence ϕ of the language is called *t-persistent* if $[|\phi|]_M = t$ and $M \sqsubseteq N$ imply $[|\phi|]_N = t$; it is called *f-persistent* if $[|\phi|]_M = f$ and $M \sqsubseteq N$ imply $[|\phi|]_N = f$. ϕ is called *persistent* if it is both t- and f-persistent. It is of obvious importance to be able to decide which sentences of the language are persistent, i.e. preserved under model extensions.

From the example above we saw that $\sim R(c_1, \ldots, c_n)$ is not persistent; on the other hand every formula containing only the strong connectives $\wedge, \vee, \neg$ is persistent. Call a formula *pure* if it contains only strong connectives. We have seen that pure implies persistent. It is a remarkable and not entirely trivial fact that *the semantic notion of persistence is characterized by the syntactic notion of purity*. This was proved by Langholm (1988):

Let ϕ be a persistent sentence, then there exists a pure sentence ψ such that $\phi \equiv \psi$ and $\neg\phi \equiv \neg\psi$ are provable

3.2.3. Higher types

We now turn to a brief discussion of *partial predicates in higher types*. In the chapter on *Montague Grammar* we have seen an approach where higher type intensional logic is used for the semantical analysis of natural languages. Is there a partial version of this theory?

Partiality in higher types has always been a troublesome issue. Kleene's theory of *partial recursive functionals in finite types* always assumed that arguments were total, otherwise one tended to lose control over the structure of subcomputations. A mathematically successful analysis was carried through by Platek (1966) (see Moldestad, 1977, for a careful analysis) through his introduction of the *hereditarily consistent objects* of higher types. But it was almost impossible to come to grips with the "intuitive" meaning of the structure of the hereditarily consistent objects. And without insight there can be no applications beyond formal calculations. Such was the state of the art within the recursion theory community for many years. Types and partiality was also a topic of interest in proof theory and foundational studies, see, e.g., Feferman (1984); for recent contributions and surveys, see also Cantini (1993). Important as these topics may be, this is not the place for a more extensive survey; we shall turn to topics at the interface of logic and linguistics.

Montague Grammar established a link between categorial grammar and higher order intensional logic; see the collection of papers by Montague in Thomason (1974). This was a "total" theory, but issues of partiality was not far away in this type of theoretical modeling; see Section 1 on sources of partiality. The "obvious" idea was to extend systems of first order partial logic to higher types. But the resulting complexities made this approach rather unattractive.

Recently we have seen a re-emergence of partiality in higher types. Muskens (1989) first recast the standard theory as a theory of relations in higher types and then showed how to extend this theory to partial relations. His motivation was to obtain a partialized version of Montague Grammar, and in this he succeeded.

Notice that this is a purely "structural" use of types, we are using type theory to describe higher order structures. There is also a "computational" side to type theory in which the objects of higher types are primarily seen as algorithms or procedures (see the references to Feferman and Cantini above). The distinction between the structural and the computational perspective is not always sharp; in our case it should be, our focus being elements, sets, sets of sets, etc...

Muskens approach was relational. Later we also got functional versions of higher types partiality. In Lapierre (1992) we find a study of a functional partial semantics for higher order intensional logic, and in Lepage (1992) we find a general study of partial functions in type theory. It is beyond the scope of this chapter to give a technical exposition of these developments. We shall, however, give a brief introduction to *partial predicates in higher types* and remark how this is related both to Montague Grammar and Situation Theory.

3.2.3.1. Types and frames. The set of *types* is defined by the following recursive clauses:

(i) e, s are *types*;

(ii) if $\alpha_1, \ldots, \alpha_n$ are *types* ($n \geqslant 0$), then $\langle \alpha_1, \ldots, \alpha_n \rangle$ is a *type*.

e is the type of individuals, s is the type of "possible worlds" or "situations".

A *frame* is a collection:

$$F = \{D_\alpha \mid \alpha \text{ is a type}\},$$

where

(i) D_s, D_e are non-empty.

(ii) $D_{\langle \alpha_1, \ldots, \alpha_n \rangle} \subseteq \text{Pow}(D_{\alpha_1} \times \cdots \times D_{\alpha_n})$,

where $\text{Pow}(D)$ is the set of all subsets of D, and $D_{\alpha_1} \times \cdots \times D_{\alpha_n}$ is the set of all n-tuples $\langle d_1, \ldots, d_n \rangle$, where $d_i \in D_{\alpha_i}$, $i = 1, \ldots, n$. Thus if $k \in D_e$, then k is an individual. If $P \in D_{\langle e \rangle}$, then $P \in \text{Pow}(D_e)$, i.e. P is a subset of D_e.

If $P \in D_{\langle s,e \rangle}$ and $w_0 \in D_s$, let

$$P_{w_0} = \{a \in D_e \mid \langle w_0, a \rangle \in P\};$$

we may think of P_{w_0} as the extension of P at "world w_0" or in the "situation w_0".

We need not include a special type for truth-values, since we always require that $D_{\langle \rangle} = \text{Pow}(\{\emptyset\})$, where $P(\{\emptyset\})$ is a set of two elements which can be identified with the values *true* and *false*.

3.2.3.2. Terms of the language are specified by the following clauses:

(i) For each type α there are constants and variables of type α.

(ii) If ϕ and ψ are terms of type $\langle\,\rangle$, then $\neg\phi$ and $\phi \wedge \psi$ are terms of type $\langle\,\rangle$.

(iii) If ϕ is a term of type $\langle\,\rangle$ and x a variable, then $\forall x\phi$ is a term of type $\langle\,\rangle$.

(iv) If A is a term of type $\langle\beta, \alpha_1, \ldots, \alpha_n\rangle$ and B a term of type β, then (AB) is a term of type $\langle\alpha_1, \ldots, \alpha_n\rangle$.

(v) If A is a term of type $\langle\alpha_1, \ldots, \alpha_n\rangle$ and x a variable of type β, then $\lambda x A$ is a term of type $\langle\beta, \alpha_1, \ldots, \alpha_n\rangle$.

(vi) If A and B are terms of the same type, then $A = B$ is a term of type $\langle\,\rangle$.

3.2.3.3. Interpretations A frame $F = \{D_\alpha\}$ is extended to a *model* or *interpretation*

$$M = \langle F, I, a\rangle,$$

by adding an *interpretation* function I which maps a constant c of type α to an element in D_α, and a *variable assignment* a which map variables of type α to D_α. We use $[|A|] = [|A|]_M$ to denote the *value* of A in the model M. $[|A|]$ is inductively defined by six clauses, corresponding to the clauses in the definition of terms:

(i) $[|c|] = I(c)$, c constant term,
$[|x|] = a(x)$, x variable symbol.

The clauses (ii), (iii) and (vi) are identical to the standard definitions in first order logic.

(iv) Let the values $[|A|]$ and $[|B|]$ be given. Then $[|AB|]$ is the subset of $D_{\alpha_1} \times \cdots \times D_{\alpha_n}$ defined by the condition

$$\langle d_1, \ldots, d_n\rangle \in [|(AB)|] \quad \text{if and only if} \quad \langle [|B|], d_1, \ldots, d_n\rangle \in [|A|].$$

To explain clause (v) we need an extra bit of notation. The value $[|A|]$ of a term A is calculated with respect to a model $M = \langle F, I, a\rangle$. Let x be a variable of type β and d an element of D_β. Let $M(x/d)$ denote the model obtained from M by modifying the variable assignment a at (possibly) one point, viz. by setting $a(x) = d$; let us denote the resulting value of a term A by $[|A|](x/d)$.

(v) $[|\lambda x A|]$ is the relation defined by:

$$\langle d, d_1, \ldots, d_n\rangle \in [|\lambda x A|] \quad \text{if and only if} \quad \langle d_1, \ldots, d_n\rangle \in [|A|](x/d),$$

for all elements $d \in D_\beta$.

To give a simple illustration, let R be a constant of type $\langle s, e\rangle$ and i_0 a constant of type s. Let $P = [|R|]$ and $w_0 = [|i_0|]$, by use of clause (iv) we see that for any $d \in D_e$: $d \in [|Ri_0|]$ if and only if $d \in P_{w_0}$, i.e. $[|Ri_0|]$ is *the extension* of R *in world* $w_0 = [|i_0|]$.

In Muskens (1992) it is shown how this theory of relations in higher types can be used to give a Montague-type semantics. Changing from functionals and applications to relations necessitates some revisions, but nothing really unexpected.

3.2.4. Partial predicates in higher types

Partiality is easily fitted into the relational framework. Let $D_1, \dots, D_n$ be sets, a *partial relation* R on $D_1, \dots, D_n$ is a pair $\langle R^+, R^- \rangle$, where $R^+, R^- \subseteq D_1 \times \cdots \times D_n$. Let $\mathrm{PPow}(D) = \mathrm{Pow}(D) \times \mathrm{Pow}(D) = \{\langle R_1, R_2 \rangle \mid R_1, R_2 \subseteq D\}$. A *frame* F *in the extended partial sense* is a collection

$$F = \{D_\alpha \mid \alpha \text{ is a type}\},$$

where D_e and D_s are non-empty sets and

$$D_{\langle \alpha_1, \dots, \alpha_n \rangle} \subseteq \mathrm{PPow}(D_{\alpha_1} \times \cdots \times D_{\alpha_n}).$$

There are a number of remarks that we ought to add in order to be technically complete and correct in every detail, in particular, in connection with the evaluation of terms in a model. Let us just note that if R is a constant of type $\langle s, e \rangle$ and i_0 a constant of type s, then $w_0 = [|i_0|]$ is an element of D_s and $[|R|]$ is a partial relation $\langle [|R|]^+, [|R|]^- \rangle$, where both $[|R|]^+, [|R|]^- \subseteq D_s \times D_e$. The interpretation of the term $[|Ri_0|]$ is the partial predicate $\langle P^+, P^- \rangle$, where $d \in P^+$ if and only if $\langle w_0, d \rangle \in [|R|]^+$, and $d \in P^-$, if and only if $\langle w_0, d \rangle \in [|R|]^-$. Thus $[|Ri_0|]$ is *the partial predicate* which is *the extension* of R *in the situation* w_0.

We have restricted our exposition to partial predicates. But there is more to partiality in types and λ-calculi than the issue of partial predicates. However, an adequate introduction to these matters is beyond the limits set for this chapter. The interested reader is referred to the current research literature; see Lapierre (1992), and Lepage (1992). We conclude with a remark on partiality in higher types and situation theory.

Partial relations in first order logic gave an analysis of some aspects of situation theory, see Fenstad, Halvorsen, Langholm and Van Benthem (1987). Partial relations in higher type can be seen as an extension, but in a way which differs considerably from current developments in situation theory; see Barwise (1989), and the chapter on *Situation Semantics* in this Handbook. In our approach we used an attribute-value formalism for the syntactic part; partiality in higher types allows you to keep *the "homomorphism"* (i.e. the structure preserving map) between *the syntactic algebra* of *categorial grammar* and the *semantic algebra* of *partial higher types*. The idea of having a "homomorphism" between the syntactic algebra and the semantic algebra has always proved appealing to the mathematically minded. In my view it is the kind of mathematical neatness which in this case needs to be resisted. Syntax is not the only input to semantic processing, see the discussion in Fenstad, Halvorsen, Langholm and Van Benthem (1987), and semantic space has a richer geometric structure than can be derived from any syntactic algebra, see Gärdenfors (forthcoming). Mathematics and logic are powerful tools in the study of natural languages, but tools must be chosen for the tasks of hand.

3.2.5. Reducibilities

It remains to add some words on the topic of *reducibility* and to explore to which extent questions about partial propositional logic and partial first-order logic can be *reduced* to or *translated* into questions about classical logic. There is an extensive literature on this topic; we shall treat only one topic related to first order logic with partial predicates. To keep technicalities to a minimum we assume once more that our *language* has variables, constants, relation symbols, the propositional connectives $\wedge, \vee, \neg$ and $\sim$ (remember that $\supset$ and $\equiv$ are definable), and the universal and existential quantifiers. In any *model* or interpretation a relation symbol R is interpreted as a partial predicate $\langle [|R|]^+, [|R|]^- \rangle$. We assume that *derivability* and *validity* notions are given.

A very simple, but basic observation on the proof theory is the following *Normal Form*: For any formula ϕ there is a formula ψ such that $\phi \equiv \psi$ is provable in the system and strong negation $\neg$ occurs in ψ only with atomic formulas $R(t_1, \ldots, t_n)$.

This Normal Form immediately admits a *translation into classical first-order logic*: Let ϕ be a formula in normal form, the translation ϕ^* of ϕ is obtained by substituting a new predicate symbol P^- for occurrences of $\neg P$ and a new predicate symbol P^+ for unnegated occurrences of P.

To establish a correspondence between partial and classical models there is one minor point to take care of. In partial logic we assume consistency in the form $[|R|]^+ \cap [|R|]^- = \phi$. In classical logic there is nothing to prevent that $[|P^+|]$ and $[|P^-|]$ have a non-empty intersection. This is taken care of by adding an extra axiom

$$\neg\exists x_1 \cdots \exists x_n \big(R^+(x_1, \ldots, x_n) \wedge R^-(x_1, \ldots, x_n)\big)$$

for each original relation symbol R. This done, there is a natural correspondence between partial models and classical models satisfying the extra axioms. *Through this correspondence, completeness and compactness for partial first-order logic is an immediate corollary of the corresponding results for classical first-order logic.*

This reduction technique was first introduced by Gilmore (1974), and later exploited by Feferman (1984). It was used in Langholm (1988), and has later been the topic of extensive studies; see Thijsse (1992), for further references. One may get the impression that this reduction "trivializes" the logic of partial predicates. But this impression is wrong as we now shall see in connection with the strong persistence theorem, see Section 3.2.2. We should also add that this reduction technique does not apply to the notion of *implicit truth*, see Section 3.1.6.

Looking closer at the proof of the strong persistence theorem we see that the translation techniques with some efforts proves the result for t-persistence, i.e. a formula ϕ is t-persistent if and only if there exists a pure formula ψ such that $\phi \equiv \psi$ is provable. Duality gives a similar result for f-persistence. This means that if ϕ is persistent, i.e. both t- and f-persistent, then there exist pure formulas ψ_1 and ψ_2 such that $\phi \equiv \psi_1$ and $\neg\phi \equiv \neg\psi_2$ are provable. More than mere reduction techniques are needed to show that ψ_1 and ψ_2 can be taken to be one and the same formula. This was proved by Langholm (1988). The intricate interplay between partial and classical logic also shows up in Langholm's analysis of *Horn Clauses in Partial logic*; see Langholm (1990).

3.2.6. Do partial structures need partial logic?

We are at the end of our discussion. We have surveyed various sources of partiality in connection with theoretical and computational linguistics. Some of these issues were "explained" within the framework of feature-valued systems and a relational theory of meaning. Moving beyond grammatical form the situation is less clear. Partial predicates turn up in a number of connections. But do partial predicates need a partial logic? The discussion in Section 3.2.5 showed that there is no easy answer. In some way this is analogous to the question whether constructive logic has something significant to add to computational mathematics beyond the classical theories of combinatorial and numerical analysis.

Let us return briefly to feature-valued systems. This theory deals with a certain class of algebraic structures. Associated with this class is a certain algebra of feature terms. This algebra can be "embedded" within first-order classical logic and standard PROLOG techniques can be used in the algorithmic study of feature-valued systems; see the Chapter on *Feature Logics* for references. This is similar to the role of constructive logic in the analysis of computational mathematics; here a possibly added value is the technique of how to extract algorithms from constructive proofs.

Can we make similar claims for partial logic? Let us grant that partial structures and partial predicates are important. Let us not argue for a possible philosophical or epistemological value of partial logic, but ask whether it is a good "algebra" for the study of partial structures. *The adequacy of this algebra* is shown through the completeness and compactness results of the logic. From the perspective of computational linguistics we would be interested in *the efficiency of this algebra* as a tool in an algorithmic analysis. A theoretical foundation for this analysis has been laid through the work of Langholm (1989); for a brief introduction see the presentation in Section 3.1.4. But we should note that in an actual implementation of a system for answering questions based on situation schemata and partial logic Vestre used the reduction theorem; see the exposition in Fenstad, Langholm and Vestre (1992). Thus our survey ends on a note of uncertainty.

References

Aanderaa, S. (1993), *A universal Turing machine*, Computer Science Logic, E. Börger et al., eds, Lecture Notes in Computer Science, Springer, Berlin.

Aczel, P. (1988), *Non-Well-Founded Sets*, CSLI Lecture Notes no. 14, CSLI, Stanford.

Allwein, G. and Barwise, J. (eds) (1993), *Working Papers on Diagrams and Logic*, Indiana University, Bloomington, IL.

Barton, G.E., Berwick, R.C. and Ristad, E.S. (1987), *Computational Complexity and Natural Languages*, MIT Press, Cambridge, MA.

Barwise, J. (1989), *The Situation in Logic*, CSLI Lecture Notes no. 17, CSLI, Stanford.

Barwise, J. and Etchemendy, J. (1987), *The Liar*, Oxford Univ. Press, Oxford.

Barwise, J. and Etchemendy, J. (1991), *Visual information and valid reasoning*, Visualization in Mathematics, W. Zimmermann and S. Cunningham, eds, MAA, Washington, DC.

Barwise, J. and Perry, J. (1983), *Situations and Attitudes*, MIT Press, Cambridge, MA.

Bell, J.L. (1988), *Toposes and Local Set Theories*, Oxford Logic Guides no. 14, Clarendon Press, Oxford.

Blamey, S. (1986), *Partial logic*, Handbook of Philosophical Logic vol. III, D. Gabbay and F. Guenthner, ed., Reidel, Dordrecht.

Cantini, A. (1993), *Logical frameworks for truth and abstractions*, Firenze, Dipartimente de Filosofia, Universita degli Studi di Firenze.

Carpenter, B. (1992), *The Logic of Typed Feature Structures*, Cambridge Univ. Press, Cambridge, UK.

Chang, C. and Keisler, H.J. (1977), *Model Theory*, North-Holland, Amsterdam.

Doherty, P. and Drainkov, D. (eds), *Partial Semantics and Non-Monotonic Reasoning for Knowledge Representation* (forthcoming).

Feferman, S. (1984), *Towards useful type-theories*, J. Symb. Logic **49**.
Feferman, S. (1991), *Reflecting on incompleteness*, J. Symb. Logic **56**, 1–49.
Fenstad, J.E., *Formal Semantics, Geometry and Mind* (forthcoming).
Fenstad, J.E., Halvorsen, P.-K., Langholm, T. and Van Benthem, J. (1987), *Situations, Language and Logic*, Studies in Linguistics and Philosophy vol. 34, Reidel, Dordrecht.
Fenstad, J.E., Langholm, T. and Vestre, E. (1992), *Representations and interpretations*, Computational Linguistics and Formal Semantics, M. Rosner and R. Johnson, eds., Cambridge Univ. Press, Cambridge, UK.
Gärdenfors, P. *Conceptual Spaces as a Basis for Cognitive Semantics*, Department of Philosophy, Lund University (forthcoming).
Gilmore, P.C. (1974), *The consistency of partial set theory without extensionality*, Axiomatic Set Theory, Proceedings of Symposia in Pure Mathematics vol. 13, part II, AMS, Providence, RI.
Gupta, A. and Belnap, N.D. (1993), *The Revision Theory of Truth*, MIT Press, Cambridge, MA.
Gurevich, Y. (1987), *Logic and the challenge of computer science*, Current Trends in Theoretical Computer Science, E. Börger, ed., Computer Science Press, Rockville, MD.
Herzberger, H. (1982), *Notes on naive semantics*, J. Philos. Logic **11**, 1–60.
Jaspars, J. (1994), *Calculi for constructive communication*, Thesis, ILLC, Amsterdam, and MK, Tilburg.
Jaspars, J. and Thijsse, E., *Fundamentals of partial modal logic*, P. Doherty and D. Drainkov, eds (forthcoming).
Johnson, M. (1988), *Attribute-Value Logic and the Theory of Grammar*, CSLI Lecture Notes no. 16, CSLI, Stanford University.
Johnson-Laird, V.P.N. (1983), *Mental Models*, Cambridge Univ. Press, Cambridge, UK.
Kamp, H. (1981), *A theory of truth and semantic representation*, Formal Methods in the Study of Language, J. Groenendijk et al., eds, MC Tract 135, Amsterdam.
Kamp, H. and Reyle, U. (1993), *From Discourse to Logic*, Kluwer, Dordrecht.
Kaplan, R.M. and Bresnan, J. (1982), *Lexical-functional grammar*, The Mental Representation of Grammatical Relations, J. Bresnan, ed., MIT Press, Cambridge, MA.
Keller, B. (1993), *Feature Logics, Infinitary Descriptions and Grammar*, CSLI Lecture Notes no. 44, CSLI, Stanford.
Kleene, S.C. (1952), *Introduction to Metamathematics*, Van Nostrand Reinholds, Princeton, NJ.
Koster, J. (1989), *How natural is natural language?*, Logic, Methodology and Philosophy of Science VIII, J.E. Fenstad et al., eds, North-Holland, Amsterdam.
Kripke, S. (1975), *Outline of a theory of truth*, J. Philos. **72**.
Langholm, T. (1988), *Partiality, Truth and Persistence*, CSLI Lecture Notes no. 15, CSLI, Stanford.
Langholm, T. (1989), *Algorithms for partial logic*, COSMOS Report no. 12, Department of Mathematics, University of Oslo.
Langholm, T. (1990), *What is a Horn clause in partial logic?*, Logics in AI. Proceedings of the European Workshop JELIA'90, J. van Eijck, ed., Lecture Notes in Artificial Intelligence 478, Springer, Berlin.
Langholm, T., *How Different is Partial Logic?*, P. Doherty and D. Drainkov, eds (forthcoming).
Lapierre, S. (1992), *A functional partial semantics for intentional logic*, Notre Dame J. Formal Logic **33**.
Lepage, F. (1992), *Partial functions in type theory*, Notre Dame J. Formal Logic **33**.
MacLane, S. (1971), *Categories for the Working Mathematician*, Springer, Berlin.
MacLane, S. and Moerdijk, I. (1992), *Sheaves in Geometry and Logic*, Springer, Berlin.
Makovsky, J. (1984), *Model theoretic issues in theoretical computer science, part I: Relational data bases and abstract data types*, Logic Colloquium '82, G. Looli, G. Longo and A. Marcja, eds, North-Holland, Amsterdam.
Martin, R.L. (ed.) (1981), *Recent Essays on Truth and the Liar Paradox*, Clarendon Press, Oxford.
Minker, J. (ed.) (1988), *Deductive Databases and Logic Programming*, Morgan Kaufmann, Los Altos, CA.
Moldestad, J. (1977), *Computations in Higher Types*, Lecture Notes in Mathematics, Springer, Berlin.
Muskens, R. (1989), *Meaning and partiality*, Thesis, University of Amsterdam.
Odifreddi, P. (1989), *Classical Recursion Theory*, North-Holland, Amsterdam.
Platek, R.A. (1966), *Foundations of recursion theory*, Thesis, Stanford University.
Pollard, C. and Sag, I. (1987), *Information-Based Syntax and Semantics*, CSLI Lecture Notes no. 13, CSLI, Stanford.
Rounds, W.C. and Kaspar, R. (1986), *A complete logical calculus for record structures representing linguistic information*, Proceedings of First IEEE Symposium on Logic in Computer Science, Boston.

Sem, H.F. (1988), *Discourse representation theory, situation schemata and situation semantics: A comparison*, Papers from the Tenth Scandinavian Conference on Linguistics, V. Rosén, ed.

Smorynski, C. (1991), *The Development of Self-Reference*, Perspectives on the History of Mathematics, T. Drucker, ed., Birkhäuser, Boston.

Tarski, A. (1956), *Logic, Semantics and Metamathematics*, Papers from 1923 to 1938, J.H. Woodger, ed., Clarendon Press, Oxford.

Thomason, R.H. (ed.) (1974), *Formal Philosophy: Selected Papers of Richard Montague*, Yale Univ. Press, New Haven, CT.

Thijsse, T. (1992), *Partial logic and knowledge representation*, Thesis, Eburon Publishers, Delft.

Urquhart, A. (1986), *Many-valued logic*, Handbook of Philosophical Logic vol. III, D. Gabbay and F. Guenthner, eds, Reidel, Dordrecht.

Van Benthem, J. (1985), *Manual of Intentional Logic*, CSLI Lecture Notes no. 1, CSLI, Stanford.

Van Fraassen, B. (1986), *Presupposition, implication and self-reference,* J. Philos. **65**.

Visser, A. (1989), *Semantics and the Liar paradox*, Handbook of Philosophical Logic vol. IV, D. Gabbay and F. Guenthner, eds, Reidel, Dordrecht.

CHAPTER 12

Mathematical Linguistics and Proof Theory

Wojciech Buszkowski

Adam Mickiewicz University, Faculty of Mathematics and Computer Science, Matejki 48/49, 60769 Poznan, Poland

E-mail: buszko@math.amu.edu.pl

Contents

HANDBOOK OF LOGIC AND LANGUAGE
Edited by J. van Benthem and A. ter Meulen

1. Introduction

In the traditional sense of the term, *mathematical linguistics* is a branch of applied algebra mainly concerned with formal languages (i.e. sets of finite strings or trees over a finite alphabet), formal grammars and automata, the latter being purely computational devices which generate (recognize) formal languages. This perspective is prevalent in all standard textbooks on the subject, to mention Hopcroft and Ullman (1979) as a most representative reference.

For readers of this Handbook it should be clear that the traditional framework mirrors old-fashioned views of mathematical modeling in linguistics, stemming from early, purely syntactic approaches in Generative Grammar and elementary tasks of syntactic description of programming languages. Modern investigations in formal linguistics are primarily occupied with semantics of natural language, and semantical problems cannot be handled by means of algebraic and combinatorial methods only. The proper world for semantics is *mathematical logic* with its deductive systems and model theory. Since Montague (1970), model-theoretic ideas have become still more significant in linguistic issues, which is reported in (Gamut, 1991; Partee, Ter Meulen and Wall, 1990; Dowty, Wall and Peters, 1981) (these are more recent textbooks on mathematical models in linguistics).

However, even the semantic turn in formal linguistics did not fully realize the significance of logical methods in linguistics: preoccupation with models suppressed any serious interest in deduction. Ironically, the combinatorial apparatus of Generative Grammar with its focusing on derivations of syntactic structures on the basis of grammatical rules was methodologically closer to logical deductive systems than the descriptive approach of Montague Grammar. One of the reasons for neglecting deduction in the early stage of natural language semantics seems to be the *formalistic* attitude of Montague and his contemporaries to the relation between logic and language. According to this view, formal languages of mathematical logic are the only correct representations of meaning structures, hence semantic description of natural language reduces to an interpretation of linguistic expressions within some (flexible enough) standard logical formalism, as, e.g., the theory of types. As a consequence, fine deductive aspects of the formalism (the codomain of interpretation) are not relevant to linguistic goals; they should bother pure logicians who sold the ready product to linguists. No surprise, classical treatises in the Montague tradition bring no really new insight into the very logic used for natural language semantics, although they successfully solve many subtle problems of interpretation. Things are different for *situation semantics*, originated in (Barwise and Perry, 1983), which offers a quite new model theory, suitable for semantic relations in natural language, but here again logical deduction plays no explicit role in semantic description.

On the other hand, a natural link between *proof theory* (i.e. the logical theory of deduction) and semantics has been established by the constructive approaches in logic (Curry, Martin-Löf) as the so-called 'formulas-as-types' interpretation or Curry–Howard correspondence: typed lambda-terms (which encode semantic structures of expressions) can be interpreted as formal proofs in Natural Deduction systems (with introduction and elimination rules for logical constants). Thus, semantic structures in the sense of Montague Grammar, being certain interpreted lambda-terms, can also be regarded as formal derivations of linguistic expressions on the basis of a logical grammar whose rules are fashioned according to the Natural Deduction format. This idea stimulates current developments in Categorial Grammar (see Moortgat's chapter), and we shall say more about this domain.

Since the very beginning in (Ajdukiewicz, 1935) (based on some ideas of Leśniewski; see Hiż, 1967) and (Bar-Hillel, Gaifman and Shamir, 1960), Categorial Grammar tries to describe a language by assigning logical types to lexical atoms (types represent syntactic or semantic categories of expressions). Types of complex expressions are derived from types of atomic expressions by a logical proof which relies on fundamental logical rules like *Modus Ponens* (infer B from $A \rightarrow B$ and A) or *Conditional Syllogism* (infer $A \rightarrow C$ from $A \rightarrow B$ and $B \rightarrow C$). These rules are interpreted in terms of type theory. For Modus Ponens, $f: A \mapsto B$ and $a \in A$ yield $f(a) \in B$, and for Syllogism, $f: A \mapsto B$ and $g: B \mapsto C$ yield $gf: A \mapsto C$. Thus, grammatical derivations are proofs in a logical system which refers to a function-argument semantics of Fregean style (with types). Accordingly, in Categorial Grammar connections between proof theory and linguistic description are quite natural and fundamental for the spirit of this discipline.

The central place of proof theory in Categorial Grammar, however, was not fully realized until the eighties. Bar-Hillel had offered it as merely an 'analytic' version of Context-Free Grammar, and this impoverishing perspective was inherited by most followers. Only Lambek (1958, 1961) essentially advanced the matter by introducing fine systems of categorial deduction (anticipating substructural logics), but this innovation was not properly understood by the contemporaries. A serious investigation of logics underlying Categorial Grammar was undertaken in the late seventies in Poland (the author, W. Zielonka), and proof-theoretic issues were mainly developed in the Netherlands by J. van Benthem, F. Zwarts, M. Moortgat and their collaborators (see Van Benthem, 1986, 1988a, 1991; Zwarts, 1986; Moortgat, 1988). Many alternative but ideologically close grammar theories have been proposed elsewhere, the most representative being Combinatory Categorial Grammar (see Steedman, 1988, 1993). Logical systems of Categorial Grammar belong to substructural logics, which enjoy nowadays an independent interest of logicians, due to their procedural interpretations (useful in computer science) and nice deductive properties (see Troelstra, 1992; Došen and Schröder-Heister, 1993).

Another area in which proofs are essential for grammatical structures is *computational linguistics* based on Prolog. Grammars are represented by Prolog programs, and grammatical derivations are simulated by executions of these programs, that means, logical proofs employing resolution and unification (see Pereira and Shieber, 1987; Gazdar and Mellish, 1989). Within this approach the idea of 'Parsing as Deduction' first entered the scene, and now it occupies a major position in all logically oriented developments of computational linguistics. The join of computational linguistics and Categorial Grammar with its rich systems of deduction results in interesting fields of current research, as, e.g., Categorial Unification Grammar (see Uszkoreit, 1986).

In this chapter there are discussed certain most characteristic links between proof theory and formal grammars. We avoid complicated problems of linguistic description; all examples are merely illustrations. We aim to persuade the reader of the generic unity of proof structures in appropriate deductive systems and syntactic and semantic structures generated by corresponding grammars. We also point out nontrivial applications of proof theory in linguistics (equivalence problems) as well, as new problems in logic suggested by linguistic interests (special deductive systems, semantic equivalence of deductive systems, special algebraic models). Although we consider various kinds of formal grammar, Categorial Grammar is our favorite reference, which is justified by its especially rich proof-theoretic resources.

In Section 2 we overview deductive systems naturally related to formal grammars. Starting from purely applicative systems, corresponding to Basic Categorial Grammars, Context-Free Grammars and Finite-State Acceptors, we pass to richer ones which employ introduction and elimination rules for conditionals and other logical constants. There are distinguished Gentzen style systems and Natural Deduction systems; the latter are further generalized to Labeled Deductive Systems in the sense of Gabbay (1991). We also handle first-order and second-order extensions of these systems, connected with Unification Systems of computational linguistics.

In Section 3 we are concerned with syntactic structures determined by proofs (grammatical derivations). The first topic is general properties of structure languages generated by purely applicative systems and methods of universal algebra applicable in this area. Here we discuss the problem of lexicalization of grammars, whose basic example is the Gaifman theorem on the equivalence of Context-Free Grammars and Basic Categorial Grammars (closely related to the Greibach Normal Form theorem for Context-Free Grammars); we also mention results on strong lexicalization (preserving structures) for Tree Adjoining Grammars of Joshi (1987). For richer deductive systems, we demonstrate fine usages of proof-theoretic ideas (cut elimination, interpolation) in equivalence results for different classes of grammars. In particular, we report the proof of the weak equivalence of Lambek Categorial Grammars and Context-Free Grammars, given by Pentus (1993a). Recent complexity results in this area are briefly surveyed.

Section 4 focuses on the Curry–Howard correspondence between Natural Deduction proofs and typed lambda-terms. We discuss special cases of this correspondence for logics stemming from grammar and fragments of the full lambda calculus. The provable equality of lambda-terms provides a semantically significant notion of equivalence of proofs. We consider the question of semantic equivalence of two different axiomatizations of the same logic (they are equivalent, if they have the same proofs up to the equality in lambda calculus).

Section 5 is devoted to algebraic models. We explain the role of residuated algebras for modeling logics defined by deduction rules and distinguish several special classes of models, suggested by intended logical or linguistic interpretations. There are discussed typical completeness and representation theorems and the role of algebraic frames for linguistic modeling.

The limited scope of this chapter does not allow us to introduce the reader in the basic notions of proof theory and mathematical linguistics. For proof theory, a good text is (Girard with Taylor, and Lafont, 1989), and for grammars and automata (Partee, Ter Meulen and Wall, 1990).

All literature references are given by the name of the authors and the year of publication.

2. Formal grammars as deductive systems

2.1. *Propositional deductive systems*

Most formal grammars, appearing in literature, can be presented as deductive systems which generate a *sequential* consequence relation $\Gamma \vdash A$, where Γ is a finite string of formulas and A is a formula, fulfilling the following conditions:

(Id) $A \vdash A$,

(CUT) if $\Gamma, A, \Gamma' \vdash B$ and $\Delta \vdash A$, then $\Gamma, \Delta, \Gamma' \vdash B$.

Typically, the relation $\vdash$ is defined as the smallest relation containing the identity axioms (Id) and a set of special axiomatic patterns $\Gamma \vdash A$ and being closed under *the cut rule*:

$$\text{(CUT)}\ \frac{\Gamma, A, \Gamma' \vdash B;\ \Delta \vdash A}{\Gamma, \Delta, \Gamma' \vdash B}.$$

The relation $\vdash$ constitutes the *deductive* part of the grammar. The *initial* part is given by a set of *lexical assumptions* $v : A$ which assign a *grammatical category* (*type*) A to a lexical atom v. Then, the expression $v_1 \cdots v_n$ is assigned category B, if there are lexical assumptions $v_i : A_i$, $i = 1, \ldots, n$, such that the pattern $A_1 \cdots A_n \vdash B$ is validated by the deductive part of the grammar.

For a *Context-Free Grammar* (CFG), formulas are *nonterminal symbols*, and the consequence relation is defined by a finite collection of axiomatic patterns $A_1 \cdots A_n \vdash A$, $n \geqslant 0$. For example, with lexical assumptions:

Joan : NP, smiles : V, charmingly : Adv,

one admits the patterns:

NP VP $\vdash$ S, V $\vdash$ VP, V Adv $\vdash$ VP,

and the resulting grammar assigns type S to expressions:

Joan smiles, Joan smiles charmingly, ... ,

where the adverb can be iterated. Usually, axiomatic patterns are called *production rules* and written $A \Rightarrow \Gamma$ rather than $\Gamma \vdash A$.

A *Basic Categorial Grammar* (BCG) invites formulas built from atomic formulas (primitive types) by means of two conditionals $\rightarrow$ and $\leftarrow$. Expressions b of type $A \rightarrow B$ (resp. $B \leftarrow A$) are interpreted as *left* (resp. *right*) *looking functors* which together with every expression a of type A form the expression ab (resp. ba) of type B; in this context, a is the *argument* of functor b. The deductive part is defined by the *modus ponens* patterns:

(MP$\rightarrow$) $A, A \rightarrow B \vdash B$, (MP$\leftarrow$) $B \leftarrow A, A \vdash B$, together with (Id) and (CUT). The resulting system is often called *the Ajdukiewicz calculus*, because of its origin in (Ajdukiewicz, 1935). Actually, Ajdukiewicz considers one conditional $\leftarrow$ but admits more than one argument, which yields formulas $B \leftarrow A_1 \cdots A_n$ written as $\frac{B}{A_1 \cdots A_n}$. The double conditional form is due to Bar-Hillel (1953) (also see Bar-Hillel, Gaifman and Shamir, 1960) and Lambek (1958). The above example, put in the BCG format, needs the lexical assumptions:

$$\text{Joan : NP, smiles : NP} \rightarrow \text{S, charmingly : (NP} \rightarrow \text{S)} \rightarrow \text{(NP} \rightarrow \text{S).}$$

Notice that the deductive part of a BCG is purely *logical* in the sense that it admits no special axioms or inference patterns, while the whole information on the particular language is provided by the initial part, and this logicality of deductions is also preserved by other kinds of Categorial Grammar to be discussed in this chapter (also see Moortgat's chapter).

Finite State Acceptors (FSAs) are closely related to BCGs of a sharply restricted form. One only admits atomic formulas (now called *states*) and unnested conditionals $A \rightarrow B$ (called *transitions*), where A, B are states. Lexical assumptions are of the form $v : A$ or $v : A \rightarrow B$. If the empty string Λ is included in the set of admissible expressions, then lexical assumptions $\Lambda : A$ must be added. An equivalent (and more standard) definition admits lexical assumptions of the form $v : A \rightarrow B$ only, but the deductive part contains special axioms $\vdash A$ which correspond to *initial states* A. The poor recognition power of FSAs can essentially be strengthened, if one uses a denumerable set $\mathcal{S}$, of states, and a finite series $f_1, \ldots, f_k$, of total recursive functions from $\mathcal{S}$ to $\mathcal{S}$. Now, each lexical atom v is assigned certain functions $f_{i_1}, \ldots, f_{i_m}$ from the latter series, and the lexical assumptions are defined as follows:

$$v : A \rightarrow B \text{ iff there is } j = 1, \ldots, m \text{ such that } f_{i_j}(A) = B.$$

The resulting system is essentially *Left-Associative Grammar* of Hausser (1989), and its recognition power is precisely the recursive languages (see Hausser, 1992).

Extended Categorial Grammars enrich MP-patterns with other logical inference rules, as, e.g., the *conditional syllogism* rules:

$$(\text{SYL}\rightarrow)\ A \rightarrow B, B \rightarrow C \vdash A \rightarrow C,$$

$$(\text{SYL}\leftarrow)\ C \leftarrow B, B \leftarrow A \vdash C \leftarrow A,$$

and the *type raising* rules:

$$(\text{TR}\rightarrow)\ A \vdash (B \leftarrow A) \rightarrow B, \qquad (\text{TR}\leftarrow)\ A \vdash B \leftarrow (A \rightarrow B).$$

The syntactic meaning of, say, (SYL$\rightarrow$) is: if expressions a, b are of type $C \leftarrow B$ and $B \leftarrow A$, respectively, then the concatenation ab is of type $C \leftarrow A$. For instance, 'every student' is of type S$\leftarrow$VP (equal to NP) and 'not' is of type S$\leftarrow$S, hence 'not every student' is of type S$\leftarrow$VP. According to (TR$\leftarrow$), each expression of type PN (Proper Noun) is also of type S$\leftarrow$(PN$\rightarrow$S) equal to NP, if one sets VP = PN$\rightarrow$S. That is the

Montague principle of lifting proper nouns to the type of Noun Phrase (see Montague, 1973). In semantic terms, MP-rules correspond to function application:

$$(\mathrm{FA}\rightarrow)\ \frac{a:A;\ f:A\rightarrow B}{(a)f:B},\qquad (\mathrm{FA}\leftarrow)\ \frac{f:B\leftarrow A;\ a:A}{f(a):B},$$

while SYL-rules to function composition:

$$(\mathrm{FC}\rightarrow)\ \frac{f:A\rightarrow B;\ g:B\rightarrow C}{fg:A\rightarrow C},\qquad (\mathrm{FC}\leftarrow)\ \frac{f:C\leftarrow B;\ g:B\leftarrow A}{fg:C\leftarrow A}.$$

The semantic meaning of (TR →) and (TR ←) is the transformations:

$$(\mathrm{FR}\rightarrow)\ \frac{a:A}{\lambda_{\rightarrow}x_{B\leftarrow A}.x(a)},\qquad (\mathrm{FR}\leftarrow)\frac{a:A}{\lambda_{\leftarrow}x_{A\rightarrow B}.(a)x}.$$

Here, we discriminate between left functions $f:B\leftarrow A$ and right functions $f:A\rightarrow B$ which give rise to application terms $f(a)$ and $(a)f$, respectively, differ in the composition order and invite two lambdas: $\lambda_{\leftarrow}$ for left functions and $\lambda_{\rightarrow}$ for right functions. This directional lambda language has been introduced in (Buszkowski, 1987a, 1988a) and thoroughly examined in (Wansing 1992). The more conservative reader may identify $f:A\rightarrow B$ with $f:B\leftarrow A$ and simplify the latter transformation to:

$$(\mathrm{FR})\ \frac{a:A}{\lambda x_{A\rightarrow B}.x(a)}.$$

According to (FR), each individual $a:\mathbf{e}$ is lifted to the function $F_a:(\mathbf{e}\rightarrow\mathbf{t})\rightarrow\mathbf{t}$ such that:

for all $g:\mathbf{e}\rightarrow\mathbf{t}$, $F_a(g)=1$ iff $g(a)=1$.

So, if one does not discriminate between sets and their characteristic functions, then F_a is the family of all sets of individuals which contain the individual a. That reminds the Leibniz idea: an individual is to be identified with the totality of properties of this individual (see the discussion in (Hiż, 1971)).

Lambek (1958) proposed a Gentzen style deductive system, providing SYL-rules, TR-rules and other patterns of that kind. We denote this system by **L**. Formulas of **L** are built from atomic formulas (variables) by means of binary logical operations $\rightarrow,\leftarrow$ and $\circ$ (product). Sequents are of the form $\Gamma\vdash A$, where Γ is a finite string of formulas and A is a formula. The axioms are (Id), and the inference rules are (CUT) and the following left and right introduction rules for logical operations:

$$(\mathrm{L}\rightarrow)\ \frac{\Gamma,B,\Gamma'\vdash C;\ \Delta\vdash A}{\Gamma,\Delta,A\rightarrow B,\Gamma'\vdash C},\qquad (\mathrm{R}\leftarrow)\ \frac{A,\Gamma\vdash B}{\Gamma\vdash A\rightarrow B},$$

$$(\mathrm{L}\leftarrow)\ \frac{\Gamma, B, \Gamma' \vdash C;\ \Delta \vdash A}{\Gamma, B \leftarrow A, \Delta, \Gamma' \vdash C}, \qquad (\mathrm{R}\leftarrow)\ \frac{\Gamma, A \vdash B}{\Gamma \vdash B \leftarrow A},$$

$$(\mathrm{L}\circ)\ \frac{\Gamma, A, B, \Gamma' \vdash C}{\Gamma, A \circ B, \Gamma' \vdash C}, \qquad (\mathrm{R}\circ)\ \frac{\Gamma \vdash A;\ \Delta \vdash B}{\Gamma, \Delta \vdash A \circ B},$$

where Γ is nonempty in (R$\rightarrow$) and (R$\leftarrow$). Lambek proved *the cut-elimination theorem*: each sequent derivable in **L** possesses a derivation not applying (CUT) (a *cut-free* derivation); see Moortgat's chapter for the proof. Since the conclusion of each introduction rule stores all the formulas appearing in the premises, then the cut-free form of **L** admits a standard decision procedure. Further, **L** possesses *the subformula property*: if $\Gamma \vdash A$ is derivable, then there is a derivation of $\Gamma \vdash A$ such that all formulas appearing in this derivation are subformulas of those appearing in $\Gamma \vdash A$.

From the logical point of view, **L** is a nice representative of *substructural logics*, i.e. logics resulting from dropping structural rules (Thinning, Contraction, Permutation) in Gentzen style systems for classical and intuitionistic logic (see Došen and Schröder-Heister, 1993). Actually, Lambek's proposal was the first one in the history of this subject. From the point of view of this chapter, it is important as a paradigm for sequential systems corresponding to grammars which incorporate a nontrivial logic of type change (*dynamic type assignment* in terms of Van Benthem (1986, 1991); see the chapters by Muskens, Van Benthem, Visser and Moortgat). Many systems discussed here are variations of the Lambek calculus. An especially important system is **LP**, i.e. the Lambek Calculus with Permutation:

$$(\mathrm{PER})\ \frac{\Gamma, A, B, \Delta \vdash C}{\Gamma, B, A, \Delta \vdash C},$$

introduced in (Van Benthem, 1986) for its natural relation with a fragment of the lambda calculus (see also (Van Benthem, 1987b) and Section 4 of this chapter). In **LP**, $A \rightarrow B$ and $B \leftarrow A$ are deductively equivalent, hence they reduce to one conditional; also $A \circ B$ is equivalent to $B \circ A$.

Observe that product types $A \circ B$ can be used to model *Generative Grammars* with production rules $\Gamma \vdash \Delta$ within the framework of sequential consequence relations, restricted to sequents $\Gamma \vdash A$. Namely, the rule:

$$A_1 \cdots A_m \vdash B_1 \cdots B_n$$

is to be replaced with:

$$A_1 \cdots A_m \vdash B_1 \circ \cdots \circ B_n.$$

Precisely, the deductive part is the $\circ$-fragment of **L** (with (CUT)) enriched with special axioms of the above form. Using (L$\circ$) and (R$\circ$), one easily proves the associativity of $\circ$:

$$(\mathrm{AS})\ (A \circ B) \circ C \vdash A \circ (B \circ C), \qquad A \circ (B \circ C) \vdash (A \circ B) \circ C,$$

and consequently, all parentheses in $B_1 \circ \cdots \circ B_n$ may be omitted.

An alternative way is to use formulas with $\rightarrow, \leftarrow$ and $\circ$ but to admit only the left introduction rules for conditionals and the both introduction rules for product (plus (CUT)). Then, the production rule above can be modeled by the axiomatic pattern:

$$\vdash A_m \rightarrow (A_{m-1} \rightarrow \cdots \rightarrow (A_1 \rightarrow B_1 \circ \cdots \circ B_n) \cdots).$$

So, *context-sensitive* rules $C, A_1 \cdots A_m \vdash C, B$ give rise to axioms:

$$\vdash A_m \rightarrow (A_{m-1} \rightarrow \cdots \rightarrow (C \rightarrow C \circ B) \cdots),$$

while context-free production rules $A_1 \cdots A_m \vdash B$ to product-free axioms:

$$\vdash A_m \rightarrow (A_{m-1} \rightarrow \cdots \rightarrow (A_1 \rightarrow B) \cdots).$$

Now, the only nonlogical elements of the deductive part are the special axioms resulting from production rules, while all inference patterns are logical. Since (CUT) is allowed, (L$\rightarrow$) and (L$\leftarrow$) can be replaced with (MP$\rightarrow$) and (MP$\leftarrow$).

Instead of Gentzen style systems of the above form we can employ Natural Deduction systems (ND-systems), based upon *introduction* and *elimination rules* for logical operations (also originated in Gentzen's staff). The ND-system for **L** is given by axioms (Id), the introduction rules (I$\rightarrow$), (I$\leftarrow$) and (I$\circ$) equal to (R$\rightarrow$), (R$\leftarrow$) and (R$\circ$), respectively, and the following elimination rules:

$$(\mathrm{E}\rightarrow)\ \frac{\Gamma \vdash A;\ \Delta \vdash A \rightarrow B}{\Gamma, \Delta \vdash B},$$

$$(\mathrm{E}\leftarrow)\ \frac{\Gamma \vdash B \leftarrow A;\ \Delta \vdash A}{\Gamma, \Delta \vdash B},$$

$$(\mathrm{E}\circ)\ \frac{\Gamma, A, B, \Gamma' \vdash C;\ \Delta \vdash A \circ B}{\Gamma, \Delta, \Gamma' \vdash C}.$$

Again, the resulting system is closed under (CUT) (the proof is much easier than for the case of Gentzen style systems: one proceeds by induction on derivations of the conclusion of (CUT) in the (cut-free) ND-system, and the induction hypothesis is directly applied to one of the premises of introduction/elimination rules, since the cut-formula A must appear in a premise).

ND-systems will thoroughly be discussed in Section 4, because they are naturally related to the typed lambda calculus (the Curry–Howard correspondence), and consequently, to the logical semantics based on type theory. Here, we only note a particular property of these systems: no logical transformation is performed within antecedents of sequents. Precisely, all inference rules perform a logical transformation on the succedent formulas together with a purely structural transformation on the antecedent strings. For instance, (E$\rightarrow$) applied to sequents $\Gamma \vdash A$ and $\Delta \vdash A \rightarrow B$ applies the MP-rule to formulas

$A, A \to B$ and concatenates strings Γ and Δ, and (I$\to$) applied to sequent $A, \Gamma \vdash B$ introduces the conditional $A \to B$ on the right and drops the left-most occurrence of A on the left.

This property of ND-systems has been exploited by Gabbay in his framework of *Labeled Deductive Systems* (LDSs); see (Gabbay, 1991, 1993). An LDS operates on *labeled formulas* of the form $s : A$ such that A is a logical formula and s is a label. Inference rules perform a logical operation on formulas and, at the same time, an algebraic operation on labels. Each ND-system is an LDS whose labels are strings of formulas (write $\Gamma : A$ for $\Gamma \vdash A$). From the linguistic perspective, LDSs are much expedient to model formal grammars as deductive systems which directly refer to language expressions in the process of deduction.

For example, each BCG can be simulated by an LDS with labeled formulas $X : A$ such that X is a string of lexical atoms and A is a formula (in the language of $\to, \leftarrow$). Lexical assumptions $v : A$ take the part of axioms, and MP-rules are replaced with (labeled) elimination rules for conditionals:

$$(\text{LE}\to)\ \frac{X : A;\ Y : A \to B}{XY : B}, \qquad (\text{LE}\leftarrow)\ \frac{X : B \leftarrow A;\ Y : A}{XY : B}.$$

Clearly, this LDS-format is equivalent to the afore-discussed MP-format. Axiomatic patterns $A_1 \cdots A_n \vdash B$, characteristic of CFGs, give rise to labeled rules:

$$\frac{X_1 : A_1; \ldots ; X_n : A_n}{X_1 \cdots X_n : B},$$

and again they can be replaced with axioms:

$$\Lambda : A_n \to (A_{n-1} \to \cdots \to (A_1 \to B) \cdots),$$

where Λ is the empty label. Since LDSs cannot directly represent left/right introduction rules of Gentzen style systems and ND-systems, the action of the latter rules must be executed in an indirect way, using labeled rules of the above form, which will be exemplified later on.

Logic suggests further enrichments of systems, discussed above. For instance, the conjunction $\wedge$ can be added with Gentzen style rules:

$$(\text{L}\wedge 1)\ \frac{\Gamma, A, \Gamma' \vdash C}{\Gamma, A \wedge B, \Gamma' \vdash C}, \qquad (\text{L}\wedge 2)\ \frac{\Gamma, B, \Gamma' \vdash C}{\Gamma, A \wedge B, \Gamma' \vdash C},$$

$$(\text{R}\wedge)\ \frac{\Gamma \vdash A;\ \Gamma \vdash B}{\Gamma \vdash A \wedge B},$$

as well as the disjunction $\vee$ with dual rules:

$$(\text{L}\vee)\ \frac{\Gamma, A, \Gamma' \vdash C;\ \Gamma, B, \Gamma' \vdash C}{\Gamma, A \vee B, \Gamma' \vdash C},$$

$$(\mathrm{R}\vee 1)\ \frac{\Gamma \vdash A}{\Gamma \vdash A \vee B}, \qquad (\mathrm{R}\vee 2)\ \frac{\Gamma \vdash B}{\Gamma \vdash A \vee B}.$$

Categorial grammars based on **L** with $\wedge$ have been studied in (Kanazawa, 1992) (also in Buszkowski, 1985, 1986a; Van Benthem, 1991; and others). Disjunction is less popular in linguistics, partly due to the fact that the above rules are too weak to formalize the complete theory of Boolean join (the distributivity of $\wedge$ over $\vee$ and the converse one cannot be derived in this framework); to get the completeness, one should pass to 'classical' sequents $\Gamma \vdash \Delta$, with the conjunctive reading of Γ and the disjunctive reading of Δ, but such sequents are not clearly related to grammatical rules. Regarding negative information invites formulas $\neg A$. In (Buszkowski, 1995), **L** is enlarged by De Morgan negation with the axioms of *double negation*:

$$(\mathrm{A}\neg 1)\ A \vdash \neg\neg A, \qquad (\mathrm{A}\neg 2)\ \neg\neg A \vdash A,$$

and the rule of *transposition*:

$$(\mathrm{TRAN})\ \frac{A \vdash B}{\neg B \vdash \neg A}.$$

The constructive negation $\neg A = A \rightarrow \bot$, being characteristic of intuitionistic logic and considered in different substructural logics, seems to lack any reasonable linguistic sense.

Modal logics can be applied to grammar in different ways. Following Keenan and Faltz (1985), the category A may be associated with a subcategory A', having special properties; for instance, PN is a subcategory of NP, and PN-expressions but not all NP-expressions are semantically interpreted as ultrafilters (*John* fulfills either VP, or non-VP, but *every student* may fulfill neither). We can write $A' = \Box A$ and assume the pattern $\Box A \vdash A$ together with the semantic principle:

$$D(x_{\mathrm{VP}}) \notin D(y_{\Box\mathrm{NP}}) \quad \text{iff} \quad D(\text{non-}x_{\mathrm{VP}}) \in D(y_{\Box\mathrm{NP}}),$$

where $D(x)$ stands for the semantic denotation of the expression x.

Recently, several authors follow the idea of Girard (1987) who uses S4-style modalities (called: exponentials) to allow a controlled version of Thinning and Contraction in substructural logics. For the noncommutative product $\circ$, a special modal operator $\Box$ admits (controlled) permutation $\Box A \circ \Box B \vdash \Box B \circ \Box A$; also a nonassociative product may admit associativity in the scope of (appropriate) modalities. An advanced theory of multimodal systems applied to grammar is mainly due to Moortgat (1995) (also see Morrill, 1994; Hepple, 1994; Kurtonina, 1995), and the chapter by Moortgat contains a detailed discussion. Further, we note that also operators $\rightarrow$, $\leftarrow$, $\circ$ etc. are modal operators in a general sense: they are non-Boolean operators on a Boolean algebra, hence the metalogic of modal logics can be involved in the metatheory of all systems, considered above. This line of thought is especially explicit in (Van Benthem, 1991) with continuation in (Kurtonina, 1995), and similar logical approaches can be found in, e.g., Došen (1988–89), Dunn (1991, 1993) and Ono (1993).

2.2. *Beyond propositional logic*

All systems, considered above, are propositional logics. More subtle linguistic goals invite first-order logics and higher-order logics. The tradition of natural language processing in PROLOG employs first-order extensions of production grammars. Thus, types S, NP, VP etc. are supplied with arguments, say, $\mathrm{S}(x, y)$, $\mathrm{NP}(x)$, $\mathrm{VP}(x, y)$, where x is Number (values: Singular, Plural) and y is Tense (values: Simple Present, Simple Past etc.), and the basic production rule NP VP$\vdash$S is refined to:

$$\mathrm{NP}(x)\ \mathrm{VP}(x, y) \vdash \mathrm{S}(x, y).$$

The generation process involves unification of arguments of category predicates. The rule (CUT) must be replaced with the *condensed* cut rule:

$$(\mathrm{CUT}^{\star})\ \frac{\Gamma, A, \Gamma' \vdash C;\ \Delta \vdash B}{\sigma(\Gamma), \sigma(\Delta), \sigma(\Gamma') \vdash \sigma(C)},$$

where σ is a most general unifier (mgu) of A and B.

Good representatives of first-order grammars are *Metamorphosis Grammars* of Colmerauer (1978) and *Definite Clause Grammars* of Pereira (see Pereira and Shieber, 1987). In the latter case, grammatical rules are first-order versions of context-free production rules. They are treated as PROLOG clauses (Horn formulas of first-order logic), hence the underlying consequence relation is not sequential, but it is the standard Tarskian consequence relation. In particular, in the clause $A_1 \cdots A_n \vdash B$ neither the order, nor the multiplicity, of formulas $A_1, \ldots, A_n$ is essential. Accordingly, the parsing tree determined by the generation process must be controlled by an extra argument. Thus, the rule NP VP$\vdash$S is implemented as:

$$\mathrm{NP}(x, T)\ \mathrm{VP}(x, y, T') \vdash \mathrm{S}(x, y, (T, T')),$$

where T, T' are the trees for the NP-part and the VP-part, respectively, and (T, T') is the tree for the sentence. Recently, Pereira develops a theory of first-order grammars based on substructural logics in which the sequence structure of $A_1 \cdots A_n$ is explicitly accounted (see Pereira, 1991).

In the same way, richer deductive systems with conditionals and other logical operators can be extended to the first-order format, and this is a leitmotive of *Categorial Unification Grammar* (see Uszkoreit, 1986). However, first-order substructural logics have not been sufficiently analyzed, as yet, except for linear logics of Girard (1987) (also see Troelstra, 1992). For instance, little is known about the first-order version of the Lambek calculus. Modern approaches of that kind generalize predicates to so-called *feature structures* which require unification of a much more sophisticated form (see the chapter by Rounds). A recent paper by Shieber, Schabes and Pereira (1995) provides a thorough survey of parsing strategies for different kinds of grammars based on deductive systems, including CFGs, Definite Clause Grammars, Combinatory Categorial Grammars, Tree Adjoining Grammars and others.

On the other hand, interesting investigations have been carried out in second-order systems, connected with grammars. Here, one unifies not only arguments of predicates but also formulas, treated as polymorphic types. For the simplest example, booleans 'not', 'and' etc. can be applied to arguments from different categories: beside the basic category S, one applies them to Noun Phrases, Verb Phrases, Determiners, Adjectives, Adverbs and other *Boolean* categories, i.e. those categories which are semantically represented as classes of functions into the set of truth values. Consequently, one assigns the polymorphic type $X \leftarrow X$ to 'not' and the polymorphic type $(X \rightarrow X) \leftarrow X$ to 'and', 'or' etc., where the variable X ranges over Boolean types. Again, the generation process of such grammars involves unification, now unification of polymorphic types. The corresponding logics result from replacing (CUT) with (CUT*) in systems, discussed above. ND-systems for these logics are closely related to the second-order lambda calculus, a system extensively studied in theoretical computer science due to its significance for semantics of functional programming (see Girard, with Taylor and Lafont, 1989; Klein and Van Benthem, 1987). From this perspective, it is natural to consider propositional logics with quantifiers (binding propositional variables) whose origin can be traced back to Leśniewski's *protothetic*. The cut-elimination theorem for the Lambek calculus with quantifiers has been proven in (Emms and Leiss, 1993).

Unification of types with variables is also a basis of learning procedures for categorial grammars, elaborated in (Buszkowski, 1987a; Van Benthem, 1987a; Buszkowski and Penn, 1990; Kanazawa, 1994; Mariciniec, 1994). *A language sample* is a finite set of expressions assigned some types (expressions are partly analyzed as functor-argument structures; see Section 3). If we assign variables to argument substructures whose type is unknown, then all functor substructures can be assigned types (with variables), according to the rule: if XY is of type B, and X (resp. Y) is the argument of type A, then the functor Y (resp. X) is of type $A \rightarrow B$ (resp. $B \leftarrow A$). As a result, each lexical atom appearing in the sample is assigned a finite set of variable types. An appropriate unification algorithm yields most general grammars compatible with the input sample. Buszkowski (1987b) considers deterministic grammars (then, the algorithm provides the most general deterministic grammar compatible with the sample or replies NO, if there exists no deterministic grammar compatible with it), while Buszkowski and Penn (1990) regard nondeterministic grammars (then, the algorithm always generates at lest one most general grammar compatible with the sample), and Marciniec (1994) employs negative postulates in language samples (the given expression is not of type A). Kanazawa (1994) uses these algorithms to prove interesting theorems on identification of categorial languages in the limit. Van Benthem (1987a) discusses closely related problems of solving 'equations': for a sequent $\Gamma \vdash A$, containing variable subtypes, we look for a substitution of constant types for variables which makes this sequent derivable in the given logical calculus. The problem is decidable for the Ajdukiewicz Calculus and for the full positive logic (by Curry's stratification algorithm), but its decidability for most substructural logics remains open.

3. Proofs and syntactic structures

In this section we discuss the role of proof theory for the analysis of syntactic structures generated by different formal grammars. We show that proof theoretic ideas and methods are essential for understanding fundamental properties of structure generation and can be used to prove nontrivial theorems concerning strong and weak equivalence of grammars.

3.1. String languages and tree languages

We consider three kinds of syntactic structure: strings, phrase structures and functor-argument structures (fa-structures). If V is a lexicon (an alphabet), then *strings* on V are finite sequences of members of V. $V^\star$ (V^+) denotes the set of (nonempty) strings on V. The set $\mathrm{PS}(V)$, of *phrase structures* on V, is defined by the recursive clauses:

(PS.1) $V \subseteq \mathrm{PS}(V)$,
(PS.2) if $X_1, \ldots, X_n \in \mathrm{PS}(V)$, $n > 1$, then $(X_1, \ldots, X_n) \in \mathrm{PS}(V)$.

The set $\mathrm{FS}(V)$, of *fa-structures* on V, is defined as $\mathrm{PS}(V)$ except for putting $(X_1, \ldots, X_n)_i$, where $i = 1, \ldots, n$, in the second clause: the subscript i indicates the substructure X_i as the functor, while the remaining substructures take the part of arguments, of the structure $(X_1, \ldots, X_n)_i$. Often, one confines herself to binary structures ($n = 2$).

Phrase structures are determined by derivations in CFGs. In the LDS format, one defines the relation $X : A$ (the phrase structure X is assigned type A) by the following recursion:

(D.1) $v : A$, if $v : A$ is a lexical assumption,
(D.2) if $A_1 \cdots A_n \vdash A$ is a production rule and $X_i : A_i$, for $i = 1, \ldots, n$, then $(X_1, \ldots, X_n) : A$.

Here, we assume $n > 1$. For $n = 1$, we assume: if $A \vdash B$ is a production rule and $X : A$, then $X : B$ (so, unary rules do not affect the structure). Actually, each CFG can easily be modified to a CFG without unary rules.

For BCGs, derivations are essentially MP-deductions, and the corresponding structures are fa-structures. The definition differs from the above in replacing (D.2) with:

(D.2 $\rightarrow$) if $X : A$ and $Y : A \rightarrow B$, then $(XY)_2 : B$,
(D.2 $\leftarrow$) if $X : B \leftarrow A$ and $Y : A$, then $(XY)_1 : B$.

In the more traditional setting of Ajdukiewicz (1935) and Bar-Hillel (1953), multiple-argument types give rise to the clause:

(MD.2) if $Y : (A_1 \cdots A_m) \rightarrow B \leftarrow (C_1 \cdots C_n)$ and $X_i : A_i$, for $i = 1, \ldots, m$, $Z_i : C_i$, for $i = 1, \ldots, n$, then $(X_1, \ldots, X_m, Y, Z_1, \ldots, Z_n)_{m+1} : B$.

To handle multiple-argument structures, it is expedient to write:

$$(A_1 \cdots A_n)_i \text{ for } (A_1 \cdots A_{i-1}) \rightarrow A_i \leftarrow (A_{i+1} \cdots A_n),$$

which means that types are identified with fa-structures over the set of atomic types. Then, (MD.2) can be rewritten in the form:

(MD.2) if $X_j : A_j$, for $j = 1, \ldots, n$, $j \neq i$, and $X_i : (A_1 \cdots A_n)_i$, then $(X_1, \ldots, X_n)_i : A_i$.

Clearly, phrase structures and fa-structures defined in this way imitate proof trees in the corresponding deductive systems. If S is a designated atomic type of the CFG (resp. BCG) G, then the *P-language* $PL(G)$ (resp. *the F-language* $FL(G)$) is defined as the set of all phrase structures (resp. fa-structures) X such that $X : \mathrm{S}$ holds true. The obvious forgetting transformation maps fa-structures into phrase structures and F-languages into P-languages, hence $PL(G)$ can be defined for the BCG G as well. Finally, dropping all structure markers changes phrase structures and fa-structures into plane strings (frontiers of the structure trees), which yields the notion of *a language* of the grammar G: the set of strings which are frontiers of structure trees X with $X : \mathrm{S}$. The language of G is denoted $L(G)$. Grammars G_1, G_2 are *weakly equivalent* (resp. *P-equivalent, F-equivalent*), if $L(G_1) = L(G_2)$ (resp. $PL(G_1) = PL(G_2)$, $FL(G_1) = FL(G_2)$). Two classes of grammars are *weakly equivalent* (resp. *P-equivalent, F-equivalent*), if they generate the same families of string languages (resp. P-languages, F-languages).

A traditional issue of mathematical linguistics is to characterize string and structure languages, generated by different classes of grammars, and to establish the weak and strong equivalence of some classes. Certain basic results can be obtained by elementary algebraic methods which exploit the properties of the absolutely free algebra of phrase structures or fa-structures and congruences in this algebra.

Given a P-language $L \subseteq \mathrm{PS}(V)$, *the basic congruence* $\sim_L$ in the algebra $\mathrm{PS}(V)$ is defined as follows:

$$X \sim_L Y \text{ iff, for all } Z \in \mathrm{PS}(V),\ Z[X] \in L \text{ iff } Z[Y] \in L.$$

Here, $Z[X]$ denotes the structure Z with a designated occurrence of the substructure X, and $Z[Y]$ results from replacing X with Y in Z. $S(L)$ denotes the set of all substructures of structures from L. By *the size* of L, $s(L)$, we mean the maximal number n such that $(X_1, \dots, X_n) \in S(L)$, for some $X_1, \dots, X_n \in \mathrm{PS}(V)$.

The classical result of Thatcher (1967) characterizes the P-languages generated by CFGs as those P-languages $L \subseteq \mathrm{PS}(V)$ for which V is finite, $s(L)$ is finite and $\sim_L$ is of finite index (there are finitely many equivalence classes of $\sim_L$). Accordingly, that is precisely the class of tree languages recognized by Finite State Tree Automata (see Gécseg and Steinby, 1984). We sketch the proof. Let G be a CFG. We consider $L = PL(G)$. The relation $X : A$ is defined, as above. Since there are only finitely many nonterminal symbols in G, then the congruence:

$$X \sim_G Y \text{ iff, for all nonterminals } A,\ X : A \text{ iff } Y : A,$$

is of finite index. Further, $\sim_G \subseteq \sim_L$, and consequently, $\sim_L$ is of finite index. The number $s(L)$ is not greater than the maximal length of the antecedents of production rules in G, hence also $s(L)$ is finite. Conversely, let $L \subseteq \mathrm{PS}(V)$, where V is finite, be a P-language with $s(L)$ finite and $\sim_L$ of finite index. One defines a CFG G whose nonterminal symbols are equivalence classes of $\sim_L$. The lexical assumptions are $v : A$ such that $v \in A$ (A is a set of structures!), and production rules are $A_1 \cdots A_n \vdash A$ such that $(A_1, \dots, A_n) \subseteq A$ and $n \leqslant s(L)$. Here, $(A_1, \dots, A_n)$ is the quotient operation given by the congruence $\sim_L$ from the free algebra operation $(X_1, \dots, X_n)$. By induction on the complexity of X one easily shows: $X : A$ iff $X \in A$. Thus, with a new nonterminal symbol S and rules $A \vdash \mathrm{S}$, for all $A \subseteq L$, one obtains: $X : \mathrm{S}$ iff $X \in L$, which yields $L = PL(G)$.

For BCGs, analogous problems have been studied in (Buszkowski, 1986b, 1988a). Auxiliary notions are needed for fa-structures. *A path* (resp. *an f-path*) in $A \in \mathrm{FS}(V)$ is a sequence $A_0, \ldots, A_n$, of substructures of A, such that A_{i+1} is an immediate substructure (resp. the functor) of A_i, for all $i = 0, \ldots, n-1$ (n is the length of the path). *The f-degree* of the F-language $L \subseteq \mathrm{FS}(V)$, $d_f(L)$, is the maximal length of f-paths in fa-structures from L. $\sim_L$ and $s(L)$ are defined as for P-languages. We confine ourselves to binary structures, hence $s(L) \leqslant 2$. One obtains the following result, for F-languages $L \subseteq \mathrm{FS}(V)$, with V finite:

(T.1) $L = FL(G)$, for some BCG G, if, and only if, $\sim_L$ is of finite index, and $d_f(L)$ is finite.

The 'only if' part is proven, as for CFGs; $\sim_G$ is of finite index, since $X : A$ can hold only if A is a subformula of a formula appearing in lexical assumptions, and $d_f(L)$ is not greater than the maximal length of f-paths in formulas (types) appearing in these assumptions (remind that types are fa-structures). For the 'if' part, one defines the BCG G in the following way. Atomic types are equivalence classes of $\sim_L$ and a new atomic type S. A relation $X : A$ is defined by recursion on the complexity of type A:

(G.1) $X : p$, if $X \in p$, for atomic types p and $X \in \mathrm{FS}(V)$, and $X : \mathrm{S}$, if $X \in L$,
(G.2 $\rightarrow$) if $(XY)_2 : B$ and $X : p$, then $Y : p \rightarrow B$,
(G.2 $\leftarrow$) if $(XY)_1 : B$ and $Y : p$, then $X : B \leftarrow p$,

where p is atomic and A is arbitrary in (G.2)-clauses. Since $d_f(L)$ is finite, this construction never assigns infinitely many types to one structure. The lexical assumptions are $v : A$ (provided by this constructions), and there are only finitely many such assumptions. The relation $X : A$ determined by these assumptions and rules (D.2 $\rightarrow$), (D2. $\leftarrow$) is precisely the relation defined by (G.1), (G.2 $\rightarrow$) and (G.2 $\leftarrow$). Thus, for the BCG G determined by these assumptions (with S as the designated type), we obtain $L = FL(G)$. An analogous theorem holds for the multiple-argument format, with the finiteness of $s(L)$ added to the conditions of (T.1).

The order of type A, $o(A)$, is defined, as follows:

$$o(p) = 0, \text{ for atomic } p,$$

$$o(A \rightarrow B) = o(B \leftarrow A) = \max(o(B), o(A) + 1).$$

The order of a BCG G, $o(G)$, is the maximal order of types appearing in lexical assumptions of G. Observe that $o(A) \leqslant 1$, for all types A produced by the clauses (G.1), (G.2 $\rightarrow$), (G.2 $\leftarrow$), hence $o(G) \leqslant 1$, for the grammar G defined above. Using (T.1), we obtain a strong equivalence theorem:

(T.2) each BCG is F-equivalent to a BCG of order at most 1.

In a similar way, one obtains many other results of that kind. For example, each BCG is F-equivalent to a BCG G satisfying $\sim_G = \sim_{FL(G)}$; the latter condition corresponds to Husserl's idea that grammatical categories (here, equivalence classes of $\sim_G$) are the same as substitution classes determined by the language (here, equivalence classes of $\sim_{FL(G)}$). Also, P-languages of BCGs are precisely the P-languages $L \subseteq PS(V)$ which are of finite index and the minimal distance from each node to a leave is bounded for the P-language (we think of phrase structures as trees).

Comparing the above with Thatcher's characterization of phrase languages of CFGs, we see that BCGs generate a proper subclass of the latter. The Gaifman theorem, first published in (Bar-Hillel, Gaifman and Shamir, 1960), establishes the weak equivalence of BCGs and CFGs. It immediately follows from the above remarks that each BCG is P-equivalent, hence also weakly equivalent, to some CFG. The converse statement is nontrivial. An algebraic proof of this statement can be given by studying the algebra of phrase structures (see Buszkowski, 1988b). Fix a CFG G; we may assume G be in the Chomsky Normal Form, that means, all production rules of G are of the form $A, B \vdash C$. Thus, $PL(G)$ consists of binary trees. Using the convention of associating parentheses to the left, each binary phrase structure can uniquely be represented in the form:

$$vX_1 \cdots X_n, \text{ where } v \in V,\ n \geqslant 0,\ X_i \in PS(V).$$

Define a transformation X^T from $PS(V)$ to $PS(V)$, by setting:

$$(vX_1 \cdots X_n)^T = \big(v\big(X_1^T\big(X_2^T \cdots \big(X_{n-1}^T X_n^T\big) \cdots\big)\big)\big).$$

Observe that X and X^T live on the same string, and $d_f(X^T) \leqslant 2$, for any $X \in PS(V)$ (now, think of phrase structures as fa-structures in which functors always occupy the left position). By Thatcher's theorem, $\sim_{PL(G)}$ is of finite index, and one can show that the transformation $X \mapsto X^T$ preserves this property, that means, $\sim_{PL(G)^T}$ is also of finite index, where:

$$PL(G)^T = \{X^T \colon X \in PL(G)\}.$$

Since $d_f(PL(G)^T) \leqslant 2$, then, by (T1), there is a BCG G' such that $FL(G') = PL(G)^T$. Clearly, $L(G') = L(G)$. We have shown that each CFG is weakly equivalent to some BCG.

Notice that the nontrivial direction of the Gaifman theorem is based upon a transformation of the given CFG to a grammar which produces phrase structures of a uniformly bounded degree. In the theory of production grammars, this transformation is known as the reduction of the CFG to the Greibach Normal Form. As a matter of fact, the Greibach Normal Form theorem for CFGs is almost the same as the Gaifman theorem.

The transformation of a CFG to the Greibach Normal Form or to an equivalent BCG is a particular case of *lexicalization*: reducing grammatical rules to structures assigned to lexical items (anchors), while some general (i.e. independent of the given language) rules govern the composition of structures into more complex structures. The lexicalization provided by the Gaifman theorem and the Greibach Normal Form theorem is weak in the sense that the lexicalized grammar preserves merely strings but not structures of the initial grammar (notice that the structure X^T essentially differs from X, although both structures live on the same string). Strong lexicalization of CFGs can be accomplished by means of Tree Adjoining Grammars (TAGs) (see Joshi and Schabes, 1992), based on some rules of tree substitution and adjunction: each finitely ambiguous CFG is P-equivalent to some lexicalized TAG, and each finitely ambiguous TAG is P-equivalent to some lexicalized TAG. For a general discussion of TAG's and other Mildly Context Sensitive Grammars, see Joshi (1987), Vijay-Shanker, Weir and Joshi (1987) and Partee, Ter Meulen and Wall (1990). Later on we mention similar results concerning Lambek style grammars.

Powerset algebras of formulas are defined in the following way. By $T(G)$ we denote the set of types appearing in G (nonterminal symbols for the case of a CFG and subtypes of the types occurring in lexical assumptions for the case of a BCG). In the powerset $P(T(G))$ one defines the operation:

$$U_1 \circ U_2 = \{C \in T(G)\colon\ (\exists A \in U_1,\ B \in U_2) A, B \vdash C\},$$

for $U_1, U_2 \subseteq T(G)$. The subalgebra of the algebra $(P(T(G)), \circ)$ generated by all sets:

$$T_G(v) = \{A \in T(G)\colon\ v : A \text{ is a lexical assumption}\}$$

is denoted $TA(G)$ and called *the type algebra* of the grammar G. The mapping h from $PL(G)/\sim_G$ to $TA(G)$, given by:

$$h([X]) = \{A \in T(G)\colon\ (X : A) \text{ holds in } G\},$$

is an isomorphism of the quotient-algebra $PL(G)/\sim_G$ onto the algebra $TA(G)$. Now, $TA(G)$ is a finite algebra, and it can effectively be constructed for the given G. Many properties of grammars can be expressed as properties of their type algebras, and the latter admit an effective verification. For example, the Husserl condition $\sim_G = \sim_{PL(G)}$ is equivalent to the fact that the identity is the only congruence $\sim$ on $AT(G)$ which satisfies the compatibility condition:

$$\text{if } U_1 \sim U_2 \text{ then } \mathrm{S} \in U_1 \text{ iff } \mathrm{S} \in U_2.$$

For any grammar G, one can effectively construct a grammar G' such that $PL(G) = PL(G')$ and G' fulfills the Husserl condition. If G_1, G_2 fulfill this condition, then $PL(G_1) = PL(G_2)$ if, and only if, the mapping:

$$h(T_{G_1}(v)) = T_{G_2}(v), \quad \text{for all } v \in V$$

can be extended to an isomorphism from $TA(G_1)$ onto $TA(G_2)$ which maps $\{U \in TA(G_1)\colon\ \mathrm{S} \in U\}$ onto $\{U \in TA(G_2)\colon\ \mathrm{S} \in U\}$. Consequently, the P-equivalence problem is decidable, both for CFGs and BCGs, and similarly for the F-equivalence problem for BCGs (see Buszkowski, 1987c).

It is known that the weak equivalence problem for CFGs is undecidable, which yields the undecidability of the same problem for BCGs (use the constructive proof of the Gaifman theorem, to be described below).

3.2. Proof theory and generative capacity

Grammatical structures, discussed above, are naturally related to proof trees in deductive systems, underlying grammars, but we have applied methods of universal algebra rather than proof theory. Below, we shall consider more subtle problems which invite genuine proof-theoretic aspects of these systems.

We focus on stronger systems, admitting introduction rules for conditionals (the Lambek calculus is a typical example). If a system admits rules (E$\rightarrow$), (I$\rightarrow$), then it is completely determined by unary patterns $A \vdash B$, derivable in this system, and the only rule (E$\rightarrow$). For, if $A_1, \ldots, A_n \vdash B$ is derivable, then, by (I$\rightarrow$), the unary pattern:

$$A_n \vdash A_{n-1} \rightarrow (A_{n-2} \rightarrow \cdots \rightarrow (A_1 \rightarrow B) \cdots)$$

is derivable as well, and $A_1, \ldots, A_n \vdash B$ can be derived from the latter and (Id), by (E$\rightarrow$). Derivations based on (E$\rightarrow$), (E$\leftarrow$) and unary patterns determine tree structures according to (D1), (D2$\rightarrow$), (D2$\leftarrow$), and the clause for unary transitions:

(D3) if $X : A$, and $A \vdash B$ holds, then $X : B$.

Thus, $FL(G)$ and $PL(G)$ can be defined also for grammars G based on **L** and similar systems.

An interesting property of grammars based on **L** and its extensions is *structural completeness*: for any string in $L(G)$, all possible structures living on this string are derivable (that means, for any structure, there is a proof which determines this structure). To show this fact, one uses the **L**-derivable patterns:

$$\text{(AS)}\ A \rightarrow (B \leftarrow C) \vdash (A \rightarrow B) \leftarrow C, \quad (A \rightarrow B) \leftarrow C \vdash A \rightarrow (B \leftarrow C)$$

together with (TR$\rightarrow$) and (TR$\leftarrow$) from Section 2. (TR$\rightarrow$) and (TR$\leftarrow$) enable one to interchange functors and arguments. For assume $[X, Y]_1 : B$ is derivable. Then, for some A, also $X : B \leftarrow A$ and $Y : A$ must be derivable. Using (TR$\rightarrow$) and (D3), we obtain:

$$Y : (B \leftarrow A) \rightarrow A,$$

and consequently, $[X, Y]_2 : B$ holds, by (D2$\rightarrow$). In a similar way, we infer $[X, Y]_1 : B$ from $[X, Y]_2 : B$. Consequently, for systems admitting Type Raising, $FL(G)$ can be identified with $PL(G)$; precisely, $FL(G)$ contains all possible fa-structures which live on phrase structures from $PL(G)$.

Now, (AS) change $[[X, Y], Z] : B$ into $[X, [Y, Z]] : B$, and conversely. For assume $[[X, Y], Z] : B$. By Type Raising, one can arrange the derivation in a form which yields $[[X, Y]_2, Z]_1 : B$. There must be subderivations:

$$X : A,\ Y : A \rightarrow (B \leftarrow C),\ Z : C.$$

Using (AS), (D3), one infers $Y : (A \rightarrow B) \leftarrow C$, which yields $[X, [Y, Z]_1]_2 : B$, by (D2$\leftarrow$) and (D2$\rightarrow$). Forgetting functor marks, we obtain $[X, [Y, Z]] : B$. The converse transition is similar. Consequently, for grammars G whose deductive part admits both (AS) and Type Raising, $FL(G)$ and $PL(G)$ can be identified with $L(G)$ in the sense that the structure languages contain all possible structures living on the elements of the string language. In particular, F-equivalence and P-equivalence problems reduce to the weak equivalence problem.

The Non-Associative Lambek Calculus, introduced in (Lambek, 1961), avoids the associativity of formula concatenation: in patterns $\Gamma \vdash A$, Γ is not a string of formulas but a bracketed string of formulas, i.e. a phrase structure whose leaves are formulas. Inference rules take the following forms:

$$(\mathrm{E}\rightarrow)\ \frac{\Gamma \vdash A;\ \Delta \vdash A \rightarrow B}{[\Gamma, \Delta] \vdash B},$$

$$(\mathrm{E}\leftarrow)\ \frac{\Gamma \vdash B \leftarrow A;\ \Delta \vdash A}{[\Gamma, \Delta] \vdash B},$$

$$(\mathrm{I}\rightarrow)\ \frac{[A, \Gamma] \vdash B}{\Gamma \vdash A \rightarrow B},$$

$$(\mathrm{I}\leftarrow)\ \frac{[\Gamma, A] \vdash B}{\Gamma \vdash B \leftarrow A}.$$

One easily shows that (TR $\rightarrow$) and (TR $\leftarrow$) are derivable in this weaker version of **L**, but (AS) are not derivable. It follows that the corresponding grammars G preserve $PL(G) = FL(G)$, but not $L(G) = PL(G)$. Actually, it has been proven in (Buszkowski, 1986b) and (Kandulski, 1988a, 1988b) (for the system with product) that these grammars are P-equivalent to BCGs: they generate the P-languages of finite index and finite degree. On the contrary, their string languages $L(G)'s$ must be the context-free languages, and consequently, they may be of infinite index (with respect to the basic congruence in $V^\star$ determined by the string language).

The P-equivalence of Non-Associative Lambek Grammars and BCGs is a good example of a theorem which relies upon fine proof-theoretic properties of the deductive system. One of the leitmotives of proof theory is normalization of proofs: each proof can be reduced to a normal form which has some nice computational features. Later on we shall discuss normalization in ND-systems parallel to normalization in the lambda calculus. The equivalence theorem we consider here requires another normalization procedure. We neglect the product. First, the Non-Associative **L** can be axiomatized by the only rules (E $\rightarrow$) and (E $\leftarrow$), (CUT) and axioms schemes (Id), (TR $\rightarrow$), (TR $\leftarrow$) together with all unary patterns which arise from the latter three patterns by means of the following monotonicity rules:

$$(\mathrm{M1})\ \frac{A \vdash B}{C \rightarrow A \vdash C \rightarrow B},\ \frac{A \vdash B}{A \leftarrow C \vdash B \leftarrow C},$$

$$(\mathrm{M2})\ \frac{A \vdash B}{B \rightarrow C \vdash A \rightarrow C},\ \frac{A \vdash B}{C \leftarrow B \vdash C \leftarrow A}.$$

Now, the axiomatic pattern $A \vdash B$ is said to be *expanding* (resp. *reducing*), if A is less (resp. more) complex than B. For instance, (TR$\rightarrow$) and (TR$\leftarrow$) are expanding, while their (M2)-transformants are reducing. We state the key normalization lemma: if $A_1, \ldots, A_n \vdash B$ is derivable, then there are formulas A'_i, $i = 1, \ldots, n$, and a formula B' such that:

- $A_i \vdash A'_i$, $i = 1, \ldots, n$, are derivable by means of reducing patterns and (CUT),
- $A'_1, \ldots, A'_n \vdash B'$ is derivable by means of (E$\rightarrow$) and (E$\leftarrow$),
- $B' \vdash B$ is derivable by means of expanding patterns and (CUT).

Further, each proof in the above axiomatization of the system can be transformed into a derivation of the latter form without changing the phrase structure determined by the proof tree. Clearly, the first, reducing part of the normal derivation can be replaced by affixing new lexical assumptions $v : A'_i$, if $v : A_i$ in the original grammar. Then, for proving $A_1, \ldots, A_n \vdash$S, the third, expanding part of the normal derivation disappears (since the complexity of S is minimal), and consequently, nonassociative Lambek derivations are equivalent to purely applicative derivations with finitely extended lexical assumptions.

Accordingly, categorial grammars based on the Nonassociative Lambek Calculus can be lexicalized with preserving structures. Kandulski (1993, 1995) proves similar results for grammars based on the nonassociative **LP**, which yields lexicalization of CFGs whose production rules are invariant under permutation (of the body) provided that the phrase structures produced by the grammar are of a bounded degree.

A very nice example of a proof-theoretic argument for an equivalence theorem is the proof of the weak equivalence of CFGs and Lambek Categorial Grammars (LCGs), i.e. grammars based on the full **L**, given in (Pentus, 1993a). Let us note that this problem, first mentioned in (Bar-Hillel, Gaifman and Shamir, 1960), remained open many years, and there appeared several partial results in this direction and some deficient proofs of the theorem.

Since Cohen (1967), it was known that each CFG is weakly equivalent to some LCG. By the Gaifman theorem and (T2), each CFG is weakly equivalent to a BCG G with $o(G) \leqslant 1$. For sequents $A_1, \ldots, A_n \vdash$S such that $o(A_i) \leqslant 1$, $i = 1, \ldots, n$, the derivability in **L** is equivalent to the derivability in the Ajdukiewicz calculus (in the Gentzen style form of **L**, no derivation of these sequents uses rules (I$\rightarrow$) and (I$\leftarrow$)). Accordingly, each BCG of order at most 1 is weakly equivalent to the LCG which is the same as the BCG except for taking **L** as the deductive part. Unfortunately, Cohen's attempt to prove the converse statement has began the series of deficient proofs of the equivalence theorem (see the discussion in (Buszkowski, 1985)).

The proof given in (Pentus, 1993a) employs certain basic properties of **L** as a strongly substructural logic. The first of them is *an interpolation lemma*, proved in (Roorda, 1991). For atomic types p and types A, by $\rho_p(A)$ we denote the number of occurrences of p in A, and by $\rho(A)$ the number of all occurrences of atomic types in A. In a similar way, we define $\rho_p(\Gamma)$, $\rho(\Gamma)$, where Γ is a string of types. Let $\Gamma, \Delta, \Gamma' \vdash B$ be a sequent derivable in **L** with $\Delta \neq \Lambda$. *An interpolant* of Δ in this sequent is a type A such that the sequents $\Delta \vdash A$ and $\Gamma, A, \Gamma' \vdash B$ are derivable in **L**. The Roorda lemma is the following:

(L1) if $\Gamma, \Delta, \Gamma' \vdash B$ is derivable, then there is an interpolant A of Δ such that, for any atomic type p, $\rho_p(A) \leqslant \max(\rho_p(\Delta), \rho_p(\Gamma, \Gamma', B))$.

The proof of (L1) proceeds by induction on cut free derivations in the Gentzen form of **L**.

The second useful property of **L** is *the independence of branches* of any cut free proof. Observe that axioms (Id) can be restricted to atomic formulas A. Then, in any cut free proof one can replace atomic formulas occurring in axioms (that means, on the leaves of the tree) with their copies in such a way that no two different leaves refer to the same formula. Then, each sequent appearing along the proof tree becomes *special*, that means, each atomic formula has either zero, or two occurrences in it. Clearly, the original proof can be regained from the modified one by substituting original atomic formulas for their copies. In particular, we obtain:

(L2) each sequent derivable in **L** arises from a special sequent derivable in **L** by substitution of atomic types for atomic types.

Notice that the independence of branches is characteristic of *multiplicative* substructural logics whose representatives are, e.g., **L** and **LP**, but it does not hold for *additive* systems. The rule (R$\wedge$) requires the same atomic types along the subtrees corresponding to the premises $\Gamma \vdash A$ and $\Gamma \vdash B$, while the rule (R$\circ$) admits quite independent premises $\Gamma \vdash A$ and $\Delta \vdash B$; so, $\wedge$ is referred to as an additive connective, while $\circ$ is referred to as a multiplicative one.

A type is said to be *thin*, if each atomic type has either no occurrences, or one occurrence in it. A sequent is said to be *thin*, if it is derivable in **L**, it is special, and each type occurring in it is thin. Notice that if $A_1, \ldots, A_n \vdash A$ is a special sequent derivable in **L**, and we replace each type A_i by its interpolant A'_i, and type A by an interpolant A' of $A_1, \ldots, A_n$, then the resulting sequent $A'_1, \ldots, A'_n \vdash A'$ is thin. For each double occurrence of an atomic type p in type A_i or A exhausts all occurrences of p in the former sequent (it is special!), hence p does not appear in the interpolant.

By $\pi(A)$ we denote the set of atomic types appearing in A. We need the following combinatorial property of thin sequents:

(L3) if $A_1, \ldots, A_n \vdash A_{n+1}$, $n \geqslant 2$, is a thin sequent, then there is $2 \leqslant k \leqslant n$ such that $\pi(A_k) \subseteq \pi(A_{k-1}) \cup \pi(A_{k+1})$.

In the proof of (L3) one employs an interpretation of **L** in free groups. Consider the free group generated by atomic types and interpret $A \circ B$ as $A \cdot B$, $A \to B$ as $A^{-1} \cdot B$, and $A \leftarrow B$ as $A \cdot B^{-1}$. Then, if $A_1, \ldots, A_n \vdash A$ is derivable in **L**, then $A_1 \cdots A_n = A$ holds true in the free group. As a consequence, we obtain the following:

($\star$) there is no thin sequent $\Gamma, A, B, C, \Gamma' \vdash D$ such that some atomic type p occurs in both A and C, and some atomic type q occurs in both B and Γ, Γ', D.

Suppose the contrary. The true equality $\Gamma \cdot A \cdot B \cdot C \cdot \Gamma' = D$ contains p precisely in A and C. Thus, p occurs in A and p^{-1} in C, or conversely. The atom q in B occurs in precisely one of the forms q, q^{-1}. The interval between the two occurrences of p does not reduce to 1 in the free group, and consequently, the equality does not hold.

Now, (L3) is proved by induction on n. For $n = 2$, we put $k = 2$: clearly, each atomic type in A_2 must appear in either A_1, or A_3, since $A_1, A_2 \vdash A_3$ is thin. Consider $n > 2$. If

$k = 2$ satisfies the desired inclusion, then the thesis is true. So, assume the inclusion does not hold for $k = 2$. Accordingly, some atomic type $q \in \pi(A_2)$ has the other occurrence beyond the string A_1, A_2, A_3. Let B be an interpolant of A_1, A_2 in the sequent. B is thin, and the sequent $B, A_3, \ldots, A_n \vdash A_{n+1}$ is thin. By the induction hypothesis, we find a number $3 \leqslant k \leqslant n$ such that $\pi(A_k) \subseteq \pi(A_{k-1}) \cup \pi(A_{k+1})$ (if $k = 3$, we replace A_{k-1} by B). If $k > 3$, then our thesis holds. If $k = 3$, then $\pi(A_3) \subseteq \pi(B) \cup \pi(A_4)$ and $\pi(B) \subseteq \pi(A_1) \cup \pi(A_2)$ (B is an interpolant!). By ($\star$) no atomic type p in A_3 can appear in A_1, which yields $\pi(A_3) \subseteq \pi(A_2) \cup \pi(A_4)$.

We are ready to prove *the binary reduction lemma*. By $T(P, m)$ we denote the set of all types A such that $\pi(A) \subseteq P$ and $\rho(A) \leqslant m$.

(L4) Let $A_1, \ldots, A_n \vdash A_{n+1}$, $n \geqslant 2$, be a sequent derivable in **L** such that $A_i \in T(P, m)$, for all $1 \leqslant i \leqslant n + 1$. Then, then there are a number $2 \leqslant k \leqslant n$ and a type $B \in T(P, m)$ such that both $A_{k-1}, A_k \vdash B$ and $A_1, \ldots, A_{k-2}, B, A_{k+1}, \ldots, A_n \vdash A_{n+1}$ are derivable in **L**.

First, we prove (L4) under the assumption that the sequent in question be thin. Take $2 \leqslant k \leqslant n$ as in (L3). By $\#(K)$ we denote the cardinality of the set K. We proceed by induction on n. For $n = 2$, we put $B = A_{n+1}$. So, assume $n > 2$. We consider two cases.

Case I. $k < n$. Then, $\pi(A_k) \subseteq \pi(A_{k-1}) \cup \pi(A_{k+1})$. We consider two subcases.

Case I.1 $\#(\pi(A_{k-1}) \cap \pi(A_k)) \geqslant \#(\pi(A_k) \cap \pi(A_{k+1}))$.

Let B be an interpolant of A_{k-1}, A_k. Then, sequents $A_{k-1}, A_k \vdash B$ and $A_1, \ldots, A_{k-2}, B, A_{k+1}, \ldots, A_n \vdash A_{n+1}$ are derivable in **L**. We show $B \in T(P, m)$. Clearly $\pi(B) \subseteq P$, so we only need $\rho(B) \leqslant m$. That holds by the following calculation:

$$\begin{aligned}
\rho(B) &= \#(\pi(A_{k-1}) - \pi(A_{k-1}) \cap \pi(A_k)) + \#(\pi(A_k) - \pi(A_{k-1}) \cap \pi(A_k)) \\
&= \#(\pi(A_{k-1}) - \pi(A_{k-1}) \cap \pi(A_k)) + \#(\pi(A_k) \cap \pi(A_{k+1})) \\
&\leqslant \#(\pi(A_{k-1}) - \pi(A_{k-1}) \cap \pi(A_k)) + \#(\pi(A_{k-1}) \cap \pi(A_k)) \\
&= \#(\pi(A_{k-1})) = \rho(A_{k-1}).
\end{aligned}$$

The first equality holds, since $A_1, \ldots, A_n \vdash A_{n+1}$ is thin, and consequently, the thin type B contains precisely those atomic types which appear in A_{k-1} or A_k but not in both. The second equality holds by the inclusion from (L3). The first inequality holds by the assumption of Case I.1, and the remaining equalities are obvious.

Case I.2 $\#(\pi(A_{k-1}) \cap \pi(A_k)) < \#(\pi(A_k) \cap \pi(A_{k+1}))$.

The argument is similar except that one interchanges the roles of A_{k-1} and A_{k+1}.

Case II. $k = n$. Then, $\pi(A_n) \subseteq \pi(A_{n-1}) \cup \pi(A_{n+1})$. Subcase II.1 analogous to I.1 (with $k = n$) is treated as above. Subcase II.2 analogous to I.2 (with $k = n$) requires another reasoning. Let C be an interpolant of $A_1, \ldots, A_{n-1}$ in the sequent in question. Then, C is a thin type, and sequents $A_1, \ldots, A_{n-1} \vdash C$ and $C, A_n \vdash A_{n+1}$ are thin. If we prove $C \in T(P, m)$, then our thesis holds, by the induction hypothesis applied to $A_1, \ldots, A_{n-1} \vdash C$ (**L** is closed under (CUT)!). Denote $\Gamma = A_1, \ldots, A_{n-1}$. We have $\pi(C) \subseteq P$ and:

$$\begin{aligned}\pi(C) &= \pi(\Gamma) \cap (\pi(A_n) \cup \pi(A_{n+1}))\\ &= (\pi(\Gamma) \cap \pi(A_n)) \cup (\pi(\Gamma) \cap \pi(A_{n+1}))\\ &= (\pi(A_{n-1}) \cap \pi(A_n)) \cup (\pi(A_{n+1}) - \pi(A_n) \cap \pi(A_{n+1})).\end{aligned}$$

The first equality holds, since C is an interpolant of Γ. The second equality is obvious. The third equality holds, by the inclusion from (L3) and the fact that $A_1, \ldots, A_n \vdash A_{n+1}$ is special. Now, we calculate:

$$\begin{aligned}\rho(C) &= \#(\pi(C))\\ &= \#(\pi(A_{n-1}) \cap \pi(A_n)) + \#(\pi(A_{n+1})) - \#(\pi(A_n) \cap \pi(A_{n+1}))\\ &< \#(\pi(A_{n-1}) \cap \pi(A_n)) + \#(\pi(A_{n+1})) - \#(\pi(A_{n-1}) \cap \pi(A_n))\\ &= \#(\pi(A_{n+1})) = \rho(A_{n+1}),\end{aligned}$$

where the inequality holds by the assumption of Case II.2, and the remainder is obvious. We have shown $\rho(C) < m$, hence $C \in T(P, m)$, which finishes the proof of (L4) for thin sequents.

We prove (L4) for arbitrary sequents. By (L2), we find a special sequent $A'_1, \ldots, A'_n \vdash A'_{n+1}$, derivable in **L** and such that there is a substitution σ (substituting atoms for atoms) with $\sigma(A'_i) = A_i$, for all $1 \leqslant i \leqslant n+1$. For each $i = 1, \ldots, n$, let B_i be an interpolant of A'_i, and let B_{n+1} be an interpolant of $A'_1, \ldots, A'_n$, in the latter sequent. Then, $B_1, \ldots, B_n \vdash B_{n+1}$ is a thin sequent. Let P' be the set of atomic types occurring in $A'_1, \ldots, A'_n \vdash A'_{n+1}$. Clearly, $A'_i, B_i \in T(P', m)$. By (L4) for thin sequents, there are a number $2 \leqslant k \leqslant n$ and a type $B' \in T(P', m)$ such that sequents $B_{k-1}, B_k \vdash B'$ and $B_1, \ldots, B_{k-2}, B', B_{k+1}, \ldots, B_n \vdash B_{n+1}$ are derivable in **L**. Since $A'_i \vdash B_i$, for $i = 1, \ldots, n$, and $B_{n+1} \vdash A'_{n+1}$ are derivable in **L**, then, by (CUT), sequents $A'_{k-1}, A'_k \vdash B'$ and $A'_1, \ldots, A'_{k-2}, B', A'_{k+1}, \ldots, A'_n \vdash A'_{n+1}$ are derivable in **L**. Put $B = \sigma(B')$. Then, $B \in T(P, m)$, and the thesis of (L4) holds true, since the derivability in **L** is closed under substitution.

The Pentus theorem easily follows from (L4). Fix an LCG G. Let P be the set of all atomic types appearing in lexical assumptions of G (as subtypes), and let m be the maximal $\rho(A)$, for types A appearing in these assumptions. Then, the CFG G' with the same lexical assumptions and the production rules being the **L**-derivable sequents $A, B \vdash C$ and $A \vdash B$, for all $A, B, C \in T(P, m)$, satisfies $L(G') = L(G)$. Production rules $A \vdash B$ can be eliminated by affixing lexical assumptions v :S, for each atom v such that, for some type A, $v : A$ is a lexical assumption of G, and $A \vdash$S is derivable in **L**. We have proven:

(T3) LCGs are weakly equivalent to CFGs.

As shown in (Kanazawa, 1992), categorial grammars based on the Lambek Calculus with additive conjunction $\wedge$ surpass the area of CF languages: some non-CF intersections of CF languages can be generated by these grammars. For the system **LP**, it is known that each permutation closure of a CF language can be generated by a categorial grammar based on **LP** of order at most 1 (see Buszkowski, 1988a; Van Benthem, 1988a). The problem of if **LP**-grammars generate precisely the permutation closures of CF languages remains open. Notice that although (L1) and (L2) hold for **LP**, the proofs of (L3) and (L4) cannot be repeated, even if one admits rearrangements of the antecedent string. The sequent:

$$(p \leftarrow q) \leftarrow r,\ (r \leftarrow s) \leftarrow t,\ (t \circ q) \leftarrow u \vdash (p \leftarrow s) \leftarrow u$$

is thin (in **LP**), but each interpolant of two antecedent types (not necessarily adjoint) contains four atomic subtypes, which exceeds $m = 3$ determined by the sequent. That breaks down the key idea of the proof of (L4) for thin sequents.

It follows from (T3) and the Gaifman theorem that LCGs are weakly equivalent to BCGs. A further refinement of the above arguments yields (see Buszkowski, 1996):

(T4) each LCG G (without product) is weakly equivalent to some BCG G' whose lexical assumptions $v : B$ fulfill the condition: for some type A, $v : A$ is a lexical assumption of G, and $A \vdash B$ is derivable in **L**.

We say that G' is a lexical extension of G.

The key idea is a proof of the Gaifman theorem with the aid of **L**. An effective construction of a BCG G_2 weakly equivalent to the given CFG G_1 can be described as follows. We assume G_1 is in the Chomsky Normal Form. To each nonterminal symbol p of G_1 we assign a finite set $I(p)$, of product-free types, by the clauses:

(I0) $\mathrm{S} \in I(\mathrm{S})$,

(I1) if $p, q \vdash r$ is a production rule of G_1, then we put both $p \to r$ and $(p \to t) \leftarrow (r \to t)$ into $I(q)$, for all nonterminals t,

(I2) if $A \in I(p)$ on the basis of (I0), (I1), then, for any nonterminal q, we put $A \leftarrow (q \to p)$ into $I(q)$.

The lexical assumptions of G_2 are assignments $v : A$ such that, for some nonterminal p, $v : p$ is an assumption of G_1, and $A \in I(p)$. One shows $L(G_1) = L(G_2)$. The proof of $L(G_1) \subseteq L(G_2)$ is combinatorial and uses regular subderivations of derivations in G_1; actually, derivations in G_2 which simulate derivations in G_1 use (MP$\leftarrow$) only. The inclusion $L(G_2) \subseteq L(G_1)$ admits a logical argument whose essential step is:

(L5) if $A \in I(p)$, then $p \vdash A$ is derivable in the system **L** (with (CUT)) enriched with the production rules of G_1 as new axioms.

For (I0), $\mathrm{S} \vdash \mathrm{S}$ is (Id). For (I1), $q \vdash p \to r$ holds, by (I$\to$), and $p \to r \vdash (p \to t) \leftarrow (r \to t)$ holds, by (SYL$\to$) and (I$\leftarrow$). For (I2), if $p \vdash A$ holds, then $q \vdash A \leftarrow (q \to p)$ holds, by (TR$\leftarrow$) and the monotonicity rule (M1). We prove $L(G_2) \subseteq L(G_1)$. Assume $v_1 \cdots v_n \in L(G_2)$. Then, $A_1, \ldots, A_n \vdash \mathrm{S}$ is derivable by MP-rules with lexical assumptions $v_i : A_i$, $i = 1, \ldots, n$. Consider an auxiliary grammar G_3 whose lexical assumptions are those of G_1 and the deductive part is the enriched **L**. Clearly, $v_1 \cdots v_n \in L(G_3)$. Now, $L(G_3) =$

$L(G_1)$, which yields the desired inclusion. The latter equality can be proved by a model-theoretic argument: grammatical categories in the sense of G_1 determine a model for the enriched **L**, and consequently, everything which holds for G_3 must also hold for G_1; the converse is obvious. An alternative, proof-theoretic argument is based on the fact that the enriched **L** admits cut elimination, provided that new axioms $p, q \vdash r$ are replaced by new rules:

$$\text{(NR)} \ \frac{\Gamma \vdash p; \ \Gamma \vdash q}{\Gamma, \Delta \vdash r}.$$

A cut free proof of a sequent $p_1, \ldots, p_n \vdash p_{n+1}$, where all p_i are atomic, must be totally based on rules (NR) and axioms (Id), which is essentially a derivation in G_1. That yields $L(G_3) \subseteq L(G_1)$.

To prove (T4) we need a version of (L4) for product-free types: it has been proven in (Buszkowski, 1996) that, if $A_1, \ldots, A_n$ are product-free, and A_{n+1} is atomic, then the type B can be chosen product-free. Accordingly, for the given LCG G (without product), a weakly equivalent CFG $G^\star$ is based on the lexical assumptions of G and the production rules $A, B \vdash C$ such that $A, B, C \in T(P, m)$ are product-free and $A, B \vdash C$ is derivable in **L**. Now, we apply the proof of the Gaifman theorem on the basis of **L**. Take $G_1 = G^\star$, and construct G_2 as above. Observe that the enriched **L** equals **L**, since the production rules of $G^\star$ are derivable in **L**. Thus, by (L5), if $v : B$ is a lexical assumption of G_2, then, for some type A, $v : A$ is a lexical assumption of $G^\star$ (hence of G), and $A \vdash B$ is derivable in **L**. Therefore, G_2 is a lexical extension of G.

Theorems (T3) and (T4) exemplify nontrivial proof-theoretic methods in mathematical linguistics. Arguments essentially involve such typically proof theoretic ideas, as cut elimination, interpolation, independence of branches in a proof tree, and others. As shown above, also the Gaifman theorem can be obtained with the aid of cut elimination in the Lambek Calculus enriched with new axioms. In (Buszkowski, 1982a), similar tools have been applied to prove that categorial grammars based on the product-free Lambek Calculus enriched with finitely many new axioms can generate arbitrary recursively enumerable languages, and consequently, the derivability from hypotheses in **L** is undecidable. Below, we give one more example of that kind beyond the world of categorial grammar.

Recursive Transition Networks (RTNs) are extensions of FSAs in which one admits basic transitions $A : B \to C$ such that A, B, C are states (see Gazdar and Mellish, 1989). Then, lexical assumptions $v : A \to B$ can be dropped; the only lexical assumptions admissible take the form $v : A$, where v is a lexical atom, and A is a state. Like FSAs, RTNs consume strings of lexical atoms from the left to the right, and transitions are executed as follows. The subinterval Y of the string XYZ is treated as an atom which yields the transition $Y : B \to C$ provided the RTN assigns some state A to Y such that $A : B \to C$ is a basic transition. Less formally, after the RTN has consumed the initial interval X and reached state B, it alters the mode: starting from an initial state, it proceeds along the string, until state A will be reached for the source string Y; then, the RTN skips Y and continues the run, starting from state C. RTNs are suited to model recursive constructions in language. For example, the RTN defined by:

- Axiom: $\Lambda \vdash I$ (the initial state),

- Lexical assumptions: Mary, John, Jim: NP; sees, knows: V; that: WH,
- Transitions: NP: $I \rightarrow A$, VP: $A \rightarrow S$, V: $I \rightarrow B$, WH: $B \rightarrow C$, $S : C \rightarrow$ VP, NP: $B \rightarrow$ VP,

where A, B, C are auxiliary states, assigns type S to strings:

- Mary sees John,
- Mary sees that John knows that Mary knows Jim,
- Mary sees that John knows that Mary sees that John knows that Mary knows Jim,

and so on. Consider the second string. Starting from I, the RTN assigns A to *Mary*. The transition VP: $A \rightarrow S$ is activated. So, the string *sees that John knows that Mary knows Jim* must be assigned state VP. Starting from I, *sees that* is consumed with outcome C, again one alters the mode to recognize *John knows that Mary knows Jim* in type S, which activates the transition $S : C \rightarrow$ VP.

It is known that RTNs are weakly equivalent to CFGs. We show that this equivalence can be proved with the aid of rule elimination theorems for appropriate LDSs.

The LDS corresponding for the given RTN is defined by:

- Axioms: $\Lambda : A$, for initial states A,
- Identity assumptions: $A : A$,
- Lexical assumptions: $v : A$,
- Transitions: $A : B \rightarrow C$,
- Rule (LE$\rightarrow$),

together with *the labeled cut rule*, which handles the recursive steps in RTN-runs:

$$\text{(LCUT)}\ \frac{XAZ : B;\ Y : A}{XYZ : B},$$

where X, Y, Z are strings of lexical atoms and states, and A, B are states.

For the given CFG (in the Chomsky Normal Form), we construct an equivalent LDS by replacing production rules $A, B \vdash C$ by unary patterns $B \vdash A \rightarrow C$. In the LDS, these patterns are executed by *U-rules*:

$$\frac{X : B}{X : A \rightarrow C}.$$

The LDS is defined by:

- Axioms $\Lambda : A$, for Λ-rules $\Lambda \vdash A$,
- Identity assumptions: $A : A$,
- Lexical assumptions: $v : A$,
- U-rules,
- Rule (LE$\rightarrow$).

There is a one-to-one correspondence between RTNs and CFGs, if we identify states with nonterminals and transitions with U-rules. The equivalence of the RTN with the corresponding CFG follows from the fact that that both the LDSs described above yield the same labeled formulas $X : A$. Denote these systems by LRTN and LCFG, respectively. Let LRTN' equal LRTN enriched with U-rules, and let LCFG' equal LCFG + (LCUT). Clearly, LRTN' and LCFG' are identical systems. The equivalence of systems LRTN and LCFG is a straightforward consequence of the following elimination theorems:

(T5) (LCUT) can be eliminated from every derivation in LCFG'.

(T6) In LRTN', U-rules can be eliminated from any derivation of $X : A$ with A atomic.

The proof of (T5) goes by an easy induction on derivations of the premises of (LCUT). For (T6), assume the U-rule:

$$\frac{Y : C}{Y : B \to D}$$

be applied in a derivation of $X : A$ in LRTN'. Since $B \to D$ is not atomic, then $Y : B \to D$ must be a premise of a next rule; this rule can be neither (LCUT), nor an U-rule, hence it must be (LE$\to$) with the other premise $Z : B$. We modify the derivation: first, we apply (LE$\to$) to premises $Z : B$ and $C : B \to D$ (it must be a transition of LRTN), which yields $ZC : D$, and second, we apply (LCUT) to premises $ZC : D$ and $Y : C$, which yields $ZY : D$, as in the initial derivation.

3.3. *Other topics*

Equivalence theorems are special instances of combinatorial properties of formal languages which are closely related to fine aspects of deduction. Let us point out other issues of that kind.

Closure properties. Tree languages of CFGs are closed under Boolean operations, which easily follows from the Thatcher theorem. For BCGs, the complementation must be restricted to trees of a bounded degree. Effective constructions of grammars which yield the join, the meet etc. of two given tree languages (with explicitly given grammars) can be performed with the aid of type algebras. Analogous constructions for string languages (join, homomorphism, substitution) are quite standard; usually, they can more easily be accomplished for CFGs than for BCGs. However, deductive properties of **L** may help to show certain closure properties of context-free languages. For instance, the latter languages are invariant under *the cyclic closure*:

$$L^{\circ} = \{YX : XY \in L\}.$$

From the results discussed above, it follows that each context-free language L equals $L(G)$, for some LCG G, restricted to types with $\to$ only. For any type A, let A^p denote the type $(A \to p) \to p$, where p is a fixed, atomic type. If $\Gamma = A_1, \ldots, A_n$, then $\Gamma^p = A_1^p, \ldots, A_n^p$. Using the Gentzen form of $\mathbf{L}_{\to}$ (i.e. **L** restricted to $\to$), one easily proves:

(L6) if $\Gamma, A \to B \vdash p$ is derivable in $\mathbf{L}_{\to}$, then there are strings Γ', Γ'' such that $\Gamma = \Gamma', \Gamma''$, and both $\Gamma', B \vdash p$ and $\Gamma'' \vdash A$ are derivable in this system,

(L7) $\Gamma, \Delta^p \vdash p$ is derivable in $\mathbf{L}_{\rightarrow}$ if, and only if, $\Delta, \Gamma \vdash p$ is derivable in this system.

Now, we expand G to G^p in the following way. Each atom v is supplied with a copy v^p, with lexical assumptions $v^p : A^p$ whenever $v : A$ is in G (we assume p be a new atomic type and the designated type of G^p). By (L6) and (L7), $L(G) \cup L(G^p)$ consists of all strings XY^p such that $YX \in L$, and the latter language is context-free. Consequently, L° is also context-free, as a homomorphic image of a context-free language. Similar type transformations have been used in (Emms, 1993) to describe some extraction phenomena in natural language.

Non-CF languages. Since $a^n(bc)^n$ $(n > 0)$ is context-free, but $a^n b^n c^n$ is not, and the latter equals the intersection of the permutation closure of the former with the regular language $a^\star b^\star c^\star$, then context-free languages are not closed under permutation. As shown in (Friedman, Dai and Wang, 1986), some non-CF languages can be generated by BCGs admitting a restricted permutation: $A, B \leftarrow A \vdash B$ is admissible in certain cases (also see Emms, 1993). As mentioned above, all permutation closures of CF languages are generated by **LP**-grammars (actually, of order at most 1). One way to show this fact is to observe that, if Γ consists of types of order at most 1, than $\Gamma \vdash p$ is derivable in **LP** if, and only if, Γ is a permutation of a string Δ such that $\Delta \vdash p$ is derivable in **L**. Van Benthem (1988a) gives an alternative proof which exploits regular expressions. First, using Parikh vectors, one shows that permutation closures of CF languages are the same as permutation closures of regular languages. Second, one proves that, for any regular language L, the permutation closure of L is generated by some **LP**-grammar, by induction on the regular expression which denotes L.

Complexity problems. We briefly survey complexity problems connected with logically oriented grammars. It is well-known that the membership problem for context-free languages can be solved in time polynomial in the size of the input string and the grammar (Hopcroft and Ullman, 1979). Kanovich (1991) proves that the decision problem for **LP** is NP-complete, which yields the NP-completeness of the recognition problem for **LP**-grammars. For noncommutative systems some interesting results have been obtained by Aarts (1994, 1995) and Aarts and Trautwein (1996). The decision problem for the product-free Nonassociative Lambek Calculus is polynomial, and so is the recognition problem for the corresponding categorial grammars, while analogous results for **L** have only been proven for types of order at most 2. These results use techniques of proof normalization (within the Gentzen format).

4. Proofs and semantic structures

4.1. Type-theoretic semantics

Montague (1974) and Cresswell (1973) are the foundations of logical semantics of natural language based on the theory of types. The standard formalism is the typed lambda calculus (see Turner's chapter). We recall basic notions. Types are formulas with only one conditional $\rightarrow$. For each type A, there are denumarably many variables $x_A, y_A, z_A, \ldots$, of type A. For each type A, one defines *terms* of type A by the recursive clauses (we write $t : A$ for 'term t is of type A'):

(TER1) variables of type A are terms of type A,
(TER2) if $s : A \to B$ and $t : A$, then $(st) : B$,
(TER3) if $s : B$ and $x : A$, then $(\lambda x.\, s) : A \to B$.

The constructions in (TER2) and (TER3) are *application* and *lambda abstraction*, respectively.

In semantics, atomic types A are associated with nonempty, pairwise disjoint sets D_A. Then, for the complex type $A \to B$, $D_{A \to B}$ is defined as the set of all functions from D_A to D_B. The set D_A is called *the ontological category* of type A. Given an assignment α, of variables in categories of appropriate type, each term $t : A$ determines a unique value $\alpha(t) \in D_A$:

(VAL2) $\alpha((st)) = \alpha(s)(\alpha(t))$,
(VAL3) $\alpha((\lambda x.\, s)) =$ the function $f : D_A \mapsto D_B$ such that $f(a) = \alpha[x/a](s)$, for every $a \in D_A$.

We fix atomic types **e**, of entities (individuals), and **t**, of truth values. If, for every type A, one adds the identity symbol $=_A$ of type $A \to (A \to \mathbf{t})$ with the meaning postulate:

$$\alpha(s =_A t) = 1 \quad \text{iff} \quad \alpha(s) = \alpha(t),$$

then the resulting language is as powerful, as logic of infinite order (we write $s = t$ for $((= s)t)$). Montague's Intensional Logic additionally admits an atomic type **s**, of possible worlds (indices, contexts and so like), which is needed for intensional constructions, but we omit these matters here.

In linguistics, it is expedient to supply this language with constants $c_A : A$ which are (interpreted) words of the language in question (with an obvious modification of (TER1)). For instance, we stipulate:

(PN) John, Mary: **e**,
(N) girl, student: $\mathbf{e} \to \mathbf{t}$,
(V) works, sings: $\mathbf{e} \to \mathbf{t}$,
(TV) loves, hates: $\mathbf{e} \to (\mathbf{e} \to \mathbf{t})$,
(Det) every, some: $(\mathbf{e} \to \mathbf{t}) \to ((\mathbf{e} \to \mathbf{t}) \to \mathbf{t}))$,
(B) not: $\mathbf{t} \to \mathbf{t}$, and, or: $\mathbf{t} \to (\mathbf{t} \to \mathbf{t})$,
(Adj) smart, handsome: $(\mathbf{e} \to \mathbf{t}) \to (\mathbf{e} \to \mathbf{t})$.

The logical structure of sentences and other complex expressions of natural language can be encoded by means of complex terms, as exemplified below:

(1) John sings; (sings John): **t**,

(2) John loves Mary; ((loves Mary) John): **t**,

(3) works and sings; $\lambda x_{\mathbf{e}}$. ((and (works $x_{\mathbf{e}}$))(sings $x_{\mathbf{e}}$)): $\mathbf{e} \to \mathbf{t}$,

(4) every student sings; ((every student) sings): **t**.

Only in (4) the term preserves the grammatical order of words. Cresswell (1973) admits the reverse application $(ts):B$, for $s:A \to B$ and $t:A$, which enables us to rearrange (1)–(3):

(1′) (John sings): **t**,
(2′) (John (loves Mary)): **t**,
(3′) $\lambda x_{\mathbf{e}}.$ (((works $x_{\mathbf{e}}$) and) (sings $x_{\mathbf{e}}$)): $\mathbf{e} \to \mathbf{t}$.

Actually, Cresswell's convention is not needed, if we apply Type Raising. For any term $t:A$, the term $t^B:(A \to B) \to B$ is defined by:

$$t^B = \lambda x_{A \to B} \cdot (x_{A \to B} t).$$

The combinatorial effect of Type Raising is the interchange of functors and arguments. Thus, (1)–(3) can be represented by the terms:

(1″) (John$^{\mathbf{t}}$ sings): **t**,
(2″) (John$^{\mathbf{t}}$ (loves Mary)): **t**,
(3″) $\lambda x_{\mathbf{e}}.$ (((works $x_{\mathbf{e}}$)$^{t \to t}$ and)(sings $x_{\mathbf{e}}$)): $\mathbf{e} \to \mathbf{t}$.

In this way, lambda terms represent semantic structures of natural language expressions. If denotations of lexical atoms (words) are fixed, then denotations of complex expressions can be computed according to their semantic representations, expressed by means of lambda terms. More interesting examples of this procedure can be found in any textbook on Montague Grammar, as, e.g., Gamut (1991) and Dowty, Wall and Peters (1981) (also see Moortgat's chapter).

4.2. *Proofs versus lambda terms*

We focus on connections between semantic structures and proof theory. The fundamental link is constituted by *the Curry–Howard correspondence* between typed lambda terms and proofs in ND-systems (see Girard with Taylor and Lafont, 1989). The logic of *positive implication* can be axiomatized in the ND-form by axioms (Id) and the following introduction and elimination rules for $\to$:

$$(\mathrm{PI}\to)\ \frac{\Gamma \vdash B}{\Gamma/A \vdash A \to B},$$

$$(\mathrm{PE}\to)\ \frac{\Gamma \vdash A \to B;\ \Delta \vdash A}{\Gamma, \Delta \vdash B}.$$

As above, Γ and Δ stand for finite strings of formulas. In (PI$\to$), Γ/A denotes a string which arises from Γ, after one has dropped a number (possibly zero) of occurrences of A. Notice that rule (PE$\to$) is the same as (E$\leftarrow$) from Section 2, if we write $B \leftarrow A$ instead of $A \to B$.

For any term t, by $\Gamma(t)$ we denote the string of types of free occurrences of variables in t (the string strictly reflects the horizontal order of occurrences of free variables in t). Then, each term $t : A$ encodes an ND-proof of the sequent $\Gamma(t) \vdash A$. (TER1) encodes the one step proof of $A \vdash A$, (TER2) corresponds to (PE $\rightarrow$), and (TER3) to (PI $\rightarrow$) (the assumption A dropped from Γ corresponds to the variable x_A bound by the new lambda abstractor). Conversely, each ND-proof can be encoded by some lambda term.

The Curry–Howard correspondence between lambda terms and proofs extends to a correspondence between lambda conversion (i.e. the logic of the lambda calculus) and normalization in ND-systems. The (extensional) equality $s = t$ of terms s and t is generated by the axiomatic equalities:

$$\lambda x.\, s = \lambda y.\, s[x := y], \tag{α}$$

$$((\lambda x.\, s)t) = s[x := t], \tag{β}$$

$$\lambda x.(sx) = s, \tag{η}$$

where in (α) y is free for x in s and not free in s, in (β) t is free for x in s, and in (η) x is not free in s. We also add standard rules of equality (substitution of equal terms for the same variable yields equal terms). The term t is said to be *normal*, if it contains no *redex*, i.e. a subterm of the form given on the left hand side of (β) and (η). *Lambda reduction* is the procedure of replacing redexes by their *contracta*, i.e. the terms on the right hand side of (β) and (η). The typed lambda calculus admits *strong normalization*: for any input term, each series of consecutive lambda reductions terminates with an outcome being a normal term which is unique (for all reduction runs) up to alphabetic variants (i.e. α-equalities). For the given term s, the unique normal term t such that $s = t$ is called *the normal form* of s.

Reduction steps in the typed lambda calculus correspond to normalization steps for ND-proofs in the sense of Prawitz (1965). The β-step mirrors the following transformation of ND-proofs. Let $\mathcal{D}$ be a proof of $\Gamma \vdash B$ whose last rule is (PE $\rightarrow$) with premises $\Gamma_1 \vdash A \rightarrow B$ and $\Gamma_2 \vdash A$ (so $\Gamma = \Gamma_1, \Gamma_2$). Also, let $\Gamma_1 \vdash A \rightarrow B$ results from (PI $\rightarrow$) with premise $\Gamma_1' \vdash B$ (so $\Gamma_1 = \Gamma_1'/A$). We form the proof $\mathcal{D}'$ of $\Gamma' \vdash B$ as follows. If no occurrence of A is dropped in (PI $\rightarrow$), then $\Gamma' = \Gamma_1$, and $\mathcal{D}'$ is the subproof of $\mathcal{D}$ which yields $\Gamma_1' \vdash B$. Otherwise, in the latter proof (represented as a tree with assumptions positioned on the leaves) we replace each dropped assumption A with a copy of the subproof of $\mathcal{D}$ which yields $\Gamma_2 \vdash A$. The resulting string Γ' differs from Γ at most in the order and multiplicity of occurrences of formulas from Γ_2, which does not restrict possibilities of application of further rules in the tree. The η-step mirrors a much simpler transformation. Namely, the rule (PE $\rightarrow$) with $\Delta = A$ (so, the right premise is the axiom (Id)) followed by the rule (PI $\rightarrow$) with premise $\Gamma, A \vdash B$ and conclusion $\Gamma \vdash A \rightarrow B$ is replaced by the subderivation which yields the left premise of (PE $\rightarrow$). A successive application of these transformations along an ND-proof of formula A (i.e. sequent $\vdash A$) eventually leads to a normal proof of this formula in which no conclusion of (PI $\rightarrow$) is used as the left premise of (PE $\rightarrow$), and no instance of (PE $\rightarrow$) whose right premise is

(Id) is directly followed by (PI$\rightarrow$) (dropping the A coming from (Id)). Normal proofs are closely related to cut free proofs in Gentzen style systems. Clearly, normal proofs are represented by normal lambda terms.

From the linguistic point of view, the Curry–Howard correspondence supplies logical semantics with computational procedures based on ND-systems: ND-proofs are computations of semantic structures. In interpreted terms, constants (words) take the part of free assumptions (instead of free variables in the above description). For instance, the semantic structure of *not every student*, which we regard as a negative NP of type $(\mathbf{e} \rightarrow \mathbf{t}) \rightarrow \mathbf{t}$, can be represented by the term:

$$\lambda x_{\mathbf{e}\rightarrow\mathbf{t}}.\ (\text{not}\ ((\text{every student})\ x_{\mathbf{e}\rightarrow\mathbf{t}})),$$

where *not* appears in its basic type $\mathbf{t} \rightarrow \mathbf{t}$. Denote $A = \mathbf{e} \rightarrow \mathbf{t}$ (the type of *student* and x), $B = A \rightarrow \mathbf{t}$ (the type of NP), $C = A \rightarrow B$ (the type of *every*) and $D = \mathbf{t} \rightarrow \mathbf{t}$ (the type of *not*). The above term corresponds to the following ND-proof:

(P1) $C, A \vdash B$, by (Id), (PE$\rightarrow$); every student: B,
(P2) $C, A, A \vdash \mathbf{t}$, by (Id), (PE$\rightarrow$); every student x: $\mathbf{t}$,
(P3) $D, C, A, A \vdash \mathbf{t}$, by (Id), (PE$\rightarrow$); not every student x: $\mathbf{t}$,
(P4) $D, C, A \vdash A \rightarrow \mathbf{t} = B$, by (PI$\rightarrow$); not every student: B.

The role of ND-proofs as semantic computations has been thoroughly examined by van Benthem in a series of publications, the most representative being (Van Benthem, 1986, 1987b, 1988a, 1988b, 1991). Below we sketch main lines of this theory.

The full power of positive implication is too great for semantic purposes. Structural rules Thinning (T), Contraction (C) and Permutation (P):

$$\text{(T)}\ \frac{\Gamma \vdash A}{\Gamma, B \vdash A},$$

$$\text{(C)}\ \frac{\Gamma, A, A \vdash B}{\Gamma, A \vdash B},$$

$$\text{(P)}\ \frac{\Gamma, A, B, \Gamma' \vdash C}{\Gamma, B, A, \Gamma' \vdash C},$$

are derivable in this system, and they give rise to derivable sequents:

(T′) $A \vdash B \rightarrow A$,

(C′) $A \rightarrow (A \rightarrow B) \vdash A \rightarrow B$,

(P′) $A \rightarrow (B \rightarrow C) \vdash B \rightarrow (A \rightarrow C)$.

Transformations (T′) and (C′) are not semantically plausible: according to (T′), each sentence (type $\mathbf{t}$) would also act as a verb phrase (type $\mathbf{e} \rightarrow \mathbf{t}$), and according to (C′), each transitive verb (type $\mathbf{e} \rightarrow (\mathbf{e} \rightarrow \mathbf{t})$) would also act as an intransitive verb (type

$\mathbf{e} \to \mathbf{t}$). Van Benthem (1986) introduces a system free of Thinning and Contraction; in the above axiomatization, the rule (PI $\to$) is restricted by the constraint: exactly one occurrence of A is to be dropped. Thus, the restricted rule admits the form:

$$(\mathrm{PI}\to)\ \frac{\Gamma, A, \Gamma' \vdash B}{\Gamma, \Gamma' \vdash A \to B}.$$

The system **LP** is axiomatized by (Id), (PE $\to$) and the restricted (PI $\to$) with the additional stipulation $\Gamma, \Gamma' \neq \Lambda$. Dropping the latter constraint yields a stronger system **LP1** which amounts to the logic BCI (see Ono, 1993) and the implication fragment of Intuitionistic Linear Logic (see Troelstra, 1992). **LP** is equivalent to the product-free Lambek Calculus enriched with Permutation. Proofs in **LP** are encoded by lambda terms fulfilling the following conditions:

(CON1) each subterm contains a free variable,
(CON2) each lambda abstractor binds a variable free in its scope,
(CON3) each lambda abstractor binds at most one occurrence of a variable in its scope.

This fragment of the lambda language is expressible enough to provide such fundamental semantic transformations, as Type Raising and Composition, and their variants given by monotonicity rules (M1), (M2). It is closed under lambda conversion, and consequently, strong normalization holds for both **LP** and the restricted lambda calculus. Observe that, for **LP**, the β-step of proof normalization yields a string of assumptions Γ' which differs from the original string Γ at most in the order of formulas.

If we reject (CON1), then the resulting lambda language corresponds to **LP1**. Rejecting (CON2) introduces Thinning, and rejecting (CON3) introduces Contraction. Thus, varying the above structural constraints and the corresponding structural rules we obtain several conditional logics, including **LP**, BCI, BCK, BCIW and others, related to appropriate fragments of the lambda calculus by the Curry–Howard correspondence (see Buszkowski, 1987a). Each of these systems admits strong normalization.

Notice that term (3) which exemplifies the role of *and* as a predicate conjunction does not obey (CON3). So, Contraction is needed for Booleans acting on types different from **t**, which provides a semantic justification for systems stronger than **LP**. However, a free usage of Contraction would have unpleasant consequences, witness the above remark on transitive verbs acting as intransitive verbs. It follows that Contraction should be admitted for some but not all grammatical constructions. That is the leitmotive of multimodal systems proposed in (Moortgat, 1995; Moortgat and Oehrle, 1994). The unique concatenation which underlies both standard syntactic structures and logical sequents discussed above splits into several different concatenation modes, each of them being governed by a different logic (see Moortgat's chapter for details).

Clearly, not only Contraction and Thinning but also Permutation is not plausible for semantic description. Since (P) is admissible in **LP**, it overgenerates syntactic structures: if a string of words can be given a semantic structure $t : A$, then also every permutation of this string can be given a structure of type A. Further, due to (P$'$) whose lambda representation is:

$$\lambda x_B . \lambda y_A . ((z_{A\to(B\to C)} y_A) x_B),$$

each binary relation (type $\mathbf{e} \to (\mathbf{e} \to \mathbf{t})$ can be transformed into its converse. So, *John loves Mary* admits the deviate reading *John is loved by Mary.* Thus, Permutation must be restricted as well. Accordingly, noncommutative systems, considered in Sections 2 and 3, are of some significance for semantics. In (Buszkowski, 1987a, 1988a), the lambda language adequate for systems with two conditionals $\to$ and $\leftarrow$ has been proposed: two lambda abstractors $\lambda^{\to}$ and $\lambda_{\leftarrow}$ correspond to types $A \to B$ and $B \leftarrow A$ (precisely, either of the clauses (TER2) and (TER3) splits in two clauses, one for $\to$ and one for $\leftarrow$; details are left to the reader). ND-proofs in **L** are represented by those terms of the bidirectional lambda language which satisfy (CON1) and the following analogue of (CON2) and (CON3): each $\lambda^{\to}$ (resp. $\lambda^{\leftarrow}$) binds precisely the left-most (resp. right-most) occurrence of a free variable in its scope. The Curry–Howard correspondence and normalization for bidirectional systems have been studied in (Wansing, 1992). For **L**, **L1**, β-steps of proof normalization yield the outcome string Γ' equal to the input string Γ.

4.3. *Fine aspects of semantics*

Van Benthem (1986) finds a nice semantic application of normalization in **LP**. Each semantic structure of an expression is called *a reading* of this expression. Two readings s, t are said to be *equivalent*, if $s = t$ holds in the lambda calculus (then, s and t denote the same object under any assignment in all models of the calculus). The Van Benthem theorem is the following:

(T1) on the basis of **LP** and the corresponding fragment of the lambda calculus, each expression admits finitely many nonequivalent readings.

The key observation is that there are only finitely many (up to alphabetic variants) normal terms t which encode a proof of the sequent $\Gamma \vdash A$ in **LP**. Since every reading is equivalent to a normal reading, then (T1) is true. This theorem fails for systems with Contraction, but it holds for bidirectional systems **L**, **L1** etc.

Above, we have discussed semantic structures produced by ND-proofs. It is also reasonable to study similar questions for other kinds of logical systems. We shall consider Gentzen style systems and Hilbert style systems.

Semantic structures generated by Gentzen style systems connected with the Lambek calculus have been studied in (Moortgat, 1988) and (Hendriks, 1993). The architecture of Gentzen systems does not exactly agree with formation rules of lambda terms, hence interconnections are less obvious. For instance, the left introduction rule for $\to$:

$$(\mathrm{PL}\to)\ \frac{\Gamma, B, \Gamma' \vdash C;\ \Delta \vdash A}{\Gamma, A \to B, \Delta, \Gamma' \vdash C},$$

is reflected by the following substitution operation on terms:

$$\frac{s[x_B]: C;\ t: A}{s[(y_{A\to B}t)]: C},$$

and the rule (CUT) is reflected by:

$$\frac{s[x_A]:B;\ t:A}{s[t]:B}.$$

The right introduction rule (PI $\rightarrow$) corresponds to lambda abstraction. Starting from basic terms $x_A : A$, Gentzen style proofs generate terms according to the above operations. There arises a natural problem of *semantic equivalence* between Gentzen systems and ND-systems: do they generate the same semantic structures up to lambda conversion? This problem has been solved in positive in (Moortgat, 1988) and (Hendriks, 1993) for the Lambek calculus and its several variants:

(T2) Cut-free Gentzen proofs are semantically equivalent to ND-proofs.

The key idea is a semantic proof of the cut elimination theorem for both kinds of systems: semantic constructions given by cut-free proofs are closed under the construction corresponding to (CUT). Hendriks (1993) also considers the so called *spurious ambiguity problem*: do any two different proofs of the same sequent yield nonequivalent readings? He finds a special axiomatization of **L** in a Gentzen style form which possesses this property.

Hilbert-style systems admit a number of formulas as axioms and the only inference rule:

$$\text{(MP)}\ \frac{A \rightarrow B;\ A}{B}.$$

In the lambda calculus, that corresponds to fixing a number of closed terms (combinators) and generating other terms by application only, which is the framework of combinatory logic. Thus, the combinators:

$$\text{S}\ \lambda x.\lambda y.\lambda z.\,((xz)(yz)),\ \text{type: } (A \rightarrow (B \rightarrow C)) \rightarrow ((A \rightarrow B) \rightarrow (A \rightarrow C)),$$

$$\text{K}\ \lambda x.\lambda y.\,x,\ \text{type: } A \rightarrow (B \rightarrow A),$$

generate the full logic of positive implication, while the logic BCI is generated by the combinators:

$$\text{B}\ \lambda x.\lambda y.\lambda z.\,(x(yz)),\ \text{type: } (B \rightarrow C) \rightarrow ((A \rightarrow B) \rightarrow (A \rightarrow C)),$$

$$\text{C}\ \lambda x.\lambda y.\lambda z.\,((xz)y),\ \text{type: } (A \rightarrow (B \rightarrow C)) \rightarrow (B \rightarrow (A \rightarrow C)),$$

$$\text{I}\ \lambda x.\,x,\ \text{type: } A \rightarrow A.$$

Combinatory terms are formed out of combinators and variables (constants) by application ((TER2)). Representation of semantic structures in the form of combinatory terms is the approach of Combinatory Categorial Grammar (CCG), developed in (Steedman, 1988, 1993; Szabolcsi, 1983) and others, with origins in (Curry, 1961) and (Shaumyan, 1977).

Clearly, combinatory terms encode Hilbert style proofs, hence Hilbert systems are proper deductive systems of CCG.

Combinators are closed terms (they do not obey (CON1)), and consequently, the corresponding logics admit sequents with empty antecedents. For logics restricted to sequents with nonempty antecedents, as, e.g., **L** and **LP**, Hilbert style forms must be modified. Axioms are replaced with unary consequence patterns, and combinators are replaced with terms containing a free variable. For instance, the axiomatic base for **LP** is given by:

$$\mathrm{B}x\ \lambda y.\lambda z.(x(yz)),\ \text{pattern: } B \to C \vdash (A \to B) \to (A \to C),$$

$$\mathrm{C}x\ \lambda y.\lambda z.((xz)y),\ \text{pattern: } A \to (B \to C) \vdash B \to (A \to C),$$

$$\mathrm{I}x\ x,\ \text{pattern: } A \to A$$

together with all patterns arising from the above by monotonicity rules (M1) and (M2) (for $\to$ only). These rules correspond to the following operations on terms:

$$\text{(M1)}\ \frac{s[x_A]:B}{\lambda y_C \cdot s[(z_{C\to A}y_C)]:C \to B},$$

$$\text{(M2)}\ \frac{s[x_A]:B}{\lambda x_A \cdot (y_{B\to C}s[x_A]):A \to C}.$$

We also need (CUT) (substitution on terms) and (MP); in the presence of (CUT), (MP) can be accomplished by the single pattern $A \to B, A \vdash B$, represented by the term $(x_{A\to B}y_A):B$. Accordingly, the construction of terms which represent Hilbert proofs is more complicated than for the case of standard Hilbert systems; not only application but also substitution and some forms of lambda abstraction are involved. Lambda abstraction cannot be eliminated, since rules (M1), (M2) cannot be replaced by any finite set of additional axiomatic consequence patterns. The latter fact is the content of the following theorem:

(T3) neither **L**, nor **LP** can be axiomatized by any finite number of consequence patterns with (CUT) as the only inference rule.

The proof of (T3) for **L** is in (Zielonka, 1981) and for **LP** in (Buszkowski, 1987a). This theorem has some direct significance for linguistics. Many authors considered categorial grammars whose deductive system was an axiomatic extension of the Ajdukiewicz calculus: for instance, one used (MP), (SYL), (AS) or other combinations. It follows from (T3) that none of these systems is deductively equivalent to **L** or **LP**.

On the other hand, the infinite Hilbert axiomatization of **LP**, presented above, is semantically equivalent to its ND-form. To prove that the Hilbert form of **LP** is deductively equivalent to its ND-form it suffices to show that the latter is closed under the rule (PI $\to$) (with only one assumption dropped). Clearly, that is a kind of *the deduction theorem* for the Hilbert system: to prove the conditional $A \to B$ one may prove B from the hypothesis A. As emphasized in (Lambek, 1993), the deduction theorem for Hilbert systems is the same as *the combinatory completeness* of the corresponding system of terms: for every term $t:B$ in the system with free variables $x_A, y_1, \ldots, y_n$, the system also contains a term $t:A \to B$ with free variables $y_1, \ldots, y_n$ such that $(tx_A) = s$ (by lambda conversion). In the language of proofs, if s is a proof of B from the assumption A (and possibly others), then there exists a proof t of $A \to B$ (from the other assumptions) such that the proof (tx_A) of B is semantically equivalent to s. One can show that systems of terms generated by Hilbert forms of **LP**, **LP1** (i.e. BCI), **LP1** with Contraction (i.e. BCIW), and so on, are combinatorily complete, and consequently, Hilbert forms are semantically equivalent to ND-forms (they provide the same semantic structures up to lambda conversion). Let us stress that combinatory completeness is needed to establish the semantic equivalence between a Hilbert system and an ND-system, that means, the equivalence of proofs in both systems, while to show merely the deductive equivalence, that means, the equivalence of consequence patterns derivable in both systems, one only needs the deduction theorem. In practice, proofs of the latter usually give a hint for the proof of combinatory completeness.

To exemplify the above, we prove the combinatory completeness of BCI, and precisely, of the system of combinatory terms formed out of combinators B, C and I and variables by application only. Let $s:B$ be a combinatory term (in the system) which contains exactly one occurrence of $x:A$. We construct a combinatory term $t:A \to B$ in which x is not free and such that $(tx) = s$ (so, $t = \lambda x{\cdot}s$). If s is x, then t is combinator I. Consider s equal $(s's'')$. If x occurs in s' (hence not in s''), then we construct an appropriate term t' for s' and define t as the term $((\mathrm{C}t')s'')$. Then:

$$(((\mathrm{C}t')s'')x) = ((t'x)s'') = (s's'').$$

If x occurs in s'' (hence not in s'), then we construct an appropriate term t'' for s'' and define t as the term $((\mathrm{B}s')t'')$. Then:

$$(((\mathrm{B}s')t'')x) = (s'(t''x)) = (s's'').$$

For other systems we proceed in a similar way (caution: for systems obeying (CON1), one cannot freely use combinators).

At the end, we mention further problems, not discussed here in detail. Grammars based on systems with more logical constants require an extended lambda calculus for semantic description (see Lambek and Scott, 1985; Girard with Taylor and Lafont, 1989; Troelstra, 1992). Polymorphic types with quantifiers $\forall XA$, $\exists XA$ are treated in the second order lambda calculus. Van Benthem (1991) considers the lambda calculus with Booleans, suitable for a simple treatment of Boolean connectives acting on different categories. Standard models can be generalized to Cartesian closed categories which are the most flexible format for type theoretic semantics (see Lambek, 1988). The quoted book by Van Benthem is the best reference to these issues from the point of view of linguistics.

Semantic structures considered here account for the construction of denotations of complex expressions from denotations of lexical items. Logical properties of these structures, in particular: their role in valid inferences, strongly depend on the peculiar denotations of lexical items. There are possible more sophisticated approaches in which certain especially relevant properties of lexical denotations are exhibited in semantic structures.

Sánchez Valenzia (1991) enriches **LP** with monotonicity marking. For instance, the determiner *every* is assigned type $\mathrm{N}^- \to (\mathrm{VP}^+ \to \mathbf{t})$, and the determiner *some* is assigned type $\mathrm{N}^+ \to (\mathrm{VP}^+ \to \mathbf{t})$, which means that the former is downward monotone in the first argument and upward monotone in the second argument, while the latter is upward monotone in both arguments. There are also provided rules for the propagation of monotonicity markers along deduction trees in **LP**, which enable one to deduce the status of a complex expression as a negative or positive expression. Dowty (1994) extends this framework to a general theory of negative polarity and concord marking in semantic description.

5. Proof theory and algebraic models

5.1. Residuated algebras and Kripke frames

In Section 3 we have discussed some algebras connected with syntactic structures determined by proofs in the deductive part of grammars. Here we consider algebraic models of deductive systems underlying grammars. Algebraic models of logical systems are a traditional domain of metalogic. Substructural logics relevant to the theory of grammar give rise to special algebraic structures: residuated algebras.

Recall that *a groupoid* is a pair $(M, \circ)$ such that M is a nonempty set, and $\circ$ is a binary operation on M. *A residuated groupoid* is a structure $(M, \circ, \Rightarrow, \Leftarrow, \leqslant)$ such that $(M, \circ)$ is a groupoid, $\leqslant$ is a partial ordering on M, and $\Rightarrow, \Leftarrow$ are binary operations on M which fulfill the equivalences:

$$\text{(RG)}\ a \leqslant c \Leftarrow b \text{ iff } a \circ b \leqslant c \text{ iff } b \leqslant a \Rightarrow c,$$

for all $a, b, c \in M$. If $(M, \circ)$ is a semigroup (i.e. $\circ$ is associative), then the above structure is called *a residuated semigroup*.

Residuated groupoids and semigroups are naturally related to sequential deductive systems, discussed above. The operation $\circ$ corresponds to the grouping of formulas in a string, and $\Rightarrow, \Leftarrow$ correspond to conditionals $\to$ and $\leftarrow$. Observe the obvious parallelism between the equivalences (RG) and inference rules:

$$\frac{\Gamma, B \vdash C}{\Gamma \vdash C \leftarrow B}, \qquad \frac{\Gamma \vdash C \leftarrow B}{\Gamma, B \vdash C},$$

$$\frac{A, \Gamma \vdash C}{\Gamma \vdash A \to C}, \qquad \frac{\Gamma \vdash A \to C}{\Gamma, A \vdash C}.$$

These rules are derivable in the Nonassociative Lambek Calculus; left rules are simply (I$\leftarrow$) and (I$\to$), while right rules are derivable by, say, (E$\leftarrow$), (E$\to$) and (Id) (in the nonassociative system, Γ is a bracketed string of formulas, and Γ, B, A, Γ denote the bracketed concatenation). In the presence of (Id) and (CUT), the above rules are equivalent to (I $\leftarrow$), (I $\rightarrow$), (E $\leftarrow$) and (E $\rightarrow$). Clearly, (CUT) is algebraically interpreted as the monotonicity of $\circ$:

(M$\circ$) if $a \leqslant b$, then $c \circ a \leqslant c \circ b$ and $a \circ c \leqslant b \circ c$

which is true in every residuated groupoid.

By *a model* we mean a pair $(\mathcal{M}, \alpha)$ such that $\mathcal{M}$ is a residuated groupoid (with universe M) and α is an assignment of formulas (with $\circ, \rightarrow, \leftarrow$) in M, satisfying the conditions:

(1) $\alpha(A \circ B) = \alpha(A) \circ \alpha(B)$,

(2) $\alpha(A \rightarrow B) = \alpha(A) \Rightarrow \alpha(B)$,

(3) $\alpha(B \leftarrow A) = \alpha(B) \Leftarrow \alpha(A)$.

Clearly, α is uniquely determined by its values for atomic formulas. For bracketed strings Γ, the value $\alpha(\Gamma)$ is defined by the recursive clause:

$$\alpha(\Gamma, \Delta) = \alpha(\Gamma) \circ \alpha(\Delta).$$

The sequent $\Gamma \vdash A$ is said to be *true* in the model $(\mathcal{M}, \alpha)$ if $\alpha(\Gamma) \leqslant \alpha(A)$. If one admits sequents with empty antecedent, then $\mathcal{M}$ is supposed to have the unit element 1 with $1 \circ a = a \circ 1 = a$, for all $a \in M$, and she stipulates $\alpha(\Lambda) = 1$. The sequent is said to be *valid* in the frame $\mathcal{M}$, if it is true in all models $(\mathcal{M}, \alpha)$.

Basic completeness theorems are the following:

(T1) Sequents derivable in the Nonassociative Lambek Calculus (resp. with empty antecedents) are precisely those which are valid in all residuated groupoids (resp. with the unit).

(T2) Sequents derivable in **L** (resp. **L1**) are precisely those which are valid in all residuated semigroups (resp. with the unit).

Soundness is easily proved by induction on derivations in the system. For the case of **L**, completeness follows from the fact that the Lindenbaum algebra of **L** is a residuated semigroup. Recall that the Lindenbaum algebra consists of equivalence classes of the relation:

$A \sim B$ iff both $A \vdash B$ and $B \vdash A$ are derivable in **L**,

and $\circ$, $\Rightarrow$, $\Leftarrow$ are standard quotient-operations corresponding to operation symbols $\circ$, $\rightarrow$, $\leftarrow$. We also define:

$$[A] \leqslant [B] \quad \text{iff} \quad A \vdash B.$$

If we set $\alpha(A) = [A]$, for every formula A, then $\Gamma \vdash A$ is derivable in **L** if, and only if, $\alpha(\Gamma) \leqslant \alpha(A)$ holds true in the Lindenbaum algebra, which yields the completeness. For other systems, we proceed in a similar way (for **L1** and related systems, the unit must be added to the Lindenbaum algebra or the constant **1** must be added to the system with obvious axioms and rules).

Stronger systems, considered in this chapter, admit quite analogous algebraic models with additional assumptions on the underlying frame:

Permutation $a \circ b = b \circ a$,

Contraction $a \leqslant a \circ a$,

Thinning $a \circ b \leqslant a$.

For instance, **LP** is complete with respect to commutative residuated semigroups, BCI (i.e. **LP1**) is complete with respect to commutative residuated monoids, and BCIW is complete with respect to commutative residuated monoids fulfilling $a \leqslant a \circ a$, for all elements a. Notice that, in each case, the system in question is even strongly complete with respect to the corresponding class of models: if Φ is a set of additional axiomatic sequents, then $\Gamma \vdash A$ is derivable in the extended system (with (CUT)) if, and only if, $\Gamma \vdash A$ is true in all models in which all sequents from Φ are true.

If more than one concatenation mode is admitted, as in multi-modal systems of Moortgat (1995), then the appropriate algebraic frame is *a residuated algebra*: an abstract algebra $(M, \mathcal{F}, \leqslant)$ such that $\mathcal{F}$ is a set of operations on M, $\leqslant$ is a partial ordering on M, and for each n-ary operation $f \in \mathcal{F}$ there exist n-ary operations f/i, $i = 1, \ldots, n$, fulfilling the equivalence:

$$\text{(RA)}\ f(\vec{b}, a_i, \vec{c}) \leqslant a \quad \text{iff} \quad a_i \leqslant (f/i)(\vec{b}, a, \vec{c}),$$

where $\vec{b}$ is the string $a_1, \ldots, a_{i-1}$, and $\vec{c}$ is the string $a_{i+1}, \ldots, a_n$, for all $a_1, \ldots, a_n, a \in M$. Clearly, f/i is uniquely determined by f and is called the i-th residuation of f. If $\mathcal{F}$ consists of the only operation $\circ$, then we obtain a residuated groupoid with $\circ/1 = \Leftarrow$ and $\circ/2 = \Rightarrow$. Appropriate generalizations of the Lambek Calculus and various completeness theorems for them can be found in (Kołowska-Gawiejnowicz, 1995).

Residuated algebras are closely related to Kripke-style frames based on ternary relations (see Došen (1992), Dunn (1993)). In the tradition of modal logics, formulas are interpreted as subsets of a universe U, of possible worlds. We consider frames (U, R) such that R is a ternary relation on U. For sets $X, Y \subseteq U$, we define operations $\circ$, $\Rightarrow$, $\Leftarrow$, as follows:

$$\text{(K}\circ\text{)}\ X \circ Y = \{z \in U\colon\ (\exists x \in X)(\exists y \in Y)\, R(x, y, z)\},$$

$$\text{(K}\Rightarrow\text{)}\ X \Rightarrow Y = \{y \in U\colon\ (\forall x, z)(\text{if } x \in X \text{ and } R(x, y, z) \text{ then } z \in Y)\},$$

$$\text{(K}\Leftarrow\text{)}\ Y \Leftarrow X = \{y \in U\colon\ (\forall x, z)(\text{if } x \in X \text{ and } R(y, x, z) \text{ then } z \in Y)\}.$$

The structure $(P(U), \circ, \Rightarrow, \Leftarrow, \subseteq)$ is a residuated groupoid; Dunn (1993) calls it *the concrete residuated groupoid* over the frame (U, R). There are several ways to prove the completeness of the Nonassociative Lambek Calculus with respect to the class of concrete residuated groupoids. Soundness follows from (T1). For completeness, one can construct the canonical frame (U, R) such that U is the set of all formulas, and $R(A, B, C)$ holds, if, and only if, $C \vdash A \circ B$ is derivable. The canonical assignment:

$$\alpha(p) = \{A \in U\colon\ A \vdash p \text{ is derivable}\},$$

satisfies: $\alpha(\Gamma) \subseteq \alpha(B)$ iff $\Gamma \vdash B$ is derivable (see Kurtonina, 1995).

Another way applies the representation theorem:

(T3) each residuated groupoid is isomorphically embedable into a concrete residuated groupoid.

Dunn (1993) proves (T3) by methods similar to well known representation theorems for Boolean algebras, distributive lattices etc. Let $(M, \ldots)$ be a residuated groupoid. We define U as the set of upper cones on M, i.e. sets $\nabla \subseteq M$ such that, for all $x, y \in M$, if $x \in \nabla$ and $x \leqslant y$ then $y \in \nabla$. The relation R is defined by:

$$R(\nabla_1, \nabla_2, \nabla_3) \quad \text{iff} \quad (\forall x \in \nabla_1)(\forall y \in \nabla_2) x \circ y \in \nabla_3.$$

Then, the mapping $h(x) = \{\nabla \in U\colon\ x \in \nabla\}$ is a monomorphism of the residuated groupoid $(M, \ldots)$ into the concrete residuated groupoid over (U, R). Similar representation theorems hold for residuated semigroups, commutative residuated semigroups, residuated monoids etc. with respect to ternary frames obeying additional conditions on the relation R. Also, residuated algebras (of arbitrary signature) are embedable into concrete residuated algebras over frames $(U, \{R_t\}_{t \in T})$; precisely, the n-ary operation f_t of the algebra corresponds to the $n+1$-ary relation R_t in the frame.

Modeling substructural logics by ternary frames establishes a natural link with modal logics. In (Kurtonina, 1995), mutual connections between Lambek systems and modal logics are studied in detail, especially the resulting correspondence theory (properties of R expressible by Lambek sequents) and Salquist–van Benthem theorems on first-order translations of modal formulas.

5.2. *Powerset frames*

For linguistics, an especially significant class of frames are powerset frames. Let $(M, \cdot)$ be a groupoid. For $X, Y \subseteq M$, we define:

$$(\mathrm{P}\circ)\ X \circ Y = \{x \cdot y\colon\ x \in X,\ y \in Y\},$$

$$(\mathrm{P}\Rightarrow)\ X \Rightarrow Y = \{y \in M\colon\ (\forall x \in X)\, x \cdot y \in Y\},$$

$$(\mathrm{P}\Leftarrow)\ Y \Leftarrow X = \{y \in M\colon\ (\forall x \in X)\, y \cdot x \in Y\}.$$

The structure $(P(M), \circ, \Rightarrow, \Leftarrow, \subseteq)$ is a residuated groupoid; we call it *the powerset residuated groupoid* over the groupoid $(M, \cdot)$. Clearly, powerset frames are special concrete frames with $U = M$ and:

$$R(x, y, z) \quad \text{iff} \quad x \cdot y = z.$$

If $(M, \cdot)$ is a semigroup, commutative semigroup, monoid etc., then the powerset residuated groupoid over $(M, \cdot)$ is a residuated semigroup, residuated commutative semigroup, residuated monoid etc., respectively.

The standard linguistic interpretations of powerset frames are *language frames* (L-frames). The basic semigroup is the free semigroup $(V^+, \cdot)$, where $\cdot$ is the concatenation operation V^+ (i.e. the set of nonempty strings over the lexicon V). The powerset residuated semigroup $(P(V^+), \circ, \Rightarrow, \Leftarrow, \subseteq)$ consists of (Λ-free) languages over V. If the empty string is admitted, V^+ is to be replaced with $V^\star$ (i.e. the set of all strings over V), and the resulting powerset frame $(P(V^\star), \circ, \Rightarrow, \Leftarrow, \{\Lambda\}, \subseteq)$ is a residuated monoid (*the powerset residuated monoid* over the free monoid $(V^\star, \cdot)$).

More general frames are obtained by restriction the universe of strings. Let $U \subseteq V^+$ be nonempty. For $X, Y \subseteq U$, we define:

$$\text{(RP}\circ\text{)}\ X \circ Y = \{x \cdot y \in U\colon\ x \in X,\ y \in Y\},$$

$$\text{(RP}\Rightarrow\text{)}\ X \Rightarrow Y = \{y \in U\colon\ (\forall x \in X)(\text{if } x \cdot y \in U \text{ then } x \cdot y \in Y)\},$$

$$\text{(RP}\Leftarrow\text{)}\ Y \Leftarrow X = \{y \in U\colon\ (\forall x \in X)(\text{if } y \cdot x \in U \text{ then } y \cdot x \in Y)\}.$$

The frame $(P(U), \circ, \Rightarrow, \Leftarrow, \subseteq)$ is a residuated groupoid; it is called *the restricted L-frame* over the set $U \subseteq V^+$. If U fulfills the condition:

$$\text{if } x \cdot y \cdot z \in U \text{ then } (xy \in U \text{ iff } yz \in U),$$

for all $x, y, z \in U$, then $(P(U), \ldots)$ is a residuated semigroup. The latter condition holds true, if U is closed under concatenation or closed under nonempty subintervals. Restricted language frames can be regarded as powerset frames over special (non-free) groupoids or semigroups. We enrich U with a new element T, and we extend $\cdot$ to be defined on $U \cup \{T\}$ by setting: $x \cdot y = T$, if $x \cdot y \notin U$, for all $x, y \in U \cup \{T\}$. Then, the restricted language frame $(P(U), \ldots)$ is isomorphically embedable into the (unrestricted) powerset frame $(P(U \cup \{T\}), \ldots)$, by sending $X \subseteq U$ to $X \cup \{T\}$.

Powerset operations $\circ$, $\Rightarrow$, $\Leftarrow$ in the L-frame $P(V^+)$ are standard operations on languages: the language concatenation and the left and right residuations of languages. For languages $L, L' \subseteq V^+$, the left (resp. right) residual $L \Rightarrow L'$ (resp. $L' \Leftarrow L$) consists of left looking (resp. right looking) functors from L to L' in the sense of Lambek (1958). Mathematical linguistics beyond the world of Categorial Grammar more often uses duals of these operations:

$$L \Rightarrow_d L' = \{y \in V^+\colon\ (\exists x \in L)\, x \cdot y \in L'\},$$

$$L' \Leftarrow_d L = \{y \in V^+\colon\ (\exists x \in L)\, y \cdot x \in L'\}.$$

Clearly, $\Rightarrow_d$, $\Leftarrow_d$ can be defined from $\Rightarrow$, $\Leftarrow$:

$$L \Rightarrow_d L' = -(L \Rightarrow -L'), \qquad L' \Leftarrow_d L = -(-L' \Leftarrow L),$$

where $-L = V^+ \setminus L$ (i.e. the complement of L to V^+). Let us mention a recent result by Pratt (1991): the equational theory of regular expressions becomes finitely axiomatizable, after one has added residuals $\Rightarrow$, $\Leftarrow$ to Kleene operations $\circ$, $\cup$, $(\cdot)^*$ (without residuals, it is not finitely axiomatizable).

Restricted L-frames appear to give a more realistic description of functor categories in natural language. For a baby example, adjectives are assigned type VP$\Leftarrow$VP by semantic reasons, but that enforces us to accept their unlimited iteration in VPs, as, e.g., *smiles charmingly*, *smiles charmingly charmingly* etc., which is typical for formal languages. If U consists of all strings which contain no repetition of (adjoint) words, then the restricted L-frame $P(U)$ simply removes iterations from the universe of admissible expressions. This move resembles Chomsky's usage of *filtration principles* which repair overgeneration of the basic grammar (see Chomsky, 1982). A more thorough discussion of restricted L-frames and other negative constraints in Categorial Grammar can be found in (Buszkowski, 1995). We also note that restricted L-frames with finite U can be applied to prove the finite model property of certain substructural logics (see Buszkowski, 1997).

Typical completeness theorems concerning powerset frames are the following:

(T4) **L** (resp. **L1**) is strongly complete with respect to powerset residuated semigroups (resp. monoids) over arbitrary semigroups (resp. monoids) (the same for nonassociative systems with groupoids (resp. groupoids with unit) instead of semigroups (resp. monoids)),

(T5) the product-free **L** (resp. **L1**) is strongly complete with respect to L-frames over free semigroups (resp. monoids) (and similarly, for nonassociative systems),

(T6) **L** (resp. **L1**) is weakly complete with respect to L-frames over free semigroups (resp. monoids).

Theorem (T4) follows from (T1) and (T2) on the basis of the appropriate representation theorem:

(T7) each residuated semigroup (resp. groupoid, monoid) is isomorphically embeddable into a powerset residuated semigroup (resp. groupoid, monoid).

Interestingly, (T7) cannot be proven in the standard way, applied in the proof of (T3) above. If $(M, \ldots)$ is a residuated groupoid, and U is the set of cones, then, for $\nabla_1, \nabla_2 \in U$, we define:

$$\nabla_1 \cdot \nabla_2 = \{z\colon\ (\exists x \in \nabla_1)(\exists y \in \nabla_2)\ x \circ y \leqslant z\}.$$

$(U, \cdot)$ is a groupoid (it is a semigroup, if $(M, \ldots)$ is a residuated semigroup). However, the mapping $h(x) = \{\nabla \in U\colon\ x \in \nabla\}$ is merely a monomorphism of the $\circ$-free part of $(M, \cdots)$ into the $\circ$-free part of the powerset frame $(P(U), \ldots)$. For $\circ$, we only have the inclusion $h(x) \circ h(y) \subseteq h(x \circ y)$.

A proof of (T4) and (T7) was given in (Buszkowski, 1986a) with applying proof theoretic techniques. One applies an LDS with formulas $t\colon A$ whose intended meaning is: in the powerset model $(P(M), \alpha)$, the element $t \in M$ belongs to the set $\alpha(A) \subseteq M$. The labels t are recursively defined as follows:

(1) all formulas are labels,

(2) if s, t are labels, then st is a label,

(3) if s is a label, and A, B are formulas, then $(s, 1, A \circ B)$ and $(s, 2, A \circ B)$ are labels.

We say that label s *reduces to* label t, if t arises from s by a finite number of reduction steps, each of them replacing a *redex* $(u, 1, A \circ B)(u, 2, A \circ B)$ by its *contractum* u. The Church–Rosser property holds for this notion of reduction, and consequently, every label s reduces to a unique irreducible label $s^\star$. Intuitively, if s reduces to t, then s and t represent the same element of M.

The LDS admits the following axioms and rules (of labeled introduction and elimination of logical constants):

(LId) $A : A$,

(LI$\circ$) $\dfrac{s : A;\ t : B}{st : A \circ B}$,

(LE$\circ$) $\dfrac{s : A \circ B}{(s, 1, A \circ B) : A}$, $\dfrac{s : A \circ B}{(s, 2, A \circ B) : B}$,

(LI$\Rightarrow$) $\dfrac{sA : B}{s : A \to B}$, (LE$\Rightarrow$) $\dfrac{s : A;\ t : A \to B}{st : B}$,

(LI$\Leftarrow$) $\dfrac{As : B}{s : B \leftarrow A}$, (LE$\Leftarrow$) $\dfrac{s : B \leftarrow A;\ t : A}{st : B}$,

together with the additional rule for reduction:

(R) $\dfrac{s : A}{t : A}$, if s reduces to t.

Further, if Φ is a set of sequents of the form $A \vdash B$, then each sequent from Φ gives rise to the corresponding rule:

(RΦ) $\dfrac{s : A}{t : B}$.

One proves that this LDS is a conservative extension of $\mathbf{L} : A \vdash B$ is derivable in $\mathbf{L}$ if, and only if, $A : B$ is derivable in the LDS, and similarly for extensions of $\mathbf{L}$ by a set Φ, of new axioms. One constructs a canonical model $(P(M), \alpha)$, as follows. The set M consists of all irreducible labels (it contains all formulas of $\mathbf{L}$). For $s, t \in M$, we set $s \cdot t = (st)^\star$ (i.e. the unique irreducible term which st reduces to). Then, $(M, \cdot)$ is a semigroup. We consider the powerset frame $P(M)$ and the canonical assignment:

$$\alpha(p) = \{t \in M \colon\ t : p \text{ is derivable in the LDS}\}.$$

One proves:

$$\alpha(A) = \{t \in M\colon\ t\colon A \text{ is derivable in the LDS}\},$$

for all formulas A of **L** (induction on A; for $A = B \circ C$, rules (LE$\circ$) are needed to show that, if $s \in \alpha(B \circ C)$, then $s = s_1 \cdot s_2$, for some $s_1 \in \alpha(B)$ and $s_2 \in \alpha(C)$, which is the key reason for employing the LDS instead of **L**, since **L** admits no analogue of (LE$\circ$)).

Using (RΦ), one easily shows that $(P(M), \alpha)$ is a model for Φ. Further, it satisfies the canonical equivalence: $\Gamma \vdash A$ is true in $(P(M), \alpha)$ if, and only if, $\Gamma \vdash A$ is derivable in **L** enriched by new axioms from Φ. Accordingly, if $\Gamma \vdash A$ is not derivable, then it is not true in some powerset model for Φ, which directly yields (T4). To prove (T7), we fix a residuated semigroup $\mathcal{A} = (A, \circ, \Rightarrow, \Leftarrow, \leqslant)$. We assume there is a one-to-one mapping which to any $a \in A$ assigns an atomic formula p_a, and all atomic formulas are of this form. An assignment μ is given by $\mu(p_a) = a$. Let Φ consist of all sequents $A \vdash B$ such that $\mu(A) \leqslant \mu(B)$. We consider the canonical model $(P(M), \alpha)$, constructed above, for **L** enriched by Φ and define a mapping $h\colon A \mapsto P(M)$, by setting $h(a) = \alpha(p_a)$, for all $a \in A$. One easily checks that h is a monomorphism from $\mathcal{A}$ to the powerset residuated semigroup $P(M)$. Analogous constructions can be performed for other kinds of substructural logics and powerset frames, and Kołowska-Gawiejnowicz (1995) discusses the general case of abstract algebras.

Results like (T5) can be obtained with the aid of simple canonical frames of the following form. Let $(M, \cdot)$ be the free semigroup of all nonempty finite strings of formulas (without product). In the powerset frame $P(M)$, the canonical assignment α is defined by: $\alpha(p)$ equals the set of all strings $\Gamma \in M$ such that $\Gamma \vdash p$ is derivable in **L** enriched by Φ (i.e. a set of product-free sequents). Then, the same equality holds for any formula A (without product) substituted for p. Consequently $(P(M), \alpha)$ satisfies the canonical equivalence above, which yields the strong completeness of the product-free **L** with respect to powerset frames over free semigroups. Similar arguments can be provided for **L1**, **LP** and other systems (see Buszkowski, 1982a, 1986a; Van Benthem, 1988a). (T6) requires much more sophistication, since canonical models of the latter form do not satisfy the canonical equivalence, if product is admitted in formulas. Actually, **L** is not strongly complete with respect to L-frames, and consequently, it is not true that each residuated semigroup is embedable into an L-frame. A pretty complicated proof of (T6) has been given in (Pentus, 1993b) who approximates a powerset model by means of partial models, closely related to restricted L-frames, discussed above.

5.3. *Gentzen-style Labeled Deductive Systems*

Labeled Deductive Systems for Lambek-style calculi (also with modal operators) are extensively studied in (Kurtonina, 1995). While the LDS for **L**, described above, uses Natural Deduction rules of introduction and elimination of logical constants, Kurtonina's systems follow the format of Gentzen calculi with left and right introduction rules. We present a system $\mathbf{NL}^l$ (the labeled Nonassociative Lambek Calculus), which is a modified version of Kurtonina's system related to ternary frames. Labels are labeled trees, represented as formal terms, defined by the following recursion:

1) atomic labels are labels,

2) if a is an atomic label, and s, t are labels, then $r(a, s, t)$ is a label.

We think of $r(a, s, t)$ as a tree whose root is labeled by a and s, t are the two subtrees raising from the root. The sequents of $\mathbf{NL}^l$ are labeled sequents of the form:

$$a_1 : A_1, \ldots, a_n : A_n \vdash t : A,$$

where $a_1, \ldots, a_n$ are atomic labels, and t is a label whose leaves are labeled by $a_i's$ (in the order indicated by the antecedent), and all internal atomic labels are pairwise distinct and different from $a_i's$, and $A_1, \ldots, A_n, A$ are formulas (of **L**). Intuitively, t represents a composition of expressions $a_1, \ldots, a_n$ of type $A_1, \ldots, A_n$, respectively, which yields the complex expression of type A. The axioms and inference rules of $\mathbf{NL}^l$ are:

(Id) $a : A \vdash a : A$,

$$(\mathrm{L}\rightarrow)\ \frac{X_1, c : B, X_2 \vdash s : C;\ Y \vdash t : A}{X_1, Y, a : A \rightarrow B, X_2 \vdash s[r(c, t, a)/c] : C},$$

$$(\mathrm{R}\leftarrow)\ \frac{b : A, X \vdash r(c, b, t) : B}{X \vdash t : A},$$

$$(\mathrm{L}\leftarrow)\ \frac{X_1, c : B, X_2 \vdash s : C;\ Y \vdash t : A}{X_1, a : B \leftarrow A, Y, X_2 \vdash s[r(c, a, t)/c] : C},$$

$$(\mathrm{R}\leftarrow)\ \frac{X, b : A \vdash r(c, t, b) : B}{X \vdash t : B \leftarrow A},$$

$$(\mathrm{L}\circ)\ \frac{X_1, a : A, b : B, X_2 \vdash s : C}{X_1, c : A \circ B, X_2 \vdash s[c/r(c, a, b)] : C},$$

$$(\mathrm{R}\circ)\ \frac{X \vdash s : A;\ Y \vdash t : B}{X, Y \vdash r(a, s, t) : A \circ B}.$$

Here, X, Y (also with subscripts) stand for finite strings of labeled formulas $a : A$. In (L$\rightarrow$), c does not occur in the right premise, a does not occur in premises, and $s[r(c, t, a)/c]$ denotes the substitution of $r(c, t, a)$ for c in s, and dually for (L$\leftarrow$). In (R$\rightarrow$), b occurs neither in X, nor in t, and X is nonempty, and similarly for (R$\leftarrow$). In (L$\circ$), $r(c, a, b)$ occurs in s, and $s[c/r(c, a, b)]$ denotes the substitution of c for $r(c, a, b)$ in s. In (R$\circ$), a does not occur in the premise.

It is easy to show that, if $X \vdash s : A$ is derivable in $\mathbf{NL}^l$, then all atomic labels in X are distinct. Further, the tree structure of s can be transferred to X: replace a_i with A_i, and drop the labels of internal nodes. Thus, each derivation in $\mathbf{NL}^l$ determines a derivation in the Nonassociative Lambek Calculus in the following Gentzen style form (given in (Lambek, 1961)):

(Id) $A \vdash A$,

$$(\mathrm{L}\rightarrow)\ \frac{\Gamma[B] \vdash C;\ \Delta \vdash A}{\Gamma[[\Delta, A \rightarrow B]] \vdash C}, \qquad (\mathrm{R}\leftarrow)\ \frac{[A, \Gamma] \vdash B}{\Gamma \vdash A \rightarrow B},$$

$$(\mathrm{L}\circ)\ \frac{\Gamma[[A, B]] \vdash C}{\Gamma[A \circ B] \vdash C}, \qquad (\mathrm{R}\circ)\ \frac{\Gamma \vdash A;\ \Delta \vdash B}{[\Gamma, \Delta] \vdash A \circ B},$$

and rules (L$\leftarrow$), (R$\leftarrow$) dual to (L$\rightarrow$), (R$\rightarrow$). Here, the antecedents of sequents are bracketed strings of formulas, as in the Natural Deduction system, discussed in Section 3. Conversely, if $\Gamma \vdash A$ is derivable in the above system, and $A_1, \ldots, A_n$ is the yield of Γ, then, for some labels $a_1, \ldots, a_n, t$, the labeled sequent $a_1 : A_1, \ldots, a_n : A_n \vdash t : A$ is derivable in $\mathbf{NL}^l$. Consequently, $\mathbf{NL}^l$ is equivalent to the Nonassociative Lambek Calculus, in a sense.

Kurtonina (1995) uses $\mathbf{NL}^l$ (actually, a slightly different system) to provide an alternative proof of the completeness of the Nonassociative Lambek Calculus with respect to concrete residuated groupoids (ternary frames). Her idea is to take a nonderivable labeled sequent $X \vdash t : A$, and to mark all antecedent formulas $a_i : A_i$ by T (the truth) and the formula $c : A$ (c is the root of t) by F (the falsity). The term t determines an initial ternary relation R which consists of all triples (a, b, c) such that $r(a, s_1, s_2)$ appears in t, for some labels s_1, s_2 with roots b, c, respectively. By affixing Henkin witnesses, the initial T–F set of formulas is extended to a complete T–F set with respect to a larger relation R', and the latter determine a model which verifies all $a_i : A_i$ but falsifies $c : A$, while $c : A$ should be true, if $A_1, \ldots, A_n \vdash A$ were satisfied by the model. The method can easily be generalized for multi-modal systems in the sense of Moortgat (1995): one uses different relation symbols r_i for different relations R_i representing different composition modes. Similar results for other substructural logics have been obtained by d'Agostino and Gabbay (1994).

From the linguistic point of view, the interesting property of $\mathbf{NL}^l$ is that the system provides a parsing procedure for grammars based on Lambek style calculi. If $a_1, \ldots, a_n$ are lexical atoms, assigned types $A_1, \ldots, A_n$, respectively, and $a_1 : A_1, \ldots \vdash t : A$ is derivable in $\mathbf{NL}^l$, then t can be read as a parse tree for the string $a_1, \ldots, a_n$ assigned type A by the given derivation. This parsing procedure has been projected for deductive systems in the Gentzen style form, but it can be adjusted to ND-systems and other logical formalisms (also see Moortgat's chapter).

Dynamic logic interprets operation symbols $\circ, \rightarrow, \leftarrow$ as the composition, the weakest postspecification and the weakest prespecification, respectively, of programs (actions, procedures). In the extensional setting, programs are represented as binary relations $R \subseteq U \times U$, where U is a universe of states (thus, R is the relation between input states and output states, determined by the program). The operations are defined as follows:

(D$\circ$) $R \circ S = \{(a, b) : (\exists c)((a, c) \in R \wedge (c, b) \in S)\}$,

$$(\mathrm{D}\Rightarrow)\ R \Rightarrow S = \{(c,b) : (\forall a)(\text{if } (a,c) \in R \text{ then } (a,b) \in S)\},$$

$$(\mathrm{D}\Leftarrow)\ S \Leftarrow R = \{(a,c) : (\forall b)(\text{if } (c,b) \in R \text{ then } (a,b) \in S)\}.$$

One easily checks that $(P(U \times U), \circ, \Rightarrow, \Leftarrow, \subseteq)$ is a residuated monoid. Consequently, **L1** is sound with respect to relational frames of that kind (by (T2)). The completeness of **L1** with respect to relational frames has been proven in (Andréka and Mikulás, 1994) by a direct construction, and Kurtonina (1995) obtains this result with the aid of an appropriate Labeled Deductive System with sequents of the form:

$$(a_0, a_1) : A_1, (a_1, a_2) : A_2, \ldots, (a_{n-1}, a_n) : A_n \vdash (a_0, a_n) : A,$$

where $a_0, \ldots, a_n$ are pairwise distinct labels. Systems like **L** require relativized frames $P(T)$ such that $T \subseteq U \times U$ is a transitive relation, and in (D$\Rightarrow$) (resp. (D$\Leftarrow$)) one stipulates $(c,b) \in T$ (resp. $(a,c) \in T$). Pankrat'ev (1994) proves the completeness of **L** with respect to relativized relational frames with the aid of a Labeled Deductive System extending the LDS for powerset residuated semigroups, discussed above (the quoted paper by Andréka and Mikulás contains another proof). For linguistics, relational frames may be useful to model dynamic semantics for natural language in which expressions are interpreted as processors of information (see the chapter by Muskens, Van Benthem and Visser).

5.4. L-frames and grammars

Above, we have considered different algebraic frames corresponding to logical systems related to grammars with the emphasis on completeness and representation theorems and the application of LDSs. At the end of this section, we briefly discuss connections between L-frames and grammars.

Models based on L-frames (L-models) can be defined as indexed families of languages $L_A \subseteq V^+$, fulfilling the equalities:

$$L_{A \circ B} = L_A \circ L_B, \qquad L_{A \to B} = L_A \Rightarrow L_B, \qquad L_{B \leftarrow A} = L_B \Leftarrow L_A,$$

for all formulas A, B. On the other hand, for any grammar G and formula A, we define L_A^G = the set of all strings (of terminals) which are assigned type A by G. For CFGs, the only logical constant may be $\circ$ with inference rules (L$\circ$), (R$\circ$) and (CUT) and special axioms $A_1, \ldots, A_n \vdash B$. Then, the equality:

$$L_{A \circ B}^G = L_A^G \circ L_B^G,$$

holds true, which means that the hierarchy L_A^G agrees with the interpretation of $\circ$ in L-frames. Further, the family L_A^G is the least solution of the postulates expressed by special axioms ($\vdash$ is interpreted as set inclusion), that means, we have $L_A^G \subseteq L_A$, for any family L_A satisfying these postulates.

Grammars essentially involving conditionals, especially categorial grammars, are not so directly compatible with L-frames. The equalities:

$$L^G_{A\to B} = L^G_A \Rightarrow L^G_B, \qquad L^G_{B\leftarrow A} = L^G_B \Leftarrow L^G_A,$$

do not hold, in general, if even G is based on a system complete with respect to L-frames, as, e.g., **L**. Consequently, the hierarchy L^G_A can be incompatible with any L-frame. Thus, for a grammar G, it is reasonable to define an L-model L^A_G as the unique L-model determined by the initial condition $L^p_G = L^G_p$, for all atomic formulas p. The grammar G is said to be *correct*, if $L^G_A \subseteq L^A_G$, for every formula A, and *complete* in the set F, of formulas, if $L^G_A = L^A_G$, for all $A \in F$. If the deductive part of G is sound with respect to L-frames, then G is correct if, and only if, $v \in L^A_G$, for any lexical atom v such that $v : A$ is a lexical assumption of G. Further, if G is complete in the set of formulas appearing in lexical assumptions, then G is correct.

In (Buszkowski, 1982a) it has been shown that not every LCG is correct, and no LCG is complete in the set of all formulas. That also holds for weaker systems, as, e.g., BCGs, and similar results can be obtained for grammars based on **L1**, **LP** etc. with respect to appropriate frames. Consequently, grammars provide a merely approximate description of L-models. Interestingly, for LCGs, the following equivalence holds true: G is correct if, and only if, the family L^G_p, for atomic p, is the least solution of lexical assumptions of G. Further, by affixing new words to the lexicon, each LCG can be expanded to a correct LCG, and the expansion is conservative, that means, expressions over the old lexicon are assigned no new types.

References

Aarts, E. (1994), *Proving theorems of the Lambek calculus of order* 2 *in polynomial time*, Stud. Logica **53**, 373–387.

Aarts, E. (1995), *Investigations in logic, language and computation*, PhD Thesis, University of Utrecht.

Aarts, E. and Trautwein, K. (1996), *Non-associative Lambek categorial grammar in polynomial time*, Math. Logic Q. **42**, to appear.

Abrusci, M., Casadio, C. and Moortgat, M. (eds) (1994), *Linear logic and Lambek calculus*, Proc. 1st Rome Workshop 1993, OTS/DYANA, Utrecht, Amsterdam.

Ajdukiewicz, K. (1935), *Die syntaktische Konnexität*, Stud. Philos. **1**, 1–27.

Andréka, H. and Mikulás, S. (1994), *Lambek calculus and its relational semantics*, J. Logic, Lang., Inform. **3**, 1–38.

Bar-Hillel, Y. (1953), *A quasi-arithmetical notation for syntactic description*, Language **29**, 47–58.

Bar-Hillel, Y., Gaifman, C. and Shamir, E. (1960), *On categorial and phrase structure grammars*, Bull. Res. Counc. Israel **F 9**, 155–166.

Barwise, J. and Perry, J. (1983), *Situations and Attitudes*, Bradford Books, Cambridge, MA.

Buszkowski, W. (1982a), *Compatibility of a categorial grammar with an associated category system*, Z. Math. Logik Grundlag. Math. **28**, 229–238.

Buszkowski, W. (1982b), *Some decision problems in the theory of syntactic categories*, Z. Math. Logik Grundlag. Math. **28**, 539–548.

Buszkowski, W. (1985), *The equivalence of unidirectional Lambek categorial grammars and context-free grammars*, Z. Math. Logik Grundlag. Math. **31**, 369–384.

Buszkowski, W. (1986a), *Completeness results for Lambek syntactic calculus*, Z. Math. Logik Grundlag. Math. **32**, 13–28.

Buszkowski, W. (1986b), *Typed functorial languages*, Bull. Polish Acad. Sci. Math. **34**, 495–505.

Buszkowski, W. (1986c), *Generative capacity of nonassociative Lambek calculus*, Bull. Polish Acad. Sci. Math. **34**, 507–516.

Buszkowski, W. (1987a), *The logic of types*, Initiatives in Logic, J.T. Srzednicki, ed., Nijhoff, Dordrecht.

Buszkowski, W. (1987b), *Discovery procedures for categorial grammars*, Categories, Polymorphism and Unification, Klein and Van Benthem, eds, University of Amsterdam.

Buszkowski, W. (1987c), *Solvable problems for classical categorial grammars*, Bull. Polish Acad. Sci. Math. **35**, 373–382.

Buszkowski, W. (1988a), *Generative power of categorial grammars*, Categorical Grammars and Natural Language Structures, R.T. Oehrle, E. Bach and D. Wheeler, eds, Reidel, Dordrecht.

Buszkowski, W. (1988b), *Gaifman's theorem on categorial grammars revisited*, Stud. Logica **47**, 23–33.

Buszkowski, W. (1995), *Categorial grammars with negative information*, Negation. A Notion in Focus, H. Wansing, ed., Gruyter, Berlin/New York.

Buszkowski, W. (1996), *Extending Lambek grammars to basic categorial grammars*, Proof Theory and Natural Language, D. Gabbay and R. Kempson, eds, J. Logic, Lang., Inform. (special issue).

Buszkowski, W. (1997), *The finite model property for BCI and related systems*, Stud. Logica, to appear.

Buszkowski, W., Marciszewski, W. and Van Benthem, J. (eds) (1988), *Categorial Grammar*, Benjamin, Amsterdam.

Buszkowski, W. and Penn, G. (1990), *Categorial grammars determined from linguistic data by unification*, Stud. Logica **49**, 431–454.

Chomsky, N. (1982), *Concepts and Consequences of the Theory of Government and Binding*, MIT Press, Cambridge, MA.

Cohen, J.M. (1967), *The equivalence of two concepts of categorial grammar*, Inform. and Control **10**, 475–484.

Colmerauer, A. (1978), *Metamorphosis grammars*, Natural Language Communication with Computers, L. Bolc, ed., Springer, Berlin.

Cresswell, M.J. (1973), *Logics and Languages*, Methuen, London.

Curry, H.B. (1961), *Some logical aspects of grammatical structure*, Structure of Language and Its Mathematical Aspects, R. Jakobson, ed., AMS, Providence, RI.

D'Agostino, M. and Gabbay, D. (1994), *A generalization of analytic deduction via labelled deductive systems I: Basic substructural logics*, J. Automat. Reason., to appear.

Došen, K. (1988–89), *Sequent systems and groupoid models*, Stud. Logica **47**, 353–385; **48**, 41–65.

Došen, K. (1992), *A brief survey of frames for the Lambek calculus*, Z. Math. Logik Grundlag. Math. **38**, 179–187.

Došen, K. and Schröder-Heister, P. (eds) (1993), *Substructural Logics*, Oxford Univ. Press, Oxford.

Dowty, D. (1994), *The role of negative polarity and concord marking in natural language reasoning*, Proc. Semantics and Linguistic Theory IV, M. Harvey and L. Santelmann, eds, Cornell University, Ithaca.

Dowty, D., Wall, R. and Peters, S. (1981), *Introduction to Montague Semantics*, Reidel, Dordrecht.

Dunn, J.M. (1991), *Gaggle theory: An abstraction of Galois connections and residuation, with applications to negation, implication and various logical operators*, Logics in AI, J. van Eijck, ed., Springer, Berlin.

Dunn, J.M. (1993), *Partial gaggles applied to logics with restricted structural rules*, Substructural Logics, K. Došen and P. Schröder-Heister, eds.

Emms, M. (1993), *Extraction covering extensions of Lambek calculus are not CF*, Proc. 9th Amsterdam Colloquium, 269–286.

Emms, M. and Leiss, H. (1993), *The Cut-elimination theorem for the second-order Lambek calculus*, DYANA-2 Research Report, Amsterdam.

Friedman, J., Dai, D. and Wang, W. (1986), *The weak generative capacity of parenthesis-free categorial grammars*, Boston University Technical Report.

Gabbay, D. (1991), *Labelled Deductive Systems I*, CIS München, Munich.

Gabbay, D. (1993), *A general theory of structured consequence relations*, Substructural Logics, K. Došen and P. Schröder-Heister, eds.

Gamut, L.T.F. (1991), *Logic, Language, and Meaning*, Univ. of Chicago Press.

Gazdar, G. and Mellish, C. (1989), *Natural Language Processing in Prolog. An Introduction to Computational Linguistics*, Addison-Wesley, Workingham, UK.

Gécseg, F. and Steinby, M. (1984), *Tree Automata*, Akadémiai Kiadó, Budapest.

Girard, J.Y. (1987), *Linear logic*, Theor. Comput. Sci. **50**, 1–102.
Girard, J.Y. with Taylor, P. and Lafont, Y. (1989), *Proofs and Types*, Cambridge Univ. Press, Cambridge, MA.
Hausser, R. (1989), *Computation of Language*, Springer, Berlin.
Hausser, R. (1992), *Complexity in left-associative grammar*, Theor. Comput. Sci. **106**, 283–308.
Hendriks, H. (1993), *Studied flexibility. Categories and types in syntax and semantics*, PhD Thesis, University of Amsterdam.
Hepple, M. (1994), *Labelled deduction and discontinuous constituency*, Linear Logic and Lambek Calculus, M. Abrusci, C. Casadio and M. Moortgat, eds, Utrecht, Amsterdam.
Hiż, H. (1967), *Grammar logicism*, The Monist **51**, 110–127.
Hiż, H. (1971), *On the abstractness of individuals*, Identity and Individuals, M. Munity, ed., New York Univ. Press, New York.
Hopcroft, J.E. and Ullman, J.D. (1979), *Introduction to Automata Theory, Languages and Computation*, Addison-Wesley, Reading, MA.
Joshi, A.K. (1987), *An introduction to tree adjoining grammars*, Mathematics of Language, A. Manaster-Ramer, ed., Benjamin, Amsterdam.
Joshi, A.K. and Schabes, Y. (1992), *Tree-adjoining grammars and lexicalized grammars*, Tree Automata and Languages, M. Nivat and A. Podelski, eds, Elsevier, Amsterdam.
Kanazawa, M. (1992), *The Lambek calculus enriched with additional connectives*, J. Logic, Lang., Inform. **1**, 141–171.
Kanazawa, M. (1994), *Learnable classes of categorial grammars*, PhD Thesis, Stanford University.
Kandulski, M. (1988a), *The equivalence of nonassociative Lambek categorial grammars and context-free grammars*, Z. Math. Logik Grundlag. Math. **34**, 41–52.
Kandulski, M. (1988b), *Phrase structure languages generated by categorial grammars with product*, Z. Math. Logik Grundlag. Math. **34**, 373–383.
Kandulski, M. (1993), *Normal form of derivations in the nonassociative and commutative Lambek calculus with product*, Math. Logic Q. **39**, 103–114.
Kandulski, M. (1995), *On commutative and nonassociative syntactic calculi and categorial grammars*, Math. Logic Q. **41**, 217–235.
Kanovich, M.I. (1991), *The Horn fragment of linear logic is NP-complete*, ITLI Prepublication series X-91-14, University of Amsterdam.
Keenan, E.L. and Faltz, L.M. (1985), *Boolean Semantics for Natural Language*, Reidel, Dordrecht.
Klein, E. and Van Benthem, J. (eds) (1987), *Categories, Polymorphism and Unification*, Univ. of Amsterdam.
Kołowska-Gawiejnowicz, M. (1995), *Powerset residuated algebras and generalized Lambek calculus*, Math. Logic Q., to appear.
Kurtonina, N. (1995), *Frames and labels. A modal analysis of categorial inference*, PhD Thesis, University of Utrecht.
Lambek, J. (1958), *The mathematics of sentence structure*, Amer. Math. Monthly **65**, 154–170.
Lambek, J. (1961), *On the calculus of syntactic types*, Structure of Language and Its Mathematical Aspects, R. Jakobson, ed., AMS, Providence, RI.
Lambek, J. (1988), *Categorial and categorical grammars*, Categorical Grammars and Natural Language Structures, R.T. Oehrle, E. Bach and D. Wheeler, eds, Reidel, Dordrecht.
Lambek, J. (1993), *Logic without structural rules (Another look at Cut elimination)*, Substructural Logics, K. Došen and P. Schröder-Heister, eds, Oxford Univ. Press, Oxford.
Lambek, J. and Scott, P.J. (1985), *Introduction to Higher-Order Categorical Logic*, Cambridge Univ. Press, Cambridge, MA.
Marciniec, J. (1994), *Learning categorial grammars by unification with negative constraints*, J. Appl. Non-Classical Logics **4**, 181–200.
Montague, R. (1970), *Universal grammar*, Theoria **36**, 373–398.
Montague, R. (1973), *The proper treatment of quantification in ordinary English*, Approaches to Natural Language, J. Hintikka, J. Moravcsik and P. Suppes, eds, Reidel, Dordrecht.
Montague, R. (1974), *Formal philosophy*, Selected Papers of R. Montague, ed., by R. Thomason, Yale Univ. Press, New Haven, CT.
Moortgat, M. (1988), *Categorial Investigations. Logical and Linguistic Aspects of the Lambek Calculus*, Foris, Dordrecht.

Moortgat, M. and Oehrle, R.T. (1994), *Adjacency, dependency and order*, Proc. 9th Amsterdam Colloquium, 447–466.

Moortgat, M. (1995), *Multimodal linguistic inference*, Deduction and Language, R. Kempson, ed., The Bulletin of the Interest Group in Pure and Applied Logics (special issue).

Morrill, G. (1994), *Type Logical Grammar*, Kluwer, Dordrecht.

Oehrle, R.T., Bach, E. and Wheeler, D. (eds) (1988), *Categorial Grammars and Natural Language Structures*, Reidel, Dordrecht.

Ono, H. (1993), *Semantics for substructural logics*, Substructural Logics, K. Došen and P. Schröder-Heister, eds.

Pankrat'ev, N. (1994), *On the completeness of the Lambek calculus with respect to relativized relational semantics*, J. Logic, Lang., Inform. **3**, 233–246.

Partee, B.H., Ter Meulen, A. and Wall, R.E. (1990), *Math. Methods Linguistics*, Kluwer, Dordrecht.

Pentus, M. (1993a), *Lambek grammars are context-free*, Proc. 8th Annual IEEE Symposium on Logic in Computer Science, Montreal.

Pentus, M. (1993b), *Lambek calculus is L-complete*, ILLC Report, University of Amsterdam.

Pereira, F.C. (1991), *Semantic interpretation as higher-order deduction*, Logics in AI, J. van Eijck, ed., Springer, Berlin.

Pereira, F.C. and Shieber, S.M. (1987), *Prolog and Natural Language Analysis*, CSLI Lecture Notes no. 10, Chicago Univ. Press, Chicago, IL.

Pratt, V. (1991), *Action logic and pure induction*, Logics in AI, J. van Eijck, ed., Springer, Berlin.

Prawitz, D. (1965), *Natural Deduction*, Almqvist & Wiksell, Stockholm.

Roorda, D. (1991), *Resource logics: Proof-theoretical investigations*, PhD Thesis, University of Amsterdam.

Sánchez Valenzia, V. (1991), *Studies on natural logic and categorial grammar*, PhD Thesis, University of Amsterdam.

Shaumyan, S. (1977), *Applicational Grammar as a Semantic Theory of Natural Language*, Edinburgh Univ. Press.

Shieber, S.M., Schabes, Y. and Pereira, F.C. (1995), *Principles and implementation of deductive parsing*, Technical Report TR-11-94, Harvard University.

Steedman, M. (1988), *Combinators and grammars*, Categorial Grammars and Natural Language Structures, R.T. Oehrle, E. Bach and D. Wheeler, eds, Reidel, Dordrecht.

Steedman, M. (1993), *Categorial grammar, tutorial overview*, Lingua **90**, 221–258.

Szabolcsi, A. (1983), *ECP in categorial grammar*, Manuscript, Max Planck Institute, Nijmegen.

Thatcher, J.W. (1967), *Characterizing derivation trees of context-free grammars through a generalization of finite automata theory*, J. Comput. System Sci. **1**, 317–322.

Troelstra, A.S. (1992), *Lectures on Linear Logic*, CSLI Lecture Notes no. 29, Stanford.

Uszkoreit, H. (1986), *Categorial unification grammar*, Proc. 11th International Conference on Computational Linguistics, Bonn.

Van Benthem, J. (1986), *Essays in Logical Semantics*, Reidel, Dordrecht.

Van Benthem, J. (1987a), *Categorial equations*, Categories, Polymorphism and Unification, Klein and Van Benthem, eds, University of Amsterdam.

Van Benthem, J. (1987b), *Categorial grammar and lambda calculus*, Mathematical Logic and Its Applications, D. Skordev, ed., Plenum Press, New York.

Van Benthem, J. (1988a), *The Lambek calculus*, Categorial Grammars and Natural Language Structures, R.T. Oehrle, E. Bach and D. Wheeler, eds, Reidel, Dordrecht.

Van Benthem, J. (1988b), *The semantics of variety in categorial grammar*, Categorial Grammar, W. Buszkowski, W. Marciszewski and J. van Benthem, eds, Benjamin, Amsterdam.

Van Benthem, J. (1991), *Language in Action. Categories, Lambdas, and Dynamic Logic*, North-Holland, Amsterdam.

Vijay-Shanker, K., Weir, D.J. and Joshi, A.K., *Characterizing structural descriptions produced by various grammatical formalisms*, 25th Meeting of the Association for Computational Linguistics (ACL'87).

Wansing, H. (1992), *The logic of information structures*, PhD Thesis, University of Amsterdam.

Zielonka, W. (1981), *Axiomatizability of Ajdukiewicz–Lambek calculus by means of cancellation schemes*, Z. Math. Logik Grundlag. Math. **27**, 215–224.

Zwarts, F. (1986), *Categoriale grammatica en algebraische semantiek*, PhD Thesis, University of Groningen.

CHAPTER 13

Formal Learning Theory*

Daniel Osherson

DIPSCO, Istituto San Rafaelle, Via Olgettina 60, I-20132 Milano, Italy
E-mail: osherson@ratio.hsr.it

Dick de Jongh

ILLC, University of Amsterdam, Plantage Muidergracht 24, 1018 TV Amsterdam, The Netherlands
E-mail: dickdj@fwi.uva.nl

Eric Martin

LAMII, Universite de Savoie, avenue de Savoie 41, BP 806, F 74000, Annecy Cedex, France
E-mail: martin@esia.univ-savoie.fr
WWW-page: ava.univ-savoie.fr

Scott Weinstein

University of Pennsylvania, Department of Philosophy, Suite 460, 3440 Market Street, Philadelphia, PA 19104-3325, USA
E-mail: weinstein@cis.upenn.edu

Contents

*Research support was provided by the Office of Naval Research under contracts Nos. N00014-87-K-0401 N00014-89-J-1725 and by the Swiss National Science Foundation under grant number 21-32399.91. *Correspondence to D. Osherson, DIPSCO, Istituto San Rafaelle, Via Olgettina 60, I-20132 Milano, Italy.*

HANDBOOK OF LOGIC AND LANGUAGE
Edited by J. van Benthem and A. ter Meulen

1. Introduction

The present chapter is devoted to formal models of language acquisition, and of empirical inquiry more generally. We begin by indicating the issues that motivate our study and then describe the scope of the chapter.

1.1. Empirical inquiry

Many people who have reflected about human intellectual development have noticed an apparent disparity. The disparity is between the information available to children about their environment, and the understanding they ultimately achieve about that environment. The former has a sparse and fleeting character whereas the latter is rich and systematic. This is especially so in the case of first language acquisition, as has been pointed out repeatedly.[1] A similar disparity characterizes other tasks of childhood. By an early age the child is expected to master the moral code of his household and community, to assimilate its artistic conventions and its humor, and at the same time to begin to understand the physical principles that shape the material environment. In each case the child is required to convert data of a happenstance character into the understanding (implicit or explicit) that renders his world predictable and intelligible.

Little is known about the mental processes responsible for children's remarkable intellectual achievements. Even elementary questions remain the subject of controversy and inconclusive findings. For example, there is little agreement about whether children use a general-purpose system to induce the varied principles bearing on language, social structure, etc., or whether different domains engage special-purpose mechanisms in the mind.[2] Although some suggestive empirical findings are available (Gleitman, 1986; Johnson and Newport, 1989; Newport and Supalla, 1989), the matter still engenders controversy (e.g., Bickerton, 1981).

The disparity noted above for intellectual development has also been observed in the acquisition of scientific knowledge by adults. Like the child, scientists typically have limited access to data about the environment, yet are sometimes able to convert this data into theories of astonishing generality and (apparent) veracity. At an abstract level, the inquiries undertaken by child and adult may be conceived as a process of theory elaboration and test. From this perspective, both agents react to available data by formulating hypotheses, evaluating and revising old hypotheses as new data arrive. In the favorable case, the succession of hypotheses stabilizes to an accurate theory that reveals the nature of the surrounding environment. We shall use the term "empirical inquiry" to denote any enterprise that possesses roughly these features.

It is evident that both forms of empirical inquiry – achieved spontaneously in the early years of life, or more methodically later on – are central to human existence and cultural evolution. It is thus no accident that they have been the subject of speculation

---

[1] See, for example, Chomsky (1975), Matthews (1984), Hornstein and Lightfoot (1981). A review of empirical findings on first language acquisition is available in (Pinker, 1990).

[2] For discussion, see Chomsky (1975), Osherson and Wasow (1976).

and inquiry for centuries, and of vigorous research programs within several contemporary disciplines (namely, Psychology, Artificial Intelligence, Statistics and Philosophy). We shall not here attempt to synthesize this vast literature but rather limit ourselves to a single line of investigation that descends from the pioneering studies (Putnam, 1965, 1975; Solomonoff, 1964; Gold, 1967; Blum and Blum, 1975). It is this tradition that appears to have had the greatest impact on linguistics, and to a limited extent on epistemology.[3]

Our topic has been named in various ways, often as "Formal Learning Theory" which we adopt here usually without the qualifier "Formal". Central to the theory is the concept of a *paradigm* (or model) of empirical inquiry. The inquiry in question might be that of a child learning language, or of a scientist investigating nature. Every paradigm in the theory has essentially the same stock of component concepts, which we now explain.

1.2. Paradigms

A paradigm offers formal reconstruction of the following concepts, each central to empirical inquiry.

(1) a. *a theoretically possible reality*

b. *an intelligible hypothesis about reality*

c. *the data available about any given reality, were it actual*

d. *a scientist (or child)*

e. *successful behavior by a scientist working in a given, possible reality*

The concepts figure in the following picture of scientific inquiry, conceived as a game between Nature and a scientist. First, a class of possible realities is specified in advance; the class is known to both players of the game. Nature is conceived as choosing one member from the class, to be the "actual world"; her choice is initially unknown to the scientist. Nature then provides a series of clues about this reality. These clues constitute the data upon which the scientist will base his hypotheses. Each time Nature provides a new clue, the scientist may produce a new hypothesis. The scientist wins the game if there is sufficient guarantee that his successive conjectures will stabilize to an accurate hypothesis about the reality Nature has chosen.

Different paradigms formalize this picture in different ways, resulting in different games. Whether a particular game is winnable depends, among other things, on the breadth of the set of possible realities. Wider sets make successful learning more difficult, to the point of impossibility. The dominant concern of Learning Theory is to formulate an illuminating characterization of the paradigms in which success is achievable.

---

[3] Within linguistics, relevant papers include (Wexler and Culicover, 1980; Borer and Wexler, 1987; Lasnik, 1989; Matthews, 1989; Truscott and Wexler, 1989). Within epistemology, see, for example, Kelly and Glymour (1993), Earman (1992, Chapter 9).

1.3. Scope of the chapter

Contemporary Learning Theory has two principal branches, which may be termed "recursion theoretic", and "model theoretic". They are distinguished, as indicated, by the tools used to define and study paradigms. The recursion theoretic side of the discipline is older and better developed. The next three sections overview some principal results. A few proofs are lightly sketched, just for "feeling". The others may be found in (Osherson, Stob and Weinstein, 1986c). A more complete survey will be available in (Sharma, Jain, Royer, Martin, Osherson and Weinstein, to appear). Concerns about recursion theoretic modeling are voiced in Section 5, and the alternative perspective is introduced. The subsequent five sections are devoted to Learning Theory from the point of view of model theory. We have chosen to follow one particular line of research, ending with some new results (proofs are given in the appendix). The material presented here is intended to be illustrative of central ideas and concepts; a comprehensive survey is not attempted. More systematic coverage is available in (Sharma, Jain, Royer, Martin, Osherson and Weinstein, to appear).

2. Identification

There is no better introduction to Learning Theory than presentation of its most fundamental paradigm. Such is the goal of the present section, whose essential ideas are due to Gold (1967). To proceed, we consider in turn the components of paradigms listed in (1).

Realities. Possible realities are represented by nonempty, r.e. subsets of non-negative integers. (The non-negative integers are denoted by N in the sequel.) Thinking of such sets as potential natural languages, the paradigm is usually called *language identification,* and the sets themselves "languages". It will be convenient in what follows to drop the "language" qualifier when referring to identification.

Hypotheses. Intelligible hypotheses are the r.e. indices for languages, relative to some background, acceptable ordering of the Turing Machines (see (Machtey and Young, 1978) for "acceptable ordering").

Data. To specify the data that Nature makes available about a given language L, we rely on the following terminology. An ω-sequence of natural numbers is called a *text.* The set of numbers appearing in a text t is denoted $content(t)$. Text t is said to be *for* L just in case $content(t) = L$. After choosing L as reality, Nature presents the scientist with an arbitrary text for L, that is, an infinite listing of L with no intrusions or omissions. If L has at least two elements, the class of texts for L is uncountable.

Let t be a text for L. The initial finite sequence of length n in t is denoted $t[n]$. $t[n]$ may be thought of as an "evidential position" since it contains all the data about L made available by t at the nth moment of inquiry. The set $\{t[n] \mid n \in N \text{ and } t \text{ is a text}\}$ of all evidential positions is denoted SEQ. Note that SEQ is the set of all finite sequences of natural numbers and hence is recursively isomorphic to N.

Scientists. A "scientist" is any function (not necessarily total or recursive) from SEQ to N, where the latter are conceived as r.e. indices. Thus, a scientist is a system that converts its current, evidential position into an hypothesis about the language giving rise to his text.

Success. Success is defined in stages.

DEFINITION 2. Let scientist Ψ, text t, and $i \in N$ be given.

(a) Ψ *converges on* t to i just in case for all but finitely many $n \in N$, $\Psi(t[n]) = i$.

(b) Ψ *identifies* t just in case there is $i \in N$ such that Ψ converges to i on t, and i is an index for *content*(t).

(c) Ψ *identifies* language L just in case Ψ identifies all the texts for L.

(d) Ψ *identifies* a collection $\mathbf{L}$ of languages just in case Ψ identifies every $L \in \mathbf{L}$. In this case $\mathbf{L}$ is said to be *identifiable*.

Thus, Ψ identifies $\mathbf{L}$ just in case for every text t for any $L \in \mathbf{L}$, Ψ identifies t. Note that any singleton collection of languages is trivially identifiable (by a constant function). Scientists (and children) are challenged only by a wide range of theoretical possibilities.

To illustrate, the collection $\mathbf{F}$ of finite sets is identifiable by Ψ defined this way: For all $\sigma \in SEQ$, $\Psi(\sigma)$ is the smallest index for *content*(σ), where the latter is the set of numbers appearing in σ. $\mathbf{F}$ has the interesting property that no extension is identifiable (Gold, 1967), whereas every other identifiable collection can be extended to another one. The collection $\mathbf{L} = \{N\} \cup \{N - \{x\} \mid x \in N\}$ is also unidentifiable, whereas it is easy to define a scientist that identifies $\mathbf{L} - \{N\}$.

To prove the non-identifiability facts cited above, we rely on the "locking sequence" lemma. Its basic idea is due to Blum and Blum (1975).

DEFINITION 3. Let scientist Ψ, language L, and $\sigma \in SEQ$ be given. σ is a *locking sequence* for Ψ and L just in case:

(a) $\Psi(\sigma)$ is defined; and

(b) for all $\tau \in SEQ$ drawn from L that extend σ, $\Psi(\tau) = \Psi(\sigma)$.

Intuitively, σ locks Ψ onto its conjecture $\Psi(\sigma)$, in the sense that no new data from L can lead Ψ to change its mind.

LEMMA 4. *Let language L and scientist Ψ be such that Ψ identifies L. Then there is a locking sequence σ for Ψ and L. Moreover, $\Psi(\sigma)$ is an index for L.*

A proof is given in Section 12.1.

Now suppose that scientist Ψ identifies some infinite language L. By the lemma, let σ be a locking sequence for Ψ and L, and let t be a text that consists of endless repetitions of σ. By the choice of σ, Ψ converges on t to an index i for L. Since L is infinite, i is not for *content*(t) since the latter is finite. Hence, Ψ fails to identify some text for a finite language, and thus does not identify $\mathbf{F}$. This is enough to show that no scientist identifies a proper extension of $\mathbf{F}$, as noted above. The nonidentifiability of $\{N\} \cup \{N - \{x\} \mid x \in N\}$ is shown similarly.

More generally, Lemma 4 allows us to provide the following characterization of identifiability (see Osherson, Stob and Weinstein, 1986c, Section 2.4, for the simple proof).

PROPOSITION 5 (Angluin, 1980). *Let collection $\mathbf{L}$ of languages be given. $\mathbf{L}$ is identifiable if and only if for all $L \in \mathbf{L}$ there is finite $D_L \subseteq L$ such that for all $L' \in \mathbf{L}$, if $D_L \subseteq L'$ then $L' \not\subset L$.*

3. Remarks about the identification paradigm

Identification evidently provides a highly simplified portrait of first language acquisition and of empirical inquiry generally. Learning theorists have exercised considerable ingenuity in refining and elaborating the basic paradigm in view of more realistic models. Illustrations will be provided in the next section. First it may be useful to comment on a few aspects of the bare paradigm defined above.

3.1. Possible realities as sets of numbers

Limiting possible realities to r.e. subsets of N is mathematically convenient, and has been a feature of much work in Learning Theory.[4] The numbers are to be conceived as codes for objects and events found in scientific or developmental contexts. The details of such coding reflect substantive hypotheses concerning the kind of phonological, semantic, and other information available to children about the ambient language, or about the character of the data that drives scientific research. Unfortunately, mathematical studies of learning often neglect this aspect of formalization, simply starting with N as the base of inquiry. Until Section 6 we shall follow suit.

Some sets of numbers are "single-valued", in the sense of Rogers (1967, Section 5.7). By limiting attention to collections of single-valued, r.e. sets, one treats the important problem of synthesizing a computer program from examples of its graph (as in Shapiro, 1983). Indeed, there have been more studies of function learning than of pure language learning (see Sharma, Jain, Royer, Martin, Osherson and Weinstein, to appear). In view of our present concern with natural language, no more will here be said about function learning (except for a remark in Section 4.9).

3.2. Reliability

The concepts of accuracy and stability are central to identification. Identifying a text t requires the scientist to ultimately issue an index i that enumerates *content* (t) and then to remain with i for the remainder of t, that is, it requires eventual accuracy and stability of the scientist's hypotheses. When we consider collections of languages a third concept arises. To identify collection **L**, a scientist Ψ must succeed on any text for any member of **L**. In this sense, Ψ is required to be a reliable agent of inquiry, succeeding not just on a happenstance collection of texts, but on all of them. Being able to reliably stabilize to an accurate conjecture is the hallmark of scientific competence in all of Learning Theory, and alternative paradigms provide varied reconstructions of these concepts. Kindred notions of reliability are studied in epistemology (e.g., Goldman, 1986; Kornblith, 1985; Pappas, 1979), which is one reason Learning Theory is considered pertinent to philosophical investigation (as in Kelly, 1994).

There is another aspect of successful performance that is pertinent to defining realistic models of language acquisition and of inquiry generally. Discovery should be reasonably

[4] An exception is Kugel (1977), who drops the r.e. requirement.

rapid. The identification paradigm imposes no requirements in this connection, since successful scientists can begin convergence at any point in a text (and at different points for different texts, even for the same language). However, other paradigms build efficiency into the success criterion (as in Daley and Smith, 1986).[5]

One requirement on scientists that is usually *not* imposed by Learning Theory is worth noting. To succeed in identification, the scientist must produce a final, correct conjecture about the contents of the text he is facing. He is not required, however, to "know" that any specific conjecture is final. To see what is at issue, consider the problem of identifying $\mathbf{L} = \{N - \{x\} \mid x \in N\}$. Upon seeing $0, 2, 3, 4, \ldots, 1000$ there are no grounds for confidence in the appealing conjecture $N - \{1\}$ since the next bit of text might contradict this hypothesis. The identifiability of **L** does warrant a different kind of confidence, namely, that systematic application of an appropriate guessing rule will eventually lead to an accurate, stable conjecture on any text for a member of **L**.

Distinguishing these two kinds of confidence allows us to focus on scientific success itself, rather than on the secondary question of warranted belief that success has been obtained. Thus, the fundamental question for Learning Theory is:

What kind of scientist reliably succeeds on a given class of problems?

rather than:

What kind of scientist "knows" when it is successful on a given class of problems?

Clarity about this distinction was one of the central insights that led to the mathematical study of empirical discovery (see Gold, 1967, pp. 465–466).[6]

3.3. *Comparative grammar*

In the linguistic context, possible realities are the languages that children might be called upon to master. Now it seems evident to many linguists (notably, Chomsky, 1975, 1986) that children are not genetically prepared to acquire any, arbitrary language on the basis of the kind of casual linguistic exposure typically afforded the young. Instead, a relatively small class **H** of languages may be singled out as "humanly possible" on the basis of their amenability to acquisition by children, and it falls to the science of linguistics to propose a nontrivial description of **H**. Specifically, the discipline known as "comparative grammar" attempts to characterize the class of (biologically possible) natural languages through formal specification of their grammars; and a *theory* of comparative grammar is a specification of some definite collection. Contemporary theories of comparative grammar begin with Chomsky (1957, 1965), but there are several different proposals

[5] Efficiency is of paramount concern within the "PAC-learning" approach to inductive inference (see Anthony and Biggs, 1992). PAC-learning is less relevant than Formal Learning Theory to language acquisition by children, and is not treated here. For one attempt to relate the two approaches, see Osherson, Stob and Weinstein (1991a).

[6] In "finite learning" scientists are allowed but a single conjecture so their attachment to it can be considered stronger than is the case for identification. See Jain and Sharma (1990b) for an illuminating study.

currently under investigation (see Wasow, 1989; and J. Higginbotham's chapter in this Handbook).

Theories of linguistic development stand in an intimate relation to theories of comparative grammar inasmuch as a theory of comparative grammar is true only if it embraces a collection of languages learnable by children. For this necessary condition to be useful, however, it must be possible to determine whether given collections of languages are learnable by children. How can this information be acquired? Direct experimental approaches are ruled out for obvious reasons. Investigation of existing languages is indispensable, since such languages have already been shown to be learnable by children; as revealed by recent studies much knowledge can be gained by examining even a modest number of languages (see Van Riemsdijk and Williams, 1986).

We might hope for additional information about learnable languages from the study of children acquiring a first language. Indeed, many relevant findings have emerged from child language research. For example, the child's linguistic environment appears to be largely devoid of explicit information about the nonsentences of the target language (see Brown and Hanlon, 1970; Demetras, Post and Snow, 1986; Hirsh-Pasek, Treiman and Schneiderman, 1984; Penner, 1987). The acquisition process, moreover, is relatively insensitive to the order in which language is addressed to children (see Newport, Gleitman and Gleitman, 1977; Schieffelin and Eisenberg, 1981). Finally, certain clinical cases suggest that a child's own linguistic productions are not essential to mastery of the incoming language (Lenneberg, 1967). These facts lend a modicum of plausibility to the use of texts as a model of the child's linguistic input. Other pertinent findings bear on the character of immature grammar, which appears not to be a simple subset of the rules of adult grammar but rather incorporates distinctive rules that will be abandoned later (see Pinker, 1990).

For all their interest, such findings do not directly condition theories of comparative grammar. They do not by themselves reveal whether some particular class of languages is accessible to children or whether it lies beyond the limits of their learning. Learning Theory may be conceived as an attempt to provide the inferential link between the results of acquisitional studies and theories of comparative grammar. It undertakes to translate empirical findings about language acquisition into information about the kinds of languages assimilable by young children. Such information can in turn be used to evaluate theories of comparative grammar.

To fulfill its inferential role, Learning Theory offers a range of models of language acquisition. The models arise by precisely construing concepts generally left vague in studies of child language, namely, the five concepts listed in (1). The interesting paradigms from the point of view of comparative grammar are those that best represent the circumstances of actual linguistic development in children. The deductive consequences of such models yield information about the class of possible natural languages.

Many of the paradigms investigated within the theory have little relevance to comparative grammar, for example, studies bearing on team-learning (Daley, 1986; Jain and Sharma, 1990b; Pitt, 1989). On the other hand, considerable effort has been devoted to paradigms which bear on aspects of language acquisition. For purposes of illustration, the next section is devoted to refinements of the Identification paradigm.[7]

4. More refined paradigms

Refinements of identification can alter any or all of the five components of paradigms, (1a)–(1e). We limit ourselves here to some simple illustrations bearing on the concepts:

- scientist (or child);
- data made available;
- successful inquiry.

More comprehensive surveys are available in Angluin and Smith (1983), Osherson, Stob and Weinstein (1986c), Sharma, Jain, Royer, Martin, Osherson and Weinstein (to appear). The latter two references provide proofs for claims made in this section.

4.1. Memory limitation

It seems evident that children have limited memory for the sentences presented to them. Once processed, sentences are likely to be quickly erased from the child's memory. Here we shall consider scientists that undergo similar information loss. The following notation is used. Let $\sigma \in SEQ$ be given (SEQ is defined in Section 2). The result of removing the last member of σ is denoted by σ^- (if $length(\sigma) = 0$, then $\sigma^- = \sigma = \emptyset$). The last member of σ is denoted by σ_{last} (if $length(\sigma) = 0$, then σ_{last} is undefined).

The following definition says that a scientist is memory limited if his current conjecture depends on no more than his last conjecture and the current datum.

DEFINITION 6 (*Wexler and Culicover, 1980*). Scientist Ψ is *memory limited* just in case for all $\sigma, \tau \in SEQ$, if $\Psi(\sigma^-) = \Psi(\tau^-)$ and $\sigma_{\text{last}} = \tau_{\text{last}}$, then $\Psi(\sigma) = \Psi(\tau)$.

Intuitively, a child is memory limited if her conjectures arise from the interaction of the current input sentence with the latest grammar that she has formulated and stored. The stored grammar, of course, may provide information about other sentences seen to date. To illustrate, it is not hard to prove that the class of finite languages is identifiable by memory limited scientist. Thus, it is sometimes possible to compensate for memory limitation by retrieving past data from current conjectures. Nonetheless, memory limitation places genuine restrictions on the identifiable collections of languages, as shown by the following proposition.

PROPOSITION 7. *There is an identifiable collection of languages that is not identified by any memory limited scientist.*

---

[7] For further discussion of the role of Learning Theory in comparative grammar see Osherson, Stob and Weinstein (1984), Wexler and Culicover (1980). Other constraints on theories of comparative grammar might be adduced from biological considerations, or facts about language change. See Lightfoot (1982) for discussion.

We give an idea of the proof (for details, see Osherson, Stob and Weinstein, 1986c, Proposition 4.4.1B). Let E be the set of even numbers, and consider the collection **L** of languages consisting of:

(a) E,

(b) for every $n \in N$, $\{2n+1\} \cup E$, and

(c) for every $n \in N$, $\{2n+1\} \cup E - \{2n\}$.

It is easy to verify that **L** is identifiable without memory limitation. In contrast, suppose that memory limited Ψ identifies E, and let $\sigma \in \mathit{SEQ}$ be a locking sequence for Ψ and E. Pick $n \in N$ such that $2n \notin \mathit{content}(\sigma)$. Then, Ψ will have the same value on σ and σ extended by $2n$. From this point it is not difficult to see that Ψ will fail to identify at least one text for either $\{2n+1\} \cup E$ or $\{2n+1\} \cup E - \{2n\}$. Hence, Ψ does not identify **L**. As is common in results of this form one may now further establish that there are uncountably many such identifiable classes of languages not identified by any memory limited scientist.

Proposition 7 shows that, compared to the original paradigm, the memory limited model of linguistic development makes a stronger claim about comparative grammar, imposing a more stringent condition on the class of human languages. According to the refined paradigm, the human languages are not just identifiable, but identifiable by a memory limited learner. Of course, this greater stringency represents progress only if children are in fact memory limited in something like the fashion envisioned by Definition 6.

4.2. Fat text

It may be that in the long run every sentence of a given human language will be uttered indefinitely often. What effect would this have on learning?

DEFINITION 8.

(a) A text t is *fat* just in case for all $x \in \mathit{content}(t)$, $\{n \mid t(n) = x\}$ is infinite.

(b) Let scientist Ψ and collection **L** of languages be given. Ψ *identifies* **L** *on fat text* just in case for every fat text t for any $L \in \mathbf{L}$, Ψ identifies t. In this case, **L** is *identifiable on fat text.*

Thus, every number appearing in a fat text appears infinitely often. It is easy to prove that every identifiable collection **L** of languages is identifiable on fat text, and conversely.

Fat text is more interesting in the context of memory limitation. The following proposition shows that the former entirely compensates for the latter.

PROPOSITION 9. *Suppose that collection* **L** *of languages is identifiable. Then some memory limited scientist identifies* **L** *on fat text.*

4.3. Computability

The Turing simulability of human thought is a popular hypothesis in Cognitive Science, and the bulk of Learning Theory has focused on scientists that implement computable functions. Obviously, any collection of languages that is identifiable by computable scientist is identifiable *tout court*. The converse question is settled by the following.

PROPOSITION 10. *Let S be any countable collection of functions from SEQ to N (conceived as scientists). Then there is an identifiable collection* $\mathbf{L}$ *of languages such that no member of S identifies* $\mathbf{L}$.

One argument for 10 proceeds by constructing for each $Q \subseteq N$ an identifiable collection $\mathbf{L}_Q$ of languages such that no single scientist can identify two such classes. The proposition then follows from the fact that there are uncountably many subsets of N but only countably many Turing machines. (See Osherson, Stob and Weinstein, 1986c, Proposition 4.1A, for details.)

The assumption that children are Turing simulable is thus a substantive hypothesis for comparative grammar inasmuch as it renders unlearnable some otherwise identifiable collections of languages (assuming the empirical fidelity of the other components of the identification paradigm, which is far from obvious). On the other hand, under suitable assumptions of uniform recursivity of the class of languages, the characterization of (ineffective) identifiability offered by 5 can be transformed into a characterization of identifiability witnessed by Turing-computable scientist (see Angluin, 1980; and for applications Kapur, 1991; Kapur and Bilardi, 1992).

It might be thought that Proposition 10 points to a complexity bound on the languages that co-inhabit collections identifiable by computable scientist. However, the following proposition shows that such a bound cannot be formulated in terms of the usual notions of computational complexity, as developed in (Blum, 1967).

PROPOSITION 11 (Wiehagen, 1978). *There is a collection* $\mathbf{L}$ *of languages with the following properties.*

(a) *Some computable scientist identifies* $\mathbf{L}$.

(b) *For every r.e. $S \subseteq N$ there is $L \in \mathbf{L}$ such that S and L differ by only finitely many elements (that is, the symmetric difference of S and L is finite).*

One such collection turns out to consist of all languages L whose least member is an index for L. This collection is easily identified (indeed, by a Turing Machine that runs in time linear in the length of the input), and an application of the recursion theorem shows it to satisfy 11(b). This argument is Wiehagen's (see Osherson, Stob and Weinstein, 1986c, Proposition 2.3A).

Once alternative hypotheses about scientists have been defined and investigated it is natural to consider their interaction. We illustrate with the following fact about memory limitation (Definition 6).

PROPOSITION 12. *There is a collection* $\mathbf{L}$ *of languages with the following properties.*

(a) *Some memory limited scientist (not computable) identifies* $\mathbf{L}$.

(b) *Some computable scientist identifies* $\mathbf{L}$.

(c) *No computable, memory-limited scientist identifies* $\mathbf{L}$.

4.4. Consistency, conservatism, prudence

At the intuitive level, learning theorists use the term "strategy" to refer to a policy for choosing hypotheses in the face of data. Formally, a strategy is just a subset of scientists, such as the class of memory-limited scientists. Further illustration is provided by the next definition, which relies on the following notation. The finite set of numbers appearing in $\sigma \in SEQ$ is denoted $content(\sigma)$. If scientist Ψ is defined on σ, then the language hypothesized by Ψ on σ is denoted $W_{\Psi(\sigma)}$ (notation familiar from Rogers, 1967).

DEFINITION 13. Let scientist Ψ be given.

(a) (Angluin, 1980) Ψ is *consistent* just in case for all $\sigma \in SEQ$, $content(\sigma) \subseteq W_{\Psi(\sigma)}$.

(b) (Angluin, 1980) Ψ is *conservative* just in case for all $\sigma \in SEQ$, if $content(\sigma) \subseteq W_{\Psi(\sigma^-)}$ then $\Psi(\sigma) = \Psi(\sigma^-)$.

(c) (Osherson, Stob and Weinstein, 1982) Ψ is *prudent* just in case for all $\sigma \in SEQ$, if $\Psi(\sigma)$ is defined then Ψ identifies $W_{\Psi(\sigma)}$.

Thus, the conjectures of a consistent scientist always generate the data seen so far. A conservative scientist never abandons a locally successful conjecture. A prudent scientist only conjectures hypotheses for languages he is prepared to learn.

Conservatism has been the focus of considerable interest within linguistics and developmental psycholinguistics.[8] The prudence hypothesis is suggested by "prestorage" models of linguistic development (as in Chomsky, 1965). A prestorage model posits an internal list of candidate grammars that coincides exactly with the natural languages; at any moment in language acquisition, the child is assumed to respond to available data by selecting a grammar from the list. Regarding consistency, it is likely not a strategy adopted by children since early grammars are inconsistent with most everything the child hears; on the other hand, consistency is a property of learners that has attracted the attention of epistemologists (e.g., Juhl, 1993; Kelly, 1994).

Consistency and conservatism are substantive strategies in the following sense.

PROPOSITION 14.

(a) *There is a collection of languages that is identifiable by computable scientist but by no consistent, computable scientist.*[9]

(b) (Angluin, 1980) *There is a collection of languages that is identifiable by computable scientist but by no conservative, computable scientist.*[10]

In contrast, we have the following fact about prudence.

PROPOSITION 15 (Fulk, 1990). *Suppose that collection* **L** *of languages can be identified by computable scientist. Then* **L** *can be identified by computable, prudent scientist.*

Indeed, the prudent scientist can be constructed uniformly from an index for the original one (Kurtz and Royer, 1988). Fulk's proof proceeds by showing that every class of languages identified by a computable scientist can be extended to a similarly identifiable collection with an r.e. index set. Proposition 15 then follows easily (see Osherson, Stob and Weinstein, 1986c, Lemmas 4.3.4A,B).

---

[8] See Berwick (1986), Baker and McCarthy (1981), Mazurkewich and White (1984), Pinker (1989, 1990).

[9] For more information about consistency and cognate notions, see Fulk (1988).

[10] See Kinber (1994) for thorough analysis of conservatism and related concepts.

4.5. Noisy and incomplete texts

Although it appears that children's linguistic environments are largely free of grammatical error (Newport, Gleitman and Gleitman, 1977), imperfections of two sorts are bound to arise. On the one hand, ungrammatical strings might find their way into the corpus; on the other hand, certain grammatical strings might be systematically withheld. Texts with simple forms of these defects may be defined as follows.

DEFINITION 16. Let language L and text t be given.

(a) t is a *noisy* text for L just in case there is finite $D \subset N$ such that t is an (ordinary) text for $L \cup D$.

(b) t is an *incomplete* text for L just in case there is finite $D \subset N$ such that t is an (ordinary) text for $L - D$.

(c) Scientist Ψ identifies L *on noisy text* just in case for every noisy text t for L, Ψ converges on t to an index for L. Ψ identifies collection $\mathbf{L}$ of languages *on noisy text* just in case Ψ identifies every $L \in \mathbf{L}$ on noisy text.

(d) Scientist Ψ identifies L *on incomplete text* just in case for every incomplete text t for L, Ψ converges on t to an index for L. Ψ identifies collection $\mathbf{L}$ of languages *on incomplete text* just in case Ψ identifies every $L \in \mathbf{L}$ on incomplete text.

It is easy to see that noise and incompletion interfere with learning languages differing only finitely from each other. A more substantial fact is the following.

PROPOSITION 17. *There is a collection* $\mathbf{L}$ *of languages with the following properties.*

(a) *Every* $L \in \mathbf{L}$ *is infinite.*

(b) *Every distinct pair of languages in* $\mathbf{L}$ *is disjoint.*

(c) *Some computable scientist identifies* $\mathbf{L}$ (*on ordinary text*).

(d) *No computable scientist identifies* $\mathbf{L}$ *on noisy text.*

A parallel fact holds for incompletion. Indeed, it is shown in Fulk, Jain and Osherson (1992, Theorem 1) that incompletion is substantially more disruptive for identification than is noise.

4.6. Exact identification

The dictum that natural languages are learnable by children (via casual exposure, etc.) has a converse, namely, that nonnatural languages are not learnable. We are thus led to consider a variant of identification in which successfully learning collection $\mathbf{L}$ entails identifying $\mathbf{L}$ and no more. But a complication arises. It may be that certain degenerate languages (e.g., containing but a single word) can be learned by children, even though we do not wish to classify them as natural.

There are findings to suggest, however, that children are not inclined to learn profoundly inexpressive languages. Some of the evidence comes from studies of children raised in pidgin dialects (Sankoff and Brown, 1976); other work involves the linguistic development of sensorily deprived children (Feldman and Goldin-Meadow, 1978; Landau and Gleitman, 1985). If we accept the thesis that learnability implies expressiveness, then it is appropriate to define the natural languages as exactly the collection of learnable languages.

Within Learning Theory these ideas give rise to the following definition.

DEFINITION 18 (*Osherson and Weinstein, 1982a*). Let scientist Ψ and collection $\mathbf{L}$ be given. Ψ identifies $\mathbf{L}$ *exactly* just in case Ψ identifies $\mathbf{L}$ and identifies no proper superset of $\mathbf{L}$.

The requirement of exact identification interacts with hypotheses about strategies. This is illustrated by comparing Proposition 15 with the following.

PROPOSITION 19. *There is a collection* $\mathbf{L}$ *of languages with the following properties.*
(a) *Some computable scientist exactly identifies* $\mathbf{L}$,
(b) *No prudent, computable scientist exactly identifies* $\mathbf{L}$.

More generally, exact identifiability by computable scientist is possible only in the circumstances described below.

PROPOSITION 20. *Let collection* $\mathbf{L}$ *of languages be given. Some computable scientist exactly identifies* $\mathbf{L}$ *if and only if* $\mathbf{L}$ *is* Π^1_1 *indexable and some computable scientist identifies* $\mathbf{L}$.

The Π^1_1 indexability of $\mathbf{L}$ here means that there is a Π^1_1 subset of N that holds indexes for just the members of $\mathbf{L}$. We note that 19 is a corollary to 20. For, there are computably identifiable, properly Π^1_1 collections of languages whereas any collection that is identified by prudent, computable scientist is r.e. indexable. (See Osherson, Stob and Weinstein, 1986c, Section 7, for discussion.)

4.7. *Efficiency*

First language acquisition by children has struck many observers as remarkably rapid.[11] It is thus pertinent to examine paradigms in which success requires efficient use of data. To define a simple paradigm of this character, we use the following terminology. Let scientist Ψ, text t, and $n \in N$ be given. Suppose that Ψ converges on t to index $i \in N$. Then n is called the *convergence point* for Ψ on t just in case n is smallest such that Ψ conjectures i on all initial segments of t of length n or greater. If Ψ does not converge on t we take the convergence point to be ∞.

DEFINITION 21 (*Gold, 1967*). Let scientists Ψ_0 and Ψ_1, and collection $\mathbf{L}$ of languages be given.
(a) Ψ_0 identifies $\mathbf{L}$ *strictly faster* than Ψ_1 just in case:
(i) both Ψ_0 and Ψ_1 identify $\mathbf{L}$;
(ii) for every text t for every $L \in \mathbf{L}$, the convergence point for Ψ_0 on t is no greater than that for Ψ_1 on t;

[11] But not everyone. See Putnam (1980).

(iii) for some text t for some $L \in \mathbf{L}$, the convergence point for Ψ_0 on t is smaller than that for Ψ_1 on t.

(b) Ψ_0 identifies $\mathbf{L}$ *efficiently* just in case Ψ_0 identifies $\mathbf{L}$, and no scientist Ψ_1 identifies $\mathbf{L}$ strictly faster than Ψ_0.

The next proposition shows that the three strategies examined in Section 4.4 guarantee efficient learning.

PROPOSITION 22. *Suppose that scientist Ψ identifies collection $\mathbf{L}$ of languages. If Ψ is consistent, conservative and prudent then Ψ identifies $\mathbf{L}$ efficiently.*

The preceding proposition can be used to show that in the absence of computability constraints, efficiency imposes no restriction on identification (see Osherson, Stob and Weinstein, 1986c, Section 4.5.1). In contrast, the work of computable scientists cannot always be delegated to efficient, computable ones.

PROPOSITION 23. *There is a collection $\mathbf{L}$ of languages with the following properties.*

(a) *Some computable scientist identifies $\mathbf{L}$.*

(b) *For every computable scientist Ψ that identifies $\mathbf{L}$ there is a computable scientist that identifies $\mathbf{L}$ strictly faster than Ψ.*

A rough idea of the proof may be given as follows (see Osherson, Stob and Weinstein, 1986c, Proposition 8.2.3A for details). Suppose that $Q \subset N$ is an r.e., nonrecursive set, and that Ψ's speed is aided by quickly deciding whether $n \in N$ belongs to Q. Then Ψ cannot do this for at least one n since otherwise Q would be recursive. Hence, there is a scientist strictly faster than Ψ which has built-in information about this n but which otherwise behaves like Ψ.

4.8. *Stability and accuracy liberalized*

Identification proposes strict criteria of hypothesis stability and accuracy (in the sense of Section 3.2), and many liberalizations have been examined. For example, weaker criteria of stability might allow successful learners to switch indefinitely often among indices for the same language, or alternatively, to cycle among some finite set of them (Osherson and Weinstein, 1982; Jain, Sharma and Case, 1989). Weaker criteria of accuracy might allow a finite number of errors into the final conjecture (Case and Smith, 1983), or else allow the final conjecture to "approximate" the target in a variety of senses (Fulk and Jain, 1992; Royer, 1986). These and other liberalizations have been studied extensively, both separately and in combination. For a review of findings, see Sharma, Jain, Royer, Martin, Osherson and Weinstein (to appear).

4.9. *Identifying the child's program for language acquisition*

Whereas the child's task is to discover a grammar for the ambient language, the task of developmental psycholinguists is to discover the mental program animating the child's efforts. By focusing on the child's learning program rather than on what it learns, we may attempt to define paradigms that illuminate the prospects for success in discovering the mechanisms of first language acquisition. In this case the learner is the psycholinguist and her data may be conceived as the graph of the acquisition function implemented by the child. Successful inquiry consists of converging on the graph to an index for the child's learning function. A less stringent requirement is convergence to a program that identifies at least as many languages as children do, irrespective of its similarity to the child's method. This latter success criterion is called "weak delimitation".

We would like to know how wide a class of potential children can be identified or weakly delimited. If the class is narrow, there may be no reliable means of investigating first-language acquisition. Success in psycholinguistics would depend in this case upon the fortuitous circumstance that the child's learning function falls into the small class of possibilities for which our scientific methods are adapted.

In (Osherson and Weinstein, 1995) it is shown that some narrow classes of potential children can be neither identified nor weakly delimited. One such class consists of just those children that identify less than three, nonempty languages, none of them finite.

5. The need for complementary approaches

A quarter century of research within Formal Learning Theory has provided suggestive findings for both epistemology and linguistics. It seems fair to say, however, that its impact on the latter discipline has as yet been meager, despite efforts to confront theories of comparative grammar with results about learning (as in Berwick, 1986; Osherson, Stob and Weinstein, 1984; Truscott and Wexler, 1989; Wexler and Culicover, 1980). One reason for the lack of interaction is the abstract character of learning theoretic results. Indeed, the majority of findings remain true under recursive permutation of N, and hence have little to do with the grammatical structure of natural language.

A more recent tradition of research on learning shows greater promise in this regard. For example, Shinohara (1990) considers languages defined via elementary formal systems (EFS's) in the sense of Smullyan (1961). He proves that for any $n \in N$, the class of languages definable by length-bounded EFS's with at most n axioms is computably identifiable. From this it follows that for any $n \in N$, the class of languages with context-sensitive grammars of at most n rules is similarly identifiable. Another notable finding is due to Kanazawa (1993). He shows that the class of classical categorial grammars assigning at most k types to each symbol is identifiable by computable scientist in the sense of Definition 2, above. As Kanazawa notes, it follows that the entire class of context-free languages is similarly learnable, provided that texts are enriched with information about the type-ambiguity of each symbol. (For further results, see Kanazawa, 1994.)

Results like the foregoing are of potentially greater interest to linguistic theory than those bearing on arbitrary r.e. sets. However, research in the new tradition has yet to investigate the special character of children's learning, e.g., its memory-limitation and resistance to noise. These are just the topics given greatest attention in the older literature.

To understand a second reason for Learning Theory's lack of impact on linguistics, let us recall that comparative grammar is supposed to contribute to the theory of innate ideas. In particular, the universal elements of grammar, invariant across natural languages, correspond to what the prelinguistic child already knows about the language into which he is plunged. Extensive debate has arisen about the form in which such knowledge might be lodged in the infant's mind – and even whether it should be called "knowledge" at all, instead of simply "predisposition" (see, for example, Chomsky (1975), Matthews (1984), Putman (1967), Stich (1978)). To address the issue squarely, let us conceive of the child's innate preparation to learn language as a prestored message that characterizes the class of potential natural languages. Then it is difficult to locate this message within the learning paradigms of the Putnam/Gold/Solomonoff tradition. There are just classes of languages in play, under no particular description. Given specific assumptions about data-presentation and so on, either the child can learn the languages or not. There is no innate starting point in sight.[12]

To remedy this shortcoming, some recent paradigms have conceived of innate knowledge as a first-order theory in a countable language (e.g., Osherson, Stob and Weinstein, 1991b, 1992). In the usual case, the innate theory is not complete; otherwise, there is nothing to learn and there would be no linguistic variation across cultures. So the child's task is to extend the innate theory via new axioms that are true of the particular language spoken in his environment. Consequently, these paradigms consider a single sentence in the language of the original theory, and ask what sort of learning device could determine the truth-value of the sentence by examining data from the environment. The environment is assumed to be consistent with the child's background theory, which thus serves as prior information about the range of theoretical possibilities.

The remainder of the chapter provides details about this approach. To keep the discussion manageable, it is limited to a single strand of inquiry, leaving several relevant studies aside (e.g., Glymour and Kelly, 1989; Kelly and Glymour, 1993). The work to be discussed was stimulated by the seminal papers (Glymour, 1985; Shapiro, 1981, 1991).

We proceed as follows. Background ontology and basic concepts occupy Section 6. An elementary but fundamental paradigm is described in Section 7 and some basic facts presented. More sophisticated paradigms are advanced in Sections 8 and 9. Their relevance to first language acquisition is taken up in Section 10. Unless noted otherwise, verification of examples and proofs of propositions are given in the appendix to this chapter.

6. Ontology and basic concepts

6.1. Overview

The paradigms in the remainder of this chapter are embedded in a first-order logical framework. By this is meant that the "possible worlds" in which the scientist might find herself are represented by relational structures for a first-order language. Moreover, the hypotheses that the scientist advances about her world are limited to sentences drawn

[12] A preliminary attempt to communicate "starting points" to learners within a recursion theoretic framework is reported in (Osherson, Stob and Weinstein, 1988).

from the same language. Generalizations are of course possible (as in Kelly and Glymour (1992), Osherson and Weinstein (1989a), for example), but our aim here is to exhibit significant results within the simplest framework possible.

6.2. Language, structures, assignments

We fix a countably infinite collection $\mathbf{D}$ of individuals $\mathbf{d}_0, \mathbf{d}_1, \ldots$. $\mathbf{D}$ is the domain of all structures to be considered in the sequel. In particular, given a set T of first-order sentences, *mod*(T) denotes the class of structures with domain $\mathbf{D}$ that satisfy T. The exclusion of finite models from the remainder of the discussion is only for convenience. In contrast, the exclusion of uncountable models is necessary to avoid unresolved conceptual questions (see Osherson and Weinstein 1986, Section 6.1).

By a "**D**-sequence" is meant an ω-sequence onto $\mathbf{D}$ (i.e. with range equal to all of $\mathbf{D}$). Given $\mathbf{D}$-sequence d and $i \in N$, d_i denotes the ith member of d, and $d[i]$ denotes the initial segment of length i in d. The set $\{d[i] \mid d \text{ is a } \mathbf{D}\text{-sequence and} i \in N\}$ of all finite initial segments of $\mathbf{D}$-sequences is denoted $\mathbf{D}^{<\omega}$.

We also fix a language $\mathcal{L}$ with a countable set VAR $= \{v_i \mid i \in N\}$ of variables. The vocabulary of $\mathcal{L}$ is assumed to be finite and include only constants and relation symbols (including identity).[13] The sets of $\mathcal{L}$-formulas and $\mathcal{L}$-sentences are denoted by $\mathcal{L}_{\text{form}}$ and $\mathcal{L}_{\text{sen}}$, respectively. The set of free variables occurring in $\varphi \in \mathcal{L}_{\text{form}}$ is denoted $\mathit{var}(\varphi)$. We use *BAS* to denote the set of basic formulas, that is, the subset of $\mathcal{L}_{\text{form}}$ consisting of atomic formulas and negations thereof.

A **D**-sequence d will be used to assign objects from $\mathbf{D}$ to variables in VAR. In particular, for every $i \in N$, $d(v_i) = d_i$. Similarly, the finite sequence $\bar{d} = (d_0, \ldots, d_n) \in \mathbf{D}^{n+1}$ corresponds to the finite assignment $\{(v_0, d_0), \ldots, (v_n, d_n)\}$. By *domain*$(\bar{d})$ is meant the set of variables that $\bar{d}$ interprets, i.e. $\{v_i \in \text{VAR} \mid i < \mathit{length}(\bar{d})\}$.

6.3. Environments

DEFINITION 24. Let structure $\mathcal{S}$ and **D**-sequences d be given. By the *environment* for $\mathcal{S}$ and d is meant the ω-sequence e such that for all $i \in N$, $e_i = \{\beta \in \mathit{BAS} \mid \mathit{var}(\beta) \subseteq \mathit{domain}(d[i]) \text{ and } \mathcal{S} \models \beta[d[i]]\}$. An *environment* for $\mathcal{S}$ is an environment for $\mathcal{S}$ and d, for some **D**-sequence d. An *environment* is an environment for some structure.

Thus, an environment is a sequence of ever-more-inclusive, finite, consistent sets of basic formulas. (The sets are finite by our choice of $\mathcal{L}$.) It is as if Nature chooses elements from $\mathbf{D}$ one by one, and after each selection tells us everything she can about the new element and its relation to all the previously chosen elements. For example, suppose that

[13] The exclusion of function symbols is for convenience only. Their presence would slightly complicate the definition of environments, below.

the predicates of $\mathcal{L}$ are $\{=, R\}$, and that structure $\mathcal{S}$ interprets R as $\{(\mathbf{d}_i, \mathbf{d}_j) \mid i < j\}$. If $\mathbf{D}$-sequence d is $\mathbf{d}_0, \mathbf{d}_1, \mathbf{d}_2, \ldots$ then the environment for $\mathcal{S}$ and d begins this way:

$$\left\{\begin{matrix} v_0 = v_0 \\ \neg Rv_0v_0 \end{matrix}\right\} \left\{\begin{matrix} v_0 = v_0 & v_1 \neq v_0 \\ v_1 = v_1 & Rv_0v_1 \\ v_0 \neq v_1 & \neg Rv_1v_0 \\ \neg Rv_0v_0 & \neg Rv_1v_1 \end{matrix}\right\} \left\{\begin{matrix} v_0 = v_0 & v_2 = v_2 & v_2 \neq v_1 & Rv_0v_1 & \neg Rv_1v_1 \\ v_1 = v_1 & v_0 \neq v_2 & \neg Rv_1v_0 & Rv_0v_2 & \neg Rv_2v_2 \\ v_0 \neq v_1 & v_2 \neq v_0 & \neg Rv_2v_0 & Rv_1v_2 & \\ v_1 \neq v_0 & v_1 \neq v_2 & \neg Rv_2v_1 & \neg Rv_0v_0 & \end{matrix}\right\} \cdots$$

The following lemma is straightforward (a proof appears in (Osherson and Weinstein, 1986)).

LEMMA 25. *Let environment e and structures $\mathcal{S}$ and $\mathcal{U}$ be given. If e is for both $\mathcal{S}$ and $\mathcal{U}$ then $\mathcal{S}$ and $\mathcal{U}$ are isomorphic.*

6.4. Scientists

The finite segment of length i in environment e is denoted $e[i]$, and the set $\{e[i] \mid e$ is an environment and $i \in N\}$ is denoted SEQ (there is no risk of confusion with our previous use of SEQ in Section 2). Since $\mathcal{L}$ is a finite relational language, SEQ is a collection of finite sequences of finite subsets of a fixed countable set; hence, SEQ is countable.

A (formal) scientist is defined to be any function from SEQ to $\mathcal{L}_{\text{sen}}$. According to this conception, scientists examine the data embodied in finite initial segments of environments, and emit hypotheses about the underlying structure in the guise of first-order sentences.

DEFINITION 26. Let $\theta \in \mathcal{L}_{\text{sen}}$, environment e, and scientist Ψ be given. Ψ *converges* on e to θ just in case $\Psi(e[i]) = \theta$ for all but finitely many $i \in N$.

6.5. Solvability for environments

To succeed in a given environment, we require the scientist's hypotheses to stabilize to a single, true, interesting sentence. The idea of stabilization is defined by 26, above. Rather than attempt to formalize the concept of "interesting sentence", we leave it as a parameter in the definition of scientific success. The parameter takes the form of a subset X of sentences, which count as the interesting ones.

DEFINITION 27. Let $\mathrm{X} \subseteq \mathcal{L}_{\text{sen}}$, scientist Ψ and structure $\mathcal{S}$ be given. Suppose that environment e is for $\mathcal{S}$. Then Ψ X-*solves* e just in case there is $\theta \in \mathrm{X}$ such that:

(a) Ψ converges on e to θ, and

(b) $\mathcal{S} \models \theta$.

It is Lemma 25 that renders clause (b) unambiguous: up to isomorphism, $\mathcal{S}$ is the unique structure for which e is an environment.

EXAMPLE 28. For $\theta \in \mathcal{L}_{\text{sen}}$, let $\mathrm{X} = \{\theta, \neg\theta\}$. Then, scientist Ψ X-solves environment e for structure $\mathcal{S}$ just in case Ψ converges on e to whichever of θ, $\neg\theta$ is true in $\mathcal{S}$. This choice of X yields the paradigm of "truth-detection", analyzed in (Glymour and Kelly, 1989; Osherson, Stob and Weinstein, 1991b).

Other choices of X are discussed in (Osherson and Weinstein, in press; Osherson, Stob and Weinstein, 1992).

6.6. *Solvability for structures*

All of the paradigms discussed below share the foregoing apparatus. They differ only in the definition given to the idea of solving a given structure $\mathcal{S}$. In each case a scientist will be credited with solving $\mathcal{S}$ if she solves enough environments for $\mathcal{S}$, but the paradigms differ in their interpretation of "enough". The first (and simplest) paradigm conceives the matter in absolute terms: To solve $\mathcal{S}$ the scientist must be able to solve all of its environments. Subsequent paradigms offer probabilistic conceptions.

A scientist Ψ solves a collection $\mathcal{K}$ of structures just in case Ψ solves all the structures in $\mathcal{K}$. This is a constant feature of our paradigms, regardless of how the solution of individual structures is defined. Of particular interest is the case of elementary classes of structures, picked out by a first-order theory. The results discussed below bear principally on this case.

6.7. *Relation to language acquisition*

Let us relate the concepts discussed above to the child's acquisition of a first language.

The collection X of sentences represents alternative, finitely axiomatized theories of some circumscribed linguistic realm, for example, well-formedness or pragmatic force. Each member of X provides an adequate description of a potential human language (relative to the realm in question). The description is "adequate" in the sense of representing the implicit knowledge accessible to mature speakers. The child's task is to find a member of X that is true of the particular language presented to him.

The class $\mathcal{K}$ of structures embodies the range of linguistic realities for which children are genetically prepared. These realities are the "human" or "natural" ones, in the terms of Section 3.3. If $\mathcal{K}$ is elementary, then the child is assumed competent for any linguistic situation that satisfies a certain theory. The theory can thus be conceived as a component of Universal Grammar, embodying linguistic information available innately to the child at the start of language acquisition.

Environments represent the linguistic data from which a theory can be inferred. In this perspective, **D** might consist of vocalic events (perhaps with associated context) which are classified by the predicates of $\mathcal{L}$. For example, if the theories in X bear on pragmatic force, then predicates might code the intonational contours of utterances, the apparent emotional state of the speaker, etc. Note that environments give direct access to "negative data", whereas this is often assumed not to be a feature of linguistic input to children (see the discussion in Section 3.3, above). To exclude negative data from environments it suffices to restrict their content to atomic formulas, suppressing basic formulas containing negations. We have not adopted this convention since it is unclear whether negative evidence is lacking in linguistic realms other than syntax; in learning the semantics of quantifiers, for example, negative feedback might be available from the failure to communicate an intended meaning. In any event, it remains to determine how well our theorems transfer to the case of "positive environments".

Formal scientists play the role of children. Their mission is to stabilize to a true theory drawn from X. In the model of Section 7 it will be assumed that children achieve such stability with perfect reliability, i.e. no matter how the data are presented. The models of Sections 8 and 9 admit the possibility that language acquisition fails when data are presented in an unlikely order.

Suppose that we've established a linguistic realm of interest (e.g., well-formedness). Suppose furthermore that X holds the kind of theories achieved by adults for that realm. Then, a nontrivial property can be attributed to the class of natural languages, namely, X-solvability in the relevant sense. The paradigms now presented provide alternative definitions of X-solvability.

7. First paradigm: Absolute solvability

The idea of solving an environment was formulated in Definition 27 above. To solve a structure, our first paradigm requires the scientist to solve all of its environments. Subsequent paradigms adopt a probabilistic stance.

7.1. *Solving arbitrary collections of structures*

DEFINITION 29. Let $X \subseteq \mathcal{L}_{\text{sen}}$ and scientist Ψ be given.

(a) Ψ X-*solves* structure $\mathcal{S}$ just in case Ψ X-solves every environment for $\mathcal{S}$.

(b) Ψ X-*solves* collection $\mathcal{K}$ of structures just in case Ψ X-solves every $\mathcal{S} \in \mathcal{K}$. In this case, $\mathcal{K}$ is said to be X-*solvable*.

For the examples to follow, we suppose that $\mathcal{L}$ is limited to a sole binary relation symbol R (plus identity).

EXAMPLE 30. Let $X = \{\theta, \neg\theta\}$ for $\theta = \forall x \exists y Rxy$ ("there is no greatest point"). We describe the extensions of R in a collection $\mathcal{K} = \{\mathcal{S}_j \mid j \in N\}$. $R^{\mathcal{S}_0}$ is the successor function $\{(\mathbf{d}_i, \mathbf{d}_{i+1}) \mid i \in N\}$. For $j > 0$, $R^{\mathcal{S}_j}$ is $\{(\mathbf{d}_i, \mathbf{d}_{i+1}) \mid i < j\}$. Then $\mathcal{K}$ is not X-solvable.

EXAMPLE 31. Let $\mathcal{K}$ be as defined in Example 30. Given $n \in N - \{0\}$, let

$$\theta_n = \exists x_1 \cdots x_{n+1}(Rx_1x_2 \wedge \cdots \wedge Rx_nx_{n+1} \wedge \forall y \neg Ryx_1 \wedge \forall z \neg Rx_{n+1}z),$$

i.e. there is an R-chain of length exactly n. Then, for all $n \in N - \{0\}$, $\mathcal{K}$ is X_n-solvable, where $X_n = \{\theta_n, \neg\theta_n\}$. The simple proof is left for the reader.

EXAMPLE 32. Let T be the theory of linear orders (with respect to R). Let $\Lambda = \exists x \forall y Rxy$ ("there is a least point"), $\Gamma = \exists x \forall y Ryx$ ("there is a greatest point"), and $\mathrm{X} = \{\Lambda, \neg\Lambda\}$. Then $mod(T \cup \{\Lambda \vee \Gamma,\ \neg(\Lambda \wedge \Gamma)\})$ is X-solvable whereas $mod(T)$ is not.

For verification of Example 32, see Osherson, Stob and Weinstein (1991b, Example 5). Additional examples are given in (Osherson and Weinstein, 1989b; Osherson and Weinstein, in press).

Example 32 reveals that inductive inference within our paradigm does not amount to "waiting for deduction to work". For, no $\sigma \in SEQ$ implies either Λ or $\neg\Lambda$ in the models of $T \cup \{\Lambda \vee \Gamma,\ \neg(\Lambda \wedge \Gamma)\}$. The latter class is nonetheless $\{\Lambda, \neg\Lambda\}$-solvable.

7.2. *Solving elementary classes of structures*

The theory of solvability has a simple character when limited to first-order definable classes of structures (as in Example 32, above). The theory defining such a class may be conceived as a scientific "starting point" since it embodies all the prior information that is available about a potential environment. In this case there is a computable learning method that is optimal, even compared to methods embodied by noncomputable scientists. We state the matter precisely in the following proposition (whose formulation presupposes familiarity with the arithmetical hierarchy and in particular with the notion of a Σ^0_2 subset of $\mathcal{L}_{sen}$).

PROPOSITION 33. *Suppose that* $\mathrm{X} \subseteq \mathcal{L}_{sen}$ *is* Σ^0_2. *Then there is an oracle machine* M *such that for all* $T \subseteq \mathcal{L}_{sen}$, *if* $mod(T)$ *is* X*-solvable, then* M^T X*-solves* $mod(T)$.

The proposition follows immediately from the following lemmas. Their statement requires a preliminary definition, along with the following notation: $\varphi \in \mathcal{L}_{sen}$ will be called "$\exists\forall$" if it is existential-universal in form; either or both sets of quantifiers may be null.

DEFINITION 34. Let $\mathrm{X} \subseteq \mathcal{L}_{sen}$ and $T \subseteq \mathcal{L}_{sen}$ be given. X is *confirmable* in T just in case for all $\mathcal{S} \in mod(T)$ there is $\varphi \in \mathcal{L}_{sen}$ such that:

(a) φ is $\exists\forall$,
(b) $\mathcal{S} \models \varphi$, and
(c) for some $\theta \in \mathrm{X}$, $T \cup \{\varphi\} \models \theta$.

LEMMA 35. *Let a* Σ^0_2 *subset* X *of* $\mathcal{L}_{sen}$ *be given. Then there is an oracle machine* M *such that for all* $T \subseteq \mathcal{L}_{sen}$, *if* X *is confirmable in* T *then* M^T X*-solves* $mod(T)$.

LEMMA 36. *Let* $\mathrm{X} \subseteq \mathcal{L}_{sen}$ *be given. For all* $T \subseteq \mathcal{L}_{sen}$, *if* $mod(T)$ *is* X*-solvable, then* X *is confirmable in* T.

Lemma 35 is an exercise in "dovetailing" and Σ^0_2-programming, some of the basic ideas already appearing in (Gold, 1965; Putman, 1965). A complete proof in a closely related paradigm is given in (Osherson and Weinstein, in press). We do not repeat it here. (Lemma 36 is proved in Section 12.5, below.)

In (Osherson, Stob and Weinstein, 1991b) the following corollary is derived from Lemma 36 and a weaker version of Lemma 35.

COROLLARY 37. *Let $\theta \in \mathcal{L}_{\text{sen}}$ and $T \subseteq \mathcal{L}_{\text{sen}}$ be given. Then mod(T) is $\{\theta, \neg\theta\}$-solvable if and only if both θ and $\neg\theta$ are equivalent over T to existential-universal sentences.*

As an immediate consequence of Corollary 37 and (Chang and Keisler, 1977, Theorem 3.1.16), we obtain the following fact, demonstrated independently in (Kelly, 1994) (cited in Earman, 1992, Chapter 9).

COROLLARY 38. *Let $\theta \in \mathcal{L}_{\text{sen}}$ and $T \subseteq \mathcal{L}_{\text{sen}}$ be given. Then mod(T) is $\{\theta, \neg\theta\}$-solvable if and only if θ is equivalent over T to a Boolean combination of existential sentences.*

We note in passing that Proposition 33 can be extended to no regular logic stronger than the predicate calculus which meets the Löwenheim–Skolem condition. See Osherson, Stob and Weinstein (1991b, Section 4).

8. Second paradigm: Probabilistic solvability

In the present section and the next we conceive of environments as created by a stochastic process. In particular, the entities in our universal domain **D** are assumed to be delivered for inspection via independent, identically distributed sampling according to a probability law which may be unknown to the scientist. The associated paradigm measures successful performance in probabilistic rather than all-or-none fashion, and thus differs from most earlier investigations of scientific discovery within a model-theoretic context. It also takes a different approach than that offered in (Gaifman and Snir, 1982) inasmuch as probabilities are attached to the countable set **D** rather than to uncountable classes of structures. Within the recursion-theoretic literature on inductive inference, related paradigms are treated by Angluin (1988) and Osherson, Stob and Weinstein (1986b, Chapter 10.5).

The core idea of our paradigm is to allow scientists to fail on "small" sets of environments, namely, of measure 0. It will be seen that such liberalization has no effect on the solvability of elementary classes of structures. Moreover, the universal machine for absolute solvability is universal in the present setting as well.

8.1. Measures over environments

The class of all positive probability distributions over **D** is denoted **P**. ($P \in \mathbf{P}$ is positive just in case $P(d) > 0$ for all $d \in \mathbf{D}$.) Given $P \in \mathbf{P}$, we extend P to the product measure over $\mathbf{D}^\omega$ (as reviewed, for example, in (Levy, 1979, Section VII.3)). Given a structure $\mathcal{S}$, this measure is extended to sets E of environments for $\mathcal{S}$ via their underlying **D**-sequences . That is, the P-measure of E is the P-measure of $\{d \in \mathbf{D}^\omega \mid \text{for some } e \in E, e \text{ is for } \mathcal{S} \text{ and } d\}$. (All sets of environments measured below are Borel.)

In what follows we ignore members of $\mathbf{D}^\omega$ that are not onto **D**. This is because the class of such sequences has measure zero for any $P \in \mathbf{P}$, by the positivity of P (for discussion see Billingsley (1986, Chapter 4)). Recall from Section 6.2 that **D**-sequences are, by definition, onto **D**. The following lemma is easy to demonstrate.

LEMMA 39. *Let structure $\mathcal{S}$ be given, and let E be the class of environments for $\mathcal{S}$. Then for all $P \in \mathbf{P}$, E has P-measure 1.*

8.2. Success criterion

To give probabilistic character to scientific success we modify only the concept of solving a structure. The same success criterion as before applies to individual environments (see Definition 27).

DEFINITION 40. Let $\mathrm{X} \subseteq \mathcal{L}_{\mathrm{sen}}$, $\mathbf{P}_0 \subseteq \mathbf{P}$, and scientist Ψ be given.

(a) Let structure $\mathcal{S}$ be given. Ψ X-*solves* $\mathcal{S}$ *on* $\mathbf{P}_0$ just in case for every $P \in \mathbf{P}_0$, the set of environments for $\mathcal{S}$ that Ψ X-solves has P-measure 1.

(b) Let collection $\mathcal{K}$ of structures be given. Ψ X-*solves* $\mathcal{K}$ *on* $\mathbf{P}_0$ just in case Ψ X-solves every $\mathcal{S} \in \mathcal{K}$ on $\mathbf{P}_0$. In this case, $\mathcal{K}$ is said to be X-*solvable* on $\mathbf{P}_0$.

If $\mathbf{P}_0$ is a singleton set $\{P\}$, we drop the braces when employing the foregoing terminology.

Of course, if $\mathbf{P}_0, \mathbf{P}_1$ are classes of distributions with $\mathbf{P}_0 \subseteq \mathbf{P}_1$ then X-solvability on $\mathbf{P}_1$ implies X-solvability on $\mathbf{P}_0$. Lemma 39 implies that if Ψ X-solves $\mathcal{K}$ (in the absolute sense), then Ψ X-solves $\mathcal{K}$ on $\mathbf{P}$. Definition 40 thus generalizes the absolute conception of solvability.

EXAMPLE 41. Let $\mathcal{L}$, X, and $\mathcal{K}$ be as described in Example 30. Let $\mathbf{P}_0 \subset \mathbf{P}$ be any class of distributions such that for all $i \in N$, $glb\{P(\mathbf{d}_i) \mid P \in \mathbf{P}_0\} > 0$. Then $\mathcal{K}$ is X-solvable on $\mathbf{P}_0$.

A recursion-theoretic analogue of the contrast between Examples 30 and 41 appears in (Osherson, Stob and Weinstein, 1986c, Proposition 10.5.2.A). Further analysis is provided by Angluin (1988).

8.3. Comparison with absolute solvability

Examples 30 and 41 show that absolute and probabilistic solvability do not coincide for arbitrary collections of structures. However, for *elementary* collections of structures things are different. In this case the same concept of confirmability (Definition 34) governs solvability in both the absolute and probabilistic senses. This is revealed by the next two lemmas, which parallel Lemmas 35 and 36. The first is an immediate consequence of Lemmas 35 and 39.

LEMMA 42. *Let a* Σ^0_2 *subset* X *of* $\mathcal{L}_{\mathrm{sen}}$ *be given. Then there is an oracle machine* M *such that for all* $T \subseteq \mathcal{L}_{\mathrm{sen}}$, *if* X *is confirmable in* T *then* M^T X-*solves mod*(T) *on* $\mathbf{P}$.

LEMMA 43. *Let* $\mathrm{X} \subseteq \mathcal{L}_{\mathrm{sen}}$ *be given. Then for all* $P \in \mathbf{P}$ *and* $T \subseteq \mathcal{L}_{\mathrm{sen}}$, *if mod*$(T)$ *is* X-*solvable on* P *then* X *is confirmable in* T.

Lemmas 42 and 43 directly yield the following proposition.

PROPOSITION 44. *Suppose that* $\mathrm{X} \subseteq \mathcal{L}_{\mathrm{sen}}$ *is* Σ^0_2. *Then there is an oracle machine* M *such that for all* $P \in \mathbf{P}$ *and* $T \subseteq \mathcal{L}_{\mathrm{sen}}$, *if mod*$(T)$ *is* X-*solvable on* P *then* M^T X-*solves mod*(T) *in the absolute sense (hence* M^T X-*solves mod*(T) *on* $\mathbf{P}$, *as well).*

As a corollary we obtain:

COROLLARY 45. *Let $\theta \in \mathcal{L}_{\text{sen}}$ be given. Then for all $T \subseteq \mathcal{L}_{\text{sen}}$ the following conditions are equivalent.*

(a) *$mod(T)$ is $\{\theta, \neg\theta\}$-solvable.*

(b) *$mod(T)$ is $\{\theta, \neg\theta\}$-solvable on* **P**.

(c) *For some $P \in \mathbf{P}$, $mod(T)$ is $\{\theta, \neg\theta\}$-solvable on P.*

(d) *θ is equivalent over T to a Boolean combination of existential sentences.*

9. Third paradigm: Solvability with specified probability

So far in our discussion we have considered the natural-nonnatural boundary to be sharp. A more liberal attitude would define the natural languages as those for which there is some positive probability of successful acquisition by children, and recognize that different members of this class are associated with different probabilities. Such is the approach of the present section. We preserve the assumption of a sharp distinction between success and failure in any given environment, but allow the class of environments that lead to success to have measure between 0 and 1.

Formulation of this idea requires reflection about the case in which success is not achieved. In particular, we rely on the following hypothesis, which is substantive but strikes us as plausible. When the acquisition process breaks down, we assume that the child fails to converge to any grammar, rather than stabilizing to an incorrect one.

It may be interesting to view the foregoing hypothesis from a normative perspective (that is, independently of the empirical question of its veridicality for children). A scientist who solves a given structure with small probability is worse than useless if he exhibits high probability of misleading an external observer. In particular, it is misleading to converge to a false theory; for in this case the mistaken theory appears to be held with confidence, and risks being accredited. If the probability that the scientist misleads us this way is high, and the probability of genuine success low, it might be better to show him no data at all.

9.1. *Definitions and principal theorem*

These considerations suggest the following definitions.

DEFINITION 46. Let scientist Ψ, structure $\mathcal{S}$ and environment e for $\mathcal{S}$ be given. Ψ *is misleading* on e just in case Ψ converges on e to $\theta \in \mathcal{L}_{\text{sen}}$ such that $\mathcal{S} \not\models \theta$.

Given $X \subseteq \mathcal{L}_{\text{sen}}$, if Ψ X-solves structure $\mathcal{S}$ then Ψ is not misleading on any environment for $\mathcal{S}$. Definition 46 is inspired by the concept of "reliability" from the recursion theoretic literature (see Blum and Blum, 1975).

DEFINITION 47. Let $r \in [0, 1]$, $X \subseteq \mathcal{L}_{\text{sen}}$, $\mathbf{P}_0 \subseteq \mathbf{P}$, and scientist Ψ be given.

(a) Given structure $\mathcal{S}$, we say that Ψ X-*solves $\mathcal{S}$ on $\mathbf{P}_0$ with probability* r just in case the following conditions hold for all $P \in \mathbf{P}_0$.

(i) The set of environments for $\mathcal{S}$ that Ψ X-solves has P-measure at least r.[14]

(ii) The set of environments for $\mathcal{S}$ on which Ψ is misleading has P-measure 0.

(b) Given collection $\mathcal{K}$ of structures, we say that Ψ *X-solves* $\mathcal{K}$ *on* $\mathbf{P}_0$ *with probability* r just in case Ψ X-solves every $\mathcal{S} \in \mathcal{K}$ on $\mathbf{P}_0$ with probability r. In this case, $\mathcal{K}$ is said to be X-*solvable* on $\mathbf{P}_0$ with probability r.

Clause (a-ii) of the definition embodies our hypothesis that acquisition failure results in nonconvergence. On the normative side, it renders useful any scientist whose chance of success is positive. In particular, the hypotheses of such a scientist lend themselves to aggregation within a larger scientific community (see Jain and Sharma, 1990a; Osherson, Stob and Weinstein, 1986a; Pitt and Smith, 1988, for discussion of aggregating scientific competence).[15]

Definition 47 generalizes the earlier paradigms. This is shown by the following lemma, which follows immediately from our definitions.

LEMMA 48. *Let* $P \in \mathbf{P}$, *scientist* Ψ, $\mathrm{X} \subseteq \mathcal{L}_{\text{sen}}$, *and structure* $\mathcal{S}$ *be given. If either*

(a) Ψ *X-solves* $\mathcal{S}$ *or*

(b) Ψ *X-solves* $\mathcal{S}$ *on* P

then Ψ *X-solves structure* $\mathcal{S}$ *on* P *with probability* 1.

The present conception of scientific success has a "zero-one" character, as revealed by the following proposition.

PROPOSITION 49. *Let* $\mathrm{X} \subseteq \mathcal{L}_{\text{sen}}$, $\mathbf{P}_0 \subseteq \mathbf{P}$, *and collection* $\mathcal{K}$ *of structures be given. Then* $\mathcal{K}$ *is* X-*solvable on* $\mathbf{P}_0$ *with probability greater than* 0 *if and only if* $\mathcal{K}$ *is* X-*solvable on* $\mathbf{P}_0$.

From Proposition 44, Corollary 45, and Proposition 49 we have the following immediate corollaries.

COROLLARY 50. *Suppose that* $\mathrm{X} \subseteq \mathcal{L}_{\text{sen}}$ *is* Σ^0_2. *Then there is an oracle machine* M *such that for all* $P \in \mathbf{P}$ *and* $T \subseteq \mathcal{L}_{\text{sen}}$, *if mod*$(T)$ *is* X-*solvable on* P *with probability greater than* 0, *then* M^T X-*solves mod*(T) *in the absolute sense.*

COROLLARY 51. *Let* $\theta \in \mathcal{L}_{\text{sen}}$ *be given. Then for all* $T \subseteq \mathcal{L}_{\text{sen}}$ *the following condition is equivalent to* (a)–(d) *of Corollary* 45.

(e) *For some* $P \in \mathbf{P}$, *mod*(T) *is* $\{\theta, \neg\theta\}$-*solvable on* P *with probability greater than* 0.

10. Empirical evaluation

The paradigms discussed above provide at best a crude picture of first language acquisition by children. We provide a partial list of their deficiencies.

[14] Recall from Section 8.1 that the measure of a set of environments is defined via their underlying **D**-sequences.

[15] We note that the aggregation problem is distinct from "team learning" in the sense of Daley (1986), Jain and Sharma (1990b), Pitt (1989). The latter paradigm requires only that a single scientist arrive at the truth, not that divergent opinions be unified into a correct one.

(a) The linguistic data available to children are not adequately represented by the formal concept of environment. The issue of negative information was already noted in Section 6.7, above. In addition, the concept of probabilistic solvability portrays data as arising via identically distributed, stochastically independent sampling. It is easy to see that real language does not arise in this way (for discussion see Angluin, 1988; Osherson, Stob and Weinstein, 1986b).

(b) Except for computability, our paradigms provide no constraint on the class of formal scientists whereas the inductive mechanisms of children surely operate under severe limitations. At the least, we can assume that children have limited memory for the precise form of spoken sentences, and that the time devoted to processing any given datum is recursively bounded. Building these constraints into formal scientists alters the collections of structures that can be solved.[16]

(c) The criterion of solvability is both too weak and too strong compared to actual language acquisition. It is too strong in requiring selection of $\theta \in \mathrm{X}$ that is "exactly" true in the underlying structure. Since the grammatical theories issuing from normal language acquisition are not likely to be entirely accurate reflections of the input language, more realistic paradigms would incorporate a suitable notion of "approximate truth" (for discussion of this notion, see Kuipers, 1987; Osherson, Stob and Weinstein, 1989). On the other hand, solvability is too weak inasmuch as it imposes no requirements on the number of data that must be examined before convergence begins. In contrast, the rapidity of first language acquisition is one of its striking features. Note also that solvability for individual environments is defined here as an all-or-nothing affair. In reality, children might harbor random processes that yield only probable success within any fixed set of circumstances.[17]

As seen in Section 4, the foregoing issues (among others) have begun to be addressed within the recursion theoretic tradition in Learning Theory. In contrast, their exploration within a first-order framework has hardly been initiated.

11. Concluding remarks

Apart from concerns about first language acquisition, the model theoretic paradigms discussed in this chapter may be examined from an epistemological point of view. For example, Proposition 33 indicates that there is an upper bound on scientific competence, at least for elementarily defined starting points (in the sense of Section 7.2). Moreover, this bound is already reached by a Turing Machine whose sole recourse to an oracle is to determine the axioms of the background theory. The theorem might thus be relevant to the thesis T according to which human mentation is computer simulable. Although T might imply various bounds on human knowledge or capacity, Proposition 33 provides one sense in which the scope of scientifically attainable knowledge is not affected by the status of T.[18] Corollary 50 provides an even stronger sense.

[16] Preliminary work on restricted classes of scientists within the model theoretical perspective is reported in (Gaifman, Osherson and Weinstein, 1990; Osherson and Weinstein, 1986).

[17] For an analysis of random processes in learning, see Daley (1986), Pitt (1989).

[18] For discussion of the machine simulability of thought, see Glymour (1992, Chapter 13) and references cited there.

Theorem 33 raises questions about the character of first-order logic itself. To what extent is the theorem linked to the special properties of the predicate calculus? Are there analogous theorems for stronger logics? Inversely, are all of the deductive consequences of first-order logic necessary for conducting scientific inquiry, including such inferences as $p \models p \vee q$ (sometimes thought to have an odd character (Schurz and Weingartner, 1987))? Some preliminary results that bear on these questions are presented in (Osherson, Stob and Weinstein, 1991b, Section 4; Osherson and Weinstein, 1993).

12. Appendix: Proofs

12.1. Proof of Lemma 4

We restrict attention to scientists that are total functions; that no generality is lost follows from (Osherson, Stob and Weinstein, 1986c, Proposition 4.3.1A,B). Assume that Ψ identifies L but no locking sequence for Ψ and L exists. Moreover assume that $a_0, a_1, a_2, \ldots$ is an enumeration of L. We now construct in stages a special text t for L.

Stage 0: Start t with a_0.

Stage $n+1$**:** Suppose that $t[m_0]$ has been constructed at stage n. By assumption, this sequence is not a locking sequence. So, it can be extended by elements of L to some τ such that either $\Psi(\tau)$ is not an index for L or $\Psi(\tau) \neq \Psi(t[m_0])$. Let τ followed by a_{n+1} be the segment of t constructed in the present stage.

It is easy to see that t is a text for L, and that Ψ does not converge on t to an index for L. Hence Ψ does not identify L, contradicting our assumption.

12.2. Notation

The following notation will be helpful in the sequel. Given **D**-sequence d and structure $\mathcal{S}$, we let $[\mathcal{S}, d]$ denote the environment for $\mathcal{S}$ and d. Given structure $\mathcal{S}$ and $\bar{d} \in \mathbf{D}^{<\omega}$ of length $n \in N$, we let $[\mathcal{S}, \bar{d}]$ denote $e[n]$, where $e = [\mathcal{S}, d]$ and d extends $\bar{d}$. For example, with $\mathcal{S}$ and d as in Section 6.3, $[\mathcal{S}, d[3]]$ is displayed just above Lemma 25 (ignoring the ...). It is helpful to note that for structures $\mathcal{S}, \mathcal{U}$, and $\bar{d}, \bar{u} \in \mathbf{D}^{<\omega}$, $[\mathcal{S}, \bar{d}] = [\mathcal{U}, \bar{u}]$ iff $\mathcal{S}$ restricted to $\bar{d}$ is isomorphic to $\mathcal{U}$ restricted to $\bar{u}$.

12.3. Model-theoretic locking sequences

In the model-theoretic paradigms the following version of the locking sequence lemma is used. It has been demonstrated elsewhere in diverse forms (e.g., Osherson and Weinstein, 1982, Lemma B; Osherson, Stob and Weinstein, 1991b, Lemma 24). The proof resembles that for Lemma 4, and we do not rehearse it here.

DEFINITION 52. Let scientist Ψ, structure $\mathcal{S}$, and $\bar{d} \in \mathbf{D}^{<\omega}$ be given. $\bar{d}$ is a *locking sequence* for $(\Psi, \mathcal{S})$ just in case:

(a) $\Psi([\mathcal{S}, \bar{d}]) \in \mathcal{L}_{\text{sen}}$, i.e. Ψ is defined on $[\mathcal{S}, \bar{d}]$, and

(b) for all $\bar{d}' \in \mathbf{D}^{<\omega}$ that extend $\bar{d}$, $\Psi([\mathcal{S}, \bar{d}']) = \Psi([\mathcal{S}, \bar{d}])$.

LEMMA 53. *Let* $\mathrm{X} \subseteq \mathcal{L}_{\text{sen}}$, *scientist* Ψ, *and structure* $\mathcal{S}$ *be given. Suppose that* Ψ *X-solves every environment for* $\mathcal{S}$. *Then there is a locking sequence* $\bar{d}$ *for* $(\Psi, \mathcal{S})$. *Moreover,* $\mathcal{S} \models \Psi([\mathcal{S}, \bar{d}])$.

12.4. *Proof of Example* 30

Suppose that Ψ X-solves $\mathcal{S}_0$. Then, because $\mathcal{S}_0 \models \theta$, Lemma 53 implies the existence of $\bar{d} \in \mathbf{D}^{<\omega}$ such that:

(54) for all $\bar{d}' \in \mathbf{D}^{<\omega}$ that extend $\bar{d}$, $\Psi([\mathcal{S}_0, \bar{d}']) = \theta$.

Choose $i \in N$ large enough so that $\mathcal{S}_i \models [\mathcal{S}_0, \bar{d}]$. Let **D**-sequence h extend $\bar{d}$. Then it is easy to verify that:

(55) for all $j \geqslant \mathit{length}(\bar{d})$ there is $\bar{d}' \in \mathbf{D}^{<\omega}$ of length j such that:

a. $\bar{d}'$ extends $\bar{d}$, and

b. $[\mathcal{S}_i, \bar{h}_j] = [\mathcal{S}_0, \bar{d}']$.

By (54) and (55), Ψ converges on $[\mathcal{S}_i, h]$ to θ. It follows that Ψ does not X-solve $\mathcal{S}_i$ since $\mathcal{S}_i \not\models \theta$.

12.5. *Proof of Lemma* 36

We rely on the following notation.

DEFINITION 56. Let structure $\mathcal{S}$ and $\bar{d} \in \mathbf{D}^{<\omega}$ be given.

(a) The set

$$\{\pi \in \mathcal{L}_{\text{form}} \mid \pi \text{ is universal, } \mathit{var}(\pi) \subseteq \mathit{domain}(\bar{d}), \text{ and } \mathcal{S} \models \pi[\bar{d}]\}$$

is denoted by $\forall$-*type*$(\bar{d}\ \mathcal{S})$.

(b) The set

$$\{\pi \in \mathcal{L}_{\text{form}} \mid \pi \text{ is existential, } \mathit{var}(\pi) \subseteq \mathit{domain}(\bar{d}), \text{ and } \mathcal{S} \models \pi[\bar{d}]\}$$

is denoted by $\exists$-*type*$(\bar{d}\ \mathcal{S})$.

Let scientist Ψ, $\mathrm{X} \subseteq \mathcal{L}_{\text{sen}}$, and $T \subseteq \mathcal{L}_{\text{sen}}$ be such that Ψ X-solves *mod*(T). We suppose that T is satisfiable and $\mathrm{X} \neq \emptyset$ (the other cases are trivial). By Lemma 53 choose $\bar{d} \in \mathbf{D}^{<\omega}$ and $\theta \in \mathrm{X}$ such that:

(57) a. $\bar{d}$ is a locking sequence for $(\Psi, \mathcal{S})$, and

b. $\Psi([\mathcal{S}, \bar{d}]) = \theta$.

It is sufficient to show that there is $\varphi \in \mathcal{L}_{\text{sen}}$ such that:

(58) a. φ is of form $\exists\forall$,

b. $\mathcal{S} \models \varphi$, and

c. $T \cup \{\varphi\} \models \theta$.

FACT 59. *Suppose that $\mathcal{U} \in mod(T)$ and sequence $\bar{u}$ are such that $length(\bar{u}) = length(\bar{d})$ and $\exists$-type$(\bar{u}, \mathcal{U}) \subseteq \exists$-type$(\bar{d}, \mathcal{S})$. Then $\mathcal{U} \models \theta$.*

PROOF. Suppose that $\mathcal{U}$, $\bar{u}$ satisfy the assumptions, and let $\bar{u'}$ extend $\bar{u}$. Let $\chi \in \mathcal{L}_{\text{form}}$ be the conjunction of the basic formulas in $[\mathcal{U}, \bar{u'}]$. Then

$$\mathcal{U} \models \exists x_{length(\bar{u})} \cdots \exists x_{length(\bar{u'})-1} \chi[\bar{u}].$$

Hence, because $\exists$-*type*$(\bar{u}, \mathcal{U}) \subseteq \exists$-*type*$(\bar{d}, \mathcal{S})$, $\mathcal{S} \models \exists x_{length(\bar{u})} \cdots \exists x_{length(\bar{u'})-1} \chi[\bar{d}]$. Hence, some extension $\bar{d'}$ of $\bar{d}$ of the same length as $\bar{u'}$ satisfies $[\mathcal{S}, \bar{d'}] = [\mathcal{U}, \bar{u'}]$. So, by (57)a, $\Psi([\mathcal{U}, \bar{u'}]) = \Psi([\mathcal{S}, \bar{d'}]) = \Psi([\mathcal{S}, \bar{d}])$. We infer immediately that:

(60) $\bar{u}$ is a locking sequence for $(\Psi, \mathcal{U})$.

From the same equality (with $\bar{u'} = \bar{u}$) and (57b), we obtain:

(61) $\Psi([\mathcal{U}, \bar{u}]) = \theta$.

Finally, Fact 59 follows from (60), (61) and the assumptions that $\mathcal{U} \in mod(T)$ and Ψ X-solves *mod*(T). □

Using Fact 59, we now show that:

FACT 62. *$T \cup \forall$-type$(\bar{d}, \mathcal{S}) \models \theta$.*

PROOF. By the Löwenheim–Skolem theorem it is sufficient to show that θ holds in any countable model $\mathcal{U} \in mod(T)$ in which $\forall$-*type*$(\bar{d}, \mathcal{S})$ is satisfied by a sequence $\bar{u}$ of the same length as $\bar{d}$. So assume that $\mathcal{U}$ and $\bar{u}$ are such a model and sequence. Then $\exists$-*type*$(\bar{u}, \mathcal{U}) \subseteq \exists$-*type*$(\bar{d}, \mathcal{S})$. Hence, by Fact 59, θ holds in $\mathcal{U}$. □

By compactness there is a finite subset Π of $\forall$-*type*$(\bar{d}, \mathcal{S})$ such that

(63) $T \cup \Pi \models \theta$.

To witness (58), let φ be the existential closure of the conjunction of Π. Then, φ can immediately be seen to satisfy (58a,b). That φ satisfies (58c) follows directly from (63).

12.6. *Proof of Example* 41

Let $\mathbf{P}_0$, X and $\mathcal{K}$ be as specified in the example.

Given $i, j \in N$, let $A_{i,j} \subset \mathbf{D}^\omega$ be the collection of **D**-sequences d such that not all of $\mathbf{d}_0, \ldots, \mathbf{d}_i$ occur in $d[j]$. By the assumption on $\mathbf{P}_0$, let strictly increasing $f : N \to N$ be such that for all $i \in N$ and $P \in \mathbf{P}_0$, $P(A_{i,f(i)}) < 1/2^i$. So for each $P \in \mathbf{P}_0$, $\sum_i P(A_{i,f(i)})$ converges. Hence, by the first Borel–Cantelli lemma (Billingsley, 1986, Theorem 4.3):

(64) $P(\limsup_i A_{i,f(i)}) = 0$ for every $P \in \mathbf{P}_0$.

Via the definition of $A_{i,j}$, (64) yields:

(65) For every $P \in \mathbf{P}_0$ the class of **D**-sequences d such that

$$\{\mathbf{d}_0, \ldots, \mathbf{d}_i\} \not\subseteq \mathit{range}(d[f(i)])$$

for infinitely many $i \in N$ has P-measure 0.

Define scientist Ψ as follows. For all environments e and all $j \in N$:

(a) if $j \in \mathit{range}(f)$ and $\bigwedge e[j]$ implies the existence of an R-chain of length at least $f^{-1}(j)$, then $\Psi(e[j]) = \theta$; (since f is strictly increasing, $f^{-1}(j)$ is well-defined).

(b) if $j \in \mathit{range}(f)$ and $\bigwedge e[j]$ does not imply the existence of an R-chain of length at least $f^{-1}(j)$, then $\Psi(e[j]) = \neg\theta$;

(c) if $j \notin \mathit{range}(f)$, then $\Psi(e[j]) = \Psi(e[j-1])$ (unless $j = 0$, in which case $\Psi(e[j]) = \forall x(x = x)$).

Now let $\mathcal{S}_j \in \mathcal{K}$ be given, with $j > 0$. Let **D**-sequences d and environment e for $\mathcal{S}_j$ and d also be given. Then for all but finitely many $i \in N$, $\bigwedge e[f(i)]$ does not imply the existence of an R-chain of length at least i (because there is no such chain). Hence, case (b) above arises for a cofinite subset of *range*(f) whereas case (a) arises for only a finite subset of *range*(f). It follows that Ψ converges to $\neg\theta$ on e. Hence, Ψ X-solves $\mathcal{S}_j$, so Ψ X-solves $\mathcal{S}_j$ on $\mathbf{P}_0$.

Regarding $\mathcal{S}_0$, let e be for $\mathcal{S}_0$ and d. Call e "bad" just in case for infinitely many $i \in N$, $\bigwedge e[f(i)]$ does not imply the existence of an R-chain of length at least i. It follows directly from (65) that for every $P \in \mathbf{P}_0$, the class of bad environments for $\mathcal{S}_0$ has P-measure 0. Hence, the P-probability is 1 that case (a) arises for a cofinite subset of *range*(f) whereas case (b) arises for only a finite subset of *range*(f). Thus, for every $P \in \mathbf{P}_0$, Ψ converges to θ on a class of environments for $\mathcal{S}_0$ of P-measure 1, so Ψ X-solves $\mathcal{S}_0$ on $\mathbf{P}_0$.

12.7. *Proof of Lemma 43*

Our demonstration of Lemma 43 proceeds via the following definition and propositions.

DEFINITION 66. Let $P \in \mathbf{P}$ be given. The class of $P' \in \mathbf{P}$ such that for some permutation $\pi : N \to N$, $P' = \{(\mathbf{d}_i, P(\mathbf{d}_{\pi(i)})) \mid i \in N\}$ is denoted *PERM*(P).

PROPOSITION 67. *Let* $\mathrm{X} \subseteq \mathcal{L}_{\text{sen}}$, $P \in \mathbf{P}$, *and* $T \subseteq \mathcal{L}_{\text{sen}}$ *be given. If* $mod(T)$ *is* X*-solvable on* P *then* $mod(T)$ *is* X*-solvable on* $PERM(P)$.

PROPOSITION 68. *Let* $\mathrm{X} \subseteq \mathcal{L}_{\text{sen}}$, $P \in \mathbf{P}$, *and* $T \subseteq \mathcal{L}_{\text{sen}}$ *be given. If* X *is not confirmable in* T *then for some* $P' \in PERM(P)$, $mod(T)$ *is not* X*-solvable on* P'.

To obtain Lemma 43 from the foregoing, let $\mathrm{X} \subseteq \mathcal{L}_{\text{sen}}$, $P \in \mathbf{P}$, and $T \subseteq \mathcal{L}_{\text{sen}}$ be given, and suppose that $mod(T)$ is X-solvable on P. Then by Proposition 67, $mod(T)$ is X-solvable on $PERM(P)$. So, by Proposition 68, X is confirmable in T.

It remains to prove the two propositions.

12.7.1. Proof of Proposition 67

Suppose that scientist Ψ X-solves $mod(T)$ on P, and let $\mathcal{S} \in mod(T)$ be given. Let π be any permutation of N, and let $P' = \{(\mathbf{d}_i, P(\mathbf{d}_{\pi(i)})) \mid i \in N\}$. It suffices to show that Ψ X-solves $\mathcal{S}$ on P'.

Given **D**-sequence d, let $\pi(d)$ be its permutation (via the indexes of **D**) under π. Given subset D of **D**-sequences, let $\pi(D) = \{\pi(d) \mid d \in D\}$. Since the measure of a collection of **D**-sequences is determined only by the probabilities applying to each coordinate (and not by their names), we have:

(69) For every set D of **D**-sequences, $P(\pi(D)) = P'(D)$.

Let $\mathcal{S}'$ be the structure whose vocabulary is interpreted in the following way. For individual constant c, $c^{\mathcal{S}'} = \mathbf{d}_{\pi(j)}$ iff $c^{\mathcal{S}} = \mathbf{d}_j$. For n-ary relation symbol R, $(d_{\pi(j_1)}, \ldots, d_{\pi(j_n)}) \in R^{\mathcal{S}'}$ iff $(d_{j_1}, \ldots, d_{j_n}) \in R^{\mathcal{S}}$. Evidently, $\mathcal{S}' \in mod(T)$ since $\mathcal{S}$ and $\mathcal{S}'$ are isomorphic. Hence:

(70) Ψ X-solves $\mathcal{S}'$ on P.

Let D be the set of **D**-sequences d such that Ψ X-solves $[\mathcal{S}', \pi(d)]$ on P. By (70), $P(\pi(D)) = 1$, so by (69) the proof is completed if we show that for almost every $d \in D$, Ψ X-solves $[\mathcal{S}, d]$ on P'. However, this follows immediately from the following fact, easy to verify: for all **D**-sequences d, $[\mathcal{S}', \pi(d)] = [\mathcal{S}, d]$.

12.7.2. Proof of Proposition 68

The proposition follows from a stronger result demonstrated in (Martin and Osherson, to appear); to avoid a lengthy argument, we refer the reader to the latter source.

12.8. Proof of Proposition 47

The right-to-left direction of the proposition is immediate. For the other direction, Let $\mathrm{X} \subseteq \mathcal{L}_{\text{sen}}$, collection $\mathcal{K}$ of structures, and $\mathbf{P}_0 \subseteq \mathbf{P}$ be given. Suppose that scientist Ψ X-solves $\mathcal{K}$ on $\mathbf{P}_0$ with probability greater than 0. We shall exhibit scientist Ψ_0 that X-solves $\mathcal{K}$ on $\mathbf{P}_0$. For this purpose some definitions and facts are needed.

DEFINITION 71.

(a) Given $n \in N$ and **D**-sequences d, the tail of d that begins at d_n is denoted d^n.

(b) Given structure $\mathcal{S}$, we denote by $\widehat{\mathbf{d}}_{\mathcal{S}}$ the class of **D**-sequences d such that for some $n \in N$:

(i) $range(d^n) = \mathbf{D}$, and
(ii) Ψ X-solves $[\mathcal{S}, d^n]$.

FACT 72. *For all $\mathcal{S} \in \mathcal{K}$ and $P \in \mathbf{P}_0$, $P(\widehat{\mathbf{d}}_{\mathcal{S}}) = 1$.*

PROOF. Let $P \in \mathbf{P}_0$ and $\mathcal{S} \in \mathcal{K}$ be given. By choice of Ψ, let $\widehat{\mathbf{d}}$ be a measurable class of **D**-sequences such that:

(73) a. for all $d \in \widehat{\mathbf{d}}$,
(i) $range(d) = \mathbf{D}$,
(ii) Ψ X-solves $[\mathcal{S}, d]$.
b. $P(\widehat{\mathbf{d}}) > 0$.

By (73a), $\widehat{\mathbf{d}} \subseteq \widehat{\mathbf{d}}_{\mathcal{S}}$, so (73b) implies $P(\widehat{\mathbf{d}}_{\mathcal{S}}) > 0$. It follows immediately from Kolmogorov's zero–one law for tail events (Billingsley, 1986, Theorem 4.5) that $P(\widehat{\mathbf{d}}_{\mathcal{S}}) = 1$. □

By Definition 47 and the choice of Ψ we also have:

FACT 74. *Let $P \in \mathbf{P}_0$, $n \in N$, and $\mathcal{S} \in \mathcal{K}$ be given. Let $\widehat{\mathbf{d}}$ be the class of **D**-sequences d such that Ψ is misleading on $[\mathcal{S}, d^n]$. Then $P(\widehat{\mathbf{d}}) = 0$.*

As a final preliminary, we make use of the following definition and fact.

DEFINITION 75. Let σ be the initial finite segment of length m in some environment e. Let scientist Ψ also be given. The *score for Ψ on σ* is the smallest $j \in N$ such that $\Psi(e[i]) = \Psi(\sigma)$ for all i with $j \leqslant i \leqslant m$.

Intuitively, the lower the score for Ψ on σ, the greater sign Ψ gives of having begun its convergence within σ. We record two obvious facts about score.

FACT 76.

(a) *Suppose that scientist Ψ converges on environment e. Then there is $s \in N$ such that for all $k \in N$, the score for Ψ on $e[k]$ is bounded by s.*

(b) *Suppose that scientist Ψ does not converges on environment e. Then for every $s \in N$ there is $\ell \in N$ such that the score for Ψ on $e[k]$ exceeds s if $k \geqslant \ell$.*

In what follows we assume the existence of a uniform recursive procedure which converts finite initial segments of environments into new segments that "start over" at a specified position n. That is, for all structures $\mathcal{S}$, **D**-sequences d, and $m \in N$, the procedure converts $[\mathcal{S}, d[m]]$ into $[\mathcal{S}, b[m - n]]$ where $b = d^n$ (if $m < n$, we take $b = d$, so $[\mathcal{S}, d[m]]$ remains unchanged). It is easy to verify the existence of this procedure.

Facts 72, 74 and 76 make it clear how to construct the desired scientist Ψ_0. We provide an informal description. Let E be an enumeration of $N \times N$.

Given incoming environment e, Ψ_0 works in stages to create ever longer initial segments $e^0, e^1, \ldots$ of e, where e^i is the environment that "starts over" at position i of e. At stage zero we have $\Psi_0(\emptyset) = \Psi(\emptyset)$. Between two stages, while not enough of e is available to proceed to the next stage, Ψ_0 repeats its last conjecture on each new position in e. At the nth stage ($n \geqslant 1$), Ψ_0 has examined enough of e to construct the initial segments of length n for each of $e^0, \ldots, e^n$. Let these initial segments be denoted $\sigma^0 \cdots \sigma^n$. Let (x, y) be the first pair enumerated in E such that $x, y \leqslant n$ and Ψ's score on σ^x is y. Then at the nth stage Ψ_0 conjectures $\Psi(\sigma^x)$. Intuitively, Ψ_0 looks for a tail of e on which Ψ's conjectures appear eventually to stop changing. For each (x, y) in turn, Ψ_0 conjectures that one such tail is e^x and that Ψ's hypotheses on e^x stopped changing at position y. This conjecture is kept until Ψ's score on some initial segment of e^x is shown to be greater than y.

To see that Ψ_0 X-solves $\mathcal{K}$ on $\mathbf{P}_0$, let structure $\mathcal{S} \in \mathcal{K}$, environment e for $\mathcal{S}$, and $P \in \mathbf{P}_0$ be given. By Fact 72 the probability (according to P) is 1 that there is $n \in N$ such that e^n is also an environment for $\mathcal{S}$ and that Ψ X-solves e^n. Call such a tail of e "good", the others "bad". By Facts 74 and 76 the probability is 1 that Ψ's scores on initial segments of any bad tail e^x eventually defeat any hypothesis (x, y). It is thus straightforward to verify that Ψ_0 converges on e to $\Psi(\sigma)$ for some σ with the following properties:

(a) σ is an initial segment of a good tail e^n of e, and

(b) for all extensions τ of σ in e^n, $\Psi(\tau) = \Psi(\sigma)$.

Since e^n is a good tail, for this σ we have $\Psi(\sigma) \in$ X and $\mathcal{S} \models \Psi(\sigma)$. Hence with probability 1, Ψ_0 converges on e to a sentence of X true in the underlying structure $\mathcal{S}$. This completes the proof.

We note that straightforward modifications to the foregoing proof demonstrate the following version of Proposition 49.

PROPOSITION 77. *Let $\mathbf{P}_0 \subseteq \mathbf{P}$, recursive* X $\subseteq \mathcal{L}_{\text{sen}}$, *and collection $\mathcal{K}$ of structures be given. Suppose that some computable scientist Ψ* X*-solves $\mathcal{K}$ on $\mathbf{P}_0$ with probability greater than* 0. *Then there is computable scientist Ψ_0, constructible in uniform recursive fashion from Ψ, that* X*-solves $\mathcal{K}$ on $\mathbf{P}_0$.*

References

Angluin, D. and Smith, C.H. (1983), *A survey of inductive inference: Theory and methods*, ACM Comput. Surv. **15**(3), 237–269.

Angluin, D. (1980), *Inductive inference of formal languages from positive data*, Inform. and Control **45**(2), 117–135.

Angluin, D. (1988), *Identifying languages from stochastic examples*, Technical Report YALEU/DCS/RR-614, Yale University, Dept. of Computer Science, New Haven, CT.

Anthony, M. and Biggs, N. (1992), *Computational Learning Theory*, Cambridge Tracts in Theoretical Computer Science vol. 30, Cambridge Univ. Press, Cambridge, MA.

Baker, C.L. and McCarthy, J. (eds) (1981), *The Logical Problem of Language Acquisition*, MIT Press, Cambridge, MA.

Berwick, R. (1986), *The Acquisition of Syntactic Knowledge*, MIT Press, Cambridge, MA.

Bickerton, D. (1981), *The Roots of Language*, Karoma, Ann Arbor, MI.

Billingsley, P. (1986), *Probability and Measure*, Wiley, New York (2nd edn).

Blum, L. and Blum, M. (1975), *Toward a mathematical theory of inductive inference*, Inform. and Control **28**(2), 125–155.

Blum, M. (1967), *A machine independent theory of the complexity of the recursive functions*, J. Assoc. Comput. Mach. **14**(2), 322–336.

Borer, H. and Wexler, K. (1987), *The maturation of syntax*, Parameter Setting, T. Roeper and E. Williams, eds, Reidel, Dordrecht.

Brown, R. and Hanlon, C. (1970), *Derivational complexity and the order of acquisition in child speech*, Cognition and the Development of Language, J.R. Hayes, ed., Wiley, New York.

Case, J. and Smith, C. (1983), *Comparison of identification criteria for machine inductive inference*, Theor. Comput. Sci. **25**, 193–220.

Chang, C.C. and Keisler, H.J. (1977), *Model Theory*, North-Holland, Amsterdam (2nd edn).

Chomsky, N. (1957), *Syntactic Structures*, Mouton, Berlin.

Chomsky, N. (1965), *Aspects of the Theory of Syntax*, MIT Press, Cambridge, MA.

Chomsky, N. (1975), *Reflections on Language*, Pantheon.

Chomsky, N. (1986), *Knowledge of Language: Its Nature, Origin and Use*, Praeger, New York.

Daley, R. and Smith, C. (1986), *On the complexity of inductive inference*, Inform. and Control **69**, 12–40.

Daley, R.P. (1986), *Inductive inference hierarchies: Probabilistic vs pluralistic*, Lect. Notes Comput. Sci. vol. 215, 73–82.

Demetras, M., Post, K. and Snow, C. (1986), *Feedback to first language learners: The role of repetitions and clarification questions*, J. Child Lang. **13**, 275–292.

Earman, J. (1992), *Bayes or Bust?*, MIT Press, Cambridge, MA.

Feldman, H., Goldin-Meadow, L. and Gleitman, S. (1978), *Beyond Herotodus: The creation of language by linguistically deprived deaf children*, Action, Symbol, and Gesture: The Emergence of Language, A. Lock, ed., Academic Press, San Diego.

Fulk, M. (1988), *Saving the phenomenon: Requirements that inductive machines not contradict known data*, Inform. and Comput. **79**(3), 193–209.

Fulk, M. (1990), *Prudence and other conditions on formal language learning*, Inform. and Comput. **85**(1), 1–11.

Fulk, M.A. and Jain, S. (1992), *Approximate inference and scientific method*, Inform. and Comput. (to appear).

Fulk, M., Jain, S. and Osherson, D. (1992), *Open problems in systems that learn*, J. Comput. System Sci.

Gaifman, H. and Snir, M. (1982), *Probabilities over rich languages*, J. Symb. Logic **47**, 495–548.

Gaifman, H., Osherson, D. and Weinstein, S. (1990), *A reason for theoretical terms*, Erkenntnis **32**, 149–159.

Gleitman, L. (1986), *Biological dispositions to learn language*, Language Learning and Concept Acquisition, W. Demopoulos and A. Marras, eds, ABLEX, Norwood, NJ.

Glymour, C. (1985), *Inductive inference in the limit*, Erkenntnis **22**, 23–31.

Glymour, C. (1992), *Thinking Things Through*, MIT Press, Cambridge, MA.

Glymour, C. and Kelly, K. (1989), *On convergence to the truth and nothing but the truth*, Philos. Sci. **56**.

Gold, E.M. (1965), *Limiting recursion*, J. Symb. Logic **30**(1), 28–48.

Gold, E.M. (1967), *Language identification in the limit*, Inform. and Control **10**, 447–474.

Goldman, A. (1986), *Epistemology and Cognition*, Harvard Univ. Press, Cambridge, MA.

Hirsh-Pasek, K., Treiman, R. and Schneiderman, M. (1984), *Brown and Hanlon revisited: Mothers' sensitivity to ungrammatical forms*, J. Child Lang. **11**, 81–88.

Hornstein, N. and Lightfoot, D. (eds) (1981), *Explanation in Linguistics*, Longman, London.

Jain, S. and Sharma, A. (1990a), *Finite learning by a team*, Proc. 3rd Annu. Workshop on Comput. Learning Theory, Morgan Kaufmann, San Mateo, CA, 163–177.

Jain, S. and Sharma, A. (1990b), *Language learning by a team*, Proceedings of the 17th International Colloquium on Automata, Languages and Programming, M.S. Paterson, ed., Springer, Berlin, 153–166.

Jain, S., Sharma, A. and Case, J. (1989), *Convergence to nearly minimal size grammars by vacillating learning machines*, Proc. 2nd Annu. Workshop on Comput. Learning Theory, R. Rivest, D. Haussler and M. Warmuth, eds, Morgan Kaufmann, San Mateo, CA, 189–199.

Johnson, J.S. and Newport, E.L. (1989), *Critical period effects in second language learning: The influence of maturational state on the acquisition of English as a second language*, Cogn. Psych. **21**, 60–99.

Juhl, C. (1993), *Bayesianism and reliable scientific inquiry*, Philos. Sci. **60**, 302–319.

Kanazawa, M. (1993), *Identification in the limit of categorial grammars*, Technical report, Department of Linguistics, Stanford University.

Kanazawa, M. (1994), *Learnable classes of categorial grammars*, PhD Thesis, Department of Linguistics, Stanford University.

Kapur, S. and Bilardi, G. (1992), *On uniform learnability of language families*, Inform. Process. Lett. **44**, 35–38.

Kapur, S. (1991), *Computational learning of languages*, Technical Report TR 91-1234, Department of Computer Science, Cornell University.

Kelly, K.T. and Glymour, C. (1992), *Inductive inference and theory-laden data*, J. Philos. Logic **21**(4).

Kelly, K.T. and Glymour, C. (1993), *Theory discovery from data with mixed quantifiers*, J. Philos. Logic.

Kelly, K.T. (1994), *The Logic of Reliable Inquiry*, MIT Press, Cambridge, MA.

Kinber, E. (1994), *Monotonicity versus efficiency for learning languages from texts*, Technical Report 94-22, University of Delaware, Department of Computer and Information Sciences.

Kornblith, H. (ed.) (1985), *Naturalizing Epistemology*, MIT Press, Cambridge, MA.

Kugel, P. (1977), *Induction, pure and simple*, Inform. and Control **35**, 276–336.

Kuipers, T.A. (ed.) (1987), *What is Closer-to-the-Truth?*, Rodopi, Amsterdam.

Kurtz, S.A. and Royer, J.S. (1988), *Prudence in language learning*, Proc. 1st Annu. Workshop on Comput. Learning Theory, D. Haussler and L. Pitt, eds, Morgan Kaufmann, Los Altos, CA, 143–156.

Landau, B. and Gleitman, L. (1985), *Language and Experience*, Harvard Univ. Press.

Lasnik, H. (1989), *On certain substitutes for negative data*, Learnability and Linguistic Theory, R.J. Mathews and W. Demopoulos, eds, Kluwer, Dordrecht.

Lenneberg, E. (1967), *Biological Foundations of Language*, Wiley, New York.

Levy, A. (1979), *Basic Set Theory*, Springer, Berlin.

Lightfoot, D. (1982), *The Language Lottery*, MIT Press, Cambridge, MA.

Machtey, M. and Young, P. (1978), *An Introduction to the General Theory of Algorithms*, North-Holland, New York.

Martin, E. and Osherson, D., *Elements of Scientific Discovery*, to appear.

Matthews, R.J. (1984), *The plausibility of rationalism*, J. Philos. **81**, 492–515.

Matthews, R.J. (1989), *Learnability and linguistic theory*, Learnability and Linguistic Theory, R.J. Matthews and W. Demopoulos, eds, Kluwer, Dordrecht.

Mazurkewich, I. and White, L. (1984), *The acquisition of dative-alternation: Unlearning overgeneralizations*, Cognition **16**(3), 261–283.

Newport, E.L. and Supalla, T. (1989), *A critical period effect in the acquisition of a primary language*, Science.

Newport, E., Gleitman, L. and Gleitman, H. (1977), *Mother i'd rather do it myself: Some effects and noneffects of maternal speech style*, Talking to Children: Language Input and Acquisition, C. Snow and C. Ferguson, eds, Cambridge Univ. Press, Cambridge, MA.

Osherson, D. and Wasow, T. (1976), *Species specificity and task specificity in the study of language: A methodological note*, Cognition **4**(2), 203–214.

Osherson, D. and Weinstein, S. (1982a), *A note on formal learning theory*, Cognition **11**, 77–88.

Osherson, D.N. and Weinstein, S. (1982b), *Criteria of language learning*, Inform. and Control **52**, 123–138.

Osherson, D.N. and Weinstein, S. (1986), *Identification in the limit of first order structures*, J. Philos. Logic **15**, 55–81.

Osherson, D. and Weinstein, S. (1989a), *Identifiable collections of countable structures*, Philos. Sci. **18**, 1–42.

Osherson, D. and Weinstein, S. (1989b), *Paradigms of truth-detection*, J. Philos. Logic **18**, 1–42.

Osherson, D. and Weinstein, S. (1993), *Relevant consequence and scientific discovery*, J. Philos. Logic **22**, 437–448.

Osherson, D. and Weinstein, S., *On the danger of half-truths*, J. Philos. Logic, in press.

Osherson, D. and Weinstein, S. (1995), *On the study of first language acquisition*, J. Math. Psychol. **39**(2), 129–145.

Osherson, D., Stob, M. and Weinstein, S. (1982), *Learning strategies*, Inform. and Control **53**(1), 32–51.

Osherson, D.N., Stob, M. and Weinstein, S. (1984), *Learning theory and natural language*, Cognition **17**(1), 1–28.

Osherson, D., Stob, M. and Weinstein, S. (1986a), *Aggregating inductive expertise*, Inform. and Control **70**(1), 69–95.

Osherson, D., Stob, M. and Weinstein, S. (1986b), *Analysis of a learning paradigm*, Language Learning and Concept Acquisition, W. Demopoulos and A. Marras, eds, Ablex, Norwood, NJ.

Osherson, D.N., Stob, M. and Weinstein, S. (1986c), *Systems that Learn: An Introduction to Learning Theory for Cognitive and Computer Scientists*, MIT Press, Cambridge, MA.

Osherson, D., Stob, M. and Weinstein, S. (1988), *Synthesising inductive expertise*, Inform. and Comput. **77**, 138–161.

Osherson, D.N., Stob, M. and Weinstein, S. (1989), *On approximate truth*, Proc. 2nd Annu. Workshop on Comput. Learning Theory, Morgan Kaufmann, San Mateo, CA, 88–101.

Osherson, D., Stob, M. and Weinstein, S. (1991a), *New directions in automated scientific discovery*, Inform. Sci.

Osherson, D., Stob, M. and Weinstein, S. (1991b), *A universal inductive inference machine*, J. Symb. Logic **56**(2), 661–672.

Osherson, D., Stob, M. and Weinstein, S. (1992), *A universal method of scientific inquiry*, Mach. Learning **9**, 261–271.

Pappas, G. (ed.) (1979), *Justification and Knowledge*, Reidel, Dordrecht.

Penner, S. (1987), *Parental responses to grammatical and ungrammatical child utterances*, Child Dev. **58**, 376–384.

Pinker, S. (1989), *Markedness and language development*, Learnability and Linguistic Theory, R.J. Matthews and W. Demopoulos, eds, Kluwer, Dordrecht.

Pinker, S. (1990), *Language acquisition*, Invitation to Cognitive Science: Language, D. Osherson and H. Lasnik, eds, MIT Press, Cambridge, MA, 199–241.

Pitt, L. and Smith, C. (1988), *Probability and plurality for aggregations of learning machines*, Inform. and Comput. **77**, 77–92.

Pitt, L. (1989), *Probabilistic inductive inference*, J. Assoc. Comput. Mach. **36**(2), 383–433.

Putnam, H. (1965), *Trial and error predicates and a solution to a problem of Mostowski*, J. Symb. Logic **30**(1), 49–57.

Putnam, H. (1967), *The 'innateness hypothesis' and explanatory models in linguistics*, Synthese **17**(1), 12–22.

Putnam, H. (1975), *Probability and confirmation*, Mathematics, Matter and Method, Cambridge Univ. Press.

Putnam, H. (1980), *'What is innate and why'*, The Debate between Jean Piaget and Noam Chomsky, M. Piatelli-Palmarini, ed., Harvard Univ. Press.

Rogers, H. (1967), *Theory of Recursive Functions and Effective Computability*, McGraw-Hill, New York.

Royer, J. (1986), *Inductive inference of approximations*, Inform. and Control **70**, 156–178.

Sankoff, G. and Brown, P. (1976), *The origins of syntax in discourse: A case study of tok pisin relatives*, Language **52**, 631–666.

Schieffelin, B. and Eisenberg, A. (1981), *Cultural variation in children's conversations*, Early Language: Acquisition and Intervention, R. Schiefelbusch and D. Bricker, eds, Univ. of Park Press, Baltimore, MO.

Schurz, G. and Weingartner, P. (1987), *Verisimilitude defined by relevant consequence-elements. A new reconstruction of Popper's idea*, What is Closer-to-the-Truth?, T.A. Kuipers, ed., Rodopi, Amsterdam.

Shapiro, E.Y. (1981), *A general incremental algorithm that infers theory from facts*, Proc. of the Seventh Internat. Joint Conf. on Artif. Intell. vol. 1, Morgan Kaufmann, Los Altos, CA, 446–451.

Shapiro, E.Y. (1983), *Algorithmic Program Debugging*, MIT Press, Cambridge, MA.

Shapiro, E.Y. (1991), *Inductive inference of theories from facts*, Computational Logic: Essays in honor of Alan Robinson, J.-L. Lassez and G. Plotkin, eds, MIT Press, Cambridge, MA.

Sharma, A., Jain, S., Royer, J., Martin, E., Osherson, D. and Weinstein, D. (to appear), *Systems that Learn* (2nd edn).

Shinohara, T. (1990), *Inductive inference from positive data is powerful*, Proc. 3rd Annu. Workshop on Comput. Learning Theory, Morgan Kaufmann, Los Altos, CA, 97–110.

Smullyan, R.M. (1961), *Theory of Formal Systems*, Princeton Univ. Press, Princeton, NJ.

Solomonoff, R.J. (1964), *A formal theory of inductive inference: Part 1*, Inform. and Control **7**, 1–22.

Stich, S. (1978), *Empiricism, innateness, and linguistic universals*, Philos. Stud. **33**(3), 273–286.

Truscott, J. and Wexler, K. (1989), *Some problems in the parametric analysis of learnability*, Learnability and Linguistic Theory, R.J. Matthews and W. Demopoulos, eds, Kluwer, Dordrecht.

Van Riemsdijk, H. and Williams, E. (1986), *Introduction to the Theory of Grammar*, MIT Press, Cambridge, MA.

Wasow, T. (1989), *Grammatical theory*, Foundations of Cognitive Science, M. Posner, ed., MIT Press, Cambridge, MA.

Wexler, K. and Culicover, P. (1980), *Formal Principles of Language Acquisition*, MIT Press, Cambridge, MA.

Wiehagen, R. (1978), *Characterization problems in the theory of inductive inference*, Proc. of 5th Colloquium on Automata, Languages, and Programming, Springer, Berlin, 494–508.

CHAPTER 14

Nonmonotonicity in Linguistics

Richmond H. Thomason

Intelligent Systems Program, University of Pittsburgh, Pittsburgh, PA 15260, USA
E-mail: thomason@isp.pitt.edu

Contents

HANDBOOK OF LOGIC AND LANGUAGE
Edited by J. van Benthem and A. ter Meulen

1. Nonmonotonicity and linguistic theory

Unlike many other chapters of this *Handbook*, this contribution is more an intimation of new opportunities than a survey of completed developments. Fulfilling the promise of these opportunities will require the creation of a group of theoretical linguists who are also familiar with some of the details of a complex and often bewildering new area of logic. I will try to provide an outline of the logical issues, with pointers to the literature, to indicate some of the applications in linguistics, and to provide references to the work that has already been done in applying nonmonotonic logic in linguistics.[1]

1.1. Monotonicity and nonmonotonicity are properties of logical consequence

Associated with any logic there is a consequence relation $\vdash$, between sets of formulas and formulas. Interpreted proof theoretically, $\Gamma \vdash A$ means that there is a hypothetical proof, or deduction, of A from Γ. Interpreted model theoretically, $\Gamma \vdash A$ means that A is true in every model of Γ.

Some properties of the logical consequence relation will vary from logic to logic:

$$\{A \to B, \neg A \to B\} \vdash B,$$

for instance, will hold in Boolean logics, but not in constructive logics, such as intuitionistic logic. Other properties of logical consequence relations seem very basic, and hold quite generally. Among these very general properties is monotonicity:

$$\text{If } \Gamma \vdash B \text{ then } \Gamma \cup \{A\} \vdash B.$$

This property says that the logical consequences of a set of hypotheses grow monotonically in relation to the hypotheses; in other words, adding new information A to the hypotheses Γ can't result in the retraction of any consequence B.

The monotonicity property follows trivially from the definitions of provability and validity that are used in familiar systems of logic. Proof theoretically, we use the fact that mathematical proofs only depend on the *presence* of information, and are not sensitive to its *absence*: if $\mathcal{P}$ is a proof relative to a set Γ of hypotheses, then $\mathcal{P}$ is also a proof relative to any larger set $\Gamma \cup \Delta$. Model theoretically, we use the fact that every model of $\Gamma \cup \Delta$ is also a model of Γ.

Nonmonotonicity is simply the failure of monotonicity. So nonmonotonicity is a property of the consequence relation – and a system of logic is said to be nonmonotonic if its consequence relation has the nonmonotonicity property. Nonmonotonicity is intimately connected with *default inferences*. Suppose we want to infer B unless A is known, and that Γ does not entail A. If we elect to satisfy this need by altering the logical consequence relation, we then have a failure of monotonicity: we would have $\Gamma \vdash B$, but not $\Gamma \cup \{A\} \vdash B$.

[1] I will try to make information on the topics discussed in this chapter available though World Wide Web and anonymous ftp; this seems to be the best way to deal with changes in this rapidly developing field. My current e-mail and World Wide Web addresses are thomason@isp.pitt.edu and http://www.pitt.edu/~thomason/thomason.html.

1.2. Motivating nonmonotonicity

Although defaults are a part of life, we are supposed to avoid them in mathematics (and in theoretical science in general). The standards for mathematical proof are designed so that what is proven will never need to be retracted under any possible assumptions. Mathematicians are trained not to claim theorems until their proofs have covered all the possible cases; any exceptional cases in which the result does not hold have to be formulated and explicitly excluded in the statement of the theorem. In retrospect, we can see the fundamental status of monotonicity in symbolic logic as a byproduct of the early emphasis in symbolic logic on mathematical reasoning.

The need to formulate and investigate nonmonotonic logics arose out of a recognition that other forms of reasoning are not always subject to this constraint, together with a reluctance to explain away the nonmonotonic effects by using mechanisms, such as probability, that are orthogonal to logical consequence. Most of the recent motivation for this work has been associated with research programs in Artificial Intelligence (AI) that stress the importance of formalizing common sense reasoning,[2] and that seek to apply logical techniques to formalize the knowledge involved in reasoning tasks like planning and problem solving.

Closed world reasoning provides a simple example of the need for nonmonotonicity, and still may remain the most widespread application of nonmonotonic reasoning. This type of reasoning arises whenever we think that we have been given complete information on a given topic. In such cases, we are willing to answer "no" to a question on a topic when we fail to find a reason for it in our data.[3]

In planning my time, for instance, I may carefully write down all my appointments and deadlines in a calendar. But no matter how meticulous I am, I won't try to enter all the things that I *don't* have to do. I take this information to be implicit in my calendar; I infer that I don't have an appointment at 1 pm today by noticing that there is no appointment entered for 1 pm in my calendar. This "closed-world" inference makes the calendar's consequence relation $\mid\!\sim$ nonmonotonic.[4] If T is my current calendar and A is 'Dentist appointment at 1 pm', we have $T \mid\!\sim \neg A$. But we do not want to have $T \cup \{A\} \not\mid\!\sim \neg A$. When the hypothesis is added that I have a dentist appointment at 1pm, it would of course be wrong to continue to infer that I don't have a dentist appointment at that time.

1.3. Nonmonotonicity and linguistics

The origins of nonmonotonic logics in AI share a motive with a research tradition that attempts to see linguistic meaning as a systematic source of insights into thought and reasoning. This tradition goes back at least to Wilhelm von Humboldt's work in the Nineteenth Century; it continued into this century with linguists such as Otto Jespersen and philosophers such as Ernst Cassirer. More recent linguistic work attempts to link this

[2] See Hobbs and Moore (1985).

[3] In the simplest form of closed world reasoning, these "questions" will correspond to positive and negative literals.

[4] Here we follow the common practice of using $\mid\!\sim$ for nonmonotonic consequence.

tradition to formal logic.[5] Because the projects of formalizing basic areas of common sense reasoning and of providing logical tools for interpreting natural language are so closely related, this is perhaps the most obvious application for nonmonotonic logics in linguistic theory, and there is a growing body of work in linguistic semantics that makes use of nonmonotonic logic. The matter is pursued in Section 7, below.

But the relations between nonmonotonic logic and linguistic theory are much more pervasive than this; nonmonotonicity can be recognized in many areas of linguistic research that have little or nothing to do either with meaning or common sense. Every area of linguistics encounters generalizations that have exceptions. As long as linguistic theory lacks direct a way to represent such generalizations, they can't be expressed in the theories that explain them. In practice, this often means that the generalizations are saved by *ad hoc* maneuvers.

Most of the available applications of nonmonotonicity in linguistics have been developed by computer scientists, or by linguists with computational interests. See, for instance, Gazdar (1987) for an excellent survey of applications of default reasoning in various areas of linguistics; Gazdar has also played a central part in the development of DATR, a system for representing morphological information that makes use of defaults.[6] For a more recent general paper exploring these applications, see Briscoe, Copestake and Lascarides (1995). There is a fairly extensive literature devoted to motivating uses of defaults and nonmonotonic reasoning in reasoning about lexical information and describing systems that use this sort of information in managing the lexicon. For instance, see Boguraev and Pustejovsky (1990), Briscoe, De Paiva and Copestake (1993), Daelemans (1987), De Smedt (1990), Flickinger (1987), Flickinger and Nerbonne (1992), Krieger and Nerbonne (1993), Russell, Carroll and Warwick (1991), and Shieber (1986).

But I think that the computational slant of much of this work is accidental. It may have more to do with the fact that computational linguists are less bound to traditional linguistic theory, and are more likely to be familiar with the new logical formalisms, than with any intrinsic connection between computation and defeasible theories of language. (Indeed, nonmonotonic logic has been used so far more as a theoretical than an applied tool.)

This chapter will not exclude computational applications, but it is also meant to make a case for a more radical suggestion: *that nonmonotonic logics are not only useful for representing common sense reasoning, but also provide appropriate foundations for some scientific theories, and in particular for linguistics.*

The claim that some sciences study exceptionless rules, while others must deal with rules that have exceptions, goes back to Aristotle's works in the methodology of science. But Aristotle placed the latter sciences in a vulnerable position by failing to provide any logical foundation for them, and by basing the separation between the two on a false cosmology. Now, we may be in a better position to articulate a science that deals with defeasible rules. The nonmonotonic logics provide the missing foundation, and linguistics gives us a well developed theoretical domain that is rich in defeasible rules. The

---

[5] Much of the work in Montague grammar has this goal; see Bach (1989) for a good general work that is explicit about this motivation for "natural language metaphysics".

[6] See Evans and Gazdar (1989a, 1989b, 1990) and Evans, Gazdar and Moser (1994).

larger project is challenging: the logics are complex and diverse, there are methodological problems,[7] and the sheer size of the project is frightening. But it is a tremendous opportunity for a strategic innovation in scientific methodology. This larger project is certainly not going to be much advanced without strong motivations within the discipline, so in the remainder of this chapter I will concentrate on case studies that provide the motivation.

2. Overview of nonmonotonic reasoning

Let me explain my expository predicament. Many readers of this *Handbook* will not be familiar with nonmonotonic logic. But (due mainly to intensive work by logically minded researchers in AI) the technical dimension of the topic has matured rapidly – without, however, generating any consensus on a single approach. I will not try here to provide even a barely adequate technical introduction to this area; instead, I will sketch a map, with pointers to the literature. What follows is not really an adequate introduction to the theory of nonmonotonic reasoning. I tried to produce a guide, with references to the places where a more adequate introduction can be found.

As usual with any new field, it is hard to avoid consulting the primary research articles. But readers who want a more systematic general introduction to the topic could consult either Ginsberg (1988a), Besnard (1989), Brewka (1991), or Davis (1990, Section 3.1). Reiter (1988) provides a briefer overview.[8]

The only specific approach to nonmonotonic logic that I will discuss in any detail is Reiter's default logic.

2.1. Default logic

This approach, due to Raymond Reiter (see Reiter, 1980) is relatively conservative from a logical standpoint and yet exemplifies many of the themes of nonmonotonic logic. Therefore it can be used as an model for illustrating the features and problems of this area of logic. That is what I will try to do in this section. But default logic is important in its own right, and represents one of the better developed areas in nonmonotonic logic. The introduction that follows will orient readers to the ideas, I hope, but will not begin to develop technical details. For these details, readers may want to consult Reiter (1980), Besnard (1989), Brewka (1991, Chapter 3), and the references from the last two of these.

---

[7] See Section 5.1, below, for a discussion of some of these.

[8] Ginsberg (1988a) is a collection of early articles in the area. Ginsberg's introduction to the volume remains one of the best ways to become better acquainted with the subject. Its readability and coverage make up for the fact that it is now somewhat out of date. A recent general work, (Brewka, 1991), covers most of the topics that would be of importance to those interested in linguistic applications. I recommend these two general introductions. And see below for references to more specialized sources.

2.1.1. *Elements of default logic*

A default theory is formed, according to Reiter, by adding new rules of inference, called *default rules*, to a first-order theory. These rules have the form

$$\frac{A:B}{C}, \quad \text{where } A,\ B, \text{ and } C \text{ are ordinary first-order formulas.} \tag{2.1}$$

The informal interpretation of such a rule is that C can be concluded provided A has been concluded and B can be consistently assumed. Thus, if B is a tautology, such a default rule specializes to a familiar monotonic rule with premiss A and conclusion C.

Defaults are not first-class citizens of default logic: they appear only as rules, not as formulas that enter into logical constructions or can themselves enter into inferential relations. Thus, it makes no sense in default logic to negate a default, to conjoin it with something, or to ask what defaults follow from a given default theory. There is one striking disadvantage to this limitation. Almost all useful default rules are general, and one wants to capture this generality using a universal quantifier. But it is illegitimate to write things like $(\forall x)\ [Bird(x) : Flies(x)/Flies(x)]$.[9]

So default logic doesn't provide a direct way of capturing the rule that birds fly – everyone's stock example of a default. This limitation can be circumvented by treating $Bird(x) : Flies(x)/Flies(x)$ as an abbreviation for a rule scheme, the set of all defaults of the form $Bird(t) : Flies(t)/Flies(t)$, where t is any closed term. In many papers on default logic and similar topics, the authors speak as if defaults involved predicates rather than closed formulas; this way of speaking has to be understood as an appeal to this schematic device.

The special case

$$\frac{A:B}{B} \tag{2.2}$$

where B and C are identified, which is called a *normal default*, is particularly important: this amounts to concluding B by default on condition A. It may well be that all the applications of default logic that might be valuable in linguistics would involve only normal defaults; if so, this would be very pleasant, since these defaults constitute a special case that is better behaved in many ways than the general one where arbitrary default rules are allowed.

We can think of a *default theory*, then, as a pair $\langle T, D\rangle$, where T is a first order theory and D is a set of default rules. The novel logical component is D; what is new here is the dependency of these rules not only on the provability of certain formulas but on the *nonprovability* of others. (To say that B can be consistently assumed is to say that $\neg B$ is not provable.)

The generalization may seem straightforward at first glance, but on closer examination the motivating idea contains a circularity. Provability depends on the notion of a correct proof; a proof is a series of steps in which the rules have been correctly applied; but

[9] We will often write defaults in this linear notation.

in order to tell if a rule has been correctly applied we have to already know what is provable in order to apply consistency tests.

In monotonic logics, this same circularity is present: to proceed from A to B in a proof, A must be provable. Here the circularity is so harmless that it is hardly noticeable; it is removed by a simple recursion on length of proof. But if proofs are generalized to depend on nonprovability, it is not so easy to banish the circularity. A closer analysis of the logical situation shows that in this more general case we will have to make several changes, which taken together represent fairly fundamental departures from the classical idea of logical consequence: (1) we can't expect constructive accounts of proof, except in some special cases, (2) we must give up the determinism of monotonic logic, and replace it with the idea that a theory can support different but mutually exclusive choices of appropriate conclusions, (3) we have to be prepared to find that some theories are incoherent, in that they allow no coherent conclusion sets to be derived.

The first point should be surprising to those who thought that nonmonotonic reasoning was motivated by a need for efficient reasoning. Readers who have this impression may want to glance again at the earlier motivation for nonmonotonic logic in Section 1.2. I tried there to provide reasons having to do with the need for natural representations and appropriate reasoning. These reasons are independent of efficiency considerations. I believe that it is best to think of nonmonotonic formalisms as logical specifications of valid reasoning. As in most other areas of AI, one has to be cautious in making cognitive claims about these formalisms, and it may be necessary to introduce heuristics or approximations if efficient implementations are wanted. From a logical standpoint, the nonconstructivity of nonmonotonic logics is not a novelty; nonconstructivity is also a feature of monotonic higher-order logics. But the other peculiarities of nonmonotonic logic require a more profound rearrangement of our logical expectations.

The second point is illustrated by a famous example of Reiter's, in which defaults conflict: we have the following two default rules, which say that if Nixon is a Quaker he is a pacifist and if Nixon is a Republican he is not a pacifist. And our monotonic axioms tell us that Nixon is a Quaker and a Republican.

$$D_1 = \left\{ \frac{Quaker(n) : Pacifist(n)}{Pacifist(n)}, \frac{Republican(n) : \neg Pacifist(n)}{\neg Pacifist(n)} \right\},$$

$$T_1 = \{Republican(n) \wedge Quaker(n)\}.$$

It's important to realize that the potentiality for cases like this does not mean that the theories that produce the conflicts are incoherent or inadequate in any way. The example is chosen to make this clear; the defaults it contains are perfectly plausible. On any broad interpretation of defaults – as norms or as generally reliable rules – we can't require that when a system of defaults contains potentially conflicting conclusions to be drawn, we will never encounter cases in which the conflicting rules are applicable. Even when we attempt to reduce conflicts between rules by some sort of scheme that assigns priorities to defaults, we can't be sure that conflicts will never arise. Of course, a default theory might be so full of spurious conflicts that it is unusable; but even then it will not be strictly inconsistent.

When conflicts arise that cannot be resolved in any principled way, the conflicting conclusions are equally reasonable. It is very natural in these cases to say that both choices represent correct ways of drawing conclusions from the theory. This makes the relation of logical consequence nondeterministic, and requires us to associate multiple, competing conclusion sets with a default theory. Reiter calls these conclusion sets *extensions*. It's helpful to think of the resulting account of logical consequence as a generalization of proof theory. In monotonic proof theory, proofs are central: taking together the conclusions of all the proofs produces the set of consequences. In default logic, we have to somehow characterize the conditions under which proofs are mutually coherent, in that they represent the same choices of competing defaults. We then define an extension by taking the conclusions of a coherent family of proofs.[10]

We want to say that two proofs are mutually coherent if a single policy is exercised throughout both. We represent this idea of a policy by imagining that, prior to the proof process, we have guessed at the conclusions we want to draw; we choose a logically closed set E^* of formulas to guide the consistency judgments that are required when a default rule is applied. In effect, we are guessing at the results of our proof procedure before we apply it, and are using this guess to guide our application of default rules.

We can now define the set NM-Proofs(D, T, E^*) of proofs that are generated by a default theory $\langle D, T\rangle$ and policy set E^*. First, some notation: where T is a first order theory, M-Theorems(T) is the set of first order consequences of T.

DEFINITION 2.1 (*NM-Proofs*(D, T, E^*)).

(1) $\langle\,\rangle \in$ NM-Proofs(D, T, E^*).

(2) If $\langle A_0, \ldots, A_n\rangle \in$ NM-Proofs(D, T, E^*), then $\langle A_0, \ldots, A_n, A_{n+1}\rangle \in$ NM-Proofs(D, T, E^*), where $A_{n+1} \in$ M-Theorems$(T \cup \{A_0, \ldots, A_n\})$.

(3) If $\langle A_0, \ldots, A_n\rangle \in$ NM-Proofs(D, T, E^*), then $\langle A_0, \ldots, A_n, A_{n+1}\rangle \in$ NM-Proofs(D, T, E^*), where for some B and some $i \leqslant n$, $A_i : B/A_{n+1} \in D$ and $\neg B \notin E^*$.

Clause (1) of this definition initializes the E^*-proofs by admitting the empty sequence as a proof. Clauses (2) and (3) allow E^*-proofs to be extended by rules of proof: Clause (2) provides for monotonic consequence, and Clause (3) allows closure under defaults that are compatible with the policy E^*.

The set NM-Theorems(D, T, E^*) of theorems that result from such a coherent set of proofs is – just as in classical logic – the set of provable formulas. (But in this case the proofs are relativized to a single policy.)

DEFINITION 2.2 (*NM-Theorems*(D, T, E^*)). NM-Theorems$(D, T, E^*) = \bigcup\{A : A$ occurs in some $\mathcal{P} \in$ NM-Proofs$(D, T, E^*)\}$.

Not every set of theorems that results from guessing an E^* will correspond to an extension: our guess may be incorrect! This can happen in two ways: E^* may be too

[10] Those familiar with the details of default logic will realize that I am not using Reiter's original definition here, but am referring to an early theorem characterizing extensions. This characterizing theorem, I believe, is easier to relate directly to intuitions about consequence, and I prefer to work with it.

small; it may fail to contain consequences that follow legitimately from $\langle T, D\rangle$. Or E^* can be too big: it can contain some of these consequences. In the former case, E^* will be larger than NM-Theorems(D, T, E^*), and in the latter case, E^* will be smaller than NM-Theorems(D, T, E^*). Thus, we define an extension as a self-proving guess: if you guess it, it then returns itself as a set of theorems.

DEFINITION 2.3 (*Extension of* $\langle T, D\rangle$). E is an extension of $\langle T, D\rangle$ if and only if $E =$ NM-Theorems(D, T, E).

For instance, in the default theory $\langle T_1, D_1\rangle$ given above, consider the following sets of formulas.

$$A = \text{The set of all formulas.}$$
$$E_2 = \text{M-Theorems}(T_1 \cup \{\mathit{Pacifist}(n)\}).$$
$$E_3 = \text{M-Theorems}(T_1 \cup \{\neg\mathit{Pacifist}(n)\}).$$

Now, (1) $\emptyset$ is not an extension of $\langle T_1, D_1\rangle$, because NM-Theorems$(T_1, D_1, \emptyset) = A$; $\emptyset$ does not provide enough information to prevent both of the incompatible defaults from applying. And (2) A is not an extension, since NM-Theorems$(T_1, D_1, A) =$ M-Theorems(T_1); because nothing is consistent with A, this guess blocks every default from applying. But (3) E_2 is an extension, since the only default it licenses is the one whose conclusion it already contains. And similarly, E_3 is also an extension.

In this case, then, though we can't regard a theory that involves competing defaults as having a single, determinate set of consequences, we can give an account of multiple coherent consequence sets that is a recognizable generalization of the monotonic notion of consequence. Built into the idea of extension that we have been presenting here is a *credulous* approach to reasoning with defaults: the assumption is that an extension should use as many default rules as can consistently be applied.[11]

In general, we can't assume that an arbitrary default theory has any extensions at all. This means that some syntactic possibilities may be proof-theoretically incoherent. We won't provide examples or go into details on this matter: examples and discussion can be found in (Reiter, 1980) and (Besnard, 1989, Section 7.1).

2.1.2. Some refinements of default logic

Model theory. There are several ways to provide a model theory for default logic. The most straightforward method, due to W. Łukaszewicz, associates with a normal default (2.2) a function that takes a set $\mathcal{M}$ of first-order models into one of its subsets – the set of models that satisfy the default.[12] The extensions of a normal default theory $\langle T, D\rangle$ are then characterized as limits obtained by applying these functions to the set of models of T.

[11] Another approach to extensions is based on the *skeptical* idea that it is best to suspend judgment when presented with conflicting rules. But the simplest way to implement this skeptical idea is to take the intersection of all credulous extensions; which makes the credulous approach seem more fundamental.

[12] M belongs to this subset in case either A is false in some member of $\mathcal{M}$ or B is false in every member of $\mathcal{M}$, or B is true in M.

Another method, due to Kurt Konolige and developed further by others[13] yields a model theory indirectly, by way of a translation of default logic into autoepistemic logic. (See Section 2.2 for a brief discussion of autoepistemic logic; all that needs to be said now is that this is approach uses modal logic.) The idea is to represent a default (2.1) with a modal formula $[\Box A \wedge \Diamond B] \rightarrow C$. The extensions of default logic then correspond to certain *strongly grounded expansions* of the associated modal theory. A model theory can now be obtained for default logic by appealing to the possible worlds semantics for modal logic.

Konolige's idea provides a way of converting defaults to first-class logical citizens: as we noted, they appear in autoepistemic logic as conditional formulas, such as $[\Box \mathit{Bird}(\mathit{Tweety}) \wedge \Diamond \mathit{Flies}(\mathit{Tweety})] \rightarrow \Box \mathit{Flies}(\mathit{Tweety})$. This enables us to examine the inferential properties of defaults; but unfortunately the results are disappointing. For instance, (because of the use of the material conditional in formalizing defaults), (2.2) implies $A \wedge C : B/B$. This, of course, seems to undermine the whole idea of nonmonotonicity. We should probably conclude that default logic is not designed to provide an account of the inferential interrelationships among defaults, and this is reflected in its modal semantics.

Preferences among defaults. Extensions are treated as equal in default logic; if this restriction is taken seriously, any preferences that a reasoner may have among competing defaults have to be treated as extralogical. But in developing realistic applications of nonmonotonic logic, one soon discovers a need to express priorities among defaults, so that when a conflict arises one default may override another. Many of these preferences have been proposed for various domains; but the single example that is most important for linguistic applications is *specificity.* According to the specificity criterion, when two defaults conflict and one of them is more specific than the other, the former should override the latter. For normal defaults, the natural criterion of specificity is this: $A : B/B$ is more specific than $A' : B'/B'$ in the context of a default theory $\langle T, D\rangle$ if A is a logical consequence of $T \cup \{A'\}$.

The stock example of specificity is Tweety the penguin. In this example, T consists of $\forall x[\mathit{Penguin}(x) \rightarrow \mathit{Bird}(x)]$ and $\mathit{Penguin}(\mathit{Tweety})$, and D consists of the two normal default schemes

$$\frac{\mathit{Bird}(x) : \mathit{Flies}(x)}{\mathit{Flies}(x)} \quad \text{and} \quad \frac{\mathit{Penguin}(x) : \neg \mathit{Flies}(x)}{\neg \mathit{Flies}(x)}.$$

If no principle of specificity is added to the definition of extension, this default theory will have two extensions: one in which Tweety flies, and one in which Tweety does not. But on the most natural interpretation of the example, the default rule $\mathit{Penguin}(x) : \neg\mathit{Flies}(x)/\neg\mathit{Flies}(x)$ is intended to mark an exception to the more general default $\mathit{Bird}(x) : \mathit{Flies}(x)/\mathit{Flies}(x)$; and on this interpretation, the first extension is anomalous and unwanted.

One way to introduce priorities into default logic is by iterating the extension construction, applying more preferred defaults first. For simplicity, assume that there are

[13] See Konolige (1988) and Marek and Truszczynski (1989).

only two rankings for defaults: more preferred (priority 1) and less preferred (priority 2); let D_1 be the set of defaults of priority 1 and D_2 be the set of defaults of priority 2.

Using Definition 2.3, construct the set $\mathcal{E}_1$ of extensions of $\langle T, D_1\rangle$. Then, for each $E \in \mathcal{E}_1$, construct the set $\mathcal{E}_1^E$ of extensions of $\langle E, D_2\rangle$. The collection $\bigcup\{\mathcal{E}_1^E : E \in \mathcal{E}_1\}$ is the set of all extensions, subject to the prioritization constraints.[14]

2.2. *Autoepistemic logic*

Some of the very earliest work in nonmonotonic logic exploited modal logic.[15] The basic idea – to use possibility to represent the notion of consistency that is involved in the application of a default – is very natural. But a clear, straightforward theory did not emerge until other approaches had been developed.[16]

The intuitive interpretation of the modal operator $\Box$ is belief; and deontic **S5** (i.e. the system **KD45** of Chellas (1980, p. 193)) is the underlying modal logic. The idea is to represent a default like

(1) 'Tweety flies if she is a bird'

as

$$[\Box Bird(Tweety) \wedge \Diamond Flies(Tweety)] \to \Box Flies(Tweety).$$

Thus, on this approach, defaults represent constraints on an agent's beliefs: "If I believe that Tweety is a bird, and have no reason to think that Tweety doesn't fly, let me believe that Tweety flies".

So far, there is no nonmonotonicity; all this has been carried out in **DS5**, which is a monotonic logic. Nonmonotonicity is introduced by following through on the idea that we are interested in theories that represent the beliefs of an agent with introspective powers. This means that the propositions in the theory should be beliefs, and the propositions *not* in the theory should be nonbeliefs. Thus, a logically closed set of sentences E is said to be *stable* if $E \subseteq \Box E$ and $\overline{E} \subseteq \neg\Box E$, where $\Box E = \{\Box A : A \in E\}$, $\neg\Box E = \{\neg\Box A : A \in E\}$, and $\overline{E}$ is the complement of E.

The stable sets represent the epistemic states of ideal introspective agents. We now want to define the states that are justified by a set of premisses T. (Note that T can contain modal formulas, so that defaults as well as facts are incorporated in the premisses; because defaults can conflict, there may be more than one state that is rationally justified by T.) We want to ensure that the *only* beliefs in this state are ones that are somehow licensed by T. This is done by letting E be *grounded in* T if for all $A \in E$, $T \cup \Box E \cup \neg\Box\overline{E} \vdash A$; a *stable expansion* of E is then a stable set that is grounded in E. Stable expansions play a role in autoepistemic logic that is analogous to that of extensions in default logic.

[14] See Brewka (1993, 1994), and Delgrande and Schaub (1994) for more discussion of prioritized defaults.

[15] See McDermott and Doyle (1980).

[16] See Moore (1985), in which the theory is motivated and reformulated; see Konolige (1988) and Levesque (1990) for refinements and developments.

2.3. Circumscription

Circumscription attempts to provide a formalization of nonmonotonic reasoning that is close to familiar logics. Rather than maximizing conclusions, circumscription aims at minimizing certain semantic values: in particular, the extensions of certain predicates. Minimization constraints on predicates can be expressed in second-order logic: for instance, let $A(p)$ be a formula containing occurrences of a second-order variable p. We can then express the claim that a one-place predicate P is the smallest possible predicate satisfying $A(p)$ as follows:

$$A(P) \wedge \forall p\big[A(p) \rightarrow \big[\forall x\big[p(x) \rightarrow P(x)\big] \rightarrow \forall x\big[p(x) \leftrightarrow P(x)\big]\big]\big].$$

(This says that P satisfies A and any predicate that also satisfies A and is included in P is equivalent to P.) Thus, second-order logic provides the logical foundation for circumscription theory.

In the earliest versions of circumscription, the motivation for minimization was a sort of closed world assumption; assume that objects that can't be inferred from your data aren't there at all. In later versions, certain predicates are listed as abnormalities, and these abnormalities are minimized. As abnormalities were used to formalize more complicated domains, more powerful methods of circumscription were felt to be needed, and the framework evolved into something much more complex and flexible than the original versions.

Though in the usual applications this logic is extensional and only second-order, it is quite easy to generalize the underlying logic for circumscription to Montague's Intensional Logic. Because it mates well with the higher order semantic apparatus of Montague Semantics, circumscription may appeal to linguists interested in semantic applications of nonmonotonic reasoning; in fact, I will use circumscription below in illustrating applications of nonmonotonic logic in lexical semantics.

The following example illustrates the simplest kind of circumscription, "Single-predicate global circumscription". We consider a theory incorporating the defeasible rule that birds fly; the theory also contains the claims that Tweety is a bird and Opus is a nonflying bird. To do this, we invoke an abnormality predicate $Ab1$; we declare that any nonflying bird has this property; and we then use circumscription to minimize $Ab1$ with respect to the theory. In order to carry out the circumscription, the theory must be packed into a single formula; we can only circumscribe theories that are finitely axiomatized.

The formula T that axiomatizes the theory is presented as a function $T(P_1, \ldots, P_n)$ of its constituent predicates. In our example, $T(Ab1, Bird, Flies)$ is the formula:

$$\begin{aligned}&\forall x\big[\big[Bird(x) \wedge \neg Flies(x)\big] \rightarrow Ab1(x)\big]\\ &\quad\wedge Bird(Tweety)\\ &\quad\wedge Bird(Opus)\\ &\quad\wedge \neg Flies(Opus)\\ &\quad\wedge \neg Tweety = Opus.\end{aligned}$$

In circumscribing $T(Ab1, Bird, Flies)$, we need to decide what to do with the predicates *Bird* and *Flies;* do we vary them, or hold them constant? In this case, we get the most natural results by holding *Bird* constant and allowing *Flies* to vary; this corresponds to the most likely situation, in which we know what the birds are, but are using a certain amount of guesswork about what things fly. The result of circumscribing $Ab1$ in T, varying *Flies* and holding *Bird* constant, is

$$T(Ab1, Bird, Flies) \wedge \forall p, q[T(p, Bird, q) \to p \not\subset Ab1],$$

where '$p \not\subset Ab1$' is short for $\exists x[p(x) \wedge \neg Ab1(x)] \vee \forall x[p(x) \leftrightarrow Ab1(x)]$.

In many simple cases the circumscribed theory is equivalent to something that is much easier to understand; our example is equivalent to the result of adding $\forall x[[Bird(x) \wedge \neg x = Opus] \to Flies(x)]$ to T.

Model theoretically, circumscription is an operation that takes a theory (which has many models) into a circumscribed theory, which in general also will have many models. The formulas valid in the circumscribed theory will be those that are true in *all* of the latter models.

This approach to nonmonotonic logic was developed by John McCarthy;[17] much of the technical work in this area has been carried out by Vladimir Lifschitz.[18] In the most advanced versions of the theory, Lifschitz introduces a formal framework in which circumscriptive policies, especially policies about variation of predicates in minimization, can be expressed.

2.4. *Model preference theories*

There is a very direct and natural way to render the model theoretic definition of logical consequence nonmonotonic. According to this definition, Γ implies A when every model of Γ satisfies A. But to have expectations is to ignore certain models. Therefore, we can represent a nonmonotonic reasoner as a function *expected* from sets of models to subsets of these sets (the subsets that are viable after expectations have ruled some possibilities out). We can then say that a set Γ of formulas, with corresponding set $\mathcal{M}$ of models, nonmonotonically implies A when A is satisfied by all models in *expected*$(\mathcal{M})$.

Yoav Shoham explored this idea, concentrating on the special case in which a partial ordering is given on models (representing epistemic preferences), and *expected*$(\mathcal{M})$ is the set of models that are minimal in $\mathcal{M}$ with respect to this ordering.[19] He is able to show that this idea delivers a very general semantical framework for nonmonotonic logic that can account for many of the leading approaches.[20]

[17] See, for instance, McCarthy (1980).

[18] See Lifschitz (1986, 1989).

[19] See Shoham (1988).

[20] To appeal to preferences among models assumes that some policy has been applied that systematically resolves conflicts among defaults. Note that this theory delivers a single, unitary notion of logical consequence rather than competing families of consequences (or extensions). For this reason, there is no very good model here of unresolved reasoning conflicts.

A version of model preference semantics has recently been used to provide an interpretation of DATR, the approach to formalizing morphology and implementing morphological processing that was mentioned above in Section 1.3; see Keller (1995). This semantics is not quite the same as Shoham's classical version, since it also involves partial models.

Shoham's ideas should seem familiar to readers who are acquainted with the logic of conditionals, where the idea is to interpret a conditional $A > B$ as true at a world in case A is true at all the "most preferred" worlds at which A is true. Though, of course, models and possible worlds are not the same, and there was much confusion between the two in the early days of modal logic, there are strong analogies – and in particular, it is often possible to build a modal logic that to some extent "reflects" model-theoretic structure. We have already seen one example of this, since autoepistemic logic is just such a reflection of default logic.

The model preference theories, then, provide a natural transition to the conditional approaches to nonmonotonic logic.

2.5. *Conditional theories*

I will assume here a general familiarity with the logic of conditionals. For further information on this topic, see Chapter 17.

A primary purpose of conditional logic, as developed by Robert Stalnaker and David Lewis, was to provide a logical account that accommodated nonmonotonicity in the antecedents of conditionals. This phenomenon is very similar to the ones that motivated nonmonotonic logic: consider, for instance, the fact that (2a) does not imply (2b).

(2) a. 'If I were a bird, I could fly'.
b. 'If I were a penguin, I could fly'.

Despite these similarities, the developers of conditional logic never entertained the idea of making the logical consequence relation nonmonotonic; the conditional logics are all straightforward versions of modal logic, featuring a connective $>$ in which $A > C$ does not imply $[A \wedge B] > C$. Although in these logics, if $\{A\} \vdash C$ then $\{A, B\} \vdash C$, this is independent of the behavior of $>$, since of course we do not have a version of the deduction theorem and its converse for $>$.

The earlier work in nonmonotonic logic did not make any direct use of conditional logics. But starting with Delgrande (1988), there is a growing literature that seeks to develop a conditional-based approach to nonmonotonicity. These approaches explore alternatives that are quite diverse, but they all relax one constraint that the standard conditional logics observed: they no longer treat conditional *modus ponens*,

$$\frac{A, A > B}{C},$$

as valid. Assuming the most natural correspondence between conditionals and defaults – i.e. assuming that, for instance, (1) is represented as a conditional

$$Bird(Tweety) > Flies(Tweety) -$$

it is clear why *modus ponens* has to go. To accommodate defaults, we have to provide for the possibility that the antecedent is true and the consequent is false. Without allowing for this possibility, we can't accommodate even the simplest examples, such as Tweety and Nixon, since these involve conflicting defaults whose antecedents can easily be true. We are interested, then, in conditional logics that stand to the familiar conditional logics as deontic modal logics stand to alethic logics. This relaxed conditional has two natural interpretations: as a logic of conditional belief, or as a logic of conditional epistemic norms. (These interpretations, of course, are closely related.)

Readers interested in this topic should study the work of Craig Boutilier.[21] Though, as far as I know, there have been no applications of Boutilier's work in linguistics, another conditional approach – commonsense entailment, due to Nicholas Asher and Michael Morreau – has been applied in several areas of interest to linguists. The remainder of this section will be devoted to their approach. For accounts of the logical theory, readers should consult Asher and Morreau (1991), Morreau (1992a, 1992b). For a related, much simpler theory, see Morreau (1995). For an approach to conditional entailment that is similar in motivation but different in logical development, see Geffner and Pearl (1992).

Commonsense entailment, unlike most other approaches to default logic, aims explicitly at the highest degree of "nonmonotonic commitment". Defaults are treated as first-class logical citizens, and the aim is to explicate their logical interrelationships. This is a very ambitious goal, and it comes as no surprise that the theory itself is rather complicated. In brief outline, these are the ideas.[22]

Like autoepistemic logic, the theory is deployed in two stages; (1) a monotonic modal logic, and (2) a phase in which a nonmonotonic consequence relation is added. The modal logic of the first phase interprets the conditional using a function * from possible worlds and sets of possible worlds to possible worlds; $A > B$ is true at a world w if and only if $*(w, [\![A]\!]) \subset [\![B]\!]$. Like most possible worlds theories, the theory identifies propositions with sets of possible worlds. At each world, then, $>$ takes a proposition into an arbitrary Kripke-style modal operator. Thus, this is the most general possible sort of conditional logic that can be based on a possible worlds approach, on the assumption that, for each antecedent, a conditional delivers a sort of necessity operator at each world. The idea here is that * picks out the worlds in which the antecedent is true in a way that is epistemically normal.

Two conditions are imposed on *:

(3) a. $*(w, \mathbf{p}) \subseteq \mathbf{p}$.

b. $*(w, \mathbf{p} \cup \mathbf{q}) \subseteq *(w, \mathbf{p}) \cup *(w, \mathbf{q})$.

Condition (3a) is easy to motivate; it is common to all conditional logics that the consequent is to be evaluated in certain preferred worlds in which the antecedent is true. Condition (3b) says that any normal $\mathbf{p} \cup \mathbf{q}$ world is either a normal $\mathbf{p}$ or a normal $\mathbf{q}$ world. This condition is harder to motivate; but in (Morreau, 1992b, pp. 126–128), it is shown that it validates a nonmonotonic version of the specificity principle.[23]

[21] See, for instance, Boutilier (1992).

[22] The presentation follows the formulation of Asher and Morreau (1991).

[23] Asher and Morreau argue that specificity needs to be captured in terms of the underlying logic. In most other nonmonotonic formalisms, specificity appears as (possibly one of many) priority constraints on defaults, if it is captured at all.

In the second phase of the project, ideas that have already appeared in connection with other nonmonotonic formalisms – possible worlds models of epistemic states and a notion of extension – are combined to furnish an account of nonmonotonic consequence. The account invokes two new devices: an operation of normalization and a special epistemic state.

(i) The operation *normalize* takes an epistemic state **s** and a singular proposition $\mathbf{p}(\mathbf{P}, \mathbf{d})$[24] into an epistemic state *normalize*$(\mathbf{s}, \mathbf{p}(\mathbf{P}, \mathbf{d}))$. Normalization is defined in terms of the epistemic normality operator $*$; it cancels out worlds in which **d** is not as normal as possible, compatible with **s** and the assumption $\mathbf{P}(\mathbf{d})$.

(ii) **Bliss** is a sort of minimal epistemic state.

Using normalization, a construction can be defined like the constructions of extensions in default logic. The construction inputs an epistemic state **s** and a set Γ of hypotheses. A set $\mathcal{P}$ of singular propositions is associated with a premiss set,[25] and is well ordered. The normalization construction then iteratively applies normalization, beginning with the epistemic state **s** and choosing singular propositions from the well ordering. From the least fixpoint of the construction, we can recover an epistemic state $\mathbf{s}'$, from **s** and Γ; this state will in general depend on how the singular propositions are ordered. Finally, commonsense entailment is defined by taking the formulas that hold in all extensions beginning with the epistemic state **s** resulting from updating **Bliss** with Γ: Γ nonmonotonically implies A if and only if $\mathbf{s}' \subseteq [\![A]\!]$, for all information states obtained by ordering the singular propositions in Γ and applying the successive normalization construction to the epistemic state $\mathbf{s}'$ and these ordered singular propositions.

Asher and Morreau are able to show that this definition has a number of interesting properties. Among these, *defeasible modus ponens* is particularly important from the standpoint of the theory of conditionals: under certain independence conditions on A and B, $\{A, A > B\}$ nonmonotonically implies B. The importance of this result lies in the fact that with it, one can hope to axiomatize a domain using conditionals for which *modus ponens* is logically invalid, and nevertheless to be able to extract defeasible conclusions from the axiomatization using *modus ponens*.

2.6. *Inheritance*

Inheritance hierarchies (or inheritance networks, or inheritance graphs) at first glance look very different from logic-inspired approaches like those that we have discussed until now. And in fact they originated in a very different tradition, inspired in part by neurological modeling and parallel processing. But as the ideas have developed, inheritance networks have come to resemble familiar logics – and that is how they will be presented here.

A general survey of work in inheritance networks is available in (Thomason, 1992), which tries to be comprehensive, and is still more or less up to date. Another survey,

[24] Where **d** is an individual and **P** is a property – i.e. a function from individuals to propositions – the corresponding singular proposition $\mathbf{p}(\mathbf{P}, \mathbf{d}) = \{w : w \in \mathbf{P}(\mathbf{d})\}$.

[25] I do not give details here, since this part of the definition is somewhat *ad hoc*.

containing a detailed comparative treatment of many inheritance policies, can be found in (Horty, forthcoming). With these references in place, I will try to be very brief.[26]

2.6.1. Strict taxonomic inheritance

We begin with monotonic or *strict* inheritance: this will provide a simple introduction to notation, and to techniques for defining inheritance. This form of inheritance is limited in two ways: (1) there is no nonmonotonicity, and (2) the only relations between concepts that can be expressed are inclusion (or subsumption, or "is-a") and exclusion (or contradiction).

An inheritance network (with positive and negative strict is-a links only) is a labeled directed graph Γ. We can think of Γ as a set of labeled edges (or *links* of various types) between vertices (or *nodes*). We associate a set of statements with such a network. An *inheritance definition* for the network defines a consequence relation $\rhd$ between networks and statements; we write $\Gamma \rhd A$ to say that statement A is a consequence of network Γ. In the case of strict taxonomic inheritance, all links have either the form $x \Rightarrow y$ or the form $x \not\Rightarrow y$. The statements associated with such a network have the form $\text{IS}(x, y)$ or the form $\text{ISNOT}(x, y)$. (We use capital letters to distinguish strict from defeasible statements; nonmonotonic networks will allow defeasible statements of the form $\text{is}(x, y)$.)

The inheritance definition for these networks is a simple induction.[27] In effect, we are characterizing the inheritable statements as the smallest set closed under the following rules.

DEFINITION 2.4 (*Strict inheritance*).

(i) If $x = y$ or $x \Rightarrow y \in \Gamma$ then $\Gamma \rhd_1 \text{IS}(x, y)$, and if $x \not\Rightarrow y \in \Gamma$ then $\Gamma \rhd_1 \text{ISNOT}(x, y)$.

(ii) $\Gamma \rhd_1 \text{ISNOT}(y, x)$ then $\Gamma \rhd_1 \text{ISNOT}(x, y)$.

(iii) If $\Gamma \rhd_1 \text{IS}(x, y')$ and $\Gamma \rhd_1 \text{IS}(y', y)$ then $\Gamma \rhd_1 \text{IS}(x, y)$.

(iv) If $\Gamma \rhd_1 \text{IS}(x, y')$ and $\Gamma \rhd_1 \text{ISNOT}(y', y)$ then $\Gamma \rhd_1 \text{ISNOT}(x, y)$.

Inheritance definitions yield prooflike constructions, but here "proofs" take on a graph-theoretic character and correspond to certain paths through networks. For instance, it's easy to verify that $\Gamma \rhd_1 \text{IS}(x, y)$ if and only if $x = y$ or there is a pathlike sequence of links $x_1 \Rightarrow x_2,\ x_n \Rightarrow \cdots \Rightarrow x_{n+1}$ in Γ, with $x_1 = x$ and $x_{n+1} = y$. Inheritance definitions are usually path-based, and the theory itself can't be developed very far without going into considerable detail concerning inheritance paths.[28] But in this presentation of

[26] It is easy to get distracted by esoteric details in this area, so whenever possible I will make simplifications for the sake of exposition, in an effort to get beyond systems that are very weak expressively to ones that could be potentially applied to linguistics. Because of this simplifying strategy, I will be using some inheritance formalisms that diverge from the ones that have been most discussed in the literature. I will try to mark the divergences when they occur.

[27] In fact, this is an induction over the monotonic distance from node x to node y. This distance is the maximum of the positive and the negative monotonic distance from x to y. The positive monotonic distance is the length of the shortest chain of positive links from x to y. The negative monotonic distance is the length of the shortest chain of links consisting of a positive chain from x to x', and a positive chain from y to y', where x' and y' are connected by a negative link.

[28] This was one reason why I first became interested in inheritance theory. I didn't feel satisfied with the motivation of the expressively strong, semantically based approaches, and felt that inheritance graphs would provide a level of granularity at which the intuitions could be better developed. I still believe that there is still some truth in this, thought the complexity of the theoretical issues that have emerged is somewhat discouraging.

inheritance theory, I will concentrate on inductive definitions of $\Gamma \mathrel{|\!\!>} A$, where Γ is a network and A is a statement in an appropriate "network language".

It is best to think of the strict networks as expressively limited logics for subsumption and disjointness relations between concepts; individuals can be treated as individual concepts.[29] The inheritance definition provides for reflexivity and transitivity of subsumption, for the symmetry of exclusion, and for a form of *modus tollens*. Despite the simplicity of the rules, the logic is nonclassical. Because statements $\text{IS}(x, y)$ are only provable when there is a path connecting x and y, the semantics of negation in networks is four-valued and so incorporates a limited amount of "relevance"; see Thomason (1987) for details.

2.6.2. Simple mixed inheritance

Now consider networks in which defeasible links $\rightarrow$ are also allowed. These networks contain positive and negative strict subsumption links and positive defeasible subsumption links. Negative defeasible links are not needed; these have the form $x \rightarrow y\,\sigma$, where σ is a strict negative path.

The inheritance definition is an induction on the longest path from x to y, where the size of a path is measured by the number of defeasible links it contains. For this quantity to be defined in a network, we must make a strong acyclicity assumption: that if any path through the network contains a cycle, then the path must contain only strict links. Even though such acyclicity assumptions are somewhat awkward, dispensing with them raises problematic theoretical considerations. There are examples showing that if unrestricted cycles are allowed, nets can be constructed in which there simply is no sensible account of inheritance.[30]

Definition 2.5 assumes the above definition of $\mathrel{|\!\!>}_1$. Clauses labeled as "strict" in the definition are applied before defeasible clauses whenever this is compatible with the outermost induction on degree.[31]

DEFINITION 2.5 (*Mixed inheritance*).

(i) (*Strict.*) If $\Gamma \mathrel{|\!\!>}_1 \text{IS}(x, y)$ then $\Gamma \mathrel{|\!\!>}_2 \text{is}(x, y)$.

(ii) (*Strict.*) If $x \rightarrow y \in \Gamma$ and not $\Gamma \mathrel{|\!\!>}_2 \text{ISNOT}(x, y)$ then $\Gamma \mathrel{|\!\!>}_2 \text{is}(x, y)$.

(iii) (*Strict.*) If $\Gamma \mathrel{|\!\!>}_2 \text{is}(x, y')$ and $\Gamma \mathrel{|\!\!>}_2 \text{IS}(y', y)$ then $\Gamma \mathrel{|\!\!>}_2 \text{is}(x, y)$.

(iv) (*Strict.*) If $\Gamma \mathrel{|\!\!>}_2 \text{is}(x, y')$ and $\Gamma \mathrel{|\!\!>}_2 \text{ISNOT}(y', y)$ then $\Gamma \mathrel{|\!\!>}_2 \text{isnot}(x, y)$.

(v) (*Defeasible.*) If $\Gamma \mathrel{|\!\!>}_2 \text{is}(x, y')$ or $\Gamma \mathrel{|\!\!>}_2 \text{IS}(x, y')$, and $y' \rightarrow y \in \Gamma$, then $\Gamma \mathrel{|\!\!>}_2 \text{is}(x, y)$ if (a) $\Gamma \not\mathrel{|\!\!>} \text{ISNOT}(x, y)$ and (b) for all v, v' such that $\Gamma \mathrel{|\!\!>}_2 \text{is}(x, v)$ and $v \rightarrow v' \in \Gamma$ where $\Gamma \mathrel{|\!\!>}_2 \text{ISNOT}(v', y)$, there are w, w' such that $\Gamma \mathrel{|\!\!>}_2 \text{is}(x, w)$, $\Gamma \mathrel{|\!\!>}_2 \text{IS}(w, v)$, $w \rightarrow w' \in \Gamma$, and $\Gamma \mathrel{|\!\!>}_2 \text{IS}(w', y)$.

The crucial part of this definition is clause v. To understand this clause, compare the verbal presentation with Figure 2.1. Clause v specifies when a subsumption relation (strict or defeasible) can be extended through a defeasible link $y' \rightarrow y$ to complete a path from x to y, thereby producing a defeasible conclusion $\text{is}(x, y)$.

---

29 Throughout this chapter, 'concepts' are monadic concepts of individuals. I will use *Capitalized-Italic* words or phrases for concepts, except when feature structures are under discussion, when I will use SMALL CAPITALS.

30 See Horty (forthcoming).

31 See Horty and Thomason (1988).

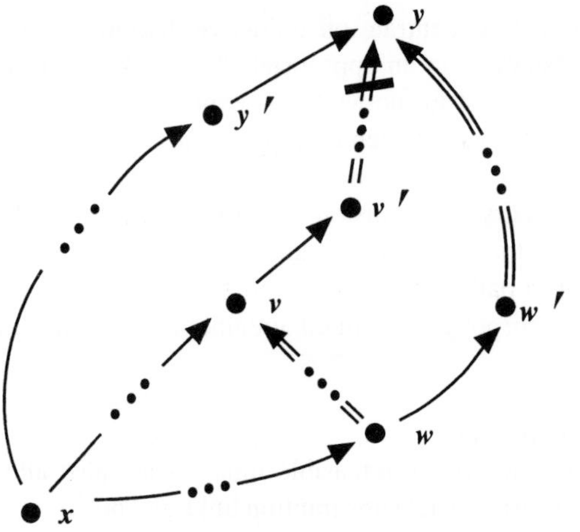

Fig. 2.1. Skeptical inheritance.

The conclusion holds as long as there is no viable competing conclusion. A competing conclusion isnot(x, y) arises when there is an established subsumption relation is(x, v), and a link $v \to v'$ from v to a v' that is strictly inconsistent with y. And the conclusion isnot(x, y) is viable if it is not preempted by a more specific reason to the contrary. Such a preempting reason consists of a node w such that is(x, w) and IS(w, v) hold, with a link $w \to w'$ from w to a w' that is strictly subsumed by y.[32] Thus, in Figure 2.1, the path from x through y' to y is good in case for every conflicting path like the one from from x through v to y, there is a preempting path from x through w to y.

This inheritance definition is skeptical, in the sense that it withholds conclusions in case of an unresolved conflict between between defaults. In the following example, for instance, neither the conclusion is(*Quaker-Republican*, *Pacifist*) nor the conclusion is(*Quaker-Republican*, *Nonpacifist*) follows.

Much of the conceptual complexity of inheritance theory derives from problems of conflict resolution. But these complexities can be ignored in many linguistic applications, since linguistic subsystems – at least, subsystems that are synchronically stable – seem to resist conflicts that are not resolved by specificity. This feature makes linguistic systems particularly attractive as applications of inheritance theory.

Systematic preference for more specific defaults is built into almost all inheritance definitions. To see how Definition 2.5 accomplishes this, compare Figure 2.3 with Figure 2.2.

2.6.3. *Strict inheritance with roles*

Although you can provide a sort of outline of the conceptual hierarchy of a domain using only taxonomic links, such formalisms lack the expressive power to reason adequately

[32] Note that the specificity path must be strict. This is the major difference between this inheritance definition and that of Horty, Thomason and Touretzky (1988).

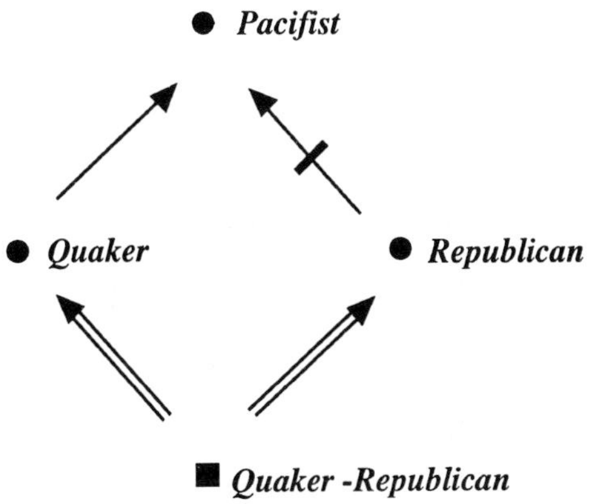

Fig. 2.2. Unresolved conflict.

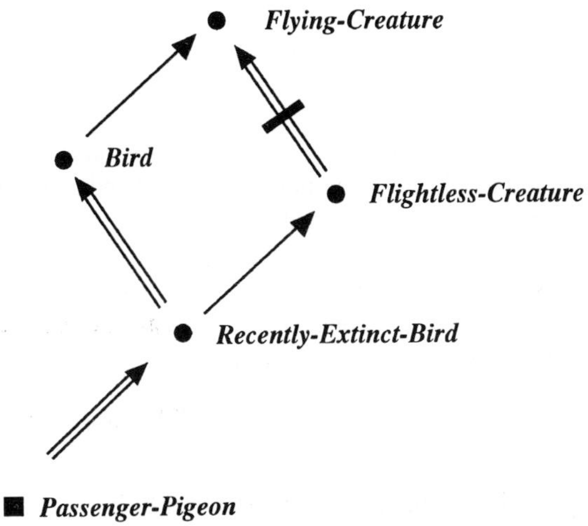

Fig. 2.3. Conflict resolved by specificity.

about the structure of domains in an interesting way. The very powerful nonmonotonic formalisms discussed above in Sections 2.1–2.5 provide this expressive power in one way. But more constrained formalisms are also worth exploring. It is always of logical interest to explore the possibilities of formalizing a domain with limited resources, and this is especially important in the nonmonotonic arena, where the more expressive systems are not even axiomatizable and basic logical issues are not yet fully understood.

In inheritance approaches, expressive power is increased by adding role links to the formalism, as well (perhaps) as some specialized relational links. The ideas involved in networks with roles, feature structures, and frame-based knowledge representation

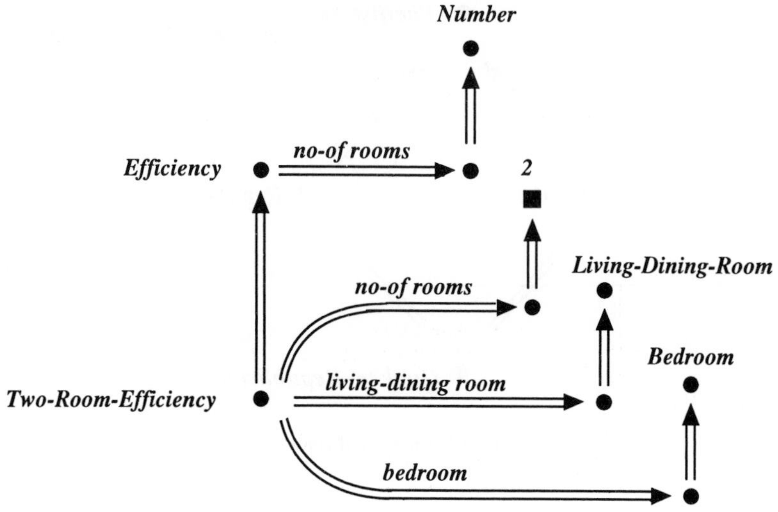

Fig. 2.4. Two-room efficiency apartments.

formalisms[33] are very similar. All of these *role formalism* approaches seek to use functional expressions to capture a limited amount of relational and quantificational reasoning. All of the approaches incorporate, to a greater or lesser extent, (1) conventions for diagramming information, (2) algorithms for computing the reasoning functions, and (3) a logical specification of the valid reasoning.

The general idea has no intrinsic connection with linguistic representations or reasoning. Consider, for instance, the following definition:

> A *Two-Room-Efficiency* is an apartment with two rooms: a *living-dining-room* and a *bedroom.*

Role formalisms seek to organize such information by bringing out the hierarchical relations between concepts. We can begin by saying that *Two-Room-Efficiencies* are *Efficiencies,* that the *number-of-rooms* of an *Efficiency* is a *Number,* that the *living-dining-room* of a *Two-Room-Efficiency* is a *Living-Dining-Room,* and that the *bedroom* of a *Two-Room-Efficiency* is a *Bedroom.*

The relationships between concepts in our examples can be diagrammed as follows.

Here, we are appealing to relations of "having" between concepts, as well as to relations of "being". Efficiencies have bedrooms, and this is represented as a relation between the *Two-Room-Efficiency* concept and the concept *Bedroom-of-a-Two-Room-Efficiency.* There is a *Bedroom* concept, which is invoked when we say that the bedroom of an *Efficiency* is a *Bedroom,* but there is also a *bedroom* role, which can be thought of as a partial function on individuals (and derivatively, as a function on concepts).[34]

---

[33] See Winston (1984, Chapter 8).

[34] Since the distinction between concepts and roles can be confusing, I've elected to capitalize references to concepts.

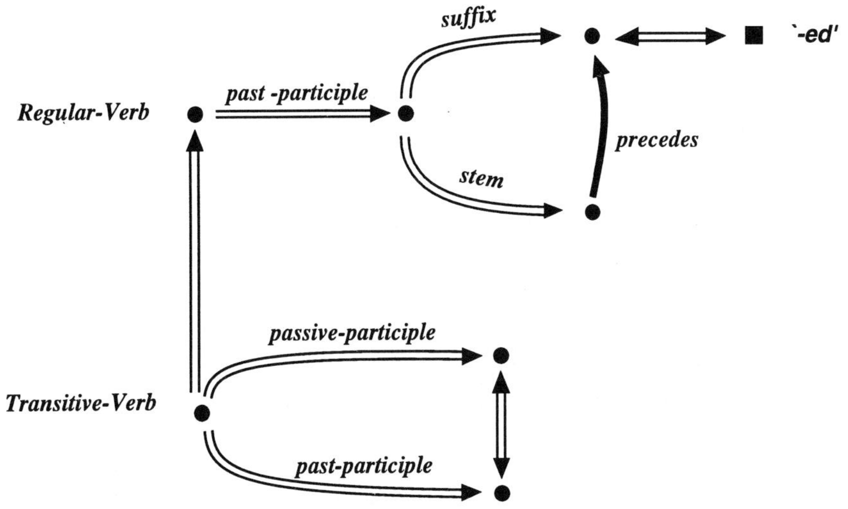

Fig. 2.5. English passive participles.

The labeled links in the diagram are *role links*. The *number-of-rooms* role, for instance, corresponds to a function taking a dwelling into its number of rooms. This diagram also distinguishes between individuals (which are best thought of as *individual concepts*) and other concepts; the former appear as squares, the latter as circles. Inheritance networks with roles may also incorporate relational links, as well as role links: for instance, a logical relation of equality (corresponding to reentrancy in feature structures), or relations like linear precedence of morphemes, that apply to special-purpose types.

The formal theory of networks with roles – especially the nonmonotonic theory – has not been developed as much as one would like. Informal remarks can be found in (Winston, 1984) and (Fahlman, 1979). Formalizations of the monotonic case can be found in (Thomason and Touretzky, 1990) and (De Guerreiro, Hemerly and Shoham, 1990). Not much has been done towards formalizing the nonmonotonic case. I hope to remedy this at some point in the future – but here I can only sketch some of the ideas and show their relevance to linguistic concerns.

The diagram above indicates how these relational notions might be used to formalize information about the English passive participle. In this diagram solid, labeled arrows are used for relations other than subsumption relations. Thus, the diagram tells us that the past-participle of a Regular-Verb[35] consists of a stem and a suffix, that the suffix is '-d', that the stem precedes the suffix, and that the passive-participle of a Transitive-Verb is the same as its past-participle.

With the addition of role links and identity, the interpretation of nodes as concepts is affected. It would not do in Figure 2.5 to treat *Transitive-Verb's-past-participle* and *Transitive-Verb's-passive-participle* as mere sets. For then, the relation of equality would

[35] We are still working in a monotonic framework, so we aren't yet in a position to deal with irregular verbs as exceptions.

have to denote equality of the sets. And then, to take a numerical example, the equality relation would hold between *Integer's-predecessor* and *Integer's-successor*, since the sets are the same. But this is not the intended interpretation of equality; in Figure 2.5, for instance, the meaning of the equality link is that a *Transitive-Verb's-past-participle* is the same as the *Transitive-Verb's-present-participle*.

I prefer an interpretation of nets with roles in which concepts, as well as roles, are interpreted as partial functions. In Figure 2.5, for instance, part of the intended interpretation would go as follows.

- '*Regular-Verb*' denotes the partial function that is the restriction of the identity function to the domain of regular verbs;
- '*past-participle*' denotes the partial function that is defined on individuals with past participles and that takes these individuals into their past participles;
- '*suffix*' denotes the partial function that is defined on individuals with suffixes and that takes these individuals into their suffixes;
- '*Regular-Verb's-past-participle's-suffix*' denotes the partial function that is defined on regular verbs and that takes individuals into the suffix of their past participle.

Negation can be added explicitly to role formalisms such as this, in the form of negative links. Or it can be added as it is in feature structure formalisms, by invoking the *unique names assumption* – that distinct individual nodes implicitly denote distinct individuals. In either case, the informal semantics that was sketched above for roles would have to be complicated, because of the considerations mentioned in Section 2.6.1.

2.6.4. Mixed inheritance with roles

Inheritance systems with roles and relations contain multiple link types; and since any strict link type can be made defeasible, there are a great many ways to extend a strict inheritance system with roles to mixed systems that contain defeasible link types. A choice that seems particularly suitable for many linguistic purposes has strict equality as its only strict relational link type, defeasible is-a and equality as its only defeasible link types, and introduces negation by means of the unique names assumption; this would suffice to formalize the inflectional properties of the Dutch verb that are discussed in Section 5.3, below. The example given there should also help to illustrate how mixed inheritance with roles should work in one moderately complex example.

I have not tried here to specify even the system of strict inheritance with roles, contenting myself with an informal presentation of the semantics for part of the positive theory. Since the logical issues concerning the formalization of defeasible inheritance with roles are more complex and are still unclear in some ways, I won't attempt a formal account. As I explained in footnote 1, I will try to make further information on these topics available by means of the Internet.

3. Nonmonotonicity and feature structures

3.1. Classical feature structures and unification

Unification-based grammars (or, more generally, constraint-based grammars) provide a good starting point for describing the issues that arise when nonmonotonicity is to be integrated into a linguistic formalism. Two reasons contribute in particular to this explanatory advantage: (1) because these grammar formalisms are intended to be used for automatic natural language processing, they are generally formalized with more care than approaches intended solely for linguistic purposes, and (2) their connection to processing algorithms is better understood. These features of the monotonic formalisms make it easier to see the shape of the corresponding nonmonotonic representations and reasoning. Fortunately, this class of theories is very general, and includes a number of approaches that have been extensively used for describing languages and for implementing natural language processing systems. For an overview of these grammar formalisms, including historical material, see Shieber (1992, Chapter 2).

Feature structures serve as a fundamental representation device in these formalisms, and *unification* of feature structures serves as a fundamental reasoning process. The broad idea is to think of linguistic units as information items. Information can be combined; linguistic theories constrain the possible combinations. The applicable notion of information is intended to be very general, and perhaps even universal for purposes of linguistic representation; thus, we can think of information items as words, phrases, or linguistic units of any kind.

These ideas are made more concrete by adopting an approach that, like inheritance with roles and frame-based knowledge representation systems, eschews relations in favor of functions, identity, and monadic predicates. Some things can be very naturally represented on this approach: 'Barbara's hair is red', for instance becomes 'The value of BARBARA for the feature HAIRCOLOR is RED', and 'Andy and Barbara are (full) siblings' becomes 'The values of ANDY and of BARBARA for the feature MOTHER are the same', and 'The values of ANDY and of BARBARA for the feature FATHER are the same'.

Of course, some things are less easy to put in this form than others – in the final analysis, though, the limits of this representation policy are a matter of what complexity and abstractness you are willing to put up with in your features and values. For instance, to represent 'Andy and Barbara are married', you need to invoke married couples as values; to represent 'Alice likes Ben more than Anne' (on either reading), you might invoke degrees of liking. This policy of value inflation reaches a systematic extreme in Alonzo Church's formulation of higher-order logic; here, to represent 'Andy is older than Barbara', you invoke a function OLDER THAN whose values are functions from individuals to truth values.

If value assignments were defined at all arguments, different information units couldn't combine consistently. Thus, value assignments are partial functions. At points where a feature value is undefined, either the feature is inappropriate or the value is in some way unknown or indeterminate. As usual when partial functions are allowed, there is a temptation to use a nonclassical logic to systematize things: various alternatives have been tried with respect to feature structures.[36]

The constraint that is presupposed in applying this idea to linguistic theory, I suppose, is that the features and values that come up when linguistic information is represented in this way should be linguistically natural and explanatory. (In specific approaches, other constraints might be added: for instance, that there should only be finitely many features and values.)

[36] See Chapter 8, Section 3.

In Chapter 8, Rounds finds the linguistic origin of this approach in the use of feature-based representations in phonology, and ascribes the idea to Chomsky and Hale (1968), which certainly systematized and popularized this sort of mechanism in phonology. But the idea has come up so often, in so many fields, that it is hard to pinpoint a historical source.

According to the standard account of feature structures, an information item will involve (perhaps among other things) an assignment of values to certain features, and declarations of identity for certain pairs of feature paths. The values of these features may be information items, which in turn will involve values for certain features. If we trace out these relations we obtain a graph whose nodes are information items. The arcs of the graph are labeled with features; an arc of the graph relates an information item to the value for this item of the feature whose label it bears. We can think of atomic values, such as truth values, or RED in the the above example, or PLURAL, as degenerate information items all of whose feature values remain undefined. The graph representation provides a useful way of associating algorithms with information items.

Unification is the fundamental operation of putting together the information in feature structures. If two feature structures are incompatible, they have no unification; otherwise, unification combines their value assignments and identities. See Chapter 8, Kay (1992), and Shieber (1986) for examples, detailed definitions, and theoretical development.

So much for the classical approach to feature structures and unification.

3.2. Need for nonmonotonic unification

In his broad motivation of feature-based grammar formalisms,[37] Stuart Shieber lists *partiality, equationality*, and *modular structure* as the broadly desirable characteristics that motivate these formalisms. Modularity, in particular, is obtained by separating out distinct feature values, across which generalizations can be stated. To motivate nonmonotonic unification, we extend Shieber's notion of modularity to include *maintainability*. If we think of a grammar formalism as a knowledge resource that needs to be engineered, updated, and validated, we may not only wish appropriate generalizations to be expressible, but to be natural and nonredundant, so that natural constraints need only be stated once. This goal enhances the formalism's maintainability because, if things that intuitively count as a single generalization are entered in many separate places in a grammar, the grammar becomes difficult to check for integrity, and changes in the grammar are more liable to contain errors.

These concerns lead to the idea of organizing information into more and less general types; generalizations can then be attached to general types, and these generalizations can be inferred (or inherited) at more specific types without having to be stated explicitly there. This conforms well with the basic architecture of feature structures and unification:

(1) The items that are described by feature structures can either be specific (e.g., they can be particular words or phrases, like 'these') or general (e.g., they can be linguistic types, like "definite determiner").

[37] Shieber (1992, Chapter 2).

(2) The operation of inheritance is a special case of unification – unification of the more specific item with the more general one from which it inherits.

With this addition, feature structure formalisms become related to similar ideas in other areas of knowledge representation and theoretical computer science: in inheritance theory, in taxonomic logics, and in type hierarchies for general purpose formal languages. This is a large topic, and it is difficult to provide comprehensive references, but see Shieber (1992) and Carpenter (1992); the latter of these two works, especially (as the title indicates) concentrates on combining a type hierarchy with feature structure formalisms.

The modifications described so far could be carried out using a monotonic inference mechanism; the need for nonmonotonicity lies in the fact (to which we alluded in Section 1.3) that many linguistic generalizations are most naturally stated as defeasible generalizations. If, for instance, we describe the generic English verb so that the suffix of its past tense form is '-d', we will then have to unify this with an item like 'freeze' whose past tense suffix is '-∅'. With monotonic unification, this operation will fail.

Of course, we can restore monotonicity by bringing the exceptions explicitly into the statement of the rules. For instance, we could introduce a type of regular verbs, and a type of strong verbs, and move the generalization about past tense suffix '-d' to regular verbs. We can then handle the example by classifying 'freeze' as a strong verb. But in doing this, we have impaired naturalness by having to create a distinct type for each generalization that has a peculiar pattern of exceptions. Also, maintainability is threatened, because (unless we treat regularity as a default, which defeats the goal of monotonicity) we have to explicitly classify each specific lexical item with respect to the generalizations that it satisfies. This is not a large price to pay with relatively small systems, but with full-scale grammars and realistic lexicons it is much more natural to attach default information to general types, attaching only exceptional information to specific lexical items. To carry this through, however, we need to provide a characterization of default unification.

3.3. *Bouma's default unification*

The project of Bouma (1992) is to define a nonmonotonic unification operation $\sqcup$. Intuitively, $A \sqcup B$ is the result of combining the information in the feature structures A and B, treating all the information in A as default information that is overridden by B. This interpretation is natural if we think of B as lexical information, while A is the template for a linguistic type. Bouma offers several definitions of the appropriate unification operation and investigates their properties; the first definition is fairly straightforward (take the most specific generalization of A that is compatible with B and unify this classically, i.e. strictly, with B), but the later definitions get rather complex because of difficulties raised by reentrancy, i.e. by path equality.

Bouma is able to show that default unification can handle a number of linguistically interesting cases. This formalization of nonmonotonic unification is rather restrictive in its representational power. For instance, it doesn't enable us to differentiate between strict and default information that may be contained in a general template. And it gives no account of how to unify two items that may conflict, when neither is more specific than the other. In general, it may happen that we want to unify two structures, which contain conflicting defaults that are not reconciled by any priorities. (This is the point of the Nixon Diamond.) Also, it may happen that overriding information is contributed by both structures. Consider a case in which the concept NATIVE-SPEAKER-OF-ALBANIAN is combined with BORN-IN-KANSAS. The first item strictly contains the information *Native-Speaker-of-Albanian* and by default contains the information *Not-Born-in-the-USA*. The second item strictly contains the information *Born-in-the-USA* and by default contains the information *Not-a-Native-Speaker-of-Albanian.* By ruling out such cases Bouma, in effect, is assuming that in the linguistic applications that he envisages, inheritance is "orthogonal", in the sense of Touretzky (1986).[38]

In fact, morphological and lexical information in diachronically stable linguistic systems does seem to be organized so as to avoid unresolvable conflicts between defaults. But taking too much advantage of orthogonality in seeking to define defeasible unification will make the resulting theory more restrictive, and may make it harder to relate it to work in nonmonotonic reasoning, which treats such unresolvable conflicts as central.

3.4. *Young and Rounds' nonmonotonic sorts*

Subsequent work by William Rounds and collaborators[39] develops a more radical approach to defeasibility in grammar formalisms, by reworking feature structure representation so that strict information is kept separate from defeasible information. The formalism is a generalization of *typed feature structures* (also known as *sorted* feature structures), as in (Carpenter, 1992).

DEFINITION 3.1 (*Typed feature structure*). Let $\mathcal{S}$ and $\mathcal{F}$ be finite, nonempty sets (the sets of types and of features), and let $\preceq$ be a reflexive partial order on $\mathcal{S}$ such that every subset of $\mathcal{S}$ with a lower bound has a greatest lower bound. Then a typed feature structure $\mathcal{FS}$ on the signature $\langle \mathcal{F}, \mathcal{S}, \prec \rangle$ consists of: (1) A finite, nonempty set Q (the nodes of the $\mathcal{FS}$), (2) A designated element r of Q (the root of the $\mathcal{FS}$), (3) A partial function δ with $\delta(q, f) \in Q$ where $q \in Q$ and $f \in \mathcal{F}$ (the feature value function of the $\mathcal{FS}$), (4) A function θ from Q to $\mathcal{S}$ (the typing function of the $\mathcal{FS}$).

According to the definition, a feature structure is a directed graph in which the nodes (which are mere abstract locations) are connected by arcs labeled with features; the labeled arcs are determined by the feature value function. We assume that this graph is connected, and rooted in r; frequently, the graph is also assumed to be acyclic.

The types induce a specificity ordering on nodes; when $q \preceq q'$, q represents a more specific concept than q'. Young generalizes this more or less standard account by adding

[38] Touretzky defined orthogonality assuming that the only way in which overriding can occur is through specificity; but in a more general setting, it amounts to restricting conflict between two items to cases in which information from one of the structures overrides all conflicting information from the other.

[39] See Young (1992) and Young and Rounds (1993). The first paper introduces the basic theory of nonmonotonic sorts, and the second develops it and relates it to Reiter's default logic. The following discussion is mainly a summary and explanation of the second of these papers. For later developments, see Young (1994), Rounds and Zhang (1995), Rounds and Zhang (forthcoming), Zhang and Rounds (forthcoming), and Rounds and Zhang (unpublished).

a set of defaults. The idea here is somewhat like Reiter's default logic, where a theory is partitioned into a classical part and a set of default rules: a nonmonotonic type consists of a strict type and a set of defaults (here represented as a set of types).[40] A natural unification operation can be defined on these generalized types.

DEFINITION 3.2 (*Nonmonotonic types and unification*). A nonmonotonic type is a pair $\langle s, \Delta\rangle$, where $s \in \mathcal{S}$ and for all $s' \in \Delta$, $s' \preceq s$. The nonmonotonic unification of nonmonotonic types $\langle s, \Delta\rangle$ and $\langle s', \Delta'\rangle$ is $\langle s \sqcap s'\rangle\{t \sqcap s \sqcap s' : t \in \Delta \text{ or } t \in \Delta'\}$.

The requirement that $s' \preceq s$ for $s' \in \Delta$ makes sense if we think of the defaults associated with a type as ways of further specifying the strict information in the type; but it wouldn't in fact make any formal difference if this condition were dropped, since defaults that conflict with the strict information in a type will be automatically overridden.

Default unification of feature structures can then be characterized in terms of unification on the types, by a definition that parallels the monotonic case.[41] This approach is more general than Bouma's in several respects: in particular, it is easily possible for incompatible types to appear among defaults of a nonmonotonic type.[42] Therefore, the problem of multiple conclusion sets that was mentioned above in Section 2.1.1 arises; Young and Rounds solve this by defining the *solutions* of a nonmonotonic type; these are monotonic types that stand to nonmonotonic types as extensions stand to default theories in Reiter's default logic. In fact, Young and Rounds develop the analogy formally by presenting a nonmonotonic version of the Kasper–Rounds logic for feature structures,[43] and showing that the solutions of a type correspond to extensions of this logic. This logical line of thought is developed further in (Rounds and Zhang, 1995; Rounds and Zhang, forthcoming; Zhang and Rounds, forthcoming; Zhang and Rounds, unpublished).

Rounds and Young provide one linguistic example: inflectional properties of the German verb. The facts in question are that middle verbs are a subtype of verbs, and strong verbs are a subtype of the middle verbs. The default past tense suffix for verbs is '-te' and the default past participle suffix for verbs is '-t'; the past participle prefix is 'ge-'. For middle verbs, the past tense suffix is '-en', and for strong verbs, the past tense suffix is -$\emptyset$. The lexical item 'spiel' is a verb; 'mahl' is a middle verb, 'zwing' is a strong verb. This information is readily encoded using the apparatus of nonmonotonic types: the type for VERB, for instance, is the ordered pair whose first member (containing the strict information) is the type corresponding to PAST:PARTICIPLE:PREFIX:'-ge', and whose second member (containing the default information) is the set consisting of the types corresponding to PAST:TENSE:SUFFIX:'-te' and PAST:PARTICIPLE:SUFFIX:'-t'. The example shows that the system is capable of formalizing some of the lexical defaults that are needed to characterize an inflectional system.

The very pleasant formal properties of this work are possible because of a number of simplifying assumptions. Nodes cannot enter into hierarchical relationships, as in inheritance networks.[44] All hierarchical relationships are strict; there is no default subsumption.

---

[40] A set of types is needed here (rather than a single, conjoined type) because some of the defaults may well be mutually inconsistent.

[41] See, for instance, Carpenter (1992, pp. 45–47).

[42] In this formalism, incompatibility is nonunifiability; it is not expressed by means of a negation operator.

[43] See Chapter 8.

[44] See Thomason and Touretzky (1990).

There is no account of path identity. And – perhaps the most severe restriction – the only way that overriding that can occur in this theory is for strict information to override conflicting default information. However, it is not difficult to think of linguistic cases where there can be three or more layers of overriding by conflicting, increasingly specific defaults.[45]

3.5. More recent work

At present, work in the theory of default unification has not yet produced a system that provides satisfactory logical foundations for a suitably expressive system. The work of Young and Rounds has the desirable logical properties, but it is not clear how to extend these to a formalism that provides for more reentrancy and more flexible overriding of defaults. Research in closely related areas is similarly incomplete. Inheritance theory provides useful insights, but the complexities of inheritance definitions have prevented a satisfactory formulation of nonmonotonic inheritance when roles and identity are present; also, the semantics of nonmonotonic inheritance remains problematic.

The most recent attempt to extend the theoretical results with which I am familiar is described in (Lascarides, Asher, Briscoe and Copestake, 1994). This paper approaches the problem of default unification using the theory of commonsense entailment, discussed above in Section 2.5. A conditional theory based on possible worlds can be applied to feature structures in a rather natural way by using the modal approach to feature structure logic.[46] Since Lascarides, Asher, Briscoe and Copestake (1994) is at present an unpublished manuscript representing work in progress I will not discuss details, except to note that the paper envisages a number of applications of the theory besides the ones that concentrate on morphological information. In particular, the authors have in mind applications in lexical semantics and in the semantics-discourse interface.

Anyone interested in research in nonmonotonic feature structures should realize that the issues are very similar to those that arise in attempts to introduce defeasibility into taxonomic logics or classification-based knowledge representation systems. See, for instance, Quantz and Royer (1992) and Baader and Hollunder (1992).

4. Applications in phonology

Though the phenomena of phonology provide many plausible instances of defeasible reasoning, the opportunities for actually applying nonmonotonic logic to this area of linguistics are limited by the need for preliminary foundational work. Such applications require a degree of formalization that is not really to be found in the area at present. As usual, the task of providing these formalizations can require rethinking substantive

[45] Here is a case from two-level English morphophonemics: underlying 'y' corresponds by default to surface 'y'; but before a morpheme boundary it corresponds by default to 'i'; but in some foreign loan words, such as 'Sonys', it corresponds to surface 'y' before a morpheme boundary.

[46] See Blackburn (1992) and Chapter 8, Section 3.2.

issues in phonology. The recent work in this direction[47] still leaves much room for more development. Also, this work has mainly been carried out by computational linguists, and it is not clear to what extent efforts in this direction will engage the interests of mainstream linguistic phonologists. For these reasons, this section has to be fairly speculative.

4.1. *Declarative formalisms*

Nonmonotonic formalisms arose in AI out of a sense that procedural approaches are unsatisfactory in many respects. Purely procedural solutions to the representation of knowledge were felt to be neither easily communicable nor understandable; also, without a specification of correct reasoning, it may be much more difficult to extend a solution or adapt it to new problems, because the consequences of changes will not be transparent. For reasons such as this, the knowledge representation community tends to prefer representation systems that have a clear semantics.

Dependence of a solution on the order of the procedures by which it was maintained is one of the hallmarks of a procedural approach. The order of the steps of a proof is immaterial, so long as the rules of wellformedness for a proof of A are observed. But care must be taken with the order of steps in a program, since in general the order has an independent effect on the resulting machine state.

By this criterion, phonological formalisms modeled on (Chomsky and Halle, 1968) (SPE) are certainly procedural, since they involve derivations whose outcome depends on the order in which rules are applied. Therefore, rule ordering constraints have to be imposed in a separate part of the theory.[48]

Though there are important differences between the goals of linguists and those of computer scientists, the idea of seeking less procedural approaches should have the same strong motivations in phonology that it does in other theoretical areas of cognitive science. If such approaches can be shown to be as adequate on linguistic criteria as procedural alternatives, many linguists might find them preferable because of the formal and practical advantages that go along with declarative, semantically articulated formalisms.

Since many central phonological phenomena are intuitively defeasible, nonmonotonic approaches provide a promising way to develop a declarative formalism that also is linguistically plausible.

4.2. *Making phonological theories declarative*

The most obvious ways of making SPE-like phonological theories more declarative depend on substantive phonological assumptions. Just as some SPE-style systems might be equivalent to finite state transducers, some systems might be reformulable in terms

[47] See Bird (1990), Scobbie (1991), Bird and Ellison (1994), Mastroianni and Carpenter (1994), Bird and Klein (1994), and Bird (1995).

[48] Some phonologists have challenged the need for rule ordering (largely because of appeals to economy of methods rather than to declarativism). See Vennemann (1972). But this group is a minority; most phonologists believe in the classic arguments for rule ordering.

of declarative constraints. *Two-level* theories[49] provide the simplest way of doing this, by replacing SPE-style rules with declarative constraints on a predicate *Underlies*(x, y) which provide a theory of the admissible pairings of underlying with surface forms. Reformulations such as this depend on there being a constant limit to the number of intermediate levels of representation (0 in the case of a two-level reformulation, and in general $n-2$ in the case of an n-level reformulation). This technique is not fully general, since there is no limit in principle to the number of intermediate levels that could be invoked by an SPE-like theory.[50]

Applications of the " 'elsewhere' principle"[51] are a natural source of defaults in two-level phonology. For instance, two-level theories usually treat any difference between underlying and surface forms as a deviation from the norm; this means that in stating a theory, only the deviations need to be stated explicitly. But such defaults have mostly been accommodated procedurally in two-level phonology: e.g., they may be implemented in a two-level finite state compiler, but are not incorporated in the linguistic theory itself. In a recent paper,[52] Gerald Penn and Richmond Thomason describe a procedural method of capturing the 'elsewhere' principle in two level phonology, which appeals to an abstract device called a "default finite state transducer". They conjecture that in linguistically natural cases these devices can be modeled declaratively in a prioritized form of Reiter's default logic, but the details of the representation have not yet been worked out.

4.3. *Underspecification theory*

There is a long tradition in logic dealing with the management of partial information. The ideas from this tradition combine very naturally with ideas from nonmonotonic logic: you can think of defaults as rules for filling in information gaps.[53] In phonology, these ideas have been applied informally in *underspecification theory,*[54] which uses partial feature assignments to characterize underlying forms, and invokes default rules in deriving surface forms (e.g., the rule that an otherwise unspecified underlying vowel is realized as schwa).

Unfortunately, the default rules that are readily extracted from underspecification theory are too simple to be very interesting from a logical standpoint.[55] But opportunities for more sophisticated applications of nonmonotonic logic would doubtless emerge from collaborative work between logicians and phonologists working in this area. There are many good opportunities at the moment for productive collaborations of this kind: that is one of the chief messages, of course, of this chapter.

[49] See Sproat (1992, Sections 3.3–3.5) for information and references.

[50] SPE could, of course, be reformulated by leaving the number of levels unbounded. Since first-order predicates can only take a finite number of arguments, this would force us to use a set theoretic representation of arbitrary sequences of intermediate forms – in effect, the procedural derivations would be admitted into the ontology. Though the resulting theory might be technically declarative, I think it would be linguistically implausible.

[51] This is the term used by linguists for the reasoning principle that more specific defaults should override less specific defaults.

[52] Penn and Thomason (1994).

[53] For examples of this sort of logical approach, see Veltman (forthcoming) and Ginsberg (1988c).

[54] See, for instance, Archangeli (1988).

[55] See Bird and Calder (1991) for a survey of such rules.

4.4. *Optimality theory and prosodic phenomena*

The recent approach known as *optimality theory,* which has mainly addressed issues in prosodic phonology,[56] displays many interesting cases of constraint interaction, but is less easily related to any existing logical theory of nonmonotonic reasoning. Like other constraint-based approaches to grammar, the approach assumes a mechanism that generates a large number of candidate surface forms for a given input: constraints then filter out the unwanted candidates. On this approach, however, the fully grammatical forms are those that, in competition with the alternative candidates, minimally violate the constraints.[57]

In stressing constraint competition, and in allowing forms to be grammatical even though they violate certain constraints, optimality theory touches on themes from nonmonotonic logic. The inspiration of optimality theory, however, comes from a combination of constraint-based grammar and connectionism, rather than from the world of logic and defeasible reasoning, and as far as I know, optimality theory has not been formalized using a nonmonotonic formalism. However, I suspect that the similarities are more than impressionistic; the idea of minimizing constraint violations matches well the motivation of circumscription, and I believe that optimality theory could be faithfully formalized using the techniques for prioritizing sources of abnormality that are discussed in (Lifschitz, 1989, Section 14). Whether such a project would advance the phonological enterprise is another matter; I am not sure that formalizations of this sort would yield results that would seem useful to the phonologists. But interesting results might well emerge from such formalizations, and in any case it would be interesting from a methodological standpoint that a high-level formalism that emerged out of connectionist insights can be captured using one of the standard nonmonotonic formalisms.

5. Applications in morphology

It is very natural to state morphological rules so that they admit exceptions. For instance, if we wish to treat

(4) The plural of a noun with stem x is $x +$'s'

as a rule of English morphology, we then have exceptions like 'deer' and 'children'. A nonmonotonic formalism for morphology therefore has very strong motivations in linguistic intuition. If we wish to think of items like (4) as genuine rules, rather than pre-scientific generalizations, we are in fact inevitably committed to a nonmonotonic approach.

56 See Smolensky and Prince (1993) and McCarthy and Prince (1993).

57 Minimal violation is defined in terms of a ranking of the constraints; form A is better than form B in case A satisfies the highest-ranking constraint on which the two forms differ.

5.1. Implications for linguistic theory: A preliminary examination

Think of an inflectional morphological rule as a constraint (which may be general or *ad hoc*), concerning the relation between an abstract specification of an inflected form and its surface realization. Axiomatizing a representative sample of such morphological rules, using any of the standard nonmonotonic logic formalisms, would be a relatively straightforward exercise.[58] In a conditional logic, (4) and one of its exceptions could be formalized as follows.

(5) a. $\forall x[\mathit{Plural\text{-}Noun}(x) > \exists y[\mathit{Suffix}(x,y) \wedge \mathit{Phonology}(y) = \text{`s'}]]$.

b. $\exists x[\mathit{Plural\text{-}Noun}(x) \wedge \mathit{Phonology}(x) = \text{`children'}$
$\wedge \exists y[\mathit{Suffix}(x,y) \wedge \mathit{Phonology}(y) = \text{`ren'}]]$.

Exercises such as this show that nonmonotonic formalisms can be brought to bear on morphological domains. Whether these ideas can be used to illuminate theoretical issues in morphology depends on whether such examples can be systematically deployed in a way that genuinely advances the theoretical issues. This much more difficult project of systematically developing morphology on a nonmonotonic basis has not, as far as I know, been carried out. It would involve foundational work as well as original work in morphology. Rather than pursuing this matter here, I'll only point out that the options that are opened up by a nonmonotonic formalism do seem to provide important new ways of looking at the linguistic issues. Here is one example.

In a monotonic setting, the universal quantifier is the only appropriate resource for formalizing a generalization. But in formalizing generalizations in a nonmonotonic setting, we will have to judge whether the generalization is strict or defeasible. It would pretty clearly be wrong to treat "Transitive verbs can take a direct object" as defeasible, or "The past tense form of a verb consists of the verb stem and the suffix '-ed' " as strict. But in many cases, there is room for judgment. For instance, take the generalization that the underlying form of an English plural noun has a plural suffix. We can either take this generalization to be strict, and formalize it as

(6) $\forall x[\mathit{Plural\text{-}Noun}(x) \rightarrow \exists y\, \mathit{Plural\text{-}Suffix}(y,x)]$,

or we can interpret it defeasibly, and formalize it as

(7) $\forall x[\mathit{Plural\text{-}Noun}(x) > \exists y\, \mathit{Plural\text{-}Suffix}(y,x)]$.

On the former axiomatization it will be inconsistent to suppose that there are any plural nouns without plural suffixes. So, to save the generalization, we are forced to treat plurals like 'deer' as having a null suffix. That is, we have to postulate something like the following claim:

(8) $\exists x[\mathit{Plural\text{-}Noun}(x) \wedge \mathit{Phonology}(x) = \text{`deer'}$
$\wedge \exists y[\mathit{Plural\text{-}Suffix}(y,x) \mathit{Phonology}(y) = \emptyset]]$.

[58] In particular, the axioms corresponding to morphological rules present no difficulties. In many nonmonotonic formalisms, however, it may be awkward to secure a preference for more specific defaults; this is why a nonmonotonic conditional approach is particularly suitable for this task.

But in a nonmonotonic setting, we have another option. We can say that plurals like 'deer' lack a suffix – our lexical entry for 'deer' can contain (or entail) the following claim:

(9) $$\exists x\big[\mathit{Plural\text{-}Noun}(x) \wedge \mathit{Phonology}(x) = \text{'deer'} \\ \wedge \neg\exists y\big[\mathit{Plural\text{-}Suffix}(x, y)\big]\big].$$

If the evidence is limited to pairings of English noun stems with their plural forms, then both formalizations match the evidence. To distinguish between these two formalizations, we must either find other linguistic evidence that can be brought to bear on the issue, or establish conventions which favor one of the two.

Arnold Zwicky has criticized the widespread practice in linguistics (and especially in areas that are influenced by fashions in syntax) of saving generalizations by postulating *ad hoc* levels of representation at which the generalizations hold.[59] Though he is able to point to many cases where the technique is abused, the force of Zwicky's criticisms is weakened without a demonstration that natural, intuitive generalizations will be forthcoming in a monotonic framework that entirely eschews the use of levels of representation to preserve the generalizations. One can of course hope that good generalizations will be forthcoming under harsher conditions. But if this hope fails, we are faced with an unpleasant dilemma: either we can have a modular theory with appealing local generalizations, but which is cumbersome and *ad hoc* at a more general level, or a more unified theory in which generalizations apply broadly but are neither natural nor well motivated.

Nonmonotonic foundations for morphology offer a third alternative. If a rule is defeasible, we do not need to invoke new levels of representation to protect it from apparent exceptions. Apparent exceptions can simply be treated as real exceptions, and we can proceed to look for subregularities among the exceptions. In a nonmonotonic theoretical context, conservatism about the propagation of hidden representations turns into the following policy:

(10) When given a choice between (1) formulating a linguistic generalization strictly, and preserving it by postulating a hidden construct, such as a new level of representation or a null item, and (2) formulating the generalization defeasibly, prefer option (2) unless the hidden construct is independently well motivated.

Genuine linguistic problems can't be defined away by logical maneuvering, though they can be relocated. To be clear where we stand, we need to ask where the conflict between the plausibility and generality of linguistic rules will reappear in a nonmonotonic framework. The relocated problem, I think, is the question of how to decide under what conditions a defeasible generalization is tenable. A few counterexamples do not threaten a defeasible rule; an overwhelming concurrence of counterexamples make it untenable. But many linguistic rules will be somewhere in the middle, and here the criteria are more difficult to apply; therefore, it becomes harder to decide between competing theories. This problem has occasionally surfaced in the form of sweeping criticisms of nonmonotonic formalisms.[60] Although the difficulty is genuine, it is too soon to tell how much of an

[59] The criticisms appear in several recent works; see Zwicky (1986) and Zwicky (1989), for instance.

[60] For instance, this is one way of reading the argument in (Brachman, 1985).

obstacle it will be in formulating linguistic theories; the main question seems to be how successful we can be in agreeing on viability criteria for nonmonotonic generalizations.

As far as I know, no one has attempted to develop a systematic account of morphology on nonmonotonic foundations, using one of the general-purpose nonmonotonic logics. But the project is promising. The logical and linguistic resources are well enough understood, and – as I argued above – the introduction of defeasible rules provides theoretical alternatives that are well worth exploring.

5.2. Taking procedures into account

The general-purpose nonmonotonic logics are very powerful, and are not immediately connected with sound and complete inference procedures of any kind, much less with procedures that are efficient. But morphology is a relatively constrained domain; and morphological processing, as part of a larger task like natural language interpretation, seems to call for inference procedures that are highly efficient, even in the presence of rather large lexical knowledge bases.

To look at the task of formalizing natural language morphology as one of designing representations that will describe the phenomena, will facilitate generalizations about the domain, and also will support efficient core procedures (such as recognition of an underlying form, when presented with a surface form), is to see the problem from the standpoint of knowledge representation and reasoning.[61] Though research in knowledge representation is far from producing a complete system that could be applied to representation problems in linguistics, or even in morphology, it has certainly produced ideas and partial results that interface well with linguistic purposes, and that can be applied piecemeal. In fact, we have a number of instances in which they are already being applied in this way.

The following considerations reflect on the expressive features that would be desirable in a system for representing and managing morphological information, and on related algorithmic requirements.

Hierarchical structure and inheritance reasoning. Let's assume that any tool for representing information about words should provide for hierarchical structuring of the relevant concepts, and also allow some form of inheritance reasoning. The advantages of storing information at the most general appropriate concept and allowing it to be inferred at more specific concepts are pretty general. They show up in almost any area where general reasoning is combined with a relatively large amount of data; object-oriented programming and object-oriented databases, as well as many knowledge-related applications in AI are examples.[62] For the need for concept hierarchies and inheritance in lexical applications, see, for instance, Briscoe (1993), Copestake (1993), and Krieger and Nerbonne (1993). But – as Section 2.6 illustrates – the complexity of inheritance depends on the other

[61] Linguists, of course, are also interested in "linguistic adequacy", or ability to explain phenomena at a very general level. I haven't added this to my list because this is not a typical goal of knowledge representation, though it is certainly compatible with the more typical goals.

[62] See, for instance, Meyer (1988) and Zdonik and Meyer (1990).

constructs that are integrated with hierarchical reasoning. And here, there is a lot more to be said about the requirements of linguistic applications.

Definitions and classification. Even linguists who work with fairly informal theories often use definitions to organize concepts, and the ability to define concepts and reason appropriately with definitions should rate highly on our list of desirable features. For instance, it should be possible to define a third person singular noun as a noun that is third in person and singular in number, or (to sharpen the attribute-value grammar flavor) to say that a third-person singular noun is a symbol whose value for the attribute CAT is N, whose value for the attribute NUMBER is SINGULAR, and whose value for the attribute PERSON is THIRD.

Once a definition is declared, a defined concept should automatically be positioned in the hierarchy of concepts so that the definition will determine appropriate relations to the other concepts. For instance, we want all the strict information that applies to the concept SINGULAR-NOUN to apply to the concept THIRD-PERSON-SINGULAR-NOUN; and we want all the strict information that attaches to THIRD-PERSON-SINGULAR-NOUN to apply to any symbol whose value for the attribute CAT is N, whose value for the attribute NUMBER is SINGULAR, and whose value for the attribute PERSON is THIRD.

We will have a much better notion of the expressive and algorithmic complexity of morphological information if we can characterize the constructs that are needed to define the concepts that are required by a morphological theory. A reliable characterization could only emerge from an extensive process of trial-and-error formalization. But at least we can indicate here the sort of constructs that are likely to be needed.[63]

Value assignment. We need to be able to specify that a feature takes a certain value. This construct, of course, was used in the example definition of the concept THIRD-PERSON-SINGULAR-NOUN.

Boolean connectives. The need for conjunction is pervasive; this construct was also used in our initial example. In classification-based knowledge representation, the use of negation and disjunction is often limited. But they occur in many natural morphological examples. Consider the following example, from (Aronoff, 1976, p. 60).

> Citing an unpublished work of Emonds, Chapin states that the distribution of these affixes [English nominal suffixes '#ment' and '+Ation'] is by and large governed by phonological properties of the base: verbs with the prefixes 'eN-' and 'be-' take '#ment'; verbs ending in oral or nasal stops take '+Ation' ('starve', 'sense', 'fix'); verbs with a liquid preceded by a vowel take '+Ation' ('console', 'explore'). All others take '#ment'.

The use of disjunction is evident in characterizing these root classes. Cases in which negation is used to define a residue class ("all others" here) are especially difficult to eliminate.

---

[63] All of these constructs have been studied in connection with taxonomic logics; see Woods and Schmolze (1992) and the references there. The trend in this area has been to implement expressively weak systems, and a system supporting all of the constructs mentioned below would be expressively strong.

Equality and quantification. Universally quantified equations are familiar from unification-based grammar formalisms. The need for this sort of construct can also be directly motivated by morphological considerations. For instance, this is precisely what is meant by *syncretism*,[64] where, for instance, a rule is wanted to the effect that two inflected forms are always identical (as, for instance, plural accusative and dative forms are in German). Similarly, universal quantifications of the form

$$\forall x[\text{TYPE}_1(x) \leftrightarrow \text{TYPE}_2(\text{PATH}(x))]$$

are generally useful for purposes of knowledge representation.[65] And generalizations of this kind are needed in morphology: the constraint that in Arabic, all roots have the form $C\,V\,C$ is an example, and (if an example with a nonempty path is wanted) so is the constraint that for the class of English verbs with regular perfective forms, the root of the plural form is identical to the root of the present form.

String types and their properties. Many morphological constraints deal with the order of morphemes in words. The rule that the English derivational suffixes '-al', '-ize', and '-tion' occur in that order, so that 'verbalization' is a word, but not 'verbization-al' is an instance. Such constraints might well enter into definitions. For instance, in Pĩraha (an Amazonian language), a word is a phrase consisting of a (possibly compound) root, followed by any number of sixteen suffixes – and these suffixes have to occur in a fixed, linear order.[66]

To deal with such constraints, morphological definitions need to include constraints on string types.[67] Of course, as soon as a construct is added to the definitional apparatus, the appropriate reasoning has to be integrated into the classifier. Adding strings raises a number of problems, but the computational issues have at least been explored in a preliminary way, in connection with a project that attempts to apply classification to plans.[68] Details can be found in (Devanbu and Litman, 1991), where classification algorithms are developed for a classification-based system supporting string types.

Once defeasibility is added to such a system, as well as the other constructs that we have mentioned, the logical details of what is wanted are not entirely clear. It is, of course, possible to specify the system in one of the general-purpose nonmonotonic logics, such as circumscription theory, but because of the power of these logics this does not provide any assurance that there will be sound and complete algorithms for basic operations such as unification, classification, or even inheritance.

---

[64] If the term is used without historical connotations, as it is in (Spencer, 1991).

[65] This is a special case of what is known as "value restriction" by in classification-based systems.

[66] Personal communication, Dan Everett.

[67] The Pĩraha constraint might then emerge as a definition of a word as a string of morphemes such that (1) its first element is a root, and (2) the list of its remaining elements is a sublist of a certain 12 element list of morphemes. This bare definition, of course, would need to be augmented, by assignment of appropriate attributes to words: e.g., prosodic attributes, semantic attributes, and the like.

[68] In Artificial Intelligence, plans are recipes that license certain sequences (i.e. strings) of actions; this is why string types are needed for extensions of classification to cover planning. This is another instance of close interrelationships between the sorts of reasoning that are needed for linguistic applications and general purpose reasoning.

The goal of designing such a system has emerged in three separate research fields: inheritance, taxonomic logics, and grammar formalisms. The work in inheritance starts with very simple nonmonotonic formalisms, so here the problem appears as one of adding relational reasoning, Boolean constructs, and the like to the basic systems. This has turned out to be surprisingly difficult. I said in Section 2.6.4 that a lot of my own work in this area is still unpublished because I don't feel that I have been able to think the issues through. In the taxonomic logic community, the desirability of adding defeasibility and classification is somewhat controversial.[69] But see Quantz and Royer (1992) and Baader and Hollunder (1992) for work that explores the issues that arise in this area when nonmonotonicity is added. We discussed the issues that arise from the perspective of unification grammar formalisms in Section 3, above.

This research area seems to be problematic because of the proliferation of logical theories of nonmonotonicity and the relatively undeveloped state of the intuitions that are needed to sort them out. But another reason for the difficulty is that our initial intuitions lead to formalisms that range from totally noncomputable to relatively intractable. There has been some success in finding implementable special cases of nonmonotonic theories, but it is hard to point to even a single application area in which these special cases might be useful.[70] For this reason, the domain of linguistic morphology is a very promising area of investigation for the nonmonotonic logic community. It is rich in logical texture and provides a good variety of defeasible generalizations; and there are useful applications in natural language processing. There are a number of special purpose systems that implement complex applications in some detail.[71]

But at the same time, the area is sufficiently complex to offer many genuine challenges to the theoretical community.

5.3. An example: The Dutch verb

The ideas in Figure 5.1 derive originally, I believe, from De Smedt (1984); similar treatments of Germanic verb morphology have also appeared in the DATR literature, and in the literature on default unification, though the example is seldom presented in its full complexity. This beautiful example illustrates complex interactions between defaults, specificity, and the logical properties of identity. It was this example that convinced me that linguistic applications could illuminate logical issues in nonmonotonic reasoning, and that the logical theories might be useful in illuminating the organization of lexical information. Figure 5.1 is a more or less straightforward rendering of the account of De Smedt (1984) in the graphical notation of inheritance theory.

Figure 5.1 declares inflectional information about three types of Dutch verbs: Verbs, Mixed Verbs, and Strong Verbs. Double shafted arrows contain strict information; single shafted arrows contain defeasible information. Single headed unlabeled arrows are is-a

---

[69] See Brachman (1985).

[70] The situation looks better if you count negation as failure in logic programming as an application area, but this application didn't arise directly out of the work in nonmonotonic logics.

[71] See Evans and Gazdar (1990), De Smedt (1990), and Daelemans (1987).

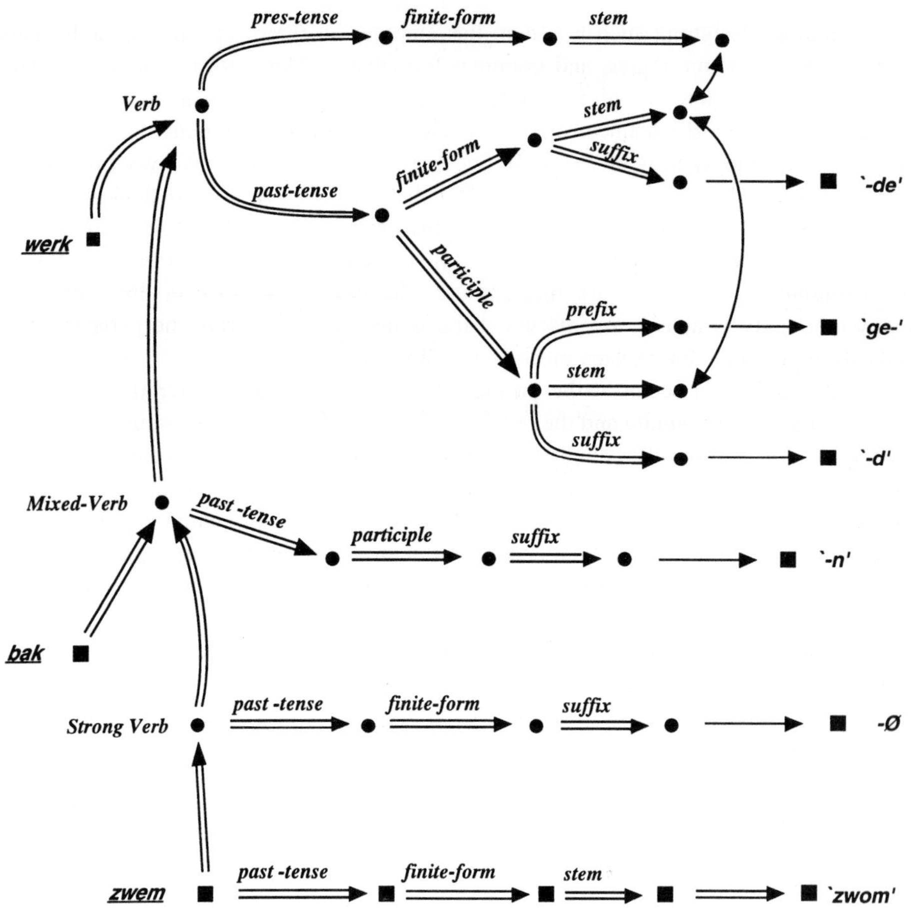

Fig. 5.1. The Dutch verb.

links; double headed unlabeled arrows are identity links.[72] Labeled arrows represent attribute links. Information attaching to general types is always general; i.e. it is always implicitly universally quantified. Squares represent objects and circles represent concepts.

Some information in the network is left implicit. We assume that the *present-finite-stem* of each *Verb* evaluates to the citation form that serves as the label for the *Verb* (so that there is an implicit is-a link[73] from bak to 'bak' that serves to evaluate the *present-finite-stem* of the verb bak). And we assume that individuals with different quoted labels are different (so that there is an implicit strict exclusion link from '-n' to '-d').

[72] Note that these diagrams differ from feature structure diagrams in representing identity explicitly; there is no literal reentrancy.

[73] Identity links to individuals do not need to be distinguished from is-a links, since for individual concepts subsumption is the same as identity.

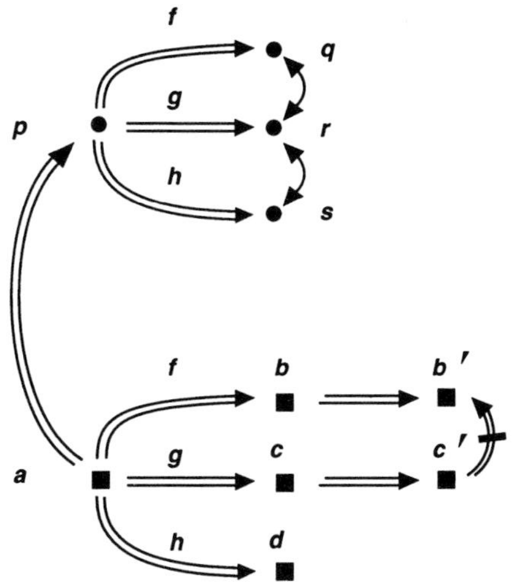

Fig. 5.2. Focusing on part of the Dutch verb.

Figure 5.1 directly contains, for instance, the information that *Mixed-Verbs* are necessarily *Verbs,* that *Verbs* have *present-finite-stems,* that the *present-finite-stem* of a *Verb* is in general the same as its *past-finite-stem,* and that the *past-participle-suffix* of a *Mixed-Verb* is in general '-n'. And there are a number of implicit inferences. We can infer by inheritance, for example, that the *past-participle-stem* of 'bak' is 'bak', and (allowing more specific defaults to override less specific ones) that the *past-participle-suffix* of 'bak' is '-n'.

Perhaps the most interesting inference produced by this network is the evaluation of the *past-participle-stem* for 'zwem'. It is 'zwom', so that (using other inferences delivered by the network) the past participle of this verb will be 'ge-zwom-n'.[74]

Since 'zwem' is classified as a verb, the network also provides a path that evaluates its *past-participle-stem* to 'zwem'. But this path is overridden by the path that produces 'zwom'. The simplified diagram in Figure 5.2 focuses on the reasoning here. In this diagram, **f** represents the path *present-finite-stem,* **g** represents the path *past-finite-stem,* and **h** represents the path *past-participle-stem.* The diagram makes it clear that the inherited default identity between **b** and **c** is overridden by the strict exclusion between **b′** and **c′**. (In all formalizations of default reasoning, strict information overrides competing default information.) However, the identity between **c** and **d** is unopposed, and should be inherited.

In the earlier discussion of inheritance I didn't provide a general inheritance definition to cover this case. As far as I know, there is none provided in the inheritance literature, though I have explored the some of the issues in unpublished work. The example is important because it produces nontrivial, interesting reasoning in a linguistically interesting

[74] This is an analysis of the underlying form; a regular morphophonemic rule of epenthesis produces the surface form 'gezwomen'.

example from morphology, and because it shows that an assumption that is incorporated in the assumptions and notation of the unification grammar community is not appropriate in a nonmonotonic setting. Note that this example depends essentially on breaking the transitivity of a default identity. In order to represent the reasoning appropriately, *it is essential not to represent identity of path values using reentrancy.* That is, in a nonmonotonic setting we need to represent identities "intensionally" as links between different locations, rather than as pointers to the same location.

6. Syntax

The need for applications of nonmonotonicity is probably harder to demonstrate conclusively for syntax than for any other area of linguistics, and it is not easy to find syntactic phenomena that make sophisticated demands on nonmonotonic logic; so this section will be brief.

Bouma (1992) provides a useful list of reasons for introducing nonmonotonicity into syntax.[75] Bouma cites the following applications:

(i) Exceptional rules,
(ii) Feature percolation principles, and
(iii) Gapping.

A syntactic rule that held by default but failed to apply in certain cases would of course be a direct source of nonmonotonicity in syntax. As far as I know, however, it is hard to argue convincingly for such rules; the difficulty is in finding compelling arguments that a nonmonotonic solution is clearly superior to spelling out the exceptional cases explicitly in the statement of the rule.

Of the cases that Bouma mentions, (ii) is probably the strongest. But though fairly convincing intuitive arguments can be given for making the "head feature convention" hold by default,[76] the use of defaults doesn't seem to result in a theory that is interestingly different.

7. Applications in semantics

In Section 1.3 I mentioned ways in which the project of using nonmonotonic logic to formalize common sense overlaps with the efforts of linguists to provide a logical framework for natural language metaphysics. Several works have already appeared that explicitly pursue projects of this sort, such as Asher (1992) (which has to do with the interpretation of progressive aspect) and Morreau (1992b) (which has to do with generic constructions).[77] The connection between cases such as these and defeasible reasoning is

[75] Bouma is thinking of constraint-based grammars, but even so, the list provides a reasonably comprehensive view of opportunities for defeasible rules in syntax.

[76] This convention says in effect that a phrase will share feature values with its head.

[77] There is a general discussion of nonmonotonic formalisms in connection with the semantics of generics in (Krifka, Pelletier, Carlson, Ter Meulen, Chierchia and Link, 1995, pp. 58–63). The upshot of this is that while nonmonotonic logic may have something to contribute, it is not the whole story.

very natural, but in both cases the formal treatment is rendered problematic by elements of context-sensitivity that are also enter into the interpretation of these constructions in ways that are not yet, I think, very well understood.[78]

One of Richard Montague's original goals for semantic theory was to provide a framework that would enable the meanings of semantically complex words to be specified by means of *meaning postulates*. Intensional Logic was meant to serve as a vehicle for stating such postulates; and in fact Montague's most extended argument for the appropriateness of Intensional Logic for semantic purposes was, essentially, that it allowed one to write meaning postulates relating derived nominals to the verbal elements from which they are derived.[79]

Of course, this area has received further attention. But despite major achievements such as Dowty (1979), it seems to me that Montague's goal of providing an adequate foundation for lexical semantics has not been realized in subsequent work. The part of the field that is formalizable is small in relation to the richness of semantic relations between words; and many researchers in lexical semantics aren't convinced that formal methods are able to come to grips with what is linguistically important in the area.

These considerations provide good motivation for exploring extensions of Montague's logical framework, and evaluating the extensions by testing their adequacy as resources for lexical semantics. I believe that a nonmonotonic extension of Intensional Logic is one of the most promising such ideas.[80] The most natural vehicle for this project is circumscription theory. (I have already mentioned that a higher-order, intensional version of John McCarthy's circumscription theory yields a formalism that is particularly close to Montague's original framework; see Thomason (1990) for more details.)

The need for a nonmonotonic theory is illustrated by notions such as causality, agency, telicity, and ability, which are pervasive in word formation processes. Here, I will only try to sketch some of the relevant issues.[81]

7.1. Causality

Causality is pervasive in word formation processes; but despite its centrality, it is generally treated as a primitive in linguistic semantics. Part of the difficulty here is that causality is an elusive notion that belongs more to common sense than to more readily formalized domains. (Philosophers have often pointed out that there seems to be no direct element of causality in the more developed physical sciences.) Nonmonotonic logics offer at least some hope for a deeper logical analysis, though the issues here remain somewhat problematic. See Shoham (1988, 1990, 1991), Simon (1991), and Geffner (1992).

---

[78] Some light may be shed on these matters by the development of a separate theory of contextual effects. In this regard, see Guha (1991). The issues explored in this dissertation are becoming quite popular, and we can expect to see more research in this area. How relevant it will be to the concerns of linguists remains to be seen.

[79] Montague (1969, pp. 148–155).

[80] See Thomason (1991) for background.

[81] This is part of an ongoing project; for more information, see Thomason (1991, 1994).

7.2. *Agency and telicity*

When it is analyzed at all these days,[82] agency involves some underlying element of necessity – with the consequence that for an act to be performed by the agent, the agent must do something that makes the result inevitable. Words for acts, however, are often lexically related to terms for goals which will *normally, but not inevitably* be achieved by invoking certain procedures. Thus, it seems wrong to say that in a case in which (1) An agent invokes the normal procedure for closing a door, and (2) The door in fact closes in the expected way, the agent didn't in fact close the door, because a gust of wind might have prevented the door from closing. These considerations suggest that nonmonotonic logic might provide a more adequate foundation for dealing with agency and telicity.

7.3. *Resultatives*

One of the first constructions to be carefully studied in connection with the logical semantics of lexical decomposition is exemplified by the semantic relation of the verb 'hammer' and adjective 'flat' to the phrase 'hammer flat'. There is a fairly extensive treatment of the phenomenon in (Dowty, 1979). He offers an analysis of 'x hammers y flat' that amounts to 'x causes y to become flat by hammering on it'.

However, this sort of definition misses something: these constructions also incorporate manner to some extent. They imply that the action is done in the usual way. Thus, for instance, if Fritz causes the metal to become flat by hammering on it as a signal for Natasha to run it through a metal press, he certainly caused it to become flat, but didn't hammer it flat.

If I say simply that Fritz used a hammer to make the metal flat, you would be entitled to assume that Fritz used the hammer in a normal way. It is just this sort of normality that seems to be incorporated in resultative constructions: 'Fritz hammered the metal flat' means 'Fritz used a hammer on the metal in the normal way (with respect to the event type of hammering) to make it flat'. We could encode this using a predicate, *normal*(x, y), which is true of an event e and an event type ϕ if and only if e is carried out in a normal manner with respect to expectations pertaining to ϕ. For instance, Fritz's hammering on the metal was not a normal event with respect to expectations attaching to hammering. (Notice that the relevant sort of normalcy is conventional; it is pretty normal to use a hammer to pull nails, but wrong to say 'Fritz hammered the nail out of the floor'. It's also worth noticing that the information about normalcy that is needed in such examples is exactly the sort of information that is needed for practical planning.)

Though the modification that I am suggesting to Dowty's meaning postulate for 'hammer flat' does not involve the use of a nonmonotonic logic, it does help to provide some independent motivation for the need in lexical semantics of the normality (or abnormality) predicates that are required by a circumscriptive theory.

[82] See, for instance, Belnap and Perloff (1990).

7.4. *The -able suffix*

Among the semantic patterns that occur fairly commonly with the *-able* suffix is an "action-outcome" meaning, exemplified by 'believable', 'detectable', 'soluble', and 'transportable'. Here, the interpretation seems to be that a "test action" will normally result in the indicated outcome. (The appropriate test action is inferred somehow; probably commonsense knowledge is involved in the inference.) To call a story believable is to say that a person will believe the story when told it, under normal circumstances.

Nonmonotonic logic (and especially the versions that use a form of commonsense entailment) delivers a natural formalization for this lexical meaning relation. The fact that using such an approach provides some hope hope of giving necessary and sufficient conditions of the meaning of, say, 'x is water-soluble' in terms of 'x dissolves in water' has some historical importance in connection with the analysis of dispositionals.[83]

7.5. *Other applications*

Accounting for *polysemy* (systematically related meanings of lexical items) has emerged as one of the most important problem areas in lexical semantics.[84] Predicting patterns of polysemy for lexical items can involve nonmonotonic inheritance. More interestingly, the interpretation of polysemous words in context certainly calls for some form of reasoning that is broadly nonmonotonic; but it is not clear to me at this point whether one of the nonmonotonic logics, or other methods – such as abduction or probabilistic reasoning – are most appropriate for this task. See Kilgarrif (1995) for an approach using nonmonotonic inheritance.

8. Applications in discourse

Defeasibility was implicitly recognized as characteristic of discourse phenomena in even the earliest attempts to separate discourse effects from what is conventional in language. Grice (1989), which for many years was circulated in various unpublished forms, and has been highly influential in the theory of discourse, uses defeasibility as a way of testing whether an interpretive effect is conventional or nonconventional.

Though discourse is thus a very natural application area for defeasible reasoning, it is only recently that we have seen any very systematic attempts to use nonmonotonic reasoning to formalize the phenomena. As we might expect, we find much the same outcome that we see in other cases where nonmonotonic formalisms are applied to phenomena with complex interacting defaults: we can achieve some success in formalizing regularities in limited domains, but it is difficult to obtain similar results in a very general way. And in general, formalisms that are less principled in their design may be more robust in actual applications.

I will briefly describe some representative work that has been done in this area.

[83] For more details, see Thomason (1994).

[84] The literature on this topic is fairly extensive; but see, for instance, Pustejovsky (1991).

8.1. Speech acts

The reasons for importing nonmonotonicity into a theory of speech acts are much the same as those that motivated nonmonotonic theories of planning and action in general. The conclusions that should be inferred about the state of the world (or the state of a conversation) after an act has been performed will in general be defeasible. Without a nonmonotonic formalism, it is very difficult to see how to axiomatize a realistic planning domain, because the ways in which an effect may fail to be achieved, or in which a background condition may fail to continue to hold after the action has been performed, are practically impossible to enumerate.[85]

Appelt and Konolige (1988) represents an attempt to formalize speech acts using ideas similar to those used in planning problems. The work builds on earlier monotonic axiomatizations by Levesque, Cohen, and Perrault of speech acts, and on Perrault's nonmonotonic reformulation of this work. The central idea of the monotonic formulations in (Cohen and Levesque, 1985, 1987; Cohen and Perrault, 1987) is to axiomatize speech acts in such a way that theorems can be proved to support the efficacy of certain speech acts in achieving their conventional goals. In the case of assertion, for instance, this means that there will be a theorem to the effect that the utterance of a declarative sentence expressing p will result in a state in which the hearer believes p.

There is a dilemma close to the surface of this line of research. On the one hand, one needs to be able to prove these "efficacy" theorems, since otherwise the planning agent will not have the beliefs that it needs about the consequences of actions in order to plan effectively. On the other hand, the theorems will either be false or will involve conditions beyond the agent's control – for instance, there will be countless ways in which the hearer may fail to believe p, even though the appropriate sentence has been uttered.

Reacting to this difficulty, C. Raymond Perrault provides a nonmonotonic solution, in which the theory of speech acts is reformulated using Reiter's default logic; rules such as the declarative rule formulated above are then treated as defaults.[86] In later work, Appelt and Konolige (1988) provide an improved formulation of the idea using Konolige's hierarchical autoepistemic logic. This work has also been implemented in a discourse planner.

As far as I know, all of the work done in this area is able to model only the effects of speech acts that are more or less direct, or "conventional", as J.L. Austin would put it. This work does not provide the means to plan implicatures, for instance. If Grice was at all correct about the rational source of implicatures, a much more detailed and complex model of the hearer's reasoning process would be needed in order to provide a theoretical basis for this sort of speech act.

8.2. Recognizing intentions and discourse structure

Turning to the other side of the discourse process, let's consider the interpretation of utterances.

[85] In the literature on nonmonotonicity, this is called the *ramification problem.* See Ginsberg (1988b).
[86] See Perrault (1990).

8.2.1. Interpretation as abduction

A large part of the reasoning task in interpreting utterances that are part of larger communicative units is the assignment of appropriate relations to the utterances. For instance, the task of interpreting the following discourse isn't over even when each sentence has been correctly interpreted; it is also necessary to determine whether (a) and (b) are items in a list of disadvantages of fossil fuel, or whether (b) is a reason for (a).

(a) Fossil fuel is expensive.

(b) It pollutes the environment.

There is some disagreement in the field about whether there are discourse relations that need to be inferred at the multisentential level by some sort of knowledge intensive parsing, or to what extent this is a special case of inferring speaker intentions: but in either case one is dealing with plausible hypotheses about the meaning, which are highly defeasible.

The abductive approach of Hobbs, Stickel, Appelt and Martin (1993), implemented in SRI's TACITUS system, models understanding a text as the process of producing a proof that leads from given information to an interpretation of the text. (In simple cases, the interpretation may simply be the proposition or propositions expressed by the text. In more complex cases, the interpretation may involve other elements, such as the proposition that the text is coherent.) Auxiliary hypotheses may need to be added in providing this proof; the idea, then, is that these hypotheses are part of the interpretation of the text (or of what the speaker meant by the text).

In this system, abduction is viewed as the process of finding a minimally (or relatively) inexpensive proof. Part of the process of knowledge representation, therefore, consists of axiomatizing domain information using familiar logical tools. This task is declarative, relatively domain independent, and is grounded in representation techniques that are fairly objective. The other part of the process, which consists in assigning costs to proofs, is more problematic in these respects.[87] And, though Hobbs and his colleagues have explored how to treat a wide variety of discourse phenomena using their abductive apparatus, the applications that they have implemented, as far as I know, have not yet tried to treat all of these problems simultaneously.

Nevertheless, the ideas have been implemented to produce natural language understanding systems that are remarkably successful in several different tasks and domains. Even though the theory of this version of nonmonotonic reasoning is not yet worked out in a way that connects it successfully with the best theoretical work in nonmonotonic reasoning, its power and its success in applied areas make it a highly important development. As Gazdar says in (Gazdar, 1987), we should beware of simplistic models of the relation between theory and applications in linguistics. We should not expect work in any major area of artificial intelligence, including natural language processing, to proceed smoothly from general theories to applications, or expect new theories to emerge smoothly from successful applications. We are unlikely, I think, to obtain robust relations between theory and applications without independent work in both directions.

---

[87] See pp. 132–137 of Hobbs, Stickel, Appelt and Martin (1993) for a discussion of the issues.

8.3. *Discourse and commonsense entailment*

In a number of recent papers, Asher, Lascarides, and Oberlander have developed an application of a theoretically motivated approach to nonmonotonic reasoning to the problem of inferring discourse relations from texts.[88] The idea is to use commonsense entailment[89] to formalize defaults concerning the temporal interpretation and coherence of texts. Assume a sentence-level interpreter that assigns an event (or more generally a state or event, an "eventuality") e_A to a sentence A.

In their rules, they take event time to be incremented with each new sentence by default: this would explain why in a text like

Linda drove to work.
She entered her office.
She picked up the telephone.

we assume that three events occurred in temporal sequence. In formalizing this, the temporal inference is mediated by a discourse relation of *Narration*. The default assumption is that sentences in sequence are in this discourse relation; a separate axiom ensures that the corresponding events are temporally ordered.

Narration 1: $\mathit{Subtext}(A, B) > \mathit{Narration}(A, B)$.

Narration 2: $\mathit{Narration}(A, B) \to e_A \prec e_B$.

However, the default can be overridden in a number of ways. For instance, in a case like

Linda drove to work.
She got in her car.
She found a parking place near her office.
She entered her office.
She picked up the telephone.

we do not want to infer that Linda drove to work before she got in her car. To provide for this, we appeal to another discourse relation of *Elaboration.* We postulate that elaboration implies temporal *non* precedence and that normally when e_B is a preparatory condition for e_A, A and B stand in the *Elaboration* relation.

Elaboration 1: $[\mathit{Subtext}(A, B) \wedge \mathit{Preparation}(e_B, e_A)] > \mathit{Elaboration}(A, B)$.

Elaboration 2: $\mathit{Elaboration}(A, B) \to e_A \not\prec e_B$.

To apply these rules to our text, we need to know that Linda's getting in the car is a preparatory part of Linda's driving to work. This is clearly based on the everyday knowledge that in general getting into a car is a preparatory condition for driving somewhere; this domain information would somehow license a default to the effect that if contiguous sentences B and A in a text express events of this kind, i.e. if e_B is an event of getting into a car and e_A is an event of driving the car somewhere, then B is an elaboration of A in the text.

[88] See Lascarides and Oberlander (1991), Lascarides and Asher (1991, 1993a, 1993b).
[89] See Asher and Morreau (1991), Morreau (1992a, 1992b), and Section 2.5 of this chapter.

In the presentations that I have seen of this approach to discourse relations, the needed information is simply posited in the required form. In this case, for instance, two things are needed: the domain fact that the events stand in the *Preparation* relation, and the discourse inference that when the events in question stand in this relation, the sentences are in an *Elaboration* relation.

Discourse Rule 1:

$$[\mathit{Subtext}(A,B) \wedge \mathit{Express}(A,e_A) \wedge \mathit{Express}(B,e_B) \\ \wedge \mathit{Preparation}(e_B,e_A)] > \mathit{Elaboration}(A,B).$$

Domain Fact 1: $\mathit{Preparation}(e_B,e_A)$.

Notice, however, that to infer Domain Fact 1, we will need to know that e_A is an event in which Linda drove her car to work; in other words, we will have to perform an instance of the discourse inference that Hobbs et al. call *coersion* in (Hobbs, Stickel, Appelt and Martin, 1993). This, and examples that are generated by considering almost any realistic text, make it clear that in order to apply the ideas, it will be necessary to have an account in this framework not only of inferred discourse relations but of a wide range of other interpretive processes.

Based as it is on commonsense entailment, the main device available to this approach of resolving competing defaults is specificity of default rules. It remains to be seen whether in a reasoning domain as complex as this, this approach to conflict resolution will be manageable even in moderately complicated domains and reasoning tasks. It will be very interesting to compare the success of this approach with that of the more flexible, but less principled abductive approach, as efforts are made to formulate them for comparable domains. The results should be important not only for discourse, but for applied nonmonotonic reasoning in general.

8.4. Modeling presupposition and implicature

Computer scientists have initiated several projects that make use of nonmonotonic formalisms to improve on theories that have been presented in the philosophical and linguistic literature of discourse phenomena. Robert Mercer applied default logic to the theory of presupposition, and Jacques Wainer developed a circumscriptive theory of implicature phenomena. See Mercer and Reiter (1982), Mercer (1987, 1988), and Wainer (1991).

8.5. Mutual defaults

Richmond Thomason has explored the use of *mutual defaults* (defaults about conversation that are mutually believed by the speaker and hearer in modeling ideas about conversation due to Robert Stalnaker and David Lewis.[90] These philosophers treat certain conversational variables (such as what has been established at a given point in the

[90] See Thomason (1990).

conversation) as information that is dynamically updated and maintained by the participants in a conversation. To preserve conversational coherence, it is important to show that the conversational participants can maintain the same view of the conversational context throughout a normal conversation in which various speech acts are performed; Thomason's paper uses a version of circumscription theory based on Montague's Intensional Logic (rather than on extensional second-order logic) to model a very simple example. The author hoped that using a more elaborate theory of mutual defaults, it would be possible to model the effects of some conversational implicatures, but it appears that that the conversational phenomena are too complex to model with even these very powerful formal tools.

References*

Appelt, D. and Konolige, K. (1988), *A practical nonmonotonic theory for reasoning about speech acts*, 26th Annual Meeting of the Association for Computational Linguistics: Proceedings of the Conference, Association for Computational Linguistics, 170–178.

Archangeli, D. (1988), *Aspects of underspecification theory*, Phonology **5**, 183–207.

Aronoff, M. (1976), *Word Formation in Generative Grammar*, MIT Press, Cambridge, MA, 1976.

Asher, N. and Morreau, M. (1991), *Commonsense entailment: A modal theory of nonmonotonic reasoning*, Proceedings of the Twelfth International Joint Conference on Artificial Intelligence, J. Mylopoulos and R. Reiter, eds, Morgan Kaufmann, Los Altos, CA, 387–392.

Asher, N. (1992), *A default, truth conditional semantics for the progressive*, Ling. and Philos. **15**, 469–508.

Bach, E. (1989), *Informal Lectures on Formal Semantics*, State Univ. of New York Press, Albany, NY.

Baader, F. and Hollunder, B. (1992), *Embedding defaults into terminological knowledge representation systems*, Principles of Knowledge Representation and Reasoning, B. Nebel, C. Rich and W. Swartout, eds, Morgan Kaufmann, San Mateo, CA, 306–317.

Belnap, N. and Perloff, M. (1990), *Seeing to it that: A canonical form for agentives*, Knowledge Representation and Defeasible Reasoning, H. Kyburg et al., eds, Kluwer, Dordrecht, 167–190.

Besnard, P. (1989), *Default Logic*, Springer, Berlin.

Blackburn, P. (1992), *Modal logic and attribute value structures*, Diamonds and Defaults, M. de Rijke, ed., Kluwer, Dordrecht, 19–65.

Bird, S. and Calder, J. (1991), *Defaults in underspecification phonology*, Default Logics for Linguistic Analysis, H. Kamp, ed., DYANA Deliverable R2.5.B, Stuttgart, 129–139.

Bird, S. (1990), *Constraint-based phonology*, PhD Dissertation, University of Edinburgh, Edinburgh, Scotland.

Bird, S. (1995), *Computational Phonology: A Constraint-Based Approach*, Cambridge Univ. Press, Cambridge, UK.

Bird, S. and Ellison, T. (1994), *One level phonology: Autosegmental representations and rules as finite automata*, Comput. Ling. **20**(1), 55–90.

Bird, S. and Klein, E. (1994), *Phonological analyses in typed feature structures*, Comput. Ling. **20**, 455–491.

Boguraev, B. and Pustejovsky, J. (1990), *Lexical ambiguity and the role of knowledge representation in lexicon design*, Proceedings of the 13th International Conference on Computational Linguistics, Helsinki, 36–42.

Bouma, G. (1992), *Feature structures and nonmonotonicity*, Comput. Ling. **18**, 165–172.

Boutilier, C. (1992), *Conditional logics for default reasoning and belief revision*, Technical Report KRR-TR-92-1, Computer Science Department, University of Toronto, Toronto, Ontario.

Brachman, R. (1985), *I lied about the trees or, defaults and definitions in knowledge representation*, Artif. Intell. Mag. **6**, 80–93.

Bresnan, J. (ed.) (1982), *The Representation of Grammatical Relations*, MIT Press, Cambridge, MA.

Brewka, G. (1991), *Nonmonotonic Reasoning: Logical Foundations of Commonsense*, Cambridge Univ. Press, Cambridge, UK.

*For an explanation of the abbreviations of journal titles in this bibliography, please see p. xxi.

Brewka, G. (1993), *Adding priorities and specificity to default logic*, DMG Technical Report, Gesellschaft für Mathematik und Datenverarbeitung, Sankt Augustin, Germany.

Brewka, G. (1994), *Reasoning about priorities in default logic*, Proceedings of the Twelfth National Conference on Artificial Intelligence, B. Hayes-Roth and R. Korf, eds, AAAI Press, Menlo Park, CA, 940–945.

Briscoe, T. (1993), *Introduction*, in Briscoe et al. (1993), pp. 1–12.

Briscoe, T., De Paiva, V. and Copestake, A. (eds) (1993), *Inheritance, Defaults, and the Lexicon*, Cambridge Univ. Press, Cambridge, UK.

Briscoe, T., Copestake, A. and Lascarides, A. (1995), *Blocking*, in Saint-Dizier and Viegas (1995), pp. 273–302.

Carlson, G. and Pelletier, F.J. (eds) (1995), *The Generic Book*, Chicago Univ. Press, Chicago.

Carpenter, B. (1993), *Skeptical and credulous default unification with applications to templates and inheritance*, in Briscoe et al. (1993), pp. 13–37.

Carpenter, B. (1992), *The Logic of Typed Feature Structures*, Cambridge Univ. Press, Cambridge, UK.

Chellas, B. (1980), *Modal Logic: An Introduction*, Cambridge Univ. Press, Cambridge, UK.

Chomsky, N. and Halle, M. (1968), *The Sound Pattern of English*, Harper & Row, New York.

Church, A. (1940), *A formulation of the simple theory of types*, J. Symb. Logic **5**, 56–68.

Cohen, P. and Perrault, C.R. (1987), *Elements of a plan-based theory of speech acts*, Cogn. Science **3**, 117–212.

Cohen, P. and Levesque, H. (1987), *Rational interaction as the basis for conversation*, Technical Report, Center for the Study of Language and Information.

Cohen, P. and Levesque, H. (1985), *Speech acts and rationality*, 23rd Annual Meeting of the Association for Computational Linguistics: Proceedings of the Conference. Association for Computational Linguistics, 49–59.

Copestake, A. (1993), *Defaults in lexical representation*, in Briscoe et al. (1993), pp. 223–245.

Daelemans, W. (1987a), *Studies in language technology: an object-oriented computer model of morphophonological aspects of Dutch*, PhD Dissertation, Katholieke Universiteit Leuven.

Daelemans, W. (1987b), *A tool for the automatic creation, extension, and updating of lexical knowledge bases*, Proceedings of the Third Conference of the European Chapter of the Association for Computational Linguistics, Copenhagen, 70–74.

Daelemans, W., De Smedt, K. and Gazdar, G. (1992), *Inheritance in natural language processing*, Comput. Ling. **18**, 205–218.

Davis, E. (1990), *Representations of Commonsense Knowledge*, Morgan Kaufmann, Los Altos, CA.

De Smedt, K. (1984), *Using object-oriented knowledge-representation techniques in morphology and syntax programming*, Proceedings, Sixth European Conference on Artificial Intelligence, Elsevier, Amsterdam, 181–184.

De Smedt, K. (1990), *Incremental sentence generation: A computer model of grammatical encoding*, PhD Dissertation, Katholieke Universiteit te Nijmegen. Also, Nijmegen Institute for Cognition Research and Information Technology Technical Report 90-01, 1990.

Delgrande, J. (1988), *An approach to default reasoning based on a first-order conditional logic: Revised report*, Artif. Intell. **36**, 63–90.

Delgrande, J. and Schaub, T. (1994), *A general approach to specificity in default reasoning*, Principles of Knowledge Representation and Reasoning, J. Doyle, E. Sandewall and P. Torasso, eds, Morgan Kaufmann, San Mateo, CA, 146–157.

Devanbu, P. and Litman, D. (1991), *Plan-based terminological reasoning*, Principles of Knowledge Representation and Reasoning, J. Allen, R. Fikes and E. Sandewall, eds, Morgan Kaufmann, San Mateo, CA, 128–138.

Dowty, D. (1979), *Word Meaning and Montague Grammar*, Reidel, Dordrecht.

Evans, R. and Gazdar, G. (1989a), *Inference in* DATR, Proceedings, Fourth Meeting of the European Chapter of the Association for Computational Linguistics, Manchester, 66–71.

Evans, R. and Gazdar, G. (1989b), *The semantics of* DATR, Proceedings, Seventh Conference of the Society for the Study of Artificial Intelligence and the Simulation of Behaviour, A. Cohn, ed., London, 79–87.

Evans, R. and Gazdar, G. (eds) (1990), *The* DATR *papers*, Technical Report, Cognitive Studies Programme, The University of Sussex.

Evans, R., Gazdar, G. and Moser, L. (1994), *Prioritized multiple inheritance in* DATR, in Briscoe et al. (1993), pp. 38–46.

Fahlman, S. (1979), *NETL: A System for Representing and Using Real-World Knowledge*, MIT Press, Cambridge, MA.

Flickinger, D. (1987), *Lexical rules in the hierarchical lexicon*, PhD Thesis, Stanford University.

Flickinger, D. and Nerbonne, J. (1992), *Inheritance and complementation: A case study of easy adjectives and related nouns*, Comput. Ling. **18**, 269–310.

Gazdar, G. (1987), *Linguistic applications of default inheritance mechanisms*, Technical Report, Cognitive Studies Programme, The University of Sussex, 1985. Linguistic Theory and Computer Applications, P. Whitelock et al., eds, Academic Press, New York.

Gazdar, G., Klein, E., Pullum, G. and Sag, I. (1985), *Generalized Phrase Structure Grammar*, Blackwell, Oxford, England and Harvard Univ. Press, Cambridge, MA.

Geffner, H. (1992), *Default Reasoning: Causal and Conditional Theories*, MIT Press, Cambridge, MA.

Geffner, H. and Pearl, J. (1992), *Conditional entailment: Bridging two approaches to default reasoning*, Artif. Intell. **53**, 209–244.

Ginsberg, M. (ed.) (1988a), *Nonmonotonic Reasoning*, Morgan Kaufmann, Los Altos, CA.

Ginsberg, M. (1988b), *Introduction*, in Ginsberg (1988a), pp. 1–23.

Ginsberg, M. (1988c), *Multi-valued logics: A uniform approach to reasoning in artificial intelligence*, Comput. Intell. **4**, 265–316.

Grice, H.P. (1989), *Studies in The Way of Words*, Harvard Univ. Press, Cambridge, MA.

Guerreiro, R.A. de T., Hemerly, A. and Shoham, Y. (1990), *On the complexity of monotonic inheritance with roles*, AAAI-90 (Proceedings of the Ninth National Conference on Artificial Intelligence). AAAI Press and MIT Press, Menlo Park, CA, and Cambridge, MA, 627–632.

Guha, R. (1991), *Contexts: A formalization and some applications*, Technical Report STAN-CS-91-1399, Stanford University Computer Science Department.

Hobbs, J., Stickel, M., Appelt, D. and Martin, P. (1993), *Interpretation as abduction*, Artif. Intell. **63**, 69–142.

Hobbs, J. and Moore, R. (eds) (1985), *Formal theories of the commonsense world*, Ablex, Norwood, NJ.

Horty, J. (1994), *Some direct theories of nonmonotonic inheritance*, Handbook of Logic in Artificial Intelligence and Logic Programming, vol. 3: Nonmonotonic Reasoning and Uncertain Reasoning, D. Gabbay, C. Hogger and J. Robinson, eds, Oxford Univ. Press, 111–187.

Horty, J. and Thomason, R. (1988), *Mixing strict and defeasible inheritance*, Proceedings of AAAI-88, Morgan Kaufmann, Los Altos, CA.

Horty, J., Thomason, R. and Touretzky, D. (1988), *A skeptical theory of inheritance in nonmonotonic semantic nets*, AAAI-87 (Proceedings of the Sixth National Conference on Artificial Intelligence), vol. 2, Morgan Kaufmann, Los Altos, 358–363.

Horty, J. and Thomason, R. (1990), *Boolean extensions of inheritance networks*, Proceedings of AAAI-90, Morgan Kaufmann, Los Altos, CA.

Horty, J. and Thomason, R. (1991), *Conditionals and artificial intelligence*, Fund. Inform. **15**, 301–324.

Kaplan, R. (1987), *Three seductions of computational linguistics*, Linguistic Theory and Computer Applications, P. Whitelock et al., eds, Academic Press, London, 149–188.

Kay, M. (1992), *Unification*, Computational Linguistics and Formal Semantics, M. Rosner and R. Johnson, eds, Cambridge Univ. Press, Cambridge, UK, 1–29.

Keller, B. (1995), *DATR theories and DATR models*, Proceedings of the 33rd Meeting of the Association for Computational Linguistics, Morgan Kaufmann, San Mateo, CA, 55–69.

Kilgarrif, A. (1995), *Inheriting polysemy*, in Saint-Dizier and Viegas (1995), pp. 319–335.

Kiparsky, P. (1973), *Elsewhere in phonology*, A Festschrift for Morris Halle, S. Anderson and P. Kiparsky, eds, Holt, Reinhart and Winston, New York, 93–106.

Konolige, K. (1988), *On the relation between default and autoepistemic logic*, Artif. Intell. **35**, 343–382.

Krifka, M., Pelletier, F.J., Carlson, G., Ter Meulen, A., Chierchia, G. and Link, G. (1995), *Genericity: An introduction*, in Carlson and Pelletier (1995), pp. 1–124.

Krieger, H.U. and Nerbonne, J. (1993), *Feature-based inheritance networks for computational lexicons*, in Briscoe et al. (1993), pp. 90–136.

Lascarides, A. and Oberlander, J. (1991), *Temporal coherence and defeasible knowledge*, Proceedings of the Workshop on Discourse Coherence, Edinburgh.

Lascarides, A. and Asher, N. (1991), *Discourse relations and common sense entailment*, Proceedings of the 29th Meeting of the Association for Computational Linguistics, 55–63.

Lascarides, A. and Asher, N. (1993a), *Temporal interpretation, discourse relations and common sense entailment*, Ling. and Philos. **16**, 437–494.

Lascarides, A. and Asher, N. (1993b), *Lexical disambiguation in a discourse context*, Unpublished manuscript.

Lascarides, A., Asher, N., Briscoe, T. and Copestake, A. (1994), *Order independent and persistent typed default unification*, Unpublished manuscript.

Lewis, D. (1973), *Counterfactuals*, Harvard Univ. Press, Cambridge, MA.

Levesque, H. (1990), *All I know: A study in autoepistemic logic*, Artif. Intell. **42**, 263–309.

Lifschitz, V. (1986), *Pointwise circumscription*, Proceedings of AAAI-86, Morgan Kaufmann, Los Altos, CA, 406–410.

Lifschitz, V. (1989), *Circumscriptive theories*, Philosophical Logic and Artificial Intelligence, R. Thomason, ed., Reidel, Dordrecht, 109–159.

Łukaszewicz, W. (1985), *Two results on default logic*, Proceedings of the Ninth International Joint Conference on Artificial Intelligence, A. Joshi, ed., Morgan Kaufmann, Los Altos, CA, 459–461.

Marek, W. and Truszczynski, M. (1989), *Relating autoepistemic and default logics*, Proceedings of the First International Conference on Principles of Knowledge Representation and Reasoning, R. Brachman, H. Levesque and R. Reiter, eds, Morgan Kaufmann, Los Altos, CA, 276–288.

Mastroianni, M. and Carpenter, B. (1994), *Constraint-based morpho-phonology*, Proceedings of the First Meeting of the Association for Computational Phonology, Association for Computational Linguistics, 13–24.

McCarthy, J. (1980), *Circumscription – a form of nonmonotonic reasoning*, Artif. Intell. **13**, 27–39.

McCarthy, J. and Prince, A. (1993), *Prosodic morphology I*, Technical Report TR-3, Center for Cognitive Science, Rutgers University Center for Cognitive Science.

McDermott, D. and Doyle, J. (1980), *Nonmonotonic logic I*, Artif. Intell. **13**, 41–72.

Mercer, R. and Reiter, R. (1982), *The representation of presuppositions using defaults*, Proceedings of the Fourth National Conference of the Canadian Society for Computational Studies of Intelligence Conference, Saskatoon, 107–107.

Mercer, R. (1987), *A default logic approach to the derivation of natural language presuppositions*, Doctoral Thesis, Department of Computer Science, University of British Columbia. Available as Technical Report TR 87-35, Department of Computer Science, University of British Columbia.

Mercer, R. (1988), *Using default logic to derive natural language presupposition*, Proceedings of the Canadian Society for Computational Studies of Intelligence Conference, Edmonton.

Meyer, B. (1988), *Object-Oriented Software Construction*, Prentice-Hall, New York.

Moore, R. (1985), *Semantical considerations on nonmonotonic logic*, Artif. Intell. **25**, 75–94.

Montague, R. (1969), *On the nature of certain philosophical entities*, Formal Philosophy: Selected Papers of Richard Montague, R. Thomason, ed., Yale Univ. Press, New Haven, CT, 148–187. (This paper was originally published in 1969.)

Morreau, M. (1992a), *Epistemic semantics for conditionals*, J. Philos. Logic **21**, 33–62.

Morreau, M. (1992b), *Conditionals in philosophy and artificial intelligence*, PhD Dissertation, University of Amsterdam, Faculteit Wiskunde en Informatica.

Morreau, M. (1995), *Allowed inference*, Proceedings of the Fourteenth International Joint Conference on Artificial Intelligence, Morgan Kaufmann, San Mateo, CA, 1466–1473.

Penn, G. and Thomason, R. (1994), *Default finite state machines and finite state phonology*, Proceedings of the First Meeting of the Association for Computational Phonology, Association for Computational Linguistics, 33–42.

Perrault, C.R. (1990), *An application of default logic to speech act theory*, Intentions in Communication, P. Cohen, J. Morgan and M. Pollack, eds, MIT Press, Cambridge, MA, 161–185.

Pollard, C. and Sag, I. (1987), *Information-Based Syntax and Semantics*, CSLI, Stanford, CA.

Prince, A. and Smolensky, P. (1993), *Optimality theory: Constraint interaction in generative grammar*, Technical Report TR-2, Center for Cognitive Science, Rutgers University Center for Cognitive Science.

Pustejovsky, J. (1991), *The generative lexicon*, Comput. Ling. **17**, 409–441.

Quantz, J.J. and Royer, V. (1992), *A preference semantics for defaults in terminological logics*, Principles of Knowledge Representation and Reasoning, B. Nebel, C. Rich and W. Swartout, eds, Morgan Kaufmann, San Mateo, CA, 294–305.

Reiter, R. (1980), *A logic for default reasoning*, Artif. Intell. **13**, 81–132.

Reiter, R. (1988), *Nonmonotonic reasoning*, Exploring Artificial Intelligence, H. Shrobe, ed., Morgan Kaufmann, San Mateo, CA, 439–482.

Rounds, W., *Feature logics*, This Handbook, Chapter 8.

Rounds, W. and Zhang, G.-Q. (1995), *Domain theory meets default logic*, Logic Comput. **5**, 1–25.

Rounds, W. and Zhang, G.-Q., *Logical considerations on default semantics*, J. Artif. Intell. Math., forthcoming.

Rounds, W. and Zhang, G.-Q., *Suggestions for a non-monotonic feature logic*, Unpublished manuscript, currently available by anonymous ftp from ftp.cwi.nl in directory pub/rounds.

Russell, G., Carroll, J. and Warwick, S. (1991), *Multiple default inheritance in a unification-based lexicon*, 29th Meeting of the Association for Computational Linguistics: Proceedings of the Conference, Association for Computational Linguistics, 211–215.

Saint-Dizier, P. and Viegas, E. (eds) (1995), *Computational Lexical Semantics*, Cambridge Univ. Press, Cambridge, UK.

Scobbie, J. (1991), *Attribute value phonology*, PhD Dissertation, University of Edinburgh, Edinburgh, Scotland.

Sells, P. (1985), *Lectures on Contemporary Syntactic Theories*, Center for the Study of Language and Information, Stanford, CA.

Shieber, S. (1986), *An Introduction to Unification-Based Approaches to Grammar*, CSLI Lecture Notes no. 4, Univ. of Chicago Press, Chicago.

Shieber, S. (1987), *Separating linguistic analyses from linguistic theories*, Linguistic Theory and Computer Applications, Academic Press, London, 1–36.

Shieber, S. (1992), *Constraint-based Grammar Formalisms: Parsing and Type Inference for Natural and Computer Languages*, MIT Press, Cambridge, MA.

Shoham, Y. (1988), *Reasoning about Change: Time and Causation from the Standpoint of Artificial Intelligence*, MIT Press, Cambridge, MA.

Shoham, Y. (1990), *Nonmonotonic reasoning and causation*, Cogn. Science **14**, 213–252.

Shoham, Y. (1991), *Remarks on Simon's comments*, Cogn. Science **15**, 300–303.

Simon, H. (1991), *Nonmonotonic reasoning and causation: Comment*, Cogn. Science **15**, 293–300.

Spencer, A. (1991), *Morphological Theory*, Cambridge Univ. Press, Cambridge, UK.

Sproat, R. (1992), *Morphology and Computation*, MIT Press, Cambridge, MA.

Stalnaker, R. and Thomason, R. (1970), *A semantic analysis of conditional logic*, Theoria **36**, 23–42.

Steedman, M. and Moens, M. (1987), *Temporal ontology in natural language*, Proceedings of the 25th Annual Conference of the Association for Computational Linguistics, Association for Computational Linguistics, 1–7.

Thomason, R., Horty, J. and Touretzky, D. (1987), *A calculus for inheritance in monotonic semantic nets*, Methodologies for Intelligent Systems, Z. Ras and M. Zemankova, eds, North-Holland, Amsterdam, 280–287.

Thomason, R. (1990), *Propagating epistemic coordination through mutual defaults I*, Proceedings of the Third Conference on Theoretical Aspects of Reasoning about Knowledge, R. Parikh, ed., Morgan Kaufmann, San Mateo, CA, 29–39.

Thomason, R. and Touretzky, D. (1990), *Inheritance theory and networks with roles*, Principles of Semantic Networks, J. Sowa, ed., Morgan Kaufmann, Los Altos, CA, 231–266.

Thomason, R. (1991), *Logicism, artificial intelligence, and common sense: John McCarthy's program in philosophical perspective*, Artificial Intelligence and Mathematical Theory of Computation, V. Lifschitz, ed., Academic Press, San Diego, 449–466.

Thomason, R. (1992), NETL *and subsequent path-based inheritance theories*, Comput. Math. Appl. **23**, 179–204. Reprinted in *Semantic Networks in Artificial Intelligence*, F. Lehmann, ed., Pergamon, Oxford, 179–204.

Thomason, R. (1994), *Non-monotonic formalisms for lexical semantics*, Unpublished manuscript. Currently available via http://www.pitt.edu/~thomason/thomason.html.

Touretzky, D. (1986), *The Mathematics of Inheritance Theories*, Morgan Kaufmann, San Mateo, CA.

Veltman, F. *Defaults in update semantics*, J. Philos. Logic. Forthcoming as of December, 1995.

Veltman, F. *Conditionals*, This Handbook, Chapter 17.

Vennemann, T. (1972), *Phonological uniqueness in natural generative grammar*, Glossa **6**, 105–116.

Wainer, J. (1991), *Uses of nonmonotonic logic in natural language understanding: Generalized implicatures*, PhD Dissertation, The Pennsylvania State University, State College, PA.

Winston, P. (1984), *Artificial Intelligence*, 2nd edn, Addison-Wesley, Reading, MA.

Woods, W. and Schmolze, J. (1992), *The* KL-ONE *family,* Comput. Math. Appl. **23**, 133–179. Reprinted in *Semantic Networks in Artificial Intelligence,* F. Lehmann, ed., Pergamon, Oxford, 133–179.

Young, M. (1992), *Nonmonotonic sorts for feature structures,* Proceedings of AAAI-92, San Jose, CA, 596–601.

Young, M. (1994), *Features, unification, and nonmonotonicity,* PhD Thesis, University of Michigan, Ann Arbor, MI.

Young, M. and Rounds, W. (1993), *A logical semantics for nonmonotonic sorts*, Proceedings of ACL-93, Columbus, OH, 209–215.

Zdonik, S. and Maier, D. (1990), *Readings in Object-Oriented Database Systems*, Morgan Kaufmann, San Mateo, CA.

Zhang, G.-Q. and Rounds, W. *Non-monotonic consequences in default domain theory*, J. Artif. Intell. Math., forthcoming.

Zwicky, A. (1986), *The general case: Basic form versus default forms*, Proceedings of the Twelfth Annual Meeting of the Berkeley Linguistics Society, V. Nikiforidou et al., eds, Berkeley Linguistics Society, Berkeley, CA, 305–314.

Zwicky, A. (1989), *What's become of derivations? Defaults and invocations*, Proceedings of the Fifteenth Annual Meeting of the Berkeley Linguistics Society, K. Hall et al., eds, Berkeley Linguistics Society, Berkeley, CA, 303–320.

Part 3
Descriptive Topics

Introduction

This final Part contains some of the central topics that are studied in natural language. Our selection has been oriented towards areas with an established logical tradition, such as *Quantifiers*, *Plurals* or *Temporality*. But we have also included cases where the most appropriate logical key to the field is still a point of controversy, such as *Generics* or *Questions*. In all this, we have not striven for exhaustive coverage of linguistics, nor even of the semantics of natural language. For some recent surveys of topics in semantics, see also the "Handbook of Semantics" as well as Part 4 of the "Handbook of Philosophical Logic" – especially the new expanded version. We have tried to include samples of semantics, but also of pragmatics, witness the chapter on *Presupposition*. One of the recurrent themes at the interface of Logic and Language is the division of labor between semantics and pragmatics. With the advent of context-dependent notions of interpretation (conspicuous in many of our chapters), this has led to close collaboration between specification of static truth-conditional content, a core concern in classical semantics, and presuppositional content, a core topic of pragmatics. The chapters on *Presupposition* and *Questions* address how these various aspects of informative content can be integrated in a comprehensive account of meaning and interpretation.

Even so, there are many areas of natural language left uncovered here. As remarked in the Introduction, we had to omit planned chapters on Intensionality and Conditionals, for which we must therefore refer to existing treatments. Also, we foresee that new areas of linguistic investigation will soon open up to the logical style of analysis. In particular, this is true for higher levels of aggregation. For example, *discourse models* and their processing strategies are a case in point. But we also envisage that current logical theories will be of use in the analysis of larger textual entities, hypertexts and documentary information systems.

In descriptive applications of logic to natural language, connections with computer science turn up at every corner. The *Questions* chapter mentions analogies with querying of databases, and likewise, the *Presuppositions* and *Generics* chapters feed into central concerns of artificial intelligence. Likewise, the *Temporality* chapter demonstrates how conceptual distinctions regarding aspect in natural languages may be linked up with computational implementation, and maintenance of temporal databases. Eventually, discourse processing will demand sophisticated computational architectures, where the ideas of dynamic semantics (cf. the chapter on *Dynamics*) may prove essential.

In all, we hope this final Part gives the reader a taste of the robust linguistic facts to be explained by logical analysis. Perhaps even more importantly, we hope it conveys the subtlety of an initial 'modeling' stage whose importance is being acknowledged more and more in computer science and related disciplines. We mean the careful conceptual analysis and argument that must precede any choice of a logical paradigm, which can only then be developed internally in the mathematical ways demonstrated in Part 2. Practitioners of this field are often experts at such modeling tasks, and these skills will no doubt have an impact beyond their particular linguistic motivation.

Johan van Benthem
Alice ter Meulen

CHAPTER 15

Generalized Quantifiers in Linguistics and Logic*

Edward L. Keenan

Department of Linguistics, University of California at Los Angeles, 405 Hilgard Av., Los Angeles, CA 90095-1543, USA
E-mail: ekeenan@ucla.edu

Dag Westerståhl

Department of Philosophy, Stockholm University, 106 91 Stockholm, Sweden
E-mail: dag.westerstahl@philosophy.su.se

Commentator: J. van der Does

Contents

*We wish to thank the editors, the participants at the workshop 'Integrating Logic and Linguistics' in Amsterdam December 1993, and in particular Jaap van der Does, for helpful comments on this chapter.

HANDBOOK OF LOGIC AND LANGUAGE
Edited by J. van Benthem and A. ter Meulen

0. Introduction

In the past 15 years the study of generalized quantifiers has deepened, considerably, our understanding of the expressive power of natural language. It has provided answers to questions which have arisen independently in language study, and it has raised, and often answered, new questions, ones that were largely inconceivable without the basic concepts of generalized quantifier theory. In turn our new linguistic understanding has prompted some novel mathematical questions (and an occasional theorem) whose interest derives, in part at least, from their natural interpretation in a non-mathematical domain.

In this paper we survey these linguistic results and we synthesize and extend the mathematical observations they have given rise to, relating them to independent work from logic.

By way of historical perspective (see Westerståhl (1989) for detailed discussion up to 1987), it was Montague (1969) who set in motion the work we report on here. That work first told us how to interpret simple Noun Phrases (e.g., *John*) directly as functions mapping predicate denotations to {*True, False*}, that is as generalized quantifiers (a terminology not used by Montague). But it was only in the early 80's that linguistic applications of generalized quantifier theory came into their own, in several cases due to joint work between linguists and logicians. The first and most influential paper here was Barwise and Cooper (1981). Higginbotham and May (1981) also appeared at that time (focusing on certain types of polyadic quantification which became more important later), and early versions of Keenan and Stavi (1986) circulated, influencing later formal developments. The latter, especially Van Benthem (1984, 1986), concerned both original constraints on natural language quantifiers and the interpretation of that work in a more classical logical setting. Two collections that reflect the status of this work by the late eighties are Van Benthem and Ter Meulen (1985) and Gärdenfors (1987). A survey of research issues in generalized quantifier theory in the early 90s, many of them with a linguistic flavor, is Van Benthem and Westerståhl (1994).

The rapid and cumulative development of this line of work by the end of the eighties also enables us to find earlier works which anticipated several of the ideas to become important later. We note Fenstad (1979) and Altham and Tennant (1975) in particular (the latter anticipating recent work, discussed here, on polyadic quantification), which drew explicitly on the logical notion of generalized quantifiers from Mostowski (1957) and Lindström (1966).

We should stress however that research into the nature of quantification in natural language has most certainly not been limited to the work we survey here. We do not touch upon the work on 'unselective binding' initiated in (Lewis, 1975) and developed, e.g., in (Heim, 1982) and within Discourse Representation Theory (Kamp and Van Eijck, this volume). Nor do we consider the differential pronoun/variable binding of different sorts of Noun Phrases, a topic of considerable linguistic interest and one that is pursued for example within DRT and various approaches to dynamic logic (Muskens and Van Benthem, this volume; see also the collections (Van der Does and Van Eijck, 1991) and (Kanazawa and Piñon, 1994)). Finally we do not treat specifically of plurals and group level quantification of the sort discussed in (Lønning, this volume) and (Van der Does, 1992, 1994a). Let us turn now to the work we do consider.

1. Generalized quantifiers in natural language: Interpretations of noun phrases and determiners

We are primarily concerned here with the semantic interpretation of NPs (Noun Phrases) like those italicized in (1)–(3). (We extend our concerns in Section 2.)

(1) *John* laughed; *Neither Bill nor Fred* smiled.

(2) *All poets* daydream; *No healthy doctor* smokes; *Most linguists* are bilingual.

(3) *More students than teachers* work hard; *Not as many boys as girls* did well on the exam.

These NPs have combined here with P_1s (*one place predicates*) like *laughed* and *work hard* to form Ss (*sentences*). P_1s express properties of objects and we limit ourselves to *extensional* NPs, ones which distinguish between properties only if different objects have them. So given a universe E of objects we treat P_1s as denoting subsets of E. Ss denote 1 (*true*) or 0 (*false*) and NPs denote *type* $\langle 1 \rangle$ (*generalized*) *quantifiers* over E, namely functions from P(E), the power set of E, into $\mathbf{2} = \{0, 1\}$. This set is noted [P(E) $\rightarrow$ **2**] and called TYPE$\langle 1 \rangle$. In general we write $[X \rightarrow Y]$ for the set of functions from X into Y.

In (2), *all, no*, and *most* are Det_1s (*one place determiners*). They combine with (property denoting) common noun phrases like *linguist, healthy doctor*, ... to form type $\langle 1 \rangle$ expressions. Semantically they map P(E) into TYPE$\langle 1 \rangle$ and so are quantifiers of type $\langle 1, 1 \rangle$ (over E).

In (3), *more...than* and *not as many...as* are of type $\langle\langle 1, 1 \rangle, 1\rangle$. We call them Det_2s. They combine with pairs of property denoting expressions to form NPs, and are interpreted as maps from P(E) $\times$ P(E) into TYPE$\langle 1 \rangle$. We study these types in turn.

Quantifiers of these types can equivalently been viewed as *relations* between subsets of E. For example, a type $\langle 1, 1 \rangle$ function F in [P(E) $\rightarrow$ [$P(E)$ $\rightarrow$ **2**]] corresponds to the binary relation Q between sets defined by $QAB \Leftrightarrow F(A)(B) = 1$. The relational view on quantifiers is common in logic. The functional view fits better into a compositional semantics for natural language, and later we will see that it also allows some natural generalizations to functions that do not correspond to relations between sets.

1.1. *Type $\langle 1 \rangle$ quantification*

Given a type τ and a natural language L the following questions are considered in Section 1:

Q1. Syntactically, what sorts of expressions of type τ does L provide?

Q2. Are there constraints on which functions of type τ may be denoted in L? Viz., for arbitrary E and arbitrary F of type τ, is there an L expression which may be interpreted as F?

Q3. Does L distinguish subclasses of expressions of type τ in any syntactically or semantically regular way? More generally, what generalizations does L support regarding expressions of type τ, and are they valid for all natural languages?

We focus on Q2 and Q3, exemplifying answers to Q1 as we go along. We assume an arbitrary universe E held constant throughout our discussion unless noted otherwise.

Important insights into the nature of TYPE$\langle 1\rangle$ in English build in part on the order relations carried by the domain and range of these functions. The relation is $\subseteq$ in the case of P(E). Independent of our concern with quantifiers we use this relation in stating semantic properties of P_1s. For example manner adverbs like *loudly* are *restricting* in that for any P_1 denotation B, **loudly**$(B) \subseteq B$, whence *John laughed loudly* entails *John laughed.* (We note nonce denotations in boldface.)

Equally it is with respect to the subset relation that the interpretations of conjunctions and disjunctions of P_1s are defined as greatest lower bounds (glbs) and least upper bounds (lubs) respectively. Thus the denotation B of *both laughed and cried* is the glb of $X = \{\mathbf{laugh}, \mathbf{cry}\}$. That is, B is a lower bound for $X (\forall A \in X,\ B \subseteq A)$ and it is greatest among the lower bounds (for all lower bounds C for $X, C \subseteq B$). In a similar way the denotation of *either laughed or cried* is the lub for X. Also we use later that P(E) is complemented. Thus *not laugh* denotes $-$**laugh**, that is, $E -$ **laugh**.

Similarly the set $\mathbf{2} = \{0, 1\}$ comes equipped with a natural order relation, $\leqslant$, the *implication order.* For $x, y \in \mathbf{2}$ we say that $x \leqslant y$ iff an arbitrary conditional sentence *if P then Q* is true whenever P denotes x and Q denotes y. So $x \leqslant y$ iff $x = 0$ or $x = y = 1$. And as with P_1s, it is in terms of the order relation that denotations of conjunctions and disjunctions of Ss are characterized as glbs and lubs (given by the truth tables for conjunction and disjunction respectively). Also **2** is complemented, the complement function being given by the truth table for negation.

Thus type $\langle 1\rangle$ functions map one poset (partially ordered set) to another and may thus be classified according to their monotonicity properties. Standardly:

DEFINITION 1.1.1. Let A and B be partially ordered sets and F a function from A into B.

a. F is *increasing* (= *order preserving*) iff $\forall a, b \in A,\ a \leqslant b \Rightarrow F(a) \leqslant F(b)$.

b. F is *decreasing* (= *order reversing*) iff $\forall a, b \in A,\ a \leqslant b \Rightarrow F(b) \leqslant F(a)$.

c. F is *monotonic* iff F is increasing or F is decreasing.

An expression is called *increasing* (*decreasing, monotonic*) iff it is always interpreted as an increasing (decreasing, monotonic) function. And we claim:

GENERALIZATION 1.1.1. *Lexical* (= *syntactically simple*) *NPs are monotonic – in fact monotonic increasing with at most a few exceptions.*

To check informally that an NP is increasing, verify that when substituted for X in paradigms like (4), changing plurals to singulars as appropriate, the resulting argument is valid – that is, the third line is true in any situation in which the first two are true.

(4) All socialists are vegetarians.
X are socialists.
∴ X are vegetarians.

The lexical NPs of English are mainly the *proper nouns* (PNs): *John, Mary, ..., Siddartha, Chou en Lai, ...* (this set is *open* in that new members may be added without changing the language significantly). Lexical NPs also include listable sprinklings of (i) personal pronouns – *he/him*,... and their plurals *they/them;* (ii) demonstratives – *this/that* and *these/those*; and (iii) possessive pronouns – *his/hers* ... */theirs*. Some grammarians would include "indefinite pronouns" such as *everyone, everybody, someone, somebody, noone*, and *nobody*, but these appear to have internal syntactic structure (e.g., *everyone* consists of the independent expressions *every* and *one*). We might also include some (restricted) uses of Dets as NPs, e.g., *all* in *A good time was had by all, some* in *Some like it hot*, and *many* and *few* in *Many are called but few are chosen*, though such uses seem limited to fixed expressions or to constrained contexts in which, in effect, a noun argument of the Det is provided. Thus an S like *All read the New York Times* is bizarre unless context makes it clear what *all* is quantifying over, e.g., students, students in my class, etc.

We note (cf. Q1) that PNs may be structured, as with first and last names: *John Smith*; titles of address: *Mistress Mary, Doctor Jones*; sobriquets: *Eric the Red, Charles the Bald*; adjectives: *Lucky Linda, Tricky Dick*; and appositives: *the philosopher David Hume*.

Of the lexical NPs mentioned above, PNs (structured or not), the pronouns and demonstratives are increasing. Only *few, noone*, and *nobody* are not increasing, and they are decreasing. Thus, with only limited exceptions lexical NPs in English are monotonic increasing. By contrast the NPs in (5) below are not monotonic.

(5) a. every student but not every teacher, every student but John, exactly five students, between five and ten cats, no student but John, John but neither Bill nor Sam, most of the students but less than half the teachers,

b. either fewer than five students or else more than a hundred students, approximately a hundred students, more students than teachers, exactly as many students as teachers.

Thus Generalization 1.1.1 is a strong empirical claim – many functions denotable by NPs in English are not denotable by lexical NPs. Keenan (1986) presents further constraints of this sort.

Generalization 1.1.1 has a companion generalization at the level of type $\langle 1,1\rangle$ Det_1s: type $\langle 1\rangle$ expressions built from lexical Det_1s are monotonic, usually increasing, though **no, neither**, and **few** build decreasing type $\langle 1\rangle$ quantifiers.[1] See (19a) for some lexical Det_1s of English.

We offer another monotonicity generalization shortly, but first we consider the quantifiers denotable by proper nouns. We call those quantifiers *individuals*:

DEFINITION 1.1.2. For each $b \in E$ define I_b from $\mathrm{P}(E)$ into $\mathbf{2}$ by setting $I_b(A) = 1$ iff $b \in A$ (equivalently, I_b is the set of subsets of E containing b). A type $\langle 1\rangle$ quantifier F is a (Montagovian[2]) *individual* iff $F = I_b$ for some $b \in E$.

[1] Sometimes a numeral Det_1 like *ten* appears to denote **exactly ten** rather than **at least ten**. It can be argued that this interpretation is not the basic one. But if it should be taken as basic, the generalization says instead that expressions built from lexical Det_1s denote either monotonic quantifiers or conjunctions of such quantifiers (**exactly ten** = **at least ten** & **at most ten**).

[2] Montague (1969) innovated this notion of proper noun denotation.

So where *John* denotes I_j, *John walks* will be true iff $I_j(\mathbf{walk}) = 1$; that is, iff $j \in$ **walk** – just the classical truth conditions for such Ss. Clearly individuals are increasing: if $A \subseteq B$ then $b \in A \Rightarrow b \in B$, so $I_b(A) = 1 \Rightarrow I_b(B) = 1$, so $I_b(A) \leqslant I_b(B)$. In fact individuals preserve, and are exactly the functions that preserve, the entire Boolean structure of $\mathrm{P}(E)$.[3]

Observe, (1b) and (6), that type $\langle 1 \rangle$ expressions allow the formation of Boolean compounds in *and/but, or, not*, and *neither ... nor* with significant freedom:

(6) a. *Either both John and Sue or else both Sam and Mary* will represent us at the meeting.

b. *Neither John nor John's doctor* wanted to ignore the report.

c. *John and some student* just came in.

d. *Just two teachers and not more than ten students* attended the meeting.

e. *More than a hundred students but not a single teacher* attended the rally.

f. *All the doctors and all the nurses but not more than half the patients* had the radio on.

Unsurprisingly, TYPE$\langle 1 \rangle$ is a Boolean lattice. The order relation $\leqslant$ is given pointwise: $F \leqslant G$ iff $\forall A \in \mathrm{P}(E),\ F(A) \leqslant G(A)$. We note for later reference:

(7) Given $\leqslant$ defined on TYPE$\langle 1 \rangle = [\mathrm{P}(E) \to \mathbf{2}]$,

a. $\mathbf{0}$ maps all $A \subseteq E$ to $0, \mathbf{1}$ to 1. $\mathbf{0}$ and $\mathbf{1}$ are called *trivial*.

b. For $K \subseteq$ TYPE$\langle 1 \rangle$,
the glb of $K, \wedge K$, is that map sending $A \in \mathrm{P}(E)$ to 1 iff each $F \in K$ maps A to 1,
the lub of $K, \wedge K$, maps a subset A of E to 1 iff for some $F \in K,\ F(A) = 1$.

c. For $F \in$ TYPE$\langle 1 \rangle$, $\neg F$ is that map sending each $A \in \mathrm{P}(E)$ to $E - F(A)$.

d. Besides these Boolean operations, quantifiers have another form of negation, called *inner negation* or *post-complement*, defined, for $F \in$ TYPE$\langle 1 \rangle$, as the map $F\neg$ sending $A \in \mathrm{P}(E)$ to $F(E - A)$.

Post-complement corresponds to verb phrase negation. For example, *At least three students don't smoke* means that the complement of **smoke** is in **at least three students**, i.e. that **smoke** $\in$ (**at least three students**)$\neg$.

We may now answer Q2 above for TYPE$\langle 1 \rangle$. Namely, for E finite, English does present enough NPs to permit any type $\langle 1 \rangle$ function to be denoted. And all we need is the capacity to denote each of finitely many individuals and to form Boolean compounds of NPs.

---

[3] The individuals are exactly the complete homomorphisms from $\mathrm{P}(E)$ into $\mathbf{2}$. We see directly that $I_b(-A) = -I_b(A)$ and $I_b(\wedge_i A_i) = \wedge_i I_b(A_i)$. For the converse: if h is a complete homomorphism from $\mathrm{P}(E)$ into $\mathbf{2}$ then the set of subsets of E that h is true of is a principal ultrafilter, and thus generated by an atom $\{b\}$, whence $h(A) = 1$ iff $\{b\} \subseteq A$ iff $b \in A$ iff $h = I_b$. Thus proper noun denotations are characterized up to isomorphism in terms of their properties as type $\langle 1 \rangle$ quantifiers.

GENERALIZATION 1.1.2 (Type $\langle 1\rangle$ Effability). *Over a fixed finite universe each type $\langle 1\rangle$ quantifier is denotable by an English NP.*

PROOF. Let E be finite and $F \in [\mathrm{P}(E) \to \mathbf{2}]$ arbitrary. We show how to build an NP in English which may be interpreted as F.

(i) For each $B \in \mathrm{P}(E)$ define $F^B : \mathrm{P}(E) \to \mathbf{2}$ by: $F^B(A) = 1$ iff $A = B$. Clearly

$$F = \bigvee \{F^B \mid B \in \mathrm{P}(E) \;\&\; F(B) = 1\}.$$

Moreover,

$$\forall B \in \mathrm{P}(E),\ F^B = \bigwedge_{b \in B} I_b \wedge \bigwedge_{b \notin B} \neg I_b.$$

Thus F is a Boolean function of individuals.

(ii) Since E is finite any F^B is expressible by a Boolean compound of individual denoting NPs like *John and Bill and Sam but not Frank or Joe or Moe*. Hence any F over a finite E is denotable by a finite disjunction of such NPs.[4] □

Type $\langle 1\rangle$ Effability tells us that in designing semantic interpretations for English expressions we cannot limit (over finite universes) the set in which type $\langle 1\rangle$ expressions denote. By contrast there do appear to be very general constraints limiting the possible denotations of type $\langle 1, 1\rangle$ expressions (Section 1.2.2).

Note that Type $\langle 1\rangle$ Effability is a *local* claim. It does not say that English can denote an arbitrary functional F which associates with each (finite) universe E a type $\langle 1\rangle$ quantifier. Such a claim would concern *uniform definability* (cf. Section 1.2.4). Type $\langle 1\rangle$ Effability simply says that once E (finite) is given then for any $F \in \mathrm{TYPE}\langle 1\rangle$ we can ad hocly cook up an English expression which could be interpreted as F.

We turn now to our second monotonicity generalization. It exemplifies a case where the study of generalized quantifiers has enabled us to make progress on a problem which arose independently in generative grammar.

---

[4] Our argument seems to assume that English presents indefinitely many proper nouns, which is in fact doubtful. Here is a more careful statement of (ii) which does not assume this. We show that English presents enough independently interpretable NPs so that the members of any finite set of individuals can be simultaneously denoted.

Consider NP_n, $n \geqslant 1$, where NP_1 = *John* and NP_{n+1} = *the one person who admires* NP_n. Suppose $E = \{a_1, \ldots, a_k\}$. Interpret *John* as I_{a_1} and interpret *admires* as $\{\langle a_{i+1}, a_i\rangle \mid 1 \leqslant i < k\}$. So for each $1 \leqslant i < k$, NP_{i+1} = *the one person who admires* NP_i denotes $I_{a_{i+1}}$ (For $m > k$, NP_m denotes $\mathbf{0}$ in $[\mathrm{P}(E) \to \mathbf{2}]$). So $\forall B \subseteq E$, F^B is denoted by NP^B = [X and Y], where X is the (finite) conjunction of the NP_j, $j \leqslant k$, which denote individuals true of B, and Y = *neither* Y_1 *nor* Y_2 *nor* ... where the Y_i run through the (finitely many) NP_j, $j \leqslant k$, which denote individuals false of B. Thus an arbitrary F of type $\langle 1\rangle$ over a finite universe is denotable in English by a finite disjunction of NP^Bs, taken over the B that F maps to 1. (Note that part (ii) above embodies an empirical claim regarding the grammaticality of English expressions.)

Negative polarity items (npi's). To characterize the set of expressions judged grammatical by native speakers of English, we must distinguish the grammatical expressions (8a) and (9a) from the ungrammatical (= asterisked) (8b) and (9b).

(8) a. John hasn't ever been to Moscow.

b. *John has ever been to Moscow.

(9) a. John didn't see any birds on the walk.

b. *John saw any birds on the walk.

Npi's, such as *ever* and *any* above, do not occur freely; classically (Klima, 1964) they must be licensed by a "negative" expression, such as *n't* (= *not*). But observe:

(10) a. No student here has ever been to Moscow.

b. *Some student here has ever been to Moscow.

(11) a. Neither John nor Mary saw any birds on the walk.

b. *Either John or Mary saw any birds on the walk.

(12) a. None of John's students has ever been to Moscow.

b. *One of John's students has ever been to Moscow.

The *a*-expressions here are grammatical, the *b*-ones are not. But the pairs differ with respect to their initial NPs, not the presence vs. absence of *n't*.

The linguistic problem: define the class of NPs which license the npi's, and state what, if anything, those NPs have in common with *n't/not*.

A syntactic attempt to kill both birds with one stone is to say that just as *n't* is a "reduced" form of *not* so *neither...nor...* is a reduced form of [*not* (*either...or...*)], *none* a reduction of *not one*, and *no* a reduction of *not a*. The presence of *n*- in the reduced forms is thus explained as a remnant of the original *not*. So on this view the licensing NPs above "really" have a *not* in their representation, and that is what they have in common with *n't*. Moreover NPs built from *not* do license npi's:

(13) Not a single student here has ever been to Moscow.
Not more than five students here have ever been to Moscow.

However, as Ladusaw (1983) shows, this solution is insufficiently general: The initial NPs in the *a*-sentences below license npi's; those in the *b*-sentences do not. But neither present reduced forms of *not*.

(14) a. Fewer than five students here have ever been to Moscow.

b. *More than five students here have ever been to Moscow.

a. At most four students here have ever been to Moscow.

b. *At least four students here have ever been to Moscow.

a. Less than half the students here have ever been to Moscow.
b. *More than half the students here have ever been to Moscow.

An hypothesis which does yield correct results is a semantic one discovered by Ladusaw (1979, 1983), building on the work of Fauconnier (1975, 1979). (See also Zwarts, 1981.)

GENERALIZATION 1.1.3 (The Ladusaw–Fauconnier Generalization (LFG)). *Occurrence within the argument of a decreasing function licenses negative polarity items, but occurrence within the argument of an increasing one does not.*

To check that an NP is decreasing verify that (15) is valid when substituted for X.

(15) All linguists can dance.
X can dance.
∴ X is a linguist (are linguists).

This test shows that the NPs in (10)–(14) which license npi's are decreasing whereas those that do not are not. Further the LFG yields correct results on expressions like (16) and (17) below, not considered by Ladusaw or Fauconnier.

(16) No player's agent should ever act without his consent.
*Every player's agent should ever act without his consent.
Neither John's nor Mary's doctor has ever been to Moscow.

(17) None of the teachers and not more than three of the students have ever been to Moscow.

(16) draws on the fact that possessive NPs, ones of the form [X's N] such as *John's doctor*, inherit their monotonicity from that of the possessor X. Viz., X'*s doctor* is increasing (decreasing) if X is. (17) is predicted since conjunctions (and disjunctions) of decreasing NPs are decreasing.

The LFG is pleasingly general. Denotation sets for most categories in English are ordered (Keenan and Faltz, 1985), so expressions in these categories are classifiable as increasing, decreasing or non-monotonic. We may expect then to find npi licensers in many categories, and we do.

A crucial case is that of ordinary negation *not* (*n't*). In general it denotes a complement operation in the set in which its argument denotes. For example, at the P_1 level *didn't laugh* denotes E – **laugh**, the set of objects under discussion that are not in the **laugh** set. So **not (n't)** maps each $A \subseteq E$ to $E - A$ and is easily seen to be decreasing. Generalizing, the binary operator **neither...nor** is decreasing on each argument (regardless of the category of expression it combines with). Thus we expect, and obtain, npi's in cases like (18):

(18) Neither any students nor any teachers attended the meeting.
John neither praised nor criticized any student.

Thus the LFG finds an independently verifiable property which NPs like *no student* have in common with simple negation. For further discussion see Nam (1994) and Zwarts (1990).

Observe finally that whether an NP of the form [Det + N] is increasing, decreasing or neither is determined by the choice of the Det, not that of the N: if *no student* licenses npi's so does *no cat*. In later sections we shall be concerned to characterize other classes of NPs studied by linguists – e.g., "definite" vs. "indefinite" ones – and again, whether an NP of the form [Det + N] is definite or indefinite in the relevant sense is, like its monotonicity properties, determined by its choice of Det. This array of facts is consistent with and even supportive of recent work in generative grammar (Abney, 1987; Stowell, 1991) which would treat, e.g., *every* as the "head" of the phrase *every man* (and assign it the category DP for "Determiner Phrase", though in this paper we retain the more traditional terminology).

1.2. Type $\langle 1, 1\rangle$ *quantification*

This is the best studied of the types we consider and includes those expressions which correspond most closely to generalized quantifiers in formal logic. (19) presents some fairly simple Det_1s and (20) some more complex ones whose use is exemplified in (21) and (22).

(19) a. some, a, all, every, each, no, several, most, neither, the, both, this, these, my, John's, many, few, enough, a few, a dozen, ten,

b. the ten, John's ten, at least/more than/fewer than/at most/exactly/only ten, only John's, more than enough, just enough, all but ten, half the, half John's, infinitely many, about/approximately two hundred, almost every/no, nearly a hundred, too many, not enough, surprisingly few, most of John's, a large/even number of, a third of the, less than ten per cent of the, between five and ten, hardly any,

(20) no more than ten, not more than half the, most but not all, at least two and not more than ten, neither John's nor Mary's, either fewer than five or else more than a hundred, no child's, most male and all female, more male than female, not one of John's, more of John's than of Mary's, John's biggest, John's third, no/every...but John, all but finitely many, seven out of ten, just finitely many, the first (next, last)...to land on the Moon, the most difficult...to talk to, whatever...you find in the cupboard, not one... in ten.

(21) a. *At least two but not more than ten* students [will get scholarships].

b. *Most male and all female* doctors [read the New England Journal].

c. *More male than female* students [laughed at John's costume].

d. *More of John's than of Bill's* articles [were accepted].

(22) a. *Every* student *but John* [attended the party].

b. *Whatever* dishes *you find in the cupboard* [are clean].

c. *The easiest* village *to reach from here* [is still a hundred kilometers away].

d. *The first* man *to set foot on the Moon* [was Alfred E. Newman].

e. *John's biggest* cat [is fat].

The Det_1s above include many that appear to be mathematically unruly. In Section 1.2.1 we find a property which identifies the "logical" Dets, which will be singled out for special study, but our initial concern is with the larger class, and this for several reasons.

First, there are several non-trivial semantic properties, such as Conservativity and Extension (Section 1.2.2) shared by basically all the Det_1s noted above, so the large class is less unruly than it appears to be. Second, many generalizations of linguistic interest use subclasses of Det_1s which include both logical and non-logical ones. And third, apparent alternative linguistic analyses of the complex Det_1s above are problematic in practice. One might claim for example that in (23a) we need not interpret *more male than female* as a Det_1, rather we just interpret (23a) as (23b) from which we derive it by some syntactic transformation.

(23) a. more male than female students.

b. more male students than female students.

But this approach does not give consistently correct results. (24a,b) are paraphrases, like (23a,b), but (25a,b) are not.

(24) a. more male than female students at Yale.

b. more male students at Yale than female students at Yale.

(25) a. more male than female students at a certain Mid-Western university.

b. more male students at a certain Mid-Western university than female students at a certain Mid-Western university.

Finally, we treat the italicized expressions in (22) as complex Det_1s since their two parts do not occur independently with the same interpretation. In (22a) the exception phrase *but John* basically constrains the choice of prenominal expression to *every* and *no*. (Moltman, 1996; von Fintel, 1993; Hoeksema, 1989; Reinhart, 1991.) In (22b) prenominal *whatever* forces the presence of a postnominal expression: **John cleaned whatever dishes.* In (22c,d) the absence of the postnominal expression forces (at best) a context dependent interpretation of *easiest village* and *first man* (?Adam?) and the presence of superlatives like *easiest*, and "ordinals" like *first, last*, and *next* forces the choice of *the*: **Most easiest villages*, **Each first man*. In (22e) if we interpreted *biggest* as forming a complex common noun with *cat* excluding *John's* then *John's biggest cat* would denote the biggest cat (which John would just happen to possess). But it doesn't. John's biggest cat might be small as cats go. Rather we evaluate the superlative *biggest* with respect to the property *cat which John has.*

We do however exclude from consideration non-extensional Dets like *too many* and *not enough*. (26a) and (26b) may have different truth values in a context in which (possibly unbeknownst to everyone) the doctors and the lawyers are the same individuals.

(26) a. Not enough doctors attended the meeting.

b. Not enough lawyers attended the meeting.

By contrast replacing *not enough* by *exactly ten* in (26) yields Ss which must have the same truth value when the doctors and the lawyers are the same. So *exactly ten* is extensional.

(27) *Some non-extensional Dets*: too many, far too many, surprisingly few, enough, not enough, a large number of, ?many, ?few.[5]

1.2.1. Logical quantifiers

Familiar "logical constants" like *every, some, no* and *exactly one* as well as Dets like *the ten, just finitely many*, and *less than half the* are distinguishable from their more unruly cousins above in being both "logical" and "constant" (see Westerståhl, 1985; Van Benthem, 1984). First, some sample denotations.

(28) a. $\mathbf{all}(A)(B) = 1$ iff $A \subseteq B$.

b. $\mathbf{some}(A)(B) = 1$ iff $A \cap B \neq \varnothing$.

c. $\mathbf{no}(A)(B) = 1$ iff $A \cap B = \varnothing$.

d. $\mathbf{exactly\ one}(A)(B) = 1$ iff $|A \cap B| = 1$.

e. $\mathbf{the\ ten}(A)(B) = 1$ iff $|A| = 10$ and $A \subseteq B$.

f. $\mathbf{just\ finitely\ many}(A)(B) = 1$ iff for some natural number n, $|A \cap B| = n$.

g. $\mathbf{less\ than\ half\ the}(A)(B) = 1$ iff $|A \cap B| < |A - B|$.

So we interpret the S *All poets daydream* as **all(poet)(daydream)**, which is true iff the set of objects in E which are poets is a subset of the set of objects which daydream.

In the same spirit we invite the reader to provide denotations for *more than ten, at most ten, all but ten, all but finitely many, two of the ten, uncountably many, less than ten per cent of the*, and *two out of three*.

Now the quantifiers in (28) are *permutation invariant*, [6] meaning, informally first, that they ignore the identity of individuals. Formally, we have

DEFINITION 1.2.1. Given E, $F \in \text{TYPE}\langle 1,1\rangle$ is *permutation invariant* (PI, or more precisely, PI_E) iff for all permutations π of E and all $A, B \subseteq E$, $F(\pi A)(\pi B) = F(A)(B)$.

Of course by πA we mean $\{\pi b \mid b \in A\}$.[7] And for $R \subseteq E^k$, $\pi(R) = \{\pi d \mid d \in R\}$, where $\pi\langle d_1, \ldots, d_k\rangle = \langle \pi d_1, \ldots, \pi d_k\rangle$. Finally $\pi(F)$ itself is that type $\langle 1,1\rangle$ map sending each πA, πB to $F(A)(B)$. So

$$F \text{ of type } \langle 1,1\rangle \text{ is PI iff for all permutations } \pi \text{ of } E,\ \pi(F) = F.$$

[5] Keenan and Stavi (1986) dismiss *many* and *few* as non-extensional. Barwise and Cooper (1981), Westerståhl (1985) and Lappin (1988) attempt an extensional semantic analysis.

[6] The term is from (Van Benthem, 1984). Keenan and Stavi (1986) use *automorphism invariance* thinking of the relevant functions as Boolean automorphisms of $P(E)$.

[7] In general, we write either fa or $f(a)$ for the value of the function f at the argument a.

That is, the PI elements of TYPE$\langle 1,1\rangle$ (in fact of any denotation set) are just the fixed points of the (extended) permutations of E (extend to the identity map on **2**).

In studying PI quantifiers it is helpful to note that (1), for $A, B \subseteq E$, A may be mapped to B by a permutation of E iff $|A| = |B|$ and $|-A| = |-B|$. Either condition alone suffices when E is finite but both are necessary when E is infinite. And (2), the "lifts" of the permutations π of E to maps: $\mathrm{P}(E) \to \mathrm{P}(E)$ as above are exactly the Boolean automorphisms of $\mathrm{P}(E)$. So PI functions are just those which respect the Boolean structure of $\mathrm{P}(E)$.

One checks directly that the quantifiers in (28) are PI. We take being PI to be a necessary ingredient of logicality. However, PI is a "local" condition. We need not compare universes to see if it holds. But PI expressions normally satisfy a stronger *isomorphism invariance* condition which is *global*. To see the intuition, imagine a Det_1 D interpreted as **every** if $7 \in E$ and as **some** otherwise. For each E, D denotes a PI quantifier over E, but in a statable sense it is not the same quantifier for all E. Expressions like *all, exactly one*, etc. are not fickle in this way. The statement that they are not requires a global perspective in which the interpretation of a Det takes the universe as a parameter. So we now think of, e.g., **all** as a functional mapping each E to a type $\langle 1,1\rangle$ quantifier $\mathbf{all}_E$ over E, one whose value at a pair A, B of subsets of E is 1 iff $A \subseteq B$. Indeed, this global perspective is natural for all Det denotations:

DEFINITION 1.2.2. A *(global) generalized quantifier of type* $\langle 1,1\rangle$ is a functional Q which maps each universe E to a (local) quantifier Q_E of type $\langle 1,1\rangle$ over E.

Now the PI property generalizes to global quantifiers as follows. First, if F is a type $\langle 1,1\rangle$ function over E and π a bijection with domain E, then, just as before (when π was a permutation, i.e. $\pi E = E$), $\pi(F)$ is that type $\langle 1,1\rangle$ function over πE sending each $\pi A, \pi B$ to $F(A)(B)$, for all $A, B \subseteq E$.

DEFINITION 1.2.3. A global generalized quantifier Q of type $\langle 1,1\rangle$ is *isomorphism invariant* (ISOM) iff for all E and all bijections π with domain E, $Q_{\pi E} = \pi(Q_E)$.

Standardly, logicality is identified with ISOM.[8] If Q is ISOM it is PI_E for all E, but the converse fails as the example just before Definition 1.2.2 shows (consider E and π such that $7 \in E - \pi E$). One may verify directly that the Det denotations in (28) are ISOM; a simpler method will be given in Section 1.2.2.

Definitions 1.2.2 and 1.2.3 extend to type $\langle 1\rangle$ quantifiers in an obvious way (in fact to quantifiers of any type). But note that NP denotations are usually *not* ISOM or even PI. The reason is that they typically involve particular N denotations (sets) – *all horses, the ten boys, two of the ten poets* – or PN denotations (individuals) – *Eve or Harry, John's friends*. But the latter denotations are rarely PI. For example, a subset A of E is PI iff for all permutations π of E, $\pi A = A$, and this holds only when $A = E$ or $A = \varnothing$. Similarly, most NP denotations are not PI. With Det_1 denotations, on the other hand, the N is not fixed but an *argument*, and this is what allows them to be ISOM. But Det_1s that

[8] The ISOM (and PI) property can be extended to function(al)s of all types. For type $\langle 1,1\rangle$ quantifiers, the term "logical" is in the literature sometimes taken to stand for ISOM + CONS + EXT; cf. Section 1.2.2.

do involve a fixed N or PN, such as *John's, no... but Eve, most male and all female*, will typically not be ISOM.

To find ISOM type $\langle 1\rangle$ quantifiers we need to look at mathematical or logical languages such as predicate logic and its extensions. For example,

(29) a. $\exists_E(A) = 1$ iff $A \neq \varnothing$,

b. $\forall_E(A) = 1$ iff $A = E$,

c. $(\exists_{\geqslant n})_E(A) = 1$ iff $|A| \geqslant n$,

d. $(Q^R)_E(A) = 1$ iff $|A| \geqslant |E - A|$ (the Rescher quantifier),

e. $(Q^C)_E(A) = 1$ iff $|A| = |E|$ (the Chang quantifier)

(note, however, that $\exists$ and $\forall$ are denotations of the NPs *something* and *everything*, respectively).

So much for logicality, but what about "constancy"? Minimally, this should mean that the interpretation is uniquely determined given the universe E, as holds for the quantifiers in (28) and (29). Thus, taking a *model* to be a pair $\mathbf{E} = \langle E, m\rangle$ where E is a universe and m a function associating with each lexical expression a denotation of appropriate type, an expression s is *constant* in this sense if for all models $\langle E, m\rangle$ and $\langle E, m'\rangle$ with the same universe, $m(s) = m'(s)$. We note that constancy in this sense implies PIness:

(A) If s is constant then for all models $\langle E, m\rangle$, $m(s)$ is PI.

For example, let D be a constant Det of type $\langle 1, 1\rangle$, and π a permutation of E. Then $m(\mathrm{D}) = \pi m(\mathrm{D})$ (by constancy) $= \pi(m(\mathrm{D}))$ (by the definition of composition). But this latter equation says that $m(\mathrm{D})$ is PI, by the condition for PIness given immediately after Definition 1.2.1.

However expressions might be logical without being constant. Consider for example the interpretative latitude afforded by the "approximative" Dets in (30):

(30) around/about/approximately a hundred, nearly/almost a hundred, more or less a hundred, ?several, ?a few.

If the number of students in my physics class is the same as the number of sparrows on my clothesline then the Ss *About a hundred students are in my physics class* and *About a hundred sparrows are on my clothesline* must have the same truth value. With the possible exceptions of *several* and *a few* the Dets in (30) seem to be *cardinal* and thus PI. Cardinal Dets are ones whose value at a pair A, B just depends on the cardinality of $A \cap B$:

DEFINITION 1.2.4. For each E, $F \in \mathrm{TYPE}\langle 1, 1\rangle$ over E is *cardinal* (CARD or CARD_E) iff $\forall A, A', B, B' \subseteq E,\ |A \cap B| = |A' \cap B'| \Rightarrow F(A)(B) = F(A')(B')$.

One readily verifies that $\mathrm{CARD}_E \subseteq \mathrm{PI}_E$. Now one way to account for the "vagueness" in *about a hundred* would be to require that in any given context it be interpreted as say *a hundred plus or minus n*, for some $0 \leqslant n \leqslant 6$. So in some contexts it means a hundred plus or minus two, in others a hundred plus or minus three, etc. We would then have a functional Q which maps each E to a *set* Q_E of type $\langle 1,1\rangle$ quantifiers over E. For such functionals, the ISOM condition is expressed just as in Definition 1.2.3, but now $\pi(Q_E) = \{\pi(F) \mid F \in Q_E\}$. Accepting this analysis we then have Dets which are logical in the sense of satisfying ISOM but not constant in that their interpretation is not uniquely determined given the universe, though the latitude allowed within a given E is limited to a small range within the PI quantifiers over E.

On the other hand, the present notion of constancy need not exhaust the sense in which common Dets are seen as constants. Varying an earlier example, imagine a Det D which was interpreted as **every** when $|E| < 10$, and as **some** when $|E| \geqslant 10$. D is ISOM and its interpretation is uniquely determined by the universe. But there is an intuitive sense in which its interpretation is still not *the same* on all universes.

We turn now to two very general properties of Dets, ones that hold we claim for all the extensional expressions in (20). One of these properties captures at least part of the just mentioned idea of a Det being interpreted the same on all universes.

1.2.2. Conservativity and extension: General constraints on Det denotations

In evaluating Ss of the form $[\mathrm{Det}_1\ \mathrm{N}]+\mathrm{P}_1$ we are thinking of the Det as mapping the noun argument to a type $\langle 1\rangle$ function, one that takes the predicate argument to *true* or *false*. Now the role of the noun argument in this computation is quite different from that of the predicate one. Informally we note,

> (*Domain Restriction*) In evaluating $[\mathrm{Det}_1\ \mathrm{N}]+\mathrm{P}_1$, the noun property delimits the objects we need to consider. It suffices to know which of them have the predicate property and which do not. But we need not consider individuals which lack the noun property.

The domain restricting role of the noun property has no obvious analogue among the properties of quantifiers studied in mathematical languages. Quantifiers, like $\forall x$ and $\exists y$, are understood as quantifying over the entire intended universe of discourse (and so paraphrase the NL expressions *every individual* and *some individual* of type $\langle 1\rangle$, not $\langle 1,1\rangle$). But NLs are inherently multi-purpose. We use them to talk about anything (enriching vocabulary as needed). And the noun arguments of Dets function to delimit "on line", as we speak, the range of things we are talking about. In logic, domain restriction of $\forall x$ and $\exists y$ to a set A is achieved using $\forall x(Ax \to \cdots)$ and $\exists y(Ay \wedge \cdots)$ instead, i.e. effecting type $\langle 1,1\rangle$ quantification by means of type $\langle 1\rangle$ quantification and logical operators. But (i) this added logical complexity is not used in NLs, and, more importantly, (ii) while the reduction works for *every* and *some*, there are many Dets, as we will see, for which there simply is no such reduction.

The apparently simple notion of Domain Restriction is expressed in the literature as the conjunction of two independent properties, *conservativity* and *extension*.

Conservativity. Early work (Barwise and Cooper, 1981; Higginbotham and May, 1981; Keenan, 1981) recognized that Dets satisfied a condition now called *conservativity*:

DEFINITION 1.2.5. $F \in \mathrm{TYPE}\langle 1,1\rangle$ is *conservative* (over E) iff $\forall A, B, B' \subseteq E$,

$$\text{if } A \cap B = A \cap B' \text{ then } F(A)(B) = F(A)(B').$$

An equivalent and commonly given defining condition is that $\forall A, B \subseteq E$,

$$F(A)(B) = F(A)(A \cap B).$$

CONS (or CONS_E) is the set of conservative functions of $\text{TYPE}\langle 1,1\rangle$ over E. A global type $\langle 1,1\rangle$ quantifier Q is *conservative* iff each Q_E is conservative (or each F in Q_E is conservative for the case when Q_E is thought of as a set of type $\langle 1,1\rangle$ functions over E).

The underlying intuition is that to know whether Det A's are B's it is sufficient to know which individuals have A and which of those A's have B (an intuition built into the interpretation of quantifiers in DRT; cf. (Kamp and Reyle, 1993, p. 317)). Knowing about B's that lack A is irrelevant. One checks directly that the functions exhibited in (28) are conservative. And it is conservativity that guarantees the logical equivalences in (31).

(31) a. Most cats are grey $\equiv$ Most cats are cats and are grey.

b. John's cats are black $\equiv$ John's cats are cats and are black.

The apparent triviality of these equivalences may suggest that conservativity is a weak constraint, but this is not the case. An easy computation (e.g., Van Benthem, 1984) shows

(32) For $|E| = n$, $|\text{TYPE}\langle 1,1\rangle_E| = 2^{4^n}$ and $|\text{CONS}_E| = 2^{3^n}$.

Thus in a universe with just two objects there are $2^{16} = 65{,}536$ elements in $\text{TYPE}\langle 1,1\rangle$, only $2^9 = 512$ of which are in CONS. So conservativity rules out most ways a natural language might associate properties with NP denotations. For example, quantifiers like those in (33) are not conservative (the first two, which are ISOM, have been studied in mathematical logic).

(33) a. $M(A)(B) = 1$ iff $|A| > |B|$.

b. $I(A)(B) = 1$ iff $|A| = |B|$ (the Härtig quantifier).

c. For each $b \in E$, $H_b(A)(B) = 1$ iff $b \in B - A$.

Thus we do not have the equivalent of TYPE⟨1,1⟩ effability. But we do have:

GENERALIZATION 1.2.1 (Keenan and Stavi, 1986). *Over a finite universe E, all elements of* CONS_E *are denotable by an English* Det.

As an aid to counting subsets of TYPE⟨1,1⟩ of interest and in proving effability results like Generalization 1.2.1 we note that $\text{TYPE}\langle 1,1\rangle$ is a complete and atomic (ca) Boolean algebra (BA) and in general subsets **B** of interest, like CONS, are ca subalgebras of TYPE⟨1,1⟩. So $|\mathbf{B}| = 2^m$, where m is the number of atoms of **B**. Keenan and Stavi compute that there are $3^{|E|}$ atoms in CONS_E. And to show finite effability it is enough to show that any finite number of atoms is denotable. Taking (finite) disjunctions then gives the effability result.

It is also fair to wonder just how we support the claim that the diverse Dets in (20) always denote in CONS.[9] Of course in part we sample. But this sampling is supported by more systematic observations. Namely,

(34) a. lexical Det_1s are conservative, and

b. the major ways of building Dets from Dets preserves conservativity.

The lexical or near lexical Det_1s of English are given in (19a) above. Of ways of building complex Dets we note four. First,

(35) The trivial functions $\mathbf{0}_{\langle 1,1\rangle}(A)(B) = 0$ and $\mathbf{1}_{\langle 1,1\rangle}(A)(B) = 1$, all $A, B \subseteq E$, are in CONS.

(36) Second, conservativity is preserved under definition by cases in terms of conservative functions. For example, **the ten** $\in$ CONS given that **every** and **0** are.

$$\textbf{the ten}(A) = \begin{cases} \textbf{every}(A) & \text{if } |A| = 10, \\ \mathbf{0}_{\langle 1,1\rangle}(A) & \text{otherwise.} \end{cases}$$

Third, and crucial for non-logical Dets like *John's ten*, composition with restricting functions preserves CONS. More explicitly,

(37) a. $f : \mathrm{P}(E) \to \mathrm{P}(E)$ is *restricting* iff $\forall A \in \mathrm{P}(E),\ f(A) \subseteq A$.

b. For $F \in$ CONS and f restricting, $F_f \in$ CONS, where

$$F_f(A)(B) =_{\text{df}} F(f(A))(B).$$

From (36) and (37) we infer immediately that **John's ten** and **none of John's ten** defined below are conservative:

(38) $$\textbf{John's ten}(A) = \begin{cases} \textbf{every}(A \textbf{ which John has}) \\ \qquad\qquad \text{if } |A \textbf{ which John has}| = 10, \\ \mathbf{0}_{\langle 1,1\rangle}(A) \quad \text{otherwise.} \end{cases}$$

(We write A **which John has** for the set of $b \in A$ which John stands in the *has* relation to, where this relation is given by the context (model). To show conservativity it suffices that the map sending each A to A **which John has** is restricting.)

(39) $$\textbf{none of John's ten}(A) = \begin{cases} \textbf{no}(A \textbf{ which John has}) \\ \qquad\qquad \text{if } |A \textbf{ which John has}| = 10, \\ \mathbf{0}_{\langle 1,1\rangle}(A) \quad \text{otherwise.} \end{cases}$$

Finally, CONS is closed under the pointwise Boolean functions. So the denotations of the expressions in (40) are in CONS given that denotations of the Dets they are built from are.

[9] For some questionable cases see Keenan and Stavi (1986), Johnsen (1987), and the more systematic discussion in (Herburger, 1994).

(40) not more than ten, at least ten and not more than a hundred, neither fewer than ten nor more than a hundred, most but not all, neither John's nor Mary's, most male but only a few female, most of John's and all of Mary's.

One shows many of the unruly looking expressions in (20) to be conservative by showing that they are expressible as some combination of definition by cases, restrictions, or Boolean functions of conservative functions.

Now, stepping back from our discussion, we see that Conservativity expresses part of what is covered informally by Domain Restriction. Conservativity says that we may limit our consideration of objects with the predicate property to those which also have the noun property. But Domain Restriction says more. It says that in evaluating S = [Det N] + P_1 we need not consider any individuals that lie outside the extension of the noun argument. Leafing through the OED we will not find some archaic Det *blik* with the sense that *Blik cats are black* is true iff the number of non-cats is 3. Yet the F in (41) is conservative.

(41) $F(A)(B) = 1$ iff $|-A| = 3$.

So the denotations of the English Dets given earlier satisfy additional constraints, challenging perhaps the effability claim (34) of Keenan and Stavi (1986). But the needed constraints are global. Once we fix a finite E, the F in (41) is expressible. To see this, note that the functions in (42) are conservative, all n, m.

(42) **at most** n **of the** $m(A)(B) = 1$ iff $|A| = m$ and $|A \cap B| \leqslant n$.

Now for $|E| < 3$, the F in (41) is just $\mathbf{0}_{\langle 1,1\rangle}$ which is CONS. If $|E| \geqslant 3$, E finite, let m be such that $|E| - m = 3$. Then the F in (41) is denoted by **at most** m **of the** m.

The type of global constraint we need to eliminate quantifiers like that in (41) was first given in (Van Benthem, 1984), and is called *extension*.

DEFINITION 1.2.6. Let Q be a global type $\langle 1,1\rangle$ quantifier. Then Q satisfies *extension* (EXT) iff $\forall E, E'$ with $E \subseteq E'$, $Q_{E'}$ is an extension of Q_E.

To say that **every** satisfies Extension (which it does) is to say that whenever $E \subseteq E'$ the function $\mathbf{every}_{E'}$ extends the function $\mathbf{every}_E$. That is, $\forall A, B \subseteq E$, $\mathbf{every}_E(A)(B) = \mathbf{every}_{E'}(A)(B)$. So quantifiers that satisfy EXT must make the same decision regarding a pair A, B of sets regardless of what the underlying universe is. The F in (41), treated as a functional $F_E(A)(B) = 1$ iff $|E - A| = 3$, fails Extension. Set $E = \{a, b, c\}$ and $E' = \{a, b, c, d\}$. Then $F_E(\varnothing)(\varnothing) = 1$ but $F_{E'}(\varnothing)(\varnothing) = 0$, so $F_{E'}$ does not extend F_E. Similarly the quantifier Q below fails Extension

(43) $$Q_E = \begin{cases} \mathbf{every}_E & \text{if } E \text{ is finite,} \\ \mathbf{infinitely\ many}_E & \text{if } E \text{ is infinite.} \end{cases}$$

Note that Extension is equivalent to the following condition:

(44) $Q_E(A)(B) = Q_{E'}(A)(B)$, all $E, E' \supseteq A, B$.

Reason: $Q_E(A)(B) = Q_{E \cup E'}(A)(B) = Q_{E'}(A)(B)$. So we see that Extension indeed captures a notion of universe-independence, or put differently, of having the same interpretation in different universes, i.e. a notion of *constancy*.[10]

We have so far been somewhat sloppy distinguishing global and local quantifiers: the underlying universe of a local quantifier has often been tacitly understood but not explicitly given. Now we see that for quantifiers in EXT such sloppiness can be formally justified. If Q is a global quantifier satisfying Extension and A, B are sets, we may drop the subscript and simply write

$$Q(A)(B) = 1$$

meaning "for some E with $A, B \subseteq E$, $Q_E(A)(B) = 1$". Extension guarantees that this is equivalent to "for all E with $A, B \subseteq E$, $Q_E(A)(B) = 1$", or, if we have a particular universe E' with $A, B \subseteq E'$ in mind, to "$Q_{E'}(A)(B) = 1$".

Consider now typical non-logical Dets like *John's ten* or *most male*. To interpret these as ordinary global quantifiers we think of *John*, the *has* relation, and the *male* property as fixed in advance. Then, for example, **most male** is that functional which maps each E to the quantifier $\textbf{most male}_E(A)(B) = 1$ iff $|\textbf{male} \cap A \cap B| > |(\textbf{male} \cap A) - B|$, all $A, B \subseteq E$. This is a CONS and EXT (but not ISOM) global quantifier.

However, it may seem more natural to treat *most male* not as a constant, but as an expression whose interpretation varies with the interpretation of *male*, which we can think of, given a universe E, as any subset of E. This treatment would give us a new source of "ambiguous quantifiers" of the kind introduced in Section 1.2.1, i.e. functionals Q mapping each E to a *set* Q_E of type $\langle 1,1 \rangle$ quantifiers over E.[11] Letting, for $X, A, B \subseteq E$, $\textbf{most}X_E(A)(B) = 1$ iff $|X \cap A \cap B| > |(X \cap A) - B|$, we could then interpret *most* here by

(45) $\quad \textbf{most}^+_E = \{\textbf{most}X_E\colon\ X \subseteq E\}.$

In the case of *most male*, the set **male** selecting the right element of $\textbf{most}^+_E$ is given directly in the model, whereas for *John's ten*, which can be treated similarly, the *has* relation is more contextual.

The alternative account sketched here allows treating *most male* and *John's ten* using logical quantifiers. Indeed, although the quantifiers $\textbf{most}X_E$ are not ISOM (except for $X = \varnothing$ or $X = E$), the "ambiguous" $\textbf{most}^+$ is ISOM, in the extended sense formulated in Section 1.2.1: if π is a bijection with domain E, $\pi(\textbf{most}X_E) = \textbf{most}\pi X_{\pi E}$, from which it readily follows that $\textbf{most}^+_{\pi E} = \pi(\textbf{most}^+_E)$, as required.

These quantifiers also satisfy a generalized version of Extension:

DEFINITION 1.2.7. Let Q be a functional mapping each E to a *set* Q_E of type $\langle 1, 1 \rangle$ quantifiers over E. Q satisfies *extension* (EXT) iff $\forall E, E'$ with $E \subseteq E'$,

[10] Yet the intuitive idea of constancy, also discussed at the end of Section 1.2.1, may involve more. For example, EXT is straightforwardly extended to type $\langle 1 \rangle$ quantifiers, but then $\forall$, defined by $\forall_E(A) = 1$ iff $A = E$, does not satisfy EXT. But we would be reluctant to conclude that $\forall$ is not a (logical) constant. Perhaps the right conclusion is instead that EXT is only reasonable for Det denotations.

[11] The term "ambiguous quantifiers" is from (Krynicki and Mostowski, 1993), who discuss a similar notion of quantifiers from a logical perspective.

(i) each $F \in Q_E$ extends to an $F' \in Q_{E'}$,
(ii) each $F' \in Q_{E'}$ is an extension of some $F \in Q_E$.

Clearly this collapses to Definition 1.2.6 when each Q_E is a unit set. And the basic intuition is the same: let F be one of possibly many interpretations of a Det D over E, and now add some elements to E yielding E'. F must "adapt": it must assign truth values to some new pairs (A', B') of subsets of E' that were not subsets of E, and there may be many ways to do this for the same reason that there were many ways to interpret D in the first place. But the original decisions F made about pairs (A, B) of subsets of E can still be made, because F's decision just depended on A and B (in fact given conservativity, just on A and $A \cap B$) not on things that lay outside them. That is, F must have an extension (and possibly many) in the enlarged universe E'.

Going the other way, if F' makes decisions about all the pairs (A', B') of subsets of E', then for any $E \subseteq E'$, it has made decisions about pairs (A, B) of subsets of E. And its decisions there have just been based on A and B, not on things outside them, so if we eliminate things outside them it can still make the same choice. That is, the restriction of F' to pairs (A, B) of subsets of E is a possible interpretation for D over E, which is just what (ii) says.

Logicality revisited. Our study of ISOM Dets is made more tractable by limiting ourselves to ones that are both CONS and EXT. Note that ISOM is independent of these conditions. For example the quantifier Q given by $Q_E(A)(B) = 1$ iff $|-A| = |-B|$ is ISOM but neither CONS nor EXT. Observe now,

PROPOSITION 1.2.1. *A global type* $\langle 1, 1\rangle$ *(ordinary) quantifier* Q *is in* CONS $\cap$ EXT $\cap$ ISOM *iff* $\forall E \forall A, B \subseteq E\ \forall E' \forall A', B' \subseteq E'$,

$$(|A \cap B| = |A' \cap B'| \text{ and } |A - B| = |A' - B'|)$$
$$\Rightarrow Q_E(A)(B) = Q'_E(A')(B').$$

Thus, given Conservativity and Extension, ISOM Dets base their decision at a pair A, B on the two quantities $|A \cap B|$ and $|A - B|$.[12] Using Proposition 1.2.1 one easily verifies that the quantifiers in (28) are ISOM. The atoms of $(\text{CONS}\cap\text{EXT}\cap\text{ISOM})_E$ are the maps (**exactly** $n \wedge$ **all but** m) which send a pair A, B to 1 iff $|A \cap B| = n$ & $|A - B| = m$, all cardinals n, m with $n + m \leqslant |E|$. And the Dets in $(\text{CONS} \cap \text{EXT} \cap \text{ISOM})_E$ are the lubs of these atoms. Note that these claims do not require that E be finite. (In finite models the atoms are expressible by the Dets **exactly** n **of the** m, for $n \leqslant m$, but in the infinite case we cannot reconstruct $|A \cap B|$ from $|A|$ and $|A - B|$.)

[12] The fact that such quantifiers on finite universes can be identified with binary relations between natural numbers allows a useful and perspicuous representation of them, and of many of their properties, in the so-called tree of numbers; cf. Westerståhl (1989).

Domain Restriction revisited. Conservativity and Extension are independent. F in (41) is CONS but fails EXT, I in (33) satisfies EXT but fails CONS. And we have: Conservativity + Extension = Domain Restriction. Can we find a conceptually unified condition on the role of the noun argument which yields conservativity and extension as special cases?

One answer to this query uses the logical notion of *relativization*. For each (global) type $\langle 1 \rangle$ quantifier Q we can define a type $\langle 1,1 \rangle$ quantifier Q^{rel} which simulates in the verb argument the behaviour of Q over the universe determined by the noun argument:

DEFINITION 1.2.8. The *relativization* of a global type $\langle 1 \rangle$ quantifier Q is the global type $\langle 1,1 \rangle$ quantifier Q^{rel} given by $Q^{\mathrm{rel}}_E(A)(B) = Q_A(A \cap B)$ for all E and all $A, B \subseteq E$.

FACT 1.2.2. *A type* $\langle 1,1 \rangle$ *quantifier is* CONS + EXT *iff it is equal to* Q^{rel} *for some type* $\langle 1 \rangle$ *quantifier* Q.

To see this, one verifies directly from the definitions that Q^{rel} is always CONS and EXT. In the other direction, if Q' is CONS and EXT, define the type $\langle 1 \rangle$ *counterpart* Q of Q' by $Q_E(B) = Q'_E(E)(B)$. Then $Q' = Q^{\mathrm{rel}}$, since $Q^{\mathrm{rel}}_E(A)(B) = Q_A(A \cap B) = Q'_A(A)(A \cap B) = Q'_E(A)(A \cap B)$ (by EXT) $= Q'_E(A)(B)$ (by CONS).

Thus, the Domain Restricted type $\langle 1,1 \rangle$ quantifiers – among which we claim to find all Det_1 denotations – are precisely the relativizations of type $\langle 1 \rangle$ quantifiers. Indeed their type $\langle 1 \rangle$ counterparts are often familiar:

(46) a. **every** $= \forall^{\mathrm{rel}}$,

b. **some** $= \exists^{\mathrm{rel}}$,

c. **at least** $n = \exists^{\mathrm{rel}}_{\geqslant n}$,

d. **most** $= (Q^{\mathrm{R}})^{\mathrm{rel}}$ (Q^{R} was defined in (29)),

e. **John's** $= Q^{\mathrm{rel}}$, where Q interprets the NP *everything that John has*,

etc.

Generalization. In evaluating Ss of the form [Det N] + P_1 the noun argument is distinguished from the verb one in determining the domain restriction. A type notation reflecting this asymmetry in the arguments would be $\langle\langle 1 \rangle,1 \rangle$. The standard notation $\langle 1,1 \rangle$ rather reflects the common view in which Det_1s denote simply binary relations over $\mathrm{P}(E)$. But the functional view we have been using generalizes more naturally than the relational view in two directions.

First, the statements of Conservativity and Extension do not depend on the range of type $\langle 1 \rangle$ functions, they merely say that under certain conditions $Q_E(A)(B) = Q_{E'}(A')(B')$. The functional view then enables us to say without change that interrogative Dets such as *which?* and *whose?* are conservative and satisfy extension. Conservativity for example just says that **which**?$(A)(B) =$ **which**?$(A)(A \cap B)$, that is *Which p's are q's?* asks for the same information as *Which p's are both p's and q's?*, which is correct. So Conservativity yields the equivalence of the (a,b) questions in (47).

(47) a. Which roses are red? b. Which roses are roses and are red?

a. Whose cat can swim? b. Whose cat is a cat that can swim?

Second, the noun argument of Det_1s forms a type $\langle 1\rangle$ constituent (NP) with the Det_1, one that occurs as an argument of transitive and ditransitive verbs, as in *No teacher criticized every student* and *John gave every teacher two presents*. These facts will prompt us in Section 2 to generalize the type $\langle 1\rangle$ functions to ones taking $(n+1)$-ary relations as arguments yielding n-ary ones as values, not just functions taking unary relations to zero-ary ones as at present.

For further extensions of these ideas to predicate modifiers of various sorts we refer to the reader to Ter Meulen (1990), Loebner (1986). Here we turn to:

1.2.3. Basic subclasses: Intersective (existential) & co-intersective (universal)

The (local) value of a Det_1 denotation F at A, B depends at most on $A \cap B$ and $A - B$. If $F(A)(B)$ depends only on $A \cap B$ we call F *intersective*; if $F(A)(B)$ depends only on $A - B$ we call F *co-intersective*.

DEFINITION 1.2.9. Let $F \in [\mathrm{P}(E) \to [\mathrm{P}(E) \to \mathbf{2}]]$. Then,

(a) F is *intersective* iff

$$\forall A, B, A', B' \subseteq E,\ A \cap B = A' \cap B' \Rightarrow F(A)(B) = F'(A')(B').$$

(b) F is *co-intersective* iff

$$\forall A, B, A', B' \subseteq E,\ A - B = A' - B' \Rightarrow F(A)(B) = F'(A')(B').$$

Equivalently, F is co-intersective iff $F\neg$ is intersective (where $F\neg(A)(B) = F(A)(E - B)$).

We write INT (or $\mathrm{INT}_E\langle 1,1\rangle$) and dually CO-INT (or $\text{CO-INT}_E\langle 1,1\rangle$) for the set of intersective (co-intersective) functions of type $\langle 1,1\rangle$ over E.

(48) a. *Some intersective* (= *Generalized Existential*) Dets *in English*.
Cardinal: some, no, a, at least n, more than n, exactly n, between n and m, fewer than n, at most n, infinitely many, forty odd, forty or more, about forty, at least two and at most ten, not more than ten.
Non-PI: more male than female, exactly five male, no...but John.

b. *Some co-intersective* (= *Generalized Universal*) Dets *in English*.
every, all but n, all but at most n, every...but John, almost all.

Where *John* denotes an individual I_j, **no...but John** (as in *No student but John laughed*) maps A, B to 1 iff $A \cap B = \{j\}$ and thus is intersective. **every...but John** maps A, B to 1 iff $A - B = \{j\}$ and so is co-intersective. Indeed, **every...but John** = (**no...but John**)$\neg$. In many cases (though not all; cf. Westerståhl, 1989), the post-complement of a Det_1 is given by another Det_1: **some**$\neg$ = **not every**,

every$\neg$ = **no**, (**at most four**)$\neg$ = **all but at most four**, (**exactly six**)$\neg$ = **all but six**, (**more than half**)$\neg$ = **less than half**, (**exactly half**)$\neg$ = **exactly half**.

INT and CO-INT are basic subclasses of Dets in several respects. We note first,

PROPOSITION 1.2.3 (Keenan, 1993).

(i) *Both* INT *and* CO-INT *are ca subalgebras of* CONS. CARD *is a ca subalgebra of* INT. *In fact,* CARD = INT $\cap$ PI, *when E is finite (but not when E is infinite).*

(ii) *For A =* INT *or* CO-INT, *the function * from A into* $[\mathrm{P}(E) \to \mathbf{2}]$ *given by* $F^*(B) = F(E)(B)$, *is an isomorphism. Also,* INT *is isomorphic to* CO-INT *via the function that maps F to $F\neg$.*

(iii) INT $\cap$ CO-INT = $\{\mathbf{0}_{\langle 1,1\rangle}, \mathbf{1}_{\langle 1,1\rangle}\}$.

Proposition 1.2.3 (i) guarantees that Dets like *at least two but not more than ten* are intersective given that the ones they are built from are.

Proposition 1.2.3 (ii) says that INT and CO-INT are very limited types of Dets, each being isomorphic to TYPE$\langle 1\rangle$, the set of possible NP denotations. One computes that of the 2^{3^n} conservative functions only $2^{2^n+1} - 2$ are generalized universal or existential. For example, for $|E| = 3$, $|\mathrm{INT} \cup \mathrm{CO\text{-}INT}| = 510$ and $|\mathrm{CONS}| > 130$ million. Still, in addition to generalizing the standard notions of existential and universal quantification, INT and CO-INT are fundamental subsets of CONS in two respects: (i) they generate all of CONS under the Boolean operations (Theorem 1.2.4) and (ii) they are precisely the type $\langle 1,1\rangle$ quantifiers which do not make essential use of the Domain Restricting property of their noun arguments (Theorem 1.2.5).

THEOREM 1.2.4 (Keenan, 1993; Keenan and Stavi, 1986). *For each E,* CONS_E *is the complete Boolean closure of* $\mathrm{INT}_E \cup \mathrm{CO\text{-}INT}_E$.

Leading up to our second result, observe that (classically) (49a) and (49b) are logically equivalent.

(49) a. Some students are vegetarians.

b. Some individuals are both students and vegetarians.

This equivalence says that for Det = *some* we may eliminate the restriction (students) on the domain of quantification, compensating by an appropriate Boolean compound in the predicate. But if *some* is replaced by *most* in (49a) we find no analogue of (49b). *Most* then appears *inherently sortal*: we cannot eliminate restrictions on its domain of quantification, compensating by some Boolean modification of the predicate. Just which Dets in English are inherently sortal in this sense?

DEFINITION 1.2.10. F of type $\langle 1,1\rangle$ is *sortally reducible* iff there is a Boolean function h of two variables such that $\forall A, B \subseteq E$, $F(A)(B) = F(E)(h(A,B))$. Otherwise, F is called *inherently sortal*.

THEOREM 1.2.5 (Keenan, 1993). *A conservative F is sortally reducible iff F is intersective or F is co-intersective.*

The class of intersective Dets also provides a fair solution to a properly linguistic problem. To state the problem with generality we shall anticipate Section 1.3 and generalize the notion *intersective* to Dets of type $\langle\langle 1,1\rangle,1\rangle$. Recall that we treat expressions like those italicized in (50) as Det_2s – they combine with two common nouns to form a type $\langle 1\rangle$ expression:

(50) a. *More* students *than* teachers attended the party.
b. *Every* man *and* woman jumped overboard.
c. *The same number of* students *as* teachers signed the petition.

A type $\langle\langle 1,1\rangle,1\rangle$ Det is *intersective* if the truth value of an S it builds depends only on the intersection of the predicate property with each of the noun properties. So *more... than* in *More dogs than cats are in the garden* is intersective since the truth of the S is determined given the two sets **dog** $\cap$ **in the garden** and **cat** $\cap$ **in the garden**. Formally,

DEFINITION 1.2.11. A function F mapping k-tuples of subsets of E to $[\mathrm{P}(E) \to \mathbf{2}]$ is *intersective* iff for all $(A_1, \ldots, A_k)$ and $(B_1, \ldots, B_k)$ and all sets C, C', if $A_i \cap C = B_i \cap C'$, all $1 \leqslant i \leqslant k$, then $F(A_1, \ldots, A_k)(C) = F(B_1, \ldots, B_k)(C')$.

Of the Det_2s in (50) one verifies that *every...and* is not intersective but *more...than* and *the same number of...as* are, as are cardinal comparatives in general, e.g., *fewer...than, exactly as many...as, more than twice as many...as.*

Now consider *Existential There* Ss like those in (51):

(51) a. There wasn't more than one student at the party.
b. Are there more dogs than cats in the garden?
c. There was noone but John in the building at the time.

Such Ss affirm, deny or query the existence of objects (e.g., students) with a specified property (e.g., being at the party). NPs like *more than one student* which naturally occur in such Ss will be called *existential* NPs. So the NPs italicized in (52) are not existential.

(52) a. *There wasn't *John* at the party.
b. *Were there *most students* on the lawn?
c. *There wasn't *every student* in the garden.

The linguistic problem: define the set of existential NPs in English. And a good first approximation to an answer here is Generalization 1.2.2. (See Barwise and Cooper (1981) for a related approach, the first properly semantic one in the literature, and see Reuland and Ter Meulen (1987) for an overview of recent work on this thorny linguistic issue.)

GENERALIZATION 1.2.2. *The* NPs *which occur naturally in Existential There* Ss *are (Boolean combinations of) ones built from intersective* Dets.

Generalization 1.2.2 correctly predicts the judgments in (51) and (52) as well as those in (53):

(53) a. There are the same number of students as teachers on the committee.

b. There aren't more than twice as many children as adults at the party.

c. There are at least two dogs but not more than ten cats in the yard.

d. *There are two out of three students on the committee.

e. *Was there every student but John in the building at the time?

f. *There weren't John's cats in the garden.

Turning now to Dets which are neither intersective nor co-intersective there are at least two classes of interest: the "definite" ones, and the properly proportional ones.

Partitives and definite NPs. We consider *partitive* NPs like *at least two of the students, all but one of John's children* and *most of those questions.* Most linguists treat them as having the form [Det_1 of NP], and more generally [Det_k (of NP)^k], like *more of the boys than of the girls.* See Ladusaw (1982) and references cited there for discussion of partitives in a linguistic setting.

The linguistic issue: For which choices of NP is the partitive [Det_1 of NP] grammatical? Some partial answers:

(54) a. *at least two of* X is a grammatical NP when X = the boys; the ten or more boys; these boys; these ten boys; John's cats; John's ten or more cats; my cats; the child's toys; that child's best friend's toys; his toys.

b. *at least two of* X is ungrammatical when X = each boy; all boys; no boys; the boy; some boys; most boys; exactly ten boys; ten boys; no children's toys; most of the houses; at least nine students; more students than teachers; five of the students.

Thus whether an NP of the form Det_1+ N occurs grammatically in the partitive context [*two of* ___] depends significantly on *its* choice of Det_1 (which is in part why we suggested to treat, e.g., *most of those* in *most of those questions* as a complex Det_1 of the form [Det_1 of Det_1]). Det_1s acceptable here were first characterized semantically in (Barwise and Cooper, 1981). Extending their analysis slightly, and adapting it to "ambiguous quantifiers", we have

DEFINITION 1.2.12. A functional Q mapping each E to a set of type $\langle 1,1\rangle$ quantifiers over E is *definite* iff Q is non-trivial and $\forall E \forall F \in Q_E\ \forall A \subseteq E,\ F(A) = \mathbf{0}$ or $F(A)$ is the filter generated by some non-empty $C \subseteq A$. If C always has at least two elements Q is called *definite plural.*

NB: to say that $F(A)$ is the filter generated by C is just to say that $F(A)(B) = 1$ iff $C \subseteq B$ (that is, iff $C - B = \varnothing$). In this respect definite Dets resemble co-intersective ones. They differ from them in placing additional conditions on their first argument. For example, **the ten** $(A)(B) = 1$ iff $A - B = \varnothing$ *and* $|A| = 10$.

(55) *Some definite plural* Det_1s.

the ten, the two or more, the_{pl}, John's ten, John's two or more, $\text{John's}_{\text{pl}}$, these, these ten, those ten or more, John and Bill's ten, his ten,...

Note that *every* is not definite and *the one*, and *John's one* are definite but not definite plural.

GENERALIZATION 1.2.3. *An* NP X *is grammatical in plural partitive contexts iff* X = [Det N] *where* Det *is semantically definite plural or* X *is a conjunction or disjunction of such* NPs.

We note that NPs such as *this student and that teacher* are excluded by this definition (though by certain other criteria in Linguistics it would count as definite plural).

1.2.4. Proportionality quantifiers and logical definability

A question that has arisen now and then in linguistics is: Can semantic interpretations for natural language be given in first-order logic? Various authors (e.g., Boolos, 1981, 1984; Hintikka, 1973; Gabbay and Moravcsik, 1974) have presented sometimes subtle, often debated, arguments to show that the answer was negative. However, the theory of generalized quantifiers provides a straightforward and undisputable argument (for the same answer): even if we restrict attention to finite universes, it can be proved by standard model-theoretic techniques (cf. Barwise and Cooper, 1981) that the denotation of *most* (in the sense of **more than half**) is not first-order definable. And nothing in this proof crucially distinguishes **more than half** from **more than two thirds** or other ISOM type $\langle 1,1\rangle$ quantifier whose value at a pair A, B properly compares $|A \cap B|$ with $|A|$ (or $|A - B|$).

More formally, let us take the *properly proportional* quantifiers to be, for $1 \leqslant n < m$, those (CONS and EXT) type $\langle 1,1\rangle$ functions taking A and B to 1 iff

$$(56) \qquad \frac{|A \cap B|}{|A|} > \frac{m}{n} \left(\text{or } \frac{|A \cap B|}{|A|} \geqslant \frac{m}{n}\right).$$

This captures the denotations of, e.g., *most, at least half, half the, more than ten percent of the*.

PROPOSITION 1.2.6. *The properly proportional quantifiers are not first-order definable (even when we restrict ourselves to finite universes).*

Clearly Proposition 1.2.6 extends immediately to negations of properly proportional quantifiers, like the denotations of *less than a third of the, at most ten percent of the*. It also extends to non-trivial meets and joins of these functions, like the denotations of *exactly ten percent of the, between two fifths and three fifths of the*. (The intent of *properly* here is to exclude non-proper proportions as in *at least* 100% *of the*, and *at least zero per cent of the*.)

Note that here we are talking about global quantifiers and uniform definability. A type $\langle 1,1\rangle$ quantifier Q is *first-order definable* iff there is a first-order sentence ϕ whose non-logical symbols are exactly two unary predicate symbols P_1 and P_2, such that for any interpretation (model) $\mathbf{E} = \langle E, A_1, A_2\rangle$, where $A_1, A_2 \subseteq E$,

$$(57) \qquad Q_E(A_1)(A_2) = 1 \Leftrightarrow \langle E, A_1, A_2\rangle \vDash \phi.$$

So the same definition ϕ works in every universe.[13] For example, obviously **at least two** is first-order definable, since $|A_1 \cap A_2| \geqslant 2$ is expressed by the first-order sentence

$$\exists x \exists y (x \neq y \wedge P_1 x \wedge P_1 y \wedge P_2 x \wedge P_2 y)$$

and similarly **all but at most two** is first-order definable by

$$\forall x \forall y \forall z (P_1 x \wedge P_1 y \wedge P_1 z \wedge \neg P_2 x \wedge \neg P_2 y \wedge \neg P_2 z \rightarrow x = y \vee y = z \vee x = z).$$

And the result above says that when $Q =$ **most**, for example, there exists *no* first-order sentence of the required kind such that (57) holds.

In fact, much stronger undefinability claims hold, some of which are linguistically relevant. To formulate these, we need to consider definability *in terms of* certain given quantifiers. To see some examples, note first that **most** is definable in terms of **more...than** of type $\langle\langle 1,1\rangle,1\rangle$:

(58) $\quad$ $\textbf{most}(A_1)(A_2) = (\textbf{more} A_1 \cap A_2 \textbf{ than } A_1 - A_2)(E)$

since most A_1's are A_2's iff more A_1's who are A_2's than A_1's who are not A_2's exist. From (58) it is clear that if we had a first-order sentence defining **more...than**, we could construct another one defining **most**. Hence, **more...than**, and in general the non-trivial comparative Dets of type $\langle\langle 1,1\rangle,1\rangle$ (cf. Section 1.3), are not first-order definable.

For another example, on finite models (not on infinite ones), the quantifiers I and M from (33) are definable in terms of **most**. For, first

(59) $\quad$ $I(A)(B) = 1 \text{ iff } M(A)(B) = M(B)(A) = 0$

so I is definable in terms of M, and second, for finite A, B we have

(60) $$\begin{aligned} M(A)(B) = 1 \text{ iff } & |A| > |B| \\ \text{iff } & |A - B| > |B - A| \\ \text{iff } & \textbf{most}((A - B) \cup (B - A))(A - B) = 1. \end{aligned}$$

This notion of definability can be made precise with the concept of a *logic with generalized quantifiers* (Mostovski, 1957; Lindström, 1966). Let Q be a quantifier of type $\langle 1,1\rangle$, or more generally of type $\langle 1,\ldots,1\rangle$ with k 1's, $k \geqslant 1$ (in this context there is no need to separate noun arguments from verb arguments). The logic $\mathrm{L}(Q)$ is obtained from first-order predicate logic by adding the new formation rule

(61) $\quad$ if $\phi_1, \ldots, \phi_k$ are formulas and x is a variable then $Qx(\phi_1, \ldots, \phi_k)$ is a formula

(here Qx binds each free occurrence of x in each of $\phi_1, \ldots, \phi_k$), and a corresponding clause in the truth definition:

[13] Note that a first-order definable quantifier is automatically ISOM, since first-order sentences are invariant for isomorphic models.

(62) $\mathbf{E} \models Qx(\phi_1, \ldots, \phi_k)\,[g]$ (i.e. the assignment g satisfies $Qx(\phi_1, \ldots, \phi_k)$ in the model $\mathbf{E}$ with universe E) iff $Q_E((\phi_1^{\mathbf{E},x,g}), \ldots, (\phi_k^{\mathbf{E},x,g})) = 1$,

where $\phi_i^{\mathbf{E},x,g}$ is the subset of E defined by ϕ_i relative to x and g:

$$\phi_i^{\mathbf{E},x,g} = \{a \in E\colon\ \mathbf{E} \models \phi_i[g(x/a)]\}$$

($g(x/a)$ is like g except that x is assigned to a). Likewise, one defines logics $\mathrm{L}(Q_1, \ldots, Q_n)$ where $Q_1, \ldots, Q_n$ are given quantifiers (of arbitrary types).

Finally, a quantifier Q of type $\langle 1, 1\rangle$ is *definable in* $\mathrm{L}(Q_1, \ldots, Q_n)$ iff (57) holds for some $\mathrm{L}(Q_1, \ldots, Q_n)$-sentence ϕ (similarly if Q is of type $\langle 1, \ldots, 1\rangle$).

For example, our statement above that (58) defines **most** in terms of **more...than** becomes the claim that **most** is definable in L(**more...than**), by means of the sentence

$$\textit{more... than}\ x(P_1x \wedge P_2x,\ P_1x \wedge \neg P_2x,\ x = x).$$

Similarly, from (60) we see that M is definable (for finite E) by the L(**most**)-sentence

$$\textit{most}\ x((P_1x \wedge \neg P_2x) \vee (P_2x \wedge \neg P_1x),\ P_1x \wedge \neg P_2x).$$

Recall now from Section 1.2.2 (Fact 1.2.2 and (46)) that each CONS and EXT type $\langle 1, 1\rangle$ quantifier Q' has a type $\langle 1\rangle$ counterpart Q, such that $Q' = Q^{\mathrm{rel}}$. If Q' is definable in terms of its type $\langle 1\rangle$ counterpart, i.e. if Q^{rel} is definable in $\mathrm{L}(Q)$, then the type $\langle 1\rangle$ counterpart is semantically sufficient. And this holds for many Det_1 denotations, for example,

(63) a. **every** $= \forall^{\mathrm{rel}}$ is defined by $\forall x(P_1x \to P_2x)$.

b. **some** $= \exists^{\mathrm{rel}}$ is defined by $\exists x(P_1x \wedge P_2x)$.

c. **all but at most three** $= (\exists_{\leqslant 3}\neg)^{\mathrm{rel}}$ is defined by $\exists_{\leqslant 3}x(P_1x \wedge \neg P_2x)$.

If similar definitions could be given for all Det_1 denotations then at least from a logical point of view type $\langle 1\rangle$ quantification would be enough. But it was proved in (Barwise and Cooper, 1981) that not only is **most** not first-order, it is not even definable in terms of its counterpart Q^{R}. Generalizing,

PROPOSITION 1.2.7. *The properly proportional quantifiers are not definable in terms of their type* $\langle 1\rangle$ *counterparts (even when we restrict ourselves to finite universes).*

This strengthens Proposition 1.2.6 (if Q^{rel} is not definable in $\mathrm{L}(Q)$ it is certainly not first-order definable), and shifts the focus from first-order definability to the semantic necessity of type $\langle 1{,}1\rangle$ quantification for natural language. (For techniques by means of which Propositions 1.2.6 and 1.2.7 can be proved in a rather straightforward manner, see Westerståhl, 1989, Section 1.7.)

More can be said. Note that in (63) all the type $\langle 1\rangle$ quantifiers are first-order definable, and either increasing or decreasing. Indeed we have the

THEOREM 1.2.8 (Westerståhl, 1991; Kolaitis and Väänänen, 1995). *Let Q be a monotonic type $\langle 1\rangle$ quantifier. Then, over finite universes, Q^{rel} is definable in* $\mathrm{L}(Q)$ *iff Q is first-order definable.*

It can be seen that Proposition 1.2.7 follows from Theorem 1.2.8 and Proposition 1.2.6. But the strongest possible generalization of Propositions 1.2.6 and 1.2.7 is due to Kolaitis and Väänänen (1995) and uses advanced finite combinatorics for its proof.[14] It shows that this kind of non-definability for properly proportional Det_1s really has nothing to do with their type $\langle 1\rangle$ counterparts; no type $\langle 1\rangle$ quantifiers at all will do! Thus in a very strong and precise sense, type $\langle 1, 1\rangle$ quantification is necessary for natural language.

THEOREM 1.2.9. *Let Q be a properly proportional* Det_1 *denotation. Then for no finite number of type $\langle 1\rangle$ quantifiers $Q_1, \ldots, Q_n$ is it the case that Q is definable in* $\mathrm{L}(Q_1, \ldots, Q_n)$*, even over finite universes.*

1.3. Type $\langle\langle 1, 1\rangle, 1\rangle$ quantification

This type of quantification has been less well studied than type $\langle 1, 1\rangle$, the main studies being (Keenan and Faltz, 1985; Beghelli, 1992, 1994). Here we simply show how the basic concepts for type $\langle 1, 1\rangle$ quantifiers extend to this type. (3), (50) and (53a–c) give some examples in this type. Others are given in (64) and (65); some sample denotations are given in (66).

(64) a. [*Almost as many* teachers *as* students] attended the meeting.

b. [*Five more* students *than* teachers] attended.

c. [*Some student's* hat *and* coat] were on the table.

d. [*More of John's* dog's *than* cats] were inoculated.

e. [*Exactly four* students *and two* teachers] objected to the proposal.

f. [*At least three times as many* students *as* teachers] forgot the meeting.

(65) fewer...than, not nearly as many...as, proportionately more...than, a greater percentage of...than, John's two...and three, exactly half the...and a third of the, fewer...than, not more than ten times as many...as, the ninety-two...and, ten per cent fewer...than.

(66) a. (**fewer** A **than** $B)(C) = 1$ iff $|A \cap C| < |B \cap C|$.

b. (**at least twice as many** A **as** $B)(C) = 1$ iff $|A \cap C| \geqslant 2 \cdot |B \cap C|$.

c. (**every** A **and** $B)(C) =$ **every**$(A)(C) \wedge$ **every**$(B)(C)$.

[14] Kolaitis and Väänänen (1995) prove the theorem for the quantifiers I and M, but Väänänen has pointed out (p.c.) that the methods generalize to other proportions, e.g., the quantifier $QAB \Leftrightarrow |A| = m \cdot |B|$. This gives the result for **more than** $1/mth$ **of**, and similarly for other properly proportional Det_1 denotations.

d. (**exactly two** A **and three** B)$(C) = 1$ iff $|A \cap C| = 2$ and $|B \cap C| = 3$.

Our type notation $\langle\langle 1,1\rangle,1\rangle$ taken from Beghelli (1992, 1994), contrasts with $\langle 1,\langle 1,1\rangle\rangle$ used for *more...than* in (67a) and $\langle\langle 1,1\rangle,\langle 1,1\rangle\rangle$ in (67b).

(67) a. More students came early than left late.

b. More students came early than teachers left late.

In (67a) there is just one noun property, **student**, and two predicate properties, **came early** and **left late**. No part of (67a) functions as a type $\langle 1\rangle$ expression. Similarly in (67b) there are two noun properties, **student** and **teacher**, and two predicate properties, **came early** and **left late**. Again however (67b) presents no expression of type $\langle 1\rangle$. We will not consider these types further here, but only note that their existence does indicate a direction in which our current analyses could be generalized (see Beghelli, 1994).

We write $\langle 1^2,1\rangle$ for $\langle\langle 1,1\rangle,1\rangle$ and in general given E, TYPE$\langle 1^k,1\rangle$ is the set of functions from k-tuples of subsets of E to type $\langle 1\rangle$ functions over E. Det$_k$s denote in TYPE$\langle 1^k,1\rangle$. The major notions used in discussing Det$_1$s extend straightforwardly to Det$_k$s. For example,

(68) For F of type $\langle 1^k,1\rangle$,

a. F is CONS iff $\forall A_1,\ldots,A_k,B,B' \subseteq E$, $(F(A_1,\ldots,A_k)(B) = F(A_1,\ldots,A_k)(B')$ if $A_i \cap B = A_i \cap B'$, all $1 \leqslant i \leqslant k)$.

b. F is CO-INT iff $\forall A_1,\ldots,A_k,B_1,\ldots,B_k,C,C' \subseteq E$, $(F(A_1,\ldots,A_k)(C) = F(B_1,\ldots,B_k)(C')$ if $A_i - C = B_i - C'$, all $1 \leqslant i \leqslant k)$.

c. A functional Q satisfies EXT iff $Q_E(A_1,\ldots,A_k)(B) = Q_{E'}(A_1,\ldots,A_k)(B)$, all E,E' with $A_i,B \subseteq E,E'$, all $1 \leqslant i \leqslant k$.

And we observe that the expressions of type $\langle 1^k,1\rangle$ considered in the literature satisfy Conservativity and Extension.[15] The most natural expressions in type $\langle 1^2,1\rangle$, the cardinal comparatives like *more... than* are intersective.

2. Polyadic quantification

So far we have discussed *monadic* quantification: the arguments of the quantifiers are *sets*, being interpretations of nouns and intransitive verbs. But NPs can also be objects (and indirect objects) of transitive (ditransitive) verbs, for example,

(69) *Most critics* reviewed *just four films*.

[15] Further, as Jaap van der Does has observed (p.c.), there are easy generalizations of Proposition 1.2.3 and Theorem 1.2.4 to type $\langle 1^k,1\rangle$ quantifiers. He also discusses Theorem 1.2.5 on sortal reducibility; here a proper generalization appears to be harder to find.

(70) *At least three girls* gave *more roses than lilies* to *John.*

Clearly, the interpretations of the (italicized) NPs and the verb in these sentences are somehow compositionally *combined* to form the interpretation of the whole sentence. Below we will discuss extensively this and other modes of combining quantifiers. But forgetting for the moment about these combinations, we *could* also give the interpretations as in the previous simpler examples, with *one* quantifier applied to many arguments. Some of these arguments are then relations, not sets. We call such quantifiers *polyadic*.

The quantifier in (69) is then applied to two noun arguments **critic** and **film**, and one verb argument **reviewed**. Its type would be $\langle\langle 1,1\rangle,2\rangle$, since it is (over E) a function taking two subsets of E to a function from binary relations on E to truth values, namely, (in one of the readings of (69)) the function F defined by

(71) $F(A,B)(R) = 1$ iff
$$|\{a \in A\colon\ |\{b \in B\colon\ Rab\}| = 4\}| > |\{a \in A\colon\ |\{b \in B\colon\ Rab\}| \neq 4\}|$$

for $A, B \subseteq E$ and $R \subseteq E^2$.

Likewise, consider (70). It has three NPs and a ditransitive verb. The first NP involves one noun, the second two, and the third none. To put this information in the type notation, we might write the type

(72) $\langle\langle 1, 1^2, -\rangle, 3\rangle$.

Semantically, a function of this type takes three subsets of E and one ternary relation on E to a truth value. Or, it takes one subset of E to a function from two subsets of E to a function from ternary relations on E to truth values. Indeed, there are many equivalent ways of describing this object. For polyadic quantifiers in general, the relational view used in logic is often the simplest: then the type is simply $\langle 1,1,1,3\rangle$, and the quantifier is (over E) a relation between three sets and a ternary relation. But then of course the information about the number of NPs and their respective nouns is lost.

The polyadic quantifier involved in (the most natural reading of) (70) is defined by

(73) $G(A,B,C)(R) = 1$ iff
$$|\{a \in A\colon\ |\{b \in B\colon\ Rabj\}| > |\{b \in C\colon\ Rabj\}|\}| \geqslant 3$$

for $A, B, C \subseteq E$ and $R \subseteq E^3$.

The functions F and G give correct truth conditions for (69) and (70). The issue then is to give an account of how these polyadic functions result from the monadic functions used in the NPs. For example, there are three monadic functions involved in (70) – the type $\langle 1,1\rangle$ **at least three**, the type $\langle 1^2,1\rangle$ **more...than**, and the type $\langle 1\rangle$ **John** – and somehow these three yield G in (73). Put slightly differently, the three type $\langle 1\rangle$ functions **at least three girls**, **more roses than lilies**, and **John**, yield the type $\langle 3\rangle$ function G(**girl**, **rose**, **lily**). In the next section we will see that this kind of combination of type $\langle 1\rangle$ functions can be described simply as *composition*, provided we allow a natural extension of the concept of a type $\langle 1\rangle$ function. This results in a general operation on arbitrary monadic quantifiers which we call *iteration*.

2.1. Iteration

2.1.1. Extending the domains of type ⟨1⟩ quantifiers

There are various accounts in the literature of the semantics of sentences like (69) with a transitive verb and quantified subject and object phrases, starting with Montague's (cf. Partee, this volume and Janssen, this volume) where transitive verbs are interpreted as higher type functions which take type ⟨1⟩ quantifiers as arguments. Here, on the other hand, we let transitive verbs simply denote binary relations between individuals, and "lift" type ⟨1⟩ quantifiers so that they can take such relations as arguments. The value should then be a unary relation. Similarly, to handle (70) we need to apply a type ⟨1⟩ function to a ternary relation yielding a binary one. Thus, type ⟨1⟩ quantifiers *reduce arity by* 1: they take an $(n+1)$-ary relation to an n-ary one. Informally for example, in *John reviewed just four films* we think of the NP *just four films* as semantically mapping the binary relation **reviewed** to the set of objects that stand in the **reviewed** relation to exactly four films; that is we interpret it as follows:

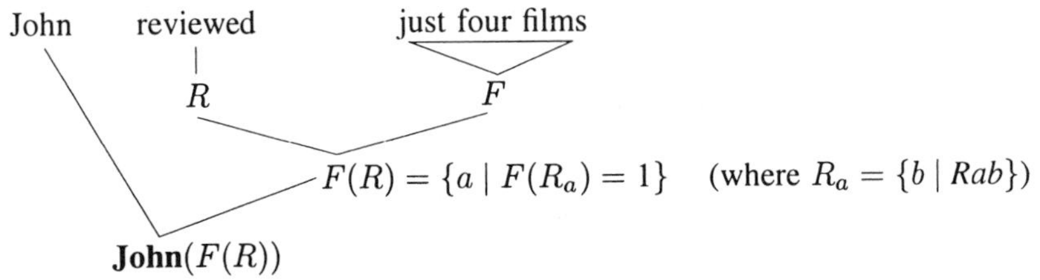

We call the class of all such functions AR$\langle -1\rangle$: a general definition follows.

Fix a universe E. In what follows we let $\mathbf{R}_n = P(E^n)$, the set of n-ary relations over E, $n > 0$, and $\mathbf{R}_0 = \mathbf{2} = \{0, 1\}$.

DEFINITION 2.1.1. For $k \geqslant 1$,

$$F \in \left[\bigcup_n \mathbf{R}_{n+k} \to \bigcup_n \mathbf{R}_n\right] \text{ is in AR}\langle -k\rangle$$

if

$$\forall R \in \mathbf{R}_{n+k}\ F(R) \in \mathbf{R}_n \quad (n \geqslant 0).$$

Also, let

$$\text{AR} = \bigcup_{k\geqslant 1} \text{AR}\langle -k\rangle.$$

We want to treat type ⟨1⟩ quantifiers as a particular kind of AR$\langle -1\rangle$ functions. Just which degree 1 arity reducers do we need as denotations of English expressions? These issues are pursued in (Ben-Shalom, forthcoming) and will just be touched upon enough here to help the reader realize that the obvious answers are not adequate. Now AR$\langle -1\rangle$ includes many functions whose values at relations of high arity is completely independent of their values at lower arities. It seems unlikely that we need all these functions as possible denotations for English NPs. But a lower bound on the degree 1 arity reducers needed are the "lifts" of maps from $\mathbf{R}_1 = \mathrm{P}(E)$ into $\mathbf{R}_0 = \mathbf{2}$, defined in (76) below.

The following notation will be used. If $R \in \mathbf{R}_n$, $0 \leqslant k < n$, and $a_1, \ldots, a_k \in E$,

(74) $$R_{a_1 \cdots a_k} = \{(a_{k+1}, \ldots, a_n) \in E^{n-k} \mid Ra_1 \cdots a_n\}.$$

Note that when $k = 0$, $R_{a_1 \cdots a_k} = R$. We also observe that

(75) $$(R_{a_1 \cdots a_k})_{b_1 \cdots b_m} = R_{a_1 \cdots a_k b_1 \cdots b_m} \quad (k + m < n).$$

Now suppose F is a type $\langle 1\rangle$ quantifier over E, i.e. a function from $\mathbf{R}_1$ to $\mathbf{R}_0$. We extend F to a function in AR$\langle -1\rangle$, also denoted F, by

(76) For $R \in \mathbf{R}_{n+1}$, $F(R) = \{(a_1, \ldots, a_n) \in E^n \mid F(R_{a_1 \cdots a_n}) = 1\}$.

The extended F is still called a type $\langle 1\rangle$ quantifier. So type $\langle 1\rangle$ quantifiers map unary relations to truth values as before, but they now also map $(n+1)$-ary relations to n-ary ones. But their values at the $(n+1)$-ary relations are determined in a particular way from their values on the unary relations. Thus we may define a type $\langle 1\rangle$ quantifier just by stating its values on the subsets of E as before.

Now we can correctly interpret (69), using the (extended) type $\langle 1\rangle$ quantifiers **most critics** and **(just) four films**, as follows:

(77) **most critics** (**four films** (**reviewed**))
$= $ **most critics** ($\{a \in E \mid$ **four films** (**reviewed**$_a) = 1\}$)
$= $ **most critics** ($\{a \in E \mid$ **four films** ($\{b \in E \mid$ **reviewed**$ab\}) = 1\}$)
$= F$(**critic**, **film**) (**reviewed**),

where F is from (71).

Similarly we calculate the interpretation of (70) (where G is from (73)):

(78) **at least three girls** (**more roses than lilies** (**John** (**gave**)))
$= $ **at least three girls** (**more roses than lilies** ($\{(c, b) \mid$ **John**(**gave**$_{cb}) = 1\}$))
$= $ **at least three girls** ($\{a \mid$
more roses than lilies ($\{(c, b) \mid$ **John** (**gave**$_{cb}) = 1\}_a) = 1\}$)
$= $ **at least three girls** ($\{a \mid$ **more roses than lilies** ($\{b \mid$ **John** (**gave**$_{ab}$)
$= 1\}) = 1\}$)
$= $ **at least three girls** ($\{a \mid$ **more roses than lilies** ($\{b \mid$ **gave**$abj\}) = 1\}$)
$= G$(**girl**, **rose**, **lily**)(**gave**).

Ben-Shalom (forthcoming) gives the following direct characterization of the extended type $\langle 1\rangle$ quantifiers:

FACT 2.1.1. *Let $F \in$ AR$\langle -1\rangle$. F is an extended type $\langle 1\rangle$ quantifier iff* $\forall n, m \geqslant 0$, $\forall R \in \mathbf{R}_{n+1}$ $\forall S \in \mathbf{R}_{m+1}$ $\forall a_1, \ldots, a_n, b_1, \ldots, b_m \in E$,

$$R_{a_1 \cdots a_n} = S_{b_1 \cdots b_m} \Rightarrow ((a_1, \ldots, a_n) \in F(R) \Leftrightarrow (b_1, \ldots, b_m) \in F(S)). \qquad (*)$$

When $m = 0$ (and so $S_{b_1 \cdots b_m} = S$), $(*)$ is to be understood as

$$R_{a_1 \cdots a_n} = S \Rightarrow ((a_1, \ldots, a_n) \in F(R) \Leftrightarrow F(S) = 1).$$ [16]

From this it follows that

$$\forall R \in \mathbf{R}_{n+1}\ \forall a_1, \ldots, a_n \in E,\ (a_1, \ldots, a_n) \in F(R) \Leftrightarrow F(R_{a_1 \cdots a_n}) = 1.$$

Hence, if F satisfies $(*)$ it is an extended type $\langle 1 \rangle$ quantifier. Conversely, one verifies that all extended type $\langle 1 \rangle$ quantifiers satisfy $(*)$.

The interest of Fact 2.1.1 stems from the fact that English presents expressions which semantically map $\mathbf{R}_2$ to $\mathbf{R}_1$ but fail to satisfy $(*)$. They do however satisfy natural generalizations of $(*)$. Good examples are referentially dependent expressions such as *himself, his doctor*, etc. We will return to these in Section 2.2.5.

2.1.2. Composition and iteration of quantifiers

It is clear already from (77) and (78) that (extended) type $\langle 1 \rangle$ functions can be composed. To make this precise we note first that the class AR of all arity reducers is *closed under composition* in the sense that if $F \in \mathrm{AR}\langle -k \rangle$ and $G \in \mathrm{AR}\langle -m \rangle$, then $F \circ G = FG \in \mathrm{AR}\langle -(k+m) \rangle$:[17] if $R \in \mathbf{R}_{n+k+m}$, then $G(R) \in \mathbf{R}_{n+k}$, so $FG(R) = F(G(R)) \in \mathbf{R}_n$. Note that composition is associative,

$$F(GH) = (FG)H$$

so we don't need parentheses. Thus, the notation

$$F_1 \cdots F_k$$

makes sense. In particular, we have

(79) If $F_1, \ldots, F_k \in \mathrm{AR}\langle -1 \rangle$, then $F_1 \cdots F_k \in \mathrm{AR}\langle -k \rangle$.

Next we observe that the extension of type $\langle 1 \rangle$ quantifiers to $\mathrm{AR}\langle -1 \rangle$ in the previous subsection works in exactly the same way for type $\langle k \rangle$ quantifiers, according to the following definition, which generalizes (76).

DEFINITION 2.1.2. Every type $\langle k \rangle$ quantifier $F \in [\mathbf{R}_k \to \mathbf{R}_0]$ (for $k \geqslant 1$) extends to a function in $\mathrm{AR}\langle -k \rangle$, also denoted F, by letting, for $R \in \mathbf{R}_{n+k}$,

$$F(R) = \{(a_1, \ldots, a_n) \in E^n \mid F(R_{a_1 \cdots a_n}) = 1\}.$$

There is a corresponding generalization of the characterization given in Fact 2.1.1. Now let F be a type $\langle k \rangle$ quantifier and G a type $\langle m \rangle$ quantifier. To compose F and G

[16] If we stipulate $(b_1, \ldots, b_m) = \varnothing$ when $m = 0$, and $1 = \{\varnothing\}$, this follows from $(*)$.

[17] Writing FG is a slight but convenient abuse of notation. Indeed, the domain of FG is not the domain of G but rather $\bigcup_n \mathbf{R}_{n+(k+m)}$, so we are really composing F with the *restriction* of G to $\bigcup_n \mathbf{R}_{n+(k+m)}$.

(in that order), extend the functions to $\mathrm{AR}\langle -k\rangle$ and $\mathrm{AR}\langle -m\rangle$, respectively, by Definition 2.1.2, and then compose as usual, which gives a function in $\mathrm{AR}\langle -(k+m)\rangle$. Restricted to $\mathbf{R}_{k+m}$, this is the type $\langle k+m\rangle$ quantifier given by

$$FG(R) = F(\{(a_1, \ldots, a_k) \in E^k \mid G(R_{a_1\cdots a_k}) = 1\}),$$

for $R \in \mathbf{R}_{k+m}$. If on the other hand we start with this type $\langle k+m\rangle$ quantifier – call it H, so

$$H(R) = F(\{(a_1, \ldots, a_k) \in E^k \mid G(R_{a_1\cdots a_k}) = 1\})$$

– and then extend H to $\mathrm{AR}\langle -(k+m)\rangle$ by Definition 2.1.2, one can verify that this is precisely the extension of F composed with the extension of G. This shows that our notion of composition is robust. Summarizing,

FACT 2.1.2. *If F is a type $\langle k\rangle$ quantifier and G a type $\langle m\rangle$ quantifier, the composition of F with G is the type $\langle k+m\rangle$ quantifier FG given by*

$$FG(R) = F(\{(a_1, \ldots, a_k) \in E^k \mid G(R_{a_1\cdots a_k}) = 1\}),$$

for $R \in \mathbf{R}_{k+m}$. Also, the extension of FG to AR $\langle -(k+m)\rangle$ *is the composition of the extension of F to* AR $\langle -k\rangle$ *with the extension of G to* AR $\langle -m\rangle$.

For example, in (77) we composed the type $\langle 1\rangle$ quantifiers **most critics** and **four films**, resulting in the type $\langle 2\rangle$ quantifier $F(\textbf{critic}, \textbf{film})(R) = \textbf{most critics}(\{a \in E \mid \textbf{four films}(R_a) = 1\})$.

Fact 2.1.2 takes care of composition of polyadic quantifiers without noun arguments. In fact we can easily extend this operation to (practically) all the polyadic quantifiers we consider in this chapter, i.e. polyadic quantifiers with k noun arguments ($k \geqslant 0$) and one verb argument. Just *fix the noun arguments* and apply Fact 2.1.2. We call this more general operation *iteration*. For example, (77) also indicates the iteration of the type $\langle 1,1\rangle$ quantifiers **most** and **four** to the type $\langle\langle 1,1\rangle, 2\rangle$ quantifier F.

It is convenient to use a superscript notation for quantifiers resulting from fixing the noun arguments. So we write $\textbf{most}^A$ for $\textbf{most}(A)$, $\textbf{four}^{\textbf{critic}}$ for $\textbf{four}(\textbf{critic})$ (or **four critics**), and $F^{\textbf{critic, film}}$ for $F(\textbf{critic}, \textbf{film})$. Thus, the iteration of **most** and **four** to F is given, for $A, B \subseteq E$ and $R \subseteq E^2$, by

(80) $$F(A,B)(R) = F^{A,B}(R) = \textbf{most}^A\textbf{four}^B(R),$$

where, for each A and B, the right hand side is well defined by Fact 2.1.2.

For a slightly more involved example, let G be of type $\langle 1,1\rangle$ and H of type $\langle\langle 1^2,-\rangle, 2\rangle$. Then the iteration of G and H, also written GH, is the type $\langle\langle 1, 1^2, -\rangle, 3\rangle$ quantifier given by

(81) $$GH(A,B,C)(R) = G^A H^{B,C}(R),$$

for all $A, B, C \subseteq E$ and all $R \in \mathbf{R}_3$. In general,

DEFINITION 2.1.3. If F has n noun arguments and one k-ary verb argument, and G has l noun arguments and one m-ary verb argument, the *iteration* FG or $F \circ G$ is the quantifier with $n + l$ noun arguments and one $(k + m)$-ary verb argument given by

$$FG(A_1, \ldots, A_n, B_1, \ldots, B_l)(R) = F^{A_1,\ldots,A_n} G^{B_1,\ldots,B_l}(R)$$
$$= F^{A_1,\ldots,A_n}(\{(a_1, \ldots, a_k) \in E^k \mid G^{B_1,\ldots,B_l}(R_{a_1 \cdots a_k}) = 1\})$$

for $A_1, \ldots, A_n, B_1, \ldots, B_l \subseteq E$ and $R \in \mathbf{R}_{k+m}$.

Observe that composition is a special case of iteration, and that iteration too is an associative operation. For example, the quantifier G in (73, 78) is

$$G = \textbf{at least three} \circ \textbf{more...than} \circ \textbf{John}.$$

What about the inverse scope reading of sentences such as (69), *Most critics reviewed four films*? Though there is a linguistic issue as to when such readings are possible and how one arrives at them, they are easily *represented* in the present framework: simply permute the order of iteration. However, this brings up a perhaps subtle point of our notation that we have so far been silent about. When we represent the interpretation of (69) using a polyadic quantifier $F^{\textbf{critic, film}}(\textbf{reviewed})$, or composing monadic quantifiers, $\textbf{most}^{\textbf{critic}}(\textbf{four}^{\textbf{film}}(\textbf{reviewed}))$, it is understood that **critic** is linked to the first argument of **reviewed** (the reviewer), and **film** to the second argument (the thing reviewed). But which argument is first and second is purely conventional; we have simply *stipulated* that the order in which the noun arguments are given corresponds to the order of the arguments of the relation (= the verb argument).

This means that the inverse scope reading of (69) must be rendered

(82) $\textbf{four}^{\textbf{film}}(\textbf{most}^{\textbf{critic}}(\textbf{reviewed}^{-1}))$

(where $R^{-1}ab$ iff Rba), so that again the first (leftmost) noun argument **film** is linked to the first argument of the relation $\textbf{reviewed}^{-1}$, i.e the thing reviewed, etc. So (82) says, as it should, that there were exactly four films such that the number of critics who reviewed them was greater than the number of critics who didn't.

In general, a permutation of the (n) monadic quantifiers in an iteration corresponds to a permutation of the (n) arguments of the relation argument, by our convention. Note that if we had used a more logical language (rather than an informal set theoretic one), the 'problem' would have disappeared, since the relevant links are carried by the bound variables instead:

(83) *most* x(*critic*(x), *four* y(*film*(y), *reviewed*(x, y))).

(84) *four* y(*film*(y), *most* x(*critic*(x), *reviewed*(x, y))).

2.1.3. Properties of iterations

There are a number of recent studies of iteration, notably Van Benthem (1989), Keenan (1992, 1993), Ben-Shalom (1994), Westerståhl (1994, 1996). We review here some of their results.

The properties ISOM and EXT extend directly to polyadic quantifiers of the types considered here. CONS also extends in a natural way. Instead of a general definition we give a characteristic example, again using the type $\langle\langle 1, 1^2, -\rangle, 3\rangle$. Here there are three NPs, linked to the corresponding arguments of the 3-place verb argument R. The first NP has one noun argument A, the second two, B and C, and the third none. So CONS should restrict the first argument of R to A, and the second to B and C in the sense of (68) in Section 1.3, i.e. to the *union* of B and C (note that $(B \cap D = B \cap D' \;\&\; C \cap D = C \cap D') \Leftrightarrow (B \cup C) \cap D = (B \cup C) \cap D')$. The third NP gives no restriction. Thus, we define

(85) F of type $\langle\langle 1, 1^2, -\rangle, 3\rangle$ is *conservative* iff for all $A, B, C \subseteq E$ and all $R \in \mathbf{R}_3$, $F^{A,B,C}(R) = F^{A,B,C}((A \times (B \cup C) \times E) \cap R)$. As usual, a global quantifier Q is conservative if each Q_E is conservative.

(Note that with this definition, a type $\langle k\rangle$ quantifier is vacuously conservative.)

The following shows that iteration is well behaved with respect to these basic properties of quantifiers.

FACT 2.1.3. *If the monadic* $F_1, \ldots, F_k$ *are* CONS (EXT, ISOM), *then so is the iteration* $F_1 \cdots F_k$.

Certain other properties of monadic quantifiers also extend to our polyadic case. We use again our standard example:

(86) Let F be of type $\langle\langle 1, 1^2, -\rangle, 3\rangle$:

a. F is *increasing* (*decreasing*) iff for all $A, B, C \subseteq E, F^{A,B,C}$ is increasing (decreasing).

b. F is *intersective* iff for all $A, B, C, A', B', C' \subseteq E$ and all $R, R' \in \mathbf{R}_3$, if $(A \times (B \cup C) \times E) \cap R = (A' \times (B' \cup C') \times E) \cap R'$, then $F^{A,B,C}(R) = F^{A',B',C'}(R')$.

FACT 2.1.4. *If* F, G *are increasing (decreasing, intersective), so is* FG.

Next, we see how iteration relates to *negation*. Post-complements of our polyadic quantifiers are obtained, as before, by taking the complement of the verb argument. Thus for F of type $\langle\langle 1, 1^2, -\rangle, 3\rangle$,

(87) $(F\neg)^{A,B,C}(R) = F^{A,B,C}(E^3 - R)$.

The *dual* of F is the complement of its post-complement: $F^{\mathrm{d}} = \neg(F\neg)$. One verifies that $F^{\mathrm{d}} = (\neg F)\neg$ and that all these negation operations are idempotent: $F = \neg\neg F = F\neg\neg = F^{\mathrm{dd}}$.

FACT 2.1.5. *For all quantifiers* F, G: (i) $FG = (F\neg)(\neg G)$; (ii) $\neg(FG) = (\neg F)G$; (iii) $(FG)\neg = F(G\neg)$; (iv) $(FG)^{\mathrm{d}} = F^{\mathrm{d}}G^{\mathrm{d}}$.

Call a type $\langle k \rangle$ quantifier G *positive* if $G(\varnothing) = 0$. For example, **some dog, most cats, John, Mary's three bikes, more students than teachers** are positive, but **no dean, at most three professors** are not. From Fact 2.1.5 (i) we see that if a type $\langle k \rangle$ quantifier H is an iteration FG, we may always assume that G is positive, a simple but useful fact.

The next few results concern the 'product behavior' of iterations, which is rather characteristic and will enable us to see how few properties of binary relations are expressible by type $\langle 1 \rangle$ quantifiers. Cartesian products, i.e. relations having the form $R_1 \times \cdots \times R_k$, rarely if at all occur as denotations of verbs, but they are useful technically. For example, as illustrated in (Keenan, 1992), and as explained by the Product Theorem below, the behavior of a quantifier on products can sometimes be used to prove that it is *not* an iteration.

First, we note that iterations 'decompose' into their components on products.

FACT 2.1.6. *If F is of type $\langle k \rangle$, G of type $\langle m \rangle$, G positive* (*recall that this is no restriction*), *and $R \in \mathbf{R}_k$, $S \in \mathbf{R}_m$, then*

$$FG(R \times S) = 1 \quad \textit{iff} \quad \big(F(R) = G(S) = 1\big) \vee \big(F(\varnothing) = 1 \ \&\ G(S) = 0\big).$$

The next theorem shows that not only do iterations behave in a very simple fashion on products, they are also *determined* by that behavior. If F and G are type $\langle k \rangle$ quantifiers, we let

$$F =_{\text{prod}} G$$

mean that for all $A_1, \ldots, A_k \subseteq E$, $F(A_1 \times \cdots \times A_k) = G(A_1 \times \cdots \times A_k)$.

THEOREM 2.1.7 (Product Theorem (Keenan, 1992)). *Let $F_1, \ldots, F_k, G_1, \ldots, G_k$ be of type $\langle 1 \rangle$. Then $F_1 \cdots F_k =_{\text{prod}} G_1 \cdots G_k$ implies $F_1 \cdots F_k = G_1 \cdots G_k$.*

Finally, we consider the following (related) issue: Given $F = F_1 \cdots F_k$, where the F_i are of type $\langle 1 \rangle$, to what extent are $F_1, \ldots, F_k$ determined by F? We know they cannot be uniquely determined, since by Fact 2.1.5 (i) inner and outer negations can be distributed in certain ways over $F_1, \ldots, F_k$ without changing F. Another obstacle is that one of the F_i may be trivial; this will in fact make F trivial, and so its components cannot be recovered. We repeat the notion of triviality used here (cf. Section 1.1, (7)):

(88) A quantifier G is *trivial* on E if G is constant, i.e. it either maps all (appropriate) arguments to 1 or all arguments to 0.

As it turns out, triviality and distribution of negations are the only obstacles. Call the pair of sequences $F_1, \ldots, F_k$ and $G_1, \ldots, G_k$ *balanced*, if for $1 \leqslant i \leqslant k$, $F_i(\varnothing) = G_i(\varnothing)$. This rules out 'facing negations' as in the following two logically equivalent sentences, where the subject NPs are post-complements and the object NPs are complements of each other:

Each student read at most six plays.

No student read more than six plays.

THEOREM 2.1.8 (Prefix Theorem (Keenan, 1993; Westerståhl, 1994)). *Suppose that $F_1, \ldots, F_k$ and $G_1, \ldots, G_k$ are balanced, that each F_i and G_i is non-trivial and of type $\langle 1 \rangle$, and that $F_1 \cdots F_k = G_1 \cdots G_k$. Then $F_i = G_i$, for $1 \leqslant i \leqslant k$.*

Using the Prefix Theorem one may show by direct calculation that very few type $\langle 2 \rangle$ functions (on a given finite universe) are iterations of type $\langle 1 \rangle$ quantifiers. Specifically over a universe E with cardinality n the number of type $\langle 2 \rangle$ functions is

$$2^{2^{n^2}}$$

and the total number of iterations of type $\langle 1 \rangle$ quantifiers is

(89) $$2^{2^{n+1}-1} - 2^{2^n+1} + 4.$$

For example in a model with 2 individuals there are $2^{16} = 65536$ type $\langle 2 \rangle$ functions only 100 of which are iterations of type $\langle 1 \rangle$ quantifiers. Thus very few of the properties of binary relations are expressible by iterations of the kind of functions denotable by subjects of intransitive verbs. We will see moreover that English presents many ways of expressing some of these other type $\langle 2 \rangle$ functions.

2.2. *Other polyadic quantifiers*

If iterations were the only polyadic quantifiers encountered in natural languages, we could safely say that natural language quantification is essentially monadic: iterations are built from monadic quantifiers, and moreover in a way which is easily described by a compositional semantics. Recent studies, however, have uncovered several types of polyadic quantification which cannot be treated as iterations. Some of these are seen to involve other modes of combining monadic quantifiers into polyadic ones. Others are, so far, merely examples with a certain structure.

In this situation, the issue of whether quantification in natural languages is *essentially* monadic becomes non-trivial. The question has two aspects. One is a matter of *grammar*: to what extent, if at all, does an adequate grammar for, say, English, need to take polyadic quantification into account? The other aspect is one of *expressive power*. Are there things which can naturally be *said* with polyadic quantifiers but which cannot be expressed at all with monadic ones?

In this section we briefly list a number of examples of polyadic quantifiers which have been claimed to occur in the interpretations of (mostly) English sentences, but which are not iterations. Most of the examples come from (Keenan, 1992), to which we refer for additional examples, elaborations and references. The issue of the expressive power of these quantifiers will be taken up in Section 2.3.2.

With each sample sentence below a polyadic quantifier will be associated. We use the convention that quantifier G_m corresponds to sentence no. (m). The sentences usually have two NPs and a transitive verb; Ben-Shalom (1994) extends several of these example types to sentences with ditransitive verbs and three NPs. As before, a universe E is assumed given unless otherwise stated, and $A, B, C, \ldots$ range over subsets of E, whereas $R, S, \ldots$ range over binary relations on E.

2.2.1. 'Different' and 'same'

An NP containing *different* or *same* is often dependent on another NP in the sentence in a way which cannot be described by iteration.

(90) Different students answered different questions (on the exam).

(91) Every boy in my class dates a different girl.

(92) Every student answered the same questions.

A reasonable interpretation of (90) uses the type $\langle\langle 1,1\rangle,2\rangle$ quantifier G_{90}:

$$G_{90}^{A,B}(R) = 1 \quad \text{iff} \quad \forall a,b \in A(a \neq b \Rightarrow B \cap R_a \neq B \cap R_b).$$

(There may also be a condition that $|A| > 1$; this is omitted in G_{90} and in similar cases to follow.) This could be varied: we might require that $\forall a,b \in A(a \neq b \Rightarrow B \cap R_a \cap R_b = \varnothing)$. Van Benthem (1989) suggests a weaker (non-first-order definable) reading:

$$H_{90}^{A,B}(R) = 1 \quad \text{iff} \quad R \text{ includes a 1–1 function from } A \text{ to } B.$$

But this is compatible with there being a set B of questions such that each student answered each question in B and no others (provided B is large enough), so that, in fact, all the students answered the same questions! A much stronger requirement (implying those suggested so far) would be that $R \cap (A \times B)$ *is* a 1–1 function from A to B.

For (91), it seems we can take $G_{91} = G_{90}$. For (92),

$$G_{92}^{A,B}(R) = 1 \quad \text{iff} \quad \forall a,b \in A(a \neq b \Rightarrow B \cap R_a = B \cap R_b).$$

There are variants of (91) and (92) with other subject NPs, e.g.,

(93) At least four boys in my class date the same girls

$G_{93}^{A,B}(R) = 1$ iff $\exists C \subseteq A[\textbf{at least four}^A(C) = 1$
$\& \forall a,b \in C(a \neq b \Rightarrow B \cap R_a = B \cap R_b)]$

which suggests the following general construction, where H is a type $\langle 1,1\rangle$ quantifier:

(94) $F^{A,B}(R) = 1$ iff $\exists C \subseteq A[H^A(C) = 1$
$\& \forall a,b \in C(a \neq b \Rightarrow B \cap R_a = B \cap R_b)]$.

Then, for example, G_{92} is obtained from (94) with $H =$ **every**.[18]

---

[18] (94) gives the simplest generalization. Jaap van der Does pointed out (p.c.) that a drawback is that it only works for increasing H (in the right argument), whereas the construction should work for decreasing or non-monotonic quantifiers (**four**, **at most four**). He proposes the two 'lifts'

(i) $L_1^{A,B}(R) = H^A\{a \in E \mid \exists b \in A(a \neq b \wedge B \cap R_a = B \cap R_b)\}$,

(ii) $L_2^{A,B}(R) = H^A\{a \in E \mid \forall b \in A(a \neq b \rightarrow B \cap R_a = B \cap R_b)\}$,

instead, and conjectures that the choice between these is related to the monotonicity behaviour of H. Note that with $H =$ **every**, L_2 correctly gives G_{92}, whereas with $H =$ **no** one needs to use L_1. In fact, the relation between these 'weak' and 'strong' readings and monotonicity seems interestingly similar to regularities observed for donkey sentences in (Kanazawa, 1994) and in (Van der Does, 1994b).

2.2.2. Exception anaphora

Consider

(95) John criticized Bill and noone else criticized anyone else.

(96) John didn't praise Mary but everyone else praised everyone else.

(97) Every man danced with every woman except Hans with Maria.

What (95) means is given simply by

$$G_{95}(R) = 1 \quad \text{iff} \quad R = \{(j, b)\}$$

and G_{96} is similar. This cannot be obtained as an iteration of the quantifiers **noone except John** and **noone except Bill** (cf. Section 2.3). We do have, however,

(98) $$G_{95}(R) = 1 \text{ iff } (\textbf{noone except John})(\textbf{some}(R)) = (\textbf{noone except Bill})(\textbf{some}(R^{-1})) = 1.$$

For (97) we get

$$G_{97}^{A,B}(R) = 1 \quad \text{iff}$$
$$(h, m) \in A \times B \;\&\; \forall (a, b) \in A \times B((a, b) \in R \Leftrightarrow (a, b) \neq (h, m)).$$

Moltmann (1996), from which (96) and (97) are taken, discusses which quantifiers allow this sort of exception constructions, and gives a semantics for *except*. Again, G_{97} is not an iteration, but as in (98) it can be written as a conjunction; one verifies that

(99) $$G_{97}^{\textbf{man},\textbf{woman}}(R) = 1 \text{ iff}$$
$$(\textbf{every man except Hans})(\textbf{every woman}(R))$$
$$= (\textbf{every woman except Maria})(\textbf{every man}(R^{-1}))$$
$$= 1.$$

2.2.3. Resumption

By the *resumption* of a monadic quantifier we mean, informally first, the polyadic quantifier which results from application of the original quantifier to k-tuples, usually pairs, instead of individuals. This of course presupposes the global notion of quantifier, where Q with *each* domain E associates a quantifier Q_E over E. Thus, Q also associates a quantifier to E^k.

Various instances of resumption in natural languages have been noted. For one example, resumption underlies the treatment of donkey sentences in 'classical' DRT; cf. for example Kanazawa (1994) and Van der Does (1994b). For another, Van Benthem (1983) and May (1985) consider Ss like

(100) No man loves no woman,

which seems to have one reading that there is no man-woman pair in the **love** relation. This is not an iteration, but the following resumption is:

(101) Every man loves every woman.

Such examples seem to be rare, cf. Liu (1991), but they suggest that the binary resumption of a type $\langle 1,1\rangle$ quantifier Q should be the quantifier Q' given by

$$Q'^{A,B}_E(R) = Q^{A\times B}_{E^2}(R)$$

(note that $A \times B$ and R are sub*sets* of E^2) and thus be of type $\langle\langle 1,1\rangle, 2\rangle$. However, other examples indicate that this is not general enough.

(102) Most twins never separate.

(103) Most lovers will eventually hate each other.

(104) Most neighbors are friends.

Here it is reasonable to construe the Ns as denoting sets of pairs, and *most* as quantifying over these pairs.[19] In (102), **separate** is not a property of individuals, and so cannot apply to individual twins. Of course, for pairs it can be defined in terms of a binary relation **separate from**, and (102) is equivalent to a sentence quantifying over individuals. But this does not work for (103) (which is due to Hans Kamp and appears in (Westerståhl, 1989)): a person may belong to several lover pairs, and there is no obvious way to reduce (103) to monadic quantification.

Thus, *most* in these examples denotes a type $\langle 2,2\rangle$ quantifier, namely, the old **most** applied to pairs. This motivates the following definition.

DEFINITION 2.2.1. If Q is of type $\langle 1,1\rangle$, the *k-ary resumption* of Q, $\mathrm{Res}^k(Q)$, is defined for $R, S \subseteq E^k$ by

$$\mathrm{Res}^k(Q)^R_E(S) = Q^R_{E^k}(S)$$

and similarly for other monadic types.

For example, for all $R, S \subseteq E^2$, $\mathrm{Res}^2(\mathbf{most})^R(S) = 1$ iff $|R\cap S| > |R-S|$. And (100), (101) can be construed with $\mathrm{Res}^2(\mathbf{no})$ and $\mathrm{Res}^2(\mathbf{every})$, respectively, and $R = A \times B$.

A final type of example comes from (Srivastav, 1990), according to whom the the following sentences in Hindi,

(105)	jis	laRkii-ne	dekhaa	jis	leRke-ko	usne	usko	cahaa
	WH	girl-erg	saw	WH	boy-acc	she	him	liked

(106)	jin	laRkiyone	jin	leRkoko	dekha,	unhone	unko	cahaa
	WH	girls-erg	WH	boys-acc	saw,	they	them	liked

[19] Actually, unordered pairs rather than ordered ones, but this just divides the quantities involved by 2. Quantification over unordered pairs in effect is quantification over sets or *collections*, or perhaps *groups*, a subject treated in detail in Lønning, this volume. Indeed, using collective quantification, slightly different analyses of (102)–(104) have been proposed.

have the truth conditions given by

$$G_{105}^{A,B}(R,S) = 1 \quad \text{iff} \quad |(A \times B) \cap R| = 1 \;\&\; (A \times B) \cap R \subseteq S,$$
$$G_{106}^{A,B}(R,S) = 1 \quad \text{iff} \quad (A \times B) \cap R \text{ is an injection } \&\; (A \times B) \cap R \subseteq S.$$

Thus, if $F^A(B,C) = 1 \Leftrightarrow |A \cap B| = 1 \;\&\; A \cap B \subseteq C$, then

$$G_{105}^{A,B}(R,S) = \mathrm{Res}^2(F)^{A \times B}(R,S),$$

and similarly for G_{106}.[20] Srivastav (1990) notes that this is similar to certain English constructions with interrogative quantifiers:

(107) Which dog chased which cat?

(108) Which dogs chased which cats?

An appropriate answer here presents a *pair* of a cat and a dog (or a set of such pairs), not an individual cat or dog.

2.2.4. Independent quantification: Branching and cumulation

An iteration FG introduces a scope dependency of G on F (for most F and G; cf. Zimmermann, 1993; Van Benthem, 1989). But there are also scope-independent ways to combine F and G. Hintikka (1973) proposed that *branching* quantification occurs in English, starting a debate which still goes on. Hintikka discussed the so-called Henkin quantifier, but since Barwise (1979) the issue has focused also on branching of monadic generalized quantifiers.[21] Here there are more easily convincing examples of branching in English, but on the other hand it is not quite clear what a general definition of branching looks like. See Sher (1990), Liu (1991), Spaan (1993) for recent discussion. Here we consider only the case which is most uncontroversial for English and where there is unanimity over the definition, namely, branching of *increasing* monadic quantifiers.

DEFINITION 2.2.2. Suppose $F_1, \ldots, F_k$ are increasing (in the verb argument) type $\langle 1, 1\rangle$ quantifiers. The *branching* of $F_1, \ldots, F_k$, $\mathrm{Br}(F_1, \ldots, F_k)$, is the type $\langle 1^k, k\rangle$ quantifier defined, for $A_1, \ldots, A_k \subseteq E$ and $R \subseteq E^k$, by

$$\mathrm{Br}(F_1, \ldots, F_k)^{A_1,\ldots,A_k}(R) = 1 \quad \text{iff}$$
$$\exists X_1 \subseteq A_1 \cdots \exists X_k \subseteq A_k [F_1^{A_1}(X_1) = \cdots = F_k^{A_k}(X_k) = 1$$
$$\& \; X_1 \times \cdots \times X_k \subseteq R].$$

Similarly for other monadic types.

[20] This monadic F is of type we have not considered in this paper: it involves two predicates so its type would be $\langle 1, \langle 1, 1\rangle\rangle$ – cf. Section 1.3, (67a,b).

[21] The Henkin quantifier can be defined as the branching, as in Definition 2.2.2 below, of the (increasing) type $\langle 2\rangle$ quantifier $\forall\exists$ (defined by $\forall\exists(R) = 1$ iff $\forall a \in E\ \exists b \in E\ Rab$) with itself, i.e. $\mathrm{Br}(\forall\exists, \forall\exists)$.

Here is one of Barwise's examples.

(109) Quite a few of the boys in my class and most of the girls in your class have all dated each other.

This is not equivalent to any of the iterations

(110) Quite a few of the boys in my class have dated most of the girls in your class,

(111) Most of the girls in your class have dated quite a few of the boys in my class,

nor to the conjunction of these two. Instead, it means that there is a set of boys in my class, containing quite a few of them, and a set of girls in your class, containing more than half of those girls, such that for *any* pair (a, b) of a boy a in the first set and a girl b in the second, a and b have dated each other. That is,

$$G_{109} = \mathrm{Br}(\textbf{quite a few},\ \textbf{most}).$$

The formal expression of the fact that branching is scope-independent is the following (for $k = 2$), which is immediate from the definition.

(112) $\mathrm{Br}(F_1, F_2)^{A_1,A_2}(R) = \mathrm{Br}(F_2, F_1)^{A_2,A_1}(R^{-1})$.

This is of course far from true (except in a few exceptional cases) if $\mathrm{Br}(F_1, F_2)$ is replaced by F_1F_2.

Another case of independent quantification is the cumulatives first discussed by Scha (1981). Consider

(113) Forty contributors wrote thirty-two papers for the Handbook.

Reasonably, this does not mean that each of the 40 contributors wrote 32 papers for the Handbook (the reading given by the iteration), but rather that each of them wrote some paper (perhaps more than one, perhaps jointly with other contributors) for the Handbook, and that each of the 32 papers were authored by some of these contributors. This leads to the following definition, which we again state for the 'cumulation' of k monadic quantifiers.

DEFINITION 2.2.3. Let $F_1, \ldots, F_k$ be type $\langle 1, 1\rangle$ quantifiers. If $A_1, \ldots, A_k \subseteq E$, $R \subseteq E^k$, and $1 \leqslant i \leqslant k$, let

$$R^i = \{a_i\colon\ \exists a_1 \in A_1 \cdots \exists a_{i-1} \in A_{i-1} \exists a_{i+1} \in A_{i+1} \cdots \exists a_k \in A_k R a_1 \cdots a_k\}.$$

The *cumulation* of $F_1, \ldots, F_k$, $\mathrm{Cum}(F_1, \ldots, F_k)$, is the type $\langle 1^k, k\rangle$ quantifier defined by

$$\mathrm{Cum}(F_1, \ldots, F_k)^{A_1,\ldots,A_k}(R) = 1 \quad \text{iff} \quad F_1^{A_1}(R^1) = \cdots = F_k^{A_k}(R^k) = 1.$$

Similarly for other monadic types.

For $k = 2$ we can express this by

(114) $\mathrm{Cum}(F_1, F_2)^{A_1,A_2}(R) = 1$ iff
$F_1^{A_1}(\mathbf{some}^{A_2}(R)) = F_2^{A_2}(\mathbf{some}^{A_1}(R^{-1})) = 1,$

and we see that $G_{113} = \mathrm{Cum}(\mathbf{forty}, \mathbf{thirtytwo})$. Again, independence holds:

(115) $\mathrm{Cum}(F_1, F_2)^{A_1,A_2}(R) = \mathrm{Cum}(F_2, F_1)^{A_2,A_1}(R^{-1}).$

2.2.5. Argument and predicate invariant functions
Consider

(116) John criticized himself.

(117) Mary praised every student but herself.

(118) Bill blamed his teacher.

The functions needed to interpret these, for example, $\mathbf{self}(R) = \{a \mid a \in R_a\}$ and $(\mathbf{every\ but\ self})^B(R) = \{a \in B \mid R_a \cap B = B - \{a\}\}$ are functions from $\mathbf{R}_2$ to $\mathbf{R}_1$, but they are not (extensions of) type $\langle 1 \rangle$ quantifiers. They do however satisfy a natural weakening of the characteristic invariance condition for type $\langle 1 \rangle$ quantifiers given in Fact 2.1.1:

(119) $F \in \mathrm{AR}\langle -1 \rangle$ is *predicate invariant* iff $\forall R, S \in \mathbf{R}_{n+1}\ \forall a_1, \ldots, a_n \in E$,
$R_{a_1 \cdots a_n} = S_{a_1 \cdots a_n} \Rightarrow ((a_1, \ldots, a_n) \in F(R) \Leftrightarrow (a_1, \ldots, a_n) \in F(S))$.[22]

Returning to the issue mentioned in Section 2.1.1 of which degree 1 arity reducers are needed, one shows that over a finite E all predicate invariant maps from $\mathbf{R}_2$ to $\mathbf{R}_1$ are denotable in English. Whether the class of functions needed for NP interpretations should be further enlarged is a matter of current investigation. See also Reinhart and Reuland (1993) for a recent discussion of reflexives in a linguistic setting.

An equally natural weakening of that condition in Fact 2.1.1 is *argument invariance*:

(120) $F \in \mathrm{AR}\langle -1 \rangle$ is *argument invariant* iff
$\forall R \in \mathbf{R}_{n+1}\ \forall a_1, \ldots, a_n, b_1, \ldots, b_n \in E$,
$R_{a_1 \cdots a_n} = R_{b_1 \cdots b_n} \Rightarrow ((a_1, \ldots, a_n) \in F(R) \Leftrightarrow (b_1, \ldots, b_n) \in F(R))$.

This condition holds of another interesting class of anaphors in English, exemplified by

(121) John read more books than Tom (did).

[22] The notions of predicate and argument invariance are from (Ben-Shalom, forthcoming). **self** and **every but self** clearly satisfy the predicate invariance condition for $n = 1$. For the general case we need to extend these functions to $\mathrm{AR}\langle -1 \rangle$. For example, for $R \in \mathbf{R}_{n+1}$, $\mathbf{self}(R) = \{(a_1, \ldots, a_n) \mid a_1 \in R_{a_1 \cdots a_n}\}$. This will handle sentences like *Mary protected Bill from herself* and *Mary protected herself from Bill* (but not *Mary protected Bill from himself*).

(122) Most students know more girls than every teacher (does).

To analyze these, let, for $B \subseteq E$ and $R \subseteq E^2$, $more^B(R)$ be the binary relation given by

(123) $(a,b) \in more^B(R)$ iff $|B \cap R_a| > |B \cap R_b|$,

so that $G^B_{121}(R) = 1$ iff $(j,t) \in more^B(R)$. Then, for any type $\langle 1 \rangle$ quantifier F, define the function

(124) $(\textbf{more } B \textbf{ than } F)(R) = \{a \mid F((more^B(R))_a) = 1\}$.

One verifies that this function is argument invariant (for each B and F),[23] and that

$$G^B_{121}(R) = \textbf{John}((\textbf{more } B \textbf{ than Tom})(R)).$$

$$G^{A,B,C}_{122}(R) = \textbf{most}^A((\textbf{more } B \textbf{ than every}^C)(R)).$$[24]

2.2.6. *Comparative dependent Det$_1$s*

(125) A certain number of professors interviewed a much larger number of scholarship applicants.

Clearly there are context-dependent factors here, but a first approximation could be

$$G^{A,B}_{125}(R) = 1 \quad \text{iff} \quad |\text{dom}(R \cap (A \times B)| < |\text{ran}(R \cap (A \times B)|.$$

Dependencies of this sort are frequent when the NPs occur in different Ss, as in *A few students came to the party early, but many more stayed late.*

2.2.7. *Reciprocals*

The semantics of reciprocals is a complex matter; cf. Langendoen (1978) for a classical discussion, and Dalrymple, Kanazawa, Mchombo and Peters (1994) for a recent systematic proposal. Here we only give a few examples to show that they often generate polyadic quantifiers. A simple kind of reciprocal English S can be given the form Det$_1$ N V RECIP, where Det$_1$ is often but not always a definite plural (Definition 1.2.12), V a transitive verb, and RECIP is *each other*. So Det$_1$ denotes a quantifier F, N a set A, and V a relation R. *each other* can be described as denoting a relation between a subset B of A and R, EO(B,R) (or a type $\langle 1,2 \rangle$ quantifier), although not always the same relation. Consider

(126) Most of the boys in your class like each other.

(127) The members of the board were chatting with each other.

---

[23] Again, a suitable extension to AR$\langle -1 \rangle$ is needed.

[24] The analysis also shows that, if we were willing to let not *read* but *read more books than* be the predicate in (121), and interpret it with (123), and similarly for (122), then these sentences would be iterations.

(128) My books are piled on top of each other.

(126) can be read as saying that there is a set B of boys in your class, containing more than half of those boys, such that any two distinct boys in B like each other. So

$$\mathrm{EO}(B,R) \quad \text{iff} \quad \forall a,b \in B\ (a \neq b \Rightarrow Rab).$$

But in (127) it doesn't seem necessary that each pair of board members were chatting; a number of 'chatting subsets' of the set of board members suffices, provided each subset has at least two members, their union is the the whole set of board members, and each member belongs to one of these subsets. More simply, this can be expressed as

$$\mathrm{EO}(B,R) \quad \text{iff} \quad \forall a \in B \exists b \in B\ (a \neq b\ \&\ Rab\ \&\ Rba).$$

The reciprocal relation in (128) is more complex; suffice it to note here that there can be several piles of books, and we need to say something like that the 'piled on top of' relation restricted to each pile is a linear order.

The simplest of these cases leads to the following definition.

DEFINITION 2.2.4. Let F be a type $\langle 1,1\rangle$ quantifier which is increasing in the verb argument. We define a type $\langle 1,k\rangle$ quantifier Ram^k by, for $A \subseteq E$ and $R \subseteq E^k$,

$$\mathrm{Ram}^k(F)^A(R) = 1 \quad \text{iff}$$
$$\exists X \subseteq A[F^A(X) = 1\ \&\ \forall a_1,\ldots,a_k \in X(a_1,\ldots,a_k \text{ distinct } \Rightarrow Ra_1\cdots a_k)].$$

Thus, $G_{126} = \mathrm{Ram}^2(\mathbf{most})$. The notation comes from the fact that these quantifiers are already familiar in mathematical logic under the name of 'Ramsey quantifiers'. (Then $A = E$ and F is some cardinality condition, say, $F^E(B) = 1$ iff B is infinite.)

2.3. *Polyadic lifts*

The list of examples in the previous section indicates that polyadic quantifiers in natural languages are often built in systematic ways from monadic ones. The canonical way is iteration, but we found several other *polyadic lifts*: resumption, branching, cumulation, etc. Another operation, implicit in some of the examples, yields what Van Benthem (1989) calls *unary complexes* as defined below (a slight generalization of Van Benthem's concept).

DEFINITION 2.3.1. Given type $\langle 1,1\rangle$ quantifiers $F_1,\ldots,F_n$, a *unary complex* (of degree k, $1 \leqslant k \leqslant n$) is a quantifier defined, for $A_1,\ldots,A_k \subseteq E$ and $R \subseteq E^k$, by a Boolean combination of sentences of the form

$$H_1 \cdots H_k^{A^*}(R^*) = 1,$$

where $H_1, \ldots, H_k$ are among $F_1, \ldots, F_n$, A^* is a permutation of the sequence $A_1, \ldots, A_k$, and R^* is the relation obtained from R by the corresponding permutation of its arguments (so that A_i is always linked to the ith argument of R; cf. the end of Section 2.1.2). If Φ is a fixed such Boolean combination, the resulting type $\langle 1^k, k\rangle$ quantifier is denoted $\mathrm{UC}^k_\Phi(F_1, \ldots, F_n)$.

So unary complexes are Boolean combinations of iterations, but we can iterate in any order and link any of the given quantifiers to any argument of the relation. Iterations themselves are unary complexes, but there were other examples in the previous section. The exception anaphora in Section 2.2.2 yielded polyadic quantifiers that were unary complexes: (98) says that G_{95} is a unary complex of **noone except John**, **noone except Bill**, and **some**, and (99) that G_{97} is a unary complex of **every except Hans**, **every except Maria**, and **every**. Furthermore, cumulations (Definition 2.2.3) are a special kind of unary complexes: $\mathrm{Cum}(F_1, \ldots, F_k)$ is a unary complex of $F_1, \ldots, F_k$, and **some**.

2.3.1. Properties of the lifts

Below we list six polyadic lifts, with a specification of to which type the arguments (of type $\langle 1,1\rangle$) are lifted. Interestingly, some of these are already familiar from other contexts; Ramsey quantifiers were mentioned above, and branching has also been studied in mathematical logic. Further, resumption has recently turned up in the attempts in computer science to find a logical characterization of the class of Polynomial Time problems (cf. Dawar, 1993).

lift	*from types*	*to type*
$\mathrm{It}(F_1, \ldots, F_k) = F_1 \cdots F_k$	k times $\langle 1,1\rangle$	$\langle 1^k, k\rangle$
$\mathrm{UC}^k_\Phi(F_1, \ldots, F_n)$	n times $\langle 1,1\rangle$	$\langle 1^k, k\rangle$
$\mathrm{Res}^k(F)$	$\langle 1,1\rangle$	$\langle k, k\rangle$
$\mathrm{Br}(F_1, \ldots, F_k)$	k times $\langle 1,1\rangle$	$\langle 1^k, k\rangle$
$\mathrm{Cum}(F_1, \ldots, F_k)$	k times $\langle 1,1\rangle$	$\langle 1^k, k\rangle$
$\mathrm{Ram}^k(F)$	$\langle 1,1\rangle$	$\langle 1, k\rangle$

These cover many of the examples in Section 2.2; in addition to what has already been stated, we note that the Ss with *different* and *same* in Section 2.2.1 may be interpreted using Ram^2 – cf. (94).[25] Furthermore, the operations are well behaved in the following sense:

FACT 2.3.1. *Each of the lifts above preserves CONS, EXT, and ISOM.*[26]

Polyadic quantifiers or polyadic lifts also have characteristic properties which do not have monadic counterparts. We mention four such properties below. For simplicity, we assume, first, that $k = 2$, second, that the noun arguments have been fixed so that we can think of our lifts as applying to (one or more) type $\langle 1\rangle$ quantifiers and resulting in a type

[25] The list is not intended to be complete. For example, another lift was defined in Section 2.2.5, (124).

[26] Straightforward, noting the following: (a) CONS for the type $\langle k, k\rangle$ case is defined by immediate analogy to the type $\langle 1,1\rangle$ case; (b) $\mathrm{Br}(F_1, \ldots, F_k)$ is always CONS, regardless of $F_1, \ldots, F_k$; (c) For Ram^k, define CONS by: for all A and R, $\mathrm{Ram}^k(F)^A(R) = \mathrm{Ram}^k(F)^A(A^k \cap R)$. Then Ram^k is always CONS.

Table 1

Lift	*Independent*	*Convertible*	*Decomposing*	*Oriented* (if ISOM)
It	No	No	Yes	Yes
UC^2_Φ	No	No	No	Yes
Res^2	–	Yes	No	Yes
Br	Yes	No	Yes	No
Cum	Yes	No	Yes	Yes
Ram^2	–	Yes	No	No

$\langle 2\rangle$ quantifier, and, third, that the universe is finite (this is not essential but simplifies the formulation of orientedness).

The first property, (order) *independence*, was already mentioned in Section 2.2.4, but is repeated here. It amounts to invariance under permutation of the quantifiers that are arguments to the lift. A related property is *convertibility*, which is invariance under permutation of the arguments of the relation the lifted quantifier applies to (for $k = 2$ this means replacing R by R^{-1}). This is a property that, like the following two, applies to any type $\langle 2\rangle$ quantifier, whereas independence is a property of the lift itself. Spaan (1993) introduced the notion of being *decomposing*, a kind of 'product behavior' we already found with iterations. Finally we have the property of being *oriented* from (Van Benthem, 1989) (Van Benthem calls this 'left & right oriented'), which is characteristic for unary complexes of ISOM quantifiers.

DEFINITION 2.3.2.

(i) An operation O that lifts two type $\langle 1\rangle$ quantifiers to a type $\langle 2\rangle$ quantifier is *independent* if, for all arguments F_1, F_2, $O(F_1, F_2) = O(F_2, F_1)$.

(ii) A type $\langle 2\rangle$ quantifier H is *convertible* if, for all $R \subseteq E^2$, $H(R) = H(R^{-1})$.

(iii) A type $\langle 2\rangle$ quantifier H is *decomposing* if, for all $A, B, A', B' \subseteq E$, $(H(A\times B) = H(A' \times B') = 1) \Rightarrow H(A \times B') = 1$.

(iv) A type $\langle 2\rangle$ quantifier H is *oriented* if, for all $R, S \subseteq E^2$, if $\forall a \in E(|R_a| = |S_a|$ and $|R_a^{-1}| = |S_a^{-1}|)$ (i.e. if each $a \in E$ has as many R-successors (-predecessors) as it has S-successors (-predecessors)), then $H(R) = H(S)$. If only $|R_a| = |S_a|$ ($|R_a^{-1}| = |S_a^{-1}|$) is required, H is called *right (left) oriented.*

Table 1 summarizes the distribution of these properties over our six polyadic lifts. To simplify matters slightly, we only consider the result of applying the lifts to *positive* quantifiers (cf. the comment after Fact 2.1.5 in Section 2.1.3). So a 'Yes' at a table entry means that the corresponding lift of *any* positive type $\langle 1\rangle$ quantifiers has the property in question, and 'No' that there are positive arguments for which the lift fails to have the property.

Westerståhl (1994, 1996) provide further information on the logical properties of these polyadic lifts. To understand polyadicity in natural languages better, one would like to know precisely what characterizes the various lifts, i.e. results of the type: F is a type

$\langle k \rangle$ branching iff F is **P**, where **P** is some informative structural property.[27] Scattered facts of this kind are known – for example, F is a resumption iff it is both left oriented and right oriented – but the general picture is not yet clear. In addition, it would be nice to have a systematic and reasonably complete description of the lifts, one which both covers most of the examples that occur, like those in Section 2.2, and is organized in a perspicuous way; perhaps by generating the set of lifts needed from a small number of fundamental operations.

2.3.2. Expressive power of the lifts

Questions of expressive power can be conveniently phrased as questions of *definability*: Is the polyadic Q definable from the monadic $Q_1, \ldots, Q_n$? Such a question is relative to a range of allowed definitions. This can be specified by a formal language in which the defining sentences must be phrased. Q can be definable from $Q_1, \ldots, Q_n$ relative to one language but undefinable in another. The choice reflects, and makes precise, the kind of expressive power one has in mind.

A positive answer to a definability question requires one to produce an adequate definition of Q in terms of $Q_1, \ldots, Q_n$. To prove *un*definability is harder. It is not enough that repeated attempts to find a definition of Q have failed. One must *prove* that none of the usually infinitely many sentences in the language can do the job. The more complex our formal language is, the harder it becomes to prove such things. On the other hand, if we succeed for a complex language, we get undefinability for free in all its less complex sublanguages.

Query: Is natural language quantification essentially monadic? This question, then, is only as precise as the definitional framework we have in mind. In addition, we must say in terms of which monadic quantifiers putative definitions should be phrased. For a polyadic lift $O(Q_1, \ldots, Q_n)$, there are basically two choices: either we look at definability in terms of $Q_1, \ldots, Q_n$, or we allow *any* (finite number of) monadic quantifiers in the definition. For undefinability, the second choice is preferred since it gives a stronger result, though one that is usually harder to prove.

Below we will consider three definitional frameworks, each one reasonable for independent reasons, and see that in each case the query receives a clear negative answer: monadic quantifiers do not suffice. Note that the notion of definability used here is *global*, i.e. independent of the domain. If Q can be defined from $Q_1, \ldots, Q_n$ over a domain E, then the *same* definition should work for other domains as well. This is in contrast with the local notion of *effability*, which was discussed in Section 1.1.

Is Q an iteration? Perhaps the simplest and most natural definability issue concerning a polyadic quantifier Q is whether or not it is an iteration. Let Q be of type $\langle 1^2, 2 \rangle$. Then the question is: Are there *any* type $\langle 1, 1 \rangle$ Q_1 and Q_2 such that $Q = Q_1 Q_2$? If F is of type $\langle 2 \rangle$ we ask instead for two type $\langle 1 \rangle$ quantifiers. Recall that iteration of type $\langle 1, 1 \rangle$ quantifiers was defined in terms of composition of type $\langle 1 \rangle$ quantifiers, by fixing the noun arguments (Definition 2.1.3). So if Q is of type $\langle 1^2, 2 \rangle$ and there are A, B such

[27] This approach is taken successfully to another kind of quantifier lifts, namely, lifts from distributive to plural quantification (or lifts from quantification over individuals to quantification over sets), in (Van der Does, 1992, 1994a). Perhaps the two kinds of lifts can fruitfully be viewed from a unified perspective.

that $Q^{A,B}$ is not an iteration, it follows that Q is not an iteration. Thus, for undefinability it suffices to consider quantifiers without noun arguments.

We remarked at the beginning of Section 2.2 that issues of expressive power really have two aspects: a grammatical one, and the logical one we are pursuing here. But the iteration question combines the two, since iterations straightforwardly allow for compositional semantic rules. This is why it is such a natural question from a linguistic point of view.

But the answer to this question is in most cases an emphatic NO. Using the machinery presented in Section 2.1.3, Keenan (1992) shows that

(129) Practically all of the examples given in Section 2.2 are *unreducible*,

which means precisely that they are *not* iterations. Ben-Shalom (1994) develops a general method for showing unreducibility, which applies to these examples and many more. And Westerståhl (1994) pinpoints (under certain conditions) exactly the very few cases when resumptions, branchings, and cumulations are iterations.

Still, even if iterations are ubiquitous in natural languages, there are other ways to combine quantifiers which have obvious natural language counterparts. Most conspicuous here are the Boolean combinations. Adding these, we arrive at the next version of our question.

Is Q a unary complex? For Q of type $\langle 1^2, 2\rangle$ this is the following question: Are there type $\langle 1,1\rangle$ quantifiers $Q_1, \ldots, Q_n$ and an appropriate Boolean combination Φ such that $Q = \mathrm{UC}^2_{\Phi}(Q_1, \ldots, Q_n)$? This has not been studied as much as the corresponding issue for iterations.[28] It can be shown with the methods mentioned above that many unary complexes are not iterations. For example, cumulations are unary complexes but (usually) not iterations. But are branchings and resumptions unary complexes?

Restricting attention to ISOM type $\langle 1,1\rangle$ quantifiers – and we saw in Section 1.2 that this is not an unreasonably severe restriction – we see from Table 1 that unary complexes are oriented. Not so branchings; in fact, branchings are very seldom oriented, and so it follows (cf. Van Benthem (1989)) that

(130) Branching quantifiers are only rarely unary complexes.

As to resumptions, $\mathrm{UC}^2_{\Phi}(Q_1, \ldots, Q_n)$ and $\mathrm{Res}^2(Q)$ are not even of the same type, so the issue seems trivial. However, it was noted in Section 2.2.3 that there is a type $\langle 1^2, 2\rangle$ quantifier, say Res*(Q), which is closely related to $\mathrm{Res}^2(Q)$ and in fact sometimes suffices for resumptive English Ss:

$$\mathrm{Res}^*(Q)^{A,B}(R) = \mathrm{Res}^2(Q)^{A\times B}(R).$$

From Table 1 we can see that orientation will not help distinguish resumptions (in the * sense) from unary complexes. Nevertheless, it follows from a result in (Westerståhl, 1994) that

(131) Res*(**most**) is not a unary complex of type $\langle 1,1\rangle$ ISOM quantifiers

and it is clear that the same holds for other properly proportional quantifiers, cf. Section 1.2.4.

[28] The characterization of unary complexes given in (Van Benthem, 1989) is a local one, and does not concern uniform definability.

Is Q definable in $L(Q_1, \ldots, Q_n)$? In Section 1.2.4 we mentioned the notion of a logic $L(Q_1, \ldots, Q_n)$ obtained by adding to first-order logic arbitrary monadic quantifiers $Q_1, \ldots, Q_n$. In fact, with a little more attention to the variable-binding mechanism, this works for polyadic quantifiers as well (cf., for example, Westerståhl, 1989). Now the previous two definability questions in fact concern a restricted class of sentences in such languages. For, an iteration of two type $\langle 1 \rangle$ quantifiers Q_1 and Q_2 is precisely the type $\langle 2 \rangle$ quantifier defined by the sentence

$$Q_1 x Q_2 y R x y$$

in the language of $L(Q_1, Q_2)$. Similarly, unary complexes correspond to a well-defined class of sentences. From a logical point of view, it is natural then to allow *any* sentence in $L(Q_1, \ldots, Q_n)$ as a definition. This is our final and most general notion of definability.

For any type τ, let the *arity* of τ (and of the quantifiers of that type) be the greatest natural number in τ. Let $\mathbf{Q}_n$ be the class of quantifiers of arity $\leqslant n$. So $\mathbf{Q}_1$ is the class of monadic quantifiers. Finally, let $L(\mathbf{Q}_n)$ be the logic obtained by adding all quantifiers in $\mathbf{Q}_n$ to first-order logic. If O is a polyadic lift, we have the following basic definability questions:

(I) Is $O(Q_1, \ldots, Q_n)$ definable in $L(Q_1, \ldots, Q_n)$?

(II) Is $O(Q_1, \ldots, Q_n)$ definable in $L(\mathbf{Q}_1)$? More generally, for a $(k+1)$-ary $O(Q_1, \ldots, Q_n)$, is it definable in $L(\mathbf{Q}_k)$?

It is clear that for $O = \text{It}, \text{UC}^k_\Phi, \text{Cum}$, the answer to (I) (hence to (II)) is YES. These operators are not essentially polyadic in the present sense. But for Br, Res^k, and Ram^k the answer is NO.

In Westerståhl (1989) it is proved with standard model theoretic methods that $\text{Br}(\mathbf{most}, \mathbf{most})$ and $\text{Res}^2(\mathbf{most})$ are not definable in $L(\mathbf{most})$, not even on finite domains. The result about $\text{Res}^2(\mathbf{most})$, and the previously mentioned result that $\text{Res}^*(\mathbf{most})$ is not a unary complex, have recently been strengthened:

THEOREM 2.3.2 (Luosto, 1994). *Under* ISOM, $\text{Res}^*(\mathbf{most})$ (*and hence* $\text{Res}^2(\mathbf{most})$) *is not definable in* $L(\mathbf{Q}_1)$, *even on finite domains.*

The proof uses advanced finite combinatorics. This is so far an isolated result. For branching and Ramsey quantifiers, more general answers to question (II) have been obtained, and we end by stating these. First we need to introduce the concept of a *bounded* increasing quantifier.

Restrict attention to ISOM quantifiers on finite domains. Then, on a domain E, an *increasing* type $\langle 1 \rangle$ quantifier Q is characterized by one single number, m_E = the smallest $n \leqslant |E|$ such that for some $A \subseteq E$ with $|A| = n$, $Q_E(A) = 1$ (cf. Proposition 1.2.1). So for all $A \subseteq E$, $Q_E(A) = 1$ iff $m_E \leqslant |A|$. m_E depends only on $|E|$, but can of course be different for different size domains. Then the global quantifier Q can be identified with the function f_Q from natural numbers to natural numbers such that $f_Q(|E|) = m_E$. For example, $f_\exists(m) = 1$, $f_\forall(m) = m$, and $f_{Q^R}(m) = m/2 + 1$.[29] But

[29] If m is even, otherwise $(m+1)/2$. The Rescher quantifier Q^R was defined in (29d), Section 1.2.1.

Q need not behave the same on different size domains; let for example H be given by $f_H(m) = 2$ if m is even, and $= 3$ if m is odd.

We say that Q is *unbounded*, if $\forall n \exists m (n \leqslant f_Q(m) \leqslant m - n)$; otherwise Q is *bounded*. For example, $\forall$, $\exists$, and H above are bounded, but Q^{R} is unbounded.

Now suppose Q is of type $\langle 1, 1\rangle$ and satisfies CONS and EXT. We saw in Fact 1.2.2 that such a Q is the relativization of a unique type $\langle 1\rangle$ quantifier Q_1. Moreover, Q is increasing (in its right argument) iff Q_1 is increasing. We extend the notion of boundedness to Q, saying that Q is *bounded* iff Q_1 is bounded. So **every** and **some** are bounded, but **most** is unbounded. More generally, the properly proportional (Section 1.2.4) quantifiers are increasing and unbounded.

THEOREM 2.3.3 (Hella, Väänänen and Westerståhl, 1994). *Restrict attention to* ISOM *quantifiers on finite domains. Suppose Q is an increasing type $\langle 1, 1\rangle$ quantifier satisfying* CONS *and* EXT. *Then*

(i) $\mathrm{Br}(Q, Q)$ *is definable in* $\mathrm{L}(Q)$
iff $\mathrm{Br}(Q, Q)$ *is definable in* $\mathrm{L}(\mathbf{Q}_1)$
iff Q *is bounded.*

(ii) $\mathrm{Ram}^{k+1}(Q)$ *is definable in* $\mathrm{L}(Q)$
iff $\mathrm{Ram}^{k+1}(Q)$ *is definable in* $\mathrm{L}(\mathbf{Q}_k)$
iff Q *is bounded.*

Thus, for a properly proportional quantifier Q, $\mathrm{Br}(Q, Q)$ and $\mathrm{Ram}^2(Q)$ are not definable in $\mathrm{L}(Q)$, in fact not even in $\mathrm{L}(\mathbf{Q}_1)$.

Conclusion. We have seen that in terms of three natural notions of expressive power, monadic quantifiers are *not* sufficient to express the quite common constructions exemplified in Section 2.2 involving polyadic quantifiers. The technical results are quite clear (and quite satisfactory) on this point. On the other hand, the considerable range of polyadic quantifiers we have discussed above are quite generally built in regular ways from monadic quantifiers. It may well be then that the range of polyadic quantifiers accepted by natural languages is constrained in just these ways.

GENERALIZATION 2.3.1. *Polyadic quantification in natural languages in general results from lifting monadic quantifiers.*

References

Abney, S. (1987), *The English noun phrase in its sentential aspect*, PhD Dissertation, distributed by MIT Working Papers in Linguistics, 20D-219 MIT, Cambridge, MA.

Altham and Tennant, N. (1975), *Sortal quantification*, Formal Semantics of Natural Language, E. Keenan, ed., Cambridge Univ. Press, Cambridge, MA.

Barwise, J. and Cooper, R. (1981), *Generalized quantifiers and natural language*, Ling. and Philos. **4**, 159–219.

Barwise, J. (1979), *On branching quantifiers in English*, J. Philos. Logic **8**, 47–80.

Beghelli, F. (1992), *Comparative quantifiers*, Proc. of the Eighth Amsterdam Colloquium, P. Dekker and M. Stokhof, eds, ILLC, University of Amsterdam.

Beghelli, F. (1994), *Structured quantifiers*, Dynamics, Polarity and Quantification, M. Kanazawa and C. Piñon, eds, CSLI Lecture Notes, Stanford, 119–145.

Ben-Shalom, D. *Semantic trees*, UCLA PhD Dissertation (in progress).

Ben-Shalom, D. (1993), *A tree characterization of generalized quantifier reducibility*, Dynamics, Polarity and Quantification, M. Kanazawa and C. Piñon, eds, CSLI Lecture Notes, Stanford, 147–171.

Boolos, G. (1981), *For every A there is a B*, Ling. Inq. **12**, 465–467.

Boolos, G. (1984), *Non-first orderizability again*, Ling. Inq. **15**, 343.

Dalrymple, M., Kanazawa, M., Mchombo, S. and Peters, S. (1994), *What do reciprocals mean?*, Proceedings of SALT IV, M. Harvey and L. Santelmann, eds, Rochester, NY (to appear).

Dawar, A. (1993), *Generalized quantifiers and logical reducibilities*, J. Logic Comput. (to appear).

Fauconnier, G. (1975), *Polarity and the scale principle*, Papers from the Eleventh Regional Meetings of the Chicago Linguistic Society, Univ. of Chicago.

Fauconnier, G. (1979), *Implication reversal in natural language*, Formal Semantics for Natural Language, F. Guenthner and S. Schmidt, eds, Reidel, Dordrecht.

Fenstad, J.-E. (1979), *Models for natural languages*, Essays on Mathematical and Philosophical Logic, J. Hintikka et al., eds, Reidel, Dordrecht, 315–340.

Gabbay, D. and Moravcsik, J. (1974), *Branching quantifiers and Montague-grammar*, Theor. Ling. **1**, 139–157.

Gärdenfors, P. (ed.) (1987), *Generalized Quantifiers. Linguistic and Logical Approaches*, Reidel, Dordrecht.

Heim, I. (1982), *The Semantics of definite and indefinite noun phrases*, PhD Thesis, University of Massachusetts.

Herburger, E. (1994), *Focus on noun phrases*, Proc. of WCCFL XII, P. Spaelti, D. Farkas and E. Duncan, eds, CSLI Lecture Notes, Stanford (to appear).

Higginbotham, J. and May, R. (1981), *Questions, quantifiers, and crossing*, Ling. Rev. **1**, 41–79.

Hintikka, J. (1973), *Quantifiers vs. quantification theory*, Dialectica **27**, 329–358. Reprinted: Ling. Inq. **5** (1974), 153–177.

Hoeksema, J. (1989), *The semantics of exception phrases*, Proc. of the Seventh Amsterdam Colloquium, ITLI, Amsterdam.

Hella, L., Väänänen, J. and Westerståhl, D. (1994), *Definability of polyadic lifts of generalized quantifiers*, to appear.

Johnsen, L. (1987), *There-sentences and generalized quantifiers*, Generalized Quantifiers. Linguistic and Logical Approaches, P. Gärdenfors, ed., Reidel, Dordrecht, 93–107.

Kamp, H. and Reyle, U. (1993), *From Discourse to Logic*, Kluwer, Dordrecht.

Kanazawa, M. (1994), *Dynamic generalized quantifiers and monotonicity*, Dynamics, Polarity and Quantification, M. Kanazawa and C. Piñon, eds, CSLI Lecture Notes, Stanford, 213–249.

Kanazawa, M. and Piñon, C. (eds) (1994), *Dynamics, Polarity and Quantification*, CSLI Lecture Notes, Stanford.

Keenan, E.L. (1981), *A Boolean approach to semantics*, Formal Methods in the Study of Language, J. Groenendijk et al., eds, Math. Centre, Amsterdam, 343–379.

Keenan, E.L. (1986), *Lexical freedom and large categories*, Studies in Discourse Representation Theory and the Theory of Generalized Quantifiers, J. Groenendijk et al., eds, GRASS 8, Foris, Dordrecht.

Keenan, E.L. (1992), *Beyond the Frege boundary*, Ling. and Philos. **15**, 199–221.

Keenan, E.L. (1993), *Natural language, sortal reducibility and generalized quantifiers*, J. Symb. Logic **58**, 314–325.

Keenan, E.L. and Faltz, L. (1985), *Boolean Semantics for Natural Language*, Reidel, Dordrecht.

Keenan, E.L. and Moss, L. (1985), *Generalized quantifiers and the expressive power of natural Language*, Generalized Quantifiers, J. van Benthem and A. ter Meulen, eds, Foris, Dordrecht, 73–124.

Keenan, E.L. and Stavi, J. (1986), *A semantic characterization of natural language determiners*, Ling. and Philos. **9**, 253–326.

Klima, E. (1964), *Negation in English*, The Structure of Language, J.A. Fodor and J.J. Katz, eds, Prentice-Hall, Englewood Cliffs, NJ.

Kolaitis, Ph. and Väänänen, J. (1995), *Generalized quantifiers and pebble games on finite structures*, Ann. Pure Appl. Logic **74**, 23–75.

Krynicki, M. and Mostowski, M. (1993), *Ambiguous quantifiers*, Manuscript, Dept. of Mathematics, University of Warsaw.

Ladusaw, W. (1979), *Polarity sensitivity as inherent scope relations*, PhD Dissertation, University of Texas at Austin.

Ladusaw, W. (1982), *Semantic constraints on the English partitive construction*, Proceedings of the First West Coast Conference on Formal Linguistics, D. Flickinger et al., eds, Stanford Linguistics Association, Stanford University.

Ladusaw, W. (1983), *Logical form and conditions on grammaticality*, Ling. and Philos. **6**, 389–422.

Langendoen, D.T. (1978), *The logic of reciprocity*, Ling. Inq. **9**, 177–197.

Lappin, S. (1988), *The semantics of 'many' as a weak determiner*, Linguistics **26**, 977–998.

Lewis, D. (1975), *Adverbs of quantification*, Formal Semantics of Natural Language, E. Keenan, ed., Cambridge Univ. Press, Cambridge, MA, 3–15.

Lindström, P. (1966), *First-order predicate logic with generalized quantifiers*, Theoria **35**, 186–195.

Liu, F. (1991), *Branching quantification and scope independence*, Generalized Quantifier Theory and Applications, J. van der Does and J. van Eick, eds, Institute of Logic, Language and Information, Amsterdam, 315–329.

Loebner, S. (1986), *Quantification as a major module of natural language semantics*, Studies in Discourse Representation Theory and the Theory of Generalized Quantifiers, J. Groenendijk et al., eds, GRASS 8, Foris, Dordrecht.

Luosto, K. (1994), *Hierarchies of monadic generalized quantifiers* (to appear).

May, R. (1985), *Interpreting logical form*, Ling. and Philos. **12**, 387–435.

Moltmann, F. (1996), *Resumptive quantification in exception sentences*, Quantifiers, Deduction, and Context, M. Kanazawa, C. Piñon and H. de Swart, eds, CSLI Lecture Notes, Stanford, 139–170.

Montague, R. (1969), *English as a formal language, in Montague, R.*, Formal Philosophy, R. Thomason, ed., Yale Univ. Press, New Haven, CT, 1974.

Mostowski, A. (1957), *On a generalization of quantifiers*, Fund. Math. **44**, 12–36.

Nam, S. (1994), *Another type of negative polarity item*, Dynamics, Polarity and Quantification, M. Kanazawa and C. Piñon, eds, CSLI Lecture Notes, Stanford, 3–15.

Reinhart, T. (1991), *Non-quantificational LF*, The Chomskyan Turn, A. Kasher, ed., Blackwell, Cambridge, MA.

Reinhart, T. and Reuland, E. (1993), *Reflexivity*, Ling. Inq. **24** (4), 657–720.

Reuland, E.J. and Ter Meulen, A. (1987), *The Representation of (In)definiteness*, MIT Press, Cambridge, MA.

Scha, R. (1981), *Distributive, collective and cumulative quantification*, Formal Methods in the Study of Language, J. Groenendijk et al., eds, Amsterdam, 483–512.

Sher, G. (1990), *Ways of branching quantifiers*, Ling. and Philos. **13**, 393–422.

Spaan, M. (1993), *Parallel quantification*, Report, Institute for Logic, Language and Information, LP-93-01, University of Amsterdam.

Srivastav, V. (1990), *Multiple relatives and polyadic quantification*, Proceedings of the Ninth West Coast Conference on Formal Linguistics, A.L. Halpern, ed., Stanford Linguistics Association.

Stowell, T. (1991), *Determiners in NP and DP*, Views on Phrase Structure, K. Leffel and D. Bouchard, eds, Kluwer, Dordrecht.

Ter Meulen, A. (1990), *English aspectual verbs as generalized quantifiers*, Proceedings of the Ninth West Coast Conference on Formal Linguistics, A.L. Halpern, ed., Stanford Linguistics Association, 347–360.

Van Benthem, J. (1983), *Five easy pieces*, Studies in Model Theoretic Semantics, A. ter Meulen, ed., Foris, Dordrecht, 1–17.

Van Benthem, J. (1984), *Questions about quantifiers*, J. Symb. Logic **49**, 443–466.

Van Benthem, J. (1986), *Essays in Logical Semantics*, Reidel, Dordrecht.

Van Benthem, J. (1989), *Polyadic quantifiers*, Ling. and Philos. **12**, 437–465.

Van Benthem, J. and Ter Meulen, A. (eds) (1985), *Generalized Quantifiers*, Foris, Dordrecht.

Van Benthem, J. and Westerståhl, D. (1994), *Directions in generalized quantifier theory*, ILLC Research Report LP-94–06, University of Amsterdam. (To appear in Studia Logica.)

Van der Does, J. (1992), *Applied quantifier logics*, Dissertation, University of Amsterdam.

Van der Does, J. (1994a), *On complex plural noun phrases*, Dynamics, Polarity and Quantification, M. Kanazawa and C. Piñon, eds, CSLI Lecture Notes, Stanford, 81–115.

Van der Does, J. (1994b), *Formalizing E-type anaphora*, Proceedings of the 9th Amsterdam Colloquium, P. Dekker and M. Stokhof, eds, ILLC, University of Amsterdam, 229–248.

Van der Does, J. and Van Eijck, J. (eds) (1991), *Generalized Quantifier Theory and Applications*, Institute of Logic, Language and Information, Amsterdam. Reprinted and extended as *Quantifiers, Logic and Language*, CSLI Lecture Notes, Stanford, 1996.

von Fintel, K. (1993), *Exceptive constructions*, Nat. Language Semantics **1**(2).
Westerståhl, D. (1985), *Logical constants in quantifier languages*, Ling. and Philos. **8**, 387–413.
Westerståhl, D. (1989), *Quantifiers in formal and natural languages*, Handbook of Philosophical Logic vol. IV, D. Gabbay and F. Guenthner, eds, Reidel, Dordrecht, 1–131.
Westerståhl, D. (1991), *Relativization of quantifiers in finite models*, Generalized Quantifier Theory and Applications, J. van der Does and J. van Eick, eds, Institute of Logic, Language and Information, Amsterdam, 187–205.
Westerståhl, D. (1994), *Iterated quantifiers*, Dynamics, Polarity and Quantification, M. Kanazawa and C. Piñon, eds, CSLI Lecture Notes, Stanford, 173–209.
Westerståhl, D. (1996), *Self-commuting quantifiers*, J. Symb. Logic **61**, 212–224.
Zimmermann, E. (1993), *Scopeless quantifiers and operators*, J. Philos. Logic **22**, 545–561.
Zwarts, F. (1981), *Negatief polaire uitdrukkingen I*, Glot **4**, 35–132.
Zwarts, F. (1990), *The syntax and semantics of negative polarity*, Views on the Syntax–Semantics Interface II, S. Busemann, ed., to appear.

CHAPTER 16

Temporality

Mark Steedman

Department of Computer and Information Science, University of Pennsylvania, Philadelphia, PA 19104-6389, USA
E-mail: steedman@cis.upenn.edu

Commentator: A. ter Meulen

Contents

HANDBOOK OF LOGIC AND LANGUAGE
Edited by J. van Benthem and A. ter Meulen

1. A case-study in knowledge representation

In thinking about the logical and computational semantics of temporal categories in natural languages, issues of temporal *ontology*, or metaphysics, must be distinguished from issues of temporal *relation*. Categories of the first kind determine the sorts of temporal entities that can be talked about – examples that are discussed below include various kinds of states and events. We shall be concerned with what Cresswell (1990), following Quine (1960), calls the "ontological commitment" of the semantics – that is, the variety of types that can be quantified over, or otherwise formally operated upon. Temporal relational categories determine the relations that may be predicated over such entities – examples to be discussed include temporal order, inclusion and overlap, together with various causal, teleological, and epistemic relations. Some of these relations depend for their identification upon inference from discourse structure and context. It follows that we must distinguish a third kind of phenomenon, that of temporal *reference*. These three distinct but interrelated kinds of phenomena are considered in turn in the three main sections of the paper that follow.

As in any epistemological domain, neither the ontology nor the relations should be confused with the corresponding descriptors that we use to define the physics and mechanics of the real world. The notion of time that is reflected in linguistic categories is only indirectly related to the common-sense physics of clock-time and the related Newtonian representation of it as a dimension comprising an infinite number of instants corresponding to the real numbers, still less to the more abstruse representations of time in modern physics.

This observation may not seem too surprising, since it is only a more extreme version of Russell and Wiener's observation of the need to distinguish between external and individual representations of time. However, the particular conceptualization of temporality that underlies language is by no means obvious. Like the concept of an entity or individual discussed elsewhere in this volume by Lønning, it is confounded with practical aspects of our being in the world of a kind that physics does not discuss. In particular, it is confounded with notions of teleology that are explicitly excluded from even the most informal and common-sense varieties of physics. On the assumption that linguistic categories are fairly directly related to underlying conceptual categories (for how else could children learn them), it is to the linguists that we must turn for insights into the precise nature of this ontology.

In this connection it may seem surprising that the present paper is confined to analyses of English temporal categories. However, it will soon be apparent that we cannot analyze the categories of English without appealing to notions of underlying meaning that are closely related to a level of knowledge about events that is independent of the idiosyncracies of any particular language. The paper returns briefly to the question of the universality of this semantics in the conclusion.

Because of this psychological grounding of the natural semantics of temporality, a certain caution is appropriate in assessing the relevance to linguistic inquiry of systems of logic and computational theory that trade under names like "Tense Logic". Such logics frequently come with very minimal ontologies, restricted to states and Newtonian instants, or to the simplest kind of interval, and similarly minimal, purely temporal, relations among them. Their authors are usually careful to stress that their systems do not reflect linguistic usage. Their *raison d'être* is analogous to that of Peano's axioms in arithmetic – that is, to characterize the metamathematical properties of physical time. Such concerns are not necessarily those of the working linguist or computational linguist, who is mainly interested in performing inference. One does not calculate via proofs in Peano arithmetic.

Many properties of natural language semantics, particularly those involving the notion of discourse *context*, are most directly modeled by dynamic processes. Since computer programs are a very direct expression of procedures, many of the logical frameworks that we shall find most useful draw upon ideas from computer science and studies in artificial intelligence as frequently as from the declarative logical tradition itself. In particular, many recent formalisms invoke the computer scientist's concept of a *side-effect* or update to a database, in order to talk about the changing context of reference, including the temporal variety. This move introduces notions of non-monotonicity, of a kind discussed by Thomason elsewhere in the volume. We shall combine this notion with the modal logicians' device of an *accessibility relation*, defining a structure on models, where models are databases, or *partial* models, in what has come to be called *dynamic logic*.

In developing an account of this very diverse and ramifying literature, it will sometimes be necessary to concentrate on one of these approaches, and there may be a danger of temporarily losing sight of the others. Nevertheless, they will meet up again as the chapter proceeds, for linguists, computer scientists and logicians are linked in this venture like mountaineers roped together during a climb. Sometimes the lead is taken by one, and sometimes another, but progress will in future, as in the past, only be made by the team as a whole.

2. Temporal ontology

2.1. Basic phenomena and descriptive frameworks

The first thing to observe about the temporal ontology implicit in natural languages is that it is not purely temporal. To take a simple example, the English perfect, when predicated of an event like *losing a watch*, says that some contextually retrievable *consequences* of the event in question hold at the time under discussion. (Such consequences have sometimes been described under the heading of "present relevance" of the perfect – cf. Inoue (1979). In restricting the perfect to this single meaning, English differs from most other European languages, in which the perfect also acts as a past tense.) Thus, conjoining such a perfect with a further clause denying those consequences is infelicitous:

(1) I have lost my watch (# but I have found it again).

In this respect the English perfect (unlike the perfect in many other languages) stands in contrast to the more purely temporal tenses, such as the past, which make no comparable claim about the consequences of the core event:

(2) Yesterday, I lost my watch (but I (have) found it again).

Further evidence for the claim that the perfect is concerned with causal effects or consequences, and that the availability of such "contingencies" depends upon world knowledge is provided by examples like the following. Example (3)a, below, is one in which no obvious consequences are forthcoming from the knowledge base. Example (3)b is one in which all the obvious consequences of the core event are consequences *for Einstein*, which our knowledge tells us cannot still hold. Both examples are therefore anomalous unless supported by rather unusual contexts.

(3) a. # I have breathed.

b. # Einstein has visited New York.

It is because categories like the perfect are not purely temporal that it is usual to distinguish them from the tenses proper as "aspects". Another aspect whose meaning is not purely temporal is the progressive or imperfective. The predication that it makes concerning the core event is a subtle one. While the progressive clearly states that *some* event is ongoing at the time under discussion, it is not necessarily the event that is actually mentioned. Thus in (4)a, below, there seems to be a factive entailment about an event of writing. But in (4)b, there is no such entailment concerning an event of writing a sonnet, for (4)b is true even if the author was interrupted before he could complete the action.

(4) a. Keats was writing $\models$ Keats wrote.

b. Keats was writing a sonnet $\not\models$ Keats wrote a sonnet.

Dowty (1979) named this rather surprising property of the progressive the "imperfective paradox", and we shall return to it below. It reflects the fact that events like *Keats writing*, unlike those like *Keats writing a sonnet*, are what White (1994) calls *downward entailing*, which we can define as follows:

(5) A proposition ϕ holding of an interval t is downward entailing if it entails that ϕ also holds of all subintervals of t down to some reasonable minimum size.

The imperfective paradox is the first sign that we must distinguish various types or sorts of core event in natural language temporal ontology.

The key insight into this system is usually attributed to Vendler (1967), though there are precedents in work by Jesperson, Kenny and many earlier authorities including Aristotle. Vendler's taxonomy was importantly refined by Verkuyl (1972, 1989), and Dowty (1982, 1986), and further extended by Hinrichs (1985, 1986), Bach (1986), Moens (1987), Smith (1991), Krifka (1989, 1992), Jackendoff (1991), and White (1994). The following brief summary draws heavily on their work.

Vendler's original observation was that a number of simple grammatical tests could be fairly unambiguously applied to distinguish a number of distinct aspectual categories. The term "aspectual" here refers to the intrinsic temporal profile of a proposition, and such categories are to be distinguished from the *sentential* aspects, the perfect and the progressive. For this reason they are often referred to under the German term *Aktionsarten*, or action-types. Vendler talked of his categorization as a categorization of *verbs*, but Verkuyl and Dowty argued that it was properly viewed as a classification of the *propositions conveyed by* verbs and their arguments and adjuncts – that is, of propositions concerning events and states.

We will consider just four tests used by Vendler and those who followed, although there are others. The first is compatibility with adverbials like *for fifteen minutes*. The second is compatibility with adverbials like *in fifteen minutes* and the related construction *It took (him) fifteen minutes to ...* . The third is the entailment arising from the progressive. The fourth is compatibility with the perfect.

Vendler identified a category of event such as *arriving*, *reaching the top* or *finishing a sonnet*, which he called *achievements*. These events are characterized by being instantaneous, and by resulting in a distinct change in the state of the world. They can be detected by the fact that they combine happily with *in*-adverbials, do not combine with *for*-adverbials, do not carry a factive entailment under the progressive, and combine happily with the perfect.

(6) a. Keats finished the sonnet in fifteen minutes.

b. # Keats finished the sonnet for fifteen minutes.

c. Keats is finishing the sonnet ($\not\models$ Keats will have finished the sonnet).

d. Keats has finished the sonnet.

Achievements are to be contrasted with a category of events like *walking*, *climbing* and *writing*, which Vendler called *activities*. Activities are extended in time, and do not seem to result in any very distinct change in the state of the world. They can be detected by the fact that they combine with *for*-adverbials but not with *in*-adverbials, that the progressive does carry a factive entailment, and that they are distinctly odd with the perfect.

(7) a. Keats wrote for fifteen minutes.

b. # Keats wrote in fifteen minutes.

c. Keats is writing ($\models$ Keats will have written).

d. # Keats has written.

Both of these categories are to be contrasted with a third category of event such as *writing a sonnet* or *flying to Paris*. Vendler called such events *accomplishments*. They superficially have the same test profile as achievements:

(8) a. Keats wrote *In Disgust of Vulgar Superstition* in fifteen minutes.

b. # Keats wrote the sonnet for fifteen minutes.

c. Keats is writing the sonnet ($\not\models$ Keats will have written the sonnet).

d. Keats has written the sonnet.

(See Garrod (1954, p. 532) for some historical background to this example.) However, accomplishments differ from achievements in being extended in time, like activities. As a consequence, they differ in entailments when combined with *in*-adverbials and progressives. In (8)a and c it is *part of* the event (namely the writing) that respectively takes fifteen minutes and is reported as in progress. It is precisely *not* part of finishing itself that takes fifteen minutes in (6)a, or is in progress in (6)c. It is some other event. In fact it is presumably an event of writing, since the overall entailments of the two pairs of sentences are very similar. Because of this relation, both Verkuyl and Dowty proposed that accomplishments should be regarded as composites of an activity and a culminating achievement.

Vendler also identified a class of *states*. States are characterized syntactically by being almost the only propositions that can be expressed in English by simple present tense. (The exceptions are performatives like the following, which in all other respects are archetypal achievements):

(9) I name this ship the *Nice Work If You Can Get It.*

States differ from events in that they lack explicit bounds. Some lexical concepts are states, notably those expressibly using the copula, as in (10)a, below. The progressives and perfects considered above, as well as certain predications of habitual action, are also archetypal states, as in (10)b, c, and d:

(10) a. Keats is a genius.

b. Keats is looking into Chapman's Homer.

c. I have lost my watch.

d. I work for the union.

It should be stressed that any claim that an event like *Keats writing* is intrinsically an activity is no more than a convenient shorthand. It is true that *in most contexts* the following sentence is odd.

(11) Keats wrote in fifteen minutes.

However, as Dowty pointed out for a related example, in a discourse context in which the speaker and the hearer both believe that Keats is in the habit of writing a sonnet to time every Sunday, and the speaker knows that on the particular Sunday under discussion, say 23rd December 1816, Keats took fifteen minutes at it, then the utterance is felicitous. Such examples show that aspectual categories like activity and accomplishment are *ways of viewing* a happening, rather than intrinsic properties of verbs and the associated propositions, or of objective reality and the external world.

The fact that the same form of words can convey more than one aspectual category, provided contextual knowledge supports this view of the passage of events, is the first clue to an explanation for the imperfective paradox. The semantics of the progressive must demand an activity as the only event type that it can map onto the corresponding progressive states. When combined with an accomplishment, as in example (8)c, it must first *turn it into* an activity, by decomposing the accomplishment into its components, and discarding the culminating achievement. When combined with an achievement, as in (6)c, it must first turn it into an accomplishment, identifying an associated activity from the knowledge base and the context. Then the original achievement can be discarded. Such an account would explain the fact that in normal contexts examples (6)c and (8)c hold of identical situations.

Events can turn into activities by turning into an *iteration* of the core event.

(12) Chapman sliced the onion (into rings).

Such iterations may themselves iterate (as in *slicing onions*), and in the progressive may be predicated of a time at which one is not performing the core event at all:

(13) I am slicing the onions.

Such iterated activities are investigated by Karlin (1988). A similar transition to a habitual state can occur if, to extend an earlier example, Keats not only writes sonnets to time, but also regularly manages it in fifteen minutes or less. Under these circumstances he can say the following on an occasion on which he is not writing at all:

(14) I am writing a sonnet in fifteen minutes (these days).

There is more to NPs like *the onions* and *a sonnet* in the above examples than may meet the eye. Verkuyl and Dowty also pointed out that some similar protean shifts in aspectual category of the event conveyed by a sentence depended upon the semantic type of the nominal categories involved as arguments of the verb. Thus *Chapman arriving* is an archetypal achievement, which happens to be resistant to combination with a *for*-adverbial, because the state that it gives rise to seems to preclude iteration, as shown by (15)a, below. But *visitors arriving* is necessarily an iteration, as in (15)b.

(15) a. # Chapman arrived all night.
b. Visitors arrived all night.

Such aspectual changes, which include several further varieties that cannot be considered here, may compose indefinitely, especially under the influence of stacked adverbial modifiers, as in:

(16) It took me two years to play the "Minute Waltz" in less than sixty seconds for one hour without stopping.

The complexities of this kind of aspectual type-shift or "coercion" are very thoroughly explored by the authors already cited. Accordingly we will pass over further details here, merely offering the chart shown in Figure 1, by way of an informal summary. The chart divides the aspectual categories into states and events, the latter being subdivided into four sorts, based on two features representing the semantic properties of *telicity*, or association with a particular change of state, and *decomposability*. The latter property is often referred to as "durativity", but it is really to do with decomposition into sub-events, rather than temporal extent. To Vendler's three event categories we follow Miller and Johnson-Laird (1976) in adding a fourth, atomic atelic, category, here called a *point*. (They are what Smith (1991) calls "semelfactives".) These authors suggest that events like *stumbling* and *breathing a sigh of relief* may be basic concepts of this type, but the real significance of the category is to act as a way-station, where the internal structure of an event is "frozen" on the way to being iterated or turned into a consequent state by the perfect. Arrows indicate permissible type-transitions, with annotations indicating the nature of the aspectual change. Some of these, like iteration, are "free", provided that the knowledge base supports the change. Others, like the transition to a consequent state (*constate*) or a progressive state (*progstate*), can only occur under the influence of a particular lexical item or construction, such as the perfect or the progressive. Such

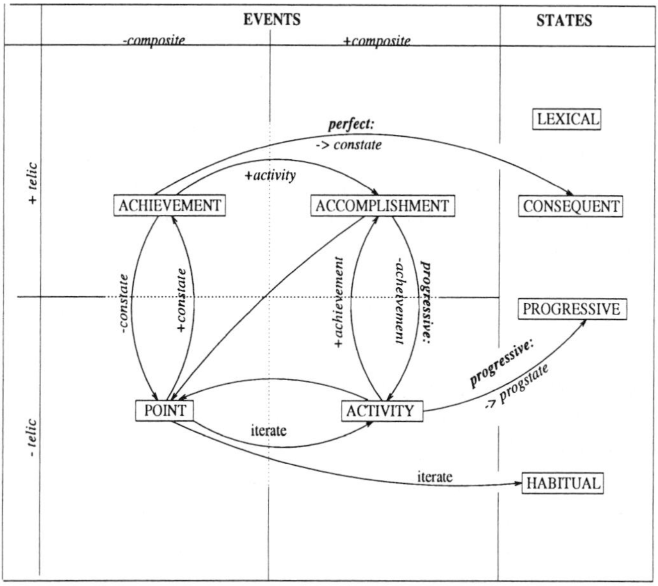

Fig. 1. A scheme of aspectual coercion (adapted from Moens and Steedman, 1988).

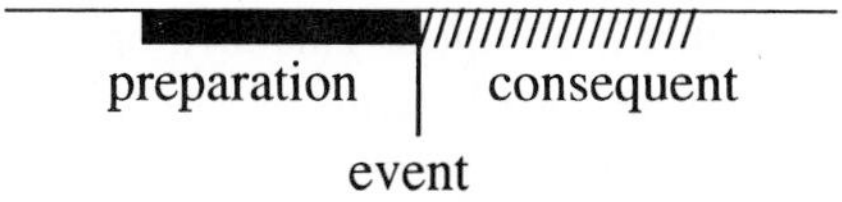

Fig. 2. The event nucleus (adapted from Moens and Steedman, 1988).

restrictions are indicated by bold-face annotations. A more extensive system of coercions and lexically-based restrictions has been developed by Pustejovsky (1991).

Whether free or lexically determined, these type-changes appear to reflect a knowledge representation in which events of all kinds are associated with a *preparation*, or activity that brings the event about, and a *consequent*, or ensuing state, in a tripartite data-structure proposed by Moens (1987) that can be viewed as in Figure 2. This structure, or "nucleus" can be regarded as composed of the types described in Figure 1. Thus the preparation is an activity, the consequent is the same kind of state that the perfect gives rise to, while the event itself is an achievement. (The nucleus itself is therefore closely related to the category of *accomplishments*.) Each of these components may itself be compound. Thus the preparation may be an iteration of some kind, the consequent state may identify a chain of consequences, and the core event may itself be a complex event, such as an accomplishment. The tripartite nucleus has been adopted and used extensively in the DRT theory of *Aktionsarten* of Kamp and Reyle (1993, pp. 557–570 *et seq.*) – cf. the chapter by Kamp in the present volume, Blackburn, Gardent and De Rijke (1993), and Gagnon and Lapalme (1995).

2.2. *Logical and computational approaches*

So much for the natural history of temporal ontology: how do we formalize this quite complex ontology? Simplifying somewhat, two basic approaches can be distinguished in this voluminous literature.

The first approach is to attempt to define the neo-Vendlerian ontology via quantification over more or less classical Priorian instants, or their dual, intervals. Bennett and Partee (1972), Taylor (1977), Cresswell (1974), Dowty (1979), Heinämäki (1974), Bach (1980), Galton (1984), and the computational work of McDermott (1982), Allen (1984), Crouch and Pulman (1993), and McCarty (1994) are of this kind.

This approach was extremely important in opening up the territory to include temporally extended events, which had largely been ignored in the situation calculus and modal-logic based approaches (see the discussion below). However, the recursive structure of events that follows from the ontology illustrated in Figure 1, and in particular the problems of granularity and non-continuity in iterated events, mean that some of the definitions of *for*-adverbials and related categories in Dowty's treatment can be criticized, as he himself has pointed out (Dowty, 1979, preface to second edition).

The second approach is to take certain types of events themselves as primitive, without any appeal to notions like truth of a predicate over an interval or set of instants. Such events involve a temporal extension, which for connected continuous events is an interval (or equivalently a pair of points, but modifiers like "slowly" are predications of the event rather than the interval that it occupies. This then opens up the further possibility of defining relations between event-sorts in terms of various lattices and sort hierarchies. The algebraic event-based approach was pioneered by Kamp (1979, 1983), and characterizes the work of Bach (1986), Link (1987), Hinrichs (1985, 1986), Ter Meulen (1984, 1986), Dowty (1986), Krifka (1990), Eberle (1990) and White (1993, 1994), and builds upon Carlson's (1977), Link's (1983) and Landman's (1991) accounts of the ontology of entities. The work of Davidson, as developed in Parsons (1990), and of Jackendoff (1991) as formalized by Zwarts and Verkuyl (1994), can also be seen as belonging to this school.

The latter approach can be seen as a logical continuation of the earlier work, for Dowty (1979) had observed the parallel between the telic/atelic distinction in the event domain, and the count/mass distinction in the entity domain. Not only is the downward-entailing property characteristic of both activities and mass terms: the involvement of mass or count terms as arguments can also determine the event type of a proposition, as in the following minimal pair.

(17) a. Chapman drank beer (for an hour/#in an hour).

b. Chapman drank two pints of beer (#for an hour/in an hour).

The technicalities involved in these different accounts are considerable, and somewhat orthogonal to the main concerns of the chapter. We will pass over them here, referring the interested reader to the chapter in the present volume by Pelletier for technical background, and to White (1994, Chapter 2) for a recent comprehensive review and one of the few extensive computational implementations of a system of this kind.

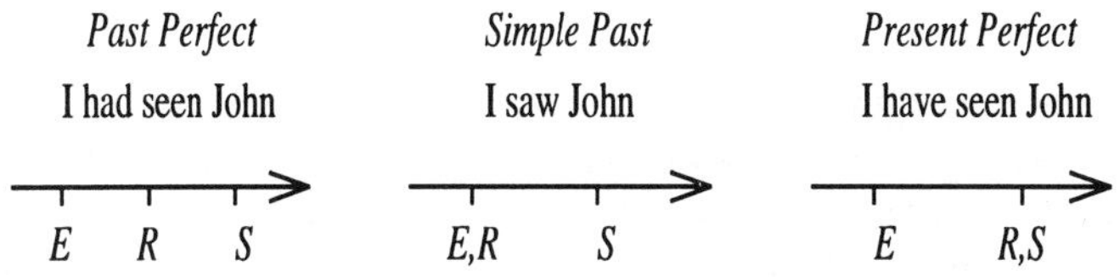

Fig. 3. Past vs. Perfect (from Reichenbach, 1947).

3. Temporal relations

3.1. Basic phenomena and descriptive frameworks

Having established an ontology, or taxonomy of temporal types, we turn to the relational apparatus. The linguistic system that conveys temporal relations between individuals of these different sorts comprises in English the subsystems of tense, (progressive and perfect) aspect (which we have so far only treated in terms of their effect upon ontological type), and modality.

3.1.1. Tense

The most fundamental of these systems is tense. In the case of tense, as in the case of propositional aspect or *Aktionsart*, there is one early modern piece of insightful descriptive work which most theories build upon, and which those who ignore seem doomed to reconstruct. This work is contained in two short and highly elliptical sections in Reichenbach's *Elements of Symbolic Logic* (1947, Chapter VII, Sections 48 and 51). (Again there are direct precedents in work by Jespersen and Cassirer.)

Reichenbach can be read as making two points about temporal expressions. The first is that there is a referential or extensional relation between propositions and facts or events, expressible by the inclusion of events or times as values of bound variables. This observation is the direct antecedent of Davidson's theory (cf. Davidson, 1967, pp. 115–116) and much subsequent work in formal semantics (cf. Parsons, 1990, p. 5), and is less directly related to the situation calculus of McCarthy and Hayes (1969, cf. pp. 498–500) and much subsequent work in artificial intelligence and computer science, discussed below.

Reichenbach's second point is more specifically linguistic. He argued that the tense system could be understood as a predication not over two times, "now" and "then", but rather over *three* underlying times. These times he called S (speech point), R (reference point), and E (event point). E can be thought of as the temporal extension of the proposition itself – essentially the Davidsonian **e**, or its modern equivalent, generalized to cope with the kind of ontological questions that concerned us in the last section, as for example in work discussed earlier by Parsons (1990) and Schein (1993). S can, as its name suggests, be thought of as the speaker's time of utterance (although we shall see that it must be generalized to cover embedded times of utterance and narrative point-of-view). Reichenbach's real innovation was the reference point, which can be identified with the notion "the time (or situation, or context) that we are talking about". It is easiest to convey the idea by example. Reichenbach offers the diagrams in Figure 3, in which the arrow indicates the flow of time, to show the distinctions between the past perfect, the simple past (or preterit) and the present perfect (all of which he includes under the heading of "tenses of verbs"). The important insight here is that the simple past is used to make a statement about a past time, whereas the perfect is used to make a statement about the present, as was noted earlier in connection with the "present relevance" property of examples like (1).

As Isard and Longuet-Higgins (1973) have pointed out, this claim is consistent with the observation that past tense, unlike the perfect, demands that the past reference point be explicitly established, either by a modifier, such as a *when* clause, or by the preceding discourse. Thus (18)a, below, is inappropriate as the first utterance of a discourse, except to the extent that the reader *accommodates* a temporal referent, in Lewis' (1979) sense of that term – that is, *introduces* an appropriate individual in the database, as one often must at the beginning of a modern novel. But (18)b is appropriate, on the assumption that the hearer can identify the time in the *when* clause:

(18) a. # Chapman breathed a sigh of relief.
b. When Nixon was elected, Chapman breathed a sigh of relief.

(In many North American dialects of English, the past tense does double duty for the perfect. I am assuming that this reading is excluded in this case by the most readily accessible aspectual category of *breathing a sigh of relief*.)

The fact that the discourse can establish the "anchor" for the reference point has led a number of authors, including McCawley (1971), Partee (1973, 1984), Isard (1974), Bäuerle (1979), Hinrichs (1985), Webber (1988), Song and Cohen (1988), Abusch (in press), and others to identify tense, and by implication R, as "pronominal" or otherwise anaphoric in character.

We should distinguish this referent-setting function of such adverbials from the aspect-setting function that we encountered in Section 2, concerning *Aktionsarten*. The adverbials like *in fifteen minutes* and *for fifteen minutes* were there predicated over the *event* point E. In the cases to hand, they are predicated over R. Many of the adverbials that relate two propositions temporally, particularly *when* clauses, do so by identifying or predicating a relation over the reference points of the two clauses, via what Reichenbach called the "positional use of the reference point". The following are all cases of this kind.

(19) a. In ten minutes, I looked at my watch.
b. When Chapman arrived, the band was playing *Nice Work If You Can Get It*.
c. After Einstein arrived in Princeton, he may have visited Philadelphia.

We return to the anaphoric role of tense in a later section.

With the benefit of the discussion in the earlier sections, we can go a little further than Reichenbach, and say that the predication which the perfect makes about the reference point, present or past, is that the consequent state that is contingent upon the propositional referent E holds at the reference point R.

Reichenbach extended his account of tense and the perfect to the progressives and futurates, including habituals, and to sequence of tenses in compound sentences. Some

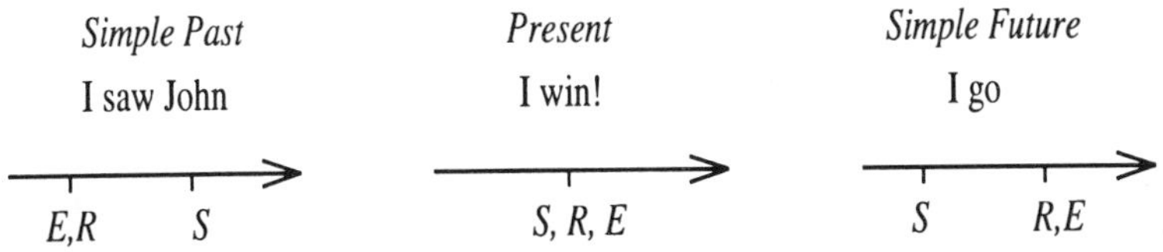

Fig. 4. The tenses.

of the details of his original presentation are unclear or incorrect. For example, the exact relation of E and R in the past progressive is unclear, possibly because of a typographical error. The account of the futurates does not correctly separate the respective contributions of tense and modality. The account of sequence of tense in compound sentences omits any discussion of examples with subordinate complements requiring more than one S and/or R, such as *He will think that he has won*. He similarly seems to have failed to notice that there is a *second* "narrative" pluperfect, involving an embedded past tense, relative to a *past* speech point, distinct from the true past perfect. It is the only realization that English affords for the past tense of indirect speech, or *oratio obliqua*, exemplified in examples like the following:

(20) I had arrived in Vermilion Sands three months earlier. A retired pilot, I was painfully coming to terms with a broken leg and the prospect of never flying again. ...

This pluperfect cannot be the past tense of a perfect, as perfects like *# I have arrived in Vermilion Sands three months ago* are infelicitous (for reasons discussed by Moens and the present author (1988)). It is rather a past tense *of a past tense*, identifying the proposition *I arrived in Vermilion Sands three months before now* as uttered by a narrator with their *own* now. (Most of Reichenbach's own examples of the pluperfect are in fact of this other kind.)

For these and other reasons the following account is something of a reconstruction of Reichenbach's theory. (See Hornstein, 1977, 1990; Enç, 1981, 1987; Kamp and Rohrer, 1983; Caenepeel, 1989; Smith, 1991, Chapter 5; and Crouch and Pulman, 1993 for related proposals. See also the discussions of Lascarides and Asher, 1993b; and Kamp and Reyle, 1993, below.)

According to this view, English and presumably other languages can be seen as having three tenses in the narrow sense of the term – the familiar past, present, and future tenses, in all of which the Reference point R and the event point E coincide. The past tense is, as we have seen, one in which the pair R, E precedes S. The present tense (which we noted earlier is in English restricted as far as events go to performative acts like naming and promising) is one in which all three coincide. The true future tense in English (as opposed to other languages) is realized by the syntactic present tense, as in *I go to London* (*next Tuesday*) and is symmetric to the past tense, with the pair R, E later than S, as in Figure 4 (cf. Hornstein, 1977, 1990). Here I depart from Reichenbach himself, and Bennett and Partee (1972), who regarded the future as not merely the mirror image of the past tense, but as combining the characteristics of a tense and a futurates aspect,

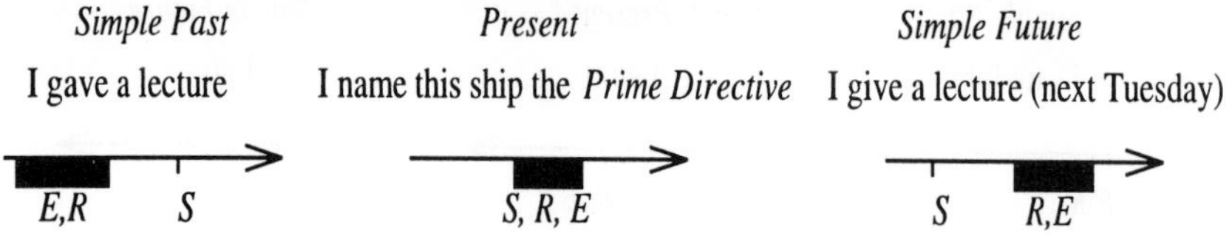

Fig. 5. The tenses for composite events.

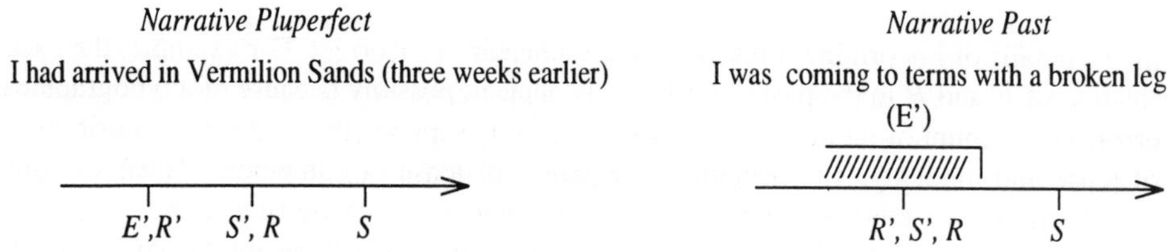

Fig. 6. The narrative tenses.

mirroring the perfect. Smith (1991, p. 246) also regards what is here called the simple future as having a *present* reference point. Nevertheless, the claim that it is a pure tense, with R co-temporal with E, is supported by the observation that the futurate is anaphoric, like the past, with exactly the same need for an "anchored" reference point. Hence (21)a, below, is inappropriate when discourse-initial, whereas the anchored (21)b is fine (cf. (18)):

(21) a. # Harry moves to Philadelphia.

b. Next Tuesday, Harry moves to Philadelphia.

The modal future, *I shall go* should be understood as identical to the simple future as far as Reichenbach's underlying times are concerned, with the modal itself contributing meaning of a quite orthogonal kind, which we shall discuss in a separate section below.

The ontology of events discussed in the previous section should be viewed as an ontology of the Reichenbachian E, so that the past and (simple or modal) future tenses can be applied to durative or composite events, as in Figure 5. (On the assumption that the performative achievement performed in saying "I name this ship the *Prime Directive*" lasts at least as long as the utterance, the present too can be regarded as having an extended R.) With the simple tenses, as opposed to the sentential aspects considered below, the reference point R continues to be *coextensive* with E for durative or composite events.

The reference point R itself is nevertheless distinct from E, and not a part of this ontology. Davidsonians accordingly distinguish it from the Davidsonian **e** (Parsons, 1990, p. 209, uses **I** for essentially this purpose in discussing tenses and temporal adverbials).

We noted earlier that past tense has a second meaning in English that is predicated of propositions in which the speaker's reference point R *coincides with* an epistemic point of view S' that is not the same as the speaker's present S, in the novellistic device of *oratio obliqua*. The syntactic past and pluperfect in the earlier example (20)

Past Counterfactual

If I had won (I would now be rich)

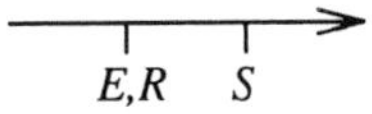

Fig. 7. The counterfactual pluperfect.

are therefore represented by the diagram in Figure 6. This analysis is related to one proposed by Kamp and Rohrer (1983) (cf. Kamp and Reyle, 1993, p. 593), and by Hwang and Schubert (1992), all of whom postulate multiple reference points to cope with related observations. The present account differs only in preserving Reichenbach's insight that for each reference point R there is an S.

The existence of these narrative or quotational tenses in English may explain the phenomenon of "sequence of tense", in which complements of tensed verbs like *said* and *thought* tend to "inherit" the tense of the matrix verb. As Hornstein (1990, Chapter 4) points out, this phenomenon is naturally captured in a Reichenbachian framework by similarly assuming that each tensed clause has its own S, R, E triple. The embedded S', which is naturally thought of as an embedded utterance point, or (more generally) an embedded epistemic point of view, is then coincident with the matrix event E, the event of utterance or epistemic consciousness. However, in the grammar of English, embedded clauses are specified to be semantically like quoted present tensed utterances, with past tense denoting the structures in Figure 6. S and R in these relational structures then coincide with S and R in the matrix clause. Thus a and b, below, mean that Chapman said something like "I arrived in Vermillion Sands three months ago", and "I am painfully coming to terms with a broken leg", just like the narrator in the following examples:

(22) a. Chapman said that he had arrived in Vermillion Sands three months earlier.
b. Chapman said that he was painfully coming to terms with a broken leg.

The fact that English complement verbs specify only quotational complements is what makes English a relatively strict "sequence of tense (SOT) language". However, this is a syntactic convention, rather than a semantic necessity, and other languages (such as ancient and modern Greek) may allow (or insist upon) the basic tenses in these contexts.

One further remark about quotational and complement pluperfects is in order. They are in fact ambiguous in English, since besides the narrative pluperfect illustrated in Figure 6a, they may denote the narrative past of a perfect, obtained by replacing the progressive state in (22)b by a perfect, or consequent, state, as in the following variant:

(23) Chapman said that he had just broken his leg.

Such an account of sequence of tense phenomena is essentially equivalent to the accounts of Enç (1981) and Dowty (1982), who invoke related notions of "anchoring".

We shall return later to the fact that past tense is also used in English to mark *counterfactuality* of the core proposition with respect to the reference point, as in the following conditional sentence.

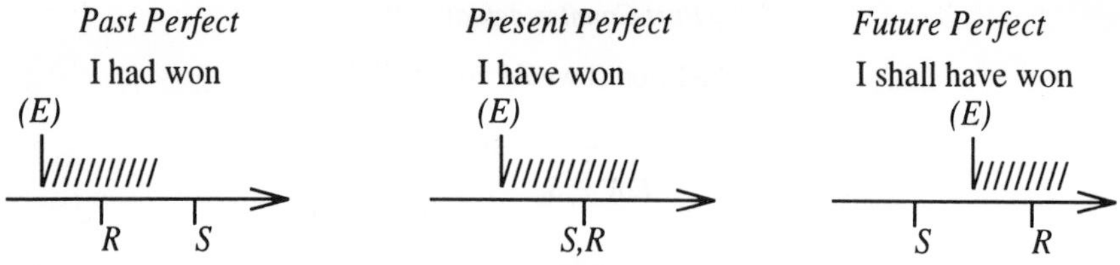

Fig. 8. The perfect.

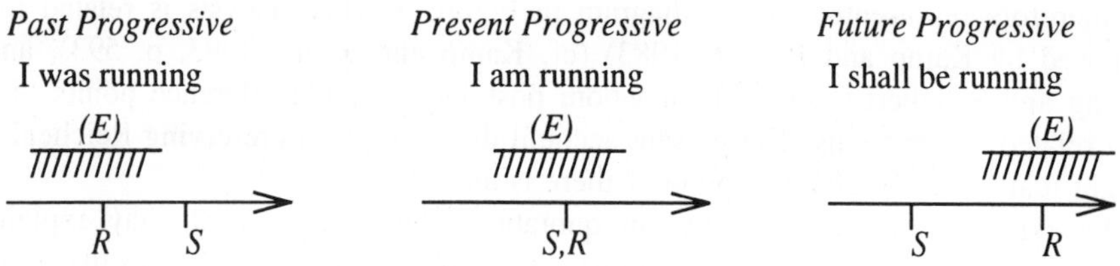

Fig. 9. The progressive.

(24) If he were taller, he could reach the book himself.

(Some languages have a distinct subjunctive mood for this purpose. English retains a distinct subjunctive in the first person of the copular verb *be*.) When the reference point itself is past, this means that counterfactuals also surface as pluperfects. We shall have more to say about the counterfactual relation of E to R below. However, as far as purely temporal relations go, their temporal profile is the same a past tense, as in Figure 7. Because of this multiplicity of functions of English past tense, Isard (1974) and Lyons (1977) suggest that syntactic past tense should be identified with a non-temporal semantic primitive *REMOTE*, rather than a time as such.

3.1.2. The perfect and the progressive

With the tenses established as in Figure 4, we can see that the perfect and the progressive (both of which we saw earlier to be states, rather than events) compose correctly with tense, as in Figures 8 and 9. In the case of the former, the reference point R lies within a Consequent State, derived from the original event E, which must in the terminology of Section 1 be an achievement. In the case of the progressives, R lies within a Progressive State, derived from the original event E, which must in the terminology of Section 1 be an activity. In neither case does E in the sense of the event directly figure in the representation. It is the (progressive or consequent) state derived from the event E, here indicated by hashing, that is predicated of R. Unlike the tenses with E, R is not coextensive in temporal terms with such states, but temporally included within them. The position of the event E relative to S and R is not in fact fully determined by the perfect and the progressive – hence its appearance in brackets in the figures. This becomes important in the case of the future perfect, in which the relation of E to S may be either prior or posterior. (Here we depart slightly from standard Reichenbachian accounts such as Hornstein (1990).)

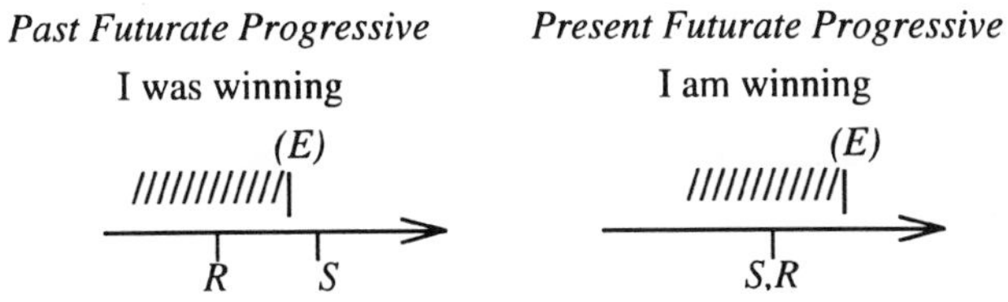

Fig. 10. The futurate progressive.

Both in the tenses and the aspects the core event E may be derived from a different event category E', via type coercion. For example, the achievement of *winning the race* can turn into a corresponding accomplishment, by the knowledge-based association of a characteristic preparatory activity, such as running. The progressive can then strip off the original achievement, to leave the bare activity, which is then mapped onto the corresponding state, which is predicated of R, the time under discussion. This explains the possibility of "futurate" progressives like a, below:

(25) a. I am winning!
b. I was winning.

As Smith (1991, p. 247) reminds us, (25)a is not really a predication about winning. It is simply a present progressive of an activity culminating in winning, which in Reichenbachian terms looks like Figure 10. Since E, the original achievement of winning, is not predicated of any underlying time, we seem to be even closer to a resolution of the imperfective paradox, which applies to both present (including futurate), and past, progressives. However, to get to that point we must consider the third temporal-relational system, that of modality.

3.1.3. Epistemic and deontic modality

The modal verbs of English, such as *will, must*, and *may*, like those of many other languages, carry two distinct senses. The first concerns such notions of necessity, possibility, inferability, or predictability of the core proposition, and is usually referred to as "epistemic" modality. The following are some examples for which this is the only readily accessible interpretation:

(26) a. It must have died.
b. That will be the mailman.
c. She may be weary.

The other set of senses concerns notions like feasibility and permissibility of the core proposition, and ability and obligation of the agent, and is usually referred to as "deontic" modality. Some relatively unambiguous examples are the following:

(27) a. You must sit down.
b. You may smoke.
c. I can do the Boogaloo.

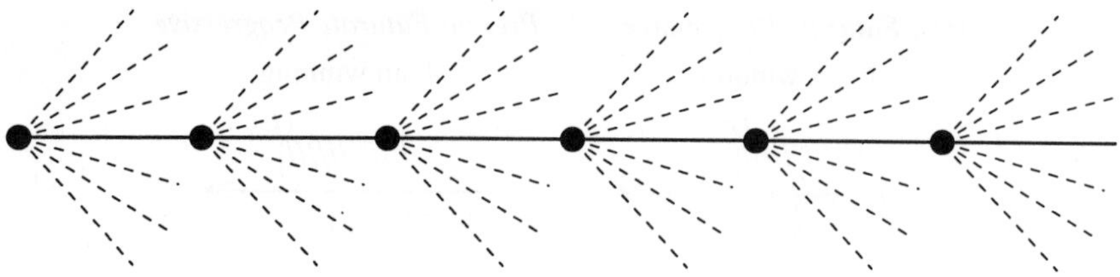

Fig. 11. Modal temporal structure.

While the pairs of senses subsumed under a verb like *must* are clearly related, the relation is indirect and appears to be somewhat arbitrarily conventionalized. While many of the deontic modals can be viewed as creating or explaining the corresponding epistemic state, there are a number of complications and lacunæin the system as a whole. For present purposes we shall consider the deontic modals as essentially distinct from the epistemic modals.

Because of their involvement with necessity and possibility, the epistemic modals differ from the systems of tense and sentential aspect in requiring us to consider more than one domain of reference or classical model. It was possible to capture the semantics of *Aktionsart*, tense, and sentential aspect in terms of a single deterministic world history, represented informally as a time-line in Reichenbach's diagrams. Instead we must think of the flow of time as a tree, so that any particular history (such as that of the real physical universe) becomes a path of branching points in a discrete graph of states, each of which gives rise to alternative continuations, which themselves branch into alternatives. Such a tree can be pictured as in Figure 11. We use bold lines and states to indicate the states and transitions of actual time. It should be noted that this representation does not distinguish the future history from the past in this respect. This reflects the fact that the simple future tense, which in English we have seen is realized as the present, treats the future as determinate. Of course, in actual fact, our access to past history is different in kind to our access to the future. There is a privileged set of past states which are distinguished as the actual history of the world, and we can only make more or less well-informed guesses about which states will turn out to be actual in future. We shall return to the consequences of this observation in the later section on modality.

We shall see below that this structure is closely related to the modal logician's notion of an *accessibility relation* over possible worlds (although the logicians frequently regard such "worlds" as including entire histories – that is, of comprising many states). It will be important to ask then how states should be represented, and what defines this relation. (For the present purpose, as in other computational applications of modal logic (cf. Goldblatt, 1992), the accessibility relation is the central construct in a modal logic.) However it is important first to see that the modal verbs, seen as predications over the elements in such structures, are straightforwardly compatible with the Reichenbachian view of tense and modality.

First, we must be clear that such structures are different from the continuous temporal dimension that is implicit in the earlier figures. We must now think of time as a (partial) ordering on discrete states corresponding to instants at which changes to a model occur (or can occur).

We could in principle think of such states as densely packed, mapping to the real numbers. When modal logics of the kind discussed below have been used to model physical time according to the special theory of relativity, they have represented time in this way – cf. Van Benthem (1983), Goldblatt (1980). (The latter achieves the *tour de force* of axiomatizing the Minkowski chronsynclastic infundibulum as a modal logic – see Van Benthem (1995) for discussion.) However, for linguistic and computational purposes, we shall invariably be interested in much sparser temporal structures. Sometimes (particularly when thinking about the theory of digital computation) states in these structures correspond to the cycles of a clock – that is, to the integers rather than the reals. In linguistics and related AI tasks like planning, we may be concerned with even sparser representations, in which only *changes* of state are represented.

We will continue to defer the discussion of how this is to be done formally. We may note however that in the latter case, transitions between points in the structure 11 are naturally associated with *events* that precipitate those changes. For example, this would be a natural way of representing the history of a board game of simple moves like *W:P-K4*, as Isard (1974) does. We shall see later how to generalize this representation to durative or composite events.

The Reichenbachian underlying times S and R can provisionally be identified with points in this structure, which will now support modality in the following way (again we go beyond anything specifically claimed by Reichenbach here).

We saw in earlier sections that the possibility of present epistemic modal statements like (28)a, below, is most naturally captured by assuming that the models or databases representing nodes in the structure specify *partial* information about worlds. A similar proposal has frequently been made for more standard model-theoretic semantics – cf. Hintikka (1962), Kripke (1965), Van Fraassen (1971), Kratzer (1977), Turner (1981), Veltman (1983), Cresswell (1985, Chapter 5; 1988), and Landman (1986). It is also central to the notions of Discourse Representation Structure in DRT and of "situation" in situation semantics – see Kamp and Reyle (1993), Barwise and Perry (1983), and Cooper (1986).

This observation can be extended to the domain of relations when we observe that modals and conditionals are essentially predications about R. In (28)a, below, the modal is predicated about a present R. Example (28)b is predicated of an R in the past.

(28) a. She may be weary.
b. Einstein may have visited Philadelphia.

(Being infinitival, this past shows up as a perfect. However it is clear that we are dealing with the modalization of the past reference point, rather than of a present perfect, because the corresponding declarative perfect, below, is pragmatically anomalous, for reasons discussed in Section 1.

(29) # Einstein has visited Philadelphia.

So the predication must be over R.)

Such "modal pasts" do in general require the reference point to be previously established or accommodatable. This can be seen in the fact that they are compatible with temporal adverbials like *yesterday*, which present perfects in general are not, as we have noted:

(30) a. She must have visited Philadelphia yesterday.

b. # She has visited Philadelphia yesterday.

One way to capture the above facts is in terms of the assumption that R is a partial model or database of the kind discussed above. Modals like *may* assert that the reference point in question is *consistent with* extension by the core proposition. Modals like *must* assert that the reference point in question implicates the core proposition under some argument or line of reasoning, as proposed by Kratzer (1991) and Stone (1994).

All of the above examples involve modal predications over *states* of one kind or another. To capture the meaning of epistemic modal predications over events, as in the following example, we must generalize the above apparatus.

(31) (If you take my queen), you may win the game.

This implies that the reference point must include or give access to the entire accessible subtree of futures after the core event. This suggests that the reference point is more like the nucleus of Figure 2 than like a situation or a time. We shall return to this point below.

I have already argued that in connection with the non-modal future tense that English and other languages treat the future part of the structure in Figure 11 symmetrically with the past, as having a determined set of states constituting actual future history. Of course, our information about future actuality is in fact limited, and our knowledge merely probabilistic. Because of this practical fact of human existence, the most common kinds of statement about the future are modal, so it is not too surprising that the modal system is in English somewhat confounded with the future component of the tense system. Nevertheless, in sentences like the following, we should clearly distinguish the contribution of the modal in (32)a, below, from the fact that it is predicated of a future reference point, as has been pointed out by Boyd and Thorne (1969) in connexion with examples like (32)b, below, where the same modal is predicated of a present reference point:

(32) a. You will marry a tall dark stranger.

b. It's late. Your mother will be worried about you.

(This point was also a subject of lively debate among 19th century linguists, as Verkuyl (1989) has shown.)

3.1.4. Counterfactuals

The system of linguistic modality is closely related to that of counterfactuality in conditionals, which in English is marked by past tense, and which will turn out to be central to the resolution of the imperfective paradox.

In order to capture the meaning of counterfactual implication, and hence causation, Lewis suggested that the meaning of counterfactuals in sentences like the following depends on the notion of *similarity* between possible worlds in a modal structure like Figure 11.

(33) If you had taken my queen, you would have won the game.

The proposal was that P (*your taking my queen*) in the situation W under discussion counterfactually implies Q (*your winning the game*) (written $P\Box\!\!\rightarrow Q$) if among all the worlds accessible from W satisfying P, all the ones that are most similar to W also satisfy Q. (It should be observed here that "worlds" are entire world histories, not the transitional states of the situation calculus.)

This works well for the example to hand, because the only counterfactual world is the one that results from your taking the queen instead of making the move you actually made. By definition it is the most similar counterfactual world, so provided all continuations of the game result in your winning the game, the claim is true.

However, as Fine (1975) pointed out, not all actions are like this. His example was the following:

(34) If Nixon had pushed the button, there would have been a nuclear war.

This statement might well be true, despite the fact that worlds in which that least monotonic of presidents pressed the button, but war did not ensue, seem to be more similar to the actual world, on the reasonable assumption that nuclear war changes just about everything. Thomason and Gupta (1980) point out that Lewis' account is compatible with an alternative notion of closeness over worlds, defined in terms of causality, a suggestion that we shall return to below, in discussing the situation calculus of McCarthy and Hayes, and its extensions.

The problems of modality and counterfactuality are closely related to the imperfective paradox, which will be recalled as arising from the existence of occasions of which it can be claimed that *Keats was crossing the road*, in spite of the fact that he was hit by a truck before the action could be completed. The problem for possible worlds semantics is precisely the same as the problem of counterfactuals, namely to specify the worlds which are most similar to the actual one, differing only in relevant respects. To specify this in terms of worlds themselves is very difficult: as Vlach (1981) pointed out, there are a great many world-histories that differ in minor respects from the actual one, but where Keats is still hit by the truck. As Landman (1992) has pointed out, there are cases of world-histories which differ from the actual world *only* in that Keats is not hit by the truck, but in which Keats would nevertheless not have succeeded in crossing the road – as when there is a second equally inattentive truck right behind. Even if there were an infinite number of such trucks, requiring an infinitely different world for Keats to succeed, it still seems true that *Keats was crossing the street* if that is what he intended, and if our knowledge of the world supports no other obstacle to the causal realization of that intention. Even more strikingly, (to adapt another of Landman's examples), it seems *not* to be true in any of these situations to make this claim if Keats did *not* have that intention, or if there is some other obstacle to its realization. If he knew perfectly well that he could not possibly get to the other side, and set out with suicidal intentions, or if he intended to turn around just short of the opposite kerb and come back again, or if he fully intended to cross but was unaware of a glass wall in the middle of the road, then the claim is false. Yet, apart from the intention itself, and its consequences for Keats' projected future actions, the counterfactual worlds are all identical.

Because of these difficulties, most theories of the progressive have invoked a function mapping possible states onto *relevant* continuations. Dowty (1979, p. 148) "reluctantly" assumed a primitive function *Inr*, mapping world-time indices onto "inertia worlds". Landman (1992) defines a function C which maps an event e and a world index onto their "continuation branch", invoking a primitive function R which maps such pairs onto event-indexed inertia worlds or "reasonable options". Some related ideas have been invoked within the DRT camp (cf. Roberts, 1989).

However, both Inr and R are unanalysed, and the involvement of intention makes it seem unlikely that there could be any definition other than one in terms of an action-based accessibility relation.

3.2. *Logical and computational approaches*

So much for the natural history of temporal relations: how do we formalize them? We should at this point distinguish two kinds of question that are somewhat confounded in the computational literature. One is the use of abstract computations to do the same job as a traditional model theoretic semantics. The other is the efficient implementation of such a semantics, to minimize costs such as search. In this section, we shall first develop a Kripke-like semantics including a representation of states and the accessibility relation. We shall then consider an efficient representation of this semantics, which builds in certain "inertial" properties of the world as it is conceptualized by human beings, via a constrained use of defaults. Finally we shall consider a reformulation of this system in terms of dynamic logic.

We noted a resemblance between the structures like Figure 11 and the notion of a *frame* in the standard semantics of Kripke (1972) for a modal logic. A frame is a structure defined in terms of *a set of worlds or states* W and an *accessibility relation* ρ over them. For the present purpose, the worlds or states can be thought of as classical models of the kind used in first-order predicate calculus (that is, sets of individuals and relations, possibly typed or sorted), except that we shall assume that states which happen to have the same individuals and relations may nevertheless be distinct. One can then define $\Box p$ ("necessarily p"), to mean that p necessarily holds in a state $s \in W$, just in case p hold in every state accessible from s. Similarly, $\Diamond p$, ("possibly p"), can be defined to hold in s if p holds in at least one state accessible from s under ρ. In most modal logics, these operators are duals, interdefinable via negation.

Possible worlds are generally assumed by modal logicians to include entire histories of the universe of discourse through many different states. However, this assumption is based on a view of time that is not the one pursued here, and for present purposes it is more useful to identify the elements under the accessibility relation with single states, as the computer scientists tend to. The accessibility relation can be any relation whatsoever, but for present purposes it is appropriate to think of it as defining the ways in which one state of the world can lawfully turn into others.

In taking advantage of this affinity between the linguistic phenomena and modal logic, we must be careful to avoid being distracted by two related concerns that have greatly occupied modal logicians. One is an interest in distinguishing between necessary propositions, such as theorems of arithmetic, and contingent ones, such as the fact that this sentence happens to have been written at 5.25 p.m on an October evening. This notion is naturally captured in a logic in which the accessibility relation is *reflexive, transitive*, and *symmetric* – that is, an equivalence relation under which all worlds in W are accessible to all others. (This is the modal logic known as $S5$.) However, this distinction may not be particularly relevant to everyday reasoning, which typically concerns an uncertain world. It does not appear to be reflected in the linguistic ontology.

The second is the representation of physicists' notions of time and causality. The mere fact that quantum theory discusses processes which reverse the arrow of time and causality does not entail that a theory of the knowledge involved in linguistic semantics should do the same. The logics we shall consider have an accessibility relation which is *asymmetric*, reflecting the directionality of the flow of time and causality. (They are therefore somewhat more like the modal logic known as $S4$, although in fact their accessibility relation will turn out to be more restricted still.)

3.2.1. The situation/event calculus

While modal logics offer an elegantly terse notation for quantifying over states or models, many of them, probably including all those of interest for linguistic purposes, can be simulated in entirely first-order terms, via the technique of "reification", which takes possible states themselves to be individuals that can be quantified over, represented either by constants t_i, t_j etc, or by more complex terms.

One such reified modal logic is the "situation calculus" of McCarthy and Hayes (1969). This system was developed within a computational framework for reasoning about actions, and is interesting from the point of view of our earlier assumption that the linguistic categories need to be based in a theory of action rather than of time. One of the most useful and attractive features of the situation calculus was the use of *terms* like $\mathit{result}(\mathit{arrive}(\mathit{person}), s)$ as individuals denoting situations or states as functions of other situations. Functions like *result* were called *situational fluents* by McCarthy and Hayes. Such terms can be used in rules like the following to transparently capture the notion that a person is present in the situation that results from their arriving:

(35) $\forall s, \forall \mathit{person}, \mathit{present}(\mathit{person}, \mathit{result}(\mathit{arrive}(\mathit{person}), s))$

This particular logic (which is, as McCarthy and Hayes point out, quite closely related to von Wright's (1964, 1967) "logic of action") embodies only the most minimal ontology of states (represented by predicates that hold over situations, such as $\mathit{present}(\mathit{person}, s)$) and atomic actions (represented by expressions like $\mathit{arrive}(\mathit{person})$). We shall look in a moment at some descendants of the situation calculus which attempt to include a richer ontology.

McCarthy and Hayes were interested in the use of such rules to construct plans of action, via inference. For example, given the following rules, one might expect to be able to infer a successful plan for bringing about a situation s in which three blocks satisfy the condition $\mathit{on}(a, b, s) \wedge \mathit{on}(b, c, s)$:

(36) a. $\mathit{clear}(a, s_0) \wedge \mathit{clear}(b, s_0) \wedge \mathit{clear}(c, s_0)$

b. $$\begin{aligned} &\forall x, \forall y, \forall s, \mathit{clear}(x, s) \wedge \mathit{clear}(y, s) \wedge x \neq y \\ &\rightarrow \mathit{clear}(x, \mathit{result}(\mathit{puton}(x, y, s))) \\ &\qquad \wedge \neg \mathit{clear}(y, \mathit{result}(\mathit{puton}(x, y, s))) \\ &\qquad \wedge \mathit{on}(x, y, \mathit{result}(\mathit{puton}(x, y, s))) \end{aligned}$$

The formulæ say, first, that everything is *clear* in a particular situation s_0, and second, that if two distinct things x and y are clear in a situation s, then in the situation that results from putting x on y in that situation, x is on y, x is clear and y is no longer clear. (The rule embodies the idea that only one thing at a time can be manipulated, in stipulating that y is no longer clear.)

Using standard inference rules of conjunction elimination, modus ponens, etc., we might expect to be able to prove the following, in which the situational terms neatly describe the sequence of putting b on c, then putting a on b:

(37) $$on(a, b, result(puton(a, b, result(puton(b, c, s_0))))) \\ \wedge\, on(b, c, result(puton(a, b, result(puton(b, c, s_0)))))$$

As yet, this doesn't quite work. While we can prove the intermediate result $on(b, c, result(puton(b, c, s_0)))$ (which looks useful) we cannot go on to prove the first conjunct, because the formulæ in (36) do not capture the fact that a remains clear after putting b on c. Nor can we prove the second conjunct, because the same formulæ fail to capture the fact that b remains on c after putting a on b.

McCarthy and Hayes point out that we can fix this by adding further "frame axioms" to the effect that if u is on v in a situation s, then u is still on v in the situation that results from putting something x on something y, so long as u is not the same as x. Similarly, if u is clear in s, it is still clear after putting something x on something y, so long as u is not the same as y:

(38) a. $\forall u, \forall x, \forall y, \forall s, clear(u, s) \wedge u \neq y \rightarrow clear(u, result(puton(x, y, s)))$

b. $\forall u, \forall v, \forall x, \forall y, \forall s, on(u, v, s) \wedge u \neq x \rightarrow on(u, v, result(puton(x, y, s)))$

The addition of these rules allows the proof (which is suggested as an exercise) to proceed to completion.

Such a system, whose affinities to von Wright's logic of action we have already remarked upon, seems to offer a very natural expression for states and the accessibility relation between them. However, as McCarthy and Hayes were aware, for computational purposes, this logic seems cumbersome. If we want to represent a less trivial universe with more state predicates and more actions or action sequences, we shall need a frame axiom pairing every predicate with every action. This exacerbates the search problem for the computational purposes that originally motivated the situation calculus.

It also somehow misses the point as a representation of action. The way we think of actions is precisely as local operations that affect just a few properties, leaving most facts unchanged. There seems to be something wrong with a notation that would make it no more inconvenient to define a highly distributed event which inverted the truth value of every fact about the world. Even the action of dropping a hydrogen bomb doesn't do *that*. McCarthy and Hayes christened this the "frame problem", and discuss a number of possible solutions, including one which they attribute to Rescher (1964), which was to assume that *all* facts that held at the start of an action held in its result, and then to eliminate any inconsistencies via what would now be recognized as a "Truth Maintenance" system (Doyle, 1979; De Kleer, 1984). However, they did not in this early paper offer a definitive solution. The search for a solution has engendered much research, not least their own (for example, McCarthy, 1977).

A solution that was related in spirit to Rescher's was nevertheless at hand in work that was being done contemporaneously in robot planning. The idea was to build into the model itself the "inertial" property just identified. The simplest way to do this is to specify actions in terms of the facts about the that world that become untrue and the new facts that become true when they occur. One computationally convenient way to do this is to represent the starting state of the world as a collection of facts, and to represent actions in terms of a triplet. Each such triplet consists of 1) a list of *preconditions* that must hold if the action is to apply in the current state, 2) *deletions* or facts that become false in the state that results from the action, 3) *additions* or facts that become true in that state. The history of an episode up to any given state can then be determined from the current state and the sequence of actions that led to it. Any earlier state can be fully determined by running the sequence of additions and deletions backwards to the relevant point.

It is not clear who first proposed this idea, because its transparent representation in terms of "assignment", database "updates" and other computational side-effects makes it almost the first thing a computer scientist would think of as a representation for action. It usually goes by the name of the "STRIPS solution" to the frame problem, because it was first made explicit in the context of a robot action planner by that name (Fikes and Nilsson, 1971).

It is also natural for this purpose to further economize by representing the state of the world solely in terms of *positive* truths, and to represent the (generally much larger) set of negative facts via a "closed world assumption" (Reiter, 1978), according to which any fact that cannot be proved true is assumed by default to be false. (It should be noted that this move demands that everything true be provable, if consistency is to be maintained.)

3.2.2. *A declarative solution*

Although the STRIPS representation of actions was originally thought of in non-declarative terms, Kowalski (1979, circulated in 1974) showed it to be elegantly realizable in entirely declarative terms, via the introduction of the closed world assumption and a more radical use of reification to simulate modal quantification. (See Nilsson (1980, pp. 308–316) for a more extensive discussion of Kowalski's proposal.) He proposed a predicate *holds*, which applies to a proposition, represented as a term, and a state. The earlier state (36)a can therefore be written as follows:

(39) $$\mathit{holds}(\mathit{clear}(a), s_0) \wedge \mathit{holds}(\mathit{clear}(b), s_0) \wedge \mathit{holds}(\mathit{clear}(c), s_0)$$

The action of putting x on y can be represented as a STRIPS rule, as follows. The preconditions are defined by the following rule which says that if you can get at x and you can get at y, the preconditions for putting x on y hold:

(40) $$\begin{array}{l}\mathit{holds}(\mathit{clear}(x), s) \wedge \mathit{holds}(\mathit{clear}(y), s) \wedge (x \neq y)\\ \rightarrow \mathit{preconditions}(\mathit{puton}(x, y), s)\end{array}$$

(In this rule, and henceforth, we adopt a convention whereby universal quantification over bound variables is left implicit.) The new facts that result from the action of putting x on y can be defined as follows:

(41) a. $holds(on(x,z),s) \rightarrow holds(clear(z), result(puton(x,y),s))$

b. $holds(on(x,y), result(puton(x,y),s))$

Kowalski assumes negation as failure, and so avoids the need to state explicitly that y is no longer clear. This fact is implicit in the following frame axiom, which is the *only* frame axiom we need for the action of putting x on y. It says that any fact which holds in s holds in the result of putting x on y in s *except* the fact that y is clear, and the fact that x was on something else z (if it was).

(42) $$holds(p,s) \wedge (p \neq clear(y)) \wedge (p \neq on(x,z)) \\ \rightarrow holds(p, result(puton(x,y),s))$$

Note that there is an assumption implicit in the use of inequality (rather than a related notion involving implication) that p is a term rather than a formula like $graspable(y) \wedge on(x,y)$. This assumption is in effect a restriction to Horn logic, in which the consequent may not include conjunction, disjunction, implication or negation, modulo the reification.

Kowalski's proposal was followed by much work on tense using reified calculi (Allen, 1984; McDermott, 1982; Kowalski and Sergot, 1986). It was also closely related to the notion of "circumscription of qualifications" – see McCarthy (1977, esp. p. 1040), and much other subsequent work, collected and reviewed in Ginsberg (1987). In particular, Reiter (1991) shows how the restricted frame axioms or "successor state axioms" can be derived automatically. We can now define a predicate *poss*, closely related to the familiar modal operator $\diamond$, over the set of possible states, via the following rules, which say that the start state s_0 is possible, and the result of an action in a state is possible if its preconditions hold:

(43) a. $poss(s_0)$

b. $poss(s) \wedge preconditions(action, s) \rightarrow poss(result(action, s))$

The earlier goal of stacking a on b on c can now be realized as the goal of finding a constructive proof for the following conjunction

(44) $$poss(s) \wedge holds(on(a,b),s) \wedge holds(on(b,c),s)$$

These rules can be very straightforwardly realized in Prolog, and can be made to yield a proof (although the search problem of finding such proofs automatically remains hard in general) in which

(45) $$s = result(puton(a,b), result(puton(b,c), s_0))$$

This technique restores declarativity to the logic embodying the STRIPS solution. There is a sense in which – despite the involvement of the closed world assumption – it also restores monotonicity, for so long as we do not add new facts (like some previously unsuspected object being present, or a familiar one having fallen off its support) or some new rule or frame axiom (say defining a new action or stating a new precondition on an old one) then we can regard negation-as-failure as merely efficiently encoding classical negation.

Of course, in the real world we *do* learn new facts and rules, and we encounter exceptions to the closed world assumption of complete knowledge. These problems are known in AI as the *ramification problem* (that is, that actions may have indefinitely many unforeseen consequences that our default model does not and cannot predict) and the *qualification problem* (that actions may have indefinitely many preconditions that our default model does not and cannot anticipate). In many recent papers, the frame problem is assumed to include these further problems. However, if we are in possession of an efficient default model which works reasonably well most of the time, it may well be wiser to regard the problem of coping with new information as residing outside the logic itself, in the truth-maintenance or "housekeeping" system. Rather than coping with ramification and qualification in the logic itself, we should think in terms of a system of truth-maintaining transitions between entirely monotonic logics.

Related techniques and their relation to ramification and qualification in a narrower sense of *known* or anticipated causal or contingent relations between events are further explored by Schubert (1990, 1994), and Reiter (1991, 1993). The Horn clause form and closed world assumption of the present system offer some hope of computational efficiency (cf. Levesque, 1988). (This is not of course to claim that it solves the explosive search problem implicit in *finding* plans.)

The STRIPS version of the situation calculus, with one class of situational fluent and one class of state-predicate, did not embody any of the ontological richness discussed in earlier sections. However, a number of systems subsequently generalized the situation calculus to deal with richer event ontologies. Allen (1984) was the first to do so, defining a number of reifying predicates of which the most basic were *HOLDS* and *OCCURS*, respectively relating properties and events to intervals. Events could be events proper, or processes, after the Vendler-like scheme of Mourelatos (1978), those events that in other systems are points or instants being represented as very short intervals, unlike instants in the related extension of the situation calculus proposed by McDermott (1982), which introduced further temporal types such as "chronicles". Galton (1990) proposes an elegant revision of Allen's theory in these respects, according to which Allen's processes correspond to progressive states in the terms of the earlier sections. A number of causal and temporal predicates allowed events and times to be related in ways that permitted a treatment of phenomena such as inaction, propositional attitudes and interacting subgoals in plans. Steedman (1982) defines the durative or composite event categories in terms of instants of starting, stopping and (in the case of accomplishments) culminating, using a STRIPS-like representation to handle the related progressive states, which (like perfects, habituals etc.) are treated as inertial properties of intervening times. (A similar approach has recently been advocated by Lin (1995) and Lin and Reiter (1995).) All of these approaches are closely related to the "event calculus" of Kowalski and Sergot (1986), itself a descendant of Kowalski's earlier work on the situation calculus, although their own ontology of events was still more minimal than these other approaches.

If possible states are defined as databases of facts exploiting a closed world assumption, then the above definition of the accessibility relation in terms of actions is essentially identical to the branching modal frame identified in Figure 11 in the last section. We noted there that in order to capture linguistic modality we seemed to need *partial*, or underspecified, states.

The accessibility relation in question is (in a sense) *transitive*, but it is *asymmetric* (and therefore *irreflexive*) – that is, a partial order. This relation defines an even weaker logic than $S4$, which has a transitive and *antisymmetric* accessibility relation.

We have already noted the similarity to the system of von Wright (1967). The states in this structure are *counterfactual* in the sense that the actions or action sequences that take the place of situational fluents, generating the successors of any given state, are disjunctive, and only one of them can correspond to the actual history of events. In this respect, our system has some affinities to proposals by Stalnaker (1968, 1984), Thomason (1970), and Lewis (1971, 1973a), and the related computational work of Ginsberg (1986). However, the definition of accessibility and counterfactuality in terms of events rather than states avoids the problem with some of these accounts that was noted earlier in connection with Fine's example (34), repeated here:

(46) If Nixon had pushed the button, there would have been a nuclear war.

According to the event-based system, there is exactly one counterfactual world in which Nixon pressed the button, rather than doing whatever else he did, and its accessibility is defined by the action itself. (Cf. Stalnaker, 1984, Chapter 7, esp. pp. 133–134.)

Such a system similarly resolves the imperfective paradox. We noted earlier that Inr and R were unanalysed in the systems of Dowty and Landman. However, in the present system they can be identified with the event-based accessibility relation proposed here. Since that appears to be the *only* accessibility relation that we need, the event-based account appears to have an advantage. In fact, to make the identification of these inertial functions with the accessibility relation itself seems to be a very natural move within all of these theories, particularly in view of the close relation in other respects that Dowty notes between his theory and the logic of action. (Cf. Dowty, 1979, p. 144.) Thomason (1991, p. 555) also notes the close relation between inertia worlds and the situation calculus, and suggests a rather different analysis in terms of defaults in a non-monotonic logic.

This is not of course to claim that the situation calculi described above solve the problem of representing causality, agency, and the like, (although here too von Wright (1967) made a start). Shoham (1988a), Morgenstern and Stein (1988) and Stein (1991, pp. 117–118), in contrast to Ginsberg (1986) and Ortiz (1994), eschew counterfactuals *and* situation-calculus like systems in favor of some more general notion of the accessibility relation based on *causality* (usually on several distinct causal operators, including as *enabling, generating* and *preventing* as well as simple causation). Schank (1975), Wilensky (1983), and Lansky (1986) are also important in this connection.

3.2.3. Dynamic semantics

There is another way of looking at all of these variants of the situation/event calculus. To the extent that the accessibility relation is defined in terms of a number of different events or causal primitives, possibly a large number, it is possible to regard each of these as defining its own distinct accessibility relation, possibly differing from others in properties like transitivity. Such systems can then be viewed as instances of the "dynamic" logics that were developed in the first place for reasoning about computer programs – see Pratt (1979), Harel (1980), and Goldblatt (1992), and the chapter by Van Benthem in the present volume. The application of various forms of dynamic logic in knowledge representation and natural language semantics has been advocated by Moore (1980), Rosenschein (1981), Webber (1983), Pednault (1989), and Scherl and Levesque (1993). (It should be noted that this original notion of dynamic logic is not the same as the "dynamic predicate logic" (DPL) of Groenendijk and Stokhof – see below.)

Dynamic logics relativize the modal operators to individual actions, events, or programs. For example, if a (possibly nondeterministic) program or command α computes a function F over the integers, then we may write the following:

(47) $$n \geqslant 0 \to [\alpha](y = F(n))$$

(48) $$n \geqslant 0 \to \langle\alpha\rangle(y = F(n))$$

The intended meaning of the first of these is "for $n \geqslant 0$, after every execution of α that terminates, $y = F(n)$". That of the second is (dually) that "there is an execution of α which terminates with $y = F(n)$".

While all of the calculi that we have considered so far are ones in which the elementary programs α are *deterministic*, dynamic logics offer a framework which readily generalizes to concurrent and probabilistic events, offering a notation in which all of the theories discussed here can be compared. (In some of these, the modal operators $[\alpha]$ and $\langle\alpha\rangle$ are no longer interdefinable – cf. Nerode and Wijesekera, 1990.)

The particular dynamic logic that we are dealing with here is one that includes the following dynamic axiom (the operator ; is *sequence*, an operation related to composition, and to von Wright's T):

(49) $$[\alpha][\beta]P \to [\alpha;\beta]P$$

In this we follow Moore (1980, Chapter 3) and Rosenschein (1981). The situation calculus and its many variants can be seen as reified versions of this dynamic logic.

We achieve an immediate gain in perspicuity by replacing the reified notation in (50)a, below, by the equivalent dynamic expression (50)b.

(50) a. $\mathit{holds}((\mathit{on}(a,b) \wedge \mathit{on}(b,c)), \mathit{result}(\mathit{puton}(a,b), \mathit{result}(\mathit{puton}(b,c), s_0)))$

b. $[\mathit{puton}(b,c);\mathit{puton}(a,b)](\mathit{on}(a,b) \wedge \mathit{on}(b,c))$

Kowalski's "vivid" version of STRIPS can be very simply represented in this logic. The initial state of the world is as follows:

(51) $$\mathit{clear}(a) \wedge \mathit{clear}(b) \wedge \mathit{clear}(c)$$

The axiom defining the preconditions of $\mathit{puton}(x,y)$ is now directly definable in terms of the predicate *possible*, which can now be identified with a subtly different modal operator, which applies to events, rather than states:

(52) $$\models \mathit{clear}(x) \wedge \mathit{clear}(y) \wedge (x \neq y) \to \mathit{possible}(\mathit{puton}(x,y))$$

The consequences of $\mathit{puton}(x,y)$ are now written as follows:

(53) a. $\models \mathit{on}(x,z) \to [\mathit{puton}(x,y)]\mathit{clear}(z)$

b. $\models [\mathit{puton}(x,y)]\mathit{on}(x,y)$

The frame axiom is written as follows:

(54) $\models p \wedge (p \neq clear(y)) \wedge (p \neq on(x,z)) \rightarrow [puton(x,y)]p$

(Again the use of inequality presupposes the Horn Logic property that p is a positive literal.)

The transitive part of the possibility relation is now reduced to the following:

(55) $\models possible(\alpha) \wedge [\alpha]possible(\beta) \rightarrow possible(\alpha;\beta)$

This fragment preserves the virtues of Kowalski's treatment in a modal notation. That is, the following conjunctive goal can, given a search control, be made to deliver a constructive proof where $\alpha = puton(b,c); puton(a,b)$. (The proof, which solely involves backward-chaining on the consequents of rules, is suggested as an exercise):

(56) $possible(\alpha) \wedge [\alpha](on(a,b) \wedge on(b,c))$

The suppression of state variables in dynamic logic affords some improvement in perspicuity over the related proposals of Kowalski, McCarthy, Schubert, and Reiter that it is here used to capture, and makes it easier to extend the calculus.

The above example only concerns non-composite or "non-durative" events, like the original situation calculus. However, the following dynamic Horn clauses begin to capture the composite events discussed earlier, along the lines suggested by Steedman (1982), Moens (1987) and White (1994). (The example is greatly simplified, and omits many rules needed to capture even this small domain completely.) First we need axioms defining the consequent and preconditions for *starting* and *stopping*.

(57) a. $\models [start(p)]in\_progress(p)$

b. $\models not(in\_progress(p)) \wedge preconditions(p) \rightarrow possible(start(p))$

c. $\models p \rightarrow [start(q)]p$

(58) $\models in\_progress(p) \rightarrow possible(stop(p))$

We also need a frame axiom for *stopping* (which could be derived as in Reiter, 1991):

(59) $\vdash p \wedge (p \neq in\_progress(q)) \rightarrow [stop(q)]p$

This axiom is not as strong as it looks. It merely says that the only state to change in this state transition is the in-progress state in question. Of course $stop(q)$ may have further ramifications, such as causing some other process to stop, but these must be mediated by relations between *events* not states. Such known ramifications should be explicitly represented in the logic. This raises the question of how concurrency is to be represented in dynamic situation or event calculi. We will return briefly to this question below, but it should be noted that this problem, like that of relating events to chronology or clock-time, is likely to be considerably simplified by the fact that the primitive events in these calculi are all instantaneous.

Finally we need a definition of the progressive, coercing achievements to accomplishments and accomplishments to preparatory activities. (Note that in (60)b, below, we assume, in line with the discussion in Section 2.1, that accomplishments can be represented by terms relating an activity and a culminating achievement. These sorts are here represented as terms in lieu of a proper system of sorts.)

(60) a. $\models in\_progress(p) \rightarrow progressive(activity(p))$

b. $\models preparation(q, p) \wedge progressive(activity(p))$
$\rightarrow progressive(accomplishment(activity(p), achievement(q)))$

c. $\models preparation(q, p)$
$\wedge\, progressive(accomplishment(activity(p), achievement(q)))$
$\rightarrow progressive(achievement(q))$

These rules say that the progressive of an activity *act* is true if *act* is in progress, that of an accomplishment is true if the progressive of its component activity is true, and that the progressive of an achievement is true if the progressive of an accomplishment made up of the achievement and its preparatory activity is true – cf. Figure 1.

The following query asks for a plan α yielding a state where Keats is finishing writing the sonnet *In Disgust of Vulgar Superstition*:

(61) $possible(\alpha) \wedge [\alpha]progressive(achievement(finish(write(keats,\ sonnet))))$

(The function *finish* maps an accomplishment onto its culminating achievement, and is distinct from *stop*, the endpoint of an activity.) To find the plan, we must assume that the knowledge base also makes explicit the relation between *finishing* an activity and its characteric preparation, the activity itself, implicit in the nucleus of Figure 2. (To simplify the example, we assume that the preparation for finishing writing a sonnet is just writing it, although in real life it is a little more complicated than that.)

(62) $\models preparation(achievement(finish(e)), activity(e))$

If we assume that events of Keats writing has no preconditions, then the accessibility relation implicit in definition (55) gives rise to a proof where

(63) $\alpha = start(write(keats,\ sonnet))$

A further simplification in the example is the assumption that all instances of writing a sonnet are preparations for finishing it. In more complicated domains, such as the traditional road-crossing domain that was used earlier to introduce the imperfective paradox, we shall want to distinguish particular instances of preparatory activities like walking that are associated with goals like reaching the other side of the road from similar activities that are not associated with such goals. This can be done via the same *preparation* relation, provided that we further individuate events via Davidsonian indices. Such individuation is also of course necessary to distinguish distinct events with the same description, and to identify which *start* belongs with which *stop* among distinct durative events of the same type. We will continue to pass over this complication here.

The proof that generates the above plan (which is again suggested as an exercise) does not involve the subgoal of showing $[\alpha]finish(write(keats,\ sonnet))$. Indeed the proof would be quite consistent with adding the denial of that fact, because the variable *ach* in rule (60) is not involved in the antecedent, capturing the imperfective paradox.

Of course, asking for a plan to bring about a situation in which Keats is finishing writing *In Disgust of Vulgar Superstition* is slightly artificial, because such states are extensive, and there may be several such plans. For example, consider the effect of adding the following rule defining the consequences and preconditions of arriving.

(64) a. $\models [arrive(x)]present(x)$

b. $\models not(present(x)) \rightarrow possible(arrive(x))$

c. $\models p \rightarrow [arrive(x)]p$

The accessibility relation (55) now allows

(65) $\alpha = start(write(keats,\ sonnet)); arrive(x)$
$\alpha = start(write(keats,\ sonnet)); arrive(x); arrive(y)$
...

As plans, these are rather foolish, because of well-known inherent limitations in the simplest STRIPS planners, although incorrect plans such as the following are still correctly excluded for the goal in question:

(66) $\alpha = start(write(keats,\ sonnet)); arrive(x); stop(write(keats,\ sonnet)$

Part of the problem is that we are not yet distinguishing true consequences, including ramifications or causal relations among events themselves, from facts that are merely coincidentally true in the state that results, because of the inertial property of the frame axiom. Nor are we distinguishing causal relations *between* event sequences from mere temporal sequence.

We can remedy this shortcoming by distinguishing the temporal sequence operator (i.e. ;) from a causal or contingent sequential operator, which we will follow Moens and Steedman (1988) in writing as @, because of its relation to one of Lanski's (1986) operators. (A related proposal to involve causality as a primitive is made by Lin (1995).) Accordingly, we need to add some further rules parallel to (55), reflecting a relation of modal necessity across sequences of events, including the following:

(67) $\models (possible(\alpha) \wedge [\alpha]necessary(\beta)) \rightarrow possible(\alpha @ \beta)$

We now add a rule saying that anyone else being present implies that Keats must stop writing:

(68) $\models present(x) \wedge (x \neq keats) \wedge in\_progress(write(keats, y))$
$\rightarrow necessary(stop(write(keats, y)))$

We can now search for plans which make an event of Keats stopping writing necessarily occur, like (69)a, below, as distinct from those that merely make it possible, like (69)b, by constructively searching for a proof for an event sequence α such that $possible(\alpha @ stop(write(keats, y)))$:

(69) a. $\alpha = start(write(keats, y)); arrive(x)$

b. $\alpha = start(write(keats, y))$

Again the examples are artificial: their usefulness for an account of tense and temporal anaphora will become apparent in the next section.

There is a close relation between $[\alpha]$ and von Wright's "and Next" operator T, which is often written $\bigcirc$ in other temporal logics – cf. Goldblatt (1992, Chapter 9). Von Wright's operator in turn has its origin in deontic logic (cf. Thomason, 1981), and there is in general a considerable affinity between deontic logic and dynamic logic. The interesting property of the system for present purposes is that it represents causally or contingently related sequences of actions.

Such a logic can be captured in the kind of axiomatization standard in the literature on dynamic logic – Harel (1980, p. 512 et seq.) provides a model which can be adapted to the more restricted deterministic logic that is implicit here by omitting some axioms and adding a further axiom of determinism. (See p. 522 et seq. I am indebted to Rich Thomason for suggesting this approach.) However, such a toy needs considerable further work to make it into a linguistically interesting object. In particular, it stands badly in need of a type system of the kind discussed in Section 2. We must also extend it to capture the fact that not only states but events may be simultaneous, and that events may in particular be embedded within other events. We are likely to find ourselves needing to express a variety of distinct causal and modificational relations between events, as Shoham (1988a) and other authors cited earlier have suggested, rather than the single contingent von Wrightian relation, and needing to introduce some coindexing device equivalent to Davidsonian **e** variables. We also need to relate the contingent sequences to clock-time. Some of these extensions are touched on in the next section, which considers how to bring this apparatus more appropriately under the control of language, by making it refer to an actual historical sequence of events.

4. Temporal reference

4.1. Basic phenomena and descriptive frameworks

In the discussion so far, we have largely ignored the question of how the Reichenbachian reference point is represented and accessed, and the anaphoric nature of tense. Several logical and computational approaches have explored this possibility.

Temporal anaphora, like all discourse anaphora and reference resolution, is even more intimately dependent upon world knowledge than the other temporal categories that we have been considering. In order to control this influence, we will follow the style of much work in AI, drawing most of our examples from a restricted domain of discourse. We will follow Isard (1974) in taking a board game as the example domain. Imagine that each classical model in the structure of Figure 11 is represented as a database, or collection of facts describing not only the position of the pieces in a game of chess, and the instantaneous moves at each frame, but the fact that at certain times durative or composite events like *exchanging Rooks* or *White attacking the Black Queen* are in progress across more than one state.

Consider the following examples from such a domain:

(70) a. When I took your pawn, you took my queen.

b. I took your pawn. You took my queen.

The *when*-clause in a, above, establishes a reference point for the tense of the main clause, just as the definite NP *Keats* establishes a referent for the pronoun. Indeed the *when*-clause itself behaves like a definite, in that it seems to presuppose that the event of *my*

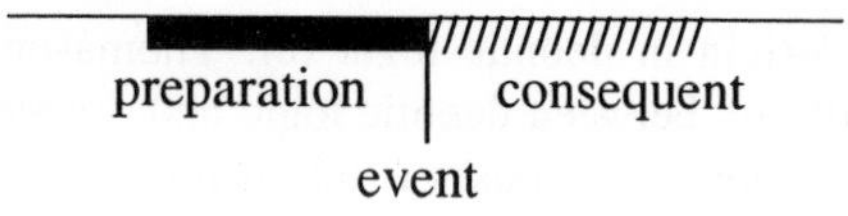

Fig. 12. The nucleus again.

taking your pawn is identifiable to the hearer. (Of course, the reader will have effortlessly accommodated this presupposition.) The first sentence in (70)b, above, behaves exactly like the *when* clause in setting the reference point for the second. The only difference is that the simple declarative *I took your pawn* itself demands a previously established reference point to be anaphoric to, whereas the *when* clause causes a new reference point to be constructed.

As has been frequently noticed, the state to which the tense in *you taking my queen* refers in (70)a, above, is not strictly the state in which *I took your pawn*. It is the state that *resulted from* that action. However, it is not invariably the case that the temporal reference point moves on in this way. Most obviously, a stative main clause is primarily predicated of the original reference point of the *when*-clause:

(71) When I took your pawn, I did not know it was protected by your knight.

(Presumably, the ignorance in question may have ended with that very move.) Events also may be predicated of the original reference point, rather than moving the action on:

(72) When I took your pawn, I used a rook.

In fact, as Ritchie (1979) and Partee (1984) have pointed out, in strictly temporal terms, we can find main clauses that *precede* the reference point established by a *when* clause:

(73) When I won my only game against Bobby Fischer, I used the Ruy Lopez opening.

These phenomena arise because the temporal referent is *not* strictly temporal. Rather than being a time or an interval, it is (a pointer to) an event-nucleus of exactly the kind that was used earlier to explain the aspectual sort hierarchy and possible coercions among the *Aktionsarten*. That is, it is a structure of the kind shown in Figure 2, repeated here as Figure 12. It will be recalled that the preparation is an activity, the consequent is a (perfect) state, and that the core event is an achievement. (Recall that any event-type can turn into an achievement via the sort-transition schema in Figure 1.)

In the terms of our modal frame, the preparation of an event is the activity or action that led to the state in which that achievement took place. The consequent is the consequent state, and as we saw in the earlier discussion of the modals, includes the entire subtree of states accessible from that state. The referent-setting effect of a *when*-clause can then be seen as identifying such a nucleus. The main clause is then temporally located with respect to the nucleus. This may be by lining it up with the core event itself, either as a property of the initial state, as in example (71), or as a property of the transition itself, as in (72). Alternatively, since accessibility is defined in terms of the subsequent actions, the actual subsequent action is a possible main clause, as in (70). Or the main clause may be located with respect to the preparation, as in (73). Which of these alternatives a given example gives rise to is a matter determined by the knowledge representation, not by rules of the semantics.

On the assumption that the consequent in the nuclear referent includes the entire subtree of future states, the information needed by conditionals, modals, and other referent-setting adverbials will be available:

(74) a. If you take my queen, you may win.

b. If you had taken my queen, you might have won.

c. Since you took my queen, you have been winning.

All of this suggests that states or partial possible worlds in a logic of action deriving ultimately from von Wright and McCarthy and Hayes, with a much enriched ontology involving a rather intimate connection to the knowledge-base, are appropriate candidates for a Reichenbachian anaphoric account of tense and temporality. But this does not tell us how the temporal referent is set up to act as a referent for anaphora.

4.2. Logical and computational approaches

It is possible in principle to embody a Reichenbachian account in a pure modal logic, say by developing "multi-dimensional" tense logics of the kind used by Nerbonne (1984) (see Van Benthem, 1991, 1995, Section III.3). However, the event-based calculus over counterfactual partially specified states discussed in Section 3 offers a promising candidate for a representation of Riechenbach's reference point R, in the form of deterministic event sequences $[\alpha]$. This opens up the possibility of applying the general modal apparatus developed so far, not only for quantifying over states, but to act as the temporal link between sentences and clauses, as in *when*-clauses and multi-sentence discourse.

Most computational approaches have equated sentential temporal anaphora with *discourse* temporal anaphora, rather than any structurally bound variety. Thus Winograd (1972), Isard (1974), and the present author treated the establishment of temporal (and pronominal) referents as temporary side-effects to a single STRIPS-like database. A reference-point establishing *when*-clause or conditional had the effect of setting the database to the state of the world at the (in Isard's case, possibly counterfactual) time in question. The way this was actually done was to "fast-forward" (or -backward) the world to the situation in question, using the history of events to carry out the sequence of updates and retractions necessary to construct the state of the world at the reference point.

Within the situation calculus and its descendants including the dynamic version, this strategem is unnecessary. The history of events is a sequence such as the following:

(75) $$start(write(keats, sonnet)); arrive(chapman) \\ @stop(write(keats, sonnet))$$

The referent of a *when*-clause, such as *When Chapman arrived*, is simply the sequence up to and including $arrive(chapman)$, namely:

(76) $start(write(keats,\ sonnet)); arrive(chapman)$

To identify the referent we need the following definition of a relation we might call *evoke*. This is merely a logic-programming device which defines a search for a deterministic event sequence of the form $[\alpha;\beta]$ or $[\alpha@\beta]$ over a history in which the sequence operators are "left-associative" (we only give the rules for the operator ; here):

(77) a. $\models evoke((\alpha;\beta),(\alpha;\beta))$

b. $\models evoke((\alpha;\beta),\gamma) \rightarrow evoke((\alpha;\beta),(\gamma;\delta))$

Evokable α are by definition possible, even for counterfactual histories.

The referent-setting effect of *when* can now be captured to a first approximation in the following rules, which first find the current history of events, then *evoke* a suitable reference point, then test for the appropriate relation *when*. (Again this is a logic programming hack which could be passed over, and again there are two further rules with @ for ; that are omitted here):

(78) a. $\models state(\gamma) \wedge S(history) \wedge evoke((\alpha;\beta), history) \wedge [\alpha;\beta]\gamma \rightarrow when(\beta,\gamma)$

b. $\models event(\varepsilon) \wedge S(history) \wedge evoke((\alpha;\beta@\varepsilon), history) \rightarrow when(\beta,\varepsilon)$

The predicate S determines the Reichenbachian speech point, which is an event or sequence of events. $S(history)$ is assumed to be available in the database, as a fact. The first rule, a, applies to *when* sentences with state-type main clause propositions, and says that $when(\beta,\gamma)$ is true if γ is a state, and you can *evoke* an event sequence ending in β after which γ holds. The second applies to *when* sentences with event-type main clauses, and says that $when(\beta,\varepsilon)$ is true if ε is an event and you can *evoke* an event sequence whose last two events are β and then ε. The question a, below, concerning the ensuing state, therefore translates into the query b:

(79) a. When Chapman arrived, was Keats finishing writing *In Disgust of Vulgar Superstition*?

b. $when((\alpha; arrive(chapman)),$
$progressive(achievement(finish(write(keats,\ sonnet)))))$

The progressive is, it will be recalled, a state, so in our greatly simplified world, this is true, despite the fact that under the closed world assumption Keats did not finish the poem, because of the earlier elimination of the imperfective paradox.

A *when*-question with an event in the main clause, as in a, below, translates as in b:

(80) a. When Chapman arrived, did Keats stop writing *In Disgust of Vulgar Superstition*?

b. $when((\alpha; arrive(chapman)), stop(write(keats,\ sonnet)))$

In the case to hand, this last will yield a proof with the following constructive instantiation:

(81) $when((start(write(keats,\ sonnet)); arrive(chapman)),$
$stop(write(keats,\ sonnet)))$

In either case, the enduring availability of the Reichenbachian reference point for later simple tensed sentences can be captured on the assumption that the act of *evoking* a new referent causes a sideffect to the database, causing a new fact (say of the form $R(\alpha)$) to be asserted, after any existing fact of the same form has been removed, or retracted. (We pass over the formal details here, merely noting that for this purpose a blatantly non-declarative STRIPS-like formulation seems to be the natural one, although we have seen how such non-declarativity could in principle be eliminated from the system. Lin and Reiter (1995) show how such a process of "progressing" the database can be defined on the basis of the declarative representation.)

The representation captures the fact that Keats stopped writing the poem *because* Chapman arrived, whereas Chapman merely arrived *after* Keats started writing, not because of it.

Of course, it will be clear from the earlier discussion that such a system remains oversimplified. Such sentences also suggest that the event sequences themselves should be considerably enriched on lines suggested in earlier sections. They need a system of types or sorts of the kind proposed by various authors discussed in Section 2. They should also be structured into *nested* structures of causal or, more generally, contingent sequences.

Since we have also observed that main clause events may be simultaneous with, as well as consequent upon, the *when* clause event, events must also be permitted to be simultaneous, perhaps using the connective $\cap$ introduced by Peleg (1987) to capture the relation between embedded events like *starting to write "In Disgust of Vulgar Superstition"* and *starting to write*, generalizing the above rules accordingly. Partial ordering of events must also be allowed. The inferential possibilities implicit in the notion of the nucleus must be accommodated, in order to capture the fact that one event may cause the preparation of another event to start, thereby embodying a non-immediate causal effect.

Very little of this work has been done, and it may be unwise to speculate in advance of concrete solutions to the many real problems that remain. However the limited fragment outlined above suggests that dynamic logic may be a promising framework in which to pursue this further work and bring together a number of earlier approaches. In this connection, it is perhaps worth remarking that, of the seven putative limitations of the situation calculus and its relatives claimed in the critical review by Shoham and Goyal (1988b, pp. 422–424), five (limitation to instantaneous events, difficulty of representing non-immediate causal effects, ditto of concurrent events, ditto of continuous processes, and the frame problem) either have been overcome or have been addressed to some extent in the published work within the situation calculus. Of the remaining two (the qualification problem and the ramification problem) the ramification problem in the narrow sense of *known* causal effects of actions has been addressed above and by Schubert and Reiter. In the broader sense of *unanticipated* contingencies or ramifications, and similarly unanticipated preconditions, or qualifications, these problems have not been overcome in *any* framework, possibly because they do not belong in the logic at all.

The non-computational approaches to temporal anaphora, in contrast, to those just described, have tended to equate all temporal anaphora with structurally bound anaphora. DRT treats temporal referent(s) much like nominal referents, as localized side-effects. This mechanism is used to extend the scope of the temporal referent beyond the scope that surface syntax would most immediately suggest, in much the same way that the scope of nominal referents is extended to capture such varieties of nominal anaphor as "donkey pronouns", and the approach is generalized to modals and conditionals by Roberts (1989), and Kamp and Reyle (1993). They, like Dowty (1986), assume that events invariably move the temporal reference point forward while states do not – cf. Kamp and Reyle (1993, p. 528), which in general is not the case. (Indeed in the case of the latter authors, this assumption is somewhat at odds with their adoption elsewhere of a nucleus-like structure over events – cf. p. 558.) However, both note the oversimplification, and their theories remain entirely compatible in principle with the present proposal to bring this question under the control of context and inference, perhaps along lines suggested by Lascarides and Asher (1993a), who incorporate persistence assumptions of the kind discussed above.

Interestingly, Groenendijk and Stokhof (1991, p. 50) show how the scope-extending mechanism of DRT can be captured straightforwardly in a first-order variety of dynamic logic, dynamic predicate logic (DPL – cf. Dekker (1979), and the chapter on 'Dynamics' in the present volume.) While DPL is quite distantly related to dynamic logic in the sense that the term is used here, the mechanism that Groendijk and Stokhof propose, which directly models the side-effects implicit in assignment to variables, seems to be generalizable to the DRT treatment of inter-clause temporal anaphora and the Reichbachian reference point, suggesting a way to unify all of the approaches discussed here.

5. Conclusion

The analysis so far has built solely upon observations from English. Nevertheless, the claim that the semantics outlined above depends directly upon the conceptual representation of action and contingency suggests that this semantics might be universal, despite considerable differences in its syntactic and morphological encoding across languages. Discussion of the evidence for this claim would take us beyond the scope of this essay. However, the available reviews of this extensive literature (e.g. Dahl, 1985; Smith, 1991) seem to lend some support to the following brief observation on this question.

Benjamin Lee Whorf once observed that the auxiliaries and inflections associated with verbs in Amerindian languages appeared to be semantically quite unlike the corresponding categories in English and other European languages. The Amerindian categories seemed to be more concerned with various aspects of the speakers' evidential and consequential relation to events, rather than the strictly temporal relations which Whorf assumed were implicated in the corresponding devices of English. He suggested, controversially, that these differences reflected differences in modes of thinking about events and time.

The work described above suggests that such differences across languages are superficial. Ironically, the English tense/aspect system seems to be based on semantic primitives remarkably like those which Whorf ascribed to Hopi. Matters of temporal sequence and temporal locality seem to be quite secondary to matters of perspective and contingency. This observation in turn suggests that the semantics of tense and aspect is profoundly shaped by concerns with goals, actions and consequences, and that temporality in the narrow sense of the term is merely one facet of this system among many.

Such concerns seem to be the force that determines the logic that is required to capture its semantics as the particular kind of dynamic system outlined above, whose structure is intimately related to knowledge of action, the structure of episodic memory, and the computational process of inference.

6. Further reading

The literature on temporality and representation of causal action is vast, and I am painfully aware of having been forced to pass over entirely or to treat rather superficially a great deal of important and relevant work. Besides numerous chapters in the present volume referred to in the text, the following sources are offered as a means of entry to a more extensive literature.

Hughes and Cresswell (1968) remains an important source for early axiomatic approaches to modal logic, and its early historical development. Van Benthem (1983) is a very readable survey of Tense Logic, with particular attention to the effects of different ontological commitments, including those related to the representation of various views of time implicit in modern physics. A number of papers in Volume II of Gabbay and Guenthner's (1984) *Handbook of Philosophical Logic* cover recent developments, including those by Bull and Segerberg, Burgess, Thomason, Van Benthem, and Åqvist. Harel (1980) in the same volume and Goldblatt (1992) are resources for dynamic logic and related systems, including temporal logic. Kamp and Reyle (1993) discuss tense and aspect within DRT. Groenendijk and Stokhof (1991) discuss the expressibility of DRT in dynamic predicate logic. The early paper by McCarthy and Hayes (1969) remains an excellent review of modal logic from a computational perspective, and is one of the few sources to explicitly relate computational and logical approaches, as is Nilsson's elegant 1980 text. The invaluable collections of readings in artificial intelligence, non-monotonic reasoning, and planning respectively edited by Webber and Nilsson (1981), Ginsberg (1987), and Allen, Hendler and Tate (1990) are sources which reprint many of the computational papers discussed above, and much other recent work in AI knowledge representation which it has not been possible to survey here. Galton (1987) is a recent collection of essays bringing together logicians and computer scientists on the question of temporal representations. The special issue on tense and aspect of *Journal of Computational Linguistics* (Volume 14.2) is another source for computational linguistic approaches. Dahl (1985) and Smith (1991) survey the tense and aspectual systems of a considerable number of languages from a linguistic standpoint similar to that presented here.

Acknowledgements

An early draft of some parts of Sections 3.2 and 4.2 appeared in a different form as Steedman (1995). I am grateful to Johan van Benthem, Pat Hayes, Stephen Isard, David Israel, Mark Johnson, Alex Lascarides, Alice ter Meulen, Marc Moens, Charlie Ortiz, Jong Park, Len Schubert, Matthew Stone, Rich Thomason, Bonnie Webber, and Michael

White for advice and criticism. They are not to blame for any errors that remain. Support was provided in part by NSF grant nos. IRI91-17110, and IRI95-04372, DARPA grant no. N660001-94-C-6043, and ARO grant no. DAAH04-94-G0426.

References

Abusch, D. (in press), *Sequence of tense and temporal de re*, Ling. and Philos. (to appear).

Allen, J. (1984), *Towards a general theory of action and time*, Artif. Intell. **23**, 123–154.

Allen, J., Hendler, J. and Tate, A. (1990), *Readings in Planning*, Morgan Kaufmann, Palo Alto, CA.

Asher, N. (1990), *A default truth conditional semantics for the progressive*, Ling. and Philos. **15**, 469–598.

Bach, E. (1980), *Tenses and aspects as functions on verb-phrases*, Time, Tense, and Quantifiers, C. Rohrer, ed., Niemeyer, Tübingen.

Bach, E. (1986), *The algebra of events*, Ling. and Philos. **9**, 5–16.

Barwise, J. and Perry, J. (1983), *Situations and Attitudes*, Bradford, Cambridge, MA.

Bäuerle, R. (1979), *Tense logics and natural language*, Synthèse **40**, 225–230.

Bennett, M. and Partee, B. (1972), *Towards the logic of tense and aspect in English*, Published by Indiana University Linguistics Club 1978, System Development Corporation, Santa Monica, CA.

Blackburn, P., Gardent, C. and De Rijke, M. (1993), *Back and forth through time and events*, Proceedings of the 9th Amsterdam Colloquium, December, ILLC, University of Amsterdam, 161–175.

Boyd, J. and Thorne, J. (1969), *The semantics of modal verbs*, J. Ling. **5**, 57–74.

Brennan, V. (1993), *Root and epistemic modal auxiliary verbs*, PhD Dissertation, University of Massachussets, Amherst.

Caenepeel, M. (1989), *Aspect, temporal ordering, and perspective in narrative fiction*, PhD Dissertation, University of Edinburgh.

Carlson, G. (1977), *Reference to kinds in English*, PhD Dissertation, University of Massachussets, Amherst.

Cooper, R. (1986), *Tense and discourse location in situation semantics*, Ling. and Philos. **9**, 17–36.

Cresswell, M. (1974), *Adverbs and events*, Synthèse **28**, 455–481.

Cresswell, M. (1985), *Structured Meanings*, MIT Press, Cambridge, MA.

Cresswell, M. (1988), *Semantical Essays*, Kluwer, Dordrecht.

Cresswell, M. (1990), *Entities and Indices*, Kluwer, Dordrecht.

Crouch, R. and Pulman, S. (1993), *Time and modality in a natural language interface*, Artif. Intell. **63**, 265–304.

Dahl, Ö. (1985), *Tense and Aspect Systems*, Basil, Blackwell, Oxford.

Davidson, D. (1967), *The logical form of action sentences*, The Logic of Decision and Action, N. Rescher, ed., Univ. of Pittsburgh Press, Pittsburgh.

De Kleer, J. (1984), *Choices without backtracking*, Proceedings of the 4th National Conference on Artificial Intelligence, 79–85.

De Swart, H. (1991), *Adverbs of quantification: A generalised quantifier approach*, PhD Dissertation, Rijksuniversiteit Groningen.

Dekker, P. (1979), *Transsentential Meditations: Ups and Downs in Dynamic Semantics*, PhD Dissertation, University of Amsterdam, ILLC dissertation Series, 1993, no. 1.

Dowty, D. (1979), *Word Meaning and Montague Grammar*, Reidel, Dordrecht. (Second edition 1991.)

Dowty, D. (1982), *Tenses, time-adverbs, and compositional semantic theory*, Ling. and Philos. **5**, 23–55.

Dowty, D. (1986), *The effects of aspectual class on the temporal structure of discourse semantics or pragmatics?*, Ling. and Philos. **9**, 37–62.

Doyle, J. (1979), *A truth maintenance system*, Artif. Intell. **12**, 231–272.

Eberle, K. (1990), *Eventualities in natural language understanding systems*, Sorts and Types in Artificial Intelligence, K. Bläsius, U. Hedtstück and C. Rollinger, eds, Springer, Berlin.

Enç, M. (1981), *Tense without scope*, PhD Dissertation, University of Madison, Wisconsin.

Enç, M. (1986), *Towards a referential analysis of temporal expressions*, Ling. and Philos. **9**, 405–426.

Enç, M. (1987), *Anchoring conditions for tense*, Ling. Inq. **18**, 633–657.

Fikes, R. and Nilsson, N. (1971), *STRIPS: A new approach to the application of theorem proving to problem solving*, Artif. Intell. **2**, 189–208.

Fine, K. (1975), *Critical notice of Lewis*, Counterfactuals, Mind **84**, 451–458.

Gabbay, D. and Guenthner, F. (eds) (1984), *Handbook of Philosophical Logic,* vol. II, Reidel, Dordrecht.

Gagnon, M. and Lapalme, G. (1995), *From conceptual time to linguistic time*, Comput. Ling. (to appear).

Galton, A. (1984), *The Logic of Aspect*, Clarendon Press, Oxford.

Galton, A. (ed.) (1987), *Temporal Logics and Their Applications*, Academic Press, New York.

Galton, A. (1990), *A critical examination of Allen's theory of action and time*, Artif. Intell. **42**, 159–188.

Garrod, H. (1954), *Commentary on Keats' sonnet 'Written in disgust of vulgar superstition'*, Keats' Poetical Works, H. Garrod, ed., Clarendon Press, Oxford. (2nd edn 1954.)

Ginsberg, M. (1986), *Counterfactuals*, Artif. Intell. **30**, 35–81.

Ginsberg, M. (1987), *Readings in Nonmonotonic Reasoning*, Morgan Kaufmann, Palo Alto, CA.

Goldblatt, R. (1980), *Diodorean modality in Minkowski spacetime*, Stud. Logica **39**, 219–236.

Goldblatt, R. (1992), *Logics of Time and Computation*, CSLI/Chicago Univ. Press, Chicago (2nd edn).

Groenendijk, J. and Stokhof, M. (1991), *Dynamic Predicate Logic*, Ling. and Philos. **14**, 39–100.

Harel, D. (1980), *Dynamic logic*, Handbook of Philosophical Logic, vol. II, D. Gabbay and F. Guenthner, eds, Reidel, Dordrecht.

Heyting, A. (1956), *Intuitionism: An Introduction*, North-Holland, Amsterdam.

Heinämäki, O. (1974), *Semantics of English temporal connectives*, PhD Dissertation, University of Texas, Austin.

Hinrichs, E. (1985), *A compositional semantics for aktionsarten and NP reference in English*, PhD Dissertation, Ohio State University.

Hinrichs, E. (1986), *Temporal anaphora in discourses of English*, Ling. and Philos. **9**, 63–82.

Hintikka, J. (1962), *Knowledge and Belief*, Cornell Univ. Press, Ithaca, NY.

Hornstein, N. (1977), *Towards a theory of tense*, Ling. Inq. **8**, 521–557.

Hornstein, N. (1990), *As Time Goes By: Tense and Universal Grammar*, MIT Press, Cambridge, MA.

Hughes, G. and Cresswell, M. (1968), *Introduction to Modal Logic*, Methuen.

Hwang, C. and Schubert, L. (1992), *Tense trees as the fine structure of discourse*, Proceedings of the 30th Annual Meeting of the Association for Computational Linguistics, 232–240.

Inoue, K. (1979), *An analysis of the English present perfect*, Linguistics **17**, 561–590.

Isard, S. (1974), *What would you have done if ...*, Theor. Ling. **1**, 233–255.

Isard, S. and Longuet-Higgins, H.C. (1973), *Modal Tictacto*, Logic, Language and Probability, R. Bogdan and I. Niiniluoto, eds, Reidel, Dordrecht, 189–195.

Jackendoff, R. (1991), *Parts and boundaries*, Cognition **41**, 9–46.

Kamp, H. (1979), *Events, instants, and temporal reference*, Semantics for Different Points of View, R. Bäuerle, U. Egli and A. von Stechow, eds, Springer, Berlin.

Kamp, H. and Rohrer, C. (1983), *Tense in texts*, Meaning, Use, and Interpretation in Language, R. Bäuerle, C. Schwarze and A. von Stechow, eds, De Gruyter, Berlin, 250–269.

Kamp, H. and Reyle, U. (1993), *From Discourse to Logic*, Kluwer, Dordrecht.

Karlin, R. (1988), *Defining the semantics of verbal modifiers in the domain of cooking tasks*, Proceedings of the 26th Annual Meeting of the Association for Computational Linguistics, 61–67.

Kowalski, R. (1979), *Logic for Problem Solving*, North-Holland, Amsterdam.

Kowalski, R. and Sergot, M. (1986), *A logic-based calculus of events*, New Generation Computing **4**, 67–95.

Kratzer, A. (1977), *What must and can can and must mean*, Ling. and Philos. **1**, 337–355.

Kratzer, A. (1991), *Modality*, Semantics: An International Handbook of Contemporary Research, A. von Stechow and D. Wunderlich, eds, De Gruyter, Berlin.

Krifka, M. (1989), *Nominal reference, temporal constitution, and quantification in event semantics*, Semantics and Contextual Expressions, R. Bartsch, J. van Benthem and P. van Emde Boas, eds, Foris, Dordrecht, 75–115.

Krifka, M. (1990), *Four thousand ships passed through the lock: Object-induced measure functions on events*, Ling. and Philos. **13**, 487–520.

Krifka, M. (1992), *Thematic relations as links between nominal reference and temporal constitution*, Lexical Matters, I. Sag and A. Szabolcsi, eds, CSLI/Chicago Univ. Press, Chicago.

Kripke, S. (1965), *Semantical analysis of intuitionistic logic I*, Formal Systems and Recursive Functions, Crossley and M. Dummett, eds, North-Holland, Amsterdam.

Kripke, S. (1972), *Naming and necessity*, Semantics of Natural Language, D. Davidson and G. Harman, eds, Reidel, Dordrecht.

Landman, F. (1986), *Towards a Theory of Information*, Foris, Dordrecht.

Landman, F. (1991), *Structures for Semantics*, Kluwer, Dordrecht.

Landman, F. (1992), *The progressive*, Nat. Language Semantics **1**, 1–32.

Lansky, A. (1986), *A representation of parallel activity based on events, structure and casusality*, Proceedings of the Workshop on Planning and Reasoning About Action, Timberline Lodge, Mount Hood, OR, 50–86.

Lascarides, A. and Asher, N. (1993a), *Temporal interpretation, discourse relations, and commonsense entailment*, Ling. and Philos. **16**, 437–494.

Lascarides, A. and Asher, N. (1993b), *A semantics and pragmatics for the pluperfect*, Proceedings of the Annual Meeting of the European Chapter of the Association for Computational Linguistics, Utrecht, NL, 250–259.

Levesque, H. (1988), *Logic and the complexity of reasoning*, J. Philos. Logic **17**, 355–389.

Lewis, D. (1971), *Completeness and decidability of three logics of counterfactual conditionals*, Theoria **37**, 74–85.

Lewis, D. (1973a), *Causation*, J. Philos. **70**, 556–567.

Lewis, D. (1973b), *Counterfactuals*, Harvard Univ. Press, Cambridge, MA, 556–567.

Lewis, D. (1979), *Scorekeeping in a language game*, J. Philos. Logic **8**, 339–359.

Lin, F. (1995), *Embracing causality in specifying the indirect effect of actions*, Proceedings of the 14th International Joint Conference on Artificial Intelligence, Montreal, August 1995, 1985–1991.

Lin, F. and Reiter, R. (1995), *How to progress a database II: The STRIPS connection*, Proceedings of the 14th International Joint Conference on Artificial Intelligence, Montreal, August 1995, 2001–2007.

Link, G. (1983), *The logical analysis of plurals and massterms*, Meaning, Use, and Interpretation in Language, R. Bäuerle, C. Schwarze and A. von Stechow, eds, De Gruyter, Berlin, 302–323.

Link, G. (1987), *Algebraic semantics of event structures*, J. Groenendijk, M. Stokhof and F. Veltman, eds, Proceedings of the 6th Amsterdam Colloquium.

Lyons, J. (1977), *Semantics, vol. II*, Cambridge Univ. Press, Cambridge, MA.

McCarthy, J. and Hayes, P. (1969), *Some philosophical problems from the standpoint of Artificial Intelligence*, Mach. Intell. **4**, B. Meltzer and D. Michie, eds, Edinburgh Univ. Press, Edinburgh, 473–502.

McCarthy, J. (1977), *Epistemological problems of artificial intelligence*, Proceedings of the 5th International Joint Conference on Artificial Intelligence, 1038–1044.

McCarty, T. (1994), *Modalities over actions I: Model theory*, Proceedings of the 4th International Conference on Principles of Knowledge Representation and Reasoning, Bonn, Germany, 437–448.

McCawley, J. (1971), *Tense and time reference in English*, Studies in Linguistic Semantics, C. Fillmore and T. Langendoen, eds, Holt, Rinehart and Winston, New York, 96–113.

McDermott, D. (1982), *A temporal logic for reasoning about processes and actions*, Cogn. Science **6**, 101–155.

Miller, G. and Johnson-Laird, P. (1976), *Language and Perception*, Cambridge Univ. Press, Cambridge, MA.

Moens, M. (1987), *Tense, aspect and temporal teference*, PhD Dissertation, University of Edinburgh.

Moens, M. and Steedman, M. (1988), *Temporal ontology and temporal reference*, Comput. Ling. **14**, 15–28.

Moore, R. (1980), *Reasoning about knowledge and action*, PhD Dissertation, Cambridge MA, MIT, published as TN-191, SRI International, Menlo Park, CA.

Morgenstern, L. and Stein, L. (1988), *Why things go wrong: A formal theory of causal reasoning*, Proceedings of the 7th National Conference on Artificial Intelligence, AAAI, 518–523.

Mourelatos, A. (1978), *Events, processes and states*, Ling. and Philos. **2**, 415–434.

Nerbonne, J. (1984), *German temporal semantics: Three-dimensional tense-logic and a GPSG fragment*, PhD Dissertation, Ohio State University, Columbus, OH.

Nerode, A. and Wijesekera (1990), *Constructive concurrent dynamic logic I*, Technical Report 90-43, Mathematical Sciences Institute, Cornell University, Ithaca.

Nilsson, N. (1980), *Principles of Artificial Intelligence*, Tioga, Palo Alto, CA.

Ortiz, C. (1994), *Causal pathways of rational action*, Proceedings of the Twelfth National Conference on Artificial Intelligence, 1061–1066.

Parsons, T. (1990), *Events in the Semantics of English*, MIT Press, Cambridge, MA.

Partee, B. (1973), *Some structural analogies between tenses and pronouns in English*, J. Philos. **70**, 601–609.

Partee, B. (1984), *Nominal and temporal anaphora*, Ling. and Philos. **7**, 243–286.

Pednault, E. (1989), *ADL: Exploring the middle ground between STRIPS and the situation calculus*, Proceedings of the 1st International Conference on Principles of Knowledge Representation and Reasoning, R. Brachman et al., eds, Morgan Kaufmann, Palo Alto, CA, 324–332.

Peleg, D. (1987), *Concurrent dynamic logic*, J. Assoc. Comput. Mach. **34**, 450–479.

Pratt, V. (1979), *Process logic*, Proceedings of the 6th Annual ACM Conference on Principles of Programming Languages, 93–100.

Prior, A. (1967), *Past, Present and Future*, Clarendon Press, Oxford.

Pustejovsky, J. (1991), *The syntax of event structure*, Cognition **41**, 47–82.

Quine, W. (1960), *Word and Object*, MIT Press, Cambridge, MA.

Reichenbach, H. (1947), *Elements of Symbolic Logic*, Univ. of California Press, Berkeley, CA.

Reiter, R. (1978), *On closed world databases*, Logic and Databases, H. Gallaire and J. Minker, eds, Plenum, New York, 119–140.

Reiter, R. (1991), *The frame problem in the situation calculus: A simple solution (sometimes) and a completeness result for goal regression*, AI and Mathematical Theory of Computation: Papers in Honour of John McCarthy, V. Lifshitz, ed., Academic Press, New York, 359–380.

Reiter, R. (1993), *Proving properties of states in the situation calculus*, Artif. Intell. **64**, 337–351.

Rescher, N. (1964), *Hypothetical Reasoning*, North-Holland, Amsterdam.

Ritchie, G. (1979), *Temporal clauses in English*, Theor. Ling. **6**, 87–115.

Roberts, C. (1989), *Modal subordination and pronominal anaphora in discourse*, Ling. and Philos. **12**, 683–721.

Rosenschein, S. (1981), *Plan synthesis: A logical perspective*, Proceedings of the 7th International Joint Conference on Artificial Intelligence, Vancouver, 331–337.

Schank, R. (1975), *The structure of episodes in memory*, Representation and Understanding, D. Bobrow and A. Collins, eds, Academic Press, New York, 237–272.

Schein, B. (1993), *Plurals and Events*, MIT Press, Cambridge, MA.

Scherl, R. and Levesque, H. (1993), *The Frame Problem and knowledge-producing actions*, Proceedings of the 11th National Conference on Artificial Intelligence, Washington, AAAI, 689–695.

Schubert, L. (1990), *Monotonic solution of the frame problem in the situation calculus: An efficient method for worlds with fully specified actions*, Knowledge Representation and Defeasible Reasoning, H. Kyburg, R. Loui and G. Carlson, eds, Kluwer, Dordrecht, 23–67.

Schubert, L. (1994), *Explanation closure, action closure, and the Sandewall test suite for reasoning about change*, J. Logic Comput. (to appear).

Shoham, Y. (1988), *Reasoning about Change*, MIT Press, Cambridge, MA.

Shoham, Y. and Goyal, N. (1988), *Temporal reasoning in AI*, Exploring Artificial Intelligence, H. Shrobe, ed., Morgan Kaufmann, Palo Alto, CA, 419–438.

Smith, C. (1991), *The Parameter of Aspect*, Reidel, Dordrecht.

Song, F. and Cohen, R. (1988), *The interpretation of temporal relations in narrative*, Proceedings of the 7th National Conference of the American Association for Artificial Intelligence, 745–750.

Stalnaker, R. (1968), *A theory of conditionals*, Studies in Logical Theory, N. Rescher, ed., Basil Blackwell, Oxford.

Stalnaker, R. (1984), *Inquiry*, MIT Press, Cambridge, MA.

Steedman, M. (1982), *Reference to past time*, Speech, Place, and Action, R. Jarvella and W. Klein, eds, Wiley, New York, 125–157.

Steedman, M. (1995), *Dynamic semantics for tense and aspect*, Proceedings of the 14th International Conference on Artificial Intelligence, Montreal, 1292–1298.

Stein, L. (1991), *Resolving ambiguity in non-monotonic reasoning*, PhD Dissertation, Brown University, Providence, RI.

Stone, M. (1994), *The reference argument of epistemic must*, Proceedings of the International Workshop on Computational Semantics, Tilburg University, The Netherlands, 181–190.

Taylor, B. (1977), *Tense and continuity*, Ling. and Philos. **1**, 199–220.

Ter Meulen, A. (1984), *Events, quantities, and individuals*, Varieties of Formal Semantics, F. Landman and F. Veltman, eds, Foris, Dordrecht.

Ter Meulen, A. (1986), *Locating events*, Foundations of Pragmatics and Lexical Semantics, J. Groenendijk, D. de Jonge and M. Stokhof, eds, Foris, Dordrecht.

Ter Meulen, A. (1995), *Representing Time in Natural Language: The Dynamic Interpretation of Tense and Aspect*, MIT Press, Cambridge, MA.

Thomason, R. (1970), *Indeterminist time and truth-value gaps*, Theoria **36**, 246–281.

Thomason, R. (1981), *Deontic logic as founded in tense logic*, New Studies in Deontic Logic, R. Hilpinen, ed., Reidel, Dordrecht.

Thomason, R. (1991), *Logicism, AI, and common sense: John McCarthys program in philosophical perspective*, AI and Mathematical Theory of Computation: Papers in Honour of John McCarthy, V. Lipschitz, ed., Academic Press, New York, 449–466.

Thomason, R. and Gupta, A. (1980), *A theory of conditionals in the context of branching time*, Philos. Rev. **88**, 65–90.

Turner, R. (1981), *Counterfactuals without possible worlds*, J. Philos. Logic **10**, 453–493.

Van Benthem, J. (1983), *The Logic of Time*, Kluwer, Dordrecht.

Van Benthem, J. (1991a), *General Dynamics*, Theor. Ling. **16**, 159–172.

Van Benthem, J. (1991b), *Language in Action*, North-Holland, Amsterdam.

Van Benthem, J. (1995), *Temporal logic*, Handbook of Logic in Artificial Intelligence and Logic Programming, D. Gabbay et al., eds, Clarendon, Oxford.

Van Fraassen, B. (1971), *Formal Semantics and Logic*, Macmillan, New York.

Veltman, F. (1983), *Data semantics*, Truth, Interpretation, Information, GRASS 3, J. Groenendijk, M. Janssen and M. Stokhof, eds, Foris, Dordrecht.

Vendler, Z. (1967), *Linguistics in Philosophy*, Cornell Univ. Press, Ithaca.

Verkuyl, H. (1972), *On the Compositional Nature of the Aspects*, Reidel, Dordrecht.

Verkuyl, H. (1989), *Aspectual classes and aspectual composition*, Ling. and Philos. **12**, 39–94.

Vlach, F. (1981), *The semantics of the progressive*, Syntax and Semantics **14**, P. Tedeschi and A. Zaenen, eds, Academic Press, New York.

Vlach, F. (1993), *Temporal adverbials, tenses, and the perfect*, Ling. and Philos. **16**, 231–283.

von Wright, G. (1964), *Norm and Action: A Logical Enquiry*, Routledge & Kegan Paul, London.

von Wright, G. (1967), *The logic of action – a sketch*, The Logic of Decision and Action, N. Rescher, ed., Univ. of Pittsburgh Press, Pittsburgh.

Webber, B. and Nilsson, N. (1981), *Readings in Artificial Intelligence*, Tioga, Palo Alto, CA.

Webber, B. (1983), *Logic and natural language*, IEEE Computer, Special Issue on Knowledge Representation, 43–46.

Webber, B. (1988), *Tense as discourse anaphor*, Comput. Ling. **14**, 61–73.

White, M. (1993), *Delimitedness and trajectory of motion events*, Proceedings of the 6th Conference of the European Chapter of the Association for Computational Linguistics, Utrecht, 412–421.

White, M. (1994), *A computational approach to aspectual composition*, PhD Dissertation, University of Pennsylvania, Philadelphia.

Wilensky, R. (1983), *Planning and Understanding*, Addison-Wesley, Reading, MA.

Winograd, T. (1972), *Understanding Natural Language*, Academic Press, New York.

Zwarts, J. and Verkuyl, H. (1994), *An algebra of conceptual structure: An investigation into Jackendoff's conceptual semantics*, Ling. and Philos. **17**, 1–28.

CHAPTER 17

Presupposition*

David Ian Beaver

Department of Philosophy/ILLC, University of Amsterdam, 1012 CP Amsterdam, The Netherlands
E-mail: dib@illc.uva.nl

Contents

*This chapter was completed with the financial support of Monika Kiraly. The manuscript has benefited from comments of Patrick Blackburn, Virginia Brennan, Gennaro Chierchia, Dimitris Dimitriadis, Gerald Gazdar, Willem Groeneveld, Martin Jansche, Ewan Klein, Emiel Krahmer, Anke Ludeling, Rob van der Sandt, Andreas Schöter, Paul Schweizer, Luca Storto, Henk Zeevat, et al. and the editors of the Handbook.

HANDBOOK OF LOGIC AND LANGUAGE
Edited by J. van Benthem and A. ter Meulen

1. Introduction

In conversation, much is presupposed, or taken for granted. The linguistic and philosophical theories which will be discussed in this chapter vary in the extent to which they involve definitions of presupposition which are close to this informal use of the word, and there is no single technical definition of *presupposition* which will satisfy all theorists.[1]

A particular point of dispute has been whether presupposition is best thought of as a semantic or a pragmatic notion, or whether indeed such notions must coexist. In a semantic theory presupposition is usually defined as a binary relation between pairs of sentences of a language. What makes this relation semantical is that it is defined or explicated in terms of the semantic valuation of the sentences, or in terms of a semantic notion of entailment. Thus a definition in terms of semantic valuation might, following Strawson, say that one sentence (semantically) presupposes another if the truth of the second is a condition for the semantic value of the first to be *true* or *false*. In pragmatic theories the analysis of presupposition involves the attitudes and knowledge of language users. In extreme cases such as Stalnaker's (1974) account, presupposition is defined without any reference to linguistic form: Stalnaker talks not of the presuppositions of a sentence, but of the *speaker's presuppositions*, these being just those propositions which are taken for granted by a speaker on a given occasion. Other pragmatic theories are less radical, in that linguistic form still plays an essential role in the theory. The majority of well-developed pragmatic theories concern the presuppositions not of a sentence (as in semantic theories) or of a speaker (as in Stalnaker's theory) but of an utterance.

In the late seventies the lack of an agreed definition was a subject of much debate, and perceived by some as a stumbling block preventing further progress in the field. However, since then there has been much progress (even without an agreed definition) as should become clear in the coming sections. The semantic/pragmatic debate is little aired nowadays, since so many researchers espouse hybrid theories on which the labels *semantic* and *pragmatic* are hard to pin.

---

[1] On a historical note, there is disagreement as to the first use of a technical notion of presupposition. Seuren (1994a) notes that a well known paradox offered by Aristotle's contemporary, Eubulides of Miletus, the so-called *Paradox of the Horned Man*, is based on a presuppositional effect. Caffi (1994), writing in the same volume as Seuren, traces presupposition "back to Xenophanes, quoted in Aristotle's *Rhetoric* ..., via Port Royal ... and John Stuart Mill". Despite these mentions of Aristotle, and despite the very, very, very long running debate as to whether Aristotle favored a departure from bivalence, the following is an example of Aristotle expounding a view that runs contrary to any semantic notion of presupposition: "For manifestly, if Socrates exists, one of the two propositions 'Socrates is ill', 'Socrates is not ill' is true, and the other false. This is likewise the case if he does not exist; for if he does not exist, to say that he is ill is false, and to say that he is not ill is true". (From Aristotle's *Categories* (Aristotle, 1950, Chapter 10:13b, pp. 27–35).) Larry Horn provided me with a convincing reference to an invocation of a concept of presupposition by a medieval scholar. See the passage around line 100 of Petrus Hispanus' *Tractatus Exponibilium*, in Mullally (1945): "Prima est quod diction reduplicativa *praesupponit* aliquod praedicatum iness aliqui subiecto et denotat quod illud super quod adit immediate sit causa inhaerentiae illius". (My emphasis.) The recent philosophical study of presupposition is generally recognized to have started with Frege's remarks in *On Sense and Meaning* (Frege, 1984b), which are not explicitly related to the work of any predecessor.

What the different theories that have been proposed over the years have in common is not a single notion of presupposition, but a more or less accepted set of basic data to be explained, and a more or less accepted set of linguistic constructions to which this data pertains. The data includes such tired examples as 'Have you stopped beating your wife?' and 'The King of France is not bald.', in which the relevant constructions, or *presupposition triggers*, include the aspectual verb 'stop', the possessive 'your' and the definite 'the'.

With regard to the first example, one may say that the proposition that the addressee has beaten his wife is given a special status. Similarly, many theorists would argue that the proposition that there is a King of France has a special status in the second example. Perhaps such propositions are taken for granted. Perhaps they are propositions that must be true for utterances of the examples to carry meaning. Perhaps they are both. Whilst there is no agreed technical definition of *presupposition*, there is agreement that the goals of presupposition theory must include determining the special status of such propositions, and explaining why and under what conditions this status obtains.

In the remainder of Section 1 some further basics are discussed, and the foundations are laid for the presentation of different accounts. Then we dive head-first into the depths of presupposition theory. One of the main insights of the last few decades of study of presupposition is that the phenomenon is heavily influenced by the dynamics of the interpretation process. Therefore, I have divided systems according to the way in which such dynamism is manifested. Section 2 "Static Accounts: Multivalence and Partiality" concerns models in which the dynamics of the interpretation process plays no role, and where the possibility of presupposition failure is tied to the presence of extra truth values in a multivalent (or partial) semantics. In Section 3: "Context Dependence and Part-Time Presupposition" models are presented in which the context of evaluation influences which presuppositions are projected, models involving an *inter-sentential dynamics* where the context of evaluation is modified with each successive utterance. In Section 4 "Context Change and Accommodation" theories are discussed in which *intra-sentential dynamics* plays a crucial role, with sub-sentential constituents being seen as having their own dynamic effects on the context of evaluation used for other constituents, and a process of accommodation allowing presuppositions themselves to produce sophisticated additional modifications. In writing this chapter I have tried to bring out the relationships between different theories, and Section 5 "Syntheses" is devoted entirely to this goal. Section 6 "Empirical Issues" rounds off the chapter with a more data-driven comparison.[2]

[2] The reader is also pointed to a number of excellent previous surveys: Levinson (1983) provides a gentle introduction to the important issues. Soames (1989) has provided an excellent overview article, whilst Van der Sandt's discussion in Van der Sandt (1988, pp. 1–154) is not only insightful but also has been unsurpassed for breadth of coverage. The relevant chapters of the Chierchia and McConnell-Ginet (1990) introduction to semantics are also to be recommended. Recently some shorter overview articles have appeared, by Horn (1994, 1995) and Seuren (1991), as well as the collection of encyclopedia entries Caffi (1994), Seuren (1994a, 1994b, 1994c). Contemporary PhD theses are of course a mine of information: see for instance the literature overviews in Bridge (1991) and Marcu (1994), both of which are strong concerning more computationally oriented accounts of presupposition, and especially Geurts (1994) and Schöter (1995).

1.1. The presupposition triggers

The class of English presuppositional constructions is commonly depicted as including those in the following list. Note that the references given include authors who would not agree with the presuppositional classification.

Definite NPs. The main references for the famous Russell–Strawson debate which centered on whether definites should be seen as presuppositional are (Strawson, 1950, 1964; Russell, 1905, 1957). The literature is enormous, but see, e.g., the following selection: Hawkins (1976), Clark and Marshall (1981), Van Eijck (1993), Heim (1982), Kadmon (1990), Neale (1990). The class of definites may be taken to include proper names, possessives, 'this'- and 'that'-clauses, and wh-phrases (some of which could alternatively be thought of as embedded questions, and are often analyzed as having category other than NP).

Quantificational NPs presupposing existence of a non-trivial quantificational domain. See, e.g., De Jong and Verkuyl (1987), Lappin and Reinhart (1988), von Fintel (1995), or, e.g., Bergmann (1981) for an example of a formal system where such presuppositions are built in.

Factive verbs and NPs presupposing truth of the propositional complement. For example, 'regret', 'know', 'the fact that X' and 'the knowledge that X'. There is a large literature on factives, starting with the Kiparskys' landmark (Kiparsky and Kiparsky, 1970). There has been much discussion as to whether *cognitive factives* (which concern knowledge of facts) and *emotive factives* (which concern emotional attitudes towards facts) manifest different presuppositional behaviour, as first suggested by Karttunen (1971a). See, e.g., Klein (1975), Gazdar (1979a), Stalnaker (1974). Other work on factives includes, e.g., Postal (1972), Zuber (1977), Peterson (1979).

Clefts. An it-cleft 'it was x that y-ed' is argued to presuppose that something 'y-ed'. Similarly for wh- and pseudo-clefts. See, e.g., Prince (1986), Delin (1989, 1992), Ramsey (1992).

Wh-questions presuppose existence of an entity answering the question, or speakers expectation of such an entity. See, e.g., Belnap (1969), Prince (1986) and Groenendijk and Stokhof's chapter on questions in this volume.

Counterfactual conditionals, presupposing falsity of the antecedent. See Karttunen (1971c), the discussion of subjunctives in Kasper (1992), and the arguments against there being a presupposition in Karttunen and Peters (1979).

Intonational stress. Destressed or unstressed material is sometimes thought to induce a presupposition, so that, e.g., 'X y-ed' with stressed 'X' might presuppose that somebody 'y-ed'. See, e.g., Halliday (1967), Chomsky (1971), Prince (1986), Reinhart (1982), Sgall, Hajičová and Benešová (1973), Sgall (1995), Horn (1986), Blok (1993), Gawron and Peters (1990), Rooth (1995).

Sortally restricted predicates presuppose rather than assert that their arguments are of the appropriate sort. For example, 'dream' presupposes animacy of its subject, and predicative use of 'a bachelor' presupposes that the predicated individual is adult and male. Also sometimes referred to as *categorical* restrictions. See, e.g., Fillmore (1971a), Seuren (1988a).

Signifiers of actions and temporal/aspectual modifiers. Most verbs signifying actions carry presuppositions that the preconditions for the action are met. These could be conceived of as a special case of sortal restriction. Modifiers such as the verbs 'stop' and 'continue', and adverbs such as 'still' are discussed more often in the literature: all of them can be seen as placing presuppositional requirements on the initial state. The modifiers may be clausal, as in 'before' and 'after' clauses. See Van der Auwera (1993), Lorenz (1992), Heinämäki (1972), Ter Meulen (1995).

Iterative Adverbs such as 'too' and 'again' are said to presuppose some sort of repetition. These are discussed, e.g., in Kripke (m.s.), Zeevat (1994), Kamp and Rossdeutscher (1994), Rossdeutscher (1994). Iteratives occur in other syntactic classes (e.g., the determiner 'another', and, relatedly, the noun modifier 'other'), and may even be seen as extending below the lexical level to the morpheme 're-'.

Others. Various other presupposition triggers have been identified, for instance Karttunen's *implicatives* (Karttunen, 1971b) (e.g., 'manage', 'succeed'), Fillmore's *verbs of judging* (e.g., 'criticize') (Fillmore, 1971b), the *focus-sensitive* particles 'even' and 'only'[3] (Horn, 1969; Krifka, 1992), discourse connectives such as 'although' and 'because', non-restrictive relative clauses (which pass the negation test, yet are invariably used to convey new information) and Keenan's pragmatic felicity conditions (e.g., use of polite forms) (Keenan, 1971).

1.2. Projection/Heritability

Frege's (1.1) (Frege, 1984a) has (1.2) as one of its implications, but it is no surprise, given some knowledge of classical logic, that (1.2) does not follow from any of (1.3)–(1.5), in which (1.1) is embedded under negation, in the antecedent of a conditional and within a modal possibility operator respectively.

[3] Apart from 'even' and 'only', the iteratives mentioned above, 'too' and 'again' are also combine being focus sensitive and presuppositional. Here I would like to make an observation, namely that the presuppositions associated with many of the focus sensitive particles are closely related to the presupposition of the underlying focused sentence. Consider the following:

(i) Mary hit JOHN.
(ii) Mary only hit JOHN.
(iii) Mary even hit JOHN.
(iv) Mary also hit JOHN.

The focus carrying sentence (i) is sometimes supposed to carry a presupposition 'Mary hit X'. Yet something of this form is also presupposed by (ii)–(iv): for (ii) X is John, for (iii) X might be some set of people, and for (iv) X is someone other than John. One is clearly tempted to say that at least part of the presupposition normally said to be associated with the focus sensitive particles is in fact derived not from those particles but from the underlying focus sentences.

(1.1) Whoever discovered the elliptic form of the planetary orbits died in misery.

(1.2) Somebody died in misery.

(1.3) Whoever discovered the elliptic form of the planetary orbits did not die in misery.

(1.4) If whoever discovered the elliptic form of the planetary orbits died in misery, he should have kept his mouth shut.

(1.5) Perhaps whoever discovered the elliptic form of the planetary orbits died in misery.

However, consider (1.6), which Frege claims to be presupposed by (1.1). Strikingly, (1.6) seems to be implied by (1.1), but also by all of (1.3)–(1.5). We may say that one implication of (1.1) is *inherited* or *projected* such that it also becomes an implication carried by the complex sentences in (1.3)–(1.5), whereas another implication of (1.1) is not inherited in this way.

(1.6) Somebody discovered the elliptic form of the planetary orbits.

This takes us to the curse and the blessing of modern presupposition theory. Certain implications of sentences are inherited more freely to become implications of complex sentences containing the simple sentences than are other implications, and such implications are commonly called presuppositions. In its guise as curse this observation is called (following Langendoen and Savin) *the presupposition projection problem*, the question of "how the presupposition and assertion of a complex sentence are related to the presupposition and assertions of the clauses it contains" (Langendoen and Savin, 1971, p. 54). The problem can be seen as twofold. Firstly we must say exactly what presuppositions are inherited, and secondly we must say why. But the observation is also a blessing, because it provides an objective basis for the claim that there is a distinct presuppositional component to meaning, and a way of identifying presuppositional constructions, a linguistic test for presupposition on a methodological par with, for instance, standard linguistic constituency tests.

To find the presuppositions of a given grammatical construction or lexical item, one must observe which implications of simple sentences are also implications of sentences in which the simple sentence is embedded under negation, under an operator of modal possibility or in the antecedent of a conditional. To be sure, there is nothing sacred about this list of embeddings from which presuppositions tend to be projected, and the list is certainly not exhaustive. The linguist might equally well choose to consider different connectives, or non-assertive speech acts, as with the question in (1.7) or the imperative in (1.8).[4]

[4] Questions have been considered as test-embeddings for presuppositions by Karttunen. The behaviour of presuppositions in imperatives is discussed by Searle (1969, p. 162). Burton-Roberts suggests the following generalization of the standard negation test for presuppositions: "Any formula equivalent to a formula that entails either p or its negation, and the negation of any such formula, will inherit the presuppositions of p." (Burton-Roberts, 1989b, p. 102). Such a generalization seems problematic. For if we allow that a contradiction entails any sentence, then it follows that a contradiction presupposes everything. But any tautology is standardly equivalent to the negation of a contradiction, so all tautologies must presuppose everything. Further, if a tautology is entailed by any other sentence, it immediately follows that every pair of sentences stands in the relation of presupposition. I fear Burton-Roberts presupposes too much.

(1.7) Did whoever discovered the elliptic form of the planetary orbits die in misery?

(1.8) Ensure that whoever discovered the elliptic form of the planetary orbits dies in misery!

Returning to projection *qua* problem rather than *qua* test, it is often forgotten that, from a semantic perspective, the projection problem for presuppositions fits quite naturally into a larger Fregean picture of how language should be analyzed. The projection problem for presuppositions is the task of stating and explaining the presuppositions of complex sentences in terms of the presuppositions of their parts. The larger problem, which strictly contains the presupposition projection problem, could naturally be called "the projection problem for meanings", i.e. the problem of finding the meanings of complex sentences in terms of the meanings of their parts. Of course, this larger problem is conventionally referred to under the general heading of *compositionality* (for discussion of which, see Chapter 7 in this Handbook).

1.3. From projection data to theories of projection

Much research on presupposition to date, especially formal and semi-formal work, has concentrated on the projection problem. This article reflects that bias, and is concerned primarily with formal models of presupposition projection. Other important issues, such as the nature of presupposition itself, the reasons for there being presuppositions in language, and the place of presuppositions within lexical semantics, are addressed here only insofar as they are relevant to distinguishing alternative projection theories. To facilitate comparison, I will present most theories in terms of an artificial language, what I will call the language of a *Presupposition Logic* (henceforth *PrL*). This is just the language of Propositional Logic (*PL*) with an additional binary operator notated by subscripting: a formula ϕ_ψ should be thought of as 'the assertion of ϕ carrying the presupposition that ϕ'.[5] I will occasionally delve into modal and first order variants of PrL, and also into a presuppositional version of Discourse Representation Theory.

Translations will be very schematic. For instance, 'The King of France is bald' will be analyzed as if it had the form ϕ_ψ, with ψ being understood as the proposition that there is a unique French King and ϕ being understood as a (bivalent) proposition to the effect that there is a bald French King. I do not wish to claim that ϕ_ψ is a good translation of 'The King of France is bald', or even that it is in general possible to isolate the presupposition of a given construction (here given as ψ) from the assertion (here ϕ): some theories do make such an assumption, and others do not. I only claim that the way in which the theories (as I will present them) treat my translations provides a fair characterization of how the theories (as originally presented) would handle the corresponding English examples.

[5] Elsewhere (see, e.g., Beaver (1995)) I have preferred to use a unary presupposition connective. For most of the systems to be presented, this is not significant, since the relevant unary and binary connectives are interdefinable. Krahmer (1995) has used a binary presupposition connective with the notation adopted here, and in the case of trivalent logics the semantics to be given for that connective coincides with Blamey's *transplication* (Blamey, 1989).

There are two main sources of data to use as desiderata when comparing theories of presupposition: felicity judgements, and implications between sentences. The standard tests for presupposition are, as I have said, based on the latter. To use felicity judgements, one requires a theory which divides sentences (or discourses) into good and bad, just as a generative grammar does. But theories of presupposition tend not to make such an explicit division.[6] Thus the principal goal of a theory will be seen as the formalization of a notion of implication (entailment/necessitation/consequence) between formulae of PrL which takes presuppositional implications into account. In some cases felicity judgements can act as desiderata within this framework, if it is supposed that the reason for a discourse's infelicity is that it implies things which hearers have difficulty accepting.

This notion of implication will be denoted $\Vdash$ to distinguish it from classical entailment $\models$. The presuppositionally sensitive implication relation $\Vdash$ should be expected to be weaker than $\models$, in the sense that there will be more $\Vdash$-valid inference patterns than $\models$-valid ones. A proposition may be $\Vdash$-implied if it follows either as a result of classically recognized patterns of reasoning, or as a result of reasoning connected to presupposition, or indeed as a result of some combination of these. Thus, for instance, we may record the fact that the presupposition of a simple negative sentence projects in the absence of extra context in terms of the following datum: $\neg(\phi_\psi)\Vdash\psi$, where ϕ and ψ are taken to be logically independent (i.e. $\phi\not\Vdash\psi$ and $\psi\not\Vdash\phi$). Although theories of presupposition can generally be formulated in terms of a $\Vdash$ relation with little or no loss of descriptive adequacy, many theorists have preferred to divorce presupposition from semantic entailment. So for various systems a relation of presupposition between sentences, denoted by $\gg$, will be directly defined. For these systems one could of course define $\Vdash$ in terms of $\models$ and $\gg$, perhaps most obviously (under a restriction to single premise, single conclusion implications) by: $\Vdash = (\models \cup \gg)^\star$ (i.e. the relation $\Vdash$ is the closure under iteration of the relations $\models$ and $\gg$).[7]

2. Static accounts: Multivalence and partiality

If the accounts to be discussed in this section differ as to the precise refinement from classical interpretation which they utilize, they none the less share a basic approach to presupposition projection: (1) Presuppositions are constraints on the range of worlds/models against which we are able to evaluate the truth or falsity of predications and other semantic operations, or against which this evaluation is legitimate. (2) If these constraints are not met, semantic undefinedness, or illegitimacy of the truth-value, results. (3) Presupposition projection facts associated with a given operator are explained in terms of the relation

[6] One exception is the theory developed in Van der Sandt's doctoral thesis (Van der Sandt, 1982, 1988, 1989).

[7] Some might maintain that presuppositional inferences are of a quite different character to the 'ordinary' truth-functional implications formalized in classical logic, but I do not take this to be an argument against presenting the goal of presupposition theory in similar terms as might be used to state the goal of classical logic. '$\Vdash$' is just a relation between sentences (or sets of sentences), regardless of the extent to which it depends on the familiar paraphernalia of classical logic (semantic valuations, axiomatization, etc.). In some theories, presuppositions of a sentence are analyzed relative to a context. But in all of the theories that will be discussed, this context is itself linguistically supplied, and could be thought of as consisting of just the sequence of sentences Σ which are extra premises in an argument of the form $\Sigma, \phi\Vdash\psi$.

between the definedness/legitimacy of that operator and the definedness/legitimacy of its arguments.[8]

In what follows I will firstly consider truth-functional partial and trivalent systems (those which may be given in terms of truth tables), then a non-truth-functional supervaluation system, and finally the two-dimensional approach (which effectively uses four values).[9]

2.1. *Trivalent accounts*

In a trivalent logic, where the semantic valuation of a formula ϕ with respect to a world w (here written $[\![\phi]\!]_w$) may take any of the three semantic values, typically thought of as true, false and undefined $(t, f, \star)$, presupposition may be defined as follows:

DEFINITION 2.1 (*Strawsonian presupposition*). ϕ presupposes ψ iff for for all worlds w, if $[\![\phi]\!]_w \in \{t, f\}$ then $[\![\psi]\!]_w = t$. We write $\phi \gg \psi$.

A model here, and for most of this chapter, is taken to be a pair $\langle W, I\rangle$ where W is a set of worlds, and I is an interpretation function mapping a pair of a world and an atomic proposition letter to an element of $\{t, f\}$. Let us assume a Tarskian notion of logical consequence as preservation of truth ($\phi \models \psi$ iff for all worlds w, if $[\![\phi]\!]_w = t$ then $[\![\psi]\!]_w = t$). Let us further assume that a negation $\neg$ is available in the formal

---

[8] In this section I have concentrated on the traditional static departures from Boolean interpretation. Recently a number of other systems which involve non-standard static logical systems have been proposed, although the application of these systems to natural language is in many ways informed by the dynamic systems of Section 4, below. I am thinking of the proposals to deal with presupposition in *property theory* (Ramsey, 1992; Fox, m.s.), constructive type theory (Krause, 1995), and also of situation theory. But note that whilst situation theorists have used partial semantics to deal with presuppositional phenomena such as definites, quantifier domain restriction and questions (see, e.g., Gawron and Peters, 1990; Cooper, 1993; Ginzburg, 1995), there is, to my knowledge, not yet any proposal in situation theory which has been proffered as a theory of presupposition *per se*.

[9] I was once horrified to hear a group of presupposition theorists arguing bitterly about whether the treatment of presupposition should use a partial or a trivalent logic. There may be philosophical significance to the choice between partial and trivalent systems, and it may be that there are applications (like the treatment of the semantical paradoxes) where it really makes a difference whether the semantical universe contains only two values for the extension of a proposition or is in some way richer. But it seems unlikely that the decision to use a partial or trivalent logic has significant empirical consequences regarding presupposition projection. In general, relevant aspects of a model of presupposition projection presented in terms of either a trivalent logic or a partial logic are straightforwardly reformulable in terms of the other with no consequences for the treatment of presupposition data. I will collapse the terms *trivalent* and *partial*: the symbol $\star$ may be understood either as a third truth value, or as a failure to define a truth value. In so doing I assume what I take to be the conventional use of the term *partial logic* by logicians (see, e.g., Blamey, 1989), whereby, for instance, versions of both Kleene's strong and weak systems are sometimes referred to as partial logics. Seuren (1985, 1990a) offers an alternative characterization whereby only Kleene's weak system (Bochvar's internal system) would count as a gapped/partial logic. This is because he implicitly limits consideration to systems which are truth functional in a strong sense, such that a compound formula can only have a value defined if the valuation of all the arguments is defined. On the other hand, Burton-Roberts (1989a) offers a system which he claims to have the only *true* gapped bivalent semantics, and which just happens to contain exactly the connectives in Kleene's strong system! Given a lack of consensus among such forceful rhetoricians as Seuren and Burton-Roberts, it is perhaps unwise to stick one's neck out.

language which is interpreted classically with respect to classically valued argument formulae, mapping true to false and *vice versa*, but which preserves undefinedness. This results in a so-called *choice* negation (as in Definition 2.4 below). Given these notions of consequence and negation, it is easily shown that the above definition of presupposition is equivalent to the following:

DEFINITION 2.2 (*Presupposition via negation*). $\phi \gg \psi$ iff $\phi \Vdash \psi$ and $\neg\phi \Vdash \psi$.

These, then, are the standard approaches to defining presupposition in three-valued logics. One author who offers a significant deviation from these definitions is Burton-Roberts (1989a). He defines two separate notions of logical consequence, *weak* consequence, which is just the notion $\Vdash$ above, and *strong* consequence, which is closer to classical implication than $\Vdash$ (e.g., no non-trivial formulae are strongly entailed by both a formula and its negation). For one proposition to strongly entail another, the truth of the first must guarantee the truth of the second, and the falsity of the second must guarantee the falsity of the first. Let us denote strong consequence by $\models_s$, where: $\phi \models_s \psi$ iff (1) $\phi \Vdash \psi$, and (2) for all worlds w, if $[\![\psi]\!]_w = f$ then $[\![\phi]\!]_w = f$.[10] Burton-Roberts suggests that presuppositions are weak consequences which are not strong consequences:

DEFINITION 2.3 (*Burton-Roberts presupposition*). $\phi \gg \psi$ iff $\phi \Vdash \psi$ and $\phi \not\models_s \psi$.

This seems an attractive definition, and is certainly not equivalent to the standard definitions above. However, it has some rather odd properties. For example, assuming this definition of presupposition and Burton-Roberts' quite standard notion of conjunction, it turns out that if ϕ presupposes ψ, then ϕ presupposes $\psi \wedge \phi$. Let us assume that 'The King of France is bald' presupposes 'There is a King of France'. According to Burton-Roberts' definition it must also presuppose 'There is a King of France and he is bald', which seems completely unintuitive. More generally, if ϕ presupposes ψ then according to this definition it must also presuppose the conjunction of ψ with *any* strong consequence of ϕ.[11] I see no reason why we should accept a definition of presupposition with this property.

---

[10] Wilson (1975) took a definition of consequence like $\models_s$ as fundamental, and used it as part of her argument against semantic theories of presupposition. In a more technically rigorous discussion, Blamey (1989) also suggests that the strong notion should be the basic one.

[11] Burton-Robert's system uses Kleene's strong *falsity preserving* conjunction, whereby a conjunction is true if and only if both conjuncts are true, and false if and only if at least one conjunct is false. The following argument then shows that a proposition must presuppose any conjunction of a presupposition and a strong entailment:

(i) Suppose $\phi \gg \psi$ in Burton-Roberts system.
(ii) Then (a) $\phi \Vdash \psi$, and (b) $\phi \not\models_s \psi$.
(iii) From (ii), $[\psi]_w = f$ and $[\phi]_w \neq f$ for some world w.
(iv) Suppose $\phi \models_s \chi$.
(v) By definition of $\models_s$, we have that $\phi \Vdash \chi$.
(vi) By (iiv), (v) and definitions of $\wedge$, $\Vdash$, it follows that $\phi \Vdash \psi \wedge \chi$.
(vii) Relative to the same model M, where ψ is false, falsity preservation of $\wedge$ tells us that $\psi \wedge \chi$ is false.
(viii) Since there is a model (M) where ϕ is not false and its weak entailment $\psi \wedge \chi$ is false, it follows that $\phi \not\models_s \psi \wedge \chi$.
(ix) Hence $\phi \gg \psi \wedge \chi$ in Burton-Roberts system. □

Moving back to the standard definitions, the presupposition projection behaviour of various three-valued logics will now be examined. A simple picture of presupposition projection is what is known as the *cumulative hypothesis* (cf. Langendoen and Savin, 1971) according to which the set of presuppositions of a complex sentence consists of every single elementary presupposition belonging to any subsentence. As far as the projection behaviour of the logical connectives is concerned, such a theory of projection would be modeled by a trivalent logic in which if any of the arguments of a connective has the value $\star$, then the value of the whole is also $\star$. Assuming that combinations of classical values are still to yield their classical result, this yields the so-called *internal Bochvar* or *weak Kleene* connectives (Bochvar, 1939; Kleene, 1938):

DEFINITION 2.4 (*The weak Kleene or internal Bochvar connectives*).

$\phi \wedge \psi$	t	f	$\star$
t	t	f	$\star$
f	f	f	$\star$
$\star$	$\star$	$\star$	$\star$

$\phi \rightarrow \psi$	t	f	$\star$
t	t	f	$\star$
f	t	t	$\star$
$\star$	$\star$	$\star$	$\star$

$\phi \vee \psi$	t	f	$\star$
t	t	t	$\star$
f	t	f	$\star$
$\star$	$\star$	$\star$	$\star$

ϕ	$\neg\phi$
t	f
f	t
$\star$	$\star$

A naive version of the cumulative hypothesis, such as is embodied in the definition of Bochvar's internal connectives, is not tenable, in that there are many examples of presuppositions not being projected. Let us consider firstly how this is dealt with in the case that has generated the most controversy over the years, that of negation.[12] In a trivalent semantics, cases where presuppositions of sentences embedded under a negation are not projected are normally explained in terms of a *denial* operator (here $\sharp$) such that when $[\![\phi]\!]_w = \star$, $[\![\sharp\phi]\!]_w = t$. Typically the following *exclusion* (sometimes called *weak*) negation operator results:

It should be mentioned that the above is not the only definition of presupposition that Burton-Roberts offers: it seems to be intended as a definition of the elementary presuppositions of a simple positive sentence. Presuppositions of compound sentences are given by a relation of *Generalized Presupposition*. This notion, which will not be discussed in detail here, is essentially the same as a notion of presupposition used earlier by Hausser (1976). It says that one formula presupposes another if falsity of the second creates the possibility of undefinedness for the first.

[12] Horn's article (1985) provides an excellent overview of treatments of negation and considers cases of presupposition denial at length. For a longer read, his (Horn, 1989) is recommended. Extensive discussion of negation within the context of contemporary trivalent accounts of presupposition is found in the work of Seuren (1985, 1988b), and Burton-Roberts (1989a, 1989c). Burton-Roberts publications sparked considerable controversy, to a degree surprising given that Burton-Roberts, though innovative, presents what is essentially a reworking of the quite well worn trivalent approach to presupposition. The refreshingly vehement debate provides the definitive modern statements of the alternative positions on negation within trivalent systems: see Horn's (1990) and Burton-Roberts' reply (Burton-Roberts, 1989b), Seuren's (1990a) and Burton-Roberts' reply (Burton-Roberts, 1990), and Seuren and Turner's reviews (Seuren, 1990b; Turner, 1992).

DEFINITION 2.5 (*Trivalent exclusion negation*).

ϕ	$\sharp\phi$
t	f
f	t
$\star$	t

Since there apparently exist both cases where a negation acts, in Karttunen's terminology, as a *hole* to presuppositions (allowing projection) and cases where it acts as what Karttunen called a *plug* (preventing projection), the defender of a trivalent account of presupposition appears not to have the luxury of choosing between the two negations given above, but seems forced to postulate that negation in natural language is ambiguous between them. Unfortunately, convincing independent evidence for such an ambiguity is lacking, although there may at least be intonational features which mark occurrences of denial negation from other uses, and thus potentially allow the development of a theory as to which of the two meanings a given occurrence of negation corresponds.[13]

There is a frequently overlooked alternative to postulating a lexical ambiguity, dating back as far as Bochvar's original papers. Bochvar suggested that apart from the normal mode of assertion there was a second mode which we might term *meta-assertion*. The meta-assertion of ϕ, $A\phi$, is the proposition that ϕ is true: $[\![A\phi]\!]_w = t$ if $[\![\phi]\!]_w = t$ and $[\![A\phi]\!]_w = f$ otherwise. Bochvar showed how within the combined system consisting of the internal connectives and this assertion operator a second set of *external* connectives could be defined: for instance the external conjunction of two formulae is just the internal conjunction of the meta-assertion of the two formulae (i.e. $\phi \wedge_{\text{ext}} \psi =_{\text{def}} A(\phi) \wedge_{\text{int}} A(\psi)$), and the external negation of a formula is just the exclusion negation given above, defined in the extended Bochvar system by $\sharp\phi =_{\text{def}} \neg A(\phi)$. Thus whilst the possibility of declaring natural language negation to be ambiguous between $\neg$ and $\sharp$ exists within Bochvar's extended system, another possibility would be to translate natural language negation uniformly using $\neg$, but then allow that sometimes the proposition under the negation is itself clad in the meta-assertoric armour of the A-operator.

There is no technical reason why the Bochvarian meta-assertion operator should be restricted in its occurrence to propositions directly under a negation. Link (1986) has proposed a model in which in principle any presupposition can be *co-asserted*, where coassertion, if I understand correctly, essentially amounts to embedding under the A-operator. Such a theory is flexible, since it leaves the same logical possibilities open as in a system with an enormous multiplicity of connectives. Link indicates that pragmatic factors will induce an ordering over the various readings, although he does not formalize this part of

[13] If the *raison d'etre* of a trivalent denial operator is to be yield truth when predicated of a non-true and non-false proposition, then in principle some choice remains as to how it should behave when predicated of a simply false proposition. Thus the denial operator need not necessarily have the semantics of the exclusion negation, although, to my knowledge, only Seuren has been brave enough to suggest an alternative. Seuren's preferred vehicle for denial is an operator which maps only $\star$ onto t, and maps both t and f onto f. I know of no other negation discussed in the literature for which double negation produces a constant f-function. Seuren has marshaled considerable empirical evidence that negation is in fact ambiguous, although the main justification for his particular choice of denial operator is, I think, philosophical.

the theory. Presumably a default must be invoked that the A operator only occurs when incoherence would result otherwise, and then with narrowest possible scope.[14]

So far we have only considered cases where presuppositions of each argument are either definitely projected to become presuppositions of the whole, or definitely not projected. Fittingly, in the land of the *included* middle, there is a third possibility. The presupposition may, in effect, be modified as it is projected. Such modification occurs with all the binary connectives in Kleene's *strong* system (Kleene, 1945, 1959):

DEFINITION 2.6 (*The strong Kleene connectives*).

$\phi \wedge \psi$	t	f	$\star$
t	t	f	$\star$
f	f	f	f
$\star$	$\star$	f	$\star$

$\phi \to \psi$	t	f	$\star$
t	t	f	$\star$
f	t	t	t
$\star$	t	$\star$	$\star$

$\phi \vee \psi$	t	f	$\star$
t	t	t	t
f	t	f	$\star$
$\star$	t	$\star$	$\star$

ϕ	$\neg\phi$
t	f
f	t
$\star$	$\star$

To see that under this definition it is not in general the case that if ϕ presupposes π then $\psi \to \phi$ presupposes π, we need only observe that if $[\![\psi]\!]_w = f$ then $[\![\psi \to \phi]\!]_w$ is defined (and $= t$) regardless of the valuation of ϕ. Presuppositions of the consequent are weakened, in the sense that in a subset of worlds, those where the antecedent is false, undefinedness of the consequent is irrelevant to the definedness of the whole. However, in those worlds where the antecedent is not false, the presuppositions of the consequent are significant, so that presupposition failure of the consequent is sufficient to produce presupposition failure of the whole.[15]

To complete the definition of a trivalent PrL semantics a binary presupposition connective can be added. A formula ϕ_ψ introduces undefinedness whenever ψ is not true:

DEFINITION 2.7 (*Trivalent presupposition operator*).

ϕ_ψ	t	f	$\star$
t	t	$\star$	$\star$
f	f	$\star$	$\star$
$\star$	$\star$	$\star$	$\star$

[14] Observe that in Link-type theory the lexical ambiguity of negation which is common in trivalent theories is replaced by an essentially structural ambiguity, and in this respect is comparable with the Russellian scope-based explanation of projection facts. Horn (1985, p. 125) provides a similar explication to that above of the relation between theories postulating alternative 3-valued negations and theories involving a Russellian scope ambiguity.

[15] Cf. the discussion of conditional presuppositions in Section 6.3, below.

The presuppositional properties of the strong Kleene logic may be determined in full by inspection of the truth tables, and can be summed up as follows:

FACT 2.8. *Under the strong Kleene interpretation, if* $\phi \gg \pi$ *then:*

$$\begin{aligned}
&\neg\phi \gg \pi, \\
&\phi \wedge \psi \gg \psi \to \pi, \\
&\psi \wedge \phi \gg \psi \to \pi, \\
&\phi \to \psi \gg (\neg\psi) \to \pi, \\
&\psi \to \phi \gg \psi \to \pi, \\
&\phi \vee \psi \gg (\neg\psi) \to \pi, \\
&\psi \vee \phi \gg (\neg\psi) \to \pi.
\end{aligned}$$

If models are restricted to those where ψ is bivalent, Fact 2.8 gives the maximal presuppositions in the sense that the right hand side represents the logically strongest presupposition, all other presuppositions being $\models$-entailed by it.

2.2. *Supervaluations*

Van Fraassen's method of *supervaluations* enables a partial treatment of presupposition to remain faithful to classical logic, although in fact the technique is of sufficient generality that it could equally be used to introduce partiality into non-classical logics.[16] The name *supervaluation* reflects the idea that the semantics of a formula reflects not just one valuation, but many valuations combined. Suppose that we have some method, let us call it an *initial partial valuation*, of partially assigning Boolean truth values to the formulae of some language. Van Fraassen's idea is to consider all the ways of assigning total valuations to the formula which are compatible both with the initial partial valuation and with principles of classical logic: call these total valuations the *classical extensions* of the initial partial valuation. A new partial valuation, let us call it the *supervaluation*, is then defined as the intersection of the classical extensions, that valuation which maps a formula to *t* iff all the extensions map it to *t*, and maps a formula to *f* iff all the extensions map it to *f*. To justify the approach, it is helpful to think of $\star$ as meaning not "undefined", but "unknown": the values of some formulae are unknown, so we consider all the values that they *might* conceivably have, and use this information to give the supervaluation.

It will now be shown how this technique can be used in the case of PrL, but it should be noted that the application will be in some respects non-standard. Supervaluation semantics is normally given for systems where partiality arises in the model. Here it will be assumed that the model provides a classical interpretation for all proposition letters, and

[16] Supervaluations are introduced by Van Fraassen (1969, 1975). There are a number of good presentations designed to be accessible to linguists, e.g., in McCawley (1981), Martin (1979) and Seuren (1985). For an application of supervaluations see Thomason (1972).

that partiality only arises in the recursive definition of the semantics, specifically with regard to the binary presupposition connective. To simplify, let us restrict the language by requiring that both arguments of any compound formula ϕ_ψ are atomic proposition letters. The notion of an *extension* to a world which will be used is odd in the sense that a world is already total with respect to interpretation of atomic proposition letters. The extension provides a valuation for presuppositional formulae: it is as if we were considering formulae ϕ_ψ to be 'extra' atomic formulae. Since there are many such presuppositional formulae, and two ways of providing a classical value to each one, there are many extensions for each world. The following three definitions give a set of extension functions for a world, a recursive redefinition of the semantics in terms of these extensions, and the resulting supervaluations.

DEFINITION 2.9 (*Extensions of a world*). The set of extensions of w is denoted EX(w), where EX(w) = $\{\langle w, \pi\rangle \mid \pi$ maps every formula of the form ϕ_ψ, for atomic ϕ and ψ, to an element of $\{t, f\}$ under the restriction that if the interpretation of ψ with respect to w is t (i.e. $I(w, \psi) = t$), then π $\pi(\phi_\psi) = I(w, \phi)\}$.

DEFINITION 2.10 (*Total valuation functions*). A classical extension $\langle w, \pi\rangle$ provides a total valuation function $\mathrm{TV}_{\langle w,\pi\rangle}$ according to the following recursive semantics: atomic formulae are valued using the interpretation function (supplied by the model) with respect to w, formulae of the form ϕ_ψ have value $\pi(\phi_\psi)$, and other compound formulae are interpreted using the classical truth-tables in terms of the $\mathrm{TV}_{\langle w,\pi\rangle}$ valuation of their parts.

DEFINITION 2.11 (*Supervaluations*). The supervaluation with respect to the world w, SUP(w), is a partial valuation defined by SUP(w) = $\bigcap \mathrm{TV}_{\langle w,\pi\rangle}$.[17] The set of supervaluations S with respect to a model w is $\{s \mid \exists w \in W\ s = \mathrm{SUP}(w)\}$.

To see that supervaluations are partial, consider the formula $A \wedge A_B$ with respect to SUP(ω), where A is true and B is false in the world ω. Some of the extensions of ω will make A_B true, and others will make it false, and likewise some valuations will make $A \wedge A_B$ true and others will make it false. Thus the intersection of the extensions will map $A \wedge A_B$ to the third value, $\star$. On the other hand, undefinedness does not always project. For example SUP(ω) gives $A \vee A_B$ the value t, since the left disjunct is true in w, and thus also true in all extensions, from which it follows that the disjunction is true in all extensions.

The supervaluation semantics is non-truth-functional. That is, the supervaluation of a compound cannot be calculated from the supervaluation of its parts. Consider SUP(ω) for the formulae (i) $A_B \vee \neg(A_B)$ and (ii) $A_B \vee (A_B)$, again supposing that A is true and B is false in ω. Although SUP(ω) makes both A_B and $\neg(A_B)$ undefined, it gives $A_B \vee \neg(A_B)$ the value t. The reason for this is that in all the extensions where A_B is true, $\neg(A_B)$ is false, and *vice versa*. Thus in every extension to ω one of the disjuncts of formula (i) is true, so the formula as a whole is true in every extension, and thus

[17] If V is a set of valuation functions, $\bigcap V$ is that function such that: $(\bigcap V)(\phi) = t$ if $\forall v \in V\ v(\phi) = t$; $= f$ if $\forall v \in V\ v(\phi) = f$; and $= \star$ otherwise.

in SUP(ω) as well. On the other hand, formula (ii) is given the supervaluation $\star$ with respect to ω, since there are some extensions where both disjuncts are false, so that the formula as a whole is false, and some extensions where both disjuncts are true, so that the whole formula is true. Since the extensions do not maintain a concensus as to the value of (ii), it cannot be bivalent. Thus both (i) and (ii) are disjunctions where the disjuncts have the same value with respect to SUP(ω), but the disjunctions have different values with respect to SUP(ω). This establishes the non-truth-functionality of the supervaluation semantics for PrL.

Despite this non-truth-functionality, some general principles of truth-value inheritance are followed, and an imprecise truth-tabular characterization of the supervaluation semantics is sometimes given: this can be helpful when comparing to other partial and trivalent approaches.

DEFINITION 2.12 (*Truth-table approximation to supervaluation semantics*). [18]

$\phi \wedge \psi$	t	f	$\star$
t	t	f	$\star$
f	f	f	f
$\star$	$\star$	f	$(f/\star)$

$\phi \rightarrow \psi$	t	f	$\star$
t	t	f	$\star$
f	t	t	t
$\star$	t	$\star$	$(t/\star)$

$\phi \vee \psi$	t	f	$\star$
t	t	t	t
f	t	f	$\star$
$\star$	t	$\star$	$(t/\star)$

These tables show that for the most part supervaluation semantics resembles the Strong Kleene semantics, providing a value whenever there are classical truth-functional grounds for assigning a value. For instance, a disjunction is true if one of the disjuncts is true, regardless of the value of the other disjunct. But the supervaluation semantics differs from the Strong Kleene when both arguments to a connective are undefined. In this case, the supervaluation semantics takes the principle of maximizing bivalence to its limit, sometimes managing to attribute bivalence even though both argument values are undefined.

To what logic does supervaluation semantics lead? It is natural to define $\models$ using preservation of truth with respect to supervaluations, i.e. $\phi \models \psi$ iff for every supervaluation s in S, if $s(\phi) = t$ then $s(\psi) = t$. The resulting logic is distinctly presuppositional. For instance, it is easily verified that both $\phi_\psi \models \psi$ and $\neg(\phi_\psi) \models \psi$. Further, the presuppositional properties are comparable with those of the Strong Kleene system, so that presuppositional implications are commonly weakened. But what marks the supervaluation definition of $\models$ out from all the others considered in this chapter is that all classical argument patterns remain valid. For instance the law of the excluded middle $\models \phi \vee \neg\phi$ holds for any choice of ϕ.[19] This takes us to one commonly made observation which never ceases to amaze me: supervaluation semantics can yield a system in which the law of the excluded middle holds, but in which bivalence fails, even for disjunctions.

[18] The tables for negation and the presuppositional connective are as in Definitions 2.6 and 2.7, respectively.
[19] I write $\models \psi$ if for all χ, $\chi \models \psi$.

2.3. *Two dimensions*

There are no obvious empirical reasons for using more than three truth values in the treatment of presupposition, and thus Occam's razor commonly makes trivalent semantics the preferred basis for a multivalent treatment of presupposition.[20] However, quite apart from the fact that four-valued logics are sometimes thought to be technically more elegant than their three-valued cousins, the use of four truth values affords theorists the space to pursue a *divide and conquer* strategy, separating issues of presupposition from those of classical truth and entailment. The idea was developed independently, but in rather different forms, by Herzberger (1973) and Karttunen and Peters (1979), Herzberger's formulation having been further developed by Martin (1977) and Bergmann (1981). The semantic domain is considered as consisting of two two-valued coordinates (*dimensions*), which I will call *assertion* and *presupposition*.[21] Thus, if the four values are represented using a pair of binary digits, with the first representing the assertion, and the second the presupposition, then, for instance, $\langle 0, 1\rangle$ will mean that the assertion is not satisfied, although the presupposition is.

Treating a four valued semantics as consisting of two Boolean coordinates allows for a straightforward introduction of the tools of classical logic to study an essentially non-classical system, and this enabled Karttunen and Peters to provide compositionally derived two-dimensional interpretations for a fragment of English using the classical IL of Montague (cf. Partee's chapter in this volume). To illustrate the approach, let us suppose that expressions of English are associated with two translation functions, $\mathcal{A}$, and $\mathcal{P}$. $\mathcal{A}$ maps expressions to IL formulae representing the assertion, and $\mathcal{P}$ likewise maps to an IL representation of the presupposition. Given that the assertion and presupposition of an expression are assumed by Karttunen and Peters to have identical IL types, and that for English sentences this type is that of truth values, the two dimensional interpretation of a sentence S relative to an IL model M and assignment g will be $\langle [\![\mathcal{A}(S)]\!]_{M,g}, [\![\mathcal{P}(S)]\!]_{M,g}\rangle$. Now we might associate with conditionals, for instance, the following translation rule pair:

$$\mathcal{A}(\text{If S1 then S2}) = \mathcal{A}(\text{S1}) \to \mathcal{A}(\text{S2}),$$
$$\mathcal{P}(\text{If S1 then S2}) = \mathcal{P}(\text{S1}) \wedge \mathcal{P}(\text{S2}).$$

This particular rule pair, defines a notion of implication comparable with the Bochvar internal implication. If we associate the value $\langle 1, 1\rangle$ with t, $\langle 0, 1\rangle$ with f, and the remaining two values both with $\star$, then a sentence 'If S1 then S2' will take the value $\star$ just

[20] Cooper (1983) presents an interesting empirical justification for the use of a fourth value, suggesting that whilst the third value is used to represent presupposition failure, a fourth value is required to signal acts of presupposition denial. This idea, which enables Cooper to give some explanation of cancellation effects without postulating an ambiguity of negation (or other operators) has not, to my knowledge, been taken up elsewhere.

[21] What are here called *assertion* and *presupposition* are for Herzberger *correspondence* and *bivalence*, and for Karttunen and Peters *entailment* and *conventional implicature*. The theories differ considerably in philosophical motivation, in that whilst Herzberger's could be reasonably termed a semantic account, Karttunen and Peters' is not presented as such. However, the fact that Karttunen and Peters give a pragmatic explication of their second dimension of evaluation is irrelevant to most of the technicalities.

in case either S1 or S2 takes this value, and otherwise will take the standard classical value.[22]

The same approach is extendible to other types. Let us suppose that a sentence of the form 'The guest Xs' involves the assertion of the existence of a guest with property X and presupposition of the uniqueness of the guest, and that a sentence of the form 'y curtsied' carries the assertion that y performed the appropriate physical movement, and the presupposition that y is female. Then assuming appropriate basic translations, constants *guest, curtsied* and *female*, and meaning postulates guaranteeing that, for instance, the constant *curtsied* stands in the correct relation to other constants relevant to the physical act of curtseying, part of the derivation of the meaning of the sentence 'The guest curtsied' might run – departing somewhat from Karttunen and Peters' original system – as follows:

$$\begin{aligned}
\mathcal{A}(\text{the guest}) &= \lambda X[\exists y\, guest(y) \wedge X(y)],\\
\mathcal{P}(\text{the guest}) &= \lambda X[\exists y\, guest(y) \wedge \forall z[guest(z) \rightarrow y = z] \wedge X(y)],\\
\mathcal{A}(\text{curtsied}) &= curtsied,\\
\mathcal{P}(\text{curtsied}) &= female,\\
\mathcal{A}(\text{the guest curtsied}) &= \mathcal{A}(\text{the guest}).\mathcal{A}(\text{curtsied})\\
&= \lambda X[\exists y[guest(y) \wedge X(y)]](curtsied)\\
&= \exists y[guest(y) \wedge curtsied(y)],\\
\mathcal{P}(\text{the guest curtsied}) &= \mathcal{P}(\text{the guest}).\mathcal{P}(\text{curtsied})\\
&= \lambda X[\exists y[guest(y) \wedge \forall z[\text{guest}(z) \rightarrow y = z]\\
&\qquad \wedge X(y)]](female)\\
&= \exists y[guest(y) \wedge \forall z[guest(z) \rightarrow y = z] \wedge female(y)].
\end{aligned}$$

This results in the assertion that a guest curtsied, and the presupposition that there is exactly one guest and that guest is female. The approach seems quite general, but Karttunen and Peters observe, in a by now infamous footnote, that there is a problem associated with their interpretation of existentially quantified sentences. According to their theory, a sentence of the form 'An X Ys' carries the assertion that an individual in

[22] This two dimensional version of Bochvar's internal implication is found in some of the systems proposed in (Herzberger, 1973). Note that the other Bochvar internal connectives can be defined similarly, such that in each case the assertion is defined entirely in terms of the assertion of the arguments, and the presupposition is defined entirely in terms of the presuppositions of the arguments. This yields what is termed (following Jankowski) a cross-product logic. However, both Herzberger and Karttunen and Peters also define operators for which this property does not hold. For instance, the two dimensional version of Bochvar's assertion operator considered by Herzberger, thought of as a semantics for the English 'it is the case that' locution, could be defined:

$$\begin{aligned}
\mathcal{A}(\text{it is the case that } S) &= \mathcal{A}(S) \wedge \mathcal{P}(S),\\
\mathcal{P}(\text{it is the case that } S) &= T.
\end{aligned}$$

Here the assertion is defined in terms of both the assertion and presupposition of its argument.

the assertional extension of X has the property given by the assertional component of Y. Further, the sentence carries the presuppositions (1) that some individual is in the presuppositional extension of X, and (2) that some individual in the assertional extension of X is in the presuppositional extension of Y. What might be referred to as *the presuppositional binding problem* is that there is no link between the variables bound in the assertion and in the presupposition. In particular, there is no guarantee that any entity satisfies both the assertional and the presuppositional requirements.

For instance, the sentence 'Somebody curtsied' will be given the assertion $\exists y\, person(y) \wedge curtsied(y)$, i.e. that somebody performed the physical act of curtseying, and the presupposition $\exists y\, person(y) \wedge female(y)$, i.e. that somebody is female. Crucially, this fails to enforce the common-sensical constraint that the person who curtsied is female. One possible fix would amount to making all presuppositions also assertions, which is standard in some of the accounts to be considered in the next section. In fact, as will be discussed there, there is a separate reason to make presuppositions also part of the asserted content, for without this one cannot easily explain why although presuppositions are commonly defeasible, presuppositions of simple positive sentences are not. If the presupposition is also part of the assertion, then the reason for this indefeasibility has nothing to do with the presuppositional dimension itself, but derives from the fact that one cannot ordinarily deny one's own assertions, or make assertions which one knows to be false.

2.4. Pragmatic extensions

Little if any recent work has advocated a pure multivalent/partial account of presupposition. Rather, even where multivalence/partiality is taken as the core of a treatment of presupposition, it is usually assumed that some pragmatic component will be required in addition:

- Karttunen and Peters (1979) assume that conversational implicatures will strengthen some of the weak presuppositions generated.
- Link (1986) assumes a mechanism whereby a presuppositional expression can sometimes be *co-asserted*. Whether an expression is indeed co-asserted must be controlled by pragmatic factors (cf. discussion of the floating-A theory, above).
- Seuren (1985) embeds a trivalent system which he terms "PPC(3)" (consisting of a mixture of Kleene Weak and Strong connectives plus an extra negation and implication) within a general theory of discourse interpretation. Further, he supposes that a mechanism of *backward suppletion* (similar to that which is below called *accommodation*) will repair the discourse context in cases of presupposition failure.
- Burton-Roberts (1989a) discusses a *meta-linguistic* use of negation which he argues enables treatment of cancellation cases without postulation of a lexical ambiguity of negation. He also provides essentially pragmatic argumentation to establish whether the falsity of a sentence's presupposition leads to the undefinedness of the sentence.
- Kracht (1994) argues that processing considerations can influence the way in which a connective is interpreted, and in this way reasons to each connective having multiple (trivalent) realizations.

3. Context dependence and part-time presupposition

The theories to be discussed in this section have two things in common. Firstly, they are, in a sense, the only true projection theories: the set of presuppositions associated with the utterance of a complex sentence is a subset of the set of elementary presuppositions of that sentence.[23] We can thus say that these theories define (relative to a context) a projection function which determines for each elementary presupposition whether it is projected or not. Secondly, this projection function is context sensitive. Whereas for the theories discussed in the previous section presupposition was understood as a binary relation between sentences, the theories to be discussed now involve definitions of presupposition as a three place relation between a pair of a sentence and a context of evaluation.[24] The context is understood to be created partly linguistically, as a result of previous utterances, and thus the models allow for dynamic effects: the context in which one sentence is evaluated will generally be different from the context in which the following sentences are understood.[25]

The accounts discussed in this section involve *part-time* presupposition (the term is used in Karttunen (1974)), theories where unwanted presuppositions appear to vanish. One can identify two means of producing this effect, which may be termed *cancellation* and *filtering*. These are commonly regarded as opposing approaches to the treatment of presupposition, but the two are closely related variations on a single theme: (1) The grammar and lexicon together encode a way of calculating for each simple sentence a set of *potential presuppositions*. (2) The set of presuppositions of a complex sentence is a subset of the union of the potential presupposition sets of the component sentences. Call this subset the *projection set*. (3) The calculation of the projection set is sensitive to linguistic context (conceived of as a set of sentences), and relies on one or both of the following two strategies. The first such strategy can be termed *Local Filtering*. Here, for each subsentence S consisting of an operator embedding further subsentences as arguments, S not only carries its own potential presuppositions, but also inherits a subset of the potential presuppositions of the arguments. In the second strategy, here called *Global Cancellation*, pragmatic principles determine a function from tuples consisting of the context, the set of potential presuppositions, the assertive content of the sentence, and a set of Gricean implicatures of the sentence, to that subset of the potential presuppositions which is projected.

---

[23] Even the Bochvar Internal connectives do not form a projection theory in this strong sense, since logical consequences of presuppositions are themselves presupposed, although they may not be amongst the elementary presuppositions.

[24] Alternatively, if an utterance is defined as a pair of a sentence (or set of sentences) and a linguistic context, then presupposition becomes a two place relation between an utterance and a sentence.

[25] The first of the accounts discussed in this section, Karttunen's model is context dependent, but Karttunen is not explicit about how the context arises. His theory requires that "the presuppositions of a compound that involves logical connectives are, in general, definable only in relation to a given set of other sentences" (Karttunen, 1973, p. 183). This dependence on a contextually given set of sentences distinguishes the theory sharply from any purely partial or multivalent approach to presupposition. Gazdar, whose theory is discussed in Section 3.2, below, was the first to make explicit the way in which such a set of sentences can be built up dynamically in the process of discourse understanding.

3.1. *Plugs, holes and filters*

Karttunen (1973, p. 178) introduced the following taxonomy:

Plugs: predicates which block off all the presuppositions of the complement sentence [examples include 'say', 'mention', 'tell, ask'];

Holes: predicates which let all the presuppositions of the complement sentence become presuppositions of the matrix sentence [examples include 'know', 'regret', 'understand', 'be possible', 'not'];

Filters: predicates which, under certain conditions, cancel some of the presuppositions of the arguments [examples include if-then, 'either-or', 'and'].[26]

Karttunen's 1973 paper provides two related models of projection: the second model can be seen formally as a generalization of the first. Definition 3.1, below, gives a function $\mathcal{P}$ which maps every formula of a language onto a set of formulae which are its presuppositions relative to a context C. This context, what Karttunen calls "a set of assumed facts" should here be a set of formulae, and the first version of Karttunen's model is obtained simply by assuming the context to be empty. The language over which Definition 3.1 is given is PrL with the addition of two sets of one place operators **H** and **P**, corresponding to hole predicates and plug predicates respectively.

DEFINITION 3.1 (*Karttunen '73 presuppositions with respect to a context* c).

$$\begin{aligned}
\mathcal{P}_c(p) &= \emptyset \quad \text{(for atomic } p\text{)},\\
\mathcal{P}_c(\phi_\psi) &= \{\psi\} \cup \mathcal{P}_c(\phi) \cup \mathcal{P}_c(\psi),\\
\mathcal{P}_c(O\phi) &= \emptyset \quad \text{(for } O \in \mathbf{P}\text{)},\\
\mathcal{P}_c(O\phi) &= \mathcal{P}_c(\phi) \quad \text{(for } O \in \mathbf{H}\text{)},\\
\mathcal{P}_c(\neg\phi) &= \mathcal{P}_c(\phi),\\
\mathcal{P}_c(\phi \wedge \psi) &= \mathcal{P}_c(\phi \to \psi) = \mathcal{P}_c(\phi) \cup \{\chi \in \mathcal{P}_c(\psi) \mid c, \phi \not\models \chi\},\\
\mathcal{P}_c(\phi \vee \psi) &= \mathcal{P}_c(\phi) \cup \{\chi \in \mathcal{P}_c(\psi) \mid c, \neg\phi \not\models \chi\},\\
\phi \gg_c \psi &\ \textit{iff}\ \psi \in \mathcal{P}_c(\phi),\\
\phi \gg \psi &\ \textit{iff}\ \phi \gg_\emptyset \psi.
\end{aligned}$$

The first five clauses of this definition are straightforward: atomic formulae, by assumption, have no presuppositions; a formula ϕ_ψ presupposes ψ and anything that ϕ or ψ presupposes; a plug embedding a formula carries no presuppositions, whilst a hole (of which internal negation is an example) carries just the presuppositions of its sentential argument. The binary connectives, which act as filters, are more interesting. Firstly, conjunction and implication. These carry all the presuppositions of the first argument, but only those presuppositions of the second argument which are not entailed by a combination of the context and the first argument. Consider the following:

[26] In the later version of Karttunen's theory discussed in Section 4, filters not only cancel presuppositions, but modify them.

(3.10) If David wrote the article and the knowledge that ([i] he wrote it/[ii] no decent logician was involved) disturbs the editors, they'll read the manuscript very carefully.

The presupposition that David wrote the article, triggered in the right hand conjunct of the antecedent of (3.10)(i), is canceled. Even ignoring the context (i.e. setting it to the empty set so as to get the first version of Karttunen's 1973 model), this result is predicted. The LF of (3.10)(i) has the general form $(\phi \wedge \psi_{\phi}) \to \chi$.[27] Since the left conjunct of the antecedent entails the presupposition of the right conjunct, the presupposition is filtered.

It is easy to find formulae for which, in the absence of a special context, filtering does not occur. For instance on Definition 3.1 we have (for independent atomic formulae ϕ, ψ, χ, π) that $(\phi \wedge \psi_{\pi}) \to \chi \gg \pi$. Thus, in the absence of a special context, (3.10)(ii) is predicted to presuppose that no decent logician was involved (in writing the article).[28] But if a context C contains (or entails) $\phi \to \pi$, then the presupposition is filtered: $(\phi \wedge \psi_{\pi}) \to \pi \gg_{C} \pi$.

There remains unclarity in Karttunen's filtering theory. What is the status of the "set of assumed facts"? Should this set contain only propositions which are commonly known to all interlocutors, or can it contain propositions which only the hearer, or perhaps only the speaker, take to be common? And what is the status of a presupposition: is it also some sort of assumed fact? What makes it hard to say what presuppositions really are in this account, as well as providing some empirical problems, is that a formula may have contrary presuppositions. For instance the following sentence (of a type originally discussed by Hausser (1976)) contains two instances of factive constructions, 'knows' and 'is upset', but the presuppositions conflict with each other, and are generally taken not to be projected:

(3.11) Either Fred knows he's won or he's upset that he hasn't.

If we analyze (3.11) as having the form $\phi_{\psi} \vee \chi_{\neg\psi}$, the set of presuppositions predicted by the above definition is $\{\psi, \neg\psi\}$, which is peculiar.

3.2. Global cancellation

The model presented by Gazdar (1979a), like Karttunen's revised filtering model, is context sensitive, provides an account of the presuppositions of utterances rather than sentences, and predicts the presuppositions of an utterance to be a subset of the potential presuppositions of the component sentences. Unlike Karttunen's model, the presuppositions are not calculated by bottom-up filtering but by a global cancellation mechanism. All the potential presuppositions of component sentences are collected together into one set, and from that set are removed any members which conflict with (1) propositions in

[27] ϕ is 'David wrote the article', ψ is the assertive component of 'the knowledge that he wrote it disturbs the editors', ϕ being the presuppositional component, and χ is 'the editors will read the manuscript very carefully'.

[28] ϕ, ψ and χ are as before, and π is 'no decent logician was involved'.

the previous context, (2) the entailments of the utterance, (3) various implicatures associated with the utterance, or (4) each other. Those potential presuppositions surviving this tough selection process go on to become full presuppositions of the utterance.

The basic idea that something cannot be presupposed if that would conflict with implicatures of the utterance is already found in Stalnaker's work (Stalnaker, 1974, pp. 207–210). Further, Soames proposed independently of Gazdar that defeat by implicature should be the central notion of a theory of presupposition projection: "A speaker who utters a truth-functional compound, question or epistemic modal indicates that he is presupposing all of the presuppositions of its constituents unless he conversationally implicates (or explicitly states) otherwise." (Soames, 1979, p. 653.) Kempson (1975), Wilson (1975), and Atlas and Levinson (Atlas, 1976, 1977; Atlas and Levinson, 1981) had all recognized that conversational factors determine whether or not a presupposition is projected, although their general strategy was of trying to find implicature-based explanations of all cases where presuppositions do project, rather than assuming by default that they project and only seeking implicature-based explanations of cases where presuppositions are canceled.

Gazdar's theory of presupposition, however, provides the first formalization of this type of account. It is set within a dynamic model of meaning, in which discourse contexts – sets of propositions – are progressively updated with the information in succeeding utterances. Note that the dynamism is found only at the level of texts, and does not extend downwards to the interpretation of the constituents of sentences. In this respect Gazdar's model contrasts with the accounts of presupposition proposed by Karttunen (1974) and Heim (1983a), as well as with the accounts of anaphora proposed by Kamp (1981), Heim (1982, 1983b) and Groenendijk and Stokhof (1991), all of which employ dynamic interpretation at the subsentence level.

Central to Gazdar's model is his notion of *satisfiable incrementation*. The satisfiable incrementation of a context X with a set Y of propositions is just the original context plus all those propositions in Y which cannot introduce inconsistency, where a proposition y *cannot introduce inconsistency* just in case all consistent subsets of $X \cup Y$ are still consistent after addition of y. The following definition (close to Gazdar's) results:

DEFINITION 3.2 (*Consistency, satisfiable incrementation*).

$$\text{cons}(X) \textit{ iff } X \not\models \bot,$$
$$X \cup ! Y = X \cup \{y \in Y \mid \forall Z \subseteq (X \cup Y)\ (\text{cons}(Z) \rightarrow \text{cons}(Z \cup \{y\}))\}.$$

For example, if $X = \{p, q\}$ and $Y = \{\neg p, r, s, \neg s\}$, with all atomic formulae assumed logically independent, then $X \cup ! Y = \{p, q, r\}$. The proposition $\neg p$ cannot be added because it is inconsistent with X, s cannot be added because there are consistent subsets of $X \cup Y$ (e.g., $\{p, q, \neg s\}$) which become inconsistent when s is added to them, and similarly for $\neg s$.

Gazdar is concerned with reasoning about the hearer's knowledge of the speaker. For that reason a Gazdarian context is just a set of epistemic formulae, formulae of Hintikka's logic of knowledge and belief (Hintikka, 1962). The symbol $\models$ will now represent entailment in this logic, and K can be thought of as 'the speaker knows that'.

The need for an epistemic logic arises from the treatment of implicatures, some of which are inherently epistemic. The discussion below, unlike Gazdar's original theory, will be restricted to one class of epistemic implicatures, so-called *clausal* implicatures. For instance, a sentence 'if Mary's happy then she is singing' carries a clausal implicature that the speaker does not know whether Mary is in fact happy. More generally, when an utterance does not decide the truth of some embedded sentence there is an implicature that the speaker does not know whether that embedded sentence is true.

Definition 3.3, below, begins with the potential presuppositions PP(ϕ) of a formula ϕ and the potential implicatures PI: both of these definitions utilize a function 'sub' which is assumed to map a formula onto the set of all its non-presuppositional subformulae.[29] The potential presuppositions are just those subformulae occurring as subscripts (i.e. as second argument to the presuppositional connective), and potential implicatures are triggered by any subformula for which the formula as a whole neither entails the subformula nor its negation. Using the notation ϕ' to mean a formula of PrL with all the instances of formulae ϕ_ψ replaced by $\phi \wedge \psi$, what we may call *the assertion of* ϕ, a function $\star\phi$ is defined. This maps a context C onto a new context which is just C with the proposition that the speaker knows ϕ' added, and then all the compatible potential implicatures added. The full update of C with a formula ϕ is given by $C + \phi$, which is just $C \star \phi$ with all the compatible presuppositions added. Finally, we arrive at definitions of presupposition: $\phi \gg_C \psi$ holds just in case ψ is added to the context in the presuppositional stage of the update of C with ϕ, and $\phi \gg \psi$, if that is so for an empty context.[30] Additionally a presuppositionally sensitive notion of implication, $\Vdash$, is also defined:

DEFINITION 3.3 (*Gazdarian presuppositions*).

$$
\begin{aligned}
\mathrm{PP}(\phi) &= \{K\psi \mid \text{for some } \chi,\ \chi_\psi \in \mathrm{sub}(\phi)\},\\
\mathrm{PI}(\phi) &= \{\neg K\psi \wedge \neg K\neg\psi \mid \psi \in \mathrm{sub}(\phi) \text{ and } \psi \text{ not of form } \alpha_{13} \text{ and } \phi \not\models \psi\\
&\qquad\qquad \text{and } \phi \not\models \neg\psi\},\\
C \star \phi &= C \cup \{K\phi'\} \cup ! \mathrm{PI}(\phi),\\
C + \phi &= C \star \phi \cup ! \mathrm{PP}(\phi),\\
\phi \gg_C \psi \ &\mathit{iff}\ C + \phi \models \psi \text{ and } C \star \phi \not\models \psi,\\
\phi \gg \psi \ &\mathit{iff}\ \phi \gg_{\emptyset} \psi,\\
\phi \Vdash \psi \ &\mathit{iff}\ \emptyset + \phi \models \psi.
\end{aligned}
$$

---

[29] For concreteness define
(i) $\mathrm{sub}(\phi\,\Omega\,\psi) = \{\phi\,\Omega\,\psi\} \cup \mathrm{sub}(\phi) \cup \mathrm{sub}(\psi)$ for Ω one of $\rightarrow$, $\vee$, $\wedge$;
(ii) $\mathrm{sub}(\neg\phi) = \{\neg\phi\} \cup \mathrm{sub}(\phi)$;
(iii) $\mathrm{sub}(\phi) = \{\phi\}$ for atomic ϕ;
(iv) $\mathrm{sub}(\phi_\psi) = \{\phi_\psi\} \cup \mathrm{sub}(\phi)$.

[30] The definition of presupposition is at variance with that given by Gazdar (1979a, p. 133), who defines the presuppositions as those potential presuppositions which are in the final context. But then note that 'Mary won and knows it' would presuppose that Mary won, which is unintuitive. On the other hand, the definition used here is also open to criticism: potential presuppositions in simple positive contexts *never* become presuppositions because they are also entailed.

The reader should verify that under these definitions presuppositions project in simple cases of embedding. Further, cancellation is correctly predicted in a wide range of cases, for instance the following:

(3.12) The King of France is not bald: there is no King of France.

(3.13) If the King of France is bald, then I'm a Dutchman: there is no King of France.

(3.14) I don't know that Louis is bald.

(3.15) If David wrote the article then the knowledge that he wrote it will confound the editors.

Let ψ be the proposition that there is a French King, and ϕ be the proposition that this individual is bald. Then the first example, (3.12), becomes $\neg(\phi_\psi) \wedge \neg\psi$. Cancellation is correctly predicted: $\neg(\phi_\psi) \wedge \neg\psi \not\models \psi$. Note that in the absence of further information presuppositions project from negative sentences, so that the first clause alone does imply the existence of a French King: $\neg(\phi_\psi) \models \psi$.

In (3.13) (as uttered by, say, an Englishman) the presupposition of the definite in the first sentence, that there is a French King, is once again canceled.[31] On the assumption that the consequent of the conditional is intended as obviously false, and may be translated as if it were simply a contradictory proposition represented by $\bot$, we derive a translation $(\phi_\psi \rightarrow \bot) \wedge \neg\psi$. The Gazdarian account again correctly predicts cancellation: $(\phi_\psi \rightarrow \bot) \wedge \neg\psi \not\models \psi$. Under the translations given here it is scarcely surprising that (3.12) and (3.13) manifest similar projection properties, but note that under some accounts this could be seen as problematic. I am thinking here of theories (like the partial and multivalent theories considered earlier) that explain the occasional failure of presuppositions to project from under negations by postulating an ambiguity of negation. Under this analysis the ordinary presupposition-projecting translation of the first clause of (3.12) alone would in fact use a different negation to that involved in the cancellation reading of the whole example. This position on negation is consistent, but as the beginnings of a general account of the phenomenon of cancellation it is at least tested by examples like (3.13). For to explain cancellation in (3.13), the supporter of an ambiguity hypothesis would presumably have to postulate ambiguity of the English conditional. One then wonders where this multiplication of ambiguities will end: could all embedding constructions end up ambiguous between projecting and canceling interpretations? This would be an unattractive result.

Example (3.14) is a historically interesting type of cancellation sentence which led some theorists, starting with Karttunen (1971a), to postulate that there is a class of attitude verbs, the so-called *semi-factives*, which in some cases fail to carry a presupposition. Gazdar (1979a, pp. 153–154) was able to show that his theory could be used to formalize an alternative explanation arising with Stalnaker (1974). Take K to be a modal operator translating 'I know', and translate 'I know that Louis is bald' as $K(\phi)_\phi$, where ϕ is the

[31] Kay (1992), contra my own intuitions, sheds doubt on whether an example like (3.13) has a cancellation reading. The example would still be of interest, but, if Kay's data is right, (3.13) is a counterexample to Gazdar's theory (and presumably to Kay's own development of Gazdar's theory) rather than providing support. Clearly more empirical work is needed!

proposition that Louis is bald. Updating with the formula's assertion results in a context containing $\neg(\phi \wedge K(\phi))$, which in Hintikka's logic entails $\neg K(\phi)$. This is sufficient to prevent the potential presupposition $K(\phi)$ from being projected. It is crucial to the argumentation that the formula explicitly concerns the speaker's beliefs, and it is correctly predicted that whilst cancellation takes place in (3.14), it does not in the structurally similar 'Marie doesn't know that Louis is bald'. Likewise, no cancellation is predicted if 'know' is substituted for a factive verb that does not assert something about the speaker's knowledge: 'I don't regret that Louis is bald' does imply that the speaker takes Louis to be bald. So the cancellation in (3.14) does not take place because of any special non-presuppositional meaning of 'know', as Karttunen would suggest, but because the ordinary lexical semantics of 'know' means that it can be used to address issues relevant to projection.

In Example (3.15), translated as $\phi \rightarrow \psi_\phi$, a potential implicature is generated by the occurrence of ϕ in the antecedent of the conditional, which results in $\neg K\phi$ being added to the context. This is sufficient to block projection of the potential presupposition $K\phi$. A similar cancellation effect would be derived for the earlier Example (3.10)(i), but, as will be seen later, this type of clausal-implicature dependent cancellation does not always produce the right results.

3.3. The pre- in presupposition

In what sense is Gazdar's theory an account of 'presupposition'? I do not mean to suggest that it does not provide an account of presuppositional data. I merely mean that the account does not bear any relation to the fairly intuitive notion of presuppositions as previous assumptions. Indeed, since presuppositions are the last things to be added in Gazdar's definition of update, perhaps it would be more natural to call them *post-suppositions*. To me, at least, the major achievement of the theory first presented in Van der Sandt's thesis (Van der Sandt, 1982), which only appeared in English somewhat later in Van der Sandt (1988), is that it does succeed in reconciling ideas from Gazdar's cancellation account with what I take to be the intuitive notion of presupposition. I will term Van der Sandt's 1982/88 account his *cancellation* theory, to distinguish it from his later DRT-based theory.

One crucial but disarmingly simple insight could be said to drive Van der Sandt's cancellation theory. Suppose a sentence S can be coherently uttered in a context σ, and that one of the constituents of S carries a potential presupposition expressible using the sentence P. If in σ the text made up of P followed by S is coherent, then utterances of S in σ will carry the presupposition P, i.e. P is projected, and otherwise P is canceled (see Van der Sandt, 1988, pp. 185–189). For example, the sentence S= 'If Mary is married then her husband is away.' does not presuppose that Mary has a husband, since the the discourse consisting of 'Mary has a husband.' followed by S is strange.

Coherence of a discourse, what Van der Sandt expresses as "acceptability in a context", here comes down to the requirement that every clause is both consistent and informative. And it is in this definition that we see a synthesis of ideas of context change originating with Stalnaker and Karttunen with an otherwise quite Gazdarian account. Acceptability of a sentence S in a context σ is the requirement that for each clause S′ appearing in S (other than within a presuppositional expression) σ neither entails S′ nor entails the contrary of S′. If this requirement is not met, then S will not be a maximally *efficient* (i.e. compact) way of communicating whatever information it conveys in that context, since some subclauses will add no new information in their local context. I simplify by taking a context to be a set of sentences, although Van der Sandt allows for contexts to contain certain additional information.

DEFINITION 3.4 (*Presuppositions in Van der Sandt's cancellation account*). Given that all the potential presuppositions (or *elementary presuppositions* in Van der Sandt's terminology) of S are collected in the set π, the presuppositions of S in context σ are those propositions ϕ such that:

(i) $\phi \in \pi$;
(ii) For any $\psi \in \pi$, $\sigma \cup \{\phi, \psi\} \not\models \bot$;
(iii) S is acceptable in the context $\sigma \cup \{\phi\}$.

Although there are problems associated with this definition,[32] the intuition is clear, as the treatment of as treatment of (3.16) should illustrate:

(3.16) If Mary is sleeping then Fred is annoyed that she is sleeping.

Suppose that the context is empty. For (3.16), π is just the singleton set {*Mary is sleeping*}, the one potential presupposition being triggered by the factive 'annoyed'. We can test whether the potential presupposition is actually presupposed by adding it to the context and checking that all the subsentences in (3.16) not appearing in presuppositional expressions are neither entailed nor contradicted in the resulting context. Since the resulting context {*Mary is sleeping*} entails one of the subsentences, i.e. the antecedent of the conditional, we can conclude that the proposition that Mary is sleeping is not being presupposed, for if it were then (3.16) would be inefficient, and hence unacceptable.

Aside from Van der Sandt's proposal, there are by now a number of other theories which utilize Gazdar's approach of making presuppositions true by default. Mercer's cancellation account (Mercer, 1987, 1992) takes Gazdar's insight that presuppositions *normally* project, and are only canceled as a result of conflict with context or implicatures, and formalizes that by explicitly encoding Gazdar's potential presuppositions as default inference rules within Reiter's Default Logic. Unlike Gazdar, Mercer explicitly formulates his theory in terms of a notion of presupposition sensitive implication, that notion of implication being drawn directly from Default Logic. Indeed, Mercer describes his theory as not being a theory of presupposition projection *per se*, but as a theory of presuppositional inference. Other cancellation accounts include those of Bridge (1991), Gervas (1995), Gunji (1981), Horton (1987, 1988), Marcu (1994), Morreau (1995), and Schöter (1994, 1995). These accounts exhibit considerable technical and descriptive variation, but all center on presuppositions being defeasible inferences.

[32] See my (Beaver, 1995) and Burton-Roberts review article, (Burton-Roberts, 1989c), for discussion of problems with Van der Sandt's definition of presupposition.

4. Context change and accommodation

We have already seen that the cancellation theory of Gazdar (1979a), although based on a classical static semantics, involves pragmatic mechanisms controlling the evolution of a set of accepted propositions. Whereas in Gazdar's account meanings are derived statically, and dynamic effects become important only secondarily, in the accounts now to be discussed meaning itself is conceived of dynamically. We will be concerned with accounts which extend the inter-sentential dynamism of Gazdar's account by employing dynamism intra-sententially, so that the context of evaluation of a given clause is determined not only by previous sentences, but also by the dynamic interpretation of other parts of the same sentence.

The dynamic models of presupposition that will be considered all run along the following lines: (1) A context is comparable to a partial model, with respect to which some propositions are satisfied, some are falsified, and others are neither satisfied nor falsified. For some, these contexts may be understood as mental representations of discourse information. Sentences are interpreted as update operations mapping contexts to contexts. (2) When evaluating a complex syntactic expression in a certain context, the semantics of the functor should determine what input contexts are used locally in the evaluation of the argument expressions. Basic projection facts are explained by assuming that a complex expression is only admissible in a context if the the argument expressions are all admitted in their local input contexts. (3) A mechanism of *accommodation* may modify contexts so as to guarantee admissibility of presuppositional expressions.

4.1. From projection to satisfaction

Karttunen's 1973 definition of presupposition involved "a set of assumed facts", utterance presuppositions being calculated relative to such a set. However, it is not clear how the set of assumed facts and the set of (utterance) presuppositions are to be understood, and what, from a philosophical perspective, is meant to be the relation between them. In Karttunen (1974), Karttunen brilliantly resolved these difficulties, essentially by turning the projection problem, as then conceived, on its head. Instead of considering directly how the presuppositions of the parts of a sentence determine the presuppositions of the whole, he suggests we should first consider how the global context of utterance of a complex sentence determines the local linguistic context in which the parts of the sentence are interpreted, and derive from this a way of calculating which global contexts of utterance lead to local satisfaction of the presuppositions. He gives a formal definition of when a context satisfies-the-presuppositions-of – or *admits* – a formula. A simple sentence p will be admitted in a context C (here written $C \rhd p$) if and only if the primitive presuppositions of p are satisfied in C, where the natural notion of contextual satisfaction is just classical entailment, and C is just a set of formulae. When a complex sentence is evaluated in some context, however, presuppositions belonging to the parts of the sentence need not necessarily be satisfied in that context. For example, if a sentence S of the form "p and q" occurs in a context C, the conditions for S to be admitted in C are that p is admitted in C and q is admitted in a new context produced by adding

p to C. Note that essentially the same idea was independently developed by Stalnaker (1973, p. 455). Definition 4.1, below, shows how the approach can be applied to PrL:

DEFINITION 4.1 (*Admittance*).

$$\begin{aligned}
C \rhd \phi_\psi &\ \textit{iff}\ C \models \psi \textit{ and } C \rhd \phi,\\
C \rhd p &\quad \text{for any atomic } p,\\
C \rhd \neg\phi &\ \textit{iff}\ C \rhd \phi,\\
C \rhd \phi \wedge \psi &\ \textit{iff}\ C \rhd \phi \textit{ and } C \cup \{\phi\} \rhd \psi,\\
C \rhd \phi \rightarrow \psi &\ \textit{iff}\ C \rhd \phi \textit{ and } C \cup \{\phi\} \rhd \psi,\\
C \rhd \phi \vee \psi &\ \textit{iff}\ C \rhd \phi \textit{ and } C \cup \{\neg\phi\} \rhd \psi.
\end{aligned}$$

Presupposition may be formally defined as follows:

DEFINITION 4.2. The presuppositions of a formula are those formulae which are satisfied in every context that admits it:

$$\phi \gg \psi \ \textit{ iff } \ \forall C \ \ C \rhd \phi \Rightarrow C \models \psi.$$

The empirical motivation Karttunen presents for this theory is much the same as for his earlier theory. For instance, consider the formula $(\phi \wedge \psi_\phi) \rightarrow \chi$, which was given as a translation for (3.10)(i). Admittance of the whole formula in a context C depends on admittance of the formula ψ_ϕ in a local context $C \cup \{\phi\}$: but this is guaranteed irrespective of C. Thus the formula as a whole is admitted in all contexts, and there is no non-trivial presupposition.

This is more or less the result that would have obtained in the earlier theory, but note the "more or less" caveat. Whereas Karttunen's 1973 theory predicts no presupposition for this example, the 1974 theory predicts that all tautologies are presupposed by every formula. Furthermore, when the 1974 theory does predict a non-trivial presupposition, all the entailments of that presupposition are also presuppositions themselves, unlike in the 1973 theory. This difference is revealing, for it shows that (Karttunen, 1974) is not a filtering model: the presuppositions of a sentence are not in general a subset of the elementary presuppositions of its parts. Furthermore, the difference is not just that entailments of presuppositions are predicted to be presupposed.[33] Here is a summary of the presupposition projection properties arising from Definitions 4.1 and 4.2:

FACT 4.3. *If ϕ presupposes ψ then:*
(i) $\neg\phi$, $\phi \wedge \chi$, $\phi \rightarrow \chi$ *and* $\phi \vee \chi$ *all presuppose* ψ,
(ii) $\chi \wedge \phi$ *and* $\chi \rightarrow \phi$ *presuppose* $\chi \rightarrow \psi$,
(iii) $\chi \vee \phi$ *presupposes* $\neg\chi \rightarrow \psi$.

[33] Geurts has also drawn attention to differences between Karttunen's earlier and later accounts. Incidentally, note the following anomolous case of a formula which carries a non-trivial presupposition on the 1973 model, but not on the 1974 model: $\phi \rightarrow (\psi \rightarrow \chi_{\phi\wedge\psi})$, presupposing $\phi \wedge \psi$ on the 1973 model.

It can be seen that when a presupposition trigger is found on the right-hand side of a connective, a conditional presupposition results, although this conditional will not in general be one of the elementary presuppositions itself. So a concrete case where the 1973 and 1974 theories vary is the formula $\phi \rightarrow \psi_\chi$. With null context, and ϕ, χ logically independent, the 1973 model predicts the presupposition χ, whereas the 1974 theory predicts the conditionalized presupposition $\phi \rightarrow \chi$.[34]

4.2. Context change potential

In Karttunen's 1974 model it is unclear what the relationship is between the definition of admittance for an expression and the semantics of that expression. Judging from the developments in Karttunen and Peters (1979), one might conclude that admittance conditions and semantics are separate and unrelated parts of a grammar, but some authors see this as a weakness of the theory. Gazdar (1979b, pp. 58–59), who does not distinguish between Karttunen's various accounts, caricatures Karttunen's justification for why presuppositions sometimes disappear as "Because those presuppositions have been filtered out by my filter conditions". Gazdar suggests that an explanatorily adequate model should not only stipulate filtering conditions, but provide independent motivation for why those conditions are as they are. Although it is difficult to give any definitive characterization of exactly when a theory of presupposition is explanatorily adequate – and Gazdar's rhetoric provides no such characterization – it is at least clear that it would be desirable to justify a particular choice of filtering or admittance conditions. Heim (1983a) attempts to provide such a justification, and at the same time to clarify the relationship between admittance conditions and semantics. In particular, Heim provides a method of stating semantics, based on the approach developed in Heim (1982), in such a way that admittance conditions can be read off from the semantic definitions without having to be stipulated separately. Heim's semantics involves a significant deviation from the classical Tarskian

[34] The PrL admittance definition does not cover Karttunen's full treatment of predicates taking propositional complements. He divided these into three classes: verbs of saying (e.g., *say, announce*), verbs of propositional attitude (e.g., *believe, want*), and others. On Karttunen's account, the simplest cases are the first and the third: presuppositions triggered within the complement of a verb of saying do not impose any constraint on the context of utterance, whilst for members of the third class all presuppositions must be satisfied. Thus "John says that the king of France is bald" should be acceptable in any context, and "John knows that the king of France is bald" should only be acceptable in contexts where there is a (unique) king of France. For a sentence with propositional attitude verb as matrix, Karttunen argues that it is the beliefs of the subject of the sentence which are crucial: for a context A to admit the sentence, the beliefs of the subject in that context must satisfy all the presuppositions of the propositional complement. Thus "John hopes that the king of France is bald" should be satisfied in contexts where it is satisfied that John believes there to be a king of France. In favor of this analysis is the fact that the sentence "Although France is not a monarchy, John believes that there is a reigning French king: he hopes that the King of France is bald", although contrived, is felicitous. The syntax of PrL could be enriched with formulae $\alpha(\phi)$ for α taken from one of three sets of predicates $\mathcal{S}$, $\mathcal{A}$ and $\mathcal{F}$ (for *Saying, Attitude* and *factive*, respectively). I will ignore members of the *other* class apart from factives. Assuming that *believes* $\in \mathcal{A}$, and further assuming that neither verbs of saying nor verbs of propositional attitude induce any new presuppositions, the following are essentially Karttunen's acceptability conditions: (1) for $\alpha \in \mathcal{S}$, $C \rhd \alpha(\phi)$; (2) for $\alpha \in \mathcal{A}$, $C \rhd \alpha(\phi)$ *iff* $\{\psi \mid C \models \mathit{believes}(x, \psi)\} \rhd \phi$; (3) for $\alpha \in \mathcal{F}$, $C \rhd \alpha(\phi)$ *iff* $C \models \phi$.

approach, in that rather than viewing meaning as a static relation holding between language and truth in the world, she takes the meaning of an expression to be a method of updating the information state of communicating agents. I will now present Heim's insights in terms of PrL, the reader being referred to the chapter on Dynamic Semantics in this volume for a more careful discussion of the dynamic semantic approach.[35]

In Definition 4.4 a dynamic semantics is given for PrL. Formulae are interpreted as relations between information states, the intuition being that if a pair $\langle\sigma,\tau\rangle$ is in the denotation of a formula, then it is possible to update the state σ with the formula to produce the state τ. Information states are fashioned after the conception in Stalnaker (1979) as sets of possible worlds, the idea being that the set of worlds in an information state represents the set of different ways the world could be whilst maintaining consistency with all the available information. There are several ways we could answer the question of exactly what an information state is supposed to be a state of, it being left open for the moment whether a state represents the information of some particular agent, such as a hearer, or represents the commonly agreed information, or *common ground*, of a group of communicating agents. The clause for atomic propositions in 4.4 says that to update a state with an atomic proposition, all the worlds incompatible with the proposition must be removed, it being assumed that the model provides an interpretation function mapping each proposition to a corresponding set of worlds. The next clause says that to update with a conjunction it is necessary to update sequentially with the left and then the right conjunct, and the final clause says that to update with the negation of a formula one must find the set of worlds that is compatible with the formula, and remove these from the information state.

DEFINITION 4.4 (*Semantics of an update logic*). For all models $\mathcal{M}$ and information states σ,τ, the relation $[\![.]\!]^{\mathcal{M}}$ (sub-script omitted where unambiguous) is given recursively by:

$$\begin{aligned} \sigma[\![p_{\text{atomic}}]\!]\tau \ &\textit{iff}\ \tau = \{w \in \sigma \mid w \in F(p)\},\\ \sigma[\![\phi \wedge \psi]\!]\tau \ &\textit{iff}\ \exists v\ \ \sigma[\![\phi]\!]v[\![\psi]\!]\tau,\\ \sigma[\![\neg\phi]\!]\tau \ &\textit{iff}\ \exists v\ \ \sigma[\![\phi]\!]v\ \wedge\ \tau = \sigma\backslash v. \end{aligned}$$

One may add extend this language with clauses for implication and disjunction using the following suitably chosen classical equivalences:

DEFINITION 4.5 (*Defined connectives*).

$$\begin{aligned} \sigma[\![\phi \rightarrow \psi]\!]\tau \ &\textit{iff}\ \sigma[\![\neg(\phi \wedge (\neg\psi))]\!]\tau,\\ \sigma[\![\phi \vee \psi]\!]\tau \ &\textit{iff}\ \sigma[\![\neg(\neg\phi \wedge \neg\psi)]\!]\tau. \end{aligned}$$

[35] The move to a dynamic semantic style of presentation for Karttunen–Heim type theories was made by Van Eijck (1993), Zeevat (1992) and myself (Beaver, 1992). More recent work along these lines may be found in Beaver (1994a, 1995), Chierchia (1995), and Krahmer (1993).

A state σ is said to satisfy a formula ϕ (written $\sigma \| \!\!= \phi$) if and only if the state is a fixed point of the formula. This means that updating the state with the formula will add no new information. One formula ϕ entails another ψ (written $\phi \| \!\!= \psi$) if any update with the premise formula produces a state for which updating with the second adds no information.[36]

DEFINITION 4.6 (*CCP satisfaction and entailment*).

$$\sigma \| \!\!= \phi \ \textit{iff} \ \sigma [\![\phi]\!] \sigma,$$

$$\phi \| \!\!= \psi \ \textit{iff} \ \forall \sigma, \tau \sigma [\![\phi]\!] \tau \Rightarrow \tau \models \psi.$$

Over the standard connectives, the entailment relation is extensionally identical to the classical relation. But the full logic including presuppositional constructions is non-classical, e.g., in the sense that classical Gentzen sequents are no longer valid. The following definition captures the intuition that presuppositions place constraints that an input context must satisfy in order for there to be an update:

DEFINITION 4.7 (*CCP semantics of the presupposition connective*).

$$\sigma [\![\phi_\psi]\!] \tau \ \textit{iff} \ \sigma \| \!\!= \psi \ \textit{and} \ \sigma [\![\phi]\!] \tau.$$

For the full language, conjunction is not commutative: e.g., the denotations of $\phi \wedge \phi_\psi$ and $\phi_\psi \wedge \phi$ are different, and the second entail formulae which the first does not. The following justifies the claim that Karttunen's admittance conditions, and thus his notion of presupposition can be read off from the semantics:

FACT 4.8. *Define Heimian admittance by $\sigma \rhd_H \phi$ iff $\exists \tau \ \sigma [\![\phi]\!] \tau$. Then the Karttunen notion of presupposition, $\gg$ in Definition 4.2 is recoverable (analogously to 4.2 itself) as:*

$$\phi \gg \psi \ \textit{iff} \ (\forall \sigma \ \sigma \rhd_H \phi \ \textit{iff} \ \sigma \| \!\!= \psi).$$

To see the CCP semantics in action, suppose we were to make the philosophically controversial claim that a statement 'X knows S' presupposes S and asserts that X believes S. Then 'Elspeth knows that Fred is happy' might be represented as $bel(e, happy(f))_{happy(f)}$. Write this formula, where *happy(f)* and *bel(e,happy(f))* are atomic propositions, as ϕ. Let the model contain only four worlds, 1–4, such that Fred is happy in the first two (i.e. $\mathcal{I} = \{1, 2\}$), and Elspeth believes that Fred is happy in the first and the third. Consider update of the state $\{1, 2\}$ with ϕ. It is necessary firstly to check that *happy(f)* is satisfied, which it is: $\{1, 2\} \models$ *happy(f)*. The state must then be updated with *bel(e, happy(f))*. Since this proposition holds in world 1 but not in world 2, the final output is the state $\{1\}$. In contrast, the formula ϕ does not define an update from input state $\{1, 3, 4\}$ in this model, since $\{1, 3, 4\} \not\models$ *happy(f)* and if a presupposition is not satisfied, updating is blocked. In fact in this model the update relation corresponding to the denotation of ϕ defines only

[36] See the chapter on Dynamic Semantics in this volume for discussion of alternative notions of entailment.

the updates $\{1,2\} \Longrightarrow \{1\}, \{1\} \Longrightarrow \{1\}, \{2\} \Longrightarrow \{\}$. There are no updates from states containing worlds 3 or 4, since the presupposition is not satisfied in any of these states. More generally, if Fact 4.8 is taken as the definition of presupposition for this system, then for arbitrary models it will be the case that $bel(e, happy(f))_{happy(f)} \models happy(f)$.

Note the distinction between *presupposition failure* and *update with contradictory information*: whereas there is no state that can be obtained by updating $\{1,3,4\}$ with ϕ, there is a state which can be obtained by updating $\{2\}$ with ϕ. However, this output state is the empty set, there being no worlds in the model compatible with all the information the agent has. It is also worth noting that for this system the definition of presupposition via admittance is equivalent with one of the standard semantic notions of presupposition introduced above:

FACT 4.9. *ϕ presupposes ψ iff $\phi \models \psi$ and $\neg\phi \models \psi$.*

The reason for this lies in the clause for the interpretation of negation, from which it may be seen that the negation of a formula defines an update just in case its positive counterpart does. It is thus obvious that if 'Elspeth doesn't know that Fred is happy' is represented as $\neg\phi$, then 'Elspeth doesn't know that Fred is happy' has the same presuppositions as 'Elspeth knows that Fred is happy'. The reader may care to verify that in the above model, the denotation of $\neg\phi$ defines only the updates $\{1,2\} \Longrightarrow \{2\}, \{1\} \Longrightarrow \{\}, \{2\} \Longrightarrow \{2\}$, mapping states in which it is established that Fred is happy, but not established whether Elspeth believes this, to states where it is both established that Fred is happy and that Elspeth does not believe this.

4.3. *Quantifying-in to presuppositions*

It is not obvious how to extend the cancellation and filtering accounts considered in Section 3 to enable them to deal with open presuppositions, that is, presuppositions containing a free variable. Heim showed how this might be achieved in the Context Change model. We will consider her approach presented in terms of an extension to the above propositional logic, and then look at a well known problem with that approach, and, briefly, one solution.

One could imagine introducing variables into the above system in a relatively conservative fashion, maintaining classical notions of scope and binding.[37] The approach Heim took, developed from that in her thesis, was more radical, and allows for binding of variables which fall outside of the conventional scope of their introducing quantifier. This

[37] Assuming the model provided appropriate interpretation functions $\mathcal{I}$ and domain $\mathcal{D}$, we might add the following clauses:

$$\sigma[P(x_1, \ldots, x_n)]_f \tau \text{ iff } \tau = \{w \in \sigma \mid \langle w, f(x_1), \ldots, f(x_n)\rangle \in \mathcal{I}(P)\},$$
$$\sigma[\exists x \phi]_f \tau \text{ iff } \exists d \in \mathcal{D}\ \sigma[\phi]_{f[x \mapsto d]} \tau.$$

Here interpretation is with respect to an assignment function, and $f[x \mapsto d]$ denotes the interpretation function differing from f maximally through mapping x onto the object d in the domain. The reader is left to consider how Definitions 4.4–4.7 might be modified.

non-standard treatment of variables was originally motivated in terms of pronominals in donkey and intersentential anaphora, but given the tight relationship between presupposition and anaphora, to which we shall turn later, it is also of relevance to presupposition, most obviously for definite descriptions.

Models will now be triples $\langle W, \mathcal{D}, \mathcal{I}\rangle$, where W is a set of worlds, $\mathcal{D}$ is a domain of individuals (here assumed constant across worlds) and $\mathcal{I}$ maps n-ary predicates onto sets of $(n+1)$-ary tuples, where the first element of the tuple is understood as a world index. Heim utilizes *sequences*, such that given a set of variables $\mathcal{V}$, a sequence is just a partial assignment function mapping a subset of $\mathcal{V}$ onto elements of $\mathcal{D}$. A Heimian information state is a set of sequence-world pairs where each sequence has the same domain of variables. Each pair encodes one possibility for how the world is and which objects in that world are under discussion.

Before coming to the technicalities, let us consider a simple example: update with 'a woman curtsied', which will be represented as $\exists x\ (woman(x) \wedge curtsied(x)_{female(x)})$. Suppose that there are only two worlds in the model, w_1 and w_2, and that the domain contains only two individuals *elspeth* and *fred*, such that in both worlds *elspeth* is a *woman* and *female* but *fred* is not. Thus, for example, $\mathcal{I}(woman) = \{\langle w_1, elspeth\rangle, \langle w_2, elspeth\rangle\}$. Suppose that *elspeth curtsied* in w_1 but not w_2. A minimal state of information with respect to this model will be one containing both worlds and where no individuals have been introduced. If we represent a sequence as a list of mappings of the form "var$\mapsto$object", such that the empty sequence is just an empty list [], then such a minimal state will be $\{\langle[], w_1\rangle, \langle[], w_2\rangle\}$. Update of this state begins with extension with valuations for x, which produces a state $\{\langle[x \mapsto elspeth], w_1\rangle, \langle[x \mapsto elspeth], w_2\rangle, \langle[x \mapsto fred], w_1\rangle, \langle[x \mapsto fred], w_2\rangle\}$, a state in which although the value of x is under discussion, there is no information about what this value is. Updating this state with *woman*(x) removes sequence-world pairs which do not map x onto an object in the extension of *woman*, to produce $\{\langle[x \mapsto elspeth], w_1\rangle, \langle[x \mapsto elspeth], w_2\rangle\}$, a state which still contains the same information about what the world is like as the initial state, but which additionally determines that the variable x is mapped to *elspeth*. Given that x is now established to be *female*, the presuppositional formula *female*(x) is satisfied. If there had been any sequence-world pairs which did not map x onto a *female*, update would have failed. Finally, updating with *curtsied*(x) removes one sequence world pair to produce the state $\{\langle[x \mapsto elspeth], w_1\rangle\}$.

Following earlier formulations of Heim's insights into DPL-like systems,[38] we arrive at definitions for predication and for existential quantification like those in Definition 4.10 below. The clause for predication is analogous to that for atomic propositions in Definition 4.4. Those sequence-world pairs which are incompatible with the predication are removed. The remaining sequence-world pairs are those where the extension of the predicate contains the tuple made up of the world and the objects onto which the sequence maps the argument variable. The interpretation of statements "$\exists x\phi$" involves extending a state with all possible valuations for that variable, and then removing all those sequence-world pairs which are incompatible with ϕ. One sequence-world pair $i = \langle f, v\rangle$ extends

[38] See the Dynamics chapter for details of DPL, introduced in (Groenendijk and Stokhof, 1991). Dekker (see, e.g., Dekker, 1993) provides a reformulation using partial assignments, and Beaver (1992) draws in the presuppositional aspects of Heim's proposal.

another $j = \langle g, w\rangle$ with respect to the variable x (written $i >_x j$) if $v = w$, f and g agree on all variables apart from x, but f additionally provides a valuation for x. An information state can be updated with $\exists x\phi$, by extending each of the sequence-world pairs in the state with x and updating the result with ϕ.

DEFINITION 4.10 (*Predication and quantification*). [39]

$$\begin{aligned}\sigma[\![P(x_1,\ldots,x_n)]\!]\tau \ &\textit{iff}\ \tau = \{\langle f,w\rangle \in \sigma \mid \langle w, f(x_1),\ldots,f(x_n)\rangle \in \mathcal{I}(P)\},\\ \sigma[\![\exists x\phi]\!]\tau \ &\textit{iff}\ \{i \mid \exists j \in \sigma \wedge i >_x j\}[\![\phi]\!]\tau,\\ \sigma[\![\forall x\phi]\!]\tau \ &\textit{iff}\ \sigma[\![\neg\exists x\neg\phi]\!]\tau.\end{aligned}$$

As things stand the definitions for satisfaction of a formula in a state and for the interpretation of negation are inadequate, since they fail to account for cases where the formula introduces a new variable.[40] If R is a Context Change Potential (i.e. a binary relation between information states) then call $\downarrow R$ the closure of R, a CCP like R except for not introducing any new variables.[41] This leads to the modified definitions for negation and satisfaction in 4.11. The propositional clause for conjunction in 4.4 still makes sense at the first order level, modulo a reinterpretation of the notion of *state*. The definitions for entailment (4.6) and for the semantics of implications, disjunctions (4.5) and the presupposition operator (4.7) are also preserved, except that they are defined in terms of the new clauses for negation and satisfaction.

DEFINITION 4.11 (*Negation and satisfaction*).

$$\begin{aligned}\sigma[\![\neg\phi]\!]\tau \ &\textit{iff}\ \exists v\ \ \sigma\downarrow[\![\phi]\!]v\ \wedge\ \tau = \sigma\backslash v,\\ \sigma|\!\models\phi \ &\textit{iff}\ \sigma\downarrow[\![\phi]\!]\sigma.\end{aligned}$$

[39] As observed in (Dekker, 1993), the logic of the resulting system is simplified if requantification over the a variable is forbidden. In the current set up, we might define a function "dom" which mapped a state onto the set of variables given valuations in that state, and then add an extra constraint on the clause for addition of a discourse marker. Similarly, the predication clause in Definition 4.10 seems inappropriate in case a predication is evaluated in a state that does not provide valuations for all the predicated variables, and an extra clause can be added requiring this. We arrive at the following:

$$\begin{aligned}\sigma[P(x_1,\ldots,x_n)]\tau \ &\textit{iff}\ \{x_1,\ldots,x_n\} \subseteq \mathrm{dom}(\sigma)\\ &\wedge \tau = \{\langle f,w\rangle \in \sigma \mid \langle w, f(x_1),\ldots,f(x_n)\rangle \in \mathcal{I}(P)\},\\ \sigma[\exists x\phi]\tau \ &\textit{iff}\ x \notin \mathrm{dom}(\sigma) \wedge \{i \mid \exists j \in \sigma \wedge i >_x j\}[\phi]\tau.\end{aligned}$$

In this system we might say, loosely, that a predication *presupposes* familiarity of the arguments, and that a quantification *presupposes* non-familiarity of the quantified marker.

[40] To see the problem, observe that the negation of a formula is defined in terms of set subtraction of the set resulting from update with the formula from the input state. But if the formula introduces a new variable, then the result of updating with it will be a disjoint set from the input, so that a negation could only define an identity update.

[41] Let us say that one sequence-world pair extends (">") another if some finite sequence of extensions of the first produces the second. Now we can define $\sigma \downarrow R\ \tau$ *iff* $\exists v\ \ \sigma R v\ \wedge\ \tau = \{i \in \sigma \mid \exists j > i\ j \in v\}$. That is, the closure of an update relation allows update of a state σ to a new state τ, where τ is that subset of sequence-world pairs in σ which have extensions in some update with the unclosed relation.

There is a problem in Heim's approach regarding the interaction of quantifiers with presuppositions, and in the current presentation this problem manifests itself as the following fact:

FACT 4.12. *If ϕ presupposes π, then $\exists x\ \psi \wedge \phi$ presupposes $\forall x\ \psi \rightarrow \pi$.*

Suppose that (4.7a) is given the crude translation in (4.7b).

(4.7) a. A plane just landed.

b. $\exists x\ \mathit{plane}(x) \wedge (\mathit{on\text{-}ground}(x)_{\mathit{was\text{-}airborne}(x)})$.

By Fact 4.12, Example (4.7b) will be predicted to carry the presupposition $\forall x\ \mathit{plane}(x) \rightarrow \mathit{was\text{-}airborne}(x)$. So, contrary to intuition, the sentence is predicted to carry the presupposition that *every* plane, and not just the one that landed, was airborne. To understand why the universal presupposition occurs, consider how a state would be updated with (4.7b). Firstly the variable x is initialized, to produce a state in which there are sequences mapping x onto every object in the domain. Then the proposition $\mathit{plane}(x)$ is added, removing all those sequence-world pairs where x is not mapped onto a plane: call the result σ. Next we arrive at the presupposition $\mathit{was\text{-}airborne}(x)$, and update can only continue if this is satisfied in σ. For this to be the case every sequence-world pair in σ must map x onto an object that was airborne. But since for any world still in contention, there are sequences in σ mapping x onto every plane in that world, the proposition $\mathit{was\text{-}airborne}(x)$ will only be satisfied if in every world in σ, every object which is a plane in that world is an object which was airborne. Thus we arrive at a universal presupposition.

To some extent this problem is idiosyncratic. There are dynamic systems combining treatments of presupposition and quantification, such as those of Van Eijck (1993), Krahmer (1995) and Chierchia (1995), where existential sentences do not lead to universal presuppositions. In some of these systems the notion of an information state is quite different from Heim's, and this is at the heart of the different predictions that arise. However a Heimian semantics like that presented above can be adapted so as to avoid problematic universal presuppositions without any alteration to the notion of an information state. It suffices to make alterations either to the semantics of the quantifiers or to the presupposition connective. As discussed in my (Beaver, 1994a), a modification to the quantifiers can arguably be motivated on independent grounds. However modifying the presupposition connective, essentially the move made in (Beaver, 1992), is perhaps the simpler. Suppose that the function *worlds* maps a Heimian context onto the set of worlds involved in that context: $\mathit{worlds}(\sigma) = \{w \mid \exists f \langle w, f\rangle \in \sigma\}$. Then one possibility would be to redefine the presupposition connective as in Definition 4.13, such that a formula ϕ_ψ allows update to continue just in case update with ψ would not remove any worlds from the input context. By contrast, the earlier definition above was stricter, requiring not only that update with ψ preserves the worlds in the input, but also that it preserves all the sequences associated with those worlds.

DEFINITION 4.13.

$$\sigma[\![\phi_\psi]\!]\tau \text{ iff } \exists v \sigma[\![\psi]\!]v \text{ and } \mathit{worlds}(\sigma) = \mathit{worlds}(v) \text{ and } v[\![\phi]\!]\tau.$$

Under this Definition 4.12 no longer holds, and existential sentences yield existential presuppositions. This shows that the problems with Heim's account of presupposed open propositions are not as intractable as has been suggested (cf. Soames, 1989) in the literature.[42]

4.4. Accommodation

> "... ordinary conversation does not always proceed in the ideal orderly fashion described earlier. People do make leaps and short cuts by using sentences whose presuppositions are not satisfied in the conversational context. ... But ... I think we can maintain that a sentence is always taken to be an increment to a context that satisfies its presuppositions. If the current conversational context does not suffice, the listener is entitled and expected to extend it as required. He must determine for himself what context he is supposed to be in on the basis of what is said and, if he is willing to go along with it, make the same tacit extension that his interlocutor appears to have made." (Karttunen, 1974, p. 191.)

The process Karttunen here describes, whereby a "tacit extension" is made to the discourse context to allow for update with otherwise unfulfilled presuppositions, is what Lewis later called *accommodation* (Lewis, 1979).[43] Theories which utilize a mechanism of accommodation, are not classical *static* theories of meaning, but rather theories about the dynamics of the interpretation process.

Two questions are central to understanding the characteristics a theory of accommodation might have:

(Q1) Given that the interpretation of a discourse involves not one linguistic context, but a series of contexts corresponding to different parts of the interpretation process and different parts of the discourse's meaning, in which context should accommodation occur?

(Q2) Given some decision as to the context in which accommodation occurs, exactly how should a hearer determine what the new context is supposed to be?

---

[42] Space permitting, it would have been appropriate to have also discussed the interaction with quantification in the context of other accounts of presupposition. Note that all systems which split presupposition and assertion into separate components of meaning, such as Karttunen and Peters' system, Karttunen's 1973 filtering account and Gazdar's cancellation account, face serious problems in this regard, but that some other approaches, such as that based on a trivalent logic, can be naturally extended to provide an account of quantified presuppositions. Discussions of systems that allow for interaction of quantification and presupposition are found, e.g., in Cooper (1983), Lehrner and Zimmermann (1983), Beaver (1994a), Beaver and Krahmer (m.s.), Krahmer (1994, 1995), Van Eijck (1993), Van der Sandt (1992).

[43] Stalnaker (1972, p. 398) expresses similar sentiments to those in the above Karttunen quotation, commenting that presuppositions "need not be true", and that in some cases a "Minor revision might bring our debate in line with new presuppositions". Interestingly, in the same paragraph Stalnaker talks of certain things being "accommodated" in the light of new presuppositions, although what he is describing here is not how we change our assumptions (the Lewisian notion of "accommodation"), but how *after* we have changed our assumptions we may reinterpret earlier observations.

Heim (1983a) was the first author to recognize the significance of the first question, noting that quite different effects could result according to which point in the interpretation of a sentence accommodation occurs. In the Heim/Karttunen account one can distinguish two types of context. There is the *global* context which represents the information agents have after complete interpretation of some sequence of sentences of text, but there are also *local* contexts, the contexts against which sub-parts of a sentence are evaluated.

Updating a context σ with a conditional $\phi \rightarrow \psi$ involves local contexts which we may notate $\sigma + \phi$ and $\sigma + \phi + \psi$ which are involved during the calculation of the update. Suppose that ψ contains some presupposition which is unsatisfied in the context $\sigma + \phi$, so that σ does not admit the conditional. In that case accommodation must occur, adjusting one of the contexts involved in the calculation so that ψ is admitted in its local context of evaluation. This might take the form of directly updating the local context in which ψ is to be evaluated with some formula α, so that the final result of updating with the context would not be $\sigma \backslash (\sigma + \phi \backslash (\sigma + \phi + \psi))$, but $\sigma \backslash (\sigma + \phi \backslash (\sigma + \phi + \alpha + \psi))$: this would be called *local accommodation*. On the other hand, an agent might backtrack right back to the initial context, add a formula β to the global context, and then start the update again. This is termed *global accommodation*, and the result of updating would be $(\sigma + \beta) \backslash (\sigma + \beta + \phi \backslash (\sigma + \beta + \phi + \psi))$. There is at least one other possibility. The agent might just backtrack as far as the evaluation of the antecedent, and add some extra information, say γ, into the context in which the antecedent is evaluated, producing a result like $\sigma \backslash (\sigma + \gamma + \phi \backslash (\sigma + \gamma + \phi + \psi))$. Since this last option involves accommodation into a context intermediate between the global context and the context in which the problematic presuppositional construction is actually evaluated, it can be termed *intermediate accommodation*. Clearly the Heimian view on accommodation is highly procedural, and the exact options which are available for accommodation will be dependent on the details of how updating actually occurs, such processing details not being fully specified by the CCP alone.

The Heimian answer to (Q1), then, is that accommodation might take place at any time during the interpretation process such as to ensure later local satisfaction of presuppositions. Put another way, accommodation might potentially take place in any of the discourse contexts used in the calculation of a sentence's CCP. Unfortunately, Heim has not provided a detailed answer to (Q2). The first theory of accommodation which provides a fully explicit answer to both questions is that of Van der Sandt (1992).

4.5. *Accommodation as a transformation on DRSs*

In Van der Sandt's theory Heimian contexts are replaced by explicit discourse representations.[44] Consequently, whereas for Heim accommodation must consist in augmenting a set of world-sequence pairs, Van der Sandtian accommodation is simply addition of

[44] Van der Sandt is not the only one to have provided an account of presupposition in DRT, but his is the most developed account of projection, and others, such as Kamp and Rossdeutscher's (Kamp and Rossdeutscher, 1994; Rossdeutscher, 1994) (which is more detailed concerning the lexical source of presuppositions) are closely related. For details of DRT, the reader is referred to Kamp (1981), Kamp and Reyle (1993) and Chapter 3 of this Handbook.

discourse referents and conditions to a DRS. This difference could be minimized if the CCP model were presented in terms of Heimian *filecards*, cf. Heim (1982, 1983b), so that accommodation would consist of either creating new filecards, or adding conditions to existing ones. Regarding (Q1), Van der Sandt's theory shares the flexibility of Heim's. If a presupposition lacks an antecedent in a DRS, Van der Sandt allows accommodation to take place in any discourse context that is accessible from the site of the trigger. Thus once again we can talk of *local accommodation*, meaning accommodation in the DRS where the trigger is represented, *global accommodation* meaning addition of material in the global DRS, and *intermediate accommodation* meaning addition of material in any DRS intermediate on the accessibility path between the global DRS and the site of the trigger.

Van der Sandt's answer to (Q2), the question of what is accommodated, is as simple as it could be: if a trigger has an antecedentless presupposition, then accommodation essentially consists of transferring the discourse markers and conditions of the presupposition from the trigger site to the accommodation site.

Before Van der Sandt's accommodation mechanism can be detailed, the more basic parts of his theory must be discussed, showing how cases not requiring accommodation are treated. Van der Sandt's principle claim is that presupposition triggers are *anaphoric* at the level of discourse representation. The theme of anaphoricity will be taken up again in Section 6.1, below. For the moment it suffices to realize that the heart of the theory involves a structural relation between the position at which a presupposition trigger is represented in a DRS, and the point at which its *antecedent* is represented. The antecedent must be represented somewhere along the *anaphoric accessibility path* from the representation of the trigger, this condition being exactly the same requirement as is placed on anaphoric pronouns and their antecedents in standard DRT. The treatment of (4.8) should illustrate.

(4.8) Fred is escaping, but Mary doesn't realize that somebody is escaping.

Initially a DRS like the following, in which the presence of a presupposition is indicated using a double thickness box, is constructed:

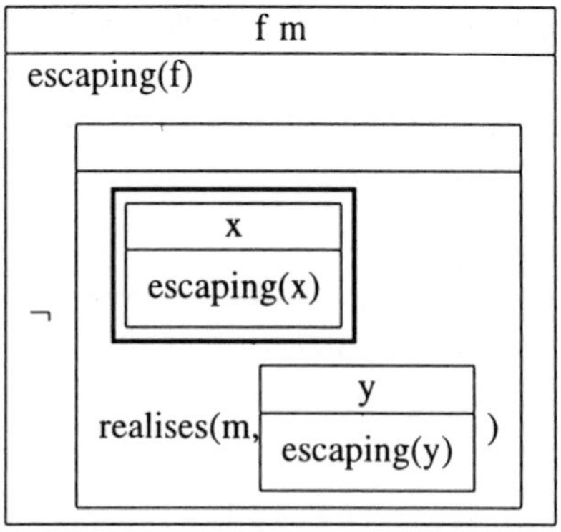

The global DRS is accessible from within the negation. The marker x can be resolved with the marker f, and in this case both the universe of the presupposition (now f) is accessible in the global universe, and the condition in the presupposition is accessible as a global condition. Thus the presupposition has an antecedent. The double-lined presupposition box, which plays no further role in DRS construction, and does not enter into the model theoretic interpretation of the completed DRS structure, is simply removed.

Note that it would make little difference to the treatment of (4.8) if the word 'somebody' had been replaced by 'he'. Van der Sandt thus provides an interesting twist to the DRT treatment of noun phrase semantics, since in his extended DRT an indefinite (when embedded in a presuppositional environment) can act anaphorically.

Now we come to accommodation. An example will illustrate the power of the accommodation mechanism and at the same time illustrate an analogy that might be drawn between Van der Sandt's theory and a transformational account of syntax, Van der Sandt's equivalent of *move-*α being an operation on DRSs.

(4.9) If Mary chose the Chateau Neuf, then she realizes it's a good wine.

Assuming, just so that we can concentrate on the treatment of the factive 'realizes', that 'Mary' and 'the Chateau Neuf' and 'it' are simply represented as discourse markers, the following DRS is derived:

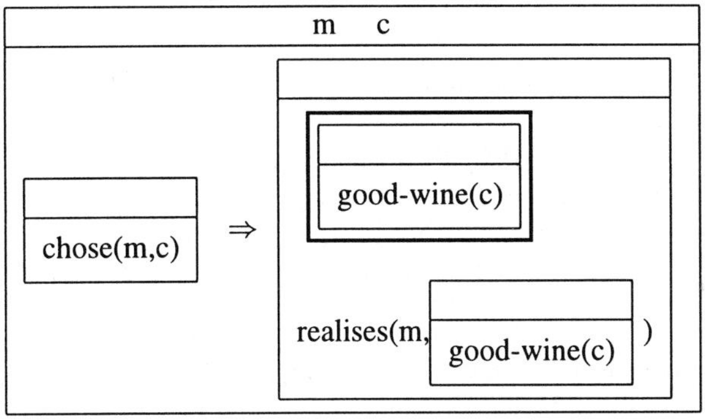

To produce a DRS in which there is no antecedentless presupposition, a transformation must take place whereby α, the presupposition [][good-wine(c)],[45] is moved to one of the three sites accessible from the site of the trigger, producing the following three representations:

Global Accommodation (Gloss: 'CN is good, and if Mary orders it then she realizes it's good.')

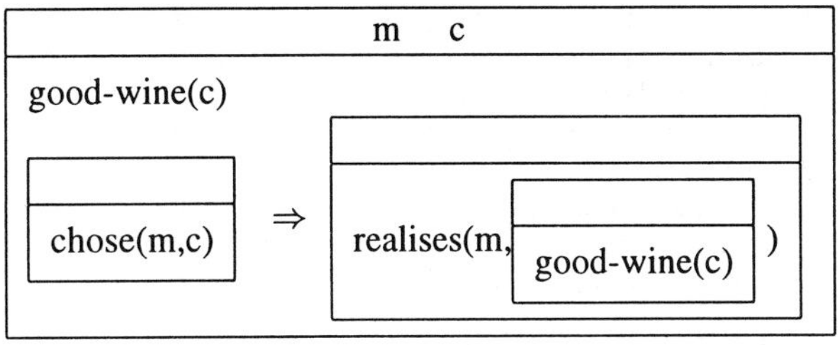

[45] When giving DRSs in the running text, I use a linear notation, whereby [a,b][p(a,b),q(a)] represents a DRS which introduces markers a and b, and has conditions p(a,b) and q(a).

Intermediate Accommodation (Gloss: 'If CN is good and Mary orders it, then she realizes it's good.')

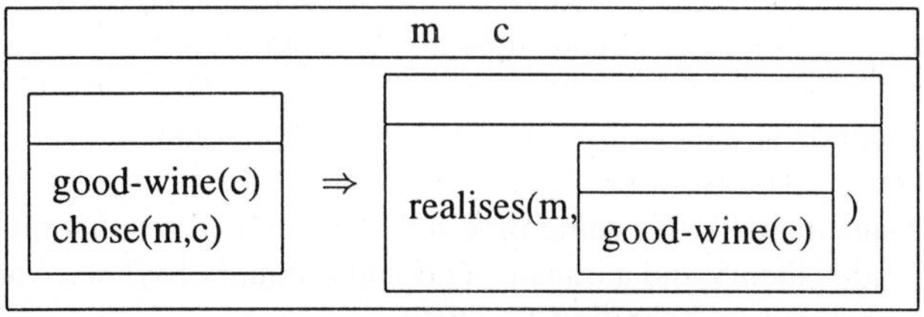

Local Accommodation (Gloss: 'If Mary orders CN then it's good and she realizes it's good.')

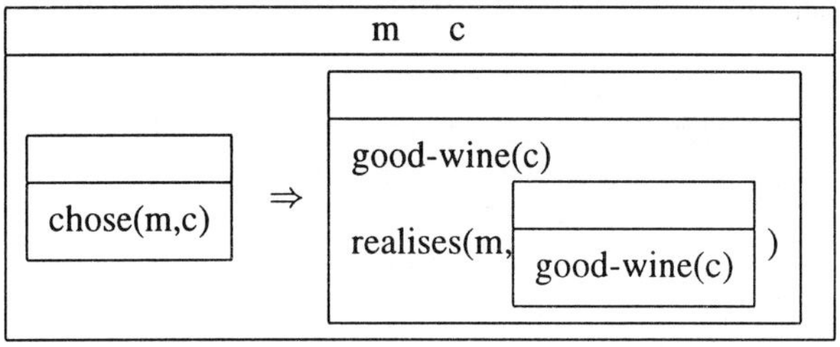

Given all these forms of accommodation, and, in Van der Sandt's theory, additional options when resolution is possible, how are we to decide which treatment is preferred? Heim offered only one heuristic: "I suggest that the global option is strongly preferred, but the local option is also available in certain circumstances that make it unavoidable." (Heim, 1983a, p. 120) Van der Sandt provides much more detail. He offers a number of constraints that any solution must obey, and also suggests a group of preferences between alternative solutions that satisfy those constraints, including a preference for global over local accommodation.[46] The following versions of the preferences and constraints are at some points revised, but I think capture Van der Sandt's intentions:[47]

[46] In earlier versions of Van der Sandt's theory the preferences between solutions were stated less explicitly, as side effects of a general algorithm for treating presuppositions. This algorithm, which he termed the "anaphoric loop" consisted of the following steps: on encountering a presupposition, firstly check each DRS along the accessibility path from the trigger, moving successively outwards, and attempting to resolve the presupposition, and if after reaching the top box no resolution site has been found, check each box in the reverse direction (i.e. from the top box to the trigger site) attempting to accommodate. Thus resolution is attempted first, and only if that fails is accommodation attempted.

[47] In particular, the presentation of constraints here differs considerably from, for instance, the presentation in (Van der Sandt, 1992). Firstly, Van der Sandt gives two consistency constraints, but these are both subsumed under the one constraint given here. Secondly, Van der Sandt's formulations of informativity and consistency constraints seem to involve a notion of local entailment of sub-DRSs, although I am not aware of such a notion ever having been formalized. Thus his equivalent of my *local informativity* (given as (iii)a on p. 167) is "Resolving [a DRS] K_0 to [produce a new DRS] K_1' does not give rise to a structure in which ... some subordinate DRS is entailed by the DRSs which are superordinate to it". Whilst he does not formalize what it

DEFINITION 4.14 (*Absolute constraints on Van der Sandtian solutions*).

(i) Trapping. If a presupposition containing a discourse marker d is triggered in an environment where d is bound, the presupposition will be resolved or accommodated at a site from where the relevant binding occurrence of d is accessible.

(ii) Global Informativity. If some DRS K is incremented with information from a new sentence, such that after solution of all presuppositions the new DRS is K', then $K \not\models K'$.

(iii) Local Informativity. No sub-DRS is redundant. Formally, if K is the complete DRS structure and K' is an arbitrarily deeply embedded sub-DRS, K' is redundant if and only if $\forall M, f \ (M, f \models K \ \rightarrow \ M, f \models K[K'/\top])$. Here $K[K'/\top]$ is a DRS like K except for having the instance of K' replaced by an instance of an empty DRS, and $\models$ denotes the DRT notion of *embedding*.

(iv) Consistency. No sub-DRS is inconsistent. Formally, if K is the complete DRS structure and K' is an arbitrarily deeply embedded sub-DRS, K' is locally inconsistent if and only if $\forall M, f \ (M, f \models K \ \rightarrow \ M, f \models K[K'/\bot])$. Here $K[K'/\bot]$ is a DRS like K except for having the instance of K' replaced by an instance of an inconsistent DRS.

DEFINITION 4.15 (*Preferences between Van der Sandtian solutions*).

(i) Resolution is preferred to accommodation.

(ii) One resolution is preferred to another if the first is more local (i.e. closer to the site of the trigger).

(iii) One accommodation is preferred to another if the first is more global (i.e. further from the site of the trigger).

I will illustrate these constraints with some examples. Firstly, trapping:

(4.10) Nobody regrets leaving school.

Initially the following DRS might be constructed:

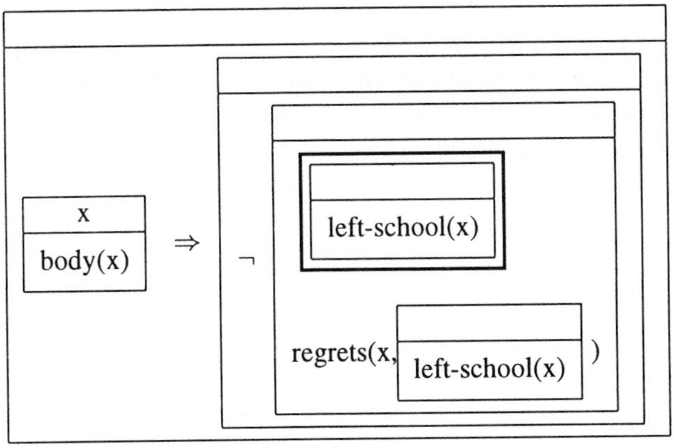

is for a DRS to be entailed by the DRSs which are superordinate to it, the formalization of local informativity given here, in terms of the standard notion of DRS embedding and a simple syntactic operation on DRSs, hopefully ties up that loose end, and is in the spirit of the definitions used in Van der Sandt's formalization of the notion of *acceptability* in his earlier non-DRT work.

The presupposition cannot be accommodated globally because the discourse marker x would become unbound. The next most preferred accommodation site is in the antecedent box. This produces the final structure, the meaning of which can be glossed as 'Nobody who leaves school regrets having left school':

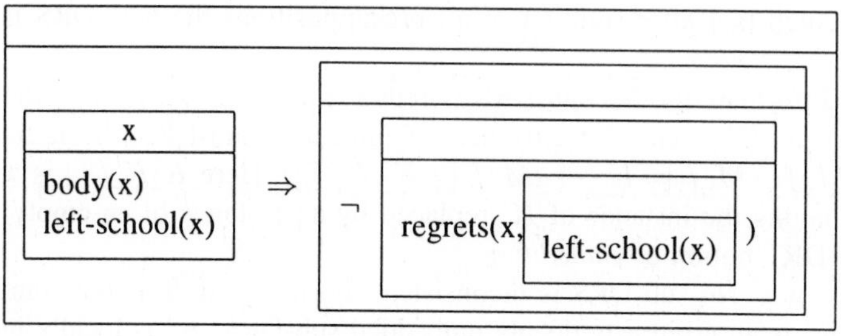

Next, application of the informativity constraint. This is exemplified by (4.11):

(4.11) If Jane is married then her husband is on holiday.

Global accommodation of the presupposition that Jane has a husband (triggered by 'her husband') would produce the following DRS:

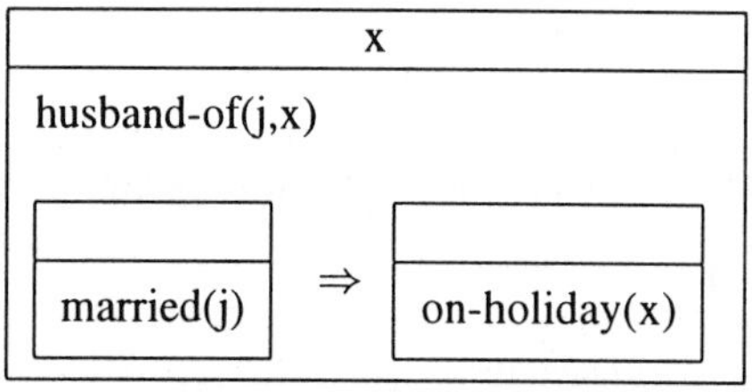

But, on the assumption that models are constrained by meaning postulates in such a way that if somebody has a husband then they are married, this DRS breaks the informativity constraint: replacing the DRS in the antecedent of the conditional, [][married(j)], by the empty DRS [][] would not alter the range of models in which the global DRS could be embedded. Thus, once again, intermediate accommodation is preferred, producing a structure glossable as 'If Jane is married to x, then x is on holiday':

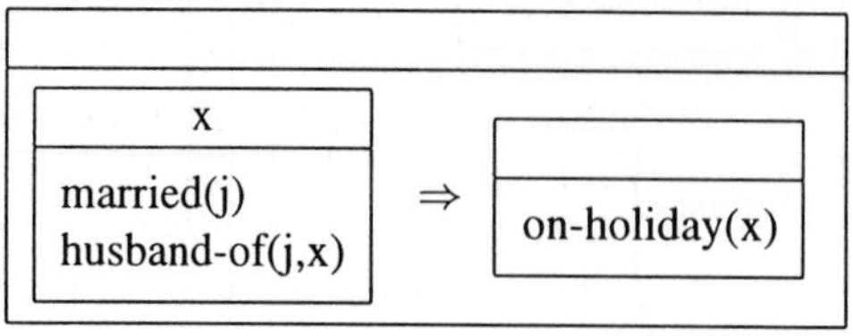

The next two examples, which I will not discuss in detail, illustrate the consistency and global informativity constraints, respectively:

(4.12) Either Jane is a spinster, or else her husband is on holiday.

(4.13) Jim is Fred's friend, and Fred is married. He is married too.

The reader should verify that for (4.12), the consistency constraint prevents global accommodation of the presupposition that Jane is married, forcing local accommodation, and that for (4.13) the global informativity constraint prevents resolution of the variable associated with 'he' to the discourse marker for Fred.[48]

Van der Sandt's DRT-based model of presupposition gets right the cases which Gazdar's theory handles well (i.e. where presuppositions are either explicitly denied, or appear to be out-competed by implicatures) *and* the cases which Karttunen's theories handle well (typically where a presupposition is entailed in its local context). Note that below, in Section 5.1, a combined Gazdar–Karttunen theory is presented, following work of Soames, which is comparable to Van der Sandt's DRT-based model in this respect. However, *none* of the cancellation accounts discussed, *none* of the various theories proposed singly or in joint work by Karttunen, and *neither* the combined Gazdar–Karttunen theory *nor* Soames own combined model provides an adequate account *either* of presupposed open propositions and their interaction with quantifiers, *or* of Kripkean cases of anaphoric presupposition. Van der Sandt's model treats both of these phenomena.[49]

4.6. Accommodation as context selection

Accommodation may be thought of procedurally, as an algorithmic repair strategy for mending discourse representations in the face of presupposition failure. This is how the first versions of Van der Sandt's DRT theory were presented (but see Van der Sandt and Geurts, 1991), and how the approach to accommodation presented by Fauconnier (see Section 5.5, below) is conceived. The current section concerns a declarative treatment of accommodation. This treatment extends the CCP model in a way related to proposals I have made elsewhere (Beaver, 1992, 1995, m.s.): here I beg the reader's forgiveness for my self-indulgence. In the extended model, accommodation is not naturally thought of as a repair strategy, but as a normal part of the communicative process whereby hearers monotonically gain information about speakers' beliefs.

In order to communicate effectively a speaker must make some assumptions about the common ground of information between the conversational participants, to take some information for granted. Presuppositions can be taken to reflect the assumptions about the common ground that the speaker has made (or, sometimes, wishes to appear to have made). The common ground assumed by the speaker can be modeled as a Stalnakerian context, a set of worlds, but a hearer cannot know which set of worlds this is. So a hearer's information about the speaker's assumptions can be modeled, so as to incorporate this uncertainty, as a set of Stalnakerian contexts. These contexts, all those which *might* accord with the speaker's assumptions, will be termed *epistemic alternatives*, and a set of

[48] Note that in Van der Sandt's system pronouns are treated in the same way as standard presupposition triggers, except that the presupposed DRS associated with a pronoun (something like [x][]) is assumed to contain insufficient conditions to support accommodation.

[49] For further critical discussion of Van der Sandt's DRT account see (Beaver, 1995, 1994b). For extensions to the theory, see Saebo's (1996) and Geurts' (1994)

epistemic alternatives will be called an *alternative set.* When a new sentence is uttered, with accompanying presuppositions, the hearer learns more about the speaker's assumptions, and is able to eliminate – 'filter out' – those epistemic alternatives which cannot correspond to the speaker's assumptions. Those alternatives which remain after this filtering must be updated with the information in the new sentence, and this produces a new alternative set to use when the next sentence is uttered. In this way, both presuppositions and assertions may be informative, although they inform on different levels: whereas assertions, following Stalnaker, are understood as filtering worlds, presuppositions filter sets of worlds.

In the following three definitions, Σ ranges over alternative sets (so $\Sigma \in \mathcal{P}(\mathcal{P}(W))$), and a notion of update of an alternative set with a PrL formula, $\Sigma + \phi$, is defined in terms of the earlier CCP semantics (Definitions 4.4, 4.5 and 4.7). Note that the definition of the update function "+" is given in terms of the $[\![.]\!]$-relation by a standard 'lifting' technique, the so-called *subset* construction (cf. the discussion in Fernando's (1995)). Satisfaction of a formula relative to an alternative set $\Sigma \models \phi$, as at the lower CCP level, is given by a fixed-point construction. Finally a notion of entailment is given, whereby ϕ entails ψ relative to an alternative set Σ if the update of Σ with ϕ satisfies ψ.

DEFINITION 4.16 (*Accommodating update, satisfaction and relativized entailment*).

$$\begin{aligned} \Sigma + \phi &= \{\sigma \mid \exists \tau \in \Sigma\ \tau[\![\phi]\!]\sigma\}, \\ \Sigma &\models \phi \ \textit{iff}\ \Sigma + \phi = \Sigma, \\ \phi &\models_\Sigma \psi \ \textit{iff}\ \Sigma + \phi \models \psi.^{50} \end{aligned}$$

To see how this approach to accommodation might be applied, consider the following two examples containing the factive 'the knowledge that':

(4.14) If David wrote the article then the knowledge that no decent logician was involved (in writing the article) will confound the editors.

(4.15) If David wrote the article then the knowledge that David is a computer program running on a PC will confound the editors.

Both examples have the general form $\phi \to \psi_\pi$. Yet the examples contrast in terms of the assumptions that a speaker would presumably be making. For example (4.14) the conditional presupposition $\phi \to \pi$ predicted by the CCP model, i.e. that if David wrote the article then no decent logician was involved, is easily defensible. However, for (4.15) some might say that the presupposition that David is a computer program simply projects, and is not conditionalized. Within the context selection model such a contrast may be predicted, whilst still allowing that the underlying presupposition is a conditional. Suppose firstly that it is plausible that David is not a good logician, and that the conditional 'if David wrote the article then no decent logician was involved', that is $\phi \to \pi$, is also quite plausible. Then we might expect some epistemic alternatives to

[50] Note that relativised entailment can be defined equivalently but more directly, without the intermediary step of defining +, as: $\phi \models_\Sigma \psi$ *iff* $\forall \sigma \in \Sigma\, \forall \tau\ \sigma[\phi]\tau \Rightarrow \tau \models \psi$.

include this information. It is easily verified that relative to an alternative set Σ which contains such alternatives, $\phi \to \psi_\pi$ entails $\phi \to \pi$, but does not entail π. So for the first example the conditionalized presupposition emerges (albeit as an entailment, since I have not here defined a notion of presupposition relative to an alternative set). Now the second example. Reinterpreting π as 'David is a computer program running on a PC', it can be argued that whilst it is *a priori* plausible that π holds, a speaker is unlikely to assume the conditional that David is a computer program if he wrote the article, i.e. $\phi \to \pi$, without assuming π itself. Relative to an ordering which contains alternatives where π holds, but in which for all alternatives where π does not hold $\phi \to \pi$ also does not hold, we will have that $\phi \to \psi_\pi$ entails π, but does not entail $\phi \to \pi$. Thus it can be seen that under certain quite strong assumptions about what is intrinsically plausible, the context selection model may predict that a conditionalized presupposition is effectively strengthened, as if the embedded presupposition had projected in the first place.

A few remarks are in order. Firstly, a sharp cut-off line between plausible and implausible alternative sets is difficult to justify. For this reason in the full model, such as discussed in (Beaver, 1995, m.s.), the set of alternatives is replaced with an ordering over alternatives. It is then only necessary to justify that some alternatives are more plausible than others, and not that some are inherently so implausible that they are not even considered. Secondly, note that whatever the shortcomings of the simple context selection model presented here, it does at least allow both for embedded presuppositions becoming full entailments and for presuppositions remaining only in weak conditionalized form. A model which does not allow for any conditionalized presuppositions, such as the cancellation and filtering models, will have difficulty with examples like (4.14), of which we will see yet more variants shortly. Note that the context selection model may be thought of as an attempt to cash out the suggestion by Karttunen and Peters (1979) that conditionalized presuppositions may sometimes be strengthened by conversational implicatures.[51]

5. Syntheses

Theories of presupposition continue to proliferate. It is rarely clear what the relationship between different theories is, and not always easy to say whether progress is being made either technically or descriptively. In fact there has been both technical convergence and an increasing amount of agreement as to what the central problems are. Indeed, one of my primary aims in writing this chapter has been to show the great extent to which convergence and synthesis have already occurred within what is apparently a quite disparate field, as well as hopefully demonstrating of the possibility of such unifying development in the future. The very fact that it has been possible to present different theories in a relatively uniform format – albeit that this sometimes involved riding roughshod over the philosophical proclivities of the original authors – shows many of the differences between theories to be superficial. To cite a particular case of convergence in what has been discussed, observe Van der Sandt's use within a cancellationist account of

[51] For criticism of Karttunen and Peters, and of the context selection model, see Geurts (1994, 1996), and for yet more discussion see (Beaver, 1994b).

Karttunen's notion of local context (cf. Section 3.3).[52] Or observe the various similarities between the theories of Heim and Van der Sandt that have been discussed. In this section we will consider a number of other ways in which theories can be compared from a technical viewpoint, or new theories synthesized.[53]

5.1. *Cancellation and filtering*

The cancellation and filtering theories are largely complementary in terms of which data they get right. Having observed this complementarity, Soames (1982) proposed a synthesis of Gazdar's account with the later versions of Karttunen's account in (Karttunen, 1974; Karttunen and Peters, 1979). However, as mentioned earlier, the later versions of Karttunen's theory are not filtering theories in the sense defined above. The presuppositions that a complex sentence is predicted to have are not a subset of the potential presuppositions of its parts. This complicated Soames' attempt to unify the insights of the two account in a single theory. To give an idea of the difficulties faced, ask yourself this question: when looking for a synthesis between two accounts, where the first account makes all presuppositions members of the set of potential presuppositions, and the second account does not, should the resulting theory be expected to make all presuppositions members of the set of potential presuppositions? (Soames in fact answers in the negative.)

A much simpler integrated theory, but one which still preserves Soames' insight of complementarity, could be formed by combining the Karttunen 1973 theory, as discussed above, with Gazdar's. The most obvious way to join the two theories so as to address

[52] Van der Sandt's later DRT account also has dynamic features reminiscent of Karttunen's proposals. The dynamics of the DRT account can be said to reside in at least three aspects of the theory: the (extended) DRS construction algorithm, the standardly dynamic DRT semantics of implication and quantifiers, and the statement of anaphoric accessibility conditions. The notion of accessibility is implicitly directional, in that it is invariably defined using an anti-symmetric relation, and reflects Karttunen's conditions on context incrementation. We might restate accessibility conditions in a way that brings this out. Say that a DRS α is a pair $\langle \alpha_0, \alpha_1 \rangle$, with α_0 a set of discourse markers and α_1 a set of conditions. Define $var(\alpha)$ as the set of markers mentioned in the conditions α_1, and take the context σ of any sub-DRS to be a set of discourse markers: this should be thought of as the set of markers external to a DRS which are accessible from within it. The markers of a DRS α in a context σ are completely accessible, written $\sigma \succ \alpha$, if $var(\alpha) \in \alpha_0 \cup \sigma$. Then the following two rules state whether the variables in the sub-DRSs of negations and implications are accessible:

$$\sigma \succ \neg\alpha \text{ iff } \sigma \succ \alpha,$$
$$\sigma \succ \alpha \rightarrow \beta \text{ iff } \sigma \succ \alpha \textit{ and } \sigma \cup \alpha_0 \succ \beta.$$

These rules, which must be extended to allow for Van der Sandt's notion of accessibility of DRS conditions as well as DRS markers, are obviously close to Karttunen's admissibility conditions, as given above (Definition 4.1), although differences will arise with conjunction and disjunction. See Zeevat's (1992) for a reformulation of Van der Sandt's DRT account which truly brings out the similarities with dynamic theories in the Karttunen–Heim tradition.

[53] It is arguable that the degree of convergence runs deeper than is detailed here. For instance, I give no direct comparison between multivalent and cancellationist accounts of presupposition. In fact there are now a number of theories which model the defeasibility of presuppositions using non-Boolean semantic valuations, such as those of Schöter (1994, 1995) and Marcu (1994).

both defeat of presuppositions by inconsistency and filtering of presuppositions which are locally entailed, would simply be to take the intersection of the set of presuppositions predicted by each of the two models. One would need first to strip the epistemic operators from Gazdar's presuppositions, or add such operators to Karttunen's, but I take this to be a trivial task. It would be natural to identify Karttunen's set of assumed facts with the incoming context in Gazdar's model. Such a joint Gazdar–Karttunen model provides a formidable account of presupposition, combining relative simplicity with a clear improvement over the original cancellation and filtration accounts (as will be seen in Section 6.3).

5.2. Trivalent and dynamic semantics

The thesis, descending from the work of Frege and Strawson, that presupposition projection should be explained as inheritance of semantic undefinedness, seems to find an antithesis in the suggestion that presupposition projection arises from (pragmatically justified) principles of context change. However, Peters (1977) provided a synthesis, observing that the presupposition inheritance properties derived in (Karttunen, 1974) could be duplicated in a system with a trivalent semantics, and thus do not depend on the dynamicity of Karttunen's account. The connectives in Peters' trivalent system, which I will refer to as the *Peters' connectives* (but which Krahmer (1993) terms the *Middle Kleene* connectives), can be used to show the relationship between the dynamic logics developed in the current work and trivalent logics. Note that the correspondence breaks down once we move to a quantificational logic, since the dynamic systems discussed manifest quantifier-scope properties not found in any standard trivalent system.

The Peters' connectives may be likened to the strong Kleene connectives, except that if the left-hand formula under a binary Peters' connective is undefined, then the whole formula is undefined:

DEFINITION 5.1 (*The Peters' connectives*). The 3-valued interpretation of a complex formula ϕ relative to a world w, written $[\![\phi]\!]^3_w$, is given by recursion over the following truth tables:

$\phi \wedge \psi$	t	f	$\star$
t	t	f	$\star$
f	f	f	f
$\star$	$\star$	$\star$	$\star$

$\phi \rightarrow \psi$	t	f	$\star$
t	t	f	$\star$
f	t	t	t
$\star$	$\star$	$\star$	$\star$

$\phi \vee \psi$	t	f	$\star$
t	t	t	t
f	t	f	$\star$
$\star$	$\star$	$\star$	$\star$

ϕ	$\neg\phi$
t	f
f	t
$\star$	$\star$

The following definitions and facts than establish that notions of entailment in the three valued and dynamic systems coincide extensionally. It follows as a corollary that definitions of presupposition in terms of entailment also coincide for the two systems.

DEFINITION 5.2 (*Entailment in the 3-valued system*). Let $[\![\phi]\!]_3^w$ be defined using the Peters' connectives and the trivalent interpretation of the presupposition operator given in Definition 2.7. Then trivalent entailment is given by:

$$\phi \Vdash_3 \psi \quad \textit{iff} \quad \forall w \in W,\ [\![\phi]\!]_3^w = t \ \Rightarrow\ [\![\psi]\!]_3^w = t.$$

DEFINITION 5.3 (*Entailment in the update system*). Let $[\![.]\!]_u$ be as in $[\![.]\!]$ of Definitions 4.4, 4.5 and 4.7. Then dynamic entailment is given by:

$$\phi \Vdash_w \psi \quad \textit{iff} \quad \forall \sigma \subseteq W,\ \sigma[\![\phi]\!]_u\sigma \ \Rightarrow\ \sigma[\![\psi]\!]_u\sigma.$$

FACT 5.4. $\phi \Vdash_3 \psi$ *iff* $\phi \Vdash_w \psi$.

A proof is given in (Beaver, 1995).[54]

5.3. *From cancellation to accommodation*

Accommodation provides one of the great unifying themes of modern presupposition theory, since many theories of presupposition which were not originally proposed as accommodation theories can be thought of in terms of accommodation. In a sense cancellation is the inverse of global accommodation. Heim (1983a), after suggesting her enhancement of the CCP model with an account of accommodation, makes the following observation:

> Note that by stipulating a *ceteris paribus* preference for global over local accommodation, we recapture the effect of [Gazdar's] assumption that presupposition cancellation occurs only under the threat of inconsistency.

I find this stunning. With one short remark buried in a terse paper Heim offers a simple synthesis between the two antitheses of 1970's presupposition theory, namely the Karttunen 1974 derived model which her paper uses as its base, and Gazdar's cancellation account. Perhaps implicit in Heim's remark is the idea that global accommodation of an elementary presupposition may be identified with what was termed *projection* in earlier models. In this case whenever accommodation is not global, we have the effect of cancellation. Looked at this way, a preference for global over local accommodation becomes a preference for projection over cancellation, and given an appropriate stipulation of the circumstances in which this preference can be overridden (e.g., in order to avoid inconsistency), the effects of a cancellation theory can be mimicked.

[54] The proof in (Beaver, 1995) concerns a system with a unary connective ∂ instead of the binary presupposition connective. However, the systems are interdefinable, with $\phi_\psi =_{\text{def}} \phi \wedge \partial\psi$, so the proof carries over directly.

In a stroke this shows a way to eliminate the bulk of existing counter-examples to the CCP model, in particular examples where a presupposition associated with an embedded trigger is eliminated by explicit denial. Further, and in common with Van der Sandt's cancellation account, Heim's remark introduces a way of thinking about Gazdar's theory that preserves his insight that default reasoning is involved in the processing of presuppositions, whilst restoring the intuition that, in some sense, presuppositions are to do with *what comes first*, with definedness conditions on the input rather than preferences on the output. Note that Van der Sandt (1988) is explicit in identifying his cancellation analysis as involving an accommodation-like mechanism, although this was not the case in his theory's first incarnation (Van der Sandt, 1982). Also note that for Heim's analogy between cancellation and accommodation theories to really drive home it is important that in the cancellation account it is assumed that presuppositions are also part of the asserted content. Entailment of presuppositions is what produces the effect of local accommodation in cases where the presupposition is globally canceled.

5.4. *The transformation from Russell to Van der Sandt*

Now let us consider a very different type of theory, that of Russell, in which alternative presuppositional readings are obtained only as a result of variations in logical scope. These scopal variations are mirrored by the alternative accommodation readings in Van der Sandt's theory, save that Russell's logical forms happened to be expressed in FOPL, whereas Van der Sandt's are expressed in the language of DRT. Russell gave few hints as to how his logical forms should be derived, and I see no obvious reason why a Russellian theory of scopal variation should not be developed where scope bearing operators are initially interpreted *in situ* to produce a first logical form, and are then moved about to produce the final logical form in a manner reminiscent of the semantic *move-α* operations of Van der Sandt's theory.[55] Thus we see that the transformation from Russell to Van der Sandt is surprisingly small.

For instance, neo-Russellian and Van der Sandt accounts allow essentially the same two readings for sentences like 'The King of France is not bald.' Taking 'ι' to be a Russellian definite description operator, the Russellian narrow scope negation reading can be represented as $\iota x[\text{k-o-f}(x)](\neg\text{bald}(x))$. Corresponding to this is the Van der Sandtian global accommodation reading in (a), below. On the other hand the neo-Russellian wide-scope negation reading, $\neg(\iota x[\text{k-o-f}(x)](\text{bald}(x)))$, is analogous to Van der Sandt's local accommodation reading, in (b).

[55] For formulations of Russellian theories of presupposition, see the work of Delacruz (1976), Cresswell (1973, pp. 168–169) and Grice (1981). Also relevant is Neale (1990), although this does not target presupposition *per se*. Kempson (1975, 1979), Wilson (1975) and Atlas (1976, 1977), whilst holding in common with Russell that there is no special presuppositional component to meaning, provide forceful arguments against the Russellian explanation of presuppositional inferences in terms of scope. For these authors, such inferences are to be explained in terms of more general pragmatic mechanisms.

(a)

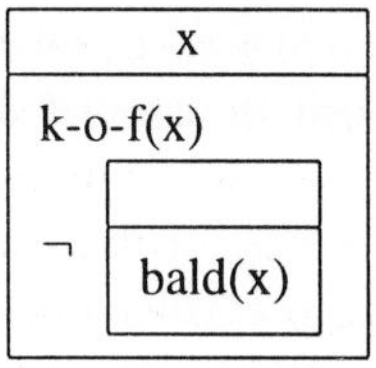

(b)

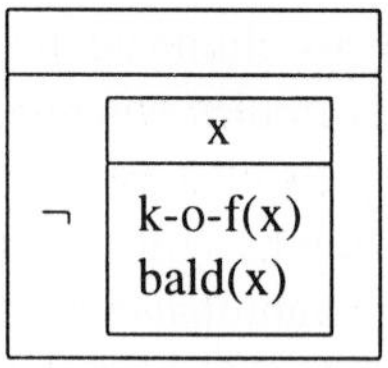

But this is not to deny that Van der Sandt's theory incorporates important innovations. Firstly, Van der Sandt's account includes not only an accommodation component, but also an anaphoric resolution component completely alien to the Russellian picture of definites. The importance of incorporating anaphoricity is discussed in Section 6.1, below. Secondly, Van der Sandt not only allows for presuppositional elements to take different *scopes*, he also provides an account of which scopes are to be preferred, and this is again something absent from the Russellian account. Thirdly, and specifically as a result of being situated in DRT, Van der Sandt's model allows for extra possibilities which would not be available to Russell. For instance, a presupposition α triggered in the consequent of a conditional may, in Van der Sandt's theory, eventually make its way to the antecedent of the conditional. Such a transformation would make no sense on the Russellian picture, since an element in the antecedent of a conditional could classically not bind material in the consequent.

5.5. *Accommodation as a journey through mental space*

Fauconnier (1985) presents a representationalist theory in which meanings are rendered in a structured collection of interconnected *mental spaces*. Mental spaces are akin to Kamp's DRS boxes (or, perhaps even more aptly, Seuren's *discourse domains*).[56]

In order to see what Fauconnier's theory of presupposition (Fauconnier, 1985, pp. 86–87) would look like in a Van der Sandtian setting, let us assume that a space is just a DRT box (i.e. a set of discourse markers and a set of conditions), and assume a DRT-like notion of accessibility. Let us say that a proposition is *supported* in a space if it is a consequence of the conditions in that space, and that a proposition is *accessible* from a space if it is a consequence of propositions in accessible (i.e. superordinate) spaces, and let us assume

[56] A few remarks should clarify the similarity of mental spaces with DRT:

(i) Like DRS boxes, mental spaces can be seen as partial models in which a set of discourse entities bear certain properties and relations to each other, but in which the extensions of many other properties and relations are left undecided.

(ii) Like DRS boxes, mental spaces are arranged hierarchically, with some boxes being seen as subordinate to others. Properties of objects in subordinate *daughter* spaces may be inherited from their *parent* spaces. However, the links between entities in different spaces are not sustained by variable binding, but by a Lewisian counterpart relation. The inter-space links between entities are analogous to the connections between discourse markers in later versions of DRT (Kamp and Reyle, 1993) where objects in intensional contexts are linked to objects outside by *anchoring* functions, these determining which objects are counterparts of which others.

(iii) Unlike Kamp, Fauconnier does not follow the Montagovian method of fragments. He does not provide a fully formalized method of constructing mental spaces for all the strings produced by a generative grammar.

(iv) Unlike in DRT, no semantic interpretation or Tarski truth definition is given for mental spaces, and no notion of logical consequence between mental spaces is defined.

a standard logical definition of *consistency* of a space, meaning consistency of the set of conditions in that space.[57] In certain cases (generally non-intensional contexts) Fauconnier also employs a notion of *compatibility*, meaning consistency of the set of conditions either in the space or accessible from it. Fauconnier's theory of presupposition can be described as a theory of presupposition flotation, whereby locally triggered presuppositions float up through as many spaces as they can without creating inconsistency.[58] I would characterize the theory as follows:

(i) Presuppositions must be supported in the local space of the trigger.

(ii) If a presupposition is accessible, then nothing further need be done.

(iii) Otherwise, the presupposition is accommodated into successively more global spaces along the accessibility path, until reaching the highest space where accommodation does not create inconsistency at the accommodation site, or incompatibility of any (non-intensional) subordinate space.[59]

It is readily seen that, at least in the Van der Sandtian form that I have presented it, Fauconnier's model will make predictions comparable to some of the other models that have been discussed. The first clause means that in a sense Fauconnier always locally accommodates, whatever else he does. This produces the effect that in a cancellation account would be derived by assuming presuppositions to be part of the asserted content. The second clause provides for something like Van der Sandt's anaphoric resolution of presuppositions. In most cases this will presumably yield filtering of entailed presuppositions as in Karttunen's '73 model. The third clause meanwhile will prevent global accommodation in case that would produce inconsistency, thus giving the effect of a cancellation theory in cases of presupposition denial.[60]

6. Empirical issues

6.1. Anaphoricity

Over the last decade a number of authors, notably Van der Sandt (1989, 1992), Kripke (m.s.) and (following Kripke) Soames (1989), have argued that there is a tight connection between presupposition and anaphora. Van der Sandt has pointed out that for every example of what might be called *discrepant anaphora*, by which I mean those

[57] The relation *supports* corresponds approximately to Fauconnier's *satisfaction*, but I refrain from using this term here since I have tended to use it elsewhere with a slightly different meaning. I have also been rather cavalier with Fauconnier's notion of *accessibility* of a proposition. I have assumed that propositions in all superordinate spaces are accessible, but Fauconnier is interested in a wide variety of intensional contexts such that (consequences of) propositions holding in parent spaces cannot in general be expected to hold locally.

[58] The flotation metaphor is used by Fauconnier himself. Coincidentally, the same metaphor is chosen by Geurts (1994) when discussing Van der Sandt's accommodation theory.

[59] I take the *incompatibility* requirement from Fauconnier's discussion of conflicting presuppositions in disjunctions (Fauconnier, 1985, p. 92).

[60] Other theories of presupposition that can be compared with Van der Sandt's in much the way as Fauconnier's are those of Dinsmore (1981b, 1992), and Schiebe (1979). Like the theories of Van der Sandt and Fauconnier, these accounts are explicitly procedural, and explicitly representational.

cases where the anaphoric link is not naturally treated using standard binary quantifiers to interpret determiners and bound variables for pronouns, parallel cases of *discrepant presupposition* can be found. To exemplify this parallelism, I give the four triples below. The (a) examples exemplify discourse anaphora, donkey anaphora, bathroom sentences and modal subordination, respectively. In each case, a corresponding example is given, as (b), in which a presupposition is triggered (by the adverb 'still') in the same structural position as the anaphor occurred, but in which this presupposition is satisfied. The third member, (c), completes the circle, showing that the argument of the presupposition trigger can itself be pronominalized with no change of meaning.

(6.1) a. A farmer owns a donkey. He beats it.
b. Wanda used to beat Pedro. She still beats him.
c. Wanda used to beat Pedro. She still does.

(6.2) a. If a farmer owns a donkey then he beats it. [*Geach*]
b. If Wanda used to beat Pedro then she still beats him.
c. If Wanda used to beat Pedro then she still does.

(6.3) a. Either there is no bathroom in this house or it's in a funny place. [*Partee*]
b. Either Wanda never beat Pedro, or she still beats him.
c. Either Wanda never beat Pedro, or she still does.

(6.4) a. Perhaps a wolf came to the door. Perhaps it ate Granny. [*Adapted from Roberts*]
b. Perhaps Wanda used to beat Pedro, and perhaps she still beats him.
c. Perhaps Wanda used to beat Pedro, and perhaps she still does.

The parallel is compelling, and furthermore similar examples are easily constructed involving all standard presupposition types. But evidence for the anaphoricity of presuppositions goes beyond cases where the presupposition is satisfied because it is in some sense anaphoric on a textual antecedent. The reverse of the coin is that, for at least some types of presupposition trigger, if a textual antecedent is not present the presupposition *cannot* be satisfied. Kripke observes that a common analysis of 'too' would make the presupposition of sentence (6.5), below, the proposition that somebody other than Sam is having supper in New York tonight. However, this proposition seems uncontroversial, so the standard account provides no explanation of why the sentence, uttered in isolation, is infelicitous.

(6.5) Tonight Sam is having supper in New York, too. (Kripke, m.s..)

Notably, (6.5) is felicitous when it follows a sentence saying of somebody other than Sam that he is having dinner in New York tonight, e.g., 'Saul is having dinner in New York tonight.' It might be argued that (6.5) places a requirement on its local context that there is a salient having-supper-in-NY-tonight event. Although one could imagine introducing event discourse markers, and some ontology of events, into the framework we have sketched so far, less effort will be required if we restrict ourselves to an alternative suggestion in Heim (1990). This is the hypothesis that (6.5) is felicitous in contexts where there is a discourse entity of which it is locally satisfied that the entity is having supper in New York tonight. Adapting from Heim somewhat, we might give the following sketch of an admittance condition for formulae ϕ *too*$_i$:

DEFINITION 6.1 (*Heimian* 'too').

$$\sigma[\![\phi \text{ too}_i]\!]\tau \textit{ iff } \sigma[\![\phi]\!]\tau, \text{ and there is some index } j \text{ such that } \sigma|\!\!\models\phi[i/j]$$

(where $\phi[i/j]$ represents ϕ with all instances of x_i replaced by x_j).

If (6.5) were indexed 'Tonight Sam$_i$ is having supper in New York, too$_i$', its translation would only be admitted in contexts where for some j, the translation of 'Tonight x_j is having supper in New York' was satisfied. We would thus expect (6.5) only to be admitted in a restricted range of contexts, but 'If Saul is having supper in New York tonight, then Sam is having supper in New York, too.' to carry no presupposition at all.

Perhaps it can be imagined how analyses like that for 'too' above could be given for other presupposition types. For instance, to make factives anaphoric, one might introduce discourse markers for propositions and facts, a development which would anyway be essential to treat propositional anaphora within texts (cf. Asher, 1993). One could then make acceptability of a factive verb with propositional complement ϕ conditional on the presence of a *factual* discourse marker, a discourse marker identifying a proposition logically equivalent to, or perhaps stronger than, ϕ, and which is satisfied in the local context.

For which presupposition triggers is an anaphoric analysis appropriate? Van der Sandt, in his DRT account, gives a straightforward answer: all presupposition triggers are anaphors. That is to say, at the level of discourse representation all presupposition triggers must have an anaphoric antecedent. Note, however, that although Van der Sandt provides a model in which 'too', in common with other triggers, can act anaphorically, this is not yet sufficient. For requiring an antecedent at the level of discourse representation is much weaker than requiring a strict textual antecedent. Van der Sandt's mechanism of accommodation will always be able to build an antecedent for a given occurrence of 'too', so an explicit textual antecedent is unnecessary. Yet this runs contra to the well established fact (Soames, 1989) that in most cases an occurrence of 'too' does require an explicit textual antecedent. A sentence like (6.5) would make a strange start to a conversation. To get the facts right, Van der Sandt would have to modify his model by removing the option of accommodation for 'too', and allowing only simple resolution and partial match. This would not be technically difficult, but it would seem unmotivated. Here those familiar with Van der Sandt's account might recall the explanation he gives of why ordinary pronouns require a textual antecedent: he says that they lack the descriptive content which accommodation requires. But in the case of (6.5) we have nontrivial information about the antecedent, corresponding to the DRS [x][not-sam(x),having-supper-in-ny-tonight(x)]. So whilst Van der Sandt's explanation of why accommodation is not triggered by pronouns seems plausible, it would wear thin if applied to the case of 'too', although one would think that the explanations for non-accommodation by pronouns and non-accommodation by 'too' should be similar.[61] Perhaps Van der Sandt's theory could be improved by not treating the class of presupposition triggers uniformly in the first place, but by actually making a separation of anaphoric and non-anaphoric triggers: an argument for this move, which anyway fits well into the fabric of Van der Sandt's account, is given in Section 6.2, below.

To conclude this section, let me point out that there is one rather common-place phenomenon which nicely demonstrates the anaphoricity of presupposition whilst confounding all the theories discussed in this chapter. This is the phenomenon of bridging. Consider the following:

(6.6) Whenever a ship docks, the captain always waves.

(6.7) As Hermione drove along the dark road, every bend presented a danger.

(6.8) If I go to a wedding the rabbi always gets drunk.

(6.9) An old woman hit me. The knuckle-duster bit deep.

In the first of these examples, the so-called *bridging description* 'the captain' would seem to be anaphoric on 'a ship'. In this particular case, one can argue that lexical information associated with the common nouns is helping provide the link, 'captain' being an inherently relational noun. One might imagine somehow stipulating that apart from when 'captain' is used with an explicit possessive clause such as 'the ship's captain' or 'the captain of the ship', the presence of a ship is presupposed, and this allows a link to be made. Example (6.7) demonstrates that the phenomenon is not restricted to definites, since here the domain restriction of a quantifier appears limited to bends in a contextually salient road. But once again, it could at least be argued that 'bend' is a relational noun, and perhaps some sort of explanation could be constructed without departing too far from existing ideas in presupposition theory. But for the following two cases, such an approach is inappropriate, since neither 'rabbi' nor 'knuckle-duster' (U.S. 'brass-knuckles') would appear to be a relational noun. It seems that when we determine on what a definite NP is anaphoric, we cannot rely only lexical information. The process linking 'rabbi' to 'wedding' must involve quite general inferencing procedures utilizing considerable amounts of world knowledge, e.g., to determine whether it is plausible that the speaker only goes to weddings where there is a rabbi. As for (6.9), whilst 'the knuckle-duster' is perhaps best classified as a bridging description, it is not even very clear what its antecedent is. The old woman, perhaps? Maybe the antecedent is not the woman, but the hitting event? Whatever the best answer, no current theory of presupposition is of much help.[62]

---

[61] Perhaps the real explanation should not be thought of in terms of limitations of the accommodation mechanism, but to do with the function of anaphoric elements themselves. If one of their chief functions were to establish textual coherence, for instance, then they could normally only achieve that goal by linking entities which had actually been mentioned. The need for accommodation would then be a sign of the failure of the text to cohere adequately. See Zeevat's discussion in (Zeevat, 1994).

[62] Some cases of bridging, those like (6.6), have been discussed in the literature. See, e.g., Bos, Buitelaar and Mineur (1995). The systems proposed by Hobbs and co-workers (Hobbs, Stickel, Appelt and Martin, 1990) probably come closest to dealing with bridging examples like those above, allowing world knowledge to be used when determining the connections between objects introduced in a text. Cf. Section 4.6 and for more on the importance of world knowledge and common-sense reasoning.

6.2. Accommodation and the taxonomy of triggers

I would like to highlight one respect in which the version of Fauconnier's theory above clearly makes different predictions from Van der Sandt's DRT account. Under Fauconnier's accommodation strategy, as a presupposition floats upwards it leaves a shadow behind (i.e. a copy of the presupposition) in every space through which it passes. But Van der Sandt's strategy depicts presuppositions as bubbling up without leaving any trace of their journey. In fact Zeevat has compared an accommodation strategy just like Fauconnier's to Van der Sandt's, although Zeevat attributes what I call Fauconnier's strategy to Heim. Distinguishing the two strategies Zeevat says (Zeevat, 1992, p. 396): "The one remaining difference [i.e. between his version of Van der Sandt's theory and his version of Heim's theory] is the question whether we should add the presupposition everywhere between the position of the trigger and the highest position where it can be accommodated, or whether we can be satisfied with adding it just once at that position." So which is the right strategy? Zeevat comes to an interesting conclusion: both are right, but for different classes of presupposition trigger. The two classes Zeevat delimits are what he calls *anaphoric* and *lexical* presuppositions. The anaphoric (or *resolution*) triggers are those "whose primary function is – like anaphora – to collect entities from the environment in order to say new things about them." (Zeevat, 1992, p. 397.) This class, which presumably at least includes definite noun phrases, and discourse particles like *too* and *again*, is the one for which Zeevat supposes the Van der Sandtian strategy to be appropriate. The following data back up his point, if the rather subtle judgements are accepted:

(6.10) a. Bill called Mary a Republican. And it is clear from Mary's diary that John insulted her too.

b. It is clear from Mary's diary that Bill insulted her.

(6.11) a. Bill called Mary a Republican. And it is clear from Mary's diary that Bill thinks that John insulted her too.

b. It is clear from Mary's diary that Bill insulted her.

c. It is clear from Mary's diary that Bill thinks he insulted her.

In Zeevat's terms, the *too* in (6.10)(a) and (6.11)(a) is used because the speaker is collecting up a property which he takes to already be realized in the context, the property of insulting Mary, and saying something new about the extension of that property. I would say that on hearing either (6.10)(a) or (6.11)(a) a hearer would normally conclude that the speaker thinks that Bill insulted Mary, presumably in the act of calling her a Republican. So it would seem that 'Bill insulted Mary' – or the proposition that the event of Bill calling Mary a Republican is identical to an event of Bill insulting Mary – is globally accommodated. But (and I hope readers can convince themselves of this) I do not think that on the basis of (6.10)(a) a hearer would conclude that the speaker believes (6.10)(b). This is just what would be predicted on Van der Sandt's strategy, since the local context to the trigger, the mental space set aside for what is clear in Mary's diary, would not need to contain the presupposition. Similarly, I do not think a hearer of (6.11)(a) would necessarily infer that the speaker believes either of (6.11)(b) or (6.11)(c), although these propositions are certainly compatible with what the speaker has said. Thus the presupposition arguably skips over both the space assigned to what Bill thinks in Mary's diary, and the space assigned to what is clear in Mary's diary, just as Van der Sandt predicts. On the other hand, on Fauconnier's strategy both (6.11)(b) and (6.11)(c) would be inferred.

The *lexical triggers* are those where the presupposition is a condition on the application of a concept, so that the presupposition must hold in any context where the trigger is applied if the application of the concept is to be meaningful. Factive verbs are presumably in this class. From this definition of lexical triggers, we can see that the presupposition should be expected to hold not only at the highest accommodation site, but also locally. Zeevat goes further in requiring lexical presuppositions to hold Fauconnier fashion in all the intermediary contexts, and the following examples perhaps provide some support for this analysis:

(6.12) a. Bill called Mary a Republican. And it is clear from Mary's diary that she realized that he had insulted her.
b. It is clear from Mary's diary that Bill insulted her.

(6.13) a. Bill called Mary a Republican. And it is clear from Mary's diary that Bill thinks she realized that he had insulted her.
b. It is clear from Mary's diary that Bill insulted her.
c. It is clear from Mary's diary that Bill thinks he insulted her.

That (6.12)(b) follows from (6.12)(a) seems indisputable. (6.13)(a) is obviously a more complicated case, and requires considerably more effort to comprehend. But my feeling is that both (6.13)(b) and (6.13)(c) do follow from it, in accordance with Zeevat's prediction that the Fauconnier (or Heim) algorithm is appropriate in this case.[63]

6.3. *Projection from binary connectives*

Consider the following group of four five-way examples, some of which have already been discussed ((i–v) are understood according to the list beneath the examples):

(6.14) If David wrote the article then the knowledge that (i/ii/iii/iv/v) will confound the editors.

(6.15) If David wrote the article and the knowledge that (i/ii/iii/iv/v) disturbs the editors, they'll read the manuscript very carefully.

[63] Cases like (6.13) constitute counterexamples not only to Van der Sandt's theory, but to any theory where accommodation occurs at only one site. As discussed above, all the cancellation and filtering theories can be thought of as falling into this class. The problem will typically occur whenever a lexical presupposition is embedded under an operator which is itself embedded in an intensional context. For instance, 'Fred thinks Mary doesn't know that she won' involves the lexical presupposition trigger 'know' embedded under a negation operator itself embedded under 'thinks'. The example suggests not only that Mary won, which is predicted by cancellation theories, but also that Fred thinks she won, which is not predicted by these accounts.

(6.16) If the knowledge that (i/ii/iii/iv/v) disturbs the editors and David wrote the article, they'll read the manuscript very carefully.

(6.17) Either David didn't write the article, or the knowledge that (i/ii/iii/iv/v) will confound the editors.

i = 'the article is written'

ii = 'he (i.e. David) wrote the article'

iii = 'he (i.e. David) wrote the article whilst blindfolded and juggling torches on horseback'

iv = 'no decent logician was involved (in writing the article)'

v = 'David is a computer program running on a PC'

Let us adopt a convention with respect to the proposition letters p, P, π, it being assumed that models are restricted such that $P \models \pi \models p$: all other proposition letters are assumed logically independent. So, given that we only consider the presuppositions associated with the factive 'the knowledge that', (6.14)(i–iii) have the forms $P \rightarrow \phi_\pi$, $\pi \rightarrow \phi_\pi$ and $p \rightarrow \phi_\pi$, respectively.[64]

The theories which have been discussed in this chapter are broadly in agreement as regards (6.14)(ii), $\pi \rightarrow \phi_\pi$, predicting (with the exception of Weak Kleene/Bochvar External) no non-trivial presupposition. The mechanisms behind the prediction vary. For instance, the Karttunen '74 and Heim accounts rely on the antecedent setting up a context within which the presupposition of the consequent is satisfied, Van der Sandt's DRT analysis is similar, albeit that logical satisfaction is replaced by anaphoric dependency. But Gazdar's account relies on an implicature triggered by the antecedent canceling the presupposition of the consequent.

If the antecedent of the conditional is stronger than the presupposition as in (6.14)(i), then the Heim, Karttunen '74 and Van der Sandt still predict no non-trivial presupposition, but Gazdar allows the presupposition to project. I take it that Gazdar's prediction is incorrect here, although it should be noted that the effects of prosody can make the judgement difficult.[65]

If the presupposition of the consequent is logically stronger than the antecedent as in (6.14)(iii), Gazdar predicts cancellation, since the implicature that the antecedent is not known to be true conflicts with the presupposition. And this seems a justifiable result, for it is intuitively correct that the presupposition (iii) does not in fact project in this case.[66]

[64] The contrast between CCP-style theories and cancellationist accounts with respect to sentences of form $P \rightarrow \phi_\pi$, $\pi \rightarrow \phi_\pi$ and $p \rightarrow \phi_\pi$ is discussed in the introduction to Heim's (1983a).

[65] If (6.14)(i) is uttered with stress on 'David' (and possibly with destressing of 'the article is written') then we do appear to get projection of 'the article is already finished'. But then it could be argued that focusing in the antecedent was itself triggering the presupposition. See Van der Sandt (1988) and Geurts (1994) for some arguments that in cases like this the presupposition may sometimes project, and Beaver (1994b) for some further discussion of the relevance of prosody.

[66] Note that Karttunen's '73 theory incorrectly predicts full projection of the presupposition in this case, in the absence of a special context, although the theory correctly predicts no projection for (6.14)(i) and (6.14)(ii). The combined Gazdar/Karttunen theory discussed in the previous section would agree with Gazdar here, since it always predicts the weakest of the results given by either Gazdar or Karttunen '73.

Karttunen '74 and Heim do predict a substantive presupposition, $p \to \pi$, paraphraseable as: 'if David wrote the article then (iii)'.

It does seem that this conditional follows as a consequence of (6.14)(iii). But here note that on the assumption that presuppositions are also asserted in their local context of evaluation, this will follow from classical reasoning: Gazdar's model predicts that $p \to \pi$ is entailed by $p \to \phi_\pi$, although not presupposed. This effect disappears with regard to the (6.15) variants. For (6.15)(i–v) the presuppositional behavior of the Heim, Karttunen '74 and Gazdar models is just as for (6.14)(i–v). In particular, with regard to (6.15)(iii), $(p \wedge \phi_\pi) \to \psi$, Gazdar predicts cancellation, whereas Heim and Karttunen '74 predict the conditional $p \to \pi$. Crucially, this conditional does not follow as an entailment in Gazdar's model, so the contrast between the accounts is quite clear.[67] I take it that the conditional $p \to \pi$ does in fact follow from (6.15)(iii), so we have an argument for preferring the Heim and Karttunen '74 models.

Here the reader should recall the earlier discussions of (6.14)(iv,v) in Section 4.6 (there (4.14) and (4.15)). These examples both have the form $\phi \to \psi_\pi$, the presupposition of the consequent not being *a priori* related to the antecedent. The Heim and Karttunen '74 theories predict a conditional presupposition $\phi \to \pi$ for both of these examples, as indeed they do for (6.15)(iv,v). On the other hand, and in the absence of any special previous context, the cancellation models, Karttunen's '73 filtering model and Van der Sandt's DRT model all predict projection of π. The conditionalized presupposition is intuitive for the (iv) variants, whilst simple projection seems appropriate for the (v)-s. It would seem that both classes of theories are in serious trouble. One solution might be obtained by strengthening the conditional presuppositions of the Heim and Karttunen '74 theories, perhaps along lines suggested by Karttunen and Peters in (Karttunen and Peters, 1979), or along those discussed above in Section 4.6. Another approach might involve somehow weakening the presupposition given by those theories which yield simple projection, although at present I am not aware of any concrete proposals that might achieve such weakening. What is clear is that a theory that is able to differentiate between the (iv) and (v) variants must incorporate reasoning that is of a non-absolute character, not simply about which propositions are true, or which propositions follow from which other propositions, but about which propositions are most *plausibly true* in a given utterance situation. Suggestions of Karttunen and Peters and the model discussed in Section 4.6 each provide possible beginnings for such an account, but there are undoubtedly many other ways that this might be achieved.[68]

---

[67] Whether or not Gazdar's model does predict cancellation for (6.15)(iii) depends on the definition of the implicature function. This does yield cancellation for the subformula-based definition used above, but it is not clear to me whether Gazdar's original formulation predicts cancellation. Predicting simple projection, the only other option available in Gazdar's theory, would be no improvement empirically, since it is clear that (6.15)(iii), just as (6.14)(iii), does not presuppose that 'David wrote the article whilst blindfolded and juggling torches on horseback'. Note that Van der Sandt's cancellation theory predicts cancellation for (6.15)(iii). His later DRT account predicts local accommodation in this case, which leads to an equivalent reading. For (6.14)(iii) Van der Sandt's DRT account additionally allows the possibility of intermediate accommodation, giving a reading corresponding to 'If David wrote the article whilst blindfolded and juggling torches on horseback, then the knowledge that this was so will confound the editors'. Perhaps this reading is indeed possible, but it seems unintuitive that it is, as Van der Sandt predicts, the preferred reading.

[68] The move to bring common-sense reasoning and general world knowledge into the presuppositional arena has been advocated by other authors. For instance, Eco's discussion of presuppositions in (Eco, 1994) centers

There remain two sets of examples above to be discussed. Example (6.16) differs from (6.15) in that the order of an embedded conjunct is reversed, so that the difference is of interest because which reveals further differences between theories which make sentence internal conjunction symmetric (e.g., Strong Kleene, Supervaluation, Gazdar's cancellation theory) and those that do not (e.g., Karttunen's proposals including his joint work with Peters, Heim '83). The first class incorrectly makes the same predictions for (6.16)(i) as for (6.15)(i), whereas the second class does not (but correctly predicts projection). I give (6.17) not to show differences between theories, but rather to show a common theme: theories tend to treat the (6.17) variants comparably to the equivalent versions of (6.14). But note that Van der Sandt's DRT account is an exception. Whereas it predicts a case of anaphoric dependency without any accommodation in (6.14)(i), it predicts projection of 'the article is already finished' for (6.17)(i), because in standard DRT anaphoric dependencies cannot be established across disjunctions.[69]

Projection from the so-called *logical* connectives, although the most oft studied part of the projection problem, remains an area rife with disagreement. The examples above show only a part of the problem. Symmetry of connectives with respect to presuppositional behaviour, for instance, is an issue not only with respect to conjunctions, but also with respect to conditionals and disjunctions.[70] Regarding disjunction, one should consider reversing the order of the disjuncts in the (6.17) examples above. The reversed (6.17)(ii) seems to be acceptable, if perhaps stilted. Just as for the 'forwards' version, the presupposition is apparently not projected, so we have an argument for symmetry. But consider the reversal of (6.17)(i) 'Either the knowledge that the article is already finished will disturb the editors, or David didn't write the article.' My intuition is that a projection reading is preferred for this example, unlike for (6.17)(i) itself. If this is so, it provides an argument against symmetry.

The data is clearly complex, and requires empirical work. Aside from systematic further study of examples like those considered above, I would like to close this article somewhat polemically by mentioning three respects in which future empirical work might substantially improve upon most existing research. Firstly, many of the examples given here, and elsewhere in the literature, rely crucially on intonation, and there

around the idea that "the reader has to 'fill' the text with a number of textual inferences, connected to a large set of presuppositions defined by a given context..."; Hobbs and co-workers (see, e.g., Hobbs, Stickel, Appelt and Martin (1990)) approach to definite descriptions (and to what are normally thought of as non-presuppositional constructions, for that matter) involves the introduction of a general inferential mechanism using weighted abduction, with the weights provided by a combination of world knowledge and knowledge of language; Thomason (1990) indicates that accommodation must take into account not only general world knowledge, but also reasoning about the communicative intentions of the speaker; Lorenz (1992) shows how world knowledge affects the behaviour of temporal presuppositions; and Kamp and Rossdeutscher (Kamp and Rossdeutscher, 1994; Rossdeutscher, 1994) show in detail how inferencing mechanisms involved in processing presuppositional constructions must utilize a combination of lexical and world knowledge. Kay (1992) explains apparent projection from attitude contexts not as presupposition projection, but as conversational implicature.

[69] Krahmer (1995) proposes a development of Van der Sandt's theory which would treat (6.14)(i) and (6.17)(i) identically, correctly predicting no global accommodation in either case.

[70] Detailed empirical arguments concerning symmetry of connectives are presented by Soames (1979, 1982, 1989).

is a clear need for future work to cite examples with prosodic marking.[71] A second, related area is provision of examples with explicit textual or discourse context. Note that many theorists emphasize the importance of discourse context, yet few give examples much longer than one or two sentences.[72] A third area where future research might benefit is in the use of naturally occurring examples. The use of artificial examples, as in this article, remains the predominant method amongst presupposition theorists. Yet some theorists have shown that this is not the only possible methodology. See especially Delin's use of corpora to investigate clefts (Delin, 1989, 1992), or, e.g., Prince's use of textual examples and taped discourse in (Prince, 1981). Presupposition is an ideal area for the use of corpora. Given that we have an independent method (projection tests) of identifying (likely) triggers, it should in principle be easy to trawl through a corpus using the triggers as search keys. And if, say, the interaction between presupposition and attitude reports is to be studied, then a more refined search for triggers occurring in the propositional argument of an attitude predicate would be feasible over a syntactically pre-analyzed corpus. Such work is necessary, but whether it would 'solve' existing empirical questions is another matter. Naturally occurring data is perhaps likely to throw up new empirical phenomena rather than clarifying existing areas of concern.

The behaviour of various of the systems discussed in this chapter is summarized in Table 1. The table concerns only quite simple instances of the projection problem. It does not include examples showing the way presuppositions project through quantifiers or modalities, or data demonstrating the anaphoricity of presuppositions. As a further simplification, a null context is assumed for theories which involve a contextual parameter, thus enabling a single *maximal presupposition* (the logically strongest formula entailed by the presuppositions) to be given for each theory and each example. The theories compared are Weak Kleene/External Bochvar (WK), Strong Kleene (SK), supervaluation semantics (SUP), Peters' connectives (P), Karttunen and Peters' two dimensional system[73] (KP),

[71] I give just one example of the importance of prosody. Soames (1982) has discussed examples (A) 'If Nixon is guilty, too, then Haldeman is guilty.' and (B) 'Haldeman is guilty, if Nixon is guilty too.'. He claims that whereas (B) can be read without requiring that anyone is established to be guilty, i.e. such that the presupposition in the antecedent is satisfied by material in the consequent, this is not the case for (B). On the other hand, Kay (1992, p. 359, fn. 32) mentions that if (A) is intoned with stress on 'too' and no preceding pause, the same reading is available as for (B). Neither Kay nor anyone else has explained the role of intonation here. Likewise, the reason why ordering of the sub-clause and main clause should be important is unexplained. (As a complete aside, note that 'Haldeman might be guilty, if Nixon is guilty too.', with appropriate intonation, appears to be at least as felicitous as (A). The extra embedding under a modal operator adds yet another layer of mystery, since according to conventional wisdom the modal should block anaphoric accessibility of 'Haldeman is guilty' independently of the use of a conditional.)

[72] What role does textual context play in examples like those in footnote 71, above? What after all do (A) and (B) mean? If they mean the same as it would without the 'too', then in what contexts is the 'too' appropriate? To take a different example of the relevance of discourse context, consider Landman's discussion (Landman, 1986) of disjunctions with competing presuppositions in the disjuncts, cf. (3.11), above. He claims the observed projection effects are not tied to properties of disjunctions as such, but result from a special sort of discourse subordination.

[73] KP was not presented in terms of PrL, but its relation to other systems discussed is well established. As far as the connectives are concerned, Karttunen and Peters themselves demonstrated the link between their joint system and the trivalent Peters system discussed above.

Table 1

Projection from logical connectives.

Formula	Example	Maximal Presupposition							
		WK	SK/SUP	P/K&P/K74/H	K73	G	KG	vdS	Data
ϕ_π	(1.1)	π	π	π	π	π	π	π	π
$\neg\phi_\pi$	(1.3)	π	π	π	π	π	π	π	π
$\phi \wedge \psi_\pi$		π	$\phi \rightarrow \pi$	$\phi \rightarrow \pi$	π	π	π	π	
$\phi_\pi \wedge \psi$		π	$\psi \rightarrow \pi$	π	π	π	π	π	
$\phi \vee \psi_\pi$	(6.17)(iv/v)	π	$\neg\phi \rightarrow \pi$	$\neg\phi \rightarrow \pi$	π	π	π	π	$\neg\phi \rightarrow \pi/\pi$?
$\phi_\pi \vee \psi$		π	$\neg\psi \rightarrow \pi$	π	π	π	π	π	
$\pi \rightarrow \phi_\pi$	(6.14)(ii)	π	$\top$	$\top$	$\top$	$\top$	$\top$	$\top$	$\top$
$(\pi \wedge \phi_\pi) \rightarrow \psi$	(6.15)(ii)	π	$\top$	$\top$	$\top$	$\top$	$\top$	$\top$	$\top$
$P \rightarrow \phi_\pi$	(6.14)(i)	π	$\top$	$\top$	$\top$	π	$\top$	$\top$	$\top$
$(P \wedge \phi_\pi) \rightarrow \psi$	(6.15)(i)	π	$\top$	$\top$	$\top$	π	$\top$	$\top$	$\top$
$p \rightarrow \phi_\pi$	(6.14)(iii)	π	$p \rightarrow \pi$	$p \rightarrow \pi$	π	$\top$	$\top$	$\top$	$p \rightarrow \pi$ (?)
$(p \wedge \phi_\pi) \rightarrow \psi$	(6.15)(iii)	π	$(\neg\psi \wedge p) \rightarrow \pi$	$p \rightarrow \pi$	π	$\top$	$\top$	$\top$	$p \rightarrow \pi$ (?)
$(\phi_\pi \wedge p) \rightarrow \psi$	(6.16)(iii)	π	$(\neg\psi \wedge p) \rightarrow \pi$	π	π	$\top$	$\top$	$\top$	π
$\neg\phi_\pi \wedge \neg\pi$	(3.12)	π	π	π	π	$\top$	$\top$	$\top$	$\top$
$\natural\phi_\pi \wedge \neg\pi$	(3.12)	$\top$	$\top$						$\top$
$\neg((K\pi)_\pi)$	(3.14)					$\top$	$\top$	$\top$	$\top$
$\phi_\pi \vee \phi_{\neg\pi}$	(3.11)	$\bot$	$\bot$ (SK)	$\bot$	$\bot$	$\top$	$\top$	$\top$	$\top$

Karttunen's 1974 model (K74), Heim's 1983 model minus accommodation (H), Karttunen's 1973 model, Gazdar's cancellation theory (G), the combined Karttunen/Gazdar model introduced earlier (KG), and Van der Sandt's DRT-based theory[74] (vdS).

References

Aristotle (1950), *Categories* (translator: E.M. Edghill), The Works of Aristotle, Translated into English, vol. 1, W.D. Ross, ed., Oxford Univ. Press, Oxford.

Asher, N. (1993), *Reference to Abstract Objects in Discourse*, Studies in Linguistics and Philosophy vol. 50, Kluwer, Dordrecht.

Atlas, J. (1976), *On the semantics of presupposition and negation: An essay in philosophical logic and the foundations of linguistics*, PhD Dissertation, University of Princeton.

Atlas, J. (1977), *Negation, ambiguity and presupposition*, Ling. and Philos. **1**, 321–336.

Atlas, J. and Levinson, S. (1981), *It-Clefts, informativeness and logical form: Radical pragmatics*, Radical Pragmatics, P. Cole, ed., Academic Press, New York, 1–61.

Beaver, D. (1992), *The kinematics of presupposition*, Proceedings of the Eighth Amsterdam Colloquium, P. Dekker and M. Stockhof, eds, ILLC, University of Amsterdam.

Beaver, D. (1993), *Kinematic Montague grammar*, DYANA-2 deliverable R2.2A Presupposition, H. Kamp, ed., University of Amsterdam.

Beaver, D. (1994a), *When variables don't vary enough*, SALT 4, M. Harvey and L. Santelmann, eds, Cornell, Ithaca, NY.

Beaver, D. (1994b), *Accommodating topics*, Focus and Natural Language Processing, vol. 3, R. van der Sandt and P. Bosch, eds, IBM, Heidelberg, 439–448.

Beaver, D. (1995), *Presupposition and assertion in dynamic semantics*, PhD Dissertation, University of Edinburgh.

Beaver, D. (m.s.), *An infinite number of monkeys*, Acta Linguistica Hungarica (Special edition devoted to Proceedings of the 5th Hungarian Symposium on Logic and Language), to appear.

[74] I use some latitude in interpreting how Van der Sandt's model behaves, translating into natural DRT equivalents of the formulae given, and taking the maximal presupposition to be whatever is globally accommodated.

Beaver, D. and Krahmer, E. (m.s.), *Back to the future*, University of Tilburg, manuscript.

Belnap, N. (1969), *Questions, their presuppositions, and how they can arise*, The Logical Way of Doing Things, K. Lambert, ed., Yale Univ. Press, New Haven, CT.

Bergmann, M. (1981), *Presupposition and two-dimensional logic*, J. Philos. Logic **10**, 27–53.

Blamey, S. (1989), *Partiality*, The Handbook of Philosophical Logic vol. IV, D. Gabbay and F. Guenther, eds, Reidel, Dordrecht, 553–616.

Blau, U. (1978), *Die Dreiwertige Logik der Sprache: Ihre Syntax, Semantik und Anwendung in der Sprachanalyse*, Walter de Gruyter, Berlin.

Blok, P. (1993), *The interpretation of focus: An epistemic approach to pragmatics*, PhD Dissertation, Groningen Dissertations in Linguistics 6, University of Groningen.

Bochvar, D. (1939), *Ob odnom trehznachom iscislenii i ego primeneii k analizu paradoksov klassicheskogo rasshirennogo funkcional'nogo ischislenija*, Mat. Sb. **4**. English transl.: *On a three-valued calculus and its applications to the analysis of the paradoxes of the classical extended functional calculus*, History and Philos. of Logic **2** (1981), 87–112.

Bos, J. (1994), *Presupposition as Anaphora in the Verbmobil semantic formalism*, Verbmobil Report 25, Universität des Saarlandes.

Bos, J., Buitelaar, P. and Mineur, A. (1995), *Bridging as coercive accommodation*, Working Notes of the Edinburgh Conference on Computational Logic and Natural Language Processing, E. Klein, S. Manandhar, W. Nutt and J. Siekmann, eds, Human Communications Research Centre, University of Edinburgh.

Bridge, D. (1991), *Computing presuppositions in an incremental natural language processing system*, PhD Dissertation, available as Technical Report No. 237, University of Cambridge Computer Laboratory.

Burton-Roberts, N. (1989a), *The Limits to Debate: A Revised Theory of Semantic Presupposition*, Cambridge Studies in Linguistics vol. 51, Cambridge Univ. Press, Cambridge, MA.

Burton-Roberts, N. (1989b), *On Horn's dilemma, presupposition and negation*, J. Ling. **25**, 95–125.

Burton-Roberts, N. (1989c), *Theories of presupposition*, J. Ling. **25**, 437–454.

Burton-Roberts, N. (1990), *Trivalence, gapped bivalence, and ambiguity of negation: A reply to Seuren*, J. Ling. **26**, 455–470.

Caffi, C. (1994), *Pragmatic presupposition*, The Encyclopedia of Language and Linguistics, R. Asher and J. Simpson, eds, Pergamon, Oxford.

Chierchia, G. (1995), *Dynamics of Meaning*, Univ. of Chicago Press, Chicago.

Chierchia, G. and S. McConnell-Ginet (1990), *Meaning and Grammar*, MIT Press, Cambridge, MA.

Chomsky, N. (1971), *Deep structure, surface structure and semantic interpretation*, Semantics, an Interdisciplinary Reader in Philosophy, Linguistics and Psychology, D. Steinberg and L. Jacobovits, eds, Cambridge Univ. Press, Cambridge, MA, 183–216.

Clark, H. and Marshall, C. (1981), *Definite reference and mutual knowledge*, Elements of Discourse Understanding, A. Joshi, B. Webber and I. Sag, eds, Cambridge Univ. Press, Cambridge, MA.

Cooper, R. (1983), *Quantification and Syntactic Theory*, Dordrecht, Reidel.

Cooper, R. (1993), *Generalized quantifiers and resource situations*, Situation Theory and its Applications vol. 3, P. Aczel, D. Isreal, Y. Katagiri and S. Peters, eds, CSLI, Stanford.

Cresswell, M. (1973), *Logics and Languages*, Methuen, London.

De Jong, F. and Verkuyl, N. (1987), *Generalized quantifiers: The properness of their strength*, Generalized Quantifiers: Theory and Applications, GRASS vol. 4, A. ter Meulen and J. van Benthem, eds, Foris, Dordrecht.

Dekker, P. (1992), *An update semantics for dynamic predicate logic*, Proceedings of the Eighth Amsterdam Colloquium, P. Dekker and M. Stockhof, eds, ILLC, University of Amsterdam.

Dekker, P. (1993), *Trans-sentential meditations, ups and downs in dynamic semantics*, PhD Dissertation, University of Amsterdam.

Delacruz, E. (1976), *Factives and propositional level constructions in Montague grammar*, Montague Grammar, B. Partee, ed., Academic Press, New York, 177–199.

Delin, J. (1989), *Cleft constructions in discourse*, PhD Dissertation, Centre for Cognitive Science, University of Edinburgh.

Delin, J. (1992), *Properties of* It-*cleft presupposition*, J. Semantics **9**(4), 289–306.

Dinsmore, J. (1981a), *Towards a unified theory of presupposition* (Review of (Oh and Dineen, 1979)), J. Pragmatics **5**, 335–363.

Dinsmore, J. (1981b), *The Inheritance of Presuppositions*, Benjamin, Amsterdam.
Dinsmore, J. (1992), *Partitioned Representations: A Study in Mental Representation, Language Understanding and Linguistic Structure*, Kluwer, Dordrecht.
Eco, U. (1994), *The Limits of Interpretation*, Indiana Univ. Press, Bloomington, IN.
Fauconnier, G. (1985), *Mental Spaces: Aspects of Meaning Construction in Natural Language*, MIT Press, Cambridge, MA.
Fernando, T. (1995), *Computational foundations for dynamic accounts of presuppositions*, Working Notes of the Edinburgh Conference on Computational Logic and Natural Language Processing, E. Klein, S. Manandhar, W. Nutt and J. Siekmann, eds, Human Communications Research Centre, University of Edinburgh.
Fillmore, C. (1971a), *Types of lexical information*, Semantics. An Interdisciplinary Reader in Philosophy, Linguistics and Psychology, D. Steinberg and L. Jacobovitz, eds, Cambridge Univ. Press, Cambridge, MA.
Fillmore, C. (1971b), *Verbs of judging: An exercise in semantic description*, Studies in Linguistic Semantics, C. Fillmore and D. Langendoen, eds, Holt, Reinhardt and Winston, New York.
Fox, C. (m.s.), *Existence presuppositions and category mistakes*, Acta Linguistica Hungarica, to appear.
Frege, G. (1984a), *On sense and meaning*, G. Frege, Collected Works, B. McGuinness, ed., Basil Blackwell, Oxford, 157–177. (First appeared: 1892.)
Frege, G. (1984b), *Collected Works*, B. McGuinness, ed., Basil Blackwell, Oxford.
Gamut, L.T.F. (1991), *Logic, Language and Meaning*, vol. I, Univ. of Chicago Press, Chicago.
Gawron, J. (1995), *Quantification, quantificational domains and dynamic logic*, Handbook of Contemporary Semantic Theory, S. Lappin, ed., Blackwell, Oxford, 247–267.
Gawron, J. and Peters, S. (1990), *Anaphora and Quantification in Situation Semantics*, CSLI Lecture Notes no. 19, CSLI, Stanford.
Gazdar, G. (1979a), *Pragmatics: Implicature, Presupposition and Logical Form*, Academic Press, New York.
Gazdar, G. (1979b), *A solution to the projection problem*, in (Oh and Dineen, 1979).
Geach, P. (1962), *Reference and Generality*, Cornell Univ. Press, Ithaca, NY.
Gervas, P. (1995), *Compositionality and presupposition*, Working Notes of the Edinburgh Conference on Computational Logic and Natural Language Processing, E. Klein, S. Manandhar, W. Nutt and J. Siekmann, eds, Human Communications Research Centre, University of Edinburgh.
Geurts, B. (1994), *Presupposing*, PhD Dissertation, University of Osnabrück.
Geurts, B. (1996), *Local satisfaction guaranteed: A presupposition theory and its problems*, Ling. and Philos. **19**(3), 211–257.
Ginzburg, J. (1995), *Resolving questions*, I, II, Ling. and Philos. **18**(5), 459–527; **18**(6), 567–609.
Goldberg, J., Kalman, L. and Szabo, Z. (m.s.), *Internal and external presuppositions*, Manuscript, Budapest. Draft version appears in R. van der Sandt (ed.), Reader for the Nijmegen Workshop on Presupposition, Lexical Meaning, and Discourse Processes, University of Nijmegen.
Grice, P. (1981), *Presupposition and implicature*, Radical Pragmatics, P. Cole, ed., Academic Press, New York, 183–199. Also in P. Grice, *Studies in the Way of Words*, Harvard Univ. Press, Cambridge, MA, 1989, 269–282. (Page numbers in text refer to 1989 version.)
Groenendijk, J. and Stokhof, M. (1984), *Studies in the semantics of questions and the pragmatics of answers*, PhD Dissertation, University of Amsterdam.
Groenendijk, J. and Stokhof, M. (1991), *Dynamic predicate logic*, Ling. and Philos. **14**, 39–100.
Gunji, T. (1981), *Towards a computational theory of pragmatics – discourse, presupposition and implicature*, PhD Dissertation, Ohio State University.
Halliday, M. (1967), *Notes on transitivity and theme in English*, II, J. Ling. **3**, 199–244.
Hausser, R. (1976), *Presuppositions in Montague grammar*, Theor. Ling. **3**, 245–280.
Hawkins, J. (1978), *Definiteness and Indefiniteness*, Croom Helm, London.
Heim, I. (1982), *On the semantics of definite and indefinite noun phrases*, PhD Dissertation, University of Amherst.
Heim, I. (1983a), *On the projection problem for presuppositions*, Second Annual West Coast Conference on Formal Linguistics, M. Barlow, D. Flickinger and M. Westcoat, eds, Stanford University, 114–126.
Heim, I. (1983b), *File change semantics and the familiarity theory of definites*, Meaning, Use and Interpretation of Language, R. Bäuerle, C. Schwarze and A. von Stechow, eds, De Gruyter, Berlin, 164–189.
Heim, I. (1990), *Presupposition projection*, Reader for the Nijmegen Workshop on Presupposition, Lexical Meaning, and Discourse Processes, R. van der Sandt, ed., University of Nijmegen.

Heim, I. (1992), *Presupposition projection and the semantics of attitude verbs*, J. Semantics **9**, 183–221.
Heinämäki, O. (1972), *Before*, Papers from the 8th Regional Meeting, Chicago Linguistic Society, University of Chicago, 139–151.
Herzberger, H. (1973), *Dimensions of truth*, J. Philos. Logic **2**, 535–556.
Hintikka, J. (1962), *Knowledge and Belief*, Cornell Univ. Press, Ithaca, NY.
Hobbs, J., Stickel, M., Appelt, D. and Martin, P. (1990), *Interpretation as abduction*, Technical Note 499, SRI International, Menlo Park, CA.
Horn, L. (1969), *A presuppositional analysis of* Only *and* Even, Papers from the Fifth Regional Meeting of the Chicago Linguistics Society, University of Chicago, 98–107.
Horn, L. (1985), *Metalinguistic negation and pragmatic ambiguity*, Language **61**, 121–174.
Horn, L. (1986), *Presupposition, theme and variations*, Papers from the Parasession on Pragmatics and Grammatical Theory (22nd Regional Meeting of the Chicago Linguistics Society, Part 2), University of Chicago, 168–192.
Horn, L. (1989), *A Natural History of Negation*, Univ. of Chicago Press, Chicago.
Horn, L. (1990), *Showdown at truth-value gap: Burton-Roberts on presupposition*, J. Ling. **26**, 483–503.
Horn, L. (1994), *Pragmatics, implicature and presupposition*, The International Encyclopedia of Linguistics vol. 3, W. Bright, ed., Oxford Univ. Press, Oxford, 260–266.
Horn, L. (1995), *Presupposition and implicature*, The Handbook of Contemporary Semantic Theory, S. Lappin, ed., Blackwell, Oxford.
Horton, D. (1987), *Incorporating agents' beliefs in a model of presupposition*, MSc Dissertation, University of Toronto. Available as Technical Report CSRI-201, Computer Systems Research Institute, University of Toronto.
Horton, D. and Hirst, G. (1988), *Presuppositions as beliefs*, Proceedings of the International Conference on Computational Linguistics, COLING, 255–260.
Kadmon, N. (1990), *Uniqueness*, Ling. and Philos. **13**, 273–324.
Kálmán, L. (1990), *Deferred information: The semantics of commitment*, Papers from the Second Symposium on Logic and Language, L. Kálmán and L. Pólos, eds, Akadémiai Kiadó, Budapest.
Kasper, W. (1992), *Presupposition, composition and simple subjunctives*, J. Semantics **9**, 307–331.
Kamp, H. (1981), *A theory of truth and semantic representation*, Formal Methods in the Study of Language, Part 1, J. Groenendijk, T. Janssen and M. Stokhof, eds, Mathematical Centre Tracts 135, Amsterdam, 277–322. Reprinted in J. Groenendijk, T. Janssen and M. Stokhof, eds, Truth, Interpretation, and Information; Selected Papers from the Third Amsterdam Colloquium, Foris, Dordrecht, 1984, 1–41.
Kamp, H. and Reyle, U. (1993), *From Discourse to Logic*, Kluwer, Dordrecht.
Kamp, H. and Rossdeutscher, A. (1994), *DRS-construction and lexically driven inference*, Theor. Ling. **20**, 165–235.
Karttunen, L. (1971a), *Some observations on factivity*, Papers Ling. **5**, 55–69.
Karttunen, L. (1971b), *Implicative verbs*, Language **47**(2), 340–358.
Karttunen, L. (1971c), *Counterfactual conditionals*, Ling. Inq. **2**, 566–569.
Karttunen, L. (1973), *Presuppositions of compound sentences*, Ling. Inq. **4**, 167–193.
Karttunen, L. (1974), *Presuppositions and linguistic context*, Theor. Ling. **1**, 181–194.
Karttunen, L. and Peters, S. (1977), *Requiem for presupposition*, BLS3, Proceedings of the Third Annual Meeting of the Berkeley Linguistic Society, Berkeley, CA, 266–278.
Karttunen, L. and Peters, S. (1979), *Conventional implicatures in Montague grammar*, in (Oh and Dineen, 1979), 1–56.
Kay, P. (1992), *The inheritance of presuppositions*, Ling. and Philos. **15**, 333–381.
Keenan, E. (1971), *Two kinds of presupposition in natural language*, Studies in Linguistic Semantics, C. Fillmore and D. Langendoen, eds, Holt, Rinehart and Winston, New York, 45–54.
Kempson, R. (1975), *Presupposition and the Delimitation of Semantics*, Cambridge Univ. Press, Cambridge, MA.
Kempson, R. (1979), *Presupposition, opacity and ambiguity*, in (Oh and Dineen, 1979), 283–297.
Kiparsky, P. and Kiparsky, C. (1970), *Fact*, Progress in Linguistics, M. Bierwisch and K. Heidolph, eds, The Hague, Mouton, 143–173. Also in (Petöfi and Franck, 1973), 315–354.
Kleene, S. (1938), *On a notation for ordinal numbers*, J. Symb. Logic **3**, 150–155.
Kleene, S. (1945), *On the interpretation of intuitionistic number theory*, J. Symb. Logic **10**, 108–124.

Kleene, S. (1959), *Introduction to Metamathematics*, North-Holland, Amsterdam.

Klein, E. (1975), *Two sorts of factive predicate*, Pragmatics Microfiche 1.1, frames B5–C14.

Kracht, M. (1990), *Assertivity, theme and presupposition*, Reader for the Nijmegen Workshop on Presupposition, Lexical Meaning, and Discourse Processes, R. van der Sandt, ed., University of Nijmegen.

Kracht, M. (1994), *Logic and control: How they determine the behaviour of presuppositions*, Logic and Information Flow, J. van Eijck and A. Visser, eds, MIT Press, Cambridge, MA, 89–111.

Krahmer, E. (1993), *Partial dynamic predicate logic*, ITK Research Report No. 48, University of Tilburg.

Krahmer, E. (1994), *Partiality and dynamics*, Proceedings of the Ninth Amsterdam Colloquium vol. 2, P. Dekker and M. Stokhof, eds, ILLC, University of Amsterdam, 391–410.

Krahmer, E. (1995), *Discourse and presupposition*, PhD Dissertation, ITK/TILDIL Dissertation Series, University of Tilburg.

Krause, P. (1995), *Presupposition and abduction in type theory*, Working Notes of the Edinburgh Conference on Computational Logic and Natural Language Processing, E. Klein, S. Manandhar, W. Nutt and J. Siekmann, eds, Human Communications Research Centre, University of Edinburgh.

Krifka, M. (1992), *Presupposition and focus in dynamic interpretation*, J. Semantics **10**.

Kripke, S. (m.s.), *Presupposition and anaphora: Remarks on the formulation of the projection problem*, Manuscript, Princeton University.

Lagerwerf, L. and Oversteegen, L. (1994), *Inferring coherence relations through presuppositions*, Focus and Natural Language Processing, vol. 3, R. van der Standt and P. Bosch, eds, IBM, Heidelberg, 503–512.

Landman, F. (1981), *A note on the projection problem*, Ling. Inq. **12**, 467–471.

Landman, F. (1986), *Conflicting presuppositions and modal subordination*, Papers from the 22nd Regional Meeting, Chicago Linguistic Society, University of Chicago, 195–207.

Lappin, S. and Reinhart, T. (1988), *Presuppositions of quantifiers: A processing account*, Linguistics **26**, 1021-1037.

Langendoen, D. and Savin, H. (1971), *The projection problem for presuppositions*, Studies in Linguistic Semantics, C. Fillmore and D. Langendoen, eds, Holt, Reinhardt and Winston, New York. Also in (Petöfi and Franck, 1973), 373–388.

Lehrner, J. and Zimmermann, T. (1983), *Presupposition and quantification*, Meaning, Use, and Interpretation of Language, R. Bäuerle, C. Schwarze and A. von Stechow, eds, Berlin/New York, 290–301.

Levinson, S. (1983), *Pragmatics*, Cambridge Univ. Press, Cambridge, MA.

Lewis, D. (1979), *Scorekeeping in a language game*, J. Philos. Logic **8**, 339–359. Also in R. Bäuerle, U. Egli and A. von Stechow (eds), Semantics from Different Points of View, Springer, Berlin, 1979.

Link, G. (1986), *Prespie in pragmatic wonderland: or the projection problem for presuppositions revisited*, Foundations of Pragmatics and Lexical Semantics, J. Groenendijk, D. de Jongh and M. Stokhof, eds, Foris, Dordrecht, 101–126.

Lorenz, S. (1992), *On the role of reasoning about change in the projection of presuppositions*, IWBS Report 234, IBM Germany.

Marcu, D. (1994), *A formalisation and an algorithm for computing pragmatic inferences and detecting infelicities*, PhD Dissertation, University of Toronto. Available as Technical Report CSRI-309, Computer Systems Research Institute, University of Toronto.

Martin, J. (1977), *An axiomatisation of Herzberger's two-dimensional presuppositional semantics*, Notre Dame J. Formal Logic **18**, 378–382.

Martin, J. (1979), *Some misconceptions in the critique of semantic presupposition*, Theor. Ling. **6**, 235–282.

McCawley, J. (1979), *Presupposition and discourse structure*, in (Oh and Dineen, 1979), 371–388.

McCawley, J. (1981), *Everything that Linguists always Wanted to Know about Logic (but were too afraid to ask)*, Univ. Chicago Press, Chicago and Blackwell, Oxford.

Mercer, R. (1987), *A default logic approach to the derivation of natural language presuppositions*, PhD Dissertation, University of British Columbia.

Mercer, R. (1992), *Default logic: Towards a common logical semantics for presupposition and entailment*, J. Semantics **9**, 223–250.

Montague, R. (1974a), *Formal Philosophy: Selected Papers*, R. Thomason, ed., Yale Univ. Press, Newhaven, CT.

Montague, R. (1974b), *The proper treatment of quantification*, in (Montague, 1974a).

Morgan, J. (1969), *On the treatment of presupposition in transformational grammar*, Papers from the Fifth Regional Meeting, Chicago Linguistic Society, University of Chicago, 167–77. Also in (Petöfi and Franck, 1973), 373–388.

Morreau, M. (1995), *How to derive conveyed meanings*, Working Notes of the Edinburgh Conference on Computational Logic and Natural Language Processing, E. Klein, S. Manandhar, W. Nutt and J. Siekmann, eds, Human Communications Research Centre, University of Edinburgh.

Mullally, J. (1945), *The Summulae Logicales of Peter of Spain*, Notre Dame Publications in Mediaeval Studies, Notre Dame, IN.

Muskens, R. (1989), *Meaning and partiality*, PhD Dissertation, University of Amsterdam.

Neale, S. (1990), *Descriptions*, MIT Press, Cambridge, MA.

Oh, C. and Dineen, D. (eds) (1979), *Syntax and Semantics* 11: *Presupposition*, Academic Press, New York.

Peters, S. (1977), *A truth-conditional formulation of Karttunen's account of presupposition*, Texas Linguistic Forum **6**, University of Texas at Austin.

Peterson, P. (1979), *On representing event reference*, in (Oh and Dineen, 1979), 325–355.

Petöfi, J. and Franck, D. (eds) (1973), *Präsuppositionen in Philosophie und Linguistik / Presuppositions in Philosophy and Linguistics*, Athanäum Verlag, Frankfurt.

Postal, P. (1972), *A few factive facts*, Ling. Inq. **3**(3), 396–400.

Prince, E. (1978), *The function of existential sentences in discourse*, Papers from the 14th Regional Meeting, Chicago Linguistic Society, University of Chicago, 362–376.

Prince, E. (1981), *Toward a taxonomy of given-new information*, Radical Pragmatics, P. Cole, ed., Academic Press, New York, 223–255.

Prince, E. (1986), *On the syntactic marking of presupposed open propositions*, Papers from the Parasession on Pragmatics and Grammatical Theory, 22nd Regional Meeting Chicago Linguistic Society, A. Farley, P. Farley and K. McCullough, eds, 208–222.

Ramsey, A. (1992), *Presuppositions and WH-clauses*, J. Semantics **9**(3), 251–286.

Reinhart, T. (1982), *Pragmatics and linguistics: An analysis of sentence topics*, Philosophica **27**, 53–94.

Roberts, C. (1987), *Modal subordination, anaphora and distributivity*, PhD Dissertation, University of Massachusetts at Amherst.

Rooth, M. (1995), *Focus*, Handbook of Contemporary Semantic Theory, S. Lappin, ed., Blackwell, Oxford, 271–297.

Rossdeutscher, A. (1994), *Fat Child meets DRT. A semantic representation for the opening lines of Kaschnitz' 'Das dicke Kind'*, Theor. Ling. **20**, 237–305.

Russell, B. (1905), *On denoting*, Mind **14**, 479–493.

Russell, B. (1946), *The History of Western Philosophy*, Allen and Unwin, London. (Page numbers in text refer to Counterpoint edition, Unwin, 1985.)

Russell, B. (1957), *Mr. Strawson on referring*, Mind **66**, 385–389.

Sæbø, K. (1996), *Anaphoric presuppositions, accommodation, and zero anaphora*, Ling. and Philos. **19**(2), 187–209. Also in DYANA-2 deliverable R2.2A Presupposition, H. Kamp, ed., University of Amsterdam, 1994.

Schiebe, T. (1979), *On Presupposition in complex sentences*, in (Oh and Dineen, 1979), 127–154.

Schöter, A. (1994), *Evidential bilattice logic and lexical inference*, Technical Report EUCCS/RP-64, Centre for Cognitive Science, University of Edinburgh.

Schöter, A. (1995), *The computational application of bilattice logic to natural reasoning*, PhD Dissertation, University of Edinburgh.

Searle, J. (1969), *Speech Acts: An Essay in the Philosophy of Language*, Cambridge Univ. Press, Cambridge, MA.

Seuren, P. (1985), *Discourse Semantics*, Blackwell, Oxford.

Seuren, P. (1988a), *Lexical meaning and presupposition*, Understanding the Lexicon, W. Huellen and R. Schulze, eds, Niemeyer, Tübingen, 170–187.

Seuren, P. (1988b), *Presupposition and negation*, J. Semantics **6**, 175–226.

Seuren, P. (1990a), *Burton-Roberts on presupposition and negation*, J. Ling. **26**, 425–453.

Seuren, P. (1990b), *Review article: The limits to debate, Noel Burton Roberts*, Linguistics **28**, 503–516.

Seuren, P. (1991), *Präsuppositionen*, Semantik: Ein Internationales Handbuch der zeitgenössichen Forschung / Semantics: An International Handbook of Contemporary Research., D. Wunderlich and A. von Stechow, eds, Walter de Gruyter, Berlin/New York, 287–318.

Seuren, P. (1994a), *Presupposition*, The Encyclopedia of Language and Linguistics, R. Asher and J. Simpson, eds, Pergammon Press, Oxford.

Seuren, P. (1994b), *Accommodation and presupposition*, The Encyclopedia of Language and Linguistics, R. Asher and J.Simpson, eds, Pergammon, Oxford.

Seuren, P. (1994c), *Projection problem*, The Encyclopedia of Language and Linguistics, R. Asher and J. Simpson, eds, Pergammon Press, Oxford.

Sgall, P. (1995), *Presupposition of existence and of uniqueness, and allegation*, Manuscript, Charles University, Prague.

Sgall, P., Hajičová, E. and Benešová, E. (1973), *Topic, Focus and Generative Semantics*, Scriptor Verlag, Kronberg.

Soames, S. (1979), *A projection problem for speaker presuppositions*, Ling. Inq. **10**, 623–666.

Soames, S. (1982), *How presuppositions are inherited: A solution to the projection problem*, Ling. Inq. **13**, 483–545.

Soames, S. (1989), *Presupposition*, Handbook of Philosophical Logic vol. IV, D. Gabbay and F. Guenther, eds, Reidel, Dordrecht, 553–616.

Sperber, D. and Wilson, D. (1984), *Relevance: Communication and Cognition*, Basil Blackwell, Oxford; Harvard Univ. Press, Cambridge, MA.

Stalnaker, R. (1972), *Pragmatics*, Semantics of Natural Language, D. Davidson and G. Harman, eds, Reidel, Dordrecht. Also in (Petöfi and Franck, 1973), 389–408. Pagenumbers in text refer to (Petöfi and Franck, 1973) version.

Stalnaker, R. (1973), *Presuppositions*, J. Philos. Logic **2**, 447–457.

Stalnaker, R. (1974), *Pragmatic presuppositions*, Semantics and Philosophy, M. Munitz and P. Unger, eds, New York Univ. Press, 197–214.

Stalnaker, R. (1979), *Assertion*, Syntax and Semantics vol. 9, P. Cole, ed., Academic Press, London.

Strawson, P. (1950), *Referring*, Mind **59**, 320–44.

Strawson, P. (1964), *Identifying reference and truth values*, Theoria **30**.

Ter Meulen, A. (1995), *Context and anaphoric presuppositions*, Manuscript, Indiana University.

Thomason, R. (1972), *A semantic theory of sortal incorrectness*, J. Philos. Logic **1**, 209–258.

Thomason, R. (1979), *Truth-value gaps, many truth values, and possible worlds*, in (Oh and Dineen, 1979), 357–369.

Thomason, R. (1990), *Accommodation, meaning and implicature: Interdisciplinary foundations for pragmatics*, Intentions in Communication, P. Cohen, J. Morgan and E. Pollack, eds, Bradford Books, MIT Press, Cambridge, MA, 325–363.

Turner, K. (1992), *Defending semantic presupposition*, J. Pragmatics **18**, 345–371.

Van der Auwera, J. (1993), *Already and still: Beyond duality*, Ling. and Philos. **16**, 613–663.

Van der Sandt, R. (1982), *Kontekst en Presuppositie: Een Studie van het Projektieprobleem en de Presuppositionele Eigenschappen van de Logisch Konnektieven*, PhD Dissertation, Nijmegen Institute of Semantics.

Van der Sandt, R. (1988), *Context and Presupposition*, Croom Helm, London.

Van der Sandt, R. (1989), *Anaphora and accommodation*, Semantics and Contextual Expression, R. Bartsch, J. van Benthem and P. van Emde Boas, eds, Foris, Dordrecht.

Van der Sandt, R. (1991), *Denial*, Chicago Linguistic Society II: Papers from the Parasession on Negation, University of Chicago.

Van der Sandt, R. (1992), *Presupposition projection as anaphora resolution*, J. Semantics **9**, 333–377.

Van der Sandt, R. (m.s.), *Discourse systems and echo-quotation*, Ling. and Philos., to appear.

Van der Sandt, R. and Geurts, B. (1991), *Presupposition, anaphora and lexical content*, Text Understanding in LiLOG, O. Herzog and C. Rollinger, eds, Springer, Berlin.

Van Eijck, J. (1993), *The dynamics of description*, J. Semantics **10**, 239–267.

Van Eijck, J. (1994), *Presupposition failure a comedy of errors*, Formal Aspects of Computing **3**.

Van Eijck, J. (1995), *Presuppositions and dynamic logic*, Papers from the Second CSLI Workshop on Logic, Language and Computation, M. Kanazawa, C. Piñon and H. de Swart, eds, CSLI, Stanford.

Van Fraassen, B. (1969), *Presuppositions, supervaluations and free logic*, The Logical Way of Doing Things, K. Lambert, ed., Yale Univ. Press, New Haven, CT, 67–92.

Van Fraassen, B. (1975), *Logic and Formal Semantics*, Macmillan, New York.

Veltman, F. (1986), *Data semantics and the pragmatics of indicative conditionals*, On Conditionals, E. Traugott, A. ter Meulen, Reilly and Ferguson, eds, Cambridge Univ. Press, Cambridge, MA.

Veltman, F. (1991), *Defaults in update semantics*, DYANA deliverable R2.5.C. To appear in J. Philos. Logic.

Vermeulen C. (1992), *Sequence semantics for dynamic predicate logic*, J. Logic, Lang., Inform. **2**, 217–254.

von Fintel, K. (1995), *Restrictions on quantifier domains*, PhD Dissertation, University of Massachusetts at Amherst.

von Kutschera, F. (1975), *Partial interpretations*, Formal Semantics of Natural Language, E. Keenan, ed., Cambridge Univ. Press, Cambridge, MA.

Wilson, D. (1975), *Presupposition and Non-truth-conditional Semantics*, Academic Press, London.

Wilson, D. and Sperber, D. (1979), *Ordered entailments: An alternative to presuppositional theories*, in (Oh and Dineen, 1979), 299–323.

Zeevat, H. (1991), *Aspects of discourse semantics and unification grammar*, PhD Dissertation, University of Amsterdam.

Zeevat, H. (1992), *Presupposition and accommodation in update semantics*, J. Semantics **9**, 379–412.

Zeevat, H. (1994), *A Speculation about certain triggers*, The Proceedings of the IBM/Journal of Semantics Conference on Focus vol. 3, R. van der Sandt and P. Bosch, eds, IBM, Heidelberg, 669–676.

Zuber, R. (1977), *Decomposition of factives*, Stud. Lang. **1**(3), 407–421.

CHAPTER 18

Plurals and Collectivity

Jan Tore Lønning*

Department of Linguistics, University of Oslo, PO Box 1102, Blindern, 0317 Oslo, Norway
E-mail: jtl@ilf.uio.no

Commentator: G. Link

Contents

*Thanks to the Research Council of Norway for partial support, grants no 102137/520 and 101335/410.

HANDBOOK OF LOGIC AND LANGUAGE
Edited by J. van Benthem and A. ter Meulen

1. Introduction

Plural is a grammatical notion. Common nouns in English are customarily sorted into two classes, mass nouns and count nouns. **Count nouns**, like *child, cat, car, thought*, apply to discrete objects which can be counted. These nouns have a singular and a plural form, e.g., *child–children*. Intuitively, the singular noun denotes one object, while the plural noun denotes two or more objects. **Mass nouns**, like *ink, stuff, information*, apply to non-discrete stuff, substances, abstract entities, etc. They only occur in the singular, and the determiners they take are different from the ones taken by the count nouns, e.g., *much water, two liters of water, *an information*. Many nouns occur in both classes; hence it has been proposed to consider the distinction to be between noun occurrences rather than between lexical items (Pelletier, 1975).

Collective, in contrast, we will use as a semantic notion. It applies to the meaning of certain occurrences of plural NPs as in the following examples.

(1) a. Bunsen and Kirchoff laid the foundations of spectral theory.
b. The Romans conquered Gaul.
c. The students gathered.
d. The disciples were twelve in number.
e. The soldiers surrounded the Alamo.
f. Some girls gathered.
g. Three thousand soldiers surrounded the Alamo.

The first sentence does not say that Bunsen laid the foundations of spectral theory and that Kirchoff did it, even though they both contributed. This contrasts with the sentences (2a), (2c), and (2d).

(2) a. Armstrong and Aldrin walked on the moon.
b. Armstrong walked on the moon and Aldrin walked on the moon.
c. Six hundred tourists visited the castle.
d. Some of Fiorecchio's men entered the building unaccompanied by anyone else.

Sentence (2a) says the same as (2b); (2c) is true if each one of six hundred tourists visited the castle; while (2d) has, according to Quine (1974), a reading upon which it is true if some of Fiorecchio's men each entered the castle only accompanied by other of Fiorecchio's men. We will call the most prominent reading of the plural NPs in (1) **collective** and the reading of the plural NPs in (2a), (2c), (2d) **distributive**.

The framework of modern logic, as developed by Frege and others in the second half of the last century, was able to analyze large parts of natural language. But it was soon observed that there are phenomena which are not easily accommodated. In fact, the problems to which the collectively read plural NPs gave rise were discussed already in letters between Frege and Russell in 1902, where the examples (1a) and (1b) can be found (Frege, 1980, p. 140).

The goal of this chapter is to discuss how a logical approach to natural language semantics best should be modified and extended to accommodate collective plural NPs. Distributive plural NPs and mass nouns will be considered to bring out the similarities and differences between them and the collective plural NPs. The emphasis will be on the reportive uses, while generic uses will be more or less ignored because of lack of space. (For bare plurals and genericity, see Pelletier and Asher (1996), Carlson (1977), Link (1991), Carlson and Pelletier (1995).) Moreover, there will not be much room for discussing the interactions of plurality and other phenomena, like anaphora or tense. Finally, emphasis will be on English and closely related languages. Other languages may behave quite differently. There are languages with three different numbers – dual in addition to singular and plural – and languages with no numbers at all.

Most proposals for the semantics of plurals assume some sort of **collections** – objects denoted by phrases like *Bunsen and Kirchoff* and *the soldiers* and ascribed properties like *surrounding the castle*. We will allow ourselves from the beginning to talk about *collections* as existing objects in a pretheoretical way, and return to the question on whether we can do without them in Section 6. There are two main views on the status of collections. One is to consider them to be higher-order individuals, Section 3, the other is to consider them to be first-order individuals similar to the ones described by singular NPs, Section 4.

2. Setting the stage

2.1. The rules of the game

2.1.1. Ontology

Our task is to give a formal semantic analysis. We start with recollecting some of the assumptions underlying such an approach. We assume some sort of first-order logical analysis of a core of English containing singular NPs. Central to such an analysis is the concept of a **(first-order) model**. It consists of a domain, E, and an interpretation function, $[\![\cdot]\!]$, which ascribes denotations to the words. The denotation of a name or variable is a member of E, $[\![john]\!] \in E$, the denotation of a predicate (unary relation) is a subset of E, $[\![Girl]\!] \subseteq E$, the denotation of a binary relation symbol is a relation over E, $[\![Kiss]\!] \subseteq E \times E$, etc.

Inherent to the concept of a first-order model is a certain minimal ontology, the choice to model the world as a set of individuals and properties as sets of individuals. One task in the sequel will be to extend this ontology to the collective plural NPs. This is not a purely ontological task, however, the starting point should be language. The question will be, what sort of objects are needed as denotations for such and such phrases, in our case, the plural phrases.

Each particular first-order model is intended to reflect one particular state of affairs. In addition, it models the meaning of the individual words. The underlying ontology is in a sense weak. It allows models where a book is on and under the same table at the same time. This does not reflect a possible state of affairs. The model concept of formal semantics is carried over from logic. The tasks of logic and of semantics are partly different. Logic studies inferences which are valid from structure alone, independently of ontology and the meaning of words. But in the study of the semantics of English, it seems legitimate to take into consideration the meaning of words like *under* and *on*. The strategy chosen in formal semantics has been to split semantics into two parts, the logical part which is captured in terms of what counts as a legal first-order model, and the lexical semantic part which in some way or other tries to exclude the unintended models. When extending the framework to plural NPs, a reemerging question will be exactly which phenomena are the formal semantics expected to answer and which can be said to belong to the realm of lexical semantics.

2.1.2. Compositionality

The model contains the assignment of denotations to a *finite* vocabulary. The goal for the formal semantic theory is to show how the denotation of *infinitely* many different sentences and other phrases can be constructed from this finite base. For this some sort of systematic recursive rules are needed.

Logical languages, like first-order logic, have well defined compositional semantics. By representing sentences from natural language in such a calculus, their meaning may be spelled out. But this spells out the meaning of the sentence in terms of the parts of the logical formula representing it, not in terms of the parts of the sentence itself. Montague (1973) showed how one could ascribe a systematic semantics to parts of English in a direct way, similarly as for logic (cf. Partee, 1966; Janssen, 1966). He also showed that exactly the same could be achieved through a systematic translation into a logical calculus containing lambda abstraction. The logical language would thereby contain terms corresponding to the phrases of the natural language.

The analysis of a natural language sentence may be more complex than that of a logical formula. In particular, one and the same sentence, e.g., *Every man loves a woman*, may have several readings thanks to differences in scope. Moreover, the study of anaphoric phenomena has revealed a more complex relationship between language and its interpretation currently investigated in the different dynamic approaches to semantics. In this chapter we will assume a static interpretation in the spirit of Montague and consider how it must be modified and extended to accommodate the collective readings. Most of what we will say here may be combined with a dynamic approach, while there are phenomena where plurality and dynamicity interact, in particular with respect to plural anaphora (cf. Kamp and Reyle, 1993, for an extensive treatment).

2.1.3. Logic

After proposing possible frameworks, it will be time for studying their formal properties. In this respect plurals differs from several other semantic phenomena. Plural logic did not establish itself as a field similarly to, say, modal logic. When the semantics of plurals were developed after 1970, most of the logical tools, as set theory, algebraic structures, higher-order logic, were already developed for more basic foundational studies in logic and the task for the semanticist became more to choose between these tools than to actually build them.

But there is another aspect to this history. Even though set theory, type theory, higher-order logics etc., were developed to yield a foundation to logic and mathematics and not to ascribe a formal semantic analysis to natural language, they were not developed in a vacuum. The intuition which the logicians and philosophers wanted to formalize could already be expressed (more or less vaguely) in natural languages, and the plural NPs were vital. Thus Russell (1919) introduces the chapter on classes by saying that "In the present chapter we shall be concerned with *the* in the plural: [...]" (p. 181). Hence some of the most fundamental questions in logic have all along been interwoven with the question of what the plural NPs mean.

2.2. *Plurals, but not collective*

As mentioned in the introduction, not all plural NPs are read collectively. Some behave semantically similarly to the singular ones.

(3) a. All boys like to sing.

b. Every boy likes to sing.

c. Some boys like to sing.

d. Some boy likes to sing.

Sentence (3a) and (3b) say the same. In this context, *all boys* may be interpreted by a universal individual quantifier. Similarly, (3c) and (3d) say nearly the same; the difference may be that (3c) claims that at least two boys like to sing. This can be expressed in first-order logic by formula (4a).

(4) a. $\exists u \exists v\, (u \neq v \wedge Boy(u) \wedge Boy(v) \wedge Sing(u) \wedge Sing(v))$

b. $\lambda X \lambda Y\, [\exists u \exists v\, (u \neq v \wedge X(u) \wedge X(v) \wedge Y(u) \wedge Y(v))]$

A compositional Montagovian analysis can be achieved by ascribing *some* in contexts like (3c) the interpretation (4b). Alternatively, one may extend the representation language with a constant $SOME_{PL}$ of type $((e,t),((e,t),t))$ with the interpretation $[\![SOME_{PL}]\!](P)(Q) = \mathbf{t}$ if and only if $|P \cap Q| \geqslant 2$.

By introducing more constants of type $((e,t),((e,t),t))$, which combine with terms of type (e,t) to generalized quantifiers of type $((e,t),t)$, we can similarly interpret other distributive plural NPs in sentences like (2) and (5):

(5) a. Most girls like to sing.

b. At least five thousand girls like to sing.

c. More girls than boys like to sing.

Here a possible interpretation of *most* is $[\![MOST]\!](P)(Q) = \mathbf{t}$ if and only if $|P \cap Q| > |P \cap \overline{Q}|$. For more on the interpretation of generalized quantifiers ranging over the basic domain E (see Keenan and Westerståhl, 1996).

2.3. *Collectively read NPs*

Which plural NPs may be read collectively, and in which contexts do they get this reading? The following rough classification of the singular NPs can serve as a useful background:

- **Proper nouns:** Mary, John, Rome.
- **Other definite noun phrases:** The girl, John's car, my nose.
- **Indefinite noun phrases:** A girl, one of John's friends.
- **Proper quantifiers:** Every girl.

This classification can be done on a mixture of syntactic and semantic criteria. It is meant to be theory neutral and should not be taken as a claim that definite or indefinite NPs shall not be considered to be quantifiers, but it is compatible with such an analysis.

The following is a similar rough first classification of the plural NPs which admit a collective reading.

- **Proper nouns:** Simpsons, Torkelsons.
- **Other definite noun phrases:** The girls, John's cars, my two ears.
- **Bare plural NPs:** apples, boats.
- **Other indefinite noun phrases:** some girls, two of John's friends.
- **Conjoined noun phrases:** Ann and Mary, John and two of his friends.

The plural proper nouns may behave similarly to the plural definite descriptions, e.g., *The Torkelsons bought a boat.* Notice also that a name can be conceived as singular, say as the name of a TV series, even though it is morphologically plural. The other plural definite NPs are quite similar to the singular definite NPs, except for the number. In addition, the plural NP may contain words which restrict the size of its denotation, say a numeral like *two*.

A singular indefinite NP has to contain a determiner in English, while a plural indefinite NP may be **bare** as in *John ate apples* or *Wolves attacked him.* (Bare plurals will not be covered in this chapter. See Link (1991) for a comprehensive discussion.) The indefinite NP may also contain a numeral similarly to the definite NP, e.g., *two apples*, or another determiner, e.g., *some apples*.

In addition, when two NPs are conjoined, the result requires plural agreement and is classified as a plural NP accordingly. It may be read collectively, as indicated in sentence (1a). This is the case whether the conjuncts are definite or indefinite, singular or plural.

The NPs which may be read collectively may also be read distributively, in particular if such a reading is forced by an explicit adverb, like (6c), (6d).

(6) a. Three girls brought a cake.

b. Ann and Mary brought a cake.

c. Cocke, Younger and Kasami independently discovered the algorithm.

d. They wrote a paper each.

What about the other direction? Can all plural NPs be read collectively? For an NP with the determiner *many* or *few* a distributive reading is clearly preferred as seen in (7a) in contrast to an NP where the determiner is a numeral and where a collective reading is preferred (6a).

(7) a. Many girls brought a cake.

b. Many girls gathered.

But these determiners can also occur in contexts where only a collective reading is possible, as in (7b), in which case they have to be read collectively. When it comes to determiners which cannot be read as specifying the size of a set, but which is inherently relational, like *most*, it seems even harder to find contexts where they may be read collectively, i.e. where *Most girls* α is read something like *There is a group X containing most girls and X* α. But we will not totally exclude the possibility that it can be used in a setting where only a collective reading is possible. Thus it seems hard to specify a fixed class of NPs which may be read collectively. Rather, it seems that some NPs are easily read collectively, while others may only be read collectively in contexts where other readings are impossible or highly unlikely.

As far as we can see, there is no plural determiner which does the same for the collections as *every* does for individuals, i.e. a determiner which imposes a reading corresponding to (8a).

(8) a. Every collection of boys lifted the stone.

b. Every two persons resemble each other.

c. Three bananas cost 50 cents.

d. A banana costs 20 cents.

There are, however, constructions which may entail a universal quantification over certain classes of collections, in particular classes of a certain specified size, (8b). Moreover, a reading similar to the universal one may, in certain cases, be obtained by other constructions. In particular, one may observe a "nearly universal" use of the indefinite plural NP, as in sentence (8c), which resembles a similar use of the singular indefinite NP as in sentence (8d).

Nor do the other plural determiners impose generalized quantifiers ranging over collections. The plural NP *most girls* cannot mean *most collections of girls*. Either it is read distributively, saying that most girls individually have a certain property, or, in rare cases, it may be read collectively, saying that a certain collection consisting of most girls has a certain property. See Link (1987) for more on the possibility of quantifiers ranging over collections.

There is a class of nouns which do not fit into what we have said so far, "words which denote a unit made up of several things or beings which may be counted separately" (Jespersen, 1924, p. 195), *family, crew, crowd, committee, army, nation, mob*, etc. In traditional grammar, the word *collective* is used for these words. As we have used this word for other purposes, we will call them **group-denoting**. In some respects, the group-denoting nouns in the singular behave like other words in the plural. In particular, they may in the singular combine with properties which are otherwise only ascribed to collective plural NPs, and they may show plural agreement in British English.

(9) a. The girls meet in secret.

b. *The girl meet(s) in secret.

c. The group meet in secret.

In other respects, these words behave like other nouns, they may themselves be pluralized and quantified *the groups/every group*. Moreover, they do not generate distributive readings in the same way as the plural NPs do.

(10) a. *The family own two cars each.

b. The members of the family own two cars each.

Whether a plural NP actually is read collectively or not is to a large degree determined by the context. There are several different possibilities for how the context interacts with the NP.

Collective properties are properties which entail some sort of collectivity and thereby triggers a collective reading. They can be further divided into three types.

• **Simple collective properties**, like *met in secret, collided*. These can combine with indefinite and definite plural NPs as well as conjoined NPs and induce an unambiguous collective reading. They may also combine with singular group-denoting nouns and with definite and indefinite plural group-denoting nouns. In the last case, the result is ambiguous, *The groups met in secret.*

• **Relational collective properties**, like *are friends, love each other*. These behave as the simple collective properties except that they cannot be combined with group-denoting nouns in the singular and they are unambiguous if combined with group-denoting nouns in the plural.

• **Cardinal collective properties**, like *are many, are twelve in number*. They do not combine with the group-denoting nouns in the singular, nor with simple conjoined NPs, **John and Harry are many*. Even the indefinite NPs are odd with them, *?Some girls are twelve in number*, while they do combine with definite plural NPs.

Ordinary properties. These fall into two groups.

• Properties like *bought a house, lifted five stones* which are ambiguous when combined with the definite and indefinite plural NPs and with conjoined NPs, but unambiguous when combined with singular NPs including the group-denoting NPs in the singular.

• Properties which do not seem to be ambiguous like *slept, likes to sing, wrote operas*. These combine with all NPs. Some of them may seem odd when combined with some group-denoting NPs for reasons that have to do with the meanings of the words. Observe also that the ordinary properties which are ambiguous may be disambiguated by adding an adverb, *between them/each*. The result may be a property which only combine with a plural NP which may be read collectively. But at the same time the resulting sentence is read distributively, *ate an apple each.*

3. Higher-order approaches

3.1. Ontology

The founding fathers of logic, Frege and Russell, did not restrict logic to first-order, but included higher-order variables and quantifiers as well. In such a setting, the first approach to the semantics of the collectives is evident. Let *the students* denote the same set of individuals as *student* denotes in other contexts and let *gather* and *to be twelve in number* be second-order properties. Then the sentences (1c) and (1d), can be represented as (11a) and (11b).

(11) a. $GATHER(Student)$

b. $TWELVE(Disciple)$

Here *GATHER* and *TWELVE* are second-order predicates, each denoting a set of sets of individuals. This proposal can be traced back at least to Russell (1903), cf. also the quotation from Russell (1919) cited above. To take into consideration the assumption of the use of the plural definite description, the Russellian representation would be (12a) where $TM(\alpha)$ is shorthand for (12b), where x and y are variables not occurring in α.

(12) a. $GATHER(Student) \wedge TM(Student)$

b. $\exists x \exists y\, (\alpha(x) \wedge \alpha(y) \wedge x \neq y)$

If one thinks that the claim that the collection consists of at least two individuals is rather presupposed than stated, one may accommodate for it in other ways. This is not essential for the discussions in the sequel, and we will mostly skip the claim in (12) and stick to the simpler representations as in examples (11).

Russell did little more than hint on such an interpretation. But it is easy to see that it may also be extended to other collectively read plural NPs. Thus the sentences (1e), (1f) and (1g) can be represented by (13a), (13b), and (13c), where *THREETH* is a second-order predicate representing *three thousand*, while *SURR* denotes a relation between sets of individuals and individuals.

(13) a. $SURR(Soldier, alamo)$

b. $\exists X\, (X \subseteq Girl \wedge TM(Girl) \wedge GATHER(X))$

c. $\exists X\, (X \subseteq Soldier \wedge THREETH(X) \wedge SURR(X, alamo))$

Here and throughout $(\alpha \subseteq \beta)$ in a formula is shorthand for $\forall x(\alpha(x) \rightarrow \beta(x))$, where x is a variable not occurring in α or β. For constants, the typeface convention followed is to write names of individuals in all lower-case, relations between individuals starts with a capital and the rest is in lower-case, while relations where one or more of the arguments are first-order predicates are typed in all capitals. Greek letters are used as metavariables irrespectively of type.

3.2. *Compositionality*

The interest for more systematic semantic rules emerged in the late sixties, in particular by the work of Richard Montague (1973) (cf. Partee, 1966). In 1974 two PhD Thesis appeared presenting similar ideas for interpreting collectively read plurals (Bennett, 1975; Hausser, 1974). Some related ideas were also presented by Bartsch (1973). The common core of Bennett and Hausser's proposals is the following. If we are to extend PTQ (Montague, 1973) with plural NPs, we need two new categories, the distributively read plural NPs with the same semantic type as the singular NPs, $((e,t),t)$, and the collectively read plural NPs with type $(((e,t),t),t)$. Other categories will correspondingly need several entries as summed up in the table. We simplify and assume a purely extensional version of PTQ.

	Singular or Plural distributive	Plural collective
NP	$((e,t),t)$	$(((e,t),t),t)$
VP	(e,t)	$((e,t),t)$
CN	(e,t)	(e,t)
Det	$((e,t),((e,t),t))$	$((e,t),(((e,t),t),t))$

All forms and occurrences of a CN get the same denotation. The part of the NP which yields the difference between the collective and the distributive interpretation is the Det. The following examples should suffice to illustrate how this works. The determiners are combined with plural CNs.

	Distributive	Collective
	$((e,t),((e,t),t))$	$((e,t),(((e,t),t),t))$
Some	$\lambda X\lambda Y[TM(X\cap Y)]$	$\lambda X\lambda\mathcal{Y}[\exists Z(Z\subseteq X\wedge TM(Z)\wedge\mathcal{Y}(Z))]$
Six	$\lambda X\lambda Y[SIX(X\cap Y)]$	$\lambda X\lambda\mathcal{Y}[\exists Z(Z\subseteq X\wedge SIX(Z)\wedge\mathcal{Y}(Z))]$
The	$\lambda X\lambda Y[TM(X)\wedge X\subseteq Y]$	$\lambda X\lambda\mathcal{Y}[TM(X)\wedge\mathcal{Y}(X)]$
The six	$\lambda X\lambda Y[SIX(X)\wedge X\subseteq Y]$	$\lambda X\lambda\mathcal{Y}[SIX(X)\wedge\mathcal{Y}(X)]$

Here $\alpha\cap\beta$ is shorthand for $\lambda z[\alpha(z)\wedge\beta(z)]$, while *TM* is true of a set of cardinality at least two, as in (12). First-order variables are in lower case and second-order variables are capitals, as usual, while third-order variables (sets of sets of individuals) are in calligraphic capitals.

The distributive interpretation of *some* is the same interpretation as we considered in Section 2.2. By expressing both readings syntactically in terms of *TM*, one may recognize the common semantic core of the two. The determiner consisting of the simple numeral *six* can be handled similarly. We assume the simple numeral *six* is read as *exactly six*. This is correct for the collective reading; observe that a group of exactly six men bought a boat does not exclude that also other men bought boats. For the distributive reading, it has been discussed whether an *exactly* or *at least* reading best captures the simple numeral. If one prefers an *at least* reading, the relationship between the collective and the distributive readings would be less direct.

The same noun may occur as the head of a collective or a distributive NP while the verbs are lexically marked for collectivity vs. distributivity. Some verbs are inherently distributive, like *run*, and will always be of type (e,t), whether it is in the singular or in the plural. Other verbs will be inherently collective, like *gather*, and can only occur in the plural with the collective type $((e,t),t)$. There are four different categories of transitive verbs according to whether the subject NP and the object NP are read collectively or distributively. The picture gets even more complicated by the fact that some verbs may belong to several categories. While *kiss* and *love* are distributive in both argument places, the subject NP of *surround* has to be collective, while the object NP can be either collective or distributive. A verb like *applaud* belongs, according to Bennett, to all four classes.

In addition, Bennett considered group-denoting nouns. The nouns themselves are introduced as of a new category, corresponding to the type $((e,t),t)$, and they can occur both in the singular and the plural. Thus the sentences (14a), (14b), (14c) can be interpreted as (14d), (14e), (14f), respectively.

(14) a. A group gathered.
b. Three groups gathered.
c. The groups gathered.
d. $\exists X\,(GROUP(X) \wedge GATHER(X))$
e. $\mathbf{three}(GROUP \cap GATHER)$
f. $\forall X\,(GROUP(X) \rightarrow GATHER(X))$

Here **three** is of type $(((e,t),t),t)$ saying that a set of sets has cardinality three. The way to achieve these readings is by allowing the collective VPs of type $((e,t),t)$ to occur in the singular with the same semantics as when they occur in the plural. In addition, to each determiner resulting in a singular NP or a distributive plural NP, i.e. of type $((e,t),((e,t),t))$, there is a corresponding determiner "one level up", i.e. of type $(((e,t),t),(((e,t),t),t))$, with a parallel semantics. For example, *three* when combined with a collective noun in the plural will have the interpretation $\lambda\mathcal{X}\lambda\mathcal{Y}[\mathbf{three}(\mathcal{X}\cap\mathcal{Y})]$.

This approach to the group-denoting nouns explains why they may combine with verbs that otherwise only combine with plural NPs read collectively. But it does not include a collective reading of the group-denoting nouns themselves. Both (14b) and (14c) have collective readings, which are not captured. Already Hausser (1974) noticed this problem and did for this reason not include group-denoting nouns in his fragment. Another problem is to say exactly what the identity conditions for a group or committee is. Should it be identified with the set of its members as this approach assumes? Bennett (1977) himself later raised doubts about it when it came to the more intentional ones, like *committee*.

3.3. *Logic*

3.3.1. *Second-order logic*

How much of higher-order logic is actually needed to represent plural NPs? First observe that the λ-abstraction of second- and higher-order variables is a tool for composition. In the end result they may be β-converted and will disappear. The extensions of first-order logic which will remain in the representations of full sentences are quantification over second-order variables as in the examples (13) and first-order lambda abstraction as in example (15).

(15) a. The men that love Mary gathered.

b. $GATHER(\lambda x[Man(x) \wedge Love(x, mary)])$

We will in this section disregard the group-denoting nouns. So far we have been a bit sloppy with the logical notation, mixing elements from different frameworks. We will now be precise and give a definition for a sufficient tool, choosing a relational variant of second-order logic. We refer to the following types:

DEFINITION 1 (*SOLID types*).
(a) 0 is a type.
(b) $\langle 0 \rangle$ is a type.
(c) For any n, $\langle \tau_1, \tau_2, \ldots, \tau_n \rangle$ is a type, if each τ_i equals 0 or $\langle 0 \rangle$.

Strictly speaking, (b) is a special case of (c). We will write 1 for $\langle 0 \rangle$.

DEFINITION 2 (*SOLID*). A **similarity type** X is a set of constants where each constant belongs to exactly one type from some finite set of SOLID types. The **Second-order language for representing indefinite and definite collective NPs (SOLID)** of similarity type X is defined as follows:
(a) The constants in X are terms of the corresponding type. There is a designated constant, and term, $=$, of type $\langle 0, 0 \rangle$.
(b) **Variables of type** 0: $x, y, z, x_1, y_1, \ldots$ are **terms of type** 0.
(c) **Variables of type** 1: $X, Y, Z, X_1, Y_1, \ldots$ are **terms of type** 1.
(d) If R is a term of type $\langle \tau_1, \tau_2, \ldots, \tau_n \rangle$ and $t_1, t_2, \ldots, t_n$ are terms with t_i of type τ_i for $i = 1, \ldots, n$ then $R(t_1, t_2, \ldots, t_n)$ is an **(atomic) formula**.
(e) If ϕ and ψ are formulas then so are $(\phi \wedge \psi)$, $(\phi \vee \psi)$ and $(\neg\phi)$.
(f) If ϕ is a formula and v a variable of type 0, $\exists v\, \phi$ and $\forall v\, \phi$ are formulas.
(g) If ϕ is a formula and V a variable of type 1, $\exists V\, \phi$ is a formula.
(h) If ϕ is a formula and v a variable of type 0, $\hat{v}[\phi]$ is a term of type 1.

We will call a term of the form $\hat{v}[\phi]$ a **set term**. This **set abstraction** will take the place of the λ-abstraction in examples like (15) and is included to give a direct representation of the definite plural NPs without the use of second-order quantifiers. Then the semantics:

DEFINITION 3. A **standard structure** for a SOLID language L is a pair, $\langle E, [\![\cdot]\!] \rangle$, where E is non-empty and $[\![\cdot]\!]$ is an interpretation function such that
(a) $E_0 = E$.
(b) For each type $\langle \tau_1, \tau_2, \ldots, \tau_n \rangle$, $E_{\langle \tau_1, \tau_2, \ldots, \tau_n \rangle} = \mathrm{POW}(E_{\tau_1} \times E_{\tau_2} \times \cdots \times E_{\tau_n})$, in particular, $E_1 = \mathrm{POW}(E)$.
(c) If α is a constant of type τ, then $[\![\alpha]\!] \in E_\tau$.

A **variable assignment**, g, maps variables of type 0 to elements in E_0, and variables of type 1 to elements in E_1. The **interpretation** $[\![\phi]\!]_g$ of the expression ϕ **with respect to the assignment** g is standard with respect to atomic formulas, the propositional part and quantifiers. Set abstraction is interpreted by:

(16) $$[\![\hat{v}[\phi]]\!]_g = \{a \in E \mid [\![\phi]\!]_{g_a^v} = \mathbf{t}\}$$

Second-order logic is a giant extension of first-order logic. A lot more can be said within second-order logic than within first-order logic, and a lot less can be said about it, as summed up in the following theorem

THEOREM 1. SOLID *is not compact, does not have any complete axiomatization, and does not satisfy the Skolem–Löwenheim properties with respect to the standard structures.*

A proof for this and other interesting properties of second-order logic may be found in (Shapiro, 1991) and (Van Benthem and Doets, 1983). They prove the result for more expressive languages. But the only resources beyond first-order logic exploited by the proofs are quantifiers ranging over subsets of the basic domain. Hence the proofs may be reconstructed within SOLID.

Some authors, in particular Quine (1970), claim that second-order logic is not logic but set theory in disguise. The point rests in a rigid distinction between truths of logic, which are truths defined by form alone, void of any content, and other truths. Statements in set theory presuppose the existence of sets, an ontology. They are not purely formal. Many logicians consider things differently. They are less concerned about finding *the* logic. Rather they study a whole family of different logics, extensions to first-order logic, and the properties of these logics, and then ask which logic is convenient for a particular task. As such there is no sharp border line between logical and other truths but rather a gradual shift, more in the spirit of Quine's own holistic program (cf. Van Benthem and Doets, 1983; and in particular, Shapiro, 1991). Quine's arguments against considering second-order logic as logic proper are not necessarily arguments against founding a semantics for natural language on second-order logic. As pointed out in Section 2.1.1, the intuitive semantic entailment relation of English goes beyond traditional logic and admits for ontological considerations. For our purposes, the question rather becomes how much of this entailment relation we want to model and how much ontology we are willing to include to reach this goal.

There are two possible routes to proceed to overcome the incompleteness of SOLID; to extend the class of structures or to restrict the language. We start with extending the class of structures.

DEFINITION 4. A **generalized structure (g-structure)** for a SOLID language L is a triple $\langle E_0, E_1, [\![\cdot]\!]\rangle$ where

(a) E_0 is non-empty.

(b) $E_1 \subseteq \text{POW}(E_0)$ and for each definable subset X of E_0, $X \in E_1$.

(c) The other domains and the interpretation function is as in the definition of the standard structure.

If L is a SOLID language and $\langle E_0, E_1, [\![\cdot]\!]\rangle$ a g-structure for L, $X \subseteq E_0$ is called **definable** provided it equals $\{a \in E_0 \mid [\![\phi]\!]_{g^v_a} = \mathbf{t}\}$ for some formula ϕ, variable v and assignment g.

The domain E_1 must contain the definable subsets to assure denotations for the set terms, cf. condition (16) above. Observe that often second-order languages are defined without set abstraction in which case g-structures might be defined such that E_1 is any subset of $\text{POW}(E_0)$. With respect to the g-structures, SOLID behaves pretty much like first-order logic:

THEOREM 2. SOLID *is compact and can be completely axiomatized with respect to the g-structures.*

PROOF. This was studied by Mostowski (1947) and Henkin (1950), cf. Van Benthem and Doets (1983). We will give an idea of the proof since the construction is revealing for issues to be considered in the sequel.

We start with a SOLID language L. Observe that the following schema is valid in all g-structures if Y does not occur in ϕ or ψ.

(17) $\psi(\widehat{x}[\phi]) \leftrightarrow \exists Y\,(\forall x(\phi \leftrightarrow Y(x)) \wedge \psi(Y))$

By repeated use of the schema, one can show that each formula ϕ is equivalent to a formula ϕ' without set terms. Hence we can consider set terms to be defined terms and for the rest of the proof assume that L does not contain set terms.

Introduce a new relation symbol $\in$ of type $\langle 0, 1\rangle$ and exchange all subformulas of the form $T(s)$, with s a term of type 0 and T of type 1, with $s \in T$. The resulting language L^+ can be considered a sorted first-order language with 0 and 1 as basic sorts. The predicates of type $\langle 0\rangle$ in L will correspond to constants in L^+, while the other relation symbols in L will be relation symbols in L^+. A generalized structure $\mathfrak{A}$ for L will also serve as a sorted first-order structure $\mathfrak{A}^+$ for L^+, where $\in$ is ascribed the obvious interpretation. One sees immediately that $\mathfrak{A} \models \phi$ iff $\mathfrak{A}^+ \models \phi^+$ for all sentences ϕ.

There are more structures for L^+ than those which may be derived from g-structures for L. We will therefore try to find a set of formulas Σ in L such that $\mathfrak{B} \models \Sigma^+$ if and only if there is a g-structure $\mathfrak{A}$ such that $\mathfrak{B}$ and $\mathfrak{A}^+$ ascribe the same truth value to all sentences. Let Σ contain the following:

1. A formula which claims E_0 to be non-empty, say $\exists x\,(x = x)$.

2. Equality schema: For any type $\tau = \langle \tau_1, \tau_2, \ldots, \tau_n\rangle$, relation symbol R of type τ, terms $t_1, t_2, \ldots, t_n$ and $s_1, s_2, \ldots, s_n$ where t_i and s_i are of type τ_i:

$$(t_1 \sim s_1 \wedge \cdots \wedge t_n \sim s_n) \to (R(t_1, \ldots, t_n) \to R(s_1, \ldots, s_n))$$

where $t \sim s$ is $t = s$ if t and s are of type 0 and $\forall x(t(x) \leftrightarrow s(x))$, where x is some variable that neither occurs in s nor in t, if s and t are of type 1.

3. Comprehension schema: For any formula ϕ and variable x, a formula of the following form, where Y is some variable not occurring in ϕ:

$$\exists Y(\forall x(\phi \leftrightarrow Y(x)))$$

If $\mathfrak{B} = \langle B_0, B_1, [\![\cdot]\!]^{\mathfrak{B}}\rangle$ is a sorted first-order structure for Σ^+ and $\{a \in B_0 \mid a \in^{\mathfrak{B}} b\} = \{a \in B_0 \mid a \in^{\mathfrak{B}} c\}$ for some $b, c \in B_1$ then ideally $b = c$. If identity of type $\langle 1, 1\rangle$ was part of SOLID, this could have been achieved with an extensionality schema: $(t_1 \sim s_1) \to (t_1 = s_1)$. In lack of identity, we construct the g-structure $\mathfrak{A} = \langle A_0, A_1, [\![\cdot]\!]^{\mathfrak{A}}\rangle$ for L by letting $A_0 = B_0$ and $A_1 = \{X \subseteq B_0 \mid \exists b \in B_1(X = \{a \in B_0 \mid a \in^{\mathfrak{B}} b\})\}$. Thanks to the equality schemata, this will induce a well defined interpretation function $[\![\cdot]\!]^{\mathfrak{A}}$ such that $[\![\phi]\!]^{\mathfrak{A}} = [\![\phi^+]\!]^{\mathfrak{B}}$ for all sentences ϕ. The comprehension schema will guarantee A_1 to contain all the definable subsets of A_0.

Compactness for a set of L-sentences Γ now reduces to first-order compactness of $\Gamma^+ \cup \Sigma^+$. To get a complete axiomatization for L, take as starting point a first-order axiomatization for L^+, use the inverse of the +-translation and add the set Σ. □

The Skolem–Löwenheim results carry over from the sorted first-order structures to the g-structures too. Observe, however, that these theorems would not only say something about the cardinality of E_0, but of E_1 as well. Thus if a countable SOLID language has an infinite g-model, it will have one where both E_0 and E_1 are countable.

3.3.2. Definite collective NPs

The standard structures come closest to our intuitions about the correct semantics for collective NPs, while the g-structures have a well behaved logic. There are inferences in SOLID for which it matters which class of structures are considered. Do any such inferences model inferences in English? To study this, whenever we have a g-structure we are interested in finding a standard structure as similar as possible to the g-structure and then see which formulas get the same truth value in the two.

DEFINITION 5.

(a) If $\mathfrak{A} = \langle A_0, A_1, [\![\cdot]\!]^{\mathfrak{A}}\rangle$ and $\mathfrak{B} = \langle B_0, B_1, [\![\cdot]\!]^{\mathfrak{B}}\rangle$ are two g-structures, we will call $\mathfrak{A}$ a **substructure** of $\mathfrak{B}$ and $\mathfrak{B}$ an **extension** of $\mathfrak{A}$, provided $A_0 \subseteq B_0$, $A_1 \subseteq B_1$, $[\![a]\!]^{\mathfrak{A}} = [\![a]\!]^{\mathfrak{B}}$ for all names a, and if R is of type $\langle \tau_1, \tau_2, \ldots, \tau_n\rangle$, then $[\![R]\!]^{\mathfrak{A}} = ([\![R]\!]^{\mathfrak{B}} \cap A_{\tau_1} \times \cdots \times A_{\tau_n})$.

(b) If in addition $A_0 = B_0$, $\mathfrak{B}$ will be called a **basic extension** of $\mathfrak{A}$.

(c) If $\mathfrak{B}$ is a basic extension of $\mathfrak{A}$ and $[\![R]\!]^{\mathfrak{A}} = [\![R]\!]^{\mathfrak{B}}$ for all relation symbols R, we will call $\mathfrak{B}$ a **minimal basic extension** of $\mathfrak{A}$, in symbols $\mathfrak{A} \leqslant \mathfrak{B}$.

(d) If $\mathfrak{B}$ is a standard structure and a (minimal) basic extension of $\mathfrak{A}$, we will call $\mathfrak{B}$ a **(minimal) completion** of $\mathfrak{A}$.

We first restrict attention to the definite collective NPs. Let a **SOLD language** be defined as a SOLID language (Definition 2) without second-order variables (point c) and quantifiers (point g). SOLD extends FOL with second-order relations and set abstraction. This is sufficient for representing the definite collectively read plural NPs as in example (15).

THEOREM 3. SOLD *is compact and admits a complete axiomatization with respect to the standard structures.*

PROOF. By induction on the construction of formulas, one checks that whenever $\mathfrak{B}$ is a basic extension of $\mathfrak{A}$, any SOLD sentence will have the same truth value in $\mathfrak{A}$ and $\mathfrak{B}$. Hence, if a set Γ of SOLD sentences has a g-model, it will also have a model. Compactness follows from the compactness of SOLID with respect to the g-structures. To get an axiomatization of SOLD, the following is needed:

1. A set of axioms and inference rules for the propositional part and the first-order quantifiers.
2. The equality schema introduced above.
3. (β-conversion): For all formulas ϕ, variables x and terms t substitutable for x in ϕ: $\hat{x}[\phi](t) \leftrightarrow [t/x]\phi$.

That this yields a complete axiomatization belongs to the folklore of logic. Keisler (1970) showed it for languages containing relations of type $\langle 1 \rangle$ as part of the study of generalized quantifiers, and Barwise (1978) considered relations of type $\langle 0, 1 \rangle$. More complex types does not add anything new, the proof is straightforward but tedious (Lønning, 1989). □

3.3.3. Indefinite collective NPs

Turning to the indefinite NPs, one faces two competing intuitions. We did not find any lexical items in English corresponding to universal quantifiers ranging over collections. From this we would not expect the full second-order logic to be exploited. On the other hand, we know that $\forall$ may be defined from $\exists$ and $\neg$, that the indefinites are represented by $\exists$, and that negation flourish in English.

DEFINITION 6.

(a) A SOLID formula ϕ will be called **persistent** if for all $\mathfrak{A}$, $\mathfrak{B}$ such that $\mathfrak{A} \leqslant \mathfrak{B}$ and all variable assignments f that take values in $\mathfrak{A}$: $\mathfrak{A} \models \phi[f]$ if and only if $\mathfrak{B} \models \phi[f]$.

(b) A formula ϕ is called **standard** if for all $\mathfrak{A}$, $\mathfrak{B}$ such that $\mathfrak{A} \leqslant \mathfrak{B}$ and all variable assignments f that take values in $\mathfrak{A}$: if $\mathfrak{A} \models \phi[f]$ then $\mathfrak{B} \models \phi[f]$.

A consistent set of persistent SOLID sentences, Γ, will always have a model; it has a g-model and since all the formulas are persistent, they will also be true in the minimal completion. We have already seen that the SOLD-formulas are persistent. The question is which further formulas representing English sentences are persistent and which are not. The following observation going back to Orey (1959) gives a syntactic class of formulas which are clearly persistent. If $\mathfrak{B}$ is an extension of $\mathfrak{A}$, a formula of the form $\exists X\, \phi$ may be true in $\mathfrak{B}$ and false in $\mathfrak{A}$ because all witnesses for X belongs to $B_1 - A_1$. But if $\mathfrak{A} \leqslant \mathfrak{B}$ and the formula has the form $\exists X(P(X) \wedge \psi)$ for some non-logical P, then a witness $c \in B_1$ will be in A_1 since $[\![P]\!]^{\mathfrak{B}} = [\![P]\!]^{\mathfrak{A}}$. The following definition generalizes the observation.

DEFINITION 7. For a second-order variable X, let the class of X-**securers** be the smallest class of formulas that contains all formulas ϕ such that:

(a) ϕ has the form $R(t_1, \ldots, t_n)$ for a non-logical n-ary relation symbol R and X is one of the t_i's.

(b) ϕ has the form $\alpha_1 \wedge \cdots \wedge \alpha_n$ for some $n \geqslant 2$ and at least one α_i is an X-securer.

(c) ϕ has the form $\alpha_1 \vee \cdots \vee \alpha_n$ for some $n \geqslant 2$ and each α_i is an X-securer.

(d) ϕ has the form $\exists x\, \psi$ or $\forall x\, \psi$ where x is a first-order variable and ψ is an X-securer.

(e) ϕ has the form $\exists Y\, \psi$ and ψ is both an X-securer and a Y-securer.

A formula ϕ is called **secure** if and only if in each subformula of the form $\exists X\, \psi$, ψ is an X-securer.

THEOREM 4. *All secure sentences are persistent.*

PROOF. For languages without set abstraction, this is a corollary of a more general result by Orey (1959) or it may be shown by simple induction. To handle set abstraction, we will for each formula ϕ construct a formula ϕ' without set terms such that $\phi \leftrightarrow \phi'$

is valid on all g-structures and if ϕ is secure or an X-securer then so is ϕ'. To construct ϕ', first exchange each sub-formula of the form $\hat{x}[\eta](t)$ with $[t/x]\eta$ (after possibly renaming variables). Then exchange each subformula of the form $R(\ldots,\hat{x}[\eta],\ldots)$ with $\exists Y\,(\forall x(Y(x) \leftrightarrow \eta) \wedge R(\ldots,Y,\ldots))$, where Y is a new variable not occurring elsewhere in the formula. □

A similar class of persistent formulas within the intensional logic IL of Montague (1973) was identified by Gallin (1975) who concluded that the extensional part of the PTQ-fragment is persistent.

To see the relevance of the theorem, consider the representation (13c) of sentence (1g) again, here repeated as (18b) and (18a).

(18) a. Three thousand soldiers surrounded the Alamo.

b. $\exists X\,(X \subseteq \mathit{Soldier} \wedge \mathit{THREETH}(X) \wedge \mathit{SURR}(X, \mathit{alamo}))$

c. $[_{S}[_{NP}[_{Det}\delta][_{N}\alpha]][_{VP}\beta]]$

d. $\exists X(X \subseteq \alpha' \wedge \delta'(X) \wedge \beta'(X))$

Sentence (18b) is secure, hence persistent. It is the non-logical predicate *SURR* which represents the verb *surround*, which secures X. The noun will in general not be a securer, as $[\![\alpha]\!]^{\mathfrak{A}} = [\![\alpha]\!]^{\mathfrak{B}}$, $\mathfrak{A} \leqslant \mathfrak{B}$ do not force $\{X \in A_1 \mid X \subseteq [\![\alpha]\!]^{\mathfrak{A}}\}$ to equal $\{X \in B_1 \mid X \subseteq [\![\alpha]\!]^{\mathfrak{B}}\}$. The same goes for the general case (18c), (18d). The most obvious candidates for securers are the verbs, β in (18c). A determiner, like δ in (18c), may be a securer provided it has a free interpretation and hence gets a representation, δ' in (18d), which is a non-logical predicate. A logical determiner can serve as a securer if it denotes a set of finite subsets of the basic domain, e.g., *exactly six* since $\{X \mid X \in A_1 \;\&\; |X| = 6\} = \{X \mid X \in B_1 \;\&\; |X| = 6\} = \{X \mid X \subseteq A_0 \;\&\; |X| = 6\}$. While a determiner like *two or more* will not be a securer, cf. the definition for *TM* in example (12b).

The example illustrates why simple sentences where the indefinite collective NP is argument to a verb or preposition are persistent. It also indicates a strategy for constructing non-persistent sentences; just negate the VP.

(19) a. Some boys did not lift a stone.

b. $\exists X\,(X \subseteq \mathit{Boy} \wedge \mathit{TM}(X) \wedge \neg\exists y(\mathit{Stone}(y) \wedge \mathit{LIFT}(X, y)))$

In (19b) *LIFT* is not a securer of X, and if *TM* is ascribed the logical interpretation: all set of individuals of cardinality at least two, then it is not a securer either. Formula (19b) is not persistent.

Some authors cast doubts about whether (19b) is a correct representation of (19a), however. It should be observed that it is not easy to determine what the sentence should mean. The formal fragment would easily generate four different readings depending on whether the subject NP is read collectively or distributively, and whether the negation has narrow or wide scope. Formula (19b) represents the collective reading with narrow scope negation. This reading seems the less likely one. To see why, suppose there are 10 boys present. Then there are $2^{10} - 11$, i.e. 1013, different collections consisting of two or more boys. For (19b) to be false, all these collections would have to have lifted a stone. Verkuyl (1988) says that the distinction between the collective and distributive reading vanishes when the verb is negated. In the same spirit, Link (1990) proposes to read (19a) roughly as (20a).

(20) a. There are some boys such that no one of them has participated with other boys in lifting a stone.

b. There are at least two boys who have not participated with other boys in lifting a stone.

We could have expressed this as a formula in SOLID, but the representation is much more elegant in a system which handles individuals and collections to be of the same type, cf. Section 4. Observe that sentence (20a) is equivalent to the persistent sentence (20b). We will not here try to reach any conclusion with respect to the question on whether formula (19b) represents a possible reading of sentence (19a), but rather conclude Solomonicly that to answer whether negation gives rise to non-persistent formulas, one has to determine the meaning of the negation.

In Section 2.3 we observed some effects of universal quantification ranging over collections of a specific size. Thus sentence (8) repeated as (21a) can be represented by (21b).

(21) a. Every two persons resemble each other.

b. $\forall X(X \subseteq \mathit{Person} \wedge \mathit{TWO}(X) \to \mathit{RESEMBLE}(X))$

c. Competing companies have common interests.

d. $\forall X(X \subseteq \mathit{Company} \wedge \mathit{COMPETE}(X) \wedge \mathit{TM}(X) \to \mathit{COMMON}(X))$

In (21a) *TWO* is naturally read as *exactly two*, hence a securer, and (21b) is persistent. Similarly, if (21c) from Link (1987) is read as (21d), one may simply assume that *COMPETE* is a non-logical predicate and a securer.

We have so far considered examples where the plural NP only fills one argument position within the sentence. But more may be achieved by anaphoric pronouns. Consider example sentence (22a) taken from Boolos (1984a) who symbolizes it as (22b) presupposing quantification over horses and using 0, s, F for *Zev, the sire of, is faster than*, respectively.

(22) a. There are some horses that are all faster than Zev and also faster than the sire of any horse that is slower than all of them.

b. $\exists X(\exists z(X(z)) \wedge \forall z(X(z) \to F(z,0))$
$\wedge \forall z(\forall z(X(z) \to F(z,y)) \to \forall z(X(z) \to F(z,s(y)))))$

This formula is not persistent. As Boolos points out, if (22b) is reinterpreted in standard arithmetic, reading s as the successor function and F as *greater than*, it becomes false in the standard model of arithmetic and true in all non-standard models. Boolos (1984b) also argues that sentence (2d), here repeated as (23a), which Quine (1974) represented as (23b), in addition has another reading represented as (23c), where $F(x)$, $E(x)$, $A(x,y)$ mean "x was one of Fiorecchio's men", "x entered the building", and "x was accompanied by y", respectively.

(23) a. Some of Fiorecchio's men entered the building unaccompanied by anyone else.

b. $\exists x(F(x) \wedge E(x) \wedge \forall y(A(x,y) \rightarrow F(y)))$

c. $\exists X(\exists z\,(X(z)) \wedge \forall z\,(X(z) \rightarrow F(z))$
$\wedge \forall z\,(X(z) \rightarrow E(z)) \wedge \forall z \forall y\,(X(z) \wedge A(z,y) \rightarrow X(y)))$

The second-order sentence (23c) is not equivalent to any first-order sentence, and not persistent. This can be observed by substituting $z > 0$ for $F(z)$ and $E(z)$ and $z = y + 1$ for $A(z, y)$. Then the sentence claims the existence of a set of numbers which is not well founded. Hence it is true in any non-standard model for arithmetic, but not in the standard model.

If we think that each sentence has a truth condition which can be expressed by a logical formula independently of reference to the speaker or hearer, what Kripke (1977) calls *sentence meaning*, then there does not seem to be any alternative to saying that occurrences of collective NPs in English exemplify non-persistent sentences.

Others have argued that the meaning of an utterance cannot always be reduced to sentence meaning. Sometimes, a speaker uses a definite description (Donnellan, 1966) or an indefinite NP (Fodor and Sag, 1982) with a particular referent in mind, and the utterance is then about that object. I have argued elsewhere that if one accepts the concept of referential use then (22a) and (23a) are examples of such referential uses (Lønning, 1989). If one further holds the view that the utterance is not true unless it is the object to which the speaker intends to refer which has the ascribed property, then there is no simple formula which corresponds to the utterance. The closest one would get would be to introduce a constant of type 1 for the object to which the speaker intends to refer. In that case the representation becomes persistent but not a representation of the sentence as such. In other words, the logical complexity of the collective NPs will depend on the view one holds with respect to reference and the relationship between sentence meaning and utterance meaning.

All candidates for non-persistent sentences considered so far are standard. Do the collectively read plural NPs of English exemplify even more complex logical formulas? When the language contains anaphoric pronouns, negation and universal quantification might also be expressed by conditional sentences. Boolos (1984b) considers examples which might need Π^1_1-formulas for their interpretation. One might also consider how negation and anaphora interact and whether there are general recursive mechanisms in English generating arbitrary complex quantifier prefixes. Boolos argues that any second-order sentence can be translated into English, while Lønning (1989) casts doubt on this.

4. First-order approaches

4.1. Background

We will now consider a different approach to collections, to regard them as individuals. Rather than adding levels to the logical hierarchy, add structure to the basic domain. While we traced the higher-order approach back to Russell, there might be some evidence for attributing the current approach to Frege. In the before mentioned letter to Russell, he separated the collective reading of (1a) and (1b) both from the distributive reading of (24a) and from a reading in terms of classes, as in (24b).

(24) a. Socrates and Plato are philosophers.

b. The class of prime numbers comprises infinitely many objects.

The collection is regarded as a whole, while the class is not, "Secondly, if we are given a whole, it is not yet determined what we envisage as its parts. As parts of a regiment I can regard the battalions, the companies or the individual soldiers [...] On the other hand, if we are given a class, it is determined what objects are members of it." (Frege, 1980, p. 140). Like Russell, Frege more pointed to a solution than worked it out, and should not be made responsible for any details in the proposal we present. He never published the mentioned remarks, and, as the quotation shows, he did not distinguish clearly between the plural NPs and the group-denoting NPs. Besides, Frege's system was not typed and can strictly speaking not be taken as a defense for a first-order approach, but rather for a type free approach.

Another root to this approach can be found in Lésniewski's *mereology* which inspired Leonard and Goodman's (1940) *Calculus of individuals* (see (Eberle, 1970) for a systematic overview of the formal theory). Lésniewski's goal was an alternative to set theory for the foundations of mathematics, Leonard and Goodman's aim was a formal ontology, while Lewis (1991) attempts to build a common framework for ontology and set theory.

One step in the direction from ontology towards semantics was the paper by Massey (1976) based on the calculus of individuals. The most influential paper within this paradigm is Link (1983), where algebraic structures are used. Another important source is Scha (1981), which shares many assumptions with Link but states the theory in a somewhat different framework based on sets. Mentioned should also be Blau (1981) which discussed a first-order approach to the plural definite description.

4.2. Basics

To a question like, *Who ate the chicken?*, one may answer *John* or *the girls*. This suggests that a plural NP like *the girls* should denote an object of the same type as *John*, and a VP like *ate the chicken* should have one denotation which includes both ordinary individuals and collections. To achieve this, one may regard the individual domain, E, as a subset of a larger set of objects, O, and let proper nouns denote members of E, $[\![Ann]\!] \in E$, and common count nouns in the singular denote subsets of E. The larger set, O, in addition has as members collections, like $[\![Ann\ and\ Mary]\!]$ and $[\![the\ girls]\!]$, and a VP denotes a subset of O.

Most proposals assume the domain O to be structured in a way which relates the collections to each other and to the individuals. The proposals have differed with respect to whether the structure should be expressed by set theoretic or algebraic means, and with respect to what sort of algebraic structure to choose. We think the structure should not be founded on ontological intuitions alone, but on the effect it has on the interpretation of the collective NPs. Accordingly, our strategy will be to first introduce a language for representing the collective NPs and interpretations where we assume no particular structure on O, nor assume anything about the relationship between E and O besides $E \subseteq O$. Then we will proceed to discuss constraints on the interpretations of the NPs and which structure these constraints induce on O. The language will basically be a first-order language with identity and quantifiers ranging over the whole domain O. We want to be able to restrict attention to E. One possibility is to let the first-order language be sorted with two sorts e and o corresponding to the two sets E and O. Hence e will be a subsort of o; the terms of sort e will also be of sort o. All constants and variables will belong to one of the two sorts and each argument place of a relation will have an associated sort. The intended application is to represent proper nouns by terms of sort e, simple common nouns in the singular, like *soldier*, by unary relations of type $\langle e\rangle$, while a VP will be of type $\langle o\rangle$ and a TV of type $\langle o,o\rangle$. As a convention, $x, x_1, x_2, \ldots$ will be e-variables and $y, y_1, y_2, \ldots$ will be o-variables.

To interpret the plural definite description, we will extend the language at one point:

DEFINITION 8 (*Tau*).
(a) If v is an e-variable and ϕ a formula, then $\tau v[\phi]$ is an o-term.
(b) There is a partial function T, $T : \text{POW}(E) \to O$, such that
a. If $X \subseteq E$ is definable and $X \neq \emptyset$ then $X \in \text{DOM}(T)$.
b. $[\![\tau v[\phi]]\!]_g = T(\{a \in E \mid [\![\phi]\!]_{g^v_a} = \mathbf{t}\})$.
c. In particular, for all $e \in E$, $T(\{e\}) = e$.

As an example, sentence (1e) can be represented as (25a) where x and *alamo* are terms of type e, *Soldier* of type $\langle e\rangle$ and *Surround* of type $\langle o,o\rangle$.

(25) $\mathit{Surround}(\tau x[\mathit{Soldier}(x)], \mathit{alamo})$

A minimal assumption we will keep throughout is that the definite description is extensional, if, e.g., $[\![\mathit{girl}]\!] = [\![\mathit{kind\ girl}]\!]$, then $[\![\mathit{the\ girls}]\!] = [\![\mathit{the\ kind\ girls}]\!]$. This corresponds to expressing the interpretation of τ in terms of a function T.

One notorious problem is what to do with a term like *the soldiers* when there are no soldiers. The term $\tau x[\mathit{Soldier}(x)]$ will be defined, and the first alternative is to ascribe it an interpretation by letting $\emptyset \in \text{DOM}(T)$. The proper representation of sentence (1e) should then contain the claim that there are at least two soldiers in a similar way as we did it in the higher-order approach.

(26) $$\mathit{Surround}(\tau x[\mathit{Soldier}(x)], \mathit{alamo}) \wedge \exists x_1 \exists x_2\, (x_1 \neq x_2 \wedge \mathit{Soldier}(x_1) \wedge \mathit{Soldier}(x_2))$$

The second alternative is to exclude $\emptyset$ from $\text{DOM}(T)$, stick to the representation (25) and let the extra claim be part of the interpretation schema for $\tau x[\phi]$. The extra claim may then either be stated, leading to a false statement if it is not fulfilled (Link, 1983), or presupposed leading to an undefined statement (Blau, 1981). Many proposals for the semantics of plurals have used structures where $\emptyset \notin \text{DOM(T)}$ (e.g., Link, 1990; Landman, 1989, 1991). From a semantic point of view, it does not matter whether $T(\emptyset)$ is defined, as long as it is not taken as a possible denotation for the plural NPs. But as we will see, it will affect which class of algebraic structures we end up with.

A similar discussion may be raised concerning T applied to singletons. We have here chosen the alternative to include singleton sets in the domain of T. Thereby, both definite descriptions in the singular and definite descriptions in the plural may be represented by

τ and interpreted by T. The difference between the singular and the plural will have to be captured by different additional claims in the representations; e.g., formula (26) should only be used for the plural.

While the noun in the singular, *girl*, denotes a subset of E, the noun in the plural, *girls*, will denote a subset of the larger domain O. There is a natural connection between the semantics of the plural noun and that of the plural definite description. If there are some young girls, we will assume $[\![\textit{the young girls}]\!]$ to be a member of $[\![\textit{girls}]\!]$. Conversely, we may assume all members of $[\![\textit{girls}]\!]$ to be composed from individual girls in this way. We will introduce a new symbol $*$ into the formal language to model the plural nouns, such that

DEFINITION 9 (*Star*).
(a) If ϕ is a formula and v an e-variable then ${}^*v[\phi]$ is a relation of type $\langle o\rangle$.
(b) $[\![{}^*v[\phi]]\!]_g = \{T(X) \mid X \subseteq \{a \in E \mid [\![\phi]\!]_{g_a^v} = \mathbf{t}\} \;\&\; X \in \textsc{Dom}(T) \;\&\; X \neq \emptyset\}$.

Sentence (1f) can be represented

(27) $\exists y({}^*x[\mathit{Girl}(x)](y) \wedge \mathit{Gather}(y))$

As we assumed $T(\{g\})$ to be defined and equal to g for $g \in E$, $[\![\mathit{Girl}]\!]$ will be a subset of $[\![{}^*x[\mathit{Girl}(x)]]\!]$, i.e. each individual girl will belong to $[\![{}^*x[\mathit{Girl}(x)]]\!]$. This seems appropriate if *girls* in the NP *no girls* is represented by ${}^*x[\mathit{Girl}(x)]$. Similarly, Kamp and Reyle (1993) show that dependent plurals include simple individuals in their denotations. A sentence like *every mother loves her children* entails that mothers who have only one child love it. Again some representation which includes both individuals and collections are appropriate. On the other hand, by choosing this interpretation of ${}^*x[\mathit{Girl}(x)]$ in example (27), something more must be added to the formula to express that the NP *Some girls* refers to a collection consisting of at least two individuals, similarly as we proposed in the second-order approach and for the plural definite description in formula (26).

To interpret the collective conjunction, we introduce a binary operator, $+$, defined on O, such that $[\![\textit{Hillary and Bill}]\!] = [\![\textit{Hillary}]\!] + [\![\textit{Bill}]\!]$ and a corresponding function symbol, $\oplus$, written infix.

DEFINITION 10 (*Oplus*).
(a) If t and s are o-terms, then so is $t \oplus s$.
(b) A structure contains a function $+ : O \times O \to O$, and $[\![t \oplus s]\!] = [\![t]\!] + [\![s]\!]$.

Sentence (1a) can be represented by the following formula where *Lfs* is shorthand for *laid the foundations of spectral theory*.

(28) $\mathit{Lfs}(\mathit{bunsen} \oplus \mathit{kirchoff})$

Observe that this same operator can handle conjunction between collections, *the secretaries and the assistants* or between an individual and a collection *Bill and his secretaries*. If we were to introduce conjunction in the higher-order framework of Section 3, we would have to handle these cases separately.

We will call a language as described in this section, with the two sorts e and o and the special symbols τ, $*$ and $\oplus$ a **first-order language for plurals (FOLP)**. A structure for a FOLP language can be written $\langle O, E, T, +, [\![\cdot]\!]\rangle$ where $[\![\cdot]\!]$ interprets the nonlogical symbols.

4.3. Ontology

Plural definite descriptions and collective conjunction have more semantic properties than what is reflected by these quite general structures. We will consider some possible constraints on the functions T and $+$ to capture these intuitions. There are three possible constraints on $+$:

C1 (**Commutativity**). *For all* a *and* b *in* O: $a + b = b + a$.
C2 (**Idempotency**). *For all* a *in* O: $a + a = a$.
C3 (**Associativity**). *For all* a, b, *and* c *in* O: $((a + b) + c) = (a + (b + c))$.

The assumption underlying constraint (C1) is that *Hillary and Bill* and *Bill and Hillary* denote the same collection and are ascribed the same collective properties. If every doctor is a lawyer and every lawyer is a doctor, *the lawyers and the doctors* and *the doctors* should denote the same, hence idempotency (C2). An NP like *Ann, Mary and Frances* is interpreted by repeated use of $+$. Associativity together with commutativity will then assure it to have the same denotation as *Mary, Frances and Ann*. We consider possible counter examples in Section 4.7.

One type of structure often used for interpreting plural NP's is semilattices. A **partially ordered set** is a set X together with a binary relation $\leqslant$ on X which is reflexive, transitive and anti-symmetric. A partially ordered set is a **join-semilattice** if any two elements a, b have a least upper bound c, i.e. $a \leqslant c$ and $b \leqslant c$ and for all d, if $a \leqslant d$ and $b \leqslant d$ then $c \leqslant d$. This least upper bound, or supremum, is called the **sum** or **join** of a and b, in symbols often written $a \vee b$. Similarly, a partially ordered set is a **meet-semilattice** if any two elements have a greatest lower bound called **meet** or **product** (in symbols $a \wedge b$) and a **lattice** if it is both a join-semilattice and a meet-semilattice. It is a standard observation in lattice theory that a semilattice can be defined from the join operation as from the ordering:

THEOREM 5. *If* $a \leqslant b$ *is defined on* O *by* $a+b = b$, *then* $\langle O, \leqslant\rangle$ *becomes a join-semilattice with* $+$ *as join if and only if* $+$ *is commutative, idempotent and associative.*

For a proof of this and other lattice theoretical results in the sequel, consult a text book like Grätzer (1978) or Landman (1991). Thus, to say that the domain is a semilattice amounts to nothing else than saying that conjunction has these three properties. We will use $\mathcal{SL}$ to denote the class of structures satisfying the three constraints.

We turn to the function T and the following possible constraints:

C4 (**Supremum**). $T(X) = \bigvee X$ *for all* $X \in \mathrm{DOM}(T)$.
C5 (**Generation**). *For each element* $o \in O$ *there is an* $X \subseteq E$ *s.t.* $o = T(X)$.
C6 (**Completeness**). *Each non-empty* $X \subseteq E$ *is a member of* $\mathrm{DOM}(T)$.

On a semilattice the sum operation generalizes to any non-empty finite subset of the domain by $\bigvee\{a_1, a_2, \ldots, a_n\} = a_1 + a_2 + \cdots + a_n$. If Tom, Dick and Harry are the boys and the only boys, then it is reasonable to assume that *Tom, Dick and Harry* and *the boys* denote the same. Correspondingly, one may let T be interpreted as lattice supremum as expressed by constraint (C4). The constraint (C5) claims all objects to be built up from individuals. It excludes the possibility of e.g., individuals being built up from atoms which are not individuals. From the interpretation rule for $*$, if X is a nonempty definable subset of *Girl*, it will form a collection in **Girl*. But what if X is not definable? From constraint (C6), X will form a collection whether it is definable or not.

In the literature on plurals, structures where the supremum of each non-empty set, finite or infinite, is defined, have been called **complete join-semilattices** We will follow this practice, but one should be aware that in most of the algebraic literature, the term *complete structure* entails that the relevant operations are defined for the empty set as well.

THEOREM 6. a) *If a* $\mathcal{SL}$*-structure satisfies* (C4), (C5) *and* (C6) *then* O *is a complete join-semilattice.*

b) *If in addition* $\emptyset \in \text{DOM}(T)$ *then* O *is a complete lattice.*

PROOF. Observe first that if $b \in O$ then $b = \bigvee\{e \in E \mid e \leqslant b\}$ from (C4) and (C5). Let B be a nonempty subset of O. Then $\bigvee\{e \in E \mid \exists b \in B\,(e \leqslant b)\}$ will be defined from (C6) and from the observation it will equal $\bigvee B$.

For the second part of the theorem, if $\emptyset \in \text{DOM}(T)$ then $\bigvee \emptyset = 0$ is defined from (C4). If B is a subset of O, $\bigwedge B = \bigvee\{a \in O \mid \forall b \in B\,(a \leqslant b)\}$ will always be defined. □

We will accordingly call the class of structures satisfying constraints (C1)–(C6) for **complete join-semilattice structures,** $\mathcal{CJSL}$. If $\emptyset \in \text{DOM}(T)$ we will call them **complete lattice structures,** $\mathcal{CL}$. A $\mathcal{CJSL}$-structure without a bottom element, we will call a $\mathcal{CJSL}_{+}$**-structure**. As mentioned earlier, many of the proposals from the literature assume $\emptyset \notin \text{DOM}(T)$ and make use of $\mathcal{CJSL}_{+}$- structures (e.g., Link, 1990; Landman, 1989, 1991).

The restrictions introduced so far force certain objects to be equal but do not prevent any objects from being equal. For example, there are $\mathcal{CJSL}_{+}$-structures where *john, bill, harry, dick* all denote different objects, still *bill* $\oplus$ *john* and *harry* $\oplus$ *dick* denote the same. To avoid this, the following constraint may be added:

C7 (Free). *For all* $X, Y \in \text{DOM}(T)$: *if* $T(X) = T(Y)$ *then* $X = Y$.

If this is added to the other constraints, E will be called a set of **free generators** for O as a complete join-semilattice (see Landman, 1989).

THEOREM 7. a) *A* $\mathcal{CL}$*-structure* $\langle O, E, [\![\cdot]\!]\rangle$ *satisfies* (C7) *if and only if* O *is a complete atomic Boolean algebra with* E *the set of atoms.*

b) *A* $\mathcal{CJSL}_{+}$*-structure satisfies* (C7) *if and only if* O *is the substructure of a complete atomic Boolean algebra with* E *the set of atoms one gets by deleting the bottom element.*

PROOF. From constraint (C4), T is a homomorphism from $\langle \text{DOM}(T), \cup\rangle$ to $\langle O, +\rangle$. From (C5), T is onto O. If T in addition is injective, (C7), then the two structures are isomorphic. From (C6) $\text{DOM}(T) = \text{POW}(E)$, and $\langle \text{POW}(E), \cup\rangle$ is a complete atomic Boolean algebra with $\{\{e\}\colon e \in E\}$ the set of atoms. □

We will accordingly call these two classes of structures $\mathcal{CABA}$ (**complete atomic Boolean algebra**) and $\mathcal{CABA}_{+}$, respectively. The models and language we end up with are quite similar to (a part of) those proposed by Link (1983, 1991). There is a difference between FOLP and the language used there, LP, with respect to which symbols are basic and which ones are defined. Another difference is that the denotation of a singular common noun is not necessarily a set of atoms in Link's proposals. The interpretation of the plural phrases remain similar, however, $[\![the\ P]\!] = \bigvee [\![P]\!]$ and $[\![{}^*P]\!] = \{\bigvee Y \mid Y \neq \emptyset \ \&\ Y \subseteq [\![P]\!]\}$.

In the literature on collective readings, some proposals are based on lattices (e.g., Link, 1987), while others are given in terms of Boolean algebras (e.g., Link, 1983). The reason to use Boolean algebras in other contexts is the wish to model all the connectives; disjunction, negation as well as conjunction. The only Boolean connective used in constructing collective NP's is *and*, but the proposition shows that it has a function to use Boolean algebras as models; they are special kinds of join-semilattices that put special constraints on the behavior of the join operation (cf. Landman, 1989, 1991; Lønning, 1989; and Link, 1990).

Each complete atomic Boolean algebra is isomorphic to a power set of some set and each $\mathcal{CABA}$-structure corresponds to a **power set structure** $\langle O, E, \bigcup, \cup, [\![\cdot]\!]\rangle$, where $O = \text{Pow}(X)$ and $E = \{\{i\}\colon i \in X\}$ for some set $X \neq \emptyset$, where $[\![\tau v[\phi]]\!]_g = \bigcup(\{a \in E \mid [\![\phi]\!]_{g^v_a} = \mathbf{t}\})$ and $[\![a \oplus b]\!]_g = [\![a]\!]_g \cup [\![b]\!]_g$. Similar structures were proposed by Scha (1981). If semantics is viewed first and foremost in terms of entailment, then there is no difference between the two model concepts. If one, on the other hand, thinks that semantics carry some deeper ontological commitments, and that the use of sets forces one to a certain ontological view, then one might claim there to be a difference (cf., Massey, 1976; Link, 1983, 1984; Lewis, 1991).

We gave an example which motivated the freeness constraint (C7). But observe that a consequence will be that two NPs like *the window parts* and *the windows* cannot get the same denotation if there are window parts which are not windows. At this point, we depart from the mereological tradition, where the sum formation is thought of as the summation of physical stuff (Leonard and Goodman, 1940). Blau (1981) discusses the injectivity of T for examples like *the cards* and *the decks of cards*, and concludes that it should be possible for the two to get the same denotation. Hence, T should not be injective. In a footnote added in print, however, he casts doubt on the identification because of the effect of predicates like *are counted*. Link (1983) includes two different preorders on the plural domain, the individual or i-ordering corresponding to the injectivity of T, and the material or m-ordering which could identify *the windows* and *the window parts*.

4.4. *Compositionality*

The interpretations described so far are compatible with different approaches to the syntax-semantics interface, whether Montague grammar, generalized quantifiers or DRT. We will sketch an extensional Montagovian approach to bring out the similarities and differences to the higher-order proposal from Section 3.2. Both e and o will be basic types besides t, and e is a subtype of o. A VP will be of type (o, t), whether it is collective or distributive, a noun in the singular will be of type (e, t), and the determiner *every* will be of type $((e, t), ((o, t), t))$ with the interpretation $\lambda X_{(e,t)} \lambda Y_{(o,t)} (\forall x_e (X_{(e,t)}(x_e) \rightarrow$

$Y_{(o,t)}(x_e)))$. When it comes to the plural NPs, like *three girls*, one possibility is to assume two different entries, one collective and one distributive, both of the type $((o,t),t)$ (but see Section 5.1). As the plural nouns when read distributively are handled exactly as the singular nouns, plural nouns will get the same interpretation as the corresponding singular noun, of type (e,t). The effect of the collectivization, $*$, will be incorporated into the collective determiner. The two interpretations of the determiners will then be as in (29a) and (29b), where *Three*(y) claims that y has exactly three different individuals as parts.

(29) a. $\lambda X_{(e,t)} \lambda Y_{(o,t)}\, [\mathit{Three}(\tau x[X_{(e,t)}(x) \wedge Y_{(o,t)}(x)])]$

b. $\lambda X_{(e,t)} \lambda Y_{(o,t)}\, [\exists y_o\, ({}^*X_{(e,t)}(y_o) \wedge Y_{(o,t)}(y_o) \wedge \mathit{Three}(y_o))]$

One might try to incorporate the collective conjunction into this framework, as a conjunction of two quantifiers of type $((o,t),t)$. But as the natural type of the conjunction is to conjoin terms of type o, it seems more natural to depart from the Montagovian approach of handling all NPs as quantifiers and rather let definite and indefinite NPs get type o and let the existential quantifier be introduced by a larger context (cf. Hoeksema, 1983; Lønning, 1987b). This is the way the collective readings are handled in DRT (Kamp and Reyle, 1993).

How should the group-denoting nouns be accommodated in the first-order approach? There are several alternatives depending on how one answers the following question. Should a group, a committee, a set be identified with its members; e.g., should *the committee* and *the members of the committee* denote the same object?

If one answers *no* to this question, then the group-denoting nouns may be handled as other nouns, i.e., as of type (e,t) (e.g., Barker, 1992). Such an approach makes no attempt at explaining semantically why group-denoting nouns in the singular may cooccur with verbs in the plural. A sentence like (30a) will not be excluded on structural semantic grounds and maybe neither on syntactic grounds. The strangeness of the sentence will be ascribed to the meaning of the involved words, cf. that (30b) is well formed.

(30) a. ? John surrounded Alamo.

b. The wall surrounded the city.

If one, on the other hand, finds it correct to always identify *the committee* and *the members of the committee*, one possibility is to represent *committee* by a predicate of type (o,t). This will explain why the group-denoting NP in the singular agrees with a plural verb. On the other hand, it does not explain why such an NP may also agree with a verb in the singular. This approach will come close to Bennett's proposal considered in Section 3.2, except that it will be easy to consider the collective reading of *the committees*, as well, by interpreting the plural definite description as the supremum operator on O, and not only on E. This process will stop in the sense that it will identify the "new" collections with "old" ones, e.g., given some group of committees of women, the following NPs will all get the same denotation: *the women who are members of a committee*, *the committees*, *the group of committees* (cf. Section 4.7).

4.5. Logic

A FOLP language extends a first-order language with expressions of the form $\tau v[\phi]$ and $^*v[\phi]$. To get an axiomatization corresponding to the quite general structures in Section 4.2, we could start with a first-order axiomatization and add schemata expressing the extensionality of τ, the interpretation of τ with respect to the singletons, and the relationship between τ and $*$. We will not give the details, but move on to the more restricted structures considered in Section 4.3. We consider the following schemata where t, s, u vary through all terms, ϕ, ψ through all formulas and x and y through all e-variables and o-variables, respectively. $t \preceq s$ is shorthand for $t \oplus s = s$.

(A1) $t \oplus s = s \oplus t$
(A2) $t \oplus t = t$
(A3) $(t \oplus s) \oplus u = t \oplus (s \oplus u)$
(A4) $\exists x\, \phi \to (\forall x\, (\phi \to x \preceq \tau x[\phi]) \wedge \forall y\, (\forall x\, (\phi \to x \preceq y) \to \tau x[\phi] \preceq y))$
(A5) $\forall y\, (y = \tau x[x \preceq y])$
(A6) $\exists x\, \phi \to (\tau x[\phi] = \tau x[\psi] \to \forall x\, (\phi \leftrightarrow \psi))$

The first three schemata correspond exactly to the first three constraints. On the $\mathcal{SL}$-structures, if $\emptyset \notin \text{DOM}(T)$, (A4) corresponds to (C4), and it is not too difficult to see that (A4) and (A5) correspond to (C4) and (C5), and that (A6) corresponds to (C7). If $\emptyset \in \text{DOM(T)}$, one gets similar correspondences by deleting the antecedent in (A4) and (A6).

We will soon see that it is not possible to express the completeness constraint (C6) within FOLP. On the other hand, the theorems we showed for the structures satisfying (C1)–(C6) have variants based on (C1)–(C5). Thus in a structure satisfying (C1)–(C5), each definable subset of the full domain O will have a supremum, and we will refer to the class as the **definable complete join-semilattice** structures, $\mathcal{DCJSL}$. If in addition $\emptyset \in \text{DOM}(T)$, the structure will be a lattice where each definable subset has both a supremum and an infimum, hence a **definable complete lattice** structure, $\mathcal{DCL}$. If a $\mathcal{DCL}$-structure also satisfies (C7), it will be a Boolean algebra, hence a **definable complete Boolean algebra** structure, $\mathcal{DCABA}$. Such a structure will correspond to a **generalized set structure** $\langle O, E, \bigcup, \cup, [\![\cdot]\!]\rangle$ where there is a set X such that $E = \{\{x\} \mid x \in X\}$ and $O \subseteq \text{POW}(X)$. If $\emptyset \notin \text{DOM}(T)$ and (C1)–(C5), (C7), one gets the substructure of a $\mathcal{DCABA}$ where the bottom element is deleted, hence a $\mathcal{DCABA}_+$-structure. All these results follow by inspecting the proofs for the similar results when (C6) is included.

The easiest way to get an axiomatization of FOLP with respect to the considered classes of structures is by observing that (C4), and hence (A4), expresses two claims; that each definable subset of E has a supremum and that $\tau x[\phi]$ denotes this supremum. The first part, call it (C4′), can be expressed by:

(A4′) $\exists x\, \phi \to \exists y_2\, (\forall x\, (\phi \to x \preceq y_2) \wedge \forall y_1\, (\forall x\, (\phi \to x \preceq y_1) \to y_2 \preceq y_1))$

If this holds, the term $\tau x[\phi]$ can be considered a defined term by the repeated use of (31a). Similarly $^*x[\phi]$ may be defined by (31b) provided (C1)–(C5) hold.

(31) a. $R(\ldots, \tau x[\phi], \ldots) \leftrightarrow \exists x\, \phi \wedge \exists y_2\, (\forall x\, (\phi \to x \preceq y_2)$
$\wedge \forall y_1 (\forall x (\phi \to x \preceq y_1) \to y_2 \preceq y_1) \wedge R(\ldots, y_2, \ldots))$

b. $^*x[\phi](y) \leftrightarrow \forall x\,(x \preceq y \rightarrow \phi) \wedge \exists x\,(x \preceq y)$

THEOREM 8. FOLP *is compact and has complete axiomatization with respect to the classes of structures:* $\mathcal{DCJSL}$, $\mathcal{DCL}$, $\mathcal{DCJSL}_+$, $\mathcal{DCABA}$, $\mathcal{DCABA}_+$.

PROOF. Since the terms which are not strictly first-order can be considered to be defined terms, it reduces to showing that the classes of structures mentioned can be defined within the sorted first-order language with the binary function symbol $\oplus$. The axiom schemata discussed above show how this can be done. □

At this point the reader probably recognizes certain similarities to the second-order framework in Section 3.3, in particular, the similarities between the power set structures and hence also the $\mathcal{CABA}$-structures and the standard structures for SOLID, and between the $\mathcal{DCABA}$ and generalized set structures and the g-structures for SOLID:

THEOREM 9. FOLP *is not compact, does not have any complete axiomatization, and does not satisfy the Skolem-Löwenheim properties with respect to* $\mathcal{CABA}$*-structures, nor with respect to* $\mathcal{CJSL}$*-structures.*

PROOF. Given a SOLID language L without set abstraction, and let Σ^+ be the translation into the corresponding first-order language L^+ with the symbol $\in$ of sort $\langle 0, 1\rangle$ considered in the proof of Theorem 2. We will define a corresponding FOLP language L^* and translation from L^+ (and L) into L^* by exchanging the two disjoint sorts $0, 1$ with the sorts e, o, respectively, and translating the atomic formula $t^+ \in S^+$ in L^+, derived from $T(s)$ in L, into $t^* \leqslant S^*$ in L^* (where t^+ is of sort 0, S^+ of sort 1, t^* of sort e and S^* of sort o). The rest of the translation is structure preserving.

From a given structure $\mathfrak{A} = \langle A, [\![\cdot]\!]\rangle$ for L we shall construct a power set structure, $\mathfrak{A}^* = \langle O, E, \bigcup, \cup, [\![\cdot]\!]^*\rangle$ for L^* as follows. Let $O = \mathrm{POW}(A)$ and $E = \{\{a\} \mid a \in A\}$. Let $f : A \cup \mathrm{POW}(A) \rightarrow \mathrm{POW}(A)$ be defined by $f(x) = \{x\}$ for $x \in A$ and $f(X) = X$ for $X \subseteq A$. Define $[\![\cdot]\!]^*$ by $[\![t^*]\!]^* = f([\![t]\!])$ if t is a constant of sort 0 or 1, and $[\![R^*]\!]^* = \{\langle f(x_1), f(x_2), \ldots, f(x_n)\rangle \mid \langle (x_1), (x_2), \ldots (x_n)\rangle \in [\![R]\!]\}$, for relation symbols R. One may prove by induction that $\mathfrak{A} \models \phi$ if and only if $\mathfrak{A}^* \models \phi^*$.

Each power set structure $\mathfrak{B}$ for L^* can be seen to be of the form $\mathfrak{A}^*$ for some L-structure $\mathfrak{A}$. Hence the results follow for the power set structures and for the $\mathcal{CABA}$-structures. Since a structure belongs to $\mathcal{CABA}$ if it belongs to both $\mathcal{CJSL}$ and $\mathcal{DCABA}$ the result also follows for the $\mathcal{CJSL}$-structures, and similarly for the classes $\mathcal{CL}$, $\mathcal{CJSL}_+$ and $\mathcal{CABA}_+$. □

Observe that the correspondence between standard structures for L and power set structures for L^* can be extended to a correspondence between g-structures for L and $\mathcal{DCABA}$-structures for L^*. One might also construct a translation in the other direction, from a FOLP language L and into a SOLID language L^S, which yields a similar equivalence between classes of structures (Lønning, 1989). This translation may be done such that e-variables translate into first-order variables and o-variables translate into second-order variables and may be used for studying the properties of fragments of FOLP. Consider the part of FOLP used for the definite NPs, i.e. τ-terms and e-quantification, but no o-quantification. If a set of sentences from this fragment has a $\mathcal{DCABA}$ model, one where T is a partial function, any completion to a full $\mathcal{CABA}$ structure where T is total will be a model as well. This fragment will be compact and admits a complete axiomatization also with respect to the classes $\mathcal{CABA}$ and $\mathcal{CJSL}$.

The discussion of the indefinites carries over, too. Concepts like securer, and secure formula can be defined by translation.

(32) a. $\exists y({}^{*}Boy(y) \wedge Tm(y) \wedge Meet(y))$

b. $\exists y(\exists x_1(x_1 \preceq y) \wedge \forall x_1(x_1 \preceq y \rightarrow F(x_1, 0))$
$\wedge \forall x_2(\forall x_3(x_3 \preceq y \rightarrow F(x_3, x_2)) \rightarrow \forall x_3(x_3 \preceq y \rightarrow F(x_3, s(x_2)))))$

In formula (32a) the verb *Meet* is a securer of y, while **Boy* is not. That *Boy* gets the same denotation in a structure and its extension does not secure that **Boy* does. In sentence (32b), a representation of sentence (22) from Section 3.3.3, the variable y is not secured, however. In other words, the results with respect to the complexity of the entailment relation between English sentences are the same whether we model them in the second-order logic or in this first-order theory.

4.6. *Mass terms*

There are obvious semantic parallels between mass nouns and plural count nouns; consider the similarities between the sentences (1e) and (33a) and between (1g) and (33b).

(33) a. The water surrounded the castle.

b. Three thousand tons of water surrounded the castle.

We will call the readings of these mass NPs **collective**, as well. Observe that even though there are many quantities of water, *the water* picks out a unique object. Moreover, an NP like *the water that John drank*, will also denote a unique quantity, the sum of the quantities of water that John drank, which is again a quantity of water. This reflects a well known and universally accepted property of mass nouns, what Quine (1960) has called **the property of referring cumulatively** (p. 91): "any sum of parts which are water is water". A similar property may be observed for plural nouns: if you add some horses and some other horses then you still have some horses (Link, 1983). In contrast to the higher-order approach, the algebraic first-order approach allows for a similar treatment of mass terms as of plurals.

One way to do this goes as follows. Let the domain of quantities, Q, be a complete join-semilattice. Let a mass noun, like *water*, denote a complete sub-semilattice, i.e. a set of the form $W \subseteq Q$ where for each non-empty $Y \subseteq W$, $\bigvee Y \in W$, and let $[\![\textit{the water}]\!] = \bigvee [\![\textit{water}]\!]$. This will correspond to the denotation of a plural noun, e.g., $[\![{}^{*}x[Horse(x)]]\!]$ is a complete sub-semilattice generated from $[\![Horse]\!]$, and $\bigvee [\![Horse]\!] = \bigvee [\![{}^{*}x[Horse(x)]]\!]$. The difference between mass nouns and plurals will be that $[\![Water]\!]$ will not necessarily be generated from a set of atoms. Correspondingly, we will not assume the join-semilattice Q to be atomic. What might be more surprising is that it is hard to find good arguments for claiming it to be non-atomic, as well.

To analyze both mass terms and plurals, the two models should be integrated in some way, e.g., by considering both O and Q to be subsets of one big domain, D, where a VP denotes a subset of D. There have been several different proposals for how the countable domain shall be considered in this larger setting. One possibility is to let D be a complete join-semilattice, E the atoms in D, and O the set generated from E as explained earlier. Other possibilities comprise to let E also contain non-atoms (Link, 1983) or to not include one set of individuals, but rather let each count noun choose its own individuals (Krifka, 1989).

Should the denotation of a mass term be more constrained? A property of mass terms which has been more disputed than the cumulative reference is **distributive reference**: "Any part of something which is water is water". Quine (1960, p. 99), e.g., rejects this property because "There are parts of water too small to count as water". To see the formal consequences of this, observe that if W is both cumulative and distributive it will equal a set of the form $\{x \mid x \leqslant w\}$ for some w. If then $P = \{x \mid x \leqslant p\}$ for some p, $\bigvee W = \bigvee P$ entails $W = P$, i.e., the definite description becomes injective. Without distributivity, however, a possible case is that $[\![$*furniture*$]\!] \neq [\![$*wood*$]\!]$, but $[\![$*the furniture*$]\!] = [\![$*the wood*$]\!]$. This may model a situation where all furniture is made out of wood and all wood is made into furniture; there may still be pieces of wood which are not pieces of furniture.

As in the plural case, one may ask whether the definite description is injective. There have been two different views depending on how *part of* is read. One may follow Quine and the mereological tradition and read it *material part of* and reject distributive reference. Or one may read it in a more abstract sense and say that Quine's observation is not semantically relevant (Bunt, 1976, 1985; Lønning, 1987a), in which case one will not necessarily claim that $[\![$*the furniture*$]\!] = [\![$*the wood*$]\!]$ in the example above, cf. the discussion on whether $[\![$*the windows*$]\!]$ and $[\![$*the window parts*$]\!]$ should be identical. Link (1983) made a compromise where he read *part of* as *material part of* in the mass domain, but not in the plural domain (cf. Section 4.3).

As the mass noun denotations are not generated from atoms in the same way as the denotations of the plural count nouns, injectivity is not sufficient to introduce a Boolean structure. But there may be other reasons. If John drank some of the water, but not all of the water, there will be many quantities of water that he partly drank and partly did not drink. If *did not drink* is ascribed the complement set of $[\![$*drank*$]\!]$ as denotation, then it will contain all the mixed quantities including $[\![$*the water*$]\!]$, hence $[\![$*the water that John did not drink*$]\!] = [\![$*the water*$]\!]$. But this is not correct. What we want is something like the maximal quantity of water which is such that John did not drink any part of it. This and similar arguments have been given for ascribing the mass domain a Boolean structure (Roeper, 1983; Lønning, 1987a). Then the set of quantities $[\![$*that John did not drink*$]\!]$ may be interpreted as $\{x \mid x \leqslant \overline{\bigvee [\![\textit{that John drank}]\!]}\}$.

Purdy (1992) uses a different approach where the denotations of the mass nouns are slightly different from complete sub-semilattices, and shows that this induces a Boolean structure on the set of possible mass noun denotations.

Does the mass NP in addition to the collective reading also show a reading corresponding to the distributive reading in the count case? Consider sentence (34a) with its similarity to the distributive (34b).

(34) a. John drank most of the water.

b. John ate most of the apples.

c. *Most of the water weigh 3 kilos.

d. Most of the apples weigh 3 kilos.

e. ?Most of the water surrounds the castle.

Most of the water cannot be analyzed by counting quantities. One cannot count all the quantities of water that John drank, nor are there any well defined minimal, disjoint quantities corresponding to individuals which may be counted. Rather what (34a) claims is that the maximal quantity of water that John drank, which equals the sum of all the quantities of water he drank, counts as most of the water. Sentence (34c) seems odd, if at all well formed. It seems like the predicates which may easily co-occur with quantified mass NPs refer themselves both cumulatively and distributively (Lønning, 1987a). As these readings seem to claim that both a quantity and its parts have a certain property, we will call it **homogeneous**. Roeper (1983, 1985) studied homogeneous readings of the logical quantifiers *all* and *some* in a logical setting, including sentences with several NPs, like (35a). Lønning (1987a) studied more general quantifiers like (35b), but only with monadic predicates. Thereby the system became decidable.

(35) a. All water is denser than some alcohol.

b. John drank two liters of beer.

These quantified mass NPs can be considered a generalization of the concept of generalized quantifiers from only considering the cardinalities of the involved sets to considering measures on the sets, cf., *two liters of*. This subject remains to be scrutinized in the same systematic way as the generalized quantifiers on the count domain, cf. Keenan and Westerståhl (1996).

4.7. Alternatives

So far, one particular set of constraints on the interpretations leading to the $\mathcal{CABA}$-structures have been assumed. Several of these constraints have been challenged, in particular the associativity of the conjunction (Hoeksema, 1983).

(36) a. (Blücher and Wellington) and Napoleon fought against each other near Waterloo.

b. Blücher and (Wellington and Napoleon) fought against each other near Waterloo.

There is a difference between Wellington fighting with Blücher against Napoleon or with Napoleon against Blücher. Hoeksema therefore proposed to treat conjunction roughly as set formation and let the two NPs denote something like $\{\{b, w\}, n\}$ and $\{b, \{w, n\}\}$, respectively. In principle, the conjunction process could be iterated. Thus one would need all the hereditary finite sets generated by the basic individuals as possible denotations.

The group-denoting nouns may lead to a similar move for definite descriptions. As remarked earlier, Bennett's (1975) approach cannot capture the collective reading of the group-denoting nouns themselves. But there is no problem to introduce third-order objects: sets of sets of individuals and third-order properties that are ascribed to third-order objects. The process does not stop, however. As Chierchia (1982) observes, if *the group of groups of boys* denotes a third-order object, *the group of groups of groups of boys* will have to denote a fourth-order object, and so forth. In principle, objects of every finite type are needed. Instead of doing this in a logic of higher and higher types, it can be done in a first-order setting with a set theoretical domain.

DEFINITION 11. Let A be a set of basic objects or *urelements*. By the **set universe above** A, in symbols $\mathcal{V}_A$, we mean the usual:

(a) $A_0 = A$.
(b) $A_{n+1} = A_n \cup \{X \subseteq A_n\}$.
(c) $A_\beta = \bigcup_{\alpha<\beta} A_\alpha$, for β a limit ordinal.
(d) $\mathcal{V}_A = \bigcup_{\alpha\in On} A_\alpha$, where *On* is the class of ordinals.

DEFINITION 12. Call a structure for FOLP, $\langle O, E, +, T, [\![\cdot]\!]\rangle$, a **hierarchical set structure** provided there is a set A of basic elements and

(a) $O \subseteq \mathcal{V}_A$.
(b) $T(X) = X$ for all subsets X of E such that $|X| \geqslant 2$.

This a very general concept which may be further constrained, in particular with respect to the relationship between E and O. If E equals A, we get roughly the $\mathcal{CABA}$-structures. At the other end, we may want E to contain as much as possible. This will make possible the sketched treatment of the group-denoting nouns. A similar interpretation was proposed by Landman (1989).

Some care should be taken here. If a word like *entity* denotes E and one wants to interpret the description *the entities*, history has taught us that we may run into problems if we let this again denote a member of E. Since there cannot be a set of all sets, *the entities* cannot be an entity. Hence E cannot equal O. Moreover E must be a subset of $\mathcal{V}_A$, while O may be a proper class.

We will conclude with a more general comment on Russell's paradox. Given $E \subseteq O$ and T a partial function $T\colon \mathrm{POW}_{\geqslant 2}(E) \to O$, we know already from Cantor that the following properties are incompatible

a. T is total.
b. $E = O$.
c. T is injective.

The properties are pairwise compatible, however. What we have pursued in this section is the possibility of keeping (a) and (c) and giving up (b). On the other hand, one may get (b) if one is willing to give up totality or injectivity.

5. Reading plural NPs

5.1. Collective and distributive readings

We will now consider in some more depth how the plural NPs should be interpreted in the formal models introduced so far, a question which is mainly independent of whether a first-order or higher-order approach is chosen. We have throughout assumed a two way ambiguity between collective and distributive readings. In Section 3.2 we considered the cause of this to be an ambiguity in the plural NP and furthermore in the plural determiner. This was Bennett's (1975) approach to the indefinite NPs; his approach to the definite NPs was a little different, but we will not consider it here. In Section 4.4 we considered a similar treatment within the first-order framework.

It is a problem for proposals which try to locate the difference between the collective and the distributive reading to an ambiguity in the NP that the same NP may be read both collectively and distributively, as pointed out already by Hausser (1974) who came up with the following example.

(37) The horses gather and graze.

Hausser's own proposal, which we will not consider here, was based on an ingenious use of quantifying-in. Another alternative is to locate the distribution effect to the meaning of the intransitive verb *graze*.

(38) a. For all non-empty $X \subseteq E$, if $X \in [\![GRAZE]\!]$ then $X \subseteq [\![Graze]\!]$.

b. For all non-empty $X \subseteq E$, if $T(X) \in [\![Graze]\!]$ then $X \subseteq [\![Graze]\!]$.

We have here given the constraint both in a version for the second-order framework (38a) and a version for the first-order framework (38b). One might consider whether there should be an implication also in the other direction, e.g., if $X \subseteq [\![Graze]\!]$ then $X \in [\![GRAZE]\!]$, a discussion which is on the side of our main issue. Exactly how the constraint should be implemented depends on one's view with respect to lexical constraints. One possibility is to use $*$ to mark the representation of certain distributive verbs, say $^*x[Graze(x)]$ (Link, 1983).

A similar approach could be used for explaining certain distributions involving transitive verbs.

(39) a. The squares contain the circles.

b. Every circle is contained in some square.

c. Hammerstein, Rodgers and Hart wrote musicals.

Scha (1981) gave a context where (39a) can be interpreted as (39b). The intended reading is obtained from a collective interpretation of both NPs in (39a) through an (optional) meaning postulate associated with the lexical entry of *contain*. Sentence (39c) may also be true, though it has been claimed that it is neither fully collective nor distributive (Gillon, 1987). None of the men wrote any musical all by himself, nor did all three of them collaborate on one. But Hammerstein and Rodgers together wrote (at least) one musical and the same did Hart and Rodgers. This situation may be described with a collective interpretation of both NPs and a more detailed analysis of the lexical meaning of the verb.

One cannot get everything this way.

(40) The boys carried the piano upstairs and got a cookie as reward.

Whatever one does to the verb *get*, with a collective interpretation of *the boys*, only one cookie is given out. A third type of proposal has therefore been to locate the ambiguity to the VP, but not in the lexical verb meaning. Instead one introduces an operator on VPs.

DEFINITION 13 (*Distribution operator*).
(a) If ϕ is a formula and v an o-variable then ${}^{D}v[\phi]$ is a relation of type $\langle o \rangle$.
(b) $[\![{}^{D}v[\phi]]\!]_g = \{b \in O \mid b \neq 0 \;\&\; \forall a \in E\,(a \leqslant b \rightarrow [\![\phi]\!]_{g^v_a} = \mathbf{t})\}$.

This D-operator will correspond to an explicit floated quantifier as *each* in *got a cookie each*. Thus, if γ represents *got a cookie, got a cookie each* is represented ${}^{D}v[\gamma(v)]$. This interpretation is also an optional reading of *got a cookie*, where no explicit *each* is present. Such an approach was first proposed by Link (1991, written in 1984) and developed further by Lønning (1987b) and Roberts (1987). She gave the following example sentence (41).

(41) Five insurance associates gave a \$25 donation to several charities.

The sentence has a reading where only five insurance associates were involved, they gave the donations collectively, but each charity received \$ 25. The example indicates that the D-operator should not only be applied to properties which correspond to syntactic constituents, it will interact with other scoping operators, like quantifiers.

Observe that for this to work on a $\mathcal{CJSL}$ structure, it has to be a $\mathcal{CABA}$, or more generally, T must be injective. Assume to the contrary that we allow *john* $\oplus$ *harry* $=$ *dick* $\oplus$ *tom*. Then it will be impossible for John and Harry to each get a cookie unless also Dick and Tom each get a cookie. But observe that if E is the set of atoms in a Boolean structure, as we have assumed, $*$ and D will be equivalent.

For the definite plural NPs, this approach will yield the same result as the ambiguous NP approach, but not necessarily for the indefinite NPs. Consider a sentence like (42a) with its collective representation (42b). With an ambiguous NP, the distributive reading is expressed by (42c); with a D-operator it is (42d) which is equivalent to (42e), but not necessarily to (42c). To see this let α' be *woman*, δ' be *five*, and β be true about exactly six women. Then (42d) yields a true sentence and (42c) a false one.

(42) a. $[_{\mathrm{S}}[_{\mathrm{NP}}[_{\mathrm{Det}}\,\delta'][_{\mathrm{N}}\alpha']][_{\mathrm{VP}}\,\beta']]$
b. $\exists y({}^{*}\alpha(y) \wedge \delta(y) \wedge \beta(y))$
c. $\delta(\tau x[\alpha(x) \wedge \beta(x)])$
d. $\exists y({}^{*}\alpha(y) \wedge \delta(y) \wedge {}^{D}\beta(y))$
e. $\exists y({}^{*}\alpha(y) \wedge \delta(y) \wedge \forall x \preceq y\,(\beta(x)))$

The two interpretations are equivalent whenever δ is monotone increasing, i.e. if for all $b, c \in O$, $b \in [\![\delta]\!]$ and $b \leqslant c$, $c \in [\![\delta]\!]$, e.g., *three or more*. In general only (42d) will entail (42c) (Lønning, 1987b). It is rather obvious that for a non-increasing determiner, like *at most five*, it is the *exactly* reading in (42d) and not the *at least* reading in (42c), which is the correct one.

To sum up, all three proposals: the ambiguous NP, the lexical analysis of the verb, and the D-operator analysis have their problems. One possibility is to assume both the D-operator and the ambiguous NP, and get three different readings of sentences with indefinite NPs. The problem for such a solution is to explain why we do not experience a three way ambiguity. Another alternative is to stick to the ambiguous VP only, and claim that the *exactly* effect is pragmatic, generated by some Gricean principles.

Finally, in frameworks with a more flexible relationship between syntax and semantics, one might possibly get one's cake and eat it too. Thus Kamp and Reyle (1993) initially (their Section 4.1.5) discuss two approaches to distribution which can be classified as DRT implementations of the ambiguous NP and the D-analysis. But finally (their Section 4.4.4), they come up with a third proposal which may be used for VP-conjunction and at the same time yield an *exactly* reading. Link (1993) gives an alternative proposal for overcoming the problems of the *exactly/at least* distinction with a D-operator.

Related to the relationship between the collective and the distributive readings are also the so-called **intermediate readings** between collective and distributive, as in (43a) and (43b) where the girls collectively got \$10 000 for the match and so did the boys.

(43) a. Mary and Eve and Bill and Tom got \$10 000 for the match.
b. The girls and the boys got \$10 000 for the match.
c. The young cows and the old cows were separated.

These readings have together with the **structured group reading** of (43c) where the old cows are separated from the young cows, cf. also example (36), been used as arguments for imposing more structure on the domain (Link, 1984; Landman, 1989; cf. Section 4.7). Schwarzschild (1992), on the other hand, argues that collective readings will do and that the structuring of the separation in (43c) should be ascribed to pragmatic principles.

5.2. *Neutral readings*

Can all possible readings of plural NPs be characterized in terms of the collective and distributive readings? Scha (1981) considered a second type of collective reading, in addition. Sentence (44a) may be true even though it is not the case that there is one gathering involving all the boys, but where there are several gatherings and the total number of boys involved in these equals six. This can be spelled out as (44b), and the general form of the NP will be as in (44c). We allow ourselves here to use a mixture of object- and metalanguage, but hope the result is sufficiently clear. We will call this a **neutral** reading.

(44) a. Six boys gather.
b. $|\{x \in E \mid x \leqslant \bigvee\{y \mid {}^{*}Boy(y) \wedge Gather(y)\}\}| = 6$

c. $\lambda X[\delta(\bigvee\{y \mid {}^*\alpha(y) \wedge X(y)\})]$

d. $\lambda X[\exists y({}^*\alpha(y) \wedge \delta(y) \wedge y = \bigvee\{y_2 \mid y_2 \leqslant y \wedge X(y_2)\})]$

Interpretations similar to (44b) have been proposed by several authors under different names: The *partitional* reading (Higginbotham, 1980), the *pseudo partitional* reading (Verkuyl and Van der Does, 1991) and the *minimal cover* reading (Gillon, 1987). The proposals differ in detail, e.g., with respect to whether boys participating in gatherings with individuals that are not boys should be counted. We will not discuss all the different options, except for one. There is a certain similarity between (44c) and the *exactly* distributive reading, and one may imagine an alternative *at least* neutral reading as in (44d). In parallel with the distributive readings, (44c) will always entail (44d), while the other direction will hold for monotone increasing δ. The *at least* reading (44d) may be derived from a collectively read NP by a lexical analysis, cf., example (39c), or by some operator similar to the *D*-operator, the *exactly* analysis cannot.

Observe also that to a certain degree the collective and distributive readings are amplifications of the neutral ones; the *exactly* distributive reading (42c) entails the *exactly* neutral reading (44c), the *at least* distributive reading (42d) entails the *at least* neutral reading (44d), and the collective reading (42b) entails the *at least* neutral reading (44d). Van der Does (1993) discussed in more detail the logical relationship between these readings and also other variants of the neutral readings under various assumptions concerning the monotonicity type of δ.

In spite of the differences of detail between the proposed neutral readings, we think the intuitions underlying these proposals are the same. The proposals should not be counted as different readings but rather as different ways to interpret one and the same reading. Even Van der Does (1993), starting out with three candidate neutral readings, concluded that only one of them should count as a genuine reading.

Is the neutral reading a separate reading of the plural NP, or should it be accommodated in other ways, e.g., by vagueness? The first possibility is, as Scha (1981) did for the indefinite NPs, to say that the plural NPs are three ways ambiguous. They have a collective (42b), an (*exactly*) distributive (42c) and an (*exactly*) neutral reading (44c). A problem for such an approach is the following observation.

(45) a. Three boys bought a book.

b. Three men wrote musicals.

c. Three hundred soldiers gathered.

Sentence (45a) has a collective and a distributive reading, but not the neutral reading. It cannot be used for expressing that two boys collectively bought one book and a third boy bought another book. In sentence (45b) and (45c), however, we may observe a neutral reading. But then it is not obvious that we in addition see a collective and a distributive reading in these examples, when the neutral reading will do. The problem is to explain why the NP is three ways ambiguous when there are no contexts where we can find a three way ambiguity, and moreover to explain how the context selects the right readings and exclude the wrong ones.

The second possibility, which was proposed by Verkuyl and Van der Does (1991), is to take the clue from the entailment relationship between the readings to the extreme, and to say that we only need the weakest reading, the neutral one. This approach also faces a problem in explaining why (45a) cannot be true in the described situation.

The third possibility is to only stick to the collective and the distributive reading and to try to ascribe the neutral reading to the meaning of the involved verb (Link, 1991). It is interesting to compare the distributive and the neutral reading at this point. A lexical analysis of the verb is not sufficient for the distributive readings because distribution may involve scope over other NPs in the sentence. The neutral readings, on the other hand, is impossible in cases where scope is involved as exemplified by (45a). The problem for this approach is similar as for the D-operator approach to the distributive reading. It generates the *at least* rather than the *exactly* reading.

The claim that the neutrally read NPs cannot take scope over other NPs has not been universally accepted, though. It has given rise to some lively discussion between Gillon (1987, 1990) and Lasersohn (1989), where Gillon (1990) argues that there are examples where one may find neutral readings taking scope over other NPs.

5.3. *Cumulative readings*

What happens if a sentence contains several plural NPs? If we assume that each of the NPs can be read collectively or distributively, sentence (46a) becomes four ways ambiguous. If a reversed scope reading is possible, the total number becomes seven – if both NPs are collective there is no scope involved. Introducing the neutral readings increases the number further. Several authors have raised doubts about natural language being this ambiguous, but there has not appeared any formal proposals for how the number should be reduced. We will consider the opposite question, whether what we have done so far is sufficient for representing all the possible readings of the sentences with several plural NPs.

(46) a. Two examiners marked five papers.

b. Six hundred Dutch firms use five thousand American computers.

c. Two hundred delegates from ten countries were gathered for one week.

Scha (1981) claims sentences (46a) and (46b) to have additional readings, called **cumulative**, where sentence (46b) says that the total number of Dutch firms using an American computer is six hundred and the total numbers of American computers used by Dutch firms equals five thousand. This may be spelled out by something like (47a) in the first-order setting.

(47) a. $\mathit{Sixh}(\bigvee\{y_1 \mid {}^*\mathit{Comp}(y_1) \wedge \exists y_2\,({}^*\mathit{Firm}(y_2) \wedge \mathit{Use}(y_1, y_2))\})$
$\wedge\, \mathit{Fiveth}(\bigvee\{y_2 \mid {}^*\mathit{Firm}(y_2) \wedge \exists y_1({}^*\mathit{Comp}(y_1) \wedge \mathit{Use}(y_1, y_2))\})$

b. $\exists y_1(\mathit{Sixh}(y_1) \wedge {}^*\mathit{Comp}(y_1) \wedge \exists y_2(\mathit{Fiveth}(y_2) \wedge {}^*\mathit{Firm}(y_2)$
$\wedge\, y_1 = \bigvee\{y_3 \leqslant y_1 \mid \exists y_4 \leqslant y_2(\mathit{Use}(y_3, y_4))\}$
$\wedge\, y_2 = \bigvee\{y_4 \leqslant y_1 \mid \exists y_3 \leqslant y_1(\mathit{Use}(y_3, y_4))\}))$

Formula (47b) could have been obtained from a double collective reading by a further analysis of the verb. It is entailed by the simple double collective reading and also by (47a), but not the other way around. Again the same *at least/exactly* conflict may be observed. The cumulative reading raises problems for a strict compositional analysis. Scha's (1981) proposal is to simultaneously combine the two NPs and the transitive verb. Logically, however, the cumulative reading does not introduce anything new, it can be expressed by well known tools.

Whether the cumulative reading represents a separate reading has also been discussed. If one considers a sentence like (46c) then an *exactly* effect seems to be observed. Each delegate has to come from one of the ten countries. Each of the ten countries has to be represented by at least one delegate. And the sentence is most often not felicitous in contexts where there are altogether five hundred delegates and twenty countries represented even though exactly two hundred of the five hundred delegates are all the delegates from ten of the represented countries. This is quite similar to the *exactly* effect we observed for the distributive readings.

We have in this section considered some issues in the reading of plural NPs, but there are many more issues discussed in the literature which space prevents us from considering, including **partitive constructions**, like *two of the cars*, **reciprocals**, like *the professors hate each other*, in particular, the relationship between the reciprocals and the collectively read NPs, cf. example (36) and (49). Mentioned should also be collective readings with relational nouns, *Mary's and John's daughters* (Eschenbach, 1993), and **plural anaphora** which have, in particular, been discussed within DRT (Kamp and Reyle, 1993).

6. Non-denotational approaches

6.1. Reducing the collective readings?

We have so far assumed existence of collections in one form or another. But are they really necessary for modeling plural NPs? In this section we will consider attempts at explaining some of the readings we have so far classified as collective without the use of collections. Some of the earlier semantic literature (e.g., Gil, 1982; Kempson and Cormack, 1981) propose four different readings of a sentence containing two plural NPs, like the ones from example (46).

(48) a. $\exists X(\mathit{TWO}(X) \wedge X \subseteq \mathit{Examiner} \wedge \forall x \in X$
$(\exists Y(\mathit{FIVE}(Y) \wedge Y \subseteq \mathit{Paper} \wedge \forall y \in Y(\mathit{Mark}(x,y)))))$

b. $\exists Y(\mathit{FIVE}(Y) \wedge Y \subseteq \mathit{Paper} \wedge \forall y \in Y$
$(\exists X\,(\mathit{TWO}(X) \wedge X \subseteq \mathit{Examiner} \wedge \forall x \in X(\mathit{Mark}(x,y)))))$

c. $\exists X(\mathit{TWO}(X) \wedge X \subseteq \mathit{Examiner} \wedge \exists Y(\mathit{FIVE}(Y) \wedge Y \subseteq \mathit{Paper}$
$\wedge \forall x \in X(\forall y \in Y(\mathit{Mark}(x,y)))))$

d. $\exists X(\mathit{TWO}(X) \wedge X \subseteq \mathit{Examiner} \wedge \exists Y(\mathit{FIVE}(Y) \wedge Y \subseteq \mathit{Paper}$
$\wedge \forall x \in X(\exists y \in Y(\mathit{Mark}(x,y))) \wedge \forall y \in Y(\exists x \in X(\mathit{Mark}(x,y)))))$

These correspond to readings encountered already. The first two are the double distributive readings, while the last two, called the *strong group reading* and *the weak group reading*, respectively, may be obtained from a double collective reading by a lexical analysis of the verb. What is common to all these readings is that even though one quantify over sets of individuals, the objects that actually are counted, and which in particular enter the *mark* relation, are simple individuals. Thus the readings are explained in terms of – or reduced to – facts about simple individuals.

One may wonder whether all collective readings may be reduced in this way. Most of the newer literature on plurals will say no. Even the sentence (46a) may become true in a situation where there are papers which were not marked by any single examiner; say, they marked half the paper each. This is not reflected by any of the readings in (48). And throughout we have seen many similar examples with other relations like *gather* or *own*, which cannot be reduced to properties of individuals.

6.2. *Branching generalized quantifiers*

A formula in first-order logic is normally interpreted from outside and inward. Hence, a quantifier will depend on a quantifier with wider scope. There have been extensions of first-order logic with partially ordered prefixes where the dependence relation between the quantifiers is more complex (see Hintikka and Sandu, 1996), and there has been a lively discussion on whether natural language exemplify such non-linear readings of the familiar quantifiers, $\forall$ and $\exists$. What is more relevant here is Barwise' (1979) claim that branched readings are more easily found with other natural language quantifiers like *most* or *at least three*. He proposed two schemata for interpreting such quantifiers, one to be applied when both quantifiers are monotone increasing, which will interpret sentence (49a), symbolized as (49b), as (49c), and another one which should be applied when both quantifiers are monotone decreasing, which will interpret (49d), symbolized as (49e), as (49f).

(49) a. Most linguists and most logicians respect each other.

b. $\begin{pmatrix} \mathit{MOST}(\mathit{Linguist})\ x \\ \mathit{MOST}(\mathit{Logician}) y \end{pmatrix} (\mathit{Respect\_each\_other}(x, y))$

c. $\exists X \exists Y (\mathit{MOST}(\mathit{Linguist})(X) \wedge \mathit{MOST}(\mathit{Logician})(Y)$
$\wedge X \times Y \subseteq \mathit{Respect\_each\_other})$

d. Few linguists and few logicians respect each other.

e. $\begin{pmatrix} \mathit{FEW}(\mathit{Linguist}) x \\ \mathit{FEW}(\mathit{Logician})\ y \end{pmatrix} (\mathit{Respect\_each\_other}(x, y))$

f. $\exists X \exists Y (\mathit{FEW}(\mathit{Linguist})(X) \wedge \mathit{FEW}(\mathit{Logician})(Y)$
$\wedge (\mathit{Respect\_each\_other} \cap (\mathit{Linguist} \times \mathit{Logician})) \subseteq X \times Y)$

The interpretation of the two NPs in sentence (49a) as branching monotone increasing quantifiers (49c) is similar to the strong group reading (48d) or what can be obtained by a collective interpretation of both NPs and a further analysis of the transitive verb. The interpretation of the monotone decreasing quantifiers (49f) is remarkable similar to the cumulative interpretation. One difference is that the branching proposal assumes that the relation should be ascribed to individuals only, while the cumulative interpretation also considers what went on between collections. But if the stars are removed from the representation in formula (47a), it will be a first-order representation which corresponds to (49f) in the higher-order framework provided δ is monotone decreasing. But there is a difference in when they are applied. Cumulative readings is thought as an option for non-decreasing determiners, like simple numerals, as well.

The proposal to interpret some occurrences of plural NPs in terms of branching quantifiers is not by itself an argument against collections. As for the proposals considered in the last section, there are uses of plural NPs not covered by such an approach.

6.3. *Rejecting collections*

In a series of papers George Boolos (1984a, 1984b, 1985) has rejected the necessity of assuming collections (1984b, p. 442): "Abandon, if one ever had it, the idea that use of plural forms must always be understood to commit one to the existence of sets (or "classes", "collections", or "totalities") of those things to which the corresponding singular forms apply". But at the same time, he argued that there are occurrences of plural NPs which may be paraphrased into second-order logic, but not into first-order logic (cf. Section 3.3.3 above). Boolos' solution to these apparently incompatible claims is to rethink the semantics of second-order logic. The sentence (22), e.g., is about horses, about one horse being the sire of another horse or being faster than another horse. But the sentence is not about collections of horses. It is not necessary to enrich the ontology to interpret the sentence. The only thing that has to be enriched are the rules for interpreting formulas in the models. Boolos' approach has certain similarities to the branching quantifiers. The branching quantifiers may be represented in terms of a second-order formula which interpretation one may think of in terms of sets. But these quantifiers may alternatively be thought of as an extension to a first-order language which may still be interpreted in a first-order model through additional interpretation rules. Similarly, second-order formulas in general can be considered as such extensions to first-order logic. Boolos (1985) presents a formal proposal for how the second-order quantifiers may be interpreted in a first-order model.

One may say that Boolos' main goal is different frrm what we have considered this far. It is not as much to state the correct semantics of plural NPs in natural language, as the correct semantics of second-order logic. The fact that there are natural language sentences corresponding to second-order formulas is then taken as a clue for translating monadic second-order logic into natural language, while the ease with which we understand plural NPs is taken as the clue for the semantics of natural language, which then induces the semantics of the second-order logic.

The current space forbids a satisfactory presentation of Boolos' views and a full discussion of whether one may do without collections, but we will consider some issues. The formal language Boolos considers can be regarded as a sublanguage of SOLID. It extends first-order logic with second-order variables and quantifiers. The relation symbols considered are all of type $\langle 0, 0, \ldots, 0 \rangle$, however. There are no relation symbols of type $\langle 1 \rangle$. Second-order variables and constants occur in predicate position, but never in argument position. Thus the representation of sentence (1c) as

(50) $GATHER(Student)$

is beyond what can be expressed in the fragment. Moreover, there is no obvious way to extend Boolos' interpretation schema to such formulas and the whole SOLID. What we have taken to be genuine collective readings cannot be described. The readings that may be captured in the fragment are the ones where the properties distribute down to individuals in some way or other.

An argument in favor of Boolos' view is the following. Russell's paradox has taught us that there cannot be a set which has as members all sets that are not members of themselves. Still, the definite description *the sets that are not members of themselves* is all right. If we take a plural definite description in general to denote a set, this description should denote a set as well, and we are in for problems. The defense a set based, or, more generally, a collection based, approach may take to this attack goes as follows. It is necessary to distinguish between an "inner" and an "outer" interpretation. Seen from within a model, something counts as a set if and only if it belongs to $[\![Set]\!]$. Since $[\![Set]\!]$ will not belong to $[\![Set]\!]$ sentence (51) will simply be false – even though $[\![Set]\!]$ is a set when seen from outside the model.

(51) The sets are a set.

This corresponds to saying that the exact meaning of the word *set* is not a part of formal semantics. One should not accept all truths of set theory to count as semantic or logical truths. Whether it is philosophically satisfactory to let the denotation of the word *set* be different from its real extension is another question. There is a striking parallel to axiomatic set theory. Axiomatic set theory, i.e. the discourse about sets, must admit as possible models so-called *inner models* where the domain itself is a set in what is regarded as the full domain of set theory.

7. Further directions

There are many issues relating to plurals that we have not considered or only mentioned in passing. One is the generic use of plurals and the use of plurals to refer to kinds. Another is the relationship between events and plurals, where several issues arise. Which readings do sentences with plural NPs have when tense is considered? What about sentences like (52) studied by Krifka (1990), where the same ship may have to be counted more than once?

(52) Three hundred ships passed the lock last year.

Events are also essential in the approaches to plurality by Lasersohn (1988) and Schein (1993). Should events themselves have a similar structure to the collective domain and how shall models with both events and collections be framed?

At several places in this chapter we have seen how the analysis of plurals interact with some of the most fundamental questions concerning the relationship between logic and language. Firstly, what counts as a reading of a sentence, how should ambiguity be distinguished from vagueness? The basic intuition about an ambiguity between a collective and distributive reading of plural NPs yields an explosion in the number of readings for sentences containing several plural NPs. Still it seems difficult to restrict this number in any principal way.

Secondly, where shall the borderline between semantics and pragmatics be drawn? In Section 3.3.3 we saw that for sentences with indefinite plural NPs, a speaker's meaning in terms of a referentially used NP might be logically less complex than a sentence meaning where one tries to capture an attributive use.

This interacts with the third issue; what is the borderline between semantics and logic, and how much ontology and word meaning belong to formal semantics? This question shows up in the interpretation of *part of*, the question regarding whether different plural descriptions may denote the same object, and the question regarding how the group-denoting nouns best should be handled.

And fourthly, the semantics of plural NPs is interwoven with some fundamental problems related to set theory and higher-order logic, as we pointed out already in the introduction, and as pointed out by Boolos. The use of plural NPs is fundamental to how we reason about logic.

Acknowledgement

I am grateful to Jens Erik Fenstad, Godehard Link, Helle Frisak Sem and Jarle Stabell for helpful advices at different stages in the preparation of this manuscript.

References

Barker, C. (1992), *Group terms in English: Representing groups as atoms*, J. Semantics **9**, 69–93.

Bartsch, R. (1973), *The semantics and syntax of number and numbers*, Syntax and Semantics vol. 2, J.P. Kimball, ed., Seminar Press, New York, 51–93.

Barwise, J. (1978), *Monotone quantifiers and admissible sets*, Generalized Recursion Theory II, J.E. Fenstad et al., eds, North-Holland, Amsterdam, 1–38.

Barwise, J. (1979), *On branching quantifiers in English*, J. Philos. Logic, **8**, 47–80.

Bennett, M.R. (1975), *Some extensions of a Montague fragment of English*, Dissertation, distributed by the Indiana University Linguistics Club.

Bennett, M.R. (1977), *Mass nouns and mass terms in Montague grammar*, Linguistics, Philosophy, and Montague Grammar, S. Davis and M. Mithun, eds, Univ. of Texas Press, Austin, 263–285.

Blau, U. (1981), *Collective objects*, Theor. Ling. **8**, 101–130.

Boolos, G. (1984a), *Nonfirstorderizability again*, Ling. Inq. **15**, 343.

Boolos, G. (1984b), *To be is to be a value of a variable (or to be some values of some variables)*, J. Philos. **81**, 430–449.

Boolos, G. (1985), *Nominalist platonism*, Philos. Rev. **94**, 327–344.

Bunt, H. (1976), *The formal semantics of mass terms*, Papers from the Third Scandinavian Conference of Linguistics, F. Karlsson, ed., Academy of Finland, Turku.

Bunt, H. (1985), *Mass Terms and Model-Theoretic Semantics*, Cambridge Univ. Press, Cambridge, UK.

Carlson, G. (1977), *A unified analysis of the English bare plural*, Ling. and Philos. **1**, 413–457.
Carlson, G.N. and Pelletier, F.J. (eds) (1995), *The Generic Book*, Univ. of Chicago Press, Chicago.
Chierchia, G. (1982), *Nominalization and Montague grammar: A semantics without types for natural languages*, Linguist. and Philos. **5**, 303–354.
Donnellan, K.S. (1966), *Reference and definite descriptions*, Philos. Rev. **75**, 281–304.
Eberle, R.A. (1970), *Nominalistic Systems*, Reidel, Dordrecht.
Eschenbach, C. (1993), *Semantics of number*, J. Semantics **10**, 1–31.
Fodor, J.D. and Sag, I.A. (1982), *Referential and quantificational indefinites*, Ling. and Philos. **5**, 355–398.
Frege, G. (1980), *Philosophical and Mathematical Correspondence*, G. Gabriel et al., eds, H. Kaal, trans., Basil Blackwell, Oxford.
Gallin, D. (1975), *Intensional and Higher-Order Modal Logic. With Applications to Montague Semantics*, North-Holland, Amsterdam.
Gil, D. (1982), *Quantifier scope, linguistic variation, and natural language semantics*, Ling. and Philos. **5**, 421–472.
Gillon, B. (1987), *The readings of plural noun phrases in English*, Ling. and Philos. **10**, 199–219.
Gillon, B. (1990), *Plural noun phrases and their readings: A reply to Lasersohn*, Ling. and Philos. **13**, 477–485.
Grätzer, G. (1978), *General Lattice Theory*, Academic Press, New York.
Hausser, R.R. (1974), *Quantification in an extended Montague grammar*, Dissertation, University of Texas, Austin.
Henkin, L. (1950), *Completeness in the theory of types*, J. Symb. Logic **15**, 81–91.
Higginbotham, J. (1980), *Reciprocal interpretation*, J. Ling. Res. **1**, 97–117.
Hintikka, J. and Sandu, G. (1996), *Game-theoretical semantics*, Handbook of Logic and Language, J. van Benthem and A. ter Meulen, eds, Elsevier, Amsterdam, 361–410.
Hoeksema, J. (1983), *Plurality and conjunction*, Studies in Modeltheoretic Semantics, A.G.B. ter Meulen, ed., Foris, Dordrecht, 63–83.
Janssen, T.M.V. (1966), *Compositionality*, Handbook of Logic and Language, J. van Benthem and A. ter Meulen, eds, Elsevier, Amsterdam, 417–473.
Jespersen, O. (1924), *The Philosophy of Grammar*, Univ. of Chicago Press, Chicago.
Kamp, H. and Reyle, U. (1993), *From Discourse to Logic*, Kluwer, Dordrecht.
Keenan, E. and Westerståhl, D. (1996), *Quantifiers*, Handbook of Logic and Language, J. van Benthem and A. ter Meulen, eds, Elsevier, Amsterdam, 837–893.
Keisler, H.J. (1970), *Logic with the quantifier 'there exists uncountably many'*, Ann. Math. Logic **1**, 1–93.
Kempson, R.M. and Cormack, A. (1981), *Ambiguity and quantification*, Ling. and Philos. **4**, 259–309.
Krifka, M. (1990), *Four thousand ships passed through the lock: Object-induced measure functions on events*, Ling. and Philos. **13**, 487–520.
Krifka, M. (1989), *Nominal reference, temporal constitution and quantification in event semantics*, Semantics and Contextual Expressions, R. Bartsch, J. van Benthem and P. van Embde Boas, eds, Foris, Dordrecht, 75–115.
Kripke, S. (1977), *Speaker's reference and semantic reference*, Contemporary Perspectives in the Philosophy of Language, P.A. French et al., eds, Univ. of Minnesota Press, Minneapolis, MN, 6–27.
Landman, F. (1989), *Groups*, Ling. and Philos. **12**, 559–605, 723–744.
Landman, F. (1991), *Structures for Semantics*, Kluwer, Dordrecht.
Lasersohn, P.N. (1988), *A semantics for groups and events*, Dissertation, Ohio State University, Columbus.
Lasersohn, P. (1989), *On the readings of plural noun phrases*, Ling. Inq. **20**, 130–134.
Leonard, H.S. and Goodman, N. (1940), *The calculus of individuals and its uses*, J. Symb. Logic **5**, 45–55.
Lewis, D. (1991), *Parts of Classes*, Basil Blackwell, Oxford.
Link, G. (1983), *The logical analysis of plurals and mass terms: A lattice-theoretical approach*, Meaning, Use and Interpretation of Language, R. Bäuerle, C. Schwarze and A. von Stechow, eds, Walter de Gruyter, Berlin, 302–323.
Link, G. (1984), *Hydras: On the logic of relative constructions with multiple heads*, Varieties of Formal Semantics, F. Landaman and F. Veltman, eds, Foris, Dordrecht, 245–257.
Link, G. (1987), *Generalized quantifiers and plurals*, Generalized Quantifiers. Linguistic and Logical Approaches, P. Gärdenfors, ed., Reidel, Dordrecht, 151–180.
Link, G. (1990), *First order axioms for the logic of plurality*, To appear in Link (forthcoming).

Link, G. (1991), *Plural*, Semantik. Semantics, A. von Stechow and D. Wunderlich, eds, Walter de Gruyter, Berlin.

Link, G. (1993), *Ten years of research on plurals – where do we stand?*, To appear in Link (forthcoming).

Link, G. *Algebraic Semantics for Natural Language*, CSLI Lecture Notes, Stanford (forthcoming).

Lønning, J.T. (1987a), *Mass terms and quantification*, Ling. and Philos. **10**, 1–52.

Lønning, J.T. (1987b), *Collective readings of definite and indefinite noun phrases*, Generalized Quantifiers. Linguistic and Logical Approaches, P. Gärdenfors, ed., Reidel, Dordrecht, 203–235.

Lønning, J.T. (1989), *Some aspects of the logic of plural noun phrases*, Dissertation, Dept. of Mathematics, University of Oslo, Cosmos preprint no. 11.

Massey, G. (1976), *Tom, Dick and Harry, and all the King's men*, Amer. Philos. Q. **13**, 89–107.

Montague, R. (1973), *The proper treatment of quantification in ordinary English*, Approaches to Natural Language, K.J.J. Hintikka, M.E. Moravcsik and P. Suppes, eds, Reidel, Dordrecht.

Mostowski, A. (1947), *On absolute properties of relations*, J. Symb. Logic **12**, 33–42.

Orey, S. (1959), *Model theory for higher order predicate calculus*, Trans. Amer. Math. Soc. **92**, 72–84.

Partee, B.H. (1966), *Montague grammar*, Handbook of Logic and Language, J. van Benthem and A. ter Meulen, eds, Elsevier, Amsterdam, 5–91.

Pelletier, F.J. (1975), *Non-singular reference: Some preliminaries*, Philos. **5**, 4. Reprinted: F.J. Pelletier (ed.) (1979), *Mass Terms: Some Philosophical Problems*, Reidel, Dordrecht, 1–14.

Pelletier, F.J. and Asher, N. (1996), *Generics and defaults*, Handbook of Logic and Language, J. van Benthem and A. ter Meulen, eds, Elsevier, Amsterdam, 1125–1177.

Purdy, W.C. (1992), *A variable-free logic for mass terms*, Notre Dame J. Formal Logic **33**, 348–358.

Quine, W.V.O. (1960), *Word and Object*, MIT Press, Cambridge, MA.

Quine, W.V.O. (1970), *Philosophy of Logic*, Prentice-Hall, Englewood Cliffs, NJ.

Quine, W.V.O. (1974), *Methods of Logic*, Third Edition, Routledge & Kegan Paul, London.

Roberts, C. (1987), *Modal subordination, anaphora, and distributivity*, Dissertation, University of Massachusetts.

Roeper, R. (1983), *Semantics for mass terms with quantifiers*, Nous **17**, 251–265.

Roeper, R. (1985), *Generalisation of first-order logic to nonatomic domains*, J. Symb. Logic **50**, 815–838.

Russell, B. (1903), *The Principles of Mathematics*, George Allen & Unwin, London. (Second edition 1937.)

Russell, B. (1919), *Introduction to Mathematical Philosophy*, George Allen & Unwin, London.

Scha, R. (1981), *Distributive, collective and cumulative quantification*, Formal Methods in the Study of Language, J.A.G. Groenendijk, T.M.V. Janssen and M.B.J. Stokhof, eds, Mathematical Centre Tracts 136, Amsterdam, 483–512.

Schein, B. (1993), *Plurals and Events*, MIT Press, Cambridge, MA.

Schwarzschild, R. (1992), *Types of plurals individuals*, Ling. and Philos. **15**, 641–675.

Shapiro, S. (1991), *Foundations without Foundationalism. A Case for Second-Order Logic*, Clarendon Press, Oxford.

Van Benthem, J. and Doets, K. (1983), *Higher-order logic*, Handbook of Philosophical Logic vol. 1, D. Gabbay and F. Guenthner, eds, Reidel, Dordrecht, 275–329.

Van der Does, J. (1993), *Sums and quantifiers*, Ling. and Philos. **16**, 509–550.

Verkuyl, H.J. (1988), *Aspect, quantification and negation*, Proceedings of the Sixth Amsterdam Colloquium. April 13–16 1987, J. Groenendijk, M. Stokhof and F. Veltman, eds, ITLI, University of Amsterdam, 353–372.

Verkuyl, H.J. and Van der Does, J. (1991), *The semantics of plural noun phrases*, Generalized Quantifier Theory and Applications, J. van der Does and J. van Eijck, eds, Dutch Network for Language, Logic and Information, Amsterdam, 403–441.

CHAPTER 19

Questions

Jeroen Groenendijk and Martin Stokhof

ILLC/Department of Philosophy, University of Amsterdam, 1012 CP Amsterdam, The Netherlands
E-mail: groenend@illc.uva.nl, stokhof@illc.uva.nl

Commentator: J. Ginzburg

Contents

HANDBOOK OF LOGIC AND LANGUAGE
Edited by J. van Benthem and A. ter Meulen

1. Preliminary

In common parlance, the term *question* is used in at least three different ways, which, in order to avoid misunderstanding, will be distinguished terminologically in this chapter. First of all, the term may be used to refer to a particular type of sentences, characterized (in English) by word order, intonation, question mark, the occurrence of interrogative pronouns. In the sequel such sentences will be referred to by the term *interrogative sentences*, or *interrogatives* for short. Another way of using the term *question* is to refer to the speech act that is typically performed in uttering interrogative sentences, i.e. to denote a request to an addressee to provide the speaker with certain information, a request to answer the question. The phrase *interrogative act* will be used to refer to such speech acts. An interrogative act can be described as the act of asking a question. In this description a third use is made of the term *question*, viz., the one in which it refers to the 'thing' which is being asked, and which, as a consequence, may be (partially) answered. This object can be viewed as the semantic content, or sense, of an interrogative. In what follows, the term *question* will be reserved exclusively for this latter use. Of course, several people have doubted that there are such things as questions in this restricted sense of the word. To establish that there are, and to argue that they constitute the primary domain for a logical and semantical theory is one of the main aims of this chapter.

It should be noted at the outset that although questions are typically asked and answered, one can also do a lot of other things with them: one can discuss them, wonder about them, formulate them, etc. Such acts are typically reported by indicative sentences. Hence questions are not exclusively tied to either interrogative sentences, or to the speech act of asking a question. Note furthermore that an interrogative sentence need not always be used to ask a question, i.e. to perform an interrogative act, witness so-called 'rhetorical questions'. And questions can also be asked by other means than through the use of interrogative sentences. Example: 'Please, tell me why there is something rather than nothing'. Or: 'I hereby request you to let me know why there is something rather than nothing'. Similar observations pertain to answers, by the way: an answer may, but need not be expressed by an indicative sentence. So-called 'rethorical questions' are not interrogative but assertive acts, and are often used to formulate an answer to a question.

Be that as it may, the relation between interrogatives and questions is obviously more than coincidental: in reality it is pretty hard to ask questions without using interrogatives at some points. And likewise, answering a question without the use of indicatives seems not to be the default case. A proper theory of the meaning and use of interrogatives should account for this.

Just like indicative sentences, interrogatives come in two forms: on their own, and embedded. The former are often referred to as 'stand alone' interrogatives. Note that in the examples just given, in which a question is asked by means of a sentence in the imperative mood or in the indicative mood, rather than by the use of a proper interrogative, embedded interrogatives occurred. If it is assumed that both stand alone and embedded interrogatives express questions, then questions are around also when the speech act of asking a question is made by non-interrogative means.

This points towards the existence of questions as a separate kind of entity, to be distinguished both from the linguistic object that an interrogative sentence is, and from the pragmatic entity that the act of asking a question constitutes. No one will deny the reality of the latter kinds of entities, but, as was already remarked above, for various reasons many have disputed the existence of questions as a separate semantic category. The study of interrogative sentences obviously belongs to the syntactic part of linguistics, and the study of interrogative acts to that of pragmatics, in particular to speech act theory. Questions, conceived of as is done here, i.e. as the senses of interrogative sentences, or as the contents of interrogative acts, would constitute the domain of a semantics, or logic, of questions. But the existence of this realm is yet to be established.

2. Setting the stage

The semantics of interrogatives is a strange affair. It seems fair to say that in a sense it is an underdeveloped part of natural language semantics. Part of the reason for that, it seems, is that there is no standard framework that is generally acknowledged as providing a common starting point for semantic analyses of various phenomena within the field. No set of concepts exists that can be used to formulate and compare rival analyses. In fact, there even seems no clear communis opinio on what constitutes the subject of investigation in the first place. Clearly this forms a stumbling block for real progress.

For indicative sentences such a common framework is available, viz., that of some variety of denotational semantics. This framework provides some starting points and concepts that various analyses can exploit, even when they want to deviate from it. In other words, denotational semantics provides us with a picture, which can be applied, filled in, modified (up to distortion, in some cases), and so on. Elements of the picture are familiar, almost 'common sense' ideas such as the following. The meaning of a sentence is given by its truth conditions. The meaning of subsentential expressions resides in the contribution they make to the meanings of sentences. Synonymy is identity of meaning, entailment comes down to inclusion of meaning. Thus this framework establishes the reality of certain types of objects and of certain relationships between them. The term *proposition* is generally used to refer to the truth conditional content of a sentence. Likewise, *property* refers to the content of a predicative expression, and so on.

Calling denotational semantics a 'common framework' does not imply that everyone subscribes to it in all details. However, it is important to note that even those who challenge the established view, e.g., the situation semanticists, or the dynamic semanticists, acknowledge that traditional denotational semantics provides a viable framework which is adequate as a semantic theory for at least a certain variety of formal languages and for interesting fragments of natural language. Few would deny that, e.g., first order logic and its standard semantics, or possible worlds semantics for modal predicate logic, are systems that give useful and interesting insights in certain aspects of the meaning of central parts of language, including natural language. It is in this sense that classical denotational semantics provides a common frame of reference for sometimes radically divergent alternative views. It is precisely such a common frame of reference that seems to be lacking when one switches from the analysis of indicatives to that of interrogatives.

The difference seems to lie in this, that in discussing indicatives a distinction is made between the contents of a sentence and the act that is performed by uttering it, with no questions asked.[1] One is usually not bothered by the fact that indicative sentences are typically, though not exclusively, used by speakers to make assertions, to inform hearers, and so on. That is to say, one abstracts away from the (typical) use of indicatives, assuming that their contents can be studied (relatively) independently. Likewise, the specific goals that speakers try to achieve in making assertions, and the strategies they follow in doing so, are considered to be irrelevant in that respect, too. One may acknowledge the importance of these issues from the point of view of an overall theory of language use, and nevertheless consider it justified to abstract away from these pragmatic aspects of meaning, and to concentrate on the informative, propositional content of indicative sentences as such.

When one comes to consider the semantics of interrogatives, however, this perspective is *not* generally adopted. One of the reasons may be the following. By and large, formal semanticists have directed their attention almost exclusively to the analysis of indicatives. In this their enterprise bears the traces of its logical ancestry. Certainly this may have given people – proponents and opponents alike – the impression that the notions of truth and falsity are at the heart of logical semantics. Observing that these notions indeed do not apply to non-assertive uses of language, some have rushed to the conclusion that the semantics of sentence types that are typically employed in performing non-assertive speech acts, are outside the reach of logical semantics, which would be reason enough to doubt its viability as (part of) an overall theory of natural language meaning.

Others, who would like to deny this conclusion, but who share the assumption on which it is based, have seen themselves forced to somehow 'reduce' non-indicatives to indicatives. One popular line of defense is that logical semantics can ignore non-indicatives, precisely because logic is only concerned with propositional content, and the content of an interrogative is a proposition just like that of an indicative. Indicatives and interrogatives, it is claimed, have a different mood, but their logical content is the same. The (unmistakable) difference between the two is not one of meaning, i.e. a matter of semantics, but solely one of use, i.e. it belongs to pragmatics. There are several variants of this type of parrying questions, but, as will be argued below, none of them is very convincing. For one thing, such reductionist' approaches do not do justice to the fact that whereas indicatives[2] can be said to be true or false irrespective of the particular use they are put to, this does not hold for interrogatives. Yet, in the case of the latter, too, there are aspects of content which can be separated from the particular ways in which they are used. If this observation is correct, a reduction of (the contents of) interrogatives to (the contents of) indicatives is fundamentally on the wrong track.

Where does this leave one? It seems that in order to argue that the development of a logical semantics of interrogatives is a viable enterprise, two views must be shown to be inadequate: one that says that they can be analyzed fruitfully only at the level of interrogative acts, and one that holds that there is no significant difference between indicatives and interrogatives, at least as far as semantic content

[1] Nowadays, that is. But the distinction did present a problem to Frege, who wrestled with the difference between asserted and non-asserted propositions, and distinguished them notationally in his Begriffsschrift.

[2] Barring perhaps explicit performative sentences.

is concerned. It is important to note that one may hold both views at the same time. Specifically, one may adduce the second view as an argument for holding the first.

If the proper arguments against these positions can be produced, this will in effect show *ex negativo* that a separate domain of questions, in the technical sense introduced above, exists. A subsequent task is to approach this domain in a more positive way, i.e. to give an indication of the phenomena that a semantics of interrogatives has to deal with, to outline various approaches that have been tried, and to provide an assessment of the main results.

By and large, it is by such considerations that the remainder of this chapter is organized. First the pragmatic view, that interrogatives can be studied fruitfully only at the level of speech acts, is considered and scrutinized. The approach here is mainly direct. An attempt is made to show that this view in effect presupposes a semantic theory of questions. The other line of reasoning, according to which there are no semantic differences between indicatives and non-indicatives, is dealt with along the way, in a more indirect fashion. Various theories that instantiate aspects of the pragmatic view are briefly characterized and discussed, but since our main interest is systematic and not historic, we focus on one particular instance.

Then we move to a discussion of semantic views. First we sketch an approach that starts out from some rather strict postulates concerning interrogatives and answers. The adequacy of the result is discussed with reference to some general methodological considerations. Then a similar kind of view is developed from a different starting point. First we consider whether, and if so how, interrogatives can be added to the language of propositional logic. One of the results of this investigation establishes the essentially intensional nature of the notion of a question. Next we consider the addition of interrogatives to the language of predicate logic, and show that, given some general requirements, the resulting analysis resembles the approach developed earlier in important respects. After a brief discussion of the goals and characteristic issues of logical and computational approaches we turn to a survey of the main semantic approaches that can be found in the linguistic literature. Then we turn to a description of some key data, empirical phenomena that any semantics of interrogatives has to cope with, explaining how the various approaches are motivated by them. Finally, we discuss some other empirical issues, and we end by briefly pointing out directions for future research.

Throughout, our main goal is not to give an exhaustive list of all the analyses and variants that have been proposed over the years, but to provide the reader with a systematic argument that there is such a thing as a semantics of interrogatives, and with a general characterization of its contents.[3]

Finally, the reader should be warned that the discussion that follows will not proceed in a strictly linear fashion. At certain points in the discussion of certain theories reference must be made to views that have not been treated in detail (yet). In an overview like this, where like a bird one spirals up and down, now trying to get a global view of the territory and now scrutinizing some part of it, such 'circularities' cannot be avoided.

---

[3] Two excellent overviews are those of Bäuerle and Zimmermann (1991) and Higginbotham (1995). The overview of Harrah (1984) deals almost exclusively with logical approaches.

3. The pragmatic approach

A general characterization of the pragmatic point of view, which was given above, was that it holds that the meaning of interrogative sentences in natural language can be studied fruitfully only at the level of the (speech) acts that are typically performed by uttering such sentences. This point of view can be argued for both in a more principled manner, and in a more ad hoc fashion. The principled approach springs forth from a theoretical view on natural language meaning as such. It holds that the speech act is the primary unit of semantic analysis, and that the meanings of sentences and subsentential expressions must be analyzed in terms of the part they play in such acts. Other analyses are not likewise theoretically motivated. They stay within the tradition of logical semantics (broadly conceived), but hold that at the level of semantic content no distinction between indicatives and interrogatives can, or need be made, and that hence the difference in meaning must be accounted for at another, i.e. pragmatic level.

Before turning to a detailed discussion of (one version of) the principled approach, let us briefly consider some of the forms that pragmatically oriented analyses have taken. In what follows we will not deal with the details of the various theories that have been proposed,[4] but will try to indicate what has inspired them, and what weaknesses they share. Essentially, all these analyses are what might be called ‘paraphrase theories’. They analyze the meaning of interrogatives not on the level of semantics proper, but through a paraphrase of what is taken to be their typical use, i.e. by taking recourse to the level of pragmatics. In what exactly they take this paraphrase to consist, and in the way in which they implement it within a semantic framework, the various analyses distinguish themselves from each other, but this is the assumption they share: the meaning of an interrogative is given by an expression which describes its typical use.

One of the more obvious ways of implementing the paraphrase view is by making a (grammatically inspired) distinction between the *mood* of a sentence, and its *radical*. This approach has been taken by, among others, Frege (1918) and Stenius (1967). The radical is the (propositional) content of the sentence, the mood the way in which this content is presented. Thus the indicative ‘John is coming to the party, too.’ and the interrogative ‘Is John coming to the party, too?’ share their radical, and differ in mood. The first sentence presents the content, viz., the proposition *that John is coming to the party, too*, in the assertive mood, whereas the same content is presented in the interrogative mood in the second example. As Frege (1918, p. 62) puts it:

> Fragesatz und Behauptungssatz enthalten denselben Gedanken; aber der Behauptungssatz enthält noch etwas mehr, nämlich eben die Behauptung. Auch der Fragesätz enthält etwas mehr, nämlich eine Aufforderung.

The indicative mood indicates that the thought expressed[5] is asserted, i.e. is presented as true. The interrogative mood corresponds to an exhortation, viz., to affirm or to deny the truth of the thought expressed. Only sentences which express a thought can be thus analyzed. Hence, Frege claims,[6] this analysis is not applicable to what he calls

[4] See the overviews referred to above.

[5] Which in this context can be equated with the propositional content.

[6] *ibid.*

'Wortfragen', which are interrogatives such as 'Who is coming to the party?'. Such sentences Frege calls 'incomplete', presumably because they do not express a thought. Thus his reductionist approach is limited in scope. This points towards a general problem. All speech act type approaches, and in this respect the mood-radical view is similar, assume that interrogatives involve the expression of an attitude (of asking, or requesting, or not knowing, or telling) towards some kind of entity, which is what the attitude is an attitude towards. The problem is to find one kind of entity that will serve this purpose both for sentential interrogatives, and for interrogatives containing a *wh*-phrase. If one takes one's lead from the attitude, some propositional kind of entity, such as a Fregean thought, easily suggests itself. But this will do only for the first case, not for the second one.

Another line that has been explored in the literature is what might be called the 'performative approach', defended, among others, by Lewis and Cresswell (see, for example, Lewis, 1970; Cresswell, 1973). The meaning of an interrogative, it is claimed, is given by an explicit performative paraphrase of the illocutionary act performed. On this view the interrogative 'Is John coming to the party, too?' means the same as: 'I hereby ask you whether John is coming to the party, too'. One obvious problem with this analysis, when taken as an analysis of the meaning of interrogatives, is that it must be assumed, to avoid circularity, that the meaning of embedded interrogatives can be specified independently. This assumption seems unattractive, if not unlikely. The analysis as such has never been worked out in sufficient detail to solve this problem.

A third kind of analysis, also starting from a semantic point of view and in some respects quite akin to the performative approach, is what is often dubbed the 'epistemic-imperative' approach, mainly associated with the work of Åqvist and Hintikka (see, for example, Åqvist, 1965; Hintikka, 1976, 1983). According to Åqvist's original analysis, the meaning of our sample interrogative can be paraphrased as 'Let it be the case that I know whether John is coming to the party, too'. Hintikka opts for a similar analysis and gives the following paraphrase: 'Bring it about that I know whether John is coming to the party, too'.

Both paraphrases display the imperative and epistemic elements involved. A remarkable feature of this variant is that it ties the meaning of interrogatives to the existence of a state of (partial) ignorance of the speaker. As a precondition on the proper use of interrogatives this might be defensible, although it implies that the use of interrogatives in circumstances where this condition is not met (such as in exam-situations) has to be explained as somehow deviant. Such an account seems possible, which is not to say that this view on such uses is necessarily correct. But by building this condition into the meaning proper of interrogatives, the present approach faces a different, and more difficult task, viz., of somehow accounting for the fact that interrogatives can be used felicitously in circumstances in which the condition is not met *without an apparent shift in meaning*.

It should be noticed, in defense of the proponents of this analysis, that their primary objective is not a systematic account of the meaning (and, perhaps, the use) of interrogative constructions as they appear in natural language. Rather, they want to develop a systematic logic of questions as abstract, logical objects (which, to be sure, is inspired by properties of natural language interrogatives). Various other aspects of the analyses of Åqvist and Hintikka bear witness to this.

For example, Hintikka analyzes interrogatives in a basic two-part fashion, which is reminiscent of the mood-radical distinction, which he calls the 'request part' and the 'desideratum'. According to this scheme, the sample interrogative used above is divided into the request part 'Bring it about that' and the desideratum 'I know whether John is coming to the party, too'. Thus interrogatives share their request part (up to differences with stem from the presuppositions of the desiderata) and are differentiated according to their desideratum. The imperative operator is sensitive to the presupposition associated with an interrogative. For example, a simple constituent interrogative such as 'Who came to the party?' has as its presupposition 'Someone came to the party', and the imperative operator is restricted by the assumption that this presupposition is fulfilled. Different kinds of interrogative constructions have different presuppositions.[7]

What is interesting to note from the perspective of a semantics of natural language interrogatives is that in Hintikka's analysis embedded interrogatives take priority over stand alone interrogatives: the former occur in the paraphrase of the meaning of the latter. This seems unnatural. The problem that arises is how to supply a semantics of the paraphrase which does not presuppose an independent semantics of the embedded part. This is a general problem with the kind of paraphrase theories we are dealing with here. Hintikka tries to work his way around this problem by giving a special treatment of the epistemic operator *know* combined with a *wh*-complement. Thus, 'I know whether John is coming to the party, too' is further analyzed as 'I know that John is coming to the party, too, or I know that John is not coming to the party, too'. Thus, 'know whether' is analyzed in terms of the familiar 'know that'. Notice that this analysis does not ascribe a meaning to the embedded interrogative as such, but only provides an analysis for the combination of embedding verb and embedded interrogative.

Whether this move is descriptively adequate or not is not what is at stake here.[8] The point is rather that as an analysis of the natural language construction it goes against a strong intuition, and a major methodological principle. The intuition is that the meaning of direct interrogatives is somehow prior to, or at least not dependent on, that of sentences containing their embedded counterparts. Correspondingly, one would like to uphold, if possible, the methodological principle of compositionality, which dictates that the meaning of a compound expression be construed as a function of the meanings of its component parts. That the embedded interrogatives in paraphrases of the kind we encountered above, are independent parts, both syntactically and semantically, can be argued for by pointing out that they can be moved ('Whether John was coming to the party, too, was what he asked me'), can function as the antecedent of anaphoric expressions ('Mary still wondered whether John was coming to the party, too, but Bill knew it'), and so on. Thus, it seems that, at least from the perspective of natural language, one would prefer an analysis which treats embedded interrogatives as distinct parts of the construction in which they occur. But then paraphrase theories run into a serious difficulty. For it seems most natural to treat the independent meaning assigned to an embedded interrogative

---

[7] See Hintikka (1983, p. 174 ff).

[8] One obvious problem is with such embedding verbs as *wonder*, which do not admit of a straightforward paraphrase along these lines.

on a par with that of its stand-alone counterpart, which makes the paraphrase treatment of the latter patently circular. For better or worse, it seems that on the basis of fairly general considerations, one is forced to abandon the paraphrase approach, and to treat the meaning of interrogatives as *sui generis*.[9]

This summary indication of the various forms that paraphrase analyses may take, shows that they are not without problems. Trying to elucidate the semantics of interrogatives, these analyses resort to what are essentially paraphrases of the pragmatics of these constructions, i.e. of the way in which they are typically used. But in doing so, the problem of specifying an independent semantic content of interrogatives can not be avoided altogether, it seems. In view of this, one might well think that perhaps a more principled approach, which starts from the assumption that meaning as such has to be defined in terms of use, might fare better. Therefore, we will concentrate in the remainder of this section on the more principled approach. The main objections to the latter also apply to the former, as will be pointed out along the way. As we will argue, the pragmatic point of view, although certainly not without an intuitive appeal, is not able to account for some simple, but basic facts. This in itself provides ample reason to reject the pragmatic approach as such, and to investigate whether taking a truly semantically oriented point of view will enable one to do better in this respect.

3.1. Starting points

Speech act theory, as it was developed systematically in the pioneering work of Searle in the late sixties, which in its turn depended heavily on Austin's work on performativity, provides a more principled approach than the ones discussed above. It starts 'from the other end', as it were, and regards the act performed by the utterance of a sentence as the primary unit of semantic analysis. Combined with the observation that assertion is but one among the many acts that can be performed through the use of language, this view radically opposes the 'propositional bias' supposedly inherent in traditional logical analysis.

Interrogatives as such have been given due attention in Searle's original work (Searle, 1969), but the concrete analyses he provides there do not really extend the coverage of the proposals discussed above. The main advantage of Searle's analysis seems to lie in this that it is carried out in a systematic framework, which takes the pragmatic point of view as its starting point in the analysis of natural language as such. As said, its empirical coverage remains rather limited, and it does not contain a principled discussion of how it relates to other types of analyses of interrogatives.

It is in these two respects that the work of Vanderveken (1990) constitutes an important step forward in the development of a pragmatic analysis of interrogatives. Especially through its discussion of logical and semantical theories, Vanderveken's work provides a much more detailed picture of what a speech act analysis of interrogatives amounts to. Also it poses some interesting challenges for semantic theories, which will be important for a proper assessment of the latter. For these reasons we will discuss Vanderveken's work in some detail.

[9] This point was argued for forcefully by Nuel Belnap jr, in the form of his celebrated 'independent meaning thesis'. See Belnap (1981).

3.2. General framework

Vanderveken formulates a general semantic framework, which he views as a conservative extension of Montague's universal grammar. His aim is not to develop speech act theory as a rival of truth-conditional semantics, but to provide 'a systematic unified account of both the truth conditional and the success conditional aspects of sentence meaning' (Vanderveken, 1990, Volume i, p. 11). However, in this general framework the speech act point of view prevails: 'My fundamental hypothesis is that complete illocutionary acts [...] are the primary units of literal meaning in the use and comprehension of natural languages' (*ibid.*). The system of illocutionary logic that Vanderveken aims to develop, characterizes the space of possible illocutionary acts.[10] This 'transcendental' (Volume i, pp. 55–56) tool, also called 'general semantics', can then be applied in the description of sentence meaning in natural languages. That truth conditional semantics alone will not suffice, Vanderveken argues by pointing out that, e.g., 'John will do it.', 'Please, John, do it!' and 'If only John would do it.', express the same proposition with respect to some context of utterance, but are used to perform different illocutionary acts with different forces. The illocutionary component, Vanderveken concludes, is an integral part of linguistic meaning. Not all languages relate to the space of possible illocutionary acts in the same way. Linguistic analysis will reveal a variety of relationships that exist between the types of sentences and other expressions that a given language displays and the kinds of illocutionary acts that are typically performed by (literal) utterances of them.

The characterization of the realm of possible illocutionary acts proceeds recursively. Elementary illocutionary acts are of the form $F(P)$ and consist of an illocutionary force F and a propositional content P. Besides elementary illocutionary acts, Vanderveken acknowledges also complex ones, such as conditional illocutionary acts, illocutionary negation, etc.[11] These complex illocutionary acts can not be reduced to elementary ones. Complex speech acts are built using illocutionary connectives, and by means of certain performative verbs. The details of this aspect of Vanderveken's illocutionary logic need not concern us here, so we will refrain from further discussing it.

What *is* relevant is the distinction between *success conditions* and *satisfaction conditions*. The first type of condition determines whether a speaker through an utterance of a sentence has indeed succeeded to perform the corresponding illocutionary act. For example, certain conditions must be fulfilled for a speaker to have made a request by uttering 'Please, pass me the salt'. Success conditions are determined by the illocutionary force F of an illocutionary act. Satisfaction conditions depend on its propositional content P. Thus, in the above example the satisfaction conditions specify that the request is satisfied if the hearer has realized the situation characterized by the propositional content, viz., that the hearer passes the salt. In this example the satisfaction condition has what is called a 'world-to-word' direction of fit: in order for the satisfaction condition to be fulfilled the world has to fit the words. The other direction, the 'word-to-world' fit, is

[10] Vanderveken uses Austin's term 'illocutionary act' in distinction to the term 'speech act', which covers more ground (see below). According to Austin's original formulation an illocutionary act is 'an act [performed] *in* saying something' (Austin, 1962, p. 99).

[11] See Volume i, pp. 24–25, for further details.

characteristic for the satisfaction condition of assertions: for an assertive illocutionary act to be satisfied its propositional content should match an existing state affairs, i.e. it should be true.

An interesting problem arises when we consider the satisfaction conditions of interrogative illocutionary acts. Vanderveken classifies such acts as *directive* speech acts, along with requests (Volume ii, p. 11). That implies that the satisfaction condition of an interrogative act has the world-to-word direction of fit: it requires the hearer to make true the propositional content of the interrogative. The question then arises what this propositional content is. We will come back to this later on.

3.3. *Criticisms of the semantic approach*

After this very summary sketch of the aims of Vanderveken's enterprise, let us now turn to the more concrete issue of the critical remarks he makes on more traditional semantic approaches. Here a distinction can be made between logically oriented approaches, which aim at the development of a pure logic of questions, without paying attention to the relationship with natural language, and more linguistically oriented work, for example within the framework of an (extended) Montague grammar. According to Vanderveken both lines of investigation share a common methodology, which is largely due to Belnap:[12] all analyses 'tend to identify a *question* with a set (or a property) of possible *answers* to that question' (Volume ii, p. 9). Moreover, the various analyses also 'tend to identify answers with propositions or other senses' (*ibid.*). Vanderveken refers to this as a theoretical *reduction* of questions to senses, and distinguishes the following principles on which such a reduction is based:

(i) To understand a question is to understand what counts as an answer to that question.

(ii) An answer to a question is an assertion or a statement.

(iii) An assertion is identical with its propositional content.

Of course, he notes, these principles leave considerable lee-way for actual analyses: e.g., Hamblin (1973) identifies a question with the set of propositional contents of its possible answers, whereas for Karttunen (1977) it is the smaller set of its true answers. And in some other variants, e.g., Hausser (1983), answers are identified with the senses of noun phrases rather than those of sentences.

Vanderveken's main objection is that this type of approach is *reductionistic*: questions are not treated as constituting a category in their own right, but are reduced to other types of entities, viz., propositions. Thus, this methodology does not take illocutionary force into account, or, rather, it reduces illocutionary force to sense. And this is incompatible with the main motivation of speech act theory. Accordingly, Vanderveken argues that the three principles mentioned above are incompatible with basic facts of language use.

However, it is not that obvious that (all of) the theories Vanderveken mentions aim at a reduction of illocutionary force to sense. (And even if they pretend to do so, it remains to be seen whether they really have to be taken that way, i.e. whether the results they obtain

[12] According to Vanderveken. But cf. the Hamblin postulates, discussed in Section 4.1.

really depend on this avowed starting point.) Rather, it seems that the primary aim of theories in this tradition is to characterize a notion of (cognitive) content for interrogative language use, c.q., for interrogative sentences. And the underlying assumption seems to be that one can do so without subscribing to a reductionist methodology, i.e. without claiming that once the contents of interrogatives have been characterized an illocutionary analysis of their function is superfluous. For can one not do truth conditional semantics for assertive language, without claiming that this makes a speech act analysis superfluous?

This is not to say that Vanderveken's characterization of the theories in this tradition is completely off the mark. Indeed, (some version of) the first of the three principles Vanderveken distinguishes seems to be subscribed to, be it sometimes only implicitly, by most protagonists of erotetic logic. The basic semantic intuition underlying this is the following. To understand an indicative sentence, i.e. to grasp the contents of an assertive act, is to know under what conditions it is true. Similarly, to understand an interrogative sentence, i.e. to grasp the contents of an interrogative act, is to know under what conditions it is answered. As indicatives are associated with truth conditions, interrogatives are linked to answerhood conditions. But it should be noted at the outset that this leaves very much undetermined: although the association of answers with propositions is an obvious one, it is by no means necessary. Answers can be given in many different ways, even if we consider only linguistic means to do so. Exclamations, subsentential expressions such as noun phrases ('Who did you meet there?' 'Some linguists.') or prepositional phrases ('How did you get here?' 'By train.'), but also non-indicative sentences ('Did you really hear him say that?' 'Would I lie to you?') may be used to answer interrogatives. So, although indeed some analyses concentrate on answers expressed by indicative sentences, this restriction does not follow from the basic intuition described above.

Hence, Vanderveken's second and third principles are not necessarily subscribed to by an erotetic logician who adheres to the first one. Nevertheless, what would make one think so? There is a chain of associations at work here. Clearly, whatever linguistic (or non-linguistic) form they have, answers convey information, in a broad sense. An interrogative act is a request to tell the hearer something (not necessarily something he does not already know). And, by definition, an answer is something that does that, i.e. something that conveys information which is pertinent to the request. From a semantic perspective, propositions are the natural 'units of information'.[13] Of course, the concept of a proposition is a theoretical one: unlike linguistic expressions, or speech acts, propositions are not observable entities. Thus, the assumption of their existence has to be licensed in some other way, e.g., by reference to their usefulness in descriptive and explanatory contexts. One of these is the speech act analysis of assertive acts, or the semantic analysis of indicative sentences. Here, it is commonly assumed that what an assertive act conveys, or what an indicative sentence means, is a proposition. But notice that it is only when we *define* the notion of a proposition in such a way, i.e. as that what is expressed by an assertion, that Vanderveken's second and third principle make sense. But obviously, no such conception is forced upon us by adherence to the first principle. A simple observation makes clear that we had better refrain from this identification of

[13] Which does not mean that the concept is used uniformly. Various divergent analyses exist, but they all share the idea of a proposition as a unit of information.

propositions with contents of assertions, or indicative sentences: in the examples given above the function of the various linguistic expressions in the context of the preceding interrogatives can very well be described as that of 'conveying a proposition'.

In view of the above, it seems that Vanderveken's charge of 'reductionism' is unwarranted, at least in this sense that the idea that interrogatives be analyzed in terms of answers, or answerhood conditions, in itself does not lead to a reduction of interrogatives to assertions. There seems to be room for a perspective on the meaning of interrogatives according to which a consistent and useful distinction can be made between an analysis of their contents, at the level of semantics, and one of the interrogative acts typically performed by the use of them, at the level of pragmatics. The semantic analysis is carried out in terms of answers, but these should be taken to be the contents of whatever linguistic expressions that can be used to answer questions, which are not tied exclusively to assertions as a separate kind of speech act.[14]

Another claim that Vanderveken makes in the context of his charge of reductionism is interesting to consider, for it, too, seems to rest on a misapprehension if not of concrete analyses, then at least of the potential thereof. What Vanderveken suggests is that erotetic logicians in their reductionist' enthusiasm identify questions with (sets of) propositions, viz., the propositions expressed by (true) answers. But this is only true in a certain sense, and only for some of them. In this context it is important to keep track of the distinction between sense and denotation. For ordinary indicative sentences, those which are normally used to make assertions, the standard analysis identifies their sense with a proposition, and their denotation in a particular world or context with a truth value. The reductionist principles that Vanderveken ascribes to semantic analyses might suggest that interrogatives receive the same kind of propositional sense, and hence, contrary to the most basic intuitions, would denote truth values. But as we saw above, the sense of an interrogative is identified with answerhood conditions, not truth conditions. To the extent that these answerhood conditions are explicated in terms of propositions, the denotation of an interrogative in a particular world or context would not be a truth value, but rather a proposition (or a set thereof), viz., the proposition(s) that in that context would be expressed by a true answer. And, its denotation being of such a propositional nature, the sense of an interrogative, conceived of in the usual way as a function from contexts to denotations, would be a propositional concept, rather than a proposition.

In view of this observation it is clear that Vanderveken's charge of reductionism is misdirected, also for analyses which do make use of propositions: such analyses do not reduce the contents of interrogatives to that of indicatives. The contents ascribed to both are different, and the differences correspond to the difference between truth conditions and answerhood conditions. Here the pragmatic distinction between the kinds of speech acts typically performed by the use of interrogatives and indicatives is reflected in the type of their semantic contents, as is to be expected. By no means should the acknowledgement of a distinct kind of semantic object to serve as the contents of interrogative sentences be taken as an implicit argument that a speech act analysis of interrogative acts is no longer needed. But it does amount to the claim that, speech act theory or no speech

[14] Needless to say that a speech act analysis of interrogative acts according to which they can be (should be) reduced to assertive acts, stands in need of justification, too.

act theory, interrogatives are distinguished not only through their illocutionary force, but also through their contents, which is related to, but distinct from the contents of assertions. What needs to be noted is that this claim, at least at first sight, seems at odds with the central thesis of speech act theory that all (elementary) illocutionary acts are of the form $F(P)$, where F is the illocutionary force, connected with conditions of success, and P is the propositional content, to be explicated in terms of satisfaction conditions. Semantic analyses of the kind outlined above would lead one to conclude that interrogative illocutionary acts do not have a proposition as their content, but rather some kind of propositional concept, to which the notion of satisfaction does not seem to apply. We return to this point below.

We conclude that Vanderveken's main criticism, that semantic analyses which analyze the contents of interrogatives in terms of answers are reductionist in nature, is unfounded.[15] However, the perspective of speech act analysis leads him to formulate some other points, which constitute interesting challenges for an overall theory. One thing Vanderveken notes is that full sentential linguistic answers to interrogatives are not necessarily assertions (p. 10). For example, the interrogative 'Do you confirm his nomination?', can be answered by a so-called declaration: 'Yes, I hereby confirm it'. And similar things can happen in case of such interrogatives as 'Do you promise to come?', which can typically be answered with a performative 'Yes, I promise to be there'. An approach which analyzes interrogatives in terms of answers, ànd which identifies answers with assertions is in trouble here. But as we pointed out above, the latter move is not necessary. Still, it remains to be seen in what way a semantic analysis of interrogatives in terms of answers will be able to cope with examples such as these. For it seems that such approaches *are* wedded to the idea that answers provide information. That is, they seem to presuppose that answers, whatever illocutionary act is performed by the use of them, have propositional content. To what extent such examples as cited above fit this scheme is not obvious. The performative sentences provide information, but not in the sense intended. One way to account for this is to uphold that this is in fact due to the interrogatives. For example, one might say that such an interrogative as 'Do you promise to come?' does not request the hearer to provide information, but asks for a promise. (Cf., the contrasting 'Did you promise to come?') Or consider the interrogative 'What shall we have for dinner tonight?'. This interrogative is typically used to elicit some discussion or suggestions about what to eat tonight. (Cf., the contrasting 'What are we having for dinner tonight?') In view of such examples it may make sense to distinguish informative from non-informative interrogatives. The latter do not primarily ask to provide information, but to perform some other action, even though either a positive or a negative answer will also provide the information that the action will, or will not, be performed. The challenge to semantical theories of the kind outlined above now is to come to grips with this phenomenon. One move might be simply to restrict the application of the theory to informative interrogatives. But this seems unsatisfactory. Another position one could take is to generalize and say that what all interrogatives have in common is that they present some potential alternatives. In the case of informative interrogatives

[15] To be sure, we refer here to what such analyses in principle are forced to acknowledge. This does not mean that there may not be proponents of this approach which *do* have reductionist aims.

these are alternative ways the world is like, in the case of non-informative ones such as those mentioned above, the alternatives concern actions of the hearer.

Another point that Vanderveken raises and that constitutes a challenge for any theory is the following. Interrogative acts are just one type of illocutionary acts embedded in a whole field of linguistic acts which are interrelated in various ways. Hence, a logic of questions can not be an isolated affair, but should be integrated within a general logic of illocutionary acts. An exposition of how Vanderveken wants to realize this, would take us to far afield. Suffice it to notice that, as is not unusual, Vanderveken takes the use of an interrogative sentence to constitute a kind of request, the contents of which he describes as follows: 'A speaker who asks a question requests the hearer to make a future speech act which is a (non-defective or true) answer to that question' (Volume ii, p. 11). Requests are considered to be a subclass of directives, which are a basic type of illocutionary act. In this way, Vanderveken wants to account for the systematic relationships that exist between interrogative acts and other illocutionary acts. The challenge for a semantic theory is, of course, *not* to provide such an account itself, but rather to lend itself to it. Granting that there is such a thing as a logic of illocutionary acts, in which interrogatives are to be treated as a kind of requests, a semantic analysis of the contents of interrogative sentences must be such that it can be embedded in such a logic. But, of course, this demand does not exclude the existence of a logic of questions, not as acts of requesting, but as the particular kind of semantic objects that constitute the cognitive contents of interrogative sentences.

And we may even take a stronger position with regard to the relationship between the two. Vanderveken recognizes that a logic and semantics of the contents of assertive language use is important, and is part of a richer illocutionary logic. Would not the same hold for the logic and semantics of the contents of interrogative language use? One argument for that would be that an illocutionary analysis of interrogatives will need to appeal to questions as the contents of interrogatives, i.e. that a logic of questions is needed as a preliminary for a pragmatic analysis. That this is indeed the case may in fact be argued on the basis of the illocutionary paraphrases that Vanderveken and others give of interrogative acts.

3.4. Questions as requests

What does Vanderveken's analysis of interrogative acts amount to? As we saw above, the illocutionary force of an interrogative act is that of a request of the speaker to the hearer. The propositional content is special: the request is that the hearer perform a future speech act which is a correct answer to his question. Thus, an explicit performative paraphrase would be something like the following: 'I (hereby) ask you to answer (the question) Q', where Q is some specific interrogative. Paraphrasing in terms of an explicit directive of the request type we would get something like: 'Please, tell me Q', with Q the same as above.

What needs to be noticed is that in such paraphrases interrogatives again appear, not as illocutionary acts, but as entities which characterize the contents thereof. Thus, it would seem that a specification of the propositional contents of interrogative acts can not get around acknowledging the existence of questions as semantic objects, given that, as Vanderveken recognizes, the content of a whole is determined by the contents of its parts.

This conclusion runs contrary to Vanderveken's intentions. It is no coincidence, perhaps, that the one particular example that is provided (Volume ii, p. 158) concerns a simple sentential interrogative: 'Is it raining?'. In such examples, it is indeed possible to avoid reference to anything like questions as semantic objects. Informally, the analysis amounts to the following: 'I request that you assert that it rains or deny that it rains'. This does indeed seem to avoid the introduction of questions. But it is not quite obvious that Vanderveken's treatment is correct as far as it goes, nor that it can be generalized. As for the first, asking a question is not simply a request to the hearer to make one of two assertions *at his or her liberty*. What we want is not merely some claim, but the truth: we want to know whether it is raining, not merely to be told that it is, or that it is not. Thus, a more adequate paraphrase along Vanderveken's lines would be: 'I request that if it rains, you assert that it rains, and if it does not rain, you deny that it rains'. Granting that this modified paraphrase is more correct, it is still not so easy to see how this strategy of paraphrasing questions away, can be applied generally. There seem to be different kinds of interrogatives, and different kinds of contexts in which they occur, that defy this analysis. To start with the latter, the modified paraphrase is adequate for certain contexts, such as *request*, *know*, *tell*, and the like. But as a paraphrase for interrogatives embedded under such verbs as *wonder*, or *investigate*, the result is clearly incorrect. And moreover, not all direct interrogatives seem to bend to the reduction as easily as simple sentential interrogatives. Consider a simple constituent interrogative such as 'Which students have passed the test?'. The following paraphrase suggests itself: 'I request that for each student that if (s)he passed the test you assert that (s)he passed the test, and if (s)he did not pass the test, you deny that (s)he passed the test'. But this will not quite do. For the proposition we want to be asserted should also claim of the person who passed that (s)he is a student, which is something this analysis leaves out of consideration. And notice that a more straightforward paraphrase, such as 'I request you to tell me which students passed the test', where the question occurs in the content explicitly, potentially avoids this problem, since it allows us to build this into the content itself. Thus it seems that Vanderveken's strategy of avoiding an appeal to questions as contents of interrogatives in his analysis of the meaning of stand alone interrogatives fails. Acknowledgement of this type of semantic objects simply can not be avoided.

And of course there is no principled reason for Vanderveken to want to avoid questions as contents to play a role in determining the propositions that present the contents of speech acts, be it asking a question or otherwise. Their existence constitutes no threat whatsoever against his general enterprise, and actually might make things easier. Embedded interrogatives play a part in many types of sentences, also simple declarative ones. In such contexts, it seems far from obvious that a speech act type of analysis is what is called for.

The above considerations suggest that the pragmatic approach, whatever its inherent virtues as an analysis of the use of interrogatives, i.e. of interrogative acts, will not do as an account of the meaning of interrogative sentences, given that we want such an account to satisfy certain requirements. For example, it seems desirable that interrogatives be treated as independent parts of sentences and that related meanings be assigned to stand alone and embedded interrogatives. But also when taken as an analysis of interrogative acts, the pragmatic approach as worked out by Vanderveken faces some difficulties which are worth pointing out.

3.5. Asking a question as a basic speech act

The above considerations criticize the pragmatic approach 'from the outside' as it were. In this section we take up an issue that constitutes an internal criticism of the analysis put forward by Vanderveken. One remarkable aspect of his analysis is that in Vanderveken's typology asking a question is not a basic speech act. It belongs to the basic type of *directives*. The illocutionary point of a directive is making an attempt to get the hearer to do something (Volume i, p. 105). Like commissives, directives have the 'world-to-words' direction of fit: their point is to make the world fit the words. The world is to be transformed by some future act, of the hearer in the case of a directive, of the speaker in the case of a commissive, in order to match (satisfy) the propositional content of the speech act. The transforming act is specified by the propositional content of the speech act. And the success of the speech act depends on the world coming to satisfy this content.

According to Vanderveken, asking a question is a special kind of directive. It is a request, which means that unlike other directives, it allows for the option of refusal. Furthermore, it has a specific kind of content: it asks for some future speech act of the hearer which gives the speaker a correct answer to her question. Notice that the 'intuitive' notion of question-as-content appears here, too, not as the (propositional) content of the act of asking a question, but embedded, as the paraphrase given just above suggests. (Note that one cannot replace 'question' again by 'request etc.', on pain of getting into an infinite regress.)

The peculiar thing to note is that the world-to-words fit that is the illocutionary point of an interrogative act, seems to be of a different kind than that of a simple request, such as 'Please, open the door for me'. The latter calls for an action that transforms the world as such, whereas asking an informative question, such as 'Will Mary come tonight?', does not. What it demands is that a change be brought about in the information state of the speaker, an effect that can typically be achieved by the performance of a speech act of assertion or denial with the appropriate content. Of course, any utterance transforms the world in this, admittedly rather trivial, sense that after the act has been been performed it has been performed. But for these kinds of speech acts that is not the real point: they require a change in information about the world, not in the world itself.

Of course, in a certain sense, the information a speech participant has about the world, and about the information of other speech participants, also forms part of the world, but it does so only in a secondary, derivative sense. The world and the information one may have about it, are clearly to be distinguished. The following consideration may perhaps clarify why. One can imagine languages that only express things about the world, *sensu strictu*, and not about information, nor about speech acts. Nevertheless, such a language may very well contain assertives, directives, maybe even commissives, and interrogatives.

And it seems that the meaning of such sentences can be stated without any overt or covert reference to information as such. In other words, the ontology of both the object and the meta-language may be stated without reference to anything but objects constructed with set-theoretical means from things in the world itself.[16]

This is a strong indication that, systematically, these levels, of the world and of information about it, are to be kept apart. Moreover, it shows that the 'merge' between denotational and pragmatic aspects of meaning that speech act theory presupposes, is not forced upon us, at the very least, and that it may even be wise to distinguish the two as much as possible. In Section 4 two examples are discussed that corroborate this point.

Now to return to Vanderveken's typology, it seems that from the perspective adopted above, there is no reason to classify interrogative acts as a subtype of directives. Assuming with Vanderveken that the latter call for an action of the hearer to change the world, their contents can indeed be identified with the specific change in the world required.[17] But assuming that interrogative acts call for an act of conveying information, and adopting the perspective that distinguishes between information and what information is about, interrogatives simply are not of the same type as directives, but rather must be regarded as constituting a basic type of speech act in their own right.[18] And one might even go further and argue that interrogative acts do not necessarily direct the hearer towards any kind of action, except perhaps that of considering the question. To ask a question and to ask someone to answer a question do not necessarily seem to be the same thing. On this view, the content of an interrogative act need not be propositional at all.

Thus it seems that we must conclude that Vanderveken's typology overgeneralizes, and does not fully do justice to the own nature of interrogatives as a separate kind of speech act.[19]

3.6. Summing up sofar

Let us take stock. In the above we have distinguished two major streams in the theory of interrogatives. One, which we dubbed the 'pragmatic approach', analyzes interrogatives

[16] Information states in dynamic semantics, e.g., are of this nature.

[17] Of course, although primarily concerned with changing the world, directives also involve a change in information. The information they convey is that the speaker wants the hearer to change the world in a certain way. And the accommodation of this piece of information, i.e. the actual change in the information state of the hearer this brings about, may even be important in bringing about what the speaker wants. For example, an explicit recognition of a certain wish that the speaker entertains on part of the hearer, may be what drives him to try and bring about the desired transformation in the world. But the important point is that this change of information does not constitute the primary point of a directive, which is directed at the world, and not at the information the hearer has about the wishes and needs of the speaker.

[18] Notice that the Åqvist/Hintikka approach explicitly recognizes that to bring about a change in the information state of the speaker is what is being requested of the hearer.

[19] Which is remarkable, in a certain sense. For did not the pragmatic approach claim to be heir to Wittgenstein's later work? But as the latter wrote (*Philosophical Investigations*, Section 14):

> Denke dir, jemand sagte: "*Alle* Werkzeuge dienen dazu, etwas zu modifizieren." [...] Wäre mit dieser Assimilation des Ausdrucks etwas gewonnen?

In this case not, it seems.

at the level of speech acts. Major proponents of this approach, in one variant or other, are Åqvist, Hintikka, Searle, Vanderveken. Within the other approach interrogatives are analyzed at the level of semantic content, i.e. interrogatives are viewed as a particular type of expressions, with a particular type of sense and denotation. The work of Belnap, Hamblin, Karttunen, Higginbotham and May, and Groenendijk and Stokhof exemplifies this trend.

Besides these a third position can be distinguished, which is a really reductionist one. It identifies interrogatives with statements, for example in Lewis' explicit performative hypothesis (Lewis, 1970). Another example is provided by the work of Tichy (1978). Here there is neither recourse to speech act theory, nor to any special type of semantic content. Plain truth conditional semantics, it is claimed, is all we need.

The argument against the third view is clear. The performative analysis is circular if not combined with an independent analysis of the meaning of embedded interrogatives. And Tichy's analysis, according to which there is no semantic distinction between interrogatives and indicatives, and which therefore must take recourse to a 'difference in pragmatic attitude of the speaker' (Tichy, 1978, p. 276) in order to keep them apart, simply fails to account for what are obvious semantic differences, such as exemplified by sentences in which interrogatives are embedded. Consider 'John knows that Bill walks' and 'John knows whether Bill walks'. If the embedded interrogative and the embedded indicative really have the same semantic value, then each of these sentences should have the same value, too. If Bill walks, and John knows this, we might say that that is indeed the case: both are true. But if Bill does not walk, and John knows this, then they differ in value: in that case the first sentence is false, whereas the second is true.

Such a simple example suffices to show that there are semantic differences between interrogatives and indicatives, and that the semantic content of interrogatives needs to be accounted for.

As said, the pragmatic approach, unlike this reductionist view, tries to do so, although it does not regard the semantic content of interrogatives as a kind of semantic entity of its own. But it encounters difficulties of its own, as we have seen. Does this mean that the pragmatic approach is wrong, and that hence only a semantic analysis can be pursued? Not necessarily. It is of some importance to notice that a priori there is no clash between the two. The case of indicatives may serve to illustrate this.

It seems that most people would agree that one can make a fruitful study of important aspects of the propositional content of assertive language use, without taking into account aspects of illocutionary force. In other words there are systematic aspects of the meaning of indicatives which can be studied independently of their use. Of course, such a semantic account will be limited, it will not cover all aspects of meaning in the intuitive sense, since some of these *are* intrinsically connected with the speech acts which are characteristically performed with indicative sentences. But granting that, most people would grant as well that there is such a thing as a 'pure semantics' of indicatives.

This point is even reinforced if we consider the pragmatic approach. For according to Vanderveken every illocutionary act is of the form $F(P)$, i.e. it has a propositional content, and nothing seems to exclude a restricted, but independent theory of propositional content as part of his overall scheme.[20]

[20] Caveat: there are sentences, such as explicit performatives, of which it seems reasonable to assume that their content can be dealt with only if both aspects of meaning are taken into account at the same time.

As the discussion above has shown, there seem to be no principled reasons for not viewing the meaning of interrogatives in the same way. They, too, have a semantic content (propositional or otherwise), which, it seems, can be studied systematically and fruitfully independent of a study of their characteristic illocutionary uses. Again, such a semantic analysis would only be part of the whole story, but a necessary, and not altogether unimportant or uninteresting one.

So it seems that no a priori considerations would prevent one from taking up the position that both approaches, the pragmatic and the semantic one, are justified in their own right, if put in the proper perspective. An overall theory of meaning has to deal with both cognitive content and illocutionary force, as two aspects of meaning. At least to some extent, it seems, both can be studied independently. When applied to interrogatives this means that one may hold that questions do constitute a separate semantic category, distinct from that of propositions. The latter being the cognitive content of assertive language (use), the former are the contents of interrogative language (use). And one can even push this a little bit further, and argue that in a speech act theory, which deals with both content and illocutionary force, the special content of interrogative language use has to be taken into account.

This may suggest a more or less traditional division of labor between semantics and pragmatics. However, it must be borne in mind that where the borderline between the two is actually drawn may change over time. For example, until recently one would, with respect to assertives anyway, make a neat distinction between truth-conditional aspects of meaning, constituting the domain of semantics, and illocutionary aspects, including conversational implicatures and the like, which were supposed to be handled in pragmatics. The development of theories of dynamic semantics has changed this picture. On empirical and theoretical grounds various people have argued that not truth, but information change potential is the core notion of semantics, thereby significantly extending its coverage. So what exactly constitutes a semantics of interrogatives is a different question than whether there is such a thing in the first place.

We take it that by now we have made it at least plausible that the latter question must be answered affirmatively. We will therefore turn in the next section to some considerations concerning the character and contents of a semantics of interrogatives

4. The semantic approach

Above we have argued that the interpretation of interrogatives in terms of the success and satisfaction conditions of performing the illocutionary act of asking a question presupposes the notion of a question as a distinct type of semantic object. In order to be able to analyze what it is to ask a question, and what counts as an answer, we have to establish what questions are. In this section we will discuss some fundamental principles which have guided much of the research into the semantics of questions over the past two decades, and we will show that they guide us towards a relatively simple, but explanatory powerful picture of what kind of semantic objects questions are. The various concrete analyses that have been put forward in the literature can be characterized in terms of variations on this one common theme. We will also discuss some criteria of adequacy which, be it often implicitly, have been used to evaluate various proposals and which direct further research. The resulting picture does have its limits, however. We will discuss some of these, and point out in which way one might try to overcome them.

4.1. *'Hamblin's picture'*

The general picture of questions as semantic objects that we are about to sketch we call 'Hamblin's picture', because we derive it from three general principles which Hamblin was the first to formulate (Hamblin, 1958). The quotes, however, are (also) scare quotes: we do not claim that Hamblin actually would agree with the outcome. In fact, his own analysis in (Hamblin, 1973) does not (quite) conform to it.

The principles in question were already referred to above, when we were discussing Vanderveken's objections to what he considers the methodology of reducing questions to answers. Hamblin's postulates read as follows:

(i) An answer to a question is a sentence, or statement.

(ii) The possible answers to a question form an exhaustive set of mutually exclusive possibilities.

(iii) To know the meaning of a question is to know what counts as an answer to that question.

In what follows we will discuss these three principles separately. In doing so, we are *not* after a reconstruction of Hamblin's intentions (recall the scare quotes), but rather want to investigate the systematic impact of the principles as such.

The main impact of Hamblin's first postulate is to turn attention away from 'surface' syntactic form. On the linguistic surface, answers often appear as subsentential phrases: for example as NPs ('Who came early?' 'John.'), PPs ('Where are you going? 'To Amherst.'), VPs ('What do you want to do?' 'Have fun.'), and so on. However, the first postulate emphasizes that the function of answers, whether subsentential or sentential, or even when provided by non-linguistic means, is to provide information, and hence that their semantic status is that of a proposition.[21]

The second postulate specifies the nature of the propositions that count as answers to a question. One thing it says is that the propositions that count as answers to a question logically exclude one another: the truth of each of the answers implies the falsity of the others. This means that individual answers are regarded as 'exhaustive' in the sense that each answer, if true, provides completely and precisely the information the question asks for. Furthermore, the postulate states that the set of answers is also exhaustive in the sense that the union (disjunction) of its members completely fills the logical space

[21] This postulate is reflected in early systems of erotetic logic in the identification of interrogatives with sets of *formulae*. To provide an answer to an interrogative is then to choose the true element(s) from the corresponding set. This syntactic set-up relates directly to the primary goal of such systems, which is not primarily the description of the semantics of interrogatives in natural language, but rather the development of formal tools, which can be put to a variety of uses, for example to query databases. (Cf., e.g., Belnap and Steel (1976, p. 2): 'our primary aim here is rather to design a good formal notation for questions and answers and a good set of concepts for talking about them'.) But here we are after a proper semantic notion, i.e. one that can be stated in terms of semantic objects, to serve as the interpretation of expressions of natural language.

defined by the question. In other words, no possible answers defined by the question are left out.

The logical space defined by a question is the space of possibilities it leaves for the world to be like. It can either be taken to be the entire logical space, or that part of it in which the presuppositions of the question are fulfilled. If in a particular situation the presuppositions of a question are not fulfilled, then, one might reason, it has no answer in that situation. In such a case, the only appropriate reply would be to express the proposition that denies that the presuppositions are fulfilled.

The picture that emerges from these two postulates, is that the possible answers to a question form a *partition* of the logical space. Taking presuppositions into account, one block in the partition has a special status, being marked as that part of logical space in which the presuppositions of the question do not hold. (Alternatively, on a non-presuppositional approach, the proposition that expresses that the presuppositions do not hold is counted as one of the answers.)

An immediate consequence of the exhaustive and mutually exclusive nature of the set of possible answers is the following: in each situation (in which its presuppositions are fulfilled) a question has a unique complete and precise true answer, viz., the unique proposition among the possible answers that is true in that situation.[22] This is not to say that this feature cannot be challenged. However, if one thinks that there are reasons to give it up, one must be willing to modify at least one of the two postulates from which it follows.

It may be worthwhile to stress at this point that the notion of answerhood that is under discussion here does not refer to linguistic objects, but to semantic objects: propositions. The existence of a unique true, complete and precise semantic answer does not imply that it can be expressed by linguistic (or other) means, nor that if it can be expressed, it can be expressed in a unique way. Also, even in case we are unable to express a semantically complete and precise answer, circumstantial pragmatic factors may still make it possible to actually convey such an answer. Likewise, pragmatic factors may determine that under different circumstances, depending, e.g., on common knowledge among questioner and questionee, different propositions are most effective in actually conveying precisely the information the question asks for. In short, the everyday observation that one and the same question can often be answered in many different ways, is not necessarily at odds with the existence of a unique true and complete semantic answer.

The importance of the third postulate, finally, is that it identifies the meaning of an interrogative with the partition of logical space which is constituted by the set of its possible answers. That is to say, questions, as semantic objects, are taken to be partitions of logical space. Notice that, Vanderveken's qualms (see Section 3.3) notwithstanding, the charge of reductionism is not justified: the meaning of an interrogative is a separate kind of entity, it is not *reduced* to the meanings of expressions which serve as answers, viz., to propositions. Of course, the two kinds of semantic objects are related: the elements of a partition are propositions. In this respect, the case of interrogatives is quite comparable to that of indicatives. Knowing the meaning of an indicative, i.e. knowing under which circumstances it would be true, obviously does not imply knowing whether it is true.

---

[22] Assuming that the question has a true answer.

Likewise, knowing the meaning of an interrogative, i.e. knowing what would count as the true answer in which situation, does not include knowing what its true answer is.

The picture that emerges from Hamblin's three postulates is extremely elegant, and (hence?) (onto-)logically compelling. But at the same time there are at least two reasons to doubt its correctness. The first one is that the picture presupposes that every question (with non-contradictory presuppositions) has an answer. This we call the 'Existence Assumption'. But, one may ask, is this assumption justified? Are there not unanswerable questions?[23]

The second objection that can be raised, is that the picture presupposes that every interrogative has precisely one true (and complete) answer in a situation (in which its presuppositions are fulfilled). This we may dub the 'Uniqueness Assumption'.[24] Are there not interrogatives with several alternative equally true and complete (equally satisfactory) answers which are not logically equivalent? Potential candidates are so-called 'mention-some' readings ('Where can I buy an Italian newspaper?') and 'choice' readings ('What do two of these computers cost?') of interrogatives, and certain types of coordinated interrogatives ('Where is your father? Or your mother?'). We will return to these issues below. For now, we want to remark only the following.

There is no a priori need to suppose that there is a single notion of a question, i.e. only one kind of semantic object that serves as the content of an interrogative. There may be several. Thus Hamblin's picture need not be interpreted as a picture of *the* essential question. One may also look upon it as a specification of the content of a particular type of interrogatives. Of course, our natural tendency would be to look for one type of object to serve as content of all the various kinds of interrogatives there are, and, sure enough, uniformity would be an important asset of an analysis. However, the possibility that questions do not form a homogeneous class should not be ruled out. And it should also be borne in mind that an assessment of a proposed analysis in semantics not only depends on its fitting all the relevant empirical facts, but also on its logical simplicity and beauty, and on its conforming to general semantic principles.

Some examples of the latter, which are important for the realm of questions, are discussed in the following section.

4.2. Criteria of adequacy

For a semantics of indicatives, the two most important criteria of adequacy are that it specify a notion of semantical identity (equivalence), and give an account of meaning inclusion (entailment). A semantic analysis is materially adequate to the extent that the equivalence and entailment relations that it accounts for are in accordance with our intuitive understanding of the meanings of the expressions involved.

---

[23] This might be a moot point. Consider the question after the truth of an undecidable mathematical proposition. Or 'paradoxical' interrogatives, such as 'Does the Liar lie?'. But the corresponding indicatives do not fit the standard circumscription of their semantics, either.

[24] Which is no other than the 'Unique Answer Fallacy' of Belnap (1982), who obviously was convinced that it is not justified. For the time being we would like to remain neutral on this point, and thus prefer to refer to this feature as an 'assumption', rather than a 'fallacy'.

Similar criteria of adequacy can be formulated for a semantic analysis of interrogatives. Thus, we require that identity criteria for questions be forthcoming, giving rise to an appropriate notion of equivalence between interrogatives. This will allow us to test the proposed analysis against our intuitions concerning when two interrogatives 'pose the same question'. Likewise we want the analysis to specify an appropriate relation of entailment between interrogatives, thus giving an account of when the question posed by one interrogative can be said to be part of the wider question posed by another.

Some decades of thinking about the semantics of indicatives have provided us with reasonably clear judgments on how we want these requirements to be met. The idea of truth conditions, alternative approaches not withstanding, has become entrenched in our intuitions, and serves as a bench mark. Equivalence and entailment defined in terms of truth conditions likewise have become part and parcel of our thinking about the meanings of declarative expressions.

With interrogatives things are perhaps not yet as clear. But something like the role that truth conditions play, is inherent in the relationship between questions and answers. No matter in what particular way we might want to account for it, the notion of a question is intrinsically related to that of an answer. Thus (intuitions about) 'answerhood conditions', though a less familiar item in our semantic vocabulary, seem a good candidate for testing analyses against. Hence, providing an appropriate notion of answerhood can be seen as another criterion for the adequacy of a theory of questions. Such an account links the semantics of indicatives and interrogatives, answers being provided by indicative expressions.

Regarding an account of answerhood as an integral part of one of questions, may also give a firmer grip on the relations of equivalence and entailment between interrogatives. If a semantic analysis specifies an appropriate notion of answerhood between the indicatives and the interrogatives of a language which accords with our intuitive understanding of when an indicative resolves the question posed by a particular interrogative, then this may give us a test for deciding whether the semantics assigns appropriate meanings to the interrogatives of the language. If two interrogatives are assigned the same meaning, then they should have the same answers under the attested notion of answerhood. And if one interrogative is predicted to entail another, then an indicative which is an answer to the first, should also be an answer to the second.

Note that although being answered by the same indicatives is a necessary condition for the equivalence of two interrogatives, it cannot always be taken to be a sufficient condition (and similarly for the relation between answerhood and entailment). It is only both a necessary and a sufficient condition in case we are dealing with a language of which we can be sure that the questions posed by its interrogatives can always be resolved by the indicatives that can be expressed in the language. To take the extreme case: if two interrogatives have no expressible answers at all, we do not necessarily want to conclude that, hence, they are equivalent.[25]

[25] As we shall see later on, this is not just a theoretical possibility. If the language of predicate logic is extended with elementary interrogatives, then even very simple and meaningful questions have hardly any expressible answers that completely resolve them. Fortunately, under suitable restrictions expressible answers are forthcoming.

Expressibility of answers is a traditional topic in erotetic logic, and it is of practical importance for the design of query systems, where the aim is to make sure that the queries that can be formulated in the language can always be appropriately answered. Likewise, it is important in this context that it is guaranteed that all information that could sensibly be obtained from an information base is expressible in a query. From this perspective one could add as an additional criterion of adequacy for a theory of questions and answers that it can shed light on the issue of expressibility of interrogatives relative to information about a particular domain, and the expressibility of possible answers relative to the interrogatives that can be expressed.

From the same perspective, there are further topics that can be addressed. Even in case a complete answer is not expressible, or when an information base (is 'aware' that it) contains only partial information, it may still be possible to come up with a partial answer. This raises the issue what under such circumstances is an optimal answer. If a semantic theory is to shed light on this, it should give rise to a notion of partial answerhood, and to a comparative notion of when one indicative gives more information about a certain question than another.

Although potentially related to practical applications, these questions can still be thought of as belonging to pure, theoretical semantics. At best, answering them could contribute to a 'static' characterization of whether a certain indicative is an optimal reply to a particular interrogative under particular circumstances. A computational semantics of interrogatives should presumably also address the 'dynamic' issue of whether and how one can effectively process a question, decide what the optimal answer is, and produce it in the most understandable way. About these latter issues we will have nothing to say, but concerning the former we at least hope to indicate that theoretical semantics may have some contribution to make here.

The criteria of adequacy discussed so far are of a general, framework independent nature. We end this section by formulating some criteria which are peculiar to a particular framework: standard denotational semantics. Within a denotational semantics, the expressions of a language are assigned semantic objects in a systematic compositional way. One may expect of an analysis along these lines that equivalence is determined by sharing the same semantic value, and that whether one expression entails the other depends on whether the value of the first is 'included' in the value of the second. The latter presupposes that the semantic values of expressions within the relevant syntactic categories come with a 'natural' relation of inclusion.[26] Finally, it may be expected that equivalence amounts to mutual entailment. These framework specific principles will be referred to as formal criteria of adequacy.[27] By default, an adequate denotational semantics of interrogatives should be no exception to these rules.

---

[26] If the semantic objects are sets, the natural relation is set inclusion.

[27] That these criteria are framework dependent is illustrated by the fact that in dynamic semantics, where the meanings of indicatives are identified with update functions, logical equivalence is not always defined in terms of identity of update functions, but in terms of a weaker equivalence relation.

4.3. Adequacy of the Hamblin-picture

That an analysis which conforms to the Hamblin-picture outlined above can be turned into an account that satisfies the adequacy criteria, of course comes as no surprise: it was designed to be that way. In particular, the third postulate forges a strong link between indicative and interrogative, thus making an account of the answerhood relation the heart of the picture. But it will be illustrative to investigate in some detail how this type of analysis complies with these requirements, if only because that will provide us with a handle on the alternatives that will be discussed later.

Since the third postulate establishes a relation between the semantics of interrogatives and that of indicatives, we must start with some assumption concerning the latter. So, suppose indicatives are assigned a proposition as semantic value, where a proposition is taken to be something that 'carves out' a particular part of logical space, viz., the part consisting of those possibilities in which the indicative holds (is true).[28] Without a need for any additional assumptions on what these possibilities are, we can stipulate that one indicative entails another iff the proposition expressed by the first carves out a part of logical space that is contained in the part carved out by the second.

In accordance with the Hamblin-picture as it was developed above, we assume that an interrogative is assigned a partition of logical space (or, alternatively, of that part of it in which its presuppositions hold). The elements of the partition are propositions, viz., those propositions expressed by possible answers. Two interrogatives are then said to be equivalent iff they make the same partition of logical space.

Entailment between interrogatives can be defined in the standard way. By '$?\phi$' we indicate an interrogative. Then we define that $?\phi$ entails $?\psi$ iff every element in the partition made by $?\phi$ is included in some element in the partition made by $?\psi$. Recalling that the elements of the partition expressed by an interrogative are intended as the propositions expressed by its answers, we note that if these propositions can be expressed in the language under consideration, this definition boils down to the following: $?\phi$ entails $?\psi$ iff every possible answer to $?\phi$ entails some possible answer to $?\psi$.

This is borne out by the following definition of answerhood. An indicative ϕ is an answer to an interrogative $?\psi$ iff the part of logical space carved out by ϕ is included in some block in the partition of logical space made by $?\psi$. Thus, an indicative answers an interrogative iff it expresses a proposition which entails one of the semantic answers to the question expressed by the interrogative. As required, this notion of answerhood is such that if two interrogatives are logically equivalent then their possible answers are the same. Likewise, if $?\phi$ entails $?\psi$ then every complete answer to $?\phi$ also is a complete answer to $?\psi$. And to the extent that the semantic answers are expressible by the indicatives of the language both implications also hold in the opposite direction.

The notion of answerhood indicated above, is a notion of complete answerhood. Next to this notion of complete answerhood, a notion of partial answerhood can be defined: ϕ partially answers $?\psi$ iff the proposition expressed by ϕ excludes at least one possible answer to $?\psi$. Complete answerhood is a limit of partial answerhood, in which every block in the partition but one is excluded. Partial answerhood determines whether a

---

[28] For convenience sake we assume that the semantics is total, but nothing hinges on this.

proposition provides relevant information about a certain question. And, in principle, we can compare answers as to the amount of relevant information that they provide concerning a certain question. On the one hand, the more possible answers are excluded, the better it is. This favors stronger propositions over weaker ones. On the other hand, if two propositions exclude the same possible answers, and one is stronger than the other, the weaker one is to be preferred, since it contains less irrelevant information, i.e. information the question does not ask for. In the end, answers which express propositions which precisely fill one block in the partition that a question makes of logical space will come out as providing the best answers. But one may be forced to compromise, either because one's information simply does not support such an optimal answer, or because the linguistic means to express such an answer effectively are lacking.

We take it that these observations suffice to show that the Hamblin-picture may lead to analyses that satisfy the adequacy criteria. Of course, the empirical import of such accounts still needs to be tested against observations concerning the meanings of actual interrogatives. What we have sketched above are the contours of an analysis, not a full-fledged theory of the semantics of the interrogative structures in a particular language. Two such concrete instances will be discussed below. In the next section we consider the case of a language of propositional logic extended with yes/no-interrogatives. In the subsequent section we discuss the predicate logical case, and extend the indicative language with elementary interrogatives asking to specify the denotation of a property or relation.

4.4. Questions in propositional logic

Above we have sketched an analysis of questions and answers which remained on a conceptual level and did not make reference to a particular language. In this section we will consider language, albeit a logical one. We will investigate how the language of classical propositional logic can be extended with yes/no-interrogatives.

Syntactically, yes/no-interrogatives are formed by prefixing a question-mark to the formulae of a standard language of propositional logic. So, there are two distinct sentential categories in the extended language: indicatives and interrogatives. The connectives only apply to indicatives. This means that the question-mark can only occur as an outermost operator. Hence, compound interrogatives do not occur in the language under consideration.[29]

The interpretation of the indicative part of the language is classical, i.e. extensional and bivalent. With respect to a model (valuation function), each indicative either denotes the value *true* or the value *false*. And the connectives receive their usual truthfunctional interpretation.

---

[29] When dealing with yes/no-interrogatives, this is no real limitation. Conjunctions of interrogatives, such as 'Does Mary come? And does Peter?', and interrogatives expressing alternative questions, such as 'Does Mary come or Peter?' cannot be answered appropriately by a simple 'yes' or 'no'. And although a conditional interrogative such as 'If Mary comes, does Peter come, too?' can sometimes be so answered, it can also be answered by 'Mary doesn't come', which shows that such interrogatives, too, are not simple yes/no-interrogatives.

What remains to be decided is how to interpret the interrogatives in the language. Of course, we might let the conceptual framework outlined above guide us here. And in the end the analysis we will come up with does conform to that. However, in the present context it is illuminating to take another route, and observe that it leads to the same result.

Forgetting about the conceptual analysis outlined above, it seems natural to raise the following issue in the present case:

> Is it possible to provide an adequate interpretation for yes/no-interrogatives by extending the standard bivalent *extensional* semantics of propositional logic?

We will argue that this question must be answered in the negative, i.e. we will show that no extensional interpretation of the question-mark operator can be provided that meets the criteria of adequacy formulated above.[30] More in particular, we will show that although it is possible to meet the criteria of material adequacy, the criteria of formal adequacy cannot be met. An extensional interpretation gives rise to materially adequate notions of answerhood, entailment and equivalence. The notion of equivalence accounts for the fact that two interrogatives are equivalent iff they have the same answers, but it is not the standard notion under which two expressions are equivalent iff they have the same semantic value.

The argument as such could be stated in a few paragraphs. However, precisely because the extensional analysis is materially fully adequate, we will work it out in some detail. The logical and semantical facts we will discuss with respect to the formally inadequate extensional semantics, will simply go through after the formal deficiencies have been repaired.

4.4.1. Yes/no-semantics

For the indicative part of the language the standard semantics specifies the truth value of an indicative ϕ in a model w as a function of its component parts, in such a way that either $[\phi]_w = 1$ or $[\phi]_w = 0$. Given that interrogatives are built from indicatives, obtaining an extensional interpretation for the question-mark operator means that we have to specify the value of an interrogative $?\phi$ in a model w in such a way that the following extensionality principle holds:

$$[\phi]_w = [\psi]_w \Longrightarrow [?\phi]_w = [?\psi]_w.$$

Since there are just two possible values for the indicatives, this means that there can be at most two values for the interrogatives. Obviously, opting for a single semantic value has absurd consequences: all interrogatives would be assigned the same meaning. Hence, we must conclude that within a bivalent extensional semantics there are exactly two possible semantic values for yes/no-interrogatives, which, moreover, are one-to-one related to the two truth values.

---

30 Although we present the argumentation against an extensional interpretation with respect to a bivalent (total) interpretation, this is not essential. A similar argumentation can be given against a three-valued (partial) extensional interpretation.

We cannot identify the semantic values for interrogatives with the truth values, since then there would be no semantic difference between an indicative ϕ and the corresponding yes/no-interrogative $?\phi$. That would bring us back to a position we have already rejected, viz., that the difference between interrogatives and indicatives is not a difference in semantic content, but resides elsewhere.

Hence, $?\phi$ should be assigned one value in case ϕ is true, and another other value, in case ϕ is false. Let us call these values **yes** and **no** respectively.

DEFINITION 4.1 (*Extensional interpretation*).

$$\begin{aligned}[?\phi]_w &= \textbf{yes} \text{ if } [\phi]_w = 1\\ &= \textbf{no} \text{ if } [\phi]_w = 0.\end{aligned}$$

As long as one remembers that **yes** and **no** are *not* the linguistic expressions 'yes' and 'no' – which do not have counterparts in this logical language, anyway – but arbitrary semantic objects, it will do no harm to refer to them as *answer values*.[31] The use of this terminology highlights that the meanings of interrogatives and indicatives are different: indicatives are related to truth, interrogatives to answers. At the same time it enables us to verbalize the semantic content of both categories of sentences in a uniform way: just as the meaning of an indicative lies in its truth conditions, the meaning of an interrogative is given by its answerhood conditions.[32]

4.4.2. Answerhood

One of the criteria of adequacy we encountered above is that the semantics give rise to an appropriate relation of answerhood between indicatives and interrogatives. We define the following notion:

DEFINITION 4.2 (*Answerhood*). ϕ is an answer to $?\psi$ iff $\forall w, w'$: $[\phi]_w = [\phi]_{w'} = 1 \Rightarrow [?\psi]_w = [?\psi]_{w'}$.

According to this definition, ϕ is an answer to $?\psi$ iff in all models in which ϕ is true, the answer value of $?\psi$ is the same, i.e. the question $?\psi$ is settled in the set of models in which ϕ is true. For trivial reasons, the contradiction is an answer to any question. However, as one would expect, it can never give a true answer to a question.

Although our basic argument in this section is that an extensional interpretation does not provide us with an adequate semantic analysis of yes/no-interrogatives, the following fact shows that the notion of answerhood that it gives rise to is materially adequate:

FACT 4.3. ϕ is an answer to $?\psi$ iff $\phi \models \psi$ or $\phi \models \neg\psi$.

[31] One way of interpreting these two values – without introducing new elements in the ontology – is as one-place truth functions: **yes** as the identity function, and **no** as the truth function corresponding to negation. In some systems of erotetic logic, yes/no-interrogatives are interpreted along these lines.

[32] Note that – whatever is wrong with it – it does not make sense to object that the yes/no-semantics is a 'reductive analysis of questions in terms of answers'. The mere fact that we refer to the semantic values of interrogatives as 'answers' is irrelevant. If that would constitute a reduction of questions to answers, then a truth conditional semantics for indicatives would be a reduction of propositions to truth values.

This fact shows that both ϕ and $\neg\phi$ are possible answers to $?\phi$.

Note that the syntax of the language guarantees that if an interrogative $?\phi$ is is a well-formed expression, then so are ϕ and $\neg\phi$. In other words, the possible complete answers to any yes/no-interrogative are expressible.

4.4.3. Formal inadequacy

The expressibility of possible answers gives us the means to test the adequacy of the analysis by checking whether the following holds:[33]

REQUIREMENT 4.4. $?\phi$ and $?\psi$ are logically equivalent iff $?\phi$ and $?\psi$ have the same answers.

From Fact 4.3, we can immediately see:

FACT 4.5. $?\phi$ and $?\neg\phi$ have the same answers.

Hence, if our semantics is to be adequate it should support the fact that $?\phi$ and $?\neg\phi$ are logically equivalent. Under the standard notion of equivalence this requires that $\forall w$: $[?\phi]_w = [?\neg\phi]_w$. But quite the opposite holds for an extensional yes/no-semantics: in each model $?\phi$ and $?\neg\phi$ have *a different* value, if the answer value of the one is **yes**, the answer value of the other is **no**.

This shows that an extensional semantics for yes/no-interrogatives, although it meets the criterion of material adequacy, viz., that it give rise to an appropriate notion of answerhood, is inadequate. It fails to meet the formal criterion that within a denotational semantics, logical equivalence amounts to identity of semantic value in each model.

4.4.4. Non-standard equivalence and entailment

In the present set-up there are two answer values, and the interrogatives $?\phi$ and $?\neg\phi$ have a different value in each model. What then do they have in common? Their *value pattern* over the set of models is the same. And in fact, this characterizes when two yes/no-interrogatives have the same possible answers:

FACT 4.6. $?\phi$ and $?\psi$ have the same answers iff $\forall w, w'$: $[?\phi]_w = [?\phi]_{w'} \Leftrightarrow [?\psi]_w = [?\psi]_{w'}$.

This observation immediately supplies us with a materially adequate criterion of identity of semantic content of two interrogatives:

DEFINITION 4.7 (*Non-standard equivalence*). $?\phi$ is logically equivalent with $?\psi$ iff $\forall w, w'$: $[?\phi]_w = [?\phi]_{w'} \Leftrightarrow [?\psi]_w = [?\psi]_{w'}$.

The notion of equivalence suggests the following non-standard notion of entailment:

DEFINITION 4.8 (*Non-standard entailment*). $?\phi$ entails $?\psi$ iff $\forall w, w'$: $[?\phi]_w = [?\phi]_{w'} \Rightarrow [?\psi]_w = [?\psi]_{w'}$.

[33] Recall from our discussion of the adequacy criteria that if some answers are not expressible, having the same answers is not sufficient for being equivalent.

This notion meets the standards that equivalence amounts to mutual entailment, and it supports the following fact, which shows its material adequacy:

FACT 4.9. $?\phi$ entails $?\psi$ iff every answer to $?\phi$ is an answer to $?\psi$.

The relations of equivalence and entailment are characterized by the following facts:

FACT 4.10.
(i) $?\phi$ entails $?\psi$ iff $\phi \equiv \psi$, or $\phi \equiv \neg\psi$ or ψ is non-contingent.
(ii) $?\phi$ is logically equivalent with $?\psi$ iff $\phi \equiv \psi$ or $\phi \equiv \neg\psi$.

So, the only 'interesting' pair of equivalent interrogatives are $?\phi$ and $?\neg\phi$.

Entailment between yes/no-interrogatives differs minimally from equivalence and is also rather 'poor'. We have already seen that $?\phi$ and $?\neg\phi$ are equivalent, so, obviously, they also entail each other. The only other entailment relation that is of interest is that any interrogative entails both $?(\phi \vee \neg\phi)$ and $?(\phi \wedge \neg\phi)$. Both have the entire space of possibilities as the only block in the partition they make. And we might call both interrogatives tautological. Any question includes the tautological question.

Entailment between interrogatives does not mirror entailment between the corresponding indicatives. For example, although $\phi \wedge \psi$ entails ϕ, not *every* answer to $?(\phi \wedge \psi)$ is an answer to $?\phi$. For, although $\neg(\phi \wedge \psi)$ is an answer to $\phi \wedge \psi$, it is not an answer to ϕ. Of course, $\phi \wedge \psi$ is an answer to both.

The poverty of the entailment relation between yes/no-interrogatives reflects that they are the atoms in the question-hierarchy induced by the entailment relation. Since there are no complex interrogatives in the language, this was to be expected.

4.4.5. An intensional semantics for yes/no-interrogatives

All seems well with the extensional semantics for yes/no-interrogatives, except for one flaw, viz., that equivalence cannot be defined in terms of having the same semantic value and that entailment cannot be defined in terms of inclusion of semantic values.

Note that the identity criterion as formulated in the definition of non-standard equivalence, can also be written as follows:

$$\forall w\colon \{w' \mid [\phi]_{w'} = [\phi]_w\} = \{w' \mid [\psi]_{w'} = [\psi]_w\}.$$

This means that if $\{w' \mid [\phi]_{w'} = [\phi]_w\}$, the set of models where ϕ has the same truth value as in w, can be taken to be the semantic value of $?\phi$ in w, equivalence can be defined in terms of having the same semantic value in each model, and entailment as inclusion of semantic values.

However, we cannot proceed in exactly this fashion. One cannot specify the semantic value of an expression *within* a certain model by referring to *other* models. An easy and standard way to get around this is to introduce the notion of a *possible world*. We identify a world w with what we used to call a model. And a model M is now a set of possible worlds. The extension of an indicative ϕ relative to a model M and a world w, $[\phi]_{M,w}$, is the truth value assigned by w to ϕ. The intension of ϕ in a model M is the set of worlds in M in which ϕ is true: $[\phi]_M = \{w \in M \mid [\phi]_{M,w} = 1\}$. A set of worlds is called a proposition, $[\phi]_M$ is the proposition expressed by ϕ in M. ϕ entails ψ iff in every model M the proposition expressed by ϕ in M is included in the proposition expressed by ψ in M, i.e. $\phi \models \psi$ iff $\forall M$: $[\phi]_M \subseteq [\psi]_M$. The interpretation of the indicative part of the language consists in a recursive specification of the extension of the indicatives of the language relative to a model and a world.

Having thus set the stage, and using the observation made above, we are ready to state the intensional interpretation of interrogatives:

DEFINITION 4.11 (*Intensional interpretation*).

$$[?\phi]_{M,w} = \{w' \in M \mid [\phi]_{M,w'} = [\phi]_{M,w}\}.$$

The extension of an interrogative in a world w is an intensional object, a proposition. It is the proposition expressed by ϕ in case ϕ is true in w, and the proposition expressed by $\neg\phi$ in case ϕ is false in w. I.e. the extension of a yes/no-interrogative is the proposition expressed by a complete and precise answer to the question posed by the interrogative. We can identify the intension of $?\phi$ in a model M, the question expressed by $?\phi$ in M, with the set of its possible extensions in M: $[?\phi]_M = \{[?\phi]_{M,w} \mid w \in M\}$. The propositions in the set are mutually exclusive, and exhaust the logical space consisting of all possible worlds in M. In other words, we have arrived at Hamblin's picture of the notion of a question as a partition of logical space: a bipartition in the case of (non-tautological) yes/no-interrogatives.

This analysis is both materially and formally adequate, as the following observations show. Entailment and logical equivalence between interrogatives, can be defined in the standard way:

DEFINITION 4.12 (*Entailment and equivalence*).

(i) $?\phi \models ?\psi$ iff $\forall M, \forall w \in M$: $[?\phi]_{M,w} \subseteq [?\psi]_{M.w}$.

(ii) $?\phi \equiv ?\psi$ iff $\forall M, \forall w \in M$: $[?\phi]_{M,w} = [?\psi]_{M,w}$.

Two interrogatives are equivalent iff they always partition the logical space in the same way. An interrogative $?\phi$ entails an interrogative $?\psi$ iff every block in the partition made by $?\phi$ is always included in a block of the partition made by $?\psi$. It cannot hold of two different bipartitions of the same logical space that every block in the one is part of some block in the other. Hence, only equivalent contingent interrogatives entail each other. And any interrogative entails the tautological interrogative, which corresponds to a partition which always has only one element, a single block consisting of the logical space as a whole.

The relation of answerhood between indicatives and interrogatives is defined as follows:

DEFINITION 4.13 (*Answerhood*). $\phi \models ?\psi$ iff $\forall M \exists w \in M$: $[\phi]_M \subseteq [?\psi]_{M,w}$.

In terms of the partition $?\psi$ makes on M, this expresses that ϕ is an answer to $?\psi$ iff the proposition expressed by ϕ in M is always a (possibly empty) part of one of the blocks in the partition made by $?\psi$.

The facts observed above in working out the extensional interpretation, concerning the relations between answerhood, entailment and equivalence remain in force, and will not be repeated. This illustrates once more that what we gain in the intensional approach is not material, but only formal adequacy. However, at the same time we hope that it also shows that formal adequacy enhances conceptual clarity.

4.4.6. Remark on coordination

An additional criterion of adequacy that can be imposed on a semantic analysis of interrogatives is that it can deal with coordination of interrogatives. Material adequacy requires that answerhood and entailment relations are appropriately accounted for. Formal adequacy requires that conjunction and disjunction of interrogatives are analyzed in the standard way in terms of intersection and union.[34]

How does the semantics presented above fare if we add coordinated interrogatives to the language? Conjunction of interrogatives ('Will John be there? And will Mary be there?') can be interpreted in a standard way: the pairwise intersection of the blocks in two partitions results in another partition. By simply conjoining the possible answers to two interrogatives, we obtain the propositions that answer their conjunction. The extension of a conjunction of two interrogatives can be defined standardly in terms of the intersection of the extensions of the conjuncts. The notions of entailment and answerhood as they were defined above give the appropriate results. For example, a conjunction of two interrogatives will entail each of its conjuncts. And an indicative is an answer to a conjunction of two interrogatives iff it is an answer to each of its conjuncts.

Disjunction of interrogatives ('Will John be there? Or Mary?') however, is another matter. To see why, it suffices to observe that taking the pairwise union of the blocks in two partitions, will usually not result in a new partition. We cannot identify the extension of the disjunction of two interrogatives with the union of the extensions of its disjuncts. It would make the wrong predictions with respect to entailment and answerhood relations.

This corresponds to the fact observed above that disjunctions of interrogatives are peculiar: they violate the Unique Answer Assumption, and it has been argued[35] that a disjunction of interrogatives, unlike a conjunction, does not express a single question. More on this below.

4.4.7. Remark on natural language

In natural language, 'negative' yes/no-interrogatives do not behave precisely the same as the interrogatives of the form $?\neg\phi$ in our logical language. Compare the following sequence: 'Is John at home? Yes (he is)./No (he isn't)', with: 'Is John not at home? Yes, (of course) he IS./No (he isn't)'. Whereas whenever $?\phi$ has a 'positive' value $?\neg\phi$ has a 'negative' value, the English interrogatives in both sequences receive the same negative answer, and the same positive answer, except for the fact that as a reply to the negative interrogative, a positive answer is marked.

The pair of logical interrogatives and the pair of English interrogatives do have in common that they express the same question. However, by using the negative interrogative in the second sequence the questioner also expresses that she is afraid to get a

[34] See Groenendijk and Stokhof (1984a, 1984b) for a more detailed discussion.

[35] See, e.g., Belnap (1982), Groenendijk and Stokhof (1984a).

negative answer to the question whether John is at home. That explains why a positive answer is marked by emphatic elements.

So, the negative linguistic element in the second sequence does not play its usual logical role of negation, but rather has a pragmatic function. One could bring forward that it is precisely the fact that from a logical semantic point of view $?\phi$ and $?\neg\phi$ express the same question, that creates the possibility for this process of pragmatic recycling of the element of negation.

4.5. *The predicate logical case*

In the previous section we only considered interrogatives which can be answered by a simple 'yes' or 'no'. Another basic type of interrogatives are constituent interrogatives such as 'Which students passed the test?', which is typically answered by listing the students that actually passed the test. One can look upon such interrogatives as asking for a characterization of the actual denotation of a particular property in case of one-constituent interrogatives, and of a relation in the case of multiple constituent interrogatives such as 'Who plays with whom?'.

Besides the possibility that constituent interrogatives ask for an exhaustive characterization of a property or relation, there is also the option that they ask to mention just one or some other number of instances. Here, we will only consider the mention-all interpretation, but we will return to the mention-some interpretation later on.

Properties and relations (between ordinary first order objects) is what predicate logic is all about, and it makes sense to consider the possibility of extending the language of predicate logic with interrogatives which inquire after which objects have certain properties and stand in certain relations.

To be able to formulate such interrogatives, it suffices to add the following rule to the syntax of predicate logic:[36]

DEFINITION 4.14 (*Syntax*). Let ϕ be a formula in which all and only the variables $x_1, \ldots, x_n$ $(n \geqslant 0)$ have one or more free occurrences, then $?x_1 \cdots x_n\phi$ is an interrogative formula.

As was the case in the propositional language, and for similar reasons, we leave complex interrogatives, including quantification into interrogatives, out of consideration.[37]

[36] For ease of presentation, we don't allow for vacuously 'querying over' a variable, and neither do we allow that interrogative formulae contain occurrences of free variables. Notice also that variables are queried over in one fell swoop, rather than one by one. The latter construction would require a syntactic rule which turns interrogatives into interrogatives. Going about the way we do here, is not a matter of principle, but of convenience.

[37] This means that, as compared to natural language, the language under consideration has limited means of expressing questions, even with respect to the particular domain it is suited for. Not only coordination of interrogatives occurs in natural language, but an interrogative sentence like 'Which student did each professor recommend?' has an interpretation where it asks to specify for each professor which student (s)he recommended. This reading, under which the sentence can be paraphrased as 'Which professor recommended which student?', seems to correspond to universal quantification into an interrogative. (But see the discussion of such cases below,

Since the rule allows for zero variables to be 'queried over', yes/no-interrogatives are just a special case. Thus we obtain interrogatives such as $?\exists x(Px \wedge Qx)$, asking whether or not there is some object that has both the property P and the property Q. As in the case of propositional logic, there are only two possibilities to be discerned.

With the aid of the same rule, we can also form interrogatives such as $?x(Px \wedge Qx)$, which is be interpreted as asking for a characterization of the extension of the complex property of being both P and Q, i.e. as asking for a complete specification of those objects which have both properties. In this case the number of possibilities equals that of the number of sets of objects that can be the value of the conjunctive predicate.

Notice that whenever the question posed by $?x(Px \wedge Qx)$ is answered, the question put by $?\exists x(Px \wedge Qx)$ is answered, too. That there are no objects that have both properties is one possible answer to the first question, which at the same time provides a negative answer to the second question. Any other possible answer to the first question, specifying some non-empty set of objects as having both properties, would at the same time imply a positive answer to the yes/no-question.[38] This means that an adequate semantics should account for the fact that $?x(Px \wedge Qx)$ entails $?\exists x(Px \wedge Qx)$.

Notice furthermore that an indicative like $(Pa \wedge Qa) \wedge (Pb \wedge Qb)$ does not count as a (complete) possible answer to $?x(Px \wedge Qx)$. The proposition expressed by that sentence only informs us that *at least* the objects denoted by a and by b have both properties, and thereby still leaves open many different possibilities for the extension of the conjunction of both properties. A question like 'Which students passed the test?' can typically be answered by 'Alfred and Bill (passed the test)', but such an answer equally typically conveys the information that *only* the students Alfred and Bill passed the test. Hence, a better candidate for a complete answer is $\forall x((Px \wedge Qx) \leftrightarrow (x = a \vee x = b))$, which specifies the extension of the conjunction of the two properties to consist only of the objects denoted by a and b. However, this will still only inform us about which *objects* have both properties to the extent that we already know which objects are denoted by a and b.

The question which object is denoted by a particular constant is posed by an interrogative like $?x(x = a)$. It asks the question who a is.[39] Again, an indicative like $\exists x(\forall y(Py \leftrightarrow x = y) \wedge x = a)$, 'a is the object which has property P', will only inform us about the identity of a to the extent that we are informed about which is the unique object that has the property P.

As a last example consider the interrogative $?xyRxy$. It asks for a specification of the extension of the relation R, i.e. it is answered by a specification of a set of pairs of objects which stand in the relation R. Obviously, whenever $?xyRxy$ is answered, $?yxRxy$ is answered also, and vice versa. Knowing who loves whom and knowing whom is loved by whom amount to the same thing. This means that an adequate semantics should account for the logical equivalence of these two interrogatives.

Section 6.4.2.) In another sense, however, it is guaranteed that any question concerning (simple and complex) relations between objects that can be formulated in the indicative part of the logical language is expressible. The paraphrase we gave of the example that seems to involve quantification into interrogatives is a case in point.

[38] So, interrogatives of the form $?x\phi$ are not interpreted as having an existential presupposition. That no objects exist that satisfy ϕ is taken to be one possible answer among the others.

[39] This is one of the meanings that natural language interrogatives of the form 'Who is A?' may have. See, e.g., Hintikka and Hintikka (1989), Boër and Lycan (1985) for discussion.

4.5.1. Intensional interpretation

If only because yes/no-interrogatives are part of the language under consideration, the argument against an extensional interpretation of interrogatives given above remains in force. As in the propositional case, it also holds for the predicate logical language that we can provide an extensional interpretation, and define notions of answerhood, entailment and equivalence which do give appropriate results, but only fail to meet the formal criterion that equivalence be defined in terms of identity, and entailment in terms of inclusion of semantic values. We will not pursue this line, but immediately present the formally adequate intensional interpretation.

As before, a model M will be identified with a set of worlds, but now, a world w is identified with an ordinary first order model, consisting of a domain and an interpretation function, assigning values to the non-logical constants of the language, relative to the domain.[40] For the indicative part of the language, the extension $[\phi]_{M,w,g}$ of a formula ϕ with respect to a model M, a world w, and an assignment g is defined in the usual way.

Interrogatives are interpreted as asking for a specification of the actual extension of a particular relation. Relative to a world and an assignment, the extension of the relation an interrogative $?x_1 \cdots x_n\phi$ asks to specify, is defined as follows:[41]

DEFINITION 4.15 (*Relational interpretation*).

$$\langle ?x_1 \cdots x_n\phi\rangle_{M,w,g} = \{\langle g'(x_1), \ldots, g'(x_n)\rangle \mid [\phi]_{M,w,g'} = 1, \\ \text{where } g'(x) = g(x), \text{ for all } x \neq x_1 \cdots x_n\}.$$

Note that in case $n = 0$, which is the case of yes/no-interrogatives, $\langle ?\phi\rangle_{M,w,g} = [\phi]_{M,w,g}$. Hence, the intensional interpretation of yes/no-interrogatives as given above now amounts to

$$[?\phi]_{M,w,g} = \{w' \in M \mid [\phi]_{M,w',g} = [\phi]_{M,w,g}\}.$$

The same schema gives appropriate results also for $n > 0$, collecting all the worlds in the model where the extension of the relation the interrogative asks to specify is the same as in the actual world w. Hence, using $?\phi$ as a meta-variable ranging over all the interrogatives of the predicate logical language, the intensional interpretation is given by:

DEFINITION 4.16 (*Intensional interpretation*).

$$[?\phi]_{M,w,g} = \{w' \in M \mid \langle ?\phi\rangle_{M,w',g} = \langle ?\phi\rangle_{M,w,g}\}.$$

---

[40] One can look upon these models as possible information states of an agent. Each possible world in a model is a way the world could be according to the information of the agent.

[41] This relational interpretation can be taken as the extensional interpretation of interrogatives in a predicate logical language. If we do so, and use analogues of the definitions of answerhood, entailment, and equivalence as they were defined with respect to the extensional interpretation of the propositional language, then we arrive at a materially adequate analysis, which only fails to meet the formal criteria concerning the notions of entailment and equivalence.

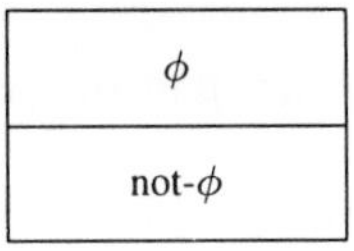

Fig. 1. Partition made by $?\phi$.

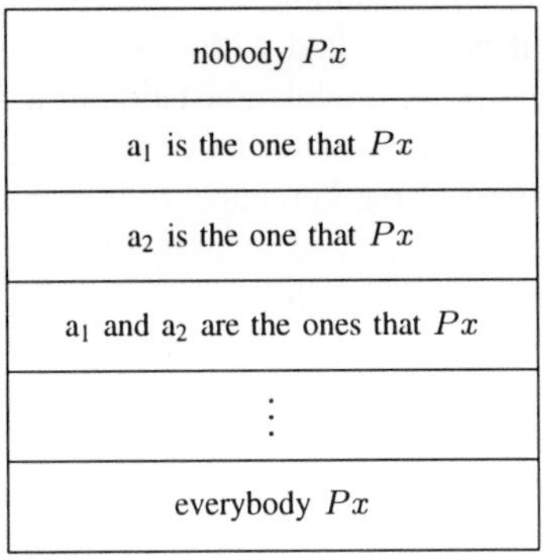

Fig. 2. Partition made by $?xPx$.

For example, the extension of $?xPx$ in a world w will be the set of all worlds in which the same objects belong to the extension of the predicate P. This set of worlds corresponds to the proposition which exhaustively characterizes the positive extension of the property P in world w. The intension $[?xPx]_M$ of $?xPx$ is then identified by the set of mutually exclusive propositions, each of which characterizes a possible extension of the predicate P relative to the model M. Their union exhausts the logical space, the set of all worlds in the model. Hence, the question expressed by $?xPx$ fits the Hamblin picture: it is a partition of logical space. There are as many blocks in the partition as there are possible extensions of the predicate P within in the model.

In general, the partition induced by an interrogative $?x_1 \cdots x_n\phi$ will consist of as many blocks as there are possible extensions of the underlying n-place relation. And each block corresponds to a proposition which characterizes a possible extension of that relation.

Partitions can be visualized in diagrams. Figure 1 illustrates the bipartition made by a yes/no-interrogative, Figure 2 is an example of a partition made by a one-constituent interrogative.

4.5.2. Entailment and equivalence

The definition of entailment can remain 'literally' the same as in the propositional case, but we formulate it in a more general way:

DEFINITION 4.17 (*Entailment*).
(i) $?\phi_1, \ldots, ?\phi_n \models_M ?\psi$ iff $\forall w \in M$: $[?\phi_1]_{M,w} \cap \cdots \cap [?\phi_n]_{M,w} \subseteq [?\psi]_{M,w}$.
(ii) $?\phi_1, \ldots, ?\phi_n \models ?\psi$ iff $\forall M$: $?\phi_1, \ldots, ?\phi_n \models_M ?\psi$.

The interrogatives $?\phi_1 \cdots ?\phi_n$ entail the interrogative $?\psi$ in a model M iff any proposition which completely answers all of $?\phi_1 \cdots ?\phi_n$ in M, also completely answers $?\psi$ in M. Logical entailment amounts to entailment in all models. Equivalence can be defined as mutual entailment between two interrogatives.

Consider the following facts, which are related to observations made above:

FACT 4.18.
(i) $?xPx \models ?\exists xPx$.
(ii) $?xPx \models_M ?Pa$, if $\models_M ?x(x = a)$.
(iii) $?xPx, ?x(x = a) \models ?Pa$.
(iv) $?xPx \models_M ?x\neg Px$, if $\models_M ?x(x = x)$.
(v) $?xPx, ?x(x = x) \models ?x\neg Px$.
(vi) $?xyRxy \equiv ?yxRxy$.

As is indicated by (i), in any model, a complete answer to the question who will be at the party cannot fail to provide a (positive or negative) answer to the question whether there will be someone at the party. As (ii) indicates, however, it does not hold quite generally that any complete answer to the question who will be at the party always provides an answer to the question whether Alfred will be at the party, too. The entailment only obtains when we restrict ourselves to a proper subset of the set of all possible models, those models in which the question who Alfred is, is already settled. Knowing who will be at the party does not imply knowing whether Alfred will be there, unless we know the answer to the question who Alfred is. Another way of saying this, as (iii) indicates, is that whenever both the question who will be at the party and the question who Alfred is are answered, the question whether Alfred will be at the party is answered, too.

Similarly, as (iv) and (v) tell us, knowing who will be at the party, is not the same as knowing who will not be there, unless we know which particular set of objects we are talking about. The latter question, of what there is, is expressed by $?x(x = x)$. Note that whereas $?\forall x(x = x)$ expresses a tautological question (i.e. $\models ?\forall x(x = x)$), $?x(x = x)$ does not. It only does so if we restrict ourselves to models which consist of worlds with the same domain.

On the relational interpretation of interrogatives, the standard notion of entailment in terms of (set) inclusion would not enable us to account for these entailments and equivalences. In general, entailments and equivalences between interrogatives which ask for the specification of relations with different numbers of arguments can not be accounted for. The (restricted) entailment between $?xPx$ and $?Pa$ is a case in point. And even with respect to two relations with the same number of arguments, one would arrive at the wrong results. We know this already from the case of yes/no-interrogatives, but the equivalence of $?xyRxy$ and $?yxRxy$, stated in (vi), is equally telling. And yet another case is the equivalence of $?xPx$ and $?x\neg Px$, restricted to a model in which the worlds have the same domain. Finally, for a case like $?x(Px \wedge Qx)$ and $?xPx$ we would predict wrongly that the first entails the second.

4.5.3. *Answerhood*

Answerhood is defined in essentially the same way as in the propositional case, except that we explicitly define a notion of answerhood restricted to a particular model, and in terms of that the more general notion of 'logical' answerhood:[42]

DEFINITION 4.19 (*Answerhood*).
(i) $\phi \models_M ?\psi$ iff $\exists w \in M$: $[\phi]_M \subseteq [?\psi]_{M,w}$.
(ii) $\phi \models ?\psi$ iff $\forall M$: $\phi \models_M ?\psi$.

Consider the following facts, related to the examples discussed above:

FACT 4.20.
(i) $\neg\exists xPx \models ?xPx$.
(ii) $\forall xPx \models_M ?xPx$, if $\models_M ?x(x = x)$.
(iii) $\forall x(Px \leftrightarrow x = a) \models_M ?xPx$, if $\models_M ?x(x = a)$.
(iv) $\forall x(Px \leftrightarrow Qx) \models_M ?xPx$, if $\models_M ?xQx$.
(v) $\forall x(Px \leftrightarrow x = a) \models_M ?x(x = a)$, if $\models_M ?xPx$.

These facts indicate that, unlike yes/no-interrogatives, constituent interrogatives do not always have expressible answers. We need expressions (or non-linguistic means) that identify (sets of) objects in order to be able to 'really' specify the extensions of properties and relations. For example, the fact that $\forall x(Px \leftrightarrow x = a)$, 'only a has the property P', is a complete answer to $?xPx$ in a model in which the question $?x(x = a)$ is already settled, reflects that it provides us with a *nominal* answer, and not with a *real* answer, unless we know already who a is.[43]

But observe that, even in case one has no idea who a is, the answer $\forall x(Px \leftrightarrow x = a)$ does provide information which is relevant to the question posed by $?xPx$. It tells us that there is an object which has the property P, that there is only one such object, and that it bears the name a. Thus, it excludes many possible answers, and it creates a new link between the questions posed by $?xPx$ and $?x(x = a)$: if the one gets answered, the other is answered also. Similarly, it can be observed that in case $\forall xPx$ or $\forall x(Px \leftrightarrow Qx)$ does not provide a complete answer to $?xPx$, it may still provide a useful partial answer by excluding many possibilities.

4.5.4. *Comparing answers*

Instead of defining a notion of partial answerhood as such, in terms of excluding certain possibilities, we concentrate on a notion which compares indicatives as to how completely

[42] If we view a model as an information state, then $\phi \models_M ?\psi$ can be read as: in the information state M' which results from updating M with ϕ, the question $?\psi$ is settled. A logical answer is such that it answers the question with respect to any information state. Similar remarks can be made about entailment and equivalence.

[43] The distinction between real and nominal answers goes back to (at least) Belnap and Steel (1976), where one can also find the observation that in many situations a nominal answer is all that is called for. Note that being provided with a real answer to the question expressed by an interrogative like $?xPx$ does not require that names for the objects in question be available, or that we be able to draw up a (finite) 'list' of such objects. A characterization in terms of a simple or complex predicate can provide a real answer as long as it rigidly specifies a certain set of objects.

and precisely they answer a certain question. First we define an auxiliary comparative notion of informativeness, which leaves precision out of consideration.

DEFINITION 4.21 (*Informativeness*).
(i) ϕ gives a partial true answer to $?\psi$ in w in M iff $[\phi]_M \cap [?\psi]_{M,w} \neq \emptyset$.
(ii) ϕ is a more informative answer to $?\psi$ in M than ϕ' iff $\forall w \in M$: if ϕ gives a partial true answer to $?\psi$ in M in w, then ϕ' does, too.

The auxiliary notion of giving a partial true answer is a very weak one: ϕ gives a partial true answer in w in M iff ϕ overlaps with the block in the partition in which w is situated. In particular, it is not required that ϕ itself be true in w, only that it be compatible with the actual true answer. Neither is it required that ϕ exclude any possible answers. Thus, even the tautology counts as a partial true answer.

Notice that the comparative notion of being a more informative answer does favor indicatives which exclude more possible answers. The contradiction then turns out to be the most informative answer to any question. Disregarding that, the most informative answers to $?\psi$ are complete answers, i.e. those ϕ such that $\phi \models ?\psi$. If ϕ and ϕ' imply the same possible answer to $?\psi$, they count as equally informative relative to the question. In terms of the absolute notion of informativeness, i.e. entailment, the one may be more informative than the other, or the one may imply the negation of the other, or they may be incomparable. If ϕ and ϕ' imply different possible answers to $?\psi$, they are unrelated with respect to their informativeness relative to $?\psi$.

Partial true answerhood and relative informativeness are put to use in the following definition, which also takes the precision of answers into consideration (the obvious relativization to a model M and a world w is omitted).

DEFINITION 4.22 (*Comparing answers*). Let ϕ and ϕ' give a true partial answer to $?\psi$. Then ϕ is a better answer to $?\psi$ than ϕ' iff
(i) ϕ is a more informative answer to $?\psi$ than ϕ'; or
(ii) ϕ and ϕ' are equally informative answers to $?\psi$ and ϕ is properly entailed by ϕ'.

According to the first clause, among the true partial answers the more informative ones, which exclude more possible answers, are preferred. The second clause favors weaker answers among equally informative ones. The sum effect is that the answer that equals that block in the partition which contains the actual world is the most preferred one. Next are those answers which are inside that block, but do not fill it completely. This means that such answers contain additional information that the interrogative does not ask for. This lack of precision is not as harmless as it may seem. An answer which *gives* a complete (or partial) true answer need not express a true proposition itself. The precise true and complete answer which fills the whole block is guaranteed to do so. Stronger, and hence over-informative answers, can express false propositions themselves. I.e. although with respect to the question posed by the interrogative they provide correct information, at the same time they may provide incorrect information with respect to some other question. This is precisely why the comparison of answers favors weaker propositions among the ones that give the same answer.

Of course, the available information may simply not support such a complete answer, in which case a partial answer is all that can be offered. The effect of the comparison is that among the answers supported by the information, those are selected that are incompatible with all possible answers incompatible with the information. There again, even though the available information may support stronger propositions, the comparison prefers the unique partial answer that completely fills the union of the blocks corresponding to the possible answers compatible with the information. Again, there is a good reason for this. The information as a whole may be incorrect at some points. But still, it may support a true partial (or complete) answer to some questions. Providing more information than an interrogative asks for, means answering other questions at the same time. But the answer given to those might very well be false. The comparison cautiously tries to prevent this.

Besides partiality of information there is another reason why proper complete (or partial) answers may not be available: it might be that they are not expressible in the language. (Or not expressible relative to the information. In discussing the notion of answerhood, we have seen that in the predicate logical case this can easily occur.) In these cases, too, we have to make do with partial or over-informative answers which are expressible, among which a choice needs to be made. In particular, to be able to provide proper answers, expressions are needed that (with respect to the information available to the questioner) rigidly identify (sets of) objects. If such expressions are lacking, a comparison among the available answers is called for. Hence, such a comparison is a necessary ingredient of any theory of questions and answers.[44]

4.5.5. Remark on natural language

It should be noted that, unlike in natural language, in this predicate logical system querying over variables is unrestricted. In natural language, however, this is almost never the case. A *wh*-phrase is usually of the form *which* CN, and even for those phrases which lack an overt CN, such as *who*, *what*, it can be argued that they are in fact restricted.

Taking our lead from quantification in standard predicate logic, we might think that restricted querying can be expressed by means of conjunction: 'Which P are Q?' would be turned into $?x(Px \wedge Qx)$. In most cases this representation is adequate, but there is a snag here. Consider the following pair of sentences:[45] 'Which men are bachelors?', 'Which bachelors are bachelors?'. Clearly, the first sentence poses a non-trivial question, which is adequately represented by $?x(Mx \wedge Bx)$. The second sentence, is trivial: it asks the tautological question. However, its representation, $?x(Bx \wedge Bx)$, is equivalent to $?xBx$, which is not trivial at all: it asks who the bachelors are. Clearly, a real extension of the syntax of the representation language is called for, if we are to be able to deal with these cases.

Up to this point we have been concerned mainly with developing an argument that purports to show that a semantic analysis of interrogatives is a viable subject. The outlines of one particular approach, based on the three Hamblin postulates, have been sketched, using two simple formal languages as pedagogical devices. But other approaches have been developed in the literature. In the remainder of this chapter we will discuss them under two headings: logical and computational theories, and linguistic theories.

---

[44] See Groenendijk and Stokhof (1984a) for some more discussion of this issue.

[45] The example is due to Stanley Peters.

5. Logical and computational theories

Although related, logical and computational theories are discussed separately, since, as we shall see, their focus is somewhat different.

5.1. Logical theories

Historically,[46] the study of interrogatives started out on logical premises. This is not surprising: the enterprise of a systematic formal semantics for natural language is of fairly recent date, and with the development of modern formal logic at the beginning of the twentieth century, it was only natural that some would want to try to extend its scope to include non-indicative expressions, among which interrogatives occupy a prominent position. Not that it was a subject which instantly drew massive attention. Except for a few isolated attempts, it was only in the fifties[47] that regular logical theorizing about interrogatives started to come off the ground, with the work of Prior and Prior (1955). Of particular importance has been the work of Hamblin, Harrah, Åqvist, Hintikka, and Belnap.[48]

Although often inspired by observations concerning natural language, logical theories were occupied with different concerns. The main objective of the work done in this tradition is to provide a set of formal tools, adequate for a formalization and subsequent analysis of the concepts of question and answer, and the relationships between them. Quite often, the analysis is set against the background of possible applications, in the sphere of question-answering, or information retrieval. Thus from the outset the concept of a 'data-base' plays a role: a typical picture is that of a questioner formulating a query, and a questionee 'looking up' the answer in a data-base and formulating it in an adequate response, which effectively answers the questioner's query.[49] It is remarkable to note that many issues that form the core of important current developments in semantics and cognitive science, such as the dynamics of meaning, update and revision of belief, are already present in these early analyses, albeit not in the form in which they shape the debate today.

This picture sets the agenda of much of the logical research. It is concerned with *expressibility* and *effectivity*, i.e. with the development of a formal language in which various types of queries and the different kinds of answers they call for, can be expressed and communicated in an effective way. The starting point in most cases is some familiar first order language, to which interrogative expressions are added and in which answers can be expressed. This language is then provided with a semantics, thus providing formal

[46] See Egli and Schleichert (1976) for an extensive bibliography which runs up to 1975.

[47] Which also saw the rise of the computer, electronic data storage, etc. As will become clear, this was one important reason for the new interest in a logic of questions.

[48] Later work of the latter two authors witnessed an increasing interest in natural language structures. This change of focus occurred in seventies, when formal approaches to natural language semantics, such as Montague grammar, started to develop. It was in that framework that the first attempts at giving a systematic semantics of natural language interrogatives were made, first by Hamblin (1973), followed by Karttunen (1977), and later by Belnap (1982), and others.

[49] See Harrah (1984, p. 725) where this perspective is introduced and discussed explicitly.

counterparts of the pre-theoretic notions to be analyzed. Remarkably, proof theoretic aspects are by and large ignored.[50]

Most logical approaches start from assumptions quite similar, and sometimes identical, to the Hamblin postulates which were taken as a starting point above (see Section 4.1).[51] Thus, questions are closely associated with answers. But in some approaches the link is not that tight. This holds especially for the analyses in the epistemic-imperative paradigm, such as those of Hintikka and Åqvist, which, as was observed earlier (see Section 3), are more in the line of the pragmatic approach. Here, one might say, questions are tied to the (desired) effect: they describe the epistemic situation that results after the questioner has updated with the answer. This is quite clear from the logical structure that is assigned to questions: e.g., 'Does John come to the party' is analyzed as 'Bring it about that I know whether John comes to the party', which can be further reduced to 'Bring it about that either I know that John comes to the party or that I know that John does not come to the party'.[52]

As we remarked, an important issue that arises from the logical point of view concerns *expressive power*: Can all questions be expressed in the language? Can all answers to a question be formulated? These issues sometimes are discussed with respect to a particular type of data-structure. In that case they are primarily design features. On a more abstract level results such as the following are obtained. Using the familiar diagonalization technique, a simple argument shows that if questions are identified with sets of formulae, being their answers, then, given some plausible assumptions concerning the number of formulae, there are more questions than can be expressed in the language.[53]

Classification, of both questions and answers, is another major concern. How do types of questions differ? What kinds of answers does a question allow? And then the relation-

---

[50] Thus Belnap and Steel (1976, p. 1):

> What is the logic of questions and answers? [...] Absolutely the wrong thing is to think it is a logic in the sense of a deductive system, since one would thus be driven to the pointless task of inventing an inferential scheme in which questions, or interrogatives, could serve as premises and conclusions. This is to say that what one wants erotetic logic to imitate of the rest of logic is not its proof theory but rather its other two grand parts, grammar (syntax) and semantics.

This is remarkable since, as was stressed above, entailment relations between interrogatives do exist, and need to be accounted for in an adequate semantics. This being the case, there seems to be no reason to exclude a priori the possibility of a (partial) syntactic characterization of both entailment between interrogatives, and the answerhood relation.

Also, it should be noted that many logical analyses are involved in syntactic issues, in this sense that the design of an adequate language, and the definition of various logical forms, is one of their main concerns.

[51] According to Belnap and Steel (1976, p. 35):

> As for questions, we rely on Hamblin's dictum (1958): 'Knowing what counts as an answer is equivalent to knowing the question.' On this insight rests the whole of our erotetic logic.

Cf., also Harrah (1984, p. 719).

[52] Again, the parallel with the current concern with dynamic interpretation is striking. In effect, Hintikka's work on game-theoretical semantics (see, e.g., Hintikka, 1983; cf., also Chapter 10) is one of the predecessors of this development. See also below, Section 6.5.2.

[53] See Harrah (1984) for a representative example of such argumentation. Notice that a similar kind of argument can be given in an intensional setting (in which it applies to propositions conceived of as sets of possible worlds). As for answers, we have seen above that already in the case of a simple predicate logical system not all answers need be expressible.

ships between these various (sub)notions have to be characterized. As for the classification of questions, here logical properties typically take priority over linguistic issues. A primary concern is always to isolate those types of questions which can be formalized, i.e. to characterize 'clear' questions which ask for some definite piece of information, and which have an answer that can be calculated, at least in principle. Again, this may differ with the kind of domain that one has in mind. Thus from a logical point of view, such interrogatives as 'Who is that man living next door?' stand in need of further analysis, because it is unclear what particular type of characterization one is asking for. With regard to answers, the distinction that is most commonly made, is that between complete and precise answers, which provide precisely the information an interrogative asks for, and partial and over-complete ones. A second distinction is that between nominal and real answers, where the former provide merely a verbal characterization, whereas the latter present a real identification of objects as a reply to a constituent question. Usually, the same distinction is made with respect to questions as such, explicitly distinguishing (in logical form) between a request for the one or the other type of answer. As far as the distinction is implemented in the syntax of the formal language, this is another example of a logical distinction which is not linguistically motivated: a natural language such as English does not distinguish between the two by providing distinct syntactic structures to represent them. From the linguistic point of view, it seems more natural to account for the difference either semantically, by assigning two distinct readings, or pragmatically, explaining it in terms of different goals and intentions.

Presuppositions of questions also receive a surprising amount of attention in erotetic logic, surprising, because as far as indicatives are concerned, logical analyses of presupposition are mainly inspired by empirical linguistic phenomena, and not by purely logical considerations. In the analysis of Belnap and Steel (1976) the meaning of an interrogative is more or less identified with its presuppositions, and also in the analysis developed by Hintikka (1976, 1983) they are essential ingredients. Roughly speaking, the presupposition of a question is the assumption that one of its possible answers is true. For questions expressed by alternative interrogatives, such as 'Do you want coffee or do you want tea?', this amounts to the requirement that the proposition expressing the exclusive disjunction of the two alternatives is true. And for questions expressed by constituent interrogatives of the form 'Which A is/are B?' this comes down to the requirement that there is at least (or precisely) one object among the A's that is a B. From an empirical, linguistic point of view, there is indeed much to say for a presuppositional analysis of alternative questions and *wh*-phrases. But from a purely logical point of view one would rather expect the reaction that, although pragmatically marked, a reply like 'None.' (or 'There are several.') is just as good an answer as any other. At least in comparable indicative cases (definite descriptions being a case in point) this is what one gets. In the end, of course, there is a 'logical' reason for reducing the meaning of an interrogative to its presupposition: the latter are of a propositional nature. In this way standard truth conditional logic and semantics can be made to apply to interrogatives.[54]

Another issue that arises has to do with *effectiveness*: here one is concerned first of all with the problem whether it is effectively decidable whether, and if so to what

[54] But notice that the problems which we noticed with strictly reductionistic approaches above (see Section 3.6), seem to arise in this context, too.

extent, a certain expression is an answer to a certain question. Again, one way to go about is to design a 'normal form' for answers, which is often derived from the logical form of the corresponding interrogatives. As regards effectiveness of questions, one may investigate what is the most efficient way to formulate certain queries. A simple example illustrating the latter problem is the following. Suppose we are interested in the question which objects have both the property A and the property B, i.e. which objects form the intersection of the extensions of the two. The queries 'Which A's are B's?' and 'Which B's are A's?' both formulate this question. But the 'search routines' they invoke are different, and that may be a reason for preferring one over the other. If A is a predicate with a much larger extension than B, it is, other things being equal, more efficient to search among the B's to find the A's, than the other way around.[55] Considerations such as these may also lead to the introduction of particular syntactic constructions to be used in formulating queries in the formal language, which do not have obvious counterparts in natural language interrogatives. An example is provided by the explicit specification of a selection size within the query, which indicates how many instances one would be satisfied with.[56]

Although perhaps not a very fashionable subject in current philosophical logic, the logical way of doing things has provided us with a wealth of insights, concepts, and, most important, with a fruitful perspective: questions and answers set against the background of exchange of information concerning some data set. Not all elements of this picture have received the same amount of attention in the work that has been done in this tradition. In particular, the dynamic aspects of the perspective that are evidently there, have been relatively ignored.

Formal semantic theories of natural language interrogatives were largely inspired by logical work (cf., above, footnote 48), but witnessed a shift in focus, which, at least initially, led to a less encompassing picture: the information exchange perspective by and large dropped from view. But with the advent of a more dynamic perspective on interpretation this is again beginning to change. Both within formal semantics as well as in cognitive science this perspective is gaining ground, and it is to be expected that some of the logical work will turn out to be quite relevant.

5.2. *Computational theories*

As was already noticed above, one of the striking features of logical theories of questions and answers is their often quite explicitly practical motivation. Many of the problems that are dealt with have a distinct 'computational' flavor, and return in a computational setting. Within computer science, research in the area of questions and answers is closely linked to data base theory and the development of query languages. More indirectly, there

[55] There is an interesting connection with generalized quantifier theory here (see Chapter 15). It seems that, in general, knowing which A's are B's is not the same as knowing which B's are A's. But something like conservativity does hold: knowing which A's are B's is the same as knowing which A's are A's that are B's.

[56] In natural language, it seems that the 'extremes', viz., mention-one and mention-all (see below), are typically formulated in the interrogative form, whereas a selection specification such as 'an odd number between 8 and 24' would rather be incorporated in an imperative structure.

is also a link with the theory of declarative programming languages, such as Prolog. A discussion of the growing literature is beyond the scope of this chapter. The reader is referred to Kanellakis (1990) for a recent overview.

The main issues that are dealt with bear a striking resemblance to the topics mentioned above, although the perspective is somewhat different. The picture is that of a certain amount of data, structured in a data base in such a way that it lends itself to efficient storage and manipulation. The problems center around the question what is the most efficient way to extract information from the data base. Obviously, the requirements imposed by the goals of efficient storage and manipulation, can, and often are, at odds with this. We typically request information from a data-base using concepts which are different from those used in storing it. Thus, the design of an efficient query language often involves a translation of one mode of representation into another. Many of the theoretical questions that are asked are related to this issue. A typical problem is that of the definability of new queries in terms of old ones, and, of paramount importance in this setting, an investigation of the complexity of this task.[57] The simplest operators defining new queries are those of relational algebras (suitably formulated). This stays within first-order logic. But also, one typically wants to compute queries which involve transitive closures of predicates, or other inductively defined constructions. This requires query languages which extend first-order logic with fixed point operators. Finally, given the nature of the task, questions of expressive power and computation are usually studied over finite data bases. This gives this account of questions the special flavor of 'finite model theory', which blends general semantic argumentation with combinatorial arguments over finite structures. Interestingly, a restriction to finite models has also been proposed independently in natural language semantics, e.g., in the theory of generalized quantifiers (see Chapter 15). The problem of giving an inductive definition of a certain set of semantic objects, too, reappears in natural language semantics, e.g., in the context of quantification over properties and functions, where on the one hand we do not want quantification to run over all objects of that type, but we also do not want to restrict it to, say, the set of objects which are lexicalized. Rather, one wants the domain to consist of the set of those functions which can be defined in terms of certain closure operations over the lexicalized ones.[58]

Quite similar questions arise in the context of declarative programming languages. Such languages can also be considered as 'query' languages: a typical Prolog program resolves a question concerning some data structure. One of the relevant issues here concerns, again, definability: Which definitions are 'save', i.e. lead to computationally tractable formalisms? Also other aspects are studied, such as that of finding an 'informative' formulation of the answer that the execution of a program provides.

It is interesting to note, finally, that some of the mathematical tools that are used in this research, viz., those of relational algebra, are also used in another setting in which information exchange is the topic, viz., that of dynamic logic (see Chapter 10). On the other

[57] A typical result regarding the latter is the following. It is known that a first order query in a fixed, finite model can be resolved in polynomial time. In 1974, Fagin (see Fagin, 1974) proved that the reverse holds, almost: any polynomially resolvable query in a finite model can be expressed in a first order language to which a limited resource of second order concepts is added.

[58] See Groenendijk and Stokhof (1983, Section 4) for a concrete example of a discussion revolving around this issue in a linguistic setting, viz., that of an account of so-called 'functional' readings.

hand, it is a moot point whether iteration and recursion occur in natural language the way they do in computation. Examples would be not so much explicit expressions denoting recursive procedures, but rather higher computational mechanisms, such as are involved in domain selection, anaphora resolution, or maintenance of discourse scheduling.

The research in these computational settings, although akin in spirit to the earlier logical work, has rapidly grown into a subject of its own. One subject area needs to be mentioned, in which logical, linguistic, and computational questions come together again. This area is devoted to the design of natural language query systems, in which 'translation' plays a role at several points.[59] First of all, a natural language interrogative has to be mapped onto an expression in some query language, which then has to be matched against a data base. Then the reverse problem has to be solved. Given the information extracted from the data base a formal expression has to be defined which answers the query. And this expression in its turn has to be translated in some natural language expression which serves as an answer to the original interrogative. If, furthermore, the fact that the questioner already has information at her disposal is taken into account, this task displays almost all aspects of questions and answers that are studied in logical, computational, and linguistic frameworks. Thus, despite the differences in outlook and techniques, it seems that to a large extent the undertaking is a common one, i.e. one in which in the end each party involved may benefit from the results of the others.

6. Linguistic theories

In this section we first provide a brief overview of the main semantic approaches in the linguistic literature. As will become apparent, such theories share certain features, but differ at other points to such an extent that they become real alternatives. Next, we sketch some empirical data that play a key role in the shaping of these alternatives, and outline how they lead to certain choices. As it will turn out, there may be good reasons for wanting to take a liberal point of view, and not succumb to the temptation to declare one of the alternatives as the only right theory. An outline of how such a more flexible approach can be incorporated in a grammar, is given. Then we complete our survey with a sketch of some other empirical issues, and with a brief outline of recent developments.

6.1. Overview

Most linguistic theories focus on the analysis of interrogative structures as such, and the analysis of answers comes into play only in the light of that. Consequently, hardly any attention is paid to matters which we saw are of paramount importance to logical and computational theories, such as expressibility of queries and of answers. The function of interrogatives and answers in information exchange is acknowledged, but most of the time it is deferred to pragmatics and does not influence the semantic analysis as such. Of prime importance for these linguistic approaches is 'to get the facts right', and that is taken to consist in giving an account of typical ambiguities that interrogatives display,

[59] A good, although not very recent example is the system described in (Scha, 1983).

their presuppositions, their behavior under embedding verbs, and so. And it is primarily in terms of their predictions on these matters that they are compared.

All semantic linguistic theories share a basic conviction, viz., that the semantic object that an interrogative expresses has to provide an account of the answers that the interrogative allows. That is, they all accept the third of Hamblin's postulates given above (Section 4.1). But they diverge as to their acceptance of the other two postulates. Thus, according to some, answers are of all kinds of linguistic categories, hence they reject Hamblin's first postulate, which says that answers have a sentential, or propositional character. Others accept it, but hold that interrogatives admit of more than one true answer, which means that they reject the second postulate, which states that answers are exhaustive and mutually exclusive. And then there are theories which accept all three.

6.1.1. Partition theories

Let us start with the latter, since they fit in with the kind of account we sketched above as the 'Hamblin picture'. As we saw above, the Hamblin-picture gives us a clean and coherent view of questions and answerhood. It presents us with a uniform and formally appealing notion of a question as a partition of a logical space of possibilities. It ties questions in a natural fashion to answers, the latter being the blocks of the partition. And it is able to account for equivalence of interrogatives and entailments between them in a standard way, i.e. without appealing to definitions of these notions which are specific for this kind of expressions. And to some extent, it is able to account for coordination of interrogatives in a likewise general fashion.

Partition theories have been developed by Higginbotham and May (1981), Higginbotham (1995), and Groenendijk and Stokhof (1982, 1983). The Higginbotham and May approach starts from the basic point of view expounded above, that a question corresponds to 'a partition of the possible states of nature', such a partition representing 'the suspension of judgment among a set of mutually exclusive and jointly exhaustive alternatives' (Higginbotham and May, 1981, p. 42). Their analysis concentrates on the derivation of interrogatives with more than one occurrence of a *wh*-phrase, such as 'Which man saw which woman?' and 'Which people bought which books?'. The details of their analysis are rather complicated, since they want to take into account what they consider to be semantic presuppositions of *wh*-phrases, in particular the uniqueness presupposition of singular *wh*-phrases. A straightforward implementation thereof wrongly predicts that 'John saw Mary and Bill saw Sue' violates the presuppositions of 'Which man saw which woman?'. In fact, Higginbotham and May argue, the uniqueness presupposition for such structures amounts to the requirement that there be a bijection between two subsets of the domains of the *wh*-phrases.[60] The derivation of such bijective interpretations, it is claimed, cannot proceed in a step-by-step fashion, introducing and interpreting one *wh*-phrase at a time, i.e. considering it as an ordinary unary quantifier. Given the uniqueness presupposition associated with a singular *wh*-phrase such a procedure would result in a reading of, e.g., 'Which man saw which woman?' in which it would presuppose that only one man saw only one woman. For single, i.e. one constituent, *wh*-interrogatives

[60] According to Higginbotham and May, there are structures in which this reading is not available, viz., those in which the domains of the two *wh*-phrases are not disjoint. An example would be 'Which number divides which number?', asked of a single list of numbers.

this is the right reading, and for some multiple *wh*-interrogatives it may also be the only reading available (cf., footnote 60). But in general this 'singular' interpretation is too strict. Derivation of the bijective interpretation, Higginbotham and May claim, requires the introduction of a binary (generally, n-ary) *WH*-operator, of which arbitrary arguments may be marked for uniqueness. This operator is of the following general form:

$$WH_n^K(x_1 \cdots x_n)$$

where K is a set of integers k such that $k \leqslant n$. When applied to a sentence of the form $\phi(x_1 \cdots x_n)$ the result is a partition with each argument x_k with $k \in K$ being interpreted uniquely. Arguments not so marked correspond to occurrences of plural *wh*-phrases, which lack the uniqueness presupposition. Thus, the representation of 'Which man saw which woman?' on the bijective reading would be the following:

$$\big[WH_2^{\{1,2\}} x, y\colon \mathtt{man}(x) \wedge \mathtt{woman}(y)\big] x \ \mathtt{saw} \ y.$$

A representation of 'Which man saw which women?', with a plural second argument, would have $WH_2^{\{1\}} x, y$ instead. One interesting thing about this analysis is that this way of deriving multiple *wh*-interrogatives seems an instance of a general quantificational mechanism, viz., that of *polyadic quantification* (see Van Benthem, 1989a; and Chapter 15; cf., also Section 4.5). In fact, in the original paper, Higginbotham and May argue that similar mechanisms provide an account of the phenomenon of crossing coreference (as in Bach-Peters sentences such as 'Every pilot who shot at it hit a Mig that chased him'). This is just one case which shows that there are interesting parallels between the analysis of *wh*-interrogatives and that of other quantifying expressions, which one would want a general theory of quantification to account for.

The partition approach of Groenendijk and Stokhof differs from that of Higginbotham and May in that it does not incorporate uniqueness presuppositions into the semantics of *wh*-phrases. They derive interrogatives from what are called 'abstracts', which express n-place relations. The semantic rule reads as follows:[61]

$$\lambda w \lambda w' \big(\lambda x_1 \cdots x_n \big(\phi(w', x_1, \ldots, x_n)\big) = \lambda x_1 \cdots x_n \big(\phi(w, x_1, \ldots, x_n)\big)\big).$$

This rule defines a partition based on an n-place relation by grouping together those worlds in which the relation has the same extension.[62] In other words, it defines an equivalence relation on the set of worlds, which holds between two worlds iff the extension of the relation in question is the same in those worlds. An ordinary indicative sentence is taken to express a 0-place relation, i.e. a proposition. Hence this rule also derives questions expressed by sentential interrogatives, viz., bipartitions.

Both approaches make (roughly) the same predictions with respect to answerhood. In particular, they are committed to what is called 'strong exhaustiveness'. This aspect will be discussed more extensively below.

---

[61] In what follows we use two-sorted type theory as a representation language. Two sorted-type theory is like the familiar intensional type theory of Montague (see Chapter 1), but allows explicit reference to and quantification over worlds.

[62] Cf., Definition 4.15 above.

6.1.2. *Sets of propositions theories*

According to the partition view an interrogative denotes its true and complete answer. In other words, its denotation is a proposition, and its sense a function from worlds to such propositions. Hence, the meaning of an interrogative is an entity of type $\langle s, \langle s, t\rangle\rangle$.[63] Other approaches take a different view: they hold that the denotation of an interrogative is a *set* of propositions, and its sense a function from worlds to such sets. Thus, they assign a different type of object to an interrogative as its meaning, viz., one of type $\langle s, \langle\langle s, t\rangle, t\rangle\rangle$.

Not all theories that assign this type of object to an interrogative interpret it in the same way, and hence they differ in what objects they actually associate with a given interrogative. For example, according to Hamblin (1973), the set of propositions denoted by an interrogative consists of its *possible* answers, whereas Karttunen (1977) lets it consist of its *true* answers. Thus a simple interrogative of the form 'Who will be coming to dinner tonight?' on the Karttunen analysis will denote in a world w the set consisting of those propositions which are true in w and which state of some person that (s)he is coming to dinner tonight:[64]

$$\lambda p\big(\exists x\big(p = \lambda w\big(\texttt{come-to-dinner}(w)(x)\big)\big) \wedge p(w)\big).$$

The propositions which make up this set each state of some individual which actually is coming to dinner that he/she is coming to dinner. On Hamblin's analysis the restriction to individuals that are actually coming to dinner is dropped.[65] Notice that in both cases the propositions are mutually compatible, which marks a principled difference with the partition theories.[66] Exactly how the individual propositions are related to answers is not entirely clear. Hamblin describes them as 'those propositions that count as answers' (Hamblin,1973, p. 46), and Karttunen looks upon them as propositions which 'jointly constitute a true and complete answer' (Karttunen, 1977, p. 20). In connection with this, it is important to note that in Karttunen's analysis the various denotations of an interrogative are also mutually compatible. This means that if we interpret the Karttunen sets as Karttunen himself suggests, the answers which his analysis defines for an interrogative are mutually compatible, too. This marks a difference with partition theories. Whereas the latter subscribe to strong exhaustiveness, Karttunen only acknowledges weak exhaustiveness. More on this below.

The main difference between Hamblin's and Karttunen's approach, which is probably the most influential analysis in the semantics literature to date, is that the former concentrates on stand alone interrogatives, whereas the latter is concerned mainly with embedded interrogatives. It is from their behavior in various embedding contexts that Karttunen derives arguments in favor of his modification of Hamblin's original proposal

[63] Where s is the type of possible worlds, t that of truth values. See Chapter 1 for more details.

[64] Application ($p(w)$) of a propositional expression (p) to a world denoting expression (w) expresses that the propositional expression is true in that world.

[65] The Hamblin set of propositions can be regained from the Karttunen interpretation simply by collecting all denotations. Likewise, a Karttunen set can be distinguished within the Hamblin set by selecting those elements which are true in a particular possible world. In this respect the difference between the two is not very essential.

[66] So Hamblin's analysis should not be confused with the Hamblin-picture!

(although he adds that he considers none of them as a 'knock-down argument' (Karttunen, 1977, p. 10)). For example, Karttunen observes that in a sentence such as 'Who is elected depends on who is running' it are the true answers (in various worlds) to the respective interrogatives that are involved, not their possible ones.

Like on the Higginbotham and May approach, interrogatives on Karttunen's analysis are the result of what basically is a quantificational process. Roughly, Karttunen defines a base level of what he calls 'proto-questions', derived from indicatives ϕ, which are of the form:[67]

$$\lambda p(p = \lambda w(\phi) \wedge p(w)).$$

Wh-phrases are regarded as existentially quantified terms. A quantificational process like that of Montague's quantifying-in then derives interrogatives from indicatives containing a free pronoun, using their proto-question interpretation. Multiple constituent interrogatives are derived in a step-by-step fashion.

Two things need to be noticed. First of all, unlike Higginbotham and May, but like Groenendijk and Stokhof, Karttunen does not build any existential and/or uniqueness presuppositions into the semantics of interrogatives. Secondly, his use of a quantificational analysis in combination with the level of proto-questions results in what are called 'de re' readings of constituent interrogatives. Cf.:

$$\lambda p\big(\exists x\big(\texttt{student}(w)(x) \wedge p = \lambda w\big(\texttt{pass-the-exam}(w)(x)\big)\big) \wedge p(w)\big).$$

This is Karttunen's translation of 'Which student passed the exam?'. Notice that the restrictor CN of the *wh*-phrase is outside the scope of the proposition. Thus such a proposition claims *of* a student that he/she comes, but not (also) that he/she is a student. More on this below.

Interestingly, the Hamblin and Karttunen analyses are not the only ones in which an interrogative is taken to denote a set of propositions. On the analysis developed by Belnap (1982) and Bennett (1979) interrogatives are assigned the same type of semantic object, but with a radically different interpretation: each proposition in the set is assumed to express a complete true answer. Hence, unlike in the Karttunen and Hamblin interpretation, the elements of the denotation of an interrogative are mutually exclusive. Accordingly, an interrogative such as 'Which student passed the exam?' will denote a singleton set. Why, then, introduce the complication of assigning them *sets* of propositions? In this way Bennett and Belnap aim to account for interrogatives which have more than one complete true answer. Examples of such interrogatives will be discussed below.

We end with noting the following characteristics of these sets of propositions theories regarding entailment and coordination. Let us start with the Karttunen analysis.[68] The standard definition of entailment in terms of inclusion predicts no entailment of 'Is Bill coming to dinner? by 'Who is coming to dinner?'. As an immediate consequence we

[67] In two-sorted type theory every context-dependent expression has an occurrence of a variable w, ranging over worlds.

[68] The following applies, *mutatis mutandis*, also to the Hamblin analysis.

note that 'John knows who is coming to dinner' does not imply 'John knows whether Bill is coming to dinner'.[69] This is related to the matter of exhaustiveness, to which we return shortly. As for coordination, it is easy to see that a standard conjunction rule, which amounts to taking the intersection of two denotations, does not make adequate predictions in certain cases. For example, given that John and Mary are different individuals, the intersection of

$$\lambda p\big(\exists x\big(p = \lambda w\, \mathtt{love}(w)(j, x)\big) \wedge p(w)\big)$$

which is the denotation of 'Whom does John love?', with:

$$\lambda p\big(\exists x\big(p = \lambda w\, \mathtt{love}(w)(m, x)\big) \wedge p(w)\big)$$

which is denoted by 'Whom does Mary love?, is empty, predicting that 'Whom do John and Mary love?' (on the conjunctive reading) does not have an answer.

As for the Bennett and Belnap approach, similar observations can be made. It, too, does not do well with regard to entailment and conjunction. It does, however, make the right predictions concerning disjunction. We return to this shortly.

6.1.3. Categorial theories

A final landmark in the landscape of semantic approaches is provided by so-called 'categorial theories'. Examples of categorial approaches can be found in work of Hausser and Zaefferer, Tichy, and Scha (see Hausser, 1983; Hausser and Zaefferer, 1978; Tichy, 1978; Scha, 1983).

Categorial theories do analyze interrogatives in terms of answers, but do not start from the assumption that the latter represent a uniform type of object. Rather, it is noted that answers are not always sentences, but may be of all kinds of categories. Also, it is observed that different kinds of interrogatives require different kinds of non-sentential answers, also called 'constituent answers'. Categorial theories focus on the relation between interrogatives and constituent answers. The existence of a categorial match between interrogatives and their characteristic constituent answers is taken to determine their category. The categorial definition of interrogatives is chosen in such a way that in combination with the category of its constituent answers, the category of indicative sentences results. Again, there is some lee-way here. Hausser, for example, takes an interrogative to be of a functional category, viz., that function which takes the category of its characteristic answers into the category of sentences. Tichy prefers to identify the category of an interrogative with that of its characteristic answers.

As a result, different kinds of interrogatives are of distinct categories and semantic types. One of the consequences of this lack of a uniform interpretation of interrogatives is that entailment relations between interrogatives of different categories cannot be accounted for by means of the standard notion of entailment, since the latter requires such interrogatives to be of the same type. More generally, since categorial theories focus on the linguistic answerhood relation, constituted by categorial fit, a semantic notion of answerhood as a relation between propositions and questions remains outside their scope.

[69] Given that Karttunen requires the subject to know every proposition in the denotation of the embedded interrogative (or, in case the denotation is empty, the proposition that it is empty). See Heim (1994) for discussion and an alternative that is meant to remedy the shortcoming noted in the text.

6.2. Key data

Up to now we have given short characterizations of various kinds of semantic theories, without going into the details of their motivation. But, surely, it must be possible to give reasons for preferring one type of approach over another? In what follows we want to discuss this matter a little further, by discussing some crucial empirical data that can be, and sometimes have been, adduced in favor of certain theories. But we must warn the reader at the outset: we are not presenting the motivations as the various proponents have given them, but discuss the matter in a systematic fashion. We know that in doing so we distort history, but we hope that the picture of the field that emerges is clear.

The starting point of our discussion will be the Hamblin-picture, i.e. that view on the semantics of interrogatives that subscribes to each of Hamblin's three postulates. As we shall see, corresponding to each of these three postulates empirical data can be adduced that provide some reason to question it. But before turning to three of them, we must point out a phenomenon that seems to lie beyond the reach of the Hamblin-approach as such.

6.2.1. Open questions

It is clear that the Hamblin-picture makes certain choices with regard to, and hence imposes certain restrictions on, its subject matter. A major one is the following. The notion of a question that the Hamblin-picture accounts for is one where the possible answers are pre-set, so to speak. The alternatives are 'already given'. In other words, giving an answer to a question is regarded as making a choice from a set of alternatives which are determined by the question itself. (In this respect there is an interesting resemblance with multiple-choice questionnaires.) This follows more or less straightforwardly from the third postulate, viz., that to know the meaning of a question is to know what counts as an answer to it. Questions such as these may be called 'informative questions'. However, if one takes informative questions as a point of departure, the picture one arrives at does not seem to apply, at least not in a straightforward way, to so-called 'open questions', which are not requests for a particular piece of information. The question addressed in this chapter, viz., the one expressed by the interrogative 'What are questions?', is probably a good example. It seems reasonable to assume that both the authors and the reader understand this question, i.e. are able to grasp the meaning of the interrogative, without there being a number of pre-set possible answers which are determined by the question itself. In this respect open questions differ from those expressed by such interrogatives as 'Who will be coming to dinner tonight?', where, depending on the domain, the set of possible answers is clear in advance ('Harry, Jane and Bill.'; 'Just Bill and Suzy.'; 'Nobody.'; and so on). Answering an open question is a creative process, one might say, where we make up the answers as we go along, and do not simply choose from a pre-established set. Notice that another distinctive feature of open questions seems to be that with them it often seems to make little sense to ask whether or not a particular answer to such a question is true or false. Rather, answers are qualified as good or bad, as more or less comprehensive, or helpful, and so on. Thus, it seems that open questions do not satisfy two assumptions which, as was observed above, are inherent features of the Hamblin-picture, viz., the Existence and Uniqueness Assumptions concerning answers.

One might say that in the case of open questions answers do not already exist, but have to be created, and that there is no unique answer to be created, but that there is an unlimited amount of not necessarily mutually inconsistent answers that can be given. So open questions do not fit the picture. Or rather, the picture does not fit them.

It seems fair to conclude that Hamblin's picture (which, to be sure, was presented by Hamblin as a proposal for a certain *methodology*) is restricted to one, albeit an important, type of questions, viz., informative questions. Whether or not this methodology is a sound one depends on whether or not open questions really are conceptually different from informative ones, a matter which has not been really settled in the literature to date. As a matter of fact, we may observe that almost all analyses are limited in that they confine themselves to informative questions.

The considerations concerning the distinction between 'open' and 'informative' questions point towards an 'external' limitation of the Hamblin-picture, suggesting that, if the observations made above are correct, it needs to be supplemented by an analysis of a different kind of questions. Other considerations, however, aim at the heart of the picture itself, purporting to show that it fails to do justice to the properties of the kind of questions it was designed to deal with, viz., informative ones. Thus it can be argued that the Hamblin-picture rests on assumptions concerning answerhood which are empirically inadequate. One assumption in particular has been attacked, for a variety of reasons, and that is the Unique Answer Assumption, i.e. the assumption that in a situation an interrogative has a unique true and complete answer.[70] In effect, many of the alternative theories that have been proposed can be understood (systematically, that is, not historically) as attempts to do without this assumption.

6.2.2. Exhaustiveness

Before turning to a brief discussion of some phenomena that can be adduced to argue that the Unique Answer Assumption is not warranted, we first mention briefly some observations that seem to support it. These observations concern certain equivalences between interrogatives that seem to be needed to get an account of the validity of certain arguments.[71] Thus, it seems that from 'John knows who is coming to dinner tonight' it follows that 'John knows whether Mary is coming to dinner tonight'. Also, it seems that, assuming that the domain is fixed over John's epistemic alternatives, i.e. that it is known to John of which individuals the domain consists, it follows from 'John knows who is coming to dinner tonight' that 'John knows who is not coming to dinner tonight'. To account for the validity of this type of inference, it seems we need the equivalence, under

[70] Note that the assumption itself can be misunderstood in a variety of ways. Although questions in the Hamblin-picture have a unique true and complete answer (if their presuppositions are fulfilled), there are still many ways in which they can be answered (truly). The notions of complete and partial answerhood discussed above illustrate this fact. Furthermore, if we take the pragmatics of question-answering into account, the range of potential answers that the theory allows for is virtually unlimited (see Groenendijk and Stokhof (1984a, 1984b) for some discussion). At the same time it brings order in this chaos by making it possible to define clearly which propositions, given particular circumstances concerning the information of the speech participants, count as optimal answers.

[71] Cf. Groenendijk and Stokhof (1982) for more elaborate discussion.

the assumption stated, of course, of interrogatives of the form $?xPx$ and $?x\neg Px$, and also the entailment between $?xPx$ and $?Pa$.[72] Hamblin's picture delivers these goods.

This feature is often discussed under the heading of 'exhaustiveness'. Usually, a distinction is made between 'weak' and 'strong' exhaustiveness. By the former we understand the requirement that a complete answer specify all true single 'instances', i.e. that it exhaustively specify the range of true partial answers. Strong exhaustiveness requires in addition a closure condition: that the answer not only in fact *give* such an exhaustive specification, but also in addition *state* that it is exhaustive. Thus, a weakly exhaustive answer provides a complete list, a strongly exhaustive answer contains in addition the closure condition stating 'and that's all, folks'. Strong exhaustiveness, thus, should not be confused with the requirement that an answer specify both the positive and the negative extension of a relation.[73] Partition theories as such are committed to strong exhaustiveness in the proper sense, but not to the latter requirement. In fact, as we saw above, the latter requirement is empirically unjustified: the equivalence of interrogatives of the form $?xPx$ and $?x\neg Px$ holds only if we assume that the domain from which the instances are drawn is fixed.[74] A phenomenon that has been suggested to constitute a counterexample to strong exhaustiveness is that of 'quantificational variability', involving adverbs of quantification, such as 'mostly', 'rarely'. See below, Section 6.4.3.

It is of some interest to note that the phenomenon of exhaustive interpretation is not restricted to interrogatives and answers. Within the semantics of plural NPs, some (see, e.g., Hendriks, 1988) have suggested that we need a 'minimal', i.e. exhaustive, interpretation of the generalized quantifiers such NPs express. Also, in the theory of topic and focus, exhaustiveness plays an important role. See, e.g., Bonomi and Casalengo (1993). In fact, as many authors have suggested, there may be an intimate relationship between questions and answers, and topic and focus. See Van Kuppevelt (1991) for systematic discussion. Rooth (1992) provides a detailed account of the relationship between Karttunen's analysis of questions and his theory of focus, which is based on 'alternative semantics'.

Moreover, the idea of exhaustiveness seems natural, not just from a strictly linguistic point of view, but also in a wider cognitive setting. In various kinds of theories which deal with information exchange and with reasoning on the basis of partial information, we can trace the idea that informational 'moves', as a rule, are to be interpreted exhaustively. That is, information is treated in a non-monotone way, i.e. it is interpreted as giving *all* information (concerning the topic in question), unless stated otherwise.[75] This ties in with the natural assumption that information exchange is structured by an 'underlying' pattern of questions and answers (cf., the relationship with topic and focus structure referred to above, see also Mayer (1990)). In effect, many specific features of discourse structure (both monological and dialogical) seem to depend on this.

---

[72] Another observation which supports this requirement is the following. We are discussing which of our friends are coming to dinner tonight. Suppose that Mary and Suzy are in fact coming to dinner tonight, but John erroneously believes that Mary, Suzy, and Bill will come. Then it seems wrong to attribute to John knowledge of who is coming to dinner.

[73] This misinterpretation has caused a lot of confusion in the literature. For discussion of these issues see Groenendijk and Stokhof (1993).

[74] Cf. also Fact 4.18, (iv), in Section 4.5.

[75] See Chapter 6, and Van Benthem (1989b).

But let us now turn to some observations that can be adduced to argue against the Unique Answer Assumption, also in order to get a better grip on the various semantic theories that have been proposed in the literature.

6.2.3. *Mention-some interpretation*

The following observation constitutes an internal criticism of the Hamblin-picture. It seems that in some situations, obviously informative interrogatives do have several, mutually compatible and equally adequate answers. Consider the following example: A tourist stops you on the street and asks 'Where can I buy an Italian newspaper?'. Clearly, she does not want you to provide her with a complete specification of all the places where Italian newspapers are sold. All she wants is that you mention *some* such place. Thus, both 'At the Central Railway Station.' and 'At the Athenaeum bookstore.' (and a host of others) each are in and of themselves complete answers, and they are mutually compatible.

Such an interpretation is often called the 'mention-some' interpretation of an interrogative, since the answers mention *some* object that satisfies the condition expressed by the interrogative. Per contrast, the interpretation that the Hamblin-picture accounts for is referred to as the 'mention-all' interpretation, since its answers specify *all* such objects. Notice that, although the subject matter of the example we gave strongly suggests a mention-some interpretation, it does not exclude a mention-all interpretation. Thus we may imagine that the interrogative is used by someone who is interested in setting up a distribution network for foreign newspapers. Clearly, such a person would use the interrogative on its mention-all interpretation, since he would regard only a list of all stores selling Italian newspapers as a complete answer.[76]

The important question that needs to be settled in order to be able to evaluate the relevance of mention-some interpretations for the Hamblin-picture is whether they constitute a distinct reading of interrogatives, or can be accounted for along other lines. To start with the latter option, one might be tempted to think that the distinction is of a pragmatic nature: circumstantial facts (concerning intentions and interests of the questioner, for example) determine whether she is satisfied with something 'less' than the complete answer that is determined semantically by the interrogative. This in effect comes down to the view that, semantically speaking, mention-some answers are not complete answers, but function so only from a pragmatic point of view. Semantically, such answers are partial, rather than complete answers: they exclude some possibilities, but do not provide an exhaustive specification. This line of reasoning, however, is difficult to maintain for the following reason. Partial answers as defined by the mention-all interpretation may also be 'negative'. For example, 'Not at the Bijenkorf.' is a partial answer to our example interrogative on its mention-all interpretation, since it excludes certain possible answers. However, such 'negative' partial answers are no good when we take the interrogative on

[76] There is, again, an interesting parallel with other instances of quantification, this time concerning 'donkey sentences'. Here, too, there are cases of structures for which a 'universal' interpretation seems to be preferred ('If Pedro owns a donkey, he beats it' seems to entail that Pedro beats all the donkeys he owns), whereas other instances which exhibit the same pattern, superficially at least, prefer an 'existential' reading ('If I have a dime, I put it in the parking meter' does not require me to put all my dimes in the meter).

its mention some interpretation, since it does not mention some positive instance, which is what, on the mention-some interpretation, is what is required.

This suggests that mention-some interpretations really are a distinct semantic reading. If we accept this conclusion, we face the following question: does the distinction between mention-all and mention-some interpretations constitute a genuine ambiguity of interrogatives? Or can the mention-all interpretation be derived from the mention-some interpretation? Or is there an underlying semantic object from which both are to be derived? Various answers can be found in the literature. Hintikka, for example, analyzes mention-all and mention-some interpretations in terms of an ambiguity of *wh*-phrases (see Hintikka, 1976, 1983). Groenendijk and Stokhof (with some hesitation, see Groenendijk and Stokhof, 1984a) turn it into a structural ambiguity. According to Belnap's analysis in Belnap (1981), mention-some interpretations are on a par with so-called choice interpretations, to be discussed below.[77] Various analyses in the line of Karttunen (see Karttunen, 1977) can be regarded as presenting the second kind of solution. To the third option we return below.

As we saw above, on the Karttunen approach the meaning of an interrogative is a function from worlds to sets of propositions. So, whereas a partition in the Hamblin-picture determines a single proposition, the Karttunen interpretation delivers a set of propositions as the denotation of an interrogative in a particular world. Both analyses relate questions to answers, but in a different way, and we may interpret this as a difference in what basic answers are.[78] According to the third postulate of the Hamblin-picture answers are mutually exclusive and together exhaustive. In other words, in each world a question has exactly one true answer. On this interpretation of the Karttunen approach, answers are mutually compatible: there may be many propositions in a given world that are a true answer. Thus, whereas the Hamblin-picture seems eminently suited to deal with mention-all interpretations, the Karttunen approach might seem to provide a good basis for dealing with mention-some interpretations. For, the propositions which make up the denotation of an interrogative in a world, each mention some object which satisfies the condition from which the interrogative was built.

The idea that suggests itself then is to regard the Karttunen semantics as the basic one, i.e. to assume that mention-some interpretations are fundamental, and to try to obtain the mention-all interpretations from it, by defining the partition in terms of the equivalence relation of having the same set of answers. However, for various reasons this strategy does not work.

First of all, it can be observed that the phenomenon of mention-some interpretations is a particular instance of something more general: mention-n interpretation. Thus, an interrogative such as 'Where do two unicorns live?' has as one of its interpretations the one in which it asks for a specification of two distinct places where one (or more)

---

[77] This identification cannot be maintained, however, for reasons discussed in Groenendijk and Stokhof (1984a), where an alternative analysis is given.

[78] Notice that we refer to 'the Karttunen approach', and not to 'Karttunen'. We do so deliberately. The point we want to make is a systematic one, and it is not intended as a reconstruction of Karttunen's actual motivation. In fact, given that Karttunen himself described the set of propositions denoted by an interrogative as 'jointly constituting a true and complete answer' we may as well take him to present the mention-all interpretation, weakly exhaustified.

unicorns can be found. Such an interpretation can be derived from the set of propositions that the Karttunen analysis provides, by introducing an operation that tells how many of the propositions will make up an answer.[79] But that means that it is not the Karttunen set that is the denotation of an interrogative, but a more basic semantic entity.

Secondly, as Heim has argued (see Heim, 1994) it does not seem possible to actually derive the right partition interpretation from the Karttunen set. The reasons behind this are complicated, and perhaps not entirely understood. One issue is that no account of 'de dicto' readings of *wh*-interrogatives can be obtained in this way, it seems.

Thus the resulting picture is rather complicated. And it becomes even more so if we look at another phenomenon that challenges the Unique Answer Assumption, viz., that of so-called 'choice' interpretations.

6.2.4. Choice-interpretation

One obvious instance in which the Unique Answer Assumption fails, is with respect to interrogatives which have a so-called 'choice'-interpretation. Prominent examples are provided by disjunctions of interrogatives, such as 'Where is your father? Or where is your mother?'. This interrogative does *not* ask for a specification of a place where your father or your mother (or, perhaps, both) can be found. Rather, its purpose is to find out about the whereabouts of either your father or your mother. Thus, it has two mutually compatible, true and complete answers. Another example of an interrogative exhibiting this kind of interpretation is 'Where do two unicorns live?', which, besides the 'mention-two' interpretation referred to above, also has an interpretation where it asks to specify of two unicorns where they live. Thus they are typically answered by indicatives of the form 'Bel lives in the wood, and Nap lives near the lake'.[80]

Disjunctions of interrogatives are not adequately accounted for in the Hamblin-picture, at least not by application of a generalized rule of disjunction. In the case of partitions, application of such a rule would amount to taking the pairwise union of the elements of two partitions, which, in general, does not result in a partition at all. The Karttunen approach, too, fails on this score. The Bennett and Belnap analysis, on the other hand, obviously is able to account for disjunction (but fails on conjunction).

A little reflection shows that all this may not be a coincidence. In general, application of a generalized rule of coordination to two objects of a certain type results in a new object of the same type. In the case of conjunction of questions we would indeed expect the result to be a new question. But in the case of disjunction this is, perhaps, not so obvious. Consider again the example 'Where is your father? Or where is your mother?'. As was remarked above, this interrogative has two mutually compatible, true and complete answers. But in this case it seems that this is due to the fact that the interrogative expresses two distinct questions, and not just one. Thus, in using such an interrogative, the questioner in effect expresses two questions, leaving the questionee the choice which of the two she wants to answer. Something similar can be said about the choice reading of the other example, 'Where do two unicorns live?'. The use of this interrogative amounts to the following: pick any two unicorns – the choice is yours – and answer for each of them the question

---

[79] See Belnap (1976) for some relevant discussion of 'completeness' of questions and answers.

[80] Belnap was the first to discuss these kinds of examples, and to stress their importance for the semantics of interrogatives. See Belnap (1982) for elaborate discussion.

where it lives. Thus this interrogative, too, does not express a single question, but two. Unlike the disjunctive example, it does not explicitly identify which two questions, but rather leaves the questionee the choice, within certain limits it sets.

What moral can be drawn from this? First of all, it seems that choice interpretations are no straightforward counterexample to the Unique Answer Assumption: if an interrogative on such an interpretation expresses more than one question, it seems we can acknowledge that it has more than one complete and true answer, while still holding on to the assumption. And actually, if we consider a slightly different example, 'What do two unicorns eat?', it seems that what we are dealing with here are two questions, each with a plausible mention-all interpretation, and thus each with a unique complete and true answer.

Secondly, the existence of this kind of interpretation, and the failure of a straightforward analysis in terms of a generalized coordination rule, indicates that interrogatives have to be analyzed at yet another level. One way to account for these interpretations is by application of a general strategy, familiar from the semantics of quantified NPs. Thus one may analyze disjunctions of interrogatives, and analogously choice interpretations, in terms of generalized quantifiers over questions, using standard coordination rules in combination with rules for lifting semantic objects.[81] An alternative analysis is the one developed by Belnap (1982) and Bennett (1979). They give up the Unique Answer Assumption (which Belnap refers to as the 'Unique Answer Fallacy') and let interrogatives denote sets of propositions, each of which constitutes a complete and true answer. Their analysis accounts for choice readings and disjunctions, but runs into problems when dealing with interpretations on which interrogatives do have a unique answer. Thus they fail to deal with conjunctions in a standard way, and also are unable to account for the entailments and equivalences which we saw the Hamblin-picture delivers.

All in all, the picture that emerges is rather varied. As we saw above, the Hamblin postulates lead to elegant and simple theories, which are capable of dealing with a range of interrogatives in a uniform way. However, such analyses also show an inherent bias towards a certain type of interpretation, the mention-all interpretation, and have problems accounting for mention-some interpretations of interrogatives. Alternative theories of the Karttunen–Hamblin type, which assign sets of propositions to interrogatives, are evidently better suited to cope with the latter, but are not able to deal with various entailments and equivalences that seem crucial for an account of a variety of phenomena, at least not in a straightforward way. The existence of choice-interpretations complicates the picture even more. Here, one of the alternatives that can be found in the literature is to add another level of analysis, viz., that of generalized quantifiers over partitions. That, however, may not be the end of the matter. In the next section we will discuss a range of phenomena that point towards yet another level on which interrogatives, it seems, must be analyzed.

6.2.5. *Constituent answers*

Starting point is the observation, already alluded to earlier on, that interrogatives may be answered not just by full sentences, but also by subsentential expressions, the so-called 'constituent answers'. Thus 'Who did John invite?' can be answered by 'John invited

[81] See Groenendijk and Stokhof (1989) for an analysis along these lines.

Peter and Mary', but also by 'Peter and Mary.' And a reply to 'Where are you going?' can be a full sentence, 'I am going to Amherst', but also a subsentential phrase: 'To Amherst.' Moreover, it seems that constituent answers are more closely tied to interrogatives than full sentential ones. Thus, 'John kissed Mary' can be an answer both to 'Whom did John kiss?' and to 'Why is Bill upset?'.[82] But 'Mary.' answers only the first, not the second.

Observations such as these have led to the development of the 'categorial approach' on interrogatives discussed above. According to the categorial view, interrogatives belong to a wide range of different categories, which correspond systematically to that of their characteristic linguistic answers. Thus, this approach is more syntax-oriented, and takes its lead from the surface syntactic properties of interrogatives and linguistic expressions that serve as answers. It is a theory that rejects the first of the three Hamblin postulates, which says that answers are sentences, or statements.

In view of that, one might be tempted, at first sight, to brush this approach aside, precisely because it is too syntactically oriented, and semantically deficient. The first Hamblin-postulate, one may reason, is beyond doubt: answers express propositions, or proposition-like objects anyway, since answers convey information. This much must be granted, it seems, but there is one aspect of the categorial view that indicates that it can not simply be disregarded. This has to do with the derivation of mention-all interpretations. Consider the sentence 'John invited Mary'. Assuming a mention-all interpretation, this sentence conveys different information if it answers different interrogatives. As an answer to 'Whom did John invite?' it states that Mary is the one (the only one) that John invited. But when it is a reply to 'Who invited Mary? it means that John was the one (again, the only one) who invited Mary. These are different propositions, which shows that in some way the proposition expressed by a sentential answer depends on the meaning of the interrogative. One way to account for that is by taking the different constituent answers, in this case 'Mary.' and 'John.' respectively, as starting point of the derivation of this single sentential answer, thus in effect treating it as ambiguous.[83] In effect this shows that also within the confines of a propositional theory the categorial viewpoint has a certain role to play, and that hence there is yet another level at which interrogatives need to be analyzed, viz., that of n-place relations.

6.3. A flexible approach?

Summing up, we see that various semantic theories analyze interrogative structures at various levels: as n-place relations, as (functions from possible worlds) to sets of (true) propositions, as partitions of a space of possibilities, and also at the level of generalized quantifiers over such entities. This is a confusing multitude of semantic objects. However, for each of these theories some empirical and methodological motivation can be given, as the foregoing survey has shown. This suggests that perhaps the search for one single

---

[82] But notice that in each case the spoken sentence will carry a different intonation contour. This provides yet another ground for believing that there is an intimate relationship between questions and answers, topic and focus, and intonation, something which has been noticed by a number of authors. See the references given earlier.

[83] See Groenendijk and Stokhof (1984b) for an analysis along these lines.

type of object which is to function as the semantic interpretation of interrogatives is misguided by an unwarranted urge for uniformity. It might well be that in some contexts (linguistic or otherwise) the meaning of an interrogative must be taken to consist of one type of object, and in other contexts it should be looked upon as being of another type. What a proper semantic theory should do then is not to look for one type of object, but to define a multitude of types and to establish systematic relationships between them.

In fact, this situation occurs not just with the analysis of interrogatives: it appears to be a justified methodology in other areas of linguistic description as well. The analysis of referring expressions, names, quantified NPs, descriptions, is a clear case in point. Here, too, it seems that we need to analyze such expressions at various type-levels, and to define adequate type-shifting rules which capture the connections. Thus, the apparently confusing multitude observed above turns out to be another instance of a familiar pattern. Flexible approaches to category/type assignment, and the associated systems of category/type shifting rules have been the subject of extensive study, especially in the context of categorial syntax with the associated type-theoretical semantics (see Chapters 1 and 2).

One of the rules needed in the analysis of interrogatives on this account we have already met above. It is the rule which turns an n-place relation into a partition. A similar rule that would deliver a Karttunen style set of propositions is easy to formulate as well. (It would differ from Karttunen's actual analysis by not proceeding in a step-by-step fashion.) Further, we need the 'Montague rule', which turns an entity of a certain type into that of a generalized quantifier over entities of that type, to account for disjunction and related phenomena. We also observed above that, apparently, no rule can be stated which transforms a Karttunen set into a partition in the Groenendijk and Stokhof style, the reason being that the latter assign de dicto readings, whereas the former provide de re specifications. And we may need yet other rules as well, to deal with other phenomena.

To what extent the various rules form a 'coherent' set is a relatively unexplored issue. Some initial work has been done in (Groenendijk and Stokhof, 1989), but many questions remain open. Yet, the emerging picture certainly seems attractive, shedding as it does the rigid 'one category – one type' attitude that has dominated semantics for quite some time. The 'polymorphic stance' has proved useful in other areas as well.

6.4. Other empirical issues

Above we have discussed mention-all, mention-some, and choice interpretations of interrogatives, constituent answers, and the various 'pictures' that they give rise to, in some detail. In what follows we will very briefly mention some other empirical issues and provide pointers to relevant literature.

6.4.1. Functional interpretations

Some interrogatives exhibit what is often called a 'functional' interpretation. An example is given by the following sequence: 'Whom does every Englishman admire most?' 'His mother.' Here the answer does not specify an individual, but a function that delivers such an individual for each entity specified by the subject term of the interrogative.

These interrogatives are also interesting because they exhibit unusual binding patterns: thus, in 'Which of his relatives does every man love?' the subject term 'every man' binds the variable 'his' which is inside the *wh*-phrase 'which of his relatives'. Functional interpretations are discussed in (Engdahl, 1986; Groenendijk and Stokhof, 1983; Chierchia, 1992-3).

Functional interpretations are not restricted to interrogatives. For example, an indicative such as 'There is a woman whom every Englishman admires' has a reading on which it can be continued by specifying, not an individual, as in: 'The Queen Mother', but a function: 'His mother'. This is a separate reading, which is also to be distinguished from the reading in which the subject NP has wide scope. (Compare 'There is a woman whom no Englishman admires' with 'No Englishman admires a woman'.) This provides yet another indication that quantification in indicative and interrogative structures exhibit quite similar patterns.

6.4.2. Pair-list interpretations

Yet another type of interpretation is the so-called 'pair-list' interpretation. Consider 'Which student did each professor recommend?'. This interrogative can be interpreted as asking for a specification of those students that got a recommendation of every professor. On this (mention-all) interpretation it is typically answered by providing a list of individuals: 'John, Mary, and Suzy'. But there is also another interpretation, on which the interrogative asks to specify for each professor which student(s) (s)he recommended. A typical answer for this reading gives a list of professor-student pairs (hence the name): 'Professor Jones recommended Bill and Harry; Professor Williams recommended Suzy and John; ...'. Notice that these answers are like those of a two-constituent interrogative. In fact, it has been argued that on its pair-list reading 'Which student did each professor recommend?' is equivalent with 'Which student did which professor recommend?'.[84]

Pair-list readings are often connected with the phenomenon of quantifying into interrogatives. See, for example, Bennett (1979), Belnap (1982). But if the above observation concerning the relation with two-constituent interrogatives is correct, a pair-list reading can not be the result of quantification of the subject NP into an interrogative. For one thing, such an analysis would not account for the 'two-constituent' nature of the answers. And it would give the subject NP a de re reading, whereas the two-constituent interrogative reads both *wh*-phrases de dicto. For argumentation along these lines, see Groenendijk and Stokhof (1984a).

An extensive discussion, also of other phenomena in which quantifiers and questions interact, can be found in (Chierchia, 1992-3), where the patterns exhibited by this interaction are related to Weak Crossover, and it is argued that pair-list readings are a special case of functional readings.[85]

6.4.3. Quantificational variability

Another phenomenon that has been related to quantification into interrogative structures is that of 'quantificational variability'. An example is provided by the following sentence: 'The principal mostly found out which students cheated on the final exam'. The

[84] Barring, perhaps, differences having to do with salience.

[85] See also Rexach (1996) for an extensive analysis using the generalized quantifier framework.

main importance of these structures seems to be their role in the ongoing debate on exhaustiveness. According to some (see, for example, Berman, 1991) they provide a counterexample: if the quantification is over students, then the principal finds about the majority of the students who cheat that they do, but she need not find out about all of them, and neither does she have to find out about all students that don't cheat that they don't.

This has been challenged (see, for example, Heim, 1994; Lahiri, 1991; Ginzburg, 1995b) on various grounds. Most opponents feel that in such structures the adverb quantifies, not over individuals, but over events, or 'cases'. Also, an attempt has been made to show how quantificational variability can be made to accord with strong exhaustiveness (see Groenendijk and Stokhof, 1993).

6.4.4. Embedding verbs

Another important set of phenomena that up to now we almost have passed over in silence concerns the classification of various types of embedding verbs. This was already a major topic in Karttunen's pioneering analysis (Karttunen, 1977), and has been subject of further study by several authors (see, e.g., Lahiri, 1991; Ginzburg, 1995a). We just mention here a few issues that have received attention.

First of all, observe that not all verbs take both indicative and interrogative complements: *know*, *tell*, *guess*, for example, take both; a verb such as *believe* combines only with indicative complements; and *wonder*, *investigate*, and the like, are restricted to interrogative complements. Furthermore, note that verbs which take both, also take 'hybrid' coordinations, as in 'John knows/revealed/guessed who left early and that Mary was disappointed'. This suggests strongly that in both the interrogative and the indicative context it is one and the same relation that is at stake, which makes an account in terms of lexical ambiguity implausible. Another interesting phenomenon has to do with factivity properties of embedding verbs. Some verbs which take both interrogative and indicative complements are factive with respect to both: 'John knows that Bill comes to dinner' implies that Bill comes to dinner, and, likewise, 'John knows whether Bill comes to dinner' implies that John knows the *true* answer to this question. Other verbs behave differently, however. Thus, whereas 'John tells whether Bill comes to dinner' does imply that John tells the true answer, it does not follow from 'John tells that Bill comes to dinner' that Bill in fact comes to dinner.

Such facts need to be explained. One way to account for the factivity phenomenon is to let interrogatives denote their true answer(s), and to distinguish between 'extensional' and 'intensional' verbs, i.e. verbs which operate on the extension of the interrogative complement, and verbs which take its intension. Thus, *know*, *tell* would take a (true!) proposition as their argument, viz., the one denoted by the question, whereas *wonder*, *investigate* take the question as such. See Groenendijk and Stokhof (1982).

A further refinement has recently been proposed by Ginzburg (see Ginzburg, 1995a), who suggests to replace the three-fold distinction just mentioned by a four-fold one: factive predicates (*know*), nonfactive resolutive predicates (*tell*), question predicates (*wonder*), and truth/falsity predicates (*believe*). The first category takes both interrogative and indicative complements, and semantically operates on propositions. The fourth category only combines with indicative complements, and operates on an individual type of entity, related to, but different from propositions. This is corroborated by the observation that such verbs also take nominal complements ('John believes the prediction Bill made'). The third category takes only interrogative complements, which express questions. Finally, elements of the second category have both indicative and interrogative complements, the latter again taken to express an individual type of entity, which is different from a question, but related to it. Ginzburg's analysis has obvious ontological ramifications, which are spelled out by him in a situation-theoretic framework, but which presumably can also be implemented in a property-theoretic setting.

6.4.5. Presuppositions

The question whether and, if so, which presuppositions are associated with interrogatives, or with *wh*-phrases has already been alluded to earlier on. We noticed that in the logical analyses of Belnap and Steel (1976) and Hintikka (1976, 1983) presuppositions are essential ingredients. They provide the means for individuating (classes of) questions. In Hintikka's approach the presupposition of a question is involved in spelling out its desideratum. Thus, alternative questions ('Is John in London, or in Paris?') are said to presuppose the truth of (exactly) one of the alternatives. Constituent interrogatives ('Who is coming to dinner?') are assumed to have existential presuppositions, viz., that there is at least one instance satisfying the predicate. In more linguistically oriented analyses, the discussion tends to focus on the uniqueness presupposition which is supposed to distinguish between singular and plural *wh*-phrases. The analysis of Higginbotham and May (1981) is a case in point. In the case of interrogatives, presupposition failure is usually said to result in the interrogative lacking a (true) answer. Other authors, e.g., Karttunen (1977), have been more indifferent.

As is the case with presuppositions of indicatives, discussion of these issues is complicated by the fact that one of the most important questions, viz., whether these presuppositions are a semantic or rather a pragmatic phenomenon, is underdetermined by our 'pre-theoretic' intuitions. Some authors distinguish negative answers from rejections ('mere replies'), but one may well wonder to what extent such distinctions are theory-loaded. Keeping this in mind, the following observations[86] may still serve to place the claim that these are straightforward semantic presuppositions in a wider perspective.

Let us start with existential presuppositions. It seems that, at least with the *wh*-phrase *who*, clear cases are actually hard to find. Of course, an interrogative such as 'Who is that?' has an existential presupposition, but it seems due to the demonstrative rather than to the *wh*-phrase. Next, consider a case such as 'Who is coming with me?'. There may be an expectation on part of the questioner that there is someone coming with her, but it does not seem to be a presupposition. For it seems that 'Nobody.' is a perfectly straight (albeit perhaps disappointing) answer, and not a rejection of the question as such.

Uniqueness presuppositions do not seem to fare much better. Consider again 'Who is coming with me?'. Does this presuppose that not more than one person is coming along, and that hence 'John and Bill.' is not an answer? It seems not. This is not to deny that expectations of uniqueness do occur. But they seem not strictly tied to singular *wh*-phrases as the following example shows. Consider the following two pairs of interrogatives:

[86] Taken from Groenendijk and Stokhof (1983).

'Which members of the cabinet voted against the proposal?' – 'Which members of the cabinet voted against the proposal?'; and 'Which member of the cabinet leaked the information to the press?' – 'Which members of the cabinet leaked the information to the press?'. The association of uniqueness seems opposite in both cases. In the first pair the plural seems neutral as regards the number of people involved, whereas in the second pair it is the singular that is neutral, and the plural is marked. An explanation can be found, it seems, by taking into account the nature of the activities involved: leaking information is typically an individual activity, whereas voting against is something one (often) does along with others. Hence, the expectations concerning (non-)uniqueness which are associated with the interrogative seem to depend (primarily) on other material than the *wh*-phrases used.

6.5. Extending the scope

The survey of theories and phenomena given in the previous sections has touched upon the main approaches and results that can be found in the literature to date, though not upon every one of them in the same detail. Thus it has provided a survey of the main stream of theorizing in this area. In what follows we want to indicate, again only briefly, what we think are two important directions for current and future research.

Whatever their differences all semantic theories considered above share certain characteristics, which are currently being challenged. One is that the semantics of interrogatives is considered from a relatively context-independent point of view. This must not be misunderstood: what we mean is not that the semantic objects assigned to interrogatives are context-independent, on the contrary. Rather, what we want to draw attention to is that it is often taken for granted that the semantic objects as such can be assigned in a relatively context-independent way. Consequently, semantic objects associated with interrogatives are in most cases total objects. Another feature that characterizes almost all existing semantic analyses is the essentially static nature of the semantics they assign to interrogatives, a feature that is no doubt connected with the frameworks in which these analyses are formulated.

Recently, semantics has witnessed a move towards more context-dependent and dynamic models of meaning. This development has occurred not just in natural language semantics, where it is connected with situation theory, discourse representation theory, and dynamic semantics, but also in more logically and computationally oriented research. From these developments a new view on meaning and interpretation is emerging, in which context, in particular the epistemic context, and context change are key notions. As such, it would seem to provide a framework that is eminently suited for an analysis of interrogatives.

6.5.1. Context-dependency and partiality

In a series of papers (see Ginzburg, 1995a, 1995b) Ginzburg has developed a theory which differs from main stream semantical theories in a rather fundamental way. Ginzburg, who formulates his approach in the framework of situation theory, discusses several phenomena which he takes to indicate that the relation of answerhood (or, as he calls it, 'resolvedness') is a partial and highly contextual one. He charges other approaches with taking a too absolute view on this relationship. This, he claims, is not just descriptively incorrect, but also theoretically unsound.

The phenomena Ginzburg discusses have to do with several aspects of the question–answer relationship. One of them concerns fine-grainedness. This seems to play a role in interpreting and answering such interrogatives as 'Where am I?', or in judging the truth of 'John knows where he is'. It depends, Ginzburg argues, essentially on the context (of utterance) exactly how these expressions must be interpreted. Thus the interrogative 'Where am I?' when uttered by someone stepping down from a plane at Schiphol Airport, obviously needs a different kind of answer than when it is uttered by someone stepping down from a taxi at the Dam square. For notice that, although both Schiphol Airport and the Dam square are located in Amsterdam, the answer 'In Amsterdam.' is not a good answer in the latter case, since it is not likely to resolve a lack of knowledge of the questioner. In that situation a more fine-grained set of answers is determined by interrogative and context.

Intentionality is another issue. It seems that the intentions of the questioner play a key role in determining what kind of answer is called for by an interrogative such as 'Who attended the lecture?': Does it call for a specification of names, roles, or yet other aspects that 'identify' individuals? Likewise, the goals and plans of the questioner must be taken into account in answering such interrogatives as 'How do I get to Rotterdam from here?'.

According to Ginzburg the essentially context-dependent character challenges exhaustiveness, even in its weak form. These phenomena certainly constitute a major challenge for existing approaches. To what extent they can be modified to be able to deal with these issues remains open for the moment. Another issue is whether these phenomena are particular to interrogatives, or rather concern interpretation in a wider sense.

6.5.2. Dynamic interpretation

As we observed above, all mainstream semantic analyses of interrogatives are cast in a static framework. The rise of dynamically oriented frameworks in semantics raises the question whether interrogatives are perhaps better analyzed in such a dynamic setting. Several attempts have already been made to cast a semantics of interrogatives in a dynamic mould. One early attempt is the work of Hintikka, who in developing his framework of game theoretical semantics (see, e.g., Hintikka, 1983) has also paid attention to dynamic aspects of the meaning of interrogatives. This seems quite natural: in the game between 'I' and 'Nature' questions have a clear function, viz., that of steering the game by determining sets of moves.[87] Hintikka has also used questions to implement a distinction in the epistemic setting as such, viz., that between information which is deduced from given data, and information which is obtained by asking questions and getting them answered. These types of information play a different role. In fact, the imperative-epistemic approach as such has a distinct dynamic flavor, although the frameworks used, those of imperative and epistemic logic, are not explicitly concerned with information change. More indirectly, dynamic aspects have been dealt with in work that is concerned

[87] There is also an obvious connection with dialogue semantics here.

with information exchange in discourse structured by question–answer patterns (see, e.g., Mayer, 1990). Also the work on pragmatic notions of answerhood (see Groenendijk and Stokhof, 1984b) must be mentioned here. Catching on to more recent developments, Zeevat (1994) combines the Groenendijk and Stokhof semantics with Veltman's update semantics (see Chapter 10).

There are several interesting empirical and methodological issues that arise here. First of all, the connection with topic–focus structures, and the relation with certain principles of discourse organization have to be explored systematically. These issues have been discussed by several authors, as we have noticed above, but not in a systematic fashion. Another topic concerns anaphoric chains across utterances, where questions seem to license more than assertions ('A man is walking in the park.' 'Does he wear a black hat?'). Also, a dynamic framework, in which information exchange is the key notion, seems to provide a natural surrounding for an account of exhaustiveness, which may be tied up with non-monotonicity of information exchange.

All in all, it seems that extending the scope of semantic theories of interrogatives, giving due attention to their context-dependent character and analyzing them in a dynamic framework, holds much promise. For interrogatives are the structures in natural language par excellence which are concerned with information and information (ex)change. To be sure, the neat distinction between semantics and pragmatics that has enabled the semantics of interrogative structures to develop into a field of its own, thereby becomes more subtle, perhaps even blurred. But that should not blind us to the reality of the intimate relationships that exist between meaning and use.

Thus, it may seem that we have come full circle, returning to where we started from, viz., the pragmatic approach. But appearances are deceiving here. For in traveling this far, we have indeed established the possibility of a semantics of interrogatives, as a field of its own. And extending its scope is not revoking its articles of faith.

Acknowledgement

We would like to thank Jelle Gerbrandy, and the participants of the Handbook Workshop, in particular Jonathan Ginzburg, James Higginbotham, and Jaakko Hintikka, for their comments. We owe a special thanks to Johan van Benthem for his many stimulating comments and suggestions, and, most of all, for his patience. Of course, thanking these people does not imply that any of them agrees with the views expressed in this chapter, or is responsible in any way for remaining errors, oversights, inconsistencies, or other flaws that it, no doubt, still contains.

References

Åqvist, L. (1965), *A New Approach to the Logical Theory of Interrogatives*, Uppsala.

Austin, J.L. (1962), *How to Do Things With Words*, Oxford Univ. Press, Oxford.

Bäuerle, R. and Zimmermann, T.E. (1991), *Fragesätze/Questions*, Semantik/Semantics: An International Handbook of Contemporary Research, A. von Stechow and D. Wunderlich, eds, de Gruyter, Berlin, 333–348.

Belnap, N.D. Jr. (1981), *Approaches to the Semantics of Questions in Natural Language. Part I*, Pittsburgh.

Belnap, N.D. Jr. (1982), *Questions and answers in Montague grammar*, Processes, Beliefs, and Questions, S. Peters and E. Saarinen, eds, Reidel, Dordrecht, 165–198.

Belnap, N.D. Jr. and Steel, T.B. Jr. (1976), *The Logic of Questions and Answers*, Yale Univ. Press, New Haven, CT.

Bennett, M. (1979), *Questions in Montague Grammar*, IULC, Bloomington.

Berman, S. (1991), *On the semantics and logical form of Wh-clauses*, Dissertation, Amherst.

Boër, S. and Lycan, W. (1985), *Knowing Who*, MIT Press, Cambridge, MA.

Bonomi, A. and Casalengo, P. (1993), *Only: Association with focus in event semantics*, Nat. Language Semantics **2**, 1–45.

Cresswell, M. (1973), *Logics and Languages*, Methuen, London.

Chierchia, G. (1992-3), *Questions with quantifiers*, Nat. Language Semantics **1**, 181–234.

Egli, U. and Schleichert, H. (1976), *Bibliography of the theory of questions and answers*, The Logic of Questions and Answers, N.D. Belnap Jr. and T.B. Steel Jr., eds, Yale Univ. Press, New Haven.

Engdahl, E. (1986), *Constituent Questions*, Reidel, Dordrecht.

Fagin, R. (1974), *Generalized first-order spectra and polynomial-time recognizable sets*, Complexity of Computation, R.M. Karp, ed., SIAM–AMS Proceedings **7**, 43–73.

Frege, G. (1918), *Der Gedanke*, Beiträge zur Philosophie des deutschen Idealismus vol. 1. (English translation: P. Geach and M. Black (1960), *Translations from the Philosophical Writings of Gottlob Frege*, Blackwell, Oxford).

Ginzburg, J. (1995a), *Resolving Questions I & II*, Ling. and Philos. **18**, 459–527, 567–609.

Ginzburg, J. (1995b), *Interrogatives: Questions, facts and dialogue*, Handbook of Contemporary Semantic Theory, S. Lappin, ed., Blackwell, Oxford, 385–422.

Groenendijk, J. and Stokhof, M. (1982), *Semantic analysis of Wh-complements*, Ling. and Philos. **5**, 175–233.

Groenendijk, J. and Stokhof, M. (1983), *Interrogative quantifiers and Skolem-functions*, Connectedness in Sentence, Discourse, and Text, K. Ehlich and H. van Riemsdijk, eds, Tilburg Univ. Press, Tilburg.

Groenendijk, J. and Stokhof, M. (1984a), *Studies on the semantics of questions and the pragmatics of answers*, Dissertation, Amsterdam.

Groenendijk, J. and Stokhof, M. (1984b), *On the semantic of questions and the pragmatics of answers*, Varieties of Formal Semantics, F. Landman and F. Veltman, eds, Foris, Dordrecht, 143–170.

Groenendijk, J. and Stokhof, M. (1989), *Type-shifting rules and the semantics of interrogatives*, Properties, Types and Meaning, vol. 2: Semantic Issues, G. Chierchia, R. Turner and B. Partee, eds, Kluwer, Dordrecht, 21–68.

Groenendijk, J. and Stokhof, M. (1993), *Interrogatives and adverbs of quantification*, Proceedings of the Fourth Symposium on Logic and Language, K. Bimbó and A. Máté, eds, Áron Publishers, Budapest, 1–29.

Hamblin, C.L. (1958), *Questions*, Australas. J. Philos. **36**, 159–168.

Hamblin, C.L. (1973), *Questions in Montague English*, Found. Lang. **10**, 41–53.

Harrah, D. (1984), *The logic of questions*, Handbook of Philosophical Logic vol. II, D. Gabbay and F. Guenthner, eds, Kluwer, Dordrecht, 715–764.

Hausser, R. (1983), *The syntax and semantics of English mood*, Questions and Answers, F. Kiefer, ed., Reidel, Dordrecht, 97–158.

Hausser, R. and Zaefferer, D. (1978), *Questions and answers in a context-dependent Montague grammar*, Formal Semantics and Pragmatics for Natural Languages, F. Guenthner and S.J. Schmidt, eds, Reidel, Dordrecht, 339–358.

Heim, I. (1994), *Interrogative complements of know*, IATL1. The Proceedings of the Ninth Annual Conference and the Workshop on Discourse of the Israel Association for Theoretical Linguistics, R. Buchalla and A. Mittwoch, eds, Jerusalem, Academon, 128–144.

Hendriks, H. (1988), *Generalized Generalized Quantifiers in Natural Natural Language*, ILLC, Amsterdam.

Higginbotham, J. (1995), *The semantics of questions*, Handbook of Contemporary Semantic Theory, S. Lappin, ed., Blackwell, Oxford, 361–384.

Higginbotham, J. and May, R. (1981), *Questions, quantifiers, and crossing*, Ling. Rev. **1**, 41–79.

Hintikka, J. (1976), *The semantics of questions and the questions of semantics*, Acta Philos. Fennica **28**.

Hintikka, J. (1983), *New foundations for a theory of questions and answers*, Questions and Answers, F. Kiefer, ed., Reidel, Dordrecht, 159–190.

Hintikka, J. (1983), *The Game of Language*, Reidel, Dordrecht.

Hintikka, J. and Hintikka, M. (1989), *The Logic of Epistemology and the Epistemology of Logic*, Kluwer, Dordrecht.

Kanellakis, P. (1990), *Elements of relational database theory*, Handbook of Theoretical Computer Science, J. van Leeuwen, ed., Elsevier, Amsterdam, 1073–1156.

Karttunen, L. (1977), *Syntax and semantics of questions*, Ling. and Philos. **1**, 3–44.

Karttunen, L. and Peters, S. (1980), *Interrogative quantifiers*, Time, Tense, and Quantifiers, C. Rohrer, ed., Niemeyer Verlag, Tübingen, 181–206.

Lahiri, U. (1991), *Embedded interrogatives and the predicates that embed them*, Dissertation, MIT.

Lewis, D. (1970), *General semantics*, Synthese **22**, 18–67.

Mayer, R. (1990), *The release of information in discourse: Compactness, compression, and relevance*, J. Semantics **7**, 175–219.

Prior, M. and Prior, A. (1955), *Erotetic logic*, Philos. Rev. **64**, 43–59.

Rexach, J.G. (1996), *Semantic properties of interrogative generalized quantifiers*, Proceedings of the Tenth Amsterdam Colloquium, P. Dekker and M. Stokhof, eds, ILLC, Amsterdam, 319–338.

Rooth, M. (1992), *A theory of focus interpretation*, Nat. Language Semantics **1**, 75–116.

Searle, J. (1969), *Speech Acts*, Cambridge Univ. Press, Cambridge, MA.

Scha, R. (1983), *Logical foundations for question answering*, Dissertation, Groningen.

Stenius, E. (1967), *Mood and language game*, Synthese **17**, 254–274.

Tichy, P. (1978), *Questions, answers, and logic*, Amer. Philos. Q. **15**, 275–284.

Van Benthem, J. (1989a), *Polyadic quantification*, Ling. and Philos. **12**, 437–464.

Van Benthem, J. (1989b), *Semantic parallels in natural language and computation*, Logic Colloquium. Granada 1987, H.D. Ebbinghaus et al., eds, North-Holland, Amsterdam, 331–375.

Van Kuppevelt, J. (1991), *Topic en comment*, Dissertation, Nijmegen.

Vanderveken, D. (1990), *Meaning and Speech Acts*, two volumes, Cambridge Univ. Press, Cambridge.

Zeevat, H. (1994), *Applying an exhaustivity operator in update semantics*, Ellipsis, Tense, and Questions, H. Kamp, ed., ILLC (DYANA-deliverable R2.2.B), Amsterdam, 233–269.

CHAPTER 20

Generics and Defaults*

Francis Jeffry Pelletier

Department of Philosophy and Department of Computing Science, University of Alberta, Edmonton, Alta., Canada T6G 2E5
E-mail: jeffp@cs.ualberta.ca

Nicholas Asher

316 Waggener Hall, The University of Texas, Austin, TX 78712, USA
E-mail: nasher@bertie.la.utexas.edu

Contents

*This paper is strongly influenced by – indeed, identically overlaps at some points – Krifka, Pelletier, Carlson, Ter Meulen, Chierchia, and Link (1995). Not all those authors agree with everything we say here, but it was through interaction with them that most of the linguistic ideas behind this paper came into existence, and we gratefully acknowledge their help. The paper also owes some of its content to work done jointly with Len Schubert: Schubert and Pelletier (1987, 1989). Other parts of this paper overlap work done jointly with Michael Morreau: Asher and Morreau (1991, 1995). We also wish to express our appreciation to the editors of this volume, Alice ter Meulen and Johan van Benthem, for their encouragement and for their comments on earlier versions of this paper.

HANDBOOK OF LOGIC AND LANGUAGE
Edited by J. van Benthem and A. ter Meulen

1. Linguistic and epistemological background

1.1. Generic reference vs. generic predication

Historically speaking, there have been two quite distinct phenomena that have been called genericity. The first is reference to a kind, a *genus*, as exemplified in (1). The italicized NPs in (1) do not denote or designate some particular potato or group of potatoes, but rather the kind Potato (*Solanum tuberosum*) itself. In this usage a generic NP is one which does not refer to an ordinary individual or object, but instead refers to a kind.

(1) a. *The potato* was first cultivated in South America.

b. *Potatoes* were introduced into Ireland by the end of the 17th century.

c. The Irish economy became dependent upon *the potato.*

NPs such as *potatoes* or *the potato* in these sentences are called kind-referring NPs (sometimes generic NPs), as opposed to object-referring NPs, and the predications in sentences involving such NPs are called kind predications as opposed to object predications.[1]

The second phenomenon commonly associated with genericity are propositions which do not express specific episodes or isolated facts, but instead report a kind of *general property*, that is, report a regularity which summarizes groups of particular episodes or facts. One common sort of generic proposition of this type occurs when the regularity holds across the individual instances of a kind; in such a case the regularity is stated as one holding for the kind itself. Examples can be found in the natural readings of the sentences in (2). Here (2a,b,c) do not state something about a specific potato, but about potatoes in general. This notion of genericity is clearly a feature of the whole sentence (or clause), rather than of any NP in it; it is the whole generic sentence that expresses regularities which transcend particular facts.

(2) a. A potato contains vitamin C and amino acid.

b. Potatoes contain protein.

c. The potato contains thiamin.

Closely related to such sentences as these are habituals, in which a regularity of action is predicated of an ordinary individual. In such cases we (mostly) intend that the regularity is predicated of the object at different times. An example is in (3), which does not report a particular episode, but a habit.

(3) Mary smokes a cigar after dinner.

---

[1] Sentences employing such kind-referring NPs are possibly what Barth (1974) has in mind by "logophoric use of the articles". She says that "*The/An M is P* is a logophoric proposition iff the article is not being used anaphorically, the NP is neither used referentially nor attributively, and this sentence does *not* mean any of:

all Ms are P; every M is P; an arbitrary M is P;

the class/set of Ms is included in the set of Ps; some M is P.

And furthermore The/An M is M has to be regarded as logically true."

It is not clear whether or not there are any logophoric sentences in this sense, at least not if some of the proposed reductions of generic NPs to quantified statements are correct.

The difference between (2) and (3) is a matter of whether one is generalizing over objects or over what an object does. In (2) we generalize over objects and say that a typical instance of such an object has a property, whereas in (3) we generalize over what an object does and say that it typically acts in a certain way. Notice then an ambiguity in such sentences as

(4) Violinists smoke after concerts

which can be seen saying either that the typical violinist has the property of smoking after each concert or as saying of all violinists that they have the habit of typically smoking after concerts. Of course it can even more naturally be seen as generalizing over *both* objects and actions, saying that the typical violinist has the property of typically smoking after concerts. Sentences like (2), (3) and (4) are called characterizing sentences (or sometimes generic sentences) since they express a characterizing property. They are opposed to particular sentences, which express particular events, properties of particular objects, and the like.[2] We therefore can distinguish characterizing predications and particular predications. Other common terms for characterizing sentences found in the literature are (g)nomic, dispositional, general, or habitual. Much of our knowledge of the world, and most of our beliefs about the world, are couched in terms of characterizing sentences. According to this attitude such sentences would be either true or false, *not* indeterminate or figurative or metaphorical or sloppy talk.

Obviously, sentences containing reference to kinds have something in common with characterizing sentences: when we refer to kinds we abstract away from particular objects, whereas when we use characterizing sentences we abstract away from particular events and facts. Furthermore, it seems natural that one way to express a general law or regularity about the specimens of a kind is to state it for the kind itself. Nonetheless, as it is argued in detail in (Krifka, Pelletier, Carlson, Ter Meulen, Chierchia and Link, 1995), it is necessary to distinguish them, since not only are there intuitive differences concerning their logical form but also there are linguistic differences between them. In this article we concentrate exclusively on characterizing sentences, since it is the phenomenon manifested by such sentences that has attracted the most interest from the logical representation wing of the artificial intelligence world. In this article we will not be concerned with the problem of delimiting characterizing sentences from kind-referring predications, nor with distinguishing all sorts of generic phenomena from non-generic phenomena. Instead we will merely assume that we know what sentences are the type of generic sentences in which we are interested; and we will proceed to investigate their semantic and logical properties. Our interest is in generic sentences of the characterizing sort, and it is these sentences that we will call generic statements in what follows.

1.2. Why are there any generic sentences at all?

A crucial feature of characterizing sentences indeed, perhaps their most interesting semantic feature and that feature which brings them to the attention of this volume is that

[2] They are also opposed to general sentences in which there is explicit quantification over particular objects manifesting particular events or properties such as *Each potato in this room was grown in Alberta.*

they admit exceptions.[3] That is, sentences in (2) and (3) are true even though there are potatoes which do not contain those nutrients and even though Mary sometimes does not smoke a cigar after dinner. In our opinion, it is precisely this feature that explains why all natural languages have generic sentences. It is an innate disposition of humans ... perhaps this is a consequence of having intelligence or perhaps it is one of humanity's survival characteristics ... that they desire to understand and characterize the world immediately surrounding them. People notice regularities in nature and form (what we might call) folk-laws to codify these regularities and to predict what the future will bring. So, although not all potatoes contain the nutrients mentioned in (2), and although Mary does not always smoke cigars after dinner, still such folk-laws are intellectually satisfying and practically useful because Mary (and potatoes) *typically* or *usually* or *normally* or *nomically* ... smokes after dinner (or contain those nutrients). Perhaps it is a feature of having finite, fallible minds that makes us often notice regularities that have exceptions, or perhaps it is more a matter of needing to be able to choose regularities quickly in order to get on with other aspects of our survival. Whatever the underlying reason, the fact is that people notice those regularities that can be used to predict actions of others and changes (or constancies) in one's environment. And such regularities commonly have exceptions; either ones that are noticed later or ones that we think we can safely ignore (for whatever reason).

Once one sees generic sentences and the role they play in guiding ordinary actions and beliefs, one discovers that such a construct is used in many different areas of academic research. For example, one can see deontic laws that have *ceteris paribus* clauses as being generic in this way; one can see presuppositions as being the exceptions to statements that don't count in the literal meaning of the statement; one can see arguments over realism/antirealism in philosophy of science as an argument over whether generic statements (with their exceptions) can ever enjoy the privileged status of a true scientific law; and one can understand the status of (legal) laws as being generic in nature as they admit exceptions and special pleas.

1.3. Generics and exceptions, two bad attitudes

From the semantic point of view it is crucial to the understanding of generics to be able to specify how the generic statement is related to the particular statements that are specific instances of it. For example, we might ask: How many exceptions can a generic statement tolerate?, or more generally, What is the relationship between a generic statement and explicitly quantified statements? In addition to the various reasonable attitudes that different theorist have taken concerning this relationship, there are two bad attitudes that are sometimes found in the literature from which we wish to dissent.

---

[3] This is not their only interesting semantic feature. In (Carlson, 1977) and (Lawler, 1973) it was pointed out that such generics seem to admit only predications where the property described is in some sense essential to the subject. Thus, *Madrigals are polyphonic* is a true characterizing statement whereas **Madrigals are popular* is not, perhaps because polyphonicity (but not popularity) is essential to madrigals. It is clear that this is related in some way to the nomic nature of generics that we discuss later, but it is far from clear how.

One attitude, an attitude taken by various logic texts and by some earlier AI practitioners, is that the generic statements are strictly speaking false, but are acceptable despite the exceptions because they are close enough to being universally true. So, *Potatoes contain vitamin C* is acceptable despite being literally false, because almost all potatoes, or all the noticeable or important ones, contain vitamin C.[4] We claim that this is not just an unhelpful way to look at the topic, but is totally incorrect. Most of our knowledge about the world is encoded in characterizing sentences, and it seems pointless to claim that such encodings are merely acceptable and not really true. Furthermore, if this were a correct attitude then one would expect that generic statements would be more acceptable or truer the fewer exceptions there be. Yet as we shall shortly see, this is not how generics act.

A second attitude that might be taken toward such exception-tolerating sentences is that they are *neither* true nor false; that these concepts simply do not apply to them. Instead, characterizing sentences are directives or rules as to how to proceed, how to draw inferences, and so on. In such a view, a characterizing statement like *Potatoes contain vitamin C* gives us information about what to expect in our experience, how to act in the presence of certain vegetables, and what to infer about the items in the grocery store namely, we should expect, and act in accordance with, and infer that: in the absence of information to the contrary, any potato we encounter will contain vitamin C. This attitude, though common in certain areas of AI, seems to have two flaws in it. First, in treating characterizing statements in effect as *rules*, as directives about what to infer, it denies truth or falsity to such statements. Instead, the relevant concept is one of truth-preservingness or of validity. Such a view denies that the classic *Snow is white* is either true or false! And it does so not because of the existence of some yellow snow or the like, but because it holds that this sentence is intended only to guide our expectations as to what color of snow we will encounter normally. It was remarked above that much (most?) of our information about the world is captured by these characterizing statements; but it would be a consequence of the present view that this information is not knowledge, since it is not true (indeed, is neither true nor false, is neither accurate nor inaccurate, etc). Instead, it would merely be a matter of directing our actions and inferences. Perhaps there are ways to ease ones conscience about this matter, but it seems very harsh.

The second conceptual difficulty with this approach is that if generic statements are neither true nor false, and instead are rules of inference, then they cannot be embedded within one another. And although some researchers have asserted that this is indeed the case and have used this claim to bolster their position, they fail to notice sentences like

(5) a. Usually, if a person smokes after dinner, he also drinks brandy before bed.

b. It is common that countries which do not honor women's rights also do not honor general human rights.

---

[4] A variant on this first bad attitude would be to claim that the acceptability of such "strictly speaking false" statements is dependent upon our ability to specify (if asked) what the exceptions are. Although the statements are strictly false, we accept them because we know where to find the exceptions. Our examples below will show that this optimistic outlook on exceptions is totally without merit.

Note that both the antecedent and the consequent of these conditionals are themselves characterizing statements (they each admit of exceptions, they each express regularities over events, etc.), and that each statement asserts there to be a generic connection between the two (the connection admits of exceptions, expresses a general regularity, etc.). Such examples seem to support strongly the view that generics are not directives or rules of inference, but instead are either literally true or literally false. We will consider this attitude and these objections again below, in Section 3.

1.4. Exceptions and generics, some other attitudes

If we adopt the view that generics *can* be either true or false, there is then a question about the logical form of generics. And this brings up once again the question of the relationship between a characterizing sentence and the specific episodes or cases of which it is a generalization. Put bluntly, we wish to know: How many exceptions can a generic statement tolerate and remain true? Different kinds of characterizing generics call for different types of cases to be relevant, and therefore determine different sorts of legitimate exceptions. This can be seen in the differences between episodic generics (where there is a regularity asserted about events),

(6) a. Tabby usually lands on her feet.

b. Marvin normally beats Sandy at ping-pong.

non-episodic generics (where there is a regularity asserted to hold over a class of objects),

(7) a. Bears with blue eyes are normally intelligent.

b. A grade school student is usually a child.

and sentences which can be seen as ambiguous between the two

(8) a. People who have a job are usually happy.

b. People who live far from their work usually drive.

(These last can be seen as saying either (a) that most people who have a job are happy [or: most people who live far from work are drivers], or (b) that a person is happy for most of the time that s/he holds a job [or: a person who lives far from work drives most of the time].)[5] We will not, however, delve into these distinctions. Instead we will concentrate mostly on the naive question of how many exceptions can be tolerated by a characterizing sentence and have it still be true. We will argue that all quantificational analyses fail: that there is no univocal quantifier which can work for all generics. We then briefly examine whether there can be some probabilistic analysis that will work;

[5] The sentences in (7) can also be seen as ambiguous: not only might it be a generalization over the objects in the class (most bears with blue eyes / most grade school children) but also as generalizing over states (such bears are intelligent most of the time but maybe sometimes change into being stupid / a grade school student is a child for most of its life). These sentences should be considered in concert with the earlier examples (2) and (4).

and again we argue in the negative: there is no sense in which a characterizing sentence asserts a unique, or even a rough, probability. Having argued against any relationship – whether quantificational or probabilistic – between generics and their instances, we offer a brief explanation of why this should be so. The failures of the quantificational and probabilistic analyses have consequences for certain AI accounts of the logical form of characterizing sentences, and we shall therefore turn to the topic of these AI techniques.

Consider these true characterizing sentences:

(9) a. Snakes are reptiles.
    b. Telephone books are thick books.
    c. Guppies give live birth.
    d. Italians are good skiers.
    e. Crocodiles live to an old age.
    f. Frenchmen eat horsemeat.
    g. Unicorns have one horn.

Obviously we understand the truth of these sentences as calling for different relative numbers or proportions of instances of the subject terms satisfying the predicate term. In (a) it is all; in (b) most; in (c) some subset of the females; in (d) some small percentage, but a greater percentage than in other countries (or maybe: the very best of the Italian skiers are better than the very best from other countries); in (e) it is strikingly few, since of the hundreds born to one female at a time, most are eaten within a few weeks of birth; in (f) there need be only a very small percentage – from the vantage point of North America, the mere fact of its happening at all is striking; and in (g) no unicorns have one horn. Examples such as these show that there is no univocal quantifier which will serve in all characterizing sentences.

Even attempts to employ vague, probabilistically-oriented quantifiers such as *most* or *generally* or *in a significant number of cases* are misguided. Consider such false characterizing sentences as

(10) a. Leukemia patients are children.
     b. Seeds do not germinate.
     c. Books are paperbacks.
     d. Prime numbers are odd.
     e. Crocodiles die before they attain an age of two weeks.

Each of these false characterizing sentences becomes true when prefixed with *In a significant number of cases*. Indeed, the actual extension of the subject within the predicate has almost nothing to do with whether the generic is true or not. Even if all children ever born in Rainbow Lake, Alberta, were left-handed, this would have nothing to do with whether

(11) Children born in Rainbow Lake, Alberta, are left-handed.

To determine the truth of (11) we would instead look to the water supply, or to the mineral deposits near the town, or to the electromagnetic fields surrounding the hospital, or to the ancestry of the parents of such children, etc., to determine whether some special causal factor was at work and made (11) a true characterizing sentence. The actual numbers or percentages of such children that are left-handed is simply not relevant, except as evidence that some other force might be at work. In this, generic statements are akin to scientific laws: they must be carefully distinguished from accidental generalizations. If it were accidentally to happen that all the remaining pandas in the world lost a leg, then even though every panda had three legs, still the characterizing sentence *Pandas have three legs* would be false. A sentence that is an accidental generalization is not a true characterizing sentence.

1.5. Generics and intensionality

Furthermore, characterizing sentences are inherently intensional, and this too is an obstacle to any extensional analysis, whether quantificational or probabilistic. Characterizing sentences like

(12) a. This machine crushes oranges,
b. Kim handles the mail from Antarctica,
c. Members of this club help one another in emergencies,

can be true despite there never being an opportunity for the generic episode to take place. (12a) can be true even if the machine is immediately destroyed upon coming off the assembly line; (12b) can be true even if there happened never to be any mail from Antarctica; and (12c) can be true even if no emergency ever occurred. Such sentences show that what is required for the truth of generics is intensional: in these cases it amounts to the design of the machine, or the job-description of the mail-sorters, or the preparedness to act in certain ways in certain situations. Surely this shows the complete implausibility of trying to capture genericity with a quantifier, no matter how inherently vague or probabilistically-determined one tries to make the quantifier. No such extensional analysis *can* be correct. One of the earliest philosophers to make this point was Bosanquet (1888), who remarked that if a generic judgment is formulated by means of the quantifier *all*, then it is helpless in the face of the most trivial exception and for this reason he used as examples only statements not containing a quantifier. (For example, Man is an animal capable of social life, A society organized on a purely commercial basis treats the working classes as little better than slaves, The bacillus is a septic organism.) His idea seems to be rather congenial to our position: we notice that *nearly all* of the Xs are Y; we notice some exceptions; but we nonetheless doubt that the nearly all could be a mere coincidence. Therefore there must be some sort of connection, however circuitous and the exceptions can be accounted for by special conditions. And to express this sort of nomic dependency we use the generic forms of bare plural (Xs are Y), indefinite (An X is Y), and definite (The X is Y).[6]

---

[6] For a discussion of Bosanquet, see (Barth, 1974, pp. 364–367).

Another reason that there must be some operator other than an implicit quantifier is that there are ambiguities in certain characterizing sentences ambiguities between different generic readings. For one thing, there is a clear ambiguity between (what might be called)[7] a habitual reading and a dispositional reading. For example,

(13) John drinks beer,

can be understood as meaning that beer is John's favorite alcoholic beverage (habitual) or that John does not object to drinking beer (dispositional). Other examples of ambiguities are illustrated by sentences like[8]

(14) a. Typhoons arise in this part of the Pacific.
  1. Typhoons in general have a common origin in this part of the Pacific.
  2. There arise typhoons in this part of the Pacific.

 b. A computer computes the daily weather forecast.
  1. Computers in general have the task of computing the daily weather forecast.
  2. The daily weather forecast is computed by a computer.

 c. A cat runs across my lawn every day.
  1. Cats in general run across my lawn every day.
  2. Every day, a cat runs across my lawn.

The 1- and 2-readings of these sentences are both generic readings, and so we need some method by which to represent this type of ambiguity. There is also a difference between readings of generics that is imposed by emphasis or focus. Consider the difference amongst (italics indicates primary stress, which can be either focal or contrastive)

(15) a. Leopards usually attack monkeys *in trees*.

 b. Leopards usually attack monkeys *in* trees.

 c. Leopards usually attack *monkeys* in trees.

 d. Leopards usually *attack* monkeys in trees.

(15a) says that when leopards attack monkeys somewhere, that somewhere is usually in trees; (15b) says that when leopards attack monkeys in, around, or near trees, it is usually *in* the tree; (15c) says that when leopards attack something in trees, it is usually monkeys; and (15d) says that when leopards are near monkeys in trees, they usually attack them. Another sort of ambiguity occurs in sentences such as

(16) Bullfighters are often injured.

---

[7] These different readings were called universal and existential by Lawler (1973), on the grounds that the first case is a quasi-universal reading and the latter case asserts an instance of John drinking beer. But we wish to move away from the extensional implications of these sentences in either of their senses and concentrate on their intensional force.

[8] The first of these sentences is from Milsark (1974), the second from Carlson (1979) where it is attributed to Barbara Partee, and the third is from Schubert and Pelletier (1987).

Clearly, often invokes some sort of implicit comparison class, and the ambiguity in (16) has also an effect on what this comparison class is. One can see (16) as saying that bullfighting is a dangerous sport and that, compared to participants in other sporting activities, bullfighters get injured in their sport more often. But one can also see (16) as saying that the sort of person who becomes a bullfighter is the sort of a person who tends generally to get injured compared to other people in their daily lives, bullfighters injure themselves more often in their daily lives. The difference here and in the other ambiguities also is what Schubert and Pelletier (1987) called the restricting cases against which the characterizing statement is made. In (16) the restricting cases can be seen as either situations in which athletes are practicing their trade, or else situations in everyone's ordinary life. In the various sentences of (15), the relevant restricting cases are those mentioned in the explanations following those examples.

1.6. Goals of an analysis of generic sentences

From a semantic point of view, there are three central goals of an analysis: (a) The analysis should give some account of the truth conditions of generic sentences, preferably one that accords with intuitive views of the truth conditions of sample generic sentences, showing how exceptions arise and in which way they can affect the truth of such statements; (b) The analysis should explain the facts about intensionality, especially the law-like nature of generic sentences and how they differ from quantified, extensional sentences; (c) The analysis must give an account of how generic sentences are used in reasoning, especially reasoning that involves the fact that such sentences admit exceptions.

Of course there are other goals one might reasonably ask of a philosophically and semantically adequate theory of generic sentences such as an account of how the analysis gives an explanation of propositional attitudes involving generic sentences, or an account of how generic sentences come to form part of the folk explanation of the universe, or an account of how generic sentences interact with other sentences in any of the fields mentioned above in Section 1.2 (ethics, legal theory, philosophy of science, etc). One might also ask for a clear statement of how the proposed semantic analysis fits in with a syntactic analysis of the same material: how can one syntactically distinguish the different partitions of the generic sentences so as to yield the various ambiguities we find in them? How can we deal with generic anaphora, since sometimes pronouns appear to refer to kinds and other times to instances of the kinds? And without doubt, there are many other reasonable expectations one might have of an adequate theory of generics. Our goals in this essay are modest, however; we concentrate only on the three goals identified in the previous paragraph, and even here we only give outlines. But we do think that the outlined answers will provide the final reasons desired, once the details are worked out.

1.7. A little notation

In general, such characterizing sentences have three parts, joined by an operator that we will simply call **GEN**: a matrix (a main clause) which makes the main assertion of the characterizing sentence, a restrictor clause which states the restricting cases relevant to the particular matrix, and a list of variables that are governed by **GEN**.[9] With such a notation we have a convenient way to represent the various readings of these characterizing sentences.

(14′) a. Typhoons arise in this part of the Pacific.

1. $\mathbf{GEN}[x](x\ \mathbf{are\ typhoons};\ \exists y[y\ \mathbf{is\ this\ part\ of\ the\ Pacific}\ \&\ x\ \mathbf{arise\ in}\ y])$.

2. $\mathbf{GEN}[x](x\ \mathbf{is\ this\ part\ of\ the\ Pacific};\ \exists y[y\ \mathbf{are\ typhoons}\ \&\ y\ \mathbf{arise\ in}\ x])$.

(13′) a. John drinks *beer.*

$$\mathbf{GEN}[x, y, s](x = \mathbf{John}\ \&\ x\ \mathbf{drinks}\ y\ \mathbf{in}\ s;\ y\ \mathbf{is\ beer}).$$

b. John *drinks* beer.

$$\mathbf{GEN}[x, y, s](x = \mathbf{John}\ \&\ y\ \mathbf{is\ beer}\ \&\ y\ \mathbf{in}\ s\ \&\ x\ \mathbf{in}\ s;\ x\ \mathbf{drinks}\ y\ \mathbf{in}\ s).$$

c. John *drinks beer.*

$$\mathbf{GEN}[x, s](x = \mathbf{John}\ \&\ x\ \mathbf{in}\ s;\ \exists y[\mathbf{beer}(y)\ \&\ x\ \mathbf{drinks}\ y\ \mathbf{in}\ s]).$$

(Again, the italicizing indicates stressed pronunciation, or focus.) The universal interpretation in (13′a) can be rendered as: In appropriate situations (for which we use the variable s, and talk about an object being in a situation) in which John drinks something, this is normally beer. The existential interpretation in (13′b) says that in appropriate situations where there is some beer available, John normally drinks it. The habitual interpretation in (13′c) says that, in appropriate situations which contain John, he will drink beer.

The list of those variables which are governed by the **GEN** operator must be allowed to vary from reading to reading, for it is here that some of the ambiguities reside. Not only is it sometimes true that the objects which are governed by **GEN** are different in the different readings, as in (14′a), but also there can be different numbers of arguments, as in (13′c) compared to (13′a) or (13′b). And one can see the ambiguity reported in (8) as a matter of having different arguments to **GEN** objects vs. situations. It is this sort of flexibility which will allow us to capture the different readings of complex generics, where a NP may be within the scopes of several **GEN** operators or explicit quantifiers, any of which may control it, so that a disambiguating syntax is required. Consider

(17) If a person occasionally contributes to a charity when he receives an appeal, he will usually receive further appeals.

Here *a charity* may be controlled by *occasionally* or by *usually*, depending on whether *further appeals* is understood as *further appeals from charities* or as *further appeals from that charity*. Disambiguations similar to those made in (13) and (14a) can be made for the sentences in (15), (16) and (17), as well as the other sentences in (14), given clever enough identification of the situations and objects, and their interrelations.

[9] This tripartite structure comes from Lewis (1975).

1.8. Generics vs. explicit statements of regularities

It has already been remarked that generic statements appear to express law-like regularities, and not mere accidental correlations. This raises some interesting questions about the possible relationship between generics and explicit statements of regularities. What is the relationship between the characterizing statement (18a) and the rest of the sentences in (18)?

(18) a. Birds fly.[10]
b. Most birds fly.
c. Usually, birds fly.
d. Birds typically fly.
e. Birds generally fly.
f. Normally, birds fly.
g. In general, birds fly.

(18a) states a generalization that follows somehow from (assumed) natural laws; it conveys nomic force. The other statements can be used to express this meaning also, but in addition they can be used to assert, on a purely extensional level, that most, or many, etc., birds can fly. This latter is *not* a generic statement – it does not have nomic force although in many cases generic statements imply or implicate these kinds of extensional statements.[11] Nonetheless, many of the analyses of characterizing statements, especially those in the AI literature, are in fact analyses of these extensional sentences. Any attempt to analyze the generic statement in terms of "most" or "the usual" falls into this category; and attempts to use "the typical" or "the normal" fall into this category also, unless these phrases are themselves given a non-extensional meaning ... an option we will consider in the next section. They simply are not analyses of generics, but rather are analyses of these extensional implications and then only in those cases where the specific generic in fact *has* this sort of extensional implication. (As opposed to some of the other types of generic statements mentioned above.) It seems to us that many of the AI theorists have merely cited those specific characterizing statements that in fact happen to have these sorts of extensional consequences, then proceeded to provide an analysis of sorts for these consequences and concluded that they thereby have an analysis of the original generic statement. It is this last inference that we challenge, and it is for this reason that we earlier gave the long list of generics that do not have this sort of extensional consequence. Of course, these AI analyses can be interesting in their own right, because these sort of extensional consequences are important and challenging. But as mentioned below, it seems that at least some of the AI theorists arrive at their analyses due to a confusion between generic nomic necessity and extensional generality.

---

[10] There is also an ambiguity in 'fly' in these sentences, between the sense that birds have the ability to fly vs. that they *are* flying. This ambiguity is heightened in those sentences with the explicit adverbial quantifiers, (b), (g). We are concerned here with the "ability to fly" sense, but the other sense of these sentences is also a generic meaning and it too requires a suitable treatment. The analysis hinted at above, with situation-variables as part of the possible arguments to the list of controlled variables seems to afford a way to accommodate this ambiguity.

[11] But not always, as various of the aforementioned examples prove.

2. Semantic analyses of generics

The **GEN** operator, and its variable-control list, is just notation. The real question is: what is the semantic interpretation of **GEN**? We have already seen that it cannot be universal quantification, nor indeed any univocal quantifier, not even a vague probabilistic quantifier. The literature contains (at least) seven other suggestions. First, the **GEN** operator might be spelled out as relevant quantification. Second, the apparent quantification embodied in generic sentences might be understood as singular predication where the subject is an abstract object. Third, the notion of prototypical entities might be employed as an improvement on the abstract object analysis. Fourth, **GEN** can be seen as a statement of a stereotype. Fifth, **GEN** might be analyzed as a modal conditional, to be interpreted in a possible world semantics. Sixth, **GEN** might be analyzed as combining with a sentence to express a constraint in the theory of Situation Semantics. And seventh, **GEN** might be given a default reasoning analysis in one form or another.

Perhaps with suitable work each of these approaches can accommodate the view that characterizing statements have nomic force and are more than mere statements of what happens more often than not.[12] We content ourselves with making brief comments on these approaches. After these comments we turn in Section 3 to a somewhat more detailed analysis of default theories and the extent to which they can be used to account for the semantic phenomena of generics.

2.1. Relevant quantification

The generic operator might be spelled out as a universal quantification over relevant entities. When a statement is made about a natural group of objects, the hearer uses world knowledge to restrict the statement to just those members of the natural group to which it can be applied in a suitable way (Declerck, 1991). For example

(19) Whales give birth to live young.
$\forall x[[\mathbf{whale}(x)\ \&\ \mathbf{R}(x)] \rightarrow x\ \mathbf{gives\ birth\ to\ live\ young}]$

will be a predication over female, non-sterile whales, as only they could possibly give birth to live young in the first place. In the formulation above, this would be expressed by specifying the restriction variable **R** in a suitable way. One obvious problem with this approach is that this principle, as it stands, can easily justify all kinds of generic sentences ... since it is easy to find restrictions which would make *any* quantification come out true. For example, the analysis could make

(20) Whales are sick

be a true characterizing sentence, since we can take **R** to be the predicate *sick*, hence to restrict the quantification to sick whales. So this approach calls for a theory of suitable restrictions, and it is unclear how or whether this can be developed. Or, if it can be developed, perhaps it would just be circular in that one can find values of **R** only if one already knows what the true characterizing sentences are.

---

[12] Of course giving an account of what happens more often than not is itself no trivial matter. But interesting as this may be, it is not the same task as giving an account of the semantics of generic statements.

2.2. *Abstract objects*

It might be supposed that generic NPs refer to an indeterminate or arbitrary object, and that characterizing statements are in fact singular statements about this object. This view has the apparent advantage of enforcing a close link between our two types of genericity: Generic NPs and characterizing sentences. But it also seems not to cover the whole range of characterizing sentences such as habituals like *Mary smokes when she is nervous* that do not appear to mention any arbitrary objects.[13] Furthermore, it is not obvious how to enforce the distinction between an accidental universal generalization and a true generic with its nomic force in any theory that appeals to arbitrary objects. In assessing the plausibility of any such analysis, much depends on what such a theory counts as an arbitrary object.

Lewis (1972, p. 203) attributes to the dark ages of logic the story:

> The phrase 'some pig' names a strange thing we may call the *existentially generic pig* which has just those properties that some pig has. Since some pig is male, some pig (a different one) is female ... the existentially generic pig is simultaneously male, female ... The phrase 'every pig' names a different strange thing called the *universally generic pig* which has just those properties that every pig has. Since not every pig is pink, grey, or any other color, the universally generic pig is not of any color. (Yet neither is he colorless since not every – indeed not any pig – is colorless) ... He is, however a pig and an animal, and he grunts; for every pig is a pig and an animal and grunts. There are also the *negative universally generic pig* which has just those properties that no pig has (he is not a pig, but he is both a stone and a number), the *majority generic pig* which has just those properties that more than half of all pigs have, and many more ...

The history of philosophy has not been kind to arbitrary objects. For example, Lewis follows the above quotation with: "The story is preposterous since nothing, however recondite, can possibly have more or less than one of a set of incompatible and jointly exhaustive properties".[14] Berkeley (1710) complained of (what he took to be) Locke's (1690) version of this theory according to which an arbitrary person (or general idea of person) would be of no particular height, of no particular sex, of no particular age, and so forth. How, Berkeley asks, can such an item represent anything in experience such as a person? Further, Berkeley continues, the whole notion seems contradictory. If the arbitrary object or general idea has just those properties enjoyed by all people, then it will be *either male or female*. But as we have seen, it is not male, nor is it female; it is either male or female, but neither male nor female. Frege (1904), commenting on the use of arbitrary numbers in mathematics, asks whether there can be two *distinct* arbitrary numbers. If not, the theory of arbitrary numbers would be useless for mathematics (which often asks us to consider two arbitrary numbers); but if so, the theory is committed to distinct objects that are indiscernible, since the alleged two arbitrary numbers share all properties. Russell

[13] Perhaps one could invoke arbitrary Mary-when-nervous objects?

[14] At least, cant have them as its properties. But of course a *set* of properties could contain contradictory properties as members, and it is this use that Lewis recommends for natural language semantics. In the theory developed in his (1972), such sets are *characters*, and are what is in the extension of noun phrases; and a character is individual in his sense just in case it is a maximal compatible set of properties so that something could possess all and only the properties in the set. Otherwise he calls the character *generic*. But this sense of the term is not what is under discussion in the present article.

(1905) points to similar difficulties with Meinongian (1904) incomplete objects, which are arbitrary objects in the sense used here.

A modern account of (universally) arbitrary objects is provided by Fine (1985), who also brings out the similarities (and differences) of his approach to that of the ε-calculus (Hilbert and Bernays, 1934; see also Routley, 1967; and Smirnov, 1976). It is possible that a similar theory of *majority* arbitrary objects or maybe even *typically* arbitrary objects could be specified along the same lines, but we do not think it would be of use in explicating natural language generics, for it would share a number of features of the actual Fine theory which we find unsuitable. In his explicit consideration of all the preceding criticisms, Fine arrives at a theory in which the principle of bivalence fails and in which disjunctions are not semantically evaluated directly by a disjunction rule (and similarly, we presume, with other connectives). Further, there needs be a distinction between (what Fine calls) generic predicates and classical predicates. It is only the generic predicates which can give rise to arbitrary objects (and thus to generic NPs). All these restrictions and caveats seem necessary to Fine's theory, and they certainly do not take away from his goal of giving an account of how to employ arbitrary objects in formal logical proofs that invoke Existential Instantiation and Universal Generalization as rules of inference. But it seems to us that it still requires a lot of further research to employ them in an account of natural language generic statements. For example, although mathematics and logic can perhaps do without bivalence in their claims concerning arbitrary numbers or arbitrary instances or arbitrary triangles, the same does not seem true of natural language generic statements. Given that one is willing to assign truth values at all to generic statements, it seems clear that any particular generic sentence is either True or is False. 'Ravens are black', 'Sally smokes after dinner', 'Birds fly', and 'Hamsters eat dogs' are each of them true ... or if one should happen not to be true, then it is false. Certainly none of them are intermediate or neither true nor false.

2.3. *Prototypes*

It can be difficult to distinguish an arbitrary object approach from a prototypical object approach, despite Barth's (1974, p. 200) claim that "the two concepts should not be regarded as logical synonyms and ... not even as closely related notions". The real difference, as we see it, is that an arbitrary object theory proposes it to be an object that is of a different nature than "ordinary objects" (especially in the sorts of properties it has), whereas prototype theories presume that prototypes are of the same nature as ordinary objects. Recall that a universally arbitrary X-object has only those properties that all Xs share, that an existentially arbitrary X-object has properties that any X has, majority arbitrary X-object would have only those properties that are enjoyed by most Xs, and that a typically arbitrary X-object would have only those properties that a typical X has. But this means that universally arbitrary X-objects, majority arbitrary X-objects, and typically arbitrary X-objects could all be *missing* properties that are necessary for (ordinary) existence. For example, although the typical human has hair, there may be no typical hair color for humans ... and so the typically arbitrary person would have hair but no hair color. Yet it is necessary that any person with hair (who exists in the ordinary sense) must have some hair color or other. A prototype theory would make different claims about such cases. It presumes that prototypes are "ordinary objects", and so the prototypical human is an ordinary human. A prototypical human will have hair, as we said; thus, a prototypical human will have some specific hair color. But since there is no prototypical hair color, it follows that there will be distinct prototypical humans (each with hair) that exemplify the different prototypically possible hair colors. It may be that one of these people will have black hair, another brown hair, another blond hair, and a fourth red hair. From this it follows that the prototypical hair color is: either black or brown or blond or red.

In the quote cited just above, Barth was complaining about Jespersen (1924), who uses the term 'generic person'[15] when talking about NPs with the indefinite article (and indefinite pronouns). Jespersen says that such an article "is a weaker version of *any* ... where a dog is taken to represent a whole class". Barth takes this to mean that an arbitrary dog is to be regarded as paradigmatic, which in turn is the "misconceived" moment in the area.

It is not so obvious to us that Jespersen is conflating arbitrary and paradigmatic objects. To us, the difference between the two is that an A-arbitrary object of type X has all and *only* the properties that A of the Xs have, whereas a paradigmatic object of type X has all the prototypical properties that Xs have, but it will also have other properties. Our idea is that for such other properties there is a prototypical object enjoying each of the various alternative properties. Thus, a prototypical person has two arms, two legs, and hair on the head; and it has these because they are the prototypical properties of people. But being male, or being female, is not such a property; thus there will be one prototype that is female and one which is male. Having blonde, brunette, red or black hair are not prototypical properties, and this will give rise to four prototypes for each of the sexes, and so on.

The prototype approach we are interested in assumes that, from among the entities which are categorized as being an instance of a certain concept, we can choose those entities which are best representations of that concept. The fundamental idea behind these approaches is that all the entities which are the most typical representatives of a concept are called prototypes ... a concept popularized in cognitive psychology especially by Rosch (1978) and Osherson and Smith (1981). A characterizing sentence is seen as a universal quantification over the prototypical elements of a concept. For example, a sentence such as *A cat has a tail* can be paraphrased as *Every prototypical cat has a tail.* If we adopt an operator **TYP** which restricts the extension of a predicate to the entities which are prototypical for that predicate, then the prototype-analysis of generics becomes:

(21) A cat has a tail.
$\forall x[\mathbf{TYP}(\mathbf{cat})(x) \rightarrow \exists y[y \textbf{ is a tail } \& \ x \textbf{ has } y]]$.

When developing a unified treatment for all characterizing sentences, however, we must assume a very general prototypicality operator, because the contents of a Restrictor can

[15] Barth says, "Jespersen's use of 'person' here is quite general and covers dogs and other logical individuals as well as human beings".

vary widely; and we must also allow such a **TYP** to be applied to predicates of different adicities. One feature of **TYP**, which has been widely noted (Smith and Osherson, 1984), is that it is not a compositional operator. For example, **TYP(pet fish)** is not a function of **TYP(pet)** and **TYP(fish)**. Note also that this operator cannot be defined in terms of sets or other extensional entities, but must be specified as an operator whose arguments are intensional expressions. For, if **GEN** were defined in terms of extensional entities, then, in a world in which all birds except penguins became extinct, the notions of typical birds and typical penguins would coincide.

But even this intensional approach does not give a fine-grained enough representation, as shown by the following true characterizing sentences:

(22) a. A duck has colorful feathers.

b. A duck lays whitish eggs.

The problem here is that only male ducks have colorful feathers, and only female ones lay whitish eggs. As the set of male and female ducks are disjoint, the predicate **TYP(duck)** does not apply to any object at all. And this would have the untoward logical consequence that *any* characterizing sentence of the form *A duck Fs* would be true (because the antecedent of the universal quantifier would always be false). Clearly, the notion of prototypicality must be relativized to the property being expressed in order to save this approach. But it is far from clear how to accomplish such a relativization.

2.4. *Stereotypes*

A related approach is to see characterizing sentences as expressing **stereotypes** (Putnam, 1975; Scribner, 1977). Look at the following contrast:

(23) a. A lion has a mane.

b. A lion is male.

Why are we ready to accept (23a) but not (23b)? Note that arbitrary lions are more likely to be male than to have a mane, since only, but not all, male lions have a mane (e.g., not male cubs). Nonetheless, (23a) is definitely true and (23b) is definitely false. Why? One possible answer is to say that (23a) but not (23b) expresses a stereotype about lions in our culture: it is part of our stereotypical knowledge about the kind *Leo leo* that it has a mane. The general idea is to break down the meaning of a lexical expression into several components, including its extension and some stereotypical properties. These properties are considered to be the core facts (about the extension of the entities) which everyone speaking the language in question must know.[16] If **GEN** expresses stereotypical knowledge, then in order to understand **GEN** we need to investigate the formation of stereotypes. But there is little hope that we will find principles of *general* logical interest in such an investigation. For example, one reason why having a mane is part

[16] Note that here, as in the case of prototypes, the stereotype of a compound expression like *pet fish* is not a function of the stereotypes of its parts, *pet* and *fish*.

of the stereotype of *lion* is that the lion is the only cat that has a mane, making this a distinguishing property for lions. Our task would be to search out other stereotype formations in which distinguishing properties play a role. But it seems unlikely that there is anything of general *logical* interest (as opposed to anthropological interest) in stereotype formation.

Another potential difficulty for a stereotype analysis arises if one assumes cultural norms are the source of stereotyping properties (Scribner, 1977). For instance, suppose it is the norm in some culture to assume that snakes are slimy. Even there, the sentence *Snakes are slimy* is a false sentence, no matter how much it is believed to be true by most members of the culture, since snakes, themselves, are in fact not slimy. That is, generics are construed as making claims about the world, rather than what is considered a cultural norm. Furthermore, a stereotype analysis cannot be the entire story, for stereotypes are tied to single words or well-known and fixed concepts, but the Restrictor of **GEN** can be made up by novel concepts as well. A sentence such as *Mary smokes when she comes home* requires a generalization over situations in which Mary comes home. This sentence can be understood and believed to be true even if the hearer does not have a stereotype about situations in which Mary comes home. If the stereotype theory were correct, **GEN** would not have a uniform interpretation after all, or, equivalently, there would have to be numerous different generic operators. In either case there is no general theory of the semantics of **GEN**.

2.5. Modal conditional approaches

The modal conditional approach uses a possible-worlds semantics in the analysis of characterizing sentences, especially treating such sentences as modal conditionals (Delgrande, 1987; Asher and Morreau, 1991; Boutilier, 1994). This seems a more promising approach than any of the foregoing approaches. For one thing, it has often been remarked that characterizing generic sentences resemble conditional sentences. (For example, a characterizing sentence such as *A lion has a bushy tail* can be rephrased as: *If something is a lion, it has a bushy tail.* And restrictive *when*-clauses, which are often used in characterizing sentences – *When a cat is dropped, it usually lands on its feet* – are similar to conditional clauses in some respects.) So the extensive literature on the modal treatment of conditionals and counterfactuals is relevant here as well. Furthermore, the philosophical literature on dispositional predicates is related to the modal approach. Dispositional predicates, like *be soluble in water*, are generally reduced to law-like sentences (*If x is put into water, it will dissolve*), and law-like sentences are in turn analyzed as modalized sentences. Thus modal approaches perhaps promise to accommodate many of our desiderata for generics.

What sort of modality should be used? Since generics resemble counterfactuals, they seem to be best handled as a sort of variably strict conditional. Counterfactuals have the property noted by Lewis (1973) that two conditionals may have contradictory consequents even though one antecedent entails the other. For example,

(24) a. If you were to drop that plate, it would break.

b. If you were to drop that plate and it were made of rubber, it would not break.

c. If you were to drop that plate and it were made of rubber and its temperature were $-40°$ C, it would break.

Analyzed in terms of nonvariable modality and a material conditional, such statements are jointly unsatisfiable, whereas intuitively we take them to be all true. Generics statements exhibit the same sort of behavior:

(25) a. Birds fly.

b. Birds that are penguins don't fly.

c. Birds that are penguins and have rockets strapped to their backs fly.

So a natural suggestion (introduced first by Delgrande, 1987) is to analyze generics in terms of some sort of quantified conditional. Delgrande (1987) first proposed that generic statements might have the logical form of a quantified conditional, and his ideas have certainly been influential in the AI community.[17] Indeed the semantics from that we propose in Section 4 is a direct descendant of his.[18]

Yet there are some problems that need to be addressed. It is most tempting to analyze the relevant type of generic sentence in terms of "the most normal possible worlds". Sentences like (25a) above would be analyzed as: *In any of the most normal possible worlds, every bird flies*. Yet it is far from clear that there is any sense at all to the notion of being "a most normal possible world" in an unrestricted sense. (Isn't ours the most normal, by definition?) And even if we restrict the notion of normality to just being normal-with-respect-to-bird-flying-ness, it still seems implausible to say that it is more normal to have all birds fly than for some of them not to fly. Is it more normal for penguins to fly? Is it really more normal if there are no penguins? Or kiwis or emu or ostriches? Or fledglings? Or clipped-winged or broken-winged or dead birds? And as sentence (22a) reminds us, if there were a world in which all ducks had brightly colored feathers then there would be no female ducks and hence no brightly-colored males. (Or would it be more normal for the female ducks to be brightly-colored??) And does (22b) presume that it would be more normal for male ducks to lay eggs?? It seems pretty clear that one overall notion of "normalcy" just is not what is called for here, for these imagined scenarios simply are *not* more normal. And as the case of the interacting defaults in (22a,b) shows, even on the extensional level it is pretty difficult to imagine how such "conflicting defaults" can be accommodated when the so-called normal worlds must choose one or the other of the groups to be eliminated as abnormal, and yet if one is eliminated then the other becomes highly abnormal because its existence depended on the existence of the other group.

[17] Other people who have advocated at least implicitly that generics be treated as some sort of conditional are Pearl (1988), who analyzes conditionals in the manner of Adams (1975) as ε-probability statements.

[18] Like most others in the AI community, Delgrande's primary interest is the formalization of commonsense reasoning and not an analysis of generics.

2.6. *Situation semantics*

According to the situation-semantic approach (Barwise and Perry, 1983), it is convenient to use domains "smaller" than complete possible worlds as conversational background. A useful domain might be one in which we look only at single turtles or only at fertilized female ducks. The fifth approach does exactly this by considering *situations* instead of possible worlds, modeling characterizing sentences as *constraints* on situations. Constraints have already been used in Situation Semantics to model conditional sentences (Barwise, 1986), and since characterizing sentences are very similar to conditionals, this constraint technique would seem to be applicable to them as well.

Constraints are relations between types of situations. A constraint such as $\Sigma \Rightarrow \Sigma'$, where Σ and Σ' are situation types, says that Σ *involves* Σ', or that whenever Σ is realized, then Σ' is realized as well, i.e. whenever there is a situation σ of type Σ there is also a situation σ' of type Σ'. The situation types may contain parameters which can be *anchored* to specific entities, locations or types. (In such an approach, parameters are similar to variables, and anchors similar to variable assignments.) An important rule is that whenever f is an anchor for Σ (i.e. $\Sigma(f)$ differs from Σ only insofar as some parameters of Σ are anchored) and we have a constraint $\Sigma \Rightarrow \Sigma'$, then we also have a constraint $\Sigma(f) \Rightarrow \Sigma'(f)$. This rule captures the dependencies between parameters, and can be used to express the dependencies in sentences with adverbial quantifiers if we analyze the variables as parameters. It is important to note that it may be the case that a constraint holds only with respect to some background **B**. Such a conditional constraint is given as $(\Sigma \Rightarrow \Sigma') \mid \mathbf{B}$, read as: Σ involves Σ', given that **B**, where **B** is a situation type as well. The background **B** can be more specific than possible worlds could possibly be. For example, in sentence (22b) **B** can be restricted to situations containing female animals because the sentence tells us something about the mode of giving birth, and therefore only female animals should count. But our considering here only situations that contain no male ducks in no way commits us to denying that there are also mating situations in which there are both male and female ducks. As with the modal approach, the pertinent background is often left unspecified; and again we must assume some rule of accommodation. We discuss such a rule below, in presenting our theory in Section 4.

2.7. *Default reasoning approaches*

The sixth approach for handling the semantics of characterizing sentences is actually a set of related approaches being developed under the rubric non-monotonic reasoning both in logic and in AI. Although this literature does not contain an explicit discussion of generic sentences, the crucial examples that guide its development are always characterizing sentences, and so, if these theories are successful, we should expect from them an adequate semantics of characterizing sentences.

There are four main accounts of non-monotonic reasoning. Consider the following example:

(26) Birds are feathered.

a. If x *is a bird* is true, and if the fact x *is feathered* can be consistently assumed, then conclude that x *is feathered* is true.

b. If x is a bird and it is not known that x is not feathered, then x is feathered.

c. If x is a bird, and x is not abnormal for a bird with respect to being feathered, then x is feathered.

d. if x is a bird, and the probability of x's flying conditional upon it's being a bird is α, then the probability that x flies is α.[19]

The reasoning in (a) is an example of a "default rule" (Reiter, 1980). This is an inference rule that allows us to reach a conclusion C (here, x *is feathered*) from a sentence A (here, x *is a bird*), given that another sentence B (the so-called justification; here, x *is feathered*) is consistent with the facts assumed so far, i.e. we cannot infer its negation from these or other facts. The reasoning in (b) is an example of "autoepistemic reasoning" (McDermott and Doyle, 1980; Moore, 1984). The various approaches which fall into this category differ with respect to the epistemic modality they invoke, as well as in certain technical details. In general, this type of approach can be characterized as reasoning with the absence of positive knowledge, and is similar to default logic in this respect. Unlike default logic, however, modalized nonmonotonic reasoning allows the default rule to be made explicit in the object language by the modal operator it *is not known that.* The reasoning in (c) represents "circumscription" or "minimal entailment" (McCarthy, 1980, 1986). The central idea is to cover all exceptions by one predicate (one stating that the exceptional cases are abnormal) and to restrict the domain of this abnormality predicate to those entities which *must* be abnormal given the positive knowledge we have. This minimization of predicate domains is called circumscription. Clearly, such an abnormality predicate must be interpreted relative to some other property. For example, the emu, Bruce, is abnormal for a bird because he cannot fly, but not abnormal in the sense of having no feathers. The reasoning involved in (d) illustrates one of the ways in which probabilistic logic may be brought to bear on the issue of reasoning with uncertainty. Authors such as Bacchus, Grove, Halpern and Koller (1993) explicitly make the link between probabilistic logic and generics in the way glossed in (d); others such as Pearl (1988) have used the probabilistic logic only indirectly – by adapting the probabilistic semantics for conditionals given by Adams (1975). In the next section we examine these four approaches in more detail.

3. Default approaches and generics

In Section 2.7 above, we briefly introduced four different ways of using default or non-monotonic reasoning formalisms as possible ways to understand the semantics of generic, characterizing sentences – or at least, as ways to understand a *part* of the semantics of such sentences. In this section we explore these methods in more detail, with particular attention to how the inner workings of these formalisms interact with the phenomena

[19] α is a number that is typically taken to be high and in the case of Pearl (1988) $1 - \varepsilon$.

of genericity. We will concentrate on two aspects of this interaction – first, what sort of truth conditional semantics, if any, these formalisms imply for generics; and second, how these formalisms account for various intuitively acceptable forms of nonmonotonic reasoning in which characterizing sentences figure as premises or as conclusions.

3.1. A general characterization of nonmonotonicity and patterns of nonmonotonic reasoning

The term 'non-monotonic' indicates that these frameworks give a formal mechanism for retracting a previous conclusion when given new evidence. Intuitively speaking, an inference is non-monotonic if the set of premises Γ generates conclusion ϕ, but the premises $(\Gamma \cup \psi)$ do not generate conclusion ϕ. For example, learning that the supermarket is open and knowing that it carries wine and that I have enough money to buy wine, I can conclude that I can buy wine. However, I might (later) learn in addition that city laws prohibit the selling of alcoholic beverages between midnight and 6:00 in the morning, and as it is after midnight now, I must retract that conclusion. And this is done without retracting any of the original premises, and without saying that the original conclusion was invalidly inferred. All the approaches we have characterized as default approaches are centrally concerned with drawing inferences, and as such differ from, e.g., the modal conditional approach which is *not* a theory of inferences but rather a theory of the truth conditions of an object language connective.

The problem of how to treat exceptions is the basic question of the enterprise. A typical problem is that we may infer from the fact that Bruce is a bird the fact that he can fly, even though there are many types of birds which are exceptions to this rule, such as kiwis, penguins, ostriches, emu, dead birds, and birds with clipped wings. We might try to include all these exceptions in our rule[20] by saying that: if Bruce is a bird that is not a kiwi, not a penguin, not an ostrich, not an emu, is not dead, doesn't have clipped wings, etc., then it can fly. But it is not possible in general to give a complete list of exceptional properties; and, in a particular case, we may not know whether the entity has an exceptional property. Still, we often reason that, if Bruce is a bird, then he can fly, and retract this conclusion at a later time if we learn that Bruce is, in fact, an emu.

Research in nonmonotonic reasoning is relevant to the semantic analysis of generic statements or characterizing sentences. Over the past twenty years, those working on nonmonotonic reasoning have isolated a number of patterns deemed to be defeasibly acceptable, though deductively invalid, reasoning; and these patterns appear to crucially use generic statements as premises. These patterns constitute, we believe, an important aspect of the use of generics, hence one which a theory of meaning for generics should capture. On the other hand, it seems incontrovertible that the acceptability of these patterns of reasoning depends upon the meaning of the generics which figure in the premises. So an adequate semantics for generics should use the truth-conditional meaning of generics to define a notion of consequence that captures and justifies these patterns of reasoning, in some sense of justification. This notion of consequence, however, is

[20] Thereby adopting the variant (mentioned in footnote 5 above) of our first bad attitude.

not to be confused with the *ordinary* notion of validity that we have referred to at least implicitly in discussing the truth conditions of generics.

Here are some of the best known patterns, listed sometimes together with a similar but invalid argument form that shows how the original pattern can be defeated. By using our **Gen** notation (suppressing the mention of some occurrences of variables), we can represent the argument form *Defeasible modus ponens* (DMP) as follows:

DMP	**The "Defeat" of DM**
$\mathbf{Gen}[x](\mathrm{A};\mathrm{B})$	$\mathbf{Gen}[x](\mathrm{A};\mathrm{B})$
$\dfrac{\mathrm{A}[d/x]}{\mathrm{B}[d/x]}$	$\dfrac{\mathrm{A}[d/x],\ \neg\mathrm{B}[d/x]}{?}$

(This is the most famous example of the default inference patterns, and is enshrined in the Tweety example.)[21] We cannot expect commonsense entailment to behave like the two displayed patterns for completely arbitrary predicates A and B. For example, if A and B are chosen to be one and the same formula, then when adding the premise $\neg\mathrm{B}(t)$ to "defeat" the modus ponens we end up with the following premises: $\forall x(\mathrm{A} > \mathrm{A}),\ \mathrm{A}(t),\ \neg\mathrm{A}(t)$. These premises *contain* $\mathrm{A}(t)$, and for this uninteresting reason $\mathrm{A}(t)$ will continue to follow (possibly along with everything else, since the premises have even become inconsistent). Similar comments may be made in connection with the other patterns of defeasible reasoning.

Another pattern is the so-called *Nixon Diamond,* the name of which stems from another famous example from the nonmonotonic reasoning literature. Unlike the preceding example, this one exhibits a *failure* to draw conclusions from conflicting defaults.

Nixon is a Quaker.
Nixon is a Republican.
Quakers are pacifists.
Republicans are not pacifists.
?

And there is the *extended Nixon diamond* in which the Nixon diamond gets added premises and a different conclusion, which now *is* validly drawn:

Nixon is a Quaker.
Nixon is a Republican.
Quakers are doves.

[21] This most celebrated and widely accepted pattern of nonmonotonic reasoning does not work equally well with all generics, however. Consider the argument,

Frenchmen eat horsemeat.
Pierre is a Frenchman.
So, Pierre eats horsemeat.

This argument does not seem so acceptable; but arguably the difference stems from an interpretation of this generic as being of a piece with the generics that Lawler (1973), we feel inaccurately, called existential. Such sentences or such readings of generic sentences are not relevant to reasoning with exceptions, and they are not captured by this semantics. It remains an open question as to what determines such readings or the preference for such readings. Perhaps a finer lexical analysis of the predicates involved will yield an answer, but this is only a guess. Perhaps the analysis suggested in Section 1.7 holds the key.

Republicans are hawks.
Doves are not hawks.
Doves are politically active.
Hawks are politically active.
―――
Nixon is politically active.

Two other important patterns are given below that researchers in AI have felt an essential part of defeasible reasoning with generics; they reflect the idea that information about subkinds should take precedence over information about the kinds which subsume them.

PENGUIN PRINCIPLE

Birds fly.	$\mathbf{Gen}[x](\mathrm{B}; \mathrm{F})$
Penguins do not fly.	$\mathbf{Gen}[x](\mathrm{P}; \neg\mathrm{F})$
Penguins are birds.	$\forall x(\mathrm{P} \rightarrow \mathrm{B})$
Tweety is a penguin.	$\mathrm{P}(\tau)$
Tweety does not fly.	$\neg\mathrm{F}(\tau)$

That penguins do not fly is a defeasible fact about penguins, a rule which admits exceptions. That penguins are birds, on the other hand, is a matter of taxonomic fact for which there are no exceptions.[22] It is interesting that swapping this taxonomic fact for the softer defeasible fact does not change our intuitions about the PENGUIN PRINCIPLE:

WEAK PENGUIN PRINCIPLE

Adults are employed.	$\mathbf{Gen}[x](\mathrm{A}; \mathrm{E})$
College students are not employed.	$\mathbf{Gen}[x](\mathrm{S}; \neg\mathrm{E})$
College students are adults.	$\mathbf{Gen}[x](\mathrm{S}; \mathrm{A})$
Sam is a college student.	$\mathrm{S}(\sigma)$
Sam is not employed.	$\neg\mathrm{E}(\sigma)$

Our comments in Sections 1.2 and 1.3 suggest – and we will argue in more detail for this in Section 3.2 – that generics must be allowed as conclusions to arguments. Once we countenance generics as conclusions to defeasible arguments, then the following patterns naturally suggest themselves.[23]

DEFEASIBLE TRANSITIVITY

Defeasibly Valid	*Defeasibly Invalid*
Birds fly.	Slow eaters enjoy their food.
Sparrows are birds.	Those disgusted by their food are slow eaters.
Sparrows fly.	Those disgusted by their food do not enjoy it.
	Those disgusted by their food enjoy their food.

[22] Such taxonomic facts are understood as being meaning postulates, or modally necessary conditionals (of the S_5 variety), or we could simply stipulate that taxonomic facts are taken to be true in all worlds.

[23] Note the difference in the following patterns from what might be called "pointwise" versions of the same arguments. DEFEASIBLE TRANSITIVITY below yields a generic statement as a conclusion whereas the pointwise defeasible transitivity would add 'x is a sparrow' as a premise and yield 'x flies' as conclusion, and would do this for each x.

DEFEASIBLE STRENGTHENING OF THE ANTECEDENT

Defeasibly Valid	*Defeasibly Invalid*
Birds fly.	Birds fly.
White birds fly.	Dead birds do not fly.
	Dead birds fly.

Finally, we mention a type of inference that is invalid in nonmonotonic logics based on conditionals but which is valid in Reiter's default logic and in McCarthy's circumscription. It is widely believed that instances of this type should be valid in any nonmonotonic reasoning system.[24] Consider first the following pattern, in which we infer that Fido, even though we know he is abnormal in one respect (he only has three legs), is hairy, and so presumed normal in another respect.

(27)

$\mathbf{Gen}[x](\mathrm{D};\mathrm{H})$	dogs are normally hairy.
$\mathbf{Gen}[x](\mathrm{D};\mathrm{F})$	dogs normally have four legs.
$\mathrm{D}[f/x],\ \neg\mathrm{F}[f/x]$	Fido is a three legged dog.
$\mathrm{H}[f/x]$	Fido is hairy.

As mentioned, this inference is widely accepted in the AI literature; nevertheless it is suspect on empirical grounds. As Elio and Pelletier (1993, 1996) mention, it seems that ordinary people are rather unhappy about drawing these default inferences about objects that are known to violate other default rules. Here, Fido violates the default rule concerning number of dog-legs; and people in general are thereby less willing to allow Fido to obey the other default rule, about dog-hair.[25] And there are other inferences that seem undeniably acceptable but which nevertheless fail for several nonmonotonic logics that are based on conditionals. For example, nonmonotonic logics that are equivalent to the rational closure defined by Lehmann (1989) fail to predict the following inference, which seems intuitively acceptable (where B, D, F, K are logically independent in a sense to be made specific later):

(28)

$\mathbf{Gen}[x](\mathrm{B};\mathrm{F})$	Birds fly.
$\mathbf{Gen}[x](\mathrm{D};\mathrm{K})$	Dogs bark.
$\mathrm{B}[t/x],\ \mathrm{D}[c/x],\ \neg\mathrm{F}[t/x]$	Tweety is a non-flying bird; Charlie is a dog.
$\mathrm{K}[c/x]$	Charlie barks.

Note the difference between the inferences (27) and (28). In (27) we have some particular object f that violates some rule, and the inference nonetheless says to infer that the object f obeys some other default rule. As mentioned, one might say that an object failing to obey one default rule is itself a reason for being less confident in that object obeying

[24] See Lifschitz (1989, Problem 3).

[25] In the present example, people probably *would* agree to this specific conclusion, but that's because they know that number of legs doesn't affect hairiness. But as an abstract *pattern*, people are unhappy about the inference.

other rules. But in (28) we have two distinct objects, one of which violates a default rule. It is difficult to see why this should have any relevance to the other object's obeying or disobeying a different default rule. And the empirical results mentioned above do not cast doubt upon these sort of cases.

As explained in (Benferhat, Dubois and Prade, 1992; Benferhat, Cayrol, Dubois, Lang and Prade, 1993), most of the known rational systems of nonmonotonic logic fail to predict this inference, because they use a ranking of all the default rules according to which rules are grouped into clusters, and these clusters are then ranked. The clusters are defined by the logical relations between the antecedents. All those rules with antecedents that either strictly or by default imply a formula that is an antecedent in another rule X are in a cluster with a higher rank than the cluster containing X has. Some of the rules in a cluster may have exceptions; in that case all the rules in the cluster are blocked from any application. The preferred model takes all the clusters down the ranking to the first cluster that has an exception and treats them as universally quantified material conditionals. In effect, the blocked rules are simply treated as atoms. In the case of (28), both rules are put in the same cluster; since one of the rules has an exception, both are rendered inert.

The failure to validate the pattern in (28) seems disastrous for any theory of the role of generics in nonmonotonic reasoning. Nonmonotonic formalisms that do not verify this pattern appear to be completely unusable, since in most realistic applications of nonmonotonic reasoning we cannot presume that there are no exceptions to any generic premises that might be added to our argument.

3.2. *Evaluation of default approaches I: Default logic and update semantics*

The default logic approach (Reiter, 1980) in (26a) differs from the other nonmonotonic approaches we consider in that it uses a formula of the meta-language rather than of the representation language to state how characterizing sentences are to be understood. For example *Birds are feathered* would be for Reiter a "normal" default rule of the form:

$$\frac{\mathrm{bird}(x)\colon\ \mathrm{feathered}(x)}{\mathrm{feathered}(x)}.$$

Informally, this rule says that if x is a bird and it is consistent to assume that it is feathered, then you may conclude that it is feathered. A set of such rules help make up a *default theory*, which is a pair containing a set of facts and a set of default rules, $\langle \mathrm{W}, \mathrm{D} \rangle$. Reiter then defines the notion of an extension of a default theory to formalize commonsense reasoning. An extension of a default theory represents a particular sort of fixed point closure of the set of facts under the default rules (for details see the chapter in this handbook by Thomason). An apparently appropriate notion of nonmonotonic consequence for reasoning about generics in this theory is to say that a sentence ϕ follows from a default theory just in case ϕ is a classical logical consequence of every extension of the default theory. This definition of nonmonotonic consequence, like the alternatives proposed below, suffices to derive fly(tweety) from the default theory

$$\left\langle \{\text{bird(tweety)}\}, \left\{ \frac{\text{bird}(x)\text{: fly}(x)}{\text{fly}(x)} \right\} \right\rangle$$

provided that we understand the default rule above as in effect the infinite set of all its instantiations when applying the notion of an extension. Thus, default logic is able to account for the pattern DMP.

Default Logic also predicts that the Nixon diamond is defeasibly invalid and the extended Nixon diamond is defeasibly valid. The Nixon diamond premises yield the following default theory

$$\left\langle \{\text{republican(nixon), quaker(nixon)}, \forall x(\text{dove}(x) \to \neg\text{hawk}(x))\}, \right.$$
$$\left. \left\{ \frac{\text{republican}(x)\text{: hawk}(x)}{\text{hawk}(x)}, \frac{\text{quaker}(x)\text{: dove}(x)}{\text{dove}(x)} \right\} \right\rangle.$$

This default theory yields two extensions, one in which Nixon is a hawk (and so not a dove) and one in which Nixon is a dove (and so not a hawk). So neither the conclusion that Nixon is a hawk nor the conclusion that Nixon is a dove follows from this default theory, given our definition of defeasible consequence for default theories.

It also predicts patterns of the form depicted in (28) and even (27) to be acceptable. It fails, however, to verify the Penguin Principle or the Weak Penguin Principle. In effect it treats the premise sets of those patterns on a par with the premise set in the Nixon diamond; it predicts that there are two extensions, one in which Tweety flies and one in which Tweety does not.[26] Influenced by Reiter's default logic, Veltman (1995) proposes a semantics in which all of the nonmonotonic inference patterns mentioned are validated defeasibly.

Default logic and its offspring do a good job at capturing those patterns of defeasible reasoning that we mentioned in the previous section. However, default logic does not provide us with an acceptable formalization of generic statements. Default rules are *rules*, and therefore are sound or unsound – rather than sentences, which are either true or false. If we analyze characterizing sentences using default rules, these sentences would not have truth values, and their meanings could not be specified by an ordinary semantic interpretation function. One consequence of being neither true nor false not being *in* the language is that characterizing sentences would therefore not talk about the world, instead they would talk about which inferences to draw. And this seems to us to be a strike against such an account.

Another possible strike against such an account is that since generics are seen as rules, not as statements, they cannot be the conclusions of arguments. But we think that generic conclusions may be among the things we should come to believe on the basis of other

[26] We note that extensions to the original default logic, such as that provided by Brewka (1991) can handle the Penguin and Weak Penguin Principles.

generic statements. In fact, one might even think it inconsistent to be willing to infer the particular conclusion *Sam flies* from the premises *Sparrows are birds, Birds fly* and *Sam is a sparrow* ... and to do this for any individual Sam, while refusing to infer the generic *Sparrows fly*. If it is true that the generic statement *Sparrows fly* summarizes facts about individual sparrows inherent flying abilities, and says something like *Individual sparrows normally fly, as a matter of nomic necessity*, how can we refuse to draw the generic as a conclusion?

Veltman (1995) in fact does claim that characterizing sentences are merely rules of inference, whose significance is not truth-conditional, but lies instead in what is called their "dynamic" meaning: the contribution which they make to how individuals update their beliefs on obtaining more information. Veltman puts his claim this way:

> The heart of the theory ... [of generics within update semantics] does not consist in a specification of truth conditions but of update conditions. According to this theory the slogan "You know the meaning of a sentence if you know the conditions under which it is true" should be replaced by this one: "You know the meaning of a sentence if you know the change it brings about in the information state of anyone who accepts the news conveyed by it".

The question of whether characterizing sentences have truth values, or whether, as Veltman supposes, they merely express rules of default inference, we take to be a very fundamental one. It is unlikely to be settled by amassing intuitive judgments of the type we brought up earlier in this Section and in Section 1, so it is of importance to look for other evidence which might bear on the issue. Here is one consideration.

If we were to accept the view, we would need to find a way to handle cases with nested **GEN** operators such as (5), or the following:

(29) A cat is healthy if it chases an object when it is moved in front of its eyes.

$$\mathbf{GEN}[x]\big(x\ \mathbf{is\ a\ cat}\ \&\ \mathbf{GEN}[y,s](y\ \mathbf{is\ an\ object}\ \&\ y\ \mathbf{is\ moved\ in\ front\ of}\ x\text{'s}\ \mathbf{eyes\ in}\ s;\ x\ \mathbf{chases}\ y\ \mathbf{in}\ s);\ x\ \mathbf{is\ healthy}\big).$$

Default rules can't work here because in such an approach the embedded **GEN**-formula would have to be spelled out as a default rule which is a statement in the meta-language, and cannot be conjoined with a sentence such as x *is a cat* in the object language as required for the treatment of the outer **GEN**-phrase. This feature of generic statements that they can be embedded or nested within other characterizing statements is not restricted to just a few formulas. Already (5) and (29) illustrate a wide range, but also consider

(30) a. People who work late nights do not wake up early.

b. People who do not like to eat out, do not like to eat out.

Sentences like these are nested in that they attribute properties which involve genericity (as expressed here by the "habitual" predicate *wakes up early*) to kinds which are defined by means of characterizing properties (*people who work late nights*). (30b) is another example of a nested characterizing sentence, this time one which arguably is logically valid.

Theories of generic meaning must be sufficiently general and provide interpretations not only for simple characterizing sentences like *birds fly*, but also for composite sentences in which genericity mixes with more genericity (as in the cases of nested characterizing sentences just mentioned), and those cases where it mixes with counterfactuality, belief, knowledge, and other propositional attitudes ... as for instance in

(31) a. John believes that cassowaries fly.

b. John knows that Mary loves kissing him, and he would be unhappy if she were to like it less.

A theory of what generics mean ought at least to extend to a theory of what they mean in such contexts. And it is extremely difficult to see how any theory denying truth and falsity to characterizing sentences can account for these phenomena.

This is where theories that assign generics truth conditions (like McCarthy's below or the one that we mention later from Asher and Morreau) differ from those which treat characterizing sentences as mere rules of default inference. Where characterizing sentences are assigned truth values it is immediately clear how to interpret nested sentences. And where the truth values are assigned in a possible worlds framework, as they are below, it is clear how to embed characterizing sentences into propositional attitudes, modal contexts, counterfactual and other conditionals, and any other constructions which have been treated within this framework.

But if characterizing sentences are interpreted as mere rules of default inference, or functions from information states to information states, it is not even clear how they could be nested even up a few levels without making the formal account phenomenally complicated. We take this to be strong *theoretical* evidence of the importance of truth conditions in a theory of what characterizing sentences mean, and a strong reminder of the danger of restricting attention to too narrow a range of the phenomena which a theory of generic meaning can be expected to explain.

If one thinks that generic statements should have truth conditions as we do, then one must look at formalisms other than default logic or those accounts of generics which, like Veltman's, are inspired by its proposals.

3.3. Evaluation of default approaches II: Autoepistemic logic

Autoepistemic logic introduced by Moore (1984) attempts to formulate "nonmonotonic reasoning" by means of a particular epistemic logic. Autoepistemic logic gives a modal translation (though not a modal conditional translation) to generic statements. A statement like *birds fly* is translated as:

$$\forall x((\text{bird}(x)\ \&\ \text{M}(\text{fly}(x))) \rightarrow \text{fly}(x)),$$

where M is an epistemic modality that means *consistent with all my beliefs*. Moore's idea, following Stalnaker (1968), is that nonmonotonic reasoning, or at least one form of nonmonotonic reasoning, can be captured by formalizing the result of an ideal agent's reflecting on his beliefs. Moore calls this a *stable autoepistemic theory*. More particularly, if T is a set of formulas in a language with one modal operator B (for 'it is believed that') that represents the beliefs of an ideally rational agent, then T is a stable autoepistemic theory if

T is closed under classical logical consequence
whenever $\phi \in T$, then $B\phi \in T$
whenever $\phi \notin T$, then $\neg B\phi \in T$

To find out whether a particular formula ϕ nonmonotonically or "autoepistemically" follows an arbitrary set of formulas X, it suffices to see whether ϕ follows classically from every stable autoepistemic expansion of X, which is simply X closed under the clauses of what it is to be a stable autoepistemic theory given above. While Moore thought that his autoepistemic logic was distinct from default logic, Konolige (1988) showed that there was a sound and complete translation from default logic into autoepistemic logic; recently, Gottlob (1993) has shown that the expressive power of standard autoepistemic logic is strictly greater than that of default logic. Autoepistemic logic does as well as (though no better than) Reiter's default logic in capturing the defeasibly valid patterns of nonmonotonic reasoning, though the techniques used by Brewka (1991) to extend default logic to capture the Penguin Principles may also be applied to autoepistemic logic.

The question central to our concerns here is, does autoepistemic logic offer an adequate interpretation of generic statements? Clearly, we think it better than that of default logic, since the autoepistemic translation of *birds fly* is a sentence that can be true or false. But the autoepistemic interpretation of generic statements has some drawbacks which we think make it unacceptable. It fails to capture the appropriate nomic connection between antecedent and consequent of a generic statement for one thing. The autoepistemic interpretation of generic statements makes such sentences as *squares are round*, *tigers are vegetables* or *numbers are animals* be true. This is so because it is not epistemically possible (for any rational agent) that a square be round or that a tiger be a vegetable, and thus those statements are true in every one of these worlds. But such generic statements are clearly false. Further, this proposed analysis makes the truth conditions of generics depend on the epistemic states of particular agents – a hypothesis with which we are uncomfortable. We believe that *birds fly* would be true even if rational agents had never existed. Perhaps there are ways to eliminate the subjectivity from the autoepistemic proposal, but we will not attempt this here. We feel that there are enough problems with this view of generic statements not to proceed any further.

3.4. Evaluation of default theories III: Circumscription

McCarthy (1980) proposed the notion of circumscription not to analyze the meaning of generics but rather to formalize commonsense reasoning. Yet because the types of inference that he took to be examples of commonsense reasoning (e.g., "Defeasible Modus Ponens") typically contain generics as premises, we can take his ideas implicitly to define a semantics of generics. To a first order language, McCarthy adds a set of one-place predicates $\{Ab_i\}$. Each predicate Ab_i represents the property of being abnormal in some respect i. The translation into McCarthy's language of circumscription of a generic like *birds fly* then is: *any bird that is not abnormal-with-respect-to-birdiness flies* or symbolically

$$\forall x((\text{Bird}(x)\ \&\ \neg\text{Ab}_i(x)) \rightarrow \text{Fly}(x)).$$

Even though this is an extensional treatment of generics, it offers significant improvements over the classical extensional translation, $\forall x(\text{Bird}(x) \rightarrow \text{Fly}(x))$. For instance, unlike the classical treatment, this treatment allows that *birds fly* may remain true even though not all birds fly, since there may be birds which are abnormal-with-respect-to-birdiness. McCarthy combines this treatment of generics with a particular approach to commonsense reasoning. To see what commonsensically follows from a set of premises containing generics, McCarthy proposes that we see what holds in those models of the premises in which the extensions of the Ab_i predicates are as small as possible. So for instance, if our set of premises are {birds fly, Tweety is a bird}, then we should look at all those models of the premises in which the extension of Ab_i above is as small as possible. Since nothing in these premises forces Ab_i to have a nonempty extension, we look at those models in which the extension is null; and in those models Tweety flies. Hence, says McCarthy, the inference from {birds fly, Tweety is a bird} to *Tweety flies* is an acceptable form of commonsense reasoning.[27] Circumscription captures all the inferences that Reiter's default logic does, but it too fails to capture the Penguin Principles. Lifschitz's development of prioritized circumscription (Lifschitz, 1985) remedies this difficulty, however.

Again although we think that research along these lines has helped elucidate commonsense reasoning and that commonsense reasoning is an important feature of the use of generics, we still feel that this proposal has some pretty clear defects as an account of the semantics of generics, and we will cite some of them in the last part of this section.

3.5. *Evaluation of default approaches IV: Probabilistic analyses*

Probabilistic analyses of generic statements and their use in nonmonotonic reasoning divide into two camps. The first approach, most recently advocated by Bacchus, Grove, Halpern and Koller (1993), uses probability statements directly to represent generics. Not only do they argue that nonmonotonic reasoning resembles probabilistic reasoning, but in particular they represent generic statements as conditional probability statements where the conditional probability approaches 1 (this has its roots in Adam's (1975) representation of a conditional sentence $A > B$ as the conditional probability statement $\Pr(B/A) > 1 - \varepsilon$). They then go on to define a nonmonotonic consequence relation that has many attractive properties. For us, however, the decision to represent natural language generics as conditional probability statements seems mistaken for the reasons we gave earlier in Section 1.3, and so we shall not consider these views further.

The other approach, exemplified by Pearl (1988), uses the probabilistic calculus to provide a semantics for a conditional, again in the manner of Adams (1975) as $\Pr(B/A) >$

[27] For more details, see Thomason's chapter in this Handbook.

$1 - \varepsilon$. And it is these conditionals that represent generic statements. This is an attractive proposal and close to the one that we shall propose in the next section. The nonmonotonic consequence relation defined by Pearl has many desirable properties. However, a difficulty with Adams's (and Pearl's) semantics for conditionals is that it is impossible to interpret conditionals with antecedents that contain conditionals within it. This casts doubt on the proposal as an adequate account of generic statements, since we have seen that nested generics (both in the antecedent and the consequent) are commonplace and perfectly acceptable. Further, Pearl's nonmonotonic consequence relation Z fails to verify either the patterns in (28) or in (27), and as we have said before, failing to validate at least the (28) pattern makes us seriously doubt that this approach can serve to capture the properties of generics in nonmonotonic reasoning.[28]

3.6. A general evaluation of default reasoning approaches

The main reason that non-monotonic logics appear to be useful for representing the meaning of characterizing statements is that they explicitly allow for exceptions to general rules, which reflects the fact that characterizing sentences typically allow for exceptions. Furthermore, there is a correspondence between the nomic quality of these characterizing sentences and the way generalizations are captured in non-monotonic logic: Part of the nomic force of characterizing sentences is that they make claims about an open (or open-ended) class of entities. For example, the sentence *A lion has a mane* does not make a claim about the closed class of all existing lions, but about every (realistically) possible lion. This excludes the possibility of simply listing the properties of the entities in question, or of formulating universal sentences and enumerating their exceptions. If it could be shown that default reasoning also embodied this feature, that would give a strong reason to favor it as an analysis.

Some nonmonotonic reasoning approaches also seems to fare well in certain cases which are problematic for the pure modal-conditional approach.[29] For example, the sentence *Ducks lay whitish eggs* does not require us to construct biologically inconsistent possible worlds in which there are no male ducks; it simply says that, when x is a duck and we have no information to the contrary (e.g., that it is a male duck), we can assume that x can lay whitish eggs.

The preceding few paragraphs state some of the attractive features of (some of) the nonmonotonic reasoning approaches in their treatments of natural language generic statements. But maybe even this much credit to the nonmonotonic logic approach is too much. For instance, isn't it *always* the case that we *do* have some information to the contrary, and yet we continue to assert the characterizing statement? Consider these characterizing statements:

(32) a. Marvin usually beats Sandy at golf.

b. Italians are good skiers.

---

[28] In (Goldszmidt and Pearl, 1990) an approach is developed that overcomes this difficulty.

[29] Of the approaches considered in the previous section, Pearl's (1990) nonmonotonic logic, which is based on understanding generics as conditionals, would have trouble with this sort of inference.

c. Bees lay millions of eggs at a time.

Clearly it would be incorrect to analyze them as

(32′) a. Given no information to the contrary, conclude that Marvin is beating Sandy at golf.

b. If x is an Italian and there is no information that would say s/he wasn't a good skier, then assume s/he is a good skier.

c. If x is a bee and there is no reason to assume it is not laying millions of eggs, then conclude that it is laying millions of eggs.

These are incorrect because there is *always* information or good reasons to the contrary, for such characterizing statements. We *know* that Marvin and Sandy are *not* usually playing golf, and so by (32′a) we would never conclude that Marvin is beating Sandy. We have an *immense* amount of information that *very, very few* Italians are world-class skiers, so we would never draw the conclusion indicated in (32′b). And we know that hardly any bees ever lay eggs, and further that when they do it is not over a very long period of time, and so we would never conclude the consequent of (32′c). But therefore it follows that the analyses in (32′) are not correct as accounts of the generics of (32).

Also, much of the default reasoning literature and many of the proposed mechanisms are stated at the extensional level. The methods yield minimal models: models where there are the fewest objects that are abnormal-with-respect-to-the-specified-predicate. Yet this is not really what is desired as an analysis of generics, for it does not honor the nomic force of generics. And even in the extensional case it yields incorrect results, for example the minimal model approach would claim that 'Birds fly, Sam is a bird ∴ Sam flies' is valid yet is defeated by the addition of 'There is a non-flying bird' as a premise. Also, little if any work has been done on the interacting defaults of the sort expressed by the sentences in (22). For these reasons, it is difficult to take seriously the work thus far completed in default reasoning as an analysis of the phenomenon of genericity. Much of the problem stems from the differing desires of AI researchers and formal semanticists. The former researchers are trying to show how to reason when we have statements that admit of exceptions. Yet this is not all there is to the semantics of generics. Indeed, it seems to us that this is less significant than issues of nomicity and of trying to specify what the relevant background against which the characterizing statement is being made, and using this information to state the truth-conditions for generic statements. And it is also less significant than the fact that differing generic statements call for radically different numbers or proportions of exceptions. Until such issues can be adequately addressed, it seems improper to investigate merely the notion of reasoning which admits exceptions and expect this to yield an answer to the semantics of generics.

For these reasons we put forward an approach to non-monotonic reasoning and the semantics of generic statements that combines insights from various of the suggestions given above, in the hopes that what was appropriate from each of those methodologies will survive. The approach, laid out in (Asher and Morreau, 1991, 1995) and (Morreau, 1992), uses a conditional logic (with a possible worlds semantics) to characterize certain aspects of generics. In particular, it allows one to specify semantic truth conditions of characterizing sentences and to do so in such a way as to allow them to enjoy their nomic force at least to the extent that nomic force and intensionality can be captured in modal logics. It combines this semantics with a non-monotonic inference relation based on situation semantics to capture default inferences involving characterizing sentences. This use of situation semantics to capture the default inferences avoids the use of minimal models (and the like) that is characteristic of circumscription and related extensional methods. In short, the theory outlined in the next section gives truth conditions to generic statements and allows these statements to have exceptions, but it separates this truth-conditional role of the semantics from the inferential role of drawing conclusions non-monotonically.

4. A formal theory of generics

Section 2 of this chapter suggests several sources for a formalization of the meaning of generics, such as: the theory of prototypes, situation theory, modal and conditional logics, and the theory of nonmonotonic reasoning. In this section, we will rehearse the requirements concerning a formal semantics for generics and then mention one theory that meets these requirements.

4.1. Requirements for the monotonic semantics for generics

We have argued that generics have truth conditions and that a semantic theory of generics should capture them. We also argued that the semantics for generics should be intensional, since extensional and probabilistic accounts succumb to difficulties that the modal approaches avoid. Our strategy is to interpret **GEN** as a conditional operator, although we need to be somewhat on the intuitive side as to what the variable-list is that **GEN** controls. Thus, from a sentence like (33a) we arrive at the logical form (33b).

(33) a. Dogs bark,

b. $\mathbf{GEN}[x](\mathbf{Dog}(x);\ \mathbf{Bark}(x))$,

or if we wish to analyze further the dispositional predicate *bark*: as itself involving a generic predication (which accords with intuitions)

c. $\mathbf{GEN}[x, s]\big(\mathbf{Dog}(x)\ \&\ \mathbf{IN}(x, s);\ \exists e(e < s\ \&\ \mathbf{Barking}(x, e))\big)$.

This logical form has the following intuitive meaning: For any object x if x is a dog and x is in an appropriate circumstance then this circumstance will normally contain an event of barking by x. So understood, **GEN** is definable by means of a universal quantifier binding some variables and a propositional conditional operator, call it $>$, linking the restrictor of **GEN** with its nuclear scope. So (33b) would, for instance, emerge as

d. $\forall x(\mathbf{Dog}(x) > \mathbf{Bark}(x))$.

Now of course, it is notoriously difficult to specify the restrictive argument for event quantification in the analysis of dispositional predicates; still, we would argue that this is an appropriate representation of the original English ... remaining vague just where the English is vague.

We now turn to some remarks concerning desiderata for the semantics of the conditional operator, >. It seems reasonable to exploit the semantics for conditional sentences developed by Stalnaker and Thomason (1967), Stalnaker (1968) and Lewis (1973), which assigns truth values to conditional sentences relative to possible worlds. Roughly then, (33c) is true at a world w just in case for every object d the set of worlds that are normal with respect both to w and to the proposition of d's being a dog is a subset of the set of worlds in which d typically is barking in the appropriate circumstances. More precisely, one can make use of a selection function * that takes worlds and propositions (sets of worlds) as arguments and returns a proposition.

$$M, w, a \models \mathrm{A} > \mathrm{B} \quad \text{iff} \quad {}^*(w, [\mathrm{A}]_{M,a}) \subseteq [\mathrm{B}]_{M,a},$$
$$\text{where } [\mathrm{A}]_{M,\alpha} = \{w \in W_M\colon\ M, w, \alpha \models \mathrm{A}\}.$$

We can think of ${}^*(w,p)$ as all the normal p worlds according to w, that is, all the worlds in which p, along with all the typical consequences of p in w, hold.

What sort of additional logical inferences do we want > to verify? One intuitive principle that a semantics for generics should validate is some sort of "idempotence" principle such as that exemplified by the following sentence:

(34) a. Dogs are dogs.

This generic, though uninteresting, strikes us as valid. And on our tentative understanding of **Gen**, we cannot imagine how such a sentence could come out as false. For anything, if it is a dog, then normally it is a dog. We account for this by FACTICITY, below.

Another pattern of logical entailment, called WEAKENING OF THE CONSEQUENT, is common to all sorts of conditionals with a modal semantics and seems obviously right. We think that it is part of the truth conditions that generics sentences like (34b) always come out true.

b. People who don't like to eat out don't like to eat out.

Our method of accounting for such sentences is by means of the principle: If B logically entails C, then the characterizing sentence *A's are B*, entails the characterizing sentence *A's are C*.

WEAKENING:[30] if $\models \forall x(\mathrm{B} \rightarrow \mathrm{C})$ then $\models \forall x(\mathrm{A} > \mathrm{B}) \rightarrow \forall x(\mathrm{A} > \mathrm{C})$

[30] The $\rightarrow$ is the monotonic material conditional of classical logic, while > is the conditional being defined. The notation is that in use in (Asher and Morreau, 1991, 1995) and (Morreau, 1992).

which can be used jointly with facticity to ensure that sentences like (34b) come out true.[31]

Finally, we take another often-adopted principle of conditional logic to be intuitively acceptable. If A's are normally B's and if C's are normally B's, then for any object, if it's either an A or a C it's normally a B. Using the bare plurals formulation, we accept sentences like the following as valid:

(35) If lions are fierce and if tigers are fierce, then (things that are) lions or tigers are fierce.

We might call this principle **OR** to reflect the fact that conjunctions of generic sentences can lead to generics whose representation in terms of **Gen** or $>$ makes the restrictor a disjunctive formula, just as with the antecedent of a classical conditional.

On the other hand, the semantics for the conditional should not support modus ponens, modus tollens, nor principles like $(\alpha \ \& \ \beta) \rightarrow (\alpha > \beta)$, which are prevalent in many conditional logics. To do otherwise would violate one of the starting points of the study of generics, the existence of exceptions. None of modus ponens, modus tollens, and the aforementioned principle honor exceptions to true conditional statements.

If we adopt the analysis of **Gen** using the conditional $>$, then we can validate or invalidate the sort of patterns of inference we have been discussing, by placing or not placing certain constraints on the selection function $*$. For instance, the constraint on $*$ known as centering below supports modus ponens for $>$, and so should *not* be adopted in a semantics for generics.

CENTERING: If $w \in p$, then $w \in {}^*(w, p)$.

Other constraints on $*$, like FACTICITY, verify the desirable idempotence inference above in (34a).

FACTICITY: ${}^*(w, p) \subseteq p$.

FACTICITY says that in those worlds where the propositions normally associated with p are true, p is also true. In other words, p is itself one of the things which normally holds when p holds. The following constraint would validate the OR principle

OR: ${}^*(w, p \cup q) \subseteq {}^*(w, p) \cup {}^*(w, q)$.

Delgrande (1987) and others like Boutilier (1992, 1994) who have used modal conditionals both to define a nonmonotonic consequence relation and (at least implicitly) to represent generic statements as well, have often opted for more constraints on the modal frames and the selection function. Were we to follow them, $>$ would reflect properties attributed by Gabbay (1985) and Kraus, Lehmann and Magidor (1990) to a nonmonotonic consequence relation. We would thus strengthen the basic logic of $>$. For instance,

[31] Starting with the instance of FACTICITY, $\forall x((\mathrm{P}x \ \& \ \neg \mathrm{E}x) > (\mathrm{P}x \ \& \ \neg \mathrm{E}x))$, we apply WEAKENING to get $\forall x((\mathrm{P}x \ \& \ \neg \mathrm{E}x) > \neg \mathrm{E}x)$, which is the relevant translation of (34b).

we can force $>$ to obey all the constraints of a "rational conditional" (Nute, 1980) by adding certain constraints on $*$. This rational conditional obeys the following principles:

CUT:	$((A > B) \,\&\, ((A \,\&\, B) > C)) \to (A > C)$.
CAUTIOUS MONOTONICITY:	$((A > C) \,\&\, (A > B)) \to ((A \,\&\, B) > C)$.
RATIONAL MONOTONICITY:	$((A > C) \,\&\, \neg(A > \neg B)) \to ((A \,\&\, B) > C)$.

If $>$ were a rational conditional, then generics would obey the following argument patterns:

(36) [CUT] Dogs bark. Dogs that bark annoy Fred. So, dogs annoy Fred.
[CM] Dogs annoy Fred and dogs bark. So, dogs that annoy Fred bark.
[RM] Dogs bark. It is not true that dogs are not hairless. So, hairless dogs bark.

We are not sure that these forms are intuitively acceptable, although Rational Monotonicity seems very plausible.[32] And so we will not impose these constraints, nor their associated inference patterns on $>$, as a part of our semantics of generics.

A final requirement on the truth conditional semantics for generics is that nestedness should also be handled satisfactorily. Earlier, we argued that sentences in whose translation the **Gen** quantifier had scope over formulas that themselves contained the **Gen** operator were not only grammatical but had determinate truth conditions. While we are unsure what principles involving nested generics the logic of **Gen** or $>$ should capture, we reject any semantics for generics in which the set of "normal" worlds is fixed in advance independently of the antecedent. In some nonmonotonic logics that define conditionals in terms of modal operators, this "independent fixing" occurs. For instance, in the logics of Boutilier (1992) based on variants of S4 or S4.3, the following principle is valid:

$$(A > B) \to ((A > \neg B) > \bot).$$

This is unacceptable in a theory of generics for it would entail the validity of:

(37) If dogs bark, then typically dogs that don't bark are frogs.

The ability to handle nested generics is also important when it comes to problems of quantification. Lehmann, for instance, notes that the following three sentences are entirely consistent:

(38) a. Elephants like zookeepers.
b. Elephants don't like Clyde.
c. Clyde is a zookeeper.

However, formalizing the first generic in a "flat" fashion using a conditional with a conjunction in the antecedent, such as

(38′) a. $\forall x \forall y((\text{Elephant}(x) \,\&\, \text{Zookeeper}(y)) > x \text{ likes } y))$,

[32] For all "generically consistent" A, i.e. where $\neg(A > \bot)$, RM as formulated above entails CM.

would entail in many conditional logics (e.g., Boutilier's) or on an extension of Veltman's (1995) approach (given an ordinary formalization of the second generic and the third premise) that in the normal worlds where e is an elephant, e does not like Clyde only if Clyde is not a zookeeper. We find this counterintuitive, but when we add some means of reasoning nonmonotonically with these premises whereby the conditionals with the logically more specific premises cancel out those with more general antecedents in case of conflict (see Section 4.2 below), we can conclude from the information given in the premises, that indeed elephant e should like Clyde. But this is intuitively what the second premise says is not true!!

Notice that if we follow rules of compositional translation from natural language familiar to linguists, we get a quite different translation for the first generic, namely:

(38″) a. $\forall x(\text{Elephant}(x) > \forall y(\text{Zookeeper}(y) > x \text{ likes } y))$.

If we adopt the constraint of weakening as we believe to be reasonable, then we get (using universal instantiation)

(38‴) a. $\forall x(\text{Elephant}(x) > (\text{Zookeeper}(c) > x \text{ likes } c))$.

Let e be an elephant and let w′ be any normal e-elephant world with respect to the world in which (38‴a) is true. Then this generic implies that, for any normal Clyde-zookeeper world with respect to w′, Clyde is liked by e in that world. Consider the translation of the second generic:

(38′) b. $\forall y(\text{Elephant}(y) > \neg y \text{ likes } c)$.

There is no incompatibility with these translations. It is true that even Clyde, in those worlds where he is a normal zookeeper, is liked by the elephants. But that is perfectly consistent with the disposition of the elephants normally not to like Clyde, as he is (in the actual world). Clyde, being a nasty zookeeper in the actual world, is normally not liked by the elephants. There is in effect a de re/de dicto distinction familiar from other intensional constructions; Clyde may, of course, have different properties in the worlds where he is a normal zookeeper from those that he has in the actual world or from those that he has in a normal e-elephant world for any elephant e. If this is right, then we see a reason for insisting that the inference, exportation, is not valid:

$$\text{EXPORTATION:} \quad \forall x(\text{A} > \forall y(\text{B} > \text{C})) \rightarrow \forall x \forall y((\text{A} \ \& \ \text{B}) > \text{C})).$$

This yields yet another reason to abjure extensional translations of generics, for in such translations (like that of circumscription) exportation is perforce valid. It also gives us a reason to not take the step often made in modal analyses of normalcy where one insists that the normal e-elephant worlds with respect to w are those worlds that *resemble* the actual world as much as is consistent with e's being a normal elephant. We note that such a constraint, in a definition of the generic conditional as in (Boutilier, 1994), would yield the unintuitive conclusion that the closest worlds compatible with e's being a normal elephant are those in which Clyde is not a zookeeper.

4.2. *Interim evaluation*

The system CE (commonsense entailment) of Asher and Morreau (1991, 1995) meets most of the desiderata above. It is a first order language augmented with a conditional connective $>$, which is interpreted in modal frames using a selection function that obeys only FACTICITY and OR. (Hence the axiomatization of $>$ contains only $(A > A)$ and $((A > C)\ \&\ (B > C)) \rightarrow ((A \vee B) > C)$.) It has two consequence relations, $\models$ and $\approx$, corresponding to classical and default consequence. The axiomatization is shown to be (argument) sound and complete in (Morreau, 1992).

We now turn to a discussion of some of the merits of this truth conditional proposal. First of all, it is nonextensional and so avoids the objections we leveled at extensional approaches. It makes generics modal but contingent, which is what we would like. That is, the truth value of a generic statement depends on worlds other than the actual one (generics are modal statements), but it may also vary from world to world (they are contingent); our generic truths may not be the generic truths of some other world. This analysis of truth conditions meets the desiderata mentioned in Section 4.1. It verifies FACTICITY, OR and WEAKENING, but it fails to verify modus ponens for $>$, and the unintuitive claims about nested conditionals that follow from Boutilier's definition of the generic conditional. This is because in our analysis of the truth conditions of generics, we do not (as Boutilier does) postulate one ordering of normal worlds relative to a given world w that must verify all the generics that are true in w. Instead, normality is captured by a set of worlds that is determined by the world of evaluation and the proposition expressed by the antecedent of the $>$ statement.

Recall, however, that in Sections 2.5 and 4.1 we made several criticisms of other modal approaches; we saw problems both in the very conception of normal worlds and in the way such proposals deal with problems of conflicting, true characterizing sentences. We noted above that some modal approaches, such as Delgrande's (1987), postulate a set of absolutely normal worlds. This leads to difficulties with (true) generic sentences like

(39) Turtles live to be a hundred years or more old,

because such a theory proposes that the most normal worlds are those where every single turtle lives to a grand old age, instead of dying while very young as the vast majority do in the actual world. Such worlds would be biologically very strange, and strike us as most implausible candidates for absolutely normal worlds. Such worlds might even violate general biological laws such as those about what would happen to turtles as a species if all of them were to be long-lived, and we think that all worlds which are normal with respect to a world w must respect the biological laws that true in w.

So let us reconsider the problems with the conception of normal worlds in the light of our new proposal for the semantics of generics. We first note that the semantics of $>$ we have sketched above does *not* presuppose *any* absolute normality order on possible worlds. In particular, we explicitly reject the idea that $*(w,p)$ is to be identified with those most normal of all possible worlds where p holds. Let us see how this semantics evaluates sentence (39) in a world w.

(39′) $\forall x(\mathrm{T}x > \mathrm{H}x)$.

For each individual d, $*$ determines, together with w and the predicate 'T', a set of normal "d-turtle with respect to w" worlds, $*(w, [\mathrm{T}](d))$. In every member of this set of normal worlds, d must have the property of living to be a hundred years or more old, but other objects that are turtles in these worlds may die, as expected, when very young.

Another problem with modal approaches is brought out by such true characterizing sentences as *ducks lay eggs*. If we accept the constraint that only female ducks can lay eggs, then apparently we must conclude, using Weakening of the Consequent, the unintuitive generic *ducks are female*. Recall also the problem of interacting defaults. The potential problem for the semantics of generics that we raised was where two intuitively acceptable generics with the same antecedent but incompatible consequents held:

(40) a. Ducks have brightly colored feathers.

b. Ducks lay eggs.

Since only males have brightly colored feathers and only females lay eggs, we see that no normal duck can have both properties. Nevertheless, it is easy to verify that in the conditional semantics that we have assigned to generic sentences, the following property holds:

$$(\forall x(\mathrm{A} > \mathrm{B})\ \&\ \forall x(\mathrm{A} > \mathrm{C})) \rightarrow \forall x(\mathrm{A} > (\mathrm{B}\ \&\ \mathrm{C})).$$

Using this principle and the intuitive translations of the two generic sentences in (40), and the knowledge that only male ducks have bright feathers and only female ducks lay eggs, and that no duck is both a male and a female, would yield the following unintuitive result:

$$\forall x(\mathrm{duck}(x) > \bot).$$

This observation poses a prima facie difficulty for the proposed modal semantics for generics. But at first glance it would appear to be part of a much more general problem of determining quantificational structures in natural language. In Section 1 above we assumed that a natural language quantificational structure has three components: the quantificational relation itself, a restrictor, and a nuclear scope; and in general, determining the restrictor of a natural language quantifier is a nontrivial matter. The problem is most immediately apparent with universal quantification where the domain of quantification is most often contextually determined. For instance, imagine a group of school students on holiday with a chaperone who calls some apprehensive parents after an outing and says,

(41) Everyone had a good time.

The chaperone does not thereby assert that every human being in the universe had a good time, which is what would follow on the usual translation for such a sentence. The inadequacy of translation of (41) is that it fails to consider the contextually sensitive nature of the domain of quantification. One way to rectify this situation is to imagine plausible content, following Lewis's (1983) ideas on accommodation and von Fintel's

(1994) ideas about quantification. On such a view, in addition to the content derived from the subject noun phrase *everyone*, we add to the restrictor a formula of the form $x \in \mathrm{A}$, where x is the variable introduced by *everyone* and the value for A is contextually specified. In the particular context of (41) used above the value for A would be the set of children and the logical form for (41) would be:

(42) $\forall x((\mathrm{Person}(x)\ \&\ x \in \mathrm{A}) \rightarrow \text{ had a good time}(x))$.

Is this strategy available to help solve the difficulty with (40a,b)? We believe that this strategy is *not* one that can in fact be used for the generic examples. First of all, (40a,b) may be perfectly felicitously be uttered in a context where there are no obvious values for a contextually specified variable. And both (40a,b) would be true in such a context. In contrast (41) in such a context (and thus without a determinate value for the set variable A in the logical form above) would truly be a universal quantification over all people. Second, attempting to create an appropriate contextual value for the parameter that is present in the logical form of (41) must not make false generic sentences magically become true ones. Consider for instance a case similar to the one in (41) where a lab technician observes fruitflies that have been genetically altered in an experiment. He observes that the altered fruitflies have five eyes. Eager to tell someone of the observation, he calls up the chief scientist. We suppose that were the researcher to recount what he had observed and then summarized with

(43) Fruitflies have five eyes,

he would have said something false. But if that is right, then the strategy of relativizing the quantification to some contextually specified set is irrelevant to accommodating generics. The problem of determining the restrictor for generics seems to be different from that for ordinary quantifiers.

We think that the proposed modal semantics in fact points the way to a proposed solution for this problem. The problem with *ducks lay eggs* is not our general understanding of the logical form of this sentence but rather our strategy for determining the antecedent of the $>$ that functions as a restrictor for the universal quantifier. So there is a sort of accommodation for generics. Our semantics, however, tells us that generic statements are modal statements, and so accommodation or further restriction of the quantification should not be done with respect to some extensionally defined parameter like the value of a set as with ordinary quantifiers, but rather with respect to some *intension*. Our view is that the appropriate restriction for a problematic generic like that in (40a) or (40b) is some subtype of the type given by the common noun that is formed into the bare plural. That is, what people really understand by (40a,b), at least when they are presented with the pair and the facts is that the universal quantifiers in each are relativized to a particular subtype. *Ducks lay eggs* is implicitly understood as *female ducks lay eggs*. On the other hand there is no natural subtype of fruitflies that would pick out just those in the experiment.

One way to test this hypothesis is to look at how speakers treat such problematic generics as (40a,b) when they exploit them in inferences. We have argued that an inference like Defeasible Modus Ponens is defeasibly valid and so should be part of a theory of generics. But many speakers express reluctance to draw even the defeasible conclusion that if Allie is a duck and ducks lay eggs, then Allie lays eggs. It would depend, they say, upon whether Allie is a male or a female duck. Similarly for (40.b) and for other cases of conflicting generics. If Defeasible Modus Ponens requires such an additional premise, then this strongly suggests that the logical form of (40.a) is not what the string itself would suggest but rather:

(44) $\forall x((\text{duck}(x)\ \&\ \text{female}(x)) > \text{lays eggs}(x)).$

We would hypothesize that such relativization of the quantifier by a type occurs only in cases where we have conflicting generic statements.

4.3. Nonmonotonic reasoning and epistemic semantics for generics

In addition to having truth conditions, generics also play an important role in plausible or nonmonotonic inference. Because we believe this role has something to do with the meaning of generics, we need to show how our theory of meaning for generics can be linked to, and help explain, the role of generics in nonmonotonic reasoning. We can exploit the truth conditional theory sketched in the previous sections to develop an epistemic semantics in which sets of possible worlds will represent information states. It is this epistemic semantics which models defeasible reasoning, and which comprises Asher and Morreau's system CE. The intuitive picture of what goes on when one reasons by defeasible modus ponens is this: first one assumes the premises *birds fly* and *Tweety is a bird*, and no more than this. Second, one assumes that Tweety is as normal a bird as is consistent with just these premises which have been assumed. Finally, one then looks to see whether one is thereby required to believe that Tweety flies or not, and finds that he does. Asher and Morreau (1995) argue that all of the plausible patterns of defeasible reasoning arise in essentially this way, from assuming just their premises, then assuming individuals to be as normal as is epistemically possible, and finally seeing whether one believes their conclusions. The details of this position can be found in (Asher and Morreau, 1995), also (Asher, 1995) and (Morreau, 1992).

To model defeasible reasoning, we will follow Asher and Morreau and build epistemic semantics using information states (which, as we said, are just sets of worlds), and two functions on these information states: updating and normalization.[33] The first of these functions is eliminative, simply removing from an information state all those possible worlds where the sentences with which one is updating are not true. Assuming just the premises of an argument can then be modeled as updating a distinguished informationally-minimal state called **0** (or the set of all the worlds in the canonical model) with those premises.

The second of these functions, normalization, codifies the notion of assuming individuals to be as normal as is consistent with premises. Individuals are assumed to be normal in certain respects, and these respects are represented by a set of propositions P.

[33] Alternatively, we could represent these information states as situations in the sense of Barwise and Perry (1983). Updating and normalization then would involve adding information to a given situation.

Normalization takes place after the just-mentioned updating function has applied. Normalizing the updating result (of updating **0** with a set of premises Γ) in every relevant respect yields a set of information states – which are the fixed points of the normalization process. The conclusions which may reasonably (though not in general validly) be drawn from premises Γ are then those sentences which are true at all the worlds in all of these fixed points. (In general, the order in which the relevant premises are considered for normalization will affect the resulting information state; and it is for this reason that we want the conclusion to hold in every fixed point of the normalization process.)

There are two algorithms one could use to generate the normalizations: a semantic method and a syntactic method. In the semantic method, one looks at each proposition defined by an instantiation of one of the antecedents of a $>$ statement that occurs in the updated premises by one of the constants that occurs in the premises (say this antecedent was instantiated to yield the proposition Fa). Given that the updating process has left us in state S, and that we want now to normalize with respect to this instantiation of a $>$ antecedent, we need to find the set of worlds in S that are normal with respect to Fa and with any $\sim$Fa worlds in S (if there are any). Normalization just throws out the abnormal Fa worlds from S, if doing so leaves us with some worlds – i.e., if the result is consistent. As mentioned, we need to do this with respect to *each* instantiation of *every* antecedent of a $>$ statement in the updated premises; and then we need to consider *every* order of normalization of premises before we can know what conclusion follows from the initial premises.

The second algorithm that we can use is the syntactic method. Normalization in effect converts $>$ statements into $\rightarrow$ statements. And the syntactic view of normalization makes this explicit. Take the theory T and consider each proposition defined by an instantiation of the antecedent (as in the semantic method). Let Fa be one of these. Normalization of T with respect to Fa is: $\mathrm{T} \cup \{(\mathrm{Fa} \rightarrow \mathrm{q}) \mid \mathrm{T} \vdash (\mathrm{Fa} > \mathrm{q})\}$, if the result is consistent. The normalization is simply T otherwise. We carry out an example of updating and normalization in the Appendix.

We shall write this notion of nonmonotonic consequence as $\Gamma \mathrel{|\!\approx}_P \mathrm{A}$. The subscript indicates the set of respects in which Γ has been normalized. $\mathrel{|\!\approx}$ is a defeasible consequence relation which generates the patterns of defeasible reasoning which we set out to capture. Also note that $\Gamma \models \mathrm{A} \Rightarrow \Gamma \mathrel{|\!\approx} \mathrm{A}$, and so commonsense entailment is supra-classical.[34]

4.4. *Patterns of reasonable and defeasible inference with generics*

In this section, we return briefly to the patterns of nonmonotonic reasoning which motivated some of the nonmonotonic formalisms for generics. Notice that these patterns are not to be thought of as completely general argument schemas, into which arbitrary generic sentences can be instantiated. Take for instance the pattern of defeasible modus ponens, which is schematically represented as: from premises $\forall x(\mathrm{A} > \mathrm{B})$ and $\mathrm{A}(t)$ follows $\mathrm{B}(t)$. But this conclusion is supposed no longer to follow if the premise $\neg\mathrm{B}(t)$ is

[34] For more details on the model theory of commonsense entailment see Asher and Morreau (1991, 1995) and Morreau (1992). For more concerning an accompanying proof theory, see Asher (1995).

added, which intuitively speaking amounts to adding the additional information that t, though an A, is not a normal A.

The following fact states conditions under which commonsense entailment captures the patterns of defeasible modus ponens:

FACT.

(i) Let $(\Gamma \cup \{\forall x(\mathrm{A} > \mathrm{B}),\ \mathrm{A}(t)\})$ be $\vdash$ consistent, and let $\{\mathrm{A}(t)\}$ be the set P of normalization respects. Then:

$$\Gamma,\ \forall x(\mathrm{A} > \mathrm{B}),\ \mathrm{A}(t) \approx\!\!|_P\ \mathrm{B}(t).$$

(ii) If $\Gamma \cup \{\forall x(\mathrm{A} > \mathrm{B}),\ \mathrm{A}(t)\} \nvdash \mathrm{B}(t)$, then if $\{\mathrm{A}(t)\}$ is the set P of normalization respects, then:

$$\Gamma,\ \forall x(\mathrm{A} > \mathrm{B}),\ \mathrm{A}(t), \neg\mathrm{B}(t) \not\approx\!\!|_P\ \mathrm{B}(t).$$

The restrictions of this FACT are sufficient to verify Defeasible Modus Ponens. A proof is contained in (Asher and Morreau, 1995), as well as in (Morreau, 1992). A similar fact establishes that commonsense entailment indeed predicts a skeptical conclusion from the premises of the Nixon Diamond but that it also predicts the conclusion that Nixon is politically active from the premises of the Extended Nixon Diamond.

By adding more constraints on *, it becomes possible to prove that other defeasible inferences can be consistently inferred within commonsense entailment.[35] The Penguin principle is captured by having the OR condition on * (see Section 4.1 above). Morreau (1992) shows that, when * is subject to this additional constraint, commonsense entailment captures the Penguin Principle in addition to Defeasible Modus Ponens and the Nixon Diamond. To capture the Weak Penguin Principle, we must add another constraint on *:

SPECIFICITY. If $*(w,p) \subseteq q$, $*(w,p) \cap *(w,q) = \emptyset$, and $*(w,p) \neq \emptyset$, then $*(w,q) \cap p = \emptyset$.

Which corresponds to the axiom:

$$((\mathrm{A} > \mathrm{B})\ \&\ (\mathrm{B} > \mathrm{C})\ \&\ (\mathrm{A} > \neg\mathrm{C})) \rightarrow (\mathrm{B} > \neg\mathrm{A}).$$

Morreau (1992) shows that commonsense entailment then still preserves the inference patterns of Defeasible Modus Ponens. But it becomes difficult to verify the other inferences model-theoretically. As we place more constraints on * it becomes more difficult to verify that our candidates for "survivor" worlds actually exist in the canonical model. So one might wish to pursue alternative lines concerning defeasible reasoning, such as done in (Asher, 1995) or in (Asher and Morreau, 1995). The idea in the latter is of ordered normalization, which corresponds closely to the strategy in prioritized circumscription (McCarthy, 1986) for capturing inferences like the Penguin Principle or the Weak Penguin Principle, where certain minimizations of extensions of predicates are performed

[35] For details see Morreau (1992).

before others. Also in extensions of Reiter's default logic (for instance, Brewka, 1991), orderings on the application of default rules are used to construct extensions that will verify these principles.

Other approaches that use conditionals as the semantic treatment of generics are the nonmonotonic logics of Delgrande (1987), Pearl's (1990) system Z, Boutilier (1994), Bacchus, Grove, Halpern and Koller (1993). All these systems verify the Penguin Principle and the Weak Penguin Principle. Lehmann (1989) provides a system, called Rational Closure, equivalent to that of Pearl's system Z but treats generics more as akin to some sort of default rule. Benferhat, Dubois and Prade (1992) provide yet another system equivalent to Lehmann's Rational Closure in which generics are thought of as constraints on an appropriate ordering of models. Often these systems are simpler than commonsense entailment and yet appear to produce equivalent results. But this only holds for simple fragments of the language and for a restricted notion of what are the acceptable defeasible patterns of reasonable inference (Asher, 1995).

What many of these simpler systems cannot do is extend readily to handle more complex forms of defeasible reasoning in which generics appear as conclusions, as well as premises. Asher and Morreau (1991) attempt to capture defeasible reasoning that has generic conclusions by complicating the normalization function. More specifically, an extra clause was added which used the behavior of * at a world to remove possible worlds from information states. So in the case of defeasible transitivity for example, possible worlds would be removed where it does not hold that *sparrows fly*. These are worlds where something is a normal sparrow without being a normal bird, and that is a possibility which this stronger notion of normalization filtered out.

We think it an extremely powerful positive feature of commonsense entailment that, unlike the theories of nonmonotonic reasoning we surveyed in Section 3, it makes the behavior of generics within patterns of nonmonotonic reasoning be determined by their truth conditional meaning. Unlike circumscription (in which generics are treated as extensional) or probabilistic theories of nonmonotonic reasoning (in which generics are treated as probability statements or statements with probabilistic quantifiers), commonsense entailment has the *prima facie* philosophical virtue of basing the acceptability of nonmonotonic reasoning patterns on a truth conditional semantics for generics that is, if we are correct, more plausible than the other alternatives.

5. Summary and conclusions

Generics attract the attention of logically-oriented scholars because the semantic phenomena surrounding them have been implicated in "default reasoning". But this implication is, upon scrutiny, rather tenuous. This article reports why the implication is tenuous and makes some suggestions as to the direction such logical accounts should take in order to accommodate generics.

We first investigated the full range of linguistic and semantic phenomena involving generics. We distinguished generic reference from generic predication – settling on the latter as relevant to default reasoning. We argued that these "characterizing statements" are either literally true or literally false – and are not therefore either "strictly false but acceptable" nor "merely directives about what sort of inferences to draw and what to expect in our experience." We then investigated the range of "exceptions" that a true generic can tolerate while remaining true, and our conclusion was that there is no unique number or proportion that will account for all the various generic statements. It follows that there is no quantifier, not even a "vague" probabilistic one, like *in a significant number of cases*, which can be used to give an account of the truth-functional force of a characterizing statement.

Part of the difficulty is that generics come with a kind of nomic force; they express a "general truth" which is enforced by some sort of law. Generics about the biological world, for example, are backed by the laws of biology; those about individual people are backed by psycho-social laws that describe what such people do. A purported generic statement which does not have such a backing is simply not true, even if the objects of which the subject is true in fact all have the property designated by the predicate. Even were it the case that all the remaining koalas in the world were to lose a paw, it still would not be true that koalas are three-pawed. For a generic statement to be true, it simply cannot report a mere accidentally true generalization.

There are two aspects to generic statements: their nomic force and their extensional consequences. In a large number of cases the extensional consequence of a generic is that most, or most of the important or noticeable or significant, instances of the subject term manifest the property indicated by the predicate. But we also noted that we cannot validly infer that any particular individual falling under the subject term has the property indicated by the predicate. As a we have indicated, not all generics have this extensional consequence; but perhaps there is an identifiable and distinguishable subset of them which do. For these types of generic statement, what would an appropriate analysis of just the extensional consequences be? We surveyed seven possibilities: relevant quantification, abstract entities, prototype theory, stereotypes, modal conditionals, situation semantics, and default theories. We found that none of the seven fared very well, but that the modal conditional and situation semantics approaches seemed to hold some promise especially as accounts of (some of) the nomic force of generic statements. The default approach fared best as an account of some of the extensional inferences we may wish to draw in the face of "generic information", and so we investigated four different approaches to default reasoning: default logic, autoepistemic logic, circumscription, and probabilistic logic.

In the end we found each of these inadequate. The problems we found ranged from incorrect prediction of conclusions to be drawn from generics, to denying truth conditional status to generics, to making dramatically incorrect predictions concerning the truth conditions of certain generics, to being unable to integrate the account with epistemic and modal logics necessary to account for the nomic force of generics.

Finally we presented Commonsense Entailment as a theory which could address many of these issues. It adopts a modal conditional analysis of generic statements, and locates the nomic force of generics in this area. But it does not posit "absolutely normal" possible worlds, nor does it locate "nonmonotonicity" there. Rather it adopts the situation-semantic strategy of judging "how much information" is in the premises of an argument, and allows that an increase here can make us wish to retract previous conclusions. Note that the generic premises continue to be true – nonmonotonicity is not to be found in denying generic statements.

After presenting the formal structure of Commonsense Entailment, we offered an evaluation of it in terms of the sort of argumentation we used against the other accounts of default reasoning as theories of generics, and we conclude that it fares well indeed. We also, however, note that there are some objections of a more general nature concerning generic statements that CE does not answer. The answer to these objections will require more investigation into the logical structure of generics.

Appendix

In Section 4.3 of the main text we presented two equivalent ways of calculating the defeasible entailments of a theory containing generics, a semantic method and a syntactic method. As an example of how our theory works, we present an extended example. Consider the theory T_0:

1a. Isis is a cat.
2a. Cats meow.
3a. Cats like to eat fish.
4a. Leonore is a cat who does not like to eat fish.
5a. Cats that like to eat fish are not fat.
6a. Cats are necessarily mammals.
7a. Mammals do not meow.

We will now see what follows from T_0 using our nonmonotonic formalism. Our theory will make defeasible predictions about particular cats like Isis and Leonore. Recall that on the syntactic theory what we do is add the instantiations of our generic statements with constants mentioned in the theory or added as witnesses for existential claims. In T_0, we have two constants: Isis and Leonore, but no existentials (hence no need for witnesses). The theory makes no links between Isis's properties and Leonore's so we may consider each of them separately. Let's consider Isis first, and the instantiations of the various conditionals to Isis.

1b. Cat(isis).
2b. Cat(isis) $>$ Meows(isis).
3b. Cat(isis) $> (\forall x)(\text{Fish}(x) > \text{Likes-to-eat}(\text{isis}, x))$.
5b. Cat(isis) $> ((\forall x)(\text{Fish}(x) > \text{Likes\_to\_eat}(\text{isis}, x)) > {\sim}\text{Fat}(\text{isis}))$.
6b. $\Box$ (Cat(isis) $\rightarrow$ Mammal(isis)).
7b. Mammal(isis) $>$ Meows(isis).

We now consider the conditionals (2) and (3), involving the antecedent Cat(isis) and consider the result of changing the main occurrences of the $>$ connectives in them into material conditionals. This theory, the $T_{\text{Cat(isis)}\rightarrow}$ theory, looks like this:

$$\text{Cat(isis)} \rightarrow \text{Meows(isis)}.$$

$$\text{Cat(isis)} \rightarrow (\forall x)(\text{Fish}(x) > \text{Likes-to-eat}(\text{isis}, x)).$$

Now the question is, are the consequents and antecedents of these conditionals consistent with our original theory? The answer is yes (which we could show by constructing a model of the original theory together with the antecedents and consequents of $T_{Cat(isis)\rightarrow}$ but we will forego that here). So according to our "syntactic" procedure for calculating defeasible entailments, we will add $T_{Cat(isis)\rightarrow}$ to our original theory, calling the result T_1. From T_1, we infer by Modus Ponens:

$$\text{Meows(isis)}$$

$$(\forall x)(\text{Fish}(x) > \text{Likes-to-eat(isis}, x)).$$

We now consider another $>$ antecedent of our theory, say

$$(\forall x)\ (\text{Fish}(x) > \text{Likes\_to\_eat(isis}, x)),$$

and collect all the conditionals entailed by T_1 with this antecedent. Beyond the instantiations of the axioms, which don't add any new information to the information state, we have just the conditional:

$$(\forall x)\ (\text{Fish}(x) > \text{Likes-to-eat(isis}, x)) > \text{Fat(isis)},$$

which we now convert into a material conditional

$$(\forall x)\ (\text{Fish}(x) > \text{Likes-to-eat(isis}, x)) \rightarrow {\sim}\text{Fat(isis)}. \qquad (*)$$

We now again test to see whether the consequent and antecedent of this conditional are consistent with T_1. Inspection shows that they are. So we add $(*)$ to T_1, forming the theory T_2, in which we infer by Modus Ponens that Isis is not fat.

The last antecedent that we must consider for Isis is Mammal(isis). It follows monotonically from T_1 that Mammal(isis), since 'cats are necessarily mammals' is a strict conditional. But it also follows in the monotonic logic of commonsense entailment (for details see Morreau, 1992) that:

$$\text{Mammal(isis)} > {\sim}\text{Cat(isis)}.$$

This conditional is a theorem of T_1 because cats and mammals have in T_1 (and in our original theory as well!) incompatible generic properties – cats meow and mammals don't. Let's now form the $\rightarrow$ theory in which all the $>$ conditionals with Mammal(Isis) as an antecedent are translated into material conditionals. This theory looks like this:

$$\text{Mammal(isis)} \rightarrow {\sim}\text{Cat(isis)}.$$

$$\text{Mammal(isis)} \rightarrow {\sim}\text{Meows(isis)}.$$

The consequents of this theory are evidently not consistent with T_2 (or even with our original theory T_0!). So we do *not* add $T_{Mammal(isis)\rightarrow}$ to T_2.

We claim that had we pursued these normalizations in a different order, we would still have arrived at T_2 as our final theory concerning Isis. One might wonder about how on a different ordering of normalizations with respect to the antecedents of $>$ conditionals in T_0 we could be assured of arriving at the defeasible conclusion that Isis is not fat. Suppose we had first considered adding to T_0 the material conditional

$$(\forall x)\ (\text{Fish}(x) > \text{Likes-to-eat}(\text{isis}, x)) \to {\sim}\text{Fat}(\text{isis}). \qquad (*)$$

$(*)$ is evidently consistent with T_0 and so could be added, but we could not yet deduce the conclusion that Isis was not fat. But once of course we add $T_{\text{Cat(isis)}\to}$ we would get the defeasible entailment. Thus, we have the following set of defeasible entailments concerning Isis – namely that she meows, she eats fish, and she is not fat.

Of course we have not yet computed all the defeasible consequences of our original theory T_0, since we have not examined any inferences concerning Leonore. So let us continue and consider the conditionals with antecedents Cat(leonore). Once again there are two:

$$\text{Cat}(\text{leonore}) \to \text{Meows}(\text{leonore}).$$

$$\text{Cat}(\text{leonore}) \to (\forall x)(\text{Fish}(x) > \text{Likes-to-eat}(\text{isis}, x)).$$

Because Leonore, unlike Isis, does not like to eat fish, according to T_0 (and hence T_2) we cannot add this set of conditionals to T_2. Normalization with the proposition that Leonore is a cat yields no new inferences. Similarly we cannot infer anything about Leonore's girth, because the antecedent of that conditional, namely

$$(\forall x)\ (\text{Fish}(x) > \text{Likes-to-eat}(\text{leonore}, x)),$$

is inconsistent with our information. But neither can we infer from Mammal(leonore) that she does not meow, because after all, she is a cat. So we end up knowing very little about Leonore. Since we could have performed these normalizations in any order while still eventually getting the same results as in T_2, T_2 represents all the defeasible entailments of the original theory T_0.

References

Adams, E. (1975), *The Logic of Conditionals*, Reidel, Dordrecht.

Asher, N. (1984), *Linguistic understanding and non-monotonic reasoning*, Proceedings of the 1984 Nonmonotonic Reasoning Workshop, American Association for Artificial Intelligence, New Paltz, NY, 1–20.

Asher, N. (1995), *Commonsense entailment: A logic for some generics*, Conditionals and Artificial Intelligence, G. Crocco, L. Farinas del Cerro and A. Herzig, eds, Oxford Univ. Press, Oxford, 115–156.

Asher, N. and Morreau, M. (1991), *Commonsense entailment: A modal theory of nonmonotonic reasoning*, Proceedings of the 12th IJCAI, Morgan Kaufmann, Los Altos, CA, 387–392.

Asher, N. and Morreau, M. (1995), *What some generics mean*, The Generic Book, G. Carlson and F.J. Pelletier, eds, Chicago Univ. Press, Chicago, IL, 224–237.

Bacchus, F., Grove, A., Halpern, J. and Koller, D. (1993), *Statistical foundations for default reasoning*, Proceedings of the 13th IJCAI, Morgan Kaufmann, Los Altos, CA, 563–569.

Barth, E. (1974), *The Logic of the Articles in Traditional Philosophy*, Reidel, Dordrecht.

Barwise, J. (1986), *Conditionals and conditional information*, On Conditionals, E.C. Traugott, A. ter Meulen, J. Snitzer Reilly and Ch.A. Ferguson, eds, Cambridge Univ. Press, Cambridge, 21–54.

Barwise, J. and Perry, J. (1983), *Situations and Attitudes*, MIT Press, Cambridge, MA.

Benferhat, S., Dubois, D. and Prade, H. (1992), *Representing default rules in possibilistic logic*, Proceedings of the 3rd International Conference on Principles of Knowledge Representation and Reasoning, J. Allen, R. Fikes and E. Sandewall, eds, Morgan Kaufmann, Los Altos, CA, 673–684.

Benferhat, S., Cayrol, C., Dubois, D., Lang, J. and Prade, H. (1993), *Inconsistency Management and Prioritized Syntax-Based Entailment*, IJCAI-93 (Chambery), 640–645.

Berkeley, G. (1710), *A treatise concerning the principles of human knowledge*, Berkeley's Philosophical Writings, D. Armstrong, ed., Reprinted, with many others of his works, together with a penetrating commentary, Macmillan, New York, 1965.

Bosanquet, B. (1888), *Logic, Or the Morphology of Knowledge*, Oxford Univ. Press, Oxford.

Boutilier, C. (1992), *Conditional logics of normality as modal systems*, AAAI, MIT Press, Cambridge, MA, 594–599.

Boutilier, C. (1994), *Conditional logics of normality: A modal approach*, Artif. Intell. **68**, 87–154.

Brewka, G. (1991), *Cumulative default logic: In defense of nonmonotonic inference rules*, Artif. Intell. **50**, 183–205.

Carlson, G.N. (1977), *Reference to Kinds in English*, PhD Dissertation, University of Massachusetts. Published 1980, Garland, New York.

Carlson, G.N. (1979), *Generics and atemporal when*, Ling. and Philos. **3**, 49–98.

Chellas, B. (1980), *Modal Logic: An Introduction*, Cambridge Univ. Press, Cambridge, UK.

Declerck, R. (1991), *The origins of genericity*, Linguistics **29**, 79–101.

Delgrande, J. (1987), *A semantics for defaults using conditional logic*, Artif. Intell. **33**, 105–130.

Elio, R. and Pelletier, F.J. (1993), *Human benchmarks on AI's benchmark problems*, Proceedings of the 15th Congress of the Cognitive Science Society, Boulder, 406–411.

Elio, R. and Pelletier, F.J. (1996), *On reasoning with default rules abd exceptions*, Proceedings of the 18th Congress of the Cognitive Science Society, San Diego.

Fine, K. (1985), *Reasoning with Arbitrary Objects*, Basil Blackwell, Oxford.

Frege, G. (1904), *Was ist eine Funktion?*, Festschrift Ludwig Boltzmann gewidmet zum sechzigsten Geurtstag, 20. Februar 1904, S. Meyer, ed., Ambrosius Barth, Leipzig, 656–666. Translation and reprint in P. Geach and M. Black, *Translations from the Philosophical Writings of Gottlob Frege*, Oxford, Blackwell, 107–116.

Gabbay, D. (1985), *Theoretical foundations for non-monotonic reasoning in expert systems*, Logics and Models of Concurrent Systems, K. Apt, ed., Springer, Berlin, 439–457.

Geach, P. (1962), *Reference and Generality*, Cornell Univ. Press, Ithaca.

Goldszmidt, M. and Pearl, J. (1990), *A maximum entropy approach to nonmonotonic reasoning*, Proceedings of AAAI-90, Boston, 646–652.

Gottlob, G. (1993), *The power of beliefs, or translating default logic into standard autoepistemic logic*, Proceedings of the 13th IJCAI, Morgan Kaufmann, Los Altos, CA, 570–575.

Heim, I. (1982), *The semantics of definite and indefinite noun phrases*, PhD Dissertation, University of Massachusetts, Amherst.

Heyer, G. (1987), *Generische Kennzeichnungen*, Philosophia Verlag, Munich.

Hilbert, D. and Bernays, P. (1934), *Grundlagen der Mathematik*, Springer, Berlin.

Jespersen, O. (1924), *The Philosophy of Grammar*, Republished 1965 by Norton, New York.

Konolige, K. (1988), *On the relationship between default and autoepistemic logic*, Artif. Intell. **35**, 343–354.

Kratzer, A. (1981), *The notional category of modality*, Words, Worlds and Contexts: New Approaches to Word Semantics, H.J. Eikmayer and H. Rieser, eds, Gruyter, Berlin.

Kraus, S., Lehmann, D. and Magidor, M. (1990), *Nonmonotonic reasoning, preferential models and cumulative logics*, Artif. Intell. **44**, 167–207.

Krifka, M., Pelletier, F.J., Carlson, G., Ter Meulen, A., Chierchia, G. and Link, G. (1995), *Genericity: An introduction*, The Generic Book, G.N. Carlson and F.J. Pelletier, eds, Chicago Univ. Press, Chicago, 1–124.

Lawler, J. (1973), *Studies in English Generics*, University of Michigan Papers in Linguistics vol. 1, Ann. Arbor.

Lehmann, D. (1989), *What does a conditional knowledge base entail?*, Principles of Knowledge Representation and Reasoning: Proceedings of the First International Conference, R. Brachman and H. Levesque, eds, Morgan Kaufmann, 212–222.

Lewis, D. (1972), *General semantics*, Semantics of Natural Language, D. Davidson and G. Harman, eds, Reidel, Dordrecht, 169–219.

Lewis, D. (1973), *Counterfactuals*, Basil Blackwell, Oxford.

Lewis, D. (1975), *Adverbs of quantification*, Formal Semantics of Natural Language, Ed. Keenen, ed., Cambridge Univ. Press, Cambridge, MA.

Lewis, D. (1983), *Scorekeeping in a language game*, Reprinted in his Philosophical Papers, vol. 1, Oxford Univ. Press, Oxford.

Lifschitz, V. (1985), *Computing circumscription*, Proceedings IJCAI-85, Los Angeles, 121–127.

Lifschitz, V. (1989), *Benchmark problems for formal nonmonotonic reasoning, v. 2.0*, Proceedings of the Second International Workshop on Non-Monotonic Reasoning, M. Reinfrank, J. de Kleer, M. Ginsberg and E. Sandewall, eds, Lecture Notes in Artif. Intell. vol. 346, 202–219.

Locke, J. (1690), *An Essay Concerning Human Understanding*. The current edition of choice is edited by P. Nidditch, Oxford Univ. Press, 1975.

McCarthy, J. (1980), *Circumscription – A form of non-monotonic reasoning*, Artif. Intell. **13**, 27–39.

McCarthy, J. (1986), *Applications of circumscription to formalize common sense knowledge*, Artif. Intell. **28**, 89–116.

McDermott, D. and Doyle, J. (1980), *Non-monotonic logic I*, Artif. Intell. **13**, 41–72.

Meinong, A. (1904), *Über Gegenstandstheorie*. Reprinted as *The theory of objects*, Realism and the Background of Phenomenology, R. Chisholm, ed., Free Press, Glencoe, 1960, 76–117.

Milsark, G. (1974), *Existential sentences in English*, PhD Dissertation, MIT, Distributed by Indiana University Linguistics Club.

Moore, R. (1984), *Possible-world semantics for autoepistemic logic*, Proceedings of the 1984 Nonmonotonic Reasoning Workshop, American Association for Artificial Intelligence, New Paltz, NY, 334–354.

Morreau, M. (1992), *Three applications of imaging*, Thesis, University of Amsterdam.

Nute, D. (1980), *Topics in Conditional Logic*, Reidel, Dordrecht.

Osherson, D. and Smith, E. (1981), *On the adequacy of prototype theory as a theory of concepts*, Cognition **9**, 35–58.

Pearl, J. (1988), *Probabilistic Reasoning in Intelligent Systems: Networks of Plausible Inference*, Morgan Kaufmann, San Mateo.

Pearl, J. (1990), *System Z: A natural ordering of defaults with tractable applications to nonmonotonic reasoning*, Theoretical Aspects of Reasoning about Knowledge (TARK III), R. Parikh, ed., Morgan Kaufmann, 121–135.

Putnam, H. (1975), *The Meaning of 'Meaning'*, Language, Mind and Knowledge, K. Gunderson, ed., Univ. of Minnesota Press, Minneapolis.

Reiter, R. (1980), *A logic for default reasoning*, Artif. Intell. **13**, 81–132.

Rosch, E. (1978), *Principles of Categorization*, Cognition and Categorization, E. Rosch and B.B. Lloyds, eds, Lawrence Erlbaum Assoc., New York, 27–48.

Routley, R. (1967), *A simple natural deduction system*, Logique et Anal. **12**, 129–152.

Russell, B. (1905), *On denoting*, Mind **14**, 479–493.

Schubert, L. and Pelletier, F.J. (1987), *Problems in the representation of the logical form of generics, bare plurals, and mass terms*, New Directions in Semantics, E. LePore, ed., Academic Press, New York, 385–451.

Schubert, L. and Pelletier, F.J. (1989), *Generically speaking, or, using discourse representation theory to interpret generics*, Property Theory, Type Theory, and Semantics vol. II: Semantic Issues, G. Chierchia, B. Partee and R. Turner, eds, Reidel, Dordrecht, 193–267.

Scribner, S. (1977), *Modes of thinking and ways of speaking: Culture and logic reconsidered*, Thinking: Readings in Cognitive Science, P.N. Johnson-Laird and P.C. Wason, eds, Cambridge Univ. Press, Cambridge, MA.

Smirnov, V. (1976), *The theory of quantification and the* ε*-calculus*, Essays on Mathematical and Philosophical Logic, J. Hintikka, ed., Reidel, Dordrecht.

Smith, E. and Osherson, D. (1984), *Conceptual combination with prototypical concepts*, Cogn. Science **8**, 357–361.

Stalnaker, R. (1968), *A theory of conditionals*, Studies in Logical Theory, N. Rescher, ed., Basil Blackwell, Oxford, 98–112.

Stalnaker, R. and Thomason, R. (1967), *A Semantic Analysis of Conditional Logic*, Mimeograph, Yale University.

Touretzky, D. (1986), *The Mathematics of Inheritance Systems*, Morgan Kaufmann, Los Altos, CA.

Veltman, F. (1995), *Defaults in update semantics*, J. Philos. Logic, forthcoming.

von Fintel, K. (1994), *Restrictions on quantifier domains*, PhD Dissertation, University of Massachusetts, Dept. Linguistics.

Logic and Language: A Glossary

Willem Groeneveld

algebra Mathematical structure consisting of a set, which is called the carrier of the algebra, together with a family of operations on the carrier set. The familiar notation for an algebra is $(A, f_1, \ldots, f_k)$, where A is the carrier, and $f_1, \ldots, f_k$ are functions on A. If $f_1, \ldots, f_k$ are the operations of some algebra $\mathcal{A}$, then the sequence of natural numbers $(n_1, \ldots, n_k)$ consisting of the arities of the operations is called the *type* or *signature* of the algebra. A simple example of an algebra is $(\mathbb{N}, +, \times)$, consisting of the natural numbers with addition and multiplication; it has type $(2, 2)$. Other well-known examples of algebras that arise in logic include:

lattices are algebras $(A, \sqcup, \sqcap)$ of type $(2, 2)$ that satisfy some specific set of equations (see (Davey and Priestley, 1990, p. 109)). The operations $\sqcup/\sqcap$ are usually called join/meet, or alternatively least upper bound/greatest lower bound, or supremum/infimum (sup/inf). An equivalent view on lattices is as an ordered set $(A, \sqsubseteq)$, where $\sqsubseteq$ is a partial order on A in which least upper bounds and greatest lower bounds exist and are unique. In logic, information is frequently assumed to have the structure of a lattice.

Boolean algebras are algebras $(A, \vee, \wedge, -, 0, 1)$ of type $(2, 2, 1, 0, 0)$; see (Davey and Pristley, 1990, p. 144) for the defining equations. Boolean algebras arise in propositional logic, in which case the carrier A is conceived as a set of propositions, $\vee$ is disjunction, $\wedge$ is conjunction, $-$ is negation, 0 is a proposition that is always false, and 1 is a proposition that is always true. Another standard example of a Boolean algebra is the algebra of subsets of some give set, in which case A is the powerset of some fixed set X, $\vee$ is union, $\wedge$ is intersection, $-$ is relative complementation, 0 is the empty set, and $1 = X$. The famous representation theorem by Stone states that every Boolean algebra is isomorphic to a subalgebra of some subset-algebra.

Lindenbaum algebras are Boolean algebras that arise in classical logic as the set of sets of logically equivalent formulae. Thus the carrier of the Lindenbaum algebra consists of all sets of the form $[\phi] = \{\psi \mid \psi \text{ is equivalent to } \phi\}$, and the Boolean operations match the connectives; e.g., $[\phi \wedge \psi] = [\phi] \wedge [\psi]$.

Boolean algebras with operators arise in modal logic. They are extensions of Boolean algebras with operators that are intended to model necessity and possibility. See (Jónson and Tarski, 1951, 1952; Marx and Venema, 1996).

relation algebras are algebras of the form $(B, \circ, \breve{}, 1)$ where B is a Boolean algebra. Concrete examples are algebras in which the carrier is of the form $Pow(U \times U)$, i.e. B is the set of binary relations over some set U. In this concrete case the operation $\circ$ is sequential composition, $\breve{}$ is converse, and 1 is the identity relation. Relation algebras are relevant to modal logic and dynamic logic (Venema, 1991).

cylindric algebras arise in the algebraic study of first order logic. They are extensions of Boolean algebras with cylindrification operations that are intended to model quantification. See: this Handbook, Chapter 7, Section 2.4.

The mathematical subject of **universal algebra** studies those properties of algebras that are independent of their type. This typically involves relations between algebras such as homomorphism, which is a structure preserving map between algebras (also see **category theory** for an abstract approach to structure preserving maps). A famous result in this subject is Birkhoff's theorem, which states that every class of algebras that is closed under homomorphisms, subalgebras and products, is definable by a set of equations; and vice versa. Universal algebra is closely related to **model theory**; the subjects share many notions and methods.

Literature: universal algebra: (Burris and Sankappanavar, 1981; Grätzer, 1968); cylindric algebras: (Henkin, Monk and Tarski, 1971, 1985); lattice theory: (Birkhoff, 1967; Davey and Priestley, 1990); Boolean algebras: (Sikorski, 1964; Stone, 1936; (Jónson and Tarski, 1951, 1952; Marx and Venema, 1996); relation algebras: (Németi, 1991; Jónson, 1991; Maddux, 1990, 1995).

ambiguity The phenomenon that a linguistic expression can be classified in more than one way. Depending on the dimension of representation, several types of ambiguity can be distinguished.

syntactic ambiguity occurs when an expression has more than one syntactic analysis. Typical examples include

1. John saw her duck.
2. Mary hit a boy with a stick.
3. Competent men and women are invited to apply for this job.
4. The horse raced past the barn fell.

The point of 4 is not that the whole sentence is ambiguous, but that its NP "The horse raced past the barn" also has category S.

semantic ambiguity consists of an expression having more than one meaning. An example is **scope ambiguity**, as in "Every woman loves a man". A limiting case of semantic ambiguity is **lexical ambiguity**. This can appear as polysemy, in which case one word is assumed to have different senses, or as homonomy, in which case different words are either written the same (homography) or sound the same (homophony).

polymorphism can be defined as categorial ambiguity. In the case of the string "duck", which is both a noun and a verb, this can be seen as homonomy. In the case of "and" as sentential conjunction or verb phrase conjunction this would count as polysemy. Polymorphism is a central issue in semantical theories that use Categorial Grammar or Type Theory (see this Handbook, Chapters 1, 2, 9).

pragmatic ambiguity can be considered as a type of ambiguity that depends only on the context of utterance. For example, it has been argued that the expression "next Thursday" is ambiguous between (a) the immediately following Thursday, and (b) the Thursday of the next week, but that this ambiguity will only arise on Monday and Tuesday (Fillmore, 1971).

derivational ambiguity This type arises in proof-based grammars when an expression has more than one derivation. Sometimes such an ambiguity is actually desirable, for example as an account of scope ambiguity.

Clearly these types of ambiguity are not unrelated. The syntactic ambiguity of (1) is triggered by the categorial ambiguity of "duck" and the corresponding case ambiguity of "her" as genitive or accusative. And (3) can be seen as a syntactically triggered form of scope ambiguity.

Ambiguity poses a serious problem for Natural Language Processing. Since ambiguities tend to multiply, the number of possible readings of which an NLP system has to keep track may become unmanageable. Moreover, in many cases the process of disambiguation involves an appeal to world knowledge, but the latter is such a vast and unsystematic body of facts that it appears infeasible to program. A current development is to work directly with underspecified semantic representations rather than to compute all possible readings (see the collection (Van Deemter and Peters, 1996)).

The multiplication of ambiguities is also a problem in the area of automated theorem proving. Here the derivational ambiguity of formulae may make the search space of possible derivations unmanageable. Thus the problem of removing spurious ambiguities (informationally equivalent derivations) becomes acute (this Handbook, Chapter 2).

In linguistics, a theoretical problem especially concerning semantic ambiguity is to find a precise demarcation from vagueness. To this end some ambiguity tests have been proposed, of which might be mentioned the paraphrase test (Pinkal, 1991) and the ellipsis test (see (Lakoff, 1970)).

In logic, ambiguities rarely occur, since logical languages are often designed with the explicit intention of avoiding them. In a logical language each symbol is taken to have a unique syntactic category, and brackets are used to avoid ambiguities in complex expressions. This is of some consequence to the approaches in logical semantics that assign meanings to natural language sentences by relating these sentences to formulae of some logical language, since this relation will have to be one-many for ambiguous sentences (or even many-many: see (Hendriks, 1993)).

Literature: (Fillmore, 1971); Chapter 8 of (Kempson, 1977), (Kooij, 1971; Lakoff, 1970; Pinkal, 1991; Van Deemter and Peters, 1996; Zwicky and Sadock, 1975).

anaphora An anaphor is an expression that can only be interpreted in virtue of a relation to another expression called its antecedent. As the name *ante*cedent suggests, the antecedent is commonly assumed to occur before the dependent item. The phenomenon that an expression can only be interpreted in virtue of a relation with an expression that occurs later in the text is usually called **cataphora**.

There is considerable divergence of opinion on, first, which relations should be called anaphoric, and second, the issue of locating the source of anaphoric dependencies either in syntax, semantics, or pragmatics. Accordingly, the description of anaphora above can only serve as a rough approximation that covers most uses of the term 'anaphora' in linguistics. Some well known examples of *antecedent/anaphor* pairs are:

1. Every farmer who owns a donkey beats *it*.
2. A man walks in the park. *He* whistles.
3. Bill likes *himself*.
4. Mary ate an apple. *So did* Peter.
5. Mary lost a red and a blue marble. Peter found the red *one*.
6. A tiger might come in. *It* would eat you first.

See: this Handbook, chapters on DRT and Dynamics.

Literature: (Chierchia, 1995; Evans, 1980; Groenendijk and Stokhof, 1991; Heim, 1982; Kamp, 1981; Pause, 1991; Reinhart, 1976, 1983).

aspect Linguistic category that labels the morphological information other than tense, polarity and agreement features in INFL (inflection). In semantics the notion often covers various kinds of information relating the speaker to what is described, including point of view (internal or external), and contextually determined reference-time. Traditionally four aspectual classes are distinguished in the 'Aristotle–Vendler classification': states (lack of change), activities (atelic events), accomplishments (telic events) and achievements (instantaneous events). Although natural languages express these aspectual classes in different kinds of constructions, it appears that all natural languages express all and only these four classes one way or another. For a comparison of different approaches to aspect see (Verkuyl, 1993). Temporal logics have been proposed to account for aspect (see (Galton, 1984)), but there is much diversity in terminology, tools and explananda. Current work in dynamic logics studies aspectual information as context-change potential (Ter Meulen, 1995).

See: this Handbook, Chapter 3 and Chapter 16.

Literature: (Galton, 1984; Ter Meulen, 1995; Verkuyl, 1993).

assignment see truth-conditional semantics.

automata theory Branch of logic and theoretical computer science that studies mathematical models of computing machines. The subject is closely connected with **formal language theory**; a common concern of these fields is the development of efficient algorithms for the automatic recognition of different types of languages. The subject is also closely related to **recursion theory** and **complexity theory**.

Some well known types of automata are the following (for precise definitions we refer to the literature):

finite state machines have a finite number of states, one of which is the initial state, and some of which are accepting states. A transition from one state to another can only be based on reading one input symbol. This next state function may be deterministic or non-deterministic. Somewhat surprisingly, this makes no difference for the recognizing power of finite state machines: they recognize exactly the **regular languages** (the Type 3 languages of the Chomsky hierarchy).

push-down automata have a finite set of states, an input tape, and a simple type of memory in the form of a push down stack, which is a finite stack of symbols. The machine can read the input tape, read the topmost symbol of the stack, remove the topmost symbol of the stack ('pop'), or put a new symbol on the stack ('push'). Push down automata recognize exactly the **context free languages** (or Type 2 languages).

linear bounded automata are a restricted type of Turing machines that recognize exactly the **context sensitive languages** (Type 1 languages).

Turing machines are at the top of the hierarchy, in the sense that they have the strongest recognizing power: they recognize the **recursively enumerable languages** (Type 0). A Turing machine has an infinite tape, conceived as an infinite string of cells. The machine can read or write a symbol in a cell, and move left or right along the tape. Turing machines are extensively used in recursion theory and complexity theory.

Literature: (Hopcroft and Ullman, 1979; Lewis and Papadimitriou, 1981; Partee, Ter Meulen and Wall, 1990).

Boolean algebra see algebra.

cataphora see anaphora.

category theory Branch of abstract mathematics that studies categories, which are defined as a collection of two kinds of entities called objects and morphisms. Typically, the objects are (structured) sets and the morphisms are (structure preserving) mappings between these sets. Category theoretical techniques are used in mathematical areas such as topology and algebraic geometry, but also in theoretical physics. In logic, category theory is applied in advanced studies in model theory and set theory, and is relevant in the model theory of intuitionistic logic.

Literature: (Goldblatt, 1984; Kock and Reyes, 1977; Lambek and Scott, 1986; MacLane, 1971; MacLane and Moerdijk, 1992; Moerdijk, 1995).

Chomsky hierarchy see formal language theory.

classical logic see logic.

common ground An important notion in linguistic pragmatics, the common ground between conversational participants refers to the set of propositions that are known (or believed) by all of them. In many cases, a stronger notion of mutual knowledge (or shared belief) is used, in which cases the propositions must also be known by all to be known by all, known by all to be known by all to be known by all, and so on.

In philosophy, mutual knowledge played an important part in Lewis's work on convention (Lewis, 1969), where it is argued that conventions can only function properly in a community if they are common knowledge. Since this applies equally well to linguistic conventions, mutual knowledge will play an important part in understanding language use as well. Several instances of this may be found in the literature. In (Schiffer, 1972) it is argued that the recognition of communicated content in a conversation, for example the calculation of a conversational implicature by the hearer, requires the notion of mutual knowledge. The notion of common ground is central in the context change theory of speech acts (see: **context change**), in particular in the pragmatic approach to presuppositions (Stalnaker, 1974; Karttunen and Peters, 1975, 1979; Gazdar, 1979; Heim, 1983). See (Smith, 1982) for a collection of papers on linguistic problems for which the notion of mutual knowledge is relevant.

Recently, the notion of common knowledge has received much attention in theoretical computer science, mainly in studies concerning communication in distributed systems. Here the notion of common knowledge is taken to be crucial for understanding processes of reaching agreement and for coordinated action. These studies have led to interesting extensions of epistemic logic with operators for common knowledge (Halpern and Moses, 1990; Fagin, Halpern, Moses and Vardi, 1995). For an analysis of common knowledge in non-well-founded set theory see (Barwise, 1989).

compactness see logic.

completeness see logic.

complexity theory A branch of computer science that studies the efficiency of algorithms and the computational difficulty of problems. The efficiency of an algorithm is measured in terms of the space or time complexity. The space complexity is a measure of the amount of memory that the algorithm needs, and the time complexity is a measure of the time that the algorithm takes. An algorithm is of space complexity $S(n)$ if there is a Turing machine that implements the algorithm that needs at most $S(n)$ cells of its tape for any input that consists of n symbols. And it is of time complexity $T(n)$ if the Turing machine needs at most $T(n)$ moves on any input of n symbols.

These measures of complexity give rise to different complexity classes. For example, $\mathit{DSPACE}(n^2)$ is the class of all problems that can be computed by a deterministic Turing machine of space complexity n^2, and $\mathit{NTIME}(\log_2(n))$ is the class of problems that can be computed by a non-deterministic Turing machine of time complexity $\log_2(n)$. An important part of the theoretical research in complexity theory concerns the establishment of hierarchy theorems, which consist in rigorous proofs that two complexity classes are different. A famous open problem in this area is the $P = NP$ problem, concerning the identity of the deterministic polynomial time class ($P = \bigcup_i \mathit{DTIME}(n^i)$) and the non-deterministic polynomial time class ($NP = \bigcup_i \mathit{NTIME}(n^i)$).

Also see: **automata theory**, **recursion theory**.

Literature: (Balcazar, Diaz and Gabarro, 1988, 1990; Bovet and Crescenzi, 1994; Hartmanis and Hopcroft, 1971; Hartmanis and Stearns, 1965; Johnson, 1990; Rabin, 1963; Van Emde Boas, 1990).

conditional The proper analysis of conditional statements is one of the oldest topics in logic. Classical logic uses truth tables for material implication (see **truth-conditional semantics**): "if A, then B" is true if either A is false or B is true. The so-called Brouwer–Heyting–Kolmogorof interpretation of intuitionistic logic (see **constructivism**) reads conditionals as stating the existence of an effective transformation from proofs of the antecedent A to proofs for the consequent B. Another strengthening emerged in modal logic, by analyzing entailment as necessary truth of the material implication (see **intensionality**). These proposals were driven by abstract intuitions concerning valid inference (cf. (Nute, 1984)).

More concretely, in natural language, different types of conditional sentence occur, including indicative conditionals stating some connection of fact ("if A, then B is the case") and counterfactuals stating what might have happened ("if A, then B would have been the case"). The latter were treated first in the philosophy of science, because of their connection with lawlike statements and explanation (Sosa, 1975). The key proposal in this tradition is the Ramsey Test, which says that to evaluate a conditional "if A, then B", one tries to add A to one's stock of beliefs consistently, performing minimal changes if needed, and then checks whether B follows from the resulting belief state. This inspired the possible worlds semantics of Lewis and Stalnaker in philosophical logic, which read a conditional "if A, then B" as stating that all A-worlds which are most similar to the current one are B-worlds (Lewis, 1973). The latter developed into a mathematical research program with non-trivial questions of completeness and representation (Burgess, 1981; Veltman, 1985). 'Non-monotonic logics' in Artificial Intelligence involve so-called default rules which show many formal similarities with conditionals. In their semantics, "most similar" is replaced here by "most preferred" in some relevant ordering (Shoham, 1988), and conditional logic comes to encode the structural behaviour of default reasoning (Gärdenfors and Makinson, 1994).

In the semantics of natural language, several more sophisticated accounts of conditionals have been proposed, including 'premise semantics' replacing possible worlds with more structured belief states (Veltman, 1976; Kratzer, 1979, 1981). This is useful for analyzing anaphora across antecedents and consequents, as in the famous 'donkey sentences' (Heim, 1982; Reinhart, 1983). This kind of anaphoric relations inspired Discourse Representation Theory, and subsequent forms of 'dynamic semantics'. Indeed, conditionals are a typical locus for dynamic phenomena. The Ramsey test presupposes a process of revision with respect to the antecedent A, whence conditional logic is also a theory of belief revision (Gärdenfors, 1988). But default conditionals have also been read as dynamifying preferential possible worlds semantics, when thought of as upgrading instructions for preference states ("increase your preference for $A\&B$-situations over *A&non B* ones"; (Spohn, 1988; Veltman, 1991)). Other neighbors of conditional logic include foundations of probability and statistics (Adams, 1975), verisimilitude (Kuipers, 1987), generalized quantifiers (Van Benthem, 1984b).

context The term 'context' has at least three distinct uses in linguistics. (1) The linguistic context of some phrase is just the surrounding linguistic material. (2) The utterance context of some statement concerns any fact that is taken to be relevant to the utterance, and may specify the speaker, the hearer, what was said, the time of utterance, the beliefs and intentions of the conversational participants, and much more. (3) In **context change** theories (see below) the term 'context' does concern the utterance context, but in the restricted sense of describing only the mutual beliefs of the conversational participants, in which case context is roughly equivalent to **common ground**.

context-dependence An expression may be context-dependent in any of the above three senses. Typically, the interpretation of pronouns may depend on linguistic context, as in "Bill knows what he likes". The interpretation of indexicals and demonstratives will depend on the utterance context, as in "I am not a crook" or "This is my car". The latter type of context dependence has inspired the philosophers Kaplan and Stalnaker to an extension of Montague's Intensional Logic that also accounts for indexicals and demonstratives. A typical observation here is that the sentence "I am the speaker" is not necessarily true, though in fact any utterance of it is true. But such a distinction cannot be made in Montague's Intensional Logic. Kaplan proposed to replace the notion of intension by the notion of *character*. A character is a function from contexts to contents, and contents are like intensions functions from worlds or indices to extensions (Kaplan, 1978; Zimmermann, 1991).

For a case of context dependence in the sense of a relation to mutual beliefs, the work of Clark and Marshall (1981) on definite reference may serve as an example. These authors argue that for the proper use of an expression like 'the man in the blue raincoat', it must not only be the case that there is a unique referent of the description, say a, but it must in fact be mutual knowledge between speaker and hearer that a is the unique referent of the description.

context change The view that assertions are operations on the context, in the sense of the common ground, was developed by Hamblin (1971), Stalnaker (1978), Gazdar (1981). In this approach the assertion of a sentence S that expresses the proposition p will change the context by adding the proposition that p to the context. This type of theory has been used to give a pragmatic explication of the notion of presupposition: if a sentence S presupposes that q, then an assertion of S is appropriate only in contexts in which q is already accepted (Stalnaker, 1974; Gazdar, 1979; Heim, 1983; Beaver, 1995).

Also see: common ground, indexicality, pragmatics, speech acts.

context free language see formal language theory.

context sensitive language see formal language theory.

constructive logic see logic.

constructivism Constructive mathematics emphasizes the actual construction of solutions to problems. Constructions are already present in Euclid's Geometry (in addition to Theorems), but their importance became a philosophical program in this century, especially, in so-called intuitionism, which replaces 'truth' by 'provability' as the basic notion of reasoning. The Brouwer–Heyting–Kolmogorof interpretation of logical constants reads them as instructions for combining proofs. The algorithmic content of this comes out best in the Curry–Howard–De Bruyn isomorphism, which matches constructive proofs with definitions of algorithms in a typed lambda calculus. Another approach to constructivism is the possible worlds semantics of Kripke, which interprets logical statements in a universe of information states, where a reasoner can move upward (Kripke, 1965). Other 'dynamic' accounts of constructivism include game-theoretical semantics (Lorenzen and Lorenz, 1979) and category-theoretic semantics (MacLane and Moerdijk, 1992). The survey par excellence is (Troelstra and Van Dalen, 1988).

convention see common ground.

conventional implicature see conversational maxims.

conversational maxims In many cases of actual conversation, the hearer is able to draw inferences on the assumption that the speaker is obeying some communicative rule, for example that the speaker is trying to be informative. These rules can be called conversational maxims. The pioneering work in this area is due to H.P. Grice (Grice, 1989), who proposed a set of rules that people who are engaged in a cooperative conversation are supposed to follow. Grice proposed a Cooperative Principle which was further explicated by four Maxims of Conversation, the Quality Maxim ('try to be truthful'), the Quantity Maxim ('be informative'), the Maxim of Relevance ('be relevant'), and the Maxim of Manner ('be perspicuous').

implicature In general, an implicature is any inference that a hearer can draw from an utterance that does *not* follow from the content of the utterance. Accordingly, such inferences are commonly considered pragmatic and non-truth-conditional.

conversational implicature A type of inference that a hearer is able to draw on the assumption that the speaker is obeying the conversational maxims. Alternatively, a piece of information that speaker is able to convey on the assumption that the hearer will recognize that the speaker is obeying the maxims. An example is the Quantity implicature from an assertion "S" to "The speaker believes that S". Grice also considered implicatures that arise from the hearers recognition that the speaker is consciously violating some conversational rule; these inferences are called floutings or exploitations.

conventional implicature A type of pragmatic inference that is not related to conversational principles, but instead is conventionally associated with some lexical item. An example considered by Grice was 'but', which he argued has the same content as 'and', but conventionally conveys some contrast between two propositions.

Literature: (Gazdar, 1979; Grice, 1989; Horn, 1972; Horn, 1973).

Cooperative Principle see conversational maxims.

counterfactuals see conditionals.

cylindric algebra see algebra.

decidability see logic, recursion theory.

definite descriptions Expressions of the form "the present king of France" or "the brother of Mary". Both in philosophy and linguistics there is an extensive literature on definite descriptions. Definite descriptions appear to require a unique referent of the description. A central problem concerns where to locate this uniqueness requirement. If it is taken to be semantical, a sentence in which a non-referring description is used, such as "The present king of France is bald", can be taken to be false, as Russell did, or to be meaningless, as Strawson held. Other positions would conceive of the uniqueness requirement as pragmatic, as a criterion of proper use. Thus it has been argued that definite descriptions have the uniqueness requirement as a presupposition, and can only be correctly used in contexts where this presupposition is satisfied. A related conception is to see definite descriptions as essentially anaphoric, in the sense that they can only be used if the previous discourse had established a unique referent for the description (see (Heim, 1982)).

See this Handbook: Chapters 3, 6 and 17.

Literature: (Donnellan, 1966; Heim, 1982; Neale, 1990; Russell, 1905, 1919, 1957; Strawson, 1950).

deixis see indexicality.

discourse Typically a continuous piece of language that consists of more than one sentence. This includes texts as well as conversations. In French structuralist philosophy, "discours" means anything that is required to make sense of any utterance, and this can in general involve anything that has occurred ever since time began.

In logical semantics the 1980's witnessed a development in which the level of analysis was shifted from the level of the sentence to the level of the text. This type of semantics is called discourse semantics. This development is represented in this Handbook by the chapter on Discourse Representation Theory (Chapter 3) and the chapter on Dynamic Semantics (Chapter 10). In linguistics there exists a longer tradition of studies on textual and conversational structure. Several approaches have been proposed here, including text grammar (Van Dijk, 1972), discourse analysis based on speech act theory (Coulthard, 1977), and many empirical studies in the field of conversation analysis (Schlegoff and Sacks, 1973; Atkinson and Heritage, 1984; Schiffrin, 1987).

domain theory Abstract mathematical theory of functions that provides a systematic way of solving recursive equations $X = \ldots X \ldots$. This is useful in the semantics of programming languages since recursive definitions of structures and procedures are very common in programming languages. Moreover, domain theory enabled a model theoretic interpretation for the untyped **lambda calculus**, by the construction of a domain D that satisfies the equation $D = [D \to D]$, where $[D \to D]$ is the set of *continuous functions* over D.

Also see: **fixed point logic**.

Literature: (Abramsky and Jung, 1992; Scott, 1982; Scott and Strachey, 1971).

dynamic logic see logic.

epistemic logic see logic.

events An event is a unit of change in the external world, whose duration is measured in an interval of time. Donald Davidson first suggested that events are needed on a par with individuals to account for the interpretation of descriptions of actions (Davidson, 1980). His influence on contemporary semantics of natural language is seen in Neo-Davidsonian event semantics, where the argument structure of certain verb classes include a first event-argument (Diesing, 1993). Events are contrasted to states, which constitute lack of change. Sometimes events are classified as telic or atelic, meaning that the way in which they are described respectively expresses information about their ending (e.g., "Jane read a book") or not (e.g., "Jane read prose"). Some authors use the term 'eventuality' to denote states and events, and reserve the notion of events for telic descriptions of change.

See this Handbook, Chapters 3 and 16.

extensionality see intensionality.

first-order logic see logic.

fixed point logic see logic.

focus In tripartite representations of information content (focus particle / focus frame / focus), focus constitutes the set of existentially quantified asserted conditions. Sometimes this is considered to be the new information, after its presuppositions have been added to the context. Virtually all English expressions can be interpreted as focus-sensitive, often facilitated by specific high pitch prosody, but there are also specific operators such as 'only' and 'even' that trigger focus-sensitive meaning. For instance, "Jane only took her mother to the movies" has several focus-sensitive interpretations, meaning that of all people Jane may have taken to the movies she took her mother; or it could mean of all the places where Jane may have taken her mother to, she took her to the movies. Focus indicates how the context is to be supplemented with alternatives to what is asserted to be the case, restricting the domain of quantifiers.

Literature: (Rochemont, 1986; Rooth, 1992, 1996; Vallduví, 1992).

formal language theory Branch of mathematical linguistics that studies mathematical properties of languages. The subject has drawn the joint attention of linguists, logicians and computer scientists. There is a close connection with **automata theory**. A much studied classification of languages is the Chomsky hierarchy (Chomsky, 1956, 1959). In this hierarchy four types of languages are distinguished. The distinction between the types is based on the properties of the phrase structure grammars that generate the languages. Such a grammar is defined as a four-tuple $G = (V, T, P, S)$, where V is a set of non-terminal symbols, T is a set of terminal symbols, P is a finite set of productions, and S is a special symbol called the start symbol. A production is a rewrite rule of the form $X \Rightarrow Y$, where X and Y are finite sequences of symbols from V and/or T, where X must be non-empty. The derivation relation $\Rightarrow^*$ is defined as the transitive closure of production relation $\Rightarrow$. Informally, V can be seen as the set of grammatical categories, T is the lexicon, P is the set of grammatical rules, and S is the category of the sentence. $L(G)$, the language generated by a grammar G is defined as the set of all strings of terminal symbols w such that $S \Rightarrow^* w$ is derivable in the grammar.

unrestricted languages These languages, which are also called Type 0 languages, are the languages that can be generated by any phrase structure grammar.

context sensitive languages Also called Type 1 languages, these languages are defined to be generated by grammars that satisfy the restriction that all productions are of the form $AXB \Rightarrow AYB$.

context free language This class of languages (Type 2) is generated by grammars that have to meet the following restriction: in every production $X \Rightarrow Y$, X may consist of only one non-terminal symbol.

regular languages or Type 3 languages, are a restricted form of context free languages: they are produced by context free grammars that are either left-linear or right-linear. A context free grammar is right-linear if in every production $X \Rightarrow Y$, Y may contain at most one non-terminal symbol, which, if present, must be the rightmost symbol of Y.

The hierarchy theorem states that the inclusions are all proper: Type $i + 1$ is a proper subset of Type i. There is also a neat correspondence of this classification with the types of automata that can recognize some particular class; see **automata theory**.

In linguistics there has been considerable discussion about the question whether natural languages are context-free or not. At present the most favored position appears to be that natural language is 'mildly' context sensitive.

Also see: **recursion theory**, **automata theory**.

Literature: (Chomsky, 1956, 1959; Hopcroft and Ullman, 1979; Lewis and Papadimitriou, 1981; Partee, Ter Meulen and Wall, 1990).

Gödel's incompleteness theorems see logic.

higher-order logic see logic.

implicature see conversational maxims.

indexicality Indexical expressions are expressions that refer to some property of the context of utterance. Examples include first and second person pronouns, space and time adverbials (*now, here*), demonstratives (*this, that*), and tense. Another frequently used term for this phenomenon is *deixis*. Both in philosophy and in linguistics there is an extensive literature on indexicality.

Also see: **context**, **pragmatics**.

Literature: (Donnellan, 1978; Fillmore, 1971, 1975; Green, 1995; Kaplan, 1978; Lewis, 1972; Lyons, 1977; Montague, 1968, 1970; Perry, 1993; Rauh, 1982; Stalnaker, 1972; Weissenborn and Klein, 1982).

intensionality The notion of 'intensionality' is used in many senses. In traditional logic and philosophy intensional notions like 'concept' or 'proposition' are discussed, while modern logic started with an 'extensional' emphasis on sets of objects falling under a concept, or ranges of values for a function. This shows in the **extensionality** principles of classical logic, which say that propositions with the same truth value, or predicates with the same extension, may be replaced by each other salva veritate. In Frege's work on the philosophy of language, 'reference' of expressions is extensional, while 'sense' is the intensional guide to the former. In the 1920's, intensional notions returned in modal logic (Lewis, 1918), the study of philosophical necessity and possibility. No single intuition governs reasoning with modalities, which shows in a landscape of proof systems for modal deduction. The central semantic account from the 1950's follows Leibniz's idea that necessity is truth in all possible worlds, with the twist that one only quantifies over all accessible worlds (Kanger, 1957; Kripke, 1959; Hintikka, 1961). Thus, intensionality is explained as multiple extension across relevant alternative situations. Possible worlds semantics has become the main vehicle for philosophical applications (including modal predication and cross-world identity of objects: (Marcus, 1961; Hintikka, 1969; Kripke, 1990)) and mathematical developments (especially, universal algebra and model theory of modal semantics: (Bull and Segerberg, 1984; Van Benthem, 1985; Goldblatt, 1993; Blackburn, De Rijke and Venema, 1996)). This framework has led to similar developments in temporal logic (Van Benthem, 1991b), epistemic logic (Hintikka, 1962), conditional logic (see **conditionals**), deontic logic (see (Åqvist, 1984)). In addition to these strands from philosophical logic, new intensional logics have arisen in computer science: dynamic logic (programs change possible states of a computer; cf. (Goldblatt, 1992; Harel, Kozen and Tiuryn, 1995)), knowledge representation (terminological languages; (Ohlbach, Schmidt and Hustadt, 1995)), and epistemic logic (distributed systems of computational agents; (Fagin, Halpern, Moses and Vardi, 1995), but also planning with limited knowledge; cf. (Moore, 1984)). The epistemic connection contains many further aspects of intensionality (cf. **common ground**).

Intensional constructions in natural language include temporal expressions, as well as intensional verbs ("seek") and propositional attitudes ("know", "believe", "doubt"), while also speech acts like questions are intensional (cf. this Handbook, Chapter 19). Montague put these at center stage (cf. this Handbook, Chapter 1), with a logical development in (Gallin, 1975). Other influential authors on intensional constructions in natural language are Lewis (1972), Cresswell (1973, 1985, 1988).

Criticisms of the multiple reference strategy toward intensionality are prominent in situation semantics (Barwise and Perry, 1983). Another alternative to the possible world analysis of intensionality is Property Theory (Bealer, 1982; Chierchia and Turner, 1988).

For a survey of developments until 1990, see (Van Benthem, 1988). As for recent developments, cf. the volumes (De Rijke, 1993, 1996), and especially for connections between the theory of meaning and dynamic semantics for modal predicate logic: (Groenendijk, Stokhof and Veltman, 1994, 1996). For junctions between the linguistic and computational traditions on epistemic logic and information exchange, cf. (Groeneveld, 1995; Gerbrandy, 1996).

intuitionistic logic see logic.

Kripke semantics see logic.

lambda calculus Originally, lambda calculus arose in foundational studies in logic as an abstract theory of functions, using only the basic operations of abstraction and application (Curry, 1930; Church, 1932, 1933). Given any term t, we can perform abstraction and obtain the functional term $\lambda x \cdot t$, or we can apply the term to an argument x and obtain the term $t(x)$. A typical axiom of lambda calculus is the rule of β-conversion, $(\lambda x{\cdot}t(x))(y) = t(y)$ (this rule is sometimes also called λ-conversion).

Attempts by Church to extend the lambda calculus with logical connectives, so that the enriched calculus may provide a foundation for mathematics, failed, since they were proven inconsistent in (Kleene and Rosser, 1935). Nevertheless the functional part of lambda calculus (which is nowadays just what lambda calculus *is*) proved very useful in a number of disciplines. Within logic itself it is relevant to recursion theory, since it is possible to explain the notion of 'effectively computable function' in lambda calculus (Church) by the concept of λ-definable function. λ-definability is equivalent to other mathematical definitions of effective computation, for example to Gödel's recursive functions (Kleene, 1936b), and to Turing computable functions (Turing, 1936, 1937).

These results, which showed that lambda calculus is capable of defining all computable functions, provided the basis of a strong interest in lambda calculus in computer science. Here the calculus became a useful theoretical tool for studying abstract problems about programming languages. But on a practical level lambda calculus also influenced the design of programming languages, most notably in LISP. Furthermore, by the strong connection between lambda calculus and programming, semantic interpretations of the former were easily transferable to semantic interpretations for the latter (see **domain theory** and **programming languages**).

For an encyclopedic monograph on λ-calculus see (Barendregt, 1984). Finally, in the area of logical semantics, lambda calculus, especially the typed version, has had a profound influence. This Handbook contains ample evidence of this influence: see Chapters 1, 2, 8, 9 and 12.

language acquisition In generative grammar a descriptively adequate grammar that accounts for all and only the intuitively acceptable expressions of a language is said to be also explanatorily adequate, when it accounts for the data concerning language acquisition, including the order in which various constructions are learned and the way in which rules are overgeneralized by young children (e.g., past tense formation is applied to strong verb forms, he walk-ed/he left-ed.) Language acquisition studies shed an interesting empirical light on to the complexity of cognitive structure and they could prove useful in increasing the psychological reality of the logical and mathematical models of the mature competence in natural language understanding.

See: this Handbook, Chapter 13.

lattice see algebra.

Lindenbaum algebra see algebra.

logic An area common to philosophy and mathematics, logic is standardly conceived as the science of valid reasoning. As as separate subject logic is very much a child of the 20th century, and it came of age mathematically through the work of Frege, Russell, Gödel, Tarski and many more (see The Handbook of Mathematical Logic and the Handbook of Philosophical Logic). A standard subdivision would have logic as consisting of **model theory**, **set theory**, **recursion theory** and **proof theory**. But recent developments have uncovered many areas of investigation that logic shares with other disciplines, most notably with computer science (see The Handbook of Logic in Computer Science), artificial intelligence (see the Handbook of Logic in Artificial Intelligence), and linguistics (this Handbook).

1. Classical logic.

The logics that have been most widely studied and applied are classical propositional logic, and classical first-order logic.

classical logic Logic that is *truth conditional.* The specific 'classical' assumptions on truth are (1) Bivalence: there are only two truth-values, 'true' and 'false'; (2) Excluded Middle: every sentence is true or false; (3) Non-Contradiction: no sentence is both true and false. A further characteristic of classical logic is that valid consequence is defined as preservation of truth: an argument $\phi_1, \dots, \phi_n/\psi$ with premises $\phi_1, \dots, \phi_n$ and conclusion ψ is valid provided that in all situations in which all of $\phi_1, \dots, \phi_n$ are true, ψ is also true. Also see: **truth-conditional semantics**.

first-order logic Refinement and extension of classical propositional logic. The refinement consists in the fact that the most simple formulae are not 'atomic', but have the structure of a predication of some n-ary relation to some n-tuple of objects. The extension consists in the addition of logical constants for quantification, the existential quantifier $\exists$ and the universal quantifier $\forall$. The qualification 'first-order' means that quantification is allowed only over objects ('entities of first order'), and not for example over sets of objects (i.e. properties) which are 'second order objects'. Also see: **truth-conditional semantics**.

2. Important concepts and results.

logical constants In a system of formal logic the logical constants are those symbols the meanings of which are regarded as fixed, as opposed to the non-logical symbols, which may have different meanings in different situations (models). Typically the logical constants are the formal counterparts of certain expressions of natural language that are crucial to reasoning, such as "not", "and", "all", "some". A general formal characteristic of logical constants of any type is that they are invariant under permutations of the domain of discourse (see (Van Benthem, 1991a)).

completeness (1) Given a syntactically defined notion of derivability $\vdash$ and some semantically defined notion of logical consequence $\models$, a completeness theorem establishes the implication: if $\Gamma \models \phi$ then $\Gamma \vdash \phi$. Thus a completeness theorem shows that the relation $\vdash$ 'completely' describes $\models$. The converse implication, if $\Gamma \vdash \phi$ then $\Gamma \models \phi$, is called a correctness theorem or a soundness theorem.

(2) A complete theory is a set of sentences T such that for all ϕ, $T \vdash \phi$ or $T \vdash \neg\phi$. This notion is sometimes called syntactic completeness, in order to distinguish it from the notion under (1).

compactness A consequence relation $\models$ is compact if $\Gamma \models \phi$ if and only if $\Delta \models \phi$ for some finite subset Δ of Γ. First-order logic is compact.

decidability and undecidability These concepts from **recursion theory** can also be applied to consequence relations. For example, the set of formulae that are valid in classical propositional logic is decidable, but the set of valid formulae of first-order logic is undecidable. Usually the statement that some logic is (un)decidable means that the consequence relation of the logic is (un)decidable.

Löwenheim–Skolem–Tarski Theorem An important theorem on first-order logic, that essentially shows the undefinability of infinite cardinalities in first-order logic. Let T be some theory in a first-order language L of cardinality $\|L\|$. The Downward Löwenheim–Skolem–Tarski Theorem states that if T has a model, then it has a model of cardinality at most $\|L\|$. The Upward Löwenheim–Skolem–Tarski Theorem states that if T has an infinite model, then it has a model of any infinite cardinality $\geqslant \|L\|$.

Lindström's Theorem is a meta-theorem that gives a characterization of first-order logic in terms of its model-theoretic properties: it sates that first-order logic is the strongest logic that satisfies the Compactness Theorem and the Löwenheim–Skolem–Tarski Theorem.

Gödel's Incompleteness Theorems The most famous results in logic to date. Gödel's First Incompleteness theorem states: Every consistent axiomatic extension of formal arithmetic is incomplete. Gödel's Second Incompleteness Theorem is: no consistent axiomatic extension of formal arithmetic can prove its own consistency (see (Gödel, 1931; Smullyan, 1992)).

3. Variations on classical logic.

constructive logics Logics that are based on constructivism, a strong undercurrent in the philosophy of mathematics, which holds that all mathematical notions and proofs should be (effectively) constructible. See **constructivism**.

intuitionistic logic Special form of constructive logic mainly due to Brouwer, Heyting and Kolmogorof. The basic philosophical point is that the notion of construction should reflect 'mathematical intuition'. The classical tautologies $\phi \vee \neg\phi$ and $\neg\neg\phi \rightarrow \phi$ are not valid intuitionistically. In intuitionistic predicate logic, the universal and existential quantifiers are not interdefinable; for example, the principle $\neg\forall x \neg\phi \rightarrow \exists x\phi$ is not intuitionistically valid. The reason is that an intuitionistic proof of an existentially quantified statement $\exists x\phi$ should provide an explicit construction of an object satisfying ϕ. See (Van Dalen, 1984; Troelstra and Van Dalen, 1988).

partial logic Logic in which the classical assumptions on truth (see **classical logic**) conditions are weakened. In many-valued logic there are more than two truth values. But also with two truth values there are possible variations: there may be formulae that are neither true or false (in which case the Principle of Excluded Middle does not hold), or there may be formulae that are both true and false (in which case the Principle of Non-Contradiction fails). See (Blamey, 1984; Langholm, 1987; Urquhart, 1984); for connections with linguistic issues see (Fenstad, Halvorsen, Langholm and Van Benthem, 1987).

4. Extensions of classical logic.

higher-order logic Logic in which quantification is possible not only over objects in the domain of discourse, but also over higher-order constructions of these objects, such as sets of objects, or sets of binary relations on objects.

second-order logic Logic that allows quantification over sets of objects and relations between objects.

modal logic Extension of propositional logic with two unary sentential operators $\Box$ and $\Diamond$ that are intended to capture the meaning of "it is necessary that" and "it is possible that". Modal logic gained a lot of momentum with the development of **Kripke semantics**, which was invented independently by Kanger, Hintikka and Kripke in the late 50's. Also see **intensionality**.

Kripke semantics A general and widely used semantics for logics with intensional sentential operators, such as modal logic, epistemic logic, tense logic and dynamic logic. A Kripke model is a structure (S, R, I) where S is some set of indexes, R is a binary relation on S, and I is an interpretation of the non-logical symbols. The interpretation of the pair (S, R) (which is also called a frame) depends on the particular logic. For example, in modal logic S is a set of possible worlds and R is an accessibility relation; in temporal logic, S is a set of points in time and R is the relation 'earlier than'. The meaning of an intensional sentential operator O is then given relative to an index in S, but relativized to other points in S via the relation R; a typical semantic clause would state that $O\phi$ is true in i if and only if ϕ is true in all $j \in S$ such that iRj.

epistemic logic The logic of knowledge and belief. Usually these logics are propositional, and sentential operators K_a and B_a are added, with intended interpretation "agent a knows that ϕ" and "agent a believes that ϕ". See (Hintikka, 1962; Fagin, Halpern, Moses and Vardi, 1995).

temporal logic The logic of temporal relations. Besides extensions of propositional logic with sentential temporal operators (such as "always in the future ..."), there are also first order logics of time. See (Goldblatt, 1992; Van Benthem, 1983).

dynamic logic Logic in which it is possible to make assertions about the behaviour of computer programs. In propositional dynamic logic there are formulae of the form $[\pi]\phi$ which express that after every successful run of program π, ϕ is true, where ϕ is some statement about the (resulting) state of the computer. There are also quantified versions of dynamic logic. See (Harel, 1984; Goldblatt, 1992; Harel, Kozen and Tiuryn, 1995).

conditional logic In many cases the natural language "if ... then ..." cannot be interpreted by the material implication (see **truth-conditional semantics**). To overcome this, conditional logics introduce new connectives that are closer to the natural language conditional operators. See **conditionals**.

fixed point logic Fixed points of a function F are those arguments X where $F(X) = X$. Fixed points are a key notion in the theory of inductive definitions (Aczel, 1977; Moschovakis, 1974), which define useful sets as fixed points of suitable operators. Suitably monotone or continuous functions always have fixed points (Scott, 1982), and hence they are also prominent in **domain theory**, which provides a semantic underpinning for the untyped lambda calculus (Barendregt, 1984). Fixed-point logics extend standard logics by adding constructors $\mu p * A(p)$, where p is a predicate occurring only positively in the formula A (see **polarity**). The latter denote the smallest solutions to the fixed-point equation $p = A(p)$, and they considerably extend the expressive power of, e.g., classical predicate logic. Many programming operations are of this nature (Harel, Kozen and Tiuryn, 1995) as are operators in computational query languages (Kannelakis, 1990). Largest fixed points are also gaining prominence in semantics, witness their use in non-well-founded set theory (see (Aczel, 1988)) and its applications (see (Barwise and Etchemendy, 1987; Barwise and Moss, 1996)).

non-monotonic logic Logic in which addition of premises may lead to withdrawal of conclusions. This will occur when the conclusion that has to be withdrawn was a default assumption, based on preferences or expectations rather than on hard facts. There is a vast body of research on this type of reasoning in Artificial Intelligence (Ginsberg, 1987; Marek, 1993; Shoham, 1988). For the connection with semantics, see this Handbook, Chapters 14 and 20.

5. Translations between logics.

Translations between theories date back to the foundations of geometry and set theory. One looks mostly at effective compositional maps sending theorems of one logic into those of another. These may satisfy:

1. if $L_1 \vdash A$, then $L_2 \vdash trans(A)$ (soundness)
2. if $L_2 \vdash trans(A)$, then $L_1 \vdash A$ (completeness)

Famous examples include translations of mathematical theories into set theory, or embeddings of classical logic into intuitionistic logic (see **constructivism**), or of intuitionistic logic into modal logic. Embeddings even exist from intensional modal logic (see **intensionality**) back into extensional classical logic (Van Benthem, 1984a). Thus, one can choose different representations of the same (linguistic) facts, and manipulate these with different logical calculi to get the same effects. The translational methodology has been applied to intensional type theories in natural language semantics (cf. Gallin, 1975). But it also applies to current dynamic semantics, witness (Muskens, 1994, 1996). Translation methods from intensional to extensional logics have become a popular tool in the literature on theorem proving (Ohlbach, 1991).

6. History of Logic.

For the history of logic before the 20th century see (Bochenski, 1956, 1961) and (Kneale and Kneale, 1962). The history of logic in this century is now amply documented in a series of handbooks. See the Handbook of Mathematical Logic (Barwise, 1977), the Handbook of Philosophical Logic (Gabbay and Guenthner, 1984), the Handbook of Logic in Computer Science (Abramsky, Gabbay and Maibaum, 1992), the Handbook of Logic in Artificial Intelligence and Logic Programming (Gabbay, Hogger and Robinson, 1993), and this Handbook.

logic programming An area in which logical formalisms are used as programming languages. Best known example is the programming language *PROLOG*, which uses a fragment of first-order logic. The basic inferential mechanism that is used is called **resolution**. The Resolution Rule for propositional logic is: from $\phi \vee \psi$ and $\neg\psi \vee \chi$ infer $\phi \vee \chi$. For predicate logic, this has to be combined with **unification** which in this case consist of a substitution that identifies two formulae: from $\phi \vee \psi_1$ and $\neg\psi_2 \vee \chi$ infer $\sigma(\phi) \vee \sigma(\chi)$, provided that σ is a substitution such that $\sigma(\psi_1) = \sigma(\psi_2)$. In formal syntax the unification of two expressions T and S can be achieved by finding a substitution α such that $T[\alpha] = S[\alpha]$. For feature structures, unification can be considered as a process of merging the information of two (or more) feature structures by finding a common more specific feature structure (see this Handbook, Chapter 8).

Literature: (Fitting, 1990; Gabbay, Hogger and Robinson, 1993; Lloyd, 1987).

logical form A concept that has been important both in logic and in linguistics. In logic the work of Russell (1905) was influential in spreading the conviction that there was a sharp contrast between logical form and grammatical form. For example, it may be argued that the sentences

1. Peter walks
2. Nobody walks

have the same grammatical form but distinct logical forms. The difference in logical form is shown in the predicate logical translations of these sentences, which are respectively Wp, a singular predication, and $\neg\exists x : Wx$, a negated existentially quantified proposition. Observations like these lead Russell to propound the 'Misleading Form Thesis': there is no one-to-one map from grammatical forms of natural language expressions to logical forms. This thesis was very influential in subsequent developments in analytic philosophy, most notably in logical positivism. The development of generalized quantifier theory, e.g., in Montague Grammar (Montague, 1974), came to shed some different light on this connection, at least for the type of example we just gave. If we interpret both "Peter" and "Nobody" as generalized quantifiers, the sentences 1 and 2 will have the same grammatical form and the same logical form $(Q(\mathit{walk}))$ and the difference in meaning will only be due to the different properties of the associated quantifiers. Thus, in Montague Grammar there is virtually no distinction between grammatical and logical form.

In linguistics the concept of logical form (LF) has played a prominent part in Chomskyan approaches to grammar. Here logical form can roughly be described as a grammatically relevant representation in which all semantic ambiguities have been resolved. Thus, for example, quantifier scope is represented at LF. Logical form has frequently been identified with D-structure. Moreover, if all ambiguities are resolved at LF, then the LF of some sentence can be taken as the meaning of the sentence, or a least as a representation that determines the meaning uniquely.

logical syntax Many linguistic theories use labeled graphs as the carriers of syntactic, semantic, morphological and phonetic information. Examples are Government Binding Theory, or Unification Grammars. On this view, a linguistic theory describes admissible graphs underlying texts or utterances. For example, a context-free grammar is a device for accepting derivation trees (satisfying 'node admissibility conditions' corresponding to its production rules). These conditions may be formulated in standard first-order logic, or with modal languages describing possible successors for the nodes. Phrase structure trees are finite modal models, with proposition letters for grammatical categories or lexical items. Thus, each grammar has its strong recognizing capacity encoded by a class of trees, and hence it corresponds effectively to a modal formula. This analogy leads to new connections between linguistics and logic. Modal languages come in a hierarchy of expressive power, which relates to the Chomsky Hierarchy of grammars (see **formal language theory**). Also, natural semantic identifications between modal possible worlds models such as 'bisimulation' encode levels of logical form for linguistic expressions. There are decidable modal logics over finite trees. 'Modal phrase structure grammar' is described in (Kracht, 1995; Blackburn and Meyer-Viol, 1994). An alternative approach uses first-order and monadic second-order languages over finite trees (Backofen, Rogers and Vijay-Shanker, 1995). Jumps in complexity for linguistic constructions in Government Binding Theory have been analyzed from this classical model-theoretic viewpoint in (Rogers, 1994). Further modal structures arise when nodes of trees are replaced by feature models (see (Carpenter, 1992); and this Handbook, Chapter 8). The result is a two-level modal logic of decorated trees, which also has connections with developments in situation theory (Barwise and Moss, 1996; Barwise and Seligman, 1997). There is a connection with dynamic semantics here, as rewrite rules are procedural in a sense, and tree models are like transition systems (see this Handbook, Chapter 10).

Löwenheim–Skolem–Tarski theorem see logic.

material implication see truth-conditional semantics.

modal logic see logic.

model theory Branch of logic that deals with the various relations between logical languages and their models. The paradigm is the model theory of first order logic, which was initiated by Tarski's truth definition, and which has reached a high degree of mathematical sophistication (Chang and Keisler, 1990). Some typical questions in model theory are the following. Given a class of models K, can we find some theory T that is true exactly in the models in K? There are several of these *definability theorems* for first-order logic. For example: (a) the class of finite models is not first-order definable; (b) the class of all infinite models is first-order definable; (c) there is no infinite cardinal number κ for which the class of all models of cardinality κ is first-order definable. Result (a) follows from the Compactness Theorem, and (c) from the Löwenheim–Skolem theorem, two famous results in model theory (see **logic**). A general result on definability is Keisler's theorem, which establishes necessary and sufficient conditions under which a class of models is definable: a class of models is first-order definable if and only if both it and its complement are closed under *ultraproducts* and *isomorphisms*.

Another usual type of question in model theory concerns the relation between some syntactic property of a formula (or a theory) and a property of models. Prime example is the Completeness theorem, which establishes the equivalence of derivability and validity (see **logic**). Other examples of this pattern are so called Preservation theorems, for example: a formula is preserved under submodels if and only if it is equivalent to a universal formula.

Abstract model theory is a general reflection on properties of logics and model theoretic results such as the Compactness theorem or Löwenheim–Skolem theorem (Barwise, 1974; Barwise and Feferman, 1985). A famous result here is Lindström's theorem, which states that first-order logic is the only *abstract* logic that has the Compactness and Löwenheim–Skolem properties.

non-monotonic logic see logic.

parsing A central concern in computational linguistics is to design and study algorithms that assign grammatical and/or semantic structures to text. This process is commonly called parsing. Several strategies of parsing have been considered: bottom up (from the lexical items up to complex structures), top down (from the complex structures down to the lexical items), and incremental (compute structure step by step, at each step adding the next item of the string). One major topic of discussion concerns the division of labor between syntax and semantics, in particular the question whether semantic and syntactic structures should be computed simultaneously or sequentially.

An influential observation on the connection between parsing and logic was made by Pereira (1983), who observed that the problem of finding a grammatical structure for a string has strong similarities to the logical problem of finding a proof for a formula. This so called 'Parsing as Deduction' paradigm is prominent in categorial and type-theoretical grammar; see this Handbook, Chapter 2.

Literature: (Carpenter, 1992; Nerbonne, 1996; Pereira, 1983; Pereira and Shieber, 1987; Rosner and Johnson, 1992; Shieber, 1986).

partial logic see logic.

performative see speech acts.

Performative Hypothesis see speech acts.

phrase structure grammar see formal language theory.

polarity A grammatical concept that signifies a systematic restriction in the distribution of a linguistic expression. **Negative polarity items** can only occur in negative contexts; they include "any", "ever", "yet". For example, "I didn't eat any bagels" is grammatical, but "I ate any bagels" is ill-formed. By contrast, **Positive polarity items** can only occur in positive contexts; they include "somebody", "already", "still". For example, "I have already finished reading" is acceptable, but "I have not already finished reading" is out. The main theoretical problem concerning polarity is to give a precise characterization of what a negative (positive) context is. This problem has been answered in various ways, syntactical (Klima, 1964; Progovac, 1993), semantical (Ladusaw, 1979; Hoeksema, 1986), and pragmatic (Baker, 1970; von Bergen and von Bergen, 1993). The semantic proposal of Ladusaw (1979) provides a nice illustration of the usefulness of logical notions in linguistics. In logic, an occurrence of a predicate P is positive (negative) in a formula ϕ if an extension (restriction) of the interpretation of the predicate preserves the truth of ϕ. Positive (negative) occurrences are also called monotonically increasing (decreasing) positions. These notions appear useful in linguistics; for example, in "I didn't eat X" the position X is decreasing, since "I didn't eat peanuts" entails "I didn't eat salted peanuts". Ladusaw's proposal is essentially that 'negative context' means 'monotonically decreasing position'. Though this proposal does not explain all data, it does appear to have a fairly wide descriptive coverage (Van der Wouden, 1994).

Literature: (Hoeksema, 1983, 1986; Horn, 1989; Ladusaw, 1979, 1996; Van der Wouden, 1994; Zwarts, 1986, 1993).

polymorphism see ambiguity.

possible worlds see conditionals, intensionality, Kripke semantics, logic.

pragmatics In the wide sense, pragmatics is the part of semiotics that studies "the relation of signs to interpreters" (Morris, 1938). In a narrower sense, linguistic pragmatics would then be the study of the relations between linguistic expressions and language users, which is roughly the conception of pragmatics of Carnap. This was narrowed down further by Bar-Hillel, who defined pragmatics as the study of languages that contain indexical or deictic terms (Bar-Hillel, 1954). The latter view is shared by Kalish (1967) and Montague (1968).

Though Morris's conception appears to be too general to be useful in linguistics, Bar-Hillel's view is arguably too narrow. There are two basic problems in defining the the subject pragmatics. First, pragmatics is concerned with meaning, but so is semantics; thus there is the problem of properly demarcating pragmatic aspects of meaning from semantic aspects. A second difficulty is diagnosed by Levinson as follows: "the term *pragmatics* covers both context-dependent aspects of language structure and principles of language usage that have nothing or little to do with linguistic structure. It is difficult to forge a definition that will happily cover both aspects." (Levinson, 1983, p. 9). See Chapter 1 of (Levinson, 1983) for a thorough discussion of several possible definitions of pragmatics. Subjects that are commonly taken to be in the scope of pragmatics are: deixis; topic-comment structure; prosody, intonation and stress; presupposition; speech acts; conversation analysis; conversational implicature.

Also see: **common ground**, **context**, **focus**, **conversational maxims**, **indexicality**, **speech acts**.

Literature: (Davis, 1991; Levinson, 1983; Mey, 1993).

programming languages In the semantics of programming languages several approaches can be distinguished. An *operational semantics* concentrates on the observable effects of a computer program, which are commonly taken to be fully given by the input–output behaviour of the program. A refinement of this approach is *process algebra*, in which intermediate states are also relevant. In *denotational semantics* the meaning of a computer program, and in fact of every construction of the programming language, is some object in a mathematical model, usually a domain (see **domain theory**). Finally an *axiomatic semantics* provides a logical calculus, in which the preconditions and postconditions of a computer program can be calculated deductively.

There appear to be no fundamental oppositions between these approaches. First, the meaning of a program in a denotational semantics could well be an 'operational' input–output function. Second, a logical system like Dynamic Logic (Harel, 1984) has an operational semantics, and its axiomatics provides a deductive machinery for calculating pre- and postconditions of (regular) programs.

Literature: (Baeten and Verhoef, 1992; Van Benthem and Bergstra, 1995; Hennessy and Milner, 1985; Meyer, 1990; Mosses, 1990; Ong, 1992; Plotkin, 1975; Scott and Strachey, 1971; Stoy, 1977; Tennent, 1991; Tennent, 1992; Wagner, 1992).

proof theory Proof theory dates back to the metamathematics of Hilbert, who wanted to describe mathematical proof combinatorially in a consistent way, so as to exclude the notorious foundational paradoxes (Smorynski, 1977). A major achievement was Gentzen's natural deduction (Gentzen, 1939, 1969), and the first major result the Cut Elimination theorem showing how predicate logic can be axiomatized with rules that incrementally build up conclusions. The resulting control over derivations allows for combinatorial analysis of deductive fine-structure. Proofs are important in intuitionistic logic (see **constructivism**), where they match descriptions of algorithms in the typed lambda calculus via the Curry–Howard–De Bruyn isomorphism. Through this link, operations on proofs such as cut elimination, match operations on lambda terms such as normalization, which amount to abstract computation. Fine-structure of proofs is prominent in linear logic (Girard, 1987), which shows how giving up the classical structural rules leads to decidable predicate logics of occurrences, which support a much richer vocabulary of logical operators. This is also the essence in applications to grammatical analysis (this Handbook, Chapter 2). Proof theory shows two faces. One is turned towards the foundations of mathematics (Schwichtenberg, 1977), with recent advances connecting up proofs with morphisms in category theory, and logics with various categorial theories (Lambek and Scott, 1986; MacLane and Moerdijk, 1992). The other face is turned towards applications in computer science and linguistics, with appropriate techniques for handling heterogeneous information, such as labeled deduction (Gabbay, 1990). An excellent sources for the whole area is (Girard, Lafont and Taylor, 1990), and an up-to-date textbook is (Troelstra and Schwichtenberg, 1996).

recursion theory Branch of logic that studies the notion of *effective computation*. The subject started with the definition of recursive functions by Gödel (1931), and was developed further by Turing, Kleene and Church. There are various different definitions of effective computability: the recursive functions defined by Gödel; the functions computable by Turing machines; the functions definable in λ-calculus; the functions computable by register machines; and still more (cf. (Bell and Machover, 1977)). A central result of the subject is that all of these alternative conceptualizations turned out to be formally equivalent. This led many to believe **Church's thesis** (also called Church–Turing thesis): every procedure that is effectively computable in the intuitive sense is in fact computable by a Turing machine.

recursive functions A particular class of functions defined on the natural numbers whose members are, intuitively, the functions for which there is a mechanical procedure for computing their values.

decidability Existence of an effective procedure for classifying positive and negative instances of a problem.

recursive axiomatizability A set of formulae Γ is recursively axiomatizable if there is a decidable set of formulae Δ, such that Γ exactly contains the logical consequences of Δ.

recursive language Language (set of strings) for which the question of whether some string belongs to the language is decidable.

recursively enumerable language Language that is accepted by a Turing machine; alternatively, a type 0 language in the Chomsky hierarchy. See **automata theory, formal language theory**.

Many expositions of recursion theory are intertwined with developments of **automata theory** and **formal language theory**. A recent development in recursion theory is **complexity theory**. Basic information about recursion theory can be found in almost any introductory book in mathematical logic (Mendelson, 1964; Enderton, 1972).

Literature: (Boolos and Jeffrey, 1989; Davis, 1958, 1965; Enderton, 1972; Gödel, 1931; Kleene, 1936a, 1952; Rogers, 1967; Schoenfield, 1971; Turing, 1936, 1937).

regular language see formal language theory.

relation algebra see algebra.

second-order logic see logic.

self-reference The phenomenon that some sentence refers to itself, as in this sentence. Though there are many instances of unproblematic self-referential sentences, such as the previous one, the famous Liar Paradox, "This sentence is not true", has puzzled philosophers ever since Antiquity. The Liar paradox caused the logician Tarski to argue that no language can contain its own truth predicate; instead, there will be a hierarchy of languages, in which the truth of sentences of level k can only be asserted by sentences at the higher level $k + 1$ (Tarski, 1956). Tarski's solution partly consists of declaring self-referential sentences to be ungrammatical. In view of the many cases of unproblematic self-referential statements, such as "This sentence consists of six words", this has been taken to be too strong a measure by many theorists. Thus many alternative solutions of the paradox have been proposed, which do allow self-reference but weaken the notion of truth. In most cases this involves a partial assignment of truth values, in such a way that some statements are neither true nor false (see the collections (Martin, 1970, 1984; Kripke, 1975; Barwise and Etchemendy, 1987).

Self-reference also plays an important part in Gödel's proof of the incompleteness of Peano arithmetic. In this proof a formula in the language of Peano arithmetic is constructed which expresses of itself that it is not provable in Peano arithmetic (see (Smullyan, 1992)).

set theory Branch of logic that studies the mathematical properties of sets. Set theory can be considered as the meta-language of logic and mathematics in general. The first systematic mathematical reflection on sets was given by Georg Cantor (Cantor, 1885). Unfortunately, Cantor was using a comprehension principle that was shown to be inconsistent by Russell (1902). Russell's discovery led to substantial research by logicians and mathematicians. These investigations led to the development of type theory (Russell, 1908), but also to formalized versions of set theory. These formal systems consist of a list of axioms in some logical language, usually the language of first-order logic. The set theories that are nowadays most widely used are ZF and ZFC (the axioms of ZF are due to Zermelo and Fraenkel; ZFC is ZF plus the axiom of Choice). A recent development is Peter Aczel's theory of **non-well-founded** sets (Aczel, 1988). This set theory allows the existence of sets that are members of themselves. In ZF such sets are prohibited by the axiom of Foundation.

Literature: (Aczel, 1988), part B of (Barwise, 1977), part IV of (Benacerraf and Putnam, 1964), (Cohen, 1966; Fraenkel, Bar-Hillel and Levy, 1973; Gödel, 1940; Jech, 1973; Kunen, 1980).

speech acts The basic tenet of speech act theory is that utterances are actions. This pragmatic view was foreshadowed by Wittgenstein's views on language-games (Wittgenstein, 1958), but the theory of speech acts is commonly attributed to the philosopher J.L. Austin (Austin, 1962). Austin argued that there are many declarative sentences that resist a truth-conditional analysis. Examples are: "I apologize"; "I give my word". The point of such sentences is not to express a proposition, but rather to perform some action. Accordingly, Austin called such sentences performatives, and distinguished then from assertions, which he called constatives. For performatives, it is nonsense to call them true or false. Instead Austin proposed to analyze the meaning of performatives in terms of felicity conditions, which are roughly the conditions in which a sentence can be properly used. Moreover, he distinguished three aspects of utterances: the locutionary act, which concerns the expression of something meaningful; the illocutionary act, which concerns the type of action being performed, such as promising or commanding; and the perlocutionary act, which relates to the effect of the utterance on the hearer(s), such as convincing or persuading. Austin's ideas were extended and systematized by the philosopher J.R. Searle in the influential (Searle, 1969). For an extension of intensional logic with speech acts, resulting in a so-called 'illocutionary' logic, see (Searle and Vanderveken, 1985; Vanderveken, 1990, 1991).

In linguistics, speech act theory has influenced theorists to propose the so-called Performative Hypothesis, which in its most simple forms states that the deep structure of every statement is of the form "I hereby PV that p", where PV is a performative verb (such as "state" or "command"), and p is the propositional content (Ross, 1970;

Sadock, 1974; Lakoff, 1972, 1975). If true, the Performative Hypothesis reduces illocutionary force to standard syntactical and semantical considerations. For the severe problems with this position, most notably the phenomenon of indirect speech acts, see the discussion in (Levinson, 1983) (Chapter 5, Sections 5.4 and 5.5).

For context-change approaches to speech acts see **context**.

Also see: **common ground**, **pragmatics**.

tense logic see logic.

tree logics see logical syntax.

truth-conditional semantics An approach to semantics in which the meaning of a declarative sentence is equated with its truth-conditions. In philosophy and logic this influential approach has a long history, that started with Aristotle, and reached the 20th century via the work of Frege, Post, Wittgenstein, Tarski, Carnap, Davidson and Montague. This tradition is classical or bivalent in the sense that there are only two truth values, 'true' and 'false'. In many-valued logics, developed by Post, Łukasiewicz and Bochvar, there are more than two truth values.

truth function A function from (a sequence of) truth values to truth values. Such a function can be of any finite arity, so if T is the set of truth values, a truth function is any function $f: T^n \to T$ for some natural number n. The meanings of connectives in classical propositional logic are truth functions.

truth table A concise way of displaying a truth-function, independently developed by Wittgenstein (1921) and Post (1920, 1921). Here are the truth tables of the classical connectives $\neg$ ("not"), $\wedge$ ("and"), $\vee$ ("or") and the **material implication** $\to$ ("if ... then ..."):

ϕ	$\neg\phi$
1	0
0	1

ϕ	ψ	$\phi \wedge \psi$
1	1	1
1	0	0
0	1	0
0	0	0

ϕ	ψ	$\phi \vee \psi$
1	1	1
1	0	1
0	1	1
0	0	0

ϕ	ψ	$\phi \to \psi$
1	1	1
1	0	0
0	1	1
0	0	1

The truth table method generalizes without problems to many-valued logics (Łukasiewicz, 1967; Rescher, 1969).

truth-functional completeness A set of truth functions X is truth-functionally complete if and only if every truth function can be defined as a composition of functions in X. Minimizing the size of X, this makes it possible to regard only a small number of connectives as basic, and to treat the remaining ones as defined. Examples of truth-functional complete sets of connectives for classical propositional logic include $\{\neg, \wedge, \vee\}$, $\{\neg, \wedge\}$, $\{\neg, \vee\}$, and $\{\bot, \to\}$, where $\bot$ is a propositional constant (a nullary truth function) that always has the value 0 (false).

assignment A function from variables to objects in the domain of discourse, invented by Tarski for obtaining a truth conditional semantics for the quantifiers in first-order logic.

satisfaction A relation between a model, a formula, and an assignment. In the familiar notation $\mathcal{M} \models \phi[g]$, the relation expresses that the formula ϕ is true in the model $\mathcal{M}$ if we fix the reference of the free variables in ϕ by the assignment g. The satisfaction relation is the key to the Tarskian semantics for first-order logic. In a slogan, "Satisfaction is the mother of model theory".

truth function see truth-conditional semantics.

truth table see truth-conditional semantics.

Turing machine see automata theory.

undecidability see logic, recursion theory.

universal algebra see algebra.

universals A universal is a property that all natural languages share. Examples include syntactic universals, such as 'every language has verbs', semantic universals such as 'every determiner is conservative' (see this Handbook, Chapter 15), or pragmatic universals concerning the grammaticalization of some illocutionary act, such as asking a question. There are also statistical universals; for example concerning the distribution of function words ("is", "of", "the") and content words ("walk", "universe", "blue", "softly"). Taken as types, the content words tend to exceed the function words by far (several hundreds of thousands vs. several hundreds); as tokens the function words occur much more frequently; the most frequently used word of English is "the" (Bolinger, 1975).

The search for linguistic universals has been a major motive in Chomskyan linguistics. In Government and Binding Theory (see this Handbook, Chapter 5) this is reflected in the methodological ideal of 'Principles and Parameters': the theory should provide universal Principles, which may contain Parameters, and actual languages or language families can then be described by filling in the Parameters.

Literature: (Chomsky, 1965; Comrie, 1989; Greenberg, 1966).

References

Abramsky, S., Gabbay, D.M. and Maibaum, T.S.E. (eds) (1992), *Handbook of Logic in Computer Science*, Clarendon Press, Oxford.

Abramsky, S. and Jung, A. (1992), *Domain theory*, Handbook of Logic in Computer Science vol. 3, S. Abramsky, D.M. Gabbay and T.S.E. Maibaum, eds, Clarendon Press, Oxford, 1–168.

Aczel, P. (1977), *An introduction to inductive definitions*, Handbook of Mathematical Logic, J. Barwise, ed., North-Holland, Amsterdam, 739–782.

Aczel, P. (1988), *Non-Well-Founded Sets*, CSLI Publications, Stanford.

Adams, E.W. (1975), *The Logic of Conditionals*, Reidel, Dordrecht.

Åqvist, L. (1984), *Deontic logic*, Handbook of Philosophical Logic vol. II, D. Gabbay and F. Guenthner, eds, Reidel, Dordrecht.

Atkinson, J. and Heritage, J. (eds) (1984), *Structures of Social Action*, Cambridge Univ. Press, Cambridge.

Austin, J.L. (1962), *How to Do Things with Words*, Clarendon Press, Oxford.

Backofen, R., Rogers, J. and Vijay-Shanker, K. (1995), *A first-order axiomatization of the theory of finite trees*, J. Logic, Lang., Inform. **4**(1), 5–39.

Baeten, J.C.M. and Verhoef, C. (1992), *Concrete Process Algebra*, Handbook of Logic in Computer Science vol. 4, S. Abramsky, D.M. Gabbay and T.S.E. Maibaum, eds, Clarendon Press, Oxford, 150–269.

Baker, C.L. (1970), *Double negatives*, Ling. Inq. **1**, 169–186.

Balcazar, J.L., Diaz, J. and Gabarro, J. (1988), *Structural Complexity, Part I*, Springer, Berlin.

Balcazar, J.L., Diaz, J. and Gabarro, J. (1990), *Structural Complexity, Part II*, Springer, Berlin.

Bar-Hillel, Y. (1954), *Indexical expressions*, Mind **63**, 359–379.

Barendregt, H. (1984), *The Lambda Calculus*, North-Holland, Amsterdam, 1984. (Revised edition.)

Barwise, J. (1974), *Axioms for abstract model theory*, Ann. Math. Logic **7**, 221–265.

Barwise, J. (ed.) (1977), *Handbook of Mathematical Logic*, North-Holland, Amsterdam.

Barwise, J. (1989), *On the model theory of common knowledge*, The Situation in Logic, CSLI Publications, Stanford, 201–220.

Barwise, J. and Etchemendy, J. (1987), *The Liar. An Essay on Truth and Circularity*, Oxford Univ. Press, New York.

Barwise, J. and Feferman, S. (1985), *Model-Theoretic Logics*, Springer, Berlin.

Barwise, J. and Moss, L. (1996), *Vicious Circles*, CSLI Lecture Notes vol. 59, CSLI Publications, Stanford.

Barwise, J. and Perry, J. (1983), *Situations and Attitudes*, Bradford Books/MIT Press, Cambridge, MA.

Barwise, J. and Seligman, J. (1997), *Information Flow in Distributed Systems*, Cambridge Tracts in Theoretical Computers Science, Cambridge Univ. Press. To appear.

Bealer, G. (1982), *Quality and Concept*, Oxford Univ. Press, Oxford.

Beaver, D.I. (1995), *Presupposition and assertion in dynamic semantics*, PhD thesis, University of Edinburgh.

Bell, J.L. and Machover, M. (1977), *A Course in Mathematical Logic*, North-Holland, Amsterdam.

Benacerraf, P. and Putnam, H. (eds) (1964), *Philosophy of Mathematics*, Cambridge Univ. Press, Cambridge, MA. (Second edition 1983.)

Birkhoff, G. (1967), *Lattice Theory*, Colloq. Publ. Amer. Math. Soc. vol. 25, 3rd edition.

Blackburn, P. and Meyer-Viol, W. (1994), *Linguistics, logic and finite trees*, Bull. IGPL **2**(1), 3–29.

Blackburn, P., De Rijke, M. and Venema, Y. (1996), *A course in modal logic*, Department of Computer Science, University of Warwick.

Blamey, S. (1984), *Partial logic*, Handbook of Philosophical Logic vol. III, D. Gabbay and F. Guenthner, eds, Reidel, Dordrecht.

Bochenski, I.M. (1956), *Formale Logik*, K. Alber, Freiburg, 2nd edition.

Bochenski, I.M. (1961), *A History of Formal Logic*, Notre Dame, IN, 1961. Translation of (Bochenski, 1956) by I. Thomas.

Bolinger, D.L. (1975), *Aspects of Language*, Harcourt Brace Jovanovich, New York, 2nd edition.

Boolos, G.S. and Jeffrey, R.C. (1989), *Computability and Logic*, Cambridge Univ. Press, Cambridge, 3rd edition.

Bovet, D.P. and Crescenzi, P. (1994), *Introduction to the Theory of Computational Complexity*, Prentice-Hall, Englewood Cliffs, NJ.

Bull, R.A. and Segerberg, K. (1984), *Basic modal logic*, Handbook of Philosophical Logic vol. II: Extensions of Classical Logic, D. Gabbay and F. Guenthner, eds, Reidel, Dordrecht.

Burgess, J.P. (1981), *Quick completeness proofs for some logics of conditionals*, Notre Dame J. Formal Logic **22**, 76–84.

Burris, S. and Sankappanavar, H.P. (1981), *A Course in Universal Algebra*, Graduate Texts in Mathematics 78, Springer, Berlin.

Cantor, G. (1885), *Beiträge zur Begründung der transfiniten Mengenlehre*, Math. Ann. **96**, 481–512. English translation: *Contributions to the Founding of the Theory of Transfinite Numbers*, Dover Publications, New York, 1915.

Carpenter, B. (1992), *The Logic of Typed Feature Structures*, Tracts in Theoretical Computer Science vol. 32, Cambridge Univ. Press, Cambridge.

Chang, C.C. and Keisler, H.J. (1990), *Model Theory*, North-Holland, Amsterdam, 3rd edition.

Chierchia, G. (1995), *Dynamics of Meaning. Anaphora, Presupposition, and the Theory of Grammar*, Univ. of Chicago Press, Chicago and London.
Chierchia, G. and Turner, R. (1988), *Semantics and property theory*, Ling. and Philos. **11**(3), 261–302.
Chomsky, N. (1956), *Three models for the description of language*, IEEE Trans. Inform. Theory **2**(3), 113–124.
Chomsky, N. (1959), *On certain formal properties of grammars*, Inform. and Control **2**, 137–167.
Chomsky, N. (1965), *Aspects of a Theory of Syntax*, MIT Press, Cambridge, MA.
Church, A. (1932), *A set of postulates for the foundation of logic*, Ann. of Math. **33**, 346–366.
Church, A. (1933), *A set of postulates for the foundation of logic*, Ann. of Math. **34**, 839–864.
Clark, H.H. and Marshall, C.R. (1981), *Definite reference and mutual knowledge*, Elements of Discourse Understanding, A.K. Joshi, B.L. Webber and I. Sag, eds, Cambridge Univ. Press.
Cohen, P.J. (1966), *Set Theory and the Continuum Hypothesis*, Benjamin, New York.
Comrie, B. (1989), *Universals and Language Typology*, Blackwell, Oxford.
Coulthard, M. (1977), *An Introduction to Discourse Analysis*, Longman, London.
Cresswell, M.J. (1973), *Logics and Languages*, Methuen, London.
Cresswell, M.J. (1985), *Structured Meanings*, MIT Press, Cambridge, MA.
Cresswell, M.J. (1988), *Semantical Essays: Possible Worlds and their Rivals*, Kluwer, Dordrecht.
Curry, H.B. (1930), *Grundlagen der kombinatorischen Logik*, Amer. J. Math. **52**, 509–536; 789–834.
Davey, B.A. and Priestley, H.A. (1990), *Introduction to Lattices and Order*, Cambridge Univ. Press.
Davidson, D. (1980), *Essays on Actions and Events*, Clarendon, Oxford.
Davis, M. (1958), *Computability and Unsolvability*, McGraw-Hill, New York.
Davis, M. (ed.) (1965), *The Undecidable: Basic Papers on Undecidable Propositions, Unsolvable Problems, and Computable Functions*, Raven Press, Hewlet, NY.
Davis, S. (ed.) (1991), *Pragmatics: A Reader*, Oxford Univ. Press, New York.
De Rijke, M. (ed.) (1993), *Diamonds and Defaults: Studies in Pure and Applied Intensional Logic*, Kluwer, Dordrecht.
De Rijke, M. (ed.) (1996), *Advances in Intensional Logic*, Kluwer, Dordrecht. To appear.
Diesing, M. (1993), *Indefinites*, MIT Press, Cambridge, MA.
Donnellan, K. (1966), *Reference and definite descriptions*, Philos. Rev. **77**(3), 281–304.
Donnellan, K. (1978), *Speaker reference, descriptions and anaphora*, Syntax and Semantics 9: Pragmatics, P. Cole, ed., Academic Press, New York, 47–68.
Enderton, H.B. (1972), *A Mathematical Introduction to Logic*, Academic Press, New York.
Enderton, H.B. (1977), *Elements of recursion theory*, Handbook of Mathematical Logic, J. Barwise, ed., North-Holland, Amsterdam, 525–566.
Evans, G. (1980), *Pronouns*, Ling. Inq. **11**, 337–362.
Fagin, R., Halpern, J.Y., Moses, Y. and Vardi, M.Y. (1995), *Reasoning about Knowledge*, MIT Press, Cambridge, MA.
Fenstad, J.-E., Halvorsen, P.-K., Langholm, T. and Van Benthem, J. (1987), *Situations, Language and Logic*, Reidel, Dordrecht.
Fillmore, C.J. (1971), *Towards a theory of deixis*, The PCCLLU Papers 3.4, 219–241. Department of Linguistics, University of Hawaii.
Fillmore, C.J. (1975), *Santa Cruz lectures on Deixis 1971*, Indiana University Linguistics Club, Mimeo.
Fitting, M. (1990), *First-Order Logic and Automated Theorem Proving*, Springer, New York.
Fraenkel, A.A., Bar-Hillel, Y. and Levy, A. (1973), *Foundations of Set Theory*, North-Holland, Amsterdam.
Gabbay, D. (1990), *Labeled deductive systems*, Manuscript, Imperial College, London.
Gabbay, D. and Guenthner, F. (eds) (1984), *Handbook of Philosophical Logic vol. II: Extensions of Classical Logic*, Reidel.
Gabbay, D., Hogger, C.J. and Robinson, J.A. (eds) (1993), *Handbook of Logic in Artificial Intelligence and Logic Programming*, Clarendon Press, Oxford.
Gallin, D. (1975), *Intensional and Higher-Order Modal Logic*, North-Holland, Amsterdam.
Galton, A. (1984), *The Logic of Aspect: An Axiomatic Approach*, Clarendon Press, Oxford.
Gärdenfors, P. (1988), *Knowledge in Flux. Modeling the Dynamics of Epistemic States*, Bradford Books/MIT Press, Cambridge, MA.
Gärdenfors, P. and Makinson, D. (1994), *Nonmonotonic inference based on expectations*, Artif. Intell. **65**, 197–245.

Gazdar, G. (1979), *Pragmatics. Implicature, Presupposition and Logical Form*, Academic Press, New York.
Gazdar, G. (1981), *Speech act assignment*, Elements of Discourse Understanding, A.K. Joshi, B.L. Webber and I.A. Sag, eds, Cambridge Univ. Press, Cambridge, 64–83.
Gentzen, G. (1939), *Untersuchungen über das logische Schiessen*, Math. Z. **39**, 176–210.
Gentzen, G. (1969), *The Collected Papers of Gerhard Gentzen*, M.E. Szabo, ed., North-Holland, Amsterdam.
Gerbrandy, J. (1996), *Dynamic epistemic semantics*, Draft, Department of Philosophy, University of Amsterdam.
Ginsberg, M.L. (ed.) (1987), *Readings in Nonmonotonic Reasoning*, Morgan Kaufmann, Los Altos, CA.
Girard, J.-Y. (1987), *Linear logic*, Theor. Comput. Sci. **50**, 1–102.
Girard, J.-Y., Lafont, Y. and Taylor, P. (1990), *Proofs and Types*, Cambridge Univ. Press, Cambridge.
Gödel, K. (1931), *Über formal unentscheidbare Sätze der Principia Mathematica und verwandter Systeme*, Monatsh. Math. Phys. 173–198.
Gödel, K. (1940), *The Consistency of the Continuum Hypothesis*, Princeton Univ. Press, Princeton, NJ.
Goldblatt, R. (1984), *Topoi. The Categorial Analysis of Logic*, Studies in Logic and the Foundations of Mathematics vol. 98, North-Holland, Amsterdam, revised edition.
Goldblatt, R. (1992), *Logics of Time and Computation (Second Edition)*, CSLI Lecture Notes no. 7. CSLI Publications, Stanford.
Goldblatt, R. (1993), *The Mathematics of Modality*, CSLI Lecture Notes no. 43, CSLI Publications, Stanford.
Grätzer, G. (1968), *Universal Algebra*, Van Nostrand, New York.
Green, K. (1995), *New Essays in Deixis: Discourse, Narrative, Literature*, Rodopi, Amsterdam.
Greenberg, J. (1966), *Universals of Language*, MIT Press, Cambridge, MA, 2nd edition.
Grice, P. (1989), *Logic and conversation*, Studies in the Way of Words, Harvard Univ. Press, Cambridge, MA and London, England, 1989. Revised version of William James Lectures at Harvard University, 1967.
Groenendijk, J. and Stokhof, M. (1991), *Dynamic predicate logic*, Ling. and Philos. **14**, 39–100.
Groenendijk, J., Stokhof, M. and Veltman, F. (1994), *This might be it*, Language, Logic and Computation: The 1994 Moraga Proceedings, D. Westerståhl and J. Seligman, eds, Stanford, CSLI.
Groenendijk, J., Stokhof, M. and Veltman, F. (1996), *Coreference and modality*, Handbook of Contemporary Semantic Theory, Chapter 7, S. Lappin, ed., Blackwell, Oxford, 179–214.
Groeneveld, W. (1995), *Logical investigations into dynamic semantics*, PhD thesis, Department of Philosophy, University of Amsterdam.
Halpern, J. and Moses, J. (1990), *Knowledge and common knowledge in a distributed environment*, J. Assoc. Comput. Mach. **37**(3), 549–587.
Hamblin, C.L. (1971), *Mathematical models of dialogue*, Theoria **37**, 130–155.
Harel, D. (1984), *Dynamic logic*, Handbook of Philosophical Logic, D. Gabbay and F. Guenthner, eds, Reidel, Dordrecht.
Harel, D., Kozen, D. and Tiuryn, J. (1995), *Dynamic Logic*, The Weizman Institute, Cornell University and University of Warsaw.
Hartmanis, J. and Hopcroft, J.E. (1971), *An overview of the theory of computational complexity*, J. Assoc. Comput. Mach. **18**(3), 444–475.
Hartmanis, J. and Stearns, R.E. (1965), *On the computational complexity of algorithms*, Trans. Amer. Math. Soc. **117**, 285–306.
Heim, I. (1982), *The semantics of definite and indefinite noun-phrases*, PhD thesis, Department of Linguistics, University of Massachusetts, Amherst.
Heim, I. (1983), *On the projection problem for presuppositions*, Proceedings of the West Coast Conference on Formal Linguistics, vol. II, J. Barlow et al., eds, Stanford Linguistics Association.
Hendriks, H. (1993), *Studied flexibility*, PhD thesis, Department of Philosophy, University of Amsterdam.
Henkin, L., Monk, J.D. and Tarski, A. (1971), *Cylindric Algebras, Part I*, North-Holland, Amsterdam. (Second edition 1985.)
Henkin, L., Monk, J.D. and Tarski, A. (1985), *Cylindric Algebras, Part II*, North-Holland, Amsterdam.
Hennessy, M. and Milner, R. (1985), *Algebraic laws for nondeterminism and concurrency*, J. Assoc. Comput. Mach. **32**, 137–161.
Hintikka, J. (1961), *Modality and quantification*, Theoria **27**, 110–128.
Hintikka, J. (1962), *Knowledge and Belief*, Cornell Univ. Press, Ithaca, NY.
Hintikka, J. (1969), *Models for Modalities: Selected Essays*, Reidel, Dordrecht.
Hoeksema, J. (1983), *Negative polarity and the comparative*, Nat. Language and Ling. Theory **1**, 403–434.

Hoeksema, J. (1986), *Monotonicity phenomena in natural language*, Ling. Anal. **16**, 25–40.
Hopcroft, J.E. and Ullman, J.D. (1979), *Introduction to Automata Theory, Languages and Computation*, Addison-Wesley, Reading, MA.
Horn, L.R. (1972), *On the semantic properties of the logical operators in English*, Mimeo, Indiana University Linguistics Club.
Horn, L.R. (1973), *Greek Grice*, Proceedings of the Ninth Regional Meeting of the Chicago Linguistic Society, 205–214.
Horn, L.R. (1989), *A Natural History of Negation*, Univ. of Chicago Press, Chicago.
Jech, T.J. (1973), *The Axiom of Choice*, North-Holland, Amsterdam.
Johnson, D.S. (1990), *A catalog of complexity classes*, Handbook of Theoretical Computer Science, vol. A, J. van Leeuwen, ed., Elsevier, Amsterdam, 67–161.
Jónson, B. (1991), *The theory of binary relations*, Algebraic Logic, H. Andréka, D. Monk and I. Németi, eds, North-Holland, Amsterdam, 245–292.
Jónson, B. and Tarski, A. (1951), *Boolean algebras with operators, part I*, Amer. J. Math. **73**, 891–939.
Jónson, B. and Tarski, A. (1952), *Boolean algebras with operators, part II*, Amer. J. Math. **74**, 127–162.
Kalish, D. (1967), *Semantics*, Encyclopedia of Philosophy, P. Edwards, ed., Collier-MacMillan, New York.
Kamp, H. (1981), *A theory of truth and semantic representation*, Formal Methods in the Study of Language, J. Groenendijk et al., eds, Mathematical Centre, Amsterdam. Reprinted in: Groenendijk et al. (eds), *Truth, Interpretation and Information*, Foris, Dordrecht, 1984.
Kanger, S. (1957), *Provability in Logic*, Almqvist and Wiksell, Stockholm.
Kannelakis, P. (1990), *Elements of relational database theory*, Handbook of Theoretical Computer Science, J. van Leeuwen, ed., North-Holland, Amsterdam, 1073–1156.
Kaplan, D. (1978), *Dthat*, Syntax and Semantics 9: Pragmatics, P. Cole, ed., Academic Press, New York, 221–243.
Karttunen, L. and Peters, S. (1975), *Conventional implicature in Montague Grammar*, Proceedings of the First Annual Meeting of the Berkeley Linguistic Society, 266–278.
Karttunen, L. and Peters, S. (1979), *Conventional implicature*, Syntax and Semantics 11: Presupposition, C.-K. Oh and D. Dinneen, eds, Academic Press, New York, 1–56.
Kempson, R.M. (1977), *Semantic Theory*, Cambridge Univ. Press, Cambridge, UK.
Kleene, S.C. (1936a), *General recursive functions of natural numbers*, Math. Ann. **112**, 727–742.
Kleene, S.C. (1936b), *λ-definability and recursiveness*, Duke Math. J. **2**, 340–353.
Kleene, S.C. (1952), *Introduction to Metamathematics*, North-Holland, Amsterdam.
Kleene, S.C. and Rosser, J.B. (1935), *The inconsistency of certain formal logics*, Ann. of Math. **36**, 630–636.
Klima, E.S. (1964), *Negation in English*, The structure of language, J.A. Fodor and J.J. Katz, eds, Prentice-Hall, Englewood Cliffs, NJ, 264–323.
Kneale, W. and Kneale, M. (1962), *The Development of Logic*, Clarendon Press, Oxford.
Kock, A. and Reyes, G.E. (1977), *Doctrines in categorial logic*, Handbook of Mathematical Logic, J. Barwise, ed., North-Holland, Amsterdam, 283–313.
Kooij, J. (1971), *Ambiguity in Natural Language*, North-Holland, Amsterdam.
Kracht, M. (1995), *Syntactic codes and grammar refinement*, J. Logic, Lang., Inform. **4**(4), 359–380.
Kratzer, A. (1979), *Conditional necessity and possibility*, Semantics from Different Points of View, R. Bauerle, U. Egli and A. von Stechow, eds, Springer, Berlin.
Kratzer, A. (1981), *Partition and revision: The semantics of counterfactuals*, J. Philos. Logic **10**.
Kripke, S. (1959), *A completeness theorem in modal logic*, J. Symb. Logic **24**, 1–14.
Kripke, S. (1965), *Semantical analysis of intuitionistic logic*, Formal Systems and Recursive Functions, J.N. Crossley and M.A.E. Dummet, eds, North-Holland, Amsterdam, 92–129.
Kripke, S. (1975), *Outline of a theory of truth*, J. Philos. **72**, 690–716. Also in R.L. Martin (ed.) (1984), *Recent Essays on Truth and the Liar Paradox*, Oxford Univ. Press, New York.
Kripke, S. (1990), *Naming and Necessity*, Blackwell, Oxford. Previous edition published in *Semantics of Natural Language*, ed. by D. Davidson and G. Harman, Reidel, Dordrecht, 1972.
Kuipers, T.A.F. (ed.) (1987), *What is Closer-to-the-Truth?*, Rodopi, Amsterdam.
Kunen, K. (1980), *Set Theory*, North-Holland, Amsterdam.
Ladusaw, W.A. (1979), *Polarity sensitivity as inherent scope relations*, PhD thesis, University of Texas at Austin, 1979. Distributed by IULC, Bloomington, Indiana, 1980; published by Garland Press: Outstanding Dissertations in Linguistics, New York.

Ladusaw, W.A. (1996), *Negation and polarity items*, The Handbook of Contemporary Semantic Theory, S. Lappin, ed., Blackwell, Oxford, UK and Cambridge, MA, 321–341.

Lakoff, G. (1970), *A note on ambiguity and vagueness*, Ling. Inq. **1**, 357–359.

Lakoff, G. (1972), *Linguistics and natural logic*, Semantics of Natural Language, D. Davidson and G. Harman, eds, Reidel, Dordrecht, 545–665.

Lakoff, G. (1975), *Pragmatics in Natural Logic*, Formal Semantics of Natural Language, E.L. Keenan, ed., Cambridge Univ. Press, Cambridge, 253–286.

Lambek, J. and Scott, P.J. (1986), *Introduction to Higher-Order Categorial Logic*, Cambridge Studies in Advanced Mathematics 7, Cambridge Univ. Press, Cambridge.

Langholm, T. (1987), *Partiality, Truth and Persistence*, CSLI Lecture Notes no. 15, Cambridge Univ. Press.

Levinson, S.C. (1983), *Pragmatics*, Cambridge Univ. Press, Cambridge.

Lewis, H.B. and Papadimitriou, C.H. (1981), *Elements of the Theory of Computation*, Prentice-Hall, Englewood Cliffs, NJ.

Lewis, C.I. (1918), *A Survey of Symbolic Logic*, Univ. of California, Berkeley.

Lewis, D. (1969), *Convention. A Philosophical Study*, Harvard Univ. Press.

Lewis, D. (1972), *General semantics*, Semantics of Natural Language, D. Davidson and G. Harman, eds, Reidel, Dordrecht, 169–218.

Lewis, D. (1973), *Counterfactuals*, Blackwell, Oxford.

Lloyd, J. (1987), *Foundations of Logic Programming*, Springer, Berlin.

Lorenzen, P. and Lorenz, K. (1979), *Dialogische Logik*, Wissenschaftliche Buchgesellschaft, Darmstadt.

Łukasiewicz, J. (1967), *On 3-valued logic*, Polish Logic in 1920–1939, S. McCall, ed., Clarendon, Oxford, 1967. Polish original published in 1920.

Lyons, J. (1977), *Semantics*, Cambridge Univ. Press, Cambridge.

MacLane, S. (1971), *Categories for the Working Mathematician*, Springer, Berlin.

MacLane, S. and Moerdijk, I. (1992), *Sheaves in Geometry and Logic: A First Introduction to Topos Theory*, Springer, New York.

Maddux, R. (1990), *The origin of relation algebras in the development and axiomatization of the calculus of relations*, Department of Mathematics, Iowa State University, Ames.

Maddux, R. (1995), *Relation-algebraic semantics*, Department of Mathematics, Iowa State University, Ames.

Marcus, R.B. (1961), *Modalities and intensional languages*, Synthese **13**(4), 303–322. Reprinted in (Marcus, 1993).

Marcus, R.B. (1993), *Modalities. Philosophical Essays*, Oxford Univ. Press, New York.

Marek, V.W. (1993), *Nonmonotonic Logic*, Springer, Berlin.

Martin, R.L. (ed.) (1970), *The Paradox of the Liar*, Yale Univ. Press, New Haven, CT. Second edition: Ridgeview Publishing Co., Atascadero, California, 1978.

Martin, R.L. (ed.) (1984), *Recent Essays on Truth and the Liar Paradox*, Oxford Univ. Press, New York.

Marx, M. and Venema, Y. (1996), *Multi-Dimensional Modal Logic*, Applied Logic Series, Kluwer, Dordrecht.

Mendelson, E. (1964), *Introduction to Mathematical Logic*, Van Nostrand, Princeton, NJ. 2nd edition 1979.

Mey, J. (1993), *Pragmatics: An Introduction*, Blackwell, Oxford.

Meyer, B. (1990), *Introduction to the Theory of Programming Languages*, Prentice-Hall, New York.

Moerdijk, I. (1995), *Classifying Spaces and Classifying Sheaves*, Springer, New York.

Montague, R. (1968), *Pragmatics*, Contemporary Philosophy: A Survey, R. Klibansky, ed., La Nuova Italia Editrice, Florence. Reprinted in (Montague, 1974).

Montague, R. (1970), *Pragmatics and intensional logic*, Synthese **22**, 68–94. Reprinted in (Montague, 1974), 119–147.

Montague, R. (1974), *Formal Philosophy*, Yale Univ. Press, New Haven. Edited by R.H. Thomason.

Moore, R.C. (1984), *A formal theory of knowledge and action*, Technical Note 320, SRI International, Menlo Park.

Morris, C. (1938), *Foundations of the theory of signs*, International Encyclopedia of Unified Science I, O. Neurath, ed., Univ. of Chicago Press, Chicago, 77–138.

Moschovakis, Y.N. (1974), *Elementary Induction on Abstract Structures*, North-Holland, Amsterdam.

Muskens, R. (1994), *Categorial grammar and discourse representation theory*, Proceedings of COLING 94, Kyoto, 508–514.

Muskens, R. (1996), *Combining Montague semantics and discourse representation theory*, Ling. and Philos. To appear.

Mosses, P. (1990), *Denotational semantics*, Handbook of Theoretical Computer Science, vol. A, J. van Leeuwen, ed., Elsevier, Amsterdam, 577–632.

Neale, S. (1990), *Descriptions*, MIT Press, Cambridge, MA.

Németi, I. (1991), *Algebraizations of quantifier logics: An overview*, Stud. Logica **50**, 485–570.

Nerbonne, J. (1996), *Computational semantics: Linguistics and processing*, The Handbook of Contemporary Semantic Theory, S. Lappin, ed., Blackwell, Oxford, UK and Cambridge, MA, 461–484.

Nute, D. (1984), *Conditional logic*, Handbook of Philosophical Logic, D. Gabbay and F. Guenthner, eds, Reidel, Dordrecht.

Ohlbach, H.-J. (1991), *Semantic-based translation methods for modal logic*, J. Logic Comput. **1**(5), 691–746.

Ohlbach, H.-J., Schmidt, R. and Hustadt, U. (1995), *Translating graded modalities into predicate logic*, Proof Theory of Modal Logic, H. Wansing, ed., Kluwer, Dordrecht, 245–285.

Ong, C.-H.L. (1992), *Correspondence between operational and denotational semantics: The full abstraction problem for PCF*, Handbook of Logic in Computer Science vol. 4, S. Abramsky, D.M. Gabbay and T.S.E. Maibaum, eds, Clarendon Press, Oxford, 269–356.

Partee, B.H., Ter Meulen, A. and Wall, R.E. (1990), *Mathematical Methods in Linguistics*, Kluwer, Dordrecht.

Pause, E.P. (1991), *Anaphora*, Semantics: An International Handbook of Contemporary Research, A. von Stechow and D. Wunderlich, eds, De Gruyter, Berlin.

Pereira, F. (1983), *Parsing as deduction*, Proceedings of the 21st Annual Meeting of the Association for Computational Linguistics, MIT, Cambridge, MA.

Pereira, F. and Shieber, S. (1987), *Prolog and Natural Language Analysis*, Univ. of Chicago Press, CSLI.

Perry, J. (1993), *The Problem of the Essential Indexical*, Oxford Univ. Press, New York.

Pinkal, M. (1991), *Ambiguity*, Semantics: An International Handbook of Contemporary Research, A. von Stechow and D. Wunderlich, eds, De Gruyter, Berlin.

Plotkin, G. (1975), *Call-by-name, call-by-value and the λ-calculus*, Theor. Comput. Sci. **1**, 125–159.

Post, E.L. (1920), *Determination of all closed systems of truth tables*, Bull. Amer. Math. Soc. **26**.

Post, E.L. (1921), *Introduction to a general theory of elementary propositions*, Amer. J. Math. **43**, 163–185. Reprinted in (Van Heijenoort, 1967).

Progovac, L. (1993), *Negative polarity: Entailment and binding*, Ling. and Philos. **16**, 149–180.

Rabin, M.O. (1963), *Real-time computation*, Israel J. Math. **1**(4), 203–211.

Rauh, G. (ed.) (1982), *Essays in Deixis*, Rodopi, Amsterdam.

Reinhart, T. (1976), *The syntactic domain of anaphora*, PhD thesis, MIT.

Reinhart, T. (1983), *Anaphora and Semantic Interpretation*, Croom Helm, London.

Rescher, N. (1969), *Many-Valued Logic*, McGraw-Hill, New York.

Rochemont, M. (1986), *Focus in Generative Grammar*, Benjamin, Amsterdam.

Rogers, H. Jr. (1967), *Theory of Recursive Functions and Effective Computability*, McGraw-Hill, New York.

Rogers, J. (1994), *Studies in the logic of trees with applications to grammar formalisms*, PhD thesis, University of Delaware.

Rooth, M. (1992), *A theory of focus interpretation*, Nat. Language Semantics **1**, 75–116.

Rooth, M. (1996), *Focus*, Handbook of Contemporary Semantic Theory, Ch. 10, S. Lappin, ed., Blackwell, Oxford, 1271–1298.

Rosner, M. and Johnson, R. (1992), *Computational Linguistics and Formal Semantics*, Cambridge Univ. Press, Cambridge.

Ross, J.R. (1970), *On declarative sentences*, Readings in English Transformational Grammar, R.A. Jacobs and P.S. Rosenbaum, eds, Ginn, Waltham, 222–272.

Russell, B. (1902), *Letter to Frege*, From Frege to Gödel. A Source Book in Mathematical Logic, 1879–1931, J. van Heijenoort, ed., Harvard Univ. Press, 1967.

Russell, B. (1905), *On denoting*, Mind **14**, 479–493.

Russell, B. (1908), *Mathematical logic as based on the theory of types*, Amer. J. Math. **30**, 222–262. Reprinted in (Van Heijenoort, 1967).

Russell, B. (1919), *Descriptions*, Introduction to Mathematical Philosophy, Ch. 16, Allen & Unwin, London, 167–180.

Russell, B. (1957), *Mr. Strawson on referring*, Mind **66**, 385–389.

Sadock, J.M. (1974), *Toward a Linguistic Theory of Speech Acts*, Academic Press, New York.

Schiffer, S.R. (1972), *Meaning*, Clarendon Press, Oxford.

Schiffrin, D. (1987), *Discourse Markers*, Cambridge Univ. Press.

Schlegoff, E.A. and Sacks, H. (1973), *Opening up closings*, Semiotica **7**(4), 289–327.

Schoenfield, J.R. (1971), *Degrees of Unsolvability*, North-Holland, Amsterdam.

Schwichtenberg, H. (1977), *Proof theory: Some applications of cut-elimination*, Handbook of Mathematical Logic, J. Barwise, ed., North-Holland, Amsterdam, 867–896.

Scott, D. (1982), *Domains for denotational semantics*, Proceedings 9th International Colloquium on Automata, Languages and Programming, M. Nielsen and E. Schmidt, eds, Springer, Berlin, 577–613.

Scott, D.S. and Strachey, C. (1971), *Toward a mathematical semantics for computer languages*, Proc. Symp. on Computers and Automata, Polytechnic Institute of Brooklyn, 19–46.

Searle, J.R. (1969), *Speech Acts*, Cambridge Univ. Press, Cambridge.

Searle, J.R. and Vanderveken, D. (1985), *Foundations of Illocutionary Logic*, Cambridge Univ. Press.

Shieber, S.M. (1986), *An Introduction to Unification-Based Approaches to Grammar*, CSLI Lecture Notes 4, CSLI, Stanford.

Shoham, Y. (1988), *Reasoning about Change: Time and Causality from the Standpoint of Artificial Intelligence*, MIT Press, Cambridge, MA.

Sikorski, R. (1964), *Boolean Algebras*, Springer, Berlin.

Smith, N.V. (ed.) (1982), *Mutual Knowledge*, Academic Press, London.

Smorynski, C. (1977), *The incompleteness theorems*, Handbook of Mathematical Logic, J. Barwise, ed., North-Holland, Amsterdam, 821–866.

Smullyan, R. (1992), *Gödel's Incompleteness Theorems*, Oxford Univ. Press, New York.

Sosa, E. (ed.) (1975), *Causation and Conditionals*, Oxford Univ. Press, London.

Spohn, W. (1988), *Ordinal conditional functions: A dynamic theory of epistemic states*, Causation in Decision, Belief Change and Statistics II, W.L. Harper et al., eds, Kluwer, Dordrecht, 105–134.

Stalnaker, R. (1972), *Pragmatics*, Semantics of Natural Language, D. Davidson and G. Harman, eds, Reidel, Dordrecht.

Stalnaker, R. (1974), *Pragmatic presuppositions*, Semantics and Philosophy, M. Munitz and P. Unger, eds, New York Univ. Press, New York.

Stalnaker, R. (1978), *Assertion*, Syntax and Semantics 9: Pragmatics, P. Cole, ed., Academic Press, New York, 315–332.

Stone, M.H. (1936), *The theory of representations for boolean algebras*, Trans. Amer. Math. Soc. **40**, 37–111.

Stoy, J.E. (1977), *Denotational Semantics. The Scott–Strachey Approach to Programming Languages*, MIT Press, Cambridge, MA.

Strawson, P.F. (1950), *On referring*, Mind **59**, 320–344.

Tarski, A. (1956), *The concept of truth in formalized languages*, Logic, Semantics, Metamathematics: Papers from 1923 to 1938, J.H. Woodger, ed., Clarendon. Polish original published in 1933.

Tennent, R.D. (1992), *Denotational semantics*, Handbook of Logic in Computer Science vol. 3, S. Abramsky and D.M. Gabbay and T.S.E. Maibaum, eds, Clarendon Press, Oxford, 169–322.

Tennent, R.D. (1991), *Semantics of Programming Languages*, Prentice-Hall, Englewood Cliffs, NJ.

Ter Meulen, A.G.B. (1995), *Representing Time in Natural Language. The Dynamic Interpretation of Tense and Aspect*, MIT Press, Cambridge, MA.

Troelstra, A. and Van Dalen, D. (1988), *Constructivism in Mathematics*, North-Holland, Amsterdam.

Troelstra, A. and Schwichtenberg, H. (1996), *Basic Proof Theory*, Cambridge Univ. Press, Cambridge.

Turing, A.M. (1936), *On computable numbers, with an application to the Entscheidungsproblem*, Proc. London Math. Soc. (Ser. 2) **4**, 230–265.

Turing, A.M. (1937), *Computability and λ-definability*, J. Symb. Logic **2**, 153–163.

Urquhart, A. (1984), *Many-valued logic,* Handbook of Philosophical Logic vol. III, D. Gabbay and F. Guenthner, eds, Reidel, Dordrecht.

Vallduví, E. (1992), *The Informational Component*, Garland, New York.

Van Benthem, J. (1983), *The Logic of Time*, Reidel, Dordrecht.

Van Benthem, J. (1984a), *Correspondence theory*, Handbook of Philosophical Logic vol. II, D. Gabbay and F. Guenthner, eds, Reidel, Dordrecht, 167–248.

Van Benthem, J. (1984b), *Foundations of conditional logic*, J. Philos. Logic **13**, 303–349.

Van Benthem, J. (1985), *Modal Logic and Classical Logic*, Bibliopolis/The Humanities Press, Naples/Atlantic Heights (NJ).

Van Benthem, J. (1988), *A Manual of Intensional Logic*, CSLI Lecture Notes no. 1, CSLI Publications, Stanford.

Van Benthem, J. (1991a), *Language in Action*, North-Holland, Amsterdam.

Van Benthem, J. (1991b), *Temporal logic*, Handbook of Logic in Artificial Intelligence, D. Gabbay, C. Hogger and J. Robinson, eds, Oxford Univ. Press, Oxford, 241–348.

Van Benthem, J. and Bergstra, J. (1995), *Logic of transition systems*, J. Logic, Lang., Inform. **3**(4), 247–283.

Van Dalen, D. (1984), *Intuitionistic logic*, Handbook of Philosophical Logic vol. III, D. Gabbay and F. Guenthner, eds, Reidel, Dordrecht.

Van Deemter, K. and Peters, S. (eds) (1996), *Semantic Ambiguity and Underspecification*, CSLI Lecture Notes no. 55, CSLI, Stanford.

Van der Wouden, T. (1994), *Negative contexts*, PhD thesis, University of Groningen.

Van Dijk, T.A. (1972), *Some Aspects of Text Grammars*, Mouton, The Hague.

Van Emde Boas, V. (1990), *Machine models and simulations*, Handbook of Theoretical Computer Science, vol. A, J. van Leeuwen, ed., Elsevier, Amsterdam, 1–66.

Van Heijenoort, J. (ed.) (1967), *From Frege to Gödel. A Source Book in Mathematical Logic, 1879–1931*, Harvard Univ. Press.

Vanderveken, D. (1990), *Meaning and Speech Aacts, Part I*, Cambridge Univ. Press, Cambridge.

Vanderveken, D. (1991), *Meaning and Speech Acts, Part II*, Cambridge Univ. Press, Cambridge.

Veltman, F. (1976), *Prejudices, presuppositions and the theory of counterfactuals*, Amsterdam Papers in Formal Grammar vol. I, J. Groenendijk and M. Stokhof, eds, University of Amsterdam.

Veltman, F. (1985), *Logics for conditionals*, PhD thesis, University of Amsterdam.

Veltman, F. (1991), *Defaults in update semantics*, ITLI Prepublication Series LP-91-02, University of Amsterdam. To appear in J. Philos. Logic.

Venema, Y. (1991), *Many-dimensional modal logic*, PhD thesis, Institute for Logic, Language and Computation, University of Amsterdam.

Verkuyl, H.J. (1993), *A Theory of Aspectuality*, Cambridge Studies in Linguistics vol. 64, Cambridge Univ. Press.

von Bergen, A. and von Bergen, K. (1993), *Negative Polarität im Englischen*, Narr, Tübingen.

Wagner, E.G. (1992), *Algebraic semantics*, Handbook of Logic in Computer Science vol. 3, S. Abramsky and D.M. Gabbay and T.S.E. Maibaum eds, Clarendon Press, Oxford, 323–394.

Weissenborn, J. and Klein, W. (eds) (1982), *Here and There. Cross-Linguistic Studies on Deixis and Demonstration*, Benjamin, Amsterdam.

Wittgenstein, L. (1921), *Tractatus Logico-Philosophicus*, Routledge and Kegan Paul (1961), London. Translation D.F. Pears and B.F. McGuinness.

Wittgenstein, L. (1958), *Philosophical Investigations*, Blackwell, Oxford.

Zimmermann, T.E. (1991), *Kontext*, Semantics: An International Handbook of Contemporary Research, A. von Stechow and D. Wunderlich, eds, De Gruyter, Berlin.

Zwarts, F. (1986), *Categoriale grammatica en algebraische semantiek*, PhD thesis, University of Groningen.

Zwarts, F. (1993), *Three types of polarity*, Semantics, F. Hamm and E. Hinrichs, eds, Kluwer, Dordrecht.

Zwicky, A. and Sadock, J. (1975), *Ambiguity tests and how to fail them*, Syntax and Semantics 4, J. Kimball, ed., Academic Press, New York.

Author Index

Subject Index